AMERICAN NATIONAL BIOGRAPHY

AMERICAN
NATIONAL BIOGRAPHY

Published under the auspices of the
AMERICAN COUNCIL OF LEARNED SOCIETIES

General Editors

John A. Garraty

Mark C. Carnes

VOLUME 2

OXFORD UNIVERSITY PRESS
New York 1999 Oxford

OXFORD UNIVERSITY PRESS

Oxford   New York
Athens Auckland Bangkok Bogotá
Buenos Aires Calcutta Cape Town Chennai
Dar es Salaam Delhi Florence Hong Kong Istanbul
Karachi Kuala Lumpur Madrid Melbourne Mexico City
Mumbai Nairobi Paris São Paulo Singapore
Taipei Tokyo Toronto Warsaw
and associated companies in
Berlin Ibadan

Copyright © 1999 by the American Council of Learned Societies

Published by Oxford University Press, Inc.,
198 Madison Avenue, New York, New York 10016
http://www.oup-usa.org

Oxford is a registered trademark of Oxford University Press

Funding for this publication was provided in part by
the Andrew W. Mellon Foundation, the Rockefeller Foundation,
and the National Endowment for the Humanities,
a federal agency.

Library of Congress Cataloging-in-Publication Data

American national biography / general editors, John A. Garraty, Mark C. Carnes
        p.   cm.
"Published under the auspices of the American Council of Learned Societies."
Includes bibliographical references and index.
1. United States—Biography—Dictionaries. I. Garraty, John Arthur,
1920– . II. Carnes, Mark C. (Mark Christopher), 1950–   .
III. American Council of Learned Societies.
CT213.A68 1998 98-20826 920.073—dc21 CIP
ISBN 0-19-520635-5 (set)
ISBN 0-19-512781-1 (vol. 2)

Printing (last digit): 9 8 7 6 5 4 3 2 1

Printed in the United States of America
on acid-free paper

BAKER, Belle (25 Dec. 1895–28 Apr. 1957), singer, was born Bella Becker in New York City's Lower East Side, the daughter of Chaim Becker, a pushcart peddler, and Sarah (maiden name unknown), both immigrants from Russia. Baker left school at an early age—most sources say nine—and went to work in sweatshops, primarily shirtwaist factories and laundries. At age eleven she landed a job as a singer at the Cannon Street Music Hall, located near her home. There she was spotted by Jacob Adler, a mainstay of Yiddish theater, who hired her as a member of his company at the Grand Theater. Baker worked for Adler for two years, both in New York City and on several out-of-town tours, and at age thirteen she was able to move her family—she was the third of eight children—to the more upscale neighborhood of Washington Heights.

Her employment at the Grand Theater came to an end when the actors' union began putting restrictions on the hours and roles of the underage Baker. She went back to work in less prestigious music halls, and it was at that point that Lew Leslie, a vaudeville promoter and producer, became her manager and began booking her in small vaudeville houses.

Baker made her vaudeville debut in Scranton, Pennsylvania, and soon was being booked in bigger vaudeville halls. In 1910 Baker married Leslie. They had no children. According to family sources, the marriage may have been contracted for business rather than romantic reasons; it enabled Leslie to avoid legal problems from traveling with the underage Baker, and it gave Baker and Leslie complete control over her business affairs.

In 1911 Baker made her major vaudeville debut at Hammerstein's Victoria Theater in New York City. By 1913 she was a vaudeville headliner. That year she made her debut at the Palace Theater in New York, the top showcase for vaudeville performers, and was an unqualified success.

Onstage, Baker, who was described as a short, plump, and dark-haired woman with a huge voice, projected a warm, approachable persona. "Her unusual personality goes right over the footlights and into the hearts of her auditors, and without knowing exactly why, you begin to regard her as your friend," said the *Toledo (Ohio) Blade* (26 Mar. 1918). She was a skilled mimic (many of her songs were sung in exaggerated Yiddish, Italian, and Irish accents), and she was adept at projecting a wide range of emotions. During her early years, critics tended to single out her comic abilities and character songs; when she was older, it was her torch songs that drew raves. In fact, she could deliver a wide range of material with aplomb. She was eventually credited with introducing 163

songs, many of them by Irving Berlin, with whom she developed a close and mutually beneficial friendship while she was still in her teens. His comedy song "Cohen Owes Me $97" was a mainstay for Baker during her early vaudeville years. Other Berlin songs that were particularly hers included "Always," "Blue Skies," and "What'll I Do?"

By 1918 Baker's earning had soared to $1,000 a week. Around this time Baker fell in love with Maurice Abrahams, a music publisher and songwriter whose hits included "Get Out and Get Under" and "Hitchy Koo." Leslie held out for a hefty financial settlement (family sources say $10,000) before he agreed to a divorce in 1919. After the divorce, however, Baker and Leslie remained friendly and occasionally worked together. Baker and Abrahams were married in 1919.

That was also the year that Baker made her first recordings and added an unusual song to her vaudeville repertoire: "Eli, Eli," sung in Yiddish, about the troubles of the Jewish people. Baker had first performed it at Adler's Grand Theater; it became a signature song after she introduced it to her vaudeville audience. Another signature song was "My Yiddische Momma."

Baker and Abraham's son, Herbert Baker (who used his mother's professional name when he started his own career as a television and movie writer), was born on his mother's birthday, 25 December 1920. In subsequent years Baker's fans heard enough about Herbert during his mother's performances to consider him something of an honorary nephew. Baker's career reached its peak in the mid-1920s, at the same time that vaudeville was beginning to show signs of decline.

In 1926 Baker made her legitimate stage debut, playing the title role in the Richard Rodgers and Lorenz Hart Broadway musical *Betsy*, produced by Florenz Ziegfeld. It proved to be an unhappy experience. Ziegfeld was simultaneously producing another show. Script problems went unresolved. As opening night approached, a nervous Baker asked Irving Berlin to supply her with an additional song. Berlin's "Blue Skies" was interpolated into the show right before opening night by Ziegfeld, who neglected to inform Rodgers and Hart of the addition. *Betsy* ran for only thirty-nine performances. Although Baker's reviews were moderately favorable and "Blue Skies" stopped the show, *Betsy*'s failure put an end to her Broadway aspirations.

Baker made her official radio debut in 1926 on WEAF in New York. Her expressive voice and use of anecdotes to set up her songs proved ideally suited for the medium. In 1929 she made her movie debut in *Song of Love*. Critics gave the movie a mixed reception, but many singled out Baker for praise. *Song of Love* did not, however, lead to more movie roles, probably because Baker did not fit into any conventional movie niche.

Abrahams died suddenly in 1931 at age forty-eight. For a year after his death Baker performed only on radio. In 1932 she scored one of her biggest hits ever with "All of Me." But with vaudeville dying, there were fewer venues for performers like Baker, and, still depressed over Abrahams's death, she could muster little interest in developing new career opportunities. In 1934, however, Baker was asked to do a two-week engagement at London's Palladium. There she scored the biggest triumph of her career. She was held over for eight weeks, then toured throughout Britain for nine months. She also had a featured role in the 1935 British movie *Charing Cross Road*.

In 1935 Baker returned to New York. Few vaudeville theaters remained, so she rekeyed her act for nightclubs, making her U.S. nightclub debut at the Varsailles Club in New York City in 1936. In 1937 Baker married Elias E. Sugarman, then the editor of *Billboard* magazine. They had no children, and their marriage ended in divorce in 1941. In 1944 she made her third and last movie appearance in *Atlantic City*.

During the 1940s Baker continued to make nightclub appearances, but their frequency declined. She still enjoyed performing but never learned to like nightclubs, and her dislike of that venue probably was a major factor in her decision to retire. Her final public performance was at the Palace Theater in 1950.

Baker died in Beverly Hills, California, where she had moved in 1953 to be closer to her son.

• Reminiscences of Baker's son, Herbert Baker, are part of the oral history holdings of Southern Methodist University in Dallas, Tex. Her son's papers and Baker's own memorabilia are in the Special Collections Department of the library of the University of California at Los Angeles. Published information on Baker is sketchy. The best overall source is Anthony Slide, *The Encyclopedia of Vaudeville* (1994). Additional information can be gleaned from contemporary newspaper articles; the Billy Rose Theatre Collection at the New York Public Library for the Performing Arts, Lincoln Center, has two clippings files on her. See also Belle Baker, "Singing Popular Songs," *Variety*, 26 Dec. 1919. Baker's granddaughter, Nicole Baker, wrote an unpublished college research paper, "Belle Baker: The Incomparable," that provides a comprehensive overview of her life.

LYNN HOOGENBOOM

BAKER, Benjamin Archibald (4 Apr. 1818–6 Sept. 1890), playwright and theater manager, was born in New York City. Little about Baker's early life is known; rumor has it that he ran away from home, arriving in New Orleans as a harness maker, later repairing cavalry gear for Sam Houston's troops in Texas. He then joined a stock company and made his debut as an actor in *Rob Roy* in February 1837 in Natchez, Mississippi. For the next two years he served as a prompter and actor in Memphis, Vicksburg, Natchez, and New Orleans.

Baker next found employment as a prompter and supernumerary for the opening of Mitchell's Olympic Theater in New York in December 1839. He remained at the Olympic for ten years, during which time he began to write scripts, beginning with the unsuccessful *Amy Lee* in 1843 and *Peytona and Fashion* in 1845. His brief *New York in 1848* premiered on 2 February 1848, introducing the character of Mose, the New York volunteer fireboy, a local tough also known as a "Bowery B'hoy." Frank Chanfrau, a former street tough himself, acted the role so successfully that Baker expanded the role and the script into *A Glance at New York*, which ran for seventy nights in 1848. The same year Baker wrote a companion play, *New York As It Is*.

While other playwrights had included "Bowery B'hoys" in previous plays, Baker's utilization of Mose the fireboy in *A Glance at New York* marked a significant advance in the emergence of character types unique to the United States on the stage. Chanfrau replicated the red shirt, plug hat, and turned-up trousers of the volunteer fireman, as well as the cockiness of the "B'hoys," many of whom regularly attended the Olympic Theater. Theater historian T. Allston Brown described the scene as Chanfrau confronted the audience: he had "a stump of a cigar pointing up from his lips to the eye . . . and his jaw protruded into a half-beastly, half-human expression of contemptuous ferocity. . . . Taking the cigar stump from his mouth and turning half-way round to spit, he said, 'I ain't a goin' to run wid dat mercheen [machine] no more!' Instantly there arose such a yell of recognition as had never been heard in the little house before." The fast-moving script contained short episodic scenes, many recognizable to the audience: the docks, a woman's bowling alley, Loafer's Paradise, and similar locales. The play scored an enormous success and stimulated dozens of imitations. Baker quickly produced other Mose plays, but only *A Glance at New York* received publication.

In 1850 Baker joined W. B. English to manage the Howard Athenæum in Boston. The next year he assumed the management of the National Theater in Washington. Catherine Norton Sinclair (Edwin Forrest's estranged wife) then engaged Baker to manage the Metropolitan Theater in San Francisco. While in California Baker led Laura Keene's company on a successful tour of the state; he then returned to the East Coast with Edwin Booth. In 1856 Baker managed Booth's first starring tour of the principal American cities. Baker and Booth became friends, Baker having been the stage manager at the old Chatham Theater when Edwin Booth unexpectedly substituted for his father as Richard III in April 1851.

In the late 1850s Baker again managed Laura Keene's company, including her production of *The Seven Sisters*, which opened in November 1860 and ran 169 performances (then considered unusually successful). In 1877 John T. Ford hired Baker to rehearse the various stock companies that performed in Ford's various southern theaters.

After two years with Ford, Baker returned to New York City, serving as a stage manager and occasionally performing. He also gave acting lessons. In 1883, to the delight of the profession, Baker was appointed assistant secretary to the Actors' Fund of America, a post he filled with great diligence and industry, overseeing the distribution of funds to indigent theater workers. His amiability endeared him to the hundreds of performers with whom he came in contact, most of whom referred to him fondly as "Uncle Ben."

After a two-week illness, Baker died at his home in New York City. His funeral was held in the Church of the Transfiguration (the Little Church around the Corner), with the pews reserved for members of the Actors' Fund, the Philadelphia Lodge of the Elks, and the St. Cecilia Lodge of the Masons, organizations to which Baker had belonged for many years. His pallbearers included such theatrical luminaries as Edwin Booth, A. M. Palmer, Joseph Jefferson (1829–1905), Lawrence Barrett, Edward Harrigan, De-Wolf Hopper, and Daniel Frohman.

• The Hoblitzelle Theater Arts Library at the University of Texas, Austin, lists Baker in its holograph file for dramatic performers. A lengthy interview with Baker is in George O. Seilhamer, *An Interviewer's Album: Comprising a Series of Chats with Eminent Players and Playwrights*, vol. 12 (1881). For Baker's dramaturgy, see William Knight Northall, *Before and Behind the Curtain* (1851); Joseph N. Ireland, *Records of the New York Stage*, vol. 2 (1867); T. Allston Brown, *History of the New York Stage*, vol. 1 (1903); Arthur H. Quinn, *History of the American Drama from the Beginning to the Civil War* (1923); and Walter Meserve, *Heralds of Promise* (1986). Substantial obituaries are in the *New York Times*, 7 Sept. 1890, and the *New York Dramatic Mirror*, 13 Sept. 1890.

STEPHEN M. ARCHER

BAKER, Carlos Heard (5 May 1909–18 Apr. 1987), educator, author, and literary critic, was born in Biddeford, Maine, the son of Arthur Baker and Edna Heard. He grew up in what he called a "yankee and the nineteenth century German" tradition and had a great passion for literature even as a child. While still a college student, he published a collection of poems, *Shadows in Stone* (1930). In 1932 he graduated from Dartmouth College and married Dorothy T. Scott. The couple had three children. He earned an M.A. from Harvard University the following year. After a short teaching stint, first at Thornton Academy in Maine from 1933 to 1934 and then at Nichols School in Buffalo, New York, from 1934 to 1936, Baker became an instructor at Princeton University, working on his doctoral degree at the same time. He received his Ph.D. from the English department there in 1940. The publication of *American Issues*, an anthology of American literature that he edited with Willard Thorp and Merle Curti in 1941, helped him to win an appointment as an assistant professor of English in 1942. With his career as both a teacher and a scholar moving along smoothly, Baker became an associate professor of English in 1946.

Through his critical book *Shelley's Major Poetry: The Fabric of Vision* (1948) Baker made his first mark as a literary scholar. Basically an interpretative account of Percy Bysshe Shelley's individual poems written between 1812 and 1822, the book traces the thoughts and ideals that have been regarded as a motivating force behind Shelley's poetry, depicting him chiefly as an intellectual and psychological, rather than a lyric, poet. What is unique about the book is the way in which Baker presents an objective account of Shelley's ideas, desires, and successes before offering his own criticism. Such a construction allows the readers of his book to compare the statements from Shelley and Baker in order to make their own judgments. The book has been considered by many as a major study on Shelley that neither a Shelley student nor a Shelley scholar can afford to neglect. The success of this book was followed by the popularity of two books Baker edited: one is a selection from William Wordsworth, *"The Prelude," with a Selection from the Shorter Poems and the Sonnets and the 1800 Preface to "Lyrical Ballads"* (1948); the other is a selection from Shelley, *Selected Poetry and Prose* (1951). These books helped Baker establish his reputation in his field. He was promoted to professor of English in 1951 and became chair of the English department at Princeton in 1952.

During this same period, Baker began devoting a considerable amount of time to a new interest in his research, Ernest Hemingway. The result was his widely acclaimed *Hemingway: The Writer as Artist*, an authorized biography. During Baker's preparation for the book, however, most biographical references were omitted because of Hemingway's opposition. Baker had to focus on the interpretation of those novels Hemingway had published up to that point. As Baker insists in the introduction, the book tries to provide "an outline of the practical esthetic assumptions with which Hemingway began and from which, with various additions and modifications, he ever afterwards operated" (*Hemingway*, p. xiv). After reading the book, Hemingway said that he admired it, except for one particular aspect: it "made too much of the symbols." New chapters were added to later editions (1956, 1963, and 1972) in order to incorporate comment on Hemingway's life and work during his later years.

From 1952 to 1957 Baker was primarily preoccupied with his administrative duties as the head of the English department and his teaching assignments as the Woodrow Wilson Professor of English, an honor that was given to him in 1953. He traveled to Europe during the 1957–1958 academic year, teaching as a Fulbright lecturer in American literature at Oxford University in Oxford, England, and at Centre Universitaire Mediterraneen in Nice, France. Nevertheless, Baker still managed to write a novel, *A Friend in Power* (1958), a story of a university professor who tries to find out how to define and face one's responsibilities. The novel was selected as one of the books to be condensed and reprinted in the summer 1958 edition of the *Reader's Digest* Book Club.

Throughout the 1960s and 1970s Baker was prolific both as a creative writer and a scholar. He won the Guggenheim Fellowship twice (1965, 1967). In addition to his frequent contributions to periodicals like *Time, Saturday Review*, and the *New York Times*, Baker wrote two novels, published a selection of his poems and a collection of his short stories, and edited two books on Hemingway, *Hemingway and His Critics: An International Anthology* (1961) and *Ernest Hemingway: Critiques of Four Major Novels* (1962). Baker also edited two selections of Romantic poetry. But the most important book he wrote in this period is *Ernest Hemingway: A Life Story* (1969), which further solidified his reputation as the leading scholar of Hemingway. He spent seven years on the project, reviewing Hemingway's letters, papers, and unpublished manuscripts, and also corresponding with Hemingway's widow and hundreds of other people. The book won high praise for its success in portraying Hemingway both as a legendary figure and a common man without imposing any conclusions, thus creating a new format in biography writing.

After his retirement from teaching in 1977, Baker continued to contribute to the studies of Hemingway and Romanticism with his *Ernest Hemingway: Selected Letters* (1981) and *The Echoing Green: Romanticism* (1984), an examination of six modern poets against the background of English Romanticism. Before he died in Princeton, New Jersey, Baker had been putting the finishing touches on his last book, *Emerson among the Eccentrics: A Group Portrait*. The manuscript was brought to press in 1996 by his daughter Elizabeth B. Carter. Beautifully crafted, this book has been hailed not only as an "intimate portrait" of Ralph Waldo Emerson but also as a detailed reconstruction of an entire era. Baker is widely known as one of America's foremost academics because of his accomplishment in teaching and his pioneering work in critical literature.

• Baker's papers are located in the Rare Books Department of Princeton University Library. In addition to books mentioned in this article, Baker wrote two novels, *The Land of Rumbelow* (1963) and *The Gay Head Conspiracy* (1973); a collection of poems, *A Year and a Day* (1963); and a short fiction collection, *The Talisman and Other Stories* (1976). He also edited works by Henry Fielding, William H. Hudson, John Keats, Samuel Taylor Coleridge, and Thomas Mann. With others Baker edited *Modern American Usage* (1966). Some interesting information about Baker's life and work is scattered throughout articles and book reviews. John Updike, "Hem Battles the Pack; Wins, Loses," *New Yorker*, 13 July 1981, pp. 96–106, and the introduction by James R. Mellow to Baker, *Emerson among the Eccentrics* (1996), are both very useful. An obituary is in the *New York Times*, 21 Apr. 1987.

AIPING ZHANG

BAKER, Chet (23 Dec. 1929–13 May 1988), jazz trumpet player and singer, was born Chesney Henry Baker in Yale, Oklahoma, the son of Vera Moser and Chestney Baker, a laborer and semiprofessional guitarist. Within two weeks after his father gave him a pawn shop trumpet, eleven-year-old Chet was picking at Harry James's "Two O'Clock Jump." In 1940 Baker's father took a job at Lockheed Aircraft, moving the family to Glendale, California. There Baker began musical training, playing in marching and dance bands. By age sixteen he had left formal education forever and joined the U.S. Army. While stationed for a year in Berlin with the 298th Army Band, he discovered jazz through the Armed Forces Network. His first major influence was Dizzy Gillespie.

Leaving the army after one stint, he studied music theory briefly and then reenlisted to join the Presidio Army Band. In San Francisco Baker spent evenings at Bop City, a jazz hot spot. Wanting no more of service life, in 1951 he went AWOL (absent without leave) and was released later that year after feigning psychological problems. Now independent, he caught the ear of Charlie "Bird" Parker in the spring of 1952 and played a three-week engagement with him at the Tiffany Club in Los Angeles; the two briefly continued to play together in other venues in other cities. In 1950 Baker married Charlaine (maiden name unknown); they had no children and divorced in 1955.

In the summer of 1952 Gerry Mulligan chose Baker to be his front-line partner in his newly formed quartet, also featuring drummer Chico Hamilton and bassist Bob Whitlock. Mulligan's "pianoless" quartet then defined, if not invented, the West Coast "cool jazz" sound of the 1950s. Best described as cool and emotionally detached, the new sound was considered intellectually complicated by some, while others thought it lacked vitality. The pioneering foursome gained attention and fame with Baker's 1952 cover of "My Funny Valentine," among the first modern jazz records to become a bestseller. British writer John Chilton noted that West Coast jazz "pleased those fans who wanted to feel part of the experimental music without any aural hardships." *Down Beat* magazine elected Baker as the new star of 1952, and in subsequent years he remained at the top of jazz polls.

In 1953 the trumpeter left Mulligan over a salary dispute, rejoined Parker briefly, and then formed his own quartet. "He went past Gerry in a sense," Dick Bock, founder of Pacific Jazz Records, recalled in an interview. "He was so bright, he had to have his own thing." That same year Baker began what became a lifetime of long years touring Europe, punctuated by intermittent returns to the United States. During this period Baker also discovered heavy drugs, became a heroin addict, and began a tragic personal odyssey that continues to evoke controversy among jazz fans.

Baker was at the peak of his popularity in the 1950s. Jazz lovers were drawn to the moody musician's square-jawed resemblance to actor James Dean, his robust build, and his musical styling, which one writer described as "haunting ruminations." Baker's understated approach was reminiscent of jazz contemporary Miles Davis. Writer Bill Kirschner noted that it "concentrates on the lower, darker octaves of the instrument and rarely, if ever, ventures above a high C" (*Down Beat*, Apr. 1984). The timbral similarity between his whispery tenor and his trumpet were liquid.

His style was to jam his horn tightly to the microphone and not use a trumpet mute, since they muffled low notes. Writer Alan Axelrod likened Baker's spare artistry to "a dry sherry. . . . What Chet Baker does is much harder than it sounds. He combines the often antithetical qualities of minimalism and warmth . . . the listener finds himself greedily savoring the satin nuances" (*Down Beat*, Mar. 1984).

In 1954 Baker tied singer Nat King Cole in a *Down Beat* readers' poll in the category of best male vocalist. In 1955 he began an eight-month tour of Europe, which was the longest overseas booking of a jazz musician at the time. While playing Paris, his pianist, Dick Twardzik, died of an apparent drug-induced heart attack. Years later Baker said that his guilt over the loss of the young musician led to his own addiction. Over time drug problems would land Baker in jail on both sides of the Atlantic, with deportations from Switzerland, Germany, and Britain. Baker married Halema Alli in 1957; they had one child before divorcing in 1964.

Baker appeared infrequently in films, notably several experimental Italian features. In 1960 the wavy-haired trumpeter was to appear as the lead in the American motion picture *All the Fine Young Cannibals*, based upon his life. However, before production he was arrested in Lucca, Italy, with his wife and two doctors and charged with possession of heroin. The others were released, while he served fifteen months and was forced to abandon his car, wardrobe, and work at the Chet Baker Club in Milan.

In March 1964 Baker was deported from Germany, following a drug arrest and forty days in a psychiatric hospital. With $1.25 in his pocket, he returned to New York. Finding a cabaret card unobtainable, he had no work for three weeks until Dizzy Gillespie intervened. Attending a performance at a Long Island nightclub, a *Time* magazine writer said that Baker "looked pained when he played and downright wounded when he sang, but his music had a bright, aggressive gusto . . . better jazz than the music his fans remembered" (17 Apr. 1964). In 1964 Baker married Carol Jackson, with whom he had three children.

During a long comeback that led him to San Francisco in 1968, Baker was almost beaten to death in what he claimed was a drug deal gone wrong. Many friends, however, believed that an acquaintance wanted to take away his means of making a living. Baker lost most of his teeth, which created a loss of natural embouchure, the articulation of lips and tongue on a brass mouthpiece. He did not play publicly for three years, was on welfare briefly, and worked as a gas station attendant.

The controversy among fans was whether Baker, with his drug problems and handicap, ever achieved the promise of his youth. Under methadone treatment for more than seven years, Baker continued to tour both continents and produce records. In 1977 he broke from methadone and that same year released an acclaimed album, *Once upon a Summertime*.

After attending a performance by the 51-year-old trumpeter, writer Maggie Hawthorn commented, "Baker is a minimalist. He has built a career on it, refining and polishing his chosen tiny patch of territory, never straying far from its well-defined limits." In later years Baker himself was dismissive of his early fame, saying, "I never really believed I deserved it. I felt that it was as though, during that period, people had, more or less just been waiting for something new" (*Down Beat*, Apr. 1978).

Baker estimated that, over his lifetime, he recorded more than 900 songs and released more than 100 albums. A year before his passing, filmmaker Bruce Weber completed *Let's Get Lost*, a definitive biographical movie. It featured clips from Baker's television and film appearances and interviews with a grizzled, yet still artful, musician, who appeared to be twenty years older than his true age.

Baker died in a fall from his second-story hotel room in Amsterdam. Police initially reported that they had found a thirty-year-old man with a trumpet on the street below. In 1989 Baker was inducted into the *Down Beat* Hall of Fame, the ninth professional trumpeter to be so honored.

• Clippings on Baker can be found in the Billy Rose Theatre Collection at the New York Public Library for the Performing Arts, Lincoln Center. Among his many recordings, Baker's best albums include *The Best of Chet Baker Sings 1953–1956* (1956); *Playboy* (1956); *Mulligan/Baker Carnegie Hall Concert*, vols. 1 and 2 (1956); and *Daybreak* (1979). See also James Gavin, *Chet Baker* (1999). Baker is extensively profiled in Robert Gordon, *Jazz West Coast* (1986), and Ted Gioia, *West Coast Jazz* (1992). An obituary is in the *New York Times*, 14 May 1988.

DON STEWART

BAKER, Daniel (17 Aug. 1791–10 Dec. 1857), minister and educator, was born in Midway, Georgia (now in Liberty County); his parents' names are unknown. Orphaned at the age of fourteen, he moved to Savannah, Georgia, where he worked as a store clerk. The religious atmosphere of Savannah had an enormous influence on this young man, and he soon chose a career in the ministry. Baker also understood the importance of an education, and in 1811 he enrolled in Hampden-Sidney College in Virginia. In 1813 he continued his education at the College of New Jersey (now Princeton University), graduating in 1815.

Since his Savannah days Baker had been involved in religious activities, and at Princeton he led prayer meetings and provoked a major revival among the students. In 1816 he married Elizabeth McRobert, and he studied theology under a Presbyterian minister, Dr. William Hill, in Winchester, Virginia. That same year Baker was certified to preach, and he traveled to various southern locations evangelizing. By 1818 he was ministering in Harrisonburg and New Erection, Virginia. He was also an outstanding school teacher, and one of his pupils, Gessner Harrison, later became a prominent professor at the University of Virginia. By 1821 Baker was the pastor of the Second Church in

Washington, D.C., a prestigious post with presidents such as John Quincy Adams and Andrew Jackson as members of his congregation. In 1828 Baker moved back to Savannah. By 1830, although his ministerial career was flourishing, he was dismayed at his lack of recent converts. Therefore, in 1831 Baker, whose skill as a revivalist was unmatched in the South, began holding revival meetings in the coastal towns of Georgia and South Carolina. These revivals were so successful that he decided to give up his post and substantial salary at the Independent Church in Savannah to become a traveling evangelist.

After holding successful revivals throughout the southern Atlantic seaboard area, Baker moved to Ohio to preach. Unlike in the South, however, in Ohio he found himself beset by abolitionists. Even though not a slave owner, he believed that slavery was sanctioned by God and that no legislative body could outlaw the institution. In addition, Ohio abolitionists continually made harsh remarks about his southern friends. Consequently Baker wanted to return to the South, and when he was offered a post in Danville, Kentucky, he immediately accepted. He moved to Frankfort, Kentucky, where he preached for three years, then to Tuscaloosa, Alabama. He also conducted revivals at major cities throughout the South, including New Orleans, Mobile, and Memphis.

In 1840, at the age of forty-nine, Baker was a prominent Presbyterian minister, and the church sent him to the Republic of Texas, which proved to be fertile ground for a man of Baker's caliber. That same year he helped organize the presbytery of Brazos, the first in Texas, and he envisioned building a college. The church, however, relocated him to Holly Springs, Mississippi, where he ministered for several years. Baker, nevertheless, was infatuated with Texas, and in 1848 he returned to Austin, holding revival meetings throughout the state and ministering in Mexico. Although citizens had earlier approved of his plans to build Austin College, nothing had been accomplished in Baker's absence, so he revitalized its development. When the college was established in Huntsville in 1849, Baker, who was a guiding force behind the school, became its president. A skillful fundraiser, he procured $100,000 in cash and thousands of acres of land for the school. He was unsuccessful in his attempts to persuade the Texas legislature to endow scholarships for students at religious schools, but his efforts did help in the passage of the 1854 bill that provided a system of public education. He was an excellent administrator, but in 1857 he resigned his post as president in order to devote more time to raising funds for the college.

In the early years of Texas, Baker's work as an educator, administrator, and fundraiser were unsurpassed. In addition, the Presbyterian girl's college at Milford and the seminary at Austin grew out of his efforts. An accomplished writer, his published works include *A Series of Revival Sermons* (1847), *An Affectionate Address to Mothers* (1850), *An Affectionate Address to Fathers* (1852), *Plain and Scriptural View of Baptism* (1853), and *Baptism in a Nutshell* (1877). Baker was such a respected educational and religious figure in Texas that both branches of the state legislature immediately adjourned upon hearing of his death in Austin. Because of his outstanding service to Texas education, Daniel Baker College was formed in 1889 in Brownwood, Texas.

• Articles on Baker's accomplishments are in Tex. newspapers and records from Austin College. The most complete assessment of Baker's life is William Mumford Baker's biography, *The Life and Labors of Daniel Baker* (1858), which was written by Baker's son and is based on Baker's own unpublished autobiography. Additional accounts are in Henry A. White, *Southern Presbyterial Leaders* (1911), and P. E. Wallace, "The History of Austin College" (master's thesis, Univ. of Texas, 1924).

CECIL KIRK HUTSON

BAKER, Dorothy Dodds (21 Apr. 1907–17 June 1968), novelist, was born in Missoula, Montana, the daughter of Raymond Branson Dodds, a businessman, and Alice Grady. Dorothy spent much of her childhood years in California, where her father worked in the oil business. She was educated at Occidental College, Whittier College, and the University of California at Los Angeles, where she received a B.A. in French in 1929, whereupon she traveled to Paris. Her travels introduced her to Howard Baker, whom she married in 1930; they had two children. At this time she also began work on a novel that with considerable addition and revision would be published some ten years later in 1943 as her second book, *Trio*. She returned to the United States and earned an M.A. in French at the University of California at Berkeley in 1934, after which she assumed a teaching position at a small preparatory school, an experience on which she based the short story "A Glance Around" (1934).

She turned her full attention to writing after leaving the teaching profession in the mid-1930s, composing several short stories dealing with topics such as the San Francisco labor strikes, her grandmother's admiration for Herbert Hoover, and the Lamson trial.

During this period Baker began to write about her favorite topic—the world of jazz. She said on one occasion, "Jazz music was one of the very few things I knew much about, and the only thing, except writing, that I had a consistent, long-term interest in." Among her favorite songs were works by Ferdinand "Jelly Roll" Morton, Louis Armstrong, Duke Ellington, and Bix Beiderbecke. The latter artist's rise to stardom and sudden fall captured her imagination as an appropriate subject for a novel, and she wrote *Young Man with a Horn* (1938). This work encompasses all the energy and passion of a young white man transfixed by the African-American art form of jazz, which he felt a natural sympathy for since he had been raised to understand black ways and attitudes as they were expressed in the music.

The manuscript won Baker a literary fellowship from Houghton Mifflin Publishers; she was awarded $1,000 and promised publication of the work upon its completion. After the novel's release the prominent literary critic Clifton Fadiman proclaimed it "darned near perfect." The book made several bestseller lists and was published in England. Baker was touted as an expert on jazz, a title she quickly renounced, claiming that "nobody is" an expert in this fluid art form. *Young Man with a Horn* was made into a film in 1950, starring Lauren Bacall and Kirk Douglas, and some critics consider it a classic in its own right.

Baker's initial success in writing led to a peak in her career in 1943 when she published her second novel, *Trio*. While this novel may not match her earlier novel in style or grace, it came on the heels of Baker's receiving a Guggenheim fellowship in 1942 and also represented her first literary work based purely on imagination. *Trio* deals with the rivalry between a sophisticated female French professor and an unsuspecting young man for the attention of a female graduate student. With its overtones of lesbianism, the subject perhaps more than the style of the work drew critical response. Baker's work again attracted the attention of Clifton Fadiman, who this time wrote dismissively of the subject matter but worshipfully of the "superb craftsmanship." John Chamberlain of the *New York Times* wrote, "No doubt Mrs. Baker had to get *Trio* out of her system. Technically speaking, the book is first-rate" (10 July 1943). Such compensatory praise of style at the expense of theme suggests that the book overstepped sexual boundaries still firmly in place in the 1940s. Jane Rule in her book *Lesbian Images* (1975) devotes several pages to a discussion of Baker's work but reminds the reader that Baker denied that her work "had anything to do with lesbianism." Baker herself downplayed the book's references to lesbianism in interviews and typically responded with a reminder that the novel "was not considered in the least immoral" by the Commonwealth Club of California, which awarded it the General Literature Gold Medal in 1943.

In her fourth novel, *Cassandra at the Wedding* (1962), Baker also refers to relationships between women but this time in a less judgmental light. Where *Trio* presents lesbianism as overtly destructive—the lesbian "villain" is disgraced and then commits suicide—in the later novel same-sex relations are simply part of the psychological puzzle from which the protagonist emerges as a stronger, more independent woman. In a redemptive image at the end of the novel, Cassandra walks across the Bay Bridge with thoughts, not of suicide, but of life and art.

Baker died in Terra Bella, California. She claimed Ernest Hemingway as her role model, and like him she wrote in a style marked by simplicity and clarity of "phrase and story." However, her work left little lasting impression on the public. Although Baker won critical and popular acclaim with her first novel, *Trio* clouded her success because it presented themes less suited for the reader at large. Still, *Cassandra at the Wedding* remains a critical gem, overlooked but worthy of reexamination, for it is here that Baker joins a powerful simplicity of style with both generosity of tone and characters of genuine psychological complexity.

• There is a tape-recorded autobiographical interview with Baker in the Oral History Collection at Columbia University. Critical reviews of Dorothy Baker's work are in the *New York Times*, 4 July 1943, p. 6; the *New Yorker*, 10 July 1943, p. 62; the *Nation*, 10 July 1943, p. 51; *Publishers Weekly*, 31 Oct. 1966, p. 87; and *Saturday Review*, 21 Jan. 1967, p. 41. Other criticism is in Jane Rule's *Lesbian Images* (1975). Biographical references can be found in obituaries in the *New York Times*, 19 June 1968, and *Newsweek*, 1 July 1968.

KELLY CANNON

BAKER, Edward Dickinson (24 Feb. 1811–21 Oct. 1861), statesman and soldier, was born in London, England, the son of Edward Baker, an educator, and Lucy Dickinson. The family emigrated to the United States in 1815 and lived in Philadelphia for about ten years. The elder Baker ran a school that young Edward attended until he secured employment as a hand loom weaver. Attracted by Robert Dale Owen's utopian community, the family moved to New Harmony, Indiana, in 1825, remaining for several years before moving briefly to Belleville, Illinois, and then pushing on to Carrollton, Illinois. Baker read law with Judge A. W. Caverly and passed his qualifying exams at the age of nineteen; he was not admitted to the Illinois bar until he reached his majority two years later. In 1831 he married Mary Anne Lee, who was a widow with two children; the Bakers had four children.

Baker enlisted in the Illinois militia during the Black Hawk War of 1832 and was elected first lieutenant. Returning to Carrollton, he decided that his opportunities for advancement in the city were limited, so he moved to Springfield. There he practiced law, and a gifted orator, he entered politics as a Whig. Before long he became a political associate and friend of Abraham Lincoln. The Lincolns held such regard for Baker that they named their second son Edward Lincoln in his honor. Baker represented Sangamon County in the Illinois General Assembly from 1837 to 1840 and served as state senator from 1840 to 1844.

Elected in 1844 to the Twenty-ninth Congress as the only Whig from Illinois, Baker took his seat in the House of Representatives on 1 December 1845. He distinguished himself by advocating the acquisition of the Oregon Country and criticizing Whig opposition to the Mexican War. While still a member of Congress, Baker raised the Fourth Regiment of Illinois Volunteer Infantry and was commissioned its colonel. Reproached for accepting salary as both a colonel and a congressman, Baker resigned his seat in December 1846 and joined his troops on the battle front. His unit participated in the siege of Veracruz; Baker assumed the leadership of the brigade when its commander, General James Shields, was wounded at the battle of Cerro Gordo.

Mustered out of service at the close of the war, Baker relocated in Galena, Illinois, and resumed his law practice. He was soon participating in politics, serving as a presidential elector for Zachary Taylor in 1848.

Despite his recent arrival, Baker was elected to Congress again, this time from the Galena district, serving from 1849 to 1851. Midwestern Whigs, especially Lincoln, urged Baker's appointment as a member of Taylor's cabinet, but the new president ignored the recommendation. Except for his support of the Wilmot Proviso and remarks censuring southerners who advocated disunion, Baker's second term in Congress was unnoteworthy. Baker declined to run for reelection. Instead he made a contract to provide construction crews for the Panama Railroad Company and left at the end of his congressional term for the isthmus. He soon contracted Chagres disease (malaria) and returned to Galena to recuperate.

Disappointed with his professional and political prospects in Illinois, Baker moved with his family to California, arriving in San Francisco in June 1852. He quickly established himself as a leading criminal lawyer and orator. He incurred the disfavor of the San Francisco Vigilance Committee in 1856, when he defended Charles Cora, a gambler accused of murder. Baker's verbal eloquence and his insistence that Cora could never receive a fair trial in San Francisco resulted in a hung jury. In September 1859 Baker delivered the funeral oration for U.S. senator David Broderick, who had recently been killed in a duel. The eulogy brought Baker national prominence. He also became active in politics once more, moving from the Whig party into the new Republican organization when it organized in California.

Following his defeat as a Republican candidate for Congress in 1859, Baker accepted an invitation to take up residence in Oregon with the understanding that he would build popular support for the Republican party there and in return be the party's candidate for the U.S. Senate at the next senatorial election. Over the opposition of Democrats led by pro-slavery vice presidential candidate Joseph Lane, Baker, a strong advocate of popular sovereignty, was elected by the combined support of Republicans and Douglas Democrats. When he arrived in Washington, D.C., to take up his senatorial duties in December 1860, Baker found himself with a new prominence because of his past close friendship with the recently elected Lincoln. Baker traveled to Springfield at the request of the president-elect to discuss the national crisis, and he was accorded the honor of introducing Lincoln to the general public at his inauguration in March 1861.

Following the surrender of Fort Sumter, Baker accepted a colonelcy in the U.S. Army with the special assignment of raising troops in Pennsylvania and New York. His efforts proved so successful that Lincoln nominated him as brigadier general in the U.S. volunteers, a promotion Baker declined because it would require that he resign as the only U.S. senator from the Pacific Coast states. His last appearance in the Senate was on 1 August 1861, when he arrived in uniform and characterized Senator John C. Breckinridge's call for calm as "words of brilliant, polished treason." Given command of the "California Regiment," Baker was ordered in October 1861 to take part in a maneuver designed to force Confederate troops out of Leesburg, Virginia. He was killed when Union forces were repulsed at Ball's Bluff, a promontory on the Virginia bank of the Potomac River. A few newspaper editors blamed Baker for the defeat because of his impetuous order to send large numbers of troops against the Confederates, but the general public and most editors believed defeat was due to misjudgements by Baker's superiors. Baker was given a public funeral in Washington, D.C.

Although Baker served as a congressman for most districts in which he lived, he left little lasting impact on them because his residence in each was so brief. His skill as an orator and his tendency to champion causes that were popular in his district account for Baker's vote-getting abilities. Aside from his untimely death, Baker is best remembered as Lincoln's friend and for his activities in California.

• Many of Baker's speeches are reprinted in *Masterpieces of E. D. Baker*, ed. O. T. Shuck (1899). The only book-length biography is Harry C. Blair and Rebecca Tarshis, *Colonel Edward D. Baker: Lincoln's Constant Ally* (1960). Shorter works or references to Baker are Joseph Wallace, *Sketch of the Life and Public Services of Edward D. Baker* (1870); Elijah R. Kennedy, *The Contest for California in 1861: How Colonel E. D. Baker Saved the Pacific States for the Union* (1912); and William D. Fenton, "Edward Dickinson Baker," *Oregon Historical Society Quarterly* 9 (1908): 1–23.

EUGENE H. BERWANGER

BAKER, Ella Josephine (13 Dec. 1903–13 Dec. 1986), civil rights organizer, was born in Norfolk, Virginia, the daughter of Blake Baker, a waiter on the ferry between Norfolk and Washington, D.C., and Georgianna Ross. In rural North Carolina where Ella Baker grew up she experienced a strong sense of black community. Her grandfather, who had been a slave, acquired the land in Littleton on which he had slaved. He raised fruit, vegetables, cows, and cattle, which he shared with the community. He also served as the local Baptist minister. Baker's mother took care of the sick and needy.

After graduating in 1927 from Shaw University in Raleigh, North Carolina, Baker moved to New York City. She had dreamed of doing graduate work in sociology at the University of Chicago, but it was 1929, and times were hard. Few jobs were open to black women except teaching, which Baker refused to do because "this was the thing that everybody figures you could do" (Cantarow and O'Malley, p. 62). To survive, Baker waitressed and worked in a factory. During 1929–1930 she was an editorial staff member of the *American West Indian News* and in 1932 became an editorial assistant for George Schuyler's *Negro National News*, for which she also worked as office manager. In 1930 she was on the board of directors of Harlem's Own Cooperative and worked with the Dunbar Housewives' League on tenant and consumer rights. In 1930 she helped organize and in 1931 became the national executive director of the Young Negroes' Cooperative League, a consumer cooperative. Baker also taught consumer education for the Works Progress Administration in the 1930s and, according to a letter written in 1936, divided her time between consumer education and working at the public library at 135th Street. She married Thomas J. Roberts in 1940 or 1941; they had no children.

Beginning in 1938 Baker worked with the National Association for the Advancement of Colored People (NAACP), and from 1941 to 1946 she traveled throughout the country but especially in the South for the NAACP, first as field secretary and then as director of branches to recruit members, raise money, and organize local campaigns. She became "something of a legend for her prowess in organizing youth chapters in the South" (Branch, p. 231). Among the issues in which she was involved were the antilynching campaign, the equal-pay-for-black-teachers movement, and job training for black workers. Baker's strength was the ability to evoke in people a feeling of common need and the belief that people together can change the conditions under which they live. Her philosophy of organizing was "you start where the people are" and "strong people don't need strong leaders." In her years with the NAACP, Baker formed a network of people involved with civil rights throughout the South that proved invaluable in the struggles of the 1950s and 1960s. She resigned from her leadership role in the national NAACP in 1946 because she felt it was too bureaucratic. She also had agreed to take responsibility for raising her niece. Back in New York City, she worked with the NAACP on school desegregation, sat on the Commission on Integration for the New York City Board of Education, and in 1952 became president of the New York City NAACP chapter. In 1953 she resigned from the NAACP presidency to run unsuccessfully for the New York City Council on the Liberal party ticket. To support herself, she worked as director of the Harlem Division of the New York City Committee of the American Cancer Society.

In January 1958 Bayard Rustin and Stanley Levison persuaded Baker to go to Atlanta to set up the office of the Southern Christian Leadership Conference (SCLC) to organize the Crusade for Citizenship, a voter registration program in the South. Baker agreed to go for six weeks and stayed for two and a half years. She was named acting director of the SCLC and set about organizing the crusade to open simultaneously in twenty-one cities. She was concerned, however, that the SCLC board of preachers did not sufficiently support voter registration. Baker had increasing difficulty working with Martin Luther King, Jr., whom she described as "too self-centered and cautious" (Weisbrot, p. 33). Because she thought that she would never be appointed executive director, Baker persuaded her friend the Reverend John L. Tilley to assume the post in April, and she became associate director. After King fired Tilley in January 1959, he asked Baker once again to be executive director, but his board insisted that her position must be in an acting capacity. Baker, however, functioned as executive director and signed her name accordingly. In April 1960 the executive director post of SCLC was accepted by the Reverend Wyatt Tee Walker.

After hundreds of students sat in at segregated lunch counters in early 1960, Baker persuaded the SCLC to invite them to the Southwide Youth Leadership Conference at Shaw University on Easter weekend. From this meeting the Student Nonviolent Coordinating Committee (SNCC) was eventually formed. Although the SCLC leadership pressured Baker to influence the students to become a youth chapter of SCLC, she refused and encouraged the students to beware of SCLC's "leader-centered orientation." She felt that the students had a right to decide their own structure. Baker's speech "More Than a Hamburger," which followed King's and James Lawson's speeches, urged the students to broaden their social vision of discrimination to include more than integrating lunch counters. Julian Bond described the speech as "an eye opener" and probably the best of the three. "She didn't say, 'Don't let Martin Luther King tell you what to do,'" Bond remembers, "but you got the real feeling that that's what she meant" (Hampton and Fayer, p. 63). James Forman, who became director of SNCC a few months later, said Baker felt SCLC "was depending too much on the press and on the promotion of Martin King, and was not developing enough indigenous leadership across the South" (Forman, p. 216).

After the Easter conference weekend, Baker resigned from the SCLC, and after having helped Walker learn his job she went to work for SNCC in August. To support herself she worked as a human relations consultant for the Young Women's Christian Association in Atlanta. Baker continued as the "ever-present mentor" (Garrow, p. 518) to SNCC civil rights workers. At a rancorous SNCC meeting at Highlander Folk School in Tennessee in August 1961, Baker mediated between one faction advocating political action through voter registration and another faction advocating nonviolent direct action. She suggested that voter registration would necessitate confrontation that would involve them in direct action. Baker believed that voting was necessary but did not believe that the franchise would cure all problems. She also understood the appeal of nonviolence as a tactic, but she did not believe in it personally: "I have not seen anything in the nonviolent technique that can dissuade me from challenging somebody who wants to step on my neck. If necessary, if they hit me, I might hit them back" (Cantarow and O'Malley, p. 82).

After the 1964 Mississippi summer in which northern students went south to work in voter registration, SNCC decided to organize the Mississippi Freedom Democratic party (MFDP) as an alternative to the regular Democratic party in Mississippi. Thousands of people registered to vote in beauty parlors and barber shops, churches, or wherever a registration booth could be set up. Baker set up the Washington, D.C., office of the MFDP and delivered the keynote speech at its Jackson, Mississippi, state convention. The MFDP delegates were not seated at the Democratic

National Convention in Washington, D.C., but their influence helped to elect many local black leaders in Mississippi in the following years and forced a rules change in the Democratic party to include more women and minorities as delegates to the national convention.

From 1962 to 1967 Baker worked on the staff of the Southern Conference Education Fund (SCEF), dedicated to helping black and white people work together. During that time she organized a civil liberties conference in Washington, D.C., and worked with Carl Braden on a mock civil rights commission hearing in Chapel Hill, North Carolina. In her later years in New York City she served on the board of the Puerto Rican Solidarity Committee, founded and was president of the Fund for Education and Legal Defense, which raised money primarily for scholarships for civil rights activists to return to college, and was vice chair of the Mass Party Organizing Committee. She was also a sponsor of the National United Committee to Free Angela Davis and All Political Prisoners, a consultant to both the Executive Council and the Commission for Social and Racial Justice of the Episcopal church, and a member of the Charter Group for a Pledge of Conscience and the Coalition of Concerned Black Americans. Until her death in New York City she continued to inspire, nurture, scold, and advise the many young people who had worked with her during her career of political activism.

Ella Baker's ideas and careful organizing helped to shape the civil rights movement from the 1930s through the 1960s. She had the ability to listen to people and to inspire them to organize around issues that would empower their lives. At a time when there were no women in leadership in the SCLC, Baker served as its executive director. Hundreds of young people became politically active because of her respect and concern for them.

• Ella Baker's papers are in the Schomburg Center for Research in Black Culture in New York City. Ellen Cantarow and Susan Gushee O'Malley, *Moving the Mountain* (1980), and *Fundi: The Story of Ella Baker*, a film directed and produced by Joanne Grant (1980), are major sources. Important background references include James Forman, *The Making of Black Revolutionaries* (1972); Clayborne Carson, *In Struggle: SNCC and the Black Awakening of the 1960s* (1981); David Garrow, *Bearing the Cross: Martin Luther King, Jr., and the Southern Christian Leadership Conference* (1986); Robert Weisbrot, *Freedom Bound* (1990); Charles Payne, *I've Got the Light of Freedom: The Organizing Tradition and the Mississippi Freedom Struggle* (1995); Mary King, *Freedom Song: A Personal Story of the 1960s Civil Rights Movement* (1987); Adam Fairclough, *To Redeem the Soul of America: The Southern Christian Leadership Conference and Martin Luther King, Jr.* (1987); Sally Belfrage, *Freedom Summer* (1965); Gerda Lerner, *Black Women in White America: A Documentary History* (1972); and Henry Hampton and Steve Fayer, *Voices of Freedom* (1991). An obituary is in the *New York Times*, 17 Dec. 1986.

SUSAN GUSHEE O'MALLEY

BAKER, Frank "Home Run." *See* Baker, Home Run.

BAKER, George (22 May 1915–7 May 1975), cartoonist, was born in Lowell, Massachusetts, the son of Harry Baker, a middle-class merchant, and Mary Portman. In 1923 the family moved to Chicago, where Baker attended Roosevelt High School. After graduation he held a succession of inconsequential jobs (truck driver, cleaner and dyer assistant, salesman, clerk) before becoming assistant (c. 1935) to a commercial artist. In 1937 he applied to Disney Studios for a job, was accepted, and moved to California. He worked in the Effects Department on full-length features such as *Pinocchio, Dumbo*, and *Bambi*. In June 1941 in the midst of the animators' strike against Disney, Baker was drafted into the army and sent to Fort Monmouth, New Jersey, for basic training, after which he was assigned to the Signal Corps to do animation for training films.

Hoping to sell a cartoon feature about army life to civilian outlets, Baker reached into "psychological reality" for his protagonist and created "an average soldier," whom Baker saw as a hapless and perpetual victim in the army's grand scheme of things. "The actual state of mind of a soldier was more authentic and real to me than his outer appearance," Baker wrote, "so therefore my character looked resigned, tired, helpless, and beaten." Unsuccessful at selling the feature, Baker gave up on the idea until the Defense Recreation Committee in New York ran a cartoon contest for soldiers in the spring of 1942; he submitted one of his cartoons and won. The resultant publicity attracted the attention of Major Hartzell Spence, who was then in New York, assembling material and a staff to produce the weekly armed forces tabloid magazine, *Yank*. Invited to submit a cartoon every week, Baker titled his feature the *Sad Sack* (employing army slang for a worthless soldier, "a sad sack of shit") and began contributing with the first issue of *Yank*, 17 June 1942. After a month or so Baker was transferred to the staff of the magazine, and he served there for the duration of World War II. *Yank* sent Baker to military installations all over the world to expose him to every possible phase of army life so that he might reflect it in the cartoon.

As perennial low man on the regimental totem pole, the Sad Sack was popular from the very start. He epitomized the frustrations and disappointments of Everyman, dragged somewhat reluctantly into a military bureaucracy he did not understand and could never master. The Sack's adventures took place entirely in pantomime; each cartoon was a series of eight to ten borderless pictures that progressively depicted the mounting dilemma of the week. Like some dumb animal being inexplicably punished for behaving in a perfectly natural way, the Sack was all the more pitiful for being mute.

The Sad Sack's personal agonies begin immediately upon his induction: when his first uniform fits him perfectly, his sergeant orders him to take it off so that he can be supplied with one that does not. The Sack always gets the worst assignments in camp. He is perpetually on K.P. ("kitchen police") duty, peeling potatoes and washing pots and pans. When he spends a whole day cleaning the latrine and making it spotless, his comrades mess it up in minutes when they return from the day's training. When he works hard, his superiors are promoted, and he gets more K.P. When he finds a girl, she deserts him for a sergeant or an officer. The Sad Sack never wins, but he never gives up either; he always comes back the next week.

Baker drew with a bold outline, which he soon began to embellish with hayey shading, creating a gritty, raunchy ambience for the feature. Human anatomy as the cartoonist portrayed it was bony and lumpy, and clothing draped on such constructions forever bagged at the knee and wrinkled everywhere. The Sack himself was a chinless apparition of comic as well as sad aspect with his sausage nose, huge ears, and meek expression; and the forces opposed to him—sergeants and officers—were lupine predators, fanged and snappish, intimidating even in appearance. The *Sad Sack* was primitive—even crude—in its visual style, but that suited the subject: a powerless cog in a machine he never made, the Sack with his sagging, rumpled, awkward physique and hangdog expression was the personification of the army's typical private, a pathetic dogface, frazzled and worn, destined to be defeated by every circumstance he encountered. Wrote Baker (in *The New Sad Sack*): "The greatest source of material for the Sack was the Army itself. . . . [A]ny idea based on the machinations of the Army, the red tape, officers or the thousands of consistent inconsistencies of the system would be accepted and understood by G.I.'s everywhere. The underlying story of the Sad Sack was his struggle with the Army in which I tried to symbolize the sum total of the difficulties and frustrations of all enlisted men."

After the war Baker left the army, married Brenda Emsley (in 1946), moved to Los Angeles, and formed Sad Sack, Inc., through which he marketed his creation. The Sack also resumed civilian life. Bell Syndicate had been distributing reprints of the *Yank* cartoons since 1945, and on 5 May 1946 it launched a Sunday *Sad Sack* comic strip with entirely new material. But it was a somewhat depressing feature. As a portrait of civilian life, the strip seemed unduly cynical and bitter: here the Sack encountered nothing but predatory con men, crooks, and heartless, conniving women, and he was victimized by their malevolent premeditation rather than by the uncomprehending and therefore comic blunderings of monumental military inefficiency. The newspaper strip ceased after a couple of years.

Baker had more success with a comic book incarnation of the Sack (for which pantomime was abandoned). Launched by Harvey Publications in the summer of 1949, *The Sad Sack* lasted into the 1980s. Initially a civilian in the book, the Sack reenlisted in the spring of 1951, and his return to army life made the comic book, aimed at a teenage audience (not at servicemen), a bestseller during the Korean War and after even though Baker no longer drew the feature (except for covers). The Sack also inspired a 1957 motion picture, starring Jerry Lewis. Although the Sad Sack secured a living for Baker until his death in Los Angeles from cancer, the Sack never again achieved emblematic status for an entire generation, as he had during World War II, when he suffered in silence as did Everyman in uniform.

• The chief source for most of the information about George Baker's life is the obituary in the *New York Times*, 9 May 1975. A few additional details can be found in Ron Goulart, ed., *The Encyclopedia of American Comics* (1990); in "Sad Sack," an article by Gordon Campbell and Mary Campbell in *Cartoonist PROfiles* 69 (Mar. 1986): 70–73; and in the front matter of the two Simon and Schuster collections of the *Yank* cartoons, *The Sad Sack* (1944) and *The New Sad Sack* (1946), especially the latter, which begins with Baker's own account of his life before and with the Sack.

ROBERT C. HARVEY

BAKER, George Fisher (27 Mar. 1840–2 May 1931), banker, was born in Troy, New York, the son of George Ellis Baker, a clerk, and Eveline Stevens. The family's roots were in Massachusetts, and Baker spent much time with his grandmother in Dedham. He attended school there until 1854, when he enrolled in the Seward Institute in Florida, New York. In 1856 he became a clerk in the New York Banking Department in Albany. In 1861 he served briefly as secretary to Governor Edwin Morgan, subsequently returning to his previous job.

As a clerk for the Banking Department, Baker became acquainted with John Thompson. When the latter organized First National Bank of New York in 1863, he asked Baker to become paying teller. In 1865 Baker became cashier and a member of the board of directors. Much of the bank's business at that time was related to selling government bonds that financed the war effort. Baker married Florence Tucker Baker (same surname but no relation) in 1869. They had four daughters and one son during the next nine years.

During the panic of 1873, First National president Samuel Thompson feared that a run by depositors might drain the bank's entire capital and surplus. Baker and vice president Frederick Thompson convinced him not to close the bank. Predicting that the bank would weather the panic, Baker offered to buy the president's First National stock. The contract they negotiated allowed Baker to pay for the stock whenever he wished, at which time Samuel Thompson would resign. The agreement made Baker the bank's dominant figure, although he did not purchase the stock and become president until 1877.

Baker built First National into one of the most important banks in the country. Much of its business focused on the purchase and sale of industrial, railroad, and government bonds; however, more and more frequently the bank dealt in corporate stocks, as Baker became a close friend and business associate of J. Pierpont Morgan. In 1879 the bank had capital of

$500,000 and surplus of $1 million. In 1901 the bank paid a dividend of $800 a share in cash and $1,100 in new stock as part of a plan to increase its capital to $10 million; surplus had already risen to $10 million. After regulators criticized the bank's stock holdings, Baker in 1908 created a securities affiliate called First Security Company, which was also capitalized at $10 million.

Because of his bank's prominence in financing corporations, many businesses asked Baker to join their boards of directors. By 1897 he was connected to thirty-one enterprises; by 1913 the number had grown to fifty-seven. Among these were U.S. Steel, American Telephone & Telegraph, Mutual Life Insurance, New York Central Railroad, Southern Railway, and Central Railroad of New Jersey.

During the panic of 1907, Morgan, Baker, and James Stillman of National City Bank organized rescue operations to prevent the failure of several important trust companies and brokerage firms in New York. Because of their actions, the monetary stringency was brief and did not precipitate a major depression.

In 1909 Baker retired as president of First National and became chairman of the board with full executive powers, a position he retained for life. This change allowed him to maintain complete control of the bank without having to handle routine business.

In 1913 Baker testified before the Pujo "Money Trust" investigation—which focused on a handful of powerful bankers suspected of controlling the growth of the American economy through their control of finance capital—and became nationally famous for the first time. He argued that owning large amounts of stock in several businesses did not mean he "controlled" them; however, he also refused to admit that he controlled First National. Baker did startle many people when he observed that the concentration of credit and money in the hands of a relatively small number of men had gone about far enough.

After the United States entered World War I, Baker was on the committee, led by Benjamin Strong of the New York Federal Reserve Bank, that managed the New York money market so that funds were available for government borrowing and the stock market. Baker often had the final say over how much each bank would contribute to the call money market. In addition, Baker committed his bank to purchasing more than $3 billion in Treasury securities between 1917 and 1925.

After 1915 Baker became a noted philanthropist, giving away an estimated $22.2 million. His single largest contribution was to Harvard University to build the Graduate School of Business Administration. In memory of his uncle, Fisher Ames Baker, he donated $2 million to Dartmouth, and to honor his parents' memory he donated $750,000 to the National Cathedral in Washington, D.C. He also gave $1 million or more to each of the following: American Red Cross, Metropolitan Museum of New York, Cathedral of St. John the Divine (New York), New York Hospi-

tal, Columbia University, New York University Medical School, and Cornell University.

Around 1920 Baker developed diabetes, but in spite of this he retained his dominant role at First National and First Security. In 1928–1929 he disregarded advice from some directors and refused to let First Security sell some of its overvalued stocks in order to repay $29 million in loans to the bank. As a result, the bank's losses were huge when the stock market crashed. Baker died in New York before market values had recovered. However, the bank had such a large surplus ($100 million in 1929) that even the crash and depression could not undermine its soundness. After mergers and name changes it survived in the 1990s as Citibank.

Baker was an outstanding representative of the bankers who helped build this country. He was always optimistic that the economy would expand, despite temporary setbacks, and he was always calm during financial panics (the bank survived four during his lifetime). He was always honest and trustworthy in his business dealings, which made him a valuable ally, and he always stood ready to aid government financing on a generous scale. As a result, he became known as the dean of American bankers during the 1920s.

• There have been two full-length biographies of Baker: Albert Bigelow Paine, *George Fisher Baker, a Biography* (1920), and Sheridan A. Logan, *George F. Baker and His Bank, 1840–1955: A Double Biography* (1981). Both of these works are hagiographic but valuable; Logan provides verbatim copies of family correspondence and oral remembrances of Baker that reveal his character and temperament. Baker's association with J. Pierpont Morgan is discussed in Vincent P. Carosso, *The Morgans: Private International Bankers, 1854–1913* (1987), and Ron Chernow, *The House of Morgan* (1990). Lester V. Chandler, *Benjamin Strong, Central Banker* (1958), discusses the panic of 1907 and Baker's work with the New York money market during World War I. For Baker's testimony before the Pujo Committee and other material on First National, see articles published in the *New York Times* in 1913. See also House Subcommittee of the Committee on Banking and Currency, *Money Trust Investigation of Financial and Monetary Conditions in the United States under House Resolutions Numbers 429 and 504* (1913), and House Committee on Banking and Currency, *Report of the Committee Appointed Pursuant to H.R. 429 and 504 to Investigate the Concentration of Money and Credit*, 62d Cong., 2d sess., 1913. An obituary is in the *New York Times*, 3 May 1931.

SUE C. PATRICK

BAKER, George Pierce (4 Apr. 1866–6 Jan. 1935), professor of drama, was born in Providence, Rhode Island, the son of George Pierce Baker, a physician, and Lucy Daily Cady, who encouraged the frail boy's interest in intellectual and cultural activities and took him to the theater from an early age. Childhood performances for family and friends and scrapbooks of clippings of touring stars he saw testify to his passionate interest.

At Providence High School he joined the Debating Society, helped found the school newspaper, wrote and recited light verse (which "made him much in demand at social gatherings"), and entertained his ailing mother, who died when he was seventeen. During a lonely freshman year at Harvard, he often attended Boston theaters. Letters to his father reveal serious, analytical interest in acting and theater's emotional appeal, which he always valued more highly than a play's literary aspects.

At Harvard, Baker studied drama within the limits of English composition or rhetoric courses. Drama courses were not then available at American universities; Baker would pioneer in developing such offerings.

Elected editor in chief of the *Harvard Monthly* for 1886–1887, Baker gained considerable personal prestige by persuading distinguished alumni to write for the young publication, vastly increasing its circulation, and turning it into a literary magazine for all New England.

Phi Beta Kappa at graduation, looking forward to life as a writer, and expecting an editorship offer from Scribner's, Baker disdained a possible instructorship at "a western university," saying "The more I have thought of teaching, the more repugnant the idea has grown." When Scribner's made no offer, the deeply despondent graduate recovered by wintering at a friend's New Mexico ranch. Returning to join his father for a London trip during Queen Victoria's Jubilee, he found Dr. Baker had cancer (he died two years later) and was unable to travel.

Touring Europe alone that summer of 1888, young Baker encountered many of his American friends, one of whom introduced him to Ibsen's works in Berlin, and later, in London, to English "Ibsenites" who became important connections to British and Continental theater circles. In London Baker learned of his appointment as instructor in English at Harvard, where he who had found the idea of teaching "repugnant" would spend the next thirty-six years.

Baker's early teaching and publications in argumentation and public address led to promotions to assistant professor (1895) and full professor (1905), but drama remained his deepest interest. In 1890 Baker took over a course introduced in 1888 by his friend and mentor Barrett Wendell. English 14, "Drama Exclusive of Shakespeare from the Miracle Plays to the Closing of the Theatres," was possibly the first such course at an American university, and Baker developed it into the first course he regarded as his own. He taught it continuously, mostly to graduate students, until 1921. Baker treated plays as scripts for actors, not as literary texts, pointing up stage effects and implicit business that might be missed by readers. This innovative approach became traditional as Baker's students introduced courses modeled on it in colleges all over the country.

In 1893 Baker married Christina Hopkinson at the vacation home of her uncle, Harvard's president, Charles W. Eliot. The couple had four children.

Baker's most famous course, a playwriting seminar introduced to Harvard in 1905–1906 after a tryout at Radcliffe, attracted national attention when *Salvation Nell*, written in the first class by junior Edward Sheldon, was produced and starred in by Minnie Maddern Fiske. Baker was in France as the 1907–1908 Hyde lecturer at the Sorbonne. Sheldon, with other students, organized the Harvard Dramatic Club to produce plays drawn largely from Baker's new course. Returning to Harvard in June 1908, Baker found ambitious student playwrights clamoring to enroll in English 47.

From 1914 to 1924 Baker held his popular 47 Workshop, an extracurricular laboratory theater whose productions in a cramped basement allowed playwrights to see their scripts fully staged, learning from Baker's comments and the written critiques required of audience members.

As the program's fame and his ambitions for it grew, Baker encountered increasing resistance from Harvard's conservative administration. After spending years consulting architects, Baker had plans for a new theater building in 1914, only to have President A. L. Lowell bar him from pursuing funds to build it. Later, permission to direct a Broadway production was refused as inappropriate for a Harvard professor.

In 1915–1916 an advanced course, English 47a, was added, and to attract mature playwrights Baker prepared the first of his annual catalogs of Harvard drama offerings: 47 Workshop productions and related English and fine arts courses—practically a "School of the Theater," though not officially recognized.

In 1924 President Lowell ordered the 47 Workshop's inadequate building restored to dormitory use. Baker resigned, accepting Yale University's offer to become professor of the history and technique of drama, chairman of America's first graduate department of drama, and director of a university theater endowed by a gift from Edward S. Harkness. Baker's resignation caused an angry uproar in the Massachusetts legislature and the press; Heywood Broun spoke for other Harvard/Baker alumni when he bitterly quipped, "Yale 47, Harvard 0."

Baker staffed his Yale department with graduates of his Harvard programs and built the theater of his dreams for it. From his base at Yale, he expanded his career-long efforts to create a fertile environment for great American drama to emerge. Among other projects, he helped organize the National Theatre Conference, which elected him its first president in 1932.

After four decades of finding and encouraging playwrights and training theater artists, teachers, and audiences, Baker retired in 1933 due to illness. *Theatre Arts Monthly* devoted its annual July "tributary theatre" issue to Baker's influence on the nation's theater. Two years later, Baker died in a New York City hospital.

Any Baker alumni list is a "Who Was Who" of American theater: playwrights Eugene O'Neill, S. N. Behrman, Sidney Howard, Philip Barry, and Albert Maltz, among others; Theresa Helburn and other Theatre Guild founders; Broadway directors from George Abbott to Elia Kazan; critics John Mason

Brown and Kenneth Macgowan; designer/teachers Robert Edmond Jones, Lee Simonson, Donald Oenslager, and Stanley McCandless; Federal Theatre head Hallie Flanagan Davis; and other leaders of community and collegiate theaters, many of whom were still working well into the second half of the century. Given the prominence and contributions of his students, George Pierce Baker can be regarded as the single most influential teacher of drama and theater in the United States in the first half of the twentieth century.

• The Harvard University Library's Theatre Collection and the Yale University Department of Drama Library contain archival materials related to Baker. His book *The Principles of Argumentation* (1893) and the two collections he edited, *Specimens of Argumentation* (1893) and *The Forms of Public Address* (1904), made his first academic reputation. His two other books result from definitive changes in direction, first toward Elizabethan and Shakespearean studies, which culminated in *The Development of Shakespeare as a Dramatist* (1907), and then toward concentrating on teaching playwrights in his *Dramatic Technique* (1919). Baker's teaching was examined in Elden T. Smith, "George Pierce Baker: A Critical Study of His Influence as a Teacher of Theatre Arts" (thesis, Case Western Reserve Univ., 1947). The most exhaustive list of Baker's published and unpublished writings, from books and plays to newspaper articles, is in Wisner Payne Kinne's meticulously annotated biography, *George Pierce Baker and the American Theatre* (1954), which also includes lists of published plays by Baker's students as well as biographical materials. Kinne documents Baker's early work staging Shakespeare on Elizabethan-style stages and highly creative writing and staging of historical pageants as well as his contributions to the establishment of Harvard University's famed Theatre Collection—all usually overlooked in brief biographical summaries. An obituary is in the *New York Times*, 7 Jan. 1935.

DANIEL S. KREMPEL

BAKER, Harvey Humphrey (11 Apr. 1869–10 Apr. 1915), juvenile court judge, was born in Brookline, Massachusetts, the son of James Baker, a merchant, and Harriet M. Humphrey. The child of a prosperous New England family with deep roots in the region, Baker did his college preparatory work at the Roxbury Latin School before entering Harvard University, where his scholarship earned him an A.B. in political science with Phi Beta Kappa honors in 1891. In college he worked as a friendly visitor for the Boston Children's Aid Society and continued to do so while attending Harvard Law School. He received his law degree and a master's in 1894, commenced the practice of law, and shortly thereafter began a lifelong connection with the Brookline law firm (later known as) Hayes, Williams, Baker & Hersey. Baker spent his first year clerking in the township's police court and then served as a special justice from 1895 until 1906, when Massachusetts governor Curtis Guild selected him to become the first judge of the newly created Boston juvenile court.

Juvenile courts were established in the early twentieth century to remove children from the criminal justice system and to provide a less adversarial setting where a sole judge could hear all of the cases involving neglected, dependent, and delinquent children. Although a bachelor, Baker epitomized the popular image of the juvenile court judge as a fatherly figure seeking to aid and rehabilitate children, instead of simply to punish them for any crimes they had committed. He was renowned for his ability to see the child's point of view as well as appreciate the parents' concerns. In a tribute, a staff member wrote, "His work proved the soundness of some of the principles of the juvenile court idea—first, that the question, 'What shall we do with the offender?' is more important than 'How shall we punish the offence?' second, before we can decide intelligently what to do with the offender we must know him; third, to know him takes time" (*Upbuilder*, p. 9). During his nine-year tenure, Baker helped to make the Boston juvenile court into a model for progressive-minded reformers, who praised him for establishing connections between the court and the city's social welfare agencies.

At annual meetings of the National Probation Association and the National Conference of Charities and Corrections, Baker shared his ideas with social welfare leaders from across the country, especially his belief in the efficacy of "private hearings" for children's cases. He helped to popularize this practice, which reduced the number of people present during the hearing of a child's case in order to protect a family's privacy. In an article about private hearings for the *Annals of the American Academy of Political and Social Science* (1910), Baker likened his role to that of a physician trying to "ascertain the facts and causes of the delinquency of the child" and argued that a more secluded setting made it easier to determine the proper remedy.

Troubled by the persistence of "baffling cases" involving children who would not reform, Baker increasingly turned his attention to the emerging psychological approaches to deviance. He helped found the Massachusetts Society for Mental Hygiene in 1914 and served as its president that year. Baker called for the construction of child guidance clinics to study and treat the difficult cases passing through the nation's juvenile courts but died of double pneumonia in Brookline before seeing juvenile justice move in this more medical direction. His death however, prompted his friends and associates to raise the funds necessary to build and endow a clinic for the Boston juvenile court. It opened in April 1917 and was named the Judge Baker Foundation in his honor. The founders declared, "There can be no finer memorial than this for one who literally gave his life in the service of the juvenile court" (*Upbuilder*, p. 2).

Baker's reputation will forever be intertwined with the early twentieth-century efforts at juvenile rehabilitation. Praised during his lifetime, the institutions his generation built came under attack during the height of deinstitutionalization in the 1960s, when juvenile courts were characterized as instruments of social control that deprived poor children of their rights. The trend in the late twentieth century has been to criminalize juvenile court procedure and to treat children, especially violent offenders, like adults. These developments suggest that Baker's principles are no longer guiding juvenile justice.

• Baker laid out his vision for juvenile justice in "Private Hearings: Their Advantages and Disadvantages," *Annals of the American Academy of Political and Social Science* 36 (July 1910): 80–84. An important source on Baker remains *Harvey Humphrey Baker, Upbuilder of the Juvenile Court* (1920); published by the Judge Baker Foundation, the volume contains a collection of his writings and a short biographical sketch by Roy M. Cushman, secretary of the foundation. For the history of juvenile justice in twentieth-century America, see David J. Rothman, *Conscience and Convenience: The Asylum and Its Alternatives in Progressive America* (1980); in Boston specifically, see Eric C. Schneider, *In the Web of Class: Delinquents and Reformers in Boston, 1810s–1930s* (1992). For contemporary assessments of Baker's life, see obituaries in *The Brookline (Mass.) Chronicle*, 17 Apr. 1915, and *The Survey* (24 Apr. 1915).

DAVID SPINOZA TANENHAUS

BAKER, Henry Brooks (29 Dec. 1837–4 Apr. 1920), public health pioneer and author, was born in Brattleboro, Vermont, the son of Ezra Baker and Deborah Knowlton Bigelow. Ezra Baker died when Henry was three. In 1849 the family (Deborah had remarried) moved to Bunker Hill, Ingham County, Michigan, and a year later moved on to Mason, the county seat, ten miles south of Lansing. Henry left home before he reached his fourteenth birthday. For the next few years he worked and attended school irregularly.

At the start of the Civil War Baker left his teaching position in southern Illinois and returned to Lansing, Michigan, to study medicine with Dr. I. H. Bartholomew. In 1861 and 1862 Baker attended medical lectures while studying chemistry at the University of Michigan.

In the summer of 1862 Baker enlisted in Company A, Twentieth Michigan Infantry, serving as a hospital steward for the next two years. He later wrote that these years were "memorable ones to him in that he was enabled to gain much practice and valuable information in surgery, being in reality an assistant at the operating table whenever and wherever there were battles in which his division was engaged" (*Portrait and Biographical Album of Ingham and Livingston Counties, Michigan*, p. 205). In July 1864 he was promoted to assistant surgeon in medical charge of the regiment. Although captured in Virginia at the Wilderness, Baker was soon released.

After the war, Baker attended the Bellevue Hospital Medical College in New York City, obtaining his M.D. in 1866. He then returned to Michigan and practiced medicine with Bartholomew for a year. In 1867 he married Fannie H. Howard, daughter of Sanford Howard, then secretary of the State Board of Agriculture at Lansing. The couple had six children. From the time of his marriage until 1870 Baker practiced in Wenona (now West Bay City).

Moving back to Lansing in 1870, Baker was appointed by the State Medical Society to a committee set up to superintend the compilation of vital statistics collected by the secretary of state. He compiled an 835-page volume of statistics of Michigan for 1870 based on the U.S. census. Baker was in charge of this committee for the next thirteen years and designed many of the medical and health-related forms and tables used by the state in this process for the next twenty years. From 1870 to 1873 he served as Michigan's first registrar of vital statistics. The original statistical work done by Baker aroused considerable interest. William A. Howard, while laying the cornerstone of the State Capitol on 2 October 1873, based much of his speech on Baker's report.

When Baker had moved to Lansing in 1870 he brought with him a bill designed to create a state board of health. This was innovative because only one or two other states had such a board at that time. Baker's bill differed from others that had been proposed elsewhere because the Michigan board was to be only advisory. Therefore, it could not be seen as usurping the functions of local boards but rather as doing "generalizing" work. The emphasis was to be on moral suasion rather than mandates. The bill was presented to the legislature for 1870–1871 but did not pass until 1873. Most of the later state boards of health were based on this "Michigan Plan." Upon establishment of the Michigan State Board of Health in July 1873 Baker was unanimously elected secretary, a position he held until 1904. In addition to the formal aspects of his work with the state board of health, Baker wrote many letters educating local officers throughout the state on public health matters.

Baker's interest in education did not remain confined to the official state network. During the period 1890–1895 he engaged upon a "campaign of education" for the general public. The production and circularization of printed matter pursuing all aspects of the campaign became so extensive that some spoke of Baker's office as the "State Literary Bureau." Baker worked especially with teachers throughout the state, either speaking himself at teacher institutes or having another member of the board do so. He also had the board sponsor carefully planned regional meetings, called Sanitary Institutes, particularly in the rural areas, to interest the general public in health matters.

As secretary of the board, Baker in 1886 made a vigorous plea for the establishment of a hygienic laboratory at the University of Michigan. This laboratory was among the earliest of its kind in the United States. The university recognized Baker's abilities by naming him the nonresident lecturer on the administration of health laws from 1898 through 1905.

The American Public Health Association elected Baker its president in 1889–1990. He was vice president of the American Social Science Association for many years. He also served as vice president of the State Medical Society for a term. The Royal Meteorological Society of England and the French Society of Hygiene later elected him to membership. One of Baker's main research interests was the relationship of climate and disease; the American Climatological Association elected him to membership.

After leaving the state's employ in 1904, Baker moved to Holland, on the western edge of Michigan, thirty miles south of Muskegon. Here he ran a private health resort until his death in Ypsilanti, Michigan.

During his three and one-half decades with the state Baker accomplished much both to elevate the professional level of public health work and to educate the general public in hygiene. He thus became the founder and promoter of public health in Michigan.

• The Bentley Historical Library, University of Michigan, contains one linear foot of Baker's papers, 1871–1900, although some of this material relates to one of Baker's sons. The Bentley also has two portraits. In addition to Baker's publications already mentioned, his annual reports of the Michigan State Board of Health contain much valuable material. Also of special interest are: "Regulation of Medical Practice," *Physician and Surgeon* 2 (1880): 481–86; "The Relations of Schools to Diphtheria and to Similar Diseases," *American Public Health Association Reports*, vol. 6 (1881); "The Relation of the Depth of Water in Wells to the Causation of Typhoid Fever," *Annual Report of the Michigan State Board of Health* (1884); "Scientific Collective Investigation of Disease," *Journal of the American Medical Association* 9 (1887): 486–91; "The Causation of Pneumonia," *Annual Report of the Michigan State Board of Health* (1885–1886); "Malaria; and the Causation of Periodic Fever," *Journal of the American Medical Association* 11 (1888): 651–63; "The Climatic Causation of Consumption," *Journal of the American Medical Association* 14 (1890): 73–85, 116–29, 152–65; and *The Relation of Preventable Disease to Taxation*, a pamphlet from the Michigan State Board of Health (1905). Descriptions of Baker and his work are found in the *American Biographical History of Eminent and Self-Made Men, Michigan Volume* (1878), pp. 8–9, and the *Portrait and Biographical Album of Ingham and Livingston Counties, Michigan* (1891), pp. 205–8 (this contains a portrait). John R. Cook, *Let in the Sunlight . . . Michigan's Heritage of Health from 1873 to the Present*, Michigan Department of Health (Dec. 1962), pp. 4–10, contains material on Baker and his methods. Many references to Baker appear in C. R. Burr, *Medical History of Michigan* (2 vols., 1930).

WILLIAM K. BEATTY

BAKER, Hobey (15 Jan. 1892–21 Dec. 1918), ice hockey player, was born Hobart Amory Hare Baker in Bala-Cynwyd, Pennsylvania, the son of Alfred Thornton Baker, an upholstery manufacturer, and Mary Augusta Pemberton, a socialite. Baker attended St. Paul's School in Concord, New Hampshire, between the ages of eleven and eighteen. His parents, who subsequently divorced in 1907, sent Baker and his older brother to this prestigious Episcopalian preparatory school in 1903. It was a school much in favor with the socialites of Main Line Philadelphia and was patterned after the so-called "public" schools of England. While there Baker came under the sporting influence of one of the masters, James Conover, his father's cousin, who established hockey as the school's most dominant sport after he had made an early trip to Montreal to purchase sticks and pucks.

Conover taught his young protégé well, and by the time Baker was fourteen he had made the school team. Those at the school at the time recalled how small and lonely Baker looked when practicing in the early days.

That untypical image did not last long; when he was an underclassman, many in the school regarded him as the finest player ever to skate at St. Paul's. By the time he was an upperclassman, a new teammate said of him, "He flew over the surface like a bird, doing inner and outer edges in wide arcs. I had seen pros play in Pittsburgh (virtually all Canadians), where I had first played hockey, but I had never seen such grace" (quoted in Davies). Baker quickly developed that essential skill of skating without looking at the puck and would frequently end practice sessions by skating through his teammates and neither glancing at the puck nor colliding into any of them.

The development of such skill levels translated into superior hockey teams at St. Paul's. Coached by Malcolm K. Gordon, the school not only provided players to Harvard, Yale, and Princeton but also competed with them on an equal level. While Baker was at St. Paul's the school defeated both Princeton and Harvard. Gordon used Baker's speed to great advantage, and in the days of seven-man hockey he created the "rover" position for Baker. Previously, the normal attacking line consisted of four men abreast, two wings, and two forwards. As a rover Baker could go wherever he wanted on the ice.

Baker remained at St. Paul's an extra year beyond his normal graduation date of 1909 to further hone his skills. He was sought after both by Yale and Princeton, but his father's status as a Princeton alumnus assured Baker's attendance there. He entered Princeton in 1910 but was ineligible for play as a freshman. Representatives of the St. Nicholas Club of New York attempted to secure his services for the 1910–1911 season, but as such play would have violated collegiate eligibility standards he restricted himself to practicing with the varsity team and with various pick-up groups.

During Baker's three varsity years (1911–1914), Princeton was intercollegiate champion twice; he served as team captain during his junior year. During his sophomore year Princeton swept to the championship, losing only once to powerful Harvard. Baker declined the team captaincy during his senior year as he held a similar post with the football squad. It hardly mattered as Princeton regained the ice hockey championship with victories in two of three games with Harvard and twice over Ottawa.

College hockey was then played in big-city arenas; Princeton used the St. Nicholas Club's rink in New York. As Baker's feats became legendary, rink operators would herald his forthcoming play by posting signs reading "Hobey Baker Plays Tonight." What the crowds would come to see was a right-handed shot with a relatively short stick that had a sharp angle between the blade and handle. Baker used his stick with pinpoint accuracy, from either the left or right, without great force. Among his typical moves as a rover were an attack through center ice, frequently after having picked up a rebound near his own net and circling it once or twice, followed by a "hook" into the opposing goal from either the right or left. Another approach he used was to fake a shot and hit the boards in the corner while passing to his center positioned near the opponent's goal. Baker's speed was far beyond that of his teammates (they frequently had difficulty keeping pace with him), and his backward skating was almost as good as his moves forward. He was equally adept at changing direction and stopped by turning his toes in rather than turning his skates ninety degrees against the direction of movement.

Baker was a model player, disdaining rough play and receiving only two penalties during his college career. He was also an outstanding football player. He excelled in returning punts on the run and in drop kicking in a defensive era in which those skills were the principal offensive weapons. It was a game characterized by forcing an opponent into a mistake that might then result in a successful field goal, a Baker specialty. Although also a fine baseball outfielder, the rules of the time prevented Baker's participation in more than two varsity sports. He was 5'9" and 160 pounds, heavily muscled, with a deep chest, highly developed knees, strong ankles, and, surprisingly, flat feet.

After graduating from college with a major in history, economics, and politics, Baker continued his hockey career with the St. Nicholas Club while working as a trainee for the J. P. Morgan bank. When the United States entered World War I he received a commission in the U.S. Army and trained as a pilot. Rising to the rank of captain, he commanded the 141st Aero Squadron in France and received both the French Croix de Guerre and the U.S. Distinguished Service Medal. Shortly before being scheduled to return to the United States after the Armistice, he was killed at Toul, France, in a farewell flight he did not have to make.

Baker was the living embodiment of the fictional Frank Merriwell of Yale transposed to Princeton. When the crowds roared, "Here he comes!" at hockey and football games, Baker was the center of everyone's attention. He could quite literally do anything athletically, while embodying all of the noble traits of decency, modesty, kindness, and courtesy.

In 1922 the indoor ice rink at Princeton was named in Baker's honor, and in 1980 an award was named for him, established by the Decathalon Athletic Club of Bloomington, Minnesota; the award is given annually to the most outstanding college hockey player in the United States. Baker was enshrined in the Hockey Hall of Fame, Toronto, Ontario, Canada, in 1945 and in the U.S. Hockey Hall of Fame, Eveleth, Minnesota, in 1973. He was the first American-developed player to be inducted into the Canadian institution. In 1977 he was also inducted into the College Football Hall of Fame, Notre Dame, Indiana.

• Information on Baker is principally in the Hobey Baker Collection, Manuscripts Division, Princeton University Library. The collection consists of letters, tape-recorded interviews, newspaper articles, and diaries gathered by John D. Davies in preparation for his biography of Baker, *The Legend of Hobey Baker* (1966). Archival materials also are located at the Hockey Hall of Fame, Toronto, Ontario, Canada, and at the U.S. Hockey Hall of Fame, Eveleth, Minn. A fictional account of his Princeton years and later is in Mark Goodman, *Hurrah for the Next Man Who Dies* (1985). See also Ron Fimrite, "A Flame That Burned Too Brightly," *Sports Illustrated*, 18 Mar. 1991, pp. 78–90. An obituary is in the *New York Times*, 27 Dec. 1918.

ROGER A. GODIN

BAKER, Home Run (13 Mar. 1886–28 June 1963), baseball player, was born John Franklin Baker in Trappe, Maryland, the son of Franklin Adam Baker, a butcher and farmer, and Mary Catherine Rust. Baker began playing baseball on the farm fields of Trappe and performed for area semiprofessional teams beginning at age nineteen, earning from $5 to $15 a week. He rejected offers from the Texas League because it was too far from home and from the Baltimore Orioles of the International League because he did not think the contract terms were fair. In 1908 he signed with Reading, Pennsylvania, of the Tri-State League, a team controlled by the Philadelphia Athletics, who called him up to Philadelphia that fall.

Baker demonstrated power and hitting ability from the start, batting .305 in 1909 and leading the American League with nineteen triples. By 1910 Athletics manager Connie Mack had assembled a formidable team that won four American League pennants in five years (1910, 1911, 1913, 1914). The team featured the "$100,000 infield" of Frank Baker at third base, Jack Barry at shortstop, Eddie Collins at second base, and Stuffy McInnis at first base. At a time when a steak dinner cost twenty-five cents, suggesting that an infield quartet might be worth $100,000 on the open market was the most outrageous evaluation an imaginative sportswriter could envision.

Baseball was still a scientific game, in which brains counted for more than brawn. Bunting, base stealing, the hit and run, and clever defensive strategies dominated the game, with low scoring the rule. Pitchers freely applied paraffin, licorice, tobacco juice, mud, or slippery elm to the ball. The same ball was used in a game until it became too mushy and lopsided to absorb further punishment. Although Baker never hit more than twelve home runs in a season, he led the American League four straight years, from 1911 through 1914. He never led both leagues in home runs; the National League's leading sluggers hit more than he did every year.

Baker's "Home Run" nickname was inspired by two home runs he hit in the 1911 World Series against the New York Giants. After the Giants won the opener, 2–1, the Athletics' Eddie Plank and New York's Rube Marquard were locked in a 1–1 contest in the second game. Baker came up to bat in the last of the sixth inning with Eddie Collins on second base and walloped a pitch over the right field wall to give the A's a 3–1 victory.

Both Marquard and Giants ace Christy Mathewson had daily ghostwritten columns appearing under their names in New York newspapers during the World Series. The next morning, Mathewson's column chided Marquard for throwing the wrong pitch to Baker, costing the Giants the game. That afternoon, Mathewson took a 1–0 lead into the ninth inning. Baker then tied the game with a homer into the Polo Grounds' stands. The A's eventually won, 3–2, in eleven innings and took the World Series in six games. Marquard then tweaked Mathewson in print for his "mistake," starting a feud between the two pitchers.

In 1912 and 1913 Baker topped the American League in runs batted in, while hitting career highs of .347 and .336. He batted .450 and hit one home run in the Athletics' five-game World Series win over the Giants in 1913.

A third major league, the Federal League, formed in 1914 and offered established players large salaries. Baker declined a $10,000 bonus from the Feds to play in Baltimore and reluctantly accepted a three-year contract from Mack. Baker never liked traveling and being away from the farm most of the summer. The A's lost the 1914 World Series in four games to the Boston Braves. Baker, unhappy that he had signed for three years and that Mack made no offer to reopen his contract, refused to report to the A's in 1915. He remained on the farm in Trappe and later that season signed as a player-manager with a semipro team in nearby Chester, Pennsylvania.

Mack, convinced that Baker would not play for him again, sold his contract to the New York Yankees that fall. Baker consistently batted near .300 for the next three years. In 1919 he led the original edition of "Murderers' Row" with ten home runs, helping the Yankees pace the league with forty-five roundtrippers.

In 1909 Baker had married Ottilie Rosa Tschantre. They had two daughters. When his wife died in 1920, Baker forsook baseball and stayed home to raise his children with the help of his sister. He then hired a housekeeper and returned to the Yankees for the 1921 season. The following year he married Margaret E. Mitchell. They had two children.

During the year that Baker had remained out of baseball, Babe Ruth came to the Yankees and changed the game forever by hitting a record fifty-four home runs, more than any other American League team's entire output. Ruth turned the Yankees into pennant winners, enabling Baker to play in his sixth and last World Series in 1922. Baker then retired from the major leagues.

Back in Trappe Baker combined baseball and farming as player-manager of the nearby Easton team in the Class D Eastern Shore League in 1924 and 1925. One evening in 1924 the most powerful right-handed slugger of all time came to his attention when Jimmie Foxx's father brought his sixteen-year-old son to Baker's home to ask for a tryout. Baker worked with the young catcher, a natural home run hitter. At the end of the 1924 season, he offered Foxx to his old team, the New York Yankees. The Yankees, skeptical of Baker's description of the teenager's potential, turned him down. Baker made the same offer to Mack, who paid the Easton club $2,500 for Foxx on Baker's word alone. Foxx preceded Baker into the National Baseball Hall of Fame in 1951. Baker was inducted in 1955.

Baker's lifetime .307 batting average and the left-handed slugger's ninety-six home runs in the deadball era overshadowed his fielding, which prompted Mack to comment, "Don't let anyone tell you that Frank Baker was just a hitter. I get a little impatient with persons who think Frank was an awkward fellow around the third-base bag. He was really a great third baseman. Look it up in the records; year after year he handled more chances than any other third baseman in the league. He had to move around to get all those total chances. People remember Baker as a home run leader; they may be surprised to hear he was also a fielding leader." In the 1990s Baker ranked tenth among all third basemen in career chances per game.

Baker worked several farms in and around Trappe and for more than twenty years served as a director of the Denton, Maryland, Production Credit Association, which lent money to farmers on Maryland's Eastern Shore. An avid duck hunter, he often hosted former players in the fall. Bill Werber, a frequent hunting companion who had also played for Mack, remarked, "Frank Baker was one of the most decent, open and honest persons I have ever met in this life." Baker died in Trappe.

• A file of clippings on Baker is in the National Baseball Hall of Fame Library in Cooperstown, N.Y. A two-part reminiscence by Baker appeared in the *Sporting News*, 9 Feb. and 16 Feb. 1955. Profiles of Baker are found in Harry Grayson, *They Played the Game* (1944), and Mike Shatzkin, The Ballplayers (1990). See also Connie Mack, *My 66 Years in Baseball* (1950), and Fred Lieb, *Connie Mack: Grand Old Man of Baseball* (1945). An obituary is in the *New York Times*, 29 June 1963.

NORMAN L. MACHT

BAKER, Hugh Potter (20 Jan. 1878–24 May 1950), forester and university administrator, was born in St. Croix Falls, Polk County, Wisconsin, the son of Joseph Stannard Baker, a land agent, and Alice Potter. His father was financially successful, and Baker grew up in surroundings that were physically comfortable and culture-filled. Both of his parents having attended college, Baker received his early schooling locally before entering Macalester College in St. Paul, Minnesota, where he remained a year before transferring to Michigan Agricultural College (now Michigan State University). He graduated with a B.S. in 1901, having also begun work in partnership with his brother, Fred Baker, in a part-time position at the federal Division of Forestry. This division, part of the U.S. Department of Agriculture, was then run by pioneer forester and future governor of Pennsylvania Gifford Pinchot. Working for the next six years on a variety of projects, including data compilation in connection with a sand dune reforestation project and the preparation of forest management plans for private timberland owners, Baker won the approval of Pinchot who, eager to expand the scope of his department, would have gladly offered Baker full-time employment.

Baker opted instead for a career in academia. Having obtained a master's degree in forestry from Yale

University (1904), he became assistant professor of forestry at Iowa State College (now University) in Ames, where he was instrumental in establishing a four-year course of study in forestry. The new professor married Fleta Paddock in 1904; they had three children. In 1907 Baker moved to the Pennsylvania State College (now University), where he served as professor of forestry in replacement of another forestry pioneer, Bernhard E. Fernow. The forestry department at Penn State was embryonic, having been founded only the previous year (1906) by Fernow, who then departed for the University of Toronto. Baker assisted with significant growth within the department, including gaining access to a 7,000-acre state forest reserve, which proved invaluable for both academic and demonstrative purposes, providing students with practical, hands-on experience.

Baker's success did not go unnoticed by officials at Syracuse University, who were eager to build up their own College of Forestry. The placement of this college on the campus of Syracuse had been a matter of some controversy. Many felt that Cornell University, the home of the state's land-grant college, should serve as host for forestry instruction. The first collegiate school of forestry in the United States had been founded at Cornell in 1898, but political controversies and mismanagement had resulted in the withdrawal of state financial support for the school by 1903. Others objected to the sectarian affiliation of Syracuse University, a private institution associated with the Methodist church. The long-standing controversy was resolved in Syracuse's favor in 1911, and Baker, who had earned a doctor of economics degree from the University of Munich in 1910, seemed the best candidate for the job of dean.

Assuming the duties of dean of the college on 1 February 1912, Baker directed the school from its modest beginnings (two instructors, a few students, and inadequate borrowed space) to a path of steady growth. He established a Forestry Experimentation Station on the southern outskirts of the city of Syracuse and purchased demonstration areas. Bolstered by a flood of applications from potential students, he made plans as early as the fall of 1912 for a separate facility for the college, which was subsequently completed and opened for classes in 1917.

A believer in specialization at the graduate level of instruction, Baker unsuccessfully attempted to implement a program leading to the degree of doctor of economics with an emphasis on forestry economics. His efforts proved more fruitful in the establishment of a five-year program that led to the master of forestry degree. Summer courses were offered in subjects ranging from forest ecology and botany to soils and woodcraft. The New York State Ranger School, founded in 1912, proved a popular subcollegiate option for students seeking careers as diverse as forest ranger, estate manager, or nurseryman. An extension department, organized in 1916, provided instruction and information to citizens throughout New York state in the form of bulletins, press releases, demonstrations, and fair exhibits. Constant battles with the state legislature over appropriations, exacerbated by continuing resentment over the issue of the location of the college, took their toll, however, and Baker resigned as dean in March 1920.

Sensing new opportunities in the field of forestry, Baker became executive secretary of the American Paper and Pulp Association. He also served as a member of the National Forestry Program Committee, an industry-oriented organization that sought, through mutual cooperation on the part of private industry, the states, and the federal government, to encourage reforestation and forest fire prevention. In 1928 Baker became manager of the Trade Association Department of the U.S. Chamber of Commerce. Also that year his wife died. In 1929 he married Richarda Sahla; no children were born of the marriage.

Baker returned to academia in 1930, once again serving as dean of the College of Forestry at Syracuse. He left, however, in 1933 to become president of Massachusetts State College in Amherst. The move was a professional advancement, and it reunited him with his brother, Ray Stannard Baker, a noted writer who had moved to Amherst in 1910. Assuming his duties in the depths of the Great Depression, Baker's administration was nevertheless one of change. He hired the first music instructor at the college in 1934 and created a Department of Economics the following year. A subject close to Baker's heart, forestry utilization, was added to the curriculum in 1933, and by 1936 courses in wildlife management were available to students. In 1938 the college trustees supported the important advance of awarding bachelor of arts degrees. Initially reluctant to expand engineering instruction, Baker later relented and in the late 1930s established a Department of Engineering. Just prior to World War II he secured funding for two badly needed new dormitories.

Baker guided the college through the difficult war years, and afterward his administration dealt with the droves of war veterans who returned to the campus with GI Bill financing. Following years of discussion and debate, on 7 May 1947 the University of Massachusetts was formally created. Baker, soon to retire because of ill health, remarked, "I shall sit on the sidelines and watch the development of the University of Massachusetts, and I see many big things ahead." His health continued to deteriorate following his retirement, and he died in Orlando, Florida.

A true leader in the development of higher education, Baker contributed to the growth and development of forestry instruction at four major universities. He is also remembered for guiding the University of Massachusetts through a major expansion in the face of both depression and warfare.

• Baker's papers are at the University of Massachusetts Archives, Amherst. Additional material on his career is in the records of the U.S. Forest Service, National Archives. The two best sources of information on his life and career remain W. Freeman Galpin, *Syracuse University II: The Growing*

Years (1960), and Harold W. Cary, *The University of Massachusetts: A History of 100 Years* (1962). An obituary is in the *New York Times*, 25 May 1950.

EDWARD L. LACH, JR.

BAKER, James (19 Dec. 1818–15 May 1898), trapper, army scout, and early settler of Colorado and Wyoming, was born in Belleville, Illinois, and grew up near Springfield. His parents were of Scots-Irish ancestry from South Carolina. With little formal schooling but adept with a rifle, Jim Baker left home for St. Louis in 1838 and signed an eighteen-month contract with the American Fur Company. On 25 May 1838 the Rocky Mountain–bound party, led by Jim Bridger, embarked on the aging steamer *St. Peter*. Leaving the Missouri at the mouth of the Kansas River, they followed what became a well-traveled route west for ninety miles to the Kaw Indian Agency, thence overland to Grand Island on the Platte. Despite encounters with suspicious Indians, the trappers arrived at the Wind River rendezvous without incident.

Baker trapped in the Green River region, in what is now southwestern Wyoming, until his contract expired. He returned briefly to Illinois, but in the spring of 1841 he joined a wagon train guided by Thomas Fitzpatrick that included Jesuit father Pierre Jean De Smet and the first Oregon-bound settlers (the Bidwell-Bartleson party). At the Green River, Baker joined a party of trappers working for Jim Bridger and Henry Fraeb. While hunting buffalo in late August along the Little Snake River, the Fraeb-led trappers were attacked by a large force of Sioux, Cheyennes, and Arapahos. At least four trappers, including Fraeb, were killed. Baker took command after Fraeb was shot and probably prevented the annihilation of the trappers. The daylong fight occurred on the Little Snake at the mouth of what became known as Battle Creek, just south of the Wyoming-Colorado line.

From 1841 to 1846 Baker ranged throughout the Rockies trapping; he participated in a horse raid into southern California in 1845–1846 and had numerous encounters with Indians, fighting with Apaches and being adopted into the Shoshoni nation. In 1847 he married a Shoshoni woman named Marina whom he helped rescue from the Blackfeet; it is known that they had one child. He continued to trap despite the decline in the fur trade.

In 1852 Baker's wife died while he was off trapping with a "last trap" organized by Kit Carson. In 1855 General William S. Harney hired him as chief of scouts at Fort Laramie, located on the North Platte River in what is now eastern Wyoming. In 1857 he guided an army column to Fort Bridger (in present-day southwestern Wyoming) during the Mormon War. From there he guided Captain Randolph B. Marcy's command across the Colorado Mountains to Fort Union in New Mexico. The force left Fort Bridger on 24 November 1857, achieved their objective despite great difficulty, and returned to Fort Bridger by 9 June 1858.

Baker briefly operated a store and ferry at the Green River Crossing of the Mormon Trail, but in 1859 he joined the Gold Rush into central Colorado. He pre-empted a quarter-section of land on 3 June 1859 and proved up on the land under the Homestead Act, officially filing on 3 December 1863. He built an adobe house at a ford on Clear Creek about four miles from Auraria (Denver) and married Mary (maiden name unknown); they had at least seven children. Baker constructed a toll bridge at Baker's Crossing. The family also kept a store and raised livestock. Baker owned an interest in a coal mine and often was engaged as a guide or interpreter. He guided Indian Bureau officials, geologists, and groups of prospectors and hunters throughout Colorado. In 1864 he lost his right thumb when a rifle exploded. Another accident left his face scarred in 1867. In the fall of 1872 he guided a party of surveyors laying out the route for the Denver & Rio Grande Railroad from Denver to Salt Lake City.

Baker sold the bulk of his Denver property in 1873 and purchased land in Carbon County, Wyoming, where he built a fortified log home near the site of the 1841 Indian fight and settled into a life of ranching. In 1897 he underwent an operation for kidney trouble. He died the following year at his home in Dixon, Wyoming, leaving his property to his surviving son and three married daughters. He was buried about a mile from Savery, Wyoming.

Baker married at least three Indian women and fathered thirteen children. After his wife Mary died, he had married her sister Eliza, and the couple had at least two children. He favored Indian dress and habits. Lean and powerful, Baker in later years sported a goatee in part to cover his scars and in his seventies still wore his mostly chestnut hair in long ringlets. In 1917 in respect for his contributions, the state of Wyoming purchased and relocated his cabin to Frontier Park in Cheyenne; this shrine to Baker was dedicated on 23 July 1917.

• Undocumented stories place Baker with Fremont's 1845 expedition, with Chivington at Sand Creek in 1864, and as a scout with Custer in 1875. An interview with Baker was published in the *Denver Tribune-Republican*, 10 July 1886. See also Randolph B. Marcy, *Thirty Years of Army Life on the Border* (1866). A biographical account by Nolie Mumey appears in LeRoy R. Hafen, ed., *The Mountain Men and the Fur Trade of the Far West*, vol. 3 (1966), pp. 39–47. Mumey's *Life of Jim Baker, 1818–1898* (1931; repr. 1972) is a worthy book-length biography.

DOUGLAS D. MARTIN

BAKER, James Hutchins (13 Oct. 1848–10 Sept. 1925), educator, was born on the family farm in Harmony, Maine, the only child of Wesley Baker and Lucy Hutchins. Rural New England instilled in Baker the values of beauty and order and the salvation of work. He acquired a moral and literary foundation from listening to his father read the Bible and Shakespeare.

Baker attended Bates College in Lewiston, Maine, and earned a B.A. (1873) and an M.A. (1876) in the classics.

After graduating from Bates College, Baker became principal of Yarmouth (Maine) High School in 1873. For health concerns, he moved to Denver, Colorado, in 1875, where he served as principal of Denver High School (East). Under his leadership the school soon developed into one of America's outstanding high schools. In 1880 Baker was elected president of the State Teachers' Association. He was aware of his school colleagues' weak voices in the National Education Association (NEA). Superintendents and heads of normal schools, rather than school principals and practitioners, strongly influenced theory and practice in secondary education. To correct that imbalance, he helped develop the association's Department of Secondary Education into an active body that ably held its ground in discussions about policy for upper level education. In 1882 Baker married Jennie V. Hilton; they had two children.

After seventeen years at Denver High School, Baker was named president of the University of Colorado. In his inaugural address, he envisioned that the university would attain a greatness equal to the best eastern institutions. Although overly optimistic since the university was little more than an academy in 1892, he defined the university's mission as bestowing on Colorado's young men and women a superior education that would equip them for responsible citizenship in a democracy. Young Coloradans need look no further than Boulder for quality education, he maintained. The state university was the capstone of the public education system and would be a true university with colleges, professional schools, and graduate courses. To fulfill the university ideal, Baker attempted unsuccessfully to establish a nonsectarian divinity school that would operate in cooperation with the university but not be governed or supported by it.

Baker realized that if the university were to succeed, it must serve the larger society, but it must not sacrifice excellence for practical ends. William Torrey Harris, philosopher and educator, influenced Baker's educational philosophy with his assertion that classical studies opened the soul "to the world of truth, rightness, and beauty." Baker pleaded for a humanism that believed "in the value of organized and transmitted knowledge" and "a culture that has a moral backbone." A classical education would empower graduates with knowledge and disciplined reason that would enable them to meet the challenges of a dynamic society. He ultimately accepted practical education's value but never gave up his classical ideals.

Baker gained national recognition with contributions in two areas: a standardization of college admission requirements, and a proposal to save at least two years of public education by allowing students to enter college earlier. The NEA's influential Committee of Ten arose from Baker's questioning of diverse academic requirements that allowed colleges to set admission standards that seemed impossible to meet; in effect, each college ruled without appeal. Harvard President Charles William Eliot chaired the committee, composed of the nation's educational leaders. Baker commented that only Eliot had enough prestige to persuade the NEA to organize such a committee and seriously examine its findings. In 1893 the committee reported an agreement on general courses of study acceptable to all colleges for admission; Baker called it a "second awakening of the high schools." The proposal that two years could be saved between high school and the beginning of college without loss of anything essential in culture or character making resulted from the Committee on Economy of Time in Education, which Baker chaired. The committee recommended the elimination of needless methodologies, time-wasting exercises, and a revision of the curriculum. The U.S. Bureau of Education published and distributed this committee's report in 1913; the recommendations helped stimulate the formation of junior high schools and junior colleges throughout America.

Baker served the University of Colorado for twenty-two years, a period in which the university expanded greatly. In 1892 there were 66 students, 32 faculty, and eight buildings with a library of 7,000 volumes; when Baker retired in 1914 students numbered 1,306 with a faculty of 200 and 21 buildings, including a library of 75,000 volumes. Perhaps more significant were the additions of graduate and professional schools, teachers' summer sessions, and a university extension division. Baker built an institution that offered a liberal arts curriculum but also addressed the students' professional aspirations.

Baker envisioned a national university that would forge a union between democracy and higher learning. He wanted culture, pure science, social justice, and absolute values to rest equally with the gods of commercial success. Education, he believed, must be the fourth estate in a democratic government. Baker's terms as president of the National Council of Education in 1892 and as president of the National Association of State Universities in 1907 further reflected his national interests and prominence. He died at St. Joseph's Hospital in Denver, after an attack of influenza and pneumonia. One of the last of the great entrepreneurial university presidents, Baker was praised as "the Dr. Eliot of the West," suggesting that his contributions to education in the West rivaled those of Harvard's noteworthy leader.

• The Archives of the University of Colorado has a box of Baker's papers. Baker published seven books: *Elementary Psychology* (1890), used as a text in secondary education; *Education and Life: Papers and Addresses* (1900); *American Problems: Essays and Addresses* (1907); *Educational Aims and Civic Needs* (1913); *American University Progress and College Reform* (1916); *After The War—What?* (1918); and *Of Himself and Other Things* (1922), which is autobiographical. Under the auspices of the State Historical and Natural History Society of Colorado, Baker edited a three-volume *History of Colorado* (1927). Michael McGiffert, *The Higher Learning in Colorado: An Historical Study, 1860–1940* (1964) presents valuable contextual information as well as a critical analysis of Baker as a university president. See also William E. Davis, *Glory Colorado! A History of the University of Colorado, 1858–1963* (1965), which has a useful bibliography, and Frederick S. Allen et al., *The University of Colorado, 1876–1976*. For background on the American university in this period, see Lawrence R. Veysey, *The Emergence of the American University* (1965), and Burton J. Bledstein, *The Culture of Professionalism: The Middle Class and the Development of Higher Education in America* (1978).

JAMES A. DENTON

BAKER, Jehu (4 Nov. 1822–1 Mar. 1903), congressman and diplomat, was born in Fayette County, Kentucky, the son of William Baker and Margaret Caldwell, farmers. In 1829 the family moved near Lebanon, Illinois, where Baker attended common schools until the age of seventeen. He then entered McKendree College and studied for several terms but did not graduate. He studied law in Belleville and, admitted to the bar in 1846, entered practice there. Three years later he shouldered the added responsibility of coediting the *Belleville Daily Advocate*. Drawing on his scholarly, legal, and editorial background, Baker gained a regional reputation as an unusually skillful orator and pamphleteer. Two effective speeches against Democratic senator Stephen Douglas and the Kansas-Nebraska Act in 1854 raised Baker's standing in the Illinois Republican party, which he strengthened with additional oratorical rebukes of secession and the southern Confederacy in 1861. In the latter year he filled his first public office, master of chancery for St. Clair County. In 1856 he married Olive Starr Wait; they had one daughter before Olive died in 1865.

Baker's national political career began in 1864, when he defeated the prominent Illinois Democrat William R. Morrison for a seat in the House of Representatives. Baker served four terms in Congress (1865–1869, 1887–1889, and 1897–1899) but was better known for his three electoral triumphs over the popular Morrison than for his deeds in office. Baker's most notable congressional service occurred in his first two terms, when Reconstruction and the impeachment of President Andrew Johnson were the chief political issues. Although he was a minor figure in the high political drama of those years, Baker's infrequent remarks were distinctive enough in their arguments, their legal and literary embellishments, and the conviction with which they were delivered to render their author a memorable figure to many of his colleagues. He was unstinting in his condemnation of former rebels and of Johnson's efforts to wrest control of Reconstruction from Congress, but he occupied a conservative position among congressional Republicans in his overall approach to Reconstruction and impeachment. He opposed Thaddeus Stevens's proposal, embodied in the Military Government Act, to treat the southern states as conquered provinces of a foreign power, objected to the voting provisions of the Louisiana Reconstruction Bill that effectively granted universal suffrage to blacks while temporarily disfranchising white rebels, and resisted the aggressive methods by which Benjamin Butler sought to impeach Johnson. On the other hand, he was a Radical on issues of money and government assistance to business, arguing for retention of greenbacks on the grounds that an inflationary currency better fit the needs of the people and cautioning against the "influence of mammoth corporations of wealth and power" (*Congressional Globe*, Thirty-ninth Cong., 1st sess., p. 276).

Baker's ideal vision of republican government and his adherence to constitutional principles as he understood them gave coherence to his seemingly disparate positions. His insistence that Confederate officials be barred from federal office reflected his belief that the "class rule and aristocracy" of the slaveholding South blunted popular education, degraded labor, and fomented rebellion. Such a danger to republican institutions had to be eradicated. When Radical Republican proposals to reconstruct the South in his view threatened basic constitutional protections, Baker objected in the name of upholding republican principles. Johnson's usurpation of congressional authority and truckling with aristocratic traitors endangered American institutions in Baker's mind, but so too did the loose constitutional basis of the Radicals' case against Johnson. Baker's vigilant concern for republican forms of government also prompted his resistance to the acquisition of Alaska. He warned Congress against the "hot haste with which 'Young America' and 'manifest destiny' would have us swallow it. Something else is needed besides swallowing, though Young America, rapt in the fine frenzy of his sophomorical spread eagle, is thoroughly ignorant of the fact" (*Congressional Globe*, Fortieth Cong., 2d sess., p. 608).

Baker's reliance on personal political principles put him outside the dominant spirit of partisan loyalty and organizational reliability that marked the "party age" of the late nineteenth century. In addition, he exhibited some of the eccentricities of the self-taught scholar. James G. Blaine noted the "peculiarities, not to say oddities, of bearing" that distinguished Baker (Blaine, *Twenty Years of Congress*, vol. 2 [1886], p. 123), a judgment seconded years later by Champ Clark. Baker left Congress in 1869 and devoted himself to law and the study of languages. In 1874 he married Mary West Robertson; their only child died in infancy. In 1876 he completed a densely annotated translation of Baron de Montesquieu's *Considerations on the Causes of the Grandeur and Decadence of the Romans* (1734), a topic in keeping with his interest in the vulnerability of republics. Baker's work was published in 1882.

Baker's talents as an orator brought him back into Republican politics in 1876, when he crisscrossed Illinois in support of the presidential bid of Rutherford B. Hayes. Baker's highly successful series of addresses prompted comparisons to the eloquent Robert Ingersoll. The *Decatur Sun* considered Baker "one of the few men who have ever lived who can be thrillingly eloquent when treating an abstruse subject." President Hayes rewarded Baker in 1878 by naming him minister to Venezuela, where he served until removed by James Garfield in 1881. Following Garfield's assassination, Baker returned to Venezuela in 1882 and remained until 1885, acting also as consul general in Caracas. During Baker's tenure, Venezuela asked the United States for assistance in resolving its border dispute with British Guiana, a future source of British-American conflict. In 1883 he became the conduit for a Venezuelan offer of alliance with the United States and widespread commercial access to Venezuelan waters. Such suggestions anticipated American imperialism but went unfulfilled in the 1880s. Grover Cleveland's election ended Baker's diplomatic career.

Baker was again elected to Congress in 1886, but he lost his seat by 100 votes in 1888. He was returned to Congress in 1896, this time as a free silver Democrat. His final term was hampered by impending blindness. He became totally blind in 1899, at which time he retired from public life. Baker died in Belleville.

• No extensive collection of Baker's papers exists, but a good collection of newspaper clippings is in the Baker Family Papers, Illinois State Historical Library, Springfield. Printed copies of Baker's most notable speeches are also available there. His Venezuela dispatches are in the Archives of the Department of State, U.S. Despatches, Venezuela, XXXI–XXXIV, Feb. 1883–May 1884, housed in the National Archives. Some of these dispatches are published in U.S. Department of State, *Papers Relating to the Foreign Relations of the United States* (1878–1885). *The United States Biographical Dictionary . . . Illinois Volume* (1876) contains some useful material. Baker's relationship to the politics of Reconstruction is explained in Michael Les Benedict, *A Compromise of Principle: Congressional Republicans and Reconstruction, 1863–1869* (1974). See Champ Clark, *My Quarter Century of American Politics*, vol. 2 (1920), for a description of the elderly Baker. Obituaries are in the *Illinois State Register*, 1 and 2 Mar. 1903, and the *St. Louis Globe-Democrat*, 2 Mar. 1903.

THOMAS R. PEGRAM

BAKER, John Hopkinson (30 June 1894–21 Sept. 1973), wildlife conservationist, was born in Cambridge, Massachusetts, the son of George Pierce Baker, a professor of dramatic literature at Harvard University and founder of the School of Drama at Yale, and Christina Hopkinson. Baker's interest in wildlife began when as a child he attended meetings and interacted with members of the Nuttall Ornithological Club and the American Ornithological Union. He became a member of both organizations in 1911. After he graduated from the Cambridge Latin School, he attended Harvard University, graduating in 1915 with a B.A. He set out to work at the National Cash Register Company that year, but World War I interrupted his employment in 1917. As a first lieutenant, Baker served as a pilot in the Air Force and spent six months overseas. When he returned, he took a job with the American International Corporation, for which he traveled extensively promoting foreign trade. In 1921 Baker married Elizabeth Dabney; the couple had two daughters.

For more than a decade, Baker was involved in finance and investment activities, both as part of the firm White, Weld & Company of New York City and as an individual investment counselor. Throughout this time, however, he had not lost contact with organizations promoting conservation and wildlife issues. He joined the Linnaean Society of New York in 1924 and was elected the society's treasurer, and in 1933 he served as its president.

Late in 1933 Baker was made chairman of the board for the National Association of Audubon Societies, created in 1886 by George Bird Grinnell, editor of *Forest and Stream*, to protect wild birds from destruction and the use of their plumage for ornamentation. Publishing *Audubon Magazine* was the initial focus of the society, which incorporated in New York State in 1897. The early membership supported the use of public education, leafleting, and sponsorship of legislation to aid wildlife preservation. The organization hoped to stop the wholesale destruction of game birds, water fowl, and specifically birds of prey, which had been perceived as "bad" birds for killing more popular song birds.

In 1934 Baker was made chief executive officer at Audubon and officially retired from the investment business to devote all of his energies to strategies that would promote the conservation of wildlife. By the late 1930s the fashion industry again promoted the use of exotic plumes on clothing and hats. The Audubon Society was instrumental in the passage of New York State legislation that outlawed their use. These early struggles were later dubbed the "feather wars," and Baker's efforts were integral in protecting a variety of wild birds from being killed. By 1952, federal restrictions banned industries from importing or using feathers of protected and endangered species.

The Audubon Societies had originally been configured as groupings of state associations that operated as regional spokesmen as the need arose. During Baker's regime, in 1940 the organization's name was changed to the National Audubon Society and a board of directors created, with individual state chapter members belonging to the national organization. This action achieved its goal of creating a more organized, more fiscally responsible society, which could attract more members and be taken more seriously by government on a local, state, and federal level. Baker also intended to broaden the scope of the society to include not only the protection of birds but also the incorporation of a sense of respect for nature and a concept of the ecology of natural resources.

Baker's initial course of action for the society was to boost membership, which stood at 3,500, and to create a more sophisticated and professionalized program of activities. To this end, he created a film series that became known as the Audubon Wildlife Films. The series enabled the society to reach an even larger audience than the traditional lecture circuit and could appeal to a wider range of age groups. His commitment to young naturalists was evident in the creation of summer camps that were headed by well-educated and trained teachers. The first such camp was the Audubon Camp on Hog Island, Maine, which opened in 1936. Eventually, three additional camps were created, one each in Connecticut, Wisconsin, and Wyoming. Extending this "learn by experiencing" technique, Baker developed the idea of a nature center that would allow groups to come by appointment to experience, either through exhibits, trail walks, guided tours, or extended programs, an approach to natural science that included conservation. Nature centers were established in El Monte, California (1939); Greenwich (1942) and Sharon, Connecticut; and Dayton, Ohio (1956).

Baker is credited with creating the research department of the National Audubon Society, which was responsible for publications and dissemination of factual information about endangered species. At various times in its history, the society supported field research to answer questions that no other national organization, branch of government, or scientific department was funding. This research took ornithologists in 1937 to the South to study the ivory-billed woodpecker and in 1939 to California to study the condor. Subsequent field research was completed on Long Island, New York, to study the black-crowned night heron and in the Florida Keys, to study the roseate spoonbill.

In 1944 Baker was made president of the society, as the organization once again went through a restructuring process. He spoke out against the use of the chemical DDT in 1945 and accurately predicted that it would prove detrimental to our natural resources, wildlife, and would, in many ways harm mankind.

Another focus of the Audubon Society under Baker's leadership was to establish sanctuaries across the United States for the protection and study of wildlife. He was largely responsible for the acquisition in 1954 of Corkscrew Swamp in southwestern Florida. Other sanctuaries established by Baker or his successors include the San Gabriel River Wildlife Sanctuary in California; Rainey Wildlife in Louisiana; the Todd Wildlife Sanctuary on Hog Island in Maine; Roosevelt Memorial, Oyster Bay, New York; and a series of island sanctuaries located on the coast of Texas.

By the time of Baker's retirement from the society in 1959, the membership had grown to over 30,000 members. His legacy also included intuitive recruitment of key personnel, such as his successor, Carl W. Buchheister, and Roger Tory Peterson, who was responsible for the standard guide books to birds. Baker stayed active in the society as a consultant for as long as his health permitted. He died in Bedford, Massachusetts.

• A small amount of Baker correspondence is located in the New York Public Library, National Audubon Society Collection, although much of the material from Baker's era of leadership was lost before it made its way to official repositories. The most comprehensive published source of information about both Baker and the National Audubon Society is Frank Graham, Jr., *The Audubon Ark* (1990), written with the benefit of Carl Buchheister's recollections. The *Audubon Magazine* contains another collaborative effort of Graham and Buchheister, "From the Swamps and Back: A Concise History of the Audubon Movement," Jan. 1973, pp. 26–36. This magazine also paid tribute to Baker with an obituary (Nov. 1973,

p. 136) and a Nov. 1969 article by Buchheister and Roger Tory Peterson that lists his accomplishments as head of the society. An obituary is in the *New York Times*, 23 Sept. 1973.

GERI E. SOLOMON

BAKER, Josephine (3 June 1906–12 Apr. 1975), dancer, singer, and civil rights activist, was born in St. Louis, Missouri, the daughter of Eddie Carson, a musician, and Carrie Macdonald. Her parents parted when Josephine was still an infant, and her mother married Arthur Martin, which has led to some confusion about her maiden name. Very little is known about her childhood, except that she was a witness to the East St. Louis riot in 1917. This event was often a feature of her talks in the 1950s and 1960s about racism and the fight for equality, which fostered the oft-repeated assertion that the family was resident in East St. Louis. Before the age of eighteen Josephine had been married twice, first to Willie Wells and then to William Baker, to whom she was married in Camden, New Jersey, in September 1921.

Josephine Baker, like many other African-American performers of the early twentieth century, began her career in "tent shows," touring musical ensembles that played mostly in the southern states. Her first success was as a comic dancer in a show starring Clara Smith, which led to her engagement in the touring company of Sissle and Blake's *Shuffle Along*. She later joined the main company of Eubie Blake's show and was billed as the "Highest-Paid Chorus Girl in the World" or as "That Comedy Chorus Girl." Her Broadway debut was in *The Chocolate Dandies* at the Colonial Theatre in September 1924, when E. E. Cummings described her as a "tall, vital, incomparably fluid nightmare which crossed its eyes and warped its limbs in a purely unearthly manner."

Subsequent appearances in New York City at the Lafayette Theatre in Harlem and in cabaret at the Plantation Club, with Ethel Waters, led to Baker's engagement as one of the featured performers in *La Revue Nègre*, an all-black show produced by Caroline Dudley, which opened at the Théâtre des Champs Elysées in Paris in October 1925. With music composed by Spencer Williams; a band led by Claude Hopkins, including Sidney Bechet; sets designed by Miguel Covarrubias; and a poster by the French painter Paul Colin that became world famous, *La Revue Nègre* was destined to become one of the key influences in Parisian theater and visual arts in the late 1920s. Baker's dancing and the choreography by Louis Douglas created a sensation that has been described and debated often. The dance critic André Levinson referred to "farouche and superb bestiality," and Janet Flanner, recalling the premiere in *Paris Was Yesterday* (1972), remembered, "The two specific elements had been established and were unforgettable—her magnificent dark body, a new model that to the French proved for the first time that Black was beautiful, and the acute response of the white masculine public."

La Revue Nègre transferred to Berlin, where its success was repeated, then Baker returned to Paris to star at the Folies Bergèrs in *La Folie du Jour*, in which she introduced her notorious dance wearing a girdle of bananas, followed by *Un Vent de Folie*. These two revues established her as one of the brightest stars of the Paris music hall. Baker's success with the theater-going public was mirrored by her social prestige as "hostess" at a nightclub named *Chez Joséphine*, which entered the annals of the legendary 1920s in Paris. Taken up by intellectuals, notably the architects Adolf Loos and Le Corbusier (Charles-Édouard Jeanneret), both of whom executed designs for her; novelists and poets Ernest Hemingway, Georges Simenon, Paul Morand, and Gertrude Stein, all of whom wrote about her; and above all by painters and sculptors, especially Paul Colin and Jean Dunand, who found in her dancing a parallel with the African influence on cubist painting and sculpture, Baker's fame was somewhat out of proportion to her actual achievements. However, as an innovative dancer, her influence over European choreographers was acknowledged by both Serge Lifar and Frederick Ashton. There are several films made in the late 1920s and early 1930s that show clearly how her fusion of ballet steps, popular American dances such as the Charleston and Black Bottom, and later elements taken from South American and Cuban dance contributed to her style, which was at once erotic and comic.

With the rise of Fascism in Germany and Italy, Baker also came to be regarded as a symbol of free-thinking radical arts. After 1930 she started to achieve equal fame as a singer, although she had already made her first records as a vocalist as early as 1927, especially in two revues at the Casino de Paris, *Paris Qui Remue* (1930), which included songs by Vincent Scotto ("J'ai deux amours" and "La petite Tonkinoise"), and *La Joie de Paris* (1932), with a number, "Si j'étais blanche!" in which she appeared in "whiteface" with a blonde wig to satirize the black-white question in the most gently good-natured way possible. Baker made a number of feature films, including *ZouZou* (1934) and *Princess Tam-Tam* (1935), and had particular success in a revival of Offenbach's opéra bouffe titled *La Créole*, at the Marigny Theatre, 1934. A return to New York in 1935–1936 at the Ziegfeld *Follies* was met with mixed, sometimes hostile, criticism despite a ballet choreographed by George Balanchine (*5 am*).

Before the outbreak of World War II Baker returned to Europe, where she married an industrialist, Jean Lion, took French nationality, and joined the League against Racism and Anti-Semitism. She and Lion separated fourteen months after their marriage.

At the outbreak of war, Baker appeared with Maurice Chevalier in *Paris-Londres* at the Casino de Paris, gave concerts for the troops, and worked as a helper with nursing organizations that dealt with refugees from the frontline. After the fall of France she went to North Africa, having been recruited by the Free French army to act as a courier and liaison officer with the Resistance. In this capacity she went three times to Spain. After the war she was awarded the Rosette de La Résistance for her work. During the Allied invasion of North Africa and the subsequent advance, Baker entertained French, British, and American troops and was a lieutenant in the Women's Auxiliary Air Force.

After the liberation of Paris, Baker returned to France and continued to work as an entertainer for the Allied forces until the end of hostilities. The French awarded her the Croix de Guerre. She worked with and in 1947 was married to French bandleader Jo Bouillon. A return with his band to the United States in 1947 was unsuccessful, but a new revue in Paris, *Féeries et Folies*, at the Folies Bergère in 1949, reestablished her name. During an extended tour of the United States in 1951, she met with a rapturous reaction, including an official "Josephine Baker Day" in Harlem (21 May), but her attempts at confrontation with hotel, café, and restaurant owners over segregation and racial discrimination eventually led to a notorious campaign against her headed by journalist Walter Winchell. Baker did not return to the United States until 1960.

In France Baker and Bouillon eventually adopted twelve children of different ethnic backgrounds as a demonstrative experiment in racial harmony, the so-called "Rainbow tribe." Housed in the Dordogne village, Les Milandes, the rest of Baker's career was devoted to promoting the idea of brotherhood and antiracism.

Baker and Bouillon parted in 1960, and financial difficulties dogged her for the remainder of her life. Although plagued by ill health and a series of heart attacks, Baker continued to perform for the rest of her life. She died in Paris, two days after appearing in a revue to celebrate the fiftieth anniversary of her Parisian debut.

Despite her original celebrity as a dancer, Baker's long recording career has left her with an equal reputation as a singer. In the sessions of the 1920s, her high, piping soubrette-style delivery makes a charming impression with the French jazz bands. A mixture of skat, operetta-style coloratura, and more conventional dance-rhythm and *sprechgesang* contrived to make her one of the most individual of the later generation of French music-hall stars. During the war she began singing with a microphone and subsequently used a more throaty, mezzo-soprano delivery more in keeping with the relaxed 1950s style epitomized by such songs as "Besamo mucho," "Brazil," and "En Avril à Paris."

Although Baker's political activities and espousal of antiracist causes were of a highly personal nature, subsequent generations have come to regard her as an important figure in the history of African-American sociology. She worked for many years as an ambassadress for the United Nations International Children's Emergency Fund (UNICEF), attended many congresses on peace and race relations, and was the first woman of American birth ever to be honored with a state funeral (at the Madeleine) in France.

• Important collections of memorabilia concerning Baker are in the Beinecke Library, Yale University; the New York Public Library's Schomburg Center for Research in Black Culture and the Library for the Performing Arts, Lincoln Center; and in the Bibliothèque de l'Arsenal in Paris. Baker collaborated on four volumes of autobiography that remain the most important sources of information about her early life. *Les Memoires de Joséphine Baker* (1927) and *Voyages et Aventures de Joséphine Baker* (1931) were both written in collaboration with Marcel Sauvage and were updated and expanded into a single volume, *Les Memoires de Joséphine Baker* (1949). *Une Vie de Toutes les Couleurs* (1935), written with André Rivollet, although a somewhat fanciful account, has more details of her childhood, and the posthumously published *Josephine* (1976), by Jacqueline Cartier in collaboration with Jo Bouillon, draws on all the earlier books as well as adds later material, including interviews with members of the "Rainbow tribe." Subsequent biographies include Lynn Haney, *Naked at the Feast* (1981), Bryan Hammond and Patrick O'Connor, *Josephine Baker* (1988), and Phyllis Rose, *Jazz Cleopatra* (1989). The fullest account by a firsthand witness of the creation of *La Revue Nègre* is in the reminiscences of Claude Hopkins, collected by Warren Vache, Sr., in the *Mississippi Rag*, Feb–Apr. 1986.

PATRICK O'CONNOR

BAKER, La Fayette Curry (13 Oct. 1825–3 July 1868), head of the U.S. Secret Service, was born in Stafford, New York, the son of Remember Baker and Cynthia (maiden name unknown), farmers. Named for the French aristocrat, the marquis de Lafayette, who aided the American cause during the revolutionary war, the youth in 1839 settled in Michigan with his parents and attended local schools. As a young man he lived in over a dozen states, including Michigan, New York, and Pennsylvania, sometimes supporting himself as a mechanic. While operating a dry goods store in Philadelphia in 1852, he married Jennie C. Curry; they had no children. The next year they relocated to San Francisco, California, where Baker worked as a general laborer and belonged to the San Francisco Vigilance Committee. His work with the vigilantes helped bring order to a city known for its gambling houses, crime, and political corruption, and Baker gained valuable experience in investigation and surveillance.

After the outbreak of the Civil War in 1861, Baker, then a resident of New York, volunteered to penetrate Confederate lines to obtain information for the Union. Dispatched clandestinely to Richmond by General Winfield Scott, Baker sought to ascertain the location and size of General Pierre G. T. Beauregard's forces around Manassas, secure data on the Black Horse Cavalry, determine what forces were in Richmond, and learn if any plans existed for an invasion of the North. Disguised as an unarmed itinerant photographer, Baker was arrested by the Confederates, who suspected him of being a secret agent. During Baker's brief incarceration, the rebel spy, Belle Boyd, attempted to trick him into revealing his identity. Posing as "Samuel Munson" of Knoxville, Baker convinced President Jefferson Davis that he was the son of a Tennessee judge, a friend of the president's orderly. Upon his return to Washington, Baker met with President Abraham Lincoln, who appointed the wily detective to inform the president about generals, officers, battles, and other pertinent war-related activities. Baker eventually gained a colonel's commission as special provost marshal of the War Department in 1862. Three years later he earned the rank of brigadier general.

Baker's years in the Secret Service were noteworthy. Heading a force that included his assistant, John Odell, and others, Baker demonstrated admirable ability as a detective, modeling himself after the French spy François Vidocq. Although an innovator of police methods, Baker often disregarded due process, search warrants, and other constitutional guarantees during the war. Defending his conduct, he claimed that a detective's professional work "forbids him to give his authority for certain acts or assign any reason for his procedure. Hence the clamor is often raised of rash and lawless abuse of power when all the time he is acting under the direct orders of the Government" (Mogelever, p. 417).

Lincoln assigned Baker to root out disloyalty in the Union military forces, and Secretary of War Edwin M. Stanton provided him with extraordinary power and large amounts of money to pursue a campaign against traitors. On one special mission for Stanton, Baker broke through enemy lines to relay information to General Nathaniel P. Banks's army. On another occasion, Baker penetrated Confederate territory to learn of troop movements and in the process uncovered a rebel plot to capture Washington, D.C. Baker's surveillance also led to the imprisonment of Louisa Buckner, who had journeyed to Washington from Virginia to purchase supplies of quinine and other goods for the Confederacy. Secretary of the Treasury Salmon P. Chase, who later served as chief justice of the U.S. Supreme Court, enlisted the chief detective to investigate charges of corruption and immorality in the Treasury Department. Baker's most famous achievement, however, was planning and leading the expedition that captured John Wilkes Booth, the actor and southern sympathizer who assassinated Lincoln.

Following the war, Baker's reputation suffered grievously. His attempt to curtail the activities of Lucy Cobb, a notorious Washington pardon broker who enjoyed ready access to the White House, led to his downfall. He warned President Andrew Johnson that "a system of manipulation and corruption are being practiced by persons holding official positions under the Government in connection with the procuring of pardons." Hearing rumors of Cobb's alleged affair with the president, Baker set a trap to catch her selling documents needed for pardons. An angry Johnson dismissed Baker for insolence, meddling, and maintaining an espionage system at the White House.

Anxious to reignite his dwindling renown, Baker testified before the House Judiciary Committee during Johnson's impeachment hearings in 1868. Baker was caught in the web of conspiracy hatched by Congressman James M. Ashley, an Ohio Republican who attempted to prove that Johnson had improperly corresponded with Davis. For his star witness, Ashley, contending that all previous presidents who died in office had been poisoned, turned to Baker, who readily complied with Ashley's request as part of his vendetta against Johnson. Baker told the House committee he had seen a purported letter written by Johnson, while military governor of Tennessee, to Davis, in which Johnson had disclosed the position of Federal forces in Tennessee and vaguely hinted at joining the rebel cause. Baker failed to produce the letter. In fact, he gave false testimony of secret letters that never surfaced, mysterious individuals who never materialized, and unsubstantiated missing pages from Booth's diary in his scurrilous endeavor to besmirch the chief executive. At one time he even failed to appear before the committee, compelling the chairman to issue a warrant for his apprehension. Committee members ultimately discounted Baker's testimony.

Baker's misleading remarks before the House committee corroborated the general impression that the former secret agent was a dubious witness. Broken in spirit and in declining health, he endured overwhelming ridicule during Johnson's impeachment trial and a financial business failure in managing a hotel in Lansing, Michigan. Less than six weeks after Johnson's acquittal by the Senate, Baker died in Philadelphia of spinal meningitis and fever.

Baker exhibited good intuition and tenacity as head of the Secret Service, an institutional predecessor of today's agency, but intoxicated by his own power and infatuated with intrigue, he in the end became his own worst enemy. A man of many sides, he was a tireless detective who could be egotistical, ruthless, and reckless, arousing much animosity in his relentless pursuits. Although many of Baker's enemies denounced him for graft and comical adventures, others in government appreciated his methods. He published a book in 1867 entitled *History of the United States Secret Service*, an important source for information on the organization of the Secret Service Bureau, leading detectives of the time, and espionage experiences of the North and South during the Civil War. The book settled some disputed aspects of the Civil War but in many cases combined truth with fiction. While his career was controversial, Baker was one of America's most colorful and daring secret service agents.

• Although Baker left no collection of letters, some papers and mementos remain in the possession of distant family members, including descendants of his brothers, sisters, and cousins. A letter dealing with Cobb is in the Andrew Johnson Papers at the Library of Congress. Additional material can be mined from the Baker-Turner papers. The two major biographies of Baker are Jacob Mogelever, *Death to Traitors: The Story of General Lafayette C. Baker, Lincoln's Forgotten Secret Service Chief* (1960), and Arthur Orrmont, *Mr. Lincoln's Master Spy: Lafayette Baker* (1966). Brief information on Baker as head of the federal Secret Service is in Hans L. Trefousse, *Andrew Johnson: A Biography* (1989); Robert F. Horowitz, *Great Impeacher: A Political Biography of James M. Ashley* (1979); Betty J. Ownsbey, *Alias "Paine": Lewis Thornton Powell, the Mystery Man of the Lincoln Conspiracy* (1993); and Donald E. Markle, *Spies and Spymasters of the Civil War* (1994). Obituaries are in the *New York Times*, the *Philadelphia Press*, and the *New York World*, all 4 July 1868; and the *New York Evening Post* and the *Washington Post*, both 6 July 1868.

LEONARD SCHLUP

BAKER, Newton Diehl (3 Dec. 1871–25 Dec. 1937), lawyer, mayor of Cleveland, Ohio, and secretary of war, was born in Martinsburg, West Virginia, the son of Newton Diehl Baker, a physician and former Confederate soldier, and Mary Ann Dukehart. Baker graduated in 1892 from Johns Hopkins University, where he first met Woodrow Wilson, and received his law degree from Washington and Lee University in 1894. In 1902 he married Elizabeth Leopold; the couple had three children.

Baker served as secretary to William L. Wilson, postmaster general in the second Grover Cleveland administration, and then moved to Cleveland, Ohio, where he became active in city and state Democratic politics. He was city solicitor under Tom L. Johnson (1901–1909) and worked for public utilities and traction reform. As the "Boy Mayor" of Cleveland (1911–1915), he continued his work for improvements in the city infrastructure and also helped restore and beautify the Cleveland lakefront. Baker entered the Wilson administration as part of an effort to cool a political situation that had become so heated during the preparedness debates of 1915 that it threatened the unity of the Democratic party and jeopardized the president's reelection. When Lindley M. Garrison resigned in February 1916 during a debate over military manpower, Baker became the expedient political choice. He was a member of the American League Against Militarism yet had worked actively for President Wilson's neutrality policies. He wanted a strong America but opposed the saber rattling of men like Theodore Roosevelt. He was no pacifist, yet he had the respect of those like Jane Addams and Oswald Garrison Villard, who were. Better yet, Baker had given little thought to military affairs and thus found it easy to accept the compromises that were worked out in the National Defense Act of 1916.

Baker was a cautious administrator and chose to maintain traditional organizational relationships wherever possible. After war was declared in April 1917, he reaffirmed equality of access and consultation in his relations with the general staff and the bureau chiefs in the War Department. He opposed efforts to lodge independent authority in civilian superagencies like Bernard Baruch's War Industries Board. Even after political pressure during the mobilization crisis of the winter of 1917–1918 forced him to strengthen War Department control over industrial mobilization and to consolidate the management of military supply and procurement in the general staff under canal builder George W. Goethals, he resisted further "root and branch" reorganization. At the end of the war, civilian agencies had eroded the War Department position, but in most important ways it still controlled the mobilization process.

The greatest innovation of the war was systematic conscription. The Wilson administration had opposed even the mention of such a notion before April 1917. However, for reasons both practical and political, once war was declared it executed a complete change in direction. Baker's support for the draft was particularly important because it persuaded many of his antimilitarist associates, who feared "selective service" would become permanent policy, that such a temporary expedient might be risked in a war for democracy. Little of the racism and anti–civil libertarianism that rose during the conflict can be traced directly to the secretary of war's office, but Baker did little to control the zeal of soldiers in the training camps, in conscientious-objector centers, or in the field. He chose to deflect and, if possible, dilute such issues, and accordingly, he was condemned for the acts of subordinates and got little credit for avoiding the cruder excesses that would undoubtedly have occurred if he had done nothing at all. Baker was less successful in resolving command issues between the War Department and the commander of the American Expeditionary Force (AEF). From the time General John J. Pershing arrived in France in June 1917, he clashed with authorities at home. In early 1918 the new chief of staff, Peyton C. March, began to insist that full policy control must be lodged in Washington. Pershing declared that the commander in the field should not be restrained in any way. Baker avoided making a decision, and the war was almost over before he clearly came to support March.

As secretary, Baker was always the president's man. He astutely handled his part of the Mexican crisis of 1916–1917 in such a way as to reduce public hysteria and help keep the control of events in Wilson's hands. He served Wilsonian wartime policy and assured the president a strong hand at the peace table by protecting the independence and physical integrity of the AEF. During two critical wartime trips to Europe, Baker negotiated agreements that determined U.S. troop strength and assured the shipping necessary to move the AEF to France. When he disagreed with the president, as he did in the debates over intervention in Russia during the summer of 1918, he loyally carried out policy once it had been established. Near the end of the war, he was prepared, if necessary, to relieve General Pershing from command in France if Pershing continued, as he had been doing, to interfere with Wilson's efforts to secure an armistice with the Germans.

Baker left public office in 1921. During the twenties, his law practice flourished, and this professional success allowed him time to render philanthropic and educational service. Still active in national politics, his plea for the League of Nations at the Democratic convention of 1924 was remembered later by Adlai Stevenson as the greatest speech he had ever heard. Baker was nominated by anti-Roosevelt Democrats for the presidency in 1932. During the thirties he served the army on various boards, including the "Baker Board" on the reorganization of the Army Air Corps. He died at his home in Shaker Heights, a suburb of Cleveland, Ohio.

To many critics, Baker's life and career were a paradox. A man of peace and a confirmed antimilitarist, he became a celebrated war leader. He had a reputation as something of a radical reformer as well as one of the significant architects of the Progressive movement, yet he died a wealthy corporate lawyer. Others have made clear his inadequacies as an organizer and administrator. All too often he let the soldiers have their way. He neither resolved the conflicts between March and Pershing nor brought the bureau chiefs under permanent central control. Still others observed that he did not support civil rights and liberties as effectively as he could have. But Baker was no crusader. He was simply a competent, humane, and compassionate man who abhorred extremes and entwined commitment to social and economic amelioration with concern for decency and order.

• The Newton Diehl Baker Papers are located in the Library of Congress. The most significant biographies include Frederick Palmer, *Newton D. Baker: America at War* (2 vols., 1931); Clarence H. Cramer, *Newton D. Baker: A Biography* (1961); and Daniel R. Beaver, *Newton D. Baker and the American War Effort 1917–1919* (1966). For other aspects of his war work, see Robert H. Ferrell, *Woodrow Wilson and World War I: 1917–1921* (1985); John W. Chambers II, *To Raise an Army: The Draft Comes to Modern America* (1987); Edward M. Coffman, *The Hilt of the Sword: The Career of Peyton C. March* (1966); Robert D. Cuff, *The War Industries Board: Business-Government Relations during World War I* (1973); David M. Kennedy, *Over Here: The First World War and American Society* (1980); Ronald Schaffer, *America in the Great War: The Rise of the War Welfare State* (1991); Donald Smythe, *Pershing: General of the Armies* (1986); and Jordan Schwartz, *The Speculator: Bernard Baruch in Washington, 1917–1965* (1981). An obituary is in the *New York Times*, 26 Dec. 1937.

DANIEL R. BEAVER

BAKER, Oliver Edwin (10 Sept. 1883–2 Dec. 1949), geographer, was born in Tiffin, Ohio, the son of Edwin Baker, a merchant, and Martha Ranney Thomas. His mother had been a schoolteacher, and because he was a frail child she supplied much of his early education. After graduating from public school Baker went on to Tiffin's Heidelberg College, where he earned bachelor's and master's degrees in 1903 and 1904, specializing in mathematics, history, botany, sociology, and philosophy. In 1905 he earned a master's degree in political science from Columbia University; from 1908 to 1912, after a year at Yale studying forestry, he did graduate work in agriculture at the University of Wisconsin, focusing on and mapping soils, climates, and agricultural production. During the summers he worked for the Wisconsin Soil Survey. Following a break from graduate school Baker returned to Madison to study economics, earning a Ph.D. in 1921 with a dissertation on land utilization. At the university two pioneering economists, Henry C. Taylor and Richard T. Ely, influenced his shift to the economics of agriculture and the economic emphasis of much of his research and writing as a geographer.

Beginning in 1912 Baker had worked in the U.S. Department of Agriculture with William J. Spillman of the Office of Farm Management, and in 1922 he joined the department's new Bureau of Agricultural Economics, headed by Henry C. Taylor. There he conducted and supervised major research projects, many of them delineating and mapping agricultural regions. He worked hard and creatively, inspired and encouraged his coworkers, and was open to suggestions from them.

Baker's work influenced geographers beyond the department. They especially admired and used his *Geography of the World's Agriculture* (1917), his six-part *Atlas of American Agriculture* (1936), his articles in *Economic Geography* (1926–1933) on the agricultural regions of North America, and his many contributions to the annual *Yearbook of Agriculture*. He served for several years as associate editor of *Economic Geography* and was a part-time professor at Clark University in Worcester, Massachusetts. He became president of the Association of American Geographers in 1932.

Working in a government agency, Baker hoped to serve more than the needs of his discipline. Geographers, he believed, should help farmers and others make better use of natural resources. Before the end of the 1920s he had grown concerned about the declining U.S. birthrate, especially among well-educated city people, and he predicted that the population of the United States would soon decline and demand for food would fall. His ideas on these subjects influenced the land and farm policies of the Herbert Hoover and Franklin Roosevelt administrations.

An agrarian philosophy permeated Baker's work. He collaborated with Ralph Barsodi, an advocate of a return to rural life, on *Agriculture in Modern Life* (1939). Critical of city life, Baker advocated a "rurban" civilization that would combine industrial and commercial employment with village and suburban living and part-time farming; he believed this would strengthen family ties, improve land-use practices, and increase the birthrate. This thinking affected his government work in that he encouraged his subordinates to investigate rural groups, such as the Amish, Mennonites, and Mormons, which seemed to offer good models. Agrarianism also influenced Baker's own family life: he and his wife, Alice Hargrave Crew, whom he married in 1925, raised four children on a large suburban plot where they could raise chickens and cows and cultivate a garden. Later he purchased a large farm, which enabled him to pursue his interest in soil conservation.

In 1942 Baker left Washington, D.C., to establish a geography department at the University of Maryland. There he recruited a strong faculty, attracted an impressive number of students, and promoted large research projects. He continued to insist that geography could and should help people solve problems, and although a "baby boom" had begun, he continued to worry about the U.S. birthrate.

Always afflicted by health problems, Baker died in his home in College Park, Maryland. His work continued to be cited by scholars for many years. A 1954 publication of the Association of American Geographers referred to *Geography of the World's Agriculture* as "the most complete array of mapped information regarding agricultural commodities ever to appear in the United States" and to Baker as "the leading agricultural geographer" of his time (James and Jones, p. 261). Some of his work, such as his population forecasts, did not hold up, and some geographers regarded his agrarianism as reactionary and regretted the large influence of his interpretation of the United States as a complex of agricultural regions. Others, however, recognized him as a pioneer who had done basic work of continuing interest and usefulness, particularly in his mapping of those regions.

• The records of the Bureau of Agricultural Economics in the National Archives house Baker's official papers. His presidential address, "Rural-Urban Migration and the National Welfare," *Annals of the Association of American Geographers* 23 (June 1933): 59–126, exemplifies his thinking. A summary of his career and a bibliography are in S. S. Visher and Charles Y. Hu, *Annals of the Association of American Geographers* 40 (Dec. 1950): 328–34. See also Thomas F. Barton and P. P. Karan, *Leaders in American Geography*, vol. 1 (1992), pp. 100–103. On his agrarianism consult Charles S. Aiken, "Expressions of Agrarianism in American Geography: The Cases of Isaiah Bowman, J. Russell Smith and O. E. Baker," *Professional Geographer* 27 (Feb. 1975): 19–29. For appraisals of Baker's contributions see Richard Hartshorne, "The Nature of Geography: A Critical Survey of Current Thought in the Light of the Past," *Annals of the Association of American Geographers* 29 (Sept.–Dec. 1939); Leonard A. Salter, Jr., *A Critical Review of Research in Land Economics* (1948); Henry C. Taylor and Anne Dewees Taylor, *The Story of Agricultural Economics in the United States, 1840–1932* (1952); Preston E. James and Clarence F. Jones, eds., *American Geography: Inventory & Prospect* (1954); and T. W. Freeman, *A Hundred Years of Geography* (1961).

RICHARD S. KIRKENDALL

BAKER, Osmon Cleander (30 July 1812–20 Dec. 1871), Methodist educator and bishop, was born in Marlow, New Hampshire, the son of Isaac Baker and Abigail Kidder. At the age of fifteen he began his studies at Wilbraham Academy in Massachusetts. Wilbur Fisk, the first major Methodist theologian to receive notice outside of the denomination, was the principal of the school, which Methodists had founded a decade earlier. While a student there in 1828, Baker was converted, joined the church, and was licensed to exhort. In 1830 he entered the first class at Wesleyan University, in Middletown, Connecticut, where Fisk, the first president, continued to have a profound effect on the young student. After Baker had spent three years at Wesleyan, ill health forced him to withdraw from the university.

In 1833 Baker married Mehitabel Perley. In 1834 he became a teacher at Newbury Seminary in Vermont, and four years later he accepted a position as principal of the institution. He joined several other professors in 1841 in offering regular theological classes; two years later a part of the seminary building was reassigned to serve as a theological school and was formally dedicated. This institutional transformation made Baker the first professor of theology in American Methodism. In 1844 he resigned from the school to serve as pastor of churches in Manchester and Rochester, New Hampshire. In 1847 Baker served as the presiding elder of the Dover district of the New Hampshire Conference. That same year the Methodist General Biblical Institute opened in Concord, New Hampshire, with Baker as professor of homiletics and Methodist discipline. He lived in Concord for the rest of his life.

At the General Conference of 1852 in Boston, Baker's fellow ministers elected him as one of four new bishops. Like other Methodist bishops, Baker spent much of his career traveling extensively to preside over the meetings of annual conferences. In 1853 he authored a short devotional book titled *The Last Witness; or, The Dying Sayings of Eminent Christians and Noted Infidels*. Baker's primary contribution to Methodism in the mid-nineteenth century was through his extensive knowledge of the constitution and laws of the Methodist Episcopal church. The hierarchical but flexible circuit system had served the denomination well for decades, and the Methodist *Discipline* had ensured some uniformity in faith and practice. Baker's *Guide Book in the Administration of the Discipline of the Methodist Episcopal Church*, first published in 1855 and revised several times thereafter, served as a standard reference for bishops and pastors as they tried to apply the *Discipline* of the church to individual churches.

During the Civil War Baker steadfastly supported the Union cause. In December 1863 Secretary of War Edwin Stanton authorized the northern Methodist bishops to seize any southern Methodist church buildings in which a loyal minister was not preaching. Baker received authority to enforce the decree in Virginia and North Carolina. In the spring of 1866 he presided over the organization of a new South Carolina Conference, composed of freedpeople and white Unionists in South Carolina, eastern Georgia, and Florida. However, the prominence of fellow bishops, like Matthew Simpson, Edmund S. Janes, and Edward R. Ames, who played a more active and visible role in national affairs, generally overshadowed Baker's episcopal career.

In 1866, while on his way to preside over the meeting of the Colorado Conference, Baker suffered a stroke. He managed to continue his trip but could only meet with the ministers in his private room. After recuperation at home, he was able to preside at a few more conferences and meet with the other bishops until 1868, when his ministry effectively ended. Baker suffered another stroke and died in Concord, New Hampshire.

• Baker's scrapbook, including some correspondence and a manuscript sermon, is in the Methodist Archives of the Perkins School of Theology at Southern Methodist University. For biographical sketches, see Matthew Simpson, ed., *Cyclopaedia of Methodism* (1878); Theodore L. Flood and John W.

Hamilton, eds., *Lives of Methodist Bishops* (1882); Frederick D. Leete, *Methodist Bishops* (1948); and Nolan B. Harmon, ed., *The Encyclopedia of World Methodism* (1974).

DANIEL W. STOWELL

BAKER, Ray Stannard (17 Apr. 1870–12 July 1946), journalist and author, was born in Lansing, Michigan, the son of Joseph Stannard Baker and Alice Potter. A descendant of pioneering stock, he grew up in St. Croix Falls, Wisconsin, where his family moved in 1875 and his father worked as a land agent. Baker later boasted that he had been brought up on the "last frontier." His mother died in 1883, but his father, a Civil War veteran, strongly impressed Baker with his rugged character, integrity, and common sense. He attended the local schools, discovered the world of books in his parents' library, and in 1885 enrolled at Michigan Agricultural College in East Lansing. In college Baker discovered a special liking for science courses and also edited the school newspaper. After receiving the B.S. degree in 1889, he returned home to work in his father's land office. In January 1892 Baker entered law school at the University of Michigan but dropped out after a few months. Meanwhile, he became interested in journalism, partly as the result of a seminar at the university. In the summer of 1892 he found a job with the Chicago *News-Record*.

Baker's years as a reporter for the *News-Record* from 1892 to 1898 were the foundation for his career as a journalist. Enterprising and industrious, he learned to approach a story directly and to write accurately and clearly. His work included many routine assignments as well as coverage of Jacob Coxey's march on Washington and the Pullman strike of 1894. He soon became, in his own words, "a special and editorial writer." Baker also began independent writing for periodicals, particularly *McClure's Magazine*, and in 1898 he left Chicago for New York to join the staff of *McClure's*. In 1896 he had married Jessie Irene Beal, the daughter of his college botany professor. They had four children.

McClure's Magazine was in the vanguard of a new style of journalism that emphasized social reality, accurate reporting, and human interest. Baker, therefore, became part of the changing field of magazine publishing. Among his first responsibilities was directing the McClure newspaper syndicate. His writing on scientific subjects for syndicated circulation resulted in the publication of his first book, *The Boy's Book of Inventions: Stories of the Wonders of Modern Science* (1899), which demonstrated his ability to make scientific phenomena intelligible to laymen. Despite his editorial responsibilities, Baker produced a stream of articles around the turn of the century, ranging from a discussion of the war of 1898 and the new American imperialism, which he approved, to sketches of contemporary leaders like J. P. Morgan and Theodore Roosevelt (1858–1919). He began to travel widely in the United States and abroad. Baker wrote not only for *McClure's*, but as a freelancer for other magazines. This profusion of articles led to the publication of several books: *Our New Prosperity* (1900), on the economic recovery at the end of the nineteenth century, *Seen in Germany* (1901), collected articles written during his travels in that country, and *Boys' Second Book of Inventions* (1903), another collection of his writings on scientific themes. Baker's reputation as a contributor to the leading popular magazines of the day grew, and he was invited to the White House to talk with Theodore Roosevelt, who liked Baker's treatment of the Rooseveltian approach and the new social issues.

As he learned more about the country's social problems, Baker, like many other journalists, encouraged reform by investigating the dark underside of American life. In 1903 he joined with Lincoln Steffens, Ida M. Tarbell, and other writers for *McClure's* in what became a nationwide crusade against corruption and lawlessness—a movement against trusts, railroad discrimination, political bosses, and so on. They engaged in what their contemporaries called "muckraking." Baker was clearly a muckraker, although not of the more sensational kind. Beginning in 1902 he investigated the use of violence against nonstriking coal miners, employer abuse in the New York garment industry, the excesses of trade unionism, the need to regulate railroad monopoly, and unsavory aspects of American politics.

Baker later undertook a critical examination of religious life in the United States that resulted in the publication of *The Spiritual Unrest* (1910). His best-known work of reportage was a series of articles on the race question, written on the basis of a trip through the South in 1907. These essays, republished in *Following the Color Line: An Account of Negro Citizenship in the American Democracy* (1908), were not, strictly speaking, a muckraking investigation. But they were a widely discussed field report on race relations and the place of blacks in America, notable for their balanced approach, comprehensive coverage, and fresh insights. Yet Baker offered no solution to the thorny problem of race in the United States, except "time, growth, education, religion, thought."

In 1906 Baker entered into an arrangement with John S. Phillips, Steffens, Tarbell, and several other journalists to purchase the *American Magazine*. The new owners hoped to develop a journal that would reflect their own tastes and that would be less sensational and more constructive than *McClure's*. They promised that the magazine would be "wholesome, hopeful, stimulating, uplifting, and . . . have a human interest on every page." The *American* enjoyed considerable success, and Baker served as one of its editors from 1906 until 1915, when he resigned. Meanwhile, his productivity as a magazine journalist continued at a high level; by the time he resigned his editorship, he had written more than 200 articles on a great variety of subjects.

Baker also began a new, experimental kind of writing. In 1907 he published *Adventures in Contentment*, the fictionalized first-person narrative of a farmer-philosopher named David Grayson, who emphasized the beauty and peacefulness of the countryside, in contrast to the harsh reality of urban life. Baker had found an alter ego in David Grayson, and the nine volumes he wrote under that pseudonym between 1907 and 1942 reflected his own idealism and Emersonian outlook. They also demonstrated Baker's desire to educate his readers. The Grayson books were popular, selling more than two million copies in the United States and abroad. The series also inspired a flood of letters to Baker, which contributed to his great satisfaction with the whole project. He later wrote that his adventures with David Grayson "have been my life, rather than my work" (*American Chronicle*, p. 241). Meanwhile, Baker's desire for a convenient base of operation and a rural refuge brought another significant change in his life. In 1910 he moved his family from East Lansing, Michigan, to Amherst, Massachusetts, which remained for the rest of his life a favorite retreat and a place of peace and quiet.

During the early decades of the twentieth century, Baker moved away from his belief in individualism and a healthy American economy toward an acceptance of collectivism, public regulation, and even government ownership. He briefly joined forces with the Socialists but soon retreated to a more moderate progressive position. After championing Theodore Roosevelt's leadership for years, Baker wrote approvingly of Republican insurgency in the administration of William Howard Taft, became a supporter of Senator Robert M. La Follette in 1911, and in the election of 1912 reluctantly voted for Woodrow Wilson. By 1914, however, he had become a confirmed Wilsonian, applauding the president's New Freedom reforms and in later years endorsing Wilson's neutrality and wartime policies.

In 1918 Baker served as a special agent of the State Department in Great Britain, France, and Italy, and at the Paris Peace Conference of 1919 he directed the American delegation's press bureau. He became a strong advocate of Wilson's work as a peacemaker and of his League of Nations, as was evident in Baker's hastily written book, *What Wilson Did at Paris* (1919). In 1922 he published a more elaborate three-volume work entitled *Woodrow Wilson and World Settlement*. Baker's involvement with Wilson continued in the mid-1920s, when he and William E. Dodd edited *The Public Papers of Woodrow Wilson* (6 vols., 1925–1927). Yet Baker had not abandoned journalism. He published *The New Industrial Unrest* (1920), wrote a number of magazine and newspaper articles in the early 1920s, and also continued writing on David Grayson. But the First World War marked a turning point in Baker's interests, and thereafter his attention shifted increasingly from the present to the past, with his historical interest focused on Woodrow Wilson.

Baker was given access to the Wilson papers before Wilson left the White House, and in 1925 Edith Wilson selected him as her husband's authorized biographer. Baker spent fifteen years on the biography, interviewing many of Wilson's family members and associates, preparing detailed memoranda, and going through the vast corpus of the Wilson papers. The first two volumes of *Woodrow Wilson: Life and Letters* appeared in 1927, and six additional volumes were published during the next twelve years. The biography was never really finished, however, as volume 8 carried the story only through the Armistice of 1918. (Baker had, of course, previously provided some coverage of the Paris Peace Conference in his *Woodrow Wilson and World Settlement*.) The early volumes received generous praise, but as the biography unfolded reviewers became more critical. This change was in part because Wilson's reputation suffered in the interwar period and his biographer was caught in the cross fire of World War I revisionism. Nevertheless, Baker's treatment of Wilson was important, and he was awarded the Pulitzer Prize for biography in 1940.

Baker continued to write until the end of his life. *Under My Elm*, the last Grayson book, came out in 1942. He also published two volumes of autobiography: *Native American: The Book of My Youth* (1941) and *American Chronicle: The Autobiography of Ray Stannard Baker* (1945). There were other demands on his time as well, including active participation in such causes as the Woodrow Wilson Foundation; yet he also found time to work in his garden, a favorite pastime. In the winter of 1943–1944 he and his wife traveled to Hollywood for the filming of Daryl F. Zanuck's motion picture *Wilson*, for which Baker served as a consultant. Baker died in Amherst, Massachusetts.

Baker was a significant journalist and author with a knack for identifying the most vital issues and developments of his day. Energetic and resourceful, judicious and dependable, with a clear and lively prose style, he was a highly successful writer. Baker became known as "America's Number One Reporter." Circumspect, soft-spoken, and thus ineffective as a public speaker, his forte was writing. His biography of Woodrow Wilson, though soon superseded by more scholarly works, was a pioneering attempt to illuminate a key figure in early twentieth-century America. Not an especially original or profound thinker, Baker nevertheless had a wide-ranging and open mind, and he was extraordinarily sensitive to his times. He was an idealist and a reformer in search of an orderly and progressive society and a faith he could live by. In many ways Baker was a prototypical progressive whose works help explain the emergence of modern America and the age of reform.

• The major collection of Baker papers is in the Library of Congress, but two other valuable collections are located in the Jones Library, Amherst, Mass., and the Princeton University library. Copies of an unpublished bibliography of Baker's writings, prepared by his daughter Rachel Baker Napier, can be found in the Library of Congress and at Princeton.

Two scholarly works are indispensable: John E. Semonche, *Ray Stannard Baker: A Quest for Democracy in Modern America, 1870–1918* (1969), which deals with Baker's career as a journalist, and Robert C. Bannister, Jr., *Ray Stannard Baker: The Mind and Thought of a Progressive* (1966), a wideranging intellectual study. Bannister also includes a useful discussion of Baker's *Woodrow Wilson: Life and Letters*. David M. Chalmers, "Ray Stannard Baker's Search for Reform," *Journal of the History of Ideas* 19 (June 1958): 422–34, is a perceptive essay. Frank P. Rand, *The Story of David Grayson* (1963), discusses the Grayson books and quotes from letters to Grayson in the Jones Library. For information on Baker's career as a muckraker, see Chalmers, *The Social and Political Ideas of the Muckrakers* (1964); Peter Lyon, *Success Story: The Life and Times of S. S. McClure* (1963); and Harold S. Wilson, *McClure's Magazine and the Muckrakers* (1970). An obituary is in the *New York Times*, 13 July 1946.

DEWEY W. GRANTHAM

BAKER, Sara Josephine (15 Nov. 1873–22 Feb. 1945), physician and public health administrator, was born in Poughkeepsie, New York, the daughter of Orlando Daniel Mosher Baker, an eminent lawyer, and Jenny Harwood Brown, one of the first Vassar College graduates. In her autobiography Baker described her father, who came from Quaker stock, as a sober, quiet man who "never uttered an unnecessary word," while her mother, "gay, social and ambitious," traced her ancestry back to Samuel Danforth, one of the founders of Harvard College. A happy child, Baker drew inspiration from both parents. Wishing to make it up to her father for not being born a boy, she became an enthusiastic baseball player and trout-fisher and read Horatio Alger stories with zest. But, as Baker wrote in her autobiography, she was also "thoroughly trained in the business of being a woman," received rigorous instruction in cooking and sewing, and cherished "Jo" from Louisa May Alcott's *Little Women* as a favorite fictional character. Though her family had intended that Baker attend Vassar, the sudden deaths of her younger brother and her father when she was sixteen drastically altered her financial prospects. Because of the delicate health of her older sister, Baker alone took on the burden of family finances. After months of painful decision making, she resolved to give up the offer of a scholarship to Vassar and use the remaining savings to attend medical school. Overcoming her mother's initial aversion to a medical career, Baker attributed a good portion of her determination to the hardened opposition of other relatives. She always relished the defiance of convention, and the stubbornness and conviction that she manifested at this time stayed with her throughout her life.

After a year of preparatory course work in general subjects, Baker enrolled in the Women's Medical College of the New York Infirmary in 1894. Founded in 1868 by Elizabeth Blackwell and Emily Blackwell, this institution had an excellent reputation and was the only regular medical school open to women in the state. It offered Baker vigorous medical training and the rare opportunity to work with outstanding female role models, such as physicians Mary Putnam Jacobi, Annie Sturges Daniel, Martha Wollstein and Emily Blackwell. Exposure to networks of successful female professionals proved crucial to Baker's development and continued after graduation in 1898, when she spent a year as intern in Boston at the female-run New England Hospital for Women and Children. Working in an out-patient clinic in the midst of Boston's worst slums, Baker encountered firsthand the subject of her future life's work: the problems of poverty and ill health among the poor. She was unsentimental about her clients ("we were dealing with the dregs of Boston, ignorant, shiftless, settled irrevocably into surly degradation") but also perceptive about the structural sources of social injustice.

Warned that it would take five years to become established, Baker nevertheless opened a private practice in New York City with fellow intern and friend Dr. Florence Laighton in 1899. When they earned only $185 in the first year, the women pressured the New York Life Insurance Company to hire them as medical examiners, which paved the way for women physicians in insurance work. In addition, Baker took a part-time position as a medical inspector for the city at a salary of $30 a month. This exposure to a group of remarkable public health officials like Drs. Walter Bensel and Herman M. Biggs drew her into the field of public health, and by 1914 she had given up her private practice entirely. In 1907 she became assistant to the commissioner of health and handled a range of problems from vaccinating against small pox to sanitation to apprehending and managing Typhoid Mary Mallon, a notorious asymptomatic carrier of the disease who, as a cook, had infected numerous people. Eventually, her interests centered on infant and child health, and in 1908 she was appointed director of the Bureau of Child Hygiene under the city health department, the first bureau of its kind in the United States, and one that her efforts had helped to create.

As bureau director, Baker made many outstanding contributions to preventive medicine and social policy. Indeed, she became perhaps the most prominent member of a cohort of women physicians who, in the first third of the twentieth century, made their mark in social medicine. One of her first accomplishments was to develop legislation, regulation, and training opportunities to control city midwives. Her efforts resulted in a significant reduction in maternal mortality and infant gonorrheal blindness. By sending school inspection nurses into slum homes to teach recent immigrants about ventilation and proper cleanliness, she brought down the incidence of infant mortality from summer diarrhea. Baker's baby health stations, which were imitative of European models, distributed pure milk, and her Little Mothers' Leagues trained preadolescent slum girls to care for younger siblings while their mothers worked. Her innovative school health program involved doctors and nurses in monitoring student health from kindergarten through adolescence and inspired similar programs in thirty-five states. By the time of her retirement in 1923, New York City had the lowest infant mortality rate of any of the major cities in America or Europe.

Baker was something of a maverick whose efforts often ran counter to a medical profession that was increasingly nervous about government incursion on fee-for-service practice. As the public health field became dominated by physician-scientists who gradually abandoned the costly and politically sensitive program of environmental reform for the more dramatic and immediate rewards of the laboratory, Baker kept her attention trained on the social context of disease. She was a consummate politician who devoted much thought to accomplishing her goals without appearing too politically radical. Her emphasis on the plight of mothers and children always muted the opposition. Increasingly recognized as a leading international authority on public health, in 1917 she became the first woman to receive a doctorate in public health from the New York University–Bellevue Hospital Medical School and lectured there annually thereafter on child hygiene. She published five books, *Healthy Babies* (1920), *Healthy Mothers* (1920), *Healthy Children* (1920), *The Growing Child* (1923), and *Child Hygiene* (1925), and contributed fifty articles to medical journals and over 200 to the popular press on the subject of preventive medicine. She served from 1922 to 1924 as a member of the Health Committee of the League of Nations and as a child hygiene consultant to the Children's Bureau of the U.S. Department of Labor, the U.S. Public Health Service, and the New York State Department of Health. In 1917 she assumed the presidency of the American Child Hygiene Association, which she had founded in 1909, and was an active member of numerous medical societies and social welfare organizations until her death.

Baker was a feminist with ties to a network of independent and unconventional women who organized themselves into a discussion group known as the Heterodoxy Club in 1912. Members included Crystal Eastman, Mabel Dodge Luhan, Rose Pastor Stokes and Henrietta Rodman. A lesbian who believed that playing down her femininity would enable her to accomplish more professionally, Baker dressed in suits and neckties and was known among the Heterodoxy Club members as "Dr. Joe." She was an active suffragist and presided over the American Medical Women's Association in 1935.

A towering figure in the field of public health in the first half of the twentieth century, Baker retired during the last years of her life to her farm at Bellemead, New Jersey, where she lived with her partner, the novelist and writer Ida Wylie, and the physician Louise Pearce. She died in New York City.

• There is no biography, but Baker's witty autobiography, *Fighting for Life* (1939), is a helpful source. See also Noah D. Fabricant, ed., *Why We Became Doctors* (1954), pp. 129–31, for a short sketch. For her professional activities, see [unsigned], "Dr. S. Josephine Baker," *Medical Women's Journal* (July 1935): 199; Alice Stone Woolley, "Tributes to Dr. S. Josephine Baker," *Women in Medicine* (July 1946): 24–26; and a feature story on Dr. Baker in the New York *World-Telegram*, 21 Jan. 1942. Especially informative is Leona Baumgartner's biography in *Notable American Women* (1971). For Baker's relationship with the Heterodoxy Club and more on her lesbianism, see Judith Schwarz, *Radical Feminists of Heterodoxy* (1986). Francis Kobrin provides context for Baker's accomplishments regarding midwives in "The American Midwife Controversy: A Crisis of Professionalization," *Bulle-

tin of the History of Medicine (1966): 350–63. See chapter 10 of Regina Morantz-Sanchez, *Sympathy and Science: Women Physicians in American Medicine* (1985), for her work in public health. An obituary is in the *Journal of the American Medical Association*, 17 Mar. 1945.

REGINA MORANTZ-SANCHEZ

BAKEWELL, Benjamin (1 Aug. 1767–19 Feb. 1844), glass manufacturer, was born in Derby, England, the son of Joseph Bakewell and Sarah Woodhouse. At the age of fourteen he was apprenticed to a haberdasher in Derby, and at the completion of his training in 1788 he went to London to work as a salesman in a mercer's shop. Three years later he opened his own store, selling primarily French goods. That same year Bakewell married Anne White; they had four children. The French Revolution began in 1789 and interrupted the flow of goods, however, and Bakewell immigrated to the United States with his wife and family in 1794.

On arriving in New York City, Bakewell opened another import business. In 1798 he and his brother William established a very successful brewery in New Haven, Connecticut, that burned in 1804. Bakewell returned to New York City to resume his import business only to suffer losses during the economic difficulties of the Jefferson administration.

Thus in September 1808 Bakewell ventured west of the Alleghenies to seek his fortune. His capital was supplied by Benjamin Page and Thomas Kinder. They seized the opportunity to take over a foundering glassworks that had been established the year before in Pittsburgh, Pennsylvania, by George Robinson and an English glass blower, Edward Ensell. In late 1808 the firm, originally known as the Pittsburgh Flint Glass Works, was reestablished as Bakewell and Ensell, with Bakewell as the operations manager and Ensell as the expert glass blower. Ensell left the partnership in 1809, but Bakewell continued the factory as Benjamin Bakewell and Company, also known as B. Bakewell and Company. Forced to learn the glass making business after Ensell's departure, Bakewell apparently mastered the craft quickly. Under a variety of names, the firm would continue in operation nearly seventy-five years. It was probably the first company in the United States to produce cut and engraved glass tablewares, and it later produced plain and molded tablewares, flint glass, and pressed glass. Bakewell's, as the firm was and is known colloquially, was widely renowned in its own time for the fine quality of its wares, produced in large quantities for markets in North America, particularly in Ohio, the West, Southwest, and even in Mexico.

In 1813 the company became known as Bakewell, Page, and Bakewell, after the inclusion of Benjamin's son Thomas. The firm received medals for cut glass at both the 1824 and 1825 exhibitions of the Franklin Institute in Philadelphia, and it exhibited regularly there for many years. In 1827 Bakewell's son John also joined the firm, in 1832 Benjamin Page retired, and in 1836 the firm changed its name to Bakewells and Company.

Bakewell's was most famous during Benjamin Bakewell's lifetime for its cut and engraved wares, produced perhaps as early as 1808, when William Peter Eichbaum, a German immigrant craftsman who was trained in France, subcontracted with Bakewell to produce magnificent cut chandeliers. By about 1815 Bakewell's established its own glass-cutting shop, which was operated by English, French, and Belgian craftsmen, including the master craftsman Alexis Jardelle. In 1817 Bakewell's produced decanters, tumblers, and wineglasses for President James Monroe's use in the White House. They made many commemorative flasks, such as the "American System" flask, and other presentation pieces honoring the marquis de Lafayette and other notables. In the mid-1820s Bakewell's was also among the first glasshouses to experiment with pressing glass, a time- and labor-saving method in which molten glass is placed into a mold and pressed into shape with a plunger. They obtained a patent for the process in 1825. In 1829 they supplied a large order of cut glass for President Andrew Jackson.

When testifying before a congressional committee on tariffs in 1828, Bakewell noted that his factory employed directly "about 60 hands; of whom about 20 or 25 are boys. The residue are able-bodied men" (quoted in Kumm, p. 127). Perhaps a dozen of his employees were engravers and ornamenters at any one time. He recalled that he had "at first, great difficulties . . . in searching for the proper materials, and in obtaining suitable workmen," but that he had "surmounted all difficulties" through "capital, skill, industry, economy, judgment, and a market." He obtained most of his materials locally, and found that steam power was more reliable and economical than water power in cutting glass.

Deming Jarves, in his *Reminiscences of Glass-Making* (1865), noted that "We may well consider Mr. Bakewell as the father of the flint-glass business in this country; for he commenced work in 1808, and by untiring efforts and industry brought it to a successful issue." Jarves's comment reiterated the high praise Bakewell's glass had consistently received. Elias Pym Fordham, in his *Personal Narrative of Travel* (1817), for example, observed that "Mr. Bakewell's works are admirable. He has excellent artists, both French and English. His cut glass equals the best I have seen in England." Mrs. Anne Royall observed in 1829 in *Mrs. Royall's Pennsylvania*, that Bakewell's

is entirely devoted to the manufacture of white or flint glass, and has succeeded in producing the best specimens of this article ever made in the United States. The admiration of this glass is not confined merely to home observers, but the great amount of it which has been exported testifies the reputation it enjoys abroad; and there is scarcely a stranger visits Pittsburgh, who is not desirous of taking a peep at Bakewell's Glass House. . . . The quality, variety, beauty, and brilliancy of the endless piles of glass at Bakewell's is the greatest show I ever saw.

After Benjamin Bakewell's death in Pittsburgh in 1844, the firm was known as Bakewell, Pears, and Company, with the addition of John Palmer Pears, and it would operate under this name until 1882. Unfortunately, Bakewell's glass was not ordinarily marked, and thus it is often difficult to identify his products today. With the exception of a few marked pieces and others in the White House and other collections with documented provenance, scholars usually can only attribute certain wares of the appropriate date, form, and style to his shop.

• For genealogical information on Bakewell, see B. G. Bakewell, comp., *The Family Book of Bakewell, Page, Campbell* (1896), and Mary E. Bakewell, "The Bakewell Glass Factory," *Antiques* 53, no. 3 (Mar. 1948): 220–21. Early references to Bakewell's factories are in Thomas C. Pears, Jr., "The First Successful Flint Glass Factory in America: Bakewell, Pears & Co. (1808–1882)," *Antiques* 11, no. 3 (Mar. 1927): 201–5. See also Rhea Mansfield Knittle, "Concerning William Peter Eichbaum and Bakewell's," *Antiques* 11, no. 3 (Mar. 1927): 205–6, and Marguerite Kumm, "Bakewell Testimony," *Antiques* 44, no. 3 (Sept. 1943): 127–28. Bakewell is profiled in George S. and Helen McKearin, *American Glass* (1941) and *Two Hundred Years of American Blown Glass* (1950). Lowell Innes, *Pittsburgh Glass, 1797–1891: A History and Guide for Collectors* (1976), contains numerous illustrations and an extensive bibliography. See also Arlene Palmer, "American Heroes in Glass: The Bakewell Sulphide Portraits," *American Art Journal* 11 (Jan. 1979): 4–26.

GERALD W. R. WARD

BALABAN, Barney (8 June 1887–7 Mar. 1971), motion picture executive, was born in Chicago, Illinois, the son of Israel Balaban, a grocer, and Goldie Manderbursky. At age twelve Balaban began working as a messenger for Western Union, then worked at various jobs until the mid-1910s when he settled as a bookkeeper at the Western Cold Storage Company. With his father, brothers, and a friend (soon thereafter brother-in-law), Sam Katz, Balaban launched the Balaban & Katz movie theater company in 1912. During the next decade Balaban & Katz redefined movie exhibition; the company's Chicago-based movie palaces became the talk of the film business and enabled Balaban to quit his day job. Thereafter, whenever he worked, Balaban managed the corporation's books and created many of the principles of modern movie accounting and record keeping.

By 1925, with air-conditioned movie palaces dominating motion picture exhibition throughout Chicago and the surrounding states of Indiana, and Wisconsin, Balaban & Katz ranked as the most successful, most profitable, and most initiated movie exhibitor in the world. That year Paramount Pictures, the largest moviemaking and distribution company in the world, merged with Balaban & Katz and moved Katz to New York City to run the newly named Publix theater empire. Balaban remained in Chicago to run Paramount's operations there which centered on the score of Balaban & Katz 4,000-seat picture palaces.

Only in 1929, when it was clear that the Paramount takeover had made him a millionaire, did Balaban marry Tillie Urkow; they had three children.

If it had not been for the Great Depression, Balaban might have remained in Chicago, a successful but not-very-famous regionally based movie theater executive. The depression, however, nearly drove Paramount (and its subsidiary Publix) out of business and cost Katz his job. In July 1936 the shareholders of the newly reorganized Paramount Pictures Corporation called Balaban to New York to run the streamlined company. He proved so successful that a decade later Paramount again ranked as the most profitable and powerful of movie corporations. Balaban knew how to take advantage of the good times that returned to the film business during the 1940s.

Throughout the late 1930s, and into the 1940s and 1950s, Paramount Pictures operated a studio in Hollywood, an international network for worldwide distribution, and a chain of nearly a thousand theaters. Indeed, more than any other movie company, Paramount held dominion throughout the U.S. heartland, with theaters in midwestern cities from Chicago to Detroit and towns across the South from Florida to Texas.

Balaban stood at the top of this corporate colossus. To increase cash flow, during the late 1930s he signed up stars from other media—most notably Bing Crosby and Bob Hope—and turned them into box-office giants. Balaban also skillfully milked distribution profits from world bookings, and he introduced buttered popcorn sales to generate greater revenues.

Balaban kept a tight lid on costs. For example, he required his approval of such expenditures as a wig for Crosby to a new popcorn machine for a Peoria theater. With revenues ever rising and costs held down, Balaban's strategy led to an increasing profitable corporate bottom line and made him the darling of Wall Street. Indeed, in 1946 Paramount Pictures earned a record $39.2 million, a figure unmatched for another generation and never exceed by a Hollywood company before the coming of television.

By the mid-1940s Balaban had formulated a strategy for producing popular films to fill Paramount Pictures' theaters. He placed his own man, Y. Frank Freeman, atop the Melrose Avenue studio lot in Hollywood. Thereafter, he and Freeman, through daily phone conversations and regular studio visits, made the movies that throughout the 1940s generated the highest international return of all movie companies.

Balaban and Freeman turned Crosby and Hope into the most popular movie stars of the 1940s. Many observers may not associate Crosby and Hope primarily with success in movies, yet by the measure of box-office receipts their films made Paramount millions of dollars. Crosby starred in *Holiday Inn* (1942), *Going My Way* (1944), *The Emperor Waltz* (1948), and *A Connecticut Yankee in King Arthur's Court* (1949). Hope appeared in a series of comedies from *My Favorite Blonde* (1942) and *My Favorite Brunette* (1947) to *Monsieur Beaucaire* (1946) and *The Paleface* (1948). Together, they became famous for their "Road" movies. Through the 1940s, Crosby's and Hope's names on marquees always meant full houses, and Balaban used them—and others, such as Gary Cooper, Betty Hutton, and Ray Milland—to make his company the most profitable in movie history up to that time. Cecil B. DeMille, Billy Wilder, and Preston Sturges, as director-producers, also made Paramount hit after hit.

Balaban did not rely solely on feature films for corporate success. Paramount's newsreels were considered the best in the business, and its Popeye the Sailor cartoons were highly popular. Critics have never considered these and other Paramount efforts classics to be praised, but Balaban was unconcerned with critical approval. He kept his eye on the box-office take, not on cinematic greatness. As a result, Paramount Pictures maintained its corporate supremacy with films that infatuated fans of the time, although many of those pictures are forgotten today.

Ever a corporate realist, Balaban in 1938 began to consider television as the next new technology for mass entertainment. With his sponsorship that year of DuMont's developmental efforts, he tried to position Hollywood as the central player in the emerging business. He reasoned that exhibition of special televised events (sports, for example) would simply add to Paramount's ability to draw customers to its theaters. But World War II called a halt to television experimentation. Balaban did sponsor theater television in the late 1940s, presenting boxing matches and Big Ten college football games. Revenue rarely exceeded costs. During the 1950s Balaban sponsored pioneering experiments with pay-TV at home. Again, revenues never exceeded costs. He was ahead of his time, since such companies as Home Box office would not make a success of pay-TV until the late 1970s.

In 1948 the U.S. Supreme Court forced Paramount to sell its theatre chain, and the studio began a period of trying to adjust as simply a studio producer and distributor. Balaban innovated VistaVision, a widescreen process, and sold Paramount's inventory of movies to advertising-based television, and he labored to make Paramount a television production factor that would feed the networks. It was not that he did not see television coming; he simply could not figure out a way to dominate the industry as Paramount Pictures had long dominated the film business. But in the early 1960s Paramount's bottom line began to turn red, and so Balaban retired. His stepping down placed Paramount "in play," and, after a great deal of corporate struggle, the company in 1966 was taken over by Gulf + Western in the first of what turned out to be the complete remaking of Hollywood ownership by conglomerate absorption.

Balaban retired and died in Byram, Connecticut.

Although he has largely been forgotten by a industry he led for a generation, Balaban made significant contributions to the development of the motion picture business. In the 1920s he and his associates taught the world how to make moviegoing a mass cultural activity by locating theaters near middle-class areas,

building opulent picture palaces, creating magnificent live stage shows, and innovating air-conditioning. But he made his greatest contribution by fashioning movie companies into streamlined businesses, aping modern management techniques of other industries and producing a sound corporation that Wall Street praised and heavily funded. In short, Balaban was among the handful of individuals who fashioned the movie corporate enterprise we take for granted today.

• Barney Balaban left no papers and wrote little for the public record. Thus, the institutions that he helped build must be examined through more general works. The rise of Balaban & Katz is described and analyzed in Douglas Gomery, *Shared Pleasures* (1992). For his brother's view of what happened, see the privately published *Continuous Performance* (1942), written by his brother A. J.'s wife, Carrie. Also consult John Douglas Eames, *The Paramount Story* (1985), and I. G. Edmonds and Reiko Mimura, *Paramount Pictures and the People Who Made Them* (1980). For the place of Paramount in the Hollywood film industry, see Gomery's *The Hollywood Studio System* (1986). For a detailed account of how Barney Balaban lost Paramount, see Robert Sobel, *The Rise and Fall of the Conglomerate Kings* (1984).

DOUGLAS GOMERY

BALANCHINE, George (22 Jan. 1904–30 Apr. 1983), ballet choreographer, was born Georgii Melitonovich Balanchivadze in Saint Petersburg, Russia, the son of Meliton Balanchivadze, a composer, and Maria Nikolaevna Vasil'eva. Balanchine was of Georgian extraction on his father's side; for this reason, he later insisted that his character owed more to Mediterranean culture than to Slav. He began piano lessons at the age of five, studying first with his mother, and was accepted into the ballet section of the Imperial Theater School, Saint Petersburg, in 1913. His financially straitened parents were motivated principally by the chance to secure him a free education. In addition to full board, the school offered a complete academic program as well as the finest dance instruction in the country; graduation guaranteed an income for life, first as a dancer, then as a teacher or coach, all subsidized by the tsar. As was customary for students, during his second year Balanchine performed with the Imperial Ballet troupe on the stage of the famed Maryinsky Theater; this crystallized his desire to dance. The ballet that so inspired him was *The Sleeping Beauty*.

Although his training was interrupted for more than a year by the Bolshevik Revolution, in 1921 Balanchine graduated with honors from the renamed Petrograd Theater (Ballet) School and was accepted into the corps de ballet of the State Theater of Opera and Ballet (formerly Maryinsky). He had begun to choreograph while still a student, and in 1919, in addition to his ballet studies, he enrolled in the Petrograd Conservatory of Music, receiving what was probably the most thorough music education of any twentieth-century choreographer.

Balanchine became the most prolific and arguably the most influential choreographer of this century.

Unlike several other revolutionaries in the field—Martha Graham or Merce Cunningham, for example—he did not discard the classical ballet but used it as a point of departure. An outstanding feature of his choreography was its musicality, and he was often far in advance of his time in his selection of scores (*Ivesiana*, Charles Ives, 1954; *Agon*, Igor Stravinsky, 1957; *Episodes*, Anton Webern, 1959). His collaboration with Stravinsky over more than fifty years resulted in some of Balanchine's undisputed masterpieces, including *Apollo, Orpheus, Firebird, Agon, Movements for Piano and Orchestra, Duo Concertant*, and *Violin Concerto*.

A hallmark of Balanchine's mature work was his frequent use of a wide range of concert music—compositions by Bach, Mozart, Tchaikovsky, Chabrier, Brahms, Ravel, Monteverdi, Mendelssohn, Vivaldi, Richard Strauss, Gluck, Schumann, and Fauré, among many others. He also embraced such popular masters as John Philip Sousa and George Gershwin, and he did not shy away from folk melody, *musique concrète*, or twelve-tone music.

In Petrograd in 1923, he presented an evening of his experimental works with the Young Ballet, a small group he had organized outside official auspices. At least one of his early innovative works was danced on bare feet, another without musical accompaniment. A second experimental evening was denounced by the state theater management, and in 1924, with three other dancers and some musicians, Balanchine left Russia (by then the Soviet Union). Under the name Principal Dancers of the Russian State Ballet, the four performed for a few weeks in Berlin, the Rhineland, and London; after a Paris audition, they were engaged by Serge Diaghilev for his renowned Ballets Russes, and, in deference to Western audiences, at Diaghilev's insistence Georgii Balanchivadze became Georges Balanchine. (In English programs, his Christian name was often given as George; his surname was sometimes spelled Balanchin). Although hired as a dancer, Balanchine soon was tapped as a choreographer as well; in all he choreographed ten ballets for Diaghilev, in addition to opera divertissements and restagings of older ballets. It was here he created *Apollon Musagète* (1928, also known as *Apollo*), which remains in the current repertory. This ballet was notable for its neoclassic style, which has been defined as "classicism seen through new eyes." Taking classical technique as his base, Balanchine subjected it to various inversions, "distortions," reaccentuations, and unexpected sequences of steps, which resulted in a greater dynamism of movement and a modification of academic correctness. In *Apollo*, he used turned-in positions of the legs, angular arms, geometric configurations, syncopated movements, and even the "contractions" later identified with the modern-dance pioneer Martha Graham. These were not to be found in any ballet classroom. He continued these tendencies throughout his career, further and further extending the vocabulary. In some later ballets, the classical foundations are less obvious, but they are always either apparent or implied. In an additional departure from tradition,

Balanchine's Apollo was not the noble Sun God, but a "wild, half-human youth who acquires nobility through art" (Francis Mason, ed., *Balanchine's New Complete Stories of the Great Ballets* [1968], p. 21). For Diaghilev, Balanchine also choreographed *Le Fils Prodigue* (*The Prodigal Son*; Sergei Prokofiev, 1929), an Expressionist dance-drama owing more to the gymnast and the acrobat than to the ballet classroom. In the lead role, Balanchine cast Diaghilev's histrionic favorite Serge Lifar; as his seducer (the Siren), he chose a tall, slim, elegant, and long-legged soloist, Felia Doubrovska, clearly the prototype of the "Balanchine ballerina" famous in later years. "Taller is better because you see more" was Balanchine's view of the feminine ideal.

After Diaghilev's death and the collapse of his troupe in 1929, Balanchine choreographed two noteworthy ballets for the newly formed Ballets Russes de Monte Carlo, *Cotillon* (Chabrier), for Tamara Toumanova, and *Concurrence* (Auric), both in 1932. With Boris Kochno he then formed a short-lived troupe, Les Ballets 1933, which disbanded after about four weeks of performances in Paris and London but was notable for providing Balanchine with his first opportunity in the West to create an entire repertory of his own. Of the six ballets presented (none of which has survived), all were by Balanchine, and all were new. During the brief life of Les Ballets 1933, Balanchine was introduced to the young American arts patron Lincoln Kirstein, a meeting that would change the lives of both as well as the history of ballet in the United States.

Although there was little activity on the American scene to encourage such a notion, Kirstein invited Balanchine to come to the United States to create a school and a company devoted to classical ballet. Without concrete prospects in Europe, Balanchine accepted, and the two founded the School of American Ballet in 1934 and a series of companies that in 1948 led to the formation of the New York City Ballet.

Balanchine's first choreography for Americans was his rhapsodic *Serenade* (Tchaikovsky, 1935), now in repertories throughout the world. Rather than the conventional series of display pieces for stars, it is a continuously flowing, kaleidoscopically changing dance fabric in which each member of the group has a separate and integral role. Although Balanchine, in using individual dancers as soloists, always displayed the greatest sensitivity to their particular abilities, an even more notable characteristic of his works is the full participation of the corps de ballet, evident first in *Serenade* and later, for example, in *Symphony in C* (1947) and his restaging of *Swan Lake*, act 2 (1951). *Serenade* has no story; it remains Balanchine's earliest surviving statement of his belief in the autonomy of choreography.

At first, American audiences, drawn to large, post-Diaghilev ballet troupes exuding an aura of Russian glamour and temperament, were not receptive to Balanchine's ideas. It took him and Kirstein fifteen years to found a permanent company. In the meantime, there was a series of impermanent groups, including an unsatisfactory residency at the Metropolitan Opera. Balanchine also kept busy choreographing for Broadway, movies, and other ballet companies. His comic ballet *Slaughter on Tenth Avenue*, for the Richard Rodgers and Lorenz Hart musical *On Your Toes* (1936), was an early example of the use of dance to further the plot of a musical comedy.

From 1944 to 1946, Balanchine was chief choreographer of the Ballet Russe de Monte Carlo (an American company, despite its name). It was during these years, without a stable company of his own, that Balanchine created three of his most bracing classical works, *Concerto Barocco, Ballet Imperial* (both 1941), and *Symphony in C. Concerto Barocco* was plotless; its only "subject" was the dance and its relation to the music. It requires from dancers a purity of line and a restraint in deportment in keeping with the almost religious nature of the music, together with the abandon to accentuate the "jazzy," syncopated aspects of Bach's complex rhythmic structure, particularly since Balanchine often set steps against the music. In *Ballet Imperial*, he sought to duplicate the grand manner of the nineteenth-century full-evening classics, but without the lengthy story and pantomime, and created a one-act ballet of brilliant technical display—Russian in style, but geared to the sensibility of contemporary Americans.

In 1946, with Kirstein, he founded Ballet Society, a chamber dance company dedicated to the production of new works. Its opening program concluded with *The Four Temperaments*, to a score Balanchine had commissioned from Paul Hindemith several years before. In this work, Balanchine used classically trained dancers, with their turnout, high leg extensions, pirouettes, and arabesques, but he manipulated them in a decidedly unclassical manner. Feet were flexed, hips thrown out, and limbs nearly ripped from torsos in movements that were both brutal and virtuosic. Although *Apollo* could be considered its distant forebear, for the most part the choreographic vocabulary of the *Four Temperaments* is unique.

In 1948, Ballet Society presented *Orpheus*, an intimate work created by the collaborative efforts of Balanchine, Stravinsky, and the designer Isamu Noguchi, who set the work not in classical Greece but in an unspecified archaic era. Balanchine departed from his normal concern with inventive movement to create a tender and plangent love story to Stravinsky's luminous score. The success of the work led to an offer for Balanchine and Kirstein to form a resident dance company for the City Center of Music and Drama, and the New York City Ballet was born.

Its beginnings were modest; there were performances one or two nights a week in a theater converted from a Masonic temple. Balanchine soon brought the new troupe to public notice with his production of *Firebird* (1949), which featured sets of jewel-like brilliance by Marc Chagall and starred Maria Tàllchief, who moved with uncommon speed and dash—one of the new breed of American ballerina. His restaging of

Swan Lake, act 2, in 1951 was a signal that the New York City Ballet would not exist on novelties alone but would honor the past as well the future. To this end, Balanchine choreographed *The Nutcracker* in 1954 (only the second full-length version of that classic to be mounted in the United States), setting a standard for the more than two hundred productions of *Nutcracker* now mounted annually in the United States. His ballet, seen twice on national television, assured the financial future of his still-struggling company. In 1957, with *Agon*, his last active collaboration with Stravinsky, Balanchine achieved the quintessential expression of his reductive aesthetic. Nicknamed "the IBM ballet" for its spare rigor and concentrated movement, in which all possible elaboration was stripped away, *Agon* was a surprise success with audiences, indicating that Balanchine's vision that dance could stand alone was beginning to find acceptance.

From its humble beginnings, the New York City Ballet grew to well over one hundred performers, with the largest operating budget by far of any ballet company in the country. In 1950, the first of many European tours was undertaken, gaining the troupe international recognition, and in 1962 the company toured the Soviet Union, marking Balanchine's first visit to his homeland since his emigration. In 1964, the company moved from City Center to the larger and better-equipped New York State Theater in New York City's Lincoln Center, the first in the country designed expressly for dance performances.

What gave the New York City Ballet its distinctive profile and forward momentum was the presence of Balanchine, not only as a creative impetus but as an inspiring teacher. He demanded of his dancers a particular vividness of muscular response and a special rough grace more associated with athletes than with sylphs. The typical Balanchine "look" is sleek, unmannered, and kinetically supercharged, heightened by Balanchine's frequent use of the leotard—a virtual second skin—as a costume. But he could also work in a lush, romantic vein (*La Valse, Brahms-Schoenberg Quartet, Liebeslieder Walzer*); experimentally (*Opus 34, Ivesiana*); and lightheartedly, especially when drawing on American themes (*Western Symphony, Who Cares?*). A late work, *Robert Schumann's 'Davidsbündlertänze'* (1980), struck many observers as a very personal contemplation of mortality. Balanchine's fluency enabled him to dash off any number of classical display pieces; in most, his debt to Marius Petipa, master of nineteenth-century Russian classicism, is evident. And, contrary to his popular reputation, he choreographed a number of story ballets, such as *A Midsummer Night's Dream, Harlequinade*, and *Coppélia*. Several works of his late years—notably *Mozartiana, Chaconne, Diamonds*, and *Vienna Waltzes*—were choreographed around the seamlessly fluid movement style of Suzanne Farrell. In his full-length *Don Quixote* (1965), he sometimes performed the role of the Don— a man seeking an ideal—to Farrell's Dulcinea.

Thanks to Balanchine's example, the New York City Ballet was always a "choreographer's company," and this was never better displayed than during the historic Stravinsky Festival of 1972. In a single week, the company presented twenty-two new ballets, of which ten were by Balanchine. Of these, *Divertimento from 'Le Baiser de la Fée', Symphony in Three Movements, Violin Concerto*, and *Duo Concertant* are considered major and enduring creations.

Balanchine became a U.S. citizen in 1939. He was married four times, to the dancers Tamara Geva (c. 1923), Vera Zorina (1938), Maria Tallchief (1946), and Tanaquil Le Clercq (1952). All of his marriages ended in annulment or divorce, and with none of his wives did he have any children. He also had close relationships with the dancers Alexandra Danilova (late 1920s), Suzanne Farrell (mid-1960s), and, toward the end of his life, Karin van Aroldingen. He died in New York City. In his will he left the performing rights to his ballets to those—mostly dancers—who had worked with him through the years. Among the many awards he received were New York City's Handel Medallion (1970), the Légion d'Honneur (France, 1975), Kennedy Center Honors (1978), Knight of the Order of Dannebrog (Denmark, 1978); and the Presidential Medal of Freedom (1983).

In all, Balanchine created over four hundred dances, including work for television, opera, movies, and the commercial theater. He continued to choreograph almost to the time of his final hospitalization for Jakob-Creutzfeldt disease, a fatal neurological disorder, in November 1982. For his revolutionary innovations, extraordinarily prolific output, and humanity, Balanchine has been compared to Mozart and Picasso. Lincoln Kirstein, who functioned as Balanchine's associate for fifty years (he was general director of the New York City Ballet from its inception until his retirement in 1989), has said of Balanchine, "He enlarged the language."

• A complete *catalogue raisonné* of Balanchine's works, including a bibliography, list of roles performed, and tours undertaken by the New York City Ballet as well as its special festivals, can be found in *Choreography by George Balanchine* (1984). Two of Balanchine's rare articles on his work are "Notes on Choreography," *Dance Index* 4 (Feb.–Mar. 1945): 20–31, and "The Dance Element in Strawinsky's Music," *Dance Index* 6 (Oct.–Dec. 1947): 250–56. Balanchine's views on ballet technique are examined, with numerous photographs, by one of his most accomplished ballerinas, Merrill Ashley, in *Dancing for Balanchine* (1984). The best biography is Bernard Taper's *Balanchine*, 3d ed. (1984), although Richard Buckle's *George Balanchine: Ballet Master*, in collaboration with John Taras (1988), has the advantage of Lincoln Kirstein's early diaries as source material. Kirstein's own account of his years with Balanchine, with profuse photos of Balanchine's work by Martha Swope, is to be found in *The New York City Ballet* (1973), which he later expanded in paperback (without illustrations) to include the years 1973–1978 (1978); the early years in the company's history are traced in Anatole Chujoy's *The New York City Ballet* (1953). Nancy Reynolds's *Repertory in Review: Forty Years of the New York City Ballet* (1977) examines one by one every ballet produced by the New York City Ballet and its predecessor companies by Balanchine and all the other choreographers who worked with the troupe from 1935 to 1977, while insightful analyses of selected Balanchine ballets appear in Kirstein's *Movement and Metaphor: Four Centuries of Ballet* (1970). Finally, distinguished critical appraisal of Balanchine's work is provided in the collected dance writings of Edwin Denby (1987); Arlene Croce's collected writings (1977, 1982, 1987); and the reviews of John Martin and Anna Kisselgoff, chief dance critics for the *New York Times*.

Anyone truly interested in Balanchine's work should consult available films and tapes, including five programs of "Dance in America," plus a two-part documentary of his life, and several programs in the series "Live from Lincoln Center" and "Great Performances," all of which were produced for public television. The Dance Collection of the New York Public Library for the Performing Arts at Lincoln Center lists 305 Balanchine entries under "Film and Video," some partial and of poor quality, some excellent.

NANCY REYNOLDS

BALCH, Emily Greene (8 Jan. 1867–9 Jan. 1961), peace activist, sociologist, and Nobel Peace Prize winner, was born in Jamaica Plain, Massachusetts, the daughter of Francis Vergnies Balch, a lawyer, and Ellen Maria Noyes. She was in the first graduating class at Bryn Mawr College, earning her degree in 1889. After studying privately for a year with sociologist Franklin H. Giddings, Balch won Bryn Mawr's highest honor, the European Fellowship. This enabled her to study economics for a year (1890–1891) at the Sorbonne in Paris, where she did research on the French system of relief to the poor.

During this period millions of recent European immigrants were facing poverty and overcrowding in American cities. In response, a new generation of college-educated reformers (particularly women) established "settlement houses" in immigration slums, where they developed an innovative range of services to meet the newcomers' needs. In addition, seeking to bridge what they saw as growing and dangerous divisions in American society, many of these reformers made their homes in the settlement houses. Soon after Balch's return to Boston, in 1892, along with some Wellesley College faculty members, she founded Boston's first settlement, Denison House; Balch became both a resident of the house and its first head. That year she met one of the pioneers of the settlement-house movement, Jane Addams, who became her lifelong colleague. In 1984 Balch represented Boston's Central Labor Union at the national convention of the American Federation of Labor. She also helped organize the Federal Labor Union, an alliance of Boston workers, reformers, and labor leaders. She later participated in the founding of the Women's Trade Union League (WTUL) in 1903 and the next year helped organize the Boston WTUL, which she later served as president.

In 1895 Balch decided to enter college teaching, hoping, as she said, to "awaken the desire of women students to work for social betterment." After studying briefly at Harvard Annex (now Radcliffe College) and the University of Chicago and spending a year at the University of Berlin, she obtained a job grading papers in the economics department at Wellesley, and she began teaching there the following semester. In 1900 she taught Wellesley's first course in sociology, and three years later she was promoted to associate professor. In 1904–1905 Balch spent a year's leave studying immigration in Austria-Hungary and in Slavic neighborhoods in the United States. Her book on the subject, *Our Slavic Fellow Citizens* (1910), remained a standard work in the field for many years. She was named chair of the Department of Economics and Sociology in 1913. Meanwhile, she continued to serve on many state boards and committees that dealt with issues such as child welfare, juvenile delinquency, industrial education, immigration, and the minimum wage.

The outbreak of World War I in August 1914 turned Balch's attention to the issue that would absorb her for the rest of her life: world peace. In September she joined other reformers in organizing the American League for the Limitation of Armaments (later renamed the American Union against Militarism and ultimately named the American Civil Liberties Union). The following year, with Addams and forty other members of the Women's Peace Party, Balch braved German U-boats to attend an international conference of women at The Hague. After the meeting participants traveled to several noncombatant countries to propose a conference of neutral nations; Balch visited Scandinavia and Russia. Back in the United States, she and Addams met with President Woodrow Wilson to urge him to support the proposal, but he declined. With Addams and Alice Hamilton, a fellow activist, Balch published *Women at The Hague* (1915).

During her sabbatical leave in 1916–1917, Balch attended the unofficial Conference for Continuous Mediation in Stockholm financed by Henry Ford; she took a leading role in both the Collegiate Anti-Militarism League and the pacifist Fellowship of Reconciliation and continued her work with the Union against Militarism. When the United States entered the war in the spring of 1917, she obtained an additional year's leave without pay to continue her work; among other things, she helped organize the People's Council of America for Peace and Democracy. Now that the United States was involved, many former activists abandoned the peace movement—opposing the war became increasingly controversial. In 1918 Balch was dismissed from the Wellesley faculty. Although the decision officially was blamed on her extended absences, faculty and students protested it strongly, and considered it punishment for Balch's position against the war.

Finding herself, as Balch said later, "with my professional life cut short and no particular prospects," she joined the editorial staff of the *Nation*. She also published *Approaches to the Great Settlement* (1918), offering her ideas for peace. The war ended, and the women who had attended The Hague conference in 1915 reassembled in 1919 in Zurich, where they organized the Women's International League for Peace and Freedom (WILPF), with Addams as president and Balch as secretary treasurer. Balch established the new organization in Geneva, devoting most of the rest of her life to it, though ill health forced her resignation as secretary in 1922. She was the WILPF's chief representative to the League of Nations, served briefly as organization secretary again in 1934, and in 1937 succeeded Addams as honorary international president. While Balch focused principally on disarmament, she also worked on drug control, international aviation, League reform, treaty revision, and mediation in the Spanish civil war. Her report on Haiti in 1927 helped persuade the United States to end its longtime occupation of the island. In addition, she helped generate support for the awarding of the Nobel Peace Prize to Addams in 1931.

Balch, who had been born a Unitarian, became a Quaker in 1920. Nevertheless, after what she described as a "painful mental struggle," in the late 1930s she concluded that war was necessary to stop fascist aggression. Although she acknowledged that her position was "neither very definite, not very consistent," she remained active in the WILPF during World War II, assisting refugees, defending the rights of conscientious objectors, advocating for interned Japanese Americans, and developing proposals for postwar international cooperation. In 1946 she and ecumenical leader John R. Mott were awarded the Nobel Peace Prize jointly. Balch gave nearly all her prize money to the WILPF. Illness prevented her from attending the award ceremony, but two years later she delivered her acceptance speech in Norway. Thereafter, until her death in Cambridge, Massachusetts, she continued to travel, write, and lecture on peace and international cooperation. She never married.

Balch described herself as "the plainest of New England spinsters," but her humor, judgment and tact endeared her to all who worked with her. As a reformer she exemplified the idealism and energy of the Progressive movement. As a teacher she helped awaken a generation of students to the critical social issues of their time. And as an activist for peace she showed, in the words of her Nobel award, that "defeat gives new courage for the struggle to those who have within them the holy fire."

• Balch's papers are in the Swarthmore College Peace Collection. Additional archival material can be found in the papers of the Geneva office of the WILPF at the University of Colorado, Boulder, and in the Wellesley College Archives. Besides the books mentioned above, Balch wrote *Manual for Use in Cases of Juvenile Offenders and Other Minors* (1895), *Occupied Haiti* (1927), *Vignettes in Prose* (1952), and a book of poems, *The Miracle of Living* (1941). In addition, most of her writings, both published and unpublished, are collected in *Beyond Nationalism: The Social Thought of Emily Greene Balch*, ed. Mercedes Randall (1972). Biographical sketches are John Herman Randall, Jr., *Emily Greene Balch of New England*, a 1946 WILPF pamphlet; Olga S. Opfell, *Lady Laureates* (1978); and Irwin Abrams, *The Nobel Peace Prize and the Laureates* (1988). An obituary is in the *New York Times*, 11 Jan. 1961.

SANDRA OPDYCKE

BALCH, Emily Tapscott Clark. *See* Clark, Emily Tapscott.

BALCH, Hezekiah (1741–Apr. 1810), Presbyterian minister, was born near Deer Creek, Harford County, Maryland, the son of John Balch, a farmer. His mother's name is unknown. During childhood Balch moved with his parents to Mecklenburg County, North Carolina, and in 1758 he entered the College of New Jersey, largely through the influence of the Reverend John Rodgers, a noted Presbyterian clergyman who had conducted an evangelistic tour through the southern colonies. Following his graduation, Balch taught school briefly in Fauquier County, Virginia, but soon decided to study for the ministry. He was licensed to preach on 11 August 1768 by the New Castle (Del.) Presbytery. Returning to Virginia, he was ordained by the Hanover Presbytery, 8 March 1770, and spent his first years as an itinerant evangelist in both Virginia and North Carolina. When the Orange Presbytery was formed from Hanover later that year, Balch became one of its constituting members. At some point during the decade of the 1770s (the sources differ as to the exact year), he ministered briefly to a Presbyterian congregation in York County, Pennsylvania, but by 1782 he had returned to the South.

Responding to the need for ministerial services in the southern back country, Balch moved sometime between 1782 and 1785 to the newly founded town of Greeneville, in an area of the southern Appalachians that today is in Tennessee. His arrival brought to three the number of Presbyterian ministers on the southern frontier (the other two were Charles Cummings and Samuel Doak) and thus permitted the formation of the Abingdon Presbytery in 1785. The first dozen years of Balch's ministry were remarkably successful. Concentrating his efforts at the Mount Bethel Church in Greeneville, he soon transformed it into the largest congregation in the Holston-Tennessee valley. Active in political affairs as well as church polity, Balch joined with fellow Presbyterian ministers Doak and Samuel Houston in supporting the movement to create a new state of Franklin, which led to a bitter controversy in the press with the Reverend William Graham of Liberty Hall in Virginia. Balch was also a strong advocate of Isaac Watts's version of the psalmody as a replacement for the older and less felicitous edition of Francis Rous. A sermon Balch preached in the autumn of 1786 on the subject before the Abingdon Presbytery, "Gospel Liberty in the Praise of God," was so well received that it was printed by the church court and widely circulated.

Recognizing the demand for educational institutions on the frontier, Balch applied for and received a charter for the creation of Greeneville College on 20 August 1794, the first action of the newly created legislature of the Southwest Territory, later to become Tennessee. The campus was a large farm about three miles from Greeneville, and initially Balch was the sole member of the faculty. In 1795 Balch traveled throughout the East in search of funds for support of his institution. In Newport, Rhode Island, he met the Reverend Samuel Hopkins, a disciple of Jonathan Edwards. Hopkins is best known for his development of a modified and less rigorous form of Calvinism called the "New Divinity," which argued that sinful man could take the initiative in seeking out God and moving toward redemption rather than being totally dependent on the will and action of God. Attracted to Hopkins's views, Balch introduced them on the Tennessee frontier, arousing a storm of protest and acrimony, much of it led by Doak. Called before the Abingdon Presbytery on heresy charges, Balch successfully defended himself, although five disgruntled ministers withdrew temporarily from the presbytery.

Meanwhile, the Synod of the Carolinas had submitted Balch's case to the General Assembly of the Presbyterian Church, where it was heard in Philadelphia in May 1798. The assembly found Balch to be in "serious error" in several points of his doctrine and required him to renounce his views and be publicly admonished. When four dissident elders from the Mount Bethel congregation appeared in Philadelphia, charging that Balch had improperly installed church officers friendly to his cause, the assembly admonished the elders and called upon all parties to unite with Balch in a spirit of harmony.

The matter came to a dramatic climax upon the return of Balch and the elders to Tennessee. Apparently Balch announced to his congregation that he had been acquitted by the assembly and proclaimed himself to be "five hundred thousand" times stronger in his beliefs. The meeting became disorderly, and angry dissidents in the congregation locked Balch out of the church. For some three months he preached to his followers under trees near the graveyard. Balch's faction ultimately won legal control of the building and took on the name of Harmony Church, while his opponents, who seem to have been a majority of the congregation and nearly all of the elders, retained the name Mount Bethel and moved to another structure elsewhere in Greeneville.

The Synod of the Carolinas took up the controversy in the fall of 1798 and found Balch guilty of duplicity in his actions, suspending him from the ministry. The four elders were also suspended for the "impropriety and irregularity of their course." Balch was later restored to good standing, and in an effort to separate Balch from his opponents, the synod redrew presbyterial boundaries, placing him with three other ministers in the new presbytery of Greeneville in 1800. The controversy was finally put to rest in 1804, when Abingdon Presbytery, which contained the Mount Bethel Church, was transferred to the Synod of Virginia, while the members of Greeneville Presbytery were placed in Union Presbytery, where Balch had amicable relations. The division left Harmony Church, which had once been the largest congregation on the Tennessee frontier, in such a weakened state that it never fully recovered, and Mount Bethel soon became the larger church.

The last ten years of Balch's life were marked by declining health and vigor. In 1805 the Reverend Charles Coffin of Newburyport, Massachusetts, who had first met Balch during his New England trip, came south to assist in the administration of Harmony Church and Greeneville College. Within two years he had completely taken over Balch's responsibilities. Balch appears to have shared the antislavery sentiments common among many early settlers in the Tennessee back country, for in January 1807 he freed the three slaves he then owned.

Balch's first wife, Hannah Lewis, with whom he had six children, died about 1808. Balch then married Ann Lucky, with whom he had no children. Balch died in Greeneville.

A gifted evangelist, Balch appears to have been an individual whose personality aroused both strong loyalties and antipathies. His conduct was often immoderate, and close friends, including Coffin, acknowledged him to have been imprudent and indiscreet. In his memoirs of Balch, Coffin wrote: "His intrepidity was a bad counsellor in the moment of provocation and temptation. . . . When the fear of God was suspended in its rule over his lofty and intrepid soul, he feared nothing in the universe; and . . . Satan was at his elbow to take some advantage of him."

Balch's importance lies in the establishment of Greeneville College, the first chartered institution of higher learning west of the southern Blue Ridge, and in his introduction of the New Divinity theology into the region. These views spread among Presbyterians of East Tennessee and contiguous states in the early nineteenth century to such an extent that a significant New School presence came into being in the southern Appalachians following the split within the Presbyterian denomination in 1837 between Old School and New School parties.

• Primary materials on Balch are in the records of the Synod of the Carolinas and the presbyteries of Abingdon and Union, located at the Presbyterian Historical Society, Philadelphia, Pa., and at the Presbyterian Study Center, Montreat, N.C. No collection of Balch's works, published or unpublished, has survived, and sources on his life are few. The most complete is the entry in William Buell Sprague, *Annals of the American Pulpit*, vol. 3 (1857–1869). Family information is in Thomas Willing Balch, *Balch Genealogica* (1907). Also useful are Ezra Hall Gillett, *History of the Presbyterian Church in the United States of America* (2 vols., 1864); Ernest Trice Thompson, *Presbyterians in the South*, vol. 1 (1970); and Richard Harrison Doughty, *Greeneville: One Hundred Year Portrait* (1975).

WILLIAM J. WADE

BALDERSTON, John Lloyd (22 Oct. 1889–8 Mar. 1954), dramatist and journalist, was born in Philadelphia, Pennsylvania, the son of Lloyd Balderston, a British doctor, and Mary Alsop, an American. He attended local Philadelphia schools. Early transatlantic travels prefigured his internationally varied career. In 1911 Balderston became the New York correspondent for the *Philadelphia Record*. From 1914 through 1918

he covered World War I from London for the McClure Syndicate, becoming a student of military tactics. He stayed on as information director for the U.S. Committee on Public Information in Great Britain and Ireland.

Balderston's one-act play *The Genius of the Marne* (1919) portrays Napoleon's ghost appearing to Marshal Joffre, the French commander at the battle of the Marne, during September 1914, as Paris's fate hangs in the balance. Napoleon suggests that Joffre use the tactics that Napoleon had used at the Marshes of St. Goud a century earlier. With regard to the play philosopher George Moore wrote, "Mr. Balderston seems to think that a man of genius is but the mouthpiece of a voice speaking from beyond," a remark that foreshadowed Balderston's later preoccupation with the mysteries of time. *A Morality Play for the Leisure Class* (1920–1921, produced 1931), a one-act fantasy of the afterlife, asserts that any life without struggle and meaningful work is hell.

From 1920 to 1923 Balderston edited the *Outlook*, a literary-political weekly that published writings by authors such as J. B. Priestley, Arnold Bennett, James Stephens, and Hilaire Belloc, as well as Americans H. L. Mencken and Walter Lippmann. In 1921 Balderston married Marion A. Rubicam, a theatrical designer; they had one child. At the *Outlook*, Balderston was pro-American at a time when American motives were under European fire. He defended President Warren G. Harding and American "simple-mindedness" in general, and he advised against the Anglo-Japanese naval alliance. Balderston also chided those who condemned the United States's insistence on war debt repayment, noting that Britain had "done very well out of the war" territorially; the United States had "settled for an atoll."

From 1923 to 1931 Balderston headed the New York *World*'s London bureau, traveling to Europe and the Near East. In 1925 he reported the opening of the tomb of Tutankhamen. He published a secret British cabinet report identifying Russia—not Germany—as the likely enemy in a future war. Covering the League of Nations, he urged U.S. intervention in Europe's woes.

Balderston's dramatic career bloomed in 1926. He collaborated with J. C. Squire, editor of the *London Mercury*, on *Berkeley Square*. Inspired by the Henry James fragment "The Sense of the Past," the play follows a twentieth-century American with a love for old things who inherits his ancestors' London house. He then proceeds to "escape" temporarily, through a fold in time, to the eighteenth century and assumes an ancestor's identity. Rejected by the Theater Guild as "a play for metaphysicians," it proved a popular success in London. A 1929 production of *Berkeley Square*, starring Leslie Howard, was a Broadway hit.

On the opening night of *Berkeley Square* G. K. Chesterton led an onstage discussion of the play's ideas. Critic James Agate praised Balderston's ability to stir "the dry bones of Relativity with something human." Of Peter Standish's reciprocated love for Helen, who reads the future in his eyes, Agate added, "There is fragrance in the young spirit knowing that it cannot encounter love this side of the grave, pathos in the lover who lives too late." With *Berkeley Square*, Balderston proved himself an intensely spiritual, often humorous romantic with a command of concrete experience and vocabulary, able to popularize complex ideas and to dispel disbelief. American expatriate actress Mary Ellis called his mind "oblique."

In 1927 Balderston joined Irish actor-author Hamilton Deane in adapting Deane's London star vehicle *Dracula* for its New York production, which introduced Rumanian actor Bela Lugosi. On Broadway and on tour, *Dracula* played for three years. Balderston's published version was purchased by Universal Studios for director Tod Browning's 1931 film. In the popular mind Balderston's work virtually obliterated the 1899 Bram Stoker original.

In 1930 Balderston collaborated with Peggy Webling in London to adapt Mary Shelley's *Frankenstein* for Deane. Although it closed after seventy-two performances, *Frankenstein* was not dead. The 1932 Boris Karloff film *Frankenstein*, directed by Briton James Whale and written by Robert Florey, was based on Webling and Balderston's drama. (The typescript credits Balderston for "composition," but his name did not appear on screen.)

Balderston's collaborative ability, combined with his knowledge of history and war, his romanticism and cosmopolitanism, and his jousting, bantering dialogue made him a natural screenwriter. When the New York *World* ceased publication in 1931, he went to Hollywood. He was a writer for Universal Studios from 1931 to 1936. For Karloff he wrote *The Mummy* (1932), for Howard the screen version of *Berkeley Square* (1934), for Peter Lorre *Mad Love* (1935), and for Whale, Karloff, and Elsa Lanchester *The Bride of Frankenstein* (1935). The last, a poignant, inventive, and funny film, can be called the gem of this golden age of horror films.

Turning to history and romance, Balderston gained "respectability" and was twice nominated for Academy Awards, first for *Lives of a Bengal Lancer* (1935). The film inspired novelist George MacDonald Fraser, whose childhood was spent during the Raj, to write, "Its . . . atmosphere is more evocative for me than any other film of India." He was again nominated for an Oscar for *Gaslight* (1944), his adaptation of Patrick Hamilton's Broadway hit. Balderston adapted works by James Fenimore Cooper, Joseph Conrad, and Anthony Hope. Balderston's 1937 adaptation of Hope's novel of Ruritania *The Prisoner of Zenda* (1894) was virtually unchanged in the 1952 remake; both are among the screen's romantic classics. Balderston also wrote the biographical film *Tennessee Johnson* (1942) and wartime films such as the naval drama *Stand By for Action* (1942).

In 1936 Balderston returned to the London stage, adapting Lajos Zihaly's *Farewell Performance* into a preposterous comedy-drama. Mary Ellis portrayed an actress whose emotionally extravagant life threatens to kill her. Believing that the aged are peaceful, the character "retires," adding decades to her years ("I am the only old woman who has never been middle-aged") so well that new, unwanted romantic entanglements arise, proving that she might as well die onstage—or at least in a dressing room.

In 1952 Balderston lectured in drama at the University of Southern California. He transformed his failed 1932 play *Red Planet* into a science fiction film and collaborated with Sybil Bolitho on *A Goddess to a God*, a book of imaginary letters between Julius Caesar and Cleopatra. In 1953 he dramatized *A Goddess to a God* for the British Broadcasting Corporation. The work offers Cleopatra's tragic, at times humorous, vision of one world ruled in morality and eternal peace by the two lovers, the true heirs of Ptolemy and Alexander the Great. Balderston was preparing a theatrical version of *A Goddess to a God* at the time of his death in Beverly Hills, California.

A *Punch* review of *Berkeley Square* said that Balderston was often "ingenious, witty, mysterious and eerily fantastic" (13 Oct. 1926). His interests were broad, his speculations lively. He sought and entertained the largest of audiences.

• Balderston's screenplays are in the library of the American Film Institute, Los Angeles. His unpublished adaptation of Lajos Zihaly's *Farewell Performance* is no. 15266 LC in the Lord Chamberlain's collection at the British Library, London. Ordinarily, Balderston's plays were published in both the United States and Britain. He is treated in *Who's Who in the Theater* listings and in autobiographies such as contemporary Eric Maschwitz's *No Chip on My Shoulder* (1957). George MacDonald Fraser, *The Hollywood History of the World* (1988), deals with several of Balderston's films. James Moore, "John Balderston," in the *Dictionary of Literary Biography*, vol. 26 (1984), pp. 24–29, is the most extensive treatment of his screenplays, and it lists others' discussions of his horror films.

JAMES ROSS MOORE

BALDWIN, Abraham (22 Nov. 1754–4 Mar. 1807), founding father, legislator, and founder of the University of Georgia, was born in North Guilford, Connecticut, the son of Michael Baldwin, a blacksmith, and Lucy Dudley. Lucy died from complications following the birth of her fifth child in 1758, and ten years later Michael started another family with Theodora Wolcot. From this second marriage Abraham gained seven siblings, one of whom, Henry, attained prominence in 1830 as an associate justice of the U.S. Supreme Court.

The Baldwin family was among the intellectuals of Connecticut society. Realizing the value of an education, Michael made major financial sacrifices to send his children to school. The debt he incurred was substantial enough that Abraham would later work to help repay it and to furnish his siblings with their educational costs. In 1768, at the age of fourteen, Abraham entered Yale College and graduated in 1772. For the next three years he studied theology in preparation for becoming a clergyman. In 1775 he was granted a license to preach and accepted the position of tutor at Yale. In 1779 he resigned the tutorial position to become a full-time army chaplain in the Continental army.

Upon completing his military service, Baldwin relocated in 1784 to Georgia. Within a year he gained admission to the state bar and began serving in the Georgia House of Representatives. The state legislature made Baldwin one of the trustees of the college endowment, a position well suited to his interests and talents. One of Baldwin's first long-term projects in this role dealt with the establishment of a state educational system and the founding of Franklin College, which later grew into the University of Georgia. His interest in promoting education substantiates the claim made by biographer Henry C. White that Baldwin came to Georgia "seeking neither land nor fortune. He came as a missionary in the cause of education" (White, p. 54).

Baldwin's early work in the Georgia legislature earned him the respect of his colleagues, and in 1785 he was one of three men to represent Georgia in the Continental Congress. From 1785 to 1788 Baldwin led the Georgia delegation. Although he was a transplanted New Englander, Baldwin fought fiercely for the right of states to decide the slavery issue for themselves. While he recognized that there were compelling moral arguments against slavery, he was firmly convinced that Georgia's economic survival depended on the perpetuation of the institution. Believing that government under the Articles of Confederation was extremely inefficient, Baldwin desired a stronger but unrestrictive governing body. The protection of slavery remained one of his primary concerns during the Convention.

In 1787 Baldwin was among the delegates appointed to the U.S. Constitutional Convention. He served on four of the six major committees to resolve controversies during the Convention: the committee on the representation of the small and large states in the national legislature; the committee on the assumption of states' debts by the national government; the committee on slavery and the navigation acts; and the catch-all committee on deferred issues. Although Baldwin was not a leader in the debate at Philadelphia, he played a yeoman role in committee work and contributed in significant ways to the enduring frame of government hammered out during the summer of 1787.

In 1799 Baldwin joined the ranks of the U.S. Senate, and beginning in 1801 he served intermittently as the presiding officer of that body. He championed a strong national government with sufficiently flexible powers to deal with those problems of trade, taxation, currency, and diplomacy that had plagued the Confederation. Baldwin was a conservative, strict-constructionist Republican, but he allowed his conscience rather than the party's political dogma to guide him.

Baldwin worked resolutely to create an enduring plan of education for Georgia. Working under the New England premise that education was an essential component of an effective democracy, the Georgia leg-islature in 1784 reserved land for an academic institution and appointed a board of trustees, of which Baldwin was a member, to oversee the project. With advice from colleagues, Baldwin composed the legislation establishing Franklin College and was Georgia assemblyman when the legislature extended a charter in 1785. Baldwin's work earned him the title Father of the University of Georgia. Acknowledgment of his primary role in establishing the facility came in 1786 when Baldwin was chosen president of the college. In 1801 he resigned to concentrate full-time on politics, but he continued to oversee the institution's progress by remaining on the board of trustees until his death.

Baldwin's personal attributes of integrity, intelligence, and affability, combined with his inspired work ethic, propelled his political career and earned him the respect of his peers. He possessed the personality, temperament, and character needed for political success. Baldwin was a statesman rather than a politician, and he cared deeply about improving educational and economic opportunities for his constituents. With his education and managerial ability he might have become a wealthy man, but he never made money a goal. He was much more interested in creating a political structure that would provide the fullest measure of economic opportunity, justice, and prosperity for his countrymen. His quiet generosity was apparent early on when he contributed to the education of his siblings. After a brief illness Baldwin died unmarried in Washington, D.C., while serving as president pro-tempore of the Senate.

• Baldwin left few writings to document his life. Of the limited papers from his political career, the principal collection is at the University of Georgia. Other miscellaneous manuscript collections are at Sterling Memorial Library, Yale University, and at the Beinecke Rare Book and Manuscript Library of the Sterling Memorial Library. In addition, the University of Georgia retains copies of government documents relating to Baldwin's career. Two comprehensive biographies of Baldwin, Henry C. White's *Abraham Baldwin* (1926) and E. Merton Coulter's *Abraham Baldwin: Patriot, Educator, and Founding Father* (1987), provide extensive information on Baldwin's developmental years and career as a statesman. A good account of the impact and legacy of Baldwin's role in the early education movement in Georgia is Keith Whitescarver's "Creating Citizens for the Republic: Education in Georgia," *Journal of the Early Republic* 13 (1993): 455–79. Three brief overviews of Baldwin are found in Forrest McDonald's *We the People: The Economic Origins of the Constitution* (1958), Clinton Rossiter's *1787: The Grand Convention* (1966), and Fred Taylor Wilson's *Our Constitution and Its Makers* (1937). Other somewhat briefer and scattered accounts of Baldwin's career are in William Omer Foster, Sr., *James Jackson: Duelist and Militant Statesman 1757–1806* (1960), and Robert E. Brown, *Charles Beard and the Constitution* (1956).

APRIL D. FOLDEN

BALDWIN, Billy (30 May 1903–25 Nov. 1983), interior decorator, was born William Williar Baldwin, Jr., in Baltimore, Maryland, the son of William Baldwin, an insurance executive, and Julia Bartlett. He was brought up in a well-to-do, traditional family in the affluent section of Roland Park. He graduated from the Gilman Country School for Boys, and went on to Princeton University to study architecture. However, he dropped out because he preferred "spending time in New York at museums and galleries and [doing] things" (*New York Times*, 26 Nov. 1983). From his earliest years Baldwin cared passionately about his surroundings; at age twelve he redecorated his bedroom, and much later he could recall all the details of rooms he had known as a child. He credited his father as a role model for his impeccable tailoring, donning his small spare frame with the same verve with which he decorated his own rooms. With the exception of a brief unhappy stint at his father's insurance agency and several years in the Army Medical Corps during World War II, Billy Baldwin's career was dedicated to the decorating profession. He began his training at C. J. Benson & Co., a local Baltimore decorating firm; by the late 1920s he had built up a considerable clientele. His personal charm and wit, in addition to his skill as a ballroom dancer, made him a success with the social elite.

Ruby Ross Wood, one of the outstanding decorators of the day, was the most important mentor for Baldwin. Baldwin moved to New York City in 1935 to become her assistant, and he remained with the firm until her death in 1950. From Wood he learned the guiding principles of the profession. He credited her influence on his taste, which stressed "the importance of the personal, of the comfortable, and of the new" (*New York Times*, 26 Nov. 1983). Another of her decorating principles that he adopted was nothing should stand out or jump out at you in a room. Baldwin was one of the first men to be hired by a woman in the female-dominated interior design profession, and his success was a key factor in opening the profession to men. In 1952 he reorganized Wood's firm and brought in Edward Martin as a partner; subsequently the company became known as Baldwin, Martin, and Smith with the addition of Arthur E. Smith.

Baldwin's finely crafted rooms were timeless statements because he created a balance between the formalities of high style with the realities of modern life, adapting his instincts as a modernist within the framework of the classical traditional look. While eliminating the superfluous, his flexibly arranged rooms had a sense of ease and a quality of graciousness sometimes attributed to his southern background. An admirer of the brilliant palette of the painter Henri Matisse, he filled many of his rooms with fresh blues, pinks, and greens, which were often combined with white furniture.

The firm of Woodson Wallpapers, founded by Baldwin's friend Woodson Taulbee, specialized in producing Baldwin's innovative designs. Among his most noted trademarks were dark lacquered walls, the armless slipper chair with a slightly angled back, and swing-arm wall-mounted brass lamps. Other signature pieces included square rattan-wrapped tables and chairs adapted from the 1930s designs of Jean-Michel Frank. Baldwin's preference for a tidy understated look extended to the use of cotton materials over ostentatious silks, white paper lampshades rather than silk ones, shutters or bamboo matchstick blinds in lieu of sheer curtains, and books as decorative elements—all of which gave his rooms what became known as the American style.

Many of Baldwin's clients figured prominently in the world of society and fashion: among them were the Paul Mellons, William and Barbara Paley, Greta Garbo, Horst, Jacqueline Kennedy Onassis, and Diana Vreeland. His thorough understanding of the cosmopolitan world of his clients and his sensitivity to the elegant women who adorned his beautiful rooms contributed greatly to his enduring success. One of his most celebrated commissions during the peak of his career in the 1950s and 1960s was Cole Porter's suite in the Waldorf Towers. While the drawing room was furnished with delicate French furniture arranged on antique carpets, the library had shiny tortoise-shell vinyl walls and brass bookshelves. Responsive to innovative design trends in Europe, Baldwin created rooms that reflected the glamour of his clients but always maintained a sense of order and proportion.

Baldwin's design work was primarily residential, with a few exceptions such as the 1963 commission for the hairdresser Kenneth Battelle, whose salon became a fashion statement after Baldwin decorated it with a profusion of patterned fabrics. As Baldwin's reputation grew his talents extended to other aspects of the design profession. At the behest of Van Day Truex, the influential designer who headed the Parsons School of Design, Baldwin lectured to students from 1946 to 1952, the only academic venture of his career. His one theatrical opportunity came in 1956 to create a fashionable London drawing room for the New York production of the play *The Reluctant Debutante*. During the 1960s he wrote about decorating for the newspaper columnist Eugenia Sheppard. He retired in 1972 and moved to the island of Nantucket, where he had summered most of his life. He never married.

Baldwin's legacy can be detected throughout much of American interior design today. He was known as the dean of American interior decorators, and his career lasted from the 1920s to the 1970s. His taste and sense of style were a great influence on the generation of designers following World War II. His sensible, versatile style was widely published in magazines such as *House and Garden* and *Vogue*. He also wrote two books, *Billy Baldwin Decorates* and *Billy Baldwin Remembers*. He died in Nantucket.

• The firm of Baldwin, Martin, & Smith became Arthur E. Smith, Inc., and it retains the records and scrapbooks of the Baldwin archives. His autobiography, *Billy Baldwin*, written with Michael Gardine, was published posthumously in 1985. Cleveland Amory wrote the introduction to *Billy Baldwin*

Decorates (1972). See also Mark Hampton, *Legendary Decorators of the Twentieth Century* (1992). An obituary is in the *New York Times*, 26 Nov. 1983.

PAULINE C. METCALF

BALDWIN, Evelyn Briggs (22 July 1862–25 Oct. 1933), arctic explorer, was born in Springfield, Missouri, the son of Elias Briggs Baldwin, an army captain, and Julia Cornelia Crampton. His father served in the Thirty-sixth Illinois Infantry Volunteers in the Civil War and later became a farmer. His mother died when he was four years old. Raised on his father's Kansas farm, Baldwin attended high school in nearby Oswego and received a B.S. from North-Western (later North-Central) College in Naperville, Illinois, in 1885. After graduation Baldwin spent a year in Europe, supporting his pedestrian and bicycle travels by writing a subscription newspaper, *Europe Afoot*.

Returning to Oswego, Baldwin worked between 1887 and 1891 as a high school principal, instructor at the Teachers' Normal Institute, and superintendent of Oswego city schools (1890–1891). During the summers he toured California, Yellowstone, and other western U.S. locales and lectured about his U.S. and European travels on Chautauqua circuits. In 1892 he joined the U.S. Weather Bureau as an assistant observer. While posted at the Nashville, Tennessee, station he applied to join Lieutenant Robert E. Peary's 1893–1894 North Greenland expedition and was accepted as the expedition meteorologist.

Baldwin's first arctic experience was not without its strains. Wintering at Anniversary Lodge, Baldwin objected to the "licentiousness practiced" by other expedition members with Eskimo women, vowing, in one of his 1893 diary entries, to "not forget my manhood and professions" of Christian religion, Masonry, and Knight Templarism. As one of the several members who left the expedition after a year, Baldwin also publicly disagreed with Peary's subsequent characterization of their departure as disloyal. Nonetheless, motivated by "an intense desire to explore," Baldwin actively pursued arctic exploration, taking periodic furloughs from his weather bureau job. In 1897, for example, he traveled to Spitsbergen in an unsuccessful attempt to join the ill-fated Andrée arctic balloon flight and spent several months on the arctic island. And in 1898–1899 he served as meteorologist and second-in-command of the Walter Wellman expedition, on which he explored the westward reaches of the Franz Josef archipelago and "discovered" Alexander Graham Bell Island.

As a means to raise money for his own polar expedition, Baldwin lectured and wrote *The Search for the North Pole* (1896). He attracted the financial support of William Ziegler, a New York baking powder manufacturer, who underwrote the 1901–1902 Baldwin-Ziegler Arctic expedition. Resigning his position at the weather bureau, Baldwin transferred to the U.S. Signal Corps as an inspector-at-large, on indefinite leave, before leaving for the Arctic. During the expedition's first year, the party, along with some 400 dogs

and fifteen Siberian ponies, wintered on Franz Josef Land at Camp Ziegler, from where the expedition members established supply depots along the coasts, gathered scientific information, and took the first arctic motion pictures. Many of the dogs died over the winter, and running low on coal fuel, Baldwin sought aid. Particularly entranced with balloon technology, he had contracted with Baldwin Bros. Government Aeronautical Engineers Balloon Manufacturers of Quincy, Illinois, to provide message balloons. In June Baldwin released the hydrogen-filled balloons with messages attached to cork buoys, hoping that relief ships would bring emergency coal supplies. The first message, however, was not picked up until seven months later; the canistered messages periodically turned up well into the 1930s.

In July the expedition was forced to return to Norway. Leadership disputes among the Swedish sailing master, Norwegian ice pilot, and Baldwin also marred the success of the expedition. Although Baldwin had anticipated leading the expedition for another year, Ziegler recalled him to New York and sent Anthony Fiala to replace him. The following year, a bitter Baldwin testified against Ziegler in a baking powder trust case in St. Louis. For several years Baldwin attempted unsuccessfully to raise financial backing for a four-year expedition to float in the arctic ice floe from the Bering Strait over the pole to Greenland.

Baldwin never returned to the Arctic, but he continued to engage in arctic exploration controversies. He initially supported Frederick Cook's North Pole claim over Peary in the extended public Cook-Peary controversy—he published "Positive Proof of Dr. Cook's Attainment of the Pole" as an appendix in Cook, *My Attainment of the Pole* (1913), and, with Cook's cooperation, worked on an extended manuscript—but he later repudiated his support. He pursued prospecting and mining ventures in Colorado and Canada, lectured on his arctic experiences in New York, Connecticut, and California, and worked as an accounting clerk in New York and Pennsylvania. In 1915, after traveling through New Hampshire as a lecturer for the Commission for Relief in Belgium, he informed the government that he had been contacted in New York by German officials who he claimed asked him to carry letters and dispatches on an anticipated trip to Belgium. Since this wartime practice of using couriers on neutral ships contributed to the recall of German military attaché Franz Von Papen and naval attaché Karl Boy-Ed in December 1915, Baldwin considered his refusal a patriotic contribution.

After working during World War I as a laborer and inspector at several Ordnance Department plants in New Jersey and Pennsylvania, Baldwin moved to Washington, D.C., where he clerked in various government offices—primarily the U.S. Shipping Board and the Office of Naval Records and Library—for the remainder of his life. Baldwin, who never married, avidly undertook genealogical work and was a member of the New York Biographical and Genealogical Society. He also compiled data in support of his futile requests for monetary recognition of his arctic activities and other patriotic work. Shortly after his required retirement in 1933, Baldwin was killed by an automobile in Washington, D.C.

• Baldwin's papers, in the Library of Congress, include correspondence, journals, and reports from the Baldwin-Ziegler expedition. His Peary expedition scientific manuscripts and journals are located in the Peary papers, National Archives; his preliminary reports are included in Robert E. Peary, *Northward over the "Great Ice,"* vol. 2 (1898), pp. 175–203. Baldwin's genealogical notes and correspondence are located in the Baldwin Family Papers at the New York Genealogical and Biographical Society Library, New York City. An overview of "The Meteorological Observations of the Second Wellman Expedition" was published in *National Geographic Magazine*, Dec. 1899, pp. 512–16; more detailed meteorological records include a report of the same title in the U.S. Department of Agriculture, Weather Bureau, Report of the Chief of the Weather Bureau (1899–1900) pt. 7, and "Auroral Observations on the Second Wellman Expedition Made in the Neighborhood of Franz Josef Land," *Monthly Weather Review* 29 (Mar. 1901): 107–15. Baldwin's published accounts of the Baldwin-Ziegler expedition are "How I Hope to Reach the North Pole," *McClure's Magazine*, Sept. 1901, pp. 415–22; and "The Baldwin-Ziegler Polar Expedition," a three-part article in *World Wide Magazine*, Jan.–Mar. 1903, pp. 396–402, 432–36, 587–93. A front-page article on Baldwin's death in the *Washington Post*, 26 Oct. 1933, is the most complete obituary.

KATHERINE G. MORRISSEY

BALDWIN, Faith (1 Oct. 1893–19 Mar. 1978), novelist, was born in New Rochelle, New York, the daughter of Stephen Charles Baldwin, a well-known trial lawyer, and Edith Hervey Finch. At age three she moved to Manhattan and then, at seven, to Brooklyn Heights. Baldwin was able to read by the time she was three years old. She attended Brooklyn Heights Academy and finishing school in Brooklyn and in Briarcliff Manor, New York. At six she wrote a drama called *The Deserted Wife* and had her first poems published in the *Christian Advocate* when she was only eleven. She lived in Germany during World War I (1914–1916) with her mother's close friend.

In 1920 Baldwin married Hugh Cuthrell, a pilot in the U.S. Navy who later became president of Brooklyn Union Gas Company. The couple had four children. Baldwin lived for many years on "Fable Farm," a fourteen-room house that had been built in 1800, near Norwalk, Connecticut, but she moved to a smaller home in the last years of her life.

Immensely popular during the depression years, Baldwin is now better known for her productivity than for the excellence of her prose. She admitted preferring reading to writing, and one reviewer said her work was "inspired by Faith, produced in hope, and not always received with charity." Nonetheless, from the publication of her first book, *Mavis of Green Hill*, in 1921, she averaged two books per year during most of her long career, reportedly typing the manuscripts herself, quickly but inaccurately. When people (especially women) felt depressed by economic woes and

political unrest, they escaped with a Baldwin novel, full of romance and certain solutions. Her heroines always ended up with the "right" man after solving the dilemma of which one was "right." They achieved a balance between work and home responsibilities, usually by recognizing the importance of the latter over the former. So effective was this formula that in 1936, one of the worst years of the American economy, Baldwin earned $300,000. A *New York Times* article once called her "one of the most successful writers of light fiction." She also wrote two novels under the pseudonym Amber Lee and two volumes of short stories. One of her best novels is *American Family* (1934), which tells the history of her own family and focuses on her grandparents, who worked in China as missionaries. A contemporary *New York Times* reviewer said this novel was "solidly conceived and worked out with unmistakeable sincerity. It firmly establishes Faith Baldwin's claim to be considered a serious novelist." A *Saturday Review* critic said "one must recognize the pictorial truth of her various atmospheres and characterizations." Baldwin admitted, however, to some poetic license with the novel, saying, "I am no historian, I am merely a teller of tales."

Baldwin sold her first serial to *Good Housekeeping* in 1927 and also contributed to *Women's Home Companion*, *Cosmopolitan*, and *American* magazine. She earned as much as $55,000 for serial rights to a novel. From 1958 through 1965 she wrote a regular column for *Woman's Day*.

Eight of Baldwin's novels were made into films with major actors. These included *Week-end Marriage* (1932); *Wife versus Secretary* (1936), starring Henry Fonda, Clark Gable, and Jean Harlow; *Comet over Broadway* (1938); and *Queen for a Day* (1951).

Sometimes called an autobiography, Baldwin's 1958 book *Testament of Truth* is actually a Christian reminiscence. It speaks to her love of nature and family, and of her religious faith. She says of her religion and her life, "Maybe I'm a reactionary, but I like tradition." She repeats this idea in her dedication to *Take What You Want*, a 1970 novel that she called a "confection, or meringue." She says it "was written in a reactionary spirit because I have so long been reading serious, important literature concerned with Problems, and starred with the now-commonplace four-letter words (the writers have forgotten there are others, such as 'love' and 'hope')."

A peaceful, noncontroversial person, Baldwin once told an interviewer that she loathed "all violent exercise except swimming." She preferred quiet activities like walking in the woods and noted that "books have been meat and drink to me." She died at home in Norwalk, Connecticut.

• Baldwin wrote more than 100 novels. Some titles not mentioned in the text are *Laurel of Story Stream* (1923), *Magic and Mary Rose* (1924), *Three Women* (1926), *Departing Wings* (1927), *Alimony* (1928), *The Office-Wife* (1930), *Skyscraper* (1931), *White Collar Girl* (1933), *Men Are Such Fools!* (1936), *Twenty-four Hours a Day* (1937), *Enchanted Oasis* (1938),

Temporary Address: Reno (1941), *Breath of Life* (1942), *He Married a Doctor* (1944), *The Lonely Man* (1964), *Evening Star* (1966), *The Velvet Hammer* (1969), *One More Time* (1972), *No Bed of Roses* (1973), *Thursday's Child* (1976), and *Adam's Eden* (1977). Her books of poetry (mainly inspirational) are *Sign Posts* (1924) and *Widow's Walk*.

Entries on Baldwin are in *Twentieth Century Authors 1942* and *Contemporary Authors: New Revision Series*, vol. 4. Articles about her appear in *Time*, 8 July 1935, and *Writer*, May 1940. An obituary is in the *New York Times*, 19 Mar. 1978.

ELAINE FREDERICKSEN

BALDWIN, Henry (14 Jan. 1780–21 Apr. 1844), U.S. Supreme Court justice, was born in New Haven, Connecticut, the son of Michael Baldwin, a blacksmith, and Theodora Wolcot. Baldwin received an LL.D. from Yale College in 1797. Thereafter, in Philadelphia, he studied law with Alexander J. Dallas, the first reporter of the U.S. Supreme Court.

Having gained admission to the bar, Baldwin set out for Ohio but settled in Pittsburgh, where he quickly gained social and political prominence. Practicing in all counties of western Pennsylvania, he was known for intelligence, indefatigability, and a ribald sense of humor. In 1802 Baldwin married Marianne Norton; they had one child. After the death of his first wife, he married Sally Ellicott; they had no children. They established a second home in Crawford County, Pennsylvania, from which he was elected to the U.S. House of Representatives in 1816. Reared as a Federalist, Baldwin's entry into politics often put him at odds with rural Jeffersonian Republican party regulars. In Congress he pressed for protective tariffs, incurring the enmity of states' rights advocate John C. Calhoun; more important, his defense of General Andrew Jackson's military actions solidified a lasting political alliance. Ill health forced Baldwin's resignation from Congress in 1822, but six years later he energetically supported Jackson's presidential candidacy. He expected to be confirmed as secretary of the Treasury, but Calhoun, now vice president, proffered instead a more sympathetic Pennsylvanian, Samuel D. Ingham.

With the death of Justice Bushrod Washington in 1829, Jackson nominated Baldwin to the Supreme Court, passing over Pennsylvania chief justice John Bannister Gibson and Horace Binney of the Philadelphia bar. Baldwin was confirmed with only two dissenting votes (both from antitariff South Carolina senators).

Jackson loyalist though he was, Baldwin, like Justice John McLean, nonetheless voted against the president in support of the national bank. In his freshman years, Baldwin also voted with Chief Justice John Marshall in the Georgia Indian suits, concurring in *Worcester v. Georgia* (1832) that federal control over the Indian tribes was exclusive.

Even before the departure of Bushrod Washington, the cohesion of the Marshall Court, especially from 1813 to 1826, had begun to wane. In its final decade under Marshall, from 1825 to 1835, the Court was less likely to produce decisions uniformly upholding federal power and the rights of private property. Baldwin

played a role in this transition. When the Supreme Court first heard *Charles River Bridge v. Warren Bridge Co.* in 1831, Baldwin alone, by his own account, favored the claims of the competing Warren Bridge Company, which had challenged an alleged Massachusetts legislative monopoly granted to Charles River Bridge. Marshall may have sided with Baldwin, indicating a growing acceptance of state legislative authority to regulate business.

On major constitutional issues, Baldwin's views are generally consistent over fourteen years. He supported unobstructed interstate commerce and, at the same time, sought to preserve the rights of the sovereign states; he regarded slaves as private property. When federal power was pitted against state sovereignty, Baldwin argued against expansion of the former. The vehemence of this position first appeared in a dissent in *Ex Parte Crane* (1831) in which he argued (here *contra* Marshall) against the extension of federal court jurisdiction to issue writs of mandamus.

After the 1837 term, when several cases held over from the Marshall Court were decided (e.g., *Charles River Bridge v. Warren Bridge Co.*), Baldwin published an extended pamphlet, *A General View of the Origin and Nature of the Constitution and Government of the United States . . .* (repr. 1970), in which he presented his concurring opinions as well as a "full explanation of what may be deemed my peculiar views of the constitution" (p. 1).

In constitutional interpretation, Baldwin is best described as a moderate, since (as his treatise seeks to explain) he eschewed the extremes of autonomous state sovereignty and of expanded federal supremacy. He placed himself in a middle category: those "who were willing to take the Constitution . . . as it is, and to expound it by the accepted rules of interpretation" (p. 37). With political sensitivity (by "justly considering . . . political power"), the Supreme Court should serve as an arbiter of federal versus state powers. Baldwin could not, perhaps, resolve in his own mind passionate support for federal tariffs and for state sovereignty; resolution could come only through the middle ground. Baldwin's key votes between 1830 and 1844 reveal him as a moderate, pronorthern justice in cases dealing with the role of corporations, federal-state relations, and slavery.

Baldwin's judicial temperament manifested an abrasive individuality, rather than teamwork or cohesion, the hallmark of the Marshall Court; in 1831, for example, he dissented seven times, violating a long-standing norm of Court unanimity and harmony nurtured by the chief justice. Just as he was a maverick loner, he preferred separate opinions. Because of strained relations with Richard Peters, the court reporter, these were often published privately or many years later. Sociable and well liked early in his career, Baldwin grew increasingly eccentric and, on occasion, violent in outbursts. He may have suffered from obsessive-compulsive syndrome, a condition characterized by social isolation and repeated activities, or rituals, self-soothing devices used to fill an emotional emptiness caused by underparenting, which was exacerbated in his final years by financial problems. He died, penniless, of paralysis in Philadelphia.

• Baldwin's papers, difficult to read because of illegibility, are scattered in the Crawford County (Pa.) Historical Society, Allegheny College, and the Baldwin Family Collection at the Huntington Library, San Marino, Calif. His Supreme Court papers, with annotated case commentary, are in the National Archives. Useful too are the papers of federal judge Joseph Hopkinson, with whom Baldwin served on circuit, in the Historical Society of Pennsylvania, Philadelphia. Baldwin also published *Reports of Cases Determined in the [Third] Circuit Court of the United States* (1837).

Frank Otto Gattell, "Henry Baldwin," in *The Justices of the United States Supreme Court*, vol. 1, ed. L. Friedman and F. Israel (1969), is the best essay on Baldwin's political and judicial careers, and it includes representative court opinions. Gattell commented (p. 580) that "Baldwin's historiographical anonymity is almost complete." Similar, more succinct, and largely repetitious essays come from Carl Brent Swisher, *The Taney Period*, vol. 5 of the *Oliver Wendell Holmes Devise History of the Supreme Court of the United States* (1974); Hampton L. Carson, *The History of the Supreme Court of the United States with Biographies* (1902), pp. 279–81; Martin Siegel, *The Taney Court*, vol. 3 of *The Supreme Court in American Life* (1987), pp. 258–60; Robert D. Ilisevich, "Henry Baldwin," in *The Supreme Court Justices*, ed. Clare Cushman (1993); and Robert G. Seddig, "Henry Baldwin," in *The Oxford Companion to the Supreme Court of the United States*, ed. Kermit L. Hall (1992). Swisher relied extensively on personal papers and correspondence.

The standard article on Baldwin's political career, with useful family information, is Flavia M. Taylor, "The Political and Civil Career of Henry Baldwin," *Western Pennsylvania History Magazine* 24 (1941). Consult also Ilisevich, "Henry Baldwin and Andrew Jackson: A Political Relationship in Trust?" *Pennsylvania Magazine of History and Biography* 120 (1996).

For useful analysis of Baldwin's judicial behavior, particularly his effect on the Marshall Court unanimity and cohesion in its final years, see G. Edward White, *The Marshall Court and Cultural Change 1815–1835* (1991), pp. 408–12; Stanley Kutler, *Privilege and Creative Destruction: The Charles River Bridge Case* (1971), pp. 172–79; R. Kent Newmyer, *The Supreme Court under Marshall and Taney* (1968), pp. 84–88; John R. Schmidhauser, "Judicial Behavior and the Sectional Crisis of 1837–1860," *Journal of Politics* 4 (Nov. 1961); and Seddig, "John Marshall and the Origin of Supreme Court Leadership," *Journal of Supreme Court History* (1991): 77–82.

ROBERT G. SEDDIG

BALDWIN, James (2 Aug. 1924–30 Nov. 1987), author, was born James Arthur Baldwin in Harlem, in New York City, the illegitimate son of Emma Berdis Jones, who married the author's stepfather, David Baldwin, in 1927. David Baldwin was a laborer and weekend storefront preacher who had an enormous influence on the author's childhood; his mother was a domestic who had eight more children after he was born. Baldwin was singled out early in school for his intelligence, and at least one white teacher, Orrin Miller, took a special interest in him. At PS 139, Frederick Douglass Junior High School, Baldwin met black poet Countee Cullen, a teacher and literary club adviser there. Cullen saw some of Baldwin's early poems and warned

him against trying to write like Langston Hughes, so Baldwin turned from poetry to focus more on writing fiction. In 1938 he experienced a profound religious conversion at the hands of a female evangelist/pastor of Mount Cavalry of the Pentecostal Faith, which he later wrote about in his first novel, *Go Tell It on the Mountain* (1953), in his play *The Amen Corner* (1968), and in an essay in *The Fire Next Time* (1963). Saved, Baldwin became a Sunday preacher at the nearby Fireside Pentecostal Assembly.

In 1938 Baldwin entered De Witt Clinton High School in the Bronx; he graduated in 1942. There Baldwin was challenged intellectually and was able to escape home and Harlem. He wrote for the school magazine, the *Magpie*, and began to frequent Greenwich Village, where he met black artist Beauford Delaney, an important early influence. Torn between the dual influences of the church and his intellectual and artistic private life, Baldwin finally made a choice. At age sixteen he began a homosexual relationship with a Harlem racketeer and later said he was grateful to the older man throughout his life for the love and self-validation he brought to the tormented and self-conscious teenager. As a preacher, Baldwin considered himself a hypocrite. At this same time, he discovered that David Baldwin was not, in fact, his real father and began to understand why he had felt deeply rejected as a child and had hated and feared his father. Fearing gossip about his homosexual relationship would reach his family and church, Baldwin broke with both the racketeer and the church. Now eighteen, he also moved away from home, taking a series of odd jobs in New Jersey and spending free time in the Village with artists and writers, trying to establish himself. He returned home in 1943 to care for the family while his stepfather was dying of tuberculosis. A few hours after his father's death, his youngest sister was born, named by James Baldwin, the head of the family. The Harlem riot of 1943 broke out in the midst of this family upheaval, all of which Baldwin described eloquently in *Notes of a Native Son* (1955).

After his father's funeral Baldwin left home for the last time, determined to become a writer. In 1944 he met Richard Wright, who helped him get a Eugene F. Saxon Fellowship to work on his first novel, then titled "In My Father's House." He gave part of the $500 grant to his mother and tried to start his literary career. Although Baldwin's first novel was rejected by two publishers, he began to have some success publishing book reviews and essays, establishing a name and a reputation. At the same time, he had difficulty extracting himself from the influence of Richard Wright, who became for Baldwin the literary father that he had to reject as David Baldwin had been the punishing stepfather to be overcome. With what was left of the Rosenwald Fellowship he had received in 1948, Baldwin, frustrated by the fits and starts of his writing career and tired of America's racism, bought a one-way air ticket to Paris and left the United States on 11 November.

In Paris, Baldwin met writers such as Jean-Paul Sartre, Jean Genet, and Saul Bellow. He garnered notice as a critic with the essay "Everybody's Protest Novel," which came out in *Partisan Review* in 1949. Although mostly a critique of Harriet Beecher Stowe's *Uncle Tom's Cabin*, this was the first of a series of three essays in which Baldwin attacked his literary mentor, Wright. Baldwin followed with "Many Thousand Gone" in 1951 and, after Wright's death, "Alas Poor Richard" in 1961. But not until he took himself, his typewriter, and his Bessie Smith records to a tiny hamlet high in the Swiss Alps in 1951 did Baldwin begin to work in earnest on his first and best novel, *Go Tell It on the Mountain*. In this autobiographical family novel, fourteen-year-old John Grimes undergoes an emotional-psychological-religious crisis of adolescence and is "saved." *Go Tell It on the Mountain* explores the histories and internal lives of John's stepfather Gabriel, mother Elizabeth, and Aunt Florence, spanning the years from 1875 to the depression and including "the Great Migration" from the South to Harlem. It was well received and was nominated for the National Book Award in 1954; Baldwin said in an interview with Quincy Troupe that he was told it did not win because Ralph Ellison's *Invisible Man* had won in 1953 and America was not ready to give this award to two black writers in a row.

Baldwin won a Guggenheim grant to work on a second novel, published in 1956 as *Giovanni's Room*, about a homosexual relationship and with all-white characters in a European setting. Baldwin's American publisher turned it down for its honesty, so Baldwin had to publish *Giovanni's Room* first in London. It was a book Baldwin had to write, he said in an interview with Richard Goldstein, "to clarify something for myself." Baldwin went on to say, "The question of human affection, of integrity, in my case, the question of trying to become a writer, are all linked with the question of sexuality." The central character, David, a young American living in Paris, is forced to choose between his fiancée, Hella, and his male lover Giovanni. David rejects Giovanni, who is later tried and executed for the murder of an aging homosexual. Racked with guilt, David reveals his true homosexual nature and breaks his engagement, making Giovanni the injured martyr and moral pole in the novel.

Baldwin's first collection of essays, *Notes of a Native Son*, appeared in 1955. These autobiographical and political pieces made Baldwin famous as an eloquent and experienced commentator on race and culture in America. Here he says on his father's funeral,

This was his legacy: nothing is ever escaped. That bleakly memorable morning I hated the unbelievable streets and the Negroes and whites who had, equally, made them that way. But I knew that it was folly, as my father would have said, this bitterness was folly. It was necessary to hold on to the things that mattered. The dead man mattered, the new life mattered; blackness and whiteness did not matter; to believe that they did was to acquiesce in one's own destruction. Hatred,

which could destroy so much, never failed to destroy the man who hated and this was an immutable law. (Bantam ed. [1968], pp. 94–95)

Baldwin returned periodically to the United States throughout the 1950s and 1960s, but never to stay. He first visited the South in 1957 and met Martin Luther King, Jr. In 1961 he published the collection of essays *Nobody Knows My Name: More Notes of a Native Son*. By 1963 he was prominent enough to be featured on the cover of *Time* magazine as a major spokesman for the early civil rights movement after another collection of essays, *The Fire Next Time*, arguably Baldwin's most influential work, appeared. His first play, *Blues for Mr. Charlie* (1964), a fictionalized account of the 1955 Mississippi murder of fourteen-year-old Emmett Till, followed. In *The Fire Next Time* Baldwin effectively honed his prophetic, even apocalyptic rhetoric about racial tensions in America, fusing his themes of protest and love. During this period Baldwin had also published his third novel, *Another Country*, in 1962. His influence in national politics and American literature had reached a peak.

Another Country took Baldwin six years to complete; it eventually sold 4 million copies after a slow start with negative reviews. It is considered to be Baldwin's second-best novel. In it Baldwin portrays multiple relationships involving interracial and bisexual love through a third-person point of view. Again he looks for resolutions to racial and sexual tensions through the power of love. The characters, however, often have trouble distinguishing sex from love and sorting through their attitudes toward sex, race, and class. Though successful, the novel is somewhat unwieldy with nine major characters, dominated by black jazz drummer Rufus Scott, who commits suicide at the end of the first chapter. The conclusion leaves readers with the hope that some of these troubled characters can achieve levels of self-understanding that will allow them to continue searching for "another country" within flawed and racist America. As Nigerian writer Wole Soyinka wrote in 1989,

In the ambiguities of Baldwin's expression of social, sexual, even racial and political conflicts will be found that insistent modality of conduct, and even resolution, celebrated or lamented as a tragic omission—love. . . . James Baldwin's was—to stress the obvious—a different cast of intellect and creative sensibility from a Ralph Ellison's, a Sonia Sanchez's, a Richard Wright's, an Amiri Baraka's, or an Ed Bullins'. He was, till the end, too deeply fascinated by the ambiguities of moral choices in human relations to posit them in raw conflict terms. His penetrating eyes saw the oppressor as *also* the oppressed. Hate as a revelation of self-hatred, never unambiguously outward-directed. Contempt as thwarted love, yearning for expression. Violence as inner fear, insecurity. Cruelty as an inward-turned knife. His was an optimistic, grey-toned vision of humanity in which the domain of mob law and lynch culture is turned inside out to reveal a landscape of scarecrows, an inner content of straws that await the compassionate breath of human love. [Troupe, pp. 11, 17–18]

With the death of Martin Luther King, Jr., and the change in the civil rights movement of the late 1960s from integrationist to separatist, Baldwin's writing, according to many critics, lost direction. The last two decades of his life he spent mostly abroad, particularly in France, which may have increased his distance from America in his work. In the essay collection *No Name in the Street* (1972), Baldwin discussed his sadness over the movement's waning. At the same time, he found himself the subject of attacks by new black writers such as Eldridge Cleaver, much like his own rejection of Richard Wright in the 1950s. *The Devil Finds Work* (1976) is Baldwin's reading of racial stereotypes in American movies, and *The Evidence of Things Not Seen* (1985), an account of the Atlanta child murder trials, was unsuccessful, although the French translation of this book was very well received. Baldwin also wrote a series of problematic novels in his later years: *Tell Me How Long the Train's Been Gone* (1968), *If Beale Street Could Talk* (1974), and *Just above My Head* (1979). In these novels Baldwin seems to go over the familiar ground of the first three novels: racial, familial, and sexual conflicts in flawed, autobiographical plots. He never again achieved the mastery of his first novel, *Go Tell It on the Mountain*, one of the key texts in all of African-American literature and of American literature as a whole.

After Baldwin died on the French Riviera, his funeral was celebrated on 8 December 1987 at the Cathedral of St. John the Divine in New York, where Maya Angelou, Toni Morrison, Amiri Baraka, the French ambassador Emmanuel de Margerie, and other notables spoke and performed. Baldwin has generally been considered to be strongest as an essayist, though he published one outstanding novel, and weakest as a playwright because he became too didactic at the expense of dramatic art. His achievements and influence tended to get lost in the sheer productivity of his career, especially as his later work was judged not to measure up to his earlier work. After his death scholars were able to look at Baldwin's contribution with perspective and a sense of closure, and his literary stature grew accordingly.

• Baldwin's personal papers and manuscripts are in the James Weldon Johnson Collection, Beinecke Rare Book and Manuscript Library, Yale University; the Berg collection at the New York Public Library; and the Schomburg Center for Research in Black Culture, New York Public Library, among other repositories. Books by Baldwin not mentioned above include *Going to Meet the Man* (1965), *A Dialogue: James Baldwin and Nikki Giovanni* (1971), *One Day When I Was Lost: A Scenario Based on Alex Haley's "The Autobiography of Malcolm X"* (1972), *A Rap on Race* (with Margaret Mead [1973]), *Little Man, Little Man: A Story of Childhood* (1976), *Jimmy's Blues: Selected Poems* (1983), *The Price of the Ticket: Collected Nonfiction* (1985), and *Perspectives: Angles of African Art*, ed. James Baldwin et al. (1987). There are a number of biographies, including David Adams Leeming, *James Baldwin: A Biography* (1994); James Campbell, *Talking at the Gates: A Life of James Baldwin* (1991); and W. J. Weatherby, *James Baldwin: Artist on Fire* (1989). Books on Baldwin and his work include Trudier Harris, *Black Women in the Fiction of James Baldwin* (1985); Horace A. Porter, *Stealing the Fire: The Art and Protest of James Baldwin* (1989); and Jean François Gounard, *The Racial Problem in the Works of Richard Wright and James Baldwin* (1992; translated from French). Some earlier studies are Stanley Macebuh, *James Baldwin, a Critical Study* (1973); Karen Moller, *The Theme of Identity in the Essays of James Baldwin* (1975); and Therman B. O'Daniel, *James Baldwin: A Critical Evaluation* (1977). There are also several collections of critical essays on Baldwin's work, among them Fred L. Standley and Nancy V. Burt, eds., *Critical Essays on James Baldwin* (1988), and Keneth Kinnamon, ed., *James Baldwin: A Collection of Critical Essays* (1974). For interviews, see Standley and Louis H. Pratt, eds., *Conversations with James Baldwin* (1989), and Quincy Troupe, ed., *James Baldwin: The Legacy* (1989). The best bibliography of works by and about Baldwin is in Horace A. Porter, *Stealing the Fire* (1989), which includes a long list of bibliographies, dissertations, and obituaries as well as primary and secondary works; for bibliographies, see also Troupe, *James Baldwin*, and Standley, ed., *James Baldwin: A Reference Guide* (1980). Obituaries are in the *New York Times*, 2 Dec. 1987, *Washington Post*, 5 Dec. 1987, and the *New York Review of Books* 34 (Jan. 1988): 8.

ANN RAYSON

BALDWIN, James Mark (12 Jan. 1861–8 Nov. 1934), psychologist and philosopher, was born in Columbia, South Carolina, the son of Cyrus Hull Baldwin, a businessman and sometime federal official, and Lydia Eunice Ford. Baldwin entered Princeton as a sophomore in 1881. There, under President James McCosh, he was exposed to both the old-style Scottish mental philosophy and the new experimental psychology of Wilhelm Wundt, a juxtaposition whose inherent contradictions helped shape much of his later intellectual career.

Graduating with the A.B. in 1884, Baldwin traveled to Germany on the Green Fellowship in Mental Science. He spent one semester in Wundt's Leipzig laboratory and another studying Spinoza under Friedrich Paulsen in Berlin. Returning to Princeton in 1885 as an instructor in French and German, Baldwin translated Théodule Ribot's *German Psychology of To-day* (1886) and published his first important paper, "The Postulates of a Physiological Psychology" (1887), which offered a framework for mental science built from the Scottish mental philosophy, the metaphysics of Spinoza, and the new psychology.

In 1887 Baldwin was appointed to a professorship in philosophy at Lake Forest University in Illinois, where he remained for two years. In 1888 he married Helen Hayes Green and completed a doctorate at Princeton. His first book, *Handbook of Psychology: Senses and Intellect* (1889), marked the beginning of Baldwin's transition from mental philosopher to experimental psychologist and led to his being offered the Chair of Logic and Metaphysics at the University of Toronto.

At Toronto, Baldwin established Canada's first laboratory of experimental psychology, and completed the second volume of his *Handbook* (1891). He initiated quantitative, experimental research on infant development that resulted in a series of papers on infant reaching and led him to adopt a more evolutionary view of the mind. In 1893 he returned to Princeton, where he held the Stuart Chair in Psychology and established a new laboratory. In 1895 he published his most important theoretical contribution to psychology, *Mental Development in the Child and the Race*.

In *Mental Development*, Baldwin articulated a biological theory of intellectual growth conceived as a process of adaptation. Assuming that organisms naturally relate to objects by acting on them, he argued that all such action is characterized by principles of "habit"—the organism's retention of that which is worth repeating—and "accommodation"—the organism's ability to vary its activity in relationship to circumstance and thereby "secure progressively . . . [more] useful reactions." "Circular reaction"—repetition of action with variation and selection—constitutes an invariant, functional mechanism through which the mind develops toward a more adequate apprehension of reality. *Mental Development* influenced several generations of scholars, most notably the Swiss psychologist Jean Piaget, who made extensive use of Baldwin's ideas in his seminal *Origins of Intelligence in Children* (1936).

During this period Baldwin cofounded the *Psychological Review* with James McKeen Cattell and began to extend his evolutionary, functional perspective to questions of social psychology. This culminated in the publication of *Social and Ethical Interpretations in Mental Development: A Study in Social Psychology* in 1897. The first book in English with the subtitle "social psychology," *Social and Ethical Interpretations* transferred the principle of circular reaction from the domain of action to that of interaction. Baldwin's central argument was that consciousness of self develops in the context of and reflects social interaction with the other just as consciousness of the other reflects consciousness of self, a view that influenced George Herbert Mead, among others.

In 1896, along with C. Lloyd Morgan and Henry Fairfield Osborn, Baldwin articulated the concept of "organic selection," an evolutionary principle that came to be known as the "Baldwin effect." In its most developed form, organic selection referred to the notion that acquired adaptations supplement natural selection in the evolutionary process. Adaptive behaviors acquired in the course of experience differentially increase the survival rate of organisms born with hereditary variations that favor those acquisitions. Over time, therefore, acquired adaptations can become congenital.

In 1897 Baldwin served as president of the American Psychological Association. His presidential address was a milestone in the development of evolutionary epistemology. Baldwin argued that "the discovery of truth . . . [is] an adaptation to a given set of data. . . . Truth is what is selected under the control of the system of established thoughts and facts, and assimilated

to the body of socially acquired knowledges and beliefs."

Baldwin also edited the *Dictionary of Philosophy and Psychology* (1901–1905). Fifty of the best minds of the day, including William James, John Dewey, Charles Sanders Peirce, Hugo Münsterberg, Edward Titchener, and Pierre Janet, contributed systematic definitions for major concepts in philosophy and psychology. Baldwin's work on this project elevated his international profile, increased his interest in the development of logic, and triggered a move away from empirical psychology toward philosophy.

In 1903 he resigned his psychology position at Princeton to become professor of philosophy and psychology at Johns Hopkins. There he founded another major journal, the *Psychological Bulletin*, and began work on *Thought and Things . . . or Genetic Logic* (1906–1911), a three-volume analysis of the development of cognition. The first volume focused on prelogical thought, imagery, memory, play, and the rise of meaning. The second volume analyzed discursive thought, reflection, the development of logical meaning, and implication. The final volume discussed "hyper-logical" operations believed by Baldwin to be expressed in aesthetic experience. Dense, conceptually difficult, encumbered by an unrestrained tendency to neologism, and appearing when psychology was struggling to free itself from philosophy, *Thought and Things* was little read and less appreciated.

In 1908 disaster struck. At the pinnacle of his career, Baldwin was arrested in a raid on a Baltimore bordello and forced to resign from Johns Hopkins. The ensuing scandal led to his being ostracized from American psychology. From 1909 to 1912 Baldwin divided his time between Mexico City, where he was associated with the School of Higher Studies at the National University, and Paris. In 1910 he was elected to succeed William James as correspondent of the Academy of Moral and Political Sciences, Institute of France.

With the outbreak of World War I, Baldwin actively promoted U.S. entrance into the war. In 1916 he wrote "Message from Americans Abroad to Americans at Home," which was widely circulated by the American Rights League. He also published *American Neutrality, Its Cause and Cure* (1916) and delivered the Herbert Spencer Lecture at Oxford, in which he attacked German political ideology. That year Baldwin also survived a German torpedo attack on the French passenger ship *Sussex* as it was crossing the English channel.

Throughout the war Baldwin worked diligently in a variety of charity and relief efforts mounted on behalf of the French people. For this, in 1917, he was decorated with the Legion of Honor. With U.S. entry into the war, he helped organize a Paris branch of the American Navy League, serving as its chair until 1922. After the armistice, he maintained informal academic contacts and spent time in preparation of his memoirs, published in 1926 as *Between Two Wars (1861–1921)*. He died in Paris.

Baldwin was not only one of the most important figures in the history of his discipline, he was one of its most sophisticated thinkers. Although by the late 1920s American psychology was committing itself to experimental empiricism, Baldwin's ideas later returned to psychology indirectly, through the work of Piaget and others interested in genetic logic and evolutionary epistemology.

• Only a few Baldwin papers are known to be extant. These are in the Princeton University Library. Additional correspondence can be found in the papers of William James, Hugo Münsterberg, George M. Stratton, Edward B. Titchener, and Robert M. Wenley. Baldwin's "postulates" appeared in the *Presbyterian Review* 8 (1887): 427–40. His infancy papers are "Origin of Right or Left-Handedness," "Right-Handedness and Effort," and "Infant Psychology," all in *Science*, 16 (1890): 247–48, 302–3, and 351–53. The Spencer Lecture was published under the title *The Super-State and the "Eternal Values"* (1916). Other major works include *Development and Evolution* (1902), *Fragments in Philosophy and Science* (1902), *The Individual and Society* (1911), *History of Psychology* (1913), and *Genetic Theory of Reality* (1915). *Between Two Wars* (1926), which reprints selected correspondence, is the best biographical source. Baldwin's autobiography in *A History of Psychology in Autobiography*, vol. 1, ed. Carl Murchison (1930), provides a retrospective account of his work. The best general secondary source is John M. Broughton and D. John Freeman-Moir, eds., *The Cognitive-Developmental Psychology of James Mark Baldwin* (1982). On Baldwin's social theories, see Eugene C. Holmes, *Social Philosophy and the Social Mind* (1942), and Vahan D. Sewny, *The Social Theory of James Mark Baldwin* (1945). On his genetic epistemology, see James Russell, *The Acquisition of Knowledge* (1978). On his organic selection, see Robert J. Richards, *Darwin and the Emergence of Evolutionary Theories of Mind and Behavior* (1987). For an early, but premature, assessment of Baldwin's influence, see Edwin G. Boring, *A History of Experimental Psychology* (1929).

ROBERT H. WOZNIAK

BALDWIN, John (13 Oct. 1799–28 Dec. 1884), manufacturer and philanthropist, was born in North Branford, Connecticut, the son of Joseph Baldwin, a blacksmith, and Rosanna Meloy. Baldwin's parents, devout Congregationalists, espoused antiliquor, antitobacco, and antislavery beliefs, which he, too, would champion. He had a conversion experience and became an evangelical Methodist at eighteen. After briefly attending an academy during his late teens, Baldwin taught school in New York, Maryland, and finally Litchfield, Connecticut. In January 1828 he married Mary D. Chappel of New London, Connecticut, herself a Methodist of humble station. They had seven children.

In spring 1828 he settled on a 200-acre tract in Middleburgh Township (later Berea), Ohio, established a farm, and built several water-powered mills. He promoted religion and reform in various ways, espousing Methodism and temperance, and promoting two reform-minded communities. The first was the Community of United Christians, a communitarian settlement designed for professing Christians who shared their property and wealth while preserving the family unit

and abiding by the settlement's temperance and antitobacco regulations. Briefly successful, it succumbed to a combination of falling land values during the panic of 1837 and criticism of its lifestyle by the Methodist church in Ohio. The second was the Lyceum Village and Berea Seminary, organized in 1837 after Josiah Holbrook's Lyceum plan. The Village never prospered, failing about 1845. A conventional school (the Berea Seminary) did evolve out of these experiments, with Baldwin supplying the building and providing employment opportunities for students.

Having given much of his money and land to underwrite these reformist enterprises, Baldwin was virtually bankrupted by their failure. He later claimed to have sought solace through a month-long series of special prayers in which he pledged that he would devote the bulk of his fortune to religious work if he were to become wealthy. His answer was a sudden inclination to inspect the rock underlying part of his property. There he discovered sandstone, which he knew to be the source for producing grindstones. His land had a plentiful supply, so he built his fortune by developing a grindstone industry in Berea. Baldwin's success came not from being the first producer of grindstones, but from introducing efficiency to their production. When he entered the business in the late 1830s, the rocks were cut, chiseled, and drilled by hand for local consumption. Mechanically adept, he conceived of a water-powered lathe to cut and drill the stones, which greatly decreased the labor and time involved in production. He also maximized efficiency in his mills and manufactories and in the mining of his quarries because he built and supervised them himself.

An entrepreneur as well as a mechanic, during the 1840s Baldwin introduced his grindstones in New York City, where they were judged superior to the French stones previously in use. Baldwin's response to the growing market was twofold: he became a promoter of railroad service to Cleveland (through Berea), and he began to lease land and water rights to others so that they might manufacture grindstones. The income from his industries allowed him to take advantage of rising Ohio land prices by buying and selling tracts throughout the remainder of his career. Thus Baldwin built Berea into the grindstone capital of America, in the process accumulating a modest fortune himself.

Financially successful by the early 1840s, he kept his vow "to appropriate my entire income, aside from the necessaries of life for myself and my family, to the cause of benevolence." Baldwin turned his attention to supporting education connected with the Methodist church. He became the founder of the Baldwin Institute, a coed academy open to all races, chartered in 1845 on his land in buildings he built, financed by gifts of his quarry land. The Institute produced few graduates, in part because of the growth of public education in Ohio, so its trustees sought reorganization, culminating in 1856 with the chartering of Baldwin University, newly underwritten with more Baldwin money. He also helped support a German department attached to the university to instruct German Methodists who had settled in the area (the German Department separated from Baldwin University in 1863 to become German Wallace College, but it merged again to form the present Baldwin-Wallace College in 1913).

The generosity Baldwin showed toward Methodist higher education attracted notice. No sooner was his Ohio university launched than he was invited to participate in a similar project in Kansas. There, Methodist promoters urged him to finance the already proposed Baker University by purchasing town lots at a site they named for him in northeast Kansas, where the school would be located. In agreeing, Baldwin united his philanthropy with his business acumen by establishing steam-powered mills in Baldwin City, thereby creating another source of income. Baker University opened in 1858, but Baldwin's enthusiasm for Kansas diminished after the death of his son, who had come to teach there. He returned to Berea without finishing his work on the mills, first leasing them to others and then selling most of them during the Civil War.

After the war Baldwin gave more quarry land to the Berea college, left the management of his Ohio enterprises to one of his sons, and in 1867 bought a 1700-acre sugar plantation in Louisiana, ostensibly because he sought a warmer climate in which to spend his old age. Again combining business acumen with philanthropy, he revived the sugar mill, brought financial improvement to the whole community (named Baldwin in his honor), and made his land and money available to Methodists to found two coed schools, one for each race. (He wanted an integrated school, but public sentiment would not permit it.)

In his later years, essentially retired from business, Baldwin continued to promote education. Learning from missionaries that there were no schools for English-speaking Methodists in India, he sent $3,000 to the church there in 1880, which founded Baldwin High Schools for each sex in Bangalore, South India. He gave forty acres of his Louisiana land to Baldwin University just months before he died in Baldwin.

Baldwin's life demonstrated many of the characteristics common to Christian reformers of the nineteenth century. His evangelical bent, his flirtation with utopian idealism, his espousal of many causes, and his settling among westering Yankees identified him with thousands of his contemporaries. But Baldwin differed from most in his mechanical aptitude and entrepreneurial spirit, which enabled him to become a successful industrialist, supplying the money necessary to turn his religious faith and reformist zeal into the creation of two colleges and several high schools. He was, as he often put it himself, a practical Christian.

• Baldwin's papers, including personal correspondence and business records, are in the Western Reserve Historical Society, Cleveland, Ohio. The only biography, uncritical and lacking citation, is A. R. Webber, *Life of John Baldwin, Sr., of Berea, Ohio* (1925). Helpful in establishing the details of Baldwin's utopian activities are David Lindsay, "A Backwoods Utopia: The Berea Community of 1836–37," *Ohio Historical Quarterly* 65 (1956): 272–96, and Henry O. Shel-

don, *A Lecture Delivered before the Society for the Promotion of Useful Knowledge upon the Lyceum System of Education, with Some Account of the First Lyceum Village, Berea, Ohio* (1842). On Baldwin's educational enterprises, see Virginia Gatch Markham, *John Baldwin and Son Milton Come to Kansas: An Early History of Baldwin City, Baker University and Methodism in Kansas* (1982), and an unpublished manuscript by Clyde E. Feuchter et al., "A History of Baldwin University and German Wallace College" (1945), housed in Ritter Library, Baldwin-Wallace College.

DAVID W. ROBSON

BALDWIN, John Brown (11 Jan. 1820–30 Sept. 1873), Virginia legislator and Confederate congressman, was born near Staunton, Augusta County, Virginia, the son of Briscoe G. Baldwin, a lawyer and judge, and Martha Steele Brown. Baldwin lived his entire life in Staunton, an urban center in the fertile Shenandoah Valley. After attending the University of Virginia between 1836 and 1839, he studied law for two years with his father and soon developed his own practice. In 1842 Baldwin married Susan Madison Peyton; they had no children.

Baldwin was elected as a Whig to the House of Delegates in 1845 (Augusta County was a Whig citadel in a generally Democratic state). He was defeated for reelection, however, because he opposed dominant public sentiment in the district, which wanted the legislature reapportioned according to white population rather than the "mixed" basis of population and property, including slaves, preferred by Baldwin and most eastern Virginians.

Baldwin held no public office in the latter 1840s or 1850s, but he remained a sought-after political speaker, especially in eastern Virginia. In 1860 he campaigned for former Tennessee senator John Bell, presidential candidate of the Constitutional Union party, who won a narrow statewide plurality.

Soon afterward Baldwin was elected to represent his home county in the Virginia Convention of 1861. There Baldwin and George W. Summers of Charleston led the nascent Union party, composed principally of former Whigs. He frequently participated in floor debate and also delivered a prodigious three-day Union oration.

The most controversial event in Baldwin's life occurred on 4 April 1861, when he met secretly with President Abraham Lincoln at the White House. The Baldwin interview came about when Secretary of State William H. Seward urgently requested that Unionists in the Virginia Convention send a spokesman to meet with the president. Seward concealed from Baldwin the full circumstances that prompted the summons— that Lincoln had decided to risk a resupply mission to Fort Sumter in the harbor of Charleston, South Carolina, and that peace hung by a thread. Baldwin pleaded with Lincoln to remove U.S. troops both from Fort Sumter and from Fort Pickens, offshore from Pensacola, Florida, the one other point in the seceded states that remained in Federal hands. By demonstrating his pacific intentions, Lincoln could hold the Upper South in the Union and give antisecessionists there "a stand-point from which we can bring back the seceded states," Baldwin assured the president. Lincoln instead expressed reservations and hinted obliquely that he intended to try to feed the troops at Fort Sumter. Baldwin, who had gone to Washington "full of hope and confidence" about finding some basis for reaching "an understanding with Mr. Lincoln," returned to Richmond "much depressed and disappointed."

According to Baldwin, Lincoln never offered to evacuate Fort Sumter in exchange for adjournment of the Virginia Convention, nor did he make any "overture" from which Baldwin "could infer it." Several days later, however, the president certainly did tell several visiting Virginians, among them the unconditional Unionist John Minor Botts, that Baldwin had summarily rejected an explicit offer to that effect. Botts concluded that Baldwin and his friends conspired to prevent Lincoln's offer from becoming known to the convention. The evidence suggests that Lincoln gave Botts a misleading version of his interview with Baldwin.

Virginia's secession and the start of the Civil War further depressed Baldwin. Deploring the "rabid" fever that seized many former Unionists, he voted against secession and predicted that "we are in danger of emerging from this revolution anything but a free people." Baldwin nevertheless accepted appointment as inspector general of the state volunteers. Soon he was appointed colonel of the Fifty-second Virginia Infantry, raised at Staunton, which he commanded in the Allegheny campaigns in the fall of 1861. While still on duty in November 1861, Baldwin was elected over two opponents to the First Confederate Congress. He was reelected in May 1863, defeating the incumbent Virginia governor, John Letcher.

Baldwin, who served from February 1862 until March 1865, played an active role in the Confederate House. He usually voted to give President Jefferson Davis broad military authority to prosecute the war. At the same time, however, Baldwin sought to mitigate the impact of warfare on the civilian population and to maintain southern food output. He voted to exempt various classes of agricultural producers from military service. By the last months of the war in early 1865, he was more ready than most to acknowledge the hopelessness of the war effort and to seek a negotiated surrender.

Baldwin's most sustained public role occurred immediately following the war. Elected to the House of Delegates of the restored state government in October 1865, he was selected two months later as Speaker. "Conservative" ex-Confederates, typically former Whigs who had opposed secession, dominated the so-called Baldwin legislature.

In February 1866 the Joint Committee on Reconstruction took testimony from a number of Virginians, among them Baldwin. There the erstwhile Unionist denied that he had concealed from the Virginia Convention of 1861 a peace overture from Lincoln. Baldwin also insisted that defeated Virginians accepted the results of the war and were working to establish equal civil rights for blacks and whites. He strongly objected, however, to any extension of political rights to blacks.

With near unanimity, the Baldwin legislature spurned the proposed Fourteenth Amendment, which would have reduced the representation of former Confederate states that did not allow black voting and would also have disqualified from office many prominent ex-rebels. In response, Congress soon moved to abolish the existing governments in the South and to require approval of the Fourteenth Amendment. By the winter of 1867–1868, a Republican-dominated constitutional convention met to lay the foundations for a new Virginia government.

The adroit Baldwin and his brother-in-law, Alexander H. H. Stuart, were among the principals on the so-called Committee of Nine, organized in December 1868, whose initiatives ended Reconstruction in Virginia. They agreed to accept universal suffrage as long as voters had the opportunity to strike the proscriptive test oath and disfranchisement clauses of the new constitution. The Committee of Nine also masterminded the nomination for governor of conservative Republican Gilbert C. Walker. The adoption of the modified constitution and the election of Walker in July 1869 made Virginia the first ex-Confederate state to fall into Conservative hands.

Baldwin's health deteriorated after 1869, and he died in Staunton. Blessed with a prodigious memory, a keen intellect, and a large measure of self-confidence, Baldwin was a gifted speaker and debater. His talents as an attorney were legendary; he likewise vaulted to prominence when holding elective office, most notably during the great crisis of 1860–1861. However unsuccessful their efforts, Baldwin and the Virginia Unionists attempted to avert a mighty conflagration. Nothing during Baldwin's eventful wartime and postwar career approached the significance of the hour he spent at the White House in April 1861.

• There is no collection of Baldwin papers, nor is there a biography. A sketch of his life written by J. A. Waddell is in *History of Augusta County, Virginia*, ed. J. Lewis Peyton (1882). On Baldwin's key role in the secession crisis, see *Interview between President Lincoln and Col. John B. Baldwin, April 4th, 1861: Statements & Evidence* (1866); Baldwin's testimony to the Joint Committee on Reconstruction, 10 Feb. 1866, 39th Cong., 1st sess., H. Doc. 30, vol. 2, Serial 1273, pp. 102–9; George H. Reese, ed., *Proceedings of the Virginia State Convention of 1861* (4 vols., 1965); and Daniel W. Crofts, *Reluctant Confederates: Upper South Unionists in the Secession Crisis* (1989). Baldwin's activities during Reconstruction are explained by Richard Lowe, *Republicans and Reconstruction in Virginia, 1856–70* (1991), and Jack P. Maddex, Jr., *The Virginia Conservatives, 1867–1879: A Study in Reconstruction Politics* (1970). An obituary is in the Stanton *Spectator and General Advertiser*, 7 Oct. 1873.

DANIEL W. CROFTS

BALDWIN, John Denison (28 Sept. 1809–8 July 1883), minister and journalist, was born in North Stonington, Connecticut, the son of Daniel Baldwin and Hannah Stanton, farmers. When he was seven, the family suffered financial reverses and moved to Chenango County, on the upstate New York frontier, and survived seven difficult years before returning to Connecticut. Baldwin attended a village school for three years, then enrolled at Yale College, supporting himself by part-time schoolteaching. He studied briefly at Yale's school of law but shifted to the school of divinity. He completed the theological course in 1834; five years later, he was awarded an honorary master of arts. In April 1832 he married Lemira Hathaway; they had four children.

From 1834 to 1849 Baldwin served as minister at a series of small Connecticut Congregational churches. In his sermons, he developed the vigorous literary style that was to serve him later in his newspaper work. He was known for introducing variegated information into his presentations, especially stories about pets.

While still a minister, he entered politics as a free-soiler, opposed to the extension of slavery into territories that had not yet been granted statehood, and was sent to the Connecticut legislature in 1847 as a representative from North Killingly. Subsequently, he was a principal organizer of the state's Free Soil party. In 1849 he abandoned the ministry to become the editor of the state Free Soil newspaper, the *Charter Oak*, later called *The Republican*. As a member of the General Assembly, he sponsored the bill creating Connecticut's first teacher's college.

In 1852 Baldwin went to Boston, Massachusetts, to become editor, manager, and part owner of the *Daily Commonwealth*, an antislavery newspaper affiliated with the abolitionist Samuel Gridley Howe. As editor, he worked closely with Senators Charles Sumner and Henry Wilson and aided in the creation of the Republican party. He edited the *Daily Commonwealth* until its final issue in September 1854.

Baldwin bought, edited briefly, and then sold a small Cambridge, Massachusetts, newspaper before founding the newspaper that was to occupy the rest of his life. In 1859, with his two sons, he acquired the *Worcester (Mass.) Daily Spy*, descended from the illustrious *Massachusetts Spy*, the revolutionary war newspaper founded by patriot printer Isaiah Thomas. The Baldwins soon restored the run-down newspaper to prosperity and put up a new building opposite the town hall in Worcester. Still aligned with the antislavery and Republican causes, Baldwin argued his positions so authoritatively that the *Spy* became known as the "Worcester County Bible" by friends and as "the lying *Spy*" by the opposition.

Baldwin continued to combine newspaper editing with politics. Serving as a delegate to the 1860 Republican National Convention, which nominated Abraham Lincoln for president, he was credited with proposing the vice presidential candidate, Hannibal Hamlin of Maine. When the Civil War started, Baldwin firmly supported Lincoln's effort to restore the Union by force, counseling the government to avoid "every dream of compromise with treason."

In 1862 Baldwin was elected a Republican member of Congress from the Worcester district. In the House of Representatives, he served on minor committees and did not speak frequently, but the speeches he made were notable. He spoke eloquently on state sovereignty and treason (1864) and on the role of Congress in Reconstruction (1866). In his most widely praised address, in January 1868, he not only defended the entitlement of freed slaves to "human rights" but envisioned a multiracial nation based on equality of opportunity.

His position on civil rights has sometimes led historians to place him among the Radical Republicans who favored harsh Reconstruction policies. But on other questions he tended to be moderate, most notably in voting against impeaching President Andrew Johnson. He was soon punished for this action; three months later the Republican district convention nominated a younger man, George F. Hoar, for his seat, although Baldwin had won four-fifths of the vote in the previous election. He left the House in 1869.

Abruptly ushered out of politics, Baldwin never returned. He became something of a recluse, concentrating on his work as an amateur scholar in archaeology and genealogy and leaving the *Spy*'s management increasingly to his sons. After his death in Worcester he was widely praised in New England newspapers for his pursuit of the old-fashioned journalism of sound opinion rather than news, steadfastness rather than brilliance. The *Springfield Union* tacitly recognized that he had outlived the issue that most strongly motivated him when it wrote: "He was a pioneer free soiler when it did not pay to speak for human rights, and happily he lived to see slavery abolished" (Staples, p. 100).

• A few papers of the Baldwin family and records of the *Worcester Daily Spy* are in the American Antiquarian Society, Worcester, Mass. Baldwin offered a brief account of his own life in his *Record of the Descendants of John Baldwin, of Stonington* (1880). His books include *The Story of Raymond Hill and Other Poems* (1847), *Prehistoric Nations* (1869), and *Ancient America: Notes on American Archaeology* (1872); he also compiled genealogies of the Denison and Stanton families of Stonington. Biographical articles include Samuel E. Staples, "Hon. John Denison Baldwin, A.M.," *Proceedings of the Worcester Society of Antiquity for the Year 1883* (1884): 90–101; Ellery Bicknell Crane, ed., *Historic Homes and Institutions and Genealogical and Personal Memoirs of Worcester County, Massachusetts*, vol. 1 (1907), pp. 309–12; Charles Nutt, *History of Worcester and Its People*, vol. 4 (1919), pp. 752–54; and James Boylan, "A Forgotten Editor from Stonington: John Denison Baldwin," *Historical Footnotes: Bulletin of the Stonington Historical Society* 19 (Aug. 1982): 1, 3, 8. Baldwin's editorship of the *Daily Commonwealth* is recounted in Albert P. Langtry, ed., *Metropolitan Boston*, vol. 2 (1929), 539–41. On the *Worcester Spy*, see Ellery Bicknell Crane, ed., *History of Worcester County, Massachusetts*, vol. 1 (1924), pp. 402–4, and Abijah P. Marvin, *History of Worcester in the War of the Rebellion* (1870). Baldwin's congressional career is analyzed in Michael Les Benedict, *A Compromise of Principle: Congressional Republicans and Reconstruction, 1863–1869* (1974); Benedict, *The Impeachment and Trial of Andrew Johnson* (1973); David Donald, *The Politics of Reconstruction,*

1863–1867 (1965); and George F. Hoar, *Autobiography of Seventy Years* (1903). An obituary is in the *Worcester Spy*, 9 July 1883.

JAMES BOYLAN

BALDWIN, Joseph Glover (21 Jan. 1815–30 Sept. 1864), attorney and author, was born in Friendly Grove Factory, Virginia, the son of Joseph Clarke Baldwin, a mill owner, and Eliza Cook. He was educated at Staunton Academy (Virginia), where he learned Latin and read widely in English and American authors. He left school at fourteen and became a clerk in the chancery court. This experience turned him toward a legal career, and after private study and law school he qualified as a lawyer at twenty. Baldwin also worked for a time as a newspaperman in Virginia and suffered a disappointment in love. In March 1836 he set out for the "Southwest"—specifically Alabama and Mississippi.

In the 1830s frontier conditions still prevailed in Alabama and Mississippi. Because of a fairly primitive legal system, social fluidity, roguery, conflicting land claims, and the rugged, semi-lawless world of men on the make, there was plenty of business for lawyers, and Baldwin became successful. He settled first at De Kalb, Mississippi, in April 1836; moved to Gainesville, Alabama, in July 1837; and lived there, practicing law, until 1850, when he moved to Livingston, Alabama. These were years of increasing prosperity and political involvement: in 1843 he was elected as a Whig to the Alabama legislature, and in 1849 he lost a race for Congress. Baldwin married Sidney Gaylard White in 1839; they had six children.

In 1850 or 1851 Baldwin began writing "sketches" of his experiences in the Southwest. These were published in the *Southern Literary Messenger* and, in 1853, appeared in book form as *The Flush Times of Alabama and Mississippi*. The contents include memoirs, character sketches of vivid personalities, and informal accounts of backwoods law; perhaps most memorably, they present Ovid Bolus, Esq., a character whose natural ability at lying brings humor and vitality to Baldwin's work. *Flush Times*, for which Baldwin is chiefly remembered, is a notable contribution to the genre of southwestern humor: mostly written by learned men about unlearned ones and published to the world *outside* the raw southwestern territory, the sketches and tales of this body of work emphasize the funny side of roguery, colorful violence and deception, and utilitarian ethics. They influenced Mark Twain, whose early sketch "The Dandy Frightening the Squatter" is in the southwestern tradition.

By the early 1850s Baldwin was turning toward California. Although he had never been to California, in 1853 he published a sketch in the *Southern Literary Messenger* called "California Flush Times," a purported emigrant's letter. He seems to have been drawn by the same kinds of opportunities—practicing law on the raw edge of civilized life and the possibilities of advancement offered by the flush times that followed the gold rush—as those that had brought him to Alabama

and Mississippi. By August 1854 he was in San Francisco. He soon became a busy and respected attorney. In September 1858 he was elected associate justice of the California Supreme Court, in which capacity he served until 1862.

Baldwin's literary career, meanwhile, had not ended. In 1854 he published a series of sketches of American politicians (Thomas Jefferson and Andrew Jackson among them), called *Party Leaders*. This is an able book, serious and well written, with strong beliefs, but without the setting and humor of *Flush Times*, for which Baldwin has always been best known.

In 1860 Baldwin was a candidate before the legislature for the U.S. Senate but was not selected. From then until his death he practiced law and oversaw his business interests, including mine holdings in Nevada. Perhaps in 1864 he began writing "The Flush Times of California," which was left unfinished and published only in 1966.

During the Civil War, Baldwin and his wife sympathized with the Confederacy, while one son and many friends were pro-Union. His son Joseph, Jr., died of tuberculosis at twenty, in 1864, and the next month Baldwin himself died in California, after a minor operation; the cause of death was tetanus or the opiates given him for his pain.

Baldwin's temperament was conservative. George W. Polhemus, the author of the biographical sketch that introduces *The Flush Times of California*, reports that he was given to melancholy and fits of temper. A slaveowner, a states' rights Whig, and then a Democrat, Baldwin distrusted the mob; in *Party Leaders* he writes with some disdain of Jefferson's democratic beliefs. His writing is elegant in an eighteenth-century way, full of allusions and Latin phrases (many of them naturally drawn from his legal practice). As standards, he appeals to the classical writers and to Burke, Byron, and Samuel Johnson, and there is something Johnsonian both in his prose, with its balance and sonority, and in his traditionalist, often pessimistic attitude toward human life. In his best work, *The Flush Times of Alabama and Mississippi*, Baldwin's conservatism and reserve set off the raucous events he describes and introduce an ironic margin between the *narration* of the book and the crudity of the contents.

• The New York Public Library contains two collections, Robert MacDonald Lester's "Papers on Joseph Glover Baldwin" (materials for an unfinished biography) and the Joseph G. Baldwin Papers, including Baldwin's correspondence. There is no published biography of Baldwin, but see Robert Bain and Joseph Flora, eds., *Fifty Southern Writers Before 1900* (1987), which includes bibliographical information; George W. Polhemus, "Biographical Sketch of Joseph G. Baldwin," in *The Flush Times of California* (1966); and James H. Justus's introduction to *The Flush Times of Alabama and Mississippi* (1987), which also contains considerable autobiographical writing. An obituary appears in the *Sacramento Daily Union*, 3 Oct. 1864.

MERRITT MOSELEY

BALDWIN, Loammi (21 Jan. 1745–20 Oct. 1807), civil engineer, was born in Woburn, Massachusetts, the son of James Baldwin, a carpenter and shopkeeper, and Ruth Richardson. (Some sources give his birthdate as 10 Jan. 1744.) After attending the local grammar school, Loammi was apprenticed in the carpentry trade. As a teenager Baldwin worked in the family's stores in Woburn and Boston. By 1767 Baldwin was engaged as a pump maker and cabinetmaker, in addition to helping in the family stores. In 1771 he and his friend Benjamin Thompson, later Count Rumford, attended the lectures of Professor John Winthrop at Harvard College and conducted home experiments based on these lectures. Largely self-taught, Baldwin focused his studies on mathematics and hydraulics. He married Mary Fowle in 1772. They had five children.

At the beginning of the American Revolution, Baldwin enlisted in the Continental army as a major and was soon thereafter commissioned a lieutenant colonel. He was later promoted to the rank of colonel of the Twenty-sixth Army Regiment and served in Boston, New York, and New Jersey, participating in the attack on Trenton of 25 December 1776. Health problems led to his resignation, and he received an honorable discharge in 1777.

Upon returning home to Woburn, Baldwin served in the Massachusetts General Court in 1778–1779 and again from 1800 to 1804. In 1780 he was appointed sheriff of Middlesex County, a position he held until 1794. His first wife having died, in 1791 he married Margery Fowle, her cousin; they had two children.

In 1793 Baldwin began his association with the Middlesex Canal, one of the nation's early important civil engineering projects. Chartered in 1793, this 28-mile waterway connected the Merrimack River with the Charles River and Boston. Designed to assure Boston its commercial position with inland New England communities, it cut through Baldwin's native Middlesex County. As one of the first artificial waterways to be built in the United States, and not a simple river improvement project, the Middlesex influenced the design of later American canals.

Baldwin played an important role as a promoter of the canal, as well as its principal engineer. As an investor, Baldwin had a financial interest in the company's success. This financial interest in the company was not atypical for engineers in the period. Listed as one of the chartering members of the canal, Baldwin served on the board of directors as first vice president. As a director from 1794 to 1804, Baldwin assisted Samuel Thompson on the first survey for the canal. After an early survey was deemed inaccurate, Baldwin was appointed superintendent of the Middlesex Canal in 1794, despite his lack of professional canal experience. With this position Baldwin's reputation as an engineer became intertwined with his financial interest in the company. Soon after his appointment, the board of directors sent Baldwin to study canals in Pennsylvania and Virginia. He was also ordered to secure the assistance of William Weston, the famed British canal engineer, then working in Pennsylvania. Baldwin lured Weston to Massachusetts in July 1794 to consult on the canal and also to train Baldwin and other canal employees in the proper use of his surveying tools. Baldwin rented Weston's tools and completed the formal survey for the Middlesex Canal with this equipment.

As superintendent Baldwin supervised the plans and construction of the canal. During the construction, five of his sons worked in various jobs on the canal. Although the initial locks were made of stone, after 1799 the uncertain financial condition of the canal company forced Baldwin to switch to wooden locks. Finally, in 1803, the entire 28-mile canal, 3½ feet deep, with twenty locks and eight aqueducts, was completed and opened for traffic. In the next two years, 1804 to 1805, Baldwin designed the Medford Branch Canal, a quarter-mile canal, with two locks, connecting the Middlesex Canal with the Mystic River.

The success of the Middlesex Canal assured Baldwin's engineering reputation and made him much in demand for other civil engineering projects in New England. In 1796 Baldwin consulted with the Proprietors of Locks and Canals, a private corporation for a bypass canal on the Merrimack River, the future location of Lowell, Massachusetts. He also designed and consulted on the construction of another bypass canal at Amoskeag, New Hampshire. In addition to canal engineering, Baldwin completed surveys for turnpike companies, including the new Concord, Stony Brook, and Montreal companies. He also surveyed and designed the town of Baldwin, Maine. He supervised the Boston harbor construction of the India Wharf, designed by Charles Bullfinch, and designed mill races and other river improvement schemes. Baldwin, however, is most closely associated with and was most proud of his work on the Middlesex Canal. Not only was this one of the earliest artificial waterways built in the United States, but its dimensions were later copied by the engineers of the Erie Canal, which itself became the American canal engineering standard.

In addition to his civil engineering work, Baldwin supervised his Massachusetts estate and achieved fame as the developer around 1794 of the "Baldwin" apple. Also called the "Woodpecker" and "Steele's Red Winter," this apple was popular for its taste and suitability for shipping.

Baldwin stands as one of the first and most influential civil engineers in New England in the eighteenth and early nineteenth century. His combining of financial investment with engineering skills was typical of American engineers of the period. His work on the influential Middlesex Canal and the training of his sons, as well as his work throughout New England, secured his reputation. In addition to Loammi, Jr., four other sons, Cyrus Baldwin, Benjamin Franklin Baldwin, James Fowle Baldwin, and George Rumford Baldwin, all worked as civil engineers for canal and railroad companies.

Baldwin was a member of the American Academy of Arts and Sciences and Harvard College awarded him an honorary masters of arts degree in 1785. He died in Woburn, Massachusetts.

• There are large collections of Baldwin papers at Baker Library of Harvard University, and at Clements Library of the University of Michigan. Both collections include professional and personal accounts. The collection at Harvard includes many reports and documents of the Middlesex Canal. For information on Baldwin's work on the Middlesex Canal, see Christopher Roberts, *The Middlesex Canal, 1793–1860* (1938). There is some information on Loammi Baldwin, Sr., in George L. Vose, *A Sketch of the Life and Works of Loammi Baldwin, Civil Engineer* (1885), although most of the book is devoted to his son. See also Frederick K. Abbott, "The Role of the Civil Engineer in Internal Improvements: The Contributions of the Two Loammi Baldwins, Father and Son, 1776–1838" (Ph.D. diss., Columbia Univ., 1952). For information on the development of civil engineering in America and the role of the engineer promoter, see Daniel Hovey Calhoun, *The American Civil Engineer: Origins and Conflict* (1960). For additional general information, see Richard Shelton Kirby and Philip Gustave Laurson, *The Early Years of Modern Civil Engineering* (1932).

FRANCES C. ROBB

BALDWIN, Loammi, Jr. (16 May 1780–30 June 1838), civil engineer, was born in North Woburn, Massachusetts, the son of Loammi Baldwin, a renowned civil engineer, and Mary Fowle. After attending Westford Academy, Baldwin matriculated at Harvard College, graduating in 1800. As a youth he had assisted his father on the Middlesex Canal. After college, his first position was in the law office of Timothy Bigelow at Groton, Massachusetts. While at Groton he designed a fire engine for the town, which was built in 1802 and operated for more than eighty years.

After being admitted to the bar in 1804, Baldwin opened his own law office in Boston but closed it just three years later when he embarked on a trip to England to study public works. In 1807 he established his engineering office in Charlestown, Massachusetts. In 1809 he published *Thoughts on the Study of Political Economy as Connected with the Population, Industry, and Paper Currency of the United States.* This pamphlet, among other thoughts, encouraged the improvement of transportation systems in the country. During the War of 1812 he was granted one of his first engineering commissions, the design of Fort Strong in the Boston Harbor in 1814. With his engineering career under way, he was in constant demand by corporations, internal improvement companies, and state and federal governments. His various assignments often overlapped each other, as he produced designs and surveys for numerous projects throughout the United States.

From 1817 to 1820 Baldwin served as principal engineer for the Virginia Board of Public Works. In this capacity he surveyed internal improvement projects proposed throughout Virginia, including surveys of the Rappahannock and Rapidan rivers, the Great Kanawha River, James River, Goose Creek, and the Richmond docks. In 1818 he and his brother Benjamin surveyed river improvement schemes in North Carolina, as well as conducting canal surveys in Kentucky, New Hampshire, Massachusetts, and Virginia. In 1819 Baldwin was appointed engineer for the Boston-Roxbury Corporation and completed the company's water-power project.

In 1821 Baldwin was appointed engineer of the Union Canal, the long-awaited project to connect the Schuylkill and Susquehanna valleys. After surveying the region, Baldwin designed a route for a 79-mile canal, which included a 739-foot long tunnel. His lock dimensions, however, were considered too large and costly by the board of directors. Baldwin departed in 1823 after a long-running controversy with the board over hiring practices and design reviews. He was replaced by Canvass White, who built the canal with the small dimensions preferred by the canal's board of directors. Although the Union Canal was completed in 1826, it never achieved the long-term success expected, in part because the boats from the connecting Schuylkill navigation system were too large for the small Union Canal locks.

In 1824 Baldwin accompanied Francis Lowell, one of the founders of the Boston Associates, on an engineering tour of Europe. Following his return in 1825 he served on the Bunker Hill Monument Committee and completed a survey for the state of Massachusetts for a proposed canal between Boston and the Hudson River. In 1826 he designed a waterpower system for the Salem Milldam Corporation, though this plan was never put into operation. Massachusetts again hired Baldwin in 1827 to survey and design a proposed railroad from Boston to the Hudson River. This project was completed by his brother James Fowle Baldwin.

From 1827 to 1835 Baldwin designed the two works considered his greatest, the government dry-docks at Charlestown, Massachusetts, and at Gosport (Norfolk), Virginia. Baldwin agreed to accept the position of civil engineer of dry docks only after carefully defining his power and responsibility for the projects. Under this arrangement Baldwin supervised the Charlestown works during the summer months, and the Norfolk project in the winter. He alternated sites with his assistant, Alexander Parris. The docks were built of granite, and the interior of the docks measured 86 feet wide by 253 feet long. Finished in 1834, these were the first dry-docks built in the United States, and the completed works were considered some of the finest and most magnificent examples of American civil engineering for the period.

While under contract with the government Baldwin also served as consulting engineer to a U.S. Navy board of commissioners studying navy yards. He also made reports on other government facilities and future facilities, including the yards at Portsmouth, New Hampshire, New York City, Pensacola, Philadelphia, and Washington, D.C.

In 1834 Baldwin published a work that studied water supplies for cities in Europe and the United States, including Boston. In 1835 his work projects included surveying the potential water power of the Androscoggin River at Brunswick, Maine. The following year he completed a water power survey for the Amoskeag Manufacturing Company, at Manchester, New Hampshire. That same year he surveyed the Altahama River in Georgia, designed and supervised the construction of Holworthy Hall for Harvard College, and served as a consulting engineer for the Louisville and Portland Canal and the Harrisburg Canal. In 1835 Baldwin was a member of the Massachusetts Executive Council, and in 1836, a presidential elector.

Baldwin's engineering firm in Boston served as one of the first training programs for engineers in the United States. His students, who included Alexander Parris, Uriah Boyden, Samuel Felton, G. J. F. Bryant, and John W. Brooks, paid for the privilege to work in his office and were subsequently reimbursed for their contributions on projects. At a time when there were only a few engineering colleges in the United States, Baldwin's office served as an important training ground for new engineers.

Long remembered for designing and supervising the construction of the first dry-docks built in the United States, Baldwin also had a significant role in numerous internal improvement projects across the nation. His biographer, George L. Vose, said of Baldwin, "There is no man among the leaders of industrial work in this country to whom we owe more" (p. 3). Working during the heyday of the American transportation revolution, Baldwin brought his expertise to a multitude of projects. Although he was not educated at an engineering school, Baldwin stands at the forefront of antebellum civil engineers and has been called the "Father of Civil Engineering in America." Baldwin was married twice, first to Ann Williams of Salem, Massachusetts. After her death in 1822 he married Catherine Beckford, a widow, in 1828. Baldwin died from a stroke in Charlestown (Boston), Massachusetts.

• Both the Baker Library at Harvard University and the Clements Library at the University of Michigan have large collections of Baldwin Family Papers. A biography of Baldwin is George L. Vose, *A Sketch of the Life and Works of Loammi Baldwin, Civil Engineer* (1885). See also Frederick K. Abbott, "The Role of the Civil Engineer in Internal Improvements: The Contributions of the Two Loammi Baldwins, Father and Son, 1776–1838" (Ph.D. diss., Columbia Univ., 1952). A chronological listing of all of Loammi Baldwin, Jr., assignments is in the appendix to Christopher Roberts, *The Middlesex Canal* (1938). Information on his term in Virginia is in the *Annual Report of the President and Directors of the Board of Public Works*; portions of the 1818 report are printed in *North American Review* (1818). Material on the dry-docks can be gleaned from the American State Papers and other congressional Reports. For material on the growth of American civil engineering, see Daniel Hovey Calhoun, *The American Civil Engineer: Origins and Conflict* (1960), and Richard Shelton Kirby and Philip Gustave Laurson, *The Early Years of Modern Civil Engineering* (1932).

FRANCES C. ROBB

BALDWIN, Matthias W. (10 Dec. 1795–7 Sept. 1866), locomotive builder, was born in Elizabethtown, New Jersey, the son of William Baldwin, a carriage maker.

His mother's name is unknown. His father's death in 1799 led to serious financial difficulties for the once-prosperous family, and Matthias, the youngest of five children, was raised in economic hardship. At age sixteen he began what he anticipated would be a career in the jeweler's trade as an apprentice to Woolworth Brothers, a jeweler in Frankford, Pennsylvania. In 1917 he moved to the Philadelphia firm of Fletcher & Gardiner, where he served as a journeyman jeweler for two years before branching off into business for himself. In 1827 he married Sarah C. Baldwin (no relation), with whom he raised five children (one of them adopted).

In 1828, casting about for new opportunities, Baldwin, along with a partner, Peter Mason, invested in the manufacture of printing machinery. At that time virtually all publishing tools and binding machines were costly, imported items. By manufacturing the machinery at their factory on Walnut Street in Philadelphia—and by utilizing innovations developed by Baldwin—the partners immediately thrived and soon expanded into the manufacture of other machine tools. Baldwin himself achieved some renown for inventing a process for placing designs on the copper cylinders used in calico printing.

The success of Baldwin & Mason led directly to Baldwin's career in steam locomotives. Unable to locate a stream engine that could provide enough power for an expanded Baldwin & Mason factory, Baldwin designed and built his own five-horsepower engine, which generated much interest. The partners began to receive orders for, and to manufacture, additional such engines, and Baldwin soon bought out Mason and devoted himself full-time to engineering.

In 1930, having heard of Baldwin's growing reputation as an inventor and manufacturer, Franklin Peale of the Philadelphia Museum contracted with him to build, for the museum, a miniature locomotive that would pull two, two-passenger cars around a circular track running around the museum. The small specialty train that Baldwin designed, based on British-built engines he had studied, was put into operation in April 1831 and immediately drew crowds to the museum. Less than a year later he was engaged by the Philadelphia, Germantown & Norristown Railroad Company to build a full-sized locomotive that would replace horse-drawn stock on the railroad. The technical hurdles that Baldwin had to overcome were immense. Skillful mechanics were hard to find, and tools at that time were inadequate for the task. Virtually every element had to be built by hand. In the process, Baldwin perfected some details, but the locomotive he built for the PG & N—called Old Ironsides for its wrought iron tires—had most of the features that were common to other engines of the period, including a wooden frame and wooden wheels.

The test run of Old Ironsides (24 Nov. 1832) was widely reported in the press. As a result, additional orders came in, and Baldwin geared his operation toward the construction of locomotives. His firm built ten more engines before 1837, when it became necessary to move to a larger plant. At this new facility Baldwin built some fifteen hundred locomotives before his death almost three decades later. During this period he expanded into a substantial foreign market, beginning with Cuba in 1838. In addition to locomotives, Baldwin sometimes took on other large engineering projects, among them the construction of an ice-breaker for the city of Philadelphia, but after Old Ironsides his primary business was always engines.

Baldwin's business success was not always constant. Economic reverses caused by the panic of 1837, for example, forced him to declare bankruptcy and it took half a decade for him to fully satisfy his creditors. Yet despite the distractions of such a severe financial crisis, Baldwin was able to concentrate on developing the locomotive. By the time his debt had been paid, Baldwin had constructed a six-wheeled gear locomotive that could haul much more freight than could any other contemporary engine.

A prominent Philadelphian active in public affairs, Baldwin was elected in 1837 as a delegate to the special Pennsylvania constitutional conventions during which he achieved some notoriety for his vehement opposition to the convention's decision to restrict suffrage to white men. Philanthropy, however, took much more of his attention. Before his death in Philadelphia, Baldwin became known as the "church builder," having donated most of the monies needed for the construction of five city churches.

• The best source for personal information on Baldwin is Wolcott Calkins, "Memorial of Matthias Baldwin," an unpublished testimonial available in the Library of Congress. Another useful source is Ralph Kelly, *Matthias W. Baldwin: Locomotive Pioneer* (1946). For technical information, see Baldwin-Lima-Hamilton Corporation, *History of the Baldwin Locomotive Works, 1831–1923*; Frederick Westing, *The Locomotive That Baldwin Built* (1966); and Edward Cressy, *A Hundred Years of Mechanical Engineering* (1937).
ALEC KIRBY

BALDWIN, Roger Nash (21 Jan. 1884–26 Aug. 1981), civil libertarian and social activist, was born in Wellesley, Massachusetts, the son of Frank Fenno Baldwin, a leather manufacturer who owned several companies, and Lucy Cushing Nash. The lines on both sides of the family went back to the Pilgrims. Baldwin attended Wellesley public schools. As a boy he lacked prowess in sports and developed interests in music, art, and nature. He was regarded as "different," which made him seek, early in life, "unconventional, nonconformist avenues of expression" consistent with the intellectual heritage of Ralph Waldo Emerson, Henry David Thoreau, and other New England icons. His family were free-thinking Unitarians.

Baldwin earned bachelor's and master's degrees from Harvard University. He became a sociology instructor at Washington University in St. Louis in 1906 and worked in a neighborhood settlement house there. He soon became chief probation officer of the local juvenile court, where he achieved a national reputation

in part through his book, written with Bernard Flexner, *Juvenile Courts and Probation* (1914).

In 1909 Baldwin attended a lecture by Emma Goldman, the anarchist, who later became an important figure in his life. Goldman opened up a new literature to Baldwin and introduced him to new sorts of people. He described them as not only anarchists but "some libertarians, some freedom lovers and some who had no label—like me." These people were bound together by "one principle—freedom from coercion," and many of them were committed to nonviolence.

In 1910 Baldwin became secretary of the Civic League of St. Louis, a reform group that addressed issues of municipal government. Baldwin said later that he got his "first impulse to civil liberties" during this period when the police denied Margaret Sanger, the birth-control advocate, the right to hold a meeting in a public hall. In St. Louis Baldwin also had his first exposure to issues of racial prejudice. After failing to obtain approval of a special course for blacks at Washington University and after white voters approved a segregationist housing ordinance, he concluded, "In cases where minority rights are concerned, you can't trust the majority."

In April 1917 Baldwin joined the American Union Against Militarism (AUAM), a New York organization of prominent reformers, writers, editors, church people, and lawyers who opposed World War I. The next month he organized the Bureau for Conscientious Objectors within AUAM to advise conscientious objectors and to help them receive favorable treatment under the new Selective Service Act. The bureau took a more aggressive stance than some AUAM directors approved and, after changing its name to the Civil Liberties Bureau, it became an independent organization. Its work broadened to include freedom of speech, press, and conscience and the defense of citizens who were prosecuted under the 1917 Espionage Act, including members of the Industrial Workers of the World (IWW), who were accused of calling strikes to obstruct the war effort.

In September 1918 Baldwin was called to register for the draft. After he "respectfully declined to appear" for a physical examination, saying that he was opposed "to any service whatever designed to help the war," he was arrested. At a hearing he made a long and eloquent statement in which he said:

I regard the principle of conscription of life as a flat contradiction of all our cherished ideals of individual freedom, democratic liberty and Christian teaching. . . . I cannot consistently, with self-respect, do other than I have, namely, to deliberately violate an act which seems to me to be a denial of everything which ideally and in practice I hold sacred.

After complimenting Baldwin for stating his position honestly, the judge sentenced him to a year in the penitentiary. Baldwin's stance earned praise from many liberal organizations, and Emma Goldman said he "has proved himself the most consistent of us all." The socialist leader Norman Thomas said that the hearing "was one of the rare experiences of a lifetime." Baldwin's time in jail was relatively pleasant, and he turned it to his advantage. He carried on an extensive correspondence, wrote poetry, and, as a trusty, worked in the prison's kitchen and garden. He also found time to start a Prisoners' Welfare League and to befriend inmates, some of whom became lifelong friends.

After his release in July 1919 Baldwin married Madeleine Doty, a writer and lawyer who was a pacifist and feminist. Less than two months later, with his wife's encouragement, Baldwin left for the West with only a few dollars to see how he would fare as an unskilled laborer. He passed several months this way, joined both the IWW and the Cooks and Waiters Union, took part in a steel strike as a union spy, and felt the satisfaction of experiencing firsthand what he had previously known only theoretically.

In January 1920, after his return to New York, he and his allies transformed the Civil Liberties Bureau into the American Civil Liberties Union (ACLU). The union's statement of purpose included reference to freedoms endangered by government repression, especially against labor—free speech, free press, the right to strike, criminal justice, immigration equity, and racial equality. As executive director, Baldwin put together a diverse board of prominent liberal activists, including Jane Addams, Helen Keller, Scott Nearing, Norman Thomas, Helen Phelps Stokes, A. J. Muste, John Haynes Holmes, Felix Frankfurter, Oswald Garrison Villard (who acted as associate director) and Walter Nelles (who acted as counsel).

Under Baldwin's direction and with the aid of volunteer lawyers, the ACLU participated in a variety of controversial cases. These included challenges to the roundup and deportation of radical aliens; the defense of John T. Scopes in the famous Tennessee "Monkey Trial" in 1925, when the case was lost but the cause won; the Sacco–Vanzetti murder case; a successful challenge to the banning of James Joyce's *Ulysses*; and the protection of the First Amendment rights of communists and socialists, union members and Henry Ford, the Ku Klux Klan and Jehovah's Witnesses. The common element, Baldwin said, was that the Constitution protected people you "feared as well as those you admired."

In the late 1920s and early 1930s Baldwin made two trips to the Soviet Union and wrote extravagant praise of that country, which he later came to regret. Although he joined no party, he worked closely with communist and other left organizations during the popular-front period of the mid-1930s. A few years later, after a change in mind, he acted decisively to remove communists and their supporters from the board of directors of the ACLU. In the most notorious case, Elizabeth Gurley Flynn, a communist leader who had been a board member from the founding of the ACLU, was removed after a celebrated "trial" at the Harvard Club of New York City. In 1940 Baldwin drafted, and the board of directors passed, a resolution that required ACLU officials to aver that they were not

adherents of communism or fascism and that they supported the civil liberties of all peoples, including those outside the United States. This resolution became, ironically, a model for government loyalty oaths that the ACLU challenged during the McCarthy period. (In the 1970s the ACLU repealed the 1940 resolution and voted to restore Elizabeth Flynn to its board of directors posthumously.)

World War II did not provoke the same pacifist protests or government repression as World War I. During the war, Baldwin was largely occupied with the legal challenge to the Roosevelt administration's decision in 1942 to round up Japanese Americans on the West Coast, many of them citizens, and send them to camps in the interior. The effort to declare these actions unconstitutional failed in the Supreme Court, although years later evidence appeared that the government concealed information that the program was not essential to national security.

In 1947 Baldwin went to Japan at the invitation of General Douglas MacArthur to help instill in the Japanese an understanding of democracy and civil liberties. The previous year Baldwin was a founder of the International League for the Rights of Man (later the International League for Human Rights). After Baldwin retired, he was the ACLU's coordinator of international work, serving as a liaison to the United Nations and participating in discussions concerning U.S. possessions and territories. For many years he taught a civil liberties course at the University of Puerto Rico.

To appreciate Baldwin's contribution, one must recall the state of civil liberties in 1920, when the ACLU was founded. Post–World War I euphoria was yielding to "normalcy" and nativism, culminating in a resurgence of the Ku Klux Klan and the Palmer Raids, mass round-ups of aliens suspected of radicalism, which often ended in trials and deportation. The Supreme Court had yet to uphold a single claim of free speech; state criminal trials were virtually beyond constitutional protection; racial minorities, women, and other disadvantaged groups found almost no judicial support; workers were unable to organize legally; and sexual privacy was forty-five years from constitutional recognition.

In 1950, when Baldwin retired as ACLU executive director, the modern foundations of the Bill of Rights were in place. Under his supervision, volunteer lawyers such as Clarence Darrow and Arthur Garfield Hays had, among other things, helped abolish the worst of company police forces, achieved initial victories for free expression and religious liberty, and assisted in laying the groundwork to end segregation in schools and other parts of American life.

Throughout his life Baldwin was an active outdoorsman. He spent weekends in a rustic house in New Jersey, where he watched birds, canoed, hiked, and observed nature. He was active in the Audubon Society as well as in the National Urban League and the National Conference of Social Welfare. Baldwin divorced his first wife in 1935 and in 1936 married Evelyn Preston, also a reformer. They had one child, and he adopted her two sons. He died in New Jersey.

That Baldwin was able to organize, lead, and put to work—for a pittance or merely a pat on the back—so many talented people speaks not only to the principles they shared but to his special character. He was cantankerous and obstinate. He was also vigorous, puckish, courtly, joyous, vain, determined, loyal, and tough. His qualities gave the civil-liberties movement, in the words of one writer, "a special blend of passion and rationality, of biting dissent and tolerance for the beliefs and causes of others."

Baldwin did not consider himself an intellectual but rather a manager, a practical man, and above all an inspirer of others. But if he was not an intellectual, he certainly was a philosopher. He knew life and he knew people. He urged everyone to live as if each individual could make a difference in a complex, stubborn, and often cruel world. He believed that each person might save the world a little, and—perhaps more important—would be saved by the effort to do so.

Baldwin was not a religious man. Nevertheless, he viewed the Sermon on the Mount as an extraordinary declaration of humanity. He patterned his pacifism after Gandhi's and, like Gandhi, he went to jail in witness to his beliefs. His life exemplified the high purposes of religion: to transmit a sense of generational continuity, of caring, and of love. He concerned himself with people not only in the mass but one by one. He genuinely cared about other people and, always with a sense of humor, gave them confidence in what they were.

• Baldwin's papers are in the Roger Nash Baldwin Papers and the ACLU Collection, Seeley Mudd Library, Princeton University. His oral history, recorded in the mid-1950s, is in the Oral History Collection, Columbia University. Peggy Lamson's *Roger Baldwin: Founder of the American Civil Liberties Union* (1976) is an extended interview with commentary. See also the interviews of Baldwin by Alan Westin, "Recollections of a Life in Civil Liberties," pt. 1, *Civil Liberties Review* 2 (Spring 1975): 39–72; pt. 2 (Fall 1975): 10–40. The annual reports of the American Civil Liberties Union, 1920–1969, published in seven volumes (1970), contain valuable material on Baldwin's work as well as his introduction, "The Meaning of Civil Liberties." Articles by and about Baldwin are in *The American Civil Liberties Union: An Annotated Bibliography*, ed. Samuel Walker (1992). See also Walker, *In Defense of American Liberties: A History of the ACLU* (1990), and *The Pulse of Freedom: American Liberties 1920–1970s*, ed. Alan Reitman (1975). A full-scale biography of Baldwin has yet to be published. Dwight Macdonald wrote a long and insightful two-part article on Baldwin in the *New Yorker*, 11 July and 18 July 1953. An obituary is in the *New York Times*, 27 Aug. 1981.

NORMAN DORSEN

BALDWIN, Roger Sherman (4 Jan. 1793–19 Feb. 1863), lawyer, governor, and senator, was born in New Haven, Connecticut, the son of Simeon Baldwin, a lawyer, judge, congressman, and mayor of New Haven, and Rebecca Sherman. Baldwin was a direct descendant of the Puritan settlers of Connecticut and the Founding Fathers of the nation. His father's family was among the original New Haven colonists, and his mother was the daughter of Roger Sherman, the Connecticut statesman who signed both the Declaration of Independence and the Constitution. After studying at the Hopkins School in New Haven, Baldwin entered Yale, graduating with honors in 1811. He began legal studies in his father's law office but completed them at the renowned Litchfield Law School. He was admitted to the bar in New Haven in 1814, and, at a time when most New Haven lawyers had offices in their homes, he opened an office in the heart of the city. For nearly half a century he worked alone, never joining a legal partnership. His mastery of the principles of law, elegant diction, and meticulous command of the English language quickly brought him respect and a large practice. He became known for his profound regard for justice as the purpose of law. In 1820 he married Emily Perkins; they had nine children.

Baldwin began a political career, which evolved alongside his legal profession, with election to the New Haven Common Council in 1826 and then the Board of Aldermen in 1828. Indicating his dislike of slavery, which he inherited from his father and grandfather, and a concern for the welfare of the black population, Baldwin, in one of his earliest cases, secured the release of a fugitive slave who had escaped from the service of Henry Clay. A former Federalist, Baldwin accepted the principles of the newly organized Whig party. He served in the Connecticut Senate, 1837–1838, and was chosen president pro tempore in his second term. He became a trustee of Yale in 1838, and he was a member of the state's house of representatives in 1840–1841.

During these years, Baldwin distinguished himself as a lawyer for the defendants in the famous "*Amistad*" case, carrying the case through the district and circuit courts of Connecticut and to the U.S. Supreme Court. The Spanish ship *Amistad*, carrying Africans kidnapped on the West Coast of Africa, was taken into New London harbor by a U.S. revenue cutter. The stolen men, who had taken possession of the ship and attempted to sail back to their native land, were placed in a New Haven jail for safekeeping. Spain demanded their return, and President Martin Van Buren, anxious to avoid an international incident and ever cautious to shore up his political position in the South, seemed ready to comply. Baldwin, concerned for the Africans, became counsel for them. When the case reached the Supreme Court, he was associated in their defense with former president John Quincy Adams. Baldwin, with "one of the most illustrious arguments ever offered" to that Court (Dutton, p. 12), secured a verdict for the Africans, and they were returned to their native land, not to the Spanish. Baldwin addressed the humanitarian and legal aspects of the case (the Africans, being stolen, were not bound by our treaties with Spain) and also the consideration of our character as a nation "established for the promotion of JUSTICE, which was founded on the great principles of the Revolution" (Dutton, p. 13). Adams, in his

Memoirs, commented on Baldwin's "sound and eloquent . . . argument," his use of "cautious terms, to avoid exciting Southern passions and prejudices" (Adams, pp. 429–30). Indeed, Justice Story noted that Baldwin's argument in the case was given greater weight than the argument of Adams.

In 1843 Baldwin was the Whig candidate for governor of his state, but the Democrats took that election. A year later Baldwin won the governorship, and in 1845 he was reelected. In carefully worded messages to the legislature, he suggested reforms relating to prison labor, corporation law, temperance, and education. Except for reestablishing state supervision over public schools, the legislature gave these suggestions little consideration. Local issues were neglected as controversy over the annexation of Texas and the presidential election of 1844 intensified. Governor Baldwin also urged the legislature to act favorably on black suffrage and to pass a law restraining citizens of the state from assisting in the capture of fugitive slaves, but Connecticut was not yet ready to take these positions. "The generally arid character of Whig accomplishment" in the Connecticut legislature did have one notable exception: property qualifications for voting were abolished (Morse, p. 323). The governor did not seek reelection in 1846 but returned to his law practice. In November 1847 he received an executive appointment to the U.S. Senate to fill a vacancy caused by the death of Connecticut senator Jabez Huntington. When the legislature convened the following year, it elected Baldwin to complete that term.

Baldwin joined senators already distinguished as debators on controversial measures relating to new territories and the extension of slavery. He had argued in Connecticut against the annexation of Texas, and as he entered the Senate, the consequent war with Mexico was in progress. He saw that war as an excuse for extending slavery and introduced resolutions opposing slavery in any new territory. Senator Baldwin also addressed the 1850 Fugitive Slave Law. His impressive speech against that law was "generally conceded to be the ablest argument in opposition to the measure delivered in the Senate" (Norton, p. 198).

Baldwin also articulated the concern shared by many as to the propriety of congressional involvement in foreign affairs. After the French monarchy was overthrown in February 1848, a resolution before the Senate tendered congratulations to the French people for establishing a republican form of government and requested that the American minister in Paris present these congratulations to the government of France. Baldwin, acutely analyzing the situation in France, pointed out that the government was not yet "in the hands of those who have been elected by the people" but still consolidated "in the hands of a Parisian regency" (*Annals of America*, vol. 7, p. 425). The senator went on to express doubts that the Congress should instigate instructions to an American minister; this, he felt, belonged in the first instance to the executive.

Baldwin was not returned to the U.S. Senate in 1851. His concept of the duty of a representative in a legislative body was to vote on his own judgment, "enlightened by the deliberations of this body" (S. E. Baldwin, p. 521). He would make no pledges and bow to no instructions. This displeased party leaders in Connecticut and cost him a second term. He then resumed a busy law practice and became active in the formation of the Republican party. In 1860 he was a member of the electoral college of Connecticut, which cast the state's vote for Abraham Lincoln. His last service to his country was as a delegate, in February 1861, to the Washington Peace Conference, which unsuccessfully tried to reconcile the slavery issue. Two years later, tall and erect, respected and still active in his profession, he died in New Haven.

• The Roger Sherman Baldwin Papers are at Yale University. His remarks in the Senate are in the *Congressional Globe*, 1847–1851, but his Senate speech on "The Executive Prerogative in Foreign Policy" is more easily found in *The Annals of America*, vol. 7 (1968). Baldwin appears in *Connecticut Reports* every year from 1816 to 1863. Simeon E. Baldwin wrote the lengthy article on his father in *Great American Lawyers*, ed. William D. Lewis (1908), which includes citations of state and federal documents. Samuel W. S. Dutton, *An Address at the Funeral of Hon. Roger Sherman Baldwin* (1863), by the pastor of North Church in New Haven, is an essential source. A eulogy and discussion of Baldwin's life, it is also a consideration of him as a lawyer and statesman, and it contains the texts of Baldwin's resolutions before the Senate on the extension of slavery and the minority report he wrote for the Washington Peace Conference. *Memoirs of John Quincy Adams Comprising Portions of His Diary from 1795 to 1848*, vol. 10, ed. Charles Francis Adams (1876), contains interesting comments on the "*Amistad*" case; see also "Argument of Roger S. Baldwin, of New Haven before the Supreme Court of the United States, in the Case of *The United States, Appellants, vs. Cinque, and Others, Africans of the 'Armistad',*" in *The African Slave Trade and American Courts*, vol. 1, ed. Paul Finkelman (1988). Frederick C. Norton, *The Governors of Connecticut: Biographies of the Chief Executives of the Commonwealth That Gave to the World the First Written Constitution Known to History* (1905), summarizes Baldwin's life and career. Jarvis M. Morse, *A Neglected Period of Connecticut's History, 1818–1850* (1933), describes a small, early nineteenth-century state, homogeneously populated and reluctant to make the reforms suggested by Baldwin. The *New Haven Journal and Courier*, 21 Feb. 1863, published resolutions of tribute passed by the New Haven bar along with insightful remarks from some of its members. An obituary by then governor Henry B. Harrison is in *Connecticut Reports* 30 (1863): 611.

SYLVIA B. LARSON

BALDWIN, Simeon (14 Dec. 1761–26 May 1851), lawyer and jurist, was born in Norwich, Connecticut, the son of Ebenezer Baldwin, a blacksmith and farmer, and Bethiah Barker. His mother died when he was a few weeks old. After a period of study with his brother the Reverend Ebenezer Baldwin in Danbury and additional schooling in Coventry and Lebanon, Baldwin attended Yale University from 1777 to 1781, a period that was interrupted by the fighting of the revolutionary war. After graduation from Yale, he taught school in New Haven and in Albany, New York, in order to support himself while deciding on a career. He became a close friend of James Kent while at Yale.

From 1783 to 1786 Baldwin was a tutor at Yale, which provided him with an income, important social connections, and more time to decide on his life's work. In 1784 he received an M.A. from Yale. Unlike his eldest brother, he rejected a clerical career. He had not experienced a personal moment of spiritual regeneration, an essential aspect of faith in the Congregational church, nor had he joined a church. Bored with divinity studies, he read law with Charles Chauncey in New Haven and Peter W. Yates in Albany in the pursuit of a practical occupation that would alleviate his straitened financial circumstances and advance his social position.

Though Baldwin was admitted to the bar in 1786, he found it difficult to build a law practice in New Haven. Connecticut had a surfeit of lawyers, and while waiting for business, he tutored young men who were preparing for college. In addition, the tall, handsome young man cultivated the social graces and enjoyed dances and the company of refined young women. In 1787 he married Rebecca Sherman, the daughter of Connecticut's prominent politician, Roger Sherman. The couple had four children, including Roger Sherman Baldwin, a future lawyer, U.S. senator, and governor of Connecticut. In order to support his growing family, Baldwin trained law students in his office and boarded them in his home. The influence of his father-in-law served to launch Baldwin's struggling legal career, and he gained several important appointments. From 1789 to 1800 he served as city clerk of New Haven, from 1789 to 1806 as clerk of the U.S. district and circuit courts for Connecticut, and in 1791 as collector of revenue in New Haven. By 1793 his finances were secure enough that he stopped taking in boarders. In 1795 he bought for $2,500 the large house in New Haven that had been the home of the Reverend Jonathan Edwards, which became Baldwin's principal residence for the rest of his life. After the death of Rebecca in 1795, he married in 1800 her sister, the widow Elizabeth Sherman Burr; they had five children.

At the turn of the century, Baldwin had established an extensive and lucrative legal practice, which was based primarily in Connecticut. A staunch Federalist, he was chosen in a special election to fill a vacant seat in the U.S. House of Representatives from 1803 to 1805. In 1805 he declined renomination even though he had served competently. More at home in the Nutmeg State than in the nation's capitol, he served as alderman in New Haven from 1800 to 1816 and 1823 and 1825 and once as mayor in 1826. In 1806 he was elected associate judge of the superior court of Connecticut and from 1808 to 1818 was judge of the Connecticut Supreme Court of Errors, the state's highest tribunal. The latter judgeship marked the zenith of his legal career, but he was removed in 1818 when opponents of the Federalist and Congregational establishment took over state government. He opposed the reformed state constitution of 1818, including the adoption of universal manhood suffrage, which he saw as a demagogic threat to the well-being of the propertied class. The decline of Baldwin's legal career coincided with the disintegration of the Federalist party in the face of a rising democratic populism. His nearly fifteen years of continuous public service ironically made it difficult for him to reestablish business connections and to build a thriving legal practice anew. Throughout the decade of the 1820s he barely made a profit at the bar and was forced to take in boarders again. A sign of his eroding influence was that in 1828 he failed to secure appointment as collector of revenue at the port of New Haven when the position went to a partisan of Andrew Jackson, the personification of the new politics.

Although he had become politically obsolete, Baldwin was actively engaged in an expansive capitalist economy. During the first decades of the nineteenth century, he was an investor in and administrator of a number of corporations, which included the Derby Fishing Company, New Haven Bank, Eagle Bank of New Haven, Savings Bank of New Haven, New Haven Fire Insurance Company, and Farmington Canal Company. He lost $4,300 in the failure of the insolvent Eagle Bank, but at the time of his death his net worth was more than $30,000. His business activities were, however, tempered by philanthropy, a type of Federalist noblesse oblige. For a brief time he owned a slave, an inheritance from his father's estate. Even so, in 1790 he championed the abolition of slavery in Connecticut and in 1791 the end of the international slave trade. In 1826 he endorsed the African Improvement Society of New Haven, an organization with links to the American Colonization Society. And in 1830 he chaired a public protest against the forceful removal of the Cherokees from Georgia. His public stewardship also involved him in the cause of temperance, education, and libraries. He was secretary of the Connecticut Academy of Arts and Sciences, a longtime official of the New Haven County Agricultural Society, and a promoter of the New Haven almshouse. Thomas Day, recorder of the state's highest court, appropriately summed up the character of the man: "Indeed the excellence of Judge Baldwin consisted in his being always the same—the same upright, deliberate, intelligent man. . . . Everybody had confidence in him whether on or off the bench" (Baldwin, pp. 355–56). He died in New Haven.

• Baldwin's papers are in the New Haven Colony Historical Society. A biography by his grandson, Simeon Eben Baldwin, *Life and Letters of Simeon Baldwin* (1919), contains a number of primary sources. Brief biographies include Dexter Franklin Bowditch, *Biographical Sketches of the Graduates of Yale College, 1778–1792*, vol. 4 (1907), pp. 178–80; *Encyclopedia of Connecticut Biography: Representative Citizens* (1917), pp. 75–76; and Dwight Loomis and J. G. Calhoun, eds., *Judicial and Civil History of Connecticut* (1895), p. 238.

LAWRENCE B. GOODHEART

BALDWIN, Simeon Eben (5 Feb. 1840–30 Jan. 1927), law professor, judge, and Connecticut governor, was born in New Haven, Connecticut, the son of Roger Sherman Baldwin, a lawyer and U.S. senator, and Emily Perkins. Baldwin entered Yale College in 1857 and graduated with a B.A. in 1861. After studying at Yale Law School and Harvard Law School from 1861 to 1863, he was admitted to the Connecticut bar and opened a solo law office in New Haven. He rapidly proceeded to build up the largest individual practice in the state by representing railroads, corporations, and wealthy individuals.

Baldwin is a remarkable example of the new breed of elite lawyer that developed during the late nineteenth century; he treated the law as a science and a grand profession rather than as a mere occupation. During the four decades that followed his admittance to the bar he was centrally involved in every aspect of the legal profession: private practice, legal education and scholarship, law reform, professional organizations, the judiciary, and politics.

The despair and loneliness of Baldwin's private life drove him to work even harder than had his natural ambition and predilection for the law. He married Susan Winchester in 1865, but by 1873 she had lapsed into an insanity so hopeless that she was institutionalized for the rest of her life. Their two children were cared for by Susan's sister, who ran Baldwin's household and died a spinster. Always lacking in sociability, Baldwin channeled all his energies into his career: "There are those to whom hard work brings its daily blessing as a banisher of sorrow," he wrote. "Melancholy is a foe to be expelled at any cost, and pre-occupation is often the only thing that avails to shut it out."

During his first years at the bar Baldwin took advantage of the long periods of inactivity between cases by compiling a complete digest of every reported Connecticut common law case. Published in 1871 after four years of grueling intellectual labor, *Baldwin's Connecticut Digest* was seven hundred pages in length and contained over 4,000 indexed cases. The *Digest* was reviewed favorably by Oliver Wendell Holmes (1841–1935) and became a daily reference work for Connecticut attorneys. It established his reputation as a legal scholar while attracting much business and enabling him to prepare cases with unusual dispatch.

In 1871 Baldwin was named counsel to the New York and New England Railroad, and by the mid-1880s he was known as one of the leading corporate and railroad attorneys in the country. Railroad corporate and trial work became the backbone of his practice, and several wealthy individuals entrusted him with the management of over $1 million. He was treated as a lawyer's lawyer: "The fact is people generally come to me only when they have some difficult and contested matter to be disposed of. Most of my cases are hard knots." His ability to pick and choose business gave him time to pursue his teaching, scholarship, and law reform efforts.

Baldwin was a major force in the reform of Connecticut's legal system in the late nineteenth century, and

his primary motive in founding the American Bar Association was to raise the standard of the profession by facilitating law reform on the national level. From 1871 to 1876 he almost singlehandedly revised Connecticut's statute book, and from 1878 to 1879 he led the revision of the state's civil rules of practice and procedure. In 1878 he extended the reach of his reform efforts by creating the American Bar Association, which he rightly considered to be his child. In the words of bar historian James Grafton Rogers, Baldwin "drafted the Constitution, guided the first steps, selected the first officers, saw to its routine on the Executive Committee, and until his presidency thirteen years later, and even afterwards, was the chief source of its projects." He served as ABA president in 1890 and later edited the first three volumes of the ABA *Journal*. At various times he also served as president of the American Social Science Association, the International Law Association, the Association of American Law Schools, the American Political Science Association, and the American Historical Association.

Baldwin believed that if he were to achieve the reputation of a great man, it would be as a law professor. Intimately connected with Yale Law School for over fifty years, he served as lecturer, professor, treasurer, and benefactor. He was one of the three New Haven lawyers who resurrected the law school following the Civil War, in 1869. In 1875 he initiated a groundbreaking graduate program and in 1894 succeeded in raising the required number of years for a law degree from two to three. In 1901 he observed in his journal: "I am inclined to think that my best life work may have been that of impressing myself and my ideas and ideals on a thousand American lawyers." When he retired from the law school in 1919, he noted that he had "been out of sympathy with my colleagues for a dozen years or more, on the question of admitting only college graduates, and of the almost exclusive use of casebooks." He nevertheless left the law school half a million dollars in his will to build a new building and endow a professorship in his name.

Baldwin was stoutly conservative in his political and social thought. He began his political life as a conservative Republican but was a leader of the Mugwump revolt in Connecticut and remained a Democrat for the rest of his life. He believed in social Darwinism, the natural rights of the individual as protected by the due process clause, the favored role of courts, and strong state sovereignty as a check on the expansion of federal authority. A member of the Connecticut Supreme Court from 1893 to 1910, he served the last four years as chief justice. Although Connecticut was a predominantly Republican state at the time, he was twice elected governor, serving from 1911 to 1915.

Baldwin's years as judge and governor were devoted largely to the defense of his conservative values against the growing forces of progressive legal and political thought. His remarkable 1910 controversy with former president Theodore Roosevelt (1858–1919) over the constitutionality of the Federal Employers' Liability Act is perhaps the best-known example of the running battle against liberalism that Baldwin conducted during the initial decades of the twentieth century. His resistance—rooted in his formalistic approach to law and government—was doomed to failure, and Baldwin often felt that the twentieth century had passed him by. In the words of Morton J. Horwitz, "few American lawyers have had more opportunities to transcend the limits of their age," but the "tragedy of Baldwin's career is that he could never mediate between his ideals and the age he lived in." He died at home in New Haven. Best remembered for founding the American Bar Association and for laying the groundwork for Yale Law School's rise to national prominence, Baldwin was one of the foremost members of America's late nineteenth-century legal elite.

• Baldwin's papers are in the Baldwin Family Collection at Yale's Sterling Memorial Library and include the nine volumes of Baldwin's private journals. The only biography is Frederick H. Jackson, *Simeon Eben Baldwin: Lawyer, Social Scientist, Statesman* (1955), which contains an extensive bibliography of Baldwin's numerous books, articles, speeches, and manuscripts. The only critical study of Baldwin's social and political thought is Forrest C. Weir, "The Social Opinions of Simeon E. Baldwin" (Ph.D. diss., Yale Univ., 1941). Neither scholar had the benefit of Baldwin's private journals, the cache of correspondence between Baldwin and Roosevelt, or the letters concerning the mental illness of Baldwin's wife. That material is explored in Charles C. Goetsch, *Essays On Simeon E. Baldwin* (1981). For a detailed analysis of Baldwin's role as a legal formalist, see Goetsch, "The Future of Legal Formalism," *American Journal of Legal History* 24 (1980): 221–56.

CHARLES C. GOETSCH

BALDWIN, William (29 Mar. 1779–31 Aug. or 1 Sept. 1819), botanist and physician, was born in Newlin, Chester County, Pennsylvania, the son of Thomas Baldwin, a minister of the Society of Friends, and Elizabeth Garretson. He attended the local schools in Chester County. Baldwin's interest in botany and medicine may have developed from his association with serious amateur botanists Dr. Moses Marshall and Humphry Marshall during the period from 1798 to 1800. After a brief interval as a teacher, Baldwin began his medical training in 1801–1802 as a pupil of Dr. William A. Todd at Downingtown, Pennsylvania. In the winter of 1802–1803 he attended Dr. Todd's medical lectures at the University of Pennsylvania, where he made the acquaintance of William Darlington, a classmate who became a life-long friend and botanical colleague. From 1803 to 1805, Baldwin continued his studies under Todd at Downingtown; and in 1805 he served as surgeon on a merchant ship to Canton, China. After his return in 1806, he enrolled to complete his medical education under Dr. Benjamin Smith Barton at the University of Pennsylvania, where he received his M.D. in April 1807. Baldwin then moved to Wilmington, Delaware, where he established a medical practice, began a study of the local flora, and established correspondence with Thomas Jefferson and botanist Dr. Henry Muhlenberg. About this time he married Hannah Webster; they had four children.

By November 1811, Baldwin's deteriorating health, attributed to consumption, compelled him to relocate to the milder climate of Georgia, where he resided at Savannah and St. Mary's. During this time he explored much of the region on foot, conducting extensive botanical studies in East Florida, western Georgia, and into the back country of the Creek Indian territory. In 1812 he visited Georgia planters John and Louis LeConte, who were amateur botanists, and the renowned South Carolina botanist Stephen Elliott. During the War of 1812, Baldwin was surgeon for the American gunboat flotilla stationed at St. Mary's. Despite his worsening health, he resumed his botanical explorations after the war, exploring St. Mary's River and the major sea islands along the Georgia coast, including Amelia, Cumberland, Jekyll, St. Simons, Sapelo, and St. Catherines. In 1815 he extended his field work to Bermuda and to Charleston, South Carolina, and from 1816 to 1817, he continued his field studies in the southeastern United States.

Baldwin returned to Wilmington in 1817 and was appointed surgeon for the U.S. frigate *Congress*, which carried a commission of "delegates" whose mission was to evaluate the potential for independence in the Spanish colonies of South America. Although Baldwin was selected for his abilities as a naturalist, his decision to join the endeavor was based in part on the hope of recovering his health. He collected plants at all stops along the coast; and, after returning to Wilmington in July 1818, he began an intense analysis of the botanical specimens accumulated during his Georgia years and from the South American sojourn. He intended to publish his findings in a work to be titled "Miscellaneous Sketches of Georgia and East Florida, to which will be added an appendix containing some account of the vegetable productions on the Rio de la Plata."

In the meantime, as plans were laid in 1818 for Major Stephen H. Long's expedition to the upper Missouri, Darlington and LeConte urged Baldwin's appointment as surgeon and botanist for the group, with Darlington writing to John C. Calhoun, secretary of war, in support of their friend's nomination. Hoping that the rigors of the trip might restore his deteriorating health, Baldwin accepted the position and departed with the Long expedition in March 1819. Other members of the group included Thomas Say as zoologist and Titan R. Peale as assistant. Recognizing his precarious condition, Baldwin wrote forbodingly to Darlington: "I shall hold out as long as I can. Whether my remains are deposited on the banks of the Missouri, or among my kindred at home, is now a matter of little consequence." From Pittsburgh, Pennsylvania, the party continued by river boat to Cincinnati, Ohio, where the expedition halted for a week for repairs and in part owing to Baldwin's continuing illness. Resuming the trip, Baldwin was so weak as to be essentially confined to the boat, and other members of the party did most of the botanical collecting for him at stops along the shore. At St. Louis, Missouri, Baldwin met the naturalist John Bradbury, who had explored much of the Missouri. By the time the expedition arrived at

Franklin, Missouri, on 15 July, Baldwin was too sick to continue and was removed from the boat to the home of John J. Lowry, where he died. Baldwin was buried at Franklin, but by 1844 his gravesite had been washed away by flood waters of the Missouri River.

Despite his experience and ability, Baldwin published only two botanical papers, one appearing in the *American Journal of Science* in 1819, and another in *Transactions of the American Philosophical Society* in 1825 both of which dealt with his discoveries in Georgia. Many of Baldwin's notes were acquired by other botanists, who acknowledged his contribution in their publications, such as John Torrey's monograph on the Cyperaceae and Asa Gray's monograph on Rhynchospora, in the *Annals of the New York Lyceum of Natural History* (1828–1836). Other data from Baldwin were used by Stephen Elliott in his *A Sketch of the Botany of South Carolina and Georgia* (1816–1824). Baldwin's herbarium was bought by Zaccheus Collins and later acquired by Lewis David von Schewinitz, who, unfortunately, destroyed all the original specimen labels prior to bequeathing the collection to the Academy of Natural Sciences in Philadelphia, Pennsylvania. Other plants collected by Baldwin were sent to A. B. Lambert and Sir James Edward Smith in England and to Muhlenberg, Elliott, and Darlington, who laid the groundwork for botanical science in the United States.

Baldwin was admired and respected by his colleagues, who felt a keen sense of loss at his untimely death. Darlington remarked that "I have never yet had the happiness to be acquainted with any man of a more amiable and upright character, more faithful in the discharge of his duties, or more zealously devoted to science and the welfare of his fellow creatures." Thomas Nuttall named the genus *Baldwinia* in Baldwin's honor, referring to him as "a gentleman whose botanical zeal and knowledge have rarely been excelled in America." Harvard botanist Asa Gray noted Baldwin's "bright hopes and high promise" as a botanist and lamented that "if he had lived, he would have outstripped all his contemporaries."

• Baldwin's papers are in the Historical Society of Pennsylvania, the Academy of Natural Sciences in Philadelphia, the Library of the Gray Herbarium at Harvard University, and the New-York Historical Society. Most of his botanical specimens are at the Academy of Natural Sciences in Philadelphia, although some are reported at the Manchester Museum at the University of Manchester, England, and a sketch of his life at West Chester State University, West Chester, Pa. He wrote *A Short Practical Narrative of the Disease Which Prevailed Among the American Seamen at Wampoa in China in the Year 1805* (1807) and *Observations on Infidelity and the Religious and Political Systems of Europe Compared With Those of the United States of America* (1809). Major sources on Baldwin include Joseph Ewan, ed., *Reliquiae Baldwinianae* (1969), which contains a biographical chronology, an extensive collection of Baldwin's correspondence, and a sketch of his life by Darlington. See also H. H. Humphrey, *Makers of American Botany* (1961), J. H. Redfield, "Some North American Botanists. VI. Dr. William Baldwin," *Botanical Gazette* 8 (1883): 233–37; John W. Harshberger, *The Botanists of Philadelphia* (1899); and Edwin James, *Account of an Expedition from Pittsburgh to the Rocky Mountains*, vol. 1 (1823).

MARCUS B. SIMPSON, JR.

BALDWIN, William Henry, Jr. (5 Feb. 1863–3 Jan. 1905), railroad executive and philanthropist, was born in Boston, Massachusetts, the son of William Henry Baldwin, a dry goods merchant, and Mary Chaffee. A direct descendant of an English settler who had arrived in Massachusetts before 1640, Baldwin grew up in a family noted for its commitment to abolition and other reforms. His father founded the Young Men's Christian Union of Boston, an adult social service organization. When Baldwin was five years old, his father retired from his successful mercantile career to serve as the union's president.

After preparatory education in Boston's public schools and the Roxbury Latin School, Baldwin enrolled at Harvard College, earning his bachelor's degree in 1885. A merely satisfactory scholar, Baldwin was an outstanding student leader, joining five clubs, editing the student daily newspaper, serving as an oarsman on his class crew, and leading the glee club and the dining association. Upon the recommendation of President Charles W. Eliot, Baldwin was offered a position in 1886 by Charles Francis Adams, Jr., the president of the Union Pacific Railroad.

After three years in various positions with Union Pacific, Baldwin had gained a reputation as a young man of great energy and ability who had, as Adams said, "quite a remarkable faculty for getting on with men." In rapid succession he became general manager of the Montana Union Railroad, an assistant vice president for the Union Pacific, general manager of Michigan's Flint and Pere Marquette Railroad, and a vice president of the Southern Railway. In 1896 he became president of the Long Island Railroad, a position he held for the rest of his life.

Baldwin might be described as the model of a Progressive businessman. Asserting that "there is a higher law than supply and demand," he strongly supported the idea of railroads run in the public interest, welcoming public scrutiny of their operations and making the commonweal a higher priority than the wishes of stockholders. Though he was not, as some of his colleagues jested, "a sort of a socialist," he saw his own industry as requiring a large degree of government regulation. Unlike many business leaders, he defended the right of workers to organize labor unions and opposed corporate efforts to eliminate unions "as the gravest social danger," in the words of his biographer. At the same time, he rejected "closed shop" arrangements.

In addition to championing new principles of business ethics, Baldwin was especially devoted to two other reforms: promoting African-American education in the South and curbing prostitution in New York City. His interest in black education led him to accept an appointment in 1895 as a trustee of Tuskegee Institute, and he quickly became a close friend of the school's principal, Booker T. Washington. ("I almost worship this man," he said of Washington on one occasion.) Baldwin was an active supporter of Robert C. Ogden's campaign for southern education (organized in 1901 as the Southern Education Board) and first president (1902–1905) of a richly endowed Rockefeller benefaction, the General Education Board.

At first, Baldwin's advocacy of black education simply combined blunt skepticism about "so-called higher education" for African Americans with enthusiastic support for the "industrial education" offered by Tuskegee and its ideological mother, Hampton Institute. In the last two years of his life, however, Baldwin became increasingly critical of his fellow philanthropists, as he developed a more complex understanding of the relationship between white and black in America. In private meetings and personal correspondence, he articulated views that he shared with Washington—namely, that supporters of the Southern Education Board and General Education Board were making too many concessions to southern white prejudice and ignoring the counsel of black educators in the South.

For five years Baldwin was the chairman of the Committee of Fifteen, a group of New York civic leaders committed to addressing the problem of prostitution in the nation's largest city. After thorough investigation, the committee issued a report, *The Social Evil, with Special Reference to Conditions Existing in New York City* (1902), which was the first of many Progressive-era vice commission reports. The report recommended a range of reforms to mitigate an evil that they did not expect to eliminate, including lessening tenement overcrowding, providing wholesome public amusements, improving "the material conditions of the wage-earning class," and decriminalizing prostitution—though not a policy of segregated red-light districts.

When Baldwin died in Locust Valley, New York, he was widely mourned—not only for his actual achievements but also for his high ideals and great promise. He had had "an inspiring career," declared an editorial in the *New York Times*. President Theodore Roosevelt and former president Grover Cleveland agreed to serve on the executive committee of a Baldwin Memorial Fund, which raised $150,000 for Tuskegee Institute.

An official biography, *An American Citizen: The Life of William Henry Baldwin, Jr.* (1910), sought to sustain Baldwin's influence and support his favored reforms. One reader powerfully influenced by Baldwin's example was Julius Rosenwald, whose reading of Baldwin's biography was the catalyst for a new phase in the Sears executive's philanthropic career, leading him eventually to create his famous southern school-building program.

In 1889 Baldwin had married Ruth Standish Bowles, the daughter of Samuel Bowles, the formidable editor of the *Springfield (Mass.) Republican*. Believing that she was continuing plans originated by her husband, Ruth Baldwin became instrumental in the founding of the National Urban League, one of the most significant groups seeking reform of modern American race relations. The Baldwins had two children. Baldwin was Unitarian in religion and a Republican in his political loyalties though he twice voted for Cleveland for president.

• Baldwin's personal papers have not been preserved, except for a few documents in the papers of William H. Baldwin III at the State Historical Society of Wisconsin. Included in this group are a 1902 speech to the Richmond (Va.) Education Association, "Why a Businessman Should Be Interested in Public Education," and comments on W. E. B. Du Bois's criticism of Booker T. Washington. The most valuable insight into Baldwin's development as a philanthropist can be found in his correspondence, especially the short, candid letters he exchanged with Washington, Robert C. Ogden, and Wallace Buttrick (of the General Education Board). For Baldwin's early understanding of black education, see his speech to the American Social Science Association, "The Present Problem of Negro Education," *Journal of Social Science* 37 (1899): 52–68. John Graham Brooks offers a laudatory picture of Baldwin in *An American Citizen: The Life of William Henry Baldwin, Jr.* (1910), but this portrait of the philanthropist misses important differences between Baldwin and other education crusaders, especially "moderate" southerners such as Edgar Gardner Murphy. Beginning with Merle Curti, *Social Ideas of American Educators* (1935), several scholars have given credence to Du Bois's claim that Baldwin's support for black education was motivated by self-interest and the hope of using skilled black workers to break the power of labor unions. For one example, see James D. Anderson, "Northern Foundations and the Shaping of Southern Black Rural Education, 1902–1935," *History of Education Quarterly* 18 (Winter 1978): 371–96. More balanced assessments are given in Nancy J. Weiss, *The National Urban League, 1910–1940* (1974); Louis R. Harlan, *Separate and Unequal: Public School Campaigns and Racism in the Southern Seaboard States, 1901–1915* (1958); and Harlan's two-volume biography of Booker T. Washington. For an overview of Baldwin's career, see Harlan's biographical sketch in *The Booker T. Washington Papers*, vol. 3 (13 vols., 1972–1984). An obituary is in the *New York Times*, 4 Jan. 1905.

ERIC ANDERSON

BALES, William (27 June 1910–8 Sept. 1990), dancer and teacher, was born in Carnegie, Pennsylvania, the son of Sam Bialystotsky and Dora (maiden name unknown), the owners of a fruit and vegetable store. Bales's older stepsisters, Anne and Gertrude, started the family's interest in theatrical performance. They studied dance in nearby Pittsburgh, then Gertrude started offering classes in their home. Bales began lessons at age fourteen in tap, acrobatics, and ballroom, but he considered the movies to be equally influential on his dancing, especially the films of Fred Astaire. Bales's mother, who was an impoverished, unschooled Russian Jewish immigrant, urged education on her first-born son. He graduated from the University of Pittsburgh in 1931 with a degree in business administration, meanwhile working at a newspaper, the *Pittsburgh Sun-Telegraph*. Then he enrolled at Carnegie Institute of Technology to pursue a second degree in what was becoming his true love, the theater. His most influential teacher there was Cecile Kitcat, who taught Dalcroze eurhythmics and was familiar with the thriving German modern dance. Bales also took ballet classes with Frank Eckl. He began to teach and to perform, first in his sister's studio, then at the Irene Kaufman Settlement House in Pittsburgh, and on the Chautauqua circuit.

Bales caught the eye of Martha Hill during a master class at a physical education conference. She headed the dance program at the new, experimental Bennington College and was aware of all that was happening in the small, intense world of modern dance. Hill told Bales about a men's group Charles Weidman was forming and suggested he audition. Bales joined the Humphrey-Weidman Dance Company in 1936. The company rehearsed mornings with choreographer Doris Humphrey and afternoons with Weidman. Bales worked in the Humphrey-Weidman company during a period when Humphrey's pioneering dance creations were becoming recognized as equal to, though stylistically very different from, those of Martha Graham. Weidman's dances consisted of sharply realized, often funny characterizations of personality. Bales's repertory included *New Dance*, *Opus 51*, and *Lynchtown*, and he was among the creators of Humphrey's studies in complex architectural movement, particularly the Bach *Passacaglia and Fugue in C Minor* (1938). A highlight of his career with the Humphrey-Weidman company was a cross-country tour of American colleges and universities in 1937–1938, an exciting venture for the dancers, most of whom had never traveled. One month each summer was spent at the influential Bennington Summer School of Dance.

During this period of important artistic creation but financial impoverishment, Bales worked for a year in the dancing chorus at Radio City Music Hall. He also assisted Weidman as a teacher and in conducting rehearsals for *Candide* (1933) on Broadway. Bales and several colleagues, including Sybil Shearer, formed a short-lived concert group, the Theatre Dance Company, which functioned roughly from August 1937 to January 1939. He also worked at Camp Tamiment in Pennsylvania, where he began to create dances, notably a solo, *Black Tambourine*, which premiered in the summer of 1940.

Hill had again influenced Bales's career when she hired him for a spring 1940 assistantship at Bennington College. His classes were popular, and he negotiated a full-time teaching contract for the 1940–1941 school year. This was the beginning of a 28-year career on the faculty of Bennington. Bales taught modern dance, composition, and production and briefly added the spice of tap dance to the course offerings. He also made his first work for a group of dancers, *Es Mujer*, to music by Carlos Chavez, which was presented during the summer session of 1941. He danced briefly as a guest artist with the Hanya Holm Dance Company and studied ballet as well as the Graham technique.

Louis Horst, critic and confidant of the modern dance movement, asked Bales to perform in a benefit for *Dance Observer* magazine, sharing a program with Jane Dudley and Sophie Maslow. Their collaboration

on the 10 and 11 March 1942 performances was so satisfying that they decided to follow up with a performance at the Ninety-second Street Y. Bales contributed his *Es Mujer* and *To a Green Mountain Boy* (1942) to the program, which included individual works by the two women and two pieces made collaboratively, *Gigue* and *"As Poor Richard Says"—A Colonial Charade*. The program was hugely successful and launched the Dudley-Maslow-Bales Dance Trio. The trio toured America extensively, offering community and college concerts until the early 1950s. Their programs were distinguished by a frequent use of American folklore and folk song, transformed by the presentational style and vocabulary of modern dance. Maslow's *Dust Bowl Ballads* and *Folksay* (both 1942) became staples of the group's repertory and brought singer Woody Guthrie to the group as a touring partner. In an oral history, Dudley remarked, "I've spoken out against what I call cooperative choreography . . . [then] I've caught myself thinking: well, that's what Bill and Sophie and I did. . . . There was the three of us pitching in and contributing our ideas." Works credited or cocredited to Bales for the trio include *Peon Portraits* (1942–1943), *Sea Bourne* (1943), *Furlough: A Boardwalk Episode* (1945), *Soliloquy* (1947), *Three Dances in Romantic Style* (1948), *Judith* (1949), and *The Haunted Ones* (1951). Bales continued an active interest in spoken theater and in 1946 designed movement for the Theatre Guild production of *The Winter's Tale*. Critic Margaret Lloyd described Bales in her *Borzoi Book of Modern Dance*: "He is tall, broad-shouldered, dark-haired, strong-featured, and manages to look his part and *move* in it. . . . He is not a lyricist." Doris Hering wrote of the Dudley-Maslow-Bales trio in *American Dancer* (May 1946) that "these three have an unconscious unity of approach with no vestige of artiness and aloofness." During these years, in 1945, Bales married actress Jo Van Fleet; their son was born in 1949.

After nearly thirty years at Bennington, in 1966 Bales was invited to form a dance department at a new campus of the State University of New York, at Purchase, which would focus on the performing arts. Here he devised a curriculum for a much larger student body than he had dealt with at Bennington, and he planned an ideal dance building with classrooms, support services, and a studio theater. He retired as dean in 1975. Bales also taught at the University of California at Los Angeles, at New York University, and at the Juilliard School and was a regular instructor at the Connecticut College Summer School of Dance and at the New Dance Group Studio in New York City. His death in New York City came after a decade of gradual decline caused by Alzheimer's disease.

• Oral histories with William Bales, and with William Bales and Jane Dudley, both conducted by Tobi Tobias, are in the Dance Collection of the New York Public Library for the Performing Arts. Margaret Lloyd, *Borzoi Book of Modern Dance* (1949), and Don McDonagh, *Complete Guide to Mod-*

ern Dance (1976), summarize the work of the Dudley-Maslow-Bales trio. Additional material is from Sali Ann Kriegsman's *Modern Dance in America: The Bennington Years* (1981), Dance Collection clippings files on the companies and individual artists, and Bennington College and State University of New York catalogs. An obituary is in the *New York Times*, 11 Sept. 1990.

MONICA MOSELEY

BALL, Charles (1781?–?), fugitive slave, soldier, and memoirist, was born on a tobacco plantation in Calvert County, Maryland, the son of slave parents whose names are unknown. When Ball was four years old his mother and siblings were sold to slave traders to settle their late master's debts; he never saw them again. Ball was sold to John Cox, a local slaveowner, and continued to live near his father and grandfather. After the sale of Ball's mother, his father sank into a deep depression, eventually escaping from slavery on the eve of his purchase by a slave trader. Ball became close to his octogenarian grandfather, a former African warrior who had arrived in Maryland around 1730.

Cox died when Ball was twelve, and the young slave worked for his late master's father until he was twenty years old. During this time Ball married a slave named Judah who worked on a neighboring plantation as a chambermaid. Ball was the subject of a two-year lawsuit between a Mr. Gibson, who purchased him from the senior Cox, and Levin Ballard, who purchased him from Cox's children; he eventually worked for the latter for three years before being sold to a slave trader from Georgia. Ball was separated from his wife and children without even being allowed to say goodbye to them. He and fifty-one other slaves, bound by neck-irons, handcuffs, and chains, were forced to travel on foot for over a month from Maryland to Columbia, South Carolina. Ball recalled in his memoir, *Slavery in the United States* (1836), "I felt indifferent to my fate. It appeared to me that the worst had come, that could come, and that no change of fortune could harm me."

In South Carolina Ball was auctioned to the owner of a large cotton plantation. Upon the marriage of his master's daughter, Ball moved to Georgia to serve her and her new husband in September 1806. After the death of his new master in a duel, however, the Georgia estate, along with its slaves, was leased in January 1807 for seven years to another man. Ball seems to have enjoyed an unusually close relationship with his new master, traveling with him to purchase cattle and horses from the Cherokee and to Savannah to buy supplies for the plantation, as well as exerting authority on the plantation as overseer. After his master died around May 1807, Ball was severely beaten by his mistress's visiting brothers; he made his first escape from slavery in August of that year.

Despite being caught and imprisoned in Virginia, where he escaped from jail, Ball successfully walked from Georgia to Maryland in a year, traveling by night and foraging for food. Reunited with his wife and children around May 1808, he worked as a freeman in Maryland, then enlisted as a seaman and a cook under Commodore Barney in December 1813. Ball was dispatched by the United States to negotiate with several hundred slaves who had escaped from slavery under British protection. Unsuccessful, Ball himself was given the opportunity to travel to Trinidad with the other "contraband." He declined on the basis that he was already free. Discharged in 1814 and widowered in 1816, Ball worked in Maryland and Washington, D.C. In 1820 he invested his savings in a farm and dairy near Baltimore. He married—this wife's name is unknown—and fathered four more children.

Ball's domestic happiness was destroyed in June 1830 when he was captured and returned to slavery by his former mistress's brother. In Milledgeville, Georgia, the residence of his new master, Ball unsuccessfully sued for his freedom. Finally he managed to escape, only to be recaptured and sold. After a week Ball once again escaped, this time heading east instead of north, to Savannah. While loading cotton on a Philadelphia-bound ship, Ball persuaded a free black sailor to allow him to stow away on the ship. Hidden among bales of cotton and equipped with only a jug of water, bread, and molasses, Ball safely made the journey to Philadelphia, emerging, undetected, free once again. Upon his arrival he was assisted by an unnamed Quaker who provided him with clothing and lodging. After a few weeks Ball returned to his home in Baltimore, only to find that his wife and children, all of whom were legally free, had been captured and sold into slavery. He never saw them again. Afraid of being enslaved again, Ball moved to Pennsylvania, where he composed his memoirs.

Ball is best known as the subject of a popular and controversial slave narrative that was printed at least six times before the Civil War, including an unauthorized, unattributed, abridged version, *Fifty Years in Chains* (1859). This novel-like account of slavery was popular not only for its subject's sensational adventures and its detailed descriptions of life in the South, but also for its restraint. Acknowledging "the bitterness of heart that is engendered by a remembrance of unatoned injuries," Ball's ghostwriter, Pennsylvania attorney Isaac Fischer, was careful to exclude "every sentiment of this kind" from his rendering of Ball's life. This editorial censorship, combined with Fischer's inclusion of anecdotes from sources other than Ball in the narrative, led both contemporary critics and recent scholars to question the authenticity of this text, and even the existence of its subject. Most agree, however, that despite its embroidery and its silences, the narrative tells the true story of a courageous man who refused to be broken by an inhuman system.

• The primary source of information about Ball's life is his ghostwritten memoir, *Slavery in the United States*. For a discussion of this narrative and its subject, see Marion Wilson Starling, *The Slave Narrative: Its Place in American History* (1981); William L. Andrews, *To Tell a Free Story: The First*

Century of Afro-American Autobiography, 1760–1865 (1986); and Charles T. Davis and Henry Louis Gates, Jr., eds., *The Slave's Narrative* (1985).

JEANNINE DELOMBARD

BALL, Ernest R. (21 July 1878–3 May 1927), pianist and composer of popular songs, was born in Cleveland, Ohio, into a middle-class family. As a young teenager he was sent by his parents to study at the Cleveland Conservatory of Music. By age thirteen he was offering piano lessons in the neighborhood; by fifteen his first composition, a march for piano solo, was completed. As a young man he moved to New York City and for several years was employed as a pit pianist in various vaudeville productions. In 1903 he secured a position as staff pianist with the famous Witmark publishing house in Tin Pan Alley. His salary, $20 per week, was a respectable wage but far below what he eventually earned as a songwriter. Early in his stay at Witmark he began composing songs.

Ball's earliest efforts were not successful, but in 1905 he composed "Will You Love Me in December As You Do in May?" The song became a nationwide hit and marked the beginning of Ball's meteoric career. The lyrics were the work of a flamboyant New Yorker named Jimmy Walker, with whom Ball would collaborate on other songs, none of which met with much success. But the "December to May" song earned each of them $10,000 in royalties during one year—an astronomical figure for the time.

Although Walker quit the music business and entered politics (he was a New York state senator and later the mayor of New York City), the "December to May" song was forever closely identified with him: it was sung at his wedding, at his inaugural, and at his funeral. The song was also featured in two Hollywood films, *Beau James* (1957), starring Bob Hope, and *The Eddie Cantor Story* (1953).

Ball collaborated with other lyricists, most notably Chauncey Olcott. Their most famous song, "When Irish Eyes Are Smiling," was recorded by, among others, Morton Downey, Kate Smith, Bing Crosby, and John McCormack. It was also featured in the movie *Coney Island* (1943).

Synchronous with his rise as an important songwriter, Ball began a career as a singer on the vaudeville circuit and often performed his own songs on stage. The Witmark company was quick to realize that it had in Ball a very profitable property and awarded him a twenty-year contract as staff composer. Thus the young man who had begun as a $20-a-week pianist rapidly became very wealthy.

Ball contributed songs to three stage shows, *Barry of Ballymore* (1910), which featured "Mother Machree," "I Love the Name Mary," and "Your Love Means the World to Me"; *The Isle of Dreams* (1913), featuring "Isle of Dreams" and "When Irish Eyes Are Smiling"; and *Heart of Paddy Whack* (1914), with "A Little Bit of Heaven."

Other songs by Ball that achieved popularity include "When Sweet Marie Was Sweet Sixteen" (1907),

"In the Garden of My Heart" (1908), "Till the Sands of the Desert Grow Cold" (1911), "Goodbye, Good Luck, God Bless You" (1916), "I'll Forget You" (1921), and his last song, "Rose of Kilarney" (1927).

Ball's melodies are mostly diatonic and remain within the range of one octave; often a high, dramatic note is achieved just before the final phrase of the song. These melodies are supported by harmonies of the sort that can be adapted to a barbershop quartet format with the addition of passing secondary dominants.

While on tour in 1927 Ball died of a heart attack in his dressing room after a show in a vaudeville house in Santa Ana, California. He was survived by his second wife, actress Maude Lambert.

In 1914 Ball was a charter member of the American Society of Composers, Authors, and Publishers (ASCAP). In 1944 a movie musical, *Irish Eyes Are Smiling*, starring Dick Haymes, featured several of Ball's songs.

Ball was the composer of more than 400 sentimental and Irish ballads, the most successful of which are reputed to have sold more than 25 million copies of sheet music. Several of his songs, including "When Irish Eyes Are Smiling," "Mother Machree," and "Let the Rest of the World Go By" (1919), have found a permanent place in the repertoire of American popular song.

• For additional information on Ball, see David Ewen, *The Life and Death of Tin Pan Alley* (1964) and *All the Years of American Popular Music* (1977).

RONALD BYRNSIDE

BALL, Frank Clayton (24 Nov. 1857–19 Mar. 1943), businessman and philanthropist, was born at "Bascomb Farm" near Greensburg, Ohio, the son of Lucius Styles Ball, a farmer, and Maria Polly Bingham, a teacher. In 1868 the family moved to Canandaigua, New York, where Ball first attended Canandaigua Academy. In 1878 he moved to Buffalo, where he lived with his uncle, a Baptist minister, who had learned of an opportunity to construct fish kits (wooden boxes used by fishermen to hold their catch) out of lumber left over from making barrels. Ball and his brother Ed entered the business and had just begun production when the building burned down, causing them to lose everything. Ball then returned to Canandaigua for another term at the academy.

The following year, at the suggestion of their uncle, Frank and Ed Ball returned to Buffalo to open an electric carpet-cleaning service. The venture proved financially unsatisfactory, so the two bought a concern making wood-jacketed glass oil cans with the aid of a $200 loan from their uncle. Although this factory also burned down, the brothers had insurance and were able to resume production. The business prospered, and three other brothers—Lucius, William, and George—joined the enterprise, now called Ball Brothers. Frank Ball became president, an office he held until his death. In 1882 the firm began to blow its own glass bodies instead of purchasing them. This proved successful, and the company expanded into the manufacture of glass fruit jars. However, after still another fire, in 1887 Ball moved the company to Muncie, Indiana, to take advantage of the availability of cheap natural gas there. In 1893 Ball married Elizabeth Wolfe Brady; they had five children.

Along with his brothers, Ball was active in local philanthropy. He spearheaded the drive to build a Young Men's Christian Association (YMCA) in 1912 and one for young women (YWCA) in 1926. The family purchased the bankrupt Muncie Normal School, which became Ball State Teachers College and gave $1 million for a gymnasium, $100,000 for an arts building, $300,000 for a girl's dormitory, and $350,000 for a boys' dormitory. The Balls donated money to build a hospital, a Masonic temple, and a golf course in Muncie as well as to institutions elsewhere.

The Balls became famous as the "X family" in Robert S. Lynd and Helen M. Lynd's *Middletown in Transition: A Study in Cultural Conflicts* (1937), a family that, the Lynds noted, dominated the town's business, intellectual, and cultural life. This created problems for the Balls, who had tried to avoid publicity and were modest concerning their many philanthropies. Frank Ball died in Muncie.

• *The Memoirs of Frank Clayton Ball* (1937) is a good guide to his early years, although it is disappointing on the reasons for the company's success. The same holds for Frederic A. Birmingham, *Ball Corporation: The First Century* (1980).

DWIGHT HOOVER

BALL, George (21 Dec. 1909–26 May 1994), lawyer and statesman, was born George Wildman Ball in Des Moines, Iowa, the son of Amos Ball, Jr., a businessman, and Jessie Edna Wildman, a schoolteacher. Amos Ball, who was largely self-educated and worked his way up the ranks to become a director of Standard Oil, encouraged nightly debates at the dinner table and weekly outings to the public library. In 1922 he moved the family to Evanston, Illinois. In 1926 George enrolled at nearby Northwestern University, where he came under the influence of Bernard de Voto, a historian who transformed the boy, as Ball recalled, into "an obnoxious little intellectual snob" who disdained the parochialism of the Midwest. In 1930 Ball received his B.A. On a trip to Europe he met Ruth Murdoch, whom he married in 1932. They adopted two boys.

Upon graduation from law school at Northwestern in 1933, Ball was recruited into Franklin D. Roosevelt's New Deal, accepting a position as counsel with the Farm Credit Administration in Washington, D.C. Soon he transferred to the Treasury Department, where he prepared briefs on tax legislation and international trade. In 1935, seeking financial security and a better understanding of legal fundamentals, he accepted an offer to return to Evanston as a tax lawyer in a private firm. But he found the work too dull and his colleagues too conservative. In 1939 he joined the Chicago firm of Sidney, McPherson, Austin, and Harper, where he gravitated to a junior partner who shared his liberalism, Adlai E. Stevenson. In 1942 Stevenson, who chaired the Chicago Council of Foreign Relations, got Ball a job with the lend-lease program in Washington. Ball then shuttled from one war-related project to another. In 1944 he went to London to direct the U.S. Strategic Bombing Survey, where he worked with John Kenneth Galbraith, the future Harvard economist. In May 1945 the two men debriefed Albert Speer, head of Adolf Hitler's procurement and production operations. Ball concluded that the Allied bombing campaign had failed to cripple German industry or to sap German morale, and the experience left him wary of received military wisdom and skeptical of the efficacy of bombing campaigns.

In 1946 Ball helped found the Washington law firm of Cleary, Gottlieb, Friendly, and Cox. Ball specialized in trade and economic developments in Europe. He became a close friend and admirer of Jean Monnet, a French investment banker and government adviser who spearheaded a campaign for European economic and political integration. Ball became a lifelong proponent of these causes. He also sought to eliminate restrictions on trade. "I felt it essential that we rid the world economy of its encrusted barnacles of trade and monetary restrictions," he wrote (*The Past Has Another Pattern*, p. 103). Moreover, Ball's widening web of political and business contacts enabled him to play a major role in the founding of the Bilderberg group, a gathering of leaders throughout the West who met annually to discuss broad issues of policy. During these years, Ball spent much of his time abroad, and relations with his family suffered.

Ball's sophisticated internationalism ran afoul of the conservative reaction of the early 1950s. He denounced McCarthyism and came to loathe Richard M. Nixon for attacking New Dealers such as Dean Acheson, Ball's former handball partner, whom Nixon labeled as "soft on communism." In 1952 Ball joined Democrat Stevenson's campaign for the presidency, though it had little chance of defeating the Republican candidate and war hero, Dwight D. Eisenhower. Ball wrote speeches and articles on behalf of Stevenson, directing most of his jabs at Nixon, Eisenhower's choice for vice president. Eisenhower won decisively. In 1956 Ball again supported Stevenson, who faced a stiff challenge from Estes Kefauver for the Democratic nomination. Ball took charge of Stevenson's decisive Florida campaign, which secured him the Democratic nomination. Stevenson again lost to Eisenhower in the general election.

Ball's political disappointments were compounded by a disastrous investment. In 1957 he and three partners purchased the *Northern Virginia Sun*. The newpaper ran up staggering losses that cost Ball nearly a half-million dollars and forced him to borrow heavily from his father's trust fund.

Ball was initially ambivalent about the election campaign of 1960. He had misgivings about John F. Kennedy's ambition and hawkish record as a Cold Warrior, but Ball had ambitions of his own and coveted a prominent position in the State Department. He was also eager to take on Nixon, the Republican candidate for president. Ball wrote articles, gave speeches, and prepared position papers on foreign policy for Kennedy, who won the election. Kennedy named Ball under secretary of state for economic affairs. On 26 November 1961, less than a year into his presidency, Kennedy dismissed Chester Bowles as under secretary of state and appointed Ball to succeed him. As under secretary of state, Ball promoted European integration, specifically the European Economic Community, and sought to eliminate trade barriers and high tariffs. His European initiatives were overshadowed by the collapse of Belgian rule in the Congo. Tribal warfare, Cold War intrigue, and a bungled United Nations intervention resulted in a makeshift American policy toward what Ball termed "that beleaguered and unhappy land" (*The Past Has Another Pattern*, p. 259).

Following the assassination of Kennedy in 1963, Ball established a measure of rapport with Kennedy's successor, Lyndon Baines Johnson. While Johnson admired the intelligence and knowledge of senior Kennedy advisers, such as Defense Secretary Robert McNamara and McGeorge Bundy, he worried about their political inexperience. Johnson was impressed that Ball, on the other hand, had done time in the political trenches on behalf of Stevenson. Yet during the culminating events—and defining failure—of Ball's career, Johnson spurned Ball's advice and followed that of McNamara and Bundy. The issue was the deteriorating situation in South Vietnam, whose U.S.-backed government appeared on the verge of collapse from the relentless pressure from the Vietcong (Communist) insurgents, backed by North Vietnam. McNamara, Bundy, and Ball's superior, Secretary of State Dean Rusk, recommended a substantial increase in the U.S. military effort. Ball disagreed, and from October 1964 through July 1965 he sent Johnson eight lengthy memos calling for American withdrawal from Vietnam. Ball became known as Johnson's "devil's advocate" in opposition to escalation of the Vietnam War.

On 21 July 1965 Johnson scheduled a special meeting to resolve the debate. McNamara, Bundy, Rusk, and all of the military men present endorsed McNamara's proposal to send 200,000 U.S. troops to Vietnam by the end of the year. Ball offered the only dissent: "We are engaged in a very perilous voyage, a very dangerous voyage. . . . We must work to cut our losses now." Escalation of the war, Ball noted in language tailored for Johnson, would fail for three reasons. The war would be protracted and American losses would be high. "I have grave doubts that any Western army can successfully fight Orientals in an Asian jungle," he declared. As American casualties mounted, he added, the American people would withdraw their support for the war, as had happened a decade earlier in Korea. Finally, he insisted that America's commitment to corrupt and unstable military cabals in South Vietnam in no way impaired American commitments to the democracies of Western Europe. Under sharp questioning from Johnson, Ball conceded that South Vietnam would likely fall to the Vietcong if the United States withdrew. McNamara and Bundy seized upon this admission. "We are better off to waffle through than to withdraw," Bundy noted. On 28 July Johnson announced in a televised address, "We will stand in Vietnam." Several hundred thousand American soldiers were sent to Vietnam by the end of the year, and many more followed.

Ball's dire predictions came true. American casualties soared, and opposition to the war mounted. In September 1966 Ball resigned quietly. "I could not share the confidence of my colleagues for a sustained period, then go out and denounce them," he later explained (*The Past Has Another Pattern*, p. 432). In January 1967 he became a senior partner in the investment firm of Lehman Brothers, but in 1968, when Arthur Goldberg resigned as ambassador to the United Nations, Johnson pressured Ball to fill the vacancy. Ball accepted the post in June 1968 but shortly afterward resigned to work on Hubert H. Humphrey's campaign for the presidency against Nixon.

Nixon won, and Ball returned to Lehman, where he cultivated business contacts in Europe and supervised several reorganizations of the increasingly fractious investment firm. During the 1970s Ball's early opposition to the Vietnam escalation conferred upon him almost oracular status as a commentator on foreign affairs. He proceeded to criticize Israeli prime minister Menachem Begin and the Likud party for holding onto Palestinian lands that had been captured in the 1967 Arab-Israeli War. He called on the United States to support United Nations resolutions to restore the Palestinian lands, and he chided Nixon and especially Henry Kissinger, Nixon's chief foreign affairs adviser, for failing to broker an Israeli pullback. Ball's criticisms of Israel and American policies in support of it had no appreciable effect, but in 1976, when Democrat Jimmy Carter was elected president and Ball was considered for secretary of state, Ball's criticisms of Israel were cited as an insuperable political liability. Though denied a regular position in government, Ball continued to offer counsel and publish articles on foreign affairs. He died in New York City.

Ball prefaced his 18 June 1965 memorandum to Johnson with the words of Ralph Waldo Emerson, "Things are in the saddle and ride mankind." You must find a way, he warned the president, "to keep control of policy and prevent the momentum of events from taking over." But the press of events in fact drove the nation into a full-throated war in Vietnam. In this policy especially but in others as well, Ball perceived that events were pushing American policies toward disaster. His prescience was his chief contribution to American statesmanship. Yet repeatedly he failed to persuade others of the nightmares he so vividly foresaw.

• Ball's personal papers are at Princeton University. His official papers are at the Kennedy Library in Boston, Mass., and the Lyndon Baines Johnson Presidential Library in Austin, Tex. Oral history interviews are available at both the Kennedy and Johnson libraries. Ball's major writings include *The*

Past Has Another Pattern: Memoirs (1982), *Diplomacy for a Crowded World: An American Foreign Policy* (1976), *Error and Betrayal in Lebanon: An Analysis of Israel's Invasion of Lebanon and the Implications for U.S.-Israeli Relations* (1984), and, with Douglas B. Ball, *The Passionate Attachment: America's Involvement with Israel, 1947 to the Present* (1992). The major biography is James A. Bill, *George Ball: Behind the Scenes in U.S. Foreign Policy* (1997). See also David L. DiLeo, *George Ball, Vietnam, and the Rethinking of Containment* (1991). Other sources include David Halberstam, *The Best and the Brightest* (1972), and Robert McNamara, *In Retrospect: The Tragedy and Lessons of Vietnam* (1995). An obituary is in the *New York Times*, 28 May 1994.

Mark C. Carnes

BALL, George Alexander (5 Nov. 1862–22 Oct. 1955), glassmaker and railroad tycoon, was born on a farm near Greensburg, Trumbull County, Ohio, the son of Lucius Styles Ball, a farmer and inventor, and Maria Polly Bingham, a teacher. Young George attended the common schools and then Canandaigua Academy in upstate New York, an institution that was probably the equivalent of a modern junior college. In 1893 he married Frances E. Woodworth, with whom he would have one child.

Ball gained his fortune, if not his fame, from the glass industry. In 1880 he joined with his four brothers, Lucius L. Ball, William C. Ball, Edmund B. Ball, and Frank C. Ball, to form Ball Brothers Company in Buffalo, New York. An uncle, George H. Ball, financed the business with a loan of $200. Frank Ball was the founding president, a position he was to hold for sixty-three years. George A. Ball was the company's secretary and treasurer and subsequently became the company's second president—at the age of eighty-one. Initially, the company purchased hand-blown glass containers and covered them with metal jackets. In 1885 the company established its own furnace for manufacturing glass. With surplus capacity, the brothers looked for other glass products to manufacture and discovered that John L. Mason's patent for a home canning jar had expired. The Balls began to manufacture a Mason-style glass jar to be used for home canning.

Following an 1886 fire that destroyed the company's Buffalo factory, the Ball brothers considered several midwestern sites for their new plant, primarily because of the cheap natural gas available in Ohio and Indiana. Frank Ball traveled to Muncie, Indiana, by train to investigate the prospects in that city. When George came later, it is said that he rode in the baggage car with his horse to ensure that the animal would receive proper treatment. The town's promise of seven acres of land, $5,000 to defray the expenses of moving from Buffalo, and free gas led the brothers to build their new facility in Muncie, where the company remained permanently headquartered. The new factory, employing 125 people, produced the first Muncie Mason jars in 1888. The jars had zinc lids, which led the company to become involved with other zinc products. The Ball Mason fruit jar became the company's major product, and the name was soon identified with quality and reliability, a factor contributing eventually to market domination. The factory was profitable from the very beginning, but during World War I, with the government encouraging home canning, the company became extremely successful and the brothers wealthy.

In addition to their company, the Ball brothers are remembered for their philanthropic efforts. They acquired a defunct private college on the edge of Muncie, constructed several buildings on the campus, and donated the facilities to the state of Indiana. To honor the family, the state named the school Ball State Teachers College (now Ball State University). Some lovingly call the institution "Fruit Jar Tech." In the 1930s the city of Muncie honored the brothers with a statue, *Beneficence*, sculpted by Daniel Chester French. The last commissioned work by French, that statue is now the symbol of the university. The brothers also gave $1 million to Indiana University and much to Hillsdale College in Michigan, where their brother-in-law was president. They donated more than half a million dollars to Riley Memorial Hospital for Children in Indianapolis and spent more than $1 million to build Ball Memorial Hospital in Muncie. In February 1933 George and Frank Ball guaranteed the deposits of the Merchants National Bank and Merchants Trust and Savings Company in Muncie at a time when banks were closing elsewhere. George Ball was chairman of the board at Merchants National Bank.

By 1935 the 72-year-old George Ball was a wealthy but little-known manufacturer of fruit jars in Muncie. His rise to fame came when Mantis James Van Sweringen and Oris P. Van Sweringen of Cleveland, Ohio, asked him to help them finance their vast $3 billion railroad empire, which was about to face bankruptcy. The Van Sweringens convinced Ball that it would not be in the nation's best interests for their railroad empire to be broken up. The companies had 25,000 employees in Cleveland alone, and many people elsewhere would lose their jobs if the Van Sweringens went bankrupt. Ball later stated: "The Van Sweringens were at the end of their string. They could not raise another dime." Ball had previously been in partnership with George Tomlinson, a friend of the Van Sweringen brothers. Tomlinson told the Van Sweringens, "There was just one man with enough shrewdness to see a good thing where Eastern bankers wouldn't, enough daring to back his own quick judgment, and enough money to help the Vans out of their fix." With an investment of only $274,682 of his own cash and about $3 million in bank loans, Ball acquired controlling interest in 246 corporations and approximately 28,000 miles of rail lines. The investment included the Chesapeake & Ohio Railroad, the Nickel Plate Railroad, the Erie Railroad, the Missouri Pacific Railroad, and many smaller lines. Also included were numerous terminals, warehouses, bus companies, mines, coal companies, real estate, and a peach orchard. The Van Sweringens had paid $100 million just to acquire the Missouri Pacific Railroad, and Ball acquired control of it and many other railroads for about the cost of two steam engines.

Ball had not intended to get involved in the railroad business; he had simply acted to help the Van Sweringens with a temporary financial problem. The transaction between Ball and the Van Sweringens, although a purchase of stock by Ball, was originally intended as little more than a temporary loan to the Van Sweringens. Ball gave the Van Sweringen brothers a ten-year buyback option, but when the two brothers died shortly after the transaction, Ball was left with a vast railroad empire that he knew nothing about. At the same time, the nation's economy was improving, and Ball's unintended stock investment began to increase in value. As a result, there was an implication that Ball had been a go-between in a doubtful transaction, and in 1936 he was called before the Senate railroad investigating committee to explain his transaction. Ball told the committee that because of the complicated financial structure, he knew little about the properties he controlled. In April 1937 he donated his stock in the railroads to the George and Frances Ball Foundation, a trust organized for educational, religious, and charitable purposes. The foundation quickly sold the stock, realizing $6,375,000 from the sale. Members of the investigating committee, headed by Senator Burton K. Wheeler, argued that Ball's donation to the foundation was a sham and should not qualify for a charitable deduction. Ball stated that he bought controlling interest in the railroads because he thought it a fine, public-spirited thing to do and that he turned it over to a charitable organization because he was "fed to the teeth with federal taxes." As he supposedly stated, "If all a man's profits are taxed away from him and he only retains his losses he loses ambition."

Ball served on the boards of directors of numerous organizations, including Borg-Warner Corporation, the Nickel Plate Railroad, Dictaphone Corporation, Kuhner Packing Company (later Marhoefer Packing), Great Lakes Portland Cement Company, Banner Furniture Company, General Household Utilities Corporation, several banks, Indiana University, Ball State Teachers College, Ball Memorial Hospital, and the Newcomen Society. He was also a Republican national committeeman from Indiana. Ball remained active to the very end, working daily at the office even after his ninety-second birthday. He died in Muncie. Near the end of his life, he reportedly said with a straight face that his reputation as a hard worker had been vastly overstated: "I never worked more than twenty-four hours in a day, and I don't now."

For the first seven decades of his life, Ball was submerged in a joint personality known as Ball brothers. By the 1920s each of the brothers was a multimillionaire, but they all remained hard workers and were conservative with money. George Ball was seemingly no different than any of his brothers. Only after three of his brothers were dead and the other quite aged did Ball's personality appear to the general public. His destiny was to be remembered, at least on the national

level, not as a glass manufacturer or philanthropist but for his investment in a failing railroad system. This man who knew little about trains became overnight the major railroad magnate of the 1930s. As with much of his money earned at the glass company, Ball allotted his capital gains to a charitable foundation that did a great deal for medical care and higher education in central Indiana.

• Information on the Ball family's early years is available in Edmund F. Ball, *From Fruit Jars to Satellites* (1960), and in Frederic A. Birmingham, *Ball Corporation: The First Century* (1980). Major articles involving railroads include Charles Wertenbaker, "Mr. Ball Takes the Trains," *Saturday Evening Post*, 6 Feb. 1937, pp. 5–6, 71–74, and Herbert Corey, "Mr. Ball's Ambition," *Nation's Business*, June 1937, pp. 84–88, 142–44. An obituary is in the *New York Times*, 23 Oct. 1955.

DALE L. FLESHER

BALL, Lucille (8 Aug. 1911–26 Apr. 1989), actress and television executive, was born Lucille Désirée Ball in Jamestown, New York, the daughter of Henry Dunnell Ball, a telephone lineman, and Désirée "DeDe" Evelyn Hunt. Stagestruck from an early age, Ball quit school at fifteen to attend New York City's John Murray Anderson/Robert Milton School of the Theater and Dance. Later accounts describe her New York years, from about 1926 to 1933, as a time of struggle that required the aspiring actress to be tough. Jobs in the chorus line of Broadway shows never seemed to pan out for Ball, who eked out a living first waitressing and then modeling. She eventually got her show-business break in 1933, when she was sent to Hollywood as a chorus girl in *Roman Scandals*, a Samuel Goldwyn film starring Eddie Cantor.

Ball frequently complained that the film industry never knew quite what to do with her. Certainly, her moves from studio to studio during her movie career indicate an uncertainty about her as a "type" (chorus girl versus housewife, vamp versus wise-cracking comedienne)—but at least she was seldom out of work. While waiting to do *Roman Scandals* (1933), she appeared in two Twentieth Century productions, *Broadway through a Keyhole* and *Blood Money* (both released in 1933). She played a number of very minor roles for Goldwyn, Twentieth Century, and Fox before being signed in 1934 as a contract player for Columbia, which was trying to form a small stock company.

Unfortunately for Ball, Columbia soon decided to disband its stock company. After a short stint as an extra at Paramount, Ball signed a contract at RKO. There she studied acting with resident coach Lela Rogers (Ginger Rogers's mother) and gradually worked her way into speaking parts. Her first big role was as a wisecracking would-be actress in *Stage Door* (1937). This spurred her promotion to star status in *The Affairs of Annabel* (1938), a film in which she burlesqued movie queens. She moved on to a more serious role in *Dance, Girl, Dance* (1940), playing a gutsy striptease artist. While working on that picture she was assigned the ingenue role in RKO's adaptation of the Broadway musical *Too Many Girls* (1940). One of the players from the Broadway production was a 23-year-old musician from Cuba named Desi Arnaz. The pair married in November 1940.

Ball thought she had hit the big time playing a bitter, crippled singer in *The Big Street* (1942). Instead, RKO released her from her contract. She moved on to Metro-Goldwyn-Mayer amid much fanfare and was encouraged to dye her brown-turned-blond hair red in order to stand out in Technicolor. Unfortunately, Ball did not fit the MGM mold. She was not a singer and thus found little work in the musicals that were an MGM staple, and her comedic talents proved a bit too common for the studio's high-toned image. She was often cast according to her looks, as a showgirl; this type allowed her little latitude or satisfaction. Leaving MGM in 1946, she freelanced for a while and finally signed a short-term contract with Columbia, taking time off to tour in a stage production, *Dream Girl*, and to star in the radio show "My Favorite Husband" from 1947 to 1951. She always had work, but her career did not really advance.

Neither did her marriage. While Ball made pictures in Hollywood, Arnaz was frequently on the road with his band. He was notorious for his womanizing, and the pair's fights were legendary. From 1943 to 1945 the couple were further separated by Arnaz's stint in the armed forces. In 1944 Ball filed for divorce, but the pair's passionate reconciliation rendered the interlocutory decree invalid.

Ball and Arnaz resealed their vows in a Catholic ceremony in 1949 and tried to find more opportunities to work together. In 1950, when CBS approached Ball in 1950 about moving "My Favorite Husband" to the nascent medium of television, she perceived a chance to work at long last with her real-life spouse, and she asked the network to cast Arnaz as her TV husband and costar. Network executives were reluctant to do so, arguing that his ethnicity would conflict with Ball's all-American image.

In order to demonstrate to CBS executives that they could impress audiences as a credible couple, Ball and Arnaz toured the country with a vaudeville routine. The success of this stage show, in which Ball played a comic figure trying to crash her way into working with Arnaz's band, helped remove network objections to his casting. Even so, the couple had to pay for the program pilot themselves under the auspices of their newly formed production company, Desilu.

In mid-1951 the Arnazes produced two offspring: Lucie Désirée Arnaz, who was born in July, and "I Love Lucy," which premiered in October. The program, which focused on the marital joys and conflicts of Cuban bandleader Ricky Ricardo and his stage-struck, no-talent wife, Lucy, rapidly became popular and stayed that way. It remained on the air for six years and never fell below number three in the ratings. It proved a gold mine in syndication decades later. Ball's comedic skills enabled the show to convey in slapstick the era's tensions between the sexes. She and Arnaz, on and off screen, were lionized in the press as an ideal couple, and she was hailed as the queen of

American comedy. Meanwhile, their production company, Desilu, made television history (and millions of dollars) with its pioneering work shooting the program on film in front of a live audience using three cameras.

The Ball-Arnaz on- and offscreen unions were further cemented in January 1953, when the two Lucys gave birth simultaneously to little Ricky Ricardo and Desi Arnaz, Jr. During the summer of 1953 Ball and Arnaz made their second feature film together, *The Long, Long Trailer*.

In the fall of 1953, however, Ball faced a challenge to her career when word got out that she had been called before the House Committee on Un-American Activities to explain her former membership in the Communist party. Ball told the committee and the American public that she had only registered in the party to please her socialist grandfather, and all allegations against her were dropped.

After capitalizing on Lucy Ricardo's pregnancy and childbirth in the 1953–1954 season, "I Love Lucy" found a gimmick for each future season. In 1954–1955 the Ricardos and their sidekicks, Fred and Ethel Mertz, went to Hollywood so that Ricky could work in films. In 1955–1956 the two couples toured Europe. In 1956–1957 Ricky purchased his own nightclub, and the now successful Ricardos eventually moved to the suburbs. At the end of that season, the program ceased regular production. Ball and Arnaz were ready to move on to other projects. Until 1960, however, they starred in several hour-long specials about the Ricardos. They also made one more motion picture together, *Forever Darling*, in 1956.

In 1958, looking to expand its production facilities, Desilu purchased the studio in which Ball and Arnaz had met, RKO. For the next couple of years Ball busied herself conducting studio acting classes modeled on those she had taken from Lela Rogers. Her marriage to Arnaz deteriorated, and in 1960, after filming the last Lucy-Ricky special, Ball filed for divorce, citing mental cruelty as grounds. Years later she would speak of Arnaz's increasing alcoholism and infidelities as the cause of the rift between them.

After a well-attended but critically unsuccessful stint on Broadway in the musical *Wildcat*, Ball surprised her fans by marrying comedian Gary Morton late in 1961. Morton was a quiet, supportive man who stood by Ball until her death. In 1962, perhaps missing the limelight, the actress returned to television in a half-hour situation comedy, "The Lucy Show," that resurrected the "Lucy" character without Ricky. Retooled as "Here's Lucy" in 1968, the program continued until 1974. Arnaz started out as the show's producer but quickly bowed out of it and of Desilu. His former wife bought him out and became chairwoman of the board in 1962.

The public Lucille Ball of the 1960s, 1970s, and 1980s was much tougher than her housewifely predecessor—as a businesswoman, running her corporation and its board meetings, and as an actress, manically controlling any production in which she took part. Rex Reed, interviewing her on the set of the 1968 film

Yours, Mine, and Ours, found her a hard-talking, bossy, dynamic figure. She developed a loathing for most contemporary film and television fare, finding it much too sexual and violent, and took pride in presenting what she considered acceptable family programming.

In 1986 Lucille Ball finally had to cease recycling her televised "Lucy" character. Amid much fanfare, ABC announced a new situation comedy starring Ball titled "Life with Lucy." The program never garnered substantial ratings after its first episode, and ABC took it off the air despite a financial commitment to several more episodes. Critics and industry commentators harshly condemned the stale humor exhibited by the aging Ball.

Lucille Ball gamely retired for good, making only occasional television appearances until her death in Los Angeles. At that point, however, she once again attracted the sort of press coverage she had enjoyed in her heyday as America's queen of comedy. Memorial tributes abounded on television and in print. The Lucille Ball evoked in these tributes was almost exclusively the Lucille Ball of the 1950s—the public figure who had loved and married Desi Arnaz, who had cavorted for the American public as the madcap, eternally black-and-white Lucy Ricardo.

• The Billy Rose Theatre Collection of the New York Public Library for the Performing Arts, Lincoln Center, has extensive clipping files on Ball's life and career. In addition, her life and work are discussed in Charles Higham, *Lucy: The Life of Lucille Ball* (1986), and Bart Andrews and Thomas J. Watson, *Loving Lucy* (1980). Ball's life is paired with that of first husband and business partner Desi Arnaz in Warren G. Harris, *Lucy and Desi* (1991), and Coyne Steven Sanders and Tom Gilbert, *Desilu* (1993). "I Love Lucy" and the Desilu company receive analysis in Bart Andrews, *Lucy and Ricky and Fred and Ethel* (1976), and Thomas Schatz, "Desilu, *I Love Lucy*, and the Rise of Network TV," in *Making Television*, ed. Robert J. Thompson and Thomas J. Watson (1990). The Rex Reed interview appears in his 1968 book *Do You Sleep in the Nude?* Tinky "Dakota" Wiseblat's "50s TV Chronicled War between the Sexes," *Hartford Courant*, 14 May 1989, appeared after Ball's death and relates her to other television housewives of the 1950s.

TINKY "DAKOTA" WEISBLAT

BALL, Thomas (3 June 1819–11 Dec. 1911), sculptor and author, was born in Charlestown, Massachusetts, the son of Thomas Ball, a house and sign painter, and Elizabeth Wyer Hall. He attended the Mayhew School until age twelve, when his father died. Needing to help support the family, Ball found work at Kimball's Boston Museum and Fine Arts Gallery, where he performed tasks that included repairing wax figures and conducting tours. Ball learned to cut silhouettes for museum visitors to supplement his income, but he described himself as exhibiting no artistic talent until he was fifteen or sixteen years old. As his interest in art grew he apprenticed himself briefly to Abel Bowen, a wood engraver. After a few months he returned to work at the museum and began painting miniatures and portraits. In 1837 he set up a small studio in Bos-

ton, where he worked hard to establish himself as a professional portrait painter. He entered art exhibitions, receiving much encouragement. He began to work in clay and found it a more interesting medium for his talent. His first work, modeled in clay and produced in plaster, was a small bust of the celebrated Swedish singer Jenny Lind (1851). Many copies were sold, and its success brought Ball orders for small-scale cabinet busts of other musicians.

At the time there were few art schools in the United States, so Ball, like other American artists, desired to study in Europe. His cabinet busts sold well, but he wanted to try life-sized busts, choosing Daniel Webster as his first subject in 1853. The bust was finished two days before Webster's death, and copies of it were in great demand. Its financial success allowed Ball to plan his long-desired trip to Europe.

In 1854 Ball married Ellen Louise Wild; they had one child. The couple traveled to Italy, where they lived in Florence, a gathering place for American and European artists and writers. Most American sculptors in Florence were self-taught and felt time spent in Europe would help them better develop their art. Ball studied masterpieces of ancient and Renaissance sculpture and learned techniques from other sculptors. He worked in clay, plaster, and marble.

After two years Ball returned to Boston and was given the commission for a large bronze equestrian statue of George Washington for Boston's Public Garden. In 1864 the plaster model was exhibited to hundreds of citizens in Boston. Because of the Civil War the Washington Statue Committee felt they should not ask for contributions, so the plaster model was placed in storage until funds could be raised to cast it in bronze. On 29 January 1869 the monument was finally unveiled and dedicated.

While on his way back to Italy in 1865 Ball heard of President Abraham Lincoln's death. "I could not free my mind from the horror of it," he wrote in his memoirs *My Three Score Years and Ten* (1891). After settling in Florence Ball began a piece to honor the slain president. The half-life-sized study of the *Emancipation Group*, also known as *Lincoln Freeing the Slaves*, depicts Lincoln standing with outstretched arms over a kneeling black man, indicating the broken chains of slavery. In 1867 Ball entered the Lincoln design for a monument in Philadelphia, but it was not selected. From 1872 to 1875 he made copies of that work in marble and bronze. In 1873 he was contacted by the Freedmen's Memorial Society, who planned a Lincoln memorial for Washington, D.C. The committee approved the *Emancipation Group* design and offered Ball $17,000 for a bronze statue ten feet high. Ball accepted the offer, realizing that every cent of the money had been contributed by freed men and women. The model for the face of the slave in this version was Archer Alexander, the last slave taken under the fugitive slave law, who was rescued from his captors. The monument was unveiled in Washington in 1876. A duplicate for the city of Boston was dedicated in 1879.

Ball continued to live in Italy. His work was in demand for portrait busts, heroic bronze monuments, marble and bronze pieces for private collections, and cemetery memorials. One of his last monuments was a colossal statue of George Washington, which was exhibited at the World's Columbian Exposition in Chicago in 1893, earning the highest honors. It now stands in the Forest Lawn Memorial Park in Hollywood Hills, California.

In 1891 Ball's wife died, and his autobiography *My Three Score Years and Ten* was published. In 1897 Ball moved from Florence to Montclair, New Jersey, with his only child, Eliza, his son-in-law, sculptor William Couper, and three grandsons. *My Fourscore Years*, a sequel to his earlier autobiography, was written in 1899–1900 but not published until 1993. He died in Montclair.

Other important sculptures by Ball are *Saint John the Evangelist* (1875), one of Ball's personal favorites; statuettes of *Daniel Webster* (1853) and *Henry Clay* (1858), now at the North Carolina Museum of Art in Raleigh; and statues of *Josiah Quincy*, the mayor of Boston (1879), now at Old City Hall in Boston; *Charles Sumner* (1878) at Boston Public Gardens; and *Daniel Webster* (1876) in Central Park, New York City, and (1886) in Concord, New Hampshire.

Ball, a self-taught artist, achieved prominence in his profession. His style was one of naturalism, which at that time dominated American art. His sculptures of historical characters are of their own period and modeled from life, paintings, or photographs. Ball's sculptures and paintings are represented in museums, public parks, cemeteries, and private collections. His work influenced monumental art in the United States well into the twentieth century.

• For more information on Ball see Wayne Craven, *Sculpture in America* (1984), and Craven, "The Early Sculptures of Thomas Ball," *Bulletin of the North Carolina Museum of Art* (Fall 1964–Winter 1965). See also William Ordway Partridge, "Thomas Ball," *New England Magazine*, n.s., 12 (1895): 291–304. Other sources include Albert T. Gardner, *Yankee Stonecutters: The First American School of Sculpture, 1800–1850* (1945), and Gardner, "The *Emancipation Group* by Thomas Ball," *Lincoln Lore*, no. 608 (2 Dec. 1940): 1. For obituaries see the *Boston Evening Transcript* and the *New York Times*, both 12 Dec. 1911.

CAROLYN R. LAFEVER

BALLANTINE, Arthur Atwood (3 Aug. 1883–10 Oct. 1960), corporate lawyer and Treasury official, was born in Oberlin, Ohio, the son of William Gay Ballantine, a professor and president of Oberlin College, and Emma Atwood. He graduated with honors from Harvard College (1904) and Harvard Law School (1907). On 19 June 1907 he married Helen Bailey Graves; they had five children.

Ballantine practiced law initially in Boston, specializing in corporate work. When the United States entered World War I, Ballantine became a "dollar-a-year man," first advising the commissioner of internal revenue on legal questions arising from the wartime tax laws, and then serving as solicitor of internal revenue, the Treasury's chief legal officer on tax issues.

His wartime record led to a significant increase in his legal business after the armistice, and in 1919 he decided to relocate in New York City. Along with several law school classmates, he founded the firm of Root, Clark, Howland & Ballantine, and later he became senior partner in its successor firm, Dewey, Ballantine, Bushby, Palmer & Wood. The firm specialized in corporate work, particularly tax and securities cases.

During the 1920s Ballantine devoted himself primarily to his law work and to enjoying the fruits of his success, such as corporate directorships and a country home at Oyster Bay on Long Island's prestigious North Shore.

In 1931 President Herbert Hoover appointed Ballantine assistant secretary of the treasury, and the following year he became undersecretary. For a political appointee, Ballantine had an unusually extensive knowledge of his field, and he found the Treasury during the depression the greatest professional challenge of his career. While he favored reducing government expenses, Ballantine, unlike Hoover, wanted the government to play a more positive role both in helping individuals and in bolstering the economic system. He helped organize the Reconstruction Finance Corporation, which funneled government loans to businesses and banks, and he also supervised the spending of $700 million in federal building projects.

Ballantine played a key role at the Treasury during the banking crisis of 1932–1933, trying to keep banks financially stable so that they would not go under. In February 1933 he tried to negotiate private loans to rescue the Union Guardian Trust Company of Detroit. When that plan collapsed, Ballantine worked with Michigan governor William A. Comstock to arrange a bank moratorium, the precursor to the banking holiday established by Franklin D. Roosevelt at the beginning of his administration.

Roosevelt and Ballantine had been at Harvard together, and at the president's request Ballantine stayed at the Treasury to help the incoming Democratic officials. He also advised Roosevelt on the bank holiday and drafted the president's fireside chat of 12 March 1933 in which he explained the plan to the American people. During the "holiday," the government closed all the banks and then reopened the ones that were financially sound. The device restored public confidence in the banking system.

Ballantine opposed the New Deal's deficit financing and large-scale building programs, and in May 1933, only two months into the new administration, he returned to private law practice. He reentered government service during World War II to undertake special projects for Secretary of the Navy Frank Knox.

After the war his law practice burgeoned, and in 1955 former New York governor and Republican presidential candidate Thomas E. Dewey agreed to join the firm. Ballantine practiced law right up until his death in New York.

• Ballantine's career is noted in the various *Reports* of the Harvard College Class of 1904; his view of the banking holiday is in "When All the Banks Closed," *Harvard Business Review* 26 (Mar. 1948): 129–43. See also Association of the Bar of the City of New York, *Memorial Book* (1961), and Susan Estabrook Kennedy, *The Banking Crisis of 1933* (1971). An obituary is in the *New York Times*, 12 Oct. 1960.

MELVIN I. UROFSKY

BALLARD, Edna Anne Wheeler (25 June 1886–10 Feb. 1971), and **Guy Warren Ballard** (28 July 1878–29 Dec. 1939), controversial founders of the "I Am" movement, were born, respectively, in Burlington, Iowa, and Newton, Kansas. Edna was the daughter of Edward G. Wheeler, reportedly a railway clerk, and Anna Hewitt Pearce; Guy the son of a farmer, Josephus Ballard, and Phebe Jane Leigh. "I Am" was a religious movement that grew at a phenomenal rate in the 1930s, became the subject of a celebrated fraud case and a landmark freedom of religion decision by the U.S. Supreme Court in the 1940s, and has since held a modest but continuing place in American spiritual life.

Guy Ballard was born into a large rural family and as a young man made his way to the Southwest. In 1916 he and Edna Anne Wheeler were married in Chicago. Ballard served as an enlisted man in the U.S. Army along the Mexican border during World War I. After the war he managed an uncle's lead and silver mine near Tucson and engaged in other mining explorations and enterprises. In the 1920s he also resided at times in Chicago with his wife, where he sold mining stock, and at times in California while she remained in Chicago. Allegations of fraud were raised in connection with the mining stock activity but were never sustained in court.

Edna Ballard became a concert harpist in 1912. During the 1920s, she also worked in a metaphysical bookstore in Chicago, the Philosopher's Nook, and edited *The American Occultist*. She and Guy Ballard both studied Theosophical and occult literature extensively. They had one son, Donald (1918–1973), who was active in the "I Am" movement in its early years.

Guy Ballard reported that while hiking on the slopes of Mt. Shasta in northern California in 1930 he encountered the comte de Saint-Germain, an eighteenth-century occultist well known in Theosophical lore as a Master. Saint-Germain taught him the Great Law of Life, emphasizing reincarnation and the power of mental affirmation. Over subsequent months Saint-Germain imparted many remarkable experiences to Ballard, showing him his past lives and introducing him to other Masters in their retreats under Mt. Shasta or the Grand Tetons. Ballard recounts these events in *Unveiled Mysteries* (1934) and *The Magic Presence* (1935), written under the pseudonym Godfre Ray King.

These works effectively combine Theosophical and "New Thought" doctrine with fast-paced narrative. Their fundamental teachings include reincarnation; affirmation of the divine "Mighty I Am" Presence; the individualized "I Am" presence centered above the head of each person; and the reality of the Ascended Masters, a hierarchy of figures like Saint-Germain and Jesus who so purified themselves that they did not undergo death but ascended to a higher state and are now prepared to help humankind. "I Am" has a strongly patriotic tone, emphasizing the destiny of the United States to become the center of a new golden age.

Guy Ballard returned to Chicago about 1932 and began classes and lectures on the teachings. Guy, Edna, and Donald were declared to be the only Accredited Messengers of the Ascended Masters; Saint-Germain, Jesus, and many others gave discourses through their lips. These lectures became the substance of subsequent books in the green-bound Saint-Germain series. "I Am" practices include meditations and chanted "decrees" or invocations for particular purposes. The movement also makes much use of color and drama.

The year 1938 marked the peak of the movement's popularity. Its followers then numbered hundreds of thousands, if not millions, in the United States; the total number of followers is uncertain since the movement did not receive formal memberships but spread its influence through lectures, sale of literature, and scattered classes. Undoubtedly the stresses of the Great Depression, controversy over the New Deal (which the Ballards fervently opposed), and growing international crises contributed to the movement's appeal. But criticism began to mount. Then, on 29 December 1939, Guy Ballard died in Los Angeles. His death disillusioned believers who thought that he, of all persons, ought to have ascended. In 1940 Edna Ballard, Donald, and a score of other leaders were indicted for mail fraud. In essence, the charge was that they had devised the "I Am" religion knowing it was fraudulent and used it as a means of soliciting money.

The case made its way to the U.S. Supreme Court in 1944. A lower court had ruled that the truth or falsity of the religion's doctrine had to be determined to decide if fraud had been committed. But the High Court's judgment, written by Justice William O. Douglas, was that power to adjudicate the truth or falsity of religious belief is not given any court or legislature under the U.S. Constitution. In an important concurring opinion, Justice Robert H. Jackson argued that, in addition, the courts cannot determine anyone's sincerity or insincerity in holding to certain beliefs. The case was returned to the lower courts, which nonetheless again convicted the Ballards et al. of fraud. When the case came back to the Supreme Court in 1946, the conviction was once more reversed, this time on the grounds that women had been systematically excluded from the jury—presumably because the prosecution thought they might be more sympathetic than men to the widowed Edna Ballard. The case was dropped.

Edna Ballard, residing chiefly in Santa Fe, delivered discourses from the Masters and led the now small and chastened but still-living movement until her death in Chicago.

• Gerald B. Bryan, *Psychic Dictatorship in America* (1940), contains much contemporary information but as an anti-"I Am" polemic should be used with caution; the "I Am" chapter in Charles S. Braden, *These Also Believe* (1949), largely follows Bryan. More recent summaries are Robert S. Ellwood, "Making New Religions: The Story of the Mighty 'I AM,'" *History Today* 38 (June 1988), and J. Gordon Melton, *Biographical Dictionary of American Cult and Sect Leaders* (1986).

ROBERT S. ELLWOOD

BALLARD, Guy Warren. *See* Ballard, Edna Anne Wheeler, and Guy Warren Ballard.

BALLARD, Martha Moore (20 Feb. 1735–19? May 1812), midwife and diarist, was born in Oxford, Massachusetts, the daughter of Elijah Moore and Dorothy Learned, farmers and innkeepers. Nothing is known about her early life and education. Though the Learned and Moore families were moderately prosperous, Martha's mother signed the only document bearing her name with a mark. Martha's father and grandfathers were town selectmen and militia officers. Her younger brother, Jonathan Moore, was Oxford's second college graduate and for a time served as librarian of Harvard College. Her uncle Abijah Moore, a graduate of Yale College, and her brother-in-law, Stephen Barton, were physicians. Presumably Martha learned her craft through working with an older midwife in Oxford.

She married Ephraim Ballard, a miller and surveyor, in 1754. They had nine children, three of whom died in the Oxford diphtheria epidemic of 1769. In 1775 Ephraim, who had already begun working as a surveyor of Maine lands, attempted to establish an inn at Fort Halifax (now Waterville, Maine) on property owned by Sylvester Gardiner, a Boston Loyalist. Within months the local revolutionary government, considering Ephraim as much a Tory as his landlord, confiscated the property. Ephraim moved downriver to Augusta (then part of Hallowell), where he leased sawmills and gristmills and made peace with the Revolution. Martha and the children joined him in 1777. In January 1785 she began the taciturn diary that establishes her place in history.

The diary not only provides an unbroken record of one woman's life in maturity and old age, it also offers powerful evidence on early midwifery, medicine, sexual mores, and household production and exchange. Between 1778 and 1812 Ballard attended more than a thousand births, achieving infant and maternal mortality rates as good as any in the United States before the 1940s. She also served as a nurse and general practitioner, treating her neighbors for common illnesses, burns, and frostbite. She processed her own medicines, sometimes purchasing ingredients from a local physician but more frequently using plants grown in her own garden or gathered from the woods and fields around her.

Ballard's "physic" was conservative. Three-quarters of the plants mentioned in the diary can be found in English herbals of the seventeenth century. She did not let blood, administer opiates, or set bones, remedies favored by male physicians of her community, but she shared their understanding of the human body. She dismissed an inexperienced young doctor who attempted to deliver babies as "that poor unfortunate man in the practise," but for the most part her relations with local doctors were cordial. They occasionally called her to observe autopsies, the details of which she recorded in her diary. She also served a quasi-judicial function in paternity suits by taking testimony from unwed mothers "in the time of travail." In 1789 she testified in the sensational trial of a judge accused of raping a minister's wife.

Ballard's life spanned an important transition in the history of obstetrics. In the early eighteenth century medicine was still a part-time specialty for learned gentlemen, a science acquired primarily through mastery of the writings of ancient authorities. Midwifery was considered a manual art best left to women unless serious complications created a medical or surgical emergency. Over the course of the century British physicians like William Smellie, William Hunter, and Charles White developed a new, more experimental obstetrics that simultaneously undermined the traditional lore of midwives and elevated the significance of manual practice. By 1820 a Massachusetts physician could write, "A man must be a universal practitioner in midwifery, before he is qualified for a practitioner in difficult cases." In his view, doctors had to become midwives, though midwives could not become doctors without destroying their moral character through contact with the dissecting room and the hospital.

These changes had little impact on Ballard's own life, but they help to explain why she left no known female successor. Her practice declined as she grew older and more feeble, but it never entirely stopped. She attended her last birth on 26 April 1812, about a month before her death in Augusta. The diary eventually descended to a great-great-granddaughter, Dr. Mary Hobart, an 1884 graduate of the Woman's Medical College of the New York Infirmary, who believed she inherited "the mantle of her gifted ancestor." Ballard's career may also have inspired Clara Barton, the founder of the American Red Cross, whose grandmother was Ballard's sister. Barton loved to tell stories about her "interesting, precise and intelligent grandmother Barton" and "her sister Aunt Ballard." Ballard's diary was largely forgotten until the 1970s, when a new interest in midwifery and in the lives of early American women helped to reclaim her story.

• The two-volume manuscript diary of Ballard, 1785–1812, is in the Maine State Library, Augusta. An abridged and expurgated version appears in Charles Elventon Nash, *The History of Augusta* (1904; repr. 1961). Robert R. McCausland and Cynthia MacAlman McCausland, eds., *The Diary of Martha Ballard 1785–1812* (1992), is a verbatim transcription of the original. Laurel Thatcher Ulrich, *A Midwife's Tale: The Life of Martha Ballard, Based on Her Diary, 1785–1812* (1990), is a full biography.

For additional context on Ballard's life and brief references to her diary, see Richard W. Wertz and Dorothy C. Wertz, *Lying-In: A History of Childbirth in America* (1977); Nancy F. Cott, *The Bonds of Womanhood: 'Woman's Sphere' in New England, 1780–1835* (1977); and Judith Walzer Leavitt, *Brought to Bed: Child-Bearing in America, 1750–1950* (1986). For European comparisons, see Hilary Marland, ed., *The Art of Midwifery: Early Modern Midwives in Europe* (1993).

LAUREL THATCHER ULRICH

BALLINGER, Richard Achilles (9 July 1858–6 June 1922), lawyer and secretary of the interior, was born in Boonesborough, Iowa, the son of Richard H. Ballinger, a lawyer, and Mary E. Norton. His father read law in the office of Abraham Lincoln and during the Civil War was regimental colonel of the Third Illinois Volunteer Cavalry. Ballinger entered Williams College in the class of 1884 and after graduation read law in an attorney's office. Admitted to the bar in 1886, he that year married Julia A. Bradley. They had two sons. He practiced law briefly in New Decatur, Alabama, but in 1890 cast his lot with the new state of Washington, admitted to the Union in the same year. He settled first in Port Townsend but soon shifted to the young city of Seattle.

Within a few years Ballinger had established a law practice and developed a reputation for probity. He became an expert on mining law and virtually all facets of the public land laws. He had numerous clients, small or middling-sized entrepreneurs, rather than a few large corporate clients. He published *A Treatise on the Property Rights of Husband and Wife under the Community . . . System* (1895) and further enhanced his reputation by compiling the codes and statutes of the state of Washington. He served as superior judge of Jefferson County (1894–1898) and in 1904 was elected mayor of Seattle on the Republican ticket.

In 1907 a Williams College classmate, James Rudolph Garfield, who was about to become President Theodore Roosevelt's secretary of the interior, invited Ballinger to become commissioner of the General Land Office. This hoary, much maligned bureau was responsible for enforcing the arcane land laws and selling public lands. For much of its history the bureau was plagued by inefficiency, frequently accused of corruption, and often racked by scandal until Ballinger instituted sweeping reforms. He reorganized the Field divisions, where much of the work of the bureau was done; carried out a great purge of aging or inefficient clerks and agents; introduced typewriters to a bureau still laboriously copying documents in longhand; shortened and simplified forms; and promoted younger men to positions of responsibility. After twelve months he resigned and returned to private life, leaving behind a transformed bureau.

Ballinger's superiors sang his praises, but some fellow bureau chiefs heaved sighs of relief. None was more relieved than Gifford Pinchot, head of the agriculture department's Forest Service, self-proclaimed architect of the Roosevelt policies for the conservation of natural resources, and a chieftain with imperial ambitions for his bureau. Ballinger and Pinchot had clashed repeatedly on the Public Lands Commission, of which Ballinger as Land Office commissioner was automatically chairman. Moreover, the Forest Service and the Land Office actually shared jurisdiction of the national forests. Pinchot's genius was to put together informal cooperative arrangements between bureaus, some in different departments, such as the Land Office and the Forest Service, with overlapping missions. The aim was to streamline the inefficient, "unscientific" organization of the federal government by creating a coordinated system. What Pinchot called "cooperation," however, Ballinger regarded as poaching, and clashes were numerous.

These differences assumed greater importance when Ballinger returned in March 1909 as secretary of the interior in the William Howard Taft administration. The stakes had grown higher during Ballinger's absence, and many hoped Garfield would be reappointed because of the unfinished work. When Ballinger was appointed instead, misgivings were grave. In the final months of the Roosevelt administration, Garfield had begun to prepare the way to introduce the Forest Service's system of regulated use of resources, already implemented in the national forests, to the public domain at large. Ballinger immediately sought to undo much of this work, which he as well as President Taft believed lacked legal authorization. Ballinger also cancelled the cooperative agreement between the Bureau of Indian Affairs and the Forest Service that had enabled Pinchot's people to manage the forests on American Indian reservations on the grounds that such agreements were illegal, thus striking at the vitals of the entire coordinated system. If the agreement between these two agencies, a model for the system, was illegal, what of the other agreements? Pinchot and his allies believed Ballinger intended to destroy the Roosevelt conservation policies, over which Pinchot exercised proprietary claims. He had to be stopped.

In August 1909 Ballinger found himself accused of malfeasance by Louis Glavis, the head of the Portland field division of the Land Office. Glavis complained that he was being rushed to complete the applications of certain coal land claimants in Alaska, known as the Cunningham group, who were tied indirectly to the Guggenheim syndicate, a notorious trust, before his investigation was complete. Glavis claimed he was being pressured by his superiors because they were being pressured by Ballinger, who had once represented the Cunningham group. In reality, Glavis's superiors had concluded that the evidence already gathered by Glavis proved the Cunningham claims were fraudulent and saw no reason for further investigation. Glavis's charges surfaced in a report, signed by Glavis but prepared in the Forest Service, submitted directly to the president by Glavis with a cover letter from Pinchot. The president authorized Ballinger to dismiss Glavis and in September exonerated Ballinger of the charges. The letter of exoneration was based on information in a memorandum prepared by a lawyer in Ballinger's own office. At that point writers in the Forest Service helped Glavis prepare an article, based on the report, published in November 1909 in *Collier's Weekly* entitled "The Whitewashing of Ballinger." The Glavis charges first emerged shortly after Taft signed the Payne-Aldrich Tariff into law and were quickly taken up by insurgent Republicans, who were ready-made allies for the disillusioned Pinchot. Shortly after the Glavis article appeared, Pinchot publicly criticized the president's decision to exonerate Ballinger and was sacked by Taft. Pinchot had deliberately engineered his own dismissal to pave the way for a congressional investigation. His access to President Roosevelt was the foundation of his great influence in conservation matters. He had rolled the dice to retain the same influence with Roosevelt's successor and lost. Now he threw in his lot with the insurgents and took his case to the public.

What the newspapers were now calling the Ballinger-Pinchot controversy was investigated in the spring by a joint committee of Congress under the chairmanship of Senator Knute Nelson of Minnesota. The hearings quickly became an inquest into the conservation policies of the Taft administration and, for his critics, the first step toward denying Taft renomination in 1912. Voting along strict party lines, the committee exonerated Ballinger again, but it was a cold victory: Pinchot had won the battle for public opinion, and, thanks largely to the clever tactics of Louis D. Brandeis, representing *Collier's Weekly* and Glavis, Ballinger's reputation was tarnished. Although actual charges against Ballinger of malfeasance and criminal activity remained unproved and on the record appear to be untrue, for Pinchot this was immaterial. His main goals were attained: to successfully portray Ballinger as an opponent of the Roosevelt conservation policies and Taft as an apostate who had turned on Roosevelt, his friend, benefactor, and patron. Perhaps the most important person who accepted this interpretation was Roosevelt. Thus the controversy contributed to the split in the Republican party in 1912 and the election of Woodrow Wilson.

Although now a political liability, Ballinger hung onto his office for another year. In March 1911 he asked to be relieved because of ill health. He returned to Seattle and resumed his law practice. He died in Seattle, never reconciled to the damage done to his cherished reputation for rectitude.

• Material on Ballinger's early life and his professional and public life is in the Ballinger papers in the University of Washington Library in Seattle. Of the numerous studies of the controversy with Pinchot, most take the side of Pinchot. An exception is an official inquiry launched by Secretary of the Interior Harold Ickes, who in the 1930s was involved in a controversy of his own with Pinchot. See Ickes, *Not Guilty: An Official Inquiry into the Charges Made by Glavis and Pinchot against Richard A. Ballinger, Secretary of the Interior, 1909–1911* (1940) and "Not Guilty! Richard A. Ballinger," *Saturday Evening Post*, 25 May 1940. For Pinchot's side see his autobiography, *Breaking New Ground* (1947). A book-length study is James Penick, *Progressive Politics and Conservation: The Ballinger-Pinchot Affair* (1968). An obituary is in the *New York Times*, 7 June 1922.

JAMES L. PENICK

BALLOU, Adin (23 Apr. 1803–5 Aug. 1890), Universalist clergyman, reformer, and founder of Hopedale Community, was born in Cumberland, Rhode Island, the son of Ariel Ballou and Edilda Tower, farmers. A largely self-educated preacher, Ballou's earliest religious experience was Calvinist in nature, and he later recalled the "very solemnizing effect" of the preaching he heard as a youth. At about age eleven, however, Ballou experienced a religious conversion, and a year later he was baptized into a Christian Connection church that emphasized a more enthusiastic and fundamentalist religiosity. Ballou developed a deep interest in religious matters over the next several years and eventually became a self-proclaimed preacher. At age eighteen, in the autumn of 1821, he was received into the fellowship of the Connecticut Christian Conference, a Christian Connection body. In 1822 he married Abigail Sayles; they had two children before Abigail died in 1829.

While enjoying success in his calling, Ballou questioned whether the Christian Connection's doctrine of destructionism, "the final doom of the impenitent wicked," was really taught in the Bible. He believed in the universal restoration of mankind, leading to his conversion, in 1822, to the Universalist faith. However, by 1830 Ballou was becoming uncomfortable with the "ultra-Universalist" position, maintained most notably by his distant relative Hosea Ballou, that no punishment would follow death. Adin Ballou asserted his alignment with the "Restorationists," who held that a purgatorial process would precede the restoration of sinners into the grace of God. In the same year he joined the Providence Association of Restorationists and agreed to edit and publish the *Independent Messenger* (1831–1839), which expressed their views. Shortly after assuming this position Ballou was dismissed from his pulpit in Milford, Massachusetts. He migrated to nearby Mendon, where he began an eleven-year ministry. In 1830 he married Lucy Hunt; they had two children. In 1831 Ballou, seven other ministers, and several laymen formed the Massachusetts Association of Universal Restorationists.

Over the next several years Ballou became increasingly concerned with the various social ills that were plaguing American society. Foremost among these were slavery, intemperance, and war. Convinced that slavery was "an awful crime against humanity and sin against God" (Staples, p. 13), he gave his first antislavery sermon on the Fourth of July 1837. The topic of abolition was a very controversial one at the time, and as Ballou persisted in raising the subject in his sermons, he found that "the unanimity of my parishioners in my favor, so emphatically declared within a year, vanished in a moment" (Ballou, *Autobiography*, p. 282). Following his declaration of abolitionist sentiment, he became interested in the peace movement. In

1838 he established contact with William Lloyd Garrison, who formed the New England Non-Resistance Society. The Garrisonians not only maintained a pacifist/nonresistance platform but also a "no government" position, which held that human governments do not serve the best interests of mankind. Ballou's increasing association with radical reformers strained his relationship with fellow Restorationists. He summarized his new views in *The Standard of Practical Christianity* (1839), wherein he advocated withdrawing from "all interference with the governments of this world." He exhorted his adherents not to vote, take part in politics, serve in the military, seek redress in the courts, or petition the legislature. On the positive side, *The Standard* encouraged all Christians "to be perfect as our Father in heaven is perfect, in all possible respects" (Ballou, *Autobiography*, p. 313). Ballou's practical social application of the Christian faith was expressed in his greatest achievement, the founding of Hopedale, which was to be the ideal community.

The Massachusetts Association of Universal Restorationists dissolved in 1841, and in January of the following year the first meeting of the Hopedale Community was held in Ballou's Mendon home. Hopedale, the first of the utopian communities founded in the decade of the 1940s (others included Brook Farm, Fruitlands, the Northampton Association, and the Oneida Community), was designed to put into effect the principles stated in Ballou's book, including "abhorrence of war, slavery, intemperance, licentiousness, covetousness, and worldly ambitions in all their forms" (Ballou, *Autobiography*, p. 311). Twenty-eight individuals began the experiment in April 1842 on 250 acres in the town of Milford, Massachusetts. The social organization of Hopedale placed a stronger emphasis on the individual than most communitarian experiments. As it evolved, members were allowed to buy individual lots upon which to build their dwellings and even to conduct business and maintain employment outside the community.

Initially, Hopedale Community flourished. Enterprises included the manufacture of hats, boxes, and shoes; painting and glazing facilities; tin works; sheet ironworks; farming; and building. Eventually, however, problems began to develop. In 1846 the community experienced a substantial financial decline and failed to make a profit as productivity fell off. A new and greatly simplified constitution was adopted on 17 July 1847 with the hope of emphasizing the spiritual aspects of the enterprise while de-emphasizing the worldly structure of it. The next several years saw a continuous effort to maintain financial solvency and to hold in balance the contending demands of individualism and community. Throughout this time Ballou published the *Practical Christian*, a bimonthly paper that served as an outlet for the expression of his reformist views.

In early 1856, with the community's membership at 110, financial reports showed that the organization was substantially in debt. Shortly after this, Ebenezer Draper and George Draper, who jointly owned three-fourths of the community's stock, withdrew to establish the Hopedale Manufacturing Company, which became very successful. Unfortunately, this was the death knell of the Hopedale Community. It continued largely as a religious organization until 1867, when Ballou founded the Hopedale Parish, which in the following year was admitted to the Worcester Conference of Congregational (Unitarian) and Other Christian Societies. Ballou remained pastor of this group until 1880. He died in Milford, Massachusetts.

Hopedale was among the most notable of all the communitarian experiments in terms of longevity and the comprehensive nature of the reforms pursued there. Ballou remained ever faithful to his basic beliefs. His writings on nonresistance were an influence on Leo Tolstoy and, according to some, Mohandas Gandhi. Overall, Ballou stands as an apt representation of that dramatic time in American social history that Henry Steele Commager so appropriately referred to as the "era of reform."

• Ballou's major works are *Non-Resistance in Relation to Human Governments* (1839), *Practical Christian Socialism* (1854), *Primitive Christianity and Its Corruptions* (1870), *Autobiography of Adin Ballou: 1803–1890* (1896), and *History of the Hopedale Community* (1897). See also Ballou, ed. and comp., *An Elaborate History and Genealogy of the Ballous in America* (1888). Writings about Ballou include C. A. Staples, *In Memoriam: Rev. Adin Ballou* (1890); Barbara L. Faulkner, "Adin Ballou and the Hopedale Community" (Ph.D. diss., Boston Univ., 1965); and Christopher W. Gregory, "Perpetual Purification and Developing Sense of Self: The Evolving Theology and Person of Adin Ballou" (Ph.D. diss., St. Louis Univ., 1990). Useful discussions are in Alice Felt Tyler, *Freedom's Ferment* (1944); David Robinson, *The Unitarians and Universalists* (1985); and Peter Brock, *Freedom from War: Nonsectarian Pacifism, 1814–1914* (1991). See also David M. Coffey, "The Hopedale Community," *Historical Journal of Western Massachusetts* 4, no. 1 (1975): 16–26. Richard M. Rollins, "Adin Ballou and the Perfectionist's Dilemma," *Journal of Church and State* 17 (1975): 459–76; and Linck Johnson, "Reforming the Reformers: Emerson, Thoreau, and the Sunday Lectures at Amory Hall, Boston," *ESQ* 37 (1992): 235–89.

LEN GOUGEON

BALLOU, Hosea (30 Apr. 1771–7 June 1852), theologian and clergyman, was born in Richmond, New Hampshire, the son of Maturin Ballou, a farmer and unpaid Baptist minister, and Lydia Harris, who came from a Rhode Island Quaker family and died when her son was two years old. Growing up in extreme poverty, Ballou had less than three years of formal schooling. A few months before his nineteenth birthday, he came forward in a revival meeting and joined his father's church. But before the year was over Ballou's interest in religion had led him to become a Universalist. Moving in with an older brother who was already a Universalist minister, Ballou prepared himself to teach and preach by attending first a community school and then a nearby academy. Despite the fact that his friends, after hearing his first sermon, delivered in 1791, doubted his "talent for such labor," Ballou preached wherever he found an open door. The next year he determined to make the ministry his career even though he had to support himself by teaching. In 1793 he went to the first of the nearly fifty New England Universalist conventions he would attend, and by the next year's session he had so impressed his colleagues that they spontaneously ordained him. In 1796 Ballou moved to Dana, Massachusetts, and in September of that year he married Ruth Washburn; they had nine children.

In addition to ministering to churches primarily in Massachusetts and Vermont (where he and his family moved in 1803), Ballou participated wholeheartedly in Universalist doctrinal controversies. His theology and original thinking shaped Universalist doctrine, particularly in three areas: its transition from a trinitarian to a unitarian belief in the nature of God, its belief that all sins would be punished on earth, and its new perspective on the doctrine of the atonement. Fitting these ideas together, Ballou gave Universalist theology more coherence.

Ballou early published two works, *Notes on the Parables* (1804), in which he stressed that one should not attempt to gain eternal life through legal righteousness, and *A Treatise on Atonement* (1805), his most influential work. In *Treatise*, he rethought the theology that John Murray, the chief founder of American Universalism, had derived from the English preacher James Relly. Rejecting the doctrine of vicarious atonement (or substitutionary sacrifice, in which Christ suffered on the cross to atone for the sins of humanity), Ballou insisted that "every sinner must bear the penalty of his own disobedience" (Allen and Eddy, p. 435) and that Christ suffered to show human beings the way to God's love. Yet Ballou believed that rather than "a wrathful deity seeking justice," God was "full of infinite love" given to all, "not reserved for a select few" (Miller, vol. 1, p. 104). John Coleman Adams, who wrote the introduction to *Treatise*'s fourteenth edition in 1902, called it "one of the great books on American theology" and "the first American book to anticipate all the essential points of . . . liberal theology" (Miller, vol. 2, p. 865).

Ballou was unable to find scriptural justification for the doctrine of the Trinity, so he rejected it and embraced unitarianism. Christ, he insisted, was not co-equal with God but was God's representative to the world. Ballou spiced his reasoning with a little humor, declaring, "If the Godhead consists of *three distinct* persons, and each of those *persons* is *infinite*, the *whole Godhead* amounts to the amazing sum of infinity, multiplied by three!" (Miller, vol. 1, p. 105). By 1805 Ballou's acceptance of unitarianism, like his view of the atonement, had "pervaded the Universalist ministry, with but few exceptions" (Miller, vol. 1, p. 105). One of these exceptions was Murray, whose Boston pulpit Ballou filled for ten Sundays in 1798. On Ballou's last Sunday, when he rose to give notice of the closing hymn, an announcement, instigated by Judith Sargent Murray, the minister's wife, rang out from the choir loft: "The doctrine which has been preached here this

afternoon is not the doctrine which is usually preached in this house" (Eddy, vol. 1, p. 509). Chagrined at the rudeness of this announcement and wanting to hear more of Ballou's revisionist preaching, some members of Murray's congregation offered to start a second Universalist church in Boston if Ballou would move there. But he discouraged them, saying, "I cannot do anything to injure Brother Murray, nor the beloved society to which he ministers" (Eddy, vol. 1, p. 511).

From 1809 until 1815 Ballou—who supported the War of 1812 despite its unpopularity in New England—preached and operated, with his grandnephew Hosea Ballou II, a small school in Portsmouth, New Hampshire. He also continued his religious controversies. "So addicted" was he "to the argumentative," a contemporary noted, "that even his prayers" were "characterized by it" (Miller, vol. 1, p. 103). After a brief stay in Salem, Massachusetts, on Christmas Day 1817, Ballou became the first pastor of the School Street Church, the newly formed Second Society of Universalists in Boston. Nearly two decades after he had first been urged to come to Boston, he settled and remained there for the rest of his life. While in Boston he engaged in frequent preaching tours, continued his writing, and became his denomination's "oracle, very nearly its pope" (Miller, vol. 1, p. 182).

In 1819 Ballou became the first editor of the *Universalist Magazine*, which became the leading denominational newspaper. In 1830, with his grandnephew Hosea Ballou, he edited the scholarly journal *Universalist Expositor*, which later was renamed the *Universalist Quarterly and General Review*. In 1834 Ballou published another major work, *An Examination of the Doctrine of Future Retribution*, which was partly an outgrowth of the Restorationist Controversy, a theological argument over whether there would be future punishment as Calvinists and the founders of Universalism had believed. After being ambivalent on the subject in 1817 and 1818, Ballou, who was one of the first Universalists to discuss the controversy formally, later said there would be no future punishment, then decided there would be a time when "the impenitent will be miserable," and finally, reverting to his former opinion, came down firmly against "any belief in punishment in a future state" (Miller, vol. 1, p. 113). Although some of Ballou's colleagues with Calvinist leanings threatened to leave the church over the controversy and used the unpleasantness surrounding it to challenge his dominant position in the church, nearly all Universalists by 1827 agreed with him that the idea of future punishment was repellent.

Called Father Ballou and very much the elder statesman of his denomination, he died in Boston. His influence, fellow Universalists maintained, was "greater on the religious mind than that of any other clergyman of the age" (Miller, vol. 1, p. 103). As a self-taught man whose writings lacked polish and whose sermons were "always and entirely argumentative," his great influence is remarkable (Miller, vol. 1, p. 103). By holding fast to truth, as he saw it, Ballou gave Universalism an undergirding it had previously lacked. For him, "truth—plain, simple, and una-dorned"—constituted "the all and the everything" (Miller, vol. 1, p. 103).

• A few of Ballou's sermons, addresses, and tracts as well as a number of the periodicals he edited are in the Massachusetts Historical Society, Boston. Some of his letters, a sermon workbook (1848), and other unpublished material is at Harvard Divinity School. For a description of these items, see Alan Seaburg, "The Universalist Collection at Andover-Harvard," *Harvard Library Bulletin* (1980): 452. Although he kept no journal and wrote no autobiography, some of Ballou's reminiscences are recorded in Maturin Murray Ballou, *Biography of Hosea Ballou by His Youngest Son* (1853), and by his former ministerial student Thomas Whittemore in *Modern History of Universalism* (1830). See also Whittemore's most detailed study, *Life of Rev. Hosea Ballou, with Accounts of His Writings, and Biographical Sketches of His Seniors and Contemporaries in the Universalist Ministry* (4 vols., 1854–1855). Other useful sources include Ernest Cassara's two books, *Hosea Ballou: The Challenge to Orthodoxy* (1961) and *Hosea Ballou and the Rise of American Religious Liberalism* (1958); Russell E. Miller, *The Larger Hope: The First Century of the Universalist Church in America, 1770–1870* (2 vols., 1971–1985); Joseph Henry Allen and Richard Eddy, *A History of the Unitarians and the Universalists in the United States* (1894, vol. 10 in the American Church History Series); and Richard Eddy, *Universalism in America: A History* (2 vols., 1886).

OLIVE HOOGENBOOM

BALLOU, Hosea, 2d (18 Oct. 1796–27 May 1861), Universalist minister and educator, was born in Guilford, Vermont, the son of Asahel Ballou and Martha Starr, farmers. His parents were hard-working, frugal, intelligent, and affectionate people, and these values shaped his personality.

Ballou's limited formal education scarcely satisfied his passion for learning, but he mastered Latin with the help of a neighboring minister and also became proficient in Greek, French, German, and Hebrew. At fifteen he worked briefly as a schoolteacher in the nearby town of Marlboro. His parents considered sending him to college but, as Universalists, were suspicious of the New England colleges, which they felt were controlled by Congregationalists and so kept him at home.

In 1813 Ballou's great-uncle, also named Hosea Ballou, invited him to assist at his private school at Portsmouth, New Hampshire. The elder Ballou was also a Universalist minister and author of the influential book on Universalist theology, *A Treatise on Atonement* (1805). Accepting the offer because he had decided to become a minister, Ballou was both able to be trained by his great-uncle and support himself. To avoid confusion with his relative he added "2d" to his name.

Ballou's ministerial career spanned three decades. His happiest and most productive pastorates were at Roxbury (1821–1838) and Medford (1838–1853), both in Massachusetts. In 1820 he married Clarissa Hatch, a childhood friend. They had seven children.

Ballou soon became an able denominational leader. He helped to organize in 1834 the Universalist Histori-cal Society and was its first president. His early interest in scholarship never waned. He wrote more than one hundred essays and several books—the most important, *Ancient History of Universalism* (1829), traced the idea of "universal salvation" from the first to the sixteenth century. He also co-edited two Universalist journals and, as the founding editor of the *Universalist Quarterly and General Review*, created the most respected of the denomination's scholarly publications.

In 1852 the Universalists, after years of wrangling, established Tufts College and chose Ballou as president, a post he held until his death at the president's house in Medford just a few days before the fifth commencement exercises. His wide-ranging activities—from fundraising to collecting library materials, from administrative routine to teaching moral science, political economy, and intellectual philosophy—enabled Tufts, an early effort at sectarian collegiate education, to take root.

Hosea Ballou 2d was the first Universalist educator and scholar to be nationally recognized and respected. His work at Tufts and his scholarship earned him two honorary degrees from Harvard College (an A.M. and S.T.D.), election to its board of overseers, and appointment by the Massachusetts General Court to the State Board of Education. The *Boston Evening Transcript*, assessing his career, said, "Dr. Ballou was probably the most learned theologian in the ranks of self-educated men in our country."

• The chief repository for Ballou manuscripts is the archives of Tufts University located in its Wessell Library. See especially the Trustee and Trustee Executive Committee minutes (1851–1861). Almost 1,600 volumes from his personal library, many of them extensively annotated in the language in which they were written, became a part of the Tufts Library shortly after his death. Additional papers (thirteen boxes), once a part of the library of the Universalist Historical Society, are in the Andover-Harvard Theological Library of the Harvard Divinity School. These include sermons (1816–1861), two chronological record books of sermons preached (1816–1855), and correspondence (1826–1861). The standard biography is Hosea Starr Ballou, *Hosea Ballou, 2nd, D.D., First President of Tufts College: His Origin, Life, and Letters* (1896). Although written by his nephew, it is nevertheless a comprehensive account but needs to be supplemented by Russell Miller, "Hosea Ballou 2d: Scholar and Educator," *Annual Journal of the Universalist Historical Society* 1 (1959): 59–79. See also Russell Miller's history of Tufts University, *Light on the Hill* (1966), and his exhaustive study of American Universalism, *The Larger Hope* (1979).

ALAN SEABURG

BALLOU, Maturin Murray (14 Apr. 1820–27 Mar. 1895), writer, editor, and publisher, was born in Boston, Massachusetts, the son of Rev. Hosea Ballou and Ruth Washburn. His father was a distinguished Universalist minister and the author of more than 100 books. Ballou attended Boston's English High School and, as a teenager, contributed travel sketches and other pieces to his cousin Hosea Ballou's religious magazines. In 1838 he published a piece in the *Olive Branch*, a weekly family story paper. Although he passed his entrance examination to Harvard, ill health forced him to withdraw. He became a clerk in the Boston post office and in September 1839 married Mary Anne Roberts. They had one child.

For health reasons Ballou and his wife traveled widely, particularly in the Caribbean. In 1843 he was employed in the Boston Custom House. His job as deputy navy agent supplied him with much practical information that he later used in his nautical adventure stories.

In 1845 Ballou proposed to Frederick Gleason, a struggling printer, that they mass distribute simple melodramatic adventure stories. Under the pen name "Lieutenant Murray," Ballou had already written *Fanny Campbell; or, The Female Pirate Captain* for a New York publisher: it sold 80,000 copies in the first few months. Gleason quickly published Ballou's *Red Rupert; or, The American Buccaneer* and *The Naval Officer; or, The Pirate's Cave* under the name of Lieutenant Murray and *The Protégé of the Grand Duke: A Tale of Italy* and *Albert Simmons; or, The Midshipman's Revenge: A Tale of Land & Sea* under the name "Frank Forester." The pamphlet novels, which sold for 12½ and 25 cents, were enormously successful. Ballou and Gleason formed a publishing house, called at one time or another Gleason's Publishing Hall and the United States Publishing Company, which published the works of J. H. Ingraham, Justin Jones (Harry Hazel), and Ann Stephens as well as additional works by Ballou such as *The Spanish Musketeer: A Tale of Military Life* (1847).

Together Ballou and Gleason, along with their contributors, established the major genres of American pulp fiction, including adventure stories set in exotic locations such as India or Spain, military stories, stories of the West with Indians and rangers, detective stories, spy stories, and tales of the sea. Ballou also wrote juvenile fiction and stories about women (women in harems, sacrificing heroines, women bandits, women as African slaves), virtuous maidens, and hard-working young men. In January 1846 Gleason founded the *Flag of Our Union*, a "bedsheet-sized" weekly family paper, with Ballou as editor. Contributors included Edgar Allan Poe (who called it "not very respectable"), Lydia Sigourney, Park Benjamin, Sylvanus Cobb, Horatio Alger, and E. Z. C. Judson (Ned Buntline). The success of the paper can be seen in the number of imitators—more than nine in Boston alone with names such as *American Union* and *Flag of the Free*. Ballou himself churned out serial after serial, poetry, editorials, and short stories for the paper. To encourage authorship so-called contests were held, but the 1848 contest for a moral tale with a prize of $150 went to "Lieutenant Murray" for a simplistic formulaic tale, *Rosalette; or, The Flower Girl of Paris*, the story of a young noblewoman who disguises herself as a flower girl to meet a heroic artisan.

Ballou's chief distinction in journalism was his founding, with Gleason, and editing of one of the earliest illustrated papers in America, *Gleason's Pictorial Drawing-Room Companion*, in 1851. Ballou hired the engraver Henry Carter (later known as Frank Leslie), who had worked for the *Illustrated London News* and had recently arrived in America. The *Pictorial*, a weekly of sixteen pages that sold for three dollars a year, had ample illustrations of foreign and American travel scenes, public figures, new buildings, natural history, and nautical and military camp scenes. Often Leslie's engravings came first, with the accompanying stories written afterwards. Ballou wrote travel series and moral essays on the editorial page. Unlike other periodicals, the *Pictorial* used no pirated works of English authors: its contributors, such as Ben Perley Poore and Caroline Orne, were all Americans.

Leslie left in 1853 to found his own rival periodicals in New York. By 1854 Ballou began outmaneuvering his partner Gleason for control of the firm. He threatened to start two competitive weeklies if Gleason did not sell his shares. Gleason announced his retirement but went on to found *Gleason's Monthly Companion* in 1872 and later died in a home for the indigent. Ballou installed a new assistant editor, began to use better paper, and housed the business in a new building. Circulation, however, lagged. Ballou tried a never-before-used expedient, inserting advertising, but quit when readers complained. He stopped publication in December 1859.

Meanwhile, in 1855, Ballou had founded America's first monthly devoted largely to fiction, *Ballou's Dollar Monthly*, to compete with Robert Bonner's *New York Ledger*. The *Monthly*, a hundred-page quarto, was advertised as "the cheapest paper in the world" and contained melodramatic adventure as well as didactic moralizing. With profits from the *Monthly*, in 1857 Ballou launched the *Weekly Novelette*, which has been said to have inspired Erastus Beadle to invent the dime novel. Only thirteen numbers of the magazine were published. In 1860 Ballou tried another pictorial, the *Welcome Guest*, which also failed. After a series of setbacks, in 1863 he sold the publishing house to his business manager's new firm, Elliott, Thomes & Talbot.

In addition to his journalistic pursuits, Ballou engaged in numerous business enterprises, including the building of the St. James Hotel in the south end of Boston. At the time of its construction, it was one of the most costly structures in Boston; later, under the name Franklin Square House, it became a boarding house for working women. Ballou also built and owned three of the largest dry goods stores in Boston and buildings, including his offices, on Winter Street.

In February 1872 Ballou; his only child Murray, president of the new Boston Stock Exchange; and other wealthy investors formed the *Boston Globe* with Ballou serving as editor and manager. In his "salutatory" editorial, Ballou promised that the *Globe* would be devoted to the "intelligent and dignified" discussion of politics and social ethics. The paper immediately began losing money—the city was oversupplied with newspapers competing for advertising—and subscribership never rose to more than 5,000. In June Ballou resigned as editor; in August Charles H. Taylor took over as editor and manager and dramatically changed the paper's appearance and substance from semiliterary to sensational. In September Ballou, again experiencing health problems, sold his shares and severed his ties to the *Globe*.

In 1879 Ballou again entered the periodical business with *Boston Budget*, a Sunday paper that lasted until 1918, and *Ballou's Magazine*, a fifteen-cent miscellany that lasted almost until his death.

Ballou traveled extensively throughout his life, journeying through the Americas, Africa, China, India, Japan, and the Pacific Islands. In 1882 he circumnavigated the globe and in 1886 voyaged to the polar regions. He wrote about his experiences in numerous travel books, including *Due West; or Round the World in Ten Months* (1884); *Due South; or Cuba Past and Present* (1885); *Under the Southern Cross; or Travels in Australia, Tasmania, New Zealand, Samoa and Other Pacific Islands* (1887); and *Due North; or, Glimpses of Scandinavia and Russia* (1887). Although better written than his fiction, Ballou's travel writing resembles much of his earlier work. In *Due South*, for example, he refers to Columbus's journals and moralizes about Spain's loss of empire: "Spain met the just fate clearly menaced by the Scriptures to those who smite with the sword." Intermingled among the historical details and didacticism are sensationalized stories of Confederate blockade runners, orgies, voodoo, and corpses that are buried at sea and land upright in coral. Ballou describes phosphorescent jellyfish, sunsets, and turtle hunting but touches lightly on each subject rather than closely investigating. A reviewer in *Nation* said of his writing: "Mr. Ballou can tell a fairly interesting story of personal observations and experiences, but he is not a writer to pin one's faith to in matters of solid information." Ballou died in Cairo, Egypt.

• In addition to numerous works of fiction published under the pen name Lieutenant Murray, Ballou published under his own name a biography, *Life-Story of Hosea Ballou, for the Young* (1854); a play, *Miralda; or, The Justice of Tacon: A Drama, in Three Acts* (1858); and eight travel books: *History of Cuba; or, Notes of a Traveller in the Tropics: Being a Political, Historical, and Statistical Account of the Island, from Its First Discovery to the Present Time* (1854), *Genius in Sunshine and Shadow* (1887), *Foot-Prints of Travel; or, Journeyings in Many Lands* (1888), *The New Eldorado: A Summer Journey to Alaska* (1889), *Aztec Land: Central America, the West Indies and South America* (1890), *Equatorial America: Descriptive of a Visit to St. Thomas, Martinique, Barbadoes, and the Principal Capitals of South America* (1892), *The Story of Malta* (1893), and *The Pearl of India* (1894). He also compiled *Treasury of Thought: Forming an Encyclopaedia of Quotations from Ancient and Modern Authors* (1872), *Pearls of Thought* (1881), *Notable Thoughts about Women: A Literary Mosaic* (1882), and *Edge-Tools of Speech* (1886).

Biographical information about Ballou and his family can be found in Adin Ballou's *An Elaborate History and Genealogy of the Ballous in America* (1888). Peter Benson has articles on "Maturin Murray Ballou" and "Gleason's Publishing Hall," in *Publishers for Mass Entertainment in Nineteenth Century America*, ed. Madeleine B. Stern (1980). Ballou's founding of the *Boston Globe* is described in Louis M. Lyons, *Newspaper Story: One Hundred Years of the Boston Globe* (1971). Ballou's periodical and fictional work are evaluated in Frank Luther Mott's *A History of American Magazines*, vol. 2 (5 vols., 1938–1968); Mary Noel's *Villains Galore: The Heyday of the Popular Story Weekly* (1954); and Madeleine B. Stern's *Imprints on History* (1956). An obituary is in the *Boston Globe*, 29 Mar. 1895.

ANN W. ENGAR

BALTIMORE, First Lord. *See* Calvert, George.

BAMBACE, Angela (14 Feb. 1898–3 Apr. 1975), labor organizer, was born in Santos, Brazil, the daughter of Antonio Bambace, a shipping company operator, and Giuseppina Calabrese. Antonio's failing health precipitated the family's return to Italy. In 1901 they emigrated to the United States, where they settled in New York City's East Harlem. Due to Antonio's ill health, Giuseppina supported the family by working in a ladies hat factory.

Upon completion of high school, Angela and her sister Maria worked in the garment industry, an occupation pursued by many Italian American women. They soon joined the ranks of union organizers for the International Ladies Garment Workers' Union (ILGWU), demanding better working conditions and fair wages. Their bilingual skills enhanced their efforts to convince Italian fathers to allow their daughters to join the union.

Angela Bambace married Romolo Camponeschi, her father's choice for her husband, in 1919. They had two children. She remained at home to care for their children until 1925 when her need to further the cause of social justice served as a catalyst for her to rejoin the labor movement in the midst of an unsuccessful attempt by communist elements to take over control of the ILGWU. The effort failed, but Bambace had made a decision. She not only supported the dissidents but also joined the Communist party, which seemed to embody the politics and activism of her closest friends in the union, Jewish radicals Clara Larson and Charles and Rose Zimmerman.

Bambace's concern with social justice also attracted her to support the cause to free the Italian anarchists Sacco and Vanzetti, imprisoned in Massachusetts. At a meeting she met Italian anarchist Luigi Quintilliano, who became her companion. Camponeschi, who did not share his wife's radical views, sued for divorce and won custody of their children by accusing her of being an unfit mother. She resumed her maiden name and bought a home in Flushing, New York, where she lived with her mother. She maintained close ties with her children for the remainder of her life.

Leaving the Communist party in 1929 after the Zimmermans were expelled as Lovestonites, Bambace continued working as an organizer for both the ILGWU and the Amalgamated Clothing Workers of America. Her efforts brought her closer to the leading Italian and Jewish union activists of the period. Embracing the New Deal policies of President Franklin D. Roosevelt, she supported his legislation to regulate industrial working conditions.

In 1934 Bambace went to Baltimore on a temporary assignment made by ILGWU president David Dubinsky. There male union members (many of them Italian American), had opposed efforts to open union ranks to women. Moving quickly and decisively, Bambace organized that city's first all women's local.

Actively supporting candidates with strong prolabor planks, such as Baltimore's representative in Congress, Thomas D'Alessandro, she opposed efforts by manufacturers to escape regulation by National Recovery Administration codes. D'Alessandro appreciated Bambace's help in his reelection bid. She also expanded the organizing activities of the ILGWU into small communities where "runaway" shops had relocated in order to avoid union influence.

Remaining in Baltimore, Bambace turned her attention to the dress and cotton shops with large numbers of women workers. As assistant manager of the ILGWU's Maryland Department, she also conducted organizing drives in outlying districts. In her personal life, she was able to bring her sons closer to her when they attended colleges in Maryland.

Bambace's responsibilities grew during World War II with the stimulation of cotton garment production in Virginia, West Virginia, and southern Pennsylvania. In 1942 she was appointed manager of the ILGWU's newly created Maryland-Virginia District. From her Baltimore office, she remained in close contact with union organizers in the field, struggling against the prejudices encountered in the Upper South—especially the anti-Semitism expressed toward the largely Jewish union leadership and field organizers and the racism directed against black members.

Bambace's success in extending union influence into unorganized areas prompted ILGWU leaders to name her district manager of the newly established Upper South Department in 1947. In 1956 she helped to organize an outpatient medical clinic for union members and the following year helped establish a pension fund. In recognition of her contributions, Bambace was elected a vice president of the ILGWU's general executive board in 1956. She was chosen to fill the spot vacated by the retirement of Salvatore Ninfo. Some suggested that she moved into an "Italian slot." Bambace was the first non-Jewish woman to hold the post, her selection reflecting the expanding role of Italians in the union.

Bambace's service extended beyond union concerns to wider community issues. She participated in war relief programs, Histradut (the Zionist labor movement), the Italian American Labor Council, Americans for Democratic Action, and the American Civil Liberties Union. In 1962 President John F. Kennedy appointed her to the Commission on the Status of Women. She retired from her post as a vice president of the ILGWU in 1972 but continued to champion the causes of labor and social justice. She died in Baltimore.

• Bambace's papers, including some personal correspondence, photographs, and clippings on her career, are at the Immigration History Research Center, University of Minnesota. Records beginning around 1939 for the Upper South Department of the ILGWU are at the union's archives in New York City. The most complete review of Bambace's career can be found in Jean (Vincenza) Scarpaci, "Angela Bambace and the International Ladies Garment Workers' Union: The Search for an Elusive Activist," in *Pane e Lavoro: The Italian American Working Class*, ed. George Pozzetta (1980). See also Salvatore Amico, *Gli Italiani e l'Internazionale dei Sarti da Donna* (1944); Marianne Alexander, "Angela Bambace, 1898–1975: Labor Organizer," in *Notable Maryland Women*, ed. Winifred Helms (1977); and A. D. Glushakow, *A Pictorial History of Maryland Jewry* (1955). An obituary is in the Baltimore *Sun*, 4 Apr. 1975.

VINCENZA SCARPACI

BAMBERGER, Louis (15 May 1855–11 Mar. 1944), merchant and philanthropist, was born in Baltimore, Maryland, the son of Elkan Bamberger, a wholesale notions merchant, and Theresa Hutzler. Bamberger attended public school in Baltimore until he quit at fourteen to become a $4-a-week clerk and errand boy in his uncles' dry-goods store, Hutzler Brothers. After two years he joined his brother Julius to work for their father, buying E. Bamberger & Company when their father retired in the mid-1870s. Leaving the position as business manager, Louis Bamberger relocated to New York City in 1887 to accumulate capital for his own retail business while working as a buyer for West Coast wholesalers.

Seeking a city with commercial potential for his new venture, Bamberger chose Newark, New Jersey. He carefully studied its layout, traffic patterns, and shopping habits. In a rare interview Bamberger explained his method:

For some time unknown to me there has been a tale current that I came over here to take care of a bankrupt stock I had bought and, finding it profitable, stayed. The truth is that I had been waiting for a location in Newark for two years, and a part of that time for this very location. I had stayed out of business two years to get just what I needed to go into business. The first thing to do was to get capital, a location, and people to work with me, the last being as essential as the two others. I had seen too many men fail because they would not wait for capital, for a location, or for that most important thing of all, business associates who could be trusted. (*American Magazine*, June 1923, pp. 72–73, 121–22)

In 1892, when Hill & Craig went bankrupt in the building of his choice, Bamberger and his partners opened L. Bamberger & Company with a bankrupt sale, adding new stock within a week.

The trio of partners, Louis Bamberger, Louis M. Frank, and Felix Fuld, brought their individual and complementary strengths to the business. Bamberger also brought $45,000 and the ethics that built customer, employee, and supplier loyalty. Frank, married to Bamberger's sister Caroline, invested borrowed money and applied his merchandising skills. Fuld contributed $25,000 and a dynamic sales and advertising ability. Caroline Frank kept house for her husband and his two bachelor partners on a commonly owned small estate in South Orange, New Jersey. After Frank's death in 1910 she married Fuld.

After studying successful retail businesses, Bamberger adopted a money-back guarantee, "because . . . this seemed to me the only way to convince the customer that I intended to be fair," and innovated price tags on all merchandise. L. Bamberger & Company positioned itself at the forefront of Newark's department stores, earning a reputation as "one of America's great stores." For his employees Bamberger provided a cafeteria, a branch of the Newark Public Library in the store, merchandising classes, and a commission in addition to a regular salary.

Bamberger and Fuld, the day-to-day manager, ran the company after Frank died. But when Fuld, the creative force behind the conservative Bamberger, died suddenly in 1929, Bamberger abruptly sold the company to competitor R. H. Macy & Company. Bamberger, at age seventy-four, believed he was "getting old and I want to be relieved of the active management and responsibility of the business which I founded. When this offer came, coming as it did from such a responsible store, I decided to accept it." From his $25-million profit, Bamberger distributed $1 million, in lieu of a pension plan, among more than 200 employees with fifteen or more years of service. Over thirty-seven years the store had grown to 3,500 employees in a sixteen-story state-of-the-art building. Bamberger continued as chairman of the board until 1939.

Bamberger, long involved in philanthropic work in Newark, planned to devote more time in retirement to his charitable activities. At a meeting of the executive committee of the Newark Museum Association in 1923, Bamberger had said, "I have felt for a long time that, inasmuch as I had made a success of my business in Newark, I owed the city something." He donated $650,000 in 1923–1924 to construct a building for the Newark Museum and later gave valuable artifacts to its permanent collection. The charitable activities of L. Bamberger & Company reflected the concerns of its chairman: music scholarships, underwriting the Newark Community Chest, regional hospitals, and national war bond efforts during World War I. Bamberger's personal largesse extended to local, national, and international Jewish charities, and secular medical, historical, and educational concerns. Among the groups benefiting from Bamberger's donations were the American Jewish Joint Agricultural Corporation, Hebrew University, Young Men's Hebrew Association and Young Women's Hebrew Association, Jewish Theological Seminary of America, and Newark Boy Scouts and Girl Scouts.

Bamberger and his sister, both childless, sought to create an educational facility that would transcend local concerns. With an initial $5 million, an additional $3 million, and bequests in their wills, they created the Institute for Advanced Study in 1930, a postdoctoral research facility based in Princeton, the first of its kind in the United States. Bamberger served as president of its board of trustees until he resigned from active participation in 1934. In her 1988 dissertation, Laura Smith Porter surmised that "for Bamberger the establishment of the Institute was symbolic of both Jewish assimilation and the responsibility of wealth, allowing him to move beyond locally focused Jewish voluntarism to philanthropy that was both national and secular in scope."

Louis Bamberger, a reserved, shy, and formal man, earned a reputation as a kind, fair, and understanding businessman. In addition to serving on the boards of various charitable organizations, he relaxed by playing golf and collecting rare books and manuscripts, including an autograph collection of the signers of the Declaration of Independence, which he donated to the New Jersey Historical Society. Bamberger, who never married, died in his South Orange, New Jersey, home.

• Bamberger Family Papers reside in descendants' private collections. Information on Bamberger's philanthropic work was reported in the *Jewish Chronicle*, the *New York Times*, and *Louis Bamberger, a Record of His Benefactions to His Community and His Country* (Newark Museum, 1934). To understand this shy man's personality, consult Frank I. Liveright's reminiscence, "One of America's Great Stores" (typescript c. 1959, at Newark Public Library), and Helen Christine Bennett's interview with him in "Do the Wise Thing If You Know What It Is—But Anyway Do Something!" *American Magazine*, June 1923. *The Municipalities of Essex County, New Jersey, 1666–1924*, vol. 3 (1925), and *New Jersey, a History: Biographical and Genealogical Records*, vol. 5 (1930), provide biographical information on Bamberger. Chapter two of Laura Smith Porter, "From Intellectual Sanctuary to Social Responsibility: The Founding of the Institute for Advanced Study, 1930–1933" (Ph.D. diss., Princeton Univ., 1988), analyzes Bamberger's creation of the institute as a transcendence of traditional Jewish philanthropy. Obituaries are in *Louis Bamberger, Honorary President of the Newark Museum: A Tribute to His Memory by His Fellow Trustees* (Newark Museum, 1944) and in the *Newark Star-Ledger* and the *New York Times*, 12 Mar. 1944.

SUSAN HAMBURGER

BANCROFT, Aaron (10 Nov. 1755–19 Aug. 1839), Unitarian minister and author, was born in Reading, Massachusetts, the son of Samuel Bancroft, a wealthy and respected landowner, and Lydia Parker. Bancroft spent his early years laboring on his father's large Reading farm. His early desire for higher education and high aptitude for learning convinced his father to send him to college. Enrolling in Harvard in 1774 at the age of nineteen, Bancroft spent the years of the revolutionary war studying for the ministry and abroad serving as a missionary. After graduating with honors in 1778, Bancroft undertook a brief study of theology with Thomas Haven, his boyhood minister. After preaching in various pulpits for a few months, Bancroft made an unusual appeal to the Massachusetts Executive Council: since his country was at war, he asked for permission to perform missionary work in Nova Scotia, Canada. With the approval of the council, Bancroft spent three years preaching to British Canadians.

Upon his return to Massachusetts in 1783, Bancroft sought to become a settled Congregational minister. He received a call to preach several sermons in Worcester, Massachusetts, but because of his growing liberal sentiments, the generally Calvinist congregation decided not to offer him its pastorate. Upon the death of the Worcester minister a year later, Bancroft again preached several sermons to the Worcester congregation. This time several of the most prominent members of the church prevailed upon their associates to make Bancroft their minister. When the town refused to assent to the appointment, the liberals formed their own Second Congregational Church and promptly installed Bancroft as minister. Ordained in February 1786, Bancroft remained the minister for many years, finally retiring in 1827.

Bancroft's long career spanned the turbulent years of doctrinal controversy and schism in Massachusetts Congregationalism. Beginning with the installation of the liberal Henry Ware as Hollis Professor of Divinity at Harvard in 1805, the Unitarian controversy was characterized by a great deal of bitterness and animosity. It ended with the liberals forming their own Unitarian denomination in 1825 and the subsequent formal disestablishment of church and state in 1833. Initially shunned for his liberal sentiments, Bancroft encountered many new opportunities as the liberal Congregational faction grew in strength, even as he regretted the split of the Standing Order of Congregational churches. By 1810, the year in which Harvard bestowed upon him a D.D., the liberals had established themselves for good in Boston and in other towns in eastern Massachusetts. After William Ellery Channing's 1819 Baltimore sermon, Bancroft and the liberals called themselves Unitarians, thus signifying their major doctrinal distinction from their orthodox brethren. Bancroft and his fellow Unitarians insisted that Jesus Christ was not divine. Accordingly, they emphasized Jesus' remarkable moral life as well as his spiritual heroism.

Bancroft's most important public function proved to be his role in the formation of the American Unitarian Association. Instrumental in its initial establishment in Boston in 1825, Bancroft served as its president for over ten years. As a leading Unitarian, Bancroft published numerous works in the course of his career. Among them were many sermons, most of which elaborated the Unitarian preoccupation with the moral teachings of the Bible. They included *A Christmas Sermon on the Doctrine of Immortality* (1818), *A Sermon on the Moral Purposes of Ancient Sacrifices* (1819), *A sermon on the Duties of Parents* (1823), and *A Sermon on the Death of John Adams* (1826). In 1822 Bancroft published his best-known work, *Sermons on the Doctrine of the Gospel*, which his friend John Adams called "a chain of diamonds set in links of gold." In addition to these works, Bancroft published a biography of George Washington, *The Life of Washington*, in 1807; it was reprinted in two volumes in 1826.

Bancroft attained several offices and honors during his long and successful ministerial career. He was elected president of many of the organizations in which he served, including the Society for Promoting Christian Knowledge, the Board of the Leicester Academy, the Worcester Bible Society, and, most importantly, the American Unitarian Association. Bancroft also served for many years on the board of the American Antiquarian Society in Worcester. Additionally, the American Academy of Arts and Sciences elected him a fellow.

Bancroft was much beloved by his congregation and the people of Worcester generally. Upon his retirement from the ministry after fifty years, the Second Congregational Church invited him to give a "farewell" sermon, which the congregation subsequently printed. Bancroft was succeeded by his colleague Alonzo Hill, who also delivered his funeral sermon. Bancroft and his wife, Lucretia Chandler, whom he had married in 1786, had thirteen children. Bancroft died in Worcester only months after the death of his wife, survived by six of his children.

Best known as the father of George Bancroft, the noted American historian, Bancroft also produced a body of professional work and publications that were important in his day and revealed admirably the interests of the Unitarian Congregational church, of which he was a leading member. His writings reflect the Unitarians' movement away from the harsher doctrines of their Calvinist forebears and toward a more rational and strictly moral set of doctrines and beliefs.

• Bancroft's papers, including many of his sermons, are located at the American Antiquarian Society in Worcester, Mass. The Andover-Harvard Divinity Library has the best collection of Bancroft's published sermons. Alonzo Hill, *A Discourse on the Life and Character of the Rev. Aaron Bancroft* (1839), offers a discussion of Bancroft's ministerial career. A short biographical sketch of Bancroft is in William Sprague, *Annals of the American Pulpit* (1865). Information on Bancroft's family history is contained in M. A. De Wolfe Howe, *The Life and Letters of George Bancroft* (1908). See Conrad Wright, ed., *American Unitarianism, 1805–1865* (1989), and Daniel Walker Howe, *The Unitarian Conscience: Harvard Moral Philosophy, 1805–1861* (1970; repr. 1988), for information on the American Unitarian Association.

PETER FIELD

BANCROFT, Cecil Franklin Patch (25 Nov. 1839–4 Oct. 1901), educator, was born in New Ipswich, New Hampshire, the son of James Bancroft and Sarah Kendall. In his early years he developed a close relationship with a Mr. and Mrs. Patch of neighboring Ashby, Massachusetts, who named him after their son who had recently died. The Patches saw to it that the boy received a good education, sending him to Appleton Academy in New Ipswich and then to Dartmouth College in Hanover, where he graduated in 1860, fourth in a class of sixty-five.

After graduation he was employed by Appleton Academy (later McCullom Institute) in Mont Vernon, New Hampshire, and served as principal for four years. He then determined to enter the ministry and in 1864 enrolled at the Union Theological Seminary in

New York City. The following year he transferred to the Andover Theological Seminary, in Massachusetts, where he graduated in 1867, making his first contact with Phillips Academy, also in Andover, by serving as an assistant teacher.

In an effort to heal the wounds of the recently ended Civil War, C. R. Robert, founder of Robert College in Constantinople, Turkey, sought to establish a "loyal Christian New England" school in the South. He chose Lookout Mountain, Tennessee, as the site and Bancroft as the school's principal. Bancroft, in the meantime, had been ordained on 1 May 1867 and one week later had married Frances A. Kittredge, one of his pupils at Appleton Academy. The newlyweds at once set out for Tennessee. However, as northern interest in Reconstruction waned, so did support for the school. In 1872, after five difficult years, the school closed. Bancroft then departed the United States to spend a year in travel and study in Europe. While there he received a telegram from the Phillips Academy trustees offering him the principalship of the school. He accepted and arrived in Andover with his family, which now included two children, in the summer of 1873. He lived in Andover for the rest of his life.

The school that Bancroft was to head was in sorry condition. The curriculum was antiquated, graduates were having difficulty getting into college, and discipline was ragged. The institution was suffering from financial difficulties, with a sizable debt, an unbalanced budget, and almost no endowment. Most important, perhaps, was the high staff turnover; between 1870 and 1875 every position was vacated at least twice. In the course of his principalship, Bancroft was to deal with all of these problems, transforming a static nineteenth-century school into a dynamic twentieth-century one. In so doing, he would set a pattern for the modern American boarding school.

Bancroft determined to make the school's centennial in 1878 the occasion for calling attention to the school's proud past. The celebration would be accompanied by a vigorous fund drive. Those attending the ceremonies included the presidents of Harvard, Yale, and other New England colleges; the governor and other officials of the state; and a number of distinguished alumni, including Oliver Wendell Holmes, of the class of 1825, who read a poem, "The School Boy," that he had composed for the occasion. The celebration accomplished all that Bancroft could have hoped: the school received valuable publicity, an endowment fund was started that soon reached $100,000, and an alumni association was established. Furthermore, the morale of the institution was greatly heightened.

Convinced that the school could not become truly great without a strong faculty, Bancroft set out to build one. Up until his time much of the teaching had been done by underpaid assistants who seldom stayed more than a year. Bancroft sought to attract strong teachers by offering them a chance to help him run the school and determine policy—a far cry from the dictatorships of earlier principals. In this he was eminently successful, with ten of his appointees staying at Andover for more than forty years. Under Bancroft, the faculty meeting, unknown hitherto, became a vital school institution.

Bancroft also realized that the curriculum, weighted heavily toward classical studies, must be modernized if the school was to keep up with its competitors. He wanted to add more science and mathematics and introduce French and German. Up until Bancroft's arrival the curriculum had been determined by the principal alone, with occasional advice from the trustees. Bancroft decided to enlist the help of leading educators from all over the country and sent his curricular proposals to college presidents and other headmasters, asking for their advice. By the end of his term, all the new proposals had been adopted. Bancroft also extended the school's traditional three-year course to four years, introduced written examinations to replace the dreaded oral exams of the past, and made most courses last a full year rather than one term.

Before Bancroft, almost all of the undergraduates had been housed in private homes in the town. Bancroft believed that all students should live on campus under faculty supervision. To achieve this goal he ordered the construction of three cottages and one large dormitory named Bancroft Hall. He also built a new science building to provide facilities for the new science courses. By the end of his term the campus had been physically as well as intellectually transformed.

As a result of the changes between 1875 and 1900, Phillips Academy doubled in size to more than 400 students, the faculty quintupled, and both the institution and its leader built a national reputation. Bancroft was invited to speak on educational matters all over the East. He was above all a "gentle" person, with an engaging sense of humor and a rare ability to get people to work for him and with him. His capacity to work hard and for long hours was remarkable; for example, he had no secretarial help and conducted all the school's business in longhand. Bancroft persevered, and by the time of his death it was clear that he had accomplished his main aim, which was to bring Phillips Academy into harmony with the educational reforms under way in the nation's colleges and generally to prepare the institution to enter the twentieth century.

• The main source for Bancroft is the sixteen boxes of his correspondence and other material in the Phillips Academy Archives. See also Frederick S. Allis, Jr., *Youth from Every Quarter, a Bicentennial History of Phillips Academy, Andover* (1979); Claude M. Fuess, *An Old New England School* (1917); and articles in the *Phillips* (later the *Andover*) *Bulletin*.

FREDERICK S. ALLIS, JR.

BANCROFT, David James (20 Apr. 1892–9 Oct. 1972), baseball player, coach, and manager, was born in Sioux City, Iowa, the son of Frank Bancroft, a Milwaukee Railroad news vendor and truck farmer, and Ella Gearhart. From 1907 to 1909 Bancroft attended Sioux City Central High School, where he played baseball. After moving to Superior, Wisconsin, at age seventeen, he married Edna H. Gisin in 1910. They had no children.

Bancroft's professional baseball career began in 1909, when he played briefly with Duluth, Minnesota, of the Wisconsin-Minnesota League. Duluth released Bancroft after two road series, but he soon became the starting shortstop with Superior of the same league. The light-hitting, 5'9½" 160-pounder was a defensive star for Superior through the 1911 season. From 1912 to 1914 Bancroft played shortstop with Portland, Oregon, of the Pacific Coast League. Teammates nicknamed him both "Dave" and "Beauty," the latter an expression Bancroft often yelled when a hurler threw a fine pitch past him.

Bancroft commenced his major league career in 1915 as the starting shortstop with the Philadelphia Phillies. As a leadoff, switch-hitting rookie, he batted .254 and sparked second-division Philadelphia to its first National League pennant. Bancroft batted .294 in the 1915 World Series, which the Boston Red Sox took four games to one. He played regularly at shortstop with the Phillies until June 1920, helping Philadelphia record second-place finishes in 1916 and 1917. Although consistently hitting below .300, Bancroft excelled at defensive play. The Philadelphia Sports Writers Association in January 1954 named him the Phillies' "all-time outstanding shortstop."

In June 1920 Philadelphia traded Bancroft to the New York Giants for shortstop Art Fletcher, pitcher Wilbur Hubbell, and cash. The Phillies already had plunged to the cellar and begun selling their star players. New York Giants manager John McGraw regarded Bancroft as baseball's "best shortstop" and immediately designated the energetic, intuitive leader as team captain. The trade paid McGraw immediate dividends, as Bancroft had six hits in a June 1920 game against his former Philadelphia teammates. The defensive mainstay led National League shortstops in putouts, assists, and double plays in 1921 and 1922, handling an incredible 984 chances in 1922. His batting average dramatically improved with the Giants, as he surpassed the .300 mark from 1921 through 1923 and attained a career-high .321 in 1922. In one 1921 game, Bancroft hit a single, double, triple, and home run. The Giants won three consecutive National League pennants from 1921 to 1923 and captured the 1921 and 1922 World Series against the New York Yankees. In those World Series, Bancroft threw out several Yankee runners rounding bases too far or attempting to take extra bases. The persistent shortstop seldom missed games with the Giants, even playing an entire 1923 contest with pneumonia. Sportswriter Frank Graham lauded Bancroft as "the greatest shortstop the Giants ever had and one of the greatest that ever lived."

In November 1923 the Giants traded Bancroft and outfielders Casey Stengel and Bill Cunningham to the Boston Braves for pitcher Joe Oeschger and outfielder Billy Southworth. McGraw allegedly traded Bancroft as a favor both to Braves president Christy Mathewson and the 32-year-old shortstop, who wanted to manage. McGraw, however, needed a place in the Giants starting lineup for twenty-year-old infield star Travis Jackson. From 1924 to 1927 Bancroft served as player-manager for Boston. Appendicitis sidelined him for over two months in 1924. He batted over .300 in both 1925 and 1926, but his talent-deficient National League club languished four consecutive seasons in the second division. In October 1927 the Braves dismissed Bancroft as player-manager. His four managerial seasons had produced a lackluster 249–363 win-loss mark. Bancroft spent his final two National League seasons as starting shortstop with the Brooklyn Dodgers.

Bancroft batted .279 during sixteen major league seasons and surpassed the .300 mark in five campaigns. Although lacking power, he utilized his speed to make 320 doubles among his 2,004 lifetime hits. Bancroft, who crowded the plate while batting, walked 827 times and scored 1,048 career runs. Defensively, he exhibited quick hands for fielding ground balls and making tags, and moved gracefully in either direction. His special skills included handling bad-hop ground balls and cutting off outfield throws. Despite having a flimsy glove, Bancroft handled nearly 12,000 fielding chances and made only 666 errors for a creditable .944 career defensive average. He has long remained the top, or one of the top, major league shortstops In average putouts (2.5) per game and average chances (6.3) per contest.

Following the 1929 season, the New York Giants signed Bancroft as a coach. He coached the Giants through the 1932 season and had hoped to replace John McGraw when the veteran manager retired that June. The Giants, however, selected first baseman Bill Terry as pilot, bitterly disappointing Bancroft. Bancroft managed three minor league seasons, piloting the Minneapolis Millers of the American Association in 1933, the Sioux City, Iowa, Cowboys of the Western League in 1936, and the St. Cloud, Minnesota, Rox of the Northern League in 1947. He completed his managerial career in the All-American Girls Professional Baseball League with the Chicago Colleens in 1948 and the South Bend, Indiana, Blue Sox in 1949.

Bancroft worked thereafter as a warehouse supervisor for Lakehead Pipe Line Company in Superior until retiring in 1956. His honors included election to the National Baseball Hall of Fame in 1971, Iowa Sports Hall of Fame in 1954, Superior Athletic Hall of Fame in 1964, Sioux City Athletic Hall of Fame in 1965, and Duluth Sports Hall of Fame in 1971. He died in Superior.

• The National Baseball Hall of Fame, Cooperstown, N.Y., and Superior Public Library, Superior, Wis., have clipping files and memorabilia of Bancroft. Family information was supplied by Frank Garretson and Paul Gaboriault. For biographical material on Bancroft, see Martin Appel and Burt Goldblatt, *Baseball's Best: The Hall of Fame Gallery* (1980); Jerry E. Clark, *Anson to Zuber: Iowa Boys in the Major Leagues* (1992); George S. May, "Major League Baseball Players from Iowa," *The Palimpsest* 36 (Apr. 1955): 133–65;

Bert McGrane, "Bancroft in Hall of Fame," *Des Moines Sunday Register*, 28 Mar. 1954; David L. Porter, *Biographical Dictionary of American Sports: Baseball* (1987); Lowell Reidenbaugh, *Cooperstown: Where Baseball's Legends Live Forever* (1983); and Robert Smith, *Baseball's Hall of Fame* (1973). Anecdotes about Bancroft appear in Frank Graham, *The New York Giants* (1952); Harold Kaese, *The Boston Braves* (1948); and Frederick Lieb and Stan Baumgartner, *The Philadelphia Phillies* (1953). Obituaries are in the *Des Moines Register*, 11 Oct. 1972, and the *Superior Evening Telegram* and the *New York Times*, both 10 Oct. 1972.

DAVID L. PORTER

BANCROFT, Edward (9 Jan. 1744–8 Sept. 1821), physician, scientist, and spy, was born in Westfield, Massachusetts, the son of Edward Bancroft and Mary Ely, farmers. The elder Bancroft died in 1746 of an epileptic attack suffered in a pigpen, two months before the birth of his younger son, Daniel. His widow married David Bull of Westfield in 1751, and the family moved to Hartford, Connecticut, where Bull operated the Bunch of Grapes tavern. Edward Bancroft was taught for a time by the recent Yale graduate Silas Deane and subsequently, in 1760, was apprenticed to a Killingworth physician. In 1763 he ran away to sea, staying briefly at Barbados and then moving to Surinam, where he was immediately employed as a plantation doctor by Paul Wentworth, owner of two sugar plantations on the Demerara River. Bancroft secured this post through the strong recommendation of a local Scottish physician, who as Bancroft's mentor fostered in him a keen interest in natural history. Bancroft remained in Surinam until 1766, when he returned to New England; in 1767 he went to London to study medicine at St. Bartholomew's Hospital.

By 1769 Bancroft was firmly established as a London physician and had achieved recognition as the author of *An Essay on the Natural History of Guiana in South America* and his pro-American tract, *Remarks on the Review of the Controversy between Great Britain and Her Colonies*. In 1770 he published a free-thinking novel, *The History of Charles Wentworth, in a Series of Letters*. Clearly autobiographical, most of the second volume is a compendium of miscellaneous information about British Guiana. J. M. S. Tomkins, in *The Popular Novel in England*, believes that Bancroft wrote the piece to utilize notes left from his earlier *Natural History*. Despite a scandalous common-law marriage to an obscure woman that produced a large family, the charismatic Bancroft moved easily in London's intellectual circles. On the recommendations of Joseph Priestley and Benjamin Franklin, he was elected to the Royal Society in 1773 and to the College of Physicians, and he was even named royal physician. His friends also found him a position as an editor of the *Monthly Review*, a popular, general-interest magazine that specialized in book reviews. Here, Bancroft covered the American scene. Meanwhile he experimented in the composition of vegetable dyes, which he believed would bring about great savings in the calico industry; he patented his process in 1775.

In 1776 Bancroft was recruited as a spy for the American cause by Silas Deane, who had been appointed by the Continental Congress as its "business agent" in France. Franklin had strongly recommended Bancroft's appointment. Following a July 1776 reunion of the two old friends in Paris, Bancroft, officially employed as a "secretary" for the American delegation, began collecting information for Deane in London. Deane considered his findings to be invaluable, but most of them appear to have been commonplace. Far more remunerative was Bancroft's compensation from Paul Wentworth, then head of the British secret service. According to a contract made with Lord Suffolk in December 1776, Bancroft was to receive a lifetime pension of £200, later increased to £500, for his services.

Although initially trusted by both sides, this double agent lost credibility in 1777 through his involvement in the "John the Painter Affair." John Aitken, a Scotsman, had devised a scheme to blow up a large part of the British fleet stationed at Portsmouth. He managed to install explosive devices in three warships, destroy a large ropewalk in the Portsmouth navy yard, and burn down a part of the city of Bristol. Pursued by the British authorities, Aitken tried to gain admittance to Bancroft's house at 4 Downing Street, London. Bancroft refused him entry but did meet him briefly at a local coffeehouse the next day. Aitken was promptly arrested, tried, found guilty, and executed. His confession named Deane as instigator of the plot but did not implicate Bancroft, who had been living at Deane's Paris lodgings when the plot was hatched. The doctor, arrested for questioning, turned state's evidence. Once released, he fled to France, where he resumed his espionage activities for both sides.

Bancroft's services to the British government proved far more useful than those rendered the American cause. He tried, without success, to convince the ministry of an impending alliance of France with the United States. From within Deane's Paris household he sent a constant stream of information to London. Learning that France and the United States had finally signed an alliance on 6 February 1778, he conveyed the news to the British government within forty-two hours. His methods of transmitting papers to the British secret service were ingenious, including the use of codes and invisible ink and the placing of messages in a hollow tree in the Tuileries Gardens. Privately, Bancroft and Deane used their inside information for profitable speculation on the stock market. Among their activities were outfitting privateers to attack British shipping, insuring ships' cargoes, investing in contraband cargoes, buying up shares in real estate speculation in the American Northwest, and manipulating war news to affect the stock market. In 1777, learning that General John Burgoyne had suffered a severe defeat, probably the battle of Bennington, Bancroft concluded that his whole military campaign would fail. He and Deane were able to anticipate the drop in investments that occurred when Burgoyne's defeat at Saratoga later became public knowledge. Bancroft and

Deane enriched themselves by selling short while prices were still high.

In 1780 Bancroft's salary was increased to £1,000, but his usefulness to the British government was waning; in 1784 he was dropped from the secret service. Desperate, he wrote a remarkable memoir to the Marquis of Carmathan on 17 September 1784 outlining his services to the government, proposing new efforts, and praying the resumption of his regular salary of £500. His request was denied, and his position was terminated.

Bancroft's friend Deane had already been removed from his office by the American Congress in August 1778 because of his use of public funds for private gain, and during two years of effort in the United States he failed to prove his innocence. Labeled a traitor, he moved first to Ghent and then, in 1783, to London, where he was supported by Bancroft. By 1789 Deane was ready to return home, buoyant with new schemes for an iron manufacturing process, steam engine development, and a canal to connect Lake Champlain with the St. Lawrence River. He also hoped to settle his accounts with Congress. In mid-September he boarded the *Boston Packet* at Gravesend, but the ship was becalmed in the Downs. While walking on deck with the captain on the twenty-second, Deane was stricken with a fatal attack, falling into a coma and dying within four hours. Rumors quickly spread that Deane had committed suicide. In 1959 Julian P. Boyd created a sensation by advancing the theory in "Silas Deane: Death by a Kindly Teacher of Treason?" that Edward Bancroft had murdered Deane through a deliberately prescribed overdose of laudanum. Boyd's evidence is largely circumstantial: that Bancroft was familiar with the use and effects of a variety of poisons; that although he did not accompany Deane to Gravesend, he had seen him in London before his departure; that he had prescribed drugs for Deane and could easily have increased the dosage; and that he was the first to call Deane's death a suicide, perhaps to divert suspicion from himself. As to motivation, Bancroft knew that when Deane arrived in the United States, he would present his papers to Congress—documents that might prove Bancroft's role in the John the Painter Affair. If this complicity became known in England, his reputation would be destroyed. The truth, of course, can never be known.

After his discharge from the British service, Bancroft continued his experimentation with dyes used in calico printing. Although a parliamentary act of 1785 earned him a monopoly on the importation and processing of oak bark dyes, a bill to extend these rights for seven years passed Commons but failed in the House of Lords in 1799. His 1794 edition of *Experimental Researches concerning the Philosophy of Permanent Colours* was expanded and reprinted in 1813. A flawed man of genius but a noted scientist, Bancroft died at Margate near London.

• It was not until the publication of the Stevens *Facsimiles* (1889–1895) that the full details of Bancroft's perfidy were uncovered. General William C. Bancroft of the British army was so angered at the revelations that he destroyed his grandfather's papers. Samuel Flagg Bemis, "British Secret Service and the French-American Alliance," *American Historical Review* 29 (1923–1924): 474–95, provides a thorough account of Bancroft's espionage, which includes the Carmathan memorial. Julian P. Boyd, "Silas Deane: Death by a Kindly Teacher of Treason?" *William and Mary Quarterly* 16 (1959), not only advances the theory that Bancroft murdered Deane but also provides much information about Bancroft's novel, *Charles Wentworth*, and his *Natural History of Guiana*. In *The Popular Novel in England, 1770–1800* (1961), J. M. S. Tomkins offers a literary interpretation of *Charles Wentworth*. Some of the Bancroft-Deane correspondence is preserved in "The Deane Papers," *New-York Historical Society Collections* (1886–1890). Leonard Labaree and William B. Wilcox, eds., *The Papers of Benjamin Franklin* (1959–), includes a running account of Bancroft's activities.

GORDON E. KERSHAW

BANCROFT, Frederic A. (30 Oct. 1860–22 Feb. 1945), historian, librarian, and philanthropist, was born Frederic Austin Bancroft in Galesburg, Illinois, the son of Addison Newton Bancroft, a businessman, and Catherine Blair. Bancroft, raised in abolitionist surroundings, attended school at Knox Academy, Knox College (1878–1881), transferred to Amherst College in 1881, and graduated a year later. He entered Columbia University's School of Political Science in 1882 to study southern history with John William Burgess. While at Columbia Bancroft campaigned for mugwump politicians, favoring civil service, tariff reform, and sound money and opposing American imperialism. His dissertation, "A Sketch of the Negro in Politics, Especially in South Carolina and Mississippi," covered the years 1865 to 1885 and was based on extensive field research in the South that Bancroft conducted in 1884. Bancroft interviewed scores of blacks and whites who had participated in Reconstruction and observed conditions in the postwar South. Based on this research Bancroft published a series of three articles titled "Notes among the Negroes" in the *New York Evening Post* (16 Jan., 10 Feb., and 18 Feb. 1885).

After receiving his doctorate in 1885, Bancroft spent almost three years studying abroad at the Universities of Berlin and Freiburg (with Hermann Eduard von Holst) and in the École Libre des Sciences Politiques in Paris. In 1888 Bancroft once again conducted fieldwork in the South, then returned to New York City to serve as an editor of the *Political Science Quarterly*. Although he lectured occasionally at Amherst, Columbia, Johns Hopkins University, and the University of Chicago, Bancroft never held a regular academic appointment.

In 1888 Bancroft was appointed librarian of the U.S. Department of State where he gained unusual access to research materials and became established in Washington's highest social circles. Noted politicians and historians, including Carl Schurz, James Ford Rhodes, Henry Adams, and Charles Francis Adams, Jr., became among his closest friends. Bancroft served in the Department of State until 1892 when he was removed by Secretary of State James G. Blaine. Supported financially by his wealthy brother Edgar, Frederic spent the remaining years of his long life as a gentleman scholar.

Bancroft researched, corresponded to numerous historians nationally, traveled, and socialized, especially at Washington's Metropolitan Club. In 1900 Columbia University historian William A. Dunning described Bancroft as "something of a *bon vivant*," who "can enjoy and can tell a good story, his own specialty being negro dialect; and is popular among the members of some of the foreign embassies" (p. 394). Despite the neoabolitionist slant of his writing, Bancroft treated blacks in a patronizing and condescending manner.

After his brother Edgar's death in 1925 Bancroft managed the family estate that he inherited. He in turn bequeathed the estate to Columbia University. Interest from the almost $2 million was used for book purchases and Bancroft prizes in American history and biography.

For all of his resources, free time, and ability, Bancroft published remarkably little. A self-proclaimed "perfectionist," he often procrastinated yet sniped at more prolific scholars. In addition to early articles in *Harper's Weekly*, *Political Science Quarterly*, *North American Review*, and elsewhere, Bancroft published *The Life of William H. Seward* (2 vols., 1900) and edited *Speeches, Correspondence, and Political Papers of Carl Schurz* (6 vols., 1913) Vitriolic and intolerant of those who disagreed with him, Bancroft in 1915 led a movement to reform the operations of the American Historical Association. In the process he needlessly alienated friends and made many enemies.

On a more constructive note, after the turn of the century Bancroft directed most of his time to researching and writing a massive multivolume history of the South. He envisioned producing a sweeping study, resembling what Thomas B. Macaulay had published on late seventeenth-century England. As in his previous research, Bancroft traveled extensively in the South to unearth primary materials and to interview whites and blacks. Despite his deep and thorough research, however, most of the immense manuscript (four holograph books) remains unpublished. Sections, mere chapters from his large manuscript, ultimately appeared as *Calhoun and the South Carolina Nullification Movement* (1928) and *Slave Trading in the Old South* (1931).

Slave Trading in the Old South is Bancroft's most important, best-known work, and it remains the standard history of the subject. It thoroughly revised Winfield H. Collins's *The Domestic Slave Trade of the Southern States* (1904) and challenged Ulrich B. Phillips's proslavery conclusions in *American Negro Slavery* (1918) and *Life and Labor in the Old South* (1929). Bancroft based his book on what were for his day fresh and original sources: slave traders' advertisements, city directories, letters, wills, court records, newspapers, and oral history testimony from ex-slaves. Strongly neoabolitionist in tone, he lashed out against

slavery and its apologists, arguing that slave breeding and slave trading were more extensive and central to the South's economy than previous scholars had assumed. The book was a significant accomplishment, especially since white southerners rarely spoke openly about slave traders and slave trading.

Aside from writing *Slave Trading* Bancroft is best remembered for leaving the generous financial gift to Columbia. In a 1908 diary entry he noted sadly a comment made by historian James Ford Rhodes: that Bancroft "knew more history and would write less, than anyone he could name" (Cooke, p. 48). Bancroft, who never married, died in Washington, D.C.

• Bancroft papers are at Columbia University. Included is his unpublished multivolume history in four manuscript books. For an early appraisal of Bancroft, see William A. Dunning's untitled article in the *Critic* 36 (1900): 393–94. On Bancroft's attempt to reform the AHA, see Ray Allen Billington, "Tempest in Clio's Teapot: The AHA Rebellion of 1915," *American Historical Review*, 78 (1973): 348–69. On Bancroft as a historian of slavery, see three works by John David Smith: "The Formative Period of American Slave Historiography, 1890–1920" (Ph.D. diss., Univ. of Kentucky, 1977), "Historical or Personal Criticism? Frederic Bancroft vs. Ulrich B. Phillips," *Washington State University Research Studies* 49 (1981): 73–86, and *An Old Creed for the New South: Proslavery Ideology and Historiography, 1865–1918* (1985). Also see Michael Tadman's introduction to the 1996 edition of *Slave Trading in the Old South*. The definitive biography is Jacob E. Cooke, *Frederic Bancroft: Historian* (1957), which includes a complete bibliography of Bancroft's publications and three previously unpublished essays by Bancroft on the colonization of blacks to Africa, Central America, and Ile à Vache.

JOHN DAVID SMITH

BANCROFT, George (3 Oct. 1800–17 Jan. 1891), scholar and diplomat, was born in Worcester, Massachusetts, the son of Aaron Bancroft, the founder of Worcester's Second Congregational Society and later president of the American Unitarian Association, and Lucretia Chandler. The eighth of thirteen children, George passed his childhood in a frugal rural household dominated by paternal activism. In 1811 he entered the Phillips Exeter Academy in New Hampshire, run by Benjamin Abbot, a family friend. Attending with a scholarship, Bancroft received a solid grounding in classics, which prepared him for Harvard, where he enrolled at the age of thirteen.

Under the presidency of John T. Kirkland, another family friend, Harvard was struggling to develop from a glorified boarding school into an institution of higher learning. Bancroft thrived in its structured environment, immersed in a curriculum fostering self-control, reasonable faith, and virtuous citizenship. Financial aid allowed him to concentrate on his studies. The seriousness of his few friends, who were among the younger faculty, rubbed off on Bancroft, and he became something of a prig. Under the tutelage of Levi Hedge and others, he acquired proper tastes in literature, a smattering of science, and a good knowledge of Greek and Latin. Moral philosophy, the underpinning of the curriculum, a mixture of Lockean rationalism and Scottish Common Sense philosophy, shaped his mental outlook. The English oration he delivered at his 1817 commencement on the dignity and philosophy of the human mind indicated his high class standing and proper outlook.

A ministerial career seemed appropriate given Bancroft's interests and education. He began the requisite M.A. studies and sought respite from theology in the novels of Sir Walter Scott and Maria Edgeworth. On Edward Everett's recommendation, Kirkland offered Bancroft the opportunity to study at the Georgia Augusta university in Göttingen, and Bancroft sailed for Europe in June 1818. His education course over four years was somewhat unfocused, but philology, biblical criticism, German and French literature, as well as ancient and oriental languages and modern history vastly broadened his intellectual horizons. Awarded a doctorate by the Georgia Augusta in 1820 but unwilling to face an uncertain future in Cambridge, Bancroft next embarked on a grand European tour, including an extended stay at Berlin to hear Hegel and Schleiermacher. He visited Paris, traveled through Italy, and met distant relations in London. Immense curiosity about America as well as letters of introduction allowed Bancroft to meet Goethe and Alexander von Humboldt, Washington Irving, and Lafayette. In June 1822 the educational pilgrimage ended, and Bancroft sailed for the United States ready to begin life in earnest.

At first Bancroft embarked on a desultory ministerial career, aware it would lead nowhere. He also antagonized several former benefactors who disagreed with his belief that a European doctorate deserved special consideration. His Georgia Augusta education was deemed fit at most for a Greek instructorship at Harvard, a one-year appointment which Bancroft was forced to accept. In an experience as unhappy as his foray into the pulpit, he joined several younger faculty members who sought to reform Harvard after European models. Their plans produced no immediate results, and in the winter of 1822, together with Joseph Cogswell, Bancroft set out to establish an intermediate educational institution patterned after the German Gymnasiums he had visited, incorporating innovative educational methods to stimulate young minds. Round Hill in Northampton was a pathbreaking experiment that appealed to parents progressive enough to entrust their boys, at sizable expense, to two young schoolmasters. In 1824 Round Hill enrolled 25 boys, and in 1827 the number had grown to 135. But the chores, administrative details, and financial worries soon forced Bancroft once again to look elsewhere for a profession. Meanwhile, the publication in 1823 of a volume of his poems had revealed budding literary ambitions.

In 1827, after an elaborate courtship, Bancroft married Sarah Dwight, the daughter of a prominent merchant-banker. Her family's social standing and political connections fueled Bancroft's ambition and increased his resources, prompting him to sever his ties with Round Hill. He wrote extensively for the *North American Review* and other magazines and translated Arnold Hermann Ludwig Heeren's *Reflections on the Politics of Ancient Greece* from German, becoming one of the main transmitters of European literature to the United States. Bancroft also began to dabble in local politics. The clergyman-schoolmaster was on his way to becoming a man of action and a scholar.

Bancroft's fluid political views attracted attention from both National Republicans and Democrats, but he wanted to publish at least the first installment of his *History of the United States* before making a serious political commitment. He began assembling materials in 1832, chiefly to explain the United States to its citizens, harnessing the past to elucidate the present. In 1834 the first volume appeared and was a great literary and scholarly achievement. Democratic in tone, it carried a reassuring message to readers worried about the future. Current upheavals, Bancroft showed, had antecedents. The United States had surmounted earlier trials and it would again. National Republicans and Democrats united in praise of the book, and the volume sold well.

Bancroft implied in the *History* that the voice of the people was the voice of God. This and several pro-Democratic pronouncements elicited overtures from local workingmen's associations as well as from the Democratic organization. After weighing options for several months, Bancroft chose to align himself with the Democratic party, whose ideology was more compatible with his views, its structure more flexible in accommodating demands, and its ranks less crowded with ambitious youngsters ready to lead. Bancroft developed an extensive friendship network with local workingmen, labor, and anti-Masonic leaders. He ran for the Massachusetts General Court as an independent, but the scurrilous opposition from the National Republicans, who tagged him a turncoat radical, contributed to his defeat and strengthened his credentials as a Democrat.

His effort to unseat Springfield's congressional representative also ended in defeat, but the irrepressible Democrat persisted in forecasting a rosy future for the state and the nation. In 1837 a financial panic exposed the shallowness of his predictions, but the death of his first wife, who never recovered from the birth of their third child, overshadowed the political aftershocks. Overcome by grief, Bancroft escaped to Montreal for a few weeks, then returned to immerse himself in party activism. Bancroft was appointed collector of the port of Boston, a post he turned into a power base, remodeling party machinery and improving its electoral chances. He also was able to use patronage to further the careers of Nathaniel Hawthorne and Orestes A. Brownson.

Bancroft moved to Boston, where in 1838 he married the widow Elizabeth Bliss, with whom he would have one child. A gracious life-style included extensive scholarly activities to prepare the next installments of the *History*, hosting foreign dignitaries, and managing Democratic party activities. In 1839 the Democrats won the governorship, thanks to Bancroft's adroit exploitation of the liquor law controversy, and the second volume of the *History*, in which Bancroft developed the Democratic message embedded in his first volume, was published the following year.

In 1840 William H. Harrison's election as president created unprecedented though temporary Democratic unity. Bancroft shrugged off troublesome questions about the nation's political system. Could *vox populi* be construed as *vox dei* when the people opted for "Tippecanoe and Tyler too"? Timorous Democrats like Brownson developed doubts, but Bancroft, embroiled at this inopportune moment in an acrimonious legal suit with the Dwights over his first wife's inheritance, thought the answer an unqualified yes. Meanwhile, the Liberty party was draining Democratic strength by exploiting slavery's political impact, which Bancroft preferred to ignore. The more his friends edged toward abolitionism, the more Bancroft distanced himself, disliking rabble-rousers, mistrustful of visionary reforms, and opposed to radical solutions.

Bancroft abandoned local for national politics. In 1844 he was a leading figure at the Baltimore Democratic National Convention, which nominated James K. Polk for the presidency. The annexation of Texas, Manifest Destiny, and the future of Oregon seemed the slogans of the hour, and Bancroft, running that year for the Massachusetts governorship, altered his political pronouncements accordingly. He campaigned for Polk in New York, tried to reconcile embittered Van Burenites, and still found time for his *History*. He lost the gubernatorial race, but Polk's victory brought Bancroft to Washington, D.C., where he joined the cabinet as secretary of the navy.

As secretary Bancroft acquired first-hand experience at conducting foreign policy in a democratic society. He also helped found the U.S. Naval Academy at Annapolis and tried to streamline the department. Bancroft was instrumental in the acquisition of California, ordering the Pacific Naval Squadron in June 1845 to occupy San Francisco and other ports in case of war, and he defended President Polk against the charge that the president was party to a nefarious southern plot to extend slavery. Bancroft believed that the Mexican War, of which he was an enthusiastic supporter, was a god-sent opportunity to enlarge the national domain for liberty. The vociferous antiwar sentiment, the shifting political alliances the war created, and the strange bedfellows it produced astounded Bancroft. After eighteen months in office he had had enough of Washington, and when Polk offered him the ambassadorship to Great Britain, Bancroft jumped at the opportunity.

Bancroft spent three years in London, where he proved himself a reliable diplomat, closely following instructions from Secretary of State James Buchanan. Bancroft ably defended U.S. policy against English criticism while moving with ease within polite society. Bancroft also followed the 1848 revolutions on the Continent and the Chartist demonstrations in London, certain that they were the death knell of the Old Regime. Meanwhile, a tribe of secretaries and friends supplied materials for the future volumes of the *History*.

News from the United States about political realignments, the rise of the Free-Soil party, and Democratic splinterings in Massachusetts augured an uncertain political future. When Whig Zachary Taylor's 1848 presidential victory ended Bancroft's service in London, Bancroft moved to New York, where, as a gentleman of means, he wrote the next four volumes of his *History*. He and his family divided their time between a gracious residence in the city and a house in Newport, Rhode Island, where Bancroft indulged his passion for roses and horseback riding. In New York he was host to prominent visitors, supported charitable associations, and observed politics from a distance. He helped shape plans for Central Park, defended animal rights, and closely followed the ups and downs of his investments.

After 1854 Bancroft resumed his public role, horrified to discover that what he had always believed an impossibility—the demise of the United States—seemed about to materialize. The *History* volumes published during this decade articulated a message to all extremists about the impossibility of deviating from the nation's providentially assigned course. They also reminded readers that progressive schemes aimed at overturning ancient abuses needed time to mature. Those who hoped to accelerate the normal pace of historical development would be disappointed. Bancroft's faith in providential guidance as well as his continued travels in the United States further reassured him that the Union ultimately could not fall apart.

When events threatened to prove otherwise, however, Bancroft fastened on the Democratic party as the last unifying, nationwide political institution. His hopes were placed successively in President James Buchanan, the Supreme Court (until the Dred Scott decision), and Stephen A. Douglas, for whom he wrote speeches during Douglas's 1860 presidential bid. Once the South seceded, Bancroft became a convert to vigorous prosecution of the war, a position he sustained throughout the conflict, amidst shifting prospects and failures that Bancroft attributed to President Abraham Lincoln's incompetence, to Republican stupidity, and to Copperhead treachery. He joined Republicans and Democrats in founding the Union League and blamed the war on a southern conspiracy. When the war's magnitude became evident, Bancroft resorted to the doctrine of affliction to justify the pain, divinely inflicted suffering a prelude to national regeneration. As the conflict expanded, he bemoaned northern defeatism and southern "fanaticism." By the summer of 1862 he opted for emancipation. The draft riots in New York in the summer of 1963 astounded him, and though still a Democrat, he voted for Lincoln the following year. In his eulogy on Lincoln before the House of Representatives in February 1866, Bancroft implied that the president had wished to punish slavery while sparing the slaveholder. Bancroft aided President Andrew Johnson in drafting his first annual message, and he supported Johnson's reconstruction policy.

The publication of the ninth volume of the *History* in 1866 embroiled Bancroft in a nasty war of words with irate grandsons of revolutionary figures who detested his current politics and his treatment of their ancestors. Johnson's offer of the post of U.S. minister to Prussia in 1867 enabled Bancroft to return to Germany, where he felt at home. While there he cultivated the acquaintance of musicians, artists, and scholars. President Ulysses Grant kept Bancroft in Berlin, where the historian witnessed first-hand Bismarck's adroit handling of opponents at home and abroad. Bancroft considered Bismarck to be Germany's George Washington and was an enthusiastic supporter of Prussia in its war with France and a vociferous defender of the newly united Germany. He remained in Berlin for seven years.

Upon his return to the United States in 1874, Bancroft settled in Washington, D.C., determined to complete his historical projects. In the remaining years of his life, he played the part of local celebrity who knew everyone worth knowing, and he was frequently called upon by prominent tourists. The tenth volume of the *History* appeared in 1874 to the customary approval, although by then younger scholars were challenging several Bancroftian interpretations of the nation's past. Undismayed, Bancroft embarked on other tasks in addition to working on the constant revisions of his *History*. The Centenary Edition appeared in 1876, in six volumes, followed in 1882 by a two-volume edition of documents relating to constitutional ratification. The last version, appearing between 1882 and 1884 and subtitled *Author's Last Revision*, incorporated the previously published volumes into a final whole. He also authored articles and notes as well as a biography of Martin Van Buren (1889). In 1885 the two-year-old American Historical Association elected Bancroft its president. By 1889 Bancroft's health had worsened, and he died in Washington.

Bancroft's *History of the United States*, a multivolume sermon, assumed the certainty of providential guidance, the transitory significance of the individual, popular conservatism, and the durability of the nation's political institutions. It documented how divinely ordained natural laws sustained growth, and it articulated a national consciousness, providing historical substantiation for an optimistic faith. A self-sustained process of orderly reform, inherent in national evolution, spared the country after 1776 the need for further revolutions. Bancroft's influence in his lifetime reflected the popularity of this message.

• The bulk of material related to Bancroft's life is divided among the Massachusetts Historical Society, the New York Public Library, Cornell University Library, and the American Antiquarian Society in Worcester, Massachusetts. The Bancroft-Bliss papers and the papers of Andrew Johnson in the Library of Congress provide additional documentation. A great deal of material is scattered among the collections of major American political and intellectual nineteenth-century figures. Lists of Bancroft's published writings can be found in Robert H. Canary, *George Bancroft* (1974), pp. 133–35. The standard biographies include Mark Anthony deWolfe Howe, *The Life and Letters of George Bancroft* (2 vols., 1908); Russel B. Nye, *George Bancroft, Brahmin Rebel* (1944); and Lilian Handlin, *George Bancroft, the Intellectual as Democrat* (1984).

LILIAN HANDLIN

BANCROFT, Hubert Howe (5 May 1832–2 Mar. 1918), businessman and historian, was born in Granville, Ohio, the son of Azariah Ashley Bancroft, a farmer, and Lucy Howe, a teacher. His formal education stopped short of college, and at age sixteen Bancroft left home to learn the book trade from his brother-in-law in Buffalo, New York. Sent to California with a valuable consignment of books, Bancroft opened his own bookstore in San Francisco in December 1856, with capital supplied by his sister and credit from several New York firms. Efficiently run, and favored by a margin between California gold and depreciated eastern currency during the Civil War, Bancroft's store proved phenomenally profitable. Within a decade, H. H. Bancroft & Co. supported extensive European travel for its proprietor and permitted him the luxury of semiretirement at age thirty-seven. In 1869–1870 he built a five-story building for his business, which expanded to include stationery, office supplies, printing, and bookbinding. He turned over the day-to-day operations to his younger brother, Albert, while he moved into the fifth floor and devoted himself to the study of history.

In the late 1850s Bancroft had developed an interest in collecting books, pamphlets, newspapers, maps, and manuscripts on early California. He had quickly increased the size of his collection during his travels to the East Coast and Europe and had enlarged its scope as he came to see California's story as connected to those of neighboring states and nations. By 1870 Bancroft's collection exceeded 16,000 volumes and extended from Panama to Alaska. When he sold it to the University of California, Berkeley, in 1905, it had grown to 60,000 volumes, plus numerous original manuscripts, and transcripts of documents and oral interviews. Early in the twentieth century the Bancroft Library won recognition as the nation's finest research repository for Mexico and the American West, but Bancroft achieved greater fame as a historian.

Writing history, Bancroft avowed, was "among the highest of human occupations." Unfettered by formal training, he drew on his businessman's experience to produce historical writing along novel industrial lines. Bancroft assembled a staff to index his library, take notes, and write initial drafts. In all, he employed over 600 people in his literary workshop, as many as fifty at a time. Bancroft calculated that the man-hours in his first work, *Native Races* (5 vols., 1874–1875), would have translated into fifty years of labor for an individual. Meanwhile, he also had underway twenty-eight more volumes: *History of Central America* (3 vols., 1882–1887), *History of Mexico* (6 vols., 1883–1888), *History of the North Mexican States and Texas* (2 vols., 1884–1889), *History of Arizona and New Mexico*

(1889), *History of California* (7 vols., 1884–1890), *History of Nevada, Colorado, and Wyoming* (1889), *History of Utah* (1889), *History of the Northwest Coast* (2 vols., 1884), *History of Oregon* (2 vols., 1886–1888), *History of Washington, Idaho, and Montana* (1890), *History of British Columbia* (1887), and *History of Alaska* (1889). Four more topical volumes on California supplemented the series, which finally ended with Bancroft's own descriptions of his life, labors, and philosophy, in two volumes of essays.

Bancroft published and promoted these thirty-nine volumes as a set, the *Works of Hubert Howe Bancroft,* and marketed them shrewdly and aggressively through subscriptions sold by teams of salesmen. Although he designed and directed the series and did considerable composition, Bancroft did not write all of his *Works*. Detractors charged that he misrepresented his authorship and that the series lacked intellectual coherence; others criticized him for demythologizing some of California's pioneers and for producing a seven-volume vanity series of biographical vignettes, *Builders of the Commonwealth* (1891–1892), whose subjects paid substantial fees for inclusion. Nonetheless, however mind-numbing their prose, Bancroft's richly detailed, documented, and massive compilations of facts, the most comprehensive history ever written of western North America, remain durable reference tools, and historians regard him as a pioneer in the use of newspapers. Bancroft's prodigious collecting of data did not extend to the national archives of Spain, Mexico, or the United States; these treasures awaited the next generation of historians.

In 1859 Bancroft had married Emily Ketchum of Buffalo, with whom he had one child, but after his wife's death in 1869 he had resisted remarriage for fear that the demands of a wife would interfere with his project. In 1876 he married Matilda Coley Griffing of New Haven, who participated in his work and with whom he had four more children. Bancroft retired at age sixty and spent the last twenty-five years of his life close to family, reading, writing, and traveling. He died in San Francisco.

• Many of Bancroft's private and business papers are in the Bancroft Library, University of California, Berkeley. In addition to his *Essays and Miscellany* and his self-congratulatory *Literary Industries,* both published in 1890, two later books of essays reveal much about his life and views: *Retrospection: Political and Personal* (1912) and *In These Latter Days* (1917). John Walton Caughey, *Hubert Howe Bancroft: Historian of the West* (1946), remains the standard biography, superseded in some respects by Harry Clark, *A Venture in History: The Production, Publication, and Sale of the Works of Hubert Howe Bancroft* (1973), which explains how production shaped content. For an analysis of Bancroft in his milieu, see Kevin Starr, *Americans and the California Dream, 1850–1915* (1973). Jo Tice Bloom, "Hubert Howe Bancroft," in *Historians of the Frontier: A Bio-Bibliographical Sourcebook,* ed. John R. Wunder (1988), pp. 56–64, offers a thorough list of Bancroft's books and pamphlets, along with a laudatory biographical sketch.

DAVID J. WEBER

BANCROFT, Jane Marie. *See* Robinson, Jane Marie Bancroft.

BANCROFT, Wilder Dwight (1 Oct. 1867–7 Feb. 1953), physical chemist, was born in Middletown, Rhode Island, the son of John Chandler Bancroft, a lawyer, stockbroker, and artist, and Louisa Mills Denny. Raised, in part, in the home of his grandfather, the historian George Bancroft, Wilder Bancroft was exposed to the vigorous expression of strong opinions from an early age. The lessons took well, and Bancroft's pungent wit, agility with words, and aggressive debating style helped make him one of the most provocative and controversial chemists of his generation.

Like his father and grandfather, Bancroft attended Harvard College, where he played football and studied English and chemistry. After graduating in 1888, he remained at Harvard for one year as an assistant in chemistry and then went abroad for four years of advanced study at Strasbourg, Leipzig, Berlin, and Amsterdam. This tour gave Bancroft an opportunity to hear the lectures of many of the leaders of European science and to work in the laboratories of two of the founders of physical chemistry, Wilhelm Ostwald (Leipzig) and J. H. van't Hoff (Amsterdam). Bancroft returned to Cambridge in 1893 with a doctorate from Leipzig (1892), great enthusiasm for physical chemistry, and an expertise that was still rare on the western side of the Atlantic.

After teaching as an assistant and instructor at Harvard for two years, Bancroft was appointed assistant professor at Cornell. In 1895, shortly after receiving his appointment to the Cornell faculty, Bancroft married Katherine Bott of Albany, New York.

Conscious of the need to proselytize for a new discipline, Bancroft embarked on an ambitious program to make Cornell a leading center for undergraduate and graduate work in physical chemistry. Together with another young faculty member, Joseph E. Trevor, Bancroft developed a broad array of new courses and founded the first English-language journal devoted to the new science, the *Journal of Physical Chemistry.* With funds from the Carnegie Institution of Washington and, sometimes, from his own pocket, Bancroft arranged research assistantships for graduate and postdoctoral students. His showmanship on the lecture stage and irreverent wit commanded the attention of undergraduates; graduate students responded to his encyclopedic command of the chemical literature, his intellectual generosity, and his insistence that neither mathematical acumen nor experimental diligence could substitute for clear and independent thought. Bancroft's energetic work led to recognition at home and abroad: promotion to professor in 1903, the presidency of the American Electrochemical Society in 1905 and 1919, the presidency of the American Chemical Society in 1910, and honorary memberships in the chemical societies of England, Poland, and France.

Although Bancroft supervised experimental research on many topics, including the electrodeposition of metals, the composition and properties of alloys, and the chemistry of dyes and photographic emulsions, he was best known for his pungent reviews and his iconoclastic surveys of the literature of physical chemistry. Prior to World War I, when most physical chemists were preoccupied with the study of equilibrium in homogeneous systems, especially dilute aqueous solutions, Bancroft stressed the importance of the study of heterogeneous systems, of which alloys are one example. Here he invested great effort in publicizing the uses of the phase rule of J. Willard Gibbs (1839–1903), which shows how the number of phases and components of a system determine the number of degrees of freedom in that system at equilibrium.

After wartime service as head of the editorial section of the Chemical Warfare Service, Bancroft focused on promoting the study of colloids, substances that will not pass readily with a solvent through membranes that are permeable to dissolved mineral salts. Decrying his colleagues' obsession with "ideal systems," Bancroft saw colloid chemistry as "the chemistry of everyday life" because it dealt with the behavior of such common substances as paints, inks, proteins, and dairy fats. Through his editorial work Bancroft did much to stimulate the study of colloids, but by aligning himself with those who saw proteins as multimolecular aggregates rather than molecules of definite proportions, Bancroft put himself on the losing side of one of the great chemical debates of the 1920s. During the early 1930s he did his reputation further damage by tracing drug addiction, schizophrenia, and aging to the coagulation of colloids in the protoplasm of nerve cells. His flimsy evidence for such claims and his advocacy of sodium thiocyanate as a remedy for the supposed changes in the condition of cellular colloids led to reprimands in the pages of the *Journal of the American Medical Association* and elsewhere.

Bancroft retired from teaching at Cornell in 1937, five years after having been pressured by colleagues into resigning as editor of the *Journal of Physical Chemistry*. In 1938 he was struck by an automobile on the Cornell campus and suffered injuries from which he never fully recovered. Bancroft died in Ithaca, leaving five children and scores of admiring students— "Banty's men," as they sometimes called themselves. Although Bancroft's professional judgments were sometimes erratic, he was a skillful teacher, a shrewd critic of conventional opinion, and a talented mediator between basic and industrial science.

• A large collection of Bancroft's papers, including correspondence and lecture notes, is in the Cornell University Archives. Most of Bancroft's articles and reviews appeared in the *Journal of Physical Chemistry*. He wrote two books, *The Phase Rule: A Treatise on Qualitative Chemical Equilibrium* (1897) and *Applied Colloid Chemistry, General Theory* (1921). Biographical sketches by friends and former students include Alexander Findlay, "Wilder Dwight Bancroft, 1867–1953," *Journal of the Chemical Society* (1953): 2506–14, which has been reprinted in *Great Chemists*, ed. Eduard Farber (1961), pp. 1245–61; H. W. Gillett, "Wilder D. Bancroft," *Industrial and Engineering Chemistry. News Edition* 24 (1932): 1200–1201; and C. W. Mason, "Wilder Dwight Bancroft," *Journal of the American Chemical Society* 76 (1954): 2601–2. Bancroft's career and its context are treated at length in John W. Servos, *Physical Chemistry from Ostwald to Pauling: The Making of a Science in America* (1990).

JOHN W. SERVOS

BANDELIER, Adolph Francis Alphonse (6 Aug. 1840–18 Mar. 1914), archaeologist, ethnologist, and historian, was born in Bern, Switzerland, the son of Adolphe Eugène Bandelier, a jurist and banker, and Marianne Senn, widow of Colonel Adrian Ritter, a Swiss army officer who served as a tutor in Russia— possibly at the Russian court. In 1847 Bandelier's father, disagreeing with the Swiss parties in power following the Sonderbund war, traveled to Brazil. Finding, however, that he disliked Brazil's slave-based society, he moved to the Swiss community of Highland, Illinois, where his wife and son joined him in 1848. In Highland, Bandelier was tutored at home. His mother died in 1855. In 1861 he married Josephine Huegy, daughter of one of his father's banking partners. The couple had no children. Bandelier referred to French as his "native language" and preferred to pronounce his name Bahn-duh-lee-ay, but he appears to have been even more fluent in German.

Though employed in his father's bank, which he hated, Bandelier's initial interests were scientific (minerology, geology, meteorology). He found little time, however, for scientific experiments and turned instead to the study of the history and native populations of Spanish America, teaching himself Spanish to read works on the subject. He was strongly influenced by ethnographer Lewis H. Morgan, who became his mentor.

Between 1877 and 1880 Bandelier published several monographs on the early Mexicans. After suffering a nervous breakdown in 1880, he obtained, with the help of Morgan, an appointment from the Archaeological Institute of America to study Indians in New Mexico. This appointment enabled him to break with the bank and begin what he felt was his true life's work.

From Santa Fe, New Mexico, Bandelier traveled often, on foot and on horseback, to Mexico, where he studied Indian vestiges and worked in the Mexico City archives. On one of these trips, in 1881, Bandelier became a Catholic through the sponsorship of his friend, Mexican scholar Joaquín García-Icazbalceta.

In 1885 Bandelier's father's bank failed. Bandelier, Sr., hurriedly left town, another partner was absent, and the third committed suicide. Bandelier, who was in Highland at the time, was held responsible and was forced to turn over all family assets to the creditors. He returned to Santa Fe practically penniless.

Because the Archaeological Institute had just terminated his employment, owing to a lack of funds, in 1886 Bandelier accepted a commission from Archbishop Salpointe to write a history of the colonization and missions of the borderlands area, as a gift from the Archdiocese of Santa Fe to Pope Leo XIII for his golden jubilee. The book was written in French with 502 illustrations, mostly watercolors by Bandelier himself, with the exception of one showing the Zuñi war gods, attributed to his friend, ethnologist and anthropologist Frank Hamilton Cushing. Among these illustrations were also a number of photographs, and several maps and blueprints. This book, translated by Madeleine Turrell Rodack as *History of the Colonization and Missions of Sonora, Chihuahua, New Mexico, and Arizona to the Year 1700*, in seven parts, has not yet been published in its entirety.

In 1886 Cushing obtained for Bandelier an appointment as historiographer for the Hemenway Expedition, organized to study southwestern archaeology. Meanwhile Bandelier was working on a novel, *The Delight Makers*, first written in German as *Die Köshare*, about the Indians of Frijoles Canyon near Santa Fe, which was published in English in 1890. It received excellent reviews, but the income from it still seems to have disappointed Bandelier. It only became a success after his death and was reprinted in four different editions from 1916 to 1971. Language tutoring and contributions to various journals supported him until he found employment in May 1892 with the Villard Expedition, funded by railway magnate Henry Villard to conduct archaeological studies and collect antiquities in Ecuador, Peru, and Bolivia.

Bandelier's wife died in Lima in December 1892. A year later he married Fanny Ritter, also of Swiss origin, whom he had met in South America. Herself a potential scholar, who spoke at least four languages, showed great aptitude for archaeological field work, and possessed excellent writing ability, she helped him greatly in his work. In 1903 the couple left South America for New York, where he arranged his notes for the Museum of Natural History, which had taken over the Villard project. He lectured at Columbia University and published his *Islands of Titicaca and Koati* (1910) under the auspices of the Hispanic Society of America. He was appointed research assistant for the Carnegie Institution in 1911 after a cataract operation improved his eyesight, which had been failing since 1909.

After another trip to Mexico for archival research, Bandelier and his wife left in 1913 to work in the archives of Seville in Spain. There Bandelier almost immediately fell ill and died. He was buried there, but his remains were returned to Santa Fe in 1977.

Bandelier was a natural scholar, an indefatigable worker, and a prolific writer. At least 150 books and articles by him have been published. He was also an excellent artist, illustrating the papal gift with watercolors of Indian costumes, pottery, lithics, and ground plans of ancient pueblos. He was a self-trained man in a day when information was scarce in his field. His favorite occupation was searching through ancient archives. But he felt that the historian should also go into the field to confirm his archival research. The field worker, in turn, should examine the documents concerning the subject of his study. In this belief that archaeology, anthropology, and ethnology went hand in hand with history, creating a new dimension that led to knowledge, Bandelier was a pioneer.

• Bandelier's original journals, including the unpublished South American portion, with other papers and memorabilia, are in the History Library, Museum of New Mexico, Santa Fe. Summaries and quotes from letters concerning his family's U.S. immigration are in Madeleine Turrell Rodack, "Adolph Bandelier and the Swiss Connection," *Reflections: The Papers of the Archaeological Society of New Mexico* 14 (1988). Her translation of the largely unpublished *History of the Colonization and Missions of Sonora, Chihuahua, New Mexico and Arizona to the Year 1700* (French original in the Vatican Library), is in the archives of the Arizona State Museum Library, University of Arizona, Tucson. Three chapters only of the English translation appeared in the spring 1988 edition of the *Journal of the Southwest*, published by the Southwest Center at the University of Arizona in Tucson. An introductory volume by Ernest J. Burrus, SJ, published by the Jesuit Historical Institute in Rome in 1969, does not include the text but include a portfolio of forty of the illustrations. The Jesuit Historical Institute also published, in 1967, the French text of parts 1 and 2, with English footnotes, ed. Ernest J. Burrus, SJ, and Madeleine Turrell Rodack. Slides of the illustrations are in Special Collections, University of Arizona Library; the Pius XII Memorial Library at St. Louis University; the Bancroft Library, University of California, Berkeley; and the Amerind Foundation, Dragoon, Ariz. The principal sources of information on Bandelier are in his *Southwestern Journals*, vols. 1 and 2, ed. Charles H. Lange and Carroll L. Riley (1880–1884), and vols. 3 and 4, ed. Lange et al. (1885–1892). Volume 4, in particular, contains a comprehensive bibliography and numerous sources on his background. Biographical sketches can be found in Ernest J. Burrus, *History of the Southwest: A Study of the Civilization and Conversion of the Indians in Southwestern United States and Northwestern Mexico from the Earliest Times to 1700, by Adolph F. Bandelier, vol. 1: A Catalogue of the Bandelier Collection in the Vatican Library* (1969), Edgar A. Goad, *A Study of the Life of Adolph Francis Alphonse Bandelier, with an Appraisal of His Contributions to American Anthropology and Related Sciences* (Ph.D. diss., Univ. of Southern California, 1939), and Leslie A. White, *Pioneers in American Anthropology: The Bandelier-Morgan Letters, 1873–1883* (2 vols., 1940). Obituaries are in the *Nation*, 26 Mar. 1914, and *American Anthropologist* 16 (1914).

MADELEINE TURRELL RODACK

BANGS, Frank C. (12 Oct. 1833–12 June 1908), actor, was born in Alexandria, Virginia, the son of David Barnwell Bangs and Margaret Cannon. As a teenager, he worked on a Washington, D.C., newspaper as a typesetter and writer; then, urged by his mother, he studied briefly for the ministry. But from the age of thirteen, he was determined to be an actor, reportedly after seeing Junius Brutus Booth in performance as Richard III.

He made his first appearance at the National Theatre in Washington, D.C., on 27 September 1851 playing with the Ravel Troupe as the lover in a pantomimic piece called *The Miller and His Men*. The troupe then hired him to play what were at that time called "general utility" roles in the National's stock company. At the end of his first season he was advanced to "walking gentleman," a position limited to minor roles with few or no lines. After two seasons at the National, he went to Ford's Theatre in Baltimore for two seasons, playing juvenile lead roles such as Romeo and

Claude Melnotte. He did two seasons at the Arch Street Theatre in Philadelphia, then moved on to the Green Street Theatre in Albany, where he became a leading man. Afterward he played short engagements in Baltimore, Washington, D.C., and Richmond.

On 22 April 1858 he made his New York debut as Gilbert Gates in J. G. Burnett's *Blanche of Brandywine* at Laura Keene's Theatre. He remained with Keene's company for the season and subsequently was in the company at Wallack's Theatre in New York, one of the finest stock companies in the city. His last role before the Civil War was that of the villain Jacob McCloskey in Dion Boucicault's *The Octoroon*.

Bangs joined the Confederate army and served with the Third Virginia Regiment, advancing in rank from private to brevet brigadier-general. He was captured and imprisoned at Hilton Head in the last year of the conflict. After his repatriation, he was engaged as a leading actor at the National Theatre, where his first stage appearance was as the heroic rebel William Tell. Before his opening appearance, two Washington newspapers, the *Star* and the *Republican*, questioned the propriety of Bangs's engagement at the National because of his Confederate service. He also received letters threatening physical injury if he should appear in Washington. But he was supported by the Washington *Globe* and the *National Intelligence*, by several military officers, and by members of the cabinet, since he had, like many former Confederate officers, taken an oath of allegiance to the United States. He played William Tell and continued to play leading roles. He was engaged in November 1868 to play a supporting role in a play called *After Dark* at Niblo's Garden in New York. While the production was in rehearsal, however, the actor who was playing the leading role of Old Tom was killed in an accident, and Bangs was transferred to his part. It proved very successful for him during the play's three-month run, one of the longest on the New York stage to that time.

The New York theater managers Albert M. Palmer and Henry C. Jarrett then offered him the title role in *Julius Caesar*, but Bangs wanted to play Mark Antony. When his negotiations with Jarrett and Palmer failed, he abruptly retired from the stage. Settling in Philadelphia, for the next two years he taught the art of reading and oratory, coached local dramatic societies, and gave a series of lectures on mental philosophy and readings from great dramatists and poets.

In the winter of 1870, however, he returned to the stage, playing in support of Charles Albert Fechter and Carlotta Leclercq at the Boston Theatre in *Hamlet*, *Ruy Blas*, and *The Lady of Lyons*. Then Edwin Booth engaged him for his new Booth's Theatre company. In a scenically splendid revival of *Julius Caesar* at Booth's Theatre in 1871–1872, Bangs first played Mark Antony. Later in the run, when Booth himself assumed the role of Mark Antony, Bangs took on that of Brutus. He afterward played in support of several stars, including Lawrence Barrett and Adelaide Neilson.

In 1874 Bangs made a starring tour on his own in *The Soldier's Trust*, an adaptation of a French play, *Le Vieux Corporal*, written for the famous French Romantic actor Frédéric Lemaître. Several months into the tour, however, during a performance in Cleveland, Bangs tore the muscles in one of his legs so severely that he had to be removed from the stage on a stretcher. The remainder of the tour was canceled, and Bangs returned to Philadelphia to recuperate. On recovering, he was engaged by Jarrett and Palmer to play Mark Antony in their own elaborate production of *Julius Caesar* at Booth's Theatre.

The next season at the same theater, Bangs played the title role in a spectacular revival of *Sardanapalus*. The *New York Herald*'s critic savaged this production, noting that Bangs's "principal office . . . is to fill up waits between the marching and the dancing and form a central figure in the tableaux." Perhaps sarcastically, the critic praised the actor's legs, which he described as "beauties in their blue silk encasements." Bangs survived such criticism. The following year he made a starring tour of the South playing Shylock, Virginius, and Mark Antony. After the success of Henry Arthur Jones's *The Silver King* at Wallack's Theatre in 1883, he was engaged to play Wilfrid Denver in a road tour of this production. After this tour he played John Strebelow in Bronson Howard's *The Banker's Daughter* at the Union Square Theatre, subsequently touring in this role as well. In the 1880s Bangs appeared in a number of starring vehicles, including J. H. Wilkins's play *St. Marc, the Soldier of Fortune* and an adaptation of Jules Verne's *Michael Strogoff*. He also toured as James Ralston in Charles Young's *Jim, The Penman* and as Colonel Preston in Augustus Thomas's *Alabama*. In 1883 Bangs married Le Grove Singer, but they were subsequently divorced. During the season of 1890–1891, he toured with the company of Joseph Jefferson and William Florence, playing Lord Duberly in *The Heir-at-Law* and Sir Anthony Absolute in Sheridan's *The Rivals*. In 1897–1898 Bangs appeared in the Fifth Avenue Theatre as Colonel Wyckoff Ransom in the popular melodrama *A Southern Romance*, adapted from Dolly Higbee's novel *In God's Country*. In the next season he played Captain Oliphant in support of Stuart Robson in Augustus Thomas's comedy *The Meddler* at Wallack's Theatre. In the latter part of his career he played supporting roles in such pieces as *The Christian*, *The Choir Invisible*, *The Eternal City*, and *The Gentleman from Indiana*. He died in Atlantic City.

During his long career, spanning over fifty years, Bangs established a solid reputation as a reliable and versatile actor but as a supporting player rather than as a leading actor or a star. His experience was thus more representative of the profession at that time than were the stellar careers of Edwin Booth and Lawrence Barrett. Working in several major stock companies, touring productions from city to city, and always playing a wide range of roles—from Shakespeare and Sheridan to turn-of-the-century melodramas and farces—Bangs had a career that typified the life of the workaday professional actor in the last half of the nineteenth century.

• Perhaps the best overview of Frank C. Bangs's career is in John Bouvé Clapp and Edwin Francis Edgett, *Players of the Present*, pt. 1 (1899), pp. 24–26. Obituaries are in *The Clipper* (New York), 20 June 1908; *The Era* (London), 11 July 1908; the *Boston Transcript*, 13 June 1908; the *New York Dramatic Mirror*, 20 June 1908; and the *New York Times*, 14 June 1908.

DANIEL J. WATERMEIER

BANGS, John Kendrick (27 May 1862–21 Jan. 1922), humorist, editor, and lecturer, was born in Yonkers, New York, the son of Francis Nehemiah Bangs, a lawyer, and Frances Amelia Bull, and the grandson of Nathan Bangs, a Methodist clergyman. His ancestors were domineering and ferocious personalities whose achievements overshadowed Bangs's career, and his perennial reluctance to take either religion or law seriously can be seen as a mild rebellion.

Bangs entered Columbia University in 1879 and, from 1881 until his 1883 graduation, wrote prolifically under a variety of pseudonyms for the *Acta Columbiana*; he edited the *Acta* in 1882 and 1883. After receiving his Ph.B. (philosophiae baccalaureus or bachelor of philosophy) in political science, he studied law in his father's office but began writing humorous sketches for New York humor magazines *Puck* and *Life*, joining the latter as assistant editor in 1884. In 1886, soon after the death of his father, Bangs married his first cousin Agnes Lawson Hyde; they had four children, three of whom survived into adulthood, before her death in 1903.

From 1888 to 1901 Bangs published freely in and was editorially affiliated with the magazines in the Harper group. He joined the prestigious *Harper's New Monthly Magazine* in 1888, writing a regular column titled "The Editor's Drawer." He simultaneously edited the "Facetiae" section of *Harper's Bazar* and soon became editor of the humor section for *Harper's Young People*; from 1899 to 1901 he edited *Harper's Weekly*. In addition, he served briefly as first editor of *Munsey's Magazine* during 1889, and he edited the American edition of *Literature*, also owned by the Harper group, during 1899. Partially because of his influential editorial position, and partially because of his gregarious nature, Bangs became important as a figure in the fin de siècle New York literary clubs. His friends (many of whom were also published in the Harper magazines) included Arthur Conan Doyle, Rudyard Kipling, William Dean Howells, Hall Caine, Richard Harding Davis, Theodore Roosevelt, and Mark Twain. In 1894 he ran for mayor of Yonkers, losing by a mere 207 votes, and during 1896–1897 he was vice president of the Yonkers Board of Education.

Bangs's association with the Harper magazines concluded in 1901. Harper's had been reorganized, and the new management objected to Bangs's coverage of the Spanish American War: Bangs supported the actions of his friend Theodore Roosevelt and wrote approvingly of the American activities in Cuba, rather than condemning them as he was supposed to.

After Bangs left the Harper publications, his literary career declined. Though an occasional piece succeeded, his work was no longer bestselling. He had to sell much of his property, including his collection of rare books, and in 1907 he moved to Ogunquit, Maine, his property apparently near that of Sarah Orne Jewett. He married Mary Blakeney Gray on 27 April 1904. From 1907 until his death, Bangs freelanced as a writer and earned his living as a professional speaker, repeatedly delivering lectures such as "The Evolution of the Humorist: From Adam to Ade" and "Salubrities [*sic*] I Have Met." During World War I, he gave hundreds of lectures on behalf of the war effort; the French government awarded him the chevalier of the Legion of Honor for his efforts. Following the war he wrote and spoke in support of Warren G. Harding and returned briefly to France to assist in rehabilitating devastated areas. In 1921 he became ill during his Christmas vacation in Atlantic City, New Jersey; he died there following an operation for intestinal sarcoma.

Though Bangs wrote poetry, drama, juveniles, and nonfiction, the first of his nearly seventy books was *The Lorgnette* (1886), an anonymous collection of social jests illustrated by *Life* artist S. W. Van Schaick. It received mixed reviews; Bangs himself was not pleased with it, calling it "a pronounced failure—flat, stale, and unprofitable." Prior to writing prose fiction, Bangs received some recognition as a playwright; his first play, *Katharine: A Travesty* (1888), a comic adaptation of *The Taming of the Shrew* set to music adapted from Gilbert and Sullivan, was moderately successful, and Bangs thereafter wrote a number of original plays. Despite occasional triumphs, as in the 1904 *Lady Teazle*, which starred Lillian Russell, the stage was not Bangs's forte, and his plays, though occasionally amusing in situation, lack dramatic tension. Bangs's poetry and juvenile books are no more memorable. His poems appeared in dozens of magazines, and from January 1913 until his death, he contributed a daily verse to the newspapers in the McClure syndicate; although he wrote an estimated 10,000 verses, he was at best a facile rhymer. His juveniles, many of which feature the character "Jimmieboy" (based on Bangs's eldest child, John Kendrick Bangs, Jr.), tell stories that are extraordinarily slight.

Bangs's friends were among the best and most noted writers of late nineteenth-century America, but his fiction, though literate, does not exemplify or follow any contemporary literary movement, though its frequently episodic structure may be loosely allied with such earlier literary models as Chaucer and Boccaccio. His first novel, the anonymously published *Roger Camerden: A Strange Story* (1887), was an attempt at writing seriously about insanity, but despite an interesting premise, it is dull and overly cerebral. Bangs's remaining works have rightly been described by contemporary critic Everett F. Bleiler as "overlong and empty," a charge that is especially true of Bangs's second novel, *Toppleton's Client: or, A Spirit in Exile* (1893), which climaxes in a naive young lawyer losing his body to a fiendish usurper.

Bangs's collection of supernatural fiction, *The Water Ghost and Others* (1894), was notable for presenting ghosts as objects of humor rather than terror. This reversal of tradition was also present when Bangs reached bestseller status with two novels set in Hades, *A House-Boat on the Styx* (1896) and *The Pursuit of the House-Boat* (1897). In these, Hades is pleasant, and the House-Boat is the social club of the Associated Shades, whose members are famous literary and historical characters. Shakespeare thus discusses drama with Hamlet and wrangles with Sir Walter Raleigh, Francis Bacon, and Nero over the authorship of his plays; Noah complains about the dinosaurs aboard his ark; and the Baron Münchhausen tells Charles Darwin and David Livingstone about talking with monkeys. Like so much of Bangs's work, these novels are slight, padded, and unmemorable. A sequel, *The Enchanted Type-Writer* (1899), in which a typewriter receives missives from James Boswell and Xanthippe, is even weaker, though the Xanthippe sections are oddly protofeminist. Bangs's best fiction is the series of humorous stories featuring a character ironically named "the Idiot." This person—young, handsome, articulate, and clever—is anything but idiotic as he spars verbally with staid opponents and, as Bangs's mouthpiece, offers mild social commentary. In *Three Weeks in Politics* (1894), the Idiot tells of Bangs's failed mayoral campaign, and in *The Idiot* (1895), the Idiot impresses his fellow boarders by quoting as Swinburne a delightful pastiche of his own composition.

Bangs's published nonfiction is varied and ranges from private publications in celebration of Mark Twain's birthday to *From Pillar to Post; Leaves from a Lecturer's Note-Book* (1916), an anecdotal account of some of the personalities and situations he encountered while earning his living as a lecturer; it is arguably Bangs's finest work. Though he failed to win public office, Bangs remained interested in politics and wrote occasionally on contemporary political subjects in works such as *Why I Am for Harding. By a Man Who Wanted Wood* (1920). He wrote a burlesque biography of Napoleon, *Mr. Bonaparte of Corsica* (1895), numerous book reviews (some of which are surprisingly acute), and dozens of light essays. He was capable of perceptive self-analysis, stating in the introduction to a later edition of *A House-Boat on the Styx*,

I must confess . . . that among the books I have written I do not find the *House-Boat* the least tolerable. To speak quite frankly, my own style of humor—if humor it may be, and many there are who say that it is distinctly otherwise—is not the kind I most admire. . . . For continuous, satisfactory reading, I prefer Shakespeare, Milton, and others whose methods differed somewhat from my own.

Bangs was an intelligent, literate man who deliberately wrote fluff, only occasionally permitting hints of a more serious, more socially conscious man to filter through his prose. His 1901 "A Glance Ahead. Being a Christmas Tale of A.D. 3568," for example, reveals that he was well aware of contemporary racial problems. He chose not to grapple with such serious issues in his fiction, however, preferring instead to write parodies of contemporary bestsellers and the works of his friends and to joke about incompetent Irish servants and relationships in boarding houses, all the while celebrating the mores of the New York upper class. He thus epitomizes the light humor of the wealthy, white Protestant New Yorker of the 1880s and 1890s, and while none of his more famous contemporaries said a bad word about him, neither did they have anything else to say. He was a perfect product of his time, whose slight and uncontroversial works will remain unread and unremembered.

• Most of the Bangs family papers are held by the Beinecke Library at Yale University (YCAL MSS 47), and William K. Finley's excellent finding aid is Internet accessible. The only book-length treatment of Bangs is Francis Hyde Bangs's hagiographic and often vague *John Kendrick Bangs: Humorist of the Nineties* (1941); Francis H. Bangs's "John Kendrick Bangs, Humorist of the Nineties," *Yale University Library Gazette* 7, no. 3 (Jan. 1933): 53–76, and Jacob Blanck's "John Kendrick Bangs" in the *Bibliography of American Literature*, vol. 1 (1955), contain the only bibliographies of Bangs, but both are incomplete. Bangs's supernatural writings are discussed by Everett F. Bleiler in *Supernatural Fiction Writers: Fantasy and Horror*, ed. Everett F. Bleiler (1985). Robert Reginald and Mary Burgess summarize the *House-Boat* novels in *Survey of Modern Fantasy Literature*, ed. Frank N. Magill (1983). Bangs was the subject of numerous newspaper articles during his lifetime, but he is virtually unstudied as an author or influence. Obituaries are in the *New York Times*, the *New York Tribune*, and the *New York Herald*, 22 Jan. 1922.

RICHARD J. BLEILER

BANGS, Nathan (2 May 1778–3 May 1862), Methodist itinerant and missionary society founder, was born in Stratford, Connecticut, the son of Lemuel Bangs, a blacksmith, schoolteacher, and surveyor, and Rebecca Keeler. In 1782, the family moved to Fairfield, Connecticut, and then in 1791, to Stamford, New York. Bangs received little formal education as a youth, but in 1799 he was hired to teach school in Niagara, Canada. Although baptized in the Anglican communion, in Canada Bangs was drawn to Methodism because of its emphasis on inner religious experience. He became licensed as a Methodist itinerant in 1801 and labored tirelessly to spread the Methodist vision, first in Upper Canada from 1801 to 1804, and then in the province of Quebec from 1804 to 1812. He is regarded as the founder of Methodism in Quebec. In 1806, Bangs married Mary Bolton; they had at least two children.

When the War of 1812 erupted between the United States and Britain, hostilities also grew between the United States and Canada, which was then a British colony. Since some U.S. leaders had called for an invasion of Canada as part of the war strategy, U.S. citizens living in Canada became suspect. As a result, Bangs felt compelled to return to the United States, and in 1812 he moved to New York City, where he became a Methodist pastor and presiding elder. Within a few years of his arrival in New York, Bangs wrote two books attacking Calvinist doctrine, *Errors of Hopkinsianism* (1815) and *Examination of the Doctrine of Predestination* (1817). In both, he asserted that humans possess a will that is free to accept or reject God's salvation through Christ and argued against the Calvinist view that God chose some for salvation and some for damnation without any human choice or response in the matter. Except for a one-year tenure as third president of Wesleyan University in Connecticut from 1841 to 1842, Bangs resided in the New York area from 1812 until his death.

In 1820, Bangs accepted an appointment as manager of the Methodist Book Concern, the publishing arm of the Methodist Episcopal Church. He streamlined its business operations and raised the standards of material published. He also began to edit the *Methodist Magazine* (later called the *Methodist Quarterly Review*) and then the *Christian Advocate and Journal*. Both publications were intended to appeal to laity and clergy alike, and Bangs used them to promote the theological emphases of Methodism, especially its advocacy of free will and human involvement, in salvation as opposed to the Calvinist notion of predestination.

A founder of the Methodist Missionary Society in 1819, Bangs became its salaried secretary (administrative head) in 1836. He oversaw Methodist expansion in upstate New York and also worked to upgrade educational standards for Methodist clergy and to strengthen denominational authority internally. Historians credit Bangs as a major force in shaping the structure of American Methodism, helping it shed its early image as a frontier sect promoted by zealous but theologically unsophisticated preachers. His *Vindication of Methodist Episcopacy* (1820) and four-volume *History of the Methodist Episcopal Church* (1838–1840) ardently defended Methodist polity, particularly the power of bishops. In these books, Bangs revealed his conviction that religious conversion was essential to becoming civilized, through he saw civility primarily as acceptance of Euro-American cultural mores. Ironically, his history virtually ignored the controversy over slavery that would divide American Methodism in 1844.

After his brief presidency of Wesleyan University, Bangs served in several Methodist churches in New York until he retired in 1852. At the time of his death in New York, Bangs was regarded as one of the most influential Methodists of his generation.

• Letters from Bangs are in the Ezekiel Cooper Collection of Early Methodist Manuscripts at Garrett-Evangelical Theological Seminary, Evanston, Illinois. Among Bangs's other works are *Christianism* (1809), *The Reformer Reformed* (1818), *The Life of the Rev. Freeborn Garrettson* (1829), *History of Missions* (1832), *Letters to a Young Preacher* (1835), *An Original Church of Christ* (1837), *Life of James Arminius* (1843), *Present State, Prospects, and Responsibilities of the Methodist Episcopal Church* (1850), and *Necessity, Nature, and Fruits of Sanctification* (1851). There is no analytical biography, but see Abel Stevens, *Life and Times of Nathan Bangs* (1863), and Alexander H. Tuttle, *Nathan Bangs* (1909), for helpful but uncritical appraisals. A more recent, unpublished study is Richard E. Herrman, "Nathan Bangs: Apologist for American Methodism" (Ph.D. diss., Emory Univ., 1973).

CHARLES H. LIPPY

BANISTER, John (1650–May 1692), clergyman and naturalist, was born at Twigworth in Gloucestershire, England, the son of John Bannister, a commoner, occupation unknown; his mother's name is also unknown. He was educated at Magdalen College, Oxford, where he received his B.A. in 1671 and M.A. in 1674. He stayed on at Magdalen as a clerk and then chaplain until 1678. At Oxford, Banister trained for the clergy and studied natural history, compiling the "Herbarium siccum Jo. Banister," an unpublished herbal with 374 folios of pressed specimens from Oxfordshire, parts of which appeared in Robert Plot's *Natural History of Oxford-shire* (1677). He attracted the attention of powerful men, including Robert Morison, professor of botany at Oxford (from 1669), and Henry Compton, who became bishop of Oxford (1674), then bishop of London (1675).

In 1678 Banister traveled through the Caribbean and on to Virginia, evidently using funds provided by English patrons. Whether his appointed task in Virginia was religious or scientific is unclear. His status as "missionary" seemingly indicated religious ministration to the colonists (which Banister performed) rather than preaching to the Native Americans. In any case, Banister devoted himself to natural history. He quickly won support from members of Virginia's elite, including William Byrd I, who was among the growing number of learned colonists who, if they had a scientific bent, were correspondents of the Royal Society and also corresponded with other British men of learning.

Banister's familiarity with plants of many parts of the world—England, America, Africa, and continental Europe—suited him to contemporary botany, which depended on the gathering and describing of specimens rather than theorizing about them. In America, Banister collected a wealth of information, mostly on Virginia plants. He also did painstaking work on insects and snails, discussed the commercial cultivation of tobacco, and made ethnological observations of Virginia's aboriginal inhabitants. Banister eventually sent specimens of about 340 species of plants to England and provided Virginia flora to Bishop Compton (for his Fulham Palace gardens) as well as to other correspondents. Banister also preserved specimens of one hundred insects and twenty mollusks and made about eighty beautiful sketches of plants. He began an ambitious "Natural History of Virginia," following the system outlined by Greek philosopher Empedocles (also used by Jose de Acosta in his influential 1590 natural history of Spanish America), in which subjects were divided among the four classical elements.

Banister maintained contact with Compton and Morison as well as with the Royal Society and the Temple Coffee House Botany Club (which took shape in the early 1690s), which had overlapping constituencies. Aside from his patrons, Banister's most important intellectual contact was with John Ray, another naturalist connected with the Royal Society. Ray solicited information from Banister to prepare his own *Historia Plantarum* (begun 1682, published 1686–1704). English patronage proved inadequate, and Banister was forced to look for other resources. These he found by entering the plantation elite of Virginia. In 1688 Banister married a widow, Martha (surname unknown); two years later he imported thirty-five servants, including two African slaves; and then on the basis of the colony's headright system, which gave acreage to settlers according to the number of dependents in their households, Banister claimed 1,735 acres in Bristol Parish of Charles City County. Banister's position in the local learned gentry was confirmed by his listing among the founders of the College of William and Mary.

Banister had thus established his livelihood and a basis for his researches, along with a position as head of a respected Virginia family. He had little time, however, to enjoy his success. While on a 1692 expedition led by Byrd along the Roanoke River, Banister was accidentally shot by a companion, Jacob Colson. Despite the legal finding of death by misadventure, for some time after Banister's death the official explanation of his demise was that he died from a fall, probably to protect Colson from public rebuke. He was survived by his again-widowed wife and an infant son, John; Martha Banister would marry Stephen Cocke in 1694, and young John Banister became a protégé of William Byrd II.

Because of Banister's early death, he did not publish any work based on his considerable number of specimens. Nevertheless, Banister's intellectual labors had a legacy surviving his death, and his collections, drawings, and notes were used by others. Many of his papers and his herbarium were sent to Bishop Compton; they eventually went to Sir Hans Sloane and the British Museum. These documents included material on the Caribbean and Virginia as well as Banister's original plant catalog, dated 1678. Other papers may have remained in Virginia and possibly were destroyed in a later fire at the Banister home.

Much scientific work of the late seventeenth and early eighteenth centuries was based on Banister's empirical foundations—whether attributed to him or not. Some of his writings appeared in the Royal Society's *Philosophical Transactions*. Significant portions of Robert Beverley's *History and Present State of Virginia* (1705) quoted without attribution from two of Banister's treatises on Virginia; parts of John Oldmixon's *British Empire in America* (1708) then repeated these sections of Banister by way of Beverley. Naturalists Martin Lister and James Petiver also used Banister's materials. Johann Frederick Gronovius, *Flora Virginica* (1739, 1743), listed most of Banister's plants, though Gronovius gathered some of these references at second hand or third hand, partly from the work of John Clayton. More significantly, Banister contribut-

ed to research that culminated in the Linnaean system of classification. John Ray was the most important conduit between the work of Banister and the achievements of Linnaeus. Ray utilized Banister's materials before and after Banister's death, continuing the seventeenth-century method of empirical description of phenomena. This method stood in contrast to the later emphasis on theory and system that took final form in Linnaeus's scientific taxonomy. Linnaeus quarreled with Ray's method but utilized the data that had, in part, derived from Banister. In 1736 Linnaeus saw Banister's specimens in Sloane's collections and at Oxford.

In addition to the survival of his Virginia family and the utilization of his work by later scholars, Banister gained lasting fame by having a botanical genus named after him. In the 1720s William Houston gave the generic name *Banisteria* to several species of tropical plants. The name, spelled *Bannisteria*, was adopted by Linnaeus in his *Genera Plantarum* (1737) and then as *Banisteria* in *Species Plantarum* (1753). *Banisteria* now encompasses about seventy species of the Malpighiaceae.

• The bulk of Banister's papers are in the Sloane manuscripts of the British Museum. His treatises and catalogs are reprinted in Joseph Ewan and Nesta Ewan, *John Banister and His Natural History of Virginia, 1678–1692* (1970), which also contains an excellent discussion of Banister's life and works. Banister is placed in a wider context in Raymond Phineas Stearns, *Science in the British Colonies of America* (1970).

JOYCE E. CHAPLIN

BANISTER, Zilpah Polly Grant. *See* Grant, Zilpah Polly.

BANKHEAD, John Hollis (13 Sept. 1842–1 Mar. 1920), politician, was born in Moscow, Alabama, the son of James Greer Bankhead, a planter and soldier, and Susan Hollis. Born and raised on his father's plantation in pioneer country, John Hollis received little schooling but supplemented his formal education with extensive reading. At the outbreak of the Civil War, he enlisted in Company K, Sixteenth Alabama Infantry Regiment. With that regiment, Bankhead participated in battles at Fishing Creek, Perryville, Stones River, Shiloh, and Chickamauga and was wounded on several occasions. His exemplary courage did not go unnoticed. Following the battle of Fishing Creek, he was promoted to third lieutenant, and after the battle of Shiloh he was appointed captain. A dour, towering figure, Bankhead was thereafter known as Captain John to his family and close friends.

Following the war, Bankhead returned to Alabama and was elected to the state legislature from Marion County, where he served from 1865 to 1867. During this immediate postwar period, he began his association with General Nathan Bedford Forrest's Ku Klux Klan, which was organized by ex-Confederates to oppose Republican policies and maintain white supremacy. After his brief stint in the Alabama legislature, he left politics to resume his life as a farmer. In 1866 he married Tallulah James Brockman; they had five children. Bankhead returned to politics as a state senator, serving in 1876–1877, and supported General John T. Morgan in his election to the U.S. Senate. Bankhead succeeded Morgan in this position thirty years later. In 1880–1881 Bankhead again served as a member of the Alabama House, this time impressing Alabama governor James Edward Cobb with his legislative and organizational skills. The following year Cobb appointed Bankhead warden of the state penitentiary, a position he held for four years. Under his wardenship, several reforms were initiated, including the abolition of the small cells as sleeping quarters and the disuse of the instruments of torture that characterized the "dark ages" in the prison system in Alabama.

On 13 September 1886, at the Fayette Court House, Bankhead was nominated to Congress by the Democratic convention of the Sixth Congressional District, and he was elected to that office in November. While serving continuously from 1887 to 1907, he was a member of the Committee on Public Buildings and Grounds that oversaw the construction of the Library of Congress in Washington. Also a member of the Rivers and Harbors Committee, Bankhead oversaw extensive improvements to the Warrior River in Alabama. A reservoir constructed at the mouth of that river now bears his name. In August 1906 Bankhead was nominated in the Alabama Democratic primary to assume that state's next vacancy in the U.S. Senate. Upon the death of Senator Morgan in June 1907, the Alabama state legislature confirmed Bankhead's nomination. After taking his seat in the U.S. Senate, Bankhead began an exhaustive campaign to increase federal cooperation with the states in the construction of highways and succeeded in securing the first federal aid in building roads in every state in the Union. After ten years his efforts were rewarded by the passage of the Bankhead Good Roads Bill, which carried an appropriation of $75 million. In recognition of his services, one of the transcontinental highways was named in his honor. The "Bankhead Highway" begins in Washington, D.C., at the "Zero Stone," marking jointly the beginning of the Bankhead and the Lincoln highways, and terminates in San Diego, California. In 1912 Bankhead managed the presidential campaign of fellow Alabamian Oscar Underwood, chairman of the House Ways and Means Committee and the first post–Civil War era presidential candidate from the Deep South.

Toward the end of his career, Bankhead continued to press for the development of the nation's water resources. He collaborated with Senator Underwood in securing the construction of the Wilson Dam at Muscle Shoals, Alabama, a model for the regional planning and development projects adopted later under the Tennessee Valley Authority. He also enjoyed the rare honor of being joined in Congress by one of his sons, William Brockman Bankhead, who was elected in 1916 to the House of Representatives, where he rose to national prominence as Speaker twenty years later. Another son, John Hollis Bankhead, Jr., served in the

U.S. Senate from 1931 to 1946. The famous stage actress Tallulah Bankhead was William Bankhead's youngest daughter. The elder Bankhead died in Washington, D.C. He had served for thirty-three years in the two houses of Congress and was the oldest Confederate veteran to sit in the U.S. Senate. Throughout his career, Bankhead was an ardent and effective advocate of internal improvements and, for the last fifteen years of his life, a pioneer in the good roads movement.

• A collection of Bankhead's official correspondence and papers is at the Alabama Department of Archives and History. The primary authority on Bankhead is the sketch by his son-in-law Thomas M. Owen in *History of Alabama and Dictionary of Alabama Biography*, vol. 1 (1921; repr. 1978). For more personal and anecdotal information on Bankhead and his family, see Tallulah Bankhead, *Tallulah: My Autobiography* (1952), and Lee Israel, *Miss Tallulah Bankhead* (1972). An obituary is in the *New York Times*, 2 Mar. 1920.

MATTHEW T. PEARCY

BANKHEAD, John Hollis (8 July 1872–12 June 1946), lawyer, businessman and U.S. senator, was born in Moscow in Lamar County, Alabama, the son of John Hollis Bankhead (1842–1920), a farmer and later U.S. senator, and Tallulah Brockman. After spending his childhood in Wetumpka and Fayette, Alabama, he received an A.B. from the University of Alabama (1891) and an LL.B. from Georgetown University (1893). In 1894 Bankhead married Musa Harkins of Fayette, with whom he had three children. Settling in Jasper, he became a lawyer for the Alabama Power Company and for leading railroads. From 1911 to 1925 he was president of the Bankhead Coal Company, a firm founded by his father, which owned one of Alabama's largest mines.

From 1903 to 1905 Bankhead served a term in the Alabama House of Representatives, where he wrote legislation disenfranchising most black voters. In 1926 he entered the U.S. Senate race but lost the crucial Democratic primary to Hugo L. Black. During the race, Black attacked Bankhead's long association with the Alabama Power Company. Bankhead became convinced that his association with corporations had cost him the election, and ever afterward he identified himself with the welfare of the cotton farmer. In 1930 Bankhead received the regular Democratic nomination for the Senate but was challenged in the general election by incumbent J. Thomas Heflin, who ran as a "Jeffersonian Democrat." With the support of Alabama's larger business leaders (called the "Big Mules"), corporations, and "dry" elements, Bankhead won by 50,000 votes. Although Heflin contested the election, a Senate committee ruled in Bankhead's favor, and in the spring of 1932 he was seated.

Entering Congress in the midst of the Great Depression, Bankhead was particularly sensitive to the poverty of the rural South, whose cotton farmers were plagued by overproduction and low prices. In his own Alabama, between 1920 and 1930 the number of individually owned farms had decreased by over 20 percent. By 1930 tenants operated more than 65 percent of the farms in the state. Nicknamed "Parity John," Bankhead was always provincial to the extreme, evaluating most issues—foreign and domestic—in terms of their effect on commodity prices, and on that of cotton in particular.

A backer of Franklin D. Roosevelt even before FDR won the Democrats' 1932 presidential nomination, Bankhead became soon after the election the new president's liaison with cotton farmers, on whom Bankhead's political life increasingly depended. He served as the administration's leader in handling the processing tax of the Agricultural Adjustment Act (AAA) of 1933, a measure that assessed millers, ginners, packers, and canners. He claimed credit for the policy of paying farmers to plow up a quarter of their fields. The Bankhead Cotton Control Act of 1934, co-sponsored in the House by his brother William Bankhead, imposed strict marketing quotas to limit production by large farmers. In February 1936 the law was repealed on Roosevelt's recommendation after the Supreme Court had declared the 1933 AAA unconstitutional, and Bankhead himself privately admitted that the measure had failed. As coauthor of the Agricultural Adjustment Act of 1938, Bankhead included a provision by which Congress established legal machinery for farmers to control cotton production and marketing. Thanks to Bankhead and his senatorial allies, the government now provided a special fund for parity payments, required the Commodity Credit Corporation (CCC) to put cotton into loan when the price fell below 52 percent of parity (the level of farm prices existing in the boom years 1909–1914), and gave the CCC the option of insuring cotton. In 1941 Bankhead successfully secured legislation that guaranteed loans on cotton production of up to 85 percent of parity.

Bankhead sponsored other measures to aid the southern farmer. Unlike so many legislators from his region, Bankhead sought to aid tenants, sharecroppers, and migrants as well as the better-off planters. His Subsistence Homestead Act, part of the National Industrial Recovery Act of 1933, included $25 million to relocate slum dwellers to the countryside. In 1937, together with Representative Martin Jones, Bankhead sponsored the Farm Tenancy Act. Under its terms, Congress established the Farm Security Administration (FSA), which extended rehabilitation loans to farmers, granted loans at 3 percent interest to enable selected tenants to buy family-sized farms, provided a fund for the purchase and retirement of submarginal land, and aided migrants by establishing sanitary camps. One of the more controversial of the New Deal agencies, during its seven year life the FSA spent over $1 billion, much of it in the form of loans; helped launch medical care cooperatives; and distributed a significant share of its benefits to blacks. Yet, bitterly opposed by large farm corporations and southern landlords, the FSA was always underfunded, and, in comparison to the scope of rural poverty, its concrete accomplishments were small.

No friend of blacks, Bankhead participated in filibusters against antilynching legislation, abolition of the poll tax, and the establishment of a permanent fair employment practices commission. In August 1942, following a disturbance in Jacksonville, Florida, he urged Army Chief of Staff George C. Marshall to keep black troops out of the South.

In 1936 Bankhead won reelection easily, enjoying the backing of powerful farm groups and organized labor. He voted against Roosevelt's "court-packing" plan but quietly supported the great bulk of New Deal legislation as well as the president's interventionist foreign policy. In 1940 he supported his brother William, who had become House majority leader, in his abortive bid for the Democratic vice presidential nomination. Just before the party convention opened, Bankhead—irritated by Roosevelt's silence in regard to the nomination—privately referred to FDR as "the most selfish men [sic] of all who have risen to the presidency."

During World War II, Bankhead often broke with the president. For example, he led the fight to exempt farm laborers from the draft and to destroy consumer subsidies. In 1943 his effort to exclude soil benefit payments in determining parity met with a presidential veto that was not overridden. Bankhead fought administration measures to draft farm laborers, sought to lift price controls from most agricultural products, and opposed any subsidy for food processors. He said candidly that while he did not oppose subsidies in principle, processors and distributors were undeserving. His perfunctory effort in 1944 to secure the vice presidential nomination met with defeat. When he died in Bethesda, Maryland, he had just been accused by columnist Drew Pearson of having profited in cotton futures, a claim that was never substantiated.

Bankhead was an amiable, bespectacled, portly man, whose ungainly body was topped by a bald head. Rumpled-looking and invariably wearing a seersucker suit, he was known for his old-style courtesy.

• The Bankhead Family Papers, including those of John Bankhead 2d, are located in the Department of Archives and History, Montgomery, Ala. See also the Owen Family Papers located there; the Franklin D. Roosevelt Papers, Franklin D. Roosevelt Presidential Library, Hyde Park, N.Y.; and Department of Agriculture records, National Archives, Washington, D.C. The most comprehensive study is Jack Brien Key, "John H. Bankhead, Jr.: Creative Conservative" (Ph.D. diss., Johns Hopkins Univ., 1964). The most succinct treatment is Evans C. Johnson, "John H. Bankhead 2nd: Advocate of Cotton," *Alabama Review* 41 (Jan. 1988): 30–58.

JUSTUS D. DOENECKE

BANKHEAD, Tallulah (31 Jan. 1902–12 Dec. 1968), actress, was born into an illustrious political family in Huntsville, Alabama, the daughter of William Bankhead, a U.S. representative and, from 1936 to 1940, Speaker of the House, and Adelaide Eugenia Sledge. Shortly after Bankhead's birth her mother died, and Tallulah was sent to Jasper, Alabama, to be raised by grandparents and occasionally by her father. Though the family was Episcopalian, Bankhead and her elder sister, Eugenia, were educated at Catholic girls' schools in Virginia, New York, Washington, D.C., and Alabama. At an early age Bankhead displayed the flamboyant personality for which she became famous.

A feisty and strong-willed child, Bankhead dreamed of a career in show business. In 1917 she won a screen opportunity contest sponsored by *Picture Play* magazine, first prize being a bit part in the film *Thirty a Week*, which was released in 1918. The prize took her to New York City, where she moved into the Algonquin Hotel and made a striking impression on the members of the famed literary and social circles that congregated there. Bankhead had bit parts in three minor films, but she had her heart set on the stage. Her first stage role in *The Squab Farm* (1918) was followed by her first lead role, in *39 East*, which led to five years of moderate success in various productions.

Bankhead sailed for England in 1923, and she took London by storm with her role in *The Dancers*. The play's phenomenal success fueled eight years of fame on London's stages; Bankhead's uninhibited stage personality attracted crowds despite the mediocrity of the scripts. Indeed, audiences flocked to see this racy blond temptress with the trademark baritone voice. *The Dancers* ran an impressive 344 performances. Bankhead was the toast of the town during the midtwenties, taking care to maintain her risqué and glamorous image onstage and off.

News of Bankhead's success in London traveled quickly to the United States, and in 1931 Paramount Pictures offered her a five-picture contract. The studio apparently sought to market her as an exotic seductress, but ironically she played docile victims of fate rather than the wanton women audiences had clamored to see her play in London. Bankhead failed to catch the public eye, and the experience left her exhausted. In 1933 she returned to New York from Hollywood for a rest. Shortly thereafter she was diagnosed with advanced gonorrhea that required massive surgery, after which she returned to London to recuperate. Bankhead's reckless lifestyle had begun to catch up with her.

In June 1934 Bankhead returned to New York to star as Judith Traherne in an unsuccessful production of *Dark Victory*, a role Bette Davis later played in the Warner Bros. film version. *Dark Victory* was the first of many coincidences between Bankhead's career and that of Davis. By the 1950s their rivalry was a familiar topic on Bankhead's own radio show, though the two women privately denied any hostility. In 1935 Bankhead starred in *Rain*, which found success with drama critics but ran only twenty-seven nights. Several months later she appeared in *Something Gay* and the following year played the lead in *Reflected Glory*.

In 1937 Bankhead married actor John Emery, who bore a remarkable resemblance to actor John Barrymore. They had no children. The couple had envisioned themselves as a glamorous acting team, but their first production, *Antony and Cleopatra*, dashed

these hopes. Critics praised Emery but criticized Bankhead, whose lack of formal training was painfully apparent. The marriage ended in divorce in 1941.

Bankhead achieved her hallmark critical success in 1939 starring as Regina Giddens in Lillian Hellman's *The Little Foxes*. She received both *Variety*'s Best Actress award and the New York Drama Critics Circle award for the best acting of the year. The play marked another coincidence between the careers of Bankhead and Davis, who starred in the film version because Bankhead lacked box office stature.

In 1942 Bankhead again received the Best Actress award from *Variety*, this time for her role in the Pulitzer Prize–winning *Skin of Our Teeth*, which also brought her another New York Drama Critics Circle award. She moved to rural New York and purchased an estate she named "Windows." There she entertained an astonishing number of regular guests. Longtime friend and actress Estelle Winwood moved in for a time, as did actress Patsy Kelly.

Bankhead returned to the public eye in 1944 in her first and only real screen success, *Lifeboat*, directed by Alfred Hitchcock, for which she won the New York Film Critics' Best Actress award. The following year she appeared in the motion picture *A Royal Scandal*, directed by Otto Preminger, and in 1948 she starred in a lengthy run of Noël Coward's *Private Lives*. Bankhead announced her retirement from Broadway in 1950, only to launch the next phase of her career, as radio host of "The Big Show," a talk show featuring appearances by celebrities such as Jimmy Durante, Groucho Marx, Ethel Merman, Edith Piaf, and the Ink Spots. The Radio Editors of America named Bankhead 1951's Woman of the Year for her work on the enormously popular program.

Throughout her life Bankhead was an enthusiastic supporter of the Democratic party. She was a member of several political committees dedicated to defending American values. She campaigned vigorously for Franklin Roosevelt's policies and U.S. involvement in World War II and devoted considerable time to U.S. tours, radio broadcasts, and fundraising events supporting the war effort.

Bankhead embraced her public role as a camp personality. Fans expected shocking, outrageous behavior, and she delivered. In 1952 she made her television debut hosting NBC's short-lived "All-Star Revue." During the same year she published a bestselling autobiography (largely ghostwritten by publicity agent Richard Maney) and made guest appearances on popular television programs such as "The Steve Allen Show" and "The Lucille Ball–Desi Arnaz Show." She also performed a nightclub act for the Sands Hotel in Las Vegas, released a recording of the songs "I'll Be Seeing You" and "You Go to My Head," and did a lecture tour in 1951.

In the final decade of her career she made several attempts to return to legitimate theater. Most of these efforts flopped, although in 1958 she achieved modest success with *Crazy October*, and in 1961 she received a Tony award for her work in *Midgie Purvis*. In 1964 she attempted a final comeback in Tennessee Williams's *The Milk Train Doesn't Stop Here Anymore*, which closed after only four nights. The role she played, that of a has-been actress suffering from a life of drugs, alcohol, and sexual excess, had been written, sadly, with Bankhead in mind. Bankhead made her last appearance as a professional actress on an episode of "Batman" in 1967, though her final public appearance was as a guest on "The Tonight Show" in May 1968. She died in New York City.

• Press clippings and material regarding Bankhead's family history are in the Alabama Department of Archives and History, Maps and Manuscripts Division. The Walter Hampden–Edwin Booth Theatre Collection and Library in New York City houses an uncataloged collection of scripts, letters, and photographs. Brendan Gill's *Tallulah* (1972) includes a complete list of films, plays, screen tests, and television and radio appearances. See also Dennis Brian, *Tallulah, Darling* (1980); Jeffrey L. Carrier, *Tallulah Bankhead: A Bio-bibliography* (1991); Lee Israel, *Miss Tallulah Bankhead* (1972); and Kieran Tunney, *Tallulah—Darling of the Gods: An Intimate Portrait* (1973). An obituary is in the *New York Times*, 13 Dec. 1968.

JENNIFER M. BARKER

BANKHEAD, William Brockman (12 Apr. 1874–15 Sept. 1940), lawyer and Speaker of the House of Representatives, was born in Moscow, Alabama, the son of Senator John Hollis Bankhead (1842–1920), a farmer, and Tallulah Brockman. He was the younger brother of U.S. Senator John H. Bankhead (1872–1946) and the father of actress Tallulah Bankhead. Bankhead graduated from the University of Alabama in 1892 and Georgetown School of Law in 1895. He then made brief forays as an actor in New York and as a lawyer in Huntsville, Alabama, before joining his brother John in the practice of law in Jasper, Alabama.

Bankhead served briefly as a prosecutor (1910–1914) and ran unsuccessfully for Congress in 1914. Following this initial defeat, the Alabama legislature, influenced by the younger John Bankhead, smoothed the way for Will's election to Congress as a Democrat in 1916 by creating a new district (from which he was later reelected eleven times). A loyal supporter of the Woodrow Wilson administration, Bankhead was overshadowed in the years of Republican dominance during the 1920s. His primary interests while in Congress lay in House rules, vocational education, health, labor, and agriculture. He also pursued the grants-in-aid principle, pioneered by his father, of giving aid to states for specified purposes, usually on a matching basis.

In the 1928 presidential election, Bankhead supported his party despite the unpopularity in the South of the Democratic nominee, Alfred E. Smith. After many prohibitionists bolted the party, Bankhead urged that the bolters be invited to return without penalty. Although Democratic party leaders rejected his advice, he and his brother were rewarded for their loyalty by John's election to the Senate in 1930.

The early years of the Great Depression made Bankhead more amenable to government spending. He aided the new Democratic Speaker in reaching a tenuous agreement with President Herbert Hoover to cooperate in a public works program. This bipartisanship was only partially successful, however, as Hoover scaled down Democratic plans. Bankhead pleased his coal-mining constituency by voting for the Norris–La Guardia Anti-Injunction Bill, a measure opposed by many conservative southern Democrats.

Like most southern congressmen, Bankhead had originally favored private operation of Muscle Shoals on the Tennessee River for the production of fertilizer. By the late 1920s, however, Bankhead and the southern delegation had come to favor government operation, primarily for the production of electric power. The Tennessee Valley Authority, based on this approach, was established in 1933 soon after President Franklin D. Roosevelt's election, with the almost unanimous support of southern congressmen, including Bankhead.

The extensive legislation necessary for implementation of the New Deal catapulted the Bankhead brothers into the limelight as champions of Roosevelt's program. The brothers became a highly effective legislative combination with the powerful support of President Roosevelt and the American Farm Bureau Federation. In 1933 Will Bankhead became de facto chairman of the Rules Committee upon the illness of Congressman Edward W. Pou, and he was named chairman in 1934. In Congress, Bankhead served mainly as a facilitator rather than an initiator, but he joined his brother in sponsoring the Bankhead Cotton Control Act, the only measure to bear his name. Bankhead was elected House Democratic majority leader in 1935 immediately after a heart attack—the nature and extent of which were not generally known. He did not resume full duties until January 1936. In June of that year, he was elected Speaker.

Roosevelt's domestic proposals in his second term irritated many southerners, but Bankhead, despite reservations, supported them. These measures included the proposed court-packing and executive reorganization bills as well as the Wage and Hours Act. War measures, popular in the South, were beginning to overshadow the New Deal, and Bankhead supported President Roosevelt's defense program as well. In January 1938, he helped defeat the Ludlow Resolution, which would have required a popular vote for a declaration of war. He also supported the administration's unsuccessful efforts to remove the 1937 Neutrality Act's restrictions on munitions sales. With the outbreak of war in 1939, he vigorously supported the addition of "cash and carry" provisions to the neutrality legislation, permitting the United States to supply needed matériel to the Allies.

In 1940, before Roosevelt's own plans to seek a third term became clear, competing factions in Alabama joined in promoting Bankhead as a candidate for president. He agreed to run, but only on a New Deal platform. When it became apparent that Roosevelt would run, Bankhead's backers supported the Speaker for vice president. The president was evasive but suggested that Bankhead was too old and his health too fragile. To head off Bankhead's candidacy, the Alabamian was named the Democratic National Convention's keynote speaker. The president's choice for vice president, Henry A. Wallace, was far from popular, and many anti-Roosevelt delegates supported Bankhead as an alternative. Bankhead received 329 votes but lost the nomination. He accepted defeat gracefully and agreed to open the Democratic campaign in Baltimore on 10 September, but he was stricken with an abdominal hemorrhage before he could give his speech. He died in Bethesda, Maryland.

Although less able than his brother, Will Bankhead was a legislative craftsman whose oratorical ability, amiable temperament, and parliamentary skill smoothed the way for the passage of New Deal legislation. While some southern Democrats supported the New Deal out of party loyalty more than conviction, Bankhead genuinely believed that its programs offered a constructive response to the problems of the era.

• The Alabama Department of Archives and History in Montgomery is a rich source of manuscripts and other materials related to Bankhead. The best source on Bankhead's life is Walter J. Heacock, "William Brockman Bankhead: A Biography" (Master's thesis, Univ. of Wisconsin, 1952). See also Heacock, "William B. Bankhead and the New Deal," *Journal of Southern History* 21, no. 3 (1955): 347–59, and Evans C. Johnson, "John H. Bankhead: Advocate of Cotton," *Alabama Review* 41, no. 1 (1988): 30–58.

EVANS C. JOHNSON

BANKS, Charles (25 Mar. 1873–1923), banker and businessman, was born in a log cabin in Clarksdale, Mississippi, the son of Daniel Banks and Sallie Ann (maiden name unknown), poor African-American farmers. Banks grew up in extreme poverty but was educated in the local public schools and later attended Rust University in nearby Holly Springs. Returning to Clarksdale, he speculated in land and cotton. After marrying Trenna A. Booze of Natchez, Mississippi, in 1893, Banks engaged her brother, Eugene P. Booze, as his apprentice, teaching him how to trade cotton and to work his general store, Banks & Co. In 1904 Banks and Booze resettled in the black-owned town of Mound Bayou. Temporarily leaving the merchandising business, Banks established the Bank of Mound Bayou, owning roughly two-thirds of its stock and serving as cashier as well as operating head. Several years later, in 1909, Banks and Booze founded the Farmer's Cooperative Mercantile Company. Capitalized at $10,000, the firm, which Booze managed, sold reasonably priced goods to area farmers until, for a variety of demographic as well as economic reasons, it closed its doors in 1922.

Located about halfway between Memphis and Vicksburg in the Mississippi delta, Mound Bayou was then one of the most promising examples of a unique phenomenon in early twentieth-century American history: a town founded, run, and largely governed by African Americans. Established in 1886 by Isaiah T. Montgomery, Mound Bayou stood for two decades of economic and civic opportunity for black Americans. Though situated in the Deep South, the town epitomized Booker T. Washington's vision of self-help, and the bank of Mound Bayou—itself sufficiently unusual, since relatively few black-owned banks had been established throughout the United States by that time—enabled local residents to become economically independent of the larger white community. In 1907 Washington wrote a lengthy article in *World's Work* in which he praised Mound Bayou, the Bank of Mound Bayou, and Charles Banks in particular for the example and potential they demonstrated for all African Americans. Despite the bank's early success, however—by 1910 it had more than $100,000 in assets and was housed in a two-story building—the Bank of Mound Bayou failed in the recession of 1914. Within eighteen months Banks and Montgomery had started a second bank, called Mound Bayou State Bank. This lending institution remained solvent for a decade but only partially met the community's demand for credit.

Banks and Montgomery, the wealthiest and most powerful figures in Mound Bayou, were principal spokesmen for Washington's policies and were instrumental in the founding and for many years the operation of Washington's National Negro Business League, established in 1900. Banks served as third vice president of the organization from 1901 to 1905 and as first vice president from 1907 until his death. Banks was also organizer and president of the league's Mississippi branch and was politically active with the so-called Black and Tan Republicans in Mississippi.

Another of Banks's economic ventures was the Mound Bayou Loan and Investment Company, which he established and ran with William Thornton Montgomery, Isaiah Montgomery's older brother. This chartered financial institution, which was capitalized at $50,000 and sold shares to the public, was founded to turn a profit but also to help keep the ownership of area farmland in the hands of African Americans. This was to be accomplished by covering defaulted mortgages of area farmers with capital raised locally, thus obviating the need to seek financial help elsewhere.

The most significant of Banks's ventures in Mound Bayou was the Mound Bayou Oil Mill and Manufacturing Company, an ambitious but ill-fated project whose failure crippled Banks financially and had a devastating effect on the town. Arguing that a cottonseed oil mill operation would further the Washingtonian goal of helping southern blacks become economically independent, Banks convinced the Mississippi chapter of the National Negro Business League to sponsor the venture, an apparently winning proposition given that the town's principal economic activity was growing cotton. The mill would thus enable Mound Bayou to become a producer of cotton products as well as cotton. Banks and Isaiah Montgomery began selling shares of stock in 1908, and construction of the plant began two years later. Unfortunately there were serious problems from the outset. For one thing,

Banks and Montgomery were unable to accumulate sufficient investment capital from local blacks and had only limited success in securing funds from wealthy white philanthropists. Banks ultimately convinced Julius Rosenwald, head of Sears, Roebuck & Company, to purchase $5,000 worth of oil mill bonds and to promise to loan the venture up to $250,000. This left them short of operating capital but was enough to finish construction. The plant was dedicated in November 1912. Banks hoped the plant's opening would increase the prospect of stock sales, and there was some success along that line, but the operation was plagued by production problems. The economic recession of 1913–1914 exacerbated an already difficult situation and forced the partners to bring in B. B. Harvey, who invested in and then ran the mill. This turned out to be a death knell. Harvey, a white mill owner from Memphis, embezzled the profits and reneged on interest payments on a corporate loan from Rosenwald. Banks was unable to save the firm. Investors had lost $100,000, and the virtually new factory building remained vacant for decades.

High cotton prices caused by World War I resulted in an upsurge of business activity, but after prices returned to prewar levels, the town's economic situation was in decline. Making matters worse was the dissolution of the partnership between Banks and Isaiah Montgomery in 1917 as a result of a political dispute. The town and Banks's fortunes were intimately connected. After he and Montgomery ceased to be partners, Montgomery consolidated his holdings and no longer supported broader town ventures. Banks, who had always been more concerned with racial solidarity than had Montgomery, continued his efforts to boost the town and thus saw his fortune plummet as the town lost its vitality. In 1923, the year after the Farmer's Cooperative Mercantile Company, the town's largest retail outlet, failed, Banks died in virtual poverty. Little is known of his personal life or of the circumstances of his death.

Charles Banks was an important figure in post-Reconstruction America, and his career exemplified the interconnectedness of African-American politics and black capitalism. Taking their cue from Booker T. Washington, southern African Americans in particular pursued the ideals of uplift and black capitalism. Mound Bayou, one of the most successful of a series of all-black towns platted on the frontier of the Trans-Appalachian West, was a prime example of this type of enterprise. Banks and Montgomery brought about this growth and development by skillfully attracting new settlers and outside financial assistance through an effective boosterism laced with black nationalism. As historian Kenneth Hamilton has noted, their joint speculative endeavors "made money, heightened racial pride, and built a black town."

• No personal or family papers are available, but a large collection of Banks's letters to Washington are in the Booker T. Washington Papers at the Library of Congress. The National Negro Business League Papers, in the Robert R. Moton Collection at Tuskegee University, also contain a number of letters. See also, in that collection, the "Proceedings of the National Negro Business League," held variously at Hampton University or Tuskegee University, for a number of speeches that Banks made to the group. A clipping file in his name is at Tuskegee University. Published biographical information on Banks is scarce, but see John N. Ingham and Lynne B. Feldman, *African-American Business Leaders* (1944), for the most complete biography. Booker T. Washington wrote a biographical sketch of Banks for *American Magazine*, Mar. 1911. Banks wrote "Negro Banks of Mississippi" for *Negro Progress in a Mississippi Town*, ed. D. W. Woodward (1909). General studies on black banking in Mississippi, which touch on Banks's role in it, include Tommy Lee Johnson, "The Development of Black Banking in Mississippi" (M.A. thesis, Jackson State Univ., 1977); W. E. Mollison, "What Banks Managed by Colored Men Are Doing for Their Communities," *Colored America* 12 (Aug. 1907): 191–92; and Abram L. Harris, *The Negro as Capitalist: A Study of Banking and Business among Negroes* (1936). Much of the information on Banks comes from materials written either about the town of Mound Bayou or about Isaiah T. Montgomery or his father, Benjamin Thornton Montgomery. The best recent study is Kenneth M. Hamilton, *Black Towns and Profit: Promotion and Development in the Trans-Appalachian West, 1877–1915* (1991). See also Janet Hermann, *Pursuit of a Dream* (1981). Contemporary accounts that deal with Banks's role in the development of Mound Bayou are Hiram Fong, "The Pioneers of Mound Bayou," *Century Magazine*, Jan. 1910; Aurelius P. Hood, *The Negro at Mound Bayou* (1909); Booker T. Washington, "A Town Owned by Negroes," *World's Work*, July 1907; and G. A. Lee, "Mound Bayou, the Negro City of Mississippi," *Voice of the Negro*, Dec. 1905.

JOHN N. INGHAM

BANKS, Nathaniel Prentiss (30 Jan. 1816–1 Sept. 1894), congressman and Civil War general, was born in Waltham, Massachusetts, the son of Nathaniel P. Banks, a textile mill foreman, and Rebecca Greenwood. He attended a school for factory children until he began work in the mills as a bobbin boy at age eleven. At seventeen he left factory work to assist his father in carpentry and to learn the machinist's trade.

Disliking manual labor and seeking new friends and experiences, Banks joined a debating club, a temperance society, and a volunteer fire company in Waltham, and he organized a dramatic society good enough to perform a play in Boston in 1839. His personal magnetism, distinguished appearance, and mellow speaking voice led him toward politics. Robert Rantoul, a lawyer and reform-minded Democratic leader, became his mentor, overseeing Banks's admission to the bar in 1839 after minimal preparation, his use as a Democratic orator in 1840, and his editorships of small party weeklies in 1840–1841 and 1841–1842. In 1843 Banks received a patronage appointment in the Boston Customs House, which he held until 1849. Although a candidate for the state legislature from 1844 to 1847, his "bobbin boy" origins failed to attract working-class voters suspicious of his temperance views and middle-class aspirations.

Following an eight-year engagement, Banks in 1847 married Mary Palmer, who shared his working-class origins and ambition for upward mobility. They had four children. Banks believed the Democrats' minority position in Massachusetts, which limited his political career, could only be overcome by flexibility on issues that divided the Whigs. Although previously uninterested in the slavery issue, Banks, an ardent expansionist, in 1846 endorsed the Wilmot Proviso, excluding slavery from any lands acquired in the Mexican War. Although eschewing the Free Soil party, he received the support of some of its ex-Whig followers in the legislative race in 1848 and won. He was reelected three times. During the long months when the legislature was not in session, Banks published a newspaper, the *Rumsford Journal* (1850–1851), and held minor positions working for the state board of education and the state census, which enabled him to travel the state promoting the idea of a Democratic–Free Soil coalition.

By 1851 the coalition controlled the legislature, and Banks became Speaker. He presided for two years over a house that passed reforms, such as the secret ballot, free banking, labor lien, and general incorporation laws, and sent antislavery politician Charles Sumner to the U.S. Senate. The coalition also engineered a call for a constitutional convention in 1853 to overhaul the state's 1780 document that had helped maintain Whig dominance. Banks presided, seldom speaking on the issues but appointing committees that systematically dismantled the structure of Whig power. The final product struck many as too extreme and was defeated by the voters.

In 1852 Banks was narrowly elected to Congress, backed by Free Soilers but not by some in his own party who opposed coalition. Faced with the Kansas-Nebraska Bill, which nullified the Missouri Compromise's provision that these territories be free, Banks denounced the measure in a forceful speech, breaking with the Democratic administration. Seeking new allies, he joined a Know Nothing (anti-immigrant, anti-Catholic) lodge in the District of Columbia. In the fall of 1854 Banks retained his seat through the combined backing of Free Soil Whigs, anti-Nebraska Democrats, and Know Nothings. With support from diverse sources plus favorable reviews as a presiding officer, Banks was a logical candidate for the Speakership in the badly fragmented Thirty-fourth Congress, which assembled in December 1855. Southern opposition was fierce, and he did not emerge victorious until the 133d ballot, winning by a three-vote margin after a plurality rule had been adopted. In retrospect the outcome seemed an important "northern" victory, demonstrating the primacy of sectional over nativist issues and providing an impetus for the anti-Nebraska forces in Congress to coalesce as Republicans.

In the national spotlight Banks proved to be a tactful, skilled presiding officer over a chaotic, still badly factionalized House. Unable to dominate the American (Know Nothing) party in Massachusetts, he moved slowly toward the Republicans, presiding over a fusion meeting in the state in 1855 that preceded the formation of the Republican party there. In 1856, as the American party sectionalized over slavery, Banks was offered the presidential nomination by northern seceders from the American party at a convention timed to meet just before the Republican convention. But he declined in favor of the Republican nominee, John C. Frémont, thus drastically weakening the Americans as an opposition party to the Democrats in the North. The personal cost to Banks was a reputation for being "very ambitious" and "scheming and sinister" (Gienapp, p. 243).

In 1857 Banks was nominated for governor of Massachusetts as a Republican and won, resigning his seat in Congress. Reelected in 1858 and 1859, he worked for a broad-based party. To this end, he vetoed a bill including African Americans in the militia in order to appeal to racial conservatives, and he supported a two-year wait for naturalized citizens before granting of suffrage, which was favored by nativists. Such measures seemed immoral to radicals, who had formed the Bird Club (named after Francis W. Bird) in opposition to the governor's Banks Club. Despite strong support for educational and penal reform, Banks was unable to unify the party, dashing his hopes of becoming the Republican presidential nominee in 1860.

In 1861 Banks began a high-paying job in Chicago as resident director of the Illinois Central Railroad responsible for promoting the company's land grants to eastern investors. Offering his services to Abraham Lincoln after the firing on Fort Sumter, he was appointed a major general of volunteers despite minimal military experience. Lincoln needed such "political" generals to encourage recruiting, promote confidence in the government, and broaden support for the war. Sent first to Maryland, Banks tried to soothe local secessionists but soon began arrests in order to secure the important transportation corridor for military supplies to Washington.

Following the Union defeat at Bull Run (Manassas) in July 1861, Banks replaced General Robert Patterson in command of troops in the Shenandoah Valley. As a field commander Banks was courageous but unprepared to analyze terrain, read maps, anticipate enemy movements, or effectively use reconnaissance, and his professional staff rarely compensated for his lapses. Given these weaknesses, he had difficulty making decisions and sometimes gave ambiguous orders. Instructed to clear the valley and northern Virginia of Confederates in anticipation of General George B. McClellan's advance on Richmond in the spring of 1862, Banks instead was manhandled by Thomas J. "Stonewall" Jackson's Confederates at Winchester on 25 May and forced to retreat across the Potomac with heavy losses of men and supplies.

Reorganized into the Second Corps of General John Pope's Army of Virginia in June, Banks's forces faced Stonewall Jackson again at Cedar Mountain in August. Under Pope's orders but without proper reconnaissance, Banks attacked the Confederate left. The rebels, who had a 2 to 1 numerical advantage, faltered, then drove back Banks's troops, who suffered heavy losses. Although investigated by the Joint Committee on the Conduct of the War, Banks defended his command decisions, and President Lincoln reassigned him to Louisiana, where political as well as military skills were needed.

Banks arrived in New Orleans in December 1862 with fresh recruits and supplies and orders to help reopen the Mississippi River and pacify the local Confederates. Seeking to demonstrate the superiority of a moderate strategy to that of General Benjamin F. Butler, a Massachusetts Radical whom he replaced, Banks released political prisoners, allowed churches to reopen, eased trade restrictions to the interior, and announced a plan for contrabands (escaped slaves of disloyal owners) to work for their old masters under sharecrop agreements on plantation lands. Neither African Americans nor Radicals liked sharecropping, reminiscent in many details of traditional slavery. The promise of schools, financed by the sale of confiscated property, and individual garden plots on plantation land for the contrabands eventually secured their cooperation. Banks also recruited at least eighteen regiments of African-American soldiers, the Corps d'Afrique, although he reversed Butler's policy of appointing black officers and permitted many forms of discrimination. Nonetheless, these soldiers were the first African Americans in the war to prove themselves in combat (at Port Hudson in 1863).

Salmon P. Chase's Treasury Department agents, who claimed jurisdiction over confiscated slave property, worked toward African-American suffrage, an immediate new constitution, and the overthrow of the planter elite as the basis for political reorganization. Banks, who hated the thought of revolutionary change, held back, promoting elections under Louisiana's prewar constitution stripped of its provisions regarding slavery. While his control of patronage and the army helped moderates to win, Radicals were enraged. To appease them, President Lincoln insisted the long-delayed constitutional convention produce a liberal document. Despite pressure from Banks to include limited African-American suffrage as desired by Lincoln, however, the constitution merely forbade slavery and promised schools for both races without enfranchising any African Americans. Even so, Louisiana whites regarded the document as unspeakably radical, and their lackluster support for Banks's policies spelled doom for congressional recognition of Banks's reorganized government. The attempt to involve moderates in a real Reconstruction had failed.

On the military front, Banks turned his attention in the spring of 1863 to Port Hudson, the Confederate stronghold anchoring one end of a 200-mile stretch of the Mississippi still controlled by the Confederates. Although the position had been lightly defended upon his arrival in New Orleans, he delayed operations against it for six months to pursue his political agenda. Failing to cooperate with General Ulysses S. Grant at Vicksburg as ordered, Banks suffered heavy losses in poorly planned attacks on Port Hudson on 27 May and 14 June. The garrison capitulated on 9 July, however, when news of Vicksburg's surrender arrived. Banks received the thanks of Congress for opening the Mississippi, but most observers credited Grant with the real victory.

In 1864 General Henry W. Halleck ordered Banks to begin operations along the Red River to seize Confederate cotton and establish a base in Texas to prevent French intervention in Mexico. Banks reluctantly assented, drawing troops temporarily from other commands. Faced with unfavorably dry weather for a river expedition, Banks pushed ahead anyway and was defeated by Confederates under General Richard Taylor at Sabine Crossroads on 8 April in a bungled attempt to take Shreveport. Although he was able to delay the Confederate pursuit at Pleasant Hill, Banks's retreat became more desperate as the Red River fell, endangering the gunboats and transports that constituted his supply lines. The disastrous campaign, which accomplished nothing, led to Banks's replacement as military commander in Louisiana in May 1864 and brought him once again before the Committee on the Conduct of the War for an embarrassing grilling. He retained his rank and nonmilitary duties, however, until he was mustered out of the army in August 1865.

Banks initially hoped for a postwar political career in Louisiana. He sought to make amends with Louisiana's Radicals by endorsing African-American suffrage in July 1865, but his prospects for office dimmed. When his old congressional seat in Massachusetts became available owing to a resignation, he hurriedly returned to Massachusetts in September 1865. Appealing to labor reformers by announcing support for the eight-hour day, he regained his seat, which he held until 1873.

Believing that Reconstruction was dependent on cooperation between the president and Congress, Banks sought to temper congressional legislation regarding the South. He resisted impeaching President Andrew Johnson until the third and final time the issue came before the House. In return the president rewarded him with control of the Boston Port patronage. With Johnson's near removal, however, Banks shifted to a more aggressive stand on Reconstruction, endorsing the Fifteenth Amendment and the ouster of Georgia's congressional delegation for violations of Reconstruction measures.

Serving as chair of the Committee on Foreign Affairs from 1865 to 1873, Banks felt excluded from decision making by the State Department and the Senate, with its exclusive power to approve treaties. Using his committee for publicity, he attacked the British over the *Alabama* claims and backed Irish nationalist activities (the Fenian uprising) against the British in Canada. Still an expansionist, he supported annexation of Mexico, Santo Domingo, Cuba, and Alaska. President Grant and Secretary of State Hamilton Fish considered Banks irresponsible in his refusal to follow their lead on such matters and sought to punish him through patronage restrictions.

Banks's alienation from the Grant administration led him to endorse Horace Greeley, who was running as a Liberal Republican with the endorsement of the Democrats, for president against Grant in 1872. The decision cost Banks his congressional seat, although he received 2,000 more votes in his district than did Greeley. Desperate for a means to pay off the debts his expensive lifestyle generated, Banks gave public lectures and in 1873 ran for the state senate backed by Democrats, Liberal Republicans, and a Labor Reform party. After winning, he advocated woman suffrage, reduced hours for labor, and public ownership of the Hoosac (railway) Tunnel in northwestern Massachusetts in the legislature.

In 1874 Banks was returned to Congress as an Independent. He won reelection in 1876 as a Republican, supporting merchants and industrialists in their efforts to keep the tariff from being cut. Although Banks failed to get the Republican nomination for his congressional seat in 1878, President Rutherford B. Hayes appointed him U.S. marshal for the Boston District, a position he retained until 1888. Banks treated the post as a sinecure, collecting a salary but allowing unsupervised subordinates to do the work. He chose to resign in 1888 in the face of an investigation of misuse of funds. He ran again successfully for Congress in 1888, despite showing signs of dementia. Voted a pension by Congress, he retired for good at the end of his term. He died in Waltham. Although Banks's brand of "practical" politics, which emphasized compromise on most issues, offended those more passionate about their causes, it enabled him to have an extraordinarily long career. His greatest national impact was in shaping the direction of Reconstruction in its earliest stages.

• The principal collections of Banks manuscripts are at the Library of Congress and the Illinois State Historical Library. Smaller collections are at Duke University and Louisiana State University. War Department records from Banks's administration in La. are in RG 107 in the National Archives. A biography is Fred H. Harrington, *Fighting Politician: Major General N. P. Banks* (1948). On Mass. politics see Dale Baum, *The Civil War Party System* (1984). Banks's role in national politics in the 1850s is discussed in William E. Gienapp, *The Origins of the Republican Party* (1987). Peyton McCrary, *Abraham Lincoln and Reconstruction: The Louisiana Experiment* (1978), discusses Banks's role in Reconstruction. See Lawrence Lee Hewitt, *Port Hudson* (1987), and Ludwell H. Johnson, *Red River Campaign* (1958), on his military career and Michael Les Benedict, *A Compromise of Principle* (1974), on his congressional career. An obituary is in the *New York Times*, 2 Sept. 1894.

PHYLLIS F. FIELD

BANNEKER, Benjamin (9 Nov. 1731–19 Oct. 1806), farmer and astronomer, was born near the Patapsco River in Baltimore County in what became the community of Oella, Maryland, the son of Robert, a freed slave, and Mary Banneky, a daughter of a freed slave named Bannka and Molly Welsh, a freed English indentured servant who had been transported to Maryland. Banneker was taught by his white grandmother to read and write from a Bible. He had no formal education other than a brief attendance at a Quaker one-room school during winter months. He was a voracious reader, informing himself in his spare time in

literature, history, religion, and mathematics with whatever books he could borrow. From an early age he demonstrated a talent for mathematics and for creating and solving mathematical puzzles. With his three sisters he grew up on his father's tobacco farm, and for the rest of his life Banneker continued to live in a log house built by his father.

At about the age of twenty Banneker constructed a striking clock without ever having seen one, although tradition states he may once have examined a watch movement. He approached the project as a mathematical challenge, calculating the proper sizes and ratios of the teeth of the wheels, gears, and pinions, each of which he carved from wood with a pocket knife, possibly using a piece of metal or glass for a bell. The clock became a subject of popular interest throughout the region and many came to see and admire it. The timepiece operated successfully for more than forty years, until his death.

After his father's death in 1759, Banneker continued to farm tobacco, living with his mother until she died some time after 1775. Thereafter he lived alone, his sisters having one by one married and settled in the region. They attended to his major household needs. His life was limited almost entirely to his farm, remote from community life and potential persecution because of his color, until the advent of new neighbors.

In about 1771 five Ellicott brothers of Bucks County, Pennsylvania, purchased large tracts of land adjacent to the Banneker farm and began to develop a major industrial community called Ellicott's Lower Mills (now Ellicott City, Maryland). They initiated the large-scale cultivation of wheat in the state, built flour mills, saw mills, an iron foundry, and a general store that served not only their own needs but also those of the region. They marketed their flour by shipping it from the port of Baltimore. Banneker met members of the Ellicott families and often visited the building sites to watch each structure as it was being erected, intrigued particularly by the mechanisms of the mills.

George Ellicott, a son of one of the brothers, who built a stone house near the Patapsco River, often spent his leisure time in the evenings pursuing his hobby of astronomy. As he searched the skies with his telescope, he would explain what he saw to neighbors who came to watch. Banneker was frequently among them, fascinated by the new world in the skies opened up by the telescope. Noting his interest, in 1789 young Ellicott lent him a telescope, several astronomy books, and an old gateleg table on which to use them. Ellicott promised to visit Banneker as soon as he could to explain the rudiments of the science. Before he found time for his visit, however, Banneker had absorbed the contents of the texts and had taught himself enough through trial and error to calculate an ephemeris for an almanac for the next year and to make projections of lunar and solar eclipses.

Banneker, now age fifty-nine, suffered from rheumatism or arthritis and abandoned farming. He subsequently devoted his evening and night hours to searching the skies; he slept during the day, a practice that gained him a reputation for laziness and slothfulness from his neighbors.

Early in 1791 Banneker's new skills came to the attention of Major Andrew Ellicott, George's cousin, who had been appointed by President George Washington to survey a ten-mile square of land in Virginia and Maryland to become the new site of the national capital. Major Ellicott needed an assistant capable of using astronomical instruments for the first several months of the survey until his two brothers, who generally worked with him, became available. He visited Ellicott's Lower Mills to ask George to assist him for the interim, but George was unable to do so and recommended Banneker.

At the beginning of February 1791 Banneker accompanied Major Ellicott to Alexandria, Virginia, the point of beginning of the survey, and was installed in the field observatory tent where he was to maintain the astronomical field clock and use other instruments. Using the large zenith sector, his responsibility was to observe and record stars near the zenith as they crossed the meridian at different times during the night; the observations were to be repeated a number of nights over a period of time. After he had corrected the data he collected for refraction, aberration, and nutation and compared it with data in published star catalogs, Banneker determined latitude based on each of the stars observed. He also used the transit and equal altitude instrument to take equal altitudes of the sun, by which the astronomical clock was periodically checked and rated.

Banneker had the use of Major Ellicott's texts and notes, from which he continued to learn, and spent his leisure hours calculating the ephemeris for an almanac for 1792. In April, with the arrival of Major Ellicott's brothers, Banneker returned to his home. He was paid the sum of sixty dollars for his services and travel. Ellicott was paid five dollars a day exclusive of room and board while his assistant surveyors were paid two dollars a day. Banneker still supported himself primarily with proceeds from his farm.

Shortly after his return home, with the assistance of George Ellicott and family, Banneker's calculations for an almanac were purchased and published by Baltimore printers Goddard & Angell as *Benjamin Banneker's Pennsylvania, Delaware, Maryland and Virginia Almanack and Ephemeris, for the Year of Our Lord, 1792 . . .* ; a second edition was produced by Philadelphia printer William Young. The almanac contained a biographical sketch of Banneker written by Senator James McHenry, who presented Banneker's achievement as new evidence supporting arguments against slavery.

Shortly before the almanac's publication, Banneker sent a manuscript copy of his calculations to Thomas Jefferson, secretary of state, with a covering letter urging the abolition of slavery. Jefferson replied, "No body wishes more than I do to see such proofs as you exhibit, that nature has given to our black brethren, talents equal to those of the other colors of men, and that the appearance of a want of them is owing merely

to the degraded condition of their existence. . . . No body wishes more ardently to see a good system commenced for raising the condition both of their body & mind to what it ought to be." The exchange of letters between Banneker and Jefferson was published as a pamphlet by Philadelphia printer David Lawrence and distributed widely at the same time that the almanac appeared. Promoted by the abolitionist societies of Pennsylvania and Maryland, the almanac sold in great numbers.

Encouraged by his first success, Banneker continued to calculate ephemerides for almanacs that were published for the succeeding five years and sold widely in the United States and England. A total of at least twenty-eight editions of his almanacs were published, largely supported by the abolitionist societies. Although he continued to calculate ephemerides each year until 1804 for his own pleasure, diminishing interest in the abolitionist movement failed to find a publisher for them after the 1797 almanac.

Although he was not associated with any particular religion, Banneker was deeply religious and attended services of various denominations whenever ministers or speakers visited the region, preferring meetings of the Society of Friends. He was described as having "a most benign and thoughtful expression," as being of erect posture despite his age, scrupulously neat in dress. Another who knew him noted, "He was very precise in conversation and exhibited deep reflection." Banneker died in his sleep during a nap after having taken a walk early one Sunday morning a month short of his seventy-fifth birthday. He had arranged that immediately after his death, all of his borrowed texts and instruments were to be returned to George Ellicott, which was done before his burial two days later. During his burial in the family graveyard on his farm, his house burst into flames and was destroyed. All that survived were a few letters he had written, his astronomical journal, his commonplace book, and the books he had borrowed.

The publication of Banneker's almanacs brought him international fame in his time, and modern studies have confirmed that his figures compared favorably with those of other contemporary men of science who calculated ephemerides for almanacs. Long thought lost, the sites of Banneker's house and outbuilding have been the subjects of an archaeological excavation from which various artifacts have been recovered. Banneker has been memorialized in the naming of several institutes and secondary schools. Without the limitation of opportunity because of his regional location and the state of science in his time, Banneker would undoubtedly have emerged as a far more important figure in early American science than merely as the first black man of science.

• The earliest biographical account of Banneker is a short sketch by Senator James McHenry, "A Letter from Mr. James McHenry . . . Containing Particulars Reflecting Benjamin Banneker, a Free Negro," published in Banneker's first almanac and reprinted in *American Museum* 12, no. 2

(Sept. 1791): 185–87. This was followed by John H. B. La-trobe's contemporary account, "Memoir of Benjamin Banne-ker, Read Before the Historical Society of Maryland," *Mary-land Colonization Journal*, n.s. 2, no. 23 (1845): 353–64. Martha Ellicott Tyson, "A Sketch of the Life of Benjamin Banneker, from Notes Taken in 1836. Read by J. Saurin Norris Before the Maryland Historical Society, October 5, 1854" and *Banneker, the Africa-American Astronomer: From the Posthumous Papers of Martha E. Tyson* (1884), are both based on personal recollections of a daughter of George Elli-cott who had known Banneker in her lifetime and had collect-ed data from others who had known him; Norris was her nephew-in-law. A brief, relatively accurate account is Mon-cure D. Conway, "Banneker, the Black Astronomer," *Southern Literary Messenger* 23, n.s., vol. 2 (July 1856): 65–66. The first book-length account of Banneker is a novel-ized biography for children by Shirley Graham, *Your Most Humble Servant* (1949), based on the few basic facts about his life embroidered with romantic speculation. A comprehen-sive biography is Silvio A. Bedini, *The Life of Benjamin Ban-neker* (1972), based on Banneker's personal papers, cor-respondence, and manuscripts, most of which are privately owned. It also includes a survey of all published sources and a scientific analysis of his mathematical calculations.

SILVIO A. BEDINI

BANNER, Peter (fl. 1794–1828), builder-architect, was born in England. Very little is known about Ban-ner's childhood or family life. He had at least one son, Peter Jr., who lived for a time in Worcester, Massa-chusetts, where his own son, George H., was born in 1834. G. N. Gage wrote in his *History of Washington, N.H.* (1886) that his grandfather was an Englishman who immigrated to Boston in 1794.

Although Banner is considered one of the most-tal-ented professionally trained architects who practiced in New England in the early nineteenth century, his career is less than well documented, and few buildings are firmly associated with his name. Some historians have claimed that he was trained as an architect in England before coming to the United States, but the evidence for this assertion is indirect. Documentary evidence indicates that at the very least he had had for-mal training in the building trade. He is listed in the New York City Directory between 1795 and 1798 as a house carpenter and master-builder. He is identified in the 1806 Boston directory as an architect, and anec-dotal evidence suggests that Banner had training in this profession. For example, in the *Life and Letters of Charles Bulfinch* (1896), Ellen S. Bulfinch claimed that Park Street Church in Boston was built in 1810 "from the design of Peter Bonner [sic], an English architect." Similarly, in 1865 W. W. Wheildon published his *Memoir of Solomon Willard* (designer of the Bunker Hill Monument) in which he identified Banner as an architect who practiced in England before coming to the United States. The term architect, however, had little specific meaning in the Americas of the late eight-eenth and early nineteenth centuries and usually was ascribed to anyone who could conceive and execute a building plan and associated ornamentation. Certainly Banner worked in the tradition of house builders who designed and directed construction, often in collabora-tion with the client and sometimes using pattern books as a guide. Whether he had formal training as an archi-tect is open to question, but work associated with him suggests that he certainly was acquainted with the principles of classical design.

The two buildings most often attributed to Banner are the Eben Crafts house (1805) in Roxbury, Massa-chusetts, and the Park Street Church (1810) in Boston. In his book *Charles Bulfinch, Architect and Citizen* (1925), C. A. Place doubted that Banner had a role in the Crafts house, but to some historians the spatial ar-rangement of the house and its classical detailing sug-gest the direct influence of contemporary English design. Consequently, Fiske Kimball, in his *Domestic Architecture of the American Colonies and of the Early Republic* (1922), attributed the design entirely to Ban-ner. There is more evidence to indicate that Banner designed Park Street Church. W. W. Wheildon, in his *Memoir of Solomon Willard*, identified Banner as the architect as well as the chief carpenter employed on the project, and some historians consider the steeple design to have been inspired by Christopher Wren's tower for St. Bride's Church on Fleet Street in Lon-don. Like the Craft house, the steeple of Park Street Church differs from any other in New England and is considered to be more English in its classical detail and composition. Banner has also been credited with designing the American Antiquarian Society building in Worcester, Massachusetts (1819; destroyed in 1910). Formal comparisons alone, however, do not necessarily suggest Banner as the architect of these buildings, and no documentary evidence exists to prove conclusively that he was the designer. The only building that can be conclusively attributed to Banner is the Old South Parsonage Houses (1809) in Boston. Records of the Old South Church prove that Banner won the design competition over other competitors, including Asher Benjamin.

Banner's career as an architect received renewed at-tention during the 1920s, at the height of the colonial revival, an early twentieth-century aesthetic that fo-cused attention on buildings from the eighteenth and early nineteenth centuries. Historians of this period sought to attribute authorship to these buildings and in so doing cited anecdotal evidence and otherwise in-explicable formal similarities as proof of an architect's involvement. Such is the case with Peter Banner. Ban-ner's involvement in many projects such as Park Street Church is very probable, but more research needs to be done before his role is secured in the architectural history of the United States. No record of place and date of Banner's death is extant.

• The only information on Banner's family life comes from G. N. Gage's *History of Washington, N.H.* (1886). Banner's career as a builder and craftsman is traced in the city directo-ries of New York (1795 to 1798) and Boston (1806 and 1828). Some early histories identify Banner as an English architect: W. W. Wheildon in *Memoir of Solomon Willard* (1865); Fiske Kimball in *Domestic Architecture of the American Colonies and of the Early Republic* (1922); C. A. Place in *Charles Bulfinch, Architect and Citizen* (1925); and J. Jackson, *The Development of American Architecture, 1783–1830* (1926).

CLIFTON C. ELLIS

BANNING, Margaret Culkin (18 Mar. 1891–4 Jan. 1982), writer, was born in Buffalo, Minnesota, the daughter of William Edgar Culkin, a Duluth newspaper executive, and Hannah Alice Young. She attended Vassar College, where she was elected to Phi Beta Kappa, and graduated in 1912. Pursuing an interest in social work, she attended Russell Sage College on a fellowship in 1912–1913, then spent the following academic year at the Chicago School of Philanthropy, which awarded her a certificate in 1914 for completion of its program. That same year she married a Duluth lawyer, Archibald T. Banning, Jr. The couple, who were divorced in 1934, had four children, two of whom survived into adulthood.

As a wealthy young woman who also had a strong sense of civic responsibility, Margaret Culkin Banning pursued a life that extended beyond conventional expectation. Stirred by the spirit of social reform that informed the early twentieth century, she was an active volunteer in organizations that welcomed participation by women of her class, including the Junior League of Duluth, the American Association of University Women, and the League of Women Voters; later she served on the boards of the city symphony and the public library.

Early in her marriage, Banning also made room in her active life to pursue a career as a writer. Her first novel, *This Marrying*, the story of a young woman who breaks away from her middle-class background to become a journalist, was published in 1920; it was widely and favorably reviewed, and it even received a brief notice in the [London] *Times Literary Supplement*, which called it "a bright and busy story." Over the next sixty years Banning wrote thirty-nine books, most of them novels. She was also the author of more than 400 short stories and personal essays, most of which appeared in leading national magazines, including *Good Housekeeping*, *McCall's*, *Ladies' Home Journal*, *Saturday Evening Post*, *Atlantic Monthly*, *Harper's*, and *Reader's Digest*.

Banning's books, stories, and essays nearly always dealt with civic, moral, and social issues—including race relations, birth control, and mixed marriages—and their particular effects on women. Virtually the only exception was her novel *Mesabi* (1968), a tale of the mining industry inspired by her second husband, LeRoy Salsich, a mining company executive whom she married in 1944. Banning's last published novel, *Such Interesting People*, appeared in 1979, when she was eighty-eight.

In some ways writing for Banning was another expression of her philanthropic nature. As she told one interviewer in middle age, each of her writings had been inspired by "a glimmer of truth" that she had seen and decided to "pass along." Banning's fictional plots, like the arguments of her essays, offered a mes-

sage that was at once politically liberal and socially conservative; she was open and nonjudgmental, and ultimately commonsensical, in her assessment of human predicaments. A lifelong Republican whose political values were formed at a time when the Republican party was the voice of reform in the United States, she seemed to speak to and for a majority of American women, or at least to express commonly held views, until the 1960s.

Among Banning's best-known writings were two works of nonfiction, a book and an article. Her *Letters to Susan* (1936), a collection of letters ostensibly addressed to college women, discussed such topics as drinking, petting, and early marriage; the *New York Times* reviewer praised the book for its "practical helpfulness" and "calm good sense." "The Case for Chastity," an article Banning wrote for the *Reader's Digest* in 1937, evoked an enormous positive response and created one of the strongest demands for reprints in the magazine's history.

A lifelong supporter of women's rights as well as a popular writer, Banning was a much sought after public speaker who appeared regularly before audiences around the country, speaking not only about women's issues but on other topics of social concern. In the aftermath of World War II she traveled to England to study the conditions of women and subsequently spent several years working in refugee camps in Austria and Germany.

Banning maintained homes throughout her adult life in Duluth and in Tryon, North Carolina. Although she set aside a sparsely furnished room in each home for her writing, she claimed to be able to compose anywhere and wrote many of her books and essays during frequent travels in the United States, Europe, and South America. Banning died in Tryon a month before her ninety-first birthday. At the time of her death she was writing another novel, which was never published.

Although Banning was nationally well known for more than half a century, she maintained a certain reserve about her private life, including her Roman Catholic religious affiliation; the relatively rare interviews that she granted invariably focused on her work, her writing as well as her civic activities. However, this reticence was most likely a consequence of her upbringing and the then-prevalent belief that well-bred women did not talk about personal matters.

• For additional biographical information on Banning, see the article in *Current Biography* (1940) and brief background sketches in *Saturday Review of Literature*, 11 Apr. 1936 and 12 June 1937; *Saturday Evening Post*, 29 Aug. 1936; and *Independent Woman*, May 1939. An obituary is in the *New York Times*, 6 Jan. 1982.

ANN T. KEENE

BANVARD, John (15 Nov. 1815–16 May 1891), panoramist, scene painter, and poet, was born in New York City, the son of Daniel Banvard, a building contractor and amateur artist of French ancestry. His mother's name is unrecorded. Banvard attended school until he was fifteen; an early talent for drawing was nurtured by his father. His youthful enthusiasm for poetry was encouraged by Samuel Woodworth, a versifier of local renown. Undoubtedly influenced by the variety of entertainments available in New York, Banvard opened a juvenile museum that included a diorama with a "Sea Scene" and a naval battle.

In about 1830 Banvard's father died; his mother and sisters joined his brother Joseph, a clergyman, in Boston. In September 1831 Banvard left for the West, stopping in Louisville, Kentucky. After a brief stint as an apothecary clerk, he received commissions to decorate gardens and paint theater scenery in Louisville, but they were not very remunerative. By 1832 Banvard had banded together with several friends to "seek anew his fortune" (*Description of Banvard's Panorama* [1847], p. 4) along the Ohio and Mississippi rivers in a flatboat. It is unclear precisely how Banvard made a living for the next several years, but by the fall of 1836, in New Harmony, Indiana, on the Wabash River, he had equipped a large flatboat with a chamber and seats for the presentation of dioramic paintings he had prepared. Taking the boat all the way to the Gulf of Mexico, Banvard and his friends were marginally successful in the presentations. Banvard sold his interest in the boat and continued as an itinerant scene painter and dioramist in cities all along the western rivers. He briefly managed a museum in St. Louis; however, it was several mercantile speculations that earned him the few thousand dollars of capital he needed to realize a long-standing ambition to paint a huge moving picture of the major sites on the shores of the Mississippi. For more than a year, beginning in the spring of 1840, Banvard sailed down the river in a little boat, stopping to sketch the most interesting scenery on either side. Finishing his preparatory work in New Orleans, he returned to Louisville and built a large studio, filling it with reams of cotton canvas ordered from mills in Lowell, Massachusetts. The first version of the panorama, containing thirty-eight scenes and measuring about 12 feet high by 1,300 feet long, took four years to complete and represented views on the Mississippi from New Orleans to the mouth of the Ohio River.

Rain and weak publicity resulted in a poor showing at Banvard's debut with the panorama on 29 June 1846. After closing the show for several months, Banvard reopened in October for two weeks and attracted extravagant praise from the local press. Having already fed eastern newspapers with items about the panorama's creation, he soon moved the show to Boston and opened the panorama at Amory Hall, where it enjoyed a sensational run of nine months. The moving picture attracted an audience of 250,000 people, with profits reported to have been as high as $70,000. It was not long before Banvard was arranging for special trains to bring audiences to Boston from the countryside. Massachusetts governor George Briggs persuaded the state legislature to pass a resolution commending Banvard for his "genius and enterprise" in creating a work of such "immense extent," "truthfulness to Nature," and "great variety of . . . scenery and objects"

(*Description of Banvard's Panorama* [1847], pp. 43–46).

Banvard had a genius for enterprise that to some extent exceeded his artistic prowess. His surviving paintings and the observations of his critics indicate that, despite the panorama's topographical accuracy, its artistic merit rose at best to the level of scene painting. Banvard himself was one of the show's chief assets, for he cultivated a colorful lecture style that he brought to each presentation of the picture. A British critic who later saw the panorama in London reported: "Upon a platform is seated Mr. Banvard, who explains the localities as the picture moves, and relieves his narrative with Jonathanisms and jokes, poetry and patter, which delight his audience mightily" (*Illustrated London News*, 9 Dec. 1848). The poetry was mostly Banvard's own, some of it set to music that was played on a pianoforte by Elizabeth Goodnow, a Boston musician who in 1847 or 1848 became Banvard's wife and eventually the mother of his five children.

In another nine-month run in New York beginning in December 1848, some 175,000 more people saw the panorama. Banvard added a section illustrating the Missouri River in anticipation of taking his show to London in September 1848. His way paved by Yankee curiosity shows such as P. T. Barnum's Tom Thumb and George Catlin's Indian exhibitions, Banvard opened at Egyptian Hall in Picadilly. The Mississippi panorama remained in London for eighteen months, attracting 600,000 Britons and earning, in April 1849, a command performance for Queen Victoria and Prince Albert at Windsor Castle. The queen bestowed on Banvard "a special mark of her royal approbation." In London, Banvard added sections of the Ohio River and the western bank of the Mississippi to the panorama. He eventually began exhibiting two separate paintings, both showing the Missouri River, one portraying the Ohio and the western bank of the Mississippi, the other depicting the eastern bank. Banvard exhibited the earlier version in Scotland, then in Paris for three months in 1850. When it was returned to Britain, the two panoramas were shown as a single exhibition in England and Ireland through 1852.

In Britain, Banvard began to be challenged by American imitators with their own Mississippi River panoramas, most notably John Rowson Smith, who staked his "four-mile painting" against Banvard's "three miles of canvas." The two blasted each other's claims in the press, but the panoramic fever in Britain had by now reached such a pitch that Banvard, Smith, and several other competitors managed to prosper. Once Banvard had completed his original design for a panorama of the three great western rivers, he embarked on an entirely new mission. Said to have been inspired by a sermon he heard in London in 1849, he left the management of his British exhibitions to agents and set out on a year-long pilgrimage through the Middle East in 1850, making sketches for a gigantic moving picture of the Holy Land. Commencing the painting in London in March 1852, Banvard finished it in New York and began performances in December

1852 in his "Georama" on Broadway. The Holy Land panorama included scenes in present-day Lebanon, Syria, and Israel and culminated in a tour of Jerusalem. Though the work did not attract the critical notice that the Mississippi panorama had enjoyed, it was seen in New York and the principal cities of the East, including Boston, Baltimore, and Philadelphia, for more than ten years. During this time Banvard brought back his Mississippi panorama, later including illustrations of Civil War campaigns on the river. With the wealth he had acquired Banvard built a grandiose castle he called "Glenada" in Cold Spring Harbor, Long Island, where he lived with his family for twenty-five years. The eventual loss of his fortune began with the erection of a new theater on Broadway in 1867, where the Mississippi River panorama was released for a third time. By then the popularity of the picture had waned, and Banvard eventually turned the management of the theater over to impresarios, who began producing plays there. The Mississippi River panorama was brought back one more time in New York, at Broadway and Thirty-third Street in 1881, but the show did not replenish Banvard's means. In 1883 he retired with his family to Watertown, South Dakota. Ever the entrepreneur, he produced one more moving panorama, of the burning of Columbia, South Carolina, during the Civil War, but it was only shown locally. He died in Watertown.

Banvard's renown scarcely outlasted his final departure from New York, and his moving panoramas, like most others, have long since vanished. Still, his significance for the culture of his milieu should not be underestimated. The panorama vogue he instigated at mid-century had remarkable repercussions in literature and the fine arts. Writers such as Charles Dickens, Henry Wadsworth Longfellow, John Greenleaf Whittier, Henry David Thoreau, Herman Melville, and Mark Twain all acknowledged the phenomenon of the moving panorama and the originality of Banvard specifically, and several adopted either comparable subject matter or panoramic formal devices in their writing. Despite his humble origins and unschooled style, Banvard was the sole American artist of international renown around 1850. He was the first to treat frontier American subject matter on a monumental scale. Only later did landscape painters Frederic Church, Albert Bierstadt, and Thomas Moran address frontier subjects in their grandiose easel paintings, which were often shown as paid-admission landscape theater spectacles. The American moving panorama popularized by Banvard constituted the most conspicuous pictorial expression of Manifest Destiny in pre–Civil War America.

• Banvard's surviving papers, including an autobiographical fragment, part of an 1848–1850 diary narrating his experiences in England and Paris, and a scrapbook of reviews of his Mississippi River and Holy Land panoramas, are in the Minnesota Historical Society, St. Paul. The society also preserves some of Banvard's paintings. The programs for the Mississippi panorama, *Description of Banvard's Panorama of the Mississippi River* (1847), *Description of Banvard's Panorama of the* *Mississippi and Missouri Rivers* (1849), *Description of Banvard's Panorama of the Mississippi, Missouri and Ohio Rivers* (1852), and *Description of Banvard's Geographical Painting of the Mississippi River* (1862), contain sketches of his early life. Banvard's career is narrated most thoroughly and authoritatively in Joseph Earl Arrington, "John Banvard's Moving Panorama of the Mississippi, Missouri, and Ohio Rivers," *Filson Club History Quarterly* 32 (July 1858): 207–40. See also John Francis McDermott, *The Lost Panoramas of the Mississippi* (1958), for an extensive treatment of the size, content, and reception of Banvard's Mississippi River panorama; Richard Altick, *The Shows of London* (1978), for Banvard's effect on the panoramic arts in England; and Dorothy Dondore, "Banvard's Panorama and the Flowering of New England," *New England Quarterly* 11 (Dec. 1938): 817–26, for the effect of Banvard's Mississippi panorama on contemporary literary culture.

KEVIN J. AVERY

BANVARD, Joseph (9 May 1810–28 Sept. 1887), Baptist clergyman and author, was born in New York City, the son of Daniel Banvard, a businessman. His mother's name is unknown. When Banvard was in his early twenties, his father lost his savings in a failed business venture and died shortly after, leaving the family in financial difficulties. His younger brother, the painter John Banvard, then left the family home, and Banvard himself soon moved away to study theology.

Banvard's chief education as a young man was completed at the South Reading Academy, after which he attended Newton Theological Institution, graduating in 1835. There was no academic degree given to graduates at that time, but the course of study indicates the equivalent of a master of divinity degree. He was ordained on 26 August 1835 and began an eleven-year tenure as pastor of the Second Baptist Church in Salem, Massachusetts. Afterward, Banvard held pastorates in various towns in and near New England. For five years he preached in Boston, for two years in West Cambridge, for three years in Pawtucket, and for five years in Worcester. In 1866 he was elected president of the National Theological Institute in Washington, D.C., a school for African-American clergymen and teachers, but he left the post within a year. He then accepted a pastorate at the Baptist church at Paterson, N.J., where he remained for ten years before accepting his final pastorate in Neponset, Massachusetts, where he died. There is no indication that Banvard ever married.

Though Banvard wrote on a variety of subjects, he is most important for his historical publications, many of which are concerned with the history of colonial America. In the preface to his 1880 book, *Southern Explorers and Colonists*, he explains his fascination with colonial America when he claims that the period "abounds in incidents of a highly romantic nature." Indeed, his prose often seems motivated by his love of the adventure tale rather than any desire to document accurately a broader-reaching historical account of this period in American history. Such a history, he claims, "would be a work so voluminous as, by its magnitude, to deter many from its perusal." By focusing on "the trials and struggles of the early settlers as they contended with the climate and the elements, with the savage Indian, or with famine and disease," Banvard felt he could provide "a far more vivid conception of the lights and shadows of colonial life than could be derived from a mere general outline."

Banvard was in most cases careful to cite his historical sources, which range from the armchair travel narratives of Hakluyt to the histories of Smith, Bancroft, and Hillard. Among his most important historical publications are *Plymouth and the Pilgrims* (1851), *Tragic Scenes in the History of Maryland and the Old French War* (1856), *Novelties of the New World* (1852), *Soldiers and Patriots of the American Revolution* (1876), and *Southern Explorers and Colonists* (1880).

The second major element of Banvard's writing derives from his interest in religious matters. Along with his interest in the romantic and adventurous elements of history, he also believed that "the past is filled with waymarks for the guidance of the present and the future," and many of his historical writings focus on such religious and spiritual lessons. His numerous publications on Daniel Webster, one of which "designed for American youth," emphasize Webster's religious conviction, and his *Priscilla; or, Trials for the Truth* (1854) is a historical account of the Puritans and Baptists.

It was for his religious publications that Banvard seems to have been most noted during his lifetime. Among them are *The Christian Melodist* (1850), a collection of hymns that was reprinted at least four times during the first ten years of its existence, and *John Flavel: Golden Gems for the Christian* (1843), a selection of essays by Rev. Flavel, a contemporary of Banvard. Many of Banvard's religious writings are directed toward children, including *A Pictoral Question Book on Incidents in the Life of Our Savior* (1853), the *Topical Question Book* (1841), the "Infant Series" (c. 1844), and the "Little Pilgrim Series" (1869–1871), all collections of booklets and essays designed for use in Sabbath schools.

Throughout his lifetime, Banvard also maintained an interest in natural history, and his writings include essays and pamphlets on birds, insects, and fish. He was chosen as an honorary member of the Boston Society of Natural History as well as of the Worcester County Natural History Society, and he was president of the Historical Society of Passaic County, New Jersey.

A eulogy given at Banvard's funeral praised him for his work as pastor and as writer and historian for the Baptist church, but the sheer breadth of his work is also to be noted. Specifically, it is his interest in using American history as a resource for entertainment and instruction, both for secular and religious purposes, that establishes him as an important figure in nineteenth-century letters.

• Many of Banvard's papers are in the Library of Congress, Washington, D.C., and at the American Baptist Historical Society, Chester, Pa. For a complete listing of his writings and publications and the libraries that own them, see Edward Starr, *Baptist Bibliography*, vol. 2 (1952), pp. 69–74. A brief discussion of his early life appears in a book about his brother, *Banvard; or, The Adventures of an Artist* (1848). Obituaries are in the *Boston Transcript*, 1 Oct. 1887; the *Salem Gazette*, 7 Oct. 1887; and the annual reports of the New Jersey and Massachusetts Baptist state conventions for 1887.

SARA J. FORD

BAPST, John (7 Dec. 1815–2 Nov. 1887), missionary and educator, was born at La Roche in the canton of Fribourg, Switzerland, the son of a prosperous farmer. He received a classical education at the Jesuit College of Fribourg and entered the Society of Jesus in 1835. Two years after his ordination in 1846 the Jesuits were expelled from Switzerland as the result of a brief war in which Swiss Catholics were defeated by Swiss Protestants. Though his success in theological studies seemed to destine him for a career as a professor of theology, Bapst was sent to the United States as a missionary to the Penobscot Indians in Old Town, Maine. It was a daunting assignment since he knew neither English nor the Abnaki language of the Indians. However, with the help of an Indian girl who knew French, he was able to communicate with the natives and learn their language, which he felt somewhat resembled Hebrew.

After Bapst had spent three years at Old Town, the bishop of Boston, John Fitzpatrick, whose jurisdiction then included Maine, asked the Jesuit to assume a wider responsibility that included French and Irish Catholics scattered through much of Maine. Father Bapst moved his headquarters first to Eastport and later to Bangor, and the Jesuit superior gave him two priest assistants.

Many of the Protestant people of Maine appreciated Bapst's hard work, especially his vigorous promotion of temperance. But there were pockets of bigotry where the Know Nothing movement, hostile to immigrants, especially Catholics, was active. In the town of Ellsworth, Father Bapst was harassed, the school where he taught Catholic children was vandalized, and an attempt was made to burn down his church. At a meeting called by sympathetic Protestants to discuss these outrages, the Know Nothings outnumbered the spokesmen for tolerance and passed a resolution, filed in the town records, ordering Father Bapst not to enter the town again under threat of physical harm. When the priest insisted on returning, he was seized by a mob, carried out of town on a rail, stripped, tarred and feathered, and tied to a tree around which underbrush was piled. Some of the mob tried to set the brush afire, but Bapst's life was spared when the supply of matches ran out before a fire could be ignited. The priest was freed from the tree, dragged back to town, and warned that if he remained to say Mass the next day he would be killed. Bapst was taken to a Catholic home where several men of his congregation spent hours removing the dreadful covering that had been placed upon him. Despite the threats Father Bapst held services and preached the next day, but for his safety a leading Protestant took him to his home and the following morning drove him by carriage to Bangor.

Fair-minded Protestants, especially in Bangor and Portland, were shocked by the barbaric treatment of the priest. In Bangor a civic reception was held for the courageous Jesuit and a watch given him to replace the one taken by his tormentors. The mistreatment of Father Bapst at Ellsworth was obviously a defining experience in his life, and the national reports of the outrage caused some backlash against the radical Protestant Know Nothing movement.

In 1860, after a year spent at Holy Cross College in Worcester, Massachusetts, Father Bapst became rector of a seminary located temporarily in the building just completed for the projected Jesuit college in Boston. In 1863 the charter for Boston College was granted, and Bapst became the first president.

It was a tribute to Father Bapst's personality and leadership that, though his mastery of English was imperfect, he was chosen as the president of an institution whose students, supporters, and faculty were almost exclusively Irish Catholics. His celebrity as a near-martyr undoubtedly commended him to the new and burgeoning Catholic population of Boston.

Attached to Boston College, under Father Bapst's rectorship, was one of the most imposing Catholic churches built in Massachusetts in the nineteenth century, the Church of the Immaculate Conception. Completed four years before the founding of the college, the church carried a heavy debt, which was naturally a challenge to Bapst, who had no experience in dealing with high finance. However, the congregation rallied around their pastor, and he was able to remove the debt during his six-year term of office.

Despite his imperfect command of English, Father Bapst was a popular preacher because of his earnestness and charity. When he hesitated, reaching for the appropriate English word, his audience silently and sympathetically joined his search for the apt word. Bapst was confessor to Bishop Fitzpatrick and to a number of the priests of the diocese. But he also won Protestant friends, the most distinguished being the famous Civil War governor of Massachusetts John H. Andrews. In an ironic twist of fate, Bapst converted Nathaniel Shurtleff, Jr., whose father was Boston's Know Nothing mayor.

When Father Bapst's six-year term ended, he left Boston College a vital institution full of promise. In 1869 Bapst was appointed superior of the Jesuit mission of New York and Canada, a position he held for four years. From 1873 to 1877 Bapst was back with the Boston College community but this time in his popular role as confessor and spiritual guide in the church. In 1877 the bishop of Providence entrusted St. Joseph's parish to the Jesuits, and Father Bapst was named pastor. During his three-year tenure he built a debt-free school for 600 children. His health began to fail, and he was returned to Boston College where he served as spiritual father. Signs of a mental infirmity clouded his last years. After resting at the Jesuit noviti-ate in Maryland for several years, in 1885 he was sent to Mount Hope Retreat in Baltimore under the care of the Sisters of Charity. He died there two years later. His Jesuit contemporaries believe that Bapst's unhappy last days were haunted by the memory of his traumatic experience in Ellsworth in 1854. Bapst Library at Boston College honors the university's founding president.

• Bapst's correspondence is in the archives of Georgetown University. An extensive profile containing many of Bapst's letters is found in "Father John Bapst, a Sketch," *Woodstock Letters* 17 (1888): 219–29, 363–73; 18 (1889): 305–19; 20 (1891): 61–68. For Bapst's years in Maine see William L. Lucey, *The Catholic Church in Maine* (1957). An account of Bapst's presidency of Boston College is given in Charles F. Donovan et al., *History of Boston College* (1990). An obituary is in *Woodstock Letters* 16 (1887): 324–25.

CHARLES F. DONOVAN

BAQUET, Achille (15 Nov. 1885–20 Nov. 1956), early jazz musician, was born in New Orleans, Louisiana, the son of Theogene V. Baquet, a cornetist, music teacher, and leader of the Excelsior Brass Band of New Orleans, and Leocadie Mary Martinez. A clarinetist and younger brother of George Baquet (also a clarinetist), Achille was reputed to be both a successful teacher and an instrumentalist and was known to have been active both in early jazz and brass bands when jazz was first developing in New Orleans. Although a creole, his light skin color allowed him to pass for white. Consequently, he was known to have performed with both black and white bands, including "Papa" Jack Laine's, Ernest Giardina's Ragtime Band, and with members of the Original Dixieland Jazz Band (before it left New Orleans in 1916).

No information exists about the extent of Baquet's formal education; however, it is presumed that he was exposed to some musical instruction at an early age by virtue of his musical family. Nevertheless, like so many other New Orleans musicians of that period, he was initially an "ear" musician before he began lessons with Santo Juiffre at the Orpheum Theater in New Orleans. Later, while still a young man, Baquet developed a reputation of his own as a teacher of music fundamentals. In *Brass Bands* (1977), William J. Schafer maintains that Baquet, along with another creole, the trombonist Dave Perkins, worked with Laine's bands to impose order on the members' "ear playing," and in the process they taught many musicians to read music.

Baquet's most significant professional move came in 1918 when he answered the summons of pianist Jimmy Durante to join him in New York City for an engagement at the Alamo Cafe on West 125th Street in Harlem. Durante, a ragtime pianist and singer, was assembling a New Orleans–style jazz band and had learned of Baquet from Nick La Rocca of the Original Dixieland Jazz Band. Durante's new group, known as the Original New Orleans Jazz Band, was a five-piece band that played at the College Inn on Coney Island and continued on at the Alamo for some years after Baquet left. In November 1918 the band recorded for the

Okeh label and subsequently for the Gennett label in 1919 and 1920. Unlike his older brother George, Achille is not well represented on recordings; only a relatively small number have survived. But from his investigation of the Baquet brothers and Achille's 1919 recordings for Gennett, Alan Barrell (*Footnote*, 1986) concludes that Achille possessed "an exceptional clarinet technique—[and was] beautifully mobile and accurate in hitting the notes."

Although Achille Baquet lived into his early seventies, whatever contributions he made as a jazz musician occurred during the formative years of his career. Durante's Original New Orleans Jazz Band was one of the earliest jazz bands to play New York, and contemporaries compared them very favorably with La Rocca's Original Dixieland Jazz Band of that same period. Yet for reasons unknown, fame smiled on one and eluded the other. In addition, little is known of Baquet in his later years, other than that he moved to Los Angeles in 1920, where he became a member of Local 47 of the American Federation of Musicians. It is unknown whether he ever married or had children.

The recognition that was bestowed on some of his contemporaries from New Orleans somehow escaped Baquet, and he died in Los Angeles, one of the many largely uncelebrated early jazz musicians who failed to attain more than a parochial reputation. Still, enough evidence exists through his recordings and from the testimony of those who knew both him and his playing, to place him among the founding generation of creole musicians from New Orleans. By virtue of their participation as early performers at a time when few models existed, they, like Baquet, are regarded as pioneers in the development of early jazz.

• Achille Baquet receives passing notice in some of the primary studies on early jazz, but the most complete examination of him and the Baquet family is in three articles by Alan Barrell in *Footnote*. In "B Is for . . . Baquet," *Footnote* 17, no. 3 (Feb.–Mar. 1986): 4–24, Barrell summarizes all known printed references to the Baquet family and presents a complete discography of Achille Baquet. "Back to Baquet," *Footnote* 17, no. 4 (Apr.–May 1986): 10–12, amends information in the first article, with additions by David Phillips, and contains corrections to the discography. Barrell's "The Baquets—Some Concluding Notes," *Footnote* 18, no. 2 (Dec.–Jan. 1987): 4–14, contains additional information by both Phillips and Paul A. Larson. A number of errors appearing in earlier publications that concern the Baquets, in particular Achille Baquet's association with Jimmy Durante and the Alamo Cafe, are corrected in Jean-Christophe Averty, "A Look at Lizana," *Storyville* 146 (June 1991): 50–53.

CHARLES BLANCQ

BAQUET, George (1883–14 Jan. 1949), clarinetist and jazz musician, was born in New Orleans, Louisiana, the son of Theogene V. Baquet, a music teacher and the leader of the Excelsior Brass Band of New Orleans, and Leocadie Mary Martinez. Baquet and his younger brother, Achille, were descendants of "downtown" creoles, whose musical training was more closely allied to the traditions of the French musical conservatory— a musical heritage at that time held to be far superior to

that of the "uptown" jazz musicians. At age fourteen, George was already playing E-flat clarinet with the Lyre Club Symphony Orchestra, a twenty-to-thirty-piece creole ensemble directed by his father. He later received additional training from legendary Mexican-born clarinetist Luis "Papa" Tio, who, with his brother Lorenzo, was among the founding members of the New Orleans school of clarinetists, a group that included Johnny Dodds, Albert Nicholas, Omer Simeon, and Barney Bigard.

Baquet is known to have played with the Onward Brass Band in 1900, with Manuel Perez's Imperial Orchestra between 1901 and 1902, and with Buddy Bolden and Frankie Dusen sometime before 1905. In 1902 he left New Orleans to tour with P. T. Wright's Nashville Student Minstrels but returned around 1905 to join the orchestra of John Robichaux, an "uptown" creole and a rival of Buddy Bolden's, who led one of the most popular and successful prejazz ensembles of that period. During the years 1905–1914 Baquet was in great demand as a member of the Magnolia, Olympia, and Superior orchestras. He departed for Los Angeles in 1914 to join the Original Creole Orchestra—perhaps the first group of early jazz-playing New Orleanians to expose a national audience to the music. Their music was jazz only in an embryonic sense. The element of ragtime was still strong, improvisation was minimal, and the feeling of rhythmic swing—so important in later jazz—was only partially developed. In addition, the group, including cornetist Freddie Keppard, played more vaudeville than dance venues (in Los Angeles they were even featured during the intermissions of prizefights), and they toured extensively on the Orpheum Circuit, a chain of vaudeville theaters whose hub was the Orpheum in San Francisco. Fearing that their material would be copied and objecting to the low pay, Keppard supposedly refused Victor's offer to record them while in New York, thus allowing the Original Dixieland Jazz Band the distinction, a few months later, of becoming the first band to make a jazz recording.

Baquet moved to Philadelphia in 1923 for an engagement with the Lafayette Players at the Dunbar Theater. There he would live for the next twenty-nine years, performing regularly for fourteen years at Wilson's Café on Walnut Street and also as a member of the Earle Theater Pit Orchestra—a venerated jazz senior among local musicians, but one who, on occasion, still recorded with nationally known artists. During this period, Baquet appeared on recordings with vocalists Bessie Smith and Clara Smith and in July 1929 recorded at least nine titles with Jelly Roll Morton's Red Hot Peppers during their sessions for RCA at the latter's Camden, New Jersey, plant.

A stroke in 1945 prompted his return to New Orleans, where he lived with his sister. Contrary to some earlier accounts, a second stroke occurred in New Orleans, not Philadelphia, and he died there in Flint Goodridge Hospital. He was never married.

Like his younger brother Achille, George Baquet became the focus of considerable legendry over the years. He personally confirmed the assertion that he was one of the two clarinetists on the fabled Buddy Bolden cylinder, supposedly made in the early years of the century. Had it been located, the much-sought-after cylinder might have shed an entirely new light on the nature of early jazz, as it would have predated the recordings of the Original Dixieland Jazz Band by more than twenty years. Baquet is also reputed to have been a teacher of Sidney Bechet and to have been the first to play the clarinet obligato in the New Orleans classic "High Society."

Baquet's contemporaries generally remember him as the possessor of a full, round tone and a legato style of playing associated with the first generation of jazz clarinetists from New Orleans. In his informative article in *Footnote* ("B Is for . . . Baquet"), Alan Barrell identifies Baquet and his generation as the progenitors of the modern reed sound of the 1930s. He credits New Orleanian Jimmy Noone (whose similar tone and full, legato style made him Baquet's replacement in the Original Creole Orchestra) as being the model for the young Benny Goodman and later reed players (among them Irving Fazola, Eddie Miller, and Barney Bigard—all from New Orleans) as being heavily influenced by Baquet's reed jazz style as they developed the new saxophone sound in orchestras led by Duke Ellington, Glenn Miller, Benny Goodman, and Bob Crosby.

• Baquet's early career is outlined in Fred Ramsey's "Vet Tells Story of the Original Creole Orchestra," *Downbeat*, 15 Dec. 1940, but the most extensive account of George Baquet is contained in a series of articles by Alan Barrell in *Footnote*. In "B Is for . . . Baquet," *Footnote* 17, no. 3 (Feb.–Mar. 1986): 4–24, Barrell gives a discography (excluding reissues), summarizes the most accessible printed references to the Baquet family, and reprints a letter of Baquet's to Dr. Edmond Souchon, dated 3 Mar. 1948, along with the notes that Baquet used when he addressed the New Orleans Jazz Club on 17 Apr. 1948. "Back to Baquet," *Footnote* 17, no. 4 (May 1986): 10–12, contains additional information on Baquet's recordings with Bessie Smith, Clara Smith, and Jelly Roll Morton, as well as a list of his original compositions. In "The Baquets—Some Concluding Notes," *Footnote* 18, no. 2 (Jan. 1987): 4–14, Barrell supplements the earlier articles with additions by Paul A. Larson and David Phillips.

CHARLES BLANCQ

BARA, Theda (1885?–7 Apr. 1955), stage and screen actress, was born Theodosia Goodman in Cincinnati, Ohio, the daughter of Bernard Goodman, an immigrant Polish Jew who began as a tailor and eventually owned a garment factory in Cincinnati, and Pauline Louise de Coppet, a French immigrant who sold women's cosmetics prior to her marriage. In 1917 the family legally changed its name to Bara, taken from de Coppet's Swiss father, Francis Bara de Coppet. Theda Bara attended the University of Cincinnati before moving with her family to New York City in 1905. There she appeared in small parts in various stock companies and briefly as a movie extra under the name Theodosia de Coppet. In 1914 she met director Frank Powell, who cast her (renamed Theda Bara) in the role of the vampire for his motion picture *A Fool There Was* (1915), based on Rudyard Kipling's poem "The Vampire." This film, in which she utters the famous line, "Kiss me, my fool," made Bara a star, and the Fox Film Company signed her to a long-term contract.

Bara was the first silent screen femme fatale and the first actress to be called a "vamp" (for her vampire-like sexual persona). Fox promoted and exploited her siren image by creating a publicity campaign for Bara that was to become the prototype for the Hollywood studio system's star-making machine. Press agents were hired to concoct an exotic background that would account suitably for her flamboyant, mysterious persona. It was said that she had been born an Arab princess in the Sahara desert, that she possessed supernatural powers, and that she was a reincarnation of many evil women of the past. She dyed her hair black, wore heavy indigo makeup, and appeared in public surrounded by symbols of evil and death such as human skulls, serpents, and ravens. Her name was said to be an anagram for "Arab Death." She was publicly denounced in churches throughout the country, and several groups, including the Better Films Committee of the Woman's Club of Omaha, Nebraska, attempted to ban the showing of her films. Such attempts served only to enhance Bara's exotic stature and the popularity of her films.

From 1915 to 1919 Bara appeared in thirty-nine films, mainly playing variations of the vampish man-killer in such roles as Cleopatra, Salome, Mata Hari, and Carmen. By 1917 she commanded $4,000 a week, and her popularity almost single-handedly established the Fox Film Corporation as a major Hollywood studio. By 1919, however, Bara's star had faded. Audiences began to tire of the fabricated, overblown image she had cultivated. When her contract at Fox expired she left Hollywood to appear in a 1920 Broadway melodrama called *The Blue Flame*. Her performance was greeted with derision, however, prompting *New York Times* drama critic Alexander Woolcott to write, "She displays a fine self-possession which enabled her to proceed last evening with unflinching gravity even when the audience lost control of itself and shook with laughter." Despite the play's failure on Broadway, Bara continued with a road tour, and audiences flocked to see the silent film star in person. Although she continued to search for film work in the years between 1920 and 1926, her only role was in the unsuccessful 1925 melodrama *The Unchastened Woman*. Her final film appearance was in a comedy short, *Madame Mystery* (1926), codirected by Stan Laurel, in which Bara lampooned her old vamp character.

In 1921 Bara had married Charles J. Brabin, who directed her last three films at Fox. They retired from show business and spent their remaining years living in Beverly Hills, California. They had no children. Bara died in Los Angeles after a long bout with cancer.

Bara's mass appeal to early film audiences established an iconic image of a powerful, dangerous, sexually liberated woman who seduced and destroyed weaker men. Beginning with Bara's work in the early years of cinema, Hollywood's fascination with the femme fatale has endured through generations of film-makers, stars, and audiences. Although the cartoonish absurdity of Bara's portrayals is obvious in retrospect, these pioneering characterizations can be seen as progenitors of the more complex and enigmatic women who appear decades later in such genres as film noir. Perhaps not surprisingly, Bara was more popular among women than men during her career in the silent film era, and she reputedly received hundreds of letters a week from women seeking advice on matters of love and marriage. Ironically, Bara was uneasy with her exotic screen image and, unlike the vamp she portrayed, lived a quiet, simple life.

• Collected papers on the Goodman/Bara family, including Bara's early years, may be found at the Cincinnati Public Library. Her film career is recorded in clippings from the Robinson Locke Scrapbooks (vol. 31) and Bara's own scrapbooks in the Billy Rose Theatre Collection at the New York Public Library for the Performing Arts, Lincoln Center. See also DeWitt Bodeen, *From Hollywood: The Careers of 15 Great American Stars* (1976); Norman J. Zierold, *Sex Goddesses of the Silent Screen* (1973); Alexander Walker, *The Celluloid Sacrifice: Aspects of Sex in the Movies* (1967); and C. Lockwood, "Priestess of Sin, Theda Bara," *Horizon* 24, no. 1 (1981). An interesting analysis of the "vamp" as a Hollywood icon appears in Molly Haskell, *From Reverence to Rape* (1974). Earlier accounts of Bara's life may be found in Mary B. Mullett, "Theda Bara, Queen of the Vampires," *American Magazine*, Sept. 1920; Terry Ramsaye, *A Million and One Nights* (1926); Upton Sinclair, *Upton Sinclair Presents William Fox* (1933); and Louella Parsons, *The Gay Illiterate* (1944). An obituary is in the *New York Times*, 8 Apr. 1955.

MICHAEL ABBOTT

BARAGA, Frederic (29 June 1797–19 Jan. 1868), first Roman Catholic bishop of Marquette and Sault Ste. Marie, Michigan, was born Irenaeus Frederic Baraga at the castle of Malavas, on the hereditary estate of his mother, near the village of Dobrnic in Slovenia in the Austrian province of Carniola, the son of John Nepomuc Baraga and Maria Katharine Josefa de Jencic, farmers. Educated in the provincial capital of Ljubljana, Baraga went to Vienna to study law in 1816 and there came under the influence of the Redemptorist priest Clement Maria Hofbauer. Having decided to become a priest, Baraga renounced his claim to the family lands in favor of his brother-in-law and was ordained for the diocese of Ljubljana in 1823. A popular preacher and confessor, he compiled a prayer book in Slovenian that was in use throughout the nineteenth century.

Baraga volunteered for the American missions and was accepted into the diocese of Cincinnati. In 1831 he was sent to Arbre Croche (Harbor Springs), Michigan, near the northern end of Lake Michigan, whence he served the American Indians on either side of the lake. Adept at languages, Baraga learned the Ottawa tongue of his parishioners and published a prayer book in their language. Transferred to the present site of Grand Rapids, Michigan, in 1833, Baraga organized a parish among the American Indians. There he encountered opposition from Protestant missionaries, who accused him of stealing their converts, and from traders, whose liquor traffic with the American Indians he denounced. In 1835 he was reassigned by his bishop to La Pointe at the western end of Lake Superior. For the next thirty-three years he worked among the Ojibway Indians and the white settlers in the Upper Peninsula of Michigan and on the shores of Lake Superior. He was the first Catholic priest to visit many of the American Indians around Lake Superior since the Jesuit "blackrobes" had been there in the seventeenth century.

Baraga returned to Europe in 1837 to raise money for his missions and while there published six books: a catechism and a life of Christ in both the Ottawa and Ojibway languages and a work on the history and character of the Indian missions in America that appeared in French, German, and Slovene. The publications in the American-Indian languages were widely circulated in the United States and Canada. In 1850 Baraga published a grammar and in 1853 a dictionary of the Ojibway language, both of which are still consulted.

In 1843 Baraga transferred his base to L'Anse in Michigan's Upper Peninsula, whence he could serve both the American Indians and the white settlers who were attracted to the Keweenaw Peninsula by the discovery of copper. He was ordained a bishop in 1853 and appointed vicar apostolic of Upper Michigan. When the diocese of Sault Ste. Marie was created in 1857, he was named as the first bishop. The see was transferred to Marquette, Michigan, in 1865.

Baraga's journeys and feats of endurance in the wild, sparsely populated territory of Upper Michigan were the stuff of legend. He learned to travel like the American Indians, eating and sleeping as little as possible, and he often walked forty miles a day on snowshoes. He abjured the use of liquor and did not eat meat. Baraga suffered a crippling stroke in 1866 during the Second Plenary Council of Baltimore. He returned to Marquette, where he died.

• Baraga manuscripts are scattered in more than ten repositories in Europe and North America, but the Bishop Baraga Association of Marquette, Mich., has collected copies of all known documents by and pertaining to Baraga. A microfilm copy of Department of the Interior records relating to the sale of mission lands near Grand Rapids, Mich., is in the University of Notre Dame Archives, as is a microfilm copy of the manuscript collection of the Bishop Baraga Association. A published edition of Baraga's diary from 27 June 1852 to 16 July 1863 is *The Diary of Bishop Frederic Baraga, First Bishop of Marquette, Michigan*, ed. Regis M. Walling and N. Daniel Rupp (1990). Although it lacks source notes, Bernard J. Lambert's biography of Baraga, *Shepherd of the Wilderness* (1967), is based on the documents gathered by the Bishop Baraga Association. Maksimilijan Jezernik, *Frederick Baraga* (1968), is based on the archives of the Congregatio de Propaganda Fide in Rome and fully notes the sources used. Both biographies list the relevant archival collections as well as works about Baraga in English, German, and Slovene. Chrysostomus Verwyst, *Life and Labors of Rt. Rev. Frederic Baraga* (1900), is an early English account of Baraga's life.

James T. Connelly

BARANOV, Aleksandr Andreevich (1746–16 Apr. 1819), Russian colonizer of North America, was born in Kargopol, Russia. His parents' names are unknown. In his early years he was engaged in trade in Moscow and St. Petersburg and in 1780 went to Irkutsk where he founded a glass factory and a distillery.

Having derived encouragement from the local authorities, Baranov built a fortified settlement on an arm of the Anadyr River, where about thirty fur traders hunted and traded with the Chukchi inhabitants for walrus ivory and baleen. At some point, however, the Chukchi became displeased with the newcomers' behavior and destroyed the new settlement.

So the ruined Baranov was forced to sign a contract with a rich merchant and fur trader, Grigory Ivanovich Shelekhov, on 15 August 1790 in Okhotsk to become the manager of his possessions in America. Immediately thereafter, Baranov sent his wife Matrena (maiden name unknown) and his two children to his native Kargopol; he never saw them again. Then he sailed on the galliot *Tri Sviatitelia* (Three saints) for Kodiak, now in Alaska. En route the ship was wrecked at Unalaska in the fall of 1790, and it was June 1791 before Baranov reached Kodiak Island. In the American colonies Baranov kept a mistress Anna Grigorevna, a daughter of an Aleutian toion (chief), Grigori Raskashchikov. He married Anna Grigorevna after his wife died in 1806; she gave birth to two children. Apparently Baranov also had one more daughter (probably with a woman named Katherina).

In 1792 Baranov transferred the headquarters of Russian America from Three Saints Bay to Pavlovskaia harbor (on Chiniak Bay) and began to take an active part in the expansion of Russian influence in the Northwest of America. Baranov founded settlements on the Alaskan coast, explored new territories, searched for minerals, developed trade with the native inhabitants, established connections with the Bostonians, and developed the fur trade in every possible way.

In 1793 he founded Voskresenskaia gavan (Resurrection harbor) on Chugach Bay, where *Phoenix*, the first ship built by the Russians in North America, was constructed under the direction of James Shields.

On 24 September 1794, during Baranov's administration, an Orthodox mission headed by Archimandrite Ioasaf arrived on Kodiak and began very actively to spread Christianity among the natives. In one year 6,740 persons were baptized, and 1,573 marriages were performed. In 1796 the first Orthodox church, Holy Resurrection, was built on American soil. Archimandrite Ioasaf severely criticized Baranov and Russian fur traders in general for their cruel treatment of the natives.

The islanders became part of Baranov's labor force as well as his army. With their help he established outposts in Tlingit territory and later in California.

In the summer of 1799 Baranov sailed on the ship *Olga* to Sitka, where he founded a new settlement, the fortress of Saint Arkhistratig Mikhail. However, in June 1802 well-armed Tlingit Indians attacked this settlement, killing about 25 Russians and 200 Aleutians and destroying a new ship. Only in the autumn of 1804 was Baranov able to recapture the island with support from the sloop *Neva*. Soon he built a new fortified post, Novo Arkhangelsk, which after August 1808 became the capital of Russian America and the home for Baranov as the chief manager of the colonies. After the Russian-American Company was founded on 8 July 1799, Baranov was appointed manager of the American colonies, a post he held until 1803, and he served as the chief manager, or governor, from 1803 to 1818.

At the beginning of the nineteenth century, systematic contacts with U.S. traders were established. More and more Russian colonies became dependent on U.S. traders for supplies. Baranov's transactions with Jonathan Winship, William Davis, John Ebbots, George Washington Ayres, and others were valued in the tens of thousands of dollars. For both sides joint hunting expeditions near the shores of California were profitable. An example of this benefit was Baranov's contract with Captain Ayres of the ship *Mercury*, who received a special work force (twenty-five kayaks with Aleutians). In 1812, following Baranov's instructions, his assistant Ivan Aleksandrovich Kuskov founded the fortress and settlement of Ross in California, only fifty miles north of San Francisco, and in 1815 Dr. Georg Anton Schäffer was sent off to the Sandwich (Hawaiian) Islands, where he made an unsuccessful attempt to take possession of Kauai.

Because of declining health and old age, in January 1818 Baranov was replaced as chief manager of Russian America by a career naval officer, Captain Lieutenant Leontii Andreanovich Gagemeister. In November 1818 Baranov sailed for St. Petersburg on the ship *Kutuzov* but died near Java in the Sunda Strait.

• Baranov's papers are in the Manuscript Division of the Russian State Library in Moscow and some other repositories, including the Russian-American Company Collection in the Archive of the Foreign Policy of Russian Empire. For additional information, see K. T. Khlebnikov, *Life of Baranov* (1835; trans. 1973); Hector Chevigny, *Lord of Alaska: Baranov and the Russian Adventure* (1942); Nikolai N. Bolkhovitinov, *The Beginnings of Russian-American Relations, 1775–1815* (1975); and R. A. Pierce, *Russian America: A Biographical Dictionary* (1990).

N. N. Bolkhovitinov

BARBADOES, James G. (c. 1796–22 June 1841), was an abolitionist and community activist. Nothing is known of the circumstances of his birth, early life, and education, although his surname may indicate West Indian origins.

Barbadoes emerged as an important figure in the small but influential African-American community in Boston's West End by the mid-1820s; from 1821 to 1840 he operated a barbershop in Boston. He was a prominent member of the African Baptist church and of African Lodge #459, the preeminent black fraternal organization in the nation. An amateur musician applauded for both his vocal and instrumental talents, he performed regularly before local audiences. But he was best known as an "indefatigable political organizer."

In 1826 Barbadoes joined with the controversial essayist David Walker and several others to organize the Massachusetts General Colored Association (MGCA), which over the next few years led local protests, corresponded with race leaders throughout the North, supported the emerging African-American press, and petitioned the U.S. Congress for an end to slavery in the nation's capital. Barbadoes served as secretary of the organization. He continued to hold a prominent place among Boston blacks in the 1830s. He was one of the founders and officers of the Boston Colored Temperance Society, which sought to convert local blacks to total abstinence from alcoholic beverages as a means of deflecting white criticisms and conserving community resources. And he represented Boston blacks at the 1833 and 1834 black national conventions.

After the conversion of William Lloyd Garrison to the cause of immediate abolition in 1830, Barbadoes became a devoted supporter and colleague of the Boston editor. He was one of the first African Americans to gain a prominent place in the new interracial antislavery movement that Garrison helped create. One of three blacks to attend the 1833 founding convention of the American Anti-Slavery Society (AASS) in Philadelphia, Barbadoes enthusiastically signed the organization's Declaration of Sentiments. He served on the board of managers of the AASS during its first four years. But he proved even more important to the movement at the local and regional levels. In 1833 Barbadoes helped bring the membership of the MGCA into the New England Anti-Slavery Society (NEASS), making the AASS affiliate into a racially mixed body.

Barbadoes used this new forum to publicize the kidnapping and incarceration of free black sailors in southern ports, making his white colleagues aware of the problem for the first time. Barbadoes knew about the problem firsthand. His brother Robert had been imprisoned in New Orleans for five months in 1815 until word reached family and friends in Boston. In 1834 Barbadoes was named to the board of counselors of the NEASS. He remained active in the movement through the end of the decade. When the antislavery movement began to fracture in 1839–1840 over questions of political action and women's role, with many abolitionists viewing the Garrisonian positions as too extreme, Barbadoes emerged as one of Garrison's strongest defenders.

Like Garrison, Barbadoes was a vocal critic of African colonization schemes, including the American Colonization Society's plan to resettle American blacks in Liberia, throughout the 1830s. Yet in 1840, disillusioned by a lack of progress in the struggle for emancipation and equality in the United States, he began to explore the possibility of migrating to a more hospitable location in the Caribbean. At first he promoted a venture in British Guiana (now Guyana), acting as secretary to a group of Boston blacks authorized by the colonial government to recruit African-American settlers. Later in the year, contrary to the advice of many of his friends, Barbadoes and his family were among thirty Bostonians who migrated to St. Ann's Parish in Jamaica to participate in a venture devoted to the culture and manufacture of silk. It was sponsored by the Jamaica Silk Company, which had recently been organized by Boston entrepreneur Samuel Whitmarsh. Barbadoes joined the enterprise, "hoping to better his condition." But the venture developed slowly and Barbadoes soon perceived that he had been duped by the flattering representations of company agents. Even worse, two of his children died of malaria and Barbadoes himself soon succumbed to the disease. His widow Rebecca and their surviving children returned broken and destitute to their Boston home.

• Dozens of documents relevant to Barbadoes's careers as an abolitionist and African-American community activist can be found in issues of the *Liberator* (1831–1841). His testimony on the kidnapping of free black sailors is in David L. Child, *The Despotism of Freedom; or, The Tyranny and Cruelty of American Republican Slave-Masters, Shown to Be the Worst in the World* (1833). Brief biographies of Barbadoes are in Rayford W. Logan and Michael R. Winston, eds., *Dictionary of American Negro Biography* (1982); and C. Peter Ripley et al., eds., *The Black Abolitionist Papers*, vol. 3 (1991). The Jamaican silk venture is discussed in Douglas Hall, *Free Jamaica, 1838–1865: An Economic History* (1959). Obituaries are in the *Liberator*, 20 Aug. 1841, and the *Tenth Annual Report of the Massachusetts Anti-Slavery Society* (1842).

ROY E. FINKENBINE

BARBARIN, Paul (5 May 1899–17 Feb. 1969), jazz drummer, was born Adolphe Paul Barbarin in New Orleans, Louisiana, the son of Isidore John Barbarin, a coachman for undertakers, and Josephine Arthidore. The Barbarins were a distinguished musical family. Paul's father played alto horn with the Onward, Excelsior, and Tuxedo brass bands and recorded with Bunk Johnson in 1945. Paul's brothers were Louis, a drummer in New Orleans long associated with Papa Celestin; Lucien, also a drummer; and Willie, a cornetist. Barbarin's nephew was jazz musician Danny Barker.

Having begun to play by using two forks on kitchen chairs, Barbarin was later arrested for drumming his sticks too loudly on the neighbor's steps; such was his skill that on his performing in court the judge dismissed the case, paid him fifty cents (his first professional income), and sent him home. Around 1915 he began working as a freight elevator operator to earn money for a drum set, and this purchase led to his accompanying Buddy Petit, Sidney Bechet, and Jimmie Noone. An astute observer, he retained and later recounted engaging memories of these early years of New Orleans jazz.

Going north to Chicago in 1917, he worked in the stockyards by day and as a musician by night. He joined bassist Bill Johnson at the Royal Gardens early in 1918. The band included King Oliver and Noone; Freddie Keppard and Bechet also joined for a time. Barbarin toured into Canada with the Tennessee Ten, a musical comedy show, and he led a band in Connecticut before returning to Chicago to join Keppard briefly, then Noone. Barbarin and Noone married sisters; by his own account, Barbarin married Onelia Thomas in September 1922 while playing with King Oliver, although at that time Oliver's drummer was Baby Dodds. In any event, Barbarin and his wife returned to New Orleans in 1923, initially staying with Barney Bigard while the two men joined a band including Luis Russell and Albert Nicholas at Tom Anderson's Cabaret. Barbarin also began playing with the Onward and Excelsior brass bands in which he marched with a snare drum before switching to bass drum. He later joined the Tuxedo Brass Band.

Nicholas, Bigard, Barbarin, and Russell left for Chicago late in 1924, all but Russell to join Oliver at Lincoln Gardens, but the dance hall burned down, and they began working only in February when Oliver introduced his Dixie Syncopators, now including Russell, at the Plantation Cafe. Bigard recalled that during this period Barbarin began using a gimmick of New Orleans drumming: he would pick up the snare drum during the last part of "Tiger Rag" and shout, "Hold that tiger" through the drumskins. Barbarin's drumming with the Dixie Syncopators was not well recorded except for a consistently prominent cymbal on many titles and clomping sounds from the temple blocks on "Wa-wa-wa" (1926). His contribution was nonetheless crucial. This is nowhere more evident than on "Deep Henderson" (1926), when Barbarin with a single chunky cymbal stroke pulls the band back into place after Russell had allowed the rhythm to go astray in his piano solo.

Barbarin remained with Oliver until mid-1927, eventually touring to New York and then to Baltimore, where the band broke up. Barbarin and Henry "Red" Allen went home to join pianist Walter Pichon at the Pelican Cafe in New Orleans. Later that same year Barbarin returned to New York to join Russell at the Nest Club. He remained in the band until early in 1932, in the process making recordings under Russell's own name (including "Muggin' Lightly," 1930); he also recorded under the leadership of Louis Armstrong (including "St. Louis Blues," 1929), Oliver, Allen, and J. C. Higginbotham, the last two being members of Russell's orchestra. Allen remembered the Russell band as "the most fiery band I ever heard. . . . It had the finest rhythm section, with Pops Foster on bass and Paul Barbarin on drums especially inspiring to the soloists."

After working in New York with lesser-known bands, including Pichon's and his own, Barbarin returned home to lead his Jump Rhythm Boys. He re-

corded with Russell again in New York in 1934 and then rejoined Russell's big band, with Armstrong taking over its leadership in 1935. Armstrong, "when discussing drummers, singled out Barbarin as an exceptional timekeeper." Recordings from this period capture his drumming better than before. Additionally, on several titles from 1938 a decision evidently was made to feature Barbarin, whose musicality had generally been kept from the spotlight. Among these, "Jubilee" offers solos based on military snare drum rudiments, juxtaposed with a conventional swing rhythm accompaniment; "I Double Dare You" includes a classic example of syncopated New Orleans parade drumming in support of solos by trombonist Higginbotham and tenor saxophonist Bingie Madison. Ironically, this same year Barbarin was fired, his job given to Big Sid Catlett.

At home once again, he led bands, joined Joe Robichaux's New Orleans Rhythm Boys, and worked with Pichon and Red Allen before leaving with Allen for a year in Chicago and on the West Coast (1942–1943). In Springfield, Illinois, he led a band in 1943, and he worked with Bechet in 1944, when his wife's illness brought him back home. Thereafter he was based in New Orleans, leading bands, playing in parades, and teaching at the Grunewald School of Music. He also worked with Art Hodes in Chicago in 1953 and performed in New York, Los Angeles, and Toronto. As a member of brass bands he was celebrated for the manner in which he danced while playing bass drum. He died while leading the Onward Brass Band in a carnival parade on St. Charles Avenue in New Orleans.

The leading figure in one of the most distinguished musical families in New Orleans, Barbarin had a modest career as a composer. "Bourbon Street Parade" became a part of the standard repertory in the revival of New Orleans jazz; he recorded it as a sideman with George Lewis in 1951 and later on numerous occasions. As a leader, he recorded a number of his other compositions, including "The Second Line." His significance, though, was as a drummer, and he approached his own sessions as he would any other, filling a supportive, subsidiary role. In this manner he made his impact on jazz, particularly in affiliations involving Luis Russell.

• One interview of Isidore Barbarin (7 Jan. 1959) and Louis Barbarin (13 May 1962) and at least five of Paul Barbarin (27 Mar. 1957–7 Sept. 1963) are in the archives of Tulane University; for transcripts on microform, see *New York Times Oral History Program: New Orleans Jazz Oral History Collection* (1978), nos. 4–5, and (1979), no. 46, chap. 15. An interview surveying his life was published by John Norris, "Paul Barbarin," *Eureka* 1, no. 1 (1960): 23–27. Entries on family members and brass bands appear in Samuel Barclay Charters, *Jazz: New Orleans, 1885–1963* (1963). Parts of an unfinished autobiography, focusing on his youth and offering a colorful and articulate social history of early New Orleans jazz, is in Clint Bolton, "All Gone Now," *New Orleans Magazine* 5, no. 8 (1971); repr. in *Second Line* 24 (Winter 1972): 19–23 and (Spring 1972): 19–21. Full listings for recordings that the Barbarins made in their hometown appear in Tom

Stagg and Charlie Crump, *New Orleans: The Revival* (1973). Considerable detail on the family appears in Danny Barker, *A Life in Jazz*, ed. Alyn Shipton (1986).

Albert J. McCarthy examines in detail the history and recordings of Russell's band in "The Big Band Era: 2. Luis Russell," *Jazz Monthly* 6, no. 6 (1960): 9–12; this is reworked in his book *Big Band Jazz* (1974), pp. 80–85, which includes a particularly complimentary assessment of Barbarin's contribution. Although Barbarin does not figure prominently, a few enlightening comments are scattered through Martin Williams, *Jazz Masters of New Orleans* (1967). A dramatic account of his death appears in Jack V. Buerkle and Danny Barker, *Bourbon Street Black* (1973), pp. 181–82. Barney Bigard recollects his years with Barbarin in *With Louis and the Duke: The Autobiography of a Jazz Clarinetist*, ed. Barry Martyn (1985). An account of his association with King Oliver appears in *Walter C. Allen & Brian Rust's "King" Oliver*, rev. Laurie Wright (1987). John Chilton, *Who's Who of Jazz: Storyville to Swing Street* (1985), supplies the most reliable single chronology of his life, although even here some details may be disputed.

BARRY KERNFELD

BARBER, Donn (19 Oct. 1871–29 May 1925), architect, was born in Washington, D.C., the son of Charles Gibbs Barber and Georgiana Williams. He grew up in New York City; attended Holbrook Military Academy in Briarcliff, New York; and went on to the Sheffield Scientific School at Yale, graduating in 1893. Afterward Barber returned to New York to work for Carrère & Hastings and to attend architectural courses at Columbia University. A protégé of John M. Carrère, he was sent to Paris in 1894 to study at the École des Beaux-Arts. He became the ninth American to receive a *diplôme*, in 1898. Profoundly influenced by his *atelier* education, Barber helped develop a similar curriculum in the United States as a founding member of the Society of Beaux Arts Architects. He rounded out his apprenticeship at the office of Cass Gilbert and Lord & Hewlett before beginning a New York practice in 1900. Only a year before he had married his Paris sweetheart, Elsie Yandell of Kentucky, and had established a summer residence for his family in White Plains, New York.

Barber seemed destined for national leadership in his profession. Described in one obituary as "strong and sturdy, wholesome and gentle, well-bred and a man to tie to," he impressed many important architects and patrons with his character and education. Drawn to monumental civic architecture in the classical tradition, he distinguished himself in such early works as the Connecticut State Supreme Court Building in Hartford (E. T. Hapgood, Associated Architects, 1900). That major commission led to additional work in Connecticut, including buildings for Aetna and Travelers insurance companies, the Hartford National Bank, the Connecticut State Library, the Berzelius Society building in New Haven, and country houses in Greenwich. His major New York buildings were the Central Branch YMCA (c. 1913–1917), the Institute for Musical Art (1910, now the Manhattan School of Music), and the Cotton Exchange (1923). Barber's early public architecture was characterized by rigorous attention to proportion, Beaux-Arts axial planning, and scholarly use of classical ornament.

He was active in professional circles and as a teacher, editing the *Architectural Yearbook* (1912); serving as president of the Architectural League of New York (1925) and of the Society of Beaux Arts Architects (1909–1910); and running his own small academy, the Atelier Donn Barber. Here he was able to employ the French pedagogy of architectural composition he so admired in his Paris school years as a means of teaching aspiring American designers.

Following a lull in work during the First World War, Barber sought to regain his stride with a major New York building, the towering Broadway Temple project, designed in 1924–1925. This speculative skyscraper combined a church on the lower levels with a hotel and stores above–to make the religious institution "self supporting, and even profit producing." In 1923 Holabird and Roche had executed a similar building in Chicago, the Chicago Temple, which combined secular and religious programs in one edifice, while in 1921 Bertram Goodhue had proposed a "Convocation Tower" for Madison Square to be the tallest building in the world.

Barber raised some $2 million for the Broadway Temple project and published renderings by the talented perspectivist, Hugh Ferris, in *Pencil Points*, to arouse public interest. The design of this massive setback skyscraper, with classical overtones, indicated that Barber was evolving a more abstract mature style akin to the work of Walker & Gillette or Shreve, Lamb and Harmon, designers of many of New York's Art Deco skyscrapers. News of Barber's sudden death after a brief illness at his home in New York City shocked the architectural profession and stopped one of the great visionary projects of the twenties. Obituaries lamented the loss of one of America's leading designers, when "he was at the very zenith of his power," as the *American Architect* observed.

Barber was survived by his wife, a musician who later became president of the Manhattan School of Music, and four children. He was a fellow of the American Institute of Architects, an honorary member of the Royal Institute of British Architects, and an affiliate of the French Society of Beaux Arts Architects.

• Short biographies of Donn Barber may be found in Mark Alan Hewitt, *The Architect and the American Country House, 1890–1940* (1990), p. 268, and Allison Sky and Michelle Stone, *Unbuilt America* (1976), p. 28. Obituaries appear in the *New York Times*, 30 May 1925; the *Yale University Obituary Record* (1925); the *Journal of the American Institute of Architects* 13, no. 7 (1925): 274; the *Architectural Record* 58, no. 1 (1925): 86; and the *American Architect* 127 (1925): 537–38.

MARK ALAN HEWITT

BARBER, Francis (26 Nov. 1750–11 Feb. 1783), revolutionary war officer and schoolmaster, was born in Princeton, New Jersey, the son of Patrick Barber, a farmer and county judge, and Jane Frasher (also spelled Fraser or Frazer). His parents had immigrated from County Longford, Ireland, in 1735. In 1764, while Barber was attending the College of New Jersey (now Princeton), the family moved to a 200-acre farm in Ulster County, New York. Upon receiving his A.B. in 1767, Barber and Stephen Van Voornees established a school at Newbridge, near Hackensack, New Jersey. Considered an able scholar in the ancient languages, especially Greek, Barber was named the master of the Elizabethtown Academy (a Latin grammar school) in 1771. Alexander Hamilton studied under Barber's tutelage during the winter and spring of 1773. At Elizabethtown, Barber fell in with a Presbyterian-Whig circle that included such patriots as William Livingston, who became the state of New Jersey's first governor. On 26 January 1773 Barber married Mary Ogden; she died in October of the same year, and no children are known. Barber lived with his father-in-law, Robert Ogden, until he went off to fight in the revolutionary war.

Barber joined the militia as a lieutenant and on 22 January 1776 participated in the daring capture of a British supply ship, the *Blue Mountain Valley*, that had been driven by a storm into Princess Bay near Sandy Hook. On 26 January 1776 Barber was appointed a major, the third in command of the Third New Jersey Regiment. The regiment was one of four such units that formed the New Jersey Brigade of Continental army troops, under the command of Brigadier General William Maxwell until July 1780 and afterward commanded by Elias Dayton. On 26 November 1776 Barber was promoted to lieutenant colonel.

When the rest of the New Jersey Brigade was assigned to the Canadian campaign in early summer 1776, Barber and the Third Regiment saw duty along the Mohawk Valley, protecting settlements from potential Tory and Indian raids. After the retreat from Canada, Barber and his regiment joined forces with the other American troops at Fort Ticonderoga and Mount Independence, at the lower end of Lake Champlain. The brigade returned to New Jersey about the time of the battle of Trenton but did not participate in that engagement. During the winter and spring of 1777, while most of George Washington's army was encamped at Morristown, Barber and his fellow New Jersey Continentals harassed British army units, chiefly foraging expeditions, in New Jersey. This little war of attrition was quite successful, resulting in severe shortages in food and hay supply for the British army in New York City and at several posts the enemy held in New Jersey.

Barber probably fought with the New Jersey Brigade in the battles of Brandywine (11 Sept. 1777) and Germantown (4 Oct. 1777), although his exact whereabouts at the time have not been fully established. At the Valley Forge encampment, Barber, as one of four subinspector generals, serving under General Friedrich Wilhelm von Steuben, helped in the new training of the troops. In March 1778 he married Anne "Nancy" Ogden, a cousin of his first wife; they had three children.

Fighting along with the few New Jersey troops who were actually in combat during the battle of Monmouth, Barber was wounded by a musket ball piercing his right ribs. He and the brigade then returned to duty similar to that of the previous year, guarding against British raiding parties crossing the Hudson River into New Jersey.

Barber and the New Jersey Brigade joined the expedition of General John Sullivan against the Iroquois Indians during the summer of 1779. On 26 May 1779 he was appointed deputy adjutant general for the Western (Sullivan's) army. At the battle of Newton, 29 August 1779, in which a group of Iroquois Indians and Tories were defeated, Barber's right ear had "a little skin and flesh" taken off by a musket ball. After the Indian campaign, Barber again assumed military duty in the Elizabethtown, New Jersey, area. He saw action at Connecticut Farms (now Union), New Jersey, on 7 June 1780 and at Springfield on 23 June 1780. During October and November 1780 he served as a deputy adjutant general under General Nathanael Greene at West Point. On 1 January 1781 he was transferred to the First New Jersey Regiment.

The New Jersey Brigade had a record of discontent among the ranks, and Barber and his fellow field officers were long at odds with their commander, General William Maxwell, whom they considered incompetent, although this actually was far from being the case. Jealousy of immediate superiors was a common trait among the officer corps. Maxwell resigned in July 1780, and afterward the New Jersey troops became even more restless, largely owing to deficiencies in clothing and pay. In January 1781 200 New Jersey Continentals mutinied at Pompton, New Jersey. Barber was placed in charge of a detachment to quell the uprising, backed up by troops of General Robert Howe, who ringed the camp of the mutineers. Barber surrounded the rebels at night and ordered them to assemble without arms. He court-martialed three insurgent leaders on the spot and had a firing squad execute two of them, reprieving the third.

In February 1781 Barber and five companies of the New Jersey Brigade were appointed to Lafayette's command, to oppose a British invasion of Virginia. Barber did not accompany Lafayette to Virginia at that time but joined Lafayette's troops in summer 1781. With General Anthony Wayne, he fought at the battle of Green Spring, near Williamsburg, on 6 July, against part of Cornwallis's army. At the siege of Yorktown, Barber was an aide-de-camp to Lafayette. He initially was afforded the honor of leading a charge on a British redoubt on 14 October, but Alexander Hamilton, having appealed to Washington directly, was given this responsibility instead. Barber, nevertheless, was in the thick of the action and while wresting a standard from a British color bearer was cut on the lip by a bayonet. For his bravery, Lafayette presented his sword to Barber and accepted Barber's in return.

Barber was stationed, 6 November 1782, at the New Windsor cantonment of the Continental army. On 7 January 1783 he was promoted to colonel and commandant of the Second New Jersey Regiment. In the afternoon of 11 February 1783 while a mile from camp, riding toward his quarters to pick up his wife for a visit with Martha Washington, he entered an area where soldiers were cutting down trees; a trunk fell on Barber, and he died instantly. Commented Lieutenant Colonel Benjamin Walker in a letter to General Steuben the next day, "thus has an unhappy accident deprived the Army of one of its most excellent Officers—& Society of one of its best Members."

Barber was regarded as a brave and able officer. He would have achieved higher rank were it not that New Jersey fielded a single brigade for the Continental army, with others having more seniority in rank than he. He appears to have had an aristocratic air about him. Wrote a fellow New Jersey officer, Ebenezer Elmer, Barber "is a bold, soldierly smart officer but rather of a monarchical temper and haughty carriage."

• Barber's military correspondence is scattered among many collections, including the Dreer and Gratz collections, Historical Society of Pennsylvania, and the George Washington Papers, Library of Congress. The best biographical article, Mrs. Russell Hastings, "The Barbers of Orange and Albany Counties, N.Y., and Elizabethtown, N.J.," *New York Genealogical and Biographical Record* 62 (1931): 3–22, has information on depositories for Barber's papers at the time of writing but unfortunately does not identify owners of private collections. For a good biographical summary, see "Francis Barber," in James McLachlan, *Princetonians, 1748–1768: A Biographical Dictionary* (1976). Of lesser value are Callahan J. McCarthy, "Lieutenant-Colonel Frances Barber: Elizabethtown Patriot and Hero," Union County Historical Society, *Proceedings* 2 (1923–1934): 127–36, and James C. Connolly, "Francis Barber of the Revolution," *Journal of the American Irish Historical Society* 26 (1927): 228–33. For Barber's early years and military duty in and around Elizabethtown, see Theodore Thayer, *As We Were: The Story of Old Elizabethtown* (1964). Barber's role in the Sullivan campaign is covered in Louise W. Murray, ed., "Order Book of Lieut. Col. Francis Barber, 26 May 1779–6 Sep. 1779," in *Notes from the Craft Collection in Tioga Point Museum on the Sullivan Expedition of 1779* (1929); the order book is also in the New Jersey Historical Society, *Proceedings* 65–67 (1947–1949). The Lafayette connection is found in Stanley J. Idzerda, ed., *Lafayette in the Age of the American Revolution*, vols. 3–4 (1980–1981). See also *The Papers of William Livingston*, ed. Carl E. Prince et al. (5 vols., 1979–1988).

HARRY M. WARD

BARBER, Jesse Max (5 July 1878–23? Sept. 1949), African-American journalist, dentist, and civil rights activist, was born in Blackstock, South Carolina, the son of Jesse Max Barber and Susan Crawford, former slaves. Barber studied in public schools for African-American students and at Friendship Institute in Rock Hill, South Carolina, where he graduated as valedictorian. In 1901 he completed the normal school course for teachers at Benedict College in Columbia, South Carolina, and afterward entered Virginia Union University in Richmond. There Barber was president of the literary society and edited the *University Journal*. In 1903 Barber earned an A.B. and spent the summer after graduation as a teacher and traveling agent for an industrial school in Charleston, South Carolina.

By November 1903, however, Barber had moved to Atlanta to accept an offer from a white publisher, Austin N. Jenkins, to assist in launching a new literary journal, the *Voice of the Negro*, which was addressed to a national audience of African Americans. Initially listed as its managing editor, Barber joined J. W. E. Bowen of Gammon Theological Seminary as coeditor by March 1904. Bowen was a senior figurehead, however, and Barber served as the operative editor. Peter James Bryant, Joseph Simeon Flipper, and Henry Hugh Proctor, all prominent Atlanta pastors, were associate editors. The *Voice of the Negro* was a monthly periodical of high quality, carrying articles by such major African-American figures as John Edward Bruce, W. E. B. Du Bois, T. Thomas Fortune, Archibald H. Grimké, Pauline Hopkins, Kelly Miller, William Pickens, William S. Scarborough, Mary Church Terrell, and Fannie Barrier Williams. Although the journal offered little fiction, it featured the poetry of William Stanley Braithwaite, Benjamin Brawley, James D. Corrothers, and Georgia Douglas Johnson as well as the art of John Henry Adams and William E. Scott.

Barber and the *Voice of the Negro* were engaged in the struggle between Booker T. Washington's advocacy of industrial education for African Americans and his accommodationist approach to racial politics, on the one hand, and W. E. B. Du Bois's insistence on the full exercise of civil rights by African Americans and a classical education for a black elite. The first issue of the *Voice of the Negro* included an article by Booker T. Washington, and Washington's secretary, Emmett J. Scott, was the journal's fourth associate editor until August 1904, leaving after Barber objected to Washington's editorial interference. The *Voice of the Negro*'s anti-Washington tone became more evident early in 1905 with the publication of W. E. B. Du Bois's attack on "hush money" used by Washington to control the black press, accompanied by an editorial attack on the "downright soulless materialism" of the Tuskegeean's policies. Washington struck back with complaints to the periodical's white owners, who had also published his autobiography, *Story of My Life and Work*. In September 1905 the *Voice of the Negro* endorsed the Niagara Movement, which was organized by Du Bois, Barber, and others to protest African Americans' loss of civil rights; four months later, the journal endorsed the Georgia Equal Rights League, which had similar objectives. *Voice of the Negro* was under attack by Washington-allied black journalists, such as Benjamin Davis of the *Atlanta Independent* and T. Thomas Fortune of the *New York Age*. In June 1906 the publication's white owners offered the *Voice of the Negro* for sale just as it reached its maximum circulation of 15,000 in sales and subscriptions.

From 22 to 26 September 1906 white mobs swept across Atlanta, brutally attacking black people in the streets. Once white civilians were under control, the police entered the black community and disarmed its defenders. On 23 September John Temple Graves of the *Atlanta Georgian* telegraphed an account of the riot to the editor of the *New York World*, placing total blame on the African-American community. Barber replied with a letter to the editor of the *World* blaming the racial sensationalism of venal politicians and the yellow journalism of men like Graves. His letter was signed "A Colored Citizen," but white Atlantans discovered the name of its author and gave him a choice: leave town or face severe legal retribution. Barber fled from the city, taking the *Voice of the Negro* with him to Chicago, where he continued its publication as *The Voice* for a year. In October 1907 the journal was sold to T. Thomas Fortune and ceased publication.

After the sale of *The Voice*, Washington's intervention cost Barber positions as editor of a newspaper, the *Chicago Conservator*, and as a teacher in Philadelphia. Barber discussed the possibility of launching a periodical for John E. Milholland's Constitutional League and addressed a session of the National Negro Political League, which was organized by William Monroe Trotter, J. Milton Waldron, and Bishop Alexander Walters in 1908 to challenge Republican hegemony among African-American voters. In 1909 Barber attended the National Negro Conference in New York, which led to the founding of the National Association for the Advancement of Colored People (NAACP). When Du Bois began editing the organization's journal, *The Crisis*, Barber served as a contributing editor for three years.

Choosing a career in which Washington could not pursue him, however, Barber entered the Philadelphia Dental School of Temple University in 1909. He graduated in 1912 and began practicing dentistry in the city. In 1912 Barber married Hattie B. Taylor, a Philadelphia public school teacher. After her death, he married another teacher, Elizabeth B. Miller.

Barber served as vice president and then president of the Philadelphia branch of the NAACP in its first decade. During the 1920s he was also a member of its national board of directors. In 1922 Barber and T. Spotuas Burwell began a series of annual journeys to John Brown's grave in North Elba, New York, and organized the John Brown Memorial Association with the intention of garnering resources for a monument in honor of the famous abolitionist. As president of the association, Barber delivered the dedication address at a service in which its monument was unveiled in 1935. Although Barber continued to practice dentistry, he engaged in little public activism after the dedication. Nine months after the death of his wife, Barber died in Philadelphia.

• There is no known collection of Barber's papers nor is there an autobiography, but important information about him is in *The Booker T. Washington Papers*, ed. Louis R. Harlan et al. (1972–1989); *The Correspondence of W. E. B. Du Bois*, ed. Herbert Aptheker (1973–1978); and unpublished documents in the Washington papers at the Library of Congress. William Pickens, "Jesse Max Barber," *The Voice* 3 (Nov. 1906): 483–88, and *Who's Who of the Colored Race* (1915) are useful contemporary biographical sources. Among secondary sources, see August Meier, *Negro Thought in America 1880–1915: Racial Ideologies in the Age of Booker T. Washington* (1963); Charles Crowe, "Racial Violence and Social Reform: Origins of the Atlanta Race Riot of 1906," *Journal of Negro History* 53 (July 1968): 234–56; Crowe, "Racial Massacre in Atlanta: September 22, 1906," *Journal of Negro History* 54 (Apr. 1969): 150–73; Harlan, "Booker T. Washington and the *Voice of the Negro*, 1904–1907," *Journal of Southern History* 45 (Feb. 1979): 45–62; Abby Arthur Johnson and Ronald M. Johnson, *Propaganda and Aesthetics: The Literary Politics of Afro-American Magazines in the Twentieth Century* (1979); Penelope L. Bullock, *The Afro-American Periodical Press, 1838–1909* (1981); and Alfred A. Moss, Jr., *The American Negro Academy: Voice of the Talented Tenth* (1981). Obituaries are in the *Philadelphia Independent*, 1 Oct. 1949, and the *Philadelphia Tribune*, 24 Sept. and 4 Oct. 1949.

RALPH E. LUKER

BARBER, John Warner (2 Feb. 1798–22 June 1885), wood and copper engraver, was born in East Windsor, Connecticut, the son of Elijah Barber, a farmer, and Mary Warner. At thirteen, he took the responsibility of helping his mother to support the family after his father died and worked the small family farm. At age fifteen, he was apprenticed to the engraver Abner Reid, who made labels for cotton goods, soap stamps, playing cards, handbills, toy books, and other children's goods. Reid was also a bank note engraver and, like most American engravers at the time, did fairly simple work. After serving his apprenticeship to Reid, Barber eventually advanced from journeyman to master status and opened his own engraving establishment in 1823 in New Haven. In 1822 he married Harriet Lines; they had one daughter. Harriet died in 1826. The following year Barber married Ruth Green; they had three daughters and two sons.

Much of Barber's work during the early 1820s was confined to the same type of commercial engraving as Reid, but the expanding New Haven economy furnished him with enough business not only to make a living but also to have ample time to apply his engraving skills to literary endeavors. His entry into the publishing world coincided with an expanding market of middle-class readers. New Haven was a particularly good locale for Barber because it was the home of Yale University. Not only could the faculty and students of Yale be relied upon to buy books, but their families and the staff of the growing university could also provide a ready market.

Barber said that his primary ambition was to "preach the Gospel by means of pictures." Five of his first seven publications had religious themes, and his *New England Primer* incorporated engravings of Christian stories to teach reading. Four of these works were directed toward children. Although Barber was a religious man, he was also aware that children's literature was a rapidly growing market, especially among the educated middle class.

Barber's most productive work, however, was in history. In 1827 he traveled around the country in a horse and wagon, interviewing witnesses to local historical events and collecting data from books, newspapers, gravestones, and other sources that he thought would yield useful information on the nation's past.

He published his findings in *Historical Scenes in the United States* and illustrated his text with his own engravings of scenes of America's early settlement. Although the book was not well received, Barber's use of local data became the methodology of his future historical work. He was more successful in 1831 with *History and Antiquities of New Haven*, which was followed in 1836 by a history of Connecticut. In 1839 he published *Massachusetts Historical Collections*, then in 1840 entered into a partnership with Henry Howe to write a history of New York State, which was followed by *Historical Collections of the State of New Jersey* in 1844. The team of Barber and Howe followed the same formula that was initially successful for Barber: they traveled around gathering material and conducting interviews, primarily of old people. They then compiled their data and divided states into geographic or political sections, described each with statistics, anecdotes, or long quotations from printed sources, and illustrated the material with engravings. The results were collections of history and folklore. Their goal was "to give faithful representations, rather than picturesque scenery, or beautiful specimens of art."

Barber was largely self-educated and never claimed to be engaged in rigorous historical scholarship. His work, however, has been valuable to historians, folklorists, and those engaged in American studies. The sheer volume of engravings that he produced makes him a unique figure in the mid-nineteenth century, and the mass of anecdotes that he collected on local levels has been fruitfully mined by later scholars. Barber died in New Haven, Connecticut.

• For information on Barber, see John T. Cunningham, "Barber and Howe: History's Camp Followers," *New Jersey History* 102 (1984): 64–72; William Dunlap, *History of the Rise and Progress of the Arts of Design in the U.S.* (1918); Sinclair Hamilton, *Early American Book Illustrators and Wood Engravers* (1968); and W. J. Linton, *The History of Wood Engraving in America* (1882).

MICHAEL T. JOHNSON

BARBER, Ohio Columbus (20 Apr. 1841–4 Feb. 1920), was born in Middlebury, Ohio, the son of George Barber, the founder of a match manufacturing company, and Eliza Smith. Ohio Barber began working in his father's company at age sixteen, first within the factory and later as a traveling salesman responsible for the states of Indiana, Michigan, and Pennsylvania. He became a partner in 1860 and two years later took over primary control of the company from his father. In 1864 the business became a public stock company under the name of the Barber Match Company. In October 1866 Barber married Laura L. Brown; they had one child.

The Barber Match Company was among the leading match production companies in the United States, and it was at the technological forefront because of its relatively early conversion from human to machine production during the late 1860s and early 1870s. In 1881 the company merged with its three largest competitors and multiple smaller firms to form the Diamond Match Company. Comprised of thirty-seven factories, the newly formed corporation was responsible for nearly 85 percent of the U.S. market. From 1881 to 1885 Barber served as vice president of the company and as its president from 1888 to 1913. Under his leadership, the firm continued to dominate the U.S. market. It began vertical integration of production by creating strawboard and paperboard plants and by obtaining its own sawing and woodworking mills. It bought wood paper and chlorate of potash directly from producers. Efficiency was further increased by the consolidation of production into large factories. In 1891 Barber founded Barberton, Ohio, outside Akron, where one of the firm's largest factories was established; its production capacity replaced thirty earlier factories. The largest match production facility in the world was built by Diamond in Liverpool, England, in the 1890s. The company also owned plants in Peru, Switzerland, Chile, and Germany.

In 1898 the Diamond Match Company secured the patent rights to a new match making process invented by two French chemists. Previously, white phosphorus had been the combustible agent used in matches, but extensive exposure to this compound was discovered to cause necrosis of the jawbone and teeth. Factory workers, Barber's own employees, were at the greatest risk. The new process replaced white phosphorus with a harmless sesquisulphide of phosphorus. (The company voluntarily surrendered its patent rights in 1911 when the use of white phosphorus was banned for health reasons.) Barber resigned from the presidency in 1909, serving instead as president of the board until his death. Following the death of his first wife, Barber married Mary F. Orr in December 1915; they had no children.

In addition to the Diamond Match Company, Barber was involved in several other business ventures. He created the American Straw Board Company, which produced straw board for use in, among other things, matchboxes; it ran twenty-six mills and produced 400 tons of strawboard per day. He also established the Diamond Rubber Company, which was later sold to B. F. Goodrich. He helped to found the First National Bank of Akron, of which he was president, and constructed the Akron and Barberton Belt Line Railway. Other investments included the Stirling Company, the Western Cereal Company, and the General Fire Extinguisher Company.

One of Barber's last projects was the development of an agricultural teaching institution situated on the 3,500-acre Anna Dean Farm near Akron. The farm featured 1,000 livestock, including the largest herd of Guernsey cows in the world. After his death the farm was bequeathed to Western Reserve University and became the O. C. Barber Industrial and Agricultural School. The bulk of his estate, its value estimated at $4.5 million, was donated to improve the school. He died in Barberton, Ohio.

• For further information, see G. Frederick Wright, *Representative Citizens of Ohio* (1913); Herbert Manchester, *Dia-*

mond Match Company (1935); S. A. Lane, *Fifty Years of Akron and Summit County* (1892); O. E. Olin, *Akron and Environs* (1917); O. C. Barber, "The Match Industry," in C. M. Depew, *One Hundred Years of American Commerce* (1895); and William Franklin Fleming, *America's Match King: Ohio Columbus Barber, 1841 to 1920* (1981), published by the Barberton Historical Society. An article on the creation of the occupational and agricultural school is in the *New York Times*, 26 Feb. 1920. An obituary is in the *New York Times*, 5 Feb. 1920.

ELIZABETH ZOE VICARY

BARBER, Red (17 Feb. 1908–22 Oct. 1992), sports broadcaster, was born Walter Lanier Barber in Columbus, Mississippi, the son of William Lanier Barber, a storytelling locomotive engineer, and Selena Martin, a teacher and grammarian whose family ran the local newspaper. When Red was ten years old, the Barbers moved to Sanford, Florida, after a boll weevil invasion destroyed the Mississippi cotton crop and hence the state's economy. In Sanford, a truck-farming area north of Orlando, Barber played football and baseball, ran track, and graduated in 1926 at the top of his high school class. The namesake and distant relative of the poet Sidney Lanier, he dreamed of becoming an English professor; however, after high school he worked at odd jobs, including truck driving, swamp clearing, and celery picking. "It took me two years of doing day labor, menial tasks, to understand that I really needed education," he would say later. He enrolled at the University of Florida at Gainesville in September 1928, earning money for tuition by participating in ROTC (Reserve Officers' Training Corps) and holding part-time jobs as a janitor and waiter.

Barber's first radio broadcast, soon after the Great Depression began, was the reading of an agriculture professor's scholarly work, "Certain Aspects of Bovine Obstetrics," on campus station WRUF. This performance landed him a $50-a-month full-time job, which he held from 1930 to 1934. Using his given name of Walter Barber, he served as disc jockey, interviewer, newsman, and play-by-play announcer. He quit college in June 1930; married Lylah Murray Scarborough, a student nurse he met at the school infirmary, in 1931; and spent vacations traveling the country, looking for a better job with a bigger station. Four years to the day after starting with WRUF, the Cincinnati Reds asked him to broadcast their games for $25 a week. On opening day 1934 the 26-year-old Barber—who did not even know how to fill out a scorecard—broadcast the first major league baseball game he had ever seen.

The Reds of the mid-1930s were not champions, but their new owner, Powel Crosley, Jr., had access to the public through the two radio stations he owned, and Cincinnati's new general manager, Larry MacPhail, was an expert promoter. This combination allowed Barber to achieve a series of firsts. On 9 June 1934 he broadcast from aboard the first airplane ride taken by a baseball team, when the Reds traveled to Chicago. On 24 May 1935 he was at the microphone in Cincinnati when President Franklin D. Roosevelt flipped on the lights for the major leagues' first night game. The game was also the first-ever sports event on the Mutual Broadcasting network, which then consisted of four "super stations"—Crosley's WLW in Cincinnati, WGN in Chicago, CKLW in Detroit, and WOR in New York—and showcased Barber in its broadcast of the 1935 and 1936 World Series. "Ol' Redhead," as Barber came to be known, prided himself on his unbiased, journalistic approach to the game and for his command of the language, which he laced with folksy southern expressions. He also knew when not to talk; after a big play, he was not afraid to be silent and to open his microphone so that the radio audience could hear the cheering crowds.

Barber followed MacPhail to the Brooklyn Dodgers after the 1938 season. In hiring Barber as the Dodgers' radio announcer, MacPhail was the first to break the long-standing agreement that the three New York teams would not broadcast games for fear of reducing the number of paying fans. Barber reported from "the rhubarb patch," as he called Ebbets Field, from 1939 to 1953. It was there that he became beloved. His southern drawl and honeyed homespun phrases—"Sittin' in the catbird's seat" for being in control of a game, "Oh, doctor!" for a heart-stopping play, "rhubarb" for an argument—made him the "verce" of all Brooklyn. He was immortalized in popular culture and in the memories of millions. Stickball-playing children who had never been south of Coney Island took on a Mississippi drawl while announcing their own exploits. While in Brooklyn Barber continued his string of milestones. He called major league baseball's first televised game, a Saturday doubleheader, in Brooklyn on 26 August 1939. During the broadcast he also ad-libbed the first-ever television commercials. Later that year, he did play-by-play of the first televised football games.

After World War II Edward R. Murrow hired Barber as director of sports for CBS radio, and Barber held the post for nine years. During this time he hosted a nightly show, coordinated national coverage of college football, and served as the only radio reporter to cover the 1948 Winter Olympics in St. Moritz, Switzerland. He continued to work for the Dodgers, by now under the management of Branch Rickey, and was considered instrumental to fan acceptance of Jackie Robinson, the first African American to play in the major leagues. Initially, Barber was against integration. When he first heard of Rickey's plan, Barber—a southerner raised in a segregated world—decided to quit. Upon reflection, however, Barber realized his role was simply to report, and he did so in 1947 as Robinson risked death threats to earn Rookie of the Year honors and to help the Dodgers win the National League pennant. Afterward Barber permanently changed his views regarding African Americans and segregation.

Barber quit the Dodgers after the 1953 season, the result of a dispute with owner Walter O'Malley over contract terms for his broadcast of the World Series. He was then hired by the cross-town Yankees to work with head broadcaster Mel Allen. Powered by legends such as Mickey Mantle, Roger Maris, Don Larsen, and Whitey Ford, the Yankees had won an unprecedented five consecutive World Series titles under Casey Stengel. Barber notched another broadcasting milestone in 1961 when he announced Maris's record-breaking sixty-first home run of the season. But after the team was sold to CBS in 1964, Barber's broadcasting colleagues were fired and replaced by two former players, Phil Rizzuto and Jerry Coleman. Former St. Louis Cardinals catcher Joe Garagiola was hired as a fourth broadcaster, and Barber—who was both respected and resented as a demanding professional who had no tolerance for work he deemed less than perfect—now shared the booth with three former athletes who had no broadcast training. In 1966, with the once-powerful Yankees in the cellar of the ten-team American League, Barber was fired for his candor in reporting a record-low paid attendance of 413 in the game of 23 September.

The move by the Yankees ended Barber's 33-year career as a major league play-by-play broadcaster. He declined an offer to broadcast the St. Louis Cardinals' games with Jack Buck and instead gave speeches and wrote newspaper columns and five of his six books. He continued his work as a lay reader in the Episcopal church and preached in hospitals, in prisons, and on USO tours to Vietnam and to other countries. He enjoyed watching his only child, Sarah Lanier Barber, fulfill his dream by becoming an English professor. Barber also attracted a new generation of fans through weekly commentaries on the National Public Radio (NPR) show "Morning Edition." From 1981 until his death in Tallahassee, Florida, he spoke live in more than 600 four-minute segments on topics ranging from cats to camellias to the classics to Casey Stengel.

Barber's honors included his 1978 induction into the broadcasting section of the National Baseball Hall of Fame in Cooperstown, New York, and a George Polk Award for his work for NPR. And in 1983, fifty-three years after dropping out of college, he reenrolled at the University of Florida for the summer and earned his B.A. in interdisciplinary studies.

In his 62-year career Barber brought high professional standards, erudite observations, and his signature southern style to sports broadcasting. He was a gentlemanly pioneer who did play-by-play for five All-Star Games and thirteen World Series. Standing apart from the "Gee Whiz" school of broadcasters, who openly rooted for their teams as well as announced their games, Barber resisted the temptation of becoming a booster and maintained journalistic objectivity. As Stanley Marshall, former president of Florida State University, eulogized, "If Red Barber had not emerged, he would have had to be invented."

• Barber donated his papers to the University of Florida at Gainesville Libraries. The university archives' Department of Special Collections houses thirty boxes of memorabilia, photos, and papers, including clippings, correspondence, and original book manuscripts. The collection also contains untranscribed video and audio tapes of selected broadcasts. Other items were given to the school's College of Journalism and Communication; to WRUF, the campus station; to the school's Red Barber Newsroom; and to WFSU, the public radio station in Tallahassee, Fla. Details of Barber's career can be gleaned from his six books, *The Rhubarb Patch* (1954); *Rhubarb in the Catbird Seat*, co-written with Robert Creamer (1968); *Walk in the Spirit* (1969); *The Broadcasters* (1970); *Show Me the Way to Go Home* (1971); and *1947—When All Hell Broke Loose in Baseball* (1982). His wife wrote an autobiography, *Lylah* (1985). Other baseball broadcasters and writers discuss Barber, including Ernie Harwell, *Tuned to Baseball* (1985); Roger Kahn, *The Boys of Summer* (1972); Curt Smith, *Voices of the Game* (1987); and Tommy Holmes, *The Dodgers* (1975). Bob Edwards recalled his weekly NPR sessions with Barber in *Fridays with Red: A Radio Friendship* (1993).

MARY JANE ALEXANDER

BARBER, Samuel (9 Mar. 1910–23 Jan. 1981), composer, was born in West Chester, Pennsylvania, the son of Samuel LeRoy Barber, a physician, and Marguerite McLeod, an amateur pianist and sister of the noted opera singer Louise Homer. At age six, he first took lessons on the cello but quickly gave it up for piano study. In 1917 he wrote his first music composition, *Sadness*, for piano. Four years later, he tried to compose an opera, *The Rose Tree*, with a libretto by the family's cook, after he saw his aunt appear with Enrico Caruso in *Aida*. He worked during his adolescence as an organist at the Westminster Presbyterian Church in West Chester. When he was fourteen, he entered the recently established Curtis Institute of Music in Philadelphia, whose founder, Mary Louise Curtis Bok, was a family friend. His father, president of the West Chester school board, pushed through a singular regulation that allowed time off from school on Fridays to students who wished to study music. As far as is known, Barber was the only student to take advantage of the ruling.

After graduating from high school in 1926, Barber formally enrolled at the Curtis Institute, studying piano with Isabelle Vengerova, conducting with Fritz Reiner, voice with Emilio de Gogorza, and composition with Rosario Scalero, a proponent of nineteenth-century lyricism. He earned his bachelor of music degree in 1932. A year afterward, he took voice lessons from John Braun in Vienna. Beginning with his student years at Curtis, Barber made frequent visits to Europe, aided by Pulitzer Traveling Fellowships. Although Barber would make a few public appearances as a baritone soloist and do some teaching at the Curtis Institute, he found such work uncongenial. His main efforts went into music composition. Monetary assistance at first came mainly from his parents and decreased greatly during the Great Depression. But by then his reputation as a composer was growing. Soon, grants, commissions, awards, performance fees, and royalties were providing a comfortable livelihood and financial independence.

Barber was unsympathetic to the dissonant avant-garde music of his day and for the most part wrote fairly assimilable music not far removed from its nine-teenth-century Romantic antecedents. When Barber was asked many years later why he never embraced the modern experimental styles, he replied: "Why should I? There's no reason music should be difficult for an audience to understand." His craftsmanship and sense of form were always impeccable. His enormous musical talent and individual expression found outlets in pronounced lyricism, warm harmony, an approachable style, and grateful, idiomatic writing for instruments and voices—factors that made him a favorite with performers and the general music public. He was preeminent as a composer of art songs, writing them throughout his creative life. The example of his aunt, Louise Homer, his training as a vocalist, and his love of melody predisposed him to the genre. The first songs, "Sometime" and "Why Not?," were completed in 1917; his last songs, "Now I Have Fed and Eaten Up the Rose," "A Green Lowland of Pianos," and "O Boundless, Boundless Evening," appeared in 1974. Although after 1944 he did venture more into dissonance, nontriadic harmony, increased chromaticism, and simultaneous multiple tonalities, he remained basically a conservative artist.

While enrolled at the Curtis Institute he met his lifelong friend Gian Carlo Menotti and composed his first piece to achieve wide success, the *Overture to the School for Scandal* (1933), premiered by Alexander Smallens and the Philadelphia Orchestra. Works from his student years include the effective *Dover Beach* (1931) for voice and string quartet, based on a poem by Matthew Arnold, and the lyrical Cello Sonata (1932). Two other early compositions were well received: *Music for a Scene from Shelley* (1933) and the Symphony no. 1 (1936), in one movement, written in Rome after Barber was awarded the Prix de Rome. The symphony was given its initial performance in Rome, by Bernardino Molinari and the Augusteo Orchestra, in December 1936, and was played in Cleveland a month later, by Artur Rodzinski and the Cleveland Orchestra.

In 1935 Barber met the famous conductor Arturo Toscanini in Italy and showed him his music. Though notorious for avoiding contemporary music in general and American music in particular, Toscanini liked Barber's music and in 1938 conducted the NBC Orchestra in his *First Essay for Orchestra* and *Adagio for Strings*, an event that brought Barber lasting fame. The latter work, arranged from his Quartet for Strings (1936) and soon recorded by Toscanini, has remained an international success. Audiences have appreciated its beautiful singing passages and have been moved by its intimations of deep sadness. Two more *Essays* followed in 1942 and 1978. In recognition of his creative achievements, the National Institute of Arts and Letters elected Barber a member in 1941, as did the American Academy of Arts and Letters in 1958.

Drafted into the U.S. Army in 1943, Barber served as a corporal in the air force, for which service he wrote and dedicated his Symphony no. 2 (1944), which was criticized after its premiere by Serge Koussevitzky and the Boston Symphony because he had introduced a novel electronic instrument that imitated the sound of radio signals. Although in 1947 Barber revised the symphony and moderated its realistic effects, the work never satisfied him. However, he did extract its second movement, now entitled *Night Flight*, for independent performance. Unusual for Barber was the increased dissonance and weakening of traditional tonality that characterized much of the symphony's music and signaled a turn to a bolder style.

In the years following his discharge in 1945, Barber received several important prizes, including two Pulitzers, and substantial commissions. He composed the ballet *Medea (The Cave of the Heart)* for Martha Graham; and the operas *Vanessa*, in four acts, with a libretto by Menotti, and *Anthony and Cleopatra*, in three acts, with a libretto by Franco Zeffirelli, for the Metropolitan Opera. *Vanessa*, intricate in form and remarkable for the large variety of subtle to strong feelings it evoked, was well received by audiences and critics and won the Pulitzer Prize for music in 1958. Tense dramatic scenes were underlined with a free use of dissonance, with ambiguous tonality, and on occasion with singing that was indefinite in pitch—neither speech nor song. It was revised in 1978. *Anthony and Cleopatra*, commissioned to inaugurate the new Metropolitan Opera House at Lincoln Center, fared less well. The libretto proved too ponderous, the production by Zeffirelli too elaborate. Its premiere in 1966 was afflicted by mishaps on the stage and by poor acoustics. Critics and audiences gave it a lukewarm reception. A new version was completed in 1975, in which the music was revised, the acts were shortened, and the staging was simplified. It was staged at the Juilliard School of Music and won a great deal more public support.

Barber's outstanding works are *Knoxville: Summer of 1915* (1948) for voice and orchestra, with text by James Agee; the Piano Sonata (1949); the Concertos for Violin (1941), for Cello (1946), and for Piano (1962); the *Hermit Songs* (1953) on ancient Irish texts, for voice and piano; and the *Prayers of Kierkegaard* (1954) for soprano, chorus, and orchestra. The Cello Concerto won the New York Critics' Circle Award in 1947; the Piano Concerto won Barber his second Pulitzer Prize.

Barber, who never married, died in New York City following a protracted bout with cancer and during a celebration of his seventieth birthday by the international music world. Barber had a genius for composing melodious music that was marked by vitality, was grateful to the ear, and was capable of moving the general music public deeply.

• Most of Barber's music manuscripts and some of his papers are held by the Music Division of the Library of Congress; memorabilia and some scores are in the Curtis Institute of Music; newspaper clippings and other materials related to Barber are in the Chester County (Pennsylvania) Historical Society; some letters are in the Moldenhauer Archives in Spokane, Washington. A study of his life and music up to the early 1950s is contained in Nathan Broder, *Samuel Barber*

(1954). Also useful are Don A. Hennessee, *Samuel Barber, A Bio-Bibliography* (1985), and Barbara Heyman, *Samuel Barber, the Composer and His Music*, (1992). Other sources of information are the *Current Biography Yearbook* for 1945 and 1963, as well as Richard Jackson and Barbara Heyman, "Barber, Samuel" in *The New Grove Dictionary of American Music* (1986). An obituary written by Donal Henahan is in the *New York Times*, 24 Jan. 1981.

NICHOLAS E. TAWA

BARBER, Virgil Horace (9 May 1782–27 Mar. 1847), clergyman and educator, was born in Simsbury, Connecticut, the son of Daniel Barber, an Episcopal minister, and Chloe Owen Chase. He studied for the ministry at Dartmouth College (1801–1803), while teaching at Cheshire Academy, where he had begun his formal education. In 1805 he was ordained a deacon of the Episcopal church in Waterbury, Connecticut; two years later, upon ordination to the priesthood, he became its pastor. That same year he married Jerusha Booth; they had four daughters and a son.

In 1814 Barber resigned his position in Waterbury, and the family moved to Fairfield, New York, where Barber became pastor of the Episcopal community and headmaster of an academy. A little more than two years later, he converted to Roman Catholicism. Forced because of his conversion to abandon his position in the school as well as in the church, he opened a new school in New York City at the invitation of Benedict Fenwick, the vicar general of the Catholic diocese, who had been instrumental in Barber's conversion. There his wife and children also became Roman Catholics. Barber still felt a strong call to priesthood, despite the Latin rite's rule of celibacy for its clergy, and eventually the couple determined to seek a separation that would provide for their children while both parents took up religious vocations. In the spring of 1817 the Barbers received permission from church authorities to enter religious communities in Georgetown, District of Columbia—he the Jesuits and she the Visitandines. In February 1820 they pronounced their vows of poverty, chastity, and obedience in the Georgetown Visitation chapel. All of their children eventually followed them into religious life.

Following his ordination as a Catholic priest in December 1822, Barber was sent to Claremont, New Hampshire, to minister to a new community of converts, mostly from the Union Episcopal Church of the town, where his father had been pastor from 1795 to 1818. Daniel Barber too had converted to Catholicism, and he had brought many of his congregation with him. The father and son built a church and school, which quickly prospered. Within three years the Barbers had gathered a parish of more than 150 converts.

In its initial year the Claremont Catholic seminary, the first school founded by Catholics in northern New England, had more than fifty students, both Catholic and Protestant. By 1828 six Claremont students had begun studies for the priesthood; an equal number had entered convents. Benedict Fenwick, now bishop of Boston, told Barber's religious superior that his

"zeal as a missionary is great . . . I wish I had twenty more like him in my Diocese." Virgil Barber saw his academy and preparatory seminary as a key to the expansion of Roman Catholicism beyond its traditional stronghold in the South, across the United States. "The hope of the Society [of Jesus] in this country," he pleaded in 1824, "must be planted in New England. Here, and not at the south, schools of learning meet with every encouragement & here subjects for the society may be found in abundance."

Despite Barber's pleas, the Jesuits in the United States had neither the human nor material resources to support his seminary. Forced to suspend the operations of the school in 1825 owing to a lack of faculty and funds, Barber ranged widely over New England and Canada, searching for patrons to revive and expand his school, either in Claremont or elsewhere. Finally he secured enough support to reopen an enlarged academy in the spring of 1827, but the spartan conditions (the school had neither fuel nor a cook by the winter) drove out almost all the boarders. In addition, his father, brother, and sister turned against him; they tried to reclaim the land the father had given Barber for the church and school and spread stories accusing him of immoral behavior. Although an apparent majority of the congregation claimed the accusations were groundless, Barber's Jesuit superior, convinced that his family was making it impossible for him to work effectively, ordered him to close the church and school at the beginning of 1828. At Bishop Fenwick's urging, Barber's Jesuit superiors then commissioned him to minister to the Catholic Penobscot Indians in eastern Maine. There he founded a church and school under government auspices and was largely responsible for inducing the Penobscots to abandon their nomadic life for an agrarian one.

A new college begun by the Jesuits in Frederick, Maryland, needed teachers, and in the summer of 1830 Barber was sent there, despite his and Fenwick's protests. For the next twelve years he taught scripture and did pastoral work in various Jesuit schools and parishes in Maryland and Pennsylvania. In 1845 he suffered a severe stroke that incapacitated him until his death in Georgetown.

The Barber family's experience was a dramatic instance of the movement of middle-class Americans to Roman Catholicism in the early national period—a conversion that carried many of them, like the Barbers, into religious leadership within the American Catholic community. Virgil Barber's own educational and pastoral initiatives in New Hampshire prefigured the emergence of New England as a Catholic center.

• The correspondence of Virgil Barber is in the archives of the Maryland Province of the Society of Jesus, housed with the Special Collections at Lauinger Library, Georgetown University. A brief biography is Hudson Mitchell, "Virgil Horace Barber," *Woodstock Letters* 79 (1950): 297–334. On his work in New England see Louis de Goesbriand, ed., *Catholic Memoirs of Vermont and New Hampshire* (1886); Benedict Joseph Fenwick, *Memoirs to Serve for the Future: Ecclesiastical History of the Diocese of Boston* (1978); Vincent A.

Lapomarda, *The Jesuit Heritage in New England* (1977); and Robert H. Lord et al., *History of the Archdiocese of Boston in the Various Stages of Its Development, 1604–1943*, vols. 1 and 2 (1944).

ROBERT EMMETT CURRAN

BARBOUR, Clarence Augustus (21 Apr. 1867–16 Jan. 1937), clergyman and educator, was born in Hartford, Connecticut, the son of Heman Humphrey Barbour, a probate judge, and Myra Barker. Barbour received his A.B. from Brown University in 1888. At Brown he was elected to Phi Beta Kappa, chosen Senior Class Day orator, and received many other honors. He also taught in the evening public school program of Providence and, during his senior year, served as principal of the Richmond Street Evening School, supervising sixteen teachers who taught 400 pupils. In 1891 he completed his B.D. at Rochester Theological Seminary, was ordained to the Baptist ministry, and accepted a call as the pastor of the Lake Avenue Baptist Church in Rochester, New York. His decision to enter this field was perhaps influenced by his father's efforts to improve the welfare of convicts and reform drunkards. The same year he married Florence Isabelle Newell; they had four children.

During his eighteen-year pastorate in Rochester, Barbour played an active role in civic and religious affairs in the city. As president of the Young People's Society of Christian Endeavor in 1897–1898, he promoted and influenced youth ministry in Rochester. Speaking frequently at cultural meetings, church gatherings, and school functions, Barbour developed a reputation as an engaging and inspiring orator. Serving as the vice president of the Rochester Good Government Club, a nonpartisan citizens' organization, from 1894 to 1902, he worked to elect honest, civic-minded candidates and to end the spoils system of ward politics and boss rule. By giving speeches and serving on committees he helped to reform the Rochester public schools. By 1910 the city's schools had organized classes for children with special needs, established night classes, offered many commercial and technical courses, provided extensive training for teachers, actively involved parents, and had become a model for many other public systems.

Barbour's successful ministry in Rochester led the YMCA to offer him employment in 1909 as associate secretary of the International Committee's Religious Work Department. In this capacity he traveled extensively to promote cooperation between the YMCA and local congregations, and he helped to organize the Men and Religion Forward movement of 1911–1912. The movement sought to base American economic and social practices more firmly upon biblical principles and values and to motivate men to play a more active role in the church. It consisted primarily of mass meetings and seminars held for eight days in each of seventy-six major North American cities and in over 1,000 smaller communities between September 1911 and April 1912. Attended by nearly 1.5 million people and sponsored by thousands of Protestant con-

gregations, the movement emphasized evangelism, social service, boys' work, missions, and Bible study. In addition to leading one of its traveling ministry teams, Barbour edited the history of the movement, entitled *Making Religion Efficient* (1912).

Barbour was promoted to executive secretary of the YMCA's Religious Work Department in 1914, but he resigned the following year to become president and professor of homiletics at Rochester Theological Seminary, an institution he had served as a trustee since 1896 and as president of the board during 1913–1915. From 1917 to 1919 the seminary granted him a leave of absence to organize and supervise the ministry of the War Work Council of the YMCA in army camps throughout the United States. During his presidency of the seminary the library was expanded, the endowment was increased by $500,000, and the faculty was strengthened. Barbour played a major role in the negotiations that led to the merger of the Colgate and Rochester Theological Seminaries to become Colgate Rochester Divinity School in 1928, with new buildings and a new campus in Rochester.

Barbour served as the first president of the new institution but resigned the next year to become the tenth president of Brown University, succeeding William H. P. Faunce. During his seven years as president he reorganized the administration; strengthened the faculty by raising salaries and recruiting distinguished scholars; broadened the curriculum by adding new courses in art, music, psychology, and linguistics; expanded graduate programs in the arts and sciences; traveled widely to publicize the work of the university; increased the endowment; and continued the policy of selective admissions. During 1931–1932 Barbour spent nine months as one of the fifteen members of the Laymen's Foreign Missions Inquiry, which studied missions programs in India, Burma, China, and Japan. Its report, entitled *Re-thinking Missions* (1932), recommended greater autonomy for Asian congregations and improvement of theological education. Its positive attitude toward non-Christian religions and stress on humanitarian programs rather than evangelism provoked considerable controversy among American Protestants.

In addition to his effective work as a pastor, civic leader, YMCA secretary, professor, and president, Barbour was in great demand as a speaker, wrote dozens of books and articles, belonged to numerous organizations, and received many honors. During the last twenty-five years of his life he spoke often at colleges, universities, preparatory schools, churches, and clubs across the country. He edited *The Bible in the World of Today* (1911), a volume used in connection with the Men and Religion Forward movement, which defended the supremacy and the significance of the Bible, explained how the Bible was written, and discussed how reading the Scriptures promoted spiritual growth. Barbour also penned *Principles and Methods of Religious Work for Men and Boys* (1912), which described various methods used by the YMCA to promote prayer, religious education, Bible study, religious meetings, personal evangelism, community extension, and social service. In addition, he compiled and edited *Fellowship Hymns* (1910) and prepared the *Service Song Book* (1917), which included Scripture readings and prayers designed to be used by soldiers and sailors during World War I. He served on the executive committee of the Rhode Island YMCA (1929–1935), as a director of the Rhode Island Branch of the National Economy League (1933–1937), and on the national council of the Boy Scouts of America. He was an active Mason (thirty-third degree, grand chaplain of the grand lodge of New York, 1905–1909, and of the grand lodge of Rhode Island, 1935–1937). He served as president of the Northern (now American) Baptist Convention in 1916–1917 and represented the denomination at a congress of the Baptist Union of Great Britain and Ireland in Cardiff, Wales, in 1924. The Clarence Augustus Barbour School in Hartford was named for him. He died in Providence.

A man of great energy and determination, Barbour was deeply committed to "the Book of books," "the mightiest power on earth" (*The Bible in the World of Today*, p. 31). His lifelong goal was that minds might "be informed and quickened, faith strengthened and genuine Christian character established" in those to whom he ministered (*The Bible in the World of Today*, p. vi). His talent as an organizer and administrator enabled him to successfully direct an urban congregation, a major department of an international Christian ministry, a prominent seminary, and a renowned university.

• For Barbour's work as a seminary president, see Orrin Judd, *An Historical Sketch of Colgate-Rochester Divinity School* (1963); the *Rochester Theological Seminary Bulletin*'s *Anniversary Volume* of 1925; "Farewells to President Barbour," *Colgate-Rochester Divinity School Bulletin* 1 (May 1929): 237–39; Conrad H. Moehlman, "In Appreciation of President Barbour," *Colgate-Rochester Divinity School Bulletin* 1 (May 1929): 240–50; and "Appreciations of President Clarence A. Barbour," *Colgate-Rochester Divinity School Bulletin* 9 (May 1937): 237–44. To understand the context and significance of his work with the Men and Religion Forward movement, see Gary Scott Smith, "The Men and Religion Forward Movement of 1911–12; New Perspectives on Evangelical Social Concern and the Relationship between Christianity and Progressivism," *Westminster Theological Journal* 49 (1987): 91–118. Blake McKelvey, *Rochester: The Quest for Equality, 1890–1925* (1956), discusses the role Barbour played in the city's civic affairs during these years. An obituary is in the *New York Times*, 17 Jan. 1937.

GARY SCOTT SMITH

BARBOUR, George Brown (22 Aug. 1890–12 July 1977), geologist and educator, was born in Edinburgh, Scotland, the son of Dr. Alexander Hugh Freeland Barbour (at one time president of the Royal College of Surgeons) and Margaret Nelson Brown. Barbour received his preparatory school education at Merchiston Castle School in Edinburgh. In 1904–1905 he studied organ at Marburg University in Germany and in 1911 received an M.S. with honors in classics at Edinburgh. During a visit to China on his postgraduate trip around the world, Barbour experienced the turmoil surrounding the fall of the Manchu dynasty and was inspired to become a missionary in China. In 1914 he entered St. John's College, Cambridge, to complete a second M.S. that would qualify him in science and prepare him to contribute to the modernization and advancement of Chinese society.

After leaving Cambridge, Barbour served in World War I, first in Flanders with the Friends Ambulance Unit (1914–1916) and later as quartermaster in the ambulance unit of G. M. Trevelyan, the British historian. In 1919, after training for a commission, he returned to the Italian front. He was decorated with the 1914 Medal, popularly referred to as the Mons Star, a British medal issued to all who served in Belgium or France during 1914.

In 1920 Barbour married Dorothy Dickinson, the first woman to graduate in religious education at the Union Theological Seminary (N.Y.) and a faculty member at the Hartford Theological Seminary. That same year the couple went to China under the auspices of the London Missionary Society. There they joined the large group of Europeans and Americans assigned to educational and research organizations. Dickinson continued her career in religious education and was closely associated with her husband's work in China. The couple had three children.

Barbour was professor of geology at Peking National University in 1920–1921, before moving on to a professorship in applied geology at Peiyang University in Tientsin (Tiajin) for one year. From 1923 to 1932 he served as professor of geology at Yenching University in Peking (Beijing), a Christian university supported by British, Canadian, and American missionary efforts. He also held a concurrent appointment in the National Geological Survey of China. In 1927, during his tenure at Yenching, Barbour traveled to the United States to comply with residence requirements for obtaining a Ph.D. at Columbia University. He was doubtless encouraged in making the decision by Amadeus Grabau, who at that time was the leading geological professional in China and a former professor of geology at Columbia. Barbour received his Ph.D. at Columbia under C. P. Berkey in 1929 (he also served as a lecturer in Berkey's classes while working toward his degree) and returned to Yenching with credentials that enhanced his professional status.

In 1932, in the face of continuing warfare and civil turmoil in China, Barbour decided to return to the United States, serving as a visiting lecturer at the University of Cincinnati (1932–1933). From 1934 to 1937 he was an honorary lecturer at the University of London and served as an acting professor at Stanford University in 1935. Also in 1935 his *Physiographic History of the Yangtze Valley* was published, providing a geologic background for Quaternary paleontologic studies. Barbour was given the Gill Memorial Award of the Royal Geographical Society in 1937. Also in 1937, at the urging of Nevin M. Fenneman, he rejoined the faculty at the University of Cincinnati as associate professor of geology, becoming full professor in 1938 and emeritus professor in 1961. Concurrently, between 1938 and 1958 he served as dean of the College of Arts and Sciences at Cincinnati.

Barbour continued to distinguish himself in his academic endeavors and in his affiliations with professional scientific societies, making important additions to the scientific research and literature in his field of study. He served as geologist on the University of California South African Expedition in 1947. Supported by the Viking Fund of the Wenner-Gren Foundation for Anthropological Research, Barbour contributed pioneering studies of the geological setting of primitive early primate human precursors in South Africa. He was president of the Ohio Academy of Sciences in 1948–1949 and a fellow of the Geological Society of America, the Association of American Geographers, the Association of Physical Anthropologists, the Royal Society of Edinburgh, and the Royal Geographical Society.

In 1954 Barbour published *Free*, a memorial biography of his son Freeland (known as "Free"), who had died while a student in medical school. In 1961–1962 Barbour was a visiting professor at Duke University and in 1964–1965 a visiting professor at the University of Louisville.

Barbour was a geomorphologist and stratigrapher whose most significant work relates to unraveling the geologic associations of primitive hominids in China and South Africa. Perhaps his most important contribution was the part he played in investigations of Quaternary vertebrates in China—especially while conducting field research with Pierre Teilhard de Chardin, Davidson Black, C. C. Young (Yang Chung-chien), and Pei Wen-chung at the *Sinanthropus pekinensis* (Peking man) locality at Chou-Kuo-Tien. Barbour developed a strong rapport with Teilhard de Chardin, who had been sent to China by his religious order, the Jesuits, because of his controversial philosophical approach to the relationship between religion and science. Barbour's *In the Field with Teilhard de Chardin* (1965), describes the work that he did with Teilhard in China in the 1920s and 1930s, as well as his loose collaboration with Teilhard on African problems in the 1940s and 1950s. Among Barbour's important works describing his field work in China are *Geomorphology of the Kalgan Area* (1929); "The Loess Problem of China" (*Geology Magazine* 67 [1930]: 458–75); and "Physiographic Stages of Central China" (*Bulletin of the Geologic Society of China* 13, no. 3 [1934]: 455–68). *In China When . . .* (1975) is a collection of letters written by his wife, his own letters, journal abstracts, and notes from his China years. Barbour died in Cincinnati, Ohio.

• A biographical account is S. A. H., "George Brown Barbour," *Geological Society of London, Annual Report for 1978* (1978), p. 28. An obituary is in the *New York Times*, 13 July 1977.

RALPH L. LANGENHEIM, JR.

BARBOUR, James (10 June 1775–7 June 1842), planter and politician, was born in Orange County, Virginia, the son of Thomas Barbour, a wealthy planter, and Mary Pendleton Thomas. Because his family suffered financial reverses during the Revolution, Barbour did not receive a college education. After preparatory study in rhetoric and the classics at a local academy, he apprenticed himself to a Richmond lawyer. In 1793, when he was only eighteen years old, he was admitted to the Virginia bar and began practicing law in Orange and neighboring counties. Two years later he married Lucy Johnson, daughter of a prominent local planter. They established a country seat at "Barboursville," near Montpelier, where they raised five children.

Politically ambitious, Barbour used a successful law practice and good family connections, including close ties to James Madison (1751–1836), to win election to the Virginia House of Delegates in 1798. There he led the attack on the unpopular Alien and Sedition laws and served with John Taylor (1753–1824) of Caroline as one of the principal advocates for the Virginia Resolutions of 1798 drafted by Madison as a legislative protest to accompany Jefferson's Kentucky Resolutions. His eloquent speech assailing the Sedition Act and other Federalist measures was praised by Republican legislative leaders and attracted the favorable attention of Jefferson. His strong defense of Jeffersonian Republican doctrine—strict construction of the Constitution, states' rights, and minimal government—endeared him to Madison, Thomas Jefferson, and other Republican leaders. Befriended by both Madison and Jefferson, he rose rapidly to a position of leadership in the legislature and in the Virginia Republican party. His election in 1809 to the speakership of the House of Delegates was followed three years later by his elevation to the governorship of Virginia. For three terms during the troubled war years he provided strong leadership, for which he was rewarded in 1814 with election to the U.S. Senate.

By 1815 Barbour had become convinced that the restrictive political philosophy articulated in the Virginia and Kentucky Resolutions, which came to be revered as the "Doctrines of '98," was inadequate for governing the nation that emerged from the War of 1812. The United States was no longer the simple agrarian republic that Jefferson had idealized in 1800. Its society and economy had become more complex. The demands of modern capitalism, especially for banking, massed capital, roads and canals, protective tariffs, and other special incentives to encourage manufacturing and commerce, were challenging agrarian primacy. Along with Henry Clay and other postwar nationalists, who were becoming impatient with the Old Republican emphasis on agrarianism, states' rights, and constitutionalism, Barbour recognized the need for a more dynamic and imaginative government, one that would encourage national growth and expansion in the area of commerce and manufacturing as well as agriculture.

In the Senate Barbour helped to expand the role of the national government. He played a major role in gaining Senate approval of the bill chartering the Second Bank of the United States. The foremost Senate advocate of internal improvements, he steered John C. Calhoun's Bonus Bill through the upper house. When that bill was vetoed by President Madison, Barbour tried unsuccessfully to get a constitutional amendment authorizing a national network of roads and canals. He supported a stronger military establishment, a moderate protective tariff, and other nationalist measures that he thought the postwar United States required. The Missouri Controversy momentarily checked his nationalist course. A large slaveholder, he opposed restrictions on slavery in Missouri. As the crisis mounted and disunion threatened, however, he subordinated sectional to national interests and championed compromise, playing an important role in working out the details and securing its acceptance both in the Senate and in Virginia.

A popular orator and able parliamentarian, Barbour enjoyed considerable influence in the Senate. As a friend and supporter of Presidents Madison and James Monroe, he often served as their spokesman in the Senate. He worked closely with the administration in guiding legislation through Congress, and as chairman of the Senate's important Foreign Relations Committee he helped shape foreign policy. In 1819 he was elected president pro tempore.

In 1825 John Quincy Adams appointed Barbour secretary of war. In this capacity he loyally supported the nationalist program of the president, including his ambitious system of internal improvements. Barbour's energetic supervision of the National Road's construction, his support of the Panama Congress (which many southerners thought would abolish slavery), and his vigorous defense of the Creeks and Cherokees against the cupidity of the Georgia government, irrevocably alienated his conservative, states' rights Virginia constituents. In Virginia Old Republicans joined Jacksonians to defeat Adams in his 1828 reelection bid. Barbour resigned his cabinet position in 1828 and accepted an appointment as minister to England. His mission was short-lived, however, for a year later he was recalled by the triumphant Jacksonians.

Throughout his political life Barbour actively pursued agricultural interests. His plantation, Barboursville, was a model of good management and progressive farming. One of the wealthiest planters of the central Piedmont, his neoclassical home designed by Jefferson overlooked a plantation of 5,000 acres of rolling hills and rich bottomland. Barbour strongly espoused scientific farming techniques and developed agricultural innovations to prevent soil erosion and restore the land's fertility. As president of the Albemarle Agricultural Society, and later as organizer and president of the Virginia Board of Agriculture, he urged the state's farmers to adopt improved agricultural practices. His efforts to promote the diffusion of useful knowledge extended beyond agriculture. He promoted efforts to establish a system of public education in Virginia and worked closely with Jefferson to secure funding for the University of Virginia. He sponsored

legislation to abolish dueling and imprisonment for debt and advocated various reforms to improve economic and social conditions of his state and nation.

In retirement Barbour remained politically active. He was chairman of the 1831 National Republican Convention that nominated Clay for president. Throughout the decade he repeatedly backed the Kentuckian in his presidential aspirations. In December 1839 Barbour chaired the Whig convention that nominated William Henry Harrison for president and actively participated in the first successful Whig presidential campaign. During the contest his health began to fail, and he died at Barboursville soon thereafter.

Among southern politicians of his day, Barbour was an anomaly. He was a Jeffersonian Republican who moved from a strict-constructionist, states' rights position in 1798 to a nationalist position after the War of 1812, a position he maintained until his death. He avoided the regional particularism into which such contemporaries as John Randolph (1773–1833), Taylor, Nathaniel Macon, and other doctrinaire Jeffersonian Republicans fell. They viewed Jeffersonian political philosophy as fixed dogma, which they tried to impose on the national government to restrain its power. Barbour viewed the same philosophy as organic doctrine that must evolve and change over time. A pragmatic politician rooted in southern agrarianism, he grafted to the dominant political philosophy of his day those elements of the nationalist creed he deemed necessary for governing a dynamic, changing nation.

• The most important collection of Barbour's papers, consisting of personal letters, farm ledgers and journals, business records, and political correspondence, is at the University of Virginia's Alderman Library. A smaller but very important collection of several hundred political letters, involving correspondence between Barbour and such nationally prominent political leaders as Clay, Madison, Daniel Webster, and others, is housed at the New York Public Library. There are scattered Barbour items at Duke University; Huntington Library, San Marino, Calif.; the Library of Congress; Virginia State Library; and the state historical societies of Alabama, Maine, Massachusetts, and Virginia. The only comprehensive study of Barbour is the biography by Charles D. Lowery, *James Barbour, A Jeffersonian Republican* (1984). Contemporary accounts and sketches of Barbour may be found in John Quincy Adams, *Memoirs*, ed. Charles Francis Adams (12 vols., 1874–1877); Stephen Collins, *Miscellanies* (1842); Henry W. Hilliard, *Politics and Pen Pictures at Home and Abroad* (1892); Jeremiah Morton, *Eulogy upon the Late Governor Barbour* (1842); and [George Watterson], *Letters from Washington, on the Constitution and Laws, with Sketches of Some Prominent Public Characters of the United States. Writings during the Winter of 1817–1818 by a Foreigner* (1818).

CHARLES D. LOWERY

BARBOUR, Philip Pendleton (25 May 1783–25 Feb. 1841), congressman and jurist, was born in Orange County, Virginia, the son of Thomas Barbour, a planter and member of the House of Burgesses, and Mary Thomas. His father was a leader of the revolutionary movement in Virginia during the 1770s; his mother had prominent family ties. These important family connections contributed to Barbour's rise to political prominence in the early 1800s.

Economic reverses caused by the Revolution deprived Barbour of the education that was normally accorded sons of the Virginia gentry. From the local Episcopalian minister he obtained a rudimentary education that enabled him to pursue an independent course of reading and study in preparation for a career in law. In October 1800, shortly after he gained admission to the Virginia bar, he moved to Kentucky, where he set up a practice in Bardstown. The deficiencies of his legal training quickly became apparent. In the summer of 1801 he returned to Virginia, borrowed money to attend the College of William and Mary, and spent one session studying law under the distinguished jurist St. George Tucker. In 1802 he opened a law office at Gordonsville in Orange County. Two years later he married Frances Todd Johnson, the daughter of a successful Orange County planter; they had seven children.

Barbour's practice flourished. In 1812, the year that his brother James Barbour became governor of Virginia, Philip was elected to the Virginia House of Delegates. During his brief tenure in the legislature, he served on both the judiciary and the finance committees and vigorously supported legislation for waging war with England. In 1814 he was elected to Congress, where he served continuously until 1825.

Barbour's decade of service in the House of Representatives coincided with James Barbour's two terms in the Senate. The brothers differed sharply in their political views. James was a staunch nationalist who supported Henry Clay's American System. Philip was a strict constructionist who adamantly opposed the postwar nationalism of the Republican party. He fought the national bank bill, opposed federally funded internal improvements, voted against the protective tariff after 1816, opposed all efforts to restrict the expansion of slavery during the controversy leading up to the Missouri Compromise, and consistently resisted every effort to enlarge the power and authority of the national government. He forsook the Republican majority and joined with John Randolph (1773–1833), John Taylor (1753–1824), Spencer Roane, and other doctrinaire Virginians to defend the narrowly restrictive "Principles of '98." These principles, which were enshrined in the Kentucky Resolutions of 1798 and the Virginia Report of 1800, had become sacred dogma to Old Republicans, of which group Barbour was an articulate member. State sovereignty, strict construction of the Constitution, and limited government were his watchwords. The force and acuity of his constitutional arguments, the orthodoxy of his views, and his effectiveness in debate made Barbour one of the ablest congressional spokesmen for Old Republicans. In 1821, when Clay was not a member of Congress, conservatives succeeded in electing Barbour Speaker of the House, a position that he held until Clay returned to the House and reclaimed the speakership two years later. Barbour did not stand for reelec-

tion in 1824 and retired from Congress at the end of the year.

Barbour returned to Virginia with the expectation of resuming his law practice on a full-time basis, but he was soon appointed judge of the General Court for the Eastern District of Virginia. He continued in this position until 1827, when his Orange County political constituents, who desired a strong voice to oppose the nationalist policies of the John Quincy Adams administration, convinced him to stand again for election to Congress. Elected without serious opposition, he fulfilled his constituents' expectations with his unremitting attack on the Adams government, which his brother James served as secretary of war. He opposed Adams's proposal for a national university, a national astronomical observatory, and an ambitious program of internal improvements funded by the national government. Conservative southern congressmen tried unsuccessfully to reelect him Speaker of the House. As a longtime critic of the nationalist tendencies of the Republican majority and especially of the ultranationalism of Adams, Barbour gravitated naturally to the ranks of the incipient Democratic party. Among the first of Virginia's Old Republicans to do so, he declared his support of Andrew Jackson for president in 1828 and worked hard to gain his election. At the Virginia constitutional convention of 1829–1830, over which he presided as president, Barbour sided with the conservative eastern slaveholders and against the western Virginians who petitioned for apportionment of representation based solely on the white population of the state.

Barbour's staunch support of Jackson in 1828 and afterward gave him claim to consideration for a federal appointment. He was mentioned as a possible cabinet member or a potential justice on the Supreme Court. His first appointment came in 1830, when he was named judge of the Federal District Court for Eastern Virginia. In 1836 Jackson appointed him to the Supreme Court at the same time that he named Roger Taney chief justice. Southern conservatives were overjoyed by Barbour's appointment. Thomas Ritchie of the Richmond *Enquirer* wrote that Barbour, "the pride of the Democracy in Virginia," was "eminently fitted to adorn [the Supreme Court] with his talents and enlighten [it] with his inflexible and uncompromising states' rights principles." Nationalists such as Adams, who viewed Barbour as a "shallow metaphysical hair-splitter," were not so happy. Approved by a Senate vote of 30 to 11, Barbour took his seat on the Court at the beginning of its 1837 term. Generally he followed Taney's lead and supported his efforts to redirect the Court away from John Marshall's nationalist course. He did not sit on the bench long enough to have much impact on the Court's direction or to compile a distinctive judicial record. The most important opinion he wrote was *City of New York v. Miln* (1837), which buttressed the Court's earlier *Charles River Bridge* decision by upholding the right of the state to regulate corporations when necessary for achieving the well-being of the community. His tenure was cut short when he died suddenly of heart failure in Washington, D.C. His colleague Justice Joseph Story described him as "a man of great integrity, of a very solid and an acute understanding, of considerable legal attainments (in which he was daily improving), and altogether a very conscientious, upright, and laborious judge, whom we all respected for his talents and virtues, and his high sense of duty."

• The Philip Pendleton Barbour Papers are at the Virginia Historical Society in Richmond. A few letters and business items are in the James Barbour Papers at the University of Virginia and the New York Public Library. There is no biography of Barbour. A sketch of his life by P. P. Cynn is in the *John P. Branch Historical Papers of Randolph-Macon College* 4 (June 1913): 67–77. Charles D. Lowery, *James Barbour: A Jeffersonian Republican* (1984), contains much information about him but only as the lives of the two brothers overlapped. A good account of Barbour's political and judicial career is Frank Otto Gatell, "Philip Pendleton Barbour," in *The Justices of the United States Supreme Court, 1789–1969: Their Lives and Major Opinions*, vol. 1, ed. Leon Friedman and Fred L. Israel (1969). See also Carl B. Swisher, *History of the Supreme Court of the United States: The Taney Period, 1836–1864* (1974).

CHARLES D. LOWERY

BARBOUR, Thomas (19 Aug. 1884–8 Jan. 1946), naturalist and museum director, was born on Martha's Vineyard, Massachusetts, the son of William Barbour and Julia Adelaide Sprague. The Barbours lived in New York City, but William Barbour, an international businessman dealing primarily in linen thread manufacture, often traveled, sometimes accompanied by his family. Thus, by the time he was eight, Thomas Barbour had visited various natural history museums in Europe. Also in his youth he began to collect reptiles and amphibians, both in the Adirondack Mountains during the summers and one winter at his grandmother's house in Florida. In New York Barbour spent a lot of time at the Bronx Park Zoo as it was being developed in the late 1890s; there he begged zoo officials to let him have deceased reptiles for his collection. After a visit to the Museum of Comparative Zoology at Harvard University when he was fifteen, Barbour decided that he would someday become director of that facility.

Barbour entered Harvard in 1902 and received an A.B. in zoology in 1906. That same year he married Rosamond Pierce, and they promptly traveled to India, Burma, Malaya, China, Netherlands Indies, and New Guinea, spending a long time in the East Indies collecting reptiles and many other animals. Connections through his father's business made it possible for the couple to reach remote areas. The Barbours had six children.

The East Indies collection became the basis of Barbour's Ph.D. dissertation. He received an A.M. in zoology from Harvard in 1908 and a Ph.D. in 1910 with a dissertation titled "A Contribution to the Zoogeography of the East Indian Islands." By then he had published about forty titles, mostly on reptiles and amphibians. In 1910 Barbour became associate curator of

amphibians and reptiles at the Museum of Comparative Zoology, serving under Samuel Garman, who was also responsible for the collection of fishes. In 1925 Barbour was appointed curator of the herpetological department. Following the forced retirement in 1927 of Samuel Henshaw as director, Barbour attained his goal of becoming director of the Museum of Comparative Zoology, as well as being made director of all the Harvard University museums. The next year he was appointed professor of zoology at Harvard, and in 1944 he became Alexander Agassiz Professor of Zoology.

Barbour set out to revitalize the museum that had been in decline from 1910, when its second director Alexander Agassiz had died. "I *like* to run things," he said, according to Romer (1964). A wealthy man, he had offered to help with museum programs earlier, but Henshaw had rebuffed him. As director, Barbour promptly contributed to programs and collecting trips and brought in further donations from wealthy patrons. His first steps were to modernize the work rooms and to improve facilities for the staff. He then saw to improvements in the public exhibits and enlarged the collections. As a biologist, he was especially aware of the value of type specimens from which original taxonomic descriptions are made. He published a list of those in his museum's extensive collections, and he obtained available type specimens from other facilities. Because he disliked cold weather, it became Barbour's custom to spend the late winter months in tropical regions, including Florida, Cuba, many islands of the Caribbean, Panama, Mexico, and Africa. On these trips he collected archaeological items as well as many biological specimens of his own interests for Harvard's Peabody Museum.

Cuba was of special interest to Barbour from his first visit in 1908. On many return trips he collected reptiles, amphibians, birds, bats, and cave animals. During World War I he took a special intelligence assignment in Cuba for the U.S. government. With Charles T. Ramsden he wrote "The Herpetology of Cuba" in 1919 (*Memoirs of the Museum of Comparative Zoology* 17, no. 2:71–213), and he published on the birds in 1923 and 1943. As museum director, he helped develop a botanical garden, Atkins Institute, at Soledad, Cuba, under the auspices of Harvard's Arnold Arboretum; it has since been appropriated by the government of Cuba.

Barbour was active in establishing in 1923 the Barro Colorado Laboratory in the Panama Canal Zone, an island refuge for many local animals in Gatun Lake that had been created when the Panama Canal was built. He provided funds for a small laboratory and housing and served as an official of the reserve until his death. This 3,600-acre property, the Canal Zone Biological Area, has been operated by the Smithsonian Institution since 1946.

Barbour's research projects were most extensive on amphibians and reptiles of tropical regions, with an emphasis on their taxonomy and distribution. Of special interest to him were geckos, anoles, and terrapins.

Using his own large collections from West Indies islands he proposed origins for certain reptiles and amphibians from South America and others from Central America by way of land bridges. This was prior to acceptance of the concept of continental drift, which has clarified some questions of geographic distribution of species.

Barbour's publications came to about 400 titles, of which about half were on reptiles. He described many genera and species, and several of his works were major regional summaries. With Leonhard Stejneger he published *Check List of North American Amphibians and Reptiles* in 1917, which was considered very useful by his colleagues and was updated in four editions. Many of Barbour's later publications were chatty reminiscences of collecting local wildlife and lore and were well received by a general audience.

Barbour was a large man in stature—a "corpulent explorer," he called himself—with great energy, enthusiasm, and a prodigious memory. He encouraged many young scientists from many institutions by providing facilities at his own museum and sometimes his own funds for their collecting. Another example of his generosity was his purchase of a farm in Florida that was a remarkable site for fossil mammals, which he donated to the University of Florida for further studies. British herpetologist Arthur Loveridge noted in an article in *Herpetologica* after Barbour's death that Barbour was largely responsible for developments that led to the manufacture of antivenin for snake bite. Barbour was elected to the National Academy of Sciences in 1933. He served as president of the New England Museum of Natural History from 1924 to 1927 and was elected to several noted scientific societies. He died in Boston, Massachusetts.

• Barbour's papers are divided between Special Collections at the Museum of Comparative Zoology and Harvard University Archives. His Ph.D. dissertation was published in *Memoirs of the Museum of Comparative Zoology* 44 (1912). Some of his popular books were *Naturalist at Large* (1943), *That Vanishing Eden* (1944), *A Naturalist in Cuba* (1945), and *Naturalist's Scrapbook* (1946). Biographical information is in James L. Peters, *Auk* 65 (July 1948): 432–38; Henry B. Bigelow, National Academy of Sciences, *Biographical Memoirs* 27 (1952): 12–45, with bibliography; and Alfred S. Romer, *Systematic Zoology* 13, no. 4 (1964): 227–34. For additional information see obituaries in the *New York Times*, 9 Jan. 1946; *Herpetologica* 3, pt. 2 (1946): 33–39; *American Naturalist* 80 (Mar. 1946): 214–16; *Anatomical Record* 95 (Aug. 1946): 12–15; and *Proceedings Linnean Society of London for 1945–1946* (30 Jan. 1947): 63–65.

ELIZABETH NOBLE SHOR

BARCLAY, Thomas (12 Oct. 1753–21 Apr. 1830), Loyalist and British commissioner and consul general was born in New York City, the son of the Reverend Henry Barclay, rector of Trinity Church, and Mary Rutgers. His father was of Scottish and Dutch ancestry, and his mother was of Dutch descent. Both families descended from ancestors who settled in New York and New Jersey during the seventeenth century. Barclay in 1768 entered King's College (now Columbia)

where his father had been a founding trustee. Following graduation in 1772, he studied law under John Jay and was admitted to the bar in 1775. His marriage to Susanna De Lancey in the same year further strengthened his ties with the New York establishment. Shortly after marriage, he began the practice of law in Ulster (now Orange) County.

Because of his staunch loyalty to the Crown, Barclay was driven from his home by the American revolutionaries in 1776. He joined the British army in that year and was commissioned a captain when the Loyal American Regiment was organized in 1777. For gallantry in the British attacks on Forts Clinton and Montgomery in 1777, Barclay was promoted to the rank of major. In 1779 the New York legislature attainted him for high treason, and his property was confiscated. In 1780 and 1781 he served with the Provincial Corps of Light Infantry, under General Alexander Leslie in Virginia, and under Lord Rawdon in South Carolina, where he was wounded. Captured in 1781 by the French fleet off the Chesapeake while attempting to carry dispatches to Lord Cornwallis, Barclay was paroled and allowed to return to New York.

When the British evacuated New York in 1783, Sir Guy Carleton requested Barclay's assistance in the resettling of Loyalists in Nova Scotia where his regiment was disbanded. Settling first at Wilmot and then at Annapolis Royal, Barclay engaged in farming, land speculation, and the practice of law. With a growing family (there were eventually twelve children), Barclay was often hard pressed financially during these early years, though he drew the half-pay of an inactive army officer until 1799 and was awarded £2,000 by the Loyalist claims commissioners for the loss of his New York property.

Barclay's abilities were recognized in Nova Scotia, and he was elected in 1785 to the General Assembly, over which he presided as Speaker from 1789 to 1799. On the outbreak of the Anglo-French War in 1793, Barclay's military experience was remembered, and he was named lieutenant colonel of the Royal Nova Scotia Regiment. Colonel Barclay, the title by which he was thereafter known, also served for a time as adjutant general of the provincial militia.

In 1796 Barclay was named the British member of the arbitration commission under Article IV of Jay's Treaty to determine the boundary between Maine and New Brunswick by determining which river was the true St. Croix River, its mouth and source. He was chosen for this important assignment because of his loyalty and his knowledge of the American scene, along with his varied military, legal, and political experience. The wisdom of the appointment was demonstrated by his good judgment and strict attention to British interest in the deliberations of the commission between 1796 and 1798.

Barclay's appointment in 1796 was the beginning of twenty-six years of service as a British representative in Anglo-American affairs. Shortly after the conclusion of the St. Croix arbitration, he became in 1799 the British consul general in New York for the eastern states. The appointment meant a return to his native city, where he remained until his death. In addition to the usual consular duties, Barclay was often concerned during the Anglo-French Wars with matters arising from belligerent-neutral rights and obligations. The violation of American territorial waters by British men-of-war, the desertion of British seamen, and the attempts to recover them by impressment from American ships caused Barclay much trouble. The Americans generally respected him for his fairness and conciliatory efforts, but on several occasions mobs in New York threatened violence to him and his consulate. From his vantage point at New York, Barclay was an important source of intelligence for British cruisers operating off New York, though he urged naval officers to refrain from improper conduct in their encounters with Americans. When war came in 1812 Barclay went to England, but he returned in 1813 as agent for the care and exchange of British prisoners of war. Required by the State Department to conduct the agency at Bladensburg, Maryland, he found the strict regulations irksome and resigned in 1814.

On the restoration of peace, Barclay returned to the New York consulate in 1815. He soon relinquished his consular duties, however, to become a member of the Anglo-American commission, under Articles IV and V of the Treaty of Ghent, to determine the ownership of islands in the Bays of Fundy and Passamaquoddy and to fix the boundary from the source of the St. Croix River north and west to the junction of 45 degrees north latitude with the St. Lawrence River. In the matter of the islands Barclay faithfully represented the British interest in the commission, and a satisfactory agreement was reached in 1817. The question of the northeastern boundary was more intractable, as Barclay had foreseen, and the commission in 1822 ended its sessions in disagreement.

Barclay's service with the boundary commission from 1816 to 1822 marked the end of his public life. For nearly fifty years he served the British interest in the United States without losing the respect and good will of the Americans. This service was suitably rewarded by the crown, which granted him an annual pension of £1,200. Amid family and friends, he quietly spent his last years in New York, the city of his birth and the scene of much of his career. Until the end there he remained a loyal British subject, but as a descendant wrote, he was by descent and birth, marriage and residence, "essentially an American, and not an Englishman." At the time of his death the New York press praised him as "an exemplary citizen, conspicuous for piety, charity, honesty, and liberality."

• A full-length biography of Thomas Barclay has yet to be published, though the biographical sections in George Lockhart Rives, ed., *Selections from the Correspondence of Thomas Barclay* (1894), are valuable. Other than the letters printed in Rives, a small collection of Barclay papers is in the New-York Historical Society in New York City. Brief sketches of Barclay appear in Lorenzo Sabine, *The American Loyalists* (1847), and Gregory Palmer, *Biographical Sketches of Loyalists of the American Revolution* (1984). Barclay's service as

consul general and commissioner is documented in the FO 5 and FO 115 series in the British Public Record Office. Documents concerning Barclay's service as a member of the commissions created under Article IV of Jay's Treaty and under Articles IV and V of the Treaty of Ghent may be found in John Bassett Moore, ed., *International Adjudications, Modern Series* (6 vols., 1929–1933). There is a good discussion of Barclay's role in the Jay Treaty commission by Bradford Perkins, *The First Rapprochement: Great Britain and the United States, 1795–1805* (1955), and of his role in the Ghent Treaty commission in A. L. Burt, *The United States, Great Britain and British North America* (1940). Alexander Clarence Flick, *Loyalism in New York during the American Revolution* (1901), is an important background study. Barclay's obituaries in the *New York Evening Post*, 21 and 22 Apr. 1830, review his long career.

MALCOLM LESTER

BARD, John (1 Feb. 1716–30 Mar. 1799), physician, was born in Burlington, New Jersey, the son of Peter Bard, a judge, and a woman whose maiden name was Marmion (first name unknown). When Bard's father died prematurely, his mother was left to support her seven children with very few resources. Nevertheless, John received a grounding in the classics and deportment under a Scottish tutor named Annan.

At the age of fourteen or fifteen, Bard was apprenticed to a Philadelphia surgeon named John Kearsly. A harsh master, Kearsly put his apprentices to work at menial tasks and subjected them to severe punishments and austere living conditions. James Thacher reports that Bard stayed only for the sake of Mrs. Kearsly, who was kind to him, and that he stole time to study his medical books late at night and in the hours before dawn.

The time of his apprenticeship was not unrelievedly bleak, however. During those seven years Bard made the acquaintance of Benjamin Franklin. Bard joined Franklin's social club and wrote to him throughout his life. He also met Mrs. Kearsly's niece, Suzanne Valleau, whom he married sometime between 1730 and 1746. They had four children. One of their sons, Samuel, became a well-known physician in his own right.

Bard began his own practice in Philadelphia but moved to New York in 1746 at the suggestion of Benjamin Franklin. Bard soon became one of the leading physicians in the city, where he was known for his sharp wit and charming manners. He showed an interest in public health and in 1759 put his interest to use. The passengers on board a Dutch ship newly arrived in New York harbor were infected with a "malignant fever." The city asked Bard to inspect the ship and take measures to prevent the spread of the disease. Bard removed the sick from the ship and housed them in a hospital outside the city limits; however, the entire medical staff, with the exception of Bard, soon fell ill themselves. Bard then proposed a quarantine hospital, to be located on Bedloe's Island in the harbor, to prevent future epidemics. The hospital was built, and in 1759 Bard became the health officer and served as the director. His other public health appointments included a post as surgeon to British sailors stationed in New York; he held this post until his retirement in 1778.

Bard contributed to medical education and research with both his writings and public lectures. In 1750 he and his colleague Peter Middleton performed the first public dissection of a human body in the American colonies. David Hosack, professor of medicine at the New York College of Physicians and Surgeons and Samuel Bard's medical partner, wrote in the *American Medical and Philosophical Register* of 1812, "The body of Hermmanus Caroll, executed for murder, was dissected in this city by two of the most eminent physicians of that day, Drs. John Bard and Peter Middleton, and the blood vessels injected for the instruction of the youth then engaged in the study of medicine."

Bard reported one of his most unusual cases in a letter to a British colleague, John Fothergill. Fothergill read the letter, entitled "A Case of Extra-Uterine Foetus," at a 1760 meeting of physicians in London. The letter was published in *Medical Observations and Inquiries* in 1762. The article describes the case of a 28-year-old woman who delivered one healthy infant. After the delivery, she experienced abdominal swelling, pain, and fever. Bard determined that the cause was likely to be a tumor and proposed surgery. When he opened her abdomen, he discovered and removed a macerated full-term fetus. The patient made a complete recovery. Bard's other writings include several articles on yellow fever and one on malignant pleurisy. All of these writings were published in the *American Medical and Philosophical Register*.

In 1778 Bard retired from practice and moved to a farm in Hyde Park, New York. However, the fallout from the revolutionary war depleted his financial resources, and he was forced to return to practice in New York City in 1783. When the Medical Society of the State of New York was established in 1788, Bard was unanimously elected its first president. His last contribution to his profession came in 1795, when he delivered an address to the society on the "sudorific" method of treating yellow fever by inducing the patient to sweat copiously and thus drive the disease from the body. While his proposal was controversial, it was more effective than other methods and was widely adopted. Bard retired for the second time in 1798. He died at his home in Hyde Park.

Bard was one of the leading physicians of his time. In addition to being a pioneering sanitarian, he worked to improve medical education through his presidency of the Medical Society of the State of New York and, most notably, by performing before an audience of medical students the first human dissection in America. He was, by all accounts, a charming, thoughtful, and well-read man, who made real contributions to improving the position of the medical profession in America.

• A biographical sketch of Bard by David Hosack and John Francis appears in *American Medical and Philosophical Register* 1 (1811): 61–67. James Thacher included an entry on Bard in his *American Medical Biography* (1828), which contains a portrait and brief excerpts from several of Bard's letters. Information on John Bard can also be found in biographies of his son Samuel. John M'Vickar's *Life of Samuel Bard* (1822) reproduces a number of John Bard's letters.

REBECCA TANNENBAUM

BARD, Philip (25 Oct. 1898–5 Apr. 1977), physiologist, was born in Hueneme, California, the son of Thomas Robert Bard, a land and oil developer and one term senator, and Mary Beatrice "Molly" Gerberding of San Francisco, the youngest child of Christian Otto Gerberding, who arrived in San Francisco from Bremen, Germany, in 1850.

Sent by his father to the Thacher School in Ojai, California, Philip was unmotivated academically and more interested in horses and baseball. Two years in the Stanford unit of the American Army Ambulance Corps during World War I matured his outlook and sharpened his purpose. Admitted to Princeton on academic conditions that he achieve at least average grades, he graduated in 1923 with highest honors in biology after studying with E. Newton Harvey and Edwin Grant Conklin. Princeton did not admit married students when Bard entered; nevertheless, after his freshman year he was granted special permission, and he and Harriet Hunt of Pasadena married in 1922. The couple would have two children.

Bard was inspired to become a mammalian physiologist by Newton Harvey's undergraduate course in general physiology. Harvey's clear thinking and elegant experimental design especially impressed him. During a year's graduate fellowship with Harvey, Bard applied to Harvard's Division of General Medical Sciences to study for a Ph.D. with Walter Cannon. Walter Alvarez, a longtime family friend of the Bards in California, had worked at Harvard in the Cannon laboratory and had mentioned Cannon even before Philip reached Princeton.

Philip flourished at Harvard, where distinguished senior faculty in Dr. Cannon's department included Alexander Forbes, Alfred Redfield, and Cecil Drinker. The equally impressive junior faculty included Hallowell Davis, William Castle, and Harold Himwich.

"Sham rage" was Cannon's term for the anger, displayed on slight provocation, of cats deprived of cerebral cortex. For Bard's Ph.D. research Cannon suggested that he attempt a localization of the central nervous system structures necessary for the full expression of sham rage. Bard successfully demonstrated that only a surprisingly small column of central nervous system proved necessary for sham rage. Bard's "A Diencephalic Mechanism for the Expression of Rage with Special Reference to the Sympathetic Nervous System" was completed in 1927. Following his success with sham rage, Bard investigated other aspects of brain reduction for the next fourteen years.

In 1928 Bard accepted an assistant professorship in biology at Princeton, where, in addition to taking over Newton Harvey's course in general physiology, he would have a laboratory with facilities for experiments in mammalian physiology. One of his provocative experiments at Princeton involved a fully decorticate cat that displayed rage and fear and, when in estrus, the full pattern of sexual behavior. Later this observation was extended into several other species in which only a hypothalamic island was necessary, along with sufficient estrogen, for occurrence of all the components of sexual behavior. At Princeton Bard was on his own without anyone to share his interests or help plan experiments; Cannon surmised this was true and kept in touch constantly, sending notes or letters regularly and frequently mentioning new articles to read.

But Bard felt intellectually isolated at Princeton, and in 1931 he registered strong opposition to "certain administrative policies at Princeton," the details of which he scrupulously kept secret; he resigned immediately from the Princeton faculty. Alfred Redfield had just moved to a professorship in biology at Harvard, and Cannon offered Bard a position as assistant professor of physiology and tutor in normal medical sciences. In Bard's role as tutor, eight first-year students joined him for elaborate laboratory projects, read the literature pertinent to them, and were spared the more diffuse laboratory exercises of the general course. This was ideal for Bard, and he found pleasure and satisfaction in his academic freedom. With David Rioch, an accomplished neuroanatomist from Johns Hopkins who joined Harvard's anatomy department, Bard studied in detail the behavioral capacity and deficiencies in four cats from whom neocortex and additional forebrain was removed. In a letter to Bard six years later, Cannon spontaneously praised this landmark study, which set new standards for thoroughness and objectivity in laboratory studies of animal behavior.

In his first two years at Harvard (1931–1933), Bard also began to study the basic neural control of two groups of postural reactions, hopping and placing responses. Chandler McC. Brooks, Bard's first graduate student at Princeton, followed him to Harvard and collaborated immediately in this postural reflex research.

In 1933 Bard was startled to receive a letter from President Joseph Ames of Johns Hopkins University, offering him the chair and professorship of their physiology department, which was originally held by William Howell (a Bard hero). The 34-year-old Bard had published just five papers, of which only three were investigative, and he felt that many would consider his appointment unexpected and strange. His colleagues at Harvard, knowing of Cannon's impending retirement, did not want to lose Bard, and Joseph C. Aub of the Department of Medicine led efforts to keep him in Boston. However, Cannon knew Johns Hopkins was the right move for Bard and sensed, accurately, that Bard's career would be remarkable. "I could not help wishing for you a position of great strategic advantage. That you will have at Johns Hopkins," he wrote to Bard.

In 1934 Bard accepted President Ames's offer, and he and his family moved to Baltimore, Maryland. He served as departmental chairman for twenty-nine years and continued for twelve more years as professor emeritus, exerting a profound influence on colleagues, students, and the institution itself. He was persuaded by President Detlev Bronk, Alfred Blalock, and A. M. Harvey to serve as dean, which he did from 1953 to 1957 while continuing his professorship. The added responsibilities often placed cruel demands on his time, but his service as dean was distinguished by the high standards he set for grant submissions. When there was a sudden plethora of National Institutes of Health and other funds, he refused to sign weak or inappropriate grant requests. At the same time he never lost his warm and affectionate interest in individuals at all levels—students, staff, and animal keepers—and his good humor was pervasive.

The physiology department at Johns Hopkins had only four members of the teaching staff when Bard became chairman; they were joined by Chandler Brooks from Harvard as well as Clinton Woolsey, Vernon Mountcastle, and Elwood Henneman, all three of whom were diverted from training in neurosurgery or surgery to join the young department. During World War II, at the request of the National Academy of Sciences, Bard and others studied the neurophysiology of motion sickness. No practical help to affected troops came from their work, but their studies made clear the primacy of vestibular and cerebellar function in motion sickness.

After World War II, cathode ray oscilloscopes and recording of electrical activity from single nerve units revolutionized neurophysiology. The Hopkins department, with Wade Marshall's help, began early to photograph oscilloscope tracings of stimulated nerve action potentials. Cerebral cortical mapping by Bard and Woolsey and thalamic mapping of sensory units by Henneman and Mountcastle followed quickly. Woolsey extended the technique to describe, for the first time, cerebro-cerebellar connections.

Bard's interests extended outside of science. He was a board member of the Rockefeller Institute for Medical Research when it was converted to Rockefeller University, and he was active in many affairs, including the board of trustees of the Thacher School, to which he and his brothers contributed often. With Chandler Brooks he served on the board of the International Foundation in Englewood, New Jersey. Bard contributed to three editions of J. J. R. Macleod's *Physiology in Modern Medicine* (7th ed., 1935; 8th ed., 1938; 9th ed., 1941), and he edited two editions of C. V. Mosby's *Medical Physiology* (10th ed., 1956; 11th ed., 1961).

Dr. Bard received honorary degrees from Princeton, Washington and Lee, and the Catholic University of Chile. He was a member of the National Academy of Sciences and the American Philosophical Society.

Harriet Hunt Bard died in 1964 of a massive coronary occlusion, and in 1965 Philip married Janet Rioch, the sister of his collaborator at Harvard and a good friend of both Harriet and Philip. They were together happily for ten years until Janet died of pancreatic cancer. Both Bard households were known for gracious hospitality and enduring, totally committed friendship. In 1976 Bard married Colleen Gillis, the widow of a close friend. He died in Santa Barbara, California, of metastatic cancer.

• Many of Bard's letters are in private hands; the Bard Archives at Harvard has a copy of his doctoral thesis. His autobiographical article, "The Ontogenesis of One Physiologist," *Annual Review of Physiology* 35 (1973): 1–16, is worth careful reading. Bard's study with David Rioch was published as "A Study of Four Cats Deprived of Neo-Cortex and Additional Portions of the Forebrain," *Bulletin of the Johns Hopkins Hospital* 60 (1937): 73–147. Bard displayed the strength of his brain reduction research in "The Hypothalamus and Central Levels of Autonomic Function," Association for Research in Nervous and Mental Diseases, *Proceedings of the Association* 20 (1939): 551–79; this includes Bard's classic definition of a central nervous system center. Bard presented a paper at a centennial symposium honoring Cannon, published as *The Life and Contributions of Walter Bradford Cannon, 1871–1945: His Influence on the Development of Physiology in the Twentieth Century*, ed. Chandler McC. Brooks et al. (1975); the paper displays Bard's esteem for Cannon as well as Cannon's influence on Bard's career. Obituaries are in the *Baltimore Sun* and the *Oakland (Calif.) Tribune*, both 7 Apr. 1977, and the *Baltimore News-American*, 8 Apr. 1977.

TIMOTHY S. HARRISON

BARD, Samuel (1 Apr. 1742–24 May 1821), physician and teacher, was born in Philadelphia, Pennsylvania, the son of John Bard, a physician, and Suzanne Valleau. Convinced by his good friend Benjamin Franklin that New York City offered a better opportunity for professional advancement, John Bard moved his family there in 1746 and soon became one of its leading physicians.

At the age of fourteen, Samuel entered King's College (now Columbia University) as a pupil of Leonard Cutting, a professor of classics. During his first year at King's College, Bard suffered from an attack of fever and was sent to spend the summer months at "Coldengham," the country estate of his father's friend Cadwallader Colden, the lieutenant governor of New York. At Coldengham, Bard became good friends with the lieutenant governor's daughter, Jane Colden, who was a botanist and a correspondent of Linnaeus; she introduced him to the elements of botany for which he acquired a taste that he held throughout his life.

Bard began his medical career as an apprentice to his father. With the help of his father's friend John Fothergill, he became a pupil at St. Thomas's Hospital, London, in 1761. After completion of his tenure at St. Thomas's Hospital, Bard enrolled in the medical school at Edinburgh University. In addition to medicine, he was tutored at Edinburgh in French, Latin, and drawing. Bard received his medical degree in 1765, writing a dissertation on the effects of opium on the human system. Bard's research for his dissertation included experiments on himself as well as on his roommate. As a student Bard was awarded a prize for

assembling the best herbarium of plants indigenous to Scotland.

Bard went into practice with his father in New York City in 1765 and was introduced to the latter's extensive circle of patients. In 1770 Bard married his cousin Mary Bard, with whom he had three children. In 1772 Bard took over the medical practice when his father retired to his country house in Hyde Park, New York.

Interested in improving the education of American physicians since his student days at Edinburgh and impressed by what fellow student John Morgan had achieved in Philadelphia (founding the first medical school in America at what is now the University of Pennsylvania), Bard and several other physicians founded in 1767 New York's first medical school—the country's second—at King's College. Bard was named professor of theory and practice of medicine, and in 1769 he delivered the medical school's first commencement address. Besides lecturing on theory and practice of medicine at the college, Bard also taught a course on chemistry. The medical school closed in 1776 because of the revolutionary war.

With the outbreak of the war, Bard, a Loyalist at the beginning of the conflict, moved his family from New York City to Shrewsbury, New Jersey. Leaving his medical practice behind, Bard attempted to recoup his lost income by manufacturing salt. Hard-pressed economically when this venture failed, he moved his family back to New York City, which was then under British occupation. Despite his early Loyalist sympathies, the gentlemanly Bard maintained the admiration and respect of many in the city, whatever their political leanings. He gradually regained his lucrative practice. When the newly created federal government resided in New York, he served as President George Washington's personal physician; assisted by his father, Bard removed a carbuncle from Washington's thigh in 1787.

In 1785 Columbia College—as King's College was renamed—reestablished its medical school, and Bard was appointed a trustee and dean and reappointed professor of the theory and practice of medicine. He also filled the vacant chair of natural philosophy and offered clinical lectures at the newly erected city hospital. In 1813 Columbia's medical school was annexed by the College of Physicians and Surgeons. Bard was appointed the new school's first president, a post he held until his death.

Looking forward to retirement and wishing to leave his practice in able hands, in 1795 Bard took into partnership David Hosack, a colleague on Columbia's medical faculty. Three years later he left his practice to Hosack and retired to Hyde Park. When a yellow fever epidemic broke out in New York City in 1798, Bard returned temporarily to assist in combating the epidemic. Bard himself was attacked by the fever but survived. Soon after his retirement to Hyde Park Bard was elected the president of the Dutchess County Medical Society. An intensely devout Episcopalian, he founded in 1811 the Church of St. James at Hyde Park.

During his twenty-three years of retirement, Bard immersed himself in farming and agricultural research. In 1806 he was elected president of the Agricultural Society of Dutchess County. He also became involved in the merino sheep craze that hit the United States during the first decade of the nineteenth century. Bard's concern with the diseases of merino sheep and sheep in general led him to write *A Guide for Young Shepherds* (1811).

Outside of a few articles and addresses, Bard published very little in medicine. Attracted to midwifery early in his career, he became a successful accoucheur. His *A Compendium of the Theory and Practice of Midwifery* (1807) was the first textbook on obstetrics written by an American. The country's standard work in the field for decades, Bard's *Compendium* went through five editions.

Besides his academic affiliations, Bard was also involved with other New York medical, scientific, and cultural organizations. He was one of the founders of the Society for the Promotion of Agriculture, Manufactures, and Useful Arts (1794); a trustee and secretary of the Society Library of New York; and one of the founders (1804) and later an honorary member (1808) of the New-York Historical Society.

Bard was beloved by his patients and highly esteemed by his colleagues as a practitioner. According to one of his memorialists, Henry William Ducachet, it "was unfashionable to be sick without being visited by Dr. Bard." Very solicitous of his patients' well-being, Bard often advised them in their spiritual as well as their medical affairs. Conservative in his medical philosophy, Bard eschewed the medical theories and systems of his time. He firmly believed that experience was the physician's best guide to medical practice. Bard rejected the heroic therapeutics of bleeding and purging practiced by many of his colleagues. To him, allowing nature to run its course was the safest regimen for a physician to advocate. Concerning the education of this country's physicians, Bard favored preliminary schooling in classical literature and an extensive knowledge of ancient medical authors as a requisite for graduation.

Bard died at Hyde Park, just twenty-four hours after his wife's death. When he died Bard was one of the country's prominent figures in obstetrics as the result of his popular textbook and was widely recognized for his work on behalf of American medical education.

• Manuscript collections concerning Bard's life and career are in the Bard College Library at Columbia University, the New-York Historical Society, and the New York Academy of Medicine. Useful biographical studies include Henry W. Ducachet, "A Biographical Memoir of Samuel Bard, M.D., LL.D., Late President of the College of Physicians and Surgeons of the University of New-York; with a Critique upon His Writings," *American Medical Recorder* 4 (1821): 609–33; John M'Vickar, *A Domestic Narrative of the Life of Samuel Bard, M.D., LL.D.* (1822); James P. White, "Samuel Bard," in *Lives of Eminent American Physicians and Surgeons of the Nineteenth Century*, ed. Samuel D. Gross (1861); and J. Brett Langstaff, *Dr. Bard of Hyde Park* (1942). See also William

Frederick Norwood, *Medical Education in the United States before the Civil War* (1944), and David C. Humphrey, "The King's College Medical School and the Professionalization of Medicine in Pre-Revolutionary New York," *Bulletin of the History of Medicine* 49 (1975): 206–34, for Bard's activities on behalf of medical education in New York.

THOMAS A. HORROCKS

BARD, Thomas Robert (8 Dec. 1841–5 Mar. 1915), businessman and politician, was born in Chambersburg, Pennsylvania, the son of Robert McFarland Bard, a lawyer, and Elizabeth Parker Little. His father died when Thomas was nine, putting the family in somewhat straitened circumstances and placing adult responsibilities on the eldest of two sons. Bard began the study of law after graduating from the Chambersburg Academy in 1859, but a worsening family financial situation compelled him to seek more immediately remunerative employment on a railway survey crew.

During the Civil War Bard displayed his devotion to the Union through a number of close calls as a transportation agent for the Cumberland Valley Rail Road in Hagerstown, Maryland. In late 1864 Colonel Thomas A. Scott of the Pennsylvania Railroad hired Bard to manage his holdings in southern California. Arriving in San Francisco in January 1865, Bard soon began work for Scott's California Petroleum Company, of which he shortly became superintendent, in Santa Barbara County. This initial round of oil exploration frustrated by failure, Bard's duties turned to serving as Scott's land agent, earning handsome commissions on sales, rentals, and grazing and crop leases. He built a wharf at Point Hueneme, southeast of Santa Barbara, in 1871, subsequently realizing impressive profits as a grain broker. Bard also located and platted the nearby townsite of Hueneme and continued to invest in small-scale oil ventures, real estate, and sheep raising, among other enterprises.

Bard made a success of his first run for political office in 1867 as a Republican candidate for county supervisor, a position he held until 1872. In 1873 Bard was appointed to a commission established by the state to organize Ventura County and won election in 1874 to a three-year term on the new county's board of supervisors. Meanwhile, Bard played an increasingly central role in state Republican politics in addition to lobbying on behalf of Colonel Scott's Texas and Pacific Railroad, a potentially bothersome competitor to Collis P. Huntington's Southern Pacific.

In 1876 Bard married Mary Beatrice Gerberding, a daughter of *San Francisco Evening Bulletin* founder Christian Otto Gerberding. His bride also happened to be his sister-in-law, as Bard's brother Cephas—who had joined his sibling in California in 1868—had earlier wed Mary Gerberding's older sister. After honeymooning in Europe, the newlyweds occupied the recently completed house near Hueneme that Bard dubbed "Berylwood."

The Southern Pacific's powerful political influence and his Democratic opponent's electoral shenanigans cost Bard a seat in the state senate in 1877. Thereafter, he forsook running for office but remained a quiet, though influential, presence in county and state politics, consistently working to counteract the Southern Pacific political machine. A total abstainer since 1878, Bard also devoted himself to low-key exertions on behalf of temperance. In 1884 he attended the Republican National Convention in Chicago as a James G. Blaine delegate.

The 1880s real estate boom in southern California netted Bard some salutary profits, chiefly through the organization of the Simi Land and Water Company and the Las Posas Land and Water Company, while another key development occurred in 1886 with the incorporation of the Sespe Oil Company, with Bard as president. By 1890 Bard was president of two other Ventura County oil companies, the Mission Transfer Company, of which Sespe purchased control in 1887, and Torrey Canyon Oil Company, incorporated in 1889. Angling to get in on the growing fuel-oil market in both Los Angeles and San Francisco, Bard and his partners built a twenty-mile pipeline from the Mission Transfer refinery in Santa Paula to near Bard's wharf of Hueneme. Finally, in October 1890, Bard consolidated his oil interests with the incorporation of the Union Oil Company of California, of which he was also the first president.

In 1900, after ten years of steady profits but increasingly fractious relations with some fellow directors, Bard sold his shares in Union and embarked on the last phase of his political career. Bard reluctantly allowed his name to be placed in nomination for U.S. senator when the California legislature convened in January 1899. He endured a thirteen-month deadlock before divided anti–Southern Pacific Republicans finally united, paving the way for his election in February 1900. During his truncated term (1900–1905), Bard quietly but effectively exerted himself on behalf of California's Native American peoples, the conservation of public lands, and the Newlands Reclamation Act of 1902. The temporary reassertion of Southern Pacific domination in California precluded any hope of reelection by the 1905 legislature.

Nonetheless, Bard's election in 1900 had served as a harbinger of California's progressive Republican revolt against Southern Pacific control in 1910. The former senator played significant ideological and financial roles in the emergent uprising that coalesced in the creation of the Lincoln-Roosevelt League in 1907. Hiram W. Johnson, echoing Bard's strictures to concentrate exclusively on cleansing the Republican party and the state of Southern Pacific influence, rode league support to victory in the 1910 gubernatorial campaign. While not in agreement with the progressives' designs for instituting direct democracy, Bard solidly supported Governor Johnson and his fellow reformers.

Such was not the case concerning the Progressive party presidential candidate Theodore Roosevelt in 1912. Roosevelt had earned Bard's enmity by failing to support antirailroad Republicans in earlier efforts to stymie the Southern Pacific machine. Unable to vote for the stalwart Republican incumbent William Howard Taft, who was not on the ballot in California, Bard engaged in the previously unthinkable by voting for Democrat Woodrow Wilson.

In his last years Bard had a new Berylwood mansion constructed, indulged his floricultural pretensions within the estate's impressive gardens, and enjoyed the company of his wife and seven children. He died at Berylwood. Over the course of his fifty years in private business and public life, Bard influenced the development of southern California into the dominant section of that state and had a profound impact on turn-of-the-century reform politics, particularly in California.

• Bard's papers are housed in the Henry E. Huntington Library in San Marino, Calif. The definitive biography is W. H. Hutchinson, *Oil, Land, and Politics: The California Career of Thomas Robert Bard* (2 vols., 1965). For a more detailed consideration of Bard's involvement with California progressives, see Hutchinson, "Thomas Robert Bard and the Lincoln-Roosevelt League" (M.A. thesis, Chico State College, 1962). An obituary is in the *Los Angeles Times*, 6 Mar. 1915.

FRANK VAN NUYS

BARDEEN, John (23 May 1908–30 Jan. 1991), physicist, was born in Madison, Wisconsin, the son of Charles Russell Bardeen, an anatomist and dean of the University of Wisconsin Medical School, and Althea Harmer. Bardeen received his early education at an experimental school in Madison, and after skipping the fourth, fifth, and sixth grades he entered the University High School. He then transferred to Central High School, from which he graduated in 1923. In his youth Bardeen was a champion swimmer and billiard player despite a tremor that he had suffered since infancy. In 1924 he entered the University of Wisconsin, where in 1928 he earned a degree in electrical engineering with mathematics and physics as his minor studies. While an undergraduate, he worked in the engineering department of the Western Electric Company (the predecessor of Bell Telephone Laboratories). Bardeen received an M.S. in electrical engineering in 1929 from Wisconsin, having carried out experiments on the applied physics of radiation from antennas. In 1930 he went with one of his advisors, Leo J. Peters, to work for the Gulf Research and Development Corporation in Pittsburgh, Pennsylvania. There they worked to develop new techniques for analyzing maps of magnetic and gravitational field strength to facilitate locating oil deposits. Bardeen enrolled in 1933 at Princeton University, where he studied mathematics under the quantum physicist Eugene F. Wigner, which led to his study of the quantum theory as applied to solids. His thesis for his Ph.D. in 1936 was on the attractive force that holds electrons within metals. A year before finishing his dissertation, Bardeen obtained a fellowship for postdoctoral work at Harvard University, where he worked until 1938 with John Van Vleck and Percy W. Bridgeman on electrical conduction and cohesion in metals.

Bardeen married Jane Maxwell in 1938, and they had two sons and a daughter. During World War II, between 1941 and 1945, Bardeen worked as a civilian for the Naval Ordinance Laboratory in Washington, D.C., studying the magnetic fields of ships and submarines as they moved through salt water to better understand how to design mines, depth charges, and mine sweepers.

In 1945 Bardeen joined Walter H. Brattain and William Shockley of the Bell Telephone Laboratories to search for semiconductor devices that could rectify and amplify electric signals. Semiconductors, such as silicone and germanium, possess electrical resistance between that of insulators and metal conductors. The goal of Shockley's group was to develop what is now called a field-effect transistor. They were attempting to apply an electric field to a semiconductor that would influence the flow of electrons within the material. In this way Shockley hoped to use the electric field to control the flow of electrons in a region of the semiconductor and thereby modulate the current flowing through the device. Such a device (transistor) would have the capability of amplifying an electric signal because a small signal applied (applied voltage) would produce a large flow through the semiconductor.

All of the initial attempts using an applied external electric field failed. Bardeen, after studying the problem, suggested that the externally applied electric field was prevented from exerting its effect as it was blocked by electrons trapped at the surface of the semiconductor. After numerous experiments on the effects of heat, cold, light, and thin films on semiconductors in electric fields, Bardeen, Brattain, and Shockley obtained an adequate understanding of the semiconductor's surface properties, allowing them to construct the first working transistor in 1947.

The point contact transistor was their first design, and it consisted of two small wires called "cat's whiskers" attached to one end of a germanium block. These two contacts were named the emitter and collector. A third contact made at the bottom of the block was called the base. Instead of using an externally applied electric field, this transistor used a current flowing through the emitter and the base to control a larger current flowing from the emitter to the collector. Later the design was changed to the junction transistor, the point contacts were eliminated, and the emitter and the collector were constructed from semiconductor materials "doped" with specific impurities that increased the density of "electrons and holes." It was not until silicone replaced germanium, however, that field effect transistors became practical.

Transistors functioned in a manner similar to vacuum tubes, which used a small electric signal in one circuit to control a relatively large current in a second circuit. Because transistors are rugged, small, and have a low energy requirement, they soon replaced vacuum tubes. In time with improved technology, it became possible in the early 1970s to place thousands of transistors in a single silicone chip. Such chips permitted the construction of the microcomputer, hand-held calculator, sophisticated control instruments, and many other medical and home electronic devices. In 1956 Bardeen, Brattain, and Shockley shared the Nobel Prize in physics "for their research on semiconductors and their discovery of the transistor effect."

After this work on the transistor Bardeen began work on superconductivity, which had been discovered by the Dutch physicist Heike Kamerlingh Onnes in 1911 when he observed that some metals lose all resistance to the flow of electricity when their temperature is lowered to a few degrees above absolute zero.

Electric currents consist of electrons moving in particular directions. Loosely held electrons are forced to move when an electric field is created by an applied voltage. Many electrons being loosely held by a metal atom are forced to vibrate because of their heat content and random scattered motion. These movements produce resistance to the flow of electrons. Reduction of thermal motion by cooling decreases the resistance to electric flow. When all electron motion is stopped at absolute zero, resistance should be zero. The surprising finding of Onnes was that resistance disappeared at temperatures above absolute zero when some thermal vibration remained. For years there was no explanation for this phenomenon. In 1933 the German physicist Walther Meissner discovered that superconductors are perfectly diamagnetic, which prevented the penetration of a magnetic field into their interior. In contrast, a paramagnetic material attracts a magnetic field, so when it is brought into the region of a diamagnetic material they repel each other. A magnetic material placed over a superconductor will hover on a cushion of magnetic repulsion. If the applied magnet field is sufficiently strong, the superconductor will lose its superconductivity and behave like an ordinary magnet.

In 1935 Fritz London suggested that diamagnetism was a fundamental property of superconductors and that it might be a quantum effect. In 1950 several American investigators discovered that isotopes of some metals would become superconductors at different temperatures and that the critical temperature producing the effect was inversely proportional to the atomic mass. From previous studies, Bardeen knew that the only effect of different atomic masses on the properties of a solid body were variations in the propagation of vibrations within the body. This led him to suggest that superconductivity of a metal involved an interaction between conduction electrons (those relatively free to move) and the vibration of the atoms in the metal body. This link (of the conductive electrons to atomic vibration) coupled the electrons to each other.

Subsequently, Leon N. Cooper in 1955 and J. Robert Schrieffer in 1957 joined Bardeen in this work. Cooper was able to show that an electron moving through the regular structure of a metal attracts nearby positively charged atoms, thereby slightly deforming the crystal lattice and momentarily increasing the positive charge. This increased positive charge attracts a second electron, and the two electrons become paired.

Being indirectly bound together, they distort the crystal lattice. In this way many electrons throughout the metal become joined into pairs (called Cooper pairs). Schrieffer applied his mathematical knowledge and solved the problem. With this information Bardeen, Schrieffer, and Cooper were able to show in 1958 that the Cooper pairs interact to compel many of the free electrons in a superconductor to flow in unison. The superconducting electrons, as London had guessed, form a single quantum state that encompasses the entire metal body. The temperature at which superconductivity appears represents the amount of reduction in thermal vibration necessary to allow the influence of the Cooper pairs to predominate in coordinating the movement of electrons in the metal. Since the deviation of even one electron from the common stream would destroy the integrity of the quantum state, such disturbance is unlikely, and the superconducting electron drifts collectively without loss of energy. They used their theory to predict successfully superfluidity in helium 3 at temperatures near absolute zero. This overthrew the theory that superfluidity was impossible in isotopes with an odd number of nuclear particles.

Bardeen, Cooper, and Schrieffer received the 1972 Nobel Prize in physics "for their jointly developed theory of superconductivity, usually called the BCS theory." The superconductivity theory has had far-reaching effects on the theory of electronic technology.

In 1959 Bardeen joined the Center for Advanced Study at the University of Illinois. In 1975 he became professor emeritus. In his leisure time Bardeen enjoyed travel and golf. Throughout his career, Bardeen, in addition to being the only scientist to receive two Nobel Prizes in the same field, was awarded many other distinguished awards. Bardeen died in Boston, Massachusetts.

• A collection of Bardeen's personal papers is at the University of Illinois, Champaign-Urbana. Biographical sketches of Bardeen include William K. Stuckey, "John Bardeen: A Profile," *Saturday Review of Science* (Mar. 1973): 30–34, and *Sketches in National Geographic Society, Those Inventive Americans* (1971); *Biographical Encyclopedia of Scientists* (1981); and *Notable 20th Century Scientists* (1995). For information on Bardeen's Nobel Prizes, see *Who's Who of Nobel Prize Winners*, 2d ed. (1991); *Science* 178 (3 Nov. 1972): 489–91; and *Nobel Prize Winners* (1987). An obituary is in the *New York Times*, 31 Jan. 1991.

DAVID Y. COOPER

BARDEN, Graham Arthur (25 Sept. 1896–29 Jan. 1967), U.S. congressman, was born in Sampson County, North Carolina, near Turkey township, the son of James Jefferson Barden and Mary James. After Graham's early years on the family farm, the Bardens moved to Burgaw so the children could attend high school. Following graduation from Burgaw High School, Barden enrolled in the University of North Carolina at Chapel Hill. World War I intervened, and he enlisted in the navy about a month before the armistice. Discharged after five months of service, he returned to the university, where he earned his LL.B. in

1920. After passing the state bar examination, he taught and coached at New Bern High School to earn money for a law library. The next year he established his first law practice with a friend. He married Agnes Foy in 1922. They had two children. In 1931 he left his law firm to practice with his wife's brother-in-law.

In 1932 Barden was elected as a Democrat to the North Carolina House of Representatives. There he built a statewide reputation both for supporting adequate funding for all levels of education and for being economy-minded. He won election to the U.S. House of Representatives in 1934.

When Barden arrived in Washington, D.C., in 1935 as the freshman representative of coastal North Carolina's Third District, he was assigned to the Committee on Education, which allowed him to pursue his primary interest, and the Committee on Rivers and Harbors, which enabled him to secure tangible benefits for his coastal constituents. Because of his loyalty to the Franklin D. Roosevelt administration, Barden was chosen by the House leadership in the Seventy-fifth Congress (1937–1938) as an "official objector" to monitor all bills on the private and consent calendars in order to weed out those lacking merit. He was rewarded for his diligence with an assignment to the Labor Committee. As a champion of Roosevelt's efforts to cut domestic spending and increase defense outlays, he rejected the "idea that the Federal government is some sort of spiritual Santa Claus having a treasury without bottom and always full of money" (Puryear, p. 27). He maintained this philosophy throughout his career.

During World War II, as the wounded came home and as work-related injuries increased, Barden began to advocate vocational rehabilitation. After disputes among veterans groups in the Seventy-seventh Congress (1941–1942) derailed his bill to fund rehabilitation, he revised it and saw it enacted in the next Congress as the Barden–La Follette Vocational Rehabilitation Act.

By 1943 Barden had enough seniority to chair either the Library Committee or the Education Committee. He chose the latter, because it positioned him to push his interests in both education and vocational rehabilitation. It was combined with the Labor Committee in 1947 to form the Committee on Education and Labor. In May 1950 John Lesinski, Sr. (D.-Mich.) died, and Barden became the third chair of the committee, a post he first held until January 1953, when the Republicans took control of Congress, and again from 1955 until he retired in 1961.

Barden left his imprint on the nation and on Congress as Education and Labor chair. By both deed and reputation he was staunchly conservative. "Suspicious of bigness in any form," he distrusted bureaucracy, big government, and "giveaway" programs (Puryear, p. 227), consistently opposing legislation that embodied those characteristics. Holding traditional southern attitudes toward labor, he regarded unions as "inherently evil organizations interfering with free enterprise" (Reeves, p. 57) and supported legislation allowing state "right to work" laws, which were antithetical to unions. His views on states' rights coincided: "The federal government has a job to do, but it must not interfere in the business of state governments" (Reeves, p. 57). The U.S. Supreme Court decision *Brown v. Board of Education of Topeka* (1954) reinforced his convictions that with federal aid came federal interference, thus leading to charges of bigotry from his detractors. Barden joined nearly one hundred southern congressmen in signing the "Southern Manifesto," a pledge to use all lawful means to reverse the *Brown* decision. In 1956 he wrote to a constituent, "The action of the Supreme Court has almost frightened me away from any type of Federal assistance to public schools" (Puryear, p. 112). Nevertheless, when such aid was forthcoming, he fought efforts to deny it to schools in states that allowed racial segregation in education, especially since North Carolina was among them. Columnist Drew Pearson cited Barden as "the biggest headache for Democrats in Congress" because he was "sitting directly in the path of new school houses" (Puryear, p. 109). To counter the accusations of racial prejudice, Barden emphasized his record of opposition during his law practice to the Great Tiger Klan, one of eastern North Carolina's "imitators and emulators of the Ku Klux Klan" (Puryear, p. 5).

His views on separation of church and state led to allegations that he was anti-Catholic. His resolute stance against federal aid to private and parochial schools led to a well-publicized dispute in which Francis Cardinal Spellman, archbishop of New York, labeled him "a new apostle of bigotry" (Puryear, p. 83). As chair of Education and Labor, Barden had the ability to block legislation and did so with gusto. Many people thought he used his position to impede progress on important social problems by thwarting all federal aid to education and working to restrain the activities and power of labor unions (Reeves, p. 58).

Presiding in an era when committee chairs had few limits on their power, Barden employed a variety of tactics to obstruct. They included calling few committee meetings or hearings, controlling the committee's agenda, refusing to recognize his opponents to speak, stacking hearing witnesses in his favor, declaring the absence of a quorum and adjourning committee meetings to preclude legislative consideration, conspiring with other committee chairs to block legislation if it emerged from committee despite his opposition, controlling staff, failing to appoint certain members to subcommittees, and killing legislation by declining to refer bills to subcommittees or assigning them to hostile subcommittees. Barden's actions precluded most legislation of any national significance from emerging from the committee. With few exceptions, most reported bills either amended previous laws or were narrow in scope and only benefited small groups, such as longshoremen, agricultural workers, or people with particular disabilities (Reeves, p. 49).

In the late 1950s, to counteract Barden's obstructionism, the House leadership stacked the committee with liberal Democrats. They revolted against Barden in 1957 and again in 1959, forcing the adoption of committee rules to make the process more democratic and to weaken the chairmanship. Four significant pieces of legislation soon emerged, including two landmark education bills and two labor bills concerning labor-management reporting and disclosure and welfare and pension benefit plans.

As chair, Barden was instrumental in stopping or delaying legislation that embodied principles contrary to his philosophy of minimal federal involvement. He used the resources of the chairmanship masterfully to bottle up federal aid to education bills and legislation favorable to organized labor. Barden died in New Bern, North Carolina.

• Barden's papers are in the Duke University Library, Durham, N.C. Elmer Puryear, *Graham A. Barden: Conservative Carolina Congressman* (1979), is the most comprehensive source of biographical information. Barden's activities as chair are detailed in Andrée E. Reeves, *Congressional Committee Chairmen: Three Who Made an Evolution* (1993). An obituary is in the *New York Times*, 30 Jan. 1967.

ANDRÉE E. REEVES

BARDIN, Shlomo (Dec. 1898–16 May 1976), Jewish educator, was born Shlomo Bardinstein in Zhitomir, Ukraine, the son of Haim Israel Bardinstein and Menia Weissburd, members of Zhitomir's Jewish bourgeoisie. After completing his secondary education at the Zhitomir School of Commerce in 1918, he left Russia for Palestine, which was probably when he shortened his name to "Bardin." From 1920 he worked as an administrative assistant at the Hebrew Secondary School in Haifa before leaving in 1923 for the University of Berlin, where he studied history and economics. Two years later he entered University College in London for a year's study of English. Bardin returned to Haifa in 1926 and spent two years teaching at the Hebrew Boarding School. He went to New York City in 1928 and was accepted as a graduate student at Columbia University's Teachers College. At Columbia he studied comparative education with progressive educators who urged him to research the Danish Folk High School to examine its creative use of music to reach disaffected youth. He received his M.A. in 1930. In 1931 Bardin married a sculptor, Ruth Jonas, daughter of a wealthy Brooklyn lawyer; the couple would have two children.

Bardin received his doctorate in philosophy in 1932, the same year he published his dissertation, *Pioneer Youth in Palestine*. The book examined Zionist youth movements in Palestine and their role in creating a new socialist society, building cooperative settlements, reclaiming the soil, and developing a religion of labor. Returning to Palestine, in 1933 Bardin established Haifa Technical Institute modeled on the advanced scientific training offered youth at Brooklyn Technical High School. Five years later he started Haifa Nautical School as a branch of the Technical Institute, but he left Palestine for the United States in 1939 to earn money and stayed after World War II began. In 1943 Bardin became an American citizen.

Bardin's credentials as an educator and Palestinian Jew made him an ideal director of the American Zionist Youth Commission, established in 1939. He quickly adopted U.S. Supreme Court justice Louis Brandeis's Zionist philosophy blending Americanism, especially its democratic frontier spirit, and Zionism, understood as a movement to build a Jewish homeland, to shape a summer leadership training program for young adults aged eighteen to twenty-five. Bardin told an interviewer he wanted "to give the young a feeling of belonging; . . . to make him feel at ease as a Jew in an American environment." Established in Amherst, New Hampshire, in 1941, the summer institute synthesized aspects of Bardin's youth and education into a viable and innovative leadership program: his early memories of Zhitomir; his adult years in the land of Israel and its pioneering values associated with the kibbutz cooperative; his study of experimental musical methods of Danish folk high schools; and his enthusiasm for American "bull" sessions of discussion.

Bardin turned the camp into a surrogate Jewish homeland by making campers responsible for their physical needs, as in a kibbutz. In addition to daily lectures, classes, study and song, there was gardening and physical labor. Camp ran on a rigorous schedule with rest, recreation, and workshops each afternoon and structured evening programs. Bardin made the sabbath the highlight of the week. He composed new sabbath songs, let lay leaders guide participatory worship services and discuss the Torah instead of rabbi's sermons, designed dramatic rituals to bid farewell to the sabbath, and included women as equal members of the congregation. He recruited talented individuals to lead and teach, including philosopher Horace Kallen, musician Max Helfman, and dancer Katya Delakova. Ruth Bardin ran the camp's art program.

In 1943 Bardin transferred his entire program to the Poconos, having named it the Brandeis Camp Institute in honor of the justice after his death. Bardin subsequently opened a southern camp in North Carolina and a western camp in the Simi Valley, not far from Los Angeles. Eager to build an institution in his own image, Bardin soon divorced the camps from their Zionist sponsorship and established a separate camp organization. He also reinterpreted Zionism not as settling in the Jewish homeland in Israel but as returning to "the spiritual center of one's mind." Bardin's experiential education reached Jews across the denominational boundaries of Reform, Conservatism, and Orthodoxy, and the one-month camp experience often transformed young people. "Give me twenty-eight days, and I'll give you an experience that will last a lifetime," Bardin would tell campers, many of whom testified that camp made them become active Jews.

After Bardin moved to Los Angeles in 1951, he focused his energies almost exclusively on the west coast camp, which could stay open throughout the year. In 1952 he initiated programs for couples, a summer camp for young children, stag and sorority weekend institutes, and family holiday activities. Bardin attracted members of the Hollywood movie industry, including writers and producers, who lent him their services, helped him design pageants, and created often eclectic Jewish rituals to dramatize his values. With the closing of the two eastern camps by 1953 and his divorce, Bardin's life, persona, and vocation became intertwined completely with the Brandeis Camp Institute. He even made his home at camp.

Bardin wrote relatively little after publishing his second book, *Jews and the Sea*, in 1943 on the occasion of the graduation of the first class of the Haifa Nautical School. The short essays treated the historic role of Jews as navigators, their contemporary activities as fishermen, and their participation as sailors in the British and American navies. Bardin concentrated his efforts on making the Brandeis Camp Institute a living laboratory for his ideas on experiential learning. In the 1960s a steady stream of professionals came to analyze his unique program to learn from his success in intensifying the Jewish identity of young American Jews. In succeeding years, as more American Jews became estranged from Judaism, Jewish educators increasingly accorded respect to Bardin's emphasis on the sabbath and participatory learning as well as his use of music, dance, and drama to foster Jewish identification. Boston Hebrew College gave him their Philip W. Lown distinguished service award in 1974. Although he did not create a movement, Bardin was an important pioneer of alternative Jewish education in the United States. After his death in Los Angeles, the camp was renamed the Brandeis-Bardin Institute. As Gerson D. Cohen, chancellor of the Jewish Theological Seminary of America, observed in the *New York Times* (12 Aug. 1973), "I see here truly a kind of native institution, for Brandeis [Camp Institute] is clearly an American response to the American environment in Jewish terms."

• Shlomo Bardin's papers, including interviews with him, tapes of lectures and speeches, newspaper clippings, and records of the Brandeis Camp Institute, are in the House of the Book, Brandeis-Bardin Institute. An early article by Bardin, "The Brandeis Camp Institute," in *Jewish Education* 17 (June 1946): 26–27, describes his goals and program. Deborah Dash Moore devotes twelve pages to Bardin and the institute in *To the Golden Cities* (1994). Bruce Powell, "The Brandeis-Bardin Institute" (Ph.D. diss., Univ. of Southern California, 1979), discusses Bardin as an educator. In the summer 1976 issues after Bardin's death, Trude Weiss-Rosmarin in the *Jewish Spectator* and Leonard Fein in *Moment* wrote about him and the Brandeis Camp Institute.

DEBORAH DASH MOORE

BARKER, Benjamin Fordyce (2 May 1818–30 May 1891), physician, was born in Wilton, Maine, the son of John Barker, a physician, and Phoebe Abbott. Barker received a B.A. from Bowdoin College in 1837. In 1838 he began a two-year apprenticeship under physician Henry I. Bowditch in Boston and worked at the U.S. Marine Hospital in the neighboring town of Chelsea. Barker received an M.D. from Bowdoin Medical College in 1841. Suffering from a pulmonary disease, Barker took Bowditch's advice to settle in a climate more conducive to his health than that of his native state. Barker settled in Norwich, Connecticut, where he initiated his medical practice in 1841. During the William Henry Harrison presidential campaign, Barker, who supported the Whig party, "stumped" for Harrison throughout Connecticut. A biographer of Barker, James Chadwick, claimed that Barker had made "a speech in a different town every night for three months" (Chadwick, p. 553). In his leisure time, Barker pursued musical interests, singing tenor in the church choir and composing several melodies. In September 1843 he married Elizabeth Lee Dwight; they had one son.

Barker and his wife set sail for Le Havre, France, on 1 October 1844, and during the following winter term, he attended many medical lectures and clinics in Paris. While in Paris, Barker took a special interest in obstetrics and gynecology and became an intimate friend of master clinician Armand Trousseau. Barker maintained contact with many Parisian practitioners throughout his life.

Returning to the United States in 1845, due to a family illness, Barker resumed his practice in Connecicut. He accepted a professorship at Bowdoin College in 1846 but resigned after one year when he deemed this position to hinder his private practice. He then returned to Connecticut and served as president of the Connecticut Medical Society in 1848. His presidential address, "Some Forms of Disease of the Cervix Uteri," attracted wide acclaim and prompted an invitation for Barker to join the faculty of the College of Physicians and Surgeons of New York. He accepted this offer but delayed his move to New York City until 1850. Upon his arrival, he joined physicians Abraham L. Cox, R. Ogden Doremus, and Horace Green in incorporating the New York Medical College, and was appointed to the chair of obstetrics. According to Chadwick, "It was while lecturing in this school that he strained his voice and ever after labored under the disadvantage of having only a hoarse whisper at his command, due to partial paralysis of one of the vocal cords" (Chadwick, p. 554). Barker was appointed obstetric physician to Bellevue Hospital in 1854 and eventually terminated his connection with New York Medical College in 1857. Four years later, he became a charter member of the Bellevue Hospital Medical College as well as the college's professor of clinical midwifery and diseases peculiar to women, a position he held until his death. Over subsequent years, he also became a consulting physician to New York City's Nursery and Child's Hospital, St. Elizabeth's Hospital, the Cancer Hospital, and Women's Hospital.

Barker helped found the American Gynecological Society, which he served as its first president in 1876–1877. He was a member of the New York Academy of Medicine and served as its president from 1879 to 1885. Barker also belonged to the Century Club, the American Geographical and Statistical Society, American Bible Society, St. John's Guild, the Church Temperance Society, the Charity Organization Society, the Physicians Mutual Aid Association, the Metropolitan Museum of Natural History, the Royal Society of Greece, and the Anglo-American Society of Paris, at whose 1890 annual meeting he served as president, in absentia. Barker also held memberships in the New York County Medical Society, the New York Obstetrical Society, the New York Pathological Society, the New York Medical and Surgical Society, the Medico-Legal Society, the London Medical Society, and the London and Edinburgh Obstetrical Societies. He served a term as president of the Medical Society of the State of New York in 1856.

Barker gained widespread renown, becoming the nation's best known obstetrician. Biographer Chadwick claimed he did not, however, "enter into the domain of surgery, transferring to others all cases requiring the use of the knife." In 1861 Barker hailed anesthesia as the most wonderful discovery made in obstetrics for the "feeling of safety and immunity" it offered "from the greatest of all suffering that human nature is called upon to endure" Harold Speert, *Obstetrics and Gynecology in America: A History* [1980], p. 41). Several reports suggest that he introduced the use of the hypodermic syringe into American medicine. His chief written contribution, *The Puerperal Diseases* (1874), ran through many editions and was translated into French, German, Italian, Spanish, and Russian. Having had exceptional opportunities for the study of puerperal diseases, Barker hoped, through this book, to share his valuable experiences. Although he argued that "to ascertain what the nature of puerperal fever is," physicians faced "a greater diversity of opinion than exists in regard to any other disease," he nevertheless concluded that the "evidence" supported his believe that puerperal fever was a contagious disease (p. 441).

An acquaintance of American and European literati and political leaders, Barker was not too proud, in the words of a witness, to "bend over and kiss upon her forehead a poor woman in the hospital who had just undergone a severe operation." Barker made annual trips to Europe for thirty years. During these travels he pursued his writing interests and called on his intimate friends, including Charles Dickens and William Makepeace Thackeray. Barker died in New York City.

• Among Barker's formal addresses, first published in particular societies' journals and later reprinted as monographs, are *A Plea For Hospitals* (1851), *Remarks on Puerperal Fever before the New York Academy of Medicine, October 7th 1857* (1857), *On the Comparative Use of Ergot and the Forceps in Labor* (1858), *On the Use of Anaesthetics in Midwifery* (1861), *On Seasickness: A Popular Treatise for Travelers and the General Reader* (1870), and "Influence of Maternal Impressions of the Foetus," *Transactions of the American Gynecological Society* 11 (1887): 152–96. Three contemporary memoirs that provide insight into Barker's life are James R. Chadwick, "In Memoriam. Fordyce Barker, M.D., LL.D.," *Transactions of the American Gynecological Society* 16 (1891): 551–58; Henry C. Coe, "In Memoriam. B. F. Barker," *New York Journal of*

Gynecology and Obstetrics 1 (1891): 112–18; and William T. Lusk, "Memoir of Fordyce Barker, M.D., LL.D.," *Transactions of the New York Academy of Medicine*, 2d ser., 8 (1892): 286–302. An obituary is in the *New York Times*, 1 June 1891.

PHILIP K. WILSON

BARKER, James William (5 Dec. 1815–26 June 1869), nativist political leader, was born in White Plains, New York. Little is known about Barker's early life except that he worked in New York as a clerk and later opened there his own dry goods business, whose success made him quite wealthy. By the early 1850s Barker was active in the New York Whig party.

Unbeknownst to most of his fellow Whigs, Barker was also active in a nativist fraternal organization, the Order of United Americans (OUA). Hoping to expand their influence, the OUA infiltrated New York City's tiny, secretive Order of the Star Spangled Banner (OSSB). Like the OUA, the OSSB sought to curtail the political power of immigrants and Catholics, and when the OUA's members gained control of the OSSB in 1853 they installed Barker as state president. Under the leadership of Barker and other OUA veterans, the OSSB expanded enormously. By the end of 1854 the OSSB, which by this point was universally referred to as the "Know Nothings" (apparently because their members were required to feign ignorance when queried about the organization), could boast more than one million members nationwide.

Barker played an important role in the Know Nothings' expansion. In May 1854 he reunited the faction-riddled organization and assumed the post of national president, and it was in the five succeeding months that the Know Nothings enjoyed their most rapid growth. Although the expansion of the OSSB resulted from political and religious controversies over which he had little control, Barker did see to it personally that nativist issues remained a part of political debate. When New York City officials arrested anti-Catholic lecturer Daniel Parsons for speaking in public without a license in December 1853, for example, Barker helped organize a protest rally in City Hall Park.

Perhaps Barker's most significant act as a Know Nothing leader was his transformation of the organization into an independent political party. Before New York's 1854 state elections, the Know Nothings had usually supported for office candidates who had already been nominated by one of the existing political organizations. Yet having failed to secure the Whig gubernatorial nomination for a Know Nothing, Barker, in his capacity as New York Know Nothing president, encouraged the order's members to "strike down the 'old politicians'" by nominating their own candidates. Although the Know Nothings' gubernatorial nominee, Daniel Ullmann, placed third in the election, Barker's action set a precedent that most Know Nothings would follow in subsequent elections. More importantly, Barker's move produced election results in New York and Massachusetts that convinced most Whigs that their fractured organization was hopelessly moribund, thus helping to complete the destruction of the second American party system.

Barker's personal fame also peaked in the fall of 1854, when New York City Know Nothings nominated him for mayor. Although four candidates entered the race, Barker's chief rival for the post was Democrat Fernando Wood. As the candidate of a secret fraternal organization, Barker did not conduct a public campaign, depending on word of mouth and the Know Nothing network of lodges to promote his candidacy. Barker also received support from the city's temperance organizations, because the Know Nothings had made known their intention to close saloons on Sundays and put immigrant drinking establishments out of business. Even some temperance and anti-corruption reformers, realizing that only Barker or Wood could win the election, endorsed the Know Nothing in an attempt to prevent the notoriously corrupt Wood from prevailing. On election day, however, Wood defeated Barker by a small margin (20,003 votes to 18,547 out of nearly 60,000 votes cast). Barker claimed that his defeat resulted from an article that appeared in the New York *Tribune* just days before the election claiming that he had set fire to his own store in order to cheat his insurance company. After the election, Barker sued the *Tribune* for libel, and the suit was eventually settled out of court.

Although Barker's rise to political prominence came about quickly, he lost that influence nearly as fast. Early in 1855 various presidential aspirants began positioning themselves for the Know Nothings' 1856 nomination. Barker supported shipping magnate George Law, but most Know Nothing leaders preferred former president Millard Fillmore, and Fillmore's backers proceeded to oust Barker from the order's national presidency in June 1855. When Fillmore captured the Know Nothing nomination, Barker refused to endorse him and campaigned instead for Republican nominee John C. Frémont. Like many other prominent former Know Nothings, Barker also stumped for Abraham Lincoln in 1860. In that year Barker moved to Pittsburgh, where he soon became one of the city's leading dry goods merchants, although he continued to maintain a residence in New York City as well. Shortly before his death, he was elected president of the Eclectic Life Insurance Company. He died, never having married, in Rahway, New Jersey.

• Barker's life must be pieced together from a variety of sources. A few facts concerning his involvement in the OUA can be found in the Order of United Americans Scrapbook at the New York Public Library. His Know Nothing career is best chronicled in Louis Dow Scisco, *Political Nativism in New York State* (1901), although some additional information can be found in Thomas J. Curran, "The Know Nothings of New York" (Ph.D. diss., Columbia Univ., 1963); and Tyler Anbinder, *Nativism and Slavery: The Northern Know Nothings and the Politics of the 1850s* (1992). For the New York mayoralty election of 1854, see Jerome Mushkat, *Fernando Wood: A Political Biography* (1990). Information concerning

Barker's career after the Know Nothings is contained in obituaries in the New York *Herald*, 27 June 1869, and the *New York Times*, 27 June 1869.

TYLER ANBINDER

BARKER, Jeremiah (31 Mar. 1752–4 Oct. 1835), physician, was born in Scituate, Massachusetts, the son of Samuel Barker and Patience Howland, farmers. Barker's early education under the Reverend Mr. Cutter, a Congregational minister, was followed by his study of medicine under Bela Lincoln of Hingham, Massachusetts, from 1769 to 1771. A graduate of Harvard College who had studied medicine under Ezekiel Hersey and in London hospitals and who had received an M.D. from Kings College, Aberdeen, Lincoln had had an unusually academic medical education for the period, a fact that would have a positive influence on Barker's own medical training.

In 1772 Barker was summoned to Lincoln County in the District of Maine to help with an epidemic of malignant fever in Newcastle. A year later he returned to Barnstable, Massachusetts, where he practiced medicine until 1779. He was a ship's surgeon on the ill-fated Penobscot (Bagaduce) expedition in 1779. In an 1806 letter to physician Benjamin Rush, Barker wrote, "I saved a good assortment of medicine from the flames of our ships . . . [which] gave me some advantage, as medicine was scarce." With this "advantage" he settled in Gorham, Maine, where he practiced from 1780 until 1789, when his house burned. He then moved to the Stroudwater section of Portland, where he practiced until his retirement in 1818. Barker was a member of the Massachusetts Medical Society and one of the founders of the Maine Medical Society. He continued his lifelong habit of writing and corresponding until his death in Gorham.

In 1775 Barker married Abigail Sturgis Gorham of Barnstable, with whom he had four children. Abigail was the sister of Judge William Gorham, whose family had been deeded land in the District of Maine called Gorhamtown (later Gorham). Having found "the air on Cape Cod injurious to my constitution and physicians being numerous," Barker wrote, "I removed to Gorham" ("A History of Diseases in the District of Maine," p. 2). In 1790, the year of Abigail's death, Barker married Judge Gorham's sister-in-law, Susanna Garrett, with whom he had one child. After Susanna's death in 1794, he married Eunice Riggs, who died in 1799. (The medical histories of his first three wives can be found in "A History of Diseases in the District of Maine.") Judge Gorham died in 1805, and in 1808 Barker married Gorham's widow, Temperance.

Barker was an early observer and recorder of "the habits, customs and manner of living among the first settlers of this part of the state (District of Maine) . . . always carrying pen, ink and paper . . . [and thus] collect[ing] considerable historical facts." His 1806 letter to Rush relates that:

The first white inhabitants of Maine, being chiefly poor and illiterate, lived and conducted, for a time, in a very similar manner as the Indians did. Their exercise was great, their food simple and wholesome, consisting chiefly of Indian Corn and salted pork, sometimes Beer. Rum could be procured only in small quantities; and happy would it have been for them and their posterity had this *continued* to be the case. . . . Of late years meat cattle have been reared in abundance, and lavishly eaten in the interior towns. Rum too is conveyed into the country towns, as it were, through aquaducts; but none is lost for want of throats.

Barker carried on extensive correspondence with the medical men of his day, including Benjamin Rush; Samuel Latham Mitchill, physician, philosopher, and founder and editor of the *Medical Repository*; and Lyman Spalding, founder of the *United States Pharmacopeia*. Studying epidemics and carrying out a few experiments, Barker followed the medical science and chemistry of the day and was willing to risk scorn if a new therapy, such as his use of alkali for fever, seemed to be valuable. This is a good example of his efforts to apply the findings of the newly emerging science of pneumatic chemistry to the practice of medicine. "In the summer of 1795," Barker wrote, "after reading M. Lavoisier's chemical works, and making some experiments on putrid animal matter . . . it occurred to my mind . . . that the exciting cause of fever was a virulent acid often generated in the stomach from substances undergoing putrid fermentation." The point is not whether Barker's theories were valid but that he was trying to practice scientifically and to document his results. His early work on this subject was published in the *Medical Repository* in 1799.

Barker's major work, written between 1797 and 1831, is "A History of Diseases in the District of Maine, Commencing in 1735 and Continued to the Present Time . . . To This Is Annexed an Inquiry into the Causes, Nature, Increasing Prevalency, and Treatment of Consumption, Which Is Maintained to Be Curable . . . Written So As to Be Intelligible to Those Who Are Destitute of Medical Science." Although never published, it survives in manuscript form. In the first of two volumes, Barker describes the living conditions and the medical community of Cumberland County as he found them in 1780. He includes excerpts relating to epidemics and disease from 1735 to 1780, quoting from *Extracts from the Journals Kept by the Reverend Thomas Smith . . . Selected by Samuel Freeman Esq.* (1821). The remaining chapters of volume one are divided into discussions of various epidemics and diseases, such as malignant fevers, pneumonia, puerperal sepsis, apoplexy, dropsy, hydrophobia, and cancer. Barker presents 100 patients of his own, most by name, including their clinical presentations, treatments, outcomes, and occasionally the results of autopsy findings. He then excerpts the historical and contemporary medical literature to justify his diagnosis and treatment. Volume two is devoted to the prevention, diagnosis, and treatment of consumption; again he excerpts and interprets the historical and current literature, to which he adds his own cases. This careful documentation of the use of relevant medical literature is unusual and is therefore a rare and valuable example of the changing contemporary medical thinking.

Barker "practiced physic" from his homes in Stroudwater and Gorham, Maine, and cared for his patients from Bath to Biddeford, a distance of over forty miles. He brought medical books to the bedside "when engaged in extraordinary & difficult cases" (Barker's 1806 casebook) and always had a notebook in hand. His observations describing clinical findings, treatments, and outcomes of diseases and epidemics in the District of Maine can be found in his medical case books of 1771–1796 and 1803–1818 as well as in eleven articles published between 1798 and 1807 in the *Medical Repository*, the first U.S. medical journal. His unpublished manuscript is an unusually detailed account of a country practice, far from the centers of "elite" medicine. Taken together, Barker's writings are a valuable resource for those who study New England life, nutrition, public health, epidemics, and other aspects of health, disease and healing. As such, he is regarded as Maine's first medical historian.

• Barker's papers, at the Maine Historical Society (Collection 13), contain correspondence, his case books from 1771 to 1818, and his unpublished manuscript, "A History of Diseases in the District of Maine." The first public reference to Barker's planned book appears in the *Medical Repository* 1 (1798): 114, and subscription proposals for the book are found in four Maine newspapers between 1807 and 1829. Among Barker's articles in the *Medical Repository* are "On the Febrifuge Virtue of Lime, Magnesia and Alkaline Salts in Dysentery, Yellow-Fever and Scarlatina Anginosa. In a Letter from Dr. Jeremiah Barker, of Portland, (Maine) Dated May 30, 1798," 2, no. 2 (1799): 147–52; "Obstinate Eruption over the Whole Surface of the Body Cured by Chalk (Alkaline Earth, or Carbonate of Lime)," 2, no. 2 (1799): 412–13; and "Use of Alkalies in Cancer. Extract from a Letter of Dr. J. Barker to Dr. Mitchill, Dated Portland (Maine), March 12, 1801," 4 (1801): 415–16. A controversy over the prevention and cure of puerperal fever between Barker and Dr. Nathaniel Coffin of Falmouth was published in the *Falmouth Gazette and Weekly Advertiser*, 12, 19, and 26 Feb. and 5 and 12 Mar. 1785. A three-page letter from Barker to Benjamin Rush, dated 22 Sept. 1806, provides biographical information as well as some insight into Barker's medical philosophy and his use of alkaline salts in fever (vol. 2, Rush MSS, p. 28, Historical Society of Pennsylvania). Two biographical essays were written by James Alfred Spalding: "After Consulting Hours: Jeremiah Barker, M.D., Gorham and Falmouth, Maine 1752–1835," *Bulletin of the American Academy of Medicine* 10, no. 3 (June 1909): 1–24, and an entry in *Maine Physicians of 1820* (1928), pp. 31–33. See also Hugh Davis McLellan, *History of Gorham, Maine* (1903), pp. 396–98.

RICHARD J. KAHN

BARKER, Mary Cornelia (20 Jan. 1879–15 Sept. 1963), schoolteacher and teachers' union leader, was born in Rockmart, Georgia, the daughter of Thomas Nathaniel Barker, a teacher and small businessman, and Dora Elizabeth Lovejoy, a teacher. After spending her early years in rural Rockmart, Barker moved with her family to Atlanta, where she attended the public schools. She went on to Agnes Scott College in Decatur, Georgia, from which she received a diploma for completing the normal course in 1900.

Barker began teaching in small towns close to Atlanta and then taught at the Decatur Orphans' School. In 1904 she started teaching in the Atlanta public schools and rapidly moved up through the elementary grades, becoming an elementary school principal in 1921. She moved to the principalship of the John B. Gordon School in 1923 and stayed in that position until her retirement in 1944.

Barker was active in the formation of the Atlanta Public School Teachers' Association (APSTA) in 1905. The early years of the APSTA were devoted to the pursuit of a salary scale for white teachers. In 1919, however, in the midst of a dispute with the board of education, it affiliated with both the American Federation of Teachers (AFT) and the Atlanta Federation of Trades. Barker was initially cautious about union affiliation but soon plunged deeply into union activities.

Barker was secretary of the APSTA in 1919, and two years later she was elected to the first of two terms as president, following which she became first vice president for another two years. In 1920 she became a delegate to the Atlanta Federation of Trades, the city's central union organization. She also was a frequent APSTA delegate to the American Federation of Teachers national conventions. In her presidency, as well as in later years, she adopted an approach to teacher unionism that emphasized improving the professional image and responsibility of teachers as well as increasing their remuneration and other occupational rewards. Barker was successful in helping to build the APSTA (Local 89) into the largest AFT local of the 1920s. She pursued her professional agenda for the APSTA through a variety of educational activities for its members, including lectures, a public speaking course, and a continuing education program for teachers. She lobbied successfully to obtain in 1922 a tenure law for teachers, and she advocated autonomy for teachers in their classrooms. She also sought a voice for teachers in educational policy and a code of ethics for them.

Barker was a strong advocate of religious and racial tolerance in society and schools, a position that won her few friends among local teachers and teacher unionists. Similarly, her "professional" approach to teacher unionism, that is, her advocacy of tenure and autonomy, in the APSTA failed to garner wide support from the members. After her years in office her influence in the APSTA waned as a group of more traditional leaders, who were willing to cooperate completely with the school administration rather than to influence its approach to teachers, took control. This completely accommodationist unionism stood in stark contrast to Barker's agenda and approach to unionism.

Barker served as president of the American Federation of Teachers from 1925 to 1931. At the beginning of her presidency the AFT was in the midst of a sharp membership decline, as was the larger labor movement, due to the post–World War I "red scare" and intensified by business and government's successful antiunion drive. Her major accomplishment as AFT president was to prevent decline in membership. By 1931 the number of members had doubled from what it was when she assumed the presidency. As AFT president her agenda included social reform issues, such as child labor legislation and teacher tenure laws, the protection of academic freedom for teachers, worker education, and negotiations policies to govern relations between teachers and school authorities. Similar to her earlier situation in the APSTA, her influence in the national union diminished substantially after her presidency. Her opponents in the APSTA controlled the leadership of that association in the 1930s and 1940s as well as the selection of delegates to the national conventions and the positions they would take on issues.

Barker was particularly interested in the adult education movement of organized labor and workers' education, and she sought to adapt it to the needs of teachers, particularly the women teachers who made up the large majority of union members. She was active in developing the Summer School for Women Workers in Atlanta, Georgia, a facility for training young women from the textile, tobacco, and other industries in the principles of the labor movement and other studies. She worked with the summer school from its founding in 1927 until her retirement.

Barker's orientation marked her as a woman who was well ahead of her times. Her willingness to advocate unpopular causes, her wide ranging objectives for teacher unionists, and her work among young women workers all exemplified her foresight. It was her misfortune, as it was of most of those who adopted views like hers, that she was far "ahead" of those who comprised the rank and file of the teacher unions that she headed. She died in Atlanta, Georgia.

• The Mary Barker Papers are housed in the Special Collections Department of the Emory University Library in Atlanta. She is discussed briefly in Marjorie Murphy, *Blackboard Unions: The AFT & the NEA, 1900–1980* (1990). Her work in the Summer School for Women Workers is depicted in Joyce Kornbluh and Mary Frederickson, eds., *Sisterhood and Solidarity: Workers' Education for Women, 1914–1984* (1984). See also Wayne J. Urban, *Why Teachers Organized* (1982), and Joseph W. Newman, "A History of the Atlanta Public School Teachers' Association, Local 89 of the American Federation of Teachers, 1919–1956" (Ph.D. diss., Georgia State Univ., 1978). An obituary is in the *American Teacher*, Feb. 1964, p. 19.

WAYNE J. URBAN

BARKER, Ruth Mildred (3 Feb. 1897–25 Jan. 1990), Shaker trustee, was born in Providence, Rhode Island, the daughter of James P. Barker and Ruth Jackson. Her father died in 1903, and that year, unable to care for Mildred, her mother took her to the Alfred, Maine, community of the United Society of Believers in Christ's Second Appearing, informally known as the Shakers. Barker, who came to be known as Sister Mildred, grew up within the Alfred community,

signed the covenant, and worked primarily as a caretaker of young girls. She moved to Sabbathday Lake, southwest of Lewiston, Maine, in 1931 with the consolidation of the two communities.

Barker was named trustee at Sabbathday Lake in 1950 and held the financial and business position until her death. For her work in the preservation and interpretation of Shaker artistic and material culture, particularly of the musical tradition, she was recognized in 1965 by the Catholic Art Association, in 1971 by the Maine Arts Commission, and in 1983 as a Master Traditional Artist by the National Endowment for the Arts and the Smithsonian Institution.

In 1961 Barker and Theodore Johnson, a member of the Sabbathday Lake community, established the *Shaker Quarterly*, the last official Shaker publication, to which she contributed many articles, obituaries, and reminiscences. She also published several books and pamphlets on Shaker history in Maine and led efforts to restore the Sabbathday Lake library building to house Shaker manuscripts and materials.

Recognized as the spiritual leader of the Maine Shakers, Barker disagreed with the 1965 Canterbury decision to close the membership covenant, arguing in articles and in public addresses that the Shaker message was neither dying nor a failure. Since the early nineteenth century, when there were as many as twenty Shaker communities in seven states, membership had steadily declined, which had led to many community closings. By 1960, just two Shaker communities remained, one in Canterbury, New Hampshire, the other in Sabbathday Lake. Resisting the popular identification of Shaker belief with Shaker material culture, Barker was often quoted as saying that she did not want "to be remembered as a chair." It was religious principles that had made the material objects possible, she asserted, claiming that Shakers still sustained a viable, if small, community and that they would persist in the future in what she called "new spirals of spiritual life." Barker died at the Shaker community in Sabbathday Lake, Maine. Two years after her death the community had approximately ten members.

• The Sabbathday Lake Shaker Community holds tape recordings of Barker's oral histories along with manuscripts and other personal memorabilia. Her books include *The Sabbathday Lake Shakers: An Introduction to the Shaker Heritage* (1985) and *Holy Land: A History of the Alfred Shakers* (1986). For a sample of her writing, see "Home Notes from Sabbathday Lake, Maine," *Shaker Quarterly* 12 (Winter 1972): 138–46, and the reprint of her 1960 talk to the Shaker Historical Society in Shaker Heights, Ohio, "Light and Truth Forever," *Shaker Quarterly* 19 (Spring 1991): 6–7. See, as well, Gerard Wertkin, *The Four Seasons of Shaker Life* (1986), and Daniel W. Patterson, *The Shaker Spiritual* (1979). For a copy of her obituary, tributes to her, and a reprint of Barker's 1965 address to the Auburn (Maine) Historical Society, "We Have Kept the Faith," see the R. Mildred Barker memorial edition, *Shaker Quarterly* 18 (Spring 1990).

JANE F. CROSTHWAITE

BARKLEY, Alben William (24 Nov. 1877–30 Apr. 1956), vice president of the United States, was born in a log cabin in a community named Wheel, between the villages of Lowes and Fancy Farm, in Graves County, Kentucky, the son of John Wilson Barkley and Electra Smith, tenant tobacco farmers. Named Willie Alben, the "Willie" for two uncles, he changed his name as soon as he could (as he put it, as soon as he was old enough to assert himself), letting it be known that he was Alben William "and no foolishness!" Barkley grew up in poverty, working on the farm. He did not graduate from high school but managed to enroll in a tiny Methodist institution, Marvin College, in Clinton, Kentucky. Upon graduation in 1897 he sold cookware to pay his way through law school. The crockery cracked upon use, and he was reduced to going back to purchasers and paying them for their losses out of his own pocket. He managed to borrow $200 to attend a year of law school, 1897–1898, at Emory College (now Emory University), then located in Oxford, Georgia. Lacking means to continue, he taught a few months at Marvin and thereupon moved to Paducah, where, with a few shirts, fifty cents in change, and a letter of introduction to a local lawyer, he began reading law. He was admitted to the Kentucky bar in 1901 and had his last formal instruction in law during a summer at the University of Virginia in 1902. The next year he married Dorothy Brower, with whom he had three children.

Barkley quickly gained a reputation in Paducah as a public speaker. In 1905 he ran on the Democratic ticket for his first public office, county attorney, and won. Four years later he was elected county judge. He ran successfully for the U.S. Congress in 1912 and thereafter was reelected, his seat soon becoming so secure that in the early 1920s he purchased a house in Washington. In 1926 he won the seat of Republican senator Richard P. Ernst. That year his opponent's campaign slogan was "Coolidge needs Ernst." Barkley answered back, "If Coolidge needs Ernst, it is proof enough that Kentucky does not need him."

On both the state and national levels, Barkley's political views came in part from his upbringing. He never forgot his rural penury and his fight to obtain even the rudiments of an education. He thus favored lower national tariffs (to enable tobacco growers to purchase manufactured articles cheaper), regulation of railroads (which otherwise might gouge rural Kentuckians), and government assistance with road building. To this in the beginning he added a certain conservatism. His outlook was broadened by his experience on the national scene, especially acquaintance with President Woodrow Wilson, whose arrival in Washington in March 1913 coincided with his own. He met Wilson a month after entering Congress, and the two were immediately drawn to each other; both were from border states of the South, and both were lawyers. Barkley did not have Wilson's academic background, and in a sense their relationship was that of student and teacher. Wilson's far more polished politics persuaded Barkley of the need to understand political life on the national level, to sense national needs and not simply the rules governing politics in Kentucky. The president's New Freedom legislation, the apogee of Democratic progressivism, gave Barkley a ready-made program, to which he became deeply committed. When opponents of the Keating-Owen Child Labor Act of 1916 argued that preventing interstate commerce in goods made by children under the age of sixteen would reduce the power of the states, Barkley declared, "I am getting a little tired of hearing the standpats of both sides of the Chamber hide behind an antiquated interpretation of the doctrine of states' rights." Many years later, after he had known seven presidents, he would still maintain that Wilson was the greatest.

During the Republican era in the 1920s, Barkley did his best to stem the tide of reaction. In 1922, rebutting the Harding administration's claim to have returned life to a pre-Wilsonian perfection, he said that if Republicans had returned America to normalcy "then in God's name let us have abnormalcy." It may have been the stuffiness of the national scene after March 1921 that turned his attention momentarily to Kentucky politics, causing him to run for the governorship in 1923. He lost to a seasoned candidate who died a few weeks after the primary. Instead of asserting his right to the nomination, however, he let his late rival's friends choose a successor and campaigned for him, which not merely maintained party unity but set the scene for his own successful Senate campaign three years later.

The coming of the Great Depression prepared the way for the election of Franklin D. Roosevelt to the presidency in 1932, and the Kentucky senator played an important role in the years that followed. Barkley was keynoter of the national convention in 1932, a choice Roosevelt made to ensure both a first-rate speech and Kentucky support. As the president's lieutenant in the Senate during the intensely active years of New Deal legislation, Barkley stood behind Roosevelt's legislative program, supporting him on everything save the Bonus Bill, when along with many of his fellow senators he voted to override a presidential veto and give the World War I veterans the early bonuses they requested. He was again the keynoter during the Democratic convention of 1936.

In 1937, just when the administration-sponsored bill to enlarge the Supreme Court was before the Senate, the Democratic majority leader Joseph Robinson died, and in a dramatic election Barkley was chosen by a single vote to replace him. In subsequent weeks and months, as the Kentuckian defended the proposed reorganization of the judiciary and the Court bill floundered, he found himself almost adrift on the seas of Senate discontent. It was the low point in his Senate career. His conservative enemies denounced him as a party hack. Loyalty to the president and to his own progressive and New Deal principles made it difficult for the senator to defuse such criticism. Perhaps as a reward, Roosevelt hinted that Barkley might receive the Democratic presidential nomination in 1940, and the senator was willing. The president, however, decided to take the nomination himself.

It was during Roosevelt's third term that Barkley's reputation in the Senate rose to its height. In February 1944, after the majority leader had done his best to negotiate a tax bill acceptable to the administration, the president airily announced he would veto it, adding in his veto message, "It is not a tax bill but a tax-relief bill, providing relief not for the needy but for the greedy." Barkley thereupon created one of the most emotional scenes ever witnessed in the Upper House. "That statement," he shouted, " . . . is a calculated and deliberate assault upon the legislative integrity of every member of the Congress of the United States." He resigned as majority leader and urged his fellow senators to override the veto. Roosevelt immediately backed down, protesting that he had never meant to attack the Kentucky senator's integrity or that of other members of Congress and that he hoped the Democratic senators would reelect the majority leader immediately and unanimously—which they did.

Thereafter age constituted Barkley's principal political problem. Roosevelt refused to support him for the vice presidential nomination in 1944 because of age—Barkley was sixty-six that year. Had the senator been nominated he would have won along with Roosevelt and inherited the presidency the next year. The man who received the nomination in 1944, Senator Harry S. Truman, did choose Barkley as his running mate in 1948, but because of Barkley's age he was only offered the post after Justice William O. Douglas of the Supreme Court turned it down. In 1952 the senator made a last try for the great prize, the presidency, only to be told awkwardly by his allies in the labor movement that he was too old.

As a candidate for the vice presidency in 1948 and occupier of that office for the next four years, Barkley performed vigorously. Campaigning with an airplane, he flew 150,000 miles and made 250 speeches in thirty-six states. Once in office, he endeared himself to his fellow citizens. After he mentioned his grandson's suggestion that he add two "e's" between the initials "V.P.," he became widely known as "the Veep." In this role he often helped the administration carry its program to the people. He championed the North Atlantic Treaty, signed in 1949, the Korean War when it broke out in 1950, and doughtily supported the dismissal of General Douglas MacArthur in 1951. In domestic matters he went down the line for Truman's Fair Deal. His first wife died in 1947, and in 1949 he added to his public attraction, and to his private happiness, by courting and marrying a St. Louis widow thirty years his junior, Jane Rucker Hadley.

In 1954, the year after he left the vice presidency, Barkley won election to the Senate. He returned bereft of all seniority but did not mind. He continued the hectic pace he had set for himself many years before, speaking, socializing, and traveling with gusto. Little more than a year later he died—on the podium, as he might have wished, in Lexington, Virginia, in the midst of a speech before an enthusiastic crowd of students at Washington and Lee University.

Barkley's career was marked by almost uninterrupted electoral success in his native state. In national politics he excelled both in congressional committees and as a public speaker. Beloved in his later years, he inspired some critics to think him ponderous, but behind his senatorial bonhomie lay much good judgment, a quality he dedicated both to his party and the nation.

• The Barkley papers are at the University of Kentucky. The writer Sidney Shalett taped Barkley for many hours, the transcripts of which are in the Barkley papers; he also collaborated in *That Reminds Me* (1954), an informative, anecdotal memoir. There is no full biography of Barkley. An excellent short account is James K. Libbey, *Dear Alben: Mr. Barkley of Kentucky* (1979). See also Polly Ann Davis, *Alben W. Barkley: Senate Majority Leader and Vice President* (1979), and Jane Barkley, *I Married the Veep* (1958). An obituary is in the *New York Times*, 1 May 1956.

ROBERT H. FERRELL

BARKSDALE, Ethelbert (4 Jan. 1824–17 Feb. 1893), editor and U.S. and Confederate congressman, was born in Smyrna, Rutherford County, Tennessee, the son of William Barksdale and Nancy Lester. Ethelbert Barksdale was the younger brother of William Barksdale (1821–1863), commanding general of the Mississippi brigade in the Army of Northern Virginia, who was killed at the battle of Gettysburg. Ethelbert Barksdale moved to Mississippi while still in his teens and soon followed his brother William into journalism and Democratic politics. He married Alice Harris in 1843. Whether they had any children is unknown.

Barksdale settled in Yazoo City, Mississippi, where from 1845 to 1850 he edited the *Democrat*. In 1850 he moved to Jackson, Mississippi, where until 1861 he edited the *Mississippian*, at that time perhaps the most influential newspaper in the state. His first political office came in 1860, when he was chosen as a delegate to the Democratic National Convention. Like most of his fellow Mississippi Democrats, Barksdale was a strong advocate of the expansion of slavery into the western territories. After it became clear that the Democratic Convention would not endorse a plank protecting slavery in the territories and would nominate Stephen A. Douglas of Illinois for president, Barksdale, along with the other members of the Mississippi delegation, walked out of the convention. At the later convention of southern Democrats, Barksdale supported the nomination of John C. Breckinridge and actively campaigned for his election in 1860. While Barksdale had not always been a secessionist, he regarded the election of Abraham Lincoln as sufficient grounds for the slave states to leave the Union.

In 1861 Barksdale was elected to the First Confederate Congress, and in 1863 he was reelected to a second term. In the Confederate Congress he usually backed the positions of Jefferson Davis. While Barksdale was a proponent of states' rights, he supported as wartime emergency measures the suspension of habeas corpus, martial law, conscription, and a tax on agricultural products.

When the war ended, Barksdale returned to Jackson and resumed his career as a newspaperman, now editing the influential *Clarion*. Unlike many of his fellow Democrats, Barksdale advised cooperation with the policies of Reconstruction, and he favored granting some civil rights to the freedmen. Cooperation, he wrote in the *Clarion*, was the only option. Otherwise, he feared, Radical Republicans would capture complete control of the state government. To avoid this, he counseled, Democrats should register, vote, and cooperate in reconstructing the state. Nonetheless, as Reconstruction progressed, Barksdale's spirit of cooperation waned. At the constitutional convention of 1868, the Republicans denied the right to vote or to hold office to anyone who had supported secession or the Confederacy. Barksdale called these proscriptive provisions "the most sweeping, the most infamous, the most vindictive measure of proscription which has yet been passed."

Despite his early stance as a "cooperationist," Barksdale remained a staunch and partisan Democrat, serving as a delegate to the Democratic National Conventions of 1868, 1872, and 1880. He served as chairman of the State Democratic Executive Committee from 1877 to 1879. He also supported the efforts of Democrats to overthrow Reconstruction and Republican rule in Mississippi by violence and intimidation.

In the election of 1875, Mississippi Democratic leaders led a revolution that won full control of the legislature, which then proceeded to impeach and remove Republican governor Adelbert Ames and most of the members of his administration. Barksdale had supported the "revolution of 1875" and its conservative Democratic leaders, L. Q. C. Lamar, James Z. George, and Edward C. Walthall. In the following year, however, Barksdale emerged as a critic of the conservative faction of planters and railroad lawyers who dominated the post-Reconstruction Democratic party. He was politically active in pressing the demands of small farmers for such reforms as inflation of the money supply, railroad regulation, and better public education.

Led by the continued domination of the Democratic party by corporate lawyers and large planters and his own advocacy of small farmer issues, Barksdale challenged the conservative leaders of the party in the senatorial contest of 1880. The fight erupted over who would succeed Blanche K. Bruce, a Republican elected during Reconstruction who had died. Barksdale announced for the seat, and a contest developed in the Democratic caucus between Barksdale and the followers of conservative Lamar. Barksdale finally threw his support to George, who was elected, thereby thwarting Lamar's candidate, Walthall.

One year later similar contests developed over Lamar's Senate seat and the governorship; the result was further estrangement between the two factions. Throughout the 1880s Barksdale continued to support small farmers against the continued domination of the Democratic party by the conservative George-Lamar faction. While not a delegate to the constitutional convention of 1890, Barksdale, in editorials, questioned the provisions that were put into the constitution to discriminate against blacks in voting and holding office.

Barksdale ran as the Farmers' Alliance candidate against Senator George in 1891. The campaign and its outcome were especially bitter for Barksdale and his small farmer followers. After the election one expert believed that pro-Barksdale candidates had been "counted out" in the popular vote to choose the legislators who selected the new senator. George won.

The bitter senatorial contest of 1891 was symptomatic of a deep division within the Democratic party between the conservatives, who controlled the machinery of the party, and the small farmers of the hills, whose voting strength threatened to unseat the conservatives. As long as the fight remained an internecine struggle within the Democratic party, Barksdale sided with the small farmers. When some small farmers and their leaders left the party to support the third-party Populist movement, Barksdale refused to go with them and remained steadfast to the Democrats. His death in Jackson spared him the tumultuous political struggles that attended the rise of populism.

• Barksdale is mentioned extensively both as a journalist and a politician in Albert D. Kirwan, *Revolt of the Rednecks: Mississippi Politics, 1876–1925* (1951). Two articles dealing with Barksdale as a political figure are Willie D. Halsell, "Democratic Dissensions in Mississippi, 1878–1882," *Journal of Mississippi History* 2 (1940): 123–35; and Owen Peterson, "Ethelbert Barksdale in the Democratic National Convention of 1860," *Journal of Mississippi History* 14 (1952): 257–78. Halsell, "The Bourbon Period in Mississippi Politics, 1875–1890," *Journal of Southern History* 11 (1945): 519–37, is an excellent treatment of the period when Barksdale was a leader of the small farmers.

JOHN RAY SKATES

BARKSDALE, William (21 Aug. 1821–3 July 1863), congressman and Confederate officer, was born in Rutherford County, Tennessee, the son of William Barksdale and Nancy Hervey Lester, farmers. He was educated in the local schools and briefly attended the University of Nashville. After his father's death, William and his three brothers moved in 1837 to Mississippi, where they began separate careers. William settled near Columbus, read law, was admitted to the bar, and invested in land and a small number of slaves before he was twenty-five years old. During the Mexican War, he was appointed captain and served as a commissary officer under General Zachary Taylor. He saw no military action, and when he was discharged in September 1848 he returned to Columbus. In 1849 Barksdale married Narcissa Saunders of Louisiana; she brought twenty slaves, horses, mules, and several wagon loads of household goods into the family. In 1860 Barksdale owned thirty-six slaves, a plantation, and several small farms. He and Narcissa had two children.

Barksdale entered state politics as a moderate Democrat in 1850, and he spoke for the Union and the Compromise of 1850, especially the Fugitive Slave Act. Two years later, local politics led him to support the states' rights position. He was elected to Congress in 1852 and served four consecutive terms. As a congressman he supported the Kansas-Nebraska bill, which gave tacit approval to popular sovereignty and repealed the Missouri Compromise. Rumors and speculation erroneously indicated that he accompanied Preston Brooks during the attack on Charles Sumner. Barksdale supported a southern transcontinental railroad and internal improvements for Mississippi, including roads, railroads, and a marine hospital at Vicksburg. He opposed reopening the African slave trade in 1858, and he fought against the 1859 tariff bill because he thought it was protectionist and detrimental to southern interests.

Barksdale viewed the Republican party in 1856 as the party of "black Republicanism," and he vehemently opposed John C. Frémont. Three years later, Barksdale believed that John Brown's (1800–1859) raid was a direct outgrowth of Republican philosophy and doctrine. Although he was not a delegate to the 1860 Democratic convention, he supported William L. Yancey's proslavery position and endorsed John C. Breckenridge's presidential bid. Barksdale supported secession after Abraham Lincoln was elected, and when Mississippi seceded in January 1861 he resigned from the Congress. The Mississippi Secession Convention recommended that the state's congressional delegation be named as their congressmen to the new government. Before that was accomplished, the Montgomery Convention became the First Confederate Congress, with the convention's delegates seated as congressmen. In lieu of continuing congressional service, Barksdale was appointed commissary general for the Army of Mississippi.

In May 1861 Barksdale resigned his commissary general appointment and was elected colonel of the Thirteenth Mississippi Infantry Regiment. Ordered to Virginia, he received his baptism of fire at First Manassas (Bull Run) where his regiment lost only two men in battle. Subsequently, when ten soldiers died of typhoid fever and about two hundred others became ill during the epidemic, Barksdale began drinking and was temporarily removed from command. He was returned to duty after a court of inquiry recommended no further proceedings against him.

As commander of the Thirteenth Mississippi, Barksdale saw action near Balls Bluff in October 1861 and took part in the Peninsular campaign the following April. In Richard Griffith's Mississippi Brigade, Barksdale was not actively engaged until Savage Station; he was named brigade commander in June 1862, when Griffith was killed. Two days later Barksdale led a late-afternoon charge on Malvern Hill. When his color-bearer fell, Barksdale seized the flag and led the attack until the battle ended. He was promoted to brigadier general in August 1862 and served in Lafayette McLaws's division of James Longstreet's corps.

During the Confederate invasion of Maryland, which ended with the battle of Antietam (Sharpsburg), Barksdale was with Thomas J. "Stonewall" Jackson's corps at Harpers Ferry in western Virginia, and on 16 September his brigade hurriedly marched to Sharpsburg. They covered thirty miles in fourteen hours and reached Dunkard Church with fewer than 800 men. Barksdale helped hold the Confederate center against the late-morning Union attack on 17 September, but the brigade sustained heavy casualties.

Barksdale's brigade held the south bank of the Rappahannock River during the battle of Fredericksburg in December. After slowing the Union advance for sixteen hours, Barksdale withdrew to Marye's Heights. During the Battle of Chancellorsville in May 1863, Barksdale's men held Marye's Heights before being driven out by John Sedgwick's forces.

With Longstreet during the second day at Gettysburg, Barksdale faced Sickles's salient, which included artillery in the Peach Orchard. In the late afternoon, the charging Mississippi Brigade followed their commander and overran the Union battery; they then continued up Cemetery Ridge, until point-blank canister fire drove them back. Federal troops found the mortally wounded Barksdale near the crest and took him to their lines, where he died.

• Letters from William Barksdale are in the Ethlebert Barksdale Papers, Department of Archives and History, Jackson, Miss.; his military career is documented in the Compiled Service Record of Brigadier General William Barksdale, National Archives, Washington, D.C. Specific military actions are described in James Dinkins, "Barksdale's Mississippi Brigade at Fredericksburg" and "Griffith—Barksdale—Humphreys Mississippi Brigade," *Southern Historical Society Papers* 32 (1904): 17–25 and 251–74. See also James Longstreet, Lieutenant General, C.S.A., "'A Sixth Time They Charged': The Battle of Fredericksburg," in *Battles and Leaders of the Civil War*, ed. Ned Bradford (1956). Barksdale's association with the Brooks-Sumner attack is clarified in Raymond W. Tyson, "William Barksdale and the Brooks-Sumner Assault," *Journal of Mississippi History* 26 (May 1964): 137–40. See also James W. McKee, "William Barksdale: The Intrepid Mississippian" (Ph.D. diss., Miss. State Univ., 1966).

HARRY P. OWENS

BARLOW, Francis Channing (19 Oct. 1834–11 Jan. 1896), lawyer and soldier, was born in Brooklyn, New York, the son of the Reverend David Hatch Barlow, a Unitarian minister, and Almira Penniman, who were divorced in 1849. Barlow was raised by his mother and spent his youth living in Massachusetts. Graduating first in the Harvard class of 1855, Barlow journeyed to New York City, working briefly as a private tutor. In 1856 he undertook the study of law and was admitted to the bar in April 1858.

On 19 April 1861, just one week after the outbreak of the Civil War, Barlow's devotion to the Union and abolitionist sympathies compelled him to enlist as a private in the Twelfth New York Militia for three months' service. The following day he was married to Arabella Wharton Griffith; they had no children. Mrs.

Barlow subsequently volunteered as a nurse with the U.S. Sanitary Commission in order to be near her husband. Promoted to first lieutenant on 2 May 1861, Barlow saw service with his regiment in the Shenandoah Valley; the unit was never engaged in battle and was mustered out of service on 5 August 1861.

Barlow reentered the service on 6 November 1861, accepting a commission as lieutenant colonel of the Sixty-first New York Volunteer Infantry. Promoted colonel of the same regiment on 14 April 1862, he led his unit throughout the Peninsular campaign. In the regiment's first engagement at Fair Oaks, 1 June 1862, Barlow's cool handling of his unit allowed it to escape from an exposed position between the lines. Though a stern disciplinarian, his leadership abilities quickly won him the respect of his troops. "The men cheered me violently during the fight and when we came out," he later wrote with pride. The affair also earned Barlow favorable notice from his superior officers, marking him as a rising star in the Army of the Potomac. He continued to distinguish himself during the Seven Days' campaign, taking an active part in the battles of White Oak Swamp, Glendale, and Malvern Hill.

Commanding the Sixty-first and Sixty-fourth New York Infantry at the battle of Antietam on 17 September 1862, Barlow was severely wounded in the groin but was nursed back to health by his wife, who tended him on the field of battle. Barlow's conduct at Antietam earned him promotion to brigadier general on 19 September. Rejoining the army in the spring of 1863, he commanded the Second Brigade, Second Division, Eleventh Corps, at the battle of Chancellorsville, where his unit saw little action. On 23 May 1863 he was given command of the First Division, Eleventh Corps, which he led with distinction at the battle of Gettysburg. There, on 1 July 1863, he was shot in the left side while endeavoring to withdraw his troops from their position north of town. The administrations of his wife, who once again tended him on the field of battle, were greatly responsible for saving his life.

Returning to the army in April 1864, Barlow was given command of the First Division, Second Corps, which he led throughout the Virginia campaigns of 1864. On 12 May 1864, he was given responsibility for leading the assault on the Confederate salient, known ever after as the "Bloody Angle." The attack was successful, resulting in more than 5,000 Confederate casualties, most of whom were captured, along with between eighteen and twenty pieces of artillery. Barlow continued to display his military prowess and personal courage at the battle of Cold Harbor and during the Petersburg campaign. His "highly meritorious and distinguished conduct" throughout the campaign won him promotion to brevet major general on 1 August 1864.

The hard campaigning, combined with the news of his wife's death in July 1864, finally took their toll on Barlow. The following month he was granted an extended leave to recover his health, and he spent several months in Europe. Returning to the army on 1 April 1865 he was given command of the Second Division,

Second Army Corps, which he led in pursuing the Confederate retreat to Appomattox Court House. On 25 May 1865 he was promoted to major general, full rank, but he resigned from the army on 16 November 1865.

That same month Barlow was elected New York secretary of state, holding that position from 1866 to 1868. In October 1866 he married Ellen Shaw; they had three children. In May 1869 Barlow was appointed U.S. marshal for the southern district of New York, serving until October of that year. In the summer of 1869, by order of President Ulysses S. Grant, he was entrusted with all U.S. military and revenue forces in New York, New Jersey, and New England in order to prevent American sympathizers from shipping men and arms to aid Cuban insurgents in their revolt against Spanish rule. He was completely successful in breaking up these expeditions. In 1871 he was one of the founders of the New York Bar Association, the first organization of its kind in the country, and was a member of its executive committee for the first two years after its founding.

Barlow was one of the four prosecutors of the "Tweed Ring" in the summer of 1871 and thereafter directed the prosecution as state attorney general, holding that office in 1872–1873. Following the presidential election of 1876, he was appointed by President Grant as one of the delegation sent to Florida to observe the count of that state's electoral votes. Though a Republican, Barlow strongly disagreed with the declared result, which favored Rutherford B. Hayes, a member of his own party. Barlow spent the remainder of his life as a business lawyer in private practice. He died at his home in New York City.

Barlow's fame lies chiefly in his contributions as a soldier. General Nelson A. Miles believed him "utterly devoid of the sensation of fear, constantly aggressive, and intensely earnest in the discharge of all his duties." Yet his efforts as a public servant should not be ignored, for, as Miles also noted, Barlow's "integrity of purpose, independence of character, and sterling honesty in the assertion of what he believed to be right and just, made him a marked man among public men."

• Barlow's correspondence is in the Francis Channing Barlow Papers, Massachusetts Historical Society; the Samuel Bowles Papers and the Alexander S. Webb Papers, Yale University Library; the John B. Bachelder Papers, New Hampshire Historical Society; and the Samuel J. Tilden Papers, New York Public Library. Barlow's published writings consist of two items: an address entitled "Capture of the Salient May 12, 1864," in the *Military Historical Society of Massachusetts Papers*, vol. 4: *The Wilderness Campaign of May-June 1864*, (1905), and a brief sketch of his postwar life in *Apocrypha concerning the Class of 1855 of Harvard College*, ed. Edwin H. Abbot (1880). Two brief biographical sketches of Barlow exist: Edwin H. Abbot, "Francis Channing Barlow," *Harvard Graduates Magazine* (June 1896), and the State of New York, *In Memoriam: Francis Channing Barlow, 1834–1896* (1923), published on the occasion of the erection of Barlow's statue at the Gettysburg National Military Park. Obituaries are in the *New York Herald*, 12 Jan. 1896, and the *Boston Transcript*, 13 Jan. 1896.

ROBERT GARTH SCOTT

BARLOW, Joel (24 Mar. 1754–26 Dec. 1812), businessman, diplomat, and poet, was born in Redding, Connecticut, the son of Samuel Barlow and Esther Hull, fairly well-to-do farmers. Barlow was born the second-to-last child in a large family. Given the size of the family and their farm, Barlow could receive formal education only from the local minister, an education probably interspersed with farm chores. When Barlow was eighteen, his father arranged for his schooling at Moor's Indian School (now Dartmouth) in Hanover, New Hampshire. Barlow began his studies there in 1772, yet his father's death shortly thereafter made it necessary for Barlow to return home. He entered Yale College with the class of 1778. At Yale Barlow began to give evidence of an interest in poetry, in moral and political philosophy, and in science as a key to the improvement of the human condition. His first published poem, a broadside publication, was a satire in pseudobiblical verse about the bad food served in Yale commons. Although he wrote poems throughout his college days, Barlow's best-known college verses were verse orations delivered at two Yale commencements, *The Prospect of Peace* (1778) and *A Poem, Spoken at the Public Commencement at Yale College* (1781).

Barlow's college years were interrupted by the revolutionary war, in which he took part as chaplain of the Third Massachusetts Brigade. The chaplain's post enabled him to continue writing poetry at the encouragement of family and friends. His secret engagement in 1779 to Ruth Baldwin, whose father wished her to select a more practical suitor, caused the two young people a good deal of concern, for secret engagements in Connecticut were punishable at law. They eventually married in 1781, and their marriage endured until his death; they had no children. When the war (and thus his chaplainship) ended, Barlow sought patrons for his writing and opened a printing and stationer's store in Hartford.

Barlow considered himself destined—if he could only find the right topic—to be the epic poet of the United States. Looking for something that would appeal to a wide American audience, he searched through possible topics for long poems, from Jesus as the Messiah to epic battles from the Bible. Finally, with a little nudging from his former college tutor, Joseph Buckminster, who advised against biblical themes, Barlow settled on the Columbian "discovery" of the Americas. In 1787 he published *The Vision of Columbus*, an epic poem in nine books, ranging spatially and temporally from South America through North America and from the point of contact of Europeans and native peoples to the era just after the Revolution, culminating in a celebration of the future progress of the Americas in the arts, the sciences, and international commerce. The subscription list of the book was long, and it included such eminent Americans as George Washington and Benjamin Franklin as well as Louis XVI, king of France. Barlow became one of the first well-known English-speaking poets to discuss Columbus's entrance to the Americas as if it had been a heaven-granted mission that would, as the success of the American Revolution demonstrated, assist what was considered the necessary progress of all people.

In addition to this major publication success, Barlow was selected in 1787 by the Scioto Associates, a group of businessmen interested in selling to Europeans lands in present-day Ohio, to be their European representative. He sailed for Europe in 1788, embarking on a career that would last only several months but that would provide Barlow the opportunity to meet many of the most influential people in England and France, including Thomas Paine, who became a lifelong friend, William Blake, Richard Price, Joseph Priestley, Mary Wollstonecraft, the marquis de Lafayette, and Brissot de Warville. When the Scioto venture ended in a debacle for the French émigrés to the United States and in public shame (with Barlow exonerated of blame) for the scheming land-grabbers among the Scioto Associates, Barlow entered a career path more familiar to him—journalism and poetry on social and political themes—as the Bastille fell in France and the French Revolution advanced.

Barlow's seventeen years abroad gave him the intellectual freedom and impetus to pursue projects that would not have been condoned in conservative, Federalist America. With the onset of the French Revolution in 1789, Barlow initiated what would be a long career in social and political propaganda. Ruth Barlow joined him in France and then in England in 1790, yet he moved from England to France and back again as the currents of revolution ebbed and flowed. Barlow's writings during these turbulent years suggest a twofold concern: to show that revolution was a necessary outcome of an immoral and decrepit system of monarchic tyranny and to indicate to people of both the lowest and highest social stations that peaceful revolution was possible if peaceful revolution was what both groups sought. These two concerns are evident whether one is reading his poem "The Conspiracy of Kings" (written and published during the winter of 1791–1792, in response to the conservative British backlash against revolutionary events in France) or his polemic tracts in prose *Advice to the Privileged Orders in the Several States of Europe, Resulting from the Necessity and Propriety of a General Revolution in the Principle of Government* (1792) and *A Letter to the National Convention of France, on the Defects in the Constitution of 1791 . . .* (1792).

As one of the few Americans abroad at this time who played an active role in the political crises unfolding, Barlow had an especially favorable influence, precisely because he was a U.S. citizen, over young working men. Indeed, his influence was similar to the sway held by Thomas Paine and, later, William Blake, with both of whom Barlow collaborated as part of the circle of radical free-thinking writers supported by London printer and bookseller Joseph Johnson. Like his friends Paine and Wollstonecraft, Barlow sought to contradict Edmund Burke's *Reflections on the Revolution in France* (1790), a stubborn, emotive, and conservative response against the French Revolution written by one who had been a friend to American independence. Also like Paine, and with George Washington, Barlow was named during the first days of the French National Assembly a French citizen, an honor shared with few Englishmen and Americans. Encouraged to run for political office as the assembly was redistricting French lands, Barlow took a public tour to Savoy to campaign for an office in that area. While on tour, he wrote and published (in the spring of 1793) "The Hasty-Pudding," a poem that at once marked an affection for agricultural and domestic simplicity while commenting on the more worrisome turns of the French Revolution. Like his French and English friends and acquaintances, Barlow worried that the French king was taken prisoner, but he nonetheless remained optimistic about the outcome of the Revolution. When the king and royal family were killed and some of his closest friends and acquaintances (such as Brissot de Warville and Thomas Paine) were taken prisoner, Barlow wrote from Paris in May 1794 to Ruth Barlow, who had remained in London, "I meddle with no more politics." He witnessed the death of Brissot at the guillotine.

In part to escape the untenable situation in France, Barlow entered a shipping business in Hamburg, where he moved with Ruth Barlow, and in the years 1794 and 1795 they amassed a great fortune running several trading docks. As a U.S. citizen, he could deal commercially in a politically neutral position between France and other European countries seeking goods from around the world. While in Hamburg, Barlow met the celebrated German poet Friedrich Gottlieb Klopstock, whose work, along with other German writers Barlow was reading, caused him to comment in a letter to Ezra Stiles, president of Yale College, that German writings are "more numerous, and perhaps more excellent than those of any other modern nation." The Barlows returned to Paris, just after the Jay Treaty was negotiated between the United States and England and a truce reached between Portugal and Algiers. With their increased wealth and their social connections, they took up with key diplomats for the United States, including James Madison.

Barlow's international connections, his business acumen, and his knowledge of many languages—along with some old friends from the American Revolution—brought him an important and trying appointment as minister to Algiers in 1796. His mission was to seek the release of American prisoners taken captive by Algerian pirates. While Napoleon was entering his first large campaign, driving Austrians out of northern Italy, Barlow was wallowing in plague-ridden Algiers, creatively managing affairs so that 119 American prisoners would be released from their ten years of slavery. Barlow's Algerian mission—to create treaties that would free the Mediterranean of piracy and to ensure

the release of all prisoners taken captive by pirates—lasted until he succeeded in late 1797. He returned to Ruth Barlow in France; the Barlows bought a house in Paris and became patrons of the arts and sciences—and of Robert Fulton, artist, civil engineer, and inventor, who became fond of the Barlows, appreciated their financial support, and lived with them periodically over the course of several years.

By 1805 the intellectual climate in the United States had shifted so that it seemed more accommodating to the liberal, progressive tendencies Barlow espoused. The Barlows returned to the United States in 1804 and established themselves in the Washington community made inviting by the presidency of their friend Thomas Jefferson. They bought a large house that they called "Kalorama" and to which they invited many of Washington's artists and artisans. The Barlows remained in Washington in social and intellectual prominence, while Barlow himself tinkered with a number of literary projects and met with political leaders. In 1806 he published *Prospectus of a National Institution*, in which he proposed, too much before its time, a national institution in the United States for the arts and sciences. Offering to open their files to him, his friends Jefferson, James Monroe, and James Madison encouraged Barlow to write a history of America. He considered this project carefully but instead continued with Robert Fulton a long poem titled "The Canal: A Poem on the Application of Physical Science to Political Economy," designed to promote the nation's interest in and the development of technologies for social improvement and environmental change. In 1807 Barlow published *The Columbiad* (1807), a ten-book and much-reworked version of his 1787 *Vision of Columbus*. In the later poem the events of the American Revolution are developed more fully and enhanced; the Revolution as a whole carries less progressivist millennial import and far greater significance as a means for the advancement of the arts and sciences. The Christian trinity is entirely replaced with a triad of "equality, free election, and federal band." This triad becomes, by book ten—after the people of the world trample in the dust "the mask of priesthood and the mace of kings"—"one centred system, one all ruling soul" that would "live thro the parts and regulate the whole." To today's readers, the diction might sound stilted and unimaginative; for Barlow's readers, it was meant to indicate the high importance of this epic theme. The poem was beautifully printed into a book that was probably more popular as a showpiece of the bookmaker's craft than as a prophetic poem about the American experience.

Barlow might have preferred to think of himself as an author, but his career as a diplomat was not over. He was called on once again, this time by his friend President Madison in 1811, to negotiate a treaty with Napoleon. In December 1812, attempting to get Napoleon's signature on a minor treaty with the United States, Barlow located him in Russia, fleeing back to France only slightly in advance of his tattered and defeated army. The Russians were chasing Napoleon back through Wilna and then to Warsaw. First attempting to catch him and then tracking his backward steps, Barlow caught pneumonia in the rigorous and icy journey. Barlow's disgust at Napoleon and at the outcome of what he had once considered a glorious revolution is evident in a poem found among his private papers and first published in the twentieth century, "Advice to a Raven in Russia." Denouncing the destruction of war, Barlow described the frozen corpses left behind while Napoleon retreated: "Mere trunks of ice, tho limb'd like human frames," which, frozen in gory silence, "cannot taint the air, the world impest." Such was the bleak, last poetic picture created by one who, in his Yale commencement poem, *The Prospect of Peace*, had begun so assuredly on the conclusion of the American Revolution with the proclamation, "The closing scenes of Tyrants' fruitless rage,/ The opening prospects of a golden age,/ . . . Wake the glad song, and claim th'attentive ear."

At the time of his death in Zarnowiec, Poland, Barlow was in the middle of planning a multivolume edition of his collected writings. Little could he have known that by the middle of the twentieth century, his epic poems would be criticized for their stiffness, and his quickly written poem, "The Hasty-Pudding" (published in Europe in 1793 and in the United States in 1796), would be the most popular of his writings. Despite Barlow's youthful hopes to remain known to posterity for his literary accomplishments, his international political involvements seem, from this perspective, far more crucial. No one before Joel Barlow had managed—for more than a century—to free Algerian prisoners. It was Barlow who saved Thomas Paine's *Age of Reason* from the French police who took Paine to prison. Barlow's intellectual pursuits influenced scientific goals such as canal building and the development of steam engines. His project of a national institution (an idea sponsored by others, such as his childhood friend Noah Webster and Benjamin Franklin before them both) was prominently promoted in Washington by Barlow's very presence there. Each accomplishment alone suggests Barlow's importance. All of his endeavors, combined with his writings, provide an important example of preindustrial, nationalist concerns of progressive members of the elite class.

• Barlow had a wide personal and professional correspondence; manuscripts and letters in Barlow's hand are scattered in different repositories across the United States. By far the largest collection of Barlow's manuscripts is at the Houghton Library, Harvard University, but this is by no means an exclusive collection. Other distinguished collections are at the Beinecke Library, Yale University; the Library of Congress; and the John Carter Brown Library, Brown University. Barlow's publications are many; they include poems and prose tracts, translations of French writers, and writings published originally in France, some of them in French. In addition to the publications mentioned above, Barlow published several other important items, *An Elegy on the Late Honorable Titus Hosmer* (1782), *A Translation of Sundry Psalms Which Were Omitted in Doctor Watts's Version* (1785), *An Oration, Delivered . . . at the Meeting of the Connecticut Society of the Cincin-*

nati (1787), *The Second Warning or Strictures on the Speech Delivered by John Adams, President of the United States at the Opening of Congress . . . in November Last* (1798), *Joel Barlow to His Fellow Citizens of the United States* (1800, 1801), and *Letter to Henri Gregoire* (1809). His translations from French include J. P. Brissot de Warville's *New Travels in the United States of America, Performed in 1788* (1792) and, with Thomas Jefferson, Constantin Volney's *A New Translation of Volney's Ruins; or, Meditations on the Revolution of Empires* (2 vols., 1802).

Charles Burr Todd, *Life and Letters of Joel Barlow, LL.D., Poet, Statesman, Philosopher* (1886), the first full-length biography, contains many errors. It has been superseded by two studies of Barlow's early years, Theodore A. Zunder, *The Early Days of Joel Barlow . . .* (1934), and Victor Clyde Miller, *Joel Barlow, Revolutionist, London, 1791–92* (1932), along with the comprehensive critical biography by James Woodress, *A Yankee's Odyssey: The Life of Joel Barlow* (1958). Of the several dissertations on Barlow, Milton Cantor, "The Life of Joel Barlow" (Columbia Univ., 1954), is excellent as a biographical source. See also Kenneth Ray Ball, "A Great Society: The Social and Political Thought of Joel Barlow" (Ph.D. diss., Univ. of Wisconsin, 1967), and Carla Mulford, "Joel Barlow's Letters, 1775–1788" (Ph.D. diss., Univ. of Delaware, 1984).

CARLA J. MULFORD

BARNABEE, Henry Clay (14 Nov. 1833–16 Dec. 1917), singer and actor, was born in Portsmouth, New Hampshire, the son of Willis Barnabee and Mary (maiden name unknown). His father was a stagecoach driver who became an innkeeper. Willis Barnabee's wife was cook, and his adolescent son Henry was odd-jobs man and at times bartender.

Henry Clay Barnabee's talent was not encouraged by his parents, who distrusted the morality of the musical theater. Only after his father's death in 1862 did Barnabee become a fully professional performer. Long before that, however, he had sung in church choirs (he would continue as the bass of Boston's Church of the Unity Quartet for thirty-three years) and had given well-received recitations. Meanwhile he worked as a clerk in a local dry-goods store, learning business methods that he would later put to use as part owner of the Boston Ideal Opera Company and its successor, the Bostonians.

Barnabee first visited the professional theater on a trip to Boston when he was seventeen, where he saw Lucius Junius Booth in John Howard Payne's tragedy, *Brutus*. When Barnabee moved to Boston in 1854, still a dry-goods clerk, he went to as many plays as possible, analyzed the performances, and paid particular attention to those of William Warren, who represented his ideal comic actor. He also took voice lessons, joined the Handel and Haydn Society, and enrolled in a declamation class.

In 1859 Barnabee married Clara George, socially a step above him; they had no children. When the Civil War broke out, Barnabee tried to enlist, only to be rejected because of a defective eye. He was forced to content himself with playing benefits for Union causes, taking small amateur roles at the Boston Museum, and joining an emergency rifle corps. In 1865 a doctor told him to forsake the dry-goods business for his stomach's sake, whereupon he made a professional concert debut at Boston's Music Hall; in November 1866 he first appeared on the regular stage in a benefit program at the Boston Museum, where he sang and acted with William Warren in J. M. Morton's farce *Box and Cox*.

The next year Barnabee toured in a duologue, or sketch for two performers, called *Too Late for the Train*, and in a popular one-man show, *A Patchwork of Song and Story*, while also organizing the Barnabee Concert Troupe. These productions played at lyceums, a label which represented respectable, educational entertainment. Barnabee next appeared as Ben Kush in Julius Eichberg's *The Two Cadis*, the rest of the small cast being amateurs, and in the title role of Eichberg and Benjamin E. Woolf's one-act operetta, *Sir Marmaduke; or, Too Attentive by Half*.

By 1878 the completely professional singing actor (or acting singer) had earned $15,000, so he and his wife went to England, where they saw Gilbert and Sullivan's newly produced *H.M.S. Pinafore*. Barnabee made copious notes, which were invaluable when he was offered the role of Sir Joseph Porter with the new Boston Ideal Opera Company. Although American audiences had already seen innumerable pirated *Pinafores*, the Boston Ideals (as they were known) proved extraordinarily successful. Critics complimented Barnabee for his quiet but effective manner, his eschewing of broad comedy in favour of delicate humor. *Pinafore* ran for a record nine weeks and led to the production of Franz von Suppé's *Fantinitza*, originally an 1876 Viennese operetta. While Barnabee did not wholly sever relations with his concert company for another five years, he now played more operetta with the Ideals, including the comic leads in other Gilbert and Sullivan works.

Managerial problems within the Ideals led Barnabee and two fellow actors, W. H. MacDonald and Tom Karl, to form a new troupe, the Bostonians, with a core of former "Ideals." Ensemble playing and high standards had been important to the old company and became the keynote of the Bostonians, who also emphasized "clean," i.e., nonsuggestive, performances. At first they included operas in their repertory, but these were soon dropped in favour of operettas. In them Barnabee proved "excruciatingly funny"; his manner was comparatively quiet, and he had discovered W. S. Gilbert's principle that comedy arose when actors took their own absurdities seriously. He relied on his long, mobile face and a "sombre dryness that contrasts oddly with the frivolity of operatic wit" (Strang, p. 176). Moreover, in spite of almost incapacitating stage fright, he gave the appearance of ease.

Increasingly interested in light opera composed by Americans, the Bostonians decided to produce Reginald De Koven and Harry B. Smith's second collaboration, *Don Quixote*, originally written for but not played by DeWolf Hopper. Opening on 18 November 1889 at the Boston Theatre, it had an indifferent reception. As Barnabee said in his memoirs, the galleries "expected extravagant fun . . . and were disappointed; while the

high-brows resented the un-literary liberties. . . ." Moreover, the comedian could not cope physically with such situations as the fight with a windmill. The Bostonians looked elsewhere and accepted Smith and De Koven's proposition for a Robin Hood light opera, which was produced in Chicago on 9 June 1890. Even though its first performance was makeshift, it proved to be the Bostonians' greatest success, prominent in their repertory until they disbanded in July 1904. Barnabee described his role (the Sheriff of Nottingham) as the "crowning of my humble career." He played it more than 1,900 times. Thereafter, the Bostonians premiered a number of other American works, including Victor Herbert's first operetta, *Prince Ananias*, in which Barnabee was "simply inimitable," and his *Serenade*. But none achieved the "everlasting" popularity of *Robin Hood*, not even Smith and De Koven's sequel, *Maid Marian* (1902). By 1904 Barnabee, having spent all his savings to keep the Bostonians going, turned to vaudeville to recoup some of his losses. His debut on 26 August 1904 was well received, but scarcely a month later he tore the ligaments in a knee and was out of the bills. Nevertheless, in 1905 he returned in a "Musical Satire" titled *Cloverdell*, which unfortunately collapsed when its tour manager absconded.

Two enormous benefits in 1906 and 1907 provided Barnabee with enough to live on and demonstrated how beloved the performer had become. They filled his soul, according to his autobiography, "with joy unspeakable." Unfortunately, however, his wife died on Christmas Day 1909. In his later career Barnabee had achieved the soubriquet Dean of Comic Opera for both his excellent bass voice and his restrained but very funny style of acting. When he died in Jamaica Plain, Massachusetts, he had seemingly become aesthetically obsolete, as musical comedy replaced the American operettas that he had done so much to foster. Yet his belief that "the art of acting is the art of seeming natural," that words take precedence in composition over music, and that comedy is funnier when played seriously would, in the new century, prove that his Sheriff's "eagle eye" looked forward, not back.

• Barnabee and his wife collected a great mass of memorabilia throughout most of his career, including reviews, letters, photographs, and playbills, that is now housed in the Portsmouth, N.H., Public Library and described by Martha Schmoyer LoMonaco in "Treasures in the Attic: Gleanings from the Private Archive of Henry Clay Barnabee," *Performing Arts Resources* 16: 93–102. Paul Mroczka drew heavily on these archival materials for his as yet unpublished, illustrated doctoral dissertation, "Henry Clay Barnabee: Change and Stasis in America" (Tufts Univ., 1993), in which Clay's career is discussed in terms of his changing theatrical, social, and industrial milieu. Barnabee's autobiography, *My Wanderings: Reminiscences of Henry Clay Barnabee, Being an Attempt to Account for His Life, with Some Excuses for His Professional Career*, ed. George Leon Varney (1913), provides a foundation for any discussion of Barnabee's character and achievements, although some details are not completely accurate. Lewis C. Strang's chapter on Barnabee in *Celebrated Comedians of Light Opera and Musical Comedy in America* (1901) treats the comedian less enthusiastically than does Frank A.

Munsey in "The Dean of Light Opera," *Munsey's Magazine*, Mar. 1895. For background on the operettas performed by the Boston Ideal Opera Company and the Bostonians, one might begin with Morris Bacheller, "The Bostonians," *Munsey's Magazine*, Aug. 1892. Jane W. Stedman's "'Then Hey! For the Merry Greenwood'; Smith and deKoven and *Robin Hood*," *Journal of Popular Culture*, no. 3 (Winter 1978): 432–45, publishes the plot and some lyrics from *Robin Hood*.

JANE W. STEDMAN

BARNARD, Chester Irving (7 Nov. 1886–7 June 1961), telephone executive, foundation president, and management theorist, was born in Malden, Massachusetts, the son of Charles H. Barnard, a machinist, and Mary E. Putnam. His mother died when Chester was five. Apprenticed as a piano tuner, he worked his way through preparatory school at Mount Hermon Academy in Northfield, Massachusetts, and won a scholarship to Harvard, where he supplemented his income by tuning pianos and running a small dance band. He studied economics and languages but failed to receive a degree because he lacked a laboratory science course, which he felt he could not complete and yet "do all the work I had to do to eat." In 1909 he was employed by American Telephone and Telegraph Corporation (AT&T) in the statistical department, studying the rate-setting practices of European telephone companies. He married Grace Frances Noera in 1911. They had one child.

Barnard's expertise in rate-setting practices led to his appointment to the United States Telephone Administration during World War I. After the war he worked at AT&T headquarters and gave seminars on rate-setting practices to corporate executives. He was promoted to assistant vice president and general manager of the Bell Telephone Company of Pennsylvania in 1922. In 1925 he was promoted to vice president of Pennsylvania Bell and in 1927 became president of New Jersey Bell.

Although Barnard was a busy executive, his intellectual curiosity led him to read the writings of economists and sociologists and to express his notions about organizations. His best-known work, *The Functions of the Executive* (1938), was an expansion of eight lectures given at the Lowell Institute in Boston in 1937. To Barnard, the study of organizations had been obstructed by too much emphasis on the nature of the state and the church and the concomitant stress on the origin and nature of authority. Most research had focused on social unrest and reform and had included "practically no reference to formal organization as the concrete social process by which social action is largely accomplished." Social failures throughout history, he felt, were due to the failure to provide for human cooperation within organizations. In *Organization and Management* (1948), a collection of speeches and articles, he presented his views on personnel relations, the functions and pathologies of status systems in organizations, leadership, and executive education. The human relations pioneer Fritz Roethlisberger recalled that Barnard was "the one and only executive in capacity who could not only run a successful organization but could also talk intelligently about what he was up to in the process."

Barnard's enthusiasm for organizational work carried over to his work in numerous not-for-profit foundations. He served as president of the United Service Organizations for National Defense (USO) (1942–1945); as president of the General Education Board of the Rockefeller Foundation (1948–1952); as chairman of the National Science Board (1950–1956); and as chairman of the National Science Foundation (1952–1954). He was also a frequent adviser to government agencies. Illustrative of this service were his membership on the Hoover Committee on the Reorganization of the Executive Branch of the Federal Government, the Task Force on Personnel and Civil Service—the Second Hoover Commission, and the Atcheson-Lilienthal Committee on the Control of Atomic Energy.

He continued to serve and advise numerous community and educational organizations in New Jersey until his death in New York City.

• Manuscripts and copies of Barnard's published and unpublished articles, letters, and speeches are in the Barnard Collection, Baker Library, Harvard University. A complete bibliography of Barnard's published and unpublished writings may be found in William B. Wolf, *The Basic Barnard: An Introduction to Chester I. Barnard and His Theories of Organization and Management* (1974). Barnard's place in management history may be found in Daniel A. Wren, *The Evolution of Management Thought*, 3d ed. (1987). Biographical information and a comprehensive listing of Barnard's service in the not-for-profit sector is in William B. Wolf, "Chester I. Barnard," in *The Golden Book of Management*, ed. Lyndall F. Urwick and William B. Wolf, rev. ed. (1984).

DANIEL A. WREN

BARNARD, Daniel Dewey (11 Sept. 1796–24 Apr. 1861), lawyer, congressman, and diplomat, was born in East Hartford, Connecticut, the son of Timothy Barnard, a county judge, and Phebe Dewey. Barnard's early years were spent on the family farm near Hartford, Connecticut. When he was twelve the family moved to Mendon, New York (near Rochester). His formal education started with a year at Lenox Academy, after which he transferred to Williams College, where he graduated in 1818.

After graduation Barnard returned to Rochester and worked as a clerk in a law office. He practiced law in Rochester after being admitted to the bar in 1821. He became district attorney for Monroe County in 1825. That same year Barnard married Sarah Livingston, the daughter of Henry Gilbert Livingston, a man of means and the great-grandson of Robert G. Livingston, the first Lord of Livingston Manor. She died in 1829, and in 1832 he married Catherine Walsh of Albany. He had one child with his first wife and another with his second.

Barnard was elected to Congress as a National Republican in 1826, serving one term as the representative from the Rochester area, a fast-growing manufacturing center that included many entrepreneurs. In

Congress Barnard identified himself as a supporter of John Quincy Adams and spoke out on the major issues of the day. He supported a protective tariff and a national program of internal improvements. His views on slavery, however, were more complex. In a speech before Congress in February 1827, he stressed his belief in the humanity of the slave and that he considered slaves to be men. However, he also looked forward to colonization—removing blacks to Africa—as the best means for dealing with slavery. He also was careful to point out that he intended no hostility toward the South. After serving one term in Congress, he traveled through Europe and then returned to Rochester, where he resumed his law practice in 1829.

Barnard moved to Albany, New York, in 1832. As the seat of state government, it appeared an ideal place to further his political ambition. He ran for Congress as a Whig in 1834 and was defeated. He was elected to the state assembly in 1837 and one year later ran successfully for Congress on the Whig ticket. He served three terms and when the Whigs were in power, chaired the Judiciary Committee.

During this second stint in Congress, Barnard supported Henry Clay's brand of Whiggery and in particular his American System. Barnard was an economic and political nationalist who believed in positive action by the federal government and in an interpretation of the U.S. Constitution that supported economic nationalism. He was a lifelong defender of protective tariffs, federally sponsored internal improvements, and a national bank. However, his nationalistic outlook did not extend to federal interference with slavery, an issue on which he continued to favor state sovereignty.

Through his many writings and speeches, Barnard expressed his opposition to the politics of Andrew Jackson. He never accepted the newer politics of the Jacksonian era, with its appeal for mass support. Whether advocated by Whigs or Democrats, he favored the paternalistic and patrician approach in which gentlemen stood for office. He was a constant critic of Jackson and believed that government by the Jacksonians would bring chaos to an otherwise orderly society.

In the 1840s Barnard was a strong critic of the Mexican War, which he called an "executive war," meaning that proper consultation with Congress had been lacking. In contrast with many Whigs who were antislavery, he was a staunch antiabolitionist. He also fought against the temperance movement and against legislation to benefit labor and the poor. He was a chief spokesman in New York as well as throughout the nation for the conservative proslavery branch of the Whig party, and he opposed the Whig leaders Thurlow Weed and William Henry Seward.

In 1850 Barnard was appointed U.S. minister to Prussia by President Millard Fillmore. While in Berlin his main tasks were to attend social functions and ease any difficulties experienced by Americans traveling in Prussia.

When he returned to Albany from Berlin in the fall of 1853, he continued to enjoy a reputation as a lecturer and frequently addressed educational and literary societies. He used his lectures, many of which were published, to outline his belief in the importance of education, the duty of the scholar toward society, and the inevitability of progress. His philosophy was grounded in his own brand of conservatism, the central theme of which was his belief in determinism and the desirability of slow evolutionary change as opposed to radical reform movements. These ideas had been consistently expressed in his speeches and writings. In his Phi Beta Kappa address at Union College in 1837, he lashed out at those who wanted to sweep away all differences in society. He decried the attempt "to bring all the distinctive qualities of the human character to a [common] level . . . by depressing those which are . . . noble, and exalting such as are . . . low. . . . God has made men to differ in intellectual endowment, as in stature and aspect . . . some among them are always fitted for high employment and great affairs, and many are not." In his later years he grew increasingly concerned about the rapid pace of social change and continued to oppose what he stressed in this speech as a tendency toward leveling the society.

During the 1850s the differences within the New York Whig party became more extreme. Barnard continued to oppose the antislavery Conscience Whigs of the North and asked that there be no interference with slavery in the South. When the Weed branch of the party joined with the Republicans, Barnard would not go along and instead suggested a reorganization of the Whig party into a compromise and conservative party. As a Cotton Whig, he continued to stress his fear that the slavery issue would have a divisive effect on the Whig party and on the nation as a whole. Accordingly, he strongly opposed the Republican party and in his later years called on conservatives to support the Democrats and, even later, the Constitutional Union ticket.

No longer optimistic about the future of his country, in 1855, in a letter to Hamilton Fish, he discussed his concern about the republic and disunion. He saw the Republicans as a party that would keep the slavery issue alive and force the South to take action. Hence his prediction that if the Republicans were elected, disunion would follow. He believed that, if left alone, slavery would eventually disappear. He died in Albany in April 1861. On the day of his death, the newspaper headlines were devoted to the war—a war he had predicted and feared.

Born to wealth, Barnard was educated in the classical tradition and reared as a strict Protestant. His life exemplified the dilemma of a committed conservative confronted with a rapidly changing society.

• The major Barnard manuscript collection is in the Daniel Dewey Barnard Papers in the New York State Library. Other Barnard manuscripts are in the private collection of Mrs. John DeWitt Peltz of New York City as well as papers in the Rochester Historical Society Library, the Library of Congress, the New-York Historical Society, and the New York Public Library. The only biography of Barnard is Sherry H. Penney, *Patrician and Politics: Daniel Dewey Barnard of New York* (1974), which also includes a full list of Barnard's more than seventy published articles and speeches. Articles on Barnard include Penney, "Dissention within the Whig Ranks," *New-York Historical Society Quarterly* 59 (Jan. 1975): 71–92, and Arthur Ekirch, Jr., "Daniel Dewey Barnard, Conservative Whig," *New York History* 45 (Oct. 1947): 420–39. Obituaries are in the Albany *Evening Journal*, 24 Apr. 1861, and the Albany *Argus*, 26 Apr. 1861.

SHERRY H. PENNEY

BARNARD, Edward Emerson (16 Dec. 1857–6 Feb. 1923), astronomer, was born in Nashville, Tennessee, the son of Reuben Barnard and Elizabeth Jane Haywood. Barnard's parents were very poor, and his father died three months before Edward was born. His mother, who brought him and his older brother Charles up alone, began teaching Edward to read from the Bible when he was very young. With no more than two months' schooling, however, Barnard went to work full-time at the age of nine to support his mother and brother. His job, in a Nashville photographer's studio, involved keeping a huge solar "camera" pointed at the sun, the light source for making enlarged prints. Barnard thus learned for himself the apparent daily motion of the sun and its changes through the year resulting from the earth's orbital motion. He advanced to doing all kinds of photographic work in the studio and became an expert in photographic techniques. Barnard tried to study academic subjects on his own, but, as he lacked even the most basic resources, it was very difficult for him. At the age of eighteen he acquired from a boyhood friend a volume by the Reverend Thomas Dick, a writer of sermons and popular articles on astronomy, with "moral and religious reflections" on the wonders of the universe. This book started Barnard on his career in astronomy. An older friend made a two-inch telescope for him from a secondhand spyglass tube and a lens he bought, and with it Barnard began observing the phases of Venus, the four moons of Jupiter that Galileo had discovered, and the craters, mountains, and rills on the moon.

In 1877 Barnard bought a five-inch astronomical telescope, which cost him $380, two-thirds of his annual salary, and with it he began serious observing on his own, recording all that he saw. Later that same year he wangled an introduction to Simon Newcomb, the most famous astronomer of the time, who was in Nashville for a scientific meeting. Barnard asked how he could make himself useful in astronomy; Newcomb replied that he should learn mathematics and French. Barnard, depressed, tried for a time to follow this stern advice, but with little success. However, Newcomb had also advised him that he could try to discover comets with his telescope, and this suggestion Barnard pursued avidly and very successfully. Working in the studio all day and studying on the nights when the moon made the sky too bright, he otherwise searched for comets and reported the finding of his first new one in 1881. For this discovery he received a prize of $200 given by H. H. Warner, a patent-medicine entrepreneur and astronomy devotee, for each newly found

comet. The award provided a sizeable and welcome addition to Barnard's yearly income. Earlier that same year he had married Rhoda Calvert, the sister of one of his fellow workers at the studio; they were to have no children. With the Warner prize money Barnard bought a lot, which he mortgaged to build his first small house, where he, his wife, and his mother lived. He continued to search tirelessly for comets and found several more, each of which helped pay off the mortgage on the "comet house," as it became known in Nashville.

Barnard was an extremely keen-eyed visual observer who studied all the planets carefully and reported and documented the new features and changes on most of them. In 1882 he began publishing descriptions of his observations in astronomical journals, thus making himself known to the professionals in the field.

In 1883 Barnard received a fellowship from Vanderbilt University, in Nashville, under which he served as the assistant in charge of its astronomical observatory and became a special student in mathematics. This status exempted him from any degree requirements, and Chancellor L. C. Garland's plan was that sometime in the future Barnard would become the professor of astronomy. His stipend was $500, together with the use of a house on the campus rent-free. By then Barnard was corresponding regularly with several astronomers and occasionally attending scientific meetings. With his keen eyes he was discovering at the telescope faint nebulae that previous observers had been unable to see.

In 1887 Edward S. Holden, who was to become the director of Lick Observatory on Mount Hamilton in northern California as soon as its 36-inch refractor, the largest telescope in the world, was completed, offered Barnard a position on its initial staff. By now his mother was dead, and he seized the opportunity. He resigned his Vanderbilt fellowship and arrived in San Francisco nine months before the telescope was ready for use. As soon as the observatory opened on 1 June 1888, he started work and within three months discovered two more comets there, using its smaller twelve-inch telescope. But his main work was wide-field photography of the Milky Way, which he pioneered. He used a six-inch portrait lens in a camera mounted on a small telescope, which he guided to follow the motion of the stars across the sky. The photographs he obtained with this "Willard lens" showed the myriads of stars in the Milky Way and many dark markings seen against them. At first he thought they were tunnels, devoid of stars, pointing toward the sun, but he gradually came to realize that they revealed the presence of clouds of dark matter, interstellar dust clouds, silhouetted against the rich star fields. This was one of his outstanding discoveries.

At Mount Hamilton Barnard came to dislike Holden, who was a martinet and not at all successful as a research scientist. Their personalities clashed from the moment the observatory opened. Barnard especially resented that Holden assigned him regularly to observe with the twelve-inch refractor, but reserved the

36-inch for himself and the other senior members of the staff. Barnard felt that Holden wasted the telescope time the director assigned himself, and he eventually complained to the regents of the University of California, who ruled in Barnard's favor. They directed Holden to let him use the 36-inch refractor one night a week, and just a few months later, in September 1892, with it Barnard discovered the tiny fifth satellite of Jupiter, Amalthea. This completely unexpected new result made him and Lick Observatory briefly famous. Barnard became a celebrity and began traveling and giving popular lectures on astronomy. He continued his Milky Way photography and prepared a volume of plates of star fields and comets, all taken with the Willard lens, which was published years later.

In 1895 Barnard, tired of the struggle with Holden, accepted a position at Yerkes Observatory, then still being built at Williams Bay, Wisconsin, for the University of Chicago. Its forty-inch refractor, now the largest in the world, went into operation in 1897, and Barnard was one of the first to observe with it. He remained on very good terms with the first director, George Ellery Hale, and his successor, Edwin B. Frost. Barnard succeeded in persuading Catherine Wolfe Bruce, a wealthy recluse, to provide funds to build a wide-field photographic telescope for him to use to continue his work on the Milky Way. It had a ten-inch lens, designed and made to the state of the art of the time, which thus produced considerably larger-scale photographs than the earlier telescope he had used at Lick. Barnard took this Bruce photographic telescope to Mount Wilson and in eight months in 1905 obtained a majority of the plates that were published in his posthumous atlas of the Milky Way. Back at Yerkes, he took the remainder of the plates for it and observed assiduously with the forty-inch refractor, obtaining excellent photographs of globular clusters and smaller nebulae. Yet ironically this pioneer of astronomical photography persisted in trying to measure the minute motions of stars in globular clusters by old-fashioned visual methods, a program that his younger colleague, Frank Schlesinger, had long ago proven could be carried out much better photographically.

Barnard also obtained excellent photographs of the sun's corona at several solar eclipses, beginning with one in California in 1889. His cool nerves and excellent photographic skills enabled him to get the most out of any telescope he used.

In his later years Barnard suffered increasingly from health problems, notably diabetes. Still he observed whenever he could; all of his social engagements he made with the proviso that he would leave if the skies cleared and the telescope was assigned to him. He was famous for climbing up the big observatory dome on a long ladder in the middle of the night to chip off the ice if the slit though which the starlight would enter was frozen shut. Barnard's wife died in 1921, and the spark went out of his life. His niece and scientific assistant, Mary R. Calvert, cared for him until his death at his home in Williams Bay. He had gone farther in astronomy with less formal education than anyone of his

generation and had made numerous discoveries by the old visual methods and the new photographic ones.

• The most complete collection of Barnard's letters is in the Special Collections Department, Vanderbilt University Library. There are other large collections of his papers in the Mary Lea Shane Archives of the Lick Observatory, University Library, University of California, Santa Cruz, and in the Yerkes Observatory Archives, Williams Bay, Wis. Barnard published his best wide-field photographs taken at Lick Observatory in "Photographs of the Milky Way and of comets made with the six-inch Willard lens and Crocker telescope in the years 1892 to 1895," *Publications of the Lick Observatory* (1913): 1–45, and his later work along this line was published in *A Photographic Atlas of Selected Regions of the Milky Way*, with E. B. Frost and M. R. Calvert (1927). The best published sources on his life and scientific career is the excellent biography by William Sheehan, *The Immortal Fire Within: The Life and Work of Edward Emerson Barnard* (1995). The memorial biography by Edwin B. Frost, "Edward Emerson Barnard 1857–1924," National Academy of Sciences, *Memoirs* 21 (1924): 19th Memoir, 1–32, was written soon after his death and contains a complete bibliography of his published scientific papers and books.

DONALD E. OSTERBROCK

BARNARD, Frederick Augustus Porter (5 May 1809–27 Apr. 1889), scientist and university president, was born in Sheffield, Massachusetts, the son of Robert Foster Barnard, an attorney, and Augusta Porter. He attended school at the Saratoga Academy across the state border in New York and then at the Stockbridge Academy, where he was a classmate and friendly rival of Mark Hopkins, later president of Williams College. In 1824, at age fifteen, Barnard entered Yale, where men on his mother's side had traditionally been educated. He was the youngest member of his class and its best student in mathematics. In later life, like most of his generation of university-builders, Barnard had little good to say about his own collegiate education. Rampant alcoholism, inaccessible professors, and "students as distressing moral wrecks" figure prominently among his retrospective complaints. What training in mathematics he acquired was through "almost literal self-education." That this was the same Yale its president and faculty stoutly defended in their *Yale Faculty Report* in 1828 speaks to the contemporary divergence in educational views between faculty and students, to Barnard's later souring on his undergraduate experience, or, more likely, to both.

Barnard turned to teaching upon graduation in 1828, although not necessarily as a career choice. He began at the Hartford Grammar School, which served as a training ground for Yale tutors, where for two years he taught ten- to thirteen-year-olds mathematics and celestial navigation. While in Hartford he began building an extensive network of friends that he sedulously maintained through correspondence throughout his lifetime. There, too, he first experienced a partial loss of hearing, a hereditary condition perhaps brought on by respiratory problems. The onset of this lifelong condition effectively ended any thoughts he had of becoming a lawyer; however, he did not consider his condition as preventing a career in teaching, as is evidenced by his acceptance in 1830 of a one-year appointment as a tutor at Yale.

When Barnard began tutoring, the traditional Yale system required that a tutor stay with and provide all instruction for the same section of the freshman class through its first three years. In proposing to his fellow tutors that he take on all the instruction in mathematics for all members of the freshman class, and that the other tutors similarly identify themselves by a teaching "specialty," Barnard quietly effected a significant change in the academic culture. His arrangement quickly became the rule. No longer was a disciplinary specialization something that occurred much later in a Yale tutor's teaching career with the bestowal of a professorial chair. In widening the gap between tutors and students, Barnard had pointed Yale—and the rest of American higher education—to the future.

For all his early success as an educational reformer, Barnard's deteriorating hearing obliged him to give up his Yale tutorship after a year to return to Hartford, this time as a teacher of deaf children at the Connecticut Asylum for Education of the Deaf and Dumb. In 1832 he moved to the New York State Institution for the Deaf and Dumb, where his growing reputation as a skillful teacher of the deaf preceded him. That Barnard himself suffered from deafness gave him an insider's understanding of the handicaps under which his students labored, while a natural facility with languages (he eventually spoke eleven) undoubtedly contributed to his effectiveness. An 1834 article published in the *North American Review* describing his instructional methods gave him national recognition in this challenging field. But Barnard continued to think of himself principally as a mathematician. An 1837 article in Benjamin Silliman's *American Journal of Science*, "On the Aurora Borealis," indicated his availability for a respectable scientific appointment. None was available at Yale, particularly with his recent switch from his family's Calvinist Congregational church to the Episcopal church fashionable among his New York friends. Yale's President Jeremiah Day did, however, recommend Barnard for the position of professor of mathematics and natural philosophy at the recently opened University of Alabama in Tuscaloosa. Barnard received the appointment and set sail from New York for Mobile in the summer of 1837.

Barnard was very slow to adapt to his new and decidedly rustic circumstances in Tuscaloosa. His deafness presented a persistent problem, both in class and with faculty and townspeople. So did his occasional public drinking to excess, a tendency that persisted until his marriage in 1847 to a 23-year-old visitor to Alabama from Ohio, Margaret McMurray. According to local lore he proposed when drunk. Thereafter he became a conspicuous nonimbiber. The marriage produced no children.

During his eighteen years in Alabama, Barnard worked hard through public lectures and demonstrations to interest the citizens of his adopted region in supporting mathematical and astronomical studies.

He specifically urged the building of an observatory in Tuscaloosa. These latter efforts culminated in 1846 with the opening of the Alabama state observatory, only a year after Harvard had opened the nation's first. Barnard gained notoriety from his spectacular public demonstrations; for example, he commandeered the recently vacated state capitol and suspended a pendulum from its 200-foot-high rotunda to replicate Foucault's experiment that demonstrates the earth's orbital rotation. Such efforts endeared him to scientific colleagues in New Haven and Cambridge ("The Lazzaroni," an informal network of scientists who sought in the 1840s and 1850s to give direction to American science) who were organizing the American Association for the Advancement of Science, in which Barnard was a charter member at its founding in 1847 and of which he subsequently became president (1860–1864). When not teaching and meeting his obligations throughout the South as a leading spokesman for science, Barnard filled in as Tuscaloosa's photographer and its de facto newspaper editor.

Barnard's relations with the University's president, Basil Manly, were never cordial. Neither Manly's religion—he was a Baptist—nor his politics—those of a southern nationalist—attracted him to the hard-of-hearing Episcopalian Whig from the North. In 1854 they had a public falling out over two issues, student discipline and curricular reform. In response to public pressure, Manly spoke out against the faculty-enforced policy that required student bystanders at disruptions to identify the ringleaders or be expelled and spoke in favor of such students' merely swearing to their noninvolvement. Barnard opposed this change as depriving the faculty of the only coercive power they had in their losing battle with rebellious undergraduates. Manly also favored an elective system in which individual performance was graded along the lines advanced by Brown University's Francis Wayland in his *Thoughts on the Present Collegiate System* (1842) and partially implemented by President Josiah Quincy at Harvard, although he was politically astute enough to identify the reforms with Thomas Jefferson. In a series of "Letters on College Government," Barnard defended the traditional performance evaluations of his Yale undergraduate days, where all classes were required and individual grades were not assigned. Manly prevailed on both issues, and Barnard avoided being forced out by resigning from the university to accept an appointment as professor of physics, astronomy and civil engineering at the University of Mississippi. The precariousness of his professional position can be inferred from his decision, upon arriving in Oxford in 1856, to become ordained as an Episcopal priest.

Barnard remained at Oxford for seven years, the last three as university chancellor. Questions were raised at his coming about his being "unsound on the slavery question," but his testimony to the trustees (and the fact that he owned slaves) gave his local critics few grounds to challenge his regional loyalties. Only with the university's closing in 1861 upon the state's secession from the Union and the commencement of the

Civil War did Barnard reveal to scientific contacts in the North his Unionist sentiments. Visiting with his wife in Norfolk, Virginia, when Union troops overran the town, Barnard used the occasion to pass through Union lines and continue north to Washington, D.C., where his younger brother John was in charge of Union troops protecting the capital. Once out of the South, Barnard declared both his allegiance to the Union—most fulsomely in his "Letter to the President of the United States by a Refugee"—and his availability for employment beyond his temporary position at the U.S. Coastal Survey. Friends had already brought him to the attention of the Columbia College trustees, who were then in search of a new president. In 1864 he was appointed the tenth president of Columbia College.

Barnard's career as president of Columbia extended over a quarter century, second only in length to that of Nicholas Murray Butler (1902–1947). During his tenure Columbia College was transformed from a sleepy institution with an enrollment of some 150 undergraduates, drawn almost entirely from New York City's Episcopal establishment, to Columbia University in the City of New York (although officially not so designated until 1896). The university, with graduate and undergraduate enrollments approaching 2,000 and a burgeoning Ph.D. program, had ambitions that were soon to number it among the world's leading universities. This noted, Barnard has seldom been accorded equal billing with Harvard's Charles William Eliot or Daniel Coit Gilman of Johns Hopkins, both of whom he preceded in his presidency, or even with Chicago's William Rainey Harper, who came later, as among the great American university-builders. Even among his Columbia colleagues he has often been viewed as less important than some influential trustees, among them Samuel Ruggles, or enterprising and self-promoting faculty, chief among these the political scientist John W. Burgess. This assessment, understandable given his earlier academic conservativism and his physically infirm appearance during much of his Columbia presidency, is unfair. By the time he came to New York he had left far behind any residual loyalties to "the old time college" and was a thoroughly up-to-date academic reformer. Early on in his presidency, he used his *Annual Reports* to document the decline in college attendance (1866) and to question the centrality of the classics (1872). Later he used the *Reports* to align Columbia with the reform-minded in Baltimore and Cambridge and against the academic advocates of the status quo in New Haven and Princeton.

In his support for coeducation Barnard was conspicuously ahead of his presidential contemporaries, his trustees, and his faculty. His 1879 *Annual Report* forthrightly called for admission of women to Columbia College. In 1883 he succeeded in securing from a reluctant board and an openly hostile faculty an experimental arrangement by which young women might receive off-campus instruction from Columbia faculty and then sit for Columbia College exams. This arrangement satisfied no one, including the twenty-eight women who enrolled between 1883 and 1888. Burgess actively lobbied against any more gestures toward coeducation, arguing that such a change would transform Columbia into a women's seminary, and a "Hebrew women's seminary" at that.

In 1888 several prominent New Yorkers, chief among them Annie Nathan Meyers, presented the Columbia trustees with a proposal for establishing a women's college resembling Harvard's recently adopted "Annex," which later became Radcliffe. While falling far short of full coeducation, which had been the ultimate goal of Meyers, the proposal for a separate but affiliated nonresidential institution for women had the support of most advocates for the cause of women's higher education in New York. Barnard, however, opposed it as a half-way measure that would indefinitely keep Columbia from becoming fully coeducational. Only after Columbia's trustees supported the "annex" proposal and its backers offered to name it after him did Barnard lend his support—and name—to the new institution. In 1889, six months after Barnard's death in New York City, Barnard College opened its door across the street from Columbia. It is ironic that Barnard has as his most visible memorial a woman's college whose creation he only reluctantly supported and whose operations he never observed. Yet on another level Barnard College is a most apt memorial to one of the more active participants in the heroic age of American higher education who, albeit belatedly and incompletely, came to identify with its enduring promise of liberation.

• Some of Barnard's presidential papers are to be found in Special Collections and the Columbiana Room, Columbia University. The principal source of information on Barnard's life is John Fulton, *Memoirs of Frederick A. P. Barnard* (1896), the materials for which were compiled by Barnard's widow and include several autobiographical sketches Barnard published during his lifetime, as well as extended excerpts form official documents. William J. Chute, *Damn Yankee! The First Career of Frederick A. P. Barnard* (1978), takes Barnard's biography down to his Columbia appointment and makes good use of manuscript materials in Tuscaloosa and Oxford.

ROBERT A. McCAUGHEY

BARNARD, George Grey (24 May 1863–24 Apr. 1938), sculptor, was born in Bellefonte, Pennsylvania, the son of Joseph H. Barnard, a Presbyterian minister, and Martha Gray Grubbe. Before his seventeenth year, George had moved with his family first to Waukosha, Wisconsin, and later to Chicago and Kankakee, Illinois, and to Muscatine, Iowa. In 1880 Barnard entered the Chicago Academy of Design, the forerunner of the Chicago Art Institute. There he studied under academy founder Leonard Volk, Volk's son Douglas, and sculptor David Richards. Richards introduced Barnard to plaster casts of works by Michelangelo and instilled in him a desire for European study.

Upon his arrival in Paris in 1883 Barnard enrolled in the atelier of the academic sculptor Pierre-Jules

Cavelier at the École des Beaux-Arts. He became a central figure in a group of American artists that consisted of sculptors George E. Bissell, Frederick MacMonnies, and Lorado Taft, and painter William Dodge. In 1886 Barnard met Alfred Corning Clark, an heir to the Singer Manufacturing Company fortunes, who immediately offered Barnard financial support. Barnard moved into spacious new quarters and withdrew from the École. A scholar of Norwegian mythology and a patron of the arts and opera, Clark bought or otherwise commissioned Barnard's first important work, *Boy* (1884) and *Brotherly Love* (1886–1887), both marble, and *Norwegian Stove*, a large porcelain relief begun in 1886 that illustrates the Nordic legend of the Creation. The most significant Clark purchase was *Je sens deux hommes en moi*, or *The Two Natures of Man* (1888–1894), a heroic marble group representing two nude male figures. Inspired by a line from Victor Hugo, the statue, now in the Metropolitan Museum of Art, allegorizes the popular fin de siècle theme of the conflicted soul. *The Two Natures* was exhibited and enthusiastically reviewed at the salon of the Champs de Mars in Paris in 1894. Admirers of Barnard's work, including the sculptor Auguste Rodin, compared him to the young Michelangelo.

Against the advice of Clark and his artist friends, who thought that the United States provided no creative freedom, Barnard returned to the United States in the summer of 1894 to wed Edna Monroe, the daughter of Lewis B. Monroe, the dean of the School of Oratory at Boston University. They settled in Washington Heights in upper Manhattan, where Barnard maintained a studio; the couple occasionally summered at the Monroe estate in Dublin, New Hampshire, the site of an art colony. They had three children. Barnard continued to work on small private commissions and on several large figurative pieces conceived in Paris, including *The Hewer* (1895–1902, marble), and *The God Pan* (1895–1898), which was originally intended for a fountain in New York's Central Park and is now owned by Columbia University. Barnard won a medal for *The Two Natures* at the 1901 Pan-American Exposition in Buffalo and for *The God Pan* at the St. Louis World's Fair in 1904. But a series of misunderstandings among Barnard, governing committees, and architectural supervisors denied him important public commissions. The quarrels isolated Barnard from his prospering Beaux-Arts colleagues, and the great success that Barnard had expected upon his return to the United States never materialized.

Around the turn of the century Barnard made the acquaintance of a loose-knit group of liberal writers, editors, academics, and performance artists. Through the Monroes, Barnard met dramatist-poet Percy W. MacKaye, who became his most lasting friend. Barnard also maintained longtime friendships with journalist Ida M. Tarbell, editor Albert Shaw, and editor-diplomat Walter H. Page. In the hopes of inspiring a patriotic ode to the United States, Isadora Duncan danced before Barnard in 1908. They hoped to produce a figurative tableau entitled "I See America Dancing."

The first of two large commissions that revived Barnard's career came in 1902. He was asked to create two large marble groups made up of nude figures to flank the staircase of the newly erected Capitol of Pennsylvania at Harrisburg. Separated into *Love and Labor: The Unbroken Law* and *The Burden of Life: The Broken Law*, the two groups dramatize the virtues of labor over special interest capitalism and celebrate progressive political views in the context of the Last Judgement. Work on the commission began in 1903 at Moret-sur-Loing near Fontainebleau, France, but the project was suspended in 1906, when charges of corruption encumbered Barnard's $300,000 portion of the building contract. Even though Barnard defaulted on specifications, a volunteer committee of receivers arose to handle Barnard's financial obligations and saw the project to completion. The works were first publicly displayed at the Paris Salon in 1910, where they were admired by Theodore Roosevelt. Once in place, they were dedicated at the Pennsylvania state capitol on 4 October 1911, which was officially declared "Barnard Day."

In 1911 Cincinnati philanthropist Charles P. Taft, brother of President William Howard Taft, commissioned Barnard to execute a statue of Abraham Lincoln. Completed in 1916, the statue was erected in Cincinnati in March 1917. The thirteen-foot-high bronze, which portrays Lincoln as a stooped, disheveled figure attired in wrinkled, ill-fitting clothes, was widely criticized for defaming America's greatest hero. Its detractors also noted that the uncouth, beardless Lincoln resembled a laborer more than a world-renowned statesman. When Charles Taft decided in 1917 to send duplicates of the statue to London's Parliament Square and to riot-torn Petrograd, Russia, a national outcry, led by Lincoln's son Robert Todd Lincoln, demanded that Woodrow Wilson's administration stop the shipment. The Russian project was suspended almost immediately; in 1919 the Lincoln statue designated for London was diverted to Manchester, England, while a duplicate of a more dignified Lincoln statue, previously made for the city of Chicago by Augustus Saint-Gaudens, was erected on the London site. A third copy of Barnard's Lincoln was privately commissioned in 1922 for Louisville, Kentucky.

Barnard's later years were consumed by speculative schemes that in their service to the broad theme of world peace combined sculpture with grandiose theatrical settings. His most extravagant plan envisioned the transformation of the northern end of Manhattan into a giant sculpture park akin to the Athenian Acropolis. As a starting point, Barnard completed work in 1933 on a plaster version of *The Rainbow Arch*. Like the Harrisburg stair groups, the arch divides sets of nude figures, representing refugees, into "good" and "bad" communities, each singly revealing the effects of peace and war. A journalist noted that when describing his concept, Barnard spoke with a "burst of lofty madness and consecration" (Pickering, *Arts and Decoration*, pp. 34–35).

Barnard was also renowned as a collector of medieval art. While waiting out the Harrisburg fiasco in Moret, he began gathering and selling fragments of French Romanesque and Gothic monasteries, well in advance of the popular reappraisal of medieval art. The core pieces of Barnard's personal collection, including the cloisters of Saint-Michel-de-Cuxa, were installed in a brick structure known as the Cloisters, built next to Barnard's Washington Heights residence. The building was opened to the public in 1914 to benefit widows and orphans of French sculptors. In 1925 the contents were purchased by John D. Rockefeller and were deeded to the Metropolitan Museum of Art. The treasures were then reassembled in the Cloisters Museum in Fort Tryon Park. Barnard thereupon began building and stocking a second museum, the Abbaye, whose contents eventually passed into the collection of the Philadelphia Museum of Art.

Barnard had a powerful hold over many of his acquaintances. Marion MacKaye remembered the reaction of those who one evening heard him describe his discovery of a wax imprint of Michelangelo's thumb in the Sistine Chapel: Barnard's listeners were convinced that "he could be anything, make cities, anything; he is such a powerful, marvelous creator" (quoted in Ege). Despite his magnetic presence, Barnard's sculpture, with few exceptions, presents a cold and somewhat mechanical interpretation of the human form. In a time when the passionate creations of Rodin best summarized modern sensibilities, Barnard remained essentially a neoclassicist and a moralist. He died in New York City.

• Barnard's papers are at the Philadelphia Museum of Art, the Bellefonte Historical Society in Bellefonte, Penn., the Pennsylvania State Archives in Harrisburg, and the Kankakee County Historical Society, Ill. The largest single collection of Barnard's work is at the George Grey Barnard Museum at the Kankakee County Historical Society.

For biographical information, see W. A. Coffin, "George Grey Barnard," *Century Magazine* 53 (1897): 877–82; Katherine Roof, "George Grey Barnard: The Spirit of the New World in Sculpture," *Craftsman* 15 (1908): 270–80; A. B. Thaw, "George Grey Barnard, Sculptor," *World's Work* 5 (1902–1903): 2837–53; and W. M. Van der Weyde, "Dramas in Stone: The Art of George Grey Barnard," *Mentor* 11 (Mar. 1923): 19–34. For evaluations of Barnard's work, see the following articles by Harold E. Dickson: "Barnard's Sculptures for the Pennsylvania Capitol," *Art Quarterly* 22, no. 2 (Summer 1959): 126–47; "Origin of the Cloisters," *Art Quarterly* 28, no. 4 (1965): 252–75; "The Other Orphan," *American Art Journal* 1 (Fall 1969): 109–15; "Log of a Masterpiece," *Art Journal* 20 (Spring 1961): 139–43; "George Grey Barnard's Controversial Lincoln," *Art Journal* 27 (Fall 1967): 8–15; and "Barnard and Norway," *Art Bulletin* 44 (Mar. 1962): 55–59. See also Ruth Pickering, "American Sculptor—George Grey Barnard," *Arts and Decoration* 42, no. 1 (Nov. 1934): 34–35, and Arvia M. Ege, *The Power of the Impossible: The Life Story of Percy and Marion MacKaye* (1992).

FREDERICK C. MOFFATT

BARNARD, Hannah Jenkins (1754–27 Nov. 1825), disowned Quaker minister, was born in Dutchess County, New York, the daughter of Valentine Jenkins and his wife (name unknown), farmers. Reared a Baptist in the Hudson River valley, Hannah Jenkins became a convinced Friend at the age of eighteen and in 1779 married a widower with three children, Peter Barnard, originally from the Nantucket Quaker community but then a struggling wagoner in Hudson; the couple was active in the local monthly meeting. They had no children together.

Hannah Barnard was mostly self-educated, reading deeply, according to one report, in the works of French revolutionaries. Recognized as a minister by her meeting, she won note for forceful and eloquent sermons among both Friends and others. She traveled extensively in New England and her native state to testify to the truth she found through reading, meditation, and prayer. Once her views became controversial, she was damned as an infidel and tarred with Unitarianism by fellow believers, but no contemporary hints of such liabilities survive. On the contrary, upon seeking approval in 1797 for a religious trip to the British Isles, her request was granted by monthly and quarterly meetings and even the New York Yearly Meeting.

Barnard was determined and democratic, confident, like generations of her Quaker forebears, of the rectitude of her religious leadings. When she crossed the Atlantic in 1798, she and her traveling companion, Elizabeth Coggeshall, undertook visits to Friends meetings in England, Scotland, and Ireland. Winning acclaim even among Methodists, Barnard first abraded the leadership of the London Yearly Meeting in May 1799 by insisting that Friends open their meetinghouses to ministers of other denominations in return for the same consideration from them. When visiting the homes of Friends, she refused to sit with her hosts until they included their servants. In Ireland she encountered some Friends who opposed the rise of evangelicalism and denigrated the growing stress in biblical literalism. Gravitating to the side of these "New Lights," she began to question openly such orthodox doctrines as the virgin birth of Jesus and his vicarious atonement. More fundamental still, she doubted that God had commanded the ancient Jews to make war on their enemies, thus undermining the authority of the Bible itself. Wars, she insisted, occurred because of human passions and not because God ordered them.

These ideas did not offend Irish Quakers, who endorsed Barnard's labors, but a different reception awaited at the powerful yearly meeting in London in May 1800. Not only did the English ministers refuse to approve her proposed journey with Coggeshall to Germany—a rebuke provoked by David Sands, also an itinerant from New York—but they also ordered her to cease preaching and return home. The formal charge centered on her alleged denial of the Scriptures, while pamphleteers attacked her as a deist supporter of Thomas Paine, an atheist. She did not bend, appealing her sentence, and defended herself with her usual eloquence. She refused money to pay her fare home lest she be seen as acceding to the London Friends' decree.

Back in Hudson late in 1801, Barnard demanded that her meeting deal with her alleged transgressions. They responded by silencing her as a minister and in June 1802 disowned her, decisions that appeals to the quarterly and yearly meetings could not reverse. She occasionally attended her former meeting, but requests to use the local meetinghouse for gatherings of a peace society that she organized at the time of the War of 1812 were rebuffed. In 1820 she published *Dialogues on Domestic and Rural Economy, and the Fashionable Follies of the World*, a booklet featuring a didactic discussion between Lady Homespun and Miss Jenny Prinks. It served as a vehicle for her views on topics as diverse as spendthrifts to *Paradise Lost*, which she considered an assault on womanhood. Despite continued calumnies and charges of Unitarianism by Friends, she apparently never united with that sect. She died at her home in Hudson.

Barnard's disownment caused a major stir in the small world of the Society of Friends, if for no other reason than that she was the only Quaker ever disowned because her principled opposition to war led her to question the authority of the Scriptures. A traditional Friend in her approach to the Bible, her theological position did not differ markedly from that of another New Yorker, Elias Hicks, whose name was attached to the Quaker separations of 1827 and 1828, after Barnard's death. Her strength of character and determination, her eloquence, and her constancy remained with her, even as she also retained a broad tolerance exemplified by Lady Homespun's warning that novels were not as dangerous for young women as superstition and religious fanaticism.

• Letters from and about Barnard are included in the Preston family papers, in possession of Ann Preston Vail, Middletown, N.Y. Numerous documents concerning Barnard's conflict with Quakers can be found in Thomas Foster, *A Narrative of the Proceedings in America, of the Society Called Quakers, in the Case of Hannah Barnard* (1804). For a contemporary sketch of the controversy in London, with documents, see *The Records of Recollections of James Jenkins*, ed. J. William Frost (1984), pp. 339–80. The most complete biographical sketch is David W. Maxey, "New Light on Hannah Barnard, a Quaker 'Heretic,'" *Quaker History* 78 (1989): 61–86.

H. LARRY INGLE

BARNARD, Henry (24 Jan. 1811–5 July 1900), educator and editor, was born in Hartford, Connecticut, the son of Chauncey Barnard, a sea captain and farmer, and Betsey Andrews. Barnard spent his formative years in Connecticut and graduated from Yale in 1830. Immediately after college he taught school in Pennsylvania for a year and loathed it. He then read law and was admitted to the Connecticut bar in 1834; however, he never practiced. During the winter of 1832–1833 he spent three months in Washington, D.C., where he met many of the leading political figures of the day,

and then traveled in the South. Still lacking direction, he embarked on a grand tour of Europe in March 1835; the impetus for the trip was his selection as one of the Connecticut delegates to the London international peace congress. While in England he was introduced to a number of the foremost Whig intellectuals, politicians, and reformers; at the time he seemed to be primarily interested in the cause of prison reform. After touring England he spent six months on the Continent before returning home to attend his ailing father.

After his return home Barnard, well-educated, traveled, and financially comfortable, was recognized as a rising young man of the Whig party in Connecticut. He was elected to the state legislature in 1837 and then reelected the next year. In the legislature he played the role of the humanitarian reformer and by his second term adopted the reform of the common school as his cause. In 1838 he was instrumental in securing the passage of a law establishing a permanent Board of Commissioners of the Common Schools. Barnard was appointed its secretary and held the post until the board was abolished in the partisan battles of 1842.

Barnard used the ill-defined position of secretary to initiate state supervision of the common schools, a course of action entirely consistent with the centralizing tendencies of his party. Like his political peers he saw the schools as agencies of moral reform, but increasingly he emphasized the social role of schools in a democracy. Schools, he repeatedly said, should not be regarded as common because they were cheap but because they were for all, within the reach of the poor yet attracting the well-off by their excellence. Barnard also articulated a comprehensive scheme of schooling for the entire community. In addition to public schooling from the primary grades (with female teachers) through high school (he advocated separate schools for "colored" children as well as evening schools for working children), he proposed publicly supported libraries, museums, lyceums, and lecture series.

It was the duty of the board to report to the legislature on the condition of the common schools, and it was the responsibility of the secretary to investigate those conditions. Given the embryonic nature of bureaucracy, Barnard relied on exhortation and on the existence and service of the many members of the local Friends of Education throughout the state. Through statewide meetings, lectures, and school inspections, he brought education to the fore of public discourse; through diligent gathering of statistics and insistence on annual reporting he collected and published vast amounts of information. And constantly he pressured the localities to improve the supervision of the schools. He argued for gradation of schools and for the better preparation of teachers, and when the legislature declined to fund a normal school, Barnard held the first class for teachers in the state. Finally, as authorized by the legislature, he edited four volumes of the *Connecticut Common School Journal* (1838–1842), filled with local and national material (such as Calvin Stowe's report on the schools of Prussia), moral advice, practical hints for teachers (with heavy doses from the Swiss educational reformer Pestalozzi), designs for schoolhouses, and suggestions for texts and apparatus.

During 1838–1842 Barnard helped to found the Hartford Young Men's Institute and to revitalize the Connecticut Historical Society, whose secretary he remained for many years. He published the first of his many works, and, through his activity in the American Institute of Instruction, he developed a national reputation. His vast correspondence reveals ties to all of the leading lights in the antebellum school reform movement.

The Board of Commissioners was abolished in 1842, the victim of the Democratic victory in the election. Although Barnard professed to be devastated, he had been freed to do what he loved—to travel throughout the country, visiting his network of college and reformer friends, and to collect information for a history of education in the United States. The projected history was delayed, however, by an invitation from the governor of Rhode Island to conduct a survey of the condition of the schools in that state.

The results of Barnard's survey were conveyed to the Rhode Island state legislature in a report in 1844. It echoed the standard litany of common school reformers: the "evils" of inadequate schoolhouses and texts; the desirability of better record keeping, longer school days, and gradation in the schools; and the necessity of training teachers. The school law subsequently adopted by the legislature created the position of commissioner of the public schools (to which Barnard was appointed in 1843), appropriated money from the state for teacher salaries, assigned supervisory duties to the towns rather than the smaller school districts, and established rudimentary certification for teachers. It also guaranteed free schooling for poor children. Barnard married Josephine Desnoyers of Detroit in 1847. They had five children.

During his tenure in Rhode Island (1843–1849) Barnard may well have reached the pinnacle of his powers. By taking advantage of a nascent reform movement he created a commissionership of considerable force and inaugurated a system of school supervision in a state that had consistently feared the encroachment of government. He sponsored a series of institutes for teachers and published, in conjunction with the Rhode Island Institute of Instruction, three volumes of the state educational journal as well as his book on *School Architecture* (1848). But he was never wholeheartedly committed to Rhode Island and spent considerable time in his native state. He increasingly left administrative tasks to his subordinates in Providence, and in 1849 he finally resigned to return to Connecticut.

By mid-century Barnard apparently had become more ambitious. He negotiated to succeed educator Horace Mann, who had been elected to Congress, as secretary to the Massachusetts Board of Education and also sought a professorship at Brown or Yale. And he was active in Hartford, promoting a high school. When a bill establishing the state normal school passed the Connecticut legislature in 1849, the trustees

selected Barnard to be the principal, a position combined with that of state superintendent of the common schools. Under Barnard's leadership the normal school provided a form of higher education for young men and women who were experienced teachers in the common schools and who had not previously had the means or the opportunity for further schooling. Three men and two women were in the first graduating class in 1851, and more than 500 teachers enrolled for some portion of the year during the first three years. Far more teachers, however, attended the institutes that Barnard sponsored in the eight counties of the state. The normal school, the institutes, and the teachers' association (founded by the graduates of the school) introduced an embryonic sense of professionalism among the teachers—a cause Barnard constantly advocated.

By mid-century Barnard had achieved a national and an international reputation. He was a candidate for the presidencies of both the Universities of Michigan and Indiana. His advice was frequently sought on matters of school organization and architecture, and he was constantly asked to recommend teachers. He lectured widely, especially in the Midwest, and in 1853 he served as president of the American Association for the Advancement of Education (AAAE), an organization he had helped to found. He corresponded with prominent continental reformers; trips to Europe in 1851 and 1852 gave him the opportunity to meet some of them. His publications in this period focused on familiar themes: *Normal Schools, and Other Institutions, Agencies, and Means Designed for the Professional Education of Teachers* (1851); *Tribute to Gallaudet: A Discourse in Commemoration of the Life, Character and Services, of the Rev. Thomas H. Gallaudet* (1852), a eulogy to his mentor; *National Education in Europe* (1854); and *Reformatory Education: Papers on Preventive, Correctional and Reformatory Institutions and Agencies, in Different Countries* (1857). In 1855 he also commenced publication of the massive *American Journal of Education*, a labor of love that occupied him until 1880.

In 1858 Barnard was elected chancellor of the University of Wisconsin and agent for the state's normal schools. He developed a cohesive plan for higher education in the state, combining a liberal arts curriculum for the first two years at the university with professional training in seven separate schools for the final two years. The normal department was to be, he said, "the crowning feature of the state system for the professional training of teachers." Barnard scheduled a series of teachers' institutes during the eighteen months he held office in Wisconsin but made no lasting contribution to the state's educational development. The death of one of his children and his devotion to his publishing ventures and to Connecticut kept him away from Wisconsin for more than half of his time there, and he never moved his family to Madison. By 1860 he was chancellor in name only, and he resigned early in 1861.

For the next five years Barnard remained in Hartford and concentrated on his scholarly work. He was attempting to create a corpus of professional literature for the increasing number of teachers in the country. Issues of the *Journal* appeared with some regularity, and he published five major books: *Memoirs of Teachers, Educators and Promoters and Benefactors of Education, Literature and Science* (1859), *Pestalozzi and Pestalozzianism* (1859), *Papers for the Teacher* (5 vols., 1859–1862), *English Pedagogy: Education, the School and Teacher in English Literature* (1862), and *Armsmear: The Home, the Arm, and the Armory of Samuel Colt* (1866). Many of these works were published as second editions by the author, an admission that much of the material had appeared previously in his periodical.

Yet Barnard still had national ambitions, and he sought a federal appointment. He served a brief stint with the Census Bureau, a position well suited to his passion for statistics, and he hoped, but failed, to become a regent of the Smithsonian Institution. He was appointed a member of the Board of Visitors at the U.S. Military Academy at West Point in 1863 and of the Naval Academy in Newport in 1864. More and more he utilized the pages of his *Journal* as a national voice for teachers and their state associations and to promote the cause of a stronger federal role in education, a position consistently advocated by the reformers of the AAAE.

In 1866–1867 Barnard served as the principal of the newly reopened St. John's College in Maryland. He submitted a comprehensive plan for the development of the college that introduced new subjects to the classical course, made liberal education the foundation and preparation for subsequent professional study, and integrated the common schools with higher education in the state. But Barnard remained at the college less than a year, moving to nearby Washington, D.C., to head the new national Department of Education.

A coalition of national educators and Republicans in Congress, who advocated a stronger federal government and who saw federal support for schools in the South as one of the features of Reconstruction, drafted the bill creating the Department of Education in 1867. Barnard, despite strong competition, was selected by President Andrew Johnson to be the first commissioner of education. The new commissioner set to work with characteristic enthusiasm and grandiose schemes although he had very limited powers. Unfortunately his shortcomings as an administrator and his frequent visits to Hartford during his tenure limited his effectiveness and played into the hands of his political rivals.

Barnard did submit the required report on the state of education in the nation to Congress in 1868 but only after considerable pressure from his mentors. It was a hasty job, mostly republication of material from the *Journal*. A second report, on education in the District of Columbia, completed in 1870, was, on the other hand, an outstanding document that proposed an articulated system of public schools; governance was to be centralized under an incipient hierarchy of professionals who would share authority with parents and

teachers. The teachers were to be appointed after appropriate examination and were to be subjected to a form of evaluation. This *Report* continued and expanded the scheme introduced in Barnard's Connecticut and Rhode Island days—a centralized and inclusive system of schooling from elementary through higher and technical teacher training under the leadership of professional educators. The *Report* also marked the end of Barnard's public career. A national mood of retrenchment, the impeachment of President Johnson, the political manipulations of his rivals, and his almost belligerent ineptitude culminated in his dismissal and the demotion of the department to the status of a bureau in 1870.

Barnard then retired to Hartford and never again held public office. By this time he had achieved status as the "Nestor of American Education," the grand old man of the cause of the common schools. He continued to publish the *Journal*, although it appeared sporadically, and individual volumes lacked cohesion. He reprinted many of his previous publications, on familiar subjects, probably because of financial necessity. He also made repeated attempts to concentrate on the long-delayed history of education; as late as 1897 he wrote to a publisher about the project.

In his retirement Barnard lived as he had throughout his active life. He traveled to Europe with his family and frequently attended professional meetings in this country. His publications were submitted to various international expositions by the government, and he proudly reported in the pages of the *Journal* about the medals awarded to him. A gala celebration in Hartford marked his eighty-sixth birthday, and until his death other birthdays were occasions for affectionate greetings from his devoted followers. At the meeting of the National Education Association in 1900, shortly after his death, he was eulogized by his successors in the national school leadership.

It is difficult to depict Henry Barnard, the private person. He was clearly a man of warmth who enjoyed the friendship of scores of his fellow reformers. But of his family, and especially of his marriage, there is far less evidence. Josephine Barnard apparently was a dutiful and affectionate spouse who ran the household in Hartford, enduring her husband's frequent absences with little complaint. Her Catholicism may have been more of a stress on the marriage than either could admit; Barnard mentioned her religion frequently. Barnard scarcely referred to his children in his correspondence. Two of his daughters died in childhood, and his son, a lawyer like his father, died shortly after his marriage and the birth of Barnard's granddaughter. The two surviving Barnard daughters remained unmarried and took care of their father until his death in the house in which he was born.

Barnard should justly be remembered along with Horace Mann as one of the preeminent educational reformers of the antebellum period. Like his peers he advocated the improvement of public schooling, primarily for moral purposes, and the creation of a rudimentary centralized school system. He held innovative ideas about higher education and about the role of the federal government. But he was a failure as an administrator and never completed the work of the major positions he accepted. He was a promoter of teachers, their preparation, and their organization, although he continued to view teaching as a mission more than as a true profession. His image of schools was based on his childhood experiences, and he had very little comprehension of the real world of the classroom teacher and less of the world of the urban school. He demonstrated slight interest in curriculum, other than occasional articles on vocal music and the necessity of physical exercise. His concern for pedagogy was limited to discussions of school apparatus and the need for moral instruction. He did, however, publicize the works and ideas of Pestalozzi, thereby introducing a progressive element into educational discourse in the United States long before the movement of that name. He is most remembered as a scholar and especially as the editor of the massive *American Journal of Education*, although it never became the manual for teachers he had hoped it would. His work, the *Journal*, and the many individual volumes can be criticized from contemporary historiographical standards; nevertheless, they remain an important source for much of the modern scholarship in educational history and stand as a monument to Barnard's attempt to create a field.

In the final analysis Barnard must be viewed in several lights. He was a transitional figure, a mid-century reformer standing between the first generation missionaries for schools and the highly trained and self-conscious administrators of the Progressive Era. He was a curiously static figure, a man whose message scarcely varied in the thirty years of his public life, although many of his initial proposals were surprisingly innovative. Finally, he was an intender, a man of grand design and limited execution.

• The major archive of the Henry Barnard Papers is in the Fales Library at the Elmer Holmes Bobst Library of New York University; a smaller collection is in the Watkinson Library of Trinity College in Hartford, Conn. For the most part these collections contain letters to Barnard; few from him remain, but some may be found in the Henry Barnard and Elias Loomis Papers (Beinecke Rare Book and Manuscript Library, Yale University), the Horace Mann Papers (Massachusetts Historical Society, Boston), the Lyman Draper Collection (State Historical Society of Wisconsin at Madison), the Daniel Coit Gilman Papers (Johns Hopkins University), and the Special Collections at James P. Adams Library (Rhode Island College, Providence). Most biographies of Barnard have been based on his own accounts of his works, including Noah Porter's summary of Barnard's Connecticut work, "Henry Barnard," *Connecticut Common School Journal* 2 (Jan. 1855), and John D. Philbrick's repetition, "Henry Barnard: The American Educator," *New England Magazine*, n.s., 1 (May 1886). Will S. Monroe intended to be the official biographer, and Barnard entrusted his correspondence to him. Monroe's resultant *Educational Labors of Henry Barnard* (1893) is uncritical, but his 1897 bibliography is useful. Amory D. Mayo, "Henry Barnard," *Report of the Commissioner of Education, 1896–1897* (1898), chap. 16, and Bernard C. Steiner, *Life of Henry Barnard* (1918), see Barnard as a heroic

figure, whereas later scholars paint conflicting portraits. In his introduction to *Henry Barnard on Education* (1931), John Brubacher sees his subject as a progressive; Merle Curti, *The Social Ideas of American Educators* (1935), emphasizes Barnard's conservatism; Anna Lou Blair, *Henry Barnard: School Administrator* (1937), depicts him anachronistically as a modern school professional. The most balanced account is in Vincent Lannie's introduction to his *Henry Barnard: American Educator* (1974), although Lannie tends to perpetuate the traditional laudatory view. Richard Emmon Thursfield completed an exhaustive study, *Henry Barnard's "American Journal of Education"* (1945), but not the biography for which his work was a prelude. An important modern biography is Edith Nye MacMullen, *In the Cause of True Education: Henry Barnard and Nineteenth-Century School Reform* (1991). A collection of accolades is in National Education Association, *Journal of Proceedings and Addresses*, Fortieth Annual Meeting (1901): 395–408.

EDITH NYE MACMULLEN

BARNARD, John (6 Nov. 1681–24 Jan. 1770), Congregational clergyman, was born in Boston, Massachusetts, the son of John Barnard and Esther (maiden name unknown). His father, a housewright, rose to be town selectman in 1701. Information about Barnard's colorful life is available because at the age of eighty-five he wrote a charming, untitled autobiography at the request of fellow divine Ezra Stiles, president of Yale College. Although this work is self-serving and perhaps unreliable at times, it is the only significant source on his life and reveals much about eighteenth-century Massachusetts.

As a boy Barnard was both scholarly and mischievous. He claimed to have read the Bible three times, but his pranks hindered long-time Boston schoolmaster Ezekiel Cheever from getting his lessons across to the other lads at the Boston Latin School. Graduated in 1700 from Harvard College, which he stated made him as idle as his fellows, he cataloged Boston's library in 1702, preached occasionally in Massachusetts, and served as one of five chaplains on an unsuccessful expedition to conquer French Port Royal in Acadia (Nova Scotia), where he got in trouble for playing cards.

Barnard sailed for England in 1709 as chaplain of a ship commanded by John Wentworth of the prominent New Hampshire mercantile and political family. Much of his account of the voyage tells of spirits he drank and his fine companions. He found the English knew nothing of America—one lady complimented him on how well he spoke the language after being in the country only a short time. Although he preached to several dissenting congregations, he wore a wig and sword and was taken for a courtier. Barnard turned down an offer to be chaplain to Lord Wharton, the viceroy of Ireland, and refused to recommend what he considered to be a host of "obsequious and cringing" candidates for the ministry from Scotland and Ireland for jobs in New England on the legitimate ground that many Harvard graduates—including himself—could not obtain livings.

Returning to New England in 1710, Barnard lost out on a position at Boston's Brattle Square Church by one vote: his friendship with controversial governor Joseph Dudley was no advantage. After preaching in different places from time to time, in 1714 he finally obtained a pulpit at Marblehead, Massachusetts, where he remained for the rest of his life. The congregation had been deadlocked on whether to appoint Barnard or Edward Holyoke, so the town built a second meetinghouse to accommodate both men. Holyoke became president of Harvard College in 1737; Barnard was not a candidate. Barnard married Anna Woodbridge in 1718; they had no children.

Barnard was a bastion of the Old Lights, or opponents of the Great Awakening, which convulsed New England in the early 1740s. Attacking the New Lights, who stressed salvation through faith alone and believed that salvation was assured through an emotional experience of the Holy Spirit, Barnard published *A Zeal for Good Works* in Boston in 1742. He argued for "zeal guided by knowledge, tempered with prudence, and accompanied with charity." A convention of Boston ministers used his remarks in *The Testimony of the Pastors of the Churches . . . against Several Errors in Doctrine, and Disorders in Practice* (1743), and his pamphlet was reprinted in Glasgow, Scotland, in an effort to thwart the spread of this transatlantic movement that stressed personal infusion of faith and undermined the authority of settled ministers in their congregations. Closer to home, Barnard claimed that his preaching and writing kept the churches in and around Marblehead from falling into "disorder and confusion."

Into old age Barnard "spoke with energy upon every subject, as though he would impress the rising generation that grey hairs were the mark of wisdom, not of weakness" (John Eliot, *Biographical Dictionary* [1809], pp. 43–44). Throughout his life he was a good Massachusetts patriot. During his youthful voyage to England, he recommended for province agent the effective Jeremiah Dummer, who argued that the New England charters were held "not on account of grace from the throne but [by virtue of] a contract between the king and our fathers." When King George's War with France (1744–1748) occurred, Barnard's militant sermons used Cato's cry from ancient Rome—"Carthage must be destroyed!"—to urge the demolition of the French fortress at Louisbourg, Nova Scotia. In 1764, when the library of Harvard College burned down, Barnard donated his own substantial collection to rebuild it. Donors to the library continue to join the John Barnard Associates. Barnard's opinions on the imperial crisis of the 1760s, unfortunately, are not known.

Barnard enjoyed excellent health until his eyesight began to fail in 1768. He preached his last sermon on 8 January 1769 and died a year later in Marblehead. Thanks to his readable autobiography, the history of provincial Massachusetts can be experienced through the eyes of a perceptive clergyman who seemed equally at home in cosmopolitan London as the fishing village where he spent most of his life.

• Barnard's papers do not exist or have not been found. His untitled autobiography appears in Massachusetts Historical Society, *Collections*, 3d ser., 5 (1836): 177–245. His writings include *Elijah's Mantle: A Sermon Preached at the Funeral of the Rev. Samuel Cheever* (1724); *Ashton's Memorial: An History of the Strange Adventures, and Signal Deliverances, of Mr. Philip Ashton, Who . . . Made His Escape from the Pirates . . .* (1725); *A New Version of the Psalms of David* (1752); and *Sermon at the Ordination of William Whitwell: A Discourse* (1762). A complete list of Barnard's published writings may be found in Clifford Shipton's *Sibley's Harvard Graduates*, vol. 4 (1933), pp. 501–14.

WILLIAM PENCAK

BARNARD, John Gross (19 May 1815–14 May 1882), soldier, engineer, and scientist, was born in Sheffield, Massachusetts, the son of Robert Foster Barnard and Augusta Roberta Porter. He was the younger brother of the distinguished educator Frederick Augustus Barnard, president and chancellor of the University of Mississippi and president of Columbia College (now Columbia University) in New York City. Barnard graduated second in his 1833 class of the U.S. Military Academy and was commissioned in the Corps of Engineers. He married Jane Elizabeth Brand, who died in 1853. He married Anna E. Hall Boyd in 1860.

Barnard's early military career was occupied with work on coastal fortifications. He was in charge of the defenses of Tampico and surveyed the battlefields around Mexico City during the war with Mexico, and he did railroad survey work at the mouth of the Mississippi River following the war. Barnard was superintendent of West Point in 1855–1856 and then assumed direction of the fortifications of New York. By the outbreak of the Civil War he was a major of engineers and served as chief engineer to General Irvin McDowell, commander of Union forces in the First Bull Run (First Manassas) campaign. McDowell planned his battle on Barnard's reconnaissance. General George B. McClellan (1826–1885) subsequently appointed Barnard chief engineer of the Army of the Potomac with the rank of brevet brigadier general. During the Peninsula campaign Barnard conducted the siege of Yorktown and directed engineering operations for the approach to Richmond. His most noteworthy achievement would follow his assignment in April 1861 as chief engineer of the Washington defenses.

On the orders of McClellan Barnard directed construction of the first great modern fortification in American military history. The Civil War came at the transition from masonry to earthen fortifications in response to the introduction of rifled weapons. Barnard built the Washington defenses on the principles of complex field fortifications as presented by West Point professor Dennis Hart Mahan in *Complete Treatise on Field Fortification* (1836). The most notable precedent was the Russian engineer Franz E. Todleben's construction of an earthen fieldworks system for the defense of Sebastopol during the Crimean War.

By October 1864 Barnard's single line of field works encompassed Washington, Georgetown, and Alexandria and consisted of 60 forts and 93 batteries, totaling

25,799 yards, with 35,711 yards of infantry covered way and implacements for 1,447 guns. At the time its armament consisted of 762 guns and 74 mortars. These defenses had the effect of making Washington more an armed camp protected by field works than a traditional fortified city with masonry walls. As a consequence of competing demands for troops and work parties and a diminishing threat to Washington, the defenses were never fully manned, and Barnard struggled constantly to sustain the construction and its repair. Despite these operational problems, the construction of the Washington fortifications is one of the great engineering feats of American military history.

In 1864 Barnard declined nomination by Abraham Lincoln as chief of the Corps of Engineers. In June 1864 General Ulysses S. Grant appointed Barnard to his staff as chief engineer of the armies in the field. Barnard finished the war as a brevet major general and colonel in the Corps of Engineers.

Barnard had a distinguished postwar military, engineering, and scientific career. He served as a member of the joint board of the army and navy on harbor defenses and torpedoes, as a senior member of the Board of Engineers for Permanent Defenses, and as a member of the Lighthouse Board. He wrote extensively on the Civil War and on a wide range of engineering, mathematical, and scientific subjects. His best-known work was his justly celebrated *A Report on the Defenses of Washington* (1871). He was also one of the founders of the National Academy of Sciences, established during the war in 1863. His distinction as a scholar-soldier was recognized by honorary degrees not only from Yale but also from the heart of the former enemy, the University of Alabama.

• For Barnard's activities as chief engineer of the Army of the Potomac through the Peninsula campaign see his *Report of the Engineer and Artillery Operations of the Army of the Potomac, from Its Organization to the Close of the Peninsula Campaign* (1863). See also Barnard's *The Confederate States of America and the Battle of Bull Run* (1862). There is no biographical study of Barnard. An excellent study of the Washington defenses that details his role is Benjamin Franklin Cooling, *Symbol, Sword, and Shield: Defending Washington during the Civil War* (1975). For published documentary sources see U.S. War Department, *The War of the Rebellion: A Compilation of the Official Records of the Union and Confederate Armies* (128 vols., 1880–1901).

EDWARD HAGERMAN

BARNARD, Kate (23 May 1875–23 Feb. 1930), Progressive reformer and politician, was born Catherine Anna Barnard in Alexandria, Nebraska, the daughter of John P. Barnard, a lawyer and real estate speculator, and Rachael Mason Shiell. Shortly after Barnard's birth her family moved to the small frontier town of Kirwin, Kansas, where her mother died in 1877. She attended public school in Kirwin until the mid-1890s, when she and her father moved to the new territory of Oklahoma. The experiences of her early adulthood resemble those of other women Progressives in at least two ways. First, she was introduced to politics by her father, a local politician. Second, she tried several lines of work before she became a reformer. From 1896 to 1899 she taught in rural schools; then, in 1902 she exchanged teaching for stenography. Startled by the degree of poverty in her own neighborhood in Oklahoma City, she decided in the fall of 1905 to conduct a campaign to clothe the community's poor. The crusade gained her public recognition and convinced her of the importance of volunteer associations. She resuscitated a local charity organization and was appointed its matron in December 1905. She began to realize that unionization could be another weapon with which to combat poverty and, consequently, became a deputy organizer for the International Women's Union Label League.

Like other Progressives, Barnard decided that attacking the root causes of poverty required legislation and political activism. In 1906 she persuaded delegates to the Oklahoma constitutional convention to incorporate some of the latest social justice ideas into the constitution. The convention created the office of commissioner of charities and corrections. Because of Barnard's effectiveness in mobilizing public opinion for social justice reforms, the office was made open to women on the assumption that it would be filled by her. Oklahoma Democrats eagerly nominated her, and although women were not allowed to vote in Oklahoma, Barnard garnered more votes than any other candidate and became the first woman elected to a major state office. Taking office in November 1907, she accepted industrialization and urbanization as the wave of the future in the new state, but she was determined to divorce exploitation and abuse from economic and social advancement. She admired social science experts and induced some of the nation's leading progressives to draft legislation for the Oklahoma legislature. She also insisted that Christian ethics required exertion to bring about the Kingdom of God on earth. Although her election to a state office had thrust her into formal politics, she did not enlarge the scope of women's reform interests. "In my limited sphere as a woman, I naturally confine myself especially to those laws that effect the childhood of the state, and those that tend to better the condition of the poor and unfortunate of our state."

During her first term in office (1907–1910) she compiled the most impressive record of accomplishment of any state-level social justice Progressive. Her lobbying and politicking resulted in the nation's first compulsory education law with a provision for mothers' pensions, a child labor law, laws creating a three-tier prison system, and a juvenile court law. She pressured legislators into adopting laws that safeguarded laborers, created a state employment service, and protected the property rights of married women. Her widely publicized exposés in 1908 and 1909 of conditions in prisons and asylums led to reform in the treatment of convicts and the insane. Equating feminism with public endorsement of woman suffrage, Barnard did not think of herself as a feminist. She refused to identify herself with woman suffrage during the constitutional convention or during a statewide referendum on that issue in 1910. Although Barnard did not object to women voting, she did not believe that woman suffrage had developed enough momentum to be politically viable in Oklahoma. Furthermore, she was accomplishing her reform goals with the support of an exclusively male electorate. "I may become a very ardent woman's rights partisan some day. . . . If the time should come when our men do not stand for relieving the needs of the poor and helpless then I might put on a stove-pipe hat and draw on a pair of boots and go to the polls and work to defeat them." Barnard did, however, hold some strongly feminist views. She contended that women should achieve self-autonomy and economic independence, and she believed in greater educational and vocational opportunities for women.

After her re-election in 1910, Barnard's political fortunes declined. Her popularity began to suffer after she launched an extended effort to protect the property of Indian orphan children, a cause toward which many Oklahomans were indifferent, if not antagonistic. The election of 1910 cost her many legislative allies as the state was swept by a wave of political and fiscal conservatism. A hostile legislature attacked a number of state officials, including Barnard. From 1911 to 1913 physical and emotional illnesses kept her from her office for long periods, and from 1913 onward the state's most influential newspaper, the *Daily Oklahoman*, previously supportive, increasingly ignored or criticized her. Choosing not to run again in 1914, Barnard gradually retreated into private life. She died alone in an Oklahoma City hotel, all but forgotten by the Oklahomans who had once applauded "Miss Kate." Barnard's career vividly demonstrates the vital role that women played in Progressive era reform. Her leadership provided much of the impetus for Oklahoma's notable record of reform in the realm of social justice, and her successes catapulted her into national prominence.

• Letters and papers concerning Barnard's public career are in the Department of Charities and Corrections collection at the Oklahoma State Archives. No full-length biography of Barnard presently exists, but Suzanne Jones Crawford and Lynn R. Musslewhite have written a number of essays about Barnard, which include "Progressive Reform and Oklahoma Democrats: Kate Barnard vs. Bill Murray," *The Historian* 53 (Spring 1991): 473–88, and "Kate Barnard, Progressivism, and the West," in *An Oklahoma I Had Never Seen Before: Alternative Views of Oklahoma History*, ed. Davis Joyce (1994). For earlier essays on Kate Barnard see Keith Bryant, Jr., "The Juvenile Court Movement: Oklahoma as a Case Study," *Social Science Quarterly* 49 (Sept. 1968): 368–76, and K. Bryant, Jr., "Kate Barnard, Organized Labor and Social Justice in Oklahoma during the Progressive Era," *Journal of Southern History* 35 (1969): 145–164.

SUZANNE JONES CRAWFORD
LYNN R. MUSSLEWHITE

BARNES, Albert (1 Dec. 1798–24 Dec. 1870), Presbyterian pastor, was born in Rome, New York, the son of Rufus Barnes and Anna Frisby (also spelled Frisbie), farmers. After attending Fairfield Academy in Con-

necticut, Barnes entered the senior class at Hamilton College. His reading of Thomas Chalmer's entry on the "Evidences of Christianity" in *The Edinburgh Encyclopedia* and a Presbyterian revival on campus during 1819 led Barnes to abandon his early ambition to become a lawyer. Upon graduation the next year, Barnes returned home where he joined the local Presbyterian church before leaving to attend Princeton Theological Seminary.

At Princeton Barnes studied under conservative Calvinists Archibald Alexander and Samuel Miller. He developed a close relationship with Miller, serving for a time as private tutor to Miller's children. Barnes graduated from Princeton in 1823 and filled several pulpits along the eastern seaboard as a probationer after 23 April 1823, when the New Brunswick Presbytery licensed him. He married Abby Ann Smith in 1824; they had three children.

The First Presbyterian Church in Morristown, New Jersey, called Barnes as pastor in November 1824, and the following February the New Brunswick Presbytery ordained him. An early advocate of the newly emerging Sunday School movement, Barnes established a Sunday School in his own church but soon became concerned that Sunday school teachers lacked adequate resources for teaching. Consequently, he began a commentary series, *Notes: Explanatory and Practical* (1832–1853), to fill this gap. This series, which he finished only shortly before his death, achieved great success. By 1856 nearly four hundred thousand volumes had been sold.

Barnes became active in the temperance movement while in Morristown, publishing in 1828 *Essays on Intemperance*. He credited his preaching against alcoholic beverages with leading to the closing of seventeen out of nineteen local distilleries and the end of alcohol sales at eighteen of twenty nearby shops. They also sparked a revival between November 1828 and January 1829. Revivals would become a central part of Barnes's ministry because he emphasized the pastor's evangelistic responsibilities in the pulpit and stressed the need for individuals to reach out for their salvation.

On 8 February 1829 Barnes preached his most famous sermon, *The Way of Salvation* (1830). The sermon propounded the main tenets of what would become known as New School Presbyterian theology. Although Barnes had been trained at Princeton Seminary, the cradle of Old School Presbyterianism, he did not accept its theological perspective. In *The Way of Salvation* Barnes credited God entirely for the salvation of humanity, yet he denied that Adam's offspring bore personal guilt for Adam's original sin, even though after his sin Adam and humanity both were prone to sin. Barnes also challenged the idea that human beings could have no hope of obeying the biblical law and the doctrine of substitutionary atonement, which proposed that Christ died on the cross as a substitute for sinful humanity. In place of substitutionary atonement, Barnes subscribed to a governmental theory that suggested Christ had died to preserve God's moral order. Like other New School proponents, Barnes stressed the need for individuals to strive for their salvation in order to appropriate Christ's act of atonement, and he insisted that atonement was available to all rather than only to a divinely selected few.

On 22 March 1830 the First Presbyterian Church of Philadelphia called Barnes as their pastor. His installation on 25 June evoked protest from Philadelphia Presbytery members who challenged his orthodoxy. In 1831 the presbytery condemned Barnes's *Way of Salvation*, but after an appeal the General Assembly ruled that the sermon was not heretical, even though it contained "a number of unguarded and objectionable passages."

Between 1830 and 1837 rising animosity between Old and New School Presbyterians centered in Philadelphia. When Barnes published his *Notes, Explanatory and Practical on the Epistle to the Romans* in 1834, Old School opponents initiated the charge of heresy against him. Although his presbytery exonerated Barnes, his opponents appealed the verdict to the Synod of Philadelphia, and Barnes was suspended in October 1835. The 1836 General Assembly reversed Barnes's suspension, but one year later a General Assembly dominated by the Old School faction effectively excised a majority of New School Presbyterians from the Presbyterian Church in the U.S.A. (PCUSA) by abrogating an 1801 Plan of Union with Congregationalists. Barnes and a frustrated contingent of New School commissioners to the 1838 General Assembly walked out. They then met in Barnes's church to form their own Presbyterian Church U.S.A.

Barnes served the PCUSA (New School) as moderator of the Third Presbytery in 1838, the Synod of Pennsylvania in 1841, and the New School General Assembly in 1851. He chaired the Presbyterian Publication Committee from 1852 to 1870 and served on the board of the Presbyterian Minister's Fund from 1845 until his death. Although Lyman Beecher asked Barnes to join the Lane Seminary faculty in Cincinnati, he declined the offer, serving instead on the boards of Lincoln University and Union Theological Seminary in New York City. In 1867 Barnes gave the first Ely Lectures at Union. These addresses were published under the title *Lectures on the Evidences of Christianity in the Nineteenth Century* (1868).

Throughout his pastoral career Barnes vigorously supported sabbath observance and antislavery. Believing that the sabbath was the foundation for the strength of Christianity, Barnes opposed Sunday mail, newspapers, and travel, preferring himself to walk to church each Sunday. While still in Morristown he was involved in the American Colonization Society. Barnes never joined an antislavery society, but he published works against slavery, among them *An Inquiry into the Scriptural Views of Slavery* (1846) and *The Church and Slavery* (1857). In these he declared the Fugitive Slave Acts in direct and open conflict with any law of the Bible, and he condemned his Old School opponents for their "damaging silence" on the issue of slavery. By 1862 he had abandoned the idea of colonization, and in 1865 he supported the Fourteenth Amendment to the Constitution.

After 1852 severe health problems, particularly deteriorating eyesight, plagued Barnes's ministry. These difficulties required several leaves of absence from his pastorate. Nevertheless, during this period Barnes continued to publish. He retired from his Philadelphia pastorate on 18 November 1867. In 1870, only a few months after the reunion of the Old and New School Presbyterians, Barnes died in Philadelphia.

• Letters, manuscript sermons, and drafts of Barnes's published works are located at the Pennsylvania Historical Society and the Presbyterian Church (USA) Archives, both in Philadelphia. Barnes's more substantial publications, in addition to those cited above, were *Practical Preaching* (1833) and *Practical Sermons* (1841), *The Apostolic Church, an Inquiry into Its Organization and Government* (1855), *Sermons on Revivals* (1841), *Essays on Science and Theology* (1855), and *The Atonement in Its Relation to Law and Moral Government* (1859). Barnes wrote two autobiographies, *Life at Three-Score* (1859) and *Life at Three-Score and Ten* (1871). From 1830 to 1840 the *New York Observer* published complete reports of the ecclesiastical controversies surrounding Barnes. No published biography exists, but one dissertation provides a primary and secondary bibliography; see Edward Bradford Davis, "Albert Barnes—1798–1870: An Exponent of New School Presbyterianism" (Th.D. diss., Princeton Theological Seminary, 1961). For other biographical material, see S. J. Baird, *History of the New School* (1868); George Junkin, *The Vindication, Containing a History of the Trial of the Rev. Albert Barnes* (1836); and George M. Marsden, *The Evangelical Mind and the New School Presbyterian Experience* (1970).

MILTON J COALTER, JR.

BARNES, Albert Coombs (2 Jan. 1872–24 July 1951), collector, educator, and entrepreneur, was born in Philadelphia, Pennsylvania, the son of John Jesse Barnes, a butcher, and Lydia A. Schafer. Barnes's father lost his right arm in the Civil War, and his ability to support his family proved sporadic. However, Albert's mother, to whom he was devoted, was hardworking and resourceful. Among his most vivid childhood memories were the exuberant black religious revivals and camp meetings he attended with his devout Methodist parents. Accepted at the academically demanding Central High School, which awarded bachelor's degrees, his early interest in art was stimulated by his friendship with the future artist William Glackens. Graduating from Central with a B.S. degree in 1889, Barnes played semiprofessional baseball to help support himself and earned a medical degree from the University of Pennsylvania in 1892. On completing his internship he decided not to practice medicine.

Barnes had always excelled in chemistry, and he shifted his attention to the chemical aspects of physiology. He visited Europe in the summer of 1893 and returned again in 1894–1895 to work in clinical medicine and physiology at the University of Berlin. He also pursued his interests in philosophy and psychology. By 1897 he had become the director of sales and advertising for Philadelphia's leading pharmaceutical company, H. K. Mulford. Germany was the center of the lucrative chemical industry, and in 1900 Barnes was sent to Heidelberg, where he briefly studied pharmacology and philosophy and recruited the chemist and pharmacologist Hermann Hille. In 1901 Barnes married Laura Leighton Leggett, the daughter of a wealthy and established Brooklyn family. The couple had no children. By 1902 Barnes and Hille had left Mulford to establish their own company. With Barnes's awareness of the needs of the medical marketplace and Hille's technical expertise, they produced an improved silver compound with strong antiseptic properties called Argyrol. Doing the sales and marketing himself, Barnes made his fortune by aggressive worldwide distribution and vigorous legal protection of his product.

Terminating his partnership with Hille in 1908, Barnes continued to produce Argyrol in his small factory of largely black workers. Applying his psychological knowledge to secure employee loyalty and efficiency, the paternalistic Barnes launched a private social experiment, educating his employees in the principles of psychology and expanding their horizons with the study of literature, philosophy, and art. It was here, in a factory with paintings on the walls, that Barnes first developed his theories on the appreciation and understanding of art.

By the time the A. C. Barnes Company was sold in 1929, Barnes's expanding art collection had become his all-consuming interest. In 1912 he had sent William Glackens, who had introduced him to impressionism and postimpressionism, to Paris to infuse Barnes's traditional collection with contemporary work. Glackens returned with works by Vincent Van Gogh, Pierre-August Renoir, Paul Cézanne, Pablo Picasso, and others. Barnes took up the philosophical challenge presented by these paintings, developing into a champion of "the modern attitude toward painting." Becoming a discriminating and curious collector, he read voraciously and was eager to learn, debate, dispute, and bargain. Although independent in his judgments, he was influenced by individuals such as the writer and collector Leo Stein and the dealers Ambroise Vollard and Paul Guillaume. The latter introduced him to African art.

In 1922 Barnes established the Barnes Foundation "to promote the advancement of education and appreciation of the fine arts." In March 1925, as the foundation's galleries, designed by Paul Philippe Cret, were completed, Barnes's *The Art in Painting* was published. Here he explained how to banish subjective judgments by using the objective and predictable scientific method. He focused on art's universal elements of line, light, color, and space and their relationships, and he explained that these elements created art when their unique combination became richly expressive of common human experience or values. Barnes believed art was not only for the wealthy, the educated, or the art establishment but rather was a profound and powerful human experience accessible and intelligible to anyone who had "learned how to see." Although in-

debted to the ideas of William James, Clive Bell, George Santayana, Bertrand Russell, and most significantly, his longtime mentor and correspondent John Dewey, Barnes created a unique formulation. The educational program of the foundation included "the common man," whom Barnes and Dewey saw as the power behind democratic society.

Barnes wrote numerous essays for periodicals and exhibition catalogs, and with Violette De Mazia, the director of education of the art department and vice president of the foundation, he produced *The French Primitives and Their Forms* (1931), *The Art of Henri Matisse* (1933), *The Art of Renoir* (1935), *The Art of Cézanne* (1939), and *Ancient Chinese and Modern European Painting* (1943). *The Journal of the Barnes Foundation* ran from April 1925 to April 1926.

Barnes's collection of more than 2,000 works ultimately encompassed not only masterpieces of European and American modernism but also works from the Chinese, Islamic, African, African-American, and Native American traditions. It also included examples of the Old Masters, the Egyptians, the Ancients, and a large collection of decorative arts. His displays of objects were organized according to formal and expressive similarities rather than the more traditional organizational elements of date, place of origin, type, or medium. Barnes's diverse collection manifested his passion for art and reflected his analytical approach to understanding and appreciating art. His iconoclastic temperament was drawn to the masters of French modernism who sought to create a new way of seeing, experiencing, and understanding art. As a result his collection was particularly rich in masterpieces by Claude Monet, Édouard Manet, Henri de Toulouse-Lautrec, Georges Seurat, Van Gogh, Paul Gauguin, and Douanier Rousseau as well as works by Amedeo Modigliani and Barnes's own discovery, Chaim Soutine. It also contained an extensive selection of Picasso's early works, but the quality and quantity of works by Renoir, Cézanne, and Henri Matisse was unparalleled anywhere.

In 1950 Barnes amended the foundation's by-laws to empower the African-American Lincoln University to appoint the foundation's trustees. In 1926, in honor of his support of French modernism, the French government made Barnes a chevalier of the Legion of Honor and in 1937, an officer. Barnes was killed in an auto accident in Phoenixville, Pennsylvania, en route from his Chester County home, "Ker-Feal," to his home in Merion, Pennsylvania.

Barnes's continual disputes with institutions and individuals were legendary, and he could often be abusive, both privately and publicly, with those he considered his enemies. Although capable of extreme generosity, his personality was highly contentious. The by-laws he created for his foundation limited access to the collection and spawned repeated controversy and litigation. Still, Barnes's superior artistic sensibility, his intellectual acuity and ambition, and his drive left the legacy of a truly great collection.

• Much has been written about Barnes that is controversial and contradictory. Misinformation and hearsay have been printed, along with incorrect information he disseminated himself. A definitive and fully documented biography will require many years of research. Important primary sources are the Barnes Foundation Archives, Merion, Pa. (limited access); Albert C. Barnes–Horace Mann Bond Correspondence, Lincoln University Archives, Lincoln Univ., Oxford, Pa.; and the Archives of American Art, Washington, D.C. For understanding Barnes's convictions about art see Albert C. Barnes, *The Art in Painting* (1925), and John Dewey, Barnes et al., *Art and Education: A Collection of Essays* (1929). Enormous numbers of press clippings and popular articles chronicle Barnes and the controversies surrounding him. For selections from the collection and the archive see "A Passion For Art: Renoir, Matisse, and Dr. Barnes," CD-ROM, Corbis Pub. Publishing. Published sources include William Schack, *Art and Argyrol: The Life and Career of Dr. Albert C. Barnes* (1960); Henry Hart, *Dr. Barnes of Merion: An Appreciation* (1963); and Howard Greenfield, *The Devil and Doctor Barnes: Portrait of an American Collector* (1987). The latter includes a note on sources. Two brief but useful essays are Richard J. Wattenmaker, "Dr. Albert C. Barnes and the Barnes Foundation," and Anne Distel, "Dr. Barnes In Paris," in *Great French Paintings from the Barnes Foundation* (1993). Wattenmaker cites many of Barnes's periodical publications.

CAROL EATON SOLTIS

BARNES, Charlotte Mary Sanford (1818–14 Apr. 1863), playwright and actress, was born in New York City, the daughter of John Barnes and Mary Greenhill, British actors who achieved success on the New York stage as early as 1816. At age three Charlotte appeared on stage in her mother's arms in *The Castle Spectre*; her official debut came in 1834 as Angela in the same play at the Tremont Theater in Boston.

Through her parents' influence Barnes obtained several important roles at an early age, including Juliet to her mother's Romeo in Philadelphia in 1834. Attracted to tragic roles, she later starred as Juliet and as Hamlet in England in 1842. In 1847 she married Edmond S. Conner, a successful actor and manager of theaters. For a time they combined her dramatic and his managerial talents with considerable success at Philadelphia's Arch Street Theater, but Barnes never enjoyed first-rank status playing heroines on the American stage. Her career was hampered, according to Joseph Ireland in *Records of the New York Stage* (1867), by certain "physical defects," including a weak voice, an uncommanding figure and presence, nearsightedness, and wandering eyes. She was, says Ireland, much more suited to "parlor" performances or to playing young boys, for which her slight figure and soft voice were appropriate.

Although she worked occasionally as an actress throughout her life, Barnes's most important contribution was as a writer and adapter of plays. Several have not survived in manuscript or printed form, including an early attempt, *The Last Days of Pompeii* (1835), based on a novel by Bulwer-Lytton. Her best-known drama, *Octavia Bragaldi; or The Confession*, opened at the National Theater, New York City, in November 1837. This tragedy in blank verse was loosely based on a notorious 1825 crime of passion in Kentucky. Ann Cooke had been seduced by Colonel Solomon P. Sharpe, a state legislator. When her brothers refused to avenge this act, Ann Cooke convinced Jereboam Beauchamp to take revenge in exchange for an agreement to marry him. After Sharpe refused to duel Beauchamp, Beauchamp murdered him. Cooke committed suicide, and Beauchamp was hanged. The crime caught the imaginations of a number of writers, and Barnes knew at least two adaptations of the story, Thomas H. Chivers's *Conrad and Eudora* (1834) and some scenes from Edgar Allan Poe's *Politian* (1835). Like Poe, Barnes chose to transport the events to another time and place, choosing late fifteenth-century Milan for her setting. The heroine Octavia, originally played by Barnes, is deserted by Castelli, who has seduced her by means of a false marriage and who later presumably dies in battle. Octavia then marries Bragaldi and lives contentedly, until she discovers that Castelli is yet alive, has remarried, and has sullied her reputation with lies about her wantonness. Octavia convinces Bragaldi to avenge her dishonor by murdering Castelli. Both Octavia and Bragaldi die as the play ends.

In the preface to her *Plays, Prose and Poetry* (1848), Barnes acknowledged her dependence on the Kentucky tragedy, pointed out what aspects of her drama were original, and underscored the thematic message of her play—"the lamentable results of revenge, even under circumstances which in the world's opinion serve in some degree to palliate it." The play, although uneven, includes some effective blank verse passages and clearly shows Barnes's mastery of theatrical techniques and dramatic structure. She noted in her preface that the play's initial reception in New York City was helped by her parents' reputations and by her own youth, but that its later success in Britain owed nothing to these influences. She also claimed that the drama had been performed more than fifty times on both sides of the Atlantic.

Although *Octavia Bragaldi* remained her most successful effort, Barnes authored several other works, the most notable being *The Forest Princess; or, Two Centuries Ago* (1844), a drama based on the Pocahontas legend and first played in Liverpool. Plays about Pocahontas had already become familiar American fare, but earlier dramas had concentrated on the supposed rescue by Pocahontas of Captain John Smith. Barnes included an interesting final act set in England in 1617, in which Pocahontas also rescues her British husband, John Rolfe, jailed by King James I for his support of Sir Walter Raleigh. At the play's end Pocahontas envisions the glorious future of America, including George Washington with the Genius of Columbia. Barnes was proud of her research in the British Museum, on which she based this act.

Other plays by Barnes include *LaFitte; or, The Pirates of the Gulf* (not extant), first presented at the New Orleans Theatre in 1837, with Barnes as the young male lead; *A Night of Expectations* (1848; not extant), based on a French novel, first presented at the Arch Street Theater in Philadelphia in 1850, with Barnes in the leading role, although it may have played earlier in Britain and Ireland; and *Charlotte Corday*, adapted from Lamartine's *Histoire des Girondins* and Dunamoir and Clairville's *Charlotte Corday*, with Barnes playing the leading character at the play's debut at the Arch Street Theater in 1851.

Barnes's reputation rests on her relative success with poetic drama in the two plays still available for reading today, *Octavia Brigaldi* and *The Forest Princess*. Both show considerable mastery of play construction, theatrical techniques, and poetic conventions. Importantly, Barnes was a successful American playwright prior to the Civil War, at a time when few women attempted to write for the theater. She died in New York City.

• An informative but brief biographical entry appears in Alice M. Robinson et al., *Notable Women in American Theater: A Biographical Dictionary* (1989). Short critical estimates are in Walter Meserve, *Heralds of Promise: The Drama of the American People during the Age of Jackson, 1829–1849*; and Hal J. Todd, "America's Actor-Playwrights of the Nineteenth Century" (Ph.D. diss., Univ. of Denver, 1955). A nearly-contemporary account of Barnes as an actress is in Joseph N. Ireland, *Records of the New York Stage from 1750 to 1860*, vol. 2 (1867). Some works of Barnes, including her two surviving plays, are in her *Plays, Prose and Poetry* (1848); its preface provides some insight into her motives and goals for writing drama.

DELMER DAVIS

BARNES, Djuna (12 June 1892–19 June 1982), writer, was born Djuna Chappell Barnes in Cornwall-on-Hudson, New York, the daughter of Wald Barnes (born Henry Budington, recorded as Buddington), a musician, and Elizabeth Chappell. She was raised mostly in her birthplace, Fordham, and Huntington, Long Island, New York. The Barnes family, which believed in sexual freedom, included four brothers by Djuna's mother, plus Wald's mistress Fanny Faulkner and their three children; they were supported largely by Wald's mother, Zadel Barnes Budington Gustafson, a journalist and suffragist. Djuna's parents and grandmother Zadel tutored the children, especially in the arts. With the blessing of her father and grandmother (over the objections of her mother), at seventeen Djuna eloped with a soap salesman, Percy Faulkner, brother of Fanny Faulkner, but stayed with him only a few weeks. Djuna attended school sporadically, if at all; later she attended Pratt Institute (1913) and the Art Students League of New York (1915), studying life drawing and illustration.

When the divorce of her parents in 1912 obliged Barnes to help support her mother and brothers, she began her career in journalism. Starting in 1911 she wrote and illustrated many stories, plays, poems, journalistic articles, and interviews for newspapers and magazines such as the New York *Morning Telegraph Sunday Magazine*, *All-Story Weekly*, and *Vanity Fair*.

Some of Barnes's illustrations were in the style of Aubrey Beardsley, connoting an air of decadence.

In 1915 Barnes published *A Book of Repulsive Women*, a poetry chapbook of eight poems and five drawings describing in depressing terms the lesbian life. A more serious stage of her career began when she published stories in *The Little Review* (1918–1921). Her first collection of stories and poems, titled simply *A Book* (1923), was recycled in later years as *A Night among the Horses* (1929), where three stories were added, and *Spillway* (1962).

From her early Greenwich Village days, Barnes was bisexual, unmarried, and involved with numerous partners. Around 1914–1916 she was the lover of Ernst "Putzi" Hanfstaengl, a Harvard graduate from Munich who in the 1930s became Adolf Hitler's minister for the foreign press. During this time she was also associated with the Provincetown Theater, where she wrote a few plays and acted in minor roles. Among her friends were Carl Van Vechten, who photographed her; Eugene O'Neill; Frank Harris; Alfred Stieglitz; poets Elsa von Freitag Loringhoven and Mina Loy; actresses Mary Pyne and Helen Westley; and other New Yorkers in the arts. In 1918–1919 she lived with journalist Courtenay Lemon. During these early years Barnes was a highly paid journalist who was preparing herself for a literary career. In her personal life she was desperately unhappy, feeling that life was a cruel joke, an attitude often expressed in her writings.

In 1920 Barnes was sent to Paris by the editor of *McCall's* magazine to observe and write about the expatriate scene. There she came to know some of the greatest writers and artists of the age, including Gertrude Stein, Ernest Hemingway, Sinclair Lewis, Robert McAlmon, Ezra Pound, and James Joyce. During the early 1920s Barnes continued to write numerous stories, short closet dramas, and poems for various periodicals, but what caught the attention of the expatriates was her racy satire on Natalie Clifford Barney and her lesbian circle, called *Ladies Almanack* (1928), privately printed with bawdy illustrations by the author. Barnes had not intended it to be published, merely wishing to sell the work privately to pay a hospital bill.

In 1928 she also published *Ryder*, a comical family history also illustrated by the author, which describes their unusual living arrangements, Barnes's early life on the Huntington farm, and the London literary salon of her grandmother Zadel, who knew the family of Oscar Wilde and other artists and political radicals. Some chapters are in the style of Chaucer's *Canterbury Tales*. *Ryder* also describes the day when Djuna's father was told by his mother that he had to choose between his wife Elizabeth and his mistress Fanny.

Barnes's greatest work was her tragic novel *Nightwood*, which was based on her eight-year love affair with Thelma Ellen Wood, an artist from St. Louis, Missouri. They met in Paris in 1921 or 1922 and had a tempestuous though passionate relationship. Eventually Wood left Barnes for Henriette McCrea Metcalf and a new life in New York and Connecticut. Metcalf is satirized in *Nightwood* as Jenny Petherbridge, who "was a widow, a middle-aged woman who had been married four times. Each husband had wasted away and died; she had been like a squirrel racing a wheel day and night in an endeavor to make them historical; they could not survive it" (p. 65). In *Nightwood* the Djuna figure (Nora) tells her departing lover, "'In the resurrection, when we come up looking backward at each other, I shall know you only of all that company.'" Her ex-lover responds, "'Don't wait for me'" (pp. 58–59). Out of the pain of this rejection, *Nightwood* was written.

Much of *Nightwood* was written or revised in the company of art patron Peggy Guggenheim and her literary bohemian circle. Barnes's friend Emily Holms Coleman helped secure the novel's acceptance by T. S. Eliot, who was an editor with the publishing firm Faber and Faber in London. Eliot wrote the introduction to *Nightwood*, which appeared in 1936.

From the late 1930s to about 1950 Barnes was severely alcoholic and produced little work, but she conquered her malady and in 1958 published *The Antiphon*, a play written in a literary style resembling that of Shakespeare and the Jacobean playwrights. The play was translated into Swedish by Dag Hammarskjöld and his friend Karl Ragnar Gierow, director of Sweden's Royal Dramatic Theatre, and it premiered in Stockholm. Set in an English country house resembling that of Barnes's mother, *The Antiphon* is a family tragedy; the characters and themes bear a strong resemblance to those of Barnes's own family. Miranda, the Djuna figure, has been treated with cruel contempt for her artistic life by brothers who have chosen to become crass American businessmen. Their mother, Augusta, has been deceived into believing that the sons care for her and becomes distraught when Miranda proves this belief wrong. However, Miranda's chief grievance is that in early years her mother stood aside to allow her daughter's rape. Infuriated by her sons' abandonment of her and by her daughter's successful demonstration of her guilt, at the play's end Augusta crushes Miranda's skull with a curfew bell and falls dead at her side. In a 1961 letter to Willa Muir, Barnes wrote, "I wrote the Antiphon with clenched teeth, and I noted that my handwriting was as savage as a dagger."

In September 1940 Barnes moved into Patchen Place, in Greenwich Village, and remained there until her death. Other than *The Antiphon*, Barnes produced little coherent work other than a few poems, though she worked nearly daily at her writing. Her final creation was *Creatures in an Alphabet* (1982), a bestiary. Although in her last years Barnes was often caustic and bitter, she was a fascinating raconteur who had a small circle of devoted friends.

• The most important collection of Barnes's manuscripts and letters is in the McKeldin Library, University of Maryland, College Park; the correspondence of Barnes to Emily Holms Coleman in the Special Collections Department of the University of Delaware library is also significant. Cheryl J.

Plumb reedited *Nightwood* (1995). Several volumes of early Barnes have been published by Sun and Moon Press: *Smoke and Other Early Stories* (1982), *Interviews* (1985), *New York* (1989), *At the Roots of the Stars: The Short Plays* (1995), *Poe's Mother: Selected Drawings* (1995), and *The Collected Stories of Djuna Barnes* (1996). Biographies are Andrew Field, *Djuna: The Formidable Miss Barnes*, rev. ed. (1985), and the more comprehensive Phillip Herring, *Djuna: The Life and Work of Djuna Barnes* (1995). See also the "informal memoir" by Hank O'Neal, *Life Is Painful, Nasty and Short . . .* (1990), and Kyra Stromberg, *Djuna Barnes, Leben und Werk einer Extravaganten* (1989). Important criticism includes an issue of the *Review of Contemporary Fiction* (1993); Mary Lynn Broe, ed., *Silence and Power: A Reevaluation of Djuna Barnes* (1991); Louis F. Kannenstine and Allan Smith, *The Art of Djuna Barnes: Duality and Damnation* (1977); Cheryl J. Plumb, *Fancy's Craft: Art and Identity in the Early Works of Djuna Barnes* (1986); and James B. Scott, *Djuna Barnes* (1976). An obituary is in the *New York Times*, 20 June 1982.

PHILLIP HERRING

BARNES, Harry Elmer (15 June 1889–25 Aug. 1968), historian and sociologist, was born on a farm near Auburn, New York, the son of William Henry Barnes, Jr., a farmer, teacher, and later a prison guard, and Lulu C. Short. After graduating from high school in 1906, Barnes spent several years as a construction laborer and principal of a two-room village school in Montezuma, a small canal town in central New York. From 1909 to 1913 he attended Syracuse University, from which he graduated summa cum laude with a bachelor's degree in history. From 1913 to 1915 Barnes was instructor in sociology and economics at Syracuse, which awarded him an M.A. for work on the development of social philosophy from Plato to Comte. From 1915 to 1917 he was a graduate student at Columbia University, during which time he held a fellowship that allowed him to research at Harrow University from fall 1916 through early spring 1917, and in the subsequent academic year he taught at Columbia and Barnard. In 1918 he received a Ph.D. in sociology from Columbia University; his dissertation focused on the history of the New Jersey prison system. In 1916 he married Grace Stone; they had one child. After divorcing Stone eleven years later, he married Jean Hutchison Newman in 1935.

Barnes's academic career included posts at Clark University (1918–1919, 1920–1923), the New School for Social Research (1919–1920 and visiting lecturer from 1922 to 1937), Smith College (1923–1930), and Amherst College (1923–1925). From 1929 to 1934 he was an editorial writer for the Scripps-Howard Newspaper Alliance, and in 1931 he began a column that he eventually titled "The Liberal Viewpoint." From 1934 to 1940 he was columnist, editorial writer, and book reviewer for the chain's flagship, the *New York Telegram* (in 1931 the *World-Telegram*). Beginning in 1940, Barnes engaged in freelance writing for such journals as the *Progressive* while he held visiting academic appointments at the University of California (Berkeley), Colorado College of Education, Temple University, the University of Colorado, Indiana University, the

State University of Washington, and Hartwick College.

Incredibly prolific, Barnes wrote over thirty books, well over a hundred essays, and over six hundred book reviews. His primary topic, revisionism concerning both world wars, generated his greatest fame while subjecting him to bitter attack. Upon American entry into World War I, Barnes was a strong interventionist who contributed propaganda for such extremist pro-war groups as the National Security League and the American Defense Society. Among his efforts was a small book coauthored with businessman Charles Altschul, *The American Revolution in Our School Textbooks* (1917), which called for the rewriting of texts to stress a common Anglo-American heritage; a pamphlet, "America's Peril from Germany's Aggressive Growth" (1917); and an article, "Democracy," in the *Encyclopedia Americana* (1918), which accused Germany of launching an aggressive war.

Recanting five years after the war was over, Barnes wrote a series of articles and reviews in the *New Republic, Current History*, the *American Mercury*, and the *Christian Century*, in which he increasingly found the struggle rooted in France's desire to avenge the Franco-Prussian War and Russia's quest to control the Turkish Straits. His book *The Genesis of the World War* (1926; repr. 1927, 1929) exculpated a supposedly beseiged Germany of any war responsibility. In his introductory chapter, Barnes found the conflict rooted in such impersonal factors as overpopulation and Social Darwinism, but much of the succeeding narrative involved a search for villains. Here he stressed the role of Raymond Poincaré, the French president, and Aleksandr Izvolsky, the Russian ambassador to Paris. According to Barnes, British foreign minister Sir Edward Grey made war inevitable by backing France and Russia; conversely, German Kaiser Wilhelm II was one leader who continually strove for peace. The book was praised by such American historians as Carl Becker, William Langer, Ferdinand Schevill, and Preserved Smith. Charles A. Beard offered a more cautious appraisal, and Presson Slosson and Bernadotte Schmitt attacked it strongly, as did British scholar J. W. Headlam-Morley. When, in the summer of 1926, Barnes traveled to Europe, he found himself lionized by such German revisionists as Max Montgelas, Hermann Lutz, and Alfred von Wegerer and strongly welcomed by the exiled kaiser at Doorn.

To meet accusations of factual errors and unsubstantiated inferences, Barnes gathered a collection of hostile reviews, his own rejoinders, and some of his earlier articles for publication as *In Quest of Truth and Justice: De-Bunking the War-Guilt Myth* (1928). Here Barnes called William Stearns Davis "the distinguished historical novelist of the University of Minnesota," labeled the letters of E. Raymond Turner "Pedantry and Pomposity," and accused Schmitt of living "in daily dream of being mistaken for a member of the detestable Teuton race." Langer and Schevill lauded the work, but former allies Becker and Smith found his attack *argumentum ad hominem*, and many historians who were disturbed by his personal insults and polemical views started to ostracize him. Although debate over *Genesis* and *Quest* lasted throughout the 1920s, the books always lacked the stature of Sidney Bradshaw Fay's *The Origins of the World War* (1928) and Luigi Albertini's multivolume *The Origins of the War of 1914* (1952–1957).

A foe of U.S. intervention in World War II before Pearl Harbor, Barnes again offered a revisionist critique after the war had ended. By the 1950s, he was claiming that President Franklin D. Roosevelt deliberately withheld vital intelligence from the U.S. military commanders at Pearl Harbor. In privately printed pamphlets, Barnes defended the views of David L. Hoggan, a Harvard-trained historian who asserted that it was Lord Halifax, not Adolf Hitler, who was primarily responsible for the launching of World War II in September 1939. Barnes secured research subsidies for Hoggan, whose book *Der Erzwungene Krieg: Die Ursachen und Urheber des zweiten Weltkriegs* (The Imposed War: The Origins and Originators of the Second World War; 1961), published in West Germany (Eng. trans., *The Forced War: When Peaceful Revision Failed* [1989]), met with a devastating critique by German historian Hermann Graml. In private Barnes fostered the work of Paul Rassinier, a French medieval historian and geographer who denied that Germany had instituted any death camps. From 1945 on, Barnes critiqued America's Cold War policies, finding some justice in Soviet expansion and fearing the militarization of the United States. By the 1960s Barnes's brand of revisionism had become so outlandish that only a miniscule number of historians took him seriously.

Barnes also espoused "the New History," a movement that centered on the rewriting of all history in light of contemporary problems and that stressed the social and economic underpinnings of particular events. Advanced first by such older scholars as James Harvey Robinson, James T. Shotwell, Carl Becker, and Charles A. Beard, the New History defined its mission as centering not so much on what had happened but on how things had taken place. From Robinson's courses at Columbia, Barnes discovered the gap between technological and institutional change, and from his Columbia mentor Shotwell, he learned that progress depended on technological emancipation from the decadent institutions of throne and altar.

Barnes's *The New History and the Social Sciences* (1925) indicated how the major social sciences could assist the historian, while his *History and Social Intelligence* (1926) warned against nationalistic perspectives. His textbooks—*The History of Western Civilization* (1935), *Economic History of the Western World* (1937), *An Intellectual and Cultural History of the Western World* (1937; repr. 1941, 1965)—epitomized this approach, having as their premise the use of history to demolish such superstitions as religion and capitalism that had supposedly imprisoned humanity for ages.

In some ways, Barnes's revisionism was closely connected to the New History. In his preface to *Quest*, he wrote that "historical research is of little or no value unless its results have some actual bearing on the improvement of the wellbeing of man in some aspect of his life." In fact, according to Barnes, research on the war's origins would be sterile if it did not result in "the remaking of Europe." War, he always maintained, was the nemesis of reform, and in the 1920s he asserted that the "myth" of German war guilt, which led to the heavy reparations burden, had to be punctured in order to secure a true Wilsonian peace. Yet, because his other writings had stressed long-term trends and thereby repudiated the notion of personal culpability, his critics accused him of betraying the very New History principles he had espoused.

Barnes soon became famous for his attacks on traditional political, social, and economic institutions. The bane of American life, he said, was "cultural lag," a concept popularized by sociologist William F. Ogburn. By this term, Barnes simply meant that scientific and technological advances had outstripped traditional mores and practices. Writing in *Scientific Monthly* (Sept. 1940), Barnes said, "We stand today with our mechanical foot in an airplane and our social foot in an ox-cart." His *Living in the Twentieth Century* (1928) attacked "the herd instinct" and espoused an extreme form of behaviorism. *Can Man Be Civilized?* (1932) argued that a genius could transcend conventional moral standards. In *The Twilight of Christianity* (1929), Barnes claimed that supernatural religion, which he said was always "man-made," was responsible for much of the world's cruelty. *Social Institutions in an Era of World Upheaval* (1942) included the claim that private property had stifled all social reform. Barnes's crusades included a strong welfare state; nationalization of banking, railroads, and electric utilities; scientific management; plural voting for exceptional individuals; euthenasia; eugenics; cabinet government; full state-supported medical care; civil liberties; and the loosening of sexual taboos. At the same time, he attacked capitalism, censorship, "the herd instinct," and all forms of theism.

Loving shock value for its own sake, Barnes was an iconoclast par excellence. He was, however, also a child of the Enlightenment, always maintaining that society could be planned on rational lines. If human beings were far from perfectable, institutions could be made so, and through biological and environmental reforms, a rational citizenry could be developed.

Given such views it was hardly surprising that Barnes developed an expertise in criminology. In such books as *The Repression of Crime* (1926), *The Story of Punishment* (1930), and *New Horizons in Criminology*, with Negley K. Teeters (1943; repr. 1951, 1959), Barnes attacked capital punishment, claimed that prisons bred crime, and called for the replacement of the jury system by a panel of trained experts. During World War II, he served as historian and consultant of the Prison Industries Branch of the War Production Board, for which he wrote a report, *Prisons in Wartime* (1944).

Finally Barnes was an encyclopedist as well as a reformer, producing several massive compilations of data on the history of the social sciences, which are still valuable today. These works include *A History of Historical Writing* (1937; repr. 1962, 1963); *Social Thought from Lore to Science*, with Howard Becker (1938; repr. 1952, 1960); and *Historical Sociology: Its Origin and Development* (1948).

Combining the roles of scholar and popularizer, Barnes was as much at home in the pages of H. L. Mencken's *American Mercury* as in *The Encyclopedia of the Social Sciences*. He could tailor his remarks to fit his audience, writing about the origins of World War I in a relatively temperate tone for readers of the *Nation* and *Foreign Affairs* but sounding downright demagogic in addressing the German Americans who subscribed to George Sylvester Viereck's *American Monthly*. Yet he was always, as historian Carl Becker noted, a "learned crusader," who served as the intellectual engagé throughout his entire life. Polemical to the extreme, Barnes thrived on controversy and ascribed base motives to opponents. Few people professionally associated with him totally escaped his barbs. Neither an original thinker nor an archival researcher, he continually took positions that were, at best, oversimplified, exaggerated, and one-sided.

Though Barnes is best remembered for the many brands of revisionism, it always remained his Achilles heel. From 1941 on, even his visiting academic appointments were in the field of sociology, and no history department of a major university ever asked him to join its ranks. According to his biographer Roy C. Turnbaugh, Jr.,

His work as a revisionist revealed a very pragmatic, even opportunistic streak toward the truth. Since his goal as a revisionist was the establishment of a stable and peaceful international system, every other consideration was secondary to this. Truth tended to become a part of the means toward this end, and since the same facts were marshalled in opposing array by those engaged in this battle, Barnes naturally gave the facts the construction which was most favorable to his cause.

Barnes might be best understood as an unreconstructed progressive, who carried the reformist torch even when many of his causes, such as eugenics, sexual freedom, and anticlericism, were becoming obsolete. His insistence on playing the role of "prophet" became increasingly out of fashion as history and sociology became more professionalized. His lasting work lies in the history of social thought; few contributions to this field have been more thorough. He died at his home in Malibu, California.

• The Barnes papers are located in the Revisionist History Collection of the University of Wyoming, Laramie, Wyo. In addition to the works already cited, Barnes's sociological works include *Society in Transition* (1939; repr. 1952) and *The American Way of Life*, with Oreen M. Reudi (1942). Among Barnes's history textbooks are *World Politics in Modern Civilization* (1930) and *Survey of Western Civilization* (1947). His anthology *Perpetual War for Perpetual Peace* (1953) offered a bitter denunciation of the foreign policy of Franklin D. Roosevelt. The most comprehensive study of Barnes is Roy Carroll Turnbaugh, Jr., "Harry Elmer Barnes: The Quest for

Truth and Justice" (Ph.D. diss., Univ. of Illinois, 1977). Arthur Goddard, ed., *Harry Elmer Barnes: Learned Crusade* (1968), is a highly appreciative anthology on all aspects of Barnes's life and work. For work on Barnes's revisionism, see Warren I. Cohen, *The American Revisionists: The Lessons of Intervention in World War I* (1967); Richard T. Reutten, "Harry Elmer Barnes and the 'Historical Blackout,'" *Historian* 33 (Feb. 1971): 202–14; Justus D. Doenecke, "Harry Elmer Barnes," *Wisconsin Magazine of History* 56 (Summer 1973): 311–23; and Roy C. Turnbaugh, "Harry Elmer Barnes and World War I Revisionism: An Absence of Dialogue," *Peace and Change* 5 (Fall 1978): 63–69. See also Turnbaugh's "The FBI and Harry Elmer Barnes," *Historian* 42 (May 1980): 385–98. For Barnes's stress on "relevance," see Justus D. Doenecke, "Harry Elmer Barnes: Prophet of a 'Usable' Past," *History Teacher* 8 (Fall 1975): 265–76, and "The New History and the New Sociology: Harry Elmer Barnes," *Social Science* 53 (Spring 1978): 67–77. A lengthy obituary is in the *New York Times*, 28 Aug. 1968.

JUSTUS D. DOENECKE

BARNES, James (28 Dec. 1801–12 Feb. 1869), railroad executive and soldier, was born in Boston, Massachusetts, the son of Captain William Barnes and Jane (maiden name unknown). He was educated at the Latin School of Boston and went into business after graduation; but he desired a military life and in 1825 secured an appointment to the U.S. Military Academy at West Point. Barnes was an excellent student and graduated fifth in the illustrious class of 1829, which included Robert E. Lee and Joseph E. Johnston. Following graduation he was commissioned a second lieutenant in the Fourth Artillery. After a brief assignment as a French instructor at the academy, he was stationed at Fort McHenry, Maryland. He subsequently served in the Black Hawk Expedition of 1832, although he did not see active service, and was at the garrison at Charleston Harbor, South Carolina, during that state's threatened secession in 1832–1833. Barnes returned to West Point in 1833 to teach infantry tactics until his resignation on 31 July 1836.

After departing from the army, Barnes embarked on a career in railroading. He secured a position as assistant engineer of the Western Railroad, from Massachusetts to New York, and was subsequently elevated to chief engineer and superintendent. In 1848 he took the job of chief engineer of the Sea-Board and Roanoke Railroad, running from Norfolk, Virginia, to Weldon, North Carolina. He also supervised the construction of several different railroads in New York, Illinois, Indiana, and Missouri between 1848 and 1857.

At the outbreak of the Civil War, although sixty years old Barnes immediately made his services available and received a commission as colonel of the Eighteenth Massachusetts Infantry. He trained his regiment in the fall of 1861 and the spring of 1862 while serving in the defense of Washington, D.C. In the spring of 1862 he accompanied the army to the Virginia Peninsula and participated in the Peninsula campaign. He subsequently served in the second Manassas campaign, where his regiment was heavily engaged, and the Maryland campaign, where his command was held in reserve. Following the battle of Antietam, Barnes was placed in command of a brigade in the Fifth Corps. He was promoted to brigadier general of volunteers on 29 November 1862 and led his command through the battles of Fredricksburg and Chancellorsville. One member of the brigade wrote that during this time Barnes "secured the esteem and confidence of his subordinates and the admiration and regard of his soldiers." At Gettysburg, Barnes temporarily assumed command of his division in the absence of the regular division commander. He led his division into the "wheatfield" on 2 July, where it saw severe fighting. The historian of one of his regiments wrote that Barnes "rode valiantly amid the thickest of the fray, encouraging, persuading, directing with that same courageous judgment which had ever been his distinguishing characteristic."

Although Barnes was personally very brave he did not command his brigades with much success. Late in the action he received a wound that forced him to relinquish command of the division on 3 July. He was granted a leave of absence to recover from his wound and returned to Springfield, Massachusetts. When well enough to return to active duty, he was assigned to court-martial duty, and then, from September 1863 to January 1864, he commanded the defense of Norfolk and Portsmouth, Virginia. Barnes apparently suffered from poor health and he was again assigned to court-martial duty until his appointment on 2 July 1864 to command the prison at Point Lookout, Maryland. He remained there until the end of the war, when he returned to Massachusetts, but his health had been greatly impaired by the war.

In 1868 Barnes served as a member of a special commission to examine and report on the Union Pacific Railroad line. Never having married, he died in Springfield, Massachusetts. Barnes's success in the railroad industry was such that he could have comfortably avoided the war. But in spite of his age he offered his services and served creditably in the field until his Gettysburg wound and poor health forced him into less active service.

• Barnes's personal papers are at the New-York Historical Society. For his official military correspondence and reports during the Civil War, see *The War of the Rebellion: A Compilation of the Official Records of the Union and Confederate Armies* (128 vols., 1880–1901). His professional military record is contained in G. W. Cullum, *Biographical Register of the Officers and Graduates of the United States Military Academy*, vol. 2, 3d ed. (1891). For a perspective on how Barnes was seen by the men he commanded, see *History of the Corn Exchange Regiment* (1888). Barnes's performance at Gettysburg is examined in detail in Harry Pfanz, *Gettysburg: The Second Day* (1987). Barnes defended himself against the criticism of his performance at Gettysburg in correspondence that was published in Richard A. Sauers, *A Caspian Sea of Ink: The Meade–Sickles Controversy* (1989).

D. SCOTT HARTWIG

BARNES, James Martin (8 Apr. 1886–25 May 1966), professional golfer, was born in Lelant, Cornwall, England. His parents' names are unknown. As a boy he was an apprentice and then assistant professional golfer at the West Cornwall Golf Club. He immigrated to the United States in 1906 and took up residence in San Francisco. Later he became a naturalized citizen, although he frequently returned to his homeland to play in the British Open championship.

Barnes's nickname, "Long Jim," came from his height of 6'4" and his ability to hit a golf ball a long way. His first notable victory came in 1908 when he won the Pacific Northwest Open. He achieved further notice with a fourth-place finish in the 1913 U.S. Open and wins at the Western Open in 1914 and the North-South Open in 1916. Barnes was one of the founders and original members of the Professional Golf Association (PGA) and became its first champion in 1916. The next PGA tournament was not held until 1919 because of World War I; Barnes repeated as champion. By 1921 he was regarded as one of the best golfers in the world, with additional victories in the Western Open in 1917 and 1919 and the North-South Open in 1919. Barnes married Caroline Haggerty in the early 1920s; the couple had two children.

The peak of Barnes's golfing ability came in the 1921 U.S. Open, held at the Columbia Country Club in Chevy Chase, Maryland. Barnes left his competition far behind when he won by nine strokes. President Warren G. Harding, who had played golf with Barnes in Florida, followed play on the course and then presented Barnes with the championship trophy.

Barnes traveled to Great Britain in 1925 for his sixth attempt to add the British Open title to his victories. He won the prestigious title because of two factors beyond his control. First, he played early on the last day of competition and posted his score. As a result, he was not bothered by the unruly crowds that swarmed over the Prestwick course in Scotland to cheer on local favorite MacDonald Smith. Second, Smith collapsed to an 82, allowing Barnes to win by one stroke. Newspapers at the time commented more on the Smith failure than on the Barnes victory.

The 1925 British Open marked the last major win for Barnes. He remained a touring professional through 1930 and played in his final U.S. Open in 1932. Between 1916, when the PGA was founded, and 1932 Barnes won 18 tournaments and had 14 second-place finishes in the United States. At age fifty-three he won the 1939 New Jersey Open. During his career Barnes served as head professional golfer at clubs on Long Island and in Pelham, New York. His final post was at the Essex County Country Club in West Orange, New Jersey.

At his prime Barnes was a straight driver and hit the ball as far as anyone. His early training on the Cornish coast was evident whenever there was wind on the golf course. In spite of his acknowledged talents Barnes never sought publicity and remained comparatively unknown to the general public. He was a quiet man who preferred to play in silence with a sprig of clover (which became his trademark) clenched between his teeth.

Barnes authored a book of visual instruction, *Picture Analysis of Golf Strokes* (1919). It was the first golf book to use high speed photography and featured a full page of pictures analyzing key points in a golf swing.

At the time of his 1925 British Open victory, a *New York Times* columnist wrote, "No golfer ever took golf more seriously than Jim Barnes. It's a crime to Barnes to play a careless shot, even in practice." Contemporary and rival Gene Sarazen remarked that Barnes "was a damn fine golfer with a solid all around game." Barnes died in East Orange, New Jersey.

Barnes does not rank in the very top echelon of golfers, such as Walter Hagen or Bobby Jones. Nonetheless, he remains one of few golfers to win every major professional championship.

• An interview with Barnes, titled "Jim Barnes: A President's Champion," is in the *USGA Journal*, May 1964. Material on his career and accomplishments can be found in Al Barkow, *The History of the PGA Tour* (1989); George Peper and the editors of *Golf Magazine, Golf in America: The First One Hundred Years* (1988); and Robert Sommers, *The U.S. Open: Golf's Ultimate Challenge* (1987). Comments on the personality and ability of Barnes, not entirely complimentary, are in Gene Sarazen with Herbert Warren Wind, *Thirty Years of Championship Golf* (1950). An obituary is in the *New York Times*, 26 May 1966.

LEWIS H. CROCE

BARNES, Joseph K. (21 July 1817–5 Apr. 1883), U.S. Army medical officer and surgeon general, was born in Philadelphia, Pennsylvania, the son of Joseph Barnes, for many years a judge of the Philadelphia district court. His mother's name is not known. After attending a private school in Northampton, Massachusetts, Barnes entered Harvard University but was unable to complete his studies there because of poor health. After studying medicine with U.S. Navy surgeon Thomas Harris, later the navy's surgeon general, he began attending lectures in medicine at the University of Pennsylvania, from which he received his M.D. in 1838. He then served a year as a hospital resident in Philadelphia and another year as physician to that city's poor. The date of his marriage to Mary Fauntleroy is unknown; they had no children.

Barnes entered the U.S. Army Medical Department on 15 June 1840. After a brief assignment at the U.S. Military Academy at West Point, he served in Florida during the struggle against the Seminole Indians from late 1840 to 1843. He was then assigned to Fort Jesup in Louisiana, where he served until 1846 when he joined the troops preparing to invade Mexico under Brigadier General Zachary Taylor. In the course of his subsequent service under General Taylor and later under Major General Winfield Scott, he took part in every major battle of the Mexican War until the fall of Mexico City in September 1847.

During the thirteen years following the end of the Mexican War, Barnes served at many posts across the U.S. and was promoted to surgeon, a position that carried with it the rank of major after medical officers were granted rank in 1847. With the outbreak of the Civil War in 1861, Barnes was ordered from his post at Fort Vancouver on the West Coast to serve Union forces fighting along the Missouri River. In 1862 he was ordered to Washington, D.C., to serve as attending surgeon, in which capacity he cared for army and government personnel working in the nation's capital and favorably impressed Secretary of War Edwin Stanton.

In September 1863 Barnes was required to act in the place of Surgeon General William A. Hammond when that unfortunate officer fell out of favor with Stanton. When Hammond was dismissed as surgeon general on 22 August 1864, Barnes became surgeon general in his own right and was given the rank of brigadier general. The respect that Stanton had for him enabled Barnes to act forcefully to maintain the medical department's control over the evacuation of Union sick and wounded. He was also able to encourage the collection of records and anatomical specimens initiated by Hammond. Barnes was among the physicians attending President Abraham Lincoln's deathbed after he was shot on 14 April 1865 and was responsible for the official declaration of death issued the following morning. He was also responsible for the care of Secretary of State William H. Seward, who was also the victim of an assassination attempt at this time.

In the years following the Civil War, Barnes brought to fruition Hammond's ambition to create both an army medical museum and an army medical library. The former was the ancestor of today's Armed Forces Institute of Pathology, while the latter eventually became the National Library of Medicine. Barnes was also the driving force behind achieving Hammond's goal of using the records of the Civil War to create a detailed medical history, *The Medical and Surgical History of the War of the Rebellion*, published from 1870 to 1888.

Barnes's burdens were great after the Civil War. Dissuading Congress from eliminating so many positions from the Army Medical Department that it could no longer carry out its responsibilities required constant effort, as did the need to see that the department properly collected and maintained the records necessary to determine the eligibility of veterans for disability pensions. The stress on Barnes increased in 1881 when for two months he and other medical officers struggled to save President James A. Garfield, who lay dying of gunshot wounds delivered by an assassin.

The passage of a law requiring military officers to retire at the age of sixty-five dictated Barnes's retirement on 30 June 1882. Barnes's health was already failing when he retired, and he died in Washington, D.C., less than a year later.

A modest and unassuming man, Barnes came to the office of surgeon general under particularly difficult circumstances but proved himself capable of taking up where his brilliant but abrasive predecessor had left off. Because of his ability to work with Stanton and Congress, he was able to deal effectively with the many difficult problems involved in returning the wartime medical department to peacetime status. At the same time, as heir to worthwhile projects that had been tainted by their association with his predecessor, he was able both to preserve the legacy of the Civil War for future generations and to lay the foundations that became known and respected by the scientific community throughout the world. "It is wonderful," an obituary stated, "how much work was done under his supervision, and yet how seldom his own name was obtruded upon the public."

• Ironically, although he was responsible for having *The Medical and Surgical History of the War of the Rebellion* written and published and had encouraged those serving under him in other writing projects, Barnes apparently never wrote for publication himself. There is no known collection of his papers. Biographical material concerning Barnes can be found in James A. Phalen, *Chiefs of the Medical Department, United States Army, 1775–1940* (1940); James Evelyn Pilcher, *The Surgeon Generals of the Army of the United States of America* (1905); and Mary C. Gillett, *The Army Medical Department, 1818–1865* (1987) and *The Army Medical Department, 1865–1917* (1995). An obituary appears in the *Boston Medical and Surgical Journal* 108 (1883): 355, 379.

MARY C. GILLETT

BARNES, Julius Howland (2 Feb. 1873–17 Apr. 1959), industrialist and government official, was born in Little Rock, Arkansas, the son of Lucien Jerome Barnes, a banker, and Julia Hill. Moving with his family, he attended public schools in Washington, D.C., and Duluth, Minnesota. Following his father's death in 1886, Barnes left school to take a job as office boy with the Duluth grain brokerage firm of Wardell Ames. There he rose rapidly, becoming president of the company in 1910 and subsequently reorganizing it as the Barnes-Ames Company. By 1915 Barnes-Ames was the world's largest grain exporter, and Barnes acquired other business interests, principally in shipbuilding and Great Lakes shipping. In 1896 he married Harriet Carey, with whom he had two children.

As America moved into World War I, Barnes strongly advocated collective action to control and protect the grain trade. In April 1917 he became chair of the Committee of Grain Exchanges in Aid of National Defense, and in that capacity he worked with Food Administrator Herbert Hoover to devise appropriate controls. Subsequently, he divested himself of his grain interests and went to Washington as a dollar-a-year man, initially as head of Hoover's Cereal Division and later as president of the Food Administration Grain Corporation, the agency using government funds and trade agreements to maintain a fixed price for wheat and to intervene in other grain markets. In essence, Barnes ran a huge purchasing and selling agency with enough market power to move the pricing, distribution, usage, and cultivation of grain toward goals set by the war managers. By war's end the agency had bought and sold over 150 million bushels of wheat and substantial amounts of other grains, and it continued to function in the immediate postwar period. As the U.S. Grain Corporation, it became the major fiscal agency for Hoover's American Relief Administration as well as the instrument through which Barnes, the nation's wheat director, made good the promised price guarantees for the 1919 wheat crop. Not until June 1920 did Barnes end his war work, and memory of it continued to shape his ideas about business and government.

Also significant for Barnes's future was his wartime association with Hoover. In 1919 and 1920 he worked to secure the Republican presidential nomination for Hoover, even going so far as to join in purchasing the *Washington Herald* and later serving as a convention floor manager. From 1922 to 1924, as president of the U.S. Chamber of Commerce and an influential figure in the International Chamber, he worked with Secretary of Commerce Hoover on projects intended to reduce industrial waste, mitigate cyclical unemployment, improve grain marketing, develop internal waterways, and bring financial stability to postwar Europe. As an "industrial statesman," he preached, as Hoover did, an enlightened associationalism that would allegedly curb governmental growth by entrusting the management of economic and social progress to public-minded and scientifically informed business, professional, and occupational groups. This was the theme in numerous speeches and in some forty pamphlets bearing such titles as *Modern Industry and Individualism* (1922), *The Opportunity of Business Leadership* (1923), and *Self-Government in Business* (1926).

While extolling the "new business," Barnes also expanded his own holdings. In the 1920s he reacquired his interests in Barnes-Ames, retained those in shipping and shipbuilding, and added new ones in paper production, banking, and packaging. In addition, he organized and headed the Klearflax Linen Rug Company (later Klearflax Linen Looms), which put into operation his invention of a way to manufacture linen rugs from discarded flax straw. By 1929, when he began two years as board chairman of the U.S. Chamber of Commerce, he held offices in ten corporations and was widely viewed as one of the nation's leading industrialists.

Given these attachments and achievements, it was logical that Barnes should play a key role in testing Hoover's associationalism under depression conditions. In late 1929 President Hoover persuaded him to head the National Business Survey Conference, a Chamber of Commerce agency that tried unsuccessfully to implement the pledges of wage maintenance and expanded investment spending that Hoover had secured at a series of business conferences. Barnes also helped Hoover organize a similar agency intended to expand construction, and in 1931, as chair of the Executive Committee of the National Conference on Construction, he helped organize a further attack on construction impediments. He disagreed, however, with Hoover's farm and antitrust policies, especially with the new Farm Board's treatment of grain dealers and the Justice Department's prosecution of various types of trade association activity. These matters occasioned a temporary break with Hoover, leading to Barnes's

exclusion from the later phases of Hoover's recovery effort. Nor did Barnes's business ventures fare well during the depression. He lost heavily in the crash of 1929, ceased to be a major grain exporter, spent a frustrating two years (1930–1932) accomplishing little as president of the General Bronze Corporation, and by 1932 was pinning his hopes on new holdings in the insurance industry.

In his later years Barnes's major interest was in promoting the St. Lawrence Seaway, a project he had been interested in since 1905. From 1944 to 1948 he served as president of the St. Lawrence Association, helping to pave the way for legislation that made possible the opening of the seaway a month after his death. He also spent much of his remaining fortune on this promotional campaign and on civic and recreational programs for Duluth, leaving an estate of only $52,000.

In appearance and personality, Barnes was an impressive figure, tall and erect, muscular but fine featured, and adept at combining boosterish sentiments with shrewd business sense and well-developed organizational skills. He is remembered chiefly as the "Hoover man" who tamed the grain markets of World War I, but he also played a significant role in the associationalist project of the 1920s and the actions leading to public disenchantment with it during the Great Depression. He died in his hotel suite in Duluth.

• The main body of the Barnes papers, including his unpublished memoirs, are at the St. Louis County Historical Society in Duluth. Barnes materials are also at the Herbert Hoover Presidential Library, at the Hoover Institution of War and Peace at Stanford, and in the U.S. Grain Corporation records at the National Archives. The most useful biographical sketches are DuBois K. Wiggins, "Spent a Billion and Saved It," *Paterson (N.J.) Chronicle*, 11 July 1926, and John N. Ingham, "Julius Howland Barnes," in *Biographical Dictionary of American Business Leaders* (1983). Also useful for various aspects of Barnes's career are Frank M. Surface, *The Grain Trade during the World War* (1928); Albert U. Romasco, *The Poverty of Abundance: Hoover, the Nation, the Depression* (1965); Gary Dean Best, *The Politics of American Individualism: Herbert Hoover in Transition, 1918–1921* (1975); Carlton Mabee, *The Seaway Story* (1961); and George H. Nash, *The Life of Herbert Hoover: Master of Emergencies, 1917–1918* (1996). An obituary is in the *New York Times*, 18 Apr. 1959.

ELLIS W. HAWLEY

BARNES, Mary Downing Sheldon (15 Sept. 1850–27 Aug. 1898), educator, was born in Oswego, New York, the daughter of Edward Austin Sheldon, an educator, and Frances Anna Bradford Stiles. After completing her early education in the public schools of Oswego, she entered the Oswego Normal and Training School, where she finished the classical course in 1868 and the advanced course the following year. While at Oswego, Sheldon was greatly influenced by her father, who as principal of the school had molded the institution into a leading center of Pestalozzian-based education. Following graduation, she taught at the Normal and Training School in Oswego for two years before entering the sophomore class at the University of Michigan in September 1871. One of the first female students to attend the university, Sheldon was originally interested in the natural sciences. Having taken two history courses under Professor C. K. Adams, however, she was invited to teach Greek, Latin, and botany as well as history at the Normal and Training School upon her graduation in 1874. Denied the chance to teach her first love, physics, she "revenge[d] herself by applying scientific methods to history" (Barnes, quoted in Keohane, p. 68).

Successfully established as a teacher of history, Sheldon moved to Wellesley College in 1876. At Wellesley, Sheldon implemented the radical, new "seminar" method of historical instruction she had experienced at Michigan. Eschewing the use of textbooks and rote recitation that was then in vogue, Sheldon reproduced primary source material, which she then gave to her students for study and reflection. Classes were kept small, and class time was largely devoted to discussion. Her instructional methods "aimed to do two things: First, to give the students enough information to give them a clear intellectual appreciation of the general development and characteristics of European history; second, to train them to think and feel historically, to deal thoughtfully and sympathetically with historical fact" (Barnes, quoted in Keohane, p. 68).

Student reaction to the new instructional method was enthusiastic, but Sheldon's health gave out from overexertion, and she was compelled to leave her post after two and a half years. Following a year of rest and feeling the need for additional training, she journeyed to Europe and the Near East, where she spent two years in travel and also studied modern history at Newnham College, Cambridge, England, under the direction of Professor J. R. Seeley.

Upon returning to the United States in 1882, Sheldon resumed teaching in Oswego. She married Earl Barnes, a history teacher at an academy in Hoboken, New Jersey, in 1884; they had no children. During the next several years Mary Barnes refined her teaching methods and outlined them in her first book, *Studies in General History*, in 1885. In this book, she attempted to adapt her primary source method of instruction to the American high school history classroom. She also published *Studies in General History: Teacher's Manual* (1886) as a guide to high school instructors in the proper use of her methods. While her methods won support among some educators and students, they provoked criticism from others. Some objected to the time-consuming demands of the new method; others, perhaps reacting to the term "seminar," questioned the wisdom of raising college and high school students to the equality of status with the instructor that was implicit in standard graduate-school seminars. Some instructors, still clinging to the concept (prevalent in the early eighteenth century) of academic instruction in which character development enjoyed hegemony over the development of intellectual capacities, even resented the new method's success in promoting analytical and critical thinking.

In the face of both acceptance and criticism, Barnes continued to write, study, and travel. In 1891 she and her husband (who had taught history at Indiana University from 1889 to 1891) moved to Stanford University, where he became a professor of education and she accepted the position of associate professor of history in March 1892, becoming the first female faculty member at the school. The couple had combined efforts in 1891 to produce *Studies in American History*, which further outlined her theories of classroom instruction. During her years at Stanford, Barnes adapted her instructional methods for both collegiate- and elementary school–level teaching and discussed her theories in *Studies in Historical Method* (1896).

Barnes and her husband resigned from the Stanford faculty in 1897, intent on travel and study in Europe. Following a period of time in France and Italy, they visited England, where the recurrence of organic heart disease led to her death in London following an operation. Following Barnes's wishes, her husband took her body to Rome, where she was buried in the Protestant cemetery.

Mary Barnes was an educational pioneer. Her classroom teaching techniques were far in advance of her time and greatly influenced the development of modern teaching methods. Her greatest legacy was the increased scrutiny given to classroom texts, and in the increased emphasis on the use of primary sources in historical studies.

• The papers of Mary Sheldon Barnes are divided between the archives of the State University of New York at Oswego and Mr. and Mrs. Joseph Barnes of Cornwall Bridge, Conn. The best source of information on her life and career remains Robert E. Keohane, "Mary Sheldon Barnes and the Origin of the Source Method of Teaching History in the American Secondary School," *American Heritage* 2, no. 3 (Oct. 1948): 68–72, and 2, no. 4 (Dec. 1948): 109–12. Additional sources include Dorothy Rogers, *Oswego: Fountainhead of Teacher Education* (1961), and Edward Howard Griggs, *Earl Barnes: A Life-Sketch and an Address* (1935). Obituaries include Katherine Lee Bates, "In Memoriam," *Wellesley College Magazine*, Oct. 1898, and William S. Monroe's in the *Journal of Education*, 15 Sept. 1898.

EDWARD L. LACH, JR.

BARNES, Pancho (22 July 1901–c. 29 Mar. 1975), airwoman, was born Florence Leontine Lowe in San Marino, California, the daughter of Thaddeus Lowe, Jr., and Florence Mae Dobbins. The uninhibited character of Barnes's adult life contrasts sharply with the conventionality of her background and upbringing. Born into a wealthy California family and educated at several private and convent schools, she was married at the age of nineteen to the Anglican vicar of Pasadena, C. Rankin Barnes, in 1921, giving birth to her only child, William, the same year. The marriage was not successful and the couple quickly separated, although they did not divorce until 1941. The death of her mother in 1924 made Barnes financially independent, enabling her to embark upon a life of adventure. Capitalizing upon her childhood training as a horsewoman, she obtained work as a double for several Hollywood actors in horseback scenes, as well as providing occasional screenwriting assistance to her childhood friend Erich von Stroheim. Her film career was interrupted by a stint in 1927 as a deck hand aboard a cargo vessel that was briefly impounded by the authorities of the Mexican port of San Blas during the Cristero rebellion, an experience that earned her the nickname by which she was to be known for the rest of her life.

In the summer of 1928 Barnes began to take flying lessons and characteristically began performing in air shows and offering parachute jumps while still an inexperienced student pilot. Gaining her commercial license the following year, she proceeded rapidly to air racing, participating in the first coast-to-coast contest for women, or "Powder Puff Derby," in competition with such noted airwomen as Louise Thaden and Amelia Earhart. She enjoyed a measure of success as a racing pilot, setting a women's world speed mark of 196.19 miles per hour in a Travel Air Model R "Mystery Ship" in August 1930, only to be deprived of the record shortly afterward by Ruth Nichols. Barnes, however, possessed neither the resources nor the temperament for serious competitive flying—a pursuit that exacted an alarmingly high toll on machines and pilots alike—and participated in her last race in 1931.

The onset of the Great Depression severely curtailed Barnes's primary sources of income, aviation and movie work. After an unsuccessful bid in 1932 as a nonpartisan candidate for a Los Angeles County supervisor's seat, she liquidated her remaining assets and bought a desert ranch, "Oro Verde," near Muroc, California, some fifty miles north of Los Angeles. There she and her teenage son supplied agricultural produce to the personnel of the rudimentary aviation testing facility operated by the Army Air Corps and the Lockheed Aircraft Company four miles away. Barnes also opened an air training school at the ranch, securing a contract in 1940 to train civilian cadets, and supplemented her income by flying in bootleg alcohol from Mexico. With the onset of the Second World War her business boomed, as Muroc became one of the largest and most isolated test and training facilities in the country. By the late 1940s Barnes had expanded her ranch complex to include a motel, dance hall, restaurant, coffee shop, and two bars. The most controversial part of the establishment, however, was the ambiguously named "Happy Bottom Riding Club," whose main attractions—although it did, in fact, hire out horses—were the exotic dancers and "hostesses" recruited by Barnes to cater to her male customers. While in later years she indignantly disavowed any personal involvement in, or knowledge of, prostitution at her ranch, a determinedly Nelsonian blind eye was habitually turned to the "bustling and hustling" that took place at her Wednesday night bacchanalias.

The 1940s were Barnes's best years, as virtually every civilian and military test pilot of note passed through her establishment. In 1953, though, her fortunes plummeted when the Air Force moved to acquire her land for a new runway by compulsory purchase, a step she interpreted as a backdoor maneuver to close down her ranch on morals grounds. Prolonged litigation followed, and although she emerged in 1956 with a substantial monetary settlement, most of the proceeds were dissipated in a series of unwise investments. An attempt to re-create her establishment in a new location at Cantil failed, as did marriages to her second, third, and fourth husbands, Robert Hudson Nichols (1941–1945), Joseph D. Shalita (1945–1946), and Eugene S. McKendry (1952–1966), each ending in divorce. Impoverished and debilitated by a long struggle with breast cancer, Barnes spent her last years living alone in a trailer at Boron, California, where she was found dead in March 1975.

Barnes was one of the more flamboyant figures of the heroic age of American aviation. In succession a debutante, actress, deck hand, air racer, barnstormer, bootlegger, and rancher, she gained her greatest notoriety as the proprietor of a riding club cum bordello patronized by test pilots at the Muroc Dry Lake facility (now Edwards Air Force Base) in the 1930s and 1940s. Barnes's personality made an indelible impression on all who encountered her. No respecter of conventions, or of persons; spectacularly profane, "never using a five- or six-letter word when a four-letter word would do" (Chuck Yeager); and possessed, in the memorable description of her friend Glennis Yeager, of a "face like a mud fence," she was truly comfortable only in the company of her circle of hard-drinking, boisterous young pilots, whom she alternately abetted in the commission of various forms of adolescent mayhem and watched over with a protective eye. Her hard-bitten and abrasive style was tempered by a softness of heart that manifested itself in countless unadvertised, and occasionally reckless, acts of generosity. The combination of exasperation and deep affection she typically evoked from her intimate acquaintances was neatly encapsulated after her death by one of her former hostesses, Dallas Morley: "Pancho was an ornery, nasty, ugly person. But I loved her."

• A small collection of Barnes papers, including some autobiographical fragments, is in the possession of Mrs. Barbara Hunter Schultz, Lancaster, Calif., whose *Pancho: The Biography of Florence Lowe Barnes* (1996) is the most detailed life available. Ted Tate's *The Lady Who Tamed Pegasus: The Story of Pancho Barnes* (1986) is unreliable. See also Edwards Air Force Base History Office, *Pancho Barnes, An Original: 1901–1975* (1982); Chuck Yeager and Leo Janos, *Yeager* (1985); and the biographical article in the *Los Angeles Times*, 17 Nov. 1985.

R. M. DOUGLAS

BARNES, William Harry (4 Apr. 1887–15 June 1945), physician and otolaryngologist, was born in Philadelphia, Pennsylvania, the son of George W. Barnes, a menial laborer, and Eliza Webb. Young Barnes and his two sisters lived poverty-stricken lives on Lombard Street, a very poor area of the city. He decided at an early age to become a physician, a decision unheard of and regarded as preposterous in his neighborhood. His parents tried to discourage him from pursuing what to them seemed like an absolutely impossible dream for a poor black youth, hoping rather to get him to focus his attention on getting realistic employment. Determined, he walked ten miles every day to and from school and from his after-school work as a porter and messenger for jewelry shops. During summers he worked as a porter in hotels. Seeing people who lived a far different and more elegant lifestyle than his own galvanized him to work himself out of poverty. In 1908 he graduated from Philadelphia's Central High School with a collegiate bachelor of arts degree and decided to compete for a four-year scholarship to medical school offered by the University of Pennsylvania. He spent the entire summer of 1908 in serious study, took the competitive examination, passed it, and became the first black person to ever win that scholarship. Four years later, in 1912, he received an M.D. and began an internship (1912–1913) at Douglass and Mercy hospitals in Philadelphia. Also in 1912 he married Mattie E. Thomas; they would have five children.

Barnes then established several long-term relationships with hospitals and other medical facilities in and outside of Philadelphia. From 1913 to 1945 he was an ear, nose, and throat staff physician at Douglass Hospital; in 1921 he was chief of otolaryngology at Jefferson Medical School Hospital in Philadelphia; and from 1913 to 1922 and again in 1931 he was lecturer in bronchoscopy at Howard University Medical School in Washington, D.C. At this time he was also a registrant of the American College of Surgeons. In 1918 he served as acting assistant surgeon for the U.S. Public Health Service. In spite of a heavy schedule of professional responsibilities and a professionally stultifying racial environment, especially for black physicians, he managed to develop and maintain a growing private medical practice between 1922 and 1945. In 1922, against the advice of friends, associates, and relatives, he limited his medical practice to diseases of the ear, nose, and throat, making him the first black medical specialist in the United States. In the early 1930s he organized and headed the Department of Bronchoscopy at Mercy Hospital. He found time to do postgraduate work at Douglass and Mercy hospitals (1921), the University of Pennsylvania (1924, 1926), the University of Paris, and the University of Bordeaux (1924). In addition to formal course work he also took advanced medical training in bronchoscopic technique from internationally known specialists, such as Sebileau and Baldenbeck in Paris, Moure in Bordeaux, Unger in New York, and Schatz and Lukens in Philadelphia. Barnes was the first black physician to master the technique of bronchoscopy. He was also the first black granted certification by an American medical certifying board, the American Board of Otolaryngology (1927), and therefore the first black physician officially recognized as a medical specialist in the United States.

Barnes was a medical and community activist who worked hard to increase the flow of medical information, and its accessibility and availability to his people. In addition he made great efforts to upgrade medical practice and standards among black physicians. One of his highest priorities was to improve general living conditions within black communities because he was acutely aware of the connection between decent housing and good public health. He was the thirty-seventh president of the National Medical Association (1935–1936), a parallel organization created by black physicians in 1895 because they were denied membership in the American Medical Association. Barnes was an active participant in NMA annual meetings, which he turned into teaching forums by presenting papers and performing demonstration surgical procedures. In 1931 Barnes founded the Society for the Promotion of Negro Specialists in Medicine, and from 1931 to 1933 he served as the organization's executive secretary. A member of Philadelphia's Zoar Methodist Church, where he regularly taught Sunday school and for fifteen years was president of the board of trustees, he there organized a well-baby clinic and taught first aid. At other churches in the community he also set up and taught first aid classes. He founded the Zoar Community Building and Loan Association and served as its president from 1925 to 1945. A proponent of integration in public housing, he was one of the original members of the Philadelphia Housing Authority and served as its assistant secretary-treasurer from 1937 to 1945.

Barnes was a medical innovator. Between 1913 and 1938 he invented the hypophyscope, an instrument for visualizing the pituitary gland by accessing it through the sphenoidal sinus; invented a lingual tonsillectome, a specialized scalpel used in performing tonsillectomies; developed a surgical modification of the Myles lingual tonsillectomy procedure; developed surgical procedures for more effectively treating tonsillar abscesses; and created improved medical record-keeping procedures for patient records. He was an early riser and practitioner of strict punctuality. When chairing meetings he would begin at the appointed time regardless of who was, or was not, present. His surgical operations were often scheduled for seven o'clock in the morning, to the annoyance of his staff and nurses.

Barnes belonged to and was an officer in many civic and professional organizations, including the American Medical Association, when membership became possible in the late 1920s to early 1930s; the American Board of Otolaryngology; the Negro Specialists Society, which he served as executive secretary from 1931 to 1938; the Philadelphia Academy of Medicine and Allied Sciences, of which he was president for three years in the early 1930s; the National Association for the Advancement of Colored People; and the Citizen's Republican Club, where he was president of the Forum Commission in the 1930s. He died in Philadelphia, Pennsylvania.

Barnes was an indefatigable worker who personally involved himself in every aspect of medical and community life. His personal motto, which he often expressed, was "failure comes from within"; in his view, therefore, failure could be controlled and eliminated. He proved by his own example that in spite of growing up in poverty, and regularly experiencing incredible barriers and obstacles throughout most of the rest of his life, he could achieve his lofty goals even though no one else close to him thought that he could. Having done that he actively tried to help as many other people as possible obtain a better life for themselves.

• A listing of Barnes's technical writings (1913–1939) is in *National Medical Association Journal* 47 (1955): 64–66, 69. A testimonial from colleagues is in "The President Elect," *National Medical Association Journal* 26 (1934): 176. A description of his invention is found in *Laryngos* 27 (1927): 379–80. See also Vivian Ovelton Sammons, *Blacks in Science and Medicine* (1990), pp. 20–21.

BILL SCOTT

BARNET, Charlie (26 Oct. 1913–4 Sept. 1991), jazz and popular bandleader and saxophonist, was born Charles Daly Barnet in New York City, the son of Willard Barnet and Charline Daly. Both parents played piano. Barnet evidently inherited his father's ear for music, but his parents divorced when he was two years old, and Willard Barnet never saw his son again. Barnet and his mother lived with her parents. His grandfather Charles Frederick Daly was executive vice president of the New York Central Railroad, and Barnet lived comfortably in New York hotels and apartments, and a summer home.

Although his mother wanted him to study piano, Barnet preferred drums. He attended several schools, including Berkeley-Irving on Eighty-third Street and, at age twelve, the Riverdale Country School, a boarding school where he studied piano for two years and first played saxophone. He began on C-melody sax but switched to tenor sax after hearing Fletcher Henderson's orchestra with Coleman Hawkins, who became his greatest influence as a soloist. He next attended Blair Academy in Blairstown, New Jersey. After moving with his family to California, he went to live with relatives in the Chicago area and briefly attended New Trier school in Winnetka, Illinois. Running off to New York, he worked for a few weeks as a theater usher before being returned to his grandmother. He re-enrolled at Berkeley-Irving but spent most of his time working as a saxophonist rather than studying.

In the summer of 1929 Barnet made his first trip as a musician on an Atlantic cruise. He traveled throughout the South, Southwest, and southern California, and discographies credit him with playing chimes on the several recordings of "Ring Dem Bells" that Duke Ellington made in Hollywood in August 1930. By this point in his life Barnet was already an alcoholic, a light drug user, a gambler, and a notorious practical joker.

In 1933 Barnet formed a big band for a three-month residency at the Paramount Hotel Grill in New York, broadcasting nationally via the CBS network. That year he also held jobs with xylophonist Red Norvo, one or the other serving as leader. In 1934 he formed another band for the Park Central Hotel's Cocoanut Grove. Arranger, bandleader, and multi-instrumentalist Benny Carter recorded with the band in March and sat in occasionally as a trumpeter in the summer.

That fall, under Norvo, Barnet recorded solos on "I Surrender, Dear" and "The Night Is Blue" in a swing group that included the not-yet-famous clarinetist Artie Shaw and pianist Teddy Wilson. In November, on Carter's recommendation, Barnet's ensemble became the first white orchestra to play at the Apollo Theater in Harlem; in later years he appeared there regularly.

The band went on tour after this first Apollo engagement, and while in New Orleans in January 1935 they recorded Carter's scores for "Devil's Holiday" (as "On a Holiday") and "Nagasaki." Back in New York, Barnet married Joyce O'Day, a model, and then asked for a divorce almost immediately. Fleeing to Miami and Havana, he eventually worked as a gigolo during pre-divorce negotiations.

In 1936 Barnet attempted to become a movie actor, but he never got further than bit parts in *Love and Hisses* (1937) and *Sally, Irene and Mary* (1938). In the summer of 1936 he returned east and formed a band to play at the Glen Island Casino, where he introduced a singing group, the Modernaires. They recorded "Make-Believe Ballroom," the first theme song used on disc jockey Martin Block's famous radio show of that name. African-American trumpeter Frankie Newton recorded with Barnet in 1937.

Barnet's second marriage was to Shirley Lloyd, a singer, in 1938. After a quick annulment, he married Betty Lorraine, a showgirl, that same year and then again secured an annulment. Also in 1938 he formed a band for a job at the Famous Door nightclub in New York, with arrangements written by Billy May and Andy Gibson. Barnet had taken up alto saxophone after admiring Johnny Hodges's playing with Ellington, and he added soprano sax when May began writing for it. The group held an engagement at the Paramount Theater, during which time Barnet had a much-discussed romance with actress Dorothy Lamour.

Barnet explicitly imitated Ellington's orchestral style, which he admired deeply, and Count Basie's big band was also a strong influence. But Barnet's band of 1939–1941 was best known for a hugely successful instrumental theme arranged by May, "Cherokee" (1939), which showed off the leader's Hawkins-like tenor playing and featured sprightly, swinging "riffs" (little repeated melodic patterns) tossed between sections of the band. Other notable recordings included "The Gal from Joe's," "The Duke's Idea," "The Count's Idea," "The Right Idea" (all from 1939), "Pompton Turnpike," "Redskin Rhumba," singer Mary Ann McCall's rendition of "Wanderin' Blues" (all 1940), and "Harlem Speaks" (1941).

During this period of his greatest popularity, Barnet held further residencies in the New York area before traveling across the country to open in August 1939 at the Palomar Ballroom in Los Angeles. Five weeks later this venue burned to the ground. The band lost all of its instruments and music, but Basie, Ellington, and Carter contributed replacement scores, and the band toured back east for residencies in Boston and New York. On the strength of "Cherokee," Barnet's band broke the house attendance record at the Apollo Theater and then toured an African-American theater circuit before resuming general touring. His fourth marriage was to Harriet Clarke, a singer, in November 1940; they had a son, his only child, and then separated.

Early in 1941 Barnet discovered and featured a young African-American singer, Lena Horne, who recorded the moody ballads "Good-for-Nothin' Joe" and "You're My Thrill." Barnet subsequently hired a number of notable African-American jazz instrumentalists: trumpeters Peanuts Holland, Al Killian, Howard McGhee, and Roy Eldridge; trombonist Trummy Young; pianist Dodo Marmarosa; and bassist Oscar Pettiford. Other band members from this period included trumpeter Neal Hefti, clarinetist Buddy De-Franco, pianist Ralph Burns, guitarist Barney Kessel, and singer Frances Wayne. In New York Barnet recorded Burns's arrangements of "The Moose" (1943) and "Drop Me off in Harlem" (1944), the latter featuring Eldridge. In the Los Angeles area he recorded "West End Blues" and another hit instrumental theme, "Skyliner," while also performing "Skyliner" in the film short *Melody Parade* and appearing in two feature-length movies, *Jam Session* and *Music in Manhattan* (all 1944).

After divorcing Clarke, Barnet married Rita Merritt in October 1946. He made further film appearances in *The Fabulous Dorseys* (1947) and *A Song Is Born* (1948). His band continued with trumpeters Clark Terry, Jimmy Nottingham, and Doc Severinson in 1947, and trumpeters Maynard Ferguson, Rolf Ericson, and Severinson, bassist Eddie Safranski, and drummer Tiny Kahn, who arranged "Over the Rainbow," all in 1949.

The early to mid-1950s brought five more marriages and increasingly less significant jobs, as the big band era died away. Barnet's eleventh and final marriage, in 1958, was to Betty Thompson, with whom he stayed permanently. They settled in Palm Springs, moving to San Diego for summers. Apart from a prolonged period of big band work from 1966 to 1967, during which time alto saxophonist Willie Smith was with the band, Barnet mainly led a sextet or septet. Gradually he retired from music to concentrate on flying, fishing, golfing, and horseracing. He died in San Diego. Writer Leonard Feather visited him and in one source reported the death as Tuesday night, 3 September, but the precise time was slightly later, at 12:14 A.M. on 4 September.

In his autobiography Barnet presents himself as somewhat of an upper-class, real-life parallel to Jack Kerouac's fictional character Dean Moriarty, celebrating African-American jazz while living a life in which his drug use, gambling, and practical jokes seem moderate by comparison to his uncontrolled alcoholism and irresponsible, exploitive relationships with women. Evidently many people think this sort of overwhelmingly ugly self-portrait makes for good reading, and surely it is accurate to a considerable extent: trumpeter McGhee recalled one especially painful instance of Barnet's excessive insensitivity, as he refused McGhee a $30 raise while McGhee was watching him gamble away thousands of dollars. Nonetheless, one must admire Barnet as a talented, dedicated, indefatigable, tasteful bandleader. Recognizing the significance of African-American creativity in jazz, he popularized such musical conceptions for mainstream white audiences, and he was a pioneer in creating racially integrated bands.

• Tapes and transcripts of Barnet and McGhee's oral histories are at the Institute of Jazz Studies, Newark, N.J. Some useful sources include Charlie Barnet with Stanley Dance, *Those Swinging Years: The Autobiography of Charlie Barnet* (1984; repr. 1992); Leonard Feather, "Barnet Took Basie's Beat, Duke's Harmonics," *Down Beat*, 21 Sept. 1951, pp. 2–3, 16, 19; Feather, "Whatever Happened to Charlie Barnet?" *Down Beat*, 11 Apr. 1963, p. 14; Jim Burns, "Lesser Known Bands of the Forties: No. 4 Charlie Barnet," *Jazz Monthly*, no. 161 (July 1968): 10–12; and Burns, "Charlie Barnet," *Jazz Monthly*, no. 183 (May 1970): 9–12. See also Ian Crosbie, "Clap Hands, Here Comes Charlie," *Jazz Journal* 26 (May 1973): 10–12, and (July 1973): 25–28; Albert McCarthy, *Big Band Jazz* (1974); George T. Simon, *The Big Bands*, 4th ed. (1981); Morroe Berger et al., *Benny Carter: A Life in American Music*, vol. 1 (1982); and Paul B. Matthews, "Eddie Bert Interview: Part One," *Cadence* 18 (Jan. 1992): 15–16. For musical analysis, see Gunther Schuller, *The Swing Era: The Development of Jazz, 1930–1945* (1989). Catalogs of Barnet's recordings are by Ernie Edwards et al., *Charlie Barnet and His Orchestra* (1965; rev. 2d ed., 1970), and Charles Garrod, *Charlie Barnet and His Orchestra* (1973; rev. 2d ed., 1984). Obituaries are in the *Los Angeles Times*, 5 Sept. 1991, and the *New York Times*, 6 Sept. 1991.

BARRY KERNFELD

BARNETT, Claude Albert (16 Sept. 1889–2 Aug. 1967), entrepreneur and journalist, was born in Sanford, Florida, the son of William Barnett, a hotel worker, and Celena Anderson. Although his parents separated when he was young, Barnett came from a proud black family, especially on his mother's side. He attended elementary school in Chicago and in Mattoon and Oak Park, Illinois, where he frequently lived with his mother's family. He went to Oak Park High School near Chicago and worked as a houseboy for Richard W. Sears, cofounder of Sears, Roebuck and Co.

After Barnett's graduation, Sears offered him a job with his company, but Barnett's mother insisted that he continue his education and sent him to Tuskegee Institute, from which he graduated in 1906 with a degree in engineering. While at Tuskegee, Barnett absorbed the principles of thrift, hard work, self-help, industrial training, and economic progress promulgated by its founder, Booker T. Washington. Those principles influenced Barnett's life as he sought economic security in numerous business ventures, promoted black business development, and emphasized the importance of the black consumer market to major corporations.

Returning to Chicago from Alabama after graduating from Tuskegee, Barnett found employment in the post office, which he left in 1915 because of ill health.

After dabbling in several businesses, he started his own advertising agency, the Douglas Speciality Company, which sold mail-order portraits of famous black men and beautiful black women, and he cofounded the Kashmir Chemical Company, which manufactured Nile Queen cosmetics. On a trip to California in 1918, Barnett made arrangements with the *Chicago Defender* newspaper to sell advertising space as a way to pay for his travel. The black press had grown enormously during World War I and the Great Migration, when the largest number of African Americans ever left southern farms and small towns for cities in the North and the South. Black urbanization helped to support growing black businesses such as cosmetics and insurance that provided advertising revenues for black newspapers.

After his trip west, Barnett made a proposal to the *Chicago Defender* to sponsor a black news service. Its owners believed that they had sufficient sources for national news and rejected his proposal. In March 1919 Barnett started the Associated Negro Press (ANP) in the office of the Kashmir Chemical Company with the motto "Progress, Loyalty, Truth." At the time, all black newspapers were published weekly, so the ANP was able to be a mail service rather than a wire service, providing black newspapers with much-needed information about African Americans. ANP began with eighty subscribers, practically all the black newspapers and a few white papers. It cost $25 to join the service and a monthly fee of $16 or $24 depending on the level of service provided. At the $24 level, ANP dispatched releases twice a week, on Monday and Friday, while at the $16 level, ANP supplied only a Friday release. Subscribers agreed to credit ANP in their newspapers for each article, to send ANP important news about their communities, and to forfeit membership if they were more than sixty days in arrears in paying for the service.

Operating costs for the news service were minimal. ANP releases were run off on a mimeograph machine. Each week the staff produced about seventy pages of copy, including news stories, opinion pieces, essays, poetry, book reviews, cartoons, and occasional photographs. Barnett wrote some stories using the pen name Albert Anderson (a combination of his middle name and his mother's maiden name). ANP compiled news stories from a variety of sources, including black newspapers, the white press, special correspondents, and news releases from government agencies, foundations, organizations, and businesses. It developed one of the most comprehensive files of news stories about African Americans. Despite its minimal operating costs, Barnett struggled to keep ANP afloat because subscribers generally lagged behind in their payments. To produce revenue, Barnett took advertising space in the papers in lieu of news service payments. He then sold the space to advertisers through his companies, Associated Publishers Representatives and later the National Feature Service.

Barnett was elected a trustee of Tuskegee Institute in 1932, one of the first graduates to serve on the board of trustees, a position that he held for the next thirty-three years. He was also president of the board of trustees of Chicago's Provident Hospital, director of the Supreme Liberty Life Insurance Company, a member of the Red Cross's national board of governors, and trustee of the Phelps-Stokes Fund. During the late 1920s and early 1930s, he was secretary of the publicity committee for the Colored Voters Division of the Republican National Committee. He was in charge of the Republican party's publicity campaign for the Negro vote and promoted stories favorable to the Republicans, which raised the ire of some ANP subscribers. With the election of Franklin D. Roosevelt in 1932 and the popularity of Eleanor Roosevelt among African Americans, Barnett broke with the Republican party.

In 1934 Barnett married the well-known concert singer and actress Etta Moten, who had three daughters from a previous marriage. For a time, he managed her career. After appearing on Broadway in the lead role in *Porgy and Bess*, Moten's career soared, and she had to secure a full-time agent. Barnett and his wife visited Africa for the first time in 1947. They became avid collectors of African art and much sought-after speakers on Africa to black civic, fraternal, and religious organizations in the United States.

During World War II, Barnett wrote many articles about the corrosive effects of segregation in the military and is credited with playing a significant role in desegregating the armed forces. The secretary of agriculture, Claude R. Wickard, a Democrat, appointed him as one of his special assistants in 1942, a post that he held under succeeding secretaries of agriculture until the Republicans regained the White House in 1952. He and Frederick Patterson, another special assistant and the president of Tuskegee Institute, sought black access to U.S. Department of Agriculture employment; educational, health, and insurance programs for black farmers; and federal aid to black agricultural colleges.

At its height in 1945, the ANP employed eight persons at its Chicago headquarters in addition to Barnett and had 112 subscribers to its services. Barnett held the position of director and employed a full-time editor, deputy editor, editor for Africa, and a contributing editor, a part-time secretary, a sports writer, a music reviewer, and a theater critic. The ANP became the oldest and the largest black newspaper service in the United States.

ANP opened a Washington, D.C., office during World War II and later an office at the United Nations in New York City. Part-time correspondents in Hollywood and other cities were paid by the column inch for their published material. Many featured columnists were not paid but published with ANP in exchange for exposure of their ideas to a national black audience. In 1959 Barnett organized the World News Service, which sent approximately fifteen pages of copy each week to more than two hundred subscribers in Africa at its peak. With the rise of the civil rights movement in this country, many white newspapers began to increase their coverage of African Americans, and the wire services carried more information about black communities. Major news organizations started hiring black correspondents, many of whom had their start with ANP. Growing competition, financial problems, and failing health forced Barnett to retire in 1964 and to close the ANP. He died of a cerebral hemorrhage in Chicago.

Barnett created a means for the black press to receive national news about African Americans. ANP set professional standards for the black press, demonstrated the need to examine national issues as they affected African Americans, and helped to nurture black journalists, who were well prepared to take on assignments with the mainstream media after the success of the civil rights movement. Barnett developed a national forum for black news and opinion and thereby played an influential role in the struggle for racial equality.

• Barnett's papers and the ANP files are in the Archives and Manuscripts Department of the Chicago Historical Society with most of them available on microfilm. Lawrence D. Hogan, *A Black National News Service: The Associated Negro Press and Claude Barnett, 1919–1945* (1984), is a useful study of the ANP within the context of the black press in twentieth-century America. See also Hogan, "A Case of Mistaken Identity," *Editor & Publisher*, 17 Nov. 1984. Linda J. Evans, "Claude A. Barnett and the Associated Negro Press," *Chicago History* 12 (Spring 1983): 44–56, is an excellent biographical sketch of Barnett. An obituary is in the *New York Times*, 3 Aug. 1967.

ROBERT L. HARRIS, JR.

BARNETT, Ross Robert (22 Jan. 1898–6 Nov. 1987), governor of Mississippi, was born on a farm in the Standing Pine community of Leake County in central Mississippi, the son of Virginia Ann Chadwick and John William Barnett, a Confederate veteran, farmer, and part owner of a cotton gin. He worked his way as a barber through high school and Mississippi College, from which he graduated in 1922. He taught high school for two years in Pontotoc before studying law. After receiving a law degree from the University of Mississippi in 1926, he practiced law in Jackson and gained a reputation for his success in civil damage suits. In 1929 he married Mary Pearl Crawford; they had three children.

Barnett served as president of the Mississippi Bar Association in 1943–1944 and as president of the local bar for six years. He entered elective politics in 1951 by running unsuccessfully for the Democratic nomination for governor. In a libel suit growing out of the Willie McGee rape case, Barnett in 1954 won a verdict for a Laurel woman against the communist *Daily Worker*. He failed in another gubernatorial campaign in 1955. An ardent segregationist and white supremacist, Barnett in 1956–1957 volunteered his legal services to people charged in the violent opposition to school desegregation in Clinton, Tennessee. Supported by the White Citizens' Council, to which he belonged, he led in the 1959 Democratic gubernatorial primary,

easily won the primary runoff, and was elected in November without opposition.

In his inaugural address on 19 January 1960, Barnett called for economic development of the state and pledged to defend racial segregation "at all costs." As governor he took scores of trips to recruit industry, supported a right-to-work law, and worked for other legislation attractive to industry. "The Good Lord was the original segregationist," Barnett maintained. "He made us white, and He intended that we stay that way." He opposed the civil rights stands of the Democratic and Republican presidential candidates in 1960 and advocated the slate of unpledged electors that carried the state. Later Barnett criticized the John F. Kennedy administration's civil rights activities, especially its voting rights lawsuits and its aid to the freedom riders.

The most important events of Barnett's administration involved James Meredith's struggle to enroll at the University of Mississippi. When a federal judge on 13 September 1962 ordered the university to admit Meredith, Barnett pledged over statewide radio and television: "No school will be integrated in Mississippi while I am your Governor. Every public official, including myself, should be prepared to make the choice tonight whether he will submit or whether he is willing to go to jail. . . . If there is any official who is not prepared to suffer imprisonment for his righteous cause, I ask him now to submit his resignation." Two days later Barnett began secret telephone negotiations with Attorney General Robert F. Kennedy, seeking a solution to their impasse over Meredith.

At Barnett's request, the state board of trustees on 20 September transferred to the governor its power to act on Meredith's application, and later that day Barnett, at the university in Oxford, personally refused admission to Meredith. Barnett on 25 September refused to let Meredith register when he appeared at the board office in Jackson. Inclement weather the next day prevented Barnett from flying to Oxford, but Lieutenant Governor Paul B. Johnson took his place and blocked Meredith. The U.S. Court of Appeals for the Fifth Circuit found Barnett in contempt on 28 September.

In continuing negotiations with the Kennedy administration, Barnett pledged to maintain peace and oppose violence, but the irresolute governor backed out of several tentative agreements to admit Meredith. He finally did agree to have Meredith brought to campus on Sunday, 30 September 1962. From Jackson that evening Barnett called on the people "to preserve peace and avoid bloodshed." After rioting broke out on the university campus, however, an intransigent Barnett declared, "We will never surrender." Even though he had in his dealing with the Kennedy administration acquiesced in Meredith's enrollment, the governor proclaimed, "I will never yield a single inch." Within weeks the federal government began contempt proceedings against Barnett. In 1964, after Barnett had left the governor's office, the U.S. Supreme Court ruled against allowing a jury trial for Barnett, but later the case was dropped.

Barnett continued to practice law in Jackson until 1984 and in 1967 ran unsuccessfully for governor. He died in Jackson. At Barnett's death, the *Jackson Clarion-Ledger* observed that he had been a man of "misguided integrity" in defending racial segregation that was "legally and morally wrong." To the end Barnett thought "I was right. . . . I'm proud of what I've done."

• Barnett's papers are in the Mississippi Department of Archives and History. Erle Johnston, a journalist and political supporter, wrote *I Rolled with Ross: A Political Portrait* (1980) and *Mississippi's Defiant Years, 1953–1973* (1990). Important secondary works relevant to Barnett include Neil R. McMillen, *The Citizens' Council: Organized Resistance to the Second Reconstruction, 1954–64* (1971), and Earl Black, *Southern Governors and Civil Rights: Racial Segregation as a Campaign Issue in the Second Reconstruction* (1976). Helpful obituaries are in the *Jackson Clarion-Ledger*, 7, 8, and 9 Nov. 1987, and the *New York Times*, 7 Nov. 1987.

CHARLES W. EAGLES

BARNEY, Alice Pike (14 Jan. 1857–12 Oct. 1931), artist and arts patron, was born in Cincinnati, Ohio, the daughter of Samuel Napthali Pike, an arts patron and successful businessman, and Ursula Muellion "Ellen" Miller. She grew up and was educated at various schools in Cincinnati and New York City, her family having moved there in 1866. Although Barney courted the famous British explorer Henry Morton Stanley, in 1876 she married Albert Clifford Barney, who became the administrator of the extensive Pike estate. They had two daughters, Natalie Clifford, born in 1876, who was openly lesbian and known for her literary efforts and Parisian salon, and Laura Alice (Dreyfus), born in 1879, who was a social activist and follower of the Bahai faith. Albert died in 1902, and Alice surprised friends and family by marrying 24-year-old Christian Dominique Hemmick in 1911. She divorced Hemmick in 1920.

Barney's artistic fame rests on her portraits in oils and pastels and on her other figurative works. Training that prepared her for her endeavors included formal study in Paris with Charles-Émile-Auguste Carolus-Duran in 1887, 1896, and 1900 and with James McNeill Whistler from 1898 to 1899. Barney created a pastel sketch of Whistler in 1898 (*James McNeill Whistler*, National Museum of American Art) that stood out in its time for its unique assessment of the artist's personality. Although unfinished, it captures Whistler as a benevolent older gentleman at a time when many considered him to be overbearing.

The waning symbolist movement also influenced Barney's style, especially the work of John White Alexander, Edmund-François Aman-Jean, and Lucien Levy-Dhurmer. Barney appreciated the imagination and theatricality of symbolism and incorporated these traits into works such as *Woman Clothed with the Sun* and *Babylon* (both 1901, National Museum of American Art). These works were companion pieces Barney based on verses from the book of Revelation. *Woman Clothed with the Sun* portrays a draped figure holding the sun to her chest, which glows like an incandescent bulb. The light casts an ethereal light on her face and illuminates the curve of her body through her robe. The figure stands hunched over, as if protecting her burden from snakelike creatures who bear down on her from a night sky. She wears a crown of twelve stars in her hair, and the moon shines in a puddle at her feet. *Babylon* portrays an Egyptian woman seated on a throne surrounded by demons. A nude female slave lies at her feet. The woman wears a menacing expression heightened by dark swirling forms behind her head. Barney executed both pieces in softly blended pastels, a medium that adds to the pieces' otherworldly effects.

Barney's striking pastel portraits of her daughter Laura as *Medusa* and *Lucifer* (both 1902, National Museum of American Art) also reveal symbolist influence. Companion pieces as well, both works, which portray Laura's head and shoulders, capture powerful emotional states. In *Medusa*, Laura's expression is horror, and in *Lucifer*, fury. In *Medusa*, Laura's hair billows around her face as snakes stream from her head. The primary colors are icy blues and blacks. In *Lucifer*, Barney portrays Laura's hair as fire. Oranges and browns dominate the composition.

Barney also created portraits in a traditional mode. A good example of this style is her oil painting of her husband Albert called *The Fur Coat* (1900, National Museum of American Art). Here Barney portrays her first husband in profile against a dark background. The piece reveals Albert's advanced age and captures his fatigue while recuperating from a debilitating heart attack. In contrast to her symbolist work, the composition is strictly realistic and does not include imaginative elements.

Although the artist exhibited often in her early and middle years, including solo shows at the Corcoran Gallery of Art, Washington, D.C. (1901, 1909); Gallery Durand-Ruel, New York (1903); and M. Knoedler and Company, New York (1909), she turned her attention to other matters in the 1910s. Barney became a patron of the arts. She focused most of her attention on the cultural growth of Washington, D.C., the city she and Albert adopted as their home in 1889. In addition to writing and sponsoring ballets and theatricals for charity causes, Barney supported Neighborhood House, an industrial arts center for blue-collar workers. She also entertained at Studio House, the architecturally eclectic residence she and architect Waddy Wood designed with public rooms for exhibitions, plays, and musical events. Offices Barney held included president of the Amateur Authors' and Players' Group of Washington, D.C., and vice president of the Society of Washington Artists. While studying in Paris during 1898–1899, she hosted an arts salon in her home. In 1916, inspired by her father's gift of opera houses to the cities of Cincinnati and New York, Barney funded the building of the National Sylvan Theater, the amphitheater located on the mall near the

Washington Monument. When she retired to southern California in 1923, Barney founded and directed Theater Mart, an innovative playhouse that showcased the efforts of fledgling playwrights who otherwise would not have the opportunity to see their work performed.

Barney was a member of a new breed of eccentric upper-class woman that emerged with the rise of the "New Woman" around the turn of the century. A dramatically colorful character, she consistently challenged the boundaries of conventional female behavior. In 1909, two years before her marriage to a man thirty years her junior, she shocked Washington society with her surprise appearance in her operetta *About Thebes*. Advertising that the play contained a guest performance by a mysterious Mme. Geraldine Clifford, Barney herself was the surprise guest star and performed a sensuous dance in a revealing costume. In 1910 she drew crowds in front of her house and garnered the criticism of the Washington Watch and Ward Society by installing a nude statue of her daughter Natalie on the lawn.

Barney was one of the foremost artists and cultural leaders of Washington, D.C., during her time. Her efforts in transforming the national capital into a major center for the arts match those of patrons James Corcoran and Duncan Phillips. On a national level, her enthusiasm for the arts matches that of women such as Mabel Dodge Luhan in New York City and Taos, New Mexico; Isabelle Stewart Gardner in Boston; and Gertrude Vanderbilt Whitney in New York. Barney died in Hollywood, California. To honor their mother's name, Natalie and Laura donated Alice's artwork to the National Collection of Fine Arts (now the National Museum of American Art, Smithsonian Institution) in 1951 and set up a fund to promote the valuation of American art. They donated Studio House to the Smithsonian in 1960, and its contents in 1968. From 1960 to 1980 the house served as offices for various organizations, including the American Association of Museums and the Smithsonian Institution Traveling Exhibition Services. It also served as a guest house for scholars and other visitors. Studio House was renovated and opened to the public in 1980, an event that spurred new interest in Barney's art and accomplishments. In 1995 the Smithsonian approved the sale of Barney's home. The Friends of Alice Pike Barney Studio House formed in 1993 to prevent this action, but when their efforts failed, they rededicated themselves to finding an organization related to Barney's interests to buy the property.

• The National Museum of American Art, Washington, D.C., has 265 drawings and paintings by Alice Pike Barney, and scripts for her plays, manuscripts of her literary works, and other papers are in the Smithsonian Institution Archives, Washington, D.C. Major biographical sources include Barney's unpublished manuscript, "Stanley's 'Lady' Alice by One Who Knew" (1927), in the Smithsonian Institution Archives, and Jean L. Kling, *Alice Pike Barney: Her Life and Art* (1994).

CATHERINE MCNICKLE CHASTAIN

BARNEY, Joshua (6 July 1759–1 Dec. 1818), seaman and naval officer, was born in Baltimore, Maryland, the son of William Barney and Frances Holland, farmers. Barney left school at age ten and was sent by his father to Alexandria, Virginia, to be put in the care of a local merchant. After spending nearly one year in Virginia Barney returned to Baltimore, where he signed on as a crew member aboard a local pilot boat.

In 1772 Barney went to work with his brother-in-law Thomas Drysdale, who was engaged in trade with Ireland and England. During the next three years Barney made several voyages to Cádiz, Genoa, Liverpool, and many other European ports. During a winter passage to Nice in 1774–1775 Captain Drysdale became ill and died, and Barney took command of the vessel. He brought the ship safely to port and, after a series of complicated commercial maneuvers, managed to sell the cargo at a considerable profit. Barney returned to Baltimore in October 1775.

His arrival coincided with a movement in the Continental Congress to create a Continental navy. Among the vessels purchased by the congress was the sloop *Hornet* at Baltimore. Not able to sail as a merchant because of the war, Barney signed on aboard *Hornet*. Early in 1776 *Hornet* rendezvoused in Delaware Bay with eight other American vessels under the command of Commodore Esek Hopkins. On 17 February the fleet set sail to attack Nassau in the Bahama Islands. En route, *Hornet* ran afoul of another vessel and was damaged so badly that it had to return to the Delaware. For five months *Hornet* was either being repaired or cruising ineffectually along the coast. In the spring of 1776 Barney left *Hornet* and joined the crew of the schooner *Wasp* as master's mate. *Wasp* distinguished itself in several engagements, and in his reports to Congress the schooner's captain gave particular praise to Barney's conduct. As a result of his service aboard *Wasp*, in June 1776 Barney was commissioned a lieutenant in the Continental navy.

From *Wasp* Barney was assigned to the sloop *Sachem* as the executive officer. Here he again distinguished himself in battle when *Sachem* captured a British letter of marque out of Jamaica on 12 August 1776. As a reward, Barney was next posted to the ship *Andrea Doria*. In October he sailed for the West Indies to load a cargo of military stores at the Dutch island of St. Eustatius. During the voyage back to Philadelphia in December, *Andrea Doria* captured the British privateer *Racehorse*. Shortly after that, *Andrea Doria* took another prize, and Barney was put aboard as its master. While trying to make the Delaware capes, the prize was retaken by the HMS *Perseus*. Barney's confinement was brief. He was put ashore at Charleston and by mid-March 1777 was back in Philadelphia, as was *Andrea Doria*.

With the British effectively blockading the entrance to the Delaware, *Andrea Doria* was trapped in Philadelphia. By late spring and into the summer, the British under General William Howe (1729–1814) began their advance on the American capital. *Andrea Doria* participated in the defense of the city but to no avail;

shortly after the enemy took Philadelphia, the ship was burned to prevent capture. Barney, in command of a contingent of seamen, was ordered to Baltimore to go aboard the new American frigate *Virginia*. *Virginia* made several attempts to get to sea but was frustrated each time by the presence of a strong British naval force. On the last attempt, 31 March 1778, the ship ran hard aground on the middle ground off Hampton, Virginia. It was captured by the British frigate *Emerald*, and once again Barney was a prisoner of war.

For four months Barney was confined in New York until his exchange. He returned to Baltimore where, unable to find a berth in the Continental navy, he signed on as a privateer. Barney made successful voyages to the West Indies and France, and by October 1779 he was back in Philadelphia. On 16 March 1780 Barney married Anne Bedford, daughter of Gunning Bedford, a merchant and alderman of Philadelphia.

By October 1780 Barney was again at sea, serving as lieutenant aboard the Continental navy sloop *Saratoga*. On 8 October *Saratoga* captured a British privateer, *Charming Molly*. Barney took command as prize master and set a course for Philadelphia. Less than a week later *Charming Molly* was recaptured by the British *Intrepid*, and Barney was off to prison again, this time ending up in England in the notorious Mill Prison.

After one failed attempt, Barney managed to escape, and by March 1782 he was back in Philadelphia. Barney's high reputation influenced the Pennsylvania authorities to offer him command of the state vessel *Hyder Ally*. The ship's task was to protect Delaware Bay from the British and to convoy American merchantmen through these dangerous waters. On 8 April 1782, in a hot engagement at the entrance to Delaware Bay, *Hyder Ally* captured the *General Monk*. Barney brought his prize to Philadelphia where it was taken into the Pennsylvania navy and renamed *General Washington*. Barney was made captain and remained with the ship until the end of the war. Under his command the *General Washington* made a cruise to Havana to bring back specie and dispatches. Following that, Barney made three voyages to France carrying passengers and dispatches.

In the years following the Revolution Barney engaged in a variety of business ventures, including western land speculation. He was a firm supporter of the Constitution, and in 1794 President George Washington nominated him one of six captains in the newly established navy. Disappointed at being ranked only third, Barney declined the nomination. He returned to the merchant service, but a longing for naval service enticed him to accept the post of commodore in the navy of the French republic. He remained in this service until the fall of 1802 when he returned to the United States. When Barney received some long overdue prize money, he established himself and his three sons in business in Baltimore. In 1806 and 1810 he ran unsuccessfully for Congress.

Shortly before the outbreak of the War of 1812 Barney sold his property in Baltimore and moved to a farm in Anne Arundel County. As soon as war was declared, however, he returned to Baltimore to take command of the privateer *Rossie*. In a ninety-day cruise Barney captured four ships, eight brigs, three schooners, and three sloops valued at over $1.5 million. Albeit spectacular, this was Barney's only privateering cruise of the war. For the remainder of the conflict he was engaged in defending the Chesapeake Bay area from British attack. In this capacity he was given command of a flotilla of small vessels. When the British ascended the Chesapeake in August 1814, Barney's force was overwhelmed. Forced to abandon their vessels, Barney and his men marched toward Washington to help defend the capital against the expected British attack. In a spirited but futile effort Barney and his command of 500 seamen and marines defended their position at Bladensburg, where they were joined by militia and regular regiments. The British attack sent the Americans reeling in disorder; Barney's men, however, held their position in good form. Although eventually overcome, they put up a vigorous defense that earned them and Barney high praise.

After the war the city of Washington presented Barney with a sword to honor him for his gallant defense. Barney returned to farming at Elk Ridge, Maryland. He continued his interest in western lands, however, and in 1818 decided to sell his property in the East and move to Kentucky. He took ill during the trip west and died at Pittsburgh.

Throughout his long career Barney displayed extraordinary courage as both a naval officer and privateer. His exploits during the Revolution and the War of 1812 gave considerable support to the American cause, and his role in the defense of Washington in 1814 was one of the few bright spots in that dismal episode.

• Many of Barney's letters and official documents can be found in the Papers of the Continental Congress at the National Archives in Washington, D.C. Among the two best biographies of Barney are Mary Barney, ed., *A Biographical Memoir of the Late Commodore Joshua Barney from Autobiographical Notes and Journals in Possession of His Family, and Other Authentic Sources* (1832), and Ralph D. Paine, *Joshua Barney: A Forgotten Hero of Blue Water* (1924).

WILLIAM M. FOWLER, JR.

BARNEY, Natalie Clifford (31 Oct. 1876–2 Feb. 1972), writer and salon hostess, was born in Dayton, Ohio, the daughter of Albert Clifford Barney, a railroad car heir, and Alice Pike, a painter and philanthropist. Her childhood was spent in wealthy circles in Cincinnati and later in Washington, D.C., and Bar Harbor, Maine. She was educated at home by a French governess and in France at Les Ruches in Fontainebleau. By the turn of the century, she had decided to remain in Paris and write in French.

Barney's first work, *Quelques portraits-sonnets de femmes* (Some portraits and sonnets of women), a volume of verse illustrated by her mother, was published in 1900. Its lesbian love poetry scandalized American readers. Her mother seemed unaware of its implications but later accepted Barney's lesbianism; her father burned the plates of the book. She fell in love with English-born poetess Renée Vivien (Pauline Mary Tarn). Together they studied classical Greek and wrote various versions of Sappho's life. Using the pseudonym "Tryphé," Barney wrote a volume of pseudo-Socratic dialogues called *Cinq petits dialogues grecs (antithèses et parallèles)* (Five short Greek dialogues [antitheses and parallels]) in 1902.

In 1904 Barney and Vivien moved briefly to Lesbos in order to establish a women's school of poetry in imitation of Sappho, but the venture failed, and the two lovers parted. Shortly before Vivien's death in November 1909, Barney opened her salon at 20, rue Jacob in Paris, where writers, artists, musicians, and people of letters would gather almost every Friday for over sixty years. Guests included Jean Cocteau, Colette, Gabriele D'Annunzio, Rainer Maria Rilke, Max Jacob, Mata Hari, Rabindranath Tagore, Gertrude Stein, Guillaume Apollinaire, Isadora Duncan, William Carlos Williams, Ned Rorem, and Truman Capote. Plays and tableaux vivants were performed in the backyard near Barney's famous Doric-style Temple à l'Amitié (Temple of Friendship), guests read from or played new works, dances were held, and refreshments were served. In 1927 Barney established an Académie des Femmes (Academy of Women) to support the work of other women artists such as Djuna Barnes. Barney also raised funds to help support men of great talent, including Paul Valéry, T. S. Eliot, and George Antheil.

Barney wrote character sketches of some of her notable guests in *Aventures de l'esprit* (Adventures of the mind) (1929) and *Traits et portraits* (Traits and portraits) (1963). Her work came to the attention of the French public through the writings of Rémy de Gourmont, who devoted two books to her. Making a pun on Amazon and a riding habit she wore when she rode horses, he nicknamed her "l'Amazone" (the Amazon), a title she delighted in and employed in two volumes of epigrams, *Pensées d'une amazone* (Thoughts of an Amazon) (1920) and *Nouvelles pensées de l'amazone* (More thoughts of the Amazon) (1939) as well as on her tombstone. She was noted for her beauty (especially her blond hair and seductive blue eyes) and her charisma. She extended her wit and her warmth to all who entered her salon. She was the lover of many women, most notably American painter Romaine Brooks (née Beatrice Romaine Goddard), with whom she sustained a close relationship from the early 1910s until 1968.

As early as 1900 Barney was a vocal advocate of lesbian rights, and she wrote a strong defense of lesbianism in "L'Amour défendu" (Forbidden love) in *Traits et portraits*. She was a pacifist during World War I, but she supported Mussolini during World War II. She probably collaborated with him to some degree, as she was partly Jewish and lived in Florence during the war. She was never a feminist in the contemporary sense—preferring a salon of intellectual equals and never caring for the masses—and she believed that Mussolini shared this tenet. She died in Paris.

Barney's life inspired many fictional accounts, most notably as Vally in Vivien's *Une femme m'apparut . . .* (A woman appeared to me), as Flossie in Liane de Pougy's *Idylle saphique* (Sapphic idyll), as Flossie in Colette's Claudine series, as Valérie Seymour in Radclyffe Hall's *The Well of Loneliness* (1928), and as Evangeline Musset in Barnes's *Ladies Almanack*. Though Barney never had a sizable American readership in her lifetime, biographical interest began to grow after the mid-1970s. At first, her prescient attitude toward sexual liberation as well as her romantic escapades captured most attention. However, by the mid-1990s her reputation as a writer underwent a revival as several encyclopedias focusing on the gay and lesbian literary heritage offered serious evaluations of her work. A collection of her writings, *A Perilous Advantage: The Best of Natalie Clifford Barney*, was published in 1992, and the first translation into English of *Adventures of the Mind* was released the same year. In 1995 a documentary, *Paris Was a Woman*, placed her work alongside that of other American expatriates, such as Stein and Janet Flanner, and added to Barney's growing literary reputation.

• Letters, unpublished plays, diaries, unpublished memoirs, other manuscripts, and photographs are in the Fonds Bibliothèque Littéraire Jacques Doucet, Paris. Some letters and other manuscripts are in the Beinecke Rare Book and Manuscript Library, Yale University. Her autobiographical memoir is *Souvenirs indiscrets* (Indiscreet memories) (1960). Other major works are *Actes et entr'actes* (Acts and entr'acts) (1910), *Eparpillements* (Scatterings) (1910), *The One Who Is Legion, or A.D.'s After-Life* (1930), and *Poems & poèmes: autres alliances* (French poems and English poems: Other unions) (1920). A biography and literary study is Karla Jay, *The Amazon and the Page: Natalie Clifford Barney and Renée Vivien* (1988). See also George Wickes, *The Amazon of Letters: The Life and Loves of Natalie Barney* (1976), and Jean Chalon, *Portrait d'une séductrice* (1976) (Portrait of a seductress: The world of Natalie Barney) (1979).

KARLA JAY

BARNEY, Nora Stanton Blatch (30 Sept. 1883–18 Jan. 1971), women's rights activist, was born in Basingstoke, England, the daughter of William Henry Blatch, a brewer, and Harriet Eaton Stanton, an author, suffragist, and reformer. Her mother was the daughter of women's rights leader Elizabeth Cady Stanton. Through her mother Barney received early exposure to woman suffrage and other liberal ideas such as those of the Fabian Society, with which Barney's mother maintained contact. Barney's sister died in childhood, leaving her an only child. As a teenager she moved with her parents to New York City after her father's retirement. She graduated from the Horace Mann School and entered Cornell University in 1901; Barney became the first female graduate in civil engineering from Cornell in 1905. She had worked on a survey of New York State water resources in college;

after graduation she worked in drafting for the American Bridge Company and for the New York City Board of Water Supply.

In 1906 Barney met inventor Lockwood de Forest and undertook studies in electricity and mathematics at Columbia to become his assistant. They married in 1908 and spent their honeymoon in Europe demonstrating de Forest's inventions and securing contracts. Despite her husband's wishes, Barney continued to involve herself in de Forest's New Jersey–based business, and her critical eye was one factor in the couple's separation, which occurred in 1909, when she became pregnant. After she gave birth to a daughter, both de Forests filed for divorce, which was granted in 1912. Barney retained custody of their daughter.

Barney returned to New York City and worked, first as assistant engineer for three years for the Radley Steel Construction Company and then for the New York Public Services Commission. Around 1914 she also began doing some architectural design and real estate development on Long Island, which provided the background for her later real estate ventures.

During this period Barney worked closely with her mother, who had founded the Equality League of Self-Supporting Women in 1907 (later the Women's Political Union or WPU) and organized the first woman suffrage parade in New York City in 1910. Barney herself had organized a woman suffrage club while a student at Cornell. She was the first female member of the American Society of Civil Engineers, but when she reached the age limit of a junior member, they dropped her rather than admit her to full membership. Barney filed an unsuccessful suit, continuing the family tradition of agitation for women's equal status. She was executive secretary of the WPU and edited *Women's Political World*, which the group published. Like her mother and grandmother before her, Barney gave stump speeches, wrote, and even rode a horse across the state to publicize suffrage. When her mother resigned as president of the WPU in 1915, Barney took over the position, remaining in it until suffrage was won. Later, after the organization merged with the Congressional Union (later the National Women's Party), Barney worked for the Equal Rights Amendment.

In 1919 she married Morgan Barney, a naval architect; the couple had two children. In 1923, with funds from her father's estate, Barney moved her family to Greenwich, Connecticut, which she made the center of a real estate development business. As she built each house, she and the family moved into it until it was sold; then the family moved on to another house in progression. In 1935 she designed and moved into a permanent home in Greenwich. From there she continued her design and building business. She was appointed an engineering inspector for the Public Works Administration in 1934.

Barney's husband died in 1943. After his death and the end of World War II, Barney revitalized her interest in political issues, particularly world peace. She published a pamphlet advocating a world government made up of equal numbers of men and women representing economic and professional groups. She wrote other pamphlets on women's equality and on her grandmother, Elizabeth Cady Stanton. Barney supported Henry Wallace for president in 1948 and was investigated for her activities by the House Un-American Activities Committee (HUAC) in 1950. She denounced HUAC in her letter to a committee representative. Undeterred by the investigation, she called for a cease-fire in Korea in 1952.

Barney continued her real estate dealings until her death from a stroke in Greenwich. Always conscious of her heritage, Barney combined it with the concerns and ambitions of many twentieth-century women who sought equality in all areas of their lives, political, professional, and domestic. She both carried on and expanded, through the arenas of work and career pioneering as well as political action, the legacy of her mother and grandmother. She was truly a "life worker" for the causes and concerns in which she believed.

• Some of Barney's papers are in the Library of Congress, as are papers of her mother. Lee de Forest's papers are in the Foothills Electric Museum, Los Altos Hills, Calif. Her published works include "Discussion on 'Works for the Purification of the Water Supply of Washington, D.C.,'" *Transactions of the American Society of Civil Engineers* (Dec. 1906), as well as three pamphlets: *World Peace through a Peoples Parliament* (1944), *Women as Human Beings* (1946), and *Life Sketches of Elizabeth Cady Stanton* (1948). She also published a number of articles and letters in the *New York Times* between 1909 and 1945. Ellen DuBois, "Spanning Two Centuries: The Autobiography of Nora Stanton Barney," *History Workshop Journal* 22 (1986): 131–52, contains an autobiographical fragment and important commentary.

Barney's early life is chronicled to some degree in her mother Harriet Blatch's autobiography, *Challenging Years*, with Alma Lutz (1940). There is material on her first marriage in Lee de Forest, *Father of Radio: The Autobiography of Lee de Forest* (1950), and in Georgette Carneal, *A Conqueror of Space: An Authorized Biography of Lee de Forest* (1930). Her HUAC profile is contained in the 81st Congress, 2d session, House Report 1953 (1950), pp. 102 and 103. Obituaries are in the *New York Times*, 20 Jan. 1971, and *Civil Engineering* 41 (Apr. 1971): 87.

CYNTHIA FARR BROWN

BARNHOUSE, Donald Grey (28 Mar. 1895–5 Nov. 1960), maverick Presbyterian Bible expositor and broadcaster, was born in Watsonville, California, the son of Theodore Barnhouse, a contractor, and Jane Ann Carmichael. Raised in a devout Methodist home, Barnhouse underwent a conversion experience in 1910. Two years later he enrolled at the Bible Institute of Los Angeles (later BIOLA), headed by the prominent revivalist/theologian Reuben A. Torrey. Profoundly influenced by BIOLA's dispensational theology that emphasized the imminent return of Christ, Barnhouse graduated in 1914 and spent a short time amid the liberal atmosphere at the University of Chicago before moving to conservative Princeton Theological Seminary in 1915. At Princeton, Barnhouse earned a reputation among his peers for his pugnacious behavior and arrogance during in-class arguments with respected faculty members such as Benjamin B. Warfield. Barnhouse left Princeton at the beginning of World War I without earning a degree, enlisting in the army and rising to the rank of first lieutenant in the Signal Corps as a U.S.-based flight instructor.

Following his discharge from the military, Barnhouse became a missionary with the Belgian Gospel Mission in Brussels from 1919 to 1921. He spent the next four years in the French Alps, pastoring two small Reformed churches, studying French at the University of Grenoble, and traveling throughout Europe. In 1922 he married Ruth Tiffany, a fellow missionary; the couple had four children. Barnhouse returned to the United States in 1925, accepting the pastorate of Grace Presbyterian Church in Philadelphia. While in Philadelphia, he took graduate courses at the University of Pennsylvania and at Eastern Baptist Theological Seminary, from which he received the master of theology degree in 1927.

In that same year, Barnhouse was called to the pastorate of Philadelphia's Tenth Presbyterian Church, a position he held until his death. Uninterested in administrative detail, he used Tenth Presbyterian as a platform from which to pursue his other speaking and organizational efforts. Almost immediately, Barnhouse began broadcasting the church's vesper services, and in 1928, with the purchase of air time on the Columbia Broadcasting System, he became the first fundamentalist to broadcast over a major network. In 1931 he began a magazine, *Revelation*, and initiated a well-publicized Monday night Bible study in New York's theater district. These and other efforts increased the visibility and membership of Tenth Presbyterian and improved the church's finances. Of greater significance, Barnhouse enjoyed a growing national reputation, and by 1940—with the blessing of his congregation—he was spending six months a year on the road, frequently abroad.

While Barnhouse's literalist Bible expositions made him popular with conservative audiences, his outspoken style and his attacks on his colleagues' lack of orthodoxy rankled many within the Philadelphia Presbytery. As early as 1929, seventeen Philadelphia-area ministers asked the Pennsylvania Synod to investigate his critical statements. In 1932 the synod unanimously censured Barnhouse for bearing false witness against fellow clergy. Unrepentant, Barnhouse remained in the Presbyterian church, continuing to hammer away at denominational liberals while maintaining alliances with fundamentalists within and without the denomination.

World War II, his wife's cancer and subsequent death in 1944, and the problems of his adolescent and college-age children curtailed Barnhouse's aggressive ministry through much of the 1940s. But the creation of the nonprofit Evangelical Foundation in 1949 streamlined his many evangelistic and publishing projects and signaled a new burst of creativity and effort to enlarge his ministry. In the same year, Barnhouse moved to expand distribution of his radio program by repackaging it as the "Bible Study Hour" rather than as the broadcast of a conventional worship service and sermon. A new arrangement with NBC in the mid-1950s boosted the number of stations carrying his broadcasts to well over 400. In 1950 he discontinued *Revelation* magazine and with the help of an expanded staff created *Eternity*, a larger, more professional monthly.

In 1954 Barnhouse married Margaret Nuckols Bell. During this period he took a number of steps that suggested a softening of his attitude toward liberals and others he had once criticized. In 1953 he stunned friend and foe alike when in his famous "New Year's Resolution" in *Eternity* he vowed to be less critical of other Christians with whom he was in "95 percent agreement," admitting that "perhaps they do not like the 5 percent in me either!" In 1954 he appeared before the Philadelphia Presbytery and apologized for his previous lack of Christian love. His articles and broadcast statements during the years that followed sought a rapprochement also with the Seventh-day Adventists and the pentecostal Assemblies of God. These moves, as well as his participation in a series of television broadcasts sponsored by the National Council of Churches, his favorable review of the new Revised Standard Version of the Bible, his even-handed treatment of Karl Barth in *Eternity*, and his support for Billy Graham's ecumenical crusade policies brought him increasing condemnation from fundamentalist hardliners. However, Barnhouse never mellowed in his views on Roman Catholicism and saw the possibility of a takeover by a McCarthy-like figure with Jesuit connections as the greatest threat to national security. Increasingly hampered by diabetes in his final years, Barnhouse died in Philadelphia after surgery to remove a massive brain tumor.

The impact of his ministry among rank-and-file evangelicals through his one-man Bible conferences, *Eternity* magazine (published 1950–1989), his Bible commentaries, and his radio broadcasts (syndicated posthumously as "Dr. Barnhouse and the Bible") made Barnhouse a respected and authoritative figure in evangelical circles both during his life and for decades after his death. His combination of fundamentalism, traditional Reformed theology, and dispensational premillenial views on Bible prophecy translated well across a variety of conservative denominational lines and theological camps in the developing evangelical movement. He was in many ways a prime example of the changing ethos of conservative American Protestantism in the period between the 1920s and the 1950s as it moved from strident, no-compromise fundamentalism to the more irenic spirit of the "New Evangelicalism." Although he appropriated the style of an independent, "empire building" fundamentalist preacher, Barnhouse's stance as a loyal Presbyterian exemplifies the strong—though frequently overlooked—evangelical presence within mainline Protestant denominations in the mid-twentieth century.

• The Barnhouse papers, a substantial collection, are located in the Presbyterian Historical Society in Philadelphia; unfortunately, they have not yet been processed. Barnhouse was a prolific writer and speaker; many of his sermons and his editorial views are available in the pages of *Revelation* and *Eternity* magazines. In addition, he was the author of a number of pamphlets and books on various biblical and theological topics, including *His Own Received Him Not* (1933) and *God's Methods For Holy Living* (1940). His most influential and widely read works (several published posthumously), however, were commentaries on biblical books such as *Revelation: An Expository Commentary* (1971). Of these works, the best known are his ten volumes of commentaries on the book of Romans (1952–1964) that stemmed from a decade of radio broadcasts. His second wife, Margaret N. Barnhouse, wrote a biographical memoir of their time together, *That Man Barnhouse* (1983). Barnhouse has received little scholarly attention; the major discussion of his life is C. Allyn Russell's article "Donald Grey Barnhouse: Fundamentalist Who Changed," *Journal of Presbyterian History*, 59 (Spring 1981): 33–57. See also Alan C. Guelzo, "Barnhouse" in *Making God's Word Plain*, ed. James Montgomery Boice (1979). For additional information on Barnhouse's role in early fundamentalist broadcasting, see Ben Armstrong, *The Electric Church* (1979).

LARRY K. ESKRIDGE

BARNITZ, Albert Trorillo Siders (10 Mar. 1835–18 July 1912), poet and soldier, was born at Bloody Run, Bedford County, Pennsylvania. The names of his parents are not known. His father, a physician, died when Albert was thirteen, and the boy devoted himself to caring for his mother and siblings. Reading widely and deeply in literature, he became a self-taught poet of modest local reputation. His formal education consisted of a year at Kenyon College in 1851 and two years, 1858 to 1859, of intermittent study at the Cleveland Law College. His first marriage, to Eva Prouty in 1859, ended with her death in childbirth a year later.

Although Barnitz pursued his literary and oratorical interests throughout his life, the Civil War launched his career as a soldier. Enlisting in the Second Ohio Cavalry, he served on the Missouri-Kansas border through 1862. His education and intelligence quickly gained him a commission, and by 1863 he had risen to become his regiment's senior captain. After service in East Tennessee, his regiment joined the Army of the Potomac in the spring of 1864 and participated in all its major actions and campaigns.

After a summer's convalescence from a bullet wound received at Ashland Station on 1 June 1864, Barnitz and his regiment joined the Third Cavalry Division in the Shenandoah Valley. Here he came under command of the youthful General George Armstrong Custer. Because the Second Ohio had been allowed to dwindle in strength, Barnitz as senior captain succeeded to command of the regiment.

In the battles that marked the death throes of Lee's army, Barnitz and the Second Ohio played a conspicuous part, fighting with distinction under Custer's vigorous direction. At Saylor's Creek the Ohioans captured 12 cannon, 68 officers (including 3 generals), 891 enlisted men, 4 battle flags, and a 3-mile-long wagon train. In a charge on Appomattox Station, they seized 53 cannon, several railroad supply trains, and many prisoners. The regiment was the last to take fire and had the last casualty before Lee's surrender. Barnitz later immortalized these adventures in a 25-stanza epic poem, "With Custer at Appomattox," which he often read at veterans' reunions.

After a brief return to civil life, which he found tame and financially unrewarding, Barnitz applied for a commission in the regular army and early in 1867 was assigned as a captain and company commander to the newly authorized Seventh Cavalry, whose lieutenant colonel was his old commander, Custer. Married in East Cleveland to Jennie Platte, Barnitz and his bride at once entrained for the West, where he reported for duty at Fort Riley, Kansas.

Barnitz was one of the ablest and most conscientious officers of the Seventh Cavalry, and in operations against the Cheyenne Indians of the Central Plains he acquitted himself with distinction. His most notable service occurred in June 1867, while he was in command of Fort Wallace, Kansas. Cheyenne warriors pressed the post closely but were repulsed by the counterattacks of Barnitz's troopers.

Aside from his creditable military service, Barnitz is significant principally because of the papers he left for the enlightenment of subsequent generations. He kept a diary, and he and his wife, during the frequent separations enforced by military service, exchanged long and informative letters. Both were observant, literate, and candid in recording their impressions of people and events. Their writings afford the best inside view of cavalry service on the Great Plains and of the personnel who made up the Seventh Cavalry.

Custer figures prominently in the papers, as Barnitz's appraisal of him turned from adulation to contempt. In May 1867, for example, Barnitz wrote that Custer "spares no effort to render himself generally obnoxious" and added, "He is the most complete example of a petty tyrant that I have ever seen."

Later, under another commander, Barnitz was equally acerbic in commenting on the army's way of fighting Indians:

Regimental Commanders in these latter days are not much wiser than Braddock of the older times, and refuse to fight Indians or even follow Indians in Indian fashion. General Custer could not have existed without hearing the sweet sound of fifteen or twenty bugles at least a dozen times during the day . . . and liked to march upon the "divides" . . . and to encamp where we could have a magnificent prospect, and where campfires would look *gorgeous* from afar!

During Custer's charge on Black Kettle's Cheyenne village on the Washita River in November 1868, Barnitz sustained a near-fatal wound in the abdomen that took him out of the campaign and ultimately the army. Brevetted a full colonel for "distinguished gallantry" at the battle of the Washita, in November 1870 he was placed on the retired list for disability.

For the rest of his life, Barnitz never lost interest in the army and remained proud of his military record. Traveling extensively as a newspaper columnist, he played the role of scarred war veteran, participating zestfully in veterans' affairs and attaining a modest reputation as a raconteur and public speaker.

Albert Barnitz died in Asbury Park, New Jersey. He and Jennie, who died in 1927, are buried in Arlington National Cemetery.

• The papers of Albert and Jennie Barnitz are in the Beinecke Library at Yale University. Selections from the diaries and letters of the plains years have been edited and annotated as *Life in Custer's Cavalry: Diaries and Letters of Albert and Jennie Barnitz, 1867–68*, ed. Robert M. Utley (1977 and 1987).

ROBERT M. UTLEY

BARNUM, Gertrude (29 Sept. 1866–17 June 1948), settlement-house worker and labor reformer, was born in Chester, Illinois, the daughter of William Henry Barnum, a Cook County circuit court judge, and Clara Letitia Hyde. Growing up in suburban Chicago, Barnum had a privileged childhood. As a young adult, she appears to have rejected the dictates of her class when she refused to make her formal debut into Chicago society. At the age of twenty-five she went to the University of Wisconsin, majoring in English. However, after one year of study at which she excelled, Barnum left the university to become an activist for social change in the settlement-house movement.

In 1892 Barnum began her association with Hull-House in Chicago, founded three years earlier by Jane Addams and Ellen Gates Starr. Like many college-educated women of her generation, Barnum had few options other than marriage and motherhood. The growing settlement-house movement provided an outlet for these women at the same time that it offered much-needed services to the largely immigrant working class in the industrial cities of America. Barnum spent several years at Hull-House and eventually became head resident at another Chicago settlement, Henry Booth House. Serving in that capacity from January 1902 to June 1903, she increasingly became aware of the need for trade unionism, which, she believed, would be the most direct way to address the poverty of immigrant workers.

To that end Barnum immediately joined forces with the National Women's Trade Union League, founded in the fall of 1903 by settlement workers and trade unionists, including William English Walling and Mary Kenney O'Sullivan. The league sought to organize women workers, educate the public, and agitate for protective labor legislation. As a cross-class alliance, the league attempted to carry out its work among working-class women who were frequently seen as "unorganizable" by the American Federation of Labor, which relied instead on the support of middle- and upper-class allies such as Barnum. While many of the working-class women within the league appreciated the financial support and the important social and political connections provided by the allies, class ten-

sions remained. As national organizer during the league's first few years, Barnum was often in the midst of such disputes. In her official report for 1905, Barnum claimed that "it has not been simple to keep a 'fair game' between Trade Unionists—who chafe at the inactivity of the allies—and allies who criticize the activities of the Unionists."

Nonetheless, in her role as national organizer, Barnum assisted in the formation of local branches of the Women's Trade Union League in Boston, New York, and Chicago. She also helped direct strike activity in Troy, New York, and in Fall River, Massachusetts. In Fall River, where 30,000 textile workers, many of whom were women, went out on strike in 1905, Barnum took part in a league program that attempted to attract striking textile workers into domestic service. Most women industrial workers, despite the harsh conditions and low pay, avoided domestic service because it paid even lower wages for longer, usually indeterminate, hours. As Barnum reported in the progressive journal *Charities* (4 Mar. 1905), of the 130 Fall River women brought to Boston for domestic work, only 70 remained after a few weeks and "not more than twenty [were] happy about it."

Barnum was far from being the only ally who could not transcend the world view of her class. Working-class women such as veteran trade unionist Leonora O'Reilly were frequently frustrated by the well-meaning but often misguided attempts of their allies. In 1905 O'Reilly resigned from the league because of the patronizing attitude of many of the allies. Barnum chided her for resigning, writing O'Reilly that "fortunately everyone does not abandon us 'allies' as soon as they disagree with us and we may be useful yet." However, as national organizer for the league, it was part of Barnum's job to reach out to working-class women, and her efforts to do so were limited. In 1906, her position abolished, Barnum left the league she had helped create.

Barnum excelled at the writing of articles that drew attention to the often horrific labor conditions facing women workers during the early years of the twentieth century. Between 1905 and 1917 she wrote numerous articles that appeared in several Progressive-era journals such as *Charities and Commons*, the *Independent*, and *Outlook*. For working-class readers, she wrote short stories that stressed the importance of trade unions rather than radical politics as the solution to the exploitation of workers by industrial capitalists. Her writing abilities and her potential social contacts made her a valuable asset, and in 1911 the International Ladies Garment Workers' Union (ILGWU) appointed Barnum as its publicity agent.

In her role as publicity agent, Barnum organized boycotts both among consumers and retail outlets of goods produced by nonunion firms. Early in 1913 in New York City, she took part in the strike of the white goods' workers (those who made slips, chemises, and other undergarments), soliciting the assistance of the middle and upper classes. During this time she was also active in the woman suffrage movement as a member of the New York–based Equality League of Self-Supporting Women, founded by Harriet Stanton Blatch in January 1907. After leaving the ILGWU in 1916, Barnum continued her efforts to improve labor conditions through government service. In 1918 she became assistant director of investigations for the U.S. Department of Labor. She retired in 1919, moving to Los Angeles, California, where she died nearly thirty years later. She had never married. In her work with the Women's Trade Union League and the ILGWU, and in her writings, Gertrude Barnum demonstrated both the limitations and the possibilities of cross-class attempts to change the exploitative working conditions in Progressive-era America.

• The papers of the National Women's Trade Union League and its leaders, including Barnum, are at the Library of Congress and at the Schlesinger Library, Radcliffe College. Most are available on microfilm. For additional information on the organizations in which Barnum played a key role, see Nancy Schrom Dye, *As Equals and as Sisters: Feminism, the Labor Movement, and the Women's Trade Union League* (1980), and Carolyn Daniel McCreesh, *Women in the Campaign to Organize Garment Workers, 1880–1917* (1985). An obituary is in the *New York Times*, 19 June 1948.

KATHLEEN BANKS NUTTER

BARNUM, P. T. (5 July 1810–7 Apr. 1891), showman, was born Phineas Taylor Barnum in Bethel, Connecticut, the son of Philo F. Barnum, a farmer and storekeeper, and Irena Taylor. While attending public school in Bethel, Barnum peddled candy and gingerbread. He later wrote that he had always been interested in arithmetic and money.

Barnum's profitable understanding of human nature and the brotherliness of a practical joke may have been partly influenced by his grandfather Taylor, who bequeathed him the gloriously named Ivy Island, which at age ten Barnum discovered to be "an almost inaccessible, worthless bit of barren land" filled with bogs and snakes.

When his father died insolvent in 1825, Barnum began clerking in a general store near Bethel. Purchasing a wagonload of used bottles, he devised a money-making lottery in which the bottles served as minor prizes. It was an early example of the "economy, industry and perseverance" he preached in later life.

After spending 1826 and 1827 clerking in Brooklyn, in 1828 Barnum opened a successful fruit and confectionery store in Bethel, where one of his customers was Hackaliah Bailey, owner of a small traveling menagerie boasting the second elephant ever seen in the United States. Barnum worked as a lottery agent in Pennsylvania before resettling in Bethel. He married Charity Hallett in 1829. They had four children.

In 1831 Barnum started the *Herald of Freedom*, an abolitionist and "non-sectarian" newspaper in Danbury, Connecticut. Barnum was convicted of libel in 1833 after exposing a usurer. Released from jail, he rode home in an open coach with six horses while cannons boomed and friends sang "Yankee Doodle." The newspaper collapsed in 1834, and Barnum moved to New York City, where in 1835 he was running a boardinghouse and another grocery store.

In New York what Barnum later called "the least deserving of all my efforts in the show line" propelled him into his "true vocation." Borrowing $500 of a $1,000 purchase price, Barnum acquired the services of Joice Heth, purportedly the 161-year-old ex-nurse of "dear little George Washington," whose birth in 1732 she had attended. The seller produced a 1727 bill of sale to Washington's father that Barnum "honestly believed to be genuine."

Whatever the truth about the gnarled, toothless, and shrunken Heth, who while smoking her pipe faithfully unreeled such lore as the cherry tree tale, her appearance at New York's outdoor Niblo's Garden beginning 10 August 1835 brought Barnum $750 weekly. When Heth died a year later, an autopsy suggested that she was no older than eighty. Barnum responded to an indignant James Gordon Bennett, owner of the penny daily *New York Herald*, who felt hoaxed, by bruiting the story that Heth was really still alive; Bennett printed that, too. Heth was buried in the Barnum family plot. As Irving Wallace, one of Barnum's biographers, noted, "In an age of blue laws the harmless hoax was a safety valve and a means of amusement for the public."

Barnum next engaged a stilt-walking juggler, published as news a notice of his brilliance in an Albany newspaper, and brought him to New York. When the run foundered in Philadelphia, Barnum hired a heckler who swore he could outdo the signor; thereafter their "duel" brought the customers flocking. In partnership with Aaron Turner, who believed notoriety the best publicity, Barnum led a small circus through the South until 1836. For the next four years he was in and out of show business, losing all in a partnership in shoe blacking, bear's grease, and cologne water.

In 1841 Barnum learned that Scudder's New York Museum, for years a losing concern, was on the market. "Lacking gold," he wrote, he "intended to buy it with brass." Armed with endorsements he persuaded the building's owner to buy it for him. When Peale's Museum outbid them with a public stock issue underwritten by bankers, Barnum wrote a "variety of squibs" ridiculing "the idea of a board of broken down bank directors engaging in the exhibition of stuffed monkeys and gander skins." The issue foundered, and by 27 December Barnum was in possession; he took over Peale's collections in New York in 1842 and in Philadelphia in 1850.

Though it charged for admission, Barnum's American Museum was the first important "public" museum in the United States. Barnum boasted of getting himself out of debt within twelve months by never having "eaten a warm dinner, except on Sundays." His advertising methods included hiring a man to leave bricks here and there around town; curious, people followed the man—right into the museum. Once paying customers were inside they might be fascinated by the signs leading them to the remarkable "Egress."

Passing through its door, of course they found themselves on the street.

Barnum's policy was to spend lavishly and reap great rewards. He wrote, "I knew the only way to make a million from my patrons was to give them abundant and wholesome attractions for a small sum of money. . . . Year after year, I bought genuine curiosities [often genuinely curious, though not always the genuine article] regardless of cost, wherever I could find them in Europe or America." He brought New York its first floodlights; in 1842 large oval oil paintings "of nearly every important animal known" were placed overnight all over the building's exterior. "Barnum's Animals" lived on through the twentieth century on boxes of animal crackers.

To his museum Barnum brought "educated dogs, industrious fleas, automatons . . . living statuary, tableaux, gipsies, Albinos, fat boys . . . rope dancers . . . dioramas, panoramas, models of Niagara, Dublin, Paris and Jerusalem, the Creation, the Deluge . . . mechanical figures, fancy glass blowing, knitting machines and other triumphs in the mechanical arts."

These attractions were supplemented by a variety of entertainments in an adjacent lecture room, expanded in 1849 into a full-scale theater, which gave all-day performances of "moral plays in a moral manner" and in 1850 was able to seat 3,000 for a performance of *The Drunkard*. On the first floor balcony was played "free music for the millions."

Barnum's clientele apparently loved his "humbug." The Feejee Mermaid (1842), a small amalgamation of dried and wrinkled skin, hair, and scales that looked as if it had once been alive, had been in circulation since 1822, when an English sea captain bought it in Calcutta. Barnum posted colorful bills showing saucy mermaids and hired a man as Dr. Griffin of Pernambuco, who delivered a learned lecture. The crowds gathered.

The Woolly Horse was indeed a horse with sheep-like hair, but Barnum had not, as he claimed, acquired it from the adventurous pathfinder John C. Frémont, newly returned from the Rocky Mountains; it was instead from a farm in Indiana. The horse "with his head where his tail should be" was simply reversed in its stall; "chickens made by steam" came from eggs hatched in an incubator.

In 1842 Barnum's brother Philo introduced him to a two-foot-tall ten-year-old, Charles S. Stratton. Engaged for four weeks at $3 weekly, Stratton was exhibited at the museum as the "English General" Tom Thumb and quickly became a public favorite. Barnum's 1844 tour of England with the general (there "American General") was another turning point in his career. In 1844 British opinion of the United States was at an ebb, largely because of the negative reports of travelers such as Mrs. Trollope and Fanny Kemble and Charles Dickens's novel *Martin Chuzzlewit*, all stereotyping the Yank as crassly business-obsessed. With his blend of genial optimism, healthy skepticism, and frontierish humor, Barnum reversed the tide.

Though successful neither in Liverpool nor in London, where he was sandwiched between a short play and an opera (at least no missiles were thrown his way), Tom Thumb won British hearts by winning their queen's. After a campaign of wooing the London press, Barnum and Thumb received an invitation to Baroness Rothschild's home. Departing with a well-filled purse, Barnum concluded that "the golden shower had begun to fall." He rented London's exotic Egyptian Hall, where he began to exhibit Thumb, and in the meantime he plied the American minister Edward Everett with letters of introduction from *New York Tribune* editor Horace Greeley.

The strategy, helped along by the master of the queen's household, who had recently traveled with the Pawnee Indians, brought Barnum and Thumb three audiences at Buckingham Palace. A true Lilliputian, Thumb was bright, fresh, and attractive, very unlike the ugly dwarfs usually on exhibit in Europe. He pronounced himself "as big as anybody," sang, danced, and carried on enlightened conversation with all the courtiers.

Soon Barnum was taking $500 nightly at the Egyptian Hall. The triumphant tour eventually included Paris, where Thumb appeared in a play, and Brussels and Waterloo, where Barnum was bemused by the expert humbuggery of the souvenir-sellers.

At 6'2", Barnum made an imposing appearance on a lecture platform, his high-pitched voice selling American attitudes to the British: "[An American] never builds a house to last above a year or two because he's gone ahead in that time . . . and go ahead is our motto. Shut the fire door, sit on the safety valve and whop the sun. We've no bonds on airth can keep us back." Returning to New York in 1847 Barnum found that he had become his own best curiosity. In 1848 he built in Bridgeport, Connecticut, a mansion called "Iranistan," a fantastic replica of the Royal Pavilion in Brighton, England.

In 1850, though he had never heard her sing, Barnum brought to the United States the soprano Jenny Lind, the "Swedish Nightingale," mortgaging everything, he wrote, because of "her character for extraordinary benevolence and generosity." Barnum's advance work ("She was effectually introduced to the public before they had seen or heard her. She appeared in the presence of a jury already excited to enthusiasm in her behalf") produced a crowd of 20,000 at Lind's arrival in New York on 1 September. Soon there were Jenny Lind gloves, bonnets, riding hats, shawls, mantillas, robes, chairs, sofas, and pianos. Lind received $10,000 for her first concert, which sold $18,000 in tickets. Her 93-concert tour, which included Cuba, is credited with opening the United States to major European artists.

Between 1851 and 1856 Barnum also operated the touring Great Asiatic Caravan, Museum and Menagerie, which featured Tom Thumb, ten elephants, and other wild animals. In 1852 a Barnum troupe toured the new state of California. Two years later Barnum began delivering lectures on "The Philosophy of

Humbug" and issued the first of many versions of his *Autobiography*.

Instrumental in 1851 in the founding of East Bridgeport, Barnum became a bank president there and in 1852 a partner in a clockmaking factory. Eventually his booster spirit lured him into underwriting the Jerome Clock Company; this cost his latest fortune, and in 1855 he was forced to sell the American Museum's collection and goodwill.

Barnum's recovery from the latest debacle (and the 1857 fire that burned Iranistan to the ground) came partly because of further tours (1857–1858) with Tom Thumb, partly because real estate prices in East Bridgeport boomed, and partly because Charity Barnum had her own money. By 1859 Barnum was also giving 100 lectures yearly on "The Art of Money Getting."

Aside from "go-aheaditiveness" Barnum advocated reserving a nest-egg, wearing old clothes, taking cold baths and brisk walks, and abstaining from tobacco, "the noxious weed." He pointed out that a little advertising was a dangerous thing and noted that the one liquid a man could use in excessive qualities without being swallowed up in it was printer's ink.

Barnum reacquired the American Museum in 1860, presenting Grizzly Adams and his bears, wolves, lions, tigers, buffalo, elk, and sea lions. Though a sensation, the mountainman Adams suffered a gaping scalp wound and did not live long. In the next few years Barnum presented the first hippopotamus seen in the United States as well as several Indian chiefs, who left when they found that Barnum was making money from their exhibition. In 1863 several thousands attended the marriage of Tom Thumb to the dwarf Lavinia Warren.

Early a Jacksonian Democrat, Barnum had been asked in 1852 by Connecticut Democrats to run for governor, but secession turned him into a Republican. In 1865 he became a Connecticut legislator and on 13 July was speaking against price-gouging railroad schemes when the news came that the American Museum had burned down. He replaced it on a new site nearby. In 1867 Barnum lost his bid to become a congressman.

Barnum's *Humbugs of the World* was published in 1865. Noting that the title "prince of humbug" had first been applied to him by himself ("I made these titles a part of my stock in trade"), Barnum argued that humbuggery was "an astonishingly widespread phenomenon, whether secular, moral or religious," and if "humbugs" gave a customer his money's worth they were quite all right. Asserting that the greatest humbug—a fool—believed that everything and everybody are humbugs, Barnum concluded, "When all are kind and just and honest, want only what is fair and right, judge only on real and true evidence, and take nothing for granted, there will be no place for any humbug, harmless or hurtful."

In 1866 Barnum began a series of lectures on Success in Life, and in 1868 his second museum burned. In 1869 he filled a private railroad car with friends and took them the length of the newly opened Union Pacific Railroad. In 1870 he began to prepare a new show, combining museum, menagerie, caravan, hippodrome, and circus. He asked, "Can the Public Be Satisfied With Only 11 Camels?" The show opened in Brooklyn on 10 April 1871 before a crowd of 10,000.

Originally wagon-drawn, within the decade Barnum's circus was using sixty to seventy railroad freight cars, six passenger cars (one a Magnificent Advertising Car filled with press agents), and three engines. This "Great Travelling World's Fair" became Barnum's first two-ring circus during the 1872–1873 season, and a year later, on the principle of giving the public more than it can digest, there were three rings. By 1874 the show was housed in huge canvas tents. Barnum made sure that cheap excursion trains ran to all his stops. At the circus grounds Barnum's latest autobiography, *Struggles and Triumphs* (1869), selling at bookstores for $1.50, could be had for $1. Produced for nine cents, these sold 100,000 yearly. Barnum did not copyright the book, assuring that his words flowed everywhere.

Barnum was again in Europe when he learned of Charity's death in 1873. In 1874 he married Nancy Fish; they had no children. In 1875 Barnum was elected mayor of Bridgeport. Two years later he returned to England, lecturing on "The World, and How to Live in It." By this time his show, annually visiting 140 towns and covering 12,000 miles from Nova Scotia to California, was called P. T. Barnum's New and Greatest Show on Earth.

By 1880 Barnum was seriously threatened by a competitor, the Great London Circus, Sanger's Royal British Menagerie and Grand International Allied Shows. Run by James A. Bailey and James L. Hutchinson, this combination merged with Barnum's in 1881 to form the Barnum and London Circus.

This new "Barnum and Bailey" circus out-Barnumed Barnum, speeding up the action so that no act took more than six minutes. Although it was generally known that Barnum's main contribution to the new circus was his name, in 1882 his negotiations with the Regent's Park Zoo in London reaped the mighty Jumbo, a huge elephant (fourteen feet long, eighteen feet around, twelve feet tall, and weighing seven tons), which was the Greatest Show's major attraction until its heroic death in 1885, run over by a locomotive while saving the life of a baby elephant.

In 1887 the circus's Bridgeport winter quarters burned. Barnum took the Greatest Show to London, where it opened on 1 November 1889 at the vast Olympia and drew an initial crowd of 15,000, quickly clearing £15,000 weekly. The *Dramatic News* pronounced it "undoubtedly the most colossal exhibition ever produced in the metropolis," and Barnum was once again the fad of the season. Lecturing once more, Barnum "told yarns about Irish pilots, Irish waiters, funny deacons . . . [the *Pall Mall Gazette* called him] . . . a born storyteller, and in his hands the stalest chestnut would make you roar with laughter."

In 1890 Barnum wrote from Colorado, "I eat, sleep and walk like a boy of 16 . . . I have an old heart and the doctors cannot cure an old heart." After reading his own specially prepared obituary, Barnum died in Bridgeport. Various theatrical versions of Barnum's life followed; the most successful was the Cy Coleman musical comedy *Barnum* (1980), which ran for nearly three years on Broadway and achieved similar success in Great Britain.

• It is generally agreed that Barnum's own works give an accurate as well as colorfully characteristic account of his life and thought. Among other useful overviews are M. R. Werber, *P. T. Barnum* (1923); Harvey W. Root, *The Unknown Barnum* (1927); Irving Wallace, *The Fabulous Showman* (1959); R. Fitzsimmons, *Barnum in London* (1970); and A. H. Saxon, *P. T. Barnum: The Legend and the Man* (1989).

JAMES ROSS MOORE

BARNWELL, John (c. 1671–June 1724), frontier settler and Indian fighter, was the son of Alderman Matthew Barnwell of Dublin, Ireland, and Margaret Carberry. The elder Barnwell was killed in the siege of Derry in 1690 as a captain in James II's Irish army, which attempted to restore the last Stuart king after the revolution of 1688. The family seat, Archerstown in County Meath, was forfeited as a result of this support of James II against William and Mary.

John Barnwell arrived in South Carolina about 1701. He became a protégé of governor Sir Nathaniel Johnson, after whom his eldest son was named, and the powerful chief justice of Carolina, Nicholas Trott. He soon was given important government posts: deputy surveyor (1703), clerk of the council (1703), and deputy secretary of the council (1704). As deputy surveyor he mapped the newly settled sea islands around Port Royal Sound in 1703. It was there that he staked his claim to 4,800 acres of frontier land. This was the beginning of Barnwell's expertise in Indian affairs and interest in the settlement of the southern frontier.

On the southern frontier, Barnwell became an ally of Thomas Nairne, the first settler of St. Helena Island (1698), South Carolina Indian commissioner (1707), and aggressive British expansionist. Following Nairne's attack upon the Spanish mission settlements of West Florida in 1705, Barnwell made his own reconnaissance of North Florida in 1708. Barnwell's association with Nairne, and the influence of the southern planter families, particularly the Bulls, Bellingers, and Blakes, all of whom were leaders of the Dissenter faction in the Commons House of Assembly, turned him against his old patrons, Governor Johnson and Chief Justice Trott. Johnson and Trott were the leaders of the Anglican faction in South Carolina that succeeded in establishing the Anglican church in the province but failed to exclude the non-Anglican Dissenters from political participation in the Commons House of Assembly. After Nairne was imprisoned by the governor for high treason in 1708, Barnwell led a riot against his old friend Trott in 1709. It was the turning point in Barnwell's career. Thereafter, he was a staunch supporter of the provincial party against the Proprietors party.

Barnwell was also among the leading settlers of the southern frontier who in 1709 petitioned the Lords Proprietors for the settlement of a town on Port Royal Island. This new town was named Beaufort, for Henry Somerset, duke of Beaufort, and a new proprietor of Carolina in 1710. Beaufort, the second oldest town in South Carolina, was chartered on 17 January 1711.

When the Tuscarora War broke out in North Carolina, Colonel Barnwell was chosen to lead the South Carolina expedition of 1711–1712 to quell the uprising and save the fledgling settlements in the neighboring colony. With thirty Carolinians and 500 Indians, he assaulted the Tuscarora fort at Narhantes, near New Bern, and destroyed the Tuscarora villages in eastern North Carolina. In January 1712 he concluded a peace with the Tuscaroras. Though Barnwell's treaty left many in North Carolina dissatisfied because the Tuscaroras remained in North Carolina, he nevertheless returned to a hero's welcome in South Carolina. It was this expedition that earned him the reputation of South Carolina's premier Indian fighter and gave him the sobriquet "Tuscarora Jack."

No sooner had Barnwell returned to his southern plantations than the dangerous Yemassee War (1715–1728) broke out at Pocotaligo village. The war was the result of grievances of the southeastern tribes against the aggressive English Indian traders that had accumulated for more than thirty years. The specific grievance of the Yemassee tribe was the continued encroachment of settlers and cattlemen on Indian land established by the treaty of 1707. The Yemassee War involved the whole Creek Indian Confederation of Georgia and nearly succeeded in destroying South Carolina. One of the Yemassees' first victims was Indian agent Nairne, who was tortured and killed. Thus the mantle of leadership on the southern frontier passed to "Tuscarora Jack" Barnwell. In June 1715, Barnwell, leading the southern militia, drove the Yemassees from their villages in the Port Royal area. The Yemassees fled to Florida, where they received protection from the Spaniards at St. Augustine and continued to raid the sea islands intermittently for thirteen years. Barnwell was given command of the Carolina scout boats that patrolled the inland passage among the sea islands. With this waterborne force, he led several punitive expeditions to Florida and secured a temporary truce in 1720.

In 1719 the provincial leaders of South Carolina overthrew the proprietary governor Robert Johnson (1676–1735), replacing him with Colonel James Moore (c. 1650–1706). The new government chose Barnwell as their agent to the royal government in London in 1720. Barnwell convinced the Board of Trade to accept South Carolina as a royal colony and send General Sir Francis Nicholson to Carolina as the colony's first provisional royal governor. Barnwell also presented to the Board of Trade his plan for settling the southern frontier. The "Barnwell Plan" called for a ring of royal garrisons from the Georgia coast into Tennessee, surrounded by grants of free land to attract settlers. Returning with a company of British soldiers and using his "Carolina Scouts," Barnwell was able in 1721 to construct Fort King George on the Altamaha River at Darien, Georgia. This was the first English settlement south of the Savannah River and the genesis of Georgia.

Barnwell was a leading member of the Commons House of Assembly from 1721 to 1724. He had been chosen by the Commons House for a second mission to London when his health failed, and he died at his Port Royal Island plantation. His is the oldest grave in St. Helena churchyard, Beaufort, South Carolina. Barnwell was married to Ann Berners. They had eight children, whose descendants formed the leadership of the Beaufort community and the core of the sea island aristocracy through the colonial and antebellum eras. Among Barnwell's progeny were Senator Robert Woodward Barnwell and Senator Robert Barnwell Rhett, the "Father of Secession."

• Records of Barnwell's public and private life are in *British Public Records Office, Records Relating to South Carolina*; *South Carolina Commons House of Assembly Journals*; "Will of John Barnwell," 16 June 1724, Charleston Wills, vol. 1 (1722–1724); and "Inventory of the Estate of John Barnwell," 11 June 1724, Miscellaneous Records (1722–1724), all at the South Carolina Department of Archives and History. Secondary works on Barnwell are Patrick Melvin, "John Barnwell and Colonial South Carolina, *Irish Sword* 11, no. 42 (1973): 5–20; Stephen B. Barnwell, *Story of an American Family* (1969); A. S. Salley, "Barnwell of South Carolina," *South Carolina Historical Magazine* 2 (Jan. 1901): 47–88; and Walter Edgar and N. Louise Bailey, eds., *Biographical Directory of the South Carolina House of Representatives*, vol. 2 (1977). The Tuscarora War is recounted in Joseph W. Barnwell, ed., "The Tuscarora Expedition: Letters of Col. John Barnwell," *South Carolina Historical Magazine* 9 (Jan. 1908): 28–54. The Yemassee War is covered in Verner Crane, *The Southern Frontier* (1981), and Larry E. Ivers, "Scouting the Inland Passage, 1685–1737," *South Carolina Historical Magazine* 73 (July 1972): 117–29.

LAWRENCE S. ROWLAND

BARNWELL, Robert Woodward (10 Aug. 1801–25 Nov. 1882), educator, congressman, and U.S. and Confederate senator, was born at Beaufort, South Carolina, the son of Robert Gibbes Barnwell, a prosperous planter and Federalist member of Congress, and Elizabeth Wigg Hayne. In 1817 he entered Harvard College, where he became friendly with Ralph Waldo Emerson and Edward Everett. Following his graduation in 1821, Barnwell returned to South Carolina to read law in the Charleston office of Hamilton and Petigru. He was admitted to the bar in 1823 and formed a partnership the next year with his cousin, Robert Barnwell Smith (later known as Robert Barnwell Rhett). In 1827 Barnwell married his second cousin, Eliza Barnwell, who bore him four children.

In addition to law, Barnwell's interests included cotton planting, education, and politics. He represented Beaufort in the state house of representatives from 1826 to 1828. A Democrat, he won election to the U.S. House of Representatives in 1828 and served four years. Andrew Jackson's tumultuous administration

tested Barnwell. Jealously guarding the rights of South Carolina, in 1832 he signed the Ordinance of Nullification, which prohibited the federal collection of tariff duties within the state.

Declining to seek a third term, Barnwell resumed life on his Low Country plantation. In 1835 he accepted the presidency of South Carolina College (now the University of South Carolina) at Columbia, succeeding Thomas Cooper, whose reputation as a freethinker had contributed to declining enrollment. Barnwell restored the college's prestige and strengthened it in a number of ways. He built enrollment, emphasized the importance of the political philosophy and history departments, established chairs in Christianity and literature, enforced codes of discipline, enlarged the library, expanded the physical plant, and persuaded the state legislature to appropriate additional funds.

Citing poor health, Barnwell retired from the presidency in 1841 to return to his plantation, but he retained his interests in education and politics. He believed that the South constituted the bulwark of conservatism in the United States and that its institutions deserved protection from federal regulation. Radical abolitionism and the growing furor over the extension of slavery into new territories contributed to his fear that Southern civilization was "doomed" and "must go out in blood." He expressed in a letter his conviction that "when a country degrades itself, its citizens may abjure the country with the disgrace it has drawn upon them."

The death of Senator John C. Calhoun in 1850 opened the door for Barnwell's return to Washington. To fill the vacancy, Governor Whitemarsh B. Seabrook appointed Franklin H. Elmore, who died after only a few weeks in office. The governor thereupon selected Barnwell, who served in the Senate from 4 June to 8 December 1850. During this six-month period Congress considered the acts that collectively became known as the Compromise of 1850. Barnwell opposed a number of these proposals, particularly California's admission as a free state, which he interpreted as an attempt by Free Soilers to upset the balance of sectional power and threaten slavery. Having attended the Nashville Convention, which had met earlier that year to consider the question of Southern rights, Barnwell instead supported that convention's recommendation that the Missouri Compromise line of 36 degrees 30 minutes be extended to the Pacific Ocean. This would divide California into two states, with slavery permitted south of the partition line. Although Barnwell believed that the geographic restriction of slavery in the territories was without constitutional basis, he was willing to accept partition, believing that such an arrangement was necessary to save the Union. When this strategy failed, Barnwell proposed, as a delaying tactic, that California's entrance into the Union be postponed. Unable to prevent California's statehood, however, he came to feel that South Carolina had been rendered powerless in Congress and to doubt that the question of slavery could be settled within the constitutional framework of the Union.

Barnwell chose not to run for a return to the Senate. Gratified to return to self-imposed retirement and be relieved of the burden of making speeches, Barnwell nevertheless kept in touch with political events. More temperate than the prominent fire-eaters of his state, Barnwell in 1851 recalled the failures of Nullification and counseled against South Carolina's seceding on its own.

In 1860 Barnwell felt obliged to resume a more active political role. He served in the convention that passed an ordinance of secession following Abraham Lincoln's election, and he sat on the committee that produced the "Declaration of Immediate Causes of Secession." Subsequently, he was one of the commissioners sent to negotiate with outgoing President James Buchanan for the transfer of federal property in South Carolina. Barnwell served as a delegate to the convention of representatives of seceded states that met at Montgomery, Alabama, in February 1861. Elected temporary chairman, he signed the Confederacy's constitution. President Jefferson Davis quickly offered Barnwell the position of secretary of state, but the modest South Carolinian, citing his lack of experience in foreign affairs, declined the portfolio. He did, however, represent South Carolina in the Confederate senate for the next four years; although he usually disagreed with Davis on fiscal matters, he otherwise was generally considered a Davis supporter.

After the Civil War, Barnwell—who lost his slaves and other property during the conflict—relocated to Greenville, South Carolina. In December 1865 Governor Benjamin F. Perry secured him an appointment as professor of political science and dean of the faculty of South Carolina College (now the University of South Carolina). Conflict with the African Americans and white Republicans on the board of trustees, who wished to integrate and reorganize the school, led to Barnwell's dismissal in 1873. He subsequently headed a private school for girls in Columbia. In 1877 the state's newly-installed Democratic governor, Wade Hampton, returned Barnwell to the university, appointing him its librarian. He held this position until his death in Columbia.

A popular but sensitive man, Barnwell oscillated between careers in education and politics. At times he seemed to doubt his own abilities and long for a quiet life on his plantation, but his sense of duty and the course of events continually interrupted his private existence.

• The largest collections of Barnwell's letters are in the Robert Barnwell Rhett Papers, Southern Historical Collection, Wilson Library, University of North Carolina at Chapel Hill; and the Robert W. Barnwell Papers, South Caroliniana Library, University of South Carolina at Columbia; the latter collection contains personal and Congressional papers and correspondence relating chiefly to education. Other useful collections are the Whitemarsh B. Seabrook Papers at the Library of Congress, and the James Henry Hammond Papers at the South Caroliniana Library and the Library of Congress. Barnwell's speeches were published in the *Congressional Globe*. The two major articles on Barnwell are both by John

Barnwell: "'In the Hands of Compromisers': Letters of Robert W. Barnwell to James H. Hammond," *Civil War History* 29 (1983): 154–68; and "Hamlet to Hotspur: Letters of Robert Woodward Barnwell to Robert Barnwell Rhett," *South Carolina Historical Magazine* 77 (1976): 236–56. On his early career in education, see Daniel Walker Hollis, *University of South Carolina* (2 vols., 1951, 1956). See also John Barnwell, *Love of Order, South Carolina's First Secession Crisis* (1982); Drew Gilpin Faust, *James Henry Hammond and the Old South: A Design for Mastery* (1982); Harold S. Schultz, *Nationalism and Sectionalism in South Carolina, 1852–1860* (1950); and Laura A. White, *Robert Barnwell Rhett: Father of Secession* (1931). An obituary is in the Charleston *News and Courier*, 27 Nov. 1882.

LEONARD SCHLUP

BARON, Salo Wittmayer (26 May 1895–25 Nov. 1989), educator and Jewish historian, was born in Tàrnow, Galicia, then part of the Austro-Hungarian Empire, the son of Elias Baron, a banker, and Minna Wittmayer. Baron's orthodox, intellectually enlightened family was one of the wealthiest of the Jewish community in Tàrnow. The primary languages spoken in the household were Polish and German. Besides the Barons' holdings in the town, they also owned an estate in the country and had a share in a family oil field. Private tutors instructed Baron in both secular and religious subjects. He later studied in Kraków and then in Vienna, where he received doctorates in history (1917), political science (1922), and jurisprudence (1923). He also continued his Jewish studies at the rabbinical seminary in Vienna and soon became an instructor in Jewish history at Vienna's Jewish Teachers College.

In 1926 Baron was invited by Stephen Wise, noted Zionist leader and president of the Jewish Institute of Religion in New York City, to serve as visiting professor of Jewish history at the institute. He quickly gained attention for his revisionist writings, especially his 1928 essay, "Ghetto and Emancipation," in which he first attacked what he called the "lachrymose conception of Jewish history."

In 1930 Baron assumed the Miller Chair in Jewish History, Literature, and Institutions at Columbia University, which he held until his retirement in 1963. The position represented the second chair in Jewish studies established at an American university and the first chair in Jewish history. Throughout his Columbia career, Baron was recognized as the "dean of Jewish historians in America" and head of the most significant program for the academic training of graduate students in the field.

Baron married Jeannette Meisel of New York City, a doctoral student in economics at Columbia, in 1934; they had two children. Jeannette worked closely with her husband, providing considerable assistance in the preparation of his manuscripts. The couple soon acquired a second residence in Canaan, Connecticut, where Baron produced a great deal of his prolific writing in semi-isolation.

Baron's best-known work is his *Social and Religious History of the Jews* (1937). The original three-volume edition covered the entire scope of Jewish history from the biblical period through the time of the book's publication. The unfinished eighteen-volume second edition (1952–1983) covers only the ancient and medieval periods, ending in 1650. His other works included various studies on modern nationalism and toleration of minorities and a number of significant essays on Jewish historiography and American Jewish history, many of which were subsequently gathered into collections.

Baron's writing was characterized by his continual pursuit of historical synthesis. He wrote in the introduction to *Ancient and Medieval Jewish History* (1972), a collection of his essays, "I have dedicated my most concentrated labors to major syntheses of the Jewish historic evolution." One of his constant themes was the interrelationship between the social and religious elements in Jewish history, a theme reflected in the title of his history. He repeatedly and emphatically attacked the "lachrymose conception," insisting that Jewish suffering be placed in proper perspective and that Jews had been significant actors, not merely passive objects, in the shaping of their history. He also severely criticized the two earlier major Jewish historians Heinrich Graetz and Simon Dubnow for isolating Jewish history from the environment in which Jews lived. Baron insisted that Jewish history must be written in the context of what he called its "World Dimensions."

Taken together, Baron's aversion to the lachrymose approach and his objection to the isolation of Jewish history suggested that the study of Jewish history should be based on the same modes of interpretation used by other historians. Baron put it this way in his 1939 essay "Emphases in Jewish History" in his 1964 collection, *History and Jewish Historians: Essays and Addresses:* "There is a growing feeling that the historical explanations of the Jewish past must not fundamentally deviate from the general patterns of history which we accept for mankind at large or for any other particular national group," p. 77.

The Nazi occupation of Poland caught Baron's parents and one sister in Tarnow. Baron failed in his attempts to arrange for their migration through American authorities. Although the family was killed in June 1942, Baron was not aware of their fate until after the war, and a spirit of muted optimism prevailed in both his scholarly and communal writings during the war years.

Known for his long hours and intensive work habits, Baron became especially productive during this period, while simultaneously undertaking constant efforts to assist family members and friends still in Europe. He became particularly involved in writing on the medieval period at this time. In addition to the three-volume *The Jewish Community* (1942), Baron published during the early 1940s a series of essays on the leading medieval rabbinical figures Rashi, Saadiah Gaon, Yehudah HaLevi, and Maimonides, as well as his synthetic study, "The Jewish Factor in Medieval Civilization," and his classic article, "Modern Capitalism and Jewish Fate."

Baron's scholarly focus on medieval times during the war years derived from a number of motivations; he sought, in part, to elucidate the historical role played by scholars during times of crisis, to reaffirm his critique of the lachrymose conception despite contemporary developments, and to distinguish between the positive aspects of medieval Jewish life and the greater threats to Jewish survival that were integrally connected to modernity. Baron therefore hardly concealed himself in a medieval citadel, much of his writing at this time focusing more directly on contemporary affairs.

During these years Baron also wrote his first essays on American Jewish history and began to encourage graduate students to write in this entirely new field. By the end of the 1940s, Baron was identified as a leading figure in the new discipline. In 1949 he delivered a far-reaching address to the American Jewish Historical Society on the problems facing those who wished to undertake such research. Baron's interest in American Jewish history also derived from the wartime context. Realizing that American Jewry had inherited the mantle of world Jewish leadership, Baron sought to place its historical experience within the broader context of Jewish history. It was crucial to Baron's outlook that American Jewry not be perceived as an outside entity imposed upon the continuum of Jewish history.

In addition to excelling as a scholar and teacher, Baron was enormously active in Jewish affairs. He was longtime president of the Conference of Jewish Social Studies and editor of its journal from its inception in 1939 until his death. He also served as president of the American Jewish Historical Society from 1953 to 1955, his term coinciding with the tercentenary celebration of American Jewish life, in which he took an active role. Baron was also intermittently president of the American Academy for Jewish Research.

Although Baron did not observe traditional Jewish practices, in his writings he continued to affirm the importance of religion in the preservation of Jewish life. He also supported a number of Zionist efforts, especially the Hebrew University. However, his belief in the historical and continued significance of the Diaspora caused disagreements with some Israeli scholars, such as Yitzchak Baer, who insisted on stronger recognition of the centrality of Israel's role in Jewish life, past and present.

In 1961 Baron received widespread attention when he was called as one of the opening witnesses in the war crimes trial against Nazi Adolf Eichmann conducted in Jerusalem. In a masterly summation of the course of European Jewish history during the nineteenth and twentieth centuries, Baron depicted the European Jewish community as a resourceful people who had demonstrated considerable ingenuity in combating the critical conditions of the interwar period. His testimony, however, caused controversy because of the implication that the Nazis' crimes were all the more grave because they had sought to annihilate a cultured people. Political philosopher Hannah Arendt discussed these objections in her book *Eich-*

mann in Jerusalem: A Report on the Banality of Evil (1963).

During his retirement years, Baron worked primarily on the revised edition of *A Social and Religious History of the Jews* until the death of his wife in 1985. He then began work on his memoirs, which remained unfinished at the time of his death in New York.

Baron had an enormous impact on the field of Jewish studies in the United States. His noteworthy career and his extensive writings contributed to the field's academic legitimization, and his demanding requirements ensured the scholarly standing of his students. With the explosive growth in the field that began in the 1960s, the Baronian legacy continued to represent intensive training that combined immersion in traditional Jewish sources with a broad understanding of the historical forces at work in society at large.

Ironically, the enormous output of specific monographs by the growing number of scholars of Jewish history has resulted in the gradual dating of Baron's own work. Still, several of his monographs continue to serve as basic works on their subjects. More important, Baron's three basic historical approaches continue to be used by scholars in the field: his critique of the lachrymose conception of Jewish history; his study of the interrelationship between social and religious forces in Jewish history; and his emphasis on the interaction between the Jewish community and the societies in which Jews live.

• The Baron Collection of correspondence, manuscripts, including his unfinished memoirs, and photographs is in the Department of Special Collections at Stanford University Library. In addition to the *Social and Religious History* (1st ed., 3 vols., 1937; 2d ed., rev., 18 vols., 1952–1983), the best known of his works are *The Jewish Community* (3 vols., 1942); *The Russian Jew under Tsars and Soviets* (1964); *History and Jewish Historians, Essays and Addresses*, comp. Arthur Hertzberg and Leon A. Feldman (1964); *Ancient and Medieval Jewish History*, ed. Leon Feldman (1972); *Steeled by Adversity: Essays and Addresses on American Jewish Life*, ed. Jeannette Meisel Baron (1971). A bibliography of his writings through 1973, edited by Jeannette Baron, is in *Salo Wittmayer Baron Jubilee Volume*, ed. Saul Lieberman and Arthur Hyman, vol. 1 (1974), pp. 1–37. A study of his life and historical thought can be found in Robert Liberles, *Salo Wittmayer Baron: Architect of Jewish History* (1995). See also the assessments of Baron's work by Louis Feldman, Robert Chazan, and Ismar Schorsch in *AJS Review* 17, no. 1 (1993): 1–50. An interpretative memoir of Baron's life and writings can be found in the memorial essay in Hebrew by Lloyd Gartner in *Zion* 55 (1990): 317–32.

ROBERT LIBERLES

BAROODY, William Joseph (29 Jan. 1916–28 July 1980), policy analyst, research institute executive, and political adviser, was born in Manchester, New Hampshire, the son of Lebanese immigrants Joseph Assad Baroody, a stonecutter, and Helen Hasney. In 1935 he married Nabeeha Marion Ashooh. They had seven children. After graduating from St. Anselm's

College in Manchester in 1936, he took graduate courses at the University of New Hampshire (1937–1938) and at American University (1938).

Baroody's early career was as a state government official. In 1937 he obtained employment as an assistant statistician with the New Hampshire Unemployment Compensation Division and in 1941 was promoted to supervisor of its fiscal, research, and legislative planning sections. From 1940 to 1944 he worked with the New Hampshire Legislative Commission on Disability Benefits as a research associate, and from 1943 to 1944 he was director of the statistical division of the New Hampshire War Finance Committee.

In 1944 Baroody left state government to serve as a lieutenant in the U.S. Naval Reserve. In 1946, following World War II, he went to Washington, where he worked until 1949 for the Veterans Administration as chief of the Research and Statistics Division of the Readjustment Allowance Service. With the U.S. Chamber of Commerce between 1950 and 1953, he was associate editor of *American Economic Security* and executive secretary of its Committee on Economic Security.

Baroody was appointed executive vice president of the American Enterprise Association in 1954. Becoming the association's president in 1962, he renamed it the American Enterprise Institute for Public Policy Research (AEI). This small trade association had been founded eleven years earlier to articulate a free enterprise view of public policy. By the end of Baroody's presidency in 1978, the AEI's budget had increased from about $80,000 to about $8 million per year and its staff had increased to 125. The organization was well established as a major nonpartisan, nonprofit, conservatively inclined research institute, attracting the participation of leading scholars and policy makers.

In 1963–1964 Baroody served as a key adviser to Senator Barry Goldwater in his campaign for the Republican presidential nomination and in his fall campaign against President Lyndon B. Johnson. Among the leading conservatives who influenced Goldwater to run, Baroody was a rare Washington figure in Goldwater's inner "Arizona mafia" circle. The leading intellectual figure of the Goldwater campaign, Baroody directed its research and speech writing operation. In this capacity, he participated in drafting Goldwater's acceptance speech, in which the nominee declared, "Extremism in the defense of virtue is no vice."

Baroody's central role in the campaign was subsequently criticized by his former colleagues. Goldwater blamed Baroody for excluding from his campaign leading conservative intellectuals from the *National Review*, among them William F. Buckley, Jr., and L. Brent Bozell. According to Goldwater, Baroody was "a man who enjoyed power." The campaign manager, Denison Kitchel, whose unfamiliarity with Washington politics added to Baroody's influence, called him a "Svengali." By contrast, Karl Hess, who worked for Baroody both in the campaign and in the AEI, called him "the finest motivator of people I've ever met," although "some might say manipulator."

After Goldwater's defeat, Baroody helped found the Free Society Association, intended to promote political conservatism. Under the presidency of Kitchel, it did not enjoy the success of its rival organization, the American Conservative Union, and it quickly dissolved. Baroody did not again participate actively in elective politics, but he was a friend and confidant to other prominent Republican politicians, including Richard Nixon and Gerald Ford.

Succeeded as AEI president by his son, William J. Baroody, Jr., in 1978, Baroody became counsellor and chairman of the institute's Development Committee. He was also a member of the U.S. Catholic Bishops' Advisory Council (1973–1975), a member of the Board of Overseers of the Hoover Institution (1960–1980), and board chairman of the Woodrow Wilson International Center for Scholars (1972–1979). He died in Alexandria, Virginia.

Baroody has been lauded for promoting conservative ideas in American politics. Under his direction, the AEI supported anti-Communist foreign policy, free market economic policy, and smaller-government domestic policy. In 1980 Republican presidential nominee (later President) Ronald Reagan praised Baroody for "building an institution that said, 'Here is a place where you can develop your ideas,' that said to others, 'Here is a place you can turn to for advice,' that said to all of us who were concerned about our country's future, 'You are not alone.'"

• Baroody's papers are at the Library of Congress. A Melkite Catholic, Baroody wrote articles on ecumenism, Eastern rites, and public policy. Biographical overviews are in the American Enterprise Institute for Public Policy Research, *William J. Baroody, January 29, 1916–July 28, 1980* (1980), and Paul W. McCracken, et al., *William J. Baroody, Sr.: The Francis Boyer Lectures on Public Policy* (1981). Obituaries are in the *New York Times* and the *Washington Post*, both 30 July 1980.

ROBERT MASON

BARR, Alfred Hamilton, Jr. (28 Jan. 1902–15 Aug. 1981), museum official and art historian, was born in Detroit, Michigan, the son of Alfred Hamilton Barr, Sr., a Presbyterian minister, and Annie Elizabeth Wilson. Barr attended Princeton University, receiving a B.A. in art history in 1922 and an M.A. in the same subject in 1923. The teachers at Princeton who made the most lasting impression on him were Frank Jewett Mather, who taught Renaissance and modern art, and Charles Rufus Morey, whose course in medieval art Barr later described as "a remarkable synthesis of the principal medieval arts as a record of a period of civilization: architecture, sculpture, painting on walls and in books, minor arts and crafts." It was as a result of this course that Barr decided that the Museum of Modern Art in New York City, of which he became founding director in 1929, should be a repository of a similar record of the civilization of the twentieth century, with departments of not only painting, sculpture, and graphic art, but also architecture, industrial design, photography, and film.

From 1923 to 1924 Barr taught art history at Vassar College in Poughkeepsie, New York, where in April 1924 he organized an exhibition of modern European art. In September 1925 he entered the Harvard Graduate School as a Thayer Fellow and an assistant in the Fine Arts Department. For the academic year 1925–1926 he returned to Princeton as a preceptor in the Department of Art and Archaeology. In the fall of 1926 Barr was appointed associate professor in the Department of Art History at Wellesley College. He also enrolled in further graduate courses at Harvard, including the famous museum course taught by Paul J. Sachs. At Wellesley, Barr taught the first course in the United States devoted entirely to the history of twentieth-century art, a course remembered by Barr's friend and art historian Jere Abbott as "unbelievably ahead of its time."

In the winter and spring of 1927–1928 Barr and Abbott traveled to Germany and Russia and visited, among other things, the Bauhaus art school in Dessau. The Bauhaus publication program and the integration in its curriculum of architecture, art, and crafts were important models for what Barr accomplished at the Museum of Modern Art. His knowledge of the Russian avant-garde was unprecedented among Western art historians at that time, and it later enabled him to form a comprehensive collection of Russian twentieth-century painting and sculpture at the museum. In the fall of 1928 Barr returned to teaching at Wellesley.

On the recommendation of Sachs, in June 1929 A. Conger Goodyear, the chairman of a committee formed for the purpose of establishing a museum of modern art in New York, offered Barr the museum's directorship. He accepted, and the Museum of Modern Art opened on 7 November 1929 at 730 Fifth Avenue with a loan exhibition, Cezanne, Gauguin, Seurat, and Van Gogh. Later that month Barr met Italian art historian Margaret Scolari, and they were married in 1930. During the summer of that year the Barrs traveled in France, England, and Germany to secure loans for exhibitions of works by Daumier and Corot in the fall of 1930 and of German painting and sculpture in the spring of 1931, the first comprehensive exhibition in the United States of twentieth-century German art.

Long before painter Henri Matisse was accorded the acclaim that he received following World War II, Barr recognized him as a major master of twentieth-century art. In 1931 he mounted the first retrospective exhibition of Matisse's work.

In 1932 the museum's first exhibition of twentieth-century architecture, Modern Architecture, International Exhibition, was organized by Philip Johnson and Henry-Russell Hitchcock, with Barr as the catalyst. Barr introduced the designation "International Style" for the work of Le Corbusier, Walter Gropius, Mies Van der Rohe, Frank Lloyd Wright, and other innovative architects of the time. The exhibition introduced the new architecture to the United States and marked a major step toward acceptance of its innovations by the public as well as by the architectural profession.

On 3 May 1932 the Museum of Modern Art moved to a limestone town house rented from the Rockefeller family at 11 West Fifty-third Street. That fall Barr was granted a year's leave of absence to go to Europe, where, mostly in Italy and Germany, he looked at new work, made contacts with artists, collectors, and dealers, and scouted exhibitions. After returning he organized the first retrospective of the works of painter Edward Hopper.

In the spring of 1934 Barr wrote the catalog preface for Machine Art, directed by Johnson, the curator of the museum's Department of Architecture. The exhibition emphasized the stylistic interdependence of twentieth-century painting, sculpture, graphic art, and industrial design. It also marked the beginning of the museum's design collection. In November 1934 Barr organized Modern Works of Art, Fifth Anniversary Exhibition, in which he charted the directions the arts were taking in the United States and abroad and included works by thirty-one American artists. He devoted the greater part of 1935 to the preparation of Vincent van Gogh, an exhibition that attracted 123,339 people between 4 November 1935 and 5 January 1936.

Among Barr's many pioneering exhibitions at the museum were Cubism and Abstract Art (2 Mar. to 19 Apr. 1936) and Fantastic Art, Dada, Surrealism (7 Dec. 1936 to 17 Jan. 1937). They were the first two exhibitions in a series intended, in Barr's words, "to illustrate some of the principal movements of modern art in a comprehensive, objective, and historical manner." The third in the series was Masters of Popular Painting: Modern Primitives of Europe & America (1938); the fourth, directed by Dorothy Miller, was Americans 1943: Realists and Magic-Realists (1943); and the fifth, directed by James Thrall Soby, was Romantic Painting in America (1943). The catalogs for these exhibitions have become classic expositions of their subjects.

In December 1937 Barr acquired for the museum painter Pablo Picasso's *Girl before a Mirror* (1932), the first of many important works purchased by him with funds donated by museum trustee Mrs. Simon Guggenheim. Another major work by Picasso acquired by Barr was the seminal *Les Demoiselles d'Avignon* (1907), which was brought to the museum in 1939. During April and May of 1938 Barr worked in Paris on Trois siècles d'art aux États-Unis, a project of Goodyear, then the president of the museum. The exhibition was on view at the Musée du Jeu de Paume in Paris from 24 May to 31 July 1938 and constituted the museum's first exhibition abroad.

In June 1937, in order to allow for the construction of a new building at 11 West Fifty-third Street designed by Philip Goodwin and Edward Durrell Stone, the museum moved to the Time & Life Building at 14 West Forty-ninth Street. Exhibitions at the museum's temporary quarters included Useful Household Ob-

jects Under Five Dollars, the first in a series intended to promote good industrial design, and Bauhaus: 1919–1928, selected by Barr in collaboration with Bauhaus founder Walter Gropius and his wife Ise Gropius and installed by Herbert Bayer, a former member of the Bauhaus faculty. The opening ceremonies for the museum's new building were held in May 1939, and the occasion was celebrated with the exhibition Art in Our Time, which presented recent developments in the arts as represented in all of the museum's departments. Later that year the museum inaugurated regular film showings in its basement auditorium.

Soon after his appointment as director of the museum Barr had begun securing loans for a retrospective exhibition of works by Picasso. His efforts came to fruition in Picasso: Forty Years of His Art, which opened on 15 November 1939. It was the first of Barr's three major exhibitions dedicated to Picasso, followed in 1946 by Picasso: Fifty Years of His Art, and in 1957 by Picasso: 75th Anniversary Exhibition. All three exhibitions included Picasso's masterpiece *Guernica* (1937), which remained at the museum on loan until 1981, when it was given to Spain following the death of Generalissimo Francisco Franco.

In 1940 Barr installed at the museum thirty masterpieces of Italian Renaissance and baroque painting, which had been lent by the Italian government to the San Francisco World's Fair and were on their way back to Italy. The next year Barr directed exhibitions of painters Paul Klee and George Grosz, and in 1942 he mounted New Acquisitions: Free German Art. In the introduction to the catalog for the New Acquisitions exhibit, he wrote, "Among the freedoms which the Nazis have destroyed, none has been more cynically perverted, more brutally stamped upon than the Freedom of Art. . . . But German artists of spirit and integrity have refused to conform. They have gone into exile or slipped into anxious obscurity." Also in 1942 Barr wrote the introduction to *Painting and Sculpture in the Museum of Modern Art*, the first general catalog of the museum's collections.

At the request of Stephen C. Clark, the president of the museum from 1941 to 1946, Barr resigned in 1943 as director and assumed the position of advisory director in order to devote all of his time to writing about modern art. The museum's fifteenth anniversary exhibition, Art in Progress, in the summer of 1944 was composed of Painting, Sculpture, Prints; Design for Use; Built in U.S.A. 1932–1944; Posters; and Photography and paid tribute to Barr's accomplishments during his fifteen years as director.

In 1947 Barr was appointed chairman of the Museum Collections of Painting and Sculpture, a post he held until 1967. Even though he was no longer director, he continued to guide the museum's acquisition and exhibition policies. In 1944 Barr was responsible for the purchase of painter Jackson Pollock's *She-Wolf* (1943), the first work by Pollock to be acquired by a museum. Barr also recognized early on the importance of American artists Frank Stella, Jasper Johns, and

Andy Warhol. Upon his retirement in 1967 Barr was named counselor to the museum's board of trustees.

Beyond the walls of the museum Barr delivered the 1946 Mary Flexner lectures at Bryn Mawr College, titled "Programs and Practices in Modern Art." He served on the Visiting Committee for Fine Arts at the Fogg Art Museum of Harvard University from 1958 to 1960 and was its chairman from 1965 to 1970. From 1964 to 1970 he was also a member of the Harvard Board of Overseers. Barr received a Ph.D. from Harvard's Department of Fine Arts in 1946. In 1959 he received the American Federation of Arts fiftieth anniversary award "for being the founding father of the Museum of Modern Art and for interpreting the art of our time."

At his death Barr was acclaimed as "possibly the most innovative and influential museum man of the twentieth century." He broadened the concept of the museum to include architecture, industrial design, photography, and film, a concept that has been adopted in museums throughout the world. Few art historians have been more successful and influential than Barr in making modern art accessible to the public. In a report he prepared in 1944 on the collections of the museum, Barr stressed that "the primary purpose of the Museum is to help people enjoy, understand and use the visual arts of our time." His success in bringing this about was largely a result of the fact that in his books, exhibition catalogs, and exhibition labels he presented the history of modern art with order, lucidity, and discipline, and thus made it intelligible to an often bewildered public.

Barr combined a passionate curiosity about all works of art with an insistence on "the conscientious, continuous, resolute distinction of quality from mediocrity." The rigorous application of this distinction was at the core of his artistic decisions and judgments, and it is a distinction for which there are no criteria outside of the experience of the work of art itself. When asked by a journalist to define his criteria for awarding prizes at an exhibition, Barr answered that he had none. How then, the journalist wondered, was he going to judge the paintings? "By looking at them," Barr replied. One of the most fitting tributes to his achievements was paid by Philippe de Montebello, the director of the Metropolitan Museum of Art. Asked in 1979 what he would put in a time capsule that would reflect most accurately the fifty-year history of the Museum of Modern Art, de Montebello answered, "The eye and mind of Alfred Barr." Barr died in Salisbury, Connecticut.

• Barr's papers are in the archives of the Museum of Modern Art. Selected records and personal correspondence are also available on microfilm at the Archives of American Art. "Russian Diary 1927–28," Barr's account of his and Jere Abbott's trip to Russia, was published in *October* (Winter 1987). Barr is the author of *Cubism and Abstract Art* (1936), *Fantastic Art, Dada and Surrealism* (1936), *Picasso: Forty Years of His Art* (1939), *What Is Modern Painting?* (1943; ninth rev. ed., 1966), *Picasso: Fifty Years of His Art* (1946), *Matisse: His Art and His Public* (1951), *Masters of Modern Art* (1954), and

Painting and Sculpture in the Museum of Modern Art, 1929–1967 (1977). Thirty-five of Barr's shorter writings have been collected in Irving Sandler and Amy Newman, ed., *Defining Modern Art: Selected Writings of Alfred H. Barr, Jr.* (1986), which also contains a chronology of Barr's career and a bibliography of all his published writings. Information about Barr's life and career is contained in Dwight MacDonald's two-part series in the *New Yorker*, 12 Dec. 1953, pp. 49–82, and 19 Dec. 1953, pp. 35–72; Russell Lynes, *Good Old Modern: An Intimate Portrait of the Museum of Modern Art* (1973); Beaumont Newhall, "Alfred H. Barr, Jr.: He Set the Pace and Shaped the Style," *Art News* (Oct. 1979): 134–7; and two articles in a special issue of the *New Criterion*: Rona Roob, "Alfred H. Barr, Jr.: A Chronicle of the Years 1902–1929" (1987): 1–19; and Margaret Scolari Barr, "Our Campaigns" (1987): 23–74. An obituary by John Russell, "Alfred Barr: Museum Man of the Century," is in the *New York Times*, 23 Aug. 1981.

HELLMUT WOHL

BARR, Amelia Edith Huddleston (29 Mar. 1831–10 Mar. 1919), author and teacher, was born in Ulverston, Lancashire, England, the daughter of the Reverend William Henry Huddleston and Mary Singleton. When Barr was young, her family moved often, according to her father's assignment as a Methodist minister. Although her early education was frequently interrupted by relocations, returns on the Reverend Huddleston's investments allowed Barr to attend the best private schools wherever the church sent the family. Furthermore, reading sophisticated books and treatises to her father reinforced her formal schooling and contributed to an excellent early education. This childhood security ended abruptly in 1847, when a family friend absconded to Australia with the Reverend Huddleston's fortune, and Barr had to earn her own living as a "second teacher" at a school in Downham Market. Soon the family's monetary situation improved and enabled Barr, in 1849, to attend Normal School in Glasgow to learn the Stowe teaching method, with its emphasis on moral training, lifelong learning, and understanding rather than rote learning. Marriage, in 1850, to Robert Barr, a prosperous young Scottish wool merchant, ended her teacher-training program. Nevertheless, teaching, on a formal or informal basis, was an important part of Barr's life for the next twenty years.

Over the next three years, Robert Barr's financial situation deteriorated, and, facing bankruptcy, Amelia Barr suggested that they seek their fortune in the United States. Propelled by business opportunities, political controversy, and yellow fever epidemics, the Barrs arrived in New York in 1853, moved to Chicago in 1854, transferred to Memphis in 1856, and finally settled in Austin, Texas, in 1857, remaining there almost ten years. Barr's husband was a successful accountant in the state comptroller's office, but the Barrs' finances remained precarious due to the instability of the Texas government as a former Republic, as a Confederate state, and as a state under Reconstruction. Barr ran a school for girls during several of those years and at other times taught children in her home along with her growing family. By the time the couple left Austin, Barr had borne twelve children. Four of them had lived less than four days, and three had died before their first birthday. In 1866 Robert Barr accepted a promising position with a Galveston cotton firm, but the improved financial circumstances lasted only a short while. Barr lost her husband and her two surviving sons in the yellow fever epidemic in 1867. Another son, born later that year, died after only five days.

Devastated, but determined to provide for her three surviving daughters, one of whom was mentally retarded, Barr tried unsuccessfully to run a boardinghouse in Galveston. Deeply religious and somewhat mystic, she followed an inner voice that led her to New York City in November 1868. About three weeks later, with references in hand, she went to Ridgewood, New Jersey, to become a governess for a Mr. Libbey's sons. Through Mr. Libbey's encouragement and the advice of Henry Ward Beecher, whom she had met in Scotland, Barr published her first article, about Texas after the Civil War, in *Appleton's* in 1869. Spurred by this success, she wrote a barrage of articles on topics from travel to opera to biography, as well as short stories. Publishers found her flowing and engaging writing very agreeable to their readers, and Barr's work appeared in such magazines as *Christian Union*, *Harper's Bazar*, the *Advance*, *Ladies' Home Journal*, *Lippincott's*, *Illustrated Christian Weekly*, the *New York Ledger*, and others. Industrious, intelligent, and optimistic, Barr moved to New York in 1870 and began a full-time career as a writer.

So prodigious was Barr's output that she sometimes used pseudonyms to encourage publishers to accept more. She added poetry to her repertoire and earned $1,000 per year on that alone. In 1885 Barr published her first publicly acclaimed novel, *Jan Vedder's Wife*. During the remaining thirty-four years of her life, Amelia E. Barr published close to eighty novels, an average of more than two per year. Most of these popular, widely read books were romance novels in historical settings. Among the backgrounds she used were the American Revolution (*The Bow of Orange Ribbon*, 1886), the Texas War for Independence (*Remember the Alamo*, 1888), Oliver Cromwell's England (*The Lion's Whelp*, 1901), Peter Stuyvesant's New York (*A Maid of Old New York*, 1911), and the Crimean War (*Orkney Maid*, 1918). In addition, several novels concerned the woes of industrialization in England and Scotland and the settling of New York by the Dutch. Reviewers praised Barr for the fluent style of her narrative, the depth and accuracy of her historical research, her strong characterizations, and the wholesomeness of her work. Nevertheless, they criticized her sentimentalism, didacticism, and the inevitable happy endings, three characteristics that, no doubt, increased her popularity with her readers.

Barr's most highly acclaimed book was her autobiography *All the Days of My Life* (1913). Percy F. Bicknell said in *Dial* (1 Aug. 1913) that, although Barr's literary fame was well deserved, her autobiography was "more packed with incident and adventure, with strokes of good and ill fortune, with joy and sorrow, with love and longing, strange coincidences, curious omens and warnings, and a variety of unusual experiences ranging from the comic to the tragic, than any romance that has come from the autobiographer's prolific pen." Only death, in Richmond Hill, New York, shortly before her eighty-eighth birthday, could still that pen or that animated life.

• Some of Amelia E. Barr's more well-known books are *A Border Shepherdess* (1887); *Mrs. Barr's Short Stories* (1892); *The Maid of Maiden Lane* (1900); *The Strawberry Handkerchief* (1908); *The House on Cherry Street* (1909); *Sheila Vedder* (1911); *Three Score and Ten: A Book for the Aged* (1913); and *Songs in the Common Chord* (1919), her collected poems.

No complete biographical work exists other than Barr's autobiography. However, Barr has been the subject of two master's theses at the University of Texas: Mable Lee Merrem, "Amelia Barr, Educator" (1939), and Mary Eby Howard, "The Novels of Amelia Barr" (1943). The University of Texas has some of Barr's letters and manuscripts, as does the Texas State Archives. The latter also has "Memoirs of Amelia Barr in Austin and Galveston, 1856–1867," written by her daughter Lillie Barr Munroe.

Some articles about Amelia E. Barr include Oscar F. Adams, "The Novels of Amelia Barr," *Andover Review* (Mar. 1889), Hamilton Mabie, "Amelia Barr," *Bookbuyer* (Sept. 1891), and Hildegarde Hawthorne, "Amelia E. Barr, Some Reminiscences," *Bookman* (May 1920). Chapters on Barr appear in Edward Francis Harkins, *Little Pilgrimages among the Women Who Have Written Famous Books* (1902); Orison S. Marden, *How They Succeeded* (1901); Francis Whiting Halsey, *Women Authors of Our Day in Their Homes* (1903); and Grant Overton, *The Women Who Make Our Novels* (1918).

Amelia E. Barr's obituary appeared in the *New York Times* and the London *Times*, 12 Mar. 1919.

DOROTHY MCLEOD MACINERNEY

BARR, Stringfellow (15 Jan. 1897–3 Feb. 1982), college president, professor, and innovator in higher education, was born in Suffolk, Virginia, the son of William Alexander Barr, an Episcopal clergyman, and Ida Stringfellow. He started his undergraduate studies at Tulane in 1912 then transferred in 1914 to the University of Virginia from which he received the B.A. (1916) and M.A. (1917), both in history. During World War I he served with the U.S. Army Ambulance Service (1917) and the Surgeon General's Office (1918). After being discharged from the service, Barr studied at Oxford University as a Rhodes scholar from 1919 to 1921 and was awarded the B.A. and M.A. in modern history. In 1921 he married Gladys Baldwin; they had no children. He received the diplôme from the University of Paris in 1922; and he undertook additional studies at the University of Ghent, Belgium, where he won a fellowship in history, in 1922–1923.

Barr became assistant professor in modern European history at the University of Virginia in 1924 and was promoted to associate professor in 1927 and professor in 1930. Remaining at Virginia until 1937, Barr served as advisory editor (1926–1930 and 1934–1937) and editor (1930–1934) of the *Virginia Quarterly Review*. In 1936 Barr and Scott Buchanan, a professor of philosophy, proposed the creation of a "great books" honors program within the University of Virginia. When their proposal was rejected, both men left Virginia for the University of Chicago, where they taught and worked with the Committee on the Liberal Arts. This committee, initiated by Chicago's president Robert Hutchins and shaped by Mortimer Adler, associate professor in philosophy of law, sought to bring coherence and responsibility to undergraduate education in contrast to the undisciplined choice that they believed was characteristic of an undergraduate curriculum based on electives and a departmental major.

While Barr and Buchanan were serving on the university's Committee on the Liberal Arts, Richard Cleveland, a member of the St. John's College board of visitors and governors, asked the two men to revive the ailing college. This small private college in Annapolis, Maryland, had lost its accreditation, was heavily in debt, and was suffering declining faculty confidence in its degree standards and academic requirements. In summer 1937 Barr was named president, and Buchanan became dean, and they announced to the board and the faculty a sweeping curriculum revision, drawing heavily on their earlier proposals and projects at Virginia and Chicago. This curricular transformation replaced the elective system with a required four-year curriculum based on the study of some one hundred great books from Homer to the present, which was termed a "vision of a common liberal arts curriculum" (Grant and Riesman 1974, p. 30).

The great books curriculum at St. John's came to be identified with commitment to the neoclassic approach to curricular reform within American higher education. As such, it emphasized the classical trivium (grammar, rhetoric, and logic) as well as the quadrivium (arithmetic, music, geometry, and astronomy) but relied on works from a range of historical periods. Following a chronological progression, students read a selected list of texts based on what faculty considered to be the greatest minds, beginning with ancient Greece and progressing to the twentieth century. The reading lists may have been slow to change but were not impervious to revision. In the late 1970s, for example, readings included Homer's *Odyssey*, *The Republic* by Plato, and Lavoisier's *Elements of Chemistry* in the freshman year and Cicero, Shakespeare's *Othello*, and Darwin's *Origin of Species* in the sophomore year. Junior year assignments were drawn from such texts as Milton's *Paradise Lost*, Adam Smith's *Wealth of Nations*, and *Moby Dick* by Herman Melville. Senior year readings included such enduring works as Tolstoy's *War and Peace*, Nietzsche's *Beyond Good and Evil*, and Tocqueville's *Democracy in America*. Every year students were required to attend mathematics and language tutorials, with a music tutorial being mandatory during the second year. Science laboratories, required all four years, were led by a faculty instructor and advanced student aides.

From 1937 through 1946, while Barr was president of St. John's and a member of the board of visitors, the institution gained national prominence for its reliance on the great books approach to liberal arts education. According to Barr's 1974 retrospective, the neoclassical emphasis at St. John's was distinctive for the following reasons: "The elective system is chiefly concerned with course offerings in 'fields' of human knowledge. These course offerings in large part provide information. The St. John's Program is a return to what liberal education meant for more than 2,000 years: an education that develops the intellectual virtues or habits."

Integral to the educational program outlined by Barr and Buchanan was the elimination of conventional faculty ranks: all faculty were known as tutors, and all faculty taught all parts of the course of study. Two staples of American higher education—the academic department and the student major—also were abolished. The great books program kindled interest nationally among college and secondary school faculty and prospective students. Adopting the great books curriculum rescued St. John's by attracting a small but committed and growing pool of applicants who had solid academic credentials and, at the same time, by cultivating a sense of distinctive purpose within the college's faculty, staff, and board. With the implementation of this curriculum, St. John's began offering early admission to high school juniors. Barr further promoted the study of great books through the radio show "Invitation to Learning" between 1937 and 1940, and from 1944 through 1946 he was advisory editor for the British edition of the great books. He also wrote eleven books, ranging from histories of ancient Greece and Rome to a novel about academic life.

After leaving the presidency of St. John's College in 1946, Barr returned to Charlottesville, Virginia, where he was president of the Foundation for World Government from 1948 to 1958 and visiting professor of political science at the University of Virginia (1951–1953). He was professor of humanities at Newark College of Rutgers University from 1955 to 1964, and from 1966 to 1969 he was a fellow at the Center for Study of Democratic Institutions in Santa Barbara, California. In 1969 Barr retired to Kingston, New Jersey. Following his wife's death in 1974, Barr moved to Alexandria, Virginia. He lived in Alexandria until his death there.

Barr's increasing involvement in world affairs and international relations after 1946 represented a logical extension of his curricular reforms at St. John's College. His emphasis on the great books was indelibly linked to his respect for Socratic inquiry and for Plato's approach to education for citizenship and leadership, with emphasis on the critical discussion of public affairs. In the 1930s Barr's great books approach to liberal education was cited as the epitome of an educational counterrevolution, often contrasted with John Dewey's proposals for education in a democracy. Although few American colleges and universities adopted the St. John's model of teaching and learning, Barr's innovations enjoyed conspicuous symbolic importance in shaping national debates about what undergraduate education ought to be in the mid-twentieth century.

• Barr's concise memoir about the St. John's College experiment is "A Retrospective on St. John's," *Change* 6 (May 1974): 35, 63. A more complete chronicle of the reforms and innovations championed by Barr is J. Winfree Smith, *A Search for the Liberal College: The Beginning of the St. John's Program* (1983). His work is placed in national and historical perspective in Gerald Grant and David Riesman, "The Neo-Classical Revival: St. John's and the Great Books," in *The Perpetual Dream: Reform and Experiment in the American College* (1978). An earlier version of Grant and Riesman's research was published as "St. John's and the Great Books," *Change* 6 (May 1974): 28–34. For a concise profile of the curriculum developed by Barr, see Arthur Levine, "Great Books at St. John's—1937," in *Handbook on Undergraduate Curriculum* (1978). An obituary is in the *New York Times*, 5 Feb. 1982.

JOHN R. THELIN

BARRADALL, Edward (1704–19 June 1743), attorney general of Virginia, was born in England, the son of Henry Barradall and Catherine Blumfield, members of the English gentry. He was called to the bar at the Inner Temple. Sometime before 1730 he emigrated to Virginia and transferred his law practice to the General Court in Williamsburg. He was very successful; one of his clients was Thomas Fairfax, sixth Lord Fairfax, the proprietor of the Northern Neck of Virginia.

While acting for Lord Fairfax, Barradall drafted a most important bill that subsequently became the act of 1736, chapter 13. This bill settled the question of ownership of the Northern Neck so that the purchasers from Lord Fairfax received good common-law title. This would be crucial to the future economic development of that part of Virginia.

On 5 January 1736 Barradall married Sarah Fitzhugh, daughter of William Fitzhugh, a prominent Stafford County landholder. The couple had no children. On 30 November 1736 Barradall was elected mayor of Williamsburg. When John Clayton died in November 1737, Barradall succeeded him immediately as attorney general for the colony, judge of the vice admiralty court, and member of the Virginia House of Burgesses representing the College of William and Mary. He was also a member of the vestry of Bruton Parish Church in Williamsburg.

One of the bills that Barradall introduced in the General Assembly was enacted as the act of May 1740, chapter 3. Not long before this, a number of British convicts had been transported to Virginia, where they had continued in their antisocial ways to the great detriment of the local citizenry. This bill drafted them into the British army to fill the Virginia quota to fight the Spaniards in the West Indies. Thus were several goals accomplished with one deft stroke.

While in practice, Barradall, as was the English custom, kept notes of cases heard in court; his reports cover the years 1733 to 1741. Law reports of colonial Virginia cases are rare because the courts were composed primarily of laymen, who did not give learned opinions of the cases they decided. Barradall's reports record at length the arguments of counsel and give the brief judgments of the General Court. They record well-researched arguments that were based soundly on English precedents and skillfully presented to the court. Although these reports were known to more scholarly members of the Virginia bar such as William Green, Conway Robinson, and Thomas Jefferson, who used a few cases in his own set of reports, they were not published until 1909.

Barradall was frequently called upon to serve as an examiner of applicants to be admitted to the practice of law. In 1738 he examined Benjamin Waller, who later rose to the important position of clerk of the General Court, and in 1741 certified Edmund Pendleton (1721–1803) as a fit person to be admitted to the bar. Pendleton, who later became president of the Court of Appeals of Virginia, remembered having been "strictly examined." Other aspiring attorneys examined by Barradall were Abraham Nicholas, Gilbert Buchannon, John O'Sheal, Andrew Giles, Dudley Digges, Philip Prescott, John Chapman, and Edmund Porteus.

Barradall died in Williamsburg. He is remembered for his law reports, which are among the earliest in America. The reports give a rare glimpse of the case law of colonial Virginia and demonstrate clearly the high level of legal education and the sophistication of argument of the bar of early eighteenth-century Williamsburg, the capital of the largest British colony in America at that time.

• Barradall's reports of cases in the General Court of Virginia are published in Robert T. Barton, *Virginia Colonial Decisions*, vol. 2 (1909). For a sketch of his life, see R. Earl Nance, "Edward Barradall," in *The Virginia Law Reporters before 1880*, ed. W. Hamilton Bryson (1977), pp. 71–74.

W. HAMILTON BRYSON

BARRELL, Joseph (15 Dec. 1869–4 May 1919), geologist, was born in New Providence, New Jersey, the son of Henry Ferdinand Barrell, a farmer who traced his origins to colonial Boston, and Elisabeth Wisner, whose family had been landowners and army officers in New Jersey for 150 years. An advocate of public education and libraries, Henry Barrell was also an amateur naturalist who instilled in his son an early interest in astronomy and geology. While helping on the family farm, Joseph often collected rocks, birds, and insects from the fields.

Joseph was educated in local public schools, and then spent a year working as a teacher to save money for college tuition. After a year at the Stevens Preparatory School at Hoboken, New Jersey, Barrell enrolled in 1888 at Lehigh University, from which he graduated with high honors four years later. In 1893 he received an engineering certificate from Lehigh and stayed on as an instructor of mining and metallurgy and a graduate student in geology and practical astronomy, earning an M.S. in 1897. Barrell's academic career was then divided between Lehigh and Yale Universities. From 1898 to 1900 Barrell undertook graduate studies in geology at Yale, where he received his Ph.D. in 1900. He then returned to Lehigh, where he taught geology and biology for more than two years before returning to Yale as an instructor of geology in 1903. He married Lena Hopper Bailey in 1902; they had four children. In 1908 he was promoted at Yale to professor of structural geology, the position he held at the time of his death.

Barrell's entire professional career was spent in academic positions, but he gained considerable practical experience as well as financial compensation through summer work in mining geology. As an instructor at Lehigh, he worked on mining projects around the United States; as a graduate student at Yale he spent summers in Montana under the auspices of the U.S. Geological Survey, and continued this work as a faculty member, first at Lehigh and then at Yale. The monograph that resulted, *Geology of the Marysville Mining District* (1907), documented the structural relations of the Marysville granite batholiths and their country rocks and used them to develop a general theory of the mechanism igneous intrusion. The rocks around the batholiths were extensively metamorphosed and locally melted; Barrell suggested that this had been caused by the heat of the intrusion, which had emplaced itself by melting and assimilating the adjacent rock. Barrell's concept of "magmatic stoping" became the accepted theory and made him internationally famous.

Barrell practiced geology at a time when young men were expected to work for a decade or more on specific field-based problems before embarking on general theoretical work, and his career followed this pattern. After completing the Marysville work, he branched out into sedimentary, metamorphic, and structural geology and was soon considered the leading geological theorist of his generation. His intellectual powers were so formidable that one colleague remarked that, after speaking with Barrell, one was left with the impression of "a mind rather than a man." Barrell's interest in the structure of the earth led to his most famous and enduring contribution, a series of papers titled "The Strength of the Earth's Crust." These eight articles, published in the *American Journal of Science* between 1914 and 1915, discussed the geophysical implications of the theory of isostasy, recently advanced in the United States by geodecists John Hayford and William Bowie. Hayford and Bowie had demonstrated, on the basis of geodetic measurement and variations in the force of gravity, that the earth's crust was finely adjusted to the weight of surface loads, such as sedimentary deposits and glacial ice. Augmenting their mathematical deductions with geological evidence, Barrell argued that isostasy proved that the earth's rigid outer layer must rest on a flexible, plastic underlayer. He coined the terms "asthenosphere"—zone without strength—for the plastic underlayer, and "lithosphere"—zone of rock—for the rigid zone above it. Barrell's asthenosphere provided the *coup de grâce* to contraction theory, convincing remaining loyalists that it was no longer needed to account for dislocations of the earth's crust. It also helped to pave the way for plate tectonics. In the 1940s the existence of the asthenosphere was demonstrated by seismic studies, which showed it to be a zone of partial melting. This in turn helped to explain the mechanism by which crustal slabs move: later theorists proposed that convection currents in the asthenosphere drive the motions of the earth's tectonics plates.

Barrell was struck down in his prime—dying suddenly in New Haven, Connecticut, from spinal meningitis complicated by pneumonia just a few days after his election to the National Academy of Sciences. His death devastated his colleagues. William Morris Davis, the Harvard professor who helped found the discipline of geomorphology, described it as an "overwhelming disaster for American geology." Davis was right, for at the time of his death, Barrell was working on a solution to one of the most pressing problems of global geology: Gondwana. It had long been known that fossils and sedimentary sequences in parts of India, Brazil, and Australia were strikingly similar, albeit located on widely separated continents. In 1912 this observation became a principal motivation for Alfred Wegener's theory of continental drift, namely, that the continents had once been contiguous, forming a landmass dubbed Gondwana, but had subsequently drifted apart. Barrell, like many American geologists, was intrigued by the idea but unconvinced by Wegener's account, and he began to develop a theory of his own to account for the fragmentation of continents. Barrell's key insight was that the timing of the divergence of fossil forms in North and South America coincided with voluminous outpourings of basalt on either side of the Atlantic Ocean. He thus concluded that the basaltic intrusions were linked to the break-up of continents—indeed, that they *caused* continental break-up. Barrell suggested that if a continent were weighed down by voluminous outpourings of basalt, it would subside to form an ocean basin, thus creating ocean basins from dry land and isolating continents that had once been connected.

Barrell died before he had a chance to publish his paper on continental fragmentation, but in 1927, when the continental drift debate reached its peak in the United States, his Yale colleague Charles Schuchert arranged for posthumous publication of Barrell's "On Continental Fragmentation, and the Geologic Bearing of the Moon's Surface Features" in the *American Journal of Science* (213 [1929]: 283–314). At just this time, the British geologist Arthur Holmes suggested the idea of convection currents as the driving force of continental drift. We cannot know what would have happened had Barrell been alive to read Holmes's papers, but it seems likely that Barrell, given his formidable intellectual powers, would have seen the connection between basaltic intrusions and convection currents, enabling geologists to arrive sooner at the theory of plate tectonics.

• Barrell's personal papers have not been preserved, but material about him can be found in the Charles Schuchert Papers, Sterling Memorial Library, Yale University. Two other of Barrell's posthumous papers, "The Nature and Bearings of Isostasy" and "The Status of the Theory of Isostasy," directly follow an obituary by Charles Schuchert, "Joseph Barrell," in the *American Journal of Science* 198 (1919): 251–338. Other widely cited papers include "The Physical Effects of Contact Metamorphism," *American Journal of Science* 163 (1902): 279–96; "Rhythms and the Measurements of Geologic Time," *Bulletin of the Geological Society of America* 28 (1917): 745–904; and "The Growth of Knowledge of Earth Structure," in *A Century of Science in America*, ed. E. S. Dana (1918), pp. 153–92. For biographical materials, see Herbert E. Gregory, "Memorial to Joseph Barrell," *Bulletin of the Geological Society of America* 34 (1923): 18–28, and Charles Schuchert, "Joseph Barrell," National Academy of Sciences, *Biographical Memoirs* 12 (1927): 1–40.

NAOMI ORESKES

BARRÈRE, Georges (31 Oct. 1876–14 June 1944), flutist and conductor, was born in Bordeaux, France, the son of Gabriel Barrère, a furniture maker, and Marie Périne Courtet. As a child in Paris he played in a fife, drum, and bugle corps and began flute studies with Léon Richault. He studied at the Paris Conservatoire with Henry Altès (1889–1893) and Claude Paul Taffanel (1893–1896), who became his mentor. Barrère graduated with the *premier prix* in 1895. He remained at the Conservatoire for an additional year, studying composition with Xavier Leroux and Raoul Pugno.

In the meantime Barrère was playing first flute with the Folies-Bergère and at the Concerts de l'Opéra. He was also first flutist in the Société Nationale and played in the premiere of Debussy's *Prélude à l'Après-midi d'un faune* in December 1894.

In 1895 Taffanel assisted Barrère in establishing the Société Moderne des Instruments à Vent. This was in fact a resumption of the older man's Société de musique de chambre des instruments à vent (1879–1893). According to the tenth anniversary booklet, the Société Moderne was responsible for some sixty-one new compositions by forty European composers—among them André Caplet, Reynaldo Hahn, Vincent d'Indy, and Theodore Dubois.

In 1897 Barrère was appointed third flute of the Concerts Colonne. After a year of compulsory army service (1897–1898) he resumed his place in 1903 and was appointed to the first chair. From 1900 he played fourth flute at the Paris Opéra and taught at d'Indy's Schola Cantorum. His accomplishments were rewarded with election to the Académie Française in 1903.

In 1905 Walter Damrosch, eager to acquire French woodwind players, invited Barrère to become principal flutist of his New York Symphony. He held this position—except for one year's absence and intermittent short leaves—until 1928. With his silver flute, Barrère quickly revolutionized American flute playing, replacing wood flutes and the heavy German style with the lighter, more flexible, and brilliant French style. By World War I, the French model silver flute had become the standard in the United States.

Barrère was a frequent soloist with the New York Symphony, premiering several works, most notably Charles Tomlinson Griffes's *Poem* (1919). From 1920

to 1928 the New York Symphony was the resident orchestra at the Chautauqua Institution in upstate New York. After 1928 Barrère was first flute, frequent soloist, and assistant conductor of the Chautauqua Symphony under Albert Stoessel.

In addition to his orchestra work Barrère soon began playing recitals and chamber concerts, often with such colleagues as the harpsichordist and pianist Arthur Whiting and the violin-piano duo of David and Clara Mannes. Later collaborators included pianists Arthur Loesser, Rudolph Ganz, Harold Bauer, and Jesus Maria Sanromá, harpist Marcel Grandjany, and harpsichordists Lewis Richards and Yella Pessl.

In 1906 Barrère formed the New York Symphony Wind Instruments Club, the first step toward recreating the Société Moderne in America. He introduced New York audiences to many French works, but he also worked to cultivate a new American repertoire, inspiring new works by Griffes, Seth Bingham, John Parsons Beach, Christiaan Kriens, and others. The early concerts of the Barrère Ensemble involved ten or more musicians—double quintets were frequent—though individual numbers of a given program used fewer players. By the 1920s the most frequent configuration was a woodwind quintet.

On 22 February 1914 Barrère, cellist Paul Kéfer, and harpist Carlos Salzedo gave their first concert as the Trio de Lutèce. This group had an unusual repertoire, including baroque sonatas and arrangements by the multi-talented Salzedo, notably Debussy's *Children's Corner Suite* and Ravel's *Sonatine en trio*.

Five days later the organization that would become the Barrère Little Symphony made its debut in Carnegie Hall. This thirteen-man organization quickly became permanent, giving some New York concerts and touring after the New York Symphony season ended in the spring, often with Adolph Bolm's Ballet Intime and the Pavley-Oukrainsky Ballet, both Diaghilev offshoots. In later years Barrère's collaborators included Isadora Duncan and her protégées Ruth Page and Anita Zahn, and such musicians as baritone David Bispham and pianist Colin McPhee (two of whose Balinese flute transcriptions Barrère later recorded). Duncan wrote of Barrère and his signature piece in her autobiography, "There was a flutist who played so divinely the solo the Happy Spirits in 'Orpheus' that I often found myself immobile on the stage with the tears flowing from my eyes, just from the ecstasy of listening to him . . . "

In 1928, when the New York Symphony merged with the Philharmonic, Barrère left the orchestra to expand his Little Symphony into a much more ambitious enterprise. With financial backing from Elizabeth Sprague Coolidge, Mary Flagler Cary, and others, the orchestra undertook many cross-country tours in addition to giving adventurous New York programs. Barrère charmed audiences nationwide by chatting with them in cultivated broken English. As Winthrop Sargeant described these monologues, "Audiences found in his Mephesthelean appearance and

Gallic aplomb a sophisticated charm comparable to that of Adolphe Menjou and Maurice Chevalier."

Barrère revived historic chamber orchestra literature by Haydn, Rameau, Mozart, and Dittersdorf. But most significant, perhaps, was his work in championing American composers, including Victor Herbert, John Alden Carpenter (he conducted the premiere of the *Krazy Kat* ballet in Town Hall in 1922), Henry Hadley, Edward MacDowell, Colin McPhee, Ethelbert Nevin, Leo Sowerby, and A. Walter Kramer. He premiered three works by the African-American composer William Grant Still—*From the Black Belt* (1927), *Log Cabin Ballads* (1928), and *Africa* (1930)—and made a point of supporting women composers, including Mabel Wheeler Daniels (he premiered her *Deep Forest* in 1931) and Mary Howe.

In the 1930s Barrère founded three regular ensembles: Barrère-Salzedo-Britt, with harpist Carlos Salzedo and cellist Horace Britt; the Barrère-Britt Concertino, a quintet of flute, violin, viola, cello, and piano; and the Barrère Trio, with Britt and pianist Jerome Rappaport. Particularly with Barrère-Salzedo-Britt new music was a priority: it premiered Wallingford Riegger's *Divertissement* in 1933 (and recorded it for New Music Quarterly) and Bernard Wagenaar's *Triple Concerto* (for which the soloists wrote their own cadenzas) with Eugene Ormandy and the Philadelphia Orchestra in 1938.

Barrère bought his first Wm. S. Haynes flute in 1913 and became a prominent spokesman for that firm. In 1927 he made news with his acquisition of a gold Haynes and again in 1935 with the purchase of a platinum flute—the first in the United States. It was for this flute that Edgard Varèse wrote *Density 21.5*, which he premiered in 1936 at Carnegie Hall.

During the 1930s, Barrère premiered several other pieces: Albert Roussel's *Trio for flute, viola, and cello* (with Lionel Teritis and Hans Kindler, Prague, 1929), Wallingford Riegger's *Suite for solo flute* (League of Composers, New York, 1930), and Paul Hindemith's flute sonata (with Jesus Maria Sanromá, Library of Congress, 1936). In 1934 he was named a chevalier of the Legion of Honor.

Barrère was the key figure in establishing the Paris Conservatoire woodwind tradition in the United States. As part of his New York Symphony contract he taught at the Institute of Musical Art. In 1931 he joined the faculty of the Juilliard Graduate School, where he founded the woodwind ensemble program. (IMA and JGS later merged, becoming the Juilliard School of Music.) Barrère also taught privately. Among his most notable students were Arthur Lora, William Kincaid, Meredith Willson, Carmine Coppola, Frances Blaisdell, Samuel Baron, and Bernard Goldberg.

Barrère edited the etudes of Altès and Berbiguier (1918) and published a set of exercises, *The Flutist's Formulae* (1935). He made a number of quintet transcriptions and a piano reduction of the Griffes *Poem*, and he published many arrangements and a *Nocturne* (1913) for flute and piano, several cadenzas, a flute trio, and one song. Other works survive in manuscript.

Barrère founded the New York Flute Club in 1920, serving as president until his death, and was active in the Beethoven Association, the Bohemians, the Society for the Publication of American Music, and several other musical organizations. He participated in the Maverick Concerts in Woodstock, New York, an artists' colony where he had a summer home.

Barrère was married in France to Michelette Burani, with whom he had two sons. They divorced in 1916, and in 1917 he married Cécile Elise Allombert, with whom he had one son. He suffered a stroke in August 1941 and never again performed, but he continued to teach at Juilliard. After a second stroke, he died in Kingston, New York.

Barrère's life was a singular amalgam of French and American qualities: French charm, style, and *joie de vivre* combined with Yankee adventurousness and business skills. He put the flute on the American map as a solo instrument, ensured the universal adoption of the silver flute in this country, and engineered the renaissance of the flute in this century. He made enormous contributions to the development of woodwind chamber music, built new audiences for chamber music generally, and inspired some of the most important works written for flute prior to World War II. He also contributed significantly to the growth of chamber orchestras in the United States.

• Parts of a privately published autobiography, *Barrère* (1928), appeared in *The Flutist* 2, nos. 2–4 (1921), and in Leonardo De Lorenzo, *My Complete Story of the Flute* (1951; rev. and enl. ed., 1992). Barrère's *Nocturne* and seventeen arrangements for flute and piano are collected in *The Barrère Album* (1984), with an introduction by Frances Blaisdell. The most comprehensive information on his life appears in Nancy Toff, *Georges Barrère and the Flute in America* (1994), the catalog of an exhibition at the New York Public Library for the Performing Arts. For discography and discussion of performance style, see Susan Nelson, "Georges Barrère," *ARSC Journal* 24, no. 1 (Spring 1993): 4–48, and Susan Nelson, "The Recordings of Georges Barrère," *Flutist Quarterly* 20, no. 2 (Winter 1994/1995): 37–43. See also Frances Blaisdell, "In Appreciation of Georges Barrère," *Flutist Quarterly* 12, no. 1 (Winter 1986): 41–46; Nancy Toff, "Georges Barrère: Monarch of the Flute," *Flutist Quarterly* 20, no. 1 (Fall 1994): 46–57; Frances Blaisdell, "Georges Barrère—The Master—Remembered," *Flutist Quarterly* 20, no. 2 (Winter 1994/1995): 29–31; the pamphlet *Georges Barrère and the Platinum Flute* (1935); and Claude Dorgeuille, *The French Flute School 1860–1950*, trans. and ed. Edward Blakeman (1986).

NANCY TOFF

BARRETT, Benjamin Fiske (24 June 1808–6 Aug. 1892), pastor, writer, and publisher, was born in Dresden, Maine, the son of Oliver Barrett, a carpenter, and Elizabeth Carlton. Young Benjamin was anxious to obtain an education and took delight in mastering his preparatory studies. Through his own labor he was able to attend Bowdoin College, graduating with a B.A. in 1832. Although not raised in any Christian denomination, Barrett became attracted to Unitarianism while in college. He subsequently attended Harvard Divinity School, graduating in 1838. He was ordained in the Unitarian church that same year and assigned to a parish at Syracuse, New York.

Shortly before leaving Harvard, however, Barrett was introduced to the theological works of Emanuel Swedenborg, the eighteenth-century Swedish nobleman, scientist, philosopher, and religious visionary. Swedenborg's voluminous theological works described in detail the inner meaning of the Bible, the spiritual realms of heaven and hell, and the creation of a universal "new church." These and other teachings formed the basis of the Church of the New Jerusalem (also known as the New church, or Swedenborgian church), which views itself as inaugurating a new era of Christianity. By the winter of 1839–1840 Barrett had fully accepted Swedenborgian teachings as a new revelation. He left the Unitarians and joined the Boston Swedenborgian society, which at that time was the most flourishing New church congregation in the United States. Shortly thereafter he accepted an invitation to become the pastor of the Swedenborgian society in New York City.

In 1840 Barrett was ordained into the General Convention of the New Jerusalem and married Elizabeth Allen of Bath, Maine. The Barretts raised a family of seven children, four daughters and three sons.

After eight years in New York, Barrett accepted a call to pastor the New church society in Cincinnati. He arrived at his new parish exhausted and soon developed debilitating headaches from the humid and hot summers in the Ohio River Valley. He resigned from pastoral work after only two years of service.

Ever resourceful, Barrett soon learned the composition roofing business from a boarder in his home. He formed his own company and between 1850 and 1854 supported his family in this manner, working for brief periods in Detroit, Chicago, Milwaukee, and Minneapolis. His health restored, Barrett began to preach again in 1854. He moved his family to Brooklyn, New York, and then in 1856 to Orange, New Jersey, where he often filled the pulpit for the Swedenborgian society in New York City.

Although an able preacher, for the next several years Barrett worked to polish his skills as a writer, editor, and publisher in order to more thoroughly spread Swedenborgian ideas. His book *The Golden Reed* (1855), for example, contained quotations from Swedenborg that showed the universality and inclusiveness of New church theology. Rather than identifying the New church with a visible, organized body, Barrett sought to demonstrate that it "includes all, of whatever name or creed, whose ruling love is love of the Lord and the neighbor."

In 1864 Barrett accepted a call to his last parish, the Philadelphia New church society, where he continued his active interest in publishing. Here he founded the American New-Church Tract and Publishing Society in 1865. Through this organization, he worked out a financial arrangement with J. B. Lippincott & Company to print and sell several Swedenborgian books. Barrett also published the *New-Church Monthly* magazine between 1867 and 1870.

Doctrinal controversies with the denominational leaders, however, led Barrett to resign in 1871 from parish responsibilities, the General Convention, and the Tract and Publishing Society. He was firmly opposed, for example, to the practice of rebaptism when receiving members into the New Jerusalem church. Moreover, he did not limit the New church described by Swedenborg to a specific denomination, and he encouraged clergy from other traditions who accepted the "heavenly doctrines" of Swedenborg to remain and minister within their respective churches.

A generous anonymous benefactor led Barrett to form the Swedenborg Publishing Association in 1873, whose periodical, the *New Christianity*, he edited for several years. Under his guidance, the association published the Swedenborg Library (12 vols., 1876–1881), a condensation of Swedenborg's essential teachings, as well as other doctrinal books and pamphlets. The most popular title that Barrett expanded, edited, and published was probably Edward Madeley's *The Science of Correspondences* (1879?), which went through twenty-four printings. After Barrett's death his daughter continued the work of the association.

Barrett's last years were spent quietly in Germantown, Philadelphia, where he continued to write. He died in Philadelphia. While he was often polemic, Barrett was one of the most able and prolific defenders of Swedenborgian thought in the United States in the nineteenth century.

• Major works by Barrett not mentioned above include *Life of Emanuel Swedenborg* (1841); *Lectures on the New Dispensation* (1842); *Beauty for Ashes* (1855); *Binding and Loosing* (1857); *Letters to Beecher on the Divine Trinity* (1860); *Catholicity of the New Church and Uncatholicity of New Churchmen* (1863); *The New View of Hell* (1870); *Letters to Beecher on the Future Life* (1872); *The Golden City* (1874); *The New Church, Its Nature and Whereabouts* (1877); *Swedenborg and Channing* (1878); *The Question (What Are the Doctrines of the New Church?) Answered* (1883); *The Apocalyptic New Jerusalem* (1883); *Footprints of the New Age* (1884); *Heaven Revealed* (1885); *The New-Catholicism* (1886); *Ends and Uses* (1887); *A Cloud of Independent Witnesses* (1891); and *Maximus Homo* (1892). Full treatments of Barrett's life include *Benjamin Fisk Barrett: An Autobiography*, rev. and supplemented by G. A. Barrett (1891), and [J. R. Irelan?], *From Different Points of View: Benjamin Fiske Barrett, Preacher, Writer, Theologian, and Philosopher: A Study* (1896). See also the *New Jerusalem Messenger* 16 (Nov. 1892): 699–700. A complete list of his published works may be found in *Bowdoin College Library Bibliographical Contributions* (1891) and *Bowdoin College Library Bulletin*, vols. 1–4 (1891–1895). Barrett's ministry within the Swedenborgian church is described in Marguerite Beck Block, *The New Church in the New World* (1932; repr. 1984).

DAVID B. ELLER

BARRETT, Charles Simon (28 Jan. 1866–4 Apr. 1935), agricultural leader, was born in Pike County, Georgia, the son of Thomas Jefferson Barrett, a prominent farmer and politician, and Minerva Slade. Attending local schools only during winter, he spent his early years working on the family farm, where he developed his lifelong devotion to agriculture. After attending normal schools in Bowling Green, Kentucky, Lebanon, Ohio, and Valparaiso, Indiana, Barrett returned to his childhood home in Georgia. In 1891 he married Alma Rucker, a schoolteacher. The newlyweds settled in Upson County, Georgia, and opened a "literary school" for local children. For the next fourteen years, the Barretts devoted themselves to teaching, farming, and raising six sons.

Barrett launched his career as a farm leader in 1905, when he became the first farmer in Upson County to join the Farmers' Educational and Cooperative Union of America. Founded in Rains County, Texas, in 1902, the Farmers' Union, as it was commonly called, sought to improve the economic well-being and to increase the bargaining power of farmers by forming cooperatives throughout rural America. A visit from Newton Gresham, the founder of the Farmers' Union, convinced Barrett to serve as state organizer for the union. Elected state president in 1905, he was in 1906 elected president of the National Farmers' Union, a position he held until 1928. Two years after assuming the presidency of the National Farmers' Union, Barrett founded Union City, Georgia (named in honor of the Farmers' Union), located near a railroad center approximately fourteen miles south of Atlanta.

Described by journalist John Temple Graves in a March 1913 article in *Cosmopolitan* as "an agricultural Moses," Barrett worked with presidents of the United States during his 22-year tenure as head of the Farmers' Union. Theodore Roosevelt appointed him to the Country Life Commission, the first national commission to gather data and investigate problems of rural life in the United States; Woodrow Wilson appointed him as a delegate to the Versailles Peace Conference; and Warren G. Harding appointed him to the 1921 Conference on Limitation of Armament. Yet Barrett decided early in his career that he would never seek political office, and he shunned appointment as Herbert Hoover's secretary of agriculture in 1929. Barrett told a reporter for the *Washington Post* (17 Feb. 1919): "I set out to be an exception. I'm that exception and my word is still good with myself." He issued repeated warnings about the "scheming politician" who might use the Farmers' Union as the "stepping stone to his personal profit or his political preferment" (*Atlanta Constitution*, 7 Feb. 1908).

Barrett's down-to-earth and practical side won him popularity with the farmers of the United States year after year. In the tradition of the leaders of the Grange, the Farmers' Alliances, and the Populists, Barrett harshly criticized business and banking interests for exploiting hapless farmers. Focusing on the special needs of southern cotton planters, he delivered hundreds of speeches throughout the nation extolling the value of the staple. With hyperbolic flourish, he described cotton as "the absolute commercial despot of civilization. It is more powerful than any monarch of history, and its influence is more overshadowing than that ever wielded by the Czar of all the Russias" (Barrett, *The Mission, History and Times of the Farmers' Union* [1909], p. 49).

Barrett's flair for the dramatic also gained him great favor with farmers. For example, when in 1910 a bill to regulate cotton exchanges was before Congress, he gathered together several hundred farmers in Kansas and secured a promise from them that, when they returned home, they would write letters to Congress in support of the bill. On second thought, Barrett decided that such a promise was not good enough, and he insisted, "Let's write the letter right now." He then turned to the doorkeeper and commanded: "Lock that door, . . . and bring me the key. Nobody leaves this room until he writes the letter." The farmers used "cheap tablets and some cheap pencils" to write a batch of "hastily scribbled" letters, which were then mailed (Barrett, "Six Presidents," pp. 94–96).

Barrett's down-home style did not prevent him from advancing solid economic solutions to farmers' problems. At the Versailles Peace Conference, he proposed eight international agricultural resolutions that concluded with support for "the principle that compensation of agricultural producers on the basis of cost of production plus a reasonable profit is vital to the maintenance of a permanent agriculture" (Barrett, "Six Presidents," p. 150).

By the mid 1920s the membership and programmatic focus of the Farmers' Union had shifted from the cotton South to the corn-producing Middle West. In recognition of this fact, Barrett announced in 1927 that he would not be a candidate for reelection.

Following his retirement as president of the Farmers' Union in 1928, Barrett divided his time between working in Washington, D.C., where he wrote a column, "Barrett Speaking," for the National Service Syndicate, and his home in Union City, Georgia, where he continued to farm. He died in Union City, Georgia.

According to historian William P. Tucker, Barrett "largely personified the Union and its program" during his tenure as president (Tucker, p. 200). Similarly, historians Theodore Saloutos and John D. Hicks attribute "much of the success of the Farmers' Union . . . to Barrett's persistent and enthusiastic leadership" (Saloutos and Hicks, p. 222). As the "friend of presidents" and president of the leading farmer organization in the United States for twenty-two years, Barrett did more in behalf of ordinary, rank-and-file farmers in America than any other individual during the first three decades of the twentieth century.

• Barrett's papers, including scrapbooks with newspaper clippings, are in the possession of his granddaughter, Judy Barrett Litoff, Providence, R.I. In addition to the two works mentioned in the essay, Barrett authored *Uncle Reuben in Washington* (1923). Good biographical information is in his unpublished memoir, "Six Presidents, Six Million Farmers" (1930). Two works that discuss Barrett's role as president of the National Farmers' Union are Theodore Saloutos, *Farmer Movements in the South, 1865–1933* (1960), and Saloutos and

John D. Hicks, *Agricultural Discontent in the Middle West, 1900–1939* (1951). Also useful is William P. Tucker, "Populism Up-to-Date: The Story of the Farmers' Union," *Agricultural History* 21 (Oct. 1947): 198–208. For a contemporary assessment of Barrett, see John Temple Graves, "An Agricultural Moses," *Cosmopolitan*, Mar. 1913, pp. 512–14. An obituary is in the *Farmers Union Herald*, May 1935.

JUDY BARRETT LITOFF

BARRETT, Frank Aloysius (10 Nov. 1892–30 May 1962), Wyoming governor, congressman, and U.S. senator, was born near Omaha, Nebraska, the son of Patrick J. Barrett and Elizabeth Curran, schoolteachers. His father also worked as a mortician and court bailiff. Barrett was a Catholic and attended public schools and Creighton University, Omaha, earning an A.B. in 1913 and an LL.B. in 1916. He served for seventeen months in the Army Balloon Corps during World War I, attaining the rank of sergeant. After discharge, he married Alice Catherine Donoghue in Omaha in 1919; they had three children. After Alice's death in 1956, in 1959 he married Augusta K. Hogan.

After moving to Lusk, an oil boomtown in eastern Wyoming, Barrett quickly built up a thriving law practice. His success as an attorney soon enabled him to purchase a large cattle and sheep ranch in 1924. He also became active in local Republican politics, serving as Niobrara County attorney from 1923 to 1932, and became widely known in the state through his activities in the Wyoming Stock Growers' Association, the Wyoming Wool Growers' Association, and the Rocky Mountain Oil and Gas Association. Elected state senator in 1933, his first race for the U.S. Congress ended in defeat in 1936. Barrett ran again for Congress in 1942, this time winning narrowly with 50.7 percent of the vote. He subsequently won three more terms in office, substantially expanding his share of the vote thanks to Wyoming's growing conservatism and the personal appeal of his energetic, down-to-earth campaign style.

As a congressman, Barrett's major concern was to protect the interests of his constituents. He fought against a proposed project to deepen the Missouri River channel, which critics claimed would imperil the water supply of the upper Missouri basin states, and he supported sheep ranchers' demands for higher tariffs on wool imports. Serving on the Interior Committee, Barrett established a reputation as an expert on public lands and was a prominent advocate of greater control by western states over grazing and mineral rights on federal lands. He played a major role in the dispute over the Jackson Hole National Monument in northwestern Wyoming, which President Franklin D. Roosevelt created by executive order in 1943. Opposing the president's action because it denied states' rights and threatened grazing, hunting, and fishing privileges, Barrett introduced a bill to remove the monument. The measure was enacted by Congress in 1944 but was subsequently pocket vetoed by Roosevelt. Arguments about the economic value of conservation and its benefits for tourism eventually persuaded the local community to accept the integration of Jackson Hole within the enlarged Grand Teton National Park in 1950. Barrett also led opposition to stricter federal grazing regulations intended to conserve natural resources. In 1947 he chaired committee hearings that produced reports criticizing various federal agencies, notably the Forest Service. On national issues, especially labor rights and anticommunist measures, Barrett consistently voted in line with the right wing of the Republican party.

Elected Wyoming governor in 1950, Barrett protected oil industry interests against proposals for a severance tax. He also reduced expenditures by the state government, despite promoting legislation to create the Wyoming Oil and Gas Conservation Commission, the Wyoming Natural Resources Board, and a statewide system of farm-to-market roads. In 1952 he ran for the U.S. Senate, basing his campaign on a promise to clean up the "mess in Washington." Senator Joseph R. McCarthy campaigned on his behalf in Wyoming. Defeating three-term Democratic incumbent Joseph C. O'Mahoney with 51.6 percent of the vote, Barrett gained election on the coattails of Dwight D. Eisenhower.

As a senator, Barrett sat on both the Armed Services and the Interior and Insular Affairs committees. He continued to promote state interests and to side with the Republican right. A number of his legislative initiatives were designed to exploit the precedent of the Submerged Lands Act of 1953, which gave states control over offshore oil. He proposed that control of federal grazing lands be transferred to the states and private ranchers, that states be allowed to control western water rights, that 90 percent of oil royalties from the public domain be allocated to the western states, and that Wyoming be allowed to levy property taxes on federal parks within the state, all of which failed to win the support of the Eisenhower administration and went down to defeat. Barrett was more successful in promoting legislation to encourage the development of federal irrigation and reclamation projects and the exploitation of oil, gas, and uranium deposits in the federal domain in Wyoming. He also became deeply involved in the controversy over the proposed federal dam at Echo Park in northwestern Colorado, supporting the dam despite conservationists' opposition because no single resource was more important than water to Wyoming's economic development and population growth in the 1950s.

On national issues, Barrett's stand remained conservative. In 1954 he voted against the Senate censure of McCarthy. A trenchant critic of foreign aid, he was one of only three Republican freshmen senators to support a Democratic amendment seeking to limit military economic assistance to Indochina in the 1955 budget.

In 1958 Barrett was narrowly defeated in his reelection bid by Gale McGee, largely because of a national Democratic trend, the loss of support following the recession in Wyoming of the previous year, and columnist Drew Pearson's accusation (later retracted) that

Barrett had used his influence to help a supporter in a tax case. President Eisenhower then appointed Barrett general counsel for the Department of Agriculture and a director of the Commodity Credit Corporation in 1959. The following year Barrett resigned both positions to run in the Republican senatorial primary, but he was soundly defeated. He then returned to practice law in Lusk.

Barrett died of leukemia in Cheyenne. His political career bore testimony to the growing conservatism of his state and region in the 1940s and 1950s, to the animosity of western states to federal control and regulation and their simultaneous dependence on federal assistance to achieve economic development, and to the increasing tension between advocates of development and conservation in the West.

• Barrett's senatorial papers and a biographical clipping file are in the Western History Research Center at the University of Wyoming in Laramie; his official papers are in the Wyoming State Archives in Cheyenne. Although there is no biographical study of Barrett, his political activities are discussed in T. A. Larson, *History of Wyoming*, 2d ed. (1978); Elmo Richardson, *Dams, Parks, and Politics: Resource Development and Preservation in the Truman-Eisenhower Era* (1973); Robert Righter, "The Brief, Hectic Life of the Jackson Hole National Monument," *American West* 13, no. 6 (1976): 30–33, 57–62, and *Crucible for Conservation: The Creation of the Grand Teton National Park* (1982); and Mark W. Harvey, "Echo Park Dam: An Old Problem of Federalism," *Annals of Wyoming* 55, no. 2 (1983): 9–18. An obituary is in the *New York Times*, 31 May 1962.

IWAN W. MORGAN

BARRETT, George Horton (9 June 1794–5 Sept. 1860), actor and theatrical manager, was born in Exeter, England, the son of Giles Leonard Barrett, a popular provincial actor, and a highly esteemed tragic actress widely known in London by her professional name, "Mrs. Rivers." Barrett's father immigrated in 1796 to the United States, where after a moderately successful acting career he became manager of the Federal Street Theatre in Washington, D.C. It is believed that Barrett made his first appearance on stage in 1798 as one of the children in William Dunlap's version of Kotzebue's *The Stranger* at the Park Theatre. In October 1799 he is also reported as making his stage debut in *Laugh When You Can, Be Happy When You May* at the Federal Street Theatre in Boston. There are less reliable suggestions that his first role was as Cora's child in *Pizarro* at the Park Theatre, also in October 1799. What is clear is that he made several appearances as a small child in theaters where his mother and father were in the company. It was for his mother's benefit performance at the Park Theatre in 1806 that George Horton Barrett first made a name for himself in the part of Young Norval in *Douglas*.

Barrett's first adult appearance in New York was as Belcour in *The West Indian* in March 1822. This debut was a marked success and he went on to play eight other roles that season. Henceforth he had a full career in the theater both as an actor and a manager. As an actor

he was best known as a "light comedian" in roles such as Young Marlow and Charles Surface, although he was often called on to play a variety of roles. He was successful though not always as financially prudent as he might have been. J. N. Ireland in his *Records of the New York Stage* (1866) calls him an "intellectual and discriminating actor," and because of his elegant appearance and gracious manner he became known as "Gentleman George."

In 1825 Barrett married Anne Jane Henry, a brilliant and accomplished actress, skillful in both tragedy and comedy. She first appeared under the name Mrs. Barrett at the Bowery Theatre in 1826 in its opening production of *The Road to Ruin*. The Barretts acted together for many years and were an extremely popular couple, both professionally and socially; they had one child. W. G. B. Carson, in his *Theatre of the Frontier* (1932) includes them in the "galaxy of stars" who appeared at the theater in St. Louis during the 1839 season. They were best known for graceful and refined comedy.

A beautiful and successful actress, Anne Barrett drank heavily, and in 1840 Barrett divorced her, claiming infidelity. She died in 1853 at the age of fifty-two. Barrett soon remarried, but his second wife, a Miss Mason, with whom he had two children, died within a couple of years.

During a long career in the theater Barrett worked in a number of capacities. For a time he was a theater manager both in Boston and New Orleans (1849) and as such was responsible for the artistic and financial operation of those theaters. In 1847 he was the first acting-manager at the Broadway Theatre in New York. However, he proved to be less capable of handling the business side of theater management at this theater.

Barrett also worked as a stage manager at theaters in New York City and, for a season, in Charleston, South Carolina (1852–1853). Responsible for everything that happened on the stage, the position of stage manager was more like that of the director in today's theater. At the Bowery Theatre in New York, Barrett was at various times both theater manager and stage manager. In 1842 he was also noted as keeping a restaurant in St. Louis. But his first love was acting.

In 1833 Barrett was in New Orleans as an actor for the opening of Caldwell's new American Theatre. The managers of this theater hired some of the best actors in the United States and boasted of their talent in the local newspaper. Barrett played in most of the major American cities and made many appearances in New York and Boston. He managed to perform in eight seasons in New Orleans between 1833 and 1842. He traveled to England twice, in 1837 and 1848, where he played with some success at Drury Lane.

Barrett's acting style was relaxed and charming, and he was best in parts that allowed him to display his "manly beauty" and genteel manners. He was also known as something of an intellectual and tried to stay away from "low" comedy roles. In the winter of 1848 at the Park Theatre in New York he played Charles

Surface in a "star" revival of *The School for Scandal*. Ireland notes that he was "indisputably the best light comedian in America." Barrett appeared with most of the country's major actors, including Charlotte Cushman, for whom he played Sir Andrew Aguecheeck in *Twelfth Night* in 1850.

As Barrett grew older, fewer light comedy roles were available to him. His last engagement was at Burton's Theatre in 1854–1855, but ill health forced him to retire from the stage before the end of the season. As he had been unable to have a benefit performance while at Burton's he was given a "complimentary testimonial," or benefit evening, at the New York Academy of Music in 1855. Many of the most famous actors of the generation, including John Brougham, Charles Fisher, and Lester Wallack, presented scenes from *The Merchant of Venice* and *School for Scandal*, gave speeches, and played music in his honor. His final years were spent in poverty and ill health. Unable to perform himself, Barrett made a little money teaching elocution to young actors. He died in New York City.

• Barrett's life and work are covered in most of the major surveys of nineteenth-century American theater, especially Joseph Norton Ireland, *Records of the New York Stage* (1866); George Clinton Densmore Odell, *Annals of the New York Stage*, vols. 2–6 (1931); and Francis Courtney Wemyss, *Chronology of the American Stage from 1752–1852* (1852). A full account of Barrett's activities in New Orleans is contained in Nelle Smither, *A History of the English Theatre at New Orleans 1806–1842* (1944). His work in St. Louis is detailed in William Glasgow Bruce Carson, *Theatre of the Frontier* (1932). The work of the Barrett family in Boston is outlined in William Clapp, *A Record of the Boston Stage* (1853). More recent surveys of the period include Joseph W. Donohue, *Theatre Managers in England and America* (1971), and Weldon B. Durham, *American Theatre Companies: 1749–1887* (1986). A brief obituary is in *Wilkes Spirit of the Times*, 15 Sept. 1860.

ANTHONY R. HAIGH

BARRETT, Janie Porter (9 Aug. 1865–27 Aug. 1948), educator and social welfare advocate, was born in Athens, Georgia, the daughter of Julia Porter. Various biographical accounts indicate that Janie's parents were former slaves, while others speculate that her father was white. Little is known about either parent. During her early childhood, Janie resided in the home of the Skinners, a white family whom her mother served as housekeeper. After her mother's marriage to a railway worker, Janie remained with the Skinners, who encouraged her to further her education.

Though the Skinners suggested that she move North, Janie, at her mother's urging, attended Hampton Institute in Virginia, graduating in 1884. While at Hampton, she became convinced that it was her duty as an educated black woman to assiduously work for the betterment of all African Americans. That belief led her to teach in Dawson, Georgia, and at Lucy Craft Laney's Haines Normal and Industrial Institute in Augusta, Georgia, prior to securing a teaching position at Hampton in 1886. In 1889 she married Harris Barrett,

a cashier at Hampton Institute. They had four children.

While rearing her own children, Barrett decided to also share her skills with some neighborhood girls. Beginning with Tuesday afternoon sewing classes in her home for a few girls, she soon formed a club for "improving the homes and the moral and social life of that community." Persons of all ages and both genders were actively involved in developing skills designed to improve the quality of their lives. In time, because of the overwhelming response to the club and its activities, larger quarters were sought.

In 1902 the Barretts constructed a building on their property to house the Locust Street Settlement, as the club was then called, the first of its kind in Virginia. An auxiliary group of prominent community members raised funds to pay the center's basic expenses and to expand its programs. Northern philanthropists also contributed to the expansion. In 1903 they added a kindergarten to the growing list of services, and by 1909 the Locust Street Settlement House included five girls' and women's clubs and four boys' clubs. Students and staff from Hampton Institute provided instruction in arts and crafts, domestic arts, and agricultural science.

Barrett enjoyed a continuing relationship with Hampton Institute that resulted in a commitment by staff, faculty, and students to her social service and self-help projects. In 1907 the institute supplied stationery and other support to the Virginia State Federation of Colored Women's Clubs, founded at that year's Hampton Negro Conference. Barrett served as its first president.

After an encounter with an eight-year-old black girl who had been incarcerated, Barrett convinced the federation to adopt as its primary project the establishment of a rehabilitative home for "wayward colored" girls. In 1915 members founded the Industrial Home School for Delinquent Colored Girls at Peake in Hanover County, Virginia, set on a 147-acre farm. Initially, Barrett served as secretary of the school's interracial board of trustees. Following her husband's death in 1915, however, Barrett accepted the position of superintendent.

Under her leadership the school gained national prominence and was able to secure a state subsidy and private donations. Largely owing to Barrett's innovative administrative efforts, including the introduction of social welfare principles that nurtured the girls and guided their lives in new directions, the Russell Sage Foundation ranked the school among the top five of its kind in the United States. The reformatory school's program stressed the personal and educational development of the residents rather than punishment for their past behavior. Many of the students flourished in the environment, where good conduct was rewarded and practical skills for living were taught. The girls received vocational training that included sewing, housekeeping, and laundering. The program was designed to provide an eighth-grade education. Those who earned good deportment records for two years were eligible for parole. After their release, contact was maintained with the girls through the school's publication and personal communication from Barrett.

The school's many accomplishments and success stories brought Barrett numerous awards. Noted among her recognitions was the 1929 William E. Harmon Award for Distinguished Achievement among Negroes. The award was given by the Harmon Foundation, established in 1922 by philanthropist William E. Harmon. Because of her national reputation as an expert in child rehabilitation, President Herbert Hoover invited Barrett in 1930 to participate in the White House Conference on Child Health and Protection.

Although inundated by the school's management responsibilities, Barrett remained active with the federation and the National Association of Colored Women (NACW), serving as chairperson of the NACW executive board from 1924 to 1928. She also served on local boards such as the Richmond Urban League and, in keeping with her promotion of interracial cooperation in matters relating to racial uplift and equality, was a member of the Commission on Interracial Cooperation. The school's board, with an interracial membership, reflected Barrett's commitment to work with whites to achieve the school's goals.

Barrett remained superintendent of the Industrial Home School for Delinquent Colored Girls until her retirement in 1940. She left the school, now a model institution for those seeking to steer young black females away from delinquent behavior, to return to Hampton, Virginia, where she remained until her death there. After her death, the school she had led for nearly twenty-five years was renamed the Janie Porter Barrett School for Girls in honor of her achievements.

• There are limited published sources about Barrett. Data about her early social activism are included in the Hampton Institute records of its graduates, reports of the first and third Hampton Conferences, and the Nov. 1915, Oct. 1919, and Aug. 1920 issues of the *Southern Workman*. The most informative general overview of Barrett's life is provided in Alden Whitman's *American Reformers* (1985). Barrett's work with the Locust Street Settlement and the Virginia Industrial School for Colored Girls is highlighted in Cynthia Neverdon-Morton, *Afro-American Women of the South and the Advancement of the Race, 1895–1925* (1989). For more complete coverage of Barrett's many professional activities and her life, Winona R. Hall, "Janie Porter Barrett: Her Life and Contributions to Social Welfare in Virginia" (master's thesis, Howard Univ., 1954), remains the best source.

CYNTHIA NEVERDON-MORTON

BARRETT, John (28 Nov. 1866–17 Oct. 1938), commercial publicist and diplomat, was born in Grafton, Vermont, the son of Charles Barrett and Caroline Sanford. His father, reportedly shy and withdrawn, served for a time as a town official and a Republican state legislator but devoted most of his life to artistic pursuits. His mother, who was more outgoing, had a lively regard for politics, law, journalism, theology, and economics, and Barrett's letters to her suggest she strongly influenced him.

As an undergraduate, Barrett expressed interest in becoming a lawyer or a minister, but after his graduation from Dartmouth College in 1889 he traveled to the Pacific Coast to teach. He then gravitated toward journalism, working as a commercial publicist for newspapers in California, Washington, and Oregon. In 1891 he became the editor of the *Portland Evening Telegram*, a professional advance he attributed to "Providence." He also shifted political allegiance to the Democratic party in order to conform with his employer's views.

Subsequently Barrett cultivated as his clients business leaders who advocated commercial expansion into Asia, and he also developed an interest in a diplomatic career. Although he failed in his initial efforts to obtain a consular position, his earnestness, capability, and seriousness of purpose impressed President Grover Cleveland, who named him minister to Siam. The appointment took effect on 13 February 1894, when Barrett was twenty-seven, one of the youngest ministers ever. In that role he worked hard to expand market opportunities for the United States, but he fell victim to the patronage system when President William McKinley replaced him with a Republican. Fortuitously, while returning home at the outset of the war with Spain, Barrett stopped in Hong Kong and obtained a job with the William Randolph Hearst syndicate as a war correspondent, assigned to Admiral George Dewey's flagship. From that vantage point, he witnessed firsthand the battle of Manila Bay and the transformation of the United States into a Pacific imperial power. He later recorded his impressions in a laudatory biography of Dewey.

Driven from the Democratic party by W. J. Bryan's free silver heresies, Barrett returned to his Republican roots, going to work in 1900 for the party's speakers bureau. As a resolute champion of trade expansion by means of the Open Door, he wrote articles and delivered speeches while coveting another Asian diplomatic post. When his hopes fell through, he turned to Latin America, accepting President Theodore Roosevelt's appointment as minister to Argentina in 1903. He also served in quick succession as minister to Panama and to Colombia, all of which were places where Roosevelt's "canal diplomacy" left bitter legacies over interventionist methods. Hoping always for advancement, Barrett aspired to a position of real influence, perhaps as ambassador to Mexico or director general of the International Bureau of American Republics. This time, his dream came true.

The governing board of the International Bureau of American Republics, most likely acting on the recommendation of Secretary of State Elihu Root, elected Barrett director general in 1907. Called the Pan American Union after 1910, this organization came into existence as a consequence of the First International American Conference in Washington, D.C., in 1889 and functioned primarily as a clearinghouse for commercial information to promote trade. Once placed in charge, Barrett embarked upon a campaign to publicize his own work and to encourage U.S. business interests to expand their markets into Latin America. He also had a broader vision, seeking to move beyond commerce into the larger realm of hemispheric diplomacy.

During Barrett's tenure as director general, issues concerned with the Mexican Revolution, various Caribbean interventions, and the impact of the First World War assumed conspicuous importance. Barrett, in response, called upon Latin American countries to cooperate in the advancement of trade and goodwill, to accept Pan-American formulas as a means of achieving hemispheric unity, and to employ the Pan American Union as a kind of embryo League of Nations. Significantly, much in the fashion of President Woodrow Wilson, he conceived of a multilateral definition of the Monroe Doctrine by which to move beyond unilateral practices in policing the Western Hemisphere, possibly through joint diplomatic or military actions, for example, in Mexico. The idea never met with much success. During the First World War, Barrett advocated the vigorous cultivation of Latin American trade opportunities at a time of European weakness. Sometimes he caused irritation, especially when, on occasion, he offended Latin American sensibilities by appearing to regard the Pan American Union as an instrument of U.S. foreign policy. By the time of his resignation for personal reasons in September 1920, he had lost favor among top officials in the Wilson administration, in part because of his penchant for self-promotion. Nevertheless, as a kind of monument to his endeavors, he could look upon the Pan American Building, a magnificent edifice in Washington, D.C., constructed through his efforts with the financial aid of Andrew Carnegie.

No doubt partly because of the feelings he ruffled, Barrett never found a means of returning to public life, either as a front-line diplomat or as an elected official. The State Department closed its doors to him. For a time in 1924 he considered making a run in Vermont for the Senate, but he withdrew before the primary. He remained an officer of the Pan American Society, his own creation, and continued his role as a publicist, writing and speaking on behalf of Pan-American unity and related themes. Later he championed President Franklin D. Roosevelt's Good Neighbor Policy. After 1930 a heart condition forced him into partial retirement in Coral Gables, Florida.

In 1934, at age sixty-eight, Barrett married Mary Elizabeth Cady, the widow of an old friend from Burlington, Vermont. Essentially a business arrangement, the marriage enabled Barrett to manage family properties. His wife died in 1937. Barrett died in Bellows Falls, Vermont. Throughout his life Barrett functioned as a tireless promoter of Pan-Americanism as the means to cultivate good relations with the countries of Latin America.

• Barrett's papers are at the Library of Congress, Washington, D.C. His books include *Admiral George Dewey* (1899), *Latin America, the Land of Opportunity* (1909), *The Pan American Union* (1911), and *The Panama Canal, What It Is, What It Means* (1913). Salvatore Prisco III, *John Barrett, Progressive Era Diplomat: A Study of a Commercial Expansionist, 1887–1920* (1973), is an account of Barrett's professional career. Mark T. Gilderhus, *Pan American Visions: Woodrow Wilson in the Western Hemisphere, 1913–1921* (1986), puts his years with the Pan American Union in context. An obituary is in the *New York Times*, 18 Oct. 1938.

MARK T. GILDERHUS

BARRETT, Lawrence (4 Apr. 1838–20 Mar. 1891), actor, manager, and sometime theater historian, was born in Paterson, New Jersey, the son of an indigent Irish-born tailor whose name is variously reported as Thomas Barrett and Thomas Brannigan, though Lawrence insisted on the former. His authorized biography records only his mother's first name (Agnes), further indication of difficult early years. By the age of ten he had left home for employment in the linens department of a dry goods store in Detroit. Entirely self-educated, he was an avid reader of Shakespeare and at age fifteen turned to the stage as a career, his first role being that of Murad in *The French Spy* at the Metropolitan Theatre in Detroit (1853). The following year he was hired as a member of the stock company of the Grand Opera House in Pittsburgh, then under the management of Joseph Foster, where he had the opportunity to support such visiting stars as C. W. Couldock, a transplanted English actor, and the popular Julia Dean.

Barrett made his New York debut at Burton's Theatre on 20 January 1857 as Sir Thomas Clifford in *The Hunchback*. In the course of the month-long engagement he played a variety of roles in popular comedies and melodramas, such as Claude Melnotte in *The Lady of Lyons* and the title roles in *Fazio* and *The Stranger*. Later that season he joined William E. Burton at the Metropolitan in New York, where he supported numerous stars, notably the robust, heroic, traditional old-school actress Charlotte Cushman and the restrained, quiet, and comparatively forward-looking Edwin Booth. Barrett appears never fully to have reconciled these early and divergent influences on his acting style.

In the fall of 1858 Barrett commenced a two-season engagement with the esteemed Boston Museum stock company under William Warren, gaining valuable experience in an expanding repertory and working his way up to title roles in *Romeo and Juliet* and *Ingomar*; in the latter he was favorably and tellingly reported as culling "good scraps of acting from able actors" (quoted in Barron, p. 21). He left Warren for a season with E. L. Davenport at the Howard Atheneum (also in Boston) and left Davenport for the Walnut Street Theatre in Philadelphia, just prior to the outbreak of the Civil War. At the Walnut Street Theatre he first undertook Cassius, which he painstakingly developed into one of his most successful roles.

Barrett served for ten months with the Twenty-eighth Massachusetts Regiment before resuming his career in the fall of 1862 in Philadelphia. After a brief visit to Washington, D.C., where he reportedly met both President Abraham Lincoln and President-to-be James Garfield, he returned to Philadelphia, this time undertaking an engagement at the Chestnut Street Theatre, where the semiretired tragedian Edwin Forrest sent him encouraging notes from the audience. Barrett later returned the favor by writing an admiring biography of Forrest in 1881. Scarcely less admiring was Edwin Booth, who hired Barrett as part of his company at the Winter Garden in New York. Barrett supported Booth during the 1862–1863 and 1863–1864 seasons, winning especially favorable notice as Othello to Booth's famed Iago. (When Edwin Booth temporarily retired from the stage after his brother John Wilkes Booth assassinated Lincoln, Barrett lost for the time being a valuable professional ally.)

In between engagements with Booth, Barrett embarked on his first management ventures, taking over the Varieties Theatre in New Orleans (subsequently destroyed during the war) and presenting himself as a star attraction in the fall of 1864 as Elliott Grey in *Rosedale*. Venturing farther and farther afield from the theaters in the Northeast, he played a week's engagement in Liverpool in 1867 and then sailed to San Francisco for an engagement at McGuire's Opera House, where he hired John McCullough, a heroic actor of the Edwin Forrest school, to support him. The Barrett-McCullough combination proved a hit, and the pair opened up the California Theatre, commencing an extended (twenty-month) engagement.

By the summer of 1870 he had returned to New York, now with the successful management team of Jarrett and Palmer, who presented him as Cassius (opposite E. L. Davenport as Brutus) at Niblo's Garden. Once again he won the attention of Booth, who offered him an engagement at Booth's Theatre culminating in his portrayal as Leontes in Shakespeare's rarely performed *Winter's Tale* (Apr. 1871). The production was an extravagant one and, though well attended, lost money for Booth, whose decision to close it evoked a bitter response from Barrett. (Skinner, in *The Last Tragedian*, prints the text of Barrett's ungracious letter, bearing Booth's notation: "Preserve this as a souvenir of the blackest ingratitude.") A further series of misunderstandings over such matters as royalties, implied promises by Booth to hire Barrett again, and what Barrett took to be a slur on his acting alienated the two friends for most of the remainder of the decade. They reconciled in 1880, however, enabling them later to form a productive professional alliance.

After the close of Booth's 1870–1871 season, Barrett retained the theater to present himself in a new play, W. G. Wills's sentimental *The Man o' Airlie*. As the poet Harebell he won extraordinary praise from the critics, particularly for his simple tenderness, naturalness, and lack of exaggeration in the role, qualities scarcely identified with any of his previous work. The public, however, was less enthusiastic, and the production was a financial failure. (As producer, Booth took an $8,500 loss.) Barrett took *Man o' Airlie* on the road, playing it at the reopened Varieties Theatre in December 1871, but then immediately returned to

New York to play Cassius opposite Booth's Brutus, in what remains one of the most famous and successful productions (eighty-three performances) of *Julius Caesar* ever staged. Thus encouraged to expand his classical repertory, he proceeded to feature himself (back at the Varieties) as Shylock, Richard III, Richelieu (in the Bulwer-Lytton play), Raphael in *The Marble Heart*, and Alfred Evelyn in *Money*. On 30 January 1874 he first played Lear (at the Varieties), taking the production to New York the following year. At the end of 1875 he opened as Cassius in Jarrett and Palmer's spectacular revival of *Julius Caesar*. The production closed after 103 performances, breaking Booth's 100-performance Shakespearean record as Hamlet.

In 1877 Barrett embarked on a project to promote new plays by American dramatists, beginning with his encouragement of the novelist William Dean Howells to write *A Counterfeit Presentment*, which Barrett premiered at the Grand Opera House in Cincinnati on 11 October 1877. Others in this vein included Howells's *A New Play* (later retitled *Yorick's Love*) in 1878; William Young's *Pendragon* (1881); a revival of George Henry Boker's *Francesca da Rimini*, in which E. L. Davenport had starred in the 1850s (1882); Alfred Thomson's *The King's Pleasure* (1884); Mary Russell Mitford's *Rienzi* (1885); and William Young's *Ganelon* (1889). These plays constituted, and furthered, a neo-Romantic revival in American drama even as they expanded the wide range of roles Barrett regularly undertook. The genteelism of these romantic dramas bespeaks an aspiration toward cultural legitimacy that their substance, however, failed to fulfill. With the exception of Boker's piece, the plays scarcely survived Barrett's own years on the stage.

In 1886 Barrett formed a partnership with Booth that lasted until the end of Barrett's career—indeed, until his death. Ever neglectful of his business interests, Booth welcomed Barrett's offer to take over his management. From 12 September 1886 through 18 March 1891 they criss-crossed the nation, sometimes touring separately and sometimes together in a predominantly "classical" repertory that included *Hamlet*, *Macbeth*, *Othello*, *The Merchant of Venice*, *Julius Caesar*, *King Lear*, *Richard III* (the Colley Cibber version), *Richelieu*, *Don Caesar de Bazan*, *A New Way to Pay Old Debts*, *Katharine and Petruchio*, *The King's Pleasure*, *The Fool's Revenge*, and *David Garrick*. Though not without its difficulties (notably a tiff over billing with Madame Modjeska, whom Barrett had hired as leading lady), the partnership was the capstone of Barrett's career, earning him both substantial profits ($426,000) and glowing reviews.

Even Barrett's most enthusiastic supporters were unable to celebrate his acting without some qualification. His champion, the authoritative and difficult William Winter, critic of the *New York Tribune*, judged him "not so much an impersonator as an interpreter of character." The words "noble," "true," and "fidelity" dot Winter's obituary of Barrett, in which the critic described Barrett's presence as an actor: "His stately head, silvered with graying hair, his dark eyes deeply sunken and glowing with intense light, his thin visage pallid with study and pain, his form of grace and his voice of sonorous eloquence and solemn music (in compass, variety and sweetness one of the few great voices of the current dramatic generation), his tremendous earnestness, his superb bearing, and his invariable authority and distinction—all those attributes united to announce a ruler and leader in the realm of the intellect." This is anticlimactic as a eulogy for an actor and probably speaks between the lines of a certain dustiness. (Critics often said he looked like a preacher or a priest.) Those ill disposed to him concluded that the qualities he brought to his much-praised Cassius—intellectual asceticism, querulousness, mordant bitterness—were the qualities of the man himself. Others saw beneath his austerity a true love of the theater and a sense of moral obligation to offer to his public the finest he could muster. Barrett took ill during a performance (playing De Mauprat to Booth's Richelieu) and died at his apartment at the Windsor Hotel in New York City. Barrett apparently was married and had three children, but his wife's name and the year they married are unknown.

• The chief repositories of Barrett memorabilia (including letters, personal papers, clippings, promptbooks, and financial records) are at the Harvard Theatre Collection, the William Seymour Theatre Collection at Princeton, the Walter Hampden Memorial Library at the Players (New York City), and the New York Library for the Performing Arts. There are also some materials at the Museum of the City of New York, the Brander Matthews Theatre Collection at Columbia, the Harry Ransom Center at the University of Texas, and the Boston Public Library. Some valuable holdings remain in private collections. For biographical details, see Elwyn A. Barron, *Lawrence Barrett: A Professional Sketch* (1889); Mark Bailey, "Lawrence Barrett (1838–1891)" (Ph.D. diss., Univ. of Michigan, 1942); and James Ralph Miller, "Lawrence Barrett on the New York Stage" (Ph.D. diss., Tufts Univ., 1972). William Winter wrote often about Barrett in *Life and Art of Edwin Booth* (1893), *Shadows of the Stage* (1892–1895), *Other Days* (1908), and *The Wallet of Time* (1913). Otis Skinner's biography of Booth, *The Last Tragedian* (1939), contributes backstage gossip. References to Barrett are also to be found in such useful accounts of the period as John Mason Brown, *Upstage: The American Theatre in Performance* (1930); Barnard Hewitt, *Theatre U.S.A., 1665–1957* (1959); Richard Moody, *America Takes the Stage* (1955); and Garff B. Wilson, *A History of American Acting* (1966). Obituaries are in the *New York Herald* and the *New York Times*, 21 Mar. 1891; and *The World* and the *New York Tribune*, 22 Mar. 1891.

ATTILIO FAVORINI

BARRINGER, Daniel Moreau (30 July 1806–1 Sept. 1873), U.S. congressman and diplomat, was born near Concord, North Carolina, the son of Paul Barringer, a prominent Cabarrus County landowner, and Elizabeth Brandon. He enrolled in the University of North Carolina as a second-semester sophomore in 1824 and graduated with honors in 1826. He studied law under Thomas Ruffin and began practice in Concord in 1829.

That same year Barringer was elected to the North Carolina House of Commons, where he served six consecutive terms. His major initiative was a bill to establish a new state bank to replace the existing institution, whose charter was about to expire. The measure passed the general assembly in January 1833, but the bank was never organized, because private investors objected to the provision for state control of the board of directors. Barringer was also a leader in the movement to reform the state's undemocratic constitution. He served as a delegate to the constitutional convention of 1835 but left before its adjournment on account of illness. He returned to the House of Commons in 1840 and was reelected in 1842.

Never an admirer of Andrew Jackson, Barringer opposed a resolution during the session of 1831–1832 endorsing the president's reelection. By 1834 he was a leader of the Whig forces in the general assembly, speaking out against proposals to instruct North Carolina's U.S. senators to vote for a motion expunging a resolution of censure against Jackson. In 1843 he was elected to the U.S. House of Representatives, where he served three terms. During his third term he shared a desk with Abraham Lincoln, with whom he reportedly became good friends. Though he seldom participated in the debates, he established a reputation as an effective parliamentarian. Like most Whigs, he opposed the annexation of Texas and the Mexican War. Nonetheless, he worked hard to raise a volunteer regiment from the western part of the state, believing that the failure to supply troops would result in "much unjust reflection and calumny on our State" and "cast odium on the Whig party."

In 1848 Barringer supported Zachary Taylor for the Whig presidential nomination. After the election, he was appointed as minister to Spain. Relations with that country were strained as a result of efforts by his predecessor, Romulus M. Saunders, to purchase Cuba as well as by several filibustering expeditions that were launched against Cuba from the United States. Barringer's personality suited him well for diplomacy. Quiet and dignified in demeanor, he had considerable personal charm and was a popular figure in court circles. He succeeded in restoring cordial relations with the Spanish government while, at the same time, securing the release of imprisoned American filibusters. He resigned his commission in September 1853 and traveled in Europe with his wife, Elizabeth Wethered, whom he had married in 1848, and his two children, who had been born in Spain. Three other children were born after the family returned to the United States in May 1854.

Elected to the North Carolina House of Commons in 1854, Barringer was nominated by his party for the U.S. Senate. It was an empty honor, however, since the Democrats controlled the general assembly by comfortable majorities. He opposed the principles of the American party, which replaced the Whigs as the main opposition party in 1855, and became one of the most prominent North Carolina Whigs to defect to the Democrats. Barringer announced his defection in a public letter of 6 August 1856, in which he endorsed James Buchanan for the presidency on the grounds that the Democrats were now the only "truly national" party, "the only party now in existence which can meet together, discuss and adopt principles and resolves . . . in *every and in all sections* of our country."

After Buchanan's landslide victory in North Carolina, Barringer declined an appointment as minister to Nicaragua and Costa Rica. In 1858 he moved to Raleigh and by 1860 had become a member of the Democratic Executive Committee. His rapid rise to a position of influence aroused the resentment of some old-line Democrats, who complained that former Whigs like Barringer had taken over their party. He supported Stephen A. Douglas for the presidency in 1860, and after the party split, he tried unsuccessfully to call a state convention to unite the Democrats behind one electoral ticket. He then reluctantly endorsed the John C. Breckinridge–Joseph Lane ticket.

Believing that the election of Lincoln was not sufficient reason for the South to withdraw from the Union, Barringer opposed immediate secession. As one of North Carolina's five delegates to the Washington Peace Conference, he supported the Crittenden Compromise, which would have guaranteed protection to slave property in all territory south of 36° 30′. However, he voted against the watered-down version of Crittenden's plan that was finally approved by the convention, arguing that it was not strong enough to bring back those states that had already seceded.

Barringer remained a Unionist until Lincoln's call for troops in April 1861. He served briefly as an adviser to Governor Henry T. Clarke but otherwise did not play an active part in the war. According to his pardon application, he opposed the "military usurpations" of the Jefferson Davis administration and "publicly and unhesitatingly expressed himself for peace long before the close of the War." A supporter of Andrew Johnson's plan of Reconstruction, Barringer served as a delegate to the National Union Convention in Philadelphia in August 1866. After the passage of the Reconstruction Acts in March 1867, he urged the voters of his state to cooperate with Congressional Reconstruction by participating in the election of delegates to the constitutional convention. Nonetheless, he supported the Democratic candidate for president in 1868 and served as chair of the executive committee of the North Carolina Conservative (Democratic) party from 1872 until his death. He died at White Sulphur Springs in Greenbrier, West Virginia.

Barringer's significance lies primarily in his role as a moderating force during a turbulent era in American history. Both as a Whig and as a Democrat, he was a member of "that school in politics which was 'national' in its character—devoted to the Union—the Constitution and the laws" (pardon application). His influence, along with that of other nationalistic former Whigs, prevented the North Carolina Democratic party from serving as an effective vehicle for the secession movement and later helped reconcile that party to the realities of defeat and Reconstruction.

• Barringer's family, business, and political correspondence are in the Daniel Moreau Barringer Papers, Southern Historical Collection, University of North Carolina, Chapel Hill. Other letters by Barringer, as well as references to him, can be found in Henry T. Shanks, ed., *The Papers of Willie Person Mangum* (5 vols., 1950–1956); and J. G. de Roulhac Hamilton and Max R. Williams, eds., *The Papers of William Alexander Graham* (8 vols., 1957–1992). His pardon application (RG 94, Records of the Adjutant General's Office, National Archives and Records Administration, Washington, D.C.) contains a detailed discussion of his nationalistic political philosophy and his role during the secession crisis and Civil War. For the factors behind his decision to oppose the American party and become a Democrat, see *Letters of James W. Osborne, Esq., Hon. D. M. Barringer, and A. C. Williamson, Esq., Old Line Whigs of North Carolina* (1856), North Carolina Collection, University of North Carolina Library. A detailed secondary account of his life is the sketch by Daniel M. Barringer, Jr., in *Biographical History of North Carolina*, vol. 1, ed. Samuel A. Ashe et al. (1905–1917). An obituary is in the *Raleigh Sentinel*, 9 Sept. 1873.

THOMAS E. JEFFREY

BARRINGER, Emily Dunning (27 Sept. 1876–8 Apr. 1961), physician, was born in Scarsdale, New York, the daughter of Edwin James Dunning, a broker, and Frances Gore Lang. Her father left her mother with five children while he tried to recoup the family fortune in Europe. They moved to New York City before the birth of Emily's youngest brother, and while caring for her mother during his difficult birth, she developed a desire to enter the medical field.

Emily's mother felt strongly that her daughters should be prepared to support themselves as adults; she herself supported the family by taking in boarders. Emily graduated from Miss Brackett's School for Girls in 1894, planning to enter the nursing profession, but she was inspired by a lecture given by Mary Putnam Jacobi, a physician in New York City, and she realized that it was possible for her to become a doctor rather than a nurse. Henry Sage, Emily's great-uncle and founder of Cornell University, provided her financial assistance so that she could enter Cornell in the fall of 1894.

Barringer graduated from Cornell in three years. She then entered the Medical College of the New York Infirmary for Women and Children, the only orthodox medical school in New York City that accepted women. In 1899 Cornell University Medical College was founded, the Medical College of New York closed, and all its students transferred to Cornell. There, Emily met a fellow medical student, Benjamin Stockwell Barringer, whom she married in December 1904; they had two children.

After she received the M.D., Barringer's career options were limited to practicing at a women's hospital. Women were not allowed to intern in the large general hospitals in New York City. Again she sought the advice of Jacobi, who encouraged her to take a "hospital quiz" offered at Mount Sinai Hospital. She was allowed to take the quiz but was told that the results were irrelevant; the hospital would not offer her an intern position. Despite her disappointment, she kept trying and took the entrance exam to Gouverneur Hospital; though she passed with the highest score, the hospital denied her an appointment because of her sex.

Barringer began an apprenticeship with Jacobi and began to lobby the mayor's office to allow women to compete in hospital entrance examinations. In 1902 Mayor Seth Low, a reformer and former president of Columbia University, declared that women could compete freely with men on medical exams and that the top performers would be offered appointments at Gouverneur Hospital. This was one of many reform measures adopted by Low, who ran for mayor seeking to reform the corruption of Tammany Hall. Barringer initially placed high fourth on the written examination, not high enough to be allowed to take the oral exam, but she persuaded the board that her scores from the previous year should be factored into the scoring. On 1 January 1903, she became the first female doctor to intern at a New York City hospital.

The next two years at Gouverneur Hospital proved difficult for Barringer. Four senior doctors tried to force her resignation. Although the physicians persecuted her, she received strong support from other sources, such as the ambulance drivers, nurses, city policemen, and residents of New York City. As the first woman ambulance surgeon, she felt strongly that it was her duty to attend the sick, no matter where they were found. The ambulance drivers grew to respect her skill and determination. Her strong will and family support also helped her through this arduous time, and she rose through the ranks at the hospital, eventually becoming house surgeon in July 1905. During her tenure, she decided to concentrate on gynecological surgery. She received her diploma in December 1905.

After a short stay in Vienna, where both the Barringers attended classes, they returned to New York, where Emily Barringer took a position on the gynecological staff at New York Polyclinic Hospital. She was also attending surgeon at the New York Infirmary for Women and Children. She specialized in the study of venereal diseases. During World War I she was vice chairman of the American Women's Hospitals War Service Committee of the National Medical Women's Association; she spearheaded a campaign to raise money for the purchase of ambulances to be sent to Europe.

After World War I Barringer became attending surgeon at Kingston Avenue Hospital and subsequently its director of gynecology. She was a member of the American Medical Association, and a fellow of the American College of Surgeons and of the New York Academy of Medicine. In 1941 she was elected president of the Medical Women's National Association.

During World War II Barringer fought hard for women's right to obtain appointments in the Army and Navy Medical Corps. At that time women doctors were not offered commissions and had to accept positions as contract surgeons with the Women's Army Auxiliary Corps, thus denying them military benefits. Barringer felt that female physicians should be able to go where they were most needed—into combat zones. As chairman of the American Medical Women's Association's special committee on commissions for women physicians in the army and navy, she lobbied Congress and President Franklin D. Roosevelt for more than a year. In April 1943 Roosevelt signed into law the Sparkman Act, commissioning women physicians and surgeons in the Army and Navy Medical Corps and granting them the same benefits as members of the Officers Reserve Corps of the Army and Navy Reserve with the same grade and length of service.

Barringer became a physician at a time when there were comparatively few female doctors. Women were met with prejudice from medical school admission boards, hospital boards and staff, and male physicians. Barringer's vigor and determination did much to open the field of medicine to women. The early twentieth century saw a rise in the number of women physicians, but their path was difficult without the professional connections and tolerance of their male peers. She persevered because of her commitment to herself and to the medical profession. She died in New Milford, Connecticut.

• Correspondence pertaining to the Women's Medical Society of New York State is in Cornell University Libraries. Barringer's autobiography, *Bowery to Bellevue* (1950), is an important source. Her efforts to persuade Congress and President Roosevelt to allow women doctors into the army are chronicled in various issues of the *New York Times*, 1942 and 1943. Obituaries are in the *Journal of the American Medical Women's Association* 16 (1961): 958, and in the *New York Times*, 9 Apr. 1961.

LISA BROEHL GERMAN

BARRINGER, Rufus (2 Dec. 1821–3 Feb. 1895), soldier, was born in Cabarrus County, North Carolina, the son of Paul Barringer and Elizabeth Brandon. During the War of 1812, his father had attained the rank of brigadier general of militia. After attending preparatory school at Sugar Creek Academy, Barringer entered the University of North Carolina at Chapel Hill, from which he graduated in 1842. Following graduation he studied law with his brother, Moreau Barringer, then with Richmond Pearson, the future chief justice of the North Carolina Supreme Court, and subsequently opened a practice in Concord, North Carolina. He belonged to the Whig political party and won election to the state assembly in 1848 and 1850. In 1860 he was made a political elector.

Barringer fought against secession, for he "was devotedly attached to the Union and Constitution." He was a man of principle and neither ridicule nor opposition caused him to waver in his stand. He warned that if war came it would be long and bloody. For this unpopular prediction he was mocked in the streets of Charlotte. When Fort Sumter was fired upon, Barringer was one of the first in Cabarrus County to enlist, joining Company F, First North Carolina Cavalry. He was elected captain of his company soon afterward. Though lacking any military training or experience, Barringer applied himself with characteristic energy in drilling and training his company.

In mid-October 1861 the First North Carolina joined the Confederate army in northern Virginia, with whom it served to the end of the war. Barringer saw active service in the Peninsula, Second Manassas, Sharpsburg (Antietam), Fredericksburg, and Chancellorsville campaigns and in numerous cavalry actions and operations that occurred between major movements by the opposing armies. In the big cavalry battle at Brandy Station, Virginia, on 9 June 1863, Barringer received a severe wound in the face. He returned in October 1863 and received his promotion to major, which was dated 26 August 1863. During the Bristoe Station campaign on 14 October 1863, he received a wound in the thigh in action at Auburn Mills, Virginia. Barringer remained in the field and on 15 October participated in the successful ambush of Union general Judson Kilpatrick's cavalry. In the pursuit of the Federal cavalry, Barringer was severely injured when his horse fell. One month later he was promoted to lieutenant colonel. His aggressive leadership of the First North Carolina Cavalry earned the praise of General J. E. B. Stuart, who wrote that the degree of efficiency to which Barringer had raised the regiment's performance "should be called—'a pattern for others.'"

Barringer was promoted to brigadier general on 1 June 1864 and was assigned to command a cavalry brigade consisting of the First, Second, Third, and Fifth North Carolina. He led his brigade in the almost constant cavalry fighting and skirmishing that marked the 1864 campaign in Virginia. In August, while temporarily in command of Fitz Lee's division, he participated in the rout of Union forces at Ream's Station, for which he received the compliments of Robert E. Lee. On 3 April 1865, after the disastrous battle of Five Forks had forced the retreat of the Confederate army from Richmond and Petersburg, Barringer's command was ordered to hold Namozine Church, an important point about thirty miles west of Petersburg. In the ensuing engagement, Barringer was captured by scouts of Union general Philip H. Sheridan, who were disguised as Confederate soldiers. He was sent to City Point, Virginia, where he was presented to President Abraham Lincoln, who recalled Barringer's older brother Moreau, with whom Lincoln had desked in Congress. Before parting, Lincoln gave Barringer a note, addressed to Secretary of War Edwin Stanton, asking that the North Carolinian receive special consideration. Barringer was confined to the Old Capitol Prison, but thanks to Lincoln's note to Stanton, he was soon transferred to Fort Delaware. He was held there until 23 July, when he was released on parole. Throughout the war, Barringer participated in seventy-six actions, had two horses shot from under him, and was wounded three times.

Following his release from prison, Barringer moved his law practice from Concord, North Carolina, to Charlotte, where he maintained a successful practice until 1884. He was a devout Christian and, according to a biographical sketch in *Confederate Veteran*, "was a man of culture, fond of literature and history." He earned the animosity of fellow citizens by advocating a moderate view toward the Reconstruction policies of the federal government. Barringer's "directness and fearlessness of action" earned him respect, and the enmity shown toward him passed (Hill, *Confederate Military History*). He was elected in 1875 to the state constitutional convention as a Republican from a Democratic county. In 1880 he ran for lieutenant governor and lost, although he carried his own strongly Democratic county. The later years of his life were spent in farming and writing articles on the war and agriculture.

Barringer was married three times. His first marriage was to Eugenia Morrison, the sister of Thomas J. "Stonewall" Jackson's wife. Eugenia died in 1858, and Barringer subsequently married Rosalie Chunn and Margaret Long. He died in Charlotte. His son, Dr. Paul Barringer, became chairman of the University of Virginia.

Throughout his life, as a citizen or soldier, Barringer stood by his convictions and beliefs, no matter how unpopular. D. H. Hill, Jr., wrote of him, "He was tenacious of his principles, and not to be swerved from duty by any amount of ridicule or opposition."

• Barringer's papers are located at the Southern Historical Collection at the University of North Carolina at Chapel Hill. Within these papers is a detailed description of his war service that he wrote for his brother, Major V. C. Barringer, 27 Jan. 1866. For some of his wartime reports and correspondence see U.S. War Department, *The War of the Rebellion: A Compilation of the Official Records of the Union and Confederate Armies* (128 vols., 1880–1901). A full sketch of his life is in D. H. Hill, Jr., *North Carolina*, vol. 4 of *Confederate Military History*, ed. Clement A. Evans (1899). A briefer sketch, with some additional details of his life, is in *Confederate Veteran* 10 (1901): 69–70.

D. SCOTT HARTWIG

BARRON, Clarence Walker (2 July 1855–2 Oct. 1928), financial journalist, was born in Boston, Massachusetts, the son of Henry Barron, a teamster, and Elana Noyes. He was educated at the Prescott Grammar School in Charlestown, Massachusetts, and Boston's English High School, where he distinguished himself by writing prize-winning essays on railways and civil service reform. Preparing for a journalism career, Barron supplemented his writing talents by teaching himself shorthand, an activity he later would call "the best training for young men in practical life" (*They Told Barron*, p. xix). In 1875 he took a job with the *Boston Daily News* and, later that year, became a reporter for the Boston *Evening Transcript*. At first, he covered everything from street crime to gubernatorial politics, but he later convinced the *Transcript* to increase its financial coverage beyond providing stock quotes. Barron subsequently established the paper's financial section. His insightful analysis of Boston's fiscal woes impressed his readers. An acquaintance remembered, "He could find a dozen first rate stories in an incident like a change in dividend where the financial pages of general newspapers found nothing but the bare fact" (*Wall Street Journal*, 4 Oct. 1928). Barron remained with the *Transcript* for eleven years, but after an indecorous remark concerning the *Transcript*'s parent company, he left the paper. His founding in 1887 of the *Boston News Bureau* marked the beginning of modern financial journalism.

Based on the idea that men needed business news many times each day, the *News Bureau* consisted of handbills delivered by messenger as often as they were printed. Eventually the several daily items were printed together on a single sheet, and the *Boston News Bureau* evolved into a newspaper. Barron's understanding of Boston's financial state led to his first book, *Boston Stock Exchange* (1893), co-written with Joseph G. Martin. Still, he longed to expand his influence beyond Boston. He soon organized a news exchange with the New York firm, Dow, Jones, and Company, then publishing financial bulletins and the fledgling *Wall Street Journal*. In 1896 Barron founded the daily *Philadelphia Financial Journal* (later the *Philadelphia Financial News* [1895–1901] and the *Philadelphia News Bureau* [1901–1929]). In 1900 he married a widow, Jessie M. Barteaux Waldrom, who died in 1918.

Barron's journalistic efforts were financially successful, and in 1901 he further expanded his influence by acquiring control of Dow, Jones, and Company, thus taking over the Dow-Jones news service and the *Wall Street Journal*. Barron recognized that the paper could be much more than a stocks-and-bonds trade sheet. During the next twenty years, he turned the *Wall Street Journal* from a local paper with a circulation of a few thousand into the authoritative, nationwide financial daily it would remain throughout the century. He saw the paper as a way to educate the public about the value of securities and finance, and he expanded its contents to include detailed, yet easy-to-understand, explanations of how the world of finance operated, stories exposing shady financial dealings, and useful advice about the best stocks in which to invest. He was one of the earliest journalists to encourage public investment in oil. Barron also felt that it was the journalist's responsibility to inform stockholders about their companies, and he made the *Wall Street Journal* reflect his desire to faithfully serve the investment public. His personal motto became the paper's: "The Truth in its proper service." His unwavering convictions sometimes made him a difficult employer, however. Editor William Peter Hamilton recalled, "He could be almost cruelly frank at times and he was impatient of second rate work or second rate thinking . . . Stupidity and carelessness not only irritated him; they genuinely grieved him. He felt that some one was falling short of those ideals of service which he had set for himself and expected as a matter of course from his colleagues" (*Wall Street Journal*, 4 Oct. 1928).

Barron's writing style was straightforward and unadorned. While he always considered himself a newspaper reporter first and foremost, Barron wrote several books including *The Federal Reserve Act* (1914), a dis-

cussion of the principles of the new banking act; *The Audacious War* (1915), which explored economic aspects of World War I; *The Mexican Problem* (1917), which detailed Mexico's oil wealth; *War Finance* (1919); and *A World Remaking of Peace Finance* (1920), which discussed postwar finance, economic reconstruction, and war reparations. The last two books were the result of Barron's many wartime and postwar journeys to Europe, where he advised several European leaders, including Kaiser Wilhelm and former Czar Nicholas II. Barron also published several pamphlets that consisted of his speeches to various organizations, reprints of his most inspired *Wall Street Journal* articles, and religious essays reflecting his Swedenborgian views.

In 1921 he founded *Barron's*, the national financial weekly. During the twenties, he simultaneously served as editor of *Barron's*; president of Dow, Jones, and Company; publisher of the *Wall Street Journal*; manager of the *Boston News Bureau* and the *Philadelphia News Bureau*; and president of the advertising agency Doremus and Company. In addition, Barron was active in public service. Although his business responsibilities often kept him in New York, he remained a Bostonian throughout his life. He was chairman of the Cohasset Harbor Improvement Committee and of the Massachusetts Inland Waterways Commission and was a member of the Massachusetts governor's Special Commission on Municipal Expenditures.

Colorful and gregarious, Barron was a welcome guest at the best dining establishments at home and abroad. His zest for good living, however, prompted many weight-reducing visits to a Battle Creek, Michigan, sanitarium, where he died.

Many of the eulogies for Barron emphasized his journalistic honesty. Guy M. Walker remarked, "He was absolutely incorruptible. Neither his voice nor his pen could be stopped when revealing financial dishonesty or economic sophistry" (*Wall Street Journal*, 4 Oct. 1928). Barron deserves recognition as the father of modern financial journalism. Throughout his career, he ably served the American public by using his reporting skills and financial insights to help readers make sound investment decisions.

• Arthur Pound and Samuel Taylor Moore, eds., *They Told Barron* (1930) and *More They Told Barron* (1931), contain much biographical material, though poor organization hampers their usefulness. See also *New England Historical and Genealogical Register* 83 (1929): 468–69. Obituaries, tributes, and reminiscences are in the *Wall Street Journal*, 4 and 5 Oct. 1928, and the *New York Times*, 3 and 4 Oct. 1928.

KEVIN J. HAYES

BARRON, James (1769–21 Apr. 1851), naval officer, was born in Virginia, the younger of two naval sons of James Barron, a merchant captain and officer of the Virginia navy in the Revolution, and Jane Cowper. The older son, Samuel Barron, also commanded in the U.S. Navy and was senior to James. James Barron began his sea service before the age of twelve on board his father's ship in the Virginia service. He was commissioned a lieutenant in the U.S. Navy in 1798, presumably having sailed in merchant vessels in the intervening years, since he would be known throughout the service for his masterful seamanship. In 1790 he married Elisabeth Mosely Armistead, another Virginian; the Barrons' first child, Jane, was born in 1791.

Barron's first naval appointment was as third lieutenant in the frigate *United States* under the navy's senior captain, John Barry (1745–1803). In October 1798 his skill saved the ship during a violent storm, and his captain recommended his promotion. He received his captain's commission in 1799, but his first command was unlucky: the *Warren*'s officers and crew had been decimated by yellow fever on a previous cruise and suffered the same fate under Barron. He, too, was stricken with the disease and probably with malaria as well, because he suffered periods of fever throughout his life.

After this Barron served in a number of naval ships, mainly as a flag captain under the respective squadron commodores in the Mediterranean during the war with Tripoli. Between cruises, in 1803, he supervised the building of one of the navy's first gunboats. It was during this period that a midshipman described him as "in the line of his profession . . . extremely clever" and "one of the experienced and able seamen in the service." He was also said to be "a man of warm passions, but good natured withall." His most important Mediterranean service was under the command of his brother, when he effectively ran the squadron for many months while Samuel Barron suffered from severe liver disease. At the same time, he incurred the enmity of Captain John Rodgers (1773–1838), who aspired to the squadron command and thought James Barron was merely encouraging Samuel Barron to retain command in order to thwart Rodgers's ambitions. There was a threatened duel, but in the end the quarrel was allowed to subside.

Unfortunately for this consummate master of seamanship, he is most often remembered for two tragic events. The first was the so-called "*Chesapeake-Leopard* incident" in June 1807. Barron had been given command of the Mediterranean Squadron and was sailing from Hampton Roads in his flagship, the frigate *Chesapeake*, when the ship was stopped by the somewhat heavier British frigate *Leopard*, whose commander demanded the surrender of several supposed deserters from His Majesty's Navy. Not prepared for resistance, the *Chesapeake* had just left port on what was expected to be a peaceful cruise, its anchor cables were not yet stowed, and some of its late-arriving stores were lying about the decks. The powder cartridges, wads, matches, and other accoutrements of the great guns were not ready. When Barron rejected the demand for the deserters, however, the British commander fired into the *Chesapeake*, which could fire only one gun in retaliation and was forced to surrender. The *Leopard*'s officers then mustered the *Chesapeake*'s crew, removed five accused deserters, and left the American frigate to limp back into port with its dead and wounded. The outcry in the United States was piercing. Diplomatic relations with Great Britain reached a new low, and the memory of this incident was probably a major contributor to the American decision to declare war on Great Britain in 1812. Tardily, the British admitted wrongdoing and returned two of the men taken from the *Chesapeake*, but they did not reach Boston until after the declaration of war.

It would probably be fair to say that James Barron was made a scapegoat for American humiliation. The court-martial which tried him was headed by his long-time personal enemy, Commodore Rodgers, and Captain Stephen Decatur (1779–1820) sat as a member, even though he had publicly declared beforehand that he thought Barron was at fault in the incident. The court found Barron negligent in not preparing his ship for the possibility of a hostile encounter and sentenced him to a five-year suspension without pay. He left the country, and although his suspension expired in 1812, he remained in Europe, engaged in commercial trading, and did not return to the United States until after the end of the war in 1815, asserting in his defense that he could not afford to return. He probably did not expect to be actively employed in any case, and as it turned out he never commanded a naval ship again.

The second unhappy event for which Barron is remembered is the duel he fought with Commodore Decatur at Bladensburg, Maryland, in March 1820. The sources of Decatur's enmity toward Barron have never been fully clarified. In the months before the duel, he had gone out of his way to impugn Barron's character and courage, provoking the challenge that finally came. In the exchange of shots, Decatur was mortally wounded; Barron's wounds were severe, but he survived. The death of the popular Decatur brought Barron's reputation to a new low. He continued in the navy until his death, on half pay or in a series of shore commands, usually the less significant ones. Ironically, when he died at Norfolk, Virginia, Barron was the senior officer of the U.S. Navy.

• The major collection of papers of James and Samuel Barron is in the Earl Gregg Swem Library at the College of William and Mary in Williamsburg, Va. William Oliver Stevens, *An Affair of Honor: The Biography of Commodore James Barron, U.S.N.* (1969), is the only extant biography. See also W. M. P. Dunne, "Pistols and Honor: The James Barron–Stephen Decatur Conflict, 1798–1807," *American Neptune* 50, no. 4 (1990): 245–59, for an account of those officers' early acquaintance and some possible reasons for their subsequent quarrel. For a modern assessment of the duel itself and the incidents leading up to it, see David F. Long, "William Bainbridge and the Barron-Decatur Duel: Mere Participant or Active Plotter?" *Pennsylvania Magazine of History and Biography* 103, no. 1 (1979): 34–52, as well as Long's biography of Bainbridge, *Ready to Hazard: A Biography of Commodore William Bainbridge, 1774–1833* (1981). In addition to the published proceedings of the court-martial following the *Chesapeake-Leopard* incident, there is an extensive secondary literature.

LINDA M. MALONEY

BARRON, Jennie Loitman (12 Oct. 1891–28 Mar. 1969), suffragist, lawyer, and judge, was born in Boston, Massachusetts, the daughter of Morris Loitman, a needle trades worker and later an insurance agent, and Fannie Castelman, a needle trades worker. From her Russian immigrant parents, Jennie Loitman learned the value of education. She graduated from grammar school at age twelve and from Boston's Girls High School at age fifteen. While in high school she worked as an after school "hand" in a shoe factory. She taught Americanization classes in the evening and sold copies of William Shakespeare's works door to door to pay her way through Boston University, where she received three degrees, an A.B. in 1911, an LL.B. in 1913, and an LL.M. in 1914.

While attending Boston University, Barron organized the student Women's Suffrage Association and became its first president. She was a sought-after speaker on suffrage and other issues of women's rights throughout the region. After suffrage was achieved, she became active in the League of Women Voters and began a twenty-year campaign to enable women to serve on Massachusetts juries.

Upon admission to the bar in 1914, Barron entered private law practice. In 1918 she married Samuel Barron, Jr., beginning a long personal and professional partnership. The couple maintained a joint law practice until Jennie Barron was appointed to the bench.

In 1925 Jennie Barron ran successfully for the Boston School Committee. Her campaign stressed her experience as a mother, a teacher, and a lawyer and urged voters to "Put a Mother on the School Committee." She became the first woman to serve on that body in over twenty years. In 1927 she was elected treasurer by her colleagues. As a member of the school committee she was best known for her campaign for adequate facilities to accommodate Boston's school-age population. She was also an advocate for women and girls, urging equal pay for female teachers, appointment of a female Yiddish-speaking attendance officer, maintaining the position of "girls' adviser," and building a modern, adequately-sized Girls High School. She surprised many observers in 1929 when she declined to run for reelection, citing the demands of her law practice.

Barron's career was marked by an impressive array of firsts. In 1929 she became the first woman appointed a master in civil litigation by the Massachusetts Superior Court. During 1934–1935 she served as assistant attorney general. In this capacity she became the first woman to present a case before a Massachusetts grand jury as well as the first woman to prosecute major criminal cases. She was credited with recovering several million dollars owed the state from estates.

In 1934 Barron was appointed a special, part-time justice in the district court system, where she became known for her expertise on the law. When she was appointed to the municipal court in 1937, she became the first full-time woman judge in Massachusetts. Judge Barron presided in municipal court for over twenty years, until she was elevated to the superior court in 1959, where she served until her death.

During her career on the bench, Barron was known in Boston as the "judge with a heart." Her courtroom ran more slowly than those of other judges because she took time to understand the parties and their disputes. Barron referred to her court as a clinic and believed that "judges should be social engineers as well as scholars and judges" (*Boston Daily Globe*, 5 Feb. 1959). In criminal cases she was known for her innovative sentencing, requiring community service or counseling in conjunction with probation rather than a jail sentence. In civil cases, she was known for facilitating settlements. "To me, the most satisfying disposition of a case is to see people understand each other and iron out their difficulties mutually," she told one interviewer (*Boston Sunday Globe*, 14 Dec. 1947). Her special interests on the bench were domestic relations and juvenile delinquency.

In 1955 Barron was the only woman among the seventeen-member U.S. delegation to the first United Nations Conference on Crime. At the conference she argued that juvenile delinquency resulted from a lack of the three A's—affection, approval, and acceptance—and advocated better-staffed juvenile courts and programs to educate young people for their roles as parents.

Throughout her life Barron saw her family as central. She had three daughters and seven grandchildren. Upon being named National Mother of the Year in 1959, she remarked, "All the rest in life are 'fringe benefits,' in relation to family, children and grandchildren" (*Providence Evening Bulletin*, 5 May 1959). She frequently said that her most important degree was the one she received from her husband, Mrs., and credited her success to her cooperative husband.

In addition to her professional endeavors, Barron was active in several civic and philanthropic organizations, including American Jewish Congress, Beth Israel Hospital Women's Auxiliary, Hadassah, Massachusetts Association of Women Lawyers, and the National Conference of Christians and Jews. Her hobbies included public speaking and travel. The Barrons visited all five continents, often serving as informal goodwill ambassadors for the United States.

Barron was a path breaker in many respects. When she graduated from law school, women could neither vote nor serve on juries. She demonstrated by her accomplishments as well as by her words that civic life would be enriched by women's contributions. At the same time she reminded men and women that their family responsibilities were primary. She seemed to view her role as a judge as an extension of her maternal role, teaching appropriate behavior to those who for some reason failed to learn it earlier in life. She died in Boston.

• Barron's papers are at the Schlesinger Library of Radcliffe College and include some correspondence; newspaper clippings; texts of some of her speeches; and a copy of the League of Women Voters pamphlet, "Jury Service for Women," that she wrote. The Communications Library at Boston University has newspaper clipping files. An article on Barron by Polly Welts Kaufman in *Notable American Women of the Modern Period* (1980) contains information about Barron's parents and early life not available elsewhere. See also "Mother Is a Judge," *National Business Woman*, Aug. 1959, pp. 4–5, 29. An obituary is in the *Boston Globe*, 28 Mar. 1969.

JILDA M. ALIOTTA

BARROW, Clyde Chestnut (24 Mar. 1909–23 May 1934), and **Bonnie Parker** (1 Oct. 1910–23 May 1934), bandits known as Bonnie and Clyde, were born, respectively, in Teleco and Rowena, Texas. Clyde was the son of Henry Barrow and Cummie (maiden name unknown), farmers; Bonnie, the daughter of Charles Parker, a brick mason, and Emma (maiden name unknown). One of eight children, Clyde Barrow grew up in extreme poverty. His parents were tenant farmers until 1921, when they moved to the Dallas area, where neither his mother nor his illiterate father managed to significantly improve the family's prospects. Never a devoted student, Clyde quit school at age sixteen and followed his older brother Ivan "Buck" Barrow into delinquency and petty theft. In 1926 the two were arrested when a police officer observed a flock of stolen turkeys jumping about in the back seat of their automobile. Buck claimed full responsibility and served several days in jail; Clyde was released. By 1929 Clyde and Buck were robbing filling stations and cafés around Dallas. That year Buck was sentenced to four years in the Huntsville State Prison for burglary, and Clyde received a suspended sentence for car theft.

In January 1930 Clyde met Bonnie Parker, probably at the home of a mutual friend in Dallas. Her father's death in 1914 had brought difficult times for Bonnie, her mother, and her two siblings, but nevertheless as a young girl she was a successful student, winning prizes for essays, spelling, and recitation. At the age of sixteen she married Roy Thornton. They lived together only sporadically and separated permanently after he received a five-year prison sentence for robbery in 1929. Her 13 January 1928 diary entry summed up her dissatisfaction with a life she saw as dull and empty: "Sure am blue. Everything has gone wrong today. Why don't something happen. What a life!" Bonnie, as she later put it, was "bored crapless."

Clyde represented deliverance to Bonnie, and the two moved into a small furnished room in Dallas. Within a few months police arrested Clyde for the robbery of a Waco grocery; he was convicted of robbery and sentenced to two years in the Waco jail. In early March 1930 he escaped with the aid of a pistol probably smuggled in by Bonnie. Soon recaptured, Clyde was sent to the notorious Eastham Prison Farm. Paroled on 8 February 1932, he reportedly vowed, "I'll die before I ever go back into a place like that." Later that month he wrecked a stolen car while being chased by police after the burglary of a Kaufman, Texas, hardware store. He escaped, but Bonnie was caught and spent three months in jail before being released on

the basis of insufficient evidence. In the intervening months Clyde committed a number of armed robberies, several accompanied by Ray Hamilton, an acquaintance from his childhood gang. In a Hillsboro, Texas, jewelry store holdup Clyde or an accomplice killed the proprietor. In July he and Hamilton killed a sheriff and his deputy outside a barn dance in Atoka, Oklahoma.

Exploits of the late summer and fall of 1932 brought Bonnie and Clyde, now reunited, national notoriety. In Carlsbad, New Mexico, they took captive a local sheriff who had begun investigating their stolen car. In what would become a pattern, they abused him verbally, locked him in his own handcuffs, and took him for a long ride before releasing him frightened but otherwise unharmed. "Tell your people that we ain't a bunch of nutty killers, sheriff," Clyde reportedly told him, "just down home people tryin' to get through this damned Depression with a few bones." October raids on a bank and the National Guard armory in Abilene, Texas, were widely attributed to the gang. During a grocery store robbery in Sherman, Texas, Clyde killed the resistant proprietor.

That December, Clyde killed a Temple, Texas, man who attempted to stop the gang from stealing his Ford. In January he killed a Dallas deputy sheriff. Shortly thereafter the gang took as a hostage a Missouri state trooper who had pulled them over for a traffic violation. When the gang dropped him off a hundred miles away, unharmed, Bonnie advised him, he told reporters, to find a "new line of work where you won't meet such dangerous people as us."

In March 1933 the gang was joined by Clyde's brother Buck, on parole, and his wife, Blanche. Their reunion turned violent on 13 April when Joplin, Missouri, police, acting on a tip, raided their apartment. Two detectives were killed during a fierce shoot-out, and the gang careened away in a stolen car. Inside the hideout police discovered a large arsenal, jewelry from a recent robbery, and, more important to the gang's subsequent fame, a poem by Bonnie and two rolls of snapshots of the gang posing playfully with a variety of menacing weapons. Among the photos was one of Bonnie holding a shotgun on a "captured" Clyde. Even more widely published in the nation's newspapers was a shot of a cigar-champing Bonnie, revolver in hand, leaning casually on one of the gang's stolen cars. (Later, oddly regretful about this particular violation of conventional propriety, Bonnie told a captive to "tell the public that I don't smoke cigars. It's the bunk.")

Bonnie's poem, "Suicide Sal," the tale of a heroic outlaw woman, was widely published in the nation's press, after which she responded with more verse, which she mailed to several newspapers:

You have heard the story of Jesse James,
Of how he lived and died.
If you are still in need of something to read,
Here's the story of Bonnie and Clyde.

Her epic managed to be at once boastful:

> . . . those who squeal
> Are usually found dying or dead.

self-justifying:

> If they try to act like citizens,
> And rent them a nice little flat,
> About the third night they are invited to fight,
> By a submachine gun, rat-tat-tat.

and mawkish:

> Some day they will go down together,
> And they will bury them side by side.
> To a few it means grief,
> To the law it's relief,
> But it's death to Bonnie and Clyde.

Literary abilities notwithstanding, Bonnie and Clyde had become celebrity criminals of the first order.

Adding to the gang's notoriety was yet another hostage exploit in late April 1933. A Ruston, Louisiana, undertaker attempted to prevent Clyde from stealing his new Chevrolet. The gang took the undertaker and his girlfriend captive, driving them for several hours into Arkansas. After Bonnie learned his occupation, the man later told reporters, she said to him, "When the law catches us, you can fix us up."

Fame intensified the gang's encounters with law enforcement. Clyde, Buck, or William Daniel Jones killed the Alma, Texas, town marshal while he was pursuing the gang after the robbery of a local bank. Shortly thereafter, in July, a posse of about a dozen men surrounded the gang in a Platte City, Missouri, cabin camp. A barrage of fire enabled the gang to make its escape. Buck Barrow, however, was seriously wounded by a gunshot to the head, and most of the others received minor injuries. The gang was soon sighted near Dexter, Iowa, and a force of lawmen, a National Guard unit, and vigilantes, numbering about one hundred, converged on the gang in a deserted amusement park. Bonnie and Clyde escaped a withering fusillade, but Buck was mortally wounded and Blanche taken into custody.

On 16 January 1934 the gang was believed to have aided the escape of Ray Hamilton, Henry Methvin, and several other convicts from the Eastham Prison Farm. Bonnie and Clyde, now the most notorious and sought-after fugitives in the country, eluded a force of hundreds of lawmen and vigilantes near Muskogee, Oklahoma, in February. Reacting to the death of a guard wounded at Eastham, prominent Texans called for drastic measures. Lawmen received considerable support in their call for a $2,500 "Wanted Dead" reward to be posted for the two; Clyde in particular was considered a "mad dog" who deserved no better. More moderate voices prevailed, however, and a $2,500 "Dead or Alive" poster was issued.

In February 1934 the head of the Texas prison system hired Frank Hamer, a former Texas Ranger with a reputation for ruthless efficiency, to hunt the pair down. His manhunt came to fruition on 23 May. Methvin, seeking immunity from prosecution, aided Hamer in setting up a trap along a road near Gibsland, Louisiana. When Bonnie and Clyde arrived at the site, Hamer and his five-man posse poured 167 rounds of ammunition into their vehicle, killing the pair instantly.

A penchant for killing—especially lawmen—and a flair for appealing to the emotions of working people contributed to the notoriety of Clyde Barrow and Bonnie Parker far more than their monetary gain: their largest haul was probably less than $1,500. Americans had long been both appalled and enthralled by outlaws, and Bonnie and Clyde fascinated a public tuned into the mass media and the new culture of celebrity. Their deeds and words—in addition to Bonnie's poetry, Clyde reportedly wrote a famous testimonial to Henry Ford extolling the virtues of the Ford V-8 for people in his "business"—captured the public imagination as effectively as the public relations campaign of any Hollywood star. Americans were fascinated by the shattering of conventional gender rules personified by Bonnie—a petite, attractive, fashionable blonde who robbed banks, was photographed smoking cigars, and had a man's name tattooed on her thigh. Moreover, the deep depression of the early 1930s undoubtedly contributed to the seductiveness of a pair of young lovers who defied the powerful forces of a hostile world.

• E. R. Milner, *The Lives and Times of Bonnie and Clyde* (1996), is the most reliable biography. David E. Ruth, *Inventing the Public Enemy: The Gangster in American Culture, 1918–1934* (1996), explores the values promoted in mass media portrayals. The duo's ambush was widely reported in the press.

DAVID E. RUTH

BARROW, Edward Grant (10 May 1868–15 Dec. 1953), baseball executive, was born in Springfield, Illinois, the son of John Barrow, a grain dealer, farmer, and Civil War veteran, and Effie Ann Vinson-Heller. Heading west to take advantage of the Homestead Act's land grant to veterans, the family settled in Nebraska when Barrow was two. But they ultimately settled in 1877 outside Des Moines, Iowa.

In 1884 Barrow quit high school because of his father's illness and took a job as a clerk on a local newspaper where in various capacities (including advertising manager) he worked for the next six years. As supervisor of newsboys, Barrow hired Fred Clarke, whom he was to call his "first baseball discovery." Clarke went on to a Hall of Fame career as a player and manager. Barrow was a star athlete, showing excellent skill as both a boxer and a baseball pitcher, but he hurt his arm while still a teenager and never played or boxed professionally. Also an aficionado of the stage, Barrow often covered sporting and theatrical events for newspapers.

In 1890 Barrow moved to Pittsburgh with his brother Frank with the hope of making a living selling soap. "We figured Pittsburgh was a place that needed a lot of cleaning up," Barrow wrote in his memoirs, *My Fifty Years In Baseball* (1951). Although the business did not succeed, Barrow found a job as the assistant manager of the Staley Hotel. Clientele from the sporting and theatrical communities frequented the Pittsburgh hotel, and Barrow made many friends, among them the concessionaire Harry M. Stevens. Stevens offered Barrow a partnership in his growing national food, drink, and game program business, but in a move that Barrow often regretted financially, he turned down Stevens and chose to start a career as a minor league baseball manager.

In his first season, 1895, Barrow won a pennant in Wheeling, West Virginia. In 1896 he managed the Paterson, New Jersey, team in the Atlantic League and also signed that year for Paterson Honus Wagner, the future Hall of Fame shortstop whom Barrow considered "the greatest all-around ballplayer who ever lived." On the Fourth of July 1896, Barrow brought his Paterson team to play a night game in Wilmington, Delaware.

From 1897 until 1899 Barrow served as president of the Atlantic League, where, to build attendance, he approved such crowd-pleasing attractions as hiring a woman pitcher and utilizing heavyweight champions John L. Sullivan and James J. Corbett as an umpire and first baseman, respectively. "I did many things I never would have done in later years," Barrow wrote.

At the turn of the century, Barrow had a chance to invest in vaudeville, but he turned it down. Instead, he became manager and quarter-owner of the Toronto franchise in the Eastern League. His team won the pennant in 1902, and then in 1903 Barrow managed Detroit in the newly established American League. Because of front office interference, he resigned during the 1904 season and piloted Montreal in the Eastern League for the rest of the year. In 1905 he was manager for Indianapolis in the American Association, and he managed Toronto again in 1906, after which he left baseball to run a Toronto hotel for the next three years.

Barrow's first wife, Alice Calhoun, whom he had married in 1898, died in 1910. Two years later he married Frances "Fannie" Taylor, with whom he had one child.

In 1910 Barrow returned to baseball as field manager of Montreal. In December of that year, the team owners elected him league president, where he served with distinction through 1917. He presided over many improvements in the league, including a name change to the International League, the raising of the league's status within organized baseball to a Double-A classification, and the growth in respect for and professionalism of the umpiring staff.

Barrow's greatest challenge came during the 1914 and 1915 seasons when the Federal League, attempting to establish itself as a third major league, signed many International League players and competed directly for fans in such International League cities as Baltimore and Newark. Of the competition, Barrow wrote: "It was a baseball war that was every bit as damaging, if not more so, than the shooting kind." After the 1915 season, the Federal League disbanded, and the International League survived. "I never took a

player who had jumped back into the International League," Barrow wrote. "No Federal Leaguer ever got an inch of International League territory or one cent of International League money."

After the 1917 season Barrow spurned a salary cut and resigned as International League president, but he quickly found work as field manager of the Boston Red Sox. In 1918 the Red Sox won the pennant and the World Series, and Barrow became especially proud of having the distinction of being the only front office executive to win a World Series as a field manager. In 1919, at the urging of Harry Hooper, his star outfielder and team captain, Barrow shifted Babe Ruth, an outstanding southpaw pitcher, to a permanent role as an everyday outfielder.

After the 1920 season Barrow was hired as business manager (a position later called general manager) of the New York Yankees. The team was a divided franchise whose co-owners, Colonels Jacob Ruppert and Tillinghast "Cap" Huston, never agreed on anything. For the next quarter-century Barrow would oversee the greatest baseball dynasty in history. The Yankees would win fourteen pennants and ten World Series championships under him, including consecutive pennants from 1921–1923, 1926–1928, 1936–1939 (also winning four consecutive World Series in this span), and 1941–1943.

Barrow acted decisively. He forbade squabbling co-owners Ruppert and Huston from going into the clubhouse to berate the manager and players after a loss. Barrow brought Paul Krichell with him from Boston, a coach and former player who became an invaluable talent scout, discovering Lou Gehrig, among other stars. Barrow supervised the construction of Yankee Stadium, which opened in 1923, the year that the Yankees won their first World Series. That same year Barrow arranged for a loan from his friend, Stevens, that helped to buy out Colonel Huston and made Colonel Ruppert the sole owner until his death in 1939, at which time Barrow became the Yankees' president as well as general manager.

Ruppert gave Barrow complete control over baseball matters. Barrow inherited Miller Huggins as field manager and supported him fully until Huggins's premature death in 1929. When Huggins in 1925 fined Babe Ruth $5,000 for insubordination, Barrow said, "Don't back down." When Ruth suggested that he should be named manager, Barrow uttered a famous retort, "He can't manage himself."

Barrow brought in Joe McCarthy to manage the Yankees in 1931, and during McCarthy's sixteen-year tenure, Barrow came to consider him the best manager in baseball history. In his memoirs he praised McCarthy's axiom: "Temperament—or disposition—is the most important thing in baseball." In 1932 Barrow hired George M. Weiss, a veteran minor league operator, as farm director of the Yankees, and for the next twenty-five years and more, the Yankee farm system was second to none in feeding talent to the parent club.

Nicknamed "Cousin Ed" by most ballplayers, Barrow shunned the spotlight, preferring that the players get newspaper headlines. But behind closed doors he made players, stars and journeymen alike, know who was boss. Before Gehrig's fatal illness was diagnosed, he told the first baseman to begin to look for other work. He effectively withstood young star Joe DiMaggio's salary demands, often using the press to label DiMaggio as an ingrate.

In 1945 Barrow resigned as Yankee president and was named chairman of the board by Larry MacPhail, the new owner of the Yankees who, unlike Barrow, craved publicity. At MacPhail's urging, Barrow reluctantly introduced night baseball to Yankee Stadium. In 1947 Barrow gave up all links to the franchise. Considering himself too old to accept a feeler to become commissioner of baseball, he went into retirement in Port Chester, north of New York City. He died in Rye, New York. In the summer before his death, he was enshrined in the Baseball Hall of Fame.

Although he was the embodiment of baseball's establishment, he did bring in such innovations as allowing fans to keep foul balls, which he recommended in Boston in 1918, and placing numbers on the backs of players' uniforms in New York, which he introduced to the Yankees in 1929. During Barrow's New York regime, such phrases as "Murderer's Row" and "Break Up the Yankees!" became familiar to millions of Americans. "Next to Ban Johnson, founder of the American League," the *Sporting News* eulogized, "Barrow was the most vital non-playing figure in the history of the game."

• There is a Barrow file in the National Baseball Library at Cooperstown, N.Y., but there is no known repository of Barrow papers. Barrow's autobiography, *My Fifty Years in Baseball*, contains entertaining, pertinent stories, and although a memoir, it refreshingly lacks the usual self-serving tone. A valuable source for descriptions of Barrow and his early bosses with the Yankees, Colonels Huston and Ruppert, is Frank Graham, *The New York Yankees: An Informal History* (1961). For Barrow's longtime relationship with Babe Ruth, the valuable sources are Robert Creamer, *The Babe: The Legend Comes to Life* (1974); Lawrence Ritter and Mark Rucker, *The Babe: A Life in Pictures* (1988); and Marshall Smelser, *The Life That Ruth Built* (1975). For Barrow's dealings with other Yankee stars, see Ray Robinson, *Iron Horse: Lou Gehrig in His Time* (1990), and Jack B. Moore, *Joe DiMaggio: A Bio-Bibliography* (1986). The story of Barrow's participation in the 1896 night baseball game is told in Michael Gershman, *Diamonds: The Evolution of the Ballpark* (1993).

LEE LOWENFISH

BARROWS, Isabel (17 Apr. 1845–25 Oct. 1913), ophthalmologist, stenographer, and reformer, was born Katharine Isabel Hayes in Irasburg, Vermont, the daughter of Scottish immigrants Henry Hayes, a physician, and Anna Gibb, a schoolteacher. The family moved to Hartland and then Derry, New Hampshire, where Isabel Hayes graduated from Adams Academy. In 1863 she married William Wilberforce Chapin, a Congregational minister. The following year the couple traveled to India for a missionary assignment. Less

than a year after arriving in India, William Chapin died of diphtheria. Six months later Isabel Chapin returned to the United States. She moved to Dansville, New York, where she worked as a bath assistant at a water-cure sanatorium.

In 1866 she became engaged to Samuel June Barrows and moved with him to New York City, where she studied medicine and he worked as a stenographer for several newspapers. After their marriage in 1867, Isabel Barrows devoted several months to studying shorthand. In the fall of 1867 the couple moved to Washington, D.C., where Samuel Barrows worked as a stenographic secretary for Secretary of State William H. Seward. The following summer Isabel filled in for her husband for several weeks when Samuel was ill, becoming the first woman to work for the State Department.

In 1869 Isabel Barrows moved back to New York City to enroll in the new Woman's Medical College of the New York Infirmary for Women and Children while her husband remained at his job in Washington. Later that year she traveled to Austria to study ophthalmic surgery for a year at the University of Vienna. In 1869 Barrows returned to Washington, D.C., where she began a private practice and taught ophthalmology at the School of Medicine of Howard University in Washington, D.C. She also resumed her work as a stenographer, becoming the first woman to work in that capacity for congressional committees.

In 1873 Isabel Barrows discontinued her medical practice, teaching duties, and stenographic work and moved to Cambridge, Massachusetts, to join her husband, who had entered Harvard Divinity School. Shortly thereafter the couple had a daughter. In 1875 the family traveled to Leipzig, Germany, where Isabel Barrows studied Italian, French, and German and Samuel Barrows studied music and political economy. After a year in Germany they moved to Dorchester, Massachusetts, where Samuel Barrows became pastor of Meeting House Hill, the oldest Unitarian congregation in the state (the couple had become Unitarians in 1871). In 1880 he became editor of the Unitarian weekly *Christian Register*, a position he held for sixteen years. During this time Isabel Barrows assisted her husband in various editorial tasks at the newspaper's Boston office and worked in various social reform organizations. From the late 1880s to the early 1900s she served as a stenographer and editor for the National Conference of Charities and Correction, the National Prison Association, and for various conferences on social reform.

In 1896 Samuel Barrows was elected to Congress as a Republican but was subsequently defeated for reelection. He then took the position of secretary of the Prison Association of New York. In 1900 the couple moved to Staten Island, New York. Isabel Barrows continued to be active in prison reform and other "progressive" activities and in 1909 traveled to St. Petersburg to plead for the release of Catherine Breshkovsky, an imprisoned Russian revolutionary. While she was in St. Petersburg her husband died. A month after returning to New York for the funeral, Barrows traveled again to Russia to resume her work on behalf of Breshkovsky and then to Paris to take her husband's seat at the International Prison Congress. For the rest of her life she wrote and organized conferences on prison reform and various international issues. Barrows died in Croton-on-Hudson, New York.

A woman of remarkable accomplishments, Barrows combined pioneering careers in ophthalmology and stenography with substantial contributions to the reform movements of the Progressive Era.

• Madeleine B. Stern, *So Much in a Lifetime: The Story of Dr. Isabel Barrows* (1964), is a comprehensive biography, while an abbreviated version can be found in Stern's *We the Women* (1963).

THADDEUS RUSSELL

BARROWS, John Henry (11 July 1847–3 June 1902), minister and college president, was born near Medina, Michigan, the son of John Manning Barrows, a Congregational minister and college professor, and Bertha Anthony Butler, a teacher. He was educated by his parents and in the preparatory department of newly opened Olivet College, where his father became professor of natural science in 1860. Barrows graduated from the college in 1867 and with his brother Walter spent 1867–1868 at Yale Divinity School and the following year at Union Theological Seminary. His brother's ill health then forced them to leave school and join their family in Osage County, Kansas.

Barrows supplied local pulpits, wrote for area newspapers, and served for a year as county superintendent of schools. After another year as acting pastor of First Congregational Church, Springfield, Illinois, Barrows left in the spring of 1873 for a yearlong tour of Europe. On his return he entered Andover Theological Seminary but departed after 1874–1875 without graduating. He was ordained and installed as pastor of Eliot Congregational Church in Lawrence, Massachusetts, on 29 April 1875 and on 6 May married Sarah Eleanor Mole of Williamstown, Massachusetts, whom he had met on board ship two years earlier. The couple had five children. After briefly serving Maverick Congregational Church in East Boston in 1880, Barrows entered his last and most prestigious pastorate, Chicago's First Presbyterian Church (1881–1896). (Congregationalists and Presbyterians shared a common Reformed heritage, and both clergy and laity have moved easily between the two denominations since the colonial period.)

Having by this time become a liberal Presbyterian, Barrows was involved in various local theological controversies with the conservative party of that denomination. Always impressed by the oratory of Wendell Phillips and Henry Ward Beecher, Barrows himself became a popular preacher and well-known public figure in the Chicago area. In 1889 he joined the World's Congress Auxiliary of the World's Columbian Exposition. Organized by lawyer and Swedenborgian layman Charles Carroll Bonney, the auxiliary was authorized by the corporation managing the upcoming Chicago's world's fair to organize a series of international conventions to complement the technologically oriented displays of the exposition itself. Bonney appointed Barrows chair of the auxiliary's department of religion, a local committee comprising ministers from fourteen Protestant denominations, a Reformed rabbi, and the Roman Catholic archbishop. Among the denominational and other religious congresses sponsored by Barrows's department was a seventeen-day capstone event bringing together representatives of all the major religions that Barrows, drawing on Tennyson's phrase "the parliament of man," called a "parliament of religions." Contemporary observers believed that Barrows's leadership in planning (1890–1893) and chairing the World's Parliament of Religions (11–27 Sept. 1893) contributed significantly to its success.

The parliament featured 216 presentations from scholars or representatives of all of the world's major religions and many of the varying traditions within them. Although two-thirds of the speakers represented Protestant Christianity and many of them reflected the assumptions of the culturally dominant American Protestant mainstream, the parliament nonetheless exposed its American audiences to an unprecedented spectrum of beliefs and practices. Not only were Catholicism and Judaism—with Protestantism the major American religious traditions of the twentieth century—well represented, but the forty-one confident and unapologetic presentations by Asians, among the most widely reported events of the exposition, pointed toward the increasing religious diversity that would characterize the United States in the twentieth century.

Barrows's involvement in the parliament shifted his interest from the Protestant pastorate to the encounter of religions with each other, and this shift transformed him into a new kind of liberal Protestant exponent of Christian evangelism. While avoiding the denigration of other religions and cultures that he thought was typical of earlier foreign missionaries, Barrows presented to a popular audience a view of modern Protestantism as the final form of all religion but in the context of an inter-religious discussion that he believed would allow Protestantism to express itself in new ways and to expand in new places.

In 1894 Caroline E. Haskell, a member of Barrows's church, made major gifts to the University of Chicago to create there the Haskell Lectureship on Comparative Religion and the Haskell Oriental Museum, and the Barrows Lectureship on the Relations of Christianity and the Other Religions, the last to be given in India. Barrows was appointed professorial lecturer in comparative religion at the university in 1893 and held the position until his death, giving the Haskell lectures seven times between 1895 and 1901. He was thus an early, if marginal, participant in one of the pioneer programs in the study of world religions as well as a popular advocate of using the academic approach for evangelistic purposes.

The encounter of world religions was now Barrows's central interest, while many in his congregation felt that First Church needed the pastor's full attention. The church declined to grant him a leave of absence in order to deliver the first Barrows lectures in India, and they parted amicably in February 1896 when Barrows resigned his position. He spent much of 1896 preparing his lectures in Göttingen, Germany, and five months delivering them in India, Sri Lanka, and Japan from December 1896 to April 1897. After his return he preached and lectured widely on missions in India and on comparative religion—including the Morse lectures at Union Theological Seminary and a Dudleian lecture at Harvard Divinity School—and published *Christianity, the World Religion* (1897), *A World Pilgrimage* (1897), and *The Christian Conquest of Asia* (1899).

In November 1898 the trustees of Oberlin College, looking for a public figure with an academic reputation, administrative experience, and widespread personal contacts, persuaded Barrows to accept the presidency of the college at which his parents had met and been educated. Leaving academic matters to the faculty, and condoning the continuing liberalization and secularization of campus life, Barrows spent three and a half years promoting the Oberlin tradition to the public and potential donors. He presented the needs of the college as energetically as he had championed the World's Parliament of Religions and the expansion of Christianity. The half-million-dollar goal of his successful 1899 endowment campaign (which elicited gifts from Mrs. Haskell and the Rockefellers) became the standard for Oberlin fundraising in the twentieth century. Barrows set the stage for the revitalization and modernization of Oberlin during the 25-year term of its next president, mathematics professor and liberal theologian Henry Churchill King.

After a speaking tour in California and Chicago, Barrows contracted pneumonia in May 1902 while returning home from the Presbyterian General Assembly meeting in New York. He died in Oberlin several weeks later, a month before his fifty-fifth birthday.

• Papers by and about Barrows dating from 1889 to 1905 are in the Oberlin College Archives. Mary Eleanor Barrows published a full-length biography of her father, *John Henry Barrows: A Memoir* (1904), which includes extensive quotations from Barrows's sermons, lectures, publications, and personal papers. Another significant treatment of Barrows is the *Dictionary of American Biography* article by Shailer Mathews, prominent liberal theologian and dean of the University of Chicago Divinity School.

The two volumes of World's Parliament proceedings that Barrows edited and published immediately after the event, *The World's Parliament of Religions: An Illustrated and Popular History of the World's Parliament of Religions, Held in Chicago in Connection with the World's Columbian Exposition* (1893), constitute the "official" record of the parliament. Selections from that have been reprinted in *The Dawn of Religious Pluralism: Voices from the World's Parliament of Religion, 1893*, ed. Richard Hughes Seager (1993). On the historiography and significance of the parliament, see Seager, "Pluralism and the American Mainstream: The View from the World's

Parliament of Religion," *Harvard Theological Review* 82, no. 3 (1989): 301–24.

Barrows's other publications include *Spiritual Forces in American History* (1889), *Henry Ward Beecher, the Shakespeare of the American Pulpit* (1893), and *The Ideals of Christian Education: The Argument for the Christian College* (1899). The last of those represents his advocacy of Oberlin, and his presidency there is described in Donald M. Love, *Henry Churchill King of Oberlin* (1956), and John Barnard, *From Evangelicalism to Progressivism at Oberlin College, 1866–1917* (1969).

ROBERT A. SCHNEIDER

BARROWS, Samuel June (26 May 1845–21 Apr. 1909), minister, reformer, and editor, was born in New York City, the son of Richard Barrows, a printer, and Jane Weekes. He was four when his father died and nine when his mother asked her husband's cousin, printing-press innovator Richard Hoe, to give her son a job. The boy worked for Hoe as a messenger and telegrapher until he was eighteen, by which time he had taught himself shorthand. During the Civil War, rejected by the navy because of poor health, he worked for several organizations as a stenographer before going to a Hydropathic Sanitarium in Dansville, New York. In return for treatment, he served as secretary to the manager, Dr. James C. Jackson. There he met his future wife, the recently widowed Isabel Hayes Chapin, a young medical student. The Barrowses were married in Brooklyn by Henry Ward Beecher in 1867.

They had one daughter. While Barrows labored first as a reporter for the *New York Tribune* and then as private secretary to Secretary of State William H. Seward in Washington, D.C., his wife completed her medical studies in New York and, for a year, in Vienna. Barrows continued his formal education at Hoe's employee night school, at Cooper Union, and at Columbian University in Washington. Raised a devout Baptist, Barrows discovered the writings of Theodore Parker and William Ellery Channing in Washington libraries and embraced Unitarianism.

In 1871 Barrows moved to Cambridge, Massachusetts, to attend Harvard Divinity School, while Isabel treated diseases of the eyes at Freedman's Hospital and carried a small private practice in Washington, D.C. During the summers of 1873 and 1874, he rode with Generals David S. Stanley and George A. Custer in Montana and the Dakotas on *Tribune* assignments. After completing his studies and spending a year with his wife in Leipzig (1875–1876), Barrows accepted a call from the First Parish of Dorchester, Massachusetts. Four years later he was appointed editor of the Unitarian weekly, the *Christian Register*. With his telegraphy, shorthand, and reportorial skills and his experience from 1877 to 1880 reviewing foreign periodical literature for the *Unitarian Review and Religion Magazine*, he was ideally suited for the job.

In Barrows's sixteen years as editor, the weekly improved its format, enlarged its readership, and engaged in lively debate on almost all religious and reform fronts. Barrows fought strenuously for civil service, rejoicing with the passage of the initial law and defending its efficacy. Patronage appointees, he told Congress in 1898, did "not expect to support the Government. . . . They expected the Government to support them."

The cause of Native Americans was also close to Barrows's heart; the Barrowses included a young Indian boy in their family for several years before he died of tuberculosis. Barrows believed that Indians should leave their reservations and be exposed to white civilization in order, he wrote in 1890, "to be assimilated." He visited and wrote about Indian schools at Hampton, Virginia, and Carlisle, Pennsylvania, and, in Congress, served on the Indian Affairs committee. "Let the Indians take up their home among white people," he urged in 1898.

Barrows consistently advanced the rights of women in the home, in the factory, as delegates to the American Unitarian Association, and in business. He supported the Harvard Annex, a precursor to Radcliffe College, as "opening a side door to the University." At some future time, he speculated in 1884, "girls may enter the *front* door," like the boys. He took issue with Francis Parkman's attack on woman suffrage, calling the prohibition an "actual injustice . . . that most demands redress." Women should be permitted to "fulfill their duties toward the State" as they do in the home and the church. A total abstainer, Barrows enthusiastically supported the temperance movement in his weekly and other periodicals; a prohibition "that public sentiment does not sustain," he wrote prophetically in 1883, is like "a musket without a soldier." His 1908 series in the *Outlook* made him "a formidable figure in the new discussion" of that issue, a friend observed after his death.

Well before Booker T. Washington received national recognition for promoting vocational education for African Americans, Barrows was corresponding with him. "I believe in you and your work," he wrote in January 1891 and began raising money for Tuskegee Institute, hiring an African-American "typewriter" to handle the "Tuskegee department" of his paper. Barrows's paternalistic interest in the welfare and education of blacks predated and outlasted his tenure as editor.

Barrows resigned his editorial post after he was elected to the House of Representatives in 1896 from the tenth district of Massachusetts. His one term in Congress was a rear-guard action against tariffs on Greek currants and on foreign books and works of art, and for famine relief in India and the movement of Native Americans off their reservations. His articulate speeches and light humor drew applause and laughter, but this was not enough for a Republican to win a second term in a highly Democratic district.

After the Senate rejected Barrows as President William McKinley's nominee for librarian of Congress, Barrows dedicated the last decade of his life to prison reform. As the corresponding secretary of the New York State Prison Association, he became, according to the *New York Times*, "a penologist of world-wide fame" (28 May 1909). Drawing on almost twenty years of active interest in prisons, he shook off the organization's debt-ridden lethargy and shaped a positive national force for prison reform. His annual reports were models of clarity and persuasion, reflecting data and perceptions collated during his peregrinations to Albany as well as to Washington, prisons all over the country, and Europe. With some success he promoted the adoption of parole, probation, indeterminate sentences, civil service for prison employees, and better prison structures. As the U.S. representative to the International Prison Conference from 1895, he interacted with the world community and undertook several detailed studies, which the federal government published. He was president-elect of that body when he died.

His personal life was a model of organized activity. He was a skilled artisan in metals, a composer, an organist and chorister, a poet, a student of ancient and modern Greece, a linguist in at least five languages, a frequent European traveler, a military chaplain, and a fisherman. He and his wife worked side by side at the *Register* and in other endeavors, but the pinnacle was their annual summer camping experience by Canada's Lake Memphremagog. Confident of the restorative powers of "the mountain and the sky, the forest and the sea," they wrote what was probably the first American book on family camping, *The Shaybacks in Camp: Ten Summers under Canvas* (1887).

Barrows's reputation faded quickly after his death in New York City. Except perhaps for prison improvement, no single reform bears his mark, but a host of issues owe their sustained vitality to his wise and witty observations in newspapers, periodicals, speeches, and books. Civil service, temperance, justice for minorities, rights of women and children, liberal theology, the primacy of intellectual activity, and, above all, the celebration of rational thought in society represent, a eulogist proclaimed, "the uncrowned decent living of this man[,] at once a harmony and a social force."

• The Barrows Family Papers are at Houghton Library, Harvard University. Isabel C. Barrows, *A Sunny Life: The Biography of Samuel June Barrows* (1913), includes a partial listing of his articles, books, and reports. The weekly he edited, his articles for contemporary periodicals, his books, and his reports to the U.S. Congress on prisons, crime, and the courts (S. Doc. 273, 55th Cong., 2d sess. [1899]; H. Doc. 459, 56th Cong., 1st sess. [1900]; H. Doc. 566, 56th Cong., 1st sess. [1900]; and H. Doc. 701, 58th Cong., 2d sess. [1904]) comprise a revealing corpus. The latter report (1904) focuses on children's courts and was reprinted in 1973 with an illuminating preface by James T. Curran. See also Barrows's report to the U.S. Department of State titled *New Legislation Concerning Crimes, Misdemeanors, and Penalties* (1900); and his annual reports for the New York State Prison Association. The memorial minute and eulogy in vol. 64 (1909) is detailed; the reports of Barrows's memorial service are more useful than the sketchy obituaries in the *New York Times* and the *New York Tribune*, 22 Apr., 28 May 1909. His parish ministry is briefly described in Katherine Gibbs Allen, ed., *Sketches of Some Historic Churches of Greater Boston* (1918), pp. 205–6. At least one sermon, *Light out of Darkness: A Sermon* (1879), has been published. His editorial valedictory in *Christian Register*, 1 Apr. 1897, is helpful. His books include *A Baptist Meeting House: The Staircase to the Old Faith; The Open Door to the New* (1885); *The Doom of the Majority* (1890); *The Isles and Shrines of Greece* (1898); and, with Eliot Lord and John J. D. Trenor, *The Italians in America* (1905).

LESLIE H. FISHEL, JR.

BARRUS, Clara (8 Aug. 1864–4 Apr. 1931), physician and author, was born in Port Byron, New York, the daughter of John William Barrus, a traveling salesman, and Sarah Randall, a schoolteacher. She began her education at the Port Byron Academy, where three years before her graduation she decided to become a physician. She felt women physicians were scarce and were needed to "treat modest girls who refused treatment from a man" (*A Life Unveiled*, p. 156). Barrus's father solicited a Dr. Barnard, a local physician, to serve as Barrus's preceptor for two years. She studied *Gray's Anatomy*, boxes of human bones, and recited or visited patients with Barnard on Saturdays. She graduated as class valedictorian from the academy in 1884. Her intended commencement address was to have been "What Is Woman?" which Barrus described as her "revolt against the prevailing ideas about woman's inferior place in nature and in society" (*A Life Unveiled*, p. 165). Following her instructor's request not to read this essay at commencement remained one of her life's disappointments.

To earn money for college Barrus became a "regular" teacher in the Port Byron area for two terms. She also worked with her father at the local post office before entering Boston University in 1884. While in college, several of her letters to her family describing literary events and excursions in and around Boston were published in the village paper. She received an M.D. from Boston University in 1888 and later reflected in her autobiography that during her studies "I thought then, and still think, that there is nothing in the study or practice of medicine that need make a woman less womanly. It ought rather to make her more so" (*A Life Unveiled*, p. 189). After graduation, she practiced private medicine for four years in Utica, New York. During this time, she shared an office with Dr. Susan Wyeth and lived a very frugal lifestyle. In 1893, at the urgent request of the superintendent of the Middletown State Homeopathic Hospital for the Insane in Middletown, New York, Barrus decided to enter a new field of medicine, care of the insane, for which she felt she had a "strong leaning." She served as assistant physician at Middletown Hospital until 1910. During this time Barrus also served for eighteen years as professor of psychiatry at the Women's College of New York City. Barrus authored her first medical text, *Nursing the Insane*, in 1908, and in 1912 she opened a private sanitarium in Pelham, New York. In 1914 the sanitarium closed, and she ceased her practice.

During her time in Utica, Barrus was introduced to the work of naturalist John Burroughs, who would have an important influence on her later life. The two met in 1902, and thereafter she often visited with Burroughs and his wife and others at Woodchuck Lodge in Roxbury, New York, or traveled with them to the West to visit naturalist and explorer John Muir. Barrus became a lecturer on many literary and outdoor themes, particularly on the work of Muir and Burroughs. She wrote "With John O'Birds and John O'Mountains in the Southwest" in 1910, detailing her experiences with these two great naturalists as they explored Adamana, Arizona. (It was published in *Century* 80 [Aug. 1910]: 521–28.) Her first work about Burroughs was a brochure titled *The Retreat of a Poet Naturalist* (1905). Other brochures followed, including *Our Friend John Burroughs* (1914), *John Burroughs: Boy and Man* (1920), and *My Dog Friends* (1928). Upon Burroughs's death in March 1921 and under conditions of his will, she was named his literary executor and official biographer. Subsequently, Barrus organized and directed the Burroughs Memorial Association from 1921 until 1931. She edited two essays by Burroughs, *Under the Maples* (1921) and *The Last Harvest* (1922), as well as editing *The Heart of Burroughs' Journals* (1928). She published Burroughs's official biography, *The Life and Letters of John Burroughs*, in 1926. She completed the proof sheets and index of *Whitman and Burroughs, Comrades* the week of her death. Barrus, who never married, died at the home of her sister, Katherine Johnson, in Scarsdale, New York.

Through her literary writings, lectures, and books, Barrus has unquestionably provided rich insights to John Burroughs, a great American literary naturalist. Equally, her medical writings and autobiography provide innumerable insights into her life as an intelligent, educated woman physician during a period in history when it was not popular for women to be physicians. In the introduction to her autobiography, John Burroughs alerts readers "to expect the unexpected from this demure, enigmatic creature who, though preserving her own individuality, is so like all girls of her time and race" (p. ix).

• A detailed account of Barrus's early life can be found in her autobiography *A Life Unveiled* (1922), in which the descriptions of her nineteenth-century medical schooling and early medical practice experiences are exceptional. Barrus's extensive personal correspondences to Mr. and Mrs. J. E. B. Greene are available at the Henry Ford Museum, Greenfield Village Library, Greenfield Village, Mich. Her portrait is in *The Bookman* 9 (1914): 244. Barrus's other publications include "Insanity in Young Women," *Journal of Nerve and Mental Diseases* 21 (1896): 365–78; "A Singer of the Night," *Outlook: A Family Paper* (N.Y.), 8 Aug. 1903, p. 896; and "In the Yosemite with John Muir," *Craftsman* 23 (12 Dec. 1912): 324–35. An obituary is in the *New York Times*, 5 Apr. 1931.

BARBARA A. VANBRIMMER

BARRY, John (1745?–13 Sept. 1803), shipmaster and naval officer, was born in County Wexford, Ireland. His parentage is uncertain: his father was a farmer, and his mother's maiden name was Kelly. Apprenticed on a Wexford merchantman as a cabin boy in 1755, he diligently applied himself to the naval profession. Philadelphia became his permanent home in 1760; he became a devoted patriot and successful shipmaster. On 31 October 1767 he married Mary Cleary. The union produced no children before she died in 1774. In November 1775 he relinquished command of the 200-ton *Black Prince*, which Congress had purchased from Robert Morris, to enter the service of the rebellious colonies. Renamed *Alfred*, with Barry's help it became the first ship in the Continental navy. Recognizing his potential, Congress made Barry the captain of the brig *Lexington* on 14 March 1776.

Initially assigned to safeguard colonial commerce along the mid-Atlantic coast, he departed Philadelphia on 28 March 1776. On 6 April 1776 *Lexington* engaged the British sloop *Edward* for about eighty minutes. Barry captured *Edward* near the Virginia Capes, thus achieving the first naval victory for the Americans. News of this victory greatly enhanced the rebels' morale, and in correspondence dated 11 April, John Hancock's Marine Committee lauded his "zeal and bravery." Barry distinguished himself again on 28–29 June, when he led his crew in a gallant action off Cape May that prevented a gunpowder cache from being captured by the British. By August Barry had seized two more sloops, *Lady Susan* and *Betsey*, off the Virginia coast. Congress rewarded him with command of the frigate *Effingham*, then under construction at Philadelphia.

Many unfortunate circumstances, including a shortage of supplies and the harsh winter of 1776–1777, prevented *Effingham* from being brought into action against the British. Nonetheless, Barry contributed by offering his services to General George Washington. He raised an artillery battery comprised mostly of volunteer seamen. The battery's main armaments were cannons that they removed from *Effingham*, which the unit used most notably in the battles of Trenton and Princeton, 26 December 1776 through 3 January 1777.

Barry returned to Philadelphia and assumed duties as the senior naval officer in February. While still waiting for *Effingham*'s completion, he courted Sarah Austin, and in 1777 they were married. This happy union produced no children. Anxious to harass the British, then in control of the Delaware, Barry raised a squadron of small boats and interdicted British supply lines, seizing many articles for the Continental army. Washington commended him for this campaign in a letter dated 12 March 1778, in which he recognized Barry's "glory" and "bravery." Before it was ready for sea duty, however, the *Effingham* was destroyed during the British capture of Philadelphia in September 1777, in order to prevent the British from capturing it.

In September 1778 Barry briefly commanded the frigate *Raleigh*. On 25 September HMS *Experiment* and HMS *Unicorn* intercepted *Raleigh*. The battle lasted several days, and although Barry inflicted some damage on the British vessels, he was forced to run his ship aground on Wooden Ball Island near Penobscot

Bay. A court-martial later acquitted him of any wrongdoing in taking this action, and his reputation remained untarnished.

Congress recognized Barry's fortitude on 5 September 1780 by placing its finest vessel, *Alliance*, under his charge. In February 1781 he carried Colonel John Laurens, special envoy of the Continental Congress, and Thomas Paine to L'Orient, France. Capturing the privateer *Alert* en route, Barry's frigate delivered Laurens on 30 March. The return trip was eventful. *Alliance* captured two privateers, *Mars* and *Minerva*, on 2 April, and two merchant vessels on 2 May. On 23 May Barry encountered the combined challenge of HMS *Atalanta* and *Trespassy*. Because no wind prevailed, the sloops engaged *Alliance* without fear of reprisal. During the battle shrapnel struck Barry's left shoulder. Although wounded and outmaneuvered, he refused to yield, and when the wind picked up and the weather gauge favored Barry, he was able to maneuver his ship and, eventually, capture the British ships. In the fall of 1781 Barry refitted *Alliance* and transported the Marquis de Lafayette to France. He then sailed to Havana, where he performed important service in the Caribbean. In March 1782 he was responsible for convoying much-needed gold from Cuba; although challenged by the British en route, Barry's squadron accomplished its mission. He commanded *Alliance* until the end of the war and participated in several actions, including the final naval engagement of the Revolution against HMS *Sybil* on 10 March 1783 off Cape Canaveral.

After the war, Barry helped to improve the young Republic. He championed the cause of seamen excluded from the postwar benefits afforded to soldiers and petitioned the Congress to this effect. He also helped persuade congressmen that a new federal system should replace the Articles of Confederation. In June 1787 he became the master of *Asia*, a 292-ton merchant ship, and made one profitable trip to China (17 December 1787 through 4 June 1789).

Congress created the U.S. Navy on 27 March 1794, and Barry accepted his appointment as senior captain on 1 July. On 7 August he began to superintend the construction of his frigate, *United States*, which was put to sea in July 1798, and served as his flagship of the West Indies squadron during the Quasi-War with France. Under his leadership and direction, from December 1798 through 19 April 1799, the fledgling U.S. Navy provided security for American commercial interests and displayed the emerging power of the United States in the Caribbean. Barry was effective in reducing piracy and French naval presence in the area. His main action in the conflict occurred on 3 February 1799, when *United States* captured the infamous French privateer *L'Amour de La Patrie* near Martinique.

After transporting American peace envoys to France, Barry returned to Guadalupe and reassumed command of the squadron until the end of the conflict in 1801. It was during this time that many young naval officers, including James Barron and Stephen Decatur, developed under his command. "Barry's boys" were among the most brilliant stars of American naval heritage, especially in the Barbary Wars and the War of 1812.

Barry returned to his home in Philadelphia and continued to serve his country as the senior navy officer. Although suffering from a severe asthmatic condition, he routinely gave the navy valuable guidance and leadership until his death in Philadelphia. Barry was a beacon of steadfast resolve and dynamic effectiveness during very trying times in the history of the United States. Biographers have sometimes embellished his reputation for honor, courage, and commitment, but he clearly deserves to be considered the patriarch of the American navy.

• Barry's papers are in the Philadelphia Maritime Museum Library; a published guide, *The Barry-Hayes Papers, A Descriptive Guide*, processed by Mary Beth Reed and Dorothy Schneider (1991), is an excellent reference tool. Three published naval history documentary collections provide significant detail about the operational activities of Commodore Barry in three wars. These include William J. Morgan, ed., *Naval Documents of the American Revolution* (1964–1986); Dudley W. Knox, ed., *Naval Documents Related to the United States Wars with the Barbary Powers* (1939); and Knox, ed., *Naval Documents Related to the Quasi-War Between the United States and France* (1935–1938), all three of which were published by the Naval Historical Center. The first biographical sketch of Commodore Barry appeared in *Port Folio*, July 1813. William Bell Clark, *Gallant John Barry* (1938), is the most authoritative, complete, and objective secondary source. See also Francis E. Benz, *Commodore Barry, Navy Hero* (1950), Joseph Gurn, *Commodore John Barry, Father of the American Navy* (1933), and Leonard Wibberley, *John Barry, Father of the Navy* (1957), although these are not wholly reliable sources. John A. McManemin, *Captains of the Continental Navy* (1982), describes Barry's revolutionary war service. See also Luke Matthewman, "Narrative of Lieut. Luke Matthewman of the Revolutionary Navy," *New York Packet* (1787), reprinted in *The Magazine of American History with Notes and Queries* 2 (1878): 175–85. An obituary is in the *National Intelligencer and Washington Advertiser*, 19 Sept. 1803.

ROBERT G. BAKER

BARRY, Leonora (13 Aug. 1849–15 July 1930), labor leader, was born Leonora Marie Kearney in Kearney, County Cork, Ireland, the daughter of John Kearney and Honor Brown. When Kearney was three, the family sailed for the United States and settled on a farm in Pierrepont, New York, not far from the Canadian border. She grew up there, but upon her mother's death and father's remarriage, she determined to set out on her own. Though only fifteen, she arranged for a year of preparatory study with the head of a girls' school in a neighboring town and obtained her teacher's certificate. She spent the next several years teaching in a rural school.

In 1871 Leonora Kearney married William E. Barry, a painter and music teacher who had also emigrated from Ireland. The couple moved frequently, from Potsdam, New York, to Haydenville, Massachusetts, to Amsterdam, New York. In 1881 Barry's husband

died. As she later explained, "I was left, without knowledge of business, without knowledge of work, without knowledge of what the world was, with three fatherless children looking to me for bread" (quoted in Flexner, p. 197). Her oldest child died shortly thereafter. To support the remaining two, the young widow first tried earning her living as a seamstress but found the work too hard on her eyes, so she went to work in a local hosiery mill, earning only eleven cents a day. In 1884, seeking a remedy for the miserable conditions experienced by unskilled workers like herself, Barry joined the local women's assembly of the Knights of Labor. Her timing was opportune, for the organization was just entering the brief period during which it would achieve its largest membership and greatest national impact.

Barry rose quickly within the Knights hierarchy, progressing from master workman of her own assembly to leadership of the district assembly, which included fifty-two locals. At the regional convention in 1886, she was selected as one of five people to represent the district at the national general assembly. One of only sixteen women among 660 delegates attending that convention, Barry joined a women's committee set up to consider a report on female labor that had been commissioned the previous year. The committee concluded that a new Woman's Work Department should be established to investigate "the abuses to which our sex is subjected by unscrupulous employers" as well as to "agitate the principles which our Order teaches, of equal pay for equal work and the abolition of child labor" (Flexner, p. 196). The general assembly accepted the committee's proposal along with its recommendation that Barry be named to head the new department.

Besides undertaking the huge investigative tasks of her new position, Barry carried the broader responsibility of speaking for women workers in a labor movement—and an economy—run primarily by men. Leaving one of her children in a convent school and the other with her sisters-in-law, she traveled constantly for the next several years. Her goal, she said, was to free "from the remorseless grasp of tyranny and greed the thousands of underpaid women and girls in our large cities, who, suffering the pangs of hunger, cold and privation, ofttimes yield and fall into the yawning chasm of immorality" (quoted in Foner, p. 84). She set certain limits on her role; for instance, despite her passionate interest in securing Pennsylvania's first Factory Inspection Act, she refused to "go lobbying around a state Capitol or buttonholing legislators" because she thought it inappropriate behavior for a lady. Nevertheless, she played a significant role in winning passage of the inspection bill in 1889. She also maintained a voluminous correspondence, helped establish several cooperative factories, organized a number of new women's locals, helped bring in more members to existing male and female locals, compiled the first national statistics on women's labor, and galvanized groups around the country with more than five hundred rousing fact-filled speeches. Besides speaking to labor organizations on labor issues, she also addressed middle-class women, sometimes promoting woman suffrage and temperance but usually reminding them "to give your attention and some of your assistance to the root of all evil, the industrial and social system that is so oppressive, . . . which has brought the once fondly-loved mother to the position of the twelve and fourteen-hour toiler of today" (quoted in Foner, p. 86).

By the late 1880s the Knights had an estimated 65,000 female members, of whom nearly one-third were enrolled in assemblies that included both men and women. Besides the craft-workers' locals, there were assemblies for domestic servants and for housewives. Union cooperatives offered women jobs and affordable goods, and boycotts initiated by the Knights supported the interests of the many female members who worked in the garment industry. The organization was also breaking new ground in gathering information about women's work. Between 1887 and 1889, Barry presented three landmark reports to the annual general assemblies, documenting the conditions endured by laboring women and children and calling on the men of the organization to "uproot the corrupt system that is making slaves . . . of those who by right of divine parentage we must call sisters" (quoted in Foner, p. 89).

Barry's capacity to accomplish her goals was limited by the kinds of problems encountered by most unionists, including employers' freedom to bar organizers from their premises and the reluctance of better-paid workers to make common cause with those at the bottom of the ladder. In addition, as Barry observed, women were particularly difficult to organize because many of the younger ones expected marriage to take them out of the factory, because of the "foolish pride" that made some women shrink from joining a union, and because many of the worst-off workers had developed a "habit of submission and acceptance without question of any terms offered them, with the pessimistic view of life in which they see no ray of hope" (quoted in Flexner, p. 199).

Barry faced organizational obstacles as well. In the backlash following a wave of strikes and reprisals in 1886, the Knights had entered a period of rapid decline. Moreover, many men disliked seeing a woman take so prominent a role in labor organizing. Barry was criticized by some male members of the organization and by a number of Catholic priests, including Father Peter McEnroe, who called Barry "Lady Tramp" and condemned the "vulgar, immoral society" that had sent her out on her travels. The head of the Knights, Terence Powderly, defended Barry, but he suggested privately to her that she "waste no more time" on organizing men. Leading members of the organization began insisting that the Women's Work Department be abolished, and with his whole organization in disarray Powderly offered weakening resistance. Losing heart, Barry submitted her resignation at the 1889 convention, expressing discouragement with the slow rate of progress, questioning the value of organizing women separately, and recommending that her department be closed down. Her resignation was refused, but a few months later she was notified that the organization's straitened finances would require her to stop traveling and concentrate only on organizing women in the Philadelphia area.

Barry worked within this limited scope for a year, but in April 1890 she left the organization to marry Obadiah Read Lake, a proofreader and telegraph editor for the *St. Louis Globe-Democrat*. The disintegrating Knights identified one possible successor—the only woman to attend the 1890 convention—but when she declined the offer, the Woman's Work Department was abolished. Moving to St. Louis, Leonora Barry Lake took up the life of the middle-class lady volunteer. She did speak on "The Dignity of Labor" to the woman's congress at the World's Columbian Exposition in Chicago (1893), but most of her energies went to charity work, especially within the Catholic community. She also continued her support for woman suffrage, helping in the 1893 campaign that won the vote for women in Colorado. Above all, she dedicated herself to temperance, and—once Prohibition was enacted—to the rigorous enforcement of the Volstead Act. She was a leader and frequent speaker for the Catholic Total Abstinence Union of America and belonged for many years to the Woman's Christian Temperance Union. A dramatic and entertaining lecturer who never used a prepared text, she won a wide following on the Chautauqua circuit, speaking under the name of Mrs. Barry-Lake or sometimes Mother Lake.

In 1916 Barry-Lake and her husband went to live with her sister in Minooka, Illinois, near Joliet. After her husband died in 1923, she continued lecturing until 1928, when cancer of the mouth forced her to end her speaking career. She died in Minooka.

Because Barry-Lake's career with the Knights of Labor ended badly in 1890, it is possible to underestimate the significance of what she and the organization accomplished. If the Knights' success in organizing women was not all that Barry-Lake hoped, it considerably exceeded the level achieved in earlier periods, or for some years in the future. Indeed, continued progress might well have been made, despite internal opposition, had the organization itself not fallen on hard times. As for Barry-Lake, she deserves more credit for the Knights' achievements in this area than any other individual. Her energy turned a tiny department into a national program, her zeal inspired thousands, and her capacity to master complex information produced a series of reports that scholars still turn to when they want to know what it meant to be a working woman in Gilded Age America.

• Barry left no personal papers, but documentation of her activities can be found in the *Proceedings* of the Knights of Labor, 1887–1889, and in the papers of Terence V. Powderly, Catholic University of America, Washington, D.C. See also Eleanor Flexner, *Century of Struggle: The Woman's Rights Movement in the United States* (1959); Philip S. Foner, *Women and the American Labor Movement: From the First Trade Unions to the Present* (1979); Joyce Maupin, *Labor Heroines: Ten*

Women Who Led the Struggle (1974); David Montgomery, *The Fall of the House of Labor* (1987); and John B. Andrews and W. D. P. Bliss, *History of Women in Trade Unions*, vol. 10 of *Report on Condition of Woman and Child Wage Earners in the U.S.* (Senate Document 645, 1911).

SANDRA OPDYCKE

BARRY, Philip (18 June 1896–3 Dec. 1949), playwright, was born Philip James Quinn Barry in Rochester, New York, the son of James Corbett Barry, the owner of a marble and tile business, and Mary Agnes Quinn. He attended Nazareth Hall Academy, a Roman Catholic private school, Rochester's East High School, and Yale University. His father's death the year after Philip's birth motivated Barry's second Broadway production, *The Youngest* (1924). In 1905 he published a short story, "Tab the Cat," in the *Rochester Post Express* and completed a full-length play entitled "No Thoroughfare" before finishing middle school. Even with tutoring Barry failed the entrance examinations to Yale and was admitted on a conditional basis. At Yale he contributed poetry and short stories to the *Yale Literary Magazine* and read Arthur Schnitzler, J. M. Barrie, Henrik Ibsen, and Gerhart Hauptmann.

When the United States entered World War I Barry tried to enlist but was rejected because of poor eyesight. He left Yale in April 1918 to work in the Communications Division of the State Department in Washington, D.C., but transferred to the American embassy in London from May 1918 to February 1919. Barry returned to Yale and received the B.A. in June 1919. During his final semester his one-act play, *Autonomy*, "which was meant to be a bitter political satire, based on the Wilsonian theory of autonomy of nations" (Hamm, p. 7), was produced in a bill of three one-acts by the Yale Dramatic Association.

In 1919 Barry enrolled in Professor George Pierce Baker's famous 47 Workshop at Harvard and learned stagecraft while writing *A Punch for Judy*, a three-act comedy about a young man who playfully sues his sweetheart for breach of contract. In March he began working as a copywriter at the A. W. Erickson advertising firm in New York City, turning down an editorship at *Ainslee's Magazine*. He returned to Baker's workshop in September 1921, a decision that was seminal to his career as a professional playwright. During the 1921–1922 academic year he acquired disciplined writing habits and completed his first two Broadway plays: *The Jilts* (renamed *You and I*) and *Poor Richard* (later retitled *The Youngest*). In 1922 he married Ellen Marshall Semple, and when the couple returned from a European honeymoon in September Barry was awarded the Herndon Prize of $500 plus a Broadway production of *You and I*, the best full-length play written at the workshop in 1921–1922. In November 1922 *Scribner's Magazine* published his last short story, "Meadow's End." The couple had three children, one of whom died in infancy.

You and I, a comedy about a would-be artist who gives up his career for marriage, opened at the Belmont Theatre on 19 February 1923 to a successful run of 170 performances. First National Studios in Hollywood bought the rights and released the film in 1931 as *The Bargain*. On 22 December 1924 Barry's second Broadway play, *The Youngest*, opened at the Gaiety Theatre. Based on events in Barry's life, the play is about a young man who good-naturedly holds his family in thrall after acquiring a controlling interest in the family fortune because of his father's early death. The play, a mild success, ran for 104 performances.

In a Garden, which followed within a year at the Plymouth Theatre, was Barry's first attempt to depart from the pleasantries of his earlier work. Lissa, based on a character in "Meadow's End," unable to endure her husband's manipulation, leaves him to "find" herself. The plot intrigues of the play confused critics and the public. *White Wings*, an allegorical fantasy, opened at the Booth Theatre on 15 October 1926. As the last of the White Wings (street cleaners who sweep up after horses), Archie Inch confronts the onslaught of the automobile and must inevitably accept love and an accommodation with progress. Though the fantasy had a coterie of followers, it baffled critics. Barry had helped to lure Professor Baker away from Harvard to become the head of the Yale University Theatre. On 12 February 1927 Barry addressed a conference at Yale and with good humor commented ironically on the failure of his last two efforts: "I am now busy on a manuscript which will, I hope, contain enough that is of promise to decide Mr. Baker to readmit me to the Workshop" (*The Dramatist and the Amateur Public*, p. 3).

In November 1927 *John*, a turgid, verse-like drama about John the Baptist, closed after only eleven performances, but a month later *Paris Bound* opened at the Music Box Theatre in New York City and was an immediate hit, running for six months. Audiences and critics lauded Barry's wit and felicitous dialogue. The theme—that an occasional, meaningless act of adultery cannot and should not destroy the spiritual love of a marriage—caused a stir but added considerably to the box-office receipts. Barry later sold the movie rights to Pathé for $17,500. *Cock Robin*, a tongue-in-cheek collaboration with Elmer Rice intended to demonstrate their ability to write commercially successful mystery potboilers, opened at the Forty-eighth Street Theatre on 12 January 1928, amused audiences and critics, and ran for one hundred performances.

At his villa in Cannes in France Barry worked on a new play that he called *The Dollar*, renamed *Holiday* at its New Haven tryout on 18 November 1928. This high comedy had the Barry hallmarks of wit, charm, and sophistication plus the story of a young man giving up wealth and marriage to a venal young woman in order to keep his dignity and morality. The opening at the Plymouth Theatre in New York on 26 November was a rousing success. The play ran for 229 performances and became a staple of anthologies and summer stock. The screen rights were sold to Pathé for $35,000. Within thirteen months Barry had had four of his plays produced on Broadway—a remarkable feat.

Barry suffered private losses fairly close together: his mother died in 1927, his infant daughter in 1933 soon after birth, and his oldest brother, Edmond, in 1934. After 1929 he spent half the year at his villa in Cannes and during his visits to the residence of his friend Gerald Murphy met expatriates, writers, and artists of the "lost generation." From this point on the majority of Barry's ensuing plays seem darker in tonality, less brimming with an earlier youthful exuberance. *Hotel Universe*, his ninth Broadway production, graphically reveals the influence on Barry of the physical and intellectual environment of Murphy's Cap d'Antibes home. Reviewers dealt very harshly with the play, which opened on 14 April 1930 at the Martin Beck Theatre. Despite its verbal and dramatic brilliance, critics thought it was filled with murky Freudianism, philosophical meanderings about the nature of God, man, and the universe, "appalling mystical chitchat . . . mangled Einstein . . . [and] some of the more repulsive varieties of New Thought." (Krutch, pp. 170–71). It closed after eighty-one performances.

Tomorrow and Tomorrow, Barry's tenth Broadway production, opened on 13 January 1931, ran for 206 performances, and stimulated critical debate. The title comes from *Macbeth* and the theme from the Bible. The leading female character having become an "earth-mother"—adored by both lover and husband—chooses to remain with the weaker man who needs her more. Add in the possibly misinterpreted theme that adultery and infidelity can be forgiven—perhaps even condoned—if the acts somehow keep a marriage together, and Barry had a hit going. Paramount paid $80,000 for the play's screen rights. *The Animal Kingdom* opened a successful run on 12 January 1932. Barry reworked the eternal triangle by showing a man regaining his dignity when he abandons the economic and physical enticements of his wife for the love of his *true* wife, his former mistress. Enriched by the acting of Leslie Howard, the play ran for 183 performances.

After three depressing flops—*The Joyous Season* (1934), *Bright Star* (1935), and *Spring Dance* (1936)—*Here Come the Clowns*, probably Barry's finest serious play, opened at the Booth Theatre on 7 December 1938. Adapted from his only novel, *War in Heaven* (1938), the play presents a suffering Dan Clancy who seeks a reason for the existence of so much evil in the world. He learns that the Devil won the biblical war in Heaven and has been masquerading as God ever since. Representing a cross-section of humanity, the characters include a homosexual transvestite, a lesbian, a ventriloquist and dummy, a song-and-dance couple, and a dwarf. Bowing to pressure from the Broadway community, the critics returned a second time to view the work but left believing that the play was too obscure, allegorical, and symbolic even with its brilliantly written scenes and lilting dialogue. It closed after eighty-eight performances. An off-Broadway production won an Obie in 1960.

The Philadelphia Story, Barry's most popular and successful play, opened on 28 March 1939 at the Shubert Theatre. The play is a high comedy in which Tracy Lord, a Philadelphia Main Line divorcée, learns to abandon her icy morality and rejoin the world of human warmth and weakness. Critics welcomed Barry back to the milieu of high comedy and heaped praise on Katharine Hepburn, the star. The play earned more than $2 million from a year's run on Broadway plus additional large amounts from the ensuing two-year national tour, saving the Theatre Guild from certain bankruptcy. The film of *The Philadelphia Story* that followed in 1940 and the 1956 motion picture musical adaptation, titled *High Society*, were also very successful.

Barry's anti-Axis allegorical play-with-music, *Liberty Jones*, subtitled *An Allegory with Music for City Children*, opened on 5 February 1941. Based on *The Wild Harps Playing*, an idea Barry had been developing since 1936, *Liberty Jones* became on the stage an oversymbolic allegorical attack on fascism. It closed after twenty-two performances. *Without Love*, a second vehicle for Katharine Hepburn, opened on 10 November 1942 at the St. James Theatre. Its characters resemble those in *The Philadelphia Story*, and the political intrigues echoed Barry's short stint with the government. Most of the critics felt, as George Freedley wrote in the *New York Morning Telegraph*, that the theme of Ireland siding with the Allies, even without love, made the play seem "slight, extremely unimportant and out of tune with the times" (11 Nov. 1942). A mild success, *Without Love* closed after 113 performances. Metro-Goldwyn-Mayer later produced a screenplay revolving around love, not politics.

Foolish Notion, Barry's nineteenth Broadway play, opened at the Martin Beck Theatre on 13 March 1945. The plot demonstrated the difference between reality and the acted-out fantasy each character has about the return of a husband/father reported missing in action. The critics felt it was an entertaining star vehicle for Tallulah Bankhead but lacked sufficient clarity. Closing after 104 performances, the production continued on in a successful nationwide tour. Four years later, *My Name Is Aquilon*, Barry's uninspired adaptation of Jean Pierre Aumont's sex comedy *L'Empereur de Chine*, which had been presented the previous season in Paris, opened on 9 February 1949 and closed after thirty-one performances.

Barry had high hopes for his last play, *Second Threshold*, which he had worked on for more than eleven years. On 3 December 1949, the day after he submitted the play to the Theatre Guild, Barry suffered a fatal heart attack. His friend Robert Sherwood edited the work for production, leaving the first act intact but cutting and revising the second half extensively. Barry's twenty-first Broadway production, *Second Threshold* opened at the Morosco Theatre on 2 January 1951. In it Josiah Bolton estranges himself from his friends and family so they will feel no loss after his suicide. His daughter learns of his plans and threatens to follow after. Bolton recognizes his responsibility to his daughter and himself and crosses a "second threshold" by choosing life. Without Barry's revisions the play did not quite evolve into an effective study of world weariness induced by absence of love and human associations. The production ran for 126 performances, with critics appreciating the play's mature, civilized qualities.

Barry's serious work was seldom taken seriously. As John Gassner observed, "The Great Ironist has had his way with Philip Barry by giving him an enviable talent for the capers of comedy and a great desire to write serious drama but reserving all the success for the light fantastic toe" (*Best Plays*, p. 412). Barry's reputation as a skilled playwright of sophisticated comedy rests primarily on the great success of three works: *Paris Bound*, whose "brittle dialogue . . . [and] unconventional attitude toward adultery . . . were pure Barry, the *real* Barry"; *Holiday*, whose scintillating dialogue and "purposeful dramatic nonsense" convinced critics "that in this aspect Barry excelled all other American playwrights"; and *The Philadelphia Story*, one of the most popular American comedies of the twentieth century, which restored to Broadway "once more the Barry that critics and a large segment of the public wanted, the Barry of high comedy" (Roppolo, pp. 58, 62, 92).

Philip Barry was a working playwright who, in the fashion of the "old school," almost succeeded in bringing a new play to Broadway each year. When he died in his home in New York City, surrounded by his family, he had already submitted for production a new play for a new season.

• The Philip Barry Papers are in the Beinecke Rare Book and Manuscript Library at Yale University. See also his *The Dramatist and the Amateur Public* (1927). Joseph P. Roppolo, *Philip Barry* (1965), is a useful, fast-paced study of Barry. For Barry's awareness of psychodrama see W. David Sievers, *Freud on Broadway: A History of Psychoanalysis and the American Drama* (1955). Lawrence Langner, *The Magic Curtain* (1951), illuminates the production histories of Barry's plays at the Theatre Guild. See also Gerald Hamm, "The Drama of Philip Barry" (Ph.D. diss., Univ. of Pennsylvania, 1948), and David C. Gild, "An Historical and Critical Study of the Serious Plays of Philip Barry" (D.F.A. diss., Yale Univ., 1969). For drama criticism of Barry's plays see Joseph Wood Krutch, *The American Drama since 1918: An Informal History* (1939; rev. ed., 1957); John Gassner, ed., *Best Plays of the American Theatre*, 2d ser. (1947); Gassner, *Masters of the Drama*, 3d ed., rev. (1954); and Gassner, *The Theatre in Our Times* (1954). An obituary appears in the *New York Times*, 4 Dec. 1949.

DAVID C. GILD

BARRY, Thomas (27 July 1798–11 Feb. 1876), actor and stage manager, was born in England. Nothing else is known about his birth, parentage, childhood, or education. He made his first appearance in the United States on 16 December 1826 at the Park Theatre, New York City, in the title role in August von Kotzebue's *The Stranger*. Following a brief stage career in Brighton, England, Barry tried and failed to establish himself as a star in tragic roles on the American stage, but he did become popular in comic roles, such as the duplicitous Joseph Surface in Richard Brinsley Sheridan's *The School for Scandal*, in various productions of

which he performed for many years, and the weak and vacillating scoundrel in melodrama. Reportedly handsome with a graceful figure, Barry benefited as well from having a full and mellow voice and exquisite judgment in conceiving his part and rendering his lines, but he was accused of indiscreet exaggeration in moments of high drama. Barry continued with the Park Theatre company until 1833, during which time he was also an occasional visiting star at the rival Chatham Garden Theatre.

Barry's fame rested on his extraordinary ability as a stage manager, a role he assumed at the Park Theatre a few months after his arrival in 1826. Chronicler Joseph N. Ireland observed that Barry's "correct taste and excellent judgment were soon perceptible in the order, elegance, and liberality of his arrangements" (vol. 1, p. 513). Barry excelled in staging scenic spectacles, such as *Faustus* (1827) by George Soane, with music by Sir Henry Rowley Bishop and Charles Edward Horn, and operas, such as Thomas Arne's *Artaxerxes* (1828). In 1833 Barry left New York and the Park Theatre for Boston, where he managed the Tremont Theatre company for six artistically successful but financially ruinous seasons. Although by that time Barry was reputably the nation's most capable stage manager, his regimen of stars, including Mr. and Mrs. John Wood, Ellen Tree (Mrs. Charles Kean), and Edwin Forrest, in high-brow plays and operas garnered public and journalistic approval but lost money every year. His theater, built to mirror the balance of classes in a democracy, offered too few seats in the expensive dress circle to permit him to capitalize on the wealth of the audience he needed to serve.

In 1839 Barry returned to New York to join the Bowery Theatre company, to whom he provided invaluable aid in the production of new dramas. In 1841 he rejoined the Park Theatre company, where his expert stage management slowed the decline of a decaying theater with a reputation for English stodginess. After the Park Theatre burned in 1848, Barry led the displaced actors to the Bowery Theatre, where he starred briefly in *The Stranger*. Barry then produced his own topical spectacle, *The Battle of Mexico*, which ran a few nights at the Bowery.

Following a stint from 1848 to 1851 as manager at Purdy's National Theatre in Boston, Barry assumed the position of stage manager at New York's Broadway Theatre, then the nation's most pretentious venue for stars. The Broadway, modeled after London's Haymarket Theatre, seated 4,500 and was the largest theater ever built in New York to that time. The Broadway bill included American (especially Forrest) and English stars in standard dramas, comedies, and farces, visiting companies in English and Italian opera and French ballet, melodramatic spectacles, and Irish comedians. To make the gigantic theater profitable, the management needed to offer something for everyone. Special productions under Barry's direction, such as W. T. Moncrieff's *The Cataract of the Ganges* and Shakespeare's *A Midsummer Night's Dream*, inspired by the extraordinary success of a revival at Sadler's

Wells in 1853, anchored the chaotic season of 1853–1854, which was characterized by too many, too brief engagements and was Barry's last at the Broadway Theatre.

He returned to Boston in 1854 to manage the Boston Theatre stock company. The Barry formula for a forty-week season included about twenty weeks of work for the resident stock company, unembellished by stars; four or five stars (each with some nationalistic or ethnic quality) in one- or two-week stands; and Italian and English opera companies and French ballet and English pantomime groups in brief stands. The financial anchor of each season was the spring spectacle, directed by Barry. Its four- to six-week run provided the management with most of its annual profit. Barry continued with the Boston Theatre stock company until 1859, when, at age sixty-one, he went into semiretirement, reemerging in 1868 for two seasons as manager of Selwyn's Theatre company in Boston. His last turn was at New York's Bowery Theatre in 1871, when he concluded a season with a company reviving old melodramas.

Barry was married twice, both times to actresses. His first wife died in 1854. His second wife was the former Clara Biddles. He died in Boston.

In Barry's era, stage managers were in charge of the few rehearsals that a new piece or an exceptionally complicated revival might receive before it was presented to the public and thus were precursors of the modern functionary known as the director. Stage managers established theatrical production practices in response to forces then at work in the profession of the player. From the earliest days of the professional player on the English stage, performers enacted a role according to traditions originating from the playwright's verbal instructions to the first player of a part. Business or byplay, line readings, costumes, indeed everything relevant to a role's function in the drama emanated from these instructions. Subsequent generations of performers learned the role by observing and imitating the creator of the role and those he taught. This mode of operation—well suited to a guild of artisans functioning within the confines of a city or small region where the growth of the number of theater companies was suppressed by law—became less viable in the nineteenth century, when professional theater spread geographically, and players entered the profession without the benefit of a lengthy apprenticeship at the feet of a master of playing traditions. Cues in the script rather than the playwright's instructions became the keys to a correct and effective performance. Changes in the habits and interests of theatergoers also mitigated against tradition and in favor of making each production more culturally relevant. Thus arose the need for an interpreter of the text, a functionary whose consciousness displaced or amended that of the author in "instructing" the performers and adapting the script to the exigencies of a new time, place, and audience. Thomas Barry, a master of the emerging craft of the director in the antebellum American theater, filled this need.

• Accounts of Barry's activities and achievements are in Joseph N. Ireland, *Records of the New York Stage* (3 vols., 1866; repr. 1965); George C. D. Odell, *Annals of the New York Stage*, vols. 3–9 (1927–1949); William W. Clapp, Jr., *A Record of the Boston Stage* (1853; repr. 1969) and "The Drama in Boston," in *Memorial History of Boston*, ed. Justin Winsor, vol. 4 (1881); Eugene Tompkins, *The History of the Boston Theatre* (1908); and Garrett H. Leverton, *The Production of Later Nineteenth Century American Drama* (1936).
WELDON B. DURHAM

BARRY, William Farquhar (18 Aug. 1818–18 July 1879), soldier, was born in New York City, the son of Caroline M. (maiden name unknown). The full name of his father, who died when Barry was a youth, is unknown. Tutored by his mother, who gave him an "unusual knowledge" of the classics, Barry also attended high school in New York before entering the U.S. Military Academy in 1834. Four years later he graduated in the upper third of his class. He was posted to the Second U.S. Artillery, and his initial service was on the Canadian border during that country's "Patriot War" (1837–1838). In 1840, while stationed at Buffalo, New York, he married Kate McKnight.

At the outset of the Mexican War, Barry in 1847 accompanied his regiment to Tampico, where he fell seriously ill. Once he recovered he served on the staff of Major General Robert Patterson during the siege of Veracruz and, after the fall of Mexico City, became an aide-de-camp to Major General William Jenkins Worth. Promoted to captain in 1852, Barry fought the Seminoles in Florida and performed occupation duty during the sectional strife in Kansas Territory. Late in 1856 he was detailed, along with Brevet Majors Henry J. Hunt and William H. French, to revise the light artillery tactics of the army. Published in 1860 as *Instruction for Field Artillery*, the new tactics were widely used in both the Union and Confederate ranks.

Barry began the Civil War helping defend Fort Pickens, Florida, one of two U.S. garrisons in Confederate territory that did not fall into enemy hands. On 14 May 1861 he was promoted to major in the Fifth Artillery. Early in July 1861 he led the most famous light artillery unit in the army, Battery A, Second United States, to Washington, D.C. His field rank, seniority, and reputation as an administrator gained him command of the artillery attached to Brigadier General Irvin McDowell's Army of Northeastern Virginia.

At First Bull Run (First Manassas), 21 July 1861, Barry commanded ten batteries and a two-gun section of another. Although he performed competently in the morning's fighting, early in the afternoon he committed a major blunder that helped turn the tide against McDowell's forces. Deploying eleven of his cannons in an exposed position atop Henry House Hill, he failed to support them in timely fashion and forbade them from firing on an approaching column, which he took for Union troops. As his subordinates suspected, the newcomers proved to be Confederates, who killed or disabled thirty-two Union artillerymen, captured nine guns, and helped stampede the Federal army into retreat.

Atoning for his mistake, Barry did a fine job of protecting McDowell's withdrawal to Washington. This performance recommended him to McDowell's successor, Major General George B. McClellan, who on 27 July named Barry chief of artillery of the Army of the Potomac. Although denied tactical control of the units assigned to him, Barry over the next eight months oversaw their growth from 30 guns, 650 men, and 400 horses to 520 cannons, 12,500 cannoneers, and 11,000 mounts. At Barry's insistence, his superior attached to the army one-half of the batteries in the regular service, imparting a core of professionalism enjoyed by no other Civil War command. For his "industry and zeal" in helping make the artillery the most effective combat arm of the Army of the Potomac, Barry on 20 August 1861 was promoted to brigadier general of volunteers.

Barry performed creditably in an administrative role during McClellan's ill-starred Peninsula campaign of March–July 1862. When the campaign ended, he was transferred at his own request to Washington, initially serving on the staff of the chief of ordnance, Brigadier General James W. Ripley. In mid-September 1862 Barry took command of the artillery in the forts that encircled the capital while also assuming the duties of inspector of artillery and commander of the Artillery Camp of Instruction. As if these duties did not sufficiently occupy him, he served on numerous ordnance and fortification boards.

Barry remained in Washington until 20 March 1864, when he became chief of artillery to Major General William T. Sherman, commander of the Military Division of the Mississippi. Although on paper he commanded 530 guns and more than 16,000 men, Barry served mainly in an administrative capacity during the Atlanta campaign. Illness forced him to miss Sherman's March to the Sea. After recuperating, he participated in the Carolinas campaign, which terminated with the surrender of the Confederate forces under General Joseph E. Johnston. In April 1865 Sherman complimented Barry for "the efficiency of the artillery" in Georgia and the Carolinas "and the good care taken of horses and guns."

By the war's close, Barry had received the brevet of major general in both the volunteers and the Regular Army. In December 1865 he was promoted to full colonel in his original outfit, the Second Artillery. The following year he returned to the Canadian border, where he commanded U.S. troops during the Fenian uprising. In 1867 he organized the Artillery School at Fort Monroe, Virginia, and for a decade labored "assiduously and successfully" as its commandant. He died while commanding Fort McHenry in Baltimore Harbor.

Upon his death Barry was eulogized as one of the finest artillery organizers and administrators of the nineteenth century, a judgment that history has sustained. As a field commander, he ranks below his colleague Hunt, who replaced Barry as artillery commander of the Army of the Potomac. A more accomplished scholar than Hunt, Barry published many reports and learned papers, and in 1863 he coauthored with Brigadier General John G. Barnard a history of the artillery and engineer operations of McClellan's army through the Peninsula campaign.

Barry and Hunt share credit for the organizational and operational effectiveness displayed by the Union artillery in the major theaters of operations. A subordinate of both men praised them equally for keeping the artillery a cohesive force, free of the meddling of infantry leaders: "But for these two officers the batteries would have still been scattered about, attached to divisions and brigades any where and every where that a general officer had sufficient personal influence to get a battery assigned to his command."

• A small body of Barry's personal papers, mainly telegrams sent to him at Fort McHenry in 1877, is in the Maryland Historical Society, Baltimore. Some of his wartime correspondence is in the Henry Jackson Hunt Papers at the Library of Congress and in the James Duncan Papers in the U.S. Military Academy Library, West Point, N.Y. A few of Barry's campaign reports are in *The War of the Rebellion: A Compilation of the Official Records of the Union and Confederate Armies* (128 vols., 1880–1901), notably vol. 2 (First Bull Run); vol. 11, pt. 1 (the siege of Yorktown); vol. 38, pt. 1 (the Atlanta campaign); and vol. 47, pt. 1 (the Carolinas campaign). William E. Birkhimer, *Historical Sketch of Artillery* (1884), notes Barry's contributions to Civil War artillery administration. More recent studies covering aspects of Barry's war service include L. Van Loan Naisawald, *Grape and Canister: The Story of the Field Artillery of the Army of the Potomac, 1861–1865* (1960), and Edward G. Longacre, *The Man behind the Guns* (1977). Thomas Osborn, *The Fiery Trail: A Union Officer's Account of Sherman's Last Campaigns*, ed. Richard Harwell and Philip N. Racine (1986), offers a brief commentary on Barry's service in 1864–1865. A detailed obituary is in the *Baltimore Sun*, 19 July 1879.

EDWARD G. LONGACRE

BARRY, William Taylor (5 Feb. 1784–30 Aug. 1835), politician, jurist, and postmaster general, was born in Lunenburg County, Virginia, the son of John Barry, a revolutionary war veteran and farmer, and Susannah Dozier. The family moved to Kentucky, apparently in 1796, and settled in Fayette County. Following a course of study in law at William and Mary College, Barry was admitted to the Kentucky bar and set up practice in Lexington in 1805. That same year he married Lucy Waller Overton, with whom he would have two children before her premature death.

At age twenty-two Barry entered politics when he accepted an appointment as commonwealth's attorney for Fayette County. In 1807 and 1809 he was elected to the lower house of the Kentucky General Assembly. From August 1810 to March 1811 he filled a vacancy in the U.S. House of Representatives. For a period during the War of 1812, Barry acted as secretary and aide-de-camp to Kentucky governor Isaac Shelby, with the rank of major, and was present at the decisive battle of the Thames in October 1813. In Kentucky the following year he was elected Speaker of the lower house of the general assembly.

Chosen by the state legislature to complete an unexpired term, Barry served in the U.S. Senate from December 1814 to May 1816, when he resigned and returned to Kentucky to accept appointment as a circuit judge. In 1817 he was elected to the state senate. There, in the midst of a devastating state banking and financial crisis, he emerged as the spokesman of the Relief faction, which advocated legislative intervention between creditors and debtors as well as currency enhancement.

In August 1820, following a bitter campaign centering on the money issue, Barry was elected lieutenant governor. In that position he argued forcefully and successfully for the establishment of a state-funded Bank of the Commonwealth. He also chaired a six-member legislative committee that had been appointed to study the status of public education in other states. The Barry Committee gathered a wealth of information, primarily from the New England states, New York, and South Carolina, as well as insightful letters from John Adams, Thomas Jefferson, James Madison, Robert Y. Hayne, and others. The committee report to the general assembly in 1822 recommended the creation of a system of free public schools. However, partisan wrangling coupled with a lean economy doomed any hope of implementing a common public school system. As historian Thomas D. Clark has written, "For Kentucky the adoption of the central implications of the Barry Report might well have been turned into a magnificent landmark for public educational beginnings in Kentucky" (Clark, pp. 178–79).

His four-year term as lieutenant governor at its end in 1824, Barry intended to resume the practice of law and to become a professor at Transylvania College in Lexington, where he had taught law and politics intermittently for several years. Instead he became embroiled in a bitter fight over the state judicial system. In January 1825 the general assembly, controlled by the Relief forces, abolished the existing state court of appeals (known as the "Old Court") and mandated in its place a panel consisting of a chief justice—Barry—and three associates. This "New Court" operated for just under two years; in December 1826 the Relief partisans were defeated and the Old Court system was "restored."

In January 1828 the Democratic state convention in Frankfort nominated Barry for governor. His opponent on the National Republican ticket, Thomas Metcalfe, a stonemason, eked out a 700-vote majority. Barry's unwavering support of Andrew Jackson in the presidential contest that year did not escape "Old Hickory's" notice. When Jackson entered the White House in March 1829, he named the Kentuckian postmaster general and elevated that position to cabinet status for the first time.

Throughout his six-year tenure as postmaster general, Barry served as a lightning rod of sorts for the president. By 1830 accusations of mismanagement and favoritism in the operation of the post office were being widely circulated. In 1834 and 1835 both houses of Congress conducted investigations of Barry's administration of the department. Though there had been numerous instances of abuse and lax bookkeeping, none of the offenses could be directly attributed to Barry, who insisted that he was the victim of partisans intent on destroying the president himself.

Physically and emotionally shaken by the attacks against him, Barry determined to resign from the cabinet. On 10 April 1835 he submitted his resignation but immediately accepted Jackson's offer of a diplomatic post as minister to Spain. As he journeyed to assume his new office he died unexpectedly in Liverpool, England. He was survived by his second wife, Catherine Armistead Mason, the daughter of U.S. senator Stevens T. Mason of Virginia, whom he had married in 1812 and with whom he had four children. Barry's body remained buried in Liverpool until 1854, when the Kentucky legislature formally requested its return. On 8 November 1854 he was reinterred in the section of the Frankfort Cemetery reserved for the commonwealth's "distinguished dead."

• There is no extensive collection of Barry letters. The most useful small holdings are those of the Kentucky Historical Society in Frankfort and the Filson Club Historical Society in Louisville. Additional correspondence appears in "Letters of William T. Barry," *William and Mary College Quarterly Historical Magazine*, 1st ser., 14 (1906): 19–23; Cheryl Conover, "'To Please Papa': The Letters of John Waller Barry, West Point Cadet, 1826–1830," *Register of the Kentucky Historical Society* 80 (Spring 1982): 183–212; and Conover, "Kentuckian in 'King Andrew's Court': The Letters of John Waller Barry, Washington, D.C., 1831–1835," *Register of the Kentucky Historical Society* 81 (Spring 1983): 168–98. An analysis of Barry's role in state education reform is found in Thomas D. Clark, "Kentucky Education through Two Centuries of Political and Social Change," *Register of the Kentucky Historical Society* 83 (Summer 1985): 173–201. Reflections on Barry's career and influence are in *Obituary Addresses Delivered upon the Occasion of the Re-Interment of the Remains of Maj. Wm. T. Barry* (1855).

THOMAS H. APPLETON, JR.

BARRYMORE, Ethel (16 Aug. 1879–18 June 1959), actress, was born Ethel May Barrymore in Philadelphia, Pennsylvania, the daughter of Maurice Barrymore, an actor, and Georgiana Drew, an actress. The second of three children (her brothers Lionel and John also distinguished themselves on stage and screen), Ethel was born into a family whose theatrical roots reached back four generations. Her mother, a spirited and popular comedienne, had married Maurice Barrymore (born Herbert Blyth in India), a handsome and fast-living matinee idol who had come to the United States from England in 1874. But Ethel would know neither parent well. Her grandmother, Louisa Lane Drew, one of the nineteenth century's leading comediennes and theater managers, was the family matriarch and a dominant figure in her granddaughter's life, particularly as her parents frequently were on tour.

Although born into a strongly Episcopalian family, Georgiana's conversion to Roman Catholicism led her to have Ethel baptized a Catholic, and at age six she was sent to live in a convent school in Philadelphia. At thirteen Ethel accompanied her mother to California where Georgiana was to convalesce from a bout with tuberculosis. Her mother's death soon thereafter thrust adult responsibilities on Ethel, and for the rest of her life she assumed a maternal role toward her brothers. Family fortune changed in another way. Returning to the convent school in autumn 1892, Ethel was informed a few months later that her grandmother had given up management of the Arch Street Theatre and that she must leave school and begin acting. "Suddenly there was no money, no Arch Street Theatre, no house, and I must earn my living," she recalled in her autobiography. She sacrificed her early dreams of a career as concert pianist to immediate necessities.

Although her acting experience was limited to childhood theatricals with her brothers, Barrymore joined her grandmother's Canadian tour of Sheridan's *The Rivals*. She soon learned the rigors of the road, experiencing even the humiliation of sneaking out of a hotel with the company for want of money. Nor did the Barrymore name always exempt her from the drudgery of making the rounds at theatrical agencies. Yet family ties did prove valuable. Her uncle John Drew, Jr., then a reigning star of drawing room comedies, prevailed on producer Charles Frohman to give her apprentice roles. She successfully understudied Elsie De Wolfe's Kate Fennel in *The Bauble Shop* (1894), which led Frohman to give her the part in a touring company. As a coquettish maid in John Drew's *Rosemary* (1895), she displayed the charm that would propel her to stardom.

An invitation from William Gillette to appear in his London production of *Secret Service* (1897) proved to be a decisive moment in Barrymore's career. Not only did London audiences take to her, but English society threw open its doors to this American cousin. With her wide interests and unaffected yet sophisticated manner, she charmed England's social and artistic elites. A series of English suitors (including Winston Churchill) sought her hand through the years. One of these was Laurence Irving, whose celebrated father, Henry Irving, offered her roles in *The Bells* (1897) and *Peter the Great* (1898).

Barrymore returned to the United States in 1898 to discover that her English reception had made her an American celebrity. Frohman, America's leading theatrical producer, added her to his stable of stars. In 1900 he cast her as Madame Trentoni in Clyde Fitch's social comedy *Captain Jinks of the Horse Marines*. Its Broadway debut the next year was a sensation, thrusting Barrymore into stardom and making her a fashion trendsetter for young American women. She continued under Frohman's management until his death in 1915, playing with her "rare and radiant girlhood" the eternal ingenue in second-rate plays such as *Cousine Kate* (1903), *Alice-Sit-by-the-Fire* (1905), *Her Sister* (1907), and *Lady Frederick* (1908).

Although Barrymore enjoyed the adulation of stardom and the easy entrée into high society, she grew restless playing juveniles. Her attempt at Nora in *A Doll's House* (1905) failed. It remained for marriage, motherhood, and the vehicle of Arthur Wing Pinero's *Mid-Channel* (1910) to elevate her to more mature dramatic roles. This part was followed by other successes in *The Shadow* (1915), Edna Ferber's *Our Mrs. McChesney* (1915), and, most notably, Zoë Akins's *Déclassée* (1919), which enjoyed long runs in New York and on tour.

The early 1920s, however, also saw the dissolution of her marriage, which had taken place in 1909, to socialite Russell Griswold Colt. The union had produced three children, who remained with their mother. The first half of the decade also brought some stage failures, particularly the harsh reception given to her attempt at Shakespeare's Juliet in 1922 (although she was better received a few years later as Ophelia and Portia). Winning critical acclaim in *The Second Mrs. Tanqueray* (1924), two years later she found her best vehicle of the 1920s, Somerset Maugham's comedy *The Constant Wife*, in which she enjoyed three years' success. At the end of the play's run the Shubert Brothers lured her to their management with the construction of the Ethel Barrymore Theatre, which she inaugurated in 1928 with the opening of *The Kingdom of God*.

The depression ushered in the most difficult period in Barrymore's career. *Scarlet Sister Mary* (1930) failed disastrously, and no other suitable roles came along in following years. Compounding her professional difficulties was acute financial distress (including an ongoing battle with the IRS over unpaid taxes) and a drinking problem, which made her a risk to put on stage.

To survive the thirties she reverted to two familiar strategies of the past. One was to return to the vaudeville stage, which she had done intermittently since 1912 in the one-act play *The Twelve-Pound Look* (1933). The other was to venture again to Hollywood. Although she had made several silent films beginning in 1914, she had publicly let her scorn of Hollywood be known. But financial need and the chance to act with both brothers (for the only time) led her to accept MGM's offer to make *Rasputin and the Empress* in 1932. Radio also came to her financial rescue, as she did a series of her old stage roles for NBC in 1936.

After appearing in a series of weak vehicles during the late 1930s, Barrymore's career took an abrupt turn for the better in 1940 in Emlyn Williams's *The Corn Is Green*. Her portrayal of Miss Moffat, a Welsh schoolteacher, became perhaps her most acclaimed role. The play ran in New York and on the road for three years, interrupted in 1944 to allow her to make the film *None But the Lonely Heart* (for which she received the Academy Award as best supporting actress).

The 1940s would become Ethel Barrymore's decade. Having salvaged a career that apparently was over in the early 1930s, she won new critical and public acclaim and an adulation known to few other American actresses, being once again touted as "first lady of the theater." But Barrymore would appear in only one further theatrical production of note, *Embezzled Heaven* (1944). A serious bout of pneumonia and various film offers led her to permanently move to southern California. She acted in twenty films (always in prominent supporting roles) from 1946 through 1957, most notably *The Spiral Staircase* (1946), for which she received another Academy Award nomination, and *Night Song* (1947). Two more Oscar nominations as best supporting actress followed for *The Paradine Case* (1947) and *Pinky* (1949). In the early 1950s she did some radio work and made several television appearances, even briefly hosting her own series, "The Ethel Barrymore Theater." She died in Los Angeles.

Barrymore epitomized stylish elegance. "Of all the people I have known," said the author Eliot Janeway, "Ethel was the most urbane, the most civilized, the most interested, the most articulate." These qualities also defined her stage presence. Her acting attained depth in the 1920s and a technical mastery that enabled her to maintain superb performances, even after long runs. She also had a much-admired (and imitated) voice and an imperious bearing that commanded respect, and her beauty remained scarcely diminished to the end of her life. By birth and manner, she represented the grand tradition of American theater, whose passing coincided with her career.

• The major archival material on Ethel Barrymore resides in the Robinson Locke Scrapbooks at the Billy Rose Theatre Collection of the New York Public Library/Lincoln Center. Barrymore's autobiography, *Memories* (1955), lacks serious reflection on her life. The most astute biography (a collective biography of Ethel, Lionel, and John) is Margot Peters, *The House of Barrymore* (1990). Hollis Alpert, *The Barrymores* (1964), is likewise a collective portrait. Good short sketches are found in *Notable American Women* (1980) and *Notable Women in the American Theatre* (1989). An obituary appears in the *New York Times*, 19 June 1959.

BENJAMIN MCARTHUR

BARRYMORE, Georgie (21 May 1856–12 July 1893), actress, was born Georgiana Emma Drew in Philadelphia, Pennsylvania, the daughter of John Drew and Louisa Lane, actor-managers. Bred by theater people who traditionally claimed descent from strolling players in Shakespeare's time, Georgie Drew came by her abilities naturally. (Her formidable mother did not advocate theatrical careers for her four children after her husband's early death in 1862.) As manager of Philadelphia's venerable Arch Street Theatre, Louisa Drew was not only a national theatrical eminence but also a social force locally. She raised her children to be ladies and gentlemen, enrolling them in private Episcopal academies and at socially acceptable dancing and riding schools, seldom providing access to her professional world.

Georgie, however, blond and blue-eyed and possessing her mother's strength of will and her father's impish spirit, would not be restrained. On 21 October 1872, at age sixteen, she made her acting debut as Leona in *The Ladies Battle*. The Philadelphia audience

greeted her warmly, not only because she was her mother's daughter but because she took gracefully to the stage with a guileless way of tossing lines. The daughter of the Drews perfected her craft as leading lady to the likes of Edwin Booth, Lawrence Barrett, and John McCullough, great stars who played guest engagements with her mother's resident company.

But the end of an era was at hand. In the spring of 1875 Louisa Drew was forced to end the time-honored stock system at her theater, thereafter running a more expedient "combination house" for traveling companies, a financial necessity she deplored. Georgie joined Augustin Daly's popular Fifth Avenue Theatre company in New York, where her older brother, John Drew, was already making a name for himself. She made an auspicious New York debut in April 1876, replacing Jeffreys-Lewis as Mary Standish in Daly's long-running *Pique*.

On 31 December 1876 in her mother's home, Georgie married Maurice Barrymore, Daly's leading man from England, inaugurating one of the theater world's most passionate, protean couplings. During the next six years as they acted together and apart, they had three children, Lionel Barrymore, Ethel Barrymore, and John Barrymore who would ensure their parents' immortality. A match in every way for her witty, worldly husband, Georgie Drew Barrymore, as she was now billed, kept pace professionally. Her naturalism was something new and welcome to nineteenth-century audiences used to more formal styles of comedic interpretation. Her husband exploited this unique quality in the role he created for her in his tragedy *Nadjezda* (1884). "As the American girl, Eureka Grubb," wrote William Winter, the dean of New York drama critics, in his *Tribune* review, "Mrs. Georgie Drew Barrymore is in her element. The 'slang' is a little startling to the audience, and when she says, 'Did I win? Did I hit the ceiling?' the house gives a gasp and then a long, loud roar of merriment." Eureka as written and played was a revelation in stage ingenues—a nouveau riche miner's daughter—witty, with a smattering of slang, warmhearted, and aware of the possibility of rewarding sexual exchanges between ladies and gentlemen.

Georgie Barrymore filled a rare niche in theatrical circles as an independent, outspoken woman, "a woman," observed the New York *Dramatic Mirror*, "with a fund of animal spirits and *fin de siècle* repartee." Her brilliant husband was not the only person she challenged line for line. During his 1882 lecture tour, Oscar Wilde was denigrating callow America at a gathering in the studio of artist Robert Blum. "So you see," Wilde concluded, "America is a most uninteresting place—no antiquities, no curiosities."

"My dear Mr. Wilde," Barrymore countered, "we shall have the antiquities in time"—she scanned him pointedly—" and we are already importing the curiosities."

Barrymore filled a similar niche onstage, sought by the era's foremost comedians to lend grace and split-second timing as their leading lady. She won her greatest success opposite William H. Crane in *The Senator*, a very modern comedy of Washington political life by David Lloyd and Sydney Rosenfeld. "The daughter of Mr. and Mrs. John Drew; the sister of John and Sidney, and the wife of Maurice Barrymore—in short, the clever member of a clever family—Georgie Drew has, for several seasons, been promising to take the lead as a comedienne. Now she has taken it," decided the New York *Spirit of the Times* after the 13 January 1890 opening. "As handsome as a picture, exquisitely dressed, brimming over with fun and an actress to the tips of her fingers, she captured the audience at once and kept them in roars of laughter." Barrymore was forced to leave the cast for a few days in May when a difficulty in breathing, diagnosed as a touch of bronchitis, hindered her performance.

She rallied, accepting a lucrative offer to join Charles Frohman's Comedians at Proctor's Theatre on 27 August 1891 in William Gillette's new comedy *Mr. Wilkinson's Widows*. She followed that hit with *Settled out of Court* (1892), in which she captivated New York and the road as Frohman's Comedians toured the country. In San Francisco she won further plaudits in the American premiere of W. Lestocq's *The Sportsman* (1892), playing, according to the *Chronicle*, with "a spirit, a life and a breeziness and a perfection of farce acting." She repeated the triumph in New York on 14 February 1893, inspiring the *Journal* critic to conclude that she "could draw humor from the heart of a stone." It was her last role. Coughing and shortness of breath recurred, and her concerned husband, on the advice of doctors that continued to misdiagnose consumption as bronchitis, sent her to Santa Barbara, California, to recuperate in the sun. Their thirteen-year-old daughter was with her mother when she succumbed. "Oh, my poor kids," Barrymore cried out before the end, "What will ever become of them?"

Death brought a premature end to the potentially stellar career of Georgie Drew Barrymore. She left a legacy of naturalistic acting far ahead of its time and a destiny of extraordinary theatrical achievement for her "poor kids."

• For further study of Barrymore, see the memoirs of her children: Ethel Barrymore, *Memories* (1955); John Barrymore, *Confessions of an Actor* (1926) and *We Three* (1935); and Lionel Barrymore, *We Barrymores* (1951). James Kotsilibas-Davis, *Great Times Good Times: The Odyssey of Maurice Barrymore* (1977), covers Barrymore's life in detail, while comprehensive family surveys include Hollis Alpert, *The Barrymores* (1964), and Margot Peters, *The House of Barrymore* (1992).

JAMES KOTSILIBAS-DAVIS

BARRYMORE, John (14 or 15 Feb. 1882–29 May 1942), actor, was born John Sidney Blyth Barrymore in Philadelphia, Pennsylvania, the son of Maurice Barrymore and Georgiana Drew, actors. The third of three children, Barrymore would become the most conspicuous member of America's "Royal Family" of actors. Wild as a youth, he frequently received disciplinary action at the many elementary schools he attended; one such

experience led to what he believed would be his life's calling. "I was punished by remaining the whole day in an empty schoolroom with a big book," he recalled to his biographer Alma Power-Waters. "It was *Dante's Inferno*. At first I was bored and then resentful, but upon seeing the beautiful illustrations by Doré my interest was aroused, and a new urge was born within me. I wanted to be an artist."

Barrymore traveled with his father to England in 1898 and enrolled at King's College at Wimbledon Common and later at London University and the Slade School of Art to pursue training in art. Returning in 1900, he joined the *New York Evening Journal* as a cartoonist. Pressure to join the family "trade," however, was growing; in early 1901, he accompanied his father in a playlet called *A Man of the World*, and in October of that year, his sister Ethel talked him into appearing in a Philadelphia staging of *Captain Jinks of the Horse Marines*, his first full-length play. Following his dismissal from the *Evening Journal* around May 1902, he reluctantly began working his contacts in the theatrical world.

Barrymore soon joined a touring company in Chicago headed by McKee Rankin, a distant relative, and appeared in *Magda* as a minor character saddled with sluggish one-liners. Although his performance in a follow-up play was even less memorable (he uttered only one line), producer Charles Frohman decided to put Barrymore in his first Broadway play, the lightweight comedy *Glad of It*, which opened in December 1903.

Barrymore's work in this play attracted the attention of William Collier, a premiere comic actor. About to launch a Broadway production of *The Dictator*, Collier cast Barrymore as a drunken telegrapher. *The Dictator* played to great acclaim, and many critics praised Barrymore's performance. A highly successful *Dictator* tour followed from September 1904 to July 1905, and Barrymore, after appearing in several other plays, rejoined Collier's company in early 1906 for another tour. The troupe happened to be in San Francisco en route to Australia when the 1906 earthquake struck. The first shock roused Barrymore from bed, and the second threw him into the bathtub. Later, after Barrymore was trying to reach Oakland, military troops recruited him to help clear the roads. "It took a convulsion of Nature to get him into a bathtub and the United States Army to make him work," mused his uncle, John Drew.

Barrymore eventually completed the Australian tour and returned to America for several new roadshows, including one his sister arranged in 1907. Ethel included a staging of *A Doll's House* within this tour and cast him as the syphilitic Dr. Rank. Although distracted by the Stanford White murder trial underway in New York (he was once romantically linked to Evelyn Nesbit, wife of the accused killer), Barrymore handled his first dramatic assignment well.

Also in 1907 Barrymore landed his first leading role in *The Boys of Company "B"*. Although his next play, *Toddles*, proved a failure, Barrymore scored a major success with *A Stubborn Cinderella*. He devoted a whole year to this play, appearing in hundreds of performances before it closed in May 1909. Barrymore hit his stride as a comic actor in what was to be his longest running play, *The Fortune Hunter*. This play, about a charming New York con man hoping to marry into money, opened that fall and played for 345 performances before Barrymore took it on the road from September 1910 to June 1911. At the start of the tour, Barrymore engaged in what some believed was a little fortune hunting of his own by marrying socialite Katherine Harris.

Barrymore met with only moderate success on the stage during the next few years, and perhaps in response he made his first feature film, *An American Citizen* (1914), for the Famous Players company. It proved such a hit that the studio cast him in nine slapstick farces from 1914 to 1919. These films contrasted with his newfound interest in more serious drama, which began with *The Yellow Ticket*, a 1913 play about prostitution in Russia, and *Kick in*, a 1914 crime melodrama.

By 1916 Barrymore had gravitated further from comedy by starring in John Galsworthy's grim drama of misguided legal retribution, *Justice*; audiences and critics responded well to his makeover as a serious actor. This turn in Barrymore's career was not the only significant thing to come out of *Justice*; a costar introduced him to a young society woman named Blanche Oelrichs, who wrote poetry under the pseudonym of Michael Strange. The mutual attraction was immediate, and the two would wed in 1920, less than three years after his divorce from Katherine Harris. Barrymore and Strange would have one daughter.

Justice led to a string of other high-minded, well-received dramas: *Peter Ibbetson* in 1917, *Redemption* in 1918, and *The Jest* in 1919. He also turned a corner in the movies by starring in such serious works as *The Test of Honor* (1919) and *Dr. Jekyll and Mr. Hyde* (1920). Barrymore was still working on this latter film and *The Jest* when he began rehearsals for his first Shakespearean play, *Richard III*. With Barrymore cast as the gnarled, black-armored title character, the play proved an immensely popular draw. He collapsed from the physical and psychological challenges of the role after only several weeks but remained justly proud of his work.

After taking a much-needed break, Barrymore convinced producer Arthur Hopkins to mount a Broadway production of *Hamlet*. After months of work, Hopkins and Barrymore opened it in late 1922. Perhaps as a reaction to his sensitive characterizations in earlier plays, Barrymore decided to play his new character as a man's man. "Hamlet was a normal, healthy, lusty young fellow who simply got into a mess," said he. Critics agreed with his interpretation, universally praising the production as the best *Hamlet* they had seen.

His work also caught the attention of Warner Bros. executives, who signed him to appear in *Beau Brummel*. Shot during the summer of 1923, this tale of a dandy's rise and fall was Barrymore's first film made in California. Returning east, Barrymore reopened *Hamlet* in November 1923 and toured with it for several months. *Hamlet* and *Beau Brummel* brought him accolades aplenty, but Barrymore wanted something more. With an enormous amount of press attention, he daringly brought *Hamlet* to London where it opened in 1925. Receiving a huge number of favorable reviews during the show's run there, he was now riding the crest of his popularity. Impressed by all the attention, Warner Bros. signed him to a major three-film deal even before he departed London.

The first production was an adaptation of *Moby Dick* called *The Sea Beast*. Exercising his right to choose his leading lady, Barrymore selected an alluring young woman named Dolores Costello. They would become so enchanted with each other that they would marry shortly after his divorce from Michael Strange in May 1928.

After completing *The Sea Beast*, Barrymore began work on what would be remembered as the first feature film with a synchronized soundtrack: *Don Juan*, a loose adaptation of the Lord Byron poem. He followed his third contracted film, *When a Man Loves*, with three moneymakers distributed by United Artists. Although now financially well-off, Barrymore wanted to recapture some of his former glory and revived one of his most famous roles, Richard III, which he enacted in a scene for the 1929 Warners film anthology *The Show of Shows*.

Barrymore completed five more movies for Warner Bros., and, when his contract expired, the MGM studio immediately signed him on. His films there included *Grand Hotel*, a star-studded production that saw Barrymore play a destitute baron to Greta Garbo's fading ballerina, and *Rasputin and the Empress*, which featured the combined talents of Barrymore and his siblings. He also appeared in David Selznick's *State's Attorney*, *A Bill of Divorcement*, and *Topaze* before returning to MGM for several more films. At the expiration of his MGM contract in 1933, Barrymore became a journeyman movie actor.

This latest career twist led to some of his best film work: Universal's *Counsellor-at-Law* in 1933 and Columbia's *Twentieth Century* in 1934. Despite these successes, Barrymore found it increasingly difficult to live and work in Hollywood. His alcoholism was no secret among his peers, and he and they discovered that a major side effect was a frequently failing memory. In addition, his marriage to Dolores Costello and relationship with their two young children were rapidly collapsing. Believing Costello wanted to have him judged mentally incompetent, the actor fled to New York.

Hospitalized in early 1935 for bronchitis and the flu, Barrymore found an intriguing stranger at his door, Elaine Jacobs, a nineteen-year-old Hunter College student. Jacobs immediately hit it off with the aging Barrymore, and her mother arranged to have the convalescing actor move in with her family in New York. The young woman even changed her last name to Barrie to get "as near to Barrymore as I dared," as she noted in her 1964 memoir, *All My Sins Remembered*. He mocked his marriage by openly squiring Barrie about the city, but conflicts with his new "protégée" eventually led him to head back to California alone by train. Barrie literally pursued him, however, and even broadcast a personal appeal from a Kansas City radio station. The strategy worked, and Barrie and her mother soon found themselves staying in a southern California home Barrymore had rented for them.

Back in Hollywood, Barrymore agreed to appear as Mercutio in MGM's *Romeo and Juliet* (1936), his only Shakespearean feature film. Although his career enjoyed an upswing, his private life became even more tumultuous than usual. He and Dolores Costello divorced in October 1936, paving the way for his marriage to Barrie the following month. A public spat over her career plans led Barrie to begin divorce proceedings during the first week of 1937, but a timely reconciliation enabled her to work with her husband on several adapted Shakespearean plays broadcast that summer over NBC radio.

Barrymore continued his film work in 1937 with Paramount, but the first six movies he made bore little distinction. Things picked up in 1938 with MGM's *Marie Antoinette*, Paramount's *Spawn of the North*, and Fox's *Hold That Co-Ed*. Barrymore also turned in respectable performances in two 1939 films: RKO's *The Great Man Votes* and Paramount's *Midnight*.

Barrymore's commendable work in these latter movies may well have prompted him to do something he had not done since 1925: act in a stage play. His comeback vehicle was *My Dear Children*, about an aging ham who helps put his three daughters' lives back together and they his. Frequently ad-libbing his lines, Barrymore turned the play into a traveling circus as it toured much of the country in 1939 before opening on Broadway early the next year.

Throughout the play's run, Barrymore and Barrie continued their headline-making bickering. Barrymore finally divorced her in late 1940, but not before he appeared in *The Great Profile*, a movie spoof of their escapades that had culminated in *My Dear Children*. He parodied himself again in *Playmates* (1941). This movie, his last, amply illustrated the depths to which he had fallen; he played an alcoholic Shakespearean ham named John Barrymore.

If a saving grace to Barrymore's career existed at the time, it was his work in radio. Starting in October 1940, he made more than seventy appearances on Rudy Vallee's "Sealtest Show." This program made him an airwaves star with his dramatic and comic performances, and he remained associated with it up to his death. Indeed, he was in the Sealtest studio on 19 May 1942, when he collapsed and was rushed to Hollywood Presbyterian Hospital. He died ten days later.

Though Barrymore maintained ambivalent feelings about his profession throughout a forty-year career, he was arguably the most influential and idolized actor of his time. Appearing in more than forty stage productions, sixty films, and 100 radio programs, the charismatic Barrymore was famous for his ability to flesh out

and energize even the sketchiest roles. His alcoholic binges, four failed marriages, and self-parodying performances only added to his "Great Profile" legend, and he continues to intrigue and inspire performing arts enthusiasts decades after his death.

• Barrymore papers are held at the theater collection at the New York Public Library for the Performing Arts, Lincoln Center; the Harvard Theater Collection; the Gene Fowler Collection at the University of Colorado at Boulder; and the theater collection at the Museum of the City of New York. The most complete source is Martin F. Norden, *John Barrymore: A Bio-Bibliography* (1995), which offers a thorough assessment of the actor's work in the stage, film, radio, and audio-recording fields. Its annotated bibliography consists of more than 1,200 items, and it also contains information on over forty repositories of rare Barrymore materials. Another important text is Margot Peters, *The House of Barrymore* (1990), a heavily researched and highly readable book that contains discussions of several generations of the Drew-Barrymore clan. Less reliable are the earlier biographies: Alma Power-Waters, *John Barrymore: The Legend and the Man* (1941); Gene Fowler, *Good Night, Sweet Prince: The Life and Times of John Barrymore* (1943); Hollis Alpert, *The Barrymores* (1964); and John Kobler, *Damned in Paradise: The Life of John Barrymore* (1977). Barrymore's film work receives careful attention in Joseph Garton, *The Film Acting of John Barrymore* (1980), and James Kotsilibas-Davis, *The Barrymores: The Royal Family in Hollywood* (1981).

MARTIN F. NORDEN

BARRYMORE, Lionel (28 Apr. 1878–15 Nov. 1954), actor, composer, and artist, was born Lionel Blyth in Philadelphia, Pennsylvania, the son of Herbert Blyth, an actor who adopted the stage name Maurice Barrymore, and Georgiana Drew, an actress. His mother's family had been in the theater for generations. Lionel was raised chiefly in the Philadelphia home of his maternal grandmother, actress-manager Louisa Lane Drew. He attended various private schools until he was fifteen, when his grandmother removed him from school to act with her and his uncle Sydney Drew in a repertory road tour. After a calamitous first appearance on tour as Thomas in *The Rivals* he made his New York debut as a footman in *The Road to Ruin*, both in 1893.

Barrymore, mature-looking at six feet and 155 pounds, did not go back to school. His family was in financial straits, and on the strength of the Barrymore name and his increasing technique he was able to support himself playing in touring productions through 1894–1895, though he claimed to be uninterested in the stage as a profession. He later recalled, "I didn't want to act. I wanted to paint or draw. The theater was not in my blood, I was related to the theater by marriage only; it was merely a kind of *in-law* of mine I had to live with" (*We Barrymores*, p. 37). In 1896 he returned to Broadway with a role in *Mary Pennington, Spinster*. He also took lessons at the Art Students League in New York City. From an early age he shared the family addiction to alcohol.

After several more years of intermittent acting on tour and in stock companies, Barrymore played a romantic role in the play *Sag Harbor* (1900). The New York critics were not kind; the *New York Times* review pronounced him "too saturnine and brutal" (30 Sept. 1900). The play was not a success, and it confirmed Barrymore's dislike of roles in which he appeared recognizably as himself, a young man. If he must appear on stage, he preferred to be in character roles where he lost himself in the character's different appearance and personality. He was first hailed by critics and public for the character role of a frenzied Italian in *The Mummy and the Hummingbird* (1902), which starred his uncle John Drew. "The one vital character in the play was the organ grinder of young Lionel Barrymore. In his single short scene he exhibited a burst of genuine passion [that] made you feel it with him" (*New York Tribune*, 5 Sept. 1902).

Success in a central character part followed when he played a prizefighter, Kid Garvey, in the comedy *The Other Girl* (1903). After a season's run in New York, he toured the country in the play the following year. Between the New York run and the tour, in the summer of 1904, he married actress Doris Rankin. The couple had two daughters who died in infancy. In December 1905 he played opposite his brother John Barrymore for the first time in the one-act *Pantaloon*; another one-act play on the same bill, *Alice-Sit-by-the-Fire*, starred his sister Ethel Barrymore. Despite his successes, he still wished to be an artist, not an actor, and to pursue a growing interest in music. Also, his sister recalled in her memoirs, during the run of *Pantaloon* he developed a "nervous terror" that he would forget his lines (p. 152). After the play closed, in 1906 Barrymore and his wife left for Paris, where he was an art student for three years.

In 1909, when Barrymore's belief in himself as a painter and his funds both ran out, he returned to the United States. After playing a character role in a Chicago production of *The Fires of Fate* (1910), he left the cast abruptly to avoid the "nervous terror" of the play's New York opening; an attack of appendicitis was blamed. For the next two years he toured in vaudeville, playing in dramatic sketches with his wife and other family members, then joined D. W. Griffith's stock company of movie actors at the Biograph studio in New York City. From 1912 through 1914 he appeared as a character actor in dozens of the short films Griffith was then making as well as writing and occasionally directing. The best known of his Griffith films are *The New York Hat* (1912) and *Judith of Bethulia* (1913). He did not accompany the Griffith troupe to California in 1914 but continued to make films with other East Coast companies, including two serials with Pearl White.

In 1917 John Barrymore was preparing to appear in the title role of the play *Peter Ibbetson*. He and others pressed Lionel Barrymore to return to the stage in the play's outstanding character role, Colonel Ibbetson. Barrymore resisted, content with his steady work in motion pictures and with his artistic avocations. Ultimately he took the challenge, and his portrayal of the evil Colonel was hailed as an outstanding perform-ance, "artfully and richly played" (*New York Times*, 22 Apr. 1917).

Three more successful Broadway roles followed. In *The Copperhead* (1918), Barrymore played Milt Shanks, a Union spy during the Civil War whose true patriotism is revealed only when he has grown old despised by associates for his supposed Confederate sympathies. In 1919 he appeared with his brother in *The Jest*, a drama of Renaissance Italy, playing a viciously humorous braggart of a soldier. "It would be a rash man who ventured to set a limit on the powers of an actor [i.e., Lionel Barrymore] who has already risen so high" (*New York Times*, 10 Apr. 1919). Even more praise was given his performance as a heartless, ambitious attorney in *The Letter of the Law* (1920). The *New York Times* reviewer wrote, "it is a fascinating thing to watch with what a wealth of unobtrusive detail he brings [the role] to life" (24 Feb. 1920). In 1920 he also appeared in three films, including a screen version of *The Copperhead*.

Emboldened by this string of successes, Barrymore ventured to take the lead in a Broadway revival of *Macbeth* (1921). The production "had the distinction of being that season's—that decade's—most spectacular failure" (Peters, p. 214). Barrymore took a drubbing from critics and public alike, and he was reconfirmed in his belief that the stage was a cruelly uncertain place for him. His brother John's spectacular success in *Hamlet* the following year only deepened the emotional pain of his own failure.

Barrymore began to withdraw from the stage as a venue, though he had successes in two plays in the next few years: *The Claw* (1921), a drama of a middle-aged man's sexual enslavement to a young woman, and the Pagliacci story of *Laugh, Clown, Laugh* (1923). He also made eleven films from 1921 through 1924. *The Claw* wrought a change in his personal life: in the cast was actress Irene Fenwick, with whom he fell deeply in love. He and his wife divorced in 1922, and in 1923 he married Fenwick. His second marriage was childless. In 1925 he appeared in three Broadway productions in a row, all of them abject failures. The ignominy of these successive flops turned him finally to embrace the high pay and easy work of filmmaking. In 1925 he signed a long-term contract with Metro-Goldwyn-Mayer (MGM). His only future stage appearance was in a Los Angeles production of *The Copperhead* in 1927.

Barrymore's first years in Hollywood brought him leading roles with Greta Garbo in *The Temptress* (1926) and with Gloria Swanson in *Sadie Thompson* (1928). His talking picture debut was in *The Lion and the Mouse* (1928), in which his "knowledge of diction, linked with his splendid acting, overwhelmed the other players," said the *New York Times* (16 June 1928). Yet after this good beginning, from 1928 to 1931 he worked as a director at MGM as often as he acted. Reportedly, he had difficulties with morphine addiction in the years after an operation in 1925, in addition to the family weakness for alcohol and later a cocaine addiction. But in 1931 his performance in a bravura courtroom scene in *A Free Soul* won him an Academy Award as best actor of the season, and thereafter he worked exclusively in front of the camera.

Among Barrymore's film appearances in the 1930s were some made with his brother John: *Arsene Lupin* (1932), *Grand Hotel* (1932), *Rasputin and the Empress* (1932), *Dinner at Eight* (1933), and *Night Flight* (1933). His sister Ethel also appeared in *Rasputin*. One of the studio's top character stars, he appeared in no less than five films a year during the decade. Beginning in 1933, he also starred as Scrooge in a radio version of *A Christmas Carol* every holiday season—except when he was devastated by the death of his wife a few days before Christmas in 1936. That year John Barrymore filled in for him. When hip injuries relegated him permanently to a wheelchair in 1938, his close friend Louis B. Mayer, head of the MGM studio, saw to it that suitable roles were found for him, beginning with *You Can't Take It with You* (1938). In 1938, he also began a long run as crusty, wise old Dr. Gillespie in the fifteen films of the *Dr. Kildare* series. His striking mannerisms of voice and facial expression in the role made him a favorite subject of impersonators.

Besides film work in the 1940s, Barrymore starred on radio in the series "Mayor of the Town," 1942–1947. He also won recognition in this decade as an artist, for his etchings, and as a composer, for musical pieces performed by leading symphony orchestras. He worked at both avocations in his dressing room at the studio between scenes. His final memorable performance in a movie was as the doughty old man defying mobsters in *Key Largo* (1948). Offscreen, the aging Barrymore lived in Chatsworth, California, with relatives of his second wife who looked after him; he kept his Beverly Hills home intact, but unused, as a shrine to his late wife. His finances and tax debts became so entangled that MGM took them over entirely, simply doling him an allowance each week.

In 1951 upheavals at the studio brought the departure of Mayer and, soon after, the end of Barrymore's long association with MGM. His rambling historical novel, *Mr. Cantonwine*, was published in 1952. His final film appearance was a cameo part as himself in *Main Street to Broadway* (1953). His death in Van Nuys, California, ended a sixty-year acting career that brought him fame and distinction despite his repeated avowals that he had a lifelong "blanket aversion to acting."

• Materials on the life of Barrymore are in the Billy Rose Theatre Collection, New York Public Library for the Performing Arts, Lincoln Center. Barrymore's autobiography is *We Barrymores* (1951). Further information on him is in Ethel Barrymore, *Memories* (1955). Margot Peters, *The House of Barrymore* (1990), an important source of biographical information, includes a chronology of his stage and film appearances. His years at MGM are sketched in James Robert Parish and Ronald L. Bowers, *The MGM Stock Company* (1973). A portrait of his later life is Frederick James Smith, "Loneli-est Man in America," *New York Herald Tribune*, 4 May 1941. Obituaries are in the *New York Times* and the *New York Herald Tribune*, both 16 Nov. 1954, and *Variety*, 17 Nov. 1954.

WILLIAM STEPHENSON

BARRYMORE, Maurice (21 Sept. 1849–25 Mar. 1905), actor-playwright, was born Herbert Arthur Chamberlayne Hunter Blyth in Amritsar, India, the son of William Edward Blyth, a deputy commissioner, and Charlotte Matilda de Tankerville. At age ten, following the tradition of prominent Anglo-Indians, Herbert sailed for England to prepare for a direct appointment to the East India Company's service. Bright, spirited, athletic, and strikingly handsome, he opted instead for the less restrictive pleasures of London, becoming, to the horror of his proper Victorian family, the middleweight boxing champion of England in 1872. That same year, going from bad to untenable in the estimate of his relatives, he made his acting debut on 1 April at the Theatre Royal, Windsor, as Cool in Dion Boucicault's *London Assurance*. The actor's life more than acting itself captivated the bohemian refugee from the middle class. He toured as "G. H. Blythe," playing second leads in popular provincial fare, even managing a respectable Bassanio at Hull, where to further separate himself from his forebears he was billed as "Maurice Barrymore."

In 1874 Barry, as he came to be called, sailed to Boston, Massachusetts, where he won audiences as the romantic hero of Augustin Daly's rousing new melodrama *Under the Gaslight*, directed by its celebrated author. He enhanced his popular appeal as the dashing Captain Molyneux in the first Boston presentation of Dion Boucicault's *The Shaughraun*, inspiring the *Boston Evening Transcript* critic to observe that he embodied "all the requisites for his part, in his broad shoulders, manly stride, clean-cut features, handsome teeth, gentlemanly bearing, and refined self-possession." This comprehensive inventory did not escape Augustin Daly, who hired the new arrival as leading man for his famous Fifth Avenue Theatre company. While winning New Yorkers in such Daly hits as *The Big Bonanza* (his New York debut was 23 Aug. 1875), he participated in Edwin Booth's four-week, ten-play marathon, garnering particular praise for his Laertes to Booth's Hamlet on 25 October 1875.

Barry became a convivial regular at actors' clubs and cafes—the "Bedouin of Broadway," according to his colleague Otis Skinner. Matinee girls gazed longingly as he promenaded the lively blocks between Union and Madison squares, where most of New York's theaters were clustered. *Vanity Fair*, a popular tabloid of the day, described his impact in 1875: "Anyway, along came Barrymore, the finest looking youngster you could find in a day's ride, and with the highest spirits, the keenest wit, the completest courage that anybody ever saw in a single human envelope" (quoted in Kotsilibas-Davis, p. 71). He met his match when Georgiana Drew, the bewitching descendant of a venerable theatrical dynasty, joined the Fifth Avenue company. They were married in 1876, and, not surprisingly, punctuated their tempestuous relationship with three remarkable children—Lionel, Ethel and John.

After an ill-fated attempt at management with a touring production of Sardou's *Diplomacy*—Barry was wounded and another actor in his company killed by a Texas desperado—Barry returned to the New York stage in 1879. Among the aristocrats of acting in Wallack's Theatre company, he brought youthful vigor to such roles as the swashbuckling Count de Lancy in *A Child of State*. Acting, however, particularly as vacuous heroes, had become merely an expedient for Barrymore. Playwriting became his overriding goal after his first attempt, *Honour*, made a hit on 24 September 1881 at London's Royal Court Theatre. During his return to England, a brief affair with the fiery Polish tragedienne Helena Modjeska led to several American tours. His reputation soared as her leading man with vivid portrayals of such Shakespearean staples as Romeo, Orsini, and particularly Orlando. Nevertheless, the tours were fraught with the star's frustrated attempts to rekindle their London affair. The main casualty was *Nadjezda* (1884), the tragic masterpiece that Barry had written for Modjeska. "Mr. Barrymore has distanced all competitors, and at one bound taken the first place among America's dramatists," wrote John Bradford, the *Boston Courier* critic, in April 1884. "*Nadjezda* is, so far as my knowledge goes, the most powerful play written in English during the present generation." Judging by the response of contemporary critics, Barry's red-blooded, nihilistic tragedy might have satisfied his ambitions and galvanized the tepid theater of its time. But Modjeska used it to manipulate the playwright, presenting it on off nights and burying it in her repertoire. Court battles ensued, all performance rights reverted to Barry, and he again returned to England with Georgie and the children in tow. He participated in one of the British theater's most prestigious events—the glittering Farewell Season of Squire and Marie Bancroft at the Theatre Royal, Haymarket. Barry's London debut, encompassing revivals of such Bancroft successes as Sardou's *Diplomacy* and Reade and Taylor's *Masks and Faces*, won critics and patrons but served as a mere prelude to a Haymarket production the following season of *Nadjezda*. On opening night 2 January 1886, however, rowdy pittites, taking exception to the leading lady's German accent, undermined the performance with hooting and hissing. All was not lost. Sarah Bernhardt requested a French translation that Barry himself made and delivered. Unfortunately the wily Bernhardt gave the manuscript to her favorite French playwright Victorien Sardou, who plagiarized it as *La Tosca* and usurped the international success that should have been Barrymore's. Although he wrote six subsequent plays, the disheartened dramatist never again approached the power and potential of his beleaguered masterpiece.

He did, nevertheless, achieve his greatest fame when A. M. Palmer "specially engaged" him for his Madison Square Theatre company, which made Barry the only actor to serve respectively as leading man for the foremost nineteenth-century managers: Daly, Wallack, and Palmer. After he opened on 4 December 1888 as the gallant highwayman in Haddon Chambers's *Captain Swift*, Edward Fales Coward, the dramatic editor of the *New York World* who often deplored Barry's inconsistency, wrote that "had he done nothing else [but this and Orlando] they would still entitle him to a high place in histrionic ranks. . . . it was the genius of a true artist that made [Swift] real and human . . . strong in color, perfect in poise, and sustained in its power and beauty." He consolidated his standing as the acerbic Lord Darlington in the American premier of Oscar Wilde's *Lady Windermere's Fan* (1893) and in Augustus Thomas's *A Man of the World* (1889), a one-act play that served Barry well when he became the first major legitimate actor to headline a vaudeville bill eight years later.

After Georgie's untimely death from consumption in 1893, her distracted widower became increasingly erratic, although he managed two more resounding hits—opposite Mrs. Leslie Carter in Belasco's *The Heart of Maryland* (1895), and as Rawdon Crawley opposite Mrs. Fiske in *Becky Sharp* (1899). Two years later, following a devastating mental breakdown on the stage of New York's Lion Palace Music Hall, he was diagnosed with paresis, the final, brain-damaging stage of syphilis. Committed to a Long Island sanitarium, he spent his last four years fading in and out of coherence, scribbling indecipherable dramas. "'Alas, poor Yorick!'" quoted his friend, the author William Rideing. "Draw a veil over his frailty, for it was far outweighed by kindness and many other merits. In his character and temperament he was not unlike his own favorite of fiction—Fielding's Tom Jones—a sinner, but a very sweet one" (*Many Celebrities and a Few Others* [1912]).

Arguably the most potentially gifted actor of his generation, Barrymore dissipated his powers in convivial night rambles and vollies of wit. Heralded as the most promising among his contemporary dramatists, he lost heart after uncontrollable circumstances sabotaged his masterpiece. Yet circumstance—and genes—also led his three children to the incredible fame that ensured immortality for their ill-fated progenitor.

• For further study of Barrymore see the memoirs of his children: Ethel Barrymore, *Memories* (1955); John Barrymore, *Confessions of an Actor* (1926) and *We Three* (1935); and Lionel Barrymore, *We Barrymores* (1951). James Kotsilibas-Davis, *Great Times Good Times: The Odyssey of Maurice Barrymore* (1977), covers Barrymore's life in detail, while comprehensive family surveys include Hollis Alpert, *The Barrymores* (1964), and Margot Peters, *The House of Barrymore* (1990). An obituary is in the *New York Times*, 26 Mar. 1905.

JAMES KOTSILIBAS-DAVIS

BARTELME, Mary Margaret (24 July 1866–25 July 1954), lawyer and judge, was born in Chicago, Illinois, the daughter of Balthazar Bartelme, a building contractor, and Jeanette Hoff. She attended local schools, graduating from high school in 1882. She then attended Cook County Normal School, graduating to teach in the Chicago school system for five years. Originally she had planned a career in medicine, but a woman doctor advised against it and told her to meet with attorney Myra Bradwell instead. After a visit with Bradwell, Bartelme became convinced she should study law and enrolled in the Northwestern University Law School.

Bartelme graduated from Northwestern in 1894 as the only woman in her class to earn an LL.B. degree. Her thesis, "Spendthrift Trusts," won a prize, and Bradwell printed it in the *Chicago Legal News*. Admitted to the Illinois Bar in 1894, Bartelme took up a general law practice, specializing in probate law. She was admitted to the U.S. bar in 1896. In 1897 she was appointed a public guardian in Cook County. In this role she found suitable homes for orphaned children and helped to manage minor children's estates. She served in this capacity for sixteen years.

As an activist member of the Women's City Club, Bartelme took part in urging the passage of the Juvenile Court Act of 1899, which established the Chicago Juvenile Court, the first of its kind in the United States. Before its establishment both boys and girls accused of crimes spent their nights awaiting a hearing in the county jail among older, more hardened criminals. Especially disturbing to Bartelme were the cases of young delinquent females. Her criticism of the handling of these defendants in the courtroom led Judge Merritt Pickney to recommend that a woman hear these cases. In 1913 Bartelme was appointed to serve in that capacity, becoming an assistant to the judge, although her legal status was that of probation officer.

In her new capacity Bartelme heard the cases of delinquent girls from the ages of ten to seventeen. For their protection, she interviewed both the girls and their parents in private to determine the best course for a girl. She recommended this, and the judge rendered a final disposition of the case. Bartelme served as a girls' probation officer for ten years.

Bartelme had a great deal of sympathy for the young girls she counseled. Although charges had been brought against them she believed that there were no bad children. Rather, she characterized the girls she saw as "confused, neglected children, love-starved and resentful children." She hoped to give them what they lacked: "understanding and a fresh start—in the right direction" (*Chicago Bar Record*, p. 232). Journalists liked to quote Bartelme, and she received praise for her "judicial temperament" and her "quick and comprehensive" mind.

Bartelme objected to girls' being locked in jail, and it concerned her to see them separated from their families. In 1914 she remedied the situation by converting her house on the city's West Side into the first "Mary B Club." Fourteen residents were brought into this halfway house in the beginning; over the years the numbers fluctuated, and girls stayed for as little as six months or as much as several years. Bartelme received funding from various women's organizations for the upkeep of this group home.

Contributions were also used to provide each girl who left the home a suitcase containing underwear, toiletries, and a new serge dress. This was a continuation of a practice Bartelme had begun when sending girls to foster homes early in her career. She believed that this would help give the girl confidence to improve her life. Reporters soon christened Bartelme "Suitcase Mary." The program was a success. By her retirement in 1933, 9,000 suitcases had been distributed, and by 1991 six Mary B Clubs, which became known as Mary Bartelme Clubs, had been established.

In 1923 the Women's Bar Association of Illinois, organized in 1915 to promote women's interests, helped to convince the Cook County Republican Party to nominate Bartelme to finish the unexpired term of a Cook County circuit court judge. Winning with a margin of more than 14,000 votes, Bartelme became the state's first woman judge. The day after her election, women crowded the streets in a victory celebration. She continued to hear the cases of delinquent girls, but now with authority to dispose the cases. She was elected to a full six-year term in 1927.

Although Bartelme blamed absence of supervision in the home for juvenile delinquency, she named other social ills as contributing factors. She cited a lack of censorship in movie theaters and recommended that communities demand better-quality movies. She promoted the idea of using neighborhood schools as community centers for chaperoned dances and activities. She proposed raising the minimum age for working girls from fourteen to sixteen to keep young women in school. Although traditionalist in believing that girls should learn cooking, sewing, and housekeeping, she supported such advances as hiring women on the police force; she believed women officers could better handle situations involving young girls.

A Republican, Bartelme was an early advocate of woman suffrage and belonged to the Woman's Party, the Chicago Suffrage Club, and the League of Women Voters. She served on the Chicago Bar Association Committee and the Delinquent Children's Committee. Raised as a Protestant, she later became a Christian Scientist. She never married.

At least 2,000 girls had passed through Bartelme's clubs by the time of her retirement in 1933. She left the bench and Chicago, settling in Carmel, California, with her sister, brother, and niece. She spent her retirement in one of her favorite pursuits, gardening. She died in Carmel.

Seeing that female delinquents had special needs requiring a woman's understanding, Bartelme sought to place her young charges in the best environment possible. Confident of her belief in the basic goodness of children, she presided over a very special court where girls were truly given another chance.

• Bartelme's papers are at the University of Illinois at Chicago. A newpaper clipping file is at the Northwestern University Archives, Evanston, Illinois. Other helpful sources include "Woman's Place at the Bar," *Chicago Legal News* 43 (1911): 370; "America's Only Woman Judge Is Doing a Big Work," *New York Times Magazine*, 25 May 1913, p. 4; "The Opportunity for Women in Court Administration," *Annuals of the American Academy of Political and Social Science*, Mar. 1914, pp. 188–90; *Journal of the Illinois State Historical Society*, 17, Apr. 1924–Jan. 1925, pp. 246–47; Betsy Greenbaum, "'The Court of Another Chance' Where Judge Mary Bartelme Presides," *Woman Citizen*, Aug. 1927, pp. 12–14; Herman Kogan, *The First Century: The Chicago Bar Association 1874–1974* (1974); Adade Mitchell Wheeler and Marlene Stein Wortman, *The Roads They Made: Women in Illinois History* (1977); Marilyn A. Domer et al., *Walking with Women through Chicago History* (1981); and Karen Berger Morello, *The Invisible Bar: The Woman Lawyer in America 1638 to the Present* (1986). For the procedures of Bartelme's court, see Helen Rankin Jeter, *The Chicago Juvenile Court* (1922). A memorial appeared in the *Chicago Bar Record* 36 (Feb. 1955): pp. 232–33. Obituaries are in the *New York Times* and *Chicago Tribune*, both 26 July 1954.

MARILYN ELIZABETH PERRY

BARTELMEZ, George William (23 Mar. 1885–2 Sept. 1967), biologist, was born in New York City, the son of Theodore Bartelmez, a lumber company manager, and Caroline Osten. He received a B.S. from New York University in 1906, then remained an additional year to work as an assistant in zoology in order to earn enough money to continue his education. In 1907 he was awarded a fellowship in zoology at the University of Chicago, from which he received a Ph.D. in embryology in 1910.

After graduating, Bartelmez stayed at the university as an assistant in the Department of Anatomy and began building a collection of human embryos by acquiring specimens from local gynecologists. He also began an investigation into the auditory-vestibular system of fish and in the process developed an interest in the Mauthner cell, a relatively huge neuron, or nerve cell, with an unusual shape that, when paired with another Mauthner cell, signals most fish to start at the sound of a loud noise. At the time neurophysiologists were debating the validity of the "neuron doctrine," which held that nerve cells were discrete and functionally independent from one another and that their synapses, or connections, were not "fused" together in some way that differed from the connections between non-neurons. Bartelmez realized that the Mauthner cell's exceptionally large nerve fiber endings and its connection to twelve different types of nerve fibers should make it easy to determine the nature of its synapses and bring the debate to a close. Although the most powerful light microscope of the day showed only one cell membrane separating the Mauthner cell from a neighboring neuron, he posited that the synapse between these two cells involved the juxtaposition of two membranes in such a way that they appeared to be one. Published in 1915, his conclusion was borne out many years later by a researcher who replicated Bartelmez's experiment using an electron microscope.

In 1912 Bartelmez was promoted to instructor of anatomy, and later that year he married Erminnie Eliza Hollis, with whom he had three children. Unfortunately, in 1917 his pregnant wife was hit by an automobile; the baby was born prematurely, and his wife died eighteen months later from complications resulting from the accident. His close friends, chemist J. W. E. Glattfeld and family, welcomed Bartelmez and his three children into their household and helped him raise the children until they left home as young adults.

In 1917 Bartelmez returned to the study of human embryos when he came into the possession of a well-preserved specimen of the somite period. This stage of development takes place about twenty-one days after the fertilization of the egg and is set in motion when the mesoderm, or middle layer of tissue, begins to divide into segments, or somites, on either side of the embryonic spine; these somites later develop into vertebrae and muscles. Shortly thereafter he began collaborating with Herbert M. Evans of the Carnegie Institution of Washington on a study of the early somite period. Having been promoted to associate professor in 1919, Bartelmez concentrated initially on determining precisely when the optic and otic primordia, from which the eyes and ears form, and the cranial neural flexure, the cavity where the central nervous system begins its growth and development, begin to differentiate. By studying embryos from the presomite to late somite periods, he was able to identify the initial development of both primordia and the flexure as well as of other important embryonic features such as the trigeminal neural crest, which contains the nerves connecting the brain to the face and jaws, and the first somite. The results of this research were published in four articles between 1922 and 1926 and led to a reinterpretation of the order of events that take place during the embryonic growth and development of a human.

Although Bartelmez continued to work with human embryos throughout his career, in the mid-1920s he began to study the events of the menstrual cycle in humans and monkeys. His first research projects in this regard, involving anatomical studies of the human uterine gland cell and the endometrium, the mucous membrane of the uterus, contributed to his promotion to full professor in 1929. The results of his research into the nature of connective tissue in the human endometrium during menstruation as well as circulation in the macaque placenta were published in 1933 in the Carnegie Institution of Washington's *Contributions to Embryology* and in 1935 in *Anatomical Record*, respectively. In 1936 he married a widow with two children, Leila Beeman Arnold (they had no children together), and entered into an eighteen-year collaboration with George W. Corner and Carl G. Hartman that involved the study of menstruation in rhesus monkeys. In particular, the three studied cyclic changes in the endometrium and related these changes to the development of the corpus luteum, a ductless ovarian gland that develops after ovulation to secrete progesterone into the uterus to make it more amenable to the implantation of the fertilized ovum. In 1937 he published "a masterful and exhaustive review on the theories of menstruation" (Bodian, p. 12); this review established him as an authority on the cyclic changes in the uterus. In 1946 he showed that delayed ovulation is a significant factor in the variability of the menstrual cycle. In 1953, three years after retiring from the University of Chicago as a professor emeritus, moving to Baltimore, Maryland, and joining Corner as a consultant in the Department of Embryology at the Carnegie Institution of Washington, he demonstrated that the menstrual cycle varies in mammals in such a way that its only constant feature is bleeding. In 1956 he discovered that menstrual bleeding and the rejection of the endometrium's outer lining were caused by the constriction of its spiral arteries. He culminated his research on menstruation in 1957 with the publication of studies of the uterine blood vessels and blood vascular system in humans and monkeys as well as a paper interpreting the pregnancy cycle in terms of the menstrual cycle.

In 1957 Bartelmez moved to Missoula, Montana, so that his wife could be near her children. He also returned to the study of human embryology as a guest investigator at the University of Montana's Department of Zoology. Over the last ten years of his life, he published the results of his research into the development of the neural crest of the forebrain in mammals and the development of the visual and motor centers of the cerebral cortex in the embryonic brain.

Bartelmez was elected to the National Academy of Sciences in 1949. He served as president of the American Association of Anatomists from 1948 to 1950 and was an honorary fellow of the Chicago Gynecological Society. He died in Missoula, Montana.

Bartelmez made three major contributions to science. His work on the uterine mucous membrane led to a fuller comprehension of the menstrual cycle as well as the role played in that cycle by the various glands, blood vessels, and tissue components. His work on the Mauthner cell contributed to a better understanding of the nature of nerve tissue by shedding light on the cellular structure of synapses. His work in embryology identified distinctive features in the development of the brain and led to a fuller understanding of the sequence of events in the growth and development of the human embryo.

• Bartelmez's papers have not been located. A good biography and a complete bibliography of his work appear in David Bodian, "George William Bartelmez," National Academy of Sciences, *Biographical Memoirs* 43 (1973): 1–26.

CHARLES W. CAREY, JR.

BARTHÉ, Richmond (28 Jan. 1901–6 Mar. 1989), sculptor, was born in Bay St. Louis, Mississippi, the son of Richmond Barthé and Marie Clementine Roboteau, a seamstress. His father died when Barthé was one month old. Barthé began drawing as a child and first exhibited his work at the county fair in Mississippi at age twelve. He did not attend high school, but he

learned about his African heritage from books borrowed from a local grocer and publications given to him by a wealthy white family that vacationed in Bay St. Louis. This family, which had connections to Africa through ambassadorships, hired Barthé as a butler when he was in his teens; he moved with them to New Orleans. At age eighteen Barthé won first prize for a drawing he sent to the Mississippi County Fair. Lyle Saxon, literary critic of the *New Orleans Times Picayune*, then attempted to register Barthé in a New Orleans art school. Barthé was denied admission because of his race.

In 1924 Barthé began classes at the Art Institute of Chicago, his tuition paid by the Catholic priest Harry Kane S.S.L. Living with an aunt, the student paid for his board and art supplies by working as a porter and busboy. During his senior year, Barthé began modeling in clay at the suggestion of his anatomy teacher, Charles Schroeder. His busts of two classmates were shown in the Negro History Week Exhibition. These works, along with busts of Haitian General Toussaint L'Ouverture and painter Henry O. Tanner (first exhibited at a children's home in Gary, Indiana), were included in the Chicago Art League annual exhibition in 1928, the year of Barthé's graduation.

Barthé achieved wide recognition for his bronze busts and figures in the 1930s and 1940s. Within a year after his move to New York in February 1929, he completed thirty-five sculptures. He continued his education at the Art Students League with fellowships from the Rosenwald Foundation (1929–1930). Barthé's first solo exhibitions (favorably reviewed by the *New York Times*) were held in 1934 at Caz-Delbo Gallery in New York, Grand Rapids Art Gallery in Michigan, and the Women's City Art Club in Chicago, followed by solos in New York at Caz-Delbo (1933), Delphic Studios (1935), Arden Galleries (1939), De-Porres Interracial Center (1945), International Print Society (1945), and Grand Central Art Galleries (1947). He exhibited in numerous group shows as well, including the Harmon Foundation (1929, 1931, 1933), the New York World's Fair (1939), the Whitney Museum annuals (1933, 1940, 1944, 1945), the Metropolitan Museum of Art's *Artists for Victory* (1942), and the Pennsylvania Academy of Fine Arts' annual exhibitions (1938, 1940, 1943, 1944, 1948).

Many of Barthé's early works, such as *Masaai* (1933), *African Woman* (c. 1934), and *Wetta* (c. 1934), depict Africans. Barthé dreamed of visiting Africa: "I'd really like to devote all my time to Negro subjects, and I plan shortly to spend a year and a half in Africa studying types, making sketches and models which I hope to finish off in Paris for a show there, and later in London and New York," he remarked (Lewis, p. 11), but he never traveled there. Other works, such as *Feral Benga*, *Stevedore*, and *African Man Dancing* (all 1937), are among the first sculptures of black male nudes by an African-American artist.

In the mid-1930s Barthé moved from Harlem to mid-Manhattan for a larger studio and to be closer to major theaters because many of his clients were theatrical celebrities. Among his portrait busts are *Cyrina* (from *Porgy and Bess*, c. 1934), *Sir John Gielgud as Hamlet* (commissioned for the Haymarket Theatre in London, 1937), *Maurice Evans as Richard II* (1938, now in Shakespeare Theatre, Stratford, Conn.), and *Katherine Cornell as Juliet* (1942). Later Barthé produced busts of other entertainers, such as *Josephine Baker* (1950) and *Paul Robeson as Othello* (1975).

Barthé's largest work is an eight-by-eighty-foot frieze of *Green Pastures: The Walls of Jericho* (1937–1938), which he completed under the U.S. Treasury Art Project at the Harlem River Housing Project. His other public works of art include portraits of Abraham Lincoln (1940, New York; 1942, India), Arthur Brisbane (Central Park), Dr. George Washington Carver (1945, Nashville), and Booker T. Washington (1946, New York University).

Many of Barthé's busts, such as *Birth of the Spirituals* (1941) and *The Negro Looks Ahead* (1944), are imbued with a calm spirituality. Barthé described his representational work as an attempt to "capture the beauty that I've seen in people, and abstraction wouldn't satisfy me . . . My work is all wrapped up with my search for God. I am looking for God inside of people. I wouldn't find it in squares, triangles and circles" (Reynolds and Wright, p. 154). A strong believer in reincarnation, the artist often called himself an "Old Soul" who had been an artist in Egypt in an earlier life.

In the 1940s Barthé received numerous awards, beginning with Guggenheim Fellowships (1941–1942). In 1945 he was elected to the National Sculpture Society (sponsored by Malvina Hoffman) and the American Academy of Arts and Letters. He also received the Audubon Artists Gold Medal of Honor and the James J. Hoey Award for Interracial Justice. Additional honors included election to the National Academy of Arts and Letters (1949). The sculptor was also active in several artists' organizations—the Liturgical Arts Society, the International Print Society, the New York Clay Club, and the Sculptors Guild. Additionally, he had solo exhibitions at South Side Art Center, Chicago (1942); Sayville Playhouse, Long Island (1945); Margaret Brown Gallery, Boston (1947); and Montclair Art Museum, New Jersey (1949).

In 1950 Barthé received a commission from the Haitian government to sculpt a large monument to Toussaint L'Ouverture; it now stands in front of the Palace in Port-au-Prince. In 1947 Barthé had moved to Jamaica, where he remained through the late 1960s. His most notable works from this time are the General Dessalines monument in Port-au-Prince (1952) and a portrait of Norman Manley, the prime minister of Jamaica (1956). The Institute of Jamaica hosted Barthé's solo show in 1959. In 1964 the artist received the Key to the City from Bay St. Louis. He then sculpted contemplative black male nudes, such as *Meditation* (1964), *Inner Music* (1965), and *Seeker* (1965).

Barthé left the West Indies in 1969 because of increasing violence there and spent five years traveling in Switzerland, Spain, and Italy. He then settled in Pasadena, California, and worked on his memoirs. In 1978 he had a solo exhibition at the William Grant Still Center in Los Angeles and was subsequently honored by the League of Allied Arts there in 1981. He died in Pasadena. Following his death, a retrospective was held at the Museum of African American Art (1990). Barthé's work toured the country with that of Richard Hunt in the Landau/Traveling Exhibition, *Two Sculptors, Two Eras* in 1992. His sculpture, in the Metropolitan and Whitney Museums, the Smithsonian Institution, the Art Institute of Chicago, and numerous other collections, continues to be featured in exhibitions and survey texts on African-American art.

• The most complete (although brief) source on Barthé is Samella Lewis, *Two Sculptors, Two Eras* (1992). An early biographical account is in *Current Biography: Who's News and Why* (1940). Reproductions of Barthé's work and his contextualization in the 1930s are in Gary A. Reynolds and Beryl J. Wright, *Against the Odds: African-American Artists and the Harmon Foundation* (1989). The earliest article on the artist is William H. A. Moore, "Richmond Barthé, Sculptor," *Opportunity* 6 (Nov. 1928): 334. Art reviews include "The Story of Barthé," *Art Digest* 13 (1 Mar. 1939): 20; Winslow Ames, "Contemporary American Artists: Richmond Barthé," *Parnassus* 12 (Mar. 1940): 10–17; and Clarence J. Bulliet, "Art in Chicago," *Art Digest* 25 (1 Mar. 1951): 9. Popular coverage includes "Painter's Paradise: Ex-Sculptor Richmond Barthé Finds Peace in Sunny Jamaica," *Ebony*, July 1954, pp. 95–98.

THERESA LEININGER-MILLER

BARTHELME, Donald (7 Apr. 1931–23 July 1989), author, was born in Philadelphia, Pennsylvania, the son of Donald Barthelme, an architect and college professor, and Helen Bechtold. In 1933 the family moved to Houston, Texas, where Barthelme grew up. He attended the University of Houston off and on from 1949 to 1956, studying journalism as well as editing and contributing to the college newspaper and yearbook.

In 1951 he became a reporter for the *Houston Post*, covering cultural events and writing movie reviews. Barthelme was drafted into the U.S. Army in 1953, then sent to Korea. He edited an army newspaper. After his discharge, he returned to the *Houston Post* in 1955. Later that year he took a public relations job with the University of Houston, writing speeches for the president and editing a faculty newsletter. In 1956 Barthelme founded *Forum*, the university literary magazine. In 1959 he joined the board of directors of the Houston Contemporary Arts Museum; two years later he became director of the museum.

Barthelme moved to New York in 1962 to edit a short-lived art and literary review called *Location* that published works by Saul Bellow, Gunter Gass, and Marshall McLuhan. His first short story, "L'Lapse," was published in the *New Yorker* in 1963.

Come Back, Dr. Caligari, Barthelme's first book of short stories, appeared in 1964. Its title alludes to a 1919 expressionist film, *The Cabinet of Dr. Caligari*. The stories satirize artists, existentialism, and failed marriages. They reflect Barthelme's concern about the relation of language and reality. Indulging what he called his "secret vice" of "cutting up and pasting together pictures," the author placed a greater emphasis on experimental plot structures and word play than on traditional storytelling and characterization.

Barthelme lived in Denmark in 1965. The next year he received a Guggenheim fellowship, and in 1967 he published his first novel, *Snow White*, a parody of both the Grimm and Disney versions of the tale. His second collection of stories, *Unspeakable Practices, Unnatural Acts*, followed in 1968. Similar to *Come Back, Dr. Caligari* in technique, these stories deal with war and authority. Barthelme's prose, as evident in this quotation from "The Indian Uprising," is often surrealistic and filled with incongruous lists: "Red men in waves like people scattering in a square startled by something tragic or a sudden, loud noise accumulated against the barricades we had made of window dummies, silk, thoughtfully planned job descriptions (including scales for the orderly progress of other colors), wine in demijohns, and robes."

This type of linguistic experimentation dominates his next collection of stories, *City Life* (1970). It contains "Sentence," a work about a sentence and its typographical progress over the page. Barthelme's next book, *The Slightly Irregular Fire Engine; or, The Hithering Thithering Djinn* (1971), written for children, won a National Book Award in 1972. That year he also received the National Institute of Arts and Letters' Zabel Award, became an instructor at the State University of New York at Buffalo, and published another short story collection, *Sadness*.

In 1973 Barthelme accepted an appointment as visiting professor at Boston University. His next book, *Guilty Pleasures* (1974), was nominated for a National Book Award. It includes parody and satire as well as pieces the author called "bastard reportage" and hovers between fiction and nonfiction. Barthelme became distinguished visiting professor at the City College of the City University of New York in 1974. His next work, *The Dead Father*, was published in 1975. Its plot and characters continually shift and dissolve as they pass through multiple levels of meaning; the novel is an examination of the relationship between father and son.

Barthelme followed this book with a collection of short stories, *Amateurs* (1976). *Here in the Village*, selected nonfiction, appeared in 1978. Another collection of stories, *Great Days*, followed in 1979. About half the pieces in this book are dialogues between speakers who do not respond to one another. In the following exchange from his story "Great Days," one person comments, "To each his own. Handmade bread and individual attention." And the second answers, "You've got to have something besides yourself. A cat, too often." To which the first replies, "I could have done better but I was dumb. When you're young you're sometimes dumb."

In 1980 Barthelme became director of the Creative Writing Program at the University of Houston. *Sixty Stories*, a selection of the author's best work, which won a PEN/Faulkner Award for fiction, appeared in 1981.

Overnight to Many Distant Cities (1983) is yet another collection of Barthelme's stories that is unconventional in style and content. It differs from the others by having a narrative voice that speaks in brief interchapters. Three years later Barthelme published his third novel, *Paradise* (1986). It is a surrealistic examination of aging and popular culture. This volume was followed by two more books in 1987: Barthelme's second children's tale, *Sam's Bar: An American Landscape*, and another collection of short fiction, *Forty Stories*.

The author had three wives before marrying Marion Knox. He had a daughter from his second marriage. Donald Barthelme's death from throat cancer in Houston ended a successful and productive career. A member of the American Academy, Barthelme received the Rea Short Story Award and the Texas Institute of Arts and Letters Award. Novelist Robert Coover once described Barthelme's style as "precise, urbane, ironic, rivetingly succinct, and accumulative in its comical and often surreal juxtapositions" and his "worldview" as "bleakly comic, paradoxical, and grounded in the beautiful absurdities of language." Barthelme's writing has attracted increasing critical attention since his death, and much of his work remains in print.

• Barthelme's papers are at the University of Houston. *The King*, a novel by Barthelme, was published in 1990. Another posthumous volume is *The Teachings of Don B.: Satires, Parodies, Fables, Illustrated Stories, and Plays of Donald Barthelme* (1992). *Donald Barthelme: A Comprehensive Bibliography and Annotated Secondary Checklist* (1977), by Jerome Klinkowitz et al., is the principal bibliographical study, though it is outdated. Major critical studies include Maurice Couturier and Regis Durand, *Donald Barthelme* (1982), Lois Gordon, *Donald Barthelme* (1981), Klinkowitz, *Donald Barthelme: An Exhibition* (1991), Charles Molesworth, *Donald Barthelme's Fiction: The Ironist Saved from Drowning* (1982), Richard Patterson, *Critical Essays on Donald Barthelme* (1992), Barbara Roe, *Donald Barthelme: A Study of the Short Fiction* (1992), Wayne Stengel, *The Shape of Art in the Short Stories of Donald Barthelme* (1985), and Stanley Trachtenberg, *Understanding Donald Barthelme* (1990). Other books with significant discussion of Barthelme are Jack Hicks, *In the Singer's Temple* (1981), Larry McCaffery, *The Metafictional Muse* (1982), Paul Maultby, *Dissident Postmodernists* (1991), and Janusz Semrau, *American Self-Conscious Fiction in the 1960s and 1970s* (1986). An obituary by John Barth is in the *New York Times Book Review*, 3 Sept. 1989, p. 9.

ANDREW T. CROSLAND

BARTHOLDT, Richard (2 Nov. 1855–19 Mar. 1932), congressman and newspaper editor, was born in Schleiz, Thuringia, Germany, the son of Gottlob Bartholdt, a liberal forty-eighter (i.e., a supporter of the liberal revolutions in the German states in 1848), and Carolina Louise Wagner. Following early education in the Schleiz Gymnasium, he immigrated in 1872 to Brooklyn, New York, and gained U.S. citizenship. He returned to Germany to study law in 1877–1878. He worked as a typesetter and printer (Brooklyn, Philadelphia, and St. Louis), reporter for the *Brooklyn Freie*

Presse (1872–1877), foreign editor of the *New Yorker Staats-Zeitung* (1878–1884), and editor in chief of the German evening daily *St. Louis Tribune* (1884–1891). Bartholdt was a member of the St. Louis School Board, 1888–1892, and its president in 1891–1892. He married Caecilia Niedner in 1880. Their only child died as an infant.

Bartholdt's background as a journalist and school board member drew him into public service. His election as a Republican in 1892 to the Fifty-third Congress opened a new career, and he continued to represent the largely German-American Tenth Missouri District in the House of Representatives from 1893 to 1915. Elective office offered more opportunities for influence than the newspaper world, and he gained international recognition as an American and global peace worker.

Bartholdt initially fought against immigration restrictions and prohibition, defended the protective tariff, and favored the Spanish-American War and U.S. annexation of the Philippines. Later regretting his vote for the 1898 war with Spain, he preferred arbitration of international disputes, which the First Hague Peace Conference (1899) endorsed, and was drawn into the Inter-Parliamentary Union for Promotion of International Arbitration (IPU) and its work. He hosted the legislators who were members of this international peace organization at its 1904 annual meeting in St. Louis, which coincided with a world's fair brought to the city through Bartholdt's efforts. Then he organized the U.S. branch of IPU, serving as its president from 1904 to 1914. He rapidly gained an international reputation in the peace movement through his contacts and visits abroad and his participation in and promotion of arbitration conferences and world government.

Never a philosophical pacifist, Bartholdt gained a reputation as a leading peace apostle and observer of international affairs in the House of Representatives. Before World War I, in speeches and writings, he advocated European détente and an end to German militarism, he obtained President Theodore Roosevelt's support for the IPU September 1904 gathering in St. Louis, and he led IPU delegates at a later September 1904 White House reception, urging the president to promote a second peace conference at The Hague. Bartholdt was active in the annual Lake Mohonk (N.Y.) arbitration conferences, which began in 1895, and in drafting model arbitration treaties and plans for a world parliament. He headed the American congressional delegation to the Second Hague Conference (1907) and was a leader and/or an active member in the German-American Peace Society, the American Association for International Conciliation, the American Peace Society, and the World-Federation League. For the latter, in 1910 he sponsored a resolution, endorsed by President William Howard Taft and former president Roosevelt, on behalf of world federation.

With the outbreak of World War I, Bartholdt became the leading congressional spokesperson for American neutrality. As president of the American In-

dependence League, 1914–1917, he early challenged what he regarded as a pro-British position by the Woodrow Wilson administration and the U.S. press. In doing so he represented chiefly the German Americans and Irish Americans in the league and the German Americans in his district. Bartholdt worked for an embargo law on munitions trade and a national advisory referendum on declarations of war. The Fourth American Peace Congress, meeting in St. Louis in 1913, passed a war referendum study-resolution offered by the German-American Peace Society, and on 21 July 1914 Bartholdt introduced in Congress a war referendum resolution. Bartholdt's resolution, the first of its kind, died without action in the Judiciary Committee of the House of Representatives. Bartholdt decided against seeking reelection in 1914.

After departing Congress Bartholdt continued to work on behalf of arbitration, the war referendum, a munitions embargo, and mediation of the war in Europe, along with former secretary of state William Jennings Bryan, another war referendum advocate and opponent of intervention. Bartholdt also joined the Ford Peace Ship expedition in 1915. After the United States entered the war in 1917, he defended German Americans and others who questioned national policy. He later criticized the Versailles treaty and opposed U.S. membership in the League of Nations. During the 1931 War Policies Commission hearings in Congress, Bartholdt appealed once more for his peace program: a small military establishment, the war referendum, government manufacture of munitions, and a wartime embargo of money and munitions.

Bartholdt related his experiences as a German-American idealist, newspaperman, congressman, and peace apostle in his autobiography, *From Steerage to Congress: Reminiscences and Reflections* (1930). He discussed his unrealized hopes for European détente and avoidance of world war; his consideration of a campaign for the Senate, regarded as unrealistic for a German American once the European war began; and his disappointments with what he believed was a failed postwar peace settlement. Just before his death in St. Louis, Bartholdt received honorary membership on the faculty of the University of Jena in recognition of his lifetime efforts to improve German-American relations. His principal contributions were to the cause of international peace and to the American peace movement.

• Bartholdt's papers are in the Missouri Historical Society. In addition to his autobiography, his major writings include *The American Proposition for Peace* (1906), *International Arbitration and Peace* (1909), and *War and Its Remedy* (1910). His work in IPU is best presented in Hayne Davis, ed., *Among the World's Peacemakers: An Epitome of the Interparliamentary Union* (1907; repr. 1972). See also Warren F. Kuehl, *Seeking World Order: The United States and International Organization to 1920* (1969); David S. Patterson, *Toward a Warless World: The Travail of the American Peace Movement, 1887–1914* (1976); and Ernest C. Bolt, Jr., *Ballots before Bullets: The*

War Referendum Approach to Peace in America, 1914–1941 (1977). An obituary is in the *St. Louis Post-Dispatch*, 19, 20 Mar. 1932.

ERNEST C. BOLT, JR.

BARTHOLOW, Roberts (28 Nov. 1831–10 May 1904), physician, was born in New Windsor, Maryland, the son of Jeremiah Bartholow and Pleasants (maiden name unknown). He grew up in a well-to-do family and attended Calvert College (later New Windsor College), where he earned an A.B. in 1848, and the University of Maryland, receiving an M.D. in 1852. He then returned to Calvert College to practice medicine for two years and to teach chemistry. He took postgraduate medical courses in Baltimore in 1855 and 1856, then served as an army surgeon for four years in Utah, New Mexico, and Minnesota. The rigors of this tour of duty led to a variety of ailments, including the loss of most of his teeth. Although a southerner, he remained in the U.S. Army during the Civil War, serving as a medical examiner, advising Surgeon General William A. Hammond, supervising hospitals, and publishing *A Manual of Instructions for Enlisting and Discharging Soldiers* (1863), *Qualifications for the Medical Service* (1865), and a series of papers for the U.S. Sanitary Commission.

Bartholow married in 1864, settling with his wife Maria in Cincinnati, Ohio, where they raised five children. He served as a contract surgeon there for the remainder of the war, quickly building a substantial practice and becoming a prominent figure in the community. He published medical articles on subjects ranging from fevers and gunshot wounds to the role of sewage in the transmission of disease. He took charge of the local cholera hospital during the epidemic of 1866 and soon obtained admitting privileges and responsibilities as pathologist at other Cincinnati hospitals. He also worked as a medical examiner for a life insurance company. Over the next decade Bartholow taught medical chemistry and materia medica at the Medical College of Ohio. He published books and papers on disinfection, spermatorrhea, hypodermic medication, and other topics. He also founded his own controversial medical journal, the *Clinic*, using its pages to criticize what he considered the mistakes of other physicians and to promote his own theories.

In 1874 Bartholow published a paper in the *American Journal of the Medical Sciences* on his experiments on a young domestic worker with a malignant tumor of the scalp. Since the dura mater was already exposed and the patient's death seemed imminent, Bartholow saw an opportunity to replicate studies of electrical stimulation of brain function previously conducted by E. Hitzig and David Ferrier on animals. The patient consented but then died, perhaps as a direct result of the experiment. Many physicians in the United States and Britain found the affair scandalous; Bartholow apologized in the *British Medical Journal* and urged that no such further experiments be undertaken. Nonetheless, he retained his busy practice and was honored in 1874 by his colleagues at the Medical College of Ohio with a professorship in the practice of medicine.

Bartholow was known by his contemporaries mainly for his *Practical Treatise on Materia Medica and Therapeutics* (1876), one of the leading American texts on the practice of medicine. It illustrated his commitment to rational therapeutics based on physiological experimentation, rather than what he called "a blind empiricism," the uncritical use of traditional remedies. Bartholow sought to elevate therapeutics to a basic science, using laboratory methods to discover specific remedies such as chloral hydrate. He was seen by some as medically conservative because he did not embrace the new therapeutic nihilism that condemned medication (at least rhetorically) in favor of expectant treatment. However, his work exemplified the innovative effort to advance medical practice through laboratory research, an approach associated with many of the leading German medical scientists of his time.

In 1879 Bartholow left his lucrative Cincinnati practice to become professor of materia medica and therapeutics at Jefferson Medical College in Philadelphia, where he also served as dean of the faculty in the mid-1880s. There he became known for promoting therapeutic investigation on laboratory animals; however, he generally encouraged students to pursue the practice of medicine rather than careers in laboratory research. Bartholow built up a consulting practice in Philadelphia, while completing work on his monumental *Treatise on the Practice of Medicine* (1880) and helping to edit the reorganized journal *Medical News*. He also published *Medical Electricity: A Practical Treatise on the Applications of Electricity to Medicine and Science* (1881), which (like his other major works) was popular enough to warrant multiple editions.

Bartholow retired from his academic positions in 1893, apparently to recuperate from an acute crisis provoked by an opium addiction acquired in the course of treatment for diabetes; he had always been reclusive, preferring to limit his social life to his family circle. Although he resumed practice and literary work, he never recovered fully from this breakdown. He died in Philadelphia.

• For a bibliography of Bartholow's works see the *Index-Catalog of the Library of the Surgeon General's Office*. A small collection of papers pertaining to his military service is in RG 94, Series E-561, National Archives. The most detailed account of his life is James W. Holland, "Memoir of Roberts Bartholow, M.D.," *Transactions of the College of Physicians of Philadelphia* 26 (1904): xliii–lii. On Bartholow's place in American medicine, see John Harley Warner, *The Therapeutic Perspective: Medical Practice, Knowledge, and Identity in America, 1820–1885* (1986). See also J. P. Morgan, "The First Reported Case of Electrical Stimulation of the Brain," *Journal of the History of Medicine and Allied Sciences* 37 (1982): 51–64; and Gregory L. Holmes, "Roberts Bartholow: In Search of Anatomic Localization," *New York State Journal of Medicine* 82 (1982): 238–41.

BONNIE ELLEN BLUSTEIN

BARTLETT, Elisha (6 Oct. 1804–19 July 1855), physician, was born at Smithfield, Rhode Island, the son of Otis Bartlett and Waite Buffum. In his youth Bartlett attended a Quaker school in New York; later he studied medicine under George Willard of Uxbridge, Massachusetts, John Green and B. F. Heywood of Worcester, Massachusetts, and Levi Wheaton of Providence, Rhode Island. Bartlett also attended medical lectures in Boston and Providence. In 1826 he received an M.D. degree from Brown University and then went to study medicine in Paris, where he remained, except for brief visits to Italy and England, about twelve months. On his return to the United States in 1827, Bartlett settled in Lowell, Massachusetts, where he married Elizabeth Slater in 1829; they had no children.

While in Lowell Bartlett entered politics. He became the town's first mayor in 1836, and in 1840 he was elected to the legislature of Massachusetts, where he served two terms.

Bartlett was a teacher for much of his life. His first position, in 1832, was as professor of pathological anatomy and materia medica at the Berkshire Medical Institution in Pittsfield, Massachusetts. He held that chair until 1841, when he took the position of professor of the theory and practice of medicine at Transylvania University in Lexington, Kentucky. In 1846 he held that chair again. In the 1840s and 1850s he also taught medical subjects at the Vermont Medical College, the University of Maryland, the University of Louisville, New York University, and Columbia College of Physicians and Surgeons.

In addition to his duties as a teacher Bartlett spent much time writing, and not always on medicine. In 1838 he published "The Head and the Heart, or the Relative Importance of Intellectual and Moral Education; a Lecture, Delivered Before the American Institute of Instruction, in Lowell, Aug. 1838." In that essay he deplored the neglect of moral culture in America. He took an interest in the women of Lowell in "A Vindication of the Character and Condition of the Females Employed in the Lowell Mills, Against the Charges Contained in *The Boston Times*, and the *Boston Quarterly Review*" (1841), an essay commenting on the remarkable health of Lowell's women millworkers.

As a writer on medical subjects, Bartlett gained a substantial reputation, beginning with the *Monthly Journal of Medical Literature and American Medical Students' Gazette* (1831). His classic report on typhoid fever appeared as *The History, Diagnosis, and Treatment of Typhoid and of Typhus Fever; with an Essay on the Diagnosis of Bilious Remittent and of Yellow Fever* (1842), with three more editions in 1847, 1852, and 1857; it was the best clinical study of typhoid fever in Bartlett's time. Bartlett contributed to the literature on malaria by outlining the theories on it in his treatise on fevers. He treated malaria under the heading of "periodical fever," ascribing the illness to a poison known as malaria or "marsh miasm." Daniel Drake, another writer on malaria, believed microscopic animalcules

were the cause of the disease. Bartlett, while not necessarily accepting that hypothesis, thought the theory corresponded "to the ascertained phenomena in connection with the etiology of these diseases [periodical fever], better than most other hypotheses" (p. 348).

Another important contribution to medicine lay in Bartlett's defense of regular or orthodox physicians against the claims of homeopathy, a popular nineteenth-century therapeutic school. John Forbes, a British doctor, edited the *British and Foreign Medical Review*, in which Bartlett attacked homeopathy in January 1846. In doing so, however, he also questioned the practice of regular medicine. He argued that certainty escaped the physician, especially in therapeutics. Bartlett replied to Forbes in *An Inquiry into the Degree of Certainty in Medicine; and into the Nature and Extent of Its Power over Disease* (1848). He had earlier considered the philosophy of medicine in *An Essay on the Philosophy of Medical Science* (1844). To defend medical practice, Bartlett in 1848 discussed the treatment of pneumonia, arguing for the efficacy of bloodletting and antimonials.

Bartlett's medical philosophy emphasized reliance on observation of patients, a proclivity he gained from his study in the clinical school of Paris in the 1820s. Theories, according to Bartlett, deserved less attention than the phenomena of nature, the direct observation of which comprised the true object of science. The research and teaching of the clinical school derived from observations in the large hospitals of Paris, where there were many opportunities for the observation of patients and autopsies. Bartlett's *An Essay on the Philosophy of Medical Science* (1844) stood alone in the United States as a systematic account of the philosophy of the clinical school.

Bartlett also wrote practical contributions, notably "The History, Diagnosis, and Treatment of Edematous Laryngitis," in *The Western Journal of Medicine and Surgery* (3d ser., 5 [March 1850]: 209–40). He asserted that edematous laryngitis, when untreated by an operation, usually resulted in death. The essay drew in particular on the operations of Gurdon Buck of New York, who had cured several patients by scarifying the edematous membranes.

Bartlett also cherished a reverence for the history of medicine. In *A Discourse on the Times, Character and Writings of Hippocrates* (1852), he remarked on twenty-two centuries of medical art, beginning with the ancient Greeks.

Bartlett influenced the profession of medicine in the United States through his writings, particularly his works on fevers and philosophy. He had an excellent prose style, perhaps the best among such contemporaries as Samuel Henry Dickson, Jacob Bigelow, and J. K. Mitchell. In "Dr. Bartlett's Valedictory Address to the Graduating Class of Transylvania University, 1843," he dealt with the motives of the physician and ended his speech with the advice "to cultivate, to cherish, to strengthen the sense of moral obligation."

Bartlett died relatively young, at Smithfield, Rhode Island. He had a nervous disorder resulting in paralysis without mental impairment.

• Two informative sketches of Bartlett's life are "A Brief Memoir of Dr. Elisha Bartlett with Selections from his Writings and a Bibliography of the Same" (1878); and William Osler, "A Rhode Island Philosopher (Elisha Bartlett)," *Boston Medical and Surgical Journal* 142 (1900): 49–53, 77–82. Interesting views of Bartlett's philosophy appear in Erwin H. Ackerknecht, "Elisha Bartlett and the Philosophy of the Paris Clinical School," *Bulletin of the History of Medicine* 24 (1950): 43–60; and Lester S. King, "Medical Philosophy, 1836–1844," in *Medicine, Science, and Culture: Historical Essays in Honor of Owsei Temkin*, ed. Lloyd G. Stevenson and Robert P. Multhauf (1968), pp. 143–59. An exposition of Bartlett's ideas is in Lester S. King, *Transformations in American Medicine: From Benjamin Rush to William Osler* (1991). For a worthwhile discussion of Bartlett with a bibliography of his writings, see Donald de F. Bauer, "Elisha Bartlett, a Distinguished Physician with Complete Transposition of the Viscera," *Bulletin of the History of Medicine* 17 (1945): 85–92.

KEITH L. MILLER

BARTLETT, Ichabod (24 July 1786–19 Oct. 1853), lawyer and politician, was born in Salisbury, New Hampshire, the son of Joseph Bartlett, a doctor, and Hannah Colcord. Following the death of his father in 1800, Bartlett studied at Salisbury Academy, taught school, and then enrolled in Dartmouth College. After graduating in 1808, he studied law in Salisbury until 1811, when he opened a law practice in Durham, New Hampshire. He soon became a member of the Rockingham County bar, noted for such eminent lawyers as Daniel Webster, Jeremiah Smith, Jeremiah Mason, and George Sullivan. In one of Bartlett's early cases, *Dartmouth College v. Woodward*, he and Sullivan defended the right of the state to make the college into a state university, while Webster, Smith, and Mason acted as attorneys for the college. Arguing before the state superior court in 1817, Bartlett took the position that public corporations such as Dartmouth were subject to state control in the public interest. He and Sullivan won the case, but they were later replaced by other lawyers and were not involved when the state ruling was overturned by the U.S. Supreme Court in a much noted decision. In 1818 Bartlett moved to Portsmouth, New Hampshire, where he spent the rest of his career. He never married.

Bartlett had already shown his interest in politics and the Republican party in 1808 when he delivered a spirited Fourth of July address in Salisbury, defending Thomas Jefferson's embargo. He entered state politics in 1817 as clerk of the senate, and two years later he was elected to the house of representatives, where he served until 1822. At the request of the governor, in 1818 he prepared a comprehensive report on roads, rivers, and canals, which was part of a national survey of internal improvements. The report was presented to the state legislature in 1819, but the projects were never carried out. That same year Bartlett helped secure the passage of the Toleration Act, disestablishing the Congregational church, with an impassioned address

accusing his opponents of "bigotry" and comparing their speeches with "the thunders of the Vatican" (*New-Hampshire Patriot*, 27 July 1819). Bartlett was also solicitor of Rockingham County between 1819 and 1821 and Speaker of the house of representatives in 1821. A founder of the New Hampshire Historical Society in 1823, he was president of the society between 1826 and 1830.

Bartlett was elected to the U.S. House of Representatives in 1822 and served between 1823 and 1829. In his first speech, in January 1824, he drew attention by exchanging barbs with Henry Clay over U.S. policy toward the Greek revolution against the Turks. Bartlett irritated Clay by calling his proposal for supporting the Greeks quixotic. Determined to put the new congressman in his place, Clay patronizingly congratulated him for his "debut," and then taunted him for being frightened by Turkish "scimitars" (*Annals of Congress*, 18th Cong., 1st sess., 1173, 1177). Refusing to back down, Bartlett mocked Clay for his "loud voice . . . menacing look, and sneering gesture" (*Annals*, 1200). When Clay later hinted at a duel, Bartlett stood his ground, and nothing further was said. This exchange and others like it led some observers to compare Bartlett with Congressman John Randolph of Virginia, long famed for his fiery encounters in the House.

Bartlett also became known as a loyal defender of John Quincy Adams's administration, especially in February 1828 when the Jacksonians accused the president of spending money recklessly for the White House, diplomatic missions, and other projects. In a debate over paintings for the Capitol rotunda, Bartlett helped block Jacksonian efforts to commission a painting of the battle of New Orleans. During the same session he took the side of the Indians in a debate over their settlements in Georgia.

After returning to New Hampshire, Bartlett continued his fight against the Jacksonians at the state level. He served a term in the house of representatives in 1830 and then ran unsuccessfully for governor in 1831 and 1832. During the presidential campaign of 1832 he delivered a slashing speech in Portsmouth, accusing Andrew Jackson of having violated almost every one of his 1828 campaign promises. He warned that if the president was reelected, the American republican system would be destroyed.

Aside from serving three more terms in the state house of representatives as a Whig in 1838, 1851, and 1852, Bartlett largely gave up politics after 1832 and concentrated on his law practice, which grew to be one of the largest in the state. With Webster and Mason now in Boston, Smith retired, and Sullivan nearing the end of his career, Bartlett assumed the leadership of the Rockingham County bar. Never as learned as Mason or as intellectual as Webster, he nonetheless won case after case through his careful preparation, his "dexterity," and his "tenacity" (Bell, p. 173). Known as the "little giant" because of his small stature, he became famous for his wit and occasionally his sarcasm.

In 1850 Bartlett consented to be a delegate to the state constitutional convention and often chaired the entire convention when the members sat as a committee of the whole. At the end of the convention the delegates showed their respect for the aging attorney by adopting a resolution congratulating him for the "able manner" in which he had filled the chair and for his "judicious, well-documented and pithy remarks" from the floor (*Portsmouth Journal*, 11 Jan. 1851). During his final session in the house of representatives in 1852, he helped repeal the personal liberty law, in effect since 1846, which had hampered enforcement of the fugitive slave law.

Bartlett never approached the greatness of Webster. When Bartlett died in Portsmouth, just a year after Webster, the mayor of Portsmouth nevertheless mourned the passing of the "last of those great men" of the Rockingham County bar (*Portsmouth Journal*, 22 Oct. 1853).

• Several of Bartlett's speeches are preserved in pamphlet form at the New Hampshire Historical Society. His argument in the Dartmouth College case is in Timothy Farrar, *The Trustees of Dartmouth College against William Woodward* (1819), pp. 161–206. For genealogy see Levi Bartlett, *Sketches of the Bartlett Family in England and America* (1876). For short sketches see Charles H. Bell, *The Bench and Bar of New Hampshire* (1894), pp. 173–78; and Henry P. Rolfe, "Ichabod Bartlett," with portrait, included in John J. Dearborn, *The History of Salisbury, New Hampshire* (1890), pp. 453–56. An obituary, memorial resolutions, and addresses of the Rockingham County bar are in the *Portsmouth Journal*, 22 and 29 Oct. 1853.

DONALD B. COLE

BARTLETT, John (14 June 1820–3 Dec. 1905), editor, publisher, and lexicographer, was born in Plymouth, Massachusetts, the son of William Bartlett and Susan Thacher. Bartlett's love of words manifested itself at an early age: at three years he was reciting verses from the Bible; by nine he had read it from cover to cover. Educated in Plymouth's public schools, he left school at the age of sixteen. Soon after, he took a job at a bookbinding company that was then associated with the University Book Store serving Harvard University in Cambridge. His copious memory and love of books soon had the university faculty and students using him as a ready reference tool. "Ask John Bartlett" was the frequent answer to most questions. To help his memory, Bartlett began keeping a notebook of common phrases and quotations.

In 1849 he became the owner of the bookbinding business, being a good adviser to the authors with whom he worked. In 1851 he married Hannah Stanifield Willard, a kindred bookworm. Hannah was to help him in his two major works, her "ever-ready assistance" making them "a pastime," as John wrote in his dedication to *A New and Complete Concordance* . . . They had no children.

Demand on Bartlett's time soon encouraged him to publish his notebook, and in 1855 he had 1,000 copies of *A Collection of Familiar Quotations* printed privately. He stated that his intention was to show "the obligations our language owes to various authors for . . . 'household words.'" This run soon sold out and was followed by newer and increasingly larger editions. He also published *New Method of Chess Notation* (1857) during this time.

His new career as a publisher and writer was interrupted between 1862 and 1863, when he served as volunteer paymaster with the South Atlantic fleet of the U.S. Navy. In August 1863, however, he returned to his career by joining the publishing firm of Little, Brown and Company. Soon afterward Little, Brown published the fourth edition of *Familiar Quotations*. The ninth, the last edition that Bartlett edited, was published in 1891. Subsequent editions have earned the unofficial title *Bartlett's Familiar Quotations*, and Little, Brown has established a series using the Bartlett name, including *Bartlett's Book of Business Quotations* (1994) and *Bartlett's Book of Love Quotations* (1994).

During his time with Little, Brown, Bartlett earned a reputation as a considerate and generous editor. He became a partner in 1865 and a senior partner in 1878. Meanwhile, he pursued his own interests, publishing *The Shakespeare Phrase Book* (1882), *Catalogue of Books on Angling* (1882), and the extensive *A New and Complete Concordance; or, Verbal Index to Words, Phrases & Passages in the Dramatic Works of Shakespeare, with a Supplementary Concordance to the Poems* (1896).

Angling was a catalog of books that Bartlett had collected when he was preparing a new edition of Izaak Walton's *Complete Angler*. He donated these books to Harvard soon after the *Complete Angler* was published. Bartlett's interest in angling was not all business related, however. He presented poet James Russell Lowell with a freshly caught fish and was thus honored in the poem "To Mr. John Bartlett," which appeared in Lowell's *Under the Willows, and Other Poems* (1869). Lowell, along with the literati of turn-of-the-century Boston, admired Bartlett, probably more for his whist-playing abilities than for anything else.

A New Concordance is considered one of the landmark reference works in Shakespearean scholarship and is still useful a century after it originally appeared. Nevertheless, it is *Familiar Quotations* that remains Bartlett's greatest contribution to scholarship. A reference work that remains indispensable, it lives up to its editor's high ambitions. The sixteenth edition (1992) provides access to more than 20,000 quotations. In recognition of his scholarship he received an honorary degree from Harvard University in 1871 and was elected a fellow of the American Academy of Arts and Sciences.

Bartlett's wife became ill, probably with Alzheimer's disease, around 1895. He tried to continue with his work without her assistance, but her worsening condition soon forced him to give up. After her death in 1904, Bartlett became remote, almost reclusive in his Cambridge home. His own failing health deprived him of the joys of reading that he had documented so well in his autobiographical notebooks, but he still had his friends and companions. He died in Cambridge.

• The most complete biography of John Bartlett is Thomas Wentworth Higginson, "John Bartlett," in *Carlyle's Laugh, and Other Surprises* (1968), pp. 193–99. This is based on Bartlett's unpublished autobiographical notebooks recorded throughout his life. The manuscript is held by Harvard University Library. Bartlett's career was evaluated in the *New York Times*, 5 Dec. 1905. The paper ran a small obituary at the bottom of the front page the day before.

JOHN J. DOHERTY

BARTLETT, John Russell (23 Oct. 1805–28 May 1886), ethnologist and historian, was born in Providence, Rhode Island, the son of Smith Bartlett, a merchant, and Nancy Russell. During his first eighteen years he was schooled in Canada (Kingston and Montreal) and New York before he returned to Providence, where he worked as a bank cashier. Bartlett was married in May 1831 to Eliza Allen Rhodes; they had seven children. In 1836 he moved to New York City. With a partner he opened a bookstore in the Astor House and was soon attracting important customers such as writer Edgar Allan Poe and statesman Albert Gallatin. The bookshop helped sharpen his scholarly interests, which included ethnology and philology, and led to his publishing *The Progress of Ethnology* (1847) and *Dictionary of Americanisms* (1848).

By now Bartlett was developing well-placed friends in high circles. Gallatin, for example, mentioned him to senators Stephen A. Douglas and Thomas Hart Benton (1782–1858), while scientists Joseph Henry and Henry Schoolcraft at the Smithsonian Institution were interested in his studies. Thus, in 1850 when he sought other work for health and financial reasons, these contacts advanced his name for the commissionership of the Mexican Boundary Survey. The Treaty of Guadalupe Hidalgo (1848) at the end of the Mexican War called for a joint commission to run the new boundary line between the United States and Mexico. The Mexican commission under General Pedro García Conde had been reasonably stable from its appointment, but the United States had no such luck. Between 1848 and 1850 three U.S. chief commissioners had been appointed; the first died, the second was removed, and the third resigned before taking up his work. Bartlett, excited over the prospects of combining ethnological and scientific exploration, accepted the position on 19 June 1850. The job was a sensitive one, reflecting political and sectional tensions.

The commission, 140 men, assembled at Matagorda Bay in August and proceeded to El Paso, where they met their Mexican counterparts six weeks later. The Americans were already racked with dissension. Dismissals and replacements were necessary, but the delay gave Bartlett time to start a remarkable series of drawings and watercolors. The actual work of the survey did not begin until 24 April 1851. Shortly afterward Bartlett and García Conde determined the initial point and the subsequent westward line at 32° 22′. Their decision would lead to much controversy since this line deprived the United States of the Mesilla Valley, which was particularly desirable, if not essential, for the southern route of a transcontinental railroad. The choice of the initial point bred dissension between Bartlett and Andrew B. Gray, James D. Graham, and, later, William H. Emory, scientists on the expedition. These and other critics contended that he had surrendered a sizable chunk of territory, roughly 50 miles wide by 190 miles long, the approximate size of Massachusetts. Bartlett did what he felt was called for in the treaty, without reference to larger geopolitical questions, but the matter festered until the United States bought the parcel in the Gadsden Purchase of 1853.

The route surveyed went up the Rio Grande to Dona Ana, west and north to the Gila, and down that river to its confluence with the Colorado. The southern boundary of California had already been marked.

Throughout the entire survey and on side excursions, the U.S. commissioner continued to sketch, to collect specimens of plants and animals, and to observe languages and cultures of the native tribes. His specimens and notes were eagerly received in scientific societies such as the Smithsonian Institution.

On an excursion for supplies to the Mexican town of Ures in October, Bartlett was stricken with typhoid fever and was confined there for nearly three months. García Conde not only took ill but died in the same town. With his remaining strength, Bartlett left Ures in December, traveled via Acapulco to San Diego, and spent the winter in California. There he planned a fresh attack in the field for the next spring.

A pruned and newly equipped expedition set off in May 1853. Work began again at Fort Yuma to bridge in an easterly direction the unfinished gap between the already completed sections. Bartlett's most important ethnological observations were made during this period, when he was encamped with the Pima and Maricopa tribes. He also took some of the earliest measurements of the prehistoric pueblo ruins in the Southwest, stirring interest in future archaeology.

Anti-Bartlett factions were rising in Washington, D.C., as well as on the frontier. With no evidence, southern Democrats accused Bartlett, a northern Whig, of deliberately selling short the southern cause through his boundary decisions. When Bartlett returned to Washington after two and a half years as commissioner, he faced bitter invective and was removed from the position shortly after the Democrats took control of the government under Franklin Pierce. Emory of the Topographical Corps, a southerner who had served with Bartlett but had violently disagreed with him, was placed in charge of the survey and on its completion (the final report was issued in 1857) was granted most of the credit. Without government assistance Bartlett published his own *Personal Narrative* of the earlier expedition, a vivid, literate account of enduring value to scholars and naturalists.

In 1855 Bartlett was elected secretary of state for Rhode Island and served in that office for nearly twenty years. As such, he published *Records of the Colony of Rhode Island and the Providence Plantations* (10 vols., 1856–1865) and compiled an index to the acts of the Rhode Island General Assembly through 1862 (12 vols., 1856–1863). As a historian, he completed several volumes on the literature and memoirs of the Civil War. In the last decades of his life he was associated with John Carter Brown in the acquisition of his remarkable library of colonial Americana. Bartlett compiled a groundbreaking catalog of the collection in four volumes (1865–1882). After the death of his first wife, he married Ellen Eddy in November 1863; it is not known if they had any children.

A man of learning and erudition, Bartlett's experience on the boundary survey placed him for a time in a situation beyond his ability to control. National tensions proved too strong and his leadership capabilities inadequate to the western task; but he was a man of artistry, integrity, and thoughtful honesty, and his subsequent life as historian and bibliographer restored him to a more congenial milieu. Bartlett died in Providence, Rhode Island.

• Bartlett's papers and many of his drawings are housed in the John Carter Brown Library at Brown University in Providence, Rhode Island. His *Personal Narrative of Explorations and Incidents . . . with the United States and Mexican Boundary Commission* (2 vols., 1854) has been reprinted (1965). For his western years, see Robert V. Hine, *Bartlett's West: Drawing the Mexican Boundary* (1968). John D. Haskell, Jr., concentrated on the eastern years in a 1977 dissertation in American civilization at George Washington University, "John Russell Bartlett (1805–1886): Bookman." An obituary appeared in the Providence *Journal*, 29 May 1886.

ROBERT V. HINE

BARTLETT, Joseph (10 June 1762–20 Oct. 1827), lawyer, politician, and writer, was born in Plymouth, Massachusetts, the son of Sylvanus Bartlett and Martha Wait, whose occupations are unknown. A brilliant graduate of Harvard, class of 1782, he was one of three original members of the college's Phi Beta Kappa chapter. After graduation he briefly studied law and taught school in Salem before moving to London in 1783. From then until 1786 Bartlett's life in the British Isles was turbulent. He quickly became famous in society by shouting out from the audience at an anti-American play written by British general John Burgoyne, who surrendered his army to the rebels at Saratoga in 1777, "Hurrah, Great Britain, beaten by barbers, tailors, and tinkers." Bartlett then became acquainted with politician Charles James Fox, playwright Richard Sheridan, and the city's young rakes, in whose company he cavorted, winding up in debtors' prison. To obtain his release, he raised funds for a play of his own composition, the first work by an American to appear on the English stage. He also acted briefly in Scotland under the name of "Maitland."

Tiring of the theater, Bartlett borrowed money to ship a cargo to America, but it wrecked off Cape Cod. This misfortune prompted another of his witticisms, "He was not afraid to die but could not bear to be found dead in such an ordinary place as Cape Cod" (Willis, p. 438). In 1786 he began to study law in Boston, from which he took a brief hiatus in 1787 to serve as a captain of the Republican Volunteers, which set out to assist in suppressing Shays's Rebellion. Recalled after barely beginning to march west because the insurrection had been suppressed, Bartlett remarked that the rebels had surrendered when they heard he had taken the field against them.

Bartlett soon began to practice law in Woburn, where he "harangued in the grog-shops and at the town meetings, and at all times had the power of setting the mob in a roar" (Bell, p. 179). He painted his house black and dubbed it "the Coffin" to drum up business. He married Anna May Wetherell in 1795, but she soon left him, apparently agreeing with local residents, who had begun to use the phrase "as odd as Joe Bartlett" to describe irresponsible or drunken behavior.

In the mid-1790s Bartlett repaired to Cambridge, which he used as a base for practicing law and encouraging unruly college students to defy Harvard's authority. This cantankerousness, born of a fervent egalitarianism he borrowed from Thomas Paine, endeared him to the residents of Cambridge, who sent him to the Massachusetts House of Representatives from 1799 to 1802. Also in 1799 he gave a famous Phi Beta Kappa address in Cambridge in the form of a poem, published in 1810 as *Physiognomy*, which spoofed the Harvard faculty.

For some reason, in 1803 Bartlett left Cambridge for Saco, Maine, where he wasted no time getting into trouble again. Maine was still part of Massachusetts, and he served as a state senator in 1804 and 1805. In 1805 he took over a newspaper, the *Freeman's Friend*, which he used as a base to run for Congress in 1806, changing his political affiliation from Federalist to Democrat. He lost by six votes and became the butt of vicious satire from Nathaniel Willis, editor of the *Portland Argus*. Suing for defamation of character in 1807, Bartlett won a judgment of $1,987.45, which caused Willis, who was unable to pay, to be committed to debtors' prison. When Willis left the prison for a few minutes to get a drink of water from an outdoor pump, Bartlett then sued his sureties, who had posted bond equal to the judgment to insure Willis remained in jail. Bartlett collected that amount, also in 1807, in a lawsuit the Massachusetts Supreme Court decided in his favor on the technical ground that Willis had illegally left prison, although the justices joined just about everyone who knew him in deploring Bartlett's lack of scruples. Shortly thereafter, in 1808, he married Mercy Matthews.

Driven from Maine by public opprobrium following the suit, Bartlett next located in Portsmouth, New Hampshire, where he soon squandered his money and began to practice law again. He also wrote journalism and frankly declared his pen for sale to the highest bidder. In New Hampshire he wrote his book of over four hundred *Aphorisms* (1810), dedicated "to all my enemies, many of whom roll in wealth," assuring them that "your most *vigorous* opposition, your most *virulent* slander and most inveterate *malice* will be duly appreciated." Around this time his second wife left him, and the people of Portsmouth paid him some much-needed cash to get out of town.

Bartlett's final home was Boston, where he became evermore inebriated and scurrilous. In 1823 he made an effort to revive his fortunes by republishing *Physiognomy* and the *Aphorisms* in tandem with an essay on *The Blessings of Poverty*, the whole production incongruously dedicated to the upright John Quincy Adams. The same year he delivered a Fourth of July oration, *The Fourth of July Anticipated*, which included a poem, "The New Vicar of Bray," mocking the hypocrisy of contemporary politicians. By this time Bartlett was living on the charity of his landlady. He died in Boston, "unlamented, as he had lived unhonored . . . too degraded to regard the decencies of respectable company" (Willis, p. 444). Nevertheless, his writings are, in general, witty and can be read with pleasure, as can the story of his remarkable life.

• The Massachusetts Historical Society has a collection of materials on Bartlett prepared by Clifford K. Shipton. Useful sources are C. H. Bell, *Bench and Bar of New Hampshire* (1894), and William Willis, *The History of the Law, the Courts, and the Lawyers of Maine* (1863).

WILLIAM PENCAK

BARTLETT, Josiah (21 Nov. 1729–19 May 1795), physician and signer of the Declaration of Independence, was born in Amesbury, Massachusetts, the son of Stephen Bartlett, a shoemaker, and Hannah Webster. Josiah Bartlett attended common school and at the age of sixteen was apprenticed to study medicine under Dr. Nehemiah Ordway of Amesbury. In 1750, seeking to set up his own practice, Bartlett settled in Kingston, New Hampshire, where he won quick acceptance for his fever treatments and his personal manner and demeanor. There, he married Mary Bartlett, a cousin from Newton, New Hampshire. Eight of the couple's twelve children lived into adulthood.

Bartlett's enthusiasm for public service manifested itself first in his election as a selectman of Kingston in 1757. In 1765, leaving his medical practice in the hands of his apprentice, Dr. Amos Gale, Bartlett was elected to Kingston's seat in the General Court (New Hampshire's legislature), a post he held until the Revolution. He accepted appointments as Justice of the peace from Governor Benning Wentworth and his successor John Wentworth (1737–1820), as well as a commission in the provincial militia.

Bartlett was one of eighty-five men who met at Exeter on 21 July 1774 to form New Hampshire's first provincial congress. His representation of Kingston continued through January 1776 when he was elected by the lower house of the General Court to the Executive Council, in which he served until 1782. Because his residence burned in February 1774, Bartlett could not accept appointment to the Continental Congress but did assist John Pickering (1738–1805) in drafting

instructions to delegates John Sullivan (1740–1795) and Nathaniel Folsom. In December 1774 he actively supported the colonists' attack on Fort William and Mary in Portsmouth harbor to remove its gunpowder for patriot use. Governor John Wentworth thereupon revoked Bartlett's militia commission.

By September 1775, his house rebuilt, Bartlett had accepted the General Court's appointment to represent New Hampshire in the Continental Congress, where he fully supported independence and signed the Declaration. Bartlett served actively on many congressional committees, notably on the naval and marine committees, supporting the building of the *Raleigh*, the *Ranger*, and the *America* in the Portsmouth shipyard of John Langdon. The *Raleigh* became the first ship to be completed specifically for service in the American navy. The *Ranger* sailed under the command of John Paul Jones (1747–1792).

Bartlett held the rank of colonel of the seventh militia regiment until 1778. In December 1776 he mustered his regiment, declined reappointment to Congress, and accompanied his troops to Rhode Island where he attended the conference of New England states on military and economic affairs at Providence. In August 1777 he attended the wounded at the battle of Bennington. Early the next year, Bartlett chaired the legislative committee of the whole to debate the Articles of Confederation in the New Hampshire General Court and reluctantly accepted reappointment to the Continental Congress. On 9 July 1778 he became the only physician to have signed both the Declaration and the Articles. In 1779 Kingston elected him its delegate to the convention forming a state constitution. In June 1784 he presided over the opening of the newly constituted bicameral legislature (which included a senate for the first time) to swear in new members.

From November 1782 to January 1790 Bartlett served as a judge on New Hampshire's superior court. He supported the federal Constitution and in 1788 presided as president pro tem of the convention to consider ratification. He accepted appointment to be chief justice of the superior court (the state's highest) in January 1790 but in June found himself in a three-way contest for the state presidency. The New Hampshire House of Representatives selected him to be chief executive, and he handily won reelection in 1791, 1792, and 1793. Revisions to the state constitution in 1792 reinstated the title of governor so that Bartlett became the first in New Hampshire's current line of constitutional governors. In February 1791 Bartlett signed an act incorporating the New Hampshire Medical Society; he served as its first president until 1793. Within a year of retirement from the governorship Bartlett died in Kingston. He is buried in the cemetery next to the town's Congregational church.

Josiah Bartlett's integrity, self-confidence, and concern for human welfare won him the trust of the public and his fellow leaders. His trust in them was pervasive. Although his letters are sober, they betray an optimistic belief in the good of the revolutionary cause. In closing a letter to his wife on 24 June 1776, he noted his hope that "Kind Providence will order all things for the best, and if Sometimes affairs turn out Contrary to our wishes, we must make our selves Easy & Contented, as we are not Certain what is for the best." The abundant records of the era reveal his prodigious involvement in nearly every activity of public life in New Hampshire, while his personal papers portray his care of his medical patients and his deep and abiding love for his family. The state government that so clearly bore his stamp incorporated a town in his honor in 1790.

• Significant collections of Bartlett's papers are housed in the New Hampshire Historical Society, the New Hampshire State Library (both in Concord), and the Library of Congress. These, with others, were reproduced in 1976 in a microfilm edition by the New Hampshire Historical Society, the New Hampshire American Revolution Bicentennial Commission, and the National Historical Publications and Records Commission. A selection was published as Frank C. Mevers, ed., *The Papers of Josiah Bartlett* (1979). The most useful printed primary source is Nathaniel Bouton et al., eds., *The New Hampshire State Papers* (40 vols., 1867–1940), particularly vols. 7, 8, 20–22, and 30. An unpublished biography by Elwin L. Page, "Rider for Freedom: Josiah Bartlett, 1729–1795" (c. 1949), remains at the New Hampshire Historical Society. Levi Bartlett, *Genealogical and Biographical Sketches of the Bartlett Family in England and America* (1876), provides the most comprehensive personal information available. Other useful sources include Page, "Josiah Bartlett and the Federation," *Historical New Hampshire* 2 (1947): 1–6, and Mevers, "Josiah Bartlett," in *Physician Signers of the Declaration of Independence*, ed. George E. Gifford, Jr. (1976), pp. 99–121.

FRANK C. MEVERS

BARTLETT, Paul Wayland (24 Jan. 1865–20 Sept. 1925), sculptor, was born in New Haven, Connecticut, the son of Truman Howe Bartlett, a sculptor, teacher, and art historian, and Mary Ann White. Bartlett belongs to a generation of American sculptors who turned to France for inspiration and training. In 1880 he entered the École des Beaux-Arts as a pupil of Pierre-Jules Cavelier, supplementing his formal studies with instruction in animal sculpture from Emmanuel Frémiet. Bartlett eventually completed his training as an assistant in the studio of Auguste Rodin.

Between 1885 and 1889 Bartlett modeled his first two life-size statues, *The Bear Tamer* (Metropolitan Museum of Art, New York) and *The Indian Ghost Dancer* (Smithsonian Institution, Washington, D.C.). They reflect his search for a shared Franco-American artistic heritage and are significant for the insight they provide regarding the influence of evolutionary theory and biological determinism on late nineteenth-century depictions of race. In the spring of 1890 Bartlett married Emily Montgomery-Skinner, a young American recently arrived in Paris, and the couple set up residence in Passy, one of the more picturesque quarters of the city. There, next to his studio, Bartlett built a foundry around 1892 and began conducting experiments in lost-wax casting and patination techniques, creating a rich assortment of multicolored animal

bronzes that, as a group, represent a unique phase of his career.

In about 1895 Bartlett turned away from technical experimentation to follow a new artistic path, producing over the next thirty years an impressive series of public monuments and historical portraits, on which his reputation both then and now is largely based. Bartlett received his first major public commission in 1894, when he was chosen to execute bronze statues of Columbus and Michelangelo for the rotunda of the Main Reading Room of the nearly completed Library of Congress. Bartlett modeled the figures in Paris but sent them to New York to be cast in bronze by the Henry-Bonnard Bronze Company in 1897 and 1898, respectively.

Within a year of the installation of *Michelangelo*, Bartlett had contracted for a number of other important public commissions, including a statue of General Joseph Warren (1898–1904) for Roxbury, Massachusetts, and an equestrian statue of Lafayette (1898–1908) for the gardens of the Louvre in Paris. The *Lafayette*, a monument that reaffirmed symbolically the political and cultural bonds that had united the United States and France for more than a century, became the centerpiece of Bartlett's career.

Bartlett's early successes, particularly the *Lafayette*, rapidly earned him an impressive list of professional honors. In 1908 he was promoted to officer of the Legion of Honor—he had been made chevalier of the legion in 1895—and in 1911 he was elected corresponding member of the Institut de France. He also became a member of the American Academy of Arts and Letters in 1911 and an associate member of the Royal Academy of Belgium in 1912.

In the wake of such recognition, Bartlett found himself in demand as an instructor, and in about 1913 he began to teach at the Académie Colarossi in Paris. That same year he was made director of sculpture at the Glasgow School of Fine Arts in Glasgow, Scotland. He also assumed a more prominent role in organizations that fostered intercultural relations between France and the United States, such as the American Art Association of Paris and the American Club of Paris.

Bartlett's prestige at the turn of the century as a designer of public monuments earned him the opportunity to decorate some of the most important public structures in the United States. The more prominent of these commissions include the pediment for the New York Stock Exchange (1901–1904), a collaborative effort with John Quincy Adams Ward; the sculptural program for the north front of the Connecticut State House in Hartford (1904–1909); the six attic figures for the New York Public Library (1909–1915); and the pediment for the House wing of the U.S. Capitol (1908–1916).

In late 1908 Bartlett purchased a house in Washington, D.C., and built a large studio on the property to serve as his primary workshop in the United States. In 1913 Bartlett married Suzanne Earle Emmons—his first marriage had ended in divorce—and the couple established their primary residence in Washington. Bartlett had no children from either marriage. As a part-time resident of the city—he continued to divide his time among New York, Washington, and Paris—Bartlett became active in locally based groups, such as the American Federation of Arts. Through his membership in the federation, Bartlett met Glenn Brown, who, as secretary of the American Institute of Architects, was a leading campaigner for the preservation of Washington, D.C. Bartlett became a close friend of Brown's, contributing his time and intellectual energies to Brown's efforts to secure the architectural integrity of the city.

During and after World War I, Bartlett's professional stature in the United States expanded with his election to the National Academy of Design in 1917 and his tenure as president of the National Sculpture Society from 1917 to 1919. As NSS president and chairman of the art committee of the mayor's Committee on a Permanent War Memorial, Bartlett exercised considerable influence over the construction of the temporary *Victory Arch* (1918–1919), erected in New York to celebrate the return of General John J. Pershing and his troops to the United States.

Although the public commissions executed by Bartlett after the war never matched the significance of those of previous years, he nevertheless produced a number of notable statues, including a World War I memorial entitled *Patriotism Guarding the Flag* (1919) for Duluth, Minnesota; a statue of Benjamin Franklin (1911–1921) for Waterbury, Connecticut; one of Robert Morris (1915–1924) for Philadelphia; and one of Sir William Blackstone (1924–1925) for London, England. Bartlett died in Paris.

More than any other sculptor of his generation, Bartlett was heir to the nineteenth-century French romantic tradition. Nevertheless, he remained distinctly American, ever-conscious of the role sculpture could play in defining the artistic identity of his native country. Bartlett's belief that French art provided an essential ingredient in forging a uniquely American vision reflected his lifelong determination to discover and draw inspiration from a cultural heritage common to both countries.

• A substantial collection of Bartlett's papers, comprising personal correspondence, financial and legal documents, photographs, drawings, notebooks, and scrapbooks related to his major commissions, is in the Paul Wayland Bartlett Papers in the Library of Congress. Other significant Bartlett manuscript collections are in the office of the architect of the Capitol and Tudor Place Museum in Georgetown. The most up-to-date bibliography and chronology of Bartlett's life can be found in Thomas P. Somma, "Paul Wayland Bartlett and the *Apotheosis of Democracy*, 1908–1916: The Pediment for the House Wing of the United States Capitol" (Ph.D. diss., Univ. of Delaware, 1990). See also the biographical entries in Lorado Taft, *The History of American Sculpture* (1924); Beatrice Proske, *Brookgreen Gardens Sculpture* (1968); and Wayne Craven, *Sculpture in America* (1984). An obituary is in the *New York Times*, 21 Sept. 1925.

THOMAS P. SOMMA

BARTLETT, Samuel Colcord (25 Nov. 1817–16 Nov. 1898), Congregational minister and college president, was born in Salisbury, New Hampshire, the son of Samuel Colcord Bartlett, a trader and justice of the peace, and Eleanor Pettengill. The third of six children, Bartlett was brought up in modest circumstances, although his father's general store in Salisbury later prospered. Bartlett entered Dartmouth College in 1832 and received an A.B. in 1836. From 1836 to 1838 he was principal of the Caledonia County Grammar School in Peacham, Vermont, and from 1838 to 1839 he served as a tutor in mathematics at Dartmouth College.

In 1839 Bartlett entered Andover Theological Seminary, an institution in the forefront of the conflict between New England Calvinism and Unitarianism. Three well-known conservative theologians at Andover—Moses Stuart, Edwards Amasa Park, and Bela Bates Edwards—had an important influence on his religious perspective. Bartlett graduated in 1842 and spoke on "Exclusion of Philosophy from Christianity." In 1843 he was licensed to preach by the Andover Congregational Association and ordained at Monson, Massachusetts. He served as pastor of the Congregational Church in Monson until 1846, the first of several positions that he held as a religious leader and educator. In 1843 he married Laura Bradlee, who died a few months later. In 1846 he married Mary Bacon Learned; they had four children.

Bartlett's career pattern was in keeping with developments in the ministry during the nineteenth century. Many New England ministers lacked regular pastorates and sought enhanced careers as teachers, professors, college presidents, and secretaries of benevolent societies. In 1846 Bartlett became professor of intellectual philosophy and rhetoric at Western Reserve College in Hudson, Ohio. He was active in the organization of a Phi Beta Kappa chapter and participated in the formation of a Congregational association of churches in northern Ohio. Leaving Western Reserve in 1852, he became pastor of the Franklin Street Church in Manchester, New Hampshire. His interest in the religious and educational development of the West led to a position as pastor of the New England Congregational Church in Chicago from 1857 to 1859.

In 1858 Bartlett became professor of biblical literature at the fledgling Chicago Theological Seminary. During his nineteen-year affiliation, he organized classes, raised funds for the institution, and became a leader in the educational and religious developments in the Middle West. While at Chicago, his views on Christianity, the ministry, and the nature and value of higher education began to find expression in numerous sermons, orations, addresses, and published volumes, which he continued to produce throughout his life.

In 1877 Bartlett left Chicago Theological Seminary to become president of Dartmouth College. He oversaw important developments at Dartmouth during his years as president, but his tenure was turbulent and controversial. His notions of the presidency, of the college, and of higher learning, though in keeping with nineteenth-century traditions, came into conflict with a changing academic community and collegiate culture. Bartlett viewed himself as pastoral head of a "Christian college" (Bartlett, *Exercises*, p. 40) and thought Dartmouth should be "the great Northern New England College" (Bartlett, *Dartmouth College*, p. 11). He supported classical liberal arts education because he thought it better developed moral character which he considered the prime aim of education. His program to develop mental discipline was also traditional; it stressed "wakefulness, precision, fulness, equipoise, and docility" and opposed the narrowing tendency of "modern science" (*Exercises*, pp. 35, 26).

Bartlett's views, policies, and methods of administration clashed with the interests and aspirations of various groups within the college community who had new ideas about Dartmouth's role. In 1881 he was brought to trial to justify his educational practice. The trustees conducted this quasi-judicial hearing which was recorded by a court stenographer. The controversy received extensive press coverage. The New York Association of Alumni initiated the investigation with their memorial to the trustees, and they served as the prosecution during the trial. Throughout the trial, the alumni asserted their demands for a greater voice in governance and for a more metropolitan reputation for the college. The faculty sent memorials to the board, acted as the prime witnesses, and used the trial as a means to assert their professionalization and their claims for some sense of faculty autonomy. Members of the scientific department complained that Bartlett had questioned the equality of their program to the traditional liberal arts course. Students displayed their hostility toward the president and sent a petition to the board.

In spite of all the controversy, Bartlett survived both the trial and, nine months later, a partial vote of no confidence by the trustees. But several demands of the faculty, alumni, and students were realized by the end of his tenure or during the next administration. The alumni, for example, obtained their seats on the board, and the faculty realized to a considerable extent their demands for a more cosmopolitan, professionalized faculty. The Bartlett years also marked the introduction of a system of electives, the beautification and transformation of the physical plant (including the addition of new buildings), and an increase in the number of professorships from twenty-one to thirty-four. He resigned in 1892, after which he served as lecturer on "The Bible and Its Relations to Science and Religion" until 1898. He died at his home in Hanover, New Hampshire. Well known for his work as a minister, professor, and writer on religion and education during his lifetime, Bartlett achieved a lasting reputation as president of Dartmouth College, and especially for his trial, which brought the conflicting tendencies in higher education into public focus.

• Bartlett's papers and other archival material relating to the Bartlett presidency are in the Special Collections, Dartmouth College Library. Works by Bartlett include *An Appeal for Ministers* (1865), *Life and Death Eternal* (1866), *Future Punishment* (1875), and *The Veracity of the Hexateuch* (1897). His addresses include Inaugural Address, *Exercises in the Inauguration of Samuel Colcord Bartlett, D. D., as President of Dartmouth College, June 27, 1877* (1877), and *Dartmouth College as It Has Been, Is, Can Be, and Should Be: A Statement to Its Graduates and Friends, and to All Intelligent New Hampshire Men, at Home and Abroad, Jan. 1, 1881*. The most important biographical source is George Adams Boyd, *Three Stimsons and a Bartlett*, with family data compiled by Dorothy Stimson (1967). See also Edwin J. Bartlett, *The Descendants of Samuel Colcord Bartlett and Eleanor Pettengill Bartlett of Salisbury, New Hampshire to April 1, 1920* (1920); Levi Bartlett, *Genealogical and Biographical Sketches of the Bartlett Family in England and America* (1876); and John J. Dearborn, *The History of Salisbury, New Hampshire, from Date of Settlement to the Present Time* (1890). For an assessment of the Bartlett presidency, see Marilyn Tobias, *Old Dartmouth On Trial: The Transformation of the Academic Community in Nineteenth-Century America* (1982).

MARILYN TOBIAS

BARTLETT, William Holms Chambers (4 Sept. 1804–11 Feb. 1893), mathematician and astronomer, was born in Lancaster County, Pennsylvania, the son of very poor parents whose names are unknown. The family moved when Bartlett was young to Missouri, where he obtained his early education. While this was apparently meager, his natural abilities were noted, and at the age of seventeen, through the good offices of Senator Thomas Hart Benton, he received an appointment to the U.S. Military Academy. He graduated from West Point in 1826 at the head of a class of forty-one cadets. Bartlett's record at West Point was remarkable; he is alleged to have been the first in each of his classes and to never have received a demerit. He was commissioned as a second lieutenant in the Corps of Engineers and remained at West Point as assistant professor of engineering from 1827 to 1829. For the next five years he was on active duty involved in constructing forts in Virginia and Rhode Island, and between 1832 and 1834 he was assistant to the chief engineer of the U.S. Army in Washington, D.C. In 1834 he returned to West Point as department head and acting professor of natural and experimental philosophy. The professorship was made a regular appointment in 1836, and he held these positions until his retirement with the rank of colonel in 1871. At that time he became the actuary for the Mutual Life Insurance Company of New York, and he retired from that firm in 1889. He was one of the corporators and original members of the National Academy of Sciences in 1863.

The bulk of Bartlett's professional work is tied to his long career of teaching at West Point. In 1840 he went abroad to inspect the leading observatories in England and Europe, and on his return, he constructed a telescope at the academy. By all accounts, he was not an outstanding teacher but was liked by the cadets who enjoyed his laboratory demonstrations and the use of the telescope. Notwithstanding his lecturing ability, Bartlett wrote an impressive number of textbooks, including *An Elementary Treatise on Optics, Designed for the Use of the Cadets at the United States Military Academy* (1839); *Elements of Synthetic Mechanics* (1850); and the four-volume *Elements of Natural Philosophy* (1851–1855): *Mechanics, Acoustics, Optics,* and *Spherical Astronomy.* Bartlett's *Elements of Analytical Mechanics* (1853), generally regarded as his most important book, made full use of the calculus and was one of the first advanced expositions of engineering mechanics to be published in the United States. All of Bartlett's textbooks were popular, ran through many editions, and were widely used for many years at American colleges and West Point.

In addition, Bartlett did distinguished work in astronomy. He published observations of the Great Comet of 1843 and the partial solar eclipse of 1854. In the latter noteworthy publication, he pioneered the use of photography in obtaining quantitative astronomical results. He also gave a mathematical discussion of the comas and tails of comets (1859) and contributed a paper on the rifling of guns to the first volume of the *Memoirs of the National Academy of Sciences* (1866).

Finally, Bartlett's actuarial activities gave rise to the booklet *Interest Tables Used by the Mutual Life Insurance Company of New York for the Calculation of Interest and Prices of Stocks and Bonds for Investment* (1878). A later edition was published in 1889 under the editorship of Emory McClintock (the second president of the American Mathematical Society and Bartlett's successor at the Mutual Life Insurance Company). It has been suggested by one of his former students that Bartlett's actuarial work was of a proprietary nature and kept confidential by his employer.

Bartlett was a significant American scientific figure in his time and has been cited as perhaps West Point's most brilliant nineteenth-century graduate. His scientific publications were unusual in that research was hardly a priority at a military academy, and he still managed to combine them with his instructional duties. Bartlett and his colleagues Dennis Hart Mahan (engineering and military science) and Albert E. Church (mathematics) were major figures on the Academic Board, which was instrumental in governing and setting the course of studies at the academy. The science and electrical engineering building at West Point is named Bartlett Hall.

In February 1829 Bartlett had married Harriet Whithorne; they had eight children. One of their daughters married John M. Schofield, a future lieutenant general, who had been Bartlett's assistant in his astronomical work of 1854. Bartlett died in Yonkers, New York.

• An invaluable contemporary account of West Point and its program is given in "Report of the Commission to Examine the Organization, System of Discipline, and Course of Study at the United States Military Academy," 36th Cong., 2d sess., Sen. Misc. Doc. 3 (1860), based on a hearing held under the chairmanship of Senator Jefferson Davis. Bartlett's career is also discussed in Stephen E. Ambrose, *Duty, Honor, Country—A History of West Point* (1966), and James L. Morrison, Jr., *"The Best School in the World": West Point, the Pre–Civil War Years 1833–1866* (1986), A detailed obituary notice, which contains a list of publications, appears in the National Academy of Sciences, *Biographical Memoirs* 7 (1913): 171–93. An obituary is in the *New York Tribune,* 12 Feb. 1893.

JOSEPH D. ZUND

BARTLEY, Mordecai (16 Dec. 1783–10 Oct. 1870), congressman and governor of Ohio, was born in Fayette County, Pennsylvania, the son of Elijah Bartley and Rachel Pearshall, farmers. He attended country schools in Pennsylvania. In 1804 he married Elizabeth Welles, and five years later they migrated to Jefferson County in eastern Ohio, where Bartley farmed. The couple had at least two children. During the War of 1812 Bartley was captain of a company of volunteers and served under General William Henry Harrison. In 1814 he moved to relatively unsettled Richland County, Ohio, where he cleared land and resumed farming. Three years later Bartley was elected to the Ohio Senate, and in 1818 the legislature appointed him register of the Land Office, charged with administering the public lands reserved for the support of schools in that portion of Ohio known as the Virginia Military District.

In 1823 Bartley began eight years of service in the U.S. House of Representatives, during which he was a staunch supporter of John Quincy Adams and Henry Clay. Though not prominent in congressional debates, he served the interests of his northern Ohio district well. He secured the first federal appropriations for harbor improvements of the Lake Erie ports of Cleveland and Sandusky. As congressman he also proposed using Ohio land grants to endow a permanent school fund.

In 1830 Bartley refused nomination for a fifth term in Congress, and four years later he moved to the Richland County seat of Mansfield, where he founded a mercantile house. Moreover, in his spare time he studied law. In September 1842, at the age of fifty-eight, he was admitted to the bar.

Emerging from political retirement in 1844, Bartley won the Whig party nomination for governor of Ohio. That same year Bartley's son Thomas W. Bartley, the Speaker of the Ohio Senate, became acting governor when the incumbent Wilson Shannon resigned to become minister to Mexico. Thus Mordecai Bartley was running against Democrat David Tod to succeed his own son as governor. To complicate matters, the younger Bartley was an intense Democrat whose political views were directly opposed to those of his father. In fact, the chief focus of controversy in the 1844 gubernatorial campaign was the Bartley Law, an antibank measure that the younger Bartley had sponsored in the legislature. The elder Bartley headed a ticket dedicated to undoing this handiwork of his son.

In the 1844 campaign the Whig press presented Mordecai Bartley as "a practical farmer," referring to him as the "Richland Farmer" and "Farmer Bartley." "A tiller of the soil nearly all his life time," one Whig newspaper proclaimed, "he knows the wants and will be capable of ministering to the necessities of the vast agricultural population of Ohio" (*Ohio State Journal*, 28 Feb. 1844). The practical farmer image proved effective, for on election day Bartley defeated Tod by a narrow margin. The Whigs also captured control of the state legislature.

During Bartley's two years as governor, the chief political issue was banking. Radical Democrats, led by Thomas W. Bartley, opposed the chartering of banks, regarding them as privileged, corrupt corporations. The Whigs, however, favored the creation of banks, which they viewed as necessary to the state's prosperity. In his inaugural address, Mordecai Bartley expressed his probank sentiments, contending, "The banks of Ohio have contributed largely to her wealth and improvement." The like-minded Whig legislature established a state bank and granted charters to numerous banking corporations. Within a year, the number of banks in Ohio rose from eight to twenty-nine. In December 1845 a pleased Governor Bartley told the legislature, "Already do the people of Ohio begin to feel the influence of this [banking] system in the restoration of confidence, the revival of business, the increase of the wages of labor, and the rising prosperity of the State."

Another increasingly troublesome issue was race and slavery. Bartley urged repeal of Ohio's Black Laws, which required free blacks to post bond guaranteeing that they would not become public charges and denied them the right to testify against whites in court. In 1846 Bartley told the legislature, "I deem it my duty again to call your attention to the laws which unjustly oppress and degrade our colored population." Moreover, like many Whigs, he believed that the Mexican War, which broke out in 1846, was motivated by a desire to acquire additional slave territory. He condemned this expansionism, telling the legislature, "The Government of the United States has no right to engage in a war of aggression and conquest." Yet he felt bound by the federal Constitution to honor President James Polk's request for troops and raised three regiments of Ohio volunteers to fight in Mexico.

During his administration Bartley also clashed with the governor of Virginia over the fugitive slave issue. A band of irate Virginians came to Ohio, kidnapped three white Ohioans who had aided fugitive slaves, and took them back to Virginia, where the Ohioans were placed on trial. In a series of letters to Virginia's governor, Bartley demanded that the Virginians be turned over to Ohio authorities for trial "for the atrocious crime of kidnapping." "If a diabolical outrage of this kind" was tolerated by the Virginia authorities, Bartley warned in one letter, "be assured, sir, the friendly feelings and intercourse between the two States will be greatly endangered, and it is feared the people of Ohio will take justice in their own hands, and redress their own wrongs." Virginia eventually released the kidnapped Ohioans, but the incident was an ominous sign of the growing tension between North and South.

In 1846 Bartley declined to run for reelection and retired to Mansfield, where he practiced law. During the 1850s he became a staunch Republican, and according to his obituary, though "very infirm and feeble during the last years of his life, [he] never failed to attend the polls, whatever the weather might be, and vote the Republican ticket." He died in Mansfield, having witnessed the growth of Ohio from a frontier state to an emerging industrial dynamo. A typical Ohio Whig, he embraced internal improvements and banks, but as governor his concern for the rights of blacks and the incursions of slave power anticipated future events that were to divide the nation.

• For Bartley's messages and communications to the legislature, see *Ohio Executive Documents* for 1845, 1846, and 1847. Biographical sketches of Bartley are in Simeon D. Fess, ed., *Ohio: A Four-volume Reference Library on the History of a Great State* (1937); *The Governors of Ohio* (1954); and A. A. Graham, comp., *History of Richland County, Ohio* (1880). A summary of the political events during Bartley's gubernatorial administration is in Charles B. Galbreath, *History of Ohio* (1925). Edgar Allan Holt, *Party Politics in Ohio, 1840–1850* (1930), discusses the state politics of the 1840s. Identical obituaries are in the *Ohio State Journal* (Columbus), 12 Oct. 1870, and the *Dayton Journal*, 13 Oct. 1870.

JON C. TEAFORD

BARTÓK, Béla (25 Mar. 1881–26 Sept. 1945), composer and pianist, was born in Nagyszentmiklós, Hungary (now Sînnicolau Mare, Romania), the son of Béla Bartók, the headmaster of an agricultural school, and Paula Voit, a schoolteacher. Bartók received his first piano lessons at age five from his mother, who, after the death of Bartók's father in 1888, supported the family through a succession of teaching positions. At age nine, Bartók began composing short pieces for piano, and in 1892 he made his first public appearance as a pianist. His family settled in Pozsony (Bratislava) for five years between 1894 and 1899, and Bartók studied harmony and piano there with László Erkel and Anton Hyrtl.

From 1899 to 1903, Bartók attended the Academy of Music in Budapest. He studied piano with István Thomán and composition with Hans Koessler. Although Bartók was attracted early on to the music of Wagner and Liszt, he discovered more direction for his own stylistic development in the works of Richard Strauss. He was also influenced by a growing nationalist movement. Both influences are manifest in compositions from Bartók's student years, for example his symphonic poem *Kossuth* (1903).

While a student, Bartók commenced a successful career as a concert pianist. Following graduation, he studied and gave concerts in Berlin as well as in Vienna. Beginning in 1903 with his Violin Sonata and later with *Kossuth*, Bartók programmed concerts of his own compositions. In 1905 Bartók entered his Piano Quintet (1904), Rhapsody for piano (1904), and Violin Sonata in the Rubinstein competition in Paris, where he received only a disappointing certificate.

In 1904, while making his first notation of a Hungarian peasant song, Bartók discovered a folk music of which he, and his musical compatriots, had been virtually unaware. He then began the lifelong task of collecting, cataloging, and analyzing folk melodies, in much of which he was joined by Zoltán Kodály. Together they amassed thousands of peasant songs, some of which they published, beginning in 1906 with *Twenty Hungarian Folksongs*. Bartók's collecting extended over many years and into remote villages in his own and neighboring countries. In folk music, Bartók discovered the means to create his own uniquely Hungarian style, one that combined folk elements with the main trends in contemporary music. He was also strongly influenced by the music of Debussy, in which he found traits similar to those he admired in peasant songs, such as modal melodies and exotic harmonies.

In 1907 Bartók was appointed to a piano professorship at the Academy of Music in Budapest. In 1909 he married his sixteen-year-old student Márta Ziegler, with whom he had one child.

Bartók's interest in the folk idiom is evidenced in a large quantity of piano music including *Fourteen Bagatelles* (1908), his first Violin Concerto (1907–1908), *Two Portraits* (1909) and *Two Pictures* (1910), both for orchestra, his String Quartet no. 1 (1908), and several folk song arrangements. After the collapse of the Hungarian Music Society, formed in 1911 by Bartók and Kodály to promote contemporary Hungarian works, and the rejection of his opera *Duke Bluebeard's Castle* (1911) by the national opera competition, Bartók withdrew from public life, and his output decreased. He continued his folk music studies with increased enthusiasm.

During World War I, Bartók, exempt from the military on medical grounds, continued collecting folk music and returned to composing, producing the Piano Suite, op. 14 (1916), the String Quartet no. 2 (1915–1917), two song cycles (1915–1916), a number of pieces based on Romanian song, and his first unqualified public success, the one-act ballet *The Wooden Prince* (1914–1917).

After the war, Bartók found himself out of sympathy with the government. Restrictions on traveling hampered his collecting, and questions about his patriotism arose over his work with minority cultures. However, his status in Hungary improved as his international reputation grew considerably as a result of concert tours he made each year to England, Germany, the Netherlands, France, Switzerland, and Italy.

In 1923, after a divorce from his first wife, Bartók married Ditta Pásztory, who became a concert pianist; they had one child. Between December 1927 and February 1928, Bartók made a concert tour of the United States, during which he gave the New York premiere of his Piano Concerto no. 1. That same tour, his *Contrasts* for violin, clarinet, and piano was commissioned by Benny Goodman. He then toured the USSR (Dec. 1928–Jan. 1929). On his fiftieth birthday Bartók received the medal of the Légion d'Honneur and the Corvin Medal.

In 1934 Bartók ceased teaching and accepted a research post at the Hungarian Academy of Sciences that enabled him to devote more time to his folk music collection, which included some 13,000 Hungarian melodies. He wrote and lectured on his work and took part in international congresses.

Following *The Miraculous Mandarin* of 1918–1919, Bartók's compositions of the 1920s and 1930s include two violin sonatas (1921, 1922), *Village Scenes* (1926), the first and second piano concertos (1926, 1931), the third through sixth string quartets (1927, 1928, 1934, 1939), *Cantata profana* (1930), *Mikrokosmos* (1926–1939), Music for Strings, Percussion and Celesta (1936), Sonata for Two Pianos and Percussion (1937), the Violin Concerto no. 2 (1938), and Divertimento (1939). Of his work after 1926 Bartók observed in an interview in *Étude* (1941) that it became "more contrapuntal and also simpler on the whole. A greater stress of tonality is also characteristic of this time."

Eventually, Bartók's antipathy toward fascism and renewed questions over his political allegiance led to his decision to leave Hungary. He made another concert tour of the United States in April-May 1940 and returned the next October to stay. He was appointed to a research position at Columbia University to work with the Parry collection of Serbo-Croatian folk songs. Columbia also awarded him an honorary doctorate.

Bartók's American years were discouraging; for two years he composed no new music. With his wife he gave a few concerts, the last being the premiere of the Concerto for Two Pianos, Percussion, and Orchestra by the New York Philharmonic (21 Jan. 1943). Funding for his Columbia position was discontinued. During his final years, Bartók was supported through the help of friends and ASCAP (American Society of Composers, Authors, and Publishers). His final compositions include the Concerto for Orchestra (1943), commissioned by Serge Koussevitzky; Sonata for Solo Violin (1944), commissioned by Yehudi Menuhin; the unfinished Viola Concerto for William Primrose; and the Piano Concerto no. 3 (1945), on which he worked until the moment he was taken to a New York hospital, where he died.

Following his death, the Béla Bartók Archive was set up as a permanent department of the Hungarian Academy of Sciences. Along with Kodály, he is credited with the awakening of serious interest in the folk musics of his homeland. He did not establish a school of composition but is regarded as a major individualist and as one of the leading composers of the twentieth century.

• The principal collection of Bartók papers is located at the New York Bartók Archives in Cedarhurst, N.Y. The collection has been cataloged by Victor Bator in *The Béla Bartók Archives: History and Catalogue* (1963). Published studies by Bartók include his classic *Hungarian Folk Music*, trans. M. D. Calvocoressi (1931); his work on Romanian music in Benjamin Suchoff, ed., *Rumanian Folk Music*, vol. 5 (1967–1975); and, with A. B. Lord, *Serbo-Croatian Folk Songs* (1951). See also Suchoff, ed., *Béla Bartók Essays* (1976); and János Deményi, ed., *Béla Bartók Letters* (1971). An autobiography was published in German and Hungarian journals (1918–1927). A complete catalog of Bartók's compositions and published writings and an extensive bibliography appear in the *New Grove Dictionary of Music and Musicians*, 6th ed. (1980). A partial list of books about Bartók and his music, in English, includes: Emil Haraszti, *Béla Bartók: His Life and Works* (1938); Serge Moreux, *Béla Bartók* (1949; trans. 1953); Halsey Stevens, *The Life and Music of Béla Bartók* (1953; rev. ed., 1993); Agatha Fassett, *The Naked Face of Genius: Béla Bartók's American Years* (1958); Lajos Lesznai, *Béla Bartók* (1961; trans. 1973); Ferenc Bónis, ed., *Béla Bartók: His Life in Pictures and Documents* (1964; trans. 1972); Jósef Ujfalussy, *Béla Bartók* (1965; trans. 1971); E. Lendvai, *Béla Bartók: An Analysis of his Music* (1971); J. McCabe, *Bartók Orchestral Music* (1974), Gyorgy Kroó, *A Guide to Bartók* (1974); Todd Crow, ed., *Bartók Studies* (1976); Vilmos Juhasz, *Bartók's Years in America* (1981); T. Tallian, *Béla Bartók: The Man and His Work* (1981); Hamish Milne, *Bartók: His Life and Times* (1982); Elliott Antokoletz, *Béla Bartók: A Guide to Research* (1988); David Yeomans, *Bartók for Piano: A Survey of His Solo Literature* (1988); Malcolm Gillies, *Bartók in Britain: A Guided Tour* (1989) and *Bartók Remembered* (1991); and Paul Wilson, *The Music of Béla Bartók* (1992).

ELLEN KNIGHT

BARTON, Benjamin Smith (10 Feb. 1766–19 Dec. 1815), physician and botanist, was born in Lancaster, Pennsylvania, the son of Thomas Barton, an Episcopalian minister, and Esther Rittenhouse, the sister of the prominent American astronomer David Rittenhouse. Barton's parents died before he was fifteen. At the age of eighteen he began medical studies in Philadelphia with William Shippen. In 1785, while a member of the Rittenhouse survey that defined the boundary of western Pennsylvania, he developed an interest in the early history and language of Native Americans that he would maintain throughout his life. Never blessed with good health and suffering throughout much of his life with assorted illnesses, including gout, Barton often lacked the stamina to carry through many of the ambitious plans that he would announce. He continued his medical studies at the University of Edinburgh in 1786.

During his two years at Edinburgh, Barton won the Harveian Prize for a dissertation on the medicinal effects of the plant *Hyosciannus niger* (black henbane), was elected one of the four annual presidents of the Royal Medical Society of Edinburgh, and became a member of both the Speculative Society and the Society of Antiquaries of Scotland. He left Edinburgh in 1788 without receiving a medical degree under circumstances difficult to unravel but that seem to have been centered around his mismanagement of funds belonging to the Royal Medical Society. Confusion surrounds the question of Barton's medical degree. It appears he did almost nothing to thwart the public impression that he received his medical degree from the University of Göttingen, but no record exists of that university granting that degree to him. It can be verified, however, that he did receive a diploma or perhaps an M.D. from the Lisbon Academy in Portugal and a doctor of medicine from Christian-Albrechts University at Kiel, Germany; although he never attended the latter university he was apparently awarded the degree based on work he had done elsewhere.

Returning to the United States in the fall of 1789, Barton became a professor in the medical school at the College of Philadelphia, which in 1791 became the University of Pennsylvania, an institution with which he would maintain an association until his death. In addition to teaching botany, Barton also provided instruction in natural history, becoming one of the first professors of this subject in the nation. In 1795 he began also to teach materia medica to medical students. To aid in his teaching, Barton later published *Elements of Botany; or, Outlines of the Natural History of Vegetables* (1803). Dedicated "To the Students of Medicine in the University of Pennsylvania, and to the Lovers and Cultivators of Natural History, in Every Part of the United States," this diffuse and attractively illustrated work was the first botany text published in the United States. In 1797 Barton married Mary Pennington, with whom he had two children.

Because of his diverse scientific interests in botany, zoology, Native American ethnology, and linguistics, in 1803 Barton was asked by President Thomas Jefferson to help train Meriwether Lewis to make scientific observations during his great march to the Pacific Ocean. Barton also was selected to prepare the natural history reports of the Lewis and Clark expedition from specimens collected in lands west of the Mississippi River, but he did not complete this task because of a combination of other commitments and his failing health.

Barton's lifelong interest in the antiquity of Native Americans and their languages led to his publication in 1797 of *New Views of the Origin of the Tribes and Nations of America*. The second edition of this work (1798), dedicated to Jefferson, attempted a comparison of words in Asiatic languages with those of Native Americans with the goal of determining the origin of America's indigenous population; Barton maintained that the evidence suggested that they came from Asia.

Barton announced his intent to produce a systematic flora of North America and sponsored collecting trips by Frederick Pursch and Thomas Nuttall for this purpose. In 1806–1807 Pursch collected plant specimens in Maryland, Virginia, North Carolina, Pennsylvania, and New York for Barton's growing herbarium. Nuttall, an Englishman, became Barton's greatest collector; with Barton's support, training, and encouragement, he made extensive collections along the upper Missouri River in 1810–1811. Although Barton received many collections, he seldom found time to catalog them, and many he never systematically examined. While he built up a substantial botanical library, had access to a growing herbarium, and was located in the scientific capital of America, his teaching responsibilities and his inability to remain focused on a specific research objective prevented him from producing a fundamental work on American flora, zoology, ethnohistory, or medicine. Barton often initiated investigations of unique and significant topics and regularly possessed some initial insight of where the research might lead and the appropriate topics to be investigated. Yet few of these promising research opportunities were completed successfully.

With the death of Benjamin Rush in 1813, Barton assumed many of Rush's teaching obligations and became professor of the practice of physic in addition to teaching natural history, botany, and materia medica. Barton also maintained a small medical practice, served on the staff of the Pennsylvania Hospital, and was active in professional organizations, including the Linnaean Society of London, Royal Academy of Science of Sweden, American Academy of Arts and Sciences, and he was also a member of the Massachusetts Historical Society. From 1804 to 1809 he published and edited the *Philadelphia Medical and Physical Journal*. Barton was president of the Philadelphia Linnaean Society in 1806. From 1808 to 1812 he was president of the Philadelphia Medical Society, and from 1802 to 1815 he served as a vice president of the American Philosophical Society. He died from tuberculosis in New York City.

• The American Philosophical Society, the Academy of Natural Sciences of Philadelphia, the Library of Congress, and the Boston Public Library hold many of Barton's personal papers, correspondence, and manuscripts. A bibliography of his diffuse writings is in Max Meisel, *A Bibliography of American Natural History*, vols. 2 and 3 (1967). His life, career, and contributions are examined in his nephew W. P. C. Barton's *The Elements of Botany*, 6th ed. (1836), as well as in J. U. Lloyd and C. G. Lloyd, "Collections for an Essay towards a Materia Medica of the United States," *Bulletin of the Lloyd Library of Botany, Pharmacy and Materia Medica* 1 (1900): 1–10; Francis W. Pennell, "Benjamin Smith Barton as Naturalist," *Proceedings of the American Philosophical Society* 86 (1942): 108–22; and Jeannette E. Graustein, "The Eminent Benjamin Smith Barton," *Pennsylvania Magazine of History and Biography* 85 (1961): 423–38. The confusing question of Barton's medical degree is examined briefly in Whitfield J. Bell, Jr., "Benjamin Smith Barton, M.D. (Kiel)," *Journal of the History of Medicine* 26 (1971): 197–203. Additional studies that focus on specific dimensions of Barton's career include John C. Greene, "Early Scientific Interest in the American Indian: Comparative Linguistics," *Proceedings of the American Philosophical Society* 104 (1960): 511–17; Joseph Ewan, "Benjamin Smith Barton's Influence on Trans-Allegheny Natural History," *Bartonia* 54 (1988): 28–38; and Pennell, "The Elder Barton—His Plant Collection and the Mystery of His Floras," *Bartonia* 9 (1926): 17–34. (The journal *Bartonia* was named for Barton's nephew W. P. C. Barton.)

PHILLIP DRENNON THOMAS

BARTON, Bruce Fairchild (5 Aug. 1886–5 July 1967), advertising executive, writer, and congressman, was born in Robbins, Tennessee, the son of William Eleazar Barton, a Congregationalist minister, and Esther Treat Bushnell, an elementary school teacher. His father brought the family from Tennessee, where he had been an itinerant preacher, to Oak Park, Illinois, before Bruce was a year old, and there William Barton became pastor of the First Congregational Church. He held this post for twenty-five years, serving for a time as moderator of the National Council of Congregational Churches, and he published a distinguished biography of Abraham Lincoln. Bruce Barton was an enterprising young man: he sold newspapers at the age of nine, edited his high school paper, served as the only reporter for the Oak Park weekly, and merchandised his uncle's maple syrup so successfully that his uncle had to buy from neighbors to meet the demand. Barton enrolled in his father's alma mater, Berea College in Kentucky, in 1903, and the next year transferred to Amherst, where he sold pots and pans to pay his tuition. He graduated magna cum laude with a bachelor's degree in liberal arts in 1907 and was awarded a Phi Beta Kappa key and voted "most likely to succeed."

His academic success did little to help him find rewarding work in that depression year, however. He held a series of ill-paying jobs, serving as managing editor of a small religious paper in Chicago, the *Home Herald*, from 1907 until it failed in 1909, and of the *Housekeeper*, a newspaper targeted at homemakers, from 1910 to 1911, when it met the same fate. He learned enough about promotion from these two failures, however, to get a job as assistant sales manager for the publisher P. F. Collier & Son in New York, where he remained from 1912 to 1914. In 1913 he married Esther Maude Randall, with whom he had three children. During his time with Collier, he created his first advertising campaigns, including one for the Harvard Classics, the "five-foot shelf of books" with which, he wrote, "Dr. Eliot of Harvard" could give people the elements of a liberal education in fifteen minutes a day.

Barton became editor of the magazine *Every Week*, published by the Collier affiliate Crowell Publications, in 1914. He was no more successful than in his other editorial ventures, but by the time the magazine folded in 1918, he had become a proficient writer of inspirational articles. His profile of evangelist Billy Sunday brought Barton to the attention of the editor of the *American Magazine*, to which he became a regular contributor, and over the years he wrote hundreds of articles for national magazines such as *Redbook*, *McCall's*, *Collier's*, *Good Housekeeping*, *Cosmopolitan*, and *Reader's Digest*. He also wrote a syndicated newspaper column. His brief, upbeat essays were collected into several books with cheerful titles like *More Power to You* (1917), *It's a Good Old World* (1920), and *Better Days* (1924).

Rejected for military service, Barton took a job as publicity director for the United War Work Agencies in 1918, and during his year in that position met Roy S. Durstine and Alex F. Osborne. With a $10,000 bank loan the three formed Barton, Durstine & Osborne in 1919. It merged with the older George Batten Co. in 1928 to become the fourth largest and the best known advertising agency in the country. Batten, Barton, Durstine & Osborne, popularly known as BBD&O, with Barton as chair of the board, was to include among its clients U.S. Steel, General Electric, Lever Brothers, and General Mills, for whom Barton invented the ideal homemaker, Betty Crocker. One of the few advertising executives who did his own writing, Barton produced many of the textbook models of memorable advertising copy. For General Electric he wrote the often quoted "Any woman who is doing any household task that a little electric motor can do is working for three cents an hour," and he created a positive image of Andrew Carnegie after the steel strike of 1919 with the line "He came to a land of wooden towns and left a nation of steel." One of his most effective slogans became the motto for the Salvation Army: "A man may be down, but he is never out." Barton contributed his services to that organization, as well as to the American Heart Association, the United Negro College Fund, and the Institute for the Crippled and Disabled; for all of them he raised large sums of money.

A devout Christian, Barton often wrote on religious themes. In 1925 he produced the book *The Man Nobody Knows*, an unconventional portrait of Jesus as "the greatest advertiser of his own day" and the "world's greatest salesman." In protest against the image of "a weak and sad-faced Savior" that he recalled from Sunday school, he pictured Jesus as a dynamic, convivial figure, as well as a peerless copywriter. The book met a mixed reception: the *New York World* reviewer stated that "regarded as a historical interpretation of Christ's personality, it is probably the absurdest jumble ever put into type," and the *New York Times* grudgingly noted that "it will convince many, though others will find it often dropping into absurdity." Nevertheless, it headed the *New York Times* bestseller list for two years and remained in print for forty years. Barton wrote an interpretation of the Bible, also from the standpoint of Madison Avenue, called *The Book Nobody Knows*, in 1926, and the following year he produced his third volume of popular theology, *What Can a Man Believe?* Both were dismissed by most critics as superficial, if not actually sacrilegious—his treatment of some tenets of faith as trivial shocked fundamentalists—but both also became national bestsellers. His portrait of St. Paul, *He Upset the World* (1932), was less successful with the public.

Barton, a lifelong Republican, was elected to fill an unexpired term in Congress from New York's wealthy Seventeenth ("Silk-Stocking") District in 1937 and won a full term the next year. He campaigned vigorously, though unsuccessfully, against New Deal measures initiated by President Franklin D. Roosevelt, employing the motto "Repeal one useless law a week." Roosevelt ridiculed him and his fellow conservative congressmen Joseph W. Martin and Hamilton Fish, identifying them as the mythical firm "Martin, Barton & Fish." Barton reluctantly consented to run for the Senate in 1940 but lost the election.

Barton became president of his firm when Durstine resigned in 1939 but resumed the position of chair of the board in 1946, continuing to write much of the copy himself. His office was decorated with a large photograph of Coney Island's crowded boardwalk as a reminder of those whom their ads were aimed to reach. Unassuming in person (even the office boys at BBD&O called him "Bruce"), he was deeply respected

as the leader of an industry that he had done much to create. He retired in 1961 but continued to be regarded as the elder statesman of advertising. When he died in his home in New York City, he was honored not only for his contributions to his industry but also for the humanistic tradition his life had exemplified and promoted.

• The State Historical Society of Wisconsin in Madison has a collection of Barton's personal papers. His contribution to advertising is examined in James P. Wood, *The Story of Advertising* (1958); Joseph J. Seldin, *The Golden Fleece* (1963); Martin Mayer, *Madison Avenue, U.S.A.* (1958); Stephen Fox, *The Mirror Makers* (1984); and Warren I. Sussman, *Culture as History* (1984). His political career is discussed in Arthur M. Schlesinger, *The Age of Roosevelt*, vol. 3 (1960), and Robert S. McElvaine, *The Great Depression* (1984). See also *Printer's Ink*, 11 Nov. 1960, p. 20, and 10 Feb. 1961, p. 54ff. An obituary is in the *New York Times*, 6 July 1967.

DENNIS WEPMAN

BARTON, Clara (25 Dec. 1821–12 Apr. 1912), philanthropist, was born Clarissa Harlowe Barton in North Oxford, Massachusetts, the daughter of Stephen Barton, a farmer and local politician, and Sarah Stone. The childhood nickname "Clara" stuck, and throughout her life she was known to the world as Clara Barton. Her family had lived in New England for generations, and Barton grew up hearing stories of her ancestors' escapades during the American Revolution. Despite her family's comfortable position and local renown, however, her childhood was not happy. Her parents' troubled marriage and erratic behavior, the insanity and early death of her favorite sister, and the questionable business dealings of her brothers made for an unstable home life. When in later life she recalled her childhood, she wrote, "I remember nothing but fear."

To help overcome her shyness, her parents encouraged her to become a schoolteacher. Barton excelled at this profession, establishing immediately a sense of authority and scholastic rigor that belied her young age. Over the course of the next ten years, she did much to invigorate the schools in the townships around North Oxford, including the successful waging of a redistricting campaign that ultimately allowed workers' children to receive an education. These experiences also galvanized Barton's feminist leanings—for she demanded wages equal to those of her male colleagues when she was asked to take on schools traditionally reserved for male teachers—and gave her an early commitment to social reform.

In 1850 Barton interrupted her teaching to attend the Clinton Liberal Institute, a Universalist academy in Clinton, New York. A sense that she was out of step with the younger, less experienced students; the death of her mother; and her brother's indictment for bank robbery marred this year. She completed her academic work, however, and resumed teaching while on a visit to friends in Hightstown, New Jersey. In 1852 she moved to Bordentown, where she was hired to introduce a system of free public schools, based on the

Massachusetts model, then unknown in New Jersey. The experiment was successful, but the administration of such a system was thought to be inappropriate for a woman, and an unpopular male principal was installed. Barton left Bordentown early the next year, suffering the first of a series of nervous breakdowns that would plague her throughout her life.

After leaving Bordentown, Barton joined friends in Washington, D.C. She obtained a job as a copyist in the Patent Office, work at which she once again excelled. One of a handful of women employed at that time by the government, she conspicuously demanded—and received—a salary equal to that of the male employees. She endured several years of animosity and official harassment, later summing up the experience by saying that it "was very trying, but I thought perhaps there was some question of principle involved and I lived it through." In 1857, with the change in administration, Barton and the other female clerks were dismissed, but she regained her job with the reelection of the Republicans in 1860.

Barton was in Washington when the Civil War erupted, and she determined to play an active role to support the Union. At the outset, she gathered and distributed supplies for Massachusetts troops stationed in the capital. By the second year of the war, however, stories of privation at the front led her to seek permission to go to the battlefield. With the support of prominent Republicans, she finally obtained passes to the front from a reluctant War Department. As she wrote in a poem entitled "The Women Who Went to the Field," she had seen "in high purpose a duty to do / And the armor of right broke the barriers through."

Barton's first battlefield experiences, at Culpeper and Fairfax Station, Virginia, in July and August 1862, shocked her. She made it her business to fill as much of the medical and supply gap as she personally could and later described her work of the next three years as lying "anywhere between the bullet and the hospital." With skirt pinned up around her waist and a face blue from gunpowder, she served gruel, extracted bullets, and held the hands of the dying. During the battle of Antietam, she assisted at surgery, dressing wounds with green corn leaves when the bandages were exhausted. The chief surgeon wrote, "In my feeble estimation, General McClellan, with all his laurels sinks into insignificance beside the true heroine of the age, the angel of the battlefield." In Fredericksburg, Barton nearly lost her life while crossing the river to tend the wounded; once across she wrote she could barely step for the weight of her blood-soaked skirts. During the siege of Fort Wagner, South Carolina, in 1863 she ran a supply line, nursed soldiers suffering from malaria, and witnessed the action at Morris Island. She returned to the heat of battle during the Wilderness Campaign and served as supervisor of nurses for the Army of the James from June 1864 to January 1865. At the end of the war, she continued her service by opening an office to search for missing men and by

marking graves and establishing a national cemetery at the site of Andersonville Prison.

Barton pursued her war work alone and was never officially compensated for it, choosing to compromise neither her efforts nor her strong personality by aligning herself with the Sanitary Commission or Dorothea Dix's Department of Female Nurses. She was one of many brave fieldworkers, but her work came to have a popular recognition because of the dramatic lectures she gave between 1866 and 1868. Though she hated speaking, she mesmerized audiences across the country, publicizing her wartime role and commanding fees that were to make her financially independent for the rest of her life. A nervous breakdown cut her lecture tour short; doctors ordered her to recuperate in Europe.

While in Switzerland, Barton heard of the work of the recently formed International Red Cross and of the Geneva Convention that bound nations to uphold its principles of humane treatment of prisoners, the wounded, and civilians during wartime. She labored under the auspices of the Red Cross when war broke out between France and Prussia in 1870, ministering to refugees, devastated civilians, and wounded men. Her most notable accomplishment during these years was the organization of a work center in Strasbourg for the city's impoverished women. Another nervous disorder kept her in Europe as an invalid for several years. She returned to America in 1873, determined that the United States should become a party to the Geneva Convention.

Barton's continued ill health (in 1876 she moved to Dansville, New York, to follow a cure at the local sanatorium) hampered her early efforts to educate American leaders about the Red Cross. But over the course of nearly a decade she lobbied virtually alone for its acceptance, against a bureaucracy that believed that any agreement with a foreign nation meant compromising America's autonomy. Barton's determination and her agility at operating in the political sphere ultimately led to success. The Senate ratified the Geneva Convention on 16 March 1882, a tribute to Barton's foresight, courage, and perseverance.

For the next twenty-two years, Barton was president of the American National Red Cross. She never married and dedicated herself totally to the organization. She not only established the managerial framework for the body but adapted the principles of the Geneva Convention to American needs. Sensing that peacetime emergencies would be more compelling than war service, she began to use her society to aid in relief of natural disasters. Early activities included assistance during the Mississippi floods of 1882 and 1884 and relief after an earthquake in Illinois in 1886. Trained Red Cross nurses were used for the first time during a yellow fever epidemic in Florida in 1888. The most notable peacetime work of the early American Red Cross was at the Johnstown, Pennsylvania, flood in 1889. Here the fledgling organization provided temporary shelter, food, and clothing during the crucial weeks following the inundation of the town and gained valuable publicity for its work. "Hunt the dictionaries of all languages through and you will not find the signs to express our appreciation of her and her work," wrote the *Johnstown Daily Tribune*. Similar aid was undertaken with tornado victims in Iowa and those devastated by a hurricane off the South Carolina coast in 1893. Barton also pioneered American assistance in foreign crises, sending emergency food to Russia during the famine of 1892 and personally overseeing relief to civilians devastated by the religious wars in Turkey and Armenia in 1896.

These efforts gained wide recognition when the International Red Cross passed an "American Amendment" to the Geneva Convention in 1884. The amendment, sanctioning Red Cross activities in peacetime calamities, was a direct tribute to Barton's active vision and colored the subsequent development of the international body. The Red Cross as it is known today is largely as Barton defined and developed it.

During this period, Barton continued her larger interest in social reform. In 1883 she reluctantly served as the superintendent of the Massachusetts Reformatory Prison for Women in Sherborn, a sobering experience that reinforced the politicization of her innate feminism. What time she could spare from the Red Cross she devoted to raising the economic and political status of women. She attended rallies promoting woman suffrage, relishing her friendships with Susan B. Anthony, Lucy Stone, and other leaders. In 1888 alone, she traveled to four states on behalf of women's rights and was a featured speaker at the First International Woman's Suffrage Conference in Washington, D.C. She also worked on behalf of disenfranchised blacks, delivering a spirited speech on the subject in 1868 and aiding victims in the aftermath of the Sea Islands, South Carolina, hurricane of 1893.

The American Red Cross undertook its first wartime obligations during the Spanish-American War of 1898. The Red Cross had tried to give relief to Cubans being held in concentration camps before the beginning of actual hostilities, but the efforts had been disappointing. Once war began, the organization began fieldwork at the front and in hospitals, convalescent centers, and prison camps. Barton, at age seventy-six, had personally gone to Cuba to coordinate the Red Cross activities there, as she had personally commanded all other work. But it was clear that the task was now beyond the small coterie of workers that had carried the load for so long. The large organization needed to oversee such actions pushed the Red Cross into a more professional mold and gained increasing interest from Congress and the White House.

Moreover, Barton's controlling methods of management had begun to be noticed publicly. She had always been a strong and controversial personality. The most decorated woman in America, she counted the Iron Cross, the Cross of Imperial Russia, and the International Red Cross Medal among her trophies yet had never been officially recognized in the United States. Scandals involving nurses, funds, and the centralization of authority plagued her. In 1899 a campaign began in earnest to unseat her from the Red Cross presidency. Barton fought back stubbornly, enduring devastating personal attacks and focusing her energy on creating a final humanitarian gift: the concept of first aid, which culminated in the founding of the National First Aid Society. In 1904, however, she resigned as president of the American Red Cross at age eighty-three. She spent the remaining years of her life in quiet retirement at her home in Glen Echo, Maryland, where she died.

• The main body of Barton's papers are in the Library of Congress. Significant collections are also in the American Antiquarian Society, the Duke University Library, Huntington Library, American National Red Cross, and the Sophia Smith Collection at Smith College. Barton's own works, *The Red Cross in Peace and War* (1899), *The Story of the Red Cross: Glimpses of Field Work* (1904), and *The Story of My Childhood* (1907), are important both as firsthand accounts and for gaining her perspective. Percy Epler, who wrote *The Life of Clara Barton* (1915), and William E. Barton, author of *The Life of Clara Barton* (1922), knew Clara Barton, and their books contain valuable personal insights and anecdotal material. The most complete modern assessment is Elizabeth Brown Pryor, *Clara Barton, Professional Angel* (1987). Stephen B. Oates has written an in-depth account of Barton's Civil War service in *A Woman of Valor: Clara Barton and the Civil War* (1994), and William Conklin collected a large amount of material about the Dansville years in *Clara Barton and Dansville* (1966). See also Lavinia K. Dock et al., *History of Red Cross Nursing* (1922); Foster Rhea Dulles, *The American Red Cross: A History*; Estelle B. Freedman, *Their Sister's Keepers* (1981); and Eleanor Flexner, *Century of Struggle* (1974).

ELIZABETH B. PRYOR

BARTON, George Aaron (12 Nov. 1859–28 June 1942), Assyriologist and biblical scholar, was born in East Farnham, Quebec, Canada, the son of Daniel Barton, a farmer and blacksmith, and Mary Stevens Bull. He attended the Oakwood Seminary, Poughkeepsie, New York, becoming a minister of the Society of Friends in 1879, and graduated from Haverford College with an A.B. in 1882 and an M.A. in 1885. Around 1883 he moved to Boston, where he worked in insurance for a year, then from 1884 to 1889 taught mathematics and classics at the Friends School in Providence, Rhode Island. In 1884 he married Caroline Brewer Danforth; they adopted one child. In 1889 he entered Harvard Graduate School (M.A. 1890), where he studied Assyriology with David G. Lyon and Semitics and the Bible with Crawford H. Toy and Joseph H. Thayer. In 1891 he received his Ph.D. for a study, "The Semitic Ishtar Cult," later published in the *American Journal of Semitic Languages and Literatures* 9 (1893) and 10 (1894).

From 1891 to 1922 Barton was professor of biblical literature and Semitic languages at Bryn Mawr College, where he was noted as a distinguished teacher and a capable administrator and served as the college chaplain. His publications in cuneiform epigraphy, the most enduring portion of his extensive bibliography, began with a study of a group of Achaemenid contracts at the University Museum, University of

Pennsylvania (1899), as well as a small collection of Sumerian tablets in a private collection (1912). The following year his book *The Origin and Development of Babylonian Writing* was published in Leipzig. His major undertaking of this period was a three-volume publication of Sumerian cuneiform tablets in the Haverford College Library (1905, 1909, 1914; reissued 1918). Barton was in the forefront of those condemning the veracity of Herman Hilprecht, professor of Assyriology at the University of Pennsylvania, concerning discoveries made during the University of Pennsylvania's expeditions to Nippur. In the aftermath of the dispute, Barton studied tablets from Nippur excavated by the university and published *Sumerian Business and Administrative Documents from the Earliest Times to the Dynasty of Agade* (1915) and *Miscellaneous Babylonian Inscriptions* (1918), the latter containing important Sumerian literary manuscripts.

In 1902–1903 Barton served as director of the American School of Oriental Research in Jerusalem, publishing a volume on his experiences there, *A Year's Wandering in Bible Lands* (1904). Interested by the growing discipline of biblical archaeology, Barton participated in fieldwork and excavations in Palestine. His *Archaeology and the Bible* (1916) was a popular textbook on this subject, running through seven editions and numerous printings by 1937. It contained extensive translations and commentaries on Mesopotamian and Eqyptian texts with biblical parallels. He also published *A Sketch of Semitic Origins* (1902), wholly revised in a second edition of 1934. He prepared a commentary on Ecclesiastes for the International Critical Commentary (1908) and published a general study, *Religions of the World* (1917), which went through a third edition by 1929. He published *The Roots of Christian Teaching as Found in the Old Testament* (1902), *The Heart of the Christian Message* (1910), *Commentary on the Book of Job* (1911), and *The Religion of Israel* (1918; 2d ed. 1928), as well as numerous articles and reviews on biblical, Semitic, and Assyriological topics. Barton served as president of the Society of Biblical Literature and Exegesis (1913–1914) and of the American Oriental Society (1916–1917). From 1921 until 1934 he served as director of the American School of Oriental Research in Baghdad, although he did not visit Mesopotamia.

In 1922 Barton was appointed professor of Semitic languages and the history of religion at the University of Pennsylvania as successor to Morris Jastrow, Jr. He held that post until his retirement in 1932. Concurrently he was professor of New Testament literature at the Divinity School of the Protestant Episcopal Church in Philadelphia until his retirement there in 1937. In this connection he continued to publish works on Christianity, including *Jesus of Nazareth, a Biography* (1922), *Studies in New Testament Christianity* (1928), *Christ and Evolution* (1934), *The Apostolic Age and the New Testament* (1936), and with Baruch Weitzel, *A History of the Hebrew People from the Earliest Times to the Year 70 A.D.* (1930).

Through the impetus of Albert T. Clay, the American Oriental Society in New Haven launched an ambitious series of translations from ancient Oriental literatures. Barton contributed *The Royal Inscriptions of Sumer and Akkad* (1929), the first large collection of its kind in English. This in effect built on and updated François Thureau-Dangin's *Die Sumerischen und Akkadischen Königsinchriften* (1907), although, except in matters of bibliography, it was not a decisive advance over Thureau-Dangin's work. The series languished after Clay's untimely death, so Barton's volume remained the most substantial product of the enterprise. Barton also turned to the study of Hittite, publishing *A Hittite Manual for Beginners* (1928) and *A Hittite Chrestomathy* (1932).

Barton was an enthusiastic, conscientious teacher, noted for his breadth of interests, keen intellect, gracious manner, and lively sense of humor. Those of his students who went on to professional careers in Assyriology or Semitics could be dismayed by his lack of philological rigor and his serious consideration of hasty, even fantastic translations, as noted by Samuel Noah Kramer, *In the World of Sumer* (1986, p. 21), and Cyrus H. Gordon, *The Pennsylvania Tradition of Semitics* (1986, pp. 45–47). His scholarly and religious output was extraordinary, reflecting tireless energy and a ready pen. Barton was a member of the American Philosophical Society, the Royal Society of Arts (London), the Archaeological Institute of America, and the American Association for the Advancement of Science.

Barton left the Society of Friends in 1918 in protest of its pacifist stand in the First World War. He was ordained to the Episcopal priesthood in 1919. His first wife died in 1930, and a year later he married Katherine Blye Hagy. They had no children. After his retirement, Barton lived in Coconut Grove, Florida, spending his summers at Weston, Massachusetts, where he died.

• Barton's personal papers and correspondence are in the Bryn Mawr College Library. Other scholarly papers and manuscripts are in the archives of the University of Pennsylvania. A manuscript titled "Boston Broad Brim" and several letters are in the Haverford College Library. The manuscript autobiography, "The Bookworm," alluded to by Robert C. Dentan, *Dictionary of American Biography*, supp. 3, p. 37, has disappeared. A painted portrait and photos are also at Bryn Mawr College. Partial bibliographies of his publications appear in Morris Jastrow, Jr., et al., "Prof. George Barton: An Appreciation," *Bryn Mawr Alumnae Quarterly*, Nov. 1919, pp. 129–41 (also published separately in 1919); and Rykle Borger, *Handbuch der Keilschriftliteratur*, vol. 1 (1967), pp. 13–15. Biographical sketches by James A. Montgomery are in *American Philosophical Society Year Book* (1942), pp. 331–33, *American Journal of Archaeology* 46 (1942): 546. See also E. A. Speiser et al., *Bulletin of the American Schools of Oriental Research* 87 (1942): 2–4; and *Stowe's Clerical Dictionary of the Protestant Episcopal Church in the United States of America* (1941), p. 17.

BENJAMIN R. FOSTER

BARTON, James Edward (1 Nov. 1890–19 Feb. 1962), vaudeville performer and actor, was born in Gloucester, New Jersey, the son of James Charles Barton, an interlocutor with the West and Primrose Minstrels, and Clara Anderson, a vaudeville performer. At age two Barton was carried on stage by his parents in a production of *The Silver King*, and one can say without much exaggeration, that, aside from eating, sleeping, and pursuing his interests in sports and raising dogs, Barton was never off the stage for the rest of his life. At four he was playing Topsy in a tour of *Uncle Tom's Cabin*, and billed as "the boy comedian." He toured in an act with his parents between 1897 and 1903, completing his formal education with the sixth grade in Camden, New Jersey.

Barton loved show business from the start, and did not feel his vaudevillian parents pushed him into it: "No kid ever had a better time. I can't remember how old I was when they began teaching me funny skits, dance steps, bits of songs. I was nuts about it." When Barton went solo in his early teens, he worked chiefly in vaudeville circuits and stock companies in the South and Midwest. In 1905, at age fifteen, Barton began what turned into a four-year tour as a dancing comedian with Jeanette Dupree's *Twentieth Century Maids* for the Columbia burlesque chain. "Not the Minsky kind, the *old* burlesque," according to Barton, by which he meant something more respectable than what burlesque had become by the time of Minsky. In 1912 he married Ottilie Kleinert; they had no children.

It was only in 1919 that Barton first played New York. He had been cast in a minor role in *The Passing Show of 1919*, still in rehearsal when a strike by Actors Equity occurred. Barton took part in a benefit performance for the striking actors, and his routine near the end of the evening stopped the show, establishing him as a formidable song-and-dance man. He quickly rose to more featured spots in revues and musicals, finally becoming a frequent headliner at the Palace between 1928 and 1932. Often called "the man with the laughing feet," Barton featured in his act a comic drunk routine so realistic it led people to wonder about the performer's own sobriety. This routine became such a Barton trademark that he would incorporate parts of it into virtually every character he portrayed in a play or musical.

Once his reputation was secure in New York, Barton was in demand for roles in plays, musical comedies, and revues. During the 1920s he appeared in *The Last Waltz* (1921), *The Rose of Stamboul* (1922), *Dew Drop Inn* (1923), *The Passing Show of 1924* (1924), *Artists and Models* (1925), and *Palm Beach Nights* and *The Ziegfeld Follies of 1926*, both in 1926.

In 1928–1929 Barton toured as Skid in the road company of the play *Burlesque*. Presumably it was during that tour that he sustained injuries in a Baltimore hotel fire that left his face scarred and his nose disfigured. While he would thenceforth require considerable makeup, his altered features would not be a hindrance to his playing the three greatest roles of his career, nor to his marrying again, shortly after he and his wife divorced in 1933. His second wife was Kathryn Penman, who had been a Ziegfeld girl in the 1926 edition in which Barton had been featured.

In June 1934 Barton's career took a new direction, when he replaced Henry Hull as the profane, degenerate Georgia "cracker" Jeeter Lester in *Tobacco Road*. Over the next five years Barton played the part 1,899 times on Broadway, taking only one significant break from the play to make two films, *Captain Hurricane* and *His Family Tree*, both in 1935. The role of Jeeter as firmly proved Barton to be a serious actor as his virtuosic comedy, song, and dance routines had established him as a vaudeville headliner.

Barton's success in *Tobacco Road* led to numerous stage, film, and, later, television roles for the rest of his life, although with two notable exceptions he was usually cast (or even typecast) in supporting roles of the boozy, crusty, cantankerous sort, such as the prospector in *Yellow Sky* and the old Indian scout in the film version of Saroyan's *The Time of Your Life*.

Barton's most distinguished achievement on stage came in 1946 when he starred as Hickey in the original production of Eugene O'Neill's *The Iceman Cometh*. Brooks Atkinson of the *New York Times* called his characterization of the peace-peddling salesman "superb—common, unctuous, cheerful, and fanatical."

In 1951 Barton returned one last time to the musical stage in a starring role that gave scope not only to his singing, dancing, and acting talents, but even his legendary drunk routine: Ben Rumson, the variously hard-bitten, sentimental, and besotted prospector in Lerner and Loewe's *Paint Your Wagon*. Richard Gehman of *Theatre Arts* called Barton's performance "a magnificent personal triumph," and Atkinson extolled him in terms that reflected his longevity as a performer: "He gives one of those humorous, relaxed, lovable and masterful performances that are peculiar to actors with a long and varied experience. Without strutting or hamming, he owns the stage. There is a grandeur about the size of his acting despite the homeliness of the material" (*New York Times*, 18 Nov. 1951).

Barton was also very active in television from the mid-1950s to his death. He appeared in several drama presentations, including the Kaiser Aluminum Hour" and the "Kraft Television Theatre." He did the "Time of Your Life" for "Playhouse 90" and also frequently appeared in such series as "Naked City," "Adventures in Paradise," and "New York Confidential."

Barton's last stint on Broadway was in the title role of the unsuccessful *The Sin of Pat Muldoon* and his last film appearance, the year before his death, was in *The Misfits*, with a screenplay by Arthur Miller. Barton died in Mineola, New York, after an active career in show business that had spanned sixty-six years and every venue and media from the vaudeville and legitimate stages to film and television.

• Richard Gehman's interview, "James Barton," *Theatre Arts*, Feb. 1952 is the single best source of insights into Barton's character and his views on acting. The *New York Times* obituary, 2 Feb. 1962, contains a comprehensive account of the facts of his career, whereas the obituary in *Variety*, 21 Feb. 1962, is rather idiosyncratic, focusing on Barton's greatness as a vaudevillian and seeing his legitimate acting successes as tangential and rather inconsequential in the overall scheme of his career.

JOHN BUSH JONES

BARTON, James Levi (23 Sept. 1855–21 July 1936), missionary, mission administrator, and author, was born in Charlotte, Vermont, the son of Jacob Barton and Hannah Knowles, a daughter of a prominent Quaker family. His father farmed and worked at lumbering in several remote Vermont communities. While his father served several years in the Union army, Barton worked in the lumbermill and was the main support of his mother, whose faith profoundly influenced his life and thought. Barton's relative disinterest in theological controversy, his major concern for social improvement, and his confidence in divine presence and guidance all gave evidence of this Quaker influence. He also credited the spartan but happy years on the farm and in the workshop for preparing him for his career.

After education in local schools and academies, Barton entered Middlebury College in 1877, receiving his diploma in 1881 from President Cyrus Hamlin, who had as a missionary been the founder of influential Robert College in Constantinople. To earn his way through college, Barton worked at the *Middlebury Register*, where he developed his writing skills, and a law office, where he became familiar with procedures for handling bequests, later valuable to him in his extensive fundraising. After a year honing his persuasive skills as a salesman of "covered buggies" in Illinois, Barton entered Hartford Theological Seminary in 1882.

In college Barton had become interested in questions of science and religion, including Darwinism. He pursued his theological studies primarily as an exploration of ways in which Christianity could be related to modern thought and current issues rather than as vocational preparation for the ministry. His seminary years also opened his eyes to the wider world, and as graduation approached in the spring of 1885 he sought and received appointment by the American Board of Commissioners for Foreign Missions, the oldest of the American foreign mission agencies. In 1885 he married Flora Estelle Holmes, a distant relative of Oliver Wendell Holmes. They had two children. He was ordained to the Congregational ministry at New Haven, Vermont, on 26 June 1885, and on 1 September the young couple sailed for Constantinople.

Upon arrival in October Barton was assigned to Harput, 700 miles to the east in the interior of Turkey. For seven years he was supervisor of the many schools of the American Board in the Harput region, traveling extensively on his prized Arabian horse, Kirk. In 1888 he began to teach in the mission's theological seminary and developed a close connection with Euphrates College, founded in 1878. In 1891 Flora Barton's ill health made a furlough in the United States necessary, during which Barton was elected president of Euphrates College. Flora Barton's continuing health problems prevented their return to Turkey, and in 1894 Barton was elected foreign secretary of the American Board, serving in the Boston office until 1927. At first he carried responsibility for the missions in Eastern and European Turkey, Spain, Mexico, Austria, Japan, India, and Ceylon. In 1906 he assumed virtually full oversight of all the mission fields of the board, adding China, Africa, the Pacific Islands, and the rest of Turkey. He was assisted by other secretaries after 1920. He led major board deputations to Japan in 1895, to India and Ceylon in 1901, and to China in 1907.

Barton believed that the overseas churches founded or assisted by the board should become self-directing and self-supporting as soon as possible. This meant that higher education should assume a major place in mission programs so that indigenous Christian churches and communities could have well-trained, competent leadership among both clergy and lay people. Barton used his considerable talent for developing influential connections and for fundraising to secure some $33 million for building and developing institutions of higher education, including two medical schools. All of these were to be interdenominational, international, and nonsectarian. Each was provided with an independent board of trustees, both for governance and to secure continuing support outside of church and mission budgets. Barton served for many years as trustee of many of these institutions and others, including Middlebury College; Hartford Seminary; Peking Union Medical College; Peking University; Euphrates College; Woman's Christian College of Madras, India; Vellore Medical College, India; Foochow College; and International College, Smyrna. In addition to emphasizing education, Barton strongly supported medical and social work programs as an integral part of the Christian mission.

Barton was involved in many significant responsibilities beyond the program of his own organization. Beginning in 1914 he actively organized efforts to send relief to the Near East, eventuating in Near East Relief, the first major American relief enterprise overseas. In 1919, following World War I, he was director of the Relief Expedition to the Near East. He served in 1920 as moderator of the International Congregational Council, and in 1925 he chaired the interdenominational Foreign Missions Convention in Washington.

Barton's missionary and philanthropic responsibilities brought him into close contact with American officials, and he was involved in a number of important political negotiations, which are described in his "Autobiographical Notes." In 1921 he was sent by the Foreign Missions Conference of North America to represent missionary and philanthropic interests at the London Conference, which was framing a peace settlement for the Near East. A year later, at the instance of the American secretary of state and representing the U.S. Federal Council of Churches, he attended the Lausanne Conference following the close of hostilities between Turkey and Greece. He worked through the

American delegation to secure a National Home for Armenians in Turkey and to prevent expulsion of the Armenian and Greek minorities in Anatolia. Although he reported that "every moral issue was lost," Barton nevertheless urged ratification of the treaty as a basis for relations with the new Turkey of Kemal Atatürk. In 1924 Barton conferred with President Calvin Coolidge to defuse tension with Japan over projected American naval maneuvers in the Pacific. From 1922 to 1932 he served as a director of the Institute of Social and Religious Research, supported by the Rockefellers.

Barton lectured at several theological seminaries, including Bangor, Andover, Chicago, New Brunswick, and the Pacific School of Religion. He died in Brookline, Massachusetts.

• "Autobiographical Notes of James L. Barton" is a manuscript memoir of 339 pages in the Congregational Library, Boston, and the library of the United Church Board for World Ministries. Both libraries contain a number of his shorter writings and most of his books. In addition to numerous articles, including "Some Popular Objections to Foreign Missions," *Union Seminary Magazine*, Oct.-Nov. 1904, pp. 3–13, and "The Effect of the War on Protestant Missions," *Harvard Theological Review* 12 (1919) 1–35, he published six books: *The Missionary and His Critics* (1906), *The Unfinished Task of the Christian Church* (1908), *Daybreak in Turkey* (1908), *Human Progress through Missions* (1912), *The Christian Approach to Islam* (1918), and *The Story of the Near East Relief* (1930). Barton wrote many reports that appeared in the annual reports of the American Board and in the *Missionary Herald*. A notable example is the report of the Japan deputation of 1895, printed as an appendix to the annual report of 1896. A summary tribute by his successor, Fred Field Goodsell, is *James Levi Barton: Dynamic World Christian Statesman* (1964). C. H. Patton et al., "Dr. Barton as We Knew Him," *Missionary Herald* 132 (Sept. 1936): 407–11, 433, is an extensive obituary illustrated with portraits from all the stages of his life and including personal descriptions by several colleagues. Other tributes are in Missionary Herald, 182 (1936): 464–65, 570–72.

DAVID M. STOWE

BARTON, William (26 May 1748–22 Oct. 1831), revolutionary war soldier, was born in Warren, Rhode Island, the son of Benjamin Barton and Lydia (maiden name unknown). Information about his parents' occupations is not available. After receiving a common-school education, he entered the hat-making trade. In 1770, at the age of twenty-two, he married Rhoda Carver and lived peacefully for the next few years. In 1775, upon hearing of the battle of Bunker Hill, he joined the Rhode Island militia. He quickly showed an aptitude for leading men and rose to the rank of captain. A year later, on 19 August 1776, he was promoted to major.

In 1777 Barton developed and carried out a scheme to capture Brigadier General Richard Prescott, who commanded a British occupying force on Rhode Island, in Narragansett Bay. The year before, Prescott had been seized by the patriots and exchanged for General John Sullivan (1740–1795). Returning to British service, Prescott had taken control of Rhode Island in December 1776 and soon reinforced his reputation among Americans for overweening and arrogant conduct by making himself odious to the occupants. He established his headquarters in Newport, bullied the islanders, forced them to house his soldiers in private homes, and coerced them into giving his army other supports. Barton, after carefully selecting a small body of militiamen to assist him in seizing Prescott, on the evening of 4 July set out from Tiverton in four whaleboats. After rests at Bristol and Warwick Neck, he and his party silently rowed across Narragansett Bay on the night of 9 July, gliding unobserved under the shadow of three British frigates and landing about midway between Newport and Bristol ferry. With speed and stealth, Barton led his men inland toward the house that Prescott and a few guards occupied. After silencing the sentries, Barton's party broke in the door of Prescott's room, captured the British general, and took him away, half-clothed, across Narragansett Bay to Warwick. Upon landing, Prescott turned to Barton and remarked, "Sir, you have made a bold push to-night," to which Barton replied, "Sir, we have been very fortunate" (Fuller, p. 115).

Barton's reputation was vastly enhanced. For his exploit, Congress on 10 November 1777 thanked him, promoted him to lieutenant colonel, and presented him with a ceremonial sword. The general assembly of Rhode Island also voted its thanks. For a time he served as an aide-de-camp to General Nathanael Greene but soon returned to regular duty. Barton was afterward proud of his martial stroke against Prescott, despite his self-effacing remark to that general. It was said that during the retreat of the British from Warren in 1778, he challenged one of the enemy officers to single combat, identifying himself as "the man who took Prescott." During that same British retreat, Barton was wounded and disabled for a time. In 1779 he was appointed commander of a light corps, consisting of four companies, that had just been embodied by the Rhode Island Assembly. He served actively for the remainder of the war.

In 1788 Barton was on the losing side in the struggle of some Rhode Islanders to adopt the new federal Constitution. Although he had joined with fellow citizens in writing a letter to the national convention asserting support for a revision of the Articles of Confederation, Rhode Islanders refused to adopt the new basic law when it was presented to them. However, he was pleased two years later to serve in the state convention that finally ratified the Constitution of 1787. During these proceedings, he was chosen to serve as one of two monitors, positions reserved for "prominent members [whose] duty was to see order preserved" and to make sure "that the attention of members was not distracted from the business before them" (Staples, p. 643).

Barton's last years were blighted by a curious problem with a plot of land in Vermont. Having purchased the tract (or been given it by Congress) and apparently having settled upon it, his right to it was contested. He was assessed a judgment, which he stubbornly refused to pay. Consequently, he was made a "prisoner" by the Vermonters in the easy surroundings of a Danbury inn, where he lived for the next fourteen years without budging from what he considered a principled stance. His plight came to the attention of the marquis de Lafayette during the latter's celebrated visit to the United States in 1824–1825. Without Barton's knowledge or approval, Lafayette paid the judgment and thus allowed Barton to go free. Returning to his home state of Rhode Island, Barton settled in Providence, where he lived for the remainder of his days and died.

• Barton's manuscript account of the capture of Prescott is in the Rhode Island Historical Society. The only life is Catherine R. A. Williams, *Biography of Revolutionary Heroes: Containing the Life of Brigadier Gen. William Barton, and Also, of Captain Stephen Olney* (1839). The Prescott exploit is described by Oliver Payson Fuller, *The History of Warwick, Rhode Island, from Its Settlement in 1642 to the Present Time* . . . (1875); and Jeremiah Lewis Diman, *The Capture of General Richard Prescott by Lt.-Col. William Barton* (1877). For Barton's role in the convention of 1790, see William R. Staples, *Rhode Island in the Continental Congress 1765–1790, with the Journal of the Convention That Adopted the Constitution* (1871).

PAUL DAVID NELSON

BARTRAM, John (23 Mar. 1699–22 Sept. 1777), botanist, was born in Marple, Pennsylvania, the son of William Bartram and Elizabeth Hunt, farmers. His parents were members of the Society of Friends, and, although raised in this tradition, by 1757 Bartram had departed from Quaker teachings by opposing the pacifism of the society and by denying the divinity of Jesus. Excluded in that year from fellowship with the local community of Friends, he nevertheless continued to attend their Sunday services. After the death of his mother in 1701 and his father's immigration to North Carolina with a new wife around 1709, young Bartram remained in Pennsylvania and was raised by his grandmother and an uncle, Isaac Bartram. His formal education was limited; he was handicapped throughout his career as a naturalist by his poor grammar and inadequate knowledge of Latin.

Inheriting a farm from his uncle, Bartram prospered through the careful tilling of that land. In 1723 he married Mary Morris, with whom he had two sons before her death in 1727. After selling the farm that he had inherited, he purchased in 1728 the 102 acres along the banks of Schuylkill River near Philadelphia that he would carefully cultivate for the balance of his life. By draining the marshes, rotating crops, and fertilizing the land, Bartram obtained crop yields that far exceeded those of his neighbors. In 1729 he married Ann Mendenhall. A skilled stonemason, Bartram erected with his own hands the home in which he and his second wife would raise the nine children to whom she gave birth. Prospering as a farmer, Bartram obtained additional lands and began to create the garden that became famous for the rare plants he collected on his travels.

While Bartram's fascination with plants began early in his youth, his interest in their more technical features began late. This interest was nourished initially by his desire to understand the medicinal qualities of plants but soon evolved into a more general curiosity about the nature of American plants, their features, and their habitats and distribution. Bartram was aided in his desire to learn more about American flora by James Logan and by Joseph Breintnall, the secretary of the Library Company of Philadelphia, one of the nation's first scientific societies. Logan, a successful Quaker merchant and one of the leading scientific thinkers of the early eighteenth century, had amassed an extensive library and corresponded regularly with most of the prominent English naturalists. Learning of Bartram's interest in botanical subjects, Logan generously loaned him books on this subject from his library, introduced him to the study of Latin so that he could understand the system of Linnaeus, and provided him with instruction on the use of a microscope. Logan became Bartram's earliest botanical mentor. A friend of Benjamin Franklin and a correspondent with Peter Collinson in England, Breintnall was primarily interested in physical phenomena but provided the introduction to Collinson that allowed Bartram to become a plant collector for English naturalists; he may also have provided Bartram's initial introduction to Franklin.

Collinson, an English Quaker, was a successful merchant and member of the Royal Society with an interest in introducing foreign plants into England. By 1735 Bartram had begun a correspondence and friendship with Collinson that would last for more than three decades. Although they never met, Collinson was the singular influence in Bartram's development as a plant collector and botanist; their numerous letters reveal the fondness and respect each developed for the other. Collinson not only provided financial support for Bartram's botanical explorations but also saw that other English naturalists learned of his skills as a collector of specimens and seeds and even edited and submitted some of Bartram's letters for publication in the *Philosophical Transactions* of the Royal Society. In 1735 Bartram's description of his dissection of a rattlesnake appeared in the *Letter Book* of the Royal Society; this was his first publication. Collinson distributed the American plants he received from Bartram to Lord Petre, Sir Hans Sloane, the dukes of Argyll, Bedford, Norfolk, and Richmond, and other prominent English horticulturists and naturalists. The funds that Bartram received from these specimens allowed him to supplement his farm income and begin to plan more distant collecting trips. In 1736 Collinson developed a circle of English naturalists who agreed to support through annual subscription Bartram's collecting endeavors. That spring Bartram collected in the Rattlesnake Mountains and in the fall followed the Schuylkill River to its sources, gathering specimens as he wandered. While the initial focus was on botanical specimens, his patrons in England, and later those on the Continent, began to expand his collecting goals into most areas of

American flora and fauna. For five guineas a box, Bartram diligently collected and shipped fossils, reptiles, insects, birds, and mammals to his subscribers.

As his skills as a field naturalist developed, Bartram's trips became more extensive. In 1738 he made a five-week journey of more than 1,000 miles along the James River and into the Blue Ridge Mountains of Virginia. While exploring the natural history of that region, Bartram spent almost all of his time in the field and only one night under a roof. Four years later, in 1742, he collected along the Hudson River to the falls of the Mohawk River and then in the Catskill Mountains. In 1743 he accompanied Conrad Weiser and Lewis Evans on an expedition to Onondaga in New York with an additional natural history reconnaissance to Fort Oswego on Lake Ontario. Impressed by the details of this trip and the meticulous care with which he recorded what he observed, Collinson published Bartram's journal of this expedition in 1751 as *Observations on the Inhabitants, Climate, Soil, Rivers, Productions, Animals, and Other Matters Worthy of Notice. Made by Mr. John Bartram, in His Travels from Pensilvania to Onondago, Oswego and the Lake Ontario, in Canada.* Benjamin Franklin aided Bartram's career in 1743 by obtaining permission for him to have free access to the extensive collection of scientific books in the collection of the Library Company of Philadelphia. When Franklin became deputy postmaster general in 1751, he granted Bartram franking privileges for his correspondence. In 1744 Bartram collected once more in New York, and in 1745 he gathered specimens along the Susquehanna River. In 1754 and 1755 brief collecting trips were made to New York and Connecticut. With the cessation of the French and Indian War and the acquisition of the new territories acquired by the colonies, he had new lands for botanical exploration. In 1761 he explored, botanized, and collected along the Ohio River. He also traveled into the interior of South Carolina. By this time, his travels had taken him from Canada to Georgia.

Bartram's trips and the collections and letters he sent abroad made him famous throughout England and Europe. He was known and respected by Europe's most prominent naturalists and corresponded and shared ideas with Sloane, Mark Catesby, Carolus Linnaeus, J. J. Dillenius, John Frederick Gronovius, John Hope, Daniel Carl Solander, Peter Kalm, André Michaux, Alexander Garden, and John Fothergill. Through the intervention of Collinson, Bartram was named in 1765 botanist to the king with a stipend that was to allow him to continue his botanical investigations. While the recognition from George III's government was appreciated by Bartram, the small stipend of £50 a year was insufficient to support extensive collecting. Never truly daunted by the lack of funds, he set off in 1765 accompanied by his son William to botanize in Georgia and Florida. In Florida he traveled up the St. John's River to its sources; this was Bartram's last major trip.

While praising him for his meticulous observations and knowledge of plant communities and habitats, Bartram's admirers acknowledged that he knew far more about America's flora than he ever published. Peter Kalm, the talented Swedish naturalist, captured the essence of Bartram's strengths and weaknesses when he observed, "We owe to him the knowledge of many rare plants which he first found and which were never known before. He has shown great judgment and an attention which lets nothing escape unnoticed. Yet with all these qualities he is to be blamed for his negligence, for he did not care to write down his numerous and useful observations" (*Travels in North America*, vol. 1 [1937], p. 61). Handicapped by poor grammar, weak Latin, and a limited knowledge of systematic botany, Bartram gathered the specimens that allowed other naturalists to make significant advances in taxonomy, plant distribution, and the investigation of North American flora. In 1769 he was elected to the Royal Academy of Sciences in Sweden and in 1772 received a gold medal from A Society of Gentlemen in Edinburgh for his scientific contributions. Always seeking to advance science, he was one of the founders in 1769 of the American Philosophical Society. Through his garden, correspondence, and plant collecting, he made distinctive contributions to the growth of botanical knowledge. He died at Kingsessing, Pennsylvania.

• The Bartram papers at the Historical Society of Pennsylvania contain significant selections of his work. William Darlington's excellent *Memorials of John Bartram and Humphry Marshall* (1849) presents much of his correspondence as well as portions of his 1753 journal and a treatise on weed. Most of his letters that were not published by Darlington are in Edmund Berkeley and Dorothy Smith Berkeley's edition of *The Correspondence of John Bartram* (1992). Although Bartram did not publish the results of much of his work, a sense of his style and methods can be found in his *Observations on the Inhabitants, Climate, Soil, Rivers, Productions, Animals, and Other Matters . . . from Pensilvania to Onondago, Oswego and the Lake Ontario, in Canada* (1751) and *A Journal, Kept by John Bartram of Philadelphia, Botanist to His Majesty for the Floridas: Upon a Journey from St. Augustine Up the River St. Johns* (1767). An annotated bibliography of books and articles on Bartram is in Rose Marie Cutting, *John and William Bartram, William Byrd II and St. John de Crèvecoeur: A Reference Guide* (1976). Ernest Earnest, *John and William Bartram, Botanists and Explorers* (1940), provides a solid introduction to his life. Josephine Herbst, *New Green World* (1954), also examines Bartram's career. A succinct but perceptive examination of Bartram's contribution to botany and American science is in Raymond Phineas Stearns, *Science in the British Colonies of America* (1970), pp. 575–93.

PHILLIP DRENNON THOMAS

BARTRAM, William (9 Apr. 1739–22 July 1823), naturalist, artist, and explorer, was born in Philadelphia, Pennsylvania, the son of John Bartram, a naturalist, and Ann Mendenhall. Unlike his father, who was essentially self-taught, William Bartram benefited from a rigorous formal education at the Philadelphia Academy, where he studied history, Latin, French, and the classics. From an early age, however, his overriding interest was in nature. He spent much of his time as a young man traveling with his father to collect and draw plants and other specimens for John Bartram's overseas patrons and scientific correspondents.

In 1761 William Bartram gave up a frustrating business apprenticeship in Philadelphia and struck off on his own. He traveled to North Carolina to live with his father's half-brother, also named William Bartram, who owned a trading post at Cape Fear. Although his business acumen did not improve ("Everything goes wrong with him there," his father observed), the independence Bartram achieved during his stay in the South seemed to give him self-confidence.

When John Bartram was appointed botanist to King George III in 1765, he invited his son to join him on a year-long collecting trip in Florida, which had come under British control in 1763 and then extended as far west as the Mississippi River and as far north as the thirty-first parallel. The trip, focused primarily on the St. Johns River, inspired William Bartram to set his sights on becoming an explorer-naturalist.

When his father returned to Philadelphia in 1766, Bartram remained in Florida, hoping to start an indigo plantation near St. Augustine, but this proved unsuccessful. Discouraged, he returned to Philadelphia within a year; there he again failed at business.

At about this time John Bartram's English patron, Peter Collinson, brought William's paintings to the attention of John Fothergill. He admired them, and he became a generous patron to William Bartram, supporting his investigations from 1768 until Fothergill's death in 1780.

Bartram returned to North Carolina in 1770. From there he sent Collinson unusual plants for propagation and drawings of plants for his private collection. With Fothergill's pledge of a stipend of 50 pounds per year (plus bonuses for particularly prized specimens and drawings), Bartram was able to subsist as a naturalist. In 1773 he embarked on a four-year, 2,400-mile journey through southeastern North America; it would ensure him a permanent place in American natural history.

Bartram's southern travels are incompletely and confusingly documented, because unlike many later American exploratory trips, his had no predetermined destination. Instead, he meandered through the country as his inclination and fortunes dictated, or as opportunities for supplies and traveling companions or the political situation allowed. His primary purpose was to collect and ship to England new species of plants, but his interests were broad, and he recorded remarkably comprehensive observations of the region and its peoples. His comments on Native Americans, especially the Creek, Cherokee, and Seminole tribes, are especially valuable. He spent much of his time along the coasts of South Carolina, Georgia, and northern Florida, returning to many of the sites he had visited with his father in 1765 and 1766.

Bartram also traveled inland, across present-day Georgia, Alabama, and Louisiana, eventually reaching as far west as Point Coupee, north of Baton Rouge on the Mississippi River. On the way there along the Gulf Coast, he contracted a near-fatal illness that left him severely weakened and partially blind. Elsewhere on his journey he faced alligator attacks, hostile Indians, and many other dangers. In his published and unpublished accounts of the trip, however, Bartram tended to stress the glories of his experience and the wonders of nature rather than his misfortunes.

When Bartram left on his trip, Fothergill urged him to keep a diary to help him remember the locations and growing conditions of the plant specimens he collected. Bartram apparently did not intend to publish this, but eventually, at the urging of friends, he reworked his diaries to create the account for which he is best known today. A Philadelphia firm, James and Johnson, eventually published the book in 1791; it was the first serious work on American natural history published in postrevolutionary America. Issued under the full title *Travels through North & South Carolina, Georgia, East and West Florida, the Cherokee Country, the Extensive Territories of the Muscogulges, or Creek Confederacy, and the Country of the Chactaws Containing an Account of the Soil and Natural Productions of Those Regions, Together with Observations on the Manners of the Indians*, Bartram's book met with critical acclaim but only limited sales in the United States, where it was not reprinted until 1928. In Europe, however, it received enthusiastic critical and popular response. A 1792 London edition was quickly followed by a second edition there, and by editions in Dublin, Berlin, and Vienna in 1793, in the Netherlands in 1794 and 1797, and in Paris in 1799 and 1801.

Despite the many European and American visitors who flocked to his door, the reclusive naturalist, who never strayed far from his own garden in the years following his southern trip, was probably not aware of the full extent of his fame and influence. Bartram was one of the most widely-read American authors in Europe in the late eighteenth and early nineteenth centuries. His book directly influenced Coleridge, Wordsworth, Carlyle, and Chateaubriand—and in the United States, Emerson, Thoreau, John Muir, and many others.

When not traveling Bartram lived in the house where he was born, by the Schuylkill River on the outskirts of Philadelphia. After his father's death in 1777, he assisted his younger brother, John Bartram, Jr., in running the family's botanical garden there. He died in Philadelphia.

Through his writings and friendships Bartram encouraged the next generation of American naturalists associated with the Academy of Natural Sciences of Philadelphia (founded in 1812), to which he was elected in its first year. His most notable protégés were his great-nephew, Thomas Say, an entomologist and conchologist, and Alexander Wilson, a Scottish-born ornithologist who lived in Bartram's house while writing and illustrating his classic *American Ornithology*.

Although Bartram never married, he left intellectual offspring throughout the natural-science community, and a botanical legacy of discoveries and introduced species in gardens around the world. His positive treatment of the American landscape and his romantic writing style had a literary and philosophical influence that can still be discerned. Bartram died at his home near Philadelphia.

• Bartram's journals and fieldnotes from his famous journey have been lost, but a two-volume manuscript summary he sent to Fothergill is in the Library of the Natural History Museum, London, which also holds a large collection of his drawings and paintings and some letters. The American Philosophical Society, Philadelphia, has a copy of this manuscript (published with annotation by Francis Harper in the society's *Transactions* n.s. 32, pt. 2 [1943]), artwork, and letters. The Historical Society of Pennsylvania holds part of the manuscript of *Travels*, letters, and a daybook. The Academy of Natural Sciences of Philadelphia has a daybook and letters.

Letters of Bartram are included in Edmund Berkeley and Dorothy Smith Berkeley, eds., *The Correspondence of John Bartram, 1734–1777* (1992), and William Darlington, *Memorials of John Bartram and Humphry Marshall* (1849, repr. 1967). The Fothergill collection is reproduced with commentary by Joseph Ewan, *William Bartram: Botanical and Zoological Drawings 1756–1788* (1968). The most detailed scholarly edition of Bartram's *Travels* is by Francis Harper (1968). Thomas P. Slaughter, ed., *William Bartram: Travels and Other Writings* (1996), reprints all Bartram's published works.

For Bartram's influence on literature see N. Bryllion Fagin, *William Bartram, Interpreter of the American Landscape* (1933), and John Livingston Lowes, *The Road to Xanadu* (1927). Gregory A. Waselkov and Kathryn E. Holland Braun, *William Bartram on the Southeastern Indians* (1995), is useful, as is a bibliography, Rose Marie Cutting, *John and William Bartram: A Reference Guide* (1976). See also Thomas P. Slaughter, *The Natures of John and William Bartram* (1996), and Ernest P. Earnest, *John and William Bartram: Botanists and Explorers* (1940). The John Bartram Association administers Historic Bartram's Garden, a publicly-accessible house-museum and garden in Philadelphia.

ROBERT MCCRACKEN PECK

BARUCH, Bernard Mannes (19 Aug. 1870–20 June 1965), financier and statesman, was born in Camden, South Carolina, the son of Dr. Simon Baruch and Belle Wolfe. Place played a large role in his life. In 1881 the family moved to New York City, where his father became a prominent physician and leader in public health. Baruch graduated from the City College of New York and made his career in Wall Street, but he shrewdly maintained an identification with South Carolina through ownership of a plantation, "Hobcaw," where he entertained people with political connections that enhanced his influence in the national Democratic party. By transcending local politics, Baruch became one of the most powerful Democrats in the first half of the twentieth century.

Between 1891 and 1912, Baruch made untold millions as a self-styled Wall Street speculator, one of the fabled "lone wolf operators" of the era. Beginning with arbitrage (buying commodities such as currencies in the New York market and selling in the London market for a higher price, or vice versa), he profited from short trades (borrowing money on the anticipation of a "bear" or lower priced market) and numerous other investment stratagems—many of which, Baruch later

conceded, would have been illegal after the creation of the Securities and Exchange Commission in 1934.

Despite his reputation as a maverick investor, he participated in large-scale mining operations in the Congo with Rockefeller interests and in Mexico with the Guggenheim family. Among his most profitable investments was sulphur development in Texas, but he always maintained a romantic investment interest in railroads, even after they ceased to be highly profitable in the early twentieth century. Governments, Baruch believed, helped make markets, and in 1912 he became one of Woodrow Wilson's principal financial backers.

Wilson's election transformed Baruch's life. He never considered a political career for himself because he doubted that a Jew could succeed in Christian America. American Jews were then socially handicapped, although Baruch—tall, handsome, and soft-spoken with a trace of a southern accent—did not appear to be personally discriminated against. In 1897 he married an Episcopalian, Annie Griffen. Their three children were raised as Christians. Nevertheless, Baruch identified with Jews and would not trade in markets on the Jewish High Holidays.

Baruch remained on the periphery of the Wilson administration until after the outbreak of World War I. But he became friendly with Secretary of the Treasury William Gibbs McAdoo, himself a transplanted southerner. In early 1916, when Wilson launched a tentative preparedness drive, on McAdoo's advice he appointed Baruch to the Advisory Commission of the Council for National Defense. Baruch distinguished himself on the commission by devising ways in which the military could purchase raw materials at lower than market prices. After the United States entered the war in April 1917, Wilson named Baruch to the War Industries Board (WIB). In the summer of 1917, at McAdoo's insistence, Wilson made Baruch chairman.

During 1917–1918, Wilson's war managers worked to conserve resources and restrain prices. At the same time, the government pumped at least $1 billion into the nation's transportation systems. Along with Herbert Hoover in the Food Administration, Baruch in the WIB built a tightly run national bureaucracy that apportioned materials for civilian and war essentials while steadying prices. Paradoxically, the war agencies laid a patina of civilian individualism on government-supervised cartels in nearly every economic endeavor, thereby violating the antitrust laws. The public hailed Baruch as the "czar" of all industry. After the Armistice of November 1918, the WIB was disbanded and controls lifted. Baruch then joined Hoover and other war managers as economic advisors to Wilson at the Paris Peace Conference. There the economic liberalism of the Americans clashed with the European Entente's chauvinism, and a disappointed Baruch returned home to explain Wilson's apparent failures to win European concessions in a book ghostwritten by a young lawyer, John Foster Dulles, entitled *The Making of the Reparation and Economic Sections of the Treaty*.

In the 1920s Baruch launched a career as an influential economic policymaker and political kingmaker. Part of his power lay in his manipulation of the press. Many prominent journalists of the era depended on him for stories and for favors that the wealthy financier bestowed on friends. Baruch supported William G. McAdoo's quest for the Democratic nomination for president in 1924, but that failure discouraged him from financing other presidential candidacies before a Democratic convention. Instead, Baruch ingratiated himself with Senate Democratic leaders by significantly funding many of their campaigns for reelection. He also contributed generously to Democratic presidential campaigns.

Baruch used his purse to advance his causes. Technology and overproduction of many commodities, he believed, made a governmental role in markets necessary. He tentatively backed farm cooperatives and agricultural relief schemes. Still, he remained conservative—distrustful of government intervention in ordinary peacetime markets. After the onset of the Great Depression in 1929, he supported President Hoover's Reconstruction Finance Corporation and the idea of a national sales tax (which Congress rejected). He failed to anticipate the wave of anticonservative feeling that won Franklin D. Roosevelt the Democratic presidential nomination in 1932. Nevertheless, Baruch immediately jumped aboard Roosevelt's bandwagon, and his enthusiastic financial contributions assured him of a place of influence in the New Deal.

Ever cautious about administrative responsibility, if he could not be secretary of state, he would become an *éminence grise*. Since Roosevelt denied him the former, Baruch contented himself with the latter. He played a prominent unofficial role in the World Economic Conference in 1933. In general, however, he had quiet misgivings about the New Deal. He disliked government-imposed floors under prices, and he especially detested the administration's fiscal policies of heavy spending on public works paid for with taxes on corporation profits. By 1938 Baruch was all but alienated from Roosevelt and the Democratic party.

But war was again on the horizon, and Baruch again felt he would play a special role. Congress adopted his proposal for "cash-and-carry" neutrality as a means of supplying belligerents without accepting responsibility for financing or transporting weapons purchases. But Roosevelt would have none of Baruch's WIB-like formula for mobilization. Only after Pearl Harbor did the president adopt the total war agenda favored by Baruch.

During World War II Baruch's fame as a "Park Bench Statesman" (he told reporters that his only office was a park bench across from the White House in Lafayette Square) and "Advisor to Presidents" spread and encouraged FDR to use him as a public spokesman. In 1942 he chaired the Rubber Survey Committee, which recommended conservation and the massive development of synthetic rubber facilities. In 1943 he temporized when offered the chairmanship of the War Production Board, and he probably was relieved when Roosevelt changed his mind and gave the job to someone else. As it was, the president leaned heavily on an old crony of Baruch's, former Senator James F. Byrnes of South Carolina. Byrnes prevailed on Roosevelt to have Baruch and a Wall Street friend, John Hancock, propose postwar economic policies. In 1946 Secretary of State Byrnes persuaded Roosevelt's successor, Harry Truman, to appoint Baruch U.S. ambassador to the United Nations Atomic Energy Commission. In this post Baruch proposed creating a UN Atomic Energy Development Authority in which the United States would lodge its monopoly of atomic weaponry. The Soviets, however, vetoed the Baruch Plan.

Although he still could influence public opinion, as when he called for price stabilization during the Korean War, presidents and senators now ignored his kibitzing. Most of the politicos who had heeded him had died, and, to Baruch's chagrin and despair, their successors seemed to prefer inflation to the rigors of price stabilization. He predicted that such economic policies would lead to prices so high that social services would deteriorate, that the national debt would claim an inordinate share of the federal budget, and that industrialized foreign countries with lower standards of living such as Japan and Germany would capture increasing shares of world markets. Baruch died in New York City.

• Baruch's papers are in Mudd Library, Princeton University. An excellent book about his business career is James Grant *Bernard M. Baruch: The Adventures of a Wall Street Legend* (1983); a study of his public career is Jordan A. Schwarz, *The Speculator: Bernard M. Baruch in Washington, 1917–1965* (1981). Earlier biographies include Margaret L. Coit, *Mr. Baruch* (1957); Carter Field, *Bernard Baruch: Park Bench Statesman* (1944); and William L. White, *Bernard Baruch: Portrait of a Citizen* (1950). His memoirs appeared as *Baruch, My Own Story* (1957) and *Baruch, the Public Years* (1960). He is described in innumerable biographies, autobiographies, published diaries, and histories. The best historical study is Robert D. Cuff, *The War Industries Board: Business-Government Relations during World War I* (1973).

JORDAN A. SCHWARZ

BARUCH, Simon (29 July 1840–3 June 1921), physician and sanitarian, was born in Schwersenz, Prussia, to Polish Jews Bernhard Baruch and Theresa Gruen. His parents' occupations are unknown. He attended the Royal Friedrich Wilhelm Gymnasium in Posen for about seven years before emigrating to the United States in 1855 and settling in Camden, South Carolina, in 1859. In Camden, he apprenticed himself to Drs. Thomas J. Workman and Lynch Horry Deas. Baruch attended the Medical College of South Carolina in Charleston in 1860–1861 and completed his education at the Medical College of Virginia in Richmond in 1862, after the South Carolina school closed at the outbreak of the Civil War. His college expenses were paid by Mannes Baum, a family friend from Schwersenz, who had sponsored his emigration in 1855. Baruch became a U.S. citizen on 19 January 1871.

Baruch enlisted in the Confederate army as an assistant surgeon immediately after graduation in the spring of 1862. He served first with the Third South Carolina Infantry Battalion and later with Kershaw's Brigade under General James Longstreet. He was captured and exchanged twice before the end of the war. After a brief professional sojourn in New York City, he returned to Camden to start a practice in a countryside devastated by war. In 1867 he married Isabel Wolfe, with whom he had four children. Baruch struggled for another thirteen years to earn a living and to expand his medical knowledge in South Carolina, devoting much of his energy in 1880 to lobbying the South Carolina legislature for mandatory smallpox vaccination in the state. In 1881 he moved permanently to New York City in search of broader intellectual opportunities and a more lucrative practice.

In New York, Baruch's first job was handling eye, ear, and throat cases at North-Eastern Dispensary, which opened a Medical Polyclinic in 1882. He attended patients at the New York Juvenile Asylum (1881–1894) and in the summer handled private cases for another physician. In October 1884 Baruch became an attending physician at the Montefiore Home for Chronic Invalids, building his practice in the summertime by seeing patients at the West End Hotel. One of his most important contributions at this time was in the surgical treatment of perforation of the appendix. He was made chief of staff at Montefiore in April 1885.

In the 1890s Baruch began the sanitarian activism that resulted, in 1895, in the passage of a New York State law requiring all cities with populations over 50,000 to provide public "rain baths" (showers). He also worked with groups in other states, establishing public baths in Pittsburgh, Philadelphia, Boston, and Chicago, where one of the public baths was named after him. His bath exhibit at the Paris Exposition of 1900 won a silver medal. Baruch was influenced in his views on hydrotherapy by the popularity of this type of treatment in Europe, where practitioners such as the Silesian Vincenz Priessnitz had been reporting cures since 1829. Of these accomplishments he wrote that he had "done more to save life and prevent the spread of disease in my work for public baths than in all my work as a physician" (*New York Tribune*, 29 Mar. 1903; quoted in Ward, p. 201). In 1889 he extended this work into the treatment of typhoid, advocating the cold bath devised by Ernst Brand, which proponents claimed reduced mortality in this disease from more than 34 percent to less than 10 percent. In 1894 Baruch was elected the first president of the American Association for the Promotion of Hygiene and Public Baths. As professor of hydrotherapy at the New York Post-Graduate Medical School from 1893 to 1906, he sought to educate other physicians in the advantages of physical therapies in acute as well as chronic illnesses. In 1907 the Columbia College of Physicians and Surgeons created for him a chair of hydrotherapy in the Department of Materia Medica and Therapeutics, which he occupied until 1913.

Baruch became involved in the efforts of the state of New York to restore the famous mineral springs of Saratoga in 1909 and remained a major advocate of the project until his death. He was appointed medical editor of the *New York Sun* in 1912, a position that provided him with a popular forum for his ideas on sanitary, medical, and political issues. These were broad-ranging: Baruch supported handgun control, eugenics, temperance, vaccination, pasteurization of milk, and strict medical quarantine in harbors; he opposed suffrage and higher education for women. He was the author of more than 100 medical articles, several hundred editorials, and three books, *The Uses of Water in Modern Medicine* (1892), *The Principles and Practice of Hydrotherapy* (1898; rev. ed. 1903 and 1908), and *An Epitome of Hydrotherapy for Physicians, Architects and Nurses* (1920). During the First World War Baruch worked with his son Bernard, who was chairman of the War Industries Board, to promote military sanitation and the use of hydrotherapy in rehabilitation of wounded veterans.

When Baruch died in New York City, he was already known in medical circles in the United States and Europe as the "Apostle of Bathing"; his advocacy of hydrotherapy and public sanitation are still considered his most significant contributions to medicine.

• The Simon Baruch Papers are held by the South Caroliniana Library of the University of South Carolina in Columbia; some of his notebooks are in the Robert Woodruff Library of Emory University, Atlanta, Ga. A "Baruch Number" of the *Library Bulletin of the Medical College of the State of South Carolina* was published in September 1944, followed a few years later by Frances Hellebrandt's bibliographic survey *Simon Baruch: Introduction to the Man and His Work*, published as a Special Bulletin of the Baruch Center of Physical Medicine and Rehabilitation of the Medical College of Virginia (1950). H. H. Cunningham, *Doctors in Gray: The Confederate Medical Service* (1958), includes anecdotes of Baruch's life as a military surgeon. Marilyn T. Williams describes his advocacy of public baths in *Washing the Great Unwashed: Public Baths in Urban America* (1991). A detailed and reliable biography is Patricia Spain Ward, *Simon Baruch: Rebel in the Ranks of Medicine, 1840–1921* (1994). Baruch's entry in Solomon Kagan, *Jewish Contributions to Medicine in America* (1934), outlines his career in brief but contains significant errors. Baruch is discussed in the autobiography of his son Bernard Baruch, *Baruch: My Own Story* (1957). Numerous articles about Baruch appeared in the *New York Times* between 1889 and 1921, accessible through the Personal Names index to the newspaper. An obituary is in the *New York Times*, 4 June 1921.

RACHEL P. MAINES

BARUS, Carl (19 Feb. 1856–20 Sept. 1935), physicist, was born in Cincinnati, Ohio, the son of Carl Barus, a musician, and Sophia Möllman. Both parents had emigrated from Germany. Throughout Carl's childhood and youth the family lived in Cincinnati, his father making a modest income leading orchestral and choral productions and playing the organ in churches and synagogues. Carl's formal education included seven years of bilingual grammar school instruction (in English in the morning, in German in the afternoon). Barus distinguished himself in mathematics at Woodward High School, where he was a classmate of William Howard Taft, the future president and chief justice. Barus's informal education included extensive musical instruction from his father (music was to become a lifelong avocation), chemical experimentation in the family attic, and initiation into the use of machine tools in a neighborhood plumbing shop, where he also taught himself to temper steel by following the instructions in a German chemistry textbook.

Inspired by a friend's laudatory reports, Barus entered the Columbia School of Mines in 1874. Of this institution he later reported "that the just with the unjust were graduated as impartially as the Lord maketh his light to shine" ("Autobiography," p. 49), but he held fond memories of the school, especially the excellent laboratories and mineral collections. These, however, roused his interest not in engineering but in pure science, with the consequence that Barus left Columbia in 1876 to pursue advanced education in physics at the University of Würzburg in Germany. Working under the direction of Friedrich Wilhelm Kohlrausch, Barus earned a doctorate at Würzburg in 1879 with a dissertation on the electrical conductivity and thermoelectrical properties of steel in relation to hardness.

In 1880 Barus returned to the United States, where he was hired by Clarence King as a physicist for the U.S. Geological Survey. Barus's first year in this position took him to the mining regions of Nevada, where he undertook field investigations to locate subterranean ore deposits by measuring electrical potentials on the surface. His subsequent career at the Geological Survey was confined to the laboratory, in New York (1881–1882), in New Haven (1882–1884), and in Washington, D.C. (1884–1892). The ingenuity and fruitfulness of his geophysical experiments, especially his innovations for measuring high pressures and temperatures, gained him wide recognition at home and abroad; he was elected to the American Academy of Arts and Sciences in 1890, to the National Academy of Sciences in 1892, and in 1898 was named an honorary member of the Royal Institution of Great Britain. The American Academy presented Barus with its Rumford Medal in 1900.

After Congress eliminated Barus's Geological Survey position in 1892, he worked briefly for the Weather Bureau and the Smithsonian Institution before leaving government service entirely in 1895 to become the Hazard Professor of Physics at Brown University. Barus held this post until his retirement in 1926, serving also as dean of the graduate school from 1903. This latter position he administered faithfully but with very moderate enthusiasm. "I have been endeavoring," he stated in one official report, "to meet the wishes of my colleagues and have aimed at no originality whatever" (Shroeder, p. 31). His initial research at Brown evolved primarily out of issues raised at the Weather Bureau related to condensation and ionization in the atmosphere. Barus's fog chamber investigations of X-rays interested Ernest Rutherford but also drew harsh negative comments from C. T. R. Wilson, inventor of the cloud chamber; Barus, dismayed by the controversy, soon abandoned this line of inquiry. His later research was highly various but centered around his invention of a displacement interferometer. By careful analysis of optical interference patterns Barus was able to make sensitive measurements of physical phenomena involving small displacements. He ceased research work in 1929 but continued to teach a course on vector analysis at Brown until the year of his death. In 1887 Barus had married Annie Gertrude Howes, who was active in support of educational and social reform, writing many articles for newspapers and magazines. The couple had two children. Barus died in Providence, Rhode Island.

Barus was a central figure in the emerging physics community in the United States at the end of the nineteenth century. A founding member of the American Physical Society in 1899, he served as its fourth president from 1905 to 1906. He was one of the most skilled and resourceful experimentalists of his generation, and his pioneering inquiries in geology, metallurgy, pyrometry, high pressure physics, and colloid chemistry were acknowledged by later investigators. That Barus possessed a broad and comprehensive grasp of developments in nineteenth-century physics, including theory, is well exemplified by the scope of his book reviews and miscellaneous articles, and in particular by his address at the International Congress of Arts and Sciences in St. Louis in 1904, published in *Science* (Sept. 1905) as "The Progress of Physics in the Nineteenth Century." Barus did not, however, embrace the newly emerging attributes of physics research in the twentieth century, being uneasy with the "speculative probing and probability" that he saw as dominating the modern methods ("Autobiography," p. 182). Moreover, against the growing importance of large scale cooperative projects, he retained a nostalgic attachment to a research life in which lone investigators made their discoveries with simple handmade equipment, believing that "in the modern laboratory with its mechanicians and glass blowers, its motors and storage cells, most of the flavor of romance is lost" ("Autobiography," p. 60). His failure to cultivate graduate students further contributed to the isolation of his last two decades; few investigators were inspired to extend or even to read his results. Those who did read Barus encountered a literary style of great charm. P. W. Bridgman, explicating the historical roots of his own highly successful research program in *The Physics of High Pressure* (1931), noted simply of Barus that "there is an individual quality about his work that makes interesting reading."

• Barus's papers, including an unpublished autobiography, are in the Brown University Archives in Providence, R.I. A copy of the autobiography is also at the Niels Bohr Library, Center for the History of Physics, American Institute of Physics, College Park, Md. The most substantial biographical piece on Barus, including a complete bibliography of his publications, is by his student and colleague R. Bruce Lindsay in National Academy of Sciences, *Biographical Memoirs*

22 (1943): 171–213. Barus's tenure as dean of the graduate school at Brown is discussed in John Shroeder, "Jubilee Chapter in the History of Graduate Education at Brown University," *Books at Brown* 27 (1979): 22–35. Barus's 1904 address is reprinted in Katherine R. Sopka, ed., *Physics for a New Century: Papers Presented at the 1904 St. Louis Congress* (1986), pp. 107–43.

DAVID LINDSAY ROBERTS

BARZYNSKI, Vincent (20 Sept. 1838–2 May 1899), Roman Catholic priest, was born in Sulislawice, Poland, the son of Joseph Barzynski, an organist at the local church, a part-time watchmaker, and town publicist, and Maryanna Seroczynska. Barzynski completed the philosophy curriculum at Lublin in 1858 and the theology curriculum there in 1861. He was ordained as a diocesan priest on 27 October 1861 and began his clerical career as vicar of the parish church at Horodlo, located on the Bug River. In the summer of 1862 he was transferred to the Zamosc Collegiate Church, where he accepted the position of canon under Suffragan Bishop W. Baranowski.

During the Polish insurrection against the Russian government in 1863, Barzynski returned to Tomaszow, where he became actively involved with the Polish insurgency, organizing gun-runners in the area. He was eventually discovered by the Russians, who then arrested him and kept him under "special supervision" for six months. After his release, Barzynski fled to Austrian Poland, but having crossed the border without authorization and passport, he was again placed under arrest and jailed at Olmutz, at Inglau, and at Koniggratz. After serving a brief sentence, Barzynski moved to Paris, where he contacted other emigrant priests, among whom were members of the Congregation of the Resurrection of Our Lord Jesus Christ. The Resurrectionists had been founded in 1836 by an ambitious group of soldier-scholars—Bogdan Janski, Peter Semenenko, and Jerome Kajsiewicz—all of whom had been involved in Poland's ill-fated insurrection of 1831. Disillusioned by defeat, these future Resurrectionists committed themselves to combating the excesses of Polish messianic thinking, then prominent in the literary circles of Andrew Towianski. Moreover, the Resurrectionists were committed to the organization of community-parish systems in Polish emigrant areas, largely in urban areas abroad, which were poised to fight the effects of socialism, modernism, and materialism. Barzynski entered the Resurrectionist novitiate in Rome shortly after these initial contacts and took final vows on 18 September 1866. He would spend the remainder of his priestly life as a Resurrectionist actively involved in Polish Catholic missions in the United States.

The Reverend Vincent Barzynski moved to the United States in 1866. For a brief tenure he worked with Polish immigrants in the Galveston, Texas, diocese, then headed by Bishop Claude-Marie Dubuis. He then was granted permission to transfer to the growing Polish community in Chicago. Over the next quarter century (1874–1899), Barzynski would assume a historic role as one of the most influential Polish clergymen in the United States. Under his pastorship at St. Stanislaus Kostka in Chicago (founded in 1867), the first Polish Catholic parish in what would one day become the largest Polish immigrant settlement outside of Poland, Barzynski would zealously build up a mighty institutional structure serving the religious, educational, economic, social, and cultural needs of several hundred thousand Poles. In Barzynski's lifetime, St. Stanislaus Kostka, the flagship parish, would grow to nearly 50,000 members, making it the largest single parish in the Chicago Roman Catholic archdiocese and one of the largest in the entire United States by the end of the nineteenth century. St. Stanislaus Kostka Parish became a model for the more than two dozen other Polish Catholic parishes founded in Chicago by 1900. A major feature of the Resurrectionist community-parishes was the institution of hundreds of fraternal societies and sodalities that served the many needs of newly arrived immigrants in Chicago. William I. Thomas and Florian Znaniecki's classic five-volume sociological study, *The Polish Peasant in Europe and America* (1918; 2-vol. ed., 1927), gave extensive coverage to the inner workings of the Polish Catholic community-parish network.

Such spectacular and explosive growth came at considerable cost to unity within the Polish community in Chicago and elsewhere. Throughout his lifetime Barzynski was instrumental in building the Polish Roman Catholic Union (PRCU), founded in 1873. The PRCU gave rise to the so-called Unionists, or clerical party, which struggled to defeat the Alliancists, or national party, belonging to the Polish National Alliance (PNA), founded in 1880. The PRCU and the PNA eventually established themselves in virtually every major Polish immigrant settlement in the United States, which is why Thomas and Znaniecki referred to each as supraterritorial fraternal organizations. In substance, the Alliancists devoted themselves to ending the partitions of Poland and to restoring the independence of the Polish state, hence the term national party. The Unionists, on the other hand, were committed to strengthening the power of the Catholic church within immigrant settlements in the United States under the PRCU umbrella. These Unionists were dominated by the clergy, many of whom were strategically placed in leadership roles, hence the term clerical party. The Unionist camp, centered at St. Stanislaus Kostka where Barzynski was firmly in control, fought a twenty-year battle with the Alliancist group at nearby Holy Trinity Parish for local/national control of Polish parishes, fraternal organizations and sodalities, insurance (life), financial affairs (parish banks), membership, competing newspapers, and, eventually, political candidates for public offices.

Complicating matters was the Parish Bank (Bank Parafialny) scandal at St. Stanislaus Kostka in the late 1880s, which arose from the mismanagement of $550,475 of bank capital by Barzynski and the Resurrectionists. Because the Parish Bank's assets were made up of the savings of thousands of working-class

Poles, the Resurrectionists eventually agreed to pay back each of the depositors, but the resolution of these matters took thirty years. Despite the Resurrectionist efforts, the scandal, along with persistent feuding at the flagship Unionist and Alliancist parishes of St. Stanislaus Kostka and Holy Trinity, eventually cost Barzynski his leadership of Polish America. Laypersons at Holy Trinity Parish, in a well-publicized letter (2 Apr. 1891) to the Vatican, outlined their complaints against Barzynski and the Resurrectionists. So serious were the charges of mismanagement that the apostolic delegate to the United States was called in to negotiate the situation. After the Vatican intervened in 1893, Barzynski's power waned, though he was allowed to remain as pastor of St. Stanislaus Kostka until his death in Chicago.

By that time, however, a major schism, initiated by "Independents" at St. Hedwig Parish, had rocked the Chicago Polonia. Under the leadership of the Reverend Anthony Kozlowski, anti-Resurrectionist forces there broke away from the Chicago Roman Catholic archdiocese to form a schismatic parish at All Saints. Kozlowski's "Independent" revolt against the Resurrectionists and the Roman Catholic hierarchy eventually paved the way for the foundation of the Polish National Catholic Church in 1907—the only major schism in American Catholic history.

Later studies of the schism point to American Polonia's inability to manage the tensions involving clericals and nationalists as a root cause. Thus Barzynski's legacy was twofold: his biographers credit him with an "iron strength of will," which raised up one of the most powerful "brick and mortar" Catholic immigrant establishments in American Catholic history; yet nearly all agree that Barzynski was at the center of Polish America's most bitter intragroup struggles in the late nineteenth century. Barzynski's admirers have viewed him as an outstanding example of what it meant to be a Polish *Catholic* (with the accent on Catholic) in the 1870–1900 period, for that is how all loyal members of the PRCU identified themselves; his PNA critics, meanwhile, have claimed that he failed to understand the nationalist emphasis on what it meant to be a Catholic *Pole* and that the struggle for Polish national self-determination was a priority he subordinated to Catholic growth in the United States. The Polish American Congress eventually resolved most of the early identity crises in Polish immigrant settlements in America but not until after World War II. By then, there were more than fifty Polish Catholic parishes in the Chicago Roman Catholic archdiocese, each bearing many of the original community-parish organizations established by the Reverend Barzynski and the Resurrectionist Congregation.

• For additional information on Barzynski, see Stanislaus Siatka, *Krotkie Wspomnienie o zyciu i Dzialalnosci Ks. M. Wincentego Barzynskiego C.R.* (1901); Wladislaw Kwiatkowski, *Historia Zgromadzenia Zmartwychwstania Panskiego Na Stuletnia Rocznice Jego Zalozenia, 1842–1942* (1942); Edward Janas, *Dictionary of American Resurrectionists, 1865–1965*

(1967); and John Iwicki, *Resurrectionist Studies, the First One Hundred Years: A Study of the Apostolate of the Congregation of the Resurrection in the United States, 1866–1966* (1966). Iwicki's study contains the most comprehensive bibliography of manuscript materials and other sources on the Resurrectionists in Chicago. Also see Victor Greene, *For God and Country: The Rise of Polish and Lithuanian Ethnic Consciousness in America, 1860–1910* (1975), and Joseph John Parot, *Polish Catholics in Chicago, 1850–1920: A Religious History* (1981), especially the bibliography on pp. 269–84. Finally, see Waclaw Kruszka's groundbreaking *Historya Polska w Ameryce* (13 vols., 1905–1908).

JOSEPH JOHN PAROT

BASCOM, Florence (14 July 1862–18 June 1945), geologist and educator, was born in Williamstown, Massachusetts, the daughter of suffragist Emma Curtiss and John Bascom, a professor at Williams College. Her mother, as an officer of the National Suffrage Association wrote, "While the ballot is withheld from women and given to all other classes of citizens except idiots and criminals, it puts on womanhood an inescapable badge, and an inescapable fact, of inferiority" (quoted in Smith, p. 17). Her father advocated for coeducation and unsuccessfully raised the issue at Williams. Both parents profoundly affected the way Florence Bascom saw the world. She became the first woman in the United States to enter fully the profession of geology.

In 1874 Bascom moved to Madison, Wisconsin, when her father became president of the University of Wisconsin. In 1877 Bascom enrolled at that university, five years after it was opened to women. Despite limited access to various facilities and activities, she studied a variety of subjects and received bachelor degrees in letters (1882), arts (1882), and science (1884). Perhaps as a result of her experiences there, in a prescient remark that would anticipate equal education opportunity debates to come, Bascom wryly wrote (1925), "It is an interesting manifestation of the attitude of certain public critics toward change, that when the collegiate training of women was first on trial there were clamorous complaints that the health of young women was being wrecked; now the same class of public critics are loudly complaining that college women are Amazons."

After she graduated (1884–1885), Bascom taught at the newly founded Hampton Institute for Negroes and American Indians in Hampton, Virginia. Around this time, while she was on a trip with her father and Ohio State University geology professor Edward Orton, Orton's observations and explanations of the midwestern landscape encouraged Bascom's further study in geology. In 1885 she returned to the University of Wisconsin in Madison to study sheet gabbros in the Lake Superior district. She worked with Roland Irving and Charles Van Hise, pioneers in the field of metamorphism.

Upon receiving her master's degree in 1887, Bascom taught geology and chemistry at Rockford College in Illinois. In 1889 she began work toward a Ph.D. at Johns Hopkins University. In order to attend classes, she was required to obtain special permission and to sit behind a screen. Undaunted, Bascom worked with Professor George Williams, considered to be the first teacher of petrology in the United States, and entered the new field of petrography. Her dissertation, "A Contribution to the Geology of South Mountain, Pennsylvania," revealed the metavolcanic nature of rocks previously thought to be sedimentary. In 1893 she received the first Ph.D. granted to a woman by Johns Hopkins University, recognition that Johns Hopkins would not again bestow on a woman for eighteen years.

After receiving her Ph.D., Bascom taught for two years (1893–1895) as an "associate" at Ohio State University. Then, recruited for her research potential by Bryn Mawr's first president, James Rhoads, Bascom began in 1895 what would be a long and brilliant career at Bryn Mawr College. Occupying a space intended for storage on the uppermost floor of a building newly constructed for chemistry, biology, and physics, Bascom initiated a program in geology, a science considered to be merely adjunct to the others. Developing a teaching and research collection of more than one thousand samples over two years, Bascom convinced then president M. Carey Thomas to establish a geology department at the college in 1901.

The program grew, advanced degrees were offered, and the geology department produced the first female geologists in the nation: Ida Ogilvie, Julia Gardner, Eleanora F. Bliss Knopf, Anna Jonas Stose, Isabel Fothergill Smith, Louise Kingsley, and Katherine Fowler Billings. Of Bascom, Isabel Fothergill Smith wrote, "Florence Bascom's students feel an immense gratitude for the scholarly and stimulating way in which she opened up to them an understanding of the geological forces at work in and upon the earth; gratitude for their close association with a person of such consistency and integrity; gratitude for the pioneer woman that she was—a high-minded, resolute feminist; gratitude for her personal interest in them, and her immense generosity to them" (p. 45).

On sabbatical during 1906 in Heidelberg, Germany, Bascom studied the new field of optical mineralogy with pioneer crystallographer Victor Goldschmidt and mineralogist Heinrich Rosenbusch; it enabled her to bring back to her Bryn Mawr students the most recent analytical petrographic techniques. Bascom was promoted to full professor in 1906 and retired from Bryn Mawr (1928) after thirty-three years at the college.

The rigorous education Bascom provided her students was enabled by her lifelong active field and laboratory research with the United States Geological Survey (USGS). The first woman hired as an assistant geologist with the USGS (1896), Bascom focused her research on the complex petrology, structural geology, and geomorphology of the Mid-Atlantic Piedmont province of the Appalachian Mountains. Through geologic mapping in Maryland, Pennsylvania, Delaware, and New Jersey and microscopic study of samples that she collected in the field, Bascom contributed to the understanding of mountain-building processes in the Appalachians. Of her work Bascom wrote,

"This is *the life*, to plunge into the welcome isolation of the field, to return to the stimulating association of Bryn Mawr, to observe and in part to clear up geologic phenomena, to return to the exposition and interpretation of geologic phenomena" (quoted in Smith, p. 32). Her work, published in numerous USGS Folios, has served as sound basis for further study of this complex region.

Bascom was an early member of the Geological Society of Washington (1893) and was the first woman to present a paper before that society (1901), an event that would not occur again until 1921. She was an associate editor of the *American Geologist* and was a "starred" geologist in the first edition of *American Men of Science* (1906), which meant that she was regarded as one of the hundred leading geologists in the country at the time. She was the sole author of much of her published work. Elected a fellow of the Geological Society of America in 1894, a councilor in 1924, and vice president in 1930, she was the first woman officer of that society.

After she retired from Bryn Mawr, Bascom continued to work as a researcher at the USGS. An independent woman, she spent summers with her dogs and horses at her farmhouse in the Massachusetts Berkshires near her childhood home. She died in Northampton, Massachusetts, leaving her farm and belongings to her former student and longtime friend Isabel Fothergill Smith.

Florence Bascom was the first woman geologist in the United States. Her outstanding career as a research scientist and her self-conscious, feminist efforts in the education of young women scientists made geology a viable profession for future generations of women.

• Bascom's papers are in the Sophia Smith Collection, Smith College. Additional papers, including her field notebooks, are in the Bryn Mawr College Department of Geology; the Denison Library, Scripps College; and the State Historical Society of Wisconsin. Among Bascom's many published works are: "The Structures, Origin, and Nomenclature of the Acid Volcanic Rocks of South Mountain," *Journal of Geology* 1 (1893): 813–32; *The Ancient Volcanic Rocks of South Mountain, Pennsylvania*, U.S. Geological Survey Bulletin, 136 (1896); "A Pre-Tertiary Nepheline-bearing Rock," *Journal of Geology* 4 (1896): 160–65; "The Relation of the Streams in the Neighborhood of Philadelphia to the Bryn Mawr Gravel," *American Geologist* 19 (1897): 50–57; "Volcanics of Neponset Valley, Massachusetts," *Geological Society of America Bulletin* 11 (1900): 115–26. Useful biographical material may be found in Eleanora B. Knopf, "Memorial of Florence Bascom," *American Mineralogist* 31 (1946): 168–72; Isabel Fothergill Smith, *The Stone Lady: A Memoir of Florence Bascom* (1981); and Jill S. Schneiderman, "Growth and Development of a Woman Scientist and Educator," *Earth Sciences History* 11 (1992): 37–39.

JILL S. SCHNEIDERMAN

BASCOM, Henry Bidleman (27 May 1796–8 Sept. 1850), Methodist bishop and educator, was born in Hancock, New York, the son of Alpheus Bascom and Hannah Bidleman Houk. Poverty kept the family on the move in search of better living conditions, first in western New York, then northern Kentucky, and finally (1813) in southern Ohio. Young Bascom received some formal schooling until he was twelve years old, but penury forestalled further studies. He joined the Methodists at the age of fifteen, and two years later, in 1813, the Ohio Annual conference of the Methodist church licensed him to preach. During that year he was also admitted as preacher on trial and appointed to the Brush Creek Circuit where his newly settled parental home was situated. Bascom's gifts of imagination and powerful expression were quickly recognized as he filled various preaching circuits in Ohio, Tennessee, and Kentucky over the next decade. His travels to as many as thirty preaching places per month was tiring and often dangerous, but the itinerant evangelist persevered and impressed many with both his zeal and remarkable power of expression.

In 1823 Bascom was chosen, through the patronage of Henry Clay, to serve as chaplain of the U.S. Congress. He performed stated tasks in the capital for two years, but more important, he also enhanced his reputation as an extraordinary public speaker. Whenever Congress was not in session Bascom preached in churches and revivals. Huge crowds came to hear him in Baltimore, Maryland, and in Philadelphia and Harrisburg, Pennsylvania. The rhetorical force of his extempore prose, spoken without manuscript or notes, impressed many with the truth of his message. His exuberance and intensity dismayed some in the audience as being too florid and undignified, but throngs of listeners relished his ardent delivery, considering him an outstanding preacher.

At the end of his congressional appointment and on the heels of successful tours of northeastern cities, Bascom agreed in 1827 to become the first president of Madison College, located in Uniontown, Pennsylvania. Two years later he accepted work as an agent for the American Colonization Society. In 1832 he returned to academic surroundings as professor of moral science and belles-lettres at Augusta College in Kentucky. During his decade there Bascom finally acquired the financial security he thought necessary for marriage. In 1839 he wed "a Miss Van Antwerp of the city of New York." Various accounts of his life mention that they had two or three children. During these years he declined invitations to become president of Louisiana College and the University of Missouri. But in 1842 he became president of Transylvania University in Lexington, Kentucky, and the institution flourished under him.

In 1844 Bascom attended the quadrennial Methodist General Conference in New York City as a duly elected delegate, a post he had often filled before. When northern representatives voted that year to strip Georgia Bishop James O. Andrew of his episcopal powers because his wife was a slaveholder, southern delegates walked out of the meeting and split the church. At the request of his offended colleagues Bascom wrote a strong public protest against what many regarded as unwarranted interference in social mores and an exercise of ecclesiastical despotism. The following year he convened alongside other alienated co-religionists in Louisville, Kentucky, in order to form the Methodist Episcopal church, South. The organizational structure of this regional denomination, the first of several to emerge before the Civil War, was based largely on a report that Bascom had written earlier in anticipation of the need for such a blueprint. His participation in the schism and in organizing the new denomination underscored Bascom's status as an ecclesiastical statesman; performance in a third capacity further enhanced it. He chaired a commission that negotiated with northern representatives of the divided church in dealing with such thorny issues as property, jurisdiction, and legal responsibilities. Settlements reached on those questions earned him respect on both sides.

The Louisville convention also appointed Bascom the first editor of its new journal, the *Southern Methodist Quarterly Review*, tribute of some irony made to one whose formal education had ended before he entered his teens. Still, he labored away at the new task from 1846 to 1850, articulating much of the rationale that strove to justify a separate church that was pro-South if not openly proslavery. Southern Methodists met in 1850 at St. Louis, Missouri, for its second general conference and elected Bascom to the episcopacy. Scarcely more than a month later he presided over his first annual conference at Independence, Missouri. As he traveled toward his home in Lexington, Kentucky, he died of a sudden illness in Louisville.

• Bascom's publications include *Methodism and Slavery* (1845) and *Sermons from the Pulpit* (2 vols., 1850). Thomas N. Ralston edited *Posthumous Works*, which appeared in two volumes in 1855, expanded to four volumes in 1890. For biographical information see Moses M. Henckle, *The Life of Henry Bidleman Bascom* (1854).

HENRY W. BOWDEN

BASCOM, John (1 May 1827–2 Oct. 1911), author and educator, was born in Genoa, Cayuga County, New York, the son of John Bascom, a Congregational minister, and Laura Woodbridge. He grew up without any recollection of his father, who died in 1828. The task of a somewhat severe Puritan upbringing fell to his mother, who remained a widow. The youngest child and only son of a minister and a widow, he was reticent about religious topics and disinclined to embark upon a ministerial career, the profession most common among his male forebears. He remarked, in this connection, that "a desire to choose, stood in the way of choosing the right thing" (*Things Learned by Living*, p. 21). Struggling to balance piety and autonomy, he remained ambivalent about his vocational plans for many years.

Bascom's older sisters arranged for his early education at Homer Academy in the South. Pressured to go to Hamilton College but preferring Yale, he ended up at Williams College (his father's alma mater) as a sort of compromise. While he was never proud of the education he received there, he found much about the place to celebrate. Upon graduating from Williams in

1849 he weathered a depressing year teaching at Ball Seminary in Hoosick Falls, New York. During this time, his family-induced compulsion to train for the ministry subsided while a predilection for "the dialectics of law" increased, so he enrolled at Rochester, New York, to study law. He terminated his legal career after only eight months in a law office because the legal climate did not match his spiritual sensibilities.

Despite his aversion to the professional ministry, Bascom's religious seriousness and his interest in the Hebrew language led him to Auburn Theological Seminary in 1851. He interrupted his seminary studies in 1852 to become a tutor in rhetoric and oratory at Williams College. He married Abbie Burt the same year. This proved to be "a brief relation whose promises were unfulfilled," for Abbie died in 1854 (*Things Learned by Living*, p. 55). He left Williams to study at Andover Theological Seminary in 1854, only to return, reluctantly, to Williams as professor of rhetoric and oratory in 1855. The next year he married Emma Curtiss, with whom he had three children. To offset the drudgery of his official teaching appointment, he studied and taught philosophy and wrote voluminously, publishing six books—*Political Economy* (1859), *Aesthetics; or, The Science of Beauty* (1862), *Philosophy of Rhetoric* (1866), *Principles of Psychology* (1869), *Science, Philosophy and Religion* (1871), and *Philosophy of English Literature* (1874)—and numerous articles on political theory, moral philosophy, epistemology, metaphysics, theology, and the philosophy of religion.

Weary from nineteen years of teaching oratory and concerned that his religious independence had eroded his welcome at Williams, Bascom accepted the presidency at the University of Wisconsin, where he served from 1874 to 1887. During "the Bascom era," this remote state college was transformed into a bona fide university. Bascom developed a unique philosophy of college administration, which consisted initially of setting up a framework of effective student discipline. He supported the presence of women students and was proud of their attainments after graduation. At Wisconsin he installed himself as a regular lecturer in philosophy. This must have been a source of great satisfaction to him, for his power as a teacher was widely noted by his colleagues and students. His published books during this time included *A Philosophy of Religion; or, The Rational Grounds of Religious Belief* (1876), *Growth and Grades of Intelligence* (1878), *Ethics; or, Science of Duty* (1879), *Natural Theology* (1880), *The Science of Mind* (1881), *Words of Christ* (1883), *Problems in Philosophy* (1885), and *Sociology* (1887).

As university president Bascom sedulously guarded the spiritual component of higher education. It was not unusual during this period for a state university to formulate its mission in spiritual, even explicitly Christian, terms. Like other university presidents, administrators, and faculty of the time, Bascom viewed himself as a custodian of Christian culture, responsible for promoting the Kingdom of God on earth and nurturing Christian civilization through higher education. He considered philosophy to be a particularly apt discipline for carrying out the religious mission of the school. At the same time, he valued democratic pluralism and stood at the crossroads of theological change, favoring progressiveness over traditional orthodoxy. While he argued for the existence of a nonmaterial mental life and human spiritual nature against incipient physicalist naturalism, he also believed Christian theology to be compatible with the ascendant theory of evolution. He was a convinced supernaturalist who affirmed Christian revelation and exemplified confidence in divine providence, especially emphasizing the immanence of God in the world.

Politically Bascom was a Prohibitionist, and his public addresses in support of Prohibition fueled a preexisting condition of friction between himself and the board of regents at the University of Wisconsin. This led to his voluntary resignation in 1887, whereupon he retired to his homestead in Williamstown, Massachusetts.

At Williamstown Bascom soon ran short on funds. Williams College once again enlisted his services, this time to teach sociology and political science, until 1903. Prolific to the end, he wrote many more articles and several books, including *The New Theology* (1891), *An Historical Interpretation of Philosophy* (1893), *Social Theory: A Grouping of Social Facts and Principles* (1895), *Evolution and Religion; or, Faith as a Part of a Complete Cosmic System* (1897), *Growth of Nationality in the United States* (1899), and *God and His Goodness* (1901).

Bascom's final years were occupied with writing, sermons and other public addresses, town meetings, and leadership of the Greylock State Reservation Commission near his home. After his death at Williamstown, a lengthy memorial service was held at the University of Wisconsin, where he was accorded high praise for his teaching and character. A collection, *Sermons and Addresses*, and his autobiography, *Things Learned by Living*, were published posthumously in 1913.

• Many of Bascom's personal papers, along with copies of his articles and addresses, are preserved in the archives of the Memorial Library at the University of Wisconsin at Madison. These archives also contain records of "the Bascom era" at the university and published addresses delivered at the Memorial Service in Honor of John Bascom, 13 Dec. 1911. For a complete list of his publications, excluding two posthumously published books, see his autobiography *Things Learned by Living*. For more on the legacy of his administration, see Merle Curti and Vernon Carstensen, *The University of Wisconsin, a History: 1848-1925*, vol. 1 (1949); J. David Hoeveler, Jr., "The University and the Social Gospel: The Intellectual Origins of the 'Wisconsin Idea,'" *Wisconsin Magazine of History* (Summer 1976); and Bradley J. Longfield, "From Evangelicalism to Liberalism: Public Midwestern Universities in Nineteenth-Century America," in *The Secularization of the Academy*, ed. George M. Marsden and Longfield (1992). In chapter 6, "Evolution and Religious Controversies," of his book *A History of Philosophical Ideas in America* (1949), W. H. Werkmeister describes in detail Bascom's effort to assimilate Christian theology to the theory of evolution. An admiring sketch of his philosophical position may be found in

Sanford Robinson, *John Bascom: Prophet* (1922). See also Stan W. Jorgensen, "A Passage of Faith: The Thought of John Bascom and His Intellectual Successors" (Ph.D. diss., Univ. of North Carolina, 1976).

R. DOUGLAS GEIVETT

BASCOM, William Russel (23 May 1912–11 Sept. 1981), anthropologist and folklorist, was born in Princeton, Illinois, the son of George Rockwell Bascom, an engineer, and Litta Celia Banschbach. His father died when William was thirteen, and his mother then worked as a librarian at the Wisconsin State Historical Library in Madison to support her two children and her invalid mother. Bascom earned his B.A. in physics at the University of Wisconsin, Madison, in 1933 and continued postgraduate work in this subject at the same institution the following year. Bascom's summer employment in 1934 on an archaeological excavation reflected his shift of interest from physics to anthropology. He received an M.A. in anthropology from the University of Wisconsin in 1936. His master's thesis, "The Role of the Medicine Man in Kiowa Culture," written under the guidance of Ralph Linton, was based on field research conducted among the Kiowa Indians of Oklahoma.

Bascom continued graduate study at Northwestern University, where he studied with Melville J. Herskovits, who had a profound influence on Bascom. Bascom received a Ph.D. in anthropology in 1939 with the dissertation, "'Secret Societies,' Religious Cult-Groups and Kinship Units among the West African Yoruba," based on his research in Nigeria from 1937 to 1938. In his 1944 monograph *The Sociological Role of the Yoruba Cult-Group*, Bascom wrote: "The investigation of the 'secret societies' was also considerably facilitated by my initiation, while in *Ifè*, as a priest of *Orò* and a member of *Ogbóni*" (p. 6).

In 1939 Bascom became an instructor in the Department of Sociology and Anthropology at Northwestern University; in 1942 he served as acting chair of the department. On leave from Northwestern during World War II, Bascom carried out confidential work in Nigeria and Ghana as special assistant for the Office of Strategic Services and in other government posts. With Ralph Bunche, also of the Office of Strategic Services, Bascom published *A Pocket Guide to West Africa* (1943) for the War and Navy Departments. From March to December 1946 he was employed by the U.S. Commercial Company as chief economist in Ponape, Caroline Islands. His research resulted in *Ponape: A Pacific Economy in Transition* (vol. 8 of the Economic Survey of Micronesia [1947; repr. 1965, 1976]).

Bascom returned to Northwestern in 1946. He served as assistant professor (1946–1949), associate professor (1949–1954), and professor (1954–1957). Along with Herskovits, Bascom developed in 1948 the interdisciplinary Program of African Studies at Northwestern University, the first major African studies program in the United States.

In the summer of 1955 Bascom taught at the University of California, Berkeley, as a visiting professor in the Department of Decorative Art. In 1957 he moved permanently to Berkeley to accept a position as professor of anthropology and as director of the Robert H. Lowie Museum of Anthropology. He remained in this capacity until 1979.

Bascom earned a reputation for scholarly excellence in three related fields: art, folklore, and ethnography of both Africa and African-derived societies in the New World. One of the first American anthropologists to work in Africa, he was an authority on anthropological folklore and on Yoruba ethnography, especially on Ifa divination and African art in general. His research among the Yoruba continued throughout his professional life, from his dissertation research in 1937–1938, to fieldwork during World War II, to a 1950–1951 stay in Nigeria as a Fulbright research scholar, to more fieldwork in the 1960s. The focus of Bascom's research on the Yoruba reflects his concern with the rigorous, careful accumulation of details about daily life and his fascination for grasping the intricate details of esoteric religious rituals. In his published works on the Yoruba Bascom sought to convey their view of the world, situated within a cross-cultural, comparative framework. In addition to his solid ethnographic work, as exemplified in *The Yoruba of Southwestern Nigeria* (1969), Bascom's research focused on religious groups, as revealed in *The Sociological Role of the Yoruba Cult-Group* (1944; repr. 1969). His classic *Ifa Divination: Communication between Gods and Men in West Africa* (1969) was awarded the coveted Pitrè International Folklore Prize in 1969.

As a result of his research in Yoruba cities Bascom began calling for a reconsideration of the concept of urbanism. He argued for an approach to urbanism that took into account nonindustrial, homogeneous cities, such as the traditional urban centers all over Africa. Bascom's *Continuity and Change in African Cultures* (1959; 2nd ed., 1962), coedited with Herskovits, reflects Bascom's enduring concern with both what was traditional among African societies and what was undergoing transition.

Like Herskovits, Bascom was drawn to a study of African retentions in the African-derived societies of the New World. This was shown both in his early research among the Gullah peoples and in his last intensive research on African-American folktales that had originated in Africa. Bascom worked among the Gullah-speaking peoples of the Georgia and South Carolina Sea Islands in 1939. In 1948, with a grant from the Wenner-Gren Foundation, he conducted research over the summer and fall semesters in Cuba among the Lucumi, descendants of the Yoruba. Berta Montero, a Havana-born anthropology student at Northwestern, accompanied Bascom as a research assistant. At the end of the fieldtrip in 1948, they were married and settled in Evanston, Illinois. The couple had no children. They later returned to Cuba to study the Afro-Cuban cults in Matanzas and Havana. Over the next two decades Bascom devoted a series of articles to the remarkable continuation of Yoruba religious belief and practice in the Cuban cults.

Bascom's research in African art was guided by his love and respect for what he regarded as "the greatest contribution of Africa, and of Africans, to the world's cultural heritage" (quoted in his *African Art in Cultural Perspective*, p. 3). He began collecting Yoruba art during his first fieldtrip and continued throughout his years in Africa. Bascom housed his collection in the University of California at Berkeley's Lowie Museum of Anthropology, of which he became director in 1957, and he bequeathed his entire Yoruba collection to the museum upon his death. Bascom's *African Art in Cultural Perspective: An Introduction* (1973) provides an engrossing and accessible account of this rich area of expressive culture.

Bascom's work in folklore, grounded as it was in his African, African-Cuban, and African-American research, stresses the importance of understanding social and cultural context. From 1976 to 1982 Bascom's articles on African-American folktales originating in Africa appeared in *Research in African Literatures*; they were later published as a collection in *African Folktales in the New World* (1992). In "Perhaps Too Much to Chew?," a largely autobiographical lecture on Bascom's scholarly work that he delivered to the California Folklore Society just months before his death, Bascom referred to his study of folktales as his "new project, another apparently endless one." His reasons for engaging in this research were the same as those underlying so much of his other work, for as he said, "I believe that it is important, not only for folklorists and Afro-Americans, but for all Americans and for Africans to recognize the African contribution to American folklore" (*Western Folklore* 40 [1981]: 285–98). Bascom served as president of the American Folklore Society from 1952 to 1954 and was elected a fellow of the society.

As a teacher, Bascom was known for his quiet, knowledgeable guidance. He encouraged careful, empirical work and clarity in thought. In the program of African studies at Northwestern Bascom, along with Herskovits, guided over thirty students in the completion of their doctorates. In this alone, he had a profound impact on the scholarly study of African societies. At the University of California, Berkeley, he worked with professor of folklore and anthropology Alan Dundes in establishing the master's degree program in folklore in 1965, and he chaired the folklore committee until his retirement. From his office in the Lowie Museum, Bascom served as a patient, supportive mentor for scores of graduate students in folklore. He died in San Francisco, California.

• The William R. Bascom Papers are housed in the Bancroft Library, University of California, Berkeley. Bascom's research in African art is represented in Bascom and Paul Gebauer, *Handbook of West African Art* (1954). Bascom gives a thorough examination of narratives that are used to impart moral and ethical training in African societies in *African Dilemma Tales* (1975). He edited *Frontiers of Folklore* (1977), the proceedings of the folklore panel that he had been invited to organize for the American Association for the Advancement of Science. Bascom's important articles in the field of folklore are reprinted in his *Contributions to Folkloristics* (1981). Simon Ottenberg provides a consideration of Bascom's scholarly work in "The Anthropology of William R. Bascom," in *African Religious Groups and Beliefs: Papers in Honor of William R. Bascom*, ed. Ottenberg (1982), which also includes a bibliography. In Alan Dundes's foreword to Bascom's *African Folktales in the New World* (1992), he gives a critical appraisal of Bascom's research on African and African-American folktales. In Rosemary Lévy Zumwalt, *American Folklore Scholarship: A Dialogue of Dissent* (1988), Bascom's contributions as an anthropological folklorist are discussed, both in terms of defining the discipline and in terms of theoretical debate. An obituary that provides an overview of his life and work is in the *Journal of American Folklore* 95 (1982): 465–67.

ROSEMARY LÉVY ZUMWALT

BASHFORD, James Whitford (29 May 1849–18 Mar. 1919), Methodist bishop and missionary, was born in Fayette, Wisconsin, the son of Samuel Morris Bashford, a farmer, part-time physician, and local preacher in the Methodist Episcopal church, and his wife Mary Ann McKee. At the time of his birth in southwestern Wisconsin, the community labored under the rigors of pioneer life on the frontier; Bashford's mother once beat off with a shovel a prowling wolf about to enter their log cabin where her young child lay sleeping. Despite these early hardships, Bashford was prepared for college by one of his cousins, John P. Parkinson, who opened a school in the village of Fayette before eventually becoming a professor of mathematics at the University of Wisconsin, from which Bashford graduated in 1873, receiving the highest honors in the classical course. He then taught there as an instructor of Greek for a year before entering the School of Theology of Boston University in the fall of 1874. Earning his B.D. in 1876 and his Ph.D. in 1881, he was especially influenced by the liberal theology and sermons of Phillips Brooks, a prominent Boston theologian. In 1878 Bashford married Jane M. Field, a member of the first class of women admitted to the University of Wisconsin, from which she subsequently graduated Phi Beta Kappa in 1874. The couple had no children.

During his student days at Boston University, Bashford was pastor at Harrison Square, Boston (1875), and First Jamaica Plain (1878). After receiving his Ph.D. in 1881, he served as pastor at Auburndale, Massachusetts (1881); Chestnut Street, Portland, Maine (1884); and Delaware Avenue, Buffalo, New York (1887). Although a popular preacher, he was accused of heresy by another prominent Methodist clergyman because of his liberal theology. Bashford refused to see modern science as a foe of Christianity; many of his views were ahead of his time—radical in the 1880s but later widely accepted within Methodism. He was a pioneer in the woman suffrage movement, and an early and bold advocate of licensing women to preach within the Methodist church. His fearless crusade in the temperance cause in Portland, Maine, led to his nomination for governor of Maine on the Prohibition party ticket, which he declined because of his dedication to the ministry.

By 1889 Bashford's growing reputation as a scholar and Christian educator had induced eleven colleges to offer him their presidency. That year he accepted the last offer, the presidency of Ohio Wesleyan University in Delaware, Ohio, where he would remain until 1904. Some indication of his success as a college president in raising financial support for endowment, new buildings, and equipment, as well as increasing the standard of scholarship among the faculty, may be seen in the offer made to Bashford in 1900 of the presidency of Northwestern University, a much larger and wealthier institution. Characteristically unambitious in his aspirations, Bashford declined this offer because he believed his work at Ohio Wesleyan was not yet completed.

In May 1904 Bashford was elected a bishop with designation of his field as China. In a certain sense he had always wanted to be a missionary, and in China his enthusiasm, intelligence, unselfish devotion, and common sense were put to the test. He had a respect for China's ancient civilization and devoted himself to founding schools and medical colleges. His interest in all aspects of China's development led him in 1912 to urge President William Howard Taft to recognize the Chinese republic. When Japan secretly presented her Twenty-One Demands to China in January 1915, Bashford wrote compelling letters to President Woodrow Wilson and Secretary of State William Jennings Bryan alerting them to the dangers posed to China's territorial integrity and sovereignty. In a meeting with Wilson and Bryan when he returned to the United States in 1915 he pointed out that Japanese militarism threatened American diplomatic and commercial aspirations in Asia.

Bashford was an advocate of China's material progress and democratization, which he discussed in his book, *China: An Interpretation* (1916). In addition to numerous articles in periodicals, he published *Wesley and Goethe* (1903), *China and Methodism* (1906), *Christian Missions* (1906), *God's Missionary Plan for the World* (1907), and *The Oregon Missions* (1918). His death in Pasadena, California, marked the end of a distinguished career as scholar, bishop, missionary, and unofficial diplomat with an all-consuming interest in China.

• A primary source is his Diary of James W. Bashford, Missionary Research Library, Union Theological Seminary, N.Y. In addition to the works mentioned above, Bradford published *The Bible and Woman* (1890), *The Bible for Woman Suffrage* (1906), and *The Admission of Women to the General Conference* (n.d.). For a study of his life, see George R. Grose, *James W. Bashford: Pastor, Educator, Bishop* (1922). Monographs that discuss his role in China as a missionary/diplomat are Paul A. Varg, *Missionaries, Chinese, and Diplomats: The American Protestant Missionary Movement in China, 1890–1952* (1958); James Reed, *The Missionary Mind and American East Asian Policy, 1911–1915* (1983); and Valentin H. Rabe, *The Home Base of America China Missions, 1880–1920* (1978). See also Kenneth Scott Latourette, *A History of Christian Missions in China* (1929).

DURWOOD DUNN

BASIE, Count (21 Aug. 1904–26 Apr. 1984), jazz pianist, composer, and bandleader, was born William Basie in Red Bank, New Jersey, the son of African-American parents Harvey Lee Basie, an estate groundskeeper, and Lillian Ann Chiles, a laundress. Basie was first exposed to music through his mother's piano playing. He took piano lessons, played the drums, and acted in school skits. An indifferent student, he left school after junior high and began performing. He organized bands with friends and played various jobs in Red Bank, among them working as a movie theater pianist. In his late teens he pursued work in nearby Asbury Park, but he met with little success. Then, in the early 1920s, he moved to Harlem, where he learned from the leading pianists of the New York "stride" style, Willie "The Lion" Smith, James P. Johnson, Luckey Roberts, and especially Fats Waller, his exact contemporary.

Basie remained undecided between a stage or musical career. Until 1929 he alternatively combined playing in Harlem nightclubs and theaters (on piano and organ) and touring with bands for vaudeville and burlesque troupes, which took him as far from New York as New Orleans, Kansas City, and Oklahoma. In Kansas City during a layover in 1927 or 1928 he was stricken with spinal meningitis. After recovering, he worked solo jobs and eventually joined Walter Page's Blue Devils, a major regional dance band. The Blue Devils featured the southwestern boogie-woogie style of relatively spare blues-based melodies, effortless dance rhythms, and "swinging" syncopation (all hallmarks of the later Basie band style). Basie worked at devising arrangements for the band, assisted by trombonist-guitarist Eddie Durham. Basie's ability to read and write music improved over the years, but he continued to rely on staff and free-lance arrangers. At this time Basie lost interest in the musical stage and dedicated himself to dance music.

Kansas City, a wide-open hub of speakeasies, gambling, and prostitution, offered an active job market for black musicians who specialized in the aggressively swinging southwestern (or Kansas City) blues style. While with the Blue Devils, Basie blended this style with his New York stride piano background, and in 1929 he was hired by Bennie Moten, who led the most successful Kansas City band of the time. It was a move that Basie later called both the greatest risk and the turning point of his career. The Moten band toured extensively and played to large crowds in Chicago and New York.

About 1930, while working as Moten's second pianist and arranger, Basie married Vivian Wynn, but they soon separated and later divorced. Also in 1929 or 1930, he met a young chorus dancer, Catherine Morgan. She and Basie married in 1942 and had one daughter.

During a touring break in 1934, Basie took some Moten band musicians to Little Rock, Arkansas, for a longer-term job at a single location, after which the Moten band broke up. Back in Kansas City, Basie worked as a church organist and was preparing to join

Moten's newest group when the bandleader died unexpectedly in 1935.

Since 1928 Basie had called himself "Count" in imitation of royal nicknames used by other Harlem musicians, but only on taking over the Moten band did he bill himself by that name. Basie soon had the best players from the Moten unit working for him at the Reno Club in Kansas City. This nucleus included trombonists Dan Minor and Eddie Durham, who was the band's chief arranger during its early years; tenor saxophonists Herschel Evans and Lester Young, a key innovator in jazz history; and the inimitable blues vocalist Jimmy Rushing.

To many listeners, however, the heart of the band was its superb rhythm section: on drums, Jo Jones, a keenly knowledgeable musician who revolutionized both big band and small group drumming; on guitar, Claude Williams, who was replaced in 1937 by Freddie Green (the mainstay of the Basie group for five decades); and on bass, Walter Page, Basie's former leader. These three men, in concord with Basie's own idiomatic piano work, synchronized their playing with unmatched skill, lightening and shading the driving four-to-a-bar Kansas City beat, and infusing the band's ensemble play with supple, flowing, danceable rhythms.

In 1935 the white writer, critic, and record producer John Hammond heard a Basie radio broadcast and made arrangements to give the band national exposure. Expanding the group to thirteen men, Basie took his musicians to Chicago, where six of them made their first, classic recordings under the pseudonym (for contractual reasons) Jones-Smith, Inc. In New York City the band played at Roseland Ballroom and recorded for Decca Records, with which the inexperienced Basie signed a demanding long-term contract that paid no royalties. Included in the larger band's initial recordings was Basie's signature tune, "One O'Clock Jump," which featured the leader's slyly spare opening piano solo and the repeated, haunting melody played by the band. By this time Buck Clayton's often muted trumpet solos had become another of the band's features, and Ed Lewis on trumpet, Earle Warren on alto saxophone, and Jack Washington on baritone saxophone anchored those instrumental sections. The band later formed an association with Columbia Records, which continued into the 1940s.

The Basie orchestra had come to New York at the height of the big band era, but the band's relaxed, unembellished, freely swinging style reportedly puzzled those mostly white East Coast listeners who were enthusiasts of the strictly disciplined, thoroughly professional Benny Goodman orchestra. Hammond worked with Basie to tighten the band's section work and solo presentations. Such New York musicians as trombonists Dicky Wells and Benny Morton and trumpeter Harry Edison were hired. Billie Holiday, who already had forged her own deeply personal jazz singing style, became the band's first woman vocalist, to be replaced a year later by Helen Humes. They each joined Jimmy Rushing, who solidified his position as

the leading male blues singer of the big band era. The changes paid off in the late 1930s with successful stints at New York's Famous Door and Savoy Ballroom ("the home of happy feet"), followed by engagements in Chicago and San Francisco.

Basie later recalled that by 1940 "what that name [Count Basie] stood for now was me and the band as the same thing." The band undertook almost unceasing tours throughout the country and continued its prolific recording work. Among bandleaders Basie was matched only by Duke Ellington as a careful, tenacious master of a group of disparate individual artists. Both men were ambitious leaders who defined the basic sounds of their groups, and each of them was ready to step back and allow great freedom to their soloists. But although Ellington was a composer of major stature, Basie was the more successful in integrating his band into the lucrative, white-dominated entertainment industry of the 1940s through the 1970s.

With the start of World War II, Basie, like many bandleaders, had to cope with myriad difficulties; some of these included restrictions on travel, the musicians' union's recording ban that lasted two years, and above all the military draft's continual disruption of the band's roster. Basie again showed great skill in choosing talented replacements, at different times bringing in trombonist J. J. Johnson, trumpeter Joe Newman, tenor saxophonists Lucky Thompson, Paul Gonsalves, and Illinois Jacquet, and drummer Shadow Wilson, among others. All through the 1940s the orchestra worked at choice locations such as New York's Ritz-Carlton and Philadelphia's Academy of Music, while it also maintained nearly continuous nationwide touring. After the recording ban was lifted at the end of 1943, the band resumed making records until the close of the decade. In addition, the Basie group was featured in several Hollywood films—*Reveille with Beverly, Crazy House*, and *Top Man* (all 1943)—and made frequent appearances on Kate Smith's national radio show.

Following the war, Basie continued to revise personnel and shuffle arrangers; he allowed younger players like Wardell Gray on tenor saxophone and Clark Terry on trumpet to introduce a few new bebop ideas. But by the late 1940s the band had become relatively unadventurous. That development coincided with waning public interest in swing era orchestras, and in 1950 Basie was forced to disband.

Basie remained active for more than a year with a sextet that showcased Gray, Terry, and clarinetist Buddy DeFranco. In 1952, at the urging of singer Billy Eckstine, he assembled a new orchestra, which eventually would include Marshall Royal as first alto saxophonist and rehearsal director; the highly original trumpeter Thad Jones; tenor saxophonists Frank Foster, Frank Wess, Paul Quinichette, and Eddie "Lockjaw" Davis; Basie's longtime rhythm colleague Freddie Green; drummer Gus Johnson, soon replaced by Sonny Payne; and the blues and ballad singing of Joe Williams. Birdland, then the most thriving club for jazz in New York, served as an effective home base, and the band often played the Blue Note in Chicago and the Crescendo in Los Angeles.

This edition of the Basie orchestra placed new emphasis on arrangers and precisely played ensembles. Arrangers Neal Hefti, Ernie Wilkins, Quincy Jones, and "the two Franks" (Foster and Wess) played key roles in making the band sound more appealing to a wider audience. Basie now served a varied range of popular tastes, recording with celebrity singers such as Frank Sinatra and Tony Bennett, and featuring everything from Wild Bill Davis's crowd-pleasing arrangement of "April in Paris," to popular television theme songs, to jazz versions of rhythm and blues hits. In 1963 the Basie orchestra was featured in four bestselling albums, including two instrumental records arranged by Quincy Jones. Such popularity had not been attained by any big band since World War II, and, with rock music coming to dominate the record industry, it was a feat not to be duplicated.

Basie and his musicians had made the first of thirty successful European tours in 1954, and in 1963 they made the first of eight trips across the Pacific Ocean. Frequent national tours continued, usually reaching the West Coast twice each year. By 1961, when it performed at one of President John F. Kennedy's inaugural celebrations, the band had become part of America's official culture. Further appearances at the White House culminated in a reception for Basie in 1981, which celebrated a Kennedy Center honor for his contributions to the performing arts. He also was given a tribute, sponsored by the Black Music Association, in 1982 at New York's Radio City Music Hall.

Six years earlier, in 1976, Basie suffered a heart attack that kept him away from the band for half a year. After returning, he continued the band's touring on a reduced schedule, while work in the recording studios remained active. But various illnesses further weakened him, and a year after his wife's death, he died in Hollywood, Florida.

Basie's unique ability to inspire a large jazz band with the rhythmic drive and ease of 1930s Kansas City small combos, to select and lead an ever-changing roster of talented and complementary musicians, to adapt to rapidly evolving and diverse musical tastes while maintaining artistic integrity, to integrate his band into the mainstream of American entertainment, and to give the band matchless worldwide exposure—all show him to have been one of the major figures in twentieth-century American music.

• Basie's memorabilia and papers are still in private hands, although they have been pledged to the Hampton University Library, Hampton, Virginia. Basie's autobiography, written with Albert Murray and completed shortly before his death, is *Good Morning Blues* (1985). See also Stanley Dance, *The World of Count Basie* (1980); Chris Sheridan, *Count Basie: A Bio-Discography* (1986); and Gunther Schuller, *The Swing Era* (1989); as well as books by and about individual band members (Dicky Wells, Lester Young, etc.). An obituary is in the *New York Times*, 27 Apr. 1984.

BURTON W. PERETTI

BASS, Charlotta Spears (Oct. 1880?–12 Apr. 1969), editor and civil rights activist, was born in Sumter, South Carolina, the daughter of Hiram Spears and Kate (maiden name unknown). Before 1900 she joined her oldest brother (one of her ten siblings) in Rhode Island and worked for a newspaper. In 1910 she went to Los Angeles, California, for her health. She remained in Los Angeles except for a brief stay in New York City. She took journalism courses at Brown University, Columbia University, and the University of California at Los Angeles.

She worked for the *Eagle* in Los Angeles, the oldest African-American newspaper on the West Coast. It was edited by John Neimore, who soon had Bass running the paper. After Neimore's death, Captain Hawkins paid fifty dollars in 1912 to own the *Eagle* and gave Bass ownership in return for a promise of payment. She changed the newspaper's name to the *California Eagle*. At about this time she married Joseph Bass, a founder of the *Topeka Plaindealer* in Kansas and the editor of the *California Eagle*. Under their joint leadership, the paper grew from a four-page tabloid to a twelve-page standard-sized newspaper serving the African-American community and others in Los Angeles.

Charlotta and Joseph Bass reported the social news and waged a relentless and militant war against racial discrimination wherever they saw it. They assailed injustice in D. W. Griffith's *Birth of a Nation*, during the race riot of 1917 in Houston, in the trial of the Scottsboro boys, and in employment patterns on the railroads. They supported organizations that defended black civil rights such as the Progressive Educational Association, the Industrial Business Council, and the Home Protective Association.

When in 1925 the Ku Klux Klan sued the Basses for libel, the *California Eagle* having published a letter written by the Imperial Representative of the Klan in California exposing his plan to control an election in Watts, the Basses won the case. Once Charlotta Bass used a gun to order Klansmen out of the newspaper's office. After her husband's death in 1934, Charlotta Bass ran the paper by herself and helped end racial discrimination in the Los Angeles schools, hospitals, restaurants, unions, and telephone and transit companies. In the 1930s, she opposed restrictive covenants in housing and promoted consumer boycotts of employers who practiced racial discrimination.

A Republican party stalwart, she was western regional director of the Wendell Willkie presidential campaign in 1940. When she reached Republican headquarters in Chicago, she found "two worlds—upstairs was a world for white Republicans and down below was the world for Negro Republicans." The first African American to sit on a grand jury for the Los Angeles County Court (1943), she ran as an independent candidate but was not elected to the city council in 1945. She had called for jobs, decent housing, eradication of slums, a square deal for everyone, and "full citizenship for all the people." Because of her civil rights activities, she was called "un-American" and in 1946 was questioned by the Tenney Committee, the California version of the House Un-American Activities Committee. In the *California Eagle*, she called the Tenney Committee itself "un-American" and "fascist."

In 1947 she broke with the Republican party because of its failure to support civil rights legislation. She became an increasingly vocal opponent of the policy of containing communism. Bass helped found the new Progressive party and in 1948 served as national co-chairman of "Women for Wallace" during Henry Wallace's campaign for the presidency. She told the convention that in the Progressive party she had "found that one political world that could provide a home big enough for Negro and white, for native and foreign born, to live and work together for the same ends—as equals." Hadassah awarded Bass a life membership for her "outstanding crusading in the interest of her race."

In 1950 Bass went to Paris and to Prague as a member of the Peace Committee of the World Congress. There she supported a ban on the atomic bomb. She attended the World Student Congress in Prague and visited the Soviet Union. *Soviet Russia Today* published her article praising the Soviet Union and its lack of racial discrimination. Back in California, she stressed world peace and the banning of the bomb during her unsuccessful run for Congress on the Independent Progressive party ticket in 1950. She retired from the *California Eagle* in 1951.

In 1952 she became the first African-American woman to be nominated for vice president by a political party, the Progressive party. Vincent Hallinan, the Progressive presidential candidate, was a California attorney who was serving a jail term for contempt stemming from his legal defense of Harry Bridges, the radical labor leader. Bass and Hallinan had to go to court to get their acceptance speeches on radio and television. Although they were ignored by the major newspapers, they were covered and supported by the *Daily Worker* of the American Communist party.

During the campaign, Bass reiterated that there was little difference between the Democratic and the Republican parties. "After 80 years of voting and waiting," she said, "we are still looking for an anti-poll tax and anti-lynching bill." Bass described her program as "for civil rights, for peace, for decent jobs, for equality," and she advocated an immediate cease-fire in Korea. Her campaign literature included endorsements by Paul Robeson and W. E. B. Du Bois. Bass and Hallinan received only about .2 percent of the popular vote. Still, their campaign was a voice for civil rights and for peace in the midst of the McCarthy period. In 1956 after listening to civil rights leaders, Bass wrote to Florence Luscomb, "truly we are on the brink of a new day, a new world. I am happy, indeed, to be a weak link in the chain of events that are responsible for the new day."

In 1960 she privately published *Forty Years: Memoirs from the Pages of a Newspaper*, in which she chronicled the first settling of Los Angeles by Native Americans and African Americans and recalled the major political struggles covered by her paper. She wrote, "The two-headed monster, Segregation and Discrimination, which for more than a century has spread poverty and disease across the United States, must be entirely wiped out, destroyed, before our nation can come to the rest of the world with clean hands." Despite arthritis, she remained active locally, continuing her encouragement of young people, until her death in Los Angeles. In person and through her newspaper, Charlotta Bass was a lifelong voice for civil rights in the United States and for peace in the world.

• Bass's papers are at the Southern California Library for Social Studies and Research, Los Angeles. Her letter to Luscomb is in the Florence Luscomb Papers at the Schlesinger Library, Radcliffe College. Clipping files for 1945 are available at the Moorland-Spingarn Collection, Howard University, and for 1952 at the Schomburg Collection, New York Public Library. A full-page article about her, with photographs, is by Cecilia Rasmussen, "L. A. Scene: The City Then and Now," *Los Angeles Times*, 22 Feb. 1993. See also Gerald R. Gill, "'Win or Lose—We Win': The 1952 Vice Presidential Campaign of Charlotta A. Bass," in *The Afro-American Woman: Struggles and Images*, ed. Sharon Harley and Rosalyn Terborg-Penn (1978), and James Philip Jeter, "Rough Flying: The California Eagle (1879–1965)," paper delivered to the American Journalism Historians Association (1993). A front page article about her death and funeral services is in the *Los Angeles Sentinel*, 17 Apr. 1969.

NORAH C. CHASE

BASS, Mary Elizabeth (5 Apr. 1876–26 Jan. 1956), physician, medical educator, and historian, was born in Carley, Mississippi, the daughter of Isaac Esau Bass and Mary Eliza Wilkes. She grew up in Marion County, where her father operated a gristmill and dry goods store. The 1890s economic depression bankrupted Isaac Bass, and the family moved to Lumberton, Mississippi, to invest in pecan orchards. The Basses were pious Baptists and active in civic concerns.

Bass attended elementary and high schools in Columbia, Mississippi, assisting teachers and earning teaching certificates after her 1893 graduation. She taught in Texas and Mississippi. Her brother Charles had earned a degree from the Tulane University School of Medicine, and he encouraged Bass and their younger sister Cora to enroll in medical school. At that time no southern medical schools would accept women, and few schools in the United States welcomed female applicants. Many American women sought a medical education and qualifications to practice at foreign universities.

The Woman's Medical College of Pennsylvania had opened in 1850, and the Bass sisters applied for the fall 1900 term. Together they completed the curricula in four years. Bass worked several weeks after graduation on the college dispensary staff before moving to New Orleans, Louisiana, with her sister to establish a private practice. In New Orleans, she encountered many obstacles and was shunned and scorned by the male-dominated medical profession. Bass stubbornly pursued her profession despite male doctors' rigidly controlling access to medical facilities. Women were not allowed to practice in New Orleans' clinics or hospitals.

Bass ignored her ostracism by the male medical community, and with five women doctors she established a free clinic for women and children. Opening in 1908, the New Orleans Hospital and Dispensary for Women and Children (later called the Sara Mayo Hospital) provided crucial services. The hospital began in a house owned by one of Bass's friends and expanded into a larger facility. At that time only five American hospitals had been founded and managed by women. Bass welcomed all women physicians to use the hospital to treat impoverished women and children and provide other patients with medical care.

In December 1911 Bass and Edith Ballard were named the first two female faculty members of Tulane's medical school. Bass's career as a medical educator began with a three-year position as an unpaid assistant demonstrator of surgical pathology. Outside the classroom, she participated in the city's Equal Rights Association, demanding opportunities for women, and by 1914 Tulane accepted women in medical school perhaps because of her influence. Bass had been promoted to instructor in the laboratory of clinical medicine and was paid $500 a year. She divided her time between her university work, teaching pathology, bacteriology, and clinical laboratory diagnosis, and promoting issues regarding women and social issues. Bass acquired the rank of full professor in 1920.

During her thirty-year career as a pioneering female physician, Bass devoted her energy to advancing other women doctors in their careers. She was a valuable mentor to her students, advising them professionally and often providing financial assistance. She retired from Tulane in 1941 as emeritus professor of clinical laboratory diagnosis. Living in the Jung Hotel, Bass retained her private practice as house physician there and in the community because of the demand for doctors during the shortages of World War II.

The decade after her retirement resulted in perhaps Bass's most significant accomplishment. She collected materials about women medical professionals to preserve the history of American women physicians. Her personal archives contained hundreds of clippings, manuscripts, books, pamphlets, letters, and photographs, which she used to write essays and the column, "These Were the First," for the *Journal of the American Medical Women's Association* from 1946 to 1956. In addition to collecting works written by or about other women doctors, Bass published historical articles in medical journals.

Bass was an associate member of the American Medical Association, a fellow and life member of the American College of Physicians, an emeritus fellow of the College of American Pathologists, and a specialist certified by the American Board of Pathology. In 1913 she was the first woman elected to active membership in the Orleans Parish Medical Society. She served as secretary of that group in 1921 and vice president in 1923, and she edited its bulletin in 1939. She belonged to the Louisiana State Medical Society and was secretary for the Section of Pathology of the Southern Medical Association.

Bass joined the Women Physicians of the Southern Medical Association when it was founded in 1915 and was president of that organization from 1925 to 1927. In 1921–1922 she was the fifth president of the Medical Women's National Association (later the American Medical Women's Association). She also was affiliated with the Medical Women's International Association, the American Public Health Association, the American Association for the Advancement of Science, the History of Medicine Society, the New Orleans Academy of Science, and the American Society of Tropical Medicine.

Active in the American Association of University Professors and the International Association of University Women, Bass served as a delegate to several international forums. She traveled to the first Pan Pacific Women's Conference at Honolulu in 1928 and the 1934 Stockholm and 1937 Edinburgh conferences of the Medical Women's International Association. A Democrat politically, Bass voiced demands for suffrage and strengthened child labor laws through women's groups. She belonged to the Young Women's Christian Association and was welcomed into some of the city's more exclusive groups, including Le Petit Théâtre du Vieux Carré, Le Petit Salon, and the New Orleans Garden Society.

By 1949 Bass ceased her medical practice and returned to Lumberton, Mississippi, to supervise her ill mother's health care. In 1952 the Woman's Medical College of Pennsylvania gave her its Alumni Achievement Award, and in 1953 the American Medical Women's Association presented Bass the Elizabeth Blackwell Centennial Medal Award. She died of cancer at the New Orleans Foundation Hospital. She was buried in Lumberton with her family, and a tuition fund for women students was established in her name at the Tulane School of Medicine.

• The Elizabeth Bass Collection on Women in Medicine is at the Rudolph Matas Medical Library, Tulane University. Included in the collection is her unpublished book-length manuscript, "History of Medicine in Louisiana." Information on Bass as student and alumna is held by the Medical College of Pennsylvania, and her correspondence with Florence Sabin is at Smith College. See also her "Dispensaries Founded by Women Physicians in the Southland," *Journal of the American Medical Women's Association* (Dec. 1947): 560–61. Other sources describing Bass's contributions include Ruth J. Abram, ed., *"Send Us a Lady Physician": Women Doctors in America, 1835–1920* (1985); Gulielma F. Alsop, *History of the Woman's Medical College, Philadelphia, Pennsylvania* (1950); Thomas Neville Bonner, *To the Ends of the Earth: Women's Search for Education in Medicine* (1992); Lillian R. Furst, *Women Healers and Physicians: Climbing a Long Hill* (1997); and Mary R. Walsh, *"Doctors Wanted: No Women Need Apply": Sexual Barriers in the Medical Profession, 1835–1975* (1977).

ELIZABETH D. SCHAFER

BASS, Robert Perkins (11 Sept. 1873–29 July 1960), governor of New Hampshire, conservationist, and labor relations adviser, was born in Chicago, Illinois, the son of Perkins Bass, a lawyer, and Clara Foster. Bass's interest in politics was likely influenced by his father, who served as Abraham Lincoln's campaign manager in the 1864 presidential election. Robert Bass graduated from Harvard in 1896 and attended graduate school there for a year and Harvard Law School for a year, leaving without a degree in 1898. He moved to Peterborough, New Hampshire, to manage his family's farms in New Hampshire and extensive real estate holdings in Chicago. Despite his affluent upbringing and privileged experiences, Bass became a champion of the common worker and employed much effort to bring a more equitable distribution of corporate earnings between owners and labor.

The bulk of Bass's public work occurred early in his life. In 1904 he entered Republican politics and was elected to the New Hampshire House of Representatives. He was reelected to the house in 1906, and his identification with the progressive wing of the Republican party dates to his involvement in the organization of New Hampshire's Lincoln Republicans, or the Lincoln Club, that same year. This group of affluent and well-educated men sought to distinguish themselves from the "greedy magnates" and "selfish bosses" of the Republican party and were unified by a desire to wrest control of state politics from the Boston and Maine Railroad. Other concerns of Bass and the Lincoln Club included conservation of natural resources, passage of a direct primary law, direct election of U.S. senators, and injury compensation for industrial workers. The group's religious overtones reflect a support for social gospel principles.

Following the Lincoln Republicans' failed attempt to elect novelist Winston Churchill as governor in 1906, Bass emerged as the leader of progressive reform through his capacity as a state legislator. In 1906 he was appointed the state forestry commissioner and was successful in implementing a stricter conservation policy. He also transformed the legislative committee he chaired from an insignificant body into a high-profile bureaucratic oversight committee. His attack on corporate influence in state politics and his appeal for a direct primary law led conservative Republicans to oppose his election to the New Hampshire Senate in 1908. Successful in that race despite opposition from party leaders, Bass continued to champion progressive reform in a predominantly reactionary senate. His chief success as senator was the passage of a direct primary law in 1909, making New Hampshire the first eastern state to adopt that system.

New Hampshire's nascent direct primary law was essential to Bass's election as governor in 1910. Having seized control of party nominations from a conservative, railroad-governed oligarchy, Bass won the Republican primary by a two-to-one margin over the regular Republican candidate and went on to win the open election. Bass's election as governor received national coverage because, as his was the only successful Republican gubernatorial race east of the Mississippi River in 1910, it foretold the growing influence of the progressive wing of the Republican party. Theodore Roosevelt, a longtime friend of the Bass family, was associated with Bass's campaign and gained prestige over President William Howard Taft, whose support of eastern Republican gubernatorial candidates was ineffectual.

Bass, with the support of a progressive house, brought a bold reform package to the senate for ratification. The package included a bill to establish a workmen's compensation program, another to create a public service commission to regulate utilities and railroad companies, and legislation to further conservation in New Hampshire. Identified as a leading conservationist, Bass served as president of the American Forestry Association from 1910 to 1913. He called on fellow reformer Louis Brandeis to draft the public service commission bill and turned to another friend, Joseph Cotton, to establish a workmen's compensation act along the lines of New York's Wainright Commission. The standpat majority in the senate, however, refused to consider the legislation because of opposition to a bill designed to reign in the power of the Boston and Maine Railroad. With the legislative session drawing to a close, the Bass administration broke the impasse through skillful negotiation and succeeded in passing most of the reform measures. In 1912 Bass married Edith Harlan Bird; they had five children.

Bass's identification with the national progressive insurgency continued when he and six other Republican governors publicly encouraged Roosevelt to enter the 1912 presidential contest. Prior to that announcement, Bass met with Roosevelt several times and was influential in altering Roosevelt's controversial appeal to institute a recall of judges. Bass supported Roosevelt throughout the spring and summer and attended the Republican convention in Chicago. His political viability came to an end when he broke ranks with the Republican party to support Roosevelt's Bull Moose ticket. Bass ran for the U.S. Senate in 1914 and 1926 and in both cases failed to win the support of the Republican party in New Hampshire. Close friend and fellow progressive Republican George Rublee believed that the Republicans never forgave Bass for supporting the Progressive ticket and pointed out that, although Bass remained a great influence in Republican politics, "he never regained the power he once had in the state."

Although Bass would not again be elected to public office, his national prominence continued as a result of his skillful negotiations in labor disputes during World War I and his efforts to pacify labor-management relations in the wake of demobilization. During the war Bass served as the U.S. Shipping Board's director of the Marine Labor Board and as chair of the National Adjustment Commission. He scrutinized working conditions and pay rates for dock workers and merchant marines and arbitrated management-labor disputes in the marine industries. His evenhanded approach to disputes gained the confidence of labor representatives.

Having relied on patriotic sentiments to gain worker cooperation during the war, Bass was acutely apprehensive of labor relations following the termination of hostilities. In his final report as director of the Marine Labor Board, issued in February 1919, Bass pointed out that the "time has passed when the appeal to patriotism will have any influence," and he advocated that the federal government make a strong effort to mend relations between management and labor. He pointed out that "methods long in use by private employers in this country" had unfortunately led to "a deep hostility between the managers of industry and their employees." Bass believed that "revolutionary industrial propaganda can never be stilled by arbitrary suppression, by court decisions, by imprisonment, or by strong-armed methods," and he expressed his view that the "use of these methods constitutes a grave national danger." He argued that "enlightened, sound, and universal education" was the only "safeguard against extreme revolutionary industrial propaganda, which now threatens the industrial organization of the whole civilized world." His report was carried in national newspapers, and he spoke to groups such as the Chicago City Club in hopes of influencing a more progressive approach to labor relations.

The war's end brought a close to Bass's fifteen-year experience as a public official. He returned to Peterborough, New Hampshire, and operated a dairy farm throughout the remainder of his life. He continued to be a behind-the-scenes influence in New Hampshire politics and actively supported national conservation efforts. He was chair of the Brookings Institution from 1946 to 1949. He died in Peterborough.

• Bass's papers are in the Baker Library at Dartmouth College. Other useful collections include the Louis Brandeis Papers in the Law Library at the University of Louisville and the presidential papers of Theodore Roosevelt in the Library of Congress. Unpublished sources relating aspects of Bass's role in the Progressive movement include George Rublee's oral memoir, "The Reminiscences of George Rublee," at the Columbia University Oral History Office, and Marc McClure, "George Rublee: A Voice of Reason" (master's thesis, Univ. of North Texas, 1996). Published sources include Thomas Agan, "The New Hampshire Progressives: Who and What Were They?" *Historical New Hampshire* 34 (Spring 1979): 32–53; Jewel Bellush, "Reform in New Hampshire: Robert Bass Wins the Primary," *New England Quarterly* 35 (Dec. 1962): 469–88; and George Mowry, *The Era of Theodore Roosevelt* (1958). The key secondary work on progressivism in New Hampshire is James E. Wright, *Progressive Yankees* (1987).

MARC MCCLURE

BASSE, Jeremiah (?–c. Aug. 1725), governor of East and West Jersey, was born in England. His political enemies later belittled him as a former Anabaptist minister and brewer's clerk, but it is unknown whether his detractors were accurately describing him because no information has survived about his origins. Basse's parents evidently did not rank among the gentry, however, and his early religious sympathies seem not to have been with the Church of England. His career and writings demonstrated a good education and a sophisticated knowledge of law, but he was probably self-taught in both regards.

Basse emigrated to Cohansey, West Jersey, by 1686; he first held important office in 1692, when he became resident agent for the West Jersey Society, a recently organized company of English land speculators. The West Jersey Society possessed legal claims to one-fifth of West Jersey's unpatented real estate and to one-twelfth of all vacant lands in the neighboring colony of East Jersey. Control over the remaining areas lay with the East Jersey Board of Proprietors and with the West Jersey Council of Proprietors, both of which were composed of the leading political figures in each province. The West Jersey Society held the right of naming West Jersey's governor, which it had purchased as a separate privilege, and it could influence the choice of East Jersey's governor.

Although instructed to cooperate with the resident proprietors in surveying lands, Basse attempted to engross large tracts of valuable real estate at the expense of the West Jersey Council of Proprietors. Basse even tried to seize fiscal control of that body and so monopolize the disposition of all West Jersey lands by falsely representing himself as the proxy for a majority of its shares. Besides jeopardizing the economic interests of West Jersey's resident proprietors, who were overwhelmingly Quakers, Basse challenged their political influence over the colony's government. Neither Basse nor his deputies belonged to the Society of Friends, and they began organizing an opposition party among Calvinists and Anglicans who objected to Quaker domination of West Jersey.

Basse maintained good relations with the East Jersey Board of Proprietors, of whom few were Quakers, and he purchased shares in the organization. While visiting England in 1697, he persuaded the West Jersey Society and certain eastern proprietors then living in London to appoint him governor of both East and West Jersey. Because the governor-designate lacked sufficient property to post the £1,000 bond required by Parliament for that office, he reached the Jerseys in April 1698 without having been legally certified as chief executive.

Leaders in both provinces denounced Basse's tenure as unlawful. In West Jersey the assembly's speaker insolently told Basse that he would throw him out of the government; that the legislature would not convene when he summoned it; and that the treasurer refused to surrender his accounts to the incoming administration. When the governor's magistrates tried to hold court in Salem County, the citizens rioted and chased them from the bench.

Basse's association with East Jersey's proprietors generated widespread resentment in that province, where numerous communities were embroiled in boundary disputes and lawsuits over quitrents with the proprietors. After Basse used treasury funds to finance an expensive lawsuit seeking exemption from customs duties for Perth Amboy's merchants, most of whom were East Jersey proprietors, a massive wave of tax resistance ensued. When Basse imprisoned his two most prominent opponents at Woodbridge, an enraged crowd demolished the jail and freed them on 13 May 1699. The aftermath of the Woodbridge jailbreaking symbolized how low Basse's prestige and power had fallen, for he found himself forced to listen while his two erstwhile prisoners celebrated their freedom by firing off guns on a ship anchored safely offshore from his Perth Amboy residence.

The West Jersey Society and East Jersey's proprietors lost confidence in Basse and replaced him with Andrew Hamilton (?–1703). By December 1699, when Basse left office, his divisive policies and unpopularity had brought proprietary government into widespread disrepute and set in motion unremitting opposition to proprietary rule in both the Jerseys. By the spring of 1701, Hamilton's authority had also collapsed under a wave of jailbreakings, refusals to pay taxes, and forcible closings of the courts. On 12 August 1701 the West Jersey Society and East Jersey's proprietors petitioned the Crown to relieve them of governing their provinces by making New Jersey a royal colony.

After East and West Jersey were combined into a royal colony, Basse gained appointment to the highly profitable post of provincial secretary in 1703. He became a strong supporter of Governor Edward Hyde (1661–1723) Lord Cornbury, but his popularity sank to new depths because of his connections with Cornbury, who became widely reviled for soliciting bribes and appointing corrupt supporters who embezzled public funds and took illegal fees. Basse furthermore adopted the religious prejudices of Cornbury, a High Church Anglican who wished to exclude dissenters from royal office. He became a zealous member of St. Mary's congregation at Burlington, whose communicants included the most implacable opponents of West Jersey's Quaker proprietors, who allied with the East Jersey proprietors in the legislature to block Cornbury's policies.

Basse remained secretary after Cornbury's recall in 1708 until Governor Robert Hunter (1666–1734) rescinded his commission in 1715. He won election to the assembly in 1721 from Cape May, a small constituency that usually voted against his opponents in the proprietary party, and served until later in that year. By repudiating his past political career and advocating honest, disinterested government, he nevertheless reconciled himself with West Jersey's Quaker proprietors and their eastern proprietary allies, who dominated the colony's politics after Robert Hunter's governorship. His opportunistic shift of allegiances brought him appointments as attorney general and treasurer of New Jersey's western division in 1719. Although he successfully ingratiated himself with the colony's leaders and obtained posts of profit, Basse exercised little political influence after 1719.

Despite holding many remunerative offices and well placed to profit from land speculation, Basse never accumulated great wealth. His three children apparently received most of their estate from their mother, Elizabeth Curtis, who married Basse in 1704 on condition that she retain legal control over her own property. He died at Burlington.

• Documents concerning Basse's political career are in William A. Whitehead, et al., *Archives of the State of New Jersey*, 1st ser., vol. 2 (1881), vol. 3 (1881), and in George M. Hills, *History of the Church in Burlington, New Jersey* (1876). See also John E. Pomfret, *The Province of West New Jersey, 1609–1702: A History of the Origins of an American Colony* (1956); John W. Raimo, *Biographical Directory of American Colonial and Revolutionary Governors, 1607–1789* (1980), pp. 211–12; and Paul A. Stellhorn and Michael J. Birkner, eds., *The Governors of New Jersey, 1664–1974: Biographical Essays* (1982), pp. 33–35.

THOMAS L. PURVIS

BASSETT, Edward Murray (7 Feb. 1863–27 Oct. 1948), city planner and lawyer, was born in Brooklyn, New York, the son of Charles Ralph Bassett, a traveling peddler, and Elvira Rogers, a former school teacher. In 1871 the family moved to Watertown, New York, where Bassett attended local schools while his father sold dry goods in nearby villages. Bassett proved an excellent student and, despite his father's disapproval, he entered Hamilton College on scholarship, hoping to become a teacher of Greek and Latin. Halfway through his second year, he transferred to Amherst College, graduating with an A.B. degree and several prizes in 1884. He then taught school in New York City while attending Columbia Law School at night. After receiving his LL.B. degree in 1886, Bassett moved to Buffalo, where he and his brother established Bassett Bros., a firm that built and ran waterworks for nearby towns. In 1890 he married Annie Rebecca Preston; they would have five children. His company closed in 1892, having earned a modest profit.

Returning to Brooklyn, Bassett opened a law office and became active in the Democratic party. He served one term in Congress (1903–1905) but did not seek reelection, though he continued to serve on the county Democratic committee until 1907. His growing interest in real estate and urban development led him to serve on several planning committees and to write numerous pamphlets about traffic and rapid transit. These activities (plus his support for the campaign of his law school classmate Governor Charles Evans Hughes) led to his appointment to draft New York's first public service commission law, dealing with railroads, rapid transit, and public utilities. When the new law took effect in 1907, Bassett was appointed to the five-man Downstate Commission, covering New York City and Long Island. For the next five years Bassett spent much of his time on commission work, helping to revise the state's policies for regulating public utilities and to expand significantly the city's rapid transit system.

Visits to European cities intensified Bassett's interest in urban development and in 1909 he joined the new National Conference on City Planning. "I realized that I had found the kind of work that interested me," he wrote later, "and that it offered a vast field of progressive legislation." After he left the Public Service Commission in 1911, Bassett was involved in organizing the Brooklyn City Plan Committee, through which he helped promote various changes in rapid transit designed to encourage economic development in Brooklyn.

Bassett also began discussing with civic and business leaders the likelihood that certain centrally located subway stops in Manhattan would attract overdevelopment, fostering the very congestion that rapid transit had been intended to reduce. The group agreed that the lack of regulations governing skyscrapers greatly aggravated the problem. One of the men, George McAneny, persuaded the city Board of Estimate, on which he sat, to establish a Heights of Buildings Commission in 1913 and to appoint Bassett chairman. Once the group's report led to the necessary enabling legislation, Bassett was appointed in 1914 to chair a Commission on Building Districts and Restrictions. The zoning ordinance produced by this committee and adopted in 1916 made New York the first city in the country to assert comprehensive power over the height, area, and use of urban buildings. One important feature of the ordinance was that it was based on the city's police power, thus avoiding the time and expense involved in operating under eminent domain. Some critics objected that the new law made too few changes in existing land-use patterns, but Bassett, whom one historian calls "a practical idealist," was willing to work within the constraints he faced: first, that the new law must please the merchants and real estate men who dominated the commission, and second, that the law must be written as narrowly as possible to withstand legal challenge.

Once zoning was adopted, Bassett became counsel for a citizens' watchdog committee formed to ensure that the new law would be enforced. He continued this work until 1946. Convinced that New York's zoning law was more likely to survive legal challenges if other communities adopted similar legislation, Bassett began in 1917 traveling throughout the country, explaining zoning to legislators and business groups, helping them draft state and local laws, and trying zoning cases. He also held zoning roundtables at the annual meetings of the National Conference and chaired the U.S. Commerce Department's Advisory Committee on City Planning and Zoning, which published a Standard State Zoning Enabling Act (1924) and a Standard City Planning Enabling Act (1928). The impact of his efforts was reflected in the rapid diffusion of zoning throughout the country, especially after it was upheld by the Supreme Court in 1926. By 1941 more than 1,300 American communities had adopted some form of zoning.

Bassett helped found the American City Planning Institute in 1917 and was president of the National Conference (1928–1929). Between 1922 to 1928 he served as counsel to and authored several studies for the Regional Plan of New York and Its Environs, a massive multi-year analysis of development in the New York metropolitan area. He also published several important books, including *Model Laws for Planning Cities, Counties and States* (1935, with Alfred Bettman, Frank B. Williams, and Robert Whitten), *Zoning: The Laws, Administration, and Court Decisions during the First Twenty Years* (1936), and *The Master Plan* (1938). He practiced law with the firm of Bassett, Thompson & Gilpatric from 1902 to 1942 and with the firm of Bassett & Bassett in association with his son Howard from 1942 until his death. He also chaired the board of his local Congregational church for more than twenty years. He died in Brooklyn.

Bassett once called zoning "the best contribution of my life." His principal goal, he said, was "the prevention of congestion . . . the distribution of light and air—openness." Despite the historic changes he introduced, he was more interested in protecting existing land uses against deterioration than in promoting social change. By his later years many of his disciples had moved beyond him in recognizing both flaws and new possibilities in his approach to city planning. Yet he is rightly called "the father of American zoning." He pioneered the field and dedicated his life to it, spearheading a movement that helped shape the appearance and the economics of nearly every city in America.

• Bassett's *Autobiography* (1930) was intended for his family and deals mostly with his early life. The best sketch of his career, including excerpts from the *Autobiography*, appears in Donald Krueckeberg, ed., *American Planner: Biographies and Recollections* (1983). Useful discussions of his work appear in Richard E. Foglesong, *Planning the Capitalist City: The Colonial Era to the 1920s* (1986); T. J. Kent, Jr., *The Urban General Plan* (1964); Mel Scott, *American City Planning since 1890* (1969); Seymour Toll, *Zoned America* (1969); Robert Averill Walker, *The Planning Function in Urban Government* (1941); and William H. Wilson, "Moles and Skylarks," in *Introduction to Planning History in the United States*, ed. Donald A. Krueckeberg (1983). An obituary is in the *New York Times*, 28 Oct. 1948.

SANDRA OPDYCKE

BASSETT, John Young (12 June 1805–2 Nov. 1851), surgeon, was born in Baltimore, Maryland, the son of Isaac Bassett and Nancy Davidson. The extent of his early education is not known, but he received an M.D. from Washington Medical College in Baltimore in 1830. Following completion of medical school lectures, he and his brother Frank, an apothecary, went to Huntsville, Madison County, Alabama, where they began to operate a drug store. There, without a fortune or family influences, John Bassett slowly began to build a medical practice. Prospering modestly, on 21 April 1831 he married the daughter of a local physician, Isaphoena Thompson; they had five children who reached maturity.

By 1835 Bassett had made enough money to travel abroad to improve his medical knowledge and surgical skills. In January 1836 he embarked for Liverpool,

England. Upon arrival, he began a six-week tour of Edinburgh, Glasgow, Belfast, and Dublin. While in Edinburgh, he visited the Museum of the College of Surgeons and the Royal Infirmary, where, in the company of the professor of anatomy, James Syme, Bassett observed an operation performed by William Ferguson, who in the 1840s would become widely known as the founder of conservative surgery. After a two-week tour of London, he left for Paris.

Bassett attached himself to Alfred-Armand-Louis-Marie Velpeau, surgeon to La Charité and professor of clinical surgery at the Paris Faculty. In Paris, he studied anatomy by dissecting and surgery by attending clinical lectures and the daily hospital rounds of Professor Velpeau. Although he spent the majority of his days preparing himself for a surgical practice when he returned home, he also benefited from lectures and practical training in midwifery and lectures in medicine.

On 10 July 1836, in a letter to his wife, Bassett wrote, "This morning I received the appointment of *Externe* in La Charité under Velpeau . . . it is a real benefit and came unsolicited" (quoted in Osler, p. 8). This position, in which he gained valuable practical experience in the management of surgical patients, was a coveted appointment, but he had already spent seven months in close study and attendance on the hospital wards. After spending three more months on Velpeau's service and becoming anxious to see his wife and family, he left in mid-October 1836 to return to the United States.

Soon after Bassett resumed practice in Huntsville, professional colleagues recognized his recently acquired knowledge of surgery and medicine gained in Paris, the center of French medical teaching. His experience there with many surgical patients and his practical anatomical studies had gained him greater confidence, finer technique, and better results with his surgery than that of many of his contemporaries. An example of Bassett's advanced knowledge is shown in his 1847 treatment of a case of osteomyelitis of the tibia, in which he successfully operated on the patient whose painful extremity was cured without the usual practice of amputation. The success described in accounts of his surgical treatments of osteomyelitis is in sharp contrast to that of medical therapy at the time, and his reputation extended throughout north Alabama and adjacent counties in Tennessee.

From the beginning of his practice, Bassett had kept case records, as well as meteorological data to discover a possible relationship between epidemic disease and changes in the weather. Based on his recorded observations and experience, he contributed two papers to *Southern Medical Reports* (1849–1850, 1850–1851), a short-lived publication of Erasmus Darwin Fenner, a New Orleans, Louisiana, practitioner who had founded this and two other medical journals and organized the New Orleans School of Medicine.

Having contracted tuberculosis, Bassett sought restoration of his health in Florida early in 1851; however, with no improvement, he soon returned to his family in Huntsville and died at his home. Perhaps Bassett's greatest significance lay in his being one of the very few antebellum southern disciples of the French clinical school.

• A single letter from an apprentice, Claudius H. Mastin, M.D., containing some personal and family information has been published as an Appendix in Daniel C. Elkin, *The Medical Reports of John Y. Bassett*, Thomas (1941). Mastin wrote about his mentor's difficulties in beginning a practice in a small southern community where the majority of practitioners were well established in the local hierarchy of family, church, and politics. Genealogical information can be found in James Edmonds Saunders, *Early Settlers of Alabama . . .* (1899; repr. 1969). Sir William Osler, *An Alabama Student and Other Biographical Essays* (1908), contains a reprint of his essay on Bassett, "An Alabama Student," which originally appeared in the *Johns Hopkins Hospital Bulletin* 7 (Jan. 1896): 6–11.

EUGENE H. CONNER

BASSETT, Richard (2 Apr. 1745–16 Aug. 1815), lawyer, was born at Bohemia Ferry, Cecil County, Maryland, the son of Arnold Bassett, a tavernkeeper, and Judith Thompson. Bassett's father left the family, and lawyer Peter Lawson assumed the role of stepfather. In 1755 Lawson inherited thousands of acres of Bohemia Manor from his brother John, whose wife demanded and received a one-third share. Mary Lawson, a cousin of Bassett's mother, gave Bassett and his brother 1,000 acres each in 1765. Bassett was admitted to the Delaware bar in 1770 and moved to Dover, Kent County. He became an expert in property, libel, and inheritance law. In 1774 Bassett married Ann Ennals of Dorchester County, Maryland, and they had two daughters who survived infancy.

In July 1774 Bassett was appointed to the Kent County committee of correspondence, where he represented the conservative wing of the revolutionary movement against Great Britain. When radicals mistreated some conservatives in June 1776, Bassett—captain of a troop of cavalry—plotted but failed to obtain revenge in what became known as "The Black Monday Insurrection." Henceforth his political enemies labeled him a Loyalist, but this did not deter his active pursuit of a political career. Soon after the insurrection, Kent County elected Bassett to the state constitutional convention, where he served on committees for drafting a declaration of rights and a constitution. In October 1776 he was elected to the Legislative Council (upper house) and served until 1780, being reelected in 1777. When the legislature recessed in late 1776, Bassett was on the state Council of Safety. As a legislative councillor, he was on the committee that drafted instructions to the state's Continental Congress delegates concerning ratification of the Articles of Confederation. From 1780 to 1782 Bassett sat in the House of Assembly (lower house).

In 1782 Kent County returned Bassett to the Legislative Council, where he stayed until 1785. Allied with conservative leader George Read, Bassett consistently voted against debtor-relief measures. In 1786 the legislature appointed him to attend the interstate Annapolis Convention, called to consider America's commercial problems. In 1786 and 1787 Bassett sat in the House of Assembly, presenting more bills—many on the judicial system—than any other member. He introduced an act, adopted in 1787, that made it easier to manumit slaves and that gave manumitted slaves some economic and legal rights. He also manumitted his slaves and joined an abolition society.

Politics were not Bassett's only passion. Beginning in the late 1770s he became immersed in Methodism, the schismatic evangelical faith of his wife's family. He was a good friend of Francis Asbury, the great Methodist itinerant (later bishop), who along with other itinerants and bishops frequently visited him. Bassett's conversion experience occurred in the early 1780s. "A very fashionable" man before converting, he became a "religious enthusiast" who "lived plainly, without display or extravagance" (Williams, p. 150). In 1784 Bassett contributed $2,000 to the erection of Dover's Wesley Chapel.

In early 1787 the Delaware legislature appointed Bassett a delegate to the Constitutional Convention, which had been summoned to revise and amend the Articles of Confederation. Bassett attended but did not speak. It is known, however, that he voted against giving Congress an absolute veto over state laws. He signed the Constitution in September and voted to ratify it in the Delaware ratifying convention in December.

In October 1788 the Delaware legislature elected Bassett to the U.S. Senate. Bassett, who drew a four-year term (1789–1793), served on the select committee that drafted the Senate's rules. Dependent for counsel on fellow senator George Read, he was active in debate, especially on the Judiciary Act (1789), and he was part of a group of Senate Federalists who were disparagingly dubbed "the Lawyers." Bassett supported a strong judiciary and the rights of small states, while he opposed the assumption of state debts.

Bassett was a member of the Delaware constitutional convention of 1791–1792 to revise and amend the state constitution. Along with other conservative Federalists, he favored legislative supremacy and a government dominated by propertied men. Bassett remained interested in the judiciary, particularly the independence of judges, and he presented a motion, which failed, calling for the elimination of slavery through gradual emancipation.

Bassett's wealth increased in 1792 when he received Peter Lawson's share of Bohemia Manor following Lawson's death. The next year Bassett purchased more manor land, bringing his holdings to about 6,000 acres. Soon thereafter, he moved into the manor's great mansion. (Around 1813 he also bought a home in Wilmington.) In September 1793 he was commissioned chief justice of Delaware's Court of Common Pleas. His daughter married his protégé James A. Bayard in 1795, and the next year Bassett himself married Betsy Garnett of Talbot County, Maryland, his first wife having died several years earlier. He was elected

Delaware governor in late 1798. Bassett removed many Republicans from office, advocated the construction of a canal joining the Delaware River and the Chesapeake Bay, and encouraged criminal code revision and the erection of a prison.

In February 1801 Bassett resigned as governor upon learning that President John Adams, for whom he was a presidential elector in 1796, had appointed him a judge of the Third Circuit under the Judiciary Act of 1801. Bassett's son-in-law, a Delaware congressman, had actively lobbied for Bassett's appointment. A "midnight judge," Bassett did not hold office for long; in 1802 a Republican Congress repealed the Judiciary Act and removed the judges. Bassett was the only judge to protest publicly. In August 1802 the *Gazette of the United States* printed his protest, which appeared soon thereafter as a fifty-page pamphlet. The repeal, Bassett charged, struck at "a great *political principle*," the independence of judges; it also violated another grand axiom, the separation of powers.

Bassett devoted his remaining years to Methodism. He often attended camp meetings and sponsored two of them on Bohemia Manor. Famed Methodist itinerant Freeborn Garrettson noted: "Good Mr. Bassett seems taken up with divine things." Bassett died at his manor mansion.

• The papers of Richard Bassett are not extant. *The Protest of the Hon. Richard Bassett . . .* (1802) gives insights into his constitutional and legal philosophy. The fullest biographies are Robert E. Pattison, "The Life and Character of Richard Bassett," *Papers of the Historical Society of Delaware* 29 (1900); and Roger A. Martin, *A History of Delaware Through Its Governors, 1776–1984* (1984), pp. 80–89. For Bassett's political career, see John A. Munroe, *Federalist Delaware, 1775–1815* (1954); the published records of Delaware's Legislative Council, House of Assembly, and constitutional conventions of 1776 and 1790–1792; and William Charles diGiacomantonio et al., eds., *Documentary History of the First Federal Congress . . .* , vol. 14 (1995). For his Methodism, see John Lednum, *A History of the Rise of Methodism in America . . .* (1859), pp. 272–78; *The Journal and Letters of Francis Asbury*, ed. Elmer T. Clark et al. (3 vols., 1958); and William Henry Williams, *The Garden of American Methodism: The Delmarva Peninsula, 1769–1820* (1984). For Bohemia Manor, founded in 1661 by Augustine Herman, see George Johnston, *History of Cecil County, Maryland . . .* (1881).

GASPARE J. SALADINO

BASSO, Hamilton (5 Sept. 1904–13 May 1964), novelist, was born Joseph Hamilton Basso in New Orleans, the son of Dominick Basso, owner of a small shoe factory, and Louise Calamari, both of Italian descent. Growing up in New Orleans, Basso attended Colton Grammar School and Easton High School. In 1922 he entered Tulane University to study law. Finding himself more interested in history and literature than law, he became friends with a number of writers and intellectuals associated with the literary periodical the *Double Dealer*, including William Faulkner, Sherwood Anderson, and Roark Bradford.

In 1926, during his senior year, Basso dropped out of Tulane to work as a newspaper reporter. After a year in New York, he returned to New Orleans, where he worked, successively, for the *Tribune*, the *Item*, and the *Times-Picayune*. Autobiographical in nature, his first novel, *Relics and Angels*, was published in 1929. Its central character, Tony Clezac, a young man who leaves the North for his southern home, is the prototype of a character to which Basso returned again and again. On 2 June 1930 Basso married Etolia Simmons; they would have one son. In 1932 the Bassos moved to Pisgah Forest in western North Carolina, where they lived periodically until the early 1940s. There, Basso completed a biography of Confederate general P. G. T. Beauregard. Published in 1933 as *Beauregard: The Great Creole*, it was well received by the critics.

A story of the Civil War and Reconstruction set in Louisiana, Basso's second novel, *Cinnamon Seed*, was published in 1934. Demonstrating Basso's realistic bent and liberal point of view, it shows how relationships from the past influence those of the present and introduces the southern person of mixed blood, a character who would be seen again in some of the author's later novels. The Bassos wintered in Aiken, South Carolina, in 1934, and in his 1935 novel, *In Their Own Image*, Basso contrasted the lives of the resort town's inhabitants with those of wealthy vacationers from the North. Nevertheless, *In Their Own Image* is not a "southern" novel; its portraits of European and American characters highlight differences in manners and social relationships.

In 1935 Basso became an associate editor of the *New Republic*, to which he would contribute articles and book reviews, many of them on southern social problems, including conditions in the region's textile mills and racial injustice as exemplified in the Scottsboro case. Basso published his first commercially successful novel, *Courthouse Square*, in 1936. This novel also received high critical praise and established Basso as an important young southern writer. It focuses on a sensitive young southern novelist who has written critically about his native region. Leaving the *New Republic* in 1937, Basso went back to western North Carolina, where he renewed ties with his friend and fellow novelist Thomas Wolfe. But soon Basso and his wife were traveling again, to Italy and then to southern France in 1938.

Basso's *Days before Lent* (1939) confirmed his growing reputation as a writer of integrity, keen intellect, and stylistic accomplishment. Set in New Orleans on the eve of Mardi Gras, it combined Basso's penchant for realism with a treatment of serious contemporary issues such as environmental concerns and the importance of preventive medicine. A popular and critical success, it received the Southern Authors Award for 1940. The following year, the Bassos lived in Charlottesville, Virginia, and Hadley, Massachusetts. *Wine of the Country*, published in 1941, contrasts the coastal country of South Carolina with various locales in Massachusetts, while tracing the efforts of a young southern intellectual to make his way in the world. Appearing in 1942, Basso's next novel, *Sun in Capri-*

corn, deals with the life and times of Huey Long. It is not one of Basso's best works; though he knew Long's demagoguery well, he failed to provide the broad view necessary to portray fully a figure as complex as Long.

The Bassos moved to New York City in 1942 and then to a country home in Weston, Connecticut, the following year. Basso's literary friends at this time included Van Wyck Brooks, Matthew Josephson, Malcolm Cowley, and John Hersey. Basso was a contributing editor of *Time* magazine in 1942 and 1943 before becoming an associate editor at the *New Yorker*, to which he regularly contributed articles, biographical profiles, short fiction, and book reviews until the 1960s. In 1948, Basso provided an introduction to *The World from Jackson Square*, a collection of writings about New Orleans edited by his wife. Basso spent much of his time during the 1940s as a professional journalist, and seven years passed before his next novel, *The Greenroom*, based loosely on his prewar experiences in southern France, was published in 1949.

In 1952, Basso provided an introduction for his own abridged edition of an 1853 work by William Lewis Herndon, *Exploration of the Valley of the Amazon*. The same year, a film version of *Days before Lent* appeared under the title *Holiday for Sinners*. In 1954, Basso published *The View from Pompey's Head*, which became his first best-seller. A Literary Guild selection, it sold 75,000 copies in hardback. Employing the common theme of returning home, it brings together two settings that Basso knew well, a small city in the South and New York's publishing world. A film version of the novel was released in 1955. Elected to the National Institute of Arts and Letters in 1955, Basso was chosen in 1957 to serve as the institute's vice president.

Drawing upon Basso's considerable knowledge of southern history, *The Light Infantry Ball* (1959), the second novel in a projected but never completed trilogy about Pompey's Head, is a realistic treatment of a small southern town during the Civil War. In 1960, Basso worked on an unfinished novel about Tahiti and published a volume of travel sketches, *A Quota of Seaweed*. The following year, he left the *New Yorker*. When his friend William Faulkner died in 1962, he eulogized him in the pages of the *Saturday Review*. Basso's *Touch of the Dragon* (1964), a novel set in the Midwest, was completed while he was suffering from cancer. He died in New Haven, Connecticut.

Hamilton Basso was a southern novelist by background, development, and literary temperament. As much of his work demonstrates, he remained a realist who valued his native South as a distinct and separate part of the United States while also recognizing its shortcomings, such as a preoccupation with its tragic past.

• Basso's correspondence and manuscripts are in Yale University's Beinecke Library. Biographical information and critical material dealing with Basso's life and work can be found in James E. Rocks, "Hamilton Basso and the World View from Pompey's Head," *South Atlantic Quarterly* 71 (Summer 1972): 326–41; Clarence F. Ikerd, "Hamilton Basso: A Critical Portrait" (Ph.D. diss., Univ. of North Carolina, Chapel Hill, 1974); and Joseph R. Millichap, *Hamilton Basso* (1979). Obituaries are in the *New York Times*, 14 May 1964, and the *Illustrated London News*, 23 May 1964.

L. MOODY SIMMS, JR.

BATCHELDER, Alice Coleman (1874–17 June 1948), arts administrator and pianist, was born in Beatrice, Nebraska, the daughter of Theodore Coleman, a newspaperman, and Jennie (maiden name unknown). (She was to acquire the name Batchelder through marriage when she was thirty-nine.) During her childhood her family moved from Beatrice to Washington, D.C., then to Santa Clara, California, and finally to Pasadena, California, where her father served as city editor of the *Pasadena Star* and secretary for Throop Polytechnic Institute (later the California Institute of Technology) and where her mother was a teacher. Batchelder took organ lessons with English-born Mr. Dunster, organist at the First Presbyterian Church, and replaced him in that position when he returned to his home country. In 1894 she headed to Boston for more music training, and she studied piano and organ for two years with Benjamin Johnson Lang, who enjoyed a reputation as one of the most talented and versatile musicians of his day. Batchelder stayed in Boston for ten years; she accompanied the Cecilia Society Chorus, which Lang conducted; acted as substitute organist for the old King's Chapel when Lang was unavailable; taught piano pupils in Boston and nearby Providence, Rhode Island; and performed. Her piano recitals won rave reviews from critics in the Boston *Transcript* and *Herald*.

For unexplained reasons Batchelder returned to Pasadena in 1904, despite the fact that her teacher reportedly found her ready to appear as a soloist with the Boston Symphony Orchestra. In California she threw herself into Pasadena's musical life, giving piano lessons and playing organ at the First Methodist Church and later at the First Church of Christ, Scientist, which she then joined. Determined to maintain her concert career, she gave recitals and duet programs with her sister Sarah Coleman Bragdon, a composer. Batchelder soon launched a series of chamber music concerts, the Coleman Concerts, employing the Krauss Quartet, which consisted of string players from the Los Angeles Symphony Orchestra, including concertmaster Arnold Krauss. Batchelder performed regularly with the quartet, playing quintets by Schumann, Franck, Charles Widor, Beethoven, and Christian Sinding.

In July 1906 Batchelder and her mother traveled to Europe, where she continued her music studies for sixteen months. They lived in Berlin with her cousin Jessie Gregg Kelley and Jessie's husband, composer Edgar Stillman Kelley. She studied composition with Edgar Kelley and with composers Xavier Scharwenka and Fräulein Schwartz and took piano lessons with renowned pianist Harold Bauer in Paris for three and a half months. Batchelder returned to California and continued recruiting performers, donors, and audi-

ences for her chamber music series, still performing when needed. This Coleman Chamber Music Concert Series in Pasadena, California, is generally credited with being the oldest enduring chamber music series in the United States. Her activities during this time included teaching privately, accompanying California artists, supporting the building of a city auditorium and civic orchestra, initiating music programs for schoolchildren, and attending meetings of the Brahms Club. In 1912 she married Ernest Allen Batchelder, a well-known designer of the ceramic tiles that decorated the Arts and Crafts–style homes, public buildings, and fountains of southern California. The couple had one child.

From 1915 to 1921 the Coleman Concerts were offered under the aegis of the Pasadena Music and Art Association, but the series then regained its independent status. During the twenties, as more and more world-class artists visited California, it became possible for the series to increase the number of concerts each winter from three to eight and to showcase such impressive talents as the London String Quartet, the Mischa Elman Quartet, and the Flonzaly Quartet. In 1928 the chamber music concert series found a permanent home in the Pasadena Community Playhouse, where the concerts were held until 1965, at which time the organization moved to Beckman Auditorium at the California Institute of Technology. In 1932 the Coleman Concerts incorporated and in 1946 established a competition to recognize new talent among ensemble performers. Batchelder last performed with the series on 5 March 1939. She died in Pasadena, having served tirelessly to fundraise, promote, and improve the quality of the concert series that bore her name. Her life was devoted to shaping and securing a valuable and enduring institution in California's musical life.

• Files on Batchelder's life and work can be found at the Pasadena Historical Society, the Centennial Room of the Pasadena Public Library, and the Coleman Concerts Office in Pasadena. Batchelder is the author of *The Coleman Chamber Concerts, 1904–1944* (1944). See also William L. Blair, *Pasadena Community Book* (1943). An obituary is in the Pasadena *Star-News*, 18 June 1948.

KAREN J. BLAIR

BATE, Humphrey (25 May 1875–12 June 1936), bandleader, harmonica player, and physician, was born in Castalian Springs, Tennessee, the son of a local physician. His parents' names are unknown. A graduate of Vanderbilt University School of Medicine, Bate took over his father's practice and traveled the circuit in Sumner County, just north of Nashville. As a hobby he organized and led a string band that eventually became the first such group to appear on the pioneer country radio show the "Grand Ole Opry." His band is considered by historians to be one of the finest and most authentic of the old-time performing groups, and for years it was the cornerstone of the "Grand Ole Opry."

As a boy growing up in rural Tennessee in the 1880s, Bate listened to a variety of music but was especially fascinated with the tunes and songs that he heard from former slaves who worked on his father's farm. Songs that they played on the fiddle and banjo he adapted to the harmonica, including pieces like "Old Joe" and "Take Your Foot out of the Mud and Put It in the Sand," which he later recorded. Such songs, augmented by other old Civil War songs, fiddle tunes, vaudeville tunes, popular sheet music, and even Hawaiian songs, gave Bate a highly original and distinctive repertoire. As a teenager he would play his harmonica on the excursion boats that steamed up and down the Cumberland River, which ran near his home. This exposed him to an even greater variety of music, including ragtime, jazz, and black folk music.

Bate graduated from medical school just prior to the outbreak of the Spanish-American War, and he enlisted to serve in the medical corps during that conflict. Turning down offers to practice in larger cities, he chose to return home and become a country doctor. By the turn of the century he had formed his first band, Dr. Bate's Augmented String Orchestra, a large unit that included fiddle, banjo, guitar, harmonica, and cello—the latter occasionally used as a makeshift bass in rural string bands of the area. The band was so popular that by World War I Bate had created several auxillary bands to meet the demand in the area. He even began to play light classical music and Sousa marches for certain socials and for intermission music at theaters for silent movies. By the early 1920s his daughter Alcyone (born c. 1912) was playing piano in some of his bands.

Bate was acquainted with Nashville's Craig family, who owned the National Life and Accident Insurance Company and who started WSM radio station in 1925. Even before the station took to the air, they asked Bate and his band to perform. When WSM's opening was delayed, a rival station, WDAD, went on the air first and Bate performed on it. He thus became the first person to play country music on the radio in Nashville—several months before George D. Hay came to town and the WSM "Grand Ole Opry" was officially founded. On 20 December 1925 the *Nashville Tennessean* ran a photo of Bate's band, indicating that the group was already well established as radio favorites in the area; it also became the first published photo of any early "Opry" performer.

In January 1926, when WSM started a formal Saturday night "barn dance" show, Bate began a regular stint on the program, one that would last until his death. He routinely opened the show at 8:00 PM with "There'll Be a Hot Time in the Old Town Tonight." Early members of the band included Oscar Stone and Bill Barret (fiddles), Walter Ligget (banjo), Staley Walton and Burt Hutcherson (guitars), Alcyone Bate (piano and ukelele), and Oscar Albright (bowed string bass). In later years Bate's younger son "Buster" joined the band, playing guitar. Bate, of course, played harmonica (sometimes doubling it with the fiddle lead) and occasionally sang. Not long after the band started on WSM, program director Hay decided to give all the bands colorful "hayseed" names that

would help him publicize the show. Bate's orchestra became the Possum Hunters, and the station insisted they dress in overalls and rustic hats and boots for publicity photos. On one noteworthy occasion, the band was posed in a cornfield with Bate holding a hound dog—something that embarrassed all the musicians.

In 1928 the band traveled to Atlanta (Nashville was not yet a center for recording) to record for the Brunswick-Vocalion record company. This was to be the only time the original Possum Hunters recorded, and these twelve sides are considered classics of their genre. They included old favorites like "Old Joe" and "Ham Beats All Meat," as well as rare fiddle tunes like "Greenback Dollar," "Eighth of January," and "Throw the Old Cow over the Fence." There were comic songs like "My Wife Died on Saturday Night" and "How Many Biscuits Can You Eat" (which later became a theme song for a WSM bluegrass show). During the 1930s the band toured widely, through the South and up into the Midwest, with Uncle Dave Macon and other "Opry" stars. By now Bate's health was starting to fail, but he refused to curtail his activities; "it is my wish to die in the harness," he explained.

The end came as Bate felt his own pulse and announced he had not long to live. He died in Castalian Springs. His funeral services were held on the front yard of his family home, with hundreds of fans and former patients paying their respects. "We have lost the Dean of the 'Opry,'" Hay announced on the show, and historians have since confirmed how accurate that was. Though often overshadowed by more colorful figures like Uncle Jimmy Thompson or Uncle Dave Macon, Bate was in many ways the true founder of the "Opry." His band, the Possum Hunters, stayed on the show with varying personnel into the 1970s.

• Though Bate is mentioned briefly in most of the many histories of country music and the "Grand Ole Opry," the most detailed account of his life, drawn on lengthy interviews with his daughter Alcyone, is Charles Wolfe's *Grand Ole Opry: The Early Years* (1975). Though some of his individual 1928 recordings have appeared on reissue anthologies on both CD and LP, there has been no one comprehensive collection of them.

CHARLES K. WOLFE

BATE, William Brimage (7 Oct. 1826–9 Mar. 1905), Confederate general, governor, and U.S. senator, was born in Bledsoe's Lick (now Castalian Springs), Sumner County, Tennessee, the son of James Henry Bate and Amanda Weathered, planters. William Bate received the rudiments of education at a local school, later named the Rural Academy, which he attended until age sixteen. At that time, 1842, his father died, and Bate took a job as a clerk on the steamboat *Saladin*, which traveled between Nashville and New Orleans. When the Mexican War began, he enlisted as a private in a Louisiana regiment at New Orleans, and some sources allege he was the first Tennessean to reach Mexico. He completed the Mexican War as a first lieutenant in the Third Tennessee Volunteer Infantry.

Returning to Tennessee, Bate settled in Gallatin, where he started a Democratic newspaper, the *Tenth Legion*, and successfully ran for a seat in the state house. After serving one term, 1849–1851, he studied law for one year in the Lebanon Law School (now Cumberland Law School), graduating in 1852. Bate practiced law for two years before being elected attorney general for the Nashville District, a six-year position. In 1856 he married Julie Peete; their marriage produced four children.

An ardent Democrat, Bate was nominated for Congress in the late 1850s but refused the nomination. In 1860 he supported the southern Democratic candidate, John C. Breckenridge, and served as an elector for Breckenridge. Bate followed his state into secession in 1861, enlisting as a private in the Confederate army, Second Tennessee Volunteer Regiment. He quickly rose to the rank of captain and then colonel. Bate saw his first major action at the battle of Shiloh, where his leg was broken by a Minié ball. On 3 October 1862, while still recovering, he was promoted to brigadier general, and he was back in the field by February 1863. He saw further action in the Tullahoma campaign and at Chickamauga, and he served as a division commander at Missionary Ridge. On 23 February 1864 Bate received his last promotion, to major general. He experienced further combat and became noted for his leadership abilities at the battle of Resaca and in the Atlanta campaign. His front-line service with the Army of Tennessee continued at the battles of Franklin and Nashville. In early 1865, with the remnants of his command, he retreated into North Carolina, eventually surrendering at Greensboro with General Joseph E. Johnson. Over the course of his military service, Bate was wounded three times and reportedly had six horses killed underneath him. In June 1863 he declined the nomination for the governorship of Tennessee, saying that while an armed force threatened Tennessee, he would rather defend his state than govern it. Bate's refusal of the governorship brought him high praise and notoriety back home. He may have realized that by foregoing the nomination, if he survived the war, the governorship would be his for the asking later.

After being paroled, Bate returned to Gallatin and resumed the practice of law while maintaining an interest in state politics. Disenfranchised during Reconstruction because of his Confederate service, he nevertheless worked for the Democratic party in a number of ways. In 1868 he attended the Democratic National Convention, and in 1876 he served as an elector for Samuel J. Tilden while also serving on the Democratic Executive Committee for Tennessee. In 1875 Bate missed election to the U.S. Senate by one vote in the state legislature, losing to ex-president and former governor Andrew Johnson.

In 1882 Bate ran for governor as a low-tax Democrat, a label adopted by the state Democratic party signifying its commitment to fiscal prudence, against incumbent Republican governor Alvin Hawkins, a greenbacker; John R. Beasley; and J. H. Fussell, a "state credit Democrat," a splinter of the Democratic party. Bate defeated his opposition to become Tennessee's twenty-sixth governor and was reelected in 1884. His term is particularly remembered for his administration's repudiation of some of the state's debt. Prior to Bate, Hawkins had authorized a series of internal improvements, which were approved by the legislature and benefited the Republican-owned railroads in the state. These debts Bate repudiated. He also saw to the establishment of a state railroad commission to oversee and regulate the lines in Tennessee. In January 1887 Tennessee's legislature elected Bate to the U.S. Senate, where he joined a bloc of former Confederates in defending their region and in attempting to reverse Reconstruction era legislation. On 8 August 1893 Bate introduced legislation that repealed the supervision of state elections by special federal deputies, the last remaining Reconstruction oversight of state elections provided for under the 1867 Reconstruction Acts. His bill became law on 8 February 1894.

Bate was reelected three times to the Senate, serving on a variety of committees, such as Military Affairs, and chairing the Committee on the Improvement of the Mississippi River and Its Tributaries. At the start of his fourth term as senator, Bate attended the inauguration of President Theodore Roosevelt (1858–1919), where he caught a cold that developed into pneumonia. He died in Washington, D.C.

During the war, on 9 October 1863 then Brigadier General William B. Bate, C.S.A., was moved to near poetry in the closing remarks of his after-action report on the battle of Chickamauga Creek. "While the 'River of Death' shall float its sluggish current to the beautiful Tennessee," he penned, "and the night wind chant its solemn dirges over their soldiers graves, their names, enshrined in the hearts of their countrymen, will be held in grateful remembrance as the champions and defenders of their country who had sealed their devotion with their blood on one of the most glorious battle-fields of our revolution." This eloquent statement captures Bate's intense pride in his southern heritage as well as his commitment to the South generally and Tennessee in particular. Bate spent his life in the service of his region and his state and their people.

• Bate's papers have not been collected, although some of his correspondence can be found in scattered manuscript holdings such as the Fergusson Family Papers, the Samuel H. Stout Papers, the Robert H. Cartmell Papers, the George Washington Gordon Papers, the Wynne Family Papers, and the James Douglas Anderson Papers, all in the Tennessee State Library and Archives, Nashville. Bate's own writings and speeches can be found most easily in two places: *The War of the Rebellion: A Compilation of the Official Records of the Union and Confederate Armies*, ser. 1, vol. 30, pt. 2 (128 vols., 1880–1901); and the *Congressional Record*. Park Marshall, *A Life of William Bate: Citizen, Soldier, Statesman* (1908), remains the only biography of Bate, but it must be used carefully. Biographical information can be gleaned from *Biographical Directory of the U.S. Congresses, 1774–1989* (1989); Clement A. Evans, ed., *Confederate Military History*, vol. 8 (1899); Ezra J. Warner, *Generals in Grey: Lives of Confederate Commanders* (1959); and Joseph E. Kallenbach and Jessamine S. Kallenbach, *American State Governors, 1776–1976*, vol. 3 (1982). For a recent assessment of Bate as a military commander, see James Lee McDonough, *Chattanooga—A Death Grip on the Confederacy* (1984). An obituary is in the *New York Times*, 10 Mar. 1905.

THOMAS C. MACKEY

BATEMAN, Harry (29 May 1882–21 Jan. 1946), mathematical physicist, was born in Manchester, England, the son of Samuel Bateman, a pharmaceutical chemist, and Marnie Elizabeth Bond. Bateman attended Trinity College of Cambridge University, from which he earned on the Mathematical Tripos examination his B.A. in 1903 as senior wrangler and an M.A. in 1906.

After a year spent studying in Paris and in Göttingen he held several positions as a lecturer and tutor of mathematics at Liverpool University, Manchester University, and Bryn Mawr College. His term there coincided with that of another British mathematician, Charlotte Angas Scott. In 1912, at the end of his time at Bryn Mawr, Bateman received a fellowship to study at the Johns Hopkins University, where, under Frank Morley, he earned a Ph.D. in physics in 1913 for his dissertation, "The Quartic Curve and Its Inscribed Configurations." By this time he had published more than sixty papers, many in prominent research journals. Bateman had married Ethel Horner Dodd in 1912, with whom he had a son who died in childhood and an adopted daughter. He stayed at Johns Hopkins as a lecturer until 1917, during which time he also held jobs at the Bureau of Standards, Mount Saint Agnes College, the Weather Bureau, and the Department of Terrestrial Magnetism. In 1917 Throop College (later the California Institute of Technology) in Pasadena, California, hired Bateman as a professor of mathematics, theoretical physics, and aeronautics. He held this position until his death.

During his studies and career, Bateman displayed a wide range of mathematical interests, from geometry to integral equations. He had encountered this last subject while studying in Göttingen, in the work of the German mathematician David Hilbert. Bateman applied his ideas in this area to the problem of determining the velocity of earthquake waves at interior points of the earth. He later wrote "Report on the History and Present State of the Theory of Integral Equations" (1910) for the British Association for the Advancement of Science. Much of his research focused on differential equations and on their applications to mathematical physics. In the early part of his career, investigations into electromagnetic theory formed the background of these studies. Generalizing some ideas of noted physicists H. A. Lorentz and Albert Einstein in 1910, Bateman showed that the group of conformal transformations of four-dimensional space leaves James Clerk Maxwell's electromagnetic equations invariant. In 1915 Bateman published his first book, *The Mathematical Analysis of Electrical and Optical Wave Motion on the Basis of Maxwell's Equations*.

By the 1920s Bateman's applications of differential equations had shifted to hydrodynamics and aeronautics. He wrote 500 pages of a report for a National Research Council committee on viscous fluids and compressible flow in 1932. This report appeared in the *Bulletin of the National Research Council*, a periodical begun in 1919 as part of the NRC's post–World War I efforts to promote and support cooperative research projects. During World War II, as a member of the American Mathematical Society's War Preparedness Committee, Bateman served as the chief consultant on aeronautics.

In addition to these primary areas of study, Bateman frequently published papers in a variety of subjects, including potential theory, elasticity, and mathematical economics. Throughout all of his research, he showed a keen interest in collecting and studying integrals that solve partial differential equations and special functions of mathematical physics. His "Guide to Tables of Bessel Functions," compiled with R. C. Archibald and published in the first volume of *Mathematical Tables and Other Aids to Computation* (1944), grew out of this interest. He displayed an extensive knowledge of and memory for the relevant literature, keeping an indexed card catalog of abstracts of all the papers he had read. This thoroughness prompted one obituary writer, F. D. Murnaghan, to comment that Bateman's "books and papers bristle with references which are a veritable mine of useful source material."

Bateman's contributions and talents received formal recognition from several professional organizations. In 1928 he became a fellow of the Royal Society of London. The National Academy of Sciences elected him to membership in 1930. He served as the vice president of the American Mathematical Society in 1935 and gave the society's Gibbs Lecture, on "The Control of an Elastic Fluid," in 1943. Bateman was traveling to New York to receive an award from the Institute of Aeronautical Science when he died on a train near Milford, Utah, from coronary thrombosis.

These accolades provide some indication of the respect Bateman had earned for his research from his fellow scientists. The significance of Bateman's work lay both in his original contributions to mathematical physics and in his collections and summaries of established results and methods in his many books and reports. The breadth of his interests and the extent of his knowledge and memory classify him, in the words of mathematician Arthur Erdélyi, as "one of the principal representatives of a great school of analysts."

• Bateman's papers and correspondence are in the Archives of the California Institute of Technology. His dissertation appeared in *American Journal of Mathematics* 36 (1914): 357–86, while his summary of the current theory of integral equations was published in *British Association for the Advancement of Science* 80 (1910): 345–424. The report for the NRC committee appeared as "Hydrodynamics," *Bulletin of the National Research Council* 84 (1932): 89–634. The Office of Naval Research sponsored the Bateman Manuscript Project, which resulted in the collection of his unfinished manuscripts in the form of Arthur Erdélyi, ed., *Higher Transcendental Functions* (1953–1955) and *Tables of Integral Transforms* (1954). For a list of Bateman's other publications, see Erdélyi, "Harry

Bateman, 1882–1946," *Obituary Notices of Fellows of the Royal Society* 5 (1947): 591–618, and F. D. Murnaghan, "Harry Bateman," *Bulletin of the American Mathematical Society* 54 (1948): 88–103. An obituary is in the *New York Times*, 24 Jan. 1946.

PATTI WILGER HUNTER

BATEMAN, Kate Josephine (7 Oct. 1842–8 Apr. 1917), actress, was born in Baltimore, Maryland, the daughter of Hezekiah Linthicum Bateman, an actor and manager, and Sidney Francis Cowell, an actress, playwright, and manager. Kate, along with her talented younger sister Ellen, was introduced to the theatrical world at the age of four, playing in Thomas Morton's *Children in the Wood* in Louisville, Kentucky, on 11 December 1846. At a time when child actors were popular, the Bateman sisters, pushed by the managerial skills of their parents, began to tour the country. For the first few years the duo performed primarily in the Midwest as their parents were members of Noah Ludlow's company in St. Louis and New Orleans. In 1849, however, the Bateman family left New Orleans and headed for New York, the parents devoting most of their time to furthering—some critics say exploiting—their daughters' careers. Kate and Ellen Bateman opened in New York on 10 December 1849 performing excerpts from *The Merchant of Venice* (Kate as Portia, Ellen as Shylock), *Richard III* (Kate as Richmond, Ellen as Richard), and *Macbeth* (Kate as Macbeth, Ellen as Lady Macbeth) along with comical pieces like *The Spoiled Child*, *The Swiss Cottage*, *Little Pickle*, and others.

In 1851 the sisters toured England under the employ of P. T. Barnum. They were favorably received after performing at London's St. James Theatre. Once back in America the Bateman family headed west playing successfully at Catherine Sinclaire's Metropolitan Theatre in San Francisco and other theaters.

As the sisters grew up, however, the novelty of the act wore off, thus in 1856 the Bateman sisters retired. While Ellen Bateman married and never returned to the stage, four years later Kate Bateman began her career as an adult actress. On 19 March 1860 she opened in her mother's adaptation of *Evangeline* at the Winter Garden in New York. No longer regarded as a child star, Bateman began to play the leading lady in roles such as Juliet in *Romeo and Juliet*, Julia in *The Hunchback*, Beatrice in *Much Ado about Nothing*, and Bianca in *Fazio*, playing opposite popular leading men Joseph Jefferson and Edwin Adams.

In 1862 Bateman first appeared in what many critics considered her greatest role: Leah in *Leah the Forsaken*, adapted by Augustin Daly and produced by her father at the Howard Athenaeum Theatre in Boston. The play opened in New York on 19 January 1863 at Niblo's Garden with a supporting cast that included J. W. Wallack, Edwin Adams, and Mrs. Henrietta Chanfrau. A reviewer in the *New York Daily Tribune* on 20 January commented that in this role "many opportunities are afforded for the exhibition of those vehement effects of declamation by which Miss Bateman always appeals most strongly to her audience." Bateman became associated with the role of Leah even while other adaptations of the same German novel were being performed. Following this success Daly became for a short time something of a press agent and manager of her career. After playing Leah in Philadelphia and again in New York, Bateman took the role to London's Adelphi Theatre, opening 1 October 1863. Bateman purchased the rights to Daly's adaptation outright for $225 plus another $225 from an author's benefit she performed on 21 February 1863. Later, Daly and Bateman's father disagreed over the amount, and the New York district attorney A. Oakley Hall filed a case on Daly's behalf against the Batemans. Daly won the case, but Bateman still owned the rights to the play and continued to star in it for thirty years. Daly, however, rewrote the play in 1875 and by calling it *The New Leah* managed to avoid paying royalties to Bateman. This version, unfortunately for Daly, failed in its first week of performances.

In 1866 Bateman married an English physician, George Crowe, and from this time on performed primarily in England. The couple had one child. Her last New York appearance came as Mary Warner in Tom Taylor's play of the same name in 1889, a role written for her and originally performed in England. The *New York Daily Tribune* reported her performance as that of a "true artist."

In 1871 Bateman's father took over the management of London's Lyceum Theatre, whose company included the young Henry Irving. Bateman and her younger sister Isabel both acted opposite Irving at the Lyceum. Kate played Lady Macbeth to Irving's Macbeth in 1875, a production in which both she and Irving were judged inadequate by critics. The Lyceum passed into Irving's control in 1878, and Bateman's mother began managing Sadler's Wells Theatre where Bateman played Helen MacGregor in *Rob Roy* in 1879.

Bateman retired from the stage for a few years, then returned to play in *The American* (1891), *David* (1892), *Colonel Newcome* (1906), *Medea* (1907), and *The Younger Generation* (1912), all in London. She spent most of her life in the theater, and her daughter Sidney and granddaughter Leah Bateman Hunter kept the Bateman family theatrical tradition going: both became successful actresses. Bateman died in London.

Popular in both America and London, Bateman was known for the depth of emotion she put into each role. An obituary in the *New York Times* praised her "force of passion and emotion," which accordingly made her famous portrayals of Leah and Medea "stand out so prominently among the best stage creations of her time." This passion made up for an acting style that was often seen by critics as "cold" and even artificial. On the other hand, a critic for the *New York Daily Tribune* who witnessed her portrayal of Mary Warner reviewed her acting as showing "a deep intuitive knowledge of real mimicry . . . worthy of a true artist." While physical descriptions of Bateman are lacking, a posthumous editorial in the *New York Times* referred to her as a "beauty of the classic type," and publicity photos of her as Leah from the Harvard Theatre Collection show her long brown hair and the large animated eyes Bateman used to portray the emotional characters for which she became famous.

• Although no complete biography of Kate Bateman has been published, there is a brief publicity pamphlet written by Augustin Daly in 1863 titled *A Memoir of Miss Bateman: A Brief Chronicle of the Early Successes and Later Triumphs of the Great American Tragic Artiste.* The Harvard Theatre Collection contains clippings and obituaries from the *New York Daily Tribune* (12 Apr. 1917) and the London *Times* (10 Apr. 1917). G. C. D. Odell, *Annals of the New York Stage* (particularly vols. 5–8), and Joseph Ireland, *Records of the New York Stage* (1867), contain information concerning Kate Bateman's New York performances. Information concerning the Bateman sisters can be found in Joe Cowell, *Thirty Years Passed among the Players in England and America* (1844); Noah Ludlow, *Dramatic Life as I Found It* (1880); Walter Lemen, *Memories of an Old Actor* (1886); T. Allston Brown, *History of the American Stage* (1870); and George C. MacMinn, *The Theatre of the Golden Era in California* (1941). Information regarding her later career is in William C. Young, *Famous Actors and Actresses on the American Stage: Documents of American Theatre History* (1975); William Winter, *Brief Chronicles* (1889), *The Wallet of Time* (1913), and *Vagrant Memories* (1915); and H. Barton Baker, *History of the London Stage and Its Famous Players* (1904). Bateman's life can be viewed throughout the lives of others in Austin Brereton, *The Life of Henry Irving* (1908); Marvin Felheim, *The Theatre of Augustin Daly* (1956); and Joseph Francis Daly, *The Life of Augustin Daly* (1917). An obituary and memorial are in the *New York Times*, 12 and 13 Apr. 1917.

MELISSA VICKERY-BAREFORD

BATES, Barnabas (1785–11 Oct. 1853), reformer and activist, was born in Edmonton, England. Soon after his birth he immigrated to New England with his parents, whose names are not known. Educated for the Baptist ministry, Bates began his career in Hyannis, Massachusetts, in 1808, and then relocated to Bristol, Rhode Island, in 1814. Within a year he became master of the local Masonic lodge, and his sermons began to drift toward Unitarianism. Unhappy with these developments, his small congregation attempted to depose their pastor in 1816, but the coup was only a partial success: Bates lost his salary but kept the church, which remained empty for the next eight years. During this time, Bates parlayed his reputation as an "undeviating Republican" into government appointments as the Bristol postmaster and then as port collector. He used the latter office to thwart the efforts of some reputed local slave smugglers and thereby earned the enmity of Bristol's powerful deWolf family. At the urging of Senator James deWolf, the Senate rejected Bates's 1824 renomination as port collector.

Bates left Bristol and settled in New York City, where he opened a bookstore and began a small weekly journal, *The Christian Inquirer*, to promote "Free Inquiry, Religious Liberty, and Rational Christianity." The venture struggled to turn a profit, and by 1828 Bates had abandoned the press and the pulpit to pursue a career on the platform as an organizer of the Workingmen's party (an anti-Tammany, anti-monop-

oly faction within the New York Democratic party), and as a key figure in the organized opposition to the Sabbatarian movement. Bates contended that Sabbatarianism, which sought to shut post offices on Sundays, was an affront to the equal rights and sanctity of private conscience guaranteed by the U.S. Constitution. He helped weave together a patchwork national constituency of evangelical Baptists, Campbellites, Jews, laborers, merchants, Westerners, and freethinkers, including Orestes Brownson, Frances Wright, and Robert Owen. Bates's antisabbatarian efforts earned him the favor of Tammany Hall and Jacksonian Democrats, and he was rewarded with a position as New York's assistant postmaster between 1833 and 1836.

Bates's commitment to equal rights and unfettered commerce surfaced again in 1835 when he became treasurer of the Equal Rights Party (or "Loco Focos"), a radical antibanking and antimonopoly movement that broke from Tammany. His involvement lasted less than a year, and his departure, according to one prominent Loco Foco, deprived the nascent party of a responsible leader who acted "from a delicate, as well as profound sense of propriety." That propriety was, however, not sufficient to maintain the good will of newly elected President Martin Van Buren, and Bates lost his postmastership in 1836.

By the following year, a new cause was in the offing for Bates. In Great Britain Sir Rowland Hill had initiated his campaign for the reduction of postage for letters to the uniform rate of one penny. Bates read Hill's pamphlet and news of the campaign's success with great interest. Within a year, he was promoting a similar proposal to lower American postal rates: "The people of this country," Bates asserted "will never consent to see the subjects of Queen Victoria have cheaper postage and enjoy greater privileges than themselves."

In 1840 Bates published what he later claimed as the first argument for a comprehensive system of rate reduction in America, and he organized public meetings and petition drives for cheap postage. His proposals gained wide support but encountered stiff opposition from postal authorities. Such opposition was eventually overcome with the Post Office Act of 1845, which reduced letter postage to five cents an ounce on distances not exceeding 300 miles. The lower rates were, however, offset by rate increases for farther-traveled and ocean-bound letters. The shortcomings of the 1845 act encouraged Bates to expand his campaign by organizing the New York Cheap Postage Association in 1848 and publishing a widely read pamphlet, *A Brief Statement of the Exertions of the Friends of Cheap Postage in the City of New York*. With the passage of the Post Office Act of 1851, rates were further reduced to three cents a half-ounce for distances under 3,000 miles. Despite this, Bates vowed to continue traveling, speaking out, and organizing for lower rates. He died in 1853 while engaged in this effort in Boston.

In an age of electronic media, it may be difficult to appreciate the central role the postal system played in the social and political life of nineteenth-century

America, or to sense the urgency with which reformers such as Barnabas Bates worked to defend and expand postal operations. Bates's life and thought demonstrate how various strands of evangelical Christianity, enlightenment rationalism, and egalitarianism underwrote this commitment to the diffusion of information. His liberal faith that "the cheap diffusion of knowledge" would "break down the sectional jealousies and prejudices, preserve our political union and free institutions, and elevate and enlighten the great mass of the people" would be severely tested in the years following his death, but the institutional reforms that he helped secure would nevertheless make the continued expansion of public communication possible.

• Published writings of Bates include articles in his *Christian Inquirer* (1825–1827), *An Address Delivered at a General Meeting of the Citizens of New York, Held at Tammany Hall, December 28th, 1829, to Express Their Sentiments on the Memorials to Congress to Prevent the Transportation of the Mail and the Opening of the Post Offices on Sunday* (1830), and "Post Office Reform—Cheap Postage," *Hunt's Merchant's Magazine* (Mar. 1840). On Bates in Rhode Island, see George Howe, *Mount Hope: A New England Chronicle* (1959). On Bates and the Loco Focos, see Jerome Mushkat, *Tammany: The Evolution of a Political Machine, 1789–1865* (1971), and Fitzwilliam Byrdsall, *The History of the Loco Foco or Equal Rights Party* (1842). On the Federal Postal Service and postal reform, see Richard John, *Spreading the News: The American Postal System from Franklin to Morse* (1995). An obituary is in the *New York Tribune*, 12 Oct. 1853.

MARK G. SCHMELLER

BATES, Blanche (5 Aug. 1873?–25 Dec. 1941), actress, was born in Portland, Oregon, the daughter of Francis Marion Bates and Eliza Wren, actors, while her parents were on tour. Shortly after Blanche's birth, following a failed effort at managing a stock company, her father took the family on a five-year tour of Australia. After his death there, Blanche's mother returned to San Francisco with Blanche and a younger daughter to resume her acting career. Blanche was educated locally and was the first girl to graduate from Boys' High School in San Francisco.

At first disdaining an acting career, Blanche trained to become a teacher and was married briefly to Milton F. Davis, an army lieutenant, in 1890. After teaching kindergarten for a few years, in 1894 she accepted an offer from L. R. Stockwell, a theater manager and family friend, to perform a small role in *This Picture and That*, a one-act play by Brander Matthews, which opened in San Francisco.

Having decided to devote herself to an acting career, Bates followed her debut with a variety of roles in California stock companies. After failing to find roles in New York City, she joined T. Daniel Frawley's company in Denver as a leading lady. She toured from Salt Lake City to Portland and in 1895 opened at the newly leased Columbia Theater in San Francisco in Sir Arthur Wing Pinero's *Sweet Lavender*. She toured the West and Hawaii with Frawley's company until 1897, gaining valuable acting experience and creating such

popular roles as Mrs. Hillary in *The Senator*. After a brief engagement in New York City with the Augustin Daly company, appearing as Bianca in *The Taming of the Shrew*, in 1898 she returned to the Baldwin Theater in San Francisco to appear as Nora in the first western production of Henrik Ibsen's controversial *A Doll's House*, which received a flurry of negative reactions. Returning to the Daly company in 1899, she opened as Countess Charkoff in *The Great Ruby* but left the company abruptly, finding it "not congenial."

Under different management, she created the popular role of Miladi in *The Three Musketeers* (1899) and took on the role of Hannah Jacobs in Israel Zingwell's *Children of the Ghetto* (1899), which brought her to the attention of theatrical producer David Belasco. According to one reviewer, Belasco was charmed by her "striking personality." She became a leading lady in Belasco's company, playing the hosiery model, Cora, in the farce *Naughty Anthony* (1900). Belasco then offered her the role of Cho Cho San in *Madame Butterfly*, a performance that won her national fame and a long contract. Subsequently, she played Cigarette in *Under Two Flags*, Ouida's "romance of the French Foreign Legion," which ran for two years, and in 1902 she played Yo-san in *Darling of the Gods*, a Japanese drama by Belasco and John Luther Long, which also had a lengthy run. After touring for a few years, including playing Hedda in Ibsen's *Hedda Gabler* and Katharina in *The Taming of the Shrew* in 1904, she opened in 1905 as Minnie Smith in *The Girl of the Golden West*, her most memorable role. She was perfectly cast as the vivacious, plucky heroine, and the play, though sentimental, enjoyed a three-year run as one of Belasco's most brilliant creations. The long run, following her previous long engagements, impelled Bates to ask Belasco for more modern (and perhaps more challenging) roles. Belasco complied by offering her leads in *The Fighting Hope* (1908) and *Nobody's Widow* (1910), but neither play provided an outlet for the full extent of her acting abilities. After her marriage in 1912 to George Creel, a Denver journalist (and later chairman of the Committee on Public Information during World War I), she left Belasco's company to join the company of Charles Frohman, whose management, however, proved disappointing.

During World War I Bates acted in propaganda skits and plays and made her movie debut in 1918 in *The Border Legion*, an adaptation of a Zane Grey novel, playing a part undoubtedly inspired by her role in *The Girl of the Golden West*. One reviewer wrote, "She rides horses through wild country, shoots a man in a physical struggle and attempts to portray only the elemental emotions consistent with her environment" (*New York Times*, 29 July 1918). Although the reviewer commented that she took "naturally to the screen," a film career did not develop. She was apparently caught in the vise of typecasting, and no managers or film producers had enough vision to consider her for more challenging roles.

Never active in New York City's social circles, Bates devoted much of her time to her private life, her two children, and a farm near Ossining, New York, where she raised horses. Her acting career continued, but she never recaptured the acclaim surrounding her Belasco years. She concentrated her talent and experience on typecast roles such as plucky heroines Stella Ballantyne in *Witness for the Defense* (1913), Lillian Garson in *Half-an-Hour* (1914), Comtesse Zicka in *Diplomacy* (1914), Mrs. Palmer in *Getting Together* (1918), Medea in *Medea* (1919), in Philip Moeller's *Molière* (1919), Nancy Fair in *The Famous Mrs. Fair* (1919), one of the few parts she considered demanding, Karen Aldcroft in *The Changelings* (1923), and Maisie Partridge in *Mrs. Partridge Presents* (1925). After retiring from the stage in 1926, she returned with her husband to San Francisco, appearing once more in 1933 in New York City in a supporting role as Lena Surrege in *The Lake* with Katharine Hepburn.

She died in San Francisco. Despite her vivaciousness, talent, and professionalism, Bates was never able to fully develop as an actress because she was mainly cast in roles chosen by management for their box-office value. Although she performed admirably in plays by Shakespeare and Ibsen, she was trapped by her popularity in the less-demanding vehicles invented by Belasco. Nevertheless, her good looks, vivid personality, and ability to present emotions realistically won her enduring fame as the embodiment of Belasco's "Girl of the Golden West."

• Further information on Blanche Bates can be found in the Robinson Locke Collection of Dramatic Scrapbooks and the clippings file in the New York Public Library Theater Collection, Lincoln Center; Norman Hapgood, *The Stage in America, 1897–1900* (1901); Anthony Slide, ed., *Selected Theater Criticism*, vol. 1 (1895); *Who's Who in the Theater* (1939), which lists her stage credits; and Edward T. James, ed., *Notable American Women*, vol. 1 (1971). An obituary is in the *New York Times*, 26 Dec. 1941.

ELIZABETH R. NELSON

BATES, Edward (4 Sept. 1793–25 Mar. 1869), political leader and attorney general of the United States, was born in Goochland County, Virginia, the son of Thomas Fleming Bates, a planter and merchant, and Caroline Matilda Woodson. A Quaker, Thomas Bates was read out of meeting when he enlisted to fight in the Revolution, from which he emerged deeply in debt. Edward nevertheless grew up surrounded by slaves. After his father died in 1805, Edward received a good education at the home of his cousin Benjamin Bates in Hanover, Maryland, and then at Charlotte Hall Academy in St. Marys County, Maryland.

Bates briefly considered entering the navy as a midshipman but bowed to his mother's opposition. When the British threatened Virginia during the War of 1812, he enlisted in the militia and carried the English Tower musket his father had carried at Yorktown. Mustered out as a sergeant in late 1813, he accepted the invitation of his older brother Frederick, secretary of the Missouri Territory, to join him in St. Louis. Edward Bates read law under Rufus Easton, the most eminent lawyer in Missouri. Admitted to the bar in

1816, Bates soon had several leading St. Louis businessmen and politicians as clients.

Like many young lawyers, Bates aspired to political office. In 1820 Missourians elected him to the state constitutional convention, where he gained favorable attention and, as a result, subsequent appointment as the first attorney general of the state at the age of twenty-seven. He was elected to the state legislature in 1822 and as Missouri's sole representative in the U.S. House of Representatives in 1826. In 1823 he married Julia Coalter, with whom he had seventeen children, eight of whom did not survive early childhood.

A nationalist, a supporter of federal aid to internal improvements, and a proponent of public education, Bates cast his lot with the party of John Quincy Adams and Henry Clay. By 1828, however, the Jacksonians, led by Thomas Hart Benton (1782–1858), commanded a majority in Missouri and defeated Bates's bid for reelection to the House. As a leader of the newly formed Whig party, Bates served several terms in the state legislature during the 1830s, but his ambitions for higher office seemed doomed by Missouri's inveterate Democratic majority. Bates devoted most of his time to his growing law practice and his increasing family. In 1847 he reemerged temporarily to prominence as president of a rivers and harbors improvement convention in Chicago, where he made an eloquent speech favoring internal improvements to promote national unity and western expansion.

The Kansas-Nebraska Act in 1854 propelled Bates back into politics. Although he had grown up in a slaveholding family, he shared with Clay a hope that enlightened slaveholders would eventually commit themselves to the gradual abolition of slavery coupled with colonization of the freed slaves abroad. He sanctioned Congress's power to exclude the institution from the territories and deplored the provision of the Kansas-Nebraska Act repealing the Missouri Compromise's ban on slavery north of 36°30′N. However, Bates shunned the moral fervor of radical free soilers, whom he considered too prominent in the early leadership of the Republican party for him to feel comfortable in that party. For a time he affiliated with the Know Nothings, which aroused the ire of German-Americans in Missouri. Long after the Whig party had died, Bates continued to call himself a Whig. He presided over a corporal's-guard Whig National Convention in 1856, which endorsed the American party nominee Millard Fillmore for president.

By 1860 Bates belatedly recognized that the Whig party was gone forever. He emerged as the presidential candidate of conservative Republicans and of *New York Tribune* editor Horace Greeley, who supported Bates as an alternative to New York's William H. Seward, the favorite for the nomination. Bates's supporters argued that only he could carry the conservative antislavery states of the lower North, essential to Republican victory. Bates's flirtation with nativism and his lukewarm antislavery reputation hurt him among German-Americans and free soilers. He received forty-eight votes on the first ballot at the Republican National Convention (10 percent of the total and far short of the 233 necessary for nomination). Bates's strength eroded on subsequent ballots and Abraham Lincoln was nominated on the third.

The president-elect offered cabinet positions to his four rivals for the nomination, including Bates as attorney general. During the first part of the Civil War, Bates's counsel proved valuable to Lincoln. In 1861 Bates drafted an able opinion justifying the president's suspension of the writ of habeas corpus, which put Bates at odds with Chief Justice Roger B. Taney, who had denied the constitutionality of executive suspension in *ex parte Merryman*. Although Bates questioned the legal validity of a blockade in a conflict formally defined as a domestic insurrection, recommending instead a presidential order closing southern ports, as attorney general he successfully defended in 1863 the seizure of ships under the blockade, helping to win Supreme Court sanction of the blockade's legality.

As the war escalated in scale and scope, however, Bates's border-state conservatism fell out of step with Lincoln's total-war philosophy. Bates deplored the president's proclamation of martial law on 24 September 1862 and the military trials of draft resisters and other antiwar activists. He reluctantly approved the Emancipation Proclamation but opposed the arming of freed slaves along with any steps to grant them equal rights. He disapproved the admission of West Virginia as a separate state because he believed the process had violated constitutional requirements. Bates sided with conservatives in the tangled mesh of factional politics in his home state of Missouri, while Lincoln leaned increasingly toward the radicals.

Bates's own family was a house divided. One son fought in the Union army and another in the Confederate army. Worry, stress, overwork, and frustration with the powerlessness of civil law in a time of civil war perhaps brought on a mild stroke in May 1864. Bates recovered but resigned his office effective 1 December 1864. He expected Lincoln to appoint him chief justice to succeed Taney, who had died on 12 October 1864. When the post went instead to Salmon P. Chase, Bates returned sadly to Missouri. There he fought two more losing battles, opposing the radical state constitution adopted in 1865 because it disfranchised ex-Confederates and authorized the continued exercise of martial law against them, and supporting Andrew Johnson's Reconstruction policy. His deteriorating health led to a peaceful death at home in St. Louis.

During his tenure as attorney general Bates kept a diary, which provides important insights on the Lincoln administration. It also reflects Bates's dislike of Seward, Chase, and Edwin M. Stanton, the strongest members of the cabinet, whose forceful personalities and less conservative policies help to explain why their influence eclipsed that of Bates. The best adjectives to describe the attorney general are competent but colorless. The dynamic, revolutionary escalation of the Civil War left him behind. A remark made at Bates's funeral was appropriate to describe his career after 1862: he "belonged to a generation that had passed away."

• Most of Bates's letters and a diary he kept from 3 June 1846 to 25 Dec. 1852 are in the Missouri Historical Society at St. Louis. Additional papers are in the Western Historical Manuscripts Collection of the State Historical Society of Missouri at the University of Missouri in Columbia. Bates's diary for 20 Apr. 1859 to 30 July 1866 is in the Manuscripts Division of the Library of Congress. This diary has been published by the American Historical Association, Howard K. Beale, ed., *The Diary of Edward Bates, 1859–1866* (1933). The only full biography is Marvin R. Cain, *Lincoln's Attorney General: Edward Bates of Missouri* (1965). Bates's role in the controversy over habeas corpus and other legal issues confronted by the Lincoln administration are discussed in James G. Randall, *Constitutional Problems under Lincoln*, rev. ed. (1951); Harold M. Hyman, *A More Perfect Union: The Impact of the Civil War and Reconstruction on the Constitution* (1973); and Mark E. Neely, Jr., *The Fate of Liberty: Abraham Lincoln and Civil Liberties* (1991).

JAMES M. McPHERSON

BATES, Elisha (10 July 1781–5 Oct. 1861), Quaker controversialist and publisher, was born near Scimino, York County, Virginia, the son of Benjamin Bates and Hannah (maiden name unknown), farmers. Largely self-educated, Bates studied medicine for a time, learned printing, worked as a surveyor, and operated a Quaker school. Marrying Sarah Jordan Harrison in 1803, Bates fathered six children. From 1813 to 1816 he served as clerk of the Virginia Yearly Meeting. Circumstances, even for a farmer, surveyor, and schoolmaster, proved trying for an antislavery Quaker in eastern Virginia, particularly after Bates attracted public attention with his pamphlet *Moral and Political Observations, Addressed to the Enlightened Citizens of Virginia* (1817).

Hence that same year Bates moved with his family to Mount Pleasant, Ohio, and became clerk of the Ohio Yearly Meeting in 1819, a post he held six times in the next thirteen years. He bought a weekly newspaper, *The Philanthropist*, from fellow Quaker Charles Osborn in 1818, moderating its antislavery tone and expanding it to include essays on moral subjects as well as agriculture and mechanical arts; at one time during its five-year life it boasted agents as far away as New York and Virginia. Bates's language was often strong—"slavery," he insisted firmly, "is a violation of moral right"—and he forthrightly rejected the Missouri Compromise. Still, he opposed the colonization of manumitted blacks outside the United States, just as he disagreed with boycotts of goods produced from slave labor, a tactic favored by staunch antislavery Quakers. A moral suasionist on the slavery question, he wanted to convince masters of the peculiar institution's immorality and thus lead them to free their slaves. In 1821 Bates added a monthly, the *Moral Advocate*, to his publishing ventures. It focused on war, capital punishment, prison reform, and dueling, while he tried to organize interdenominational societies to promote his favored reforms. He also published and sold schoolbooks and spellers.

In 1825, his two journals having folded, Bates came into his own as a bulldog of evangelical Quakerism by publishing *The Doctrines of Friends*, which stressed theological similarities between Friends and other Christians; it went through numerous reprintings, including ten in England and Ireland, with one chapter translated into Welsh. The same year he edited some early Quaker writings, *Extracts from the Writings of Early Members of the Society of Friends*, including those that reflected his own evangelical bent. In quieter times his fellow believers might have realized that Bates had staked out a middle ground in the disputes between traditional Quakers, dubbed "Hicksites" by their opponents, and the evangelical or "Orthodox" wing. Aspersions from a Wilmington, Delaware, Hicksite paper, the *Berean*, pushed Bates to emphasize his evangelical side, and in the next decade he would decide to submit to the outward ordinance of water baptism. As he became more controversial, an Ohio opponent unfairly versified about his mien of rectitude, "a phiz that seems to scowl at sin, / oft veils hypocrisy within." The year Philadelphia Quakers split, 1827, he unveiled a new journal, the *Miscellaneous Repository*, which periodically over the next nine years smote the Hicksites as deists. When the Hicksites and evangelicals squared off at the Ohio Yearly Meeting in September 1828, Bates led the Orthodox withdrawal from the Mount Pleasant meetinghouse. The next August he presided over a committee of his Friends that convened in Philadelphia; he likely drew up its *Testimony of the Society of Friends on the Continent of America* (1830) to explain the Orthodox version of the faith.

By this time Bates's evangelical tastes and his reading in early Quaker sources led him to cease accusing the Hicksites of distortion; he began to question the doctrinal soundness of the Society of Friends itself. From 1832 to 1834 and again in 1836 he took his doubts to England. Through research in original documents there, he decided that Quaker founder George Fox's writings did not uphold true Christianity, in particular scriptural authority, the basis of evangelicalism. His presence and influence helped feed the small "Beaconite" secession in the London Yearly Meeting, a cause he stoutly defended in a revitalized *Repository* journal and in *An Appeal to the Society of Friends* (1836). In August 1836 his theological position had come to resemble mainstream Protestantism so much that he decided to follow biblical practice and be baptized, a course Quakers had always rejected as unnecessary. However difficult to apply disownment to a popular giant of the faith such as Bates, it was inevitable and came the following May.

Two years later Bates joined the Methodist church with the status of minister, but he never held a pastorate. In 1845 he founded the short-lived magazine *Evangelical Union* to unite individual evangelicals from other denominations. He went back to London in 1846 as a correspondent of the Pittsburgh conference of his new church. Bates's relations with the Society of Friends warmed sufficiently near the end of his life that when he died in Mount Pleasant, he was interred in the Friends burial ground. His former fellow believers found his abandonment of their practices embarrassing enough for them to ignore the whole of his career, and his contributions were nearly all overlooked and forgotten, even by historians. His career, marked by acrimony and apostasy, forecast more than a little of the Orthodox Quaker future, especially in the Midwest.

• A few of Bates's papers are housed in the Western Reserve Historical Library in Cleveland, Ohio, but the best extant sources for his life are his numerous publications, which—in addition to those mentioned above—include *Reasons for Receiving the Ordinance of Baptism* (1836), *An Address to the Society of Friends* (1836), and *An Examination of Certain Proceedings and Principles of the Society of Friends* (1837). For a biographical study, see Donald G. Good, "Elisha Bates: American Quaker Evangelical in the Early Nineteenth Century" (Ph.D. diss., Univ. of Iowa, 1967). For the Ohio Yearly Meeting, see William Taber, *The Eye of Faith* (1985). H. Larry Ingle puts Bates in his place in *Quakers in Conflict: The Hicksite Reformation* (1986). An account of Bates's last days is in *Friends Review*, 31 Aug. 1861.

H. LARRY INGLE

BATES, Joshua (10 Oct. 1788–24 Sept. 1864), merchant and banker, was born in Weymouth, Massachusetts, the son of Colonel Joshua Bates and Tizrah Pratt. Bates's father served as an officer during the Revolution. Joshua suffered from ill health as a child. He was educated by a private tutor and at the public school. When he was fifteen his father apprenticed him in the counting house of William R. Gray, the son of William Gray, a prominent New England shipowner. The major steps of Bates's early career are clear, but accounts of the precise details differ. At age twenty-one he left Gray and formed a partnership with Captain Beckford, who had previously worked for William Gray. The firm failed during the War of 1812, but Bates had won Gray's confidence and was sent to London in 1816 as Gray's general European agent. Bates handled Gray's business effectively, accumulating a unique knowledge of the leading American merchants and trades. While in France Bates met Peter Caesar Labouchere, senior partner of Hopes of Amsterdam; this eventually led to a partnership with John Baring, son of Sir Thomas Baring. Bates and Baring, with Labouchere's assistance, exploited gaps in the market left by the panic of 1825, and they prospered so well that in 1828 they were absorbed by Baring Brothers (Barings). Simultaneously, nearly all the partners in Barings died or retired, and in 1830 Bates became the managing partner of the most reputable Anglo-American merchant firm.

In the early 1830s Bates and his partners—Thomas "Tom" Baring, the leading family partner; Humphrey St. John Mildmay; John Baring; and Francis Baring—rapidly expanded the firm. Bates specialized in Anglo-American trade and commercial credits, which required tough intelligence and dogged application to push through transactions in a wide variety of commodities including cotton, grain, iron, and tallow, and in services like insurance and shipping. The *Edinburgh*

Review called him in 1833 "perhaps the most extensive, and certainly one of the best informed merchants in the country." Thomas Wren Ward of Boston, Barings's American agent and Bates's friend since youth, wrote him, "I marvel at how much you get through." Together Bates and Ward linked Barings to leading New York merchants such as Jonathan Goodhue, also originally connected with Gray. In addition, in 1813 Bates had married Lucretia Augusta Sturgis, whose family firm, Russell and Sturgis, provided valuable contacts in the Far East; the couple had two children. Russell Sturgis, Lucretia's cousin, became a partner in 1851 and eventually senior partner in 1873. Tom Baring specialized in foreign loans and investments and provided the Baring name and connections, great financial and political insight, and occasional bursts of intense hard work. His talents complemented Bates's, and they worked well together. The other partners took smaller shares of the profits and retired in the 1830s and 1840s. Bates was therefore the most active partner, controlling the most detailed operations, taking the largest share of the profits, and imposing a dour New England prudence.

Bates and Tom Baring not only piloted Barings through the trade and financial crises of the 1830s and 1840s, but also helped stabilize the Anglo-American financial community. The panic of 1837 weakened or destroyed many of their competitors, but Bates had cautiously retrenched before the storm, and the Barings emerged preeminent. They were already London agents for the U.S. government, several American state governments, and the Bank of the United States (BUS). In late 1839 Bates helped support the Bank of England and the BUS through the crisis. He commented in August 1839, "The monetary affairs . . . of England seem . . . chiefly deranged by the operations of the Bank U States and Jaudon [the BUS agent in London] should be stopped. I doubt if it is not a duty to stop him. It is better that he stop than the Bank of England should." And in January 1840 he continued, "It cannot be denied that but for the exertions of my House the Bank of England would have stopped payment as also Jaudon. and Bills on Peabody for a large amo would have gone back to America and the confusion would have been very great. I have now the satisfaction that by a bold & determined course all these evils have been averted, and the Bank [of England] is now in a strong position and it will be its own fault if it goes wrong again" (Diary, 31 Aug. 1839, 7 Jan. 1840). Simultaneously, Ward used the Baring name to prevent the suspension of the leading New York and New England banks.

During the 1840s Bates, working through Ward, persuaded several of the defaulting American state governments to resume interest payments. Bates's visits to the United States in 1841 and 1849 were tours of leading officials, including Presidents John Tyler and Zachary Taylor. In London, each American ambassador, several former or future American presidents, and hundreds of influential Americans either visited him or sought his advice. Most of Bates's energies, however, were absorbed in commercial operations. Barings aimed to import annually 80,000–100,000 bales of cotton during the 1840s and in 1845–1846 and 1855, respectively, undertook huge British and French grain orders to meet Irish and French emergencies. In addition, Bates controlled and financed many of the transatlantic packet lines: "the conviction amongst the Shipmasters and shipowners that we are always ready to assist in case of need brings pretty nearly all the freight money of the United States into our hands and it is the best business we have" (quoted in Hidy, p. 350). In a period of increasing specialization, Bates remained ready to pick up opportunities where presented. For instance, in 1845 he invested in iron mining and manufacturing in Britain, shipping the product to American railroads financed by Barings. In 1859, however, he was persuaded by the senior Liverpool partner that "the management of steamers is a business in itself and with which the less such Houses as ours have to do, the better" (quoted in Ziegler, pp. 167–68).

Bates was socially ambitious, but for a long time he was frustrated by a lack of family connections and social skills. Hence he complained bitterly to his diary in 1836 that Lord Ashburton, the former senior partner, Alexander Baring, only asked him to dinner "when some American is invited, and then my wife is not included, which is very mortifying to her" (Diary, 30 Apr. 1836). Bates himself was awkward but dryly humorous and shrewd. His wife, however, was "audaciously vulgar" and "born in a four roomed log house." He "has a trial in his wife," wrote Ward, "as great as almost any person living" (quoted in Ziegler, p. 124). Bates's breakthrough came when his only daughter Elizabeth (his only son had been accidentally shot earlier, to his very great distress) married Sylvain Van der Weyer, the Belgian ambassador in London. His son-in-law provided Bates with an entrée to the court, and by the late 1840s he was more contented. His huge London mansion near Piccadilly, on the present site of the Ritz, was, according to Ward, who visited in 1853, "Most magnificent, adequate for Royalty itself; the ceilings some 20 or 25 feet high in the drawing rooms; the walls of the rooms all lined with satin damask, and the painting white and gold" (quoted in Ziegler, p. 159). Bates also had a large country house at Sheen, near Richmond Park, where he entertained first Louis Napoleon, the future Napoleon III, and then Louis Philippe, the former king of France. Bates wrote to Ward on his career in some wonder: "I started from Weymouth with $5 in my pocket and have increased it to $4 million. . . . I am on friendly terms with King Leopold and the French Emperor, my Grand Children play with Princes and Princesses" (Queen Victoria and Prince Albert were godparents to his grandchildren, Victoria and Albert). "The world as old Rothschild used to say has been very kind to me" (quoted in Ziegler, p. 160). He became a British citizen in 1842.

Barings increased both their commercial and financial interests during the great international boom of the 1850s. Bates wrote frequently as in 1855 that he was thinking of retiring, but "then Mr Thos Baring will only attend but a short time per day . . . and the new partners . . . have no capital. I cannot therefore withdraw my capital without weakening the house too much and as I have contributed more than anyone else to make the House what it is I feel that while I have any interest in it that it should be kept up and to do so requires a capital of at least one million. . . . I have already more than enough and should retire, but the House is the first in the World and it is great fame to be at the head of it" (Diary, 11 Nov. 1855, 5 Dec. 1855). Bates therefore soldiered on despite increasing ill health and in 1858 noted proudly that Barings were London agents for the governments of Austria, Norway and Russia, Canada, New Brunswick and Nova Scotia, the United States, Chile, Buenos Aires and New Granada, and Australia; held the personal accounts of the emperor of the French and the king of the Belgians; and had 1,200 correspondents worldwide (see Ziegler, p. 164).

Hence, unlike some of the other leading financiers such as Nathan Rothschild, or the senior Barings, Bates had little time for public service. However he successfully arbitrated the disputed cases arising under the Anglo-American Claims Convention of 1853 and, by donating $100,000 in books and cash, in effect founded the Boston Public Library. In 1861 the larger part of Barings's business was still in North America, and Bates was distraught by the outbreak of the Civil War. He and Tom Baring supported the North and permitted the federal government to draw many millions on liberal terms to pay for arms and ironclads at a time when no other European house could or would have done so. By the time of Bates's death in England, the commercial business of the house had shrunk. Tom Baring and the remaining partners survived the loss of Bates's capital by concentrating on finance and amalgamating with another London house.

• Bates's career at Barings can be studied in collections in London, England; Ottawa, Ontario, Canada; and Boston, Mass. The Baring collection at ING-Barings in London is one of the most important business history collections in Britain, holding copies of Bates's private journals (10 vols., 1830–1864), diary, letter press copies of many of his outletters, and correspondence generated by the Bates and Baring partnership, 1826–1828. The Baring collection in the Canadian National Archives was formed when a substantial proportion of the Barings' correspondence relating to Canada and North America were removed to Ottawa in the mid-1920s and never returned. Finally, the Ward Family Collection at the Massachusetts Historical Society in Boston contains Bates's correspondence with Thomas Wren Ward, 1830–1857, and Thomas Ward's diaries, 1828–1855, which occasionally mention Bates.

Several useful books on Barings survey Bates's role in the firm. Ralph W. Hidy, *The House of Baring in American Trade and Finance: English Merchant Bankers at Work, 1763–1861* (1949), is a solid business history but, apart from a brief character sketch, formulaic on the detail of Bates's contribution to the Barings' decisions. Philip Ziegler, *The Sixth Great Power: Barings, 1762–1929* (1988), commissioned by Barings, contains excellent personal observation but less economic analysis. John Orbell, *A History of Baring Brothers to 1939* (1985), is a short but useful study. For Bates's early career, his role in the 1854 Anglo-American claims settlement, and his contribution to the Boston Public Library, see *The Memorial of Joshua Bates from the City of Boston* (1865) and Samuel Gray Ward, *The Ward Family Papers* (1900), pp. 90–92. Stanley Chapman, *The Rise of Merchant Banking* (1984), provides a good survey of British merchant banking, including half a chapter on Barings.

J. R. KILLICK

BATES, Katharine Lee (12 Aug. 1859–28 Mar. 1929), educator and writer, was born in Falmouth, Massachusetts, the daughter of William Bates, a Congregational minister, and Cornelia Frances Lee, a former schoolteacher. When Bates was less than a month old, her father died, leaving the family in straitened circumstances. They remained in Falmouth for a dozen years, then moved to Wellesley, Massachusetts, which would be Bates's home and professional base for the rest of her life. Although the family was unusually education-minded—Bates's paternal grandfather had been president of Middlebury College, and her mother had graduated from Mount Holyoke Seminary (later Mount Holyoke College)—poverty prevented her older brothers from continuing their schooling. Because they contributed to the family's income, however, Bates was able to complete high school and to enroll in the newly established Wellesley College, from which she received her B.A. in 1880.

After five years of teaching at the secondary level in both public and private schools, Bates returned to her alma mater in 1885 as an instructor of English. She remained an active member of the Wellesley faculty for forty years. After periods of study at Oxford and completion of her M.A. at Wellesley, she served as permanent head of the college's English department. Because the college was still very young when she began teaching there, Bates's contributions to women's higher education, to religious and academic freedom at Wellesley, and to curriculum development in her own department were both formative and highly influential. Her teaching reflected a vision of literary scholarship as a support to criticism and appreciation, a view that had an impact on several generations of Wellesley students.

Bates's reputation as a writer, a pursuit in which she engaged for monetary as well as creative rewards, was high in her own lifetime. For some four decades, she published books of poetry, such as *The College Beautiful and Other Poems* (1887) and *America the Beautiful and Other Poems* (1911); criticism and scholarship, including *American Literature* (1898) and *English Religious Drama* (1893); and juvenile literature, such as *Rose and Thorn* (1889) and *Sigurd, Our Golden Collie and Other Comrades of the Road* (1919); and an autobiography that was privately printed after her death. At the time she died, however, the general shift in taste toward stylistic experimentation and the accompanying revolt against the genteel tradition had already marked her work as "dated," paving the way for its future obscurity.

It is both fitting and ironic that Bates is remembered today for a single poem, "America the Beautiful" (1895), which, set to the tune of the hymn "Materna," has become a patriotic song that many prefer to the official national anthem. The poem is representative of her style in its adherence to mainstream nineteenth-century poetic conventions—the line of John Greenleaf Whittier, say, over that of Walt Whitman—and in its paired invocation of natural beauty and spiritual or national brotherhood. But Bates was not uncritically nationalistic. Although her lover, Katharine Coman, and close friends such as her colleague, Vida Scudder, were more committed to Progressive Era activism, the conservative Bates did join a number of organizations for social change. With Coman and Scudder she worked to found in 1890 the College Settlement Association, the first college settlement house based on English models. Her brand of patriotism recognized the flaws in turn-of-the-twentieth-century U.S. society and strove to bring that society into closer conformity with professed American ideals. Indeed, one of the lesser-known verses of "America the Beautiful" replaces "God shed His grace on thee" with "God mend thine every flaw," and Bates was prepared to admit that there was a place in this work of reparation for human effort.

Another irony in her being enshrined in history as the author of "America the Beautiful" is that, however fully American Bates may have felt herself to be, the brotherhood that her hymn celebrates was not prepared to embrace the sisterhood that she lived. Like many of her contemporaries among the first generation of faculty at the eastern women's colleges, Bates constructed and flourished in a community of women who, as colleagues and friends, developed a devoted, long-lasting network. Those who knew her well stressed her personal warmth, her witty sense of fun, and her joy in living, all qualities that were nurtured and expressed within her community of women.

Bates's relationship with Coman, who also taught at Wellesley and who organized the college's economics department, subsisted in the context of this community of women, which was created as an alternative to marriage and children. Bates and Coman were a couple from 1890 until Coman's death in 1915. They lived together for most of this time, eventually helping to plan and build a house of their own, "The Scarab," where Bates remained until her own death. The years of their partnership were at the core of Bates's dual career as educator and writer. Their relationship and Bates's loss informed the volume that is arguably Bates's strongest collection of poems, *Yellow Clover: A Book of Remembrance* (1922), which Judith Schwartz described as "one of the most anguished memorials to the love and comradeship between two women that has ever been written" (p. 59). The Clover Club, a social organization of lesbian faculty and staff at Wellesley, was later formed as a tribute to Bates's work. She retired from teaching in 1925 and was professor emeritus at Wellesley until her death. Her life was marked by bouts of ill health, caused by a weak heart, and she died of pneumonia at her Wellesley home.

• The Wellesley College Archives house Bates's papers and correspondence. Among her major works not mentioned in the text are two edited volumes: *Old English Ballads* (1890) and *English History as Told by English Poets*, with Katharine Coman (1902); *Hermit Island* (1890); *Spanish Highways and Byways* (1900); *From Gretna Green to Land's End* (1907); *Shakespeare: Selective Bibliography and Biographical Notes* (1913); *Fairy Gold* (1916); and *America the Dream* (1930). *An Autobiography in Brief of Katharine Lee Bates* was privately printed in Wellesley, Mass., in 1930. Two book-length biographies, both tending to the hagiographic in tone, are Dorothea Lawrence Mann, *Katharine Lee Bates: Poet and Professor* (1931), by a contemporary, and Dorothy Burgess, *Dream and Deed: The Story of Katharine Lee Bates* (1952), by Bates's niece. For the best modern article that focuses on the relationship with Coman but also offers biographical insights into Bates, see Judith Schwartz, "*Yellow Clover*: Katharine Lee Bates and Katharine Coman," *Frontiers* 4, no. 1 (1979): 59–67.

LILLIAN S. ROBINSON

BATES, Marston (23 July 1906–3 Apr. 1974), naturalist and educator, was born in Grand Rapids, Michigan, the son of Glen F. Bates, a farmer and horticulturist, and Amy Mabel Button. In 1916 his father moved the family to Fort Lauderdale, Florida, where young Bates was reared. An only child in a rather isolated environment, he developed an interest in insects (he collected butterflies) and an ambition to visit the tropics. He earned a B.S. in biology at the University of Florida in 1927.

From 1928 to 1931 Bates worked for Servicio Técnico de Cooperación Agrícola of the United Fruit Company in Honduras and Guatemala, first as a research assistant and then as director of the service. He left that post to do graduate work at Harvard University, where he received an A.M. (1933) and a Ph.D. (1934) in zoology.

Bates's thesis, "The Butterflies of Cuba," won him an appointment in 1935 as a research assistant at the Harvard Museum of Comparative Zoology, but he was soon granted a leave of absence to join a Rockefeller Foundation project investigating mosquito biology in Albania. He resigned from the museum in 1937 and joined the staff of the foundation's international health division. In 1939 he married Nancy Bell Fairchild; they would have four children. Also in 1939 Bates was sent to Egypt to set up a laboratory for malaria research. The project was abandoned with the outbreak of World War II, and he was transferred by the Rockefeller Foundation to direct a laboratory for yellow-fever research at Villavicencio, Colombia.

Early in the twentieth century Walter Reed had identified the mosquito *Aedes aegypti* as the carrier of yellow fever. Subsequently an immunization vaccine was developed, and the disease was thought to be under control, but epidemics broke out again in South America during the 1930s. To meet this new threat the Rockefeller Foundation embarked on an ambitious project of study and control with the aim of eliminating the disease. "It ended," wrote Bates, "by demonstrating that the original objective—the elimination of yellow fever from America—was impossible" (*Scientific Monthly*, July 1946, p. 43).

Nonetheless, the work of the Rockefeller Foundation scientists succeeded in reducing the problem of yellow fever. Under Bates's supervision the researchers at Villavicencio studied the swamps and forests in the surrounding area, demonstrating that mosquito species other than *Aedes aegypti* carried the yellow-fever virus. One was *Haemagogus*, a day-flying mosquito that lived in the forest canopy and was capable of infecting monkeys as well as humans. Knowing about *Haemagogus* and other types of mosquitoes that carried yellow fever opened the way to new steps in prevention.

On his return to the United States in 1948 Bates undertook postdoctoral work at the Johns Hopkins School of Hygiene and Public Health in Baltimore. The following year he published his first book, *The Natural History of Mosquitoes* (1949). His objective in writing the book was twofold—to organize what was known about mosquitoes and to indicate what needed to be done in the way of further research. That he succeeded in his goal is evident from the favorable reviews accorded the volume. The *American Journal of Public Health and the Nation's Health* (Dec. 1949), for example, recommended the work to all students of tropical medicine. Naturalist Edward Way Teale judged it "a solid book, factual and close-packed" (*New York Herald Tribune*, 10 July 1949).

Bates returned to work with the Rockefeller Foundation in 1949, undertaking an analysis of demographic problems from a biological point of view. The following year he was named special assistant to the president of the foundation. In 1952 Bates accepted an appointment as professor of zoology at the University of Michigan, a post he retained until his retirement in 1971.

Although *The Natural History of Mosquitoes* was lucidly written, it was too technical for the lay reader. Still, Bates firmly believed that "scientists can and ought to write in a way capable of reaching a wide and influential audience" (*Science*, 18 Apr. 1952). He was also convinced, as his wife Nancy Bell Bates wrote in *East of the Andes and West of Nowhere*, "that too many scientists are too specialized within their own fields."

Acting on these convictions, Bates published a series of lively, jargon-free volumes concerned with various aspects of nature. These included *The Nature of Natural History* (1950), *Where Winter Never Comes* (1952), *Coral Island: Portrait of an Atoll*, with Donald P. Abbott (1958), *Gluttons and Libertines: Human Problems of Being Natural* (1958), *Man in Nature* (1960), *Animal Worlds* (1963), *The Land and Wildlife of South America* (1964), and *A Jungle in the House* (1970).

Bates also published a well-received book on the population problem, *The Prevalence of People* (1955). Borrowing the cultural concept from the discipline of anthropology, he decided that despite "the underlying biological facts of reproduction and death," the "number of men, the prevalence of people, can best be understood in cultural terms."

Probably Bates's most influential popular book was *The Forest and the Sea* (1960). A nontechnical textbook of ecology, it dealt with the broad sweep of living organisms, from plants and insects to animals and humans, and their environments. "Few biologists," a reviewer wrote, "could treat such a wide range of subjects in so detailedly accurate a fashion" (*New York Herald Tribune*, 20 Mar. 1960).

In addition to his books Bates published dozens of scientific papers and articles in popular journals. Between February 1967 and January 1969 he also authored a column, "Naturalist at Large," in *Natural History*.

Bates belonged to numerous scientific and academic organizations. He was a member of the National Science Foundation and its chair (1956–1958). He served on the advisory board of the Guggenheim Foundation (1955–1958) and as a trustee of the Cranbrook Institute of Science (1952–1962). He was a member of the Pacific Science Board, the American Society of Naturalists (president, 1961), the Council on Foreign Relations, and the American Academy of Arts and Sciences. His honors included the Centennial Certificate of Merit of the University of Florida (1953), the Charles P. Daly Medal of the American Geographical Society (1967), and the Distinguished Faculty Award of the University of Michigan (1968). Bates died in Grand Rapids, Michigan.

The citation accompanying the Daly Medal recognized Bates's special attributes as a scientist. It acclaimed him as "at one and the same time biologist, zoologist, medical ecologist, naturalist, humanist, and, unquestionably, also geographer manqué." It also saluted him as "one of the too few scientists with a gift for clear and literate exposition," with a style that "displays a philosophic bent, an acuity of perception and a spark of humor that together make for delightful reading."

• The Marston Bates Papers, including correspondence, journals, and other writings, are at the Bentley Historical Library, University of Michigan. Other correspondence of Bates is in the Paul Lester Errington Papers, Iowa State University Library, Ames. For biographical information consult the Scientific Club Memorial found in the Bates Collection of the Bentley Historical Library and Bates's own books, which contain many personal references. Nancy Bell Bates, *East of the Andes and West of Nowhere: A Naturalist's Wife in Colombia* (1947), is an entertaining and informative account of the couple's life in Villavicencio. An obituary is in the *New York Times*, 5 Apr. 1974.

RICHARD HARMOND

BATES, Onward (24 Feb. 1850–4 Apr. 1936), civil engineer, was born in Saint Charles County, Missouri, the eldest son of Judge Barton Bates and Caroline Matilda Hatcher. Bates attended local schools in St. Charles County until the age of fifteen. He then began an apprenticeship at the Fulton Iron Works in Saint Louis, where he planned to learn the machinist trade. Instead he was soon hired as a draftsman by C. Shaler Smith, a prominent engineer, who made Bates an inspector of the bridge he was building over the Missouri River at St. Charles. Bates also took advantage of an opportunity to work on the Eads Bridge, one of the first to span the Mississippi and the first major steel bridge in America. The three arch spans, measuring 502, 520, and 505 feet respectively, shattered all engineering precedents, the center being by far the longest span in the world. Smith became Bates's mentor and encouraged him to pursue an engineering education at the foremost institution in the field, Rensselaer Polytechnic Institute (RPI) in Troy, New York. After only two years, Bates returned to St. Louis in 1873 to continue working on the Eads Bridge. He worked for a contractor and then as steel inspector for Eads's St. Louis Bridge Company.

Upon completion of the bridge in 1874, Bates sought employment rather than returning to RPI to complete his education. He was hired by Louis Gustav Frederic Bouscaren, assistant chief engineer of the Cincinnati Southern Railroad, as a draftsman under the immediate supervision of Charles Louis Strobel, who was in charge of developing the drawings for the longest span (517 feet) iron-truss bridge in the world at the time, the Cincinnati Southern's bridge over the Ohio at Cincinnati. Later he was promoted to bridge inspector by Bouscaren and served in this capacity until June 1877. He then went to Milwaukee, where he briefly worked with the Chicago, Milwaukee & St. Paul Railroad. In March 1878 he was hired by the Edge Moor Iron Company of Wilmington, Delaware, and was sent to Australia to secure several contracts for bridges and viaducts; the design and execution of these projects kept him in that country for more than three years. Returning in 1883, he found interim employment with C. Shaler Smith before a better opportunity, an offer of the presidency of the Pittsburgh Bridge Company, drew him away. However, in 1887 the lure of work abroad struck again, and he briefly joined a mining venture in Mexico.

Returning to the United States, Bates again worked for a short time for Edge Moor Iron Company. In February 1888 he was asked to return to another of his former employers, the Chicago, Milwaukee & St. Paul Railroad, this time as chief engineer and superintendent of bridges and buildings. He remained with the company for thirteen years, during which time he married Virginia Castleman of St. Louis in 1892. The couple had no children.

By 1901 he was confident enough of his abilities to go into private practice, and he formed Bates and Rogers Construction Company. The partnership lasted until 1907, when Bates decided to retire from active engineering and sold his share to his associates. However, he was so well respected by his former peers that he was occasionally called back to the firm to arbitrate engineering and contracting matters.

Though Bates never received a formal degree, he did receive several honorary degrees from prestigious universities including the University of Wisconsin (1897), Rensselaer Polytechnic Institute (1918), and the University of Missouri (1924). He was active in the American Society of Civil Engineers, serving as its vice president (1906–1907) and president (1909); the Western Society of Engineers, for which he was president; the Engineers Club of New York; the City Club of Chicago; the Institution of Civil Engineers of Great Britain; and the Royal Society of the Arts. He died in Augusta, Georgia, with many notable bridges to his credit and the distinction of having given substantial service to the engineering profession.

• Bates's career and contributions to civil engineering are discussed in *A Biographical Dictionary of American Civil Engineers*, vol. 2 (1991). For memoirs treating Bates, see the American Society of Civil Engineers, *Transactions* 102 (1937): 1484–87.

ERIC DeLONY

BATES, Theodore Lewis (11 Sept. 1901–30 May 1972), advertising agent, was born in New Haven, Connecticut, the son of Vernal Warner Bates, a businessman, and Elizabeth Brooke Hails. After graduating in 1924 from Yale University's Sheffield Scientific School with a B.S., Bates took a job with the Chase Manhattan Bank in New York City. Six months later the bank's advertising manager contracted pneumonia, and Bates found himself performing that job. He later recalled that, without training, he relied heavily on the advice of his "very efficient woman assistant."

Bates's entry into advertising agency work was equally fortuitous. He encountered friends at the Yale Club who disparaged bank advertising work and urged him to move to an advertising agency. George Batten, head of the New York firm that bore his name, invited Bates to join the agency in 1924; Bates accepted and took a pay cut of $60 a month.

Starting out as a general assistant, Bates soon moved into copywriting and then into account work. He handled the account of Continental Bakers and by 1934 rose to the rank of vice president. His connection to the manufacturer endured, and when Bates moved to Benton & Bowles in 1935, Continental followed him. At Benton & Bowles he also managed, among others, the account of Colgate-Palmolive.

Colgate and Continental Bakers were the first to give their business to the agency of Ted Bates & Company, Inc., which Bates founded with Rosser Reeves in December 1940. The agency grew steadily. Its initial billings (the volume of advertising it placed) of $4.5 million grew to nearly $30 million by 1951, about $170 million by 1961, and $425 million by 1971.

From the start, Ted Bates & Company specialized in packaged goods—mass-produced and mass-distributed products—which it sold through insistent, repetitive advertising. The flamboyant Reeves publicized the agency's doctrine of the Unique Selling Proposition in his 1961 book, *Reality in Advertising*. A USP was to be a distinctive product claim offering a meaningful advantage to customers that could induce them to purchase the Bates brand. Thus, Bates himself wrote the slogan for Continental Baking's Wonder Bread, "Builds Strong Bodies 12 Ways." For Colgate Dental Cream, the agency asserted that it "Cleans Your Breath While It Cleans Your Teeth." Reeves also stressed the agency's commitment to supporting research. Bates's technical staff and consultants were charged with developing Unique Selling Propositions and testing the product claims they made. Meanwhile, the agency tested its copy and campaigns extensively. It compared the proportion of consumers who knew the advertising and used the brand with the share of consumers who were unaware of the advertising but bought the product anyway. The difference measured the campaign's "copy pull." The Bates style suited the marketing context of midcentury America. Rosser Reeves was fond of saying that the typical client brought the agent two half-dollars, saying "Mine is the one on the left. You prove it's better" (Mayer, *Madison Avenue U.S.A.*, p. 53). In an era of "parity products," a successful USP could differentiate a brand from its rivals.

The agency also found ways to use the capabilities of television effectively for visually demonstrating rather than merely asserting product claims. By 1962 Bates was placing 80 percent of its advertising on television. Seeking to reach as many consumers as possible rather than concentrating on targeted audiences was an appropriate strategy for clients with large advertising budgets and hopes of selling standardized products to mass markets. Advertisers entrusted brands like Viceroy Cigarettes, Palmolive Shave Cream, Rolaids antacid, Anacin, and Carter's Little Liver Pills to Ted Bates and kept their accounts there. In its first twenty years the agency boasted that it never lost an account. Since Bates's campaigns often repeated the same commercials for years, clients sometimes did wonder what they were getting from the agency for their money. When one client asked Reeves what the 700 Bates employees were supposed to be doing, Reeves replied, "They're keeping your advertising department from changing your ad."

Bates's advertising differed sharply from the campaigns produced by David Ogilvy, the head of the rival firm of Ogilvy & Mather. Brand image, rather than a unique sales appeal, was the hallmark of Ogilvy ads for luxury products like Rolls Royce and Hathaway shirts. Yet when Ogilvy proposed his choices for an "all-star" advertising agency, he named Bates as president because he could "rivet his crystal-clear brain on pure selling." Critics of the agency objected to the "pneumatic-drill" style of its advertising, but few could claim it did not work in the post–World War II consumer boom years. For this period, Ted Bates himself exemplified the "organization man" celebrated and denigrated in the sociological and popular literature of the time. Rosser Reeves promoted the agency himself; Ted Bates promoted his clients' products.

Bates's advertising was notably aggressive and "hard sell." Yet the agency's head was private and taciturn. He called himself a quiet Maine Yankee and shunned publicity. In 1965 an *Advertising Age* profile only half-jokingly commented that "many in the ad business . . . believe there really is no such person." Even in the firm he was inconspicuous, although executives insisted that he was firmly in charge: "Ted Bates runs this shop and always has. . . . He's in everything here, one way or another, but also he's an expert at delegating authority" (*Printer's Ink*, 20 Apr. 1962). Devoted to his family, he also kept his personal life outside the spotlight. He married the Cuban-born Evelyn Turull in 1934; they had twin daughters. When *Life* asked to photograph his daughters for a story on debutantes, he reluctantly agreed but was embarrassed when he found the picture on the magazine's cover. His avocation, fishing, was also private, and he pursued it from Newfoundland to Cuba. Bates remained active in his agency throughout his life. He was a director and in 1965 was given the title of honorary chairman of the board. The title was somewhat misleading, for he continued to work regularly at the agency for several years thereafter.

In the 1960s a so-called creative revolution in the advertising business changed dominant commercial styles. Meanwhile, mass production and mass markets were giving way to market segmentation and targeted advertising strategies. These developments challenged the approach and style of Bates advertising. Yet by the early 1970s the agency's emphasis on advertising as a selling tool rather than a creative art was beginning to regain favor in the industry. Meanwhile, Ted Bates, the private man who had entered advertising by accident, never lost the respect of his business colleagues. He died in New York City while playing bridge with friends.

• There is no collection of Bates's papers. The successor agency of Backer Spielvogel Bates, Inc. has in its library a small collection of clippings, press releases, and related material on Bates, but it contains no writings by Bates himself. Nor did he give speeches or write articles for advertising trade publications. Rosser Reeves's papers are at the State Historical Society of Wisconsin; they contain an unpublished history of the agency by Martin Mayer, but access to the Mayer manuscript is closed until the year 2007. Several articles on the agency did appear in advertising journals; these include "Ted Bates & Co.: A 10-Year Report," *Tide* (4 Aug. 1950): 23–27; "Story of Ted Bates & Company," *Advertising Agency and Advertising & Selling* 45 (Nov. 1952): 65–67, 100; and "Inside Ted Bates & Co.," *Printers' Ink* (20 Apr. 1962): 31–34. A *New York Times* article, 2 Jan. 1962, and "Ad Business Is Pretty Human, Says Ted Bates," *Advertising Age* 36 (20 Dec. 1965): 40, are based on interviews with Bates. Martin Mayer, *Madison Avenue U.S.A.* (1958), has some comments on Bates but more on Rosser Reeves, as does Stephen Fox, *The Mirror Makers* (1984). Obituaries are in the *New York Times*, 1 June 1972, and *Advertising Age*, 5 June 1972.

DANIEL POPE

BATES, Walter (14 Mar. 1760–11 Feb. 1842), Loyalist, was born in Stamford, Connecticut, the son of John Bates and Sarah Bostwick, farmers. The fifth of eleven children, he was raised in an Anglican family at a time when Congregationalism was the colony's established religion. He was sixteen years old when the Revolution broke out, moved frequently during the war years, and left for Canada at age twenty-three.

Bates is significant principally for his posthumous publication. *Kingston and the Loyalists of the "Spring Fleet" of 1783* (1889; repr. 1980), a thirty-page pamphlet containing information about the experiences of Loyalist. The date of composition is unknown. Bates begins his personal narrative with the calamities of the revolutionary war years. When local Connecticut authorities learned that his three brothers had joined the British garrison, they harassed, imprisoned, and whipped the young Bates in an unsuccessful effort to learn the names of other Tories in the area. Two years later, when drafted into the Continental army, Bates fled to Long Island and joined a community of Loyalists at Eaton's Neck where he became a schoolteacher. On learning of the king's offer to Loyalists of 200 acres of land in Nova Scotia, he boarded the *Union*, lead ship of the first "spring fleet" sailing to Canada in 1783. The group landed at Belleisle Bay in New Brunswick, where, he wrote later, there was "nothing but wilderness before our eyes; the women and children *did not refrain from tears!*" Although the landscape was daunting, the Micmac Indians helped with provisions, supplying generous quantities of moose meat to the newly arrived immigrants. The band settled at the head of Belleisle Creek, establishing the town of Kingston. They divided land, including allotments for an Anglican church and a school, and quickly raised log houses. Bates drew a favorable lot in the first land division, and in 1784 he and Abigail (maiden name unknown) became the first couple in the community to be married by the Anglican minister. He worked as a farmer and a shoemaker, was a lay reader in Kingston's Trinity Church, and served Kings County for many years as a high sheriff.

Kingston and the Loyalists is a loosely organized work, with separate chapters on Bates's personal history, the fate of other Connecticut Loyalists, the founding of Kingston, a history of Kingston's Trinity Church, and incidents from Connecticut's early days. His partisan view of Connecticut history is similar to that found in the better-known work by the Loyalist minister Samuel Peters, the *General History of Connecticut* (1781). Bates's narrative is distorted but colorful, as is evident in his description of the settlement of Hartford by Thomas Hooker, who established himself, according to Bates, first by destroying the Indian settlement, next by expelling the Dutch "as a dangerous set of heretics," and then by treating the numerous sects that arose with "thundering anathemas . . . and the heated vengeance of the civil power." Appended to Bates's strong-minded narrative is the diary of Sarah Scofield Frost, a relative of his, who kept a personal account of her voyage on the ship *Two Sisters*, a vessel in the second fleet of Loyalists that headed north in the spring of 1783.

Bates spent the remainder of his life in Canada but apparently returned to Connecticut at least twice. In his only other known publication, *The Mysterious Stranger*, first printed in New Haven in 1817, Bates narrates the fascinating story of a talented thief who successfully defied all restraints in the Kingston prison and was pursued by Sheriff Bates to Simsbury, Connecticut. Another reference to Bates's return is a moving account, telling of a visit in 1838 to his much-changed birthplace, found in Rev. E. B. Huntington's *History of Stamford, Connecticut* (1868). Bates was a minor yet versatile figure among the Connecticut refugee Loyalists, one of the many of yeoman origins who brought their talents to the founding of New Brunswick. He died at Kingston.

• A brief biography of Bates is in Lorenzo Sabine, *Biographical Sketches of Loyalists in the American Revolution* (1864). Some details are included in the list of 6,000 Loyalists in Esther Clark Wright, *The Loyalists of New Brunswick* (1955). Bates's work is placed in historical context by W. H. Siebert, "The Refugee Loyalists of Connecticut," *Proceedings and Transactions of The Royal Society of Canada* 10 (1916): 75–92, and by Robert A. East, *Connecticut's Loyalists* (1974).

BARBARA E. LACEY

BATESON, Gregory (9 May 1904–4 July 1980), anthropologist, was born in Grandchester, England, the son of William Bateson, a well-known biologist, and Caroline Beatrice Durham. As a young man, Bateson was an outstanding student. He began his academic endeavors at Charterhouse School, London, where he was enrolled from 1917 to 1921. He continued his studies at St. John's College, Cambridge University, where he obtained a B.Sc. in 1925 and an M.A. in anthropology in 1930. In 1936 he married the anthropologist Margaret Mead, with whom he had one child. He divorced Mead in 1950 and in 1951 married Elizabeth Sumner; they had one child and divorced in 1958. In 1961 he married Lois Cammack; they had one child.

Having been trained as an anthropologist at Cambridge, Bateson did his first fieldwork with the Baining, the indigenous people of New Britain. Later he carried out an extensive study of the Iatmul peoples of New Guinea, which resulted in a classic publication in the history of ethnography, *Naven: A Survey of the Problems Suggested by a Composite Picture of the Culture of a New Guinea Tribe Drawn from Three Points of View* (1936; rev. ed., 1958).

The next phase of Bateson's work extended into the realms of psychology. He became influential in the study of schizophrenia, particularly in the family therapy movement. He developed and was instrumental in a great deal of research on the Double Bind Theory, which to this day is a well-known and important concept in clinical psychology. According to this fresh perspective on the etiology of schizophrenia, which Bateson generated in collaboration with Donald Jackson and J. Hayley of the Veterans Administration in Palo Alto, California, a victim can respond to neither a primary nor a secondary injunction and, in such a communicational context, learns to distort responses in such a way as to neutralize the implicit threat. Later in his life, he applied his central focus on the study of system behavior (systems theory) to the problems of biological evolution and learning. His study of human communication led him to integrate theoretically knowledge on all levels of abstraction and existence. Bateson's approach to learning was primarily toward a theory of how we learn to learn.

For most of his life, Bateson strove to develop a universal epistemology that would, in an essentially systems-theory frame of reference, give an integrated account of the capabilities of all living things to integrate information, organize and reorganize it, and communicate it outward from themselves. Bateson drew on a wide range of intellectual fields to inform and illustrate his approach, among them mechanics, electronics, mathematics, cybernetics, and information theory, as well as biology, psychology, genetics, anthropology, philosophy, and religion. Within Bateson's framework, the integrity of explanation across widely differing phenomena is accomplished through the identification of analogies and homologies. Thus, for example, to the putative question, "How is a leaf on a tree similar to a noun in a sentence," Bateson would argue, "Both grammar and biological structure are products of communicational and organizational process."

Bateson was perennially in search of the impertinent question. The reason for going into so many different areas was not to acquire the diversity of a polymath or to make a display of erudition, but to find new ways of conceptualizing basic epistemic phenomena. He was obsessed by the thought that traditional categories of thought had grown stale and, worse, that the current search for practical solutions had become utterly bogged down in this backwash of stale ideas. What was needed first and foremost were new ways of looking at the human mind and its relation to nature in the context of a universal ecological system that would include both organism and ideas.

In Bateson's later theory he argued that it is no simple matter to find new conceptual approaches. As mind is part of a larger system that includes the environment, and as the larger system is characterized by redundancy and stability, it is all too easy to fall into a thinking-as-usual approach. It is, however, possible to break out of thinking as usual through creativity, or exposure to novelty, or a combination of the two. The trick is to be constantly on the lookout, as Bateson was, for possible intellectual spurs to thinking in new ways.

But because neither creativity nor fresh experience can be planned or budgeted for, the search for the impertinent question is itself impertinent; it is a tricky, hard road to follow. Bateson's career was that of an intellectual nomad, traveling from place to place, and from one field to another, without ever settling into the safety of a secure niche and, as such, did not lend itself to academic tenure or research grants. Too often, he was offered positions not entirely appropriate of his gifts, or else he was offered posts that for reasons of intellectual conscience he could not accept. As a consequence, this gentle, sincere, warm man enjoyed neither the reputation he deserved nor the real security appropriate to his achievements until nearly the last decade of his life.

None of this was evident in Bateson's attitude toward life, and none of it comes through in his own account of his career, *Mind and Nature: A Necessary Unity* (1979). Bateson seems to have been blessed from the beginning by a deeply felt intuition that it was important to be constantly trying new things and that he was lucky to have the chance. In the search for novelty, however, Bateson was, in a certain sense, always plowing the same field. He came back to certain topics again and again. But each time that he returned, he added something new.

In his collaboration with Margaret Mead doing anthropological fieldwork, he originated the concept of "schismogenesis" to describe situations, such as mutual threat, in which the behavior of one individual serves as a signal to another to initiate more drastic behavior, which in turn serves as a signal to the first to do the same, and so on. In such a system, only a slight initial difference, a threatening gesture from one individual, causes the system to run rapidly out of control. Bateson identified two classes of schismogenic systems. These he designated as "symmetrical" and "complementary." Conditions of mutual threat, whether between animals, individual humans, nations, or races, constitute a symmetrical system: a given behavior in one entity causes the same behavior in the other. In complementary systems, a given behavior induces the reciprocal behavior in another. Dominance induces submission, sadism, masochism, haughty indifference, hopeless longing.

What distinguishes both kinds of system is that they rapidly get "stuck" and further learning does not occur. Though internally they show a hair-trigger dynamic, they are relatively static in comparison to the larger environment of which they are a subsystem. It took some time, however, for Bateson to realize that though schismogenic systems certainly can and do exist, their very nature militates against their indefinite survival. The adaptive value of such runaway systems is nil. Nature abhors schismogenesis. Between mammals of the same species, a situation of threat leads rapidly to more threat, but before the interchange gets out of hand, and real injury occurs, one or the other typically makes a submissive display.

Schismogenic systems can be distinguished from more normal systems of interaction in yet another way. In these latter systems, there is a progressive gain in organization. This gain, moreover, is on more than one level. Kicking a football is not the same as shooting baskets. But if one practices kicking a football, one is learning more than just how to split the uprights. One is also learning what it is to practice, how much discipline and concentration are needed, and so on. Recognition of this phenomenon—it has been observed in laboratory mice—and its classification and elucidation as "deutero-learning" (learning to learn) was one of Bateson's many contributions.

Essential to Bateson's outlook was a sense that even fresh ideas rapidly tend to become shibboleths. It was necessary to keep playing with ideas, to keep juxtaposing them in new combinations, if one wanted to continue to make sense. In this regard—in the combination of intellectual openness and theoretical playfulness—Bateson most resembles William James; he had as well some of that same geniality and essential gentleness of spirit.

Thus we come to another feature of Bateson's epistemology—the constant integration of concepts derived from one branch of research with problems and concepts derived from another. Through this integration, composite organisms, such as human societies, came to be viewed as similar to individual organisms, and evolutionary change as of a kind with individual learning. This multilayer integration of concepts is both method and result for Bateson. It exemplifies the power of the mind to operate across different logical categories in search of ever more relevant patterns of metaknowledge. It is also the means by which that power comes into being. Put another way, the search for the impertinent question is as endless as life. For no sooner has it generated a pertinent solution than it becomes time to push ahead and find a new impertinent question. And, one might add, it is perhaps best if this new impertinent question can be put to the solution that has just been found.

Bateson died in San Francisco, California.

• Among Bateson's most important works, in addition to those mentioned in the text, are *Balinese Character: A Photographic Analysis*, with Margaret Mead (1942); *Communication: The Social Matrix of Psychiatry*, with Jurgen Ruesch (1951); *Steps to an Ecology of Mind* (1972); and *Essays of Gregory Bateson*, ed. John Brockman (1977). Biographical accounts include M. C. Bateson, *Our Own Metaphor* (1989); David Lipset, *Gregory Bateson: The Legacy of a Scientist* (1980), which contains a bibliography; and Margaret Mead, *Blackberry Winter* (1972). See also R. W. Rieber, ed., *The Individual, Communication and Society: Essays in the Memory of Gregory Bateson* (1989), and C. Wilder-Mott and John H. Weakland, eds., *Rigor and Imagination: Essays on the Legacy of Gregory Bateson* (1981).

R. W. RIEBER

BATTERSON, James Goodwin (23 Feb. 1823–18 Sept. 1901), insurance executive, was born in Wintonbury (now Bloomfield), Connecticut, the son of Simeon Seely Batterson, a stonecutter, and Melissa Roberts. Batterson spent his early childhood around New Preston, Connecticut, where he attended the local country school and academy. Unable to afford the college education that he greatly desired, he moved around 1838 to Ithaca, New York, where he served a three-year apprenticeship in the print shop of Mack, Andrus & Woodruff and spent his evenings and free time in independent study. At his aging father's request, he then returned to Connecticut and joined his father's stonecutting business in Litchfield. Batterson read law in the office of Origen S. Seymour for a year, but family circumstances again resulted in his abandonment of formal education, and he concentrated on building up the family business. He married Eunice Elizabeth Goodwin of Hartford in 1851; they had two children.

With the continued growth of the business, Batterson relocated to Hartford, where he undertook a wide variety of tasks. His business contributed stone to a long list of buildings, including the National Capitol and the Library of Congress in Washington, D.C.; the state capitol buildings of New York and Connecticut in Albany and Hartford, respectively; mansions for the Vanderbilt family both in New York and in Newport, Rhode Island; and the Waldorf-Astoria Hotel in New York City. Batterson's firm continued to grow, and by 1860 he had established a large stoneworks in New York that produced interior marble pieces, as well as owning and operating stone quarries in Westerly, Rhode Island; New Canaan, Connecticut; and Concord, New Hampshire. Also producing outdoor stone monuments, the firm erected the National Soldiers Monument at Gettysburg and placed its work at Antietam, Galveston, and San Francisco. Batterson himself invented instruments (including a lathe for turning and polishing columns) that greatly aided his operations, and by 1875 the firm had been organized into a stock company, the New England Granite Works.

A widely traveled man of many interests, Batterson took a business trip to England in 1859 that changed the course of his life. Fascinated by British efforts at accident insurance, he enlisted the support of a group of individuals who shared his enthusiasm upon his return to the United States. Batterson was successful enough at selling the new concept to potential partners that in May 1863 he, along with nine others, petitioned the Connecticut legislature for permission to enter the business of issuing accident insurance. The Travelers Insurance Company officially opened for business in Hartford on 1 April 1864, having collected its first premium on 24 March of the same year. A local banker by the name of James E. Bolter, who had met Batterson in the Hartford post office and inquired into the new business venture, had been insured against accidental occurrences on the return trip to his home; it was the new company's first premium. The two cent payment was soon followed by a multitude of other premium payments, as Batterson aggressively promoted his new venture.

After returning from a subsequent trip to England in the summer of 1863, Batterson remarked, "The officers and directors of these [insurance] companies are of the first respectability, but still there seems to be a great want of life and energy in the direction and management. A man might travel from one end of the country to another and never hear of such an institution. In short, the business is not well advertised." Determined to avoid such mistakes at home, Batterson pioneered advertising on billboards (1873), streetcars (1868), and matchbook covers (1898). He also launched a monthly magazine—the *Travelers Record*—that emphasized the benefits of accident insurance, as well as life insurance, which the company started to sell in 1865. The company also advertised heavily on a line of calendars, in popular publications such as *Puck* and *Harper's*, and on items such as beach umbrellas and tug boats.

Batterson was intimately involved in every facet of his insurance business, serving as his own underwriter, actuary, auditor, claim adjustor, and advertising agent. The company grew rapidly and spawned a host of imitators, nearly all of which soon folded, leaving the Travelers in a dominant market position. Employers' liability insurance was added to the product line in 1889, and in 1892 the Travelers also pioneered the concept of "double indemnity," a policy provision that specified payment of double the face value of the policy in the event of death by accident. Perhaps the most significant addition occurred in 1897, when the company issued the first automobile insurance policy (to Gilbert J. Loomis of Westfield, Massachusetts, a mechanic who had built his own one-cylinder car).

Years of independent study left Batterson with many interests beyond his business. He conducted field research in geology and mineralogy and, in the process, assisted geologist James G. Percival in the first geological survey of Connecticut (1842). He later conducted similar research, with civil engineer Isambard K. Brunel, in the Nile Valley region in the winter of 1858–1859. A Republican in politics, he served as chairman of the Connecticut State Committee and was active in Abraham Lincoln's presidential campaign of 1864. His self-acquired scholarship in the classics gained him the presidency of the Greek Club of New York and allowed him to author his own translations of the *Iliad* and *Odyssey* of Homer and *The Lyrics of Anacreon*. An art patron as well, Batterson collected numerous works of the old masters, which he later presented to museums in both Philadelphia and Hartford.

Active in company affairs until his death at his home in Hartford, Batterson was a classic example of the nineteenth-century self-made man. Denied access to extensive formal education, he combined intelligence and entrepreneurial skills in founding the Travelers Insurance. A leader in the field of accident and liability coverage, the company stands as Batterson's greatest legacy.

• A small collection of Batterson's papers are at the Connecticut Historical Society. In addition to his efforts in the classics, Batterson authored *Gold and Silver as Currency in the Light of Experience, Historical, Economical, and Practical* (1896). The best source of information on his life and career is the company-produced *A History of the Travelers* (1980), by uncredited author(s). Other sources include an uncredited article in *Commemorative Biographical Record of Hartford County* (1901), and the *Travelers Record* (Oct. 1901): 4–5. Obituaries are in the *Hartford Courant* and the *Hartford Times*, both 18 Sept. 1901.

EDWARD L. LACH, JR.

BATTEY, Robert (26 Nov. 1828–8 Nov. 1895), surgeon, was born in Augusta, Georgia, the son of Cephas Battey and Mary Agnes Magruder. Battey at-

tended Richmond Academy in Augusta and then Phillips Academy in Andover, Massachusetts, from which he graduated in 1844. After graduation, Battey first worked in Detroit and then in Marshall, Michigan, before returning south to work as a drugstore clerk in Rome, Georgia. By 1849 he was the proprietor of his own drugstore and had married Martha B. Smith, with whom he would have fourteen children. While in Rome, Battey began studying medicine under his brother George M. Battey. He continued his education in Philadelphia, Pennsylvania, in 1855, first in Professor James C. Booth's School of Analytical Chemistry and then at the Philadelphia School of Pharmacy. After graduating from the Philadelphia College of Pharmacy in 1856, he attended two courses of lectures at Jefferson Medical College, from which he graduated in 1857.

Battey returned to Rome to practice surgery. In 1858 he performed a successful operation for vesico-vaginal fistula (an abnormal tract between the bladder and the vagina that usually results from tearing in childbirth). This was a new procedure, and his success brought him to the attention of many of his peers. As a result, Battey was asked to speak at the Obstetrical Society of London in 1859 about vesico-vaginal fistula. While abroad, he performed this procedure successfully at the Dublin Hospital in Ireland, on a patient who had already had five failed fistula operations. Battey traveled throughout Europe, returning home in 1860.

With the outbreak of the Civil War in the spring of 1861, Battey joined the Confederate army. He served as chief surgeon in several hospitals in the Nineteenth Regiment of Georgia Volunteers and with Hampton's Brigade.

Following the surrender of the Confederacy in April 1865, Battey returned to Rome to resume his practice. He established a Gynecological Infirmary, later enlarging this into the Martha Battey Hospital, named in recognition of his wife, who had assisted him in many operations. From 1874 to 1875 Battey served as professor of obstetrics at the Atlanta Medical College and editor of the *Atlanta Medical and Surgical Journal*.

On 27 August 1872 Battey performed an oöphorectomy (removal of the ovaries) on a thirty-year-old woman who had been an invalid for sixteen years. Since the onset of her menarche, she had suffered recurring debilitating bouts of painful rectal bleeding associated with other symptoms. With the removal of her ovaries, the woman made a dramatic recovery. Following this, Battey operated on many women with somewhat similar manifestations (severe dysmenorrhea and headaches, pelvic pain, hystero-epileptic attacks, and so forth). Over the next two decades, in more than twenty publications, he reported his results of nearly 300 cases. His purpose was to bring on the "change of life for the effectual remedy of certain otherwise incurable maladies." "Battey's Operation," as it became known, was espoused by other leading surgeons both in America, and in Europe. At its height of popularity during the 1880s, the procedure was considered a panacea for severe pelvic pain, insanity, convulsive disorders, and other forms of mental and nervous instability.

Battey was president of the Georgia Medical Society in 1879 and the American Gynecological Society in 1888 and honorary fellow of the British Gynecological Society and the Obstetrical Society of Edinburgh.

Battey's operation has been decried as one of the most egregious examples of excess by overenthusiastic surgeons. In its first decade, mortality rate for patients undergoing the operation was more than 30 percent. Nonetheless, Battey's operation contributed greatly to an understanding of disease of the female genital tract and the advancement of pelvic surgery. In addition, it helped to make more acceptable laparotomy and abdominal surgery. Perhaps most important, in the realm of clinical investigation, it led to an appreciation of the relation of the gonads to menstruation and was one of the seminal studies in reproductive endocrinology. Battey died near Rome, Georgia.

• Battey's papers and documents are archived in Special Collections, Robert W. Woodruff Library, Emory University, Atlanta, Ga. Among Battey's most important papers are "Normal Ovariotomy-Case," *Atlanta Medical and Surgical Journal* 10 (1872): 321–29; "What Is the Proper Field for Battey's Operation?" *Transactions of the American Gynecological Society* 5 (1880): 38–43; and "Battey's Operation: Its Objects, Results, Etc.," *Transactions of the Medical Society of Virginia* 10 (1887): 188–293. Discussions of the Battey Operation can be found in H. H. Carstens, "Three Cases of Battey's Operation," *American Journal of Obstetrics and Diseases of Women and Children* 16 (1883): 266–71; E. W. Cushing, "Report of a Case of Melancholia; Masturbation; Cured by Removal of Both Ovaries," *Journal of the American Medical Association* 8 (1887): 441–42; L. D. Longo, "The Rise and Fall of Battey's Operation: A Fashion in Surgery," *Bulletin of the History of Medicine* 52 (1979): 244–67. Biographies of Battey are J. A. Eva, "A Sketch of the Life and Labors of Dr. Robert Battey, of Rome, Georgia," *Virginia Medical Monthly* 15 (1878): 1–9; and T. A. Reamy, "In Memoriam, Robert Battey, M.D., LL.D.," *Transactions of the American Gynecological Society* 21 (1896): 467–72.

LAWRENCE D. LONGO

BATTLE, Cullen Andrews (1 June 1829–8 Apr. 1905), politician and soldier, was born in Powelton, Georgia, the son of Cullen Battle, a wealthy planter, and Jane A. Lamon. He moved with his parents to Irwinton (now Eufaula), Alabama, in 1836. After graduating from the University of Alabama in 1850, he studied law with John G. Shorter, who was later state governor, and was admitted to the bar in 1852. Battle soon entered a partnership with former Alabama chief justice William P. Chilton. The year before his admittance to the bar he married Georgia F. Williams, with whom he had four children.

Battle won a reputation as an orator of some repute. He entered politics and was a vocal advocate of the secessionist movement. In 1856 he was substitute elector on the Buchanan ticket, and during the 1860 Alabama Democratic State Convention, he was made a presidential elector on the motion of Senator William L.

Yancey. He and Yancey traveled across the state and to Charleston, New York, Boston, and Philadelphia on an extended speaking tour.

At the outbreak of the Civil War, Battle had little military experience. Following the John Brown raid in 1859, he offered Governor Henry Alexander Wise of Virginia a military company he had raised. Wise declined the offer, but Alabama commenced raising the "Alabama Volunteer Corps," which was to consist of ten regiments. Only two were actually formed, and Battle was elected lieutenant colonel of the Second Regiment. In January 1861 the Second Regiment was ordered to Pensacola, Florida, where it participated in the capture of the Warrington Navy Yards and Forts Barrancas and McRae. Shortly after this Alabama passed the ordinance of secession and annulled all military commissions previously granted above the rank of captain. Battle promptly shouldered a musket as a private until he was elected major of the newly formed Third Alabama Infantry. The regiment was ordered to Virginia, where it reported in early April. The colonel was then promoted and transferred west, which in turn allowed Battle to be promoted to lieutenant colonel. Assigned to William Mahone's brigade, the regiment received a brutal baptism of fire at the battle of Seven Pines (31 May–1 June), where Colonel Tennant Lomax was killed and Battle wounded. Battle acted as colonel for the remainder of 1862, but his promotion was not confirmed until 26 March 1863. His regiment was transferred to Brigadier General Robert Rodes's Alabama brigade. Because of his wound, Battle missed the Seven Days' battles (25 June–1 July), where the Third Alabama suffered severe casualties. At Malvern Hill (1 July) they incurred the largest loss of any Confederate regiment.

Battle rejoined his regiment in time for the Confederate invasion of Maryland and participated in heavy fighting at South Mountain (14 Sept.) and Sharpsburg (17 Sept.), receiving a slight wound in both battles. General Rodes singled him out for "admirable conduct" at South Mountain and recommended him for promotion, which, despite the support of Alabama politicians who also sought Battle's advancement, he was unable to obtain. Immediately before the battle of Chancellorsville, Battle was badly injured when his horse reared and fell. On the day before the battle began he attempted to ride his horse, but he reinjured his back and had to relinquish command. Believing his usefulness in the field at an end, Battle submitted his resignation. Rodes disapproved it and instead repeated his recommendation that Battle be promoted, to no avail. Just how earnestly Rodes pushed for Battle's promotion is uncertain, for the colonel was not his first choice to command the brigade when Rodes was promoted to division command.

Battle had recovered sufficiently by June 1863 to accompany his regiment for the invasion of Pennsylvania. During the fighting at Gettysburg on 1 July, Rodes reported, "The whole brigade, with the exception of the Third Alabama, was repulsed quickly and with loss." Another brigade commander, with whom

Battle's regiment cooperated, reported that Battle "rendered brilliant and valuable service." Following Gettysburg, the commander of Rodes's old brigade, Colonel Edward O'Neal (1818–1890), was removed. Despite his glowing recommendations of Battle, Rodes wanted either John B. Gordon or John T. Morgan to replace O'Neal. When he could not obtain either, Rodes again urged Battle's promotion, which was approved in August 1863.

Battle's brigade engaged in some of the fiercest fighting of the battles of the Wilderness and Spotsylvania Court House in May 1864. In mid-June part of the Confederate Second Army Corps under Jubal Early, including Battle's brigade, was transferred to the Shenandoah Valley to eliminate a Union threat to that region. Battle and his command were heavily engaged at the battles of Winchester (19 Sept.) and Cedar Creek (19 Oct.). During the initially successful assault against Philip Sheridan's army at Cedar Creek, Battle received a severe wound in the knee. The leg was to be amputated, but Sheridan's counterattack drove Early's army from the field, forcing Battle's evacuation before the operation could take place. Battle suffered through an immensely painful trip to Richmond, where he spent three months attempting to recover. His wound left him crippled and ended his field service.

Battle returned to Tuskegee, Alabama, where he resumed his law practice and reentered politics. He was elected to Congress in 1868, but his refusal to take the oath of allegiance to the federal government prevented him from taking his seat. In 1870 his name was advanced for the Democratic nomination for U.S. senator, but the probability that he would again refuse to take the oath caused his name to be withdrawn. In 1880 he migrated to New Bern, North Carolina, where he was editor of the *New Bern Journal* for some time. He spent the last two years of his life with his son, Rev. H. W. Battle, in Greensboro, North Carolina, where he died.

• Some of Battle's papers are at the Alabama Department of Archives and History. They include Battle's manuscript history of the Third Alabama, which relates many personal incidents. Battle's wartime reports and correspondence and mention of his conduct by his superiors are in U.S. War Department, *The War of the Rebellion: A Compilation of the Official Records of the Union and Confederate Armies* (128 vols., 1880–1901). J. B. Hawthorne, *Cullen Andrews Battle* (1905?), is a very rare biography. For a good sketch of Battle's life, although some of the details are incorrect, see Clement Evans, ed., *Confederate Military History*, vol. 7, *Alabama* (1899). Brief biographies are in Willis Brewer, *Alabama* (1872; repr. 1964), and the monthly *Confederate Veteran* 13 (1905): 318. Douglas S. Freeman, *Lee's Lieutenants: A Study in Command* (3 vols., 1942–1944), should be consulted for his military experience after promotion to colonel. An obituary is in the *News and Observer* (Raleigh, N.C.), 9 Apr. 1905.

D. SCOTT HARTWIG

BATTLE, Kemp Plummer (19 Dec. 1831–4 Feb. 1919), educator and college president, was born in Franklin County, North Carolina, the son of William Horn Battle, a judge, and Lucy Martin Plummer. His father served on the Superior Court of North Carolina, riding a circuit during much of Battle's early years. His mother was the chief formative influence on Battle; her wise counsel to him was, "Kemp, never be beaten if you can help it!" Battle began school in Louisburg in Franklin County. When he was eight years old, the family moved to Raleigh, and he continued schooling at the Raleigh Male Academy. The family moved to Chapel Hill in 1843, where he studied at the village school in preparation for entering the university. In September 1845, prior to his fourteenth birthday, Battle entered the University of North Carolina. He graduated in 1849 at age seventeen as one of the top students in the class, delivering the valedictory address at the commencement as his father had done in 1820.

Battle's teaching career began in 1849 when the university offered him an appointment as a tutor in Latin, a position that included teaching college Latin classes. He was later appointed as a tutor in mathematics and continued in this position until the summer of 1854. He was described by a contemporary as "peculiarly fitted by nature and education for this occupation; his mind is clear and discriminating, cultivated to a high degree; apt to learn, and patient in imparting instruction; kind and generous in his temper, he has much success as a tutor" (Ashe, p. 27). These characteristics, observed early in his career, were to prove invaluable to his later success. During his time as a tutor, he received an A.M. (1852)—although the Battle genealogy book notes that this degree, as was customary at the time, required no additional work, only the payment of certain fees. In 1882 he was granted an LL.D. from Davidson College, and in 1910 he received an LL.D. from the University of North Carolina.

After reading law under his father, who was then a professor of law at the university, Battle was admitted to the bar in 1854. In 1855 he married Martha Ann "Pattie" Battle, a distant cousin from Edgecombe County, North Carolina; they had four sons and one daughter who survived childhood. He began law practice in Raleigh in partnership with Quentin Busbee. His activities included an appointment as a director of the newly rechartered Bank of North Carolina in 1857 and an unsuccessful candidacy for the state legislature in 1860. During this time, Battle was a strong Union supporter, serving as the president of the Union Club in Wake County. After President Abraham Lincoln called for troops to keep the seceding states in the Union, however, Battle's support shifted. He served as a delegate to the State Constitutional Convention and signed the Ordinance of Secession. He later volunteered for service in the Confederate army, but he was not elected to serve. Perhaps his greatest service to the southern cause was the organization of the Chatham Railroad Company for the purpose of building a road from Raleigh to the Chatham County coal fields to supply Confederate munitions factories. He served as the president of the company from 1861 to 1866. After the war, Battle applied for and received a full pardon from President Andrew Johnson. In 1866 he was elected as the state treasurer, serving in that position until 1868, when the entire state government was replaced by U.S. military authorities under congressional Reconstruction.

Following the war, Battle engaged in varied activities designed to return his beloved state to normalcy. In the late 1860s and early 1870s he served as the president of the State Fair Association in Raleigh, combining his interests in farming and the advocacy of improved agricultural methods. He was for many years a member of the State Board of Agriculture. During this Reconstruction period, Battle became increasingly distressed over the condition of the University of North Carolina. After much turmoil in the state government as a result of Reconstruction legislation, the election of university trustees to the general assembly was reinstated in 1873; in 1874 a new board was named that included both Battle and his father. Battle was subsequently named as the secretary and treasurer.

Through efforts largely attributed to Battle, the university was reopened after being closed since approximately 1870. George T. Winston, who succeeded Battle as the university president, characterized Battle's contribution during this time: "Nothing daunted by these evils and inspired by a lifetime love of the University, Mr. Battle set vigorously to work and canvassed the State for funds. No other man would have undertaken the task, and certainly no other man could have accomplished it. He appealed to the alumni and to patriotic men not alumni, through the press, by letter and by personal interview. The result was $20,000 and the revival of the University" (H. B. Battle, p. 155). Battle also worked through the general assembly to secure additional funding for the institution.

In 1876 Battle became the president of the university, a position in which he served for fifteen years. Accomplishments during his presidency included the construction of several buildings, increased fundraising, and enhanced student enrollment. One major issue was the disbursement of the federal Land Grant Fund. The final outcome, as in many states, was the continuation of the university and the establishment of a new Agricultural and Mechanical College, today known as North Carolina State University. Battle also influenced public school teaching with the establishment of the Summer Normal School at the university in 1877. A chair of history was established during his last year as president, and he was elected to fill the position upon his retirement from the presidency in 1891. He continued as a professor of history until 1907. In his retirement he continued to write, publishing histories of his beloved university and of his own tenure as president. He died in Chapel Hill.

Battle is considered the second founder of the university because of the assistance he provided to the institution; former students and colleagues also called him the "Grand Old Man of North Carolina." At his death, both houses of the general assembly adjourned in his honor. The university faculty honored him by resolution: "He demanded truth and justice, but for

him justice was tempered by mercy. And so he went through life working, helping, and striving always to create an atmosphere of harmony. As his presence was a benediction, his memory will be an inspiration" (H. B. Battle, p. 164). Those chronicling the history of the university recognize Battle for his leadership in the rebuilding and growth of the university.

• The Battle Family Papers (1765–1955) are in the Southern Historical Collection of the Manuscripts Department of the University of North Carolina, Chapel Hill. This collection contains more than 9,000 items of papers, correspondence, and volumes. Books written by Battle include *History of the University of North Carolina* (2 vols., 1907 and 1912) and *Memories of an Old-Time Tar Heel* (1945). The latter, edited by his son William James Battle, provides coverage of his life through 1891, including his years as the president of University of North Carolina. Battle's numerous monographs and addresses provide accounts of the history of Raleigh, North Carolina, and the history of Supreme Court of North Carolina, among other topics of history, education, and financial and public questions. Other helpful sources are Herbert Bemerton Battle, *The Battle Book: A Genealogy of the Battle Family in America* (1930), and Samuel A. Ashe, *Biographical History of North Carolina* (1907).

MARY E. OUTLAW

BATTLE, William Horn (17 Oct. 1802–14 Mar. 1879), jurist and law professor, was born in Edgecombe County, North Carolina, the son of Joel Battle, a planter and manufacturer of cotton goods, and Mary Johnson. He graduated second in his class at the University of North Carolina in 1820 and studied law under Chief Justice Leonard Henderson. He and another Henderson pupil, Richmond M. Pearson, became well-known law teachers and competitors for a seat on the North Carolina Supreme Court. Impressed by Battle's legal prowess, the North Carolina Supreme Court allowed him to forego the regular examination and licensed him to practice law in all state tribunals in 1824. Battle settled initially in Louisburg, North Carolina, to practice his profession. Simultaneous farming took time from his professional labors and resulted in his going on circuit for several years with little practice. During "those slow years of constrained leisure," however, he acquired the thorough grounding in law that informed his later service as superior court judge, supreme court justice, and law professor. In 1825 Battle married Lucy M. Plummer; they had ten children.

Battle also ventured into public service. Defeated for a legislative seat in 1831 and 1832, he later served in the North Carolina House of Commons in 1833–1834 and 1834–1835. His elections attest his personal popularity, for his constituents were predominantly Jacksonian Democrats while he was a Whig. He later served as a delegate to the 1839 Whig National Convention. From 1834 to 1839 Battle was reporter to the North Carolina Supreme Court. In 1835 he served as a joint commissioner to revise the state's statutes, and in 1872–1873 he was the sole reviser of the state's statutes.

Battle served as a judge of the North Carolina superior court from 1840 to 1848. In 1848 Governor William Alexander Graham considered only judges Battle and Pearson for an interim appointment to a vacancy on the supreme court. Western Whigs demanded the appointment of Pearson, largely because of the concentration of statewide officeholders in Battle's then home county of Orange in eastern North Carolina. Pearson, they opined, "would be independent of that Raleigh clique, to which the people are getting strongly opposed." When the governor appointed Battle, Whig legislators came to Raleigh determined to elect Pearson for the permanent commission. After numerous inconclusive ballots, Battle withdrew. Chief Justice Thomas Ruffin, whom renowned legal scholar and longtime dean of Harvard Law School Roscoe Pound would call one of "the ten judges who must be ranked first in American judicial history," regretted Battle's defeat. "The whole state," Ruffin wrote, "cannot produce a man who would make her a more able and upright magistrate." Battle wrote only three opinions for the court while serving under this interim appointment.

The legislature returned Battle to the superior court in 1849 and to the supreme court in 1852. Ruffin's retirement occasioned the second supreme court appointment, and Ruffin, who "cherish[ed] the warmest interest in the reputation of the Court," urged the appointment. Battle served on the court until 1865, when the federal government declared all state offices vacant; he was immediately reelected and served until 1868, when he was defeated in the state's first popular judicial elections. Chief Justice Pearson, who had defeated Battle for the 1848 appointment, said Battle knew "more of North Carolina law than any man in the State." Accordingly, his contributions to the court's deliberations in conference were said to be invaluable. His opinions for the court (*North Carolina Reports*, vols. 40, 44–63) were noted for their logic and clarity, supported by reason and authority, and seldom overruled by subsequent decisions.

In 1841 Battle and ex-Governor James Iredell, Jr., began teaching law in Raleigh. In 1843 Battle moved to Chapel Hill and taught law in his office. In 1845 he became professor of law at the University of North Carolina, thus commencing the university's law school. Equipped only with his well-stocked mind, in a small room with six chairs, he prepared the state's future lawyers and jurists. As a professor of law from 1845 to 1868 and 1877 to 1879, he duplicated on a smaller scale the achievement of Joseph Story, who served simultaneously as associate justice of the U.S. Supreme Court and professor of law at Harvard.

Battle contributed to the biographical literature of his profession. He published memoirs of John Louis Taylor, North Carolina's first chief justice, and Leonard Henderson, a later chief justice. He gave an address on the life of William Gaston, an associate justice. A trustee of the University of North Carolina from 1833 to 1868 and 1874 to 1879, Battle urged the university's "re-establishment . . . upon a sound and . . . permanent basis" when it closed following the Civil War. When the university reopened, he encour-

aged its students to "a hearty performance of all their duties."

An active Episcopalian for forty years, Battle was a delegate to the 1865 general convention, at which he and his son Kemp Plummer Battle assisted the bishop in effecting a reunification of the Episcopal church. It was said that no layman of the South was more esteemed in church circles. Although the Battles were strongly antisecession, two of their sons died fighting for the Confederacy. Only three of Battle's children outlived him. Upon Battle's death in Chapel Hill, the community gathered at the university chapel "to pay a last honor to a learned teacher, a useful citizen . . . full of honors and ripe for his reward." Battle's greatest legacy is his inauguration of the study of law at his state's university.

• Battle's papers are located in the Battle Family Papers, Southern Historical Collection, University of North Carolina, Chapel Hill. His address given on 15 Sept. 1875, upon the reopening of UNC after the Civil War, is in the *North Carolina Journal of Education* 3, no. 3 (1875): 95–112. Biographical accounts include Joseph B. Batchelor, Address at the presentation of the portrait of Judge Battle to the North Carolina Supreme Court, 15 Mar. 1892, *North Carolina Reports* 110 (1892): 619–636; Kemp P. Battle, *Memories of an Old-Time Tar Heel* (1945); and Proceedings on the presentation of the portrait of William Horn Battle to the University of North Carolina School of Law, 8 Feb. 1923, in holdings of UNC School of Law Library, Chapel Hill. Battle's legal career is examined in Fannie M. Farmer, "The Bar Examination and Beginning Years of Legal Practice in North Carolina, 1820–1860," *North Carolina Historical Review* 29 (1952): 159–70 and "Legal Education in North Carolina, 1820–1860," *North Carolina Historical Review* 28 (1951): 271–97; and Roscoe Pound, *The Formative Era of American Law* (1938). See also W. Conard Gass, "A Felicitous Life: Lucy Martin Battle, 1805–1874," *North Carolina Historical Review* 52 (1975): 367–93; Marc W. Kruman, "Thomas L. Clingman and the Whig Party: A Reconsideration," *North Carolina Historical Review* 64 (1987): 1–18; and the William D. Valentine Papers, Southern Historical Collection, UNC Chapel Hill. Obituaries include Proceedings in the North Carolina Supreme Court in memory of William H. Battle, *North Carolina Reports* 80 (1879): 498–509.

WILLIS P. WHICHARD

BAUER, Catherine Krouse (11 May 1905–22 Nov. 1964), housing advocate and urban-planning educator, was born in Elizabeth, New Jersey, the daughter of Jacob Louis Bauer, a highway engineer, and Alberta Louise Krouse, a suffragist. Bauer graduated from Vassar College in 1926, having spent her junior year at Cornell University studying architecture. Following graduation she lived in Paris and wrote about contemporary architecture, including the work of the modernist Le Corbusier. In New York from 1927 to 1930, she held a variety of jobs and began a friendship with the architectural and social critic Lewis Mumford.

With an interest in the aesthetics of architecture and a growing concern for housing reform, Bauer traveled to Europe in 1930. Her research led to an award-winning magazine article (*Fortune*, May 1931) on the design of modern German housing. Returning to New

York in 1931, she became executive secretary of the Regional Planning Association of America and carried out research for Mumford and the planner Clarence Stein.

The publication of *Modern Housing* (1934), a sweeping account of housing in the United States and Europe, established Bauer's reputation as a leading housing reformer. Analyzing the politics, economics, design, and building of low-cost, modern housing in northern Europe, Bauer contrasted initiatives to plan for "public utility housing" with an American system of "speculative chaos" in which the private sector failed to provide sufficient housing. European reforms were due, she emphasized, to the political power of labor parties and trade union movements, not to technical expertise. She wrote, "There will never be any realistic housing movement in this country until the workers and consumers—and the unemployed—themselves take a hand in the solution" (p. 255).

From 1934 to 1937 Bauer devoted herself to building a housing reform movement in the United States, organizing local and national support for housing legislation. In 1934 she worked with labor activist John Edelman and Philadelphia trade unionists to found the Labor Housing Conference. In cities throughout the nation, Bauer brought together labor unionists, social reformers, and public officials, sparking the formation of local housing committees. She served as secretary and lobbyist for the American Federation of Labor's Housing Committee from 1935 to 1937. Working alongside housing reformers such as Edith Elmer Wood, Bauer played a pivotal role in the creation and passage of the Wagner-Steagall Act of 1937, a bill that established the government's role in providing low-cost housing through local authorities. Bauer then served as research and information director in the newly created U.S. Housing Authority until 1939. Though dissatisfied in this position, she continued to press for public housing and encouraged local housing authorities to build grass-roots support for the housing movement.

In 1940 Bauer was appointed as the Rosenberg Lecturer in Public Social Services at the University of California, Berkeley. Later that year she married San Francisco architect William Wilson Wurster; they had one child. They moved to Cambridge, Massachusetts, where Bauer conducted a housing seminar at Harvard from 1946 to 1948. Returning to the Berkeley campus in 1950, she joined the Department of City and Regional Planning. While on the faculty, she continued to write, speak, and teach about housing and urban development. She also consulted extensively with federal housing agencies, foundations, and the United Nations, served on advisory groups (including President Lyndon Johnson's urban task force), participated in Democratic party politics, and remained active in professional associations (including the National Public Housing Conference, the California Planning and Housing Association, and the International Federation of Housing and Town Planning).

In her many articles on social planning during these years, Bauer extended her analysis of public housing, cautioned against urban redevelopment, and advocated a balanced approach to metropolitan planning and development. Initially hopeful that a housing shortage during the World War II years might strengthen support for public housing, she was soon discouraged. Though a longtime proponent of large-scale planning, Bauer decried the institutional traits and "charity stigma" of high-rise housing projects. Population density, monotonous architecture, inattention to everyday human needs, and increasing social and racial isolation in housing projects had undercut support for low-cost public housing, turning even residents against it. In an influential 1957 article, "The Dreary Deadlock of Public Housing" (*Architectural Forum* 106, no. 5: 140–42, 219, 221), Bauer faulted the housing movement for having separated low-cost housing programs from the rest of federal housing policy and for having failed to adapt the principles of large-scale community design to the U.S. context in which individual homeownership was prized.

During the 1940s and 1950s Bauer wrote and spoke frequently about conflicts between housing and urban redevelopment programs. Denouncing the real estate industry's efforts to obtain public subsidies for slum clearance in order to benefit through increased land values, she maintained that decent, affordable housing must be the first priority. She urged planners to recognize the politics of planning, stressing that these conflicts were inherent to democracy and not overcome by technical expertise alone.

In the last decade of her life Bauer focused on questions of metropolitan and regional development in the United States and developing nations. Rather than seek to recapture the city of old, Bauer encouraged planners to strive for a balance of concentration and decentralization in the modern urban region by examining, for instance, what drew people to suburbs and by promoting the urban qualities that many still found attractive. Without a balanced regional approach, the modern metropolis would be threatened by even greater class and racial divisions and unmet human needs, including that of decent low-income housing.

Bauer died of a brain concussion and exposure suffered while hiking on Mount Tamalpais, just north of San Francisco. At the time of her death, she was associate dean in the College of Environmental Design at the University of California, Berkeley. Though she was not successful in building a sustained housing movement, her early insistence that modern housing was primarily a political issue, her emphasis on social planning, and her endeavor to reconcile planning and democracy distinguished her in the history of twentieth-century housing reform and the planning profession.

• After marriage, Bauer used both her maiden and married names professionally. The papers and correspondence of Catherine Bauer Wurster (1931–1964) are in the Bancroft Library, University of California, Berkeley. The State Historical Society of Wisconsin holds the Labor Housing Coalition Papers in the American Federation of Labor Collection. For an example of Bauer's housing reform work in the 1930s see "Now, at Last: Housing: The Meaning of the Wagner-Steagall Act," *New Republic*, 8 Sept. 1937, pp. 119–21. Bauer's *A Citizen's Guide to Public Housing* (1940) and "Redevelopment: A Misfit in the Fifties," in *The Future of Cities and Urban Redevelopment*, ed. Coleman Woodbury (1953), pp. 7–25, address the housing and redevelopment programs. On metropolitan development and planning, see "Framework for an Urban Society," in *Goals for Americans: Programs for Action in the Sixties*, U.S. President's Commission on National Goals (1960), pp. 225–47; Gail Radford, *Modern Housing for America: Policy Struggles in the New Deal Era* (1996), examines Bauer's leadership in housing reform. H. Peter Oberlander and Eva Newburn, "Catherine Bauer: Ahead of Her Time," *Planning* 61 (May 1995): 10–12, and Eugenie Ladner Birch, "An Urban View: Catherine Bauer's Five Questions," in *The American Planner: Biographies and Recollections*, ed. Donald A. Krueckeberg (1994), pp. 311–43, survey Bauer's work and life. For an extensive bibliography, see *Shaping an Urban Future: Essays in Memory of Catherine Bauer Wurster*, ed. Bernard J. Frieden and William W. Nash, Jr. (1969). Bauer's obituary is in the *New York Times*, 24 Nov. 1964.

ERIC FURE-SLOCUM

BAUER, Eddie (19 Oct. 1899–18 Apr. 1986), sporting goods retailer, was born on Orcas Island, Washington, the son of Jacob Bauer, a gardener-caretaker, and Marie Uhrich. Bauer spent his first years on a sparsely inhabited island, and his earliest memories centered on the hunting and fishing that supported the islanders. His parents relocated to the Seattle area when Bauer was three, and hunting and fishing became his favorite pastimes. He held various odd jobs while a boy, often at a country club where his father was caretaker. From club members and also from local Native Americans, Bauer learned techniques of marksmanship, sportfishing, and trapping that enhanced his hunting and fishing skills.

Bauer's parents separated when he was in his teens, and he worked to help support his mother. He took a job as a retail clerk at a Seattle sporting goods store, where the owner encouraged him to think creatively about ways to draw customers. Bauer determined that one way to attract customers was to establish a reputation as a master outdoorsman, reasoning that the publicity he earned would be free advertising for his employer. His plan worked, as he won numerous hunting and fishing competitions and admirers interested in duplicating his success began to seek out and follow his recommendations about sporting goods. Bauer also believed that such admirers would become frequent customers if they remained confident of the accuracy of his advice and if they were promised full refunds and prompt attention should they find fault with a recommended item. While his employer did not adopt such policies officially, Bauer was permitted to practice them and found them effective.

Increasingly devoting his energies to his job and outdoor activities, Bauer did not graduate from high school. He continued his promotional strategies by developing such skill at stringing tennis rackets that his employer put him in a store window to draw crowds. Certain that his reputation was an asset on which he could build his own business, Bauer quit his job, rented space in a nearby shop, and strung tennis rackets full-time. Less than a year later, in 1920, he had earned enough to open his own store, Eddie Bauer's Tennis Shop. Throughout the 1920s, Bauer diversified his business. He changed its name to Eddie Bauer's Sports Shop and began to carry high-quality gear for hunting, fishing, and other wilderness recreations. He attracted attention to the business by displaying freshly caught fish and large game in the windows and on the sidewalk outside. During hunting and fishing seasons, he field-tested products and made it known to his clients that he would sell only those that earned his full confidence. He also initiated the "Eddie Bauer Guarantee," which assured refunds to any customers not satisfied with products purchased at his store.

Bauer developed a series of sporting goods inventions, including uniform shuttlecocks, a racket-stringing machine, and a salmon-fishing flasher designed to attract fish to a lure (patent rights for which he granted to a friend). In 1935 he devised a quilted, goose down–insulated jacket. Inspiration for the invention came from his own experiences with hypothermia and family stories about a Cossack uncle who had stayed warm in a down-lined coat during the Russo-Japanese War. He patented the design in 1936, named the garment the "Skyliner," and began to manufacture and sell it. Competing products generally used wool or cotton batting, which were inferior to down as insulators and more cumbersome. Customers swiftly recognized the merits of down, and Bauer's sales increased almost tenfold between 1936 and 1941, aided by national advertising that drew mail-order customers from outside the Northwest. When the United States entered World War II, access to down for civilian uses was restricted by the War Production Board, but the war soon presented Bauer with new business. His company produced thousands of down-insulated flight suits and sleeping bags for the military.

In 1945 Bauer was poised to recapture the civilian market for down-insulated goods. Soldiers and pilots who had used Bauer products during the war became a large pool of potential customers. To reach such consumers nationwide, Bauer emphasized use of mail-order catalogs. Increases in many Americans' leisure time and disposable income buoyed the market for recreational goods in the 1950s and 1960s. Bauer's company continued to serve expert hunters and fishermen but increasingly drew customers from the growing ranks of casual hikers and campers.

In 1951 William F. Niemi joined Bauer as a partner in Eddie Bauer's Sporting Goods, bringing much-needed capital to help the company expand. His son, William Niemi, Jr., assumed the presidency of the company in 1968, when both Bauer and Niemi, Sr., retired. At that point, the company was restructured as Eddie Bauer, Incorporated, and collected well over a million dollars annually from mail-order sales. The company continues under that name, although General Mills purchased it in 1971 and then sold it in 1988 to Spiegel, Incorporated. These changes in ownership brought changes in corporate purpose, as the company added many retail outlets and increased fashionwear lines, while almost eliminating hunting and fishing products.

In retirement, Bauer pursued the outdoor activities that had always been at the center of his life. Married since 1929 to Christine Heltborg Bauer, with whom he had one son, Bauer maintained a home near the Redmond, Washington, headquarters of Eddie Bauer, Incorporated, as well as a home on the Olympic Peninsula of Washington State, from which he could easily fish and hunt on a regular basis. He provided some consulting and product-testing services for Eddie Bauer, Incorporated, and with coauthors contributed to recreational guides featuring his name in the titles. Bauer remained active until his wife's death in 1986, two weeks after which he died. His career had flourished as a result of growing public enthusiasm for outdoor recreation and his exceptional attention to customer service and product quality. Introducing quilted, down-insulated winter clothing was his most influential accomplishment, as consumers eventually bought such recreational gear for everyday use and popularized it as urban apparel.

• An unpublished autobiographical memoir written from Bauer's dictation is held by Eddie Bauer, Incorporated, in Redmond, Washington. Articles on Bauer include Robert Spector, "Eddie Bauer: The Man behind the Name," *Pacific Northwest Magazine*, May 1983, and Syl Jones, "Eddie Bauer: The Man behind the Name," *Family* [General Mills], Feb. 1980. A short article on Bauer is included in Joseph Fucini and Suzy Fucini, *Entrepreneurs: The Men and Women behind Famous Brand Names and How They Made It* (1985). Obituaries are in the *Seattle Post-Intelligencer*, 25 Apr. 1986, and the *New York Times*, 26 Apr. 1986.

BETH KRAIG

BAUER, Harold Victor (28 Apr. 1873–12 Mar. 1951), concert pianist and music educator, was born in New Malden, Kingston-upon-Thames, England, the son of Victor Bauer, a public accountant, and Mary Taylor Lloyd. His first piano teacher was his aunt and his first violin teacher his father. After making an initial decision to concentrate on the violin, Bauer began formal study with the prominent London teacher Adolf Pollitzer. At age ten, he made his first "public" appearance as violinist at a private concert in London; for the next decade he gave public appearances both as a violinist and as a pianist. In the musical circles of London he met pianist Graham Moore, from whom he learned about the technique of piano playing, although at the time Bauer had no thought of discontinuing his career as a violinist.

On one occasion, when he was taken to play the piano for the Polish pianist Ignace Paderewski in London, the famous pianist said, "That is very nice, but you have a lot to learn"; Bauer replied, "I wish you could hear me play the violin, I can play it better." Paderewski subsequently introduced Bauer to his friend,

violinist Wladyslaw Gorski, who, after hearing Bauer play both violin and piano told him, "You play better than I do. I think, however, that you play the piano better than you play the violin." Gorski then asked Bauer to accompany him in playing a sonata by César Franck (*Musical Quarterly* 29 [Apr. 1943]: 159). Bauer agreed; meanwhile Paderewski, who was in the process of learning a number of piano concertos, asked Bauer to play the orchestral reductions on the second piano and to practice the works with him at his home. This association with Paderewski later prompted Bauer to acknowledge that he "learned a great deal by being in the presence of this great master" but that "it cannot be said that I was his pupil" (*Musical Quarterly* 29 [Apr. 1943]: 159).

During the winter of 1894–1895, Bauer toured in Russia as accompanist for the singer Louise Nicholson, also filling out the programs with piano solos. Subsequently he returned to Europe, with Paris as a center, where he worked diligently to make a name for himself as a pianist. He realized that in order to overcome his technical deficiencies, he would need to find some means of making his playing acceptable without subjecting himself to the usual approach to technical study commonly undertaken by pianists—that is, evenness of scales, arpeggios, and "good tone." Accordingly, he decided that rather than practicing scales and other exercises, which had nothing to do with the piece at hand, he would devote himself entirely to developing his technic within the context of music itself, thereby refining his expressive powers, enhancing his phrasing, and discovering how "one note relates to other notes" (Cooke, p. 71). As he put it, "The only technical study of any kind I have ever done has been that technic which has had an immediate relation to the technical message of the piece I was studying" (Cooke, p. 65). His somewhat unorthodox approach of never studying technique independent of the musical piece produced such fine results that he became convinced that it was a mistake to practice technique at all "unless such practice should conduce to some definite, specific and immediate result" (Cooke, p. 66). As he explained to James Cooke,

Naturally, studying in this way required my powers of concentration to be trained to the very highest point. This matter of concentration is far more important than most teachers imagine. . . . Many pupils make the mistake of thinking that only a certain kind of music demands concentration, whereas it is quite as necessary to concentrate the mind upon the playing of a simple scale as for the study of a Beethoven sonata (Cooke, pp. 68–69).

Bauer adamantly believed that, correctly understood, "*technic is art* and must be studied as such. There should be no technic in music which is not *music itself*" (Cooke, p. 70).

On 30 November 1900 Bauer played the Brahms D minor Piano Concerto with the Boston Symphony under the conductor Wilhelm Gericke. From 1901 through 1902 he played again in the United States with orchestras in many of the nation's principal cities, and in 1903 and 1904 he toured in Brazil. He played in the United States and Europe as soloist and chamber musician during the following ten years, appearing with such illustrious musicians as cellist Pablo Casals and violinists Fritz Kreisler and Jacques Thibaud. Later his duo piano recitals with pianist Ossip Gabrilowitsch became highly popular. The individuality, fire, and imagination that he brought to his playing earned Bauer unanimous praise from critics and colleagues as one of the most distinguished pianists of his day.

Following the outbreak of World War I, Bauer settled in New York and became an American citizen. In 1917 he helped organize the Manhattan School of Music and in 1919 he founded the Beethoven Association, a society organized "to bring together artists of established reputation with the object of giving an annual series of concerts in a spirit of artistic fraternity." Bauer was president of the Beethoven Society from its beginning until 1939, just before the society dissolved. During his presidency the society was celebrated for the artistic quality of its concerts, which featured many outstanding artists who performed free of charge in its programs. The proceeds from the performances went to such charitable purposes as furthering the publication of Alexander Thayer's *Life of Beethoven*, supporting the MacDowell Association, a center for the arts in Peterboro, New Hampshire, facilitating the extensions of public collections of Beethoveniana, furnishing manuscript scores by great composers and reference books on musical subjects for the Library of Congress and the New York Public Library, and contributing to the building of the Festspielhaus in Salzburg.

During the height of his career (1915–1935), Bauer made nearly two hundred records and several radio appearances. Later he gave private instruction in New York and conducted master classes at the leading music schools and conservatories throughout the United States. Bauer introduced Claude Debussy's works to English audiences and arranged compositions of J. S. Bach, Johannes Brahms, Henry Purcell, and Robert Schumann for piano. Through his leadership in the Beethoven Association of New York and the Friends of Music of the Library of Congress, he did much to encourage interest in chamber music in America.

His first wife, Marie Knapp, of Stuttgart, whom he married in 1906, died in 1940. He predeceased his second wife, Winnie Pyle. Both marriages were childless. Bauer died in Miami, Florida.

• Bauer's papers are in the Library of Congress and include over 300 letters from friends and professional associates; 100 photographs; numerous concert programs, awards, press clippings, and lectures; printed music and holographs of piano arrangements; and the manuscript for his autobiography *Harold Bauer, His Book* (1948). Bauer's other works include "Self-Portrait of the Artist as a Young Man," *Musical Quarterly* 29 (Apr. 1943): 153–68, with photographs; "The Paris Conservatoire. Some Reminiscences," *Musical Quarterly* 33 (Oct. 1947): 533–42; and "Artistic Aspects of Piano Study," in James F. Cooke, *Great Pianists on Piano Playing: Study*

Talks with Foremost Virtuosos (1917). Other information on Bauer and his career may be found in Clara Clemens, *My Husband Gabrilowitsch* (1938); Adella Prentiss Hughes, *Music Is My Life* (1947); Harold C. Schonberg, *The Great Pianists: From Mozart to the Present* (1987), with photographs; and Olga Samaroff Stowkowski, *An American Musician's Story* (1939).

S. MARGARET WILLIAM MCCARTHY

BAUER, Louis Agricola (26 Jan. 1865–12 Apr. 1932), geophysicist and scientific administrator, was born in Cincinnati, Ohio, the son of Ludwig Bauer and Wilhelmina Buehler, occupations unknown. His father and mother were both brought to the United States from Germany by uncles about 1848. Bauer was the sixth of nine children. Born with no middle name, he jokingly conferred one on himself (Agricola is a Latin translation of Bauer, "farmer"). Although little more is known of the family, it is clear that they had adequate resources to send Bauer to college. He married Adelia Francis Doolittle in 1891. They had one child.

Bauer studied civil engineering at the University of Cincinnati, earning his C.E. in 1888. He had already been employed for two years, first in 1886 by a cable-car company and a railroad company, and then by the U.S. Coast and Geodetic Survey (USCGS). While an aide in the Computing Division at the USCGS from 1887 to 1892, Bauer began his transition to science. He worked under C. A. Schott, one of America's chief geomagnetic scientists since the 1850s. At the USCGS Bauer learned practical aspects of geomagnetism, including use of instruments and reduction of data. As did other American scientists, Bauer went next to Germany, where he earned a Ph.D. at the University of Berlin in 1895. He studied theoretical topics in physics and geophysics with well-known scientists, including Max Planck, Wilhelm von Bezold, and Wilhelm Foerster. These scientists served as examiners for Bauer's dissertation on the secular variation of geomagnetism, the slow change in the direction and intensity of earth's magnetism. In 1893 he met the influential magnetician Adolph Schmidt, and they began a long collaboration.

Bauer returned to the United States with a life's goal: to raise the study of earth's magnetism to the status enjoyed by other areas in the physical and earth sciences. He moved steadily and imaginatively toward this goal for thirty years. He taught mathematics and mathematical physics at the University of Chicago in 1895–1896 and in 1896–1897 became instructor in geophysics there, one of the first university positions in geophysics in the United States. Bauer became assistant professor of physics and mathematical physics at the University of Cincinnati in 1897, where among his courses was one on geomagnetism. After moving to Washington, D.C., in 1899, Bauer occasionally taught geomagnetism at Johns Hopkins University.

Bauer's greatest achievement was the organization and direction of extensive programs for the observation of earth's magnetic field. In this activity, he followed the tradition started by Sir Edmond Halley in the seventeenth century and promoted in the nineteenth century by Alexander von Humboldt and Carl Friedrich Gauss, among others. He first learned about mapping the geomagnetic field at the USCGS, and he observed magnetic variations at the Prussian geomagnetic observatory while a student in Berlin. While at Chicago and Cincinnati, he directed the geomagnetic survey of Maryland in the summers, the first complete magnetic survey funded by a state government. This survey was one of the most detailed in the world at the time, superior to those in Britain and Germany and surpassed only by that of the Netherlands.

In 1899 Bauer shifted from university employment to the USCGS to concentrate on research. As the first chief of a new Division of Terrestrial Magnetism, Bauer developed a full geomagnetic survey of the country and greatly expanded and reorganized the series of observatories for studying the temporal changes in earth's magnetism. In both these activities Bauer saw his task as keeping the United States at the highest international standard. Bauer also began a program of geomagnetic measurements on USCGS steamships.

Bauer extrapolated these three basic activities to an international scale after joining the Carnegie Institution of Washington (CIW) in 1904. He had concluded that no physical theory of earth's magnetism could be developed or tested until the magnetic elements had been mapped precisely over a significant portion of earth's surface, including the oceans, over a comparatively short period of time. The endorsement of the project by the CIW enabled Bauer to pursue his dream vigorously. Between 1905 and 1921, his Department of Terrestrial Magnetism (DTM) sponsored 130 expeditions to remote parts of the globe, and its two ships, the *Galilee* and the nonmagnetic yacht the *Carnegie*, sailed many times around the globe measuring the magnetic elements. Bauer participated in the fieldwork, traveling to Ceylon (modern Sri Lanka), Samoa, northern Canada, and Liberia and sailing on both ships. This ambitious project was the first comprehensive world magnetic survey.

Bauer's international efforts were not restricted to expeditionary science. He also organized and edited the journal *Terrestrial Magnetism* (now the *Journal of Geophysical Research*) from 1896 until the 1920s. He cultivated its international character. He included scientists of many countries among its associates and included articles in several languages. He published news of geomagnetic surveys and observatories around the globe and notes on promotions, retirements, and deaths of prominent magneticians. Bauer viewed the journal as a means of communication for an emerging specialty and as a means of building a sense of community among researchers of magnetism.

Bauer participated in numerous international scientific associations and congresses and helped organize the International Union of Geodesy and Geophysics after World War I. He was the first secretary of its Section of Terrestrial Magnetism and Electricity and edited its earliest publications. He was elected president of

the section in 1927 but was unable to serve because of a mental breakdown. His hopes for international science and his admiration for German scientists had been greatly disappointed by the war (he felt they had abandoned the internationalism of science for chauvinism), and his disappointment may have exacerbated a growing depressive condition.

Bauer's most important contributions to theory were in the physical decomposition of the earth's magnetic field (the mathematical analysis of the field based on physical theory), its statistical analysis, the determination of the ratio of causes within the earth to causes beyond it (for example, solar influences), the study of laws of secular variation and the gradual diminution of the earth's magnetization, and the correlation of solar and terrestrial phenomena. While based on the best available data, Bauer's work had a decidedly speculative element. Bauer thought he had shown that earth's rotation directly affects the magnetic field. He also concluded that part of the geomagnetic field is due to electric currents passing vertically through earth's surface, that is, perpendicularly to the surface. These and other conclusions came into doubt, some by the 1920s. Scientists in the 1950s and later, using new data-gathering technologies and computers, have been able to shed a clearer light on problems that were intractable in Bauer's lifetime. Nevertheless, Bauer's efforts provided much improved data and defined new problem areas. He published over three hundred articles and monographs.

Bauer had a strong sense of mission and obligation to his cause. He was noted for his efficiency and for his intolerance of imprecision among his subordinates. Although he delegated responsibility, he also controlled closely the lines of research at the DTM. He was described by colleagues as fiery, dynamic, and enthusiastic. Although his hopes for a separate discipline of geomagnetism were never realized, the various research areas he promoted have become central to our understanding of earth's deep structure, of continental drift, and of planetary physics.

Bauer committed suicide in Washington, D.C., after several years of depression and treatment.

• Letters and papers of Bauer are in the National Archives in the records of the U.S. Coast and Geodetic Survey and at the Carnegie Institution and its Department of Terrestrial Magnetism. Bauer materials are also in the George Ellery Hale Papers at the California Institute of Technology, Pasadena, Calif.; in the W. F. G. Swann Papers at the American Philosophical Society Library, Philadelphia, Pa.; and in the Adolph Schmidt Papers at the Forschungsbibliothek, Gotha, Germany. His scientific career is discussed and a bibliography of his scientific publications appears in a memorial number of *Terrestrial Magnetism and Atmospheric Electricity* (Sept. 1932). More recent historical articles include those by Gregory A. Good: "The Study of Geomagnetism in the Late 19th Century," *EOS: Transactions of the American Geophysical Union* 69 (19 Apr. 1988): 220–28, "Scientific Sovereignty: Canada, the Carnegie Institution and the Earth's Magnetism in the North," *Scientia Canadensis* 14 (1990): 3–37, and "Vision of a

Global Physics: The Carnegie Institution and the First World Magnetic Survey," *History of Geophysics* 5 (1994): 29–36. An obituary is in the *Washington Post*, 13 Apr. 1932.

GREGORY A. GOOD

BAUER, Marion Eugenie (15 Aug. 1887–9 Aug. 1955), composer, teacher, and advocate of modern music, was the daughter of Jacques Bauer and Julie Heyman. Her father was an amateur musician who earned his living as a grocer, and her mother was a language teacher. Born in Walla Walla, Washington, Bauer began her musical study in Portland, Oregon, where the family moved after the death of her father in 1890. Soon after her high school graduation in 1903, Bauer moved to New York City to live with her eldest sister, Emilie Frances, a pianist and music critic, who provided her with financial support and encouragement. During this period, Bauer studied piano and composition with Henry Holden Huss.

Bauer traveled to France in 1906 to continue her studies. The pianist Raoul Pugno introduced her to Nadia Boulanger, with whom she studied harmony until 1907. Boulanger was to have a profound influence on modern American composers during the decade following World War I, and Bauer was one of her first American students. Bauer returned to New York in 1907 to teach and compose; her song "Light" was premiered there by contralto Ernestine Schumann-Heink. Bauer traveled to Europe again in 1910, this time to study counterpoint and musical form with Paul Ertel in Berlin. On her return, Bauer was offered a seven-year contract for exclusive rights to her songs by the publisher Arthur P. Schmidt. During the next decade, she composed for larger and more varied musical ensembles, including women's and men's voices and a chamber ensemble of eleven instruments. Her early style, derived largely from impressionism, gradually came to include more dissonance, and she became a spokesperson for a modern, experimental idiom that incorporated dissonant note combinations and uneven rhythmic patterns. Indeed, throughout her teaching career, Bauer gave lecture-recitals in which she sought to explain modern music and to familiarize her audiences with unusual sounds.

Bauer made a third trip to Europe in 1923, where she studied fugue with André Gédalge in France and became part of the avant-garde "scene" in and around Paris. She became acquainted with many European and American composers who had gravitated to the excitement of Boulanger's studio and the cafes of the Left Bank. This trip abroad ended sadly with the illness and death of her sister in 1926.

After Emilie's death, Bauer returned to New York, where she became an editor and critic for the *Musical Leader*. She taught at New York University from 1926 to 1951, attaining the rank of associate professor in 1930; she was also a member of the Juilliard School of Music faculty from 1940 to 1944. Bauer was an active lecturer on modern music at the Chautauqua Institute from 1928 on and was a board member of the League of Composers, an organization committed to the creation and performance of experimental music through concerts and through its journal, *Modern Music*. Her own writings on musical history and aesthetics include three collaborative efforts with Ethel Peyser, *How Music Grew: From Prehistoric Times to the Present Day* (1925), *Music through the Ages: A Narrative for Student and Layman* (1932), and *How Opera Grew: From Ancient Greece to the Present Day* (1956); her own *Twentieth Century Music* (1933) and *Musical Questions and Quizzes: A Digest of Information about Music* (1941); and numerous articles in the musical press. She was honored on the occasion of her retirement in 1951 from New York University with a Town Hall concert of her works. She died in South Hadley, Massachusetts.

Marion Bauer is remembered more as a teacher and writer on music than as a composer. However, the recognition that she received at a time when women composers were hardly taken seriously is significant. She championed the cause of the American composer and of modern music.

• There has not yet been a full-length biography of Bauer. For a very good discussion of her life and works, see Christine Ammer, *Unsung: A History of Women in American Music* (1980). Other works that analyze some aspects of her career include Bauer's own autobiographical sketch in David Ewen, ed., *American Composers Today: A Biographical and Critical Guide* (1949; repr. 1979) and *Composers since 1900: A Biographical and Critical Guide* (1969; repr. 1981). See also Claire R. Reis, *Composers in America: Biographical Sketches of Contemporary Composers with a Record of Their Works* (1947); Madeleine Goss, *Modern Music Makers: Contemporary American Composers* (1952); Gdal Saleski, *Famous Musicians of Jewish Origin* (1949); and Irwin A. Bazelon, "Woman With a Symphony," *Baton* (March 1951). Obituaries appear in the *New York Times*, 11 Aug. 1955, and *Musical Leader* (September 1955).

BARBARA L. TISCHLER

BAUGHER, Henry Lewis (19 July 1804–14 Apr. 1868), college professor and president, was born in Abbottstown, Pennsylvania, the son of John Frederick Baugher, a prosperous tanner and farmer, and Anna Catharine Matter. For almost forty years his grandfather, John George Bager, was one of the pioneer German Lutheran pastors west of the Susquehanna River in Pennsylvania. After graduating from Dickinson College as salutatorian in 1826, Baugher studied at the Princeton Theological Seminary (1826–1828) and then at the recently established Lutheran Theological Seminary at Gettysburg (1828–1829). Licensed to preach in the latter year, he then became pastor of four congregations in the Boonsboro, Maryland, Lutheran parish. In 1829 he married Clara (or Clarissa) Mary Brooks; they had seven children.

In April 1831 Baugher took charge of the classical department of a secondary school operating under seminary auspices, the Gettysburg Gymnasium. When the Pennsylvania legislature transformed that institution into Pennsylvania College of Gettysburg (now Gettysburg College) in 1832, he was elected professor of the Greek language and belles-lettres. After the first president resigned in 1850, the trustees elected Baugher president of the college, a position he reluctantly accepted and in which he was still serving when he died.

During Baugher's tenure as president, the college remained small. Until 1866–1867 the college never enrolled as many as one hundred degree candidates, and the usual size of the full-time faculty was five, including Baugher. As were most of his contemporaries in other colleges, President Baugher was first among equals. His executive ability enabled him to secure the respect and support of his faculty and trustee colleagues. During his tenure the college's first successful endowment effort was undertaken. As did most presidents of his day, he continued to teach, holding the professorship of mental and moral science. Except for presidential sermons and discourses delivered to graduating classes, some of which appeared as separate pamphlets and others as articles in the *Evangelical Review*, he published little.

Deeply interested in the welfare of students, especially in their spiritual development, Baugher was long remembered as a "rigid disciplinarian." For him, strict obedience to the many rules and regulations then governing student life was indispensable for the development of good character. He was diligent in investigating infractions and requiring what were called "satisfactory acknowledgments" by guilty students. Once these were secured, he was quick to forgive and readmit students into his good graces.

Baugher was ordained a Lutheran pastor in 1833, and for the rest of his life he was an energetic member of either the West Pennsylvania or Maryland Synod. In addition, on numerous occasions he represented his regional synod at meetings of the General Synod of the Evangelical Lutheran Church in the United States. For more than thirty years he was secretary of its society that assisted poor young men in preparing for the Lutheran ministry. Between 1841 and 1852 and again from 1861 to 1866 he was pastor of Christ Lutheran Church in Gettysburg, which both college and seminary students were required to attend. He shared preaching duties with college and seminary colleagues. To the end of his days Baugher was a fervent supporter of student religious revivals.

During the Civil War battle of Gettysburg, the house Baugher's family occupied on the college campus was within Confederate lines. The Baughers successfully hid wounded Union soldiers in their basement, and the president joined faculty colleagues in ministering to the wounded and dying. Baugher was chosen to deliver the benediction at the dedication of Soldiers' National Cemetery on 19 November 1863.

Contemporaries described Baugher as a good teacher and effective preacher. He was outgoing, genial, and an excellent conversationalist with a large circle of friends. In an obituary tribute in the *Lutheran Observer*, 24 April 1868, its editor, Frederick W. Conrad, who knew Baugher well for more than thirty years, wrote about him: "Ardent in temperament, he did every thing with all his might. Frank and candid, he uttered his sentiments without fear or favor. Honest and courageous, he took his stand for the right, regardless of consequences, and rather courted than shrank from meeting difficulties and opposition."

After about a year of failing health, Baugher died, unexpectedly, in Gettysburg. A tribute in an alumni association report in 1870 accurately declared that he had been "connected with the instruction and discipline of the institution for almost thirty-seven years, actively and earnestly identified with all its interests from the beginning and largely contributing to its success and usefulness."

• Manuscript records generated during Baugher's long career that contain much information about him are in the Gettysburg College Archives, Gettysburg. For estimates by contemporaries, see John G. Morris, *Fifty Years in the Lutheran Ministry* (1878); Frederick W. Conrad, in *The Pennsylvania College Book, 1832–1882*, ed. E. S. Breidenbaugh (1882); and Henry Eyster Jacobs, in *Memoirs of Henry Eyster Jacobs . . .*, ed. Henry E. Horn (1974). For an estimate of Baugher's role in the history of Gettysburg College, see Charles H. Glatfelter, *A Salutary Influence: Gettysburg College, 1832–1985* (2 vols., 1987). Obituaries are in the *Gettysburg Star and Sentinel*, 15 and 22 Apr. 1868; the *Gettysburg Compiler*, 17 and 24 Apr. 1868; the *Lutheran Observer*, 24 Apr. 1868; and the *Decennial Report Made to the Alumni Association of Pennsylvania College, Gettysburg, Pennsylvania, June 30, 1870* (1871), p. 28.

CHARLES H. GLATFELTER

BAUM, Dwight James (24 June 1886–13 Dec. 1939), architect, was born in Little Falls, New York, the son of Fayette Baum and Alina Elizabeth Ackerman. His family was of Dutch descent and had come to New York in colonial times. Baum graduated from Syracuse University in 1909 and married Katharine Crouse of Syracuse in 1912, before moving to New York City.

Known as a hard-working and diligent professional, Baum planned his career carefully to succeed in the highly competitive environment of New York City. He settled in the small Bronx hamlet of Riverdale and built himself an attractive home in the Colonial Revival mode then becoming popular. "Sunnybank," built in 1915, was perched prominently on a hillside and partook of a number of early Hudson River Dutch building traditions. As a result of the patronage of developer Edward C. Delafield, whose Fieldston home he remodeled, Baum soon found himself busy designing suburban houses, planning a new country club (1920), and serving on the planning committee of this smart new bedroom suburb. Many of his houses were dressed in a rustic clapboard vernacular and topped by gambrel roofs—critics dubbed them "Dutch Colonial." Baum's practice flourished during the 1920s, and he soon built a special building to house his large staff near his home in Riverdale. In 1932 he was awarded the gold medal at the annual exhibition of the Architectural League of New York for the "simplicity and dignity" of his residential work.

Baum executed several major estates in the New York area, the largest being William P. Hoffman's imposing Georgian mansion in Fieldston (1922); "Wildflower," a Tudor house for theatrical producer Arthur Hammerstein in Whitestone, Long Island; and "Lawridge" (1921), his most elaborate Tudor design, for Robert J. Law in Port Chester, New York. He also designed the fanciful Venetian home, "Ca d'Zan" (1926), of circus man John Ringling in Sarasota, Florida. However, the mainstay of his lucrative practice was the smaller, single-family house planned for emerging suburbs such as Riverdale, Fieldston, Mamaroneck, and Maplewood, New Jersey. During the Great Depression, Baum demonstrated the virtue of plain, box-like two-story houses. "The greatest percentage of houses are small ones," he lamented in a magazine interview, "but they are the smallest percentage to have the best thought put into them." In 1930 he was awarded a prize by President Herbert Hoover and the Better Homes of America Association for one of his designs. He later became a consulting architect for *Good Housekeeping* magazine and designed its pavilion for the 1933 "Century of Progress" exhibition in Chicago.

Like many successful eclectic designers, Baum was something of a scholar who used his knowledge of colonial precedents to flavor the details in his houses. He published articles on early American architecture, served as a restoration architect in Charleston, South Carolina, and was a key member of the 1930s Architects' Emergency Committee. This group organized unemployed architects to document key examples of American colonial architecture threatened with demolition and eventually published the compendium *Great Georgian Houses of America* (2 vols., 1937). Baum's concern for people and the social dimensions of architecture pervaded all aspects of his work.

Baum's public buildings were generally tasteful, conservative examples of academic eclecticism. He is well represented in the city of Syracuse by the Hendricks Memorial Chapel on the Syracuse University campus. His best-known New York work, the Italian-Romanesque West Side YMCA (1930), was considered the finest facility in the United States at the time of completion. In addition to athletic and recreation spaces, it contained a hotel for 600 men and a dormitory for 300 boys. He also designed the Flushing Post Office in Queens (1932) and the delightful structures of Rye Playland in Westchester. In the mid-1930s he was appointed architect for Syracuse University's Maxwell Graduate School of Citizenship and Public affairs and served on the design committee that planned the 1939 New York World's Fair.

His career was cut short when he died of a sudden heart attack on the streets of midtown Manhattan, and his last designs had to be realized posthumously. Baum was survived by his wife and three sons. He was a member of the American Institute of Architects, the Beaux Arts Institute of Design, the National Sculpture Society, and the Architectural League of New York.

• A limited archive of photographic and manuscript material on Baum's architecture exists at the George Arents Research Library and University Archives at Syracuse University. Because Baum was the very first client of the noted photographer Samuel Gottscho, his work is well represented in the Gottscho-Schleisner collections at the Avery Library in New York City, the Museum of the City of New York, the Library of Congress, and in the hands of the photographer's executors. There are two photographic monographs, *Dwight James Baum, Architect, New York City: Architectural Catalogue* (privately printed, 1922) and *The Work of Dwight James Baum* (1927). No adequate biography has yet been prepared. On Baum's residential work, see Mark Alan Hewitt, *The Architect and the American Country House, 1890–1940* (1990), and John Taylor Boyd, Jr., "The Problem of the Small House," *Arts and Decoration* 33, no. 3 (1930): 25–28, 78–79. For his New York buildings, see Robert A. M. Stern, Gregory Gilmartin, and Thomas Mellins, *New York 1930* (1987). Obituaries are in the *New York Times* and the *New York Tribune*, 14 Dec. 1939.

MARK ALAN HEWITT

BAUM, L. Frank (15 May 1856–6 May 1919), children's author, journalist, and playwright, was born Lyman Frank Baum in Chittenango, New York, the son of Benjamin Ward Baum, a cooper and sawyer who had made a fortune in Pennsylvania oil, and Cynthia Stanton. He grew up on the family estate, "Roselawn," outside Syracuse, New York. Suffering from a congenitally weak heart, he was educated at home. A stay at Peekskill Military Academy beginning in 1868—which gave Baum a lifelong antipathy to academics and the military—ended less than two years later in his having a heart attack. Back home, he published a family newspaper and periodicals on stamp collecting and the breeding of fancy chickens. In 1881 he studied theater in New York City and joined a repertory company, then managed an opera house in Richburg, New York, from 1881 to 1882, and, with his father's financing, toured successfully with *The Maid of Arran*, a melodrama of his own composition, in 1882.

Baum married Maud Gage, the daughter of women's rights campaigner Matilda Joslyn Gage, in 1882. They had four children. He left the theater in 1883 to help establish a family business producing an axle grease. In 1888, when the business seemed doomed to fail, Baum moved his family to Aberdeen, South Dakota, to be near Maud's relatives. Baum's Bazaar, an elegant department store he opened, failed in a year. He next edited a newspaper, *Saturday Pioneer*, which folded in 1891. They moved to Chicago, where Baum briefly worked as a newspaper editor, then found more stable employment first as a traveling salesman and later as a buyer for a department store. Weary of life on the road, he founded and edited a trade magazine, *The Show Window*, for the National Association of Window Trimmers, a job that kept him at home.

Baum's career as a children's author began when his mother-in-law encouraged him to compile explanations of nursery rhymes that he had improvised for the amusement of his sons. Published in 1897, *Mother Goose in Prose* sold well because of its illustrations by Maxfield Parrish. In 1899 he collaborated with Chicago cartoonist W. W. Denslow on a large, lavishly illustrated volume of children's verse, *Father Goose: His Book*. No publisher would risk the investment; but Baum and Denslow paid for the printing, and it became a bestseller. Baum and Denslow collaborated again, in 1900, on the innovative design of the first edition of *The Wonderful Wizard of Oz*. The book's success allowed Baum to devote himself full time to a writing career. In his lifetime he produced more than eighty titles for children, as well as stage plays, songbooks, novels, and assorted specialty publications, using several pseudonyms (Louis F. Baum, Schuyler Staunton, Floyd Akers, Laura Bancroft, John Estes Cooke, Edith Van Dyne, Captain Hugh Fitzgerald, and Suzanne Metcalf). Although some were highly popular in their day (such as the Aunt Jane's Nieces series written as Van Dyne), only the original Oz story achieved the status of an American classic.

Baum's penchant for creating popular extravaganzas that cost more than they earned caused his personal fortunes to continue to shift. *The Wonderful Wizard of Oz*, adapted for musical theater complete with splendid sets and special effects, had a record 293-performance run on Broadway (1903), but expenses consumed Baum's income from the show and left him insolvent. To suit the tastes of theatergoers, the juvenile heroine Dorothy was made a young woman and given a suitor, a poet named Sir Dashemoff Daily. Comedy team David Montgomery and Fred Stone stole the show as the Scarecrow and the Tin Woodman, leading to demand for more adventures of these two characters. (The show had many imitations, the most successful of which was Victor Herbert's operetta *Babes in Toyland*.)

Baum responded to his audience's wishes by writing *The Land of Oz* (1904), which featured the Scarecrow and the Tin Woodman and introduced the character Princess Ozma, disguised as a boy for most of the story. The book succeeded, but a stage adaptation failed. Driven by popular demand and the need to make money, Baum continued the series with *Ozma of Oz* (1907), *Dorothy and the Wizard in Oz* (1908), and *The Road to Oz* (1909). In 1908 he launched an expensive multimedia project, *Fairylogue and Radio Plays*, which left him in debt. Hoping to live more cheaply, Baum moved his family to then-quiet Hollywood, California, in 1910. He tried to end the Oz series with *The Emerald City of Oz* (1910), but readers neglected his non-Oz works (such as *The Sea Fairies* [1911] and *Sky Island* [1912]). After declaring bankruptcy in 1911, he assumed the title "Royal Historian of Oz" and committed himself to producing one new Oz book per year. He wrote fourteen in all, some based on plays and tales written earlier: *The Patchwork Girl of Oz* (1913), *Tik-Tok of Oz* (1914), *The Scarecrow of Oz* (1915), *Rinkitink in Oz* (1916), *The Lost Princess of Oz* (1917), *The Tin Woodman of Oz* (1918), *The Magic of Oz* (1919), and *Glinda of Oz* (1920).

With partners, Baum formed the Oz Film Manufacturing Company, which produced several films with innovative special effects but failed in 1915. Baum had wisely not invested his own money and remained solvent. Complications following a gall bladder operation in 1918 left him bedridden. After Baum's death in Hollywood, Ruth Plumly Thompson continued the Oz series, producing nineteen more books that sustained the popularity of those authored by Baum.

Baum's stated goal in creating the land of Oz was to update the fairy tale, doing away with the standard monsters inherited from folklore and aiming to give children pleasure rather than teach them grim moral lessons. What the series does teach through the adventures of its young heroes and heroines is the development of character traits considered distinctively American: practicality, self-reliance, candor, optimism, and an attachment to home. Though full of wonders and absurdities, Oz's magic, like stagecraft, is more technological than supernatural; it is a fantasy land made of familiar American landscapes and modernized with smoking machinery. The 1939 production of *The Wizard of Oz*, one of Hollywood's all-time most beloved films, renewed Oz's popularity and Baum's place among the foremost American fantasists and children's authors.

• Baum's papers and manuscripts are housed at Columbia University. The major source on Baum's life is *To Please a Child: A Biography of L. Frank Baum, Royal Historian of Oz* (1961), by Frank J. Baum, the author's son, and Russell P. MacFall. *Baum Bugle*, a journal founded by the International Wizard of Oz Club in 1957, is an important source of scholarship. Since the 1960s many critics have taken serious interest in Baum, with articles appearing regularly in scholarly journals and chapters devoted to him in survey studies. See, for example, Roger Sale, *Fairy Tales and After: From Snow White to E. B. White* (1978), and Brian Attebery, *The Fantasy Tradition in American Literature: From Irving to Le Guin* (1980). Michael Patrick Hearn produced *The Annotated Wizard of Oz* (1973) and selected essays for a Critical Heritage book, *The Wizard of Oz* (1983). Hearn's essay collection includes Henry M. Littlefield's famous speculation, written in 1963, that *The Wizard of Oz* is a populist allegory in which the yellow brick road represents the gold standard. An obituary is in the *New York Times*, 8 May 1919.

JANET GRAY

BAUM, Vicki (24 Jan. 1888–29 Aug. 1960), writer, was born Hedwig Baum in Vienna, Austria, the daughter of Hermann Baum, a bookkeeper, and Mathilde Donat. According to her memoirs, Baum's early life was difficult, despite her middle-class surroundings. Her mother was institutionalized for mental illness and died from cancer when Vicki was young, while Hermann Baum tried to wield dictatorial control over his daughter. She escaped through reading and writing, and even had a story published at a young age in *Muskete*, a Viennese humorous weekly. However, writing was not Baum's first career; she studied harp at the Vienna Conservatory as a child and appeared with various orchestras in her teens and twenties. In 1906 she married writer Max Prels; they had no children. Incompatibility and financial woes led to divorce in 1912. Baum continued to write during their marriage and her entire musical career. In fact, Prels sold several of her stories under his name to the German magazine *Velhagen und Klasings Monatshefte*. She also published under her name during the marriage, for example in the Berlin Jewish magazine *Ost und West*.

Shortly after her divorce, Baum left Vienna to take a position with the Darmstadt city orchestra and married its conductor, Richard Lert, in 1916; they had two children. In 1914 she had published her first novel, *Frühe Schatten* (Early shadows), but Baum still considered herself a musician until she gave up this career to raise her family. At least in part to improve the family's finances, Baum then launched a second career in writing, landing *Der Eingang zur Bühne* (1920; *Once in Vienna*, 1943) in the inexpensive popular novel series of the giant Ullstein publishing house. Although she continued to turn out books for this series, she rejected Ullstein's lucrative exclusive contract because she wanted to write higher-quality fiction, and from 1920 to 1926 she authored several works that did garner some critical acclaim.

But by 1926 Baum had concluded that her family needed more money than her higher-quality work would earn, so she signed with Ullstein. Moving to Berlin—her family followed later—she became a staff writer for Ullstein publications and an editor for their glossy women's magazine. Her greatest effort, though, was put into producing well-written, middle-brow novels that possessed mass market appeal. These works did become enormously successful, and Baum emerged as a true celebrity in Berlin at the end of the "Golden Twenties."

Baum's first bestselling novel was *Stud. chem. Helene Willfüer* (1928; *Helene*, 1932). Serialized like all her popular novels in Ullstein's mass market weekly, this story of a "new woman" chemistry student caused an uproar with its modern depiction of women students, extramarital sex, and women's careers. But it was overshadowed by Baum's next novel, *Menschen im Hotel* (1929; *Grand Hotel*, 1930), which skyrocketed to international fame, especially following its publication in the United States in 1931. In part to work on the screenplay for a Hollywood version of *Grand Hotel* (which she did not write), Baum traveled to the United States in 1931, resolving to remain after a brief return to Germany in 1932, when she realized that Germany was too dangerous for a Jewish writer and her family.

While living in southern California, Baum wrote plays, stories for magazines, and scripts for companies such as Paramount and MGM. She undertook publicity tours, gave interviews, later helped sell war bonds, and traveled widely to research her novels and because she was fascinated by the cultures of other peoples. She also continued to produce—eventually in English—her trademark: popular, middle-brow novels combining well-researched realism and solid craftsmanship with melodrama and sentimentality. Examples include *Liebe und Tod auf Bali* (1937; *Tale of Bali*, 1937), depicting the conflict between Balinese natives and the Dutch colonial administration, and *The Weeping Wood* (1943), a series of loosely connected stories detailing the history of rubber. She and her family integrated themselves into the community, and her husband was named conductor of the Pasadena City Orchestra. Baum never felt truly at home in the United States, but she took U.S. citizenship in 1938 and did not consider returning to Europe to live after 1945. She died in Los Angeles.

Although Baum was a prolific writer, *Grand Hotel* was certainly most responsible for her fame. Translated into at least seventeen languages, this story has been adapted and readapted for more than sixty years. In the United States alone the number of versions is striking: from 1930 to 1931, the hit of the Broadway season; in 1932, MGM's Oscar-winning classic starring Greta Garbo, Joan Crawford, and John and Lionel Barrymore; from 1933 to 1945, an NBC, later CBS, radio serial; in 1945, MGM's remake called *Weekend at the Waldorf*, starring Ginger Rogers; in 1958, the (unsuccessful) musical *At the Grand*, starring Paul Muni; and from 1989 to 1992, *Grand Hotel: The Musical*, directed and choreographed by Tommy Tune, which ran for 1,018 performances on Broadway and won several Tony awards.

Actually *Grand Hotel*'s success came to be a burden for Baum, who felt she had been indelibly marked "the woman who wrote *Grand Hotel*" and that everything else she produced was inevitably compared to it. Although she believed that most people had missed the point of the novel, which was her ironic interpretation of modern life, it undeniably entertained millions. It also came to influence twentieth-century popular culture, for it was the first widely circulated work to employ what became a standard device in popular texts: an ensemble of characters arrives at a nuclear location; for twenty-four hours they interact in a series of dramatic incidents; then they go their separate ways.

Over the years Baum grew dissatisfied with her career, torn between her long-held belief that she could write works of higher literary quality and the need to earn money with books like *Grand Hotel*. Finally, as a test, she wrote what she thought was a higher-quality novel, a critique of contemporary American society called *The Mustard Seed* (1953), and planned to publish it under a pseudonym. But the publisher spoiled her ruse, printing it under Baum's name and even referring to *Grand Hotel* on the dust jacket, while reviewers failed to notice a difference in quality. At the end of her life, Baum seemed to come to terms with her kind of fame, calling herself a "first class writer of the second rank" in her memoirs.

• Baum's memoirs were published as *Es war alles ganz anders* (1962; *It Was All Quite Different*, 1964). Her early "better quality" novels include *Feme: Bußfahrt einer verirrten Jugend* (1927; *Secret Sentence*, 1932). Baum's middle-brow popular novels include *Zwischenfall in Lohwinckel* (1930; *. . . and Life Goes On*, 1931, dramatized as *Divine Drudge: A Play in 3 Acts*, 1934), and *Hotel Shanghai* (1939; *Shanghai '37*, 1939). As of *The Ship and the Shore* (1941), Baum wrote mainly in English, including *Marion Alive* (1942), *Hotel Berlin '43* (1944), *Headless Angel* (1948), *Danger from Deer* (1951), and *Theme for Ballet* (1958).

A book-length study on Baum is Lynda J. King, *Best-sellers by Design: Vicki Baum and the House of Ullstein* (1988), which also includes an extensive bibliography and biographical material. Other sources with bibliographical and biographical material in English are Robert Bell, "Vicki Baum," in *Deutsche Exilliteratur seit 1933*, ed. John M. Spalek and Joseph Strelka, vol. 1: *Kalifornien*, pt. 2 (1976), pp. 6–13; John M. Spalek, *Guide to the Archival Materials of the German-speaking Emigration to the United States after 1933* (1978), pp. 51–55; and Richard E. Ziegfeld, "The Exile Writer and His Publisher: Vicki Baum and Doubleday," in *Deutsche Exilliteratur: Literatur der Nachkriegszeit*, ed. Wolfgang Elfe et al. (1981), pp. 144–53.

LYNDA J. KING

BAUR, John I. H. (9 Aug. 1909–15 May 1987), museum director, curator, and art scholar, was born John Ireland Howe Baur in Woodbridge, Connecticut, the son of Paul V. C. Baur, a Yale University professor of archaeology, and Susan Whiting. Jack Baur, as he was known, attended Yale, graduating in 1932 with a degree in English. He had difficulty finding teaching jobs because of the depression, and he was lured back to Yale by an art history scholarship, although he had little background in the subject. Baur studied under Henri Focillon, the author of *The Life of Forms in Art* (1934), and architectural historian Marcel Aubert, and he received his M.A. in 1934, specializing in baroque art.

Baur was offered a position at the Brooklyn Museum as supervisor of education, and after two years he was appointed curator of painting and sculpture. Baur often explained that it was limited funds and the comparative expense of European art that led to his interest in purchasing and eventually specializing in American art. His pioneering efforts to rediscover forgotten nineteenth-century American painters led to his exhibitions on Eastman Johnson (1940), John Quidor (1942), and Theodore Robinson (1946). It was at the Brooklyn Museum that Baur met Louise Weld Chase, the assistant curator of medieval art, whom he married in 1938; they had three children.

Baur's career was interrupted by World War II, when in 1944 he entered the army as a private in the infantry. He was promoted the next year to technical sergeant in special services and helped to arrange an exhibition of soldiers' art at the National Gallery in Washington, D.C., ghostwriting a catalog foreword for Secretary of War Henry Lewis Stimson. When the war ended Baur returned to the Brooklyn Museum and his writing, publishing a long essay, "Trends in American Painting, 1815–1865," for the catalog *M. and M. Karolik Collection of American Paintings 1815–1865* (1949). He also returned to Yale as a visiting lecturer in 1950–1951.

The Library of Congress asked Baur to write a survey of twentieth-century American art for its series on American civilization. This resulted in his first book, *Revolution and Tradition in Modern American Art* (1951), and recognition as a leading scholar in American art. Baur's research for this volume often led him to the Whitney Museum of American Art, where he

became good friends with Lloyd Goodrich, then the museum's associate director. In 1952 Baur left the Brooklyn Museum to become a curator at the Whitney Museum, which was still in its original home on West Eighth Street. Two years later the Whitney moved to a new building on West Fifty-fourth Street, behind the Museum of Modern Art. Here, attendance at the museum grew from 70,000 to 270,000, and it became clear another major expansion would soon be necessary.

When Goodrich became director in 1958, Baur was appointed associate director and placed in charge of a capital campaign to raise $8 million for a new building. For the next eight years, working in close collaboration with architect Marcel Breuer, Baur orchestrated the move to a still larger space at Madison Avenue and Seventy-fifth Street. The new museum opened to the public in 1966, and two years later Baur succeeded Goodrich as director of the Whitney Museum. Under his supervision the scope of the museum's annual survey of American art greatly expanded to include artists from all across the country. In an interview with the *New York Post*, Baur stated, "The Whitney is unique in that it believes—actively believes—in the diversity of American art, that no one direction has a claim to be the only creative direction." Baur also expanded the education department, added a film and video program, and in 1973 established the museum's first satellite exhibition space, the downtown branch, in the financial district of Lower Manhattan.

In his long career Baur organized and wrote monographs for exhibitions on Loren MacIver and I. Rice Pereira (1953), George Grosz (1954), Charles Burchfield (1956), Bradley Walker Tomlin (1957), William Zorach (1959), Philip Evergood (1960), Balcombe Greene (1961), Bernard Reder (1961), Joseph Stella (1963), and John Quidor (1965). His numerous books include *American Painting in the Nineteenth Century* (1953), *ABC for Collectors of Contemporary Art* (1954), *Nature in Abstraction* (1958), and, with Goodrich, the influential *American Art of Our Century* (1961). In addition, he was a regular contributor to journals such as *Art News*, *Art in America*, *Art Digest*, and *Magazine of Art*, and he served on many of their editorial boards.

Baur retired in 1974 but remained on the museum's board as director emeritus and honorary trustee until his death. He continued to write and curate exhibitions, serving as consulting director for the Terra Museum of American Art in Chicago and then as research consultant to the Kennedy Galleries in New York, for which he wrote thirteen exhibition catalogs from 1983 to 1986. At the time of his death in Manhattan he was preparing an exhibition, New Horizons: American Painting (1840–1910), for the Smithsonian Institution's Traveling Exhibition Services that was scheduled to open in Moscow that autumn.

Baur moved the Whitney from a Greenwich Village brownstone to become a landmark institution on Manhattan's Upper East Side. He was responsible for the acquisition and exhibition of contemporary American art during a period when few art museums recognized the value of this work. Artist Helen Frankenthaler wrote of Baur, "He was simple, clear, forthright and unassuming; yet strong in his views and stood by them. Politics were not his game; rather, he quietly and firmly stood up for his goals and beliefs and took healthy chances to defend them."

• Baur's papers are in the Archives of American Art, Smithsonian Institution. Administrative papers can be found in the archives of both the Brooklyn Museum and the Whitney Museum of American Art. Baur was the subject of an exhibition and symposium, Making History at the Brooklyn Museum, at the Brooklyn Museum, 16 Apr. 1988; and in conjunction with this an article by John Russell appeared in the *New York Times*, 10 Mar. 1988. Obituaries are in the *New York Times*, 16 May 1987, and *American Art Journal*, no. 2 (1987): 84–86.

JULIE MELLBY

BAUSCH, Edward (26 Sept. 1854–30 July 1944), industrialist and inventor, was born in Rochester, New York, the son of John Jacob Bausch, an industrialist, and Barbara Zimmerman. His father, who had immigrated from Würtemberg (in present-day Germany) in 1849, opened an optical shop in Rochester in 1853 and had begun to make eyeglasses and frames, taking Henry Lomb into a partnership that would grow into the Bausch & Lomb Optical Company.

While attending a German-language elementary school and the city high school, Edward worked after hours in the family business, assisting his father in the production of the hard-rubber spectacle frames in which the firm specialized. At age fourteen he designed and built his first microscope. In 1871 he won an engineering scholarship to Cornell University but left without a degree in 1874 to enter the firm full time.

In 1875 Bausch & Lomb began the production of microscopes designed by Edward Bausch. With his two younger brothers, William and Henry, he did all the optical work on the microscopes—lens-grinding, assembly, and testing—for many years. Edward went to Philadelphia in 1876 to run the firm's exhibit at the Centennial Exposition, where he met many visiting microscopists and studied the construction and performance of instruments sent by leading European firms. When he returned home he began to design machinery that would compensate for the lack of skilled workers in America able to produce European-quality hand-crafted microscopes. His machines permitted him to reduce the price substantially. When he began, an adequate instrument cost $1,000, but in a few years Bausch & Lomb succeeded in lowering to below $200 the price of a basic microscope.

Other inventions followed. In 1882 Bausch patented a microscope specially designed to study contamination in meat; he soon added patents on microscope illuminators, microtomes, invertible microscopes, binocular microscopes, and projection apparatus. He wrote *Manipulations of the Microscope* (1885), which became a standard textbook and went through four editions by 1901, expanding from ninety-six to 202 pages. In 1902 he prepared a 37-page extract titled *The Use and Care of the Microscope*; a revised version was still packaged by Bausch & Lomb with all its microscopes as late as 1950.

Under Bausch's direction the firm began the production of photographic lenses in 1883 and became the main supplier of lenses for the Eastman Kodak Company, a relationship that lasted until 1912, when George Eastman decided to build his own optical factory. Bausch's patent of an iris diaphragm shutter won praise from Eastman, who adopted it for his cameras and became a close friend.

His trips to Europe in 1888, 1891, and 1893 permitted Bausch to visit the leading European manufacturers of scientific instruments. He was particularly impressed with the innovations of the Carl Zeiss firm of Jena and arranged to acquire American rights to produce the anastigmatic photographic lenses, prism binoculars, and range finders that Zeiss had invented. In time this led to a cooperative working arrangement in which each firm shared the inventions of the other. The contract with Zeiss was suspended during World War I but renewed in the 1920s. Despite being heavily criticized in the 1930s and 1940s for its close contacts with the Germans, Bausch & Lomb defended its actions on the grounds that the contract provided the United States with privileged access to the best European military optical technology. Before the United States entered the war, William Bausch discovered a way to produce quality optical glass, which until then had been entirely imported from Europe. In both world wars the company won official praise for its production of optical equipment for the army and navy.

Edward Bausch became vice president of Bausch & Lomb in 1899 after the death of Henry Lomb and succeeded to the presidency when his father died in 1926. In 1935 he resigned the presidency to become chairman of the board, a post he held until his death.

He was very active in civic and philanthropic affairs in his home city. He joined with George Eastman in founding the Community Chest in 1918, serving as chairman of the campaign committee for eleven years before succeeding Eastman as president. Also with Eastman he helped organize the Bureau of Municipal Research, an agency designed to aid municipal reform by providing scientific advice to local officials in the Rochester area. With his brothers and members of the Lomb family, he donated funds for construction of a science building, Bausch & Lomb Hall, on the University of Rochester campus.

A charter member of the American Microscopical Society, Edward Bausch was also chosen as a fellow of the Royal Microscopical Society. In 1936 the American Society of Mechanical Engineers awarded him a gold medal for his lifetime contributions to science and engineering, an honor he shared that year with Henry Ford.

In 1878 Bausch had married Matilda G. Morrell, whom he had met at Cornell; they had no children. Shortly before her death in 1940 the couple donated the grounds of their Rochester mansion and $523,000 to the Rochester Museum of Arts and Sciences (later called the Rochester Museum and Science Center) for a new building that was completed in 1942. Ill health confined him to his home for several years before his death there.

• The Rochester Museum and Science Center has manuscript material, family photographs, and memorabilia on Edward Bausch, his family, and the Bausch & Lomb Optical Company. William F. Peck, *History of Rochester and Monroe County* (2 vols., 1908), has biographical sketches of Edward and his father, along with a brief history of the company. Edward B. Foreman, *Edward Bausch: An Appreciation* (1933), and "Memorial Issue: Edward Bausch and William Bausch," *Bausch & Lomb Magazine* 20, no. 3 (1944), contain much biographical material. Harold A. Nichols, "A Pioneer in Vision Looks Back," *Rochester Democrat & Chronicle Sunday Magazine*, 27 Sept. 1942, is an interview written for his eighty-eighth birthday. M. Herbert Eisenhart, *J. J. Bausch (1830–1926), American Pioneer* (1948), is really a brief history of the company by Edward's successor as president of Bausch & Lomb and is very defensive about the contract with Zeiss. The *Rochester Democrat & Chronicle*, 24 Jan. 1933, has extensive coverage of the tributes to Edward Bausch at a dinner given in his honor by the Society of the Genesee in New York City the previous evening. Obituaries are in the *New York Times* and the *Rochester Democrat & Chronicle*, 31 July 1944.

MILTON BERMAN

BAXTER, Anne (7 May 1923–12 Dec. 1985), actress, was born in Michigan City, Indiana, the daughter of Kenneth Stuart Baxter, a business executive, and Catherine Wright. Her maternal grandfather was architect Frank Lloyd Wright. By the time she was ten, the Baxters had moved to New York City and Anne had announced her intention of becoming an actress. Her parents supported her ambition and enrolled her in drama school. Success came early to Baxter, who made her Broadway debut at age thirteen in *Seen but Not Heard* (1936). At the time she told a reporter, "Acting is not merely fun, it is an earnest career."

In 1938 Baxter appeared in two Broadway flops, *There's Always a Breeze* and *Madame Capet*, and was rejected for the role of Katharine Hepburn's younger sister in the Broadway version of *The Philadelphia Story*. Despite these setbacks, she was determined to become a star, and she set her sights on Hollywood. Once there, she screen-tested for the lead role in *Rebecca* but was turned down because she appeared too young. (At sixteen, she was half the age of the film's male star, Laurence Olivier.)

Darryl F. Zanuck, then head of 20th Century–Fox studios, was impressed by Baxter's screen test and signed her to a seven-year contract. She was loaned to MGM for her first film assignment, a supporting role in a minor western, *Twenty Mule Team* (1940). Baxter's subsequent roles in *The Great Profile* (1940), *Charley's Aunt* (1941), and *Swamp Water* (1941) failed to garner her much attention. Her first notable performance came when Orson Welles cast her as Lucy Morgan in *The Magnificent Ambersons* (1942), based on Booth Tarkington's Pulitzer Prize–winning novel.

Slightly overweight, Baxter was not a typical movie ingenue. She once said of herself, "I'd wanted to be in pictures ever since I was twelve, although I was fat and

pudgy, had broken my nose and was advised to wear glasses—which I never did." Even when she developed a more shapely figure, Zanuck felt she lacked sex appeal and saw her as a "librarian" type. As a result, Baxter was mainly cast in secondary, girl-next-door parts throughout this early stage of her career. During World War II, when patriotic war films were popular, her films typically portrayed her as the faithful wife or girlfriend of a soldier.

Baxter fought against being typecast as a nice homebody and scored favorable reviews for her portrayal of a malicious bride-to-be in *Guest in the House* (1945). In another radical departure from her demure screen persona, she played the alcoholic Sophie in *The Razor's Edge* (1946). The *New York Sun* reviewer wrote, "Sophie may not be the central character. She is still the one you'll remember." Baxter's performance earned her the Academy Award for best supporting actress. In a 1985 interview she called her portrayal of Sophie "my only great performance."

After her Oscar win, Baxter was again relegated to playing librarian types. She toiled in a number of unremarkable pictures before landing the plum role of Eve Harrington in *All about Eve* (1950).

Baxter gave the most memorable performance of her career as Eve, the scheming understudy who plots to take over for Broadway star Margo Channing (played by Bette Davis). She and Davis were both nominated for Oscars in the best actress category but lost to Judy Holliday. Davis and the studio had been pushing for Baxter to be nominated as best supporting actress, but Baxter refused the nomination, feeling that she had graduated from supporting roles and was as important to the film as Davis. Years later she reflected that she and Davis probably "canceled each other out" as best actress.

In 1952 Baxter left 20th Century–Fox, hoping to create a new identity as a glamour girl. She actively courted publicity, smoking cigars in public and making outrageous statements to the press ("I'd love to eat hummingbird tongues" was one) in an attempt to add spice to her image. The gambit worked, and she found herself in constant demand. She worked steadily, but most of her films were inconsequential. One exception was Cecil DeMille's epic *The Ten Commandments* (1956).

Baxter's focus shifted in the 1960s to the growing medium of television. She appeared in numerous made-for-television movies and series episodes but turned down a regular role in the series "Marcus Welby, M.D." She turned heads with a recurring character on the campy series "Batman" and earned an Emmy nomination for an installment of "Name of the Game."

Baxter returned to the stage in 1971, ironically, replacing Lauren Bacall in the Broadway musical *Applause* (1971), the musical version of *All about Eve*. The film's "Eve" had finally become Margo Channing.

Another bit of ironic casting came in 1983 when Bette Davis suffered a stroke while filming the television series "Hotel," and Baxter was hired as her replacement. Through the years, the *All about Eve* screen rivals had been rumored to be feuding, but Baxter insisted they were on friendly terms. She told an interviewer, "What I'm hoping is that now that Bette is out of the hospital, we will actually have some episodes together. I'd love to work with her again."

Baxter suffered a stroke on 3 December 1985 while Christmas shopping in Manhattan. She died there nine days later.

Baxter was married to actor John Hodiak from 1946 until their divorce in 1953. She married Randolph Galt in 1960 and temporarily gave up her acting career to live on his cattle ranch in Australia. They divorced in 1970. Her third marriage, to investment banker David Klee, began in 1977 and ended with his death less than a year later. She had three children, one with Hodiak and two with Galt.

Of her more than fifty films, only a handful were truly remarkable, yet Anne Baxter was considered one of the silver screen's finest actresses. Never a superstar, she earned a reputation as a consistently competent, intelligent performer. With *All about Eve* firmly established as a cinema classic, Baxter's place in movie history will not soon be forgotten.

• In the autobiographical *Intermission* (1976), Baxter candidly covers the period from Jan. 1959 to Mar. 1963, during which she met and married Randolph Galt and forsook her acting career to move with him to the Australian bush. Baxter is the subject of an in-depth career analysis, Karin J. Fowler, *Anne Baxter: A Bio-Bibliography* (1991). James Robert Parish, *The Fox Girls* (1971), includes a lengthy chapter on Baxter, with several photographs and a filmography. J. E. A. Bawden's lengthy profile of Baxter appeared in *Films in Review*, Oct. 1977, pp. 449–62. Other magazine and newspaper articles of note include Helen Dudar, "Anne Baxter's Road to Shakespeare," *New York Times*, 1 Aug. 1982; Cliff Jahr, "Great Hollywood Comebacks: Anne Baxter," *Ladies Home Journal*, June 1985, pp. 63–65; Judy Klemesrud, "From 'All about Eve' to All about Anne," *New York Times*, 22 Aug. 1971; Doug McClelland, "Taking Stock," *American Classic Screen*, Nov./Dec. 1977, pp. 8–12; and Philip K. Scheuer, "Anne Baxter Fights for Lighter Roles," *Los Angeles Times*, 26 June 1949. Obituaries are in the *Hollywood Reporter*, the *Los Angeles Times*, the *New York Times*, and the *Washington Post*, all 13 Dec. 1985; and *Variety*, 18 Dec. 1985.

BRENDA SCOTT ROYCE

BAXTER, Elisha (1 Sept. 1827–31 May 1899), lawyer and governor of Arkansas, was born in Rutherford County, North Carolina, the son of William Baxter, a wealthy farmer, and Catherine Lee. Elisha Baxter received a meager education in the local schools and at an early age opened a store at Rutherfordton with his brother-in-law. Baxter also tried farming. In 1849 he married Harriet Patton; they had six children.

Baxter and his family moved to Batesville, Independence County, Arkansas, in 1852. He opened a store there with his brother Taylor but went bankrupt in 1855. For a year he worked as a typographer and read law in his spare time with Hulbert F. Fairchild. In 1856 he was admitted to the bar. He first became involved in politics in 1853, when he ran successfully for mayor of Batesville. In 1854 and 1858 he was elected to the lower house of the state legislature. Baxter was a Whig in his early career, but in 1858 and 1860 he associated politically with Thomas Carmichael Hindman, a Democratic congressman from Helena who attacked the domination of the state Democratic party by a group known as the "family," appealed to the state's yeoman farmers for support, and advocated secession, even though Baxter never personally advocated disunion.

Baxter dropped his association with Hindman in 1861 and opposed secession. After Arkansas seceded, he proclaimed himself a neutral and remained at home, although he served as prosecuting attorney in the state's Seventh Judicial District. When Union forces under General Samuel Ryan Curtis arrived at Batesville in 1862, Baxter, as the community's most prominent Unionist, was offered command of a Union regiment recruited there. He refused the commission, however, because, while opposed to secession, he did not want to make war on his neighbors. After the Union army left the area, Baxter faced growing hostility from loyal Confederates because of his pro-Union stand, and he fled the state to Missouri, leaving his family behind. In 1863 Confederate cavalry under Colonel Robert C. Newton captured Baxter in Missouri, where he was working as a teacher. He was sent to Little Rock and handed over to civil authorities. Charged with treason because of his unionism, he escaped from prison before he could be tried and again fled to Missouri.

His treatment by Arkansas authorities radicalized Baxter regarding the war, and after his escape he decided to join the Union army. Following the fall of Little Rock in September 1863, he went to the state capital and requested authority from General Frederick Steele to recruit an Arkansas regiment. Steele gave him permission, and Baxter began organizing the Fourth Arkansas Mounted Infantry (Union) at Batesville. Steele also named Baxter commander of the military post there.

In the election of 1864 that created a loyal Union government under Isaac Murphy, Baxter was chosen for a position on the state supreme court. He resigned his commission as colonel of the Fourth Arkansas to accept that seat, but on 4 May 1864, before he assumed it, the legislature elected him to the U.S. Senate. Baxter presented his credentials later that month, but, as in the case of other congressmen-elect from Confederate states with loyal wartime governments, he was never seated because Congress objected to Abraham Lincoln's terms for readmission.

After the war Baxter was active in the newly formed Arkansas Republican party. Governor Powell Clayton appointed him judge of the Third Judicial District on 25 July 1868. He was named registrar in bankruptcy for the First Congressional District the next year and continued in that position until 1872, when he became the candidate for the governorship of the Republican faction led by Clayton known as the "Minstrels." Baxter ran on a platform that sustained Clayton's programs insuring law and order, developing public education, and encouraging economic development through the construction of railroads. His opponent, the Iowa carpetbagger Joseph Brooks, ran at the head of the "Brindletail" ticket backed by the Liberal faction of the Republican party and many Democrats. In a close election, Brooks claimed victory, but the election board, controlled by Clayton's men, gave Baxter the official majority. Baxter took office, but Brooks filed suit to have the results overturned in the state supreme court and in the Pulaski County [Little Rock] Circuit Court. The supreme court denied Brooks's appeal immediately, but the circuit court delayed its decision, setting up a later political conflict.

When he took office, Baxter moved away from the Clayton faction. He proposed conciliatory policies toward ex-Confederates, such as removal of the disfranchising provisions of the state constitution. He also opposed legislation that gave state bonds to railroads and refused to issue railroad bonds approved by his predecessor, thus blocking the railroad and economic development favored by many Clayton Republicans. When in 1874 he appeared ready to support the legislature in calling a constitutional convention, the Clayton Republicans dropped their support of Baxter, while Liberal Republicans and Democrats moved into his camp. Senators Clayton and Stephen Dorsey opposed Baxter by pressuring the Pulaski County Circuit Court for a decision in Brooks's case. The court made a decision favoring Brooks's claim to the governor's office and demanded that Baxter step down. Baxter refused, and a group of armed men forcibly expelled him from office. Baxter then called on his supporters to sustain him. A series of armed clashes known as the Brooks-Baxter War failed to resolve the conflict, and only a proclamation by President Ulysses S. Grant recognizing Baxter settled the dispute peaceably.

Baxter's success in 1874 allowed the Democrats, who had already regained control of the legislature, to complete their return to power. With Baxter's support, they called a constitutional convention, which wrote a new constitution and also vacated all offices, including Baxter's. Baxter left office on 12 November 1874. The Democratic convention offered him their nomination for governor, but he declined and returned to his home at Batesville, where he farmed and practiced law. His name was put forward in 1878 for the U.S. Senate in the state legislature, but he was not elected. Although he had played an important role in the conservative "redemption" of the state government, Baxter never played a major role in state politics afterward. He died at Batesville.

• Baxter wrote a short autobiography that provides some insight into his career, "Elisha Baxter's Autobiography," ed. Ted R. Worley, *Arkansas Historical Quarterly* 14 (1955): 172–75. For a short scholarly biography, see Michael Dougan, "Elisha Baxter," in *The Governors of Arkansas*, ed. Timothy P. Donovan and Willard B. Gatewood, Jr. (1981). Baxter's role in postwar politics may be seen in George H. Thompson, *Arkansas and Reconstruction: The Influence of Geography, Eco-*nomics, and Personality* (1976). Details of the Brooks-Baxter War may be found in John M. Harrell, *The Brooks and Baxter War: A History of the Reconstruction Period in Arkansas* (1893), and James H. Atkinson, "The Brooks-Baxter Contest," *Arkansas Historical Quarterly* 4 (1945): 124–49. Obituaries with considerable detail are in the *Arkansas Democrat*, 1 June 1899, and the *Arkansas Gazette*, 2 June 1899.

CARL H. MONEYHON

BAXTER, James Phinney, III (15 Feb. 1893–17 June 1975), historian, was born in Portland, Maine, the son of James Phinney Baxter, Jr., a businessman, and Nelly Furbish Carpenter. He was educated in Portland public schools, finishing his last year of high school at Phillips Academy in Andover, Massachusetts. Baxter attended Williams College in Williamstown, Massachusetts, where he majored in history and participated in debate and student government. He was elected to Phi Beta Kappa and graduated summa cum laude in 1914.

Baxter worked for a year for the Industrial Finance Corporation, a New York banking firm, before contracting tuberculosis. While recuperating in Colorado he met and married Anne Holden Strang in 1919; the Baxters had three children. Always interested in the academic field of history, Baxter determined to make it his career. He began his graduate study in Colorado, earning his M.A. in absentia from Williams in 1921. Baxter then taught at Colorado College for one year before continuing his graduate work at Harvard University, where he was awarded a second M.A. in 1923. In 1924 Baxter was granted the John Harvard Fellowship, which allowed him a year of travel.

In 1925 he began teaching at Harvard, earning his Ph.D. in diplomatic history and international relations with highest honors in 1926. His thesis, "The Introduction of the Ironclad Warship," won the Toppan Prize for best Harvard Ph.D. thesis of the year and was published in 1933. Baxter taught diplomatic history, naval history, and international relations at Harvard, and he wrote numerous articles on naval and diplomatic history, earning an international reputation in those fields. In 1931 he was promoted to associate professor and was appointed the first master of Adams House, a residence hall modeled after the traditional English college. He was promoted again in 1936 to full professor. During his years at Harvard, Baxter also served as a visiting lecturer at Lowell Institute, the Naval War College, and Cambridge University. He later lectured at the National War College, the Air War College, and the Canadian Defense College. In addition Baxter chaired the Social Science Research Council's committee on social science personnel in 1932. That committee investigated the loss of outstanding students to fields other than teaching and research. He also served on another SSRC committee that studied the poor quality of social science teaching on the secondary school level.

Baxter was offered the presidency of Williams College in 1934. Wishing to continue the work of creating Adams House he declined, but he accepted an appointment as a member of the board of trustees. In 1937 he was offered the presidency again, accepted, and served for twenty-four years. Baxter saw himself primarily as a teacher and continued to teach part time while president. He argued that "vital teaching is the essential thing" and felt a strong faculty was the key to a quality education. As president he quadrupled the college budget for instruction and improved tenure and sabbatical leave policies. Baxter was also a strong supporter of academic freedom, taking stands in defense of two controversial Williams faculty in the post–World War II period.

Baxter rose to national prominence after becoming president. He spoke out against neutrality legislation in his inaugural address in 1937 and advocated U.S. intervention in the European war in a commencement address in 1941. In the same year William J. Donovan asked him to organize the research and analysis section of the Office of the Coordinator of Information (later the Office of Strategic Services, the predecessor of the Central Intelligence Agency). Baxter recruited experts on history, geography, economics, and politics to gather information. In 1942 he took a leave of absence from Williams in order to serve as deputy director of the OSS on a part-time basis. The following year Baxter moved to Vannevar Bush's Office of Scientific Research and Development as historian, remaining there on an uncompensated, part-time basis until 1946. In 1945 Baxter began work on the official history of the OSRD, writing twenty-two of the twenty-eight chapters and taking courses on electricity and electronics to prepare himself for the task. The resultant book, *Scientists against Time*, won the Pulitzer Prize in history for 1946.

Baxter advised the federal government on education during and after the war. In 1942 he headed the Commission on Liberal Education of the Association of American Colleges, which recommended programs for the wartime and postwar education of military personnel. From 1945 to 1946 he served on a navy board to plan naval officer procurement. During these same years, Baxter was president of the Association of American Colleges and of the Society of American Historians. He also was a member of the American Council on Education and the Harvard Board of Overseers, a fellow of the American Academy of Arts and Sciences, chair of the Board of Visitors and an education adviser to the Academic Board at West Point, and a member of the historical advisory committee of the Atomic Energy Commission. He served as a trustee of Radcliffe College, Phillips Andover Academy, the American Military Institute, and the World Peace Foundation.

Baxter was an active member of the Republican party and a leader in the Eisenhower for president movement. Dwight D. Eisenhower appointed him to the Gaither Commission to study the Cold War in the 1950s. Baxter, concerned about the expansion of the Soviet Union, urged an American military build-up. In testimony before a 1960 Senate hearing he proposed the strengthening of conventional forces to wage limited warfare. Baxter retired as president of Williams College in 1960 and the next year moved to New York City to become the first senior fellow of the Council on Foreign Relations. However, he returned to Williamstown when his health began to fail in 1965. He died there ten years later after living for several years in a nursing home.

Baxter successfully combined the roles of historian, educator, and government leader. He began his professional life as a historian and continued to research and write throughout his career, earning one of the most prestigious awards in the field, the Pulitzer Prize in history. Baxter considered teaching to be the most important role of an academic. He continued to teach while serving as president of Williams and strengthened support for instruction. Baxter used his presidency to speak out on national and international issues, and he became an adviser to the Roosevelt, Truman, and Eisenhower administrations on intelligence, education, and foreign relations.

• Baxter's presidential papers, including some material relating to his historical research, are part of the Records of the Williams College President's Office in the Archives and Special Collections of the Williams College Library. Baxter's classmate and Williams College trustee William O. Wyckoff wrote a brief, retrospective article for the *Williams Alumni Review* (July 1960) on the occasion of Baxter's retirement as president, and the issue contains other material on Baxter's years at the college. An article in the *Washington Post*, 19 June 1975, at the time of Baxter's death provides a summary of his life and career.

JOEL WEBB EASTMAN

BAYARD, James Asheton (15 Nov. 1799–13 June 1880), lawyer and U.S. senator, was born in Wilmington, Delaware, the son of James Asheton Bayard, a lawyer and U.S. senator, and Ann Bassett. His family was socially and politically important, and his father was a leading Federalist during the formative years of the United States. His mother was the daughter of Delaware's chief justice Richard Bassett. Bayard and his older brother Richard Bayard, also a U.S. senator, maintained the family's prominence.

Bayard attended Princeton and Union Colleges, graduating from Union in 1818. He then studied law. In 1822 he was admitted to the Delaware bar and began a successful law practice in Wilmington. His legal reputation was soon enhanced by his handling of cases with economic and political importance, such as one concerning the Chesapeake and Ohio Canal Company. In 1823 he married Ann Francis; it is known that they had one son.

Bayard's political career began with a succession of defeats. He was an unsuccessful candidate for the U.S. House of Representatives in 1828, 1832, and 1834. Delaware politics were acrimonious: the Federalist party of his father's day was no longer viable, and Whigs and Democrats, vehemently opposing each other, fought bitterly for political control. Bayard declared himself a Democrat, having early on approved of Democratic ideas, such as opposition to high tariffs, rather than Whig ideas.

In 1833 President Andrew Jackson nominated Bayard to be one of the five directors of the Bank of the United States. He refused to serve, however, when the U.S. Senate, controlled by Whigs, rejected the Democratic president's other four nominees. Bayard almost won a bid for a U.S. Senate seat in 1838, but Delaware party politics interfered as the Delaware Senate, controlled by Whigs, refused to meet in joint session with the Democratic Delaware House to carry out the election process. That same year President Martin Van Buren, a Jacksonian Democrat, appointed Bayard the U.S. attorney for Delaware. Bayard held this position from 1838 to 1843.

In 1846 Delaware Whigs and Democrats found an issue on which they could agree, the Wilmot Proviso, prohibiting slavery in territory to be acquired from Mexico. This ultimately paved the way for Bayard to go to Congress. (The Proviso was not then adopted but the issue of slavery in the territories was heatedly debated until 1861, when Congress enacted legislation prohibiting slavery in any territory.) Both Whigs and Democrats in Delaware supported the Wilmot Proviso, and in 1851 enough members of the state legislature finally came together, on the sixteenth ballot, to choose Bayard as U.S. senator. He succeeded a Whig in that office and was returned to the Senate in 1857 and 1863.

Being a senator in the years preceding and during the Civil War was nearly as difficult as getting elected. Bayard served on the Committee on Engrossed Bills, which he chaired in the Thirty-second Congress; the Committee on Public Buildings in the Thirty-third and Thirty-fourth Congresses; the Committee on the Judiciary in the Thirty-fifth and Thirty-sixth Congresses; and the Committee on Public Buildings and Grounds in the Thirty-fifth Congress. However, issues relating to slavery were dividing the Democratic party and challenging the senator's beliefs. In 1857 the U.S. Supreme Court ruled in *Dred Scott v. Sandford* that "Negroes . . . had no rights which the white man was bound to respect," and could be taken, just like other property, into the territories.

In the election of 1860 Delaware Democrats favored the presidential candidacy of John C. Breckinridge, who supported the *Dred Scott* decision and was the choice of southern Democrats. Bayard could not support either Breckinridge or Stephen A. Douglas, the choice of northern Democrats, so he became a Republican. While Bayard retained his faith in Jacksonian ideals, he supported President Abraham Lincoln during the Civil War. However, the abolitionism of Radical Republicans caused him embarrassment in Delaware, which was still a slave state. In Congress Bayard frequently voted against antislavery legislation, predicting race problems consequent to emancipation and warning of the dangers of provoking anti-Union sentiment in the critical Border States. He spoke out for more conciliation in the Radical Republican Reconstruction policies, and he would not support such

Radical Congressional leaders as Representative Thaddeus Stevens and Senator Charles Sumner. Bayard would gradually return to the Democratic party.

When Bayard took his Senate seat to begin his third term in 1863, he objected to having to take the "ironclad" oath, which Congress legislated in the heat of war to exclude from public office individuals who would not swear to past and future loyalty to the Union. During a lengthy debate on whether or not this law applied to Congress, Bayard argued that a senator was not a civil officer within the meaning of the Constitution. A senator was, he maintained, in a position as much under the authority of his state as under the federal government. Therefore, the requirement, for members of Congress, was unconstitutional and an infringement of the rights of states. Proponents of the oath, however, led by Senator Charles Sumner of Massachusetts, were numerous enough to pass a resolution mandating that senators take the oath. Bayard felt duty bound to abide by the majority vote of 27 to 11, and he took the oath. However, he also felt he must resign from the body that passed such a rule. Addressing the Senate, Bayard said, "Your decision inflicts a vital wound upon free . . . government." Test oaths are, he continued, "demoralizing acts of tyranny . . . , the first weapons young oppression learns to handle" (Hyman, p. 235). The vacancy caused by Bayard's resignation in January 1864 was filled by George R. Riddle, who died in March 1867. Bayard was appointed to fill the vacancy and then was elected as a Democrat to serve out his own unexpired term. When he finally left the Senate in March 1869, his son Thomas Francis Bayard had been chosen U.S. senator by the Delaware legislature. Thomas Bayard served in the Senate until 1885. James Bayard died in Wilmington.

Bayard was esteemed as a constitutional lawyer and was respected for his sense of public duty. However, his belief in Jacksonian Democracy, his support for Lincoln and the Union, and his conservative attitude toward emancipation were hard to reconcile. His position as a Border State senator who switched parties was politically difficult. His senatorial career survived a dogmatic era of party politics and a war that divided his country, while he maintained his integrity and demonstrated the courage of his convictions. Bayard passed on to his son the family tradition of respect for law and the obligation of public service.

• "Though few families in our history have contributed so many members to public life as has the Bayard family . . . little from the pens of its members or concerning them has found its way into print" (Elizabeth Donnan, ed., *Annual Report of the American Historical Association for the Year 1913* [1915], p. 5). The *Congressional Globe*, 1851–1869, and the *Journal United States Senate*, 1851–69, detail the Congresses in which Bayard served. Harold M. Hyman analyzed the question of the ironclad loyalty oath in "Two Generations of Bayards Debate the Question: Are Congressmen Civil Officers?" *Delaware History* 6 (Sept. 1953): 225–36. John A. Munroe, *Louis McLane: Federalist and Jacksonian* (1973), a biography of Bayard's legal mentor and fellow Delaware politician, is useful for details of the politics of the time. Morton

Borden, *The Federalism of James A. Bayard* (1955; repr. 1968), although focusing on the father, has ten pages of bibliography and thirty-seven pages of notes that provide manuscript sources, with locations, and published sources on the Bayard family. C. E. Hoffecker, *Delaware: A Bicentennial History* (1977) places Bayard within the context of nineteenth-century Delaware. The *New York Times* published an obituary on 14 June 1880, and on 15 June 1880, the *Times* published an article discussing the political tradition of the Bayards, four generations and five members of whom served in the U.S. Senate.

SYLVIA B. LARSON

BAYARD, James Ashton (28 July 1767–6 Aug. 1815), attorney and politician, was born probably in Philadelphia, Pennsylvania, the son of James Ashton Bayard, a physician, and Agnes Hodge. Following his father's and mother's deaths in 1770 and 1774 respectively, Bayard became the ward of his uncle John Bayard, a prosperous Philadelphia merchant, and his aunt Margaret Hodge Bayard, his mother's sister, under whose guardianship he was tutored and schooled. Sometime in 1781 or 1782, Bayard entered the College of New Jersey (later Princeton University). He received his degree in 1784, graduating second in his class.

After returning to Philadelphia to study law with the noted attorneys Joseph Reed and Jared Ingersoll, Jr., Bayard was admitted to the bar in 1787 and took up residence in Wilmington, Delaware. His law practice quickly prospered. In 1795 he married Ann Bassett, daughter of Richard Bassett, successively U.S. senator, chief justice of Delaware's court of common pleas, and governor. The couple had six children.

Secure in profession and family, in 1796 Bayard commenced his political career with his election as Delaware's sole congressman. Taking his House seat in 1797 as a member of the Federalist majority, he proved himself an ingratiating politician and skilled speaker, trusted in all political camps. While a warm partisan, his Federalism was characteristically moderate, centrist, and nationalist. He shunned regional particularism and opposed slavery.

Although, for example, his maiden House speech assailed France and commended the undeclared naval war against that nation, he opposed all-out combat and backed President John Adams when Adams named a peace mission to France in 1799. Similarly, while forcefully championing passage of the Alien and Sedition Acts of 1798, he significantly advanced the Anglo-American law of free speech by successfully offering an amendment to the Sedition Act that allowed evidence of the truth of an alleged libel to be presented as a defense in criminal libel cases. As if to underscore the seriousness with which he took his role as the people's deputy, he even presented petitions to the House from his Democratic-Republican constituents protesting these acts.

Bayard's quick rise to prominence was attested by his service as one of five House members who in 1797 and 1798 investigated Tennessee senator William Blount for allegedly assisting Britain in seizing Spanish territory in the Southwest. The investigation led to Blount's expulsion from the Senate in 1797. Nevertheless, even though Blount was no longer a member of Congress, impeachment proceedings were brought against him. Bayard chaired the House committee that managed Blount's impeachment trial in 1798 and 1799 before the Senate, the first ever to be heard by that body. The trial was unsuccessful. Subsequently, Bayard led the successful effort to pass the nation's first bankruptcy act in 1800.

Unlike many leading Federalists, Bayard backed John Adams for reelection in 1800. As a result, before his retirement in 1801, Adams nominated Bayard to be American minister to France. Bayard, however, refused to accept the post after winning Senate confirmation, fearing that his possible retention by Thomas Jefferson, whose party carried the 1800 election, would appear a reward for his having been instrumental in Jefferson's becoming president.

It was by refusing in 1801 to bar Jefferson's election as president by the House of Representatives that Bayard made his most enduring contribution to the nation's history. When the Democratic-Republicans failed to coordinate casting their ballots in the electoral college and submitted an equal number of votes for Jefferson and for Aaron Burr, who was assumed to be the party's candidate for vice president, the presidential election of 1800 had to be decided in the House of Representatives. In the House, under the Constitution, in case of an electoral tie votes for president are cast by states. On the first thirty-five ballots, Jefferson secured the votes of eight states, Burr of six (all controlled by Bayard's Federalist colleagues); two states, equally divided between Federalists and Democratic-Republicans, cast no votes. Thus neither contender gained the majority of states voting—nine being needed for election. As Delaware's single representative, Bayard was in a position to give or deny the outcome to Jefferson, whom Bayard deeply distrusted. Withstanding intense pressure from fellow Federalists, Bayard precipitated a conclusion by submitting a blank ballot on the thirty-sixth ballot. Bayard's action led one other delegation to do the same and the Federalists in two others to withdraw, thus allowing Jefferson to become president with the vote of ten states. Whether or not Jefferson and some Federalists came to a tacit understanding through Bayard and others about the actions Jefferson would and would not pursue in exchange for his election has been debated ever since. Bayard, however, explained his actions simply: because, he wrote, of the "imperious necessity" of running "no risk of the Constitution," he would not "exclude Jefferson at the expense of the Constitution." By acting thus to end the nation's first major constitutional crisis, he performed one of the earliest and arguably one of the greatest acts of absolute constitutionalism in the nation's history, an act later characterized by Albert Gallatin as one of "pure patriotism" (Borden, pp. 90–91, 95).

Bayard commenced his minority party days in the House by unsuccessfully opposing repeal of the Judiciary Act of 1801, which had allowed the appointment of sixteen Federalist judges. Defeated in 1802 for re-election to a fourth term by his lifelong friend and political foe Caesar A. Rodney, he was reelected to the House in 1804, only to be chosen instead by the Delaware legislature to fill an unexpired term in the U.S. Senate, in which he served, after reelection in 1805 and 1811, until 1813.

Bayard's Senate participation was sporadic and unenthusiastic, no doubt because of his minority status. While like most Federalists he opposed the Embargo of 1807 and commercial retaliation against foreign trade restrictions and military attacks, he strongly advocated arming American vessels. While voting against the declaration of war with Britain in 1812, he supported the war once it began. No doubt for this reason, in 1813 President James Madison named Bayard to the commission to negotiate a peace treaty. After playing only a minor part in securing the 1814 Treaty of Ghent and declining the ambassadorship to Russia, he returned home. A wealthy man, he died shortly thereafter in Wilmington of "advanced necrosis of the breastbone."

Bayard was of the generation of public figures who, coming of age after the American Revolution, were left to implement it. Perhaps because he represented a small mid-Atlantic state, he was distinctive in his unwavering nationalism and constitutionalism, never yielding wholly either to partisanship or ideology. In making possible in 1801 the modern world's first peaceful transfer of power between opposing political parties, he achieved historic importance.

• No records of Bayard's birthplace seem to exist. Although both Philadelphia and Wilmington have been named by previous scholars, the former seems the most likely site, given what is known of Bayard's parents. Similarly, extant records of Princeton University do not permit a precise dating of Bayard's entry into the College of New Jersey.

The Library of Congress houses the principal collection of Bayard papers, many of which were published in Elizabeth Donnan, ed., "Papers of James A. Bayard, 1796–1815," in *American Historical Association Annual Report for 1913*, vol. 2 (1915). Other Bayard papers are in the Maryland Historical Society and the Historical Society of Delaware. The fullest study is Morton Borden, *The Federalism of James A. Bayard* (1955). For the Delaware context of his public career, see John A. Munroe, *Federalist Delaware* (1954).

JAMES M. BANNER, JR.

BAYARD, John Bubenheim (11 Aug. 1738–7 Jan. 1807), merchant and statesman, was born at Bohemia Manor, Maryland, the son of James Bayard, a merchant and planter, and Mary Asheton. He and his twin brother James Asheton Bayard were educated first by Samuel Finley at the Nottingham Institution, Maryland, then privately by the Reverend George Duffield. In 1756 Bayard entered the Philadelphia mercantile firm of John Rhea.

Bayard married Margaret Hodge, daughter of Andrew Hodge of Philadelphia, in 1759. Eight of their children reached maturity, including Margaret Bayard Smith, novelist, society leader, and renowned observ-

er of the American social and political scene between Jefferson's administration and that of William Henry Harrison. When James Asheton Bayard died in 1770 his children, including James Asheton Bayard, Jr., joined the John Bayard household and were raised and educated there. Following Margaret Bayard's death in 1780, Bayard married Mary Grant, widow of John Hodgson of South Carolina. No surviving children were born to this four-year union. Nor did a third marriage to Johannah White in 1787 produce issue.

By 1763 Bayard was a respected merchant in Philadelphia. He signed the 25 October 1765 Nonimportation Agreement as part of Pennsylvania's resistance to English policies, beginning for him an important career in committee politics. Genial and popular, he was elected to the Sons of Liberty in 1766 and the Philadelphia Committee of Inspection and Observation in 1774. In the latter he provided leadership in the Committee of Sixty-six and in the First and Second One Hundred committees, which served as executive councils for that organization. He participated in both the second Provincial Convention (Jan. 1775) and the Provincial Conference (June 1776) and chaired the 20 May 1776 public meeting that denounced the colonial assembly and demanded a constitutional convention chosen by the people. He was among those given special commissions as justices of the peace to ensure stability until a state constitution could be written and implemented, and he was named to the Board of War. Commissioned a major of the second battalion of Philadelphia Associators in May 1775, he later served at Perth Amboy and saw action at Princeton (where he fought with distinction), Brandywine, and Germantown. He was promoted to colonel in 1777.

Bayard opposed the Pennsylvania constitution of 1776, arguing that it lacked adequate checks against democratic impulses within the state. He presided over a 21 October 1776 public meeting called to protest the new state constitution and helped to prepare amendments to the constitution in the event that anticonstitutionalists should gain control of the assembly. Elected to the assembly on the Republican ticket in November 1776, Bayard proved to be one of the most talented members in that first legislature. Five times he was elected to that body and with one exception acted as its Speaker in each of those sessions. Despite his continuing qualms regarding the weaknesses of the 1776 Pennsylvania constitution, by 1777 Bayard decided to become a "Constitutionalist" and to work with the state government to guarantee the success of the Revolution. Accordingly, he put aside demands for revising the constitution until a more propitious time. Men like Thomas McKean and Joseph Reed who worked closely with Bayard in the new government chose similar paths for the same reasons. When the Pennsylvania Supreme Executive Council (SEC) was enlarged, granted broader powers, and renamed the Council of Safety in October 1777, Bayard was elevated to that board.

Bayard was elected to the SEC in 1781. Believing that he was to be named president of that body, Republicans blocked the move by insisting that his election to the council was tainted. A year before, despite opposition from the assembly, the SEC had appointed Bayard auctioneer of the city of Philadelphia, a lucrative office with substantial fees. To pacify those who complained of his dual roles after 1781, Bayard resigned from the SEC in 1782. Unappeased, the Republican-dominated assembly also removed him as auctioneer in 1783. Bayard chaired a 1784 public meeting that passed a number of resolutions fixing the exchange rate of continental paper money to specie at 75 to 1 and establishing an association to enforce the new policy. That same year he was among the directors of a proposed Bank of Pennsylvania who challenged the alleged monopoly of the Bank of North America. Rather than see a new rival destroy their exclusive operations, directors of the Bank of North America successfully absorbed their potential competitors by enlarging the bank's issue of stock and making it available to them. In 1785 Bayard was elected to the Continental Congress, where he resisted those seeking to guarantee American access to the Mississippi River. Apparently under the influence of Pennsylvania's eastern commercial interests, he aligned with New England delegates in favoring a plan whereby Spain would make commercial concessions to the United States in exchange for the United States relinquishing its use of the Mississippi River for twenty-five years.

Bayard's fortunes in Philadelphia waned after 1785. Though considered a delegate, he was not chosen to attend the 1787 federal constitutional convention. Nor was he returned to Congress in 1787. He ardently supported the new federal constitution but was disappointed in his 1789 quest for office under the new national government. In 1788 Bayard moved his family to New Brunswick, New Jersey. There he entertained a steady stream of prominent figures, most of whom shared his Federalist politics. He continued in public life, serving as mayor of New Brunswick in 1790 and as presiding judge of the Court of Common Pleas for Somerset County. Among the founders of the Society for Establishing Useful Manufactures (1791), he also acted as a trustee of the College of New Jersey (later Princeton) and as a trustee and ruling elder for the First Presbyterian Church. Bayard died in New Brunswick.

Not a major figure either in the revolutionary movement or in the politics of the early republic, Bayard nonetheless was an active and useful individual during both periods, one of many second-line leaders who shouldered the day-to-day burdens of leadership and organization in addition to military duties. His career is a reminder that those who argue that the division between the advocates and opponents of the 1776 Pennsylvania constitution was rigid and insurmountable do so at some risk. An opponent of the document in 1776, he agreed to put aside his criticisms and to work with the constitutionalist government to secure the Revolution. Only after peace with England did he eagerly embrace constitutional reforms both on the state and national levels. He died an ardent Federalist.

• Materials on Bayard's life and career are thin. A few Bayard manuscripts and papers touching on his career can be found in the Historical Society of Pennsylvania, Philadelphia. Philadelphia newspapers and the journals of the Pennsylvania assembly also provide occasional glimpses of Bayard's public life as do the records of the Supreme Executive Council, *Minutes of the Provincial Council of Pennsylvania*, Colonial Records of Pennsylvania (16 vols., 1851–1853), especially vol. 13. Letters and papers of his daughter Margaret Bayard Smith are located in the Library of Congress. James Grant Wilson, *Colonel John Bayard and the Bayard Family of America* (1885), offers a short biography and genealogical background of the subject. Other works that treat aspects of Bayard's life include the *New Jersey Historical Society Proceedings*, ser. 2, vol. 5, no. 1 (1877): 139–60, and ser. 3, vol. 2, no. 2 (1897): 100–115; Paul H. Smith, ed., *Letters of Delegates to Congress, 1774–1789* (18 vols., 1976–1991); Worthington C. Ford, ed., *Journals of the Continental Congress, 1774–1789* (34 vols., 1904–1937); Richard A. Ryerson, *"The Revolution Is Now Begun": The Radical Committees of Philadelphia, 1765–1776* (1978); and Robert L. Brunhouse, *The Counter-Revolution in Pennsylvania, 1776–1790* (1942; repr. 1971).

G. S. ROWE

BAYARD, Nicholas (1644–1711?), merchant, was born probably in Alphen, near Utrecht, in the Netherlands, the son of Samuel Bayard, a merchant, and Anna Stuyvesant. Bayard was the nephew of Peter Stuyvesant, the last Dutch governor of New Netherland. His mother Anna, Stuyvesant's sister, with her four children, accompanied the Stuyvesants to New Amsterdam in 1647. Educated by his mother in English, French, and Dutch, he began a long and lucrative political career with a post as English clerk in Stuyvesant's government. He also held posts under the English administration that commenced in 1664 and during the second brief Dutch occupation in 1673.

Bayard's career suffered a setback with the reestablishment of English control, and in October 1675 he was imprisoned for refusing to take the oath of allegiance after New Netherland was transferred to the English for the second and last time. Bayard joined with other leading Dutch burghers in seeking protection for the privileges enjoyed by the Dutch in New York before imposition of the oath. In a militant nationalist statement they petitioned Edmund Andros, the new British governor, to maintain the freedom of their church and guarantee that they would not be forced to take up arms "against any native Dutch nation." In return, they promised "full obedience." "Swearing lightly what nature and love for our own nation forbid" was so objectionable that the Dutch leaders said they would rather leave New York if their demands were refused. Instead, they were arrested. Tried and convicted of promoting rebellion, their sentence was forfeiture of their estates. The burghers protested against the sentence, later reduced to one-third of their estates, and only Bayard was imprisoned in the "hole" of the fort.

Following the loyalty oath crisis, Bayard adjusted to English rule by taking the oath of allegiance and becoming English himself. It took him ten years to win office in the English administration. In 1685 he was appointed mayor of New York City and by 1689, when Leisler's Rebellion broke out, he was the commanding officer of the New York County militia and a member of the provincial council. Few, if any, of the town's prominent anglicizing Dutch merchants who collaborated with Andros's Dominion government had become as fully integrated into the new order as the former belligerent Dutch nationalist Bayard. Yet while he continued to enjoy the spoils of high office until the close of the seventeenth century, in 1702 Bayard's career plummeted again when he was sent to trial on a charge of high treason.

The Bayard treason trial was a complex and puzzling affair that can only be understood against the backdrop of Leisler's Rebellion, one of several uprisings in the American colonies during the crisis of authority created by the Glorious Revolution. When the ruling elite proved reluctant to voice support for the new king, William of Orange, the militia and townsfolk seized the fort in his name. Jacob Leisler, a militia captain, was accused of instigating the revolt, but the Leislerians, as the rebels came to be called, claimed that Leisler took command only when Colonel Bayard refused to lead them. Bayard was imprisoned during Leisler's rule, which ended when he surrendered the fort to Governor Henry Sloughter in 1691. Bayard was to play a key role in persuading Sloughter to execute Leisler for treason, thereby incurring the enmity of the Dutch Leislerian community. A decade later, when they returned to power, the Leislerians seized the first opportunity to wreak revenge on the man they held primarily responsible for Leisler's execution. In 1701 Bayard and his "English party" faction organized a petition campaign against the new administration, accusing the government of being corrupt and of discriminating against the English faction in favor of the Dutch faction. This created the opportunity for the Leislerians to charge Bayard with violating the law passed by the general assembly in 1691 that made it high treason to attempt to "disturb the peace, good and quiet" of the government. Ironically then, the act that Bayard had supported, condemning Leisler's administration, was now being used against him.

Bayard was a shadowy, controversial figure in the complicated configurations of early colonial New York politics. But his trial can be interpreted as a drama highlighting continuing Dutch-English antagonisms in New York. Had he wished to, Bayard could have boasted a Dutch pedigree equal if not superior to that of any other colonial New Yorker. Not only was he related to Peter Stuyvesant, he could also have pointed to his 1675 stand on behalf of the Dutch nation and his record eight terms as an elder in the town's Dutch Reformed church. But by 1702 Bayard had become the leader of the English party. He had also begun attending Anglican services at Trinity Church. By thus transferring his affiliation from the Church of the Fatherland to the Anglican church, Bayard was almost fully transformed into an Englishman. At his trial he demanded an all-English jury, while denigrating as

"mean" and "ignorant" the Dutch Leislerian townsmen who were picked as jurors. In letters to the London colonial office and to placemen, he repeated these charges against the Leislerian Dutch protagonists in the trial, identifying them as his "mortal enemies."

Bayard escaped the gallows because the Leislerians, afraid of being called to account, failed to act decisively against him. After the trial, he soon faded from public life and the public records. His wife, Judith Varleth, whom he had married in 1666, was a member of a prominent Dutch family and had been imprisoned briefly for witchcraft in Connecticut. It is notable that their only child, Samuel, who was active in his father's English party, retained his links to the New York City Dutch community and sent his children to the Dutch Reformed church. Trinity Church vestry records—the last surviving public record of Bayard—list him as a vestryman for the period 1705 to 1711, when, presumably, he died in New York City.

• Bayard and a lawyer, David Jamison, wrote an account of his treason trial, *An Account of the Illegal Prosecution and Tryal of Coll. Nicholas Bayard* (1702). This publication was reproduced in Thomas B. Howell, *Complete Collection of State Trials, and Proceedings for High Treason*, vol. 14 (1816), pp. 471–516. For biographical and bibliographical references see A. Howe, "The Bayard Treason Trial: Dramatizing Anglo-Dutch Politics in Early Eighteenth-century New York City," *William and Mary Quarterly*, 3d ser., 47 (Jan. 1990): 57–89.

ADRIAN HOWE

BAYARD, Richard Henry (26 Sept. 1796–4 Mar. 1868), lawyer, senator, and diplomat, was born in Wilmington, Delaware, the son of James Asheton Bayard, a Federalist leader, and Ann Bassett. Bayard graduated from Princeton College in 1814 and then read for the law. Toward the end of the War of 1812 his studies were briefly interrupted by military service. In 1815 he married Mary Sophia Carroll, granddaughter of Charles Carroll of Carrollton, Maryland.

In 1818 Bayard was admitted to the bar in New Castle, Delaware. For the next ten years he devoted himself to his law practice in Wilmington, where his father had also practiced. The elder Bayard had assisted his son with his legal studies, and the son inherited many of the father's former clients. He quickly became prominent in his profession, and the Bayard home was a center of social activity. Bayard took part in events such as welcoming the marquis de Lafayette to Delaware in 1824 and a dinner honoring President Andrew Jackson's appointment of fellow Delawarean Louis McLane as minister to Great Britain in 1829.

In 1830 Bayard and his brother James Asheton Bayard determined to refute certain comments in Thomas Jefferson's just-published diary that cast doubt on the character of their father. The elder Bayard was one of the Federalist congressmen who, in the stalemated election of 1800, withdrew their opposition to Jefferson and thus enabled the Republican to assume the presidency. Bayard, in return, had sought assurances from Jefferson concerning "certain points of the future administration," fueling later accusations of unseemly political persuasion (quoted in Borden, p. 91). His sons gathered documents and letters that negated the allegations against their father, and in 1831 they published *Documents Relating to the Presidential Election in the Year 1801: Containing a Refutation of Two Passages in the Writings of Thomas Jefferson, Aspersing the Character of the Late James A. Bayard, of Delaware.*

In 1832 Richard Henry Bayard assumed his first political office when Wilmington adopted a city charter and elected him its first mayor. He held this position for three years. In June 1836 he was elected as a Whig to the U.S. Senate, filling a vacancy created by the resignation of Arnold Naudain.

Bayard went to Congress in time to play a role in the aftermath of one of the most controversial episodes in that body's history. President Jackson had vetoed the renewal of the charter of the Bank of the United States and in 1834 was censured by the Senate. The president's friends in the Senate, led by Thomas Hart Benton, began a campaign to vindicate Jackson and expunge the censure from the official record. Bayard firmly voiced his opposition to Benton's formal resolution to expunge. However, as Jackson's second term was ending, the resolution was passed. The manuscript journal of the 1833–1834 session was brought to the Senate and the secretary ordered to write across the censure resolution, "Expunged by order of the Senate, the 16th day of January, in the year of our Lord 1837"; Bayard condemned this as tampering with the *Journal* of the Senate of the United States.

In September 1839 Bayard resigned his Senate seat to accept the office of chief justice of Delaware. However, he was soon reelected to fill the Senate vacancy left by his own resignation, and he served again from January 1841 to March 1845. Bayard served on the Senate Committees on Private Land Claims (chair), District of Columbia, and Naval Affairs. He does not seem to have played a significant role in the Senate, nor did he leave a legacy of ideas on contemporary issues.

Not seeking another term, Bayard returned to Wilmington in 1845. He practiced law there for the next five years. His last public office was as chargé d'affaires to Belgium, representing the United States in Brussels from December 1850 until September 1853. After he returned home, Bayard continued his law practice in Delaware and Pennsylvania for fifteen years, but he was no longer politically active. He died in Philadelphia.

Like other members of his family, Bayard was trained in the law and bred in the tradition of public service. He assumed the responsibility of his legacy, enduring the divisive atmosphere of the 1830s through the 1860s and earning respect in the midst of political controversy.

• The Bayard Family Papers are in the Manuscript Division of the Library of Congress. The *Congressional Globe* (1836–1845), the *Journal of the United States Senate* (1836–1845), and the *Journal of the Executive Proceedings of the United States Senate* (1836–1845) detail the Congresses in which Bayard served. See also the *Delaware Gazette* (1824–1836), *Niles' Register* (1836–1845), and Ben Perley Poore, *Perley's Reminiscences of Sixty Years in the National Metropolis* (1886). On the pamphlet published by the Bayard brothers, see John A. Munroe, "William Plummer's Biographical Sketches of James A. Bayard, Caesar A. Rodney and Samuel White," *Delaware History* 4 (1951): 354–77; the pamphlet is available in the Library of American Civilization ultrafiche #40116. Morton Borden, *The Federalism of James A. Bayard* (1955; repr., 1968), although focusing on the father, includes a bibliography and notes that provide manuscript and published sources on the Bayard family. C. E. Hoffecker, *Delaware: A Bicentennial History* (1979), places the Bayards within the context of nineteenth-century Delaware. An obituary is in the *New York Times*, 8 Mar. 1868.

SYLVIA B. LARSON

BAYARD, Thomas Francis (29 Oct. 1828–28 Sept. 1898), U.S. senator, secretary of state, and ambassador to Great Britain, was born in Wilmington, Delaware, the son of James Asheton Bayard, a political leader and U.S. senator, and Ann Francis. The family had been politically prominent in Delaware for generations, and Thomas was educated in private schools. In 1843, when his father moved briefly to New York, Thomas found employment in a mercantile house there and, for less than a year in about 1846–1847, in Philadelphia. Although he never attended college, he at about the age of twenty began to read law in Wilmington and was admitted to the bar in 1851. He developed a successful practice in Wilmington and Philadelphia administering estates and from 1853 to 1854 served as U.S. district attorney for Delaware. In 1856 he married Louise Lee, with whom he had three sons and six daughters.

A peace Democrat during the Civil War, Bayard opposed both the war and the southern states' struggle to secede from the Union. In 1869 he was selected by the Delaware legislature to succeed his father as U.S. senator from Delaware. Because of Bayard's limited government experience, political opponents viewed his sudden elevation to high office as evidence of his Democratic family's continuing domination of state politics. In the U.S. Senate he led resistance to the Republican legislative agenda and made strident denunciations of Radical Reconstruction policies. He was also noted for consistent condemnations of subsidies for shipbuilders, high protective tariffs, and land grants to railroads. As Republicans controlled the White House and Congress during the period he served in the Senate, Bayard's role was leading opposition to initiatives rather than advancing an agenda of his own or of his party. His prominence as a Democratic loyalist earned him support from his party for presidential nominations in 1876, 1880, and 1884. However, his formal and aloof bearing prevented him from building a broad popular following. He served as a member of the electorial commission of 1877 appointed to decide the contested election of the previous year. Following the election of Grover Cleveland as the first Democratic president in almost a quarter of a century, Bayard was named secretary of state, a post he apparently accepted out of party loyalty rather than any burning ambition. Cautious and conservative, he was known for his tall, stately stature, good looks, courtly manners, and personal integrity.

Besieged by Democratic office seekers hungry for long-denied patronage positions, Bayard, a believer in civil service reform, resisted political pressures and named, for the most part, competent representatives to foreign capitals. Negotiations with Great Britain over matters related to Canada occupied much of Bayard's attention during his tenure at the head of the Department of State. In 1887 the British government welcomed his proposal for a conference in Washington to settle matters related to British possessions in North America, in particular a dispute over American fishing rights in the North Atlantic and a controversy related to hunting fur seals in the Bering Sea. Bayard led an American delegation comprised of James B. Angell, president of the University of Michigan, and Judge William Putnam of Portland, Oregon. Following protracted discussions, during which no formal records were kept to facilitate open discussions, the British delegates left for Canada to consult with government leaders in Ottawa. Bayard's studious and conciliatory manner in dealing with the British over the issue of American fishing rights off the coast of Newfoundland and Labrador led to the signing of the Bayard-Chamberlain Treaty of 1 February 1888. The agreement was assailed by critics as a surrender by the United States and was rejected in the Senate, where Republicans refused to give the Cleveland administration a foreign policy achievement during an election year. Following the seizure by the United States of three Canadian sealing vessels off the Pribilof Islands in 1885, British protests led Bayard to initiate efforts to reach an international agreement, including the Japanese and Russians, that would protect the rapidly diminishing seal herd. Canadian objections doomed Bayard's efforts. However, Bayard's steady labors to negotiate with the British and through them with their Canadian subjects on halting pelagic sealing in the Bering Sea and protection of the seal herds set the stage for future agreements.

Bayard's attempts to reach an agreement with Britain and Canada on the Alaskan boundary dispute also met with failure, and his offer of the good offices of the United States to help settle a boundary dispute between Venezuela and Great Britain was rejected. During the summer of 1887, tensions rose over Germany's expanding influence in Samoa, where the United States had a decade earlier secured the rights to establish a naval station at Pago Pago. While Bayard failed to resolve the conflicting interests of Britain, Germany, and the United States in the island, his conciliatory approach in the matter paved the way for a future settlement. In 1887 the United States secured in Hawaii the exclusive right to build a naval coaling and repair station at Pearl Harbor in exchange for reciprocal trade privileges desired by the Hawaiian planters. Bayard staunchly defended American interests in the island and rejected a British suggestion that the United States establish a form of protectorate over the islands in league with themselves and Germany.

Following a massacre of twenty-eight Chinese workers in Rock Springs, Wyoming, in 1885, Bayard expressed regrets to the Chinese minister in Washington and promised an investigation of this and other instances of anti-Chinese violence in western states. When the Chinese government demanded redress for its citizens, Bayard tried to explain that the U.S. government denied responsibility since these outrageous acts were committed by private individuals, not federal officials. On 12 March 1888 Bayard and the Chinese minister in Washington signed a treaty excluding Chinese laborers from the United States for twenty years and offering the Chinese an indemnity of $276,619 without admitting federal government responsibility. The outraged Chinese refused to ratify the treaty, and the Cleveland administration, anxious to secure western votes, responded with the Scott Bill, excluding Chinese laborers.

During the presidential campaign of 1888, a political controversy arose over an unfortunate written response the British minister to Washington, Sir Lionel Sackville-West, had made to a Republican political operative who had asked "privately and confidentially" if Cleveland's foreign policies would "favor England's interests." Lord Sackville unwisely stated that he favored the Cleveland administration's diplomacy, and when Republican campaign managers obtained the letter, they published it, claiming that the British minister's statements showed Cleveland to be a tool of Great Britain. Bayard was forced to demand the minister's recall, which the British foreign secretary, Lord Salisbury, refused to do without a full review of the incident. Bayard, while sympathetic to Lord Sackville's plight, nevertheless concurred with Cleveland's dismissal of the diplomat. The British government demonstrated its displeasure at the whole affair by refusing to name a new minister to Washington until Cleveland left office.

After Cleveland's defeat in the 1888 election, Bayard returned to his legal practice in Wilmington. In 1889, three years after his first wife's death, he married Mary W. Clymer; they had no children. With Cleveland's return to the White House in 1893, Bayard was appointed ambassador to Great Britain, becoming the first representative of the United States to hold that rank. Working to improve relations between the two countries, he enthusiastically attended to the usual social duties and impressed his British counterparts with his hunting skills and sportsmanship. At the same time he exercised caution during the Venezuelan crisis of 1895–1896, when it appeared that Great Britain might use military force to resolve a nagging dispute with the South American nation. Bayard's most controversial act while in Britain caused more consternation in the U.S. Congress than in the Court of St. James's. Addressing the issue of "Individual Freedom" before the Edinburgh Philosophical Institution on 7 November 1895, Bayard stated, "In my own country I have witnessed the insatiable growth of that form of state socialism styled 'protection', which I believe has done more to foster class legislation and create inequality of fortune, to corrupt public life . . . and place politics upon the low level of a mercenary scramble than any other single cause" (Shippee, p. 106). When his remarks were reported in the United States, a proposal for impeachment surfaced in the House of Representatives. Following partisan debate, that body adopted resolutions of censure. During his final year abroad, Bayard's health began to fail, and upon his return in 1897 he withdrew from involvement in public affairs. He died at the home of his daughter in Dedham, Massachusetts.

• Bayard's papers are in the Library of Congress and the Delaware Historical Society in Wilmington. Material on Bayard's career in the U.S. Senate and his roles as secretary of state and ambassador to Great Britain is in the *Congressional Record* and the *Foreign Relations of the United States* for the periods of his service. Also see Lester B. Shippee, "Thomas Francis Bayard, Secretary of State, March 7, 1885 to March 6, 1889," in *American Secretaries of State and Their Diplomacy*, vol. 8, ed. Samuel F. Bemis (1963); and Charles C. Tansill, *The Foreign Policies of Thomas F. Bayard, 1885–1897* (1940). A campaign biography, Edward Spencer, *An Outline of the Public Life and Services of Thomas F. Bayard* (1880), is useful only for the early life and political career of its subjects. Obituaries and related articles are in the *Wilmington, Del., Morning News*, 29, 30 Sept. and 1 Oct. 1898, and the *New York Times*, 29 Sept. 1898.

MICHAEL J. DEVINE

BAYER, Adèle Parmentier (1 July 1814–22 Jan. 1892), pioneer Catholic social worker, was born in Enghien, Belgium, the daughter of André Parmentier, a horticulturalist, and Sylvia Marie Parmentier. (The parents were distant cousins.) In 1824 the Parmentiers moved to New York City, where André (also known as Andrew) established his Horticultural and Botanic Garden in Brooklyn. The Parmentiers were devout and generous Catholics who worshiped regularly at St. James Church. There being no nearby Catholic school, Adèle was educated privately. Fluent in French and an apt pupil of English, she assisted her father in his flourishing business until his sudden death in 1830. Adèle and her mother then managed the garden for two years, after which they sold the property.

The Parmentier home became a center of refinement and hospitality. Sylvia Parmentier and her daughters supported religious causes, including missionary priests, and also contributed to social and charitable agencies. In 1839 Adèle Parmentier met Edward Bayer, a German merchant and banker, whom she married in 1841 at the first nuptial mass ever held in Brooklyn.

The Bayers and Adèle's sister Rosine Parmentier purchased tracts of land in a mountainous region of Polk County, Tennessee, in 1842. Here they established a colony of seventeen German Catholic families five years later. In 1852, when the three proprietors first visited "Vineland," or "Bayer's Settlement," as it was called, Rosine Parmentier kept a detailed and illustrated journal describing the settlers and the area's natural beauty. The colony gradually declined, however, and the land was given or sold to the settlers in 1897.

Influenced by her mother's piety and generosity and sympathetic to the needs of strangers, for forty years the childless Adèle Bayer devoted her energy and resources to the welfare of seamen. She regularly visited merchant seamen at City Hospital on Bedloe's Island, Long Island College Hospital in Brooklyn, and the Marine Hospital on Staten Island. Her fluency in several languages allowed her to converse with seamen from many nations. After the outbreak of the Civil War, she also exercised her social work at the busy New York Naval Shipyard, better known as the Brooklyn Navy Yard, which was located near her home. She met incoming ships, talked to the sailors, wrote letters for them, urged them to save some of their pay, and encouraged habits of good living. Bayer became a familiar figure as she distributed scapulars, medals, and rosaries from the large bag she always carried. Concerned about the sailors' religious duties, she persuaded Bishop John Loughlin of Brooklyn to appoint a priest to offer Sunday mass at the yard. On 28 April 1878 Bayer rang a bell to summon officers and sailors to the first mass celebrated on the USS *Minnesota*. She continued this practice each Sunday until 16 November 1890, as her handwritten list reveals. In 1888 Bayer rejoiced at the appointment of Father Charles H. Parks as the first Catholic chaplain of the U.S. Navy. Assigned to the Brooklyn Navy Yard, he served aboard the USS *Vermont*. In addition to her social work among the seamen, Bayer continued to correspond with missionary priests whose work she generously supported.

Adèle Bayer died at home. On Sunday, 13 November 1892, she was memorialized at a solemn high mass aboard the USS *Vermont* during which Father Parks paid eloquent tribute to this friend of sailors. In 1925 Professor Henry G. Bayer of New York University (no relative of Adèle Bayer) established the Parmentier-Bayer Centenary Commission to honor Adèle Bayer and her father. Diplomatic, political, and naval officials attended a morning ceremony on Saturday, 17 October 1925, at which a bronze tablet was unveiled at the receiving-ship entrance of the Brooklyn Navy Yard. It memorialized Adèle Bayer as the Guardian Angel of the Sailors. In the afternoon a bronze tablet honoring André Parmentier was unveiled at the entrance to the present Brooklyn Botanic Garden.

• The Parmentier Family Papers, preserved in the archives at St. Joseph Convent, Brentwood, N.Y., contain Adèle Bayer's correspondence and other papers. Her portrait, photographs, and memorabilia—including the bell she rang—supplement the collection. No complete biography exists. Thomas F. Meehan published two articles: "Andrew Parmentier, Horticulturalist, and His Daughter, Madame Bayer," in *Historical Records and Studies*, vol. 3 (1904), and "Adèle Bayer, née Parmentier," in *The Catholic Encyclopedia*, vol. 2 (1913). Henry G. Bayer's booklet, *A Short Biography of André Parmentier and Adèle Bayer*, was published by the Centenary Commission in 1925. Sister Mary James Lowery, "Model Lay Activity: The Brooklyn Parmentier Family" (master's thesis, St. John's Univ., 1940), includes references to Adèle Bayer. Ben H. McClary and LeRoy P. Graf, eds., "'Vineland' in Tennessee, 1852: The Journal of Rosine Parmentier," in East Tennessee Historical Society *Publications*, no. 31 (1959), pp. 95–111, describes the social experiment. Also see Roy G. Lillard, "Vineland: Polk County's Old Dutch Settlement," *Tennessee Conservationist* 53 (Jan./Feb. 1987): 19–21. Adèle Bayer is included in Margaret M. Quinn, C.S.J., "Sylvia, Adèle and Rosine Parmentier: 19th Century Women of Brooklyn," *U.S. Catholic Historian*, 5 (Summer/Fall 1986): 345–54. John Furey paid tribute in "Mrs. Bayer and Her Work in the Navy Yard," *Messenger of the Sacred Heart* 33 (May 1898): 412–17.

MARGARET M. QUINN

BAYER, Herbert (5 Apr. 1900–30 Sept. 1985), artist, industrial designer, and architect, was born in Haag (near Salzburg), Austria, the son of Maximilian Bayer, a rural government bureaucrat, and Rosa Simmer. Bayer traced his lifetime interests in nature and art to early alpine treks with his father and to watercolor landscape painting encouraged by his mother.

Bayer's developing interests in art and design fortunately coincided with significant advances in Austrian and German arts: the Vienna Secession, the Deutscher Werkbund movement, and eventually the Bauhaus. While he apprenticed during his teens in a provincial arts and crafts workshop, he aspired to the more sophisticated circles of contemporary modern urban art centers. By 1920 he was able to join the Mathildenhöhe circle of art nouveau artists in Darmstadt. With his ever-increasing sophistication in design, Bayer left the decorative style of the art nouveau behind for the more avant-garde Weimar Bauhaus by 1921. There he encountered two of the most formidable and influential figures of his career: Walter Gropius, the director and founder of the Bauhaus, and Wassily Kandinsky, a Bauhaus painter. Studying design at the Weimar Bauhaus from 1921 to 1923, Bayer moved with the school to Dessau in 1925. His career trajectory mirrored that of the school, for he advanced from student to master (teacher) at the Dessau Bauhaus from 1925 until 1928, and he expressed in his work Gropius's ideals of the fusion of art with industry.

Gropius recognized Bayer's particular talent as a graphic and industrial designer, and this direction better exploited Bayer's precisionist tendencies and ability to combine message with medium than Kandinsky's fine arts approach to painting. Gropius appointed Bayer master of the typography and graphic design workshops and assigned him the task of designing Bauhaus typography and letterheads. Through this seemingly simple but artistically valuable assignment, Bayer's own precise yet expressionistic style came to signify visually all that was the Bauhaus. Bayer's uncapitalized, sans serif typographic designs in simple black, white, and red modern page layouts, have since entered museum collections and become Bauhaus icons.

Bayer defined his work in the essay "Typography and Design," in *Concepts of the Bauhaus*, the catalog for a 1971 retrospective exhibition at Harvard University, with these words, "Typography is not self-expression but . . . is founded in and conditioned by the message it must convey." This quote captures the prime motivation of Bayer's Bauhaus-influenced ideals of objectivity over subjectivity in art and of the symbiosis of design with industry. Some of his finest works were publication designs for modernist contemporaries: for Marcel Breuer's *Metallmöbel* (1928) and José Luis Sert's *Can Our Cities Survive?* (1942). Especially emblematic was the design for his classic and repeatedly reissued publication with Walter and Ise Gropius, *Bauhaus 1919–1928* (1938). Oddly, Bayer seemed to underestimate his own graphic design talent, for despite these testimonies to his excellence as an innovator in typography and graphic design, he always insisted that he was first a painter, a medium in which he was often quite derivative and critically unlauded.

Modern design, to which Bayer had devoted his career, offended the Nazi regime. Furthermore, Bayer had married a Jewish woman, Irene Hecht. Thus, to protect both his career and his marriage, Bayer sailed with his wife and child to the United States in 1938. As a refugee, following the emigration of Walter Gropius and so many other Bauhaus artists to freedom, Bayer was relatively fortunate. Urbane New York City of the 1930s appreciated Bayer's graphic style and photomontages, symbols of his uncompromisingly modern design aesthetic. He successfully found jobs in commercial advertising, working for major firms such as J. Walter Thompson. More important, Bayer was named by museum director Alfred Barr to the prestigious position of exhibition designer for the major American landmark Bauhaus Exhibition of 1938 at the Museum of Modern Art.

Bayer's career and life at this point took off into new directions. He became a naturalized American citizen in 1944, left his first marriage, and married Joella Haweis Levy, acquiring three stepchildren. In the true American tradition of adventure, he left New York, and heeding the call to go West, the family moved in 1946 to the then-developing Rocky Mountain town of Aspen, Colorado. There Bayer became the major designer of the Aspen Institute for Humanistic Studies, a think tank and adjunct to a planned mountain resort community. Through the Aspen Institute, Bayer made the connections to American corporate patronage that dictated the direction of the second half of his career, first through employment as design director for Container Corporation of America (CCA) and later for the oil giant ARCO.

With typical American postwar zeal, CCA employed Bayer as overall design director, a kind of American derivation of the Bauhaus concept of "total designer," with responsibilities ranging from the microscale of typography to the widely disseminated scale of advertising, even including the macroscale of architecture of corporate structures. Bayer's advertising concept for CCA, "great ideas of western man," rather bland magazine page designs linking American statesmen with corporate identity, though perhaps well-intentioned by the newly American Bayer, tends to be viewed with a modicum of cynicism in retrospect. Some critics interpret much of the latter part of Bayer's life as filled with aesthetic compromise. Examination of his complete works demonstrates that Bayer had been much sharper in his early Bauhaus years, when his conflicting tendencies toward precision and expressionism had come together in his compositions; that powerful aesthetic tension had disappeared by the Aspen period. On one hand, throughout his career Bayer epitomized the Bauhaus ideal of design for industry, but on the other, his motivations seem to have been personal and monetary rather than the altruistic improvement of life through design for the common man, the Bauhaus ideal. Thus critical opinion of Bayer's complete oeuvre has been ambivalent.

Design ultimately provided Bayer with a comfortable American lifestyle, affording the son of rural Europeans the opportunity to build himself a suave American modernist wood and glass house in exclusive Aspen (1959), truly fulfilling the postwar American dream of prosperity. In Aspen Bayer continued to paint for the remainder of his life, dying in Montecito, California. He was artistically prolific, represented by New York dealer Marlborough Gallery, and his work was exhibited in galleries from New York to Denver, from London to Munich. Bayer's painting favored geometric abstractions on flat planes, with the image of the mountains a recurring theme in his work, particularly in a series of the 1950s titled Mountains and Convolutions.

Late work in still another artistic medium, however, far exceeded his painting in both style and substance: Bayer's experiments in environmental sculpture, now called "earthworks," were a real innovation in the mid-1950s. For the Aspen Institute Bayer created the first of his major outdoor structures, the giant *Grass Mound*, a spiraling, forty-foot-diameter soil sculpture reflecting the undulations of his beloved mountain vistas. In the massive environmental sculptures of the last decades of his life, Bayer insightfully continued to explore relationships of the natural world with manmade form. From the Alps to the Rockies, from typography to earthworks, the hand of Herbert Bayer left its graphic signature.

• The Herbert Bayer Collection and Archive is located at the Denver Art Museum, for which an illustrated catalog by the same title has been published (1988). Another significant repository of Bayer works can be found in the Bauhaus Collection, Busch-Reisinger Museum, Harvard University Art Museums. The most significant biography on Bayer was his own *herbert bayer: painter, designer, architect* (1967), which is both written and designed by Bayer, incorporating not only his own visual style and typography but his insistent omission of capital letters as well. Arthur A. Cohen, *Herbert Bayer: The Complete Work* (1984), followed this study to the later period of Bayer's life. See also publications of the Bauhaus-Archiv, *Herbert Bayer, Das künstlerische Werk 1918–1938* (1982), and the excellent documentary source on the period, first published in English in 1980, Hans M. Wingler, *The Bauhaus*. A thoughtful obituary is in the *New York Times*, 1 Oct. 1985.

LESLIE HUMM CORMIER

BAYES, Nora (29 Nov. 1880–19 Mar. 1928), singer and comedienne, was born Theodora Goldberg in Joliet, Illinois, the daughter of Elias Goldberg, a merchant, and Rachel Miller. The product of local public schools, which she left to enter vaudeville, the young Dora Goldberg was largely self-taught musically. She had already made her debut at the Hopkins Theatre in Chicago and had become "Nora Bayes" when, at eighteen, she received her first acclaim at the Hyde and Behman vaudeville theater in Chicago, singing comic songs in dialect while impersonating Yiddish and Irish stereotypical characters then fashionable in vaudeville.

By the 1900–1901 theater season Bayes had reached the big time in vaudeville and was performing on the Keith Circuit. At the Keith-affiliated Orpheum Theater in Brooklyn, New York, in 1902 she achieved her first major success when she introduced "Down Where the Wurzburger Flows," a comic ballad by Harry von Tilzer and Vincent P. Bryan. A chance hearing by producer Florenz Ziegfeld, who was then promoting his wife, Anna Held, led the budding impresario to engage Bayes for a new and extravagant form of musical entertainment he planned to call the *Follies*.

The first edition—the *Follies of 1907*—was premiered at the New York Theatre Roof in July 1907. As the only featured performer on the playbill and surrounded by the lavish sets and statuesque young women for which the *Follies* became famous, Bayes brought her singular blend of comedy and tragedy to a variety of ethnic-oriented comic songs. Perhaps the high point of her early career came in 1909, when she introduced "Has Anybody Here Seen Kelly?" on Broadway in the musical *The Jolly Bachelors*. Delivered in a mock Irish brogue, the song became a Bayes staple for the duration of her career. She became an overnight sensation in the 1907 *Follies* and, because of Ziegfeld's relentless promotion, she went on to achieve even greater acclaim as a comedienne in the *Follies of 1908*.

Bayes left the Ziegfeld fold a major star in 1908. Earlier, during her performances in the 1907 *Follies*, she had married vaudeville comedian Jack Norworth, who became the second and best known of her five husbands. Her other husbands were Otto Gressing, Harry Clarke, Arthur A. Gordon, and Benjamin L. Friedland. ("The Wedding March," Bayes once quipped during a tour abroad, "is my national anthem.") Between their marriage in 1907 and their divorce six years later, Bayes and Norworth toured the United States as a double act on the Keith and Orpheum circuits and also garnered rave reviews in London. Their joint appearances blended Bayes's Irish comic ballads and Norworth's tongue-twisting patter songs ("Which Switch Is the Switch, Miss, for Ipswich?" was one of his specialties) and also gave them a vehicle for introducing Norworth's own compositions, including several on which he and Bayes collaborated. One of these joint efforts, "Shine On, Harvest Moon," outlived both stars and became a popular-music standard.

During and after her marriage to Norworth, Bayes built one of the most successful stage careers of the World War I era. Alternating between big-time vaudeville engagements and touring in shows that she either produced or coproduced, she introduced a stream of popular songs by some of the leading Tin Pan Alley songwriters of the day. Most of these songs were timely but did not achieve lasting popularity. (Typical among them was "Cheer Up! Eat and Grow Thin!" by Ray Goetz, reflecting the dieting craze of the late 1910s.) But any song Bayes performed benefited from her unique delivery, both on stage and on recordings. Most of the latter were issued by the Victor Talking Machine Company and Columbia Graphophone between 1915 and 1925, including three duets that she and Norworth recorded of their own compositions ("Turn Off Your Light, Mister Moon Man," "Rosa Rosetta," and "Come Along, My Mandy," all recorded for the Victor Company).

By far the most popular of the songs that Bayes introduced at the peak of her career was George M. Cohan's stirring "Over There," which became an unofficial anthem when the United States entered World War I. Although sales figures for early recordings are often tenuous, Bayes's recorded rendition of "Over There," issued on Victor's celebrity-series blue label, reportedly sold more than any other recording of "Over There"—including one recorded several months later by the celebrated operatic tenor Enrico Caruso.

Although Cohan, Irving Berlin, and Jerome Kern wrote songs for Nora Bayes, not all of her collaborations with songwriters went smoothly. In mid-1918, after auditioning several new songs at the T. B. Harms Company, one of Tin Pan Alley's leading publishing houses, Bayes agreed to include a song called "The Real American Folk Song (Is a Rag)" in an upcoming show that she intended to produce. The song's lyrics were written by an unknown named Arthur Francis—the pseudonym of Ira Gershwin—and the music was the product of his younger brother, George. When George Gershwin auditioned the song for Bayes, she was so impressed with his piano prowess that she engaged him as her accompanist for the touring version of the musical, which came to be titled *Ladies First*. Early in the tour, however, Gershwin's intricate and inventive piano playing began to take away some of the limelight from Bayes's performing. When she began to blame Gershwin for almost anything that went wrong on tour, he kept silent. But when she ordered him to rewrite the ending of "The Real American Folk Song" to suit her tastes, Gershwin balked—and Bayes summarily fired him.

Bayes remained a headliner on the Keith Circuit well into the 1920s. When she played at the Palace, the most prestigious of Keith's Manhattan theaters, she was routinely billed as the "Extraordinarily Superlative Attraction, the Super Star, the Pre-eminent Singer with Splendid Dramatic Art, the Very Best—So Clever, in Fact, That No Rival Can Be Called a Second." Although she indeed had her rivals (especially Eva Tanguay, who had replaced Bayes in the *Follies* of 1909), one of her chief rivals, Elsie Janis, paid tribute to Bayes by including an endearing and well-received impersonation of her in Janis's own Keith Circuit appearances in the 1917–1918 season.

Much of Bayes's great success can be attributed less to her singing voice (which she described "as loud enough but throaty and not so good") and more to her ability to hold an audience. "My performances are exactly like an intimate chat," she wrote in 1917. "I can think of no better symbol to express my own feelings toward [my] audience than that of a small party seated at a friendly table." Although changing musical trends in the 1920s made her somewhat less an attraction than she had been a decade before, Bayes continued to perform well into the decade, both in the United States and occasionally in England. On 15 March 1928 she performed gratis for the indigents at Tom Noonan's Bowery Mission in New York City. She died four days later at the Brooklyn Jewish Hospital from an abdominal infection that surgery had failed to cure.

• Bayes left no memoirs but contributed occasional interviews and articles to theatrical periodicals. See, for example, "Holding My Audience," *Theatre Magazine*, Sept. 1917, reprinted in Charles W. Stein, *American Vaudeville as Seen by Its Contemporaries* (1984). She is profiled in Marian Spitzer, *The Palace* (1969); Abel Green and Joe Laurie, Jr., *Show Biz, from Vaude to Video* (1953); and Marjorie Farnsworth, *The Ziegfeld Follies* (1956). Bayes's stage performances were reviewed regularly in *Variety* and *Billboard* throughout her career. Complete information about her Victor Talking Machine Company recordings (including all that were released as well as her unissued performances) is in Ted Fagin and William R. Moran, *The Encyclopedia Discography of Victor Recordings*, vol. 3 (1997). Obituaries are in the *New York Times*, 20 Mar. 1928, and *Variety*, 23 Mar. 1928.

JAMES A. DRAKE

BAYLEY, James Roosevelt (23 Aug. 1814–3 Oct. 1877), Roman Catholic bishop, was born in New York City, the son of Guy Carleton Bayley, a physician, and Grace Roosevelt, a member of a prominent merchant family. He was the nephew of Elizabeth Bayley Seton, founder of the Sisters of Charity and the first native-born American to be canonized a saint of the Roman Catholic church. Bayley attended Amherst College but graduated from Trinity College in Hartford, Connecticut. After a year of practicing medicine he studied for the ministry in the Episcopal church and was ordained priest in 1840. After struggling with doubts over the validity of the claims of the Episcopal church to be in continuity with the church of the apostolic age, he resigned his rectorship in 1841 and was received into the Roman Catholic church in Rome in April 1842. After seminary studies in Paris and New York, he was ordained a Roman Catholic priest in

1844. He served at St. John's College (Fordham University) in New York City and as secretary to Bishop John J. Hughes of New York.

In 1853 Bayley was appointed first bishop of Newark, New Jersey. Not a controversialist, he preferred discussion and persuasion as his way of addressing contemporary controversies. In his nineteen years as bishop of the see of Newark, which was then responsible for the entire state of New Jersey, he established many parishes, missions, and parochial schools to meet the needs of a rapidly increasing Catholic population whose growth was fueled by immigration from Ireland and Germany. Dedicated to the intellectual life, Bayley founded Seton Hall College (named after his aunt and now Seton Hall University) and Immaculate Conception Seminary (now the School of Theology of Seton Hall University). During this time he was also influential in the establishment of the North American College in Rome. He is considered the cofounder of the Sisters of Charity of St. Elizabeth of New Jersey, a religious congregation dedicated to Catholic education.

Bayley's administrative duties in organizing and administering a rapidly growing diocese claimed the major portion of his time. He did not, however, neglect his scholarly interests. He lectured widely and published a *Brief Sketch of the Early History of the Catholic Church on the Island of New York* (1853, 1870) and the *Memoirs of the Rt. Rev. Simon Wm. Gabriel Brute, First Bishop of Vincennes* (1860). Although he preferred to remain in Newark, he yielded to pressure from Rome and accepted the premier see of the American church (an honorific title applied to the first diocese established in a country) and was appointed archbishop of Baltimore on 21 July 1872. Hampered by illness and the responsibilities of an extensive territory, he asked for a coadjutor archbishop to assist him. In 1876 James Gibbons was appointed to this post. While on a visit to New Jersey, Bayley died in Newark.

• The greater portion of Bayley's papers are in the Archives of the Archdiocese of Baltimore, Md. Some of the papers from his Newark period are in the Archives of the Archdiocese of Newark at Seton Hall University. The major biography is M. H. Yeager, *Life of James Roosevelt Bayley, First Bishop of Newark and Eighth Archbishop of Baltimore 1814–1877* (1947). See also W. N. Field and F. Peters, eds., *The Bishops of Newark: 1853–1973* (1978).

ROBERT J. WISTER

BAYLEY, Richard (1745–17 Aug. 1801), physician and surgeon, was born in Fairfield, Connecticut. Little is known about his parents except that his mother was French, and his father was English. Indeed, it appears that little was known even to Bayley's contemporaries. What is certain about Bayley is that he was an ambitious and innovative physician. After an early education that included French and the classics, he took an apprenticeship with the prestigious and fashionable New York physician John Charlton in 1766. Bayley studied with Charlton for three years; during that time

he successfully courted and married his preceptor's sister. They had children, but the precise number is uncertain. After completing his apprenticeship, Bayley wanted to put further polish on his medical education and in 1769 sailed to London to study with William Hunter; the famous anatomist apparently was pleased with his student. Bayley wrote to his wife in 1770 that "Dr. Hunter gives me great encouragement, and thinks that . . . I may with ease qualify myself for a practitioner in surgery in any part of the world." After three years with Hunter, Bayley returned to New York and began practice in partnership with Charlton.

After his return to America, Bayley began making his own contributions to medical knowledge. About 1774 he wrote a letter to Hunter distinguishing "fatal croup" (or diphtheria) from "putrid sore throat" (or strep throat). (This letter was later published as "A View of the Croup" in 1781.) By applying European techniques in pathological observation and autopsy, Bayley discovered that diphtheria kills its victims through suffocation, while other forms of sore throat do not. In all likelihood he was one of the first Americans to use these techniques. Bayley used his discoveries to develop a new treatment for diphtheria that soon became widely accepted. His treatment consisted of bleeding from the jugular vein to relieve inflammation; blisters applied to the throat as a counterirritant; and purges and emetics to cleanse the system.

Bayley returned to England in 1775 to spend the winter with his mentor Hunter. He remained there until the spring of 1776, when he returned to America as a military surgeon under the British general William Howe. He served in that capacity in Newport, Rhode Island, for one year, until he was forced to resign because of his wife's ill health. He returned to New York in the spring of 1777; his wife died shortly after his return. Bayley resumed his established New York practice and also gave anatomical lectures at the New York Hospital.

Bayley led an uneventful life until 1788. In April of that year, a mob, excited by rumors of grave robbing by medical students, attacked the South Wing of the New York Hospital. Bayley was one of its prime targets. The rioters viewed Bayley's well-known collection of pathological specimens as evidence of his complicity in the alleged grave robbing; they were further inflamed by whispers that Bayley had performed bizarre and cruel medical experiments on his army patients in Rhode Island. Bayley escaped unharmed, but his anatomical collection did not. The mob seized his specimens and triumphantly interred them in a nearby churchyard. The rioting continued until it was finally put down by the New York militia several days later. Despite this incident, Bayley continued his practice.

The following years brought Bayley many professional honors. In 1792 he was appointed the first professor of anatomy at Columbia College; the following year he became professor of surgery. During his time at Columbia he introduced many new surgical techniques to the American medical community. Of these techniques the most important was a new method of amputating the arm at the shoulder joint. In his biographical article James Thacher describes Bayley's amputation technique as follows: "He . . . successfully removed the arm from its glenoid cavity by the operation of the shoulder joint." Bayley was the first American known to successfully perform this operation.

In addition to his academic work, Bayley served the city of New York in several public health capacities. He was instrumental in founding the New York Dispensary, which aided the city's poor. When the city's infamous series of yellow fever epidemics began in 1795, Bayley took an interest in that disease. He wrote a well-known and widely accepted treatise on the subject, in which he declared that yellow fever stemmed from filth and decay—specifically, piles of rotting garbage and animal carcasses. The publication of this treatise led him to a seat on a physicians' committee to develop quarantine laws for the city. Bayley was appointed in 1795 to the office of health physician, the doctor who inspected incoming ships for disease before they were allowed to dock in New York Harbor.

Ironically, it was Bayley's interest in public health that led to his death. On 10 August 1801 Bayley inspected an Irish immigrant vessel that had recently arrived in the harbor. He discovered a horrifying scene inside: all the crew and passengers were acutely ill and many were dying. He supervised their removal to a quarantine hospital, then returned home. Shortly thereafter he began to feel ill and took to his bed. The illness worsened, manifesting itself with intense pain in his head and stomach. A week later, he died of the illness, yellow fever.

Thacher describes Bayley as "a perfect gentleman . . . of perfect integrity." While Bayley made a good name for American medicine in the dissecting rooms and hospital wards of Europe, it is more likely that his greatest achievement lay in bringing the best of European medical research to America and in applying those techniques to his own practice.

• Bayley's own works include "A View of the Croup," *Medical Repository* 12 (1809): 331–39, and *An Account of the Epidemic Fever Which Prevailed in the City of New York during Part of the Summer and Fall of 1795* (1796). The best biographical source is James Thacher's entry on him in *American Medical Biography* (1828). Thacher gives a detailed account of Bayley's professional life, quotes extensively from Bayley's medical writings, and cites several of his letters. On the "doctor's mob" of 1788, see Mary L. Booth, *History of the City of New York from Its Earliest Settlement to the Present Time* (1859).

REBECCA TANNENBAUM

BAYLOR, Frances Courtenay (20 Jan. 1848–19 Oct. 1920), author, was born at Fort Smith, Arkansas, the daughter of James L. Dawson, an army officer stationed at Fort Smith at the time of her birth, and Sophie Baylor. She was educated by her mother as the family moved to military posts at San Antonio and then New Orleans. Near the end of the Civil War her mother, a member of a distinguished and very tradition-conscious family, reassumed her maiden name

for herself and Frances. She then returned with Frances to Virginia, where she had grown up, living for a time with another daughter, Sophie, who was married to Confederate general John G. Walker. When the war ended the entire Walker household moved to England for a lengthy stay, where Frances was introduced to a wide circle of literary people.

Settling in Winchester, Virginia, upon her return to the United States in the late 1860s, Baylor began to write. Her anonymous play, *Petruchio Tamed*, was followed by numerous sketches and considerable verse that, under the name of a male relative, appeared in newspapers from New Orleans to London. Some of her patriotic poems became quite popular. Using her own name, Baylor also contributed to such publications as *Lippincott's Magazine*, the *Atlantic Monthly*, and the *Princeton Review*. In *Lippincott's* she published "The Perfect Treasure," a humorous account of an American family's social misadventures in England. It was followed in the same magazine by "On This Side," which, reversing directions across the Atlantic, depicted the encounters of a British family in the United States. In 1886 Baylor combined the two stories in *On Both Sides*, an Anglo-American novel of manners that was praised highly by reviewers and readers. It eventually went through eleven editions.

Baylor followed her first critical and commercial success with *Behind the Blue Ridge* (1887), a novel about the people of the nearby Blue Ridge Mountains of Virginia. Though the tone is overly sentimental and the plot often weak—characteristics common to much of her work—the customs, manners, and speech patterns of the region generally receive realistic treatment. Of all her novels, only *Behind the Blue Ridge* deals exclusively with American characters. *On Both Sides* and the novels published after *Behind the Blue Ridge*—*Juan and Juanita* (1887), *Claudia Hyde* (1894), *Miss Nina Barrow* (1897), *The Ladder of Fortune* (1899), and *A Georgian Bungalow* (1900)—involve persons of different nationalities interacting with one another. Because the story lines in these novels are weak, much of their interest derives from Baylor's social insights and her efforts to contrast the moral strengths and weaknesses of her characters.

Juan and Juanita, Miss Nina Barrow, and *A Georgian Bungalow* are juvenile fiction. The first deals suspensefully with the capture and escape of two Mexican children. It became something of a minor classic in children's literature, going through many editions. Baylor's short stories and sketches that earlier had appeared in a variety of periodicals were collected in 1889 as *A Shocking Example, and Other Sketches*.

In 1896 Baylor married George Sherman Barnum of Savannah, Georgia, where the couple lived for a short time before moving to Lexington, Virginia. After he died around 1900, Baylor returned to her family home in Winchester, where she lived quietly with her mother and sister. She periodically worked on a new novel, entitled "The Matrimonial Coolie," but it was never published. Baylor's last published work was *Remaking a Man: One Successful Method of Mental Refitting*, which appeared in 1919. She died in Winchester.

• Biographical information on Baylor can be found in Florence Walker, "A Feminine Glimpse of Miss Baylor," *Critic*, n.s., 9 (Apr. 1888): 163–64; Mildred Lewis Rutherford, *The South in History and Literature* (1906); and C. Carroll Hollis, "Frances Courtenay Baylor," *Southern Writers*, ed. Robert A. Bain et al. (1979).

L. MOODY SIMMS, JR.

BAYLY, Thomas Henry (11 Oct. 1810–22 June 1856), congressman, was born at "Mount Custis," the family estate, near Accomac Court House, Virginia, the son of Thomas Monteagle Bayly, a prosperous planter and congressman, and Margaret Pettit Cropper. The youth attended private schools before graduating from the University of Virginia in 1829. Trained as a lawyer, Bayly passed the bar in 1831 and began his practice that year in Accomack County, where he inherited the family estate. In 1838 Bayly married Evelyn Harrison May, with whom he had three children.

Bayly was elected as a Democrat to the Virginia House of Delegates in 1836, in which capacity he served until 1842. In 1837 he secured an appointment from the state assembly as brigadier general of the Twenty-first Brigade Virginia Militia. He resigned this position and his legislator's seat in 1842, when he became a circuit court judge, filling the vacancy occasioned by the appointment of Judge Abel P. Upshur as secretary of the navy in President John Tyler's administration. Two years later, in 1844, he won election to the U.S. House of Representatives to fill the seat vacated by his cousin Henry Alexander Wise, who was appointed minister to Brazil. Bayly remained in the House until his death. There he eventually gained the chairmanships of the Committee on Ways and Means in the Thirty-first Congress and the Committee on Foreign Affairs in the next two Congresses.

Although a champion of states' rights, Bayly maintained a firm commitment to the Union. A popular and independent man, he earned the respect of his constituency in eastern Virginia and that of his party in Washington. He also caught the attention of President James K. Polk, who enlisted Bayly in 1845 to write a letter to Thomas Ritchie, the elderly editor of the *Richmond Enquirer*, to persuade him to assume the editorial chair of the *Washington Union*, a new party organ. Bayly successfully accomplished this assignment.

During the congressional debate in 1846 over the Wilmot Proviso, which sought to exclude slavery from any territory acquired from Mexico during the Mexican War, Bayly, a slaveholder, endeavored to reconcile southern and northern Democrats on this controversial issue. Condemning the Wilmot Proviso as unconstitutional, he confined his remarks in a lengthy speech in the House of Representatives to the question of whether Congress, under the Constitution, had the power to prohibit slavery in the territories. He concluded that the matter could only be resolved by the federal judiciary and that he would accept the court's decision. "They are questions which Congress has no authority to settle," he said, "and they are questions which I do not wish to see introduced here or in the politics of the country. Neither the Congress nor the President can have anything to do in their solution." Although his position was not widespread, Bayly had his speech printed and distributed throughout the South. He wanted Democrats to remain united for the sake of the party principles and for the stability and endurance of the nation. In the end, he was largely responsible for aligning southern and western Democrats to defeat the Wilmot Proviso.

Bayly played an important role at the Democratic National Convention in Baltimore in 1848. He headed the Virginia delegation, a large group wielding much influence. At first the delegates divided fairly evenly among the three leading presidential contenders, Lewis Cass of Michigan, James Buchanan of Pennsylvania, and Levi Woodbury of New Hampshire. Determined to remove any differences in interpreting the doctrine of popular sovereignty (local determination of the status of slavery) and committed to the alliance between southern and western Democrats, Bayly supported Cass for president. Virginia's endorsement was crucial to the outcome, and Cass was nominated on the fourth ballot, much to Bayly's satisfaction. He also supported the platform plank that criticized all efforts to bring the slavery question before Congress. However, the Whig party won the presidential election with Zachary Taylor, a popular general, as its standard-bearer.

By 1848 Bayly was one of the leaders of the Democratic party who played a key role in the critical decisions that confronted the nation. Along with Linn Boyd of Kentucky, John McClernand of Illinois, and Howell Cobb of Georgia, he emerged in 1849 among the top finalists for the position of Speaker of the House of Representatives. Bayly eventually withdrew from the contest and supported Cobb, who as Speaker rewarded him with the chairmanship of the powerful House Ways and Means Committee.

Worried that slavery and other sectional issues were shredding the fabric of the nation, Bayly supported efforts at conciliation between North and South. In February 1850 Ritchie and Bayly met with Senator Henry Clay of Kentucky in his Washington hotel room to work out details of a compromise package to preserve the Union as well as reconcile past differences between Ritchie and Clay. Bayly argued passionately for the Compromise of 1850, a collective term of later origin that applied to five laws enacted in September. They included the admission of California as a free state and an act abolishing the slave trade in the District of Columbia. Bayly's moderate appeal for mutual concessions to stem mounting sectional grievances contrasted sharply with the positions of Senator William H. Seward of New York and Senator James M. Mason of Virginia, who read the anticompromise speech of the enfeebled Senator John C. Calhoun of South Carolina. Although Bayly's stand earned him the wrath of southern extremists, the Virginia congressman joined forces with Senator Daniel Webster of Massachusetts, Senator Clay, and President Millard Fillmore (who succeeded to the presidency in 1850 upon Taylor's death) to coalesce sentiment in favor of a settlement between North and South.

Bayly's political career reached its climax in 1850. He served six more years in Congress and became chairman of the House Foreign Affairs Committee, but deteriorating health marred his last years in Congress. In 1851 he teamed with Senator Stephen A. Douglas of Illinois to push through the House a bill providing a federal grant for the Illinois Central Railroad. Bayly played no major role in 1854 when the Kansas-Nebraska Act passed by a bipartisan combination of southern Democrats and Whigs, with such reluctant northern Democratic support as could be obtained by Douglas and President Franklin Pierce. The act, which divided Kansas and Nebraska at the fortieth parallel, incorporated the principle of popular sovereignty, a theory dear to Bayly's heart, and by implication formally established the doctrine of congressional nonintervention in the territories. Popular dissatisfaction with this act ultimately caused political realignment and the emergence of the Republican party.

Although Bayly was an advocate of slavery who defended that institution as an economic necessity protected by the Constitution, he was not a southern firebrand. He disliked both southern and northern extremists, contending that abolitionists were practicing mad schemes. Bayly put the Union first, but his accomplishments were often overshadowed by the controversies of his generation. He sought a proper division of power between the states and the national government, but he did not want slavery to destroy the country. His Federalist roots, inherited from his father, were too strong to permit a permanent separation. In the end, Bayly's moderate, Unionist stance amidst increasing sectional tensions proved to be ineffective. The era of the compromisers ended, the Whig party collapsed, the Democratic party divided, and with Abraham Lincoln's presidential victory in 1860, the Civil War began.

Known for his ready wit and firm convictions, Bayly served twelve years in the House of Representatives during a contentious period in U.S. history. His speeches may have lacked eloquence, but they were forcefully presented and substantiated by facts. Bayly's House colleague Cobb described the Virginian as a clear speaker who commanded the attention of the legislators for his talents and for the learning and research that he brought into the discussions. Bayly succumbed to consumption at Mount Custis. Upon hearing of Bayly's death at his plantation, Cobb and others in the House commented on his personal traits, prudence, moderation, constitutional construction, and friendship for the Union.

• A small collection of Bayly's letters is in the Virginia State Library and Archives in Richmond. Others are in the papers of contemporaries, including Lewis Cass (Univ. of Michigan at Ann Arbor), Mason Family Papers (Univ. of Virginia), and James K. Polk, Levi Woodbury, and John Tyler (Library of Congress). Additional material is in the Orris Applethwaite Browne Scrapbooks, Eastern Shore of Virginia Historical Society, Onancock; and Ulrich Bonnell Phillips, ed., "The Correspondence of Robert Toombs, Alexander H. Stephens, and Howell Cobb," *Annual Report of the American Historical Association for the Year 1911* 2 (1913): 138. Bayly's speeches are in the *Congressional Globe* (1845–1856). A biographical sketch is in Samuel T. Ross, "Recollections of Bench and Bar of Accomack: An Address Delivered at the Dedication of the Courthouse on June 19, 1900," *Onancock Eastern Shore News*, 25 Jan., 1, 8, 15, 22 Feb., 1 Mar. 1935. His career is mentioned in Ralph T. Whitelaw, *Virginia's Eastern Shore: A History of Northampton and Accomack Counties* (1951); and Chaplain W. Morrison, *Democratic Politics and Sectionalism: The Wilmot Proviso Controversy* (1967). Insights into the period may be gleaned from Glyndon G. Van Deusen, *The Jacksonian Era, 1828–1848* (1959); Charles Henry Ambler, *Thomas Ritchie: A Study in Virginia Politics* (1913); Holman Hamilton, *Prologue to Conflict: The Crisis and Compromise of 1850* (1964); Virginius Dabney, *Virginia: The New Dominion* (1971); Joseph G. Rayback, *Free Soil: The Election of 1848* (1970); Robert R. Russel, "What Was the Compromise of 1850?" *Journal of Southern History* 22 (1956): 492–509; James P. Hambleton, *A Biographical Sketch of Henry A. Wise* (1856), p. 344; and Craig Simpson, *A Good Southerner: The Life of Henry A. Wise of Virginia* (1992). Obituaries are in the *Richmond Dispatch* and the *Richmond Enquirer*, 27 June 1856.

LEONARD SCHLUP

BAYNE, Thomas (1824–1889), dentist and politician, was born into slavery in North Carolina and was known as Samuel Nixon before his escape from bondage in 1855. He was sold several times before being purchased by C. F. Martin, a dentist in Norfolk, Virginia. As the slave of Martin, Bayne learned sufficient dentistry to serve as the doctor's assistant and to make dental house calls. Bayne also developed bookkeeping skills and monitored the doctor's accounts.

In Norfolk Bayne became involved with the Underground Railroad. Befriending the captains of many of the schooners sailing in and out of Norfolk, he often convinced them to hide fugitive slaves aboard ship and carry them north, usually to Philadelphia or to New Bedford, Massachusetts. After conducting many other slaves through the Underground Railroad, Bayne decided to become a passenger himself in March 1855. He and three other slaves disguised themselves and hid on board a schooner bound for Philadelphia. He left behind his wife Edna (maiden name unknown) and one child, both of whom were owned by E. P. Tabb, a Norfolk hardware merchant. The ship landed in New Jersey, where Bayne was directed to Abigail Goodwin, a Quaker abolitionist. In a letter to a fellow abolitionist, Goodwin described Bayne as "a smart young man . . . well dressed in fine broad-cloth coat and overcoat, and has a very active tongue in his head," but she worried that "they will be after him soon."

He soon traveled to New Bedford, where he changed his name to Thomas Bayne and began a dentistry practice while maintaining contact with Underground Railroad agents like William Still of Philadelphia. Letters between Bayne and Still reveal that Bayne sometimes sheltered fugitives in his New Bedford home and that Still aided Bayne's advancement by sending medical and dental textbooks. In January 1860 Bayne thanked Still for his "Vigilance as a colored man helping a colored man to get such knowledge as will give the lie to our enemies." Bayne also gained renown in New Bedford as a speaker at abolitionist and temperance meetings, and he served on the New Bedford City Council in 1865.

At the end of the Civil War, Bayne returned to Norfolk, Virginia, to rejoin his family. He immediately became involved in politics, and in May 1865 he chaired a public meeting at which the participants passed eight civil rights resolutions under the title of *Equal Suffrage: Address from the Colored Citizens of Norfolk, Virginia to the People of the United States*. These resolutions pledged Virginia's loyalty to the Union, decried race discrimination as abhorrent to "patriotism, humanity, and religion," and demanded equal suffrage for black and white Americans. As a member of a committee that testified on behalf of rights for freedmen, Bayne appeared before O. O. Howard of the Freedmen's Bureau in December 1865. The following year he was among a delegation of black men from Virginia who met with President Andrew Johnson to articulate demands for civil and political rights, especially the right to vote. Bayne also testified before the Joint Committee on Reconstruction, where he urged that the rights of ex-slaves be protected and Reconstruction reforms be enforced.

An important black leader in the Virginia Republican party, Bayne served as vice president of the April 1867 state Republican convention held in Richmond, where he earned a reputation for his elegant dress and commitment to public education. He was subsequently elected as a delegate from Norfolk to the Constitutional Convention of the State of Virginia, which was charged with the task of drawing up a new state constitution that would qualify Virginia for readmission to the Union. He was one of twenty-four black delegates to the convention, which met during the winter of 1867–1868. In the convention, Bayne adamantly insisted that the residual injustices of slavery be redressed. He fervently supported the proposed state constitution's Declaration of Rights, which stated that "all men are, by nature, equally free and independent, and have certain inherent rights . . . namely, the enjoyment of life and liberty, with the means of . . . obtaining happiness and safety." In the debate that surrounded that preamble, Bayne claimed the promises of the Declaration of Independence and the Constitution for black as well as white Americans and pledged himself to a constitution "that should not have the word black or the word white anywhere in it." He repeatedly argued that the harmful aftereffects of slavery could best be combated with the protection of black voting and equal citizenship rights.

Bayne recognized education as a priority for Virginia's black community. At the Virginia state convention, he spoke out against the prejudice faced by many uneducated blacks with the reminder that white Virginians had "robbed the black man of his education, . . . taken the money and labor of the black man to support themselves in grandeur, and now they curse the black man because he is not a grammarian. They are like the hunter who shot the bird through both wings, and when it fluttered and fell, damned it because it would not rise." In reparation, Bayne proposed that Virginia's constitution ensure that "the free public schools in this State shall be open free to all classes, and no child, pupil or scholar shall be ejected from said schools on account of race, color, or any invidious distinction," but the measure was defeated as too radical.

Following the state convention, Bayne retained interest in public affairs, attending an all-black political convention in May 1869. Reconstruction soon ended in Virginia, however, and he turned increasingly to his dentistry practice. As political opportunities for black Virginians diminished, Bayne sought to maintain a public profile by engaging in periodic bouts of traveling ministry, but these efforts were cut short by the senility that plagued his later years. In 1888 he was admitted to the Central State Lunatic Asylum in Norfolk, where he died. For Bayne, as for many other freedmen and freedwomen, the promise of Reconstruction's early days, during which he played an important role in post–Civil War politics, proved brighter than the reality of Reconstruction's long-term impact.

• Information about Bayne must be gleaned from a variety of sources. William Still, *The Underground Railroad: A Record of Facts, Authentic Narratives, Letters &c.* (1872), contains some of Bayne's letters and includes a narrative of Bayne's early life, escape from slavery, and life in New Bedford, Mass. *Debates and Proceedings of the Constitutional Convention of the State of Virginia* (1868) and *Journal of the Constitutional Convention of the State of Virginia* (1867) feature Bayne's speeches, debates, and actions as a delegate to the state constitutional convention. Eric Foner, ed., *Freedom's Lawmakers: A Directory of Black Officeholders during Reconstruction* (1996), discusses Bayne's career. Accounts of Reconstruction politics in Va. often refer to Bayne. Alrutheus A. Taylor, *The Negro in the Reconstruction of Virginia* (1926), covers those aspects of political life in Va. in which Bayne was involved. Herbert Aptheker, *A Documentary History of the Negro People in the United States*, vol. 2 (1968), includes a copy of the resolutions adopted by the meeting of Norfolk African Americans that Bayne chaired. *The Negro in Virginia*, published by the Virginia Writers' Program (1940), notes press reactions to Bayne.

CHANDRA M. MILLER

BAYNE-JONES, Stanhope (6 Nov. 1888–20 Feb. 1970), physician and bacteriologist, was born in New Orleans, Louisiana, the son of Samuel Stanhope Davis Jones, a physician, and Amelia Elizabeth Bayne. His childhood was a tumultuous one, largely as a result of the struggles for his custody that followed the death of his mother in 1893 and the subsequent financial ruin and suicide of his father in 1894. Apparently at the instigation of his maternal relatives, in 1902 his last name was changed to Bayne-Jones.

In 1910 Bayne-Jones received an A.B. from Yale University and entered the Tulane Medical School. After spending most of the summer of 1911 studying at the Rush Medical School, he entered the second year of the Johns Hopkins Medical School, where he stood first in his class when he received an M.D. in 1914. He remained at Johns Hopkins to study pathology and to serve as assistant resident pathologist and in 1915 joined the Army Medical Reserve Corps as a first lieutenant. After six months of graduate work in bacteriology at Columbia University's College of Physicians and Surgeons, he became director of a new laboratory concentrating on bacteriology and immunology at Hopkins.

In April 1917, after the United States entered World War I, Bayne-Jones was promoted to captain in the Army Medical Reserve Corps. He volunteered to join members of the staff of Cleveland's Lakeside Hospital in providing medical assistance to British military forces in Europe. In this capacity, he saw action at the front, service for which the British later awarded him the Military Cross. After U.S. troops began to take an active part in the conflict, he was ordered to join them and again served at the front. Not long after Armistice Day on 11 November 1918, he was promoted to major. From January 1919 until his discharge from the army the following May he served with the U.S. Army of Occupation in Germany.

In June 1919 Bayne-Jones received a one-year appointment as associate in bacteriology at Johns Hopkins and the following June was promoted to associate professor. In 1921 he married Nannie Moore Smith; the marriage was childless. In 1922 he accepted an offer to serve as head of the Department of Bacteriology at the newly created medical school at the University of Rochester in New York, where he became responsible not only for teaching but also for handling diagnoses for the city's health department and for its two hospitals. While at Rochester he served as president of the Society of American Bacteriologists and of the New York State Association of Public Health Laboratories.

In June 1931 Bayne-Jones left Rochester to accept an appointment to serve as a residential master of one of the newly formed residential colleges at Yale University and as professor of bacteriology. In 1935 he began a five-year term as dean of the Yale School of Medicine, where he launched a health plan for medical students that proved to be the forerunner of health insurance that became common fifty years later. In 1939 he was promoted to the rank of lieutenant colonel in the Medical Corps Reserve. A year later, when the secretary of war authorized the formation of the civilian-manned Army Epidemiological Board, he became the head of its Commission on Epidemiological Survey, whose principal mission was to identify potential epidemics in the hope of preventing their actual occurrence. Late the same year he also became a member of a secret organization of civilians studying the feasibili-

ty of biological warfare with the goal of preparing defenses against it.

In fall 1941 Bayne-Jones was called to active duty. From this point onward until the end of World War II he was located mainly in Washington, D.C., and involved principally with the administrative aspects of the army's preventive medicine service. Increasingly concerned about the possibility of a major outbreak of typhus among the civilians most severely affected by the conflict, he pushed for the formation of the United States of America Typhus Commission; as its head, he organized the campaign that successfully headed off an epidemic. In 1944, at the height of this effort, he was promoted to brigadier general. He received many honors both from the American and the British military.

Bayne-Jones returned to his work at Yale in 1946. A year later he was appointed president of the board of New York Hospital–Cornell Medical College Association. In 1953 he returned to Washington, D.C., to serve as technical director of research and development for the army's surgeon general, a position from which he resigned in 1956. In 1957 he became head of an advisory group formed to create guidelines for the National Institutes of Health in Washington, D.C. His work in this capacity included participation in the drive to create the National Library of Medicine in Bethesda, Maryland. In 1958, when he was named to the Armed Forces Epidemiological Board, he again become involved in research concerning biological warfare and the development of vaccines against diseases that could be used as weapons, a role he continued in until 1965.

In 1959 Bayne-Jones briefly served as a member of the National Advisory Cancer Council, created to assist the Public Health Service in decisions concerning research and research grants. In 1962 he became a member of the Surgeon General's Advisory Committee on Smoking and Public Health, whose studies led to the conclusion in 1964 that smoking was directly related to cancer. In the final years of his life, he devoted much of his time to research and writing, and particularly to the official Medical Department histories of its activities in World War II. In 1966 he also began taping an oral history of his life, which he completed not long before his death in Washington, D.C.

As a teacher and as an expert in the field of preventive medicine, Bayne-Jones was involved with a myriad of organizations concerned with various aspects of preventive medicine and earned the respect of some of the most distinguished scientists of his time. His most significant contributions to medical science, however, were those he made as a teacher and as a leader skilled in coordinating the efforts of others, many with difficult temperaments, toward reaching a common goal.

• The bulk of Bayne-Jones personal papers are held at the National Library of Medicine in Bethesda, Md. His many publications include such books as *Man and Microbes* (1932) and *The Evolution of Preventive Medicine in the United States Army, 1607–1939* (1968). He coauthored with Hans Zinsser the 7th ed. (1934) and 8th ed. (1939) of *A Textbook of Bacteri-*

ology, a standard work on the subject. Representative of the many articles he contributed to books and journals are "Board for the Investigation and Control of Influenza and Other Epidemic Diseases in the Army," *Army Medical Bulletin* 64 (Oct. 1941): 1–22; "Reciprocal Effects of the Relationship of Bacteriology and Medicine," *Journal of Bacteriology* 21 (1931): 61–73; "A Teacher by Preference," *Science* 143 (1964): 347; and two articles in the nine-volume work, *Preventive Medicine in World War II*, ed. Ebbe Curtis Hoff, "Typhus Fever," in *Communicable Diseases*, vol. 7 (1964), and "Enemy Prisoners of War," in *Special Fields*, vol. 9 (1968). Albert E. Cowdrey's *War and Healing: Stanhope Bayne-Jones and the Maturing of American Medicine* (1992) is a full-length biography. An obituary is in the *Washington Post*, 21 Feb. 1970.

MARY C. GILLETT

BAZETT, Henry Cuthbert (25 June 1885–12 July 1950), physiologist, was born in Gravesend, England, the son of Henry Bazett, a clergyman and later a physician, and Eliza Ann Cruickshank. He attended Dover College and Wadham College, Oxford University, receiving his B.A. (1908), M.S. (1913), and M.D. (1919). He also trained at Saint Thomas's Hospital. In 1912 Bazett was awarded a Radcliffe traveling fellowship, which allowed him to spend a postgraduate year at Harvard University. He returned to England in 1913 and at the outbreak of World War I joined the Royal Army Medical Corps. In 1917 he married Dorothy Livesey; they had a son and a daughter. He served with distinction in France and in 1918, after his discharge, was appointed an officer of the Order of the British Empire.

As a patient awaiting medical treatment for acute appendicitis in France, Bazett had been able to observe the effects of cold on the body when it was in a state of shock. After this experience he wished to focus his research primarily on physiology as it related to surgery. Following the war, he returned to Oxford as a lecturer in clinical physiology. Like others who had returned from France, Bazett felt that many aspects of the university were outmoded; although he participated in an effort to make reforms, nothing changed. Unable to obtain a position that would allow him to concentrate on clinical physiology, Bazett left Oxford in 1921 and accepted an offer from the University of Pennsylvania to chair the Department of Physiology, a post that he held until his death.

From the time of his appointment, Bazett's enthusiasm for seeking knowledge won him friends. Among his colleagues he was admired for listening to descriptions of interesting experiments and vividly explaining his own experiences. When discussing science, his demeanor was like that of an excited child, and his enthusiasm never diminished as he grew older. His one problem in communicating with students was that his understanding of physiology was so clear that he skipped steps in explaining processes, leaving some listeners confused.

Bazett was fearless both in the army and in his research. He was always the first to volunteer as a subject for his human experiments regardless of the danger, and he performed many operations on himself. In an experiment to study thermal sense and body temperature control, Bazett inserted thermocouples (conductors that produce thermoelectric currents to measure temperature) in various depths under his skin and in many blood vessels. This, in conjunction with other experiments, demonstrated the importance of the venae comites in controlling body temperature. He discovered that arterial blood in the limbs that was surrounded by a network of veins, or *venous plexus*, could be cooled by the returning venous blood. Bazett showed that a temperature gradient existed, thus disproving the assumption that blood temperature was constant throughout the body. This work led Bazett to postulate that the body responds reflexively to heat and cold. Superficial receptors (Ruffine and Karuse receptors) mediate these reflexive responses, and deep receptors respond to temperature gradients. The superficial receptors, he found, increase subcutaneous venous flow when the skin is exposed to heat and shunt it away when the skin is exposed to cold. The deep receptors, on the other hand, control sweating by detecting the difference between heat produced by muscle exercise and heat applied superficially. His research proved valuable in explaining some of the peculiarities of circulation and sweating rates and helped to clearly establish the relationship between the increase in blood volume and hot environments.

Concerned for his fellow Englishmen on the brink of World War II, Bazett obtained a leave of absence from the University of Pennsylvania in 1940 to take part in the aviation medical research that was beginning in Canada. When the leader of the research team, Sir Frederick Banting, died, Bazett took his place, serving in this position from 1941 to 1943. His advice was important to the war efforts of both Great Britain and the United States, and for it he received the order of Commander of the British Empire (1946).

Considered a daredevil, Bazett had so great a disregard for his own safety that it eventually led to a heart attack. He attempted to disprove the theory that the average man could hold his breath under water for one minute. Bazett did it for two. He later died of a second heart attack on board the *Queen Mary* while traveling overseas, one year after his appointment as president of the American Physiological Society.

Bazett's experiments on blood flow and temperature change were ground-breaking discoveries that are still considered significant. He is fondly remembered for his important contributions to clinical physiology as well as for his inimitable personality.

• For further information on Bazett, see Francis Heed Adler, "Memoir of H. C. Bazett (1885–1950)," *Transactions and Studies of the College of Physicians of Philadelphia* 121 (1951–1952): 121, Wallace O. Fenn, "H. C. Bazett (1950)," *History of the American Physiological Society: The Third Quarter Century* (1937–1962), pp. 20–21; "Professor H. C. Bazett, C.B.E.," *Nature* 166 (1950): 933–34; and Lysle H. Peterson, "Henry C. Bazett, President of the APS, 1950," *Physiologist* 22 (1979): 4–5. A summary of Bazett's ideas on body temperature regulation, prepared posthumously by Peterson, is Bazette, "Theory of Reflex Controls to Explain Regulation of Body Temperature at Rest and during Exercise," *Journal of Applied Physiology* 4 (1951): 245–62. An obituary is in the *Lancet*, 19 Aug. 1950.

DAVID Y. COOPER

BAZIOTES, William (11 June 1912–6 June 1963), painter, was born in Pittsburgh, Pennsylvania, the son of Frank Baziotes, a restaurant owner and baker, and Stella Eliopoulos. Both of his parents were Greek immigrants. The family moved to Reading, Pennsylvania, in 1913. When Baziotes was about eleven years of age, a fire destroyed his family's restaurant. Taking a job as an errand boy soon after, Baziotes was exposed to the seamier side of society, and he was fascinated by the gamblers, gangsters, and boxers he came across. His wife later recalled that while he was in high school he had considered a career as a boxer. Art and literature were also important to the young Baziotes, and his friendship with Byron Vazakas, a poet in Reading, introduced him to the poetry of the French symbolists. This interest in Paul Verlaine, Arthur Rimbaud, and Charles Baudelaire stayed with Baziotes throughout his life.

After a brief job at a newspaper Baziotes served an apprenticeship at a stained-glass factory in 1931–1933. Soon he moved to New York City, where in 1933 he enrolled at the National Academy of Design. He studied there with Gifford Beal and Leon Kroll, among others. Leaving the academy in 1936, Baziotes worked for the Federal Art Project (FAP). His first assignment for the FAP was as an art instructor in New York City, a position he held until 1941, when most of the FAP was terminated. In addition to his teaching, from 1938 on he also worked for the FAP's easel painting division.

Working for the easel division allowed Baziotes to paint outside the constraints of an academic environment. Though the work done on the FAP was in the social realist vein, Baziotes was most influenced by the school of Paris, particularly the work of Joan Miró, Henri Matisse, and Pablo Picasso. Uncomfortable with the social realism then current in the art world, Baziotes "engaged in a form of late cubist painting, expressionistic and linear" (Alloway, p. 15).

In 1941 Baziotes married Ethel Copstein; they had no children. In the early 1940s Baziotes began to associate with the surrealist artists exiled because of the Second World War. Chief among his associates in New York City were Gordon Onslow-Ford and the Chilean-born Roberto Matta Echaurren. Like most North Americans, however, Baziotes never became a member of the orthodox surrealist cadre led by André Breton, though Breton had invited him to participate in the 1942 exhibition *First Papers of Surrealism*.

Baziotes had his first solo exhibition at Peggy Guggenheim's Art of this Century Gallery in New York in October 1944. Two years later he had a solo exhibition at the Kootz Gallery in New York, where he exhibited regularly until 1958. The success of his early exhibitions brought Baziotes critical acclaim. In 1947 he re-

ceived the Walter M. Campana Memorial Purchase Prize from the Art Institute of Chicago, a distinguished award for an artist of his generation, for his painting *Cyclops* (1947). An announcement of the award and an illustration of the painting appeared in both *Time* and *Life* magazines. The following year Baziotes was singled out to represent the United States at the Twenty-fourth Venice Biennale.

During the 1940s Baziotes experimented with automatism, allowing his unconscious to form his images. Out of this and other experiments he began to develop his mature style, in which the "typical forms are delicate presences, half flat, half translucent, suspended, as if in amber" (Alloway, p. 11). Critic Harold Rosenberg, in an exhibition brochure for a 1947 exhibition of Baziotes's work at the Kootz Gallery, said that "The shapes in a Baziotes canvas are covers of hidden spaces, rather than spatial forms themselves," and that a "vibration flows through his colors, whose textures seem to absorb silence as if his paints had been mixed in a meditation of sleep."

In 1948, along with fellow artists Robert Motherwell, Barnett Newman, Mark Rothko, and David Hare, Baziotes founded the Subjects of the Artists School in New York City. The founders hoped to create a new type of learning environment in which an artist could learn through exposure to the subject matter of the instructors. Eschewing the traditional concept of student and teacher, Baziotes and his fellow instructors hoped to work as collaborators with their students as they explored the creative process. For a number of reasons, including personality conflicts and lack of students, the school closed after its third term in 1949.

Probably as a result of both a falling out with the other members of the school and a general disillusionment with the art world, Baziotes became more introspective and isolated after 1949, and he retired from social aspects of the art world. Instead of traveling to artist retreats, in 1955 Baziotes and his wife began spending their summers in his childhood home of Reading, Pennsylvania.

Though less involved with his contemporaries in the art world, Baziotes continued to teach art. After the Subjects of the Artists School closed, he taught at the Brooklyn Museum Art School and New York University (1949–1952) and the People's Art Center at the Museum of Modern Art (1950–1952). In 1952 he took the position of associate professor of art at New York's Hunter College, where he remained until his death.

Of all of the abstract expressionists, Baziotes remained most faithful to his surrealistic roots. Biomorphic shapes and a soft, almost hazy palate remained dominant characteristics of his work until his death. Commenting in *Time* on the genesis of his works, Baziotes said, "Each painting comes about in a different way. Some are started with a few touches of color, others with lines. Sometimes nothing happens" (2 Feb. 1950, p. 60).

Baziotes had a lifelong interest in natural history and spent many hours at New York's American Museum of Natural History studying and sketching fossil dinosaurs. These forms later appeared in such works as *Primeval* (1952) and *Primeval Landscape* (1953). Unlike Barnett Newman or Mark Rothko, who began to use non-descriptive nomenclature for their works, Baziotes, with such late works as *Animal on Landscape* (1959) and *Serpentine* (1961), retained the surrealist convention of dream-like titles. At the same time, he commented "I try not to make my titles too esoteric. The artist Yves Tanguy, painted a picture representing a group of abstract forms on a desert and called it, "Papa, Here Comes Mama." That's a surrealist shock title; I am not at all interested in that. I try to keep my titles simple" (*Perspective No. 2*, 1956–1957, pp. 27, 29–30).

Baziotes was a sensitive and often shy man; his wife once described him to Clyfford Still as a "darkling poet." Sculptor David Hare commented that "William Baziotes was a natural painter and a natural raconteur. He talked the same way he painted, fluently, sharply, often throwing away lines in quiet gestures" (*Location* 1, no. 2 [Summer 1964]: 88). Baziotes died of lung cancer at his home in New York City.

• Major collections of Baziotes's work are located in the Metropolitan Museum of Art; the Museum of Modern Art in New York; Albright-Knox Art Gallery, Buffalo; Minneapolis Institute of Arts; Hirshhorn Museum and Sculpture Garden, Smithsonian Institution; National Museum of American Art, Smithsonian Institution, National Gallery of Art; and the Baltimore Art Museum. The extensive William and Ethel Baziotes papers are held by the Archives of American Art at the Smithsonian Institution. Biographical and critical information can be found in Lawrence Alloway's catalog to the Solomon R. Guggenheim Museum's exhibition, *William Baziotes: A Memorial Exhibition* (1965); and in the essays by Michael Preble, Barbara Cavaliere, and Mona Hadler in the exhibition catalog published by the Newport Harbor Art Museum, *William Baziotes: A Retrospective Exhibition* (1978). See also Clyfford Still's comments in *William Baziotes: Late Work, 1946–1962* (1971), an exhibition held at Marlborough Gallery Inc., New York, and David S. Rubin's catalog for the exhibition, *William Baziotes: A Commemorative Exhibition* (1987), which includes a dedication by Ethel Baziotes. An obituary is in the *New York Times*, 7 June 1963.

MARTIN R. KALFATOVIC

BEACH, Alfred Ely (1 Sept. 1826–1 Jan. 1896), magazine publisher and inventor, was born in Springfield, Massachusetts, the son of Moses Yale Beach, a newspaper publisher, and Nancy Day. His father was apprenticed as a cabinetmaker but rose through a series of businesses to become owner and publisher of the New York *Sun* in 1838. Moses Beach was also noted for a series of inventions, such as the stern-wheel steamboat and a ragcutter for papermills.

Alfred Beach was educated at the Monson Academy in Monson, Massachusetts, and joined his older brother Moses Sperry Beach at the *Sun* to learn the newspaper business from the ground up. Alfred and his brother took over ownership and operation of the paper when their ill father retired in 1848, but Alfred's interest had already turned elsewhere by 1846 when he learned that *Scientific American* magazine was for sale.

Beach convinced classmate Orson D. Munn to join him in New York City, where they founded the firm Munn & Company to purchase the magazine from Rufus Porter. At the time of purchase, in 1846, the magazine was only a four-page folio with a circulation of 200. Two years later it had a circulation of 10,000 and was the leading journal of its kind. Munn learned the business side of the publication under the tutelage of Porter, who stayed on to serve as editor for nearly a year. Beach's name was kept out of it until 1848, when his father retired from the *Sun*, and he became co-editor of the magazine with Robert McFarlane.

Beach sold his interest in the magazine to Munn in 1849 and his share of the *Sun* to his brother Moses in 1852. He founded a weekly pictorial newspaper called the *Illustrated News* in 1853, but it failed within a year. He then tried again with the *People's Journal* in 1853, which was filled with what Beach called "useful knowledge" for farmers, mechanics, inventors, and others, and also established an associated patent agency. This publication also failed after a year, and Beach returned to *Scientific American* and repurchased a one-third interest from Munn, who had already taken in another partner.

Beach resumed his previous positions as co-editor of the magazine and as supervisor of the Scientific American Patent Agency, becoming a skilled patent agent through self-study and practical experience. Beach was interested in patent rights for two reasons: his father never profited from his ragcutter because of a delay in applying for a patent, and Beach was an inventor in his own right. He invented two forms of typewriters, one of which produced raised characters on a strip for the use of the blind, winning a gold medal at the Crystal Palace Exposition in 1856.

Among his other patents was one for an improvement to tunneling shields that permitted greater maneuverability while protecting workers from cave-ins. He also devised a cable traction system for aboveground transportation in New York City, which was used for a number of years. These patents were sold for modest profits. His most ambitious project began as a pneumatic underground mail delivery system and developed into a pneumatic underground transportation system, the progenitor of the subway. An interim step was an above-ground suspended tube with an air-driven, ten-capacity car, which was exhibited with great success at the American Institute Fair in 1867 and won a first prize.

Beach organized the Pneumatic Dispatch Company in 1868 and received a charter for an underground postal delivery system from the New York legislature that year. Instead of the postal system, Beach constructed a pneumatic subway more than 300 feet long under Broadway and gave demonstrations to the general public. Beach subsequently twice failed to get Governor John Thompson Hoffman's approval on a charter for his subway; by the time a new governor did sign it, Beach was unable to raise sufficient funds to construct a useful citywide system and had to abandon his project in 1873.

Beach thereafter devoted his energies to *Scientific American* and its subsidiary publications, the *Science Record* (1872–1875), which was an annual compilation of important articles; the *Scientific American Supplement* (1876–1896); an *Export Edition* (1878–1896); a Spanish-language edition (1889–1896); and an *Architects and Builders Edition* (1885–1896), as well as to the associated Scientific American Patent Agency, which became the foremost of its day. In his role as head of the patent agency, Beach dealt with some of the most renowned inventors of his day, including Peter Cooper Hewitt, John Ericsson, Cyrus H. McCormick, and Samuel F. B. Morse. Thomas Edison brought his first successful model of the phonograph to Beach for its initial public demonstration.

The generally accepted view of the nature of science and scientific investigation was in flux during the latter half of the nineteenth century, gradually moving away from the pursuit of practicality to the pursuit of knowledge itself. Beach was a "practical" man in the sense that he looked to utility as a measure of value and resisted the differentiation of goals. What he strenuously opposed was the elitism that suggested that the common man was incapable of understanding scientific concepts. He combined those precepts in his view of the role of *Scientific American*: "The sole claim any publication can make that can entitle it to public favor is that it educates its readers. If it does not accomplish this it is a failure, unworthy of public patronage. . . . Our own paper . . . has without doubt been largely instrumental in developing the present popular taste for scientific information." The magazine therefore became a popularizer of science information by putting it in a practical context for its readers rather than a scientific journal in the modern sense. For example, readers learned about concepts of electricity and acoustics in the explanation of how the telephone worked; astronomy and the origin of the universe were discussed in conjunction with a discussion of the optics of a new 21-inch telescope.

Beach followed his educational principles in his philanthropies as well, donating money to begin a private school in Stratford, Connecticut, in 1860 and to found the Beach Institute in Savannah, Georgia, after the Civil War for the education of freed slaves. There is still an Alfred Ely Beach High School named for him there.

In 1847 Beach had married Harriet Eliza Holbrook, with whom he had two children. His wife was just returning from Europe when Beach died in New York City. His partner, Orson Munn, wrote in his diary that day, "Poor Alfred how can we get along without him? He was a unique character and had many good traits and to me and our business was an important factor."

Beach was instrumental in disseminating technical information to the general public during the years of the Industrial Revolution and in promoting the values of educational technical democracy. Little known today, his reputation as a publisher has benefited somewhat from misleading information, repeated over the years, about his contributions. In fact, although he initially set the aims of the magazine, his varied interests and responsibilities and frequent absences left the day-to-day editing to others. He often wrote editorials and occasionally pushed for the inclusion of particular articles or coverage of certain ideas, but especially in his later years, he was not the driving force behind the magazine that many have thought. Nevertheless, his magazine legacy lived on while those of others more celebrated today did not.

• The most complete source on Beach is "Alfred Ely Beach," *Scientific American* 74 (11 Jan. 1896): 18–19. This must be balanced by Michael Borut, "The 'Scientific American' in Nineteenth Century America" (Ph.D. diss., New York Univ., 1977), which contradicts some accepted views. His contributions to *Scientific American* are also reviewed in "Fifty Years of the Scientific American," *Scientific American* 88 (25 July 1896): 91–94, and "Seventy Years of the Scientific American," *Scientific American* 112 (5 June 1915): 540–43, 546. See Robert Daley, "Alfred Ely Beach and His Wonderful Pneumatic Underground Railway," *American Heritage* 12 (June 1961): 54–57, and Beach's own *The Pneumatic Dispatch* (1868) for his work in transportation. Edward Wright Byrn, *The Progress of Invention in the 19th Century* (1900), and Waldemar Kaempffert, *A Popular History of American Invention* (1924), cover his work with the typewriter. See Robert Post, "Science, Public Policy, and Popular Precepts," in *The Sciences in the American Context*, ed. Nathan Reingold (1979), for an assessment of his role in the growth of science in the nineteenth century. An obituary is in the *New York Times*, 7 Jan. 1896.

JACK COLLDEWEIH

BEACH, Amy (5 Sept. 1867–27 Dec. 1944), composer and pianist, was born Amy Marcy Cheney in West Henniker, New Hampshire, the daughter of Charles Abbott Cheney, a paper miller and, later, paper stock salesman, and Clara Imogene Marcy, an amateur pianist and singer, both from colonial New England families. In 1871 the family moved to Chelsea, Massachusetts, near Boston, and in 1875 to Boston proper. An only child, Beach was an infant prodigy with perfect pitch and total recall, an instinctive gift for the piano that showed itself at age four, and an untaught sense of harmony and form. Her general education began at home with her mother (1873–1879) and ended with three years (c. 1879–1882) at a Boston private school. Her piano studies also began in 1873 with her mother. She next studied with W. Ernst Perabo (1875–1882) and finally with Carl Baermann (1882–1886), a pupil of Franz Liszt. Her piano debut on 24 October 1883 in Boston with orchestra, at which she played Ignaz Moscheles's G Minor Concerto, won high praise from critics, one of whom stated that she "gave proof of great talent, both for technique and for interpretation." During the next two years she gave frequent recitals and appeared as soloist with the Theodore Thomas and Boston Symphony orchestras.

Beach began composing at age four. Her formal studies were limited to harmony and counterpoint with Junius Welch Hill (1881–1882). Otherwise she was self-taught in composition, following the advice of Wilhelm Gericke, conductor of the Boston Symphony Orchestra. Her first published piece, "The Rainy Day," a song written in 1880 to a text by Henry Wadsworth Longfellow, appeared in 1883. Following her marriage in December 1885 to Henry Harris Aubrey Beach, a leading Boston physician, she redirected her principal energies to composition, playing only infrequently in public. The couple had no children.

Her art songs soon became favorites among singers. One, "The Year's at the Spring" (Robert Browning), op. 44, no. 1 (1899), was sung from Boston to Australia. Concert artists, among them Josef Hoffman and Olga Samaroff, played her piano compositions, especially the brilliant "Fireflies," op. 15, no. 4. It was her larger works, however, that gained her acceptance as a member of the Boston school of composers and established her reputation: Mass in E-flat, op. 5, an hourlong work for chorus and orchestra introduced by the Handel and Haydn Society of Boston (7 Feb. 1892); *Festival Jubilate*, op. 17, for chorus and orchestra, commissioned for the opening of the Woman's Building at the World's Columbian Exposition in Chicago (1 May 1893); and especially her Symphony in E Minor (*Gaelic*), op. 32, given its premiere by the Boston Symphony Orchestra (30–31 Oct. 1896). A critic wrote that the symphony "entitles her to high rank among American composers." Boston composer George Whitefield Chadwick agreed, stating that now she was "one of the boys." During Beach's lifetime the work had dozens of performances by leading orchestras in the United States and Europe.

Other major works followed, including her Piano Concerto, op. 45 (6 Apr. 1900); Variations on Balkan Themes, op. 60, for piano; *Service in A*, op. 63 (1905–1906), a multimovement choral work for the Protestant Episcopal rite given in many churches; *The Chambered Nautilus*, op. 66, a setting of Oliver Wendell Holmes Sr.'s poem for women's chorus and orchestra (1907); and Quintet for Pianoforte and Strings, op. 67, which became her most frequently performed instrumental work. During her Boston years, she also functioned as patron, regularly introducing young musicians to leaders of Boston's musical, social, and cultural elite at her Wednesday "at-homes." Beach, who missed regular concertizing, stated that although her home life kept her in the neighborhood of Boston, "my compositions gave me a larger field. From Boston I could reach out to the world" ("Why I Chose My Profession").

Widowed in 1910, Beach went to Europe in 1911 for the first time, to reestablish her career as a performer, to have her major works played and reviewed, and not least to augment her income. She returned to the United States in the fall of 1914 with glowing reviews and a fully booked concert season. Thereafter she toured during the winters, featuring her own music, and composed during the summers. She became virtual composer-in-residence at St. Bartholomew's Episcopal Church, New York, where many of her later sacred choral compositions had their first performances.

From 1921 until her very last years she was a fellow at the MacDowell Colony. Outstanding works of the period from 1915 to her death include Theme and Variations for Flute and String Quartet, op. 80, commissioned and introduced by the Chamber Music Society of San Francisco (28 Sept. 1916); Prelude and Fugue, op. 81, for piano (1918); Quartet for Strings in One Movement, op. 89 (MS, 1921–1929); *Rendezvous* (Leonora Speyer), op. 120, for voice, violin, and piano; *The Canticle of the Sun* (St. Francis of Assisi), op. 123, for chorus and orchestra (1928); *Cabildo*, op. 149, a chamber opera in one act with libretto by Nan Bagby Stephens, given its first performance in Athens, Georgia (27 Feb. 1945); and finally her Piano Trio, op. 150 (1939). Almost all her works were published and performed, some many times. She regularly signed her works "Mrs. H. H. A. Beach."

The first successful American woman to compose large-scale art music and a heroine to many women, Amy Beach was celebrated during her lifetime as the foremost woman composer of the United States. Her early success brought her into the center of a controversy over women as composers of art music that began in 1880 and continued for decades. Her supporters considered her the person who proved that women could create works of value, while the opposition dismissed her as a rare exception. She played an active role in a second controversy over American musical nationalism that began in 1893 with Antonín Dvořák's challenge to American composers to create a distinctive national style by borrowing from Native-American and African-American music. Thereafter she quoted or wrote in the idiom of folk music in about thirty of her compositions, beginning with her *Gaelic* Symphony. Later, folk songs of the Alaskan Inuit that she quoted in the Quartet for Strings inspired a significant change in her style.

Beach's mature style is marked by a sense of the long line, an intense, often passionate lyricism, and dissonance produced by contrapuntally driven chromaticism in an extended tonal system. Frequent modulations are controlled by an unerring ear for tonal relations. Her earlier works are harmonically lush in the late Romantic tradition; her later works are leaner and more dissonant. She composed over 300 compositions, including 128 songs, 75 choral and 53 piano works, 14 chamber music compositions, and 18 works with or for orchestra.

Beach was the country's first concert pianist trained in the United States. She was also one of the first generation of American-born women to become professional instrumentalists, to receive commissions for major works, to compose a work played by the Symphony Society of New York, to have a choral composition given by the Handel and Haydn Society of Boston, and to have a symphony played by major orchestras across the country. She wrote choral compositions on commission for the world's fairs of 1893, 1898, 1904, and 1915; was invited by the French government to submit a manuscript to an exhibit at the Paris Opera (1900); was a member of *Das Comité des*

Richard Wagner-Denkmal (Berlin, 1903); had a copy of her Mass, op. 5, placed in the cornerstone of the Boston Opera House (1908); had days named for her at the Panama California Exposition in San Diego (1915, 1916); and was founder and first president of the Society of American Women Composers (1925–1929). She also was an active member of many musical and sororal organizations. Beach died in New York City.

• Major Beach collections, including manuscript and printed music, sketchbooks, correspondence, scrapbooks, diaries, and photographs, are at the University of New Hampshire at Durham, the Library of Congress, and the University of Missouri in Kansas City. For smaller collections, see Donald W. Krummel et al., *Resources of American Music History* (1981). For a catalog of her compositions, see *The New Grove Dictionary of American Music* (1986). Beach wrote a number of articles, the most important of which is "Why I Chose My Profession: The Autobiography of a Woman Composer," interview by Ednah Aiken, *Mother's Magazine*, Feb. 1914, pp. 7–8. Studies of her life and works include Percy Goetschius, *Mrs. H. H. A. Beach* (1906); Louis C. Elson, *The History of American Music* (1904; repr. 1971); Burnet C. Tuthill, "Mrs. H. H. A. Beach," *Musical Quarterly* 26 (1940): 297–310; E. Lindsay Merrill, "Mrs. H. H. A. Beach: Her Life and Music" (Ph.D. diss., Univ. of Rochester, 1963); Myrna Garvey Eden, *Energy and Individuality in the Art of Anna Hyatt Huntington, Sculptor, and Amy Beach, Composer* (1987); Adrienne Fried Block, "Why Amy Beach Succeeded as a Composer: The Early Years," *Current Musicology* 36 (1983): 41–59; and Block, "The Child as Mother to the Woman: Amy Beach's New England Upbringing," in *Cecilia Reclaimed: Feminist Perspectives on Gender and Music*, ed. Susan C. Cook and Judith Tsou (1994). On the controversy over women as composers, see Judith Tick, "Passed Away Is the Piano Girl," in *Women Making Music: The Western Art Tradition, 1150–1950*, ed. Jane Bowers and Judith Tick (1986). On Beach and musical nationalism, see Block, "Dvořák, Beach, and American Music," in *A Celebration of American Music: Words and Music in Honor of H. Wiley Hitchcock*, ed. Richard Crawford, R. Allen Lott, and Carol J. Oja (1990); and Block, "Amy Beach's Music on Native American Themes," *American Music* 8 (1990): 141–66. An obituary is in the *New York Times*, 28 Dec. 1944.

ADRIENNE FRIED BLOCK

BEACH, Frank Ambrose, Jr. (13 Apr. 1911–15 June 1988), psychologist and educator, was born in Emporia, Kansas, the son of Frank Ambrose Beach, professor of music, and Bertha Robinson. He received a B.S. in education in 1932 from the Kansas State Teachers College in Emporia, where his father taught. Although he had already developed an interest in psychology, he planned to be a high school English teacher. Because of the depression, however, Beach was unable to find a job and so continued in school at Emporia, receiving an M.S. in psychology in 1933. His thesis project was a search for color vision in rats.

Beach continued his graduate studies in psychology at the University of Chicago in 1933. There he was influenced by some of the leading psychologists and other scientists of the day, including Karl Lashley, Harvey Carr, Louis Thurstone, Paul Weiss, and C. Judson Herrick. When he ran out of funds, he took a

year off to teach high school English in Yates Center, Kansas. Returning to Chicago, Beach completed his Ph.D. in 1936. His dissertation dealt with maternal behavior in rats and how it is affected by lesions in the cerebral cortex of the brains. Because of a delay in fulfilling his language requirements, Beach's Ph.D. actually was not awarded until 1940. He spent 1936–1937 working in the laboratory of Karl Lashley, who was then at Harvard University. Also in 1936 Beach married Anna Beth Oldenweller; they had two children.

In 1937 Beach accepted a position as an assistant curator in the Department of Experimental Biology of the American Museum of Natural History in New York. There he launched a series of diverse projects to explore the neural bases, hormonal influences, and evolution of reproductive behavior. When his department chairman, G. Kingsley Noble, died in 1940, the museum was on the verge of closing the department. Beach succeeded in saving it and changing the name to the Department of Animal Behavior; he became its chair in 1942. The department was an important focus of studies in comparative psychology for many years.

Beach left the American Museum for a position in the Department of Psychology at Yale University in 1946; in 1952 he was appointed Sterling Professor. During his years at Yale, he published two important books. *Hormones and Behavior* (1948) was a groundbreaking work establishing the study of the relationship between hormones and behavior as a scientific endeavor. *Patterns of Sexual Behavior* (1951), written with anthropologist Clellan S. Ford, was a major cross-cultural survey of sexual practices. He delivered the William James lectures at Harvard in 1950–1951. While at Yale, Beach was elected president of the Eastern Psychological Association, became a charter member of the Psychobiology panel of the National Science Foundation and a member and chair of the National Research Council Committee for the Study of Problems of Sex. In 1958 he received the Distinguished Scientific Contribution Award of the American Psychological Association.

After spending the 1957–1958 year at the Center for Advanced Study in the Behavioral Sciences at Stanford University, Beach accepted a position on the faculty of the University of California, Berkeley. His wife died in 1971, and he married Noel Gaustad the following year. He remained at Berkeley the rest of his life, retiring and becoming a very active professor emeritus in 1978. At Berkeley he produced two more books, established the Field Station for Research in Animal Behavior, and greatly increased his commitment to teaching at both the undergraduate and graduate levels, receiving the American Psychological Foundation's Award for Distinguished Teaching in Biopsychology in 1985. He died in Berkeley.

Beach was especially important in serving as the "conscience of comparative psychology," helping to retain interests in a wide range of species and problem areas in the field. He provided a model of the dedicated researcher, publishing a long string of empirical studies. Even more important, however, was the succession of more integrative articles that was interspersed within this continuous, active research record. Beach had a knack for sensing the appropriate time for a new perspective or approach and presenting it in a manner that affected the subsequent activity in the field. For example, when he sensed that female sexual behavior is more complex than previously had been thought, he distinguished among proceptivity, receptivity, and attractivity in female mammals and thus facilitated a more complete picture of female sexuality.

Along with William C. Young, Beach established the field of behavioral endocrinology as a major research field. He did much research, wrote the first integrative book, and cofounded the primary journal in the field, *Hormones and Behavior*, in 1969. He did much to establish the study of sexual behavior as a viable scientific endeavor at a time when social mores made discussions of sex delicate.

Beach was a dedicated scholar, noted for devoting as much care to scholarly research and the precise use of the English language as to his detailed laboratory studies. At the same time, however, he was a very earthy man. He was a man who both enjoyed himself immensely and did much to shape psychobiology in the twentieth century.

• The largest collection of unpublished materials is in the Frank Beach Papers at the Archives of the History of American Psychology of the University of Akron, Akron, Ohio. Other materials are at the Library of the American Museum of Natural History, New York, N.Y., and in the papers of various correspondents. Autobiographical chapters appear in G. Lindzey, ed., *History of Psychology in Autobiography*, vol. 6 (1974), and J. Meites et al., eds., *Pioneers in Neuroendocrinology*, vol. 2 (1978). Biographical sketches were written by S. E. Glickman and I. Zucker, *American Psychologist* 44 (1989): 1234–35, and by D. A. Dewsbury, *American Journal of Psychology* 102 (1989): 414–20. Other relevant information can be found in the journal *Hormones and Behavior* (1988 memorial articles) and in T. McGill et al., eds., *Sex and Behavior: Status and Prospectus* (1978).

DONALD A. DEWSBURY

BEACH, Harlan Page (4 Apr. 1854–4 Mar. 1933), missionary, missions librarian, and professor of missions, was born in South Orange, New Jersey, the son of Joseph Wickliff Beach and Mary Angeline Walkley, farmers. He prepared for college at Phillips Andover Academy and graduated from Yale University in 1878. He taught at Phillips Andover Academy for two years, then entered Andover Theological Seminary, graduating (B.D.) in 1883. His father opposed his decision to be a missionary, but his mother encouraged him. He married Lucy Lucretia Ward on 29 June 1883 and was ordained to the Congregational ministry on 19 July 1883; later in the same year they were sent by the American Board of Commissioners for Foreign Missions to serve in North China. After language study he was on the staff of a high school and theological seminary at Tung-chau until December 1889, when his wife's ill health caused their return to the United States.

While in China, Beach mastered the language to the point where he served on the committee that prepared a revision of the Mandarin Bible. He is also credited with founding one of the first Young Men's Christian Associations (YMCA) in China. In his book *Dawn on the Hills of T'ang or Missions in China* (1898; rev. 1905; repr. 1907), which was a textbook for mission study classes in colleges and seminaries, Beach recounted the work of Protestant missions in China through medicine, famine relief, social reform against opium and footbinding, service to the deaf, blind, and foundlings, education, literacy, literature production and distribution. The principal goal, however, was "to preach the gospel of an all-powerful Saviour" (p. 117).

Based in Chicago, Beach spoke on missions for the American Board until June 1891; then was pastor of Lowrie Hill (Congregational) Church, Minneapolis, until May 1892, when he became an instructor, and later superintendent, of the School for Christian Workers in Springfield, Massachusetts. In June 1895 he became educational secretary of the Student Volunteer Movement for Foreign Missions, under the direction of John R. Mott, and was responsible for a program of missionary education for students. In this post he lectured widely, organized mission study classes in colleges and seminaries, produced numerous mission study books, both as author and editor, and was an editor of the *Intercollegian* magazine. He was chairman of the exhibit committee and also on the executive committee of the Ecumenical Missionary Conference at Carnegie Hall in New York in 1900. During this period his work as a statistician and compiler of atlases of foreign missions—his major contribution to scholarship—began with the publication of *A Geography and Atlas of Protestant Missions* (vol. 1, 1901; vol. 2, 1903). This was followed by *World Atlas of Christian Missions* (1911), with James S. Dennis and Charles H. Fahs; *World Statistics of Christian Missions* (1916), with Burton St. John; and *World Missionary Atlas* (1925), with Charles H. Fahs.

Yale church historian Roland H. Bainton later reported that when Beach became the first professor of missions at Yale Divinity School in 1906 "he was easily the best informed man in the world with regard to global Christianity." This post at Yale was endowed in 1914 and Beach became the first incumbent of the D. Willis James professorship in the theory and practice of missions, a position he held until he became emeritus in 1921. From 1911 he served concurrently as librarian of the Day Missions Library at Yale, also until 1921, and was honorary librarian until 1925. In the judgment of Kenneth Scott Latourette, Beach's successor at Yale, Beach's "major achievement at Yale was the enlargement and organization of the Day Missions Library," which Beach considered to be a "laboratory for missions." At Yale he was expected to spend one-third of his time visiting overseas mission fields. Thus he spent the year 1907–1908 on a world trip studying mission methods, visited the work of Yale-in-China several times, and traveled to the Middle East in 1910, Africa in 1912, and Panama in 1916. His trip to

Panama, for a conference of Protestant missionaries to South America, resulted in his report, *Renaissant Latin America* (1916). He also attended the World Missionary Conference in Edinburgh, Scotland, in 1910, where he reported to the commission on the preparation of missionaries that Yale had the largest collection of missionary literature in America.

Latourette once recalled that the Fellowship of Professors of Missions in the New England and Middle Atlantic states grew out of informal meetings to hear reports of Beach's trips. "Beach's primary concern in missions was evangelization," according to Bainton. "He believed in the finality of Christianity and shared the urgency of his age to win the world for Christ in that generation. At the same time he was not indifferent to the social impact of missions" (p. 248). Beach served on the editorial council of *Missionary Review of the World* and was a visiting lecturer on missions at Boston University School of Theology and Union Theological Seminary in New York. On the occasion of his retirement from Yale, he was described as "the encyclopaedist of missions." After leaving Yale he became lecturer in missions at Drew University Theological School until ill health forced his permanent retirement in 1928. He and his wife had no children of their own, but they adopted two sons. He died in Winter Park, Florida, and cremation took place at Orlando, Florida. In a memorial tribute to Beach, Robert E. Speer said, "His work as a missionary biographer and statistician was unique and unprecedented."

• Beach's letters and diaries are in the special collections of Yale Divinity Library. Other publications by Beach include a mission study on India, *The Cross in the Land of the Trident* (1895); a small volume of missionary biographies, *Knights of the Labarum* (1896); *Princely Men in the Heavenly Kingdom* (1903); and *Missions as a Cultural Factor in the Pacific*, prepared for the July 1927 conference of the Institute of Pacific Relations. Family history is found in the book by his brother David Nelson Beach, *Beach Family Reminiscences and Annals* (1931). A tribute to Beach on the occasion of his retirement by John Clark Archer is in *Yale Divinity News*, Mar. 1921, and an assessment of Beach's academic contribution by Roland H. Bainton is in his *Yale and the Ministry* (1957; repr. 1985). Obituaries are in the *Yale University Obituary Record* (1933), *Congregationalist*, 23 Mar. 1933; *Missionary Review of the World*, Apr. 1933; and the *New York Times*, 5 Mar. 1933.

GERALD H. ANDERSON

BEACH, Joseph Warren (14 Jan. 1880–13 Aug. 1957), educator, literary critic, and poet, was born in Gloversville, New York, the son of Eugene Beach, a physician, and Sarah Jessup Warren. After graduating from a public high school there, he attended the University of Minnesota, where his uncle Cyrus Northrop was president. He earned his B.A. in English in 1900 and moved on to Harvard University, where he received his M.A. in 1902 and his Ph.D. in 1907, both in English. At Harvard Beach studied under philosopher Charles Peirce and his thesis director, George Lyman Kittredge; the latter was described affectionately by Beach as a "benevolent dictator and terror of the un-

dergraduates." His dissertation, "The Loathly Lady" (1907), explored folkloric elements in Geoffrey Chaucer's *Canterbury Tales*.

From 1907 until 1948 Beach taught in the English department of the University of Minnesota, serving as chair from 1939 until he retired. His departmental colleague William Van O'Connor observed that Beach "lived the intellectual and literary life as purely as anyone is likely to live it." His Minneapolis home was visited by literary notables such as Carl Sandburg, Sinclair Lewis, James Stevens, and T. S. Eliot. He became a much admired and respected teacher, in part, according to Theodore Blegen, a former student and one of Beach's eulogists, because he drew out of his students their best efforts and best selves. Among his accomplishments at Minnesota, Beach himself especially valued attracting Robert Penn Warren to the English department. After retiring from the University of Minnesota Beach took a series of visiting appointments at Harvard University (1949–1950), the University of Illinois (1950–1951), the Sorbonne and Strasbourg (1951–1952), as a Fulbright scholar, Johns Hopkins University (1952–1953), and the University of Vienna (1954–1955), again as a Fulbright scholar.

Beach was an influential and prolific literary critic. Early in his career he wrote principally about the British Romantic and Victorian periods, but he later turned more toward contemporary American novels, poetry, and prose. Probably his most important critical work was *American Fiction: 1920–1940*, which provided an early defense of the modernist achievements of Ernest Hemingway, William Faulkner, John Dos Passos, Thomas Wolfe, and others. Written at the request of a friend, *American Fiction* was intended for the educated general reader. Beach wanted to show that the novelists of his time were not the pale descendants of Henry James or Nathaniel Hawthorne; rather, he argued that these authors were to America of the 1920s and 1930s what Charles Dickens was to Victorian England. Toward the end of his career Beach turned his attention to contemporary poetry, especially that of W. H. Auden; he completed the index for his *The Making of the Auden Canon* only a few days before he died.

Beach also published three volumes of poetry, a novel, *The Glass Mountain* (1930), and a book of essays, *Meek Americans & Other European Trifles* (1925). For Beach, poetry was a labor of love. Although the fruits of his labor are largely forgotten, his poems illustrate what O'Connor called his life's purpose: "to reduce his experiences to understanding [and] order." His novel undertakes a similar task. At a critical moment, the heroine assuages her critic husband's anxiety about any residual feelings she might have for her first husband by saying; "You are a better man than Max Harder. You are really good. You are aware of *others*. . . . You are capable of *understanding*. And that is the great quality in a social being, in a human being." While contrasting American and European manners and morals in *Meek Americans*, Beach explored the values that the New World and the Old share, which for Beach were compassion, charity, and human solidarity.

Beach was married twice: in 1907 in Minneapolis, Minnesota, to Elisabeth Northrop, who died in 1917, and in 1918 in Crown Point, Indiana, to Dagmar Doneghy. He had two sons with his first wife. Outside the university Beach lived a rich and happy life that complemented his professional interests. He loved the outdoors, especially time he could spend at his summer camp on the St. Croix River, and he took the opportunity to travel whenever possible, with Mexico and Italy being his favorite destinations. Beach died at home in Minneapolis.

During his lifetime Beach was one of the most eminent scholars in the United States. His judgments about the achievements of Auden, Faulkner, Hemingway, and many other modernists became received wisdom. His account of his aims as a literary critic can serve to describe what he accomplished during his life: "I do not aim so much to render final judgments and deliver certificates of greatness, which is manifestly impossible and a trifle ridiculous, as to analyze and interpret stories and poems as expressions of our humanity and as effective works of art" (quoted in Stanley J. Kuritz, ed., *Twentieth-century Authors* [1955], p. 56).

• A collection of Beach papers is in the archives at the University of Minnesota. Beach's works of literary criticism, in addition to those cited in the text, are *The Comic Spirit in George Meredith* (1911), *The Technique of Thomas Hardy* (1922), *The Outlook for American Prose* (1926), *The Twentieth-century Novel: Studies in Technique* (1932), *The Concept of Nature in Nineteenth-century English Poetry* (1936), *A Romantic View of Poetry* (1944), and *Obsessive Images* (1960); the last was edited by William Van O'Connor from an unfinished work. Beach also wrote three volumes of poetry: *Sonnets of the Head and Heart* (1903), *Beginning with Plato* (1944), and *Involuntary Witness* (1950). William Van O'Connor dedicated to Beach his edited collection of essays by distinguished critics, *Forms of Modern Fiction* (1948).

DAVID M. CRAIG
JENNIFER M. CRAIG

BEACH, Moses Yale (7 Jan. 1800–19 July 1868), journalist and inventor, was born in Wallingford, Connecticut, the son of Moses Sperry Beach and Lucretia (Stanley) Yale, farmers. (Some sources cite 15 January as his birth date.) With some common school education, young Moses demonstrated mechanical ingenuity and was apprenticed to a cabinetmaker at age fourteen. By working overtime he was able to buy his freedom in four years, and he set up a cabinet shop of his own in Northampton, Massachusetts. He married Nancy Day of Springfield in either 1819 or 1821 (sources conflict); the couple would have eight children. (It is possible that he married a second time, but the evidence is not firm.)

Beach's mind ran to mechanics rather than furniture, and he invented an engine powered by exploding gunpowder, tinkered with steam engines, and developed a rag-cutting machine for use in paper mills. The device was used for many years and would have made a fortune for Beach had he patented it. He did use its rag-cutting abilities to obtain an interest in a paper mill in Saugerties, New York, where he moved in 1829. The mill was only moderately successful.

In 1835 Beach was taken as a partner by his brother-in-law, Benjamin H. Day, on the *New York Sun*, managing the finances and the mechanical department of that pioneer penny newspaper. Day had founded the paper two years earlier and had achieved the largest circulation in New York, 22,000, when Beach joined the staff, by departing from the standard practices of the established press. Other papers were sold by subscription or at the office for six cents a copy; the *Sun* was sold by newsboys on the street for a penny. Other papers covered business news and politics; the *Sun* covered the local police courts and interesting tidbits. The small classified advertisements sold by space rates for cash also contributed to the *Sun*'s early success.

Rivalry with James Gordon Bennett's *Herald* led the *Sun* to expand its coverage of traditional business and political news and to adopt speedier and more enterprising news-gathering methods, such as special horse expresses and news boats to meet incoming ships off New York harbor. In 1838 Day, disappointed in the profits from a sluggish economy, sold his share of the paper to Beach for $40,000. By 1840 Beach had paid off his debts to Day, and the profits began to mount. The *Sun* remained the circulation leader in New York until the mid-1850s, when the *Herald*'s daily total of 57,000 surpassed the *Sun*'s 50,000. (The *Sun* still sold for a penny, while the *Herald* had raised its price to two and then three cents.)

The *Sun* was an enterprising newspaper during the 1840s under Beach's direction. He ran horse expresses and special trains to bring important news to New York in advance of the mails, and in 1842 he built a new plant for the *Sun* at the corner of Fulton and Nassau streets with a hugh pigeon house on the roof. For half a century the *Sun*'s carrier pigeons brought news from incoming ships at Sandy Hook (N.J.) and from Albany and Washington. With the development of the telegraph and the resulting rise in newsgathering costs, Beach was one of the founding partners of the New York Associated Press in 1848. His son Moses Sperry Beach was the secretary of the press association during its early years.

Although it claimed to be independent, the *Sun*'s editorial policy was usually pro-Democratic and pro-southern, like that of the *Herald*. Also like Bennett, Beach was a jingoistic expansionist, preaching Manifest Destiny from early 1845 and championing the annexation of Texas, New Mexico, and the Yucatan. He was a strong supporter of the war with Mexico, favored the acquisition of all of Mexico, and opposed the Treaty of Guadalupe Hidalgo as annexing too little territory. By 1847 he favored the annexation of Cuba, and he was rhapsodic about the revolutions of 1848 in Europe.

Beach had held an interest in transit rights across the Isthmus of Tehuantepec since 1846; he believed he could broker a peace with Mexico with the transit rights as his broker's fee. He was encouraged in this by President James K. Polk and Secretary of State James Buchanan, and on 21 November 1846, Beach was commissioned by them as a confidential agent to explore peace possibilities, with no explicit instructions. He arrived in Mexico by way of Havana in January 1847, only to learn that the transit rights had been granted to England. He managed to escape to General Winfield Scott's American army at Veracruz and from there returned to New York, his mission a failure.

Since 1842 Beach had published a pioneer compendium, *Wealth and Biography of the Wealthy Citizens of New York*, which sold for twenty-five cents and went through thirteen editions until its last in 1855. This purported to be a list of the 500 to 1,000 wealthiest New Yorkers, but it was carelessly compiled and filled with inaccuracies that went uncorrected from edition to edition. (Beach set down his own wealth in 1846 at $300,000 and that of his rival Bennett at only $100,000.) New Yorkers did not use Beach's list for serious credit ratings.

Beach had returned from Mexico in ill health. In 1845 he had taken into the *Sun* as partners his sons Moses and Alfred Ely Beach. In December 1848 he retired and turned the *Sun* over to them. (The Beaches sold it in 1868 to Charles A. Dana.) Beach lived with his considerable fortune for twenty more years in Wallingford, where he engaged in local philanthropy and continued to watch the progress of the *Sun* and the Associated Press. In 1865 he suffered a stroke and died three years later in Wallingford.

• The standard source remains Frank M. O'Brien, *The Story of the Sun*, rev. ed. (1928). On the founding of the *Sun*, see the differing interpretations of Michael Schudson, *Discovering the News: A Social History of American Newspapers* (1978), and Alexander Saxton, "Problems of Class and Race in the Origins of the Mass Circulation Press," *American Quarterly* 36 (1984): 211–35. On the rivalry with Bennett, see James L. Crouthamel, *Bennett's New York Herald and the Rise of the Popular Press* (1989). For circulation estimates and the origins of the Associated Press, see Richard A. Schwarzlose, *The Nation's Newsbrokers*, vol. 1 (1989). On Beach's expansionism and his mission to Mexico, see Frederick Merk, *Manifest Destiny and Mission in American History* (1963) and *The Monroe Doctrine and American Expansionism* (1966). On the wealthy citizens pamphlet, see Edward Pessen, "Moses Beach Revisited: A Critical Examination of His Wealthy Citizens Pamphlets," *Journal of American History* 58 (1971): 415–26. An obituary is in the *New York Times*, 21 July 1868.

JAMES L. CROUTHAMEL

BEACH, Rex (1 Sept. 1877–7 Dec. 1949), novelist and scenarist, was born Rex Ellingwood Beach in Atwood, Michigan, the son of Henry Walter Beach, a fruit farmer, and Eva Eunice Canfield, a former schoolteacher. When Beach was nine years old, he and his two older brothers accompanied their parents when they left their ill-paying farm and sailed with two neighboring families on a schooner to Chicago, into and down the Illinois River, to the Mississippi River, and on to Tampa, Florida, where they homesteaded on a farm.

Beach attended the preparatory department of Rollins College, at Winter Park, Florida, beginning in 1891, then Rollins College, where he earned his tuition money by managing a laundry. He studied well, played intercollegiate baseball, and edited and managed the school literary magazine. In 1896 he left school short of graduating. Joining his brothers, both lawyers in Chicago, he performed odd jobs for them and studied at the Chicago College of Law. He played football and water polo on teams sponsored by the Chicago Athletic Association—mainly to eat at its training table. He was 6'1″, weighed just over 200 pounds, and had a correspondingly large appetite.

In 1897 Beach went to the Klondike in search of Alaskan gold. During most of the next five years he prospected and worked in mines and at various jobs in and near Rampart City and Nome, often suffered grievously, and met with little success apart from absorbing the varied local color. He read stories Jack London set in Alaska but evidently never thought at that time of emulating them. Instead, returning to Chicago, Beach sold firebricks, lime, and cement and quickly advanced to an executive position in a brick and clay company. When a friend happened to tell him that stories about Alaska were hot-selling properties, he drafted one and sold it to *McClure's Magazine* for $50, which encouraged him to write more. In all, he placed five stories in *McClure's* in 1904. They became the nucleus of *Pardners* (1905), a collection of melodramatic tales of good and evil men seeking to wrest quick riches from an uncompromisingly brutal Alaska and the Far West. Soon writing full time, he published a five-part muckraking essay in *Booklovers' Magazine* (Jan.–May 1906). Entitled "The Looting of Alaska," it identified corrupt politicians, judges, and lawyers and explained how by "legal" maneuvers they connived to cheat tough but callow grubstakers out of their earnings.

An almost unbelievably successful and versatile career followed. Beach became a bestselling fiction writer, then a producer of movies based on his work, and finally a professional gardener and cattleman in Florida. Even before his "looting" articles began to appear, he started serializing *The Spoilers* in *Everybody's Magazine* (Dec. 1905–June 1906). This novel concerns the clash of an honest prospector (based on a real-life former reindeer herdsman named Jafet Lindeberg), a rich political boss, a crooked federal judge and his decent niece, a dance-hall hostess (based on a heart-of-gold courtesan named Julia Bulette), a shyster lawyer, a reformed outlaw, and vigilantes—all against a painterly backdrop of harsh Alaska. In book form, *The Spoilers* (1906) became a well-marketed bestseller. In 1907 in New York City, where he later invested in expensive residential property, Beach married Edith Greta Crater of Denver, the owner of a hotel in Nome, where the two had met. (The couple had no children.) Beach's next novels were *The Barrier: A Novel* (1908), about an army lieutenant's reluctance to love a woman in the Alaskan gold region because she might be part Indian, and *The Silver Horde* (1909), about would-be monopolists in Alaska's burgeoning salmon-canning industry. Readers bought and relished these books, even though critics occasionally accused Beach of exaggerating the vulgarity and brutality of Alaskan life. He lashed back with proof of his accuracy.

Meanwhile, Beach was the first American to retain movie rights to his fiction, contracted with Samuel Goldwyn of Hollywood to form his own well-paid production company, and saw *The Spoilers* in 1914—filmed anew in 1923, 1930, 1942, and 1955—as the first of fourteen of his novels reworked into movies; in addition, he wrote sixteen original film scripts. Even as he continued to mine literary gold out of his memories of Alaska, Beach was branching out with novels on other subjects. Four examples among a dozen or so will sufficiently illustrate his versatility. *The Ne'er-Do-Well* (1911) concerns a pampered college lad drugged to replace a criminal on the way to the Panama Canal region, which Beach had visited and where his hero must meet the challenge of surviving on his own. *The Net* (1912) features a hero entangled with the Mafia when his friend is murdered in Sicily (which Beach had never seen) and the dead man's fiancée follows the hero to New Orleans. *The Auction Block: A Novel of New York Life* (1914) weakly presents chorus girls' desire less for theatrical fame than for opulent husbands. And *Heart of the Sunset* (1915) details the derring-do of a Texas Ranger, his beloved, and her dissipated, dishonest husband's violent Mexican friends. All the while, Beach was continuing to transmute Alaskan tundra into golden royalties. *The Iron Trail: An Alaskan Romance* (1913) is his anticonservative novel about Alaskan coal and railroad rights, while in *The Winds of Chance* (1918) he mainly reworks Klondike material but also features a dogsled race.

Writing somewhat less in the 1920s and 1930s, Beach began agricultural experiments in Sebring, Florida. He made a third fortune, to go with his royalties and his movie earnings, by raising gladioli, Christmas lilies, and mineralized fruits and vegetables and also by helping to develop the Florida cattle industry. At one time, he owned 9,000 acres near Sebring and Avon Park. His final years were marked by illness and sorrow. From 1912 he had suffered from iritis. He endured repeated cataract and throat-cancer surgery. Two years after his wife died, Beach, long breathing through a tube in his neck, fed through another in his stomach, going blind, and in dreadful pain, shot himself to death in his Sebring bedroom.

Rex Beach led a robust and varied life. He was a popular author and club member, an esteemed hunting and fishing companion, and a generous friend and philanthropist. He advanced the cause of writers in filmdom's early days and was a successful agronomist and cattle breeder. However, he will be remembered longest for his thrilling he-man narratives set in remorseless Alaska.

• Beach's personal papers are at Rollins College in Winter Park, Fla., and at Syracuse University, Syracuse, N.Y. Other representative novels by Beach include *The Mating Call* (1927), *Jungle Gold* (1935), *The World in His Arms* (1946), and *Woman in Ambush* (1951). *Personal Exposures* (1940) is Beach's rambling, informative, and delightfully funny autobiography. Gina Macdonald's entry on Beach in *Twentieth-Century Western Writers*, ed. James Vinson (1991), has an extensive primary bibliography. S. S. McClure in *My Autobiography* (1914) praises his manuscript reader Viola Roseboro for first recognizing Beach's talent as an author. In *Writers and Writing* (1946), Robert Van Gelder reports his revealing interview of Beach. Louis Nizer, "The Most Unforgettable Character I've Met," *Reader's Digest*, Jan. 1951, pp. 33–37, is a lively sketch. Alice Payne Haskett and James Henry Burke, in their *80 Years of Best Sellers, 1895–1975* (1977), include Beach's *The Spoilers, The Barrier, The Silver Horde,* and *The Net* in their chronological lists. Abe C. Ravitz, *Rex Beach* (1994), contains the best critical treatment of Beach's writings. William R. Hunt, *North of 53°: The Wild Days of the Alaska-Yukon Mining Frontier, 1870–1914* (1974), uses much material from Beach. Three books touching on Beach and the early movie industry are Vachel Lindsay, *The Art of the Moving Picture* (1915; rev. ed., 1922), Benjamin B. Hampton, *A History of the Movies* (1931), and A. Scott Berg, [Samuel] *Goldwyn: A Biography* (1989). A lengthy obituary is in the *New York Times*, 8 Dec. 1949.

ROBERT L. GALE

BEACH, Sylvia Woodbridge (14 Mar. 1887–6 Oct. 1962), bookstore owner and publisher, was born in Baltimore, Maryland, the second of three daughters of Sylvester Woodbridge Beach, a Presbyterian minister, and Eleanor Orbison, an artist. Disinclined toward both religion and formal education, she often pleaded illness and eventually fled the Presbyterian parsonage of Princeton, New Jersey, for Europe. Beach spent 1907–1908 and 1911–1912 in Florence, 1914–1916 in Spain, and in midsummer of 1916 settled in Paris, where her father had served as associate pastor at the American Church from 1902 to 1905. Paris would remain her home until her death there forty-six years later.

During World War I Beach met her lifelong companion, Adrienne Monnier, who owned a bookshop on the Left Bank. In late summer 1917 Beach worked as a volunteer farmhand in Touraine and during the first seven months of 1919 with the Red Cross in Serbia. After her return to Paris that summer, with Monnier's assistance, she opened Shakespeare and Company bookshop and lending library at 8 rue Dupuytren on 17 November 1919. A year and a half later she moved around the corner and across the street from Monnier's bookshop, La Maison des Amis des Livres. At 12 rue de l'Odéon, Beach sold only English-language books; at No. 7 Monnier sold only French literature. Together they orchestrated much of the exchange of English and French literature for the first half of the twentieth century.

Beach's single greatest achievement was the publication of James Joyce's *Ulysses*, agreed upon on 1 April 1921, printed by Maurice Darantière of Dijon, and published 2 February 1922 in time for Joyce's fortieth birthday. Beach hired typists, presold subscriptions to the novel in order to pay the printer and support the Joyce family, and intervened with the printer so that Joyce could write nearly a third more of the novel on a series of page proofs. For a decade, until her relationship with Joyce became strained and Random House took over publication, she reprinted the novel and cared for all of Joyce's literary—and many financial—needs. She published his second collection of poems, *Pomes Penyeach*, in France (1927) and the United States (1931), and published the early reviews of what was to become his *Finnegans Wake* in a volume called *Our Examination Round His Factification for Incamination of Work in Progress* (1929), for which she wrote the introduction.

Shakespeare and Company served as a center for Joyce studies as well as for the exchange of avant-garde twentieth-century literature. Joyce called it "Stratford-on-Odéon." Beach's library cards—for she operated chiefly a lending library—afford a valuable index to the reading habits of her famous patrons, from Ernest Hemingway to Simone de Beauvoir. Beach distributed all the small expatriate publishers' books and periodicals, participating directly in three French journals. Monnier's *Navire d'argent* (June 1925–May 1926) published Monnier and Beach's translation of T. S. Eliot's "The Love Song of J. Alfred Prufrock," the first complete Eliot poem translated into French. Beach also assisted with *Commerce*, a quarterly (1924–1932), by choosing and arranging the translation of several British and American literary works, and served on the board of *Mesures* (1935–1940).

She kept her bookshop open during the difficult depression years through regular donations from Bryher (Winifred Ellerman), the English novelist, and thanks to her own abstemiousness. But the success and endurance of the bookshop resulted primarily from the force of her personality, which was characterized as much by her hospitality and loyalty (the quality Ernest Hemingway most admired) as by her sharp wit and verbal play. Janet Flanner praised her "vigorous clear mind." In 1935 her French friends, headed by André Gide, organized a support group, The Friends of Shakespeare and Company, which sponsored readings by among others T. S. Eliot, Ernest Hemingway, Stephen Spender, André Gide, and Paul Valéry. Beach finally had to close the shop at the end of 1941 during the Occupation.

While presiding over an international literary crossroads, Beach introduced William Carlos Williams to Valery Larbaud, the French translator of *Ulysses*; F. Scott Fitzgerald to André Chamson, who wrote the introduction to the French translation of *The Great Gatsby*; and Eugene Jolas to James Joyce. For a decade Jolas published portions of Joyce's last novel in his *transition* magazine. With Monnier, Beach translated Bryher's *Paris 1900* in 1938; also she translated Henri Michaux's *A Barbarian in Asia* (1949), for which she won the Denyse Clairouin Award the following year. Her awards included the French Legion of Honor in 1938.

During World War II, Shakespeare and Company remained a safe haven for its remaining library members. Beach was forced to close the shop when a German officer demanded that she sell him her last copy of *Finnegans Wake* or face the confiscation of her library. She was placed in an internment camp for six months after the United States entered the war, and, despite the urging of T. S. Eliot and others, did not reopen the bookshop after the war. She lent books from her apartment, lived on a small stipend given by a friend, and in her final official act, dedicated the James Joyce Library in the Martello Tower outside Dublin.

• Beach's papers, including all her bookshop and lending library papers, are at Princeton University's Firestone Library. The library at the State University of New York at Buffalo has many of her James Joyce papers, and her papers collected by the Monnier estate are at the Harry Ransom Humanities Research Center, University of Texas. *Shakespeare and Company* (1959), her brief memoir, includes only a handful of pages on her personal life. The first and only biography, *Sylvia Beach and the Lost Generation: A History of Literary Paris in the Twenties and Thirties* (1983), was written by Noël Riley Fitch, who also wrote "Sylvia Beach: Commerce, Sanctification, and Art on the Left Bank," in *A Living of Words: American Women in Print Culture*, ed. Susan Albertine (1994), which focuses on Beach as a businesswoman. Another valuable source for opinions of her contemporaries is the memorial edition devoted to Sylvia Beach by *Mercure de France* (1963). Hugh Ford's *Published in Paris; American and British Writers, Printers, and Publishers in Paris 1920–1930* (1975) opens with a chapter devoted to Shakespeare and Company. See also Adrienne Monnier's *The Very Rich Hours of Adrienne Monnier*, trans. with lengthy introduction by Richard McDougall (1976), *James Joyce's Letters to Sylvia Beach 1921–1940*, ed. Melissa Banta and Oscar A. Silverman (1987), and Shari Benstock's *Women of the Left Bank: Paris, 1900–1940* (1986), which focuses on the Beach-Monnier association.

NOËL RILEY FITCH

BEACH, Wooster (1794–28 Jan. 1868), physician, was born in Trumbull, Connecticut, the son of Lewis Beach. His father was of English descent and his mother's name is unknown. Beach received a scant education in a rural school. As a young man, he developed a zealous interest in reforming religious and medical practices of the time. He particularly distrusted current medical practices and was familiar with the criticisms of physicians such as Benjamin Rush. Beach married Eliza de Grove in 1823; they had five children.

Beach's obsession with finding better medical treatments led him to a successful but unlicensed country herbal physician, Jacob Tidd of Amwell in Hunterdon County, New Jersey. Beach apprenticed himself to Tidd until Tidd's death in 1825. After Tidd's death, Beach's reputation as a successful practitioner led to invitations to New York City to treat some difficult cases, which he successfully treated. Beach stated that to "detect the error of the modern practice . . . I obtained a diploma according to the law of the State of New York during the time Drs. Post, Hosack, Mott and others were professors" (Felter, p. 82). The department was under the authority of Rutgers College (later Rutgers University) in New Brunswick, New Jersey, during this period.

Because Beach began his medical career using various botanic techniques, he immediately faced hostility from the school's physicians, who practiced the allopathic or "regular" system of medicine. He rejected the accepted practices of bleeding the patient and using other harsh methods to purge the body. He also rejected as too harsh the Thomsonians' treatment, patented by Samuel Thomson in 1813, of sweating the body and purging it with strong herbs instead of minerals. Beach's treatment, which involved the use of mild herbs and roots and employed successful remedies no matter their origin, attracted many patients as well as potential students. He began instructing students in his methods at his home in 1825. In the spring of 1827, aware of the value of a hospital practice for medical observations, teaching opportunities, and new medical discoveries, Beach opened the United States Infirmary, treating over 2,100 patients in the first year. The school and clinic were expanded into the Reformed Medical Academy in 1829 and a year later became the Reformed Medical College of the City of New York. Because the school was unchartered by the state, medical degrees were not granted, and certificates that only resembled diplomas were issued. Without accreditation, the school lacked sufficient student enrollment and closed in 1838.

In 1829 Beach founded the Reformed Medical Society of the United States, the first national medical society in the country. Charter members of this society, which was headquartered in New York City, included future renowned eclectics such as John King, Thomas Vaughan Morrow, and Ichabod Gibson Jones. Frustrated by Beach's inability to obtain certification of the Reformed Medical College in New York State, the group began to search for a new location for the school. The society distributed circulars in the western territories of the United States to obtain invitations to begin a licensed medical college. Colonel James Kilbourne of Worthington, Ohio, contacted Beach concerning the Worthington Academy, a literary and scientific school of which Kilbourne was president of the board of trustees. The school had a college building and the necessary charter needed to confer accredited degrees. In 1829 the Reformed Medical College of Ohio, also known as the Medical Department of Worthington College or the Worthington Medical College, was organized. The school retains the distinction of becoming the first chartered sectarian medical school in the United States. It closed, however, in 1840, when the Ohio legislature rescinded the school's authority to confer medical degrees as a result of a community uprising over the disappearance of a body from a local grave; the body was later found on a dissecting table at the school.

Undaunted, Morrow remained steadfastly at his teaching post even when the school closed and his colleagues abandoned him. In the winter of 1842–1843 Morrow started the Reformed Medical School of Cincinnati, which in 1845 became known as the Eclectic Medical Institute of Cincinnati. This accredited school became the foundation for other eclectic institutions later organized in the United States and Canada.

Graduates of the New York, Worthington, and Cincinnati schools were designated as "botanic," "reformed," or "American" physicians; at times they were called "Beachites." It was not until the mid-1840s that the term "eclectics" began to be used by Beach's followers. Although the origin and date of the term have not been verified, Beach allegedly accepted the term after it was used to describe Beach and his followers by the Thomsonian physician Isaac J. Sperry of Connecticut. Beach is said to have replied, "You have given me the word which I have wanted; I am an Eclectic" (Wilder, p. 433).

While the various schools were evolving, Beach continued his medical activities in New York. In March 1832 he was elected as a member of the New York County Medical Society. In July of the same year, during the Asiatic cholera epidemic, Alderman John Palmer appointed Beach the health physician for poor patients in New York's Tenth Ward. Beach practiced his usual noninvasive treatment of the body by using herbs instead of purging medicinals and relying on ear-to-chest auscultation instead of a stethoscope. He claimed to have only a 20 percent mortality rate, while some contemporary physicians' mortality rate was greater than 50 percent.

Beach understood the power of publicity and became known nationally and internationally through his numerous writings, which he distributed free to many world leaders. His popular three-volume set, *The American Practice of Medicine* (1833), was the first text published in the United States that dealt with the relationship between pathological changes and disease processes. Each volume included "commonsense observations, inspirational poetry, domestic practices, popular wisdom and testimonials" (Haller, pp. 73–74). The set was condensed in 1842 to a single volume, *The Family Physician*, and was republished fourteen times. Beach claimed in the later editions to have received recognition awards and decorations from European monarchs and Harvard professors. Many physicians of the time vigorously rebuked these distinctions because they felt that Beach had not produced any original medical thoughts and had borrowed heavily from others without acknowledgment.

The status of the Eclectic Medical Institute in Cincinnati was strengthened when Beach was elected by the faculty as an honorary chair of the clinics from 1847 to 1850. During this time he was actually at Central Medical College in Syracuse, New York, lecturing on the theory and practice of medicine. In 1848 he visited England, and even though he was considered an ineffective speaker he claimed a number of converts to his cause through a series of lectures. From this endeavor came his book *The British and American Reformed Practice of Medicine* (1859). He was the founder of the National Eclectic Medical Association in 1849 and was elected its president in 1855. He also served as a corresponding member of the Medical and Surgical Society of Berlin, Germany. Beach claimed to have been an honorary member of the medical societies of Leipzig, Bamberg, and Wetterau.

Beach was a poor businessman: although he was a prolific writer, he scarcely had enough money to secure himself and his family. His relationships with other teachers of the reformed or eclectic technique became less than cordial. The accidental death of a son—whom he had hoped would carry on his reform movement—and his inability to maintain his former leadership left Beach mentally incapacitated, and he drifted into obscurity after 1855. He died in New York City.

Beach is known as the founder of American eclecticism in medicine. Although the original ideas of "eclecticism" are not practiced today, Beach's protests of invasive medical practices encouraged many to question the techniques of medical treatment of the period. More important, Beach's followers eventually helped to force the practitioners of regular medicine to organize as a profession and push for medical education standards in the United States.

• A more detailed analysis of Beach's medical influence is in John S. Haller, Jr., *Medical Protestants: The Eclectics in American Medicine, 1825–1939* (1994); H. W. Felter, *History of the Eclectic Medical Institute* (1902); and Alexander Wilder, *History of Medicine* (1901). Additional biographical information can be found in Alex Berman, "Wooster Beach and the Early Eclectics," *University of Michigan Medical Bulletin* 24 (1958): 277–86; "An Historical Sketch of the Eclectic Medical College, 1845–1911," *Bulletin of the Lloyd Library of Botany, Pharmacy and Materia Medica*, 5th ser., no. 19 (1912): 359–77; and Wilder, "Eclecticism in Medicine Defined by Eclectic Writers," National Eclectic Medical Association, *Transactions* 28 (1901): 98. An obituary is in the *New York Herald*, 30 Jan. 1868.

BARBARA A. VAN BRIMMER

BEADLE, Erastus Flavel (11 Sept. 1821–18 Dec. 1894), publisher, was born in Stewart's Patent (now Pierstown), New York, the son of Flavel Beadle and Polly Turner, farmers. In 1833 Flavel Beadle moved his family to Kalamazoo County, Michigan. After two unsuccessful years of farming, the Beadles migrated back to their native New York, working odd jobs on farms along the way. Fourteen-year-old Erastus remained for several months as a farm worker in Fredonia, New York, where he was introduced to the town's printer, from whom he learned the rudiments of the printing trade.

About 1838 Beadle was apprenticed to printers H. and E. Phinney of Cooperstown, New York. In 1846 he married Mary Ann Pennington, with whom he had three children. When their Cooperstown printing house burned down in 1847, the Phinneys decided to relocate to Buffalo. Beadle followed the firm there and began work as a stereotyper for Jewett, Thomas, and Company, publisher of the *Buffalo Commercial Advertiser*. In 1850 he and his brother Irwin began a stereotype foundry, and in 1852 Beadle began his first publication, *The Youth's Casket: An Illustrated Magazine for the Young*. By 1856 he had sold his stereotyping business and had begun publishing a new periodical, *The Home: A Fireside Companion and Guide for the Wife, the Mother, the Sister, and the Daughter*. In that year Beadle took on Robert Adams as a partner.

In August 1856 Beadle traveled to Omaha, Nebraska, hoping to make a fortune in land speculation. The following spring he returned to Nebraska to set up a real-estate office, but a sharp drop in land values thwarted any dream of riches. In October 1857 he abandoned the venture and returned to Cooperstown.

In 1858 Beadle moved to New York City with Irwin and Adams. Irwin began independently publishing a series of songbooks that sold for a dime, the first of this kind to be issued on a regular basis. The songbook series was shortly followed by other series, including recipes and dialogues. The popularity of these publications prompted Beadle to begin publishing with Irwin and Adams a series of adventure novels that sold for a dime each, the beginning of the landmark Dime Novel series. The first number appeared in June 1860, a reprint of Ann S. Stephens's *Malaeska: The Indian Wife of the White Hunter*. The Dime Novel series proved to be phenomenally successful; thousands of copies were reputedly shipped to Union soldiers during the Civil War. Within the first five years of production, about 5 million novels were sold.

In 1861 Orville Victor was hired as editor for the various Beadle series. In the same year Beadle went to London, England, to oversee the opening of Beadle's American Sixpenny Publishing House, which issued Beadle's American Library, reprinting titles from Beadle's American series in order to discourage pirated English editions. In 1866 this English branch was sold to George Routledge and Sons. In 1862 Irwin Beadle sold his share of the publishing company but shortly after began another publishing firm with George Munro, who became one of Beadle and Adams's major competitors. Adams died in 1866, leaving Beadle as the sole remaining partner of Beadle and Adams until his retirement.

Though Beadle and Adams were not the first to publish inexpensive paper-covered novels, they were the first to issue a continuous series of such novels on an established schedule. The original Dime Novel series, more than 600 issues, were sextodecimo and approximately 100 pages—30,000 words. Typical press runs began at 60,000 copies but grew considerably with the success of the series. Beadle and Adams published more than twenty-five series, including Beadle's Pocket Novels, the Fireside Library, Beadle's Dime Library, Beadle's Half-Dime Library, and the Waverley Library. While some of these were issued in the sextodecimo format, others were quarto and octavo, with smaller print and multiple columns. Beadle and Adams also issued several weekly and monthly periodicals, such as the *Saturday Journal* and the *Banner Weekly*.

While their publications included books of etiquette, national tax laws, joke books, and baseball rule books, Beadle and Adams specialized in fiction, particularly frontier stories derived from the romances popularized several decades before by James Fenimore Cooper. In the 1870s dime novelists developed the genre of the western, transforming the cowboy into a hero. In addition to introducing numerous fictional heroes, such as Seth Jones and Deadwood Dick, Beadle and Adams novels conferred mythical status on historical personages such as Kit Carson, Wild Bill Hickock, Buffalo Bill Cody, and Davy Crockett. While frontier and western fiction remained a staple of the Beadle and Adams catalog, by the early 1880s other genres began to overtake the western in popularity, such as the detective novel.

Despite complaints about the sensational nature of the typical dime novel, from the outset Beadle insisted that his novelists conform to certain standards. Directions for prospective authors included, "We prohibit all things offensive to good taste in expression and incident—We prohibit subjects or characters that carry an immoral taint." In the early years Beadle made a point of luring well-known writers such as Ann S. Stephens, A. J. H. Duganne, Mayne Reid, John Neal, and Albert W. Aiken. He also helped launch the careers of previously unknown writers such as Edward S. Ellis, Prentiss Ingraham, and Edward L. Wheeler.

In 1889 Beadle retired with a considerable fortune to a lakeside home in Cooperstown that he dubbed "Glimmerview." In 1892 he ran unsuccessfully as a Republican congressional candidate. Beadle died in Cooperstown, New York.

Beadle helped revolutionize the American publishing industry, paving the way for the mass-market paperback. While his dime novels were formulaic and sensationalistic—decidedly subliterary—they remain of interest for the social historian, comprising, according to Henry Nash Smith, an "objectified mass dream" of mid- to late nineteenth-century America.

• The New York Public Library has published *To Nebraska in '57: A Diary of Erastus F. Beadle* (1923), which not only chronicles Beadle's life from March through October 1857 but also provides an intriguing account of cross-country travel and midwestern land development in the mid-nineteenth century. The most comprehensive biographical information about Beadle is in Albert Johannsen, *The House of Beadle and Adams and Its Dime and Nickel Novels*, vol. 1 (1950). Johannsen includes a detailed account of the history of the Beadle and Adams publishing firm, as well as a comprehensive list of titles and authors in all the series. For information about Beadle's early life and career see John C. Kunzog's two-part article "The Beadle Brothers: Erastus and Irwin," *Dime Novel Roundup* 36 (Apr. 1967): 34–38, and (May 1967): 46–50. Henry Nash Smith, *Virgin Land: The American West as Symbol and Myth* (1950), offers an incisive analysis of the popular appeal of the nineteenth-century dime novel western. Michael Denning, *Mechanic Accents: Dime Novels and Working-Class Culture in America* (1987), examines the development of the dime novel industry. An obituary is in the *New York Tribune*, 20 Dec. 1894.

RANDALL C. DAVIS

BEADLE, George Wells (22 Oct. 1903–9 June 1989), geneticist and university president, was the son of Hattie Albro and Chauncey Elmer Beadle, farmers near Wahoo, Nebraska. He was raised on a small farm that was noteworthy for its sound agricultural practices. After the early death of his mother and the accidental death of an older brother, it was assumed that he would take over the farm. Instead, thanks to the beneficent influence of Bess MacDonald, a high school teacher, he went to college. Further encouraged by the mentoring of Franklin D. Keim, an agronomy professor at the Nebraska College of Agriculture, Beadle entered graduate school at Cornell University in 1927 to pursue a career in biology.

There he soon took up genetics, working under Rollins Emerson, a founder of maize genetics and teacher of a group of brilliant graduate students. Beadle quickly made important contributions, publishing fifteen papers, mainly in maize cytogenetics, from 1928 to 1932. In 1928 he married Marion Hill. They had one son; then the marriage ended in divorce in 1953. Although he wished to remain at Cornell, a postdoctoral fellowship (1931) from the National Research Council required him to move. He joined Thomas Hunt Morgan's group at the California Institute of Technology and began work on fruitfly (*Drosophila*) genetics, continuing to pursue some maize work as well. The ethos of both the Emerson and the Morgan groups was cooperative, involving the sharing of techniques, seed stocks, fly cultures, and preliminary results. Beadle's style as a leader of laboratory groups and as an academic administrator was greatly influenced by these early experiences and by his love of "hands-on" work.

Beadle continued cytogenetic work in the heady atmosphere of Caltech while seeking tools for a fundamental breakthrough, particularly regarding the mechanisms of gene action. Boris Ephrussi, a Rockefeller Foundation fellow from Paris with a background in embryology, visited during 1934. Beadle and Ephrussi decided to gamble a year's work on an attempt to integrate the findings of genetics and embryology. The two disciplines had evolved in different directions since the turn of the century, working with different techniques on different organisms, and embryologists were largely unconvinced that genetic mechanisms—gene action—could explain the control of organismal development. Working in Paris in 1935, Beadle and Ephrussi laid the groundwork for five years of intense labor on *Drosophila* (fruit flies), employing embryological techniques (transplanting imaginal disks, i.e., the primordia for various organs) to study the effects of the presence of genetically distinct tissues within a single body on development. This work yielded some major insights into gene action. In particular, it allowed dissection of a pathway by which genes control formation of an eye color pigment. Ultimately this work led to the identification of two specific products (pigment precursors) made under the control of the "wild type" (normal) variants of two genes, but not by the mutants of those genes. It also became clear that the techniques were too slow and difficult, and the biochemistry of *Drosophila* was too complex, for this program of research to go much further with the available tools.

In 1937 Beadle moved to Stanford; by 1938 he was working with the biochemist Edward L. Tatum on the *Drosophila* pigment system. Given its difficulty, they sought a simpler system with which to analyze the genetic control of biochemical processes in living cells. Beginning in 1941 (not 1940, as often appears in the literature) they found—really made—such a system using a red bread mold, *Neurospora crassa*. The principle of their investigation was straightforward, though the details were complex. The life cycle of *Neurospora* allows complete control of sexual crosses, facilitating genetic work; furthermore, *Neurospora* remains in a haploid state (i.e., with unpaired chromosomes) for many generations, reproducing asexually, so that the effects of a gene can be tested without the interference of a second, potentially variant, copy. The mold will normally grow on a so-called minimal medium consisting of a sugar, some salts, and biotin (a B vitamin). Many *Neurospora* cells with a relevant genetic defect (obtained by radiation) cannot grow on this minimal medium but can grow on a complete medium. With enough tinkering, one can locate both the genetic defect and the specific biochemical step(s) that the mold cannot manage. This allows a careful investigation of just what biochemical consequences follow from the presence of a particular variant of a particular gene. Five years of labor with a team of students and colleagues during World War II yielded mastery of this system and impressive results, bearing on both fundamental genetics and the biochemistry of nutrition. Beadle was able to maintain support for the intensive activity of his research group during the difficult days of scientific mobilization for World War II by steering their projects so as to make significant contributions to nutritional research and by employing their knowledge of mutagenesis to help improve mass production of penicillin.

For genetics, the *Neurospora* work supported the "one gene–one enzyme" hypothesis, which states that genes control the specific structure of enzymes and that the specificity of any enzyme is determined by one and only one gene. The availability of particular enzymes determines whether a cell can accomplish a step in the degradation or synthesis of some substance; thus, an account of the control of enzyme synthesis was, potentially, the beginning of an account of the genetic control of physiological functions and of organismic development. The "one gene–one enzyme" hypothesis was controversial, in part because it sought to analyze the complex phenomena of embryological development and physiological function in terms of relatively simple and isolatable biochemical steps. It proved to be an important milestone on the road toward molecular genetics, according to which, to a first approximation, a gene is a linear code (now known to be composed of DNA) specifying the sequence of amino acids that make up a protein.

The 1958 Nobel Prize for physiology or medicine was jointly awarded to Beadle, Tatum, and the latter's student Joshua Lederberg for their work in biochemical genetics, including the pathbreaking work of Beadle and Tatum on *Neurospora*. Equally important, the *Neurospora* work provided genetical methods for working with mutants to analyze the basic biology of nutrition, drug resistance, and many other fundamental traits of organisms. (Lederberg's share of the Nobel Prize in part honors his and Tatum's extension of some of the *Neurospora* techniques to bacteria.)

Once it was recognized that the growth of *Neurospora* requiring a particular substance serves as a sensitive test of the amount of that substance in a given material, useful biological assays for the presence and concentration of vitamins and amino acids in foodstuffs could be developed. This extension of Beadle and Tatum's work was important for the war effort. Their work also provided systematic means for investigating the biosynthetic pathways by which amino acids are produced and for studying dietary requirements—for example, to ascertain whether any amino acids, beyond the twenty essential ones already known, were nutritionally necessary. The work was also extended to pharmaceutical assays. Thus research in Beadle's laboratory received continuous support during the difficult years of World War II. This support enabled the laboratory to serve as a major training ground for young geneticists during the war.

In 1946 Beadle succeeded Morgan as chairman of the Division of Biology at Caltech. His administrative duties soon prevented him from continuing laboratory research. He was, however, a major force in the renovation and reorientation of the biology division, guiding it into the era of molecular biology. He facilitated the appointment of a series of brilliant investigators, maintained the strong tradition of interdisciplinary cooperation central to the Caltech ethos, and helped obtain crucial funding for, among other things, the construction of two major new laboratory buildings. In 1953 he married Muriel Barnett, a widowed writer, adopting her young son. Some years later he and Muriel coauthored a book for young people, *The Language of Life: An Introduction to the Science of Genetics* (1966). From 1960 to 1961, Beadle served as acting dean of faculty at Caltech, then left to become president of the University of Chicago (1961–1968), a post he held until he reached the mandatory retirement age.

At Chicago, Beadle was charged with steering a university in difficult circumstances through turbulent times and through the hazards of surrounding urban decay. The situation there, and the path that he chose to achieve considerable renovation of the faculty and the facilities, are well described by Muriel Beadle in *Where Has All the Ivy Gone?* (1972). The sixties were difficult times for university presidents, who had to cope with student protests over national and college policies, sit-ins (of which Chicago had its share), and racial tensions on and off campus. In addition, the university had to play an important and difficult role in the renewal of its immediate neighborhood, Hyde Park. National events as well as local ones impinged on the university: Beadle's term of office ended the year of the assassinations of Martin Luther King, Jr. and Robert F. Kennedy. In the face of all these problems, he managed to rebuild a weakened faculty and retained substantial trust among students, faculty, trustees, alumni, and the Chicago business community. He closed his presidency with the successful completion of a $160 million fundraising campaign for the university. He also served, as he had at Caltech, on numerous national committees, for example, the Council of the National Academy of Sciences (1969–1972).

At the close of his presidency, Beadle remained at Chicago as distinguished service professor and resumed work on one of the problems he studied in his youth—the origin of maize. This was the subject of three final scientific publications in 1980 and 1981. In 1982 he retired to Pomona, California, where he spent his declining years with gradually increasing disability from Alzheimer's disease.

• The Archives of the California Institute of Technology have a major collection of Beadle's papers and correspondence. There is also considerable material in the Archives of the Rockefeller Foundation. Some personal papers and speeches are in the University of Chicago Archives. Norman H. Horowitz, "George Wells Beadle, 1903–1989," in *Biographical Memoirs of the National Academy of Sciences* (1990), provides a biography and scientific bibliography. See also Beadle's Nobel lecture, "Genes and Chemical Reactions in Neurospora," *Science* 129 (1959): 1715–19, and two autobiographical essays—"Biochemical Genetics: Some Recollections," in *Phage and the Origins of Molecular Biology*, ed. John Cairns et al. (1966), and "Recollections," *Annual Review of Biochemistry* 43 (1974): 1–13. For the work with Ephrussi see Richard M. Burian et al., "The Singular Fate of Genetics in France, 1900–1940," *Journal of the History of Biology* 21 (1988): 357–402. For later phases of Beadle's career, see Norman H. Horowitz, "Fifty Years Ago: The Neurospora Revolution," *Genetics* 127 (1991): 631–35; Lily E. Kay, "Selling Pure Science in Wartime: The Biochemical Genetics of G. W. Beadle," *Journal of the History of Biology* 22 (1989): 73–101; and L. E. Kay, *The Molecular Vision of Life: Caltech, The Rockefeller Foundation, and the Rise of the New Biology* (1992). An authoritative textbook by Beadle and Alfred H. Sturtevant, *An Introduction to Genetics* (1939), represents the state of the discipline as of that date. The following review articles by Beadle summarize some of his own contributions: "The Development of Eye Colors in *Drosophila* as Studied by Transplantation," *American Naturalist* 71 (1937): 120–26; "Biochemical Genetics," *Chemical Reviews* 37 (1945): 15–96; "The Genetic Control of Biochemical Reactions," *Harvey Lectures* 40 (1945): 179–94; and "Ancestry of Corn," *Scientific American* 242, no. 1 (1980): 112–19.

RICHARD M. BURIAN

BEAL, William James (11 Mar. 1833–12 May 1924), botanist, was born in Adrian, Michigan, the son of William Beal, a pioneer farmer and builder, and Rachel S. Comstock. After obtaining his early education in a district school and a seminary, Beal attended the University of Michigan, from which he received an A.B. in 1959 and an A.M. in 1862. He then enrolled at Harvard University (B.S., 1865), where he studied with botanist Asa Gray and zoologist Louis Agassiz.

While a student at both Michigan and Harvard, Beal found it necessary for financial reasons to alternate his periods of university study with teaching. In 1863 he married Hannah A. Proud, with whom he had one child. In 1868 he obtained a professorship of botany at the University of Chicago and in 1870 he went to Michigan Agricultural College (now Michigan State University), where he was appointed professor of botany and horticulture in 1871. Beal remained at Michigan until his retirement in 1910.

In 1871 Gray had written to Beal, "I am glad you are established in Michigan. You will bring up botany . . . in all that region." Gray's expectation was entirely fulfilled: during Beal's forty years at Michigan State University, he pioneered as a teacher, researcher, and contributor to the larger scientific community. In teaching, Beal followed in the path of Agassiz, who had taught biological sciences at Harvard by the laboratory method. Beal soon established a botanical laboratory and a botanical garden. He rejected the textbook-recitation method, replacing it with what he termed the "New Botany." Students were sent out into the field to make discoveries for themselves, to find out how plants functioned, and to make critical examinations of specimens, rather than simply learning their names. He wrote of his students' work that "some of the discoveries, so far as I know, were new to science, and nearly everything was new to the members of the class."

The college's botanical building, which was built next to Beal's gardens in 1880, had no lecture room but had a large laboratory on the first floor, where seniors were equipped with microscopes, costing from thirty-five to eighty dollars; Beal believed there were only three other schools in America at the time that emphasized this kind of individual research in science. He summed up his teaching philosophy in a phrase: "To be constantly giving information in science makes intellectual tramps, and not trained investigators." Several of Beal's students became distinguished scientists, including C. S. Crandall, Eugene Davenport, C. C. Georgeson, and L. H. Bailey.

Alongside the laboratory were Beal's famous gardens—a grass garden started in 1873 and a wild garden begun in 1877. He and his students set out plants according to family, in large patches, and by the time Beal retired, there were more than 2,100 species and varieties, many of which were native to Michigan. He built a greenhouse across from the gardens and also set out an arboretum, which would eventually include 150 species of trees. He also helped to improve the physical appearance of the college by planting hundreds of specimens of trees and shrubs about the general landscape. All of these were labeled and cataloged by Beal and his colleagues, serving as an outdoor laboratory.

In his own research, Beal was particularly interested in the Poaceae family and published the two-volume *The Grasses of North America* in 1887 and 1896. His other publications include *The New Botany* (1880), *Seed Dispersal* (1898), *Michigan Flora* (1892), *Addi-*

tions to the Michigan Flora since 1892 (1898), and *History of the Michigan Agricultural College* (1915).

Beal followed another line of inquiry in his work on the hybridization of corn, in which he was influenced by English naturalist Charles Darwin's *The Effects of Cross and Self Fertilization in the Vegetable Kingdom.* Beal corresponded with Darwin and received an encouraging reply, which led to experiments from 1877 to 1880 that proved the increased vigor and productivity of corn through cross-fertilization.

In addition to dedicating himself to teaching and research, Beal found time to write dozens of articles for botanical periodicals and horticultural and agricultural papers; every year he answered hundreds of inquiries in long hand about agriculture, horticulture, and forestry. Consequently, Beal became one of the best-known members of the Michigan State faculty, both in Michigan and in neighboring states.

Because of his strong interest in the dissemination of scientific knowledge, Beal participated in the work of many scientific organizations. He was first president of the Society for the Promotion of Agricultural Science, a charter member and first president of the Michigan Academy of Science, fellow of the American Association for the Advancement of Science, secretary of the American Pomological Society, and president of the Michigan State Teachers' Association. From 1888 to 1892 he was director of the State Forestry Commission, a position to which he was named because of his concern about the state's vanishing forests and the need for conservation. In the 1870s Beal had urged that conservation practices be adopted, even though this was an unpopular idea among the many who believed the forests to be "inexhaustible." He also stressed the importance of local societies for surveying and conserving Michigan's natural heritage. When the Michigan Academy of Science was founded in 1894, Beal wrote that "Michigan is far behind many other states . . . in the study of flora and fauna. . . . Local societies for investigating this subject should be encouraged and assisted."

Throughout his career, Beal was a man of enormous vitality and energy, and he believed his constant good health was a result of hard work and Quaker-like abstemious habits. He engaged in some physical work or exercise every day and never took a vacation. At the time of his death in Amherst, Massachusetts, he was the oldest graduate of the University of Michigan and the oldest resident of Amherst. Because of his innovations in teaching science and his contributions through research and other scientific activities, Beal was one of the important pioneers in American botany of the nineteenth and early twentieth centuries.

• R. S. Baker and Jessie Beal Baker, *An American Pioneer in Science* (1925), is a short biography by Beal's daughter and son-in-law that also contains three of Beal's articles, "The New Botany," "Studying the Sciences Fifty Years Ago," and "Pioneer Life in Southern Michigan in the Thirties." Other biographical sources include Madison Kuhn, *Michigan State: The First Hundred Years* (1955), and E. G. Voss, *Botanical Beachcombers and Explorers: Pioneers of the Nineteenth Century in the Upper Great Lakes* (1978). See also Voss, "Across Michigan by Covered Wagon: A Botanical Expedition in 1888," *Michigan Botanist* 15, no. 1 (1976): 3–70. Further references are in Frans A. Stafleu, *Taxonomic Literature*, supp. II (1993), pp. 1–3; and "Beal Centennial: 1873–1973," *Michigan Science in Action* (May 1973). Obituaries are in *Science* 61 (1925): 559–60, and, by E. A. Bessey, *Botanical Gazette* 79 (1925): 103–6.

ROBERT F. ERICKSON

BEALE, Joseph Henry (12 Oct. 1861–20 Jan. 1943), legal educator, was born in Dorchester (now part of Boston), Massachusetts, the son of Joseph Henry Beale, who ran a prosperous mattress business, and Frances Elizabeth Messinger. He grew up in Brahmin Boston, graduated from Harvard College in 1882, taught for a year (1882–1883) at St. Paul's School in Concord, New Hampshire, and then returned to Harvard for postgraduate work in classics and history. He enrolled in law school in 1884 and received an LL.B. and A.M. from Harvard in 1887. During his third year in law school he was a founder of the *Harvard Law Review.*

On graduation, Beale refused an offer to serve as law secretary to Horace Gray of the U.S. Supreme Court and instead opened his own office in Boston. In 1891 he married Elizabeth Chadwick Day; they had two daughters, as well as a son who died in infancy. While in practice, Beale coedited an edition of *Sedgwick on Damages* (1891) and lectured on the subject at Harvard; he was invited to return as an instructor in criminal law in 1891–1892. Beale was appointed a full-time assistant professor in 1892 and remained on the Harvard faculty until retirement in 1938. He became a professor in 1897, Bussey Professor in 1903, Carter Professor in 1908, and Royall Professor in 1916. Beale died in Cambridge.

For nearly five decades Beale was a major figure in legal education, an influential scholar, and a teacher of many leading lawyers. He was a founder of the Association of American Law Schools in 1900 and its president in 1913–1914. He helped organize the American Law Institute in 1922 and served as its reporter on conflict of laws. He was also the first president of the American Legal History Society in 1933.

For two years (1902–1904) Beale was "on loan" from Harvard to serve as founding dean of the University of Chicago Law School. It was understood that Chicago would replicate the Harvard curriculum. A blow-up occurred, though, when it seemed Chicago might introduce subjects that Harvard did not regard as strictly legal, such as jurisprudence and taxation. Beale diplomatically patched things up (and later, back at Harvard, taught jurisprudence and taxation himself). In 1915, irked by Harvard's refusal to admit women, he founded the Cambridge Law School for Women but appears to have lost interest when his daughter dropped out to marry.

Beale was an ardent churchman, active in Christ Church, Cambridge, and in diocesan and general conventions of the Protestant Episcopal church. He served on the school committee and, for three years, on the board of aldermen of the City of Cambridge; he was also a delegate to the 1928 Republican National Convention.

A popular, energetic, and stimulating teacher, Beale could also terrify and wound. In descriptions of his teaching, the image recurs of a brilliant verbal swordsman parrying blows with a horde of student antagonists. Learned Hand, an early student, remembered that "[a]lthough the most generous and warmhearted of men, he was formidable in classroom by the impetuosity of his manner and the inexorability of his dialectic" (Hand, p. 8). There is an oft-repeated story in which Beale observed that a student's proposition was not the law in a single state; the student cited a Pennsylvania (or perhaps Massachusetts) decision, and was dismissed with the instant reply: "That's not a State; it's a Commonwealth!"

Beale would advance preposterous theories, encouraging students to challenge them. He had a penchant for trying to reconcile the irreconcilable and for bringing order out of intractably chaotic material. He was (as Justice Oliver Wendell Holmes said of Beale's teacher Langdell) a "legal theologian." Learned Hand said of Beale: "[D]eeply religious, he believed that, were we only true to ourselves, law would emerge as the will of God" (Hand, p. 8).

He refused to accept that courts make law. He maintained that law is a system of transcendent principles that provide the foundation for both legislation and judicial decision; neither legislators nor judges can change those basic principles. He was thus a favorite bête noire of the "legal realists" (the next generation of academic lawyers who came to prominence in the 1920s and 1930s) in their attacks on formalism. In Jerome Frank's *Law and the Modern Mind* (1930), legal formalism is called "Bealism." Beale was relatively unperturbed and responded with good humor, saying it was no shame for a lawyer to be thought legalistic.

Beale was not the absolute conceptualist he pretended to be. He criticized the arch-formalist Langdell for being "too academic." He had an abiding interest in legal history and recognized that law is a continually changing agency of social governance, that judges make choices (although constrained choices), and that common law is more a method of thought than a body of fixed rules. As Jerome Frank conceded, Beale was "not a consistent Bealist."

Beale taught an extraordinary variety of subjects and produced some twenty-seven books and a long list of articles. He taught and published on common carriers, contracts, conflicts, corporations, criminal law, criminology, criminal pleading and practice, equity, evidence, innkeepers, jurisprudence, legal history, municipal corporations, partnership, pleading, principles of legal liability, property, public service companies, railroad rate regulation, taxation, federal taxation, torts, suretyship, and mortgages.

He most often taught criminal law and conflicts. His casebook on criminal law went through four editions and was widely imitated. Beale helped give the subject academic respectability, but because he focused on specific crimes and defenses rather than general principles, he never brought to criminal law what it most needed—the imaginative system-building that characterized his work in other fields.

He is most closely associated with conflict of laws and had the greatest impact on that field. In his work on the Restatement of Conflict of Laws promulgated by the American Law Institute in 1934 and his magisterial *Treatise on the Conflict of Laws* (1935), he presented the subject as a unified, tightly logical system. Beale presupposed that a state's law can have no effect outside its territory but that transactions in foreign jurisdictions give rise to "vested rights," which, having been created by the appropriate law, must be recognized everywhere. The next generation of theorists had great fun attacking Beale's question-begging premises, as well as his mechanical solutions. But underlying his system was a practical concern with reducing legal costs by promoting simplicity and predictability and by ensuring that the same law would be applied to a transaction wherever suit was brought.

Beale's reputation has gone through three phases. In his lifetime he was widely regarded as author of some of the best contemporary legal scholarship. Toward the end of his career and after, he was widely ridiculed as the worst kind of formalist. More recently, he has been viewed as a good illustration of how the work of any significant figure embodies exaggerations and contradictions and contains within itself a struggle, a debate, and a dialectic.

• For biographical material on Beale, see the five memorial tributes (by Williston, Griswold, Pound, Chafee, and Frankfurter) in the *Harvard Law Review* 56 (1943): 685–703, and the dedicatory note (unsigned, by Pound) in *Harvard Legal Essays, Written in Honor of and Presented to Joseph Henry Beale and Samuel Williston* (1934), which contains a full bibliography through 1933. Vignettes of Beale as a teacher appear in Harlan B. Phillips, ed., *Felix Frankfurter Reminisces* (1960); Arthur E. Sutherland, *The Law at Harvard* (1967); and the obituary by Reginald Heber Smith in *American Bar Association Journal* 29 (1943): 147. Learned Hand's assessment appears in the first of "Three Letters from Alumni," *Harvard Law School Bulletin*, Jan. 1949, pp. 7–8. On Beale's role as founding dean at Chicago, see Frank L. Ellsworth, *Law on the Midway: The Founding of the University of Chicago Law School* (1977); on the Cambridge Law School for Women, see Robert Stevens, *Law School: Legal Education in America from the 1950s to the 1980s* (1983). Warren J. Samuels, "Joseph Henry Beale's Lectures on Jurisprudence, 1909," *University of Miami Law Review* 29 (1975): 260–333, reproduces Robert Lee Hale's class notes and provides a useful introduction to Beale's jurisprudential thinking. Tony Freyer, *Harmony & Dissonance: The Swift and Erie Cases in American Federalism* (1981), relies in part on student notes of Beale's lectures (preserved in the Harvard Law School library) to present a picture of Beale as much less of a conceptualist than he is usually supposed to be.

EDWARD M. WISE

BEAMS, Jesse Wakefield (25 Dec. 1898–25 July 1977), physicist, was born in Belle Plains, Kansas, the son of Jesse Wakefield Beams and Kathryn Wylie, farmers. Beams graduated from Fairmont College (now Wichita State University) in 1921. He spent the following year earning a master's degree in physics at the University of Wisconsin. Beams then accepted a position as an instructor in physics at Alabama Polytechnic Institute (now Auburn University). The chairman of the Polytechnic's physics department, Fred Allison, was impressed with Beams's abilities in experimental physics and encouraged him to go on for a Ph.D. at the University of Virginia. Accepting a teaching fellowship there for 1923 and 1924, Beams worked under Professor Carroll M. Sparrow, who had also been Allison's mentor.

At Sparrow's suggestion, Beams tried to measure very short time intervals—the time difference between the arrival of a light quantum and the ejection of the first photoelectron (photoelectric effect). Beams developed a technique for this measurement that later became widely used. The central feature of the apparatus was a shutter mechanism that consisted of a Kerr cell connected to delay lines of differing lengths, one of which supplied the activating voltage to the cell, while the other removed it. Driving this cycle was the potential difference across a high-intensity spark gap, which produced the light bursts used to produce the photoelectrons. Beams's apparatus was sensitive enough to allow him to ascertain that the difference must be less than 10^{-8} seconds, a milestone measurement for its day. Along the way, Beams was able to measure such things as the time interval between excitation and emission of some fluorescent spectra as well as the relative time delay, after excitation, in the appearance of different lines in particular spectra. It was for these measurements that, in 1925, Beams was awarded his Ph.D. He quickly earned the reputation of being a laboratory virtuoso for work of this sort.

Two years later, in a paper coauthored with Ernest O. Lawrence and delivered at the American Physical Society meetings, and later published as "The Instantaneity of the Photoelectric Effect" (*Physical Review* 29 [1927]: 361–62, 903), Beams and Lawrence argued that for all practical purposes, there was no measurable time difference between the arrival of photons and the ejection of photoelectrons. Their technique was an adaptation of the measurement of short time intervals that Beams had employed in his dissertation work.

Upon completion of his Ph.D., Beams was awarded a two-year National Research Council Fellowship. During the first year, he remained at Virginia. The second year of the fellowship was spent at Yale University, where Lawrence too was a National Research Fellow. They shared a common background, both coming from small, isolated farming communities, and they shared a common interest in developing practical ways of measuring short-time intervals. Their paths were to cross again during World War II, when stark differences in their personal styles—Lawrence, always the optimistic, confident extrovert and salesman, and Beams, cautious and self-deprecating, moving with measured deliberativeness—had quite different, but complementary, influences on the building of the atomic bomb.

Upon leaving Yale in the fall of 1928, Beams returned, with an appointment as associate professor of physics, to the University of Virginia, where he spent the rest of his career. In 1931 he married Maxine Sutherland, a teacher. At Virginia, Beams acquired a reputation for being a talented and concerned teacher who developed excellent rapport with his graduate students as well as being an inventive and productive researcher. Beams, who served as department chair from 1948 to 1963, is widely credited with building up the reputation of the Virginia physics department.

In 1930 Beams opened up a line of research that, more and more, would dominate his professional life. In that year he published a short article on obtaining high-speed rotation ("A Review of the Use of Kerr Cells for the Measurement of Time Intervals and the Production of Flashes of Light," *Reviews of Scientific Instruments* 1 [1930]: 780–93). Initially, as Beams himself noted many years later, his interest was piqued "when Ernest O. Lawrence and I were looking for a way to make high speed photographs of . . . phenomena of very brief duration. . . . By mounting a mirror on an air-driven motor we were able to build a high speed camera that met our needs. This was my introduction to high speed rotation" ("Ultrahigh-Speed Rotation," *Scientific American* 204, no. 4 [Apr. 1961]: 134–47).

The challenge of producing apparatus capable of higher and higher rates of rotation became the central focus of Beams's research interests. By the end of the 1930s Beams was recognized as *the* world's authority on high-speed rotation, especially with regard to applications to centrifuge technology. During that period Beams developed ultracentrifuges that featured rotors enclosed in evacuated spaces and equipped with flexible shafts that allowed the rotor to spin about its own inertial axis (after the Swedish engineer Carl de Laval). Next, the rotor, sans bearings and shaft, was magnetically suspended, using negative optical feedback to control the vertical displacement of the rotor. This was superseded by a driving system in which the rotor served as the armature of a synchronized induction motor. In time Beams and his University of Virginia group were able to produce ultracentrifuges, capable of speeds in excess of a million rotations a second, limited only by the tensile strength of the rotor itself.

After 1940 Beams became associated with two major applications of ultracentrifuges: separation of elemental isotopes and separation of so-called "organic" molecules and molecules associated with living systems. The importance and the impact of Beams's postwar work on the latter application can be measured by the fact that, in 1967, Beams was awarded the National Medal of Science for developing the technology with which viruses and other biologically active forms could be separated from their carrying media.

At the end of 1939 Beams took on the job, offered by the U.S. government's secret Uranium Committee, of adapting centrifuge techniques for the separation of the two isotopes found in natural uranium, nonfissioning uranium 238 and its rarer, but fissioning sibling, uranium 235. Between 1939 and the end of 1942, not knowing which of several techniques for isotope separation would be viable, and believing that they were in a race with the Germans, the Uranium Committee and its successor, the Manhattan Engineer District (the Manhattan Project) funded several different separation schemes. But as costs skyrocketed, the head of the project, General Leslie R. Groves, chose at the end of 1942 not to continue Beams's gas centrifuge project. Groves, a forceful and aggressive administrator, was negatively impressed with Beams's diffidence, a by-product of his revulsion of self-promotion and self-aggrandizement, and decided to go forward with other separation methods (electromagnetic separation and gaseous diffusion). After the war, work on gas centrifuge was revived and eventually, with Beams as a primary consultant, became the method of choice.

Beams formally retired in 1969 but continued his life of active research. Among his later accomplishments were an adaptation of the ultracentrifuge to the measurements of fluid density and viscosity and an ingenious modification of the Cavendish technique for determining the gravitational constant G, which had the promise of improving the accuracy of the determination by several orders of magnitude.

Beams was a highly respected member of the U.S. physics community. In 1947 he served as president of the Virginia Academy of Sciences and in 1958 was president of the American Physical Society. Besides the National Medal of Science, he was awarded the Franklin Institute's Potts Medal (1942), U.S. Naval Ordnance Development Award (1946), and the American Philosophical Society's Lewis Award (1958). A University of Virginia lectureship in biophysics in Beams's name was initiated in 1972, and in 1973 the southeastern section of the American Physical Society established the Jesse W. Beams Award for Research.

Typical for Beams, on the day that he died in Charlottesville, he was actively working on the completion of a paper with his collaborator D. W. Kupke, reporting improvements in the instrument for measuring fluid density and viscosity. Kupke later described Beams as "a quiet man who thought deep thoughts about the universe and the role of mankind, but . . . [who] did no preaching" (Gordy, p. 31).

• The most useful source of information on Beams's life is the commemoration by Walter Gordy in National Academy of Sciences, *Biographical Memoirs* 64 (1983): 3–49. Among the most significant of Beams's more than 200 professional papers are, with R. D. Boyle and P. E. Hexner, "Equilibrium Ultracentrifuge for Molecular Weight Measurement," *Journal of Polymer Science* 57 (1962): 161–74; with A. M. Clarke, "Magnetic Suspension Balance for Determining Densities and Partial Specific Volumes," *Reviews of Scientific Instruments* 33 (1962): 151–55; "Finding a Better Value for G," *Physics Today* 24, no. 5 (May 1971): 34–40; and *Early History of Gas Centrifuge in the U.S.A.* (1975), a special report of the University of Virginia and Union Carbide Oak Ridge Nuclear Division. Beams's role in the Manhattan Project is discussed in detail in Richard G. Hewlett and Oscar E. Ander-

son, Jr., *The New World, 1939–1946: A History of the United States Atomic Energy Commission*, vol. 1 (1962). An obituary by J. C. Street is in *Physics Today* 30 (Nov. 1977).

STANLEY GOLDBERG

BEAN, Joel (16 Dec. 1825–11 Jan. 1914), Quaker minister and author, was born in Alton, New Hampshire, the son of John Bean and Elizabeth Ham, farmers. Joel received his education in local public schools and in the Friends Boarding School in Providence, Rhode Island, now Moses Brown School. Although the Beans were staunch Quakers, they lived at a distance from a Friends meeting, and so Joel had considerable contact with other denominations. After finishing at Providence, he taught in Quaker schools in New England and North Carolina.

In 1855 Bean moved to Cedar County, Iowa; he was one of the first to arrive in what became a large Quaker community at West Branch. Over the next two decades, he became one of West Branch's leading citizens—farmer, teacher, and bank officer. In 1859 he married Hannah Elliott Shipley, a member of a prominent Philadelphia Quaker family of abolitionists and reformers, with whom he had two children.

In the 1860s the Beans became leaders among American Quakers. They first attracted notice with an eight-month visit to the Hawaiian Islands in 1861 touring missionary schools and churches. They also became active in Quaker Sunday school work and in peace activities in Iowa. Joel was a frequent contributor to Quaker periodicals and in 1867 became the clerk, or presiding officer, of Iowa Yearly Meeting of Friends. He was also recorded as a Quaker minister. In 1872 the Beans made a long tour of Great Britain, where they formed numerous ties with leading British Friends. From 1875 to 1877 the couple taught at the Friends Boarding School in Providence, then returned to Iowa, where Joel once again became clerk of Iowa Yearly Meeting.

Iowa Quakers were undergoing radical changes in the 1870s, changes that Joel Bean originally supported but gradually came to fear. Bean's ties were with the Gurneyite persuasion of Friends, who had emerged from a series of splits between 1820 and 1860 as the largest Quaker group in North America. The Gurneyites took their name from the well-known English Quaker minister Joseph John Gurney. Their teachings reflected the growing influence of non-Quaker evangelicals, especially those in the Wesleyan tradition, on many Friends. They were characterized by close ties with English Friends, an openness to contacts with non-Quakers in charitable and reform causes, and an increasing emphasis on evangelical theology, including a commitment to the authority of Scripture and the necessity of a definite, instantaneous conversion experience.

By the 1870s Gurneyite Friends across the United States were swept up in a wave of revivalism, which brought music, altar calls, and other hitherto unknown practices into their meetings. At the heart of this revival was the doctrine of instantaneous sanctification, or holiness—the belief that through faith humans can be freed entirely from the power and influence of sin. The doctrine had a profound and lasting impact on many Quakers, but others found such changes too radical. In Bean's last year as clerk of Iowa Yearly Meeting a number of Friends opposed to the revival, especially its teachings on holiness, left to form their own yearly meeting.

Bean had welcomed the first stirrings of revivalism in the late 1860s as hopeful signs of new life. By 1877, however, he had become skeptical, especially of the doctrine of instantaneous sanctification. Instead, he was an advocate of the traditional Quaker understanding of sanctification as gradual. The revivalists' attacks on the Quaker doctrine of the Inner Light ("that of God in every man") further alienated him. A revival at West Branch in March 1880 hopelessly divided the Quaker community there. Bean's response was an article, published in the *Glasgow British Friend* in 1881, titled "The Issue." It was a devastating critique of the revival and what Bean saw as its withering impact on Quakerism. It won acclaim from revival opponents but evoked a furious response from supporters. Believing that the situation among Iowa Friends was hopeless, and tired of conflict, the Beans decided to move to San Jose, California, where Joel's brother already lived.

The move to California did not end the Beans' involvement in controversy. They were still under the jurisdiction of Iowa Yearly Meeting, and their opponents, seeing both Joel and Hannah as hindrances to the cause of aggressive soul-saving, continued to challenge them. The opposition limited the powers of the Beans' meeting in San Jose, questioned the soundness of their ministry, and subjected them to challenges to their character and their standing as Quaker ministers.

The great crisis of Joel Bean's life came in 1893, when Iowa Yearly Meeting adopted a set of doctrinal questions for all ministers to answer. When the Beans received them, they gave affirmative answers to all but one, which dealt with eternal punishment. Joel answered that he was uncertain about this and so had never touched on it in his public ministry. Iowa Friends, however, found this a sufficient basis on which to depose the Beans as ministers.

The Iowa action created a firestorm of protest, especially among Quakers in the eastern states and in England, where the Beans were well known and respected. It was a crucial factor in alienating English Friends from the American Quaker revival. In 1898 the controversy flared anew when the Beans were dropped from membership by Iowa Friends. In this case, however, after more protests, the action was reversed.

After 1898 Joel Bean confined his Quaker activities to writing. The small meeting that he and Hannah founded at College Park (outside San Jose) became the nucleus of Pacific Yearly Meeting, the large liberal Quaker group in California. Joel Bean died in Honolulu.

• A large collection of Joel Bean papers is at the Friends Historical Library, Swarthmore College. Vital for Bean's reaction to the revival in Iowa are his letters in the Timothy Nicholson Papers, Friends Collection, Earlham College. Although Bean published no books, he was a prolific contributor to Quaker journals such as the *Friends' Review* and the *American Friend*. One of his reminiscences was edited and published by Howard H. Brinton as "The Revival Movement in Iowa: A Letter from Joel Bean to Rufus M. Jones," *Bulletin of Friends Historical Association* 50 (Autumn 1960): pp. 102–10. Secondary treatments of Bean include Catharine E. B. Cox, "Joel and Hannah E. Bean," *Quaker Biographies*, 2d ser., vol. 3 (n.d.); David C. Le Shana, *Quakers in California* (1969); Errol T. Elliott, "Joel Bean," in *Quaker Profiles from the American West* (1972); and Thomas D. Hamm, "Joel Bean and the Revival in Iowa," *Quaker History* 76 (Spring 1987): 33–49, and *The Transformation of American Quakerism: Orthodox Friends, 1800–1907* (1988). An obituary is in *The Annual Monitor for 1915: Being an Obituary of Members of the Society of Friends* (1914).

THOMAS D. HAMM

BEAN, L. L. (13 Oct. 1872–5 Feb. 1967), retail merchant, was born Leon Leonwood Bean in Greenwood, Maine, the son of Benjamin Warren Bean and Sarah Swett, farmers. Orphaned at age twelve, he lived with his brother and four sisters in South Paris, Maine, and briefly attended Kent Hill Academy and Hebron Academy. Lennie Bean worked in his brother's retail store in Freeport and in an Auburn clothing store from 1892 to 1907. In 1898 Bean married Bertha Porter, and they had two sons and a daughter. After his wife died in 1939, he married Claire L. Boudreau in 1940. Achieving little success in various business ventures, from selling soap to working in a creamery, in 1907 Bean moved to his wife's hometown, Freeport, Maine, to take over his brother Ervin's retail store.

Bean's unremarkable career changed in 1911 when he invented the leather-top, rubber-bottom Maine Hunting Shoe, which made him famous. A lifetime of hunting and fishing taught him that a practical way to keep the hunter's feet warm and dry was lacking. More importantly, Bean discovered the lucrative direct-mail sporting goods business by selling these shoes by mail to holders of nonresident Maine hunting licenses. This experiment in direct-mail merchandising was unique. According to Bean company legend, ninety of the first hundred shoes sold were returned as defective, but Bean gave each customer a full refund. However, from 1912 to 1918 Bean perfected the patented design and built his company's reputation and sales. He wrote personal letters to answer each inquiry or complaint, basing his success on the sale of quality outdoors products backed by an unconditional guarantee, a form of consumer protection made famous by larger mail-order retailers like Montgomery Ward and Sears, Roebuck.

By 1917 Bean opened a retail store on Main Street in Freeport and added other hunting and camping gear to his inventory. He personally field tested every item he sold, cultivating the image of a folksy, honest, thrifty Yankee store small enough to care about quality and customer satisfaction. The Maine Hunting Shoe remained the centerpiece of his catalogue, but his chamois cloth shirt, zipper duffel bags, Hudson Bay "point" blankets, and other camping items proved popular. These high quality goods attracted a growing number of hunters, hikers and campers as loyal customers. By 1937 the company passed the million-dollar sales mark, and in 1951 Mr. Bean converted the store to a round-the-clock operation open every day (except Christmas) to accommodate many out-of-state "sports" driving north on U.S. Route One to fishing and hunting camps.

After World War II members of the expanding Sierra Club and the Appalachian Mountain Club discovered L. L. Bean and demand increased for outdoor recreation equipment. In 1954 Bean opened a women's department and added more items for children. Maine's outdoor recreational opportunities became very popular, and visitors from cities in the Northeast began to frequent the waterways, lakes, and forests of the "vacation state." The Appalachian Trail, which begins at Mount Katahdin, and Acadia National Park in Bar Harbor also attracted increasing numbers of vacationing customers to the L. L. Bean store. By the 1960s a nationwide interest in ecology, the environment and personal fitness added to the L. L. Bean customer base, but his sales were limited by his company's old-fashioned methods (one million mailing labels were typed by hand). In the 1960s his reputation spread by word of mouth rather than advertising, and the small Freeport store was expanded many times to accommodate growing numbers of shoppers.

Until his death in Florida, Bean remained president of the L. L. Bean Company, and his booming voice was commonly heard in the rambling Freeport store. He still answered many customer inquiries with a handwritten letter, a folksy practice that continued to distinguish the company. The basic selection of merchandise that Bean had sold since 1912—woodsman's boots, chamois shirts, and tan cotton chino pants—remained unchanged, and the same design or materials for many products were still being used fifty years later. In addition to the traditional merchanise, however, the catalog contained hundreds of new items designed for outdoor leisure activities. Bean's rustic Freeport store, decorated with a stuffed moose and a trout pond, became Maine's second biggest tourist attraction, drawing more than two million visitors each year. The small specialty retail and mail-order catalogue company founded in 1912 was operated in later years by Mr. Bean's grandson, Leon A. Gorman. Despite dramatic growth in products and sales, L. L. Bean's image as the embodiment of Yankee virtue and value has continued to attract loyal customers throughout the United States and abroad.

• Bean wrote a book addressing his favorite pastimes: *Hunting-Fishing-Camping* (1942). L. L. Bean, *My Story* (1939), provides autobiographical information. See also M. R. Montgomery, *In Search of L. L. Bean* (1984). His obituary is in the *New York Times*, 7 Feb. 1967.

PETER C. HOLLORAN

BEARD, Charles Austin (27 Nov. 1874–1 Sept. 1948), political scientist, historian, and pundit, was born near Knightstown, Indiana, the son of William Henry Beard, a farmer and banker, and Mary Payne. The family was of a Quaker heritage, and Charles attended a local Quaker academy before going on to DePauw University, from which he graduated in 1898. At DePauw his teachers introduced him to modern social theorists, including Herbert Spencer, Karl Marx, Lester Frank Ward, and Alfred Marshall. He first confronted the conditions of urban and industrial life in the summer of 1896, when he visited Chicago, and the experience, according to Mary Ritter (Mary R. Beard), whom he married in 1900, "made a great imprint upon his mind and influenced his future activities" (*Making of Charles A. Beard*, pp. 14–15).

After graduation Beard went to England (1899–1901), where he studied at Oxford and devoted himself to lecturing on behalf of the labor movement. He also helped to found Ruskin Hall (now College) at Oxford, for workers. His first book, *The Industrial Revolution* (1901), was written to provide workers with a historical perspective on their own contemporary social and economic circumstances. Although not a major work, the book forecast his lifelong commitment to using scholarship for human betterment by bringing historical knowledge to bear upon present problems.

In 1902, after a brief period of study at Cornell, Beard commenced graduate work at Columbia, completing his Ph.D. in 1904 with a dissertation entitled "The Office of the Justice of the Peace in England." He was appointed lecturer in history, working under the supervision of James Harvey Robinson, with whom he wrote *The Development of Modern Europe* (1907), a textbook that exemplified the "New History," a broader civilizational approach that sought to illuminate the present. In 1907, after three years as a lecturer, he received a regular professorial appointment in the department of public law, and he inaugurated undergraduate instruction in politics at Columbia. Beard also held positions with the New York Bureau of Municipal Research and its Training School for Public Service, both of which he later directed.

In 1917 Beard resigned from Columbia, protesting the denial of free expression of political opinions at the university. The immediate stimulus for his dramatic act was the firing of faculty opposed to American participation in the world war. Beard himself supported the war effort, but he insisted that, unless opponents could be freely heard, his own support might well be suspect. The moral authority of an intellectual, he announced, demands an "independence" that is "beyond all doubt."

After his resignation, Beard increased his responsibilities at the Bureau of Municipal Research and collaborated with his friend Robinson, who also resigned from Columbia, the philosopher John Dewey, the economist Wesley Clair Mitchell, and the journalist Herbert Croly to establish the New School for Social Research. He began lecturing at the Rand School for Social Science, a center of workers education partly modeled on Ruskin Hall, and with Mary Beard he helped to establish the Workers Education Bureau. By 1921, however, he had largely withdrawn from any institutional setting for his work, establishing himself at his farm in New Milford, Connecticut.

Beard's move out of academe was facilitated by his having inherited his father's wealth, but his intellectual milieu had always been larger than the university. His habitat was civic, not merely academic. His aim was to be a teacher in a sense that extended far beyond the classroom. In 1921, writing in the *Freeman,* he declared that for "the true teacher, the restless searcher-out-of-things," the printing press had created a "greater forum than the narrow school room." Henceforth Beard understood himself as an individual voice, doing his work with the printed page. Other leaders of American social science, most notably political scientist Charles Merriam, Jr., of Chicago, were moving in a different direction, forging the modern alliance of academic scholarship, the foundations, and government agencies. Beard rejected this model. He would be beholden to no one; one of his reasons for leaving the Bureau of Municipal Research was the difficulty his "radicalism" posed for the work of fundraising. He willingly gave up the resources such institutions could supply and the power they could confer. He preferred independence. One of Beard's friends, the writer Matthew Josephson, observed that he had "never met anywhere a man who so thoroughly enjoyed his own sense of freedom or who was so jealous of his intellectual and moral independence" (*Virginia Quarterly Review* 25 [1949]: 585).

Although Beard spent only a few years in the classroom (he returned briefly for a term at Columbia in 1939 and for a year at Johns Hopkins in 1940–1941), his whole career and even his intellectual style, as Forrest McDonald has pointed out in *Pastmasters,* bear the marks of a great teacher. Whether at Columbia or in the larger society he won over his auditors and readers by being at once the knowing skeptic and the visionary idealist. There was an Olympian quality to his presence on the lecture platform; he was always the orator, never merely a speaker. Eric Goldman, who studied with Beard at Hopkins, recalled "the rugged body, the great head with the sharply outlined features, the magnificent wrath and the simple compassion, the wit lashing out against any pretension—all this made Charles Beard on the lecture platform a rousing symbol of what American liberalism wanted to be" (Beale, p. 6).

Beard's rhetoric, whether on the platform or on the printed page, achieved its power by giving architectonic form to complex issues and themes. Urgency and directness characterized his language. He expressed his ideas in spontaneous and clear form; his language never had the feel of refinement. He was this century's most influential scholar of American politics and history, and he was the most prolific as well. He wrote forty-seven books, plus seven more with Mary Beard and twenty-four with other collaborators. He published more than 150 articles and in excess of sixty scholarly book reviews. All added up to more than 20,000 pages of published prose. When he died, his books had sold more than eleven million copies; at least three remain landmarks: *An Economic Interpretation of the Constitution* (1913), *The Economic Origins of Jeffersonian Democracy* (1915), and, with Mary Beard, *The Rise of American Civilization* (1927). Other especially important ones (besides those noted below) include *American Government and Politics* (1910), *The Supreme Court and the Constitution* (1912), *The Economic Basis of Politics* (1922), and, again with Mary Beard, *America in Midpassage* (1939).

Beard's objective as a teacher, whether in the classroom or in the public realm, was to open closed minds. "When I come to the end," he once remarked, "my mind will still be beating its wings against the bars of thought's prison" (Beale, p. 7). He did not hesitate to stretch a point in the interest of provoking fresh thought and encouraging critical attitudes toward conventional beliefs. "A good teacher much exaggerate," he confided to a student (Beale, p. 224). His purpose, he told Arthur Schlesinger in 1915, was to "rough hew" the material (Nore, p. 59). That would prompt critical reflection; let others do the work of correcting errors of detail and doing "the balanced job."

Beard was always more than a scholar and pundit. He was an activist—joining picket lines in strikes, participating in various progressive causes, and working in behalf of political candidates. Indeed, Beard the Connecticut farmer wrote the legislation for that state's milk code in the 1930s in the midst of conflict among farmers and dairies.

At the time he resigned from Columbia, Beard was notorious for his book on the Constitution (a *New York Times* editorial assured the public that the resignation improved Columbia), but his reputation then rested less on his work as a historian than as a municipal expert. He had written *American City Government* (1912), the first textbook on urban politics; he was an editor of the *National Municipal Review* (1912–1914); and he was an officer in the National Municipal League. Even while at Columbia he spent three afternoons a week downtown conducting studies for the Bureau of Municipal Research and working with students in its Training School for Public Service. In terms characteristic of academic progressives, he described the aims of the bureau as "the application of continuous and experimental research" to municipal administration (C. A. Beard, *Government Research* [1926], pp. 3–4). He was the author and coauthor of several major reports on state and local administration and a strong advocate of city planning. His textbook on urban politics gave prominence to planning, which Beard defined as "the substitution of scientific organization of prudent forethought for the largely fortuitous results of real estate speculation" (*Political Science Quarterly* 26 [1911]: 714).

His stature as a municipal expert resulted in an invitation to Tokyo, where he wrote the report *Administration and Politics of Tokyo* (1922–1923). He was instrumental in the founding of the Tokyo Bureau of

Municipal Research, for which he is remembered in Japan as a founder of city planning. When Tokyo was struck by a devastating earthquake in 1923, Beard was immediately summoned by the city's authorities to advise on reconstruction policies. It was from the perspective of Japan that Charles and Mary Beard determined to write *The Rise of American Civilization,* their synthetic appraisal of American history and culture. This work—and their other coauthored works—were full collaborations between Charles and Mary. They divided up the work, with Charles primarily responsible for the political and economic themes and Mary the social and cultural ones. But they read and revised each other's work. Charles once compared their collaboration to that of two lawyers who talk through a brief and then divide the labor of preparing it.

Writing *The Rise of American Civilization* was a civic act and an affirmation of American nationalism. But it was nationalist in a particularly worldly way. That this work of giving narrative form to their understanding of American civilization was prompted by contact with another culture provides a telling insight into the Beards' sense of national affiliation. Charles Beard's idea of American distinctiveness was grounded in a firsthand and sustained knowledge of Western Europe, Eastern Europe, and Asia. He was an unembarrassed patriot, but he was proudly cosmopolitan as well, never lapsing into a parochial nationalism.

Beard's impact on the study of American history and politics was transformative. When he entered Columbia, John W. Burgess presided over the faculty of political science, and the prescribed approach to the field was narrowly juridical, formal, and abstract. Beard opened up the study of politics. He learned from such teachers as Frank Goodnow, a political scientist pioneering the study of cities, and E. R. A. Seligman, the economist; and he was especially influenced by Arthur F. Bentley's book, *The Political Process* (1908), a pioneering realistic analysis of American politics. Beard rooted political analysis not in doctrines and formal categories, but, as he put in *Politics* (1908), in "social realities" (p. 6).

For Beard humans were more than political animals, even in their political activities. It was incumbent upon political science to consider the actions of the "whole man" in political life. He emphasized the relation of economic aspects of life to politics. He learned from his early study of Marx but also from the domesticated version of Marx presented in E. R. A. Seligman's book, *The Economic Interpretation of History* (1902). For both Seligman and Beard, economic interpretation was a liberal historiography, not a Marxist one. They accepted much of Marx's rendering of political economy but not his philosophy or his revolutionary politics. When they referred to economic interest there was a certain unclarity about its meaning; usually it did not refer to class interest in a Marxian sense (in relation to the ownership of production and the commodification of labor). They emphasized sector interests (landed interest, sectional interests, commercial interests, the traction interest, and the like), and

such interests were easily assimilated into liberal pluralism.

In *An Economic Interpretation of the Constitution,* Beard associated his analysis of economic interest with James Madison's (1751–1836) discussion of the political implications of "different degrees and kinds of property" in the *Federalist Papers,* number ten. At other times, however, Beard insisted that his understanding of the connection between economics and politics was no more than the common sense heard in any midwestern parlor during his youth.

In arguing that interest or economic advantage motivated the political elite who devised and achieved the ratification of the Constitution, Beard committed an act of desacralization. This was, however, only one of his intentions, for he also aimed to reform scholarship, to "suggest new lines of historical research" (*An Economic Interp.,* p. xix). *An Economic Interpretation of the Constitution* was designed in its method to exemplify the approach to political analysis that he had outlined in *Politics* five years earlier. The law, he wrote, "is not an abstract thing"; it becomes "real" only as it intervenes in society and affects life. "Separated from the social and economic fabric by which it is, in part, conditioned and which, in turn, it helps to condition, it has no reality" (*An Economic Interp.,* p. 12). He took aim at the notion—conventional among lawyers as well as political scientists—that the Constitution proceeded in a moment of inspiration (divine or otherwise) "from the whole people" (*An Economic Interp.,* p. 10). It was, he argued, a political document, the product of historical processes and conflicts. The new republic was created because a group that stood to benefit from its own work brilliantly devised a realistic instrument of government and pushed through its ratification.

The *New York Times* denounced *An Economic Interpretation* when it appeared, as did President Woodrow Wilson, among others. But many scholars and liberals immediately recognized its political and historiographical significance. In explicitly acknowledging and building upon the work of Frederick Jackson Turner, *An Economic Interpretation* transformed historical study in the United States. If Beard's formulation of the politics of the constitutional era has not survived in its particularity, his argument that the Constitution must be understood as the product of social negotiation and conflict has become an operative assumption of scholarship.

Challenges to Beard's book have been both empirical and conceptual. Closer study of both the founders and the state ratification struggles (study he invited) has undermined the categories of interest he proposed. Moreover, his concept of economic interest has itself become less and less clear. At times he seemed to propose the narrowest kind of personal interest to explain support of the Constitution, and this has not proven to be the case. At other times he referred to a broader notion of class formation and interest, and this understanding of the era of the Revolution and the Constitution remains a fertile stimulant to research.

Subsequent scholarship has not effectively displaced his characterization of the movement for the Constitution as a conservative movement, a reaction by an elite challenged by new social groups and new political forms.

Beard's desire to make historical scholarship bear upon the present was one of the impulses behind what he and Robinson called the "New History." Existing textbooks ended their stories well before the present: European history ended with the French Revolution, and American histories rarely ranged beyond the Civil War. Such chronological restraint diminished the usefulness of history for understanding the events unfolding in the daily newspaper. In "A Plea for Greater Stress upon the Modern Period," an address to high school teachers in 1908, Beard insisted that "history which does not emerge into the living present is . . . sterile when viewed from the standpoint of public need, however diverting it may be as subject of interested speculation on the part of private persons." He was particularly concerned with the problems and possibilities of the urban and industrial society that emerged after the Civil War. His first American history textbook, *Contemporary American History* (1914), covered that period. At the Bureau of Municipal Research he confronted the urban present directly.

In his work with the bureau and in his scholarship before World War I, Beard was committed to the political efficacy of the objective fact; facts would translate directly into social progress. In the 1920s Beard came to understand the limits of this approach to knowledge and reform, and he challenged these assumptions when he found them in the monumental report of the President's Committee on Social Trends. Commissioned by President Herbert Hoover, sponsored by the Social Science Research Council, funded by the Rockefeller Foundation, and orchestrated by Charles Merriam of the University of Chicago, *Recent Social Trends* (1933) represented the highest ambitions of American social science. It aimed to guide public policy by presenting social facts in an impartial manner, thus supplying the basis for intelligent action. Beard rejected the underlying assumptions of the report, denying that the objective assembly of facts was possible and that such facts would of themselves lead to any conclusion. Facts had to be framed in compelling interpretive structures, or narratives. With *The Rise of American Civilization,* Charles and Mary Beard offered the public just such a narrative. For Charles it represented a new orientation to the public, the orientation of a writer, of a scholar no longer affiliated with institutions, of a publicist rather than an expert. He had become more the historian and less the expert in political science.

At the same time he began to reflect seriously about European theories of historicism and the problem of objectivity in historical writing. From the "new physics," invented in the first decades of the century by Albert Einstein, Neils Bohr, and Werner Heisenberg, Beard borrowed the notion of the "frame of reference" to describe the relation of facts to the author and to the reader of history. Finding support for his concern in the writings of the Italian philosopher Benedetto Croce, Beard denied that facts themselves carried any inherent interpretation. He believed that the historian's selection of facts and periodization were shaped in a significant degree by contemporary concern. This, he believed, was a virtue, a strength of historical study, not a disqualifying vice. If facts were objective, subject to empirical verification, narratives were not. Histories were, therefore, acts of interpretation.

Professional history in the United States had been founded upon German historian Leopold von Ranke's dictum that the historian's task was to "describe the past as it actually was." In "Written History as an Act of Faith" (1934) and in "That Noble Dream" (1935), Beard insisted that such was not possible. "Every historian's work—that is, his selection of facts, his emphasis, his omissions, his organization, and his methods of presentation—bear relation to his own personality and the age and circumstances in which he lives" (*Am. Historical Review* 44 [1939]: 572). Such contingent truth, it seemed to Beard, liberated historians from presumptuous and dangerous claims to absolute truth, but it also conferred heavy obligations upon them. As Beard put it in *The Open Door at Home* (1934), the historian becomes a "statesman, without portfolio, to be sure, but with a kindred sense of public responsibility" (p. 138).

To many historians, Beard's relativism threatened the foundations of their profession. It seemed to invite subjectivity. Beard's refusal of absolute truth was more threatening to the profession than was the pragmatism of John Dewey, with whom he is often associated in their common revolt against formalism. But Dewey protected his position from charges of subjectivity in a way that Beard did not. Dewey would fix truth in a contingent and relativistic world by empowering inclusive communities of inquirers, something that was recognizably related to (if not precisely assimilable to) the work of professional disciplinary communities. Beard, however, envisioned the historian as he himself worked: as a solitary maker of narratives. Always an individualist, Beard relied upon the moral integrity of the historian, not upon a professional community. Beard believed that the unattached or independent intellectual belonging to no class could and ought to project an independent social and historical vision, a notion implicit in his reasons for resigning from Columbia in 1917.

It has been fashionable among historians to argue that Beard was out of his element in philosophy and that philosophers do not take him seriously. That is a convenient way of avoiding his disconcerting ideas. Beard was in fact widely read in the relevant philosophical literature of his time as well as in the sociology of knowledge being developed by Karl Mannheim. His challenge, necessarily rephrased, still faces the profession.

The Rise of American Civilization is the most powerful narrative synthesis of American history written in the twentieth century. It is informed by an appreciation of the material resources of the United States and a faith in the capacity of social knowledge to direct the use of the wealth to humane ends, to a national collective good. It is the story of the building of an industrial society from rich agricultural foundations. The Civil War, designated the "Second American Revolution," marked the moment and the mechanism of transition.

The Beards' history proceeds from material foundations: material conditions stimulate cultural change. But the process is not mechanical; it is, in their words, "cumulative . . . complex and interacting" (*Rise of Am. Civilization,* vol. 2, p. 358). Clearly, much of the story told by the Beards is about the misappropriations and injustices associated with industrialization, but the book ends on a hopeful note, anticipating a new dawn on the horizon of history. Until the 1950s, this remarkable history was America's history—it was the touchstone of professional scholarship, it reached a wide public, and it was distilled by the Beards and by others into schoolbooks read by the nation's children.

The Beards' sympathy for the fate of the mass of Americans did not translate into an effective evocation of the actual lives of workers, slaves, immigrants, or even, despite their feminist commitments, women. Reading their pages one would scarcely guess that American society was historically multiethnic. Yet they were not blind to the issue of America's cultural pluralism. They understood that no American history could be merely a projection of their own Anglo-Saxon Protestant culture. Charles had rejected the Teutonic theories of Burgess at Columbia, and he rejected the notion of national identity as an ethnic inheritance. Instead he offered a constructed vision that might define America and provide the terms for a just society. *The Rise of American Civilization* sought to supply that vision, and in a successor volume, *The American Spirit* (1942), the Beards were more explicit in their aim of giving currency to humanistic and democratic values that they pulled out of the American past.

During the 1930s and 1940s Beard worried that the domestic reforms begun by the New Deal would be sidetracked or cut short by foreign war. In 1934, with George H. E. Smith, he wrote *The Idea of National Interest* and *The Open Door at Home,* two books urging Americans to focus upon building a humane and democratic continental nation. If national interest (or general humanity) demanded American military involvement in Europe or Asia, then, he argued, the president was obliged to be more honest, more open, and more of an educator of the public. He suspected that Franklin D. Roosevelt was retreating from this work of persuasion so crucial to a democratic polity and was instead secretly orchestrating an Asian incident that would bring the United States into the war. These writings on Roosevelt and foreign policy were widely denounced by his fellow liberals. Lewis Mumford, in particular, attacked Beard savagely, writing in a letter to the *Saturday Review of Literature* (2 Dec. 1944) that Beard was an "abettor of tyranny, sadism, and human defilement." In 1948, when Beard was honored by the National Institute of Arts and Letters with its gold medal, Mumford resigned, and the organization felt obliged to emphasize that the award was for a whole life's work.

After Vietnam, Watergate, and much else, one may look with more sympathy on Beard's suspicions about the emerging national security state and about the temptation of democratic governments to lie and to pursue secret and even illegal policies in foreign affairs. But when Beard died in New Haven, Connecticut, he was admired for his early work and shunned for his recent writings.

The Republic (1943), one of Beard's last works, was his most popular book, selling over four million copies. It was not one of his better books, but it was his favorite. One can see why; it reveals Beard in his most characteristic mode of public teacher and moralist. The book takes the form of a dialogue between Beard and an imaginary educated American citizen called Dr. Robert Smyth. Beard had a gift for sensing the questions on the minds of men and women of education and goodwill, and this book makes explicit that quality of his work, for it answered those questions in a public way. For "Dr. Smyth," as for his many readers and auditors over the years, Beard played the historian and the analyst of the present, the patriot and the critic. Here is Beard the creative skeptic, the man whom Carl Becker had etched two decades before while reviewing one of his books for the *Nation* (22 Nov. 1922): "He is an exasperated critic and a warm-hearted friend of suffering humanity. . . . Perfectly aware of human folly, he never quite loses faith in human nature."

Beard refused to be bounded, and he is a standing rebuke to the professional impulse toward insularity and specialization. While he recognized the value of monographs and acknowledged his dependence on specialized research, he asked more of scholars who would serve the public. He feared that scholars and administrative professionals, like the city planners with whom he had for so long associated professionally, were in danger of becoming wholly absorbed in narrow technical issues. In 1930, as he responded to a request for advice from Abraham Flexner, who was setting up the Institute for Advanced Study in Princeton, Beard reflected that "the older I grow, the more I feel the urgency of more thinking at the top, more bold, free, imaginative, integrating thinking" (Letter of 21 Dec. 1930, Beard Letters, Columbia Univ.).

Few historians have so effectively negotiated the borders of scholarly discourse and public discourse. Not only did he establish the research agenda of professional history for a half-century, but he also reached the public directly. He had a talent for importing the concerns of the educated public into fruitful scholarly research programs. Beard was not an original thinker, but he was always provocative and illuminating. He personified the historian as citizen. As historian Howard K. Beale wrote in memorializing him, Beard embodied "scholarship made vital in public affairs" (Beale, p. 159).

• There is no collection of Beard papers; there are miscellaneous letters scattered in various collections, the largest group of which are in the Harry Elmer Barnes Papers at the University of Wyoming Library. There are a few letters collected at Butler Library, Columbia University. Mary Beard collected some biographical material into a useful memoir in *The Making of Charles A. Beard* (1955). The best scholarly account of Beard's life and work is Ellen Nore, *Charles A. Beard: An Intellectual Biography* (1983). For an extremely perceptive appraisal by a major historian of the succeeding generation, see Richard Hofstadter, *The Progressive Historians* (1968). Howard K. Beale, ed., *Charles A. Beard: An Appraisal* (1954), contains essays by many scholars who knew him, each considering a different aspect of his career. Forrest McDonald provides a penetrating analysis of Beard's work in "Charles A. Beard," in *Pastmasters*, ed. Marcus Cunliffe and Robin W. Winks (1969), pp. 110–41. Appraisal of his historiographical ideas and procedures may be found in Morton White, *Social Thought in America* (1957); Cushing Strout, *The Pragmatic Revolt in American History: Carl Becker and Charles Beard* (1958); Lee Benson, *Turner and Beard: American Historical Writing Reconsidered* (1960); and Peter Novick, *That Noble Dream: The "Objectivity" Question and the American Historical Profession* (1988). An obituary is in the *New York Times*, 1 Sept. 1948.

THOMAS BENDER

BEARD, Frank (6 Feb. 1842–28 Sept. 1905), originator of "Chalk Talks," popular lectures illustrated with rapid chalk drawings, was born Thomas Francis Beard in Cincinnati, Ohio, the son of James Henry Beard and Mary Caroline Carter, artists. His father and his uncle, William Holbrook Beard, were well-known portrait, genre, and animal painters. His education began in Cincinnati and continued at the Academy in Painesville, Ohio, following his family's move there in the mid-1850s. He began drawing early and while still a boy sent sketches to all the major periodicals. His first cartoon was published in 1856 in *Yankee Notions*, one of America's earliest illustrated, humorous newspapers. When he was eighteen, his cartoon "Why Don't You Take It?" met with great success when published by Currier & Ives and distributed by the Republicans as a campaign document; it generated orders for over 100,000 copies. As a young adult he moved frequently, joining his brother James, an artist, in New York in 1859 and staying with family members in Cincinnati and Painesville in 1860.

At the outbreak of the Civil War he returned to Painesville to enlist in General Jack S. Casement's Seventh Ohio Regiment but was turned down because of a hearing deficiency. However, he traveled with the regiment, became good friends with the general, and considered himself "a soldier." During the 1860s he served as a special cartoonist with the Army of the Potomac for *Frank Leslie's Illustrated News* and *Harper's Weekly*, and his war sketches later served as the basis for his "100 Original Drawings" that illustrate Jesse Bowman Young's 1894 book, *What a Boy Saw in the Army: A Story of Sight-Seeing and Adventure in the War for the Union*. In 1862 he opened a studio in Cincinnati, became a member of the Sketch Club, and unsuccessfully applied for a lieutenant's commission in the

U.S. Army. He returned to New York in 1865 to work briefly as a designer and engraver before spending considerable time as a self-described "tramp." In 1867 he returned to Painesville to marry Helen Augusta Goodwin, a former schoolmate and daughter of the local Methodist minister; they settled in New York.

Beard entered the booming field of comic illustration along with Thomas Nast, Edward Jump, Joseph Keppler, and the Gillam brothers and was a mentor to Frederick Burr Opper. During the late 1860s and throughout the 1870s he was one of the most prolific cartoonists for such short-lived comic papers as *Phunny Phellow and Wild Oats* and Frank Leslie's various comic magazines, including *Budget of Fun, Jolly Joker*, and *Comic Monthly*. He gained recognition as a book illustrator in 1871 when Dr. Edward Eggleston's bestseller, *Hoosier School Master*, sold some 500,000 copies. He became more widely known in 1872 when he "profusely illustrated" Fletcher G. Welch's book, *That Convention; or, Five Days a Politician*, a humorous account of the Democratic convention in Cincinnati that nominated Horace Greeley for president. He gained additional renown in 1874 through his illustrations for Eggleston's *Circuit Rider*.

Beard's talent for humorous drawing and his interest in educational entertainment found a natural outlet with the establishment of Chautauqua, a religious, cultural, and recreational center on Lake Chautauqua, New York, in 1874. He was part of the assembly's first summer program and was listed as a regular feature during the next fifteen years, entertaining groups of all ages with his illustrated lectures or "Chalk Talks." He was known to set "the audience wild with excitement and laughter" with his rapid, inventive drawings and his own dramatic gestures. Regarded by contemporaries as both "the clown of Chautauqua" and "a serious soul" he was admired for his ability to blend humor with religion. Although he and his wife had no children, Beard took a special interest in youth education, establishing the "Children's Hour" as a daily feature in 1876 and publishing his first book, *The Chalk Lesson: The Blackboard in the Sunday School*, in 1877. He expanded his involvement with the Chautauquan movement as it began to spread across the United States in the late 1870s, and he traveled the Chautauqua circuit for seventeen years, visiting new Chautauquan sites and lecturing in nearby cities. He was heralded as "The Celebrated New York Chalk Talk Artist" and attracted admission-paying crowds in New York, Massachusetts, North Carolina, Georgia, Kentucky, and Ohio.

While employed by *Scribner's*, Beard also submitted works to the *Illustrated Christian Weekly* and the *Chautauqua Assembly Herald*. He joined the staff of the humorous Republican paper, the *Judge*, when it was founded in 1881 and was professor and chair of aesthetics and painting at Syracuse University from 1881 to 1884, where he was long remembered as "a wizard with chalk." Concerned with the effectiveness of illustration, he wrote articles on caricature, distinguishing between character artists, who, he argued, merely varied facial expressions, and true caricaturists who devoted attention to the individuality of the entire figure. He numbered William Hogarth and Thomas Nast among the former, and Gustave Doré and himself among the latter. When he became editor of the *Judge* in 1884, during the presidential campaign, between Grover Cleveland and James G. Blaine, he merged political interests with artistic rivalry and produced hundreds of caustic images parodying Nast and other Republican defectors, many of which were published as color lithographs. A few years later, when the art staff was restructured, he left the paper and shifted his attention from political to religious reform.

Beard's involvement with the *Ram's Horn*, a Methodist weekly based in Chicago, Illinois, began around 1885 and continued until his death. He submitted drawings and poetry, became an editor in 1890, and received special acclaim for his highly charged temperance cartoons. He also wrote and illustrated religious books, including *Picture Puzzles or How to Read the Bible by Symbols, Designed Especially for the Boys and Girls* (1899), *The True Life of Christ* (1899), *Fifty Great Cartoons by Frank Beard* (1899), *One Hundred Sermon Pictures* (1902), and *"Blasts" from the Ram's Horn* (1902), before his life as an educator through illustration ended suddenly when he died in Chicago of a cerebral hemorrhage.

• A collection of Beard's *Harper's Weekly* and *Ram's Horn* sketches, illustrated notes, and family records are in the Lake County Historical Society, Mentor, Ohio. Records of "Chalk Talks," published works, and scrapbook clippings of his lectures and travels are in the Chautauqua Institution Archives, Chautauqua, N.Y. His articles include "Caricature," *Manhattan* 3 (Feb. 1884): 134–43, and "The Age of Caricature," *Chautauquan* 7 (Jan. 1887): 206–7. For comparison with other cartoonists, see Roger A. Fischer, "Mugwump's Monkey: Thomas Nast, 1884 Cartoon Caricature," *Journal of the Thomas Nast Society* 4 (1990): 3–14; Albert B. Paine, *Thomas Nast: His Period and His Pictures* (1904); Stephen Becker, *Comic Art in America* (1959); and *The World Encyclopedia of Cartoons* (1980). Obituaries are in the *Chicago Tribune*, 29 Sept. 1905; *New York Times*, 30 Sept. 1905; *Painesville Telegraph*, 5 and 19 Oct. 1905; and *American Art Annual* 5 (1905–1906).

THELMA S. ROHRER

BEARD, George Miller (8 May 1839–23 Jan. 1883), physician, was born in Montville, Connecticut, the son of Spencer F. Beard, a Congregational minister, and Lucy A. Leonard. He attended Phillips Academy in Andover, Massachusetts. In 1858 he enrolled for college at Yale, graduating in 1862. After a year of medical school in New Haven, he worked for two years as acting assistant surgeon in the West Gulf Squadron of the U.S. Navy, completing medical school at New York's College of Physicians and Surgeons in 1866. During this same year he married Elizabeth Ann Alden of Westville, Connecticut, with whom he had at least one child.

Beard's brief but prolific research career following medical school touched on a wide range of topics, including the psychology of the Salem witch trials, the phenomenon of hypnotism, and the causes of and therapies for seasickness and hay fever, but he early showed intense interest in mental disease and medical electricity. He began to research the medical uses of electricity in partnership with A. D. Rockwell, a New York physician with whom he worked for many years. In 1868 Beard became a lecturer on diseases of the nerves at New York University. He began practicing at the Demilt Dispensary in New York City around 1870, specializing in nervous diseases and electrotherapeutics.

Beard founded the journal *Archives of Electrology and Neurology* in 1874. He helped to found the New York Society of Neurology and Electrology (which later merged with the New York Neurological Society), and he served often as a delegate to foreign scientific societies, including the International Medical Congress of London in 1881. Among his most significant—and most controversial—contributions to medical knowledge were his argument for the causal relationship between social phenomena and mental ailments and his assertion that the roots of mental illness lay in physical rather than moral disorder.

Beard is best known for his identification, study, and treatment of neurasthenia, a disease he named in 1869. In his popular book *American Nervousness: Its Causes and Consequences* (1881), he explained, "Nervousness is strictly deficiency or lack of nerve-force" (p. vi); that is, neurasthenia was in fact a form of "nerve-lessness." In keeping with the medical knowledge of his time, Beard assumed that the human body was a closed system fueled by nerve-force. If one area of the body became irritated or was overused, it drew more than its share of nerve-force, causing deprivation and illness in another bodily region. Although nervous debility had long been understood in this way, Beard coined the term "neurasthenia" and argued that the disease's etiology was derived from elements in its social and historical contexts (rather than only from the patient's inherent weaknesses), simultaneously granting its sufferers medical legitimacy. Because neurasthenic patients suffered from an immense variety of vague ailments with no traceable physical origin, their claims to illness had usually been dismissed as either the result of overindulgence of physical appetites or emotional foolishness and malingering. Although Beard could not prove the correctness of his theory with the technology then available, he speculated that neurasthenia was "a physical not a mental state" (*American Nervousness*, p. 17) and concluded that its sufferers deserved to be taken seriously by medical practitioners. He argued that this physical debility was brought about by the very elements in American industrial society that, he thought, marked the United States as superior to other nations and peoples: "steam-power, the periodical press, the telegraph, the sciences, and the mental activity of women" (*American Nervousness*, p. vi). The majority of neurasthenic patients were white, educated, upper-class, and urban-dwelling, so Beard concluded that this elite group of Americans, like America in relation to the rest of the world, was biologically destined for social superiority (despite their apparent physical inferiority); their highly sensitive nervous systems were a mark of higher evolution. As medical historian Charles Rosenberg explained, Beard's theory of the etiology of neurasthenia was "as much social comment as medical theory." In addition to its inherent nationalism, it "not only implied a justification of social relationships as they were, but—with seeming inconsistency—constituted an indictment of many of this society's failings," such as "premature industrialism," "materialism," and the anxious way of life that accompanied these phenomena (p. 256).

In keeping with Beard's argument for the organic origin of neurasthenia was his claim that insanity was a physical ailment with an organic cause. Along with other neurologists and social workers, he worked tirelessly within the asylum reform movement, attempting to improve treatment of the insane as well as to grant them the dignity and credibility of physical rather than moral illness. He helped to found the National Association for the Protection of the Insane and the Prevention of Insanity in 1880, insisting in a paper titled "Why We Need a National Association for the Protection of the Insane" (1880) that "it is no disgrace to be crazy" (p. 149). He and his fellow reformers in the association incurred much public censure for their views when, in 1881 and 1882, they attempted to save Charles Guiteau, the assassin of President James Garfield, from the death penalty on the grounds that he was insane and therefore not responsible for his action.

Beard's significance in his field derives from his argument for the methodical study of neurosis, his efforts to end social condemnation of its sufferers, and his understanding of the connections between mental illness and social organization. Although some viewed Beard as a charlatan, disliked his egotism, and dismissed his theory of neurasthenia as well as his work on behalf of the insane, many others in his time admired his work and his vision. Rosenberg argued that by the early 1890s Beard's theories of neurasthenia "had become part of the office furniture of most physicians" (p. 258). Even on his deathbed in New York City, Beard argued for the importance of his theories and reform efforts; he is reported to have said, "I hope others will carry on my work" (Morton, p. 134).

• A modest collection of Beard papers is in the Yale University Library. Beard's best-known writings besides *American Nervousness* are *The Medical Use of Electricity* (1867), *Our Home Physician* (1869), *Legal Responsibility in Old Age, Based on Researches into the Relation of Age to Work* (1874), and *A Practical Treatise on Nervous Exhaustion (Neurasthenia): Its Symptoms, Nature, Sequences, Treatment* (1880). For information on his life see Charles L. Dana, "Dr. George M. Beard: A Sketch of His Life and Character, with Some Personal Reminiscences," *Archives of Neurology and Psychiatry* 10 (1923): 427–35; and A. D. Rockwell, *Rambling Recollections: An Autobiography* (1920). The most thorough treatment is Charles E. Rosenberg, "The Place of George M. Beard in Nineteenth-century Psychiatry," *Bulletin of the History of Medicine* 36, no. 3 (1962): 245–59, which contains a wealth of useful bibliographical footnotes. For Beard's theories in their historical context see Barbara Sicherman, "The Uses of a Diagnosis: Doctors, Patients, and Neurasthenia," in *Sickness and Health in America: Readings in the History of Medicine and Public Health*, ed. Judith Walzer Leavitt and Ronald L. Numbers (1978), pp. 25–38. Obituaries include W. J. Morton, "Obituary: George Miller Beard, A.M., M.D.," New York," *Journal of Nervous and Mental Disorders* 10 (1883): 130–34; *Medical Register of New York, New Jersey and Connecticut* (1883): 218; and *Boston Medical and Surgical Journal* 108 (1883): 116, 325–26.

JENNIFER S. TUTTLE

BEARD, James Andrews (5 May 1903–23 Jan. 1985), cookbook author and American food authority, was born in Portland, Oregon, the son of John Beard, an assistant appraiser of the Port of Portland, and Mary Elizabeth Jones, a hotel and boardinghouse owner. Beard's formidable mother exercised a powerful influence on her only child. The enticing aromas and tastes of her kitchen dominated his memories of childhood. Recipes and food lore she taught him occupy more than half of his 1964 autobiography, *Delights and Prejudices*. She encouraged his youthful acting and singing and his dream of a career on the musical stage. After a brief attendance at Reed College, 1920–1921 (he was expelled after a homosexual incident), his mother supported his decision to study opera in London. During his two-year stay abroad, 1922–1924, he traveled to France and Italy, storing up memories of food while pursuing his musical career.

Vocal problems led Beard to abandon singing; his acting success was minimal. Not until 1938 did cooking become primary when with two partners he began a catering service for cocktail parties in mid-Manhattan. Success led to a commission to write a cookbook in six weeks' time, published as *Hors d'Oeuvre and Canapés, with a Key to the Cocktail Party* (1940). *Cook It Outdoors*, the first serious book on outdoor cookery, followed in 1941.

The World War II draft led to a six-month stay in the Army Air Corps; after his discharge he managed overseas clubs for merchant seamen from 1943 to 1945 in Puerto Rico, Rio de Janeiro, Naples, and Marseilles.

In the spring of 1946 Beard was invited to give cooking demonstrations on NBC-TV. Sponsored by the Borden Company, "Elsie Presents James Beard in 'I Love to Eat!'" made him television's first chef. "At last—a chance to cook and act at the same time" (*Delights*, p. 302). The show lasted only two years, but his reputation grew as he continued to publish. The extensive publicity that the publisher provided for *The Fireside Cook Book* (1949; rpt., *The Fireside Cookbook*, 1984) made Beard a household name; *The James Beard Cookbook*, a 75-cent paperback, became an unexpected runaway national bestseller in 1959.

Beard built on his reputation. He crisscrossed the country, lecturing and giving cooking demonstrations. He acted as a spokesman for wine and cognac importers, endorsed new culinary implements and convenience foods, and invented the field of food consulting—advising restaurants on menus and manufacturers on products. With editorial assistance he poured out magazine articles, weekly syndicated newspaper columns, and more cookbooks. In 1955 he started his own cooking school, later remodeling the kitchen of his Greenwich Village townhouse to accommodate classes. A genial, friendly man, he welcomed newcomers to the field of food writing more as colleagues than as competitors, providing book-jacket blurbs and hosting parties to introduce their books.

Critics attacked Beard's eclectic approach to food and his acceptance of new products. *Newsweek* quoted one critic in 1977 as saying, "He even admits he eats marshmallows. He's worked with all the corporations and he never knocks a product." Beard insisted he only endorsed products he liked and claimed he had refused substantial fees to praise others he had tested and found wanting. He was proud of the range of styles taught in his books and cooking school. "We have taught our pupils great French dishes, great Italian dishes, some English and Oriental dishes, and regional dishes of America. During the preparation of these, the pupils learn to make the mother sauces and variations of them; how to roast, broil, poach and bake," he wrote (*Delights*, p. 311).

The massive 877-page *James Beard's American Cookery* (1972) showed his eclecticism at its best. In 1949 he had asserted that "America has the opportunity, as well as the resources, to create for herself a truly national cuisine that will incorporate all that is best in the traditions of the many people who have crossed the seas to form our new, still-young nation" (*Fireside Cookbook*, p. 11). With more than 1,500 recipes in *American Cookery*, he set out to demonstrate what had been achieved. He drew on nineteenth-century advice books and cooking manuals; on recipe books published by church groups, missionary societies, and women's clubs; on memories of the food cooked by his mother and her friends; and on examples he had observed in his travels across the United States. He described immigrant dishes like veal parmesan that had become part of the national diet, modified to suit American palates; he noted dishes that few realized had been invented in America, such as London broil and vichyssoise; three pages documented ten regional variations on baked beans. Even critics unwilling to accept the idea of a uniquely American cuisine found this classic work impressive.

Two final cookbooks capped Beard's writing career. *James Beard's Theory and Practice of Good Cooking* (1977) takes the reader inside his cooking classroom. Focusing on the why as well as the how, fourteen chapters explain specific techniques—boiling, braising, baking, etc.—with master recipes illustrating each procedure, as well as more elaborate variations. *The New James Beard* (1981), arranged in the traditional appetizer-to-dessert chapters, complements his previous works with more than 1,000 recipes that extend the cook's range.

Reflecting his growing health problems, Beard's later books are much less lavish in their use of salt and butter. Always pudgy (despite his 6'3" frame), Beard eventually ballooned to over 300 pounds. Severe vascular and intestinal problems in the 1970s and 1980s led to a series of hospitalizations and surgical procedures before his death in New York City. Beard never married and left no survivors.

Beard was a pioneer in the culinary-awareness movement that swept the United States in the years after World War II. His cooking demonstrations, television appearances, and books both advanced and benefited from a growing interest in cooking. His favorite recipes were clear and direct, designed for the home kitchen and for the lover of good food, rather than the classic gourmet. His work gave American cuisine credibility and advanced his credo that "cooking is fun, especially good cooking" (*James Beard Cookbook*, p. 8).

• The most comprehensive public collection of manuscripts and other material relating to Beard is in the University of Wyoming American Heritage Center, Laramie, Wyo. Other significant collections are held by the Oregon Historical Society, Portland; the Eric V. Hauser Memorial Library, Reed College, Portland, Ore.; and the James Beard Foundation, New York City. His letters to Helen Evans Brown have been published as *Love and Kisses and a Halo of Truffles; Letters to Helen Evans Brown by James Beard*, ed. John Ferrone (1994). *Delights and Prejudices* (1964), his autobiography, also has a five-page index of recipes. *The James Beard Celebration Cookbook* (1990) has fragments of an uncompleted autobiography as well as memories and recipes contributed by his friends. Robert Clark, *James Beard: A Biography* (1993) and Evan Jones, *Epicurean Delight: The Life and Times of James Beard* (1990) are full-length studies. See also *Newsweek*, 11 Apr. 1977, p. 93, and *National Review*, 9 June 1972, pp. 653–54. Obituaries are in the *New York Times* and the *Washington Post*, both 24 Jan. 1985, and *New York*, 5 June 1985, pp. 68–69.

MILTON BERMAN

BEARD, James Carter (6 June 1837–15 Nov. 1913), artist, author, and naturalist, was born in Cincinnati, Ohio, the son of James Henry Beard, a portrait, genre, and animal painter, and Mary Caroline Carter. He spent his childhood there and in nearby Covington, Kentucky, then attended Miami University at Oxford, Ohio, during the mid-1850s. Later he read law in Cincinnati under Rutherford B. Hayes, the future president of the United States.

Although admitted to the Ohio bar in 1861, Beard chose to pursue a profession in the arts, a decision that directly conflicted with his father's wishes. However, this choice was undoubtedly supported by his siblings, all of whom became active as painters or illustrators, and by the friends and acquaintances he had made through his involvement in Cincinnati's cultural life. In the early 1860s he was part of the city's Sketch Club, where fellow members included the young painters Alexander Helwig Wyant and Henry Mosler, as well as Beard's brother Harry. During this same period he also befriended Jean François Edouard Hillen, a lithographer and special artist for *Frank Leslie's Illustrated Newspaper*, who perhaps influenced Beard's decision to become an illustrator. In 1862 Beard opened his own studio in the Queen City, and he was named professor of drawing and painting at the Ohio Female Seminary, a post he held until 1865. At this time he also attempted to operate his own academy of art, but this venture was short-lived.

In 1864 Beard's career was interrupted briefly by his service as a "hundred days" soldier for the Union forces, but he returned to the Cincinnati area by 25 December 1864. He married Martha J. Bray on that day; they had two children. The next several years of Beard's life are poorly documented, but it is known that his illustrations were being published in New York by 1866. However, it seems he did not leave the Cincinnati-Covington area for New York City until the early 1870s, when he became a staff artist for D. Appleton and Company and Charles Scribner's Sons.

During this time Beard also produced numerous articles and black-and-white illustrations of plant and animal life for periodicals such as *Harper's*, *Forest and Stream*, *Scientific American*, and the *Century*. In addition, he wrote and illustrated five books of his own, including two guides for art instruction, *The Artist's Manual: A Practical Handbook of Oil and Watercolor Painting and Crayon Drawing* (1877) and *Painting on China: What to Paint and How to Paint It* (1882), as well as *Little Workers: A History of God's Little Creatures that Labor without Hands* (1871), *Curious Homes and Their Tenants* (1897), and *Billy Possum* (1909), which includes some illustrations in color. Beard also provided illustrations for numerous other books, notably the McGuffey *Readers* (beginning in 1879), Theodore Roosevelt's *Hunting Trip of a Ranchman* (1885), and William Temple Hornaday's *American Natural History* (1904).

After his wife's death Beard left his home in Brooklyn and spent his remaining years in New Orleans, where he periodically wrote and illustrated articles for the *Daily Picayune* until his death.

• A collection of Beard's family letters, in addition to genealogical materials, are part of the Daniel Carter Beard Papers in the Manuscript Division of the Library of Congress. The Ohio Artists Project in Oberlin, Ohio, contains a vertical file on Beard that includes numerous short biographical articles and examples of his work that appeared in periodicals of his day. Details about his early family life can also be gleaned by reading Daniel Carter Beard's autobiography, *Hardly a Man Is Now Alive* (1939).

BRIAN L. MEGGITT

BEARD, James Henry (20 May 1811–4 Apr. 1893), artist, was born in Buffalo, New York, the son of Captain James Beard, a sailor (later a farmer), and Harriet Wolcott. The exact year of Beard's birth has been disputed, but 1811 is recorded in the family's Bible. His first artistic exposure is said to have been watching the designer and builder of a Lake Erie steamboat draw the figurehead for the vessel around 1818. Before his father died in 1823, Beard's family moved to Painesville, Ohio, where he obtained his earliest artistic training. He is said to have observed an itinerant por-

trait painter receive $10–15 for portraits, and after that artist moved on, Beard undertook similar images for $3–5 to great success. Beard may have studied with Reuben Hitchcock in Ravenna, Ohio, and in 1827 Jarvis Frary Hanks is said to have given him four lessons. Beard moved to Pittsburgh about 1828, working both as a painter and as a shipping clerk, and by 1830 he was living in Cincinnati, where he may have had further training at Franks's Academy of Fine Arts.

In Cincinnati Beard worked as a chair painter and later traveled down the Ohio and Mississippi Rivers painting portraits in Louisville and New Orleans. On 28 August 1833 he married Mary Caroline Carter, whose father ran flatboats to New Orleans; they had six children.

Beard was commissioned in 1835 to paint the battle flag of the Kentucky Volunteers for Texas Independence (Texas State Capitol), and about 1836 a now-lost portrait of a child and a dog firmly established Beard's reputation as a serious artist. Beard was the most significant painter to emerge in the 1830s in what was then the western United States. In 1837 Harriet Martineau wrote about him at some length in her *Retrospect of Western Travel* (1838). The artist thrived by painting portraits in Cincinnati, other major inland river cities, and the South, but he also began work as a genre painter. Charles Dickens, on his visit to Cincinnati in 1842, saw Beard's *Fagin* (c. 1840, Cincinnati Art Museum), the character from *Oliver Twist*.

Some of Beard's genre work had political overtones. *The Long Bill* (1839–1840, Cincinnati Art Museum) is a rustic allegory of the issues of the 1840 presidential campaign and includes portraits of William Henry Harrison serving cider and Martin Van Buren warming himself absent-mindedly by a stove. Beard had been exhibiting paintings in New York as early as 1838 and moved there in 1846 when *North Carolina Emigrants* (Procter & Gamble Art Collection) was well received at the National Academy of Design; it sold for the extraordinarily high price of $750. He was a charter member of the Century Association and was awarded an honorary professional membership in the National Academy of Design in 1848.

Beard returned in 1847 to Cincinnati, where he took an active role in the cultural life of the city. He painted both narrative subjects and portraits, although he probably discontinued experiments in sculpture; he had displayed a clay self-portrait bust at the Cincinnati Academy of Fine Arts exhibition in 1841. Among his eminent sitters were John Quincy Adams, Henry Clay, and Zachary Taylor. He painted several portraits of William Henry Harrison, both before and after his election to the presidency and premature death, including a full-length portrait (c. 1840) acquired by subscription by members of Cincinnati's Young Men's Mercantile Library Association (which also functioned as something of a civic collection). Beard's success in New York may have encouraged him to paint the monumental *The Last Victim of the Deluge* (1849, Cincinnati Art Museum), often considered his masterpiece (but now much damaged by aggressive past restorations). Exhibited in Cincinnati, Louisville, New Orleans, and New York for a fee of twenty-five cents, the picture was widely acclaimed and hung for many years in Cincinnati's Burnet Hotel.

In 1852 Beard was elected to Cincinnati's Literary Club; his list of papers presented is unrecorded (although he is documented as singing "'Feerinu,' with irresistible humor" at an informal meeting). He also completed for the club in 1855 an unfinished self-portrait by his late fellow member the artist Benjamin McConkey. He took on students, the most celebrated of whom, from 1859 until 1861, was Henry Mosler, later the first American artist to have a painting acquired by the French government.

During the Civil War Beard served as a captain in the Union army on the staff of General Lew Wallace. He was in New York in 1863, when he exhibited anthropomorphic genre paintings depicting domestic animals. The success of these works—he was known as "The American Landseer"—led him to paint them almost exclusively for the rest of his life. He moved permanently to New York in 1870 and was formally elected an academician of the National Academy of Design in 1872. Beard never traveled to Europe, turning down sponsored trips in the 1830s because he either hoped to pay for it himself or because the stipend did not include his wife. President Harrison apparently had chosen Beard for a diplomatic post in Europe, but the president's death a month into his term ended the artist's hopes of going in that role. Beard died at Flushing, Long Island.

• There is no large collection of Beard's papers. A large collection of transcribed contemporary newspaper clippings, letters, and photocopied material for an abandoned exhibition on the artist is in the artist files in the department of painting and sculpture, Cincinnati Art Museum. His significance to the art of the near Midwest has been noted in several accounts, in particular William H. Gerdts, *Art across America: Two Centuries of Regional Painting, 1710–1920* (1990). He is also concisely examined in Donald Ralph MacKenzie, "Painters in Ohio, 1788–1860, with a Biographical Index" (Ph.D. diss., Ohio State Univ., 1960), and in *The Golden Age: Cincinnati Painters of the Nineteenth Century Represented in the Cincinnati Art Museum* (1979). Dan Beard, *Hardly a Man Is Now Alive: The Autobiography of Dan Beard* (1939), written by Beard's son, provides several anecdotes of the artist's life. Contemporary sources are scarce, but Harriet Martineau, *Retrospect of Western Travel* (1838); Leon Mead, "The Apprenticeship of an Academician," *American Magazine* 9, no. 2 (Dec. 1888): 192–200; and an anonymous article in *The Art Journal* (1875): 366–68, are the most useful. Obituaries are in the *New York Tribune* and the *New York Herald*, 6 Apr. 1893.

JOHN WILSON

BEARD, Mary (14 Nov. 1876–4 Dec. 1946), public health administrator, was born in Dover, New Hampshire, the daughter of Ithamar Warren Beard, an Episcopalian minister, and Marcy Foster. At the age of twelve she contracted diphtheria and was confined to her home for an extended convalescence, during which she was cared for by a kind visiting nurse.

Deeply moved by the experience, she determined to devote her own life to nursing. She eventually dropped out of high school and then worked for several years as a private tutor in Boston, Massachusetts. In 1899 she enrolled in the New York Hospital School of Nursing. She graduated in 1903 and the next year began caring for sick people in their homes as a staff nurse for the year-old Visiting Nurse Association (VNA) of Waterbury, Connecticut.

In 1910 Beard resigned as VNA's director to work in the Laboratory of Surgical Pathology at Columbia University's College of Physicians and Surgeons, while also serving as a member of the American Society of Superintendents of Training Schools, an organization concerned with the education of nurses. Because of the urgent need for increased public health services, in 1912 she accepted the position of director of the Boston Instructive District Nursing Association (BIDNA), a charitable organization devoted to treating and preventing illness among Boston's poor. Under her direction BIDNA continued to provide basic health services, including school nursing and caring for patients with tuberculosis and other contagious diseases, while becoming increasingly involved in the delivery of prenatal and maternity care and education. In 1922, just before its merger with the Baby Hygiene Association to form the Community Health Association (CHA), BIDNA employed 116 nurses and provided care to more than 36,000 patients. As CHA's first director, Beard strove to involve local government more directly in the delivery of preventive health services, particularly for the welfare of infants.

In 1912 Beard was one of the seven founders of the National Organization for Public Health Nursing, intended to uphold sound nursing practices and education for the growing number of visiting nurse associations. She was a member of its first board of directors and served as its president from 1916 to 1919. After the United States entered World War I, she chaired the Council of National Defense Medical Board's Committee on Public Health Nursing, which encouraged the country's 6,000 public health nurses to continue their work with the civilian population instead of volunteering for military service; she also served on the National Committee on Red Cross Nursing Service.

In 1924 the Rockefeller Foundation invited Beard to join its Committee for the Study of Nursing and Nursing Education and sent her to England to conduct a study of that country's maternal health care. The next year she became special assistant to the director of the foundation's Division of Studies and oversaw the allocation of funds to nursing schools so that they could implement the higher standards of education recommended by the Winslow-Goldmark Report, the result of the committee's 1923 investigation into nursing practices and training. In 1927 she was made assistant to the director of the Division of Medical Education and charged with recruiting more college-educated women into nursing. In this role she began to take an interest in the affairs of the Association of Collegiate

Schools of Nursing (ACSN). Between 1931 and 1938, as associate director of the International Health Division, she personally investigated the state of nursing practices and training in most countries of Asia and Europe, helped to establish nursing schools in many of these countries, and arranged for more than 400 nurses from around the world to come to the United States for training.

In 1938 Beard accepted the directorship of the American Red Cross Nursing Service and set out to revitalize this important arm of the Red Cross, in addition to establishing programs for educating nurse's aides and home nurses. After the United States entered World War II, she chaired the Office of Defense Health and Welfare Service's Subcommittee on Nursing. She assumed responsibility for educating, certifying, and assigning 50,000 nurses, most of whom she recruited through the Red Cross, to military duty without depleting the ranks of the civilian nursing services or stripping nursing schools of their instructors. She also established Camp Community Emergency Nursing Services to provide maternal and child health care for military dependents, chaired the Council of National Defense's Subcommittee on Public Health Nursing, and served on the National Nursing Council.

The author of *The Nurse in Public Health* (1929), which addressed serious issues in public health nursing such as rural nursing, education, and administration, Beard was awarded honorary memberships in the Grand Council of the International Council of Nurses, the ACSN, and the Old Internationals Association, the alumnae of the Florence Nightingale International Foundation in London. Declining health forced her to retire from the Red Cross and government service in 1944. She died, never having married and without children, in New York City.

Beard played a major role in advancing the cause of nursing education. A gentle but determined administrator, she firmly believed that nurses, in addition to being caring individuals of good moral character and physical vigor, should also be well trained in the biological and social sciences, psychology, and basic education. Her ability to gain widespread acceptance and implementation of this belief constitutes her major contribution to American medicine.

• Beard's papers are in the archives of the Rockefeller Foundation, the American Red Cross, and the Cornell University Library. The significance of her work is discussed in Annie M. Brainard, *The Evolution of Public Health Nursing* (1985), and M. Louise Fitzpatrick, *The National Organization for Public Health Nursing, 1912–1952: Development of a Practice Field* (1975). Obituaries are in the *New York Times*, 5 Dec. 1946; *Time*, 16 Dec. 1946; *Public Health Nursing* 39 (Jan. 1947); and *American Journal of Nursing* 47 (Feb. 1947).

CHARLES W. CAREY, JR.

BEARD, Mary Ritter (5 Aug. 1876–14 Aug. 1958), historian, was born and reared in comfort in Indianapolis, Indiana, the daughter of Eli Foster Ritter, a lawyer, and Narcissa Lockwood. Her parents, both from families that had migrated from the Upper South, were observant Methodists and well educated (her mother had briefly taught school). Mary Ritter did not warm to religion, but shone academically, graduating as high school valedictorian and going on—as did her five siblings, following their father—to Methodist-affiliated DePauw University in Greencastle, Indiana, where she received the Ph.B. in 1897. At college she met fellow student Charles Austin Beard, and, true to her family tradition (all the Ritter children met their spouses at DePauw), married him in 1900, after a brief stint teaching German at a high school in Greencastle.

The couple departed immediately for England, where Charles had been studying at Oxford University since 1898 and had helped to found Ruskin Hall, which offered evening and correspondence courses to workers. Living in Oxford and then in Manchester, Mary Beard, who had known solid Republican comfort, confronted working-class poverty for the first time and became committed to cooperative socialism and workers' education. She read Charlotte Perkins Gilman's *Woman and Economics* (1898), the persuasive indictment of Victorian gender roles. She also read history and began to write. Her first published article, dwelling on the status of the emergent twentieth-century woman, appeared in *Young Oxford*, the journal of Ruskin Hall. Especially influenced by Emmeline Pankhurst, a close neighbor in Manchester who was soon to become renowned for suffrage militance, Beard became deeply interested in the lives and problems of women wage earners and in the vote for women as a force for change.

The Beards returned to the United States to live in New York City shortly after the birth of a daughter in 1901. Like her husband, Beard enrolled for graduate study in political science at Columbia University—a bold step for the mother of an infant—but she soon left to combine the care and education of her children (a son was born in 1907) with voluntary activities. Traces can be found of her work between 1907 and 1913 with the Rand School of Social Science, the American Socialist Society (which promoted workers' education), the Equality League for Self-Supporting Women (a suffrage group founded by Harriot Stanton Blatch), the New York Women's Trade Union League, and other progressive causes. In 1910–1911 she edited the *Woman Voter*, which was published by the Woman Suffrage Party of New York State, led by Carrie Chapman Catt. She then worked to develop a Wage-Earners' Suffrage League linked to the Woman Suffrage party, but she broke entirely with Catt in 1913 when the latter spurned the now internationally controversial Pankhurst. The same year, Alice Paul and Lucy Burns recruited Beard for the inner circle of the Congressional Union, a new militant suffrage group (later the National Woman's Party) focused solely on achieving the vote by constitutional amendment and political methods rather than by state-by-state and educational means employed by the longer-established National American Woman Suffrage Association. Beard became a prime mover in the new organization, forming strong attachments.

In the throes of suffrage activity, Beard was also beginning her vocation as researcher and writer. She collaborated with her husband on a high school civics text, *American Citizenship* (1914), which gave particular attention to girls' and women's preparation for participation in the polity. Next she completed her own first book, *Women's Work in Municipalities* (1915). This overview of the accomplishments of contemporary women's voluntary associations presaged the theme of women's constructive, world-building public endeavors that she would later develop in historical treatments. Not entirely satisfied devoting herself to an organization founded on a single issue, Beard eased herself from the top leadership of the Congressional Union in 1915. Her comment to Paul in a letter of mid-1916—"I am so much more radical than either of the old political parties that, when I get off and think, I lose my whole absorption in the one fight for enfranchisement"—suggests her persistent maverick sense of herself. After New York women got the ballot by state referendum in 1917, she left the suffrage movement and wrote a second book, *A Short History of the American Labor Movement* (1920), for the Workers' Education Bureau that she and her husband had helped found.

After World War I and the family's permanent move to New Milford, Connecticut, to a house they had acquired in 1909 and initially used as a summer retreat, Beard became known as a historian. Independent-minded, she sought to realize her ideals for a more humane society through her use of the spoken and written word. Never affiliated with any institution of higher education or group of colleagues, she depreciated her own talents and knowledge. At the same time she was highly skeptical of academic expertise, rowing against the stream of professionalization that engulfed her generation. With her husband, however, she formed an all-important partnership. In the mid-1920s, after travel to war-ravaged Europe and then to Japan and China, the Beards together wrote *The Rise of American Civilization* (2 vols., 1927), a panoramic history that stressed the natural and industrial resources of the nation, included its literature and arts, and paid more attention to women than any other survey written prior to the 1970s. *The Rise* reigned definitive for decades, selling nearly 150,000 copies. It was followed by the sequels *America in Midpassage* (2 vols., 1939), treating the 1920s and 1930s, and *The American Spirit; A Study of the Idea of Civilization in the United States* (1942), which especially showed Mary Beard's hand. The couple also wrote two U.S. history textbooks and, as a last joint endeavor, the inexpensive paperback *A Basic History of the United States* (1944), which sold over 600,000 copies.

Although her husband unfairly received the lion's share (if not all) of the credit for their joint works, there is reason to believe that Beard introduced into the collaboration the broad-ranging "civilization" concept that so distinguished *The Rise* and its sequels from preceding historians' work. She believed it necessary to go beyond the narrowly political, to "widen the frames" of history and "comprehend the wide course of civilization," in order to achieve a fully human history—that is, one that included women. These convictions, which had been developing for several decades, emerged in full flower in her first book tracing women's part in the history of Western civilization, *On Understanding Women* (1931). (She later regretted the psychological cast of the title, which was meant to convey that an understanding of women's current position depended on a knowledge of history. In 1940, when she planned a new edition—never published—it was to be called *Woman: Co-Maker of History*.)

During the depression decade, building on acclaim for *The Rise*, Beard reached her peak of productivity, activism, and influence on behalf of women's history. In rapid succession she published *America through Women's Eyes* (1933), an anthology of women's documents of U.S. history; *Laughing Their Way* (1934), a collection of women's humor coedited with Martha Bruere; a syllabus of study topics and questions for the American Association of University Women called *A Changing Political Economy as It Affects Women* (1934); and a number of articles on women's relation to the economic crisis. Having left socialism behind, Beard remained a sharp critic of capitalism. Her depression-era works showed not only her rejection of economic individualism but also her disenchantment with the feminist goal of "sex equality," which she believed did not measure up to women's tradition of civilization building. Highlighting and preserving knowledge of women's vital social contributions became so important to her that between 1935 and 1940 she headed an effort, involving dozens of donors and sponsors, to establish a World Center for Women's Archives. "Papers. Records. These we must have. Without documents; no history. Without history; no memory. Without memory; no greatness. Without greatness; no development among women," she wrote to the Howard University archivist whom she enlisted to submit African-American women's papers. She saw the World Center as a force for social and political change as much as an archive. Although ultimately unsuccessful, the project was the progenitor of major collections founded at Radcliffe and Smith Colleges during the 1940s. Beard's attempt in the early 1940s to revise the *Encyclopaedia Britannica* to include women's part in culture and history, although invited by the editor, also met frustration. During these years, she felt increasingly isolated in her mission. Her husband was vilified for his opposition to the American entry into World War II, and she, sharing his conviction that the United States should keep to its own shores, found few others who agreed with her combination of anti-Fascism and pacifism. As her public influence had depended on him, so the ignominy heaped on him shadowed her.

Admittedly "obsessed" with women, Beard had an ambivalent relation to feminism. She retained ex-suffragist friends into the 1930s and 1940s and moved in circles of women activists, but she neither supported the Equal Rights Amendment advocated by her former Congressional Union colleagues nor joined women's organizations. Until his death in 1948, her closest companion and constant sounding board was her husband. She raged against what she called the "feminist" version of history for misrepresenting the past by broadcasting a view of women as the historically subject sex. Much influenced by her reading of Victorian anthropologists who had theorized women's invention of language, farming, and the primitive arts, Beard saw women sustaining a creative and multifaceted, although underacknowledged, partnership with men throughout world history. In her zeal, she frequently interpreted the exceptional woman's achievement as possible for all; on the other hand, she gave full recognition to women's capacity for evil (manifest to her in Nazi women) as well as to their beneficent works.

Her most ambitious and best-known work, *Woman as Force in History* (1946), published when she turned seventy, elaborated these complex and sometimes mutually contradictory viewpoints and meted out acid criticism of male historians for their disregard of women's past. Shriller than *On Understanding Women* in attacking the "dogma" of women's subjection, the later work focused especially on coverture, the Anglo-American common-law doctrine that held that a married woman's legal identity (and property) merged into her husband's. Opposing the feminist contention that coverture showed male domination, Beard argued that the parallel English system of equity jurisdiction enabled married women to escape the "disabilities" imposed on them by common law. Although her book gained only modest success compared to the Beards' joint works (selling about 10,000 copies), it was one of the first works consulted when the "new women's history" began its rise in the 1960s and 1970s. Beard's research on coverture continued to fuel historiographical debate almost a half century after its publication.

Substantially founding the modern field of women's history, Beard left it an awkward legacy. Her rejection of "equal rights" as a deficient goal for women and her critique of feminism were disconcerting for later historians who adopted both. Yet she alone in her generation refused to see in men the full measure of human accomplishment and was persistently determined to put women on the historical record. She made a start at reconstructing history, valuing women's presence and words, seeking out and recognizing women's contributions to public life as well as to families. If her strong perspective had the defects of its virtues (willfully ignoring the social construction of gender hierarchy), it appealed nonetheless to subsequent historians who, like her, thought to view history through women's eyes. In line with her lifelong belief that learning was sterile unless aimed at social use, she tried to supply her contemporaries and future generations of women with a past to inspire rather than deflate them. Late in life, she published two more books, *The Force of Women in Japanese History* (1953), a result of con-

tacts she made in Japan in the 1920s, and a brief biography, *The Making of Charles A. Beard* (1955). She spent her last three years in Scottsdale, Arizona, and died in Phoenix.

• Mary Ritter Beard destroyed most of her personal papers and there is no single major collection. The largest holdings are in the DePauw University Library; the Arthur and Elizabeth Schlesinger Library, Radcliffe College; and the Sophia Smith Collection, Smith College. Beard's work with the Congressional Union can be traced in the National Woman's Party Papers, Library of Congress. Important records of the World Center for Women's Archives are in the Schwimmer-Lloyd Collection, New York Public Library.

The major treatments of Beard's life and work are Ann J. Lane, *Mary Ritter Beard: A Sourcebook* (1977); Barbara K. Turoff, *Mary Beard as Force in History* (1979); and Nancy F. Cott, *A Woman Making History: Mary Ritter Beard through Her Letters* (1991). Loretta Zimmerman, "Mary Beard: An Activist of the Progressive Era," *University of Portland Review* 26 (1974): 15–36, and Ellen Nore, *Charles A. Beard: An Intellectual Biography* (1983), are very useful on her life early in the twentieth century. For analyses of Beard's accomplishment see Berenice Carroll, "Mary Beard's *Woman as Force in History*: A Critique," *Massachusetts Review* 8, nos. 1 and 2 (Winter-Spring 1972): 125–43; Bonnie Smith, "Seeing Mary Beard," *Feminist Studies* 10 (1984): 399–416; Suzanne Lebsock, "Reading Mary Beard," *Reviews in American History* (1989): 324–39; and Nancy F. Cott, "Two Beards: Coauthorship and the Concept of Civilization," *American Quarterly* 42 (1990): 274–300. Sales figures for the Beards' books may be found in Howard K. Beale, ed., *Charles A. Beard: An Appraisal* (1954).

NANCY F. COTT

BEARD, Richard (27 Nov. 1799–2 Dec. 1880), minister and educator, was born in Sumner County, Tennessee, the son of Adam Beard, a schoolteacher, and Caty Barclay. His mother died in 1804, and his father remarried. Beard's parents were Presbyterians who came under the influence of the Second Great Awakening, a period of heightened revivalism that began at the end of the eighteenth century and extended into the early years of the nineteenth century. They later became members of the Cumberland Presbyterian church, a denomination that was a direct outgrowth of the revival movement, organized in Dickson, Tennessee, in 1810. Beard was converted and became a member of the New Hope Cumberland Presbyterian church in 1817. Beard was received as a candidate for the ministry by Nashville Presbytery in 1819, licensed in 1820, and ordained in 1822. Because his father was a teacher, Beard's education had been "more extended than usual for the time in his church" (Crisman, p. 8), but he was required nonetheless to complete a tutorial program that was a prerequisite of the presbytery for anyone studying for the ministry. Candidates for the ministry were required to read and pass examinations on certain standard texts in general education and theology. Given the circumstances of the frontier, and due to the pressing need for ministers, this kind of educational preparation was sometimes accepted by the Cumberland Presbyterian church in lieu of a college degree.

Immediately after his licensure in 1820, Beard was sent by Nashville Presbytery to "ride a circuit" in west Tennessee. After his ordination he returned to west Tennessee, serving as pastor of churches in Henry County and helping to organize Hopewell Presbytery in 1825. When his father died in 1825, leaving a number of children from his second marriage, Beard began teaching school to supplement his meager salary as a pastor in order to assist his father's family.

Described by a colleague as "slender in physique" and possessing a "manner ungainly," Beard was said to have had "an embarrassing impediment in his speech," which made his "delivery difficult." Nevertheless, his leadership abilities were soon recognized in the Cumberland Presbyterian church. He served as clerk of the 1828 meeting of Cumberland Synod, the year the decision was made to divide the church into four synods and to constitute a General Assembly. Beard subsequently served as clerk of the Cumberland General Assembly, in 1829 and 1830, and was twice elected moderator of its General Assembly, the highest office in the church, in 1845 and 1866.

Beard resigned his pastoral and teaching duties in 1830 to enter Cumberland College in Princeton, Kentucky. After his graduation two years later, he was appointed a member of its faculty as professor of languages. In 1834 Beard married Cynthia Ewing Castleman; they had five children.

It was in higher education that Beard made his greatest contribution to the Cumberland Presbyterian church. In 1838 he was appointed professor of languages at Sharon College in Sharon, Mississippi, but returned to Cumberland College as president in 1843. In 1852 he served on a commission that recommended to the General Assembly that a department of theology be established at Cumberland University in Lebanon, Tennessee. The next year he was appointed professor of theology in the newly established department, assuming the position on 13 March 1854. For the next twenty-four years, through teaching and writing, Beard helped formulate the theological stance of the Cumberland Presbyterian church, which had been described by its founders as a "medium position between the extremes of Calvinism and Arminianism." Extreme Calvinism referred to certain teachings of John Calvin (1509–1564), as formulated in the Westminster Confession, which stated that before the foundation of the world God decreed that certain persons were destined for heaven and all others were destined for hell, destinies that were irrevocably fixed. Extreme Arminianism referred to a theology associated with the teachings of Jacob Arminius (1560–1609), which held that persons were free and able to determine their own destinies in heaven or hell. "Medium theology" held that all persons are free to choose their eternal destinies but, because of their inclination to sin, are unable, without the assistance of the Holy Spirit, to choose heaven. In his writings, Beard gave definitive shape to this "medium theology." His influential little book, *Why Am I a Cumberland Presbyterian?* (1870), was both a justification of the formation of the church in 1810 and a succinct statement of the essential doctrines of a "medium theology."

At the height of his teaching career at Cumberland University, Beard published a three-volume series, *Lectures in Theology* (1860–1870). He also contributed more than thirty-five articles to the *Theological Medium*, a theological journal established by a group of Cumberland Presbyterian ministers in 1845 and published, under various names, throughout the rest of the century.

Toward the end of Beard's career, winds of theological change were moving through the Cumberland Presbyterian church, and Beard became concerned about what he regarded as departures from the church's "medium principle" in theology. He thought there was a movement toward extreme Arminianism. This meant "softening" the effects of original sin on the human will, so that persons were seen to be both free and able, without divine aid, to determine their eternal destinies. A few months before his death, in an address to the General Assembly, he opposed the movement to revise the 1814 Confession of Faith, saying, "I think that this is the sort of Confession of Faith any man needs. . . . Any conservative man can adopt it. Let it alone." Despite his pleading, three years after Beard's death in Lebanon, Tennessee, a revised edition of the Confession of Faith was adopted by the church.

• Beard's personal journal for the years 1854 to 1864 is in the archives of Cumberland University, Lebanon, Tenn. Other personal papers are in the Historical Archives of the Cumberland Presbyterian church, Memphis, Tenn. His published works, other than those cited above, include *Brief Biographical Sketches of Some Early Ministers of the Cumberland Presbyterian Church* (vol. 1, 1867; vol. 2, 1874) and *Miscellaneous Sermons, Reviews, and Essays* (1875). Copies of the *Theological Medium* are in the library of Memphis Theological Seminary, cataloged under *Cumberland Presbyterian Review*, ser. 1, 2, and 3. Published biographical materials are found in E. B. Crisman, *Biographical Sketches of Living Old Men of the Cumberland Presbyterian Church*, vol. 1 (1877); Winstead P. Bone, *A History of Cumberland University* (1935); and *Minutes of the General Assembly of the Cumberland Presbyterian Church* (1881).

HUBERT W. MORROW

BEARDEN, Romare (2 Sept. 1911–11 Mar. 1988), artist, was born Romare Howard Bearden in Charlotte, North Carolina, the son of R. Howard Bearden, a grocer, and Bessye Johnson. When Bearden was about four years old the family moved to New York, settling in Harlem, where he went to public school and his parents developed a wide network of acquaintances among the Harlem jazz musicians and intellectuals of the day. His father later became an inspector for the New York Board of Health; his mother, a civic leader. Bearden finished high school in Pittsburgh, however, having lived there for a time with his grandmother. In 1932, after two years at Boston University, he transferred to New York University, where he did illustrations for the undergraduate humor magazine and earned a B.S. degree in mathematics in 1935. For the next two years he contributed political cartoons to the *Baltimore Afro-American*. Unable to find steady work, he enrolled at the Art Students League and studied drawing with the German emigré artist George Grosz in 1936–1937.

About this time, Bearden joined the 306 Group, an informal association of black artists and writers—among them Jacob Lawrence and Ralph Ellison—who met in the studio of his cousin, the painter Charles Alston, at 306 West 141st Street. From 1938 to 1942, now beginning to paint, Bearden supported himself as a full-time caseworker with the New York City Department of Social Services (returning to this job after World War II). In 1940, at the Harlem studio of a friend, Ad Bates, Bearden exhibited some of the work he had done over the past four years, including paintings in oil and gouache, watercolors, and drawings. Taking his own studio on 125th Street, over the Apollo Theater, he started a series of paintings that evoked the rural South of his childhood. Typical of the series is *Folk Musicians* (1941–1942), painted in a bold and dramatic style with flat planes and simplified, colorful figures.

In 1944, during the war, while serving with an all-black regiment, Bearden had a solo exhibition at the "G" Place Gallery in Washington, D.C., which brought him to the attention of the influential New York dealer Samuel Kootz. Bearden's first exhibition at the Kootz Gallery, in 1945, was devoted to The Passion of Christ series, a group of semiabstract, cubist-inspired watercolors on paper. The exhibition was highly successful in terms of reviews and sales; *He Is Arisen*, purchased by the Museum of Modern Art in New York, was the first of Bearden's works to enter a museum collection. The following year, Kootz exhibited Bearden's painting *Lament for a Bullfighter*, inspired by García Lorca's poem *Lament for the Death of a Bullfighter*. Inclusion of Bearden's works in the 1945 and 1946 annuals at the Whitney Museum of American Art in New York and in the Abstract and Surrealist American Art show held at the Art Institute of Chicago in 1948 further boosted his growing reputation.

In 1951 Bearden went to Paris on the GI Bill to study philosophy at the Sorbonne. In addition to meeting the cubist masters Pablo Picasso and Georges Braque, Bearden joined the circle of black artists and writers inspired by the concept of negritude. As he later admitted, however, the most significant thing he learned during his year in France was how to relate the black experience to universal experience. Between 1952, when he returned to New York, and 1954, the year he married West Indian dancer Nanette Rohan, Bearden devoted himself mainly to music; some twenty of the songs he wrote in this period were published and recorded. Then, after his marriage (which was childless), Bearden returned to painting and set up a new studio in lower Manhattan, on Canal Street, where he lived for the rest of his life. In 1961 he showed some of his now wholly abstract oil paintings in the first of several solo exhibitions at the Cordier & Ekstrom Gallery, his dealers from then on.

Bearden, who had described art in the journal he began keeping in 1947 as "a kind of divine play" (quoted in Schwartzman, p. 217), was increasingly drawn to collage, a way of "playing" with assortments of materials to create a whole and a medium much employed by the cubists. He created his first signed collage, *Circus*, in 1961; three years later collage became his chief method of expression. The beginning of the civil rights movement and his participation in the discussions of the Spiral Group (which he cofounded in 1963) on the role of black artists in a time of new challenges coincided with this profound change in Bearden's art. In 1964 he did a series of small montages composed of fragments of reproductions cut from newspapers, magazines, or postcards and pasted onto a paper backing; these assemblages were then photographed and enlarged. The resulting "Projections," as Bearden titled them, were exhibited that year at Cordier & Ekstrom. Later, arranged in series by subject matter, they were developed into true collages. One such sequence, titled *The Prevalence of Ritual*, includes individual panels representing "The Funeral," "The Baptism," and "The Conjur Woman." Another collage series evokes Harlem street life, as in *The Dove*, a crowded assemblage of cut-out figures set against a suggestion of city buildings. The bizarrely composite figures, the abrupt shifts in scale between heads and bodies, and the arbitrary spatial relationships convey the rich, kaleidoscopic variety of the scene. Other series recall the Harlem jazz world of the 1930s (*The Savoy*, for example) and southern life (the nostalgic *Train Whistle Blues*).

As Bearden developed his collage techniques into the 1970s, he began to incorporate more of his own painted touches, in acrylics or watercolors, as well as torn pieces of paper in various hand-painted colors and bits of fabric. Spaces were opened up and thus easier to perceive. Coinciding with the start of annual visits to his wife's family home on Saint Martin, the artist's palette took on the lush colors of the Caribbean and the collage figures became overtly sensuous. One of these later collages, *The Block* (1971), a large six-panel composition, approached mixed-media work; with the accompaniment of taped gospel and blues music, children's voices, and actual street noises, it recreated the look, sounds, and "feel" of an urban street.

Besides working in collage, Bearden designed tapestries and posters; in 1968 he was represented in an international poster exhibition in Warsaw, Poland. He did sets for the Alvin Ailey Dance Company in 1977 and continued to make prints, including the colored lithographs that illustrate a 1983 edition of the work of the Caribbean poet Derek Walcott. He also created murals, such as *Quilting Time*, commissioned by the Detroit Institute of Arts and installed there in 1986. In it, the quilter and six onlookers form a frieze against a brilliantly hued tropical setting. The whole is a mosaic of glass tesserae, so combined and colored as to suggest the molding of bodies and the textures and folds of fabrics.

A large traveling retrospective of Bearden's work, organized by the Mint Museum in Charlotte, North Carolina, in 1980 and concluding its tour at the Brooklyn Museum in 1981, capped Bearden's career. Also in 1980 he taught at Yale University, one of several temporary teaching posts he held during the course of his career. Represented in every major museum in New York and in others throughout the country, he is considered to have transformed collage, generally regarded as a minor art form, into a forceful means of expression with universal appeal. "An artist for all seasons and for all humankind," Marvin Schwartzman has called him (p. 305).

Part of Bearden's legacy consists also of his multiple roles as teacher; as art director of the Harlem Cultural Council, to which he was appointed in 1964; as organizer of the landmark exhibition the Evolution of Afro-American Artists: 1800–1950, held at City College of New York in 1967; and as cofounder, in 1969, of the Cinque Gallery in New York, a showcase for younger artists from various minority groups. For these contributions, Bearden was inducted into the National Institute of Arts and Letters in 1966; he was honored by his home state in 1976 as recipient of the Governor's Medal of the State of North Carolina, and he also was awarded the National Medal of Arts in 1987 as well as honorary doctorates from Pratt Institute (1973) and Carnegie-Mellon University (1975). He died in New York City.

• The Schomburg Center for Research in Black Culture, part of the New York Public Library system, is the primary source of archival material relating to Bearden: photographs, his sketchbook and notebooks, and correspondence. The center also maintains a collection of his posters as well as examples of his other work. The Archives of American Art, in New York, houses the Romare Bearden Papers. In addition to *The Painter's Mind: A Study of Structure and Space in Painting*, written with his longtime friend, the artist Carl Holty (1969), Bearden wrote (with Harry Henderson) *A History of Afro-American Artists from 1792 to the Present* (posthumously published in 1993). Also with Henderson he did a book for young readers, *Six Black Masters of American Art* (1972). Essential monographs are Marvin Schwartzman, *Romare Bearden: His Life and Art* (1990), and *Memory and Metaphor: The Art of Romare Bearden, 1940–1987* (1991), with essays by Mary Schmidt Campbell and Sharon F. Patton. Charles Childs, "Bearden: Identification and Identity," *Art News*, Oct. 1964, is informative on the work that led up to the collages. Lynn M. Igoe and James Igoe, comps., *250 Years of Afro-American Art: An Annotated Bibliography* (1981), provides a definitive listing of monographs, exhibition catalogs, and periodical articles devoted to Bearden. An obituary is in the *New York Times*, 13 Mar. 1988.

ELEANOR F. WEDGE

BEARDSHEAR, William Miller (7 Nov. 1850–5 Aug. 1902), United Brethren minister and college president, was born on a farm outside of Dayton, Ohio, the son of John Beardshear and Elizabeth Coleman, devout members of the United Brethren church. William enlisted in the 184th Ohio Infantry in 1864 and served in the Civil War until its conclusion in 1865.

In 1869 Beardshear enrolled at Otterbein University, a United Brethren institution in Westerville, Ohio. During his freshman year he returned home temporarily to manage the family farm after the death of his father. In 1873 he married Josephine Mundhenk of Brookville, Ohio; they had five children. After completing his B.A. in 1876 (he later received an M.A. and an LL.D. from his alma mater), Beardshear served as a United Brethren pastor in Arcanum, Ohio (1876–1878), and at the Summit Street Church in Dayton, Ohio (Oct. 1880–July 1881). Between his two pastorates he began studies at Yale Divinity School in 1878, but in 1879 or early 1880 ill health forced him to withdraw and return home. Beardshear's reputation as a preacher and his commanding presence gained him widespread fame within the United Brethren church, and in 1881, at the age of thirty, he became president of Western College in Toledo, Iowa. Beardshear labored vigorously to expand the college's faculty, facilities, and enrollment, which swelled from eighty in 1881 to over 400 when Beardshear left his position in 1889. Between 1889 and 1891 he served as superintendent of schools in West Des Moines, Iowa, a job that exposed him to the challenges facing primary and secondary educators. Managing the largest school system in Iowa tested Beardshear's tact and persuasion, two qualities with which he was richly blessed.

Beardshear's varied experiences in educational administration prepared him for his appointment in February 1891 as president of Iowa State College of Agriculture and Mechanic Arts in Ames, Iowa. For the next eleven years he presided over the steady growth of the land-grant institution. The selection of Beardshear as president helped to resolve a simmering controversy that had arisen over the evolving teaching mission of the college. Members of the farming community accused Iowa State of drifting away from its initial emphasis on agricultural and mechanical arts as outlined by the 1862 Morrill Act. With Beardshear in charge the curriculum was revamped and the traditional land-grant college disciplines were given renewed attention.

Similar to his approach at Western College, Beardshear focused on developing the campus through new building projects and expansion of the faculty. The Agricultural Experiment Station was reorganized, and James Wilson, a prominent Iowa farm leader, was appointed director. New divisions in the curriculum reflected post–Civil War developments in the sciences, engineering, agriculture, and veterinary medicine. During Beardshear's tenure the school's enrollment quadrupled, reflecting the national growth in higher education characteristic of the 1890s. Largely as a result of Beardshear's lobbying, by 1902 the state legislature had begun allocating tax revenues annually in support of the institution. As president he traveled throughout Iowa speaking on behalf of the college and higher education in general. In 1898 he invited Iowans to visit the Ames campus, and over 6,000 responded. These annual Excursion Days continued thereafter for years.

Beardshear was actively involved in state and national associations. He served as president of the Iowa State Teacher's Association in 1894 and as president of the National Education Association in 1902. From 1897 to 1902 Beardshear was a member of the United States Indian Commission. His interest in local agriculture issues resulted in his appointment as president of the Iowa State Improved Stock Breeder's Association in 1899.

Beardshear was an imposing figure, over six feet tall, powerfully built, with black hair, full beard, and piercing eyes. His rural roots instilled in him a deep reverence for nature, and he enjoyed daily walks in the woods, sometimes sitting for hours at the base of a tree, reading or just gazing at the wildlife. He could be a stern disciplinarian when necessary: he banned all Greek organizations from campus in 1891 because of rioting among students. A popular speaker, Beardshear had a forceful delivery that radiated vitality and energy, and his chapel sermons were well received. Faculty and students alike trusted him, and in his daily outings he often conversed at length with those he encountered. Beardshear's vision and energy enabled Iowa State College to develop from a small rural state college into an institution of national reputation in agriculture and the sciences. He died in Ames, Iowa.

Beardshear was a deeply religious man, with an abiding concern for the education of young people. His career in academia, especially at Iowa State, can best be summed up as one of successfully building upon the solid foundations of the institutions in whose leadership he was entrusted.

• The Iowa State University archives maintain a small collection of Beardshear's papers. A collection of his speeches and writings is published in William Beardshear, *A Boy Again and Other Prose Poems* (1904). A biographical sketch, which contains reminiscences, is found in L. H. Pammel, *Prominent Men I Have Met*, vol. 2 (1927). Beardshear's years at Iowa State College are covered in Earle D. Ross, *A History of the Iowa State College of Agriculture and Mechanic Arts* (1942). Lengthy obituaries are in the *Ames* (Iowa) *Times*, 14 Aug. 1902, and the Des Moines *Register and Leader*, 6 Aug. 1902.
EDWARD A. GOEDEKEN

BEATRICE, Sister. *See* Rogers, Elizabeth Ann.

BEATTY, Bessie (27 Jan. 1886–6 Apr. 1947), radio broadcaster, journalist, and author, was born Elizabeth M. Beatty in Los Angeles, California, the daughter of Thomas Edward Beatty and Jane Mary Boxwell. Her parents had immigrated from Ireland to the Midwest and then to Los Angeles, where Thomas Beatty became a director of the first electric street railroad in the city. In 1903 Bessie Beatty matriculated at the Highland Park campus of Occidental College, determined to be a writer. She was active in campus literary societies and wrote several articles for student publications before taking a position in her senior year as a reporter for the *Los Angeles Herald*. Assigned to cover a mine strike in Nevada, she stayed for an entire year,

sending back stories that were later published as a book, *Who's Who in Nevada* (1907). She never graduated college.

Fremont Older, editor of the San Francisco *Bulletin*, was impressed by Beatty's writing and hired her as a reporter. Within a couple of years she was writing under her own byline. She was active in the struggle for woman suffrage, and when California granted women the vote in 1911, she wrote *A Political Primer for the New Voter* (1912) as a guide to the newly enfranchised. As a writer and activist Beatty supported many progressive causes, including that of Thomas J. Mooney, convicted of planting the bomb in the 1916 San Francisco preparedness day march (and eventually pardoned), and the rights of prostitutes to alternative employment when their brothels were closed by police actions. During World War I she became a foreign war correspondent for the *Bulletin*, covering events in Japan, Korea, China, and Russia. In China she wrote amid the revolutionary struggles taking place there, managing to interview leaders of the contending forces as civil war swirled around them.

From China Beatty traveled via the trans-Siberian railroad to Petrograd to cover the Russian Revolution. Arriving in June 1917 she situated herself at the heart of the struggle before touring the Russian lines on the German front. For a week she interviewed women soldiers of the Battalion of Death, while under enemy fire. Back in Petrograd she met with Trotsky and Lenin at the Smolney Institute, the center for Bolshevik activity during the revolution. While talking with Lenin, she witnessed an assassination attempt on his life.

Beatty observed firsthand the Bolshevik defeat of the Kerensky government during the October Revolution. When the cannons from the *Aurora* battleship sounded, Beatty was in the Smolney with her fellow American correspondents John Silas Reed, Louise Bryant, Albert Rhys Williams, and Alexander Gomberg; together they set out for the Winter Palace in an open truck loaded with rifle-toting revolutionaries distributing pamphlets along Nevski Prospect. Crossing the great palace square while the shooting was still taking place, they entered the Winter Palace with the Red Guard and witnessed the surrender of the Kerensky government. Later, Beatty visited the prisoners in the St. Peters and Paul Fortress at the request of Raymond Robbins of the Red Cross to ensure that they were not being ill treated.

Her sympathies during the revolution and afterward were with the Russian people. "Revolution," she wrote, "cries incessantly for larger freedom." After an eight-month stay in Russia she sailed for New York, commenting, "Mingled with my sorrow, the morning I left Petrograd was a certain exultant, tragic joy. I had been alive at a great moment, and knew it was great." Back in the United States she wrote *The Red Heart of Russia* (1918), recounting her experiences in the revolution. Called to testify before the 1919 Senate Overman Committee, which sought to demonstrate that the Russian Revolution was financed by Germany and German-American breweries in particular, she gave a spirited defense of the revolution in the face of hostile questioning. At this time she and Louise Bryant were admitted to the Heterodoxy, a radical women's organization whose membership included many of the country's outstanding feminists and writers.

Beatty's loyalty to the Bolshevik Revolution never flagged: she protested U.S. intervention in 1918, fought for U.S. recognition of the Soviet state, and was still signing petitions for Russian assistance on the eve of World War II. Leaving the *Bulletin*, she became editor of *McCalls* for three years before becoming a freelance writer and world traveler, publishing articles in the leading periodicals of the day, including the *Nation*, *Century*, the *Saturday Review*, *Asia*, *Ladies' Home Journal*, and *Good Housekeeping*. Back in Russia she boated down the Volga with Kalinin, the president of the Soviet Union, and visited with Chicherin, the Soviet foreign commissar, writing favorably of the progress being made by the Bolsheviks. In 1922 she visited Turkey, "The Bogy-Man of the Bosporus," defending that nation from what she considered to be the one-sided media criticisms of its policies as a new nation. From London she sought to calm American fears that the new Labour government under Ramsay MacDonald would mark the end of England's constitutional government.

In 1926 Beatty married the English actor William Sauter, explaining her decision to wed in an editorial in *Good Housekeeping* titled "I Would Rather Be Married Than Single." They had no children. Over the next ten years she tried her hand at many tasks, including scriptwriting for MGM, authoring a Broadway play *Jamboree* (1932), serving as American secretary of International PEN, an organization for writers, and directing the National Label Council (an organization dedicated to informing buyers that their purchases were union-made). In 1940 she began her career as a radio broadcaster, taking over the Martha Deane show from Mary Margaret McBride on WOR in New York City. Within two years her program had the largest audience of any women's show on the air utilizing a question-and-answer format, along with informal chitchat, and personal interviews. *Time* magazine called her "Mrs. Know-It-All" in a complimentary article describing her program. The recipient of broadcasting awards for her efforts to support the war on the homefront and for her contribution to women's programming (including one from the Crossley ratings organization and another from the Women's International Exposition of Arts and Industries), Beatty was at the height of her popularity when she suffered a heart attack and died in Nyack, New York.

• Most of Bessie Beatty's papers are lost; a few pieces are scattered in the Herbert Hoover Presidential Library in West Branch, Iowa; the Bancroft Library at the University of California at Berkeley; and the State Historical Society of Wisconsin. Her book *The Red Heart of Russia* (1918) is the best account of her life in Russia. See also Lisa M. Jankoski, "Bessie Beatty: One Woman's View of the Russian Revolutions," (M.A. thesis, Villanova Univ. 1989) and Zena Beth McGlashan, "Women Witness the Russian Revolution: Analyzing Ways of Seeing," *Journalism History* 12, no. 2 (Summer 1985): 54–61. An obituary is in the *New York Times* 7 Apr. 1947.

NORMAN S. COHEN

BEATTY, Clyde Raymond (10 June 1903–19 July 1965), animal trainer and circus owner, was born in Bainbridge, Ohio, the son of James Edward Beatty and Margaret Everhart, farmers. After first trying at age thirteen to run away to join the circus, he succeeded at fifteen, following his freshman year at Bainbridge High School.

Beatty joined a "Great London" circus—actually part of the Ringling Brothers and Barnum & Bailey chain—as an acrobat. By age seventeen, the 5′6″, 145-pound Beatty had begun his animal-training career—first as cage boy, then as assistant trainer. In 1923, replacing a trainer who had had a nervous breakdown, he took over an act composed of lions, leopards, and bears. By 1926 he was performing with ten lions and four tigers. In 1930 he reached a previously unheard-of total of forty (probably at least twenty-five were lions).

Beatty wrote, "The principal reason why my act is a success is that I mix lions and tigers on a big scale." Behind this appeal to his public's sense of danger lay his understanding that lions and tigers were natural enemies and that by mixing the sexes within his steel cage he further focused the animals' attention on each other rather than himself.

Though denying that he flirted with death, Beatty built his eighteen-minute act (performed twice a day for forty years) on menace and battle, sometimes between beasts who fought to the death. Beatty refused to "tame" his animals. One star, a lion named Nero, "saved" Beatty by going after a tiger who had the upper claw on the trainer, but in 1932 it was Nero's turn to attack and Beatty nearly lost a leg. Staged in arenas such as Madison Square Garden in New York City, Beatty's battles gave him national celebrity.

It is estimated that Beatty was mauled more than 100 times. "I wanted to evolve an act so dangerous that I should not have to worry about being supplanted," he once said. Dale Carnegie remarked, "Beatty would rather be gored to death than bored to death." In 1933 Beatty married Harriett Evans, a dancer who had joined the circus. By 1935 she was also an animal trainer; they had one child.

Beatty's whip-cracking, stool-thrusting, blank cartridge–shooting style—"American," by contrast to gentler European and Indian circus animal acts—was attuned to its era. His 1937 *Time* magazine cover story said, "Our civilization places too high a value on the cute and cunning." Beatty's fame coincided with that of big-game hunter Frank "Bring 'Em Back Alive" Buck and explorers of exotic lands such as Martin and Osa Johnson. Ernest Hemingway studied Beatty, likening his use of the whip to a matador's use of the cape.

Clad in white shirt and jodphurs, Beatty arranged his beasts as they charged one by one into the arena through a chute. Three tigers went onto pedestals; he gradually built the forty animals into an amphitheater of snarling onlookers. Then he set them, in various combinations, to rolling over or spinning, rolling a globe or walking a tightrope or a huge roller, lying in a perfect line, or clearing flaming hurdles. In one version, tigers leapt onto the back of galloping elephants. Briefly his audiences were "guarded" by uniformed "gun bearers," but Beatty rightly understood that his act's real attraction was its danger. He claimed to be the only Ringling Brothers and Barnum & Bailey performer who couldn't get life insurance.

Having appeared briefly with a puma in a 1924 silent film, Beatty took Nero to Hollywood for *The Big Cage* (1933). The *American Film Institute Catalog* describes its opening: "As twenty caged tigers are unloaded from a ship, one escapes when its cage falls, causing havoc on the docks until Clyde Beatty, subjugator of wild beasts, backs the tiger into a room with a chair and cane." In *The Lost Jungle* (1934) Beatty had a slightly rangier role: "On the day he is to set sail with explorer Professor Livingston for the South Sea Islands, Captain Robinson insists that his daughter, Ruth, either procure a marriage proposal from her boyfriend, Clyde Beatty, a renowned circus animal trainer, or leave with him."

The Lost Jungle's real success came as a twelve-chapter serial for the Saturday matinee audience. In 1936 Beatty starred in a fifteen-episode serial, *Darkest Africa*, battling hostile natives, lions, tigers, and a tribe of winged men called Bat Men. Scenes from these films became stock footage for later productions requiring animal battles. Beatty also starred in a network radio series dramatizing incidents in his life. He coauthored three popular autobiographical books and was included in Robert Ripley's "Believe It or Not" columns, programs, and books.

Between 1935 and 1936 a combined Clyde Beatty–Cole Brothers Circus toured the country. In 1936 and 1937 Beatty earned $3,500 weekly, performing four or five shows daily in vaudeville. In 1937 the New York Zoological Society's curator declared Beatty not guilty of cruel practices charges brought by the Humane Society. He made a triumphal 1938 Canadian tour. In 1939 the Beattys opened a tropical zoo in Fort Lauderdale, Florida. In 1944 there was a Clyde Beatty–Russell Brothers Circus, and between 1945 and 1963 Beatty ran one of the last traditional circuses. While other circuses traveled by bus and chose indoor auditoriums, the Clyde Beatty Circus, 500 employees strong, continued to arrive in fifteen railroad cars and unfurl its big tops. By his own calculations, Beatty traveled a million miles and performed for 40 million people.

Harriett Beatty died of a heart ailment in 1945, and Beatty married Jane Abel in 1951; they had one child. In his later years, Beatty performed regularly on radio and television variety programs. He died in Ventura, California, of cancer.

If George Chindahl is correct, Beatty's childhood fascination with the circus began during the midpoint of its last golden age. If Beatty is to be believed, the Midwest of his youth contained "the most passionate circus devotees I've ever met." Throughout his public life, he retained his region's speech, talking in a gravelly voice of "lahns and taggers." Beatty said that his favorite among decades of descriptions of his act came from a schoolchild assigned the task: "When they do not obey, he hits them on the head or shoots them and then they obey."

• Clyde Beatty coauthored three books: *The Big Cage*, with Edward Anthony (1933); *Jungle Performers*, with Earl Wilson (1941); and *Facing the Big Cats*, with Anthony (1965); Edward Anthony, incidentally, also co-wrote Frank Buck's books. George Chindahl, *A History of the Circus in America* (1959), is incomparably detailed, and Charles P. Fox and Tom Parkinson, *The Circus in America* (1969), is an effective update. Beatty's film exploits are covered in Ed Weiss and Ed Goodgold, *To Be Continued* (1972), and the *American Film Institute Catalog*. Beatty's obituary in the *New York Times*, 20 July 1965, is exciting and poetic.

JAMES ROSS MOORE

BEATTY, John (19 Dec. 1749–30 Apr. 1826), physician, army officer, and government official, was born in Warwick, Pennsylvania, the son of Charles Clinton Beatty, a Presbyterian minister, and Anne Reading. John attended the College of New Jersey (now Princeton University), where he was one of twenty graduates in the class of 1769. He received an A.M. there three years later. As an undergraduate, he was an original member of the school's literary club, the American Whig Society. During the interval between his two degree awards, Beatty studied medicine under Dr. Benjamin Rush in Philadelphia and practiced first in Princeton and then in Hartsville, Pennsylvania. He returned to Princeton in 1774, when he married Mary Longstreet. They had one child who survived infancy.

The outbreak of the American Revolution prompted the suspension of Beatty's medical career, as he and three brothers all volunteered for service in the patriot cause. In January 1776 John Beatty was commissioned a captain and company commander in the Fifth Pennsylvania Battalion. Beatty's battalion was soon ordered to New York, where it was assigned to build fortifications against an impending British invasion. At one of these defense works, Fort Washington on the northern edge of Manhattan Island, Beatty, then a major commanding the Sixth Pennsylvania Battalion, was captured on 16 November 1776. He endured six months of harsh confinement on board a prison ship in New York Harbor. He then spent almost a year more on parole in Flatbush on Long Island before he was exchanged in May 1778.

The remainder of Beatty's military career also proved disappointing. Shortly after his exchange, he was elevated to the rank of colonel and named commissary general to supply the needs of captured enemy prisoners for the Continental army. However, both the Continental Congress and General George Washington failed to provide him proper backing for his duties, while at the same time they insisted that he comply strictly with their instructions. Colonel Beatty reacted by conducting his task on an informal basis with his British counterparts, even permitting trade with them. As a result, on Washington's orders, he was eventually detained and subjected to a general court-martial in February 1780. The next month Beatty resigned his commission after receiving strong reprimands from both the court and from General Washington.

Following his resignation, Beatty engaged in farming and medicine before entering public service. From 1781 to 1783 he served on the New Jersey State Council. In November 1783 the New Jersey legislature elected him to serve in the Continental Congress. There he became a staunch advocate for the claims of land speculators in the western territories against the titles or charters of the larger states, and he also sought unsuccessfully to arrange for the Confederation government's ability to enforce requisitions from the states. Beatty's disillusionment over his failures in the Continental Congress led to his temporary withdrawal from politics in May 1785, but he returned in 1787 as a Federalist delegate at the New Jersey convention that ratified the Constitution of the United States. Then, as Speaker of the New Jersey Assembly in 1789 and 1790, he offered the state's congratulations to President Washington upon his assumption of office in New York City in 1789. The end of the decade found Beatty engaged in several activities in Princeton. He continued his medical practice and was active in the state medical society, he did some farming, he was a trustee of the college beginning in 1787, he held executive office in the Masonic Order, and he was an officer in the Hunterdon County militia.

Returning to public affairs, Beatty was elected to represent New Jersey's newly created Fifth Congressional District in 1792. He played an active role in the sessions of the Third U.S. Congress, meeting in Philadelphia. As a Federalist, Beatty enthusiastically supported Treasury Secretary Alexander Hamilton's fiscal programs, condemned the actions of the French minister Edmond Charles Genet, and successfully moved to mollify proposed anti-British trade legislation. His major work before leaving Congress in 1795 was his vigorous advocacy of creating a U.S. Navy Bureau within the federal government so that American commercial and neutral rights could be protected. Although Beatty was unable to secure the establishment of a Navy Department, Congress did authorize the construction of six new frigates, thanks to his lobbying.

Beatty moved with his family to Trenton after leaving Congress. Although he worked in state affairs, including the post of New Jersey secretary of state (1795–1805), for another decade, business interests dominated most of his later years. He became president of the Delaware Bridge Company that constructed Trenton's first bridge across the Delaware River. He was also a founder and later president (1815–1826) of the Trenton Banking Company, and he simultaneously dabbled in real estate. In religious matters he was an elder in the Presbyterian church and a trustee of the Princeton Theological Seminary. He retired as a trustee of the College of New Jersey itself in 1802.

Mary Beatty died in 1815, and in 1818 John married Katherine De Klyn Lalor. They had no children who survived infancy. John Beatty died at his home in Trenton. His most significant historical achievements were made within New Jersey as a prominent guiding figure in the state's early political, educational, and economic development.

• The most worthwhile manuscript material regarding Beatty is in the New Jersey State Library Archives, Princeton University and Princeton Theological Seminary Archives, Historical Society of Pennsylvania, and microfilms of the papers of the Continental Congress and the Third Congress of the United States. A concise, well-written biography is in Richard A. Harrison, *Princetonians: 1769–1775, A Biographical Dictionary* (1980). Information relating to Beatty and his family is in Eli F. Cooley, *Genealogy of Early Settlers in Trenton and Ewing, Old Hunterdon County, New Jersey* (1883); Richard P. McCormick, *Experiment in Independence: New Jersey in the Critical Period, 1781–1789* (1950); John Hall, *History of the Presbyterian Church in Trenton, New Jersey, from the First Settlement of the Town* (1859); Harold Sprout and Margaret Sprout, *The Rise of American Naval Power, 1776–1918* (1939); and Paul G. Tomlinson, *A History of the Trenton Banking Company, 1804–1929* (1929). Two articles with information relating to episodes in Beatty's career are Joseph M. Beatty, "Letters of the Four Beatty Brothers of the Continental Army, 1774–1794," *Pennsylvania Magazine of History and Biography* 44 (1920): 193–262; and Robert M. Berkhofer, Jr., "Jefferson, the Ordinance of 1784, and the Origins of the American Territorial System," *William and Mary Quarterly*, ser. 3, 29 (1972): 231–62.

SHELDON S. COHEN

BEATTY, Talley (1919–29 Apr. 1995), choreographer, dancer, and teacher, was born in Cedar Grove, Louisiana, the son of a house painter. His parents' names are unknown. In the small town of Cedar Grove, right outside Shreveport, Beatty's earliest dance influence was the legendary Katherine Dunham. When he was eleven years old, she invited him to "watch dances in progress," according to historian Joe Nash, a close friend and colleague of Beatty. Dunham was in rehearsal for Ruth Page's *La Guiablesse*, scheduled to open at the Chicago Civic Opera (1933), and was trying to keep the young boy's playing from disrupting her work. Beatty danced on stage for the first time in the opera's 1934 season and emerged as a dancer of note after studying from 1937 to 1940 at Dunham's Studio de la Danse in Shreveport. He danced the role of a priest in Dunham's *Yanvalou*, a snakelike dance in honor of the Voudoun deity Damballa, at the historic Negro Dance Evening, 7 March 1937, at the Ninety-second Street Young Men's and Young Women's Hebrew Association in New York City.

Beatty toured with the Katherine Dunham Company for nineteen years. He was in the brief 1940–1941 run of *Cabin in the Sky* on Broadway and appeared in films with the Dunham company, including *Carnival of Rhythm* (1941), *Cuban Episode* (1942), *Flamingo*

(1942), and *Stormy Weather* (1943). Beatty left Dunham's company to form a duet with the celebrated Janet Collins, who was the first black prima ballerina at the Metropolitan Opera House (1951–1954). He returned to New York around 1950. In the late 1940s he appeared in Maya Deren's innovative film *Choreography for Camera*. He danced in the 1946 revival of *Show Boat* with Pearl Primus, Joe Nash, and Alma Sutton.

Beatty's ballets have been often classified as part of a jazz idiom; however, the movements are not vernacular, and they never fall into an unidentifiable heap of clichéd gesture. In fact, his dances, which survive in the repertories of the Philadelphia Dance Company, the Dayton Contemporary Dance Company, and the Alvin Ailey American Dance Theater, are not only virtuoso tours de force but transformative excursions into human need. Beatty's sagas of city living, depicted by fast-paced moving, convoluted interactions between text and subtext, and the tensions created by social challenges, are a testimony to his choreographic facility. Beatty's legacy is part of a long tradition of dance as social commentary and as a catalyst for social change.

The *New York Times* critic Anna Kisselgoff had this to say about his work in 1989: "What is a Beatty signature? It is primarily his genius for putting technical perfection at the service of emotional expression. Inventing a jazz idiom that has the continuum of classical dancing, he has composed dance poems of urban existence. Their structure is largely abstract, creating drama through pattern and composition." Despite the fact that Kisselgoff incorrectly labels the work as "a jazz idiom," probably because he used classical jazz scores from the likes of Miles Davis, Duke Ellington, and Billy Strayhorn in his distillation of ideas and motifs, along with short, tight, isolated gestures to frame and accent large technical phrases, she is on target when she notes the structure of his dances. Beatty was a master crafter of mood and innuendo. With just the right mix of gestural mapping, speed, rhythmic thrust, and abstraction, he created dances that challenged notions of dance patterning and stylistic classification.

Beatty's first major work, *Southern Landscapes* (1947), a response to Howard Fast's book *Freedom Road*, was reconstructed on the Philadelphia Dance Company in 1992. A ballet in four sections, *Southern Landscapes* comments on the rise of the Ku Klux Klan, as black and white working-class communities sought unity after the Civil War. Between 1947 and 1955 Beatty toured with his company, Tropicana, and then created many memorable masterpieces, including *The Road of Phoebe Snow* (1959), which chronicles the journey of a luxury train that passes through the backyards of the United States, witnessing people who are alienated from themselves and their communities; and *Come and Get the Beauty of It Hot* (1960), which takes audiences through a day in the lives of Harlemites. "Toccata," the opening segment of *Beauty*, is a collage of finger-popping, body-slapping moves atop technical ploys. Dancers take to their knees, twist in diverse directions, and end, hovering, in nearly upside-down balances; "Toccata" is often performed independently. "Congo, Tango, Palace," the final section of *Beauty*, which depicts the elegance and bravura of flamenco executed in a Spanish Harlem ballroom, is also performed as a solo work. The ballet, excerpted and in its entirety, is a staple of the Dayton Contemporary Dance Company. Other ballets that span Beatty's forty-eight years of dance making include *Tropicana* (1949); *Migration* (1964); *Bring My Servant Home* (1969), a tribute to Martin Luther King, Jr.; *The Stack-Up* (1983); *A Rag, a Bone and a Hank of Hair* (1985); and *Such Sweet Morning Songs* (1990).

In addition to his work on the concert stage as a dancer and choreographer, Beatty created television specials like Duke Ellington's "Black, Brown, and Beige" for CBS in 1974 and made movement for the Broadway show *Your Arms Too Short to Box with God*, which was nominated for a Tony Award in 1977. As a teacher Beatty also made his mark in the 1960s and 1970s. Students at the Alma Lewis School of Fine Arts in Boston and the Fred Benjamin Dance Company in New York, as well as dance students in England, France, Sweden, and Israel, had the opportunity to experience his rare gifts. Beatty had a wry sense of humor, an acute awareness of the human condition, and the courage to speak from his heart and soul. His death in New York City caused a silence in the dance world. Declared a "living legend" in 1992 during the National Black Arts Festival in Atlanta, Georgia, and a recipient of the Samuel H. Scripps/American Dance Festival Award in 1993, Beatty was, indeed, a national treasure. He created more than fifty ballets that were performed by some fourteen companies in the United States, Europe, and western Asia. A member of Ballet Society (which became the New York City Ballet in 1933), Beatty not only defied the images proscribed for blacks during his time but also set a standard for performance that has become a model for contemporary dancers of all ethnic groups. Even when blacks were stereotyped as incapable of performing ballet, Beatty dared to dance and choreograph as he chose. A consummate ballet technician, he blended ballet with other ethnic styles. With the language of the body he provided blueprints of everyday life for all humanity. Beatty is sorely missed, but his spirit lives on in the dances he made and the people he touched.

• Materials on Beatty are located in the Dance Collection of the New York Public Library for the Performing Arts, Lincoln Center. See also Richard Long, *The Black Tradition in American Dance* (1989); Clive Barnes, "Dance: Beatty Winding Up City Center Season," *New York Times*, 21 May 1969; B. S. K. Bartett, "Talley Beatty Company in Vivid Performance at John Hancock Hall," *Boston Globe*, 15 Jan. 1952; "Dunham Dance Graduates," *Ebony*, June 1953, pp. 48–53; Jennifer Dunning, "Dance: Black Festival in Brooklyn," *New York Times*, 23 Apr. 1983; Lynne Fauley Emery, *Black Dance in the United States from 1619 to Today*, 2d ed. (1988); Doris Herring, "The Workshop: A New Perennial," *Dance Magazine*, July 1947, pp. 19–21; "Talley Beatty Work at ANTA," *New York Post*, 19 Apr. 1974, p. 36; "Talley Beatty and Company," *Dance Observer* 15 (Nov. 1948): 122; John

Martin, "Dance: Good Job," *New York Times*, 6 Dec. 1959, and Arthur Todd, "Dance: Riches: The Art of the American Negro Is One of Our Foremost Natural Treasures," *New York Times*, 2 July 1961.

C. S'THEMBILE WEST

BEATTY, William Henry (18 Feb. 1838–4 Aug. 1914), attorney and jurist, was born in Monclova, Ohio, the son of Henry Oscar Beatty, a lawyer, and Margaret Boone. Beatty grew up in Washington, Kentucky, but his father moved both his law practice and family to Sacramento, California, in 1853. In 1855 William returned to the East to attend a preparatory academy in Kentucky, perhaps Center College in Danville, where his uncle, Armand Beatty, was once president. William also studied at the University of Virginia for two years before returning in 1858 to his father's office to read law. Admitted to the California bar in 1861, he associated with his father's law firm.

The California practice did not last long because both father and son were drawn to Nevada by the mineral strikes. Henry Beatty moved his practice to Virginia City in 1863 and William moved shortly thereafter to Austin. William became Austin's city attorney shortly after arriving and won election as Lander County district judge in 1864. He was on the district court bench for a decade, a period in which that court's jurisdiction expanded to include White Pine County and heard some of the most complex mining litigation of its times. William Beatty's mining cases made him a recognized expert in the field in the mining West.

In 1874 Beatty married Elizabeth McKay Love; they had two children. The same year, he was elected associate justice of the Nevada Supreme Court and continued on the appellate bench until 1880, when he lost in a bid for reelection. During the last two years of his tenure on the Nevada appellate bench, he served as chief justice.

Returning to Sacramento in 1880, Beatty resumed private practice and involved himself in Republican politics. In 1888 he was elected chief justice of the California Supreme Court to serve the two years remaining in the term of the deceased Chief Justice Robert Morrison. Beatty won reelection to full twelve-year terms in 1890 and 1902. He outlived all the members of the sitting court and saw thirteen new members join it in the quarter century that followed.

Beatty's tenure on the court and his role as chief justice positioned the court for national recognition. From 1879 to 1900 the California Supreme Court witnessed more partisan tension than it had since its creation. As chief justice, Morrison had molded a great deal of consensus, but Beatty stressed judicial independence. Beatty sat on 12,614 cases and dissented in 475. His disagreements were bipartisan, turning on procedural matters. He maintained that even if the court had once sustained a position, no one should be given an uncontestable right to an unjust precedent or technicality. Beatty focused on substantive issues and was more interested in the weight of legal reasoning than consensus-building around a common partisan position. He also was willing to state his positions critically in public. His public reprimands of his colleagues was a very direct form of judicial leadership. As a result, judicial independence, not partisan accountability, became the most important feature of the state's judicial culture.

Beatty was a member of the San Francisco Bar Association, the University Club of San Francisco, Phi Kappa Sigma, and the Pacific Union and Southern clubs of San Francisco and the president of the California Water and Forest Association. He died at his San Francisco home.

• For more information see J. Edward Johnson, *History of the Supreme Court Justices of California*, vol. 1 (1963), pp. 163–70; Kermit Hall, "Dissent on the California Supreme Court, 1850–1920," *Social Science History* 11 (Spring 1987): 63–83; and "Memorial of the Life and Services of the Honorable William H. Beatty," *California Reports* 168 (1914), p. 799.

GORDON MORRIS BAKKEN

BEAUMONT, William (21 Nov. 1785–25 Apr. 1853), physician and physiologist, was born in Lebanon, Connecticut, the son of Samuel Beaumont and Lucretia Abel, farmers. Little is known about his early life, except that he attended a local common school and disliked farming. At age twenty-one he left home and settled several months later in Champlain, New York, a village near the Canadian border. For three years he taught school and read borrowed medical books in his spare time. In the fall of 1810 he moved to St. Albans, Vermont, to learn medicine as an apprentice to an established physician, Benjamin Chandler, still the most common means of acquiring a medical education. While living in the Chandler household and performing chores for the doctor, Beaumont learned by observing and doing. He rode to see patients with his preceptor, assisted in operations, compounded drugs, and occasionally filled in during Chandler's absence.

On 2 June 1812 the Third Medical Society of the State of Vermont, having examined Beaumont, recommended him "to the world as a judicious and safe practitioner." Soon thereafter Beaumont, in need of money and eager to obtain more surgical experience, enrolled in the U.S. Army as a surgeon's mate, just in time to see service in the War of 1812. With the coming of peace in 1815, he quit the army to practice medicine in Plattsburgh, New York, where he remained for about four years.

In the winter of 1819–1820 Beaumont turned over his medical practice to a cousin and reenlisted in the army as a post surgeon. His first assignment was to a fort on the island of Mackinac in Lake Huron between the upper and lower peninsulas of Michigan, where the American Fur Company had established its headquarters. During a furlough to Plattsburgh in the summer of 1821 he married a young widow, Deborah Green Platt; they had four children.

On 6 June 1822 Beaumont, who had received permission to engage in private practice on the side, was called to treat a 28-year-old French-Canadian voyageur, Alexis St. Martin, suffering from a gunshot wound in his chest. Under Beaumont's care, the man survived, but the ordeal left him with a permanent hole, or fistula, leading directly into his stomach. One day about a year after the accident, Beaumont treated St. Martin for constipation by pouring a cathartic through a glass funnel into his stomach. The success of this novel procedure apparently prompted Beaumont to begin suspending "flesh, raw and roasted, and other substances in the hole, to ascertain the length of time required to digest each." Encouraged by Surgeon General Joseph Lovell to continue taking advantage of his unique opportunity to study the process of digestion, Beaumont at various locations between 1825 and 1833 conducted hundreds of experiments on his sometimes reluctant subject, poking "different kinds of food, drinks, elastic catheters, [and] thermometer tubes" into the opening and extracting large quantities of gastric juice and chyme. In 1833 he published the results of his research under the title *Experiments and Observations on the Gastric Juice, and the Physiology of Digestion.* Appearing in the midst of a scientific debate over the nature of digestion, it offered compelling evidence in favor of a chemical theory and demonstrated the importance of gastric juice in digesting food.

The publication of *Experiments and Observations* made Beaumont a scientific celebrity at home and abroad. Americans, notorious for their dyspepsia, especially appreciated his practical dietary advice, particularly his widely reprinted table giving the average times of digestion for various foods. "Hardly a book has been published, for many years, on physiology or health," noted American physician William A. Alcott, "that has not availed itself, more or less, of his interesting facts" (*The Laws of Health* [1860], p. 142). Indeed, Beaumont's experiments on the man with a hole in his stomach remained a staple of American physiology and hygiene textbooks until the end of the nineteenth century. Yet Beaumont failed to influence the course of experimental physiology in America, largely because of the indifference of other American physicians to scientific research.

According to the *Medico-Chirurgical Review* of London, Beaumont's experiments "excited great interest in every country of the civilized world" (vol. 33 [1838]: 19). A German translation of *Experiments and Observations* appeared in 1834, and a Scottish edition followed four years later. Inspired by Beaumont's success with St. Martin, European investigators eagerly exploited persons with gastric and other fistulae to learn more about the physiology of digestion. And in the absence of human subjects with natural fistulae, they created artificial openings in animals. At the request of France's leading physiologist, Claude Bernard, an American physician visiting Paris in 1850 wrote home to Beaumont about his European influence: "The publication of your observations, exposing so clearly and analytically the physiology of the stomach, was the commencement of a new era in the study of this important organ and those associated with it. Your experiments are constantly imitated here upon

animals and by a large number of investigating physiologists, among whom M. Bernard probably stands first" (quoted in Myer, p. 289).

Beaumont, though generally respected, was at times quarrelsome, thin-skinned, and self-righteous. He professed no religion. For years after 1833 he obsessively hounded St. Martin in order to perform additional experiments, but the latter somehow managed to stay out of the frustrated physician's hands. In 1834 Beaumont, growing increasingly deaf, moved to the St. Louis area, where he resided for the last nineteen years of his life. Although formally in the army during his first years there, he built up a lucrative private practice in the city. When an unsympathetic surgeon general ordered him to Florida in 1839, Beaumont angrily resigned from the army. By the time of his death in St. Louis following an injury to his head on an icy step, Beaumont had won, in the words of a resolution passed by the St. Louis Medical Society, "the esteem of the profession of all countries." The Columbian College had awarded him an honorary M.D. (1833), and the medical societies of Michigan and Connecticut had voted him honorary membership. He had served as president of the Medical Society of Missouri and had received a special invitation to attend the organizing session of what became the American Medical Association.

• The Washington University School of Medicine Library in St. Louis houses the most extensive collection of Beaumont's papers and correspondence, but the Joseph Regenstein Library, University of Chicago, also possesses a Beaumont collection. The still standard biography is Jesse S. Myer, *Life and Letters of Dr. William Beaumont* (1912). Myer's laudatory portrayal should, however, be supplemented by two more critical pieces, Estelle Brodman, "William Beaumont: The Individual," which introduces an abridged reissue of Myer's book, *William Beaumont: A Pioneer American Physiologist* (1981); and Ronald L. Numbers, "William Beaumont and the Ethics of Human Experimentation," *Journal of the History of Biology* 12 (1979): 113–35. On Beaumont's contribution to the physiology of digestion, see Jerome J. Bylebyl, "William Beaumont, Robley Dunglison, and the 'Philadelphia Physiologists,'" *Journal of the History of Medicine and Allied Sciences* 25 (1970): 3–21. On his influence, see Numbers and William J. Orr, Jr., "William Beaumont's Reception at Home and Abroad," *Isis* 72 (1981): 590–612.

RONALD L. NUMBERS

BEAUREGARD, Pierre Gustave Toutant (28 May 1818–20 Feb. 1893), soldier, was born at "Contreras," his family's plantation in St. Bernard Parish, Louisiana, the son of Jacques Toutant-Beauregard, a planter, and Helene Judith de Reggio. At age eight he was sent to a private school in New Orleans for three years, and for four years after that he attended the French School, a private institution in New York City. Beauregard entered the U.S. Military Academy in 1834 and graduated second in the class of 1838. Commissioned a second lieutenant of engineers, he worked on various fortifications in Florida and in his native state during the years prior to the Mexican War. In 1841 Beauregard married Marie Laure Villere; they had two sons. Laure died in March 1850, giving birth to a daughter.

During the Mexican War, Beauregard served as an engineer in Winfield Scott's army and distinguished himself in several battles, including Contreras, Churubusco, and Chapultepec. He received brevets as captain and major for his conduct and was promoted to captain in the regular army on 3 March 1853. Beauregard returned to Louisiana after the war and resumed engineering duties there. He married Caroline Deslonde in 1860; she died in 1864. The couple had no children. On 23 January 1861 he became superintendent of West Point but was ordered to vacate the post two days later. Beauregard left the academy two days after the secession of Louisiana, and he resigned his commission on 20 February 1861. Governor Thomas O. Moore of Louisiana passed over Beauregard for commander of the Louisiana state forces but offered him a commission as colonel of engineers. Beauregard declined the commission and enlisted as a private in a volunteer company.

Jefferson Davis appointed Beauregard a brigadier general in the Provisional Army of the Confederate States of America on 1 March 1861 and placed him in command of the troops at Charleston, South Carolina. There Beauregard supervised the bombardment of Fort Sumter and received the surrender of its garrison on 14 April. The public acclaim Beauregard received led to his assignment to command Confederate forces near Manassas, Virginia. Though outranked by General Joseph E. Johnston, Beauregard was allowed by the latter to direct the disposition of troops for the battle of First Manassas on 21 July. The Creole general performed bravely in the engagement and had a horse shot from under him. He was promoted to full general on 13 August to date from 21 July.

Beauregard was assigned to cooperate with General Albert Sidney Johnston in the western theater in the spring of 1862. He assumed command at Corinth, Mississippi, and concentrated a force of about 40,000 men there as Johnston's line in Kentucky and Tennessee collapsed. Beauregard planned the attack on Major General Ulysses S. Grant's army at Shiloh and served as second in command to Johnston until that general's death late on 6 April. He failed to press the Confederate attack that day but was successful in holding back Federal attacks on 7 April. Falling back to Corinth, the army fortified that place, while the Union army slowly advanced against it. Beauregard ordered the evacuation of the town in late May. The following month he went on sick leave without first receiving approval from Davis, so the latter relieved him of command of the Army of Mississippi. This action exacerbated the deteriorating relationship between the two men, and Beauregard soon became a leader of the western theater generals who opposed Davis's strategy for the war.

On 19 August 1862 Beauregard was named as commander of the Department of South Carolina and Georgia. In this capacity, he supervised the defenses of Charleston and successfully repelled Union land and naval advances through the fall and winter of 1863. He also wrote *Principles and Maxims of the Art of War* (1863) while in command at Charleston. Beauregard received command of the Department of North Carolina and Cape Fear on 23 April 1864, and he renamed it the Department of North Carolina and Southern Virginia. He performed admirably in defeating Major General Benjamin F. Butler's Army of the James at Bermuda Hundred, Virginia, in May. The next month Beauregard's forces held back Union attacks on Petersburg until reinforced by troops from General Robert E. Lee's Army of Northern Virginia. Beauregard continued to serve under Lee until the fall.

Again Davis sent Beauregard to the western theater, on 17 October naming him commander of the Military Division of the West. He had the responsibility of overseeing all Confederate armies in Mississippi, Alabama, Georgia, and the Carolinas. During the next several months, General John Bell Hood's invasion of Tennessee was crushed near Nashville, and the troops facing Major General William T. Sherman's Union armies in Georgia failed to halt the advance of those forces. Beauregard, in reality, could have done little to change these situations. He assumed command of troops in South Carolina on 16 February 1865 and shortly afterward again came under the command of General Joseph E. Johnston. Beauregard was paroled after the surrender of Johnston's forces to Sherman on 18 April. He then returned to New Orleans.

Beauregard was president of the New Orleans, Jackson & Mississippi Railroad from 1865 to 1870. During that time period, he declined offers by several foreign governments to command their armies. Beauregard became manager of the Louisiana State Lottery Company in February 1877 and recouped the financial losses he had experienced previously. He was appointed commissioner of public works in New Orleans in 1888 and served for several years as adjutant general of Louisiana. Beauregard died in New Orleans, and his body was interred in the Army of Tennessee vault in Metairie Cemetery.

The controversy that swirled around Beauregard during much of his Civil War career has continued to be discussed among historians, who generally acknowledge that he had great potential as a military leader. He never lived up to that potential, in part because of petty jealousies and his own ego. No one has ever questioned his bravery on the battlefield. However, he never seemed to understand fully the realities of the Confederacy's capabilities to wage war. Beauregard correctly recognized the importance of the western theater, but his poor relationship with Davis and other generals hampered his efforts to improve the Confederacy's situation there.

• Beauregard's official and personal papers are voluminous. The largest collection of documents is in the Library of Congress, while many of his official papers are in the National Archives. Beauregard's other papers are scattered in a dozen repositories around the country; the most significant collec tion is at Tulane University in New Orleans. The best biography of Beauregard written to date is T. Harry Williams, *P. G. T. Beauregard: Napoleon in Gray* (1955). An older work by Hamilton Basso, *Beauregard: The Great Creole* (1933), is highly laudatory. Alfred Roman, *The Military Operations of General Beauregard, in the War between the States, 1861 to 1865* (2 vols., 1884), was largely written by Beauregard though attributed to his former chief of staff. Numerous articles have been written about Beauregard; the following are among the most informative: Bruce S. Hass, "Beauregard and the Image of Napoleon," *Louisiana History* 5 (1964): 179–86; Gerald Patterson, "Gustave," *Civil War Times Illustrated* 31, no. 3 (July–Aug. 1992): 28–35, 52–54; and Williams, "Beauregard at Shiloh," *Civil War History* 1 (1955): 17–34. An obituary is in the *New Orleans Picayune*, 21 Feb. 1893.

ARTHUR W. BERGERON, JR.

BEAUX, Cecilia (1 May 1855–17 Sep. 1942), portrait painter, was born in Philadelphia, Pennsylvania, the daughter of Jean Adolphe Beaux, a French émigré and silk manufacturer, and Cecilia Kent Leavitt, a governess and teacher from New York City. She was baptized Eliza Cecilia Beaux. Twelve days after her birth, Beaux's mother died from childbirth complications; her father then gave her and her sister to their maternal grandmother and aunts to raise. The Leavitt family's tenuous financial circumstances, ever present during Beaux's childhood, were eased when her aunt Emily married mining engineer William Foster Biddle and he joined the household.

Educated at home until age fourteen, Beaux attended the Misses Lyman's School for two years and then began her art training. In 1871 William Biddle arranged private art instruction for her with artist and distant relative Catharine Ann Drinker (who later became Catharine Janvier). For a year Beaux did copy work with Drinker and then completed two years of more formal art training at the short-lived art school of Francis Adolf Van Der Wielen, a Dutch artist who had emigrated to Philadelphia.

Adopting her mother's name—Cecilia Beaux—as her artistic signature, Beaux began her career in the decorative arts. In 1873 she taught art classes at Miss Sanford's School and within a year was giving private art lessons to a number of individual students. She soon expanded her efforts to commercial endeavors, making a lithograph entitled *The Brighton Cats* (1874; private collection). Its success probably brought her earliest lucrative commission executing lithographic drawings of fossils for the paleontologist Edward Drinker Cope, who was then doing work for the U.S. Geological Survey. Following a month of china-painting lessons in 1879 with French ceramist Camille Piton, Beaux began creating portraits of children on china plates. She also produced crayon, watercolor, and charcoal portraits based on photographs. Beaux's interest in portraiture developed from her experiences in the design arts.

To enhance her skills Beaux sporadically attended the Pennsylvania Academy of the Fine Arts from 1876 to 1878 but refused to study with Thomas Eakins, working instead in the school's antique, portrait, and costume classes. She continued her art training in the early 1880s in a private class, to which the artist William Sartain infrequently came to give criticism. It was under Sartain's tutelage that Beaux learned to paint, producing her first major portrait, *The Last Days of Infancy* (1883–1884; Pennsylvania Academy), for which she was awarded the Pennsylvania Academy's Mary Smith Prize in 1885. In 1888 Beaux went to Paris for a year and a half and received her final art instruction at the Académie Julian and Académie Colorossi, where her work was critiqued by Tony Robert Fleury, Adolphe-William Bouguereau, Gustave Courtois, P. A. J. Dagnan-Bouveret, and Benjamin Constant. During the summer of 1888, while painting in the Breton village of Concarneau with artists Thomas Alexander Harrison and Charles Lasar, Beaux's ambition to become a portrait painter solidified.

Beaux's painting career spanned the great age and last stage of the formal society portrait in America, and when she returned to Philadelphia in 1889 she established her reputation with beautiful grand manner paintings of her sister's children, such as *Cecil* (1892; Philadelphia Museum of Art) and *Ernesta with Nurse* (1894; Metropolitan Museum of Art), and with exquisite commissioned portraits of Philadelphia's elite, such as *Mrs. Beauveau Borie and Son Adolph* (1896; Amon Carter Museum) and *Mrs. Clement A. Griscom and Daughter Frances* (1898; Pennsylvania Academy). Beaux's standing in the Philadelphia art world was acknowledged in 1895, when she was hired by the Pennsylvania Academy to teach the school's portrait classes; she was the first woman to teach there full time and remained on the faculty until 1916.

In 1896 Beaux sent a group of paintings, including *The Dreamer* (1894; Butler Institute of American Art) and *Sita and Sarita* (1894; Musée d'Orsay), to the Parisian Salon at the Champs de Mars. Acclaimed by the critics, Beaux was made an associate of the Société Nationale des Beaux-Arts; her artistic reputation escalated to an international level; and William Merritt Chase soon declared her "the best woman painter who ever lived." Beaux continued exhibiting her work in annual exhibitions and international expositions, where she frequently won awards and prizes, including the Pennsylvania Academy's Gold Medal of Honor (1898), the Carnegie Institute's gold medal (1899), and the gold medal (1900) at the Exposition Universelle in Paris.

By 1899 Beaux had moved from Philadelphia to New York City, and by 1905 she was regularly spending summers in Gloucester, Massachusetts, where she had built "Green Alley," her summer home and studio. As one of America's most esteemed portrait painters, Beaux was now fulfilling commissions for numerous luminaries. These commissioned works include *Mrs. Theodore Roosevelt and Daughter Ethel* (1902; private collection); *A. Piatt Andrew* (1902–1903; Cape Ann Historical Association), for the Harvard economist and U.S. congressman; *Richard Watson Gilder* (1903; private collection), for the *Century Magazine* editor; and *Caroline Hazard* (1908; Wellesley College) for Wellesley College. In 1919, at the close of the First World War, the U.S. War Portraits Commission assigned Beaux her final important portrait commission, for which she produced *Cardinal Desire Joseph Mercier*, *Premier Georges Clemenceau*, and *Admiral Sir David Beatty* (all Smithsonian Institution, National Museum of American Art).

From 1918 to 1928 Beaux gave criticism in a private art class in New York, but when she broke her hip on the streets of Paris in 1924 her painting career ended. Crippled for the rest of her life, Beaux turned her energies to writing her autobiography, *Background with Figures* (1930). During the 1930s Beaux was honored for her contribution to the arts. The National Institute of Arts and Letters elected her to membership in 1930; the American Academy of Arts and Letters, in 1933. She was also awarded the National Achievement Gold Medal from the Chi Omega Fraternity in 1933. Given to "the American woman who had made the greatest contribution to the culture of the world," the medal was presented to her by first lady Eleanor Roosevelt. In 1935 the American Academy of Arts and Letters organized the first retrospective of her work, and in 1942 they awarded her a gold medal for lifetime achievement.

Beaux never married, believing that her art career was a "sacred calling" given to her as one of the few artistically gifted women willing to sacrifice marriage and family for the rewards of artistic success at the highest levels. Beaux's portraits, filled with bravura brushwork and enticing color notes, flatteringly chronicled the lives of America's upper class and were often favorably compared to the work of John Singer Sargent. Beaux died at Green Alley and was buried in the West Laurel Hill Cemetery in Bala-Cynwyd, Pennsylvania.

• Beaux's papers are in the Archives of American Art, Smithsonian Institution; the Archives of the Pennsylvania Academy of the Fine Arts, Philadelphia; and the Archives of the Corcoran Gallery of Art, Washington, D.C. There is also substantial information on Beaux in the Gilder/Palmer Family Papers in Tyringham, Mass.; and the George Dudley Seymour Papers in the Yale University Library. In addition to her autobiography, Beaux wrote a number of articles on art education, including "Why the Girl Art Student Fails," *Harper's Bazar*, May 1913; "Professional Art Schools," *Art and Progress*, Nov. 1915; and "What Should the College A.B. Course Offer to the Future Artist?" *American Magazine of Art*, Oct. 1916. Important sources on Beaux's life are Thornton Oakley, *Cecilia Beaux* (1943); Pennsylvania Academy of the Fine Arts, *The Paintings and Drawings of Cecilia Beaux* (1955); Catherine Drinker Bowen, *Family Portrait* (1970); an exhibition catalog by the Pennsylvania Academy of the Fine Arts, *Cecilia Beaux: Portrait of an Artist* (1974); and Tara Leigh Tappert, *Choices: The Life and Career of Cecilia Beaux—A Professional Biography* (1990). Beaux was also the subject of numerous articles during her lifetime, including William Walton, "Cecilia Beaux," *Scribner's*, Oct. 1897, pp. 477–85; Mrs. Arthur Bell, "The Work of Cecilia Beaux," *International Studio*, Oct. 1899, pp. 215–22; Hildegarde Hawthorne, "A Garden of the Heart—Green Alley, the Home of Miss Cecilia Beaux," *Century Magazine*, Aug. 1910, pp. 581–

87; Gutzon Borglum, "Cecilia Beaux—Painter of Heroes," *Delineator*, June 1921, pp. 16–17; and Allison Gray, "The Extraordinary Career of Cecilia Beaux," *American Magazine*, Oct. 1923, pp. 61–63, 195–98. Contemporary reassessments include Elizabeth Graham Bailey, "The Cecilia Beaux Papers," *Archives of American Art Journal* 13, no. 4 (1973): 14–19; Judith E. Stein, "Profile of Cecilia Beaux," *Feminist Art Journal* 4 (Winter 1975–1976): 25–31, 33; Tappert, "Cecilia Beaux: A Career As a Portraitist," *Women's Studies: An Interdisciplinary Journal* 14, no. 4 (1988): 389–411; and Sarah Burns, "The 'Earnest, Untiring Worker' and the Magician of the Brush: Gender Politics in the Criticism of Cecilia Beaux," *Oxford Art Journal* 15, no. 1 (1992): 36–53. An obituary is in the *New York Herald Tribune*, 18 Sept. 1942.

TARA LEIGH TAPPERT

BEAVER, Robert Pierce (26 May 1906–20 Nov. 1987), minister and missions scholar, was born in Hamilton, Ohio, the son of Joseph Earl Beaver, an employee of the Game and Fish Commission of Ohio, and Caroline Neusch. He received the B.A. and M.A. in art history at Oberlin College (1928) followed by post graduate studies at Munich (1931–1932), a Ph.D. in history from Cornell University (1933), and postdoctoral study at Yale (1938). He married his high school classmate Wilma Manessier, a kindergarten teacher, in 1927; they had three children.

Beaver was ordained to the ministry in the Evangelical and Reformed church (later the United Church of Christ) in 1932 and served pastorates in Cincinnati, Ohio, and Baltimore, Maryland, until 1938, when the denomination sent the family to China as missionaries. After language study at the College of Chinese Studies in Peking in 1938–1939, Beaver taught at the Central China Union Theological Seminary in Lingling, Hunan Province (1940–1942). In 1942, because of poor health, he was sent to Hong Kong, arriving less than twenty-four hours before the bombing of that city. He was interned in Hong Kong by the Japanese for seven months until he was repatriated in 1943. In the meantime, his wife and children had returned to the United States in 1940.

After returning to the United States, Beaver spoke in churches and conferences for the mission board and did postdoctoral studies at Union Theological Seminary and Columbia University, both in New York City. Then he taught courses in the history and theory of missions at Lancaster (Pa.) Theological Seminary (1944–1948). He was director of the Missionary Research Library (MRL) at Union Theological Seminary from 1948 to 1955 and concurrently served as research secretary of the Foreign Missions Conference of North America, which in 1950 became the Division of Foreign Missions of the National Council of the Churches of Christ in the U.S.A. Of Beaver's service at the MRL, John Bennett, then president of Union Theological Seminary said, "He was an extraordinary librarian, or rather, strategist in building a library. His scholarship was very remarkable in its breadth and in the tenacity of his hold on facts. . . . He made of the library not merely a collection of books and materials, but a center of research" (quoted in Kang, p. 165).

Beaver's productivity and influence as a missions scholar began during his tenure at the MRL. In 1950 he began publishing the *Occasional Bulletin*. This MRL periodical, which later became the *International Bulletin of Missionary Research* published by the Overseas Ministries Study Center, provided documentation and encouraged the advancement of scholarship in the study of Christian missions. While serving at the MRL, Beaver also lectured in missions at Union Theological Seminary and at Biblical Seminary (now New York Theological Seminary).

In 1955 Beaver was appointed professor of missions at the University of Chicago Divinity School, where he served until he retired in 1971 as professor emeritus. Jerald Brauer, then dean of the divinity school, said about Beaver, "Within the brief period of fifteen years at the University of Chicago he revolutionized the teaching of the history of missions" (quoted in Kang, p. 170). In postretirement (1973–1976) Beaver was director of the Overseas Ministries Study Center, then located in Ventnor, New Jersey.

He was a founding member of the Association of Professors of Missions in 1952 (president, 1956–1958) and for many years was a trustee of the Foundation for Theological Education in South East Asia. He also served on the research committee of the International Missionary Council and on the United Board of Christian Colleges in China, forerunner of the United Board for Christian Higher Education in Asia. Beaver traveled and lectured frequently in Africa and Asia. In 1957 he gave the Carey Lectures at Serampore University in India and in 1959 the Barrow Lectures in Taiwan.

A prolific author, Beaver published several pioneering studies that became standard references: *Ecumenical Beginnings in Protestant World Mission: A History of Comity* (1962), *Pioneers in Mission: The Early Missionary Ordination Sermons, Charges, and Instructions* (1966), *Church, State, and the American Indians* (1966), and especially *All Loves Excelling: American Protestant Women in World Mission* (1968; rev. 1980 as *American Protestant Women in World Mission: History of the First Feminist Movement in North America*). The proceedings of a large symposium he edited for the American Society of Missiology, *American Missions in Bicentennial Perspective* (1976), was judged by church historian Robert T. Handy to be "one of the most important books in the field of religion to arise out of the bicentennial celebration . . . a landmark in the development of missiology in America" (*Occasional Bulletin of Missionary Research* 2, no. 1 [1978]: 28). Beaver also edited *The Gospel and Frontier Peoples* (1973), the report from a large consultation he organized for the National Council of Churches that focused attention on the unfinished task of frontier missions to tribal peoples.

Warmly evangelical yet firmly ecumenical, a historian with distinguished academic credentials, Beaver was trusted across the theological spectrum and served as a "bridge person" in bringing scholars together to advance the cause of Christian mission studies. His work was marked by the range and quality of his scholarship, his attention to documentation and sources, his pioneering studies about the contribution of women in American Protestant missions, and his irenic spirit, which encouraged cooperation among scholars from different church traditions. In the period after 1960 he made a major contribution to the revival and recognition of missiology as an academic discipline in North American theological education. He died in Tucson, Arizona.

• Beaver's personal library, papers, and unclassified documents are in the library of Memphis Theological Seminary, Memphis, Tenn. A biographical tribute by Wi Jo Kang and a bibliography of Beaver's published work up to 1969 are in the festschrift *The Future of the Christian World Mission: Studies in Honor of R. Pierce Beaver*, ed. William J. Danker and Wi Jo Kang (1971; repr. in *Criterion* 10, no. 3 [1971]: 10–13). The best survey and assessment of Beaver's work is by F. Dean Lueking, "The Legacy of R. Pierce Beaver," *International Bulletin of Missionary Research* 14, no. 1 (1990): 2–5.

GERALD H. ANDERSON

BEAVERS, Louise (8 Mar. 1902–26 Oct. 1962), actress, was born in Cincinnati, Ohio, the daughter of William Beavers. Her mother's identity cannot be ascertained. As a child she moved with her musically inclined family to California, where, in 1918, she graduated from Pasadena High School. She then joined a "Ladies' Minstrel Troupe" for a year before being recognized by talent scouts.

Beavers, who would appear in more than 100 motion pictures, began her Hollywood career playing a maid to leading lady Lilyan Tashman in *Gold Diggers* (1923). Early on it was a role she had to play off screen as well as on. From 1920 to 1926 she worked first as a dressing room attendant and then as the real-life personal maid of actress Leatrice Joy. In 1927 she landed a major role in *Uncle Tom's Cabin*, followed, in 1929, by roles in *Coquette* and *Nix on Dames*. In the early 1930s she earned critical notices for her handling of subservient roles in *Ladies of the Big House* (1932), *What Price Hollywood?* (1932), *Bombshell* (1933), and *She Done Him Wrong* (1933). Big-boned, dark-skinned, and usually smiling on the screen, she was best known for playing the good-natured maid or housekeeper for such stars as Mae West, Claudette Colbert, and Jean Harlow. Typecast as a maid for her entire acting career, Beavers was seen "serving" a cavalcade of other motion picture greats, including Clara Bow, Boris Karloff, Hedda Hopper, James Stewart, Joan Crawford, Spencer Tracy, Ralph Bellamy, Ginger Rogers, Joan Blondell, Jimmy Durante, Edward G. Robinson, Humphrey Bogart, Ronald Reagan, Jane Wyman, Rosalind Russell, Henry Fonda, Bing Crosby, John Wayne, Zero Mostel, Orson Welles, Marlene Dietrich, W. C. Fields, Sidney Poitier, June Allyson, Jack Lemmon, Debbie Reynolds, Lloyd Bridges, Natalie Wood, and Pearl Bailey, among many others. As black film historian Donald Bogle has pointed out, Beavers came to epitomize the lovable, loyal, overweight "Mammy" figure seemingly capable of taking on all the troubles of the world. "She perfected the optimistic, sentimental black woman whose sweet, sunny disposition and kindheartedness almost always saved the day, the Depression era's embodiment of Christian stoicism and goodness, lending a friendly ear and hand to down-on-their-luck heroines, who knew that when the rest of the world failed them, Louise would always be there" (Bogle, p. 73).

Beavers's professional breakthrough came in her powerful portrayal of businesslike, pancake-flapping Aunt Delilah to Claudette Colbert's Bea in *Imitation of Life* (1934), a sensitive performance acclaimed by both the white and black press, many critics saying they thought she deserved an Oscar nomination. Yet what Beavers mostly won from that performance was the "Aunt Jemima" label that would stick to her forever. Despite her screen persona as a domestic, Beavers never cooked, though she did maintain a high-calorie diet to keep her weight up, and she took elocution lessons to cultivate a southern drawl. Although she was married to LeRoy Moore in the late 1950s, she never had children.

Beavers was proud to be featured in two pioneering black-cast films produced by Million Dollar Productions, *Life Goes On* (1938) and *Reform School* (1939), even though in *Reform School* her role as a probation officer was a Mammy-type character. Of note is the fact that, whereas in these films her respective characters were named "Star" and "Mother Barton," in other movies her names were usually associated with black servitude, such as "Lulu" in *The Expert* (1932), "Ivory" in *Ladies of the Big House* (1932) and *Women without Names* (1940), "Pearl" in *She Done Him Wrong* (1933), "Loretta" in *Bombshell* (1933), "Magnolia" in *Pick Up* (1933), "Imogene" in *Hat, Coat and Gloves* (1934), "Florabelle" in *Wives Never Know* (1936), "Ophelia" in *Virginia* (1941), "Ruby" in *The Big Street* (1942), "Maum Maria" in *Reap the Wild Wind* (1942), "Mammy Jenny" in *Jack London* (1943), "Bedelia" in *Barbary Coast Gent* (1944), "Petunia" in *Seven Sweethearts* (1942), "Gussie" in *Mr. Blandings Builds His Dream House* (1948), and "Mammy Lou" in *Belle Starr* (1941). More typically, however, Louise Beavers was listed in movie credits—if at all—simply as "maid" (*Night World, Street of Women,* and *Young America,* all 1932), "cook" (*Made for Each Other,* 1939), "Mammy" (*Too Busy to Work,* 1932) Aunt so-and-so (Tina in *The Lady's from Kentucky,* 1939), or "Mamie" (*Make Way for Tomorrow,* 1937).

Ending the 1940s with *Tell It to the Judge* (1949), Beavers then starred in *Girls' School, The Jackie Robinson Story,* and *My Blue Heaven* in 1950; *Colorado Sundown, I Dream of Jeannie,* and *Never Wave at a WAC* in 1953; *Goodbye, My Lady, Teenage Rebel,* and *You Can't Run Away from It* in 1956; *Tammy and the Bachelor* in 1957; *The Goddess* in 1958; and *All the Fine Young Cannibals* in 1960.

Television also played a role in the Louise Beavers profile. Following on the heels of two other prominent black actresses who had starred on the popular television series "Beulah" (Ethel Waters and Hattie McDaniel), Beavers decided to play the Henderson household's good-natured domestic. Her brief tenure, begun in 1952, lasted until the next year when the show went off the air because she decided to leave the role. Her other television credits include "Star Stage" (1956), "The Hostess with the Mostest" on "Playhouse 90" (1957), and "Swamp Fox" on "Walt Disney Presents" (1959). Perhaps it was appropriate that, after nearly three decades and more than 116 films, Beavers's final role was the "Gilbert maid," serving Bob Hope and Lucille Ball in the 1961 madcap comedy *The Facts of Life.* She died the following year in Los Angeles.

The career of Louise Beavers serves as a critical reminder of how, in the early days of Hollywood, the stock characters available to black actresses progressed from merely inhabiting the background to representing a servile and gratuitous stereotype. Just as Aunt Delilah in *Imitation of Life* selflessly shares her pancake recipe with Bea rather than cash in on it herself, Louise Beavers exemplifies the legions of other early black actresses whose talents were subordinated to the self-serving biases of the dominant society.

• For further information, see clipping files on Louise Beavers in both the New York Public Library Theatre Collection and the Academy of Motion Picture Arts and Sciences National Film Information Service Library; Donald Bogle, *Brown Sugar: Eighty Years of America's Black Female Superstars* (1980); Linda K. Fuller, "From Servile to Sassy: A Look at Hollywood's 'Maids,'" in *Beyond the Stars,* vol. 1: *Stock Characters in American Popular Film,* ed. Paul Loukides and Linda K. Fuller (1990); and James R. Nesteby, *Black Images in American Films, 1896–1954: The Interplay between Civil Rights and Film Culture* (1982). Obituaries are in the *New York Times, New York Herald Tribune, New York World Telegram and Sun, Variety,* and *Time.*

LINDA K. FULLER

BECHET, Sidney (14 May 1897–14 May 1959), jazz soprano saxophonist and clarinetist, was born Sidney Joseph Bechet in New Orleans, Louisiana, the son of Omar (or Omer) Bechet, a shoemaker and amateur flutist, and Josephine Michel. An incorrigible truant, after age eight he stopped attending school and started teaching himself clarinet. What basic education he later received came from private tutoring by a cousin. He received some clarinet training from George Baquet, "Big Eye" Louis Nelson, and Lorenzo Tio, Jr. Born with perfect pitch and an infallible musical memory, Bechet could duplicate anything he heard, and, as a result, he never learned to read music. He started playing professionally almost immediately, and his first jobs were with his brother Leonard's Silver Bells Band and the Young Olympians, a group he formed with Buddy Petit around 1909. In 1911 (or 1913) he started playing with Bunk Johnson in Frankie Dusen's Eagle Band, and he also worked regularly with Freddie Keppard, Manuel Perez, and Jack Carey. By 1914, when he joined King Oliver and Zue Robertson in the Olympia Band, he was considered the best jazz clarinetist in New Orleans. Bechet married Norma (maiden name unknown); they had no children.

In 1916, after a tour with a Clarence Williams troupe left him stranded in Galveston, Texas, Bechet toured with a carnival before returning home to work with Oliver. In the fall of 1917 he went north with a road company, but he quit in Chicago in March 1918 to join Lawrence Duhé's band at the De Luxe Café, later doubling at the Pekin Café with Tony Jackson and the Dreamland Café with Oliver. In early 1919 he was heard by Will Marion Cook, who hired him for a tour of Europe with his Southern Syncopated Orchestra. Following a short stint with Tim Brymn's band in Coney Island, New York, Bechet traveled with the Cook company to London, where the 27-piece orchestra and choral group performed at the Royal Philharmonic Hall from 4 July through 6 December 1919. The Cook program consisted mostly of heavily orchestrated concert material, but Bechet was given the penultimate slot for his own "Characteristic Blues," a nightly feature that inspired Swiss classical conductor Ernest Ansermet to write what has become one of the more widely quoted encomiums in jazz history. In a piece published in an October 1919 *Revue Romande*, Ansermet cited Bechet as "an extraordinary clarinet virtuoso" who could improvise fluently on the blues. Most significantly, he predicted that Bechet's "'own way' [of playing] is perhaps the highway the whole world will swing along to-morrow." However, despite this praise and other acknowledgments of his talent, because of unpaid back wages Bechet and five other musicians left Cook in December to work at the Embassy Club. At that time he bought his first straight soprano saxophone. By early October 1920 Bennie Peyton's Jazz Kings were performing double duty at both the Hammersmith Palais and Rector's cabaret, and, although the six-piece band did not play New Orleans jazz, Bechet improvised freely on popular dance songs, operatic arias, and rhapsodic melodies such as "The Song of Songs." The band continued to work at both places through mid-1922, when Bechet left to take his own group into the Embassy. In early September, following charges that he had assaulted a woman whom he claimed was a prostitute and a user of drugs, Bechet was found guilty and sentenced to two weeks imprisonment and deportation. Despite a petition for appeal launched by Peyton in October, the ruling was upheld, and Bechet left for New York in early November. After a brief stay with Ford Dabney's orchestra, he accepted a leading role as a saxophone-playing Chinese laundryman in *How Come*, a traveling show that also featured Bessie Smith. In early 1923 he left the show and rejoined Cook for a tour of vaudeville houses.

In early 1924 Bechet worked in the racially mixed "Black and White Revue" and played brief jobs with James P. Johnson and Willie "The Lion" Smith before going into the Kentucky Club with Duke Ellington's Washingtonians. A May through July 1925 stint with the variety show *Seven-Eleven* preceded his unsuccessful attempt at running his own Club Basha, and in September he went with *La Revue nègre*, a show fea-

turing Josephine Baker. Opening at the Théâtre des Champs-Elysées in Paris on 2 October 1925, the revue later played in Brussels and Berlin but folded when Baker left to go with the Folies Bergère. Bechet then toured Russia with Frank Withers from February through May 1926, after which he joined a reassembled *La Revue nègre* in Berlin as musical director. On the tour's conclusion, he returned to Paris in the spring of 1928 and joined Noble Sissle's orchestra at Les Ambassadeurs, after which a shooting fracas occurred that resulted in his being imprisoned for eleven months. Deported from France, he moved to Berlin, where he worked at the Haus Vaterland and appeared in a film. On 22 December 1930 he returned to New York and rejoined Sissle at the Rockland Palace.

Following a succession of theater dates, Sissle returned to Les Ambassadeurs in May 1931, while Bechet worked in Berlin and later toured with *Black Flowers* (formerly *La Revue nègre*). He rejoined Sissle in New York in September, but mounting frustration with his limited role in the band caused him to leave in early 1932 to work with Lorenzo Tio at the Nest Club in Harlem. After a very brief tour with Ellington, for which he was hired to teach Johnny Hodges his set solo on "The Sheik of Araby," Bechet formed his own sextet, which worked at the Saratoga Club and other locations before going into the Savoy Ballroom in September. The day after their opening, Bechet's New Orleans Feetwarmers recorded an exciting session for Victor that created a stir among lovers of small-band jazz, but for lack of work the group soon disbanded. Bechet next played in a trio with Willie "The Lion" Smith at Pod's and Jerry's, where Billie Holiday often came to sing. Then, with his trumpeter from the Feetwarmers, Tommy Ladnier, in early 1933 he opened a cleaning and pressing shop in Harlem. Having divorced his first wife in 1929, in 1934 Bechet married nineteen-year-old Marilouise Crawford; they had no children and were divorced after 1942.

In May 1934 Bechet rejoined Sissle in Chicago, where the band was working in a traveling company of the Folies Bergère. More years of touring and frustration followed, but in October 1938, prompted by the popularity of a series of small band records he had made months earlier, he left Sissle to concentrate on playing only jazz. His next job was at Nick's in Greenwich Village, first as the featured soloist with the Spirits of Rhythm and then as leader of his own quartet. In November he performed on Joe Marsala's jam session for the BBC, and the next month he led the reassembled New Orleans Feetwarmers at John Hammond's "From Spirituals to Swing" concert at Carnegie Hall. From July 1939 to January 1940 he led small groups at various places in the Adirondacks, and from February through May he was back at Nick's. After summering in Philadelphia, Bechet worked at the Enduro in Brooklyn, and from October through the summer of 1941 he was at the Log Cabin, the Mimo Club in Harlem, and Camp Unity, a retreat run by the Communist party in upper New York State. From

September 1939 until May 1940 he recorded with Jelly Roll Morton, Muggsy Spanier, and Louis Armstrong, and from June 1940 to October 1941 he led eight highly acclaimed New Orleans Feetwarmers sessions for Victor.

Early in 1942 Bechet appeared with Red Allen's band at Boston's Ken Club, spent the summer at Camp Unity, and played at various restaurants and nightclubs in the fall and winter. After recuperating from an illness and dental problems, he resumed steady work in March 1943 with engagements in Maryland, Pennsylvania, Massachusetts, and New York, where he worked at the Onyx Club and then at Nick's. For several months in early 1944 he led a quartet at the Club Rio in Springfield, Illinois. He was back in New York in December to record his classic "Blue Horizon" for the Blue Note label and to appear on Eddie Condon's "Town Hall Jazz Concert" broadcasts. From March through May 1945 he led a band at Boston's Savoy Café, and in July he began a series of recording dates for Mezz Mezzrow's King Jazz label. In October he collaborated with Wild Bill Davison and Art Hodes on the first of several sessions for Blue Note. Starting in February 1946, when he paired with Albert Nicholas for another classic Blue Note recording date, Bechet frequently played concerts and club sessions in and around New York and appeared regularly at Condon's and Jimmy Ryan's. In March 1947 he led a trio at Ryan's and began appearing as featured soloist on Rudi Blesh's "This Is Jazz" weekly radio series. From September 1947 through September 1949 Bechet alternated between Ryan's and Jazz Ltd. in Chicago while recording for King Jazz and Blue Note. In May 1949 he appeared in concert at the Salle Pleyel in Paris, and from October 1949 through late 1953 he divided his time between European engagements, with Paris as his home base, and New York, where he continued to appear at Ryan's and to record for Blue Note.

For several years Bechet played residencies at the Vieux Colombier in Paris and at its summer resort branch in Juan-les-Pins. In August 1951 he married Elisabeth Ziegler, his third wife, in Cannes to a citywide celebration of street floats and parading jazz bands. A month after his wedding he appeared at Chicago's Blue Note and at Storyville in Boston, and in December he was back in Paris. The couple had no children. Following a summer in Juan-les-Pins and a tour of North Africa, he spent the first half of 1953 in Europe. In August he played at the Bandbox in New York, and in September he worked with Marty Marsala at the Down Beat Club in San Francisco and with Bob Scobey at the "Dixieland Jubilee" festival in Hollywood. After a few dates in Philadelphia and Boston, he returned to France in December. Following an operation in June 1954 he was back at Juan-les-Pins and later the Vieux Colombier, from which base he resumed touring. In September 1956 he visited the British Isles and in 1957 Germany, Italy, and France. In July 1958, after playing at several other festivals, he

led an all-star American band at the World's Fair in Brussels. Later that year he was diagnosed with lung cancer, but he continued to perform, happy that his "Petite fleur" had become an international hit. In such great regard was he generally held that, on his death in Garches, a small town north of Paris where he maintained a home for his mistress and their son, more than three thousand mourners attended his funeral.

As is strikingly evident from the first recordings he made with Clarence Williams's Blue Five in 1923, as well as those pairing him with Louis Armstrong in 1924 and 1925, Bechet exhibited a commanding musical presence, one characterized by breathtaking inventiveness, sweeping passion, rhythmic drive, and emotional intensity. His tone, with its fast, throbbing vibrato and expressive timbre, remained relatively unchanged throughout his career, but by 1932 his rhythmic sense had started to anticipate the looser phrasing of the Swing Era. In his earlier years he had been a stylistic model for Johnny Dodds, Jimmie Noone, Albert Nicholas, Omer Simeon, Buster Bailey, and Johnny Hodges, but by the late 1940s his influence had spread throughout the world. Bechet's approach to slow blues ran the gamut from tender to fierce, while his innate sense of swinging time lent a majesty to his phrasing at faster tempos. Perhaps, though, it was his rhapsodic way with ballads, a legacy of both his Creole heritage and his lifelong love of opera, that appealed so much to the Gallic temperament. An unabashed romantic, Bechet always aimed for the heart. Forty years after he had deeply moved his first European audiences, he still had the verve and passion to thrill their grandchildren.

• Although Mary E. Karoley's "Sidney Bechet," *Jazz Information,* 6 Dec. 1940, pp. 8–16, is the earliest biographical treatment, the definitive critical biography is John Chilton, *Sidney Bechet: The Wizard of Jazz* (1987), a work that expands on and puts into proper sequence the chronological anomalies of Bechet's own *Treat It Gentle* (1960). The long second chapter of the posthumously published autobiography, in which Bechet discusses his "grandfather" Omar, has more to do with folk legend than history, but precisely because of the deeply touching, mythopoetic manner of his storytelling, Bechet can be forgiven. His ongoing descriptions of the emotional impact of jazz are masterpieces of metaphor and make for revealing insights into the man. The complete text of Ernest Ansermet's 1919 review of the Southern Syncopated Orchestra and of Bechet in particular is in Martin Williams, ed., *The Art of Jazz* (1960). Valuable analyses of Bechet's recordings and style are in Martin Williams, *Jazz Masters of New Orleans* (1967); Whitney Balliett, *American Musicians* (1986); Gunther Schuller, *Early Jazz* (1968) and *The Swing Era: The Development of Jazz, 1930–1945* (1989); and Richard M. Sudhalter and Bob Wilber, *Notes* to Time-Life's Giants of Jazz album of Sidney Bechet (1980), a booklet that also contains a biographical essay by Frank Kappler. The most comprehensive discographical references are Brian Rust, *Jazz Records, 1897–1942* (1982); Walter Bruyninckx, *Traditional Discography, 1897–1988* (6 vols., 1988–1989) and

Swing Discography, 1920–1988 (12 vols., 1988–1989); Tom Lord, *Clarence Williams* (1976); and Erik Raben, *Jazz Records, 1942–1980*, vol. 2.

JACK SOHMER

BECK, Claude Schaeffer (8 Nov. 1894–14 Oct. 1971), surgeon and educator, was born in Shamokin, Pennsylvania, the son of Simon Beck and Martha Schaeffer. He attended public schools in Shamokin, graduating as valedictorian of his high school class in 1911. After graduating from Millersville State Normal School in Reading, Pennsylvania, in 1914, he continued his undergraduate education at Franklin and Marshall College in Lancaster, Pennsylvania, receiving his A.B. in 1916. Inspired by one of his professors, Richard Schiedt, to enter the field of medicine, Beck enrolled at Johns Hopkins University School of Medicine, completing his M.D. in 1921.

After graduating Beck did a residency in surgery at Yale University's New Haven (Conn.) Hospital in 1922. In 1923 he was appointed the Arthur Tracy Cabot Fellow in Surgical Research at Harvard University, where he worked under Harvey Cushing, and as associate surgeon at Peter Bent Brigham Hospital in Boston, where he worked with Elliot Cutler.

When Cutler was appointed professor of surgery at Western Reserve University (WRU) and director of surgery at University Hospitals of Cleveland, Ohio, in 1924, Beck followed him as Crile Fellow in Surgery at University Hospitals and demonstrator of surgery at WRU. He was appointed in 1926 resident surgeon at University Hospitals and in 1928 attending surgeon, a position he held until he retired in 1965. Beck married Ellen Manning in 1928; they had three daughters. He was also appointed assistant professor of surgery at WRU in 1928, rising to associate professor in 1933 and professor in neurosurgery in 1940. During World War II Beck served as surgeon consultant to the Fifth Army Service Command at Fort Hayes in Columbus, Ohio; he was awarded the Legion of Merit in 1945. In 1952 WRU created the first professorship of cardiovascular surgery for Beck. He was appointed professor emeritus in 1965.

Beck first began researching the treatment of coronary disease through his work with Cutler. In 1924 Beck helped to organize the first surgical research laboratory at WRU. He also began assisting Cutler in attempting to relieve stenosis, or narrowing of the heart's mitral valve, through surgery using the cardiovalvulotome, an instrument developed at WRU's new surgical research laboratory. Although operations for mitral valve stenosis had already been performed in England, Cutler and Beck's work pioneered such research in the United States.

While doing research between 1925 and 1935 on polyserositis of the heart (chronic inflammation of the membranes), Beck began investigating the concepts of the acute and chronically compressed heart with studies on the physiology of those conditions and their surgical treatment. His medical studies of the heart's restricted ability to fill completely with blood were used to establish acute and chronic compression of the heart as clinical entities; his description of the diagnostic symptoms became known as "Beck's Triad." In addition Beck investigated other problems relating to heart surgery, including defibrillation of the ventricles, the use of anesthesia in heart surgery, techniques for suturing wounds of the heart, and penetrating and nonpenetrating wounds of the heart.

Beck's experience convinced him that many forms of heart disease could be treated using surgical methods. Embarking on an intensive study of methods for delivering additional blood to the heart muscle in the presence of coronary-artery occlusion, Beck developed the cardiopericardiopexy, a procedure designed to create a more even blood supply to the heart by the development of an alternative source of circulation. He first performed the procedure, also known as the Beck I operation, on a human patient in 1935, following extensive laboratory experiments on dogs.

Following World War II Beck became even more convinced that many forms of heart disease could be treated using surgical methods. Between 1946 and 1948 his laboratory developed the more complicated Beck II operation. Designed to convert veins of the heart into functioning as arteries by constructing a vein graft between the coronary sinus and the aorta and to stimulate the growth of intercoronary communications, the procedure preceded by twenty years the advent of coronary bypass surgery. Beck went on to perform 124 of these operations between 1948 and 1954; however, because of the operation's technical difficulties he returned to the simpler Beck I procedure.

The death of a young boy during heart surgery in 1934 inspired Beck to discover a way to reverse ventricular fibrillation, a phenomenon that causes the heart to convulse, lose rhythm, and stop pumping blood. In 1937, under laboratory conditions, Beck succeeded for the first time in defibrillating a dog's heart by applying electrical current directly to the heart muscle for a fraction of a second. In 1947 he installed an electric-shock device at University Hospitals; shortly thereafter he successfully used it to defibrillate a patient's heart that had stopped beating during a heart operation by using open-chest cardiac stimulation. As a result of this success Beck began a program to train medical personnel in cardiac resuscitation, including mouth-to-mouth ventilation and open-chest cardiac massage and defibrillation. With the development of the closed-chest method in the 1960s, in 1964 he helped to found Resuscitators of America, a volunteer organization dedicated to helping train lay rescue personnel in the new method. Beck died in Cleveland.

To Beck the heart was "the Great Northwest of surgery," and he was one of its devoted explorers. He achieved international recognition both for his own pioneering work in heart research, surgery, and cardiopulmonary resuscitation and as the director of a surgical research laboratory that was for many years the only one in the country devoted entirely to the study of the heart. Although the medical community did not always understand or embrace his advances in the new and complex field of cardiovascular surgery, Beck's work and concepts were significant advances that laid the foundations for the surgical treatment of heart disease.

• The Claude S. Beck, M.D. Papers are at the Stanley A. Furguson Archives at the University Hospitals of Cleveland; included are copies of almost all of his publications as well as a number of sound recordings. Beck also made a number of motion pictures, most of which are at the Howard Dittrick Museum of Medicine at Case Western Reserve University and have been transferred to videotape. In honor of the 100th anniversary of Beck's birth, University Hospitals published *Centennial Celebration, Claude S. Beck, M.D. 1894–1971* (1994) in association with its annual Claude S. Beck Lecture. The Cleveland Press Collection at Cleveland State University has extensive local newspaper clippings on Beck, dating from the 1930s to his death and including his obituaries in the *Cleveland Plain Dealer* and the *Cleveland Press*. The *New York Times* also carried an obituary, 15 Oct. 1971. The *Encyclopedia of Cleveland History* (1987) contains a biographical sketch.

WILLIAM BECKER

BECK, Dave (16 June 1894–26 Dec. 1993), labor union leader, was born David Daniel Beck in Stockton, California, the son of Lemuel Beck, a carpet cleaner and part-time auctioneer, and Mary Tierney, a laundress. His father, who had migrated to California from his native Tennessee in search of work, moved his family to Seattle, Washington, when Beck was four years old. Beck had dreams of becoming a lawyer but dropped out of high school at the age of sixteen to help support his chronically impoverished family. After four years of odd jobs, he found steady work driving a truck for the laundry where his mother was employed and developed a lucrative route of his own. At night he took extension courses in law, economics, and business administration at the University of Washington. Beck enlisted in the navy in 1917 and saw action as a gunner on anti-zeppelin patrols over the North Sea. While on furlough the next year, he married Dorothy E. Leschander of Seattle. The couple had one child, Warren David, who later legally changed his name to Dave Beck, Jr.

When he returned to Seattle after the war, probably in 1918, Beck found his job gone and took another driving a truck for a laundry owned and operated by the Teamsters Union, which he had joined in 1914. In two years he was made route manager, but he quit after an argument with his supervisor over working conditions and took back his original job. He was particularly successful at convincing hotel owners to deal only with laundries whose truck drivers belonged to the union and at persuading nonunion laundries to join the Teamsters. His organizational skills earned him a place on the executive board of the Seattle Laundry and Dye Drivers Local 566 in 1925. The next year he left his job driving a laundry truck and became the secretary-treasurer of the local, and in 1927 he was made its president. By then Beck's oratorical skills had attracted the notice of the Teamsters' national leaders,

and that year he was given the post of general organizer of the Pacific Northwest and British Columbia.

Beck worked aggressively to swell the ranks of his union, consolidating many previously independent locals and inducing members of other unions to join the Teamsters. In 1937 he organized the Western Conference of Teamsters and became its first president. Beck also organized workers in many fields that he felt were related to transportation and distribution, incorporating warehousemen and freight handlers into the Teamsters. He forged a labor empire described by *Newsweek* in 1957 as "a vast octopus that held fast not only truckers but department-store workers, automobile salesmen, cannery workers, undertakers, cow punchers, dry cleaners, and filling-station operators as well." He was criticized for his strong-arm tactics in raiding other unions and for forcing unorganized workers in Los Angeles into his own union by the use of boycotts and by threatening to cut off supplies.

Beck was made international vice president of the Teamsters in 1940, seven years later the title of executive vice president was created for him, and he replaced Daniel Tobin as president of the Teamsters in 1952. During his term of office he made the International Brotherhood of Teamsters, Chauffeurs, Warehousemen, and Helpers of America the world's largest and most powerful labor organization, with almost 1.6 million members. As the head of the largest union in the American Federation of Labor (AFL), Beck also became vice president and a member of the executive council of the AFL in 1953. He used both his position and his considerable business acumen to increase the union's power and wealth. It was one of his proudest claims that when he first went to Los Angeles his union had fewer than 400 members and that he brought the number to more than 100,000. He also boasted that his investment of the International Teamsters' funds had increased the union's assets by more than $14 million while he was its president.

No less shrewd in his personal finances, Beck invested money wisely in Seattle real estate and made himself a millionaire. This fact, as well as recurring allegations of involvement with organized crime, led to charges of corruption against him in 1956, and he came under investigation by the Senate Select Committee on Improper Activities in the Labor or Management Field. The chair of the committee, Senator John L. McClellan, and his chief counsel, Robert F. Kennedy, accused him of appropriating $322,000 in union funds for his own use. Beck became national news by invoking the Fifth Amendment with the formula "I refuse to give testimony against myself" 117 times during these hearings and, at a later court session, another thirty times. No charges were brought against Beck by the Senate, but he was dismissed from the American Federation of Labor–Congress of Industrial Organizations executive council for his refusal to cooperate with the rackets committee. In May 1956 he was charged by a federal court with income-tax evasion and with preparing a false return for a Teamster association, and that same year he was indicted by a Washington state court for embezzling $1,900 from the sale of a used Cadillac owned by the union.

At the end of his five-year term as president of the Teamsters in 1957, Beck chose not to run for reelection and relinquished the office to Jimmy Hoffa, one of his vice presidents. That year he was convicted of the tax-evasion charge, but the decision was reversed on appeal. In 1959 the state court found him guilty of embezzlement, and the federal court convicted him of filing a fraudulent tax return. Beck served from June 1962 to December 1964 in a Washington state prison but was pardoned by the governor of Washington for the state conviction in 1965 and by President Gerald Ford for the federal charge in 1975. He always emphatically denied his guilt on both charges.

Beck's wife died in 1961. He married Helen (maiden name unknown) in 1967. They had no children, and she died in 1977. After his release from prison, he retired on his union pension of $50,000 a year. Although a tough negotiator in union activities, he was personally cordial and was known for his full-toothed smile and warm handshake. He lived well but was moderate in his habits and never smoked or drank. Beck spent the last decades of his long life as a successful real-estate entrepreneur and community leader in Seattle, where he died. He served as an official of the Elks, an honorary member of the American Legion, the chair of the board of regents of the University of Washington, and a member of the Washington State Parole Board, and he was a popular speaker at union meetings and civic functions in Seattle.

• An admiring biography of Dave Beck, much of it in the subject's own dictated words, is John Dennis McCullum, *Dave Beck* (1976). Beck's union activities and legal difficulties were widely reported in the contemporary press. See especially *Business Week*, 22 June 1940, pp. 26–28, and 13 June 1942, pp. 86–88; *Fortune*, Dec. 1948, pp. 191–92; A. H. Baskin, "Union Leader—and Big Business Man," *New York Times Magazine*, 15 Nov. 1953, pp. 13ff.; *Newsweek*, 25 Feb. 1957, pp. 39–41; and *U.S. News and World Report*, 12 Apr. 1957, pp. 30–32. A lengthy obituary is in the *New York Times*, 28 Dec. 1993.

DENNIS WEPMAN

BECK, James Montgomery (9 July 1861–12 Apr. 1936), lawyer, solicitor general, and congressman, was born in Philadelphia, Pennsylvania, the son of James Nathan Beck, the owner of a small music publishing company, and Margaretta C. Darling. Coming from modest financial means, Beck inherited his father's interest in music and the family's Moravian antiwar and communitarian heritage, which contributed to his early pacifism and anticorporation viewpoints. Following matriculation at Philadelphia's Episcopal Academy, Beck graduated from Moravian College in Bethlehem, Pennsylvania, in 1880. After reading law, he began legal practice in 1884. From 1888 to 1892, he served as assistant U.S. attorney for eastern Pennsylvania. In 1890 he married Lilla Mitchell, daughter of a Philadelphia businessman, with whom he had two children.

Beck began his political career as an anticorporation Grover Cleveland Democrat who opposed the nomination of William Jennings Bryan in 1896. He soon joined the Republican party, however, because it offered him a promising future and social respectability. In the process he became an imperialist during the Spanish-American War; a promoter of big business whose legal clients eventually included William Rockefeller and Edward Harriman; and the assistant attorney general in the William McKinley and Theodore Roosevelt administrations. Like Roosevelt, he believed in the efficacy of federal regulation to promote a responsible Republican partnership with business in part to curb the states' occasional intrusions against corporate power. Yet in 1903 Beck so skillfully presented the government's case against the J. P. Morgan–controlled Northern Securities Company that the *St. Louis Post-Dispatch* labeled him "Roosevelt's Favorite 'Trust-Buster.'" Shortly afterward, Beck began to have second thoughts about such government activity; in 1903 he left the Justice Department to focus on a lucrative corporate law practice. He was soon preaching the doctrines of limited government and free enterprise, arguing that trust-busting was "un-American." During the financial panic of 1907, he called Roosevelt a threat to American institutions after a client, Edward H. Harriman, faced an Interstate Commerce Commission investigation.

During World War I, Beck became a leading advocate of American preparedness and an early supporter of the Allies. His *The Evidence against the Case* (1914), which indicted the Central Powers for causing the war, won him considerable notoriety. His pro-Ally and preparedness stands led to a reconciliation with Roosevelt, as Republicans moved from progressivism to "Americanism." In addition, Beck's dislike of Democratic president Woodrow Wilson's progressive program partly strengthened his opposition to Wilson's Fourteen Points and to the Versailles peace treaty. Like many Republicans, Beck favored a postwar triple entente comprised of the United States, Great Britain, and France rather than the broadly based League of Nations.

Despite the postwar rejection of Wilsonianism and progressivism, Beck found the new Republican era disappointing. Again returning to government service, he became President Warren Harding's solicitor general. In that capacity he eloquently defended the government's position in such key cases as the second child-labor law, even though reluctantly finding himself justifying the elevation of national power. Clearly, Harding-era conservatives did not always support laissez-faire enough to suit Beck, causing him to resign as solicitor general in 1925. Beck faced further disappointment when he failed to be appointed either ambassador to England or attorney general. Overall, he found the societal changes of postwar America difficult to accept. He bemoaned the "incredible frivolity and selfishness" of the times and the labor-saving machinery that had eroded the character of the individual. Nothing seemed to arouse his anger more than national Prohibition, which he viewed as a violation of individual liberty.

His opposition to Prohibition, along with the backing of Philadelphia's Republican boss Edward S. Vare, enabled Beck to win a congressional seat in 1927. Representing the squalid navy yard district of Philadelphia, Beck became a leader of anti-Prohibition congressmen and an outspoken opponent of immigration restriction. He later opposed most of President Herbert Hoover's presidential programs as either menaces to bureaucracy or as misuses of federal power. His *Wonderland of Bureaucracy* (1931) caused one reviewer to write that Beck seemed "unaware that there have been political philosophies since Herbert Spencer."

The New Deal caused Beck to reach the depths of disillusionment. He denounced the National Recovery Administration, the Agricultural Adjustment Administration, and the relief programs, believing that Franklin Roosevelt was marching the country toward Moscow. In 1934 he declined to seek reelection, maintaining that Congress had become a rubber stamp. He elected to fight the New Deal in the courts, in writings and speeches, and in political organizational work. Blaming both political parties for what he termed "Paradise Lost," he showed little enthusiasm for the prospective 1936 Republican nominee, Alfred Landon, whom he called the typical candidate of the "liberal" wing of the party. Beck died in Washington, D.C., without providing a viable conservative alternative to the welfare state.

• The Beck papers are in the Princeton University Library. Beck's many articles include "The Federal Power over Trusts," *American Academy of Political and Social Science Annals* (July 1904); "The Federal Regulation of Life-Insurance," *North American Review* (Aug. 1905); "The Pilgrims as Individualists," *New England Society Anniversary Celebration* (1933); "The Psychology of the War," *New York State Journal of Medicine* (June 1918); "The Federal Power over Intrastate Railroad Rates," *University of Pennsylvania Law Review* (Nov. 1922); and "The NRA Is Unconstitutional," *Fortune*, Nov. 1933. The only biography of Beck is Morton Keller, *In Defense of Yesterday: James M. Beck and the Politics of Conservatism, 1861–1936* (1958). See also C. H. Cramer's review of Keller's book in the *Mississippi Valley Historical Review* 6 (June 1959–1960): 335–36. An obituary is in the *New York Times*, 13 Apr. 1936.

JAMES N. GIGLIO

BECK, Johann Heinrich (12 Sept. 1856–26 May 1924), conductor, composer, and violinist, was born in Cleveland, Ohio, the son of Charles Beck, a businessman, and Rebecca Butler. He was one of five children, all boys, all of whom played the violin. He was educated in Cleveland and spent most of his life there, although he attended the Leipzig Conservatory from 1879 to 1882. He made his acclaimed European debut at the Leipzig Gewandhaus as violinist in his own String Quartet in C Minor. His diploma read in part: "In Theory Mr. Beck possesses highly advanced knowledge, in practical Composition, *a genuine gift* and a persevering, conscientious striving towards a no-

ble ideal." After his return to Cleveland he married Blandina Fellar of Tiffin, Ohio, in 1890. They had two children.

Beck undertook an active musical life. He organized the Schubert String Quartet in 1877 and later the Beck String Quartet, in which he appeared as violinist. The Schubert String Quartet gave numerous concerts during the 1880s. In 1884 the Schubert String Quartette Concert Company undertook a concert tour, with an extensive repertoire of works by Beethoven, Beck, Léo Delibes, Haydn, Mendelssohn, Anton Rubinstein, Johan Svendsen, and others. The Beck Quartet made frequent appearances during the 1890s.

Beck composed a number of piano pieces, sonatas for violin and piano, a short work for flute and piano, songs, part-songs, four string quartets (1877–1880), a string sextet (1886), other violin and cello pieces, and a number of large orchestral works. His orchestral compositions include an early symphony, *Sinbad* (1877); four overtures, one to Shakespeare's *Romeo and Juliet* (1876) and another to Byron's *Lara* (1885); *Skirnismäl* (the Lay of Skirner), a cycle of five tone poems for large orchestra (two finished); *Symphonic Scherzos* in A Major and F Major (1889 and 1895); and *Aus meinem Leben* (1917). His vocal/orchestral works include *Six Tone Pictures* for voice and orchestra (unfinished); *Deukalion*, a cantata for solo quartet, chorus, and grand orchestra on a text by Bayard Taylor; *Wie schön bist du* for tenor and grand orchestra; and *Meeresabend* for mezzo-soprano or tenor and orchestra. A number of these are incomplete. Only one of his pieces, the short *Elegiac Song* for violin and piano (undated), was published, by A. J. Peck in Cleveland, during his lifetime.

Noted critic James G. Huneker, writing in the *New York Musical Courier* (July 1888), called Beck ". . . one of the strongest of the group of young American composers, and his work is laid on lines infinitely broader than those of many of the others. He is no trifler, but a vigorous, scholarly and dramatic writer." Beck emphasized in his writing large orchestral canvasses inspired by the ideals of late German Romanticism, which were his heritage by background and training.

As a conductor Beck directed the Detroit Symphony Orchestra (a precursor of the present ensemble) for the season 1895–1896 and appeared frequently with major orchestras elsewhere, often conducting his own works. These appearances included engagements with the Boston Symphony Orchestra and the famed Theodore Thomas Orchestra. His work was heard in several major cities—Boston, New York, Philadelphia, Detroit, and Chicago. Beck conducted his "Der Freude Kuss" (Kiss of Joy), the first part of Skirnismäl, at the St. Louis Exposition in 1904. In Cleveland, Beck alternated his position at the podium with Czech oboist and conductor Emil Ring; the two men led orchestras there from 1900 to 1912. These ensembles were variously called Cleveland Symphony Orchestra, *The Cleveland Symphony Orchestra*, and Cleveland Grand Orchestra. The Cleveland Grand Orchestra played local seasons under the name of "Citizens 'Pop' Concerts"; the series from 1910 to 1912 with the Cleveland Symphony Orchestra was entitled "People's Symphony Concerts." Local artists and performing groups participated, including the Singers Club, the Cleveland Opera and Oratorio Society, and the Harmonic Club. The musical fare was lively and varied. The fifty-member orchestra's People's Symphony Concert of 9 January 1910, for example, conducted by Beck, featured concertmaster Sol Marcosson, accompanied by his wife. The program listed eight works: John Zamecnik's march *Trip to the North Pole*, Károly Goldmark's overture "Sakuntala," two movements from Saint-Saëns's Violin Concerto no. 3 in B Minor, two movements from Beethoven's *Eroica* Symphony, Victor Herbert's selection *Little Nemo*, Henryk Wieniawski's *Souvenir de Moscou* (Russian Airs), Emil Waldteufel's waltz "Woodland Dreams," and Moritz Moszkowski's *Einzugsmarsch*. The orchestras prepared the way for the founding in 1918 of the present Cleveland Orchestra, known in its first season as Cleveland's Symphony Orchestra. During this period Beck also conducted the Pilgrim Orchestral Club from 1904 to 1910 and the Elyria Orchestra from 1905 to 1907.

Shortly after Beck's death in his home city, the *Cleveland Town Topics* featured a discussion of his activities as a teacher of violin and composition. Beck taught for many years and founded the Beck Violin School. He was active in the Music Teachers National Association (MTNA) and the Ohio Music Teachers Association. A paper of Beck's read before the MTNA meeting of 3 July 1980, entitled "Orchestral Composition," discusses the history of orchestral scoring through Wagner, whom he speaks of as "the colossus." An American schooled in Germany and an heir to the German tradition, Beck worked in the larger forms for large orchestra, which the Wagner tradition represented.

Johann Beck was a well-trained performer and composer who was held in high esteem nationally as well as in Cleveland. Called on several occasions "Cleveland's Beethoven," he was a solid craftsman with high ideals who did much to develop musical values in the United States as he perceived them. He remained devoted to the European classical composers throughout his life and believed that his greatest contribution to American culture lay in emulating European achievements on these shores.

• Beck's papers, including his music in manuscript, concert programs, press clippings, sketches, and other material are in the Cleveland Public Library, where a bronze bust of him stands at the entrance to the Fine Arts Division. J. Heywood Alexander, *It Must Be Heard: A Survey of the Musical Life of Cleveland, 1836–1918* (1981), places Beck's life and work in the context of musical life in that city during the period. A recording of Beck's *Sextet* performed by members and assisting artists of the Cleveland Octet was issued by the Western Reserve Historical Society at the same time. General biographical sketches may be found in *Brainard's Musical World* 24 (Oct. 1887): 364, and 28 (June 1891): 174; *The Musician* 2 (Mar. 1897): 1; and Mary Hubbell Osburn, *Ohio Composers and Musical Authors* (1942). A discussion of Beck, which includes a score illustration from *Salammbo*, is in Rupert Hughes, *Contemporary American Composers* (1900). See also F. Karl Grossman, *A History of Music in Cleveland* (1972). An obituary is in the *Cleveland Town Topics*, 31 May 1924.

J. HEYWOOD ALEXANDER

BECK, John Brodhead (18 Sept. 1794–9 Apr. 1851), medical professor, was born in Schenectady, New York, the son of Caleb Beck, a lawyer, and Catharine Theresa Romeyn. Caleb Beck died in 1798, and Catharine Beck, powerfully committed to a thorough education for each of her five young sons, placed John in the home of her uncle, the Reverend John B. Romeyn, a Dutch Reformed theologian then living in Rhinebeck, New York. Under Romeyn's tutelage, Beck studied classical languages.

In 1804 Romeyn moved from Rhinebeck to New York City and took his sister's son with him. Five years later, John Beck entered Columbia College, where he continued to study classical and theological texts. He graduated with highest honors in 1813, then continued his classical studies in Europe. Though his upbringing and education pointed toward a theological career, Beck returned to New York City determined to study medicine. Working primarily with David Hosack, Beck completed a medical doctorate at the College of Physicians and Surgeons of New-York in 1817. In an era when most American medical theses were superficial summaries of work published in Europe or ill-supported theoretical glosses, Beck's dissertation revealed characteristics that would make its author one of the most impressive medical professors of his time: systematic logic, original research, practical experimentation, clarity of expression, and a fascination with the relationship between medicine and social policy. The dissertation dealt with infanticide, a phenomenon Beck would continue to explore for the next thirty years. The subject led him into such related issues as the length and nature of gestation, the causes and prevention of stillbirth, and the process of infant respiration.

In 1822 Beck helped establish the *New-York Medical and Physical Journal*, which served through the rest of the decade as an outlet for some of the most significant work of the period, including statistical studies of insanity and analyses of medical evidence by his older brother Theodric Romeyn Beck as well as discussions of medical chemistry by his younger brother Lewis Caleb Beck, both of whom were also building reputations as distinguished medical scientists. In 1823 much of John Beck's research on infanticide was incorporated as a separate section into the *Elements of Medical Jurisprudence*, a masterful book published by Theodric Romeyn Beck. Continuously revised through midcentury, the *Elements* appeared in several successive editions in the United States and translations in Europe, bringing the Beck brothers international acclaim. From 1835 onward, John Beck's name appeared as coauthor.

John Beck's chief scientific contributions were made in what would now be called neonatal physiology. He did extensive research on the way newborn lungs functioned and on the diffusion of chemicals in infant bodies. His ongoing research also made him perhaps the world's leading authority on abortion, accidental and intentional. He opposed the latter, even though the practice was then quite common in the United States and unregulated in New York. Beck's views directly influenced public policy when his brother Theodric Romeyn Beck became one of the principal behind-the-scenes revisors of the New York criminal code of 1828. The Becks inserted into that influential and often-copied code New York's first statutory penalties for physicians who performed certain types of abortions. Though the penalties were limited in degree and in circumstance, a policy of state regulation had begun.

In 1826 John Beck accepted a professorship at the College of Physicians and Surgeons of New-York, where he continued as professor until his death. By all accounts, Beck was a superb teacher, whose pedagogical skills and popularity with the medical students helped the college survive the vicious internecine politics of medical education in New York City. "His lectures were clear, precise, and singularly practical," reported his faculty colleague Chandler R. Gilman, "no merely specious theories, no rash generalizations, no loose assertions, found place there; all was logical, accurate, true" (p. 612). Beck taught his students to be scientific and thorough. As one of them noted while listening to Beck's 1829 lectures on forensic medicine: "always make your opinion not from one test, but from all of them" ([John Clarkson Jay], "Medical Jurisprudence by Dr. [John B.] Beck," student notebook from College of Physicians and Surgeons of New York, fall term 1829, p. 14; in Rare Book Room, New York Academy of Medicine).

Beck married Anne Tucker in 1831 (the number of children they had together is uncertain) and gained appointment as a physician to the New York Hospital in 1835. From that point forward, Beck's career combined practice, teaching, and research. A collection of his principal articles appeared as *Medical Essays* in 1843, and in 1849 he published an important treatise on *Infantile Therapeutics*, the culmination of decades of investigation. In an era when anyone could practice medicine and no one needed a license, Beck was a forceful champion of scientific research as the best basis upon which to build the nation's medical profession. He deplored the empiricism of the so-called irregular physicians and folk healers of the period, many of whom saw little benefit in scientific research. Like those who would eventually transform the American medical profession early in the twentieth century, Beck also believed that formal education was essential to professional advancement. Beck served in the highest offices of several regular medical societies, including most prominently the presidencies of the New York County Medical Society and the New York State Medical Society.

Beck began having serious health problems in 1842. From 1845 until his death, often in great pain from what was probably colon cancer, he struggled to maintain his regular duties as physician and professor. An early exemplar and influential shaper of the modern medical professional, he died probably in New York City, although some sources say Rhinebeck, New York.

• The Beck family papers are at the New York Public Library. A few student notebooks from Beck's classes have survived at the New York Academy of Medicine, which also holds a catalog of his private library. The most readily accessible overview of Beck's career by a contemporary is C[handler]. R. Gilman, "John B. Beck," in *Lives of Eminent American Physicians and Surgeons of the Nineteenth Century*, ed. Samuel D. Gross (1861). That entry is a slightly revised version of Gilman's biographical eulogy, *Sketch of the Life and Character of John Brodhead Beck, M.D., Late Professor of Materia Medica and Medical Jurisprudence in the College of Physicians and Surgeons, New York* (1851). For an assessment of Beck's impact on American abortion policy, see James C. Mohr, *Abortion in America: The Origins and Evolution of National Policy, 1800–1900* (1978), and for his impact on medical jurisprudence in the United States, see Mohr, *Doctors and the Law: Medical Jurisprudence in Nineteenth-Century America* (1993).

JAMES C. MOHR

BECK, Julian (31 May 1925–14 Sept. 1985), stage designer and author, was born in New York City, the son of Irving Beck, an auto parts salesman, and Mabel Lucille Blum, a teacher. Unlike his parents, who had struggled to overcome poverty, Julian benefited in his youth from middle-class comforts he later repudiated. In 1943 he abandoned his studies at Yale University to become a painter and writer in New York. There he met seventeen-year-old Judith Malina, whom he married in 1948 and with whom he had two children.

In the 1940s and 1950s, before becoming internationally known as a cofounder and spokesman of the radical Living Theatre, Beck was noted for his abstract expressionist paintings. He exhibited alongside other New York School artists such as Jackson Pollock, Willem de Kooning, and Franz Kline. Beck's collage-painting *Jeremiah* reflects his Jewish ancestry and upbringing. When Beck decided to make his career in theater, he sold his paintings to support the Living Theatre Collective; most of his early work has therefore been lost.

Beck's *Songs of the Revolution*—collections of his poetry published in 1963, 1969, and 1974—focus on ideas that sometimes veer away from the trivial and the pedestrian only by sheer energy and strength of conviction. His poetry takes the form of shorthand thought that occasionally explodes with hallucinatory or orgiastic intensity. In his poetry as in his prose, Beck linked the political to the life of the body: he contrasted oppression with the free experience of nonviolent sexuality, dogma with the exploration of the senses. Like the radical psychiatrist Wilhelm Reich, a main influence in his work, Beck expanded the meaning of the term politics to include the personal and the sexual. With his friend, the poet Allen Ginsberg, Beck believed that only life-affirming art could break the circle of political oppression and self-hate.

Beck is best remembered for his contribution to theater. In 1947 Beck and Malina founded Living Theatre Productions, Incorporated, in New York City to perform the modernist plays of Gertrude Stein, William Carlos Williams, Federico García Lorca, and Paul Goodman before a select audience in the couple's West End Avenue living room. Although both took on a variety of functions in the theater, Malina primarily directed, while Beck designed sets and costumes that revealed the influence of designer and theorist Frederick Kiesler. Distinctive in Beck's designs was his use of discarded material—a method inspired as much by sheer economic necessity as by choice.

The Living Theatre's innovative, iconoclastic repertoire evoked a never-abating stream of criticism that kept it constantly in the news. Although the company had found more suitable premises in 1951, lack of funds and difficulties with the tax revenue service kept it constantly on the move. In 1958 Beck abandoned his career as a painter in order to apply his organizational and artistic talents exclusively to theater. Among the company's best-known, controversial early works are Jack Gelber's *The Connection* (1959), a play about drug addicts, and Kenneth H. Brown's *The Brig* (1963), a Marine Corps prison drama. In 1961 and 1962 the Living Theatre gained international recognition after two European tours. In 1963 federal tax agents closed their 14th Street Theater in New York, and the Living Theatre became an itinerant company. Among the most important plays of that middle period were the collectively created *Mysteries and Smaller Pieces* (1964), *Frankenstein* (1965), and *Paradise Now* (1968), in which actors invaded the audience space and invited spectators to participate in the action on stage.

The company's politics changed over time. In the late 1950s the Living Theatre had opposed Cold War policies by obstructing civil defense drills. In the late 1960s it inspired and led the uprising of students, workers, and minorities. In 1970, however, the Living Theatre had to revise its strategies drastically: violent radicals of the New Left ridiculed Beck's dreamy pacifism, while the complacent Right trivialized the company's program. The company soon found itself catering almost exclusively to a smartly radical, middle-class audience. Critical success and the leftward drift of liberal culture had made Beck's experiments merely fashionable.

In reaction, the Living Theatre broke up into "cells," each independent from the mother organization but performing under the same name. In this later period Beck and Malina opted for guerrilla tactics, leading their company into the streets in search of a new audience. Among the plays wholly or partially devised by Beck during this time were *The Legacy of Cain* and *Rituals, Rites, and Transformations* (1971), *Seven Meditations on Political Sado-Masochism* (1974), and *The Archeology of Sleep* (1984).

Beck's last years were spent fighting cancer and struggling hard to keep the company afloat. Pressing financial needs led him to accept roles in Francis Ford Coppola's *Cotton Club* (1984), Brian Gibson's *Poltergeist II* (1985), and the violent television series "Miami Vice" (1985). In March 1985, shortly before his death in New York City, he performed the solo monologue of Samuel Beckett's *That Time* in a Beckett trilogy at La Mama Experimental Theater Company in New York. His performance showed him to be an actor of considerable talent.

For all his avant-garde tendencies, Beck was no theorist. He is remembered for the innovative ways in which he implemented the theories of others. His principal influence was Antonin Artaud, the French poet, actor, and critic whose Theatre of Cruelty aimed at increasing the audience's emotional involvement through a variety of shock tactics. Yet, as Beck explained in the posthumously published *Theandric* (1992), a collection of his thoughts, "Theatre of Cruelty without political objective/social action becomes its opposite, seduction to sadism." Politically, Beck occupied a position in between anarchism and socialism. To express these views theatrically, he turned for inspiration also to the political theater of Erwin Piscator and Bertolt Brecht. The result was an amalgam of highly physical acting and plain political exhortation that was to become typical for avant-garde theater in the 1960s and 1970s and that was based on the belief that political re-education had to go hand in hand with a reform of the body, site of bourgeois reticence and prudery.

Like other postwar theater reformers such as Peter Brook, Jerzy Grotowski, Robert Wilson, and Herbert Blau, Beck revitalized the stage. His courageous and creative management of the Living Theatre demonstrated the artistic potential and the admittedly precarious economic viability of a new kind of small, innovative theatrical enterprise, known as Off Broadway and Off Off Broadway because of its location away from the centers of conservative, commercial New York. In that way Beck and Malina's work smoothed the way for other experimental companies such as Joseph Chaikin's Open Theater, Richard Schechner's Performance Group, Charles Ludlam's Ridiculous Theatrical Company, André Gregory's Manhattan project, and La Mama Experimental Theater Company.

• Important primary and secondary material documenting Beck's organizing and inspiring role in the Living Theatre can be found in the Special Collections Department of the University of Iowa Libraries in Iowa City and in the Living Theatre Collection, the Kelly collection, and the Billy Rose Theatre Collection at the New York Public Library for the Performing Arts, Lincoln Center. Beck's account of the function and life of his theater company is in *Revolution and Counterrevolution* (1968); *We, the Living Theatre* (1970), coauthored with Judith Malina and Aldo Rostagno; and *The Life of the Theatre* (1972), which contains essays and short reflections on theater and politics. For interviews with Beck and Malina see Jean-Jacques Lebel, ed., *Entretiens avec le Living Theatre* (1969). Renfreu Neff, *The Living Theatre/USA*

(1970), and Pierre Biner, *The Living Theatre* (1972), assess the company's work in its early and middle period. The latter also contains a bibliography. *The Living Book of the Living Theatre* (1971) features mainly illustrations and an introductory essay by Richard Schechner. Some of Beck's essays can be found in anthologies of the counterculture (see for instance "Money Sex Theatre," in *Counter Culture*, ed. Joseph Berke [1969]) and as introductions to the company's published plays. For the latter see Kenneth Brown, *The Brig, with an Essay on the Living Theatre by Julian Beck and Director's Notes by Judith Malina* (1965). Bruce Cutler, *Two Plays of the Living Theater: The Difficult Wisdom of Nothing* (1977), contains a bibliography.

Drama Review has discussed many of the company's productions; see for example Schechner, "The Return of the Living Theatre," 13 (1969): 21–107; Paul R. Ryan, "The Living Theatre in Brazil," 15 (1971): 21–30; and Ryan, "The Living Theatre's 'Money Tower,'" 18 (1974): 9–25. See also Malina, *The Enormous Despair* (1972) and *The Diaries of Judith Malina, 1947–1957* (1984), and Jack Gelber's revealing account of Beck's lesser-known role as an administrator and fundraiser for the Living Theatre, "Julian Beck, Businessman," *Drama Review* 30 (1986): 6–29. Another important source on Beck and the Living Theatre is the alternative press; see tributes to Beck by Ira Cohen, Allen Ginsberg, Jerome Rothenberg, and Michael McClure in *Third Rail* 7 (1985–1986). An obituary is in the *New York Times*, 17 Sept. 1985.

LUC GILLEMAN

BECK, Martin (31 Aug. 1865–16 Nov. 1940), vaudeville manager, was born in German Czechoslovakia. Little is known of his early years. At about the age of eighteen he immigrated to the United States as part of a troupe of European actors. Beck's first theatrical experience was as a German actor, appearing at the Thalia Theater in New York and later with the Waldamer Stock Company in St. Louis. The group was not successful in America and soon broke up. Having no means of livelihood, Beck turned to any form of endeavor that would enable him to survive. After working at a number of menial jobs he turned up in Chicago as a waiter in a music hall where he also served as part-time bartender, earning the nickname "Two Beers Beck." The year was 1893, and the World's Fair was in full swing. Beck's previous theatrical experience came in handy, and he soon found work as a part-time stage manager. Other jobs followed, and he quickly rose to the position of house manager and then bookkeeper.

Beck's interest in theater was a natural one, and he soon moved to a larger music hall. A partnership became available, and Beck's rise in the managerial aspect of American theater began. But as the effects of the panic of 1893 set in, Beck was forced to resume his acting career; in 1895 he became a member of a vaudeville company known as Schiller's. Their tour took them to the Far West, and it was there that, forced to give up his idea of establishing a German stock company, Beck achieved his first fame as a theater manager. while the Schiller group was playing an engagement in San Francisco, Beck met Gustave Walters, owner of the Orpheum Theater, a combined saloon and music hall. Walters hired Beck to manage his theater, and under Beck the Orpheum became a huge success.

Meanwhile, a group of San Francisco businessmen, many of them interested in theater, soon became aware of Beck. Realizing that he knew more about theater than they did, they gave him virtually free rein. Beck soon acquired other theaters in California. He formed an alliance with Morris Meyerfeld, Jr., who had founded the Orpheum Vaudeville Circuit in the Far West. The two men then created the Western Vaudeville Managers Association, which, together with the Orpheum Circuit, controlled the vast majority of vaudeville theaters between Chicago and the West Coast. In 1920 Beck became president of the Orpheum Circuit.

Beck now emerged as the most successful theatrical entrepreneur west of Chicago. More cosmopolitan than most theatrical managers, he spoke six languages and was both a book and an art collector. He was an excellent judge of artistic talent, and performers generally liked him because he always treated them fairly. In 1912 he brought the great French actress, Sarah Bernhardt, to America. She played to packed houses at the then unheard of salary of $7000 a week. In this and other ways Beck helped to raise the artistic level of vaudeville. His booking strategies were innovative and his theaters the finest. As a result, the Orpheum Circuit grew substantially, numbering well over sixty theaters at the height of the vaudeville era.

Around 1906 Beck had moved to New York, where he developed a plan for a super-deluxe vaudeville theater in the heart of Manhattan. This had always been his dream, and he now undertook to make it a reality. By 1911 he had acquired a major piece of property on the east side of Broadway and 47th Street at the exact juncture where Broadway and Seventh Avenue meet. The necessary leases were signed, and construction of the Palace Theater began early in 1912. But the other New York vaudeville managers, especially Benjamin Franklin Keith and Edward F. Albee, were not prepared to sit idly by and let Beck have it all to himself. When the Palace was ready to open in March of 1913, Beck's rivals swung into action. The facts have never been fully revealed, but somehow Keith and Albee managed to wrest financial control of the Palace Theater away from Beck and reduce the latter's role to that of booking agent. It was, in short, a very successful coup. When the dust settled, Albee had control of the Palace Theater (Keith had died in 1914) and Beck's stock had been reduced to well below 50 percent.

For the next twenty years control of the crown jewel of American vaudeville theaters remained in the hands of the Keith-Albee organization and its successor, Radio-Keith-Orpheum. In 1927 Beck merged his Orpheum Vaudeville Circuit with that of Keith-Albee. One year later, financier Joseph P. Kennedy, patriarch of the Kennedy family, gained control of Keith-Albee-Orpheum, ousted Albee from power, and immediately sold the company to the Radio Corporation of America, which promptly renamed it Radio-Keith-Orpheum (RKO). Beck was excluded from the management of the new corporation. Beck's first wife was Susan Sonnenberg. Sometime after her death in 1919 he married Louise P. Heims, who survived him. Beck was the father of two daughters.

The onset of the Great Depression saw a brief revival in Beck's career. Albee died in 1930, and two years later Beck brought suit against both the Albee estate and RKO. A few weeks after the lawsuit was filed, Beck was invited to resume an active role in both the Palace Theater and the Radio-Keith-Orpheum Vaudeville Circuit. His success was short-lived. The forces allied against Beck were overwhelming: the severity of the depression, the popularity of radio and, most important of all, the conversion of every major film studio and most of the motion picture theaters in the United States to talking pictures. Vaudeville had no future, and Beck knew it; he retired in 1933. He died in New York City.

Martin Beck's legacy was twofold: his immense contribution in making vaudeville the leading form of popular entertainment in America during the early years of the twentieth century and his lifelong commitment to the legitimate theater as well. In 1924 he had built the very beautiful Martin Beck Theater, which was notable in two ways: it was the only New York legitimate theater located west of Eighth Avenue, and it was the only one that never carried a mortgage. Despite its location, it has been a very successful house. It remained in the Beck family until 1966, a fitting memorial to Martin Beck.

• The best source for information on Beck and on the building of the Palace Theater is *The Palace* (1969), written by Marian Spitzer, who worked at the Palace when it opened. Other useful volumes are Robert Grau, *Forty Years Observation of Music and the Drama* (1909) and *The Businessman in the Amusement World* (1910), both of which include material on Vaudeville and legitimate theater, as does M. B. Leavitt, *Fifty Years in Theatrical Management: 1859–1909* (1912), a comprehensive work; Joe Laurie, Jr., *Vaudeville: From the Honky Tonks to the Palace* (1953); and John E. DiMeglio, *Vaudeville, U.S.A.* (1973). Douglas Gilbert, *American Vaudeville: Its Life and Times* (1940), and Charles Samuels and Louise Samuels, *Once upon a Stage: The Merry World of Vaudeville* (1974), contain information on Beck, but both must be read with caution.

CHARLES W. STEIN

BECK, Theodric Romeyn (11 Aug. 1791–19 Nov. 1855), physician and professor, was born in Schenectady, New York, the son of Caleb Beck, a lawyer, and Catharine Theresa Romeyn, the daughter of the Reverend Derick Romeyn, a founder of Union College. After Caleb died in 1798, Catharine Beck assumed responsibility for raising their five sons.

Beck graduated from Union College in 1807. After serving apprenticeships with physicians in Albany and New York City and studying at the College of Physicians and Surgeons in New York City, he received a medical degree in 1811. In 1814 he married Harriet Caldwell; they had two children. Beck practiced in Albany for six years and also accepted an appointment in 1815 as professor of the Institutes of Medicine and lecturer in medical jurisprudence at the College of Physicians and Surgeons of the Western District of New York in Fairfield. He taught at the medical school in Fairfield until 1840, then at the Albany Medical College until 1854. Desiring a career in writing and teaching, Beck stopped attending patients in 1817. He served as principal of the Albany Academy between 1817 and 1853.

Reviewers lavishly praised Beck's most important scholarly work, *Elements of Medical Jurisprudence*, which was published in two volumes in 1823, the year of Harriet's death at the age of thirty-one. In this remarkably comprehensive work of almost 2,000 pages, Beck analyzed the legal issues associated with sexual and reproductive matters such as rape, illegitimacy, infanticide, traumatic injuries, death by unknown causes, mental illness, and poisoning. A synthesis of the European heritage and recent American experiences, the work appeared in at least twelve editions during the nineteenth century (six American, four British, one German, and one Swedish). More than any other author, Beck encouraged physician-professors to devote systematic attention to medical jurisprudence in American medical schools.

Beck took on other roles during his career. He served three terms as president of the New York State Medical Society (1827–1830) and was a member of the Board of Managers of the New York State Lunatic Asylum at Utica from 1842 until his death. He was secretary of the Board of Regents of the University of the State of New York from 1841 until his death. He also participated in organized efforts to advance the natural sciences, to develop libraries and museums, and to advocate better care for physically and mentally disabled persons. He became editor of the *American Journal of Insanity* in 1850.

A large man with dark, rumpled hair, Beck had gentle and sympathetic manners. He was devoted to his mother and two surviving brothers, John B. Beck and Lewis C. Beck, who were also distinguished physicians and authors. Beck died in Albany.

• Letters and papers written by Beck can be found in the Theodric Romeyn Beck Papers and the John Wakefield Francis Papers at the New York Public Library and in the John W. Francis Papers at the New York State Library in Albany. For a brief account of Beck's life, see J. Lewi Donhauser, "The Life and Career of Dr. T. Romeyn Beck," in *Union Worthies*, vol. 5 (1950). For an overview of the teaching of medical jurisprudence in the United States, see Chester R. Burns, "Medical Ethics and Jurisprudence," in *The Education of American Physicians: Historical Essays*, ed. Ronald L. Numbers (1980). An obituary appeared in the *Albany Evening Journal*, 19 Nov. 1855.

CHESTER R. BURNS

BECKER, Carl Lotus (7 Sept. 1873–10 Apr. 1945), historian, was born on a farm in Black Hawk County, Iowa, the son of Charles DeWitt Becker, a Union army veteran, and Almeda Sarvay. In 1884 the family moved fifteen miles to Waterloo. Becker, who had attended a small rural school, excelled at West Side High School and proceeded in 1892 to Cornell College, a Methodist school in Mt. Vernon, Iowa. A year later he enrolled at the University of Wisconsin at Madison.

Unsure of what to study at Wisconsin, Becker heard rave reviews of Frederick Jackson Turner, one of the most famous of the Progressive historians, and soon became one of his students. After receiving his B.Litt. with honors in history in 1896, he began graduate school at Wisconsin. After teaching freshman history at Wisconsin in 1897 Becker went to New York City and became a fellow in history and constitutional law at Columbia University. Before he earned his Ph.D. he accepted a short-term position as an instructor at Pennsylvania State University in 1899 and another at Dartmouth College in 1901. The year he went to Dartmouth he married Maude Hepworth Ranney of New York City; they had one child.

In 1902 Becker accepted a position as an assistant professor at the University of Kansas. While at Kansas he completed his dissertation under the direction of Turner and received his Ph.D. from Wisconsin in 1907. That year he was promoted to associate professor. Although Becker was trained as an American historian, he studied under European historians as well, thus preparing him for his position at Kansas teaching European history. As he told Turner in 1902, he was responsible for many history courses: "Greek and Roman, Medieval, Renaissance and Reformation, and English."

In 1909, after he had been promoted to professor at Kansas, Becker published his dissertation, *The History of Political Parties in the Province of New York, 1760–1776*. The book was a meticulous reconstruction of politics in a colony long known for its divisive public affairs. Influenced by Progressive concern about class relations, it soon became a classic and had an enormous impact on the study of the American Revolution. In it, Becker developed the idea that the Revolution needed to be studied as a dual movement: the revolt was an imperial struggle over "home rule," particularly over what types of rights colonists possessed but it also concerned the distribution of power in the colonies—or as Becker put it in his most famous formulation, "of who should rule at home."

At Kansas Becker honed a writing style that became as significant to the profession as any of his research. He laced his essays and letters with literary flourishes and droll wit. In a 1909 letter to Turner he noted that another young historian at Kansas was succeeding well, although he had not yet "mastered the 'Kansas language,' which develops steadily at the expense of the English." The next year he published an essay entitled "Kansas" in a festschrift presented to Turner. That essay, reprinted often, captured the essence of a state peopled by New England immigrants who withstood the battles over slavery during the bloody 1850s and emerged triumphant, the embodiment of the state's motto: *ad astra per aspera*. Yet Kansas also seemed parochial to Becker, a place where everyone conformed to certain norms and where "freaks are raised for export only."

In 1910 Becker also published "Detachment and the Writing of History" in the *Atlantic Monthly*, an essay arguing that even professionally trained historians faced massive difficulties in their attempts to become sufficiently detached from their own circumstances to render an objective portrayal of a complicated past. "The 'facts' of history do not exist for any historian," he insisted, "until he creates them, and into every fact that he creates some part of his individual experience must enter." Although the essay did not immediately have much impact on the community of historians, Becker's contention that each age made its own history undermined the central contention of nineteenth-century scholars that history should be a scientific enterprise aimed at revealing objective truth.

By the early 1910s Becker's work began to reach a wider audience and his career soared. In 1914 he became a member of the editorial board of the *American Historical Review*, a position he held until 1922. After publishing *The Beginnings of the American People* in 1915 Becker moved to the University of Minnesota in 1916. The next year he became professor of European history at Cornell University, where he remained until his retirement.

Soon after he took up his position in Ithaca Becker published other interpretive works on American history, including *The Eve of the Revolution* (1918) and *The United States: An Experiment in Democracy* (1920). In 1921 he was elected a fellow of the Royal Historical Society, the first of such honors revealing the international respect that he had acquired as historian. In 1922 Becker published perhaps the most significant book of his career, *The Declaration of Independence: A Study in the History of Political Ideas*. Here Becker subjected one of the critical documents in American history to intensive scrutiny. He explored the language and logic of the Declaration and placed it in the intellectual context of its age. Gone was the detailed research that went into his history of revolutionary New York. Becker was concerned more with ideas than with the people who promulgated them. When Alfred Knopf decided to reprint the book in 1941, Becker took the opportunity to note in the introduction that "the servile and remorseless activities" of Hitler's "bleak-faced, humorless Nazi supporters" had "forced men everywhere to re-appraise the validity of half-forgotten ideas." In a world at war he hoped that his thoughts on "the famous American character of political freedom" would find a receptive audience.

In 1923, after his *Declaration* was published, Becker was elected to the American Academy of Arts and Sciences. By the end of the decade his reputation had led to his election as the president of the American Historical Association. In 1931 Becker delivered his presidential address, "Everyman His Own Historian," to the organization. Published in 1932 in the *American Historical Review*, the essay, perhaps the most influential that he ever wrote, revealed Becker's return to the issues he had raised early in his career concerning the notion of objectivity in historical research. History, he argued, "cannot be reduced to a verifiable set of statistics or formulated in terms of universally valid mathematical formulas. It is rather an imaginative creation, a personal possession which each one of us, Mr. Everyman, fashions out of his individual experience, adapts to his practical or emotional needs, and adorns as well as may be to suit his aesthetic tastes."

In 1931 Becker traveled to Yale to deliver the Storrs Lectures, published the next year as *The Heavenly City of the Eighteenth-Century Philosophers*. Although Becker had until that point been teaching European history, this work represented a break from his previous books, all of which dealt with elements of American history. Like his earlier work, *The Heavenly City* focused on the eighteenth century, particularly on the struggles of the philosophes to supplant a world of medieval superstition with a more rational and skeptical view of events. The philosophes "renounced the authority of church and Bible," he proclaimed, yet they "exhibited a naive faith in the authority of nature and reason." *The Heavenly City* became Becker's most popular book, revealing a master stylist at home in a world of abstract ideas and able to decode them for a willing audience.

The 1930s brought Becker more honors. In 1933 he was elected to the National Institute of Arts and Letters; two years later, when he published a collection of essays, he was offered but declined the Harmsworth Professorship of American History at Oxford. In 1936 Becker was elected to the American Philosophical Society. By the end of the decade he had joined the editorial board of the *Yale Review*. He retired from his position at Cornell in 1941, although he taught for a semester at Smith College in 1942 and continued to write. His Messenger Lectures at Cornell in 1943 focused on the history of the university and were published that year. At that point, with the world at war again, Becker turned his attention to twentieth-century issues, particularly those relating to the nature of democratic societies. His final books, *How New Will the Better World Be?* (1944) and *Freedom and Responsibility in the American Way of Life* (1945), revealed his abiding concern for the fate of democracy. As he wrote in the *Yale Review* in 1940, democracies "have a life of their own apart from any particular social system or type of civilization."

By the time of his death in Ithaca Becker had produced an enormous body of writing, including sixteen books, seventy-five articles, and scores of reviews. Since his death many historians have offered critical assessments of his work, noting that Becker often repeated himself, that he was inconsistent, and that he, except in his first book, paid little attention to the lives of most eighteenth-century people. Yet he remains a central figure in the development of the nature of historical inquiry, in large measure because his own skepticism about historians' abilities is an enduring caution to any scholar who believes that he or she can offer an objective portrayal of a complicated past.

• Becker's papers are held in the Department of Manuscripts and University Archives in Cornell University's Olin Library. Over three hundred of his letters are included in Michael Kammen, ed., *What Is the Good of History?: Selected Letters of Carl L. Becker, 1900–1945* (1973), and some of his essays and reviews can be found in Phil L. Snyder, ed., *Detachment and the Writing of History: Essays and Letters of Carl L. Becker* (1958). For analyses of his work see Bernard Bailyn, "Becker, Andrews, and the Image of Colonial Origins," *New England Quarterly* 29 (1956): 522–36; Robert E. Brown, *Carl Becker on History and the American Revolution* (1970); Milton M. Klein, "Detachment and the Writing of American History: the Dilemma of Carl Becker," in *Perspectives on Early American History*, ed. Alden T. Vaughan and George A. Billias (1973); Charlotte W. Smith, *Carl Becker: On History and the Climate of Opinion* (1956); Cushing Strout, *The Pragmatic Revolt in American History: Carl Becker and Charles Beard* (1958); and Burleigh T. Wilkins, *Carl Becker: A Biographical Study in American Intellectual History* (1958). An obituary is in the *New York Times*, 11 Apr. 1945.

PETER C. MANCALL

BECKER, George Ferdinand (5 Jan. 1847–20 Apr. 1919), geologist, was born in New York City, the son of Alexander Christian Becker, a physician, and Sarah Cary Tuckerman. Becker spent his youth in Cambridge, Massachusetts, where his mother's family had strong ties to Harvard College and links to members of the Cambridge scientific community, most notably, the zoologist Louis Agassiz. Because his mother had planned his education carefully, Becker was already well acquainted with many of the leading lights of the faculty when he entered Harvard College in 1864. Influenced by Agassiz, the mathematician Benjamin Peirce, and the anatomist Jeffries Wyman, Becker matriculated at Heidelberg, Germany, after completing his bachelor's degree in 1868 and pursued work in mathematics, thermodynamics, mineralogy, and chemistry. In 1869 he received a doctorate in chemistry summa cum laude. While in Europe, he also took a "Certificate as a Practical Puddler" from the Royal Academy of Mines in Berlin and worked as a correspondent for the *New York Herald* during the Franco-Prussian war. Along with his passion for science, his concern with the practical uses of knowledge and taste for worldly adventure would endure.

Upon returning to the United States in 1871, Becker became an engineer for the Joliet Iron and Steel Company, where he investigated the design of furnaces. In 1874, perhaps to improve his health and perhaps to indulge his wanderlust, Becker accepted a position as instructor in metallurgy at the University of California in Berkeley. His duties soon led him to study the genesis and structure of the ore-bearing rocks that were important to California's economy. Becker's interest in the mineral resources of California and in broader questions that related to their formation led to a friendship with Clarence King, then the director of the U.S. Survey of the Fortieth Parallel. When King became head of the newly created U.S. Geological Survey (USGS) in 1879, he engaged Becker as one of his principal lieutenants.

Hoping to both establish the utility of the USGS and contribute to geological science, King directed Becker to conduct fieldwork in the precious metal districts of California, Nevada, and neighboring territories, which had immediate demand for reliable geological knowledge and abundant opportunities to study such general issues as ore deposition, petrogenesis, and orogeny. The most important result of this work, Becker's *Geology of the Comstock Lode and Washoe District* (1882), superseded previous studies of the richest find of precious metals in the United States. In addition to presenting a traditional description of ore bodies in this work, Becker also gave careful attention to the composition of surrounding rocks and to the complex system of faults in the locality. By joining the resources of chemistry, physics, and microscopical petrography to those of geology and classical mineralogy, his work set a standard for survey geologists.

During the 1880s, John Wesley Powell, King's successor as head of the USGS, oversaw a massive expansion of the agency. As geologist-in-charge of the survey's Pacific Division, Becker continued his work on mineral deposits, writing a monograph on the quicksilver deposits of the West Coast and supervising a study of the Eureka mines of Nevada. These studies underlined for him the importance of the faults and fissures that were abundant in the rocks of the Sierra Nevada. They were, he maintained, the avenues by which eruptive rocks moved, and the conduits for mineral-bearing waters. Becker developed a special interest in finding mathematical methods to describe the forces that caused these and other forms of rock deformation, although such theoretical pursuits were little encouraged by Powell or his colleagues at the survey.

Becker's position, like those of many other accomplished geologists, was eliminated in an orgy of congressionally dictated budget slashing in 1892. Becker used this opportunity to pursue his theoretical interests in the processes by which rocks undergo physical alteration, especially rupture. The subject was pertinent, as Becker saw it, not only to understanding the fissure systems and physical geology of the mineral-rich Sierra Nevada, but also to understanding the subterranean forces that molded the earth's surface. His extensive use of mathematics and rational mechanics in these investigations made him at once a pioneer in the study of rock mechanics and a cipher to some of his geological colleagues.

Rehired by the USGS in 1894, when his friend Charles D. Walcott became director, Becker continued theoretical work on the physical behavior of rocks. He also became a roving expert on the geology of gold fields and traveled to both Alaska and South Africa. In 1898–1899 and 1902–1903, as part of the American effort to assess the resources of its new possession, Becker also made two extended visits to the Philippines.

In June 1900 the USGS placed Becker in charge of its Division of Chemical and Physical Research, where he hoped to initiate research into the formation of ore deposits, the chemistry of metamorphism, the lithology of massive rocks, and the physical chemistry of igneous rock formation. He soon found, however, that meager appropriations and the day-to-day pressures of performing routine analyses for field geologists made sustained progress difficult. When Andrew Carnegie announced plans in 1902 to endow a new philanthropic agency to support scientific research, Becker recognized an opportunity to secure the support necessary for unimpeded work on geophysics. In cooperation with USGS director Walcott, who was also secretary of the new Carnegie Institution of Washington, Becker laid ambitious plans for a geophysical institute. These plans resulted in the establishment of the Geophysical Laboratory of the Carnegie Institution of Washington in 1905. Although Becker had helped persuade the trustees of the Carnegie Institution to build this laboratory, he was passed over for its directorship—a source of keen disappointment, which was assuaged only in part by the trustee's selection of his young assistant, Arthur Louis Day, for the post.

Becker suffered another blow in 1907, when a new director of the USGS, George Otis Smith, ordered Becker to suspend physical investigations and instead focus on more routine tasks of chemical analysis. Becker, who felt that he had been assured of the freedom to maintain a physical laboratory in his division, tendered his resignation. He spent his final years as a research associate at the Geophysical Laboratory of his founding, where he conducted experimental and theoretical studies of schistosity, elasticity, and diffusion. He died in Washington, D.C.

Becker's first marriage was to Sarah M. Barnes (date unknown). After their divorce in 1879, he married Alice Theodora Watson, who died in 1880. In 1902 he married Florence Serpell Deakins. None of his marriages produced children.

A scientist of exceptionally broad training, Becker was skilled in mathematical and descriptive methods, field and laboratory work. Geological colleagues found Becker self-assured to the point of arrogant and eccentric in his taste for mathematics. Nevertheless, his talents were recognized both through his election to the National Academy of Sciences in 1901 and his election to the presidency of the Geological Society of America in 1914. Through his monographs on ore deposits, studies of the physics of rock deformation, and work on behalf of the creation of the Geophysical Laboratory of the Carnegie Institution of Washington, Becker exerted a significant influence on the development of petrology and geophysics in America.

• A substantial collection of Becker's papers is in the Library of Congress; additional correspondence can be found in the Carl Barus Papers at Brown University and in the records of the U.S. Geological Survey in the National Archives. Useful memoirs on Becker by Arthur L. Day, *Bulletin of the Geological Society of America* 31 (1920): 14–25, and George P. Merrill, *Memoirs of the National Academy of Sciences* 21 (1926): 1–13, include bibliographies of Becker's publications. Thomas G. Manning, *Government in Science: The U.S. Geological Survey* (1967), and Stephen J. Pyne, *Grove Karl Gilbert: A Great Engine of Research* (1980), offer useful information on Becker's role in the USGS. See also John W. Servos, "To Explore the Borderland: The Foundation of the Geophysical Laboratory of the Carnegie Institution of Washington," *Historical Studies in the Physical Sciences* 14 (1983): 147–85.

JOHN W. SERVOS

BECKER, Howard Paul (9 Dec. 1899–8 June 1960), sociologist, was born in New York City, the son of Paul John Becker, a laborer, and Letitia Dickson. During Howard's infancy Paul Becker left home for several years traveling throughout North America as a prospector. At this time Howard lived with his mother in a small village in Ontario, Canada. In 1910 Howard and his mother joined the venturesome father in Nevada. In 1917 they moved to South Bend, Indiana, where father and son worked at the Dort Motor Company. Howard worked in various automobile factories and gave evidence of a promising career as an industrial engineer that stemmed in part from technical training he picked up through a correspondence course.

Although Becker had no high school education, he entered Northwestern University at age twenty-three by passing a special entrance exam. He earned two degrees from Northwestern: the A.B. (1925) and the M.A. (1926). Extensive travel in Europe complemented Becker's education. During the summer of 1923 he participated in an American-German exchange program that gave him the opportunity to travel throughout Germany with members of the German youth movement. In 1926 he returned to Germany, where he studied at Cologne under Leopold Von Wiese, Paul Honigsheim, and Max Scheler. Becker continued his studies at the University of Chicago in the Department of Sociology. He married Francis Bennett, a sociologist, in 1927; they had three children. Under the direction of Robert Park, he wrote his doctoral thesis on ancient Greece, *Ionia and Athens: Studies in Secularization* (1933). In 1934 Becker made another sojourn to Europe as a Social Science Research Council fellow. He spent several months in Paris studying under Maurice Halbwachs and traveled to Germany to make firsthand observations of Adolf Hitler's new regime.

Becker's teaching career began at the University of Pennsylvania in 1928. In 1931 he went to Smith College as an associate professor; six years later he accepted a position at the University of Wisconsin as a professor. During summers he taught at Harvard, Stanford, and Columbia. In 1951 he was a Fulbright fellow at the University of Birmingham. During World War II Becker joined the Office of Strategic Services. As leader of the Morale Operations Unit, he managed a secret broadcasting station that was engaged in "Operation Capricorn." After the war he stayed in Germany as chief of higher education in Hesse (1946–1947). He then returned to the United States to resume his academic career, serving as president of the Midwest Sociological Society (1947) and the American Sociological Association (1960).

Although Becker is best known as a sociological theorist and methodologist, he also wrote extensively about historical topics and contemporary social conditions in Germany. In *Systematic Sociology* (1932) he adapted Von Wiese's formal sociological theory for an American audience. His collaboration with Harry Elmer Barnes in the two-volume work, *Social Thought from Lore to Science* (1938), provided American social scientists with a broad awareness of historical and contemporary European social thought. Some of his most important essays on theory and method are found in *Through Values to Social Interpretation* (1950). He challenged prevailing sociological practices that defined scientific advancement in terms of the quantitative methods of survey research. Rejecting this approach as positivism, he argued for an interpretive perspective that placed the study of values at the center of sociological analysis.

Becker revised Max Weber's concept of ideal types by developing a more systematic and empirically grounded method he termed constructed types. Sociological investigation requires the use of constructed types and cultural case studies of a given society or community in a particular historical period. While most American sociologists of his day ignored historical scholarship, Becker insisted that sociology and history are necessarily complementary disciplines. He was one of the first to introduce these Weberian themes to American sociology.

Becker's major theoretical writings were devoted to developing a sacred-secular theory of social change. In the early phase of his career, he was primarily interested in studies of secularization. According to Becker, sacred societies such as ancient Greece and European peasant communities confronted forces of change (e.g., migration or increased communication), which generated inevitable secular processes. But Becker's observations of Nazi Germany in the 1930s offered new insight into a reverse process in which a secular society undergoes sacralization. In *German Youth: Bond or Free* (1946) he examined the Nazis' ability to manipulate sacred images of the fatherland. The Nazis attempted to prescribe a new sacred order. In later years, Becker became increasingly interested in the outer limits of secularization that generate reactionary movements of sacralization. Secular conditions of normlessness, Becker argued, lead to normative reactions that attempt to restore sacred prescriptions. Becker was a colorful writer. At the conclusion of *German Youth* he wrote, "For better or for worse, this is the voice of Howard Becker warbling his native woodnotes wild."

Throughout his career Becker was fundamentally interested in how the processes of change and order can be maintained in a liberal democratic society. He wrote of this problem in terms of the "balance" between sacred and secular values of a modern secular society guided by such core principles as universality, achievement, and tolerance. A stable secular democracy is based on sacred principles, but the balance between sacred and secular values never reaches a stable equilibrium. Numerous factors lie behind any sacred-secular imbalance. On the one hand, there are nonrational elements stemming from traditional beliefs and charismatic movements and, on the other hand, there are such forces as expedient rationality and excessive calculation that disenchant human life. Though Becker was committed to rational principles essential for a liberal democratic society, he realized that, in the last analysis, human commitment to a given set of values is never fully rational. Becker's analysis of the value crisis confronting liberal democracies borrowed heavily from Weber. Many of these concerns have remained central to Western sociology throughout the twentieth century. Becker died in Madison while he was still active as a professor at the University of Wisconsin.

• A collection of Becker's papers is at the University of Wisconsin, Madison. Becker wrote more than 100 scholarly articles and eight books. Some of his most representative ideas can be found in *Modern Sociological Theory in Continuity and Change*, coedited with Alvin Boskoff (1957). At the time of his death he was collaborating with John C. McKinney on the theory and method of constructive typologies; see John C. McKinney, *Constructive Typology and Social Theory* (1966). Critical appraisal of Becker's ideas are in Paul J. Baker, "A Critical Analysis of Selected Theoretical Problems in the Works of Howard P. Becker" (Ph.D. diss., Duke Univ. 1967). Obituaries are in the *American Sociological Review* 25 (Oct. 1960): 743–44 and the *American Journal of Sociology* 66 (Nov. 1960): 289–90.

PAUL J. BAKER

BECKER, Marion Rombauer (2 Jan. 1903–28 Dec. 1976), cookbook writer, arts administrator, and conservationist, was born Marion Julia Rombauer in St. Louis, Missouri, the daughter of Edgar Roderick Rombauer, a lawyer, and Irma Louise von Starkloff, a cookbook writer. Her outlook and interests were strongly shaped by a freethinking, reform-minded family. She studied art history and French at Vassar College and spent her junior year at Washington University in St. Louis, receiving a B.A. from Vassar in 1925. Hoping to find a career in modern dance or art education, she began teaching in 1929 in the art department of John Burroughs School, an experimental school in Clayton, Missouri.

After her father's sudden death in 1930 Marion Rombauer encouraged her mother—left with little money as the Great Depression spread—in the project of compiling a cookbook and selling it by mail order. The result, published at Irma Rombauer's own expense in 1931, was *The Joy of Cooking*. Her daughter, who had helped test the recipes, illustrated the work with a set of silhouette chapter headings.

In 1932 Marion Rombauer married John William Becker, a childhood friend who had just joined a Cincinnati architectural firm; they had two children. The young couple took up a host of reformist political causes in Cincinnati, where Marion Becker found another teaching position in 1932 as head of the art department at Hillsdale, a private girls' school. She quickly became active in the Regional Planning Council of Cincinnati and Vicinity, of which she served as president from 1934 to 1936, and the Better Housing League, whose annual reports chronicling the progress of efforts against substandard and ghetto housing she wrote or produced from 1938 to 1950.

As time went on Becker's concern for regional planning increasingly focused on preserving ecological resources and wild habitats. A member of the Nature Conservancy, she became a leader in many campaigns to set aside Ohio wilderness areas for preservation. Her efforts on behalf of the Lynx Prairie area (the first Ohio site acquired by the Nature Conservancy) earned her the Amy Angell Collier Montague Civic Achievement Award of the Garden Club of America in 1961. She was also honored with a Silver Oakleaf Award from the Nature Conservancy in 1974.

During much of her life Becker was also active in the field of modern art. In 1942 she became the first professional director of the recently founded Cincinnati Modern Art Society. Under her leadership the organization mounted dozens of exhibitions at the Cincinnati Art Museum that were considered models of their kind by leading museum and gallery directors. She not only conceived and produced shows of major works by artists such as Paul Klee, Alexander Calder, Fernand Léger, and Henri Rousseau but also put on eclectic, politically resonant, theme-oriented exhibitions (e.g., Look at Your Neighborhood, Shelter in Transit and Transition, Accident and Design) and other shows featuring the work of Ohio artists or holdings of local collectors. Usually she was also the writer for the ambitious descriptive/analytical catalogues accompanying the exhibits. She served as director of the Modern Art Society until 1947 and continued to be active after its 1954 reorganization in new premises as the Contemporary Arts Center.

Becker saw her political, cultural, and conservationist activities as far more important than the career for which she is chiefly known: coauthor and eventually sole author of *The Joy of Cooking*. For some years after her efforts on the first edition she was only slightly involved with the book, though she did contribute silhouette artwork to her mother's *Streamlined Cooking* (1939) and *A Cookbook for Girls and Boys* (1946). In 1948 Irma Rombauer asked her daughter to participate in the next revision of *The Joy of Cooking*, which had been published in an expanded version by the Bobbs-Merrill Company in 1936 and, after a further revision incorporating much of the *Streamlined Cooking* material, had become a national bestseller in 1943. The first Rombauer-Becker edition was published in 1951.

The 1951 edition began the gradual transformation of the book—originally an informal recipe collection enhanced by Rombauer's witty persona—into a more systematic manual reflecting Becker's interest in whole-grain cooking, health foods, nutrition, and organic gardening. The 1962 revision, prepared by Becker after her mother had suffered several strokes, was a still more radical departure in both organization and approach. Issued in the year of Irma Rombauer's death, it encompassed a wide range of dishes, including recipes drawn from French, Italian, and other cuisines, and incorporated a huge amount of information on how cooking works, in terms of techniques, equipment, types of heat, and the properties of ingredients.

Within ten years it was obvious that the 1962 revision had an extraordinary and lasting appeal to an audience attuned to the so-called gourmet revolution of the 1960s and 1970s. This version's success outstripped that of any previous edition; many food professionals regarded it as the most important culinary reference work in English. The triumph of Becker's first solo revision led her publishers to undertake two other projects conceived by her: *Little Acorn* (1966), a brief informal history of *The Joy of Cooking*, and *Wild Wealth* (1971), an ambitious book on gardening with wild plants. She considered the latter work—a collaborative effort with ecologist Paul Bigelow Sears, florist-botanist Frances Jones Poetker, and illustrator Janice Rebert Forberg—her most important.

The last and most far-reaching Becker revision of *The Joy of Cooking* appeared in 1975. Its influence as an encyclopedic manual of cookery has surpassed even that of the previous edition. Gravely ill throughout most of the work's preparation, Becker died in Cincinnati a little more than a year after it was published, having lived to see only the first hint of its success.

Marion Becker was seen by friends and associates as a woman of great zeal and energy, with a strong crusading streak. The first woman in her family to receive a college education, she early acquired a reverence for systematic study and a high-minded idea of the rational, aesthetically satisfying life lived in accordance with functional and democratic values. Her mother's cookbook became the somewhat unlikely vehicle for much that mattered to her. Some users devoted to earlier versions of *The Joy of Cooking* found her revisions pretentious and strained compared to the unforced charm of the original. On the other hand, it was only after her involvement that the book acquired much of its present usefulness as a learning tool for people interested not only in recipes but also in the reasons behind the formulas. Her frankly educational approach struck a chord that has long resonated among American cooks, both professional and amateur. More crucial from her own point of view, the cookbook enabled her to address concerns conspicuously absent from most recipe books up to that time and even now seldom found in the big kitchen bibles. Had it not been for the book, Becker's deep knowledge of plant life, reservations about the ecological effects of modern agribusiness, and concern for the future of the human food supply would have been a matter only of serious local activism. Through *The Joy of Cooking* she was able to speak of such questions to a national audience and firmly link them with the everyday practice of cooking.

• Becker's papers are at the Schlesinger Library at Radcliffe College. Early papers of the Cincinnati Modern Art Society are in the University of Cincinnati Library. Some autobiographical material appears in her *Little Acorn: The Story behind "The Joy of Cooking," 1931–1966* (1966), reprinted in slightly revised form in 1981 as *Little Acorn: "Joy of Cooking," the First Fifty Years, 1931–1981*. Biographies of Becker and her mother appear in Anne Mendelson, *Stand Facing the Stove: The Story of the Women Who Gave America "The Joy of Cooking"* (1996). Obituaries are in the *Cincinnati Enquirer* and the *Cincinnati Post*, both 30 Dec. 1976.

ANNE MENDELSON

BECKET, Frederick Mark (11 Jan. 1875–1 Dec. 1942), industrial electrometallurgist, was born in Montreal, Canada, the son of Robert Anderson Becket, a businessman, and Anne Wilson. Becket attended McGill University, graduating in 1895 with a degree in electrical engineering. Intending initially to follow a career in the electrical industry, he went to work for Westinghouse Electric and Manufacturing Co. in East Pittsburgh, Pennsylvania.

By the summer of 1896 Becket had decided to concentrate his interests in the fields of electrochemistry and electrometallurgy, and he soon took a position at a pilot plant set up by Charles E. Acker in Jersey City, New Jersey. There he worked on the production of caustic soda and bleaching powder, as well as the electrolytic preparation of a series of alkaline lead and tin alloys. In 1898 Becket enrolled at Columbia University for a formal course of study with Charles F. Chandler in physical and industrial chemistry and in metallurgy. He wrote his master's thesis on electric furnace production of metals and chemical compounds and received an M.S. in 1899.

In 1900 Becket was named chief electrician at a commercial-scale plant constructed by Acker in Niagara Falls, New York. Also in 1900 Becket married Frances Kirby, of New York City, who died within three months of a ruptured appendix. Later that year, he returned to Columbia's graduate program to study chemistry with Chandler and metallurgy with Henry M. Howe. While pursuing research for his Ph.D. dissertation on the electrical conductivity of fused salts, Becket accepted a job with the Ampere Electrochemical Company from 1902 to 1903 in Niagara Falls. Abandoning for good his academic studies, Becket worked on processes for producing high-quality metallic iron using high-temperature electric furnaces.

In April 1903 Becket and two Ampere colleagues, Lewis A. Saunders and R. A. Witherspoon, formed Niagara Research Laboratories (NRL) to conduct original research in metallurgy and finance it by serving as a consultant to outside firms. When the firm failed to turn a profit in its first years of operation, Becket's partners withdrew from the venture. Left in charge, Becket embarked on the work that would constitute his major contribution to the field of metallurgy, originating the silicon reduction process for producing low-carbon ferroalloys and alloying metals. Becket's technique of reducing ores in high-temperature electrical furnaces with silicon instead of carbon resulted in the commercial production of low-carbon alloys of chromium, vanadium, and other metals, as well as commercially pure forms of some of these metals.

Becket's work during this period provided the basis for the development of various stainless steels: ferrotungsten steels used primarily for high-speed metal-cutting tools just then coming into widespread use; ferrovanadium steel alloys used in the automobile industry; and eventually silicon metal used in aluminum alloys for airplane manufacture. Becket's new process thus became a central part of several major metallurgical developments in the twentieth century.

In September 1906 NRL was absorbed by the Electro Metallurgical Company (EMC), a new venture initiated by Edgar F. Price with financing from the Union Carbide Company. (In 1917 EMC would become part of Union Carbide.) Becket became chief metallurgist of the new company and for the next two years struggled to perfect a low-carbon ferrochromium process, relying on his engineering background to help him overcome the electrical problems presented by this task. During this period Becket acquired thirteen new patents in silicon reduction processes. His work helped EMC gain a lead of several years over European competitors in developing a large-scale production process, a lead never relinquished during Becket's tenure with the company. In 1908 Becket married Geraldine McBride of Niagara Falls; they had two children.

Frustrated that his job allowed little time for experimentation with new products or processes, Becket in 1910 won Price's approval to establish a small "experimental account, which would enable us to develop new products and also to decrease manufacturing costs." The first new product to emerge from Becket's research lab was low-carbon ferromanganese, and Becket also experimented with ferrotungsten, work that he had begun but not commercialized at NRL. His research staff continued to grow and in 1921 was reorganized as the Union Carbide and Carbon Research Laboratories, Inc., with Becket as chief metallurgist. By 1927 he had risen to president of the corporation's research laboratories in Long Island City, New York. During this period, in 1918, Becket had become a naturalized citizen of the United States.

Although Becket continued to conduct experiments and eventually acquired 125 patents in his name, he now spent the bulk of his time overseeing the research of others. Under his guidance researchers developed the processes for the manufacture of ferromolybdenum and various chromium-manganese and chromium-manganese-nickel steels. During World War I he developed a process for producing ferrozirconium, a metal used in lightweight armor plate. By 1940, the year of his retirement, Union Carbide's alloy division was producing nearly fifty different ferroalloys totaling $60 million in sales, for many of which Union Carbide was either an important or the sole producer.

Becket should be viewed as a pioneer in the development of corporate research and development in the United States. Throughout his career he supported pure research as well as applied engineering, firmly believing that "our milestones in industrial research have been based on discoveries in fundamentals." Becket's associates viewed him as particularly adept at combining business and engineering judgments in the development of commercially successful processes.

He recognized early in his career that the chemical industry was undergoing a process revolution characterized by focus on technique, the realm of the physical chemist, rather than solely on the end product, the realm of the analytical chemist.

Becket was a longtime member of the Society for Promotion of Engineering Education and the Engineer's Council for Professional Development. He was a founding member of the Electrochemical Society, serving as its president in 1925–1926, and was president of the American Institute of Mining and Metallurgical Engineers in 1933. Among his many professional awards were the Perkin Medal of the Society of the Chemical Industry (1924), the Acheson Medal of the Electrochemical Society (1937), and the National Pioneers Award of the National Association of Manufacturers in 1940.

Becket died in New York City. Through his own research, and later, through the management of other scientists' work, Becket did much to advance the fledgling electrochemical industry and the cause of corporate research and development.

• Archival information on Becket can be found at Columbia University, McGill University, and the Union Carbide Corporation. Although no full biography exists, two autobiographical accounts are very helpful for understanding Becket's career, "A Few Reflections on Forty Years of Research," *Transactions of the Electrochemical Society* 72 (1937): 14–24, and "Perkin Medal Address," *Industrial and Engineering Chemistry* (Feb. 1924): 197–205. Also useful are James H. Critchett, "Dr. Becket's Scientific and Technical Accomplishments," *Transactions of the Electrochemical Society* 72 (1937): 7–13; Martha Moore Trescott, *The Rise of the American Electrochemicals Industry, 1880–1910: Studies in the American Technological Environment* (1981); and "Union Carbide II: Alloys, Gases, and Carbon," *Fortune*, July 1941, pp. 49–56, 92. Obituaries are in *Transactions of the Electrochemical Society* 82 (1942): 34–36, and the *New York Herald Tribune*, 2 Dec. 1942.

STEPHEN H. CUTCLIFFE

BECKLEY, Jake (4 Aug. 1867–25 June 1918), baseball player, was born Jacob Peter Beckley in Hannibal, Missouri, the son of Bernhardt Beckley, a brick mason, and Rosine Nith. As a youth, Beckley played with the various semipro baseball teams in and around Hannibal. His batting prowess earned him the nickname "Eagle Eye." His professional career began in 1886 with Leavenworth, Kansas, in the Western League. Bob Hart, a former Hannibal teammate who pitched for Leavenworth, knew the club needed some new players and suggested Beckley, who became the starting second baseman. Beckley had a fine year, hitting well above .300. In 1887 he switched to first base, a position he played for the next twenty years. Early that season his contract was sold to the Lincoln, Nebraska, team where he continued to dominate Western League pitchers, maintaining a season average above .400 at a time when walks were counted as hits.

The following season Beckley played with the St. Louis club in the Western Association. His offensive showing there was lackluster, but his outstanding defensive play earned him promotion to the major league Pittsburgh Nationals. He stayed in Pittsburgh through mid-1896, although in 1890 he jumped to that city's entry in the Players League, leading that circuit in triples and finishing in the top five in several other offensive categories. His exodus was felt severely by the Nationals as the club finished with a dismal 23 wins and 113 losses. His return in 1891 helped the team improve its record, but Pittsburgh never was a contender in the National League pennant race during his tenure.

Beckley married Mollie Murphy on 31 March 1891, but seven months later she died of consumption. His only bad season with Pittsburgh came the following year. He remarried in March 1896, to Georganna Rupp. With Beckley playing below par in 1896, he was traded to the New York Giants for a younger first baseman, Harry Davis. Beckley's stay in New York was short; seventeen games into the 1897 season his contract was sold to the Cincinnati Reds. Beckley enjoyed seven good seasons in Cincinnati, but again he could not lead the club to contending status. Despite five straight seasons in which he batted above .300, the St. Louis Cardinals purchased his contract at the end of the 1903 season.

Although Beckley had a successful first year in St. Louis, batting .325, the team finished in the second division with a 75–79 won-lost record. The next two seasons saw the Cardinals get worse, and Beckley's production decreased dramatically. His batting average fell to .286 in 1905, .247 in 1906, and had sunk to a paltry .209 when the Cardinals released him early in 1907.

Beckley's former teammate Jimmy Burke, managing the Kansas City Blues of the American Association, quickly signed him as the team's starting first baseman. Beckley found new life there. He hit .365 to win the league batting title. He stayed with Kansas City for two more seasons and was named manager early in 1909, replacing his former teammate Monte Cross. Beckley himself was fired in midseason.

Beckley played two more seasons in the minor leagues, closing out his career in 1911 as player-manager of the cellar-dwelling Hannibal entry in the Central Association. He returned to Kansas City where he worked for a railway company and became a baseball umpire for college and semipro games; one college team, finding him a source of baseball wisdom, considered him "the perfect umpire." He also served as a Federal League umpire during its six-team minor league season of 1913, and he umpired the first Federal League game played in Kansas City against St. Louis on 12 July. Beckley died in Kansas City of heart disease.

Many baseball historians consider Beckley to be the best-fielding first baseman of the nineteenth century. Although he played most of his career in the days of the 130- to 140-game season, he set major league marks for the most games played at first base and most putouts and chances accepted, records that stood for more than ninety years. He led his league in putouts six times, in assists three times, and in fielding percentage three times. His 243 career triples rank him high on the all-time list. He is also credited with coining several popular baseball expressions, among them "Heads Up" and "Be Alive." Beckley was an excellent bunter with a unique style of turning his bat around as the pitcher started his delivery and then bunting with the handle out.

Despite never playing on a championship team, Beckley was one of baseball's finest first basemen. He was elected to the National Baseball Hall of Fame in 1971.

• There is a file on Beckley at the Baseball Hall of Fame in Cooperstown, N.Y. His major league career statistics can be found in *The Baseball Encyclopedia*, 9th ed. (1993), and in John Thorn and Pete Palmer, eds., *Total Baseball*, 3d ed. (1993). Also see Lee Allen, *One Hundred Years of Baseball* (1950); Harold Seymour, *Baseball, the Early Years* (1960); David Voigt, *American Baseball: From Gentleman's Sport to the Commissioner's System* (1966); and *Daguerreotypes of the Great Stars of Baseball* (1971), published by *Sporting News*. Obituaries appear in the *Kansas City Star*, the *Kansas City Journal*, and the *Hannibal Evening Courier-Post*, 26 June 1918.

BILL CARLE

BECKLEY, John James (4 Aug. 1757–8 Apr. 1807), first clerk of the United States House of Representatives and first librarian of Congress, was born in England and came to Virginia as an indentured servant at the age of twelve in August 1769. Though little is known of his family in England, Beckley's coming to America was driven more by opportunity than by poverty and came as a result of the search by John Clayton, a leading American botanist and clerk of Gloucester County, Virginia, for a scribe to assist him. Clayton made the arrangements through the mercantile firm of John Norton & Sons, of which James Withers, an uncle of Beckley, was a member.

The young Beckley lived in Clayton's home and assisted him in his office until Clayton's death in December 1773, which terminated Beckley's indenture and left him on his own at the age of sixteen. He continued to find employment as a clerk, moving to Richmond and assisting the clerk of Henrico County. As resistance to England mounted, Beckley was appointed clerk of the Henrico County Committee of Safety in November 1774, beginning a long career as the clerk of public bodies. In 1776 he was the clerk of the committee of trade of the Virginia House of Delegates, and in the following year he was elected clerk of the Virginia Senate. In October 1779 Beckley became clerk of the House of Delegates, not long after Thomas Jefferson became governor of Virginia. He served ten years in that post. By 1780 he had held twelve different clerkships—some simultaneously. During the 1780s he was also three times mayor of the city of Richmond.

Meanwhile, Beckley had been reading law and began to practice, but law never became his primary career. While in Williamsburg, Beckley was elected to Phi Beta Kappa (10 Apr. 1779), although not a student at the College of William and Mary. He was soon elected secretary of the society, and he would draw up and sign the charters for new chapters of the young scholarly society to be founded at Harvard and Yale.

Beckley journeyed to Philadelphia with Edmund Randolph in April 1787 hoping to become the secretary of the Constitutional Convention, but he failed to win the post. He was more successful the following year, when he was chosen secretary of the Virginia ratifying convention. With the Constitution ratified and the elections of 1788 over, Beckley was in New York in March 1789 campaigning to be chosen as clerk of the House of Representatives. After a tie with William Samuel Stockton, Beckley was elected on the second ballot to be the first clerk of the United States House of Representatives. Beckley married Maria Prince in New York in 1790; they had four children, only one of whom, Alfred, survived early childhood.

Beckley was an able clerk of the House. Though his early implementation of records management led him to discard many manuscript drafts of documents that scholars later would have prized, his efficiency was praised by many congressmen. Virginia's John Page affirmed that "there never was a more correct and diligent clerk . . . who so happily united Accuracy with Dispatch," and he praised Beckley for "the Facility with which he could turn to any Paper which had ever been committed to his care."

In his impact on his times, Beckley was more influential as a partisan political operative than as a skilled secretary or clerk. He shared Jefferson's distrust of Alexander Hamilton and was an early partisan of Jefferson and the Republican party. He supplied Jefferson with information that he collected in New York and Philadelphia and was an active organizer of the Republican party in Pennsylvania, while the capital was in Philadelphia from 1790 to 1800. Beckley devoted many hours to political correspondence and circulating political handbills and pamphlets, some of which he wrote himself. He was often a behind-the-scenes operative. "We have already dispersed in Circular letters, all over the States, a petition to the House of Representatives without, as yet, the smallest suspicion from our opponents," he reported to James Madison in 1795. "All our movements are kept secret until they have reached their ultimate destination, and we now meditate an address to the people in the same mode."

In 1796 Beckley managed the Pennsylvania campaign in support of Jefferson for president, employing methods innovative in a time when direct campaigning for political office was not widely accepted. In an election in which each voter was required to cast a handwritten ballot, Beckley organized committees to write tickets for presidential electors and directed the distribution of 30,000 handwritten Jefferson tickets throughout the state. He also directed the distribution of handbills and political addresses. Beckley's efforts contributed heavily to Jefferson's winning fourteen of the fifteen electoral votes of Pennsylvania in 1796.

Beckley's success in Pennsylvania was not matched nationwide. Jefferson lost to John Adams by three electoral votes, and Federalists won a majority of seats in the House of Representatives. As a result, Beckley lost his post as clerk of the House. In 1799 the newly elected Republican governor of Pennsylvania, Thomas McKean, appointed Beckley to two court clerkships with income equaling his lost position.

As chairman of the Republican committee for Philadelphia in the election of 1800, Beckley was again politically active in the presidential contest. Jefferson's victory and the election of a Republican majority in the House of Representatives led to Beckley being restored to his post as clerk of the House in 1801.

In 1802, when Congress authorized the appointment of a librarian, Jefferson promptly named Beckley to be the first librarian of Congress. Appointing an assistant to manage the small congressional library, Beckley would retain both posts until his death in Washington, D.C.

Beckley's careful administration of his office as clerk of the House of Representatives during seven of the first nine congresses of the United States made an important contribution to the compilation of the legislative record of the young republic. His activities as an early party manager, however, may have been more influential than his administrative work as clerk of the House or as librarian of Congress.

• Beckley's letters are widely scattered in the papers of recipients, including those of Thomas Jefferson, James Madison, and James Monroe in the Library of Congress and the William Irvine Papers in the Historical Society of Pennsylvania. Edmund Berkeley and Dorothy Smith Berkeley, *John Beckley: Zealous Partisan in a Nation Divided* (1973), is a comprehensive biography based on wide research. Beckley's political activities are examined in Noble E. Cunningham, Jr., "John Beckley: An Early American Party Manager," *William and Mary Quarterly*, 3d ser., 13 (1956): 40–52, and *The Jeffersonian Republicans: The Formation of Party Organization, 1789–1801* (1957). An obituary is in the (Washington, D.C.) *National Intelligencer*, 10 Apr. 1807.

NOBLE E. CUNNINGHAM, JR.

BECKWITH, James Carroll (23 Sept. 1852–24 Oct. 1917), painter, was born in Hannibal, Missouri, the son of Charles Henry Beckwith, a Chicago grocer, and Martha Melissa Owen. Beckwith's artistic education began in Chicago, where his family had moved while he was still an infant. At his father's insistence, he briefly attended several New York and Ohio military academies; however, the young boy was miserable in this environment and had to be withdrawn more than once for severe illness. Beckwith's constitution was considered delicate—as an adult, he was thin and stood 5′7″—and ill health plagued him for the rest of his life. Back in Chicago, he worked for a time in his father's store, but by age eighteen he was enrolled in the Chicago Academy of Design, studying under Walter Shirlaw and Conrad Diehl. The Chicago fire of 1871 left his family without a home or business, but it also provided Beckwith with the impetus to move to New York and continue his professional training in earnest.

In New York Beckwith enrolled at the National Academy of Design, an institution that would remain at the center of his professional career for much of the rest of his life. Studying under Lemuel Wilmarth, he immediately associated himself with a group of young painters who would later be seen as rebelling against what they felt were backward, "nativist" tendencies in the generation of American artists active during the 1850s and 1860s. During this period he received support from his wealthy great-uncle, John H. Sherwood, a New York real estate investor and art collector. With Beckwith's advice, Sherwood later built the celebrated Sherwood Studio Building (1880, destroyed) at Fifty-seventh Street and Sixth Avenue, an experimental type of apartment building combining artists' studios and living flats. The Sherwood became the residential and artistic nexus of Beckwith's cosmopolitan circle, and he came to be considered the "doyen" of this "colony." He lived and worked on the top floor of the building for over thirty years.

In October 1873 Beckwith sailed for Europe. It was a difficult decision; his diaries show that he was plagued by self-doubt and financial woes, a situation that continued throughout much of his career. Once in France, however, he stayed for five years. After being turned away from the full atelier of Isadore Pils, he entered the newly formed studio of Emile-Auguste Carolus-Duran. "Then," as he recounted in an unpublished autobiographical essay ("Souvenirs and Reminiscences"), "I think my real Art life began."

Beckwith's years with Carolus-Duran were in all respects seminal. In time, he became a favorite of the master, working as his chief assistant both privately and in the school. In 1875 he and his fellow students John Singer Sargent (Beckwith's Parisian roommate) and Frank Fowler assisted Carolus-Duran with his large ceiling decoration, *The Apotheosis of Marie de Medici*, in the Luxembourg Palace, Paris. Yet Beckwith recognized what he saw as the technical shortcomings of Carolus-Duran's method, which was characterized by flashy brushwork and vigorous paint application. Thus, when he competed for the difficult entrance exam to the École des Beaux-Arts, he sought additional basic training in drawing at the Académie Suisse. He also worked in Joseph-Florentin-Léon Bonnat's studio at night. After one unsuccessful attempt, he was admitted to the École in February 1875. Nonetheless, he continued to work primarily with Carolus-Duran. His most notable success at the time was his costume piece, *The Falconer*, exhibited at the Paris Universal Exhibition in 1878 (and donated by the artist to the Toledo Museum of Art in 1910).

During his European sojourn, Beckwith usually spent the warm months traveling with his fellow students in the country—at Fontainebleau or in Italy and Germany. It was in Munich in 1875 that he met the painter William Merritt Chase. When the two returned to settle in New York in 1878, they were received as apostles of the Paris and Munich schools, respectively, and immediately hired as instructors at the Art Students League. It was hoped that Beckwith's

demanding drawing course would invigorate the league's curriculum, whereas Chase's freer painting class was seen as a foil to the rigor of Beckwith's method. "Becky," as he was known to his friends, became a familiar fixture at the league, teaching there for almost twenty years (his connection with the Art Students League was severed in 1897, in a dispute over what he saw as a retreat from academic standards). Known throughout New York as an important pedagogue, he gave additional classes at the Brooklyn Art Guild, the Cooper-Union school, and, later, at his summer home in Onteora, New York.

Beckwith's main concern, however, was with his own work and with the American artistic profession in general. After his return from France, he began painting portraits and ideal female figures. These he showed regularly at the annual exhibitions of the National Academy of Design, beginning in 1877, and he continued to send his work there until his death. Elected an associate member in 1886 and a full academician in 1894, he served on the academy's council from 1895 to 1901 and chaired the (unsuccessful) committee to raise $600,000 for a new building. Other organizations in which he was active include the younger and more European-oriented Society of American Artists (to which he was elected in 1880), the Society of Painters in Pastel (of which he was a founder), and the American Water Color Society. With Chase he organized the benefit exhibition for the Statue of Liberty pedestal fund in 1884. He was also the prime figure in the Free Art League, an artists' campaign to lobby Congress to repeal a heavy tariff on the importation of foreign art. (At the end of his life, Beckwith reversed his views on this subject, arguing that the protective tariff was needed to make up for American collectors' reluctance to buy American art.) As a result of this service, Beckwith established a reputation as a shrewd organizer and businessman.

Despite such civic recognition, Beckwith remained insecure about his artistic abilities and resentful of his need to supplement his income with teaching. His diaries attest to continued financial anxieties well into middle age. The type of work to which he was most attracted, ideal compositions, often failed to find a buyer. His *Christian Martyr* (1881), for example, a partial view of a palm-covered recumbent female figure for which he had high hopes, remained in his studio unsold for years; he donated it to the Illinois Eastern Hospital for the Insane in 1903.

Instead, Beckwith made his living primarily through portraiture. Skilled at producing flattering, aristocratic likenesses of New York's upper-class women, he was also known for his male portraits, particularly a series of military officers. Among his best-received portraits, perhaps a result of his gregarious nature, were his likenesses of artist friends. Of these, the most celebrated were his full-length painting of William Merritt Chase (Indianapolis Museum of Art) shown in the Paris Salon of 1882, his informal view of William A. Coffin reading (1885), and his striking and boldly colored figure of William Walton (1886, Century Association), set iconically against a wall of the Sherwood Studio Building. Although not known as a muralist, he did contribute an important dome decoration, *Electricity*, to the Manufactures and Liberal Arts Building of the World's Columbian Exposition (1893).

Apart from his activities as a painter, Beckwith cultivated a media personality that kept his name constantly before the readers of New York newspapers. With his wife, Bertha Hall, the daughter of a wealthy New York dry-goods merchant and an amateur performer whom he married in 1887 (the couple had no children), he staged lavish parties and receptions in his Sherwood studio. He conducted interviews there on a variety of subjects, making authoritative and sometimes controversial pronouncements on such topics as government policy toward the arts, municipal park design, and a variety of issues relating to women's dress, beauty, and health. His picturesque clothing and grooming—unconventional light-colored suits, boldly patterned trousers, and a Van Dyck beard—as well as his dedication to the sport of fencing also contributed to the exotic and dandified image he projected.

Near the end of his life, with his work increasingly out of step with new artistic developments and his views in conflict with his fellow members of the National Academy, Beckwith withdrew for a time from New York society. In 1910, after a somewhat disappointing sale of his studio contents, he and his wife left for Europe, where they spent two years, primarily in Italy. There the artist concentrated on small landscape sketches of European gardens and architecture. Following his return to New York in 1912, he frequently exhibited these studies, particularly a Versailles series, as well as other small drawings and pastels. Occasionally he would also publish a diatribe against the nonacademic, modernist art of the day, usually in letters to the editors of New York newspapers. In 1917, while visiting with the aged painter Thomas Moran in California, Beckwith began writing his autobiography, "Souvenirs and Reminiscences." He continued writing at his summer home in Onteora, but he died in New York City soon after, leaving behind an incomplete manuscript.

Beckwith was a prominent figure in the generation of artists who returned to the United States in the 1870s and 1880s after extensive European training. In late nineteenth- and early twentieth-century art circles, his name always stood for an unwavering commitment to the highest ideals of academic art. Throughout his career, he remained true to his early French training, first as a young portrait painter fresh from years of Parisian study; then as an influential teacher of careful, accurate drawing; and finally as an uncompromising conservative bemoaning the state of modern art. Although not an active force in the American art world at the time of his death, Beckwith contributed significantly to the education of an entire generation of artists, as well as the general public, never failing to stress the Parisian academic precepts in which he had been trained.

• Beckwith's diaries (with the exception of the year 1895), his autobiographical manuscript "Souvenirs and Reminiscences," his "Record of Pictures," and various notebooks and photographic albums are housed at the National Academy of Design, New York. The entire collection has been microfilmed by the Archives of American Art, Smithsonian Institution. The diary for 1895, as well as eight scrapbooks relating to the artist's life, are in the collection of the New-York Historical Society. There is virtually no modern literature that specifically addresses Beckwith's career. Important articles published during his lifetime include "James Carroll Beckwith," *Art Amateur* 6 (Apr. 1882): 94–96; Charles William Larned, "An Enthusiast in Painting," *Monthly Illustrator* 3 (Feb. 1895): 131–37; and Robert J. Wickenden, "The Portraits of Carroll Beckwith," *Scribner's Magazine*, Apr. 1910, pp. 449–60. An obituary is in the *New York Times*, 25 Oct. 1917.

JOHN DAVIS

BECKWITH, Martha Warren (19 Jan. 1871–28 Jan. 1959), educator, folklorist, and ethnographer, was born in Wellesley Heights, Massachusetts, the daughter of George Ely Beckwith and Harriet Winslowe Goodale, schoolteachers. Beckwith was the grandniece of Lucy Goodale Thurston, one of the first company of Congregational missionaries to the island of Hawaii, and Beckwith's father had spent sixteen years in Hawaii before she was born, working as a missionary and a teacher, and then as manager of a sugar plantation. In 1874 the Beckwiths moved back to Hawaii. There Beckwith was introduced to the "cousins" society, a group formed by the descendants of the early missionaries, most of whom had intermarried, producing an intricate web of family relations. Beckwith was adopted immediately into the cousins society, through which she developed an interest in their history and in the legends and culture of early Hawaii.

Beckwith was educated on Maui at Mauanaolu Seminary and then enrolled in college preparatory institutions in Massachusetts; she graduated from Mount Holyoke College in 1893. She returned to the islands that year and taught at Punahou College in Oahu until 1895. In 1897 she returned to the mainland and took positions at Elmira College, Mount Holyoke, Smith, and finally Vassar, where she remained throughout most of her career. She began working slowly on an advanced degree in anthropology at Columbia University in New York, studying under Franz Boas; she received an M.A. degree in 1906 and a Ph.D. in 1918, again with Boas as her long-term mentor.

Anthropological folklore dominated her professional career. In 1920 she accepted a joint position at Vassar as a research professor associated with the Vassar Folklore Foundation and associate professor of comparative literature. In 1929 she received a full-time research appointment with the Folklore Institute, and the responsibilities as associate professor of comparative literature were dropped. She retired in 1938.

Beckwith's first publications reflected the research and study she had done for her advanced degrees. In 1907 she published a comparison of the dance forms of the Moqui (Hopi) and Kwakiutl Indians based on her master's degree work. Her first book, published in 1919, drew on her Ph.D. research in Hawaiian folklore and was titled *The Hawaiian Romance of Laieikawai*. Thereafter, Beckwith conducted research all over the world, studying the folklore and ethnography of black and East Indian Jamaicans (1919–1924), the Mandan and Hidatsa Indians in the Dakotas (1926–1932), and the folk festivals Americans of multiple ethnicities in the East and South as a member of the National Folk Festival Committee (1934). Her monumental *Folklore in America*, published in 1931, proved to be a valuable survey of folklore's history, theories, and methodologies. She emphasized placing folklore in its indigenous cultural context rather than interpreting folklore's stories from one's own foreign context or perspective. Folklore, she believed, should never be separated from its own culture because of its roots in geography and ethnicity as well as cultural values and traditions. Her studies of the Hopi and Kwakiutl Indians benefited from the training she had received from Franz Boas, who specialized in the languages and cultures of American Indians and who had earlier studied the Kwakiutls himself. Boas had especially encouraged women like Beckwith to take up the field of anthropology, and she continued and furthered his Kwakiutl studies. Beckwith served as president of the American Folklore Society in 1932–1933.

In 1938 she was made professor emerita of folklore at Vassar and returned to Honolulu to work at the Bishop Museum as an ethnographer. Here she became an honorary research associate, studying Hawaiian folklore. In 1940 she published perhaps her most famous book, *Hawaiian Mythology*. She was fluent in the Hawaiian language, having learned it as a young child, and her translations of myths and legends from Hawaiian into English made an important contribution to preserving the Hawaiian culture. In addition, Beckwith showed the relationships of more recent folklore to Hawaii's earliest past. In 1951 she published an analysis of the *Kumulipo* (Hawaii's creation mythology), in which she made an effort to examine the chant "in the light of Polynesian thought" rather than approaching it as a foreigner. This work, which she completed when she was eighty years old, marked another high point in her career.

Beckwith influenced a number of younger scholars associated with the Bishop Museum, such as Laura Green and Mary Kawena (Wiggin) Pukui. A diligent scholar who would ponder the possibilities of a translation for hours, Beckwith trained her selected pupils with care so that her methods could be passed on to another generation of scholars. She enjoyed a wide circle of friends throughout the islands and often joined them in "ocean-bathing" as she called it, for health. When she died in Berkeley, California, her ashes were returned to Maui for burial. Beckwith had studied and written about American folklore and folk festivals, she said, to generate "an interest in and appreciation of the varied strands of folk life," which in America enrich "our national art and add to our range of aesthetic enjoyment." She had made the study of American folk-lore into a strict scientific discipline, applying critical methodology and emphasizing the importance of language in culture, laying the foundation for her well-trained scholars to follow. An inspiring teacher, she aided in the preservation of Hawaiian culture, such as myths and chants, which enjoyed a renaissance through many of her students in the late 1970s.

• Beckwith's papers are housed at the University of California at Berkeley and at the Bernice P. Bishop Museum in Honolulu, Hawaii. In addition to the books mentioned above, Beckwith published numerous articles, including "National Folk Festival, Washington D.C., Mountain Folk Festival, Berea College," *Journal of American Folklore* 51 (1938–1939): 442–44, and "Folklore Conditions in Hawaii," *The Friend*, Sept. 1930, pp. 204–5. A brief biography offering a discussion of Beckwith's scholarship by another anthropologist is Katharine Luomala, "Martha Warren Beckwith, a Commemorative Essay," *Journal of American Folklore* 75 (1962): 341–53; see also Luomala's introduction to a reissue of *Hawaiian Mythology* (1970) for a worthwhile analysis of Beckwith's life and writings. Other biographical sketches appear in the *Directory of American Scholars* (1957), p. 49; *American Women*, vol. 3 (1939–1940), p. 6; and Barbara Bennett Peterson, ed., *Notable Women of Hawaii* (1984), pp. 26–30. An obituary is in the *Honolulu Star-Bulletin*, 4 Feb. 1959.

BARBARA BENNETT PETERSON

BEDAUX, Charles Eugene (10 Oct. 1886–18 Feb. 1944), scientific manager, entrepreneur, and fascist collaborator, was born in Charenton-le-Pont, France, a suburb of Paris, the son of Charles Émile Bedaux, a railroad engineer, and Marie Eulalie, a dressmaker. Bedaux spent his first twenty years on the streets of Paris, doing odd jobs and usually avoiding school. He attended the Lycée Louis LeGrand in Paris but did not receive a regular degree. In 1906 he left Paris to seek his fortune across the Atlantic. In the United States Bedaux worked as a dishwasher, an insurance salesman, and a sandhog with the crews building the Hudson River tunnels. He also had a stint at the New Jersey Worsted Mills in Hoboken. He became a naturalized citizen in 1908.

In 1909 Bedaux moved to St. Louis, where he was employed by the Mallinckrodt Chemical Company. It was here that he first began his inquiries into efficient production. The following year Bedaux met Wilfred Sellers, of the Sellers Kitchen Cabinet Company of Ellwood, Indiana, and the two became fast friends. Sellers recommended Bedaux's penchant for reorganization to friends in the furniture manufacturing industry in Grand Rapids, Michigan, and Bedaux was secured as a management consultant for a number of them. Between 1912 and 1916 Bedaux acted as a consultant for firms in both the United States and France. In 1916, with the financial backing of a sales entrepreneur, Frederick Brearly, he formed the Charles E. Bedaux Company of Cleveland. His first marriage, to Blanche Allen of St. Louis, ended in divorce; he then married Fern Lombard of Grand Rapids. His only child was born in 1909.

Bedaux was an entrepreneur who saw his fortune in the scientific management movement stimulated by

Frederick Winslow Taylor and Harrington Emerson. The "Bedaux system" was enormously popular in the United States, and even more so in Great Britain, because it purported to produce immediate results in increased productivity and efficiency. Bedaux claimed to have solved the problem that had plagued Taylor and other scientific managers, namely the precise relationship between work and fatigue. In his time studies, Taylor had always added an arbitrary allowance for rest. Bedaux, on the other hand, discovered a unit of work that he proudly called the "B," defined as "a fraction of a minute of work plus a fraction of a minute of rest, always aggregating unity, but varying in proportions according to the nature of the strain." This principle of "human power measurement" permitted a comparison of the efficiency of men, departments, and firms. It was also the basis for an incentive system of wage payments—the whole thrust of the Bedaux system. Ideally, the worker would receive extra wages for work in excess of the required sixty Bs per hour, and output per worker would increase by one-third.

Despite opposition from both labor and management, the Bedaux system enjoyed a remarkable international success. The history of scientific management in the post–World War I years could almost be written as the history of Bedaux. By 1939 Bedaux had opened offices in over twenty countries with more than four hundred "Bedaux engineers" applying the system in a variety of industrial settings. In the United States, his clients included the American Rolling Mills, Kodak, Standard Oil, Dow Chemical, the Diamond Match Company, General Electric, Swifts, and General Foods. But the system achieved its greatest success in Great Britain. Between 1926 and 1949 it was implemented at more than six hundred British firms; the most important application of the Bedaux method occurred at nearly all plants of the industrial giant Imperial Chemical Industries.

As a scientific manager, Bedaux was quite unlike Taylor. Whereas Taylor was always directly connected with the affairs of shop reorganization, Bedaux left the implementation of his system to his highly trained subordinates, many of whom later became consultants themselves. Bedaux was not a theorist but an entrepreneur in scientific management techniques. In this respect, he was closer in spirit to Emerson than Taylor, although Taylor clearly provided him with the basics of his system. The originality of the Bedaux system was that Bedaux knew how to market his product.

The system made Bedaux a wealthy man, and he was able to live comfortably at his château in France, courting the wealthy and influential. By the 1930s the popularity of the system in the United States began to decline. The American Federation of Labor reported that the system was little more than pseudoscientific rhetoric intended to speed up production without attention to management reorganization. In addition, Bedaux ran into personal and business difficulties with Albert Ramond, the manager of his highly successful Chicago office. By the early 1940s the Bedaux name was dropped, engineers were instructed not to mention his name on the job, and the Bedaux work unit, the "B," was replaced by the more neutral "P" (point) or "AM" (allowed minute).

Bedaux achieved international fame in 1937 when the duke of Windsor (the former King Edward VIII of England) married the American divorcée Wallace Warfield Simpson at Bedaux's château near Tours. Bedaux then arranged a German tour for the duke, who was interested in foreign labor conditions. He subsequently prepared an American visit for November 1937 in which he would accompany the duke, but the American Federation of Labor, the United Textile Workers' Union, and the New York maritime unions all denounced Bedaux for his fascist sympathies, and he canceled the trip. In 1940 Bedaux became more actively involved with the Nazi rulers of France and the Vichy government. While in Algeria he began a project to transport peanut oil more than 2,000 miles across the Sahara. In November 1942 Bedaux was captured by the Allies and brought back to the United States, where he was held in custody in Miami, Florida. While awaiting trial for treason, Bedaux committed suicide.

• The Bedaux archives are located at the Information Office of Inbucon Management Consultants, Ltd., of Haywards Heath, West Sussex, England. More than thirty rolls of microfilm contain the daily reports of Bedaux engineers in over 600 British firms between 1926 and 1950. The best introduction to the mechanics of the Bedaux system is Charles E. Bedaux, *The Bedaux Efficiency Course for Industrial Application* (1917). A precise statement of Bedaux work study can be found in the International Bedaux Company publication, *Bedaux Labor Measurement* (1928; repr. 1932), also published as *Bedaux Measures Labor*. See also two reports by the Bedaux Company, *Production Management* (1943) and *More Production, Better Morale: A Program for American Industry* (1944). The New York Public Library holds a brief file on Bedaux that includes the International Bedaux Company's *Representative List of All Bedaux Companies* (1934). An informal "History of the Bedaux Companies and Albert Ramond and Associates, Inc.," is on file at Albert Ramond and Associates (Chicago). There are two biographical treatments of Bedaux: Janet Flanner, "Annals of Collaboration: Equivalism," *New Yorker*, 22 Sept., 6 Oct., and 13 Oct. 1945, and Jim Christy, *The Price of Power: A Biography of Charles Eugene Bedaux* (1984). For Bedaux's British experience, see General Federation of Trades Unions, *Report on the Bedaux and Kindred Systems* (1932); Trades Union Congress, *The TUC Examines the Bedaux System of Payment by Results* (1933); Percy Glading, *How Bedaux Works* (1934); and two works by W. F. Watson, *Bedaux and Other Systems Explained* (1932), and *The Worker and Wage Incentives: The Bedaux and Other Systems Explained* (1934). The National Industrial Conference Board's *System of Wage Payment* (1930) and the International Labour Office's survey, *Payment by Results* (1951), contain clear expositions of the system. Modern historical treatments of Bedaux include Geoff Brown, *Sabotage: A Study in Industrial Conflict* (1984), and Craig R. Littler, *The Development of the Labour Process in Capitalist Societies* (1982). An obituary is in the *New York Times*, 20 Feb. 1944.

STEVEN KREIS

BEDFORD, Gunning (7 Apr. 1742–30 Sept. 1797), officeholder, was born in New Castle Hundred, New Castle County, Delaware, the son of William Bedford, a sadler and landowner, and Catherine Jacquett. In 1752 William Bedford, having moved his family to Philadelphia, enrolled his son in the College, Academy, and Charitable School of Philadelphia (later the University of Pennsylvania), where Gunning studied in the academy division until 1756. William's brother also lived in Philadelphia and had a son Gunning Bedford, Jr. (1747–1812), who is often confused with William's son. After Gunning Bedford, Jr., moved to Delaware in 1779, his older cousin was described as "Senior" or "the Elder." William Bedford's family resided in Philadelphia until at least 1763 and then returned to New Castle Hundred.

In 1769 Gunning Bedford married Mary Read, the sister of lawyer George Read, at whose house the ceremony probably took place, because Mary's mother opposed the match. Bedford's prospects were apparently not good. George Read hoped that Bedford would bring to the marriage the plantation on which his father lived, but such was not the case. Bedford received his father's two plantations only after his father's will was proved in 1789. The couple had no children. All of Bedford's biographers maintain that he was a lawyer, but none offers hard evidence to support this contention.

The revolutionary war and his connection to Read, leader of the state's conservatives, improved Bedford's fortunes. Delaware's conservatives were reluctant revolutionaries, largely of English descent, who did not want to change the old social order as drastically as the Scotch-Irish radicals. In May 1775 he was elected a major in the New Castle County militia. In September he became a delegate to the state council of safety, remaining until November 1776. The Second Continental Congress, acting on the council of safety's recommendation, appointed Bedford lieutenant colonel of the First Delaware Regiment of the Continental army in January 1776. Bedford served until January 1777 and saw action at the battles of White Plains and Princeton. He was wounded in the arm at White Plains and soon "tired of the service." After the regiment's colonel was killed at Princeton, Commander in Chief George Washington offered the command to Bedford, who rejected it. A fellow officer later noted that "Nature Never intended him for a Soldier." Nevertheless, in late 1777 or early 1778 Bedford became lieutenant colonel of the Second Regiment of Delaware militia and was promoted to colonel in June 1778, serving until at least 1781.

Political appointments also came swiftly. On 22 February 1777, the day he rejected Washington's offer, Bedford was appointed to a two-year term in the state's four-man privy council, an advisory body to the state's president, who presided over it. In March 1777 Bedford was named prothonotary or principal clerk of the Court of Common Pleas of New Castle County and, the next year, register for probate of wills for the county. He was regularly reappointed to these lucra-

tive positions into the 1790s. The initial appointment of register was made by Read, the state's vice president and acting president. In 1781 Bedford was commissioned a justice of the peace for New Castle County and was recommissioned in 1789.

In February 1783, after losing control of the election for the state's president, Read engineered the election of Bedford and other conservatives to the privy council, where Bedford remained until October 1785. During the 1780s the state's conservatives encouraged the legislature to promote the economy aggressively, favored lenient treatment of Loyalists, and opposed debtor legislation and paper money. They gained control of the House of Assembly in October 1786, and Bedford was appointed a delegate to the Confederation Congress. He declined the post in January 1787, ostensibly because he did not have the time to attend. Bedford actually preferred to stay in Delaware so that he could act as Read's political agent. Read, like Bedford's cousin Gunning Bedford, Jr., was elected to the constitutional convention called to meet in Philadelphia in May 1787 to revise and amend the Articles of Confederation. James Tilton, Read's bitterest enemy, was apparently alluding to Bedford when he wrote that the "Prime Minister" represented "our chief ruler" while he attended the Constitutional Convention.

In December 1787 Bedford and twenty-nine other Delaware convention delegates unanimously ratified the Constitution recommended by the Constitutional Convention. Delaware's three presidential electors, including Bedford, voted in January 1789 for Washington as president and John Jay as vice president. About the same time Read installed Bedford as boss of New Castle County's Federalists. From November 1790 to November 1791 Bedford again served as a privy councillor, replacing Read. In 1792 Bedford, a land-rich and comfortable officeholder, was elected president of the newly incorporated board of trustees of New Castle Common, an area of about 1,100 acres that was used for the benefit of the inhabitants of New Castle, the town in which Bedford lived. This same year Bedford and Delaware's other presidential electors again voted for Washington as president, but this time, apparently prompted by Read, they supported John Adams for vice president.

In late 1795 Bedford, "an old and tried friend to his country," was elected governor of Delaware, defeating Democratic-Republican Archibald Alexander of New Castle County by a vote of 2,352 to 2,142. Bedford was soundly defeated in his home county, the seat of Scotch-Irish Presbyterianism and the center of revolutionary fervor. He was a Presbyterian, but not, as one of his supporters revealed, "a Churchman"; had he been, the conservatives in Sussex County, the stronghold of wartime loyalism, and other Federalists would not have voted for him so overwhelmingly. Bedford took the oath of office in January 1796. In his legislative address the next year he called attention to only one important matter—the need to reform the harsh system of "penal jurisprudence" and replace it with a more humane system of confinement. He died in New Castle while still holding office.

• On his political, executive, and legislative activities, see Claudia L. Bushman et al., eds., *Proceedings of the Assembly of the Lower Counties on Delaware, 1770–1776, of the Constitutional Convention of 1776, and of the House of Assembly of the Delaware State, 1776–1781* (1986), and *Proceedings of the House of Assembly of the Delaware State, 1781–1792, and the Constitutional Convention of 1792* (1986). Also see "Minutes of the Council of the Delaware State from 1776 to 1792," *Papers of the Historical Society of Delaware*, vol. 6 (1887); "Minutes of the Privy Council" in the microfilm collection, "Records of the States of the United States of America," at the Library of Congress; Harold B. Hancock, ed., "Loaves and Fishes: Applications for Office from Delawareans to George Washington," *Delaware History* 14 (1970–1971): 135–58; William Thompson Read, *Life and Correspondence of George Read* (1870); John A. Munroe, ed., *Timoleon's Biographical History of Dionysius, Tyrant of Delaware, with Notes by Thomas Rodney* (1958); and Munroe, *Federalist Delaware, 1775–1815* (1954). Brief biographies of Bedford are scattered in general works on Delaware, but, since Bedford and his cousin of the same name are often confused, they should be used cautiously. The best are in Charles E. Green, *Delaware Heritage: The Story of the Diamond State in the Revolution* (1975), and Roger A. Martin, *A History of Delaware through Its Governors, 1776–1984* (1984). For the Bedford family, see Lewis D. Cook, "The Gunning Bedford Family: New Castle, Philadelphia, Baltimore," in *Genealogies of Pennsylvania Families from the Pennsylvania Genealogical Magazine*, vol. 1 (1982), pp. 21–41. Public Archives Commission of Delaware, *Delaware Archives: Revolutionary War* (3 vols., 1919); and George Herbert Ryden, ed., *Letters to and from Caesar Rodney, 1756–1784* (1933).

GASPARE J. SALADINO

BEDFORD, Gunning, Jr. (1747–30 Mar. 1812), revolutionary statesman, signer of the U.S. Constitution, and federal district judge, was born in Philadelphia, Pennsylvania, the son of Gunning Bedford and Susannah Jacquett. His upper-middle-class father was associated with the Philadelphia Carpenter's Company, a labor combination of master workers. Bedford referred to himself as Gunning Bedford, Jr., probably to avoid being confused with his notable cousin and contemporary, Colonel Gunning Bedford, Sr., governor of Delaware.

Bedford was educated at the Philadelphia Academy from 1766 to 1768 and then at Princeton, from which he received an A.B. in 1771 and an A.M. in 1774. A classmate of James Madison at Princeton, Bedford joined the American Whig Society and delivered the valedictory oration at graduation. In 1771 he married Jane Ballereau Parker, daughter of the printer James Parker. Bedford and his wife had five children, two of whom died young. After studying law in 1771–1772 with Joseph Reed, an eminent Philadelphia attorney, he in 1774 was licensed to practice law in Chester County, Pennsylvania, and in 1779 he gained admission to the Sussex County, Delaware, bar.

On 16 January 1779 Bedford wrote to Caesar Rodney, governor of Delaware, expressing his interest in being attorney general and indicating that he and his

family would move to Delaware that summer. Bedford first settled in Dover, then moved to Wilmington in 1783. On 26 April 1784 he was appointed attorney general of Delaware, and he served until 26 September 1789. In 1785 he bought a farm, "Lombardy," on Brandywine Creek above Wilmington, where he resided periodically from 1793 to 1812 and operated a model farm.

Bedford was elected three times to the Continental Congress. First elected on 1 February 1783 and reelected on 26 October 1784, he, during both terms, had poor attendance. He was elected again on 4 November 1785 but never attended that session. Elected by the legislature to the Annapolis Convention, held on 11–13 September 1786, he did not attend that meeting either. During 1786–1787 he was a delegate to the Delaware House of Representatives.

As a group, the Delaware delegation to the Philadelphia Constitutional Convention in 1787, Bedford, George Read, John Dickinson, Richard Bassett, and Jacob Broom, clearly represented the state's political values and attitudes. His fellow Delaware delegates were more conservative in their leanings than Bedford, and in national politics after 1789 they were more Federalist in their views than Bedford. At the Philadelphia Convention, Bedford initially favored only amending the Articles of Confederation, but later he adjusted his views. According to *The Records of the Federal Convention of 1787* and Madison's records, Bedford took his seat on Monday, 28 May 1787. A Georgia delegate to the convention, William Pierce, described him as "very corpulant [*sic*]" and "a bold and nervous Speaker" with "a very commanding and striking manner." Pierce thought him "warm and impetuous in his temper, and precipitate in his judgment."

Bedford took extensive notes on the debates relative to the powers of Congress and the states. Edmund Randolph argued that the Congress of the Articles of Confederation was too weak. In general, said Randolph, "Congress ought to be paramount to state legislatures" and "empowered to negative all laws that interfere with confederation." If a state disagreed, the appeal should be heard by the judiciary. Bedford and the other Delaware delegates opposed amending Article V of the Articles of Confederation, which gave each state one vote in Congress.

During the convention, Bedford played a crucial role as a small-state advocate. Missing few sessions and speaking often, he vigorously defended state sovereignty and argued for the principle of "one state–one vote" in a national legislature. He opposed the idea of a general veto of state laws because it would "strip the small states of their equal right of suffrage." He estimated that Delaware would hold only 1/90 of the total votes of the general government, whereas Pennsylvania and Virginia alone would control "1/3 of the whole." Accusing the large states of self-interest, he suggested the small states would defend themselves and offended large-state delegates by adding, "I do not, gentlemen, trust you." The Delaware legislature had strictly enjoined its delegates not to change the existing "rule of suffrage," insisting that each state should retain one vote in Congress. Consolidation, Bedford argued, was out of the question. In a confederacy, the states "must continue if not perfectly, yet equally sovereign." He made what Massachusetts delegate Rufus King characterized as the "most intemperate speech uttered in the Convention" and "challenged the large States to do their worst," suggesting that, if the large states dissolved the confederation, "the small ones will find some foreign ally of more honor and good faith, who will take them by the hand and do them justice." Bedford served actively on the eleven-member committee that drafted the Great Compromise on the issue of representation. The committee report, brought in on 5 July, called for representation in the lower house based on free population and three-fifths of the slaves and equal representation of states in the upper house.

Bedford much preferred a system of government with a strong legislative and weaker executive power. During the 1 June 1787 debates, he argued that the executive office required "peculiar talents." The country had to have an "opportunity of ascertaining his talents." "Therefore, frequent change" was requisite. Strongly opposed to the proposal for a seven-year term for the executive, he worried that the country might be "saddled" with a president who "did not possess the qualifications ascribed to him." He did not think impeachment would be a "cure for this evil" because it "would reach misfeasance only, not incapacity." On this basis, he argued "for a triennial election, and for an ineligibility after a period of nine years."

In the 2 June 1787 debates on removal of the executive from office, Bedford seconded a motion by John Dickinson to add, after the words "to be chosen by the national legislature for the term of seven years," the phrase "to be removable by the national legislature upon the request by a majority of the legislatures of the individual States." Only Delaware voted in favor of the motion; nine states voted against it.

Madison noted that during the 4 June 1787 debates on the executive veto power, Bedford opposed "every check on the Legislative" power, even the proposal of a council of revision. He preferred defining clearly the "boundaries to the Legislative Authority," which would provide security to the rights of the other branches of government. According to Madison, Bedford stated, "The Representatives of the People were the best judges of what was for their interest, and ought to be under no external controul [sic] whatever." The two houses of the legislature would sufficiently control each other without the presidential veto. He argued also that the Congress would not subvert the executive branch because the executive powers would be so well defined that the legislature "cannot overleap the bounds."

Bedford thought the clause, "no State being separately competent to legislate for the general interest of the Union," as it stood in the resolution on the general powers of Congress was formidable. On 17 July 1787 he offered an amendment to change the wording to "and moreover to legislate in all cases for the general interests of the Union, and also in those to which the States are separately incompetent, or in which the harmony of the United States may be interrupted by the exercise of individual legislation." His amendment was adopted by a 6 to 4 vote. Through this discussion and vote, the delegates, including Bedford, came to an understanding about appropriate areas of legislative jurisdiction for the states and Congress.

Bedford signed the Constitution on 17 September 1787 and was a delegate to the Delaware ratification convention. The state convention, meeting in Dover, unanimously ratified the Constitution on 7 December 1787. Bedford seemed assured that the Constitution indeed provided a system of limited government and protected the states.

During 1788–1789 Bedford served as a member of the state council from New Castle, and he was a presidential elector in 1789 and 1793. During his last year as Delaware attorney general, he critiqued a draft of the new judiciary bill before Congress. On 26 September 1789 President George Washington appointed Bedford federal district judge for Delaware, a position he held until his death.

In June 1800 Justice Samuel Chase of the Supreme Court, presiding with Bedford at a circuit court held at New Castle, declared "that a highly seditious temper had manifested itself in the state of Delaware among a certain class of people." Chase was concerned about growing opposition to the 1798 Sedition Law and attacks by James Wilson, editor of the Wilmington newspaper, *Mirror of the Times*, against President John Adams, the Sedition Law, and New England Federalists. Bedford replied to Chase, "I believe you do not know where you are, the people in this place are not pleased with the sedition law."

In his later years Bedford encouraged education as president of the trustees of Wilmington Academy. A proponent of abolition, he was an active member of the Delaware Society for Promoting the Abolition of Slavery, which also sought to protect free blacks and mulattoes. He was the main speaker at Masonic ceremonies for President Washington, and he wrote *A Funeral Oration upon the Death of Washington* (1800). Bedford served as the first grand master of the Grand Masonic Lodge of Delaware in 1806. He died in Wilmington, Delaware.

• The Gunning Bedford, Jr., Papers are in the Historical Society of Delaware. His speeches at the Philadelphia Constitutional Convention are in Max Farrand, *The Records of the Federal Convention of 1787*, rev. ed. (4 vols., 1987); see also *The Debates in the Federal Convention of 1787 . . . Reported by James Madison*, ed. Gaillard Hunt and James Brown Scott (2 vols., 1987). On his education, see Richard A. Harrison, *Princetonians, 1769–1775, a Biographical Dictionary* (1980). The most informative source on Bedford's career as a federal district judge is J. P. Nields, *Gunning Bedford, Junior* (1907). For other aspects of his life, see *Congressional Quarterly Guide to U.S. Elections* (1985). See also Merrill Jensen, *Ratification of the Constitution by the States: Delaware, New Jersey, Georgia, Connecticut* (1978); George H. Ryden, ed., *Letters to and from Caesar Rodney, 1756–1784* (1933); William Thompson Read, *Life and Correspondence of George Read* (1870); and John A. Munroe, *Federalist Delaware, 1775–1815* (1954).

RODGER C. HENDERSON

BEDINGER, George Michael (10 Dec. 1756–8 Dec. 1843), soldier, legislator, and businessman, was born in York County, Pennsylvania, the son of Henry Bedinger and Magdalene von Schlegel, innkeepers. In 1737 his grandfather had moved to Pennsylvania from the vicinity of Strasbourg in Alsace-Lorraine. At the time of George Michael's birth, the family name was spelled Biedinger and German was the language spoken at home. Late in life Bedinger was described by a contemporary as a "full blooded Virginia Dutchman."

Bedinger spent his youth in Shepherdstown, Virginia (now West Virginia), where he received a basic education. Following his father's death in 1772, he trained as a wheelwright in a concern owned by his mother. Despite his youth and early loss of his father, Bedinger enlisted for military service in 1775 for one year in a local rifle company that was sent to Cambridge, Massachusetts. Although young, Bedinger was promoted to corporal. He reenlisted in January 1777 for three months and again later that year, during which time he participated in the battle of Germantown. He returned to Shepherdstown after his service. During the winter of 1777–1778 he supported the war effort by helping supply the American troops at Valley Forge. His decision to remain at Shepherdstown was probably due to his elder brother's capture and imprisonment by the British.

During the later part of the American Revolution Bedinger's activities were split between his home in Shepherdstown and Virginia's trans-Allegheny domains. In early 1779 he accompanied a small group of friends on an expedition to Kentucky to claim western land and pursue adventure. Bedinger remained in Kentucky most of that year, residing primarily at Boonesborough despite frequent British-supported Indian attacks. That summer he joined the Kentucky militia in Colonel John Bowman's retaliatory expedition against Native American locations in Ohio. Bedinger served as adjutant and quartermaster. At the end of the year he returned to Shepherdstown. Part of 1780 was again spent in Kentucky. In 1781 Bedinger joined the American defense of Yorktown, by this time holding the rank of major. Despite several surveying trips to Kentucky, Shepherdstown remained his primary residence during these years.

In 1786 Bedinger began operating a large gristmill in Shepherdstown in partnership with his friend James Rumsey. Financially secure, Bedinger married Nancy Keene in December 1786. She died the following year giving birth to a daughter. Leaving the infant in the care of its grandmother, Bedinger soon returned to Kentucky. He received a commission as a major in the U.S. Army in 1789 and in 1791 accompanied General Arthur St. Clair's expedition against Native Americans in Ohio but because of ill health was not with the main army at the time of its disastrous defeat.

By 1792 Bedinger had taken up residence at Kentucky's Lower Blue Licks on the Licking River, where he operated a ferry, gristmill, and saltworks. In 1792 he was elected as a representative to the new state of Kentucky's assembly but soon resigned in order to accept a commission as a major in the U.S. Army. Bedinger was well regarded as a man capable of instilling order and discipline among his troops. His commission as major, however, caused jealousies among other veteran officers, causing him to take a leave of absence followed by his resignation in 1793.

In February 1793 Bedinger married Henrietta Clay, daughter of a prominent neighbor. Her parents objected to the match because of the fourteen-year difference in the couple's ages, causing them to elope. Bedinger and his second wife had nine children.

In 1794 Bedinger was elected again to the Kentucky legislature. In 1799, when the Lower Blue Licks became part of Nicholas County, he was appointed to the County Court of Quarter Sessions. He also served as county surveyor until 1803. In 1802 Bedinger, a Jeffersonian Republican, was elected to the U.S. House of Representatives, taking his seat 4 March 1803. Bedinger was a known emancipationist, believing slavery to be "an unhappy thing." As a member of Congress, he attempted to introduce legislation prohibiting further importation of slaves, but his efforts met with little interest. According to a contemporary, Bedinger found slavery a bedeviling problem, and he once supposedly proposed that "they should just get all the negroes asleep, Knock them in the head, and kill every one of them" (Draper collection, Rev. James Gallagher Interview, 15CC63). A small-scale slaveowner himself, Bedinger tried to keep slave families together, and he freed several of his slaves.

Bedinger was reelected to Congress in 1804, but believing in the rotation of office, refused to run for a third term. In 1828, though advanced in years, he ran for Congress again, unsuccessfully, as a Whig candidate and a strong proponent of internal improvements. He also wished to abolish the electoral college. His other activities during these later years included participation in the American Colonization Society. He died at the Lower Blue Licks.

• The George Michael Bedinger Papers are in the Lyman C. Draper Collection and the John D. Shane Collection, both at the Wisconsin Historical Society. The Bedinger-Dandridge family papers are in the Special Collections at Duke University. Biographical works include Danske Dandridge, *George Michael Bedinger: A Kentucky Pioneer* (1909); Charles G. Talbert, "George Michael Bedinger," *Register of the Kentucky Historical Society* 65 (1967): 28–46; William Dodd Brown, ed., "A Visit to Boonesborough in 1779: The Recollections of Pioneer George M. Bedinger," *Register of the Kentucky Historical Society* 86 (1988): 315–29; W. H. Perrin et al., *Kentucky: A History of the State* (1886); and L. F. Bittinger, *Bittinger and Bedinger Families* (1904). An obituary is in the *Louisville Weekly Journal*, 19 Jan. 1844.

ELLEN T. ESLINGER

BEE, Clair Francis (2 Mar. 1896–20 May 1983), basketball coach and writer, was born near Clarksburg, West Virginia. His parents' names and occupations are unknown. Before he was six, he suffered from tuberculosis, and a doctor advised that he spend a great deal of time outdoors. "That prescription," Bee later said, "helped to push me into sports." Bee and his friends often would sneak into a church gymnasium to play basketball. When he was six, his mother died of tuberculosis, after which Bee spent part of his boyhood on his uncle's farm in Belleville, Kansas, part in Parkersburg and Grafton, West Virginia, and the rest at Massanutten Military Academy, Woodstock, Virginia. As a sophomore at Grafton High School in 1915, he wrote what may have been one of the first short stories on basketball, "Bud's Loyalty." In 1917 he graduated from high school.

During the early 1920s, after moving to Ohio, Bee worked in a steel factory in Mansfield, and although short and wiry he played quarterback for the company team against opponents such as the Canton Bulldogs and the Massillon Maroons. He also coached football at Mansfield High School. Beginning in 1922, he attended Waynesburg College in Waynesburg, Pennsylvania, and while still a student he was the college's assistant registrar; he also coached basketball and football for several seasons. He graduated from Waynesburg in 1925. The following year he was hired to coach basketball, baseball, and football at Rider College in Trenton, New Jersey. During his five years at Rider, his basketball teams won 55 games while losing only 7. He was also an assistant to the college president, and he attended Rutgers University, where he earned a master's degree in 1932. He later earned an academic degree from Ohio State University. During his years in New Jersey, Bee found time to write several articles on zone defenses.

In 1931 Long Island University (LIU) in Brooklyn, New York, hired Bee to coach baseball and football and to serve as the school's comptroller. He attempted to propel LIU's football program into major competition, and the team played several games in Brooklyn's Ebbets Field. But the experiment failed. In 1932 Bee became head basketball coach, a position he held through 1951 (interrupted for two years in 1944–1945 when he was a commander in the U.S. Merchant Marine during World War II). During nineteen seasons his teams won 357 games and lost only 79.

Located in an industrial section of Brooklyn, LIU did not have a basketball court and played its home games at the Brooklyn College of Pharmacy's matchbox gymnasium, which became known as the "Druggist's Den." At one point LIU had a home winning streak of 139 games. Citing lax academic standards at the school, major New York teams such as St. John's, City College of New York, and New York University refused to schedule Bee's teams. In 1936, however, Ned Irish, who had been booking college basketball doubleheaders at Madison Square Garden, invited LIU to play there. LIU quickly became a national basketball power. During one span (1934–1936) LIU won forty-three games before being defeated at the Garden by a Stanford team led by Hank Luisetti. Bee's teams won two National Invitation Tournaments (1939 and 1941), a Helms Foundation national championship (1939), and twice LIU went undefeated (1937 and 1939).

A small, slightly built man, with deep-set eyes, and a bony face, Bee was considered by competing coaches to be one of the premier strategists of the game, and he continued to produce outstanding college teams in the postwar era. He developed the 1-3-1 zone defense, which was widely used in that era, and he recommended the three-second rule restricting offensive players from remaining in the foul lane. Bee married Mary Margaret Miller in 1941; they had two children.

One of Bee's goals was to become a published writer. After World War II he became prolific, turning out more than fifty books. Some were technical works on coaching and playing basketball. The Clair Bee Basketball Library, consisting of *Science of Coaching, Man to Man Defense and Attack*, and *Zone Defense and Attack*, were published in 1942; the titles were translated into Spanish, Portuguese, and French. His most popular books, however, were twenty-three Chip Hilton sports novels written for adolescents from the late forties through the seventies. Hilton was a clean-cut, idealistic, Frank Merriwell type who was based on Bob Davies, a blond, slick, ball-handling guard who played at Seton Hall in the early 1940s. The fictional character reflected the idealistic side of Bee that valued hard work, intelligence, and honesty as well as responsibility to family, church, school, friends, and even enemies.

Yet this image conflicted with the reality of big-time college athletics and basketball. The atmosphere at Madison Square Garden where LIU played many of its games was alien to a Chip Hilton. Bee, the realist, had fought and scratched to win against the toughest competition. Former players reported that he sometimes falsified grades or imported ineligible athletes to win important games.

In 1951 Bee's world was turned upside down when eight of his players were involved in a nationwide basketball scandal, and three were indicted. Sherman White, possibly the best player in the country at the time, Dolph Bigos, and LeRoy Smith confessed to taking bribes from gamblers to shave points from LIU's scores to beat the point spreads established by bookmakers. In the aftermath, LIU dropped basketball and did not resume play until 1957. Shattered by the revelations, Bee took an administrative position at the school. He later told a group of coaches that "we—you and I—have flunked. We have not done the job that was expected of us in training the young people. I am not bitter. I am hurt, hurt desperately."

In 1952 Bee became head coach of the Baltimore Bullets of the National Basketball Association (NBA); he became part owner of the team several months later. His enthusiasm for coaching had waned, however, and his teams posted a 33–113 won-lost record over three seasons. Bee sold his interest in 1954, three days before the franchise folded.

Although credit is often given to Danny Biasone, owner of the Syracuse Nationals, Bee devised the 24-second rule in the NBA, which many experts believe created a more exciting game and built stronger public support for the young league. From 1954 until 1967 Bee served as athletic director of New York Military Academy. He also ran a farm in Roscoe, New York, and he continued to write, work as a television commentator for college basketball games, and run an accounting business. In his later years, he received numerous invitations to address basketball clinics and banquets and to talk about basketball. But he had no interest in returning to big-time coaching. "I had my fill," he said. "I wouldn't want to go through all those headaches again. Not at my age. I'm just content with things as they are at school, my farm and the writing." In 1967 Bee was selected to the Basketball Hall of Fame as a "contributor." Among his outstanding players at LIU in addition to White were Art Hillhouse, Bill King, Ossie Schechtman, Marius Russo, and Dolly King. Bee died in Cleveland, Ohio, during a visit with his daughter. His books on coaching had influenced several generations of high school and college coaches, and his college coaching record of 412 wins and only 87 losses over twenty-one years was the second best in division history.

• A file on Bee's career may be found at the Basketball Hall of Fame in Springfield, Mass. See also Sandy Padwe, *Basketball's Hall of Fame* (1970); Zander Hollander, ed., *The Modern Encyclopedia of Basketball* (1969); Charles Rosen, *Scandals of '51: How the Gamblers Almost Killed College Basketball* (1978); Neil D. Isaacs, *All the Moves: A History of College Basketball* (1975); Joe Jares, *Basketball: The American Game* (1971); Jack M. McCallum, "A Hero for All Times," *Sports Illustrated*, 7 Jan. 1980, pp. 50–54, 56–60; and Ira Berkow, "Clair Bee, 85, Loves the Game," *New York Times Biographical Service*, Mar. 1981, pp. 275–76. An obituary is in the *New York Times*, 21 May 1983.

JOHN M. CARROLL

BEEBE, Lucius Morris (9 Dec. 1902–4 Feb. 1966), journalist and newspaper publisher, was born in Wakefield, Massachusetts, the son of Junius Beebe, a wealthy leather manufacturer and bank president, and Eleanor Harriet Merrick, the daughter of John Mudge Merrick, a Harvard chemistry professor. His early life was spent in comfort in the Back Bay section of Boston and in Wakefield, where his family had a 140-acre dairy farm. A clever but mischievous youth with a propensity for pranks, Beebe was expelled from two Massachusetts preparatory schools—St. Mark's in Southboro and Berkshire in Sheffield—before graduating from the Roxbury School in Cheshire, Connecticut, in 1922. At Yale Beebe wrote for the literary magazine and published a book of verse, *Fallen Stars*, as a freshman. He became well known for wearing a monocle, plus fours, and cutaways to class and keeping a roulette wheel and a well-stocked bar in his dormitory room. A militant opponent of Prohibition, Beebe donned clerical vestments to mock divinity school professor Henry Hallam Tweedy, a backer of the Eighteenth Amendment, on the stage of a local theater and was asked to leave Yale in his sophomore year. He then found employment as a correspondent for the *Boston Telegram*, a short-lived afternoon newspaper, before entering Harvard as a special student in 1924. There he resumed his mischief-making as well as his literary studies but managed to obtain his B.A. in 1927.

After spending another year at Harvard studying the poetry of Edwin Arlington Robinson under the direction of Professor John Livingston Lowes, Beebe returned to journalism as a contributor to the literary section of the *Boston Evening Transcript*. In 1929 he moved to New York and joined the staff of the *Herald Tribune*. Over the next four years he covered fires and garden club events, often in top hat and tails; wrote and edited features; and reviewed minor plays and films. The *Herald Tribune* syndicate gave Beebe his own column on the lifestyles of New York's depression-era elite in 1933. "So This Is New York" debuted in the *Philadelphia Inquirer* and became a popular feature in a number of other papers outside New York. A year later the column was installed as a Saturday-morning staple of the *Herald Tribune* itself under the revised title "This New York." At its peak, "This New York" had 2 million readers nationally.

Beebe's own fondness for dove-gray top hats, mink-lined overcoats, gold-headed canes, beluga caviar, Bollinger champagne, Corona cigars, and Rolls Royce automobiles made him the ideal chronicler of café society, which he defined as "an unorganized but generally recognized group of persons who participate in the social life of New York available to those possessed of a certain degree of affluence and manners." For ten years he made the rounds of the posh restaurants and nightclubs and attended exclusive cocktail parties, gourmet dinners, and theater first nights to report on the food, the wine, and celebrity doings in prose as ornate as his appearance. In Beebe's column, spring receptions were "vernal levees" and fancy names became "euphonious cognomens." He noted that actress Ona Munson's drawing room was "quite littered with pianos," that actress and playwright Cornelia Otis Skinner's "pet fido" was a "dog of something less than certain antecedents," and that the opening of a certain New Jersey resort was replete with "popping corks, bedizened flunkies, clamoring celebrities and the blinding noiselessness of photographers' flashes."

The flamboyant Beebe himself became a popular subject for magazines and newspapers. His friend Wolcott Gibbs wrote a flattering two-part profile ("The Diamond Gardenia") in the *New Yorker* in 1937 and other journalists had a field day with Beebe's colorful manner and style, playfully dubbing him the "orchidaceous oracle of Cafe Society" and the "purple Pepys of El Morocco." Beebe's detractors were led by rival columnist Walter Winchell, who called Beebe "Luscious Lucius." According to Brendan Gill, Winchell once ridiculed "This New York" for its numerous references to photographer Jerome Zerbe, with whom Beebe was having a homosexual affair, by writing that the column should be retitled "Jerome Never Looked Lovelier." Another critic, Kyle Crichton, labeled Beebe a "kind of sandwich man for the upper classes" for his celebration of excess. In a similar vein, columnist Dorothy Kilgallen opined that he belonged in a "platinum champagne bucket."

After "This New York" was discontinued in 1944, Beebe continued to write for the editorial and drama pages of the *Herald Tribune* for six years, wrote the "Along the Boulevards" column for *Gourmet Magazine* from 1945 to 1951 (he picked it up again from 1962 to 1966), and contributed articles to the *American Mercury*, *Collier's*, and other national publications. He also authored a number of books during his newspaper days, beginning with *Boston and the Boston Legend* (1935), an affectionate and irreverent social portrait of his hometown, which he described at one point as the scene of "some of the most gorgeous rioting, hardest drinking, most learned cursing and spectacular highbinding finance on record." A passionate railroad enthusiast who despised the airplane ("the Wright Brothers' folly"), Beebe wrote the text for and contributed photographs to a series of picture books on trains and their history, including *High Iron: A Book of Trains* (1938); *Highliners: A Railroad Album* (1940); and *Trains in Transition* (1941). He was a consultant for the motion picture *Union Pacific* (1939). In 1945 he formed a close association with Charles M. Clegg, Jr., a like-minded photojournalist, and the two collaborated on popular histories of trains and another of Beebe's fascinations, the American West, over the next twenty-one years. Among their works were *Highball: A Railroad Pageant* (1945); *Mixed Train Daily: A Book of Short Line Railroads* (1947); *U.S. West: The Saga of Wells Fargo* (1949); *Virginia and Truckee: A Story of Virginia City and the Comstock Times* (1949); *Legends of the Comstock Lode* (1950); *Hear the Train Blow: A Pictorial Epic of America* (1952); and *The American West: The Pictorial Epic of a Continent* (1955).

After Beebe left the *Herald Tribune* in 1950, he and Clegg moved west, where people were few and it was, Beebe later wrote, "still possible to drive all day and not encounter a Communist, a Congressman, or any important functionary of the federal government." They settled in Virginia City, Nevada, a virtual ghost town on the site of the long-depleted Comstock Lode, taking up residence in the gaudy Victorian home of nineteenth-century opera and theatrical impresario John Piper. Two years later they reactivated the *Territorial Enterprise*, a weekly newspaper that had been the first to run the byline of Mark Twain in the early 1860s and had been defunct since 1926. Under Beebe and Clegg the frontier paper used 1860-style type and possessed a freewheeling style. When a lady reformer caused a barroom brawl, the *Enterprise* headline screamed, "Bar a Shambles as Virtue Runs Amuck." The *Enterprise*'s editorial page, overseen by Beebe, "derided all manifestations of progress and modernity and espoused the cause of 'benevolent backward-

ness.'" When the local government threatened a legal bordello because it was operating fifty yards from a school, the *Enterprise* thundered, "Don't move the girls, move the school." Beebe's most celebrated verbal fusillade came when the Curtiss-Wright Corporation, an aviation technology giant, purchased 100 square miles of desert land near Virginia City in 1957. He attacked Curtiss-Wright's management as a "predatory posse of business-suited opportunists" seeking "a remote geographic locale in which to mount some arcane and presumably offensive Fourth of July experiments in noise and combustion." He did not relent until company managers agreed to help the city gain access to a water supply that had frozen solid during the winter.

In five years the *Territorial Enterprise* had the largest paid circulation of any weekly west of the Mississippi; counted Irving Berlin, J. Edgar Hoover, and Spencer Tracy among its subscribers; and revived Virginia City as a tourist mecca. Dressed in his low-crowned, broad-brimmed black hat; string tie; ruffled shirt; black clawhammer coat; frontier pants; and boots, Beebe himself became one of the main attractions. He even served a term on the Nevada State Board of Economic Development and was a member of the state centennial commission.

In the late 1950s Beebe and Clegg commuted between Nevada and California in a private railroad car (they owned two) replete with a marble fireplace and Venetian decor. They sold the *Territorial Enterprise* in 1960 and relocated to Hillsborough, California, a suburb of San Francisco. Beebe lived in his usual splendor and produced new books on trains, the West, and the American rich and famous and wrote pieces for *American Heritage*, *Esquire*, *Holiday*, *Playboy*, and *Town & Country*. In addition, he wrote a weekly column for the *San Francisco Chronicle*. Called "This Wild West," the column continued the witty war on American modernity begun in the *Territorial Enterprise* and contrasted sharply with the liberal views of the *Chronicle*'s editors. While other columnists derided the 1964 presidential candidacy of Senator Barry Goldwater of Arizona as one that would return America to its distant past, Beebe applauded the prospect. He longed for a time without such "disasters" as "woman's suffrage, the universal motorcar, credit cards, international airports, repudiation of the national currency, tranquilizers, freedom riders, digit-dialing, and the one-ounce martini." He died in Hillsborough.

With his exhibitionism and unabashed snobbery, Beebe was a splendid anachronism. He viewed himself as something of a Renaissance man ("not a Michelangelo but perhaps a poor man's Cellini or a road company Cosmo [sic] d'Medici") and wanted his obituaries to conclude "Everything he did was made to measure. He never got an idea off the rack."

• A good collection of Beebe's writings is *The Lucius Beebe Reader*, ed. Charles Clegg and Duncan Emrich (1966), with a useful introduction by Clegg and a biographical sketch by

Emrich. Selections from his *San Francisco Chronicle* columns were published as *The Provocative Pen of Lucius Beebe, Esq.* (1966), with an introduction by Gordon Pates. The subject supplies a short summary of his life until 1952 in the *Harvard Class of 1927 25th Anniversary Report*. His assessment of that life appears in Herb Caen's column in the *San Francisco Chronicle*, 13 Feb. 1966. Beebe's "This New York" columns can be found in the Saturday *New York Herald Tribune*, 1934–1944. Among his many books not mentioned in the text are *Aspects of the Poetry of Edwin Arlington Robinson* (1928); *Snoot if You Must* (1943); *Mansions on the Rails: The Folklore of the Private Railway Car* (1959); *The Trains We Rode*, with Clegg (2 vols., 1964–1965); and *The Big Spenders* (1966). Articles on Beebe include Wolcott Gibbs, "The Diamond Gardenia—I," *New Yorker*, 20 Nov. 1937, pp. 24–29, "The Diamond Gardenia—II," *New Yorker*, 27 Nov. 1937, pp. 25–29, and "One with Nineveh," *New Yorker*, 24 Mar. 1956, pp. 28–32; John Richmond, "Orchidaceous Lucius Beebe," *American Mercury*, Nov. 1940, pp. 309–17; and Richard Merkin, "Luscious Lucius," *GQ*, Sept. 1989, pp. 195, 202, 206. On his stewardship of the *Territorial Enterprise* and the battle with Curtiss-Wright, see "Epicure Editor Brings Missile Maker to Bay," *Business Week*, 12 Oct. 1957, pp. 192–202. See also Richard Kluger, *The Paper: The Life and Death of the "New York Herald Tribune"* (1986), and Brendan Gill, *Here at the "New Yorker"* (1975) and *A New York Life: Of Friends and Others* (1990). Beebe himself wrote the obituary that appears in the *Herald Tribune*, 5 Feb. 1966. Other important obituaries are in the *Boston Globe*, the *New York Times*, and the *San Francisco Chronicle* for the same date.

RICHARD H. GENTILE

BEEBE, William (29 July 1877–4 June 1962), naturalist, oceanographer, and zoological society executive, was born Charles William Beebe in Brooklyn, New York, the son of Charles Beebe, the owner of a paper company, and Henrietta Marie Younglove. In the late 1880s the family moved to the first of a succession of addresses in East Orange, New Jersey. Beebe, an active boy, early developed an interest in natural history, fostered in part by family travels to New England and eastern Canada. He learned to identify many kinds of wildlife, particularly birds. Young Charles (he dropped his first name in high school and was known ever after as William) entered East Orange High School in 1891 and spent five years there, taking, in addition to the regular course, six additional semester-long classes in the sciences. Once Beebe had determined on a career in natural history, his mother, a woman very ambitious for her son, made a point of seeing to it that he met most of the major natural scientists in New York City. Beebe attended Columbia University for several years (1896–1899), completing a series of courses in biology, zoology, and related subjects, but he did not receive a degree. Beebe later received two honorary doctorates of science, one from Tufts College, the other from Colgate University, both in 1928.

One of Beebe's mentors at Columbia, the paleontologist Henry Fairfield Osborn, first president of the New York Zoological Society, was instrumental in helping Beebe secure his first post, that of assistant curator of birds at the society's newly opened Zoological Park, in the fall of 1899. Beebe, who was elevated to curator in 1902, had little formal preparation in ornithology but had done a fair amount of dedicated fieldwork. The profession of aviculture was in its infancy when Beebe began making plans for housing the larger birds at the Bronx Zoo. He was criticized for the size and design of the building when it opened in 1906, but with the aid of Samuel Stacey, an experienced English zookeeper, Beebe's project achieved great success.

Beebe also took steps to establish himself as a credible working scientist, and his keenness for fieldwork became evident early in his career. His first book was *Two Bird Lovers in Mexico* (1905); this included a final chapter written by his first wife, Mary Blair Rice, whom he had married in 1902. The couple also collaborated on *Our Search for a Wilderness* (1910), an account of several trips taken to parts of Venezuela and Guyana during the years 1908–1910. Beebe and his wife, who were childless, were divorced in 1913. *The Bird, Its Form and Function* (1906), Beebe's initial technical work, was very clearly a first effort, tentative in tone. *The Log of the Sun* (1906), a compilation of pieces previously published elsewhere, was the first in a series of popular books that Beebe would turn out in the course of the next half-century.

Beebe soon began a second career of sustained field research. Visits were made to Trinidad and Venezuela (1908) and to British Guiana (1909). Later in 1909 Beebe undertook a study of world pheasant populations underwritten by Colonel Anthony R. Kuser, a trustee of the society. Beebe and his first wife made another strenuous trip to North Africa and various parts of Asia for seventeen months in 1909–1911, visiting seventeen nations; this was followed by three years of additional museum research. *A Monograph of the Pheasants*, the publication of which was delayed until after World War I, appeared in four volumes between 1918 and 1922. *Pheasants: Their Lives and Homes*, a two-volume popular version lacking only the technical descriptions, appeared in 1926. Frank M. Chapman, a leading contemporary ornithologist, described the original work as "perhaps the greatest ornithological monograph of the present century." Beebe's taxonomic arrangement of the pheasants, however, soon underwent extensive revision at the hands of other ornithologists.

Beebe returned to South America in 1915, visiting Para in Brazil and, in 1916, establishing the Society's first field station at Kalacoon and later Kartabo, British Guiana. *Tropical Wildlife in British Guiana* (1917), written with G. I. Hartley and P. G. Howes, received favorable reviews from the scientific community. Only one of several projected volumes were published. Beebe's contributions to the volume had mainly to do with birds, especially the hoatzin. This proved to be Beebe's last book dealing with birds. Because the focus of his professional interests had changed, Beebe was made director of tropical research for the Zoological Society and honorary curator of birds at the Bronx Zoo in 1916, posts he held until his retirement in 1952.

During parts of 1917 and 1918 Beebe was in France flying for the French Aviation Service. He then returned to South America and spend much of the next ten years in British Guiana, although there were interruptions for the completion of the pheasant project and trips to the Galapagos in 1923 and to both the Galapagos and Sargasso Sea in 1925. Beebe gave some attention to the fish and coral reefs in the waters around Haiti in 1927. Most of these expeditions were underwritten by wealthy trustees of the Zoological Society and their friends. In 1927 Beebe married Elswyth Ricker Thane, an Iowa-born writer. The couple had no children.

The well-publicized helmet diving done by Beebe to study fish and other marine species commenced in the Galapagos in 1925, but sustained work in the waters off Bermuda and nearby islands was not begun until 1928. A spherical diving device known as the bathysphere, financed and developed by Otis Barton, was used to make some thirty descents, the deepest being one of 3,028 feet off Nonsuch Island in 1934. This record was not exceeded for fifteen years. Beebe also rediscovered the cahow, a Bermudan bird long thought to be extinct, in 1935. Later Beebe undertook more oceanographic work off the coast of Baja California in 1936 and the Pacific coast of Central America in 1937 and 1938. A final trip to Asia took place in 1955, so that Beebe could check on the status of birds he had studied there more than forty years before.

Unable to continue his oceanographic work in Bermuda waters because of the onset of World War II, Beebe resumed his jungle research for the Department of Tropical Research in the region around Caripito, Venezuela, in 1942. Much of the work of classifying collected specimens was done at the Bronx Zoo over the next several years, but in 1945 another jungle forest research station was established at Rancho Grande, Venezuela. Beebe built one more tropical station at Simla, in the Arima Valley of Trinidad, in 1950. He remained there as director for much of the time until his retirement in 1952, and then he continued on as director emeritus until his death. He purchased the property soon after his arrival there and later presented it to the society. A final trip to Asia was made in 1955 so that Beebe could check the status of birds he had first observed there more than forty years previously.

Beebe was a prolific author and notable nature essayist who published some 800 scientific and popular articles in periodicals such as the *Atlantic Monthly* and *National Geographic Magazine*, together with nearly two dozen books. His popular titles were highly readable and sold well, even though there was an element of fiction in some of the nonscientific material they contained.

Beebe's work and his many publications unquestionably exemplified the work of the Zoological Society for many Americans, particularly young people, from the 1920s to the early 1940s. The scientific community, on the other hand, was reluctant to recognize his scientific accomplishments, owing in part to his lack of formal credentials and his success as a popular writer of natural history. Beebe received many honors, including the Daniel Giraud Elliott Gold Medal from the National Academy of Sciences, together with gold medals from the Societe d'Acclimation of France and the New York Zoological Society. He died and was buried in Trinidad.

• The Alphens Hyatt Correspondence, Princeton University, includes some unpublished letters. Beebe's other books include *Jungle Peace* (1918); *Edge of the Jungle* (1921); *Galapagos: World's End* (1924); *Jungle Days* (1925); *The Arcturus Adventure* (1926); *Pheasant Jungles* (1927); *Beneath Tropic Seas* (1928); *Nonsuch: Land of Water* (1932); *Field Book of the Shore Fishes of Bermuda* (1933), written with John Tee-Van; *Half Mile Down* (1934); *Zaca Venture* (1938); *Book of Bays* (1942); *High Jungle* (1949); and *Unseen Life of New York as a Naturalist Sees It* (1953). There were also several volumes of previously published pieces by Beebe, including *Exploring with Beebe* (1932) and *Adventuring with Beebe* (1955). He also edited *The Book of Naturalists* (1944). A full-length biography is Robert H. Welker, *Natural Man: The Life of William Beebe* (1975). See also Tim H. Berra, *William Beebe: An Annotated Bibliography* (1977); William Bridges, *Gathering Animals: An Unconventional History of the New York Zoological Society* (1974); and Donald Goddard, ed., *Saving Wildlife: A Century of Conservation* (1995). An obituary was published in the *New York Times*, 6 June 1962, as was a memorial by Lee S. Crandall in the *Auk*, Jan. 1964.

KEIR B. STERLING

BEECHER, Catharine Esther (6 Sept. 1800–12 May 1878), educator and social reformer, was born in East Hampton, New York, the oldest child of Lyman Beecher, the most prominent Evangelical clergyman of the 1820s, and Roxana Foote. At the age of ten Catharine Beecher moved with her family from the isolated and rural tip of Long Island to class-conscious Litchfield, Connecticut. There she acquired the normal accomplishments of her well-born status. When her mother died of consumption in 1816, Catharine assumed responsibility for her younger siblings, including Harriet and Henry. Later in life her close relationship with these famous siblings helped fuel her resistence to accepted conventions. Her father's remarriage to a woman for whom she had little affection deepened her spirit of independence. In the pivotal event of her young adulthood she resisted her father's pressure to experience religious conversion. Expected to undergo conversion as a part of their transition to adulthood, young women like Catharine confronted a process that required them to reject their worldly experience and place their trust in God. This Catharine could not do; she valued her experience too much. This self-assertion, combined with the independence thrust upon her when her fiancé, a young professor at Yale, perished in a sea wreck, led her to seek a career as a teacher.

Beecher's career as an educator and as a publicist for new attitudes toward women flourished in the dynamic cultural environment of pre–Civil War America. In 1823 she founded one of the new nation's most rigorous academies for higher education for women, the Hartford Female Seminary, and hitched her own star to the rising status of women as educators. In a pamphlet she urged parents to shun ornamental education for their daughters, which taught them to paint, embroider, or play the piano, and instead aim for the cultivation of lasting mental qualities, such as rationality and persistence. In 1832 she followed her father and siblings to Cincinnati, where, like them, she championed the dominance of New England evangelicism in the multicultural environment of the American West. In Ohio and other midwestern territories, New Englanders struggled with migrants from other regions for cultural supremacy. Partly to advance New England values as well as to forward her views about women, Beecher founded a school for young women. By hiring others—including her sister Harriet—to teach in her newly founded Western Female Institute, Catharine freed herself to write a series of popular books that established her reputation for astute social commentary on the place of women in American society.

Although she did not use the term, Beecher's writings advocated "domestic feminism"—that is, expanded power for women within domestic life and ancillary power in the wider society. Her views of domestic life were informed by Harriet's struggle to maintain a respectable household on the inadequate pay of her clergyman husband and, after the birth of five children in the early years of her marriage, to increase intervals between pregnancies. When, after an interval of more than five years, Harriet wrote *Uncle Tom's Cabin*, Catharine moved in with her sister and helped keep up the Stowe household.

Catharine Beecher was best known for her *Treatise on Domestic Economy*, first published in 1841 and reprinted annually through 1856. She coauthored a greatly expanded version with Harriet Beecher Stowe, *The American Woman's Home; or, Principles of Domestic Science*, which was widely reprinted between 1869 and 1873. Beecher's advice to women reflected the contemporary economic changes that were relocating male labor and much of what had formerly been household production outside the household. She advised married women to exercise greater control over domestic life, including family finances, and to value their work as an honorable calling with great significance for the future of American democracy. "The success of democratic institutions, as is conceded by all, depends upon the intellectual and moral character of the mass of the people," she wrote in *A Treatise on Domestic Economy*. "If they are intelligent and virtuous democracy is a blessing; but if they are ignorant and wicked, it is only a curse. . . . It is equally conceded, that the formation of the moral and intellectual character of the young is committed mainly to the female hand" (rev. ed. [1842], pp. 36–37). In other domestic writings, especially *Letters to Persons Who Are Engaged in Domestic Service* (1842), *The Evils Suffered by American Women and American Children* (1846), *The True Remedy for the Wrongs of Woman* (1851), *Letters to the People on Health and Happiness* (1855), and *Physiology and Calisthenics for Schools and Families* (1856), Beecher reinforced her authority as a delineator of middle-class social mores and personal development.

Beecher's domestically based expansion of women's influence competed for the loyalties of American women with the natural-rights views forged in the antislavery movement. A debate between the two perspectives occurred when, in response to the public activity of antislavery women, especially Angelina Grimké's *Appeal to the Christian Women of the South* (1836), Beecher published *An Essay on Slavery and Abolitionism with Reference to the Duty of American Females* (1837). Later, her book *Woman's Profession as Mother and Educator with Views in Opposition to Woman Suffrage* (1872) insisted that "the evils it is hoped to cure by the ballot would continue" until women's domestic labor was granted the respect accorded to male labor outside the home. Beecher's stance was not really shaped by her opposition to woman suffrage—a cause that she never felt passionately about one way or another. Instead, she was motivated primarily by the new platform that suffrage provided for her ideas about the social importance of women's domestic work and their labor as teachers.

Catharine Beecher's writings gained a wide public readership in the decades before the Civil War because they so cogently expressed new views about the expanded power of women in family life. Those views supplanted eighteenth-century notions and became the basis for modern assumptions about the place of women in American society. Beecher promoted women's domestic power by linking it with new forms of power in the public domain. Beecher's writings also gave her a modest income between 1840 and 1860, but more important to her (if less lucrative) were her efforts to feminize the teaching profession and to justify women's greater access to higher education through their "calling" as teachers. Women needed to gain access to higher education so they could bring to the nation the same benefits as teachers that they brought to family life as mothers. This theme, which also justified her own public activities, first appeared in her 1829 pamphlet *Suggestions Respecting Improvements in Education* and was subsequently orchestrated in such works as *An Essay on the Education of Female Teachers* (1835) and *The Duty of American Women to Their Country* (1845). The success of the National Board of Popular Education, which she founded in the late 1840s to place eastern women teachers in western communities, showed that her ideas were sustained by two of the most fundamental processes of change under way in nineteenth-century America—geographical expansion and the empowerment of women as the chief agents of children's socialization. Patriarchy, defined as the rule of the father, was still alive and well in the courts and other arenas of public life, but the basic shift from male to female rule in family matters was, thanks in part to Catharine Beecher's influence, well launched by 1850.

To a considerable degree, Beecher's authority on matters pertaining to education and to family life derived from her facility as an interpreter of American religious life. In an age dominated by grassroots religious fervor, she deftly channeled spiritual anxieties into commonsense moralism. Her *Elements of Mental and Moral Philosophy, Founded upon Experience, Reason and the Bible* (1831) was the first in a series of her writings that turned away from doctrinal controversies and stressed a moral system based on self-sacrifice. A code of self-sacrifice fit well with the new industrial work ethic and at the same time carried some traditional moral values forward. Seeking to replace her father's theology with "sure and universal principles that will evolve a harmonious system in which we shall all agree," she identified "self-conquest" and service to others as the highest good. Through service to others—especially as "infallible teachers of what is right and true"—women occupied the center of her moral universe. Theories of morality and religion, she thought, "are especially to be examined and decided on by woman, as the heaven-appointed educator of infancy and childhood."

Her other religious writings included *The Moral Instructor for Schools and Families* (1838), *An Address to the Protestant Clergy of the United States* (1846), *Common Sense Applied to Religion, or the Bible and the People* (1857), *An Appeal to the People on Behalf of Their Rights as Authorized Interpreters of the Bible* (1860), and *The Religious Training of Children in the School, the Family, and the Church* (1864). Her last publication, *Educational Reminiscences and Suggestions* (1874), reiterated the merger of sacred and secular themes that sustained her long career. Although Beecher's writings and her life work might appear to late twentieth-century readers to uphold the status quo, in her own time they remained controversial, since in advocating women's moral authority, she also explicitly challenged the moral authority of ministers and implicitly questioned male authority in family life.

Catharine Beecher never succeeded in her goal of establishing a home of her own. Having alienated her father's third wife, whom he married soon after the death of his second wife in 1836, she was not welcome in their home. Like other unmarried women, she resided with those of her siblings who could accommodate her, spending a few months with each until her welcome wore thin. She frequently devised projects that required her to travel, and on those occasions she lived with her supporters. In Milwaukee during the 1850s, she founded the Milwaukee Female Seminary, partly with the intention of building a retirement home there. Although she offered to contribute $3,000 toward the construction of a home for herself that could also serve as a domestic science building, the institution's trustees refused to cooperate with her proposal. A design in *The American Woman's Home* showed how "a small church, a school-house, and a comfortable family dwelling may all be united in one building, and for a very moderate sum," but the plan remained unexecuted. Beecher became adept at inviting herself into the homes of prosperous community leaders wherever she traveled. Increasingly in the 1860s she resided with Harriet at Hartford. During the year prior to her death she lived with the family of her half brother, Thomas, in Elmira, New York.

• The Beecher Family Papers at Sterling Library, Yale University, is the richest collection of Catharine Beecher's family correspondence. Her correspondence and papers can also be found at the Stowe-Day Foundation, Hartford, Conn.; the Beecher-Stowe Collection at the Schlesinger Library, Radcliffe College; the Beinecke Library, Yale University; the Cincinnati Historical Society; the Connecticut Historical Society; and the Williston Library, Mount Holyoke College. For writings about Beecher, see Kathryn Kish Sklar, *Catharine Beecher: A Study in American Domesticity* (1973); Sklar, "Catharine Beecher's *Treatise on Domestic Economy*: A Document in Domestic Feminism," in *Portraits of a Nineteenth Century Family*, ed. Earl A. French and Diana Royce (1976); Jeanne Boydston et al., eds., *The Limits of Sisterhood: The Beecher Sisters on Women's Rights and Woman's Sphere* (1988); and Mae Harveson, *Catharine Esther Beecher, Pioneer Educator* (1932). See also Marie Caskey, *Chariot of Fire: Religion and the Beecher Family* (1978); *The Autobiography of Lyman Beecher*, ed. Barbara M. Cross (1961); Lyman Beecher Stowe, *Saints, Sinners, and Beechers* (1934); Sklar, "Victorian Women and Domestic Life: Mary Todd Lincoln, Elizabeth Cady Stanton, and Harriet Beecher Stowe," in *Women and Power in American History*, vol. 1, ed. Sklar and Thomas Dublin (1991); Joan D. Hedrick, *Harriet Beecher Stowe: A Life* (1994); Gerda Lerner, *The Grimke Sisters from South Carolina* (1967); and Boydston, *Home and Work: Housework, Wages, and the Ideology of Labor in the Early Republic* (1990).

KATHRYN KISH SKLAR

BEECHER, Edward (27 Aug. 1803–28 July 1895), clergyman and educator, was born in East Hampton, New York, the son of Lyman Beecher, a prominent Congregational minister, and Roxana Foote. Although always in the shadow of his more famous father and siblings, Beecher was a leader of the New School wing of the evangelical establishment, promoting a relatively conservative political and social agenda throughout the antebellum period. Beecher grew up in the Federalist stronghold of Litchfield, Connecticut, and graduated valedictorian of his Yale College class in 1822. He then became headmaster of the Hartford Grammar School and studied briefly at Andover before returning to Yale as a tutor in 1825. A year later, at his father's urging, Beecher declined the offer of an academic position at Dartmouth College in favor of a pastorate at the prestigious Park Street Congregational Church in Boston. Four years later, Beecher's pastorate fell victim to divisions within his congregation, overwork, and intimations of his psychological instability.

Beecher was delivered from his Park Street difficulties by an invitation to become the president of Illinois College in Jacksonville, Illinois, a school founded in 1829 by a group of former divinity students known as the Yale Band. In 1830 Beecher joined the westward movement of evangelical Congregationalists committed to seizing the cultural initiative in the Mississippi Valley. The Illinois years were active ones for Beecher, taken up with teaching, fund-raising, civic activities, and ecclesiastical politics. Beecher was active in the ecclesiastical wars that pitted Old School Presbyterians against New School Congregationalists in a West nominally ruled by the Presbyterian Plan of Union of 1801. It was a battle between the hierarchical polity and creedalism of the former and the independent associations and experientialism of the latter under what was to have been a cooperative arrangement for missionary activity in the old Northwest. Beecher's involvement with the conservative wing of the antislavery cause further complicated his position, particularly after he supported abolitionist editor Elijah Lovejoy who was killed by a mob at Alton, Illinois, in 1837. Lovejoy's death occasioned what is now Beecher's best-known work, *Narrative of Riots at Alton* (1838), although at the time other accounts of the violence eclipsed the tract.

Resistance to Beecher's antislavery views exacerbated the difficulties faced by Illinois College in the wake of the panic of 1837. In 1840, as a result of the college's worsening financial position, Beecher went on a major fundraising tour of the East that, in retrospect, ushered in a transitional period in his life. Also in 1840, Beecher published in the *Biblical Repository* the first in a series of articles growing out of concerns about baptism, which he experienced prior to ordination. These articles eventuated in *Baptism, with Reference to Its Import and Modes* (1849), a historical and philological book taking the irenic position that both affusion and immersion represented apostolic baptismal practice. In 1843 Beecher helped found the Society for the Promotion of Theological and Collegiate Education at the West as a consolidated eastern fundraising vehicle for western educational institutions.

Recognizing that the center of his activities had shifted to the East, in 1844 Beecher severed his formal ties with Illinois College and accepted a call to Boston's Salem Street Church, where he embarked on an even more active career as a writer and polemicist. In 1845 he published "Dr. Beecher on Organic Sin," a series of twelve essays in the *Boston Recorder* that stressed the institutional nature of slavery and rejected radical abolitionist measures. Then, in 1849, he became editor of the *Congregationalist*, a paper that advocated Congregational and Calvinist unity and nonextension of slavery into the territories. In 1853, however, Beecher published the results of theological speculation that had privately preoccupied him since his early twenties, resurrecting the fourth-century Origenist heresy of the preexistence of souls as a solution to the problem of evil. Although reaction to *The Conflict of Ages* was muted—not to say bewildered—Beecher's career came under a cloud. Beecher threw himself into opposition to the Kansas-Nebraska Act, and his influence helped prompt his sister, Harriet Beecher Stowe, to write *Uncle Tom's Cabin*. Two years later, in 1855, at the height of the Know-Nothing party's influence, Beecher published a lengthy and virulent anti-Catholic diatribe, *The Papal Conspiracy Unveiled*, apparently aimed at earning reinstatement in the ranks of the orthodox.

Shortly afterward, in 1855, Beecher returned to the West to become pastor of the Congregational church in Galesburg, Illinois, and to lecture on church institutions at Chicago Theological Seminary. In 1860 he published *The Concord of Ages*, which failed to gain a

rehearing for his views on the preexistence of souls. In 1871, after facing down a minor show of disunity in his Galesburg congregation, Beecher returned East once again. He settled in Brooklyn, where his brother, Henry Ward Beecher, was at the zenith of his career as pastor of the Plymouth Church. Edward performed editorial tasks for Henry's paper, *The Christian Union*, and remained active in ecclesiastical affairs. Edward successfully represented his brother in the 1874 and 1876 church councils that investigated Henry's alleged misconduct with Elizabeth Tilton, and in 1878 he published his last major work, *History of Opinions on the Scriptural Doctrine of Retribution*.

Beecher remained physically and mentally active into old age; in 1885, at the age of eighty-two, he began to supply the pulpit of the Parkville Congregational Church near Brooklyn. This association lasted until 1889, when he lost a leg in a railroad accident on the way to church and became unable to make the trip. Slipping into senility, Beecher spent his last days in Brooklyn, where he probably died, although the sources are not explicit on this point. He was survived by his wife, Isabella P. Jones whom he had married in 1929, and two of their eleven children.

• The most important collections of Beecher's letters and other papers are in the Beecher-Stowe Collection of the Schlesinger Library of Radcliffe College; the Joseph K. Hooker, Katherine Stowe Day, and White Collections in the Stowe Day Library, Hartford, Conn.; the Beecher Family Collection in the Williston Library of Mount Holyoke College, Holyoke, Massachusetts; and the Beecher Family, Kingsley Family, and Yale Miscellaneous Manuscript Collections in the Yale University Archives. Charles Beecher's manuscript "Life of Edward Beecher," which contains extensive excerpts from Edward Beecher's diary, is in the Illinois State Historical Library, Springfield, Ill. A complete list of Edward Beecher's published works, running to six close-set pages, is available in the bibliographic essay in Robert Merideth, *The Politics of the Universe: Edward Beecher, Abolition, and Orthodoxy* (1968). Additional biographical material is available in Lyman Beecher, *Autobiography of Lyman Beecher*, ed. Barbara M. Cross (1961), a collection of family documents by the Beecher children; and in the excellent short biographical sketch in Marie Caskey Morgan, *Chariot of Fire: Religion and the Beecher Family* (1978). See also Marc M. Arkin, "Edward Beecher: The Development of an Ecclesiastical Career: 1803–1844" (Ph.D. diss., Yale Univ., 1983).

MARC M. ARKIN

BEECHER, Henry Knowles (4 Feb. 1904–25 July 1976), medical researcher, was born Henry Knowles Unangst in Wichita, Kansas, the son of Henry Unangst, a night watchman and carpenter, and Mary Julia Kerley. Young Henry grew up in modest circumstances in Wichita and nearby Peck, Kansas, in a family that did not place much emphasis on intellectual attainment. He worked odd jobs to pay his way at the University of Kansas, receiving an A.B. in 1926 and an A.M. in 1927 from that institution. In 1928 Henry left Kansas to enter Harvard Medical School. But, before leaving, he changed his surname to Beecher—an identifier that would be more widely recognized and admired in Boston than Unangst. He was, in fact, related to the famous abolitionist Beecher clan through his maternal grandmother, Maria Kerley, whose maiden name was Beecher.

Four years after entering Harvard Medical School, Beecher graduated cum laude with the class of 1932. After graduating Beecher accepted a prestigious two-year internship on the surgical staff at Massachusetts General Hospital (MGH). In 1935 he spent a year in Copenhagen, Denmark, studying in the laboratory of the Nobel Prize–winning physiologist August Krogh, with funding from Harvard as a Moseley Traveling Fellow. In the spring of 1936, shortly after his return from Denmark, Beecher was presented with an opportunity to serve jointly as an instructor in anesthesia at Harvard Medical School and as anesthetist in chief at MGH. The ambitious 32-year-old initially hesitated at the offer because anesthesia was not, at that time, a highly regarded medical specialty. However, Beecher did not deliberate for long; instead, he accepted the offer and committed himself to improving the standing of his newly chosen area of specialization. Beecher's commitment brought quick results. In less than a year, he had established the world's first facility devoted solely to the scientific study of problems in anesthesiology: the Anesthesiology Laboratory of the Harvard Medical School at the Massachusetts General Hospital. Beecher soon published *The Physiology of Anesthesia* (1938), which quickly became a standard text in the field and remained so for decades, through several subsequent editions. After five busy and successful years, Beecher was rewarded in February 1941 by being named the Henry Isaiah Dorr Professor of Research in Anesthesia at Harvard University—the first ever endowed chair in anesthesiology.

Beecher held this prestigious position for the next thirty years, but only months after winning his professorship the United States entered World War II. During the war Beecher took a leave of absence from Harvard and joined the army as a major in the medical corps. He served the army surgeon general as a consultant on anesthesia and resuscitation, making significant contributions to the improved handling of battlefield injuries. Beecher carried out much of his wartime research under heavy combat conditions in North Africa and Italy, including several weeks on the bloody Anzio beachhead during early 1944. Among other medical insights, Beecher discovered that morphine poisoning often occurred when repeated injections of the painkiller were given to an injured person who was chilled or in shock. He also observed that soldiers who were pumped with adrenaline and then hurt in the emergency of battle (or those who might welcome a nonfatal injury as a life-saving ticket out of combat) often did not experience pain in the same way as injured civilians. Thus, he recommended against routine battlefield administration of potentially harmful painkillers, such as morphine. For his important—and genuinely heroic—research on safer military uses of morphine Beecher was awarded the Legion of Merit.

At the conclusion of the war, he retired from the army as a lieutenant colonel.

Beecher returned to Boston, where he continued to build the anesthesiology program at Harvard and to shape MGH into a major locus for research and teaching. In the course of his career, he trained more than 300 anesthesiologists—more than fifty of these students went on to become professors of anesthesia around the world and twenty-nine others pursued academic careers in other fields. The years immediately following the war also marked a period of great personal research activity for Beecher. His clinical investigations on topics such as respiratory acidosis among surgical patients and various metabolic responses to the experience of anesthesia made many important contributions to the field of anesthesiology. But Beecher's research during this period also had broad implications for medical science. He developed a number of techniques for the quantitative measurement of subjective responses experienced by patients and experimental subjects—such as pain, thirst, nausea, and even mood—that were widely employed by other researchers. Beecher was also a pioneer in recognizing the reality and inescapability of the placebo effect in medical practice, and he was among the most influential early advocates of the need for double-blind controlled studies to account for this phenomenon in clinical research.

Toward the end of the 1950s Beecher became increasingly concerned with the ethical aspects of human experimentation, and it is in this area that he probably achieved his most lasting fame. The motivation behind this shift in focus is not entirely clear, but a number of factors might have played a role. Historian David J. Rothman has suggested that Beecher's interest in ethics stemmed from a long-standing tendency among anesthesiologists to critique the work of surgeons. "Anesthesiologists," Rothman wrote, "have a reputation for being the fifth column within medicine. Beecher belonged to the specialty that daily watches colleagues perform in the operating room and then discusses their relative strengths and weaknesses" (pp. 70–71). Rothman has also emphasized Beecher's commitment to high-quality research and his concomitant fear that unethical and dangerous research would bring discredit to the enterprise of medical science. Beecher's son, Jonathan F. Beecher, has pointed to his father's deep Christian faith (Beecher read a chapter of the Bible every day) to suggest a partial explanation for Beecher's excursion into the ethics of human experimentation. It also seems possible that Beecher harbored some guilt over experiments that had taken place under his supervision. In 1965 he made the following acknowledgment in a speech that called into question the behavior of his peers who conducted experiments with human subjects: "Lest I seem to stand aside from these matters I am obliged to say that in years gone by work in my laboratory could have been criticized" ("Ethics and the Explosion of Human Experimentation," paper delivered 22 Mar. 1965, Brook

Lodge [Mich.] Conference, "Problems and Complexities of Clinical Research," Beecher papers).

Beecher made this speech before an audience of leading science writers in a move clearly calculated to create a stir. He succeeded. Several of the nation's most prominent newspapers soon carried stories written by reporters who had attended the meeting. For example, a *Boston Globe* journalist who had heard Beecher's speech published an article headlined "Are Humans Used as Guinea Pigs Not Told?" *Globe* editors placed the piece on the front page of their 24 March 1965 issue—alongside pieces covering the third day of Martin Luther King's march from Selma to Montgomery, Alabama, and the successful flight of Gemini 3. Beecher faced harsh and immediate criticism from some of his colleagues who believed both that he had violated professional etiquette by airing his concerns in public and that he had incorrectly characterized ethically dubious clinical research as common rather than exceptional. Beecher was not deterred; indeed, a year later he published an expanded version of his 1965 speech in the *New England Journal of Medicine*. The publication of this 1966 paper, "Ethics and Clinical Research," is now recognized as a seminal event in the history of research ethics. Four years later Beecher published *Research and the Individual*, a book that stands as his magnum opus on the ethics of human experimentation.

In the late 1960s Beecher also contributed constructively to another major area of discussion within the burgeoning field of bioethics: the question of how to define death. In 1968 Beecher chaired an ad hoc committee established at Harvard to consider the delicate matter of exactly when a person could be considered dead. The committee's arrival at a persistently flat electroencephalogram (EEG) as a reasonable, reliable, and objective determinant of death was widely adopted and received as especially important in the context of growing excitement (and anxiety) over organ transplantation.

In 1969, at the age of sixty-five, Beecher stepped down as the head of anesthesiology at MGH; a year later he retired from his endowed chair at Harvard. But this transition did not mark the end of his productivity as a scholar. Most notably, Beecher embarked on a major new project with his colleague Mark D. Altschule: to produce a book-length history of Harvard Medical School in recognition of the institution's 300th anniversary. He persisted in this effort despite a personal struggle with cancer and the 1973 death of his wife, Margaret Swain, whom he had married in 1935 and with whom he had three children. Beecher died at home in Boston. He was survived by a legacy of accomplishment in medical practice, medical teaching, medical research, medical ethics, and medical history.

• Beecher's personal papers are maintained in the manuscript collection of Harvard's Francis A. Countway Library of Medicine. The history of Harvard Medical School that Beecher cowrote with Mark D. Altschule, *Medicine at Harvard: The First Three Hundred Years* (1977), gives some attention to Beecher's own career. David J. Rothman devotes a chapter ("The Doctor as Whistle-blower") of his history of bioethics, *Strangers at the Bedside* (1991), to Beecher's work in medical ethics. The *Dictionary of American Medical Biography* (1984), contains a brief but informative entry on Beecher. Beecher's son, Jonathan F. Beecher of Santa Cruz, Calif., provided additional biographical information (including his father's name change) in a telephone interview, 11 Dec. 1996. Significant biographical notices published on the occasion of Beecher's death are in *New England Journal of Medicine* 295 (23 Sept. 1976): 730; *Anesthesiology* 45 (Oct. 1976): 377–78; and the *Boston Globe* and the *New York Times*, both 26 July 1976.

JON M. HARKNESS

BEECHER, Henry Ward (24 June 1813–8 Mar. 1887), preacher and reformer, was born in Litchfield, Connecticut, the son of Lyman Beecher, a leader of the Second Great Awakening, and Roxana Foote. Following in the footsteps of his father and his five brothers, Henry Ward displayed an early interest in religion. He graduated from Amherst College in 1834, studied at Lane Seminary in Cincinnati, Ohio, and was admitted to the ministry in 1837. That same year he married Eunice Bullard White and began work at the Second Presbyterian Church in Indianapolis, where he gained a reputation as a revivalist and published in 1844 his first book, *Seven Lectures to Young Men*, a melodramatic advice book that displayed his ability to create verbal pictures of great power and persuasiveness. Beecher's reputation as a preacher in Indianapolis brought him to the attention of a group of liberal Congregational businessmen in Brooklyn, New York, who invited him in 1847 to head the newly formed Plymouth Church.

A talented writer and speaker, Beecher soon developed a strong following and became a powerful force in the New York religious press. His weekly column in *The Independent*, a widely read Congregational newspaper, promoted his genial vision of a new, Romantic, Christianity; focused on God's love for humankind; and stressed to an urban audience the regenerative power of Nature. The articles were later republished in three volumes: *Star Papers; or, Experiences of Art and Nature* (1855), *Plain and Pleasant Talk about Fruits, Flowers and Farming* (1859; repr. 1874), and *Eyes and Ears* (1862). Within his church, Beecher built a large and prosperous congregation and helped spark the revival of 1857.

As his fame as a dramatic preacher spread, Beecher in the 1850s also gained a reputation as an abolitionist. An early critic of the expansion of slavery into the western territories, he protested the passage of the Fugitive Slave Law (1850), supported his sister Harriet Beecher Stowe in her publication of *Uncle Tom's Cabin* in 1852, and became an early campaigner for the Republican party. Guns sent to Kansas in 1855 during the dispute over the new territory became known as "Beecher's Bibles," an ironic reference to them as a force for moral suasion. By 1861 he had become a power within the Republican party. As editor of *The Independent* between 1861 and 1864, he campaigned for the party, supported the war effort, urged Abraham Lincoln to issue the Emancipation Proclamation, and undertook a popular speaking tour of England that helped keep that country from joining the side of the Confederates. Beecher's political speeches, published as *Freedom and War* (1863) and *Patriotic Addresses* (1887), identified the northern war effort with God's mission: moral duty would support national destiny.

By the end of the war, Beecher had developed a national reputation as a civic leader and a preacher. Although he supported a variety of liberal political issues ranging from abolitionism and temperance to women's rights and the expansion of education, he particularly excelled as an innovative spokesman for a Romantic Christianity that stressed the presence of God in the everyday and the common place. Apple pie, fishing, a trip to the mountains, the beauty of a sunset, and the fragile globe of a dandelion seed all revealed the blessings of life, the gift from the divine. "It is the end of art to inoculate men with the love of nature," he wrote. "But those who have a passion for nature in the natural way, need no pictures nor galleries. Spring is their designer, the whole year is their artist." Speaking for the vast middle-class audience that purchased his books, read his newspaper articles, listened to his sermons, and attended his popular lyceum lectures, Beecher developed a style of discourse that emphasized familiar, everyday events. "I aim to make them feel my personality," he asserted. By this time Beecher had also cashed in on his publishing success and accepted the offer of Robert Bonner, editor of the *New York Ledger*, to write a novel. *Norwood*, published serially and later as a book in 1867, earned Beecher $24,400. The story of two pairs of young lovers caught up in the Civil War, one couple from the North, the other from the South, the novel recapitulated many of the themes of his other writings: the importance of God's love, the inspiration of the divine in nature, and the application of moral principles to everyday affairs. It was not great literature, but it spoke to the hopes and fears of his middle-class public.

By the 1870s, Beecher was at the height of his career. In addition to his novel, he published *The Life of Jesus Christ*, vol. 1 (1871) and his *Yale Lectures on Preaching* (3 vols., 1872–1874), the latter of which gave astute advice to his divinity school audience about how the preacher might compete with the explosion of printed matter at the time. Beecher's solution was to assert that the preacher should make his audience feel the force of his personality and, in essence, become a media event himself, a suggestion that he embodied in his own career. Beecher not only dominated the liberal evangelical community by editing a new religious journal, *The Christian Union* (later called *The Outlook*), and by publishing his collected sermons in a series, *Plymouth Pulpit* (19 vols., 1868–1884), he also developed a vast national following by becoming a star on the lecture circuit. In 1875, for example, he traveled 27,000 miles by rail and spoke in eighteen states and Canada, for which he was paid $60,000.

Beecher's position as one of the leading clerics of the day was abruptly challenged in 1872 when the radical feminist Victoria Woodhull asserted in her *Weekly* that Beecher had committed adultery with Elizabeth Tilton, wife of the editor of *The Independent*. The resulting scandal was aired first in a church trial in 1874 and then in a civil suit in 1875. The civil trial became a media event, which the *New York Times* and most other urban papers splashed over their front pages for six months. A hung jury exonerated the embattled preacher, and most middle-class Americans seemed to accept his innocence if, for no other reason, than the fact that a guilty verdict would impugn the emphasis on morality and progress that they, too, shared. But the conflict split his own family (one sister, Harriet Beecher Stowe, defended him while another, Isabella Beecher Hooker, thought he was guilty). The conflict also fragmented the Protestant religious community in Brooklyn and reflected deep divisions over tactics and philosophy within the women's rights movement.

Beecher finished out his career in the late 1870s and early 1880s with intensified energy. Taking up the debate over evolution that developed after the publication of Charles Darwin's *On the Origin of Species*, Beecher lectured widely on the compatibility of religion and science. Picturing himself as a "cordial Christian Evolutionist," Beecher insisted that Darwin's theory proved the existence of civilization and progress. In 1879 Beecher entered the political debate by supporting civil service reform, and in 1884 he boldly supported Grover Cleveland despite the revelation that the presidential candidate had fathered an illegitimate child. Two years later, in the midst of intense strikes, Beecher supported the right of laborers to organize into unions. When he died in Brooklyn, he was widely celebrated as one of the nation's most innovative preachers. George William Curtis, editor of *Harper's Weekly*, captured the popular response to the man when he wrote that Beecher was a man "of strong virility, of exuberant vitality, of quick sympathy, of an abounding humor, of a rapid play of poetic imagination, of great fluency of speech: an emotional nature overflowing in ardent expression, of strong convictions, of complete self-confidence; but also not sensitive, nor critical, nor judicial; a hearty, joyful nature, touching ordinary human life at every point, and responsive to every generous moral impulse" (in J. H. Tewskesbury, ed., *Henry Ward Beecher as His Friends Saw Him* [1904], p. 135).

Beecher's contemporaries and later historians have focused on his remarkable talents as preacher of a new gospel of love, a modified evangelical religion that stressed the impact of love and commitment on everyday life. As the historian Thomas Bender has suggested, Henry Ward Beecher recognized the crisis of urban culture in the late nineteenth century with its diversity, isolation, anonymity, and egalitarianism. Beecher's "most important contribution to the quest for intellectual authority and influence," according to Bender, rested on "a personalism that relied upon personality and the appearance of intimate discourse"

("The Erosion of Public Culture: Cities, Discourse, and Professional Disciplines," in *The Authority of Experts*, ed. Thomas Haskell [1984], pp. 90–91). A master at creating a sense of familiarity and personal conversations with his many audiences, Beecher articulated the hopes and fears of millions of middle-class Americans who sought moral stability in the dramatic social turmoils that convulsed American society in the middle decades of the nineteenth century.

• The major collections of Henry Ward Beecher's letters and sermon notes can be found in the Beecher Family Papers in the Yale University Library, the Beecher-Stowe Collection in the Arthur and Elizabeth Schlesinger Library on the History of Women in America at Radcliffe College, and in the Henry Ward Beecher Papers in the Library of Congress. For recent interpretations of Beecher's life and career see William G. McLoughlin, *The Meaning of Henry Ward Beecher: An Essay on the Shifting Values of Mid-Victorian America, 1840–1870* (1970); Clifford E. Clark, Jr., *Henry Ward Beecher: Spokesman for a Middle-Class America* (1978); Milton Rugoff, *The Beechers: An American Family in the Nineteenth Century* (1981); and Altina L. Waller, *Reverend Beecher and Mrs. Tilton: Sex and Class in Victorian America* (1982). An obituary is in the *New York Times*, 9 Mar. 1887.

CLIFFORD E. CLARK, JR.

BEECHER, Lyman (12 Oct. 1775–10 Jan. 1863), Protestant clergyman, was born in New Haven, Connecticut, the son of David Beecher, a blacksmith, and Esther Lyman. On his mother's death within days of his birth, Lyman was sent to the Guilford, Connecticut, farm of a maternal aunt. Catharine and Lot Benton became his foster parents; David Beecher proved to be a distant and disparaging father.

In 1795, while a junior in Yale College, Beecher became the protégé of Timothy Dwight (1752–1817), who had assumed the presidency of Yale. After undergoing a religious conversion Beecher completed his undergraduate work and stayed on to study for the ministry, becoming an ardent exponent of Dwight's rationalizing and humanistic recasting of orthodox theology. From the same source he imbibed an enthusiasm for revivals, for foreign and domestic missions, and for the cooperation of clergy and laity in philanthropic endeavors.

Called to the Presbyterian church of East Hampton, Long Island, Beecher was ordained to the Presbyterian ministry in 1799. That same year he married Roxana Foote; they had nine children. From the start of his ministry Beecher exhibited the traits that would make him one of the most revered and execrated clergymen of his generation: "for I soon found myself harnessed to the Chariot of Christ." Unquenchable optimism, finely honed skills as a revivalist and popularizer of ideas, and unstinting devotion to pastoral care perfectly suited the temper of a turbulent young country. In East Hampton Beecher enjoyed the success of a major revival and was frequently invited to preach at other churches in New York and New England. Preeminently a man of the pulpit, he worked at revitalizing mainstream Protestantism by restating

Calvinistic dogmas in terms more acceptable to nineteenth-century rationalism and individualism and by generating new institutional forms through which the churches could direct social energies, particularly voluntary societies to promote foreign and domestic missions, dissemination of tracts and Bibles, and financial support for seminaries. He heartily approved denominational cooperation, as embodied in the 1801 Plan of Union, which for a time fostered Congregational and Presbyterian unity in spreading the gospel in the new settlements.

In 1810 Beecher became pastor of the Congregational church of Litchfield, Connecticut, where he enjoyed the support of a pious Federalist elite. Prostrated by the cares of a huge and impecunious household, Roxana Beecher died in 1816. Beecher married Harriet Porter in 1817; they had four children. Beecher was instrumental in the founding and support of a host of new religious enterprises, among them the American Bible Society and the *Christian Spectator* and *Connecticut Observer* magazines. He won fame in 1825 by inveighing against "the fiery waves of intemperance" in *Six Sermons on Temperance*, which helped to mobilize a national movement to guard the moral health of the Republic. The one great idea of his generation of evangelicals was the inauguration of the Kingdom of God, a goal whose success depended upon revivals of religion and thoroughgoing moral regeneration. This millennial hope was the main impetus behind the erection of a "benevolent empire" of moral reform societies in which Protestant clergy shared power with prominent laypeople to inculcate public virtue and individual responsibility. Lobbying for positive legislation to extirpate vices was controversial; evangelicals were mindful of the antidemocratic implications of coercion and tended to view electoral politics as inescapably corrupting.

Arguing that citizens of a republic required a gospel of free will and social benevolence, Beecher, in association with Nathaniel William Taylor, claimed to retain the essentials of Calvinism but preached human agency and responsibility in seeking salvation, a development that came to be known as New Haven Theology. He was active in the founding of the Yale Divinity School (1822) to disseminate these views, "good sound Calvinism, or if you please, Beecherism and Taylorism." Beecher's version of orthodoxy avoided detailed consideration of such central tenets of Calvinism as predestination and original sin. Far better, he reasoned, to stress the ethical imperatives of active piety: "I have used my evangelical philosophy all my lifetime, and relieved people without number out of the sloughs of high Calvinism." The very flux and confusion of American culture that gave scope to such modifications produced a profound divisiveness over churchly means and ends. As doctrinal and ecclesiological divisions became more embittered, the Congregational and Presbyterian scheme of cooperation foundered, even as the two denominations fell prey to savage internal conflicts.

"Beecherism" had marked affinities to the teachings of the Presbyterian Charles Grandison Finney, whose call for immediate repentance in revival settings of fervid emotionalism caught on in western New York. His innovations, particularly the use of an "anxious bench" for sinners in the throes of public conversion and the encouragement of female-led prayer and testimony, produced great disquiet among conservative Congregational and Presbyterian clergy, especially in New England. Beecher increasingly found himself lumped with Finney and others whose orthodoxy was assailed, leading to strained relations within the New England clergy.

The new Hanover Street Church called Beecher in 1826 to Boston, where he waged a pamphlet and pulpit war against the Unitarians, whose power and influence he strove in vain to curb. To present the evangelical viewpoint, Beecher founded the *Spirit of the Pilgrims* (1828), a newspaper aimed at both clergy and laity. Among his many achievements of this period were fostering of hymnody and church music at Hanover Church, raising of funds for a host of benevolent associations, and nurturing of numerous educational and self-help organizations among the working class and professional men of the city. Anxious lest Finney's growing influence split the evangelical movement, Beecher acceded to the demands of conservative clergy to persuade Finney to abandon his "wrong measures" in favor of more decorous revival practices. A lengthy conference between the opposing groups at New Lebanon, New York, in 1827 ended acrimoniously, and rapprochement seemed unlikely. Within two years, however, Beecher gave up his opposition to Finney's revival tactics, inviting him to preach in Boston. Inexorably Beecher and those who followed his lead were identified with the liberal, or even renegade, branch of evangelicalism, which allegedly sought to bring about mass conversions through appeals to flawed human reason.

Boston also brought Beecher face to face with the rising power of the Catholic church, which he pilloried in an 1831 lecture series as steeped in Old World authoritarianism and cravings for power and thus a sworn enemy to the Republic. When anti-Catholics mobbed and burned the Ursuline convent in Charlestown, Massachusetts, he was blamed as an instigator, although there was nothing exceptionally inflammatory about his speeches in an era when much learning and ingenuity was devoted to exposing "popish plots."

The western territories now claimed his interest as a grand new mission field. Beecher was called to be the first president and professor of theology by Lane Theological Seminary in Cincinnati, Ohio, posts he assumed in 1832 over the vehement protests of "Old School" (conservative) Presbyterians who objected to his reentry into their church by way of a "New School" (liberal) presbytery. Several of his sons had already become New School ministers and were also regarded as dangerously heterodox, reinforcing a perception that the numerous, gifted, and idiosyncratic Beecher family was a force to be reckoned with. In a career marked by heated conflicts and broken alliances, Beecher nevertheless knew the immense satisfactions of being father to devoted, talented children. All seven of his sons followed him into the ministry, and three of his daughters led noteworthy public lives.

The transition to Lane was a stormy one, owing to the presence among its students of staunch abolitionists. Whereas Beecher had excoriated as "a national sin" the practice of dueling, he saw in slavery an issue that was bound to sunder national unity. Desperate to secure the seminary's prosperity and to avert potentially violent conflicts, he took a temporizing line, discouraging discussion of slavery and the social mingling with blacks that incensed white Cincinnatians. An adherent of the American Colonization Society, he believed its gradualism and program to deport freed slaves would secure the end of slavery with the least amount of social and political conflict. In 1834, seizing on Beecher's absence, the Lane trustees passed regulations that forbade debate about immediate emancipation, which Beecher could not undo. Following Theodore Dwight Weld, the vast majority deserted Lane, regrouping in Oberlin, Ohio, where they formed a rival school under abolitionist auspices. Ironically, most of Beecher's children became abolitionists, while their father continued to defend African colonization. Multiplying Beecher's tribulations, his second wife died in 1835.

Hard on this crisis came the attack of the Old School Presbyterians, who brought Beecher to trial on heresy and other grounds, citing the New Havenite doctrines he had proclaimed in preaching revivals. Abetting his accusers was a small but vocal group of New England Congregationalists claiming to preserve consistent Calvinism. Acquitted by the presbytery in June 1835, he was dragged through protracted church litigation before the charges were dropped. Far from vindicating his theology, the net effect was to deepen cleavages that led, in 1837, to a schism of the national Presbyterian church.

The economic depression of 1837 led to the withdrawal of most of Lane's financial support; but Beecher served the school until 1851, endlessly traveling east to raise money for Lane and numerous educational and moral reform organizations. His work in the West at an end, he returned to Boston with Lydia Beals Jackson, whom he had married in 1836. His collected *Works* were published in 1852–1853, and his children busied themselves transcribing the manuscripts and eliciting the reminiscences that would form the core of his *Autobiography* (1864). In 1856, his mental faculties badly dimmed, he moved to Brooklyn Heights where Henry Ward Beecher was a celebrated preacher. The coming of the Civil War saw one of his sons, James Chaplin Beecher, become colonel of a volunteer black regiment. Lyman Beecher died in Brooklyn.

• Many of Beecher's personal papers were destroyed after his death, but significant manuscript collections containing letters and other documents are located at Yale University; the

Stowe-Day Library, Hartford, Conn.; McCormick Theological Seminary, Chicago; and the Boston Public Library. The chief source for his life is the so-called *Autobiography*, of which there is a modern edition, ed. Barbara Cross (1961); both editions must be used with caution because of numerous inaccuracies owing to faulty recollection and personal bias. Vincent Harding, *A Certain Magnificence* (1991), is a sympathetic and eloquent account and the only full-dress scholarly biography. The chapters in Constance Rourke's *Trumpets of Jubilee* (1927) seem dated; and Stuart Henry, *Unvanquished Puritan* (1973; rept. 1986), is more an appreciation than a biography. Marie Caskey, *Chariot of Fire* (1978), considers the impact of Beecher's religious ideas upon his children.

MARIE CASKEY MORGAN

BEEKMAN, Henry (2 Jan. 1688–3 Jan. 1776), New York landowner and provincial assemblyman, was born in Kingston, New York, the son of Henry Beekman, a landowner and provincial assemblyman, and Johanna Lopers. Beekman was not a self-made man. His Dutch ancestors were prominent locally in the turmoil associated with the Protestant Reformation and the Dutch struggle for independence from Spain. His immigrant grandfather, William Beekman, was an administrative subordinate to the governor of New Netherland. His father was a militia leader from Ulster County whose work in preparing for possible attacks by the French during King William's War (1689–1697), plus a small gratuity to the governor, won him land grants later branded "as large as a middling county of England." These Dutchess County land grants (Rhinebeck Patent, 21,766 acres; Beekman Patent, 84,000 acres) became the basis for the younger Henry Beekman's career.

Beekman's early life is obscure. The idiosyncratic spelling in his letters suggests strongly that he grew up speaking Dutch as did most people in Ulster County at that time. He courted Joanna Livingston, daughter of the lord of Livingston manor, but her family found him unacceptable. Instead, in 1721 he married Janet Livingston, of a lesser branch of the Livingston family; they had one child survive to adulthood. After Janet's death in 1724, he married Gertrude Van Cortlandt, daughter of another major landholder, in 1726, thereby increasing his landholdings by several thousand acres.

As a landlord Beekman was indulgent, solicitous, even protective of his tenants; they were usually years behind in rent and work obligations. During the antilandlord riots of the 1760s Beekman's tenants were notably quiescent, but he did have trouble with New England migrants squatting on his lands along the Connecticut border and contesting his title. If Beekman contributed to the alleged inclination of settlers to choose other provinces over New York, it was not that he oppressed his tenants, but that in common with other great landlords he was usually disinclined to sell his lands.

As the major local landholder, Beekman was destined to serve in the colonial assembly. Elected in 1724 at age thirty-six, Beekman first drew attention to himself in 1727 when Governor William Burnet began to

act as a chancery court judge, compelling major landholders, including Beekman, to pay long unpaid quitrents (annual charges against land grants). This action was offensive to Beekman not just because it cost him money, but because the court was not authorized by New York law; it operated without a jury; and it gave the governor revenue free from legislative control while the legislators were trying to make provincial officeholders look to them and not to British officials or fees for pay. When the council, the legislature's appointed upper house, attempted to investigate the passage of an assembly resolution condemning Burnet's action, Beekman alone among those summoned defied the inquisitors, denying the right of the council to investigate the assembly. He was jailed briefly for his temerity. A new assembly then resolved unanimously in 1728 that for actions in its sessions its members were responsible to "no other Person or Persons whatsoever." Burnet's successor not only abandoned the chancery fight, he also appointed Beekman to the lucrative office of sheriff for New York County.

Beekman lost his job as New York sheriff under Governor William Cosby. Cosby in fact had reappointed him in 1732 and 1733, but then Cosby determined to suppress a newly established newspaper published by John Peter Zenger, which was very critical of his administration. To do so he first sought a grand jury indictment against Zenger for libel. Contrary to expectations, the grand jury selected by Sheriff Beekman not only refused to indict Zenger but challenged the governor's ally, Chief Justice James DeLancey, a nephew of Beekman's, to make public the case against Zenger. Thus identified with the governor's opponents, Beekman was not reappointed in 1734.

Thereafter Beekman continued to try to reduce British authority. He supported measures to increase assembly control of expenditures. He fought prosecution by "information," a practice enabling the attorney general, long since deprived of a salary, to prosecute without a grand jury indictment and to collect court fees even if he lost. In 1743 Beekman introduced a measure, which was aborted by dissolution of the assembly on the arrival of the new governor, that would have required the attorney general to post a bond for court fees before prosecuting and to forfeit his bond if he lost, as was likely in a jury trial. In 1745 he protested, as likely to "Establish arbetrary power to all the Contenant," an abortive British effort to make royal instructions absolutely binding and championed the right of the assembly to issue paper money without waiting for British approval.

Beginning in the late 1740s, Cadwallader Colden, ever the protector and increasingly the wielder of British prerogatives, deprived Beekman of his power over local appointments in Dutchess County, but despite growing local resentment of great landlords Colden was never able to dislodge him from the assembly. Assiduous in serving constituent interests and "refreshing" the voters on election days, preferring usually to "Suffer a Small Indignity than Inflame the Community," Beekman kept his post until he retired finally in 1758, bequeathing the county's assembly seats to his son-in-law and a nephew. He died at his home in Rhinebeck, New York, just six months before the Declaration of Independence, which fittingly his grandson Robert R. Livingston, one of many prominent children of his daughter Margaret, had been chosen to help draft.

• Letters from Henry Beekman appear in the Beekman Family Papers at the New-York Historical Society, and in the Henry Livingston Papers at the New York Public Library and at the Franklin Delano Roosevelt Library, Hyde Park. He receives considerable attention in Philip L. White, *The Beekmans of New York in Politics and Commerce, 1647–1877* (1956), pp. 159–207; Patricia Bonomi, *A Factious People: Politics and Society in Colonial New York* (1971), pp. 166–71; and Sung Bok Kim, *Landlord and Tenant in Colonial New York: Manorial Society, 1664–1775* (1978). Scattered references appear also in Staughton Lynd, *Anti-Federalism in Dutchess County: A Study of Democracy and Class Conflict in the Revolutionary Era* (1962), Clare Brandt, *An American Aristocracy: The Livingstons* (1986), and Henry Noble Mac-Cracken, *Old Dutchess Forever! The Story of an American County* (1956). There is a brief obituary in the *New York Gazette and Weekly Mercury*, 12 Feb. 1776.

PHILIP L. WHITE

BEER, George Louis (26 July 1872–15 Mar. 1920), historian, was born on Staten Island, New York, the son of Julius Beer, an immigrant from Germany who had a business importing tobacco, and Sophia Walter. As was the case with many second-generation immigrants, George Beer received an excellent education in the public schools of New York City. He entered Columbia College at the age of sixteen. While engaged in his studies at Columbia, Beer came into contact with a group of remarkable scholars, among them John William Burgess. Beer happened to be studying at Columbia at the very time when that institution was making a concerted effort to develop its offerings in political science. Benefiting from this synergy of talent and energy, Beer received his bachelor of arts in 1892 and proceeded to write his formidable master's essay, "The Commercial Policy of England toward the American Colonies," which was soon published in the *Columbia Studies in History, Economics and Public Law* (1893). This early start to his scholarship gave Beer a name and reputation that went ahead of him through the rest of his career and opened doors for him among the prominent scholars and teachers of his day. In 1896 he married Edith Cecilia Hellman. They had one daughter.

Unlike many of his contemporary scholars (and most of those of the twentieth century), Beer had a second string to his career. From 1893 until 1903 he worked in his family's tobacco business, where he succeeded in acquiring enough wealth to pursue his scholarship without having to engage in teaching. As a lecturer at Columbia (1893–1897), Beer had shown no great interest in teaching. He was, however, truly engaged in the pursuit of his scholarly studies, and in 1903 he retired from his mercantile pursuits and gave

himself over to the studies that he had commenced during his undergraduate days at Columbia: notably, relations between the American colonies (1607–1775) and the British Empire.

Beer wrote three books that received wide recognition and some acclaim. The first of these, *British Colonial Policy, 1754–65* (1907), was something of a classic in its field. Prior to Beer's work, most American historians had taken the tried and true method of condemning Great Britain for blunders in its relationship with the American colonies. Beer succeeded in placing the British-American relationship within a wider context (that of the entire English imperial system), and he provided a context for Americans to better understand the stresses and strains of that crucial period in the development of Britain's empire.

It might be said that Beer went backwards (at least chronologically) in his work; he then wrote *The Origins of the British Colonial System, 1578–1660* (1908), in which he traced the motives and methods for the empire back to the Tudor and Stuart days of England. Although some British scholars might have quarreled with some of Beer's conclusions, the fact remains that he had by this point become the American scholar most fitted to undertake studies of the British Empire. Beer then went to England for further research and published his third book, *The Old Colonial System, Part I* (1912), which was for many years the most complete and authoritative study made on English colonial policy during the period 1660–1688. Beer fully intended to write one more major work to complete his series, a study of English colonial policy during the crucial years of 1688–1754, but the start of World War I changed his plans.

From 1914 on, Beer became involved in the current events that were creating a maelstrom in Europe and that threatened to do the same in the United States. As a historian who had been given the unusual position of being able to influence current events, Beer made regular contributions to the *Round Table*, in which he tracked and traced the evolution of American public opinion regarding a possible entry into World War I. He wrote *The English-Speaking Peoples* (1917), which became the most widely read of his books. In this work Beer presented the possibility of a cooperative alliance between the United States and Great Britain; in so doing, he followed in the wake of Cecil Rhodes and anticipated the thoughts of Winston Churchill.

Beer became a prominent member of a group known as "The Inquiry." Formed by Colonel Edward House at the request of President Woodrow Wilson, the group examined problems of policy at the end of World War I, anticipating the peace conference at Versailles. Beer wrote a number of reports for the group, one of which was published after his death in *African Questions at the Paris Peace Conference* (1923). He was a believer in and an advocate for the mandate system that emerged during the peace conference, under which peoples around the world would be liberated step by step from their former colonial status. He was named chief of the colonial division of the American delegation at Versailles, and when the League of Nations was formed he was named head of the mandates division. Following the U.S. Senate's rejection of the Versailles treaty, Beer was unable to take his place at the League of Nations. He died in New York City.

Beer enjoyed a varied career. A second-generation immigrant, he took advantage of an excellent early education and the wealth generated by his family's business to advance early in the ranks of American scholars. Without the advent of World War I, he would likely have passed a substantial but little-noticed life in academia. Instead the pressing issues of war and peace, colonialism and imperialism, propelled him forward, owing to his great understanding of the British colonial system—a system that had developed during the eighteenth century and blossomed in the nineteenth century.

Well intentioned in his work at Versailles, Beer was nonetheless an unwitting victim (as were many of his colleagues) of his vision of the permanence of the nineteenth-century world. Beer and others failed to see that the nineteenth-century themes of empire and imperialism (especially as personified by Great Britain) would yield in the twentieth century to a much diminished England, the reduction of imperialism around the globe, and the emergence of truly independent nations in Africa and Asia. Far from being alone in his views, Beer was actually quite representative of his peers, men who had grown up during the heyday of imperialism and who could not—in spite of their best intents and wishes—imagine a world without rulers.

• Beer's books present the surest guide to understanding his historical and economic theories. Excellent commentary is provided in *George Louis Beer: A Tribute to His Life and Work in the Making of History and the Moulding of Public Opinion* (1924). An unsigned testament to Beer is in *Publications of the American Jewish Society*, 28 Nov. 1922. An obituary is in the *New York Times*, 16 Mar. 1920.

SAMUEL WILLARD CROMPTON

BEER, Thomas (22 Nov. 1888?–18 Apr. 1940), writer, was born in Council Bluffs, Iowa, the son of William Collins Beer, a corporate attorney and lobbyist, and Martha Ann Alice Baldwin. Though born in western Iowa, Thomas Beer spent most of his childhood in Yonkers, New York, with summers in Nantucket and on his grandfather's farm in Bucyrus, Ohio. Wealth and position from his father's Wall Street business gave Beer a distinct sense of social superiority, which he manifested in personal relations and cultural criticisms. Despising the bourgeoisie, the working-class masses, and the chic lifestyles of the Jazz Age, Beer projected an image of extreme conservatism and tesselated sophistication. At Yale, class of 1911, he was class poet, lifelong friend of the actor Monty Wooley, editor of the literary review, and contributor of twenty stories, essays, and poems. After college he spent five years as a dilatory student in the Columbia law school and as clerk in his father's law firm, but when his father died at his professional nadir in 1916, Beer turned

to letters. His first important short story—"The Brothers"—was published a few months later in the *Century*. The incentive for writing *Stephen Crane* he also dated as having occurred in 1916. Soon afterward Beer enlisted in the U.S. Army; first as private, but eventually promoted to first lieutenant, he served in France at the end of World War I.

A prolific writer in his prime, Beer published nearly 140 short stories—an average of more than six a year—between 1917 and 1936. Written expressly for the *Saturday Evening Post*, most of these bittersweet comedies celebrate the wholesomeness of the American heartland. Beer's settings are generally farms and small towns in upstate New York or Ohio; his prototypic hero—Adam Egg—is a muscular, laconic youth who serves as moral arbiter in resolving domestic or communal unrest. Beer's formulaic plots usually contain hints of Oedipal conflicts and sibling rivalries, but they are always agreeably resolved. His stories, like Norman Rockwell's artwork, appealed strongly to the *Post* readership in affirming the innate wisdom of common folk.

This self-proclaimed "desolating literary prostitution" earned Beer a modest fortune. His potboilers sold for as much as $3,000 each; in 1931 he earned more than $31,000. Nevertheless, success by this means embarrassed him. Beer's deportment and tastes diverged sharply from the fictional world that made him popular. A closet homosexual, he cultivated a studied urbanity and a loathing of the vulgar and the provincial. Like Petronius, his favorite Latin author, Beer sneered at convention and promoted style above morality. Alfred Kazin ranked him with other "Exquisites"—James Branch Cabell, Joseph Hergesheimer, and Elinor Wylie—who cultivated an "elaborate decadence and estheticism."

Alfred Knopf, Beer's publisher and patron, encouraged him to excel. "I have—for reasons I can hardly explain—great confidence in you," Knopf wrote responding to the submission of Beer's first novel in 1921, "and feel that your work is going to count." The three novels did not, however, live up to the publisher's expectation. *The Fair Rewards* (1922) and *Sandoval* (1924) are studies of bygone manners projected against the background of New York City in the nineteenth century. First admired for their ornate virtuosity, these novels pale when compared with the more innovative modernism of Ernest Hemingway, F. Scott Fitzgerald, and Sinclair Lewis. *The Road to Heaven* (1928), a philosophically ambitious novel, suggests a Spenglerian analysis of culture through the cousins Abner and Lamon Coe—one typifying decadent urbanity; the other, rustic vitality.

Beer's best writing is found in his nonfiction, where he displayed remarkable ability as a biographer, historian, and cultural critic. *The Mauve Decade: American Life at the End of the Nineteenth Century* (1926), an anecdotal tour de force, derives its title from James Whistler, who observed that "Mauve is just pink trying to be purple." Flamboyant, nostalgic, impudent, and cynical, *The Mauve Decade* illustrates

Beer's style at its height. What the book lacks in historical accuracy is redeemed by its vivid, incisive images of America in the 1890s. In a similar manner, *Hanna* (1929), an impressionistic biography of Mark Hanna, explores politics in the Gilded Age. Members of Beer's family were powers in the Republican party in Ohio; his father served Hanna and William McKinley as undercover agent and campaign manager. Parts of *The Mauve Decade* and *Hanna* constitute a history of the Beer family, deriving from family papers and memories, real and invented.

Beer's principal yet most problematic work is his *Stephen Crane: A Study in American Letters* (1923), the first biography of Stephen Crane and unfortunately the basis of future scholarship. Reviewers greeted Beer's *Crane* with enthusiasm, stating that it set an example for a new type of life history, devoid of hagiography and replete with dramatic appeal. However, later biographers found the book evasive and inaccurate, particularly in its misrepresentation of Crane's "marriage" to the nightclub manager and madam who called herself Cora "Taylor." Worse still, it now appears that the excerpts from approximately seventy of Crane's letters that Beer published in *Stephen Crane* and elsewhere were his forgeries and that many of the episodes and persons named in his book and essays on Crane do not exist in fact. Once trusted as a source for Stephen Crane studies, Thomas Beer is now wholly discredited.

Beer's career came to an abrupt halt in July 1937 when he broke down and was confined for fourteen months to the Hartford Retreat, a neuropsychiatric clinic, where he was treated for hypertension, insomnia, vertigo, obesity, and depression. Unmentioned in clinical records, though doubtlessly a major contributing factor, was alcoholism. When he was discharged in September 1938, Beer had two contracts pending with Knopf, but he could no longer write. Unable to earn a living, he sold his property—including his books and art collection at a devastating loss—and moved to an apartment in Manhattan. He died at the Albert Hotel in Greenwich Village, New York City, officially of a heart attack, but most likely a suicide.

• The Beer Family Papers are at Yale University, Sterling Memorial Library, Manuscripts and Archives: MS 73. The discrepancy in the date of Thomas Beer's birth is clarified in the introduction to these papers compiled by Ruth Gay and Linda Wrigley. For criticism and bibliography, see Evans Burnham Harrington, "The Work of Thomas Beer: Appraisal and Bibliography" (Ph.D. diss., Univ. of Mississippi, 1968), and William Daniel Coyle, "The Short Stories of Thomas Beer" (Ph.D. diss., Univ. of North Carolina, 1977). The most influential critique of Beer's writing is in Alfred Kazin, *On Native Grounds* (1942). For recent discussions of Beer's *Stephen Crane*, see Stanley Wertheim and Paul Sorrentino, "Thomas Beer: The Clay Feet of Stephen Crane Biography," *American Literary Realism, 1870–1910* 22, no. 3 (1990): 2–16, and John Clendenning, "Thomas Beer's *Stephen Crane*: The Eye of His Imagination," *Prose Studies* 14, no. 2 (1991): 68–80.

JOHN CLENDENNING

BEER, William (1 May 1849–1 Feb. 1927), librarian, was born in Plymouth, England, the son of Gabriel Beer and Harriet Ferguson. Little is known about his family or his youth except that he attended the Plymouth Grammar School and went to Paris in 1872 to study medicine and art. He returned to England in 1877 to study mining engineering at the College of Physical Science at Newcastle-on-Tyne (later King's College, Durham University), and two years later he joined a new company manufacturing stained glass. His interest in libraries and antiquarian subjects surfaced early. At the age of twenty he was a director of the Cottonian Library in Plymouth. He took part in local explorations of the Newcastle Society of Antiquaries and collected imprints there, which he donated to the Newcastle-on-Tyne Public Library in 1884 when he emigrated to the United States.

After a period of travel in Canada and the United States with stops in New York, Pittsburgh, Chicago, and Detroit and longer stays in Cincinnati, Opechee (Mich.), and Leadville (Colo.), he attended the first of many annual conferences of the American Library Association, in St. Louis in May 1889. In July of the following year he was appointed librarian of the Public Library of Topeka, Kansas. His employment in mining companies undoubtedly alerted him to the need for library service to working people. In Topeka he enlarged the library's collection of technical books, issued lists of books pertaining to practical subjects of interest to workers, and sponsored a series of university extension courses on electricity. He also served as secretary to the Kansas Library Association and raised $50 for the endowment fund of the American Library Association. In 1891 he accepted the librarianship of the Howard Memorial Library, which had opened two years earlier in New Orleans.

In that crescent city Beer, at the age of forty-two, was to find his niche. The library, established in 1888 as a public reference library by an endowment of Annie T. Howard, occupied a characteristic H. H. Richardson–style building on a busy circle near the business section of the city. To the general reference collection that had already been purchased, Beer added books and journals needed to make it an outstanding collection of southern history and literature. The collecting of Louisianiana was largely an uncharted field, but local collectors Gaspar Cusachs and T. P. Thompson and others had good private libraries, and the Louisiana historians Charles Gayarré and Alcée Fortier were available for advice. Beer also worked with cultural and social organizations such as the Louisiana Historical Society, the New Orleans Academy of Sciences, and the Pickwick Club. His vacations became hunting expeditions in search of Louisianiana. In 1894 he reported that he had inspected sixty libraries and nearly a hundred bookstores in a six-week tour. In his 1895 annual report he wrote that his acquisitions in London, Rotterdam, The Hague, Leyden, Berlin, Paris, Dresden, Brussels, and Antwerp made the library's collection of Louisiana history "incontestably the finest in the world."

In 1896 he also became the first librarian of the Fisk Free and Public Library and served as librarian of both the public library and the Howard library for the next ten years. Cooperation between the two libraries was encouraged by Frank T. Howard, who served as president of the public library board and secretary of the Howard Memorial Library. The Fisk Library, the last of a long series of previously unsuccessful attempts to provide library service to the city, was established on the second floor of a building five blocks from the Howard Memorial Library. Beer quickly set about organizing the library for use, beginning with fiction to attract readers. A list of 2,800 titles was issued for the public in March 1897, and other lists followed, by classes, until a complete catalog was published in January 1900. Financial support for the library improved, and the Carnegie Corporation awarded a grant of $250,000 for constructing a central library building and three branches. At this point a full-time librarian was required, and Beer chose to remain with the Howard Memorial Library.

For the next twenty-five years all Beer's energies and ingenuity were needed to stretch a book budget that seldom exceeded $500 a year. By careful and persistent soliciting of gifts and exchanges from other libraries, the United States and foreign government departments, and historical and scientific societies, he continued to develop the outstanding reference library of the southern states. Beer himself came to be, in the words of Anatole Le Braz, who visited New Orleans, "le volume le plus rare, le plus attachant, et si je ne m'abuse, le plus consulté" ("the rarest, most interesting, and, I suspect, the source most often consulted," *Revue des Deux Mondes* 51 [15 May 1919]: 324). A sample from his correspondence files includes letters from Reuben Gold Thwaites, Walter L. Fleming, John Franklin Jameson, Charles Evans, Clarence S. Brigham, the American novelist Winston Churchill, and Theodore Roosevelt.

Beer wrote some eighty-five items, although he derived more satisfaction from assisting others in their research. For example, for Francis H. Herrick he recovered seven early letters that John J. Audubon had written his father, which Herrick used in his *Audubon the Naturalist* (1917, vol. 1, pp. 154–55). Most of his own works are bibliographical notes and historical texts, discussions of librarianship, and articles on the history of New Orleans and Louisiana.

An active member of professional organizations, Beer attended fifteen conferences of the American Library Association and contributed papers to many of them. He served on the National Advisory Board of the Special Libraries Association from its inception. He was a fellow of the Library Association, a founding member of the Bibliographical Society of America, and a member of the Grolier Club, the Caxton Club, and the Bibliographical Society.

Edward Laroque Tinker remembered Beer this way: "Bushy eyebrows overshadowed tired eyes, misty-irised with age, and his whole appearance suggested a sleepy bird of prey; but this predatory impression was most misleading, for in reality he was a very kindly but caustic old gentleman."

Beer, who never married, died in New Orleans. He was remembered by few librarians but was appreciated in print by the editors of historical and bibliographical journals. The age in which the bookman and the antiquarian were held in high esteem had passed, but Beer's contribution to libraries in the South Central states outlived him. He had organized the first public library in New Orleans and had developed it into a major reference library (it is now part of the collection at Tulane University), one that attracted scholars from all parts of the country. At a time when eastern and midwestern libraries dominated the profession, Beer established a library that need bow to no other.

• Beer's papers are in the Howard-Tilton Memorial Library, Tulane University, New Orleans. Joe W. Kraus, "William Beer and the New Orleans Libraries, 1891–1927," ACRL Monographs, no. 1 (Jan. 1952), includes a bibliography of Beer's writings. "Our Frontispiece: William Beer," *Bulletin of Bibliography* 12 (May–Aug. 1923), includes the only portrait in print. Edward Laroque Tinker, "William Beer, 1849–1927," Bibliographical Society of America, *Papers* 20 (1926), pp. 77–84, is a highly personal, delightful account. Obituaries are in the *New Orleans Times-Picayune*, 2 Feb. 1927, and the *Louisiana Historical Quarterly* 19 (1927): 249–51.

JOE W. KRAUS

BEERS, Clifford Whittingham (30 Mar. 1876–9 June 1943), founder of the mental hygiene movement, was born in New Haven, Connecticut, the son of Robert Anthony Beers, a produce merchant, and Ida Cooke. He spent much of his childhood supervised by an aunt. He attended local public schools and then, at eighteen, matriculated at Yale University's Sheffield Scientific School. Shortly after he began his studies, his older brother was diagnosed with epilepsy. Fear of developing the disease haunted Beers's years at Yale; nevertheless, he graduated in 1897 with a Ph.B. After three years working as a clerk in business firms in New York City, Beers suffered a mental breakdown and attempted suicide. Hospitalized between August 1900 and September 1903 with only brief discharges, he was treated at Stamford Hall, the Hartford Retreat, and the Connecticut State Hospital at Middletown. At all of these institutions, he suffered mistreatments ranging from humiliation to physical abuse. Outraged at the untherapeutic conditions and determined, upon his release, to work to reform them, he once intentionally caused himself to be transferred to a more severe ward to experience the worst conditions the hospital had to offer, including physical abuse and fifteen consecutive hours in a straight jacket. After his release he returned briefly to the business world, intent on acquiring enough prestige and money to begin a campaign to fight for the reform of mental institutions. The stress that these ambitions induced necessitated a brief return to the Hartford Retreat for several months in late 1904 and early 1905.

After his release in January 1905, Beers wrote *A Mind That Found Itself* (1908). In addition to chronicling his illness and the mistreatments he endured, the book outlines a plan to increase and improve the therapeutic treatments in mental hospitals. It received wide critical acclaim and brought the plight of mental patients to the public's attention, evoking a sympathy for a hitherto ostracized population. In May 1908 Beers, with the help of psychiatrist Adolf Meyer, physician William H. Welch, and philosopher William James, founded the Connecticut Society for Mental Hygiene. Its threefold aim was to help prevent mental disorders, to improve the quality of care in mental health facilities, and to educate the public about issues of mental health. Its success inspired regional chapters to spring up across the United States and Canada. In February 1909 Beers established the National Committee for Mental Hygiene, based in New York City. Through extensive fundraising efforts, he secured hundreds of thousands of dollars in private donations for the committee. Its efforts to improve psychiatric treatment included extensive hospital surveys, grants for research into the causes of mental illness, programs to improve psychiatric training for medical students and social workers, and the establishment of experimental child guidance clinics. To increase public awareness of mental health issues, the committee published two quarterly magazines, *Mental Hygiene* and *Understanding the Child*, as well as numerous monographs. In June 1912 Beers married Clara Louise Jepson, who proved instrumental in aiding him in his organizational and fundraising work. They had no children out of fear of hereditary mental illnesses. The committee also cooperated with the U.S. surgeon general during World War I to detect mental instability in servicemen, resulting in a national record low rate of mental collapse in battle.

Beers's insistence on retaining tight personal control over the National Committee led to increasing conflicts with other committee members. Because of these disagreements Beers's interest shifted to international work, although he remained secretary of the National Committee. He organized the International Congress for Mental Hygiene, held in May 1930 in Washington, D.C., which was attended by representatives from fifty-three countries. It gave rise to the International Committee for Mental Hygiene, with Beers as general secretary. Beers's involvement with the National Committee was sharply reduced in 1934 when glaucoma and arteriosclerosis crippled his capacity to work. However, several years later, the then impoverished committee asked Beers to help them in critical fundraising efforts. The difficulty of this task induced in Beers a crisis of confidence, and his mental state soon degenerated into depression and paranoia. Beers committed himself to Butler Hospital in Providence, Rhode Island, in June 1939 and died there four years later of bronchial pneumonia.

As founder and figurehead of the mental hygiene movement, Beers deserves much credit for increasing public sympathy and understanding for the mentally ill. He was instrumental in beginning a public discussion of mental health, which had its most tangible ramifications in schools, especially in the hiring of guidance counselors, and in courts, by making the defendant's psychological state a legitimate factor in the deliberations and sentencing. He was not, however, a social reformer, since his motivations were grounded in personal experience rather than social consciousness or ideology.

Beers's strengths as a leader and organizer were simultaneously his weaknesses. The intensity, energy, and single-mindedness that he brought to the cause engendered his success, especially in fundraising efforts, but also eventually alienated many of his collaborators. His lifelong psychological need for the approval of authority figures made him energetic in courting the support of wealthy individuals, notably John D. Rockefeller, but also limited the focus of his appeals to a relatively small upper-class population. Following the publication of his book, Beers lost real interest in courting the sympathy of the wider public; the movement thus lacked national impact and failed to gain significant political change in the legal status of the insane.

Beers's work was primarily organizational and financial, since he lacked the medical training to speak specifically about how treatment of the insane should be effected. He did, however, appeal for aid in reintegrating the mentally ill into society after their treatment, especially with regard to employment. He proposed the establishment of halfway houses, in which the recovering patient could be monitored outside of a hospital setting. He also advocated the establishment of more mental-illness treatment facilities connected to university medical departments or to preexisting state hospitals. Beers's most fundamental objective was always to combat the gross mistreatments common in insane asylums at that time. He pleaded for protection of patients against "physical abuse, indignities, and what, in so many cases, amounts to criminal neglect."

• Beers's papers are housed in the National Foundation for Mental Hygiene in New York City. The best source for information on Beers is Norman Dain, *Clifford W. Beers: Advocate for the Insane* (1980). Wilbur L. Cross, ed., *Twenty-five Years After: Sidelights on the Mental Hygiene Movement and Its Founder* (1934), contains approximately 500 tributes to Beers. See also Albert Deutsch, *The Mentally Ill in America*, 2d. ed. (1949), chap. 15; and Robin McKown, *Pioneers in Mental Health* (1961). Posthumous tributes are in *Mental Hygiene*, Apr. 1944, and the *American Journal of Psychiatry* 100 (Apr. 1944). Obituaries are in the *New York Times* and the *New York Herald Tribune*, both 10 July 1943.

ELIZABETH ZOE VICARY

BEERS, Ethel Lynn (13 Jan. 1827–11 Oct. 1879), poet and writer, was born Ethelinda Eliot in Goshen, Orange County, New York, the daughter of Horace William Eliot, a druggist, postmaster, and justice of the peace, and Keziah Westcott. Her father was a soldier during the War of 1812 and was a direct descendant of John Eliot, the apostle to the Indians. Also of note is that her mother was the daughter of David Westcott, who was a member of the state legislature and a colonel of the state militia.

Using the name Ethel Lynn, she started at an early age to submit her writings to magazines. She was nineteen years old when she married William H. Beers in 1846; they had one son. After her marriage she published under the name of Ethel Lynn Beers.

Beers was a frequent contributor to the *New York Ledger*, edited by Robert Bonner. Her most famous piece, a poem originally published in *Harper's Magazine* on 30 November 1861 and titled "The Picket Guard," was much more widely recognized from its first line, "All Quiet along the Potomac." This poem was written as a reference for and a response to that frequently repeated dispatch during the first year of the Civil War, and it paid tribute to an unknown soldier. Although the poem was considered by some to be a bit sentimental, it did achieve wide popularity. In fact, the poem was reprinted anonymously in a southern paper more than a year later, with an attached claim that it had been found on the body of a dead Confederate soldier. Two southern writers, Thaddeus Oliver and Lamar Fontaine, both claimed authorship. However, neither was ever able to prove authorship of this or of any other poem, and Beers was able to prove its publication in *Harper's Magazine*. Lamenting over this struggle to authenticate authorship, Beers wrote in a private letter, "The poor 'Picket' has had so many claimants and willing sponsors that I sometimes question myself whether I did really write it that cool September morning after reading the stereotyped announcement, 'All Quiet,' etc, to which was added, in small type, 'A Picket Shot.'"

Beers continued to submit stories and verses to magazines, again primarily to the *New York Ledger*. Among her most popular writings were "Which Shall It Be?" a poem that deals, again in a somewhat sentimentalized fashion, with the issue of parents struggling to decide which of their children to give up for adoption. Other popular verses were "Weighing the Baby" and "Baby Looking Out for Me." Beers also authored *General Frankie: A Story for Little Folks* in 1863.

Although Beers was considered to be a happy, somewhat cheerful woman by nature who did not adhere to any particular superstitions, she was known to have one rather curious premonition: that if her poems were ever collected into a single volume, she would die upon their publication. Beers's collection of poetry, *All Quiet along the Potomac, and Other Poems*, was published in Philadelphia on 10 October 1879. One day later she died suddenly in her home in Orange, New Jersey. The cause of her death remains unknown.

• For a discussion on the authorship of "All Quiet along the Potomac," refer to James Woods Davidson's *The Living Writers of the South* (1869). See also the *New York Ledger*, 8 Nov. 1879 and 15 Nov. 1879. Obituaries are in the *New York Times*, 13 Oct. 1879, and the *New York Evening Post*, 14 Oct. 1879.

ALI LANG-SMITH

BEERY, Wallace (1 Apr. 1885–15 Apr. 1949), actor, was born Wallace Fitzgerald Beery in Kansas City, Missouri, the son of Noah Webster Beery, a policeman, and Margaret Fitzgerald. A tall, husky child (who was taunted with the name "Jumbo" by his classmates), Beery attended the Chase School through the fourth grade. A poor student, he became a frequent truant. In his early teens Beery ran away from home but voluntarily returned when his parents agreed that he could drop out of school permanently. Beery helped lay track for the Santa Fe Railroad and worked at the blast furnace of the Sheffield Nut and Bolt Co. before joining the Forepaugh-Sells Circus as an elephant handler at age sixteen. He was later employed in the same position by the Ringling Bros. Circus.

Dissatisfied with circus life, Beery moved to New York City in 1904 hoping to follow in the footsteps of his brother Noah, who was a chorus boy in musical comedies. Beery appeared in the chorus of *Babes in Toyland* (1905), *The Prince of Pilsen* (1905), and other productions. He first attracted attention when he temporarily replaced star Raymond Hitchcock in *A Yankee Tourist* (1907), a musical. For the next few years Beery toured in national productions of *A Yankee Tourist*, *The Prince of Pilsen*, and other musicals. During this period the 6′1″ Beery added even more weight to his already hefty physique and developed the burly, jowly look that would later become his trademark.

In 1913 Beery was in a production of *The Balkan Princess* that closed in Chicago. He then signed a $75-a-week contract with the Chicago-based Essanay motion picture company and made his screen debut in the one-reel farce *His Athletic Wife* (1913). For the next two years Beery stayed in Chicago and appeared in dozens of one-reel comedies for Essanay, including the *Sweedie* series in which he played a Swedish housemaid. A shortage of technical help at Essanay forced him to direct many of his early films. In 1915 Essanay sent Beery to Niles, California, to open a film studio. The venture quickly folded, and Beery moved to Hollywood to work in comedies for the Universal and Keystone film companies. In February 1916 he married Gloria Swanson, a young actress he had met while working for Essanay in Chicago. Swanson joined Beery in Hollywood where they both made films for Keystone. While her career flourished, his languished. They appeared together in *A Dash of Courage* (1916) and *Teddy at the Throttle* (1917), featuring the canine star Teddy. Beery and Swanson, who had no children, separated in June 1917 and divorced in December 1918.

Anti-German sentiment during World War I helped comedian Beery acquire a new screen persona as a villain. He played brush-cut, evil-doing "Huns" in *The Little American* (1917) and *Johanna Enlists* (1918), both starring Mary Pickford, and *The Unpardonable*

Sin (1919), starring Blanche Sweet. For the next few years Beery continued in the role of the "heavy" in films such as *The Last of the Mohicans* (1920) and Rex Ingram's *The Four Horsemen of the Apocalypse* (1921), with Rudolph Valentino. "There is no better screen blackguard than Wallace Beery. There may be more brutal ones on occasions, such as Louis Wolheim, but Beery for craft, conscienceless scheming, sinister flirtations and cold-blooded murders is probably at the top of the list of film villains," said the *New York Times* (17 Aug. 1924). He finally got to portray a heroic character in *Robin Hood* (1922), directed by Allan Dwan and starring Douglas Fairbanks as the title character with Beery as Richard the Lion-Hearted. A sequel, *Richard the Lion-Hearted* (1923), gave Beery his first starring role in a feature-length picture. The film was popular but did not establish Beery as a major star. Beery's other notable films of the 1920s are *The Sea Hawk* (1924); *So Big* (1925), a screen version of the Edna Ferber novel, *The Lost World* (1925); and *Old Ironsides* (1926).

In August 1924 Beery married Mary Arieta Gilman, an actress known professionally as Rita Gilman, who had played bit parts in *Robin Hood* and *The Sea Hawk*. The couple later adopted the orphaned daughter of one of Gilman's relatives.

Beery, who signed a contract with Paramount in 1925, returned to comedy in *Behind the Front* (1926), a popular takeoff on World War I dramas, costarring Raymond Hatton. Beery and Hatton then were reteamed in an increasingly lackluster series of similar comedies. Soon after making his first all-talking film *Chinatown Nights* (1929), Beery's contract with Paramount, along with that of many other silent era performers, was not renewed.

After a year of unemployment, Beery was hired by Metro-Goldwyn-Mayer (MGM) Pictures to replace the recently deceased Lon Chaney in *The Big House* (1930). Beery earned an Academy Award nomination for his performance as a thug who leads a prison revolt. Beery was then paired with comedienne Marie Dressler in *Min and Bill* (1930), a tear-jerking tale of a scruffy waterfront couple who fight to prevent Dressler's adopted daughter from being placed in a "proper" home. The low-budget picture became one of the biggest hits of the year, and Beery finally emerged as a major star. Beery's next important film was the sentimental *The Champ* (1931) in which he played a washed-up boxer who makes a comeback in order to win the respect of his young son (Jackie Cooper). Beery won the best actor Academy Award for *The Champ* (he shared the award with Fredric March of *Dr. Jekyll and Mr. Hyde*). Beery remained a top attraction with parts in two "all-star" productions, *Grand Hotel* (1932), a drama in which he played the villain, and *Dinner at Eight* (1933), a comedy in which he played the crude businessman husband of Jean Harlow. He worked with Dressler again in *Tugboat Annie* (1933), a popular follow-up to *Min and Bill*, and his portrayal of Mexican revolutionary leader Pancho Villa in *Viva Villa!* (1934) is regarded by many critics as

his finest screen performance. Other Beery films of this period are *Treasure Island* (1934), with Jackie Cooper; *The Mighty Barnum* (1934), in which he played the nineteenth-century impresario; and *Ah, Wilderness!* (1935), based on Eugene O'Neill's stage comedy.

Beery's gruff manner, reluctance to rehearse, and penchant for improvising dialogue caused many of his colleagues to find him "difficult." He paid little attention to Hollywood social life, preferring to spend time at his ranches in Wyoming and Idaho or piloting his own plane. After his divorce from Gilman in 1939, he successfully applied for custody of his adopted daughter.

In the late 1930s Beery's career went into decline. His roles were mostly tired reworkings of his earlier successes. MGM frequently loaned him to the newly formed and less prestigious 20th Century–Fox Pictures (in which some MGM executives had invested). Beery contributed to his own downfall by giving a number of lazy, uninspired performances. In an attempt to recapture the appeal of his films with Marie Dressler (who had died in 1934), MGM paired him with character actress Marjorie Main in a series of low-budget comedies. Other films in the later part of his career include *Stablemates* (1938), a racetrack yarn with Mickey Rooney; *The Man from Dakota* (1940), a Civil War drama with Delores Del Rio; and *A Date with Judy* (1948), a youth-oriented comedy in which he had top billing but actually played second fiddle to teenage stars Jane Powell and Elizabeth Taylor. Beery died at his home in Beverly Hills, California. His last film, *Big Jack* (1949), another in his series with Main, was released posthumously.

• Good sources of information on Beery's career are a profile by Alva Johnston in the *New Yorker*, 9 Nov. 1935, pp. 22–27, and a detailed article by Earl Anderson (with filmography by Richard E. Braff) in *Films in Review* 21 (June–July 1973): 330–57. See also David Shipman, *The Great Movie Stars: The Golden Years* (1995), and "Who's Who in the Films," *New York Times*, 18 Dec. 1932. An obituary is in the *New York Times*, 17 Apr. 1949.

MARY C. KALFATOVIC

BEHN, Sosthenes (30 Jan. 1884–6 June 1957), corporation executive, was born Louis Richard Sosthenes Behn in St. Thomas in what was then the Danish West Indies, the son of Ricardo Augusto Guillermo Behn, a businessman, and Louise Monsanto. Behn was educated in the Virgin Islands, Corsica, and at Collège Ste. Barbée in Paris. During the course of his education and travels, he became fluent in English, French, and Spanish. In 1898 Behn's family moved to New York City, where he found jobs as a messenger and later as a clerk. When Morton Trust Company, a Wall Street concern, rejected Behn for employment because he was too young, he grew a beard, changed his official birth date to 1882, and reapplied a few months later. This time he was hired and was eventually promoted to head clerk at the firm.

When he was sent to Puerto Rico on an assignment, Behn decided to remain there, where he worked with his older brother Hernand. In 1904 the two men founded their own banking and brokerage firm, Behn Brothers, with Sosthenes as president and chief operating officer. The brothers' entry into the telecommunications field was serendipitous and revealed Sosthenes's early talent at mergers and acquisitions. Although the precise date is uncertain, in 1905 or 1906 the brothers acquired South Puerto Rico Telephone from a client as payment for a debt. It was a small, rudimentary operation, but the Behn brothers parlayed their new acquisition into a profitable business and were able to merge it with the island's other telephone company, Puerto Rico General, to form Puerto Rico Telephone Company.

In 1916 the Behns took over the ailing Cuban Telephone Company and within two years turned it into a vibrant enterprise. With their reputations on the rise, Sosthenes and Hernand brought American Telephone and Telegraph to the bargaining table to form the Cuban-American Telephone and Telegraph Company; the objective was to lay a cable connecting Havana, Cuba, with Key West, Florida, which was achieved in 1919.

When the United States entered World War I, Behn immediately volunteered for the U.S. Army and was commissioned as a captain in the Signal Corps. In 1918 he saw action in France as commander of the 322d Field Signal Battalion. Promoted to lieutenant colonel, he received the Distinguished Service Medal from the United States and was recognized as a commander by the French Legion of Honor. Fiercely proud of his wartime achievements, Behn enjoyed being addressed as "Colonel Behn" for the rest of his life.

In 1920 Behn founded International Telephone and Telegraph (IT&T), offering investors in the new corporation partial ownership of the three companies it comprised (Puerto Rico Telephone, Cuban Telephone Company, and Cuban-American Telephone and Telegraph Company). By 1923 IT&T's shares were being traded on the New York Stock Exchange, and soon the company was established enough that Behn began a series of takeovers. He started in Spain, beating competition from Swedish and German companies to gain control of the country's government-owned telephone system, which was in poor condition. In order to manufacture telephone equipment in Spain, Behn purchased International Western Electric Corporation, AT&T's European subsidiary, renaming it International Standard Electric (ISE). Spain thus became the first European country to entrust its national telephone network to private hands. The acquisition of the Spanish telephone network, combined with the resources of ISE, turned IT&T from a small utility into a large concern that could both manufacture and operate telecommunications systems on a national scale. This new status emboldened Behn and put him in a position of strength as he sought new acquisitions.

Behn subsequently embarked on a flurry of takeovers. He gained control of the Mexican Telephone and Telegraph Company, the smaller of two competing telecommunications operations in Mexico. In 1927 he purchased All America Cables, which maintained telegraphic cables between the United States and Latin America and which he used as a beachhead to obtain additional concessions in the latter. Over the next two years he acquired a half dozen of South America's telephone companies in countries such as Uruguay, Chile, Brazil, and Argentina. He also expanded IT&T's holdings by gaining control of manufacturing interests in Austria, Hungary, and Yugoslavia. In 1928 Behn made two significant transactions, gaining control of Creed & Company, Ltd., a British maker of teleprinters, and acquiring Mackay Company, which operated telecommunications firms that included Postal Telegraph and Commercial Cable, a company that maintained several transoceanic cables connecting the United States with Europe and several Pacific islands. By the end of the 1920s—within less than a decade—Behn had achieved what he referred to as the "International System," a worldwide telecommunications corporation. IT&T was the archetype of the American multinational corporation, and Behn had established himself as a global businessman.

But IT&T fell on hard times during the Great Depression. Behn, mistakenly believing that the economic prosperity of the 1920s would continue, fell into debt with his whirlwind of acquisitions. With the 1929 stock market crash, IT&T's stock collapsed, and Wall Street investors' confidence in the corporation plummeted. Instead of expanding, IT&T began contracting, sloughing off operations, and closing doors at some firms. A personal blow to Behn came in 1933, when his brother and longtime business partner Hernand died. He was devastated by this loss and wore a black armband for over a year. After Hernand's death, Behn managed IT&T by himself and displayed remarkable sangfroid during the fiscal crisis, paring back expenses and instituting economies that pulled IT&T from the brink of bankruptcy. By 1936, as the U.S. economy improved, IT&T's financial situation had stabilized.

But World War II dealt another blow to Behn's international empire. Fearful of having IT&T's European telephone operations confiscated or ruined, Behn reluctantly decided to retrench operations abroad, concentrating instead on manufacturing operations in the United States. His goal for the company changed, envisioning it now as an industrial giant. Intent on producing military products for the government, Behn revamped one of his corporations to form the Federal Telephone and Radio Laboratories (Federal), constructing new facilities in New York and New Jersey. This operation, which produced devices such as telephone receivers and radio transmitters, grew rapidly and was soon IT&T's largest and most profitable firm.

A significant part of IT&T's restructuring during the 1940s involved selling off some of its foreign holdings. In 1941 Behn sold Romana de Telefoane to the Romanian government for $13.8 million. In 1945 the Spanish government bought IT&T's telephone network in Spain for $83 million, and the following year the Juan Perón government bought River Plate, IT&T's major utility in Argentina, for $94 million.

At the end of World War II, Behn was in his sixties but had no plans to retire. He wanted to acquire a domestic company to complement Federal, whose military contracts were depleted after the war. Behn assumed the title of chairman of IT&T, in addition to that of president, perhaps to heighten his stature as he sought a new acquisition. But in 1947 his leadership was challenged when a group of stockholders led by Clendenin Ryan revolted, charging Behn with incompetent management and withholding payment from stockholders. Behn was able to beat back the insurgency, but he had to make concessions that weakened his hold over IT&T, among them accommodating new stockholders and a new president, William Harrison, who were largely inimical to Behn's goals (Behn retained the title of chairman and chief executive officer). A particular area of conflict was Behn's domestic orientation; Harrison preferred to expand operations in Europe, and stockholders supported him. The clash reduced Behn's influence, and he was stripped of some corporate perquisites, such as his private limosine. These untoward developments caused Behn's confidence and influence to wane.

What further damaged Behn's position in the corporation was the failure of his new ventures. In 1949 he obtained a firm to complement Federal, Capehart-Farnsworth Television and Radio, which had a weak product line and was a risky venture. Behn also acquired the Coolerator Company, a subsidiary of Gibson Refrigerator, and poured millions of dollars into the company to develop new products. These new ventures fared poorly and repudiated Behn's business strategy. In 1954, under pressure to step aside, Behn agreed on a compromise to diminish his profile at IT&T, retaining the title of chairman but assuming a ceremonial role, while Harrison was elevated to president and chief executive officer. In 1956 Behn resigned as chairman, becoming an honorary chairman.

Behn had married Margaret Dunlap of Philadelphia in 1921. They had three children. He had become a naturalized citizen of the United States in 1927. Behn died in St. Luke's Hospital in New York City.

• Robert Sobel, *ITT: The Management of Opportunity* (1982), provides considerable information on Behn's life and work. *Current Biography* featured Behn in its 1947 volume. Obituaries are in the *New York Times*, 7 June 1957, and *Time* and *Newsweek*, 17 June 1957.

YANEK MIECZKOWSKI

BEHRENS, Henry (16 Dec. 1815–17 Oct. 1895), Roman Catholic priest and religious administrator, was born in Münstadt, Hanover, Germany. His parents' names are unknown, and he kept no record of his family or early years. In 1832 he entered the novitiate of the German province of the Society of Jesus (Jesuits) at Estavayer-le-Lac, Switzerland. He was ordained a priest on 7 August 1842.

Until the outbreak in 1847 of the Swiss civil war, Behrens served as dean of discipline and taught mathematics at St. Michael's College in Fribourg. When federal troops invaded the college, he disguised himself as a federal officer and was able to save some Jesuit property. But the entire order was expelled from Switzerland, and he was put in charge of a group of forty-one who fled to the United States aboard the ship *Providence*, arriving in New York after a forty-day voyage. The trip was hastily planned, none of them spoke English, and they were not expected by the French Jesuits who ran two colleges in New York.

In a report to his superior in Germany, Behrens wrote that the expedition had been badly managed. He finally succeeded in placing the refugees in Jesuit institutions on the East Coast and in the Midwest and then returned to Europe. Assigned to work in Westphalia in Prussia's Rhine provinces, he made his final profession of vows on 2 February 1850 and was named director of novices for the German province. In 1851 he became rector of the novitiate, located at Friedrichsburg, a suburb of Münster. He became a widely known spiritual counselor to the Rhenish Catholic nobility, where his image was that of a strong, severe, stern man, very stiff and formal, yet widely sought after.

In 1856 Behrens became provincial superior of the Jesuits in the German states and "guided the province with a firm hand" for a single three-year term. His successor wrote that Behrens had done "a great deal for the province's material advancement" and "put discipline on a proper basis." He again took up direction of the Friedrichsburg novitiate and added direction of young priests in their final year of spiritual training. During Prussia's wars with Denmark (1864) and Austria (1866), he organized Catholic chaplaincy services for the Prussian troops. In the Franco-Prussian War (1870–1871), he supervised the Jesuit priests, seminarians, and brothers who tended the wounded at military hospitals in France, but the Prussian king (later emperor) and his chief minister Otto von Bismarck opposed employment of Jesuits in the camps and hospitals and entrusted the work to the Protestant Knights of St. John, assisted by the Catholic Knights of Malta. Behrens, with the help of influential friends among the Rhenish Catholic nobility, however, fought successfully for the admission of Jesuits and Catholic sisters to the service. He also organized and monitored the security of trainloads of bandages and other medical supplies collected by Catholic women's organizations for the troops. After peace was declared Behrens was invited to ride to Berlin on Bismarck's train and was awarded the Iron Cross. But with the "Jesuit law" of 4 July 1872, Behrens was, with his fellow Jesuits, expelled from Germany. Bismarck's "Kulturkampf," his "culture conflict" with the Roman Catholic church, inaugurated for German Jesuits a 45-year-exile from their homeland that lasted until 1917.

Behrens was assigned to the German mission based in Buffalo, New York, where in 1870, Canisius College had been opened. On 22 December 1872 he became superior of the mission and rector of the fledgling college. The general superior of the Jesuits in Rome believed the Germans had been too hasty in opening the Buffalo college, which had been done without his permission, but wrote hopefully to Behrens that his "own practical sense" would put things right. Behrens was not sanguine, commenting that the situation was "as if in building a new house one were to put up the roof first," but he set to the task with a will. Staffing was inadequate, and most of the German priests spoke no English. Behrens began at the age of fifty-six studying English. His personality was "indeed strong and sturdy, at times bordering on harshness," one observer noted, while another commented of an address to the student body, "There was certainly nothing of the honey that attracts flies about Father Rector's speech this morning." But others remarked on his "great prudence and efficiency in administration." Behrens complained of anti-German prejudice among Irish priests but during his time in office "Irishers" came to account for 20 percent of the student body.

Ill health caused Behrens to be removed from both his offices in 1876, and he spent the next ten years in pastoral work, a familiar figure in Buffalo's orphanages, hospitals, and correctional institutions. He became popular with the Irish, who called him "Father Burns," and he was spiritual adviser to Bishop Stephen V. Ryan of Buffalo, who said of him, "I have a saint in my diocese, and his name is Father Behrens." Reappointed mission superior in 1886, he served until 1892.

In short order, Behrens founded St. Ignatius College (now John Carroll University and St. Ignatius High School) in Cleveland, Ohio (1886), and opened two missions for Native Americans, St. Francis among the Brulé Sioux on Rosebud Reservation (1887) and Holy Rosary among the Oglala Sioux at Pine Ridge (1888), both in South Dakota. To staff these missions he closed Sacred Heart College in Prairie du Chien, Wisconsin, turning it into a seminary. Influenza forced him into retirement in 1893 and two years later he died in Buffalo.

• Official reports from Behrens are in the Roman Archive of the Society of Jesus, Rome, Italy. An obituary notice, "Father Henry Behrens: A Sketch," is in an internal Jesuit publication, *Woodstock Letters* 25 (1896): 385–404. He is mentioned passim in Charles A. Brady, *Canisius College: The First Hundred Years* (1969); Gilbert J. Garraghan, *The Jesuits of the Middle United States* (3 vols., 1984); Donald P. Gavin, *John Carroll University: A Century of Service* (1985); and Thomas E. Harney, *Canisius College: The First Nine Years, 1870–1879* (1971).

JAMES HENNESEY

BEHRMAN, Martin (14 Oct. 1864–12 Jan. 1926), mayor of New Orleans, Louisiana, was born in New York City, the son of working-class German-Jewish parents, Henry Behrman, a cigar maker, and Frederica (maiden name unknown). The family moved to New Orleans when Martin was seven months old. His father died while his son was still too young to remember him in later years. His mother ran a dry goods

stand in the Quarter's French Market after her husband's death. She died in 1876 leaving Behrman an orphan at twelve.

After his mother's death he went to live with a relative on the west bank in a section of the city known as Algiers and quit school to work as an assistant cashier in a thrift store. Sometime during his youth he converted to Catholicism. His education consisted of about five years of schooling in a German-American private school and in public school. From his job he saved enough money to attend night school for several years, giving him the equivalent of an elementary school education. During the next decade Behrman moved into the grocery business as a clerk and traveling salesman. He briefly ran his own grocery with a partner, Peter Lawton, in 1887. That same year he married Julia Collins, daughter of John P. Collins of Cincinnati, Ohio, who was a friend of the Lawton family. The Behrmans had eleven children, only two of whom lived to be adults. They lived in a modest cottage in Algiers throughout their married life.

When the Behrman-Lawton store proved unprofitable, Behrman gave it up to take several jobs as a salesman in the wholesale grocery business. He believed that his experience as a salesman was invaluable in politics. In 1888 he was named secretary of the Fifteenth District campaign in Algiers to elect Francis T. Nicholls governor. After Nicholls's election, Behrman was given the post of deputy assessor of the city's Fifteenth District (Algiers). In addition, he was called on to help with assessments on the city's east bank in the First District (the main business district), thus putting him in contact with many prominent businessmen. Steadily, Behrman was making contacts in politics and business that would aid him in his career. To supplement his income, he took the census of Algiers in 1890. Through his knowledge of English, French, and some German, he could converse easily in the city's main language groups.

During John Fitzpatrick's term as mayor (1892–1896), Behrman served as clerk to the three most important city council committees: budget, public order, and streets and landings. He held this job until 1896. It was ideal training in city government. In the 1892 election Behrman was also elected to the school board and served three successive terms (1892–1904) on that body. In the 1896 election he ran for the state legislature but was defeated. However, the new governor, Murphy J. Foster, appointed him assessor for the Fifth District. He was reappointed to this post in 1900 by Governor William W. Heard. When stalwarts of the regular or Ring faction of the city's Democratic party regrouped in 1897 and established the Choctaw Club, Behrman was chosen to serve on its caucus. Eventually he became the leader of this political organization, which dominated city politics in the early twentieth century.

In 1898 Behrman was elected a delegate to the Louisiana Constitutional Convention, which disenfranchised the black population of the state through various voting requirements such as property qualifications and literacy tests. Behrman's attitude toward the blacks of New Orleans (who made up 27.1 percent of the total population by 1900) was openly racist and reflected the rising intolerance of many whites in Louisiana by the end of the century when Jim Crow laws began to come into effect in the state. He considered the voting restrictions against blacks in the 1898 constitution that he had helped to draft to be "the best thing done for Louisiana in my time."

In 1904 Behrman was elected state auditor, but he vacated that post to run for mayor of New Orleans, which he won. He was reelected mayor in three consecutive elections: 1908, 1912, and 1916. On the state level, as a Choctaw Club leader, member of the state Democratic Central Committee, and mayor of the largest city in the state, he was a powerful behind-the-scenes influence on the early twentieth-century governors Newton C. Blanchard, Jared Y. Sanders, and Ruffin G. Pleasant from 1904 to 1920. As mayor, Behrman concentrated on civic improvements for New Orleans; public-operated drainage and sewerage were installed, and the municipal waterworks came into operation. A vigorous campaign by municipal and federal authorities was carried on during the 1905 yellow fever epidemic to eliminate mosquitoes, carriers of the disease. Behrman also cooperated with businessmen and state officials to achieve construction of the riverfront Public Belt Railroad.

Behrman's greatest failing was his inability to accept political reforms such as civil service and to understand the motivations of opponents who were socially prominent reformers. In his memoirs, which first appeared in the New Orleans *Item* and later were edited by John R. Kemp and published in book form (1977), he calls such reformers "silk stockings" and defines the term as anyone "who knew all about municipal government because he read magazines and books and the *Life of Jefferson* and did not know where to file his complaint if the garbage man did not come around early enough to suit him" (Kemp, p. 108). Behrman nevertheless was adroit at drawing business and professional men into city affairs and always showed a talent for compromise when working with them. He was equally successful in getting the support of white labor leaders. He backed up the waterfront unions in their confrontations with steamship agents and stevedores in 1907, 1917, 1919, and 1920. Ill and out of touch with public opinion, Behrman was defeated in his fifth mayoral campaign in 1920. Some of the issues that caused his rejection at the polls included his longtime toleration of the red-light district, Storyville, until local reformers and the secretary of the navy forced city government to abolish it, his stubborn rejection of civil service, and his continued support for the outmoded ward-boss system of politics. In assessing his loss, he explained it in simple terms: "No matter what you do in public life, you still make enemies. Sixteen years of enemies is a lot of them" (Kemp, p. 316). In 1925, despite failing health, Behrman ran again and won his fifth and last term as mayor of New Orleans. He died there after only one year back in office.

In eulogies after his death, Behrman received praise from colleagues and critics alike. The *Times-Picayune*, which had always been critical of his methods but usually approved of his objectives, summed up his qualities best in calling him "a kindly citizen, a forceful leader,—and a municipal servant who made the most of his opportunities for service to the city he loved as it was given him to see and use those opportunities." Essentially he was an honest machine boss—shrewd, calculating, and tough-minded in his politics but sincerely dedicated to municipal government and public improvements.

• The most important source on Behrman is his memoirs, which appeared in the New Orleans *Item* between 22 Oct. and 25 Mar. 1923. John R. Kemp edited the memoirs, wrote an introduction and epilogue, and published them in 1977 under the title *Martin Behrman of New Orleans: Memoirs of a City Boss*. Another significant work that devotes an entire chapter to Behrman is George M. Reynolds, *Machine Politics in New Orleans, 1897–1926* (1936). William Ivy Hair, *Bourbonism and Agrarian Protest: Louisiana Politics, 1877–1900* (1969), covers politics in Louisiana during the early period of Behrman's career. Harold Zink, *City Bosses in the United States: A Study of Twenty Municipal Bosses* (1930), allows comparisons to be drawn between Behrman and the other politicians discussed in the book. John S. Kendall, *History of New Orleans* (3 vols., 1922), is old but is still the most detailed history of the city and its municipal government during Behrman's first four administrations. Eric Arnesen, *Waterfront Workers of New Orleans, 1863–1923* (1991), is a detailed history of the development of labor unions on the docks and sheds light on a topic not mentioned elsewhere too often: Behrman's relations with labor. See also a brief but well-written description of Behrman and his regime by Herman B. Deutsch, "New Orleans Politics—The Greatest Free Show on Earth," in *The Past as Prelude: New Orleans, 1718–1968* (1968), ed. Hodding Carter. An obituary is in the New Orleans *Times-Picayune*, 13 Jan. 1926.

JOY J. JACKSON

BEHRMAN, S. N. (9 June? 1893–9 Sept. 1973), playwright and essayist, was born Samuel Nathaniel Behrman in Worcester, Massachusetts, the son of Joseph Behrman, a teacher of Hebrew, and Zelda Feingold, soon after their immigration from Lithuania. Because no birth record survived, Behrman selected his own birthdate. Living in a tenement in a Yiddish-speaking neighborhood, Joseph Behrman studied the Talmud relentlessly and instructed children in Hebrew. In 1903, at about ten years of age, his son Samuel Nathaniel chanced to hear a presidential campaign address by Socialist Laborite candidate Eugene V. Debs at Worcester's Mechanics' Hall and remarked later that although he had been too young to understand the economic implications of Debs's remarks, it nevertheless "gave to all my later life an orientation it would otherwise not have had—a bias in favor of those who suffered from cruelty and callousness." Behrman eventually aligned himself with the Clark College (Worcester) Socialist Club, and his continuing commitment to humanism, coupled with a skepticism toward capitalism, is evident in his depression-era, socially oriented high comedies *Meteor* (1929), *Biography* (1932), and *Wine of Choice* (1938).

Without his parents' knowledge, Behrman at twelve passed four days in New York's theatrical district with a fellow classmate from Worcester's Classical High School. General ill health obliged him to interrupt his secondary education for two years and instead haunt the Worcester Free Public Library, where he read the unlikely combination of Horatio Alger and Shakespeare—diverse but significant influences toward his incipient life in letters. So too, Behrman at sixteen witnessed a Sigmund Freud lecture at Clark College in 1909. After a limited tour with the Poli vaudeville circuit in 1911, he studied psychology under G. Stanley Hall at Clark, where he enrolled as a special student in 1912, and thereafter submitted essays such as "Psychology and the New Philosophy of the Theatre" to the undergraduate *Clark College Monthly*. Although Behrman grew active in oratorical competition and public debate at Clark, he was suspended for refusing to register for physical education courses. He enrolled in Harvard summer school during his suspension, returned to Clark, declared a major in literature, and then with the aid of two scholarships returned to Harvard to register for George Pierce Baker's famous English 47 playwriting course and for Charles Townsend Copeland's composition class, which drew upon passages from the King James Bible as a rhetorical cornerstone.

Behrman's first commercial success occurred in 1915 when he sold a story called "La Vie Parisienne" to the *Smart Set*, edited by George Jean Nathan and H. L. Mencken. Unable to find work after graduation from Harvard in 1916, Behrman took a master's degree at Columbia in 1918, worked as an ad typist and book reviewer for the *New York Times* until 1920, wrote more short fiction, and became a public relations representative for a Texas oil man and for publishers Ben Huebsch and Thomas Seltzer. By 1921 he collaborated on the writing of short stories and some ultimately unproduced plays with Indiana prose writer and playwright J. Kenyon Nicholson, and in 1926 formed another coauthorship with established playwright Owen Davis. That year he arranged a pre-Broadway tryout of *The Second Man* (the first of his twenty New York plays) and was on his way to developing a reputation as a writer of socially conscious dramas and high, sophisticated comedy. He formed a lasting association with *New Yorker* editor Harold Ross in 1929 and became a lifelong contributor to the magazine. His plays *Serena Blandish* and *Meteor* opened in 1929, and in 1930 alone he wrote Hollywood scripts for such films as *Liliom* (based on the 1909 Ferenc Molnar play), *The Sea Wolf*, *Lightnin'*, and *He Knew Women*—a film version of *The Second Man*. Although the *New York Times* derisively called Behrman "the Molnar of Malibu Beach," he still remained active in the theater with *Brief Moment* (1931), *Biography* (1932), *Rain from Heaven* (1934), and *End of Summer* (1936).

Behrman married Elza Heifetz, sister of violin virtuoso Jascha Heifetz, in 1937, and their only child was born in Salzburg a year later, when Behrman joined Robert Sherwood, Maxwell Anderson, Elmer Rice, and Sidney Howard in forming the Playwright's Company. While he was writing scripts for Greta Garbo at MGM in 1939, his *No Time for Comedy* opened, followed by *The Talley Method* (1941), *The Pirate* (1942), and *Jacobowsky and the Colonel* (1944). Behrman's postwar plays, upstaged by his growing reputation as a prose writer, included *Dunnigan's Daughter* (1945), *I Know My Love* (1949), *Jane* (1952), *Fanny* (1954), *The Cold Wind and the Warm* (1958), *Lord Pengo* (1962), and *But for Whom Charlie* (1964). Probably his best work, at least after the 1930s, is in prose pieces like *Duveen* (1952), *The Worcester Account* (1954), *Portrait of Max* (1960), *The Suspended Drawing Room* (his only novel, in 1965), *The Burning Glass* (1968), and his memoirs, *People in a Diary* (1972). Behrman died in New York. He is best remembered today as a man of considerable charm and social grace whose work reflects those characteristics. His early penchant for leftist political posturing mellowed into a moderately liberal stance in his last decade.

• Behrman's manuscripts, along with letters, reviews, playbills, and related materials, are on deposit at the State Historical Society of Wisconsin in Madison. Lewis Williams Heniford's comprehensive and readable "S. N. Behrman as a Social Dramatist" (Ph.D. diss., Stanford Univ., 1964) assembles most of what was known about Behrman at that time. Kenneth T. Reed's *S. N. Behrman* (1975) carries his career and bibliography to the end of his life. William Klink's *S. N. Behrman: The Major Plays* (1978) offers somewhat more recent critical perspectives. An obituary is in the *New York Times*, 24 Sept. 1973.

KENNETH T. REED

BEIDERBECKE, Bix (10 Mar. 1903–6 Aug. 1931), musician, was born Leon Bix Beiderbecke in Davenport, Iowa, the son of Bismarck Herman Beiderbecke, a coal and lumber dealer, and Agatha Jane Hilton. The youngest of three children in a well-to-do musical family, Beiderbecke was only seven when he achieved local fame for his ability to sit at the piano and play by ear virtually any tune of the day. At age fifteen, having come under the spell of the music of the riverboat bands and the Original Dixieland Jazz Band, he acquired a cornet and resolved to master the instrument on his own. He quickly became fluent enough to play jobs with other young musicians. His father and mother, distressed over his increasing preoccupation with jazz and his corresponding loss of interest in academic studies, enrolled him in Lake Forest Academy, a boarding school near Chicago. Beiderbecke made a poor adjustment to the school, however, and was compelled to withdraw. At age nineteen he thus was launched on a career as a jazz hornman.

Late 1923 found Beiderbecke with the Wolverine Orchestra, an eight-piece group that soon became the rage among collegiate jazz fans in the Midwest. The band's records for the Gennett label—Beiderbecke's first recordings—and the band's appearance at the Cinderella Ballroom in New York left no doubt that the cornetist was an emerging talent of major stature. Beiderbecke quit the Wolverines in October 1924 to join the highly regarded big band of Jean Goldkette in Detroit. Although his improvised solo work was as impressive as ever, his lack of experience in sight reading led to his being fired in a matter of weeks.

Beiderbecke was very much the itinerant in 1925–1926. He gigged with Merton "Bromo" Sulser's Iowa Collegians in Iowa City and, for a mere eighteen days, was even an "unclassified" student at the university there. After a short stay in New York, where he sat in with the California Ramblers (which at that time included Jimmy and Tommy Dorsey and Red Nichols), he went to Chicago and joined the band of pianist Charley Straight. Some summer work with small Goldkette groups at resort areas in Michigan was followed by a long engagement in St. Louis with Frank Trumbauer's band. Both Beiderbecke and Trumbauer, a respected saxophonist, became regular members of the full Goldkette orchestra in May 1926. When Goldkette split his band into two units for the summer season, Beiderbecke played in the one under Trumbauer's leadership at Hudson Lake, Indiana.

The reconstituted Goldkette orchestra that made its debut in the fall of 1926 was perhaps the finest white jazz-oriented big band of the era. Outstanding arrangements by Bill Challis effectively showcased the solo capabilities of the band's hot men, among whom Beiderbecke was preeminent. Of the many records the band made for Victor, none shows Beiderbecke and the ensemble to better advantage than "Clementine (from New Orleans)," recorded only three days before Goldkette disbanded the group in New York on 18 September 1927.

With the dissolution of the Goldkette orchestra, Beiderbecke, Trumbauer, and other Goldkette sidemen joined the band organized by Adrian Rollini for the opening of the Club New Yorker. The nightclub failed in less than a month, whereupon Beiderbecke and Trumbauer became featured soloists with Paul Whiteman, the "King of Jazz." Whiteman's orchestra, comprising some thirty instrumentalists and vocalists, was a commercial dance and concert organization, not an authentic jazz band. However, Whiteman was the most successful bandleader in America. He admired jazz musicians, employing several at a time, and paid very well for their services. Moreover, both on records and in public performances, he gave his ad-lib men frequent opportunities to swing. Some of Beiderbecke's best choruses are to be heard on such Whiteman recordings as "China Boy," "Dardanella," "From Monday On," "You Took Advantage of Me," and "Sweet Sue."

Beiderbecke left Whiteman in September 1929. His health undermined by chronic alcohol abuse, he entered the Keeley Institute in Dwight, Illinois, for treatment of his addiction. He returned to his Davenport home after being discharged and, for some months, gigged with various local bands before heading for New York again. In 1930–1931 he played the "Camel Pleasure Hour" radio show and took part in recording sessions and college engagements with the Dorsey brothers and Benny Goodman. A four-day tryout with the Casa Loma Orchestra came to naught. Beiderbecke never married. He died in his apartment in Queens, a victim of lobar pneumonia and the effects of alcoholism.

Despite the brevity of the mature phase of his career, Beiderbecke is an immortal of jazz, a man whose life has assumed almost mythic proportions. Celebrated musicians who had the good fortune to hear him in his prime have characterized him as "the master," a "once-in-a-million artist." Equally enthusiastic jazz critics and historians have seen in him "the first real modernist in jazz," "a musical genius," "the great romantic legend of American jazz," and "the first great white jazz musician." Possessed of a stunningly pure, burnished tone, Beiderbecke brought to jazz a virtually unparalleled lyricism and poignancy. Harmonically, he operated at a level of sophistication that eluded the majority of his cohorts. These qualities grace the full chorus he played on Trumbauer's 1927 recording of "Singin' the Blues," a solo universally regarded as one of the great moments in recorded jazz. Beiderbecke was the composer of "Davenport Blues" (still in the repertoire of traditionalists) and of four compositions for piano that reflect something of his deep interest in modern classical music: "Flashes," "Candlelights," "In the Dark," and the famous "In a Mist."

• The definitive Beiderbecke biography is Richard M. Sudhalter et al., *Bix: Man and Legend* (1974), a prodigious effort that relies exclusively on primary sources. Additional biographical details and interpretive material may be found in Charles H. Wareing and George Garlick, *Bugles for Beiderbecke* (1958); Ralph Berton, *Remembering Bix: A Memoir of the Jazz Age* (1974); and Chip Deffaa, *Voices of the Jazz Age* (1990), pp. 52–105. Both Burnett James, *Bix Beiderbecke* (1959), and Richard Hadlock, *Jazz Masters of the Twenties* (1965), pp. 76–105, offer carefully considered analyses of Beiderbecke's musicianship and assess his impact on the development of jazz. Two feature-length films on Beiderbecke deserve mention: *Bix* (1981), directed by Brigitte Berman, a superior documentary; and *Bix: An Interpretation of a Legend* (1990), directed by Pupi Avati, a dramatic rendering of the cornetist's life that features meticulous musical recreations but departs egregiously from established facts. So far as is known, Beiderbecke himself appeared only once in a sound film, a very brief newsreel piece on the occasion of Paul Whiteman's move from Victor to Columbia Records. This treasured clip, showing Beiderbecke standing and playing through an ensemble brass passage, is the highlight of the video compilation *At the Jazz Band Ball* (1993). All of Beiderbecke's extant recordings have been brought together in the superb collection *Sincerely, Bix Beiderbecke* (1988). An obituary is in the *Davenport Democrat*, 7 Aug. 1931.

STEVEN M. KANE

BEISSEL, Johann Conrad (1 Mar. 1692–6 July 1768), religious leader, was born in Eberbach, Baden-Württemberg, Germany, the son of Matthias Beissel, a baker, and Anna (maiden name unknown). He was baptized George Konrad Beissel. His alcoholic father died two months before his birth; his mother died when he was eight or nine. Conrad Beissel was raised by his older brothers and sisters. Possibly because of recent French depredation of the area where they lived, his family was very poor. Conrad was undernourished and remained comparatively small. According to tradition, he performed remarkably well during his brief attendance at his parish school. Nevertheless, he was largely self-educated. While still a youth, Beissel was apprenticed to a master baker, who also was a capable fiddler who taught Beissel to play the violin. Beissel became a popular performer and played at weddings, country dances, and other joyful occasions. He enjoyed the notoriety and attention, especially from women.

Beissel grew to adulthood as the religious movement of Pietism, with its emphasis on prayer, Bible reading, and pious living, was spreading through his native Palatinate. Turning away from the frivolous festivities at which he had played his fiddle, he began to attend Pietist conventicles and associate with radical Pietists. These activities resulted in his banishment from the Palatinate, depriving him of both home and livelihood. After taking refuge with several Pietistic groups, he emigrated from Europe in 1720. With this background, it was almost inevitable that Beissel would seek Pietistic groups in America. After landing in Boston, he went directly to Germantown in Pennsylvania to join the Pietistic hermits who in 1694, on the Wissahickon Creek, had founded the Society of the Woman of the Wilderness. By the time Beissel arrived, however, most of the members had died or left the group. He then accepted the invitation of the Dunkard (German Baptist) leader Peter Becker to join his household and learn the weaver's trade from him. With Becker, Beissel hoped to revive the Dunkards' languishing spirituality, and he participated in Dunkard revivals during the 1720s.

Beissel became disillusioned with the Dunkards and moved west into the interior of Pennsylvania, probably in an attempt to meditate and pray without distraction. His association with the Dunkards and his charismatic personality made it impossible for him to enjoy the solitary life, however. By the early 1730s followers had gathered around him at a place that he called Ephrata on the Cocalico Creek in the Conastoga region. Forming a community of Seventh Day Baptists, they constructed communal dwellings for single women and men. Married couples lived in cabins on the fringe of the settlement. All were to remain celibate upon entering the community, consistent with Beissel's assertion that sexual intercourse was debilitating spiritually and physically. Ephrata's economy was communal, prosperous, and increasingly commercial, a result of the members' industriousness in agriculture; milling of grain, linseed oil, and wood; manufacture of textiles and paper; and printing of books. The buildings necessary to these activities were constructed adjacent to the dwellings. When prosperity threatened to undermine the members' spirituality, in 1745 Beissel reduced the economy practically to a subsistence level,

exiling Israel and Samuel Eckerling, brothers who were the community's leading economic promoters.

Beissel's primary emphasis was on spiritual development, not financial profit. He promised the Skippack Mennonites that the Ephrata printery would publish their *Martyr-Spiegel* (Martyrs' Mirror) without requiring them to purchase a minimum number of copies. Appearing in 1748, with more than 1,500 pages, it was the largest book printed in America before 1800. The printery also turned out the *Turtle-Taube* (Turtle Dove), which contained more than 400 of the community's hymns, most of which Beissel wrote. He is said to have written more than 4,000 lines of poetry, almost all of it religious, some of it set to music that he composed. For the community's worship, he developed distinctive types of choral harmony and antiphonal singing, and he frequently required the members to sing in this style on late night walks around Ephrata. In order to avoid pride and temptation, which he feared accompanied the appearance of human flesh, he required both women and men to wear hoods, women to veil their faces, and men to wear cowls similar to those of Capuchin monks. Ceilings in most buildings were low, not only because Beissel was short but also to force members to stoop in humility. Beissel required that the members make regular reports of their spiritual progress; he read the reports publicly and published some. At the community's numerical peak in the 1750s, it included about 350 residents.

Both within and without Ephrata, Beissel aroused controversy. His opposition to the institution of marriage early divided his congregation, as did his refusal to tolerate the community's money-making industries. His adoption of the Jewish sabbath and work on Sunday violated provincial laws and aroused the opposition of civil officials. That women left their husbands and homes to be with Beissel produced their husbands' ever-lasting hostility and even provoked one to attack Beissel physically. Beissel's willingness to permit women to spend nights in his cabin and his initial housing of men and women in the same building led to rumors of sexual promiscuity that prompted a neighbor to try to set fire to the cloister. As war between Great Britain and France resumed in the mid-1750s, provincial officials suspected that the liturgical music and monkish garb of Ephrata's residents masked their alliance with the Catholic French. When the British stationed troops there, Beissel assuaged their fears by sharing the contents of his well-stocked wine cellar with the officers. Opposition and declining health undermined Beissel's leadership, and his community began to decline well before his death in his cabin in the Ephrata cloister. Only the buildings and a few of the members remained by the early nineteenth century.

Nevertheless, Beissel stands out as an example of the intensely spiritual individuals who characterized dissenting religious movements in the western world, and especially Pennsylvania, during the eighteenth century. Beissel's Ephrata was one of the best-known religious communities of its time, attracting to its cloisters prominent people—both the spiritual as members and the curious as visitors. Beissel's German-language poetry has not received the attention it deserves. Scholars do study the music that he wrote and arranged, as well as the art that he inspired. The Pennsylvania Historical and Museum Commission has restored the community's buildings and administers the site for tourists to see and hear what Beissel and his followers did at Ephrata.

• Beissel left no diary, letters, or records. The major source of information about him is Lamech and Agrippa, *Chronicon Ephratense: A History of the Community of the Seventh Day Baptists at Ephrata*, trans. and ed. J. Max Hart (1889; repr. 1972), which was originally published in German (1786). "Agrippa" was John Peter Miller, Beissel's assistant, who became superintendent after Beissel's death. "Lamech" may have been Jacob Gass, but this is not certain. Additional primary material can be found in Peter Erb, ed., *Johann Conrad Beissel and the Ephrata Community; Mystical and Historical Texts* (1985). E. Gordon Alderfer, *The Ephrata Commune: An Early American Counterculture* (1985), contains an informative account of Beissel's early life, spiritual development, and leadership of his community. His "Conrad Beissel and the Ephrata Experiment," *American-German Review* 21, no. 6 (1955): 23–25, also is informative. Other works on Beissel include Walter C. Klein, *Johann Conrad Beissel: Mystic and Martinet, 1690–1768* (1941; repr. 1972); Lloyd G. Blakely, "Johann Beissel and the Music of the Ephrata Cloister," *Journal of Research in Music Education* 15 (Summer 1967): 120–38; Julius Friedrich Sachse, "The Music of the Ephrata Cloister; also Conrad Beissel's Preface to the 'Turtle Taube' of 1747," *Proceedings and Addresses of the Pennsylvania German Society* 12 (1902): 5–108; Samuel W. Pennypacker, "The Quarrel between Christopher Sower and Conrad Beissel," *Pennsylvania Magazine of History and Biography* 12 (1888): 76–96; and Guy Tilgham Holliday and Christopher E. Schweitzer, "The Present State of Conrad Beissel/Ephrata Research," *Monatschefte* 68 (Summer 1976): 171–78. The most complete but not entirely reliable treatment of the Ephrata cloisters appears in Sachse, *German Sectarians of Pennsylvania, 1708–1800* (1899; repr. 1970). James E. Ernst, "Ephrata: A History," *Pennsylvania German Folklore Society* 25 (1963), and Felix E. Reichman and Eugene S. Doll, "Ephrata as Seen by Contemporaries," *Pennsylvania German Folklore Society* 17 (1952), also contain much information on Beissel.

JOHN B. FRANTZ

BÉKÉSY, Georg von (3 June 1899–13 June 1972), physiologist, was born in Budapest, Hungary, the son of Alexander von Békésy, a member of the diplomatic service, and Paula Mazaly. He received his early education in Munich, Constantinople, and Zurich and his high school education in Budapest. He then enrolled at the University of Bern, Switzerland (1916–1920), and later at the University of Budapest, where he earned a Ph.D. in physics (1923). His doctoral research was on interference microscopy, a branch of optics. Jobs in that field were scarce at the time, and therefore he elected to work as a communications engineer in the research laboratory of the Hungarian telephone system. It was the only laboratory still equipped after World War I because the government was forced by postwar treaties to maintain the telephone and telegraph lines that crisscrossed the country.

Although the telephone lab did not have an opening for a physicist at the time, von Békésy was still hired at a small salary. He stayed with this agency for twenty-three years, except for one year that he spent at Siemens & Halske A. G. in Berlin, then a center of telecommunications development. In 1946 he immigrated to Stockholm, Sweden, where he worked at the Karolinska Institute and at the Royal Institute of Technology. Moving to the United States a year later, he went to Harvard University as a research lecturer and eventually was promoted to the rank of senior research fellow in psychophysics. In 1966 he left for the University of Hawaii, where he worked as a professor of sensory sciences until the time of his death in Honolulu. Von Békésy was basically a very simple, unassuming man who intentionally avoided the spotlight. He often said that he liked the lonely life because "concentration on one field is possible only if you are lonely to a certain degree." His obsessions in life were two: solving deafness and collecting primitive art.

Von Békésy said that he developed an interest in sound and the ear when he first heard high-pitched gypsy music as a boy in Hungary. While working for the Hungarian telephone system, he decided to study how the human ear receives sound. The basic anatomy of the ear was pretty well documented by the mid-1920s. Hearing occurs when sound waves enter the ear, strike the eardrum, and thus create vibrations that pass the leverlike bones of the middle ear and eventually are transmitted to the cochlea. The cochlea is divided lengthwise into two sections by the basilar membrane, which carries specialized hair cells that transmit the vibrations to the nerve fibers of the auditory nerve. Scientists were unsure, however, about the way the basilar membrane responded to sound pressure.

Helmholtz's theory, the standing theory at the time, stated that each fiber had a natural period of vibration and responded to sound that vibrated during that natural period. Since any sound is a combination of pure vibrations, it would vibrate a combination of fibers to send the message to the brain. Research on the ear was very difficult at the time since it was generally believed that ear tissues deteriorated rapidly after death. Von Békésy discovered that this was true only if the tissues were dehydrated and that the properties were pretty much intact as long as ears from cadavers were kept in an environment that provided 100 percent humidity. He therefore developed a special underwater microscope to observe the progress of his work closely. Most of the work was done on the acoustic organs of guinea pigs that were much smaller than those of the human being, and, as a result, von Békésy was forced to develop microsurgical tools that would not irreversibly damage the various components of the middle and inner ear.

After many years of tedious, hard work using an enlarged plastic model of the cochlea that he developed, von Békésy discounted Helmholtz's theory and demonstrated that sound vibrations are actually traveling waves that respond differently to the various areas of the basilar membrane. These areas, he determined, are not uniform; instead, the membrane is stretched tight at its base and is wider and floppier at the apex of the cochlea. He concluded, therefore, that nervous inhibition must play an important role in the way sound is perceived and is responsible for the differentiation of high- and low-pitched sounds because the brain receives information about the location of the sound from nerve fibers in the cochlea.

Von Békésy continued his research on the biomechanics of the cochlea, and his work led to significant advances in the diagnosis and treatment of hearing disorders. As a result, microsurgeons have been able to develop ways of constructing new eardrums of skin or vein tissue and are capable of replacing small bones of the ear with plastic parts.

The zenith of world recognition for his scientific work came in 1961, when von Békésy was awarded the Nobel Prize in physiology or medicine. In his ceremonial address Professor Carl Gustaf Bernhard, the Nobel Foundation representative, praised him for discoveries that "contribute most significantly to the analysis of the relation between the mechanical and electrical phenomena in the receptors which are involved in the transformation of sound into nerve impulses."

As a Nobel Prize recipient von Békésy was unique. He was the only one until the mid-1970s to work in a university until his retirement without being a professor. Only he and Joshua Lederberg managed to reach the height of inconspicuous eminence by choosing not to list their Nobel Prizes in *American Men and Women of Science*. Nevertheless he was awarded at least nine prestigious international prizes and awards, apart form the Nobel Prize, and nine honorary university doctorates and medical degrees.

Georg von Békésy never married and had no offspring. He dedicated his entire life to research on hearing. He was known to stay at the laboratory from nine in the morning to ten at night. He ate lunch at work and dinner at a restaurant before he walked home. Despite his rather limited ability to speak English on his arrival in the United States, he quickly managed to speak it fluently with a Hungarian accent supplemented by expressive gestures, and practically all of his publications were in English.

Six months after his death, the 17 January 1973 edition of the *Medical Tribune* announced that von Békésy had named the Nobel Foundation heir to his estate of $400,000 in art objects—about ten times the amount he had received from his prize. The Nobel Foundation in turn placed his art collection on public exhibition for the first time on 9 December 1974.

The obituary in the *Washington Post* (16 June 1972) described von Békésy's achievements as "a scientific basis for advances in the treatment of deafness and a tremendous contribution to the knowledge of acoustics." One day later, *The Times* (London) announced his death with the indication that von Békésy's work made it possible to differentiate between certain forms of deafness and to select the proper treatment more accurately.

• Georg von Békésy's two most important books are *Hearing: Its Psychology and Physiology* (1938) and *Experiments in Hearing*, ed. E. G. Wever (1960). Floyd Ratliff, in the National Academy of Sciences, *Biographical Memoirs* 48 (1976): 25–49, provides an excellent biography that includes a description of von Békésy's passion for the mechanism of hearing and his primitive art collection, a list of his honors, and a complete bibliography of his publications. Other information about von Békésy appears in the Nobel Foundation *Nobel Lectures, Including Presentation Speeches and Laureates' Biographies: Physiology or Medicine 1942–1962* (1964), pp. 719–48; Bernard S. Schlessinger and June H. Schlessinger, *The Who's Who in Nobel Prize Winners* (1986), p. 103; and Wasson Tyler, *Nobel Prize Winners* (1987), pp. 76–78. The most recent biographical sketch of von Békésy is by Paris Svoronos in *The Nobel Prize Winners: Physiology or Medicine* (1991), pp. 827–35.

PARIS SVORONOS

BELASCO, David (25 July 1853–14 May 1931), playwright and director, was born in San Francisco. His Portuguese Jewish parents, Humphrey Abraham Belasco and Reina Martin, were émigrés from England, where his father had been a harlequin in pantomimes. In North America his parents become shopkeepers. Raised in Victoria, British Columbia, Belasco claimed to have been educated at a monastery but actually attended the Colonial School and the Anglican Collegiate School. As a child he acted professionally, including portraying the Duke of York during Charles Kean's farewell tour of *Richard III*.

When he was eleven the family moved back to San Francisco, where Belasco expanded his theatrical interests by writing plays, completing his first when he was twelve years old. He finished his education at Lincoln Grammar School in 1871. For five years he barnstormed on the West Coast, acting and writing pirated versions of foreign dramas. In 1873 he worked as a call boy at a San Francisco theater; spent time in 1874 in Virginia City, Nevada; and then was hired by San Francisco impresario Tom Maguire, for whom he acted, adapted plays from many sources, prompted, stage managed, and directed. During the 1870s Belasco appeared in over 300 San Francisco productions and worked with some of the era's greatest stars. His most controversial production during this period was Salmi Morse's *Passion Play* (1879), starring James O'Neill; it was considered blasphemous because it showed Christ on stage. One of Belasco's early collaborators was James A. Herne. After Belasco sold his interest in their most successful work, *Chums* (1879), a romantic melodrama based on an English play, his partner, who bought him out, made a fortune with it under the title *Hearts of Oak*.

Belasco and his wife, Cecilia Loverich, whom he had married in 1873, moved permanently to New York City in 1882, when he was hired to manage the Madison Square Theatre. After giving up acting in 1880, he concentrated on playwriting and directing. One of his successes was his own *May Blossom* (1884). After a brief period back in San Francisco, he returned to New York and was employed by Daniel Frohman from 1886 to 1890 at the Lyceum Theatre, where his productions included four plays he coadapted with Henry C. De Mille. In 1888 he staged a surprisingly modern version of Sophocles' *Electra* at the American Academy of Dramatic Arts.

During this period Belasco also gained attention for training redheaded, divorced socialite Mrs. Leslie Carter as an actress, accepting her as a pupil only after she pleaded with him on bended knee. Two years went into the arduous task of making her a colorful star, and part of her fame derived from her notoriety. In the early 1890s he presented her in a series of period melodramas, several of them presented in London as well. The most successful were his and Franklyn Fyles's highly profitable American Indian melodrama, *The Girl I Left behind Me* (1893); his exciting Civil War play, *The Heart of Maryland* (1895); *Zaza* (1899), a Belasco adaptation from the French; his *Du Barry* (1901), about King Louis XV's mistress; and *Adrea* (1905), his and John Luther Long's romantic melodrama set after the fall of Rome. When Mrs. Carter remarried, Belasco felt betrayed and turned to developing other stars. Among those stars who came to fame under Belasco's tutelage was Blanche Bates, who was a sensation in Belasco's coadaptation with Long of the latter's *Madame Butterfly* (1900), Paul Potter's *Under Two Flags* (1901), and Belasco and Long's elaborate melodrama set in old Japan, *The Darling of the Gods* (1902). The only major male star he molded was David Warfield, who became famous in Lee Arthur and Charles Klein's drama about a Lower East Side Jew, *The Auctioneer* (1901); Warfield played in a number of other Belasco productions, including *The Merchant of Venice* (1922), the only classic Belasco ever staged professionally.

In 1900 Belasco—one of the most outspoken opponents of the Theatrical Syndicate then attempting to monopolize American theater production—became an independent producer. In 1902 he leased his own theater, the Republic, which he remodeled and called the Belasco. Here some of the plays already mentioned were performed, as well as *Sweet Kitty Bellairs* (1903), his adaptation of a British novel set in the eighteenth century; his cowboy melodrama, *The Girl of the Golden West* (1905); and his and Richard W. Tully's southern California romance, *The Rose of the Rancho* (1906), based on Tully's novel. Both *Madame Butterfly* and *The Girl of the Golden West* were made into operas by Giacomo Puccini. In 1907 Belasco opened the Stuyvesant Theatre, which was renamed the Belasco in 1911 (the Republic returned to its original name). From 1902 to 1931 most of Belasco's productions were offered at the Belasco and the Republic. He directed sixty-four plays during these years and produced many others as well.

The striking-looking Belasco was short, white-haired in his later years, and black-browed. Fostering the probably apocryphal image of his monastery upbringing, he wore a reversed collar like a priest, reveling in the title "the bishop of Broadway." At the second Belasco Theatre, where he lived, his office was well known for its atmospheric jumble of unusual *objets d'art*, including a Ming dais, burning incense, candles, and a desk converted from an onyx commode. Belasco's ghost is said to haunt the theater.

In addition to those already mentioned, a partial list of the plays with which he was involved during his last thirty years includes Eugene Walter's *The Easiest Way* (1909); Belasco and Alice Bradley's *The Governor's Lady* (1912); Edward Knoblock's *Marie-Odile* (1915); Belasco's Chinese melodrama *The Son-Daughter* (1920); Sacha Guitry's *Deburau* (1920); André Picard's *Kiki* (1921); Hubert Osborne's *Shore Leave* (1922); Edward Sheldon and Charles MacArthur's *Lulu Belle* (1926); and Ferenc Molnàr's *Mima* (1928). Those by Italian, French, and Hungarian authors were usually adapted by Belasco himself.

Most of the plays he wrote, directed, or produced were sensational, occasionally lurid, sentimental melodramas, making their impact through strong theatrical situations, colorful and even exotic backgrounds, and the remarkably detailed and often spectacular realism of their productions. Contemporary critics often belittled the plays while praising their realizations, and, indeed, Belasco is remembered more for his contributions to stagecraft than to dramaturgy. He was one of the earliest American master directors, and during his last two decades he concentrated on directing, as his playwriting activities diminished.

With the help of lighting technician Louis Hartmann, Belasco made many important lighting advances, particularly the abandonment of the footlights, the creation of the baby spotlight, and the use of scrim effects. He even built an expensive lighting laboratory. His sets were as lifelike (and solid) as possible, and he was known for such effects as vividly reproducing the interior of a Childs Restaurant or a cheap boardinghouse. Every element had to be as authentic as possible, including real jewelry, food, and wallpaper. Even partly seen offstage rooms were likely to get the full Belasco treatment. As a result, some productions were hindered by the time it took to shift the cluttered sets.

Belasco heightened the emotional power of his productions by carefully integrating music into them and by employing an array of naturalistic sound effects. Over thirty stagehands were used in one production to simulate the sound of an offstage storm. Belasco drilled his actors endlessly to create seamless ensemble performances. He instructed the cast in every vocal and gestural nuance of their roles and helped them create an atmosphere of believability by his microscopic attention to the minutiae of stage business.

During his lengthy career, Belasco's admirers praised the theatrical fullness of his work, while his critics dismissed his shows as claptrap. He was often in the public eye, sometimes being sued for plagiarism, sometimes battling the new actors' union, whose existence he deplored. He was a great showman who usually was in touch with public tastes, although in his final decade a rapid succession of theatrical developments made him seem increasingly a throwback to the nineteenth century. During the run of his last production, Lily Hatvany's *Tonight or Never* (1930), he died in New York.

• The finest collection of Belasco's papers is at the New York Public Library's Performing Arts division at Lincoln Center. Belasco's own *The Theatre through Its Stage Door*, ed. Louis V. Defoe (1919), is of some interest, although it is not completely reliable. For representative Belasco plays see Montrose B. Moses, ed., *Six Plays* (1928). Chief among his biographies is Craig Timberlake, *The Bishop of Broadway: The Life and Work of David Belasco* (1954). Others are William Winters, *The Life of David Belasco* (2 vols., 1918), and Lise-Lone Marker, *David Belasco: Naturalism in the American Theatre* (1975).

SAMUEL L. LEITER

BELCHER, Ernest (8 June 1882–24 Feb. 1973), ballet teacher and movie dance director, was born in London, England, the son of Mark Belcher, a butcher, and Emily (maiden name unknown). Belcher attended high school, apprenticed in an architect's office, and studied piano and painting. Belcher had no exposure to dance or theater until he was sixteen, when attendance at orchestral concerts made him realize that "expression of myself in gesture and movement was to be the great dominating force in my life." Against the wishes of his parents he began to study dance, first with the music-hall star Ethel Payne, then with Francesca Zanfretta, a well-known ballet teacher in London, and finally with Alexandre Genée, uncle and teacher of the Danish ballerina Adeline Genée. He also studied period and national folk dances with Louis d'Egville and Cormani, Spanish dances under Caroline Otero, Lopes and Tortola Valencia, and Malaganita, and Indian and oriental dances under Roshanara.

Belcher made his dance debut on 20 September 1909 at London's Alhambra Theatre in a skit he created, *Sal-Oh-My*, followed in 1910 by a Haymarket Theatre engagement in Maurice Maeterlinck's *The Blue Bird*, in which he danced and spoke. For the next four years in England Belcher had a series of female partners with whom he performed ballet and ballroom dances in private clubs and theaters. It was with a group called the Golden Dancers that he arrived in New York in 1914 and decided to stay in the United States; by the end of that year and through early 1915 he was engaged by the Keith-Orpheum circuits to present his own act. Toward the end of that period Belcher was diagnosed with tuberculosis and decided to leave New York, arriving in Los Angeles in September 1915.

In Los Angeles Belcher began teaching, opening his first studio in May 1916. In 1917 he married Gladys Basquette; they had two children of their own. Basquette's daughter was ten when they married. By 1928 he had more than 2,000 students at his studio. At that time in Los Angeles, ballet performances were a rarity and good training virtually nonexistent. Belcher developed a system of disciplined, sequential training he called the "Eight Grade System"; it relied on repetition of the same material until a certain level of proficiency was attained. Young dancers were classified as beginners or upper-classmen, and there were four grades for each. Pointe work was not allowed until students had the required strength; students taking class several times a week finished the eight-grade course in four years. In a one-year "postgraduate" course, students learned about costumes, makeup, and business and stage management, and were taught performing material.

Belcher was strict, not allowing progress to the next level until the material was mastered. Performance was of the utmost importance. Special men's classes were offered, and the school curriculum also included tap, ballroom, and Spanish dance. Teachers from all over the country came for a one-month summer course; a certificate was awarded after completion of practical and written exams.

The well-known ballerina Maria Tallchief was Belcher's pupil from 1933 to 1937, coming to him at the age of eight after having studied elsewhere. She noted in a 1964 interview that "it was good I ended up with Ernest Belcher." He was a mentor to many others who went on to have careers in dance, including Marge Champion (his daughter), Gower Champion, Carmelita Maracci, Rod Alexander, Cyd Charisse, Nanette Fabray, Maria and Marjorie Tallchief, Paul Godkin, Loren Hightower, Matt Matox, Rosita Moreno, and Gwen Verdon.

Belcher felt he had a mission to educate all Americans about ballet as an art form, and in 1921 his twenty-one consecutive ballet lessons were published in the *Los Angeles Record*. In 1927 he issued a booklet, *Basic Principles of Dancing*, that had twenty-three progressive lessons, and he wrote in the introduction, "While the basic principles in this book are absolutely legitimate for one expecting to become a professional dancer, the book was essentially produced for the thousands more than the individual." The *American Dancer* magazine carried a monthly series by Belcher about correct methods of teaching ballet from January 1931 through September 1932, and in 1935 he gave several radio interviews in which he tried to teach the general public about ballet and invited questions from the audience.

In 1918 Belcher began working for the movies when he created dance sequences for Cecil B. De Mille's *We Can't Have Everything*, and in 1925 he was given the title "Dance Director of Movieland." Although often his credits did not appear onscreen, he worked on over two hundred movies through the 1930s, including *Salome vs. Shenandoah* (1919), *A Small Town Idol* (1921), *Heroes of the Street* (1922), *Souls for Sale* (1923), *Beau Brummel* (1924), *The Phantom of the Opera* (1925), *The Jazz Singer* (1927), *General Crack* (1929), *Anna Karenina* (1935), and *The Little Princess* (1939). Film stars flocked to his studio for training in movement and assistance with dances, among them Mary Pickford, Pola Negri, John Barrymore, Ramon Novarro, John Gilbert, Marion Davies, Lillian Gish, Loretta Young, Ruby Keeler, Betty Grable, Ida Lupino, Yvonne de Carlo, and Rita Hayworth. Belcher trained

Shirley Temple over a long period of private lessons at her home during 1938–1939. Movie directors valued his ability to work in a wide variety of styles and to create dance sequences that advanced the movie action. He never sacrificed integrity or historical accuracy and did not permit low technical or artistic standards.

Belcher created concert ballets at the Hollywood Bowl from 1922 to 1934 and introduced thousands to dance. By 1955 he had given up the 36,000-square-foot studio built for him by De Mille in 1931 and taught only a few private students from then until his death in Los Angeles. Although separated from Gladys Basquette in 1942, he remained close to his children and grandchildren. In 1965 he was honored at a special ceremony in Los Angeles, joined by Ruth St. Denis and Marge and Gower Champion.

Belcher, the classical dance teacher, was way ahead of his time in terms of awareness of the importance of rhythm, expression, and new ways of moving. Modern dance did not play a large role in his school, but it was offered on a limited basis along with tap, acrobatics, physical culture, hula, ballroom, and Spanish dance.

• Special Collections at the University Research Library of the University of California at Los Angeles has material that is useful, including a Belcher Collection consisting of pictures, articles about Belcher, school catalogs, and articles written by Belcher. Biographical treatments of Belcher include Naima Prevots, *Dancing in the Sun: Hollywood Choreographers, 1915–1937* (1987), and "Ernest Belcher and American Dance," *Dance Chronicle* 10 (1987): 170–222. Two unpublished works by Renee Dunia Hawley are helpful, "Ernest Belcher: The Father of Dance in Southern California" (Belcher Collection) and "Los Angeles and the Dance, 1850–1930" (master's thesis, 1971). There are good discussions of Belcher in Ann Barzel, "European Dance Teacher in the U.S.," *Dance Index* (Apr.–June 1944): 92, and Leland Windreich, "June Roper," *Dance Chronicle* 10 (1987): 109. Earlier articles that provide insight include Faith Service, "Ernest Belcher: The Teacher of 'It,'" *Dance Magazine*, Aug. 1928, p. 18; B. Griffith, "Where Many in Movieland Get Dancing Inspiration," *Dancing Master*, Apr. 1929, p. 108; and Ruth Eleanor Howard, "Dancing Has Brought a New Angle to Talkies," *American Dancer*, Nov. 1929, pp. 14–15. Obituaries are in the *Los Angeles Times*, 27 Feb. 1973, and *Dancing Times* and *Dance Magazine*, both May 1973.

NAIMA PREVOTS

BELCHER, Jonathan (8 Jan. 1682–31 Aug. 1757), governor of Massachusetts, New Hampshire, and New Jersey, was born in Cambridge, Massachusetts, the son of Andrew Belcher, a merchant, and Sarah Gilbert. Jonathan's father was wealthy and ambitious, with business connections throughout New England. Jonathan attended the Boston Latin School, then Harvard College for an A.B. from 1695 to 1699 and for an M.A. in 1702, and he toured England and northern Europe for nearly two years and visited the British royal family in Hannover.

Following his return, Belcher in 1706 married Mary Partridge, the daughter of the New Hampshire lieu-

tenant governor. The couple had five children. Over the years Belcher and his father cut powerful figures in Boston politics. Their mercantile house often needed direct personal contacts with English politicians, and Belcher did his duty in London. His prominence led to his election to the Massachusetts Council in 1718 and his reelection in 1719, 1720, 1722, 1723, 1726, and 1727. He gained a reputation as a person of polish, dignity, and frankness. He was often too sharp for his personal good, however; he referred to rivals often in demeaning language, describing William Shirley, for instance, as that "ingrate . . . that meddler . . . that pettifogger." His cultivation of English acquaintances put him in touch with many influential politicians of the day, and he became known for his opposition to Massachusetts's inflated paper currency, his support of the Whig Restoration, and his adherence to Puritan beliefs. He corresponded with several English religious dissenters, including Samuel Shute, John Shute, Thomas Hollis, Samuel Holden, and his brother-in-law Richard Partridge, who was a Quaker. His connections and ideas helped him win appointment as governor of both Massachusetts and New Hampshire in 1729, but he first traveled to London to press his cause personally. He avoided making promises to back the English plan for a fixed salary for the governorship of Massachusetts, which the Board of Trade and Privy Council hoped would enable the governor to be independent of the obstreperous house of representatives.

In 1730 Belcher received the warm applause of the people on his return to Boston as governor, beginning a generally successful tenure of eleven years. For a time, serving two masters, the British ministry and the New England people, was a problem, but Belcher handled the situation adroitly. He chose his supporters cautiously, abandoning the powerful Elisha Cook, a radical friend of his youth, and bargained with the legislature for cooperation by not pressing for a fixed salary. His popularity grew as he cajoled interest groups, including those wanting to exploit the King's Woods, merchants desiring to trade easily with England, and religious groups favoring Puritan expressions of support (that is, groups not part of the Church of England). Belcher used the language of the colony's Puritan founders, masking his calculated attempts to control the legislature. His strongest supporters were the wealthy merchants, who, like himself, were interested in trade, a regulated currency, and good relations with England. While he stood side by side with them, he withdrew from active management of his own business establishment, putting his sons, relatives, and a host of employees in charge of an estate reportedly worth £60,000.

Until 1737 Belcher ruled effectively, even though he had some vocal opposition from David Dunbar, the surveyor of the King's Woods, for permitting local timber cutters to violate the law. He handled the pressures of administration well until his wife died in 1736. Without her restraining hand, he poured out invectives upon any challenge to his ideas. Signs of his weakness began to show when the financial community, suffering from inflation, developed plans for banks, the great merchants favoring a silver-based credit system while landowners and smaller merchants preferred to use land for security. Either plan would have relieved the difficulties of unreliable credit then affecting the economy, and a combination of the two would have materially eased exchange problems. Unfortunately, rivalry between the groups brought Belcher into the fray with his powerful if unguarded support of the merchants. Where he could, he removed the land bank supporters from office, struck out at them in the elections, and denied them entry into his presence. Emotions rose, and a group of rivals stormed off to London to plead their cause before a ministry itself experiencing instability. Belcher's English friends—Robert Walpole; Sir Spencer Compton, the earl of Wilmington; Charles Townshend—momentarily had lost power, and Belcher's enemies removed him from office in 1741. By that time Belcher and his enemies in Massachusetts had caused so much turmoil by their political tactics that revolutionary conditions were evolving.

At the height of the crisis the Board of Trade removed Belcher from both of his governorships, and an act of Parliament suppressed both banks and imposed harsh penalties on all bank shareholders. Belcher remained a powerful man in New England, but his wings were surely clipped. He decided to plead his case before the Board of Trade and some members of the English aristocracy, and his appearance in England in March 1744 brought a symbolic meeting with King George II and assurances of a future preferment. Belcher hoped for the governorship of South Carolina but was offered the military command of the fortress of Louisbourg, which he declined. In 1747 he was appointed governor of New Jersey, an offer probably inspired by his Quaker friends. In 1748 he married Mary Louisa Emilia Teal, a gracious lady of "great merit, and a handsome fortune." They had no children. Living in rural Burlington, near the "World's End," was difficult for Belcher to contemplate, but the colony had many New England inhabitants, and urban Philadelphia was only several hours away.

Belcher thought the people of New Jersey suffered from gross illiteracy, and his first project was to secure a liberal charter for the struggling College of New Jersey (now Princeton University). He helped select a permanent campus, collected money for its first building, and rounded up some New England students. At his death he donated to the college his large library of over four hundred books and a collection of portraits.

Legislative battles over such issues as land tenure, tax levies on lands owned by the proprietors, and credit controls plagued Belcher. The colony budget as a result was not passed by the legislature for periods of up to two years. The legislature refused to pay his salary, and the local politicians, who objected to direction from an outsider, pressed for his removal from office because of land squatters and tenants seeking titles to lands. Belcher relaxed his insistence on tight credit with the beginning of the French and Indian War.

Eventually he and the legislature compromised on taxes and his salary, and Belcher had some personal satisfaction in laying a foundation for a stable government. He favored the Albany Plan of Union in 1754 and strove to provide forces for the defense of the colonies in the campaigns against France in 1755 and 1756. Palsy affected Belcher's health in his mid-seventies, so the British government appointed a lieutenant governor, Thomas Pownall, to handle those duties that necessitated travel outside of the colony. Belcher was honored by the British Board of Trade as an effective voice in American colonial administration, though his lack of energy in later life led to serious problems of political control in New Jersey. He died in Elizabethtown, New Jersey.

Belcher kept letter books throughout most of his life and was apparently fond of having his portrait painted. Both John Singleton Copley and Thomas Hudson were among the artists who painted this tall man, dressed in fine clothes, always ready to issue a barbed comment. Governor of three colonies, each for over a decade, Belcher was an important colonial official of the mid-eighteenth century. He attempted to balance British and American interests, but in a manner to further his personal political career.

• Belcher left important documents of his daily life in letter books and a journal, which are preserved in the collections of the Massachusetts Historical Society. They are published in "Belcher Papers," *Collections of the Massachusetts Historical Society*, 6th ser., 6 and 7. Important printed appraisals include William H. Belcher and Joseph W. Belcher, *The Belcher Family* (1941); John A. Schutz, "Succession Politics in Massachusetts, 1730–1741," *William and Mary Quarterly*, 3d ser., 15 (1958): 508–20; Clifford K. Shipton, "Jonathan Belcher," *Sibley's Harvard Graduates*, vol. 4 (1690–1700); and Donald L. Kemmerer, *Path to Freedom: The Struggle for Self-Government in Colonial New Jersey, 1703–1776* (1940). See also Joseph J. Malone, *Pine Trees and Politics; the Naval Stores and Forest Policy in Colonial New England, 1691–1775* (1964).

JOHN A. SCHUTZ

BELDEN, Jack (3 Feb. 1910–3 June 1989), foreign correspondent, was born Alfred Goodwin Belden, Jr., in Brooklyn, New York, the son of Alfred Goodwin Belden and Mabel Kathleen Sweezey. The details of Belden's life are sketchy, starting with a childhood that he later spoke of ruefully. His parents separated when Belden was a toddler. When he was approaching his teens, his mother remarried and moved the family to Summit, New Jersey. Belden resented his stepfather and recalled that he did not feel welcome in his home.

The family had financial means and shielded Belden and his older sister from the depression. Belden—who adopted the name Jack—enjoyed his years at Adelphi Academy in Brooklyn and later at Colgate University, where he majored in geology and minored in literature. Not only eager to get away from home but also itching to travel for its own sake, he took a boat trip to South America between his junior and senior years at college. Through contacts in his stepfather's firm, Federal Paint Company, which sold nautical paint, Belden secured a position as a seaman upon graduation in 1931.

In 1933 Belden impetuously jumped ship in Hong Kong and made his way to Shanghai, where he gambled and begged money to survive. With jai alai winnings, he went to Peking (Beijing). After teaching English at a night school and doing other odd jobs, he was hired in Shanghai as a reporter with the *Shanghai Evening Post*. He subsequently became a China correspondent for United Press and in 1939 a *Time* magazine correspondent.

During this period China was beset by civil war and Japanese aggression. Like many young Americans who came to China on a lark, Belden was drawn into China's struggles. Covering the local Chinese courts for the *Shanghai Evening Post*, he learned about the privations of ordinary Chinese people. He also picked up a working knowledge of the Chinese language and traveled through the countryside.

Tillman Durdin of the *New York Times* shared the common view that Belden was "one of the great correspondents. He had a penetrating intelligence, an inborn capacity to see and depict the inner sense of what he observed" (letter to author, 20 July 1990). In addition, he was intrepid in pursuing stories and was known for being honest, the flip side of which was an inability to compromise. He also had a reputation for being difficult and troubled. In the wartime capital of Chongqing (then Chungking), he was known to pull the shades down in his room in the Press Hostel and drink for days at a time. *Time* editors objected to Belden's use of four-letter words in stories, a problem that foreign correspondent Theodore White, who had recruited Belden for the magazine, suggested the editors resolve by substituting the Chinese equivalents. Belden's friend Edgar Snow, a fellow foreign correspondent, referred to him as "mad and gifted."

Belden was in Burma when the Japanese drove the Allied forces out of that country in 1942. Rather than leaving with the other correspondents, Belden joined General Joseph W. Stilwell's epic retreat to India. While hospitalized after the march, possibly for malaria, he became what one contemporary called "the Homer of the Stilwell odyssey" by writing *Retreat with Stilwell*, published in 1943.

After his recovery, *Time* sent Belden to report on the North African front of the European theater. In September 1943 he was wounded while covering General George Patton's invasion of Salerno. In his North Africa hospital bed, he wrote two memorable cover stories for *Time*'s sister publication *Life* magazine: one about being shot in the leg and the other about falling in love with a blonde American nurse in the Italian hospital.

During a long convalescence in New York hospitals, Belden wrote a second book. *Still a Time to Die* was a searing reflection on the war, which he was anxious to see again as a journalist. Over the objections of his doctors and his editors—or so he would recall—he

managed to reach England on a Norwegian fruit ship in time to cover the invasion of Normandy. While in Paris during the liberation, in 1944 he met and married Paula Allouard, with whom he had one son.

Belden returned to China in 1946. Postwar China was described by fellow journalist Arch Steele as "a place of free spirits. You could do almost anything you pleased and you could do it on very little money" (Rand, p. 281). This atmosphere of freedom suited Belden, who was now estranged from *Life* and *Time*. (They thought he was a prima donna; he thought they mangled his copy.) He wrote *China Shakes the World* about the civil war between the Nationalists and Communists. Published in 1949, it has remained an important historical source on the period. At the time, however, the book did not do well financially. Its pro–Red Chinese sympathies were not welcome by the increasingly anti-Communist American audience. In addition Belden felt he had been cheated financially by his publisher, and he decided to give up journalism.

Although Belden's writing could be intensely personal, he was private and brooding by nature. Unlike many foreign correspondents of the period, he never wrote full-length memoirs. After the war, when his journalism career ended abruptly, even his family did not always know his whereabouts. During these postwar years he gambled in Nevada and drove a cab. He and his wife had lived together only a few months before he left by himself for China. They divorced in 1954. A second marriage, to Eleanor Stuart in 1964, produced a son but also quickly fell apart.

Eager to extricate himself from the marriage, he relocated to Paris in 1965. Friends and family were never clear how he survived, but he eked out an existence gambling and, apparently, with small sums sent by his mother, who died only shortly before he did.

He wrote occasional poetry for amusement. Although he thought about writing on foreign affairs again, nothing came of it. With Sino-American rapprochement in 1972, Belden made a return trip to China. He was uncomfortable about his Chinese hosts paying many of his bills and disillusioned about Communist rule.

In his final days he was reunited with the nurse about whom he had written in his *Life* article after being wounded at Salerno. Beatrice Weber cared for him before he died of lung cancer in a Paris hospital for the indigent.

• The Stanford University library has a collection of Belden's papers, including his China journal and notebooks from 1939 to 1940, a scrapbook of clippings from American papers, and *Time* and *Life* dispatches and notebooks. Belden wrote sketchy summaries of his life, which can be found in family files. He is mentioned in memoirs written by many of his colleagues and in various histories of the period. Two such books are Peter Rand, *China Hands* (1995), and Stephen P. MacKinnon and Oris Friesen, *China Reporting: An Oral History of American Journalism in the 1930s & 1940s* (1987). His reporting has been anthologized in the Library of America's

Reporting World War II (1995). Obituaries are in the *New York Times*, the *Los Angeles Times*, and *The Times* (London), all 6 June 1989.

JOHN MAXWELL HAMILTON
CAROLYN PIONE

BEL GEDDES, Norman. *See* Geddes, Norman Bel.

BELKNAP, Jeremy (4 June 1744–20 June 1798), Congregationalist clergyman and historian, was born in Boston, Massachusetts, the son of Joseph Belknap, a leather dresser and furrier, and Sarah Byles. After graduating from Harvard College in 1762, he taught school and studied theology with local ministers, earning a master of arts degree in 1765. In 1767 he accepted the call of a congregation in Dover, New Hampshire, to serve as its minister; he remained there for almost twenty years. Also in 1767 he married Ruth Eliot, who traded a comfortable life in Boston for the trials of a minister's wife in a rustic New England village. The couple would have six children. During the American Revolution Belknap was a patriot preacher who exhorted his parishioners to resist British plans to regulate and tax the colonists. After independence he became a moderate Federalist who championed order for both his state and the young republic and enlightened government by the educated upper classes.

In 1786 Belknap resigned from his pulpit in Dover and in 1787 accepted an invitation to become the pastor of the Long Lane Church in Boston. He was delighted to move back to his native town because he had become increasingly unhappy and estranged from his congregation in New Hampshire. His troubles in Dover began when his salary depreciated due to the inflation of the war years. His bitterness intensified when his congregation refused to grant him a substantial adjustment to help him support his growing family. Moreover, his residence in Dover made it difficult for him to pursue his love of history and his other varied interests. His new position in Boston thus enabled him to serve a congregation that appreciated his talents while he also devoted himself to his labors as a historian, scientist, man of letters, humanist, and staunch defender of the new Constitution, a plan he believed struck "at the root of such evils as we have suffered by the madness of Sovereign state Assemblies."

Belknap's most important contributions to the development of early American culture were his historical writings and his activities as a collector of primary source materials pertaining to the early history of the British-American colonies. He began his research for his multivolume *History of New-Hampshire* during the early 1770s, but the practical difficulties of subsistence, raising a family, and coping with the stresses of the revolutionary war delayed the publication of the first volume until 1784. The second and third volumes appeared in 1791 and 1792, followed by a two-volume series of essays, *American Biography*, published in 1794 and 1798. *American Biography* covers such important topics as the trend of colonization across the Atlantic, clashes between Europeans and native Indi-

ans, and the nature of the Pilgrim and Puritan missions in North America. Although trained in a Puritan tradition that stressed the role of Divine Providence in directing world history, Belknap adopted a research method and a writing style that reflected the influence of the Enlightenment. His approach was scientific, rational, and analytical, emphasizing human reason as the major force in history. Although he tried to be objective in relating the political narrative of New Hampshire and other colonies, his books reveal his revolutionary ideology and his partiality for the new national Constitution of 1787, a strong central government, and firm leadership by an educated and responsible aristocracy at both the state and federal levels. Belknap's works also include extensive sections on New England and New Hampshire geography, natural history, and the customs and folkways of the people who lived there. Particularly noteworthy are his discussions of the social and cultural lives of both white and native Indian inhabitants.

Belknap's determination to base all of his works on original documents led him to establish a repository for letters, maps, books, newspapers, and other manuscripts. He and several of his friends launched the Massachusetts Historical Society in 1791. In that year he wrote: "We intend to be an *active*, not a *passive*, literary body; not to lie waiting, like a bed of oysters, for the tide (of communication) to flow in upon us, but to *seek* and find, to *preserve* and *communicate* literary intelligence, especially in the historical way." Belknap served as the society's first corresponding secretary, collector of books and manuscripts, and editorial adviser for the initial series of its *Collections*. The first organization of its kind in the United States, it became the prototype for similar groups in many states.

During his final decade Belknap became an avid cultural nationalist and humanist. He helped to create and promote an American history, science, and literature that was distinct from European culture. As a man of letters in the young republic he was an active contributor to several early American magazines; in 1792 he published a book-length political allegory, *The Foresters*, a satirical mock-epic tale of the American Revolution and the Confederation told from a Federalist perspective. His reform activities included efforts in temperance, education, antislavery, and missionary work with indigenous peoples. When a stroke ended his life in his native Boston just after his fifty-fourth birthday, the young nation lost one of its leading literary and cultural figures. A distinguished member of the revolutionary generation, he gave the country he loved much reason to remember him.

• The vast majority of Belknap's letters, sermons, diaries, commonplace books, notebooks, rough drafts of his books, and miscellaneous pieces are in the Massachusetts Historical Society in Boston. The New Hampshire Historical Society's box of Belknap materials contains mostly family letters. Some of his correspondence has been published in the *Collections of the Massachusetts Historical Society*, ser. 5, vols. 2 and 3 (1877), and ser. 6, vol. 4 (1891). In addition to the works cited above, see the address Belknap delivered at the Massachusetts Historical Society, *A Discourse, Intended to Commemorate the Discovery of America by Christopher Columbus* (1792). His *Sacred Poetry* (1795) is a collection of psalms and hymns. *The Life of Jeremy Belknap, D.D., the Historian of New Hampshire*, by Jane Belknap Marcou (1847), is an early "life and letters" biography written by his granddaughter. The most complete account of Belknap's life is George B. Kirsch, *Jeremy Belknap: A Biography* (1982). For his achievements as a historian, see also Leonard Tucker, *Clio's Consort: Jeremy Belknap and the Founding of the Massachusetts Historical Society* (1990). Useful articles are Sidney Kaplan, "The History of New Hampshire: Jeremy Belknap as Literary Craftsman," *William and Mary Quarterly* 21, no. 1 (1964): 18–39; and three by Kirsch: "Jeremy Belknap and the Coming of the Revolution," *Historical New Hampshire* 29, no. 3 (1974): 151–72; "Jeremy Belknap and the Problem of Blacks and Indians in Early America," *Historical New Hampshire* 34, nos. 3 and 4 (1979): 202–22; and "Jeremy Belknap: Man of Letters in the Young Republic," *New England Quarterly* 54, no. 1 (1981): 33–53.

GEORGE B. KIRSCH

BELKNAP, Waldron Phoenix (12 May 1899–14 Dec. 1949), art historian, was born in New York City, the son of Waldron Phoenix Belknap, a banker, and Rey Hutchings. Both of his parents were descended from early colonial settlers, and Belknap's awareness and appreciation of his own family's history, nurtured by his parents, developed into a deep and lasting interest in American history and material culture. He graduated magna cum laude from St. Paul's School in Concord, New Hampshire, in 1916 and was admitted to Harvard that same year; he interrupted his studies to join the army shortly after the United States entered World War I. He graduated from the heavy artillery school at Fort Monroe, Virginia, in 1918 with a commission as a second lieutenant, returning to Harvard at war's end. He still was able to graduate with his class in 1920, and he then spent eight years in investment finance, working in New York, Boston, and London.

Belknap's interest lay not in banking, however, but in the practice of architecture, and he returned to Harvard to study at the School of Architecture, from which he graduated in 1933. He settled in Boston and spent the next ten years working independently in that field. His clients tended to be conservative businessmen, and so the homes he designed for them followed traditional models, although he himself admired and preferred modern styles. He returned to active duty in 1943 as a first lieutenant in the Army Air Corps and subsequently served in England with the Eighth Army Air Force Intelligence. He was promoted to captain in March 1944, but poor health forced his retirement from active duty later that year and prevented him from returning to his architectural practice when he returned to Boston. He never married.

It is not, however, as an architect that Belknap is remembered, but as an art historian. His interest in American painting, heretofore a hobby, became his central focus, and he devoted the years following World War II to a comprehensive study of colonial American painting. He had done research in this area before the war and in 1941 had written an article on

Charles Willson Peale's portraits of the de Peyster family of New York. He did not publish the article apparently because he felt that additional research might turn up some new information. His first published article (and the only one published during his lifetime), "The Identity of Robert Feke," appeared in the *Art Bulletin* in September 1947 (29, no. 3: 201–7). It was written in response to an essay by James Thomas Flexner published a year earlier. Flexner had questioned whether Feke the painter was the same person as Robert Feke, Jr., of Oyster Bay, Long Island, and, indeed, whether Feke was even a native American artist. Through a detailed review of the Feke family genealogy, Belknap was able to demonstrate conclusively that Robert Feke, Jr., of Oyster Bay was indeed Robert Feke the artist, thus establishing his birthplace and probable birthdate, neither of which had been known to art historians.

Belknap's most important work was yet to come. While researching a 1718 portrait that he had purchased of an ancestor, Johannes de Peyster, Belknap discovered that the artist (unknown to him but now believed to be Nehemiah Partridge) had copied the pose, background, and accessories from John Smith's 1708 mezzotint after a portrait by Sir Godfrey Kneller of Sir John Perceval. Through additional work at the Frick Art Reference Library and the New York Public Library he quickly saw that this was not an isolated case. In August 1949 he did further research in London's British Museum and Courtauld Institute, where he came to understand the full significance of his discovery. What he found was that the vast majority of portraits executed in America before the American Revolution owed their compositions in some way to British portrait engravings, primarily mezzotints. Hundreds of these mezzotints after portraits by the leading British painters were imported to America beginning in the early 1700s. They were the colonists' leading source of information on fine art and current fashion and served as learning tools for the colonial painter who had no access to real works of art. Belknap was able to demonstrate that each artist kept a collection of these prints and conceivably even had his sitters choose the pose they preferred.

The earliest work on colonial portraiture, conducted in the wake of the centennial of American independence in 1876, had emphasized its originality and freedom from European influences. While there were of course artists who had come over from England and the Continent bringing Old World conventions with them, the best colonial painters, it was said, had worked out their own solutions with what might be termed Yankee ingenuity. There had been clues that this was not in fact the case, but they had gone unrecognized. For example, it had been observed in 1916 that John Singleton Copley, when painting his portrait of Mrs. Jerathmael Bowers, had copied the pose, costume, accessories, and background from an engraving of Sir Joshua Reynolds's portrait of Lady Caroline Russell, changing only the face. In 1942 the discovery was made that Copley had used an engraving of

Thomas Hudson's portrait of Mary, Viscountess Andover as a model for three portraits. Art historians, believing Copley to be an isolated case, puzzled over what had led him to copy prints instead of nature.

Belknap discovered that it was standard practice for colonial artists to rely on English portrait engravings when painting a portrait. He even found that Sir Joshua Reynolds himself followed the practice. His portrait of Lady Caroline Russell, so slavishly copied by Copley, was in turn based on an earlier engraving of Catherine of Braganza, consort of King Charles II. In the eighteenth century, when "a copy of a very good picture is preferable to an indifferent original" (to quote the British artist Jonathan Richardson), colonial painters did not hesitate to borrow wholesale from engravings after the leading British or European painters, for they believed that at least some of the qualities that marked the original as a work of art would thus appear in their own paintings as well.

In July 1949, shortly before he left for England to continue his research, Belknap was invited to participate in a proposed seminar on colonial American painting. He declined, explaining that he was not yet ready to reveal the results of his research and would not be in a position to do so for at least another year. He planned to write "a series of comprehensive, illustrated articles analogous to the chapters of a full-scale book, which might or might not be published afterward in book form" (Belknap, p. xviii). After he returned to the United States, he made great progress in assembling his evidence but had not begun to write his articles at the time of his death in Boston.

His friend John Marshall Phillips, director of the Yale University Art Gallery, was familiar with Belknap's research and made public the discovery of the "mezzotint prototypes" in January 1952 at the annual meeting of the College Art Association. Scholars were made aware that early American art could no longer be viewed as having developed in a vacuum. Colonial portraits were not free of foreign influence; they wallowed in it. Belknap's work largely put an end to the jingoistic aspect of American art scholarship, as scholars came to realize that much of what had been believed about colonial painting was in fact a misunderstanding. His discovery has resulted in a better, more accurate understanding of colonial American life, art, and culture and also of the complex and fascinating relationship, both artistic and commercial, between painters and engravers in America, Britain, and Europe.

• Belknap's papers, research notes, and personal library are housed in the Belknap Library of the Henry Francis du Pont Winterthur Museum, Winterthur, Del. His most important research notes were published as *American Colonial Painting: Materials for a History* (1959). This book also contains a short biographical sketch and an account of the discovery of the mezzotint prototypes, both written by Charles Coleman Sellers. John Marshall Phillips et al., eds., *The Waldron Phoenix Belknap, Jr. Collection of Portraits and Silver . . .* (1955), also recounts Belknap's discovery.

DAVID MESCHUTT

BELKNAP, William Worth (22 Sept. 1829–12 or 13 Oct. 1890), secretary of war, was born in Newburgh, New York, the son of William Goldsmith Belknap, a career army officer, and Ann Clark. Following his graduation from Princeton in 1846, he studied law at Georgetown University. Belknap moved to Keokuk, Iowa, in 1851 and became the law partner of Ralph P. Lowe, who later became the governor of Iowa and a state supreme court justice.

In 1854 Belknap married Cora Le Roy; they had two children, neither of whom lived to adulthood. Three years later he won election to the Iowa House of Representatives for one term (1857–1858) as a Douglas Democrat. At the outbreak of the Civil War, he served as a captain in the Fifteenth Iowa Infantry, part of the Union Army of the Tennessee. Shortly after he left home for active duty in 1862, his wife died. Belknap was not only popular with his men but also received praise as a first-rate officer. At the battle of Shiloh (1862), Belknap, remembered one superior, was "always . . . in the right place at the right time." Following the Atlanta campaign, he joined William T. Sherman's army in its march to the sea. Belknap was breveted major general in 1865.

When the war ended, Belknap rejected an offer to become a commissioned army officer. Instead, he opted for the position of collector of internal revenue for the First District of Iowa. Belknap performed his duties skillfully, handling large sums of money without any suggestion of impropriety. In 1868 he married Carita "Carrie" Tomlinson, an arrangement that had far-reaching consequences for Belknap's career.

Belknap's exemplary war record led his former commander Sherman to suggest him as Ulysses Grant's secretary of war in October 1869. Belknap accepted Grant's invitation and moved immediately to Washington. The Belknaps gained quick and broad popularity among capital society, whom they entertained frequently and lavishly. On 29 December 1870 Carrie died of tuberculosis, leaving her husband with an infant boy. Belknap's sister-in-law, the widowed Amanda Tomlinson Bower, agreed to help care for the child. The infant's death the following May compounded Belknap's personal tragedy. In December 1873 Belknap married Amanda.

Belknap's contributions to the cabinet were undistinguished. He was involved with important decisions but rarely acted alone. Initially, he avoided the allegations of scandal that buffeted the Grant presidency. At the end of Grant's second term, Belknap sought to capitalize on his performance by seeking a senatorial seat representing Iowa in 1876. He lost by a wide margin. By this time Belknap found himself embroiled in a controversy that has come to symbolize the corruption associated with the Grant administration.

Controversy continues to surround the allegations that first broke in the *New York Herald* on 9 February 1876. The paper reported that "vague rumors have reached the capital" for months that sutlers supplying military posts in the West had to pay a "tax" in order to retain their lucrative posts. The *Herald* also reported that a journal "in a Western city" claimed all soldiers knew that the increased cost of goods they bought was a result of this "tax," which benefited the secretary of war.

In late February 1876 hearings before the House Committee on Expenditures in the War Department disclosed that Belknap and his wife Amanda had received money from Caleb Marsh to ensure Marsh's position as post trader of Fort Sill. Under Belknap, the War Department had assumed control of these appointments from post commanders. Those seeking such positions came to view a bribe as little more than a business expense. Belknap neither confirmed nor denied the allegations when he appeared before the committee.

Further investigation revealed that Carrie Belknap had made a financial arrangement with both the former post trader, John S. Evans, and his would-be successor Marsh. Evans kept his post but had to make a yearly payment of $6,000 each to Marsh and Carrie Belknap. Carrie received only one payment before falling ill, but she explained the arrangement to her sister before she died. At the funeral, Marsh agreed to continue the payments to Amanda, ostensibly to provide for Carrie's young son.

By 1876 congressional records estimated that the Belknaps (Carrie and Amanda) had received a total of nearly $20,000 from the arrangement. Much of this went to supplement Amanda Belknap's demanding entertaining and clothing budget. In fact, General Sherman's assessment of the scandal focused on the Belknaps' expensive social obligations.

Apparently Belknap was not caught unawares by the allegations. He shrewdly, if tearfully, tendered his resignation to Grant on the morning of 2 March. Congress immediately made plans to impeach Belknap for malfeasance. The former secretary responded that Congress did not have the authority to convict a one-time public official who was no longer in office. Despite this argument, the Democratic-dominated House voted for impeachment in an effort to further embarrass Grant and the Republicans during the upcoming elections. Despite the evidence, the question of congressional jurisdiction caused the Senate to acquit Belknap at his impeachment.

The extent of Belknap's guilt remains in question. He was never tried on the allegations of selling sutler posts. The scandal centered on the issue of his wives' financial arrangements with Marsh. It is clear that Belknap received money from Marsh for Amanda, but she had come to the marriage with considerable savings. Belknap maintained that the money represented returns on investments entrusted to Marsh. Once the New York papers broke the story, however, Belknap clearly determined that his only course of action was to resign to spare his wives—and Grant—the shame of an investigation.

Not surprisingly, the Democrats seized on the Belknap scandal in an effort to weaken Grant and the Republicans during the fall elections. Belknap steadfastly maintained his innocence during the trial and worked to clear his name in later years, yet he never gave a full account of his role in the matter. Was he simply trying to protect himself, or was he covering for his wives?

Belknap resumed the practice of law in Washington, D.C. Despite the less than conclusive results of his impeachment trial, he continued to find support among a number of influential politicians. He likewise never lost the confidence of Union veterans' groups, particularly those in Iowa. Accordingly, following his death (sometime during the night of 12 and 13 Oct.) in Washington, he was buried with full military honors at Arlington National Cemetery. The flag at the War Department was also lowered to half-mast, an act that generated controversy around the country.

• Belknap's papers are located at the Iowa State Department of History and Archives in Des Moines and in the manuscript collection at Princeton University. William Talbot of Keokuk, Iowa, also has selected Belknap manuscripts. Since he freely corresponded with many of his contemporaries, Belknap's letters can be found scattered among a number of other collections. Belknap contributed an article, "The Obedience and Courage of the Private Soldier," in *War Sketches and Incidents*, ed. Iowa Commandery, Military Order of the Loyal Legion (1893). The only full-length study is Roger D. Bridges, "The Impeachment and Trial of William Worth Belknap" (M.A. thesis, State College of Iowa, 1963), which offers a sympathetic view of Belknap. His Civil War experiences are well documented. Mildred Throne, ed., "The Civil War Diary of G. F. Boyd, Fifteenth," *Iowa Journal of History* 50 (1952): 47–82, 155–84, 239–70, 345–78, presents a favorable view of Belknap in the eyes of an enlisted man of his regiment. Further information is in the *Roster and Record of Iowa Soldiers in the War of Rebellion, 1861–1866*, vol. 2 (1908). For details of Belknap's impeachment trial, see "Proceedings of the Senate, Sitting for the Trial of William W. Belknap, Late Sec't of War," *Congressional Record*, 44th Cong., 1st sess., vol. 4 (1876). *Harper's Weekly*, the *New York Herald*, and the *New York Tribune* carried detailed accounts of Belknap's downfall in 1876. See also Robert C. Pickett, "The Malfeasance of William Worth Belknap," *North Dakota History* 17 (1950): 97–134; and Philip D. Jordan, "The Domestic Finances of Secretary of War W. W. Belknap," *Iowa Journal of History* 52 (1954): 193–202. Allan Nevins offers a useful summary of the Belknap scandal in *Hamilton Fish: The Inner History of the Grant Administration* (1937). William S. McFeely provides a more recent assessment of the episode in *Grant: A Biography* (1981).

W. BRUCE BOWLUS

BELL, Alexander Graham (3 Mar. 1847–2 Aug. 1922), inventor and educator, was born in Edinburgh, Scotland, the son of Alexander Melville Bell and Eliza Grace Symonds. Family tradition and childhood environment set him on the path to his greatest invention, the telephone. His grandfather had turned from acting to speech teaching, and his father had become eminent in the latter vocation. His mother, despite her seriously impaired hearing, was an accomplished pianist and engaged her son's interest in that form of sound communication. Edinburgh, second only to London as an intellectual center of the British Empire, excelled in science and technology, which probably stirred the boy's interest and ambition in such matters. He made a hobby of botany and zoology. Playing about a local grist mill, he took up the miller's challenge to make himself useful and devised a hand-cranked machine that took the husks off the grain—"my first invention," he later called it.

Along with a tendency to scatter his interests and energies, certain other traits influenced the course of his life. From his boyhood onward he struggled consciously to restrain a propensity toward introspection and solitude. More than his two brothers, he felt both oppressed and challenged by his imposing father's professional eminence. One of his brothers teased him about his "wish to do something great," but an undistinguished record at Edinburgh's Royal High School did little for his self-confidence. A subsequent year under the tutelege of his grandfather in London gave Bell a more solid intellectual grounding, though the separation from his contemporaries left him seeming older than his sixteen years. This precocious maturity would serve him well in his succeeding three years of private school teaching in Scotland and England.

On Bell's return from London, his father sought to rally his spirits by challenging him to collaborate with his elder brother in making a "speaking machine"—a device for mechanical production of vocal sounds. The maneuver worked. After studying a lamb's larynx given them by a butcher, the young men devised a model of the vocal organs manipulated by levers. Sounding it by blowing through a tube, they could make it emit humanlike cries. This heightened Bell's fascination with the mechanisms of speech. He followed the call further during his stint of school teaching, when he sounded tuning forks before his open mouth as he manipulated his vocal organs. Each position would amplify a different fork because of resonance. He discovered that each vowel sound is a compound of two pitches and that in a certain sequence one rises and the other falls as the sequence progresses. Moreover, he deduced the physiological basis of the phenomenon.

His elation was dampened when he learned that the great scientist Hermann von Helmholtz had recently made the same discovery. But he was intrigued by Helmholtz's device for keeping each of his tuning forks vibrating: an intermittent electrical current of the same frequency as the fork's pitch, activating an electromagnet near the fork. Bell told friends that someone, someday, would go on to transmit speech and music by telegraphy. He began tinkering with batteries and telegraphic instruments.

Meanwhile his father had realized a dream of many years by scientifically analyzing vocal sounds to develop a complete and universally applicable system of phonetic notation. Bell became adept in the system, which his father called Visible Speech, and helped win acclaim for it by public demonstrations. More than one observer pointed out its potential for teaching speech to the deaf. In 1868 Bell put the suggestion to the test with four girls at a private school in London. In the experiment's brilliant success Bell found what he ever after would consider his true calling. To the end of his days he would list "teacher of the deaf" as

his profession, notwithstanding his numerous other pursuits.

While in London, to which his parents had moved after his grandfather's death, Bell made use of the family piano. With his ear for pitch and his well-trained voice he had a knack for singing into the wires and sounding them selectively by sympathetic vibration. This suggested to him that if the different frequencies of several tuning forks were transmitted simultaneously over a single wire, they could be separated out by similarly tuned forks at the other end. Thus a number of Morse code messages might be sent at the same time over a single wire, with the prospect of immense savings for the telegraph industry.

Events crowded the idea out of Bell's mind for the time being. His younger brother had died of tuberculosis in 1867, and his older brother succumbed to the same disease in 1870. His father, having decided to migrate to Canada, persuaded his only surviving son to come along to that more bracing and healthful climate. Bell and his parents settled in Brantford, Ontario, that summer. When the elder Bell, warmly received in a series of lectures at Boston, was asked to introduce the Visible Speech method there at a new school for deaf children, he referred the offer to his son, who accepted it eagerly.

Bell arrived in Boston in April 1871. His success at the Boston school and at others in the region—a success due as much to his talent and enthusiasm as to the Visible Speech system—encouraged him to open his own private teacher-training classes in 1872. Bell's higher education consisted of a couple of courses at the University of Edinburgh in 1864 and a few more at the University of London in 1868 and 1869. But in that period the lack of more elaborate academic credentials did not preclude college teaching. Bell's demonstrated skill led Boston University to engage him as professor of vocal physiology in 1873. This gave him access to Boston intellectual circles.

Boston was an American counterpart of Edinburgh. Its oldest college, Harvard, had been joined in the 1860s not only by Boston University and Boston College, but also by the Massachusetts Institute of Technology. Boston was a center of American industry and finance, as well as literature and learning. And it was the leading center of American science and technology. In that setting Bell's interest in science and invention revived. He attended evening lectures at MIT. In October 1872 he heard the eminent English scientist John Tyndall lecture on the "undulatory theory" of light propagation. That month the newspaper in which Bell advertised his speech lessons reported that Western Union had paid handsomely for a Boston inventor's "duplex telegraph," which by an ingenious arrangement of circuits could send a message in each direction simultaneously on a single wire.

Bell's thoughts returned to his London concept of sending several, not just two, messages at once on the quite different plan of superimposed frequencies. He began experimenting by night, teaching by day, and thus confirmed his lifelong night-owl habits. In struggling with certain snags he resorted to an induced "undulatory" current, which could reproduce both amplitude and pitch, instead of an intermittent one, which transmitted pitch only. In 1874 an MIT invitation to use its laboratories introduced him to a device, the "phonautograph," that literally made speech visible by using its vibrations to trace an undulating curve on a strip of smoked glass, displaying both amplitude and frequency.

That summer at Brantford the two lines of experiment fused in his mind to form the basic principle of the telephone. He assumed, however, that vocal sounds could not vibrate an armature with enough force to induce a current capable of reproducing audible speech. Fortunately, he discussed the theoretical concept with Boston scientists, one of whom preserved notes dated October 1874.

Putting aside what he deemed an impractical notion, Bell resumed work on his "harmonic" multiple telegraph. Two events added urgency to his quest. A Boston businessman, Gardiner Greene Hubbard, whose daughter Mabel was one of Bell's deaf pupils, had projected an enterprise to compete with Western Union. The latter's acquisition of the new duplex telegraph gave Hubbard pause, but word of Bell's scheme roused him that October to offer financial backing, in which he was joined by a Salem businessman, Thomas Sanders, father of another Bell pupil. Bell's growing romantic interest in Mabel Hubbard gave him added reason to press on with the harmonic telegraph. So also did the news in November that a Chicago inventor named Elisha Gray was working along similar lines. Now having financial support, Bell resorted to Charles Williams's Boston shop for custom-made electrical apparatus. There, early in 1875, he engaged the full-time services of a bright young worker, Thomas A. Watson.

Bell and Watson labored on the harmonic telegraph that winter and spring. In February Bell hurried to the U.S. Patent Office, only to find that Gray had filed a harmonic telegraph patent two days ahead of him. Bell, however, was first with applications for important elements of such a system, but at Washington, D.C., Joseph Henry, the most eminent of American scientists and head of the Smithsonian Institution, had listened to his telephone conception with interest and urged him to give it priority over the telegraph system. Bell thought of another way to make the undulatory current, using sound waves to vary the resistance in a battery-powered circuit, though the means he tried did not work. Then, in the attic of the Williams shop on 2 June 1875, struggling with a multiple-telegraph circuit, Watson happened to pluck a steel reed that had stuck to an electromagnet. Beyond a partition, Bell heard another reed twang. At once the significance broke upon his mind: the motion of Watson's reed had induced a current that made an audible sound at Bell's end.

That summer Bell was again diverted from the telephone goal by his courtship of Mabel Hubbard. Her parents objected on grounds of her youth, and her fa-

ther insisted on priority for the multiple telegraph. Not until Thanksgiving did the young couple become engaged. In January 1876 Bell completed his telephone application. Hubbard, at last grasping the importance of the concept, took it upon himself to file Bell's application on 14 February 1876. By what seemed an extraordinary coincidence, Elisha Gray filed a similar caveat—a statement of an untested idea—a few hours after Bell's completed application. Gray, however, claimed to have had the conception in November 1875, which was more than a year after Bell's documented conception. Gray's earliest record of it was the caveat itself. Interestingly, Gray had frequented the Patent Office for several days before that, during which time Bell's notarized specifications had been the subject of admiring discussion in the office. Bell's Patent Number 174,465, often called the most valuable single patent in history, was duly issued on 7 March 1876.

Though Bell's induction-based instruments had transmitted unmistakably vocal sounds, it was a device using his concept of variable resistance, covered in the patent, that first produced an intelligible sentence—"Mr. Watson, come here, I want to see you"—on 10 March 1876. Later that month Bell also made his induction or electromagnetic model talk. Bell's father being the listener, its first word was "Papa."

Along with his Boston University classes and private instruction, Bell worked on further improving the induction model's performance. In June he gave a triumphant private demonstration to the judges at the International Centennial Exhibition in Philadelphia. With the party was Dom Pedro, emperor of Brazil, who, contrary to legend, did not exclaim, "My God, it talks!," but rather, "I hear, I hear!" Though the public took little note at the time, another member of the party, the English scientist Sir William Thompson, later awakened Europe to Bell's achievement.

In the months that followed, Bell and Watson worked to improve the telephone's performance and extend its range. Bell relished publicizing it in lecture tours. After he married Mabel Hubbard in July 1877, however, the couple sailed for England and Scotland, where they remained for more than a year. Two days before the wedding Gardiner Hubbard had led the group that organized the Bell Telephone Company, and he ran its affairs with great success during the newlyweds' absence. On their return, Bell gave up his university appointment and worked as the new company's technical adviser. That work, however, ceased entirely after the early eighties. He cheerfully admitted that it no longer appealed to him. His services remained vital to the company as a key witness in its triumphant defense of the basic patents during years of litigation against a horde of infringers and counterclaimants. Among them was Elisha Gray, who, after initially brushing off the telephone as of little value, gradually became convinced that he had somehow been cheated of a great fortune. Bell himself did not become immensely rich. In lieu of royalties he had received stock, most of which he sold at an early date. But he emerged independently wealthy.

The Bells and their two daughters moved to Washington, D.C., in 1882. In that year Bell also became a U.S. citizen. In 1886 he bought land for a summer home near Baddeck, Nova Scotia, where the family spent an increasing part of the year as time went by. By then Bell was no longer the slender, dark-haired young man who had won Mabel Hubbard. On his honeymoon he had begun putting on weight and growing a full beard. By his forties he was stout and graying. His physical presence matched his world fame: he bore himself with the majesty of a Moses and the benevolence of a Santa Claus. When he entered a room, he seemed to fill it.

Bell remained active as a teacher, an organizer, a frequent and masterful public speaker, a member of many clubs and other organizations, the sponsor for many years of a brilliant Washington salon, and the paterfamilias of a numerous and close-knit clan. Yet one of his sons-in-law said of him, "I have never known anyone who spent so much of his time alone." In Baddeck he retreated alone for weekends on a secluded houseboat, and year-round he worked and studied alone until three or four in the morning, then slept until ten or eleven, notwithstanding his wife's periodic efforts to make him diurnal. He himself tried but never quite succeeded in shaking off his tendency to solitude.

It may have been that characteristic, more than the deafness of his mother and wife, that made him empathize with the relative isolation of the deaf from society at large. His most notable scientific work dealt with deafness. He helped apply his telephone as an audiometer, and his name entered the language in the decibel—the standard measure of sound intensity. He contributed to genetics through studies of inherited propensity to deafness, of which he found some evidence. And he became a leader in the education of the deaf. In Scotland during his honeymoon, and later in Washington, D.C., he planned and directed schools for deaf children, always regretting that telephone affairs prevented long-term commitments. He became a champion, mentor, and long-time friend of the blind and deaf Helen Keller. He gave a sizable share of his income over the years to the cause of the deaf. He also gave his leadership and the weight of his eminence to conquering the solitude of deafness through the teaching of speech, the establishment of public day schools mingling deaf and hearing children, and the organizing and support of an association supporting those goals. He became the leader of those who defended oral communication by the deaf against the inroads of the more socially limited, though more natural, sign language.

All along, however, Bell resisted being bound to any single line of work. In counterpoint to his work for the deaf ran concurrent activity in technology and science. Impressed by Edison's Menlo Park "invention factory," he tried to replicate it in Washington, the difference being that, whereas Edison looked for a commer-

cial need and sought a way to meet it, Bell more often seized on a physical phenomenon and looked for a way to use it. Intrigued by the element selenium's increase in electrical conductivity with the intensity of light falling on it, Bell hired a young technician, Sumner Tainter, and in 1880 produced his "photophone," which transmitted speech by a light beam of fluctuating intensity. But its range of only a few hundred feet, and that only in the absence of fog, rain, and other obstacles, gave it no commercial value, though Bell always claimed it to be a greater invention than the telephone, doubtless because he hated to think that his career had peaked at twenty-nine.

In 1881 Bell did invent for a practical purpose: to locate an assassin's bullet in the body of the dying President James A. Garfield. His frantic efforts produced an adaptation of the induction balance that worked like a present-day mine detector and a probe combining a needle with a telephone receiver to produce a click when it touched metal. But the bullet was too deep for the first to pinpoint, and the surgeons chose not to try the probe, though afterward it was much used until superseded by X-rays. In that same summer the death of an infant son from respiratory failure drove Bell to invent a "vacuum jacket" using mechanical power to expand and contract the lungs—an anticipation of the iron lung developed for polio victims a half-century later. Also in the early eighties Bell turned the tables on Edison, who had much improved telephone reception with his carbon-button transmitter. Bell now mustered the talents of his cousin Chichester Bell and Sumner Tainter to make Edison's phonograph commercially viable. The Bell-Tainter patents brought the team several hundred thousand dollars, of which Bell's share went to endow research on deafness.

In 1891, inspired by the experiments of his friend Samuel P. Langley of the Smithsonian Institution, Bell set out to realize a goal he had dreamed of since boyhood—that of powered heavier-than-air flight. For a few years he puttered with gunpowder rockets, helicopter rotors, and little monoplanes, growing more and more certain that "flying machines are practical." In 1898 he started up the blind alley of kite flying to experiment on stability. It led him to his last notable inspiration in technology: the use of tetrahedral framework in construction—an anticipation of space-frame architecture, made famous by R. Buckminster Fuller. But though he patented, publicized, and demonstrated it, it did not catch on. Bell went on with his flight experiments, engaging a young engineer, F. W. "Casey" Baldwin as a successor to Watson and Tainter. Eventually he brought together a group of other young men, including Glenn Curtiss, organized as the Aerial Experiment Association. By then the Wright brothers had carried off the palm, but the Bell group won a secure place as pioneers in the new field. Bell's last notable technological project, begun in 1908 with the assistance of Baldwin, was to improve hydrofoil boats. In 1919 their fourth experimental craft set a world speed record that stood for ten years.

In physics Bell lacked the mathematical training increasingly necessary for theoretical work. But he was elected to the National Academy of Sciences, to which he contributed significant papers on aspects of heredity. For some thirty years at his Nova Scotia estate he carried on meticulously recorded experiments in breeding twin-bearing sheep, though without commercially significant success. He also left his mark on science as a patron and organizer. In 1881 he financed a major phase of Albert Michelson's classic experiments on the speed of light. In 1882 he rescued the foundering journal *Science* and helped finance it for nearly a decade. And not least, Bell, himself a world traveler, served from 1898 to 1903 as second president of the National Geographic Society (succeeding its founder, Gardiner Hubbard) and as a shrewd adviser to the society's magazine, edited by his son-in-law Gilbert H. Grosvenor.

Bell died at his Baddeck estate. The tablet set over his grave there includes, as he had specified, the words "Died a Citizen of the United States." Through his numerous achievements in the analysis, teaching, and transmission of speech; education of the deaf; support of major journals; and promotion of air and sea transport, runs the theme of communication and, more particularly, the conquest of involuntary solitude, even in his own nature. As his friend and sometime competitor Thomas Edison remarked at news of his death, Bell had "brought the human family in closer touch."

• The Alexander Graham Bell Papers are in the Library of Congress. No other manuscript repositories contain significant material not also found there. A full bibliography of Bell's published writings and addresses, as well as a list of his U.S. patents, is given on pages 20–29 of Harold S. Osborne, "Biographical Memoir of Alexander Graham Bell, 1847–1922," *National Academy of Sciences Biographical Memoirs* 23 (1943). The only comprehensive, scholarly biography is Robert V. Bruce, *Bell: Alexander Graham Bell and the Conquest of Solitude* (1973).

ROBERT V. BRUCE

BELL, Bert (25 Feb. 1894–11 Oct. 1959), professional football commissioner, was born De Benneville Bell in Philadelphia, Pennsylvania, the son of John Cromwell Bell, a prosperous lawyer and member of a Philadelphia Main Line family, and Fleurette de Benneville Myers. As a student at the Haverford preparatory school, Bell attained greater success as a football, basketball, and baseball player than as a scholar. In 1915 he entered the University of Pennsylvania where he played quarterback; Penn upset powerful Michigan that year but lost the Rose Bowl game to Oregon. After army service in World War I, he returned to captain Penn in 1919; the next year he left without a degree.

In the 1920s and early 1930s Bell's life lacked direction, much of it spent drinking, gambling, and pursuing chorus girls. He dabbled in a variety of business ventures, including hotel management and a brokerage firm, and served on a volunteer basis as an assistant football coach at Penn from 1920 through 1928 and at Temple University in 1930 and 1931. His court-

ship and marriage to Frances Upton, a Broadway musical comedy star, in 1934 radically altered his habits, especially since Upton insisted that he give up drinking. The couple had three children.

Bell began his long association with the National Football League in 1933 when he, along with six friends, purchased the franchise of the Frankford, Pennsylvania, Yellow Jackets for $2,500. Already located in a northeast Philadelphia neighborhood, the team was renamed and became the Philadelphia Eagles. The depression further crippled a financially shaky enterprise; between 1933 and 1936 the Eagles allegedly lost $80,000. When Bell bought out his partners in 1936 for only $4,500, he appointed himself head coach. Under his direction between 1936 and 1940, the Eagles won ten games, lost forty-four, and tied two. In 1940 Bell sold the franchise and purchased a half-interest in the Pittsburgh Steelers, where he served at various times as president, general manager, and coach. In 1946 he sold his interest in the Steelers to become commissioner of the NFL.

In 1936 Bell had persuaded his fellow owners to adopt a major innovation in player recruitment. This was a draft for the selection of college players by NFL teams in reverse order of their league standing at the end of the preceding season. The draft, Bell reasoned, would tend in the long run to equalize competition among the franchises, thereby stimulating fan interest. Although not stated publicly, the draft had the added advantage to the owners of preventing them from bidding against one another for the services of college athletes. After World War II a similar draft would be employed by professional basketball and hockey and in 1965 by major league baseball.

As commissioner, Bell used his authority broadly. He tried to improve the image of professional football by closely watching players and owners suspected of associating with gamblers. He also successfully directed the NFL through a costly rivalry with the All-America Football Conference (AAFC), organized in 1946. In 1949 the AAFC dissolved with the understanding that the Cleveland, San Francisco, and Baltimore franchises would join the NFL on terms favorable to the new teams. Along with the strong fan support that the former AAFC franchises brought with them, the arrival of such stars as quarterbacks Otto Graham and Y. A. Tittle from the AAFC added to the NFL's growing popularity. When owners could not agree on a procedure for distributing the players made available by the AAFC's collapse, Bell determined their assignment.

In the 1950s Bell laid the foundations that would soon transform professional football into the nation's most successful team sports enterprise. Unlike the independent barons of baseball, the NFL owners, who shared a long history of financial tribulations and were mostly of Irish-Catholic stock, were far more willing to delegate authority to their commissioner. Bell personally created the NFL's schedule, putting in some 400 to 500 hours per year at the task. In order to encourage close races for divisional titles, he deliberately scheduled weak teams against other weak teams and strong teams against other strong teams (based on the previous season's record). While television was destroying minor league baseball and reducing major league attendance, Bell helped ensure that it would be a boon to football. At a 1952 owner's meeting he rammed through amended bylaws that made the commissioner the virtual dictator of the NFL's television policy. Although a federal district court judge ruled in 1953 that the revised bylaws violated antitrust law, the judge implicitly upheld TV blackouts of home games. By 1959 each club averaged nearly $100,000 a year from television rights, while the TV industry converted millions into pro football fans. Bell died in Philadelphia while watching a game between his beloved Eagles and the Pittsburgh Steelers.

• The NFL office in New York City holds materials on owner actions, and the Pro Football Hall of Fame in Canton, Ohio, has a newspaper clipping file on Bell. W. C. Heinz, "Boss of the Behemoths," *Saturday Evening Post*, 3 Dec. 1957, and Al Hirshberg, "He Calls the Signals in Pro Football," *New York Times Magazine*, 23 Dec. 1958, are valuable articles. An obituary is in the *New York Times*, 12 Oct. 1959.

BENJAMIN G. RADER

BELL, Cool Papa (17 May 1903–7 Mar. 1991), Negro League baseball player, was born James Thomas Bell in Starkville, Mississippi, the son of a farmer; his parents' names are not known. Because Starkville offered few opportunities for blacks, his mother sent him to live with his sister and four brothers in St. Louis, Missouri, where he attended high school for two years and worked in a packing plant. During this time Bell played semiprofessional baseball; he was "discovered" in 1922 by the St. Louis Stars of the Negro National League, against whom Bell pitched. The Stars signed him to a $90-a-month contract.

Bell played for many different teams in the Negro Leagues, but he is generally associated with the St. Louis Stars and Pittsburgh Crawfords. Bell got the nickname "Cool" for his demeanor under pressure while pitching for the Stars at the age of 19. His manager, Bill Gatewood, added "Papa" despite his young age.

To take advantage of Bell's speed and hitting, Gatewood moved him from the mound to the outfield and taught him to switch-hit. He played for the Stars from 1922 to 1931. In 1932 he was a member of the Detroit Wolves and, when the Wolves disbanded, the Kansas City Monarchs. Then in 1933 Bell joined the Pittsburgh Crawfords, one of the greatest teams in baseball history. The Crawfords featured Satchel Paige, Judy Johnson, Oscar Charleston, and Josh Gibson, four of the greatest players in the Negro Leagues and all members of the National Baseball Hall of Fame. In 1937, when Gus Greenlee, the owner of the Crawfords, defaulted on their salaries, Bell joined Paige and a number of other Crawford players in Santo Domingo, playing for a team put together by Dominican Republic dictator Rafael Trujillo, who thought a championship would help him to consolidate power. Trujillo

kept the players under armed guard. When they fell behind in the championship series, the players feared for their lives, but they rallied to win.

For the next four years Bell played in the integrated Mexican League for $450 a month. He had his greatest year in 1940 when he won the Mexican League triple crown, hitting .437 with 12 home runs and 79 runs batted in. He also led the league in runs scored and triples and was among the leaders in doubles and stolen bases. After one more year in Mexico, he returned to the United States in 1942 to play for the Chicago American Giants and the Memphis Red Sox of the Negro American League. He played for the Homestead Grays from 1943 to 1946 and for the Detroit Stars in 1947, and he concluded his career as a player-manager with the Kansas City Stars, a farm team of the Kansas City Monarchs, from 1948 to 1950. Bell played 29 summers of professional baseball in the Negro Leagues and barnstorming in exhibitions. He also played 21 seasons of winter baseball in Cuba, Mexico, Puerto Rico, and California.

Few players were as universally respected or loved as Bell. He was one of the great players in the Negro Leagues along with legends like Paige, Johnson, Buck Leonard, Gibson, and Charleston. Players and sportswriters who saw him play unanimously conclude that he would have been a star in the major leagues if the color barrier had been lifted. Regarded by many as the fastest man to play organized baseball, he was once timed circling the bases in 12 seconds. It was said that Olympic sprinter Jesse Owens refused to race Bell.

Bell was a symbol of the aggressive style of baseball that helped define the Negro Leagues. Players stole bases and gambled on the base paths; Bell referred to it as "tricky ball." The fame of Babe Ruth and the lively baseball turned major league baseball in the 1920s into a game based more on power and less on aggressive running; as the number of home runs rose, the number of stolen bases declined. The Negro Leagues combined both elements.

Although record keeping in the Negro Leagues was suspect, it is estimated that Bell ended his career with a lifetime batting average around .340. In 54 recorded games against players from the major leagues, he hit .391. Bell estimated that he stole 173 bases in 200 games in 1933. He hit over .400 a number of times, and he was a perennial Negro League all-star, making the All-Star team every year he was eligible (1933–1936, 1942–1944).

There are a number of legends surrounding Cool Papa. Satchel Paige frequently said that Bell was so fast that he could flip the light switch and be in bed before the room was dark. In fact, there was an element of truth to this story; Bell discovered a faulty light switch and bet the unwitting Paige that he could fulfill the boast. Another story had it that Bell hit a ball up the middle and was hit by the ball as he slid into second base.

Other stories had more factual bases. In an all-star game against major leaguers, Bell scored from first base on a bunt, brushing by the catcher who still had the ball. In 1946 Bell deliberately forfeited the Negro League batting title to Monte Irvin, in order to enhance Irvin's chances of following Jackie Robinson to the major leagues. Bell was also instrumental in convincing Robinson that he could not play shortstop in the major leagues. He hit balls to Robinson's right and beat out each one, showing Robinson his arm was not strong enough to throw Bell out from the hole. He also discovered future Chicago Cubs great Ernie Banks and recommended him to Buck O'Neil, later the first black coach in the major leagues.

Bell was offered a chance to play in the major leagues for the St. Louis Browns in 1951, but he refused, citing his age. He never expressed bitterness over the injustices of the color ban. After his retirement from baseball, he spent 21 years working as a custodian and security guard at St. Louis City Hall and lived on Cool Papa Bell Boulevard, named for him in 1983.

Bell was elected to the National Baseball Hall of Fame in 1974, the fifth Negro League player so honored, preceded by Paige, Leonard, Irvin, and Gibson. In his typically selfless manner, Bell said that getting into the Hall of Fame was his greatest honor, but his "biggest thrill was the day they opened the door [to major league baseball] to the Negro."

Bell and his wife Clarabelle had one daughter, Connie Brooks, who dedicated herself to keeping the memories of the Negro Leagues and their players alive. He died in St. Louis.

• The National Baseball Library in Cooperstown, N.Y., has a clipping file on Bell. Newspapers are the best source for information about Bell and the Negro Leagues, especially African-American newspapers such as the *St. Louis American*. For more on the Negro Leagues, their personalities, and the place of Bell, see Robert Peterson, *Only the Ball Was White* (1970); Donn Rogosin, *Invisible Men: Life in Baseball's Negro Leagues* (1983); James Bankes, *The Pittsburgh Crawfords: The Lives and Times of Black Baseball's Most Exciting Team* (1991); James Riley, *The Biographical Encyclopedia of the Negro Baseball Leagues* (1994); John Holway, *Voices from the Great Black Baseball Leagues*, rev. ed. (1992); Mark Ribowsky, *A Complete History of the Negro Leagues: 1884 to 1955* (1995); Holway, *Black Diamonds: Life in the Negro Leagues from the Men Who Lived It* (1989); and David Fremon, *The Negro Baseball Leagues* (1994). See also Mike Shatzkin, *The Ballplayers* (1990); Anthony J. Connor, *Voices from Cooperstown: Baseball's Hall of Famers Tell It Like It Was* (1982); and Donald Honig, *Baseball When the Grass Was Real* (1975).

RICHARD L. PACELLE, JR.

BELL, Eric Temple (7 Feb. 1883–21 Dec. 1960), mathematician, was born in Peterhead, near Aberdeen, Scotland, the son of James Bell, a fish-curer and fruit grower, and Helen Jane Lindsay Lyall. When he was barely a year old, the family left England in 1884 for the United States. Following the death of his father in San José, California, Bell returned with his mother and older brother to England when he was thirteen. In 1898 he entered the Bedford Modern School, where Edward M. Langley inspired Bell's lifelong interest in

number theory and elliptical functions. In 1902, at age nineteen, he returned to the United States in order (as he later said) "to escape being shoved into Woolwich [home of the British Royal Arsenal] or the India Civil Service" (Bell, *Twentieth Century Authors*, p. 70).

In America, Bell was on his own but managed to support himself with a variety of odd jobs, from surviving as a ranch hand and mule skinner to working as a surveyor. After making his way to California, Bell entered Stanford University in 1902. There he succeeded in completing "all of the mathematics offered" in two years, whereupon he graduated with honors, Phi Beta Kappa. After one year at the University of Washington, he received an M.A. in mathematics in 1908, and several years later, another year at Columbia University resulted in his Ph.D. in mathematics in 1912. There his adviser was Cassius J. Keyser, who Bell admitted was "one of the main reasons for my going to Columbia." Above all, he admired the fact that "mathematics to [Keyser] was more than an interminable grind of theorems." When Keyser interviewed Bell about his plans as a graduate student in 1911, specifically how long he planned to take getting his Ph.D., Bell was blunt but accurate: "One academic year . . . my money won't last a day over ten months" (Bell, "Cassius Jackson Keyser," p. 27).

In 1910 Bell married Jessie "Toby" Lillian Smith Brown, a widow nearly six years his senior; they had one child. Meanwhile, having lectured at Harvard, Chicago, and the University of Washington (where he was a "teacher-scholar" from 1912 through 1926), in 1926 he settled at the California Institute of Technology, where he remained until his retirement in 1953. Seven years later, Bell died in Watsonville, California, not far from where he had been raised as a child.

Bell was a prolific author. In addition to more than 250 mathematical papers, many devoted to arithmetic, number theory, and elliptic functions, he published nine texts devoted either to mathematics or history of mathematics: *Algebraic Arithmetic* (1927), *Numerology* (1933), *The Search for Truth* (1934), *The Handmaiden of the Sciences* (1937), *Men of Mathematics* (1937), *The Queen of the Sciences* (1938), *The Development of Mathematics* (1940), *Mathematics, Queen and Servant of Science* (1951), and *The Last Problem* (1961). Published posthumously, this was indeed his last scientific work and was devoted to a history of Pierre de Fermat's so-called last theorem.

In addition to Bell's mathematical and historical writings, he was also a productive writer. Under his pseudonym "John Taine," he published seventeen science fiction novels, many short stories, and some poetry. *Before the Dawn* (1934), the only piece of science fiction he published under his own name, was his admitted favorite and was inspired, he once said, by the dinosaur models he remembered from his childhood in Croydon Park, on the grounds of the old Crystal Palace near London (Bell, *Twentieth Century Authors*, p. 70).

Bell was elected president of the Mathematical Association of America for 1931–1932. Earlier, his article on "Arithmetical Paraphrases" had won the association's Bôcher Prize for 1921. But his popularized histories of mathematics were his best-known writings, especially *Men of Mathematics*, which won the Gold Medal of the Commonwealth Club of California. T. A. A. Broadbent captured the essence of the man who most know from his popularizations: "He was no uncritical hero-worshiper, being as quick to mark the opportunity lost as the ground gained, so that from his books we get a vision of mathematics as a high activity of the questing human mind, often fallible, but always pressing on in the never-ending search for mathematical truth" (Broadbent, p. 443).

Historian of mathematics Kenneth O. May has written that "[Bell's] insights and provocative style continue to influence and intrigue professional mathematicians—in spite of their historical inaccuracies and sometimes fanciful interpretations" (May, p. 584). Others, however, have been more critical, objecting to Bell's usually opinionated and often prejudiced views; his description of the Russian mathematician Sophia Kovalevskaya, for example, has been denounced as an "infuriatingly patronizing, innuendo-laden mistreatment" (Cooke). Whatever may be said of the shortcomings of Bell's research and historical scholarship, however, one cannot help but admire the enthusiasm with which he promoted mathematics. He was active in organizations that supported research, teaching, and writing. While in religion and politics he has been described as an "individualist and uncompromising iconoclast" (May, p. 584), these traits were no less true of his historical works, which, ultimately, have had the greatest influence and have often served as the first introductions for many mathematicians to the history of mathematics.

• Major repositories of Bell's papers include the archives of the California Institute of Technology, the D. E. Smith Collection in the Rare Book and Manuscript Library of Columbia University, and other personal documents in the possession of Bell's son, Taine T. Bell of Watsonville, Calif. For Bell's appraisal of his adviser, see his "Cassius Jackson Keyser," *Scripta Mathematica* 14 (1948): 27–33. Until recently, most accounts of Bell's life have been based on his own autobiographical description published in *Twentieth Century Authors*, supplement 1, *A Biographical Dictionary of Modern Literature*, ed. Stanley J. Kunitz (1955), pp. 70–71. But as Constance Reid has revealed in an engrossing biography of Bell, much of this information is purely fictitious; it seems that Bell did everything he could to obscure his early family history, his father's true profession, and the fact that he had been raised in California. For an authoritative and detailed account of his life, based upon a careful study of family records and Bell's own surviving papers, see Reid, *The Search for E. T. Bell, Also Known as John Taine* (1993), which includes a complete list of personal and professional correspondence, papers, and other unpublished materials of Bell. See also T. A. A. Broadbent, "Prof. E. T. Bell," *Nature* 4763 (11 Feb. 1961): 443; Kenneth O. May, "E. T. Bell," *Dictionary of Scientific Biography*, ed. Charles C. Gillispie, vol. 1 (1970), pp. 584–85; and Roger L. Cooke's remarks about Bell in his review of an article by Ann Hibner Koblitz, "New Material

on S. V. Kovalevskaya" (in Russian), *Mathematical Reviews* (1992), review 92h01056. An obituary is in the *New York Times*, 22 Dec. 1960.

JOSEPH W. DAUBEN

BELL, Eudorus Neander (27 June 1866–15 June 1923), first chairman (a position now designated "general superintendent") of the Assemblies of God, was born in Lake Butler, Florida, one of twin sons born to George Bell and his wife (name unknown). Bell's father died in 1868, and scant references to his childhood indicate that the family was not financially secure. He worked his way through Stetson University in De Land, Florida, where he received his B.A. in 1900. After attending the Southern Baptist Theological Seminary in Louisville, Kentucky, during the academic year 1900–1901, Bell enrolled at the University of Chicago Divinity School where he was awarded the bachelor of divinity degree in 1903. Given his later involvement with Pentecostals who questioned the doctrine of the Trinity, the topic of his thesis merits notice: "The Significance of the Term 'Son of God' in Romans and Galatians." While at the University of Chicago, Bell preached twice each week at the Baptist church in the small town of Chenoa, about 100 miles south of Chicago.

After preaching in Southern Baptist churches for seventeen years, Bell heard about Pentecostalism in 1907. His curiosity prompted him to take a leave of absence from his church in Fort Worth, Texas, and to return to Chicago where he became associated with William Durham, another Baptist who had recently embraced Pentecostalism. Durham was the pastor of a mission at the intersection of West North and Sheffield avenues that was a hub for Chicago Pentecostals. Under Durham's tutelage, Bell was persuaded of the validity of the Pentecostal reading of Scripture, and on 18 July 1908 he experienced baptism with the Holy Spirit through speaking in tongues. He returned to Fort Worth where many in his congregation apparently supported his changed views. The next year he married a widow, Katie Kimbrough, and resigned his church to accept a Pentecostal pastorate in Malvern, Arkansas.

In 1909 Bell began editing a monthly magazine, *Word and Witness*. The publication helped establish him as a leader among a far-flung constituency formed by the magazine into a loose network. In April 1914 Bell was among a small group of Pentecostal pastors and evangelists who convened a council of some 300 people who were concerned about tendencies toward religious fanaticism in the movement. The council met in Hot Springs, Arkansas, and voted to create an association to facilitate advice and discipline for workers and to coordinate evangelism. Bell—who was better educated and more experienced than most of those in attendance—was elected chairman of the association, which was called the General Council of the Assemblies of God. He served from April until November, overseeing the formation of a rudimentary denomination and working especially to establish its publishing outreach, which became Gospel Publishing House.

Although he resigned as council chairman, Bell remained editor of council publications. In 1915 he identified briefly with an emerging unorthodox variation of Pentecostalism known as "Oneness." He accepted rebaptism by immersion using the words "in the name of Jesus" instead of the trinitarian formula. Pentecostals who accepted rebaptism thought that they were obeying explicit instructions given in the New Testament (Acts 2:38). Bell did not endorse the nontrinitarian views that gradually evolved among Oneness Pentecostals, who identified the Christ of the New Testament with Jehovah of the Old. He attempted, rather, to conform to New Testament usage by submitting to rebaptism using a specific formula. His rebaptism caused a considerable stir, however, as it seemed likely that others would follow his example. The survival of the Assemblies of God seemed temporarily jeopardized, but Bell reevaluated his views and remained with the organization. After a brief pastorate in Galena, Kansas, Bell moved back into denominational leadership.

One of two men who chose Springfield, Missouri, as the headquarters city for the Assemblies of God, Bell moved to Springfield with the organization in 1918. He served as the denomination's general secretary from 1919 to 1920. The 1920 General Council elected him once again to the office of chairman, a position he held at the time of his death, in Springfield.

Bell heavily influenced early Assemblies of God views. His long Southern Baptist associations apparently predisposed him toward a narrow view of the office of chairman, and he strongly favored a marked degree of congregational autonomy. As a southern Pentecostal whose roots were not in the Wesleyan-based holiness revival, he was inclined toward the non-Wesleyan views on the second work of grace that sparked one of the earliest and most divisive controversies in American Pentecostal history. Wesleyan pentecostals taught that believers should earnestly seek three distinct spiritual experiences: conversion, sanctification, Spirit baptism. Bell, like Durham, believed that sanctification was progressive rather than instantaneous, and he helped align the Assemblies of God with a non-Wesleyan stance on this pivotal doctrine. His question and answer column in one of the most influential early American Pentecostal periodicals, the *Pentecostal Evangel* (a publication that stemmed, in part, from Bell's earlier *Word and Witness*), helped clarify doctrines and articulated for Pentecostals a mode of responding to current theological and cultural issues.

• Bell's ministerial file is kept in the Assemblies of God archives in Springfield, Mo. Additional biographical information is contained in Carl Brumback, *Suddenly . . . from Heaven* (1961), and Stanley Frodsham's biographical sketch in Eudorus N. Bell, *Questions and Answers* (1923), pp. v–xi.

EDITH L. BLUMHOFER

BELL, James Ford (16 Aug. 1879–7 May 1961), corporate executive, was born in Philadelphia, Pennsylvania, the son of James Stroud Bell, a miller, and Sallie Montgomery Ford. His family relocated to Minneapolis, Minnesota, in 1888, and Bell received his early education in the public schools there. After preparing for college at the Lawrenceville School in New Jersey, he entered the University of Minnesota. Bell graduated with a B.S. in chemistry in 1901 and immediately joined his father's firm, the Washburn Crosby Company. Initially employed as a salesman in Michigan, he soon became fully acquainted with all facets of the firm's operations. He married Louise Heffelfinger of Minneapolis in 1902; the couple had four children.

By affiliating with Washburn Crosby, Bell continued a family commitment to the milling industry that had endured for six generations. He became a director of the firm in 1909, and upon his father's death in 1915 he became a vice president. When the United States entered World War I in 1917, the milling industry came under the jurisdiction of the U.S. Food Administration, and Bell, by virtue of his stature in the industry, became head of the Milling Division. In this position Bell oversaw the government's successful efforts to control both production and pricing in the milling industry. In January 1918 he also created a mechanical department within the division to furnish millers with technical assistance, and he made the Milling Division a clearinghouse of business management assistance to small independent millers. With the Milling Division's organization firmly in place, Bell joined Food Administration head Herbert Hoover on his European Food Mission in August 1918. After studying conditions among the Allies, Bell returned to the United States in the fall of 1918 and became the treasurer and general manager of the Sugar Equalization Board. He resigned from the board in March 1919 and returned to his former post at Washburn Crosby.

Following the end of World War I the milling industry, like much of the economy, faced a period of readjustment. One ominous trend was the continuing decline of per capita flour consumption among consumers; in seeking to train Americans to use flour substitutes, the federal government had succeeded too well. As a result, millers sought additional markets, and Washburn Crosby was no exception. An accidental spillage by a company nutritionist led to the development and introduction of a ready-made breakfast cereal in 1924. Dubbed "Wheaties," it was initially a poor seller until Washburn Crosby began to use radio advertising. Another company innovation was the creation in 1921 of the fictitious character Betty Crocker. First used to answer consumers' mail-in questions, by the late 1920s the character was the star of her own radio program, where culinary advice was combined with company advertisement.

After he assumed the presidency of Washburn Crosby in 1925, Bell continued the company's research efforts and, much as his father had before him, sought to maintain company profitability by expansion. Convinced of the need for a nationwide company in order to justify the ever-increasing advertising expenses, Bell was the driving force behind the creation of General Mills in 1928. Formed from the merger of Washburn Crosby with the Red Star Milling Company of Kansas, the Kell mills of Texas and Oklahoma, and the Sperry Flour Company in California, the new firm served as a holding company for the still independently operated mills. The Larrowe Milling Company of Michigan—a major producer of agricultural feeds—was added in the following year. Now nationwide in scope, the newly created General Mills possessed a great advantage in reduced transportation costs with its far-flung chain of mills.

Although general business conditions suffered greatly with the onset of the Great Depression, General Mills not only survived but thrived. While conservative management was critical to this success, ongoing research that led to new products also played a part. With continued advertising, including the use of sports figures and the slogan "Breakfast of Champions," Wheaties became a profitable item. Further diversification came with the introduction of products like Bisquick (1931), Kix (1937), and Cheerios (1941).

Bell resigned as president of General Mills in 1934 but remained a very active chair of the board. As chair he oversaw a 1937 reorganization of General Mills that resulted in its component firms being merged into a single corporate structure. By the time Bell resigned his chair in 1947, General Mills had enjoyed a steady string of profitable years, having made a profit and paid common stock dividends in each year from 1928 to 1947. The company was double the size of Pillsbury, its closest competitor. A staunch Republican, Bell had serious reservations about much of President Franklin D. Roosevelt's New Deal legislation. He was outspoken in his opposition to the Agricultural Adjustment Administration in particular, and he resigned from his seat on the Commerce Department's Business Advisory Council in July 1935 in exasperation over administration policies. By the late 1930s, however, Bell came to grudgingly accept continued government intervention in the private sector. In addition to his duties at General Mills, he served on the boards of Northwestern National Bank, American Telephone & Telegraph, Eastman Kodak, and the Pullman Company. Active in civic affairs as well, he was a trustee of the Minneapolis Society of Fine Arts and of the Dunwoody Institute. He was also a regent of the University of Minnesota and donated his book collection, consisting of early histories of business and exploration, to that institution. Active on General Mills' committee on financial and technological progress even in retirement, he died in Minneapolis two weeks after the death of his wife.

James Ford Bell built on the foundation that his father and the other leaders of Washburn Crosby had created. His vision and leadership were essential parts of the growth and development of General Mills.

• The correspondence of James Ford Bell is divided among the Hoover Institution, Stanford University, Palo Alto, California; the James Ford Bell Library at the University of Minnesota, Minneapolis; and the Minnesota Historical Society, St. Paul. An excellent secondary source on his life and career is James Gray, *Business without Boundary: The Story of General Mills* (1954). Obituaries are in the *Minneapolis Tribune* and the *New York Times*, both 8 May 1961.

EDWARD L. LACH, JR.

BELL, James Franklin (9 Jan. 1856–8 Jan. 1919), army officer, was born near Shelbyville, Kentucky, the son of John Wilson Bell, a dairy farmer, and Sarah Margaret Venable Allen. Bell matriculated at the U.S. Military Academy in September 1874 and graduated in June 1878, standing thirty-eighth in a class of forty-three members. He served as a company officer in the Seventh Cavalry on the northern Great Plains from 1878 to 1886 and spent three years as a professor of military science and tactics at Southern Illinois Normal University at Carbondale, Illinois. He became involved in a number of service reforms, including marksmanship training and physical conditioning, and he was one of the first American officers to use a sand table to teach his men tactics. In 1881 he wed Sarah Buford. The Bells had no children.

Bell participated in the Chilocco Creek, Indian Territory, maneuvers of 1889 as a member of the maneuver director's staff, and he served as the first secretary of the Cavalry and Light Artillery School (1893–1894) and as aide to Brigadier General James W. Forsyth (1894–1897). He also wrote the first U.S. Army manual on the conduct of maneuvers. Major General Wesley Merritt was so impressed with Bell that he selected him to serve as chief of military intelligence for the Philippine Expeditionary Force (later VIII Corps) during the war with Spain.

Bell personally conducted most of the negotiations with the Philippine revolutionary government of General Emilio Aguinaldo for Merritt and his successor, Major General Elwell S. Otis. After serving as chief of scouts for Major General Arthur MacArthur in the Malolos campaign of the Philippine-American War, Bell was promoted to colonel of volunteers and commanded the Thirty-sixth Volunteer Infantry. He won the Congressional Medal of Honor near Porac, Luzon, on 9 September 1899. When Aguinaldo disbanded the main Filipino army to initiate guerrilla operations, Bell shattered one of the retreating columns at Mangatarem, which led to his promotion to brigadier general of volunteers on 5 December 1899.

Bell held a series of commands in the guerrilla war that followed and in the process became the army's premier counterinsurgency expert and a brigadier general in the regular army (19 Feb. 1901). His command of the Third Separate Brigade, Department of the North Philippines (Nov. 1901–July 1902), was very controversial. To destroy one of the last remaining centers of Filipino resistance, Bell arrested all local Filipino officials, moved the entire population into garrisoned enclaves dubbed "concentration camps," and began large-scale operations in the countryside that did not cease until the Filipino insurrection leader, General Miguel Malvar, surrendered on 16 April 1902. Anti-imperialists were outraged, and, while their charges of deliberate cruelty were overblown, it was a very dirty war.

Bell returned to the United States in 1903 to become commandant of the General Service and Staff College at Fort Leavenworth, Kansas. By attracting able instructors and students, he succeeded in bringing the school back to the levels of intellectual activity it had enjoyed before being closed during the war with Spain. In 1905 he reintroduced a second year of instruction for distinguished graduates of the first year—the former called the Staff College, the latter became the School of the Line.

President Theodore Roosevelt selected Bell to be the fourth chief of staff of the U.S. Army on 14 April 1906. Bell spent much of his first two years responding to a series of domestic and international crises. He coordinated the dispatch of relief supplies to San Francisco following the earthquake there on 18 April 1906. After the outbreak of an insurrection in Cuba led to American intervention, he commanded the Army of Cuban Pacification from October through December 1906. Returning to Washington in January 1907, he directed the preparation of a joint emergency war plan against Japan and initiated a debate over long-term American strategy in the Pacific. Bell and the General Staff convinced Roosevelt that the navy should locate its main Pacific base at Pearl Harbor on Oahu rather than in the Philippines.

Bell entered office believing that the reforms of Secretary of War Elihu Root were simply a starting point for comprehensive reforms designed to permit the U.S. Army to contend with the armies of the great powers. However, rather than present a comprehensive legislative program at the beginning of his tour, he opted to press for a few reforms—separation of the coast and field artillery with a modern tactical organization for the latter, enacted into law in 1907, and a pay bill, the first increase since the Civil War, the same year. Other reforms he could push through without legislation—the creation of machine gun sections in all regiments of infantry and cavalry and minimum physical standards and annual physical tests for all officers. As president of the Board of Ordnance and Fortification he was responsible for purchasing the first military airplane and approved the creation of aero companies to support each mobilized corps. He approved the establishment of the School of Musketry (later the Infantry School), laid the groundwork for the creation of the School of Fire (later the Field Artillery School), and was chiefly responsible for shifting the mission of the Army War College from acting as a planning adjunct of the General Staff to providing officer education. With the enthusiastic support of Secretary of War William Howard Taft, Bell attempted to concentrate the scattered units of the regular army at brigade posts. Initially, he did not seek to create balanced tactical units; instead he intended to bring many units of the various branches together at a single location so that the officers could learn the capacities of branches other than their own. Bell thus facilitated the development of combined arms before the term became common.

Bell believed that the General Staff followed the German model too closely and suggested an adaptation of the French organization. In 1908 he reorganized the General Staff into two sections—the first section became an executive agent to enable the chief of staff to shape the flow of policy proposals and coordinate operations in the field, while the second engaged in the traditional General Staff tasks of intelligence collection, analysis, and planning. Bell proposed to extend that reform by incorporating both the adjutant general's and inspector general's departments in the General Staff, thus making the politically well-connected adjutant general, Major General Fred C. Ainsworth, subject to Bell's orders. Secretary of War Jacob M. Dickinson, however, vetoed the idea.

The same result occurred with Bell's comprehensive reform plan, which became enmeshed in President Taft's struggles with the progressive wing of his party. The president first postponed and then abandoned the idea. Illness, exhaustion from overwork, and injuries suffered in an automobile accident undermined Bell's efforts during his last two years in office. Discouraged about the defeat of his plans, he nevertheless created two administrative agencies that his successors put to good use—a permanent legislative liaison officer between the War Department and Congress and a public affairs officer to try to build grassroots support for reform. Bell remained on active duty until his death, but age and ill health restricted him to training and administrative positions in World War I. He died in New York City.

Bell is primarily remembered in the U.S. Army for his contributions to officer education. The education system that he helped found and promote contributed greatly to the army's success in both world wars and continues to be central to the profession of arms in the United States. He is equally important, if less well remembered, as a successful practitioner of counterinsurgency warfare and for the reform agenda that he laid down while chief of staff. By 1916 his successors, aided by the Preparedness movement, had achieved most of his goals.

• Bell's papers are scattered, but large numbers of his letters survive in the Theodore Roosevelt, William Howard Taft, Leonard Wood, and John J. Pershing papers at the Library of Congress and the Chief of Staff Army Correspondence Files for 1903–1906 and 1907–1916 at the National Archives. His brother-in-law and sometime inspector general of the army, Brigadier General Ernest A. Garlington, and his sometime aide, Major General Johnson Hagood, provide separate contemporary assessments in "James Franklin Bell," *Fiftieth Annual Report of the Association of Graduates of the United States Military Academy* (1919). Three views of his controversial reconcentration policy include John M. Gates, *Schoolbooks and Krags: The United States Army in the Philippines, 1898–1902* (1973), a strongly favorable assessment; Brian M. Linn, *The U.S. Army and Counterinsurgency in the Philippine War, 1899–1902* (1989), a more nuanced view; and Glenn A. May,

Battle for Batangas: A Philippine Province at War (1991), a critical account. Bell's contributions to postgraduate education are outlined at least in part by Timothy K. Nenninger, *The Leavenworth Schools and the Old Army* (1978), and Harry P. Ball, *Of Responsible Command: A History of the U.S. Army War College* (1983). Allan R. Millett, *The Politics of Intervention: The Military Occupation of Cuba, 1906–1909* (1968), and Richard D. Challener, *Admirals, Generals, and American Foreign Policy, 1898–1914* (1973), provide insights into the foreign relations aspects of Bell's tour as chief of staff. An obituary is in the *New York Herald*, 9 Jan. 1919.

EDGAR F. RAINES, JR.

BELL, James Madison (3 Apr. 1826–1902), abolitionist, poet, and lecturer, was born in Gallipolis, Ohio. His parents' identities are unknown. At age sixteen, in 1842, he moved to Cincinnati. While there, in 1848, he married Louisiana Sanderlin (or Sanderline), with whom he had several children, and also learned the plastering trade from his brother-in-law George Knight. Bell worked as a plasterer during the day and attended Cincinnati High School for Colored People at night. Founded in 1844 by Reverend Hiram S. Gilmore, the school had a connection to Oberlin College and was said to have given impetus to the sentiment found in *Uncle Tom's Cabin* and the cause of human freedom. Through his studies Bell was thoroughly indoctrinated into the principles of radical abolitionism.

In 1854 Bell moved his family to Chatham, Ontario, Canada, where he felt he would be more free under the authority of the British government. While continuing his trade he became involved in political activities and met and befriended John Brown. As his ally, Bell raised money and enlisted men to support Brown's raid on Harpers Ferry. He probably was one of the last people to see Brown before the raid took place.

In 1860 Bell moved to San Francisco, California, where he became involved in the fight to ensure equal education for local black children. He also took a leading and active role at various state conventions protesting laws that discriminated against blacks. At one such convention held by ministers of the African Methodist Episcopal (AME) church, Bell addressed the subjects of the role of the church and its relationship to the state. He was an active member and steward of the AME church in San Francisco. Although far removed from the battlefield, Bell worked as a crusader for abolition during the Civil War. Bell wrote some of his most rousing poems while living in California, including "Emancipation," "Lincoln," and "The Dawn of Freedom." His works were long, comprising as many as 950 lines, and were meant to be recited. His poetry has been compared to following a mountain stream whose source is unknown. Although known as a poet today, poetry came second to his activism during his lifetime.

Bell left California and moved to Toledo, Ohio, in 1865. He arrived at the time of emancipation and began to work with the freedmen, focusing his energies on the struggle for civil rights. Bell later went to Canada to visit his family and eventually moved them to Toledo. He continued to be active in the AME church, serving as superintendent of the Sunday school and as a lay worker. Active briefly in Republican politics, Bell was elected as a delegate from Lucas County to the state convention and as a delegate at large from the state of Ohio to the Republican National Convention in both 1868 and 1872. He was a vocal and enthusiastic supporter of the nomination of Ulysses S. Grant at both conventions.

Bell traveled frequently, espousing doctrines on human liberty, enjoining blacks to use their freedom responsibly, and instructing freedmen in their political and civic duties, often reciting his long poems as the method of instruction. Bishop B. W. Arnett, a friend who worked with Bell in the church, often traveled with him as he gave public readings of his poetry and lectured on educational and legal rights for black Americans. According to Arnett, no one instructed people better or had a more imposing manner than Bell. "Many a young man who was not an honor to his race and a blessing to his people received the first spark of inspiration for true greatness" while listening to Bell's poems (Arnett, p. 10).

Bell addressed many issues in his poems, including slavery, war, emancipation, and Reconstruction, often referencing historical figures, such as John Brown, or events of historical significance. Although he tended to vary the lengths of stanzas, his poems have been described as "almost identical and dull" and "without any distinctive literary quality." Many of Bell's poems were published individually and eventually compiled in Arnett's *The Poetical Works of James Madison Bell* (1901).

One of Bell's long poems, "The Progress of Liberty" (1866), was written for the third anniversary of the Emancipation Proclamation. Its 850 lines review the Civil War, the triumph of liberty, and the martyrdom of Abraham Lincoln:

> The bondsman's gloomy night has passed;
>   The slavery of this land is dead;
> No tyrant's power, however vast,
>   Can wake it from its gory bed.

It picks up later with:

> Though slavery's dead, yet there remains
> A work for those from whom the chains
> Today are falling one by one;
> Nor should they deem their labor done,
> Nor shrink the task, however hard,
> While it insures a great reward,
> And bids them on its might depend
> For perfect freedom in the end.

Bell also used poems to encourage blacks to be model citizens:

> In this yourselves must take the lead;
>   You must yourselves first elevate;
> Till then the world will ne'er concede
>   Your claims to manhood's high estate.

In addition, Bell used his works—and the reading of them—to denounce laws and policies that he deemed to be detrimental to blacks. He is said to have triumphed in his "daring, vigorous satire of President Andrew Johnson" in the poem "Modern Moses, or 'My Policy' Man" (1867). Called Bell's "most inventive and readable work" because of its "shrewd humor and irony, concrete topicality and personal emotion" (Sherman, p. 192), the poem ridicules Johnson from a personal as well as political perspective. It portrays the president as a Judas who betrayed the people by vetoing the Freedman's Bureau bill:

> Mark when that bill for the supply
> Of starving millions met his eye;
> A breadless, clotheless, houseless throng.
> Thus rendered by his nation's wrong.
> Does he the bill in haste receive
> And sign, their suff'rings to relieve?

He goes on:

> Then he in their deep hour of grief,
> Did them relieve and kept his vow;
> When with a dark and wrinkled brow,
> He stamped his veto on their prayer,
> And doomed the suppliants to despair.

In *From Slavery to Freedom*, historian John Hope Franklin argues that the overwhelming acclaim of the poet Paul Laurence Dunbar probably overshadowed the works of Bell and other black poets of his era. If not for Dunbar's fame, Bell might have been more highly regarded as a poet during an age that was critical to the political, social, and cultural development of black Americans.

• Very little has been written about Bell. The most-definitive work is Bishop B. W. Arnett, *The Poetical Works of James Madison Bell* (1901). Joan R. Sherman, in *African American Poetry of the Nineteenth Century: An Anthology* (1992), provides a short biography and a review of some of Bell's work.
MAMIE E. LOCKE

BELL, James Stroud (30 June 1847–5 Apr. 1915), businessman, was born in Philadelphia, Pennsylvania, the son of Samuel Bell, a miller, and Elizabeth Faust. He received his early education in the public schools of his native city and after graduating from Central High School joined his father's milling and flour brokerage business. Only sixteen years old when he became a part of the firm, Bell joined a line of family millers that extended back for five generations. He received a thorough training in all aspects of the business and became a partner in the newly renamed firm of Samuel Bell & Sons in 1868.

Bell remained with his father for twenty years. He married Sallie Montgomery Ford in January 1873; they had one son. The firm acted as local sales agents for the firm of Washburn, Crosby & Company, based in Minneapolis, Minnesota. This firm, which was owned by the C. C. Washburn Flouring Mills Company, had been established in Minneapolis by milling industry pioneer Cadwallader Washburn and had achieved a significant share of the flour market in the Midwest. Although the milling industry had under-

gone rapid development in the years following the Civil War—and after 1877 engaged in ever-expanding export trade as well—dark clouds loomed on the horizon. By 1888 flour prices had declined because of intense competition between millers, and the governments of Europe responded to American flour exports with stiff tariffs. As the industry faced increasingly difficult circumstances, Bell was persuaded by William Hood Dunwoody, a fellow Quaker, Philadelphia native, and miller, to join Washburn, Crosby & Company.

Bell relocated to Minneapolis in September 1888 and became managing partner of the newly reorganized firm of Washburn Martin. Conflict with Washburn's heirs led to the removal of Washburn's brother William from the management of the firm, which was again reorganized in 1889 as the Washburn Crosby Company. As president of the new firm, Bell faced numerous challenges. His water-driven power supply, the St. Anthony Falls, was controlled by William Washburn; therefore, he was often forced to use steam power to run his mills. After an English syndicate obtained control of a major competitor (Pillsbury Washburn), it appeared that Bell might lose control of his firm as well. After a bitter fight, the syndicate was defeated in 1890, and Bell was free to focus on rebuilding his company's market.

Bell saw the salvation of the Minneapolis mills in an expanded domestic market, and he spared no effort toward that end. Blessed with a gift for hiring employees who were both enthusiastic and talented, he revitalized the sales force, which soon scoured the countryside for additional business. One important success was the penetration of the St. Louis market, which had previously favored locally produced winter wheat flour (Bell's mills used spring wheat). He backed his aggressive sales force with extensive pamphlet and newspaper advertising featuring prominently the firm's famous "Gold Medal" brand. In the mid-1890s, in a move that many considered daring, Bell initiated advertising in magazines such as the *Ladies' Home Journal* as well, spending approximately $220,000 on this facet of the business by 1894.

Working in an industry that traditionally operated on narrow profit margins, Bell viewed expanded production as essential to Washburn Crosby's future. In 1903 the firm built a new mill in Buffalo, New York, which facilitated access to overseas and eastern markets and also saved the company considerable transportation expense. A second mill was added in Louisville, Kentucky, the following year, and additional branch mills soon followed at Kalispell and Great Falls, Montana. Washburn Crosby Company continued to prosper. Capital stock, which had been increased to $1,200,000 in 1899 (the same year in which the firm purchased its previously leased mills), was increased again in 1903, 1907, and in 1909, when it reached $6,000,000. Daily production, which had been 8,000 barrels a day when Bell joined the firm, reached 27,700 by 1915.

Recognized as a leader by the industry, Bell had a mixed record of dealings with the federal government. He and other millers were excited about the 1904 advent of electrical bleaching, which greatly accelerated the natural aging process that millers had traditionally followed. This enthusiasm was soon dampened when Dr. Harvey Wiley, author of the 1906 Pure Food and Drug Act, led a fight to ban the process, which produced a whiter flour with greater consumer appeal and superior baking properties, claiming that it was unwholesome. Bell had better success in opposing a Wilson administration proposal to make imported flour duty-free while retaining the tariff on wheat; his counterproposal that either both commodities be made duty-free or that the duty on wheat be retained was adopted.

Following the death of his first wife in 1905, Bell married Mrs. Mabel Sargent in 1912. He fell seriously ill the following year and, while retaining the company presidency, spent the rest of his life as an invalid before dying in Minneapolis. Bell used the experience that he gained as a member of a family of millers that stretched back through five generations. His aggressive leadership helped to place the Washburn Crosby Company and the Minneapolis milling industry in a firm position for even greater achievements under the leadership of his son, James Ford Bell. Washburn Crosby later became a part of today's General Mills.

• The papers of James Stroud Bell have apparently not survived. Secondary sources that discuss Bell and the Washburn Crosby Company are William C. Edgar, *The Medal of Gold* (1925); James Gray, *Business without Boundary: The Story of General Mills* (1954); and John Storck and Walter Dorwin Teague, *Flour for Man's Bread* (1952). Obituaries are in the *Minneapolis Tribune* and the *St. Paul Pioneer Press*, both 6 Apr. 1915, and the *New York Times*, 8 Apr. 1915.

EDWARD L. LACH, JR.

BELL, John (18 Feb. 1796–10 Sept. 1869), politician, was born in Mill Creek, Davidson County, Tennessee, the son of Samuel Bell, a farmer and blacksmith, and Margaret Edmiston. Young Bell graduated from Cumberland College in Nashville in 1814 and within two years began to practice law. In 1817 he was elected to represent Williamson County in the state senate. Before again pursuing public office, Bell relocated in Nashville, the state capital, where he became a prominent attorney.

Bell was elected in 1827 to the first of seven consecutive terms in the U.S. House of Representatives. He proclaimed himself a loyal Jacksonian but had to overcome personal opposition from the most prominent citizen in the district, Andrew Jackson, who became president one year later. Bell and his allies in the Nashville business community disapproved of the president's war against the U.S. Bank, but he was forced by overwhelming public sentiment to support Jackson's 1832 veto of the bill rechartering the bank. In 1833 Bell opposed Jackson's far less popular removal of federal deposits from the bank.

When Jackson loyalist and intrastate rival James K. Polk sought election as Speaker of the House, Bell assembled a coalition opposed to removal of the bank deposits, defeating Polk in June 1834, 114 to 78. Though not yet a Whig, Bell thereby gave the nascent Whig party its first conspicuous national victory. Proadministration gains in congressional elections in 1834–1835 enabled Polk to deny Bell a second term as Speaker in December 1835. A similar result occurred in September 1837. In December 1839 Bell narrowly lost the election for Speaker to R. M. T. Hunter of Virginia.

Meanwhile Bell masterminded the 1836 presidential candidacy of Tennessee senator Hugh Lawson White. Although White carried Tennessee and Georgia and showed some strength elsewhere in the South, northwestern Whigs supported William Henry Harrison, while those in the Northeast preferred Daniel Webster. Incumbent vice president Martin Van Buren therefore succeeded Jackson, winning a larger number of electoral votes than his three rivals combined. Only after Van Buren replaced Jackson did Bell and other white supporters in Tennessee affiliate with the Whig party.

In 1840 a far better unified Whig party challenged Van Buren, whose presidency coincided with an increasingly severe economic downturn. Bell hoped that Whigs would nominate their most charismatic leader, Henry Clay, to whom Bell was related by marriage. Instead the Whigs met in national convention in December 1839 to choose the more "available" candidate, Harrison. Elected in the memorable "log cabin and hard cider" campaign, Harrison died only one month after taking office, setting the stage for disaster. States' rights Whig John Tyler (1790–1862) of Virginia, the first vice president to fill a vacancy caused by the death of a president, refused to support the Whig economic program, which included the establishment of a new national bank. A polarizing deadlock developed between the headstrong president and Whig leaders, led by Clay. Before long most of the cabinet, including Bell, who had been appointed secretary of war, resigned to protest Tyler's apostasy.

Between 1841 and 1847 Bell held no public office. He used the interval to widen and stabilize his extensive investments in coal, railroads, and iron manufacturing, most notably the Cumberland Iron Works in Stewart County. He also attempted to block the improbable ascent of his longtime rival Polk, who in 1844 became the dark-horse Democratic nominee for president, committed to annexing Texas. Bell and Tennessee Whigs narrowly managed to deny him the support of his home state, but Polk ran well enough elsewhere to capture the prize. A year after taking office Polk led the United States to war against Mexico.

In 1847 Bell sought and won a seat in the legislature. Its Whig majority thereupon elevated him to the first of two terms in the U.S. Senate. There he attempted to quiet North-South tensions, fueled by disputes about the future of slavery in the Mexican conquest. Democrats castigated Bell for abolitionist proclivities, as they had during the 1830s when he opposed the gag rule.

Bell was among the early backers of General Zachary Taylor, who won the 1848 presidential election. Once in office, Taylor tried to end the festering controversy about slavery in the territory acquired from Mexico by transforming it into two large states, California and New Mexico, neither of which appeared likely to accept slavery. Clay then offered his famous compromise package, which tied the admission of California to several prosouthern concessions, most notably a fugitive slave law. More loyal to Taylor than other southern Whigs, Bell disdained Clay's compromise. He supported California and New Mexico statehood, suggesting that the division of Texas into two states would ameliorate southern grievances.

Taylor suddenly died in July 1850. His successor, Millard Fillmore, promoted an arrangement along the lines sketched by Clay. Amid growing evidence that Tennessee Whigs favored the Compromise of 1850, Bell climbed aboard the bandwagon and thereafter clung tenaciously to the settlement. Unlike some southern Whigs, however, Bell thought it impolitic to insist that northern Whigs accept Fillmore as the 1852 party nominee. Hoping to keep antislavery Whigs within the party, Bell readily acquiesced in the nomination of Winfield Scott, notwithstanding Scott's equivocal stance on the compromise.

Reelected to the Senate in October 1853, Bell soon faced a new sectional controversy. He believed that repeal of the Missouri Compromise, the key part of the Kansas-Nebraska Bill, needlessly alienated northern Whigs without securing anything tangible for the South in return. Characteristically, Bell vacillated before making his position known; however, in the end he resisted pressures from a southern Whig caucus and cast the only southern vote in the Senate against the bill. Only seven southern Whigs in the House—four of them from Tennessee—followed his lead.

The poisonous Kansas controversy persisted. In 1858 Bell and a handful of ex-Whigs from the Upper South opposed admission of Kansas into the Union as a slave state under the Lecompton Constitution. Once again, as in 1854, southern Democrats insisted that Bell and his allies were traitors to their region.

The final phase of Bell's political career was played out during the two years before the war. His Senate career ended in March 1859, because Democrats held a majority in the Tennessee legislature. Nevertheless, Bell's moderate stance on North-South issues made him a plausible presidential candidate, attractive to southern Whigs who lacked a connection to any national party after the collapse of the Whig party and its successor, the American party. Ex-Whigs, primarily from the Upper South, organized the Constitutional Union party, which convened in Baltimore in May 1860 and nominated Bell for president and Edward Everett of Massachusetts for vice president.

Although Bell's ticket never had any realistic prospect of winning a popular majority at the polls, many of its advocates, including the presidential candidate, hoped the election would be resolved by the House of Representatives. If Republicans failed to carry several key northern states, such as Pennsylvania and New York, and if southern Democrats split their votes between Stephen A. Douglas and John C. Breckinridge, Bell might carry enough southern states to finish among the three largest recipients of electoral votes, positioning him to emerge as the compromise choice. Bell's calculations proved to have some basis. Democratic divisions did allow Bell to carry his home state along with Kentucky and Virginia. He did gain the third-largest total of electoral votes. His relative success proved barren, however, because the Republican candidate, Abraham Lincoln, swept the North and won a decisive victory in the electoral college.

At that juncture, events swiftly rushed out of control. Immediately following Lincoln's election, secessionist hysteria gripped the South, particularly the Deep South. For more than a month Bell did nothing. Then, somewhat belatedly, he issued a cautionary public letter, pointing out that the majority of Republican voters harbored no ill will toward the South and warning that secession was an illegal and ineffectual means of redressing southern grievances.

Bell played a more assertive role in arresting secession enthusiasm in his home state. Speaking to a large audience in Nashville on 22 January 1861, Bell predicted that Lincoln would adopt a conciliatory policy toward the South. Tennessee voters, hoping for a peaceful resolution of the crisis, voted overwhelmingly against secession on 9 February. Shortly afterward Bell traveled to Washington to confer with the president-elect. Bell must have felt reassured, because he agreed to accept the Union party nomination for his old seat in the U.S. House of Representatives.

A month after the inauguration, however, Lincoln decided that he had no choice but to mount a military challenge against Deep South secessionists, who had effectively removed seven states from the Union. Lincoln's call for troops ignited a prosecession groundswell in Nashville. Initially hoping that Kentucky and Tennessee together might maintain armed neutrality, Bell soon judged that his state had no choice but to side with the South. He found his new position uncomfortable, but his cautious instincts rendered him quite unable to resist the raging torrent that engulfed Middle and West Tennessee. Even had Bell continued to oppose secession, he could not have prevented Tennessee from joining the Confederacy.

Bell ceased to play any public role after 1861. His extensive coal and iron facilities were damaged when Union forces invaded Middle Tennessee in early 1862. For the duration of the war, he became a refugee. During the final four years of his life after the end of the war, he attempted to reopen his mines and mills.

Bell was twice married, first in 1818 to Sally Dickinson. She died in 1832, leaving five children. In 1835 Bell married a wealthy widow, Jane Erwin Yeatman, who provided him with important social contacts, many slaves, and a stake in iron mining and manufacturing; they had no children. Late in life Bell became a Presbyterian. He died in Stewart County, Tennessee

Bell's career encompassed numerous paradoxes. "Dignified even to the point of aloofness," he "never possessed the common touch" (Parks, *John Bell of Tennessee*, p. 173). He made effective set speeches but lacked the quick-wittedness and mental agility to debate. He was thin-skinned and "ill suited to the give and take of political warfare" (Sellers, p. 248). Nevertheless, Bell was a skilled partisan politician. Even though three Tennessee Democrats—Jackson, Polk, and Andrew Johnson—reached the pinnacle of American politics in the middle decades of the nineteenth century, only once in the seven presidential elections between the rise of the two-party system and the outbreak of the Civil War (1836–1860) did Democrats carry Tennessee. More than any other person, Bell was responsible for the persistent strength of Tennessee's Whig party.

Yet Bell's career epitomized the sad history of the Whig party. Prevented from wielding effective national power in the 1830s and 1840s by a series of misfortunes, the party ruptured during the 1850s. When moderate southerners such as Bell attempted to hold the Union together in 1860–1861, they had neither a national party base nor a popular national leader. Their failure was both fated and tragic.

• Bell's papers are scattered and fragmentary, ensuring that he will remain more obscure than his three Democratic rivals who achieved the presidency. A few items are preserved in the John Bell Papers in the Library of Congress and in the Polk-Yeatman papers in the Southern Historical Collection, University of North Carolina at Chapel Hill. Important published letters may be found in St. George Sioussat, ed., "Correspondence of John Bell and Willie P. Mangum," *Tennessee Historical Magazine* 3 (1917): 196–200; and Sioussat, ed., "Letters of John Bell to William B. Campbell, 1839–1857," *Tennessee Historical Magazine* 3 (1917): 201–27. Counterbalancing the absence of papers is a solid biography, Joseph Howard Parks, *John Bell of Tennessee* (1950). See also two articles by Parks, "The Tennessee Whigs and the Kansas-Nebraska Bill," *Journal of Southern History* 10 (1944): 308–30, and "John Bell and Secession," *East Tennessee Historical Society Publications* 16 (1944): 30–47. Various aspects of Bell's career are covered in Charles Grier Sellers, Jr., *James K. Polk: Jacksonian, 1795–1843* (1957); Arthur Charles Cole, *The Whig Party in the South* (1912); Paul H. Bergeron, *Antebellum Politics in Tennessee* (1982); and Daniel W. Crofts, *Reluctant Confederates: Upper South Unionists in the Secession Crisis* (1989).

DANIEL W. CROFTS

BELL, Lawrence Dale (5 Apr. 1894–20 Oct. 1956), aircraft manufacturer, was born in Mentone, Indiana, the son of Isaac Bell, a lumber mill operator, and Harriet Sarber. When Bell was thirteen, his family moved to Santa Monica, California. After his graduation from Santa Monica Polytechnic High School in 1912, Bell secured his first job in aviation as an aircraft mechanic for his brother Grover E. Bell and Lincoln Beachey. Bell decided to leave aviation after the death of his brother in an exhibition flight on 4 July 1913, but one

year later he reentered the industry by taking a mechanic's position on the shop floor of the Glenn L. Martin Aircraft Company in Santa Ana, California. Bell's drive earned him rapid promotion at Martin, and he was named superintendent at the age of twenty. As superintendent, he created one of the aircraft industry's best engineering teams, centered on Donald W. Douglas, who later would found the Douglas Aircraft Company. In 1915 Bell married Lucille Mainwaring; they had no children.

In 1917 Martin Aircraft merged with Wright Aeronautics. This new company, Wright-Martin Aircraft Company, was assigned to build aircraft engines for the war effort. Both Glenn Martin and Larry Bell preferred building airframes and they left to form a new Martin Aircraft Company in Cleveland, Ohio. Bell, now vice president of the new Martin Aircraft Company, oversaw the construction of the new factory. During this period, Martin Aircraft developed the twin engine Martin MB-2 bomber that William "Billy" Mitchell would use to sink the captured German battleship *Ostfriesland* tests conducted in 1921. By the end of 1924 the relationship between Bell and Martin had become strained over Bell's desire for partial ownership of the company. Martin refused, and Bell left Martin Aircraft in 1925.

For the next three years Bell worked at a number of odd sales positions. In 1928 Major Ruben Fleet, president of Consolidated Aircraft Corporation in Buffalo, New York, offered Bell a position as sales manager. Bell's first task was to oversee the production of the PY-1 seaplane. In 1929 Fleet, pleased with Bell's performance, promoted him to vice president and general manager. In June 1935 Fleet decided to move Consolidated to San Diego, California, to take advantage of the city's year-round flying conditions. By this time Bell desperately wanted to run his own company, and Consolidated's move provided the opportunity to start one. Bell obtained financing from investors in the Buffalo area. He took advantage of the empty Consolidated factory and reserve of skilled aircraft workers that remained in Buffalo after Consolidated's departure. Bell, with Ray Whitman and Bob Woods, incorporated the Bell Aircraft Corporation on 10 July 1935.

Bell Aircraft survived its early days by subcontracting wing panels for Consolidated Aircraft. In 1938 the company designed and built its first aircraft, the twin engine *Airacuda*. Thirteen prototypes of the *Airacuda* were built for the Army Air Corps. Although production was limited to the prototypes, the aircraft gave the company a reputation for utilizing innovative design methods.

In 1938 President Franklin Roosevelt selected Bell to serve on a fifty-person commission of industrialists and military personnel to examine Europe's aircraft industry and its preparations for war. Bell was particularly impressed by Germany's aircraft industry. He would later apply some of the German production methods he studied to Bell Aircraft's assembly lines.

Following closely behind the design of the *Airacuda* was another unique Bell design, the P-39 *Airacobra*.

The Army Air Corps awarded Bell Aircraft a contract for a prototype aircraft on 7 October 1937. The aircraft XP-39 was delivered to Wright Field in Ohio in the spring of 1938 and test flown on 6 April 1938. Satisfied with the performance of the prototype, the Air Corps signed another contract to build thirteen more aircraft. A full production contract for the P-39 was signed on 10 August 1939; delivery of these aircraft to Air Corps began in early 1941. The unusual layout of this aircraft placed the single inline engine behind the pilot with a shaft driving the propeller. The *Airacobra* and its improved version, the P-63 *Kingcobra*, would become Bell Aircraft's principal export and its product for the Army Air Forces during World War II. During the war, Bell Aircraft, like many other American companies, saw a rapid increase of production, plant space, and employment. A new one-million-square-foot facility was built in Buffalo. New Bell plants were built in Marietta, Georgia, and Fort Worth, Texas, as well. The company would also subcontract airframe sections for P-51 Mustangs and B-17 Flying Fortresses, and it built 700 complete B-29 Superfortresses at the Georgia plant.

On 5 September 1941, Larry Bell and Harland Poyer, Bell Aircraft's chief engineer, met with Brigadier General Oliver Echols, chief of the Air Force Materials Division, to discuss production of America's first jet aircraft. General B. W. Chidlaw USAF (Ret.), assigned by General Henry H. Arnold to oversee the project, later explained that Bell Aircraft was selected for the project because of the company's innovative engineering staff and experience in fighter aircraft production and because "we were all well aware of Larry Bell's personal drive and boundless enthusiasm in all matters relating to Research and Development." One year later the company delivered and flew the jet-powered XP-59 *Airacomet*.

In early 1944, Major Ezra Kotcher, an engineer with U.S. Army Air Forces Development Engineering Branch, approached Bob Woods of Bell to join with the Army Air Forces and National Advisory Committee for Aeronautics (NACA) to build a transonic aircraft, the X-1. By the end of the year the initial engineering specifications were completed, though very little about transonic flight was known at the time. On 16 March 1945 Bell Aircraft signed a contract with the USAAF to build three experimental supersonic aircraft. The fuselage of the X-1 was based on the shape of a .50-caliber bullet, one of the few objects known to move faster than the speed of sound. The aircraft utilized XLR-11 rocket engines fueled by liquid oxygen and ethyl alcohol. With this aircraft, on 14 October 1947, Captain Charles "Chuck" Yeager became the first person to fly faster than the speed of sound, at Mach 1.06.

During the war Bell risked the company by backing Arthur M. Young to develop a new helicopter design, which became the Bell Model 30. Young's work would culminate on 8 December 1945 with the first flight of the much-improved Bell Model 47 helicopter. Three months later the Model 47 would be the first helicopter to receive an Aircraft Type certificate from the Civil Aeronautics Administration. In early 1951 the helicopter division was moved from the Niagara Falls plant to Fort Worth. Because of the success of the helicopter division of Bell, it would be incorporated as the Bell Helicopter Corporation on 1 January 1957. The Model 47 would see a long service life; it rescued well over 18,000 wounded soldiers during the Korean War.

Bell received a number of awards throughout his career, including the Guggenheim Medal, the Collier Trophy, the French Legion of Honor, and the President's Certificate of Merit. Throughout the mid-1950s, his health deteriorated. A stroke suffered on 24 May 1956 forced Bell to resign as company president in mid-September. He died of heart failure five months later in his hospital bed in Buffalo, New York.

• The best account of Lawrence Bell's life is Donald J. Norton's *Larry: A Biography of Lawrence D. Bell* (1981). For information on Lawrence Bell, the Bell Aircraft Company, and its aircraft, see A. J. Pelletier's *Bell Aircraft since 1935* (1992). A number of contemporary articles and company biographies can be found in Lawrence Bell's biography file, CB-105000-01, National Air and Space Museum, Washington, D.C. An obituary is in the *New York Times*, 21 Oct. 1956.

ALEX M SPENCER

BELL, Luther V. (20 Dec. 1806–11 Feb. 1862), psychiatrist and founding member of the American Psychiatric Association, was born in Francestown, Hillsborough County, New Hampshire, the son of Samuel Bell, a lawyer, governor of New Hampshire, and U.S. senator, and Mehitable Dana. After his mother's death in August 1810, Bell spent his early years with his paternal grandparents in Londonderry (now Derry), New Hampshire.

Bell graduated from Bowdoin College in 1823 and then studied medicine under the tutelage of his older brother John, a physician in New York City. Bell received his medical degree from Dartmouth in 1826, shortly before his twentieth birthday. Presumably because of concerns about personal maturity, he did not begin the practice of medicine, in Derry, until 1831. In 1834 he married Frances Clark Pinkerton; they had seven children. Also in 1834 he won the Boylston Prize of the Massachusetts Medical Society for an anti–vegetarian diet essay. Shortly after, he published two papers on general clinical medicine. In 1849 he described in the *American Journal of Insanity* a form of maniacal insanity that became known as "Bell's mania" and was briefly considered a distinct eponymic diagnostic entity.

Carrying on a family tradition of political and public service, Bell became a representative in the state government and served on a legislative committee to investigate the status of the insane in New Hampshire. In 1837, without seeking the position or being interviewed for it, Bell was invited to become the medical superintendent of the McLean Asylum for the Insane in Waverly, Massachusetts. He served in that position for almost two decades.

Bell's medical and administrative philosophy included a major emphasis on moral (i.e., psychological) treatment, with the adjunctive use of medications or mechanical restraints when necessary (the latter applied only under his personal supervision). He reported that rarely was more than 1 percent of the patient population in restraints, with none for several weeks at a time. He was concerned, also, with the proper heating and ventilating of the buildings, the comfort and nutrition of his patients, and their recreational and occupational therapy. Bell so distinguished himself in this area that in 1844 he was approached by the founders of Butler Hospital to become its first superintendent and to participate in the design of the new hospital. Rejecting the offer to become superintendent, he did travel to Europe to observe the best hospitals for the insane and returned to participate in the planning for Butler.

In 1850–1851 Bell was secretary of the Association of Medical Superintendents of American Institutions for the Insane (AMSAII), which in 1922 would become the American Psychiatric Association. In becoming the first medical specialty organization in America, preceding the formation of the American Medical Association by three years, the AMSAII made psychiatry the oldest organized medical specialty in the country. As president of the AMSAII from 1851 to 1855, Bell was a vocal critic of the customary use of statistics by asylum superintendents in their annual reports. The statistics in these reports generally focused on improvement or cure of *recent onset* cases of insanity, but modern historians have misinterpreted them to be applicable to *all* admissions, including those of long-standing, chronic cases. Bell felt that these statistics were too subjective, vague, undefined, and unreliable for scientific use. He was joined in this view by his contemporary, Isaac Ray, another founder of the AMSAII.

Bell's tenure as superintendent was, personally, of near tragic proportions. While at McLean, three of his children died, and in 1855 his wife died in childbirth. In December of that year he resigned in order to devote himself to raising his remaining four children. Bell, whose own health was not good, had some episodes of coughing up blood in the period before his resignation. He was succeeded by his assistant physician, Chauncey Booth, who shortly after became quite ill. In November 1857 Bell was recalled to take charge of the asylum and remained until March 1858, when John E. Tyler was appointed superintendent.

Unlike many of his fellow superintendents, Bell was active in party politics (Whig) while heading the McLean Asylum. In 1850 he was chosen to be a member of the executive council of the state of Massachusetts, among whose activities was that of advising the governor on questions of clemency for convicted criminals. Bell played a significant role in the denial of clemency for Harvard professor George W. Webster for the murder of Boston physician George Parkman. Bell was an unsuccessful Whig candidate for Congress in 1852 and for the office of Massachusetts governor in 1856.

Bell had a strong interest in investigating the claims of spiritualists and psychics. He was often referred to as a believer in spiritualism, but, as he told Isaac Ray, it was largely scientific curiosity and a belief that science owed it to society to investigate the alleged psychic phenomena that fueled his interest.

After several years of retirement, in 1861 Bell applied for and received a commission as a regimental surgeon with the Eleventh Regiment of Massachusetts Volunteers. Eventually he came under Union general Joseph Hooker's command and advanced in rank to brigade-surgeon and then to medical director of the division. Despite his own past medical history and the rigors of military life in the Civil War, Bell remained in good health, worked many long hours, and found time to write letters home. On the morning of 5 February 1862 he suddenly felt, in his lumbar region, an excruciating pain. He held on for six more days, requiring liberal doses of chloroform, before he died. No autopsy was performed or diagnosis made, but a slowly dissecting aortic aneurysm would be a reasonable cause of death.

Bell was among the most outstanding of the "original thirteen" founders of the American Psychiatric Association and one of the most influential psychiatrists of his time. As medical director of the McLean Asylum and as consultant to the founders of the Butler Hospital in Rhode Island and to a Massachusetts governor, he served as a bridge between the then young medical specialty of psychiatry and the lay trustees and directors of newly formed asylums. He also served successfully as an advocate for the insane to the legislatures of New Hampshire and Massachusetts and as an ambassador for psychiatry to the governor of Massachusetts.

• Bell's most often cited publication is "On a Form of Disease Resembling Some Advanced Stages of Mania and Fever, but So Contradistinguished from Any Ordinarily Observed or Described Combination of Symptoms, as to Render It Probable that It May Be an Overlooked and Hitherto Unrecorded Malady," *American Journal of Insanity* 6, no. 2 (Oct. 1849): 97–127. Two eulogies written after Bell's death, George E. Ellis, *Memoir of Luther V. Bell, M.D., LL.D.* (1863), reprinted from the *Proceedings of the Massachusetts Historical Society* 7 (1863–1864); and Isaac Ray, *A Discourse on the Life and Character of Dr. Luther V. Bell: Read to the Association of [Medical] Superintendents of North [sic] American Institutions for the Insane, at Its Annual Meeting, Providence, R.I., June 10th 1862.* (1863), provide the principal sources of information about Bell.

JACQUES M. QUEN

BELL, Mary A. (2 July 1873–20 Sept. 1941), artist, was born in Washington, D.C., the daughter of James F. Bell and Susanna County, probably laborers. Very little is known about Bell's early life. As an African American, she presumably attended segregated schools. It is unlikely that she ever received artistic training; she declared that she drew "without human teaching." She probably worked as a domestic servant, laundress, or seamstress beginning in her teenage years, and she may have traveled extensively; Bell said she "lived all around" before World War I. Since she does not appear in early twentieth-century city directories or census records in Washington, D.C., or Boston, Massachusetts, and because she apparently never married or had children, it is likely that she resided with her various employers.

By the mid-1920s Bell was working for Edward Peter Pierce, justice of the Supreme Judicial Court of Massachusetts (1914–1937), and Adele Dutaud Pierce, his wife, as a live-in domestic servant in Boston and in their summer home in Georgetown, Maine. Bell may have also worked on occasion for sculptor Gaston Lachaise and his wife Isabel. Isabel and Adele were sisters; Lachaise family papers indicate they both had a fondness for their maid. Bell maintained a friendly written correspondence with both families, signing letters, "your humble servant," after she left their employ sometime in the mid-1930s.

Around 1936 Bell moved into a lodging house in Boston. Her artistic career blossomed when she was in her sixties; she produced at least 140 drawings between 1936 and 1939. Apparently self-taught, Bell usually drew at night after working odd jobs. Most of her wax crayon and colored pencil drawings on tissue paper are delicate, fanciful courtship scenes of well-dressed white couples in elegant parlors or luxurious gardens. Yet there are also depictions of Creole beauties, regal Ethiopians, burlesque performers, penitent sinners, and loving mothers. A small narrative label in flowing script glued to the top center of a fastidiously constructed double-tissue border announces the title of each stage-like scene.

Bell regularly featured women in her work, explaining that "a woman is the cream of the earth and everybody likes cream, so I put a woman in all my drawings." Typically, a large-scale woman and a small man float in between plants and multiple horizon lines or small household furnishings, the latter perhaps traced from magazines. One exemplary work is *Proposing*, which depicts a beautiful woman seated in a parlor amidst tiny floating furniture, including a grand piano, a swag lamp, and a fringed hook rug. A Catholic who declared that God, rather than she, created her drawings—as do many self-taught artists—Bell occasionally included an oval portrait of the Virgin Mary in the background, as she does in *Proposing*. Bell explained that the Mother of God appeared in all of her drawings initially "just to introduce her to my friends; now they all know HER and I don't need to put her in pictures."

Another notable work is *American Mixtures of the Ethiopian Race*. Here, three women prance in a floral landscape. Two wear fashionable clothing, elaborate coiffures, and sparkling jewelry. The largest and fanciest figure is also the lightest skinned. Bell reflects contemporary notions of hierarchical skin tones by inscribing, "The girl in the center is Octoroon. The girl on the left, the Creole type. The [girl on the] right is

the so-called Chocolate type." The darkest-skinned woman wears a miserable sack and has unruly hair. Bell may have identified with her; the artist's monogram, a floral bell, appears just below the hem of her dress.

Such charming images depicted on fragile materials delighted a small group of patrons, mostly in the Boston area, who excitedly shared Bell's work with each other, priced at just fifty cents each. After Gaston Lachaise died in 1935, Isabel introduced Bell's art to her grandniece Ruth Pierce, a journalist, and artist Kate Buss. Buss in turn sent Bell's drawings to Gertrude Stein in Paris and to New York writer and photographer Carl Van Vechten. Van Vechten's friend, publicist Mark Lutz of Philadelphia, also became a patron, as did art critic Henry McBride. McBride then convinced artist Florine Stettheimer to purchase several pieces. Additionally, some of Isabel Lachaise's other friends took Bell's drawings on vacation to share with friends abroad. All admired Bell's flamboyant images of women and flowers, dreamlike space, vivid colors, and charming narrative.

For Stein and Van Vechten, Bell was all the more exotic and attractive because of her race and outsider status. Both befriended and supported African-American writers and performers. Van Vechten, a bisexual, was known for his photographs of Harlemites, and Stein consented to an all-black cast for the performance of her operatic *Four Saints in Three Acts*. Further, African-American writers commended her short story, "Melanctha," for its nonpatronizing attitude toward black people. Stein also collected work by both modern masters and self-taught artists and even planned an exhibition of American folk art in Paris in 1939. World War II, however, prevented this event.

While Bell did not associate with other artists and never exhibited her art, she hoped that her drawings might lead to some renown and racial uplift. She wrote to Van Vechten, who purchased more than 100 of her drawings, that she was reincarnated and that whispering spirits told her to send out her drawings and "make yourself known to the world." In 1936 Bell took six works to a movie producer, explaining that she wanted the glory of the Ethiopian race to be known to the world. The producer, apparently amused by the ambition of an elderly black domestic, informed her that her marvelous colors could not possibly be duplicated. Soon thereafter, she realized she had been duped when she received a photographic postcard of one of her drawings made by Van Vechten.

Pleased with Van Vechten's patronage, Bell offered to sign her works any way he wished, and she adopted a monogram in the shape of a floral bell at his suggestion. Yet when he and Lutz paid Bell a surprise visit in 1938, she refused to see them for unknown reasons. She also denied Van Vechten's request to photograph her, stating that she would not be photographed until she was on "Ethiopian soil." While stereotypes about a racial hierarchy according to skin color are evident in the artist's work—she believed the most beautiful women were the lightest—Bell was proud of her racial heritage. She included flags and jewelry with the Pan-African colors (red, black, green, and gold or yellow) in her art and took interest in the career of Hailie Selassie, emperor of Ethiopia.

Plagued with failing eyesight and asthma, Bell also suffered from smoke inhalation from a fire in her apartment, which forced her to move across the street in May 1938. She then hoped to secure a four-room apartment near the Charles River so that she could have a gallery of her own. Soon, however, she lost her most loyal patrons. Two of Van Vechten's friends, Edward Pierce and lawyer James Weldon Johnson, died in 1938. That year the writer officially donated his entire collection of black memorabilia to the Beinecke Rare Book and Manuscript Library at Yale University in honor of Johnson.

By mid-December 1940, Bell was institutionalized at the Boston State Hospital, a public mental health facility. She had predicted her tragic demise two years earlier: "fate has decreed a cruel ending for me." Bell died in the facility of heart disease and hardening of the arteries, complicated by psychosis. It is not known how long she was mentally ill, or whether the condition affected her art. Destitute, Bell was buried in a pauper's grave across the street from the hospital.

Recognized by such luminaries as Van Vechten, Lachaise, Stein, and Stettheimer in her own time, Bell's charming and provocative works and letters continue to offer a rare glimpse into the world of an intriguing, self-taught African-American artist. While virtually unknown to the mainstream history of art, her works are significant for their fresh vision and their social commentary on escapist romance, black skin tones, religion, and Pan-African overtones. Exhibitions of Bell's drawings were held at the Beinecke Library (1945), the Galerie Brusberg in Berlin, Germany (1986), the Chicago International Art Exposition (1987), and the Yale University Art Gallery (1991).

• Bell's papers, including thirty-four letters to Carl Van Vechten, Mark Lutz, and Isabel Lachaise along with 105 of her drawings, are part of the James Weldon Johnson Memorial Collection of American Negro Arts and Letters in the Beinecke Rare Book and Manuscript Library, Yale University. There are also small vertical files on the artist in the National Museum of Women in the Arts in Washington, D.C., and the Carl Hammer Gallery in Chicago, and some of her pieces are in private collections.

THERESA LEININGER-MILLER

BELL, Matty (22 Feb. 1899–30 June 1983), athlete and college coach and administrator, was born William Madison Bell in Alvarado, Texas, the son of Ruben Edwin Bell, a dry goods store operator, and Elizabeth Morgan. As a teenager Bell adopted the nickname Matty because he admired professional baseball pitcher Christy Mathewson. Bell grew up in Fort Worth, Texas, where he played in the backfield of the Fort Worth North Side High School football team in 1914 and 1915. He was recruited by Robert L. "Chief" Myers to attend Centre College in Danville, Kentucky. Myers drew talent heavily from the Dallas–Fort Worth area, and with local players such as Alvin "Bo" McMillin, James "Red" Weaver, Swede Anderson, Bill James, and Bell, Centre College made its presence known nationally in college football. The 1919 Centre College team had a 9–0 record, with 481 points scored, only 23 points given up, and with 5 shutouts of opponents. Under Coach Charles B. Moran, who arrived at Centre College in 1919, the school lost only three games from 1919 through the 1922 season with his talented Texas recruits.

Bell wanted to become a lawyer. However, coming from a family with extremely limited financial resources and having gone into debt to finish college, after his graduation from Centre College in 1920, Bell was unable to go directly to law school. Instead he took a job coaching football at Haskell Institute, a Native-American school in Lawrence, Kansas. In the 1920 and 1921 seasons his teams compiled a 12–5–2 record, with his 1921 team beating both University of Pittsburgh and Texas Christian University by 14–0 scores. In the 1922 season he coached at Carroll College in Wisconsin, compiling a 4–3–1 record. In 1923 he was offered a job as an assistant coach at the University of Texas, but he declined it. With the entrance of Texas Christian University into the Southwest Conference that same year, the school hired Bell as its head coach. His first two seasons at Texas Christian produced identical 4–5 records, but his next four were winning seasons, with his 1928 team posting an 8–2 record and losing only to Baylor 7–6 and 6–0 to Texas University, the Southwest Conference champion. His 1925 team was 7–1–1, beating later conference champion Texas A & M 3–0. His overall record at Texas Christian was 33–17–5, and his effective coaching made the school a recognized powerhouse in the conference.

Bell married Peggy Holt in 1929, and they had one daughter. From 1929 through 1933 Bell was the head coach at Texas A & M. However, his five seasons there produced only a 24–21–3 record with his Aggies team defeated by Texas Christian in all five contests. His best season at Texas A & M was in 1931 with a 7–3 record. In the 1933 season his team won its first four games and finished 6–3–1 overall. But Bell was fired on the basis of his disappointing overall record and because he had failed to continue the stellar winning tradition established by his predecessor, Dana X. Bible, whose teams never had had a losing season and had compiled a 70–19–9 record in eleven seasons.

In 1934 Bell served as line coach at Southern Methodist University under Ray Morrison. When Morrison left in 1934 to become head coach at Vanderbilt University, Bell replaced him as head coach of Southern Methodist. In his first season Bell directed his team, anchored by ten seniors in his starting lineup, to an undefeated 12–0 regular season record, shutting out eight opponents and giving up only 32 points while scoring 288 points. His team was ranked first nationally and won the national championship even though they lost 7–0 to Stanford University in the 1936 Rose Bowl. The most dramatic game in the 1935 season featured Southern Methodist against Texas Christian when both teams had 10–0 season records and a Rose Bowl bid at stake. The game, played in Fort Worth, was featured on a national radio broadcast with the outcome decided by a 35-yard pass play on the fourth down.

This time Bell continued a winning tradition. With the exception of the seasons in 1942, 1943, and 1944, when Bell served as a lieutenant commander in the naval reserve, he guided Southern Methodist for twelve seasons and compiled a 47–23–3 record. His career at Southern Methodist was marked by early success with the national championship in 1935 and later success in the 1947 and 1948 seasons. His 1947 team had a 9–0–1 record, with a 19–19 tie with Texas Christian in the last game of the season, and was ranked third nationally. His 1948 team had an 8–1–1 record and ranked tenth nationally. The 1948 team featured running back Doak Walker, who was an All-America selection and was awarded the Heisman Trophy. Bell's undefeated 1947 team tied an undefeated Penn State University 13–13 in the Cotton Bowl, and his 1948 team defeated the University of Oregon 21–13 in the same bowl. In 1947 he finished second to Fritz Crisler of the University of Michigan in the voting for coach of the year. The 1947 and 1948 teams claimed Southwest Conference championships, and Bell's 1940 team, with an 8–1–1 record, shared the conference championship with Texas A & M.

Bell's last season, 1949, resulted in a 5–4–1 record, with the team losing its last three games. He retired as the head coach to concentrate on his duties as athletic director, a position he assumed in 1945 and held until his full retirement in 1964.

In his coaching Bell used the standard single-wing offense as well as the innovative and wide-open offensive system of his predecessor Morrison. This system relied on the forward pass and the original double-wing formation that utilized the spread backfield with the fullback handling the ball on almost every play. This spread-offensive system featured multiple ball-handling by the backs and multiple laterals and passes. It was an exciting system because it spread the defense and opened up the field to outside running, where speed was critical. Bell was a calm leader who believed that game preparation and execution provided the basis for winning. He knew how to inspire and challenge his teams without histrionics, and he was able to utilize talent effectively and to fit players into his system.

During his coaching career Bell served on the board of trustees of the American Football Coaches Association from 1937 to 1942; he was president of the association in 1942 and 1943. In 1954 he was named an honorary life member of the AFCA. He also served on the NCAA Football Rules Committee. In his role as full-time athletic director at Southern Methodist, Bell directed the expansion of the school's intercollegiate sports program and facilities. He also directed the construction of a $2.25 million basketball arena, which opened in 1956, and converted the old gymnasium into a first-class swimming and diving facility. A major disappointment to Bell was that Southern Methodist failed to win a football conference championship during his tenure as athletic director. However, the basketball team claimed three consecutive conference championships from 1955 through 1957 and co-conference championships in 1958 and 1962. The swimming-and-diving team became a conference powerhouse, winning eight straight Southwestern Conference championships from 1956 to 1964. As athletic director Bell had the satisfaction of working closely with Morrison, who returned to Southern Methodist in 1953 as vice president for public relations and development. Bell was elected to the College Football Hall of Fame in 1955, a year after Morrison. The track facility at Southern Methodist is named the Morrison-Bell Track Stadium.

In his retirement Bell played golf and served as a scout in the Southwest for the Washington Redskins of the National Football League. He died at his home in Dallas, Texas. He was known as a man who enjoyed close and long-lasting friendships, believed in the value of intercollegiate athletics as a means of providing both education and an opportunity to develop athletic potential, and saw smaller institutions like Southern Methodist University as capable of competitive excellence during a period that saw the development of big-time athletics. In 1991 he was inducted into the Athletic Hall of Fame at Centre College.

• No collection of Matty Bell's papers exists. His daughter, Patty Bell Kendrick of Plano, Texas, has a small collection of his correspondence and papers, and the Sports Information Office at Southern Methodist University in Dallas has a substantial file of clippings. For Bell's career in college football, see Allison Danzig, *The History of American Football: Its Great Teams, Players, and Coaches* (1956); Tom Perrin, *Football: A College History* (1987); Tim Cohane, *Great College Football Coaches of the Twenties and Thirties* (1973); Temple Pouncey, *Southern Methodist Football: Mustang Mania* (1981); Harold V. Ratliff, *The Power and the Glory: The Story of the Southwest Conference* (1957); Will Grimsley, *Football: The Greatest Moments in the Southwest Conference* (1968); and Wilbur Evans and H. B. McElroy, *The Twelfth Man: A Story of Texas A & M Football* (1974). Obituaries are in the *Fort Worth Star-Telegram* and the *Dallas News*, both 1 July 1983.

DOUGLAS A. NOVERR

BELL, Philip Alexander (1808–24 Apr. 1889), abolitionist and journalist, was born in New York City (of unknown parents) and received his education there at the African Free School. He married Rebecca Elizabeth Fenwick, originally from Charleston, South Carolina, in 1832 (number of children unknown). Bell established his reputation as a civic leader in the early 1830s by participating in a wide range of activities in New York City's African-American community. He was a member of the American Anti-Slavery Society, served as New York's first subscription agent for William Lloyd Garrison's *Liberator*, and worked with the city's fledgling underground railroad to assist fugitive slaves. As chairman of the Philomathean Society and director of the Phoenix Society, Bell led the local efforts to enhance black education. He promoted the black national convention movement of the 1830s, whose goals were to promote moral reform—education, temperance, self-improvement—for northern free blacks, and represented New York City at three annual conventions.

Bell was a life-long critic of black emigration programs, particularly the proposals by the American Colonization Society to settle free black Americans in Africa. He argued that African Americans should remain in the United States and demand their rights as American citizens. He advocated political action to achieve these rights, and as a leader of the New York Political Association in the 1830s, he urged blacks to organize petition and lobbying campaigns to expand their voting rights. In the 1850s he continued to work for black enfranchisement through the black state conventions and the New York State Suffrage Association.

Bell's most notable achievement was his pioneering work in the development of the African-American press. His career in journalism spanned over fifty years, beginning in January 1837 when he was editor and proprietor of the New York City *Weekly Advocate*. Although Samuel E. Cornish assumed the editorship in March 1837, when the newspaper was renamed the *Colored American*, Bell remained closely involved with all facets of the enterprise. He helped define the *Colored American*'s racially independent and assertive character, in the process drawing criticism from white abolitionists, particularly the Garrisonians. Under the direction of Bell and Cornish, the *Colored American* gained wide circulation and became the most successful and influential black newspaper of its time. After leaving the newspaper, Bell opened an "intelligence office"—an employment service for black workers in New York City—but maintained his interest in journalism, collecting subscriptions and corresponding with several antislavery and reform newspapers, often under the pseudonym "Cosmopolite."

In 1853 Bell helped establish the first national black organization, the National Council of Colored People, and later witnessed its demise because of disagreement among its leaders at the 1855 black national convention in Philadelphia. In the early 1850s, Bell joined with twelve other prominent New York City blacks to form the Committee of Thirteen, which directed the local opposition to the Fugitive Slave Law, racial discrimination, and black emigration.

Bell continued his career as a journalist after settling in San Francisco in 1857. He assumed editorial duties with the *Pacific Appeal*, published by Peter Anderson, in 1862. Unable to resolve editorial disagreements with the publisher, Bell left the *Appeal* and in 1865 founded his own newspaper, the *Elevator*, which he described as "a Journal of Progress." His weekly newspaper primarily served blacks living on the West Coast, but he attracted a national readership by publishing reports from communities across the continent. By the 1880s he could boast that the *Elevator* was the longest running secular African-American newspaper of the nineteenth century. Bell remained in-

volved with the *Elevator* until his death. In addition to being a journalist, he supplemented his meager income by working as a real estate broker. Bell was a stalwart Republican during Reconstruction and, as described in his obituary, helped keep "the colored voters in unbroken harmony in state, municipal, and national elections." The state Republican party acknowledged his political labors in 1880 by securing him employment as assistant sergeant at arms in the California Senate.

As one of San Francisco's distinguished black personalities, Bell frequently assumed a conspicuous role in civic functions and at public ceremonies. In 1865 he served as secretary of the black state convention. He was also involved in several social organizations, including the Oakland Literary and Aid Society and a local masonic lodge. Bell nurtured an abiding interest in drama, and his reviews of theater performances appeared in several California newspapers as well as the *Elevator*. He attempted dramatic readings himself but was acclaimed more for his editorials than his oratorical skills. William Wells Brown described Bell as "an original and subtile writer" and "the Napoleon of the colored press" (p. 471). Despite his ground-breaking contributions to African-American journalism and his several business ventures, Bell achieved little financial success, spending his final years in dire poverty. He died in the Bay Area.

• Correspondence and editorials from Bell and other documents relating to his life are in the Black Abolitionist Papers and cataloged in George C. Carter and C. Peter Ripley, eds., *Black Abolitionist Papers, 1830–1865: A Guide to the Microfilm Edition* (1981). Bell is the subject of a biographical note in the *Black Abolitionist Papers*, vol. 4, *The United States, 1847–1858* (1991). See also the biographical sketch in William Wells Brown, *The Rising Son* (1874), references to Bell in I. Garland Penn, *The Afro-American Press and Its Editors* (1891). An obituary is in the San Francisco *Morning Call*, 27 Apr. 1889.

MICHAEL F. HEMBREE

BELL, Samuel (9 Feb. 1770–23 Dec. 1850), lawyer, governor, and senator, was born in Londonderry, New Hampshire, the son of John Bell and Mary Ann Gilmore, farmers. His father, a tall, rugged, hot-tempered man, was a commanding figure in his community, who served as a deacon and selectman and as a member of the New Hampshire committee of safety and provincial congress during the Revolution. After working on the farm until he was eighteen, Bell studied at a local school and attended New Ipswich Academy before entering the sophomore class at Dartmouth College in 1791. Following graduation in 1793, he studied law in Amherst, New Hampshire, under Samuel Dana. By the time Bell was admitted to the bar in 1796, he was twenty-six, tall and erect like his father, but less powerful and domineering.

Bell was an immediate success. His law practice, which he opened in Francestown, New Hampshire, grew rapidly. In 1797 he married Mehitabel Dana, the daughter of his law instructor, and by 1806 the Bells had five children and had moved back to Amherst. There he was elected president of the newly chartered Hillsborough Bank. A Republican in politics, he rose quickly through the ranks. A state representative in 1804, he became Speaker of the house of representatives in 1805 and 1806, president of the state senate in 1807 and 1808, and governor's councilor in 1809.

Bell's good fortune came to an end when the Hillsborough Bank closed suddenly in August 1809. Although the closing was due in part to a general banking panic brought on by the Embargo Act, questionable banking practices were also responsible. Within the first six months of its existence, the bank had issued $450,000 in bank notes, over three times the amount authorized by its charter. The bank, which never reopened, quickly became the subject of angry petitions, investigations, and lawsuits. As its president, Bell bore the brunt of the attacks, and as late as 1819 the so-called Amherst Bubble was used against him politically.

The bank controversy came at a bad time for Bell and his wife, for both had fallen seriously ill, and Mehitabel died in 1810. Samuel, who was suffering from consumption, recovered—gradually thanks partly to a regimen of horseback rides—on one of which he went as far west as Ohio. He did not return to public life for six years. In 1812 he moved to Chester, New Hampshire, to be close to his parents and his brother John.

When the Republicans, who had been out of favor during the War of 1812, returned to power in 1816, Bell was appointed associate justice of the state superior court. In 1817 the court, made up entirely of Republicans, ruled in favor of the act turning Dartmouth College into a state university, but two years later the decision was reversed by the U.S. Supreme Court in the famous *Dartmouth College v. Woodward* opinion. Bell was elected governor in 1819, and with the collapse of the Federalists was easily reelected until 1823. Shortly after he took office the Toleration Act was passed, reducing the power of the Congregational church by giving all Christian denominations the right to be supported by tax revenues. In his messages to the legislature Bell sought to check intemperance through licensing and taxation, called for a law requiring paupers to contribute whatever they could toward their own support, and proposed important changes in the court and militia systems. He also urged the legislature to consider ways to promote manufactures. The legislature responded with a number of modest reforms and in 1822 elected Bell to the U.S. Senate.

While he was in the Senate, Bell continued to play a major role in state politics. A new political system began to emerge with Bell and Isaac Hill at the head of rival Republican factions. Although never as clever as Hill, Bell became a capable party organizer, especially in the state and federal elections of 1828. He laid the groundwork for the campaign by sending out form letters to prominent members of his party, asking whether they favored allying with former Federalists. After they agreed to include the Federalists, Bell's National Republicans ran an effective campaign, using some of Hill's own techniques. They elected Bell's brother, John Bell, governor in March and carried the state for John Quincy Adams over Andrew Jackson in the fall. They also reelected Bell himself over Hill to the U.S. Senate.

Bell was a respected though not prominent member of the Senate. Cautious about federal legislation, he resisted a bill in 1828 to abolish imprisonment for debt and opposed preemption and graduation land bills in 1829 and 1830. Consistent with his interest in promoting manufactures, he strongly supported a protective tariff. He voted against the tariff of 1832 because it was not protective enough but accepted the compromise tariff of 1833 as the best bill possible at the time. During the financial panic of 1834 Bell presented petitions from two New Hampshire mill towns, condemning Jackson for removing the federal deposits from the Bank of the United States. But he was fighting a losing battle, for the Democrats had gained control both in Washington and New Hampshire. They had already pushed a resolution through the New Hampshire legislature calling on Bell to resign his Senate seat on the grounds that he no longer represented the people of the state. Although he ignored the resolution, he did not run for reelection and left the Senate in March 1835.

Bell spent the rest of his life on his farm in Chester. He had married Lucy Smith in 1828, and he and his second wife had four children. One of Bell's nine children was named to the New Hampshire superior court; another son was elected to the U.S. Senate; a nephew became governor; and a grandson served as a congressman. Bell was the central figure in a family that left its mark on New Hampshire life from before the Revolution until well after the Civil War. He died in Chester.

• The New Hampshire Historical Society has a small collection of Bell papers, including a brief autobiographical letter from Bell to William Cogswell (1840), as well as three of his governor's messages. His legal career is assessed by his nephew Charles H. Bell in *The Bench and Bar of New Hampshire* (1894), pp. 79–81. The failure of the Hillsborough Bank is described by Norman W. Smith in "The 'Amherst Bubble,' Wildcat Banking in Early Nineteenth Century New Hampshire," *Historical New Hampshire* 20 (Spring 1965): 27–40. For genealogy see Benjamin Chase, *History of Old Chester* (1869), pp. 468–71. An obituary is in the *Portsmouth Journal*, 18 Jan. 1851.

DONALD B. COLE

BELL, William Brown (16 Feb. 1879–20 Dec. 1950), chemical industrialist, was born in Stroudsburg, Pennsylvania, the son of Thomas Alsop Bell, a china manufacturer, and Elizabeth Dunn. Raised as a Quaker, he attended Haverford College, from which he received both a B.A. in 1900 and an M.A. in political science the following year. Bell earned a law degree from Columbia University in 1903 and in the same year married Susan Kite Alsop, with whom he had one child. Bell then passed the New York bar exam and joined the New York City law firm of Guthrie, Cravath, Henderson, and de Gersdorff. Giving up the practice of law in 1905, he worked on a newspaper in Atlantic City, New Jersey, until 1915 and then spent a year managing the Pocono Lake Preserve in Pennsylvania.

In 1917 Bell entered the chemical industry when he became associated with the Air Nitrates Corporation, which had been created by Frank S. Washburn, founder of American Cyanamid Company, as a subsidiary to construct the government's wartime hydroelectric Nitrate Plant No. 2 at Muscle Shoals, Alabama. Bell, who represented the investment interests of James B. Duke, assisted Washburn in the planning and construction of the nitrogen plant and, at the direction of the Duke interests, essentially ran American Cyanamid after Washburn fell ill in 1920. When Washburn died in 1922, Bell was selected as Cyanamid's second president and chairman of the board, positions that he held until his death.

When Bell took over the reins of American Cyanamid, it was still a relatively small chemical company. Washburn had created the company in 1907 to produce fertilizer from atmospheric nitrogen, but World War I diverted production into ammonia and nitric acid for military purposes. By the end of the war numerous foreign companies were all competitively producing similar products. With several of the company's plants and mines shut down or operating at partial capacity, "any fool could see that what we needed was diversification," Bell later explained.

In seeking to diversify Cyanamid, Bell implemented a dual strategy to develop new product lines and expand through corporate acquisition. Corporate research resulted in the development of new commercial processes for the production of prussiate of soda, dicyandiamide, guanidine rubber accelerators, and alkyd coating resins. Although the company committed $15 million to research and development between 1928 and 1940, in the late 1920s Bell turned to the acquisition of outside companies as a surer and certainly quicker way to increase financial returns. Under his leadership, in 1929 Cyanamid acquired Calco Chemical Company, producers of dyestuffs, pharmaceuticals, and coal tar intermediates; Kalbfleisch Corporation, a producer of heavy chemicals, including aluminum sulfate and products for the paper industry; and the Seldon Company, manufacturer of coal tar intermediaries and, more important, a patented vanadium catalyst used in manufacturing sulfuric acid. In 1930 it acquired Lederle Antitoxin Laboratories, a producer of antitoxins, vaccines, and biologicals, and, in 1933–1934, the Burton and American Powder Companies, both producers of explosives. These acquisitions were financed primarily through the issue and exchange of common stock and reflected a trend toward consolidation within the chemical industry during this period. Cyanamid also combined forces with Pittsburgh Plate Glass Company in 1931 to found Southern Alkali Corporation for the purposes of building a $7 million soda ash and caustic soda plant that became operational in 1934 and a liquid chlorine plant that opened in 1938.

During the 1930s, Cyanamid continued to grow through acquisitions both by subsidiaries and the parent company. Continued growth and diversification presented complex organizational and managerial problems that Bell sought to rectify by separating the company into seven divisions. In addition, Cyanamid utilized various subsidiaries to handle other operations. For example, the Chemical Construction Corporation offered design, engineering, and construction services for the heavy chemicals industry, building "turnkey" plants for clients all over the world.

Satisfied with the company's rapid expansion through acquisitions, Bell refocused his attention on research by 1936. In that year he established the Stamford Research Laboratories in Stamford, Connecticut. An early accomplishment of the revitalized research program was the 1938 development of commercial production processes for melamine resins, which had applications in hardening work surfaces and strengthening paper fibers. In 1942 the laboratories developed a liquid polyester resin, manufactured under the trade name of Laminac, which could be used in the production of lightweight structural materials that resisted weather and corrosion. Commercial development in 1940 of acrylonitrile under the trade name "acrylo" was particularly helpful to the wartime production of synthetic rubbers. After the war it was also utilized as an adhesive, as an intermediate in the production of dyes, and in paper coatings.

Bell's approach to industrial research was generally conservative, with practical product development and application foremost in mind. New research projects underwent extensive committee and executive review before receiving funding approval. Although he did not begrudge spending research dollars, Bell wanted to ensure they were well spent. As he noted in a 1940 *Fortune* article, "In research there is nothing more important than to be able to recognize 'a dead horse,' take him out of the laboratory, and bury him quickly, quietly, with the least possible expense."

Whether or not his scientists found Bell's approach to research overly restrictive, his two-pronged strategy of diversification and expansion certainly was successful. By the time of his death in 1950, Bell had transformed Cyanamid from a relatively small company with less than $5 million in sales to the fifth-largest American chemical firm with branch and sales offices throughout the world, assets of over $325 million, and net sales nearly equal to assets based on the manufacture of over 5,000 products by more than 20,000 employees.

In personality and background Bell was quietly thoughtful, modest, and reserved, as reflective of his Quaker upbringing, yet he was conservative with firmly held convictions—qualities that led him to positions of importance in the corporate, political, and civic arenas. At the time of his death, Bell was chairman or president of several Cyanamid subsidiaries and more than a half-dozen other corporations. During the depression he served as president of the Chemical Alliance, a trade organization originally developed during World War I, which sought to write the industry's codes for the National Recovery Administration. Bell also chaired the national committee for modification of the industrial section of the Securities Exchange Act in 1934. Politically a Republican, Bell was frustrated with the New Deal and served as the chairman of his party's National Finance Committee in 1936. Bell also served as a trustee of the Duke Endowment, the Sloan Foundation, and Haverford College and as a member of the advisory committee of the School of Public Health of Howard University. Bell was also president of the Manufacturing Chemists' Association (1936–1938) and a director of the National Association of Manufacturers as well as a member of the Chemists Club of New York City. He was the recipient of awards from the Society of the Chemical Industry in 1934 and again in 1939.

Bell died in Marrakesh, French Morocco, while honeymooning with his second wife, Marion Walters. (His first wife had died the previous year.) Bell left a company strongly positioned to enter the second half of the twentieth century. Much of the strength of that position can be attributed to Bell's vision of Cyanamid's need for diversification and his ability to achieve it.

• No known collection of Bell's papers exists, and there is no full-scale biography. Particularly helpful, however, in piecing together his career are Williams Haynes's *American Chemical Industry*, vols. 2 and 6 (1945) and an essay on American Cyanamid in *Fortune*, Sept. 1940, pp. 66–71, 102–6. An obituary is in the *New York Times*, 22 Dec. 1950.

STEPHEN H. CUTCLIFFE

BELLAMY, Edward (26 Mar. 1850–22 May 1898), novelist, was born in Chicopee Falls, Massachusetts, the son of Rufus King Bellamy, a Baptist minister, and Maria Putnam. One of four children raised in a strict Calvinist household, he was educated at local schools and briefly attended Union College in Schenectady, New York. As a young man, he developed a strong social interest in poverty, unemployment, and other ill effects of industrialization, which he presumably witnessed not only in the mill towns of western Massachusetts but also in Europe, where he lived for a year in 1868.

Returning to the United States, Bellamy studied law; but he soon turned to journalism, first in New York City and then back in Massachusetts, where in 1880 he founded the *Springfield Daily News*. In 1882 he married Emma Sanderson; they had two children. Desiring a literary career, Bellamy began writing stories for magazines. He wrote three romances, one of which, *Dr. Heidenhoff's Process* (1880), was admired by author William Dean Howells. A fourth novel, *The Duke of Stockbridge* (1900), which was serialized but not published in book form until after his death, was about Shays's Rebellion and clearly displayed the author's sympathies for the economic plight of the agrarian rebels.

The Gilded Age had already experienced the severe depression of 1873 and its aftermath of strikes and violence, as well as the assassination of President James Garfield in 1881 and the Haymarket riot of 1886. As the gulf widened between capital and labor, proposals of all sorts (mostly of a socialist nature) abounded to remedy the situation. One of the most popular was Henry George's economic tract *Progress and Poverty* (1879); another equally popular work was Bellamy's novel *Looking Backward 2000–1887*, which appeared in 1888.

Looking Backward 2000–1887 proposed a cure for what Bellamy saw as society's chief problem: the inequality brought on by the dominant capitalism of the age. In his view, American civilization had been transformed from its agrarian, preindustrial roots into a postbellum landscape marked by plutocracy, competition, waste, exploitation, poverty, social injustice, and strife. For Bellamy, the cure for these problems was simple: people had only to adopt and act on the universal principle of absolute economic equality.

The novel tells the story of Julian West, a young man of inherited wealth but a sensitive nature who goes to sleep one night in Boston in 1887 and awakens in the year 2000. He encounters Dr. Leete, his host and all-knowing guide, through whom he learns about the remarkable social order that now prevails. At first scarcely believing the total transformation of this world, Julian is soon convinced that a complete moral renovation of the social order has taken place. All the old ills that had divided and threatened human society in 1887 have been overcome. The concentration of capital into competing corporations and trusts has been eliminated, and the nation's wealth is now in the hands of a single national syndicate.

Also banished from society are the excessive individualism and private luxury that afflicted the earlier era, as are antisocial practices such as buying and selling. For the first time the efficiencies and economies of industrial production are devoted not to making the rich richer but to equally benefiting all of society. Cooperation has replaced competition; men and women are supremely happy in a rational, communal society. Secure from want, freed from competitive struggle, citizens no longer work for the accumulation of wealth but for the honor derived from service to the nation. Julian learns that "no man any more has any care for the morrow, either for himself or his children, for the nation guarantees the nurture, education, and comfortable maintenance of every citizen from the cradle to the grave."

How were society and its structures—not to mention human nature—so fundamentally reformed from their grievous and threatened state of 1887? Not through strikes, propaganda, direct action, or political parties but through a peaceful evolution from capitalism to socialism. The transition occurred naturally—"a triumph of common sense"—when all segments of society recognized that the principle of total equality would end the strife and guarantee life, liberty, and the pursuit of happiness for all.

Looking Backward was an unparalleled success as soon as it was published, selling thousands of copies a week in the first few years. It was also translated into several languages. Bellamy Nationalist Clubs sprang up across the country to further the author's ideas, and a monthly journal, *The Nationalist*, began publication. By 1891 public interest was so stimulated that Bellamy, a rather reclusive figure by all accounts, started up a weekly magazine called the *New Nation*, which advocated a program of political reform involving the nationalization of all industries. The novel had plenty of critics, of course. William Morris labeled it "a horrible cockney dream." Many critics were quick to point out that Bellamy's cure was an external remedy for an internal disease. Some labeled his vision as communistic and Marxian; years later others insisted it advocated fascism. As to its view of human nature, when Clarence Darrow criticized *Progress and Poverty* for "its cocksureness, its simplicity, and the small value that it placed upon the selfish motives of men," the complaints could, with equal justice, have been applied to *Looking Backward*.

By the middle of the 1890s the movement was finished; the Nationalist Clubs had folded, and Bellamy himself, now ill with tuberculosis, ceased publication of the *New Nation*. He wrote a sequel to *Looking Backward* titled *Equality*, which was published in 1897, the year before his death in Chicopee Falls. As a supplement, again in fiction form, it was meant to furnish further clarification and justification for his vision. More tract than novel, the book's success was limited.

Bellamy said that he had intended *Looking Backward* to be "a mere literary fantasy, a fairy tale of social felicity," not a work of political economics. But it was as a timely work of political speculation that the book gained its original popularity. Although to later generations Bellamy's vision has seemed naive or nostalgic, the book has continued to attract readers and commentary, from prominent literary critics, including Granville Hicks, Alfred Kazin, Lewis Mumford, Jacques Barzun, and Mark Van Doren. Articles continue to appear on Bellamy and his novel.

In *Main Currents in American Thought* (vol. 3, 1930), cultural historian Vernon L. Parrington describes the importance of *Looking Backward* as

a suggestive document of a generation that saw its finer spirits repelled by the vulgar individualism of the Gilded Age. In the long run, no doubt, its influence was slight, and the hopes of the Bellamy Nationalists, like the hopes of the Single-Taxers, were doomed to disappointment. Nevertheless, it remains as a testimony to the fact that in a blatant world of preemption, exploitation, and progress, were some who were concerned for a juster social order than the Gilded Age dreamed of—a true commonwealth that free men might build if they would.

• Bellamy's writings and correspondence are at the Houghton Library at Harvard University. The main biographical sources are Arthur E. Morgan, *Edward Bellamy* (1944); and Sylvia E. Bowman, *The Year 2000: A Critical Biography of* *Edward Bellamy* (1958) and *Edward Bellamy* (1986). Critical studies of Bellamy's work may be found in Arthur Lipow, *Authoritarian Socialism in America: Edward Bellamy and the Nationalist Movement* (1982); Stephen Kesselman, *The Modernization of American Reform* (1979); Everett McNair, *Edward Bellamy and the Nationalist Movement* (1957); D. Aaron, *Men of Good Hope* (1951); Daphne Patai, ed., *Looking Backward 1988–1888* (1988); and John L. Thomas, *Alternative America* (1983).

BRUCE R. CARRICK

BELLAMY, Elizabeth Whitfield Croom (17 Apr. 1837–13 Apr. 1900), author and teacher, was born near Quincy, Florida, the daughter of William Whitfield Croom, a plantation owner and merchant, and Julia Stephens. Elizabeth received her education in Philadelphia, at Pelham Priory, and in New York, at the Spingler Institute, under the direction of the Reverend Gorham D. Abbot. Graduating in 1856, Elizabeth had focused her interests on music, literature, and foreign languages. In 1858, she married her cousin, Dr. Charles E. Bellamy. She later gave birth to two children, a son who died at the age of four and a daughter who died in infancy. Dr. Bellamy enlisted as a surgeon in the Confederate army during the Civil War and died, while serving, in 1863. Devastated by her misfortunes, Elizabeth returned to her father's home in Eutaw, Alabama, and began teaching school.

After her mother's death in 1867, Bellamy left Eutaw and resumed her teaching career in Gainesville, Alabama. In the late 1870s, she moved to Mobile to live with her brother, Major Stephens Croom, an attorney, and soon established the Elizabeth Whitfield Bellamy Finishing School for Young Ladies. After her brother's death in 1884, Bellamy and her sister-in-law, Mary Marshall Croom, opened a new school in the family home on Augusta Street. The women converted the former servants' cottage into a one-room schoolhouse, where Croom provided a solid educational foundation for boys and girls in the elementary and intermediate grades. Meanwhile, Bellamy reestablished her finishing school in an upstairs apartment in the home. There, she continued to share her knowledge of English literature, history, and foreign languages with young women. Many of Bellamy's students gained prominence as teachers, community leaders, and writers; playwright and author Amélie Rives Troubetzkoy is only one example.

In addition to teaching, Bellamy began writing stories which appeared in *Appleton's, Atlantic Monthly, Youth's Companion*, and other journals. Under titles such as "Hannah Calline's Jim," "The Finding of Miss Clementine," "At Bent's Hotel," and "Mom Cely's Wonderful Luck," the stories portrayed various aspects of southern life. Bellamy published these early works, as well as her first two novels, under the pseudonym Kamba Thorpe. Ads for Bellamy's first novel *Four Oaks* (1867) did reveal, however, that Thorpe was a "Southern lady." "Thorpe" published *The Little Joanna* (1876), but *Old Man Gilbert* (1888) and *Penny Lancaster, Farmer* (1889) were released under the name Elizabeth Whitfield Bellamy.

Like her short stories, Bellamy's novels involved southern life. All four were fairly typical romance novels set in the period shortly before, during, or after the Civil War. Typical plot devices included complicated family relationships, former slaves who remained faithful to the master's family, and southern women who were strong and capable, yet gracious and virtuous, as they faced the exigencies caused by the Civil War. Other familiar themes in her works involved the difficulties incurred by whites and freed slaves during Reconstruction, the acceptance of former Yankees in southern society, the problems encountered by poor sharecroppers and women who farmed their own land, clouded inheritances, and the importance for women of common sense and intellect over beauty and helplessness. Frequent moments of comic relief and inevitable happy endings were also typical of Bellamy's work. While not highly acclaimed for their literary content or construction, the books and stories portrayed ways in which southerners faced their many problems during the latter half of the nineteenth century. Though classified as a romance writer or a local colorist, Bellamy did not sentimentalize the antebellum South. Instead, her works indicated an acceptance of what had come to pass and an eagerness to overcome the disruptions caused by the Civil War and to move forward.

Bellamy regarded *Old Man Gilbert* as her finest novel. Reviewed by Joel Chandler Harris and Augusta Evans Wilson, among others, it was praised, as were many of her other works, for its phonetically authentic Negro dialect and its solid characterization of the protagonist. Harris considered *Old Man Gilbert* to be "one of the most remarkable contributions that have been made to American literature since the war." In addition to writing about the South, Bellamy enjoyed sharing her appreciation of nature. Descriptions of natural settings enhanced her fiction and also appeared in articles and poems she contributed to various magazines. For example, readers could picture lush scenes of uncontrolled plant growth in undeveloped areas, relish the aromas of handpicked nosegays and the flavors of homegrown vegetables, and experience arduous wagon journeys through mud "up to the hub" in the Mississippi Bottom counties.

Bellamy continued teaching and writing throughout most of her life. She was also an enthusiastic scholar of William Shakespeare. Not only did she study his works for her own benefit and for that of her young students, but she also presented lectures to the adult community in Mobile on his life and works. The community recognized Bellamy as a French scholar, as well, and sought her help when the need for translation arose. A member of Mobile's literary circle, Bellamy enjoyed the friendships of contemporary writers Augusta Evans Wilson and Thomas Cooper De Leon. Bellamy died in Mobile.

• Bellamy's family in Mobile still holds her papers and manuscripts. Her grandnephew Stephens G. Croom and his wife, Velma, provided articles from the *Mobile-Press Register*, let-

ters to the publisher about *Old Man Gilbert*, and other sources of information used in preparing this biographical sketch. References to Bellamy can be found in Frances E. Willard and Mary A. Livermore, eds., *American Women* (1897; repr. 1973); Ida Raymond, *Southland Writers* (1870), reissued under the title *The Living Female Writers of the South* (1872); and Thomas McAdory Owen, *History of Alabama and Dictionary of Alabama Biography* (1921). An obituary is in the *Mobile Register*, 14 and 15 Apr. 1900.

DOROTHY MCLEOD MACINERNEY

BELLAMY, Joseph (20 Feb. 1719–6 Mar. 1790), Congregational minister and theologian, was born in the Cheshire section of Wallingford, Connecticut, the son of Matthew Bellamy, a prosperous landowner, and Sarah Wood, who died when he was an infant. He and ten other children were raised by his father's second wife, Mary Johnson. In 1731, at age twelve, Bellamy was sent to Yale College, from which he graduated in 1735. He then read theology with Jonathan Edwards (1703–1758), with whom he established a long friendship. At some time in 1736 Bellamy experienced what he believed to be "a saving conversion," a subtle but sure conviction that he was predestined to heaven.

In 1738, as a visiting preacher, Bellamy inspired a revival in the town of Bethlehem, Connecticut, and was invited to organize a Congregational church there. On 2 April 1740 he was ordained, and he spent the rest of his clerical career as pastor of that church. In 1744 Bellamy married Frances Sherman of New Haven; the couple had eight children. Despite the size of his family and an occasional controversy with his congregation about pay, Bellamy had sufficient income from his salary and from the lands he owned to send one son to Yale, to provide for each of his heirs, and to purchase a number of slaves.

Bellamy's ministerial career coincided with the eruption of the Great Awakening, an event that Bellamy welcomed as a work of the Holy Spirit. In order to spread the message of religious revival, Bellamy itinerated widely, throughout Connecticut and into Massachusetts, New York, New Jersey, and Pennsylvania, preaching several sermons a day, every day, for weeks at a time. From all accounts, Bellamy's commanding voice, his gift for vivid metaphor, his imposing stature, and even the coarseness of his facial features left an indelible impression upon his audiences.

When the Awakening collapsed in 1745 Bellamy blamed extremists on both sides, those who had opposed the revival from the outset and those who carried revival to emotional excess. In defense of his own middle position, Bellamy published *True Religion Delineated* in 1750, his most important publication. It is essentially a text that explains Calvinist Congregational orthodoxy as defined by Jonathan Edwards, who read the manuscript and wrote the introduction. The work established Bellamy's reputation as a theologian, a reputation he solidified over the next two decades by defending such doctrines as Original Sin and by denouncing such "unscriptural" practices as the Half-Way Covenant. Scores of young men studying for the Congregational ministry sought out Bellamy as their mentor, and Bellamy's home in Bethlehem became an informal seminary.

Bellamy opposed the Stamp Act in 1765, and his opposition to Parliament grew more militant as the American colonists moved closer to rebellion. Bellamy had long suspected that England had a design to insinuate Anglican bishops into New England, and he welcomed separation from a nation that he believed had become morally corrupt. At least two of his sons enlisted in the struggle for independence.

In 1785 Bellamy's wife, Frances, died, and he was remarried in 1786 to a widow, Abiah Storrs (née Burbank). A few months later, on 19 November 1786, Bellamy suffered a stroke that partially paralyzed him. He lived three more years but was seldom fully conscious. He died in Bethlehem and was buried in the graveyard of the First Congregational Church.

Bellamy enjoyed a transatlantic reputation as a theologian during his own lifetime, as demonstrated by the award of an honorary degree by the University of Aberdeen in Scotland in 1768. He helped formulate the "New Divinity," an elaborate explication of the theology of Jonathan Edwards that attempted to prove that a belief in the total depravity of man was compatible with a belief in the absolute goodness of God. As Calvinist orthodoxy waned Bellamy's intellectual reputation diminished, and he is read today only for historical interest. At best, he extended one or two of Edward's thoughts; at worst, he stretched them to absurdity. Where Edwards speculated that the saved might finally outnumber the damned by "hundreds of thousands," Bellamy calculated the precise ratio: 14,476 ¼ to 1. Bellamy too often entered waters above his head, arguing at various times that God would consent to his own damnation if he were capable of sinning, that God could not have created any other universe than the one he did and that sin and misery demonstrate the perfection of the universe. Consistent at all cost, Bellamy attributed his debilitating stroke to "Infinite Goodness."

Though deficient as a philosopher, Bellamy was an excellent instructor of young clergymen. When he observed one of his pupils blasting his congregation with hellfire sermons week after week with no positive result, Bellamy pointed out that it was not thunder that killed, but lightning. "Thunder less," Bellamy advised, "and lighten more."

• The most informative biography of Bellamy is Glenn Paul Anderson, "Joseph Bellamy (1719–1790): The Man and His Work" (Ph.D. diss., Boston Univ., 1971). The best published biography is the introduction by Tyron Edwards to *The Works of Joseph Bellamy, D.D., First Pastor of the Church in Bethlehem, Conn., with a Memoir of His Life and Character* (2 vols., 1987.) For a more specific study of the New Divinity, see William Breitenbach, "The Consistent Calvinism of the New Divinity Movement," *William and Mary Quarterly* 41, no. 2 (1984): 241–64. Mark Valeri argues that Bellamy's thought evolved significantly between the Great Awakening and the Revolution in "The New Divinity and the American Revolution," *William and Mary Quarterly* 46, no. 4 (1989): 741–69. Bellamy's letters and unpublished sermons are scat-

tered into many archives. The most important collection is at the Case Memorial Library, Hartford Seminary, Hartford, Connecticut, but there are important items at Yale University, the Connecticut Historical Society, the American Antiquarian Society, the New York Public Library, and the Library of Congress.

JAMES P. WALSH

BELLANCA, August (14 Mar. 1885–13 Nov. 1969), trade union and political activist, was born in Sciacca, Sicily, Italy. His father was a farmer and a baker, but little else is known of his parents or his childhood in Sicily. Bellanca attended elementary school in Sciacca and went to work at age sixteen, when he was apprenticed to a tailor and a barber in Sciacca. Some time between 1900 and 1905, he immigrated to the United States and worked as a cigar maker in Tampa, Florida, and San Francisco, California, until he moved to the Northeast. Bellanca helped found the Brotherhood of Tailors, which became an important dissident group in the United Garment Workers of America (UGWA), a conservative affiliate of the American Federation of Labor (AFL). Bellanca's own immigrant background enabled him to become an organizing force among the garment workers, a group composed primarily of Italian and Eastern European Jewish immigrants who maintained their roots in ethnic communities and cultures.

Bellanca was one of many UGWA members who felt that the AFL union's leadership was undemocratic, biased toward skilled members, and unresponsive to the demands of the majority of unskilled and semiskilled workers. Emboldened by recent strike victories, Bellanca and other leaders of this insurgency led a revolt at the UGWA's 1914 national convention and established a rival union, the Amalgamated Clothing Workers of America. Bellanca had been a key activist in the garment workers' recent struggles in Baltimore, Maryland, and New York City, and he was an important leader of secessionist sentiment in Baltimore. He became a delegate representing New York's Local 63 at the 1914 convention and thus became a founding member of the ACWA. Bellanca proved to be an exceptionally popular leader, and within two years he had become vice president of the ACWA.

Bellanca was one of several young activists who became the organizing corps of the new ACWA. He, his brother Frank Bellanca, and his future wife, Dorothy Jacobs, were part of a tight leadership group, gathered around union president Sidney Hillman, that organized strikes and planned strategy in the early years, guiding union leadership for over three decades. As the Amalgamated attempted to consolidate the remnants of UGWA unions in the years before World War I, Bellanca's union activities sent him repeatedly around the circuit of garment centers in the Northeast and Midwest. Between 1914 and 1919 Bellanca participated in ACWA leadership of strikes in Chicago, Illinois; New York City; Baltimore; and Boston and Lawrence, Massachusetts.

The ACWA's early battles involved fights with rival unions almost as often as fights with garment manufacturers, and Bellanca was frequently dispatched to organize and represent the ACWA. In 1916 Bellanca aided the ACWA in the Baltimore "battle of the scissors," one of the most dramatic and violent interunion struggles of the union's early history. In this battle the Amalgamated squared off against both the UGWA and the radical Industrial Workers of the World (IWW), which were united in a most unlikely alliance. While leading an ACWA picketline, Bellanca was ambushed and beaten by AFL and IWW workers. The matter came to a climax when Amalgamated leaders and manufacturers deliberately provoked a fight with the UGWA cutters, who were a minority of workers in a shop teeming with ACWA sentiment, by introducing Amalgamated cutters into the UGWA cutters' shop. UGWA cutters immediately attacked members of the rival union, and the UGWA cutters in turn were attacked by hundreds of ACWA workers. According to one witness, the fight escalated until 2,000 people were involved. The fight poured out of the factory into the streets, and before it ended dozens were arrested, injured, and hospitalized.

Bellanca first met Jacobs through union work in Baltimore. She was a trade union leader in her own right, and she was also an ACWA founder and member of the General Executive Board. An organizer since the age of fifteen, she became a prominent advocate of enlarging women's roles as both participants and leaders in the Amalgamated. After Jacobs and Bellanca were married in August 1918, they continued to shape ACWA leadership. Although their mutual dedication to the union sometimes interfered with their personal lives, such union marriages were common in the ACWA. The Bellancas, for example, were close personal friends of the Hillmans, also a union couple, and the four frequently spent leisure as well as working hours together.

After the early interunion battles, when the Amalgamated became more securely established, Bellanca continued to play a key role in union leadership. One historian of the Amalgamated has suggested that Bellanca may have been the most popular leader of the ACWA in the 1920s, since he consistently outpolled all General Executive Board candidates in union elections. Although Bellanca's health sometimes required him to absent himself temporarily from ACWA activities, he was a nearly constant presence in union leadership until the 1960s. He served as the vice president of the ACWA from 1916 to 1934, from 1946 to 1948, and from 1952 to 1966.

Bellanca was also a lifelong political activist. As a young man, he was active in the Socialist party in Italy, and he maintained his connections to socialist politics in the United States as a Socialist party member from 1902 to 1919. Bellanca was also an active anti-Fascist, and he helped found the Mazzini Society, an American group opposed to the dictatorship of Benito Mussolini. After World War II Bellanca helped organize aid to Italy and was twice decorated by the Italian government for his service. Like many other American labor leaders, Bellanca shifted his political allegiance to the New Deal and Roosevelt during the 1930s and 1940s. Speaking to the ACWA convention, Bellanca defended his support of Roosevelt with a reminder that the choice in 1936 was "not Franklin Roosevelt or the Socialist Party" (Asher, p. 211). Bellanca the socialist was also a realist, who wholeheartedly supported the efforts of Democrats such as Roosevelt and his personal friend Fiorello La Guardia when he felt it would benefit workers. Bellanca remained active until the very end of his life. At the age of eighty-six he helped found the Trade Union Division of the National Committee for a Sane Nuclear Policy. He died at his home in New York City.

Although in life Bellanca was perhaps overshadowed by the prominence of Sidney Hillman and the remarkable achievements of his wife, trade union histories and the correspondence of Amalgamated members attest to the critical role Bellanca assumed in forming the clothing workers union. Allegedly a man who avoided the limelight, Bellanca was nevertheless well known by his contemporaries and coworkers for his popularity among the rank and file and his unselfish devotion to his work.

• Bellanca's correspondence is included in the Records of the Amalgamated Clothing Workers of America, which are available on microfilm. Nina Lynn Asher's biography of Dorothy Jacobs, "Dorothy Jacobs Bellanca: Feminist Trade Unionist, 1894–1946" (Ph.D. diss., State Univ. of New York, Binghamton, 1982), provides an interesting account of Bellanca's personal life and the life of a union couple in the ACWA. Biographies of Sidney Hillman; histories of the Amalgamated such as Matthew Josephson, *Sidney Hillman: Statesman of American Labor* (1952), and Steve Fraser, *Labor Will Rule: Sidney Hillman and the Rise of American Labor* (1993); the Amalgamated's *ACWA Documentary History*, published biennially; and the ACWA convention proceedings provide details on the early events in Amalgamated history in which Bellanca played a key role. Some biographical details of Bellanca's early life are in a brief contemporary biographical sketch in *American Labor Who's Who* (1925) and an obituary in the *New York Times*, 14 Nov. 1969, although they provide conflicting dates of his arrival in the United States.

MICHELLE BRATTAIN

BELLANCA, Dorothy Jacobs (10 Aug. 1894–16 Aug. 1946), labor organizer, was born in Zemel, Latvia, the daughter of Harry Jacobs, a tailor, and Bernice Edith Levinson. Seeking a better life, the Russian Jewish family emigrated to America in 1900 and began a new life in Baltimore, Maryland. Dorothy's mother died a short time after their arrival.

Educated at local schools, Dorothy was hired at the age of thirteen to work in a clothing factory as a button-hole stitcher on men's coats. Seeing the problems that many female immigrant workers endured in the men's garment factories, Dorothy Jacobs shifted into action to organize workers. In a protest against the poor wages and terrible conditions at the factory, Bellanca and her co-workers mobilized by 1909, forming Local 170 of the United Garment Workers of America

(UGWA). Their numbers added to the tally of newly organized local unions of unskilled workers forming across the country. In 1914 when Bellanca became head of the local, the membership included nearly 65 percent of the machine sewers, who were mostly males.

Struggles ensued between American-born and immigrant garment workers, and as a result the UGWA split into two factions. Dorothy Jacobs brought Local 170 into the new Amalgamated Clothing Workers of America (ACWA) and became one of the local's two delegates to attend the first convention. As an activist in her organization, she ably negotiated contracts and became involved in national strikes in Chicago in 1915 and in organization drives in Philadelphia and New York City in 1917. After being the only woman elected to the general executive board of the ACWA in 1916, Bellanca was elected vice president in 1918 and served on the board for the remainder of her life.

Her marriage to August Bellanca, an Italian immigrant and fellow ACWA organizer and executive board member, in August 1918 interrupted her union activities for a short period before she began executing her duties from her New York City home. The couple had no children, and their lives revolved around labor organizing.

In the early 1920s women accounted for 60 to 70 percent of the ACWA membership, but, although they were strong in numbers, their position in the union was weak. To correct this, locals were formed in numerous cities that allocated to female members one representative on the joint board and one business agent, thus allowing women to gain leadership slots. In 1924 the ACWA moved a step further toward granting women a voice in their union's future when it founded a Women's Bureau. Dorothy Bellanca took the position as chief in 1924, but the bureau collapsed in 1926 and women's strides in the union were slowed.

A dedicated organizer, Bellanca's activities between 1932 and 1934 were concentrated in the Northeast among the shirt workers. Her efforts brought nearly 30,000 shirt workers into the ACWA. In 1933 she spearheaded a campaign in western Pennsylvania to organize workers against the sweatshop practices of low wages and poor hours for children. The resulting "baby strike," in which fourteen- and fifteen-year-old workers participated, attracted public attention.

Politically active during the 1930s, Bellanca, along with other members of the ACWA, endorsed New Deal labor policies. In order to help Franklin D. Roosevelt continue in his presidency in 1936, Bellanca along with nineteen others formed the American Labor party in New York State. The new party hoped to lure leftist voters who had refused to vote for the Tammany-controlled Democratic ticket. In 1938 Bellanca ran for a Brooklyn congressional seat under the American Labor party ticket but lost. During the next two presidential elections she continued to work for Roosevelt's reelection as the state party's elected vice chairman.

An active member of the Consumers' League of New York and the Women's Trade Union League, Bellanca also served on the CIO Textile Workers' Organizing Committee between 1937 and 1938. Named to the General Advisory Committee on Maternal and Child Welfare by Secretary of Labor Frances Perkins, she also served on a committee dealing with children's health. As a member of the Women's Policy Committee of the War Manpower Commission during World War II, Bellanca strove to bring five million women into gainful employment in war industries and to provide for their entitlement to fair wages and safety protections. In 1941 her crusade for female and racial equality led her to work with the New York State Council on Discrimination in Employment. She was appointed to the New York State War Council Committee on Discrimination in Employment in 1943. Not satisfied with the results, she and seven other members of the commission charged that their proposals had been ignored, and in 1944 they resigned. She addressed the racial issue once more when she served on the Mayor's Committee on Unity.

Concerned with the woman worker's role following World War II, Bellanca headed the Conference on Full Employment in 1944. The conference yielded a resolution to aid women in the conversion from war to civilian production, calling for gainful employment, equal pay, child care, and the complete integration of women into unions. The resolution, however, was never implemented.

A respected labor organizer, Bellanca was said to have been responsible for organizing more local unions than any other person with the ACWA. Until her death in New York City, she remained committed to bringing justice and equality to the workplace for all women and children workers.

• For biographical material see the ACWA Research Department, New York City; *Nation* (31 Aug. 1946); *Advance* (1 and 15 Sept. 1946); and *New Leader* (21 Sept. 1946). Other sources for biographies include Elinore M. Herrick, "Dorothy Bellanca: Champion of Democracy," *Woman's Press* (Dec. 1946), and "In Memoriam: Dorothy J. Bellanca," Amalgamated Clothing Workers of America, Gen. Executive Board, *Report* (1948): xx–xxii. Bellanca is referred to in Philip S. Foner, *Women and the American Labor Movement: From World War I to the Present* (1980), and Susan Ware, *Holding Their Own: American Women in the 1930s* (1982). To understand the context of Bellanca's labor activities, see Matthew Josephson, *Sidney Hillman* (1952). Obituaries are in the *New York Times* and the *New York Herald Tribune*, 17 Aug. 1946.

MARILYN ELIZABETH PERRY

BELLANCA, Giuseppe Mario (19 Mar. 1886–26 Dec. 1960), aircraft manufacturer, was born in Sciacca, Sicily, the son of Andrea Bellanca, a flour mill owner, and Concetta Merlo. Bellanca spent his childhood in Sciacca. After his high school graduation, he attended the Technical Institute of Milan, Italy. While attending school in Milan, Bellanca's interest in aviation emerged. During his third year Bellanca, with help from two friends, Enea Bossi and Paolo Invernizzi, designed and built his first aircraft. On 8 December 1909 the little biplane was ready for its first flight. The honor of this flight was given to Bellanca's partner Bossi. He promptly crashed and destroyed the aircraft on the first attempt. After graduating from the Technical Institute with a bachelor's degree in engineering, Bellanca became professor of industrial mathematics at the Royal Institute of Milan.

In 1911 Bellanca immigrated with his family to Brooklyn, New York, where he built another aircraft with his family's assistance in the basement of their home. With this aircraft, Bellanca taught himself to fly.

In 1912 Bellanca incorporated the Bellanca Aeroplane Company and Flying School. The company built the aircraft used to instruct students. His most famous student was Fiorello H. LaGuardia, who later became mayor of New York City. In 1916 the Maryland Pressed Steel Company of Hagerstown, Maryland, decided to enter the aviation business and hired Bellanca as a consulting engineer. The first aircraft built by the company was a small biplane designed by Bellanca, the C.D. During World War I, the company's interest in aircraft waned when it obtained lucrative contracts to build artillery and ammunition. Once the war ended, Maryland Pressed Steel built the second Bellanca design, the C.E. Both aircraft were commercial failures because of the glut of surplus military aircraft. With the loss of military contracts and no aircraft orders forthcoming, Maryland Pressed Steel went into receivership in 1921.

In early 1922 Bellanca moved to Omaha, Nebraska, and entered into a partnership with Victor H. Roos, who had purchased Maryland Pressed Steel's aviation assets. The first product of the Roos-Bellanca Aircraft Company was a sleek cabin monoplane, the Model C.F. In July 1922 the airplane won first prize in thirteen events at the midwestern flying meet in Monmouth, Illinois. Although the aircraft performed well, it, like the other Bellanca designs, saw limited commercial success. Also in 1922, Bellanca married Dorothy M. Brown. They had at least one son.

In fall 1923 Bellanca left Omaha and formed the second Bellanca Aircraft Company in Farmingdale, Long Island. This new company received contracts from the U.S. Air Mail Service to build efficient high-lift wings for the DH-4 airplanes going into service. By early 1925 future contracts from the Air Mail Service were not forthcoming, and Bellanca, again, had to shut down production.

In 1925 Bellanca joined the Wright Aeronautical Corporation. Wright Aeronautical would build two Bellanca designs, the Wright-Bellanca WB-1 and WB-2. Again these planes demonstrated excellent performance but would see only limited commercial success. By the end of 1926 the Wright company decided to focus on aircraft engine production. Wright sold its aircraft interest to the Columbia Aircraft Company founded by Charles Levine.

Charles Levine was interested in building specialized aircraft for record-breaking flights. On 14 April 1927 Clarence Chamberlin and Bert Acosta set a world endurance record of 51 hours, 11 minutes, in a Bellanca-designed WB-2, the *Columbia*. After this successful flight, Levine registered the aircraft for the $25,000 Orteig prize for the first nonstop flight from New York to Paris. Unfortunately for Levine and Bellanca, Charles A. Lindbergh in his small Ryan monoplane, *Spirit of St. Louis*, took off before the *Columbia* was prepared for flight. After Lindbergh's successful flight, Chamberlin, with Levine as a passenger, set a new distance record when they landed *Columbia* in Eisleben, Germany, on 5 June 1927 in an attempt to fly from New York to Berlin.

With the success of *Columbia* and after disagreements over Levine's business methods, Bellanca formed the third Bellanca Aircraft Company in Staten Island, New York, in 1927. With the reputation derived from the accomplishments of the *Columbia*, he finally had advance orders for his aircraft. The Du Pont Company wanted to enter the aviation industry, and in 1927 it approached Bellanca to move Bellanca Aircraft to a large new factory in New Castle, Delaware. Bellanca agreed to the move. However, the two parties soon had a falling out. Bellanca managed to retain control and became president of a larger and financially stronger company.

During the late 1920s and early 1930s the company continued to build specialized endurance aircraft. By the mid-1930s the company began to build the *Cruisair* series for the private aircraft market.

During World War II, Bellanca Aircraft suspended production of its civilian aircraft and subcontracted production of Boeing AT-15s and Fairchild Aircraft's AT-21s.

After the war, Bellanca Aircraft returned to private aircraft production. In 1954 Bellanca sold his interest in the company and retired to his farm near Galena, Maryland. Bellanca died in a hospital in New York City.

• A number of contemporary articles and company biographies can be found in Giuseppe Bellanca's biography file (CB-106900-01) at the National Air and Space Museum in the Smithsonian Institution. Jay Spenser, *Bellanca C.F.: The Emergence of a Cabin Monoplane in the United States* (1982), traces Bellanca's career and his aircraft designs. It focuses on the history and restoration of the Bellanca C.F. owned by the National Air and Space Museum. An obituary is in the *New York Times*, 27 Dec. 1960.

ALEX M SPENCER

BELLINGHAM, Richard (c. 1592–7 Dec. 1672), governor of colonial Massachusetts, was born in Boston, Lincolnshire, England, the son of Frances Amcotts and William Bellingham. A friend of the earl of Lincoln and a lawyer, he served as a Member of Parliament for Boston in 1628 and as recorder of the borough of Lincolnshire from 1625 to 1633. One of the original patentees of the Massachusetts Bay Charter, he immigrated to New England in 1634 with his first wife, Elizabeth Backhouse, and their only child Samuel, who would graduate with Harvard College's first class of 1642. Bellingham was immediately elected deputy governor of the colony (1635–1636), a post he held again from 1640 to 1641, from 1653 to 1654, and from 1655 to 1665. He served as an assistant on the Governor's Council (1636–1641 and 1642–1653), the colony's treasurer (1637–1640), and governor (1641–1642, 1654–1655, and 1665 until his death). He was a member of the committee that in 1648 drafted *The Laws and Liberties of 1648*, the first comprehensive code of laws in English America. According to historian Thomas Hutchinson, Bellingham and the Reverend John Cotton were the major authors of the biblically inspired code that made blasphemy and disobedience to parents capital crimes and stipulated various penalties for drunkenness, idleness, and fornication while permitting divorce, this last an unusual feature in the seventeenth century.

Bellingham led the faction opposed to John Winthrop and the majority of the upper house in the Bay Colony. Whereas Winthrop favored a populace passively acquiescing in the rule of the wealthy and powerful men who were magistrates, Bellingham sided with the deputies, the lower house, who preferred a more popular government. He was one of three magistrates, the others being Leverett Saltonstall, Jr., and Israel Stoughton, who usually opposed their colleagues. For instance, in 1643 he supported Goody (Elizabeth) Sherman's ownership of a sow she disputed with the wealthy merchant Robert Keayne, thereby provoking Winthrop's famous speech about the perils of democracy. Two years later Bellingham backed the Hingham militia's right to change their captain, a move opposed by the other magistrates, who preferred the rival candidate. Bellingham also had his dissent entered in the records of the colony in 1646, when he refused to join in squelching the petition of Robert Child, who complained that Massachusetts was violating its charter. In contradiction to the laws of England and provisions the charter required it to follow, the Bay Colony discriminated against Anglicans and non–church members (those who had not related satisfactorily how they had received salvation to their congregation). They could neither take Holy Communion nor vote in elections that chose all religious and civil officials in Massachusetts.

Yet Bellingham repeatedly won election as a magistrate at the same time as his opponents in contests allowing all freemen to vote for governor, deputy governor, and assistants. This suggests the Puritans in general were split on these issues, as indeed were their magistrates and deputies. Bellingham was the logical alternative to Winthrop as governor; indeed, he might have served more than one term after 1641 had he not done a truly bizarre deed. As a magistrate he had the authority to perform a wedding. He used this authority to marry himself in 1641 to his second wife, Penelope Pelham, with whom he eventually had four children. (His first wife had died.)

Bellingham maintained sufficient prestige, however, to retain his magistracy, and he succeeded to the governorship after Winthrop and John Leverett. He was the last survivor to whom the original charter had been granted. Bellingham staunchly defended the charter when royal commissioners arrived in 1664 to inquire into abuses, including violation of the Navigation Acts and denial of religious and political freedom to non-Puritans. His obstinacy earned him an order to return to England to explain the colony's recalcitrance, but the legislature sent two large masts for the Royal Navy in a successful attempt to divert the imperial bureaucracy to other matters.

Bellingham's last major controversy was his firm support of the First Church of Boston, which in 1669 imported from New Haven the elderly John Davenport, who was committed to the old standard of church membership (confession of saving faith) rather than admitting "Half-way" members (baptized yet still searching for assurance of conversion). The Third Church ("Old South") was formed to accommodate the "Half-way" members, but Bellingham tried unsuccessfully to have its organizers arrested. Although he was here defending the old Puritans from a liberalizing elite, Bellingham's stand was consistent with his refusal to oppose Robert Child's petition two decades earlier. In both cases he took a populist, anti-elite stance.

Even after his death in Boston, Bellingham did not cease to be controversial. To all practical purposes, his will disinherited his family, while making various bequests to support religion. Since his estate of £3,244 was the second largest probated for any Boston legislator of the seventeenth century, it is understandable that lawsuits ensued and dragged on for over a century. Another unusual incident connected with Bellingham was the execution of his sister Anne Hibbins in 1656 for witchcraft.

Bellingham was an important political figure in early Massachusetts who led a persistent grass-roots opposition, both legal and legitimate, to the Puritan consensus Winthrop and his colleagues strove to maintain. While less spectacular than the challenges of Anne Hutchinson, Roger Williams, and the Quakers, it was perhaps more important in the long run in shaping the future of the Bay Colony, since it could not be banished from the colony's borders.

• The most complete sketch of Bellingham's life is Robert Emmet Wall, Jr., *The Membership of the Massachusetts Bay General Court, 1630–1686* (1990). Wall goes into more detail in *Massachusetts Bay: The Crucial Decade, 1640–1650* (1972), which is usefully supplemented by Theodore B. Lewis, "Massachusetts and the Glorious Revolution, 1660–1692" (Ph.D. diss., Univ. of Wisconsin–Madison, 1967). Thomas Hutchinson, *History of the Colony and Province of Massachusetts-Bay*, vol. 1 (1765; repr. 1936), is still essential for many details. Also useful are *Winthrop's Journal: The History of New England, 1630–1649*, ed. James K. Hosmer (1908), and Nathaniel B. Shurtlef, ed., *Records of the Governor and Company of the Massachusetts Bay in New England* (5 vols., 1853–1854).

WILLIAM PENCAK

BELLINI, Carlo (c. 1735–June 1804), librarian and teacher, was born in Florence, Italy, the son of Leone (or Leon) Girolamo Bellini, a tradesman. His mother's name is not known, and details of his early life are sketchy. He taught in the Santa Maria School in Florence, frequented the best Florentine intellectual circles, and was a close friend of Philip Mazzei, who, like him, was a member of the Masonic Lodge "della Cucchiara."

In 1764 Bellini left Florence after his free-thinking ideas upset the Tuscan authorities. After traveling throughout Europe and visiting Germany, Spain, and France, where he taught modern languages, Bellini returned to Florence, where he worked in the tax office of the grand duke of Tuscany and married Gaspara Bonciani, a widow; there were no children.

Unable to live comfortably on the pay he received for clerking, opposed by the clergy for his indifference to religion, and ambitious to get a more intellectual position, Bellini joined Mazzei in Virginia. Accompanied by his wife, Bellini traveled by brigantine and arrived in Jamestown, Virginia, in the summer of 1774. Along with Mazzei, they went to Monticello as Thomas Jefferson's guests, then stayed at "Colle," Mazzei's neighboring plantation. During his first five years in Virginia, Bellini may have worked in Williamsburg, at that time the political and intellectual capital of Virginia and, until the Revolution, the residence of the British royal governors. In 1775 Bellini and Mazzei enlisted as volunteers in a militia regiment in Albemarle. With Jefferson's help, Bellini made a modest living from translating and tutoring. In a 1778 letter to his brother in Florence, he called himself "an ordinary soldier, a noble and glorious office!" With the outbreak of the American Revolution, the foreign correspondence of Virginia increased. On 25 March 1778 the Virginia Council of State requested "a faithful & capable person to Act as Secretary & Interpreter of the French & other foreign Languages"; in June, on Jefferson's recommendation, Bellini, "as a gentleman possessed of the requisite Qualifications for such an Office," was sworn in as a Clerk of Foreign Correspondence at 200 pounds a year. In letters to relatives in Italy, Bellini called himself "Secretary of this State of Virginia for Foreign Affairs."

In August 1778, Bellini was appointed professor of modern languages at the College of William and Mary, then the educational center of the South. His appointment to the position he would hold for twenty-four years came after the need for linguistic reform at the college was met by a 1779 reorganization in which Jefferson and other leading Virginians participated. It instituted three new chairs: modern languages, medicine, and law.

Bellini first appears in the college records as a member of the faculty in the minutes of a 29 December 1779 meeting. Besides the Romance languages (French, Italian, Spanish), he most likely taught German as well. Mazzei claimed that "Bellini knew French very well besides his own tongue, and sufficiently well German and Spanish." This statement helped to settle an uncertainty in the history of linguistic teaching in the United States. It credits Bellini with teaching college German before it was taught at Har-

vard, making William and Mary the first U.S. college to teach that language.

Bellini settled happily into Williamsburg life. He was friends with Abbé Rodin, who found Bellini so delightful "that after he had told us of his brethren we could not help regretting their absence." The only correspondent to address Jefferson as "My Dearest Thomas" (Dumas Malone, *Jefferson the Virginian* [1948], p. 285), Bellini discussed with him the social situation in Europe and the Greek and Latin classics. From 1779 to 1783 Bellini's name appears on the rolls of the Masonic Lodge at Williamsburg.

On 20 May 1780 his faculty colleagues appointed Bellini librarian at the College of William and Mary. He increased the size of the library's collection with a large stock of "ancient authors" but few modern ones. In 1781, during the British occupation of Williamsburg, Bellini remained as sole custodian of the college and its property; he later told French officers that he had been badly treated by the British. When the French army arrived in Williamsburg to prepare for the battle of Yorktown, the affable Bellini enjoyed himself, entertaining the officers who sought him out for his company and for his understanding of French society.

During the 1780s and 1790s, the faculty was forced to economize; its residential facilities were eliminated and the number of subjects taught was reduced. As professors were paid directly by the students who registered for their courses, those whose income depended solely on these fees, such as Bellini, were hit hardest.

When Bellini first started teaching at William and Mary, enthusiasm for learning languages was high and most students there acquired some fluency in French and Italian, but this did not last and the teaching of modern languages declined.

In reduced circumstances by 1789, Bellini asked Jefferson to find him a position as a clerk or translator in the Department of State. Jefferson refused. At this time Bellini also appealed to the college for money due him and quit corresponding with his family in Italy. After his wife's death in 1798, a lonely Bellini gave hospitality to a slave, Lucy, and to her two children, whom he brought from the College of William and Mary. In 1799 a student found Bellini living in an old house near the Royal Governor's Palace, very poor and afflicted by "a late paralytic attack," subsisting on wine and biscuits, and taking snuff. When Bellini's eyesight weakened, Jefferson sent him eyeglasses.

As his health worsened, Bellini stopped teaching during the 1803–1804 academic year. He died in poverty in Williamsburg. The College of William and Mary has a memorial tablet to Bellini in the Wren Building chapel, and there is a room named after him in Monroe Hall. He is important in the history of education, for he is recognized as the first professor of modern languages in a North American college.

• The College of William and Mary Archives has a considerable body of material on Bellini, including a biographical sketch by E. C. Branchi, who extensively researched Italian archives for his article "Primati italiani negli Stati Uniti: Carlo Bellini," *Il Carroccio* 27 (1928): 214–18. *The Papers of Thomas Jefferson* (1950–1992) include correspondence from Bellini. Descriptions of adventures with Bellini appear in *Memoirs of the Life and Peregrinations of the Florentine, Philip Mazzei, 1730–1816*, trans. Howard R. Marraro (1942; *Memorie della vita e delle peregrinazioni del fiorentino Filippo Mazzei*, orig. pub. 1845). Abbé Robin, *New Travels through North-America* (1784), has information on Bellini's activities during the 1781 British and French occupations of Williamsburg. See also Frank B. Evans, "Carlo Bellini and His Russian Friend Fedor Karzhavin," *Virginia Magazine of History and Biography* 88, no. 3 (July 1980): 338–54; J. E. Morpurgo, *Their Majesties' Royall Colledge; William and Mary in the Seventeenth and Eighteenth Centuries* (1976); Earl G. Swem, "Charles Bellini, First Professor of Modern Languages in an American College," *William and Mary Quarterly*, 2d ser., no. 5 (Jan. 1925): 1–29; Evans, *The Story of the Royal Charter of the College of William and Mary* (1978); Antonio Pace, "Another Letter of Carlo Bellini," *William and Mary Quarterly*, 3d ser., no. 4 (July 1947): 350–55; and Lyon G. Tyler, "Early Courses and Professors at William and Mary College," *William and Mary College Quarterly Historical Magazine*, 1st ser., no. 14 (1905): 71–83.

MARTIN J. MANNING

BELLOMONT, Earl of. *See* Coote, Richard.

BELLOWS, George Wesley (12 Aug. 1882–8 Jan. 1925), painter and printmaker, was born in Columbus, Ohio, the son of George Bellows, a builder and contractor, and Anna Smith. In 1901 Bellows entered Ohio State University, where his extracurricular activities included athletics and art. He dropped out of college near the end of his third year and in the fall of 1904 headed for New York City, where he intended to train for a professional career as an illustrator. Bellows enrolled in the New York School of Art, where William Merritt Chase was the best-known instructor but he soon came under the influence of a more charismatic member of the faculty, Robert Henri. Henri's circle, also known as the Ashcan School, was notorious during the first decade of the twentieth century for paintings of gritty, urban subject matter. Bellows gradually abandoned the stylish drawing mannerisms he had learned during his college days from copying illustrations by Charles Dana Gibson, and he began exploring the streets of New York in search of subjects that his new teacher considered closer to real life.

Bellows's first publicly exhibited pictures feature working-class children cavorting at the edge of the East River or standing idly in an alley. Other notable early subjects include the excavations for Pennsylvania Station and prizefighting scenes. The deliberate choice of indecorous urban themes and the brilliantly painted but unpolished surfaces of his canvases link Bellows with artistic radicalism and the anti-academic posture of "the Eight." Although Bellows was not included in the group of eight artists who showed their work in the famous exhibition at the Macbeth Gallery in 1908, he shared to some extent the group's reputation for artistic insurrection and was associated with its

highly publicized campaign against the art establishment and the National Academy of Design. Undoubtedly, Bellows reaped benefits from his connection with the Henri circle, which was at the forefront of the contemporary art scene. At the same time he managed to develop an independent identity, in part because of his spectacular technical facility and in part because his approach to his subjects was palatable even to conservative members of the contemporary art audience. For example, a painting such as *Stag at Sharkey's* (1909, Cleveland Museum of Art) presented boxing as a brutal sport and its fans as bloodthirsty. By thus emphasizing the tawdry nature of the subject, Bellows conveyed a judgmental view of prizefighting that correlated with the opinions of many early twentieth-century gallery-goers. Likewise, his *Forty-two Kids* (1907, Corcoran Gallery of Art), which features the nude and gangling bodies of tenement-district children playing on a city dock, conformed to a moralistic, middle-class view of poverty.

Bellows met with early success. After only four years of serious study, he succeeded in having one of his urban landscape paintings, *North River* (1908), purchased by the Pennsylvania Academy of the Fine Arts for its permanent collection. *Little Girl in White (Queenie Burnett)* (1907, National Gallery of Art), a portrait that demonstrates Bellows's debt to Edouard Manet, won him one of many awards, the National Academy's first Hallgarten Prize, in 1913. Bellows's acceptance by the academic establishment was also confirmed by his election in 1909, at the age of twenty-six, as an associate member of the National Academy of Design. He became a full academician in 1913.

In 1910 Bellows married Emma Story, the daughter of a well-to-do businessman from Upper Montclair, New Jersey; they had two children. He was also appointed as life class instructor at the Art Students League in New York City. The following year he had his first one-person show, at the Madison Gallery in New York. Bellows spent that summer on Monhegan Island, Maine, beginning a routine of leaving the city during the summer months. Eventually, he produced the majority of his paintings during his retreats to Monhegan, Ogunquit, and Camden, Maine, and finally to Woodstock, New York, where he built a modest summer home in 1922.

Bellows helped to hang the 1913 Armory Show in New York City that introduced European modernism to American art audiences. That event reconfigured the development of American art and removed Bellows and other members of the Henri circle from their prominent positions in the contemporary art world. Bellows's own work reflected the impact of his encounter with the advanced styles he had seen at the Armory Show. The experience reinforced his interest in art theory and scientific systems by which to order compositions and color choices. Before 1913 Bellows's painting method had combined thoughtful premeditation with spontaneous self-expression, but following the Armory Show he displayed a growing interest in laws of design and in carefully composing his canvases in accordance with them.

Though best known for his oil paintings, Bellows was also a powerful graphic artist, drawing inspiration from Goya and Daumier, as well as from some of his contemporary colleagues in the Henri circle who worked as newspaper illustrators. Bellows received commissions for illustrations that appeared in *Collier's*, *Everybody's*, *Harper's Weekly*, and *Century*. In 1913 he contributed illustrations to the radical magazine the *Masses*, though none of his entries were overtly political. In 1916 Bellows began making lithographs, and his work contributed to the revival of interest in the print media in the United States.

Some of Bellows's late portraits of family members, such as *Elinor, Jean, and Anna* (1920, Albright-Knox Art Gallery), and *Emma and Her Children* (1923, Museum of Fine Arts, Boston), must be considered among his finest achievements. The former garnered first prize at the Carnegie International Exhibition in 1922. The portrait of Bellows's wife and daughters, *Emma and Her Children*, displays a monumentality of structure and conception that combines subtle psychological insight with exquisite tonal harmonies and pays homage to Thomas Eakins and James Whistler, as well as to Manet and Renoir. During this period Bellows continued to work in a realistic mode that distinguished his art from the vanguard of stylistic innovation in American art, yet critical support for his paintings and prints remained strong. Less than a year after Bellows's sudden death from appendicitis at age forty-two in New York City, the Metropolitan Museum organized a major retrospective of his work, only the ninth time an American painter had been similarly recognized.

Belonging to the tradition of American realism, Bellows came to fame as a member of the Henri circle of artists. Though Bellows's style underwent a series of changes, he remained committed to the realist mode, producing vigorously brushed genre paintings, portraits, and landscapes during virtually every phase of his career.

• Correspondence, documents, and an unpublished autobiography are in the George Bellows Papers, Special Collections Department, Amherst College Library, Amherst, Mass. Notes on interviews with family members and colleagues as well as other materials collected by Bellows's biographer, Charles Morgan, are in the Morgan on Bellows Papers, Amherst College Archives. Published statements by Bellows include "The Big Idea: George Bellows Talks about Patriotism for Beauty," *Touchstone* 1 (July 1917): 269–75; and "What Dynamic Symmetry Means to Me," *American Art Student* 3 (June 1921): 4–7. Morgan's published biography, *George Bellows: Painter of America* (1965; repr. 1979), provides the facts of Bellows's life. Additional interviews are included in Frank Seiberling, Jr., "George Bellows, 1882–1925: His Life and Development as an Artist" (Ph.D. diss., Univ. of Chicago, 1948). For accounts by Bellows's contemporaries, see Robert G. McIntyre, "George Bellows—An Appreciation," *Art and Progress* 3 (Aug. 1912): 679–82; Charles L. Buchanan, "George Bellows: Painter of Democracy," *Arts and Decoration* 4 (Aug. 1914): 370–73; Louis H. Frohman,

"Bellows as an Illustrator," *International Studio* 78 (Feb. 1924): 421–25; Carlo Beuf, "The Art of George Bellows: The Lyric Expression of the American Soul," *Century* 112 (Oct. 1926): 724–29; Edmund Wilson, "George Bellows," *New Republic* 44 (28 Oct. 1925): 254–55; and Rollo Walter Brown, "George Bellows—American," *Scribner's* 83 (May 1928): 575–87. The catalog raisonné of Bellows's prints is Lauris Mason, assisted by Joan Ludman, *The Lithographs of George Bellows: A Catalogue Raisonné* (1977). Additions to the 1977 catalog and analysis is provided by Jane Myers and Linda Ayres, *George Bellows: The Artist and His Lithographs, 1916–1924*, exhibit catalog (1988). For criticism and analysis of Bellows's work, see E. A. Carmean, Jr., et al., *Bellows: The Boxing Pictures*, exhibit catalog (1982); Marianne Doezema, *George Bellows and Urban America* (1992); and Michael Quick et al., *The Paintings of George Bellows*, exhibit catalog (1992).

MARIANNE DOEZEMA

BELLOWS, Henry Whitney (11 June 1814–30 Jan. 1882), Unitarian minister, was born in Boston, Massachusetts, the son of John Bellows, a wealthy merchant, and Betsy Eames. From 1824 to 1828 he attended the Round Hill School conducted by George Bancroft in Northampton, Massachusetts, then went to Harvard, from which he graduated in 1832. He taught school in Cooperstown, New York, and served as a tutor in a Louisiana family. He graduated from Harvard Divinity School in 1837. After a brief pastorate in Mobile, Alabama, he served as minister of the First Unitarian Church in New York City from 1839 until his death. He cherished his southern experience and was proud that he and many of his congregation hailed from New England—"the mother of so many sturdy virtues," he liked to declare. But, earlier than most New Englanders, he recognized that New York had become the "central seat of power." Late in life he declared that "the largeness and variety of life" in New York "expanded my horizons."

Public-spirited and congenial, Bellows helped found the Century Club, the Union League, and the Harvard Club of New York. Late in his life, he was an active crusader for civil service reform. In August 1839 he married Eliza Nevins Townsend of New York; they had five children. She died in August 1869. Five years later in June 1874 he married Anna Huidekoper Peabody of Boston, who survived him; they had two children.

Bellows was not a systematic scholar but rather a pastor preoccupied with responding to the practical and spiritual difficulties of his flock. He was a churchman who corresponded with, and visited, Unitarian ministers across the country. He urged Unitarians in the East to support the young Antioch College in Ohio, asserting that they were "the only body of people in the country enlightened enough, rich enough, liberal enough, unsectarian enough" (*The Claims of Antioch College*, 1865). He was a publicist, founding the *Christian Inquirer* in 1846 and editing it for many years. Above all he was a preacher; twenty-five of his sermons, published in 1860 as *Restatements of Christian Doctrine*, reflect his desire both to avoid controversy with other denominations and to help Unitarians find a middle ground, between an unreflective traditionalism on the one hand, and on the other a reckless radicalism that dismissed all old doctrines as "retrogressive" and "superstitious."

Speaking at the Harvard Divinity School in 1859, Bellows gave full force to his disenchantment with the implications of Ralph Waldo Emerson's "Divinity School Address" given there twenty-one years earlier. Titled "The Suspense of Faith," Bellows's lecture insisted that Protestantism had grossly overstated the ability of the individual to find saving truth. "As an inorganic, unrelated, independent being, a man has not, and cannot have, the affections, internal experiences and dispositions which he can . . . receive in his corporate capacity." Unitarians should not be tempted to rely on a "thin, ghostly individualism" or a "meager congregationalism." Bellows declared that "institutions"—and above all the visible church—were "the only constant and adequate teachers of the masses." He stressed the importance of holy festivals and traditional liturgy. "Give back to the communion service," he declared, "the mystic sanctity" that two centuries have been trying to expel. The demand of "unchurched humanity," he concluded, was for "a new Catholic Church" that sustained "a dignified, symbolic, and mystic church organization without the aid of the State, or the authority of the Pope" (Sydney E. Ahlstrom and Jonathan S. Cherry, eds., *An American Reformation* [1985], pp. 371–97). Many Unitarians were upset, and Bellows felt obliged to acknowledge that members of his congregation had the right to decide whether any liturgical reform was desirable. He declared his faith in the processes of history, however, fully confident that the "next generation" of Unitarians would develop a ritual to which members of all liberal churches would adhere, just as the Book of Common Prayer had for centuries bound Episcopalians together.

The secession of the southern states and the consequent Civil War were frontal challenges to his reverence for institutions. He had been an early critic of slavery, but he was also appalled by the reckless attacks of many abolitionists on church and state. Once the war had begun, he enjoined all "Christian citizens" to acknowledge that the "state and nation" were "sacred" and deserved "unconditional loyalty." Far from dreading the suffering war would bring, he was sure only suffering would make Americans recognize the need for disciplined effort.

In April 1861 Bellows helped transform the Women's Central Association of Relief created by New York women—many of them from his church—into the U.S. Sanitary Commission, which under his presidency swiftly became "the largest, most powerful, and most highly organized philanthropic activity that had ever been seen in America" (Fredrickson, p. 98). Sanctioned by the Lincoln administration, the commission coordinated relief efforts, inspected camps, provided hospitals, nurses, and ambulances, and collected statistics. It also skillfully negotiated between military and civilian authorities and successfully outflanked both the individualistic approach of a Dorothea Dix and the more evangelical, but less rationally organized, philanthropies of the YMCA-sponsored Christian Commission. To protect the "army system" from "the rising tide of popular sympathy," the Sanitary Commission would, Bellows insisted, think and act scientifically, employ experts like Frederick Law Olmsted, and train women workers like Louisa Lee Schuyler to subordinate feeling to bureaucratic rationality (Bellows, "Sanitary Commission," p. 179). He convened the national board twenty-three times and was a member of the executive committee, which met in New York six times a week for four years. "I have always thanked God," he later reminisced, "for the opportunity that the Sanitary Commission gave me for trying my hand in the conception and administration of a work so wide, so urgent, so comprehensive . . . so sanctified by its ends and objects" ("First Congregational Church," p. 29). Bellows sensed the congruence of the Sanitary Commission's work with that of the International Red Cross founded in Switzerland in 1864. He was unable however, in the years after the war, to persuade the United States government to endorse the Red Cross.

Bellows felt that God meant him to use his demonstrated "organizing spirit and facility" to help change American Unitarianism from a small and uncertain denomination into a strong national church that was broad enough to enlist all "liberal Christians" but not so indifferent to its origins as to sanction either "free religion" or a resurgent Trinitarianism. Bellows's goal was to develop an organized and compact religious body. Even before the war ended he had helped create a National Conference of Unitarian Churches. As chairman of its council from 1865 to 1875 he pressed for the adoption of a statement of principles, for a fund to support new Unitarian churches, for aid to Harvard Divinity School and Antioch, and for a new journal of liberal religion. He also created a Minister's Institute to supplement divinity school instruction.

Bellows did not realize all his goals, but his friend, fellow Unitarian minister Frederic Henry Hedge, was right in calling him "our Bishop," comparing Bellows, as a father of action, to William Ellery Channing, as a father of faith, and asserting that his "organizing genius" rendered American Unitarianism "as compact as our unformulized [*sic*] theology and the right to differ . . . will allow" (Kring, p. 470). Bellows died in New York City.

• The largest collection of Bellows's papers is in the Massachusetts Historical Society. An authoritative bibliography of his books, sermons, articles, and addresses is provided in Walter Donald Kring's detailed biography, *Henry Whitney Bellows* (1979). In two sermons in 1879 titled "First Congregational Church in the City of New York," Bellows chronicled his career (first published in 1899). See also his "The Sanitary Commission," *North American Review* 98 (1864). A perceptive biographical sketch is John W. Chadwick, *Henry W. Bellows: His Life and Character* (1882). Bellows's role in the evolution of American Unitarianism is perceptively analyzed in Conrad Wright, *The Liberal Christians* (1970). His activities in the Sanitary Commission can be traced in the commission's papers in the New York Public Library and in William Q. Maxwell's political history of the Sanitary Commission, *Lincoln's Fifth Wheel* (1956). George M. Fredrickson's *The Inner Civil War* (1965) charges Bellows with subordinating Christian sympathy to the interests of a social elite and the imperatives of order and discipline.

ROBERT D. CROSS

BELMONT, Alva Erskine Smith Vanderbilt (17 Jan. 1853–26 Jan. 1933), social leader and suffragist, was born Alva Erskine Smith in Mobile, Alabama, the daughter of Murray Forbes Smith, a cotton merchant, and Phoebe Ann Desha. As a child, Alva summered with her parents in Newport, Rhode Island, and accompanied them on European vacations. In 1857 the Smiths moved to New York City, where they settled in Madison Square. Murray Smith later went to Liverpool, England, to conduct his business, and Alva, her mother, and her sisters moved to Paris. Alva attended a private boarding school in Neilly, France, for one year.

After the Civil War, the family returned to New York, where Phoebe Smith died in 1869. As Murray Smith suffered repeated losses in his business dealings, his health, too, began to fail. He died shortly after Alva's marriage to railroad heir William Kissam Vanderbilt, which took place in Calvary Church in New York on 20 April 1875. Alva and William had three children; she arranged the marriage of the eldest, Consuelo, to the English ninth Duke of Marlborough.

Alva Vanderbilt was noted for her energy, intelligence, strong opinions, and willingness to challenge convention. After her marriage, she achieved fame for her conduct as one of the richest socialites of the Gilded Age. Her renowned fancy-dress ball in March 1883 drew wide public attention and garnered social acceptance for the Vanderbilts. Together with Richard Morris Hunt, she was responsible for the design and construction of some of the period's landmark architecture and interior design, including three Vanderbilt mansions: 660 Fifth Avenue in New York, Marble House in Newport, Rhode Island, and Idlehour at Oakdale, Long Island. Her involvement in architecture continued to the end of her life and included renovations to Belcourt Castle in Newport and the fifteenth-century French Chateau d'Augerville-la-Rivière.

In 1895 Alva Vanderbilt successfully sued William for divorce, an act that was considered scandalous because of her social standing. On 11 January 1896 she married Oliver Hazard Perry Belmont, the son of financier August Belmont, in a civil ceremony in New York City. The marriage was a happy one and lasted until Oliver's death in 1908.

In 1909 Alva Belmont attended a lecture by Ida Husted Harper and embraced the cause of woman suffrage. Although she noted in her autobiography that the ordeal of her divorce "led up to [her] own rebellion against the existing order as it affected women," she also believed that her charity work in hospitals and settlement houses had influenced her philosophy. In the magazine *World Today* (Oct. 1911) she wrote, "Men and women are equal only when their opportunities for doing good are equal." With the vote women would be able to enact further social reforms. She gave strong support to labor in the 1909–1910 New York shirtwaist makers strike. She paid the bail of picketers who had been arrested and funded a large rally in the city's Hippodrome, which she addressed along with Anna Howard Shaw, president of the National American Women's Suffrage Association (NAWSA). In 1909 she joined this organization and was named an alternate delegate from New York to the International Women's Suffrage Association meeting in London.

There, Belmont observed the militancy of Emmeline Pankhurst and her followers, who would influence the depth and the form of her commitment to the cause. On her return, she paid for office space on Fifth Avenue that allowed the relocation of NAWSA offices to New York, and she funded its National Press Bureau. At the same time, she formed her own Political Equality League to seek broad support for suffrage in neighborhoods throughout the city, and, as its president, led its division of the 1912 Women's Votes Parade.

By this time, organized suffrage activity was centered on educated, middle-class white women, who were often reluctant to accept immigrants, blacks, and the working class into their ranks. Belmont's Political Equality League only partially broke with this tradition. She established its first "suffrage settlement house" in Harlem, and she included black women and immigrants in weekend retreats at Beacon Towers, her Sands Point, Long Island, home. Still, the Harlem Club women with whom Belmont associated were educated and successful. She looked down on poor black people and, in speaking before affluent whites, reiterated racist fears. She quietly contributed to the Southern Woman Suffrage Conference, which refused to admit blacks, and a decade later, the National Woman's Party, which she led, would be tainted by racism.

With the promise of Belmont's support, the Congressional Union for Woman Suffrage (CU), organized by Alice Paul and Crystal Eastman, separated from the NAWSA in 1913. Belmont then merged the Political Equality League into the CU. Now committed to defeating the incumbent party and securing the passage of the Susan B. Anthony amendment, Belmont convened a Conference of Great Women at Marble House in the summer of 1914. The Duchess of Marlborough, who promoted suffrage and prison reform in England, addressed the gathering, which was followed by the CU's first national meeting. Belmont served on the executive committee of the CU from 1914 to 1916.

In 1915 Belmont chaired the women voters' convention at the Panama-Pacific Exposition. The following year, she helped to establish the Woman's Party of voters from twelve suffrage states, which organized the first picketing ever to take place before the White House in January 1917. That March, the party merged with the CU to form the National Woman's Party, which Belmont served as a member of its executive committee from 1917 to 1920. She hoped that following the ratification of the Nineteenth Amendment, this organization would seek true party status, an idea its members rejected. Nevertheless they elected her their president, an office she held until her death. The National Woman's Party continued to lobby for new initiatives from the Washington, D.C., headquarters that Belmont had purchased for the group. She paid a salary to Alice Paul, who worked to defeat protective legislation for women. Belmont also was committed to furthering women's rights abroad. By the early 1920s, she lived in France most of the time. With Paul, she formed the International Advisory Council of the National Woman's Party and the Auxiliary of American Women abroad.

Belmont suffered a stroke in the spring of 1932 that left her partially paralyzed, and she died in Paris of bronchial and heart ailments the following January. A large contingent of suffragists honored her at her funeral in St. Thomas Episcopal Church in New York. She was buried next to Oliver Belmont in Woodlawn Cemetery, New York.

Belmont came to the cause of woman suffrage late in her life, yet she devoted tremendous energy and resources to established suffrage organizations and to the community on their behalf. Although she is not described prominently in most histories of the suffrage movement, she brought vital financial support, publicity, and most of all bold ideas to her cause.

• Alva Belmont employed two women to assist her in writing her autobiography. Sara Bard Field's research notes and first draft are in the C. E. S. Wood Collection at the Huntington Library, San Marino, Calif. A typescript by Matilda Young, written years later, is in the William R. Perkins Library at Duke University. Belmont's suffrage papers are in the Jane Norman Smith, Alice Paul, and Doris Stevens Collections at the Schlesinger Library at Radcliffe College. See also the National Woman's Party records in the New York Public Library, and the National Woman's Party Papers, which have been microfilmed, in the Library of Congress. Belmont is discussed in oral history interviews with Sara Bard Field and Alice Paul; these are in the collection of the Suffragists Oral History Office at the Bancroft Library, University of California at Berkeley. Belmont is credited with more than a dozen magazine and newspaper articles on woman suffrage; a bibliography is in Clarice Stasz, *The Vanderbilt Women: Dynasty of Wealth, Glamour and Tragedy* (1991). See also Mari Jo Buhle and Paul Buhle, eds., *The Concise History of Woman Suffrage: Selections from the Classic Work of Stanton, Anthony, Gage, and Harper* (1974); Aileen Kraditor, *The Ideas of the Woman Suffrage Movement, 1890–1920* (1965); and Eleanor Flexner, *Century of Struggle: The Woman's Rights Movement in the United States* (1959). For contemporary accounts, see Doris Stevens, *Jailed for Freedom* (1920); Inez Haynes Irwin, *The Story of the Woman's Party* (1921); and Ida Husted Harper, ed., *History of Woman Suffrage*, vols. 5 and 6 (1922). Obituaries are in the *New York Times*, 26 and 27 Jan. 1933.

KATHERYN P. VIENS

BELMONT, August (8 Dec. 1813–24 Nov. 1890), financier, politician, and sportsman, was born in Alzey, a German Rhineland village, the son of Simon Belmont, a moneylender and landowner, and Frederika Elsass. He attended a Jewish school, the Philanthropin, in Frankfurt and in 1828 began work as an office boy for the local branch of the Rothschild banking family, to which he was distantly related through marriage. He was soon promoted to confidential clerk and in 1837 was sent to Cuba to investigate that Spanish colony's stability. A stopover in New York changed the course of his life. The panic of 1837 had just struck, and the Rothschilds' New York agent had declared bankruptcy. Belmont decided to stay and established August Belmont and Company, a private banking firm that would maintain a close, long-term working relationship with the Rothschilds. Belmont's rise on Wall Street was rapid. He profited from foreign exchange transactions; commercial and private loans; corporate, real estate, and railroad investments; and as a U.S. government fiscal agent during the Mexican War. In 1849 he married Caroline Slidell Perry, with whom he had six children.

With unlimited energy and ambition and a willingness to spend money, Belmont set out early on a career in politics. Influenced mainly by his wife's uncle, John Slidell, a powerful Louisiana politician of the antebellum and Civil War periods, Belmont became the New York manager of James Buchanan's unsuccessful campaign for the 1852 Democratic presidential nomination. Franklin Pierce, the eventual nominee, won the presidency and rewarded Belmont, who had contributed generously to Pierce's presidential campaign, by appointing him minister to the Netherlands. During his tenure at The Hague (1853–1857), Belmont negotiated successfully a commercial treaty, designed to open the Dutch East Indies to American trade, and a criminal extradition treaty between the two countries. He also played a behind-the-scenes role in drafting the Ostend Manifesto (Oct. 1854), a diplomatic initiative that he hoped would lead to American acquisition of Cuba. Belmont supported Buchanan's successful bid for the 1856 presidential nomination, but when Buchanan refused Belmont's request to be named minister to Spain, the banker resigned his diplomatic post, returned to New York, and shifted his allegiance to Buchanan's major Democratic antagonist, Illinois senator Stephen A. Douglas.

Following his nomination in 1860 by the northern wing of the Democratic party, Douglas selected Belmont to run the presidential campaign as chairman of the Democratic National Committee. Following Douglas's defeat in November and his death the following June, no political heir appeared; most of the veteran Democrats in Congress were southerners who had seceded with their states. Belmont then assumed the party's national leadership in his position as chief executive officer of the existing organization and held it for twelve years. Few northern Democrats challenged him, owing to the distractions of war and the ensuing reconstruction. Belmont sided with "War"

Democrats and used his influence as an international banker to discourage the Rothschilds and other prominent European financiers from investing in or underwriting Confederate bonds. In 1862 Belmont, with Samuel J. Tilden and other leading Democrats, purchased the New York *World* and installed as editor Manton M. Marble, one of Belmont's closest, lifelong friends. Until Marble's retirement in 1876, he and Belmont succeeded in making the *World* the nation's leading Democratic organ. In 1864 Belmont helped an ally, General George B. McClellan (1826–1885), obtain the party's presidential nomination, but Abraham Lincoln easily won reelection. Belmont fought against any Democratic merger with President Andrew Johnson's National Union party in 1866. When his first choice for the 1868 nomination, Chief Justice Salmon P. Chase, refused to desert the cause of African-American suffrage, Belmont saw the prize go to former New York governor Horatio Seymour (1810–1886), who, as Belmont predicted, campaigned weakly and lost to General Ulysses S. Grant. Belmont resigned as Democratic national chairman after the 1872 national convention and gradually reduced his political activities, though he championed Delaware senator Thomas F. Bayard's presidential ambitions in the next three campaigns.

After the Civil War Belmont was a "hard money" advocate, supporting immediate resumption of specie payments and criticizing the Bland-Allison compromise of 1878. As the economy revived following the 1873 crash, Belmont's firm often joined with J. P. Morgan and Company and other major Wall Street houses in forming underwriting syndicates to facilitate the public sale of huge securities issues.

Belmont's stature also loomed large in sporting and social circles. He helped introduce thoroughbred horse racing to the United States, owned two large breeding farms, was president of the American Jockey Club from 1866 to 1887, and originated the Belmont Stakes in 1867. In 1889 and 1890 his stable led all others in the country in money earned from racing. He was famous for the gourmet cuisine served at his numerous lavish entertainments, and Lorenzo Delmonico, the chief restaurateur of high society, called him a "Maecenas of gastronomy." Belmont owned a large collection of paintings and, as an opera lover, was the first board president (1878–1884) of the Academy of Music. He died in New York City.

From the time Belmont became a naturalized American in 1844 until his death he was one of the country's richest citizens, bequeathing a fortune estimated at between $10 million and $50 million. Despite his high standing in several spheres of activity, anti-Semites frequently denigrated him as a "foreign-born Jew," even though he was married in a church into an old, distinguished American family—his wife's father was Commodore Matthew Perry—and had his children baptized as Episcopalians. He long regretted that his attainment of political power coincided, as he later recalled, with "the most disastrous epoch in the annals of the Democratic Party."

• The files of Belmont's banking house and much of his political correspondence were destroyed by fire in 1912. Most of what survived remains in private collections, though scattered letters can be found in the Library of Congress, the Massachusetts Historical Society, the New York Public Library, and the New-York Historical Society. In his lifetime, Belmont printed, for private distribution, *A Few Letters and Speeches of the Late Civil War* (1870) and *Letters, Speeches and Addresses* (1890). His letters are also accessible in manuscript collections of contemporaries, and they were used extensively in two biographies: Irving Katz, *August Belmont: A Political Biography* (1968), and David Black, *The King of Fifth Avenue: The Fortunes of August Belmont* (1981). A lengthy obituary is in the *New York Times*, 25 Nov. 1890.

IRVING KATZ

BELMONT, August, II (18 Feb. 1853–10 Dec. 1924), financier and sportsman, was born in New York City, the son of August Belmont, a banker, and Caroline Slidell Perry. Belmont graduated from Harvard in 1874 (A.B.) and joined the international banking house of August Belmont & Co. in 1875. Within eight years he was running its daily affairs and had modernized operations. He became head of the firm in 1890, following his father's death. His biggest projects included a $63 million loan floated with financier J. P. Morgan for the second administration of President Grover Cleveland and the financing of New York City's first subway. In November 1881 he married Elizabeth Hamilton Morgan, with whom he had three children.

In 1890 Belmont chaired a transit planning commission that recommended building a subway for New York, but the concept made little headway against surface and elevated streetcar line opposition until 1900, when the Rapid Transit Commission approved a publicly financed $36 million West Side subway line. When contractor John B. McDonald could not guarantee the required $6 million in security bonds and $1 million in cash to begin the project, Belmont established the Interborough Rapid Transit Construction Company to finance it. In 1907 Belmont's firm constructed a tunnel connecting Manhattan to Queens, and in 1914 he was responsible for the building of the thirteen-mile Cape Cod Canal that reduced shipping routes between Massachusetts Bay and Long Island Sound by seventy miles.

Belmont was vice president of the reform-minded National Civic Federation, but he also was deeply involved in Democratic party politics. On the local scene he supported a cross-class coalition to protect his traction interests and to safeguard horse racing from antigambling reformers. In 1904 he was titular head of the New York State delegation to the national Democratic convention, and he played a prominent role in securing the presidential nomination for Judge Alton B. Parker. He left politics after serving as a Champ Clark delegate at the 1912 convention when William Jennings Bryan attacked him and other financiers as privileged men representing special interests.

Belmont gained great renown in Thoroughbred horse racing, following in the footsteps of his father, who had founded the American Jockey Club and whose horses twice led the nation in purse winnings. The senior Belmont was considered the leading breeder of his day, and in 1882 Belmont took over his father's breeding farm, the Nursery, which when disposed of in 1890 was the largest of its era, with 131 horses being sold at auction for $639,500. The imported stallion, St. Blaise, winner of the English Derby, went for $100,000.

In 1892 Belmont reestablished the Nursery Stud, sparing little expense. His finest stallions were Hastings, a Belmont Stakes winner purchased in 1895 for $37,000, and Henry of Navarre, bought for $35,000, which subsequently won the Suburban Handicap. In 1898 Belmont dropped out of racing under his own name because of the death of his wife, ill health, and growing business commitments. His horses raced in the name of his trainer, J. J. Hyland, for two years, after which Belmont resumed full participation. In 1906, for $125,000, he purchased the English Thoroughbred Rock Sand, who became one of the greatest sires of all time. Rock Sand was later sold to a French syndicate for $250,000. Belmont, who bred hundreds of Thoroughbreds, was among the first to produce eight $100,000 winners, six by Fair Play, most notably Man o'War. However, Man o'War had not shown any great potential as a yearling and was sold in 1918 to S. D. Riddle for $5,000.

Belmont played a vital role in the governance of the turf, serving as second chairman of The Jockey Club (1895–1924), which had been organized in 1894 to protect the breeding industry and to elevate the sport. It established, interpreted, and enforced the rules of Thoroughbred racing, licensed jockeys and trainers, appointed officials, allotted racing dates, and operated the *American Stud Book*. In 1895 racing was almost banned in New York, and Belmont played an important role in passing legislation that saved the sport; the new law established a state racing commission, with Belmont as chairman, to regulate racing under Jockey Club rules.

Belmont was president of the Westchester Racing Association (WRA) that operated Morris Park from 1895 through 1904, when the club relocated to rustic Long Island. In 1905 the WRA opened the $2.4 million Belmont Park, named for his father. It was the outstanding American track, with a 1.5-mile oval raceway, a grandstand 650 feet in length, and an opulent clubhouse.

In 1908, with the future of New York racing again in doubt, Belmont shipped some horses to England, where he won the 2,000 Guineas classic. In 1910 he married Eleanor Robson, an actress. They had no children. Belmont failed to prevent Governor Charles Evans Hughes from halting racetrack gambling in 1911, but he successfully led the effort to restore the sport in 1913 under the oral system of betting.

In 1917 Belmont was commissioned a major in the U.S. Army and served in Spain, exporting supplies to France and purchasing lifestock for the military. In the following year, after the death of his son, August III, and in the face of growing business problems and

concerns with the war, Belmont lost interest in the turf and sold most of his stable to his trainer, Samuel C. Hildreth. In 1920 he resumed an active role in breeding, and he returned to racing two years later. In 1924 two of the nation's leading three year olds, Ladkin and Ordinance, raced under his colors. That year his stable won twenty-four races and earned $112,735, the most of his career. In all, Belmont saw his horses win six Belmont Stakes. After his death, the entire stock was sold for about $1,175,000 to W. Averell Harriman, Gertrude Vanderbilt Whitney, and Joseph E. Widener.

Belmont was an all-around sportsman who was an active polo player, vice commodore of the New York Yacht Club, president of the Westminster Kennel Club, and a supporter of the sport of aviation. His elite economic and social status was further reflected by a Newport summer home, a Long Island country estate, and New York's only private subway car. Belmont died in New York City.

• On Belmont's youth, see David Black, *The King of Fifth Avenue: The Fortunes of August Belmont* (1981), which is heavily based on family papers, particularly those held by August Belmont IV. Other papers are in the Belmont Family Papers, Special Collections, Columbia University. For Belmont's racing contributions, see William H. P. Robertson, *A History of Thoroughbred Racing* (1960); Dan M. Bowmar III, *Giants of the Turf: The Alexanders, the Belmonts, James R. Keene, the Whitneys* (1960); Edward C. Devereux, Jr., *Gambling and the Social Structure: A Social Study of Lotteries and Horse Racing in Contemporary America* (1980), pp. 351–52, which describes Fair Play's prowess as a sire. Valuable for Belmont's later years is Eleanor Robson Belmont, *The Fabric of Memory* (1957). For Belmont's obituary, see the *New York Times*, 11 Dec. 1924.

STEVEN A. RIESS

BELMONT, Perry (28 Dec. 1850–25 May 1947), politician and sportsman, was born in New York City, the son of August Belmont, a banker, politician, and sportsman, and Caroline Slidell Perry, daughter of Commodore Matthew C. Perry. He attended Harvard College, 1867–1872, graduating with a B.A. in history, studied Roman and civil law at the University of Berlin, 1873–1874, and enrolled in the Columbia University Law School, 1874–1876. He was admitted to the bar in 1876 and the next year entered the law firm of Porter, Lowrey & Stone. In 1878 he established his own law firm of Vinton, Belmont, and Frelinghuysen.

In 1880 Belmont was elected as a Democrat to the House of Representatives from New York and was reelected in 1882, 1884, and 1886. Assigned to the Foreign Affairs Committee, he cooperated with maritime interests, advocating what later became a standing committee on Merchant Marine and Fisheries and promoting measures to secure greater safety at sea through the eventual establishment of a permanent International Maritime Commission. He also supported civil service reform, opposed construction of an interoceanic canal through Nicaragua, and regularly denounced the growth of monopolies under Republican high-tariff policies.

In 1885 Belmont became chairman of the Foreign Affairs Committee for four years. He spoke out for consular reform overseas, and in 1888 he was instrumental in securing a joint resolution authorizing the United States to participate in France's centennial celebration of the fall of the Bastille. For this he was later made a commander of the Legion of Honor. Belmont declined renomination in 1888, and in November President Grover Cleveland appointed him minister to Spain. He served until March 1889, when he resigned upon the inauguration of a Republican president. When a vacancy occurred for a congressional seat late in 1901, Belmont, despite spirited intraparty opposition, secured his party's nomination in the coming special election. But Tammany Hall Democrats, led by Richard Croker, resented Belmont's recent criticisms of Tammany and encouraged an "independent" to enter the race. With a divided Democratic vote, the Republican candidate won the three-way contest.

During the Spanish-American War, Belmont used political and family connections to obtain a major's commission and a post as inspector general of the First Division, Second Army Corps, U.S. Volunteers. He resigned from the army six weeks later upon learning that the division would be sent to Cuba without him. As president of the National Campaign Publicity Association (1906–1911), his lobbying efforts bore fruit when Congress passed the Federal Campaign Publicity Act (1911), making secret party funds illegal. When the United States entered World War I in 1917, Belmont, at age sixty-six, again took advantage of well-placed government officials to secure a captain's commission in the Remount Service of the Army Quartermaster's Corps, getting the age limit for appointment waived in his behalf. At the war's end, he opposed American membership in the League of Nations, proposing instead an "understanding" or informal alliance with Great Britain and France to counter any future aggression.

When Belmont's father, who had introduced thoroughbred racing to the United States, died in 1890, his sons sold the family's lucrative racing stable and breeding farms at public auction, under the terms of the will. With this income and other legacies, Belmont organized his own racing stable, rented a breeding farm, and was very successful with race horses he trained for his own stable and with those he sold as yearlings to other stables. He was at various times president of the Turf and Field Club at Belmont Park, of the United Hunts Racing Association, and of the National Steeplechase and Hunt Association. He also helped introduce the sport of polo to the United States.

Belmont's father was Jewish, but the son was baptized and raised by his mother as an Episcopalian. At age ninety he converted to Catholicism. In 1899 Belmont married Jessie Ann Robbins, a wealthy New York socialite, after a divorce suit in which her husband named Belmont as co-respondent; the couple did not have children.

Though his public officeholding ended in 1889, Belmont remained in the spotlight through continued involvement in Democratic party affairs, regular pronouncements on domestic and international issues, publication of articles and short books, and numerous social activities. He was a delegate to most Democratic National Conventions from 1884 to 1912. In 1896 he joined many eastern "gold" Democrats in deserting William Jennings Bryan's presidential campaign, though he returned to support Bryan in 1900. A lifelong Democrat who came of age during Reconstruction while his father was chairman of the Democratic National Committee, Belmont rarely had kind words for any of his political adversaries. In his ninety-first year he wrote, "While not always agreeing with the leaders of my own party . . . , I have never voted for a Republican candidate, and see no reason why I ever should" (Belmont, *An American Democrat*, p. 126). He died in Newport, Rhode Island.

Belmont epitomized the second-generation inheritors of eastern wealth in the years after the Civil War. Connected to the early history of his country through his maternal grandfather, he perhaps felt duty-bound to participate in politics, which he did by running five times for a safe seat in Congress. In this respect he received only a single surprise, when Tammany Hall blocked the way. He dabbled in diplomacy and the military, devoted himself to horses, and to the end maintained his belief in the system that supported him.

• Belmont's autobiography, *An American Democrat: The Recollections of Perry Belmont* (1941), is disorganized and selectively self-serving. He wrote four relatively short books: *National Isolation an Illusion* (1924), *Survival of the Democratic Principle* (1926), *Return to Secret Party Funds* (1927), and *Political Equality and Religious Toleration* (1927). He contributed four articles to the *North American Review*: "Congress, the President, and the Philippines," Dec. 1899, pp. 894–911; "The Philippines and the Supreme Court," Mar. 1900, pp. 433–45; "Bryanism," Feb. 1901, pp. 268–75; and "Publicity of Election Contributions and Expenditures," Feb. 1905, pp. 166–85. See also Irving Katz, *August Belmont: A Political Biography* (1968). Belmont expressed his opposition to "present Populist quackeries" in an interview in the *New York Times*, 31 Aug. 1897. The same paper, in a long article, praised his "considerable success" in advocating the publicizing of national party fundraising sources (27 Nov. 1905). An obituary is in the *New York Times*, 26 May 1947.

IRVING KATZ

BELO, Alfred Horatio (27 May 1839–19 Apr. 1901), Confederate soldier and newspaper manager-publisher, was born in Salem, North Carolina, the son of Frederick Edward Boehlo, a mercantile businessman, and Amanda Fries, both Moravians. (Belo's ancestors were northern European refugees who had settled in the Piedmont area, where they changed the spelling of the family name to match its English pronunciation.) Belo attended Moravian Boys' Academy, where for four years he studied Latin, German, and geometry; a year and a half at the Masonic Institute at Germantown; and three years at the school of Dr. Alexander Wilson, a Presbyterian minister and cultural scholar, in Alamance County (N.C.). Instead of attending college, Belo succeeded his ailing father in the management of his general merchandise store, linseed oil mill, iron foundry, and roughly 450-acre farm.

As the Civil War approached, Belo opposed secession, but after North Carolina seceded from the Union, he volunteered and organized the Forsyth County Riflemen, became its captain, later commanded a battalion in the Fifty-fifth North Carolina Regiment, and became one of the youngest Confederate colonels. He was severely wounded in the battles of Gettysburg and Cold Harbor and for the rest of his life carried both the title of "Colonel" and the adverse effects of a shattered upper left arm.

After the Civil War ended in 1865, Belo rode horseback to Texas, where he worked and tutored briefly on a Waller County plantation near Houston before becoming bookkeeper for the long-established *Galveston News*, which had moved inland to Houston temporarily during the war. In 1868 he married Jeanette "Nettie" Ennis of Galveston; they had two children, a son and daughter. Belo's precise military and management skills so impressed *News* publisher Willard Richardson that in 1866 Belo became his business partner. After Richardson died in 1875, Belo became sole owner of the paper and created A. H. Belo & Company, which in 1885 established the *Dallas Morning News*.

Belo's fame rests on his innovations in business and technology and his editorial independence. He was an early user of Linotype and stereotype for production and telegraph wire and railroads for distribution of the news. He helped create the Texas Associated Press and in 1866 the Western Associated Press. At the 1872 Democratic National Convention at which Horace Greeley was endorsed for president, the *Galveston News* became the first Texas newspaper to assign its own wire correspondent to such a national gathering, held in Baltimore. In 1878 Belo installed the first telephone in Texas as a private line from his newspaper office to his home. It was also his idea to use the first special train to deliver his newspaper to subscribers in other towns. In 1884, according to his *Memoirs*, Belo's new *Galveston News* building was the first designed exclusively to put out a newspaper and the first fireproof structure in the southwestern United States. When Belo established the *Dallas Morning News* in 1885, the simultaneous publication of his two newspapers, headquartered in separate cities 315 miles apart, through the use of wire copy and the railroads was credited as constituting the first "chain" newspaper, an accomplishment that was acknowledged by Charles Dana of the *New York Sun*, William Randolph Hearst, and Lord Northcliffe of the *London Times* and *Daily Mail*; Northcliffe later called it "the greatest journalistic feat of the times" (*Galveston News*, 11 Apr. 1917).

Through his newspapers and a supplementary *Texas Almanac*, Belo promoted the growth and development of Texas agriculture and industry, land, and population. The *Galveston News*, long considered the voice of the Texas Democratic party, was the first to suggest for president the name of Grover Cleveland, with whom Belo often fished and hunted in the Adirondacks. Despite such influential connections, Belo sought to keep his newspapers politically independent so as to gain credibility with readers. He insisted that Texas state printing contracts go to the lowest bidder, and in 1892 he rejected efforts by Cleveland to appoint him minister to Austria-Hungary.

Belo eventually moved from Galveston to Dallas, but by 1895 the *Dallas Morning News* was being operated by G. B. Dealey, whom Belo had hired as an office boy in Galveston in 1874. Recurring bouts with old war wounds, malaria, and yellow fever led Belo to recede from his newspapers and take frequent recuperative, therapeutic, and socially nostalgic trips to Europe, Mexico, and the northern and eastern United States. He died at Asheville, North Carolina, and was buried at his hometown of Salem.

• Related and random material on Belo is in files of the American History Center, University of Texas at Austin; the G. B. Dealey Library in the Hall of State in Dallas (Dallas Historical Society); the G. B. Dealey Collection at the *Dallas Morning News*; and the Fikes Hall of Special Collections and the DeGolyer Library Collection at Southern Methodist University, Dallas. The major source on Belo's life is his *Memoirs of Alfred Horatio Belo* (1904), dictated by him to Charles Peabody. See also Sam Acheson, *35,000 Days in Texas: A History of the Dallas News and Its Forbears* (1938); and Lillian Davis Martin, "The History of the *Galveston News*" (1929), and Ralph H. Parker, "The History of the *Dallas Morning News*" (1930), both M.A. theses, Univ. of Texas at Austin. In addition, see Ernest Sharpe, *G. B. Dealey and the Dallas News* (1955); entries on Belo and the *Dallas Morning News* in William T. Pace, *Texas Scrapbook* (1933), and Alex E. Sweet and J. Armoy Knox, eds., *Texas Siftings* (1886); and Belo's family history in *Memorial and Biographical History of McLennon, Falls, Bell and Coryell Counties, Texas* (1893), pp. 539–40. See also the fortieth anniversary edition of the *Dallas Morning News*, 1 Oct. 1925. An obituary is in the *New York Times*, 20 Apr. 1901.

GENE A. BURD

BELTRAMI, Giacomo Constantino (1779–6 Jan. 1855), explorer, was born in Bergamo, Italy, the son of Giovanni Battista Beltrami, a Venetian customs official, and Margherita Carozzi. His early career was formed by the Napoleonic presence in northern Italy. Enamored of the ideals of the French Revolution and an admirer of Napoleon Bonaparte, Beltrami joined the militia of the Cisalpine Republic in 1796 and rose to become a vice inspector of armies. In 1807 he became chancellor of the Department of Justice of Parma and served as a judge until 1813. As the Napoleonic empire began to crumble, Beltrami retired from the bench and became a member of the Florentine salon of Louise Maximilienne Caroline, the countess of Albany and the widow of Charles Edward Stuart, better known as the "Young Pretender" or "Bonnie Prince

Charlie." Beltrami also forged important relationships with Countess Giulia Spada de Medici and Countess Geronima Compagnoni.

Because the political climate of his homeland was at that time hostile to his ideals, Beltrami left Italy in 1821. He traveled in France, Germany, and England before deciding to go to North America. He sailed from Liverpool in November 1822 and arrived in Philadelphia, Pennsylvania, on 30 December 1822. While in the United States he was able to draw funds from an account with the Baring Bank in London; the account was quite possibly created through the good offices of the countess of Albany. Beltrami went to Baltimore, Maryland, and then to Washington, D.C., where he had an impromptu meeting with President James Monroe. Beltrami traveled to Pittsburgh, Pennsylvania, which served as a point of departure for his travels in the Old Northwest (presently the American Midwest).

Beltrami proceeded to St. Louis, Missouri, and took the steamboat *Virginia* to Fort St. Anthony (later Fort Snelling) at the junction of the Minnesota and Mississippi rivers. In July 1823 Beltrami joined the exploratory party of U.S. major Stephen H. Long and headed northward from Fort St. Anthony. In the company of the American explorers, Beltrami was definitely the odd man out; he cherished thunderstorms and raging rivers while his companions simply endured them. Beltrami lamented in his letters to Countess Compagnoni that he was in the company of "people who had no idea of stopping for anything but a broken saddle" (*A Pilgrimage*, p. 318).

After an altercation with Major Long, Beltrami left the American party on 9 August 1823 and pushed southward from Pembina (on the U.S.–Canadian border) with a part-Indian interpreter and two Chippewa guides. Determined to find the source of the Mississippi River, Beltrami entered Sioux territory, whereupon his interpreter and guides deserted him. Beltrami forged on alone for several days, pulling his canoe behind him since he had not learned how to paddle. His red silk umbrella served both as a flag of civilization and as a covering for his personal effects. Beltrami met another Indian who agreed to guide him, and he continued his journey. On 28 August 1823 he came to a small heart-shaped lake that lay between the watersheds of the Red and Mississippi rivers. Beltrami named this Lake Julia in honor of Countess Giulia (who had died in 1820) and exulted that "these sources are the actual sources of the Mississippi" (*A Pilgrimage*, p. 413). In fact, he was mistaken. Nine years later Henry Schoolcraft found the actual source—Lake Itasca. But Beltrami was in good company: David Thompson (1798), Zebulon Pike (1806), and Lewis Cass and Henry Schoolcraft (1820) had all named incorrect sources.

Confident that he had achieved his goal, Beltrami returned to Fort Snelling and proceeded to St. Louis and then to New Orleans, where he wrote *La decouverte des sources du Mississippi . . .* (1824). He traveled across Mexico and then returned to the United States,

where he wrote pamphlets defending his claim. He then returned to Europe and lived in Paris (c. 1830–1834) and Germany (1834–1836) before finally returning to Italy. He lived in retirement on his estate in Filottrano and died there, several years before Italian unification was achieved.

Beltrami's romantic spirit was indicative of the European attitude toward the American wilderness. To a generation of Europeans who had been inspired by the promise of the French Revolution and the power of the Napoleonic empire, post-1815 European politics appeared both stale and regressive. Beltrami was one of a number of Europeans who came to the United States in order to experience nature firsthand. In this he was highly successful. Beltrami admired the American wilderness more than he did the young American republic and the North American Indians. It is perhaps fortunate that he witnessed American institutions before the advent of Jacksonian democracy, which might have confirmed his doubts as to the viability of the democratic experiment in North America.

As an explorer, Beltrami has received less credit than he deserves, although the state of Minnesota has named a county, a village, and a park after him. Although Schoolcraft discovered the source of the Mississippi, Beltrami deserves recognition for having floundered through brush, stream, and unknown land in search of the source. Striving to be another Christopher Columbus, Beltrami left a series of letters (published in English in 1828) that provide insight into the influence of early nineteenth-century romanticism on a European traveling in North America.

• Many of Beltrami's papers are housed at the Biblioteca Civica in Bergamo, Italy. The primary source for Beltrami's travels in the United States not already mentioned in the text is his *A Pilgrimage in Europe and America Leading to the Discovery of the Sources of the Mississippi and Bloody River . . .* (1828). See also Augusto Miceli, *Man with the Red Umbrella: Giacomo Constantino Beltrami in America* (1974). Beltrami's story is discussed in Roger Kennedy, *Rediscovering America* (1990); and Evan Jones, *Citadel in the Wilderness: The Story of Fort Snelling and the Old Northwest Frontier* (1966). For additional information, see Timothy Severin, "The Preposterous Pathfinder," *American Heritage* (Dec. 1967): 57–63; and Michael Martin, "Improbable Explorer: Giacomo Beltrami's Summer of Discovery," *Timeline* 7, no. 1 (1990): 32–43. The career of the countess of Albany is discussed in Alex Charles Ewald, *The Life and Times of Prince Charles Stuart* (1883). For a social study comparable to Beltrami's works about North America, see Theodore Dwight, Jr., *A Journal of a Tour in Italy in the Year 1821* (1824).

SAMUEL WILLARD CROMPTON

BELUSHI, John (24 Jan. 1949–5 May 1982), actor-comedian, was born in Chicago, Illinois, the son of Adam Belushi, the owner of a local restaurant, and Agnes (maiden name unknown). John was the eldest of three sons. His younger brother Jim also became an actor. An aggressive and difficult child, Belushi often got into trouble as a youngster. At Central High School in Wheaton, Illinois, however, he satisfied an intense need for attention by participating in such extracurricular activities as football, wrestling, choir, forensics, and the drama club and by playing drums in a rock 'n' roll band. In his senior year he was captain of the football team as well as homecoming king.

After graduating from high school in 1967, Belushi tried summer stock and then, to avoid the draft, attended several colleges in the Midwest; during this period he performed in a few dramatic productions, among them Arthur Miller's *The Crucible* in the role of Danforth. After two years Belushi decided that acting in plays was not for him. He wanted instead to perform his own material using a more improvisational format. Together with two friends, Tino Insana and Steve Beshakas, Belushi began to perform, in a coffeehouse setting, comedy routines that mocked conventions of the day. This led, in 1971, to an audition with Del Close, director of Second City, Chicago's renowned improvisational troupe. Belushi would later credit Close with perfecting his comedic technique and teaching him how to act within an ensemble.

Belushi's work at Second City brought him to the attention of *National Lampoon*'s Tony Hendra, who cast Belushi in his off-Broadway production of *National Lampoon's Lemmings*, a rock musical that spoofed the music industry. The revue opened at the Village Gate in Greenwich Village on 25 January 1972 with the expectation of it running for only a few weeks before embarking on a college tour. The revue's great popularity, however, kept it in New York for an extended run—ten months before sell-out crowds. For this same team Belushi wrote, directed, and acted in the weekly "*National Lampoon* Radio Hour," and on 21 February 1975 he opened off-Broadway in *The National Lampoon Show*.

This second *National Lampoon* production was not nearly as popular as *Lemmings*, but it brought Belushi to the attention of producer Lorne Michaels, who was putting together a cast for a late-night comedy show to air on NBC called *Saturday Night*. The ninety-minute show, telecast live from New York's Rockefeller Center, was made up of the same kind of irreverent, topical comedy sketches that Belushi had performed in the Chicago coffeehouse years before. Billed as the Not Ready for Prime Time Players, the ensemble, which was then made up of Belushi, Dan Aykroyd, Chevy Chase, Jane Curtin, Garrett Morris, Laraine Newman, and Gilda Radner, became a comic sensation and launched a network television institution that became the starting place for dozens of other comic actors and resulted in several spin-offs. In 1977 Belushi won an Emmy Award for his work on the show.

Belushi's characters were mostly aggressive and manic—his most popular included a grunting Samurai warrior, a Greek chef who only cooked cheeseburgers, the leader of a band of giant killer bees, and a weather forecaster who lost control during the "Weekend Update" segment and always ended with the catch phrase, "But noooooooooo!" One of his most successful character portrayals teamed Belushi with Aykroyd as "The Blues Brothers." Originally a warm-up act for *Saturday Night*, the characters became regulars on the show, then spawned an album, *A Briefcase Full of Blues* (Atlantic Records, 1978), and later a movie, *The Blues Brothers* (1980), which received mixed reviews but gained a large popular following.

In 1977 Belushi married his high school sweetheart, Judy Jacklin; they had no children. In 1979, like several other *Saturday Night* cast members before him, Belushi left the show to pursue a career in Hollywood. In his first movie release, *Animal House* (1978), he played Bluto Blutarsky, a hard-partying, rule-breaking member of an outrageous college fraternity. Although some critics decried the sophomoric humor of the film, Belushi garnered rave reviews, and the film itself became a huge hit. Unfortunately, none of his subsequent films achieved the success of *Animal House*. In *Goin' South* (1978), directed by and starring Jack Nicholson, Belushi had a small role as a mangy Chicano deputy sheriff. In *Old Boyfriends* (1979) Belushi took on his first serious role, as aging rocker Eric Katz, but despite his lauded portrayal of male arrested development, the film was a commercial failure. Belushi was first teamed up with Aykroyd on film in *1941* (1979), a spoof of the post–Pearl Harbor fear that the Japanese were about to invade California. Belushi played a crazed pilot. Neither *1941* nor Belushi's final two films, *Continental Divide* (1981) and *Neighbors* (1981), were commercial or critical successes.

Belushi's volatile nature could not bear the pressure of having to be continually funny and successful, and like many stars before and after him, he turned to drugs and alcohol in an attempt to cope. On the day of his death, a woman named Cathy Smith, a friend who kept Belushi supplied with drugs, injected him with a mix of heroin and cocaine; called a "speedball," it proved fatal. In 1983 Smith was convicted of manslaughter in connection with Belushi's death.

An intense comic, Belushi was even more intense in his personal life. He seems to have converted the aggressiveness of his youth into a manic style of comedy that became progressively more explosive as he moved from the stage to television to film. In *Wired* (1984), his timely biography of Belushi, *Washington Post* reporter Bob Woodward concluded that Belushi's extreme personality embodied the essence of the 1970s. His personal excesses have also been viewed as a reflection of the "unapologetic selfishness" that came to characterize the 1980s. Yet it was his unpredictability and his seemingly insane antics that made him such an outstanding comic. However representative he was of the drug-obsessed entertainment industry of his time, Belushi helped to develop, and make popular, an energetic and highly creative form of improvisational comedy that continues to please audiences the world over.

• In addition to Bob Woodward's *Wired: The Short Life and Fast Times of John Belushi* (1984), which was made into a movie in 1989, see Judy Belushi's *Samurai Widow* (1990); written from a personal viewpoint, it disputes some facts in Woodward's biography. For a cultural critique of Belushi's comic excesses, see Ronald L. Smith, ed., *Who's Who in Comedy* (1992). Information on Belushi's work on *Saturday Night* can be found in Michael Cader, ed., *Saturday Night Live: The*

First Twenty Years (1994). Belushi's comedic style can be seen in the numerous videotapes of *Saturday Night*, as well as the video *The Best of John Belushi* (1993). An obituary is in the *New York Times*, 6 May 1982.

MELISSA VICKERY-BAREFORD

BEMAN, Amos Gerry (1812–1874), clergyman and abolitionist, was born in Colchester, Connecticut, the son of Jehiel C. Beman, a clergyman. Nothing is known of his mother. He grew up and received basic education in Middletown, Connecticut, where his father was pastor of the African church. A Wesleyan University student, L. P. Dole, volunteered to tutor Beman after the university refused his application for admission because he was an African American. Dole and Beman suffered ridicule and harassment from other students, and an anonymous threat of bodily harm from "Twelve of Us" caused Beman to give up the effort after six months. He went to Hartford, where he taught school for four years, and around 1836 he briefly attended Oneida Institute in New York.

Beman was ordained a Congregational minister in 1839. At about this time he married a woman whose name is not known. In 1841 he became the first named African-American pastor of Temple Street African Church in New Haven, where he was to remain for seventeen years. Here he gained respect and support throughout the city from both blacks and whites. The church became a center for social, educational, and benevolent activities for the African-American community. The Temple Street church is now the Dixwell Avenue Church and is the oldest existing African-American Congregational church in the nation.

Beman was an avid supporter of temperance throughout his life. His father had organized the Home Temperance Society of Middletown African Americans in 1833, and the younger Beman served as its secretary. He was also a participant in the founding of the Connecticut Temperance Society and served two years as its president. He was a leader in 1842 in effecting a merger of the African-American temperance associations in Connecticut, Massachusetts, New York, and New Jersey into the States' Delavan Union Temperance Society of Colored People and was the principal speaker at its convention in 1845. For about a year, in 1842, Beman edited *Zion's Wesleyan*, a newspaper that provided a voice for temperance, abolition, and other reforms.

Beman was an ardent abolitionist and a member of the American Anti-Slavery Society from its founding in 1833. In 1840, with the great schism in antislavery ranks resulting from differences on women's rights, politics, and the role of the churches in the antislavery movement, Beman withdrew from the American Anti-Slavery Society. He then became one of the eight African Americans—his father was another—in the founding convention of the American and Foreign Anti-Slavery Society, for which he served as assistant secretary. In great demand as an antislavery speaker, Beman traveled more than 5,000 miles between January and August 1856, crisscrossing the northeast and

making trips into Canada and Illinois. In his churches he held regular concerts for the enslaved, which combined protest, agitation, and prayer. Beman also was a frequent contributor to the *North Star* and *Frederick Douglass' Paper*.

Civil and political rights for free African Americans also received Beman's attention and energy. He carried on a long campaign to get suffrage rights in Connecticut, and he was a leader in the Negro Convention Movement. He served as president of the national conventions that met in Buffalo in 1843 and in Philadelphia in 1854 and as vice president of the meeting in Rochester in 1853. It was at the Buffalo meeting that Henry Highland Garnet gave his famous address in which he called on the slaves to rise in revolt. Beman stepped down from the chair and spoke for more than an hour against endorsing Garnet's address. Beman carried a majority of the convention with him against force and violence. However, after John Brown's raid and capture, Beman assisted in a prayer meeting for him at the Siloan Presbyterian Church in Brooklyn, New York.

In 1841 Beman was one of the founders and served as the first secretary of the Union Missionary Society, established by African Americans to support antislavery missionary work at home and abroad. When that society joined with other organizations in 1846 to organize the American Missionary Association (AMA), Beman became a supporter and active worker for the new evangelical abolitionist organization.

In the winter of 1856–1857, Beman's wife and two of their four children died from typhoid fever. After about a year he remarried, this time to a white woman whose name is not known. As a result, he lost favor with his New Haven congregation and submitted his resignation in 1858 to accept a call to the Abyssinian Congregational Church in Portland, Maine. This church was small and poor, although it was the only church serving a community of 400 African Americans. To supplement the small salary pledged by the church, the AMA commissioned him as a city missionary. When the church failed to raise the pledged salary, and he again encountered resentment against his wife, he petitioned the AMA for a full-time commission and received an appointment in 1859 as the association's fundraising agent for New England. That year, at a meeting in Brooklyn, he was elected president of the Evangelical Association of Colored Ministers of Congregational and Presbyterian Churches.

Beman was a hard worker for the AMA, covering a territory from Maine to Sag Harbor, Long Island, visiting both white and black churches of any denomination that would admit him as an agent of an abolitionist society. He usually prefaced his appeals with lectures on such topics as "The Origin and History of the African Race" and "What the Colored People Can under God Do for Themselves." Nevertheless, his collections were small. He either resigned or his commission was allowed to expire, and in 1863 he became pastor of a struggling Congregational church in Jamaica, Long Island. There his second wife died. In 1865 he went to pastor Mt. Zion Congregational Church in Cleveland, Ohio. He married again in 1871.

Beman died in Pittsfield, Massachusetts, where he was pastor of the Second Congregational Church, which he had helped in establishing a quarter century before.

• The Beman Collection in the Beinecke Rare Book and Manuscript Library at Yale University contains clippings, pamphlets, and scrapbooks which Amos Beman organized and annotated. There are seventy-two letters and reports written by Beman from 1841 to 1869 in the American Missionary Association Archives in the Amistad Research Center at Tulane University. The most extensive treatment of Beman's life is in David E. Swift, *Black Prophets of Justice: Active Clergy before the Civil War* (1989). Robert A. Warner has written an excellent overview of Beman's life and work in "Amos Gerry Beman—1812–1874, A Memoir of a Forgotten Leader," *Journal of Negro History* 22 (Apr. 1937): 200–21. More details about his work as pastor of Temple Street African Church are in an unpublished article by Kurt Schmoke, "The History of an Urban Church: Dixwell Avenue Congregational Church, 1829–1896," located in the Whitney Library at the New Haven Colony Historical Society.

CLIFTON H. JOHNSON

BEMAN, Nathan Sidney Smith (26 Nov. 1785–6 Aug. 1871), Presbyterian clergyman and educator, was born in New Lebanon, New York, the son of Samuel Beman and Silence Douglass. Beman matriculated at Williams College in 1803 but withdrew after the second term; following a year's teaching at Fairhaven, Vermont, he continued his studies at Middlebury College. After graduation in 1807, Beman became preceptor at Lincoln Academy, Newcastle, Maine, where he studied theology with Kiah Bailey. He returned to Middlebury as tutor in 1809.

His career as an educator established, Beman began the second part of his calling, the ministry, the following year when he was ordained as pastor of the First Presbyterian Church, Portland, Maine, on 14 March 1810. Poor health forced his resignation two years later, whereupon Beman relocated to Mount Zion, Georgia, and formed both an academy and a Presbyterian church. With the exception of a single year, 1818–1819, when he was president of Franklin College in Athens, Georgia, Beman remained at Mount Zion until he assumed the pastorate of the First Presbyterian Church in Troy, New York, on 14 June 1823.

Amid the revival fires of the so-called "burned-over district" of New York State, Beman would enjoy his greatest success as an evangelist, a leader of New School Presbyterianism, and a polemicist. Over the course of his forty-year tenure at First Presbyterian, Beman, an eloquent and powerful preacher, established himself as a leader in ecclesiastical, educational, and community affairs. He became a trustee of Middlebury College in 1824 and declined an election to the presidency of that institution in 1846. He also was associated with Rensselaer Polytechnic Institute (also in Troy, N.Y.); in 1842 he was elected vice president and in 1845 president, a post he held concurrently with his pastorate until 1865.

Many of his sermons and discourses were published, some separately and some collected into volumes. *Four Sermons on the Doctrine of the Atonement* appeared in 1825 and was reprinted in England; *The Old Minister* was published in 1839. Beman could be pugnacious, his rhetoric biting. Much of his fire was directed toward the Roman Catholic church and the Protestant Episcopal church, belittling their claims of apostolic succession, the doctrine that the spiritual authority of the bishopric can be traced in a direct line to the apostles. Beman supported various social reform movements, and as the Civil War approached he stood resolutely and vociferously in the camp of those calling for the abolition of slavery.

Beman's advocacy of revival thrust him into the cauldron of Presbyterian politics in the 1820s and 1830s. Old School Presbyterians, led by Charles Hodge and the theologians at Princeton Theological Seminary, implacable opponents of revival enthusiasm, looked askance at the Arminian theology of Charles Grandison Finney, whose "new measures" had been adopted by Beman and other revival-minded Presbyterians. Beman's revivals in 1826 drew the ire of these Old School conservatives, and he was reprimanded by a convention that same year, but his stature was such that he nevertheless was elected moderator of the General Assembly five years later, in 1831.

Although Beman tried to act as peacemaker between the Old School conservatives and the New School revivalists—he brokered a meeting between the two sides at Mount Lebanon, New York, in 1827—his sympathies clearly lay with the New School, in part because of his friendship with Finney. When the Old School wrested control of the denomination in 1837 and exscinded the synods with New School sympathies, the revivalists chose Beman as leader of their New School movement. He contributed further to the cause by compiling the *Social Psalmist* (1843), a collection of hymns that was adopted by the New School Presbyterians. Beman's own contributions to nineteenth-century hymnody bear the unmistakable stamp of postmillennial optimism. An example is his hymn "Jesus! We Bow before Thy Throne": "Lord! arm thy truth with power divine. / Its conquests spread from shore to shore. / Till suns and stars forget to shine, / And earth and skies shall be no more." That refrain characterized Beman's expectations for the kingdom of God and epitomized the hopes that suffused antebellum Protestantism.

After stepping down from his pulpit and his presidency, Beman spent several years in retirement in Carbondale, Illinois, where he died.

• Beman published his complaints against the Episcopal church in *Episcopacy Exclusive: A Review of Dr. Coit's Sermon and Pamphlet* (1856), his anti-Catholic sentiments in *Letters to Rev. John Hughes* (1857). Beman's contributions to New School Presbyterianism are treated in George M. Marsden, *The Evangelical Mind and the New School Presbyterian Experience* (1970).

RANDALL BALMER

BEMELMANS, Ludwig (27 April 1898–1 Oct. 1962), writer and illustrator, was born in Meran in Tyrol, Austria (now Italy), the son of the Belgian painter Lambert Bemelmans, and Frances Fischer from Regensburg, Germany. He spent his early childhood in Gmunden on the Traunsee, Upper Austria, where his father owned a hotel. French was his first language, German his second. In 1904 his father abandoned the family, running off with Ludwig's governess. The mother moved with her two sons to her native Regensburg on the Danube, where her father owned a brewery and beer garden. Bemelmans rebelled against the strict German discipline. After repeatedly failing the first grade of the Gymnasium (equivalent to the American fifth grade), he was sent to a boarding school in Rothenburg, and after failing there as well, was apprenticed to his uncle Hans Bemelmans in Austria to learn the hotel trade. After a serious altercation with a hotel manager (the nature of which is in dispute), he was shipped off to America, where his father had become a jewelry designer.

Arriving in New York City in December 1914, Bemelmans spent the next two and a half decades in the hotel and restaurant business, from busboy to part owner of a restaurant. In 1917 he enlisted in the U.S. army, but because of his German background he was not sent to Europe. He worked in the medical corps in a psychiatric ward until he was selected for officer's training and rose to the rank of second lieutenant. In 1918 he became a naturalized American citizen.

Back in the hotel business, Bemelmans tried to establish himself as an artist. He considered himself to be a painter first and a writer second. In 1926 he published the cartoon series "The Thrilling Adventures of the Count Bric a Brac" in the *New York World*, but this cartoon was dropped after only six months. When he finally tried to leave the hotel world for good, in 1929, the depression had begun and nobody wanted to buy paintings.

In the early 1930s Bemelmans met May Massee, an editor for children's books at Viking Press, who encouraged him to write and illustrate books for children. His first work was *Hansi*, the story of a boy from Innsbruck who travels to the mountains, published in 1934. Other books followed in quick succession: *The Golden Basket* (1936), *Castle Number Nine* (1937), and *Quito Express* (1938), the last based on a visit to Ecuador.

Bemelmans married Madeleine Freund in 1934; they had one daughter. He enjoyed traveling and spent much of the 1930s in Europe. He was especially fond of Paris, which inspired him to write in rhymed verse and illustrate his classic *Madeline* (1939), the story of an enterprising school girl in Paris. Ironically, this book that was to have such a tremendous success was turned down by Viking and published by Simon and Schuster. During the last years of his life, Bemelmans created four sequels to *Madeline*: *Madeline's Rescue* (1953), *Madeline and the Bad Hat* (1956/57), *Madeline and the Gypsies* (1958), *Madeline in London* (1961), and a short "extra" for *McCall's* magazine, "Madeline's

Christmas" (1956). Other juvenile fiction from these years included *The High World* (1954) and *Parsley* (1955).

While Bemelmans was most famous for and successful with his children's books, both for their illustrations and their texts, he had a remarkable career as a writer of adult books, usually a mixture of autobiography and fiction, often in (not always connected) episodes. Most of the books, like the children's books, appeared first in magazines, either serialized or in condensed form. *My War with the United States* (1937), based on a diary by Bemelmans and written in German, draws on his experiences as a soldier in World War I. *The Donkey Inside* (1941) and *Now I Lay Me Down to Sleep* (1943) depict South America. *The Blue Danube* (1945) uses Regensburg for a story about the Nazi era. *The Eye of God* (1949) views the same period from the mountains of Tyrol, close to the Arlberg. His hotel experiences provide the material for *Hotel Splendide* (1941) and his first trip to Europe after 1945 is reflected in his book *The Best of Times* (1948).

In 1943 Bemelmans was drawn to Hollywood where he wrote the script for *Yolanda and the Thief* (MGM). He portrayed Hollywood characters and events in the satirical novel *Dirty Eddie* (1947), which apparently enraged Louis B. Mayer. In Hollywood he became a close friend of Lady Elsie Mendl who appears in books such as *To the One I Love the Best* (1955) and *How to Travel Incognito* (1952).

Bemelman's painting style has been compared to Chagall, Raoul Dufy, and the fauvists. He preferred water colors and used several techniques. As he grew older he devoted more and more time to painting and had numerous exhibitions. He also painted murals in restaurants and bars. He summed up his experiences and views in *My Life in Art* (1958). He received several awards for his books for children, notably the 1937 Newbery Honor Award for *The Golden Basket*, the 1940 Caldecott Honor Award for *Madeline*, and the 1954 Caldecott Award for *Madeline's Rescue*. He died in New York City.

Bemelmans was, to a point, a victim of his own success, being classified as primarily an author of juvenile fiction. He was in fact a remarkable humorist and a special kind of immigrant writer whose view of the United States and Europe in the 1930s and 1940s ought to be rediscovered. His art deserves serious consideration as well.

• Bemelmans's papers are mainly in the possession of his widow, Madeleine Freund Bemelmans. The best list of Bemelmans's works, including translations, magazine articles, exhibitions, and reviews of his 543 books, is provided by Murray Pomerance, *Ludwig Bemelmans: A Bibliography* (1993). Although his books were widely reviewed when they appeared, there has been little scholarly attention paid to his art and his adult books. He appears usually under the rubric "writers for children." The most comprehensive treatment of Bemelmans's books for children is Jacqueline Fisher Eastman, *Ludwig Bemelmans* (1996). See also May Massee, "Ludwig Bemelmans," *Hornbook* 20 (Aug. 1954): 263–69. For a book of selections of Bemelmans's writings, see *Tell Them It Was Wonderful* (1985), with an introduction by Madeleine Freund Bemelmans.

WULF KOEPKE

BEMIS, Samuel Flagg (20 Oct. 1891–26 Sept. 1973), historian of American diplomacy, was born in Worcester, Massachusetts, the son of Charles Harris Bemis, a newspaperman, and Flora M. Bemis. Raised on a family farm, he attended Worcester public schools and, later, Clark University, where he received a B.A. in 1912 and an M.A. in 1913. Entering the graduate program in history at Harvard University that fall, he worked with Frederick Jackson Turner and became a protégé of Edward Channing. Under Channing's direction, Bemis wrote a seminar paper on Jay's Treaty, a subject to which he later devoted his dissertation.

In 1915 Bemis went to London to complete his research. After mailing his finished dissertation to Channing, he headed for Paris and was on board the French Channel packet *Sussex* when she was torpedoed in March 1916 by a German submarine. Having endured several hours in the water, he and his precious research notes were rescued by a British destroyer. The Germans initially denied responsibility for the attack, but Bemis's testimony that he had seen the track of the torpedo helped to persuade the Wilson administration to press Germany for a pledge to end submarine warfare against passenger and merchant vessels. The "*Sussex* pledge" made by the Germans in May 1916, though qualified, did end submarine warfare for over eight months.

After receiving his Ph.D. degree in 1916, Bemis went to New Mexico to recover from the tuberculosis he had developed as a result of his immersion in the Channel. In 1917 he began teaching at Colorado College. Two years later he married Ruth M. Steele, who served as his scholarly collaborator and with whom he had one daughter. Bemis accepted an appointment in 1920 to Whitman College in Walla Walla, Washington, where he stayed until he moved back east. Bemis's years in the West impressed upon him the importance of American continental expansion, which became a major theme in his writings, but they did nothing to erase the flinty and conservative Yankee characteristics and outlook that marked his personality.

In 1923 J. Franklin Jameson brought Bemis to the Carnegie Institution of Washington as an associate research fellow. Four years later, Jameson, who by then had moved to the Library of Congress, commissioned his protégé to head a mission to photocopy records relating to the United States in European archives. This task took Bemis to Europe, primarily England, for about two years. Meanwhile, Bemis had accepted an appointment at George Washington University in 1925. His almost ten-year residence in the nation's capital allowed him to pursue an impressive program of research and publications.

After a year as a visiting professor at Harvard University, Bemis moved in 1935 to Yale University, where he remained until his retirement in 1960. Although he possessed a mischievous sense of humor and could be genial with those he knew well, as a teacher Bemis's demeanor was austere, formal, and remote. His undergraduate lectures, delivered in a grating Yankee voice, were extraordinarily lucid and marvelously organized; at least until the end of his career, he attracted large enrollments. His year-long graduate seminar was a model of its kind, and he excelled as a thesis director and critic. As a result, he had more doctoral students than any other professor of American diplomatic history of his generation.

Bemis's contributions as a scholar were enormous, and many of his writings remain standard treatments of their subjects. He published more than seventy articles, the first in 1913, as well as scores of erudite book reviews. He wrote eleven books and edited and contributed to the ten-volume series the American Secretaries of State and Their Diplomacy (1927–1929), later supplemented by additional volumes covering the more recent period, some under Bemis's editorship. In 1935 he and Grace Gardner Griffin presented a masterful *Guide to the Diplomatic History of the United States, 1775–1921*, an exhaustive compendium of primary and secondary materials. His very detailed, scholarly, and yet lucid textbook *A Diplomatic History of the United States*, first published in 1936 and revised as late as 1965, was the first truly satisfactory work of its kind. During the 1930s, his interests turned increasingly in the direction of American relations with Latin America; one outcome of this new interest was the publication of *The Latin American Policy of the United States* (1943). In addition, Bemis was a willing, helpful member of numerous professional committees throughout his career.

Valuable as these contributions were, Bemis's greatest achievements were in two other categories: his monographs based on multiarchival research and a two-volume biography of John Quincy Adams. Although not the first practitioner of multiarchival research, Bemis made the case for this approach at a time when diplomatic history was just becoming an important field of study and introduced a steady stream of graduate students to a method that they in turn passed on to others. His three best-known monographs, *Jay's Treaty* (1923), *Pinckney's Treaty* (1926), which was awarded a Pulitzer Prize, and *The Diplomacy of the American Revolution* (1935), exemplified his approach, based as they were on intensive, scrupulous research in the government archives of several countries. Bemis did relatively modest work in the private papers of his actors, especially in his earlier studies, and he paid almost no attention to the role of public opinion. Within the framework he constructed, however, the research was definitive, and Bemis's work remains not only useful but essential to students of early American diplomacy.

Although several of his earlier articles had a biographical cast, Bemis did not turn fully to biography until the 1940s. His subject was John Quincy Adams, a man with whom he had great intellectual affinity and to whom he even bore a physical resemblance. Favored by an almost unprecedented access to family papers, Bemis constructed his biography of Adams in two parts, *John Quincy Adams and the Foundations of American Foreign Policy* (1949) and *John Quincy Adams and the Union* (1956). The first volume, which he called "a diplomatic biography" and which garnered Bemis his second Pulitzer Prize, traced its subject's diplomatic career and, using Adams as a vehicle, examined the origins of America's fundamental foreign policies. Addressing primarily the postpresidential years, the second volume focused on Adams's political life and the issue of slavery but also included revealing discussions of personality, character, family life, and the American setting, making it a more expansive study than any of his other writings. Bemis's respect for Adams did not lead him into distortions; the biography is rightly praised as a model of its kind.

In 1961 Bemis became president of the American Historical Association. His presidential address, "American Foreign Policy and the Blessings of Liberty," reviewed in a generally celebratory fashion the major themes of American diplomacy, as he saw them. Bemis concluded his address, however, with a pessimistic discussion of the current state of the nation, criticizing its narcissism, self-indulgence, and unwillingness to sacrifice in the defense of freedom. President John F. Kennedy's secretary of state, Dean Rusk, was so distressed by this jeremiad that he arranged to appear at the convention to deliver a rebuttal in defense of the New Frontier.

Bemis's poor health in later years perhaps helps to explain the gloom of his presidential address or at least the depth of his feeling. The death of his wife in 1967 made life even more burdensome. He died six years later in Bridgeport, Connecticut.

While in the course of a long career the particulars of Bemis's views shifted, the major thrust of his thinking remained consistent. He believed in the didactic power of history, since "by extending our experience . . . back beyond the touch of our own lifetime, it fortifies our own judgment in dealing with problems of the present and measuring hopes for the future" (*American Foreign Policy and the Blessings of Liberty*, p. 1). He believed that the enduring values and fundamental purposes of the Unites States were revealed in its history. Not uncritical of episodes and individuals, especially after 1898, he nevertheless recounted the story of American diplomacy in a spirit of "heartfelt nationalism—sometimes amounting in the opinion of critics almost to chauvinism" (Allen, p. 203).

From this patriotic feeling flowed Bemis's celebration of American continental expansion as well as his predominantly isolationist viewpoint. He regretted, for example, the decision for empire in 1898 and the entry of the United States into European politics in World War I, although as early as 1918 he responded favorably, but briefly, to Woodrow Wilson's crusade for a League of Nations. An isolationist in the 1930s,

Bemis approved America's entry into World War II only after the fact. Later, he strongly endorsed Cold War policies. In summary, his opinions were strongly held; equally firm was his commitment to professional standards in the use of evidence. He still ranks as the leading historian of early American diplomacy.

• Bemis's manuscripts and correspondence are in the Beinecke Library, Yale University, and Albertus Magnus College. A list of his writings as well as a number of his articles and speeches, including his presidential address to the American Historical Association, may be found in his *American Foreign Policy and the Blessings of Liberty* (1962). For assessments and personal recollections of Bemis by former students, see Russell H. Bostert and John A. DeNovo, "Samuel Flagg Bemis," Massachusetts Historical Society, *Proceedings*, 85 (1973): 117–24; and Lewis Gaddis Smith, "The Two Worlds of Samuel Flagg Bemis," *Diplomatic History* 9 (1985): 295–302. Fuller treatment will be found in H. C. Allen, "Samuel Flagg Bemis," in *Pastmasters*, ed. Marcus Cunliffe and Robin W. Winks (1969), pp. 117–29.

BRADFORD PERKINS

BEN-AMI, Jacob (23 Dec. 1890–22 July 1977), actor, was born Yakov Shtshirin in Minsk, Belorussia, the son of well-to-do parents whose names are unknown. Jacob received a traditional education in public schools and was also tutored privately. He was attracted to the stage early, and with the other boys who sang with him in the synagogue choir, he frequented the local Russian theaters. At age seventeen Jacob joined the Minsk municipal Russian theater as an extra and gradually began to play bit parts. He declined the opportunity to study at the prestigious Moscow Art Theater, since working in the capital required converting to Christianity. Instead, in 1908 he joined a Yiddish theater troupe. A year later he joined forces with playwright Peretz Hirschbein in creating the Hirschbein Troupe, an artistically ambitious venture intended to ameliorate the folksy Yiddish theater and make it comparable to the literary Russian stage. Though the troupe did not last more than one season, its formation is seen as a major milestone in the development of the artistic Yiddish stage. For young Jacob it marked the beginning of a lifelong commitment to serious theater and quality drama.

Ben-Ami (the name means "son of my people") came to the United States in 1912 and worked with a variety of Yiddish companies. It is not known when he changed his surname. In 1917 he was engaged by Maurice Schwartz as a principal player at the Irving Place Theatre (later renamed the Yiddish Art Theater) in New York, the flagship company of the Yiddish theater in America. A champion of literary drama, Ben-Ami stipulated in his contract that in addition to the regular repertoire, the theater would present a serious play once a week. He was even willing to take a significant pay cut in order to support that venture. The first such production, *A Secluded Nook* by Peretz Hirschbein, was a phenomenal success, confirming the existence of a young, cultured audience. It is credited with advancing the literary Yiddish theater that flourished in the United States during the 1920s and 1930s.

In 1919 Ben-Ami founded his own Jewish Art Theater in New York City. The theater produced plays by noted Yiddish playwrights such as Hirschbein, Sholom Asch, Sholom Aleichem, David Pinski, and Osip Dimow, as well as plays by Gerhart Hauptmann, Lev Nikolaevich Tolstoy, and Sven Lange. When acting in Lange's *Samson and Delilah* (1920), Ben-Ami was "discovered" by Arthur Hopkins, who consequently cast Ben-Ami as the star in an English-language production of the Greenwich Village Theater, with a cast that included Sam Jaffe and Edward G. Robinson. Ben-Ami's debut on the English-speaking stage caused a sensation in New York. He was praised for his barnstorming acting that combined passion with self-control and for his skillful use of expressive gesticulation and revelatory silences.

Following the great success of *Samson and Delilah*, Ben-Ami appeared on Broadway in another Hopkins production, an English-language version of Peretz Hirschbein's *The Idle Inn* (1922), which led to roles in *Johannes Kreisler* (1923), *Welded* (1924), and *Man and the Masses* (1926). In the 1930s he became a mainstay of Eva Le Galliene's Civic Repertory Theatre, starring in *The Seagull* (1931), *The Cherry Orchard* (1932), and *Camille* (1932). Critics designated him "great actor" and predicted splendid achievements, which led to an impressive career but not to stardom on Broadway. Thirty-nine years after his first English-speaking debut, Ben-Ami finally participated in a true Broadway hit, Paddy Chayefsky's *The Tenth Man* (1959).

During his distinguished English-language career, Ben-Ami maintained his devotion to the Yiddish stage. He starred in the Yiddish version of *Hamlet*, as well as numerous other Yiddish plays and Yiddish translations of Russian, American, and European plays, including *Awake and Sing, Beethoven, Abe Lincoln in Illinois, Ghosts*, and *Liliom*. Ben-Ami spent much of his acting career on tour. English-language tours included great successes in *The World of Sholom Aleichem, Payment Deferred, Death of a Salesman*, and *The Diary of Anne Frank*. He played in South America, including nine seasons in Buenos Aires, in South Africa, and in Europe.

Ben-Ami last appeared on stage in 1972 in *Yoshe Kalb*, which was performed at the theater on Twelfth Street and Second Avenue. He died in New York. He had survived by eleven years his wife, Slava Estrin, an actress who translated plays from German, Russian, and Polish into Yiddish. They had one son.

• Ben-Ami's personal papers are at the YIVO Institute for Jewish Research. Nahma Sandrow, *Vagabond Stars: A World History of Yiddish Theater* (1977), is the most complete English source for information on Ben-Ami. In English see also David S. Lifson, *The Yiddish Theatre in America* (1963), and Irving Howe, *World of Our Fathers* (1975). In Yiddish the most important source is Zalmen Zylbercwaig, *Lexicon fun yidishn teater*, vol. 1 (1931).

EDNA NAHSHON

BENAVIDES, Alonso de (c. 1578–c. 1636), Franciscan missionary, was born on San Miguel in the Azores. The names and occupations of his parents are lacking. Soon after Alonso's birth, Spain annexed the Portuguese empire, including the Azores, and he later emigrated to the Spanish Indies, where he spent much of his life. In 1602 he entered the Order of Friars Minor in Mexico City. After religious training and ordination, Benavides served in a succession of positions. While a missionary at San Juan Temamatla, southeast of the viceregal capital, he learned of his assignment as superior and first agent of the Inquisition in New Mexico on New Spain's far northern frontier.

Founded in 1598 as a proprietary enterprise by a mine developer, Juan de Oñate, New Mexico had proven a bad investment. When Oñate resigned, advisers recommended abandoning the colony. Instead, the Spanish crown in 1609 assumed financial responsibility, basing its decision on the Franciscans' dubious claim of having converted to Christianity more than seven thousand Pueblo Indians. From that point forward, clashes between royal governors and friars over Pueblo labor, land, and loyalty kept the precarious colony in turmoil.

With the heavy freight wagons of the mission supply caravan, a dozen more missionaries, the newly appointed governor Felipe de Sotelo Osorio, and Benavides entered mud-built Santa Fe early in 1626. An edict of the faith announced to the colony's 1,000 or more mainly mixed-blood Hispanic settlers that the authority of the Inquisition now resided among them. Pueblo Indians, however, because of their status as Christian neophytes, were exempt. While some of Benavides's successors would wield the power of the Holy Office as a weapon against governors, Benavides concentrated on his ministry.

Zealously optimistic, Benavides presided over the founding of several new missions among sedentary Pueblo peoples and labored personally but in vain to attract the seminomadic Apaches. In 1629, when he left New Mexico for Mexico City, he expected to return. But his superiors found his hopeful progress report so convincing that they sent him instead to the royal court in Madrid as a lobbyist.

In Europe Benavides presented two book-length memorials: the first, published in 1630 at government expense, to the Spanish king Philip IV, and the second, a revised and enlarged but unpublished 1634 version, to Pope Urban VIII. The friar's intention was to win further support for the ministry of his Franciscan brethren in New Mexico and, at the same time, advance his own bid to become that colony's first bishop. These seventeenth-century observations provide a revealing window on the quixotic effort of the Franciscans to bring about a millennial kingdom on the Rio Grande.

Benavides's memorials have been called "a curious mixture of ethnography, fiction, and fable" (Reff, p. 52). Obviously the friar related details of native lifeways to show that the Franciscans were winning their battle with the devil for the hearts of the Pueblo people, and in places, he exaggerated. To seize the pope's attention at the outset, Benavides claimed more than half a million Indian conversions. Elsewhere, his figures accord more closely with other evidence. Even his description of the mission church at Pecos pueblo, "of peculiar construction and beauty, very spacious, with room for all the [more than 2,000] people of the pueblo," was thought to have been an exaggeration until the 1960s, when National Park Service archaeologists unearthed the foundations of what was unquestionably the most monumental structure ever built in colonial New Mexico.

A comparison of Benavides's fervent condemnation of Pueblo Indian sacred spaces, or kivas, as dens of devilish idolatry with the matter-of-fact inventories a century and a half later by Fray Francisco Atanasio Domínguez suggests how differently later Franciscans would view their ministry. The old crusading intolerance, out of place in the eighteenth-century colony, gave way to a fitful live-and-let-live accommodation.

In the 1630s, however, Benavides knew his audience, secular and ecclesiastical. He assured the Spanish king of mineral as well as spiritual returns, and he embellished for the pope alleged miracles demonstrating God's special favor toward the Franciscans of New Mexico. While in Spain, Benavides interviewed Mother María de Jesús de Agreda, verifying the nun's visions of being transported miraculously to the plains east of New Mexico to instill in Jumano Indians a desire for baptism.

Benavides was geopolitically astute as well, and he promoted the Counter Reformation in the New World. In his 1634 memorial he suggested importing English-speaking Irish Catholic priests, who might turn back the Protestant tide "from Virginia and the islands of North America. . . . Thus they may not only convert the heathen . . . but also the heretics who have come from England and Holland and have increased in large numbers, taking Indians for wives, and together might convert the heathen already perverted, and hinder the propagation of heresy in New Mexico." At the same time, Benavides strove to protect Franciscan New Mexico from rival Jesuits and Dominicans.

Benavides never returned to New Mexico. Named auxiliary bishop of Portuguese Goa, he evidently died on the outward voyage. His ardent rhetoric, a belated final chapter of the mendicant orders' perceived spiritual conquest of Mexico in the sixteenth century, told as much about him as about the American Indians he described. Benavides remains New Mexico's premier seventeenth-century Spanish missionary propagandist.

• *Benavides' Memorial of 1630*, trans. Peter P. Forrestal, ed. Cyprian J. Lynch (1954), and *Fray Alonso de Benavides' Revised Memorial of 1634*, ed. Frederick Webb Hodge et al. (1945), are annotated scholarly editions. Daniel T. Reff, "Contextualizing Missionary Discourse: The Benavides *Memorials* of 1630 and 1634," *Journal of Anthropological Research* 50 (1994): 51–67, analyzes the friar's perceptions in cultural-historical, rhetorical, and institutional terms. For the fascinating relationship between Benavides and the Spanish

abbess María de Jesús de Agreda, see John L. Kessell, "Miracles or Mystery: María de Agreda's Ministry to the Jumano Indians of the Southwest in the 1620s," in *Great Mysteries of the West*, ed. Ferenc Morton Szasz (1993); and Clark Colahan, *The Visions of Sor María de Agreda: Writing, Knowledge, and Power* (1994). Compare Benavides's seventeenth-century memorials with Eleanor B. Adams and Fray Angélico Chávez, eds., *The Missions of New Mexico, 1776: A Description by Fray Francisco Atanasio Domínguez with Other Contemporary Documents* (1956).

JOHN L. KESSELL

BENBRIDGE, Henry (20 Oct. 1743–Jan. 1812), portrait painter, was born in Philadelphia, Pennsylvania, the son of James Benbridge and Mary Clark, occupations unknown. Benbridge was enrolled on 11 March 1751 in the Academy of Philadelphia, where he studied through 17 July 1758. After his father's death his tuition was paid by his stepfather, Thomas Gordon, but how Benbridge originally became interested in painting is unknown. In 1758 Benbridge was instructed in painting by John Wollaston, who was in Philadelphia that year and who painted a portrait of Thomas Gordon. Several of Benbridge's paintings from this period survive, of which *The Gordon Family* is at the Pennsylvania Academy of Fine Arts in Philadelphia. These pictures show the strong influence of English engravings and Wollaston's English style but are clumsy in composition.

On reaching his majority in 1764, Benbridge received his inheritance from his father and traveled to Rome to pursue his painting studies. This opportunity was unusual for an American colonist. In 1765 he was sharing quarters there with the Irish sculptor Christopher Hewetson. Benbridge's painting technique shows the influence of the Italian painter Pompeo Batoni, under whom it is thought he studied.

In 1768 Benbridge was commissioned by James Boswell to paint a portrait of the Corsican general Pascal Paoli (Fine Arts Museums of San Francisco, Calif.). This portrait served to launch Benbridge's career, for it was shown to the court of the grand duke in Florence and then sent to England, where it was shown at the May 1769 exhibition of the Free Society of Artists.

Benbridge left Italy for England in November 1769. In London he lodged in Panton Square a few doors from the quarters of Benjamin West, where he took his meals (West's wife was a distant relative). In a letter to his mother from London, dated 23 January 1770, Benbridge wrote, "I shall presently get money enough as I am not long painting a picture, having studied an expeditious way and at the same time a correct one" (Henry Francis du Pont Winterthur Museum, Joseph Downs Manuscript Collection, no. PH. 34). There is no record, however, that Benbridge was ever one of West's pupils. Benbridge exhibited two portraits at the Royal Academy in 1770. One, number 14, was of Benjamin Franklin (unlocated).

Benbridge returned to America in the summer of 1770. He remained in Philadelphia, where he was elected a member of the American Philosophical Society in 1771. Sometime in 1772 he removed to Charleston, South Carolina. In that year he married Letitia (or Esther) "Hetty" Sage (herself a miniature painter), and his only child was born. In Charleston Benbridge was successful with the wealthy planters and merchants, with clients including Charles Cotesworth Pinckney (National Portrait Gallery, Smithsonian Institution).

Benbridge supported the American cause during the Revolution, and when Charleston fell to the British on 12 May 1780 he was taken prisoner and sent to St. Augustine, Florida. After his release by March 1783 he went to his native Philadelphia and there painted a portrait, *Bushrod Washington* (Mount Vernon Ladies Association) in April of that year. By 1784 he returned to Charleston, where he painted *The Hartley Family* (Princeton University Art Gallery). In a letter from Charleston dated 8 March 1786 to his half sister Elizabeth Saltar, he wrote, "I am much hurried with business, having had as much as I could wish for since my arrival, & no prospect of its declining as yet & which I believe won't be the case." Again on 8 December 1786 he stated in an apology for not writing, "I have been so much engaged in business, that I put off writing from one time to another 'til the Vessell sailed, and really I am so tired at Nights after sitting close to work all Day, that when I would write I want spirits to begin" (Henry Francis du Pont Winterthur Museum, Joseph Downs Manuscript Collection, no. PH. 42 and no. PH. 43). Benbridge remained in Charleston until 1790, which is the last time his name appears in the city directory there.

After leaving Charleston, Benbridge worked in Norfolk, Virginia, probably living with his son, who had moved there by 1800. Here Thomas Sully met Benbridge and commissioned a portrait of himself (unlocated) in order to receive instruction in portrait painting from Benbridge. Among several conversation pieces from this Norfolk period is *The Family of Francis Stubbs Taylor* (Museum of Early Southern Decorative Arts, Winston-Salem, N.C.).

The Baltimore directory lists "Henry Benbridge, Merchant" in the years 1810 to 1812. This is no doubt Henry Benbridge's son. If Benbridge was living with his son, there are no known paintings from this Baltimore period. Where Benbridge was living at the time of his death in January 1812 is not known, but he was buried 25 January 1812 in Christ Churchyard in Philadelphia.

Benjamin Franklin wrote to his wife from London: "Mr. Benbridge, who has so greatly improved himself in Italy as a portrait painter that the Connoisseurs in that art here think few or none excel him." Benjamin West wrote to Francis Hopkinson, "You will find him [Benbridge] an ingenious artist. . . . His merit in the art must procure him great encouragement and much esteem." Although Benbridge's work was familiar to painters such as Washington Allston and Charles Frazer, it had no effect on their painting styles. He was not known to have had any pupils other than Thomas Sully. His works remained for the most part in obscure family collections and were unknown or misattributed until the middle of the twentieth century.

• For Henry Benbridge's career and a catalog of his works see Robert G. Stewart, *Henry Benbridge (1743–1812): American Portrait Painter* (1971). For his work in Norfolk, see Carolyn J. Weekly, "Henry Benbridge: Portraits in Small from Norfolk," *Journal of Early Southern Decorative Arts* 4, no. 2 (Nov. 1978): 50–64. See also Stephen E. Patrick, "I Have at Length Determined to Have My Picture Taken: An Eighteenth-Century Young Man's Thoughts about His Portrait by Henry Benbridge," *American Art Journal* 22, no. 4 (1990): 68–81.

ROBERT G. STEWART

BENCHLEY, Nathaniel Goddard (13 Nov. 1915–14 Dec. 1981), author, was born in Newton, Massachusetts, the son of Robert Charles Benchley, a humorist, and Gertrude Darling. Benchley was brought up largely in comfortable suburbia but moved to New York City after his 1938 graduation from Harvard University, his father's alma mater, where both father and son had served as presidents of the editorial board of the Harvard *Lampoon*. He was married in 1939 to Marjorie Bradford. They had two sons, one of whom, Peter Benchley, became a bestselling author. Nathaniel Benchley reported that he really got to know his father as an adult in the late 1930s, as they spent long evenings together in the city. Eventually Benchley came to be known, like his father, as a man-about-town, hobnobbing with such figures as Humphrey Bogart (of whom he wrote a 1975 biography), John Steinbeck, and Walter Cronkite.

Benchley was a reporter for the *New York Herald Tribune* from 1939 to 1941. He enlisted in the U.S. Navy immediately after the attack on Pearl Harbor and served in the Pacific from 1943 to 1945 as an officer aboard submarine chasers.

Benchley was assistant editor of the drama department of *Newsweek* magazine from 1946 to 1947 and then launched on the freelance career that made his reputation, writing articles and stories for the *New Yorker* as well as *Life, Holiday, Esquire, Vogue, Redbook, Harper's Bazaar,* and other national magazines. His books included a well-received biography of his father (*Robert Benchley*, 1955) and numerous novels. The first, *Side Street* (1950), he adapted into a play, *The Frogs of Spring* (1953). Four of his novels were adapted to film. The best known of these were *Sail a Crooked Ship* (1960), filmed in 1961 under the same name; and his comic masterpiece *The Off Islanders* (1961), which appeared in 1965 as *The Russians Are Coming, the Russians Are Coming.* An allegory in which the crew of a stranded Russian submarine and the residents of a New England island at first are terrified by each other but eventually discover their common humanity, this work drew productively on Benchley's knowledge of American character types and of Nantucket, where he had vacationed since his childhood. A continuing concern with American history was reflected in novels covering subjects as varied as financial speculation in the early republic (*Portrait of a*

Scoundrel, 1979) and the San Francisco earthquake (*All Over Again*, 1981).

From the mid-1960s onward Benchley began to write novels aimed at children and young adults, "to get young people into the habit of reading instead of staring at the tube" (*Publishers Weekly*, 2 Oct. 1972, p. 14) and to help bridge the gap between elementary-level texts and the classics. In association with such noted illustrators as Arnold Lobel and Mamoru Funai, many of the works for children drew on Benchley's knowledge of the ecology of the natural world, particularly the sea. Other books for children and young adults explored young people's experiences of history. These included views of both sides of the beginnings of the American Revolution in *Sam, the Minuteman* (1969) and *George, the Drummer Boy* (1977) and of the first meetings between American Indians and Europeans. *Only Earth and Sky Last Forever* (1972) examined the Plains Indian wars including the battle of the Little Big Horn from the point of view of an adolescent Indian boy. It won an award from the Western Writers of America in 1973. Another young adult book, *Bright Candles: A Novel of the Danish Resistance*, was named a 1974 Notable Book by the American Library Association.

Benchley followed in part the literary track of his father, yet eventually he forged his own professional identity, not only as the author of comic novels but as a serious writer for children and adolescents. Along with the biography of his father, these many books for young people represent Benchley's greatest continuing contribution to American letters.

Benchley was a resident of Nantucket during roughly the last decade of his life, painting and continuing to write. He died in Boston.

• Nathaniel Benchley's papers are in the Mugar Memorial Library at Boston University. The Robert Benchley Papers, housed in the Billy Rose Theatre Collection at the New York Public Library for the Performing Arts, Lincoln Center, include material documenting the career of Nathaniel Benchley. Benchley published more than forty-five books. Others of particular interest include a collection of his father's works, *The Benchley Roundup, a Selection by Nathaniel Benchley of His Favorites* (1955), and the novel *Catch a Falling Spy* (1963). Other notable books for children are *Red Fox and His Canoe* (1964) and *The Strange Disappearance of Arthur Cluck* (1967), both illustrated by Arnold Lobel. Benchley's worth as a children's author is examined in *English Journal* (Sept. 1976) and *Twentieth Century Children's Authors* (1980). Obituaries include Russell Baker's in the *New York Times*, 15 Dec. 1981; the *Washington Post*, 14 Dec. 1981; *Newsweek*, 28 Dec. 1981; and *Time*, 4 Jan. 1982.

FREDERIC SVOBODA

BENCHLEY, Robert (15 Sept. 1889–21 Nov. 1945), humorist, drama critic, and actor, was born Robert Charles Benchley in Worcester, Massachusetts, the son of Charles H. Benchley, the mayor's clerk, and Maria Jane Moran. After the death of his older brother Edmund in the Spanish-American War, an event that stunned Benchley's family, Edmund's fiancée, Lillian Duryea, largely financed Robert's education. Bench-

ley attended Phillips Exeter Academy, where his bent for satire early revealed itself when his assigned essay on "a practical subject," embalming, earned an *A*. As a student at Harvard he acted in Hasty Pudding musicals and worked as an illustrator and member of the editorial board of the Harvard *Lampoon*. He was president of the board during his junior year. Caricaturist Gluyas Williams (later Benchley's witty illustrator in many works) was a fellow Lampooner. While at Harvard, Benchley was much in demand as an after-dinner speaker; among his humorous monologues were satires on contemporary explorers and politicians.

After receiving his diploma in 1913 (officially as a member of the class of 1912), Benchley edited a Curtis Publishing house organ and worked as a "welfare secretary" for a paper mill company. In June 1914 he married Gertrude Darling, whom he had announced he would marry when he was in the third grade. They soon moved to New York City, then to suburban Scarsdale. They had two sons. Benchley's first published humor appeared in 1914 in *Vanity Fair*. He worked in social service for the East Side House and the Urban League but by 1916 was a reporter for the *New York Tribune*. He then served as associate editor of the *Tribune* Sunday magazine (and was fired in May 1917 when the magazine was discontinued).

Over the next two years Benchley held a succession of jobs in New York City and Washington, D.C., as a critic and publicity agent for: *Vanity Fair*, Broadway producer William A. Brady, the U.S. Aircraft Board, the *New York Tribune Graphic* (a new Sunday rotogravure section), and the Liberty Loan. In 1919 he was appointed managing editor of *Vanity Fair* but resigned in protest in 1920 (along with Robert E. Sherwood) when Dorothy Parker was fired by the magazine for criticisms of Billie Burke (Mrs. Florenz Ziegfeld) and other show people. Resolving to live by freelance writing, he and Parker then memorably shared a tiny office and supposedly the cable address "Parkbench." The cable address was apocryphal—but indicative of the place that both would occupy in legends of New York in the 1920s.

Benchley then began a *New York World* column, "Books and Other Things," which ran through 1921, and served as drama critic for the humor magazine *Life* from 1920 to 1929. His first collection of humor, *Of All Things*, appeared in 1921. Benchley was among the Algonquin Round Table wits from 1919 into the 1930s. "The Vicious Circle" included Parker, Sherwood, Harold Ross, Alexander Woollcott, George S. Kaufman, Marc Connelly, Harpo Marx, Edna Ferber, and Russel Crouse. Many were *New Yorker* contributors after 1925.

Benchley wrote for Ross's *New Yorker* beginning in December 1925 and contributed "The Wayward Press" column under the pseudonym "Guy Fawkes." He served as the new magazine's drama critic from 1929 to 1940 and helped establish its tone of humorous urbanity. The bemused yet serious protest at the ironies of modern life that was at the center of Benchley's appeal is well illustrated in the following *New Yorker* comment: "I would like to protest the killing by a taxi-cab . . . of Wesley Hill, the angel Gabriel of "The Green Pastures" [Connelly's Pulitzer Prize–winning play based on black religion]. There was really no sense in that, Lord, and you know it as well as I do" (20 Dec. 1930).

Benchley's association with Hollywood filmmaking grew out of humorous monologues that continued the tradition of his college humor. "The Treasurer's Report" of 1922 (which he eventually delivered on Broadway as a part of the third *Music Box Revue*) was filmed in 1928 and appeared as a book in 1930. Also among his forty-eight film shorts were *The Sex Life of the Polyp* (1928) and *How to Sleep*, which received an Academy Award as best short film of 1935. In these and in much of his writing his persona was that of the decent, middle-class American—whom he characterized as the "poor boob"—born into comfort yet facing a trying modern world.

By 1938 Benchley's evolving media career had him commuting from coast to coast. He also worked as a radio emcee beginning in 1938 with the highly popular Old Gold program and cut back on his writing for the *New Yorker*. He considered himself retired from writing by 1943. His last film was made for the U.S. Navy in 1945. He died in New York City of a cerebral hemorrhage and was buried in Nantucket, where he had spent many happy summers.

• Robert Benchley's papers are in the Mugar Memorial Library at Boston University. Additional material is housed in the Billy Rose Theatre Collection at the New York Public Library for the Performing Arts, Lincoln Center. Biographies of Benchley are his son Nathaniel Benchley's *Robert Benchley* (1955), which includes a useful foreword by Robert Sherwood, and Babette Rosmond's *Robert Benchley, His Life and Good Times* (1970). Norris W. Yates, *Robert Benchley* (1968), examines his career as writer and humorist. Both the *New Yorker* obituary (1 Dec. 1945) and James Thurber's *New York Times Book Review* article (18 Sept. 1949) help to explain the continuing appeal of Benchley's life and writing. *The Benchley Roundup, a Selection by Nathaniel Benchley of His Favorites*, comp. Nathaniel Benchley (1954), and *The Best of Robert Benchley* (1983) are accessible compilations from earlier collections of his work. *The "Reel" Benchley: Robert Benchley at His Hilarious Best in Pictures* (1950) is a collection of six scripts of his film shorts. *Chips off the Old Benchley*, comp. Gertrude Benchley (1949), and *Benchley Lost and Found: 39 Prodigal Pieces* (1970) include previously uncollected material.

FREDERIC SVOBODA

BENDER, Chief (5 May 1884–22 May 1954), baseball player and manager, was born Charles Albert Bender at Partridge Lake, Crow Wing County, Minnesota, the son of Albertus Bliss Bender and Mary Razor, farmers. His father was of German-American descent, and his mother, whose tribal name was Pay shaw de o quay, was a half-white member of the Mississippi band of the Ojibwa (Chippewa). The family moved to Brainerd, Minnesota, on White Earth Indian Reservation during the 1880s, but at age seven Bender was placed in the Educational Home in Philadelphia, an Episcopal school for white and Indian orphan and destitute children. Although he returned to Minnesota in mid-1896, he soon ran away and enrolled at the Indian School in Carlisle, Pennsylvania, where he played baseball and football under the legendary coach Glenn Warner. After leaving Carlisle in February 1902, he pitched for nearby Dickinson College. That summer he played for the Harrisburg, Pennsylvania, Athletic Club, using the surname Albert to protect his college eligibility. There, he pitched a 3–1 win over the Chicago Cubs. Jess Frisinger, a scout for Connie Mack, signed him to a contract for 1903 with the Philadelphia Athletics of the American League at a monthly salary of $300.

Because Bender's dark complexion, hair, and eyes made him appear to many people as fully Indian, his Philadelphia teammates gave him the nickname "Chief," but he signed autographs "Charley Bender" and said, "I do not want my name presented to the public as an Indian, but [as] a pitcher." During his career he endured war whoops and other Indian allusions with dignity and good humor. He became the first American Indian to achieve baseball stardom.

Bender won in relief for Philadelphia on opening day in 1903 and two weeks later pitched a four-hit shutout. Thereafter, the 6'2", 185-pound right-hander pitched twelve seasons for the Athletics, although illness frequently sidelined him. In 1904, for example, he suffered from measles, tonsillitis, and "incipient" appendicitis. In that same year he married Marie Clement; they had no children.

Bender's 193–102 won-lost record with the Athletics included season victory totals of 23 (1910) and 21 (1913), victory streaks of 14 (1914) and 11 (1911), the American League pitchers' won-lost percentage leadership three times, and an almost perfect no-hitter against Cleveland on 21 May 1910. Besides helping the Athletics secure their 1905, 1910, 1911, 1913, and 1914 American League pennants, Bender won six and lost four World Series games with an overall 2.44 ERA. He pitched a shutout in the only World Series game that Philadelphia won in 1905 against the New York Giants and contributed to the Athletics' 1910, 1911, and 1913 world championships.

Bender's strengths included an excellent fastball, sharply breaking curveballs thrown overhand, outstanding control, unflappability, and thorough baseball savvy. However, extremely warm weather weakened him as a pitcher. A good batter, he occasionally pinch-hit or played in the field in a utility role. In one game in 1906 he played right field and hit two home runs. As a coach, he repeatedly discovered how opposing pitchers unwittingly gave away their intended pitches.

In the 1914 World Series Bender not only lost the first game to the Boston Braves, but he allegedly handicapped the Athletics by disobeying manager Mack's order to scout Braves' hitters during the regular season's final week. When Mack asked waivers on him, Bender moved to the Federal League in 1915, where arm trouble and poor batting and fielding by tail-end

Baltimore resulted in his 4–16 record. After relatively limited appearances with the 1916 and 1917 Philadelphia Phillies of the National League and a wartime year working in shipyards, he compiled an extraordinary 29–2 record in 1919 as player-manager for Richmond of the Virginia League. In 1925–1926 he coached the Chicago White Sox and pitched one final big league inning. He pitched and managed in the minor leagues through 1927 at New Haven, Connecticut (Eastern League); Reading, Pennsylvania, and Baltimore (International League); and Johnstown, Pennsylvania (Middle Atlantic League); coached at the U.S. Naval Academy during off-seasons from 1923 through 1928; coached for the New York Giants in 1931; and pitched at times for semiprofessional clubs, including the House of David, from 1932 until 1936.

He again worked for the Athletics from 1938 on, except in 1942 when he scouted for the New York Yankees. With the A's organization he handled public speaking and other promotional assignments; pitched batting practice; managed Wilmington, Delaware (Inter-State League), in 1940, Newport News (Virginia League) in 1941, and Savannah, Georgia (South Atlantic League), in 1946; scouted in 1945 and 1947–1950; and coached pitchers and catchers from 1951 to April 1954, when heart disease and cancer forced his withdrawal from spring training camp.

Throughout his life Bender developed expertise in such occupations as jeweler and diamond appraiser, watchmaker, and salesman of firearms, sporting goods, and men's clothing. Besides his favorite recreations, hunting and fishing, his natural athleticism led him to become an exceptional trapshooter, a rival to Christy Mathewson as baseball's best golfer, and a competitive billiards player. An educated, well-read man, he also was proficient as a painter in oils and as a gardener.

His overall major league statistics included a 212–127 won-lost total, 40 shutouts, and per game averages of 2.46 earned runs, 7.9 hits allowed, 2.1 bases on balls, and 5.1 strikeouts. These figures do not fully convey his value as a "money pitcher." Mack once said, "Whenever there is a game the fortunes of our club hang on, I send in the Chief, and he has delivered every time." Bender was elected to the National Baseball Hall of Fame in 1953. He died in Philadelphia.

• There are no biographies of Bender. The best articles are Robert Tholkes, "Chief Bender—The Early Years," *Baseball Research Journal* 12 (1983): 8–13; "Daguerreotypes: Charles Albert Bender," *Sporting News*, 21 Oct. 1937; and "Three and One, Looking Them Over with J. G. Taylor Spink" (two installments on Bender's career), *Sporting News*, 24, 31 Dec. 1942. Bender's playing record appears in *The Baseball Encyclopedia*, 9th ed. (1993); John Thorn and Pete Palmer, eds., *Total Baseball*, 3d ed. (1993), on which the statistics in this article were based; and Craig Carter, ed., *Daguerreotypes*, 8th ed. (1990), each volume indicating slightly different statistics. See also the Bender file in the National Baseball Hall of Fame Library, Cooperstown, New York. Obituaries are in the *Philadelphia Inquirer*, 23 May 1954; the *New York Times*, 23 May 1954; and the *Sporting News*, 2 June 1954.

FRANK VAN RENSSELAER PHELPS

BENDER, George Harrison (27 or 29 Sept. 1896–17 or 18 June 1961), U.S. congressman and senator, was born in Cleveland, Ohio, the son of Joseph Bender, an employee at General Electric, and Anna Sir. Bender attended West Commerce High School, graduating in 1914. With an early interest in politics, he at age fifteen collected 10,000 signatures on a petition encouraging former president Theodore Roosevelt to run for the presidency in 1912. Bender presented the petition to Roosevelt personally and was rewarded when Roosevelt wrote him with news of his candidacy for the Republican presidential nomination shortly before it was publicly announced. In 1916 Bender served as a delegate to the abortive Progressive party convention, which voted to dissolve rather than nominate its own presidential candidate. During the November election, Bender campaigned for Republican party candidates. His shifting party orientation reflected the internal divisions between "progressive" and "Old Guard" Republicans of the period from 1912 to 1916.

In 1920 he married Edna Eckhardt; they had two daughters. During his life and political career, Bender held a series of jobs and began a number of business ventures to support his family. His business career included stints as a department store advertising manager, manager of the Cleveland Stadium, and proprietor of a start-up business, the Bender Insurance Company. However, politics remained his only genuine interest. In 1920, as a Republican, he became the youngest person to win a seat in the Ohio Senate to that time. Serving until 1930, he had limited influence. He pushed unsuccessfully for the introduction of teacher tenure. Initially a strong supporter of Prohibition, his attitude changed when the police received an anonymous tip and raided his house in search of liquor. They found nothing, but Bender thereafter vehemently opposed the alcohol ban. In 1934 he founded the *National Republican* and the *Ohio Republican* magazines, which he also edited and published. After losing four bids for the U.S. House of Representatives in 1930, 1932, 1934, and 1936, he at last won in 1938. He was reelected until 1948, a Democratic electoral year. He won the seat back in 1950 and retained it for four more years.

Strongly opposed to President Franklin D. Roosevelt's foreign and domestic policies, Bender articulated his criticism in the polemical *The Challenge of 1940* (1940). The only aspects of Roosevelt's agenda that escaped Bender's censure were certain humanitarian New Deal programs, notably the Works Progress Administration, which he accepted only as a temporary measure. With the onset of the Cold War after 1945, Bender opposed the Marshall Plan and the Truman Doctrine. He did not question the necessity of helping European countries devastated by the war, but he disagreed with the idea that the U.S. government should take a direct role in channeling the relief aid. He argued that assistance for European recovery should come either through the United Nations or private relief organizations. He also fervently opposed aid to Greece and Turkey, where British influence had been strong, on the premise that U.S. involvement in the region only accommodated the "needs of a collapsing British empire" without benefiting the United States.

His reputation for strong party loyalty brought Bender the job of organizer for Ohio senator Robert Taft's candidacy for the presidential nomination at the 1948 and 1952 Republican National Conventions. His public role included arranging musical entertainment, conducting singing, leading demonstrations, and ringing cowbells. His often comic antics led to many unfairly dismissive jokes, as his opponents quickly dubbed him the "Clown Prince." This mockery did not diminish the fact that he remained a serious and influential political figure.

After Taft's death in 1953, Bender ran for and narrowly won the vacant Senate seat and served the remaining two years of its term. An avowed supporter of President Dwight D. Eisenhower, Bender consistently endorsed both Republican party and presidential initiatives. His earlier isolationist views softened considerably, and he now approved of more direct U.S. involvement abroad, including aid to countries of the former British empire. In 1956 he lost his Senate seat to Governor Frank J. Lausche, a popular Democrat. Bender then worked as special assistant to the secretary of the interior from June 1957 to May 1958, during which time he campaigned for the incorporation of Alaska as the forty-ninth state.

Bender's political career was clouded by allegations of corruption in his ties to the Teamsters' Union. He was accused of curtailing a 1956 investigation into the organization after receiving a $40,000 campaign contribution. In August 1958 union president Jimmy Hoffa hired Bender to investigate charges of corruption in the union at an initial fee of $250 a day. Subsequently this fee was lowered to $125 per week. The Senate Select Committee on Improper Practices in the Labor or Management Field looked into the accusations in autumn 1958 but recommended no actions. In his testimony during the hearings, Bender defended his behavior, saying: "When you run for office, you have to have the votes of the washed and the unwashed as well. If cats and dogs could vote I'd shake hands with them." He subsequently lost both a 1960 bid to be a delegate to the Republican National Convention and a 1961 campaign for the post of Republican precinct committeeman. Bender died in Chagrin Falls, a suburb of Cleveland.

• Bender's papers are in the Western Reserve Historical Society in Cleveland. His published speeches and articles include "The Poll Tax Disgrace," *Christian Century*, 23 July 1947; "Should the Voice of America Project Be Established by Congress?" *Congressional Digest*, Feb. 1948; and "A Faith for Fif-

ty-One," *Vital Speeches*, 1 July 1951. Two articles on Bender are "Noisiest Man on Capital Hill," *Saturday Evening Post*, 7 Aug. 1954, and "The Man with the Bell," *Newsweek*, 13 Sept. 1954. An obituary is in the *New York Times*, 19 June 1961.

ELIZABETH ZOE VICARY

BENDER, Lauretta (9 Aug. 1897–4 Jan. 1987), child psychiatrist, researcher, and educator, was born in Butte, Montana, the daughter of John Bender, a lawyer, and Katherine Irvine. Her father had moved to Montana to seek business opportunities with copper companies. Disappointed by failures, the Benders moved to Washington State and then to Hollywood, California. Bender repeated first grade three times because she suffered from a form of dyslexia. Her parents and teachers at first thought she was mentally defective but realized that she could learn by listening as well as by reading.

After that, Bender excelled in her classes. She especially liked biology in high school and considered a research career. After a year of college study, possibly in California, she transferred to the University of Chicago for her sophomore year; there she became interested in medicine. She earned her bachelor's degree in 1922 and finished a master's degree in pathology the next year. At the Rush Medical School in Chicago, she was a laboratory assistant, studying nervous system abnormalities. During graduate school, she became interested in psychiatry: "I was primarily interested in human beings and couldn't do research work with human behavior as my clinical material unless I had daily contact with patients. Research would then accumulate out of my medical practice" (Knapp, p. 83).

For medical school, Bender selected the State University of Iowa because of its neuropathology faculty. She was a research fellow in the psychopathic hospital, where Samuel T. Orton influenced her work with learning-disabled children. Bender completed her medical degree in 1926 and then spent one year in Amsterdam after receiving a Rockefeller Scholarship to study the physiology of the nervous system. She returned to the University of Chicago for a clinical residency in neurology at the Billings Hospital. At the Boston Psychopathic Hospital, Karl Bowman and C. MacFil Campbell worked with her and recommended her for advanced training at the Phipps Clinic of Johns Hopkins University Hospital.

By 1928 Bender had researched schizophrenia with Adolf Meyer, who was considered the dean of American psychiatry. In 1930 she met Paul Schilder, a Viennese psychiatrist and an associate of Freud who was visiting the clinic. Fifty years later, Bender recalled in an interview the precise time and place that she had met Schilder, admitting that she "immediately fell for him." Schilder accompanied Bender when she studied schizophrenic women who had been transferred from the clinic to Springfield State Hospital near Baltimore. She was beginning to devise tests for these uncommunicative patients.

When Schilder accepted an appointment at Bellevue Hospital in New York City, Bender took civil service examinations to secure a position at that hospital. She began as a staff member in 1930, and five years later she became the chief of PQ6, the children's unit. As the senior psychiatrist in charge of children's service, she became an authority on children's mental health. Bender's research focused on the causes of childhood schizophrenia, and she studied childhood suicide and violence.

Bender's New York environment inspired her to continue her most significant research. In 1931 she noted, "I became interested in the spontaneous production of children in the chalk drawings on sidewalks and the open pavements of parks" (*A Visual Motor Gestalt Test*, p. 14). Previously, she had adapted nine images designed by Max Wertheimer and showed them to "psychotic, regressed and defective schizophrenic patients" in the Springfield State Hospital. Bender repeated this test with adults and children at Bellevue. She realized that analysis of children's drawings could reveal delays in visual-motor and perceptual maturation.

By 1938 Bender had published *A Visual Motor Gestalt Test and Its Clinical Use*, a research monograph sponsored by the American Orthopsychiatric Association that outlined her Bender-Gestalt Visual Motor Test, a neuropsychological examination. Considered a "unique and important contribution to the field," the test presented a new approach for evaluation of patients. "Psychological experimentation often artificially disrupts perception and motility," Schilder explained in the book's preface. "This is avoided here by the simple expedient that the individual draws what he perceives." Both Bender and Schilder believed that drawings and paintings provided clues to personality problems. "All things are important in considering the cause and cure of any mentally sick child," Bender explained. "You must consider the brain structure and function, environmental factors, personality development, and heredity. In that way you can employ every available technique to do as much as possible for each child" (Knapp, p. 89). One assistant remarked that "the secret of [Bender's] success with children is that she gets down to their own level. She sits in their little chairs and digs down into their young minds and personalities for details that no one else would bother with, because she knows they are very important" (Knapp, pp. 89–90). Although her Gestalt procedure was used internationally and was critically acclaimed, Bender was disappointed by the misuse and interpretation of the test.

Bender married Schilder in November 1936; they had two sons and a daughter. Schilder credited Bender in his work, and together they attended meetings of Bellevue Hospital's Society of Psychotherapy and Psychopathology, known as the Schilder Society. Schilder was killed when he stepped into traffic after visiting Bender and their newborn daughter at the hospital. Because of the great need for doctors at Bellevue, Bender continued working, preparing her husband's manuscripts for posthumous publication. She retained their apartment and Long Island summer home and brought her children to work. Bender supervised shock treatments for schizophrenic children, wrote reports, evaluated diagnoses, and lectured at New York University, where she was a professor of clinical psychiatry and an associate attending psychiatrist at University Hospital.

Examining thousands of mentally ill children, Bender received grants from the National Institute of Mental Health and prolifically produced research articles and books, including several volumes for the Bellevue Studies of Child Psychiatry. Her *Child Psychiatric Techniques: Diagnostic and Therapeutic Approach to Normal and Abnormal Development through Patterned, Expressive, and Group Behavior* (1952) contains chapters from a manuscript, "Art and the Problem Child," that Bender wrote with Schilder before his death. They emphasized the role of art in revealing psychological issues and as a therapeutic method.

In 1953 Bender's *Aggression, Hostility and Anxiety in Children* was issued; in it she countered Freud's theory that aggression was due to a death instinct and primordial responses to frustration. Bender stated that aggression was simply a reaction to deprivation and that treatment "should be constructive or preventive, aiming at the amelioration of the developmental discrepancies" (p. 149). The next year she published *A Dynamic Psychopathology of Childhood*, revealing how psychopathological responses influence personality development. The final volume of the series, *Psychopathology of Childhood with Organic Brain Disorders*, appeared in 1956.

Bender received the 1955 Adolf Meyer Memorial Award in honor of her research of schizophrenic children. At that time, she was the director of the psychiatric research children's unit of Creedmor State Hospital in Queens Village, New York. Bender was appointed as the principal research scientist of child psychiatry in the New York State Mental Hygiene Department in 1955. She worked with the state until 1973, when she moved to Annapolis, Maryland. In 1968 Bender married Henry Banford Parks, a New York University history professor who died in 1973.

Bender taught at the University of Maryland and served as a consultant to the Children's Guild, Inc., and other groups for emotionally disturbed children as well as for the Anne Arundel County Board of Education. Throughout her career, Bender worked to improve institutional and foster care, helping to change policies regarding the adoption of infants across the country. She warned that the "basic reason for a psychopathic personality . . . is the lack of a parent-child relationship with some one adult during those first years" (Knapp, pp. 90–91). She affirmed that adoptive parents could not "compensate for the early deprivation, because the physiological patterns are set" in older children.

Encouraging women to pursue medical education, Bender's philosophy differed from many of her colleagues. She believed that a child psychiatrist should be "an active advocate, going wherever necessary to carry out this role." Bender wanted her students to formulate their own opinions even if they differed with hers, and she refused to take credit for her students' research. "As a psychiatrist, a wife, and a mother, I was able to combine my career with my family life," Bender stated. "I just did what I wanted to do from one stage to the next. . . . Though others may consider me as such, I do not consider myself as having been a pioneer in the area of women's liberation" (Shaskan and Roller, p. 33).

Bender was a member of the American Psychiatric Association, the American Neurological Association, the American Academy of Child Psychiatry, the American Association for the Advancement of Science, and the Citizen's Committee for Children of New York City, Inc. She died in an Annapolis, Maryland, nursing home.

• Bender's papers, primarily her correspondence, scrapbooks, and photographs, are held in the Brooklyn College Library's Special Collections. Alexander Tolor and Herbert C. Schulberg, *An Evaluation of the Bender-Gestalt Test* (1963), features a foreword by Bender. For further information see Stella Chess, "In Memoriam: A View of Lauretta Bender, 1899–1987," *Journal of the American Academy of Child and Adolescent Psychiatry* 26 (May 1987): 460–61; Sally Knapp, *Women Doctors Today* (1947); and Donald A. Shaskan and William L. Roller, *Paul Schilder: Mind Explorer* (1985).

ELIZABETH D. SCHAFER

BENDIRE, Charles Emil (27 Apr. 1836–4 Feb. 1897), naturalist and soldier, was born Karl Emil Bender at König im Odenwald in Hesse-Darmstadt (now in Germany). The identities of his parents are not known. At age twelve he began his studies at a theological seminary in Passy, France. Misconduct led to his departure five years later. In 1853 he immigrated to the United States and anglicized his name to Charles Bendire. The following year he joined the First Dragoons in the U.S. Army. During his second enlistment, which began in 1860, he became a sergeant and later hospital steward in the Fourth Cavalry.

In 1864 Bendire was commissioned a second lieutenant in the Second Infantry. Later that year he was transferred to the First Cavalry, where he was breveted first lieutenant "for gallant and meritorious services" at the battle of Trevillian Station, Virginia. He became a captain in 1873 and retired in 1886. In 1890 he was breveted major for gallant services in an 1877 action against the Nez Percé at Canyon Creek, Montana.

For most of his army life Bendire served in isolated posts in Arizona, California, Idaho, Montana, New Mexico, Oregon, and Washington. An avid hunter, he developed an interest in natural history, especially ornithology. After the Civil War he began to study and collect birds, eggs, and nests. Bendire's earliest writings were in the form of letters to prominent naturalists. The recipients of these descriptions—Joel A. Allen, Thomas M. Brewer, Elliott Coues, and Robert Ridgway (1850–1929)—published them in the *Bulletin of the Nuttall Ornithological Club*, *American Natu-*

ralist, and elsewhere beginning in 1872. In 1877 his articles appeared under his own name, chiefly in the *Auk* and *Ornithologist and Oölogist*. A few of his publications dealt with fish, mammals, and reptiles.

In the 1870s Bendire began donating specimens, mostly eggs, to the U.S. National Museum in Washington, D.C. His observations and collections, made in regions little known to scientists, were valued for the new information they provided on the ranges and habits of western birds. Among the new species he discovered is Bendire's thrasher, *Toxostoma bendirei*. He also established the first U.S. records of several other birds. Bendire was a founder of the American Ornithologists' Union and a member of its council.

While on leave from the army (1883–1884), Bendire served as honorary curator of the Department of Oölogy at the National Museum; he continued in this position after his retirement from the army until his death. During his tenure he meticulously arranged the museum's neglected accumulation of eggs and added to it his own collection of about 8,000.

As a writer, Bendire's major achievement was the *Life Histories of North American Birds*. He failed to complete all of the projected five or six volumes before he died. But the two volumes that were published (1892, 1896) contain information—much of it based upon his own investigations and those of his numerous correspondents—that is still valuable.

Aloof and brusque with strangers, he was helpful and warm-hearted to those who earned his respect. Bendire never married. He died in Jacksonville, Florida.

• The principal collections of Bendire's papers are in the Manuscript Division of the Library of Congress and the Archives of the Smithsonian Institution (Division of Birds, Data on Birds' Eggs and Nests, RU 1060102). The fullest account of Bendire's life is J. C. Merrill, "In Memoriam: Charles Emil Bendire," *Auk* 15 (Jan. 1898): 1–6. Other useful accounts are John Farrand, Jr., "Lieutenant Bendire's Thrasher," *American Birds* 44 (Fall 1990): 351–52, and C. Hart Merriam, "Charles E. Bendire," *Science*, n.s., 5 (12 Feb. 1897): 261–2. See also Elliott Coues, "Bibliographical Note," *Auk* 14 (July 1897): 327–9.

MICHAEL J. BRODHEAD

BENDIX, Vincent Hugo (12 Aug. 1881–27 Mar. 1945), engineer, inventor, and industrialist, was born in Moline, Illinois, the son of the Reverend Jan Bendix, a minister of the Swedish Methodist Episcopal church, and Alma Danielson. (The original family name, Bengtson, was changed to Bendix after Vincent's parents emigrated from Sweden.) At an early age Bendix moved with his family to Chicago. He had an early interest in mechanical inventions, and at age thirteen he designed a chainless bicycle. At age sixteen he left home for New York City, where he worked as an elevator operator, in a lawyer's office, and as a handyman in bicycle shops and garages. In 1901 he was hired by Glenn Curtiss, who was then building the Torpedo motorcycle. There Bendix designed and built an experimental motorcycle. He attended some night school classes in engineering, but his work experience laid his foundation in the automobile manufacturing business. Bendix married in 1902, but his wife's name is unknown. They had no children. He returned to Chicago about 1907 to work as a sales manager for the Holmsman Automobile Company.

In 1907 Bendix designed the Bendix Motor Buggy, which was called the Bendix "30." Although the enterprise was not a success, it convinced him that only the development of a mechanical starter would assure public acceptance of the motor car, especially among drivers who found hand cranking both inconvenient and hazardous.

An early electric starting motor was first introduced on the 1911 Cadillac, but it lacked a dependable mechanical link between the starting motor and the car's engine. Bendix was able to develop a workable transmission device to provide such a link, but it required, as a vital part, a triple thread screw that was difficult to produce economically and in volume.

In 1913 Bendix found that the Eclipse Machine Company of Elmira, New York, was manufacturing a bicycle coaster brake that used a triple thread screw of the kind he needed. Bendix negotiated with them, and in 1914 he gave them an exclusive license to manufacture his "transmission device for the starting of explosive motors." The device, which was marketed by Bendix under the slogan "the mechanical hand that cranks your car," was more commonly known as the "Bendix starter drive." It caught on quickly and in 1914 was installed in Chevrolet's Baby Grand touring car. From a small start of 5,500 drives in 1914 production grew to nearly 1.5 million by 1919.

In 1919 Bendix purchased the Winkler-Grimm Wagon Company facility in South Bend, Indiana, to build fire engines. When he lost out on a bid to market them, Bendix was forced to sell the plant. Nevertheless, he retained some of the nearby land, which later became the location for the future Bendix engineering works. Having divorced his first wife in 1920, Bendix in 1922 married Elizabeth Channon. They had no children and divorced in 1932.

In 1923 Bendix met Henri Perrot, an outstanding French engineer who was working on improvements in automotive brake equipment. Bendix negotiated with Perrot for the exclusive license to his shoe brake patents, as well as Perrot's interest in a brake linkage license he had granted to General Motors. With the completion of the agreement, Bendix founded the Bendix Engineering Works and was soon able to offer the American auto industry the first reliable four-wheel brake system. Bendix's continuing relations with Perrot and his subsequent contributions to the French automobile industry later led to his recognition, in 1936, by the French government, which made him knight of the Legion of Honor. In 1924 the Bendix Corporation offered its stock for public sale and that same year started manufacturing automobile brake systems in a new plant in South Bend.

In 1928 Bendix sought a majority interest in the Eclipse Machine Company. The conservative administrators of Eclipse were reluctant to deal further with Bendix because of his flamboyant lifestyle. The General Motors Corporation, however, which was at that time the largest customer for the Bendix starter drive, agreed to act as his agent in the transaction so that the deal could go through.

Over the next few years the Bendix Corporation expanded, acquiring more than 100 companies, corporations, and partnerships. Notable among these were the Scintilla Magneto Company, Pioneer Instrument Company, and Stromberg Carburetor Company. Bendix Automatic Laundry, however, was not affiliated with the corporation, although Bendix assisted the developers and let them use his name.

In 1929, although only 8 percent of the corporation's sales were in aviation products, Bendix realized the potential of the emerging aircraft industry and changed the name to the Bendix Aviation Corporation. The aviation business continued to boom until the Great Depression, when it and Bendix suffered financially. Research done by the Bendix Aviation Corporation during this period, however, led to many successful inventions and aeronautical developments that were key components in the superiority of American aircraft during World War II.

Bendix himself, however, did not fare well financially. He had a high lifestyle and invested heavily in various business ventures and real estate. His personal financial collapse came in June 1939, and all of his belongings had to be sold to pay off his bankruptcy debts.

Bendix was an amiable, energetic man with big ideas and extravagant tastes. In 1929 he contributed a large sum of money to finance a Sino-Swedish expedition to western and southwestern China. As a result, a magnificent model of the Golden Pavilion of Jehol was displayed at the 1933–1934 Chicago Century of Progress Exposition. For his support of the project, he was presented in 1929 with the insignia of the Order of the North Star by King Gustav of Sweden. He also established the Bendix Transcontinental Air Races in 1931. These flying events did much to popularize flying in the 1930s, as well as contributed technically to airplane development and design. In 1931 he was elected president of the Society of Automotive Engineers.

In 1937, after a series of financial setbacks and personnel problems, General Motors, which owned 25 percent of Bendix stock, began to take control of his corporation and changed its structure from a kind of holding company of wholly owned subsidiaries to an operating organization made up of divisions. Bendix remained as president and chair of the board of Bendix Aviation until the spring of 1942, when he finally resigned.

Undaunted, Bendix formed in 1944 a new corporation, Helicopter, Inc., later Bendix Helicopter, Inc., to develop a helicopter four-passenger sedan for production after the war. Bendix died at his home in New York City, and the project was never completed.

• The best narrative account of Bendix's activities is Rebecca Wolfe, "The Splash and Splendor of Vincent Bendix," Northern Indiana Historical Society, *St. Joseph Valley Record* 3, no. 2 (Fall 1990): 1–8. This is partially based on a manuscript by Menefree R. Clements, "King of Stop and Go, the Story of Bendix: A History, 1919–1963, in South Bend, Indiana" (1970), a draft copy of which is on deposit at the South Bend Public Library; it includes a fairly complete chronology of Vincent Bendix. The manuscript was sold to the Bendix Corporation and was never published. A shorter history of the Bendix Corporation is in A. P. Fontaine, *Where Ideas Unlock the Future: The Story of the Bendix Corporation* (1967). This is a printed address, presented by the then chair and chief executive officer of the Bendix Corporation. Some personal profiles of Bendix, including his financial problems and relations with the Bendix Corporation, are "Bendix, Sales Gladiator, Slays the Dragon Depression," *Sales Management*, 28 Nov. 1931, pp. 308–9; "Personalities in Industry," *Scientific American* 158, no. 5 (May 1938): 259; and "Biggest Blow," *Time*, 5 June 1939, pp. 73–74. Obituaries are in the *New York Times* and *South Bend Tribune*, both 28 Mar. 1945, and *SAE Journal* 53, no. 5 (May 1954): 27.

ROBERT J. HAVLIK

BENEDICT, Francis Gano (3 Oct. 1870–14 May 1957), chemist and physiologist, was born in Milwaukee, Wisconsin, the son of Washington Gano Benedict, a businessman, and Harriet Emily Barrett. In about 1878 the family moved to Orange Park, Florida, and in 1881 to Boston, Massachusetts, where Benedict attended public schools and took piano lessons because of his parents' interest in music.

After attending a lecture in Boston by chemist and assayer James Francis Babcock on "A Basket of Coal" when he was thirteen, Benedict became interested in chemistry and began experiments in his home basement. He completed high school in 1888 and studied chemistry for a year at the Massachusetts College of Pharmacy before entering Harvard University. There he took courses from the distinguished chemist Josiah Parsons Cooke, who in about 1850 had founded the Harvard chemistry department. While an undergraduate, Benedict also was an instructor at the College of Pharmacy from 1892 to 1894 and assistant to Cooke in 1893–1894. He received an A.B. in 1893 and an A.M. in 1894. He then went to Heidelberg University for a year of graduate study, mostly with chemist Viktor Meyer, and received a Ph.D. in 1895.

On his return to the United States that year Benedict began work in Middletown, Connecticut, with Wilbur Olin Atwater, who held positions in chemistry and nutrition with several organizations. Benedict soon became involved in these, which drew him into physiology. He began in 1895 as research assistant to Atwater in the chemistry department of Wesleyan University, where he advanced to instructor in 1896 and to professor in 1905. He was also physiological chemist for the U.S. Department of Agriculture from 1895 to 1907, and chemist at Storrs Experiment Station from 1896 to 1900. Benedict married Cornelia Golay in 1897; they had one child.

Benedict published more than twenty-five papers during the years at Middletown, several of them with Atwater. The two scientists began with studies of metabolism in humans, by means of equipment created by Benedict to measure oxygen consumption and heat of the body. He later said that this respiration calorimeter, "developed from the ground up," was "the most important mechanical contribution I have been privileged to make" (DuBois and Riddle, p. 69). It made possible precise measurements of heat production and loss in animals, including humans. With Atwater, Benedict also published "An Experimental Inquiry Regarding the Nutritive Value of Alcohol" (National Academy of Sciences, vol. 8, *Memoir 6* [1902], pp. 233–397), the first of several papers on alcohol, and he held a lifelong antipathy to its use.

Benedict's published results on oxygen, nitrogen, and other aspects of human metabolism drew the attention of physicians. Among them were John Shaw Billings, William Williams Keen, and William Henry Welch, who persuaded the Carnegie Institution of Washington to establish in Boston in 1907 a Nutrition Laboratory, to which Benedict was appointed director. Early that year, while the laboratory was under construction, Benedict traveled to Europe to confer with physiologists on their techniques and equipment. Funding for the new laboratory was generous, and its results could be published in long monographs financed by Carnegie Institution.

At Carnegie's Nutrition Laboratory, Benedict devised new equipment, including a smaller instrument for measuring oxygen consumption in humans. When, in about 1911, physiologist Eugene F. DuBois built a similar machine using Benedict's design, he found the equipment and methods of calculation "extraordinarily accurate" (DuBois and Riddle, p. 70). With colleagues, Benedict undertook studies on the production of heat and its regulation in humans of all ages and under assorted conditions of working, exercising, and eating or fasting. For forty years Benedict was known for his keen observation and accuracy of measurements. He defined basal metabolism in humans by gender, age, height, and weight and made comparisons of variations such as individuals with diabetes or thyroid problems. Some of his researches were on specific racial groups: "browns and blacks" in Jamaica, Mayans in Yucatan, Chinese in Manchuria and Szechwan, Samoans, and various races in Hawaii. From his studies of various categories he determined a basal metabolism in humans. With J. A. Harris he wrote "A Biometric Study of Basal Metabolism in Man" (Carnegie Institution of Washington, *Monograph No. 279* [1919]). Benedict also carried out studies on pigeons and doves, dogs, rats, woodchucks in and out of hibernation, beef steers, sheep, goats, chimpanzees, elephants, pythons, and alligators. All of these differed from humans.

Benedict's wife, who had a degree in zoology, participated in some of his work and was a coauthor on several papers. Benedict summarized much of his research on humans in *Vital Energetics: A Study of Comparative Basal Metabolism* (1938). His work on animals was published as "Animal Metabolism from Mouse to

Elephant" (a chapter in *Science in Progress*, ed. G. A. Baitsell [1939]), as well as in several papers. He also published "The Composition of the Atmosphere, with Special Reference to Its Oxygen Content" (Carnegie Institution of Washington, *Monograph 166* [1912]), which he considered his most significant work in chemistry.

Benedict visited Europe often, published in foreign journals, and maintained correspondence abroad. He was elected to the National Academy of Sciences in 1914. The National Institute of Social Sciences awarded him a medal in 1917 for "his valuable contributions to human energetics and the alcohol problem," and he received a gold medal from the University of Hamburg in 1929 for his contributions in metabolism and physiology.

When Benedict retired from the Nutrition Laboratory in 1937, he carried out his announced intent to end scientific researches and moved to Machiasport, Maine. A member of the Society of American Magicians, he enjoyed magic tricks and piano playing as hobbies. He died in Machiasport.

Equipment that Benedict developed for measuring oxygen consumption, carbon dioxide production, and heat production and its regulation in humans (as well as other vertebrates) became standard in the medical profession. His researches, which were fundamental in establishing a determination of basal metabolism in humans and in identifying factors that affected it, enabled later researchers to advance the field of physiology.

• A small amount of archival material on Benedict is at the Carnegie Institution of Washington. The Nutrition Laboratory closed in 1945. Biographies are Oscar Riddle, "Francis Gano Benedict," *American Philosophical Society Yearbook for 1957* (1958), pp. 109–13, and Eugene F. DuBois and Oscar Riddle, "Francis Gano Benedict," National Academy of Sciences, *Biographical Memoirs* 32 (1958): 66–99, with bibliography. An obituary is in the *New York Times*, 16 May 1957.

ELIZABETH NOBLE SHOR

BENEDICT, Ruth Fulton (5 June 1887–17 Sept. 1948), cultural anthropologist, was born in New York City, the daughter of homeopathic physician Frederick Fulton and Vassar graduate Bertrice Shattuck. Her father died in 1889, and Benedict spent her early childhood on the farm of her maternal grandparents near Norwich, New York. She was influenced by life on the farm and by four years in the Midwest where her mother supported the family by teaching in Missouri and in 1896 as Lady Principal (director of the girls' division) of Pillsbury Academy in Owatonna, Minnesota. Two years later, her mother took a job as superintendent of circulation at the public library in Buffalo, New York.

When Benedict entered school it was discovered that she had trouble hearing, a result of having had measles. Her family had considered her a moody child who would not answer at times when called and who was prone to unpredictable and violent tantrums, which could be effects of the hearing loss. Benedict as an adult attributed her moodiness to psychological causes, particularly withdrawal and anger as responses to the early death of her father and her mother's explosive outpouring of grief. Benedict described herself as growing up identifying with her father and thus as being fascinated by death, while psychologically she rejected her mother. It was an insightful but limited view, given her hearing problems and considering cultural influences of the late nineteenth century, an age fascinated with death and in which middle-class women were rejecting the world of their mothers and embracing the more public world of their fathers.

Benedict graduated from Vassar College in 1909 and was given an unexpected opportunity to spend a year on the Grand Tour of Europe with two other young women. She then became a paid social worker for the Charity Organization Society in Buffalo. Next she taught at private girls' schools in California until her marriage to biochemist Stanley Benedict in 1914.

From 1914 to 1918 the Benedicts lived in the New York City suburbs. She studied dance, attempted various writing projects, including a study of Mary Wollstonecraft, Margaret Fuller, and Olive Schreiner, and did volunteer work. In 1918 she enrolled at Columbia University, studying under John Dewey. At the New School for Social Research she also took courses taught by Elsie Clews Parsons and Alexander Goldenweiser and discovered anthropology. Helped by their recommendations, she did graduate work in anthropology at Columbia University under Franz Boas, receiving her Ph.D. in 1923.

For the next eight years Benedict existed on the fringes of academic life, receiving a two-year research fellowship funded by Parsons and holding part-time and temporary appointments at Columbia and Barnard College. In 1925 she became editor of the *Journal of American Folklore*, a position she held until 1940, which provided a small but steady salary and some professional recognition.

On her first field trip, to the Serrano of California in 1922, she recovered information slowly being lost as the Serrano adapted to modern American civilization. Her trip to the southwestern Zuni in 1924 to collect mythology and observe Zuni life was her first contact with a largely intact and unassimilated Native-American culture. She returned the next summer and also spent some time at Cochiti Pueblo. In 1927 she studied aspects of the Cochiti, Pima, and Mojave cultures.

In the 1920s she published "The Vision in Plains Culture" (1922), *The Concept of the Guardian Spirit in North America* (1923), originally her dissertation, and an article on the Serrano. But since the chance for an academic career seemed small, Benedict seriously considered becoming a poet. She met Louise Bogan, Leonie Adams, and other poets, and anthropologist Edward Sapir, himself a poet, also encouraged her. Her poems were published in small magazines, but after a collection was rejected for publication in 1928, she ceased to try to make a career in poetry.

In 1931, through Boas's efforts, Benedict was appointed assistant professor of anthropology at Columbia. She had separated from her husband in 1930. They had grown apart, and both of them had had extramarital affairs in the 1920s, she exploring heterosexual boundaries with her colleague Margaret Mead. Mead and Benedict remained friends all their lives, but by 1931 Benedict had met another woman with whom she lived for the next seven years, Natalie Raymond.

In 1934 Benedict published *Patterns of Culture*, one of the most influential American books of the first half of the twentieth century. In it she used the metaphor of Apollonian and Dionysian cultures to explain her idea of cultural configurations or underlying mental patterns that guide a culture; she also employed psychological characterizations of some configurations as paranoid or megalomaniac. Benedict introduced American readers to the range of possible solutions to cultural problems and issues and the relativity of cultural responses, emphasizing a nonjudgmental attitude. *Patterns of Culture* popularized the anthropological ideas of culture and cultural relativity and made them important concepts in American thinking. While explaining other cultures' underlying patterns, the book suggested new values and beliefs for twentieth-century Americans, including the central role of relativity, the potential coexistence of Chaos and Order, the importance of culture over biology, the rejection of absolute values and moral judgments, and the need to reinterpret relationships between men and women. It further argued that normality and abnormality were relative; for example, that homosexuality might be accepted as normal in one culture, abnormal in another.

Patterns of Culture helped create the Culture and Personality school in anthropology, which greatly influenced American anthropological studies in the 1930s and 1940s and provided an alternative model to British functionalism for studying cultures. The book also precipitated a kind of identity crisis in anthropology as to if and how the discipline should be defined and which methodologies were legitimate to use.

During the 1930s Benedict became increasingly responsible for the Columbia anthropology department as Boas approached retirement. Students and colleagues described her as a woman of remarkable competence and beauty. The psychologist Abraham Maslow, who met her in the 1930s, later used her as one model in working out his idea of the self-actualized person. But when Boas retired she was passed over as anthropology department chair.

Benedict led a teaching field trip in 1931 to the Mescalero Apache in the Southwest and another in 1939 to the Blackfoot and the Blood in the Northwest. She published her best-known mythological work, *Zuni Mythology*, in 1935. As an anthropologist Benedict put much energy into fighting racist ideas emanating from Nazi Germany under the guise of science. *Race: Science and Politics* (1940) dealt with stereotypes about race by presenting what was scientifically known on the subject and analyzing the causes of racism. She became acquainted with psychoanalyst Karen Horney in the 1930s and influenced the ideas of the Neo-Cul-

tural School of Psychoanalysis that Horney created. Benedict's relationship with Natalie Raymond ended sometime in 1938, and in 1939, while on sabbatical, she became involved with psychologist Ruth Valentine in a relationship that lasted for the rest of Benedict's life.

During World War II Benedict worked for the Office of War Information (OWI) preparing materials explaining Allied cultures to American soldiers and writing memoranda on ways to understand and influence enemy cultures. She also wrote a Public Affairs pamphlet, *Races of Mankind* (1943), with anthropologist Gene Weltfish. This pamphlet created a sensation when Kentucky Congressman Andrew J. May tried to block its distribution, complaining because it claimed that some African Americans were more intelligent than some Euro-Americans, including Kentuckians. The pamphlet led to a cartoon movie on race, a comic book, and a children's book under Benedict's and Weltfish's names.

After the war Benedict used information she had gathered in the OWI to write *The Chrysanthemum and the Sword* (1946), her book on Japanese culture that was read by American policymakers and that helped shape the postwar American image of the Japanese. She returned to teaching at Columbia and in 1947 organized a major project, Research in Contemporary Cultures, to study the cultures of modern nations, an idea that became popularly known as national character study. This was a controversial project because of the complexity and difficulty involved in studying a modern nation instead of a native people. She was elected president of the American Anthropological Association for 1947, and in 1948 she became a full professor at Columbia. She went to Europe in the summer of 1948 to participate in a UNESCO conference. Shortly after her return, she died in New York City before the project was completed.

• The Ruth Fulton Benedict Papers, Special Collections, Vassar College Library, Poughkeepsie, N.Y., contain the bulk of Benedict's known personal and professional papers. The Margaret Mead Papers at the Library of Congress contain information on Research in Contemporary Cultures and other aspects of Benedict's life. The Franz Boas Papers, at the American Philosophical Society in Philadelphia but also available on microfilm, contain letters from and about Benedict and her anthropological colleagues. The Elsie Clews Parsons Papers, also at the American Philosophical Society, contain letters and other material, particularly on Benedict as editor of the *Journal of American Folklore*. The Guernsey Memorial Library, Norwich, N.Y., keeps files on local families including the Shattucks and the Fultons, which contain articles from local newspapers of the period and other information. Margaret Mead, ed., *An Anthropologist at Work: Writings of Ruth Benedict* (1959), remains the classic reference work on Benedict, providing selections of letters, both published and previously unpublished articles, poetry, private journal passages, and a chronology of her life, all tied together by four biographical essays by Mead from various perspectives of Benedict's life. Ruth Limmer, ed., *What the Woman Lived: Selected Letters of Louise Bogan, 1920–1970* (1973), contains letters from Bogan to Benedict. Three good biographies of Benedict are Margaret M. Caffrey, *Ruth Benedict: Stranger in This Land* (1989); Judith Modell, *Ruth Benedict: Patterns of a Life* (1983); and Margaret Mead, *Ruth Benedict* (1974). Modell approaches Benedict as an anthropologist, while Caffrey puts Benedict in the intellectual and cultural context of her time. Mead's short book gives an overview of Benedict's life, including some of her writings. Mary Catherine Bateson, *With a Daughter's Eye: A Memoir of Margaret Mead and Gregory Bateson* (1984), talks of Mead's relationship with Benedict.

MARGARET M. CAFFREY

BENEDICT, Stanley Rossiter (17 Mar. 1884–21 Dec. 1936), biochemist, was born in Cincinnati, Ohio, the son of Wayland Richardson Benedict, a professor of philosophy and psychology at the University of Cincinnati, and Anne Elizabeth Kendrick, a teacher and author. As a boy, Benedict planned on medicine as a profession and entered the University of Cincinnati in 1902 with that goal in mind. Chemistry classes, however, piqued his interest, especially those with Junius F. Snell, the renowned analytical chemist who had himself worked with Wilbur O. Atwater in studying the chemical composition of foods and the energy requirements of human beings. As a consequence, Benedict began a productive career in analytical and biological chemistry by publishing his first paper (with Professor Snell) in 1903 when he was only nineteen, followed by nine others, all but one devoted to inorganic analyses, prior to receiving his bachelor's degree in 1906.

His graduate training was done at Yale's Sheffield School of Science, where he received his Ph.D. in 1908 under the supervision of Lafayette B. Mendel, an excellent physiological chemist of the time. During this period Benedict published three more papers, the first of which launched his career in biochemistry ("The Detection and Estimation of Reducing Sugars," *Journal of Biological Chemistry* 3 [1907]: 101–17). Within a few years he had developed the famous Benedict's Solution, used by generations of students, medical practitioners, and clinical laboratories to determine the glucose content of bodily fluids.

After one year as an instructor in chemistry at Syracuse University and another as an associate in biochemistry at Columbia University, Benedict moved to Cornell University Medical College in New York City, starting as assistant professor of chemical pathology in 1910. Two years later he was appointed to Cornell's department of chemistry, becoming professor and chairman in 1913, a position he retained until his death. Having written or coauthored nearly thirty papers by 1913, the direction of Benedict's future was clear. He focused his energies on teaching and research, sharing credit generously for works accomplished with a host of graduate students and a number of colleagues. "As a teacher . . . he stimulated colleagues, aroused the interest of students in the chemical aspects of physiology and medicine, encouraged honest ability, and fought sham and hypocrisy" (Shaffer, p. 1).

With respect to his research interests, Benedict concentrated on three areas: analytical biochemistry, nutrition, and the chemical aspects of cancer growth. In biochemical analyses, Benedict became known as both an innovator and as an improver of methods developed by others, especially those of Otto Folin, an older contemporary at Harvard's Medical School. So intertwined were these men in their efforts to develop analytical procedures to determine small amounts of non-protein substances in blood and urine that biochemist Elmer McCollum wrote in 1952, "In respect to knowledge of metabolism, historians will discuss the state of this department of science as it existed before and after Folin and Benedict" (p. 155). Folin and Benedict were certain that animal metabolism and pathology could be better understood by relating both normal and abnormal health to the presence (or absence) in blood and urine of specific chemical substances such as glucose, uric acid, creatine, and creatinine. More than a third of Benedict's papers are concerned with these substances (see, for example, "Uric Acid in Its Relation to Metabolism," *Journal of Laboratory and Clinical Medicine* 2 [1916]: 1–15). In his role as an improver he once wrote, "Folin . . . presents some material which may . . . confuse the subject of uric acid determination." Still, with his characteristic fairness, he wrote in a later part of the same paper, "Certainly, Folin's new standard [of uric acid] appears to be worthy of study" ("The Determination of Uric Acid," *Journal of Biological Chemistry* 54 [1922]: 233–38).

In the area of nutrition, Benedict was caught up in the then-current enthusiasm over vitamins. He examined the effects of radiation on the vitamins of yeast, investigated the adequacy of synthetic diets for pigeons, and studied the nutritive properties of the banana, particularly in its ability to serve as a carbohydrate and possible vitamin source for albino rats.

Benedict's many years of research into the chemistry of cancers was initially founded on his belief that diet had a significant effect on cancer growth (see, for example, "Studies in the Influence of Various Factors in Nutrition upon the Growth of Experimental Tumors," *Journal of Cancer Research* 2 [1917]: 159–78). Later he joined the ranks of other researchers who believed that the use of colloidal suspensions of heavy metals might retard malignant growths. This dietary, chemotherapeutic approach led to the testing of nearly one hundred chemical agents and, while positive results were obtained in some animals, no material was effective in treating humans. Nevertheless, such research efforts by Benedict and others helped to define the biochemical complexities of cancers and, by showing what procedures were ineffective, opened the door for different tactics that ultimately would prove to be beneficial in treating some human cancers and tumors.

Benedict wrote no textbooks or reference works. However, commencing about 1908 he served as a reviewer for *Chemical Abstracts*, and from 1912 on he supervised that journal's section on biochemistry. In addition, he was associated with the *Journal of Biological*

Chemistry almost from its inception, becoming an associate editor in 1920 and managing editor in 1925. As an editor of this journal he was able to assist a large number of researchers in clarifying not only their writing skills but also the directions of their research.

Given his teaching load and research projects coupled to his editorial responsibilities, Benedict had little time for recreational activities. He spent summers in either New Hampshire or his home in Elmsford, New York, occupying himself with amateur photography and reading philosophy. In 1914 he married Ruth Fulton, a Vassar graduate who, after a few years of marriage, obtained her Ph.D. in anthropology from Columbia University and went on to become the famous ethnologist, Ruth Benedict. The Benedicts had no children and eventually separated in 1923, keeping up a cordial relationship until he died at his home in Elmsford.

Benedict's nearly thirty years in biochemistry were highlighted by his development of Benedict's Solution, used principally to detect small concentrations of reducing sugars; by his career-long efforts to develop and improve analytical biochemical procedures; by his investigations into the relationships between diet and disease; and lastly, by his stewardship of the *Journal of Biological Chemistry*, whereby he strongly influenced not only the journal's style but also the directions of research of the journal's contributors.

• There are no known repositories of Stanley R. Benedict's papers. In addition to his publications cited in the text, some other publications that reveal Benedict's interests and skills include, with Emil Osterberg, "Studies in Creatine and Creatinine Metabolism, III: On the Origin of Urinary Creatine," *Journal of Biological Chemistry* 18 (1914): 195–214; with Kanematsu Sugiura, "A Critical Study of Vitamin A and Carcinogenesis," *Journal of Cancer Research* 14 (1930): 306–10; and with Ruth C. Theis, "A Modification of the Molybdate Method for the Determination of Inorganic Phosphorus in Serum," *Journal of Biological Chemistry* 61 (1924): 63–66.

A good biographical sketch is Elmer V. McCollum, "Stanley Rossiter Benedict, 1884–1936," National Academy of Sciences, *Biographical Memoirs* 27 (1952): 155–77, which includes a nearly complete listing of all of Benedict's writings. Another source that affords clues as to Benedict's personality and work habits is the Ruth Benedict Collection, Special Collections, Vassar College Libraries, Poughkeepsie, N.Y.

Obituary articles of significance are those of H. D. Dakin, "Stanley R. Benedict," *Science* 85 (1937): 65–66; James Ewing and George Holmes, "Resolutions Adopted by the Medical Board, 29 Dec. 1936, Memorial Hospital [later Memorial Sloan-Kettering Cancer Center], 'Stanley Rossiter Benedict, 1884–1936,'"; and Philip A. Shaffer, "Stanley Rossiter Benedict," *Journal of Biological Chemistry* 117 (1937): three unnumbered pages preceding p. 429.

STANLEY L. BECKER

BENÉT, Stephen Vincent (22 July 1898–13 Mar. 1943), writer, was born in Bethlehem, Pennsylvania, the son of James W. Benét, a career officer in the U.S. Army, and Frances Neill Rose. The Benét household was extremely literary. Benét's father, whose military specialty was ordnance, loved to read, recite, and discuss poetry. Writing some years after his death, Benét said

of his father, "He was interested in everything from the Byzantine emperors to the development of heavy ordnance, and was the finest critic of poetry I have ever known." Benét's mother was also an avid reader and the author of occasional verse. His brother, William Rose Benét, and his sister, Laura Benét, both became poets and writers of considerable stature.

Benét's childhood was spent in a series of army base homes in several parts of the United States: five years in Watervliet, New York; a year in Illinois; six years in Benicia, California; and four years in Augusta, Georgia. At the age of three, he contracted scarlet fever, which impaired his eyesight and his health for the rest of his life. His early education was conducted at home, through a system of lessons by correspondence. At the suggestion of a doctor who said he needed more social stimulation, Benét was sent at the age of twelve to the Hitchcock Military Academy in Jacinto, California. The physical bullying and humiliation he suffered there made it a traumatic experience for him, a fact that became clear when he wrote about it years later in his novel *The Beginning of Wisdom* (1921) and in several short stories. He escaped the ordeal of the military academy after one year, when the Benét family moved to his father's new command, the Augusta Arsenal in Georgia. There Benét spent four years at the Summerville Academy, a much happier time for him. He handled the schoolwork with ease and had time to read his favorite authors—William Makepeace Thackeray, Joseph Conrad, Rudyard Kipling, William Morris, Christina and Dante Gabriel Rossetti, G. K. Chesterton, and others. He wrote poetry in great abundance and with remarkable success. When he was thirteen, a poem of his won a prize from the St. Nicholas League; the next year, his ballad about Robin Hood, "A Song of the Woods," won another prize and was published in *St. Nicholas Magazine*. In 1915, before he was seventeen, he sold his first poem to the *New Republic*; a few months after that, his first book of poetry, *Five Men and Pompey*, was published by a Boston company.

After failing entrance examinations in Latin and mathematics and then passing them on a second attempt, Benét entered Yale University at the age of seventeen. Although his background was rather different from that of most Ivy League students, he was soon accepted into undergraduate literary circles at Yale and eventually became their brightest star. He was a mediocre student but an avid reader of poetry and history and a convivial member of the Elizabethan Club and other undergraduate social groups. He wrote for both the student literary magazine and the student humor magazine and became an editor for both. He won a number of literary prizes at Yale, including the honor of having his *Young Adventure: A Book of Poems* published in the Yale Series of Younger Poets in 1918. At the same time, he found success with his poetry beyond the academic world, publishing in the *New Republic*, *Century Magazine*, and *Seven Arts*.

In 1918, after the United States entered the First World War, Benét left school and tried repeatedly to enlist in the army. Rejected because of his poor eye-sight, he resorted to memorizing an eye examination chart and managed to have himself sworn in. The severity of his myopia was quickly discovered, however, and he was discharged after only three days. Determined to contribute to the war effort, he went to work for the State Department, where again his eyesight was a handicap. He resigned from his post shortly after the armistice in 1918 and returned to Yale, where, in 1919, he received his B.A. After three months working as an advertising copywriter in New York, Benét reentered Yale for graduate study. He received his M.A. in 1920, his graduate thesis consisting of a group of poems that were published as *Heavens and Earth* by a commercial publisher the same year.

Benét's year as a graduate student was irregular from a traditional academic point of view, for he took little interest in the formal study of literary history; but it was productive for him as a fledgling professional writer. His favorite course was Henry Seidel Canby's English 40, in which students were encouraged to write in numerous forms or genres, with their eyes on commercial markets. Benét continued to place his poetry in a variety of magazines; he started his first novel; he collaborated with Monty Woolley, a Yale faculty member who later became a successful actor, on an acting version of Christopher Marlowe's *Tamburlaine the Great* (1919); he helped to found the literary little magazine *S4N*; and he sold his first short stories to *Munsey's* and *Smart Set*.

In the summer of 1920, having received a traveling fellowship from Yale, Benét made his first trip to Paris, where he enrolled at the Sorbonne and worked on his poetry and fiction. It was in Paris that he met Rosemary Carr, whom he married when the couple returned to the United States in 1921. Their marriage lasted the rest of Benét's life; they had three children.

Benét's first novel, *The Beginning of Wisdom*, was published in 1921, soon followed by *Young People's Pride* (1922) and *Jean Huguenot* (1923). More importantly for his reputation as a poet, his "The Ballad of William Sycamore" was published in 1922 in the *New Republic*, and the 200-line "King David" appeared in the *Nation*. "The Ballad of William Sycamore," about a mythical pioneer, hunter, and farmer, was especially important for Benét, because it was his first success at celebrating the American past in a popular style loosely derived from folklore. "The Mountain Whippoorwill" (1925), a ballad subtitled "How Hill-Billy Jim Won the Great Fiddler's Prize," was another early success of his in this vein.

Neither his novels nor his early achievements in poetry brought Benét financial security, and he had to work hard at his writing to support himself and his family. Under the guidance of his literary agent Carl Brandt, he wrote formula short stories for magazines; he reviewed books and plays; he collaborated with John Farrar, his friend from Yale, on two unsuccessful stage dramas. He also completed his fourth novel, *Spanish Bayonet* (1926), a historical romance set in eighteenth-century Florida.

In 1925 Benét won a $2,500 grant from the Guggenheim Foundation to support the research and writing of a long historical poem on the Civil War, the poem that became Benét's magnum opus, *John Brown's Body*. Benét went to Paris to work on the book because, he said, living there was cheaper than it was at home. He conducted extensive research for the poem, much of it primary examination of diaries, memoirs, letters, and military records. In something less than two years, he compiled massive historic information on the Civil War and distilled from it a kind of modern epic in some 15,000 lines.

Doubleday, Doran and Company published *John Brown's Body* on 8 August 1928, and it was an immediate critical and popular success. Long portions of the poem were soon adapted for performance in lecture halls and theaters and on the radio. Within two years it had sold more than 130,000 copies and reached heights of popularity that no American poem had achieved since Henry Wadsworth Longfellow's *Evangeline* (1847) and *The Song of Hiawatha* (1855). *John Brown's Body* made Benét a national celebrity virtually overnight, the best-known living poet in the United States. It won the Pulitzer Prize for poetry in 1929.

In writing about the Civil War in verse that was graceful, accessible, and sometimes stirring, Benét had tapped a subject of great interest to many Americans. Admirers of the poem from all sections of the country wrote to him in appreciation for the sympathetic view he took of both his northern and his southern characters. In its first two years, the poem netted Benét about $25,000 in royalties—most of which he lost in the stock market crash of 1929.

Benét went to Hollywood in 1929 and wrote the script for D. W. Griffith's film *Abraham Lincoln*. But he disliked the movie-studio system of writing by committee and left Hollywood permanently when his twelve-week contract was fulfilled.

Benét continued to celebrate elements of the American past in popular forms, often in a style based on the oral folktale or the folk ballad. In this vein, he produced some of his most successful short stories, such as "Johnny Pye and the Fool-Killer" (1937), "The Devil and Daniel Webster" (1937), and "Doc Mellhorn and the Pearly Gates" (1938); and, with his wife Rosemary Carr Benét, *A Book of Americans* (1933), a series of lighthearted poems for children about such figures as Thomas Jefferson, Daniel Boone, Jesse James, Cotton Mather, and John James Audubon.

The fame and prestige Benét had gained with *John Brown's Body* made him greatly in demand as a literary leader and spokesman. He was elected to the National Institute of Arts and Letters in 1929 and to the American Academy of Arts and Letters in 1938. In 1933 he became editor of the Yale Series of Younger Poets, a position he held for the rest of his life. He wrote book reviews for the *New York Herald Tribune* and the *Saturday Review of Literature*. He advised publishing houses and young writers; he lectured widely and appeared at numerous writers' conferences.

The Great Depression, the rise of fascism in Europe, and the emergence of demagogues such as Huey Long and Father Charles E. Coughlin in the United States prompted Benét, for the first time, to write poetry and fiction with an angry political edge to it. He wrote a number of "nightmare" poems, expressing apocalyptic visions of social collapse, such as "Metropolitan Nightmare" (1933), "Litany for Dictatorships" (1935), "Ode to Walt Whitman" (1935), and "Ode to the Austrian Socialists" (1936) (many of which were collected in the book *Burning City* [1936]), and several short stories with conspicuous political themes, such as "Silver Jemmy" (1936), "The Blood of Martyrs" (1936), and "Into Egypt" (1939). He also published his fourth novel, *James Shore's Daughter* (1934), a critical portrayal of American plutocrats. Benét's politics were based on two fundamental themes: he favored Franklin Delano Roosevelt's New Deal, and he opposed all forms of totalitarianism.

During the 1930s Benét's health, which had never been strong, declined. In 1930 he suffered debilitating attacks of arthritis of the spine, an ailment that made much of the remaining thirteen years of his life a period of great physical discomfort. In 1939 he was hospitalized for several weeks with nervous exhaustion.

When the Second World War broke out in Europe, Benét threw himself into the task of building American national morale and of writing what he frankly called propaganda for the Allied cause. He belonged to or supported the Council for Democracy, the Civil Liberties Union, the Writers War Board, and numerous other patriotic organizations. He wrote scripts for the radio series *This Is War* and *Dear Adolf*. In 1943, at the request of the Office of War Information, he wrote a 40,000-word history of the United States, titled *America*, for publication throughout the world. In the midst of a heavy schedule of writing and public appearances, he died of a heart attack at his home in New York City.

Soon after his death, Farrar and Rinehart published *Western Star* (1943), the first book of Benét's projected nine-book narrative poem about the European settlement of North America, on which he had been working intermittently since 1937. *Western Star* won the Pulitzer Prize for poetry in 1944.

During the 1930s and 1940s, Benét was one of the best-known and most widely read American poets, respected by critical reviewers and honored in poetry workshops and university lecture halls. His poems and short stories on popular subjects from American myth and history were read, studied, anthologized, and adapted to the stage and screen. At their best, they constitute a kind of high folk art. *John Brown's Body* and collections of his better-known short stories have remained uninterruptedly in print. However, his work is seldom still included in anthologies of serious literature or studied in college literature classes. Ultimately, he will be remembered as a talented writer of middlebrow literature, comparable to Longfellow, Carl Sandburg, and Vachel Lindsay.

• Benét's papers are in the Beinecke Library at Yale University. The full-length biography is Charles A. Fenton, *Stephen Vincent Benét: The Life and Times of a Man of Letters, 1898–1943* (1958). The most nearly complete bibliography is Gladys Louise Maddocks, "Stephen Vincent Benét: A Bibliography," *Bulletin of Bibliography and Dramatic Index* 20 (Sept. 1951): 142–46; 20 (Apr. 1952): 158–60. See also Charles Fenton, ed., *Selected Letters of Stephen Vincent Benét* (1960); Parry Stroud, *Stephen Vincent Benét* (1962); and George Abbe, *Stephen Vincent Benét on Writing* (1964).

JOHN GRIFFITH

BENÉT, William Rose (2 Feb. 1886–4 May 1950), poet and editor, was born in Fort Hamilton, New York, the son of James Walker Benét, an army ordnance officer, and Frances Neill Rose. He attended the Sheffield Scientific School at Yale University, graduating in 1907. While at Yale, Benét edited the *Yale Record* and the *Yale Courant*, and he began to write poetry in earnest.

Throughout his life Benét continued the tandem efforts of poetry and editing that he began at Yale. In 1911 he joined the staff of *Century* magazine. He was promoted to assistant editor in 1914 and stayed until 1918, when he volunteered for the U.S. Signal Corps. He served as a second lieutenant in the aviation section, doing duty on the ground. After World War I ended, he returned to editing as the assistant editor for *The Nation's Business*. In 1920 he began working for the *New York Evening Post Literary Review*, where he and three others—Henry Seidel Canby, Amy Loveman, and Christopher Morley—founded the *Literary Review* as a supplement. In 1924 this same group founded the *Saturday Review of Literature*; Benét edited and wrote columns for this publication throughout the rest of his life. He also edited several books, including the *Oxford Anthology of American Literature* with Norman Holmes Pearson in 1938, *The Poetry of Freedom* with Norman Cousins in 1945, and *The Reader's Encyclopedia* in 1948. Benét's preface to *The Reader's Encyclopedia*, a compendium of information to help readers understand literary allusions, provides insight into his views of the world of literature and his role in it. He looked on literature as a cave of treasures and on himself as a guide to the glories of the cave.

I prefer to think of the book before you as a cave like the famous one stumbled upon by Aladdin. I might go on from there to describe its revelation of treasure of so many varieties and kinds, yet each in its own particular bin. For the office of a reference book is, after all, to bring some sort of order out of chaos. But it is also to present to you a well-organized supplementary memory, in one volume. The delights of such a memory may be inexhaustible; the safaris of research it can initiate, endless; the urge to literary creation which it can supply, present on every page.

During his lifelong career as an editor Benét continued to write and publish poetry. His first volume, *Merchants from Cathay*, appeared in 1913. These early poems had a romantic tone and featured exotic images and settings. By the time he published *The Burglar of the Zodiac and Other Poems* in 1918, Benét's style showed the influence of more modern subjects; however, his early preference for romanticism continued throughout his poetic career. In *From Another World*, Louis Untermeyer referred to Benét's "love of medievalism, exotic language, and a general preference for 'period pieces'" (p. 235). In 1941 Benét won the Pulitzer Prize for his autobiography in verse, *The Dust Which Is God*. *Day of Deliverance: A Book of Poems in Wartime*, published in 1944, demonstrated Benét's willingness to write patriotic, even propagandistic, poetry in support of the U.S. role in World War II. Late volumes included *The Stairway of Surprise* (1947) and *The Spirit of the Scene*, published posthumously in 1951.

Benét married four times. On 3 September 1912 he married Teresa Frances Thompson; they had three children, and she died in 1919. His second wife was Elinor Wylie, a writer; they married on 5 October 1923, and she died in 1928. His third marriage, to actress Lora Baxter, took place on 15 March 1932; they were divorced in 1937. Marjorie Flack became his fourth wife on 21 June 1941; they remained married until Benét's death in New York City.

During his lifetime Benét's poetic career was often overshadowed by that of his brother, Stephen Vincent Benét. William Benét's poetry is little known today. His work as an editor and man of letters, as a general promoter of poetry, writing, and reading, created his role in American literature. Perhaps his most important contribution is one he would have least expected to endure—his *Reader's Encyclopedia*. The third edition of the book, published in 1987, honored Benét by adding his name to the title: it is now *Benét's Reader's Encyclopedia*. A knowledge of literature that was both broad and deep made Benét the intelligent and generous person of letters his friends and colleagues remembered; Untermeyer said that Benét was "a man of generosity and ungrudging good will" who "never spoke ill of anyone" and "was never jealous" of new poetic talents (pp. 236–37).

• Benét's papers are held by Yale University's Beinecke Library. His volumes of poetry include *The Falconer of God and Other Poems* (1914), *The Great White Wall: A Poem* (1916), *Perpetual Light* (1919), *Moons of Grandeur* (1920), *Rip Tide, a Novel in Verse* (1932), *Starry Harness* (1933), *Golden Fleece: A Collection of Poems and Ballads Old and New* (1935), *Harlem and Other Poems* (1935), and *With Wings as Eagles: Poems and Ballads of the Air* (1940). He also wrote a novel, *The First Person Singular* (1922), and a collection of light essays, *Wild Goslings* (1927). He edited *The Collected Poems of Elinor Wylie* (1932), *Fifty Poets: An American Auto-anthology* (1933), and, with Conrad Aiken, *An Anthology of Famous English and American Poetry* (1945). Stanley Olson, *Elinor Wylie: A Life Apart* (1979), and Louis Untermeyer, *From Another World* (1939), provide coverage of Benét's life and career. An obituary is in the *New York Times*, 5 May 1950.

LORI J. WILLIAMS

BENEZET, Anthony (31 Jan. 1713–3 May 1784), abolitionist, educator, and reformer, was born in San Quentin, Picardy, France, to Jean Étienne Benezet and Judith de la Méjenelle, wealthy Huguenots. Because of increasing religious persecution, his family fled to Rotterdam in 1715, remaining there briefly before traveling to London where they spent the next sixteen years. It was here that Benezet may have attended a Quaker school and began his lifelong association with the Quakers. After emigrating with his family to Philadelphia in 1731, Benezet worked briefly as a merchant with his brothers and became a member of the Society of Friends. He married Joyce Marriott, a Quaker minister in 1736; neither of the couple's two children survived to their first birthdays.

Unhappy as a merchant, Benezet found his calling in teaching, a profession that would bring him significant personal satisfaction throughout his life as a result of his belief that education offered a means of reforming an increasingly competitive society. He sought to convince fellow Quakers that next to their duty to God was their duty to educate youth, a mission he later described in *Some Necessary Remarks on the Education of the Youth in the Country Parts of This and Neighbouring Governments* (1778). Many of Benezet's efforts were directed toward children with little or no access to education, such as the children of Acadian refugees who arrived in Pennsylvania in the mid-1750s. After teaching at the Germantown Academy and later at the Friends' English Public School, Benezet resigned in 1754 in order to establish the first secondary school for girls in Pennsylvania. To further the education of disadvantaged white children in Pennsylvania, he published several primers in 1778—*The Pennsylvania Spelling Book*, *A First Book for Children*, and *Essay on Grammar*—which were distributed by the Overseers of the Friends' Public Schools to Quakers and non-Quakers alike. After two decades of offering free evening classes for black students in his home, in 1770 he persuaded the Society of Friends to open an "Africans' School." Although the school's enrollment was rather low, a number of Benezet's students—among them Absalom Jones and James Forten—became important leaders of Philadelphia's black community. Benezet's lifelong devotion to the school was captured in a 1783 letter to Benjamin Franklin; referring to his role as a teacher at the school, he noted, "I know no station of life I should prefer before it."

From the 1750s until his death, amid numerous other reform projects, Benezet actively pursued an abolitionist campaign that began in Pennsylvania and soon extended across the Atlantic. His work began on the local level during the early 1750s when he and fellow Quaker John Woolman led the Philadelphia Yearly Meeting of the Society of Friends to announce its opposition to slaveholding and to publish *An Epistle of Caution and Advice, Concerning the Buying and Keeping of Slaves* in 1754. While he continued abolitionist work in Philadelphia, in 1759 he began to publish a series of influential antislavery tracts that soon reached an international audience. In *A Short Account of That Part of Africa Inhabited by the Negroes* (1762), a pamphlet that was later translated into French and German, he directly challenged assertions of innate black inferiority, stating, "Negroes are generally a sensible, humane, and sociable People; and . . . their capacity is as good, and as capable of Improvement as that of the Whites." This text was well-received in the colonies and later served as the impetus for a lengthy correspondence between Benezet and the British abolitionist Granville Sharp. Recognizing the need to attack the slave trade on an international level, Benezet directed his next tract, *A Caution and Warning to Great Britain and Her Colonies* (1766), to the British, "Especially to those in Power." Benezet's tracts were powerful and far-reaching because they compiled information from a wide range of sources, including the works of philosophers, travelers, merchants, and various experts on Africa, and because they argued from a range of religious and secular positions. Indeed, the British abolitionist Thomas Clarkson later noted in *The History of the Rise, Progress, and Accomplishment of the Abolition of the African Slave Trade* (1808), that Benezet's *Some Historical Account of Guinea* (1772), was "instrumental beyond any other work ever before published in disseminating a proper knowledge and detestation of this trade."

During the 1770s Benezet published tracts on a variety of topics, from pacifism to temperance; yet when the Philadelphia meeting finally decided in 1776 that the penalty for buying or selling slaves would be disownment, Benezet worked tirelessly to persuade reluctant Quakers to free their slaves. His successful efforts lobbying the Pennsylvania legislators saw the passage of the gradual abolition law of 1780. Indeed, throughout the latter part of his life Benezet wrote and circulated antislavery tracts; authored countless letters to political and religious leaders in addition to the monarchs of England, Portugal, and France; submitted petitions to the Continental Congress and Parliament; and inspired the work of numerous British and American abolitionists. Although Benezet's antislavery work during the 1780s found a much less receptive audience at home than it had a decade earlier, it proved very influential in Europe, particularly in England and France, where his tracts were widely circulated and reprinted even after Benezet's death in Philadelphia.

Benezet's description of himself in his will as "a teacher of the Free School for the Black People in Philadelphia," and his decision to leave the bulk of his estate to this school demonstrates that to the end he viewed himself primarily as a committed teacher, dedicated to educating those usually overlooked. Although Benezet is recognized as the most prolific antislavery propagandist of the eighteenth century, throughout his lifetime he supported and wrote about a wide variety of causes and topics, including assistance for Acadian refugees, temperance, peace, fair treatment of Native Americans, religion, educational reform, and poor relief.

• Many of Benezet's papers and materials concerning him can be found in the Haverford College Library; the Historical Society of Pennsylvania; the Swarthmore College Library; Friends' House Library, London; Arch Street Meeting House, Department of Records, Philadelphia; and the Huntington Library, San Marino, Calif. Benezet's numerous works include *Observations on the Enslaving, Importing and Purchasing of Negroes* (1759), *Thoughts on the Nature of War, and Its Repugnancy to the Christian Life* (1766), *The Mighty Destroyer Displayed* (1773), *Serious Considerations on Several Important Subjects* (1778), *A Short Account of the People Called Quakers, Their Rise, Religious Principles, and Settlement in America* (1780), and *Some Observations on the Situation, Disposition, and Character of the Indian Natives of This Continent* (1784). Many of Benezet's voluminous writings were published as parts of other books or pamphlets. The most complete biography is Nancy Slocum Hornick's "Anthony Benezet: Eighteenth Century Social Critic, Educator and Abolitionist" (Ph.D. diss., Univ. of Maryland, 1974). See also George S. Brookes's *Friend Anthony Benezet* (1937), which includes a significant collection of Benezet's letters; and Robert Vaux's early biography *Memoirs of the Life of Anthony Benezet* (1817), later revised by Wilson Armistead and published as *Anthony Benezet: From the Original Memoir; Revised, with Additions* (1859). See William C. Kashatus's "A Reappraisal of Anthony Benezet's Activities in Educational Reform, 1754–1784," *Quaker History* 78 (1989): 24–36 and Nancy Slocum Hornick's "Anthony Benezet and the Africans' School: Toward a Theory of Full Equality" *Pennsylvania Magazine of History and Biography* 99 (1975): 399–421 for useful discussions of Benezet's work in education.

AMY E. WINANS

BENIOFF, Victor Hugo (14 Sept. 1899–29 Feb. 1968), seismologist and geophysicist, was born in Los Angeles, California, the son of Simon Benioff, a tailor, and Alfrieda Widerquist. Benioff's father and mother were immigrants, from Russia and Sweden respectively. Benioff attended the public schools of Los Angeles and Long Beach, where he expressed an early interest in science. As a youth, he was particularly interested in astronomy. From 1917 until 1921, while pursuing his undergraduate studies at Pomona College, he spent his summers working as an assistant at the Mount Wilson Observatory in the San Gabriel Mountains above Los Angeles. After receiving his A.B., he accepted a job at the Lick Observatory in Santa Cruz, California, where he worked from 1921 to 1922.

Working full time as an astronomer, however, Benioff was troubled by his intolerance for the cold, nocturnal work required to observe the stars. As a result, in 1924 he secured a position with the Seismological Laboratory in Pasadena, California, one of the leading centers of the emerging study of seismology, then run by the Carnegie Institution of Washington, D.C. As an assistant physicist at the lab, Benioff was assigned the task of developing a system to drive seismological recording drums. He soon proved himself an able instrument builder, developing a new impulse motor that could measure the arrival times of seismic waves to an accuracy of .1 second. This instrument was the first of many Benioff developed during the course of a career that transformed seismology from a mostly qualitative study of the effects of earthquakes on manmade structures into a detailed, quantitative science focused on the recording and analysis of seismic wave energy. As a result of his work at the lab, Benioff decided to pursue seismology as a career. He began graduate study in seismology at the California Institute of Technology and in 1935 received a Ph.D.

Not satisfied with his early instrumental improvements, Benioff continued to strive for ways to further enhance the precision and sensitivity of seismographs. In 1931 he finished work on a variable-reluctance seismometer that allowed for extremely high magnification of small seismic movements. This feature enabled the instrument to measure both small local earthquakes and larger, distant ones. Benioff next worked on perfecting a linear strain seismograph. By responding to ground motions in a different manner from that of the traditional pendulum seismometer, Benioff's instrument allowed for the detection of different types of seismic waves, especially those generated by deep-focus earthquakes. Benioff's instruments soon were incorporated into a network of linked recording instruments throughout southern California that gave researchers at the Pasadena laboratory the ability to precisely pinpoint and gauge the relative magnitude of local earthquakes. This network contributed to many new insights into earthquake mechanics and led directly to the development, by Benioff's Caltech colleagues Charles Richter and Beno Gutenberg, of what came to be known as "the Richter scale" in 1935. This scale provided a method of ranking the intensity of different ground motions based on a logarithmic scheme, generating a single number that could represent the relative size of earthquakes.

In 1937 the Pasadena Seismological Lab was officially joined to the California Institute of Technology; Benioff was appointed to the position of assistant professor of seismology at Caltech and was soon afterward raised to associate professor. Although a member of the regular faculty, Benioff preferred his work on instruments to teaching and had relatively little formal contact with students. Researchers and graduate students sought him out, however, for his insight into the particular problems of instrumentation and the detection of seismic waves. During the Second World War, Benioff participated in a program for improving radar and sonar detection for the Submarine Signal Corporation, and during the 1950s he took part in a program for the detection of underground nuclear explosions.

During the 1940s Benioff's interests in the transmission of waves also led him to develop electronic amplifiers for the violin and cello. These "seismographic fiddles" had the same design as their conventional counterparts, except that the wooden resonance chambers were replaced by a small, aluminum container beneath the strings. Within this compartment, the musical vibrations caused a crystal to generate electrical current, which was then amplified. Benioff's instruments were hailed for producing tones of outstanding clarity and depth. From 1946 to 1962 Benioff worked as a consultant with the Baldwin Piano Company and helped them to develop electronic instruments, including a violin and a piano, based on the same principles. In his home, Benioff constructed an elaborate system of recording equipment and built a superb library of recordings. He also developed a means whereby the seismic waves of earthquakes could be played back on an audio system, allowing researchers to actually "hear" the sound of earthquakes.

Benioff also won acclaim for his contribution to a prediction made in 1949 by Beno Gutenberg, director of the Caltech seismological lab, that the Pacific Coast region was due for either a large earthquake or a series of small tremors. This prediction was based on measurements made by Benioff revealing that the subsurface strain in the central California region was building. In 1950 a series of tremors shook the lower Imperial Valley, and in 1952 a major quake took place in the region.

Later in his career Benioff became interested in the study of microseismic waves, the slight shaking of the earth's crust that goes on continually. He also worked on magnetic micropulsations, which are small geomagnetic fluctuations in the earth's magnetic field. These researches led to his work on detecting the free vibrations of the earth. Benioff's broad interests and contributions to seismology won him widespread recognition in the field. In 1950 he became a full professor at Caltech, and in 1953 he was elected to the National Academy of Sciences. He also served as the president of the Seismological Association of America. In 1964 Benioff became professor emeritus at Caltech but continued his research and consulting work. He served as adviser to both the government and private industry on issues of the seismic safety of nuclear power plants. During his career he published many significant papers on seismography, microseisms, and earthquake dynamics.

Benioff was married twice. His first marriage, to Alice Silverman, in 1928 produced three children. They divorced in 1953. That same year he married Mildred Lent, with whom he had one child.

Benioff was a great lover of nature and the outdoors. Following his retirement, he moved to Cape Mendocino in northern California to enjoy the beauty of the natural environment of that area. While there, he died suddenly of a heart attack. His contributions to seismology, especially in the development of seismic instruments, made him one of the founding figures of the modern study of earthquakes.

• Biographical information on Benioff can be found in the historical files and in several oral history interviews in the archives at the California Institute of Technology. Among Benioff's most significant scientific papers were his descriptions of his new seismographs published during the 1930s in the *Bulletin of the Seismological Society of America*. A good summary of these developments is Benioff's "Seismological Instruments Developed at the C.I.T.," *Engineering and Science* 11 (Feb. 1948): 24–25, 31. A biography of Benioff by Frank Press is in the National Academy of Sciences, *Biographical Memoirs* 43 (1973): 27–40. The best survey to date on the development of seismology in America is Judy Goodstein, "Waves in the Earth: Seismology Comes to Southern California," *Historical Studies in the Physical Sciences* 14 (1984): 201–30. An obituary is in the *New York Times*, 2 Mar. 1968.

DAVID A. VALONE

BENITES, José María (fl. 1803–1806), surgeon and eighth surgeon general of California, was born presumably in Catalonia, Spain; his date of birth, parentage, and date of death are all unknown.

Little information is available about the nine men who served as surgeon general of California during the Spanish colonial period that began with the Portola expedition, which in 1769 was sent out from Mexico to extend Spain's control up the coast, and ended about 1822. What is known, however, is that about 1800 the appallingly high mortality rate of the neophyte population, as reported annually by the Franciscan missionaries, began to trouble both the spiritual and the temporal authorities in Mexico City.

On September 1804 the viceroy, Joseph de Iturrigaray, was determined to take action by sending a letter to Monterey. The viceroy's missive directed Benites, who had assumed the duties of surgeon general during the previous year, to investigate, ascertain the causes, and report on the alarming number of deaths occurring among the soldiers, Indians, and colonists of Alta California, the territory claimed by Spain from Baja California northward.

Benites's response was immediate. Shortly after receiving the viceroy's directive, he began to tour the settlements around Monterey, observing and gathering case histories from as far north as the Mission Dolores and extending as far south as San Luis Obispo. Within three months he was able to forward a detailed account to the viceroy. His *Informe*, or *Expediente*, dated 1 January 1805, is the first official account of health conditions in Alta California written by a trained physician.

Benites identified the principal diseases that he observed on his tour as dysentery, fevers, pleurisy, peripneumonia, contagious syphilis, scrofula, and phthisis, or pulmonary tuberculosis. He attributed their etiology to a variety of conditions. Dysentery, Benites explained, resulted from drinking and cooking with impure water, from wearing unclean clothes, and from the squalor he noted in the living quarters of Indians and settlers alike. Other contributing factors Benites identified were the absence of vegetables in the daily diet of most Californians as well as a vexing proclivity to disregard both simple hygienic measures and the advice of their physician.

Benites linked the cases of syphilis, pleurisy, and inflammatory fevers found among the Soledad neophytes to the foggy and windy climate of the region. Most of the women Benites examined at San Luis Obispo were suffering from either tuberculosis or syphilis, and he seems to have been well aware of the contagious nature of these diseases. Having discovered them also at the Mission of San Juan Bautista, he ascribed their etiology to impure relations on an excessive scale, filthy health habits, the custom of sleeping huddled together with individuals who had contracted these diseases, the dissolute pursuit of pleasure, and, finally, the overuse of the temescal, or sweat house.

Benites apparently failed to recognize that a degree of personal hygiene, at least among the male native population, had long been attained through the temescals. Their neglect during the the colonial period may have contributed to the unsanitary conditions to which he attributed many of the illnesses he described, however, and the respiratory ailments he reported may have been markedly exacerbated by their use followed by a plunge in cold water. Modern practitioners who seek to deal with the health problems of one culture trained only in the medical protocols developed in another may well sympathize with him and learn from his account.

Other lessons are to be learned from Benites's *Informe*. Its reception and distribution attest to the efficiency of both mission and colonizing systems. Directed by the viceroy, a civil authority, to compile a medical survey, Benites was able to assemble his materials and submit his findings in three months. After reading the report the viceroy passed it to the treasury office for comments on its financial implications. The document was then forwarded to the Royal Medical Board, and together with the comments of its members it was sent to the bishop of Sonora, who relayed it to Father Estavan Tàpis. Tàpis, president of the California missions, wishing to derive as much benefit as possible from the medical report, circulated it to all of the missions from Soledad southward to San Diego. At each mission a Franciscan signed the circular letter attesting that he had read it thoroughly.

In a little more than a year, Benites's *Informe* had been sent to Mexico City and passed through the hands of both temporal and spiritual authorities. Thus, though never printed in its entirety, Benites's report had been widely read and distributed. At the end of his *Informe*, Benites requested the viceroy's permission to continue his tour of inspection by visiting the presidios of Santa Barbara and San Diego, but there is no evidence that he ever undertook this mission. Perhaps in recognition of his work on the survey, in November 1804 the governor increased his annual salary to 1,000 pesos.

The only other fact known about José María Benites is that he was succeeded as surgeon general in 1807 by Manuel Quijano of Madrid. When Benites left California and how he spent his life after 1807 are unknown. His historical significance lies in his description of the health and living conditions of the resident population in California as recorded in his *Informe*.

• The principal source for information about Benites is the copy of his *Informe* contained in *California Mission Document*, CMD No. 671, as well as other similar materials now in the Santa Barbara Mission Archive Library. A translation of an incomplete version of Benites's report appears in Sherburne Cook, "California's First Medical Survey: Report of Surgeon-General José Benites," *California and Western Medicine* 45 (1936): 352–54. Cook, "The Monterey Surgeons during the Spanish Period in California," *Bulletin of the History of Medicine* 5 (1937): 43–70; Doyce B. Nunis, Jr., ed., and L. Jay Oliva, trans., *A Medical Journey in California by Dr. Pierre Garnier* (1967); and Henry Harris, *California's Medical Story* (1932), survey the medical scene. Zephyrin Engelhardt, *The Missions and Missionaries of California* (1930), and

Maynard Geiger, *Franciscan Missionaries in Hispanic California* (1969), chronicle the principal mission activities of the period, while Robert F. Heizer and Albert B. Elsasser, *The Natural World of the California Indians* (1980), and Edith Webb, *Indian Life at the Old Missions* (1952), examine Indian Life in California during the same period.

YNEZ VIOLÉ O'NEILL

BENJAMIN, Asher (1773–26 July 1845), architect and author, was born in Hartland, in rural northwest Hartford County, Connecticut, the son of Asher Benjamin, a carpenter, and Elizabeth (maiden name unknown). Benjamin may have apprenticed with a local carpenter, Eliphalet King or Thomas Hayden, who added a wing to the Suffield house of land speculator Oliver Phelps. This house featured details derived from William Pain's *Practical House Carpenter* (1789), a popularization of Robert Adam's neoclassical style. According to Phelps's account book Benjamin was paid for carving the Ionic capitals of the new entrance between October 1794 and February 1795.

Later in 1795 Benjamin designed and superintended the erection of a circular staircase in the new state house in Hartford, designed by Charles Bulfinch of Boston. The method for building such stairs had only recently been published by the British architect Peter Nicholson, and years later Benjamin recalled that it "was the first circular rail that was ever made in New England."

Benjamin's earliest independent commissions were in Brookfield, Massachusetts, in the Connecticut River Valley towns of Northampton, Deerfield, and Greenfield, Massachusetts, and in Windsor, Vermont. These works blended forms found in the books of Pain and Nicholson with elements from the Boston works of Bulfinch. The Deerfield Academy (1797–1798), an austere brick block with rusticated doorways, was Benjamin's first brick building. The Windsor meetinghouse (1799–1800), built of wood, was indebted to Bulfinch meetinghouses in Taunton and Pittsfield.

While living in Greenfield, Benjamin published *The Country Builder's Assistant* (1797), thirty somewhat crudely drawn plates depicting the orders, doorways, mantels, moldings, and plans and elevations for two houses, derived largely from Pain's *Practical House Carpenter*. Its design for a meetinghouse, based on those of Bulfinch, was imitated all over New England.

Benjamin considered himself a teacher bringing the neoclassical gospel to country workmen. Indeed, while in Windsor he announced that he would teach the principles of design, construction, and architectural drawing. This would have been the earliest school of architecture in the United States, but Benjamin left town a few months later, so the school could have existed only for a short time.

In November 1797 Benjamin married Achsah Hitchcock of Brookfield, with whom he had four children. She died in Boston in January 1805, and in July 1805 Benjamin married Nancy Bryant of Springfield, Massachusetts, with whom he had four more children.

By August 1802 Benjamin was working in Boston. In that year he won a $50 premium for his design for the U.S. Marine Hospital in Charlestown, based largely on Bulfinch's Almshouse (1799–1801). In 1806 Benjamin designed and built the West Meetinghouse, a simple, squarish block fronted by a tower and cupola, inspired by Bulfinch's New North Church (1803–1804). In rapid succession Benjamin designed two other churches similar to the West Meetinghouse but even more austere in their neoclassicism: the Third Baptist Church, later known as the Charles Street Meetinghouse (1807), and the fourth building of the First Church, Boston, on Chauncey Street (1808).

Among his largest and most complex designs was the Exchange Coffee House (1806–1809). An assembly room, a dining room, coffee rooms, reading rooms, a Masonic lodge, rental offices, and a 200-room hotel were organized around the merchant's exchange itself, a lofty space soaring up to the domed roof. Though its exterior was rather ungainly, it was one of the earliest hotels and mixed-use buildings anywhere.

In 1806 Benjamin, with the stucco specialist Daniel Raynerd, published *The American Builder's Companion*, which became the principal source for the Federal style for carpenters across the eastern half of the United States. Technically the plates were far superior to those in *The Country Builder's Assistant*, and the work was much broader in scope, including Roman versions of the five orders but also novel variants of capitals and bases. Plans and elevations included town houses, country houses, a courthouse, and a meetinghouse similar to Benjamin's Old West. Ever the thrifty Yankee, Benjamin suggested that mutule blocks could be bored with holes rather than carved to resemble bells, "which will save one half the labour of making them; and, at a distance of fifteen or twenty feet, looks as well, if not better."

Benjamin soon bought out Raynerd, and for the second edition of 1811 he thoroughly revised the work, replacing the generically Roman orders with the more academically correct versions of Sir William Chambers's *Treatise on Civil Architecture* (1759). This edition also revealed Benjamin's interest in new technologies, including kitchen fireplaces with Rumford roasters and boilers based on the recent innovations of Benjamin Thompson, Count Rumford.

The recession brought on by Thomas Jefferson's embargo and the War of 1812 sharply curtailed Benjamin's practice, and from 1813 to 1823 he ran a paint store in Boston. Although little was being built in Boston, his renown brought commissions from other parts of New England. His meetinghouse in Northampton (1810–1812), built by Isaac Damon, had an interior explicitly modeled on that of the First Church, Boston, but the exterior featured his most lavishly neoclassical porch. Benjamin also provided the original design for the Center Church in New Haven (1813–1814), built by Ithiel Town. Its freestanding portico is unusual in Benjamin's oeuvre; it seems likely that

Town and the building committee changed Benjamin's plan.

When Boston adopted a new form of government with a mayor and council, Benjamin ran and was elected alderman in 1823 and 1824 as part of the "Middling Interest," an alliance of artisans and small businessmen led by Josiah Quincy. Benjamin served on the building committee for the new Faneuil Hall Market (Quincy Market), working closely with its architect, Alexander Parris.

In 1825 Benjamin declared bankruptcy and moved to Nashua, New Hampshire, where he worked as agent of the Nashua Manufacturing Company. There he supervised construction of mills and related structures, and he may have designed the Olive Street Congregational Church (1825). He was back in Boston by 1828.

With the advent of the Greek Revival, Benjamin found himself falling behind the times. For the 1827 edition of *The American Builder's Companion* he included the Greek orders along with the Roman. In *The Practical House Carpenter* (1830), he observed that "since my last publication, the Roman school of architecture has been entirely changed for the Grecian." In this work, *Practice of Architecture* (1833), and *The Builder's Guide* (1839) Benjamin illustrated Greek orders and details, and plans for churches, but no new house plans.

In the 1830s Benjamin's career as architect enjoyed a resurgence. He designed houses for such prominent Bostonians as the editor Joseph Tinker Buckingham and the noted Unitarian minister William Ellery Channing. Benjamin also designed the Fifth Universalist Church on Warren Street in Boston and the church of the Third Religious Unitarian Society in Dorchester. In December 1836 he was among the founders of the American Institution of Architecture, the forerunner of the American Institute of Architects.

Benjamin published his last book, *Elements of Architecture*, in 1843, when he was seventy years old. Much of the material was technical, but he also included a section on principles of architecture derived largely from the Scottish philosopher Archibald Alison, which emphasized the expression of fitness as the key to beauty, concepts then current in picturesque architectural theory.

In his own designs Benjamin rarely achieved the restrained elegance of his hero Bulfinch; rather, his special genius lay in the ability to present plans, elevations, and details in a manner understandable to country carpenters and urban builders alike. As a result Benjamin was largely responsible for the simple yet refined classicism that characterizes so much of early nineteenth-century American architecture. As the author of seven architectural pattern books—including the first architectural pattern book compiled by an American—which were immensely popular in the eastern half of the United States, he led two generations of American builders to the sources first of Roman and then of Greek neoclassicism, the Federal and

Greek Revival styles. Benjamin died in Springfield, Massachusetts.

• The greatest source of primary information about Benjamin is his books. Papers and drawings are scattered. The largest cache of drawings is at the Society for the Preservation of New England Antiquities in Boston. Jack Quinan compiled a list of projects and buildings and a bibliography for the *Journal of the Society of Architectural Historians* 38 (Oct. 1979): 253–56; see also Abbott Lowell Cummings, "Asher Benjamin," in the *Macmillan Encyclopedia of Architects* (1982), and William N. Hosley, Jr., "Architecture," in *The Great River: Art & Society of the Connecticut Valley, 1635–1820* (1985).

KENNETH HAFERTEPE

BENJAMIN, Harry (12 Jan. 1885–24 Aug. 1986), physician, endocrinologist, and sex researcher, was born in Berlin, Germany, the son of Julius Benjamin, a banker, and Bertha Hoffman. He became interested in human sexuality at the age of twenty, when he read August Forel's *The Sexual Question*. According to Benjamin's later associate Leah Cahan Schaefer, this book convinced him that "the existing concepts of sex were wrong and absolutely unscientific" (*Archives of Sexual Behavior* [1988]: 12).

Benjamin received his M.D. at the University of Tübingen in 1912 and planned to specialize in geriatrics and endocrinology. In 1913 he moved to the United States and studied tuberculosis at a sanitarium in New York, but he grew dissatisfied with the work and quit. He had too little cash to return home, which "was the luckiest thing," he later said, "because it forced me to remain in the United States, thereby avoiding two wars in Germany, plus the Depression and most importantly of all, Hitler" (*Archives* [1988]: 13).

In 1915 Benjamin began to meet weekly with Joseph Frankel of Columbia University in informal seminars. Frankel studied the ductless or endocrine glands, which secrete hormones important in human physiology. Frankel believed that the glands affected personality and aging; some researchers, Benjamin among them, hoped to rejuvenate the elderly with glandular injections. Benjamin also investigated the physiological effects of sex hormones from the 1920s into the 1940s. From 1930 to 1941 he served as a consulting endocrinologist to the College of the City of New York. In 1937 he and Robert Edward Lee Masters wrote a book, *Rejuvenation*.

Benjamin had married Greta Guelzow in 1925. They had no children. Benjamin spent his summers in San Francisco. In 1948 his friend Alfred C. Kinsey, the sex researcher, was in the city interviewing subjects about their sexual histories. One subject, whom Kinsey called "Barry," was an effeminate-looking 23-year-old man who wanted to change his sex. Kinsey referred Barry and his mother to Benjamin. The mother pleaded: "Look at this boy, he's not a boy! You've got to do something to help my son *be* a girl!" (Schaefer and Wheeler, p. 78). Benjamin encouraged Barry to go to Europe, where surgeons were willing to perform a then-remarkable operation, converting the genitals by removing the testicles and penis, then constructing a makeshift vagina lined with skin from the thigh. (Later transsexual procedures were more sophisticated in that surgeons created a functional vagina by inverting the penis, like turning a finger on a glove inside out.)

During the 1950s Benjamin was a founding member of the Society for the Scientific Study of Sex. Early in that decade, transsexualism made headlines when George Jorgensen, an American soldier, had a sex-change operation in Denmark and became Christine Jorgensen. Benjamin wrote to Jorgensen and, as she later recalled, "told me that he was guiding people and so forth . . . concerning transsexuality. . . . I went down to his office in Manhattan and we had a very long conference about the whole thing and it was an absolute godsend for me." She referred Benjamin to the many people who contacted her about their own sexual confusion, so "suddenly the deluge fell onto poor Harry's shoulders" (*Archives* [1988]: 24–25). Benjamin became the best-known American expert on transsexualism, a word he proposed for the obsessive urge to belong to the opposite sex. His growing transsexual clientele drove away his geriatric patients: "They made it quite clear that they didn't want to share the waiting room or their doctor with these patients," his colleague Virginia Allen later said (*Archives* [1988]: 27).

Benjamin identified different degrees of what he called "sex and gender role disorientation and indecision" (*The Transsexual Phenomenon*). They ranged from transvestites, who enjoy occasional cross-dressing but otherwise have no desire to change sex, to "true transsexuals" who are intensely uncomfortable with their genetic sex. Most transsexuals, he found, are men who wish to become women; some were so unhappy that they mutilated their genitals or attempted suicide. Benjamin provided hormone treatments to some transsexuals so their bodies would develop physical characteristics of the desired sex; for example, male-to-female transsexuals who received female hormones tended to develop a more feminine body shape, including breasts. Extreme cases were referred to transsexual surgery, which eventually became available at U.S. medical institutions. Psychotherapy, Benjamin believed, was pointless for true male-to-female transsexuals, who "harbor a female 'soul' . . . in their male body. . . . A patient like that has every right to be accepted as a woman and lead a woman's life" (Hausman, p. 123). His book *The Transsexual Phenomenon* (1966)—published when he was eighty-one years old—became the first authoritative guide to the subject of transsexualism and gender dysphoria, or dissatisfaction with one's sex.

The subject remained controversial through the remaining years of Benjamin's life. Medical and psychiatric experts debated the effectiveness of transsexual surgery in alleviating transsexuals' unhappiness. Some feminists criticized the surgery, maintaining that it reinforced social stereotypes about what constituted maleness and femaleness. Transsexuals, however, viewed Benjamin as their savior. A male-to-female transsexual, Renée Richards, said that without Benjamin, "I don't know what our fate [as transsexuals] may have been: a fragmented personality, a suicide, many possible things other than the integrated, consolidated, productive people that many of us are" (*Archives* [1988]: 23). Politically minded transsexuals launched the transgender movement to fight against legal and job discrimination; it became closely allied to the gay and lesbian rights movement. In 1984 Benjamin's colleagues in the field of transsexual therapy formed the Harry Benjamin International Gender Dysphoria Association.

Benjamin remained scientifically active to the end of his life at the age of 101. He died in New York City.

• Details of Benjamin's life appear in a memorial article in *Archives of Sexual Behavior* 17, no. 1 (1988): 1–31, with anecdotes from transsexuals and other therapists. Further biographical details are in Leah Cahan Schaefer and Connie Christine Wheeler, "Harry Benjamin's First Ten Cases (1938–1953): A Clinical Historical Note," *Archives of Sexual Behavior* 24, no. 1 (1995): 73–93. Renée Richards describes her relationship with Benjamin in her autobiography written with John Ames, *Second Serve* (1983), especially chapter 13. Benjamin's work is discussed in Bernice L. Hausman, *Changing Sex—Transsexualism, Technology, and the Idea of Gender* (1995). Benjamin opposed the persecution of prostitutes and wrote *Prostitution and Morality* (1964), republished in 1966 as *The Prostitute in Society*. The paperback edition of his book *The Transsexual Phenomenon* misidentifies him as Henry, and, he said, it contains "other typographical errors that could only be deliberate sabotage" (*San Francisco Chronicle*, 15 July 1969). An obituary is in the *New York Times*, 27 Aug. 1986.

KEAY DAVIDSON

BENJAMIN, Judah Philip (6 Aug. 1811–6 May 1884), Confederate cabinet member, U.S. senator, and lawyer, was born at Christiansted, St. Croix, West Indies, the son of Philip Benjamin, a shopkeeper, and Rebecca de Mendes. St. Croix was under British rule at the time of Benjamin's birth. He grew up in Charleston, South Carolina. Though his father's circumstances were always modest, wealthy relatives and other benefactors helped him attend Yale (1825–1827), but he left as a junior under circumstances that remain unclear.

Moving to New Orleans in 1828, Benjamin arrived with no resources except his energy and intellect. He worked for a merchant and a notary and tutored English while reading law. He was admitted to the bar shortly before his marriage in 1833 to a former student, Marie Augustine Natalie St. Martin, of a devout Catholic family. Though of Sephardic ancestry, Benjamin was a nonobservant Jew. He was ambitious, while Marie liked to socialize and preferred New Orleans society to the isolation of a busy attorney and planter's wife. It was this basic incompatibility between the couple, not religious differences, that led to his wife's move to Paris in 1845, where Benjamin saw her no more than once a year. They had one child.

Benjamin made a small fortune as a New Orleans attorney, specializing in civil and commercial law. He preferred appeals to ordinary cases and judges to juries. With Thomas Slidell he compiled the *Digest of the Reported Decisions of the Superior Court of the Late Territory of Orleans and the Supreme Court of the State of Louisiana* (1834), twenty-five volumes that included French and Spanish precedents. Among his most important causes were a series of suits arising from a slave insurrection aboard the brig *Creole* (1842), *Murdoch v. McDonogh* (1854), and *United States v. Castillero* (1860). The second case involved the will of New Orleans millionaire John McDonogh and was decided by the U.S. Supreme Court, as was the last, concerning title to a California mine.

By the early 1840s Benjamin was able to buy a half interest in "Bellechasse," a sugar plantation below New Orleans, after damaging his eyesight with overwork. He experimented with technology to improve the quality of his crop but lost his holding because of financial reverses. He was also a railroad promoter in Louisiana and Panama and speculated in South American guano.

Benjamin began his political career as a conservative Whig in 1842, serving in the lower house of the Louisiana legislature. Elected to the U.S. Senate in 1852, Benjamin was already allied with Democratic boss John Slidell. He switched parties in 1856 as Whiggery disintegrated and was reelected to the Senate in 1859. A staunch defender of the South, Benjamin was not a fire-eater, nor was he one of Louisiana's representatives at the Montgomery, Alabama, constitutional convention that formed a provisional Confederate government.

When Louisiana seceded (26 Jan. 1861), Benjamin resigned his Senate seat (4 Feb.) and returned to his law practice in New Orleans. President Jefferson Davis, whom Benjamin had once challenged to a duel after the then U.S. secretary of war insulted the senator, asked him to become the Confederacy's first attorney general. Benjamin won an apology in the earlier incident and Davis's respect; their new relationship would ripen into friendship and mutual admiration. The Confederate Senate confirmed his nomination on 5 March 1861. It was a minor post but in theory of equal cabinet status. The Confederate Justice Department preceded that of the United States (1870) and included a patent office, a bureau of public printing, and responsibility for territories.

Benjamin established his department quickly and, because of his efficiency, had time to receive foreign visitors, deal with office seekers, and handle other chores for Davis. After the government moved to Richmond, Virginia, in May 1861, there was talk by late summer of Benjamin seeking the post of secretary of war. When Leroy Pope Walker resigned, Davis appointed Benjamin as acting secretary on 17 September 1861. Since Benjamin remained attorney general for two months, the appointment was at first thought to be temporary, but the provisional Confederate Congress confirmed Benjamin in office on 21 November 1861. He worked with some success to recruit more soldiers with longer enlistments than the one-year term then common, purchased war matériel abroad, negotiated other contracts, and continued Walker's attempts to stimulate domestic industry. Unfortunately, Benjamin lacked any military experience, almost a prerequisite for success in his new office. Although urbane and courteous in person, his often brusque letters and his religious and ethnic background help to explain his unfortunate quarrels with a number of key generals, including Joseph E. Johnston, Pierre G. T. Beauregard, and most notably, Thomas J. "Stonewall" Jackson, over matters such as strategy, troop movements, control of armies, and seniority. The generals saw Davis as their commander in chief and only superior but regarded Benjamin as a civilian and an amateur at war, a political bureaucrat.

As secretary of war, Benjamin more than Davis was blamed for the loss of Roanoke Island off the North Carolina coast in February 1862. This defeat embroiled him in a bitter feud with former Virginia governor and political general Henry Alexander Wise, who had been forced to surrender the island and lost his oldest son in the battle. Wise's superior in Norfolk was partly responsible, but Davis and Benjamin had privately decided that the secretary would take the blame rather than reveal that the government had no ammunition to send Wise's force. Benjamin's congressional critics, such as Henry S. Foote and Louis T. Wigfall, and the press, notably John M. Daniel's *Richmond Examiner*, accused him simultaneously of being a mere office boy for President Davis and of being wholly responsible for various disasters. Meanwhile Benjamin had become Davis's personal confidant and a firm ally as well of Varina Howell Davis. Yet the president mentioned his closest adviser only twice in his monumental two-volume memoirs, *The Rise and Fall of the Confederate Government* (1881), a seeming contradiction that biographers have been unable to explain. Benjamin had become "the most unpopular and hated man in the Confederacy" (Patrick, p. 180) by March 1862. Widespread Confederate anti-Semitism made Benjamin an easier target than the president. Davis could not keep him at the War Department in the permanent government because of political pressure and public sentiment.

Instead, the president made Benjamin secretary of state. Benjamin assumed his third portfolio on 18 March 1862. It was still the Confederate hope that "king cotton" diplomacy would force European diplomatic recognition and even military intervention. Benjamin arranged the Erlanger loan from a Paris bank to the Confederacy in January 1863; it was the only significant European loan of the war. He also struggled to demonstrate the ineffectiveness of the Union blockade and to convince England and France that war with the United States would not result from their recognition of the Confederacy, but he failed to achieve these goals or to split the two powers. As a last resort, he persuaded Davis by 1865 to offer emancipation of the slaves in return for recognition, but this initiative came too late. Benjamin drew up the original instructions, purposefully vague, for the Confederate peace commissioners who met with Abraham Lincoln and William H. Seward at the February 1865 Hampton Roads Peace Conference, but since Davis insisted on southern independence, little was accomplished.

Speaking at an important public meeting in Richmond on 9 February 1865, Benjamin advocated freeing slaves to fight for the Confederacy. His speech caused controversy, though he was one of a number of leaders who supported the desperate measure. Always unpopular, Benjamin again bore the brunt of criticism, much of it from anti-Semitic members of Congress, but efforts to censure or remove him from office failed by a narrow margin. A few black soldiers were recruited in March 1865 and fought before the capital fell.

Benjamin evacuated Richmond with Davis's official party the night of 2–3 April 1865. The steadily dwindling band of fugitives passed through Danville, Virginia, and Greensboro and Charlotte, North Carolina. Benjamin eventually separated from Davis and his military escort after crossing the Savannah River into Georgia, shortly before the latter's capture by Federal cavalry. Donning a series of ingenious disguises, Benjamin was able to reach coastal Florida after close escapes from Union forces. He almost drowned in a storm while passing in a small boat from the Keys to Bimini. After further adventures, he reached Nassau in the Bahamas, and from there he made his way to Havana, Cuba, and finally Southampton, England.

Because of his prodigious energy and intellect, Benjamin won admission as a barrister (Lincoln's Inn) by June 1866, after only five months of study, an unprecedented accomplishment for an American. He practiced on the Northern Circuit, which included Liverpool. His *Treatise on the Law of Sale of Personal Property with Reference to the American Decisions and to the French Code and Civil Law* (1868) became the standard work. Benjamin was appointed queen's counsel for Lancashire County in 1870 and won a patent of precedence in 1872. He appeared in many landmark cases, some arising from the Civil War, including *United States v. Wagner* (1867); *United States v. McRae* (1869); *Potter v. Rankin* (1872); *Queen v. Keyn* (*Franconia* case, 1876); *London and County Banking Company v. Ratcliff* and *Castro v. the Queen* (1881); *Neill v. Duke of Devonshire* and *Earl of Zetland v. Hislop* (1882). Benjamin achieved such eminence that he eventually accepted only appeals to be argued before the House of Lords or the Privy Council. He also earned a measure of financial security for himself and his family after sixteen years of effort in the English courts. After he retired, the leaders of the British bar honored him with a banquet at the Inner Temple.

Benjamin's health declined with the onset of diabetes in May 1880, a fall from a Parisian trolley in 1881, and a heart attack at the end of 1882 that forced his retirement. He had planned to enjoy the comfort of his Paris mansion with his wife and daughter, but it was not to be. He died in Paris less than two years later.

As the most controversial and bitterly criticized civilian member of the Confederate government, particularly after Davis's postwar imprisonment by the United States made him a martyr for the Lost Cause, "the brains of the Confederacy" endured the anti-Semitism rife in nineteenth-century America and virulent in the wartime South. Some historians have claimed that Benjamin might have won Confederate independence if he had been given real freedom of action, but it is not clear what more he could have done. His motives were often indistinct, but since Benjamin kept his own counsel, he could be an enigma even to his closest associates, and he continues to defy the best efforts of biographers.

• Many of Benjamin's papers were left behind in New Orleans and Richmond and were destroyed or fell into the hands of souvenir hunters. He systematically burned other records after the war. Thus, few of Benjamin's papers survive, except for letters in private hands and items captured by Union forces and printed in *The War of the Rebellion: A Compilation of the Official Records of the Union and Confederate Armies* (128 vols., 1880–1901).

Pierce Butler, *Judah P. Benjamin* (1907), is still valuable and beautifully written. The best modern biography remains Robert Douthat Meade, *Judah P. Benjamin, Confederate Statesman* (1943), which is notable for its judicious and balanced treatment. An article in the *Times* (London), 9–10 Feb. 1883, is a lengthy appreciation on his retirement from the British bar. Rembert W. Patrick in *Jefferson Davis and His Cabinet* (1944) puts Benjamin in context and devotes far more space to him, whom he calls a "jack-of-all-trades," than to any of the seventeen other figures covered. References in older works tend toward bitter criticism, often indulging in religious and ethnic stereotypes. Examples include John Beauchamp Jones, *A Rebel War Clerk's Diary* (2 vols., 1866), and John S. Wise, *The End of an Era* (1901). Such accounts are somewhat balanced by Thomas C. De Leon, *Four Years in Rebel Capitals* (1890) and *Belles, Beaux and Brains of the '60s* (1909). Some more recent biographies suffer from filiopietism and hagiography as well as careless scholarship. William A. Tidwell et al., *Come Retribution: The Confederate Secret Service and the Assassination of Lincoln* (1988), provides persuasive if largely circumstantial evidence that Benjamin was involved in a plot with Davis, Robert E. Lee, and others in the Confederate high command to kidnap Lincoln and hold him as a hostage, forcing the North to sue for peace. If true, it might help to explain Davis's reticence in his memoirs about Benjamin's role in his cabinet. William C. Davis, *Jefferson Davis: The Man and His Hour* (1991), the best biography of the Confederate president, portrays Benjamin in a positive way and contains many details that refute the old charge that he was cold and heartless, abandoning Davis and other friends once he had reached safety in England.

MICHAEL B. CHESSON

BENJAMIN, Park (14 Aug. 1809–12 Sept. 1864), editor and author, was born in Demerara, British Guiana, the son of Park Benjamin, a New England sea captain and merchant, and Mary Judith Gall, daughter of a Barbados planter. In 1813 he was sent to live with relatives in Norwich, Connecticut. After entering Harvard in 1825 his interest turned to literature, but illness caused him to withdraw during his second year, and he completed his degree at Washington (now Trinity) College in Hartford in 1829. While there he was encouraged in his literary ambitions by George D.

Prentice, a prominent Connecticut poet and editor whose caustic wit and acerbic style made a lasting impression on the younger man.

Following his graduation, Benjamin edited a newspaper in Norwich, but when that venture failed he entered law school, first at Harvard, then at Yale. Admitted to the Connecticut bar in 1833 and to the Massachusetts bar in 1834, he settled in Boston, where he renewed friendships with former schoolmates, including Oliver Wendell Holmes, Charles Sumner, John O. Sargent, and John Lothrop Motley. Uninterested in pursuing a legal career, he became prominent in Boston's literary circles. With Holmes and Sargent he published a book of poems, *The Harbinger: A May-Gift* (1833). Though he continued to write poetry, he never surpassed these early efforts, and even these are commonplace examples of the popular verse of the time.

It was as a literary editor that Benjamin made his contribution to American letters. During the next decade he edited, sometimes briefly but always vigorously, several of the country's leading periodicals. The first was the *New-England Magazine*, a Boston monthly whose editorial staff he joined in December 1834; he became sole editor and proprietor the following March. The excellently produced magazine counted among its contributors many of the best American writers, chief among them Nathaniel Hawthorne. But financially it was unsuccessful, and Benjamin merged his magazine with the New York–based *American Monthly Magazine* in January 1836 and moved to New York City. This, too, failed, and in January 1838 Benjamin became literary editor of Horace Greeley's *New-Yorker*. In July 1839 Benjamin and another of Greeley's assistants, Rufus W. Griswold, began a mammoth-sized weekly titled *Brother Jonathan*, which specialized in sensational journalism and serial fiction. The following year Benjamin and Griswold, having quarreled with their publisher, founded a short-lived daily, the *Evening Signal*, and the enormously successful semiliterary weekly, the *New World*, whose first number appeared in June 1840.

Benjamin had finally found his métier, and he enjoyed his success immensely. Never one to avoid controversy, he entered into the literary battles of the day, which included a "moral war" directed against the sensational journalism of his rivals and a much-publicized libel suit brought against Benjamin by James Fenimore Cooper after Benjamin called Cooper, who then was under attack by the American press for his vilification of his native land in his novels, "the craziest loon that ever was suffered to roam at large without whip and keeper." But it was as a purveyor of popular fiction that the *New World* made its greatest contribution, especially through the *New World* "Extras," cheaply priced supplements large enough to accommodate within individual issues full-length novels, most of them popular foreign works that could be "pirated" by American publishers because of the lack of international copyright. Benjamin also made room for domestic fiction, including Walt Whitman's early

temperance novel *Franklin Evans* (1842), and gave far more space than did most other journals to literary criticism. Changes in postal laws, however, brought an end to the *New World* in 1845, and although Benjamin repeatedly tried to regain an editorial foothold, he spent most of his last years as a popular lecturer and a literary agent. He continued to work as hard as he did for love of the work, not financial need. Following his marriage in 1848 to Mary B. Western, daughter of a prominent New York attorney, and, soon after, the final settlement of his parents' estate, he was left financially able to enjoy his growing family, which eventually included eight children. Never defeated despite his many failures, Benjamin remained active in the literary life of his country up until the time of his death in New York City following a brief illness.

• The Park Benjamin Collection in the Butler Library at Columbia University contains his literary manuscripts, holograph letters, books, and a collection of his printed poems and the magazines edited by him. This collection was the basis of Merle M. Hoover's biographical study, *Park Benjamin: Poet and Editor* (1948), as well as Hoover's edition of Benjamin's *Poems* (1948).

THOMAS WORTHAM

BENJAMIN, Robert Charles O'Hara (31 Mar. 1855–2 Oct. 1900), journalist and lawyer, was born on the island of St. Kitts in the West Indies. Details about his early life, including the names of his parents and his education, are not known. In the fall of 1869 he arrived in New York, where he worked as soliciting agent for the *New York Star* and then as city editor for the *Progressive American*. Benjamin apparently became a U.S. citizen in the early 1870s, and in 1876 he gave speeches in support of Rutherford B. Hayes, the Republican candidate for president. He was rewarded with a position as a letter carrier in New York City but quit after nine months and moved to Kentucky, where he taught school. While there, Benjamin also took up the study of law. He continued his studies after being named principal of a school in Decatur, Alabama, and was admitted to the bar at Nashville, Tennessee, in January 1880.

Before and after his admission to the bar, the peripatetic Benjamin continued his career in journalism. In total, he edited and/or owned at least eleven black newspapers, including the *Colored Citizen* of Pittsburgh; *The Chronicle* of Evansville, Illinois; the *Nashville Free Lance* (where, as contributing editor, he wrote under the name "Cicero"); the *Negro American* of Birmingham, Alabama; the *Los Angeles Observer*; and the *San Francisco Sentinel*. When Benjamin worked at each of these papers is unclear. He was apparently in Birmingham in 1887, Los Angeles in 1888, and San Francisco in 1891. He also worked for the *Daily Sun*, a white-owned newspaper in Los Angeles.

In addition to his journalism, Benjamin also published a number of books and pamphlets that reflected the wide range of his interests. In 1883 he published *Poetic Gems*, a small collection of poetry, and in 1888 he published *Life of Toussaint L'Ouverture*. He was perhaps best known for *Southern Outrages: A Statistical Record of Lawless Doings* (1894). In 1886 Benjamin traveled to Canada on a speaking tour.

For twenty years Benjamin maintained a legal practice in the cities where he edited newspapers. One of his cases received widespread publicity: in Richmond, Virginia, in 1884 he won an acquittal of a black woman charged with murder. At a time when most white newspapers spoke of blacks in derogatory and racist terms, Benjamin's skills as a lawyer drew favorable comment from white newspapers in Richmond, Los Angeles, and Lexington.

Benjamin, however, did not court white opinion, although he well understood the risk that African Americans ran in challenging whites in civil rights, politics, and race relations. Benjamin was a vocal critic of racial discrimination and went much further than most black leaders; instead of simply denouncing Jim Crow legislation, he urged blacks to defend themselves when attacked by whites. Such an outspoken attitude led to Benjamin being forced to leave Brinkley, Arkansas, in 1879 and Birmingham in 1887. Irvine Garland Penn, author of *The Afro-American Press and Its Editors* (1891), said of Benjamin: "He is fearless in his editorial expression; and the fact that he is a negro does not lead him to withhold his opinions upon the live issues of the day, but to give them in a courageous manner."

In December 1892 Benjamin married Lula M. Robinson; they had a son and a daughter. The family settled in Lexington, Kentucky, in 1897. To the dismay of some whites, Benjamin quickly became involved in local politics. On 2 October 1900 he argued with Michael Moynahan, a Democratic precinct worker, over the white man's harassment of blacks wishing to register to vote. Late that evening Moynahan killed Benjamin. At the examining trial several days later, he pleaded not guilty by reasons of self-defense. The judge accepted Moynahan's claim and dismissed the case, even though Benjamin had been shot in the back.

Because of his militant stance, his journalism and other writings, and his legal career, R. C. O. Benjamin deserves serious attention from scholars. His tragic death is also a reminder that throughout American history even highly respected black leaders have been vulnerable to white violence.

• A few letters written by Benjamin can be found in the Booker T. Washington Papers at the Library of Congress. Copies of some of his books and pamphlets can be found in the Library of Congress, the New York Public Library, the Huntington Library, San Marino, Calif., and Stanford University. Some copies of the *Los Angeles Observer* and the *San Francisco Sentinel* are available at the Bancroft Library, University of California, Berkeley. Benjamin is profiled in William J. Simmons, *Men of Mark: Eminent, Progressive and Rising* (1887). Additional information can be found in the *Washington Bee*, the *New York Age*, the *Indianapolis Freeman*, and the white daily newspapers in the cities where he resided.

GEORGE C. WRIGHT

BENNER, Philip (19 May 1762–27 July 1832), soldier, pioneer ironmaster, and entrepreneur, was born in Chester County, Pennsylvania, the son of Henry Benner and Dinah Thomas, farmers. For Philip Benner as for many of his generation, the American Revolution was the defining experience of his early life. When his father, a vocal patriot, was imprisoned by the British, Philip went to war in the Continental army wearing a vest in which his mother had quilted guineas in case of emergency. Benner fought as a private under the command of his relative General Anthony Wayne, and the experience established his lifelong devotion to the military. Following the Revolution he was commissioned a major-general in the Pennsylvania state militia and thereafter was always known as General Benner.

After independence Benner learned the iron trade at Nutt's Forge in Coventry, northern Chester County, where some of Pennsylvania's earliest iron "plantations" were located. Sometime around 1785 Benner married Ruth Roberts; together they raised eight children. In May 1792 he purchased the land of Rock Forge in central Pennsylvania and began the task of establishing an iron business there. Bringing with him ninety-three experienced iron makers, Benner gradually improved the site, constructing first a house and saw mill in the spring of 1793 and erecting the following year an iron forge, believed to be the first forge in Centre County. Benner added a slitting mill in 1799, a second forge in 1800, and later a nail mill and a furnace. Throughout these early years Benner and his men were sustained largely by provisions imported by horseback from eastern Pennsylvania.

As his mills began to produce iron, Benner eschewed established markets along the Atlantic coast in favor of the markets emerging in the West. He began by shipping his iron products on horseback to Pittsburgh at the cost of $75 per ton. But since a ton of iron then commanded about $250 in the West, the trade was extremely profitable. The "Juniata iron" produced in his mills was widely regarded as among the finest iron produced in the charcoal furnaces of America. It won praise from Eli Whitney, who used it in his gun factory, and also helped to build Oliver Hazard Perry's fleet at Erie, Pennsylvania, during the War of 1812.

Like other entrepreneurs of his day, Benner was involved in a number of business ventures in addition to ironmaking. He was a major real estate speculator who helped develop Bellefonte, Pennsylvania; he also served as president of the Centre and Kishacoquillas Turnpike Company and owned Logan's Branch Woolen Factory. Benner, a lifelong Democrat, also founded a Jacksonian newspaper in 1827, the *Centre Democrat*, and twice served as a presidential elector, most notably for the Jackson-Calhoun ticket in 1824. He died at his residence in Spring Township, Centre County, Pennsylvania.

As a pioneer ironmaker and entrepreneur, Benner made important contributions to the growth and the geographical expansion of both the American iron industry and the nation.

• Some of Benner's business correspondence is included in the papers of William Orbison in the Orbison Family Papers at the Pennsylvania State Archives. See also Sherman Day, *Historical Collections of the State of Pennsylvania* (1843); John Blair Linn, *History of Centre and Clinton Counties, Pennsylvania* (1883); John B. Pearse, *A Concise History of the Iron Manufacture of the American Colonies Up to the Revolution and of Pennsylvania until the Present Time* (1876); Sylvester K. Stevens, *Pennsylvania: Titan of Industry* (3 vols., 1948); and James Moore Swank, *History of the Manufacture of Iron in All Ages*, 2d ed. (1892).

JOHN W. MALSBERGER

BENNET, Sanford Fillmore (21 June 1836–11 June 1898), physician and writer of popular verses and hymn texts, was born in Eden, New York, the son of Robert Bennet and Sally Kent. After spending his early years in New York, Bennet moved with his family to Lake County, Illinois. By the age of eighteen Bennet was teaching school in Wauconda, Illinois. In 1858 he entered the University of Michigan but did not complete a degree there, deciding instead to accept a position as the head of the Richmond, Illinois school district. After his marriage to Gertrude Crosby Johonnatt, Bennet moved to Elkhorn, Wisconsin, where he became co-owner and editor of the *Elkhorn Independent*.

The Civil War period marked a change in Bennet's professional life. In 1864 he sold his interest in the *Independent*. After serving with the Fortieth Infantry Regiment, Wisconsin Volunteers, from 25 May to 16 September 1864, he returned to Elkhorn, opened a drugstore, and began serious, if informal, medical study. In 1874 Bennet received a degree from Rush Medical College in Chicago. He moved back to Richmond, Illinois, where his medical practice flourished and he renewed his interest in journalism. He contributed frequently to the *Richmond Gazette* and also served as the paper's editor and publisher for a brief period.

Bennet wrote verses and collaborated often with composer J. P. Webster to create popular songs and hymns. In 1871 they published *The Signet Ring*, a popular hymn collection for which they wrote more than 100 of the pieces. The best-known Bennet-Webster collaboration is "The Sweet By and By," a hymn that has been used widely in churches throughout the United States and has been translated into numerous languages, including Chinese. In the first decade of the twentieth century, the Industrial Workers of the World (the Wobblies) used this hymn, with new words by Joe Hill, as a popular union organizing song, "The Preacher and the Slave."

In the last year of his life, Bennet published a memoir, *The Pioneer, an Idyll of the Middle West*. It describes the frontier conditions in Lake and Henry counties in Illinois that Bennet had experienced as a young teacher and journalist, and, later, as a physician. He died in Richmond, Illinois.

• For a discussion of Bennet's life and works see H. A. Kelly and W. L. Burrage, *American Medical Biographies* (1920), and the *Wisconsin Historical Society, Newspaper Catalog* (1911). An obituary is in the *Wisconsin State Journal* (Madison), 14 June 1898.

BARBARA L. TISCHLER

BENNETT, Alice (31 Jan. 1851–31 May 1925), physician and hospital administrator, was born in Wrentham, Massachusetts, the daughter of Isaac Francis Bennett, a blacksmith, and Lydia Hayden. She taught in the district schools of her hometown for four years to earn tuition for medical school, receiving her medical degree from the Woman's Medical College of Pennsylvania in 1876. Following graduation, Bennett worked at a dispensary in a Philadelphia working-class neighborhood, taught anatomy at her alma mater, and maintained a private medical practice while continuing her study of anatomy at the University of Pennsylvania. In 1880 she became the first woman to receive a doctor of philosophy degree from that university.

In the same year, Bennett was appointed superintendent of the Department for Women at the Norristown Hospital for the Insane, the first woman to hold such a position. Fellow medical practitioners such as Hiram Corson, having waged a professional and political battle in the early 1870s to allow women to participate in the medical profession in Pennsylvania, later in the decade had taken up a crusade to mandate the employment of women physicians on the staffs of all state institutions that served women. While resistance to women practicing medicine persisted in many circles, nineteenth-century ideas about women's supposed modesty and medical rationales that created causal connections between mental illness and gynecological problems persuaded some that women physicians could more effectively treat mentally ill women. Corson's success in convincing the trustees of the Norristown Hospital of such a positive result had led to Bennett's historic hiring.

Bennett served the Norristown Hospital until 1896. During those sixteen years, she recruited and trained dozens of women staff doctors, reorganized the treatment of women patients, established a system of family and community contacts, and challenged many of the traditional tenets of the psychiatric profession.

Bennett reinstituted educational and occupational therapy at the hospital (a regimen known as "moral therapy" earlier in the century) and challenged the use of drugs as sedatives. She believed that work therapy was "not inferior to drugs" and urged that a "change *out* of the hospital" might be equally effective. She spoke often and publicly against the use of restraining devices, publishing her articles in the *Medico-Legal Journal* (1884) and the *Transactions* (1884) of the Pennsylvania Medical Society. She was equally outspoken on matters concerning the diagnosis and treatment of the mentally ill in each of the official annual reports she prepared for the hospital's trustees. Bennett initiated the practice of regular gynecological examinations and treatments for her patients, a practice other women physicians in public institutions would imitate. Her experience led her to challenge the etiology of the day that drew a direct connection between women's reproductive systems and their vulnerability to mental illness.

Bennett's persistence in gaining membership in professional organizations helped to open medical and psychiatric professional organizations to women. She maintained membership in the American Medical Association, the Pennsylvania State Medical Society, the Philadelphia Neurological Society, the Philadelphia Medical Jurisprudence Society, and the Montgomery County Medical Society (in 1890 she became that society's first woman president). She held membership in the American Psychiatric Association (variously known as the Association of Medical Superintendents of American Institutions for the Insane and the American Medico-Psychological Association) and the rival National Association for the Protection and Prevention of Insanity.

In 1892 Bennett received some notoriety by allowing local and staff doctors to perform what some deemed as unnecessary gynecological surgery on nonconsenting patients. Cleared of any wrongdoing, she, nevertheless, tired of institutional and professional politics. After finishing her last three-year contract with the commonwealth of Pennsylvania, she left the superintendency in 1896.

From 1896 until 1898, Bennett was employed by the family of Cyrus McCormick (1859–1936) to care for his daughter, Mary Virginia, who suffered from chronic mental illness. Moving among the various McCormick family estates, Bennett organized not only the care of Mary Virginia, using even this idiosyncratic case as an intellectual prod for thinking about the nature of mental illness, but managed the entire household. In the face of allegations of opium addiction, Bennett resigned her position and returned to her hometown of Wrentham before once again embarking upon a private medical practice.

In 1910 Bennett moved to New York City, where she offered her services to Emily Blackwell's New York Infirmary for Women and Children. For fifteen years, she labored without remuneration, assisting in over 2,000 births.

Bennett's willingness to take an administrative position at a public institution and her perseverance in challenging both gender stereotypes and psychiatric paradigms won her a place in the history of women's professional advancement. Elizabeth Cady Stanton included Bennett in her 1886 *History of Woman Suffrage*, as did Frances Willard and Mary Livermore in their 1893 *A Woman of the Century*. Bennett died in New York City.

• There is no collection of Alice Bennett papers. Information about her years at the Norristown Hospital and her medical

and psychiatric philosophy can be gleaned from the records and annual reports of the Norristown Hospital currently housed at the Pennsylvania State Archives in Harrisburg. Her experiences with the care of Mary Virginia McCormick are documented in the extensive collection of McCormick family papers at the Wisconsin Historical Society in Madison. An analysis of Bennett's professional career can be found in Constance M. McGovern, "Doctors or Ladies? Women Physicians in Psychiatric Institutions, 1872–1900," *Bulletin of the History of Medicine* 55 (Spring 1981): 88–107. An obituary is in the *New York Times*, 1 June 1925.

CONSTANCE M. McGOVERN

BENNETT, Belle Harris (3 Dec. 1852–20 July 1922), church and ecumenical leader, was born Isabel Harris Bennett on the family plantation, "Homelands," in Madison County near Richmond, Kentucky, the daughter of Samuel Bennett and Elizabeth Chenault. Belle (as she preferred) was reared in a cultured and affluent but strict Methodist household. Her parents were descendant from early Virginia and Maryland settlers. Her paternal grandfather had migrated to Madison County around 1790 and was known as "Honest John Bennett," a Methodist itinerant, who supported himself as a farmer and tailor. Isabel Harris, her maternal grandmother, had migrated from Virginia and was related to the Chenaults, a French Huguenot family that had fled to British America to avoid religious persecution. Belle was the younger of two daughters in a family of eight children, all of whom attended the local county school. At age eleven Belle entered a private school conducted by Robert Breck, a Presbyterian minister. Next she attended Nazareth, a Catholic school, near Bardstown, then furthered her training at College Hill, Ohio. As a student she was proficient in belles lettres and the classics but as both an avid reader, especially of history, and a world traveler she continued her education throughout life. In 1916 Kentucky Wesleyan College conferred on her an honorary LL.D.

In 1875, influenced by an evangelistic meeting, Bennett joined the Providence Church (Methodist) near Richmond. In 1884 the Reverend George O. Barnes, a Presbyterian, helped her envision a life of Christian service. With her elder sister, Sue, she attended a missionary meeting in 1887 that focused her interest. The next year she was elected president of the Kentucky Conference Women's Missionary Society of the Methodist Episcopal Church, South. At the 1889 meeting of the Woman's Board of Foreign Missions she advanced the idea of creating a training school for women missionaries. Appointed project agent by the board, she became a key figure in creating Scarritt Bible and Training School, dedicated in Kansas City, Missouri, on 14 September 1892 (moved to Nashville, Tenn., in 1924).

Upon Sue Bennett's death in 1892, Belle was elected to replace her sister on the central committee of the Woman's Parsonage and Home Mission Society, a denominational agency designed to provide homes for itinerant ministers. In 1898 the General Conference authorized the formation of the Woman's Home Mission Society, and Bennett was elected its president. In 1910 the General Conference created the Board of Missions to oversee its mission work, both domestic and foreign; Bennett was elected to head the Women's Missionary Council, which the Board of Missions oversaw. She remained in this position until her death. In this role she initiated or supported the establishment of Ensley and Bethlehem community houses in urban centers, designated dormitories for women on college campuses, and advocated improved working conditions for laborers, prohibition, woman suffrage, interracial cooperation, and the extension of mission services to Africa, Latin America, Japan, Korea, and China. In 1913 she visited Brazil and subsequently Panama and China in her role as president of the Board of Missions.

Her sister's death also prompted a friend to establish, in 1896, the Sue Bennett Memorial School in London, Kentucky (today Sue Bennett College), with which Belle was intimately involved for the remainder of her life. That same year she corresponded with Lucy J. R. Meyer of Chicago to secure information about her experience in training women planning to enter religious careers. Her efforts led the Methodist Episcopal Church, South to create a deaconess order in 1902. Between 1906 and 1918 Bennett led a successful fight within her denomination for full lay rights for women. Her article "The History of the World-Wide Movement for the Liberation of Women," published in the *Methodist Review Quarterly* (Jan. 1912), was a clarion call for action. Her home conference elected her its first woman delegate to the General Conference in 1922, but due to failing health she was unable to attend.

In ecumenical activity Bennett was a delegate and speaker at the 1901 Third World Methodist Conference held at City Road, London. In 1910 she attended the International Missionary Conference in Edinburgh, Scotland, a singular event in launching the twentieth-century ecumenical movement. At the Congress on Christian Work in Latin America, held in Panama in 1916, sponsored by the Missionary Educational Movement of the United States and Canada, she chaired Commission V on "Women's Work." When both branches of episcopal Methodism created the Centenary Committee to celebrate, in 1920, the one-hundredth anniversary of the Missionary Society, Bennett was the only woman member. This celebration was a step in eventually reuniting Methodism, North and South, in 1939. The year before her death she was active at the Foreign Mission Conference held at Garden City, Long Island.

Recognition of Bennett's service is evident in the Belle H. Bennett Memorial at Scarritt College, the Bennett College in Rio de Janeiro, and the Belle H. Bennett Clinical Building of the Woman's Christian Medical College in Shanghai, China. Bennett died in Richmond, Kentucky.

• A few of Bennett's papers are in the Minerva McDaniel Library of Sue Bennett College, London, Ky. Mrs. Robert W.

MacDonnell, *Belle Harris Bennett: Her Life Work* (1928), is a major biography commissioned by the Board of Missions of the Methodist Episcopal Church, South. Noreen D. Tatum, *A Crown of Service: A Story of Woman's Work in the Methodist Episcopal Church, South, from 1878–1940* (1960), places Bennett in the context of her denomination; John Patrick McDowell, *The Social Gospel in the South: The Woman's Home Mission Movement in the Methodist Episcopal Church, South, 1886–1939* (1982), views her work within contemporary culture. In addition to entries on Bennett in the standard biographical dictionaries, Carolyn L. Stapelton, "Belle Harris Bennett (1852–1922): Model of Holistic Christianity," *Methodist History* 21 (Apr. 1983): 131–42, also is helpful. Additional material is in Rosemary R. Ruether and Rosemary S. Keller, *Women and Religion in America*, vol. 1 (1981), and Hilah F. Thomas and Rosemary S. Keller, *Women in New Worlds: Historical Perspectives on the Wesleyan Tradition* (1981–1982). Obituaries are in the *New York Times*, 21 July 1922, and the *Christian Advocate*, 28 July 1922.

FREDERICK V. MILLS, SR.

BENNETT, Constance (22 Oct. 1904–25 July 1965), actress, was born Constance Campbell Bennett in New York City, the daughter of Richard Bennett, a prominent actor, and Mabel Adrienne Morrison, an actress descended from a long line of stage performers in the Morrison and Wood families. Constance Bennett grew up the eldest of three daughters (her youngest sister Joan also became a well-known film actress) in various areas of New York City and its suburbs and attended Miss Merrill's School in Mamaroneck, New York. At age sixteen she eloped, on a dare, with University of Virginia student Chester Moorhead. Bennett's furious parents quickly separated the newlyweds by sending the bride to Europe and eventually had the marriage annulled. To keep his willful daughter out of further trouble her father encouraged Bennett's tentative acting ambitions by obtaining for her bit parts in low-budget comedies filmed in New York. This led to parts in New York–produced feature films, including the appropriately titled *Reckless Youth* (1922).

In 1923 the blond and vivacious Bennett was spotted by producer Samuel Goldwyn at the Actors' Equity Ball, where she was her father's date for the evening. After a successful screen test Goldwyn brought her to Hollywood to play a secondary role as a calculating young actress in *Cytherea* (1924). Bennett then returned to New York, where she appeared in *Into the Net*, a ten-part serial for the Pathé company. The cliffhanger plot featured Bennett as a Long Island society girl kidnapped by a crime ring. She traveled back to Hollywood and landed roles in a number of films, all released in 1925, including *My Son*, with Alla Nazimova, and *Sally, Irene, and Mary*, costarring a youthful Joan Crawford. On the strength of her performance in *Sally*, Bennett was offered (and signed) a contract with Metro-Goldwyn-Mayer Pictures, but before she made any films under her MGM contract Bennett asked that the agreement be voided. She had decided to give up her career to marry longtime beau Philip Morgan Plant, heir to a steamship and railroad fortune.

Bennett's four-year marriage to heavy-drinking Plant was spent primarily in Europe amid other fast-living young socialites. Divorcing Plant in 1929, she returned to the United States accompanied by an infant son and resumed her acting career. Under the guidance of her new paramour, Pathé executive Henri de la Falaise, the marquis de la Coudraye, Bennett signed with Pathé (which soon merged with RKO). She quickly became one of the top stars of the early sound-film era.

During her four years at RKO Bennett appeared in seventeen films, mostly melodramas aimed at class-conscious, depression-era audiences. Since the Production Code, which regulated the moral content of Hollywood films, was not yet in full effect, many of her RKO pictures had sordid plots. These included *Common Clay* (1930), in which she played a servant girl fighting for custody of her illegitimate child fathered by her employer's son; *Bought* (1931), featuring Bennett as a seamstress's daughter whose romance with a wealthy playboy (Ray Milland) is threatened by the discovery that she is illegitimate (Bennett's real-life father, in their only professional collaboration, played her illegitimate father). She also starred in *Bed of Roses* (1933) as a girl recently released from reform school who sets her cap for a rich husband only to fall in love with a young riverboat captain, played by Joel McCrea (Bennett's leading man in several pictures). The most highly regarded film in which Bennett appeared is the George Cukor–directed *What Price Hollywood?* (1932), a classic rags-to-riches story of a young waitress propelled to screen stardom at the cost of happiness. Cukor, who directed Bennett in five films, later told *Glamour* magazine that "Constance Bennett had one kind of romantic, F. Scott Fitzgerald look about her. It was the look of the Thirties—or perhaps the Thirties looked like her" (July 1963).

Bennett's icy beauty and somewhat haughty demeanor were not suited to the working-girl roles into which she was channeled. Offscreen the actress made no secret of enjoying a life of luxury during the depths of the depression. The mansion she shared with Falaise, who became her third husband in 1931 (they had no children), was a center of Hollywood social activity. Her forthright manner did not endear her to studio bosses (she was frequently likened to her handsome and opinionated stage-star father in both looks and personality). Though Bennett's films were solid box-office attractions, earning her one of the highest salaries in Hollywood, the imperious actress never won the hearts of moviegoers. When RKO decided not to renew her contract in 1933, Bennett did not protest and continued to view her acting career as something of a lark. Working as a freelancer she enjoyed a final flutter of screen success in 1937 with the hit MGM comedy *Topper*. The Norman Z. McLeod–directed film featured Bennett and Cary Grant as a sophisticated married couple killed in an auto accident after a night on the town. Fearing rejection at heaven's gate, they decide to stay on earth as ghosts to perform a good deed before offering themselves for judgment.

Bennett followed *Topper* with a popular sequel, *Topper Takes a Trip*, and a similar "screwball" comedy, *Merrily We Live*, both released in 1938.

Untroubled by her fall from stardom, Bennett gamely spent the remainder of her screen career essaying lead roles in "B" pictures and playing secondary parts in major films such as *Two-Faced Woman* (1941), which starred Greta Garbo. In 1939 she made an unsuccessful try at Broadway in Noël Coward's *Easy Virtue*. Divorced from Falaise in 1940, the next year she married actor Gilbert Roland, with whom she had two daughters before divorcing him in 1945. Bennett's fifth and final husband was an air force colonel, John Theron Coulter, whom she wed in 1946. They had no children. Though she continued to make frequent forays back into show business, including a nightclub act, a national tour in 1958 of the play *Auntie Mame*, and a brief cameo appearance in the 1954 comedy *It Should Happen to You*, directed by her old friend Cukor, Bennett spent the last two decades of her life primarily as a military wife. The still-glamorous Bennett accompanied her husband to postings in Europe and the United States. She died suddenly of a cerebral hemorrhage at the army hospital at Fort Dix, New Jersey (her husband, now a brigadier general, was stationed at nearby McGuire Air Force Base). She was buried in Arlington National Cemetery.

• A lengthy chapter in James Robert Parish, *The RKO Gals* (1974), and a detailed article by Gene Ringgold, "Constance Bennett Contributed to the Legends about the Hollywood of the '20s," *Films in Review*, Oct. 1965, pp. 472–95, are the most valuable sources of information on Constance Bennett. See also *The Bennett Playbill: Five Generations of the Famous Theater Family* by Bennett's sister Joan Bennett, with Lois Kibbee (1970), and Mary Margaret McBride, *The Life Story of Constance Bennett* (1932). An obituary is in the *New York Times*, 26 July 1965.

MARY C. KALFATOVIC

BENNETT, Edward Herbert (12 May 1874–14 Oct. 1954), architect and city planner, was born in Cheltenham, England, the son of Edwin Charles Bennett, a master mariner, and Margaret Julia Callas. Bennett emigrated to San Francisco, California, in 1890, where he apprenticed with several architects, including Robert White. In 1895, through the influence of architect Ralph Bernard Maybeck, Bennett received from philanthropist Phoebe Apperson Hearst a scholarship to attend the École des Beaux-Arts in Paris; he obtained a diploma from that institution in 1901.

After returning to the United States, Bennett worked for two leading architectural practitioners, George B. Post of New York and Daniel H. Burnham of Chicago. During his stint with Post from 1902 to 1904, Bennett assisted Burnham with an unsuccessful entry submitted to the U.S. Military Academy at West Point competition of 1903. The next year he relocated to Chicago to work for Burnham. His work included designing Chicago South Park District fieldhouses (1904–1910), drafting the *Plan of the City of San Francisco* (1905), and coauthoring the *Plan of Chicago*

(1909). The Chicago project set the standard for American city planning documents and represented a culmination of the City Beautiful Movement, which advocated efficiency and professionalism, along with the construction of parks and monumental public buildings modeled on those in Paris and other European capitals.

Burnham's mentoring launched Bennett on a career as a nationally prominent planning consultant. Bennett formed a partnership with architect William E. Parsons in 1919. In 1922 the firm became Bennett, Parsons, Frost, and Thomas after Bennett and Parsons allied themselves with architects Harry T. Frost and Cyrus W. Thomas; from 1929 until 1938 it was known as Bennett, Parsons & Frost; and from 1938 to 1944, as Bennett & Frost. Bennett served as consulting architect to the Chicago Plan Commission from 1909 to 1930. In this capacity he helped design many prominent public works projects, including Michigan Avenue Bridge (1910–1920), Grant Park and Buckingham Fountain (1915–1927), and Wacker Drive (1917–1926). Additionally, he contributed to numerous street improvements and to the locating of public buildings and monuments according to the 1909 plan. Bennett's firm created Chicago's first zoning ordinance in 1923. The partners produced plan reports and zoning ordinances for a number of private and public clients in the Chicago region. Bennett lived in the wealthy suburban town of Lake Forest with his first wife, Catherine Jones, whom he married in 1913; they had one child. Catherine Bennett died in 1925, and in 1930 he married Olive Holden Mead, a widow with two children; they had no children of their own.

Bennett and his partners also worked extensively outside Chicago. His plans for such smaller cities as Minneapolis, Minnesota (1910–1911), and Portland, Oregon (1912), resemble the 1909 plan of Chicago in their formality, monumentality, and presentation through beautifully rendered drawings. Bennett also worked on proposals for Cedar Rapids, Iowa (1910–1911, 1916), Ottawa, Ontario, Canada (1912–1915), Brooklyn, New York (1912–1915), Detroit, Michigan (1913, 1915), Pittsburgh, Pennsylvania (1914), and Denver, Colorado (1917). However, like most of the idealistic civic center, park, and city plans of the era, few of his were executed. An exception was Bennett's site plan for the 1915 Panama-Pacific International Exposition in San Francisco.

Bennett's experience led him to become a founding member of the American City Planning Institute in 1917. During the 1920s Bennett's firm became one of two dozen professional planning firms offering consulting services nationwide. In addition to civic center and park plans for Pasadena, California (1923), and Vincennes, Indiana (1928–1935), among others, the firm produced numerous reports of a more technical nature, reflecting the profession's new emphasis on zoning and traffic planning. Representative of this shift from planning for the "city beautiful" to planning for the "city functional" is the 1922 plan for St. Paul, Minnesota. Other commissions in the 1920s were obtained through Bennett's social connections and included site plans for the Knollwood Country Club in Lake Forest, Illinois (1924), and a subdivision for Vincent Astor on Long Island, New York (unexecuted, 1926–1927).

In the 1920s and 1930s Bennett participated in three especially prestigious projects of national scope. In 1922 he was selected as one of six planning experts to prepare background reports for the *New York Regional Plan*, a landmark document published in ten volumes between 1927 and 1931. In 1927 Bennett became chairman of the board of architects in charge of designing the Federal Triangle in Washington, D.C., a vast federal office building complex. Bennett, Parsons & Frost designed the Apex Building (1931–1938) for the Federal Trade Commission and the Botanic Gardens Conservatory (1931–1933) at the foot of Capitol Hill. In 1928 Bennett was selected to work on the projected 1933 Chicago Century of Progress Exposition, and he is credited with the design and codesign of six of its major structures, including the Federal Building, the Administration Building, and the Travel and Transport Building.

Throughout his career Bennett remained true to the aesthetic approach to planning and urban design that he had learned at the École des Beaux-Arts and under the tutelage of Burnham, although his firm's expertise had broadened to accommodate the profession's increasingly technical emphasis. Although not an innovator, Bennett helped establish standards and practices for the fledgling planning profession. Largely retired by the late 1930s, he spent his last years painting. Bennett died at his home in Tryon, North Carolina.

• Bennett's papers and drawings are in the Burnham Library at the Art Institute of Chicago. Other than those mentioned in the text, writings by Bennett include "City Planning," in *The Significance of the Fine Arts* (1923), published by the American Institute of Architects; and "Public Buildings and Quasi-Public Buildings," in *City Planning*, ed. John Nolen (1929). The only biography is Joan E. Draper, *Edward H. Bennett, Architect and City Planner, 1874–1954* (1982). Also see F. S. Swales, "Master Draftsman, XIV, Edward H. Bennett," *Pencil Points* 6 (Aug. 1923): 42–56; and Thomas S. Hines, *Burnham of Chicago* (1974). An obituary is in the *Chicago Tribune*, 16 Oct. 1954.

JOAN E. DRAPER

BENNETT, Floyd (25 Oct. 1890–25 Apr. 1928), aviator, was born at Truesdale Hill, Town of Caldwell (now Lake George), New York, the son of Wallace Bennett and Henrietta (maiden name unknown). At age nine he went to live with his uncle and aunt in Warrensburg, New York, where he attended public schools and did farm work. He left school at age seventeen and worked for a year in a lumber camp near Lake George to earn money to attend an automobile school in Schenectady. He then worked at the People's Garage in Ticonderoga. He eventually became co-owner but later sold his share and moved to Hague, New York, where he was employed as a mechanic in

R. F. Bolton's garage. He enlisted in the U.S. Navy on 15 December 1917, serving at naval air stations at Bay Shore, New York; Hampton Roads, Virginia; and Pensacola, Florida. In 1918 he married Cora Lillian Orkins of Ticonderoga; they had no children.

Rising to the highest enlisted rating of chief machinist's mate, aviation, by February 1919, Bennett reenlisted in July of that year and in December was sent again to Pensacola to be trained as an enlisted pilot. He was serving on the cruiser USS *Richmond* in 1925 when he applied for, and was assigned to, the Navy-MacMillan expedition to Greenland. Lieutenant Commander Richard E. Byrd, recognizing Bennett's skills and personal qualities, chose Bennett to act as pilot on a flight to the North Pole, with Byrd navigating.

At 1:55 A.M. on 9 May 1926, Byrd and Bennett took off from King's Bay, Spitzbergen, Norway, for the North Pole in a Fokker trimotor named *Josephine Ford* after the daughter of Edsel Ford, who had supported the expedition. They reached the pole at 9:02 A.M. and circled it several times before returning to land at King's Bay at 5:15 P.M., having flown 1,360 miles. Byrd later wrote that he had thought, during the flight, "I would rather have Floyd with me than any other man in the world" (*Skyward*, p. 195).

On their return to the United States, Bennett received a medal from the National Geographic Society and the keys to the city of New York. He was awarded the Distinguished Service Medal by President Calvin Coolidge and was promoted to warrant officer by act of Congress and awarded the Medal of Honor.

Byrd chose Bennett as pilot of a planned transatlantic flight, but unfortunately Bennett was severely injured in the landing crash of an aircraft designed and being flown by Anthony Fokker. His months of recuperation forced him to miss the flight.

Returning from Europe, Byrd began planning an Antarctic expedition, with Bennett to be second in command. In the spring of 1928 Bennett went to Detroit to test an aircraft the Bellanca company had built for the expedition. While he was there, three transatlantic fliers damaged their aircraft, the *Bremen*, while landing on Greenly Island in the Gulf of St. Lawrence. The *New York World* and the North American Newspaper Alliance arranged for an aircraft to fly to their rescue.

Although both were ill, Bennett and Bernt Balchen departed Detroit to deliver the parts needed to repair the *Bremen*. On landing at Ste. Agnes Flying Field, Murray Bay, Quebec, Bennett collapsed. Early reports stated that he was recovering, but his condition worsened and he was taken to the Jeffrey Hale Hospital in Quebec City. He was diagnosed as suffering from double pneumonia and pleurisy in addition to being badly run down and in generally poor physical condition.

Charles Lindbergh, responding to the need of a fellow aviator, flew through a severe blizzard to deliver serum. John D. Rockefeller, Jr., sent a message offering the full resources of the Rockefeller Institute and saying that no expense should be spared in the effort to save Bennett's life. Tragically, the serum was discovered to be useless against Bennett's type of pneumonia; he died a few days later with Byrd and Mrs. Bennett at his side. His body was escorted by the Royal Twenty-second Canadian Infantry Regiment to a train that carried it to New York City. It lay in state at the Seventy-first Armory, escorted there by the army's 161st Infantry, the Seventy-first Regiment of the New York National Guard, and the New York Police Force. Bennett was buried with full military honors at Arlington National Cemetery, near the grave of Admiral Robert Peary.

On 28 November 1929 Byrd and Balchen took off from Little America and made the first flight over the South Pole in an airplane Byrd had named the *Floyd Bennett*. At the pole they dropped an American flag from Bennett's grave.

The airport at Glens Falls, New York, not far from Warrensburg, a naval air station near the present site of Kennedy Airport, and a navy destroyer were all named in Bennett's honor.

• Abundant files of news and commentary about Bennett's career and death, published in local and regional newspapers, along with information and photographs released by the U.S. Navy, are in the Richards Library, Warrensburg, N.Y. See *Floyd Bennett*, by his widow, Cora Bennett (1932), for further information about his life. Bennett figures prominently in Richard E. Byrd's *Skyward* (1928).

VINCENT P. NORRIS

BENNETT, Gwendolyn (8 July 1902–30 May 1981), writer and artist, was born in Giddings, Texas, the daughter of Joshua Robin Bennett and Mayme F. Abernathy, teachers on a Native American reservation. In 1906 the family moved to Washington, D.C., where Bennett's father studied law and her mother worked as a manicurist and hairdresser. Her parents divorced and her mother won custody, but her father kidnapped the seven-year-old Gwendolyn. The two, with her stepmother, lived in hiding in various towns along the East Coast and in Pennsylvania before finally settling in New York.

At Brooklyn's Girls' High (1918–1921) Bennett participated in the drama and literary societies—the first African American to do so—and won first place in an art contest. She next attended fine arts classes at Columbia University (1921) and the Pratt Institute, from which she graduated in 1924. While she was still an undergraduate, her poem "Nocturne" was published in *Crisis* (Nov. 1923); "Heritage" appeared in *Opportunity* (Dec. 1923).

Bennett's poetry generally dealt with racial uplift and pride in her African heritage. "To Usward" was a tribute to the new generation and a call to those who have "a song to sing," published in both *Opportunity* and *Crisis* in May 1924. She also produced symbolist-inspired and romantic lyrics, such as "Quatrains" (1927). It expressed the tension Bennett experienced, torn between art and literature:

Brushes and paints are all I have
To speak the music in my soul
While silently there laughs at me
A copper jar beside a pale green bowl.

Over the next nine years, twenty-two of Bennett's poems appeared in *Opportunity, Crisis, Palms,* and *Gypsy.* Additional poems were published in William Stanley Braithwaite's, *Anthology of Magazine Verse for 1927 and Yearbook of American Poetry* (1927), Countee Cullen's *Caroling Dusk* (1927), and James Weldon Johnson's *The Book of American Negro Poetry* (1931).

Bennett also created cover illustrations for *Crisis* (Dec. 1923, Mar. 1924); the latter, "Pipes of Pan," was a line drawing of a young African-American man listening to music produced by nymphs and satyrs. Her covers for *Opportunity* appeared in January and July 1926 and December 1930. She also produced oil landscapes, but she rarely exhibited her work publicly.

In 1924 Bennett began teaching design, watercolor, and crafts at Howard University in Washington, D.C., and was reunited with her mother. The following year, on a $1,000 Delta Sigma Theta sorority fellowship, she studied art in Paris at the Académies de la Grande Chaumière, Julian, and Colarossi, and at the École du Panthéon. She published two short stories—"Wedding Day" published in *Fire!!* (1926), and "Tokens" in Charles S. Johnson's *Ebony and Topaz: A Collectanea* (1927). Both express the isolation and loneliness she experienced in Paris and feature African-American expatriates who remained in France after serving in World War I.

After Bennett returned to Washington, D.C., in 1926, her father died, and she lost most of the paintings and batiks she had produced abroad in a fire in her stepmother's home. She then spent two years (1927–1928) writing "The Ebony Flute," a "literary and social chit-chat" column for *Opportunity,* for which she had also written book reviews. During the summer of 1927 she also taught art classes at Nashville's Tennessee Agricultural and Industrial State College. The same year, she served as editor for the magazine *Black Opals.*

In 1928 Bennett received a scholarship to study art at the Barnes Foundation in Merion, Pennsylvania. She also married Alfred Jackson and moved to Eustis, Florida, where her husband had a medical practice. Unhappy in the segregated South, Bennett gained sixty pounds in four years and wrote little. The couple moved to Hemstead, Long Island, in 1932, and Bennett took a job with the Department of Information and Education of the Welfare Council of New York, writing feature articles that appeared in the *Amsterdam News,* the *New York Age,* the *Baltimore Afro-American,* and *Better Times.*

After Jackson died in 1936, Bennett lived alternately with her stepmother and with the sculptor Augusta Savage in New York. She worked as a teacher, then a project supervisor, in the Federal Art Teaching Project. When Savage resigned as director of the Harlem Community Art Center, a Federal Art Project endeavor, in 1939, Bennett took that position. She was also active in the Harlem Artists Guild, the National Negro Congress, the Artists Union, the Negro People's Theater, and the Negro Playwright's Company, serving on the board of directors of the last.

In 1941 Bennett gave a series of lectures on African-American arts at the School for Democracy; she also married a white Harvard graduate and fellow teacher, Richard Crosscup. Three years later, Bennett was suspended from the Art Center by the House Un-American Activities Committee (HUAC) for her leftist sympathies. She then cofounded and directed the George Carver Community School, an adult education center for African Americans in Harlem. HUAC investigated the school, and it closed in 1947. From the end of the 1940s until the late 1960s, Bennett worked for the Consumers Union as a correspondent.

Upon their retirement in 1968, Bennett and her husband moved to Kutztown, Pennsylvania, and opened an antiques store. Bennett died of congestive heart failure in Reading. She had no children.

Although she was a minor writer and artist, Bennett contributed significantly to the New Negro movement with her editing, teaching, and leadership, aiding the careers of such better-known colleagues as Aaron Douglas, Langston Hughes, and Countee Cullen.

• Bennett's papers are in the Schomburg Center for Research in Black Culture and History at the New York Public Library. Correspondence from her is in the Countee Cullen Papers in the Amistad Research Center, Tulane University; in the Woodruff Library, Atlanta University Center; in the James Weldon Johnson Collection at Yale University; and in the Alain Locke Papers, Moorland-Spingarn Research Center, Howard University. The most comprehensive study of Bennett is Sandra Govan, "Gwendolyn Bennett: Portrait of an Artist Lost" (Ph.D. diss., Emory Univ., 1980). Bennett's activities with the Works Progress Administration are addressed in Govan, "After the Renaissance: Gwendolyn Bennett and the WPA Years," *MidAtlantic Writers Association* 3 (Dec. 1988): 27–31. Her work as a writer is discussed in Ronald Primeau, "Frank Horne and the Second Echelon Poets of the Harlem Renaissance," in *The Harlem Renaissance Remembered,* ed. Arna Bontemps (1972), pp. 247–67.

THERESA LEININGER-MILLER

BENNETT, Harry Herbert (17 Jan. 1892–4 Jan. 1979), auto industry executive, was born in Ann Arbor, Michigan, the son of Verne C. Bennett, a sign painter, and Imogene Bangs, a schoolteacher. When Bennett was two years old, his father was killed in a fight. His mother later married Robert Winslow, a professor of engineering at the University of Michigan, who died a few years after the marriage. At age fifteen, Bennett moved with his mother to Detroit, where he entered the Detroit Fine Arts Academy to train as a commercial artist. Conflict at home caused him to run away and join the navy in 1909.

Bennett states in his memoir, *Ford: We Never Called Him Henry* (1951; repr. 1987), that although he enjoyed the excitement and camaraderie of military service, he had little interest in rising through the ranks of the navy. During his tour of duty he was assigned various jobs, including drawing cartoons for the navy magazine, some routine diving, and serving as a gunner on the ships *Texas*, *Ohio*, and *Nashville*. He also trained as a boxer and excelled at the sport. Bennett maintained a reputation for being quick with his fists outside the ring as well, showing little patience in the navy or elsewhere with people who annoyed him.

After his enlistment ran out in 1916, Bennett and a navy friend were involved in a fight with some customhouse officials in New York. Journalist Arthur Brisbane witnessed the brawl and took Bennett along with him to a meeting with Henry Ford, the owner of the Ford Motor Company. When Bennett first met him, Ford's River Rouge plant in Dearborn, near Detroit, was under construction. According to Bennett, Ford told him that the men building the Rouge were "a pretty tough lot," and that the company could use a man like him at the plant (Bennett [1987], p. 6).

After spending some time at the company's New York sales office, in 1916 Bennett moved to Detroit, where he worked in the Ford Motion Picture Department for several months before finally becoming Ford's personal assistant. Like most of Ford's other employees, he had no official title. Bennett states, "I guess the simplest way to define my position is to say that I was Mr. Ford's aide, his man of all work" (1987, p. 22). Some of the tasks he was assigned included the apprehension of thieves who had planned to hold up the company pay car, the recruitment of former convicts to act as security guards for the plant and for Ford family members, and service as a liaison with newspaper reporters. Ford expected Bennett to carry out orders promptly and without question, and Bennett generally did so. On 7 March 1932 several thousand unemployed workers participated in a hunger march on Ford's Rouge plant. When Bennett tried to calm the crowd, they threw rocks at him. Either Ford security men or the Dearborn police then opened fire, killing four marchers and wounding twenty others. Bennett was knocked unconscious in the ensuing confusion and had to be hospitalized.

Bennett married Eileen McClellan shortly after World War I; they had two children. In 1928, after a divorce, he married Margaret MacKensie; they had one child. A few years after his 1933 divorce from his second wife, Bennett married Esther Beattie; they also had one child.

Bennett is most famous for the role he played in the Ford Motor Company's fierce resistance to the unionization of its workers in the 1930s and 1940s. Attempts by the United Auto Workers (UAW) to organize Ford employees were met with the company's refusal to negotiate, the firing of workers who became involved in union activity, and violent attacks on UAW representatives who ventured inside the Rouge plant. In May 1937 union officials distributing leaflets at the plant were severely beaten by Ford security men, apparently on Bennett's orders. In the resulting case before the National Labor Relations Board, the company was found guilty of violating laws that protected the rights of workers to join unions. As the head of the security

forces, Bennett was sued for damages by the victims of the attack.

The company was unable to prevent workers from organizing. In 1941, after a strike forced the Rouge plant to shut down, Ford authorized Bennett to begin negotiations with the union. A few months later he signed a contract on behalf of the company that recognized the UAW as the legitimate representative of Ford employees and made numerous concessions into wages and working conditions.

In 1943 Ford appointed Bennett to the board of directors of the Ford Motor Company. Bennett ultimately presided over all personnel decisions, labor relations, and publicity and advised Ford on general policy. Within a few years, however, Ford's increasing senility and Henry Ford II's assumption of the company presidency left Bennett depressed and isolated. He left the company in September 1945.

The extent to which Bennett was responsible for labor policies and the violent conflicts that resulted at the Ford Motor Company is unclear. His autobiography leaves several gaps in information (there is no mention of the May 1937 beatings of UAW organizers, for example), but apart from these omissions it is a surprisingly frank autobiography that offers insight into the characters of both Bennett and Ford. Some historians have depicted Bennett as a clever, manipulative man who heavily influenced Ford and enjoyed almost total control over personnel matters. Others maintain that Bennett was merely the executor of orders that originated in the mind of his eccentric, suspicious, and authoritarian employer. Charles Sorensen, another Ford executive, was once startled when Ford's wife asked him, "Who is this man Bennett who has so much control over my husband?" He did not know how to tell her that "Bennett did not control Henry Ford but that the reverse was true" (Sorensen, p. 256).

Ford not only dominated at work but involved himself in his employees' personal lives as well. Bennett's first two marriages ended in divorce partly because Ford made excessive demands on his time. Bennett "literally had no existence outside the Ford Motor Company" (Bennett, p. 143).

After his retirement from Ford, Bennett moved to one of several properties he had accumulated, a 290-acre ranch in Desert Hot Springs, California. In 1969 the family moved to a ranch near Las Vegas, Nevada. Bennett died in a nursing home in Los Gatos, California.

• Some papers and oral interviews regarding Bennett's work for Ford are available at the Ford Archives, Henry Ford Museum. Details of Bennett's life and his work at Ford are outlined in Ford R. Bryan, *Henry's Lieutenants* (1993), a collective biography of Ford executives. Charles Sorensen, *My Forty Years with Ford* (1956), contains some information about Bennett and is useful for comparison with Bennett's account. Irving Bernstein, *Turbulent Years: A History of the American Worker, 1933–1941* (1970), and David Lewis, *The Public Image of Henry Ford: An American Folk Hero and His Company* (1976), both give negative portrayals of Bennett. Carl Raushenbush, *Fordism: Ford and the Workers, Ford and the Community* (1937), is a contemporary account of the labor struggles at the Ford Motor Company in the 1930s that offers some useful information about company labor policies and assesses Bennett's role and power within the organization. An obituary is in the *New York Times*, 14 Jan. 1979.

GRETA DE JONG

BENNETT, Henry Garland (14 Dec. 1886–22 Dec. 1951), university and government administrator, was born near New Hope in Nevada County, Arkansas, the son of Thomas Jefferson Bennett, a blind evangelist, and Mary Elizabeth Bright. At the age of eight, Henry was enrolled in the primary department (laboratory school) at Ouachita College in Arkadelphia, where he remained until 1907, when he received the bachelor of arts degree. Following graduation, he earned a teaching certificate, taught in a business college in Texarkana, sold textbooks, and finally entered the public educational system in Oklahoma, subsequently holding teaching or administrative positions in Boswell, Choctaw County, and Hugo. Bennett secured a master's degree from the University of Oklahoma in 1924, and Columbia University granted him the Ph.D. in 1926 for a dissertation entitled "The Coordination of the State Institutions of Higher Education in Oklahoma." In Hugo, Bennett met Vera Pearl Connell, the daughter of a lawyer and federal judge who resided in Durant. The couple were married in January 1913; they had five children.

From 1917 to 1951 Bennett served as a university president. Initially, he headed Southwestern State College in Durant. Among his lasting contributions there was the founding of the Ancient and Beneficent Order of the Red, Red Rose, an organization designed to foster appreciation for rural school teachers. In 1928 Bennett was invited to preside over the faculty of the Oklahoma Agricultural and Mechanical College (hereafter also called Oklahoma State University or OSU) in Stillwater. His tenure there was such that he eventually received recognition as one of the foremost university presidents in the United States. Bennett did all the things that successful executives do, internally; equally important, he tied OSU and the state of Oklahoma to the New Deal during the Great Depression and later World War II. Moreover, he or members of his administration assisted the Overseas Branch of the Department of the Army, the Civilian Agricultural Department of the Army, and the United Nations, especially the Food and Agriculture Organization, from 1945 to 1950. He initiated dozens of administrative and academic ties to these and other organizations, creating an international model at Oklahoma State University that later would be replicated by hundreds of institutions of higher education all over the United States.

In November 1950 Harry S. Truman appointed Bennett as the first permanent director of the Technical Cooperation Administration (TCA), with the rank of assistant secretary of state. This agency, popularly called Point Four, was the precursor of the Agency for International Development. In its early years, the TCA devised and implemented a plan to send American professors abroad to help emerging nations enter the window of the twentieth century by improving agriculture, engineering, manufacturing, and education. Initial activities were based in Africa, Asia, Europe, and some countries in Latin America. The so-called shirt-sleeve diplomats from the United States worked side by side with the indigenous population to modernize underdeveloped nations. This effort was titled "the Great Adventure in American Education," and it had much to do with facilitating educational exchanges and internationalizing the curriculum of U.S. colleges and universities.

The first major test of the Great Adventure came in Ethiopia, a North African nation whose economic jugular had been cut by the Italians during World War II. Bennett, who had been involved with food production and distribution in the world, hypothesized that the twelve inches of topsoil in Ethiopia could grow enough agricultural products to feed all of Europe, that hydroelectric power could be used for light manufacturing to decrease dependence on imports, and that a rise in the number of veterinarians could even foster the exportation of beef. He also promised the emperor Haile Selassie that the old school system would be rebuilt and that a comprehensive system of higher education, including a community college system, would be in place without delay. These latter institutions were to be staffed by Americans; however, exchange programs would be developed so that young Ethiopians could earn undergraduate and advanced degrees in the United States, returning home thereafter to form a native instructional cadre.

Shortly after a round of conferences with Selassie in the United States, Bennett left for a tour of the Middle East. Stops were scheduled in Rome, Athens, Cairo, Amman, Beirut, and Teheran. On 22 December 1951 the chartered plane crashed into the side of a mountain during a blinding snowstorm just five miles from its destination in Iran. Bennett, his wife Vera, three coworkers (A. C. Crilley, Benjamin Hardy, and James T. Mitchell), and the entire crew were found dead the next morning by Ambassador Loy Henderson. Bennett's death was mourned by many, including President Truman, members of Congress, the faculty and staff of the Oklahoma Agricultural and Mechanical College, and his family. His friend Senator Bob Kerr had once called him "a dreamer of no little Dreams" and now in eulogy added that he had a "vision as unlimited as Oklahoma sky." But perhaps Bennett himself best summarized his lifelong goals in a speech delivered in 1927: "I should like to see one generation of . . . youth reared and educated from cradle to maturity with the benefit of all that we know about medicine, health and hygiene, formal education and psychology. I should like to see one generation of . . . children grow up free from disease, social or biological, or mental malnutrition and maladjustment, in happy and healthy learning situations." Iranians marked the site of Bennett's death with a bronze sundial; Oklahoma State University dedicated a chapel on the campus in his honor; and the U.S. Congress funded one thousand international scholarships in his name.

• The largest collection of Bennett's personal papers is in the special collections of Oklahoma State University. Records pertaining to government activities are at the Harry S. Truman Library in Independence, Mo., and at the State Department in Washington, D.C. The last three chapters of Philip Reed Rulon, *Oklahoma State University* (1975), and Rulon's essay "Henry Garland Bennett: The Father of the 'Great Adventure' in University Contracts Abroad," *Red River Valley Historical Review* 2 (Summer 1975): 255–72, are the earliest scholarly treatments of Bennett's career. Jerry Gill, *The Great Adventure: Oklahoma State University and International Education* (1978), is an extension of Rulon's work. Courtney Vaughn, "The Politics of Progressive Higher Education: As Seen through the Career of Henry Garland Bennett" (Ph.D. diss., 1980), is on file in Stillwater. Newspapers published in Tulsa and Oklahoma City followed most of President Bennett's work in the Sooner State and are the best daily record of his career.

PHILIP R. RULON

BENNETT, Hugh Hammond (15 Apr. 1881–7 July 1960), soil conservationist and soil scientist, was born near Wadesboro in Anson County, North Carolina, the son of William Osborne Bennett and Rosa May Hammond, farmers.

Bennett earned a bachelor of science degree with an emphasis in chemistry and geology from the University of North Carolina in June 1903. At that time, the Bureau of Soils within the U.S. Department of Agriculture (USDA) had just begun to make county-based soil surveys, which would in time be regarded as important American contributions to soil science. Bennett accepted a job in the bureau headquarters' laboratory in Washington, D.C., but agreed first to assist on the soil survey of Davidson County, Tennessee, beginning 1 July 1903. The acceptance of that task, in Bennett's words, "fixed my life's work in soils."

The outdoor work suited Bennett, and he compiled a number of soil surveys. The 1905 survey of Louisa County, Virginia, in particular, profoundly affected Bennett. He had been directed to the county to investigate its reputation for declining crop yields. As he compared virgin, timbered sites to eroded fields, he became convinced that soil erosion was a problem not just for the individual farmer but also for rural economies. While this experience aroused his curiosity, it was, according to Bennett's recollection shortly before his death, Thomas C. Chamberlain's paper on "Soil Wastage" presented in 1908 at the Governors' Conference in the White House (published in *Conference of Governors on Conservation of Natural Resources*, ed. W. J. McGee [1909]) that "fixed my determination to pursue that subject to some possible point of counteraction."

In addition to supervising the soil surveys in the southern United States, a position he assumed at the bureau in 1909, Bennett accepted opportunities to study soils abroad and in U.S. territories. He worked in Costa Rica and Panama (1909), Alaska (1914), and Cuba (1925–1926) and served on the Guatemala-Honduras Boundary Commission (1919).

Bennett wrote steadily and increasingly about soil erosion in the 1920s in an array of journals from popular ones such as *North American Review* and *Country Gentleman* to scientific ones such as *Scientific Monthly* and the *Journal of Agricultural Research*. Eventually he succeeded in arousing national attention where others had failed. Among his writings of the 1920s, probably none was more influential than a USDA bulletin coauthored with William Ridgely Chapline titled *Soil Erosion: A National Menace* (1928). In it Bennett expressed the motivation for his later actions: "The writer, after 24 years spent in studying the soils of the United States, is of the opinion that soil erosion is the biggest problem confronting the farmers of the Nation over a tremendous part of its agricultural lands." The bulletin was not a manual on the methods of preventing soil erosion; rather it was intended to draw attention "to the evils of this process of land wastage and to the need for increased practical information and research work relating to the problem."

In answer to the need for action on soil conservation, Bennett promoted research with immediate applicability to conservation problems on the farm. Largely in response to Bennett's campaign for soil conservation, Representative James P. Buchanan of Texas attached an amendment to the 1930 appropriations bill authorizing the USDA to establish a series of soil erosion experiment stations. Bennett selected the sites for some stations and designed their research programs.

The availability of New Deal funds for emergency work programs meant that some of the funds could be directed to soil conservation. Bennett successfully argued that single practices such as the terracing of land would not succeed and that a comprehensive program to address numerous conservation problems on farmlands was needed. Having made himself the recognized expert on soil erosion, he became the director of the Soil Erosion Service in the Department of the Interior in September 1933. The agency worked with farmers to demonstrate soil conservation methods in watershed-based demonstrations. Wanting the work to have a firmer legislative foundation, Bennett successfully promoted the passage of the Soil Conservation Act of 27 April 1935, which created a Soil Conservation Service at the USDA. Bennett served as its first chief until his retirement in 1951. The agency's work and staff spread nationwide in cooperating with nearly 3,000 locally organized conservation districts. The Brown Creek Soil Conservation District covering parts of Anson and Union counties in North Carolina was the first district recognized, on 4 August 1937.

As Bennett guided the young agency, his concepts proved wise. Various disciplines, not just one, would contribute to designing conservation methods and practices for the farm, and, by the same token, no single effective conservation practice existed. Conservation farming meant rearranging the operations of the farm in the interest of conservation and productivity.

Soil conservationist worked on the land, directly with farmers, to develop conservation farm plans for the benefit of the land and the farmer.

Bennett possessed the energy and single-mindedness of an evangelist in his promotion of soil conservation. He steadily wrote articles about soil conservation and was a welcome and inspiring speaker not only at farm-field demonstrations, but also at scholarly gatherings. A contemporary, Santford Martin, noted that he "combined science with showmanship." Before congressional committees, Bennett employed tactics such as pouring water on a table to show the effect of rain on unprotected, bare soil. When a dust storm moving eastward in the spring of 1935 arrived over Washington, D.C., as he was testifying before a congressional committee on the bill that would create the Soil Conservation Service, he used the duster to dramatic effect to demonstrate the need for soil conservation. His crusading zeal brought many converts to soil conservation and made him the embodiment of the movement, the father of soil conservation.

The recipient of several honorary degrees, Bennett was also president of the Association of American Geographers in 1943 and was awarded the Frances K. Hutchinson Award by the Garden Club of America in 1944; the Cullum Geographical Medal by the American Geographical Society in 1948; and the Distinguished Service Medal by the USDA and the Audubon Medal by the National Audubon Society, both in 1947. He was a fellow of the American Society of Agronomy, the American Geographical Society, the American Association for the Advancement of Science, and the Soil Conservation Society of America. Upon his retirement, the *Raleigh (N.C.) News and Observer* opined that Bennett might come to be "recognized as the most important North Carolinian of this generation" (18 Jan. 1951).

An Episcopalian, Bennett had married Sarah Edna McCue in 1907. She died in 1909, leaving him one daughter. He married Betty Virginia Brown in 1921; they had one son and lived for many years at "Eight Oaks," a historic mid-nineteenth-century home in Falls Church, Virginia. Bennett died in Burlington, North Carolina, where his son was then living.

• Bennett's papers are in the Southern Historical Collection, University of North Carolina at Chapel Hill; the Archives of American Agriculture, Iowa State University, Ames; and in RG 114, Records of the Soil Conservation Service, National Archives, College Park, Md. Books written or co-written by Bennett include *Soils of the United States* (1913), *Soil Reconnaissance in Alaska, with an Estimate of the Agricultural Possibilities* (1915), *The Soils and Agriculture of the Southern States* (1921), *The Soils of Cuba* (1928), *Soil Conservation* (1939), and *Elements of Soil Conservation* (1947). For works about Bennett see Wellington Brink, *Big Hugh: The Father of Soil Conservation* (1951); Jonathan Daniels, *Tar Heels* (1941); and Robert J. Morgan, *Governing Soil Conservation* (1951). An obituary is in the *New York Times*, 8 July 1960.

DOUGLAS HELMS

BENNETT, Isadora (21 July 1900–8 Feb. 1980), publicist for dance and theater, was born in Canton, Missouri, the daughter of Clarence Bennett and Catherine Marshall, managers of a touring theatrical company. Bennett claimed that the circumstances of her birth were in the best theater tradition, occurring between the first and second acts of *Faust*. As a girl she lived during school terms with relatives in Springfield, Illinois. At a precocious age she won a scholarship to the University of Chicago, but soon she took a job as a cub reporter with the *Chicago Daily News*, becoming one of the first woman journalists on a major metropolitan newspaper. Bennett married Daniel A. Reed in 1919, and they moved to Columbia, South Carolina, where they founded the Town Theater. In the next several years they lived in various parts of the country, including Rochester, New York, and Hollywood, working as performers and producers as well as writing plays and theatrical journalism. Their two children became performing artists and had significant careers in the theater.

After moving to New York City in the 1930s, Bennett worked briefly for the *New York Daily News* but soon took a job in theatrical publicity with Oliver M. Sayler, who represented the director-producer Morris Gest, while Reed continued to act, write, and direct. Her first independent clients were the modern dance duet Miriam Winslow and Foster Fitzsimmons and the Spanish dancer La Argentinita. In 1939 Bennett formed an enduring professional relationship with dancer and choreographer Martha Graham. An early believer in the signal importance of Graham's work, she acted as press representative for the Martha Graham Dance Company until 1970. Another long association began in 1943 when the American Theatre Wing became a Bennett client.

Another of Bennett's clients in the late 1930s was the Mordkin Ballet, the predecessor of Ballet Theatre (now American Ballet Theatre). Through Mordkin, Bennett began a professional association with Richard Pleasant, who was manager of the Mordkin Ballet. With ballerina and heiress Lucia Chase, Pleasant envisioned a new American repertory company for ballet. On 11 January 1940 Ballet Theatre presented its premiere performance. Chase and Pleasant were codirectors of Ballet Theatre, and Bennett handled the publicity. Pleasant left the new ballet company after its second season. War service intervened as well as Pleasant's own managerial and publicity ventures, but in February 1949 Bennett and Pleasant announced their partnership in the public relations business, which continued until his death in 1961.

Pleasant brought to the public relations partnership a long association with the Perry-Mansfield Dance Camp and Festivals in Colorado. The firm represented a significant list of dance and performing arts clients, including the Royal Danish Ballet, Ted Shawn and the Jacob's Pillow Dance Festival, José Limón, Ravi Shankar, the Grand Kabuki, Doris Humphrey, Charles Weidman, Hanya Holm, the Erick Hawkins Dance Company, the Dancers of Bali, the National

Ballet of Canada, the American Ballet Theatre, José Greco, Lewisohn Stadium, Town Hall, the New York City Opera, Angel Records, and the Antoinette Perry "Tony" Awards. The Joffrey Ballet was a client from its early years, and Bennett took a participatory interest in the young company.

Bennett and Pleasant also undertook occasional production projects. One of these was the New York City Dance Theatre, an early attempt at a modern dance repertory company, presenting Weidman, Limón, Valerie Bettis, and Merce Cunningham in a 1949 season at City Center, New York. From 1954 to 1958 Bennett and Pleasant were general managers of the McCarter Theater in Princeton, New Jersey. Bennett was a founder of the Asia Society's performing arts program and from 1960 served as its executive director. She championed the creative performer. Her tone is apparent in this note to dancer Ted Shawn: "I am glad you find Shanta's [Rao] letter sweet and amusing as I do. You can see what a great person she is and all of that seeming extravagance is simple honest to God outgoing nature. It is, of course, the extravagance of the artist." Several managers and publicists trained under her supervision, including Charles Reinhart, who became director of the American Dance Festival. Choreographer Paul Taylor records in his autobiography, *Public Domain* (1987), his impression of a visit to Bennett's office: "'Yes, yes. Oh my, yes? This place is in one hell of a mess.' Her fingers are raking through her graying red hair, leaving it no less rampant. One of the buttons of her blouse is in the wrong hole. 'Things never seem to get caught up, but there's always time for my darlin'. Now tell me, what can I do for you?'" Despite her famously disheveled office and person, Bennett ran a supremely disciplined organization. She was uncompromising in taking as clients only those artists whose work she believed in absolutely and with whom she could build a mutual trust. She claimed this trust allowed "speedy coordination and plain, old efficiency." Her clients' quality as artists and her extra efforts for them guaranteed the attention of newspaper and magazine editors. One of her colleagues said, "When Isadora Bennett put her stamp of approval on it, you knew it had to be good." She wrote fluently, with wit and warmth, producing endless press releases and a huge correspondence. Bennett was honored by the dance profession with the Dance Magazine Award in 1963 and the Capezio Award in 1973. She died in New York City.

• Bennett's papers are in the Dance Collection of the New York Public Library for the Performing Arts and include some material on Richard Pleasant. Additional letters are part of the Ted Shawn manuscript collection. The Dance Collection also houses an unpublished Bennett manuscript, "The Dear Old Public: Workbook of a Publicist," prepared for the American Association of Dance Companies, which contains many anecdotes of her early career. See also Charles Reinhart, "Recalling Isadora Bennett," *Ballet News*, July 1980. An obituary is in the *New York Times*, 10 Feb. 1980.

MONICA MOSELEY

BENNETT, James Gordon (1 Sept. 1795–1 June 1872), newspaper editor, was born in Keith, Banffshire, Scotland, the son of a Roman Catholic farmer. After attending public school, Bennett at age fifteen entered the Catholic seminary at Aberdeen to train for the priesthood. He left the seminary after four years and spent the next five years reading and traveling, supported by an indulgent family, until 1819, when he impulsively decided to emigrate to the United States.

Bennett taught school for a few months in Halifax, Nova Scotia, and in Maine until he could reach Boston in 1820. He worked there for three years as a clerk at a printer and bookseller. In 1823 he was hired by Aaron S. Willington, publisher of the *Charleston* (S.C.) *Courier*, for whom he worked for ten months. He decided to make journalism his career, training here on one of the nation's best newspapers. He was responsible for news of Latin America and the Caribbean, and developed sympathy for the southern slave system.

Late in 1823 Bennett moved to New York and supported himself by freelance writing for several newspapers. In 1827 he became one of the editors of Mordecai M. Noah's *New York Enquirer*, covering politics in Albany and Washington. Noah's paper merged in 1829 with James Watson Webb's *New York Courier*, which Bennett joined as an associate editor writing on politics and banking. The *Courier and Enquirer* was the largest and most influential newspaper in the nation during the three years that Bennett was there, enterprising in its news gathering and staunchly pro–Andrew Jackson. Bennett wrote many of the editorials attacking the recharter of the Second Bank of the United States. A month after Jackson's veto of the recharter bill, the *Courier and Enquirer* switched sides, abandoned Jackson, and supported the recharter, perhaps because of timely loans from the bank.

Bennett quit the paper immediately, refusing to desert Jackson. He tried unsuccessfully to publish a small, cheap newspaper, the *New York Globe*, and failed in an attempt to buy into Francis P. Blair's (1791–1876) Washington *Globe*. In 1833 he was in Philadelphia editing the *Pennsylvanian*, a Jacksonian daily, but soon quarreled with party leaders. He returned to New York, freelancing again until 1835. By this time he was ready for his own venture, his stubborn independence accentuated by unsatisfactory experience on party newspapers.

Bennett had watched with interest the success of Benjamin H. Day's *New York Sun*, which appeared on 3 September 1833. The *Sun* was sold for a penny by newsboys on the street, unlike the traditional papers' yearly subscriptions. It was much smaller than the prevailing "blanket sheets" and focused on local human interest news, especially police court reports, neglecting the political, commercial, and foreign news of interest only to the elite. The *Sun* was a runaway success, circulating 10,000 by late 1834. The *Daily Transcript*, following a similar model, did almost as well.

Bennett believed there was room for another penny paper that would appeal to the large audience of literate middle- and working-class New Yorkers who liked the zest and local emphasis of the *Sun* and *Transcript* but wanted more foreign and national news, compressed and focused.

With $500 in capital, Bennett launched the *New York Herald* on 6 May 1835. It contained tidbits of local news, summaries of national, state, and foreign news, and a few advertisements. A week later it reappeared on a daily basis, soon adding a new feature—a Wall Street column that explained commercial and financial developments to lay readers. By the late 1830s the *Herald* and the *Sun* were the nation's largest circulation dailies. By the 1850s the *Herald*'s average daily circulation was between 50,000 and 70,000, the largest in the nation.

The *Herald* succeeded for two reasons. First, its human interest stories appealed to readers. Using the technique of sensationalism, Bennett focused on violence, crime, murder, suicide, seduction, and catastrophe in his local news coverage. He expanded the boundaries of news to include the social elite, sports (with news of horse racing, boxing, and yacht racing), religion, and whatever else he thought interesting. In 1836 his extensive and sensational coverage of the Robinson-Jewett murder case, in which a young clerk was accused of killing a beautiful prostitute but was eventually acquitted, outstripped that of Bennett's rivals and established a circulation lead for the *Herald*.

Bennett made himself a continuing story in the *Herald*, publishing many egocentric autobiographical pieces and attacking rival editors. The writing was sharp and often humorous. He treated religious developments in the same way as other news, often in a light, frivolous manner. In May 1840 he greatly overstepped the bounds of propriety with a vicious and vulgar attack on his own Roman Catholic Church. Two weeks later he announced his engagement to Henrietta Agnes Crean, an Irish immigrant and music teacher, in a front-page news story; a week later, a front-page story described his wedding.

The result of Bennett's unconventional coverage of religion, his egocentrism, and his personal attacks on rival editors was the "Moral War" of 1840. The rest of the New York press, the clergy, and business leaders tried to ruin the *Herald* by social ostracism of Bennett and a reader and advertiser boycott of his paper. The *Herald* lost circulation, not fully recovered until 1844, but it survived.

The second reason for Bennett's success was the comprehensive coverage of conventional news in the *Herald*, which by the 1840s matched that of his traditional rivals. By then the *Herald* cost two cents, and its size was enlarged. Bennett was zealous in his news gathering and quick to adopt new technology. Bigger steam presses kept up with increases in circulation and size. The staff became larger and more specialized. Regular correspondents reported from Albany and Washington as early as 1836, and in 1838 Bennett organized a network of European correspondents. The *Herald* made frequent scoops—it was the first paper to print the peace treaty with Mexico in 1848, for exam-

ple. Special reporters covered Wall Street and local government, and others reviewed cultural events. Directing all of them was Frederic Hudson, the managing editor since 1846, who was in charge during Bennett's frequent absences from New York.

Dissatisfied with the speed of the mail, Bennett established horse expresses to Washington and, during the Mexican War, a special express to New Orleans. He kept a fleet of newsboats to meet incoming ships, was quick to use the telegraph for news transmission, and helped organize the New York Associated Press in 1848.

Advertising receipts kept pace with circulation increases. Bennett required that payments be in cash in advance and that ads be changed each day so that they would always be fresh. No one was excluded, including abortionists and medical quacks. The volume of advertising made eight-page issues common by the 1850s. The income from Bennett's cash-and-carry policies provided capital for technological expansion to keep up with the increased circulation, especially in the 1850s.

Bennett professed to be politically independent, but his editorial policy was erratic. He was a jingoistic preacher of Manifest Destiny, believing that all of North America and the Caribbean would become part of the United States. He was extremely pro-South and proslavery, thus garnering unrivaled news sources in the southern states. He supported for president Democrats Andrew Jackson, James K. Polk, and Franklin Pierce, Whigs William Henry Harrison and Zachary Taylor, and Republican John Frémont. He criticized all of New York's state and local parties at one time or another but usually sided with the pro-South Hunker Democrats. Locally, he supported the outs against the incumbent administration in most elections.

The *Herald* opposed Abraham Lincoln's election in 1860 but supported the Civil War when it came. Its news gathering during the war was exceptional, with as many as sixty-three correspondents in the field at one time or another. But its editorial policy remained erratic, opposing emancipation and most of Lincoln's policies, puffing such personal favorites as General George B. McClellan (1826–1885) and endorsing no one in the 1864 presidential election. Bennett made Lincoln into a martyr following the assassination, and he supported most of Andrew Johnson's reconstruction policies.

Bennett retired from active management of the *Herald* after the war ended, turning it over to his playboy son James Gordon Bennett (1841–1918). The younger Bennett inherited the largest and most profitable newspaper in the nation, but it went into steady decline under his undisciplined direction. The elder Bennett lived in luxurious retirement until his death in New York City. He was also survived by his wife and their daughter Jeanette.

• There is no extensive collection of Bennett manuscripts. The standard accounts are Douglas Fermer, *James Gordon*

Bennett and the New York Herald: A Study of Editorial Opinion in the Civil War Era 1854–1867 (1986), and James L. Crouthamel, *Bennett's New York Herald and the Rise of the Popular Press* (1989). Different interpretations of Bennett's role in newspaper history are Helen MacGill Hughes, *News and the Human Interest Story* (1940); Dan Schiller, *Objectivity and the News: The Public and the Rise of Commercial Journalism* (1981); Michael Schudson, *Discovering the News: A Social History of American Newspapers* (1978); and John D. Stevens, *Sensationalism and the New York Press* (1991). John C. Nerone, "The Mythology of the Penny Press," *Critical Studies in Mass Communications* 4 (1987): 376–404, is an important revisionist account.

JAMES L. CROUTHAMEL

BENNETT, James Gordon, Jr. (10 May 1841–14 May 1918), newspaper publisher and editor, was born in New York City, the son of James Gordon Bennett, the founder and editor of the *New York Herald*, and Henrietta Agnes Crean. The eldest child of the man who popularized sensational journalism, Bennett grew up in an environment of wealth and privilege. He spent most of his youth abroad, educated privately by tutors and then at the École Polytechnique in Paris. Returning to the United States in 1861, he served briefly in the navy as a lieutenant during the Civil War. After the war, Bennett entered journalism seriously for the first time, working as an intern at the *New York Herald* under the tutelage of his father. Named as managing editor in 1866, Bennett assumed proprietary control of the *Herald* after his father's retirement in 1867.

At the time of his rapid succession to a position of great power at one of the country's leading newspapers, Bennett's reputation as a playboy overshadowed his journalistic pretensions. As a young man in New York City, his inherited wealth, dashing good looks, and extravagant lifestyle made him a popular member of the city's "fast set" in the post–Civil War era. A contemporary described Bennett as "the beau ideal of the man of the world and all-around daredevil." An avid sportsman, he served two terms as commodore of the New York Yacht Club. Nicknamed "Commodore" forever after, the sobriquet suited his imperious personality.

Despite his lavish social life, Bennett led the *Herald* to a new peak of popularity. Inexperienced and endowed with mediocre writing ability himself, Bennett nonetheless possessed a keen sense of the newsworthy. Recognizing a growing demand, Bennett launched an afternoon edition, the *Evening Telegram*, in 1867. However, he focused his efforts on increasing the flagging circulation of the *Herald*. He staffed the *Herald* with talented journalists, including James Creelman, Charles Nordhoff, Aloysius MacGahan, and Charles Edward Russell; famous writers such as Mark Twain and Walt Whitman also contributed to its pages.

Bennett's willingness to expend vast sums in pursuit of "hot" news stories soon proved to be successful. While retaining its sensational edge, the *Herald* became known for its coverage of breaking news, especially foreign affairs and wars. Under Bennett's direction, the *Herald* featured exclusive interviews with politicians, military men, scientists, and other celebrities from around the globe. As a result, the circulation of the *Herald* reached new heights in the 1870s and 1880s.

Bennett's dedication to exclusive news was rewarded when he assigned journalist Henry M. Stanley to go to Africa in search of David Livingstone, the Scottish missionary-explorer who had not been heard from for three years. Reflecting his determination to spare no expense, Bennett reportedly directed Stanley to "Draw a thousand pounds now, and when you have gone through that, draw another thousand, and when that is spent, draw another thousand . . . and so on; but find Livingstone!" (Carlson, p. 386). Stanley did just that in 1872, thus giving the *Herald* one of the most famous journalistic scoops of all time. Bennett later sponsored other explorations, including the ill-fated expedition by George Washington DeLong to find the North Pole in 1879. For Bennett such endeavors merely demonstrated his commitment to provide the *Herald*'s readers with all the important news of the day.

However, Bennett's capriciousness often undermined his best journalistic intentions. Autocratic by nature, he ruled his newspaper empire willfully and impulsively. He once demanded that his chief editor fire several of his most capable employees, asserting, "I want no indispensable men in my employ" (Laney, p. 37). Bennett kept a tight rein on both his employees and the content of his newspapers. Addressing new staff members, Bennett's words revealed his policy: "I am the only reader of this paper. I am the only one to be pleased. If I want the columns turned upside down, they must be turned upside down" (Laney, p. 19). Yet he could also be charitable, especially for high profile causes; the *Herald* sponsored soup lines in New York City slums in 1873 and established a relief fund for distress in Ireland in 1882. Inconsistent and increasingly eccentric, Bennett could always be counted on to do the unexpected.

Bennett's professional and personal fortunes took an unexpected turn when he was forced to leave New York in 1877. While visiting the home of his wealthy fiancée, Caroline May, a drunken Bennett reportedly relieved himself while in mixed company. The young woman's outraged brother, Frederick May, attacked Bennett several days later, beating him with cowhide in front of the Union Club. In retaliation, Bennett challenged May to a duel with pistols, which took place on 7 January. While no blood was shed, and both parties proclaimed themselves satisfied with the outcome, Bennett was ostracized as a result of the widely publicized scandal. He moved to Paris, where he lived as an expatriate for forty years. However, distance did not diminish his control of the newspapers in New York; he cabled daily instructions to his editors, and no one could be hired or fired without his approval.

Absentee ownership and competition from rising newspaper moguls such as Joseph Pulitzer and William Randolph Hearst led to the decline of Bennett's newspapers, particularly after the turn of the century. Yet Bennett continued to live extravagantly, maintaining lavish estates throughout Europe and socializing with European royalty. In 1887 he established the *Paris Herald*, known chiefly for its society news and its appeal to American expatriates, members of the international set, and tourists. It consistently lost money. However, both the *Paris Herald* and Bennett himself enjoyed a brief renaissance of sorts during World War I, when Bennett assumed personal control of the paper and successfully brought out every issue for the entire course of the war.

Bennett married Maud Potter, the widow of Baron George de Reuter in 1914. He died at his villa in Beaulieu, France, and was buried in Paris. Immediately after his death, Bennett's three newspapers were sold to Frank Munsey; the *Herald* was later absorbed into the *New York Herald Tribune*. Extravagant to the end, Bennett left a legacy of personal flamboyance and erratic professional success to the history of journalism.

• A full-length biographical treatment of James Gordon Bennett, Jr., has yet to be published, but six chapters are devoted to him in Don C. Seitz, *The James Gordon Bennetts, Father and Son* (1928). A biography of his father, Oliver Carlson's *The Man Who Made News: James Gordon Bennett* (1942), contains some information about the son. An evaluation of Bennett's career is in Richard Kluger, *The Paper: The Life and Death of the New York Herald Tribune* (1986). Anecdotal sources for Bennett's life and career are Oswald Garrison Villard, *Some Newspapers and Newspapermen* (1923); Albert Stevens Crockett, *When James Gordon Bennett Was Caliph of Bagdad* (1926); Al Laney, *Paris Herald: The Incredible Newspaper* (1947); and Richard O'Connor, *The Scandalous Mr. Bennett* (1962). A lengthy reminiscence of Bennett appears in the 19 May 1918 issue of the *New York Times*.

JULIE A. DOYLE

BENNETT, James Van Benschoten (28 Aug. 1894–19 Nov. 1978), director of the U.S. Bureau of Prisons, was born in Silver Creek, New York, the son of Edmund C. Bennett, an Episcopalian clergyman, and Mary Frances Berry, a former teacher. Bennett attended Brown University, where he received an A.B. in 1918, and served in the Army Air Corps during the closing months of World War I. In 1919 he married Marie Ettl; they had three children.

After his discharge from the army, Bennett passed the federal service examination and became an investigator for the Bureau of Efficiency, an agency designed to help streamline the federal bureaucracy. He studied law at George Washington University, graduating with an LL.B. in 1926.

Bennett's earliest achievements are among his most notable. In 1928 he was assigned to investigate and report on federal prisons. His report on the prison system led directly to the establishment of and his career in the U.S. Bureau of Prisons. He wrote of the deteriorating conditions of the prisons and the lack of a centralizing agency. The three federal penitentiaries existing at that time, Leavenworth, Atlanta, and McNeil Island, were vastly overcrowded, in part as a result of

the enactment of three federal laws promulgated since 1919: the Volstead (Prohibition) Act, the Harrison Narcotic Act, and the Dyer (Automobile Theft) Act. Bennett recommended, among other things, "the establishment of the first federal prison bureau in our history" and the building of "three new penitentiaries . . . keyed . . . to a plan of rehabilitation." In another report Bennett emphasized the importance for prison reform of providing meaningful labor for convicts.

The Hoover administration endorsed Bennett's recommendation to create a centralized bureau of prisons within the Department of Justice, and in 1929 President Herbert Hoover appointed Sanford Bates, Massachusetts commissioner of corrections, as superintendent of prisons. Bennett, whose report was instrumental in getting the bureau established, was appointed as one of three assistant directors in 1930. He helped draft the legislative proposals for prison reform that President Hoover sent to Congress, including the act to set up the Bureau of Prisons, the authorization of prison industries, the provision of education to prisoners, and the building of new prisons.

As assistant director, Bennett was responsible for the management of prison industries. With the onset of the depression, prison industries came under attack from organized labor, and Congress forbade prison-made products in interstate commerce. One of Bennett's outstanding career triumphs was the drafting of legislation that created a separate corporation with its own board and capitalization to manage prison industries. In 1934 President Franklin D. Roosevelt signed the act authorizing the Federal Prison Industries, Inc. Prison shops manufactured goods, such as mailbags, shirts, brooms, brushes, hardware, desks, chairs, and beds, for governmental markets. Bennett proclaimed the prison industrial labor rehabilitative: "Primary emphasis must be placed upon work which will train inmates in skills likely to provide them [convicts] with adequate livelihood upon release." By 1964 prison sales reached $40 million, with profits going into the Treasury as well as into more vocational training.

Upon Bates's retirement in 1937, President Roosevelt named Bennett director of the Bureau of Prisons. As director, Bennett attempted to put into effect prison rehabilitative programs then current among Progressive Era reformers, including parole, probation, abolition of physical punishment, individual treatment of convicts, and classification of prisoners as both a management and a rehabilitative tool. Shortly after Bennett's appointment as director, all bureau personnel except top management came under the Civil Service Law, a process that had started some time before, and he presided over the complete bureaucratization of the Bureau of Prisons. During his directorship, narcotics addicts were assigned from prisons to the new hospitals under the U.S. Public Health Service, and through a variety of legislative actions juveniles were separated from and treated differently from adult offenders. Also during the first ten years or so of his tenure, the number of federal prisons multiplied rapidly. Several new federal prisons were built in the late 1930s using Public Work Administration funds, and by the beginning of World War II the federal prison system had expanded its capacity to accommodate the rising number of offenders committed under federal laws.

Near the end of Bennett's directorship, in the late 1950s and early 1960s, he instituted new rehabilitative programs based on behavioral science models that were continued under his successors. These initiatives included programs for juvenile delinquents, training of counselors, and prerelease guidance centers. He successfully lobbied for the Indeterminate Sentence Act of 1958, the Prison Rehabilitation Act of 1965, and an elaboration of the Federal Youth Correction Act of 1950. Little concrete evidence suggests that these measures successfully rehabilitated convicts either at the federal or state level, but their implementation is indicative of Bennett's political success in working with Congress and the presidents.

Bennett retired from the directorship in 1964. During his more than a quarter century at the helm of the U.S. Bureau of Prisons, he proved to be a sound manager and an adroit politician and was primarily responsible for building the vast federal penal system and bureaucracy. He also closed America's most infamous prison and symbol of an era, Alcatraz, and presided over the building of the new maximum security prison at Marion, Illinois. He was active in several professional associations and was president of the American Prison Association in 1939. Among his published writings is an autobiography, *I Chose Prison* (1970), which also details his view of the history of the prison bureaucracy. His first wife died in 1967, and in 1971 he married Olympia Stone. He died in Bethesda, Maryland.

• The primary source for Bennett's career is the U.S. Bureau of Prisons papers in the National Archives. Of importance are his government reports, especially Federal Penal and Correctional Institutions, *Report* (1930); and "Prison Industries," *Proceedings of the 60th Annual Congress of the American Prison Association* (1930), pp. 135–43. The early history of the bureau from the point of view of the first director is in Sanford Bates, *Prisons and Beyond* (1936). Bennett is a prominent figure in Paul Keve, *Prisons and the American Conscience: A History of U.S. Federal Corrections* (1991). The foreword to Keve's book was written by Myrl Alexander, Bennett's successor but definitely not his choice as director. Also useful is Blake McKelvey, *American Prisons: A History of Good Intentions* (1977). Bennett is placed in the context of the history of prison reform in Larry E. Sullivan, *The Prison Reform Movement: Forlorn Hope* (1990). An obituary is in the *New York Times*, 21 Nov. 1978.

LARRY E. SULLIVAN

BENNETT, John Charles (6 Dec. 1923–5 May 1980), major general in the U.S. Army and White House aide, was born in Washington, D.C., the son of Ivan Loveridge Bennett and Ruby Jenrette. Shortly after graduating from the U.S. Military Academy at West Point in 1945, Bennett married Jean Hazelton MacKenzie. They had four children. In 1951 Bennett re-

ceived an M.A. in English from Columbia University. He received another M.A. in international affairs from George Washington University in 1964.

Bennett had a distinguished military career. He rose to the rank of general and became chief of staff of the army's Alaska Command. After retiring from the army in 1972 with the rank of major general, he became in 1973 vice president of ERA Helicopters of Anchorage, Alaska. Bennett's corporate career was short-lived, however, as later that year he joined the White House staff of President Richard M. Nixon as an assistant to the president, working directly for General Alexander M. Haig, Jr., when Haig became Nixon's chief of staff.

As deputy chief of staff under Haig, Bennett was given, among his other duties, custody of President Nixon's White House tape recordings. These tapes, recorded at various White House and Executive Office locations, were an essential ingredient in Nixon's downfall. With what *Newsweek* magazine referred to as "security befitting the crown jewels," Bennett regularly cataloged and secured the tapes in three locked vaults, which were fitted with electronic sensors to monitor any motion. Bennett was one of only three people who had access to the tapes.

In November 1973, amid the heat of the Watergate scandal and investigations of criminal wrongdoing in the Nixon administration, both Congress and the Special Prosecutor's Office subpoenaed the president's tapes, which they believed could either clear or condemn President Nixon. The president fought to retain control of the tapes, claiming that they were protected by "executive privilege," but in July 1974 the Supreme Court, in an 8–0 decision (*United States v. Nixon*), forced Nixon to surrender the recordings. These tapes contained conversations between the president and H. R. "Bob" Haldeman, his chief of staff, recorded just days after the arrest of the Watergate burglars in the Democratic Party Headquarters in the Watergate complex.

The recording of the 23 June 1972 conversation was referred to as the "smoking gun," because in it the president and Haldeman discussed ways to block the Federal Bureau of Investigation inquiry into the Watergate burglary. Nixon agreed that the Central Intelligence Agency would concoct a false story to get the FBI to back off from its investigation. This obstruction of justice was one of the many charges that would have led to Nixon's impeachment and conviction in the Senate had he not resigned in August 1974.

On 7 November 1973 Bennett testified before federal district judge John Sirica that there was an 18½-minute "gap" in one of the key tapes covering 20 June 1972, the day that President Nixon and Haldeman had their first opportunity to discuss Watergate. Court-appointed experts later concluded that this gap was the result of several intentional erasures. Additionally, several tapes subpoenaed by the special prosecutor could not be found. Because Bennett had custody of these tapes under heavy security, Judge Sirica repeatedly questioned Bennett regarding the whereabouts of the missing tapes and the possible tampering with the tapes. Bennett shed no light on these mysteries, and they remain among the many unanswered questions of the Watergate scandal.

In 1977 Bennett returned to Alaska and became vice president of the Alaska Pacific Bank in Anchorage. He rarely discussed Watergate and never explained the tape gap. Bennett's body was found along the slopes of Mount Susitna, near Anchorage, Alaska, in the wreckage of his light plane. He had left Anchorage International Airport alone in his Cessna 185 for a flight to Red Shirt Lake and Alexander Lake. Before the crash, he had sent out a distress signal, saying that the plane was going down.

For the most part, Bennett lived a life outside the glare of public notoriety. When he did receive widespread national attention, he was put on the defensive over knowledge of the possible tampering with the White House tapes. He was unable (perhaps unwilling) to clear up the confusion over the tapes, and as of the mid-1990s it was still not known who altered the Nixon White House tape recordings.

• Bennett's role in the Nixon White House is discussed in James F. Clarity, "Notes on People: White House Doubles in Brass," *New York Times*, 14 June 1973, p. 61; "Spotlight on the Tape Vault," *Newsweek*, 5 Aug. 1974, p. 24; and Anthony Ripley, "Was the Cover-Up Covered Up?" *New York Times*, 19 Jan. 1974, p. 12. An obituary is in the *New York Times*, 6 May 1980.

MICHAEL A. GENOVESE

BENNETT, John Coleman (22 July 1902–27 Apr. 1995), theologian and seminary president, was born in Kingston, Ontario, the son of William Russell Bennett, a Presbyterian minister, and Charlotte Coleman. He attended Williams College (A.B., 1924), Oxford University (A.B. in theology, 1926; M.A., 1930), and Union Theological Seminary (B.D., 1927; S.T.M., 1929). He married Anna Louesa McGrew in 1931; they had three children. He was ordained as a minister in the Congregational Christian Churches in Berkeley, California, in 1939.

Theologically Bennett stands in the tradition of liberal Protestantism. The influence of the social gospel movement is most clearly seen in *Social Salvation* (1935). But he subsequently moved away from the idealistic views of human nature and historical progress identified with certain forms of that movement to a position that he called "Christian realism" (*Christian Realism*, 1941). He believed there should be a balance between reason based upon experience and revelation in dealing with complex social issues. Empirical analysis is prerequisite both for understanding the problems themselves and for the development of effective strategies for dealing with the latter. The moral law is partially discernible through reason (natural law); for the Christian, however, it is most fully disclosed through revelation in Christ. Although Christian ethics has much in common with other forms of morality, it is finally distinguished from the latter by its demand for obedience to the love commandment. The possibility

of such obedience is grounded ultimately in faith; it includes love for all people in a universal community.

Bennett's methodology in social ethics is most fully developed in *Christian Ethics and Social Policy* (1946). His primary purpose in this series of lectures was to develop a strategy by which Christian ethics would assist in the formulation of public policy. By way of contrast, he first identified four other methods that he rejected as inadequate: the Catholic appeal both to the authority of the church and to natural law; the strategy of withdrawal from the morally ambiguous aspects of public life; the identification of Christianity with particular social programs; and the adoption of a double standard for personal and public life. As an alternative Bennett proposed a fifth strategy that emphasized the primacy of the love commandment, recognized the universality and persistence of sin, and took into account the earthly political realities of public policy. Love for the neighbor requires a sustained effort to spell out the content of this demand in the public domain.

Bennett was also involved in the ecumenical movement. At the Oxford Conference on Life and Work in 1937, he served as secretary of the section on "Church, Community, and State in Relation to the Economic Order." He was a leader in the Amsterdam (1948), Evanston (1954), and New Delhi (1961) assemblies of the World Council of Churches. *Christian Social Ethics in a Changing World* (1966), which Bennett edited, was part of a four-volume series prepared for the World Council of Churches Conference on Church and Society (Geneva, 1966). In the numerous books and articles that he wrote throughout this period, he dealt primarily with the relationship of Christian faith to economics and politics, including the state, Communism, foreign policy, and war. The ecumenical movement provided an indispensable resource for his deepening understanding of the complexity and interrelatedness of such issues on a global basis.

Bennett also worked closely with both the Federal Council of Churches and its successor, the National Council of the Churches of Christ in the U.S.A. As a member of the commission of the Federal Council of Churches, he studied the moral implications of wartime use of weapons of mass destruction (1950). He participated in the preparation of a series of volumes sponsored by the National Council of Churches on the Ethics and Economics of Society. For many years he served as a member of the departments of the church and economic life and of international affairs of the National Council of Churches.

Christianity and Communism (1949), together with new editions of that work (*Christianity and Communism Today*, 1960; 1970); *Christians and the State* (1958); *Nuclear Weapons and the Conflict of Conscience*, which he edited (1962); and *Foreign Policy in Christian Perspective* (1966) reflected Bennett's continued involvement in international affairs. In his analysis of Communism, he stressed the need to understand its origins, its concern for social justice, and the changes that had taken place in the Soviet Union and other

Communist states. He believed that such an understanding was necessary as a corrective to the view that Communism was an unchanging system of evil.

Bennett was a pacifist throughout the early and mid-1930s. His pacifism was not, however, based upon an absolute principle of nonviolence but rather upon a pragmatic assessment of war as the greatest evil threatening humankind. With the rise of Nazism and the increasing threat of aggression that it posed, he moved gradually to a "just war" position on the ground that a Nazi victory represented an even greater evil than war. In 1941 he and Reinhold Niebuhr cofounded *Christianity & Crisis* as a voice of protest against American isolationism. In the years following World War II, he was actively engaged in foreign policy debates related to the Cold War, international Communism, and the use of nuclear weapons. During this period he came to defend the possession of nuclear weapons as a means of nuclear deterrence but denounced their use on a first-strike basis.

An outspoken critic of U.S. involvement in Vietnam, Bennett was one of the cofounders of Clergy and Laity Concerned about Vietnam. He was also active in the civil rights movement. As president of Union Theological Seminary (1963–1970), he was instrumental in the establishment of contractual arrangements with Fordham University (a Roman Catholic School), whereby the two institutions began to pool professors, library resources, and credits in graduate studies in religion. During this period he also developed an academic relationship with Woodstock Theological Seminary (Roman Catholic) and Jewish Theological Seminary.

Following his retirement in 1970, Bennett moved to Claremont, California. He continued to write and was visiting professor at Claremont School of Theology (1975–1976) and the University of Southern California (1976). He died in Claremont.

• A collection of Bennett's papers is in the library of Union Theological Seminary. In addition to works cited above, his books include *The Radical Imperative* (1975) and *U.S. Foreign Policy and Christian Ethics* (with Harvey Seifert, 1977). He was coauthor of *Christian Values and Economic Life* (1954) and wrote approximately 350 articles and editorials for *Christianity & Crisis* (1941–1993). He was also a frequent contributor to other leading periodicals, including *The Christian Century*, *Christendom*, and *Religion in Life*. The best critical assessment of Bennett's theology is Edward LeRoy Long, Jr., and Robert T. Handy, eds., *Theology and Church in Times of Change* (1970). The chapter by Robert F. Beach contains an extensive bibliography of Bennett's writings. For an analysis of the basic structure of Bennett's ethics, see David H. Smith, *The Achievement of John C. Bennett* (1970), especially the section on foreign policy. Robert Handy, *A History of Union Theological Seminary* (1987), contains an account of Bennett's presidency at Union. For brief personal assessments of Bennett as an ethicist see the *Christian Century*, 17 May 1995, pp. 535–36; and 24–31 May 1995, pp. 556–57. An obituary is is in the *New York Times*, 2 May 1995.

E. CLINTON GARDNER

BENNETT, John Cook (3 Aug. 1804–5 Aug. 1867), physician, religious leader, and entrepreneur, was born in Fair Haven, Bristol County, Massachusetts, the son of John Bennett, a shipowner, and Abigail Cook. At his father's death in 1817, he moved with his mother to Ohio to stay with relatives. In 1825, after a three-year apprenticeship with a physician and an oral examination by an Ohio medical society, Bennett received his M.D. and a license to practice. That year he married Mary Barker; they had three children. There is no evidence supporting his claim to have attended Ohio University or McGill College in Montreal; he did, however, become a Freemason in 1826.

Doubling as a lay preacher, Bennett successfully lobbied Ohio's legislature to incorporate the Methodist Episcopal church in 1827. He published his first medical article in the *Western Journal of the Medical and Physical Sciences* in April 1829, followed by four other articles in the next eight months concerning cases of disease or problems during childbirth. Bennett combined traditional medicine with the vegetable remedies advocated by Samuel Thomson.

When the Ohio legislature resisted Bennett's lobbying to incorporate a Methodist college in 1830, he abruptly joined Alexander Campbell and the Disciples of Christ. In 1833 he became the president and later the chancellor of the "Campbellite" Christian College in New Albany, Indiana. To bolster the college's finances, he sold diplomas in medicine, law, divinity, and the arts and sciences to persons without training, apprenticeship, or exams. He also authorized others to issue diplomas in his name and sold diplomas from the Midwest to Boston. This was apparently the first "diploma mill" in the United States.

Early in 1834, before Campbell and the Indiana college repudiated him for selling diplomas, Bennett unsuccessfully lobbied Ohio's legislature and the Baptist church to establish a college and medical school in that state. His illicit awarding of diplomas not only embarrassed the Disciples of Christ, but also led the Ohio Masons to make an unsuccessful attempt in February to expel him.

Undeterred, in November 1834 Bennett became a professor of medicine and the faculty president of the Willoughby University in Chagrin, Ohio. Bennett retained that position for five months, after which the trustees expelled him for selling diplomas. Nevertheless, by September 1835 he was professor and president of the Sylvanian Medical College in Erie, Pennsylvania. Bennett resigned in March 1836 after granting M.D.'s to the college's four students after only five months of training.

Meanwhile, as an extension of his emphasis on Thomsonian medicine, Bennett had begun promoting the medicinal benefits of the tomato and refuting its reputation as being poisonous. Bennett's writings about the tomato in the mid-1830s were published throughout the United States and succeeded in popularizing the tomato as an edible fruit. To the end of the century, Bennett's articles about the tomato were cited in medical journals and gardening magazines as far away as Europe and Australia.

After legislators had rejected his petition to form a militia in Ohio, Bennett abandoned his wife and children in June 1838. (She had already been estranged because of his extramarital affairs.) He moved to Illinois, where he signed a petition asking the legislature to incorporate the state's first private militia.

After the incorporation of the Invincible Dragoons in February 1839, Bennett became its brigadier general in April by appointment of the governor. This began Bennett's remarkable success and notoriety in Illinois, where he became the founder and secretary of the state medical society in June 1840. In July the governor appointed him as the quartermaster general for the entire state.

Two months later Bennett moved to Nauvoo, Illinois, the new headquarters of the Church of Jesus Christ of Latter-day Saints (LDS). Nauvoo was the boom town of Illinois as a result of its geometric growth created by Missouri's expulsion of the Mormons in 1839. Seeing vast opportunities for self-advancement, Bennett converted to Mormonism and successfully lobbied the Illinois legislature to incorporate Nauvoo. Its city charter allowed extensive autonomy, including its own militia. Because Mormons voted as a bloc, nomination by church president Joseph Smith, Jr., guaranteed Bennett's unanimous election as Nauvoo's mayor on 1 February 1841. The Mormon capital was now larger than the state capital of Springfield, formerly the largest city in Illinois.

This was only the first of Bennett's rewards for helping to make Nauvoo a virtual city-state in Illinois. Within days of his mayoral election, Bennett became the major general of the newly organized Nauvoo Legion, the chancellor of the city's university, and the secretary of its Masonic lodge. In April 1841 Smith appointed him as an assistant counselor in the First Presidency of the LDS church, despite Smith's knowledge that Bennett had a reputation for adultery. In May, Judge Stephen A. Douglas also appointed the physician-mayor (and fellow Democrat) as the judicial master in chancery for Hancock County. Bennett unsuccessfully fought his dismissal as the state quartermaster general for accepting the Nauvoo Legion position.

"I'll throw a mantle of charity over your sins," Smith had proclaimed in a sermon to Nauvoo's Mormons, but this philosophy backfired with Bennett. He seduced several women and appointed them as the "spiritual wives" of anyone he sent to them for casual sex. Smith tried to avoid a public scandal by having Bennett quietly resign his civil and church positions, but the rumors soon forced the LDS president (who was also Bennett's successor as mayor) to publicly denounce Bennett in May 1842. In quick order, Bennett lost his positions in the Nauvoo Legion, the university, and the Masonic lodge. Amid the scandal he also resigned as the county's master in chancery in a possible quid pro quo with Douglas, who secured Bennett a quick divorce from his abandoned wife.

Bennett was furious at what he regarded as a hypocritical betrayal, since Smith secretly had polygamous wives of his own. By June Bennett was exposing and embellishing Nauvoo's secrets in lectures throughout the Midwest and the East. He published an expanded version of his lectures as *The History of the Saints; or An Expose of Joe Smith and Mormonism* in 1842 in Boston. In August of that year, a Mormon newspaper retaliated by referring to Bennett's bisexual conduct, and Mormon apostle Brigham Young even publicly identified Bennett's 21-year-old boyfriend. In March 1843 Bennett married Sarah Rider, whom he had met while lecturing in Massachusetts.

Bennett was now Mormonism's Benedict Arnold; yet Smith had forgiven other apostates and restored them to their church offices. That prospect probably motivated Bennett to repay his financial debts to Smith in December 1843. However, no reconciliation had occurred by the time anti-Mormons murdered Smith in June 1844. Bennett then tried to establish links with nearly every possible successor except Young, who never forgave disloyalty. Bennett forged an alleged revelation from Smith appointing Sidney Rigdon as Smith's successor. Rigdon's followers promoted the bogus revelation in 1845 even though Rigdon himself seemed embarrassed by it.

James J. Strang was the only Mormon succession advocate to accept Bennett, who became Strang's secret counselor in 1846. Although Strang's was not a military organization, he allowed Bennett to adopt the title "general-in-chief." He also ignored Bennett's expressions of his love for a young man and fellow physician while Bennett's wife remained in Massachusetts. Many of Strang's followers could not forgive Bennett's former treachery and refused to acknowledge his offices. For a year Strang supported Bennett, but he had to repudiate him in 1847 because of increasing disclosures of his sexual improprieties with women.

By the end of 1847, Bennett had returned to his wife in Massachusetts. At Plymouth he began experimenting with chloroform as an anesthetic. In 1848 he reported 127 successful surgeries performed with chloroform and promoted it in medical journals.

Often (probably erroneously) credited as the originator of the Plymouth Rock chickens, Bennett organized the first large exhibition of poultry breeders in 1849 at Boston. Poultry breeding provided him a comfortable living for the rest of his life.

Bennett began visiting Iowa in the late 1840s to spend time with the physician, Pierce B. Fagen, who had sparked his bisexual interests during Bennett's association with Strang. The man had married the daughter of railroad entrepreneur B. T. Hoxie, but Bennett moved to Iowa in 1853 to renew their association. His friend abruptly moved to California, but Bennett continued to await his return to Iowa.

After Bennett's wife joined him in Iowa, he became the postmaster of Des Moines in 1856. He was a justice of the peace in Polk City, Iowa, in 1857. During the Civil War, he was a major in Iowa's Tenth Regiment and a field surgeon in the U.S. Third Infantry. At his death in Polk City, the *Des Moines Daily State Register* noted: "For many months he was a helpless invalid, and death to him was probably a welcome visitant. He was a kind neighbor and public-spirited citizen."

• Bennett's book on poultry breeding is *The Poultry Book: A Treatise on Breeding and General Management of Domestic Fowls* (1850) Biographical works on Bennett include Andrew F. Smith, *The Saintly Scoundrel: The Life and Times of Dr. John Cook Bennett* (1997); James J. Tyler, "John Cook Bennett: Colorful Freemason of the Early Nineteenth Century," *Proceedings of the Grand Lodge of Ohio* (1947): 140–48; Smith, "Dr. John Cook Bennett's Tomato Campaign," *Old Northwest* 16 (Spring 1992): 61–75; and Smith, "'The Diploma Peddler': Dr. John Cook Bennett and Christian College at New Albany, Indiana," *Indiana History* 90 (Mar. 1994): 26–47; Also see D. Michael Quinn, *The Mormon Hierarchy: Origins of Power* (1994); Roger Van Noord, *King of Beaver Island: The Life and Assassination of James Jesse Strang* (1988); and Quinn, *Same-Sex Dynamics among Nineteenth-Century Americans* (1996).

D. MICHAEL QUINN

BENNETT, Lewis (1831–18 Jan. 1896), distance runner, was born Hagasadoni at the Cattaragus Reservation in Erie County, New York. The exact date of his birth and his parents' names are unknown. A Seneca Indian of the Snipe clan, he was given the English name Lewis Bennett. As a professional runner, he competed under the name "Deerfoot."

Deerfoot first came to public notice in 1856 when he won the purse in a five-mile race in a fair at Fredonia, New York, running the distance in twenty-five minutes, a time so fast in that period that few people believed it to be accurate. A year elapsed before he was listed again in the victory column. This time he won the ten-mile race at the same fair in the respectable time of fifty-six minutes and nineteen seconds. The next year he again ran the five-mile distance in twenty-five minutes and eighteen seconds. In the late 1850s, with another Seneca runner known as Albert Smith, Deerfoot began to compete against the professionals in Massachusetts and the New York City area.

Running races had become a popular spectator sport in the United States, partially as the result of the visits in the 1840s to this country of professional runners from England, where organized competition was far more advanced. Pedestrian contests were especially popular in the New York City and Boston areas. Running races for American Indians were part of the entertainment at county fairs in western New York State.

In 1861 George Martin, an English promoter, appeared in New York City with three professional runners to challenge the best that the United States had to offer. Deerfoot and Smith accepted the challenge but were easily outdistanced by the English professionals. However, recognizing that Deerfoot, a tall, handsome, muscular youth and an indigenous American, would be quite an attraction in England, Martin persuaded him to travel there for a series of races.

In England, Martin made every effort to convey the image of Deerfoot as an unspoiled child of the wilderness. Deerfoot was introduced to the public wearing a wolf-skin blanket and a band around his head with an eagle feather stuck in it. It was announced that Deerfoot spoke no English and that one of his handlers had to serve as an interpreter, a fabrication; Deerfoot spoke English fluently. To a public thrilled by the novels of James Fenimore Cooper, Deerfoot became an immediate sensation. Although he lost his first race in England on 9 September 1861, he won his next race and continued to win his subsequent contests, attracting larger crowds with each performance. The Prince of Wales was among the spectators at some of the races, and at one he presented Deerfoot a purse of eighteen pounds to add to his winnings.

Racing every week and sometimes more than once in a week, Deerfoot began to show signs of fatigue by December. He rested for two months and then returned to competition. The attendance at the races began to fall off, perhaps due to rumors of fixed races. Martin, Deerfoot's manager, then took his runner on tour through the northern counties, Scotland, and Ireland. Each evening Deerfoot competed in a four-mile race against professional runners who were traveling with the show, and Deerfoot won every evening. At the conclusion of the tour in September 1862 Deerfoot had run in competition more than 400 miles and had performed for more than 150,000 people. At this time, William Jackson, one of Deerfoot's traveling competitors, sued Martin for breach of contract and testified that all of the races were fixed. It is quite likely that Deerfoot's races on the tour were staged as exhibitions rather than as true competition. The results of professional pedestrian contests were often viewed with suspicion. However, in the major races in the London area, where large sums of money were wagered on the outcome of the races and as many as 5,000 spectators witnessed the contests, measures were taken that made the fixed race less common than they might have been in the rural areas. One of the most common practices to eliminate cheating was to make the elapsed time a condition of the wager.

In October 1862, when Deerfoot returned to competition in the London area, he seemed tired, running slow times and failing to finish one race. It seemed that his career was over, but a one-hour race on 27 October 1862, in which he outlasted his rivals and set a record by traveling 11 miles, 720 yards, restored his popularity. In the remaining months of his English visit his performances were erratic, sometimes winning and setting records and at other times failing to finish. In his last great race on Good Friday 1863, a twelve-mile handicap race in which Deerfoot gave the leading runners of England a head start, he set a record of 51 minutes, 26 seconds for the ten-mile distance and covered the twelve miles in 1 hour, 2 minutes, and 2-1/4 seconds, records that would stand until well into the twentieth century. In one hour he had run 11 miles, 970 yards.

After he returned to the United States Deerfoot continued to compete but failed to perform as well as he had in England. In the 1870s two Iroquois runners, Keraronwe and Daillebout, were attracting attention.

On 27 August 1870 Deerfoot was matched with and lost to the younger Keraronwe in a three-mile race. Deerfoot complained that three miles was not long enough for him. He continued to perform at county fairs, sometimes racing against other Senecas and at other times racing against horses, and traveling as far west as Chicago. His last public appearance was not as an athlete but as part of an exhibition of Native Americans in 1893 at the Chicago World's Fair. Deerfoot died on the Cattaragus Reservation, where he was buried. Three years later his remains were removed to a cemetery in Buffalo, New York, and placed next to the grave of the celebrated Seneca orator Red Jacket.

Deerfoot was one of many excellent Indian runners from western New York State who competed in professional running races from 1840 until near the end of the century, when professionalism was replaced by the amateur athletic movement. His reputation as a great runner rests on that brief period when he outran the best athletes of England and set records that endured for many years. Other Indian athletes traveled to England in subsequent years, but none achieved the success or enjoyed the popularity that Deerfoot experienced.

• Accounts of Deerfoot's pedestrian feats are covered well in the *New York Clipper* throughout his career. The *Clipper* began tracking his career when he raced at the county fairs in the Buffalo area. The *Clipper* followed his English tour for its readers by reprinting the detailed reports of his races that appeared in the London *Sporting News* and *Bell's Life in London*. Even after his return from England, when his career as a winner was over, the *Clipper* continued to chronicle his activities. See especially the *New York Clipper*, 24 Oct. 1857; 30 Oct. 1858; 23 July 1859; 13 July, 5, 12, 19, 26 Oct., 2, 16, 30 Nov., 21, 28 Dec. 1861; 4, 11, 18 Jan., 8 Feb., 8, 15, 22, 29 Mar., 5 Apr., 24 May, 25 Oct., 22 Nov. 1862; 28 Mar., 2 May, 6 June 1863; 11 June, 16 July 1864; 11 Mar. 1865; 14 Dec. 1867; 16 Nov. 1868; 3, 17 July 1869; and 27 Aug., 10 Sept. 1870. An obituary is in the *New York Times*, 20 Jan. 1896.

JOHN CUMMING

BENNETT, Michael (8 Apr. 1943–2 July 1987), musical theater director and choreographer, was born Michael Bennett Di Figlia in Buffalo, New York, the son of Salvatore Di Figlia, a machinist, and Helen Turnoff, a secretary. Bennett took weekly dance classes, studying ballet, tap, jazz and modern technique. He attended Hutchinson Central Technical High School for Boys, where he studied architectural design, but at seventeen he dropped out of school to go on a year-long European tour in a production of *West Side Story*.

Returning to the United States, he settled in New York City. He began teaching jazz classes at the June Taylor studios, and he danced in the Broadway choruses of *Subways Are for Sleeping* (1961), *Here's Love* (1963), and *Bajour* (1964); he also assisted with the choreography in *Nowhere to Go but Up* (1962). His first assignment as a Broadway choreographer was for *A Joyful Noise* in 1966, which closed after twelve performances. Despite its brief run, the show earned Bennett his first Tony award nomination for choreography. *Henry, Sweet Henry* (1967), his second choreographic effort, received another Tony nomination, but it ran for only eighty performances. Bennett's first Broadway success was *Promises, Promises* in 1968, produced by Broadway veteran David Merrick, which featured a book by Neil Simon and a score by Burt Bacharach and Hal David. The show ran for 1,281 New York performances and was a hit in London.

During the late 1960s Bennett branched out into television (the choreography for "Pinocchio" on NBC's Hall of Fame in 1968) and industrial shows. His next Broadway effort was *Coco* (1969). Based on the life of designer Coco Chanel, the musical was essentially a glorified fashion show and feature for Katharine Hepburn in her first and only musical comedy role. Although tepidly received by critics, the musical ran for some three hundred performances and displayed Bennett's ability to provide seamless transitions while furthering character development. "He works very much from character and isn't interested in the steps per se," the show's director, Harold Prince, told a reporter. "In this way, he gets the physical qualities that come from character into his dances and so eliminates that awful wrench when you go from a scene to a song and dance."

Bennett came into his own as a director and choreographer during the 1970s. In 1971 he codirected, with Prince, the musical *Follies*, which depicted the reunion of former Follies showgirls in a decrepit theater and featured a score by Stephen Sondheim. Bennett received Tony awards for codirection and choreography. He made his nonmusical Broadway directorial debut with *Twigs* (1971), by George Furth, which ran for eight months. A minor success, *Seesaw* (1973), for which Bennett received another Tony for his choreography, and a flop, Neil Simon's *God's Favorite* (1974), preceded his landmark work, *A Chorus Line* (1975).

The first musical that Bennett directed and choreographed from its inception, *A Chorus Line* represented a shift in the importance of dancers in the Broadway musical. Not only did the show use the unsung gypsies, or chorus dancers, as a metaphor for life, but the show's unusual development—evolving from taped interviews with dancers to a series of production workshops—provided an entirely new approach to conceiving a musical. One critic wrote, "The Broadway dancer became for [Bennett] the perfect embodiment of the state of Broadway, the exact opposite of the dishonesty of Watergate, and the reflection of his personal uncertainty." The close collaboration between Bennett, his cast, composer Marvin Hamlisch, librettists Nicholas Dante and James Kirkwood, and lyricist Ed Kleban, resulted in what is considered to be Bennett's finest work. *A Chorus Line* won a Tony for best musical in 1976 and a month later the Pulitzer Prize. On 29 September 1983 the show became the longest-running play or musical in Broadway history to that time. That same year *Variety* reported a worldwide gross of $260 million from the show's touring companies, which played 184 U.S. cities, ten Canadian cities, and in eight other countries. The 1985 film adaptation was a critical and financial failure. On 28 March 1990 the Broadway version of *A Chorus Line* finally closed.

Bennett married Donna McKechnie, a dancer in *A Chorus Line*, in 1976; the marriage was childless and ended in divorce two years later. Throughout his life Bennett had sexual relations with both men and women. He told *London Gay News* in 1976, "If I like someone, then I can feel for them and sex is just an extension of that feeling, whether it's a man or a woman."

Bennett's next theatrical effort, *Ballroom* (1978), based on a CBS television movie, had a cast of thirty Broadway dancers between the ages of forty and sixty. After a three-month run, the show closed at a loss of nearly $3 million, although it received eight Tony award nominations. That same year Bennett used his earnings from *A Chorus Line* to purchase an entire building in downtown Manhattan, where he and other directors and choreographers continued to develop musicals-in-progress.

Bennett rebounded from *Ballroom* with the hit *Dreamgirls* in 1981. A backstage musical loosely based on the career of the black singing group, the Supremes, the show cost $3.5 million and was Bennett's most technically elaborate effort. Some critics believed his masterful choreography broke new ground and advanced the form of musical theater. Bennett and his collaborator, Michael Peters, won Tony awards for the show's choreography.

During the mid-eighties Bennett was involved with three aborted Broadway musical projects, *A Children's Crusade*, *Chess*, and *Scandal*. *Scandal*, a contemporary musical about sex and relationships, was scheduled to open in 1985, but Bennett became ill and discontinued the project. In 1986 he withdrew as director of the musical *Chess*, stating the reason as angina pectoris. A year later, he disclosed that he was suffering from AIDS. He sought treatment in Tucson, Arizona, where he died of lymphoma, an AIDS-related cancer. His estate was estimated at $425 million, of which 15 percent was bequeathed to organizations involved with AIDS research and treatment.

Bennett's choreography, originating from musical theater traditions of the 1940s and 1950s, moved dance away from decorative production numbers to dramatic throughlines that integrated plot with other stage elements. As a person, Bennett was considered to be a contradiction. He was not an intellectual, although his choreography was highly structured and never superfluous.

• Bennett's Broadway career, especially his work on *A Chorus Line*, is treated in several books, Denny Martin, *What They Did for Love: The Untold Story behind the Making of "A Chorus Line"* (1989); Kevin Kelly, *Our Singular Sensation: The Michael Bennett Story* (1990); and Ken Mandelbaum, *A Chorus Line and the Musicals of Michael Bennett* (1989). An obituary is in the *New York Times*, 3 July 1987.

KEVIN GRUBB

BENNETT, M. Katharine Jones (28 Nov. 1864–11 Apr. 1950), philanthropist and church leader, was born in Englewood, New Jersey, the daughter of Henry Jones and Winifred Davies, natives of North Wales. Her father was a prosperous builder. Her first name was Mary, but she was known as Katharine and tended to use just an initial for her first name. Entering Elmira College in Elmira, New York, in 1881, she graduated four years later with an almost perfect academic record. After teaching in both public and private schools in her native Englewood, she was drawn into social and religious service. In 1894 she was named national secretary of young people's work for the Woman's Board of Home Missions of the Presbyterian Church (U.S.A.), commuting to its New York City office. During this period she also became a member of the governing board of the College Settlements Association, organized in 1890 by graduates of several eastern women's colleges in an effort to advance the growing settlement house movement.

In 1898 she resigned her position and on 20 July married Fred Smith Bennett, a successful New York manufacturer and merchant who lived in Englewood. Both were involved in social settlement work at Whittier House in Jersey City, and he supported her other social and religious activities; as they had no children, she soon devoted much of her time to those concerns. Bennett became a member of the board that formerly had employed her, proving herself to be a cooperative team worker and effective speaker. In 1909 she was elected board president, serving ably until 1923, when it merged with the general Presbyterian Board of National Missions. She served as vice president of the latter board for eighteen years and also was a corresponding member of her denomination's General Council, from 1924 to 1932.

Financially prosperous, Bennett traveled extensively for the cause of home missions in the United States as well as overseas. A loyal Presbyterian, she was also interested in cooperation among churches and represented her communion's interests on the interdenominational Council of Women for Home Missions (CWHM), a coordinating agency for a score of Protestant women's groups, from the time of its founding in 1908 to its merger with the general Home Missions Council (HMC) in 1940. In 1916 she was elected as the second president of the CWHM, an office she held for eight years. Her talent in presiding over meetings was much in demand; she became the first president of the interchurch Board for Christian Work in Santo Domingo (1920–1936). Bennett also became a member of several committees of the Federal Council of the Churches of Christ in America. She was the only woman on its controversial nine-member Commission on Inquiry that investigated the steel strike of 1919. The commission's unanimous report, issued in 1920 after the strike had been broken, helped bring to an end that industry's twelve-hour workday. Deeply interested in the rise of the modern ecumenical movement, Bennett was a Presbyterian delegate to the international Life and Work Conference at Oxford, England, on "Church, Community and State" in 1937.

Her concern for missions, however, never flagged; when the CWHM merged with the HMC, she was determined that missionary work among migrants and American Indians that had been done under the women's board would not be minimized, and she emphasized that determination in an address, "The Content of Home Missions," before a joint meeting of the two councils held early in 1940. She chaired a committee on Indian wardship and strongly backed the work of Edith E. Lowry, director of the migrant program, as it significantly expanded its activities in the 1940s. During her long years of leadership Bennett wrote many articles and pamphlets, often focusing on the social aspects of home missions, the plight of migrant workers, and the needs of Indians.

In the 1930s, together with many other church people of that period, she participated in the peace movement, serving on the executive board of the National Committee on the Cause and Cure of War. One of the eight leading peace societies of that decade, the committee occupied a moderate position, resisting the trend toward isolationism. Though not a conspicuous leader in the specifically women's movements of her time, she worked quietly for equal recognition of the sexes, particularly in church affairs. Along with many other Protestant leaders, she hoped and worked for the fuller Christianization of her country. She was troubled, however, by secularist trends in the culture; early in the 1940s she said, "It is not likely that any one now living will see a world as friendly to Christian and humanitarian causes as were the Eighteenth and Nineteenth Centuries, and the first decade of the Twentieth Century."

While providing notable leadership in national and international church affairs, Bennett also devoted much time and energy to activities at home, in both church (First Presbyterian) and community. She was the first president of the Englewood Civic Federation (1901–1911), which carried out many welfare and other civic projects. She took a turn as president of her city's woman's club (1902–1906) and in 1916 was a founder of the Englewood Forum, which brought prominent lecturers to the city. During World War I she chaired the local Woman's Council for National Defense and was involved in many of its activities, notably, arranging for a hostess house at nearby Camp Merritt to provide accommodations for women workers and guests of soldiers quartered there on their way overseas.

A small woman, barely over five feet tall, Bennett was long remembered by local residents for the pleasure she took in entertaining guests in her home. She relaxed by reading, playing golf, and motoring. She died at Englewood Hospital.

• Archival materials are at the Department of History, Presbyterian Church (U.S.A.), Philadelphia, in the files of both the Board of National Missions and the Federal/National Council of Churches, which are in the care of that department. The best known of her writings is the pamphlet *Home Missions and the Social Question* (1914). Obituaries are in the *New York Times*, 12 Apr. 1950, and the *Englewood Press-Journal*, 13 Apr. 1950.

ROBERT T. HANDY

BENNETT, Richard (21 May 1870–22 Oct. 1944), actor, was born Charles Clarence William Henry Richard Bennett in Deacon's Mills, Indiana, the son of George Washington Bennett, a lumber mill owner, and Eliza Leonora Hoffman. An unruly student at local schools, Bennett was put to work at age fourteen, first as a clerk in a dry-goods store and then as a night watchman at his father's lumber mill. Interested in the theater since early childhood and inspired by Edwin Booth's Hamlet, which he had seen during a visit to New York, Bennett left home at age sixteen or so to pursue an acting career. He worked as a singing waiter on a Great Lakes steamboat and as a medicine show barker until being discovered by a relative and sent back to Indiana.

Bennett's father then apprenticed him to a tailor in Frankfort, Indiana, but the headstrong young Bennett soon joined a minstrel show that was passing through town. He eventually landed in Chicago, where he made his debut in the legitimate theater in *The Limited Mail* in 1891. Bennett toured in this melodrama for more than a year, during which time he made his first New York appearance in November. By now he had selected one of his middle names as a stage name and became known as Richard Bennett. Declining an offer to take over the family lumber business, Bennett spent the next few years in stock companies in Milwaukee, Wisconsin, and Richmond, Virginia, and in Chicago-based touring companies under the management of Gustav Frohman, the brother of the powerful theatrical impresario Charles Frohman.

Bennett returned in 1897 to New York, where he appeared in the musical *A Round of Pleasure*. Hearing reports of Bennett's versatility as an actor and potential "matinee idol" from his brother, Charles Frohman gave the blond, square-jawed actor the juvenile lead in *The Proper Caper*, an adaptation of a French farce. For the next decade Bennett appeared in secondary roles in a variety of plays, mostly under the management of Frohman. These included *The White Heather* (1898), with Rose Coghlan; *His Excellency, the Governor* (1899), featuring the up-and-coming ingenue Ethel Barrymore; *The Royal Family* (1900), with Annie Russell; *Imprudence* (1902), with William Faversham; and the highly successful *The Lion and the Mouse* (1905), a topical drama of corporate influence in politics. Also in 1905 Bennett played Hector Malone, Jr., in the original American production of George Bernard Shaw's *Man and Superman*.

Bennett worked with young actress Mabel Morrison in *Royal Family*. When Morrison, the daughter of prominent actor Lewis Morrison, did not immediately reciprocate his romantic overtures, while on tour in

San Francisco Bennett hastily married a music student, Grena Heller, in 1901. The union was brief and childless; when the divorce became final in 1903 he married the now more agreeable Morrison (who later acted under her middle name Adrienne). Two of their three children, Constance and Joan, later became well-known film actresses.

Bennett reached genuine stardom when Frohman cast him opposite Maude Adams, then the nation's most popular performer, in J. M. Barrie's comedy *What Every Woman Knows* in 1908. The play enjoyed a substantial run on Broadway and a sellout national tour the following season. Bennett's good looks and brash manner (he was often compared to John Barrymore) were well suited to the role of John Shand, an ambitious young Scotsman who is too egotistical to realize that his rise in the political world is due not to his own brilliance but to the efforts of his quietly clever wife. (The events of the play were underscored by the offstage antipathy between the reserved, clean-living Adams and the garrulous, hard-drinking Bennett.)

Now established as a leading man, Bennett had starring roles in *The Brass Bottle* in 1910, *The Deep Purple* and *Passers-By*, both in 1911, and *Stop Thief* in 1912. Curtain speeches by a star were customary during Bennett's peak years of fame, and he took full advantage of the opportunity to air his opinions on social issues, such as woman suffrage and birth control. He often held court for up to half an hour after the play had ended. When Frohman rejected Bennett's idea of producing an English version of Eugene Brieux's *Les Avaries*, a frank dramatization of the horrors of venereal disease, the actor coproduced the controversial play himself in 1913 with two other backers. Under the English title *Damaged Goods*, the play was praised as a mature, nonsensational examination of a serious social problem and had a modestly successful run on Broadway with Bennett starring as a husband who discovers he has infected his wife (and consequently their baby) with syphilis. However, his production of Brieux's birth control drama *Maternity* in 1915 was not a success.

Over the next five years Bennett appeared in a number of plays and in 1915 made his first foray into motion pictures with a screen version of *Damaged Goods* for the American-Mutual Company. In 1920 he starred in *Beyond the Horizon*, Eugene O'Neill's first success. Bennett's enthusiasm for the unknown young playwright's work was instrumental in convincing the now-deceased Charles Frohman's former business manager John D. Williams to produce the play. "Richard Bennett plays with fine eloquence, imagination, and finesse," said Alexander Woollcott in the *New York Times* of Bennett's portrayal of doomed New England farmer Robert Mayo. *Beyond the Horizon* won the 1920 Pulitzer Prize for drama.

In 1922 Bennett starred as the tortured clown in the newly formed Theatre Guild's production of Leonid Andreyev's *He Who Gets Slapped*. The flamboyant Bennett chafed at the Guild's "nonstar" policy and is reported to have climbed by fire escape to the balcony of the Garrick Theatre to continue what many by then considered the outmoded practice of taking bows between acts. Despite their differing attitudes Bennett enjoyed another major success with the Theatre Guild as a wheelchair-bound grape grower in *They Knew What They Wanted* (1924). This drama by Sidney Howard became the second Pulitzer Prize–winning play (1925) in which Bennett had the leading role.

After these successes Bennett's career began to falter, owing in part to personal problems. Though never a model husband or father, Bennett had always valued his domestic life and enjoyed gardening and interior decorating. When his second marriage ended in divorce in 1925, the actor's drinking increased. A turbulent third, childless union—to Aimee Raisch Hastings, a socialite and sometime actress—lasted from 1927 to 1937 (Bennett spent part of this time out of the country to avoid legal charges of nonsupport). Bennett's last notable work in the theater was his portrayal in 1935 of Judge Gaunt, conscience-stricken to the point of insanity, in Maxwell Anderson's verse drama *Winterset*.

Though he had little respect for the motion picture industry, Bennett appeared in a number of films in character parts, most notably *Arrowsmith* (1931), *The Magnificent Ambersons* (1942), and *Journey into Fear* (1943), the last two directed by Orson Welles, who held Bennett in high esteem. Bennett died in Los Angeles, and after brief interment there his body was moved, at the request of his daughters, to the Morrison family plot in Old Lyme, Connecticut, for burial beside their mother.

• The New York Public Library for the Performing Arts has scrapbooks and clippings files relating to Bennett's career. The most complete source of information on Richard Bennett is *The Bennett Playbill: Five Generations of the Famous Theatre Family*, written by his daughter Joan Bennett and Lois Kibbee (1970). Also of value are "Richard Bennett—An Actor to Be Reckoned With," *Theatre Magazine*, Feb. 1909, pp. 64–65; "Temperament! Richard Bennett Tells of the Many Things That Upset an Actor's Nerves," *Theatre Magazine*, Oct. 1926, pp. 12, 53; and "Why Managers Don't Love Mr. Bennett," a brief interview with the actor in *Actorviews* by Chicago theater critic Ashton Stevens (1923). An obituary is in the *New York Times*, 23 Oct. 1944.

MARY C. KALFATOVIC

BENNETT, Robert Russell (15 June 1894–18 Aug. 1981), arranger, orchestrator, and composer, was born in Kansas City, Missouri, the son of George Robert Bennett, a musician, and May Bradford, a piano teacher. Bennett gave early evidence of musical talent: at age three he could peck out themes from Beethoven piano sonatas. At the age of five he began to study the piano with his mother; shortly thereafter his father provided him with instruction on a variety of orchestral instruments. Within a few years he became a member of his father's orchestra, playing whatever instrument was called for at the moment and sometimes conducting the group. By the time he was ten years old he was giving piano recitals in the Kansas City area.

The young pianist played only selections from the classical literature, as his mother strictly forbade him to play any sort of popular music.

At fifteen Bennett took up the study of harmony and counterpoint with Carl Busch, the founder and conductor of the Kansas City Symphony Orchestra. A year later Bennett began to make a living as a pianist and arranger for a variety of instrumental groups. By 1916 he had saved enough money to finance a move to New York. There he worked as a pianist in restaurants and as a music copyist for G. Schirmer & Co.

Despite a limp remaining from a childhood case of polio, Bennett was able to enlist in the army in 1917. He served for a year, first as a foot soldier and then as a dance band arranger in special services.

In 1919 Bennett boldly marched into the offices of the T. B. Harms music company and announced that he was an orchestrator in search of employment. This was uncharacteristic of Bennett, as he was normally a rather quiet, retiring person, though resolutely confident of his musical skills. The manager handed Bennett a new song by Cole Porter and said, "See what you can do with this." The song was "An Old Fashioned Garden"; it, along with Bennett's arrangement, became the biggest hit of that year.

From that moment on Bennett was much in demand as an arranger-orchestrator of Broadway shows. In the course of his career he arranged more than 300 shows, including *Rose Marie* (1924), *Show Boat* (1927), *Of Thee I Sing* (1931), *Anything Goes* (1934), *Annie Get Your Gun* (1946), *Kiss Me Kate* (1948), *South Pacific* (1949), *The King and I* (1951), *The Sound of Music* (1959), and *Camelot* (1960). Also in 1919 Bennett married Louise Edgerton Merrill; the couple had one child.

Bennett's wife encouraged him to pursue a career as a composer. He had long wanted such a career, but his hectic Broadway schedule left him little time for serious composition. Finally, in 1926, after having scored sixty musicals, he moved his family to Paris for a year and studied with renowned composer and teacher Nadia Boulanger. During that year he wrote the first of his six symphonies and submitted it to the *Musical America* composition contest; it received an honorable mention. A Guggenheim award allowed the Bennett family to return to Paris, Berlin, and London during parts of 1927–1928. In Berlin the idea of the second symphony, *Abraham Lincoln Symphony*, took shape. Bennett submitted this symphony along with another orchestral work, *Sights and Sounds*, to the RCA composition contest of 1930. The judges of the contest divided the prize money among five works: one by Aaron Copland, one by Louis Gruenberg, one by Ernst Bloch, and the two scores by Bennett.

Bennett's star was rising ever higher, and Hollywood was beckoning. He went there in 1930 and worked in the Warner Bros. studio. He returned to Hollywood later in the decade and from 1936 to 1940 was in the employ of RKO Pictures. In all, he wrote scores to thirty feature films, among the most famous of which are *Show Boat* (1936), *The Hunchback of No-tre Dame* (1939), *Rebecca* (1940), and *Oklahoma!* (1955), for which he won an Academy Award.

Returning to New York in 1940, Bennett initiated a series of network radio broadcasts called "*Russell Bennett's Notebook*," while continuing his Broadway career and composing as time permitted. He functioned as programmer, orchestrator, composer (at times), and conductor of the broadcasts. Featured on some of the programs were "Music Box Operas," which included Bennett's arrangements of well-known American songs, such as "Clementine," "My Old Kentucky Home," and "The Man on the Flying Trapeze." In a separate enterprise, Bennett scored more than eleven hours of music for the television series "Victory At Sea" (1952), with music by Richard Rodgers.

Bennett is best remembered as the dean of arranger-orchestrators of the American musical theater. Beginning in the 1920s his skill and taste in this field elevated the work of the Broadway arranger from that of a pedestrian, plodding orchestrator to a high artistic level. His work became the model against which all others would be measured. But his success in this field has somewhat obscured the fact that he composed a considerable amount of symphonic, chamber, and choral music. Bennett is known to have composed approximately seventy-five concert works, of which scarcely two dozen exist in published form. In addition to the six symphonies there are thirty-five other orchestral works, including concertos for violin (1941), flute (1946), piano (1948), woodwinds (1958), violin and piano (1963), and guitar (1970). Chamber works, numbering about eighteen, include a string quartet (*Water Music*), four solo piano works, an organ sonata, and pieces for various small ensembles. There are fourteen songs, five choral works, and four operas.

The published works are written in an accessible style: the harmonic language is rich and tonal; here and there is found the influence of jazz; the forms are carefully crafted; and the sense of orchestral color is brilliant. Some of these works were much celebrated in their day. *The Four Freedoms* (Symphony no. 5, 1943) was performed twelve times by Eugene Ormandy and the Philadelphia Orchestra in 1943 alone and at other times thereafter. Bennett was a rabid baseball fan, and two of his most popular orchestral works take up the baseball theme: *Third Symphony: In D for the Dodgers* (1941) and *Eight Etudes* (1938), dedicated to the New York Giants pitcher Carl Hubbell.

Bennett received numerous awards, prizes, and honors. In 1947 he was elected president of the National Association of American Composers and Conductors. He served as a fellow of the J. S. Guggenheim Memorial Foundation, and in 1965 he became president of the Bohemians. Bennett died in New York City.

• Bennett's writings include "Eight Bars and a Pencil," *New York Times*, 8 June 1947; "All I Know about Arranging Music," *International Musician* (1949): 9; and "A Look at Music Arranging," *Music Journal* 22 (1964): 37, 88–89. Secondary works that mention Bennett include John Tasker Howard,

Our American Music (1931; rev. ed., 1965); Clair Reis, *Composers in America* (1938); Madeleine Goss, *Modern Music Makers* (1952); and David Ewen, *The Lighter Classics in Music* (1961) and *Composers since 1900* (1969). Also useful is H. W. Wind, "Another Opening, Another Show," *New Yorker*, 17 Nov. 1951, p. 46. An obituary is in the *New York Times*, 19 Aug. 1981.

RON BYRNSIDE

BENNETT, Wilda (19 Dec. 1894–20 Dec. 1967), actress, was born in Neptune Township, New Jersey, the daughter of John Bennett, a builder, and Mary Elizabeth Crawford. Details of Bennett's early life are unknown; she initiated the legend of her running away from family and school in Asbury Park to win instant success. Later, she admitted that she had an apprenticeship in a church choir (probably the Baptist church her parents attended) and in amateur theatricals in her Jersey Shore community. She auditioned unsuccessfully for a few parts before she was chosen to play the role of Conscience in *Everywoman*, by Walter Browne, in the Henry W. Savage production, opening 27 February 1911 at Lew Field's Herald Square Theatre, New York, when she was just seventeen. She performed so well that she was the only original cast member to be selected by Sir Arthur Collins to play in the London production at the Theatre Royal, Drury Lane, which opened on 12 September 1912.

On her return to New York, she joined the illustrious cast (including Mary Pickford, Lillian Gish, and Ernest Truex) of David Belasco's production of *A Good Little Devil*, playing Queen Mab. The play was adapted by Austin Strong from the French original by Rosemonde Gérard and Maurice Rostand (wife and son of the playwright Edmond) and opened at the Republic Theatre on 8 January 1913. Following her modest success as the Fairy Queen, Bennett apparently devoted about a year to further voice and dance training, which may have helped her win her first starring role, as Ruth Wilson, a composer, in producer Joe Weber's *The Only Girl*, with music by Victor Herbert and Henry Blossom's lyrics and book (adapted from a less popular play, *Our Wives* [1912], by Frank Mandell). When the musical comedy opened at the Thirty-ninth Street Theatre on 2 November 1914, a reviewer found Bennett "perfectly" cast, "expressing a personality as exquisite as a flower." The description of her selection for her role—"If you wanted a pretty girl to sing, act and play the piano, she came to mind"—could serve as a summary of her career.

After her personal triumph in *The Only Girl* in New York and on tour, Bennett replaced Julia Sanderson on tour in the title role of *Sybil*, produced by Charles Frohman, in March 1917. Later that year she appeared as Sylva Vareska in *The Riviera Girl*, with music by Emmerick Kalman and book by Guy Bolton and P. G. Wodehouse, opening at the New Amsterdam Theatre on 24 September 1917. She "sang like a bird" and won her way into an anonymous reviewer's heart. Bennett returned to the Jersey Shore briefly to open as Lucienne Lambrissac in *The Girl behind the Gun* at the Apollo Theatre in Atlantic City during the week of 26 August 1918; the production later opened on Broadway in the New Amsterdam Theater on 16 September. For one reviewer, this production revealed "Wilda Bennett as a young American prima donna who need not give precedence to any prima donna imported from the European stage. She has beauty, youth and gaiety. She has a voice of silvery clearness, which she uses according to admirable method."

Probably her most memorable role was as Nancy Dodge in *Apple Blossoms*, which opened on 7 October 1919 at the Globe and then toured through 1920. The operetta, which featured music by Fritz Kreisler and Victor Jacobi, was based on Alexandre Dumas's *A Marriage under Louis XV*. Although Bennett was admired for her virtuosity in dancing and singing, especially in songs like "Who Can Tell," "Star of Love," and the duet "You Are Free," Fred and Adele Astaire's performance distracted attention from the star.

Bennett enjoyed a respite from operettas with her performance in *The Music Box Review*, with music and lyrics by Irving Berlin, which opened at the Music Box Theatre on 22 September 1921, a revue that proved a box office smash hit; Berlin had to prohibit preproduction performance of the show's classic, "Say It with Music," sung by Bennett and Paul Frawley. She returned to musical comedy in the role of Marianna in Frederick Lonsdale and Cyrus Wood's *The Lady in Ermine*, based on the London musical *The Lady of the Rose*, by Rudolph Schanzer and Ernest Welish. The Shubert production opened on 2 October 1922 at the Ambassador Theatre. Bennett scored a personal success singing "When Hearts Are Young," by Alfred Goodman and Sigmund Romberg.

Bennett's professionalism won her the title role in *Madame Pompadour* when she was rushed in to replace Hope Hampton, a movie star making her Broadway debut, just one week before the Broadway opening. The opulent production by Charles Dillingham and Martin Beck, with music by Leo Fall, was designed to inaugurate the Martin Beck Theatre on 11 November 1924; reviewers respected Bennett's brief preparation period for the role and complimented her on her vivacious performance. Before her last appearance in musical comedy as Folly Watteau in *Lovely Lady*, replacing Edna Leedom in May 1928, Bennett performed in vaudeville at the Palace in March 1927.

Her career was interrupted in the late 1920s by difficulties in her private life. Bennett was involved in several litigations, in particular a $100,000 alienation-of-affection suit brought by Mrs. Charles Frey. Bennett pleaded ignorance of Frey's marriage but had to pay damages, reduced to $25,000, in 1925. She was married four times, first to Robert Schable, a producer, whom she divorced in 1920. Her widely publicized marriage to her Brazilian dancing partner Abraham (Pepe or Peppy) De Abreo on 11 April 1926 in Jersey City, New Jersey, ended in divorce within two years. Her third marriage, to Anthony J. Wettach, a poloist and riding master of Elberon, New Jersey, on 15 December 1930, ended when he sued her for divorce after she struck him with a heavy sport trophy; he won his decree on 27 July 1933. Her fourth husband was Munro Whitmore, a mining engineer who died in 1960. During her last seven years Bennett lived by herself; she died in Winnemucca, Nevada.

Wilda Bennett enjoyed a brief but intense popularity through the early 1920s, setting fashion trends with her "beau catcher" curls and with the muff she carried in the wedding scene from *The Riviera Girl*. Colleagues recognized her as thoroughly professional, however temperamental she was in private life. Bennett avoided movie cameras because the "dangerous stunts" she might be asked to perform could ruin her voice; while it lasted, she was dedicated to her career in musical comedy and operettas. She advised young singers to ignore Europe as a training ground for operatic careers and to concentrate on American musical theater: "Any woman who is successful in the singing of light music has the extreme pleasure of reaching a far greater number of people and gaining a more truly national reputation than even those employed in grand opera work, unless, of course, she is a celebrated singer."

• Most of the information on Wilda Bennett was gleaned from the clippings and a scrapbook file in the Theater Collection of the New York Public Library for the Performing Arts. A good chronology of her musical comedy work is presented in Stanley Green, *Encyclopaedia of the Musical Theatre* (1976). Some reviews can be found in David Ewen, *New Complete Book of the American Musical Theater* (1970). Obituaries are in the *New York Times*, 23 Dec. 1967, and *Variety*, 27 Dec. 1967.

ELIZABETH R. NELSON

BENNING, Henry Lewis (2 Apr. 1814–10 July 1875), soldier and jurist, was born in Columbia County, Georgia, the son of Pleasant Moon Benning and Malinda Meriwether White, planters. In 1834 he graduated with honors from the University of Georgia, Athens. Soon afterward he moved to Columbus, where he was admitted to the bar. Barely two years after entering upon his profession, Benning was appointed solicitor general for his judicial circuit. In 1839 he married Mary Howard Jones, daughter of a prominent Columbus attorney with whom Benning formed a partnership. They had ten children.

A slavery and states' rights advocate in the mold of John C. Calhoun, Benning was an avid secessionist more than a decade before the Civil War began. In 1850 he called on Georgia to leave the Union and join a southern republic whose government would be controlled by Deep South politicians. Despite Benning's efforts, Georgia repudiated secession and the following year rejected his congressional bid as a southern rights Democrat.

In 1853 Benning was appointed an associate justice of the state supreme court. In that capacity he was responsible for what one biographer calls "perhaps the most vigorous and elaborate exposition of the doctrine of 'strict construction' ever set forth in a judicial pronouncement." Adjudicating *Padleford v. Savannah*, a liability suit against the city of Savannah, Benning ruled that state supreme courts were "coordinate and co-equal" with, and therefore not bound by the decisions of, the U.S. Supreme Court.

Benning's preference for immediate secession moderated by 1860, when he was a delegate to the Democratic National Convention in Charleston. Refusing to follow disgruntled "fire-eaters" who bolted the convention, he joined regular party members and served as vice president of the Baltimore Convention, which nominated Stephen A. Douglas for president. Douglas's defeat by Abraham Lincoln, however, convinced Benning that secession and war were inevitable. Thereafter he was a major force in Georgia's decision to leave the Union and in persuading the Upper South to follow suit.

Reportedly, Benning was seriously considered for a Confederate cabinet post. Perhaps because of his perceived extremist views, he was passed over. In any case, although approaching middle age he preferred to serve in a military capacity. At Columbus he recruited and organized the Seventeenth Georgia Infantry and was elected its colonel.

When sent to the Virginia front, Benning's regiment was stationed at Lynchburg before moving eastward to take part in the Peninsula campaign as a member of Brigadier General Robert Toombs's brigade, Army of Northern Virginia. During a series of holding attacks south of the Chickahominy River on 27 June 1862, the Seventeenth Georgia foiled an enemy attempt to turn Toombs's left, and at Malvern Hill, 1 July, the outfit boldly advanced through what Benning called "a very heavy fire both of artillery and musketry, grape and shell, splinters and Minié balls flying thick about us and through us, and making gaps in the ranks at every step." Despite the carnage, Benning's prudent leadership resulted in only thirty-six of his men becoming casualties.

Benning won praise at Second Manassas and Sharpsburg (Antietam), where he commanded Toombs's brigade. At Thoroughfare Gap, 28 August, his men captured a strategic peak of South Mountain, preventing Union artillery from shelling the division of Major General David R. Jones. After some initial difficulty at Second Manassas—becoming separated from part of his brigade because of an unexpectedly fierce Federal attack—he led one of his regiments, the Twentieth Georgia, in driving another enemy force "in complete rout—a huddled mass." The reunited brigade solidified its reputation for tenacity on 17 September, when for four hours it prevented much larger forces under Major General Ambrose E. Burnside from crossing Antietam Creek. In his after-action report, Benning's immediate superior cited his "coolness, courage, and skill" in holding his position until long-delayed reinforcements secured the Confederate right flank.

Only two of Benning's companies saw action at Fredericksburg, 13 December. The following spring the brigade was lightly engaged during the siege of Suffolk, Virginia. By then, however, Benning's battlefield performances had gained him permanent command of Toombs's brigade, now a part of Major General John Bell Hood's division. On 23 April 1863 Benning received an overdue promotion to brigadier general.

When the army marched to Gettysburg, Benning proved himself worthy of his honors. During Hood's 2 July assault on Devil's Den and Little Round Top, the Georgians supported the Texas brigade of Brigadier General Jerome B. Robertson, then guarded the rear of Brigadier General E. M. Law's Alabama brigade. Committed to the fighting late that afternoon, Benning led a furious assault on Devil's Den. Heeding their leader's injunction to "give them hell, boys," his brigade gouged the enemy out of its boulder-strewn position, captured three cannon, and held the disputed ground against repeated counterattacks. For their efforts the Georgians suffered more than 350 casualties, one being their commander's son and adjutant, Captain Seaborn Jones Benning. In 1874 the young man died of the lingering effects of his wound.

Benning served conspicuously during the return march to Virginia, helping block Union efforts to intersect the retreat column at Manassas Gap, Amissville, and Newby's Crossroads. In September his brigade was transferred with the rest of Hood's division to Tennessee. En route west, some of its men sacked the offices of a Raleigh, North Carolina, newspaper that had been critical of Confederate military policies. Although not personally involved in the vandalism, Benning apparently approved it. Nevertheless, he escaped censure in the official investigation that followed. This was his second brush with judicial punishment. In July 1862 he had narrowly avoided a court-martial for his defiance of the Confederate Conscription Act that had taken effect three months earlier. He had permitted the men of his original regiment, the Seventeenth Georgia, to elect their own officers, a practice forbidden under the conscription act.

In the West, Benning's men saw considerable service and lost heavily. On 20 September, at Chickamauga, where the general took a wound in the chest and had two horses shot from beneath him, his command helped widen the decisive penetration of the Union line at a cost of 488 killed, wounded, or missing. By early December, at the close of the unsuccessful effort to capture Knoxville, Tennessee, the brigade had been reduced to fewer than 500 effectives.

Benning lost more than half the remnant when his troops returned to Virginia for the fighting of May–June 1864. In the Wilderness Benning fell wounded, and he made a slow recovery. Welcome recruits and not-so-welcome draftees helped the brigade regain its strength, apparently without diluting its fighting spirit. On 29 September it held strategic Fort Gilmer on the intermediate defense line of Richmond, repulsing a series of assaults. Early the following month the command gave a strong account of itself along the Darbytown Road southeast of the capital. Its morale remained remarkably high: a few weeks before Appomattox, with Confederate fortunes at their nadir, the brigade reported one of the lowest desertion rates in the army.

After the war, Benning returned to Georgia to find his home and his possessions in ruins. He resumed his law practice to provide for a family enlarged by the addition of the widow and children of his brother-in-law, a war fatality, and the family of his recently deceased sister. The burden of caring for so many dependents, especially following his wife's death in 1867, made Benning feel "as if I had the world on my shoulders." He died in Columbus, Georgia.

Benning presented a rugged, rough-hewn appearance. His diligence as a jurist was considered exceptional, and his tenacity as a field commander earned him the nickname "Old Rock." Yet he possessed an aesthetic sensibility, evident in his reading of Greek, Latin, and English literature. He reportedly graced his conversation with apt illustrations drawn from the classics and the Bible. His command of language made him an effective orator and a skilled writer. Although national fame eluded him, his name is preserved by the U.S. Army's Fort Benning in Georgia.

• A collection of Benning's papers—sixty-five items, most of them related to his war service—is at Columbus College, Columbus, Ga. A microfilm copy is in the Southern Historical Collection at the University of North Carolina at Chapel Hill. The fullest biography is Marie W. Kerrison, "Henry Lewis Benning, State Rights Advocate and Soldier" (M.A. thesis, Emory Univ., 1937). Other biographical sources include Clement A. Evans, ed., *Confederate Military History*, vol. 6 (11 vols., 1899), William J. Northen, ed., *Men of Mark in Georgia*, vol. 3 (6 vols., 1907–1912); and Kenneth Coleman and Charles S. Gurr, eds., *Dictionary of Georgia Biography*, vol. 1 (2 vols., 1983). The origins of Benning's political philosophy are traced in James C. Cobb, "The Making of a Secessionist: Henry L. Benning and the Coming of the Civil War," *Georgia Historical Quarterly* 60 (1976): 313–25. His wartime service is followed in *The War of the Rebellion: A Compilation of the Official Records of the Union and Confederate Armies* (128 vols., 1880–1901). An informative obituary is in the *Atlanta Constitution*, 11 July 1875.

EDWARD G. LONGACRE

BENNY, Jack (14 Feb. 1894–26 Dec. 1974), comedian on radio, in films, and on television, was born Benjamin Kubelsky in Chicago, Illinois, and grew up in Waukegan, Illinois. His father, Meyer Kubelsky, only recently had come to the United States from Russia. His mother was Emma Sachs, the daughter of Lithuanian immigrants; she met her husband in Chicago through a matchmaker. Meyer Kubelsky began selling household goods from a horse and wagon traveling along the shores of Lake Michigan; he then became a saloon-keeper and eventually purchased a haberdashery shop.

On his son's sixth birthday, Benny's father presented him with a violin; Benny had wanted a tricycle. Benny became so proficient at the instrument that he soon gave concerts at a local theater. Yet he was not interested in becoming a concert violinist, nor in scholarship, and at the end of his second term in high school he was expelled for poor work. He was, however, eager to perform on the stage, and against the protests of his parents he embarked on a career in vaudeville theater at age eighteen.

Calling himself Ben K. Benny, he teamed with a professional pianist, Cora Salisbury, whose musical act was billed "From Grand Opera to Ragtime." During one of their performances he told his first joke. "The audience laughed," he later reminisced. "The sound intoxicated me. That laughter ended my days as a musician, for I never again put the violin back where it belonged except as a gag." His never-completed rendition of the tune "Love in Bloom," which always elicited laughs from audiences, became an integral part of his act. Throughout his professional career Benny would employ the violin as a comedic prop.

When the United States entered World War I, Benny enlisted in the navy and was assigned to "The Great Lakes Review," a sailors' road show. On one occasion he played a perfectly straight song from his stage repertoire, "The Rosary," and was booed. A friend quickly came on stage, as if by plan, and whispered to him, "Put the damn fiddle down and start talking!" Benny looked over the audience and ad-libbed, "I was having an argument with Dave Wolff this morning . . . " He paused, not knowing what to say next. Laughter developed. "Well . . . anyway . . . this morning, I was having this argument with Dave about . . . the Irish Navy . . . You see, I claim the Swiss Navy is bigger than the Irish Navy . . . but that the *Jewish* Navy is bigger than both of them put together. . . . "

After the war he revised his stage name, taking the name "Jack" from Jack Osterman, a highly popular comic for a short time, and labeled himself as a monologist. Over the years in performances in small-town theaters across the country he honed his talent as an ad-libber and developed a masterly sense of timing. The comedic persona that gradually emerged assumed a carefully tuned nonaggressive stance with tilted head and a routine punctuated by pauses, silences, and stares; double takes that built from wide-eyed innocence to a drawn-out "Welllll," or "hmmmmm"; and curt responses to being ribbed, such as "Now cut that out!" It has been said that he was the only radio comedian who could convulse an audience in laughter with nothing more than deadpan silence.

Benny attained Broadway status in 1926 in a big, bawdy musical revue, *The Great Temptations*, in which he introduced several acts, did a comic monologue, and played the violin. This led to jobs as master of ceremonies-monologist playing in vaudeville theaters from New York to Los Angeles. His growing reputation led Louis B. Mayer, the head of MGM, to offer him a film contract. Over the next few years Benny appeared in several films: *Hollywood Revue of 1929* (1929), *Chasing Rainbows* (1930), and *The Medicine Man* (1930). When *Hollywood Revue* was shown in Waukegan, the townspeople turned out in large numbers, led by Benny's father.

Lured back to Broadway in 1931 by a lucrative contract offered by Earl Carroll to emcee the musical revue *Vanities*, Benny temporarily suspended his movie career. His national recognition came just as radio was developing, and while in New York he was invited to appear on newspaper columnist Ed Sullivan's radio interview program. His timing and folksy brand of humor were an instant hit, and within a short time he was assigned to his own show on the National Broadcasting Company system. From 1932 until his radio show went off the air in 1955, Benny was a "national institution." Throughout the 1930s and 1940s his regular NBC Sunday evening program received the highest Hooper ratings.

Benny's radio debut occurred during the Great Depression, a time when the film and radio industries supplied entertainment fare that diverted audiences from their economic distress. Many former vaudeville entertainers headed their own shows during these years, including Eddie Cantor, George Burns and Gracie Allen, Al Jolson, Ed Wynn, and Bob Hope. In his radio performing "character," Benny was a special type of Everyman. As he observed, he had the uncanny knack of reflecting the shortcomings that people recognized in themselves or in their relatives and friends. "I try to make my character encompass about everything that is wrong with everybody," he said. "On the air, I have everybody's faults. All listeners know someone or have a relative who is a tight-wad, show-off or something of that sort. Then in their minds I become a real character."

Unlike one thrust of American humor in which the joke is directed at others, Benny's comedy made him the butt of teasing. He was the never-aging, always 39-year-old figure, suspiciously toupeed, huffy and petty, tenaciously parsimonious. But he never played the buffoon or fool. Audiences laughed at him while empathizing with his plight because his best plans were invariably thwarted. In one of his best-known scenes he was held up by a bandit who demanded, "Your money or your life!" An extended silence followed, filled with growing laughter. Finally, Benny snapped, desperately, "I'm thinking, I'm thinking."

Although his initial success was as an emcee-monologist, on radio Benny was the centerpiece of a group of performers who created an extended family called the Benny "gang." He was always the object of their raillery. There was his girlfriend, Mary Livingstone, (actually his wife, the former Sadie Marks whom he married in 1927 and with whom he adopted a daughter); Don Wilson, the rotund announcer; Phil Harris, the wisecracking orchestra leader; Eddie "Rochester" Anderson, the raspy-voiced, sassy valet and servant; Dennis Day, the naive singer; and a host of supporting figures, some of whom were created by the master of voices, Mel Blanc. Blended into the comedy was a series of sound effects that audiences came to recognize: Benny's sputtering and wheezy Maxwell car, always kept under twenty-five miles per hour by the cautious owner; his basement vault, squeaking and cranking when opened, and guarded by an old man who had been there since 1917; the pay telephone and cigarette machines in his living room that noisily gobbled up coins.

Among Benny's relationships, however, it was his interaction with Rochester that was the most extraordinary. Over time, it was his valet-servant more than anyone else who got the better of him. From his introduction into Benny's radio family in 1937–1938, Rochester constantly mocked and jived his "boss." These were liberties not previously accorded a black man in public. In a typical scene, Benny is atop a ladder trimming the Christmas tree when the doorbell rings. "There's the door, Mister Benny, you want me to answer it?" "Look Rochester," replies a sarcastic Benny, "I'm up here on the ladder, my arms are full of ornaments, so *what do you think?*" "Well," Rochester counters, "how long before you come down?" The pair became the oddest racial couple in American culture, their shared intimacies within a domestic arrangement on radio and television going far beyond the typical employer-employee association, that aided in changing the stereotype of the black male in popular culture.

During this time Benny starred in many comedy films of varying success: *Buck Benny Rides Again* (1940), *Charley's Aunt* (1941), *To Be or Not to Be* (1942), *George Washington Slept Here* (1942), *The Meanest Man in the World* (1943), and *The Horn Blows at Midnight* (1945). Of these, *To Be or Not to Be*—one of Ernst Lubitsch's finest films—is a classic of very high rank.

In 1948, because of unhappiness with NBC, Benny shocked the media world by joining with other highly popular radio comedians—"Amos 'n' Andy," Burns and Allen, ventriloquist Edgar Bergen and his dummy Charlie McCarthy, and Red Skelton—in switching his radio show to the Columbia Broadcasting System. The radio show on CBS lasted until 1955 when it was replaced by Benny's television program. At the beginning, Benny's conversion to the new television medium was difficult. His first stint in 1950 was criticized for its adherence to radio's format and lack of visual attraction. But the program eventually succeeded as the kinks were worked out, and it became a mainstay at CBS from 1960 until 1965.

Benny's shows altered the course of radio comedy. Humor emanated from story situations involving his "gang" rather than unconnected one-liners. Each show revolved around several plots, the laughter flowing from a situation that invariably involved an aspect of Benny's flawed character. A good-humored Sunday night "feud" with comedian Fred Allen, a radio satirist, constantly enlivened the comedic action. In 1936, after a ten-year-old violinist had expertly played Schubert's "The Bee," Allen ad-libbed about Benny's inability to handle the piece. On his next show Benny immediately retorted to the playful charge and countered with his own insults. Over the years the performers maintained the rivalry by appearing on each other's program. Once when Allen had delivered a particularly clever put-down line, Benny, in typical self-deprecating fashion, countered by declaring that if his own

script writers had been there, Allen could never have gotten away with it.

After his retirement from the airwaves, Benny was in constant demand. He performed in many nightclubs in Las Vegas and New York, appeared in a variety of special telecasts and programs such as "The Jackie Gleason Show," and "played" his violin at a large number of concerts to benefit musical causes: for Carnegie Hall in New York, the New Orleans Philharmonic, the San Francisco Symphony, and others. Just before his death in Beverly Hills, California, Benny played a psychiatrist in a television special, "Annie and the Hoods." He never spoke a single word as a patient chattered nonsensically. "He didn't have to," wrote critic John J. O'Connor in the *New York Times*, appraising Benny's impact on the country for more than four decades. "The radio character had become a national institution."

• Benny's extensive radio and television scripts are located in the University of California at Los Angeles Manuscript Collection. An early, useful listing of his performances can be found in David Rollin Smith, *Jack Benny Checklist: Radio, Television, Motion Pictures, Books and Articles* (1970). A highly informative work is by Milt Josefberg, *The Jack Benny Show* (1977). In the Museum of Television and Radio in New York City are examples of his radio and television programs. A retrospective on Benny by the museum also made available written documentation of his achievements: *Jack Benny: The Radio and Television Work* (1991). The impact of his shows on radio programming and race relations is analyzed in several works: Arthur Frank Wertheim, *Radio Comedy* (1979), and Joseph Boskin, *Sambo: The Rise and Demise of an American Jester* (1986). There is no critical biography of Benny, but a number of works provide intimate glimpses by family members: Mary Livingstone Benny and Hilliard Marks, with Marcia Borie, *Jack Benny* (1978), and Jack Benny and (his daughter) Joan Benny, *Sunday Nights at Seven: The Jack Benny Story* (1990). Additional information can be gleaned from his longtime agent, Irving Fein, *Jack Benny: An Intimate Biography* (1976). A lengthy, front-page obituary, along with the comments of John J. O'Connor, appears in the *New York Times*, 28 Dec. 1974.

JOSEPH BOSKIN

BENSON, Egbert (21 June 1746–24 Aug. 1833), jurist and founding father, was born in New York City, the son of Robert Benson and Catherine Van Borsum. After graduating from King's College (now Columbia) in 1765, Benson served his legal clerkship in the New York City office of the revolutionary leader John Morin Scott and was admitted to the bar in January 1769. Plagued by a lack of business, he moved from New York City as soon as he could find a community with an available clientele—Red Hook in Dutchess County—in 1772.

Besides financial gain, Benson achieved political success, which coincided with the movement for independence. As New York province evolved into a state, Benson's lawyering skills were in demand to fill the void created by the departure of Loyalist attorneys. In the war-created chaos he served simultaneously as the state's first attorney general (1777–1788) and as an assemblyman during the legislature's first four formative sessions (1777–1781). Before the state government was organized he served on the second council of safety. As attorney general Benson was an active presence in each of the state's twelve county courts, as well as the supreme court. He was in constant demand as a mediator for interstate disputes, but he could not afford to neglect his private practice, which added to the hectic pace of his schedule. Occasionally his private and public business mingled, as when he succeeded in obtaining an exemption for his client, the Dutch-owned Holland Land Company, from a state prohibition against foreign land ownership. One of his law clerks was James Kent, who became arguably the most significant figure in nineteenth-century American law. So busy was Benson that he failed to appear as a delegate to the Continental Congress in 1781, despite having agreed to accept legislative designation for the post.

The need to secure independence, combined with New York's vulnerability to British attack, caused a muting of political differences among patriots at the war's outset. While the conservative Benson associated with like-minded men, among whom were John Jay, Robert R. Livingston, Philip Schuyler, and later Alexander Hamilton, the attorney general was also a confidant of liberal governor George Clinton during the war. Once independence was achieved, however, the coalition that had guided the state through the war dissolved. Benson and his conservative associates strenuously moved for a stronger national government, as opposed to stronger state and local control, because they believed the national government would promote stability and commercial development, while catering to speculators.

Benson's role in the Constitution's adoption and implementation was remarkable, particularly since he was neither a member of the constitutional convention nor the state ratifying convention. Partly by default, he was selected by the legislature to join Hamilton as New York's delegation to the Annapolis Convention of 1786, convened to provide more effective commercial regulations under the Articles of Confederation. Benson and Hamilton audaciously led the call for a new convention to strengthen the Articles; this became the Philadelphia Convention of 1787. Benson was blamed by opponents of centralization for influencing the legislature to send Hamilton to the Continental Congress at a time crucial to getting the Philadelphia Convention called. Hamilton for his part unsuccessfully tried to get New York's delegation to Philadelphia increased from three members to five, with Benson among the names he suggested. Benson had returned to the New York assembly in the winter of 1788, and he introduced the resolution calling for a ratifying convention for the new constitution—to be selected by voters without the customary property requirement. Historians dispute how liberal this measure was, but Benson and other Federalist candidates were rejected by Dutchess County voters.

Benson was, however, returned to the first federal House of Representatives. He was active in imple-menting the new government and in the process helped to create the two-party system. He was deeply involved in crafting the enabling acts creating the executive departments, including authorizing the secretary of the treasury (Hamilton) to report annually to Congress, and he joined James Madison in asserting the president's right to remove cabinet officers. Benson and Madison split, however, over Hamilton's financial plans, for Benson was one of the secretary of the treasury's staunchest supporters. Hamilton lamented Benson's unwillingness to seek reelection after two terms. The Judiciary Act of 1789 established the federal court system, and while Benson's presence was not noticable during its passage, when Attorney General Edmund Randolph proposed revisions to the law in 1791, Benson countered with a proposal to integrate state and federal judiciaries into a single system. Benson's plan was never voted on. A constant supporter of the judiciary, Benson moved, unsuccessfully, that the chief justice immediately follow the vice president in the order of presidential succession.

On leaving Congress, and with Federalist control of state patronage, Benson was appointed to the New York Supreme Court in 1794. His former clerk, Kent, estimated that he "did more to reform the practice of that court than any member of it ever did before, or ever did since," including providing the court's first set of rules. Membership on the court also included membership on the Council of Revision, consisting of the judiciary (supreme court and chancellor) and the governor; the council wielded the veto power over all bills passed by the legislature. Benson had argued as a lawyer in the famous *Rutgers* case in 1784 that the council's reviewing process was tantamount to judicial review, and the question was still debated when the council went out of existence in 1823. Adherence to due process was important for Benson, thus he expressed a dissenting view of a bill repealing John Fitch's steamboat grant because "such Forfeiture is to arise in some due course of law." He considered the court's powers as "indispensable for preserving order and restraining and preventing usurpation and oppression," so that the right of appeal should not be eliminated "without the most clear and urgent reasons of necessity." In short, he viewed the judiciary as a bastion against the legislature. As an advocate of this tenet of the Federalist party, it was only a matter of time before Benson was appointed to the federal bench. He was particularly agreeable, since he faced mandatory retirement at age sixty, and he accepted appointment as chief judge of the second circuit, created by the Judiciary Act of 1801. The Jeffersonians repealed this Federalist measure the following year, essentially retiring Benson from public life.

Benson returned to the practice of the law. He was a founding member and first president of the New-York Historical Society. During a Federalist resurgence, he returned to the House of Representatives for a term in 1813, where he opposed the conduct of the War of 1812. Occasionally, he sallied forth into print with a pamphlet, such as *A Vindication of the Captors of Major*

Andre. Benson lived his later years at Jamaica on Long Island, where he died.

A "profane bachelor" in Hamilton's phrase, Benson was a most convivial man, who retained his intellectual faculties up to his death. In Kent's words, "he never for a moment forgot that he was a Federalist and a gentleman." Along with helping to get the state through the struggle for independence, Benson can best be remembered for his collaboration with Hamilton.

• Ironically the first president of the New-York Historical Society left very few papers, and they are in highly scattered collections throughout the country. His apprentice, colleague, and friend, James Kent, provided a brief but warm sketch, published in William Kent, *Memoirs and Letters of James Kent, LL.D.* (1898), pp. 20–22. John D. Gordan, III, ed., *Egbert Benson, First Chief Judge of the Second Circuit (1801–1802)* (1987), is a handsome little volume containing essays on Benson by David A. Nourse and Wythe Holt, as well as the Kent sketch.

DONALD ROPER

BENSON, Eugene (1 Nov. 1839–28 Feb. 1908), art critic, painter, and essayist, was born in Hyde Park, New York, the son of Benjamin Benson. His mother's name is not known. He went to New York City in 1856 to study painting at the National Academy of Design; he also learned portraiture in the studio of J. H. Wright. Taking up residence at the New York University Building, he formed close friendships with several other artists who lived there, most notably Winslow Homer. Desperately poor, Benson earned extra money by writing art criticism for the newspapers, particularly the *New York Evening Post*, for which he signed his name "Proteus." He quickly became known as a leading art critic. In 1862 he was elected an associate of the National Academy of Design, where he exhibited regularly from 1861 to 1871.

In the *Book of the Artists* Henry T. Tuckerman classified Benson as a genre painter, describing his motive as "poetical" and remarking that "the *Fireside Reveries* reminds us somewhat of [French artist Charles Theodore] Frere: a young girl sits by a stove, gazing in abstracted mood into the fire; the position and expression are full of the unconsciousness which betokens self-absorption." Benson's major contribution to American art, however, came through his criticism; as Nicolai Cikovsky, Jr., observed, Benson's goal was to formulate the principles of "a modern, national, and democratic art, derived from native materials and formed in a native language of style" (Cikovsky, p. 42).

Benson wrote approvingly of those artists who, as he explained, had been "least influenced by foreign art." These included Homer and the painters Sanford Robinson Gifford, Frederick Edwin Church, and John Frederick Kensett. He did not hesitate to denounce what he considered the meretricious, such as the overly dramatic work of two popular Dusseldorf-trained painters, Albert Bierstadt and Emanuel Leutze. With the founding in May 1866 of the journal the *Galaxy*, Benson gained a forum for his wider observations of

American life. Casting himself as a "literary frondeur"—a writer who "affronts, outrages, defies, or rails at something which time or custom has made respectable"—he charged editors with not realizing "how far the sense of conventional propriety is destructive of the literature of the people." He wrote approvingly of Edgar Allan Poe, Henry David Thoreau, and Walt Whitman, and of Rebecca Harding Davis's realistic story of social protest, "Life in the Iron Mills."

Late in 1866 Benson and Homer held a joint sale of their paintings to raise funds for a trip to France, where Benson stayed for approximately a year. His articles, Lois Fink has written, "affirmed the sensuous quality in French art so often attacked in American criticism. Writing about Parisian life and art with knowledge and sensitivity, he made a major contribution to the maturing of art literature in this country" (Fink, p. 44). In February 1869 the *Atlantic Monthly* published his pioneering article, "Charles Baudelaire, Poet of the Malign." However, his exploration of French culture did not lessen his commitment to formulate a democratic aesthetic; on 2 January 1868 the *Nation* linked him with Whitman as the leading advocates of American literary nationalism.

Benson's outspokenness, however, irked even the *Galaxy*'s tolerant editors, the brothers William C. and Francis P. Church, and Benson in turn was irked by what he saw as the Churches' editorial timidity. In 1869 he moved to New Haven, Connecticut, where he lived with Henriette Malan Fletcher, the wife of a prominent Presbyterian clergyman and missionary, James Cooley Fletcher of Newburyport, Massachusetts. By 1873 Benson and Mrs. Fletcher, whom he later married, had become permanent expatriates in Italy. The family included her son and daughter, Julia Constance Fletcher, who would gain fame as the author (under the pseudonym "George Fleming") of *Kismet* (1877) and other novels and several plays that were performed in London and New York.

They settled first in Florence, then Rome, and in 1888 in Venice, where their villa Palazzo Capello, Rio Marin, served as a model for the setting of Henry James's *The Aspern Papers*. In 1881 Benson published *Gaspara Stampa*, which told the tragic love story of that Renaissance woman poet. In a series of travel letters for the *New York Post* Benson recorded his search for neglected masterpieces of Italian art, contrasting the aesthetic and spiritual unity of an idealized Italian past with the fragmentation of modern life. They were collected in 1882 as *Art and Nature in Italy*.

Benson now painted not the meditative American girl, but the *Interior of St. Mark's*, and, as Henry James wrote to the photographer Alvin Langdon Coburn, "refined and interesting little landscapes of the Venetian country." Benson's travels provided subjects for such paintings as *Hashish Smoker in Jerusalem* and *Bazaar at Cairo*. The *London Times* remarked that his *Strayed Maskers*, which he exhibited at the Royal Academy and at the Philadelphia Centennial Exhibition, "shows judgment, command of technical procedures, and sound conception of effect, and is free from exaggeration. The artist is one of the few American painters who contribute to our Exhibitions." Although Benson had some success in finding purchasers for his work, he remained poor. He reflected on his life in Italy in two volumes of poetry, *From the Asolan Hills*, published in London by E. Mathews in 1891, and *An Old Garden*, published in Venice in 1902 by M. Fontana. An artist and critic who had promoted a native American aesthetic in spite of long residencies in Europe, Benson long since had lost touch with America and was largely forgotten at his death in Venice.

• Forty letters from Benson to Francis Pharcellus Church and his brother William C. Church, *Galaxy* editors, are in the New York Public Library. Small numbers of letters from Benson to Parke Godwin and John Ferguson Weir are in the Archives of American Art in Washington, D.C. Benson's paintings are widely scattered. Exhibition records include Maria Naylor, *Exhibitions of the National Academy, 1861–1900* (1973), and Algernon Graves, *A Dictionary of Artists Who Have Exhibited Works in the Principal London Exhibitions of Oil Paintings* (1884; repr. 1972). Scholarly treatments include Raymond Adams, "An Early and Overlooked Defense of Thoreau," *Thoreau Society Bulletin* 32 (July 1950): 1–3; Nicolai Cikovsky, Jr., *Winslow Homer* (1990); Lois Fink, "American Artists in France, 1850–1870," *American Art Journal* 5 (Nov. 1973): 32–49; Henry W. French, *Art and Artists in Connecticut* (1970), pp. 149–50; James S. Patty, "Baudelaire's First American Critic: Eugene Benson," *Tennessee Studies in English* 2 (1957): 65–71; and Robert J. Scholnick, "Between Realism and Romanticism: The Curious Career of Eugene Benson," *American Literary Realism* 14 (Autumn 1981): 242–61, which includes a bibliography of his magazine publications and books; and Clara Erskine Clement Waters and Laurence Hutton, *Artists of the Nineteenth Century and Their Works* (1916; repr. 1969). Mabel Dodge Luhan reported on Benson's life in Italy in *European Experiences* (1935). An obituary is in *Il Secolo, Gazzetta di Milano*, 11 Mar. 1908.

ROBERT J. SCHOLNICK

BENSON, Ezra Taft (4 Aug. 1899–30 May 1994), president and prophet of the Church of Jesus Christ of Latter-Day Saints (Mormons) and U.S. secretary of agriculture, was born in Whitney, Idaho, the son of George Taft Benson, Jr., and Sarah Sophia Dunkley, farmers. Benson was the great-grandson and namesake of Ezra T. Benson, one of the early leaders of the Mormons who entered the Great Salt Lake valley in 1847 with Brigham Young after the assassination of Joseph Smith, the founder of the church.

Benson's early activities centered on the church, farming, and scouting, and all three remained avid interests throughout his long life. He studied agriculture at Utah State Agricultural College (now Utah State University) and graduated from Brigham Young University in 1927 with honors. He also studied farm economics at Iowa State College (now Iowa State University). He interrupted his education to serve two years (1921–1923) as a church missionary in England. In 1926 he married Flora Smith Amussen; they had six children. Upon completion of his master's degree in farm economics, Benson served for a year as a county extension marketing agent in Idaho until his appointment as chairman of the Department of Agricultural Economics at the University of Idaho in 1927. He initiated the farm cooperative movement in Idaho in 1935 and was a pioneer in the cooperative marketing of agricultural products. Church service was an integral part of Benson's life. At no time during his adulthood did he not hold a church office or serve the church in some capacity. In the 1930s and 1940s he was stake president in Boise, Idaho, and Washington, D.C.

In 1939 Benson moved to Washington, D.C., as executive secretary of the National Council of Farmers' Cooperatives, the cooperative agriculture industry's national trade association. He served from 1939 to 1944. In 1943 he was called to serve on the Council of Twelve Apostles, the ruling body of the Mormon church. Benson remained an apostle for forty-three years, the last twelve as president of the twelve, or senior apostle. During World War II he served on president Franklin D. Roosevelt's agricultural advisory board. Although Benson was a staunch Republican and a severe critic of New Deal farm policies, Roosevelt respected his expertise and valued his candor.

In 1946 Benson was selected by the church to make an on-site assessment of surviving Mormon communities in war-ravaged Europe. For almost a year he traveled throughout Europe, and he was often the first nonmilitary visitor to devastated cities and towns on the Continent. He met with Mormon communities and delivered desperately needed supplies of food, clothing, and medicine. More importantly, as one of the highest officials of the church, his presence brought the message to Mormons in Europe that their church had not abandoned them. He remained in Europe from 1946 to 1947 as president of the church's European Mission, headquartered in London.

In 1952 president-elect Dwight D. Eisenhower named Benson to his cabinet as secretary of agriculture, a post Benson retained throughout both terms of the Eisenhower administration (1953–1961). His service as agriculture secretary was marked by controversy. His opposition to parity subsidies and soil bank programs angered many farmers, but he consistently advocated self-reliance and condemned government price supports as inimical to the working farmer's character. An uncompromising advocate of the free market, he believed that efforts by government to rescue inefficient farmers was wasteful and immoral. As the Eisenhower administration drew to a close, Benson's name was frequently mentioned in conservative Republican circles as a potential presidential or vice presidential candidate in 1960.

Following his retirement from government service in 1961, Benson remained an outspoken critic of what he viewed as the nation's dangerous drift toward socialism. He became increasingly identified with reactionary positions, labeling the civil rights movement of the 1960s as Communist-inspired, urging the repeal of the graduated income tax, and attacking détente with the Soviet Union, the women's rights movement, welfare, sex education in the public schools, and rock and roll music. His relationship with Eisenhower became strained as Benson's rightist views clashed with Eisenhower's increasingly centrist positions. For the remainder of Benson's life, the conservative faction of the Republican party held him in high esteem and advanced his name in 1968 and 1972 as a potential presidential or vice presidential candidate. However, he was not a serious candidate, and his interest and energies remained focused on the Mormon church.

From 1968 to 1970 Benson served as president of the church's Far East Mission. In 1970 he was given the responsibility of supervising the church's propriety farms and agricultural enterprises. Benson became the president, prophet, seer, and revelator of the Church of Jesus Christ of Latter-Day Saints (LDS) in 1985 upon the death of LDS president Spencer W. Kimball. In this office, Benson was the thirteenth in a direct line from Smith.

When Benson took over its leadership, the Mormon church had approximately 6 million members and was one of the fastest growing denominations in the world. Under his direction the church continued to grow at a rapid pace, and by the time of his death, church membership had further increased by almost 50 percent to approximately 9 million adherents. His tenure was marked by the establishment of seven new temples and hundreds of new stakes worldwide and by an accelerated missionary program.

To Benson's admirers his parallel careers in the Mormon church and in government service were driven by his uncompromising adherence to deeply held values: religious faith, the sanctity of the family, unswerving allegiance to free enterprise economics, unquestioned belief in the ability of the unfettered individual, mistrust of government intervention in private or corporate affairs, and a mystical devotion to the U.S. Constitution and the Bill of Rights as divinely inspired documents. To his detractors, he was an autocratic reactionary with little understanding of or sympathy for society's underprivileged and oppressed.

The last five years of Benson's life were hampered by a debilitating illness that severely restricted his energy and mobility and impaired his mental capacity. He never fully recovered from the personally devastating loss of his wife in 1992. He died in Salt Lake City.

• Of special value for their illumination of critical aspects of Benson's life and work are his books *Farmers at the Crossroads* (1956), *Freedom to Farm* (1960), *So Shall Ye Reap* (1960), *Cross Fire: The Eight Years with Eisenhower* (1962), *The Red Carpet* (1962), *Title of Liberty* (1964), *An Enemy Hath Done This* (1969), *God, Family, Country: Our Three Great Loyalties* (1974), *This Nation Shall Endure* (1977), *Come unto Christ* (1983), *The Constitution: A Heavenly Banner* (1986), *A Witness and a Warning* (1988), and *The Teachings of Ezra Taft Benson* (1988). The most comprehensive biography of Benson is Sheri L. Dew's laudatory *Ezra Taft Benson: A Biography* (1987). Also useful for background and biographical information are two profiles by Mark E. Petersen, "Ezra Taft Benson: A Habit of Integrity," *Ensign*, Oct. 1974, pp. 15–29; and "President Ezra Taft Benson," *Ensign*, Jan. 1986, pp. 2–13. Benson family history is covered in detail in Donald Benson Alder and Elsie L. Alder, *The Benson Family* (1979). For Benson's career as secretary of agriculture and in agricul-ture-related politics, see Edward L. Schapsmeier, *Ezra Taft Benson and the Politics of Agriculture* (1975). Obituaries are in the *New York Times*, 31 May 1994, and *Current Biography* 55, no. 8 (Aug. 1994): 639–40.

FREDERICK J. SIMONELLI

BENSON, Frank Weston (24 Mar. 1862–14 Nov. 1951), painter, was born in Salem, Massachusetts, the son of George Wiggin Benson, a successful cotton merchant, and Elisabeth Frost Poole. In 1880 he entered the School of the Museum of Fine Arts, Boston, where the curriculum was based on methods of instruction imported from European academies. In 1883 Benson followed a pattern established by other Museum School graduates by moving to Paris to further his education. He bypassed the prestigious École des Beaux-Arts and enrolled in the Académie Julian on rue du Faubourg St. Denis. There, under the sporadic tutelage of Gustave Boulanger and Jules-Joseph Lefebvre, Benson spent two years mastering the calculated, academic style favored in late nineteenth-century Paris salons. This approach to painting prized good draftsmanship and sound design above all else. This academic tradition was so deeply ingrained in Benson that it endured throughout his career and was passed along to his numerous pupils.

Benson was aware of the tumultuous changes in the Paris art world in the 1880s, but the avant-garde challenges mounted by the impressionists initially held little interest for him. (However, Benson did not completely ignore the impressionist movement, on rare occasions choosing to paint outdoors.) As a student in the mid-1880s he labored in vain to create paintings that would be acceptable to the juries of the conservative salons in Paris. He finally achieved some measure of success in the spring of 1885, when he exhibited *After the Storm* at the Royal Academy of Art in London.

In 1885 Benson returned to the United States, settling in his hometown of Salem, Massachusetts. He had little expectation of selling the large figural pieces he had created abroad but was disappointed when portrait commissions proved difficult to secure. In 1887 Benson accepted a teaching position at the Portland (Maine) Society of Art. The next year he participated in the important Society of American Artists show in New York City, where a portrait of Ellen Perry Peirson, *In Summer*, was well received. This work was later chosen to hang at the Paris International Exposition in 1889.

Benson married his childhood friend Ellen Peirson in the fall of 1888; they had four children. Ellen maintained their home in Salem, and he commuted daily to a rented studio in Boston. His financial security was realized in the spring of 1889, when he was appointed to the faculty of the Museum School along with his good friend Edmund C. Tarbell. They taught there until 1912 and remained affiliated with the school until 1931. During their tenure the financially troubled institution became solvent and acquired a reputation as one of the preeminent art schools in the country.

Benson and Tarbell helped gain recognition for a group of painters known collectively as the Boston school. Although they worked in a variety of styles, the Boston school artists shared a commitment to academic painting that was reflected in their technique and their choice of subject matter. The most successful artists adapted elements of the linear, hard-edged style of French academic painting and blended them with the more painterly manner of the impressionists. This synthesis resulted in a style that later came to be known as American impressionism. The Boston school was closely identified with figure painting, particularly depictions of attractive young women.

During the 1890s Benson drew attention for a series featuring women in elegantly furnished rooms reading or sewing by firelight. Benson was noted for works that seemed to mirror the aspirations of upper-middle-class American society. In an article for *Harper's Monthly Magazine* (June 1909), Charles H. Caffin described the figures in Benson's work as a type, "a cross between the exacting narrowness of Puritanism and the spiritual sensuousness and freedom of Emerson. . . . it seemed to me to embody very remarkably the ideals of this country."

In 1897, dissatisfied with the policies of the Society of American Artists, ten prominent painters, including Benson, Tarbell, John H. Twachtman, Childe Hassam, and Willard Metcalf, decided to resign from the organization and hold their own exhibitions. The shows, which began the following year, were held annually until 1917. The group became known as the Ten American Painters, preaching no particular aesthetic and dedicated to freedom of expression and experimentation rather than pleasing authorities and winning medals. A final retrospective exhibition of the group was held in 1919. Even after his death Benson remained closely linked with the Ten American Painters because many of his most celebrated oils were included in the group's shows.

In the summer of 1899 Benson painted *The Sisters*, a key impressionist work. Exhibited widely, the canvas marked a major change of direction in both subject matter and style. His depiction of children playing outdoors signaled a departure from the artificially illuminated interiors of the early and mid-1890s, while the larger brush strokes and looser application of paint heralded a new freedom of approach. Over the next two decades Benson turned repeatedly to the formal concerns he addressed in *The Sisters*, especially the use of light as it enveloped and defined figures in the outdoors. A reviewer in the 21 March 1901 *New York Daily Tribune* echoed the observations of most critics when he remarked, "The picture is full of sunshine, skilfully [sic] distributed."

By 1900 Benson was working out-of-doors on a regular basis. Within two years he had established the motif for which he is best remembered: one or more figures, silhouetted against the sky, gazing out to sea. Benson's family often served as subjects for these paintings. Writing in *Arts and Decoration* (Mar. 1911), William H. Downes described them as "gracious women and lovely children, in a landscape drenched in sweet sunlight, and cooled by refreshing sea breezes." This series, including *The Hilltop* (1903, Malden Public Library), *Summer* (1909, Rhode Island School of Design), and *Two Boys* (1926, Metropolitan Museum of Art), helped to secure Benson's reputation as a significant American painter. A large number of his best-known works were painted during this impressionist period of the 1900s and 1910s; almost all sold within a year or two of their creation. These paintings were displayed at the important annual exhibitions at major museums along the East Coast and across the Midwest and garnered numerous prizes. Museums acquired many for their permanent collections. Benson's work also appealed to individual collectors, many of whom were wealthy New Englanders drawn to images that reflected their own genteel lifestyle. Downes described it as "a holiday world, in which nothing ugly or harsh enters, but all the elements combine to produce an impression of natural joy of living."

Benson's mature paintings were done in part outdoors and have the shimmering surfaces and loose brushwork of impressionism, but his academic background mitigated against a strict imitation of impressionist techniques. Although contemporary critics applauded the spontaneity of his creations, many of his renowned outdoor canvases may have been composed in his studio from photographs and preliminary studies. Benson worked hard at his craft, and he believed that great art required creative vision as well as skill. In 1930 he commented to his daughter, "A good picture has a certain austerity, a distinction. . . . Mere craftsmanship, representing nature, does not make a picture."

Frequent sales afforded Benson a very comfortable living and further enhanced his reputation. During the winter he divided his time between painting in his Boston studio and teaching at the Museum School. Summers were spent at North Haven, Maine, an island in Penobscot Bay, where he relaxed with his family while creating some of his most famous paintings. Benson also had a partial interest in a Cape Cod hunting retreat, and he journeyed annually to a fishing camp on Canada's Gaspé peninsula.

In 1912 Benson began to experiment with etching, a medium he had not worked in since the early 1880s. Initially reluctant to exhibit his prints, Benson was astonished by the reception his new work received; his first show in 1915 at the Guild of Boston Artists sold out immediately. The vast majority were hunting and fishing scenes gleaned from decades of careful observation. The swift and positive reaction of the public was equaled by that of reviewers, who showered Benson with praise.

Benson achieved this success again in the early 1920s, when he began to paint in watercolor. Critics had hailed his black and white ink wash drawings in the 1910s, but his watercolors in the 1920s marked his transformation from a regional New England artist to an American master. *Boiling the Kettle* (1923, Art Institute of Chicago) and *The Bowsprit* (1922, Museum of Fine Arts, Boston) represent Benson's finest work in watercolor. Five years after his initial experiments with the medium, Benson received the gold medal for watercolor at the Sesqui-Centennial International Exposition, the World's Fair held in Philadelphia in 1926.

Benson continued to paint with oils, but by 1920 his art underwent yet another revision in style and subject matter. A sense of energy and action absent in the earlier canvases pervades much of his work of the 1920s and 1930s. The intimate, domestic scenes of women and children engaged in leisurely pastimes were supplanted by more expansive and dynamic compositions and traditionally male subjects, especially salmon fishing and hunting. Benson balanced this new interpretation of the outdoors with a brilliant series of interior still life paintings executed over nearly two decades, including *The Silver Screen* (1921, Museum of Fine Arts, Boston) and *Still Life* (1926, National Museum of American Art).

Benson's success continued through the 1930s and 1940s. His switch from figural subjects to sporting art enabled him to meet the requirements of an audience who increasingly viewed the Boston school as old fashioned and out of touch with modern life. Benson was remarkable for his uncanny insights into changing taste and for his ability to transform his art quickly to meet the demands of both the public and critics. Few American painters attained the critical success Benson did, and fewer still reaped the financial rewards. He was honored with more medals and prizes than any other American artist of his time.

Benson was a leader of the Boston art community at the height of its influence in the early part of the century. Perhaps his greatest legacy was the inspiration and counsel he provided for the hundreds of painters he trained at the Museum School. While doing so he helped transform a struggling art school into a major institution with an international reputation. Benson died at home in Salem, Massachusetts.

• Benson's papers are in the Benson Family Manuscript Collection in the James Duncan Phillips Library of the Peabody Essex Museum, Salem, Mass. The Archives of American Art, Smithsonian Institution, Washington, D.C., and Boston, Mass., includes extensive correspondence between Benson and a number of artists, museums, and dealers with whom he was associated. The most comprehensive assessment of his career is Faith Andrews Bedford, *Frank W. Benson: American Impressionist* (1994). Exhibition catalogs in which his work is discussed at length include William H. Gerdts et al., *Frank W. Benson: The Impressionist Years* (1988), which discusses the artist's paintings in Maine; Bedford et al., *Frank W. Benson: A Retrospective* (1989); Gerdts et al., *Ten American Painters* (1990); Sheila Dugan, *Frank W. Benson, N.A.* (1991); and Dugan, *Frank W. Benson Watercolors* (1997). For a discussion of Benson and Tarbell's friendship, see Susan Faxon Olney, *Two American Impressionists: Frank W. Benson and Edmund C. Tarbell* (1979). Vose Galleries of Boston, Mass., maintains the computerized *Frank W. Benson Catalogue Raisonné* of the artist's oils, watercolors, and pastels. Benson's prints were cataloged in Adam E. M. Paff, *The Etching and Drypoints by Frank W. Benson* (4 vols.,

1917–1929). A final volume of the series was produced by Arthur Heintzelman in 1959. For a critical discussion of the artist's graphic work see John T. Ordeman, *Frank W. Benson, Master of the Sporting Print* (1983). Obituaries are in the *Boston Daily Globe*, 15 Nov. 1951, and the *New York Times*, 16 Nov. 1951.

SHEILA DUGAN

BENSON, Oscar Herman (8 July 1875–15 Aug. 1951), educator and organizer of youth groups, was born in Delhi, Iowa, the son of P. C. Benson and Celia Ortberg, farmers. His father died when Oscar was still a child, and he became the principal support for his mother and three younger siblings. He continued to farm and took on additional jobs to pay for his education. At the age of eighteen, while working in a sawmill, he lost three fingers in an accident. His neighbors, in admiration of his determination to succeed, took up a collection that enabled him to continue his schooling. In 1898 Benson graduated from Epworth (Iowa) Seminary and Teaching College and then financed three further years of college (the State University of Iowa, Iowa State Teachers' College, and the University of Chicago) by teaching in rural schools. In 1902 he married Sadie J. Jackson; they had three children.

In 1904 Benson was appointed the county superintendent of schools in Wright County, Iowa, a position he held for six years. During this time he introduced agricultural home economics and extension teaching in Iowa, and he lectured at farmers' meetings, chautauquas, and teachers' institutes about agriculture. His main interest was in developing profit-making enterprises for rural children that would engage them in farm life and thus halt the flight to the cities. He established and encouraged a variety of youth organizations, the corn club, the dairy club, and the garden club. In 1907, while visiting a school in Lake Township, he was presented with a bouquet of four-leaf clovers. Later, during his address to the students, he drew a four-leaf clover on the blackboard and wrote an "H" on each section to stand for head, heart, hands, and health. Thus, the 4-H symbol was born.

In 1910 Benson was hired by the U.S. Department of Agriculture (USDA) to continue his work developing boys' and girls' clubs in thirty-three northern and western states. He developed a combination of contests, competitions, profits, and prizes, and the movement peaked during World War I with 251,000 club members. Encouraging children to contribute to the war effort, he was proud to claim that the club members had produced foodstuff valued at $6,019,092 during the crisis.

In a larger scheme, Benson aimed, through the club system, to improve the rural life of the United States. He saw the system as a way to develop community leadership and cooperation as well as a sense of community spirit and citizenship. He wrote, "They [the boys and girls] are trained . . . for community leadership and cooperative work of every kind and are taught that it is infinitely better to be a proprietor of farm land, farm animals, and farm machinery than to be a mere wage earner" (USDA circular no. 66, p. 38).

Also while working for the Department of Agriculture, Benson independently developed the cold pack canning method. This made it easy for canning to be completed in a farm kitchen with minimal investment of labor, fuel, equipment, and time. The department was not initially convinced of the method's viability, and Benson spent a number of years convincing the secretary of agriculture, James "Tama Jim" Wilson, to adopt the new system. It was finally officially endorsed in 1912. At this point Benson launched a nationwide conservation program to encourage home canning throughout the country, in urban as well as rural areas.

In 1920 Benson left the USDA on the encouragement of a number of northern industrialists. These men, led by Theodore N. Vail of the American Telephone and Telegraph Company, wanted Benson to formulate a program to meet the needs of ten million children in the North Atlantic states, both country and city dwellers. Benson asked for an investment of $50,000 for the first year, $100,000 a year for the subsequent four years, and a final endowment of $2 million. The sixty business leaders agreed to his terms, and Benson became the head of the Junior Achievement Bureau of the Eastern States League based in Springfield, Massachusetts.

In 1926 Benson took a position on the professional staff of the Boy Scouts of America as director of rural scouting services. His job was to expand scouting among the rural population, which meant addressing the issues of poverty, incessant labor, isolation, and the farmers' fear that too much socialization would lead the children away from the farm. Benson's response was to develop the concept of the Lone Scout, which did not cost as much as regular scouting, directed its attention largely back to agricultural issues, and did not often bring the boys into contact with strangers. During his time with the scouts, Benson also helped to develop the manual *Scouting for Rural Boys* and to introduce thirty-eight new merit badges on rural subjects. In 1927 he also started a monthly publication, the *Lone Scout*, which had a circulation of 6,000 by 1936. For all his efforts, rural scouting never became a big success; scouting continued to flourish mostly in small towns and villages. He retired in 1940.

Benson was the president of the Home Canners' Association from 1921 to 1925. He wrote a number of books, including *Agriculture and the Farming Business* (1915) and *Agriculture: A Text for the School and the Farm* (1916), both of which he coauthored with George Herbert Betts. Benson also wrote books and pamphlets dealing with such topics as homemaking, home management, canning, and instructions to the cold pack canning method. He died in Gettysburg, Pennsylvania.

• Much information on Benson is in Perry Holden's family album in Special Collections at the library of Iowa State University. Benson's useful writings include "Organization and Results of Boys' and Girls' Club Work, 1918," USDA department circular no. 66 (1920), and miscellaneous articles in *Journal of Education*, such as, "A Good Use for Free Time," Sept. 1929; "He Sold His Blood," July 1929; and "The Country Boy," July 1929. See also Selene Armstrong Harmon, "Why Theodore N. Vail Backed O. H. Benson," *World's Work*, Mar. 1921, pp. 517–20; Alfred Charles True, *A History of Agricultural Extension Work in the United States* (1928); David I. Mcleod, *Building Character in the American Boy: The Boy Scouts, YMCA, and Their Forerunners, 1870–1920* (1983); and William D. Murray, *The History of the Boy Scouts in America* (1937).

CLAIRE STROM

BENSON, William Shepherd (25 Sept. 1855–20 May 1932), naval officer, was born in Bibb County, Georgia, the son of Richard Aaron Benson and Catherine Elizabeth Brewer, planters. Benson was one of the first men from the Reconstruction South to attend the U.S. Naval Academy, graduating forty-third in a class of forty-six in 1877. After first serving on the *Hartford*, he received his commission as ensign in 1881. That same year he married Mary Augusta Wyse after converting to her Catholic religion; they had four children.

During the following three decades Benson moved slowly through the ranks of the navy with polite and competent, if uninspiring, service in a variety of posts, mainly at sea or at the Naval Academy. During this period the navy was experiencing major intellectual, strategic, technological, and administrative changes, but Benson remained far from the cutting edge; he was not counted among the era's prominent naval reformers: Stephen Luce, Alfred Mahan, Bradley Fiske, and William Sims. Benson also missed the Spanish-American War, and his one stint at the Naval War College in 1906 was limited to two months.

Only while serving as chief of staff to the Pacific Fleet (1909–1910) did Benson attract positive notice, although he did not receive a major command until his billet on the dreadnought *Utah* (1911–1913). From there, he was given command of the Philadelphia Navy Yard—a comfortable post but one that generally did not presage major advancement. Certain historical developments, however, worked to Benson's favor. By 1915 the U.S. Navy had become one of the world's largest, and along with the beginning of the First World War there was increasing pressure on the secretary of the navy to create a new position similar to the army's chief of staff. The civilian secretary, the Democratic and pacifist-leaning Josephus Daniels, resisted creating the position for fear that it would shift policy formulation from civilian to military quarters. By 1915 he could resist no longer. Instead of appointing one of the leading navy reformers, either Sims or more likely Fiske, Daniels reached down past all twenty-six flag officers and five senior captains to select Benson as the first chief of naval operations (CNO). (The reformers called for improving fire-control by increased target practice and gun-sight machinery, consolidating command at the highest levels, and improving tactics through a "scientific" study of previous wars and war-gaming.) Daniels's maneuver enabled him to accede to the demands for a chief while ensuring that the post would not become a pulpit for naval politics.

As CNO Benson set out to prepare the fleet for America's possible entry into the European war, he had to juggle logistical and manpower issues with the secretary's concern that the United States not appear too belligerent. Soon Benson received a huge boost with President Woodrow Wilson's call for a "navy second to none," which resulted in massive new battleship appropriations. These new measures, however, failed to account for the threat of the rapidly developing German submarine and had to be altered during the course of the war. In the meantime, Benson's navy participated in the large-scale interventions in Haiti in July 1915 and in Santo Domingo (now Dominican Republic) in November 1916, missions similar to those undertaken by the navy in the Caribbean during previous decades.

With Germany's reintroduction of unrestricted submarine warfare and Congress's vote for war in April 1917, Benson demonstrated his strength for organization and hard work: the fleet was mobilized within five hours of the declaration of war. The actual military conduct of the war, though, proved the inutility of battle fleets. For the most part, the German fleet generally remained bottled up, unable to engage the superior British Royal Navy. Refusing to fight, thereby protecting their fleet from severe loss or damage, the Germans made other fleets, like the American's, expensive deterrents and nothing more.

The German strategy, however, did not mean that the Allies maintained freedom of the seas. Germany had established a deadly submarine blockade around Britain, which proved remarkably effective until the introduction of serious antisubmarine warfare measures such as destroyers, mines, and especially convoys. Working with Sims as commander of U.S. Naval Forces in Europe, Benson effected these changes with what then appeared to be considerable success. At its height the U.S. Navy had over half a million men and over two thousand ships, all under Benson's command.

After the armistice, Benson served as technical advisor on naval issues for President Wilson at the Versailles Peace Conference. Upon his return he was dismayed to hear that Sims was charging naval leaders with incompetency in their war efforts. As part of his overall criticism that the navy had been woefully unprepared for war in 1917, Sims charged that Benson had been appointed first CNO based on personal and political service and not on merit. These claims, most publicly described in Sims's Pulitzer Prize–winning *The Victory at Sea* (1920), were refuted, but Benson's name was soiled. Despite such public controversies, Benson was awarded two Distinguished Service Medals (U.S. Navy and U.S. Army) as well as several major honors from Allied governments and Catholic organizations in the years following the war.

After retiring from the navy in 1919, Benson was appointed by Wilson to chair the United States Shipping Board. He diligently attempted in his new position to secure the advances that U.S. commercial shipping had made during the war; in support of this effort, he published *The Merchant Marine* in 1923. Finally, in 1928 Benson retired from public life, and in 1930 Congress promoted him to his highest wartime rank—admiral. He died in Washington, D.C.

• Much of Benson's personal correspondence was destroyed by his widow, but the Manuscript Division of the Library of Congress holds some of his papers. The National Archives includes many of his official writings, see especially Record Groups 32 (Records of the United States Shipping Board), 45 (Naval Records Collection of the Office of Naval Records and Library), and 80 (General Records of the Department of the Navy). His only major publication shied away from naval affairs, discussing instead, as indicated by its subtitle, the merchant marine as "a source of independence and strength in time of peace." Mary Klachko (with David Trask) has published a well-researched and authoritative biography, *Admiral William Shepherd Benson: First Chief of Naval Operations* (1987). See also Elting E. Morison, *Admiral Sims and the Modern American Navy* (1942). Important obituaries are in the *Baltimore Catholic Review*, 27 May 1932, and the *New York Times*, 21 May 1932, which includes comments by William V. Pratt, a successor CNO.

MARK RUSSELL SHULMAN

BENT, Charles (11 Nov. 1799–19 Jan. 1847), frontiersman, fur trapper, and Santa Fe trader, was born in Charleston, Virginia (now W.V.), the son of Silas Bent, Jr., a surveyor and jurist, and Martha Kerr. The family moved first to Ohio, then in 1806 to St. Louis, Missouri. Charles attended Jefferson College in Canonsburg, Pennsylvania, although for how long is unknown. In 1822 he joined the Missouri Fur Company of Joshua Pilcher as a clerk, and in 1825 he became a partner. The American Fur Company of John Jacob Astor proved to be too powerful a competitor, and by 1829 Bent and his partners were wholly unsuccessful in the fur trade.

Bent then turned to the Santa Fe trade. In 1829 he and his brother William led a trade caravan down the Santa Fe trail, using the Cimarron Cutoff through future western Oklahoma. They became the first persons on the trail to experiment with using oxen instead of mules to pull wagons. When the caravan was attacked by several hundred Indians, probably Kiowas, the brothers deployed a cannon and charged into the attackers, driving them off. In 1830, with Ceran St. Vrain, Bent formed Bent, St. Vrain and Company to expand trading activities. The company established offices in Taos and Santa Fe and in 1833 established Bent's Fort on the Arkansas River, between the future sites of Las Animas and La Junta, Colorado. William Bent oversaw the construction of the fort, and the location became a well-known trade site and stopover for Santa Fe trail travelers. Charles Bent spent little time there, for he usually was in St. Louis or in New Mexico handling the commercial affairs of the company.

Bent bought trade goods, especially blankets, from northern Mexican fabricators and traded these to Indian tribes for beaver pelts, bolts of calico, and Taos whiskey, while he also sent New Mexican sheep to Missouri and traded them for horses and mules. He continued to participate quite successfully in the fur trade. In 1836 two additional Bent brothers joined the firm to work at Bent's Fort. In the next few years Bent and St. Vrain established a post on the South Platte River (1837) and on the Canadian River (1842).

Bent succeeded in most of his business ventures, becoming financially comfortable and a close associate of Manual Armijo, Mexican governor of New Mexico. Bent's marriage to María Ignacia Jaramillo, the daughter of a prominent New Mexican family (in 1835 or 1836), cemented his relationship with local Mexicans and with Armijo. The couple would have three children. Bent prospered in New Mexico and constructed residences in Santa Fe and Taos. His main limitation was that he retained his U.S. citizenship and thus could not apply for land grants, available only to Mexicans; he did profit, however, when Armijo granted land to certain associates.

When the war between Mexico and the United States began in 1846, New Mexico fell under control of the U.S. Army of the West, commanded by Brigadier General Stephen Watts Kearny. Kearny knew of Bent and appointed him civilian governor of the newly conquered territory. Bent never thought of himself as anything but a U.S. citizen, despite his marriage and his association with Armijo. He was able as a consequence of his family connections to maintain a satisfactory relationship with some local Mexicans, although he warned Kearny of plots to overthrow U.S. control and even named the conspirators. In January 1847, during an Indian and Mexican rebellion in Taos against U.S. authority, Bent was killed and scalped by Mexicans.

Charles Bent was one of the most prominent Anglo-American Santa Fe traders, for he operated more profitably and successfully over a longer period than did most traders.

• For Bent's correspondence as governor of New Mexico, see Records of the War Department, Department of New Mexico, Record Copy of Letters Sent, vol. 5, Sept. 1846–1847, in the National Archives. A considerable number of earlier letters from Bent to U.S. consul Manuel Álvarez are in the Reed collection at the Museum of New Mexico in Santa Fe. See also David Lavender, *Bent's Fort* (1954); Allen Bent, *The Bent Family in America* (1900); Donna May Lewis, "The Bents and St. Vrains as Pioneers in the Trade of the Southwest" (M.A. thesis, Univ. of California, 1924); George B. Grinnell, "Bent's Old Fort and Its Builders," *Kansas Historical Society Collections* 15 (1919–1922): 102–8; and "Bent's Fort, 1844–45," *Colorado Magazine*, Nov. 1934, which includes excerpts of contemporary accounts.

JOE A. STOUT, JR.

BENT, George (7 July 1843–19 May 1918), frontiersman, soldier, and Indian interpreter, was born at Bent's Old Fort on the Arkansas River in present-day southeastern Colorado, the son of William Bent, a pioneer merchant and Indian trader, and his Cheyenne wife, Owl Woman. Named after an uncle who had been killed by Comanches on the Santa Fe Trail in 1841, George was the third of four children. When he was only four, his mother died giving birth to his sister Julia, and subsequently his father married Owl Woman's sister, Yellow Woman, who was the mother of George's half brother, Charles. George grew up bilingual and at age ten was sent with his siblings to the farm started by William Bent and his brother Charles near Westport, Missouri, where George attended school for the next four years. Albert D. Boone, grandson of Daniel Boone, served as the children's guardian during this time. In 1857, according to his accounts, George was enrolled in "the academy" at St. Louis, where he remained until the outbreak of the Civil War in 1861.

At age seventeen the pro-southern George Bent enlisted in a Confederate cavalry regiment, participating in the battles of Wilson's Creek and Pea Ridge, then in Earl Van Dorn's campaigns in Arkansas and Mississippi. At the siege of Corinth, Mississippi, he was captured and, with help from his older brother Robert, was paroled at St. Louis. Weary of the conflict, he returned with his half brother Charles to his father's new fort in the upper Arkansas Valley, where tensions between white settlers and Indians had increased. Concerned about his sons' safety, William Bent reportedly urged them to stay with their mother's people. George thus lived with the southern Cheyennes almost continuously for the rest of his life.

In 1864 Colorado posses began attacking Cheyenne villages at widely separated points. Bent felt that this was being done purposefully, to stir up the Indians and to prevent territorial troops from going east to fight Confederate forces. Thus Bent gradually became involved on the Cheyenne side and in one skirmish was falsely reported killed. Late in the summer of 1864 he and Ed Guerrier, another half-blood, wrote letters for Cheyenne leader Black Kettle to the commandant at Fort Lyon, Colorado, seeking peace. The resultant talks led to the Cheyenne encampment on Sand Creek, forty miles northeast of the fort. When Colonel John Chivington's troops attacked the encampment on 29 November, Bent was severely wounded in the hip, but he managed to escape to the Smoky Hill River and afterward to his father's ranch, where he recuperated before rejoining the Cheyenne camp on Cherry Creek, in present-day Cheyenne County, in late December.

With the Colorado frontier further inflamed, Bent took part in the first Cheyenne attack on Julesburg on 7 January 1865. Subsequently, more than 100 miles of stage stations and telegraph lines were laid waste, wagon trains plundered, and communications to the East cut off by his Cheyenne band. After a second attack on Julesburg, Bent went north with the Cheyennes and participated in two engagements at Mud Springs, Nebraska, and a skirmish with a force under Colonel William O. Collins on the North Platte. After camping on the Powder and Tongue rivers in the Sioux country, Bent joined the war party that hit Camp Dodge on the North Platte road on 3 June 1865, running off several horses. It was Bent that Lieutenant Colonel Preston

Plumb mistook for the white renegade Bill Comstock in his report on the incident.

Bent participated in the battle of Platte Bridge in July and the subsequent harassment of Colonel Patrick Edward Connor's expedition against the Cheyennes on the Powder River. Following the four-day siege of a Connor wagon train, he acted as interpreter during a parley in which the Indians were bought off with a wagonload of plunder. Bent also was in on the combined Cheyenne-Sioux attack on the Cole-Walker wing of the expedition on the Powder River, but afterward he went south again with other southern Cheyennes who were homesick for the old range. Back in Colorado, they captured some wagon trains bound for Denver on the South Platte trail and also raided along the new stage route that followed the Smoky Hill River. After crossing the Arkansas, Bent and the band struck out for the Cimarron route and were reunited with Black Kettle in late December.

In the spring of 1866 George Bent married Black Kettle's niece, Magpie, who also was Ed Guerrier's sister-in-law. Over the next two years, whenever Bent was not out hunting or raiding, the couple lived in the chief's lodge. Bent later stated that "these were happy days for us," and he always held Black Kettle in high esteem. (There is no record of the couple having children.)

In April 1867 Bent was involved in the confrontation with soldiers under General Winfield S. Hancock on the Pawnee Fork of the Arkansas, which ended futilely, although the subsequent Hancock campaign triggered more depredations by Indians who had been relatively quiet. That summer Bent joined a war party preying along the Cimarron cutoff of the Santa Fe Trail and reportedly made off with some stock. When the army invited the southern Cheyennes and other plains tribes to peace talks at Medicine Lodge Creek in Kansas, Bent deciphered the letter for Black Kettle and accompanied him as interpreter to the council where the treaty was signed on 28 October 1867. Following the council, Bent accompanied Black Kettle south of the Arkansas before leaving with Magpie to visit relatives in Colorado. That was the last they saw of the chief before he was killed by George Armstrong Custer's cavalry in the battle of the Washita on 26 November 1868.

At that point, Bent's exact movements in the Indian wars are sketchy and uncertain. While he had sometimes ridden with Roman Nose, Bent did not claim to be present at the battle of Beecher Island, in which that famous chief was killed. Nor did he admit participation in subsequent engagements, including Summit Springs in Colorado (11 July 1869) and Adobe Walls in the Texas Panhandle (27 June 1874), although his later descriptions of these well-publicized battles from the Indian perspective are detailed and quite accurate. Perhaps the tragic death of Black Kettle and that of his half brother Charles from wounds received in a fight with Pawnees in 1868 lessened his desire to war against the whites. Nevertheless, Bent's sympathy toward the Indians, especially his mother's tribe, re-

mained strong to the end. His intimate acquaintance with many important frontier figures, both Indian and white, would prove invaluable in the years to come.

After the Red River War in 1875, Bent and his wife moved to the Cheyenne Agency in the Indian Territory (Okla.), where he served as an interpreter and became a leader in his tribe's difficult transition toward the "white man's road." Later they resided at Colony, Oklahoma, where he played host to and provided valuable information for sympathetic ethnologists and writers such as George Bird Grinnell, Frederick Webb Hodge, and Ernest Thompson Seton. At that time Bent corresponded extensively with historian George E. Hyde, who eventually compiled Bent's letters into a readable first-person account of his early life and escapades with the Cheyennes. While Hyde considered Bent a highly reliable leading man "in the field of Indian history and ethnology," the manuscript lay unpublished until 1968. George Bent died at Colony and was buried in the community cemetery.

• Two sets of Bent's correspondence with Hyde and the original manuscripts from them are housed in the Yale University Library and the Denver Public Library. Other papers of George Bent are in the Colorado Historical Society repository in Denver and the Southwest Museum Library in Los Angeles, Calif. See also George E. Hyde, *Life of George Bent, Written from His Letters* (1968); George Bird Grinnell, *The Fighting Cheyennes* (1915) and *The Cheyenne Indians* (2 vols., 1924); Donald J. Berthrong, *The Southern Cheyennes* (1963); and David Lavender, *Bent's Fort* (1954).

H. ALLEN ANDERSON

BENT, Silas (9 May 1882–30 July 1945), author and editor, was born in Millersburg, Kentucky, the son of the Reverend Dr. James McClelland Bent, a Baptist minister, and Sallie Burnam. His father was at one time president of Georgetown College. Silas Bent grew up in Kentucky and was educated at public schools and Ogden College in Bowling Green, from which he was graduated in 1902.

Bent's first job after college was as a reporter for the *Louisville Herald* and *Times*. Two years later he went to St. Louis to work for the *Post-Dispatch* and the *Republic* until 1911, except for a brief stint teaching at the new school of journalism at the University of Missouri. He was one of the original faculty members at the new journalism school, which opened in September 1908, and he taught there for at least a year. Following his return to the *Post-Dispatch*, he served as assistant city editor until 1912, when he entered publicity work for the National Citizens' League, whose "sound banking" campaign helped lead to the passage of the Federal Reserve Act of 1913. Later Bent was a drama critic for *Reedy's Magazine* in St. Louis and worked briefly for the *Chicago Evening American*. He moved in 1914 to New York City, where he worked successively for the *Herald*, the *Tribune*, the *World*, and the *Times*. On the *Times* he was an editor of the Sunday magazine from 1918 to 1920. During the presidential campaign of 1920 Bent was in charge of publicity for the Democratic National Committee, where, in his words, he had an opportunity "to see how legislation and national elections are swayed by the drive of publicity agencies upon the press." From 1920 to 1922 he was associate editor of the *Nation's Business* in Washington. In 1916 Bent married Elizabeth Chism Sims of Bowling Green, Kentucky. They had no children. For many years, after about 1920, the Bents' home was "The Log Cabin," Old Greenwich, Connecticut.

Bent devoted the rest of his life after 1922 to freelance writing. Among his works are biographies of U.S. Supreme Court Justice Oliver Wendell Holmes, in 1932, and former president Zachary Taylor, in 1946, the latter titled *Old Rough and Ready* and written with a cousin, Silas Bent McKinley. Bent wrote two critical books on journalism, *Ballyhoo: The Voice of the Press* (1927), based on a series of lectures he gave at the New School for Social Research in New York City, and *Newspaper Crusaders: A Neglected Story* (1939). In *Ballyhoo*, his first book, he discussed the problems and ills of metropolitan newspapers, particularly their invasion of privacy, their sensationalism, and the "evil" influence of advertisers and chain newspaper ownership. He wrote of the press's "priestliness," comparing it to the "pretences" of the church. The church is concerned mainly with the future, he said, the press with the present, and that both were subjected to attack by the laity, often without evidence. "The history of newspapers as of religions is a history of constant conflict. Editor and priest . . . think of themselves as radiant centres of supernal wisdom, and chosen mouthpieces of its propagation." Bent said the American press had drifted away from the democratic ideals of its "most valiant defenders," Abraham Lincoln and Thomas Jefferson, and that publishers were motivated more by business interests than by their "priestly function." He feared that big journalism, run by inoffensive editors, threatened the editorial illumination needed by a self-governing democracy. In contrast, Bent believed that editors of earlier times, a number of whom he praised in *Newspaper Crusaders*, were more courageous. He included Joseph Pulitzer, William Randolph Hearst, Isaiah Thomas, Philip Freneau, editors against slavery, *New York Times* editors who opposed William M. "Boss" Tweed, and Oliver K. Bovard, managing editor of the *St. Louis Post-Dispatch* when Bent worked there. Unfortunately the book lacks scholarly depth and is but a series of short biographical impressions with no notes and a meager bibliography.

Among Bent's other books were *Strange Bedfellows* (1928); *Machine Made Man* (1929); *Buchanan of the Press* (1932), a newspaper novel set in St. Louis and somewhat autobiographical; and *Slaves by the Billion* (1938). He wrote numerous articles for magazines such as *The Nation*, *Yale Review*, the *Century*, the *Independent*, *Plain Talk*, the *North American Review*, *Harper's*, the *Atlantic*, *Collier's*, *Outlook*, and the *New Republic*. His works appeared regularly in the *Literary Digest*.

Bent died in Stamford, Connecticut, following a long illness. Irving Dilliard, a former editor of the *St.*

Louis Post-Dispatch, attributed Bent's health problems to excessive drinking. Appraising Bent's career, Frank Luther Mott, the American journalism historian, ranked *Ballyhoo* with Upton Sinclair's *The Brass Check* (1919) as among the "highly critical appraisals of the press." A prolific writer, Bent wrote on current topics thoughtfully if not always with staying power or literary skill. His work, however, is representative of much of American popular magazine journalism during the 1920s and 1930s.

• A few newspaper clippings on family members and some typed manuscripts by Bent are in the library at Western Kentucky University. Secondary sources include Simon M. Bessie, *Jazz Journalism: The Story of the Tabloid Newspaper* (1938); Earl English, *Journalism Education at the University of Missouri* (1988); Linda W. Hausman, "Criticism of the Press in U.S. Periodicals, 1900–1939," *Journalism Monographs*, no. 4 (1967), which lists many of Bent's magazine articles; Robert V. Hudson, *Mass Media: A Chronological Encyclopedia of Television, Radio, Motion Pictures, Magazines, Newspapers, and Books in the United States* (1987); Alfred McClung Lee, *The Daily Newspaper in America: The Evolution of a Social Instrument* (1937; repr. 1973); Ralph E. McCoy, *Freedom of the Press* (1968), which annotates Bent's major books; and Frank Luther Mott, *American Journalism: A History, 1690–1960*, 3d ed. (1962). An obituary is in the *New York Times*, 31 July 1945.

RICHARD F. HIXSON

BENT, William (23 May 1809–19 May 1869), frontiersman and trader, was born in St. Louis, Missouri, the son of Silas Bent, Jr., of Massachusetts, a surveyor and judge, and Martha Kerr of Virginia. William Bent began trapping on the upper Arkansas River in 1824. He was married three times. His first wife was Owl Woman, a Cheyenne, with whom he had four children. Upon her death he married her sister Yellow Woman, with whom he had one child, and on her death he married Adelina Harvey, the daughter of a Blackfoot woman and Alexander Harvey, a former fur trader on the Missouri River. (Marriage dates are unknown.)

In 1829 he joined his brother Charles, who with Ceran St. Vrain was involved in the Santa Fe trade. William continued with his brother's company, and in 1833 he supervised the construction of Bent's Fort on the north bank of the Arkansas River between the sites of the future Colorado cities of Las Animas and La Junta. The men constructed the fort to initiate increased trade of blankets, furs, and other items with the Arapaho, Comanche, Cheyenne, and Shawnee in the region. The brothers engaged in trade also with northern Mexican merchants and drove sheep back to Missouri, where they traded these for mules and horses. William Bent managed the fort for the company throughout its successful years of operation.

Bent led General Stephen Watts Kearny's Army of the West from Bent's Fort to Santa Fe at the beginning of the war with Mexico in 1846, and after the war he continued the trade business. St. Vrain retired in 1849, and William Bent became the sole owner of the company. (His brother was killed in 1847 during the war with Mexico.) Because he was disgusted with a government offer to buy his fort, Bent destroyed the original structure in 1849 and built a new post thirty-eight miles downstream. This outpost was smaller than the original Bent's Fort but was located under the shelter of a stone bluff in the Big Timbers. It was better located to trade with the Native American tribes. In 1857 he constructed yet another fort at the mouth of the Purgatoire River. This became the first permanent Anglo-American settlement in what is today Colorado. The Colorado gold rush of 1859 brought thousands of white settlers, but Bent remained uninvolved in the frenzied search for precious metals. More white settlers in the region provoked intense warfare with the Cheyenne and other tribes in the region. As Bent's sons were one-half Native American and he had always been close to the tribes, this white intrusion brought additional family and other difficulties to Bent and his enterprises.

After 1864 Bent returned east to live briefly at Westport, Kansas, where his neighbors were mountain men James Bridger and Louis Vasquez. Although Bent was not involved in the Civil War, his sons George Bent and Charles Bent fought for the Confederacy. Bent's closest friend during much of his life was the famous Santa Fe trader, trapper, and soldier Kit Carson. Although Carson remained in the West, the two friends kept in touch during the late 1860s. Bent died at Westport in 1869, surviving Carson by one year. Upon his death Bent left a fortune said to amount to $150,000 to $200,000 in property and other assets, and apparently he did not specifically leave this money to his sons. His marriage to his third wife did not last, and thus she was not in line to inherit Bent's fortune. There is no evidence that he left the money to anyone. William Bent contributed to the overall development of trade in the New Mexico–Colorado region and thus helped open the way west to thousands of white settlers.

• For Bent's own work, see William Bent, Records of the Bureau of Indian Affairs, National Archives and Records Service, Washington, D.C. For discussions of the Bent family, see Allen H. Bent, *The Bent Family in America* (1900); Donna May Lewis, "The Bents and St. Vrains as Pioneers in the Trade of the Southwest" (master's thesis, Univ. of California, 1924); and H. L. Luebers, "William Bent's Family and the Indians of the Plains," *Colorado Magazine*, Jan. 1936. There are also a number of histories of Bent's Fort, including "Bent's Fort, 1844–1845," *Colorado Magazine*, Nov. 1934; Matthew C. Field, "Sketches of Big Timbers, Bent's Fort, and Milk Fort in 1839," *Colorado Magazine*, May 1937, pp. 102–8; Leroy R. Hafen, "When Was Bent's Fort Built?" *Colorado Magazine*, Apr. 1954, pp. 105–19; Mary Prowers Hudnall, "Early History of Bent County," *Colorado Magazine*, Nov. 1945, pp. 233–47; and David Lavender, *Bent's Fort* (1954).

JOE A. STOUT, JR.

BENTLEY, Arthur Fisher (16 Oct. 1870–21 May 1957), sociologist, political scientist, and philosopher, was born in Freeport, Illinois, the son of Angeline Alice Fisher and Charles Frederick Bentley, a banker. The family moved to Omaha and then to Grand Island, Nebraska. Bentley briefly attended both York College, Nebraska, and the University of Denver, Colorado, before returning to Grand Island to work in his father's bank. In 1890 Bentley entered Johns Hopkins University to study economics and sociology. He returned again to Grand Island and, with his father, collected economic and agricultural data on the community of Harrison, Nebraska. Bentley received an A.B. in 1892. His undergraduate thesis, "The Condition of the Western Farmer as Illustrated by the Economic History of a Nebraska Township," was published the next year in the *Johns Hopkins University Studies in Historical and Political Science*.

Bentley continued his studies at Johns Hopkins, completing his thesis "The Units of Investigation in the Social Sciences." He received a Ph.D. in 1895, and his research was published in the *Annals of the American Academy of Political and Social Science*. Bentley spent a year in Europe, attending lectures in sociology and economics by influential German intellectuals at the Universities of Berlin and Freiberg im Breisgau. In *A Victorian in the Modern World* (1939), lifelong friend Hutchins Hapgood described the youthful Bentley as "a strangely vivid young man" with "a definite sense of responsibility which much of the time made him unhappy."

After completing his studies, Bentley served as an instructor of sociology at the University of Chicago. There he met John Dewey, who would later become a close collaborator. Bentley, however, had little interaction with most of his colleagues, and he left academia after a single year. He worked as a newspaper reporter and editorial writer in Chicago for the *Times-Herald* (later renamed the *Record-Herald*). While a working journalist, Bentley became intimately familiar with practical politics and pressure group activities. He married Anna Harrison, a physician and childhood friend from Nebraska, in 1899. His career in journalism offered Bentley a lot of free time for contemplation and research. From 1896 to 1908 he wrote the influential political science text *The Process of Government: A Study of Social Pressures* (1908). As the book neared completion, the periodic illnesses that had interrupted his educational career, combined with the death of his father, led to a lengthy psychological breakdown. Following his mother's death in 1911, Bentley and his wife moved to Paoli, Indiana.

The Process of Government laid the foundations for the group theory of politics. The book also promoted an empirical methodology for social science research. Bentley rejected both the formally descriptive and the prescriptive orientations common to scholarship of the day. Instead he suggested that scholars should analyze politics as a social process. Group interests serve as the central theme in understanding political activity. Though the book would later be seen as a forerunner of the behavioral revolution in political science, it remained virtually unnoticed for several decades. Bentley's insistence that systematic analysis requires accurate descriptions and postulates that lead to quantification and prediction appealed to behavioralist scholars of a later era, and his work was resurrected.

Paoli served as a rural retreat for Bentley, though he maintained an extensive correspondence with academic and political leaders. Bentley was active first in the American Red Cross and then in Progressive party politics, serving on the national party committee and chairing the Indiana state committee coordinating the presidential campaign of Robert LaFollette. He operated an apple orchard in Paoli but persisted in his research and writing on issues relating to the social sciences. Initially, Bentley extended his earlier examinations of pressure groups. His book *Makers, Users, and Masters* (1969) analyzed the economic concentration and power of American business and financial interests. It was completed in 1920 but remained unpublished until after his death.

Bentley's intellectual pursuits gradually shifted from politics to the philosophy of science. He incorporated new developments in theoretical physics and mathematics and applied them to the social sciences. *Relativity in Man and Society* (1926) adopted Albert Einstein's view that space and time were integral dimensions in which social events occur and argued that sociologists should place their own research in the context of these social events. In *The Linguistic Analysis of Mathematics* (1932) he analyzed the relationship between ordinary language and scientific symbols and notation. Bentley challenged the view that mathematics can be reduced to logical foundations and argued that foundations of the mathematical sciences must be viewed in the context of its symbols, language, and semantics. Bentley then applied this perspective to the social sciences in *Behavior, Knowledge, Fact* (1935). Here he clearly argued that human behavior must be reduced to empirical observation before the scientific method can be applied successfully to studies of social processes.

These earlier books by Bentley were appreciated by few contemporary readers. However, one scholar who expressed profound interest in Bentley's ideas was philosopher John Dewey. Dewey and Bentley forged their perspectives into a persuasive theory of logic and scientific knowledge. Their collaboration led to a series of articles that were subsequently collected in *Knowing and the Known* (1949). This volume developed the transactional approach that emphasizes the total process; individual persons and things are integrated within their social and natural processes. Independently, Bentley also published a number of articles on related topics, including linguistics and the meaning of knowledge. Twenty essays on the sociology of knowledge and the philosophy of science (including thirteen previously published) formed the anthology *Inquiry into Inquiries* (1954).

Bentley's influence was felt in a variety of disciplines, chiefly political science, sociology, psychology, philosophy, and social science methods. Bentley rejected the view of his contemporaries, and of his doctoral thesis, that the individual is the center of social relations. Instead, Bentley proposed that groups and social processes formed the units of understanding and that the individual must be understood in terms of social relationships (not the reverse). Group interests are distinct from public opinion, elites, or class interests. Groups are not static but are functional and variable. This belief led Bentley to espouse realism and objectivity in research; social scientists should focus on observable behavior, not on legal structures or moral strictures. With Dewey, Bentley rejected artificial dichotomies and emphasized process and the transactional point of view in understanding social relationships. Just as an elementary particle in physics can be understood only as part of a larger system, the individual can be known only in the context of social behavior and activity. Bentley's thought is best understood in terms of his vast influence on the direction of subsequent social science research.

Bentley's first wife died in 1924. In 1930 he married Susan W. Chipman, a family friend from Indianapolis; she died in 1942. In 1946 Bentley married Indianapolis businesswoman Imogene M. Shaw. He had no children. He returned to academia only once, as a visiting professor of philosophy at Columbia University in 1941–1942. Bentley then spent the remainder of his days in Paoli, Indiana, where he died.

Bentley challenged the intellectual and philosophical orthodoxy of his day, and his earlier works remained underappreciated for decades. Not until he was already advanced in years was Bentley acknowledged as one of the preeminent thinkers of his day. His writings are now considered classic texts in political science and the philosophy of knowledge, though his works have been cited more often than read. He was a prominent figure in the transformation of social science research, yet the iconoclast Bentley was never affiliated with an educational institution. In an obituary for the *Journal of Philosophy*, Sidney Ratner described Bentley as a scholar who "fused passion and reason" and who "carried on his scientific inquiries with more zest and energy than most of his more academically fortunate contemporaries." Bentley's influence on the advancement of scientific thought has often been indirect, yet generations of scholars returning to his writings find fresh approaches and new inspiration from the questions Bentley raised and the answers he suggested.

• An extensive collection of Bentley's manuscripts, papers, and correspondence resides in the archives of Lilly Library at Indiana University. Much of the written exchange between Bentley and Dewey is collected in Sidney Ratner et al., eds., *John Dewey and Arthur F. Bentley: A Philosophical Correspondence, 1932–1951* (1964). The Festschrift edited by Richard W. Taylor, *Life, Language, Law: Essays in Honor of Arthur F. Bentley* (1957), demonstrates Bentley's cross-disciplinary influence. Valuable assessments of Bentley's scholarship include Taylor, "Arthur F. Bentley's Political Science," *Western Political Quarterly* 5 (1952): 214–30; Paul F. Kress, *Social Science and the Idea of Progress: The Ambiguous Legacy of Arthur F. Bentley* (1970); G. David Garson, "On the Origins of Interest-Group Theory: A Critique of a Process," *American Political Science Review* 68 (1974): 1505–19; James F. Ward,

"Arthur F. Bentley's Philosophy of Social Science," *American Journal of Political Science* 22 (1978): 595–608, and *Language, Form, and Inquiry: Arthur F. Bentley's Philosophy of Social Science* (1984); and Thelma Z. Lavine, "The Process of Government," *Society* 32 (1995): 48–55. Useful biographies of Bentley can be found in obituaries by Ratner, "Arthur F. Bentley, 1870–1957," *Journal of Philosophy* 55 (1958): 573–78, and Taylor, "Arthur F. Bentley—In Memoriam," *American Political Science Review* 51 (1957): 912–13.

JAMES ENDERSBY

BENTLEY, Elizabeth Terrill (1 Jan. 1908–3 Dec. 1963), Communist party activist and government witness, was born in New Milford, Connecticut, the daughter of Charles Prentiss Bentley, a newspaper editor and department store manager, and Mary Burrill, a schoolteacher. After growing up in small towns in Connecticut, New York, and Pennsylvania, Bentley enrolled in Vassar College and in 1930 received an undergraduate degree in English. While at Vassar, she became involved in a variety of Socialist causes but did not demonstrate any interest in more radical left-wing ideas. For two years following graduation, she taught languages at the Foxcroft School in Middleburg, Virginia, but left in 1932 for Columbia University, where she earned her M.A. in Italian in 1935. While working on her graduate degree, she accepted a fellowship that took her to the University of Florence for the 1933–1934 academic year.

After returning to New York, Bentley became active in the American League against War and Fascism. Through the league and Columbia University she met several members of the Communist party and became a member in March 1935. For the next three years she worked at odd jobs and lived the life of "an average run-of-the-mill member" of the Communist party, participating in demonstrations, serving on picket lines, and attending meetings. According to her later testimony, her functions changed dramatically after June 1938, when she took a position as a secretary and research assistant for the Italian Library of Information in New York. She learned that the library was an arm of the Italian Propaganda Ministry and concluded that she could serve the Communist cause by providing information from her sources.

About this time, she met and fell in love with Jacob Golos, who ostensibly directed World Tourists, a Communist party travel agency facilitating tourist travel in Russia, but who in reality was a member of the powerful three-man Control Commission of the American Communist party and a leading Soviet agent. According to Bentley, Golos encouraged her clandestine activities at the Italian Library of Information until she lost her position in April 1939. He also convinced her to drop her official membership in the Communist party, explaining that she would thus become a more effective agent. He provided her with a cover, first making her an employee of World Tourists and later vice president of U.S. Service and Shipping Corporation, a business created with Communist party funds and designed to handle passenger and freight traffic between the United States and Russia.

From 1940 until November 1943, when Golos died of a heart attack, Bentley traveled regularly between New York and Washington, D.C., collecting information from government employees in numerous agencies, including the Treasury Department, the Board of Economic Warfare, the Farm Security Administration, the War Production Board, the Commerce Department, the Pentagon, the Office of the Coordinator of Inter-American Affairs, and even the Office of Strategic Services (OSS). Her sources worked in two espionage rings, one headed by Nathan Gregory Silvermaster, an economist with the Farm Security Administration and later the Board of Economic Warfare, and the other by Victor Perlo, an economist with the War Production Board.

Bentley also claimed that although she never met them personally, she received information through Silvermaster from Harry Dexter White, at the time director of the Division of Monetary Research in the Treasury Department and subsequently assistant secretary of the department, and Lauchlin Currie, one of President Franklin D. Roosevelt's administrative assistants. Finally, she maintained that she had a number of individual sources of information in Washington, including William Remington of the War Production Board and Maurice Halperin and Duncan Lee of OSS.

After Golos died, Bentley reported to a succession of Russian officials whom she knew only by code names, although the Federal Bureau of Investigation (FBI) later identified one as Anatoli Gromov, secretary of the Soviet embassy. Even after she ceased her activities in December 1944, she was terrified that either the FBI would uncover her clandestine activities or that the Russians might decide to eliminate her because she knew too much about Soviet espionage in the United States.

By August 1945 Bentley's fears overwhelmed her, and she began visiting FBI offices in the strange hope of discovering what they knew about her activities. She first went to the New Haven office and then in October to the New York office. Agents at both locations found her a bit bizarre, and one concluded that "possibly she was a psychopath rambling on." Still, the New York office followed up her visit and asked her to return for an interview in early November. By the time she returned, she was ready to tell all. Interviewed for more than two weeks, Bentley provided the FBI with a wealth of information, including the names of more than 150 individuals. The FBI assigned 227 agents to follow up on Bentley's allegations, concentrating on the fifty-one individuals she had named as espionage agents. These included twenty-seven people still employed by the federal government. J. Edgar Hoover, director of the FBI, found her story credible and so informed the Harry Truman White House.

In 1947 and 1948 Bentley testified before a special grand jury. No one, however, was indicted, primarily because the intensive FBI investigation had uncovered no firm corroborating evidence. Called before the House Committee on Un-American Activities, Bentley made her story public for the first time on 31 July 1948 and during interviews earlier that month with the *New York World-Telegram* that quickly drew national attention. For the next several years, she repeatedly testified before congressional committees holding hearings on Communist influence in America. She also testified at four trials, including the trial of William Remington, who in 1950 was indicted for perjury when he denied Bentley's allegations about his Communist affiliations and activities. She also testified at the trial of Julius and Ethel Rosenberg, who were accused (but not by Bentley) and later convicted of providing atomic secrets to the Soviet Union. Although Bentley never testified at the trial of Alger Hiss, she helped convince the FBI that Hiss was a Communist activist. In her original interview with the FBI in 1945, she stated that one of her Russian contacts informed her that a key State Department official was working for the Soviet Union. Although she stated that she had never met this person, she had been told that his name was "Eugene Hiss." Because the FBI had received similar accusations from Whittaker Chambers, whom Bentley did not know at the time, it concluded that she had gotten the first name wrong and made Alger Hiss the subject of intense scrutiny.

After going public in 1948, Bentley gained enormous notoriety. She became a consultant and lecturer on communism and unsuccessfully sought to transform her notoriety into a career. When her financial situation became desperate during the early 1950s, the FBI provided her a stipend of $50 a week. In the 1950s FBI officials also helped her find a position teaching Romance languages at the College of the Sacred Heart in Grand Coteau, Louisiana. She taught at the Long Lane School for Girls, a state correctional institution, in Middletown, Connecticut, from 1958 until her death in New Haven, Connecticut, following surgery for an abdominal tumor. She had never married. Often lonely and in financial difficulty, Bentley frequently asked the FBI to assist her with personal matters. These requests usually were denied.

During the late 1940s and early 1950s Bentley, along with several other disillusioned former Communists, provided the FBI, the Department of Justice, and numerous congressional committees with the material they needed to launch an anti-Communist crusade. Subsequent inquiries have revealed a few inconsistencies and numerous exaggerations in her testimony, but they have not impugned the main outline of her story. Although she died in obscurity, the "Blond Spy Queen," as she was dubbed by the tabloid press, held center stage during the decade following World War II as one of the most important ex-Communist informants in the United States.

• There is no known repository of Bentley papers. Her autobiography, *Out of Bondage* (1951), provides a broad outline of her career. A great deal of information can be found in the relevant FBI files, in her statements to congressional committees, especially the House Committee on Un-American Activities and the Senate Internal Security Subcommittee, and in her testimony at various trials, including *United States v. William Remington* (1951) and *United States v. Julius and Ethel Rosenberg* (1951). Other important sources of information are Gary May, *Un-American Activities: The Trials of William Remington* (1994); Kenneth O'Reilly, *Hoover and the Un-Americans: The FBI, HUAC, and the Red Menace* (1983); Ronald Radosh and Joyce Milton, *The Rosenberg File: A Search for Truth* (1983); Earl Latham, *The Communist Controversy in Washington: From the New Deal to McCarthy* (1966); and Herbert L. Packer, *Ex-Communist Witnesses: Four Studies in Fact Finding* (1962). An obituary is in the *New York Times*, 4 Dec. 1963.

HAROLD JOSEPHSON

BENTLEY, William (22 June 1759–29 Dec. 1819), clergyman, scholar, and journalist, was born in Boston, Massachusetts, the son of Joshua Bentley, a carpenter, and Elizabeth Paine, the daughter of a merchant. Bentley was raised in the home of William Paine, the prosperous grandfather for whom he was named, and he was educated at the Boston Latin School before entering Harvard College in 1773. After graduation in 1777, Bentley taught school. He returned to Harvard in 1780 as a tutor in Latin and Greek and prepared for the ministry. Ordained at the Second (East) Congregational parish in Salem, Massachusetts, in 1783, Bentley served in its pulpit until his death thirty-six years later.

Although Bentley stayed in Salem he gradually became famous for the encyclopedic learning he acquired. He became controversial due to his commitment to Unitarianism during the Christian revival known as the Second Great Awakening as well as for his devotion to Jeffersonian Republicanism in a profession and region where Federalists prevailed. A lifelong bachelor who was seldom distracted from study by family responsibilities or the need to provide for a wife and children, Bentley spent much of his life mastering more than a dozen European and Near Eastern languages as well as a full range of scientific, philosophical, literary, and political writings. A person of modest material appetites, Bentley assembled one of the nation's most comprehensive private libraries, one that numbered some 4,000 volumes at his death. Bentley's prodigious learning was recognized by election to the American Philosophical and Massachusetts Historical societies, by an honorary doctorate in divinity from Harvard (1819), and by an invitation from Bentley's correspondent, Thomas Jefferson, to lead the University of Virginia as its first president. Bentley's erudition as a linguist was so well known that he was once called on by Jefferson's secretary of state, Albert Gallatin, to translate the credentials of the Tunisian ambassador. Bentley expressed his keen interest in history, natural as well as human affairs, in a 75-page description and history of Salem, which the Massachusetts Historical Society published in its 1799 *Collections*.

Bentley's ambition for learning was motivated less by his concern for the advancement of scholarship than by a desire to keep himself and the public abreast of the cornucopia of knowledge that the progress of

Enlightenment learning made available. From 1794, when he began to compile news digests and commentaries for the *Salem Gazette* (later the *Impartial Register*), until his death, Bentley devoted his learning to public service by providing summaries of foreign and domestic news, including scientific discoveries, advances in education, and the publication of notable books in all fields. During his more than twenty-five years as a voluntary, unpaid journalist, Bentley wrote more than 2,000 of these news digests—nearly as many digests as he wrote sermons—in his effort to enable "all classes of readers," as he put it, to understand "the causes which produce interesting events." Bentley declined to reply to direct partisan attacks, but his Jeffersonian politics and his progressive Christianity influenced both his choice of subjects and his treatment of them. Because Bentley's summaries and comments often were excerpted and reprinted in other newspapers, his influence as an enlightened republican journalist extended throughout the United States.

Bentley's diary, which he kept faithfully from April 1784 through December 1819, reveals that while its author outwardly strove to be friendly to all, he actually held caustic views toward the orthodox clergy and Federalists who often criticized him and that he reserved particular scorn for under-educated revivalist preachers. Bentley's liberalism made him more able than any evangelical Calvinist to assist a Roman Catholic evangelist, John Thayer, and to converse with the nation's first Catholic bishop, John Carroll. Befriending Catholics was good policy, he reasoned, since good treatment of Catholics in America would promote greater tolerance for Protestants in Catholic countries.

For Bentley, tolerance was an article of faith reinforced by his long and prominent commitment to the Masonic movement in New England. Ironically, what he found hard to tolerate was the narrow intolerance he saw in evangelical Calvinists such as the Reverend Jedidiah Morse. In Bentley's only address to the Massachusetts legislature, an 1807 election sermon, after noting the imperfection of human knowledge, he declared that "the state must not then fix bounds to enquiry into religion, more than to other researches of genius." Convinced that the pursuit of progress in all forms of knowledge was among humankind's highest duties, Bentley rejected notions of fixed orthodoxy, both secular, as in standing-order Federalism, and religious, as with Trinitarian Calvinism.

When Bentley died in Salem, he was a scholarly celebrity; but because he was not an original thinker or an institution builder, his reputation faded quickly. By the twentieth century historians remembered him chiefly for his voluminous diary, a rich source for the period 1784–1819. William Bentley's importance however, transcends his immediate impact. He embodied one of the ideals of the Christian Enlightenment by developing his universal learning and putting it to the service of his community and, via his journalistic career, the new American republic.

• Bentley's manuscripts, including his diary, correspondence, more than 3,000 sermons, and a list of titles in his library at his death, are at the American Antiquarian Society in Worcester, Mass. In addition to twelve occasional addresses and sermons and a collection of psalms and hymns, during his lifetime Bentley published "A Description and History of Salem," *Massachusetts Historical Society Collections*, 1st ser., 6 (1799): 212–88. The diary, including an 1868 biographical sketch by Joseph G. Waters, a bibliography of Bentley's published works, and an 1897 address on Bentley by Marguerite Dalrymple, who had been one of his parishioners as a child, were published by the (Salem, Mass.) Essex Institute in four volumes (1905). One issue of the *Essex Institute Historical Collections*, 113 (July 1977), is devoted to "Dr. Bentley's Salem: Diary of a Town." Biographical articles include Joseph T. Buckingham, "William Bentley," in his *Specimens of Newspaper Literature*, vol. 2 (1850); four articles by Louise Chipley, "The Enlightened Library of William Bentley," *Essex Institute Historical Collections* 122 (Jan. 1986): 2–29, "William Bentley, Journalist of the Early Republic," *EIHC* 123 (Oct. 1987): 331–47, "'The Best Instruction of the People': William Bentley on the Congregational Clergy and the Republic, 1783–1819," *EIHC* 127 (July 1991): 194–210, and "The Financial and Tenure Anxieties of New England's Congregational Clergy during the Early National Era: The Case of William Bentley, 1783–1819," *EIHC* 127 (Oct. 1991): 277–96; and Richard D. Brown, "William Bentley and the Ideal of Universal Information in the Enlightened Republic," in his *Knowledge Is Power: The Diffusion of Information in Early America, 1700–1865* (1989).

RICHARD D. BROWN

BENTON, Thomas Hart (14 Mar. 1782–10 Apr. 1858), U.S. senator and congressman, was born near Hillsboro (now Hillsborough), North Carolina, the son of Jesse Benton, a lawyer and farmer, and Ann "Nancy" Gooch. Jesse Benton died in 1791, leaving eight children, considerable land, extensive debts, and an aristocratic lifestyle. The family suffered a further blow when Thomas Hart Benton, at age sixteen, was expelled from the University of North Carolina for misusing money entrusted to him by roommates. The future senator was known ever after for scrupulous honesty and belligerent defense of his honor; concern that the story of his expulsion might surface probably influenced his consistent refusals to be considered for the presidency.

In 1801 Benton's family moved to the Nashville, Tennessee, frontier in search of better fortune. There Benton taught school, became a successful attorney and state senator, and won the friendship of Andrew Jackson. In the state senate Benton secured extensive reform of the Tennessee judicial system.

During the War of 1812, Benton was elected commanding colonel of his regiment, and as Jackson's "first aid" he helped transport two thousand men by flatboat to Natchez for the defense of the region. When the secretary of war ordered this army disbanded, an angry Jackson marched his men back to Nashville. Benton went to Washington and gained reimbursement for Jackson's expenses and a regular army commission for himself. Meanwhile, however, Jackson had helped arrange a duel in which Benton's younger brother Jesse was wounded and humiliated. Benton, infuriated, fought Jackson in a sword and pistol brawl, in which Jackson was badly wounded. The general's revenge was subtle. When on two occasions the eager Colonel Benton was poised to lead his men into battle, Jackson ordered him home for recruiting duty.

Recognizing Jackson's supremacy in Tennessee, Benton moved to St. Louis, Missouri, and soon became a successful attorney, civic leader, politician, and newspaper editor. In 1817 he fought two duels with Charles Lucas, a political rival. In the second duel, fought at ten feet, Lucas was mortally wounded. Benton, full of remorse, never dueled again, despite many insults and occasional challenges.

In 1820 the popular and pugnacious Benton was elected one of Missouri's first two U.S. senators. The new senator sought validation of Spanish and French land titles in Missouri and promoted the interests of St. Louis fur traders. He proclaimed that all of Oregon extending to 49° N belonged to the United States and predicted that American democracy would spread to Asia via the Columbia River and the Pacific Ocean. He persuaded Congress to finance a road from Missouri to Santa Fe so that Mexican silver could be imported to supply the United States with sound money. The great depression of 1819 had resulted from a speculative boom fueled by excessive paper money issued by unsound banks, and Benton sought to limit bank notes and bring more specie into circulation. His efforts ultimately got the value ratio of gold to silver raised to 16 to 1, but his efforts to promote hard money failed because they were out of step with the country's need for a rapidly expanding currency.

Equally dear to the hearts of Benton's constituents were his arguments, year after year, for conveying public lands to small farmers as quickly and cheaply as possible. Eloquently describing the ownership of land as a God-given natural right, he advocated a graduation program that would annually reduce the price of government lands by twenty-five cents per acre and provide that it ultimately be given away to actual settlers. His appeal to small farmers helped keep him in the Senate for thirty years.

Benton married Elizabeth McDowell in 1821. It was a long and happy union, and he quickly became known as a "house lamb," in contrast to his reputation as a "street lion." Five of the six Benton children, who fondly remembered their father's loving attention and constant efforts to improve their education, survived to adulthood.

In 1824 Benton was reconciled with Jackson, and after 1828 he was Jackson's devoted partisan. In the Senate he fought for Jackson against the Second Bank of the United States; his arguments for hard money won him the sobriquet "Old Bullion." His ideal, in the bank war as in all else, was a simple and frugal government that spent money only for defense and western expansion; kept tariffs and taxes at a minimum; gave the national domain to private enterprise as quickly, cheaply, and fairly as possible; and granted no artificial privileges to anyone. In 1837 he was one of only a

handful who opposed the act that transferred the federal treasury surplus to the states.

In 1833 Benton opposed the Calhoun-Clay Compromise Tariff, which brought the nullification controversy to an end, because Henry Clay proposed extending tariff protection for ten more years. In 1836, when John C. Calhoun demanded that Congress reject petitions for the abolition of slavery in the District of Columbia, Benton denounced him for unnecessarily giving the petitioners a national forum. He also opposed Calhoun's efforts to allow postmasters to censor and destroy abolition literature, warning that such a policy would threaten freedom everywhere.

By the 1840s Benton's efforts, previously centered on hard money, low land prices, and other economic issues, became focused on fighting Calhoun, denouncing the extension of slavery, and protecting the Union. In 1844, when Calhoun as secretary of state signed a treaty annexing Texas and claimed that the treaty alone would prevent British-influenced abolition in Texas, Benton led the Senate fight against ratification, even though the treaty was immensely popular in Missouri. He derided the abolition threat in Texas and warned that the treaty would produce war with Mexico and sectional combat in the United States. Instead he proposed annexing Texas only after winning Mexican concurrence, making a new slave state of Texas no larger than the largest existing state, and dividing the remainder of Texas equally into slave and free territories. The slave South doomed Benton's effort.

After Congress annexed Texas by joint resolution and President James K. Polk pursued war with Mexico and negotiation with Britain over the Oregon boundary, Benton still supported American manifest destiny. He insisted that the United States was destined to expand its superior culture to the Pacific and beyond. He also believed, however, that the United States should set the world a noble example of justice toward other nations. He thus delivered an eight-hour speech to prove that 49° N rather than 54° 40′ N was the rightful boundary of Oregon and that the seizure of the Rio Grande Valley from Mexico would be wrong. This unpopular stance helped defeat Polk's efforts to make Benton the commander of American armies in Mexico, with the power to negotiate a peace treaty.

When the Wilmot Proviso against slavery in the territories acquired from Mexico produced angry debates, Benton denounced the proviso, but he also refused to support the southern demand for territorial expansion. He insisted that slavery where it existed was in no danger, while geography, climate, and the opposition of existing territorial populations would prevent its expansion. Though a slaveholder himself, Benton described the institution as an incurable evil, preserved only by racial fears and animosities. He hoped that it would ultimately disappear, but meanwhile he prayed that it would never be expanded.

In 1848 Calhoun warned that Congress would intolerably insult the South by allowing Oregon to bar slavery. Benton replied that the issue was meaningless, because slavery would never spread so far north. After many weeks of angry debate, he and Texas's Sam Houston cast the deciding votes admitting Oregon with its ban against slavery.

Meanwhile, Benton's close friend Martin Van Buren was nominated for president by the Free Soil party. Benton, however, supported Lewis Cass, the Democratic candidate, who advocated leaving the territorial slavery decision to the settlers. To Benton, Van Buren's Free Soilers were an unnecessary irritant, serving only to strengthen Calhoun and the southern radicals.

In 1849 the Missouri legislature instructed Benton to defend southern interests. The legislators would soon vote on his reelection, but the senator defied the legislature in fiery speeches throughout Missouri. He idealized the American Union as humanity's last best hope for freedom on earth and insisted that this gift to all humankind was being needlessly threatened by ambitious southerners demanding useless rights.

Benton's Unionist efforts in 1849 and in subsequent years probably contributed to the disunionists' weakness in Missouri in 1861. In 1850 his Missouri opponents attempted a reconciliation, but the old man replied that he preferred defeat to cooperation with those opposed to the Union. With the Democrats thus divided, the legislature elected a Whig senator and ended Benton's long senatorial tenure.

Before leaving the Senate, Benton cooperated with Clay in 1850 until southerners combined Clay's compromise proposals into a single omnibus bill. He argued that the omnibus could not pass, that it was prolonging and inflaming the debates, and that it was a southern ploy to give Texas most of present-day New Mexico. During the debates the much younger Henry S. Foote of Mississippi taunted Benton unmercifully for several weeks and pointed a pistol when Benton finally approached him in an unfriendly manner. The incident stirred up northern public opinion, as editors throughout the section denounced Foote as a typical southern assassin. Ultimately, amendments destroyed the omnibus, and as Benton had predicted, its various parts were passed as separate bills.

In 1852 Benton was elected to the House of Representatives. When the Kansas-Nebraska Act repealed the Missouri Compromise in 1854, Benton angrily called it a needless betrayal of a sacred agreement that had helped to preserve the Union for thirty-four years. The southern people, he insisted, had not requested it and would not benefit from it, and it would only inflame the North. In the House he also denounced federal subsidies of western railroads as cheating the taxpayers and as a source of corruption and inefficiency. He argued that the government should build and own the Pacific Railroad and lease it to private operators or that private capitalists should build it aided only by a free right-of-way through public lands.

Defeated in the 1854 congressional race, Benton continued work on his two-volume memoir, *Thirty Years' View* (1854, 1856), which he hoped would rally admiration for the Union and distrust of sectional agitators. In 1856 his long crusade against "Union-break-

ers" took on painful personal consequence when his son-in-law John C. Frémont became the first presidential candidate of the new, all-northern Republican party. While professing love for Frémont, Benton delivered twenty-one speeches supporting James Buchanan. He warned that the election of an entirely pro-northern president would bring secession and a civil war. His angered family and friends blamed him for Frémont's defeat.

In 1857 the Supreme Court, in the *Dred Scott* decision, ruled that the federal government could not bar slavery from any federal territory. Benton answered this ruling with a 192-page *Historical and Legal Examination of the Dred Scott Case* (1857), which glorified the Union, appealed for sectional peace, and denounced the decision as bad constitutional law. After finishing this book, Benton delivered appeals for understanding and peace in numerous northern cities, stretching from Chicago to New England. Although painfully injured in a train wreck near Pittsburgh, he delivered his lecture as scheduled.

Benton, dying of cancer, was determined to finish both his massive memoir and his sixteen-volume *Abridgment of the Debates of Congress* (1857–1861). He wished to make the great compromise speeches of Clay and Daniel Webster more accessible to the public, and he completed the *Abridgment* less than twenty-four hours before his death in Washington, D.C. His debts at his death exceeded his financial assets.

In an age when senators did their own research, wrote their own speeches, and developed their ideas without the aid of opinion polls, extensive staffs, or wealthy contributors, Benton was a prodigious worker and a wise public servant. Although his personal sacrifices could not prevent the Civil War, he became one of the most respected pre–Civil War statesmen.

• The only extensive collection of Benton's papers is at the Missouri Historical Society in St. Louis. Numerous scattered references are in the Martin Van Buren Papers and the Francis P. Blair Papers at the Library of Congress and in the Blair-Lee papers at Princeton University. Elbert B. Smith, *Magnificent Missourian: The Life of Thomas Hart Benton* (1958), stresses Benton's role in the sectional struggle; and William N. Chambers, *Old Bullion Benton, Senator from the New West* (1956), emphasizes Benton's career as a Jacksonian Democrat. See also Arthur M. Schlesinger, Jr., *The Age of Jackson* (1945); Robert Remini, *Andrew Jackson*, vol. 3 (1984); and Allan Nevins, *Ordeal of the Union* (2 vols., 1947). Obituaries are in the *Jefferson Enquirer*, 24 Apr. 1858, and the *New York Tribune*, 14 Apr. 1858.

ELBERT B. SMITH

BENTON, Thomas Hart, Jr. (5 Sept. 1816–10 Apr. 1879), frontier educator and legislator, was born in Williamson County, Tennessee, the son of Samuel Benton, a congressman. His mother's name is unknown. His uncle and namesake practiced law as an associate of Andrew Jackson's before moving north up the river to Missouri, where he became a prominent U.S. senator. Samuel Benton moved his family briefly to St. Louis but returned to Shelby County, Tennessee, near Memphis, when Thomas, Jr., was five. Young Thomas's studies began with his father. Later he attended and graduated from the academy in Huntington, Tennessee. He also studied the classics at Marion College, a small school in Missouri, but he did not graduate. His early education included many opportunities to travel up and down the Mississippi River between St. Louis and Memphis. Family ties gave him a strong Methodist upbringing, exposure to discussions of important events, and acquaintance with powerful political leaders of the country.

Benton sought opportunities in the West and became involved in education and politics. He went to Iowa (then part of the Wisconsin Territory) shortly after the territory was created in 1836. Settling in Dubuque, a frontier town with a population of 1,200, during the summer of 1837, Benton in 1838 established the first classical school in Iowa; he taught classics and his one assistant taught literature. Benton was a proponent of Iowa becoming the twenty-ninth state in the Union in 1846. He became a state senator and served in the new state's legislature from 1846 to 1848. Because of his scholarly nature and political acumen, he was elected to the office of superintendent of public instruction in 1848. He helped organize many levels of schooling, including the State University of Iowa, which was created by the legislature in 1847 and accepted its first students in 1855. Also during this busy period of his life, in 1851, he married Susan Culbertson. They had one daughter.

After these years as a leader in politics and education, Benton in 1854 moved across the state to Council Bluffs and worked as a banker and merchant. He prospered as a businessman until he lost his fortune in the crash of 1857 and returned to public service. Under its newly adopted constitution, Iowa had replaced the office of the state superintendent of public instruction with the secretary of the state board of education, to which post Benton was appointed in 1858. As secretary he also held the title of president of the board of trustees at the State University of Iowa, where he supported coeducation, insisting that boys and girls deserved the same benefits from the state. For more than a year he fought faculty sentiment against the idea of women in higher education and eventually won.

The looming national crisis over slavery drew Benton into the debate on the side of the Union, and his organizing talents now turned from building schools to building armies of war. Early in the Civil War he was commissioned a colonel in the Twenty-ninth Iowa Infantry. He spent the war in the Arkansas Territory, where he was military governor of Little Rock. He set up his headquarters at the home of a southern general, Albert Pike, whose library was famous. Benton's move into Pike's home prevented the destruction of these library resources. Although he left the army in October 1865 as a brigadier general, he was often called "Colonel Benton" after the war.

In these times of national expansion and government crisis, members of the influential Benton family often took complex political positions. Sometimes these stands created splits within the family. Benton's uncle Thomas Hart Benton, Sr., was a staunch Unionist who nevertheless opposed abolition. Thomas, Sr.'s daughter Jessie Benton Frémont and her husband, John C. Frémont, supported the abolitionists and were impatient with Abraham Lincoln on emancipation. Thomas, Jr., was a Jackson Democrat all his life until he became a Republican and Unionist during the Civil War. However, he also took a public stand against black male suffrage during a campaign for governor of Iowa following the Civil War. Running on a "Soldier's Ticket" in opposition to the Republicans in 1865, he lost yet garnered a large vote because of the controversial suffrage issue, his war record, public service, and widespread name recognition.

After his wife's death in 1869, Benton moved to Cedar Rapids and worked as an auditor for the Burlington-Northern Railroad. When he retired on account of poor health, he joined his daughter and sister in St. Louis. He died there at his sister's home and was buried at Marshalltown, Iowa, with masonic honors. Iowa's reputation for excellence in education owes much to Benton's early leadership.

• Materials relevant to Thomas Hart Benton, Jr., are available in the Benton drawer at the Missouri Historical Society. His reports as superintendent of public instruction are available in the *Journal of the Iowa House and Senate*, 1850–1854, and his reports as secretary of the state board of education are in *Iowa Legislative Documents*, 1860–1864. For an overview of Benton's life, see T. S. Parvin, "Thomas Hart Benton, Jr.," *Iowa Historical Record* 16 (1900). His work as an educator is discussed in Clarence Aurner, *History of Education in Iowa* (4 vols., 1914). See also Perry McCandless, *A History of Missouri, 1820–1860* (1972).

KATHLEEN S. BROWN

BENTON, Thomas Hart (15 Apr. 1889–9 Jan. 1975), painter, was born in Neosho, Missouri, the son of Maecenas Eason Benton, a politician, and Elizabeth Wise. Benton grew up in an environment of politics and conflict. He was named for his great-uncle, a U.S. senator and a prominent champion of westward expansion. His father was an outspoken midwestern populist and foe of East Coast business interests. As a child Benton often accompanied his father on his political tours into rural areas. After his father was elected to the U.S. Congress in 1896, Benton's world broadened enormously: although he continued to summer in the rural, almost primitive environment of Neosho, he henceforth spent his winters in the sophisticated, urban milieu of Washington, D.C.

From an early age Benton displayed precocity in drawing. A surviving pencil sketch of a locomotive, made when he was nine, reveals an ability worthy of a mature artist. His talent became an issue in his parent's frequent battles with each other, his father opposing the son's artistic gifts and his mother supporting them.

As a boy Benton had little exposure to actual paintings, except for the murals in the newly constructed Library of Congress. He absorbed visual ideas chiefly through newspaper cartoons and book illustrations and grew adept at drawing caricatures of figures with big heads in the manner of Clifford Berryman, the cartoonist for the *Washington Post*. This skill earned Benton his first artistic job. While sitting in a bar in Joplin, Missouri, where he was working as a surveyor in the summer of 1906, he heard of an opening for a cartoonist, applied for the job, and obtained it. Unimpressed, his father sent Benton to military school the following year; but after a single term the elder Benton relented and allowed his son to attend the Art Institute of Chicago. There Benton concentrated on pen-and-ink illustration and also showed outstanding talent for watercolor. After his second year, no longer content with becoming a commercial artist, he left Chicago to study painting in Paris, where he found himself a studio apartment and began taking classes at the Académie Julian.

Up to this time Benton had conceived of painting primarily in realistic, narrative terms. In France, however, he was introduced to impressionism and to even more radical artistic styles that concentrated on the abstract qualities of color and form. For the next twenty years he struggled to master this different approach, running the gamut of modern styles including postimpressionism, pointillism, fauvism, synchromism, and constructivism. This progression, however, was not a smooth one, and until the early 1920s Benton vacillated between modern and conservative styles, never quite finding an artistic idiom that satisfied him.

Within a few months of his arrival in France Benton had largely abandoned his classes to embark on a course of self-instruction. He alternated between copying the old masters' drawings in the Louvre and painting landscape studies outdoors to learn how to handle color. The strongest paintings of his stay in France were a group of pointillist landscapes that he executed in the south of France in the summer of 1910. Throughout this period his closest friend was the California painter Stanton Macdonald-Wright, who encouraged his most radical experiments. Unfortunately, in the spring of 1911 Benton's mother arrived unexpectedly in Paris, discovered that he was living with a French mistress, and decided to take him home. Thus, Benton's artistic development was interrupted at a crucial moment.

After spending an unpleasant year in Neosho, during which his father raged over the foolishness of his modernist ventures, Benton departed for New York, assuring his parents that he could support himself as a portraitist and commercial artist. This turned out to be wishful thinking. For the next ten years he lived a precarious existence, supporting himself with menial jobs and handouts from friends. Ralph Barton, a successful cartoonist, often provided Benton with a place to stay. For a while he designed movie sets for his friend Rex Ingram.

During this period Benton continued to experiment with modernist styles. Shortly after his arrival in New York he painted a group of still-life and figure paintings in the manner of Cézanne. But his art received a new impetus when his friend Macdonald-Wright returned from Paris, having just created a new art movement that he called synchromism—a kind of cubism with bright colors. Benton began to experiment with this approach, creating both pure abstractions and brightly colored figure paintings. Thanks to his friendship with Macdonald-Wright, he showed some of the figure paintings in the Forum Exhibition of 1916—the first group exhibition of modernist American artists. These attracted considerable attention in the press, winning for Benton his first significant recognition.

During World War I, Benton enlisted in the navy. He served at the Norfolk Naval Base, making documentary drawings of ships and machines. He later declared that this task was the first step in pushing him away from abstraction toward realism, but after his discharge he went back to his modernist experiments. Eager to give greater physical intensity to his paintings, he made constructions in paper, wood, and wire that served as models for his abstractions. Similarly, he made clay models for his figure paintings so that he could work out the formal organization of the composition. In the early 1920s he perfected this method in a series of large, semiabstract figure compositions filled with muscular, writhing figures. In February 1922 he married a spirited Italian immigrant, Rita Piacenza, who brought a new element of stability to his life and acted as his manager and dealer. They had two children.

In 1926–1927 Benton summed up his ideas on abstract composition in a series of articles in *Arts* magazine titled "The Mechanics of Form Organization in Painting." Here he outlined his techniques for designing abstract compositions, based on considerations of compositional balance, compositional connection, and visual rhythm. These articles provided much of the basis for the abstract paintings of Benton's pupil Jackson Pollock, who essentially deconstructed Benton's visual style, reducing it to its most fundamental principles of abstract design.

Benton had been generally viewed as a modernist and was even briefly patronized by Albert Barnes, the Philadelphia collector of modern art. In the early 1920s, however, he shifted toward painting the American scene. He began work on a series of wall paintings that he titled *The American Historical Epic*, portraying American history from the standpoint of ordinary people. He worked on the project until about 1928, completing eighteen paintings. He also painted portraits of colorful characters on Martha's Vineyard in which he attempted to capture a distinctive sense of place.

Perhaps most important, in 1924 Benton visited his father, who was dying of cancer in Missouri. During this visit he was flooded with memories of his childhood and of the America he had known as a boy. In 1926 and 1928 he set out on long sketching tours around the United States during which he made hundreds of drawings of steelworkers, coal miners, lumbermen, cotton pickers, river rats, oil workers, and cowboys. These trips provided much of the material for his great murals of the 1930s.

Benton burst into public awareness a few years later with his mural *America Today* (New School for Social Research), completed in 1930. Consisting of ten large panels packed with energetic figures, it established a new type of mural painting that was widely imitated and became the basis of the Works Progress Administration mural program of the 1930s. Among the novelties of Benton's style, previously unknown in American mural painting, were intense colors, bold shapes, an intense sense of sculptural form, strictly American settings, and a strong emphasis on working-class subject matter. Benton followed this work with two other murals, *The Arts of Life in America* (1932), showing ordinary Americans at play, and *A Social History of Indiana* (1933), showing industrial and social change from American Indian times to the present. These were executed for the Whitney Museum of American Art and the Indiana Pavillion of the Century of Progress Exposition in Chicago.

The sheer scale of these projects was astounding. The Indiana mural took up 3,500 square feet of wall space and contained hundreds of figures. Benton designed the project in a mere four months and painted it in just over two—the equivalent of producing an easel painting six by eight feet in size at the rate of one a day for more than sixty days in a row. Benton's work was fiercely attacked both by conservatives, who felt that his view of the United States was unflattering, and by communists, who felt that he was soft on capitalism.

In 1934 Benton was featured on the cover of *Time*, an event that established his national reputation. He was featured as the leader of the regionalist movement in American art along with two other midwestern painters, John Steuart Curry and Grant Wood. This publicity provided the impetus for ever more vicious attacks on Benton's work, and not long afterward, in April 1935, Benton decided to return to the Midwest to teach at the Kansas City Art Institute and to paint a mural for the Missouri State Capitol in Jefferson City.

Benton's Missouri mural, which he completed late in 1936, was the most personal of his mural projects, and he considered it his masterpiece. Filled with family vignettes, including a scene of his father delivering a speech, it celebrated the growth of the state while at the same time pointing out the tawdry aspects of its history. Benton unflinchingly portrayed scenes of racial and religious intolerance, of poverty and financial exploitation, and of dishonesty and political corruption.

The Missouri mural stirred up so much controversy that Benton received no more mural commissions for a decade. But he remained extremely active throughout the 1930s, producing a series of memorable easel paintings, including two controversial nudes, *Susanna and the Elders* and *Persephone*, which humorously set ancient stories in a contemporary American setting.

In 1941 Benton was fired from the Kansas City Art Institute after making tactless public remarks about homosexual staff members at the Nelson-Atkins Museum of Art in Kansas City. Nevertheless, his reputation remained intact until the end of the Second World War. After Pearl Harbor was bombed by the Japanese, Benton produced a number of paintings to support the war effort, including a grisly series titled *Year of Peril* (1941; State Historical Society of Missouri), which focused on Nazi atrocities. He also continued to produce midwestern farm scenes, such as *July Hay* (1943; Metropolitan Museum of Art, New York).

Around 1947, however, Benton's work began to come under attack from European-trained art historians, such as H. W. Janson, who published a savage attack in the *Magazine of Art* in which he compared Benton's work with Nazi painting. During the 1950s and 1960s Benton ceased to garner national attention. He fell back on local patronage and turned increasingly to landscape. When he took up mural painting again in 1947 he no longer depicted scenes from contemporary life but created historical reenactments of early American history. The most ambitious of these was *Independence and the Opening of the West* (1961) for the Truman Library in Independence. While working on this project he established a warm friendship with former President Harry Truman.

Benton published two autobiographies, *An Artist in America* (1937) and *An American in Art* (1969), the first a colorful personal reminiscence, the second a more technical account of his artistic methods. He also achieved distinction as a musician, collecting folk tunes, inventing a new form of musical notation for the harmonica that is widely used, and producing a record for Decca titled *Saturday Night at Tom Benton's*. By the end of his life he had become a kind of living old master and was often called on for interviews and television appearances. In August 1970, when he was in his eighties, *Sports Illustrated* ran an account of one of his float trips down the Buffalo River in northwest Arkansas. Active until the end, Benton died in his studio in Kansas City while looking over his last mural, *The Sources of Country Music*, which he had completed the day before.

The most controversial American artist of this century, he played a major role in shaping three separate movements of American art: the early American modernism of the 1910s and 1920s; the regionalism of the 1930s; and through his influence on his pupil Jackson Pollock, the abstract expressionism of the 1940s.

• The large collection of documents, paintings, and drawings that Benton owned at the time of his death is currently held by the Benton Trusts, UMB Bank, Kansas City, Mo. The American Art Department of the Nelson-Atkins Museum of Art, Kansas City, Mo., holds an extensive collection of writings by Benton and articles about him, which was gathered in preparation for the centennial exhibition of Benton's work in 1989. In addition to his two marvelous autobiographies, Benton was hard at work at the time of his death on a third account, "The Intimate Story," the manuscript of which is held by the Benton Trust. Benton's six articles on "The Mechanics of Form Organization in Painting," published in *Arts* beginning in Nov. 1926, summarize his theories of abstract composition and greatly influenced Jackson Pollock. The most detailed biography of Benton is Henry Adams, *Thomas Hart Benton: An American Original* (1989). Also useful are Matthew Baigell, *Thomas Hart Benton* (1974), and Adams, *Thomas Hart Benton: Drawing from Life* (1990), an account of Benton's working methods with a useful bibliography. For a forceful critical attack on Benton see H. W. Janson, "Benton and Wood, Champions of Regionalism," *Magazine of Art*, May 1946, pp. 184–86, 198–200. Benton's influence on Pollock has been discussed by Stephen Polcari in "Jackson Pollock and Thomas Hart Benton," *Arts*, Mar. 1979, pp. 120–240. An obituary is in the *New York Times*, 21 Jan. 1975.

HENRY ADAMS

BENTON, William (1 Apr. 1900–18 Mar. 1973), advertising executive, educator, and politician, was born in Minneapolis, Minnesota, the son of Charles Benton, a Congregationalist clergyman and professor of romance languages, and Elma Hixson, a schoolteacher. After brief military service in World War I, Benton attended Yale University and graduated in 1921. In 1928 he was married to Helen Hemingway. They had four children.

Starting out as an advertising copywriter in the booming business world of the 1920s, he and Yale classmate Chester Bowles founded in 1929 the Madison Avenue firm of Benton and Bowles, which quickly became the world's largest single-office advertising agency. Benton and Bowles's success was based on the use of radio as a marketing device. The firm invented soap opera ("Young Doctor Malone," "Portia Faces Life") and pioneered consumer research surveys, one of which reportedly made Benton "the world's greatest authority on the sanitary napkin."

A millionaire by 1936, Benton resigned and then became vice president of the University of Chicago, where he employed his advertising talents in developing educational radio and films, most notably the award-winning "University of Chicago Round Table" radio program. Benton also enabled the university to purchase the *Encyclopaedia Britannica*, personally providing $100,000 to complete the acquisition in 1943. As chairman and publisher of the *Britannica*, Benton expanded and diversified its publications, including the Great Books of the Western World series, all of which eventually brought the university more than $50 million in endowments and other gifts. He also gained financial control of Muzak (a radio music service that came into homes without static over telephone wires), and wired music thrived under his supervision.

Benton began his public service in 1940–1941 as a consultant to Nelson Rockefeller, then coordinator of inter-American affairs. Appointed assistant secretary of state for public affairs in September 1945, Benton spent two years overseeing the country's foreign information programs. In 1945 he gave the name "Voice of America" to the department's shortwave radio broadcasts; he administered the new Fulbright international educational exchange program, and from 1945 to 1947 helped establish the United Nations Educational, Scientific, and Cultural Organization (UNESCO).

A liberal internationalist who had become a Democrat from public service rather than partisanship, Benton assumed the duties of a U.S. senator in 1949 when his former partner, Connecticut governor Chester Bowles, appointed him to fill a vacant Senate seat. The next year Benton won election for the rest of the term against Republican Prescott Bush by a bare 1,102 votes. Although he lost his bid for reelection in 1952 by 88,000 votes, Benton earned a reputation during his short tenure as one of the Senate's leading liberals, especially distinguished for his courageous opposition to Republican senator Joseph R. McCarthy of Wisconsin.

A Fair Deal Democrat who cosponsored bills for fair employment practices, antilynching, outlawing the poll tax, and cabinet departments for health, education, and social security, Benton first denounced McCarthy in May 1950 as "a hit-and-run propagandist of the Kremlin variety." He defended former colleagues like Secretary of State Dean Acheson and Ambassador Philip Jessup against McCarthy's charges of coddling communists. As a junior "ad man" amid an assemblage of lawyers and politicians, however, Benton made little impact on his fellow legislators until August 1951. As a member of the Senate Rules Committee, Benton read an advance copy of the Maryland report, an investigation of that state's 1950 senatorial election in which outsiders, led by Senator McCarthy, had conducted a "despicable 'back street' type of campaign" that resulted in the defeat of Democrat Millard Tydings, one of McCarthy's earliest critics. The report sharply criticized McCarthy but made no specific recommendation. Fearing that the report would simply be "filed and forgotten," Benton surprised everyone by introducing an unprecedented resolution calling on the Rules Committee to investigate "whether or not it should initiate action with a view toward the expulsion . . . of Joseph R. McCarthy."

Although a dozen senators congratulated Benton after his speech, none rose to support his resolution nor did any defend him against McCarthy's blast that Benton, "a mental midget," had become "the hero of every Communist and crook in and out of government." The probe nonetheless proceeded. In 25,000 words of prepared testimony Benton addressed the investigating subcommittee headed by Senator Guy Gillette in September, citing specific cases to prove McCarthy guilty of dishonesty, corruption, and irresponsible conduct. Among Benton's claims: McCarthy had lied to the Senate about the specific number of card-carrying Communists in the State Department as alleged in his famous speech in Wheeling, West Virginia; McCarthy had "deceitfully" failed to honor his promise that he would repeat in public anything he had said on the Senate floor; McCarthy had violated Senate ethics by accepting payments from a company that was undergoing congressional investigation; finally, his notorious attack on George C. Marshall as mastermind of "a conspiracy so immense" (allegedly to encourage "Communists" in the State Department to "lose" China), should alone justify the Wisconsin senator's expulsion on grounds of mental incompetence.

Benton's resolution began the long process that eventually led to McCarthy's censure by the Senate in 1954. A friend summed up Benton's crucial role: "You were the only person in the Senate in an ideal position to go after McCarthy. You had little political background in elective office, and thus there weren't too many grounds on which McCarthy could launch an attack on you. You had the money with which to hire lawyers to defend yourself. And you weren't afraid of defeat because you had plenty of activities beckoning to you if you lost your Senate seat." Contemporary analysts attributed Benton's 1952 electoral defeat to his feud with McCarthy, but political scientists subsequently concluded that the Eisenhower landslide had determined the outcome in Connecticut.

Benton attempted a political comeback in 1958 by running unsuccessfully against Thomas J. Dodd for the Democratic senatorial nomination in Connecticut. He turned down President John F. Kennedy's offer to become ambassador to Italy in 1961, but from 1965 until 1968 he assumed ambassadorial rank as the chief U.S. member of the UNESCO executive board. His last public service was as a member of the platform committee of the Democratic National Convention in 1972.

Some five years before his death in Southport, Connecticut, in 1973, the University of Chicago honored Benton by creating a new award, the highest it had ever given to anyone—the William Benton Medal for Distinguished Service. In accepting the honor, Benton referred to himself as "an extremely *shy* fellow . . . a tactless, not too likable fellow, who all his life has worked much harder than necessary trying to make ends meet." With a career spanning business, education, publishing, and politics, a biographer quite aptly referred to "the lives" of William Benton.

• Benton's papers are in the Regenstein Library of the University of Chicago. For additional information on Benton see Sidney Hyman, *The Lives of William Benton* (1969); Richard M. Fried, *Men against McCarthy* (1976); and Howard B. Schaffer, *Chester Bowles—New Dealer in the Cold War* (1993). An obituary is in the *New York Times*, 19 Mar. 1973.

J. GARRY CLIFFORD

BERELSON, Bernard (2 June 1912–25 Sept. 1979), behavioral scientist, was born in Spokane, Washington, the son of Max Berelson, owner of a furniture business, and Bessie Shapiro. Berelson received an A.B. from Whitman College in 1934 and a B.S. (1936), an M.A. (1937), and a Ph.D. (1941), all from the University of Washington and all in library science. He was a professor of library science from 1946 and dean of the Graduate Library School at the University of Chicago until 1951.

Although he was trained as a librarian and wrote two important books on the public's use of libraries, Berelson identified himself primarily as a behavioral scientist. He revived this term from its earlier casual use by John Dewey and Arthur F. Bentley and, per-haps more than any other person, was responsible for its widespread acceptance in the United States. The Center for Advanced Study in the Behavioral Sciences in Stanford, California, which was established largely as a result of Berelson's initiative and effort, is a prime example of how the term has become institutionalized. In 1941 he married Elizabeth Durand, with whom he had two children before they divorced.

From 1941 until 1944 Berelson worked in Washington, D.C., for the U.S. government's Foreign Broadcast Intelligence Service as an analyst of opinion and morale in the German army during World War II. In 1944 he joined the Columbia University Bureau of Applied Social Research, then directed by its founder Paul F. Lazarsfeld. There he helped analyze the data from a pioneering panel study of the 1940 U.S. presidential election and was a coauthor, with Lazarsfeld and Hazel Gaudet, of the bureau's major publication, *The People's Choice* (1944; 2d ed., 1948). Another bureau study during those years—of a New York City newspaper strike—led to his innovative 1949 article, "What 'Missing the Newspaper' Means" (*Communications Research, 1948–49*, ed. Lazarsfeld and Frank N. Stanton [1949]). Other publications during this phase of Berelson's career are *Reader in Public Opinion and Communication* (1950; rev. ed., 1966), edited with Morris Janowitz; and a pioneering methods handbook, *Content Analysis in Communication Research* (1952). In 1948 Berelson married Rosalind Kean; they had three children. After they divorced, he married Ruth Palter in 1953; they had no children.

In 1951 Berelson joined the Ford Foundation as director of a program providing support for research in the behavioral sciences. The program funded a number of "propositional inventories." Berelson viewed these systematic attempts to codify what is known and not known in a particular field as essential for scientific advance. The program also supported a wide range of empirical studies, including groundbreaking research on the behavior of juries at the University of Chicago Law School. The Ford program was terminated in 1957; it is widely believed that in the tenor of those times the Ford trustees had become hesitant to support the often-controversial social sciences. After leaving the foundation, Berelson became a professor of behavioral sciences at the University of Chicago.

During his years at the Ford Foundation, Berelson participated in the analysis of another bureau voting study—this one of the 1948 U.S. presidential election—and was the senior author of the resulting publication, *Voting* (1954), with Lazarsfeld and William N. McPhee. The work contains an inventory of findings from previous voting studies in an important appendix and an influential chapter by Berelson on the meaning of the voting process for democracy. He demonstrated that, contrary to the conventional wisdom about voting, many voters are unqualified to vote, they misperceive political reality, and they often respond to irrelevant information. Berelson argued, however, that these superficially based votes reveal the necessary balance between the flaws of total commitment and total indifference in a democratic society. *Voting* remains one of the classics in advancing the central tenet of behavioral empiricism: the faith that objective, quantitative studies of how people actually behave can discover more or less invariant laws of human behavior as well as guide the formation of enlightened public policy.

In 1960 Berelson returned to the Columbia Bureau as director but found that his colleagues did not share his enthusiasm for transforming the bureau into a policy research institute. In 1961 he joined the staff of the Population Council in New York City, a foundation-supported research and training institution that had been founded by John D. Rockefeller III. This move became the defining decision of Berelson's career: although he was hired as a communications specialist and had had no prior training or special interest in population, he rose rapidly, from program director to vice president to president, and came to exert an enormous influence both on the organization itself and on the sprawling international population field. He served as president from 1968 until 1974 and then as president emeritus and senior fellow until his death in North Tarrytown, New York.

Berelson joined the Population Council at a time when U.S. foundations and the international assistance programs of the industrialized countries were turning their attention to the problems created by rapid population growth in the developing countries. He encouraged this interest among funding organizations and gave both national and international leadership to coordinating their programs. The Population Council flourished both intellectually and financially during his presidency. Its field staff gave guidance and support to the family planning programs of dozens of countries, and its numerous research publications set standards for the entire field. Berelson was the founding editor of the international journal *Studies in Family Planning*, first published by the Population Council in 1963, in which a number of his papers first appeared. His *The Great Debate on Population Policy: An Instructive Entertainment* was published by the Population Council in 1975.

Berelson was highly respected and extremely successful in the population field as an administrator, researcher, and international statesman and gained a reputation among his colleagues for his sheer intelligence. Although he considered himself to be a person of action more than of words, he published widely. His books and articles are all written in an unmistakable style that is direct and free of jargon, as is illustrated in a passage from *The Great Debate on Population Policy*: "The debate is not as it ought to be—too often repetitive, circular, untidy, pedestrian, oblique, evasive. It is too schematic, it assumes clear-cut and clearly formulated alternatives that do not exist. The point is that nothing works very well, and that goes for development as well as for family planning" (p. 25).

Berelson was in the forefront of social scientists who had concerns about the value implications of their work. He struggled particularly with the ethical complexities inherent in attempts to improve the quality of life in developing countries, and his influential contributions to research and action in this area continue to be felt. His careers as a researcher and foundation executive demonstrate that an orientation toward behavioral empiricism is quite compatible both with an interest in improving the world and a conviction that knowledge must be used carefully, with respect for the rights of people whose lives are affected.

• Many of Berelson's papers and letters are in the Rockefeller Archive Center, Pocantico Hills, North Tarrytown, N.Y. Berelson's major publications in the library field are *What Reading Does to People* (1940), with Douglas Waples and Franklyn R. Bradshaw; and *The Library's Public* (1949). His writings on the behavioral sciences include "Behavioral Sciences," *International Encyclopedia of the Social Sciences*, vol. 2 (1968), pp. 41–45; *The Behavioral Sciences Today* (1963); and *Human Behavior: An Inventory of Scientific Findings* (1964), with Gary A. Steiner. Much of the research on wartime opinion and morale in the German army is summarized in Edward Shils and Morris Janowitz, "Cohesion and Disintegration in the Wehrmacht in World War II," in *Reader in Public Opinion and Communication*, ed. Berelson and Janowitz (1950; rev. ed., 1966).

A selection of Berelson's papers on population programs and policies, including *The Great Debate*, was published in *Berelson on Population*, ed. John A. Ross and W. Parker Mauldin (1988), which also contains an extensive bibliography of his writings on population. An account of his contributions to the behavioral sciences is David L. Sills, "Bernard Berelson: Behavioral Scientist," *Journal of the History of the Behavioral Sciences* 17 (1981): 305–11. Appraisals of his contributions to the population field include Mauldin, "Bernard Berelson: A Personal Appreciation," *Studies in Family Planning* 10 (Oct. 1979): 259–62; Sheldon J. Segal, "Bernard Berelson," *Rockefeller Foundation Illustrated* 4 (Apr. 1980): 12; and Richard Lincoln, "Review of *Berelson on Population*," *Population and Development Review* 15, no. 1 (Mar. 1989): 150–53. A fascinating account of how the views on population control of Berelson and John D. Rockefeller III ultimately came into conflict is in John Ensor Harr and Peter J. Johnson, *The Rockefeller Conscience* (1991), chaps. 3 and 26.

DAVID L. SILLS

BERENSON, Bernard (26 June 1865–6 Oct. 1959), art historian, was born Bernhard Valvrojenski in Biturmansk, Lithuania, the son of Alter (later Albert) Valvrojenski and Eudice (later Julia) Mickleshanski (or Michliszanski). Many different spellings of his hometown have been recorded, including Biturmansk, Butrymanz, and Butremancz. After immigrating to Boston in 1875, the family changed their surname to Berenson. Berenson completed his undergraduate degree at Harvard University in 1887 with honorable mention in Semitic languages and English composition.

Intent on becoming a writer and novelist, Berenson set off for Europe in June 1887 for what was to be a one-year trip funded by several people who later sought his advice on art matters, including Isabella Stewart Gardner, Edward Warren, and James Burke. During his extended sojourn Berenson studied Italian Renaissance paintings throughout Europe's museums, galleries, and churches and started accumulating a monumental collection of photographs of Renaissance paintings.

While in Europe, Berenson read Giovanni Morelli's writings on Italian Renaissance art in which Morelli reattributed paintings, using his "scientific" method. According to Morelli, analytic observation of human figures in paintings revealed characteristics that could be used to authenticate works based on artists' styles. After meeting Morelli in May 1890, Berenson divined his new calling to a friend: "We shall give ourselves up to learning, to distinguish between the authentic works of an Italian painter of the 15th or 16th century, and those commonly ascribed to him."

While in England in August 1890, Berenson spent time with art historian and women's advocate Mary Costelloe, who hailed from Pennsylvania and who would eventually become his wife and professional cocontributor. A year later Mary left her husband, Irish barrister Frank Costelloe, and her two daughters to accompany Berenson on his travels.

Berenson's first book, *The Venetian Painters of the Renaissance* (1894), traced the development of Venetian art between the fifteenth and eighteenth centuries. The publication resulted from substantial reworking of one of Mary Costelloe's essays. Her detailed notes from their trips formed the index of Venetian painting, which comprised almost half the book. Generally well received, the publication established Berenson's reputation in Europe and America as an authority on the period.

Berenson defined his connoisseurial principles, stemming from Morelli's theories, in his 1894 essay, "The Rudiments of Connoisseurship (A Fragment)," anthologized in *The Study and Criticism of Italian Art, Second Series* (1902). He wrote that by subjecting a painting to a battery of "tests" used to identify similar traits in specific properties, such as eyes, hands, landscapes, and fabric folds, one could identify a painting's creator by comparing other works by the same painter. Berenson's devaluation of documentation in ascertaining authorship was his most controversial assertion. Using this "scientific" method of morphological analysis, Berenson examined the work of a relatively unknown Venetian painter in *Lorenzo Lotto: An Essay in Constructive Art Criticism* (1894).

Berenson's first foray into art consultation was locating and acquiring several impressionist works and one Renaissance painting for Burke in 1892. In 1893 a group of American collectors in Rome engaged Berenson's expertise on several paintings. By 1894 Berenson's advisory career was gaining momentum as he began a long-term relationship with American financier Theodore M. Davis.

In June 1894 Isabella Stewart Gardner embarked on a yearlong European trip, during which she and Berenson began a collaboration that lasted for thirty years, until her death. For a percentage fee Berenson located Renaissance paintings and negotiated their prices on Gardner's behalf. Gardner's aspirations to assemble the finest art collection in Boston encouraged Berenson to acquire many masterpieces that formed the nucleus of her private museum.

Published in 1896, Berenson's *The Florentine Painters of the Renaissance* surveyed artists from the fourteenth to the sixteenth centuries and introduced his theory of "ideated sensations." The Florentine artists, wrote Berenson, excelled in conveying tactile values and movement in two-dimensional representation, thus affording the viewer a unique visceral experience. Thus, a painting's formal elements should evoke life-enhancing responses from their viewers. Likewise, Berenson concluded that the artists he examined in *The Central Italian Painters of the Renaissance* (1897) specialized in illustration and "space composition," or the ability to compose a viable sense of depth within a two-dimensional construction.

The North Italian Painters of the Renaissance (1907) was the final book in his "four gospels" on Italian painters and was his hardest to complete because this selection of artists' works did not fit his theories of ideated sensations. He focused instead on the dangers of "prettiness" and the lack of life-enhancing qualities. In all of the subsequent editions of the four surveys, Berenson never altered his text. He did, however, spend the rest of his life correcting and supplementing the extensive lists of attributions at the end of each book.

After Costelloe's husband died in 1899, she and Berenson married in 1900 and settled into "Villa I Tatti," a house built in the sixteenth century just outside Florence. The Berensons, who had no children together, kept the villa for the rest of their lives, regularly entertaining American expatriates and scholars, such as Edith Wharton and Henry James, as well as European artists and writers, including Oscar Wilde and Berenson's brother-in-law Bertrand Russell. Berenson bequeathed the three-story house and his vast collection of photographs and books to Harvard University, which runs a fellowship and study program at this center for Italian Renaissance studies.

Berenson's greatest art historical contribution was published in 1903: *The Drawings of the Florentine Painters: Classified, Criticised, and Studied as Documents in the History and Appreciation of Tuscan Art with a Copious Catalogue Raisonné*. The two-volume book was widely praised for its extensive text and 180 plates of many previously unpublished drawings that shed new light on the development of these Renaissance painters. It also confirmed Berenson's reputation as an extremely thorough and knowledgeable connoisseur, for he had visited eighty museums and seventy private collections in Europe to gather his material.

Also in 1903, the Berensons traveled to the United States, where they met several important collectors, including Henry Walters in Baltimore and Peter Widener and John Graver Johnson in Philadelphia, all of whom enlisted Berenson's advisory services to enhance their collections. Berenson later wrote catalogs of Widener's and Johnson's collections (published in 1913 and 1916, respectively).

The nature of the art trade and Berenson's close association with it drew suspicion in some art historical circles. Since Berenson was paid by commissions, the more paintings he attributed to masters, the more he profited. His standard commission was 10 percent, but he sometimes took as much as one-third to one-half of the net. Berenson once sold a Pinturicchio Madonna from his own collection to Gardner at a large profit. In 1905 the Metropolitan Museum of Art bought an El Greco on Berenson's advice, unaware until afterward that he received £1,700 for the sale. He was occasionally involved in smuggling out of Italy works headed for America.

Although Berenson worked with numerous dealers throughout his lifetime, none was more notorious than Joseph Duveen. After meeting Berenson in 1906, the dealer sought the expert's imprimatur for myriad sales over the next thirty years. A formal arrangement cloaked in secrecy was initiated in 1912, with Berenson receiving 25 percent of net profits. With Berenson's attributions, often sent by wire using code names, Duveen sold many masterpieces to American collectors, including John Pierpont Morgan and Andrew Mellon. Duveen's questionable transactions (the firm had paid the U.S. Customs Service $1.8 million to settle a customs claim in 1911), bullish behavior, incessant inquiries, and disagreement over Berenson's attributions eventually led Berenson to terminate the partnership in 1937.

Berenson's later scholarly writings, none of which had as much impact as his four "gospels," included *Venetian Painting in America* (1916), *The Study and Criticism of Italian Art, Third Series* (1916), *Essays in the Study of Sienese Painting* (1918), and *Studies in Medieval Painting* (1930), as well as books on artists Stefano di Giovanni Sassetta (1909), Alberto Sani (1950), Caravaggio (1953), and Piero della Francesca (1954). His *Aesthetics and History in the Visual Arts* (1948) expanded on his theories of ideated sensations and "life-enhancing" qualities in art. He was one of six contributing writers to the inaugural issue (Jan. 1913) of *Art in America*, a magazine subsidized by Duveen to educate American collectors.

Berenson remained in Europe during both world wars. At the recommendation of his friend Edith Wharton, Berenson was employed as a translator and negotiator to the American Army Intelligence Section during World War I. Because of his Jewish heritage and anti-Fascist beliefs, Berenson was hidden by friends just north of I Tatti during World War II. His diary entries written during his exile were published in 1952 as *Rumour and Reflection, 1941–1944*.

Until his death Berenson continued consulting, primarily for dealer George Wildenstein, and writing. He regularly published articles in the Italian newspaper *Corriere della Sera*, and he wrote several books on art theory that were not well received critically, in part because he lambasted modern art trends. He died in Florence, Italy.

Among Berenson's greatest contributions to the field of art were his Italian Renaissance scholarship and his impact on American public and private collections (he once boasted that most Italian paintings had

come to America with "my visa on their passport"). He mentored many American art historians, including John Walker and Sydney J. Freedberg, who studied at I Tatti and worked at the National Gallery in Washington, D.C., as director and chief curator, respectively. Despite his vehement disdain for modern art, Berenson's formalist rather than contextual approach to art interpretation anticipated modern reductionist aesthetics propounded by formalist critics such as Clive Bell, Roger Fry, and Clement Greenberg.

• Much of Berenson's correspondence remains at the Berenson Archive, Harvard University Center for Italian Renaissance Studies, Villa I Tatti, Florence. Berenson's early books on the four regions of Italian Renaissance art were combined into one volume in 1930 titled *Italian Painters of the Renaissance*. The three-part series *The Study and Criticism of Italian Art* presents several of his early articles. *Bibliografia di Bernard Berenson*, comp. William Mostyn-Owen (1955), lists his writings complete to that date (see Samuels for additional materials). The most thorough Berenson biography is Ernest Samuels, *Bernard Berenson: The Making of a Connoisseur* (1979) and *Bernard Berenson: The Making of a Legend* (1987). Other biographic sources include Berenson's autobiography, *Sketch for a Self-Portrait* (1949), and *Forty Years with Berenson* (1966), written by his companion Elisabetta "Nicky" Mariano. See *Mary Berenson: A Self-Portrait from Her Letters and Diaries*, ed. Barbara Strachey and Jayne Samuels (1983), for Berenson's wife's contributions to his career; Colin Simpson, *Artful Partners: Bernard Berenson and Joseph Duveen* (1986), on the relationship between the art expert and the dealer; and Mary Ann Calo, *Bernard Berenson and the Twentieth Century* (1994), on Berenson's interest and influence on modern art and aesthetics. An obituary is in the *New York Times*, 8 Oct. 1959.

N. ELIZABETH SCHLATTER

BERENSON, Senda (19 Mar. 1868–16 Feb. 1954), sportswoman and physical educator, was born Senda Valvrojenski in Biturmansk, Lithuania, the daughter of Albert Valvrojenski, a worker in the timber industry, and Julia Mieliszanski. Her father emigrated to the United States in 1874, settling in Boston's West End. He changed his name to Albert Berenson and became a peddler, earning a meager wage in the Boston area. A year later Senda arrived in Boston with her mother and older brother, Bernard, who became a renowned Italian Renaissance art critic. Education was prized by the Jewish family.

Berenson attended the Boston Girls' Latin School, but because she was frail, she never completed a full year. Music and art were among her favorite subjects. She studied piano at the Boston Conservatory of Music, but she was unable to practice regularly because of a weak back. In 1890 Berenson was persuaded to improve her strength by enrolling at the Boston Normal School of Gymnastics, founded the previous year by philanthropist Mary Hemenway. She came under the influence of school director Amy Morris Homans and the program of Swedish gymnastics, a system of lightweight and scientific exercises developed by the Swedish literatus Per Henrik Ling. Though initially detesting the school, her health improved, and she became a strong advocate of the value of physical activity. During her second year Berenson was recommended for a position in physical training at Smith College in Northampton, Massachusetts. She recalled, "My indifference had changed to deep conviction, and I wanted to work only in physical education so that I might help others as I had been helped."

In 1892 Berenson began a twenty-year teaching career at Smith College, where she emphasized Swedish gymnastics and participation in sports. She helped organize a gymnastics and field association in 1893, assisted in setting up a golf course, and began teaching fencing in 1895. Berenson attended the Royal Central Institute of Gymnastics in Stockholm in 1897. On her return, she introduced folk dance into the physical education program and invited England's Lady Constance Applebee to inaugurate field hockey at Smith in 1901. In 1908 she introduced a field day at Smith that included contests in archery, basketball, clock golf, cricket, croquet, field hockey, tennis, and volleyball.

The introduction of basketball as a team sport for women was Berenson's greatest contribution to athletics. Shortly after James Naismith invented basketball in 1891 at the Young Men's Christian Association Training School at Springfield, Massachusetts, Berenson read about the game in a YMCA publication and introduced the game to Smith women in the fall of 1892. Soon, according to Berenson, it was "by far the most popular game that women play." To provide for a womanly game, Berenson modified the rules to the supposed needs of women. To avoid physical roughness and playing with abandon, she disallowed grabbing the ball from opponents. To increase the pace of the game she mandated that the ball could be retained no longer than three seconds, and it could be dribbled no more than three times. To prevent overtaxing the body and domination of play by one individual, she created "line basketball," dividing the court into three zones and preventing players from crossing the lines. These rules were incorporated into the official rules in 1899, when Berenson was chosen editor of Spalding's Athletic Library *Basket Ball for Women*. Berenson became the first American woman to edit a sport publication. She continued editing the Spalding rules for the next sixteen years. These rules, with only slight changes, remained in force until the 1960s and 1970s, when women's basketball reverted to rules similar to those followed by men.

Leaders of college women's sport emphasized the contrast between men's and women's athletics, believing the commercialized and professionalized men's model contributed little to education or the socialization process. Basketball, wrote Berenson in 1894, "has helped to develop the athletic spirit in woman. . . . It is a splendid game to cultivate physical courage." She believed that it "combined both the physical development of gymnastics and the abandon and delight of true play." Berenson led the Basketball Committee for Women from 1905 to 1917. The committee was the forerunner of the National Association for Girls and Women in Sport, an organization that for much of the twentieth century opposed highly competitive intercollegiate athletics for women. Berenson and other women leaders favored intramural athletics for the many, not intercollegiate athletics for the few.

Berenson resigned from Smith College in 1911, when she married Herbert Vaughn Abbott, an English professor at Smith. They had no children. Following her marriage, she was director of physical education at the Mary Burnham School in Northampton for a decade. She traveled widely, especially in Europe, where she studied art in France, Germany, Greece, and Italy. She lived in Northampton until 1934, five years after her husband died, when she moved to California. Berenson lived with her sister in Santa Barbara until her death there.

Berenson was an important leader of women's sport for a quarter-century, being especially important in transforming James Naismith's basketball into a woman's sport. For these contributions, Berenson was elected in 1985 as the first woman member of the Basketball Hall of Fame in Springfield, Massachusetts, and was called the "Mother of Women's Basketball."

• Berenson's papers are in the Smith College Archives. Berenson's writings include "Basket Ball for Women," *Physical Education* 3 (Sept. 1894): 106–9; *Line Basket Ball or Basket Ball for Women* (1899); *Basket Ball for Women* (1901); and *Official Basketball and Official Rating Guide for Women and Girls* (1905). Betty Spears, "Senda Berenson Abbott: New Woman, New Sport," in *A Century of Women's Basketball*, ed. Joan S. Hult and Marianna Trekell (1991), is an important source. On Berenson's career, see Agnes C. Stillman, "Senda Berenson Abbott: Her Life and Contributions to Smith College and to the Physical Education Profession" (M.S. thesis, Smith College, 1971), a major, but uncritical, source; Edith N. Hill, "Senda Berenson," *Research Quarterly* 12, supp. (Oct. 1941): 658–65, for Berenson's description of early basketball; Dorothy Ainsworth, "The Development of Athletics at Smith College," *Smith Alumnae Quarterly* 22 (Nov. 1930): 22–26, and L. Clark Seelye, *The Early Years of Smith College, 1871–1910* (1923), for a description of Smith College facilities and program; and Sylvia Sprigge, *Berenson, a Biography* (1960), and Nicky Mariano, *The Berenson Archive* (1965), for family background. An obituary is in the *New York Times*, 17 Feb. 1954.

RONALD A. SMITH

BERG, Gertrude (3 Oct. 1899–14 Sept. 1966), actress, writer, and producer of radio and television programs, was born Gertrude Edelstein in the Harlem district of New York City, the daughter of Jacob Edelstein, a Catskills resort hotel owner, and Diana Netta Goldstein, a bookkeeper and hotel kitchen manager. She was educated in public schools and showed interest in acting as a child, performing comic skits at her father's hotel. As a teenager, she took several extension courses in playwriting at Columbia University. In 1918 she married Lewis Berg, a mechanical engineer, whose work took the couple to a sugar refinery in Reserve, Louisiana. In 1921 they returned to New York, where they would live for the rest of their lives. The couple had two children.

Berg continued to work at her writing after marrying and sent several unsolicited manuscripts to radio broadcasters. In 1929 her script for *Effie and Laura*, a soap opera, was accepted for production by the National Broadcasting Company (NBC), but the program was canceled after only a single episode. She persisted, however, and made a breakthrough in 1929 with the NBC debut of *The Rise of the Goldbergs* (later shortened to *The Goldbergs*). As star, chief writer, and de facto producer, Berg received $75 per week to cover not only her salary but all production costs for the series, which was presented in fifteen-minute episodes airing Monday through Friday. It became one of the most popular shows of the radio era. By 1931 her fee had risen to $2,000 per week. A shrewd businesswoman, she maintained control of the program at a time when most radio series were the properties of advertising agencies. This enabled her to negotiate advantageous contracts; at various times *The Goldbergs* aired on the NBC, CBS, and Mutual radio networks.

On radio Berg created the character Molly Goldberg, the folk-wise, self-sacrificing matriarch of an immigrant Jewish family living in a modest Bronx apartment house. She would make the role her career-long dramatic persona, adapting it for stage, screen, and television over the course of three decades. Perhaps no other single character contributed more to making the Jewish mother an institution of American popular culture. While some critics saw Molly Goldberg as an overly sentimental amalgam of clichés of obsessive mothering, cultural assimilationism, and chicken soup philosophy, the national audience seemed to accept the character as quintessential rather than stereotypical.

Berg was extraordinarily prolific. During twenty years of radio production, she wrote and performed in thousands of episodes of *The Goldbergs*. As a producer she demonstrated an uncommon eye for talent, casting young future film stars, including John Garfield, Joseph Cotten, Anne Bancroft, and Van Heflin, to play some of the several hundred characters she introduced to the radio serial. In 1935 she produced a second radio program, *The House of Glass*, based on memories of her father's hotel, but it was only moderately successful. She also contributed scripts to *Kate Hopkins*, a serial about a nurse.

A pioneer in the area of product tie-ins, Berg capitalized on the fame of her radio character by writing Molly Goldberg short stories, stageplays, feature films, and even a cookbook. In his review of her 1948 Broadway play, *Me and Molly*, Brooks Atkinson commented, "Mrs. Berg . . . believes in the people she writes about and is not ashamed of their simplicity. . . . The result is a leisurely, intimate, cheerful portrait of interesting people and the humor is kind-hearted."

In 1949 *The Goldbergs* debuted on television as a half-hour situation comedy, broadcast live each week from New York. The program played for six seasons, airing variously on CBS, NBC, and Dumont. Berg was perhaps the only woman during this period to achieve authorship of a prime-time network television program. In 1951 the TV cast appeared in a Paramount feature film, *Molly*, which Berg co-wrote with N. Richard Nash.

Berg took a notable stand against the industrywide blacklisting of television actors that was practiced in the early 1950s. When her longtime co-star Philip Loeb, who played Molly's husband Jake, was accused of communist affiliations, Berg refused the demand of her sponsor, General Foods, to fire him, and *The Goldbergs* was promptly canceled by CBS. Loeb, however, did not want to see his colleagues lose their jobs and voluntarily quit the cast, thus saving the show. He later committed suicide.

The TV version of *The Goldbergs*, however, never achieved the popularity of the radio program. In 1955 Berg made an attempt to rework the program to contemporary concerns, renaming it *Molly* and moving the family from its Bronx apartment to a spacious house in the suburbs; nevertheless, the show was canceled in 1956. Berg then turned her attention to the stage, taking roles in such comedies as *The Solid Gold Cadillac* (1956) and *The Matchmaker* (1957). Her most memorable achievement on Broadway was her performance in *A Majority of One* (1959), co-starring with Sir Cedric Hardwicke. Her character was a familiar one, a Jewish mother from Brooklyn. However, the intensity of the play's subject matter, which includes the lingering animosities of World War II, race prejudice, and the loneliness of widowhood, stretched Berg's talents beyond the boundaries of the light comedy for which she had always been known. Her performance surprised many and won her a Tony Award as best actress of 1959.

Berg was the author of three books: a novel, *The Rise of the Goldbergs* (1931); a cookbook, *The Molly Goldberg Cookbook* (1955); and an autobiography, *Molly and Me* (1961). She received numerous awards for the positive messages of religious and racial tolerance that can be found in her work, including a Citation of Distinguished Merit from the National Conference of Christians and Jews (1950) and the Interfaith Award from the Cinema Lodge of B'nai Brith (1949). She was active in many charitable activities, winning citations from the Federation of Jewish Philanthropies, the Community Chest, the United Cerebral Palsy Association, the American Cancer Society, and Hadassah. She died of natural causes in New York City.

• Berg's papers, including many of her radio and television scripts, are at the George Arents Research Library, Syracuse University. Details of her life and work appear in her autobiography, *Molly and Me* (1961), in *Current Biography* (1941, 1960), and in a feature article in the *New York Times*, 17 Oct. 1959. David Inman, *The TV Encyclopedia* (1991), contains a complete list of Berg's television acting credits, including several dramatic roles and variety show guest appearances. An obituary is in *Current Biography*, Nov. 1961.

DAVID MARC

BERG, Joseph Frederic (3 June 1812–20 July 1871), German and Dutch Reformed clergyman, was born on Antigua in the British West Indies, the son of Christian Frederic Berg and Hannah Robinson Tempest, Moravian missionaries. Berg was the first white child born on the island. At the age of four, he was sent to England to be educated at a Moravian school in Falneck; a decade later he went to the Moravian academy in Nazareth, Pennsylvania. There he showed himself to be unusually energetic and a precocious learner, teaching chemistry at age seventeen and receiving his license to preach two years later.

In 1835 Berg received a call from the German Reformed Church in Harrisburg, but he remained there only briefly. That same year he married Eleonora Pomp; they had at least one child, a daughter. Subsequently he taught languages at Marshall College in Mercersburg, where he declined to accept the offer of a professorship. In 1837 he accepted a call from the Race Street German Reformed Church in Philadelphia.

Despite a successful pastorate, Berg became increasingly troubled by what he believed were the dangerous errors and "romanticizing tendencies" then current in his denomination. Led by historian Philip Schaff and his colleague John Williamson Nevin, the "Mercersburg Movement" within the German Reformed church encouraged an understanding of Christianity as a single, organically connected development in which each historical era, despite its errors and excesses, might be considered a legitimate bearer of the true faith. This was a viewpoint that, some believed, effectively legitimized the medieval papacy and even gave Roman Catholicism apparent parity with modern reformed Protestantism. With what today would be called ecumenical vision, Schaff and Nevin looked forward to a church in which Protestant and Catholic would one day be reconciled and united. As the editor of the militantly anti-Roman *Protestant Banner*, however, Berg passionately opposed these latitudinarian views. To him, all of Christian history from St. Paul to Martin Luther was simply "the dark ages," a term he used freely; the Protestant Reformation represented the long-awaited restoration of primitive Christianity. In broadening the prevailing view of the church, Berg believed, Schaff and Nevin were up to nothing less than the devil's work.

With Jacob Helffenstein of Germantown, Pennsylvania, Berg was a major protagonist in the celebrated but unsuccessful heresy trial of Nevin and Schaff in 1845. Berg's accusations against the two focused on their "heretical" teachings on the "spiritual real presence" of Christ in the eucharist—a teaching that for Berg, an avowed Zwinglian, was far too close to the Roman Catholic doctrine of transubstantiation. Yet Berg's dispute with the Mercersburg Movement was rooted in more than sacramental theology: he opposed every imagined hint of rapprochement with Rome, including both doctrinal matters and more practical ones such as the proper attire for clergy.

Despite his antagonists' acquittal by the York Synod in 1845, Berg continued to attack the leading Mercersburg theologians and their followers in the pulpit and the press. Biblical interpretation, the nature and import of creeds and confessions, the historical development of the church—these were the substance of ongoing debate that engendered interest well beyond the boundaries of the German Reformed church. The *Protestant Quarterly Review*, which Berg edited from 1844 to 1854, and the *Evangelical Quarterly* (1851–1861) served as outlets for his passionate opinions. During this period, he also acquired an M.D. from Jefferson Medical College.

In 1852, Berg—no doubt sensing the tide of international opinion was turning against him—finally abandoned the German Reformed church for its more conservative Dutch counterpart, taking a portion of the Race Street congregation over to his new pastorate at the nearby Second Dutch Reformed Church. His colleague Helffenstein followed suit, defecting to the Old-School Presbyterians. For a decade after 1861, Berg served as a professor of didactic and polemic theology at the Dutch Reformed Theological Seminary in New Brunswick, New Jersey; he also taught for five years as a professor at Rutgers. In addition to his numerous books, pamphlets, and tracts, Berg wrote stories for children. Although today he is remembered chiefly for his stridently anti-Catholic writings, he seems not to have been actively involved in the nativist movement per se; nevertheless Nevin characterized his stance as "theological nativism." Berg died in New Brunswick.

• Berg published a number of books that elaborated on his vehemently anti-Catholic sentiments. These include *Lectures on Romanism* (1840); *Papal Rome* (1841); *The Great Apostasy* (1842); *The Inquisition: Church and State; or, Rome's Influence upon the Civil and Religious Institutions of Our Country* (1851); and *Papal Usurpation* (1855).

ELIZABETH C. NORDBECK

BERGEN, Edgar (16 Feb. 1903–30 Sept. 1978), actor and ventriloquist, was born Edgar John Berggren in Chicago, Illinois, the son of John Berggren and Nell Swanson, stolid Swedish immigrants who lived in various places in Illinois and for a time owned a dairy farm in Michigan. From an early age Edgar was attracted to show business, especially to local fairs, circuses, and vaudeville. At age eleven he sent off a quarter for "The Wizard's Manual," which taught, among other things, "Secrets of Magic, Black Art, Mind Reading, Ventriloquism, and Hypnotism." Edgar found all of these arts attractive and shortly was performing magic tricks and ventriloquism for his family and neighborhood children.

John Berggren died when Edgar was sixteen, so he and his older brother Clarence took jobs to help their mother. Clarence eventually became an accountant, but Edgar worked in a silent movie house, where he stoked the furnace, operated the player piano, and even ran the projector on occasion. Edgar's mother hoped he would go to college and become a doctor, and he entered Northwestern University with that end in mind. Already in high school Edgar had been working as a "trickster and voice illusionist," and apparently he continued to find local engagements while in college. He switched his college major to speech but got so busy in show business that he quit before graduation, much to his mother's disappointment.

By the time he was in his early twenties, Edgar Berggren, his name now simplified to Bergen, was on the vaudeville circuit, trying various acts. Throughout the 1920s he worked steadily in vaudeville but without rising to star status. In time his most popular act became a ventriloquist routine using a dummy of a boy named Charlie McCarthy. The character and the dummy were based on a breezy, insolent, earthy, red-headed Irish kid who had sold newspapers on the street in Decatur, Illinois. Bergen worked up a series of routines with Charlie McCarthy, and after years of playing the sawdust trail and the second circuit of vaudeville, Bergen eventually got his act to the Palace in New York City, where the top acts of the day were featured.

But vaudeville was dying a slow death in the depths of the depression, and Bergen—and Charlie McCarthy—had to look for other work. For a while the pickings were slim. There were some occasional nightclub offerings, which required Bergen as well as the raffish, wisecracking newsboy to dress up in a top hat and monocle, a garb seemingly at odds with either's character. But Bergen continually improved his act. Ventriloquist and dummy appeared at the elegant Rainbow Room at Rockefeller Center. And at a Manhattan society party playwright Noël Coward caught the act, thought it good, and asked Bergen who wrote his material. "I write it myself," answered Bergen.

Bergen soon found his way into radio as did a number of other former vaudevillians, including Jack Benny, Ed Wynn, Eddie Cantor, George Burns, and Fred Allen. He and Charlie McCarthy made a guest appearance on the "Rudy Vallee Show"—their radio debut—on 17 December 1936. The routine was so popular that they were asked to return. What was originally scheduled to be a single performance became more or less regular for three months. So popular did the act become that Bergen and McCarthy got their own show in 1937 on the NBC network, and it soon became one of the great hits of radio.

By 1938 the program was the highest-rated radio program, and Bergen was receiving $200,000 a year, quite a princely sum. That year the program was broadcast on Sunday evenings, and the other networks could find nothing to go up against it. The high-toned "Mercury Theatre of the Air" of Orson Welles was on at that hour but was unable to find a sponsor. On Sunday, 30 October 1938, when Welles broadcast his famous "War of the Worlds" adaptation, radio executives were surprised to learn that many people were frightened by the program, not because of the techniques used but because everybody was supposed to be listening to "Charlie McCarthy."

The success of the program can be traced to the inexplicable appeal of a ventriloquist on radio, the one place where presumably the art could not be demonstrated at all. There were some who insisted that Bergen was not one of the best ventriloquists in the country in any case. But he had created the most successful ventriloquism act of all time on the basis of superb comedy characterization. Charlie McCarthy with his jaunty, impudent, devil-may-care manner seemed to bring out something buried deep inside everyone's character (especially that of Bergen himself, whose dignified and taciturn manner rarely showed emotion). The *New York Times* wrote in 1939, "psychologists say that Charlie differs from other dummies because he has definite spiritual qualities. His throaty almost lecherous chuckle is a haunting thing; his whole attitude of *Weltschmerz* is astonishingly real. He says things that a human actor would never say in public and gets away with them."

In the late 1930s and early 1940s many stars wanted to appear on the Bergen and McCarthy program. The most frequent and successful visitor was W. C. Fields, whose aggressive manner seemed a perfect foil for Charlie. Bergen and McCarthy also got into Fields's movies, most prominently in *You Can't Cheat an Honest Man* (1939). Their popularity was such that they also appeared in a number of other movies, usually just brief appearances, but more extensively in a few feature films such as *Charlie McCarthy, Detective* (1939).

Bergen moved into a large Beverly Hills mansion with his bewildered mother who could never quite figure out how her son had become wealthy using a dummy. In his late thirties Bergen was a tall, shy, balding, seemingly unemotional man who had never married. He seemed out of sync with the high life of the Hollywood community. Gossips suggested that it was really Charlie McCarthy who controlled Edgar Bergen, and, furthermore, it was Charlie McCarthy, not Bergen, who was endlessly chasing after pretty girls. However, at thirty-nine Bergen met Frances Westerman, a beautiful nineteen year old from Alabama, and the two married the following year. The couple had two children. Frances Bergen had a brief career as a film and television actress, and daughter Candice Bergen became a fashion model and photographer and then a film and television star.

The "Edgar Bergen and Charlie McCarthy" program continued in popularity on radio throughout the 1940s. Bergen still wrote much of his own material but added a professional staff of comedy writers. To add variety Bergen introduced two other dummies, Mortimer Snerd, a purported halfwit, and Effie Klinker, an old maid who was always trying to find a man. But Charlie continued to get top billing. At the height of the show's popularity there were Charlie McCarthy coloring books, mugs, comic strips, shirts, and, of course, smaller versions of the dummy himself that came to be owned by hundreds of thousands of children.

The program did not make a successful transition to television in the 1950s, but for a while Bergen and McCarthy hosted a comic game show called "Do You

Trust Your Wife?" Occasionally Bergen would try guest appearances on television shows or in nightclubs without Charlie but with only small success. But he continued to make occasional appearances with Charlie at county fairs, benefits, and Republican conventions. Bergen also worked as a character actor in the movies, usually playing standoffish or diffident types, as in *I Remember Mama* (1948).

Charlie McCarthy was occasionally brought out of his plush traveling case, and Bergen never completely retired. Bergen died in Las Vegas, Nevada, where he had gone to revive the old act with Charlie at Caesar's Palace. He had been suffering from a heart condition but accepted a three-week engagement. After two nights of thunderous applause with Bergen using "ad-lib" material that he had polished for over half a century, the famed ventriloquist died in his sleep. Charlie McCarthy (or one of the numerous copies of the dummy owned by Bergen) took up residence at the Smithsonian Institution in Washington, where succeeding generations can view the monocled wooden figure that once was one of America's best-known and most vivid personalities.

• A fair amount of biographical material on Bergen may be found in *Knock Wood*, an autobiography written in 1984 by his daughter Candice Bergen, who also discusses her own relationship with her father. But because she was born after his days of greatest fame, the material on his early life is sketchy. Nonetheless, this book, which is not a routine film star's book, contains an intelligent, perceptive, loving, not-always-flattering portrait of Bergen. For a good discussion of the Bergen-McCarthy act, see Jim Harmon, *The Great Radio Comedians* (1970). For a full list of the regulars on the old "Edgar Bergen and Charlie McCarthy Show," including writers, announcers, producers, and guest stars, see Frank Buxton and Bill Owen, *Radio's Golden Age* (1966). An interesting account of the show is in John Dunning, *Tune in Yesterday: The Ultimate Encyclopedia of Old-Time Radio, 1925–1976* (1976). An obituary is in the *New York Times*, 1 Oct. 1978.

GEORGE H. DOUGLAS

BERGER, Meyer (1 Sept. 1898–8 Feb. 1959), journalist, was born in New York City's Lower East Side, the son of Ignace Berger, a tailor, and Sarah Waldman, the proprietor of a candy shop. His parents, Jewish immigrants from Eastern Europe, supported their eleven children with difficulty, and Berger began his association with newspapers at the age of eight as a newsboy. The family moved to the Williamsburg section of Brooklyn a few years later, and Berger attended the Eastern District High School for two terms before leaving in 1911 to become a messenger boy for the *New York World*. He carried copy between the paper's offices in downtown Brooklyn and its main building on Manhattan's Park Row, gaining an intimate knowledge of New York City along with his $1.50 weekly salary. The job also gave him the chance to steep himself in the atmosphere of journalism. "Here I absorbed all the legends of the craft, ancient and contemporary," he wrote in *The Eight Million* (1942). "I contracted newsprint fever in this way, by a kind of osmosis. Here I learned, I think, a sounder journalism than

is taught in graver halls of learning" (Introduction, p. ix). He acquired the lifelong nickname of Mike at the *World*, where he became a night telephone operator and, by the time the United States entered World War I in 1917, the paper's head office boy.

That year, despite his extreme near-sightedness, Berger enlisted in the army, where he attained the rank of sergeant with the 106th Infantry of the American Expeditionary Force's 27th Division. He saw action in France and won the Silver Star for carrying four wounded men back to the American line through No-Man's Land with a bullet in his own shoulder. He also received the Purple Heart and the Conspicuous Service Cross.

After his discharge in 1919, Berger returned to New York and to the Brooklyn office of the *World*, where he worked as a police reporter. He left for a job as district reporter for the Standard News Service in Brooklyn in 1922 and became the syndicate's chief rewrite man. In 1926 he married Mae Gamsu, a schoolteacher; they had no children. Berger was made top rewriter with the newly established *New York Times* Brooklyn-Queens news section in 1928 and went on to become a general reporter for the *Times*. Except for an unhappy one-year interlude as a staff writer for the *New Yorker* in 1937–38, he worked for the *Times* for the rest of his life.

Berger first became known for his reports of the New York underworld and was nominated for the 1932 Pulitzer Prize for his series on the 1931 trial of Al Capone. Even more popular were his humorous and poignant vignettes of everyday life in the city. In response to his growing popularity, the *Times* assigned him to write a daily column called "About New York," which began on 9 July 1939. These affectionate, witty, and sometimes lyrical human-interest stories appeared until 1940, when they were discontinued due to a paper shortage but were resumed 19 April 1953, appearing on Mondays, Wednesdays, and Fridays until Berger's death. Collections of his columns were published as *The Eight Million: Journal of a New York Correspondent* and *Meyer Berger's New York* (1960).

Berger interrupted his coverage of New York for only a few months in the summer of 1942, when he was stationed in London, and in 1945, when he made a brief tour of the fighting in North Africa and Europe, but in both places he was more a reporter of local color than a typical war correspondent. His moving account of the first war dead to return to New York, in 1947, was hailed as a masterpiece of reporting. He was awarded the Pulitzer Prize in 1950 for his report of Howard Unruh, a 28-year-old veteran who went berserk and shot thirteen people in Camden, New Jersey, in 1949. After spending six hours tracing the course of the event and interviewing fifty witnesses in the neighborhood, Berger typed out a 4,000-word article in two and a half hours. The piece appeared without a word changed by the rewrite desk. Only much later was it learned that Berger had given the $1,000 award money to Unruh's mother.

In addition to his writing for the *Times*, Berger free-lanced extensively for national magazines such as *Harper's Bazaar*, the *Saturday Evening Post*, and *Reader's Digest*. In 1943 he collaborated with Rev. James Keller on *Men of Maryknoll*, a history of the Catholic missionary society. He also helped the Maryknoll priests with their monthly magazine and prepared a pamphlet, *Notes on Missionary Writing*, for their use. He was selected by the *Times* to write the official centennial history of the paper, *The Story of the New York Times, 1851–1951* (1951). This was a collection of anecdotes about the people who created and produced the paper rather than a formal history. Although critically acclaimed, Berger was not happy with the job, complaining that editorial restraints had prevented him from being wholly objective. Typically, his own name appears only in an appended list of *Times* Pulitzer Prize winners. Other books published by Berger included *Growth of an Ideal, 1850–1950: The Story of the Manhattan Savings Bank* (1954), a history of the New York Public Library; *New York: City on Many Waters* (1955); and *The Library* (1956).

Described by John Lardner as a "dark, frail, bespectacled, knife-faced fellow, gentle and kind," Berger was one of the best-loved and most respected figures in his profession. In 1961 was honored by the Columbia University Graduate School of Journalism with the establishment of the Mike Berger Awards. Shortly after he died in New York City, the *Times* ran a letter from a reader stating, "With Meyer Berger, New York has lost her most devoted, loving and revealing biographer. He was an eye-opener and a heart-opener for the big city."

• Berger's personal papers and notebooks are in the Columbia University Graduate School of Journalism, New York City. His work is discussed in Stanley Walker, *City Editor* (1934), Gay Talese, *The Kingdom and the Power* (1969), Turner Catledge, *My Life and the Times* (1971), and A. J. Liebling, *Liebling Abroad* (1981). See also *Harper's Bazaar*, Aug. 1943, p. 62; *Time*, 8 May 1950, pp. 70–71; *Newsweek*, 16 Feb. 1959, p. 64; John Lardner, "Mike," *Newsweek*, 23 Feb. 1959, p. 96; and John C. Devlin, "The Most Unforgettable Character I've met," *Reader's Digest*, Oct. 1959, pp. 77–81. Obituaries are in the *New York Times* and the *New York Herald Tribune*, both 9 Feb. 1959.

DENNIS WEPMAN

BERGER, Victor Louis (28 Feb. 1860–7 Aug. 1929), a founder and leader of the Socialist Party of America and a U.S. congressman, was born in the Nieder-Rehbach region of the Austro-Hungarian Empire (now Romania) to Ignatz Berger and his wife, Julia (maiden name unknown), innkeepers. Berger attended the Universities of Vienna and Budapest for two years. His family suffered economic reversals and in 1878 emigrated to Bridgeport, Connecticut. In 1881 Berger settled in Milwaukee, where he taught school. In the heavily Germanic city he emerged as a leader, initially through the *Turnverein,* an athletic club that sponsored educational and recreational activities. Drawn to politics, he joined the Socialist Labor party in 1889,

and he flirted with the Populist movement in the 1890s. Increasingly committed to Marxist ideology, he became a skillful political negotiator and organizer who, along with Eugene V. Debs, founded the Social Democracy of America in 1897 and the next year, the Social Democratic party. In 1901 Berger and Debs, along with Morris Hillquit and others who split from the Socialist Labor party, organized the Socialist Party of America, the Marxist political organization that achieved the greatest following in American history. Berger built up the Milwaukee branch of the party, its most electorally successful component, and was known as its boss.

Berger developed a local publishing empire. He was the editor and publisher of the German-language *Wisconsin Vorwaerts (Forward)* from 1892 to 1898, the *Social-Democratic Herald* from 1901 to 1913, and the Milwaukee *Leader* from 1911 to 1929, as well as a number of smaller newspapers. His newspapers helped strengthen the local socialist movement, which developed an unusually strong partnership with organized labor through the Milwaukee Federated Trades Council. The German-dominated unions became the basic constituency on which the socialists' electoral successes were built. Berger was elected to the city council in 1910 after a few unsuccessful races. That year the socialists enjoyed an electoral sweep of the city and county, winning the mayor's office and thereafter passing various social welfare and employee protection measures. That November, Berger was elected to the U.S. House of Representatives from the Fifth Congressional District of Wisconsin, encompassing Milwaukee and its environs, and became the first socialist to serve in Congress.

He married Meta Schlichting in 1897, and they had two daughters. His wife was the first socialist woman elected to public office in the United States, serving from 1909 to 1939 on the Milwaukee school board.

Berger was one of the shaping forces of the Socialist party nationally in its most successful years and was said to have introduced Debs to socialism. He was a fixture on the party's executive committee from 1901, served on both standing and ad hoc committees, and represented the party abroad at meetings of the Second International. Berger worked successfully to move American socialists away from organizing separatist, collectivist colonies toward working within society. While not a creative theoretician, he became a revisionist and reformist socialist who tried to amend Marxist theory to American conditions. He believed in collective ownership of the means of production and distribution, and he argued that the change from capitalism to socialism could be achieved successfully through electoral means. Through propaganda, education, and political reforms, and aided by existing trends toward economic concentration, he predicted the inevitable triumph of democratic socialism. While early in his career he considered that violence might be necessary to achieve a social transformation, he became convinced that a peaceful transition would occur through the nationalization of monopolies. Berger believed in the efficacy of the tactic of boring from within. Accordingly, as a member of the International Typographical Union, he worked with the existing trade union structure and the American Federation of Labor. He favored cooperation with nonsocialist reformers and tried to incorporate farmers into the socialist movement, defining them as self-employed laborers rather than landowners. Many of these positions challenged Marxist orthodoxy and led to much criticism of Berger as a reformist and an opportunist by his party's left wing. Moreover, as a bombastic and egotistical individual, his personality—along with the positions he took—often involved him in internecine controversies as he pursued principles that conflicted with party policy.

From 1911 to 1913 Berger served in the sixty-second Congress, where he chose to work within the system while trying to express socialist principles and represent American workers. He introduced nearly two dozen bills and sat on the committee exercising jurisdiction over the District of Columbia. He also sponsored measures to improve working conditions in the District, and his major piece of legislation provided for a national system of public pensions. He introduced a bill that called for the social ownership of major industries and several resolutions to convene a constitutional convention to abolish the U.S. Senate and the president's veto power. He promoted a measure to ensure the constitutional rights of J. J. and J. B. McNamara, unionists indicted and later convicted for dynamiting the *Los Angeles Times* building, and he successfully sponsored hearings on the Lawrence, Massachusetts, mill workers' strike of 1912 that helped the workers win their strike.

In other matters he condemned the stationing of troops on the Mexican border in 1916 and opposed tariff revision with Canada as meaningless to the interests of workers. He voted against restrictive immigration legislation in accord with party principles, despite his own reservations on the issue. Berger won the respect of his congressional colleagues, but he was criticized by some socialists for failing to challenge congressional procedures as insufficiently democratic. He was defeated for reelection in 1912 by a fusionist ticket engineered by Milwaukee Republicans and Democrats, and he lost again in 1914 and 1916.

Before American intervention in World War I, Berger was active in peace groups, but he also accepted the idea of wars of national self-defense, despite socialist teachings. He even endorsed a program of conscription for public service, a position for which he faced a recall motion from the party executive in 1916. In general, Berger condemned the war and tried to walk a fine line between local German loyalties and socialist analysis of the war as an economic and imperialist adventure. After the American declaration of war in April 1917, he cautiously supported his party's opposition to it.

In 1917 his newspaper, the Milwaukee *Leader,* was denied second-class mailing privileges under the Espionage Act, and in 1918 he was twice indicted for conspiracy to violate that legislation on the basis of the *Leader's* editorials. Nevertheless, he was elected to his former congressional seat in November 1918. In 1919 he was found guilty of violating the Espionage Act and sentenced to twenty years at Leavenworth by Judge Kenesaw Mountain Landis. His conviction was reversed by the U.S. Supreme Court two years later, and Berger never had to go to prison. At the height of the Red Scare the House of Representatives barred him from serving in the sixty-sixth Congress because of his criminal conviction, and it did so again when he was elected in 1919 to fill his own vacant seat. By that time he had become a critic of the Bolshevik regime in Russia and what he believed to be its dictatorial thrust. When a Socialist party schism occurred that year, he remained with the rump faction rather than joining the emerging American communist movement, and he was in the small minority that opposed any formal links to international communism.

Berger was elected to Congress in 1922, 1924, and 1926 without controversy. In those three terms he again proposed constitutional revisions and an old-age pension; introduced a measure to establish compulsory unemployment insurance; promoted civil liberties including the repeal of the Espionage Act; opposed the Volstead Act; introduced legislation that sought to limit the influence of the Ku Klux Klan; promoted public housing and conservation programs; and encouraged revision of the Versailles Treaty and recognition of the Soviet Union. In the meantime, he was a founder of the Conference for Progressive Political Action, a coalition of farmer, labor, socialist, and progressive forces, and in fact he promoted the emergence of a viable leftist party to replace the old Socialist party. Berger was defeated for reelection in 1926. He returned to Milwaukee to work in the local socialist movement and on his daily newspaper. He died there as a result of a traffic accident.

• Collections of Berger's correspondence and other papers are at the Wisconsin State Historical Society, the Milwaukee County Historical Society, the Milwaukee Public Library, and at Tamiment Library at New York University. Additional papers are located in the Socialist Party of America collection at Duke University's Perkins Library. Two collections of his articles have been published: *Broadsides* (1912) and *Voice and Pen of Victor L. Berger* (1929). A compilation of Berger's correspondence is *The Family Letters of Victor and Meta Berger, 1894–1929,* ed. Michael E. Stevens (1995). See also Sally M. Miller, *Victor Berger and the Promise of Constructive Socialism, 1910–1920* (1973). An obituary is in the *New York Times,* 8 Aug. 1929.

SALLY M. MILLER

BERGH, Henry (29 Aug. 1811?–12 Mar. 1888), animal welfare reformer, was born in New York City, the son of Christian Bergh, a shipbuilder and real estate investor, and Elizabeth Ivers. He attended schools in New York City and Columbia College but left before graduating. The next five years he spent touring Europe and developing his interest in literature and writing plays. Upon his return to the United States in 1836 he married Catherine Matilda Taylor, the daughter of wealthy English parents residing in New York City. After their father's retirement, Henry and his brother ran their father's shipbuilding business. When their father died in 1843, the brothers sold the business and divided the proceeds. Henry Bergh was now free to devote his life to literary pursuits and to the protection of animals.

Bergh and his wife settled in Europe in 1843, and he resumed writing plays and poetry. Several of his comedies were performed in England without critical success, and his satirical poem "Married Off" was published in London in 1860. Because of Bergh's knowledge of Europe, President Abraham Lincoln appointed him secretary of the American Legation in Russia. He later became acting vice consul of the legation. Bergh had been shocked by instances of cruel treatment to animals he witnessed in Europe. Dressed in his official uniform, he found that he could successfully stop St. Petersburg drivers from cruelly beating horses and donkeys. Forced to resign his post because of ill health, Bergh decided to devote himself to animal welfare work. En route to the United States, in London he visited the Royal Society for the Prevention of Cruelty to Animals, in operation for more than forty years. Bergh saw the RSPCA as the model for the American animal welfare organization he was intent on founding.

Arriving home in the midst of the Civil War, Bergh encountered little interest in and considerable hostility to his cause. After a year spent developing plans and promoting his idea among the socially and politically prominent, Bergh gave a public lecture in New York City in February 1866 on the cruelties animals suffered. Two months later, despite legislative opposition, Bergh secured from the New York state legislature a charter of incorporation for the American Society for the Prevention of Cruelty to Animals and new legislation to punish acts of cruelty to animals. Agents of the society were given the power to arrest violators of the state's anticruelty law, and Bergh was permitted legal standing to prosecute cases of animal cruelty in the city's courts. Within a few months he had secured the first arrests and convictions in the United States for cruelty to animals and received enormous press coverage for his work. Elected president of the ASPCA in 1866, Bergh served in that capacity until his death.

Henry Bergh was never content to leave the work of the society to its few paid agents. Wearing the shiny silver badge of the society, he patrolled New York City's streets, forcing passengers to disembark from overloaded horse-drawn streetcars, stopping cockfights and dogfights, arresting butchers for treating live calves cruelly and sailors for boring holes in the fins of live turtles, and exposing the feeding of garbage and spoiled milk to cows. For many of these efforts he was satirized in the popular press, and his home and the offices of the society were picketed.

In the first four years after the society was founded, Bergh personally prosecuted all violators of the state's animal anticruelty law. He lectured to agricultural societies and schoolchildren on the subject that animals were not property but had rights, which must be respected. In 1869 he arranged to have an ambulance transport injured and dying horses to an animal hospital. Up to this time, sick or injured horses had been left to die on city streets. He also invented a clay pigeon as a substitute for the live ones used in sporting practice.

Although Bergh contributed his own money to the ASPCA and volunteered his services without pay, the society at first operated with only meager funds. Initially the society was housed in two attic rooms in Lower Manhattan, but in 1871 a dying French immigrant, who had met Bergh, left his considerable fortune to the society. With this unexpected bounty the society bought a substantial building in New York City and developed an endowment fund. Bergh was also able to enlist the volunteer services of Elbridge T. Gerry, as legal counsel of the society. Together they pushed through national legislation to prevent cruelty to animals on interstate transportation. In 1873 Bergh began an eight-city lecture tour of the Midwest, which helped establish several new anticruelty societies.

Under Bergh's direction, in 1874 the society's agents rescued an abused and neglected girl from the apartment where she had been confined. Aroused by the plight of this child, called "little Mary Ellen," Bergh decided to establish a society to prevent the abuse of children, just as he had formerly founded one on behalf of animals. Bergh and Gerry founded the Society for the Prevention of Cruelty to children in 1875. Although the new society had its offices in the same building as the ASPCA, the work of the two organizations remained separate, and Bergh devoted himself to the cause of animal welfare.

In 1887 Catherine Bergh died. The next year Henry Bergh died at home in New York.

Police officer and prosecutor, lecturer and lobbyist, Henry Bergh aroused the nation's conscience about the suffering of animals at human hands. At his death he left a legacy of state and national legislation, an organization that served as a national model, and an example of ingenuity and indefatigable devotion to a once unpopular cause.

• Letters of Henry Bergh are in the Archives of the ASPCA in New York City and at the New York Historical Society. Among assessments of Bergh's contribution to animal welfare work are Sydney H. Coleman, *Humane Society Leaders in America* (1924); Roswell C. McCrea, *The Humane Movement: A Descriptive Survey* (1910); "Henry Bergh and His Work," *Scribner's Monthly*, Apr. 1879, pp. 872–84; and Clara Morris, "The Riddle of the Nineteenth Century: Mr. Henry Bergh," *McClure's*, Mar. 1902, pp. 414–22. An obituary is in the *New York Times*, 13 Mar. 1888.

ELIZABETH PLECK

BERGMAN, Ingrid (29 Aug. 1915–29 Aug. 1982), film and stage actress, was born in Stockholm, Sweden, the daughter of Justus Samuel Bergman and Friedel Adler. Bergman's father owned a successful photography shop, but he had artistic aspirations that found fruition in his daughter's career. Bergman absorbed her father's interest in the arts, but her early years of relative solitude also fostered the development of her imagination and devotion to acting. Her mother died when Bergman was three, and her father when she was twelve. At age eleven she had told her father at an outing to the theater, "that's what I'm going to do," and the relatives with whom she lived after being orphaned recalled her dreams about acting (she even found work at the Svensk Filmindustri as an extra at age fifteen). While she was not a particularly good student at the girls' school she attended in Stockholm, she found her educational métier in 1933 at Sweden's leading acting center, the school of the Royal Dramatic Theater. After a one-year apprenticeship, she left for a career in films. She made many pictures for the Svensk Filmindustri, and her role in *Intermezzo* (1936) propelled her to stardom in Sweden and ultimately in the United States.

In *Intermezzo*, Bergman plays Anita Hoffman, a pianist who falls in love with a renowned but married violinist; once the violinist leaves his family, the illicit couple travel together, although he returns home after Anita self-sacrificingly ends their relationship. In the part, Bergman solidified the role she typically portrayed through much of her early career: a naive and pure young beauty who gets entangled in a morally questionable situation but who somehow emerges with her innocence and character unbesmirched. As one biographer noted: "For her audience she sanctified behavior that the moral dictates of her time considered slightly sordid or improper." Bergman's performance in *Intermezzo* captured the attention of Hollywood producer David O. Selznick, and in 1939 Selznick launched her in a film career that took her to the heights of stardom and celebrity. She became one of the most popular actresses in America during the 1940s.

Bergman remade *Intermezzo* (1939) for American audiences, and she appeared in several more films until her role as Ilsa Lund Laszlo in *Casablanca* (1942) secured her rise to stardom. Portraying a woman torn between two lovers—the dashing, cynical American Rick Blaine (Humphrey Bogart) and her Nazi-fighting husband Victor Laszlo (Paul Henreid)—Bergman began to touch the film immortality that *Casablanca* as a whole achieved as a cult icon from World War II. (There is irony in Bergman gaining success in what was anti-Nazi propaganda; she had close relatives in Germany, made a film there in 1938 and had resisted taking part in pictures she deemed too anti-German.) Bergman's triumph in *Casablanca*, in a part that symbolized transcendent innocence and natural beauty, suggested her appeal to American audiences both during and after the war.

Bergman furthered the image of political romanticism in her next role as Maria in *For Whom the Bell Tolls* (1943), and she earned an Academy Award for her portrayal of the tortured wife in *Gaslight* (1944). She played a psychiatrist in Alfred Hitchcock's *Spell-*

bound (1945), and she reaffirmed her image of purity as Sister Benedict in *The Bells of St. Mary's* (1945). As Alicia Huberman in Hitchcock's *Notorious* (1946), she again assumed a persona tainted by immorality and shame. Huberman attempts to expiate the guilt of her father's Nazism by spying on Nazis in South America, to the point of marrying one despite her love for her American contact, played by Cary Grant; yet here too she managed to overcome such corruption through her apparently innate goodness and idealism.

The mid-1940s had witnessed Bergman's ascendance as a fine film actress. In 1944 she was the leading actress in America according to box-office statistics, and *Life* proclaimed 1945 "Bergman's Year." After filming *Notorious*, however, Bergman's career and reputation began to slide. In 1946 she freed herself from the studio system and Selznick's control and embarked on a series of ill-fated films. *Arch of Triumph* (1948) and *Under Capricorn* (1949) were commercial and critical disappointments, and *Joan of Arc*, although successful at the box office, was deemed a failure by critics. Seeking a change in direction and some excitement in her film life, Bergman contacted the Italian neorealist filmmaker Roberto Rossellini; their collaboration sparked a scandal that for years effectively ended Bergman's career in American films.

Until 1949 Bergman had masterfully managed both her film and public images; she was seen as a virtuous beauty in her career and in her personal life. She presented herself as a happily married wife and mother, with her husband Dr. Peter Lindstrom (to whom she was married from 1937 until 1950) and her daughter, Pia (born in 1938). In reality, Bergman was a woman dedicated much more to her career than to her family, and she had numerous affairs during her marriage. Bergman's illicit doings remained unexposed until her alliance with Rossellini, and the ensuing scandal illuminated as much about American mores and expectations as it did about those of the principals. By leaving the United States, her husband, and her daughter to live and work with Rossellini, Bergman betrayed the postwar ideal of domesticity. The tension she had successfully negotiated in her films between innocence and iniquity collapsed in her personal life, and Americans punished her for it.

Bergman had gone to Italy to film *Stromboli* (1950) with Rossellini, but their affair did not remain a secret for long. Not only was the scandal broken in the press, but Bergman became pregnant. From her arrival in Italy to the illegitimate birth of her son, she was subjected to constant criticism and condemnation in the United States. As her daughter, Pia, noted, her mother went "from being a saint to a tramp in a few days," and many Americans came to perceive her as a symbol for much of what was morally wrong in Hollywood. In early 1950 U.S. Senator Edwin C. Johnson denounced her on the Senate floor as "a powerful influence for evil." Such treatment for an otherwise strong and professional woman not only ruined Bergman's immediate fortunes in American cinema but sabotaged the critical and commercial potential of the several films she made with Rossellini.

Bergman remained in Italy as the scandal raged, working for her new husband (she married Rossellini in 1950 and divorced him in 1958) and having more children (twins were born in 1952). Bergman remained as active and ambitious as ever, but both her personal and working relationships with Rossellini were as tempestuous as the scandal. Bergman therefore began a "comeback" outside Italian neorealism with her title role in the U.S. production *Anastasia* (1956). Just as her character undergoes a transformation—from refugee to potential Russian princess—so did Bergman start to reclaim and repair her status in Hollywood. She garnered her second Academy Award for *Anastasia*, and she was reintegrated into the star system.

While Bergman continued to find success in both the theater and film, particularly in *Indiscreet* (1958) and *Murder on the Orient Express* (1974), for which she won her third Academy Award, good parts became rarer as she aged, suggesting the power of Hollywood's disaffection and disrespect for older actresses. She remarried in 1958, to Lars Schmidt, a theatrical producer; they divorced in the late 1970s. In films and in her private life her ambition and dedication to career had caused her to be punished, even throughout an era that evinced increasing acceptance of powerful women and sexual liberation. That such pitfalls did not deter Bergman appeared evident at the end of her life and career. As she was weakening from the cancer that killed her, she filmed the highly praised *Autumn Sonata* (1978), directed by Ingmar Bergman, and before her death in London she played the lead role in *A Woman Called Golda* (1982), a television miniseries for which she won an Emmy Award. She thus finished her career as she had begun it—with success and acclaim.

• The most comprehensive biography of Bergman is Laurence Leamer, *As Time Goes By: The Life of Ingrid Bergman* (1986), which contains a complete list of her films, plays, and television performances. Bergman's own version of her life is presented in her autobiography, written with Alan Burgess, *Ingrid Bergman: My Story* (1981). Other works of interest include John Russell Taylor, *Ingrid Bergman* (1983), Curtis F. Brown, *Ingrid Bergman* (1973), Lawrence J. Quirk, ed., *The Films of Ingrid Bergman* (1970), and Joseph Henry Steele, *Ingrid Bergman: An Intimate Portrait* (1959). An obituary is in the *New York Times*, 30 Aug. 1982.

MARGOT A. HENRIKSEN

BERGMANN, Carl (12 Apr. 1821–10 Aug. 1876), conductor, cellist, and composer, was born in Ebersbach, Saxony, the son of middle-class parents. His talent for music manifested itself early, and he was a pupil of Adolph Zimmerman at Zittau as early as 1827 and later studied with the organist-composer Adolph Hesse at Breslau. By 1842 he was playing cello and occasionally conducting the orchestra in Breslau and in these capacities toured central and eastern European cities

between 1842 and 1848. His early compositions, written before 1848, apparently included an opera and a symphony.

As a result of his support of the revolutionary movements in Germany during 1848, Bergmann emigrated to the United States in the fall of 1849. In 1850 he joined the Germania Musical Society as cellist and later served as its conductor. Between 1852 and 1854 he conducted concerts of the Handel and Haydn Society in Boston. Despite efforts by J. S. Dwight and Otto Dresel to keep Bergmann in Boston, he relinquished the Handel and Haydn Society post to Carl Zerrahn (flutist in the Germania organization until its dissolution) in 1854. In that year he first considered settling in Chicago, then returned briefly to Boston. Bergmann moved to New York City in early 1855, initially to conduct the Männergesangverein Arion (a German men's chorus).

In New York, where he spent the rest of his life, he was swiftly recruited by impresario-conductor Theodore Eisfeld. For ten seasons (1855–1865), Eisfeld and Bergmann shared the conducting duties of the New York Philharmonic. Bergmann became a major figure overnight with the Philharmonic's performance on 21 April 1855 of the overture to Wagner's *Tannhäuser*, called "the most sensational success in the orchestra's early history." This event defined Bergmann's mission as an acolyte of "Zukunftmusik" (music of the future). In addition to Wagner, among the composers championed by Bergmann were Liszt, Berlioz, Meyerbeer, Brahms, and even Tchaikovsky. Bergmann conducted the first complete performance of a Wagner opera in America (*Tannhäuser*, New York Stadt-Theater, 4 Apr. 1859) and the first American performance of Meyerbeer's *L'Africaine* (New York, Academy of Music, 1 Dec. 1865).

In addition to his Philharmonic duties and performances in the William Mason-Theodore Thomas chamber concerts, Bergmann organized his own "Sacred Concerts" (1855–1856), where his evangelical fervor for contemporary music was untrammeled by any reservations the Philharmonic may have had about the degree of "novelty" in his programs. That he was an orchestral musician himself—a so-called "artist-conductor"—endeared him to the orchestral players who knew he had come up through their ranks. When Eisfeld retired in 1866, Bergmann became the permanent conductor, the last to be elected directly by the members of the orchestra and the first to be paid a regular salary. For another five years the orchestra prospered artistically and financially under Bergmann.

Bergmann's life and career declined after 1870. Possibly a manic-depressive, he was certainly an alcoholic. The banking failure of 1873 and ensuing financial panic exacerbated a crisis within the Philharmonic. From 1864 it had to compete for audience share with a rival orchestra directed by Bergmann's protégé, Theodore Thomas, who had been concertmaster of the "Sacred Concerts" orchestra. During four seasons, as box office receipts fell, subscriptions dropped off, and the orchestra's morale deteriorated, Bergmann sank into physical and spiritual decay. The Philharmonic's board, aware of the orchestra's great affection for him, allowed him to continue, although they complained that their once-great maestro was now an unreliable wreck, "lazy, negligent, and continually overcharged with lager."

By the second half of the 1875–1876 season, Bergmann had to relinquish the direction of several concerts to violist George Matzka (once a member of the Mason-Thomas chamber group.) The Philharmonic finally requested his resignation on 24 April 1876. Concurrent with this defeat came the death of his wife (her name is unknown), and Bergmann, "in poor health for a considerable time, . . . became morose and moody. . . . He rapidly declined in health and spirits, living a solitary and retired life, and shunning the company of his former associates" (*New York Tribune*, 14 Aug. 1876). He died at the German Hospital in New York City.

During the "Bergmann era" the axis of musical life in the United States became fixed with Germany at the opposite pole. Serious music became synonymous with German music, and fledgling attempts by composers such as W. H. Fry and George Bristow to create a national American musical style were marginalized where they were not entirely abandoned. Bergmann at his best was a competent orchestral conductor whose zeal made up—for a while—for any defects in technique. His success with the New York Philharmonic was due in part to his rank-and-file understanding of orchestral conducting, and in part to his missionary-like promotion of the latest and most challenging scores from Germany. George Martin, in *The Damrosch Dynasty* (1983), called him "the first conductor, in an interpretive sense, the country had known." These qualities built the ensemble into a first-class orchestra and also had a strong influence on New York (and hence, American) taste in orchestral and operatic music.

• The location of any of Bergmann's pre-1848 compositions is unknown. He later published many arrangements for orchestra of dance music by Johann Strauss, Sr., Gungl, Lanner, and other light composers, as well as his own original waltzes, polkas, marches, etc. His principal publisher was Brainard. Considerable anecdotal material on Bergmann is in Howard Shanet, *Philharmonic: A History of New York's Orchestra* (1975). Contemporary New York and Boston papers covered Bergmann's activities closely: *Dwight's Journal of Music* has more than eighty citations for Bergmann between 1852 and 1876, including reprints of other journals' articles and reviews. These can be found indexed in *RIPM*, vol. 4, pp. 994–95. An obituary is in the *New York Tribune*, 14 Aug. 1876.

DAVID FRANCIS URROWS

BERGMANN, Gustav (4 May 1906–21 Apr. 1987), philosopher and mathematician, was born in Vienna, Austria, the son of Fritz Bergmann, an import/export merchant, and Therese Pollack. Before Bergmann took a Ph.D. in mathematics with a minor in philosophy in 1928 at the University of Vienna, he had already been invited to join the famous Vienna Circle. This group of philosophers, scientists, and mathematicians had adopted what they called logical positivism (or sometimes logical empiricism): advocating a scientific world view, they rejected traditional metaphysics and religion as meaningless and regarded ethical and aesthetic statements as only expressions of attitudes. As one of the youngest members of the Circle along with his Gymnasium classmate, the mathematical logician Kurt Gödel, Bergmann was especially influenced by the philosophers Moritz Schlick, Friedrich Waismann, and Rudolf Carnap who were members of the Circle.

In 1929–1930 Bergmann taught mathematics at the Neubau-Realschule in Vienna and the following year joined his dissertation director, Walther Mayer, in assisting German physicist Albert Einstein in his work in Berlin. Discouraged by the prospects for Jews in academia, Bergmann took a J.D. from the University of Vienna in 1935 and began work as a junior in a firm of corporation lawyers. With financial assistance from Circle member Otto Neurath, Bergmann moved to the United States in the fall of 1938 with his first wife, Anna Golwig, whom he had married in 1927 and with whom he had his only child. On the boat trip across the Atlantic, Bergmann wrote, at Neurath's request, a monograph on the Vienna Circle, published as "Erinnerungen an den Wiener Kreis: Brief an Otto Neurath," in *Vertriebene Vernunft II: Emigration und Exil Österreichischer Wissenschaft* (1987) and in English translation as "Memories of the Vienna Circle: Letter to Otto Neurath (1938)," in *Scientific Philosophy: Origins and Developments* (1993), both edited by F. Stadler (Bergmann insisted that this document be published only after his death). During this voyage he and the novelist Hermann Broch became close friends by nightly reading of their works-in-progress to each other.

After working in New York as an actuary for a few months, Bergmann was able, with a letter of recommendation from Einstein and the assistance of Circle member Herbert Feigl, who had left Vienna for the University of Iowa in the early 1930s, to obtain an appointment at Iowa, where he was to remain for the rest of his career. Bergmann began in 1939 as assistant to the psychologist Kurt Lewin in the Iowa Child Welfare Research Station. In 1940 Bergmann received a faculty appointment as assistant professor in Iowa's Department of Philosophy, and in 1943 he was given an additional appointment in the Department of Psychology. In that same year Bergmann divorced his first wife, who had been institutionalized shortly after their arrival in America, and married Leola Nelson, a scholar of American studies and a printmaker. In 1944 he became an American citizen.

With the exception of a short piece on literary theory, Bergmann's publications before his emigration were all in the field of mathematics and mainly on his specialty of topology. His reputation in philosophy was established in the 1940s and early 1950s with numerous papers in the philosophy of psychology and the philosophy of physics, and in logic and probability—an aspect of Bergmann's work that culminated in his *Philosophy of Science* (1957). In this area of philosophy Bergmann's ideas were, and remained, largely those of orthodox logical positivism. During these early years at Iowa Bergmann also established an association with the psychologist Kenneth Spence, a student of Clark Hull. (Bergmann had spent two months with Hull at Yale in the summer of 1939.) This association, which resulted in several important papers in the journals *Philosophy of Science* and *Psychological Review*, proved to be the most productive of the many associations across the country that constituted an important part of the intellectual culture of the time—the alliance between logical positivism in philosophy and behaviorism in psychology. Bergmann was named full professor of philosophy and psychology in 1950.

By the late 1940s, Bergmann had begun what was to become his most important work—studies in metaphysics, philosophy of logic, and philosophy of mind. A collection of papers published as *The Metaphysics of Logical Positivism* in 1954 resulted in his intellectual, and in a few cases personal, estrangement from other members of the Circle (most of whom had also settled in America); Bergmann insisted, contrary to positivist orthodoxy, that not only did some traditional metaphysics make sense if properly recast, but that logical positivism itself contained an implicit metaphysics.

In rejecting what he regarded as the narrow scientism of most of his colleagues in the logical positivist movement (which included many thinkers not in the Vienna Circle), Bergmann adopted the "ideal-language" method of doing philosophy. This method, of which Bergmann remains the best-known practitioner, calls for the reformulation in principle of all of the meaningful sentences of natural language into a certain kind of artificial language that allows a precision and independence from context unavailable in natural languages. In discoursing about this ideal language (a language never actually to be spoken and to be written only in fragments), the philosopher would be able clearly to formulate and, in principle, definitively to solve the traditional philosophical problems. Although the notion of an artificial language for the solution of philosophical problems originated with German philosopher Gottfried Wilhelm von Leibniz, Bergmann's form of it derives from the work of two of the century's most important philosophers, Bertrand Russell and Ludwig Wittgenstein, who, with G. E. Moore, were the most important influences on him in the early years of his metaphysical thinking. From Moore he adopted the idea that certain beliefs of everyday life (that there is a world that exists independent of our minds, for example) are the ones from which philosophy begins. Russell's primary influence was in more technical matters having to do with metaphysics, logic, and the formal structure of the ideal language, while Wittgenstein's *Tractatus Logico-Philosophicus* of 1922, which contains numerous examples of the use of the ideal-language method, was probably the single most important work for Bergmann at this time (although he eventually became the primary critic of its most important doctrine).

If in his early years Bergmann was "the most sophisticated and plausible of the positivists," as characterized by Robert Turnbull, in the 1950s Bergmann's work moved in directions that were to make him eventually, in the words of another eminent philosopher, Hector-Neri Casteñeda, "the major ontologist of recent decades." Ontology for Bergmann was the attempt to specify comprehensively what the categories of the *simple* constituents of reality are as discovered through direct experience of reality and dialectical reasoning about it. The simplest signs of the ideal language would stand for the simplest constituents of reality with the structure of reality thereby exposed in the structure of that language. Bergmann's collection of essays *Meaning and Existence* (1959) dealt with these themes and was partly responsible for his invitation by the government of Sweden to lecture at the four Swedish universities during the academic year 1961–1962. By this time, too, partly by placing many of his students as faculty in departments of philosophy and psychology in leading universities of the United States, Bergmann had brought national status to a small philosophy department in a middle-sized midwestern university.

A fundamental aspect of Bergmann's ontology was his insistence, contrary to Wittgenstein, that logic (including mathematics) is a part of reality itself and not "nothing," or just the way humans think. Papers on this theme and others were published under the title *Logic and Reality* in 1964. In philosophy of mind, by rejecting the materialism and phenomenalism of his positivist teachers, Bergmann insisted on dualism, or, as he preferred to call it, "realism," in arguing that mind and matter are each independently real and neither reducible to the other. His theory of the nature of the mind as consisting of mental acts that are intrinsically intentional, while original and profound, acknowledged the influence of the Austro-German tradition as represented by Franz Brentano, Alexius Meinong, Gottlob Frege, and Edmund Husserl. Bergmann treated these themes and others in *Realism: A Critique of Brentano and Meinong* (1967).

In 1967–1968 Bergmann served as president of the American Philosophical Association, Western (now Central) Division. In 1972, by being named Carver Professor, he was awarded the first named professorship in the College of Liberal Arts at the University of Iowa, and in 1974 he formally retired as Carver Professor Emeritus of Philosophy and Psychology. For a few years he continued to teach at Iowa his famous "History and Systems of Psychology" course, through which he had transmitted his ideas in theoretical psychology to hundreds of philosophy and psychology graduate students over the years. The main product of Bergmann's postretirement work was his posthumous *New Foundations of Ontology* (1992). Chronic illness prevented him from accepting most of the requests for lectures elsewhere that continued to come his way. He died in Iowa City.

Bergmann's social values were roughly those of classical liberalism tempered by Freudian pessimism. (He was a strong believer in the power of the unconscious and had undergone psychoanalysis himself during the Vienna years. Although he never met Sigmund Freud, he was acquainted with Freud's psychiatrist daughter, Anna Freud.) In the arts Bergmann had both devotion to and substantial knowledge of literature, painting, and music. But these matters played no direct role in his academic philosophy any more than did his extensive knowledge of European history, with the exception of the history of philosophy itself. His values were best expressed in print in a nontechnical but, for many of his readers, one of his most powerful papers, "Ideology" (*Ethics* 61 [1951]: 205–18), in which he maintained that "the ideal of an ideology-free society is a consummation devoutly to be desired, if for no other reason than the humanity, the intelligence, and the courage it takes to bear life without the support of ideological illusion. To me such a world is the only one worth living in and therefore, if necessary, worth dying for." His attempt to live a life without the illusions of religion and ideology was manifest in his daily existence.

Bergmann had a strong personality that affected people in markedly different ways. While some perceived him as harsh in his judgments and brusque in his manner, for those who knew him well he was a man of great generosity—of time and of spirit. While he and his family had suffered great indignities because of their ethnic heritage, he always remained capable of judging a person on that person's individual characteristics, as was most strikingly evidenced by his willingness to befriend and to direct the dissertation of a (non-Jewish) German student who came to America soon after the war.

Bergmann's earlier work in the spirit of logical positivism made its way into anthologies and libraries, but his later work in ontology and philosophy of mind mark him as one of the most important philosophers in the analytic tradition of the second half of the twentieth century. This later work, while having sustained interest only for a small minority even within professional philosophy, received significant attention not only in the English-speaking and other northern European countries of the analytic tradition but also in the former Soviet Union, in Germany, in Spain, and especially in his beloved Italy, with his theory of the nature of consciousness and his use of the ideal language being probably the most important topics of lasting interest. He is widely recognized within professional philosophy as one of the few, from Plato to the present, who has pursued the fundamental ontological questions so deeply.

• A complete bibliography of Bergmann's published writings can be found with his papers on deposit in the archives of the Main Library of the University of Iowa. His famous "Ideology" was reprinted in his *The Metaphysics of Logical Positivism* (1954) and anthologized elsewhere. In addition to the six books mentioned in the text, Bergmann published about 125 articles, reviews, and discussion notes. With the exception of the early articles in German-language mathematical journals, almost all of these are in professional English-language philosophical journals and anthologies; a few are in psychological journals and physics journals. There is an account of Bergmann's association with Kenneth Spence and Clark Hull in Laurence D. Smith, *Behaviorism and Logical Positivism: A Reassessment of the Alliance* (1986). The only study devoted to a comprehensive survey of Bergmann's philosophy is Laird Addis, "The Philosophy of Gustav Bergmann," *Algemeen Nederlands Tijdschrift voor Wijsbegeerte* 63 (1971): 78–98. Addis also provided an obituary in *Proceedings and Addresses of the American Philosophical Association* 61 (1987): 164–65.

LAIRD ADDIS

BERGMANN, Max (12 Feb. 1886–7 Nov. 1944), biochemist, was born in Fürth, Germany, the son of Solomon Bergmann, a coal merchant, and Rosalie Stettauer. He entered the University of Munich inclined toward botany, but his studies convinced him that biological questions required the methods of organic chemistry for their answers. Following the receipt of a bachelor's degree in 1907, he became a student of Emil Fischer, a Nobel Prize winner and the world's foremost protein and carbohydrate chemist, at the University of Berlin. He received a Ph.D. in 1911 and then served as Fischer's research assistant until the latter's death in 1919. Bergmann was a privatdocent at Berlin before going to Dresden in 1921 as director of the new Kaiser Wilhelm Institute for Leather Research and professor of chemistry at the Dresden Technical University. In Dresden he created one of the leading laboratories for protein chemistry. Bergmann was a Jew, and with the rise to power of Adolf Hitler he came to the United States. From 1934 to his death he was at the Rockefeller Institute for Medical Research in New York.

Bergmann represents the brilliant tradition of German organic chemistry applied to biological problems, a tradition he and other German émigrés brought to the United States to greatly strengthen American biochemistry in the 1930s. As a protein chemist, he wanted to understand the complex structure of proteins and how they act in living systems. This meant determining the amino acid composition of proteins, finding how these units are linked in individual proteins, and applying this knowledge to account for their biological activity. Working under Fischer, he made many basic contributions to protein and amino acid chemistry, and in Dresden he extended Fischer's program of separating and identifying the amino acid constituents of proteins.

Bergmann also assumed the even more difficult tasks of the synthesis and determination of the sequence of amino acid linkages in a protein. By 1910 Fischer had shown that amino acids combine in long chains to form peptides. Some protein chemists inferred that proteins were giant polypeptides containing thousands of amino acid residues. To establish this conjecture, Bergmann developed new and more powerful methods for peptide synthesis, and in 1932 he made the most important discovery of his Dresden period.

The synthesis of a polypeptide requires a method to form desired peptide linkages without getting undesired ones. Bergmann had to find a way to protect some amino acid residues from reacting by means of an attached group that could be removed later. With his associate Leonidas Zervas he devised the carbobenzoxy protecting group. He could now synthesize peptides using any amino acid in any sequence to produce peptides and polypeptides that more closely resembled in size and composition the naturally occurring proteins. The carbobenzoxy method eclipsed all previous methods and became essential to protein chemistry. It was an easy route to synthetic peptides, capable of incorporating amino acids hitherto impossible to use in forming peptides.

Bergmann continued these researches in New York, emphasizing two lines of investigation: expanding the carbobenzoxy method in order to form peptides for use as substrates for protein-splitting enzymes and the unraveling of the total structure of proteins. By 1937, when he became head of the chemistry laboratory at the Rockefeller Institute, Bergmann had attracted several talented biochemists to his staff. With Joseph Fruton, between 1936 and 1939, he discovered the first synthetic peptide substrates for which several enzymes had catalytic activity. When they demonstrated that the enzyme pepsin could catalyze the hydrolysis of synthetic peptides, they implicated the peptide bond in protein structure and also provided the first clear evidence that specific enzymes split peptide bonds at precise linkages in the chain in a way related to the structures of the enzyme and substrate. The discovery opened the way to the study of the mode of action of enzymes as catalysts for every biological function.

The problem of protein structure proved incapable of solution by Bergmann's methods of analysis and synthesis. He employed methods for the separation and quantitative analysis of every amino acid in a protein and tried to establish their sequence in the polypeptide chain. In 1938 he advanced a theory of systematic periodicity or recurrence in the location of every amino acid residue in the peptide chains of a protein. That this hypothesis was an oversimplification was shown by two biochemists of his own research group in 1939. Stanford Moore and William Stein collaborated in developing novel and superior methods for the quantitative analysis of amino acids in protein hydrolysates. Bergmann had to abandon his periodic theory after Moore and Stein showed him that the analytical data did not support it. World War II research on war gases interrupted this investigation, but after the war Moore and Stein perfected their methods, and by 1949 it became possible to determine the order of linking of each amino acid in a protein. Frederick Sanger in England was the first to establish the complete amino acid sequence and total structure of a protein, the hormone insulin. Moore and Stein followed with the structure of the more complex protein, the enzyme ribonuclease. These complete sequencings of amino acids in

proteins represented the fulfillment of Bergmann's research goals. Moore and Stein received the 1972 Nobel Prize for their contributions to the mapping of the molecular structure of proteins and enzymes.

Bergmann died in New York City, a victim of cancer. In 1912 he had married Emmy Miriam Grunwald, with whom he had two children. The marriage ended in divorce, and in 1926 he married Martha Suter. His research group found him to be an agreeable leader and intimate collaborator. He had many joint publications with members of the group.

Bergmann enriched American biochemistry with the skills and knowledge of the German organic chemist, and his research proved central to the study of biochemical processes. His mastery of the art of peptide synthesis and protein splitting was the starting point for modern protein chemistry and the study of enzyme-substrate interactions.

• Collections of Bergmann papers are in the American Philosophical Society Library and the Rockefeller University Archives. The majority of his publications are in German journals. He wrote with Joseph Fruton several reviews in protein and enzyme chemistry, notably "Proteolytic Enzymes," *Annual Review of Biochemistry* 10 (1941): 31–46, and "The Specificity of Proteinases," *Advances in Enzymology* 1 (1941): 63–98. Fruton's "The Synthesis of Peptides," *Advances in Protein Chemistry* 5 (1949): 1–82, covers Bergmann's findings in both Germany and the United States. For commentaries on his scientific contributions, see Garland Allen, *Life Science in the Twentieth Century* (1975); Hans T. Clarke, "Max Bergmann, 1886–1944," *Science* 102 (1945): 168–70; and George W. Corner, *A History of the Rockefeller Institute* (1964). An obituary is in the *New York Times*, 8 Nov. 1944.

ALBERT B. COSTA

BERIGAN, Bunny (2 Nov. 1908–2 June 1942), jazz trumpeter, was born Roland Bernard Berigan in Hilbert, Wisconsin, the son of William P. "Cap" Berigan, a railroad agent and then a candy and cigarette salesman, and Mayme Schlitzberg, a piano teacher. Berigan's musical studies began with his mother, who taught him piano. He made his first public appearance at age eight as a vocalist, with accompaniment by his mother. In 1922 he took part in his first jazz concert as a member of the Pennsylvanians, a band led by Merrill Owen; he played trumpet and violin and sang. He dropped out of high school in his junior year.

From the early 1920s to the early 1930s Berigan performed with numerous groups, including those of Cy Mahlberg (1923), Robert "Big Bob" Berigan (1925), and Jessie Cohen; several college bands; and the pit bands of both the Capitol and Orpheum theaters. After traveling to Philadelphia in the spring of 1928, he performed briefly with the Crusaders, a group led by violinist Frank Cornwell, before returning to Madison, Wisconsin. Beginning in 1929 Berigan performed with Al Thompson's Nighthawks, the Pete Drum and Paul Bean orchestras, Joe Schoer, Cornwell again briefly, Hal Kemp, Paul Whiteman (1932–1933), and several other groups from the late 1920s to 1933. He led his own big band in 1933. In about 1932 he had married Donna (maiden name unknown); they had two daughters.

Although his reputation as an excellent musician was well established, Berigan's career received a boost in 1934, when Benny Goodman asked him to join his band. While with Goodman, he was part of the "Let's Dance" broadcasts that began in December 1934. Thereafter he performed on the 8 and 22 December and the 5 and 12 January broadcasts of 1935. He left the Goodman band on 27 September 1935.

From 1936 to 1937 Berigan recorded extensively with several notable artists, including Bud Freeman, Dick McDonough, and Dick Stabile. He also accompanied Mildred Bailey, Billie Holiday, Louis Armstrong, and Tommy Dorsey. Among the recordings he made with the Dorsey band are "Marie" and "Song of India." With the help of Dorsey, he organized his own big band in 1937 and made several recordings, including "Cause My Baby Says It's So," featuring Berigan on vocals; a song permeated with a racial stereotype of African Americans, "All Dark People Are Light on Their Feet," featuring Ford Leary on vocals; "Frankie and Johnny"; "Mahogany Hall Stomp"; and "I Can't Get Started." All were recorded on 7 August 1937.

From 1940 until his death Berigan continued to record. He rejoined Dorsey briefly in 1940, recorded (with a studio band) a soundtrack for the film *Syncopation* in 1941, led another big band, and caught pneumonia twice before his death. Although his group was good, it was disbanded in February 1940 because of Berigan's drinking and loose management style. In addition, he had filed for bankruptcy and sometimes could not afford to meet his payroll.

Throughout his life, Berigan displayed a strong affection for Bix Beiderbecke and Juan Tizol. He recorded several transcriptions of Beiderbecke's harmonically complex piano compositions in 1938 and performed "Caravan" and "Night Song," both Beiderbecke pieces, on many occasions. On his recording of "Marie" with Dorsey, he demonstrated an ability to slur an octave from F to F, a rich tone, and a technical facility that was advanced for its time.

According to Gunther Schuller, Berigan's "strangely searching solos (on 'Slow Beef' and 'Postage Stomp'), neither linearly melodic nor rigidly harmonic, reveal an inventive, improvisational talent that was not beholden to any known model" (p. 465). Maturity, as witnessed by explorations of low notes, technical proficiency, and confidence in his ideas, can be heard in his 1930 recording of "Them There Eyes," possibly reflecting his acquaintance with the work of Louis Armstrong and Roy Eldridge. Two later recordings, "That Foolish Feeling" (1936) and "I Can't Get Started" (1937), show technical difficulty and a musically creative four-bar modulation. Berigan sang, played a free-tempo cadenza, and displayed a smooth, flowing style. He also exhibited a three-octave range, mastery of the low register, and a rich vibrato.

Although Berigan's drinking problem may well have undermined his musical success, he should be remembered for having been able to explore all registers of his instrument, to create and adapt to different styles, and to sustain a technique that was among the best of his day. He died in New York City of cirrhosis.

• A concise source for the life and discography of Berigan is Vince Danca, *Bunny: A Bio-Discography of Jazz Trumpeter Bunny Berigan* (1978). Materials that cover his life and contributions include Robert Dupuis, *Bunny Berigan: Elusive Legend of Jazz* (1993); O. Coyle, "He Gave the Kid a Break: The Discovery of Bunny Berigan," *Mississippi Rag* 2, no. 11 (1975): 10; L. Crosbie, "Bunny Berigan," *Jazz Journal* 27, no. 9 (1974): 8; J. Dapogny, "Bunny Berigan," in *The New Grove Dictionary of Jazz*, ed. Barry Kernfeld (1988); E. Jenkins and J. Kline, "Touring with Bunny," *Mississippi Rag* 10, no. 4 (1983): 1; and Gunther Schuller, "Bunny Berigan," in *The Swing Era: The Development of Jazz, 1930–1945* (1989).

EDDIE S. MEADOWS

BERING, Vitus Jonassen (Aug. 1681–8 Dec. 1741), explorer, was born in Horsens, Denmark, the son of Jonas Svendsen, a customs inspector, and Anne Petersdatter. Her family included the distinguished poet Vitus Pedersen Bering; young Vitus was named for him. Bering's half-brother Svend, given the choice between colonial service and prison after he participated in riots, chose colonial service and sailed for India in April 1696; Vitus was along as ship's boy.

In 1703 Bering joined Peter the Great's Russian navy, founded in 1697, as a second lieutenant. He had previously made a whaling voyage and a voyage to the East Indies. He had studied navigation, chart making, and geography. He was promoted to lieutenant in 1706; to captain lieutenant in 1710 with the Azov fleet; to captain third class in 1715 in the Baltic; and to captain second class in 1720.

In 1718 Bering, now a Russian citizen (Ivan Ivanovich Bering), married Anna Christina Puellse, the daughter of a merchant in Vyborg, Finland, near St. Petersburg. They had eight children by 1730, four reaching adulthood. Bering's resignation from the navy on 20 January 1724 had a financial motive: officers junior to him received raises when the Northern War ended. He left for Vyborg in February but then requested reinstatement. In October he resumed service as captain first rank. He was named to head a navy expedition to Kamchatka.

The purpose of this expedition has been debated from its beginning, when it was assumed that it was sent by Peter the Great to determine whether Asia and America were joined. Sound cartographical and literary evidence has shown that the Russians knew prior to the expedition that the two continents were separate. The main purpose of the expedition (there may have been several) was to prepare an accurate map of the route from Tobolsk to Okhotsk, and of Kamchatka and the coasts to the north, particularly in relation to a "Terra Incognita" on maps of the time.

The First Kamchatka Expedition began with thirty-four men leaving St. Petersburg early in 1725. The expedition employed more than 400 men for transporting flour, anchors, artillery, cannon, compasses, and other navigational equipment; for building ships, boats, rafts, and lodging; and for driving horses, cattle, and dogs. Reaching Yakutsk in June 1726, they found that no preparations had been made for their arrival. The horses, saddles, and packs needed to continue the expedition were not available, in spite of orders from the government in St. Petersburg that the Siberian officials were to assist the expedition. Eventually 660 horses were obtained, of which 393 survived the march to the sea (at Okhotsk). Of the 204 horse handlers, forty-six deserted, thirty-eight were discharged, five died, and twenty-seven were left behind. Lieutenant Martin Spanberg, second in command, left Yakutsk with 250 men in thirteen boats, traveling by the Lena and Yudoma rivers as far eastward as possible. In the terrible land route from there to Okhotsk, more than half the cargo was abandoned and ninety men pulled loaded sleds on foot. Of these forty reached Okhotsk, without the sleds.

Finally, in August 1727 thirty-five men in two ships left Okhotsk for Bolsheretsk, because it was late in the sailing season and the route around the southern tip of Kamchatka was unknown. The expedition and its equipment crossed the peninsula to the mouth of the Kamchatka River, traveling by boats on the rivers and on Kamchadal dogsleds overland. A new ship was built in the spring, especially for the voyage. After three and a half years, on 14 July 1728 Bering sailed north with 44 men in the *Gabriel*, a two-masted ship that was the largest built in Siberia to that time. It was sixty feet long, twenty feet wide, and seven and a half feet tall. They sailed to the north and east, proceeding slowly in order to map the coast. The route was through Bering Strait, but the American coast, visible on a clear day, was hidden by fog. In mid-August, at 67°18′N., Bering ordered a southerly course, wintering at the Kamchatka River. The *Gabriel* sailed eastward briefly in the spring of 1729 searching for land the Kamchadals said could be seen on a clear day. Not finding it, the ship sailed for Okhotsk.

Bering reached St. Petersburg on 30 March 1730 to a lukewarm reception. Members of the new Academy of Sciences interested in a northeast passage from Europe felt he should have explored the Arctic coast. The Admiralty College did not accept Bering's map and reports from the Chukchi as conclusive proof that the continents were not joined. The map made by the expedition was not sufficiently appreciated even though, as Evgenii G. Kushnarev put it, this map "was not simply relatively correct, but immeasurably more accurate than all previous maps" (p. 155). Bering proposed a second expedition, which he would lead as captain commander.

Plans for the Second Kamchatka Expedition, because of demands from the Academy of Sciences and the Senate, were extravagant. The expedition was to explore and map the arctic coast from Arkhangelsk in northwest Russia to the point in Siberia reached earlier; discover a route to Japan for trade; and explore and map lands of the North Pacific and to reach America. Members of the Academy of Sciences would participate as botanists, geologists (for precious metals), historians, and physicians to study the natural history of the lands explored.

From 1733 to his departure on the voyage to America in 1741, Bering was consumed by administration. All the problems of the first expedition were multiplied in the second, which began with 500 men. In Siberia 500 soldiers were recruited to serve the expedition. In addition, 2,000 men were hired at various times to transport supplies and build houses, ships, and roads.

Two ships, packet boats about 80 feet long, were built in Petropavlovsk, Kamchatka. On 4 June 1741, Bering with 77 men on the *St. Peter*, and Aleksei Chirikov, with 75 men on the *St. Paul*, sailed east from Avacha Bay. They searched for the mythical "Juan de Gama Land" thought to be nearby. On 20 June a storm separated the ships. Both reached America, Chirikov at the south end of the Alaska panhandle on 15 July, Bering further north the next day. Neither stayed long; Chirikov lost his two longboats and eleven of his men in attempting to land. With no way to get fresh water, Chirikov headed for home, with a crew suffering from scurvy, reaching Kamchatka on 12 October.

On July 20 Bering and the *St. Peter* were at Kayak Island for fresh water. Naturalist Georg Wilhelm Steller had less than ten hours on land to survey its natural history. The other stop Bering made in America was at the Shumagin Islands, late in August, again for water. Bering and his officers decided on 10 August to return to Kamchatka because of the late season, the scarce water supply, scurvy, and contrary winds. They gave up mapping. The men were so sick they could hardly work the ship. On November 6 land was sighted that they believed was Kamchatka. The crew pointed the *St. Peter* toward land, but it struck a reef. Miraculously it was tossed beyond the reef into shallow water. The men set up lodgings on the uninhabited island (now known as Bering Island), where they spent the winter fighting off the tame foxes and catching sea otter, whose pelts they used as money in gambling. Bering died there during their stay. Steller described him as a "friendly, quiet man, and for that reason always popular with the entire command." Bering has been called the "Russian Columbus" because of his voyage to America. The following year the men built a smaller ship from the wreck of the *St. Peter* and returned to Kamchatka, where news of the sea otter pelts they brought soon spread, setting off a Russian "fur rush" to the Aleutians and then to the mainland of North America.

• The Central State Archive of the Navy in St. Petersburg, Russia, has manuscripts on the expeditions, including reports and journals, but Bering left few writings. Peter Lauridsen, *Vitus Bering: The Discoverer of Bering Strait* (1889), trans. by Julius E. Olson from the Danish of 1885, is a laudatory biography. Frank A. Golder, *Bering's Voyages: An Account of the Efforts of the Russians to Determine the Relation of Asia and America* (2 vols., 1922), is a standard work. Boris P. Polevoi offered a new interpretation of Peter the Great's instructions for the First Kamchatka Expedition in 1970, elaborated in Raymond H. Fisher, *Bering's Voyages: Whither and Why* (1977). Carol Urness, *Bering's First Expedition: A Re-examination Based on Eighteenth-Century Books, Maps, and Manuscripts* (1986), and Evgenii G. Kushnarev, *Bering's Search for the Strait: The First Kamchatka Expedition, 1725–1730* (1990), ed. and trans. by E. A. P. Crownhart-Vaughn from the Russian of 1976, focus on the first expedition.

The success of the Second Kamchatka Expedition, particularly in mapping the Arctic, has not had the attention it deserves in books about exploration. The American voyages have been studied more, and an excellent book is *Bering and Chirikov: The American Voyages and Their Impact*, edited by O. W. Frost (1992). Modern translations and editions, with commentary, of Georg Wilhelm Steller, *Journal of a Voyage with Bering, 1741–1742*, trans. O. W. Frost and Margritt A. Engel (1988), and Gerhard Friedrich Müller, *Bering's Voyages: The Reports from Russia*, trans. Carol Urness (1986), make two accounts by participants readily available.

CAROL URNESS

BERK, Fred (25 Jan. 1911–26 Feb. 1980), dancer, was born Fritz Berger in Vienna, Austria, the son of Jacob Berger, a dairy owner, and Henrietta Blau. Berk was born into a Viennese Orthodox Jewish family to a stern father who apprenticed him at age fourteen to a goldsmith. Hunching over his metalwork led to back problems and the medical suggestion to study dance. This began a career that spanned continents and decades.

Berk, trained in the expressionist modern dance style of Gertrud Kraus, performed in the Kraus Dance Troupe in Vienna from 1931 to 1933. He later opened his own studio in Vienna and performed in his own works, winning the bronze medal for his anti-Hitler solo "The Tyrant" in the 1934 international dance competition sponsored by the International Archives of the Dance. He also performed in Holland, Italy, and Switzerland before fleeing the Nazis in 1939, first to England and then to Cuba, where he performed for two years with Kraus dancer Claudia Vall Kauffman. He was stricken with arthritis, which delayed his entry to the United States until June 1941.

In an interview for his biography, *Victory Dances* (1985), Berk said he realized positive emotions about Judaism "only when I came to the U.S. in 1941 during the Holocaust." His feelings about the importance of Jewish identity crystallized into a deep ongoing commitment to Jewish dance. In New York he discovered that Katya Delakova, also from Kraus's troupe, had survived the Holocaust; like Berk, she had lost her home and family members in the concentration camps. They were married in 1943; they had no children. Delakova and Berk formed a dance duo that had wide appeal. Their first program, "Make Way for Tomorrow," on 23 January 1944, combined American and Jewish folk music and dance. The young couple wrote in their program notes, "We speak to you of humor, heroism and love of different people until the different and the strange become your brother." They performed together for seven years in Jewish community centers, colleges, and universities all over the country, as well as at Madison Square Garden, the United Nations, the Museum of Natural History, Carnegie Hall, rallies and conferences for Jewish causes, Yiddish theaters, and in the Catskills during the summers on the borscht belt circuit.

Berk's dance work fit into the developing Americanization of Judaism, according to Joseph Blau's *Judaism in America* (1976). A new mode of Jewish identification came to the fore as American Jews dedicated themselves to Zionism, the rebuilding of the state of Israel. Israeli folk dance and dances with Jewish themes put Berk in a key place with a ready audience and eager students in all sectors of Judaism. In addition to working with Zionist youth movements and Jewish community centers, there were summer camps and the Young Men's and Young Women's Hebrew Association, especially at the 92d Street Y in New York. And for some twenty-five years he taught at Camp Blue Star's special Fred Berk Israeli Folk Dance Camp in the Blue Ridge Mountains. In the 1940s Berk and Delakova started the Jewish Dance Guild performing group; the *Dance Observer* review of January 1948 reported that the dancers were "healthy, exuberant adolescents whose zestful joie de vivre was delightfully refreshing in a season of dance which seems to be preoccupied with psychoanalysis."

Delakova and Berk toured Israel in 1949, and Delakova decided to settle there. Berk returned to the United States, where he felt he could be most effective, though Israel remained a place of inspiration for him; he returned often to Israel and lived there for a few years in the 1970s. He and Delakova divorced in 1952.

In New York, then the center of American modern dance, Berk created a three-year series of performances spanning the 1949–1952 seasons, called "Stage for Dancers," which provided stipends for the performers in fully produced concerts. He combed the New York studios for talent, combining dancers from a variety of modern dance styles and studios in performances he booked at the Brooklyn Museum, Alwin Nikolais's Henry St. Playhouse, Cooper Union, and the Masters' Institute. *Dance Magazine* wrote about him that Berk's programs have "a healthy air of adventure and discovery . . . In the 10 years he's lived in America, the Austrian born Mr. Berk viewed with no little astonishment and finally with ire the spectacle of capable dancers practicing their craft in studios year after year . . . 'I got bored with seeing the dancers sit around their studios and I decided something must be done to get them on stage.'"

In 1953 Berk also helped create and codirect, with legendary modern dancer Doris Humphrey, the first professional dance company for children, the Merry-Go-Rounders. His popular dance "Holiday in Israel" was a staple of the programming. However, owing to arthritis in his hip and unsuccessful surgery, Berk was left with a severe limp, forcing him to abandon his own dancing. Nevertheless, he continued to be active as a teacher, choreographer, researcher, and director.

From 1953 to 1980 Berk continued to promote Israeli folk dance in the United States. At the 92d Street

Y in New York, he was director of the Jewish Dance Department, where he taught all levels of Israeli folk dance, brought its creators from Israel for special workshops, created several performing groups, among them Hebraica, with a mixed Jewish–modern dance repertory, and set standards for teaching and staging Israeli folk dance. Every spring he directed the Israeli Dance Festival, first at Hunter College, then at Carnegie Hall, the Felt Forum, and Philharmonic Hall at Lincoln Center, with hundreds of youth from many Jewish youth groups participating.

From 1968 until his death in New York City, he directed the Israel Folk Dance Institute of the American Zionist Youth Foundation, which sponsored the Israel Dance Festival and enabled Berk to lead study tours of folk dancers to Israel, publish his books, and sponsor the publication *Hora*, which he edited. He also created thirteen phonograph records of Israeli folk dance music, considered the best in both America and Israel partly for their superb musicality and partly because of the concise and clearly written folk dance manuals accompanying the records. Fred Berk was a key figure in the development of modern dance in New York in the 1950s and a leading authority, as master teacher, producer of Israeli folk festivals, researcher, author, and performer, on Jewish dance in America.

• Fred Berk's papers as well as extensive hours of taped interviews with him are housed at the Dance Collection of the New York Public Library for the Performing Arts at Lincoln Center, New York City. He published several articles in *Dance Magazine* (including "Staging Folk Dance," May 1952; "A Dissenting Point of View about Folk Dance," Dec. 1957) and wrote a book for the Dance Notation Bureau, with Lucy Venable, *Ten Folk Dances in Labanotation* (1959). He edited *Hora*, a publication of Israeli folk dance, from 1968 to 1978 published by the American Zionist Youth Foundation and wrote several books, including *The Jewish Dance* (1960); *Ha-Rikud, the Jewish Dance* (1972); *The Chasidic Dance* (1975); and with Susan Reimer, *Machol Ha'am: Dance of the Jewish People* (1978). His thirteen phonograph records appeared under the Tikva, Elektra, and Michael Herman's "Folk Dance House" labels. His biography, *Victory Dances: The Life of Fred Berk*, written by Judith Brin Ingber, was published in 1985. An extensive article by Anna Kisselgoff appeared in the *New York Times* on 24 Nov. 1985, following the publication of his biography. An obituary is in the *New York Times*, 28 Feb. 1980.

JUDITH BRIN INGBER

BERKELEY, Busby (29 Nov. 1895–14 Mar. 1976), stage and film choreographer and director, was born William Berkeley Enos in Los Angeles, California, the son of Francis Enos, a stage director, and Gertrude Berkeley, a character actress. Berkeley's mother and father were associated with the Tim Frawley Repertory Company. Although they wanted to spare him the life of the theater, he soon joined them on stage. After his father's death in 1902, Berkeley became devoted to his mother, who, until her own death in 1948, remained a strong influence on him. While his mother performed with Alla Nazimova's acting company, Berkeley attended military school. After graduation, he

became an apprentice in a shoe business, but his theatrical abilities were tapped by the army during World War I when he served in France as an assistant entertainment officer, working with both the U.S. and French armies designing parade drills as well as serving as an air corps aerial observer. Berkeley called this experience his "best apprenticeship," and from it came his lifelong fascination with military formations.

After the war he made his Broadway debut as an actor in *The Man Who Came Back* (1918). Although he had no dance training, he also worked as an assistant stage manager and dance director in stock productions. In the 1923 revival of *Irene* he played the courtier Mme. Lucy and continued in the part for nearly three years on tour. His big break as a dance director came with Richard Rodgers and Lorenz Hart's *A Connecticut Yankee* (1927), followed by the same team's *Present Arms* (1928), in which he also performed, introducing the song "You Took Advantage of Me." By the end of the season he had staged five musicals in one year and was soon known as one of the "Big Four" group of young dance directors and show doctors (the others were Bobby Connolly, Seymour Felix, and Sammy Lee). In 1929 Berkeley was one of the first to produce, direct, and choreograph a musical, *Street Singer*. By this time sound motion pictures were beckoning all Broadway dance directors, and Berkeley followed the call, accepting a contract with Samuel Goldwyn to stage the dances for *Whoopee*, starring Eddie Cantor, who had recommended him to Goldwyn.

Whoopee (1930) used the stylistic elements that Berkeley would later expand on and use in nearly all of his films. He combined his limited dance knowledge with his fascination for military precision lines to create interesting patterns of movement and form. Although he was a novice at camerawork, he convinced Goldwyn to allow him, rather than the picture's director, to film his own numbers. Berkeley used only one camera rather than the customary three or four, stating, "My idea was to plan every shot and edit in the camera."

Overhead shots had been used in earlier motion pictures, but Berkeley made the camera travel above, in, out, and around the chorus girls and, for the first time on the screen, zoom in for individual closeups. When a mystified Goldwyn asked him why he was doing this, Berkeley replied, "Well, we've got all these beautiful girls in the picture. Why not let the public see them?" Goldwyn understood that logic and continued to promote a group of young women as the "Goldwyn Girls" in subsequent pictures.

Although movie musicals were no longer big moneymakers at the time, Berkeley continued to work on Eddie Cantor films for Goldwyn, including *The Kid from Spain* (1932) and *Roman Scandals* (1933). Since his contract allowed him to freelance, however, he accepted an offer from Darryl Zanuck at Warner Bros. to stage the musical numbers for *42nd Street* (1933), an attempt to revive interest in motion picture musicals. The experiment was an unqualified success and launched Berkeley on a fertile period with a succession of backstage musicals that sometimes starred Dick Powell and Ruby Keeler as the ingenues and the ubiquitous Toby Wing in supporting parts.

Outstanding numbers that Berkeley devised include the title song from *42nd Street*, where Keeler dances on a taxicab, a scene that evolves into the bustle of 42d Street and ends with a staircase of tilting skyscrapers. In *Gold Diggers of 1933* (1933) he illuminated patterns of chorus girls as glowing violins in the dark for "The Shadow Waltz," risked censorship with tin bathing suits that could be removed by can openers in "Pettin' in the Park," and memorably commented on the depression when Joan Blondell in the finale is surrounded by World War I soldiers who turn into the jobless in "Remember My Forgotten Man."

In most of these musicals Berkeley continued to create two types of numbers: lavish spectacles with hundreds of chorus girls, such as the famous "By a Waterfall" in *Footlight Parade* (1933) and the kaleidoscope of hundreds of Keeler look-alikes in "I Only Have Eyes for You" from *Dames* (1934); or ministory musicals, such as the comic romance and marriage of "Honeymoon Hotel" in *Footlight Parade* to the more serious "Lullaby of Broadway" in *Gold Diggers of 1935* (1935). In most of these films the musical numbers were supposed to take place on some theatrical stage, although, except in Berkeley's imagination, no stage could hold such presentations.

By the end of the 1930s Warner Bros. was no longer producing lavish musicals, and Berkeley moved to Metro-Goldwyn-Mayer (MGM), where he continued to work as both a choreographer and a director, especially on the series of Mickey Rooney–Judy Garland "Let's-put-on-a-show" musicals produced by Arthur Freed. These included *Babes in Arms* (1939), where Berkeley showcased them in an elaborate production called "God's Country"; *Strike Up the Band* (1940), where Berkeley's knowledge of military drills was given full scope in the title number; *Babes on Broadway* (1941), which ended with an elaborate vaudeville-minstrel show sequence; and *Girl Crazy* (1943), where he surrounded Rooney and Garland in a complex rodeo routine sung and danced to "I've Got Rhythm." On *Girl Crazy* Berkeley had been scheduled to be director-choreographer, as he had been on the previous Rooney-Garland movies, but, because of his strained relationship with Garland, he was removed from the picture after staging the one number.

Interspersed among these movies, Berkeley continued to show his talent for spectacle by staging the musical numbers for *Ziegfeld Girl* (1941), where tulle-and-feather-clad chorus girls emerged from the mist and paraded onto gigantic staircases in "You Stepped Out of a Dream," and Garland was surrounded by nearly two hundred exotically dressed young dancers, as well as a menagerie of animals, in "Minnie from Trinidad." This South American theme was carried even further when MGM loaned Berkeley to 20th Century-Fox for *The Gang's All Here* (1943), perhaps the pinnacle of the Berkeley style since the film combines the prerequisite chorus girls with color, lavish sets, elaborate costumes, and an idiosyncratic use of props and special effects.

After *The Gang's All Here*, Berkeley was involved in fewer and fewer productions, although MGM did hire him to direct (but not choreograph) *Take Me Out to the Ball Game* in 1949 for Gene Kelly, Frank Sinatra, and Esther Williams, and to stage the spectacular water ballets for Williams in *Million Dollar Mermaid* (1952), which included hundreds of streams of water, smoke effects, water slides, and Williams dropping fifty feet into a Ferris wheel of a hundred young swimmers. Berkeley worked again with Williams on elaborate air and water routines in *Easy to Love* (1953), filmed at Cypress Gardens, Florida, his first film without the controlled environment of a studio soundstage. His last film was *Jumbo* in 1962, also for MGM, where as "second unit director" he staged the circus sequences and large-scale musical numbers.

Berkeley did not have much luck in his personal life, having married six times: name unknown, married late 1920s, divorced 1930; Merna Kennedy, married 1934, divorced mid-1930s; Claire James, married mid-1930s, annulled that same year; Myra Steffin, married and annulled 1944; Marge Pemberton, married mid-1940s, divorced mid-1950s. After *Jumbo* Berkeley retired to Palm Desert, California, with his sixth wife, Etta Dunn Judd, whom he married in 1958. The late 1960s saw a revival of interest in his work, and he was invited to many international festivals and tributes where a new generation of moviegoers rediscovered his films; film scholars also began to write about his unique style as well as his influence on cinema technique. He also was invited back to Broadway to "supervise" the revival of *No, No, Nanette* in 1971, starring Ruby Keeler. Although the dance numbers and direction were really in the hands of others, contemporary reviews confirm that Berkeley's name helped certify the show's success. He died in Palm Springs, California.

Berkeley holds an unusual place in film history as the only nonperforming film dance director of the 1930s and 1940s who was recognized by the public and whose name could help sell a motion picture. Although not a dancer or a technically proficient choreographer (he never learned tap, for example; the tap sequences in his films were staged by assistants), he had a remarkable ability to choreograph with the camera and expand the horizon of cinema effects. The opposite of Fred Astaire, who insisted that the camera remain on the dancer's full figure, Berkeley used bodies more as objects for patterns and designs to fill the camera eye. Richard Day, the art director on *Whoopee*, told the young Berkeley that "the camera has one eye, not two. You can see a lot with two eyes but hold a hand over one and it cuts your area of vision." Berkeley stated that for the rest of his career this advice helped him stage numbers with "that one eye in mind."

• Berkeley is discussed in many standard texts on the motion picture, but more detailed analysis can be found in *The Busby*

Berkeley Book (1973), by Tony Thomas and Jim Terry, which includes many quotes from Berkeley and a film-by-film overview; *That's Dancing!* (1984), by Tony Thomas, which puts Berkeley in the context of screen dancer-choreographers such as Fred Astaire and Gene Kelly; and John Kobal's *Gotta Sing Gotta Dance* (1971; rev. ed. 1983), which includes rare photographs and interviews with former Berkeley dancers. Ethan Mordden's *The Hollywood Musical* (1981) has information on the Hollywood musical pre-Berkeley and a detailed analysis of the changes he made, especially in contrast to Astaire's concepts. Finally, Bob Dunn's *The Making of* No, No Nanette (1972) probes the final years of Berkeley's life in relation to the revival of this 1920s musical. Almost all of Berkeley's major films are available on videocassette, and laser disk versions frequently include footage of Berkeley in rehearsal or outtakes. An obituary is in the *New York Times*, 15 Mar. 1976.

FRANK W. D. RIES

BERKELEY, Frances, Lady (1634–1695?), influential figure in Virginia politics and society, was born Frances Culpeper in Kent, England, the daughter of Thomas Culpeper, a member of the Virginia Company, and Katherine St. Leger. Around 1650 she and her parents immigrated to the colony of Virginia. Members of her family played important roles in Virginia affairs both in the colony and at court. Her father was an original patentee of land in the Northern Neck of Virginia, while Alexander Culpeper, her brother, held an appointment as surveyor general of the colony (1671–1694), and Thomas Lord Culpeper, baron of Thoresway, her cousin, advised the Privy Council on colonial affairs and served as governor of Virginia (1677–1683).

While her family connections proved advantageous to Berkeley, her influence in Virginia was furthered through her successive marriages to three colonial governors. Her first marriage, to Captain Samuel Stephens, took place in 1652, when she was about eighteen. Stephens served as governor of North Carolina from 1667 until his death in 1669. Subsequently she inherited "Bolthrope," his 1,350-acre plantation, and, consistent with the terms of their antenuptial agreement, received absolute possession of the estate, which she soon sold. About six months after Stephens died, she married Sir William Berkeley, governor of Virginia from 1641 to 1652 and 1660 to 1677. The marriage agreement gave her a yearly income of estate in England worth £600. During this second marriage, Lady Frances Berkeley's power and influence in political affairs were very much in evidence.

Sir William and Lady Frances Berkeley lived at "Green Spring," the governor's manor house, where they regularly entertained the councillors, burgesses, and other notable members of Virginia's government and society. In 1676 Governor and Lady Berkeley faced their most difficult crisis when Bacon's Rebellion erupted. The trouble began when planters disagreed with Berkeley's policies toward Native Americans. Nathaniel Bacon, Jr., who with his wife, Elizabeth, had stayed with the Berkeleys at Green Spring when he first arrived in the colony, led an attack on peaceful Indians, contrary to the governor's orders. The governor sought to prevent further unsanctioned attacks, but Bacon, leader of the opposition, continued to challenge him, and what had begun as a dispute over policy was transformed into a rebellion against the governor.

Throughout this crisis in her husband's administration, Lady Frances Berkeley ardently supported him, vigorously defending his policies both to the colonists and the Crown. She wrote to Bacon, accusing him of ingratitude, and defended herself when rebels promised to see her wardrobe reduced to "canvas linen," the coarse cloth often worn by laborers. In June 1676 she traveled to England as her husband's emissary and arranged to have an account of the rebellion presented to the Crown. Her petition was successful: in 1677 she returned to Virginia accompanied by Sir Herbert Jeffreys, a royal commissioner, and 1,000 English troops. By the time she arrived in the colony, Bacon had died and the rebellion for the most part was over, but Berkeley continued to act on behalf of her husband. As the royal commissioners investigating the rebellion grew increasingly doubtful of the governor and his policies, they found a formidable enemy in Lady Berkeley. In response to their criticisms, she arranged for the "common hangman" to drive their coach home after visiting the Berkeleys. This constituted a deep insult to the commissioners, and they faulted Lady Berkeley for casting "public odium and disgrace" upon them, although she denied any involvement. Still, when one of them later entreated her to persuade the governor to pardon a condemned rebel, she agreed and was successful, proving herself to be a powerful ally when she so chose.

Sir William Berkeley returned to England and died there in 1677. Lady Frances Berkeley continued to resolutely promote the political interests she shared with the supporters and intimates of the late governor. In particular, her leadership in the "Green Spring faction" gained her the resentment of Jeffreys, who was then the lieutenant governor. Named for the gubernatorial home where she conducted their private meetings, the Green Spring faction also included Thomas Ballard, Robert Beverley, Edward Hill, and Philip Ludwell. The group unflaggingly antagonized Jeffreys and opposed his imperialist policies, which they saw as a threat to their own independence and autonomy within Virginia. In several letters Jeffreys complained about the extent of Berkeley's influence on Virginia government, noting that she continued to act as though her husband was living. When Thomas Lord Culpeper, Berkeley's cousin, arrived in Virginia to assume the governor's office in 1680, the Green Spring faction had reason to feel optimistic. Eventually, however, the leaders of the party—except for Lady Berkeley—were denounced.

By 1680 Lady Frances Berkeley, as she continued to be called, had married Philip Ludwell, who served as governor of North Carolina (1689–1693) and North and South Carolina (1693–1694). For the most part, the couple resided at Green Spring, and they had a pew in the Bruton Parish Church. Berkeley remained active in Virginia politics, entertaining, among others, Francis Lord Howard of Effingham, governor of Virginia (1683–1692). Although the governor removed her husband from office in 1687, he wrote very favorably of Berkeley.

Apparently Berkeley had no children, but she may have been pregnant during her marriage to Ludwell. In 1684, when she was forty-seven, both Effingham and William Byrd I made references to her indisposition due to pregnancy.

Berkeley was a powerful political influence in seventeenth-century Virginia. Her family connections in England and Virginia and her willingness to vigorously promote policies she supported gave her a stature and authority uncommon to English women in colonial North America. Her sharp mind, lively temperament, and fierce loyalties were a boon to her friends and political allies, although these same traits gained her harsh critics as well. The precise date and cause of Berkeley's death are unknown, but a fragment of her tombstone can be seen in Jamestown.

• Manuscript materials by and about Lady Berkeley can be found in the Coventry papers, vols. 77 and 78, Longleat House, Marquess of Bath, Warminster, Wiltshire; Cunliffe-Lister Muniments, Bradford, Yorkshire; Filmer Manuscripts, Kent Archives, Maidstone; Public Record Office, C.O. 1/34–48, C.O. 5/1371. The manuscript materials from English repositories may be consulted via the microfilm collections of the Virginia Colonial Records Project: see John T. Kneebone and Jon Kukla, eds., *A Key to Survey Reports and Microfilm of the Virginia Colonial Records Project* (2 vols., 1990). Genealogical information about Lady Frances Berkeley can be found in Virginia M. Meyer and John Frederick Dorman, eds., *Adventurers of Purse and Person, Virginia 1607–1624/25*, 3d ed. (1987), and Fairfax Harrison, "Proprietors of the Northern Neck," *Virginia Magazine of History and Biography* 33 (Oct. 1925): 333–58. For assessments of Lady Berkeley see Warren M. Billings, "Berkeley and Effingham: Who Cares?" *Virginia Magazine of History and Biography* 97 (Jan. 1989): 38–41, and Suzanne Lebsock, *"A Share of Honour": Virginia Women 1600–1945* (1984), pp. 25–26.

TERRI L. SNYDER

BERKELEY, George (12 Mar. 1685–14 Jan. 1753), philosopher, was born in Kilkenny, Ireland, the son of William Berkeley, a gentleman farmer, and, probably, Elisabeth Southerne. He entered Trinity College, Dublin, in 1700, organizing a society to study the work of Nicolas de Malebranche, René Descartes, Gottfried Wilhelm von Leibnitz, Thomas Hobbes, Sir Isaac Newton, and John Locke in 1705. He received his B.A. in 1704, his M.A. and a fellowship in 1707. His philosophy responds to Locke and Newton and the mathematical and scientific skepticism of their followers.

Berkeley's first philosophical publication, *An Essay towards a New Theory of Vision* (1709), denied that the mind sees distance by an innate geometry as Descartes and William Molyneux argued. This was a first step in attacking Locke's position that primary qualities (ex-

tension, size, place, and movement) exist in substances and are perceived as ideas by the mind even though the mind does not perceive the substance itself. (See *An Essay Concerning Human Understanding* [1690].) Berkeley's *Treatise Concerning the Principles of Human Knowledge* (1710) and *Three Dialogues between Hylas and Philonous* (1713) argue that neither Locke's primary qualities nor his "secondary" ones (color, heat, and sound—which are not in the substance but are effects produced in the perceiver) require or demonstrate the existence of a substance.

Briefly, Berkeley argued that all qualities attributed to substance are ideas that some mind perceives. If no quality can be proven to exist in the substance rather than in mind, then substance or matter becomes an unnecessary hypothesis; all phenomena are ideas. Berkeley also denied that anyone can coherently describe how a substance or sensation can become an idea. Thus he made his famous declaration that there exist only perceiving spirits and the passive perceived or, "existence is to be perceived or to perceive" (*esse* is *percipi* or *percipere*). What humans do not perceive does not cease to exist, because God's omniscient perception of things keeps it in being.

Berkeley meant to fight skepticism and preserve faith in the common sense of perceptions by undermining Locke's notion of a "true" substance that senses cannot perceive. If Locke's secondary qualities— heat, color, and sound—were only perceptions of the mind, then why should Locke's primary qualities— figure, motion, and rest—adhere in an unknowable substance rather than be merely further products of the perceiving mind? By placing in the mind what common sense is sure of, an object's solidity and extension, Berkeley hoped to achieve a similar certainty for heat, cold, etc. But to anyone with less faith in a God who thinks the world into being he seemed to allow for complete relativism of perception. Although usually called an idealist, Berkeley titled his ideas "the immaterialist hypothesis." The nonintuitive nature of his ideas kept them from cordial reception in his day, but they anticipated aspects of semiotics and phenomenology. His attacks on Newton's ideas of absolute space, time, and motion existing apart from each other and from objects fit well with modern science.

At Trinity Berkeley was made a sublecturer in 1710 and served as junior dean in 1710–1711 and junior Greek lecturer in 1712. His sermon *Passive Obedience* (1712) brought him under temporary suspicion of Jacobitism. In 1713 Berkeley journeyed to London, becoming familiar with Joseph Addison and Sir Richard Steele, Alexander Pope, John Arbuthnot, and Jonathan Swift, who secured his appointment as Lord Peterborough's chaplain. From 1716 to 1720 he traveled Europe as tutor to George Ashe, writing a description of the explosion of Mount Vesuvius that appeared in *Philosophical Transactions* in 1717. He wrote his *Essay towards Preventing the Ruine of Great Britain* after seeing the speculative fever of the South Sea Bubble when he returned to London in 1720. *De motu* attacked both Newton and Leibnitz. Berkeley continued to rise at Trinity: he was made senior fellow in 1717, was granted a B.D. and a D.D., was made divinity and senior Greek lecturer in 1721, and was appointed Hebrew lecturer and senior proctor in 1722. His financial situation became more secure in 1723, when Hester Vanhomrigh (Swift's Vanessa) left him half her estate.

At the same time his abiding social concern led him to project a college in the Bermudas to educate ministers from among the colonials and the black and native populations. He received letters patent from the king and subscriptions of £5,000. Even Parliament appropriated £20,000. In 1728 Berkeley married Anne Forster and sailed to Newport, Rhode Island, buying a farm, "Whitehall," where his son was born and a daughter who died shortly after. Four of his children survived infancy. His presence as a dean of the Anglican church and his regular sermons from Trinity Cathedral were well received, even in an anabaptist center like Providence, Rhode Island. Berkeley helped from a "society for the promotion of Knowledge and Virtue" and hosted the twice-yearly meeting of missionaries from the Society for the Propagation of the Gospel. He befriended Samuel Johnson, later his greatest philosophic adherent and president of King's College (today Columbia University). Interesting himself in slavery, Berkeley not only wrote on the treatment of slaves in the colonies but also bought three slaves. He thought his St. Paul's College might rescue historic Christianity and purify and preserve Western civilization. "Verses on the Prospect of Planting Arts and Learning in America" (written in 1726, published in 1752) make it clear that he had little hope for ministers whom "Europe breeds in her decay" but hoped to see in the New World "another golden Age / The rise of Empire and of Arts." When convinced that his college would never be funded, since the appropriated funds were misdirected under George II, Berkeley returned to London in 1731, donating his farm and almost a thousand books to Yale.

In Providence he had written a book that soon brought him back into the English public eye. *Alciphron; or, The Minute Philosopher* (1732) attacked Bernard Mandeville's blurring of virtue and vice in *The Fable of the Bees* (1714) and provoked Mandeville's heated response, *A Letter to Dion* (1732). In his *Theory of Vision; or, Visual Language, Vindicated and Explained* (1733) Berkeley clarified his conviction that the ideas we have of things, while merely ideas, are true because God has caused certain ideas to be associated with what we perceive; God could as easily have used another arbitrary system of ideal "signs" to denote objects. *The Analyst; or, A Discourse Addressed to an Infidel Mathematician* (1734) combated Newton's ideas. Berkeley's faith, brilliance, and friends won him appointment as bishop of Cloyne from 1734 to his life's end. He personally supervised the education of his children. At Cloyne his interest in the poor continued in *A Discourse Addressed to the Magistrates* (1738); in the practical maxims of *The Querist* (1735–1737); and in regular monetary distributions.

His fascination with the medicinal virtues of tar-water, a nostrum encountered in America, resulted in letters to Thomas Prior (1744; 1747) and "further Thoughts" on it in his *Miscellany* (1752). But *Sirus: A Chain of Philosophical Reflexions and Inquiries concerning the Virtues of Tar-water* (1744) makes the miraculous water part of a chain of being that unites heaven and earth.

Losing both his son William and his lifelong friend Prior in 1751 darkened Berkeley's life; he retired to London in August 1752, dying there five months later. Known as a man of compelling charm, purity, and goodness, Berkeley's life of useful actions contrasts curiously with his popular image as impractical and against common sense.

• The Berkeley papers are in the library of the British Museum, and some correspondence is in the Public Records Office, London. For Berkeley's works not covered in the text, see Arthur Ashton Luce and Thomas E. Jessop, eds., *The Works of George Berkeley, Bishop of Cloyne* (9 vols., 1948–1957, 1964); and his commonplace book from 1707 to 1710, *Philosophical Commentaries*, either in Alexander C. Fraser's edition (1871) or Luce's (1944). A full biography is Luce, *The Life of George Berkeley, Bishop of Cloyne* (1992). Treatments of his stay in America are A. Brayton, *George Berkeley in Newport* (1954), and Edwin Gaustad, *George Berkeley in America* (1979). Examinations of his philosophy worth consulting are George Pitcher, ed., *The Philosophy of George Berkeley* (15 vols., 1988–1989); David Berman, *George Berkeley: Idealism and the Man* (1994); and Walter Creery, ed., *George Berkeley: Critical Assessments* (1991).

HENRY RUSSELL

BERKELEY, William (3 July 1606–9 July 1677), royal governor and captain general of Virginia, was born in or near London, the son of Sir Maurice Berkeley, a well-connected gentleman of distinguished family. He was the brother of John, first Baron Berkeley of Stratton, a colonial proprietary. He entered Queen's College, Oxford, in February 1623 and received his B.A. in July 1624 from St. Edmund Hall, Oxford. Five years later, he completed his M.A. at Merton College, Oxford. A charming, intelligent, well-connected gentleman, Berkeley became a favorite of King Charles I and was created a member of the Privy Chamber. In 1632 he was appointed a Commissioner of Canadian affairs and executed the office with distinction. He authored a number of notable plays, among them *The Lost Lady, a Tragi-Comedy*, published in 1638. In July 1639 the king knighted him and on 9 August 1641 commissioned him governor and captain general of Virginia, a position that he retained except for brief interruptions until shortly before his death.

When Berkeley arrived in Virginia the following year, he unified the colony's divided political life by developing a political alliance with aristocratic Virginians. This coterie remained in power for the rest of Berkeley's administration, except for the interruption caused by Oliver Cromwell's rule in the 1650s. During his early administration, Berkeley convinced Virginians that he had their best interests at heart, working assiduously for them in a number of ways. He encouraged crop diversification, silk growing, exploration of the western reaches of Virginia's territory, and the devolution of power to the General Assembly from the Council. He also proved his worth as a military leader. In April 1644 Indians of the Powhatan Confederation launched a devastating military assault in Virginia, killing 500 of the 8,000 settlers in a single, coordinated campaign. Berkeley began to rally the colonists for a powerful militia counteroffensive but suddenly took ship for England, ostensibly to solicit aid for his beleaguered colony. Actually he wished to join the side of King Charles I in the English Civil War. After fighting with the royal armies for some months, he returned to Virginia, where in 1646 he commanded a daring militia expedition that captured Opechancanough, the Indian leader, and ended the frontier war. For this exploit, Berkeley gained the admiration of Virginians.

When the English Civil War had commenced in 1642, Berkeley had vehemently denounced Parliament's opposition to King Charles I and prevailed upon the General Assembly to do likewise. He was particularly outraged when the Roundheads executed the king in 1649, and he offered asylum in Virginia to defeated royalist gentlemen. He refused to submit voluntarily to parliamentary authority, and when Cromwell dispatched a small fleet against him, he organized military resistance. Compelled to capitulate and resign his commission, he nevertheless was granted the right to live peacefully on his Virginia plantation, "Green Spring," during the Interregnum. Upon the ascension of Charles II to the English throne in 1660, Berkeley was reappointed governor, and although the king meditated Berkeley's dismissal in 1665, nothing came of it. Probably the king did not act because of the outbreak of the Anglo-Dutch wars in that year, which necessitated Berkeley's remaining in Virginia to organize the colony's defenses. Already Berkeley had regularized and systematized the Virginia militia system, and in 1667 he put together a scratch force of merchant ships to fend off a Dutch war fleet. Six years later, he more easily repulsed a smaller Dutch squadron. In both instances, he ordered militiamen to patrol Virginia's shores and man coastal batteries to drive off landing parties. Having proved his abilities as an administrator and a brave soldier, Sir William Berkeley now stood high in the esteem of Virginians, described as "just in peace, diligent and valiant in war." About 1670 he married Frances Culpeper Stephens. They had no children.

As Berkeley aged, he became more inflexible in his attitudes. Already he had shown a lack of toleration in religion, zealously persecuting both Puritans and Quakers. Also, he had manifested unfriendliness toward education and the printing press, declaring that "learning has brought disobedience, and heresy, and sects into the world, and printing has divulged these and other libels." But his popularity among Virginians began to wane only in the 1670s, when his political control came to be perceived as too centralized and oppressive. Other problems also arose for Virginians, such as a depressed tobacco market and restraints on trade imposed by the Navigation Acts. When in 1675 and 1676, Berkeley failed to respond adequately to Indian raids on Virginia's frontiers, angry colonists led by Nathaniel Bacon began to fight the Indians on their own. Finally, after provocations by both Berkeley and Bacon, a fairly localized mutiny exploded into full-scale civil war known as Bacon's Rebellion. In August 1676 Berkeley abandoned Jamestown to Bacon's forces and fled to the Eastern Shore. From there he commandeered merchant vessels, returned in September to Jamestown, and was expelled once more. Only after Bacon died on 26 October 1676 did Berkeley negotiate an end to the uprising and restore order. Immediately, he launched a series of reprisals, including hangings and property confiscations, that created additional dissensions. Moreover, he refused to cooperate with a royal commission sent to investigate the Virginia troubles and acceded to its order to return to England only when his health was broken. He died in London before he could present his case to the king and was buried at Twickenham.

• Berkeley's *A Discourse and View of Virginia* (1663) is a useful source. Also useful are *Calendar of State Papers, Colonial Series, America and West Indies, 1675–1676* (1893) and William Waller Hening, *The Statutes at Large, Being a Collection of All the Laws of Virginia*, vol. 2 (1823). A good, short biographical sketch is Marcia Brownell Bready, "A Cavalier in Virginia—The Right Hon. Sir William Berkeley, His Majesty's Governor," *William and Mary Quarterly*, 1st ser., 18 (1909): 115–29. Jane D. Carson, "Sir William Berkeley, Governor of Virginia: A Study in Colonial Policy" (Ph.D. diss., Univ. of Virginia, 1951), and Percy Scott Flippen, *The Royal Government in Virginia, 1624–1775* (1919), analyze Berkeley's gubernatorial administration. Good accounts of Bacon's Rebellion are Mary Newton Stanard, *The Story of Bacon's Rebellion* (1907); Thomas J. Wertenbaker, *Torchbearer of the Revolution: The Story of Bacon's Rebellion and Its Leader* (1940); and Wilcomb E. Washburn, *The Governor and the Rebel: A History of Bacon's Rebellion in Virginia* (1958). Thomas J. Wertenbaker, *Virginia under the Stuarts, 1607–1688* (1914); Matthew Page Andrews, *Virginia the Old Dominion* (1937); Wesley Frank Craven, *The Southern Colonies in the Seventeenth Century, 1607–1689* (1949); Richard L. Morton, *Colonial Virginia*, vol. 1 (1960); Wesley Frank Craven, *The Colonies in Transition, 1660–1713* (1968); Edmund S. Morgan, *American Slavery, American Freedom: The Ordeal of Colonial Virginia* (1975); and Stephen Saunders Webb, *1676: The End of American Independence* (1984), provide useful background information.

PAUL DAVID NELSON

BERKENMEYER, Wilhelm Christoph (7 Apr. 1687–c. 10 Oct. 1751), colonial Lutheran minister, was born in Bodenteich, Germany, the son of Georg Berkenmeyer, a minister, and Anna Engel Rühden Pöppelbaum. His mother died eighteen months later, and his father married again in 1690. In 1708, the year after his father's death, Berkenmeyer entered the Protestant University at Altdorf, a center of Lutheran orthodoxy, from which he graduated in 1712. Pastoral candidates exceeded vacancies throughout Germany, and like many candidates, he found work as a children's tutor.

In November 1722 he was appointed lay chaplain at the Hamburg city prison. In 1725 he accepted a call from the Amsterdam consistory to become pastor of the Dutch Lutheran churches in New York and New Jersey, even though he did not yet know the language. He was ordained on 25 May in Amsterdam.

Following his arrival in New York in September, Berkenmeyer was accepted by the New York, Albany, and Hackensack congregations. He received an additional call the next year from six German congregations in the Hudson Valley. His initial challenges included a lack of hymnals and Bibles and dilapidated buildings in both New York and Albany. The New York congregation rebuilt in 1729, but Albany's congregation met at the Anglican church and in private homes until 1742. In 1727 Berkenmeyer married Benigna Sibylla Harrsch, daughter of the German pastor Josua Kocherthal (who had changed his name). The Berkenmeyers had no children.

The Hamburg ministerium sent additional clergy, and Berkenmeyer, as senior pastor, grouped congregations into parishes for them and acted as superintendent. He turned over the southern congregations to Michael Christian Knoll in 1732, and Berkenmeyer settled in Loonenburg (now Athens), from which he also ministered to Dutch congregations in Albany and Normanskill (Guilderland) and German congregations in the middle Hudson Valley. He also visited scattered German settlements from Sheffield, Massachusetts, to Herkimer on the western Mohawk. Johann August Wolf came in 1735 to the Raritan region in New Jersey, Peter Nicholas Sommer came in 1743 to the Schoharie and Mohawk valleys, and Johannes Christophorus Hartwig came in 1746 to the middle Hudson. However, unlawfully ordained and lay preachers interjected themselves into some of the widely spaced congregations, plaguing Berkenmeyer throughout his ministry.

Berkenmeyer believed that consistency in doctrine and in liturgy were essential, and he therefore prepared a set of church orders based upon those of the Amsterdam consistory but adapted to the colonial situation. The document was accepted in 1735 by the consistories at New York, Hackensack, and Albany and by delegates from Raritan. Pastors Knoll and Wolf signed it then, Sommer did later, and even the pietist Hartwig eventually did. It is orthodox, conservative, and formal. Sermons and teaching are to be based on the Bible and the Lutheran symbolic books, which include the Augsburg Confession and Martin Luther's catechisms. Only pastors from orthodox schools are to be called. Services should include a formal liturgy and use the Amsterdam prayer book of 1689. For consistency's sake Berkenmeyer later opposed the introduction into German congregations of a different, Rhineland set of church orders.

Berkenmeyer's oversight was not appreciated by everyone, and some laity referred to him and his ally Knoll as "the two popes." In 1735 Berkenmeyer organized a "classical assembly" of clergy and outside laity, which negotiated a settlement between Wolf and his congregation at Raritan, who had been at odds from Wolf's first month. However, agitation reoccurred within weeks and continued for a decade. Finally, Berkenmeyer agreed to let Knoll and Pennsylvania ministers Henry Melchior Mühlenberg and Tobias Wagner serve as arbitrators. Mühlenberg forced Wolf to resign, giving the victory to the congregation's agitators, and Berkenmeyer wrote to Mühlenberg in great anger. They were strongly opinionated men from different schools of thought. Berkenmeyer opposed pietism in any form, while Mühlenberg thought Berkenmeyer was "an old guardian and champion of liturgical forms and opponent of the power of godliness." When Hartwig joined Mühlenberg and other pietists in forming the Pennsylvania Ministerium, Berkenmeyer accused him of Moravian tendencies and denounced him in four pamphlets. He then led a synod of laity and pastors, including Knoll and Sommer, that investigated Hartwig's teachings, but the synod reached no conclusion.

Later writers have accused Berkenmeyer of not allowing a voice to laity, but this is not supported by the evidence of consistory minutes and his dealings with recalcitrant congregations. Some have also claimed erroneously that orthodoxy disappeared with the ascendance of Mühlenberg's pietism, that the classical assembly of 1735 was an unsuccessful attempt to create a perpetual synod, and that Berkenmeyer was Sommer's father-in-law.

Berkenmeyer was a voice of orthodox Lutheranism. He was unable to bind all American Lutherans to confessional doctrine, one service book, and one form of worship, but these were goals that could not be achieved, then or since. His protocols and his correspondence with church officials in Europe provide a record of the intellectual, spiritual, and material state of the church in colonial society but were long unpublished. His sentences in German are often so complex that even he sometimes loses the thread, while the difficulty of his Dutch is compounded by frequent Germanisms.

Berkenmeyer lived modestly. His Loonenburg congregation often fell short in paying his salary, and his principles did not allow him to use other church funds to make up the difference or to take individuals to secular courts over unfulfilled pledges. He surrounded himself with books, his own, the Loonenburg congregation's library, and Kocherthal's collection on loan from the church in New York. In all he housed over 500 volumes, many containing two or more works, that encompassed a wide range of subjects. One of his great disappointments was his inability to establish a school at Loonenburg for lack of a teacher. Berkenmeyer died in Loonenburg. In his will he recited his dedication to Scripture, to the ecumenical creeds, and to the symbolic books of Lutheranism.

• Berkenmeyer's records of official activities are in Simon Hart and Harry J. Kreider, trans., *Protocol of the Lutheran Church in New York City, 1702–1750* and John P. Dern, ed., *The Albany Protocol . . . 1731–1750*, trans. Hart and Sibrandina Geertruid Hart-Runeman (1971). A different but contemporary view of events is in Theodore G. Tappert and John W. Doberstein, trans., *The Journals of Henry Melchior Mühlenberg* (1942). Berkenmeyer's correspondence with the Amsterdam consistory is in A. J. F. van Laer, trans., *The Lutheran Church in New York. 1649–1772* (1946). His correspondence with the Hamburg ministerium is in Hart and Kreider, trans., *Lutheran Church in New York and New Jersey, 1722–1760* (1962). He attacked the vagabond preacher, Johann Bernhard van Dieren, in *Getrouwe Herder- en Wachter-Stem Aan de Hoog- en Neder-Duitsche Lutheriaanen in dese Gewesten* (True shepherd and watchman's voice to the German and Dutch Lutherans in these regions) (1728), and accused Hartwig of Moravian tendencies in *Geheime unt öffentliche Ansprache . . . an Herren Johann Christopher Hartwick* (Private and public address . . . about Mr. Johann Christopher Hartwick) (1749) and in *Consilium in Arena oder Mitleidens volle Antwort aufdas bitt-schreiben der hoch-teutsch luthrischen Gemeinde im Camp* (Resolved after deliberation; or compassion's full answer on this written petition of the German Lutheran congregation in the Camp) (1749?). Berkenmeyer's service in Albany is discussed in Henry H. Heins, *Swan of Albany* (1976) and his broader career in Kreider, *Lutheranism in Colonial New York* (1942). Wittenberg University's Thomas Library in Springfield, Ohio, has 226 books from his library, containing 434 works.

PETER R. CHRISTOPH

BERKHOF, Louis (13 Oct. 1873–19 May 1957), theologian, was born in Emmen, in the province of Drenthe, the Netherlands, to Jan Berkhof and Geesje ter Poorten, bakers by trade, though Jan later became a factory worker. The family moved to the United States in 1882, the peak of Dutch-American migration, and settled in Grand Rapids, Michigan, the group's emerging center. Sharing the deep Calvinistic piety of his parents, Berkhof took both his college and seminary education (1893–1900) at the Theological School of the Christian Reformed Church (later renamed Calvin Theological Seminary) in Grand Rapids. He earned a B.D. degree at Princeton Theological Seminary (1902–1904) and, after serving two Christian Reformed congregations in the Grand Rapids area, was named professor of biblical theology at the Calvin Theological Seminary in 1906. There he spent the rest of his career, switching to his preferred field of systematic theology in 1926 and serving as the seminary's president from 1931 until his retirement in 1944.

Berkhof was a staunch conservative in theological matters, devoted to the systematic, rational presentation of traditional Reformed doctrine as it had been developed in seventeenth-century Europe and adapted in the nineteenth-century Netherlands. His scholarly mentors were Geerhardus Vos, also a Christian Reformed immigrant who taught at Princeton, and Herman Bavinck, professor at the conservative Calvinists' Kampen Theological Seminary and Free University of Amsterdam in the Netherlands. Bavinck's Dutch-language theological studies provided the organization and much of the substance for Berkhof's chief work, the *Systematic Theology* of 1941 (originally published as *Reformed Dogmatics* in 1932).

Berkhof's aim in these volumes was not originality, but the concise, logical exposition of what he believed to be a fixed system of truth. He took pains to differentiate his own position from those that he thought deviated from the classic formulation, especially and emphatically those of Protestant liberalism. His talent for clear, precise condensation made *Systematic Theology* a standard textbook at conservative Reformed and evangelical seminaries in North America and the British Isles. It also became a definitive English-language reference in Europe and, in translation, has been used by a variety of evangelical Protestant institutions in Spain, Portugal, Japan, Korea, and China.

Berkhof had a pronounced influence in maintaining Reformed traditionalism in his own denomination. He taught two generations of Christian Reformed clergy and wrote voluminously in church magazines. From 1917 to 1925, he took a leading role in the denomination's theological wars against Fundamentalist dispensational premillennialism, liberal biblical criticism, and "hyper-Calvinist" denials of common grace. These battles concluded with Berkhof's traditional Reformed position triumphant and his theological authority unrivaled within the denomination. Before World War I Berkhof also published extensively on social and cultural issues, elaborating the practical application of Calvinistic principles for education, family and gender roles, and labor-management relations. In 1920–1921 he was honored with the Stone Lectureship at Princeton Seminary.

By all accounts Berkhof was a genial, reserved, and noncombative personality, highly disciplined and efficient in all his ways. He regularly led Bible studies for laity and raised six children with his two wives. In 1900 he married Reka Dijkhuis, who died in 1928, and he married Dena Joldersma in 1933. Berkhof died at Grand Rapids within a month of the centennial anniversary of the denomination whose character he, as much as anyone, defined and preserved.

• Berkhof's papers are in the archives of the Christian Reformed Church at Calvin College, Grand Rapids, Mich. His other significant works include *The Church and Social Problems* (1913); *The Christian Laborer in the Industrial Struggle* (1916); *Vicarious Atonement through Christ* (1936); *History of Christian Doctrines* (1937); *Aspects of Liberalism* (1951); and *The Kingdom of God* (1951). The best biographical sketch is Henry Zwaanstra, "Louis Berkhof," in *Reformed Theology in America: A History of Its Modern Development*, ed. David F. Wells (1985).

JAMES D. BRATT

BERKMAN, Alexander (21 Nov. 1870–28 June 1936), anarchist and political author, was born Ovsei Osipovich Berkman in Vilnius, Lithuania, part of the Russian Empire, the son of Joseph Schmidt Berkman and Yetta Natanson. His father was a wealthy leather wholesaler for the shoe industry in St. Petersburg. His mother was the older sister of Maxim Natanson, a leader of the People's Will terrorist organization, responsible for the assassination of Czar Alexander II in 1881. Berkman remained intellectually favorable to the radical political agendas of Russian Nihilist groups throughout his life. He admired those men and women who sacrificed their lives to the principle of equality for all.

The business connections of Berkman's father allowed the family to live outside the Jewish Pale Settlements legally. After the death of Joseph Berkman in 1882, however, the family was forced to leave St. Petersburg because of religious and judicial intolerance. They moved to a maternal uncle's house in Kovno, Lithuania, where Berkman attended university. His mother's death in 1886 freed Berkman from familial responsibilities and Russia. Two years later he went to Berlin, where his brother Maxim could legally attend university, then on to the United States.

Berkman read and discussed the Jeffersonian America ideas of freedom and democracy as a youth. In *Prison Memoirs of an Anarchist* (1912), Berkman wrote that at the time he believed America was "the land of noble achievement" and "the very realization of my youthful dreams" (p. 23). He arrived in New York City during February 1888, three months after the Chicago Haymarket Riot trial and executions of the four anarchists. Berkman realized that the idealized America of his dreams did not exist. He became part of the anarchist movement, joining with other first-generation immigrants, galvanized by the Chicago incidents. It was through political activities and associations that he met fellow immigrant Emma Goldman. Their shared belief in the innocence of the Haymarket anarchists was the basis for a lifelong political and personal relationship.

Berkman became a follower of the political ideas articulated by Johann Most and Joseph Puekert, German immigrants who influenced American anarchism after the Haymarket incident. As with many young idealists, Berkman felt no sacrifice was too great for the cause. He served the revolution against the state in 1892, when the Homestead, Pennsylvania, unionized steelworkers were in dispute with the Carnegie Steel Corporation over pay and union recognition to bargain. Henry Clay Frick, general manager of the Homestead plant and junior partner of Andrew Carnegie, closed the plant and locked out the workers. Frick's subsequent use of Pinkerton agents to break the strike led to armed combat within the town. Frightened, Frick asked the governor to send the state militia. Berkman's group saw this as an attempt to crush workers' rights and decided Frick must be assassinated. Because of a shortage of funds, Berkman went to Homestead alone to carry out the deed. He had one dollar in his pocket and was armed with a secondhand gun, which had been purchased for him by Emma Goldman with borrowed money. On 23 July 1892 he strode into Frick's office and fired the revolver several times, wounding Frick in the neck. After an employee wrestled him to the ground, Berkman pulled out a knife and stabbed Frick in the leg.

The resulting trial was an easy exercise for the state, since the accused never denied the charges. Berkman acted as his own counsel, believing that his action was aimed at all oppressors and therefore did not need a traditional legal defense. The state used professional witnesses, who sensationalized the anarchist aspect of the case. The arresting charge for attempted murder was expanded to three charges by the judge during the trial. These resulted in a 22-year prison sentence, of which Berkman served fourteen years. He spent ten years in solitary confinement because prison officials feared an anarchist would incite others against authority. Goldman wrote him during this time about the movement and its activities while maintaining the friendship that was a cornerstone of his life.

Berkman returned to New York in 1906 a changed man. The youthful idealism that led to an act of violence was replaced by a mature certainty that anarchism is the natural state of mankind. At this point he repudiated violence as a means to social evolution. He lectured and wrote about politics, life experiences, and injustices from an anarchist perspective. Berkman edited Goldman's *Mother Earth* from 1908 to 1915, using the journal as a forum to comment on contemporary political injustices, including the Los Angeles trial of the McNamara brothers in 1911, the Ludlow Massacre of 1913, Big Bill Haywood's ejection from the Socialist party in 1913, and Margaret Sanger's birth control campaign. He participated in anarchist groups on New York's Lower East Side, which after 1912 received the proceeds from his prison memoirs to further the cause.

During the summer of 1914 Berkman led an attack on the Tarrytown home of John D. Rockefeller over the right of free speech for labor. He was charged with inciting a riot and threatened with another prison sentence. Although the charges were dropped, Berkman remained under police surveillance. The anarchist movement decided that Berkman should lead a national lecture tour the following year in order to keep police scrutiny at a minimum. After meeting a group of enthusiastic anarcho-syndicalists in California, he established the revolutionary labor newspaper *The Blast* in San Francisco. This was another vehicle to fight other anarchist causes and U.S. involvement in World War I. Berkman was soon embroiled in controversy again when on 22 July 1916 a bomb exploded at a preparedness parade in San Francisco. Thomas Mooney, a known socialist labor agitator, was arrested. Berkman wrote editorials in Mooney's defense and toured the country enlisting union aid, even though Mooney was not an anarchist at the time. Although Berkman had returned to New York before the trial, he was implicated during the proceedings. The governor of California sought his extradition. International outcries generated by the case led to a retraction of the extradition order and a commutation of Mooney's death sentence to life in prison.

The entrance of the United States into World War I in 1917 led Berkman and Goldman to found the No-Conscription League. Both were charged with antigovernment agitation; they were found guilty, sentenced to two years' federal imprisonment, and fined $10,000. While they were incarcerated, the Bolshevik

Revolution erupted, leading to a "red scare" in America. Attorney General Alexander M. Palmer built the case for Berkman's deportation. Interviewed by government investigators, Berkman stated he recognized no government and believed, as an anarchist, he was a citizen of the world. Berkman and Goldman were deported, along with 246 men and 3 women, for political views in December 1919. Their destination was Bolshevik Russia.

Shortly after his arrival in January 1920, Berkman and other non-Bolsheviks were devastated by the lack of positive government response to differing political ideas and methods. During his two years in Russia Berkman kept a diary that would be published as *The Bolshevik Myth* in 1925. After the Kronstadt Rebellion in 1921 and the brutal manner in which Lenin's government dealt with dissidents, Berkman felt politically disillusioned. He left Russia for Stockholm, Berlin, and finally Nice. He wrote about the problems and contradictions within Russia for European journals. During his 1922 to 1924 stay in Berlin Berkman met Emmy Eckstein, who remained with him until his death. Berkman neither married nor had children.

During the last years of his life, his correspondence was full of self-doubt about a life lived for a single cause. Berkman died at home in Nice, France, by his own hand. The pain from his prostate cancer had become unbearable. An anarchist to the end, Berkman took his own life rather than be a burden to society and his friends.

Berkman lived his life as a citizen of the world. He believed that it was each individual's moral obligation to make it better. As a political writer and theorist he contributed to the social dialogue of his day, challenging governments and their very existence, regardless of personal cost.

• Berkman's papers, letters, and unpublished manuscripts are in Amsterdam at the International Institute of Social History. His published works include *What Is Communist Anarchism?* (1929), better known as *ABC of Anarchism*. The following articles by Berkman were written after he left Russia and were published in the German journal *Der Syndikalist* in 1922: "The Russian Tragedy," "The Russian Revolution and the Communist Party," and "The Kronstadt Rebellion." The best secondary works on the subject are Richard Drinnon, *Rebel in Paradise: A Biography of Emma Goldman* (1961); Emma Goldman, *Living My Life* (1931), a two-volume study with a great deal of information about and insight into Berkman's life; and Gene Fellner, *Life of an Anarchist: The Alexander Berkman Reader* (1992). An obituary is in the *New York Times*, 2 July 1936.

LINNEA GOODWIN BURWOOD

BERKNER, Lloyd Viel (1 Feb. 1905–4 June 1967), engineer, was born in Milwaukee, Wisconsin, the son of Henry Frank Berkner and Alma Julia Viel. Berkner and his two brothers were raised in the small towns of Perth, North Dakota, and Sleepy Eye, Minnesota. Berkner enrolled in a radio operator's school and served aboard ship for one year after completing his high school studies. He then entered the University of Minnesota as an electrical engineering student, receiving a B.S. in 1927 as well as a commission as an aviator in the U.S. Naval Reserve. He later took some graduate courses in physics at Minnesota and at George Washington University but earned no graduate degree. In 1928 he married Lillian Frances Fulks; they had two children.

After working briefly for the U.S. Bureau of Lighthouses installing radio navigation equipment, in 1928 Berkner joined the U.S. National Bureau of Standards (NBS), Radio Division, in Washington, D.C. Among his other duties there, he assisted Amelia Earhart in planning her first transatlantic flight. Also, on loan from the NBS, he participated in Richard Byrd's first antarctic expedition (1928–1930) as a radio operator. Berkner and many others were released from NBS in 1933 because of the economic depression, but during his years there he contributed to the development of ionospheric radio instrumentation and wrote several papers on ionospheric radio propagation, including, in 1933, the first revelations of the existence of the F1 region of ionization in the ionosphere. Berkner's assertion that he and his colleagues had first discovered and published material on the F1 ionosphere region resulted in a confrontation with the noted English radio physicist Edward V. Appleton (Nobel prizewinner for physics in 1947), who claimed that he had found it first.

In 1933 Berkner joined the staff of the Carnegie Institution of Washington's (CIW) Department of Terrestrial Magnetism (DTM), which had conducted pioneering work in radio studies and geomagnetism. The DTM would be Berkner's major employer for the remainder of his active scientific career, and he would become a protégé of Vannevar Bush, CIW president. Berkner modified and extended the automatic ionospheric radio sounding equipment used previously at the NBS and DTM and installed these sounders in Washington, D.C.; Huancayo, Peru; Watheroo, Western Australia; and Fairbanks, Alaska. Data from these radio sounding stations allowed the preparation of predictive charts for long-distance radio operating frequencies. Thus by the outbreak of World War II, most Allied forces' radio prediction data were being provided from stations established by Berkner and the DTM.

Berkner participated in the radar proximity fuse project at the Johns Hopkins University Applied Physics Laboratory, led by his former DTM chief, physicist Merle A. Tuve. Berkner's administrative talents came to the fore during World War II in the U.S. Navy, where he first headed the Radar Section (1941–1943), then the entire Electronic Materiel Division (1943–1945), of the Bureau of Aeronautics. Berkner supervised the development and introduction of important techniques to U.S. Navy aviation, including anti-kamikaze ship radar defense systems, electronic navigation and bombing, VHF radio, and other systems. During his naval reserve career, Berkner rose from second-class seaman to rear admiral and senior officer.

Immediately after World War II, Berkner served as executive secretary to Vannevar Bush on the U.S. military Joint Research and Development Board and later advised both the Defense Department and the Department of State on matters of science and military policy, including the formation of the North Atlantic Treaty Organization (NATO). Berkner saw science now as a major force in society, integrally involved with national policy, and he believed that America's scientists could and should contribute to the national need, including defense work. In 1946 the Associated Universities Incorporated (AUI) was established as the modern university consortium, and in January 1951 Berkner was named as AUI president. His duties included managing the Brookhaven National (nuclear physics) Laboratory.

Given his background in radio engineering, electronics, and geophysics, it is not surprising that Berkner pushed for U.S. expansion into the new field of radio astronomy. The United States, ironically, had pioneered this field in the 1930s, but postwar successes in this country had been achieved largely by British, Dutch, and Australian scientists. Berkner realized that tremendous technical applications would result from the associated research into antennas, data collection and display devices, and electrical circuit theory and electronics needed to advance work in radio astronomy. In 1954 he organized a large committee of noted American astronomers and physicists to plan a national radio astronomy facility. Berkner argued that radio astronomy needed large-scale research facilities comparable to those that had been constructed for nuclear physics research. His old chief and colleague Merle Tuve, believing that scientists should do pure research, and usually on a smaller scale and organized around university laboratories, was opposed to this. After two years of planning and controversy, the National Science Board awarded Berkner's AUI a contract to establish and operate a national radio astronomy facility.

Berkner was one of the most powerful scientific advisers during the administrations of Dwight D. Eisenhower. He served on the president's Science Advisory Committee and led the panel that envisioned Project Vela for the monitoring of nuclear tests on land and in the air and space. In 1950 he had proposed the idea of a third International Polar Year to be modeled on the first (1882–1883) and second (1932–1933). This idea developed into the International Geophysical Year (1957–1958) (IGY), the most important international cooperative effort in geophysics in the twentieth century. In addition to serving as vice president of the operating committee of the IGY, he directly supervised the largest U.S. IGY program, on rockets and satellites. He also organized the Space Science Board of the U.S. National Academy of Sciences and was its chairman, and he worked on the planning of the National Aeronautics and Space Administration (NASA).

The recipient of many honorary degrees, Berkner was the president of several national and international scientific and engineering societies as well as a member and treasurer of the U.S. National Academy of Sciences. In 1960 he became the first president of the Graduate Research Center of the Southwest, in Dallas, Texas, serving in that post until he suffered a heart attack in 1965. He died two years later in Dallas.

• The Berkner papers are in the Manuscript Division of the Library of Congress in Washington, D.C. Berkner coedited two books, *Manual on Rockets and Satellites*, vol. 6 of *Annals of IGY* (1958), and *Science in Space* (1961). He also wrote *The Scientific Age* (1964). Some of Berkner's scientific articles are abstracted in Laurence A. Manning, *Bibliography of the Ionosphere: An Annotated Survey through 1960* (1962). For articles concerning Berkner's life and career, see Walter Sullivan, "Profile of Lloyd V. Berkner," *ICSU Review* 3 (1961): 208–11, and Allan A. Needell, "Lloyd Berkner, Merle Tuve, and the Federal Role in Radio Astronomy," *Osiris*, 2d ser., 3 (1987): 261–88. An obituary is in the *New York Times*, 5 June 1967.

C. STEWART GILLMOR

BERKSON, Isaac Baer (23 Dec. 1881–10 Mar. 1975), educational philosopher, was born Isadore Berkson in Brooklyn, New York, the son of Henry Berkson, a merchant, and Jennie Berkman. He attended the City College of New York (1908–1912), where he received a B.A. in liberal arts, Greek, and Latin; and Columbia University and Teachers College (1912–1919), where he earned a master of arts in history of philosophy and sociology of education and a Ph.D. in philosophy and education. In 1919 he married Libbie Suchoff; the couple had three children.

In the late nineteenth and early twentieth centuries, owing primarily to political and economic instability, pogroms, and general anti-Semitism, a large mass of Eastern European Jews immigrated to the United States, especially to the New York metropolitan area, where a resulting twentyfold increase in the Jewish population made it the largest urban Jewish center in the world. A major perceived challenge of this heterogeneous, variegated community was the need to Americanize the adult population while not adversely affecting the cultural and/or religious development of the children and youth as Jews. Toward these ends, in 1908 the bulk of the Jewish community organized an umbrella group of cultural and educational organizations known collectively as New York Kehillah. Berkson held a number of positions in the Kehillah education network: teacher (1911–1913), principal (1914–1915), supervisor of the girls' preparatory schools (1916–1917), director of the first major American Jewish community center, the Central Jewish Institute (1917–1918), and supervisor of school and extension services of the Bureau of Jewish Education of New York (1919–1921). Subsequently he taught at the New York Graduate School of Jewish Social Work (1924–1926), the Jewish Institute of Religion (1926–1928, 1935–1939), Baltimore Hebrew College (1939–1940), and Dropsie College for Hebrew and Cognate Learning (now known as the Annenberg Center) (1945–1953). He was editor and founder of the *Jewish Child* magazine (founded in 1912) and the journal the

Jewish Teacher (founded in 1916). He was also the first president of the Jewish Teachers' Association of New York (founded in 1916).

A meticulous administrator and a visionary social engineer—he coined the terms *cultural pluralism* and *educational reconstructionism*—Berkson articulated his philosophy of education in "Jewish Education, Achievements and Needs" (in *The American Jew: A Composite Portrait*, ed. Oscar Janowsky [1942]), in which he described the school as "more than a preserver of old values in the light of new conceptions and new needs" and education as a process that looks "forward as well as backward" with the school serving as a "mediator between the past and the envisaged future." Working as a unit, the school and the teacher "occupy a place of leadership in the building of a more unified and better society." Thus Berkson saw the school as a major agent of societal change to be centrally controlled by the community, and he clung to this educational philosophy until his death. As early as the 1920s, however, the major cultural challenge for American Jews was no longer Americanization but rather Judaization, and the fragmentation, factionalization, and decentralization of American Jewish education that resulted from the varying approaches taken to this process made his a minority voice in the policy planning toward strengthening the Jewishness of Jewish Americans and thereby making Jews better Americans.

An advocate of informal education as an efficacious means of conducting Jewish leadership training, Berkson and two colleagues founded in 1922 one of the early private Jewish educational summer camps, Camp Modin, for the children of middle- and upper-class Jews who, because of their privileged upbringing, were destined to become leaders in the Jewish community. Located in Canaan, Maine, the camp provided for these children round-the-clock immersion in Jewish values and culture and education in Judaic studies and Hebrew.

Berkson was a cultural Zionist who also subscribed to the principles of Brit Shalom, a pacifist organization calling for a binational, Jewish-Arab state in Palestine. From 1927 to 1935 he served on the Palestine Zionist Executive in Jerusalem in the area of education and as such was de facto minister of education of the Yishuv, the Jewish community in Palestine prior to the establishment of the state of Israel. The backing of a centralized quasi-government better enabled Berkson to realize his community concept of education, and he brought order and sophistication to a hitherto unorganized, underfunded, and demoralized education network. Again, however, his was a minority position. Politically the executive was a Labor Zionist establishment, and when Chairman David Ben Gurion wanted to use teachers to block roads in order to prevent Arab workers from working on Jewish fields—cheap Arab labor was causing vast unemployment in the Jewish sector—Berkson vehemently disagreed, and this led him to decide to leave Palestine.

On his return to the United States in 1935, Berkson undertook two major evaluative surveys of Jewish education in Cleveland and New York. In 1943 he was appointed director of research for the American Zionist Emergency Council in New York City and served in that post until 1946. During the crucial World War II and postwar years leading to the establishment of the state of Israel, he edited and wrote most of the seminal *Palestine: A Study of Jewish, Arab and British Policies* (1947). Extending himself beyond the field of Jewish education, Berkson taught at the City College of New York from 1945 to 1961, during which he attained the rank of full professor in the areas of history of education and contemporary educational trends and movements. From 1965 to 1967 he taught similar topics at the University of Oregon.

Berkson wrote one book on his theories of Jewish education, *Theories of Americanization: A Critical Study with Special Reference to the Jewish Group* (1920), and four on his philosophy of general education, *Preface to an Educational Philosophy* (1940), *Education Faces the Future: An Appraisal of Contemporary Movements in Education* (1943), *The Ideal and the Community: A Philosophy of Education* (1958), and *Ethics, Politics, and Education* (1968). These books, which were fairly widely used in schools of education, counteracted the overemphasis on progressive education, which concentrated on how to teach but not what to teach. He also was a prolific author of articles and monographs.

Berkson died in New York City. Since his death, momentous changes in both the Jewish and non-Jewish world have made some of his ideas moot or even obsolete, and his vision of a united, sharing world seems more elusive today than in his day. Yet his ideas on the scope and role of education, including his conscious social engineering utilizing the school as the tool of change, have had an impact on the development of American Jewish and Israeli education and educators as well as made an imprint on general educational philosophy.

• Some of Berkson's papers are in the Zionist Archives in Jerusalem. Berkson's scholarly articles include, among many others, "Some Dewey Ideas and Their Implications for Jewish Education," *Jewish Institute Quarterly* (Jan. 1927): 13–21, (Mar. 1927): 22–32, (May 1927): 19–22; "The Hebrew Public School System and Other Jewish Educational Activities," *International Institute Educational Yearbook* (1937): 354–68; and "Experimentalism, Ethical Theory and Education," *Proceedings of the Fifteenth Annual Meeting of the Philosophy of Education Society* (1959): 124–31. The most extensive biographical work is Henry Franc Skirball, "Isaac Baer Berkson and Jewish Education" (Ph.D. diss., Columbia Univ. Teachers College, 1977).

HENRY F. SKIRBALL

BERLE, Adolf Augustus (29 Jan. 1895–17 Feb. 1971), lawyer and statesman, was born in Brighton, Massachusetts, the son of Adolf Augustus Berle, a Congregational minister, and Mary Augusta Wright. His parents began his schooling at home, and he and his three siblings won acclaim as child prodigies. Berle graduated from Harvard College at age eighteen and Harvard Law School at age twenty-one. His parents were active in the Social Gospel wing of progressive reform, providing him with beneficial political acquaintances. His first legal position was with the firm of reform lawyer and Supreme Court justice Louis D. Brandeis in Boston. Berle served as an army intelligence officer in the Dominican Republic in 1918 and at the Paris Peace Conference in 1919.

For two years in the 1920s, he lived at and provided legal services for Lillian D. Wald's Henry Street Settlement House on Manhattan's Lower East Side. In 1924 Berle formed the New York law firm Lippitt and Berle, and in 1933 he opened a Wall Street firm, Berle and Berle, specializing in corporation law. An incisive and eloquent liberal polemicist, he wrote for the *New Republic*, the *Nation*, *Survey*, and other progressive journals. His ambition, however, was to become an academic authority on the "law of corporation finance." Eschewing the growth of "legal factories" on Wall Street, Berle sought corporate retainers for his small firm while emphasizing the scholarliness of his activity. He wrote articles for law reviews and commuted to teach at Harvard Business School, aspiring to a professorship in a law school. In these endeavors he was encouraged by Beatrice Bend Bishop, the daughter of an aristocrat, whom he met in 1925 and married in 1927. They had three children.

Through a friend at Harvard Business School, economist William Zebina Ripley, Berle won a grant from the Laura Spelman Rockefeller Foundation to study corporations with an economics doctoral candidate at Columbia University, Gardiner C. Means. In 1927 he began teaching the "law of corporation finance" at Columbia. In 1928 he published his first book, *Studies in the Law of Corporation Finance*, thereby joining the "legal realism" movement, which included Jerome Frank, Herman Oliphant, Thurman Arnold and William O. Douglas. These men, like Berle, were powerful intellects who injected the social sciences into legal studies in an effort to humanize corporation law. Berle fancied himself a great social critic and aspired to be the "American Karl Marx," theorizing that managers had usurped control of capitalism from shareholders, a corporation's true owners.

In 1932 Berle and Means published *The Modern Corporation and Private Property*, in which they asserted that the concentration of wealth in just two hundred corporations tended toward oligarchic economic power that threatened self-government in American society. Their ideas were not original, but their expression of them was powerful, and their restatement was timely. In the midst of the Great Depression, the book seemed to answer the question of where capitalism had gone wrong, and its conclusions, eloquently hinting at the need for greater governmental supervision of corporations or even "state capitalism," captivated a generation of intellectuals. Reviewers celebrated it as "epoch-making," compared it with Adam Smith's *Wealth of Nations* (1776), and hailed it as an instant classic.

Subsequent generations of economists have quarreled with its premises, data, and conclusions, but, in the words of historian Thomas K. McCraw, *The Modern Corporation and Private Property* has "gained a permanent place in the life of the mind."

In 1932 Columbia University government professor Raymond Moley asked Berle to be an adviser on corporations to New York governor and presidential candidate Franklin D. Roosevelt. Berle thus joined the "brain trust" that included Moley and another Columbia professor, Rexford G. Tugwell, whose task it was to sharpen Roosevelt's ideas and draft his campaign speeches. Berle's principal contribution was the Commonwealth Club of San Francisco speech, which more than any other campaign address foretold the New Deal's planning thrust. Following his election, Roosevelt rewarded Moley and Tugwell with positions in the State and Agriculture departments, respectively. Berle preferred to return to New York, but he accepted temporary assignments during the banking crisis of 1933 and the railroad emergency later that year. Also in 1933, he accompanied Assistant Secretary of State Sumner Welles on a mission to Cuba to stabilize Havana's government.

Smitten with politics, he advised Fiorello La Guardia during the 1933 New York mayoralty race and, as chamberlain of the city from 1934 to 1938, was Mayor La Guardia's principal financial consultant. Berle masterminded the city's financial recovery from the brink of bankruptcy in 1934–1935. His strategy depended heavily upon assistance from the federal government's Reconstruction Finance Corporation and Public Works Administration, requiring continuing ties to the New Deal. Roosevelt frequently consulted him on national economic policies, and Berle responded with letters that began with the lighthearted salutation, "Dear Caesar." Lest the public misunderstand, Roosevelt asked him to desist from this playful familiarity.

In 1938 Berle accepted Roosevelt's invitation to become assistant secretary of state with a license to advise on economic policy, and he was a major witness at the Temporary National Economic Committee hearings in 1939. He immersed himself in foreign affairs, and for the rest of his life he retained a special interest in the struggles of Latin American democracy against the threats of fascists, Communists, and dictators. In the late 1930s he organized Pan-American conferences designed to fund and reinforce antifascist governments throughout the hemisphere.

During World War II, Berle ran the State Department's worldwide intelligence network. He also organized the International Civil Aviation Conference in Chicago in 1944, one of a series of conferences determining a postwar order. This conference asserted American air supremacy at a time when the United States manufactured most of the aircraft used for commercial purposes. At the conference's conclusion, Roosevelt enigmatically removed Berle from the State Department and sent him to Brazil as ambassador.

Berle consistently despised totalitarianism, being one of the first New Deal liberals to condemn a "Soviet Empire" and to describe World War II's alliance with Stalin as "a temporary confluence of interest." Yet he was not just anti-Communist. During the year he served as ambassador to Brazil, he successfully encouraged Brazilians to topple the dictatorship of Getulio Vargas. This amounted to blatant meddling in another country's internal affairs, but the cause of democracy was more important to him than the principle of self-determination.

Following his year in Brazil, Berle informally worked on occasion with the Central Intelligence Agency against communism in Europe and against dictators in Latin America. He also wrote a great many books and articles about power, corporations, and foreign affairs.

A consensus of those who knew him regarded Berle as arrogant and brilliant. Didactic in nature, he pontificated on a subject in a manner that left little room for disagreement, thereby making many enemies among New Dealers and developing a feud with his former professor, Felix Frankfurter. He was an ideological liberal and one of the founders and leaders of New York's Liberal party. However, his wife's money allowed him strong aristocratic pretensions, and in his later years his more conservative instincts manifested themselves. Short, almost gnomish in stature, he could chain-smoke his way through intricate intellectual conversations. He was obsessed with power, not necessarily for himself, but as an abstract intellectual concept that applied to organizations, societies, and empires. In 1934 his quest for control brought him into the Twentieth Century Fund, an early think tank founded by enlightened businessmen Edward A. Filene and Henry S. Dennison. In 1951 he became chairman of its board of trustees, which enabled him to influence many of its subsequent policy-making studies.

When the Democrats returned to power in 1961, many of them considered Berle the most knowledgeable man about politics in the Western Hemisphere. President John F. Kennedy made him chairman of a Latin American task force that supported the Bay of Pigs incursion and originated the Alliance for Progress, but Berle quit after six months because he wanted more authority over foreign policy. Obsessed with Cuba's Fidel Castro and communism's threat to capitalism in the Americas, Berle endorsed President Lyndon Johnson's 1965 intervention in the Dominican Republic. A vehement hawk during the Vietnam War, Berle believed that Communists had masterminded American dissent. He died in New York City, labeled by many of his old friends a quintessential "Cold War liberal."

• Berle's papers are in the Franklin D. Roosevelt Library, Hyde Park, N.Y. Most of his diary and several of his papers were published in Beatrice Bishop Berle and Travis Jacobs, *Navigating the Rapids, 1918–1971: From the Papers of Adolf A. Berle* (1973). The only biography is Jordan A. Schwarz,

Liberal: Adolf A. Berle and the Vision of an American Era (1987). His wife's memoir—Beatrice Bishop Berle, *A Life in Two Worlds* (1983)—is an engaging and lively celebration of their activities. Insights can be found in numerous books by or about New Deal figures. Elliott A. Rosen, *Hoover, Roosevelt, and the Brains Trust: From Depression to New Deal* (1977), is a useful glimpse of him. Important and excellent articles are Thomas K. McCraw, "In Retrospect: Berle and Means," *Reviews in American History* 18 (Dec. 1990): 578–96, and Richard S. Kirkendall, "A. A. Berle, Jr.: Student of the Corporation, 1917–1932," *Business History Review* 35 (Spring 1961): 43–58.

JORDAN A. SCHWARZ

BERLIN, Donovan Reese (13 June 1898–17 May 1982), aircraft designer and executive, was born in Romona, Indiana, the son of Charles N. Berlin and Maude Easter Mull, farmers. After high school at Brook, Indiana, Berlin enrolled in the Purdue University School of Mechanical Engineering in September 1916 but withdrew almost immediately when his father insisted he stay home and work the farm. He reentered the university in September 1917 and completed a B.S.M.E. on 8 June 1921. His first employment, as an assistant in the aerodynamics laboratory of the Air Service at McCook Field at Dayton, Ohio, from 1921 to 1926, launched his career in aeronautics.

As project engineer and chief draftsman for the Douglas Aircraft Company (1926–1929), he perfected his design skills before becoming chief engineer of the Valley Manufacturing Company of Glendale, California, where in 1929 he designed and built a trimotor eight-place transport that flew airmail in Guatemala for three years. From October 1929 to October 1934 Berlin served the Northrop Aircraft Division of United Aircraft Corporation at Burbank, California, where he became chief engineer. There he was involved in developing the first all-metal stressed-skin airplane in the United States, the "Alpha," which marked the revolutionary transition from wood, wire, and fabric to monocoque construction. After a brief stint with the Stearman Aircraft Company in Wichita, Kansas, Berlin returned to Northrop until moving to the Buffalo, New York, Curtiss Airplane Division of the Curtiss-Wright Corporation in 1934. In 1926 he married Helen Elizabeth Hentz in Hamilton, Ohio; they had one child.

When Curtiss offered Berlin an annual salary of $4,000, a substantial amount in the depths of the depression, he showed something of his character and personality by asking for $6,000. Two weeks passed, doubtless uncomfortably for the applicant, before Curtiss agreed to his figure. The firm had little reason to regret the decision, however, for he promptly showed his mettle as project engineer on the P-36, the first in a series of successful Curtiss pursuit planes culminating in the P-40, for which the War Department signed a large production order in April 1939, by which time Berlin had become chief engineer. In all, 13,738 P-40s were produced. Curtiss awarded the designer a $30,000 bonus for his work on the P-40. Because of its success against the Japanese, Major General Claire Chennault's American Volunteer Group (AVG), the "Flying Tigers," made Berlin an honorary member of the AVG.

Berlin was not only a gifted designer but something of an intellectual leader in the aeronautical engineering field. His particular forte was in the imaginative way he related an aerodynamically optimal design to the realities and limitations of manufacturing. In 1939, for example, when many in the profession doubted that the aerodynamic advantage of flush riveting could be achieved without prohibitive cost, he published in the *SAE Journal* the results of an extended Curtiss investigation analyzing such factors as strength, processing methods, the economies of production, and the specialized equipment and tooling required to support the feasibility of this highly significant aerodynamic advance.

By 1941 Berlin was director of engineering in the largest pursuit airplane factory in the world, a newly erected facility with a million and a half square feet of unobstructed floor space for straight line production. This expansion, made possible by export orders after the outbreak of war in Europe and President Franklin D. Roosevelt's May 1940 call for 50,000 aircraft, stimulated Berlin to think deeply about the practical problems of mass-producing airplanes. At this time the nation's aircraft production capacity was scarcely more than 15,000 units per year. Berlin and a colleague published a series of articles in *Aviation* magazine and the *SAE Journal* spelling out in detail how a fuller application of automobile industry methods, especially production tooling and the managerial attitudes that must accompany such a move, could radically increase aircraft output.

When the War Department began recruiting auto manufacturers to help with aircraft production, Berlin was a logical choice for General Motors to lure away from Curtiss, installing him in the Fisher Body Division in 1942. At Fisher he presided over the development of the XP-75, a fighter largely constructed from assemblies already in production for other aircraft. Unfortunately, this attempt to compress the time required to reach mass production failed. So many modifications were required to achieve suitable flight characteristics that the anticipated speedup in production never materialized, and the project was abandoned by the War Department after an expenditure of nearly $50 million.

Berlin left General Motors in 1947 to become vice president in the McDonnell Aircraft Corporation, where he worked on several fighter designs and ramjet engines for helicopter rotors. In 1953 he became president of the Piasecki Helicopter Corporation of Wayne, Pennsylvania, which at the time had a backlog of $175 million worth of helicopter orders arising out of the Korean War demand. Despite the boom in helicopter sales, Berlin's tenure was shadowed by corporate conflicts with Piasecki, the founder, which led to a change in corporate name to Vertol Aircraft Corporation. When Vertol was acquired by Boeing in 1960, Berlin was named vice chairman and general manager of Ver-

tol, but in 1963 Curtiss-Wright once again recruited him as vice president of corporate staff. Shortly before his retirement in 1979, he took a position with the E. F. Felt Corporation of San Leandro, California, an aircraft maintenance organization.

Berlin's crowning achievement lay in designing the P-40, one of the most widely used aircraft in World War II. Many of his innovative ideas such as the underbelly radiator were extensively adopted throughout the industry. He was a member of the Society of Automotive Engineers and the American Helicopter Society and a fellow of the Institute of Aeronautical Sciences. For two years he was a member of the Air Force Scientific Advisory Board. Berlin was a resident of Glen Mills, Pennsylvania, at the time of his death, which occurred in Middletown, Pennsylvania.

• Berlin's personal papers were largely destroyed in a house fire after his death. A short biography appears in the *Purdue Alumnus*, Oct. 1993; the Purdue University registrar's office prepared a brief biographical sketch to accompany the honorary degree the university awarded Berlin in 1953. Berlin discusses his revolution in airplane manufacturing in his article "Applying Automotive Methods to Aircraft Production," *Aviation* 40 (Jan. 1941): 42–43, 122–24, and 42 (Mar. 1941): 46–47. For a historical perspective, see "Wing Tips," *Steel*, 11 Sept. 1942, pp. 100–102, and "A Detroit Dream of Mass-produced Fighter Aircraft: The XP-75 Fiasco," *Technology and Culture* 28 (July 1987): 578–93. An obituary is in the *New York Times*, 8 June 1982.

I. B. HOLLEY, JR.

BERLIN, Irving (11 May 1888–22 Sept. 1989), songwriter and music publisher of the Tin Pan Alley era, was born Israel Baline in Tumen, in western Siberia, the son of Moses Baline, a cantor, and Leah Lipkin. Berlin was the youngest of eight children, six of whom emigrated with their parents to the United States in 1893 following a pogrom. After settling his family in a tenement on New York City's Lower East Side, Berlin's father could find only part-time employment as a kosher poultry inspector and manual laborer. The children were obliged to contribute to the family income. When not attending the local public school or receiving religious instruction at a *cheder*, "Izzy," as the youngest child was called, delivered telegrams and sold newspapers and junk on the streets. He left school after the death of his father in 1901.

Equipped with a good natural singing voice and a superb ear, Berlin supported himself by busking on street corners and in saloons, then by plugging songs in vaudeville houses. At age sixteen he became a singing waiter at the Pelham Café in Chinatown, where he taught himself to play the piano in his spare time. In 1907 he wrote his first song, "Marie from Sunny Italy," in collaboration with the house pianist, Mike Nicholson, taking "Irving Berlin" as his nom de plume and subsequently his legal name.

After the modest commercial success of the songs "Sadie Salome (Go Home)" and "My Wife's Gone to the Country (Hurrah! Hurrah!)," Berlin was employed as a staff lyricist at the Ted Snyder Music Company, where between 1909 and 1911 he collaborated with Snyder on some fifty songs. Many of these were novelty pieces with German, Italian, Irish, Jewish, and African-American protagonists, written for performance on the vaudeville stage before audiences for whom the ethnic identification and accented English of such songs were the rule of the day. In 1910 Berlin and Snyder sang several of them in the show *Up and Down Broadway*, and Berlin recorded "Oh How That German Could Love" for Columbia Records. It was "Alexander's Ragtime Band," however, written by Berlin alone and first performed by him in early 1911 for the annual *Friar's Frolic*, that brought him national and then international fame. He was made a partner in the publishing company, renamed Waterson, Berlin & Snyder. Dozens of successful songs followed, most of them by Berlin alone, including such hits as "I Want to Be in Dixie," "Do It Again," and "When the Midnight Choo Choo Leaves for Alabam'."

In February 1912 he married Dorothy Goetz, sister of his sometime collaborator E. Ray Goetz, but she died five months later of an illness contracted on their honeymoon in Havana. His successful songs to this point had been lively in tempo and comical or satirical in nature; though he had written a handful of more expressive pieces, none of these had been particularly noteworthy. "When I Lost You," however, published shortly after Dorothy's death, became the first in a long line of notable lyrical ballads, many of them in slow waltz time.

His first show for the musical stage, *Watch Your Step*, starring Irene and Vernon Castle, opened on Broadway on 8 December 1914 and was followed in 1915 by *Stop! Look! Listen!* with its hit song "I Love a Piano." Though neither show was quite his long-rumored ragtime opera, both demonstrated that Berlin's syncopated style could be adapted to a full-length stage production, and they were landmarks in the transformation of the popular theater, long associated with the working class, into an attraction for fashionable New York audiences.

Berlin next turned his attention to the revue. After being drafted into the army in 1918, he wrote *Yip, Yip, Yaphank* for performance on Broadway by an all-soldier cast, with Berlin himself singing "Oh! How I Hate to Get Up in the Morning." Proceeds went to the war effort. After writing most of the songs for the *Ziegfeld Follies* of 1919 and 1920, Berlin built at a cost of nearly a million dollars his own Music Box Theatre, where the first *Music Box Revue* opened on 22 September 1921. New editions followed in each of the next three seasons, introducing "Say It with Music," "All Alone," "What'll I Do?" and many other enduring songs.

He began publishing his show songs under his own copyright in 1914, though his other songs were still brought out by Waterson, Berlin & Snyder. In 1919 he gained complete financial and artistic control over his songs by establishing his own publishing company, Irving Berlin Incorporated. The firm prospered as a result of the continuing popularity of his own songs

and also from his acuity in recognizing and publishing potentially successful songs by other songwriters. As a charter member and an early president of the American Society of Composers, Authors and Publishers (ASCAP), the American performing rights and licensing organization, he was a leader in the successful attempt by composers and lyricists to share in the profits accruing from public performance and mechanical reproduction of their music.

His marriage in 1926 to Ellin Mackay was the subject of intense and sensational media coverage. Though this union of an immigrant Russian Jew who had once scuffled for a living on the streets of New York and the daughter of Clarence Mackay, a socially prominent millionaire telegraph magnate and a Catholic, was unusual for the day, the marriage proved to be a strong and lasting one; they had three children.

Eager to explore new avenues for the dissemination of his music, Berlin became one of the first Tin Pan Alley songwriters to embrace the medium of sound film. The first "talkie," *The Jazz Singer* (1927), featured Al Jolson singing Berlin's "Blue Skies"; his first musical comedy, *The Cocoanuts*, was made into a film in 1929; and *Mammy* (1930), starring Jolson, was based on Berlin's own unproduced play with music, *Mister Bones*.

After a sojourn in Hollywood for the production of *Puttin' on the Ritz* (1929) and *Reaching for the Moon* (1931), Berlin returned to New York to write two topical stage pieces, the satirical *Face the Music* (1932) and the innovative *As Thousands Cheer* (1933). The latter, a revue based on front-page news stories, was remarkable for its large number of effective and memorable songs, including "Easter Parade," "Heat Wave," and "Harlem on My Mind"; another, "Supper Time," was suggested by a news item about a black woman whose husband had been lynched.

None of the first films for which he had written songs had enjoyed much success, but with *Top Hat* (1935) Berlin found a formula that redefined the genre of movie musical: a cast featuring attractive and personable dancer-singers; escapist, lighthearted plots; lavish production numbers exploiting the technical potential of the movie camera; and romantic ballads with lush orchestral accompaniment. The next two decades brought a succession of his films of this sort, starring the likes of Fred Astaire, Ginger Rogers, Bing Crosby, Alice Faye, Judy Garland, Mitzi Gaynor, and Marilyn Monroe, and filled with some of his most sophisticated and enduring songs, including "Cheek to Cheek," "Let's Face the Music and Dance," "White Christmas," and "Love, You Didn't Do Right By Me." The most successful of these films were *Follow the Fleet* (1936), *On the Avenue* (1937), *Alexander's Ragtime Band* (1938), *Holiday Inn* (1942), *Blue Skies* (1946), *Easter Parade* (1948), and *White Christmas* (1954).

With the entry of the United States into World War II, Berlin wrote another revue with an all-soldier cast, *This Is the Army* (1942). After opening on Broadway, the show toured the United States and American army bases all over the world. Proceeds of the show and of the film version (1943) went to the Army Emergency Relief. In 1945 President Harry S. Truman awarded Berlin America's highest civilian award, the Medal of Merit.

Like many other immigrants who made a good life for themselves in America, Berlin was an outspoken patriot. Beginning with "They're on Their Way to Mexico" (1914), he wrote many songs supporting the United States and its institutions, including "For Your Country and My Country" (1917), "This Is a Great Country" (1940), "Song of Freedom" from *Holiday Inn* (1942), and "Give Me Your Tired, Your Poor" from *Miss Liberty* (1949). Berlin assigned the copyright for "Any Bonds Today?" (1941) to the Treasury Department, which received all royalties, and all profits from "God Bless America," written in 1918 for *Yip, Yip, Yaphank* but cut from the show and not published until 1938, went to the Boy Scouts and Girl Scouts of America. Berlin made no secret of his support for the Republican party, and his song "I Like Ike" figured prominently in Dwight Eisenhower's successful bid for the party's presidential nomination in 1952 and his subsequent election.

Berlin's first musical comedy, *The Cocoanuts*, though breaking no new ground for the genre, had enjoyed a modest run on Broadway in 1925 with a cast including the Marx Brothers. Years later, a series of shows integrated text and music more closely and enjoyed more popular and critical success. *Louisiana Purchase* (1940) is a satirical parody of southern political demagoguery, set in the Louisiana of Huey Long. *Annie Get Your Gun* (1946) is Berlin's most successful work for the musical stage and has been judged one of the top musical comedies of all time. With Ethel Merman in the role of Annie Oakley and packed with more hit songs than any musical of the era, including "Anything You Can Do (I Can Do Better)," "There's No Business Like Show Business," "The Girl That I Marry," "They Say It's Wonderful," and "You Can't Get a Man with a Gun," the show had a Broadway run of 1,147 performances, an even longer run in London, numerous revivals by road companies all over the world, and a film version in 1950. *Miss Liberty* (1949) was less favorably received, but *Call Me Madam* (1950), a satire of diplomatic life in Washington, was greeted with critical praise and ran for eighteen months on Broadway, then became a hit movie in 1953.

Like many other Tin Pan Alley songwriters and performers, Berlin had little empathy for the new styles and genres of the postwar era, particularly rock 'n' roll. Little was heard from him in the decade following the success of *Call Me Madam*, but in 1962 he wrote another musical comedy, *Mr. President*, and a cluster of songs for a projected film, *Say It with Music*. The musical had only a modest first run and received little critical praise, however, the film was never produced, and Berlin's public career was at an end.

Though Berlin continued to write songs for the next two decades, these remained unpublished and were known only to family and a few friends. Honors and recognition of his accomplishments continued to come his way, including a special medal from President Eisenhower in 1954, a network television spectacular organized by Ed Sullivan to commemorate Berlin's eightieth birthday (with an appearance by then President Lyndon Johnson), and an ASCAP-sponsored concert of his music in Carnegie Hall when he reached the age of one hundred. Berlin died at his home in New York City.

Berlin's career spanned virtually the entire Tin Pan Alley era, and he made major contributions to each of its genres: ballads suitable for performance in the home by amateurs, comic and satirical songs for vaudeville and revue, production numbers and romantic ballads for films, and musical comedies. Alec Wilder characterized him as "the best all-around, over-all song writer America has ever had, the master of the entire range of popular song" (Wilder, p. 120), and the obituary in the *New York Times* the day after his death rhapsodized that he "set the tone and tempo for the tunes America played and sang and danced to for much of the 20th century." The number of his songs achieving commercial success while at the same time penetrating deeply and lastingly into the American consciousness is unmatched by that of any other songwriter, and "White Christmas" is the single most commercially successful song of all time, having sold more than 360 million recorded units, of one performance or another, by 1992.

Berlin was a thoroughly professional and highly self-critical songwriter, revising lyrics and music as many times as necessary to get a song just right. He published nearly a thousand songs in his lifetime but withheld many times that number from publication because he was not completely satisfied with them. Like most songwriters who learned their trade in the early days of Tin Pan Alley, he was a self-taught musician who played the piano mostly on the black keys and dictated songs to staff musicians rather than notating them himself. Despite persistent rumors that he played the piano with only one finger and that his songs were written by staff arrangers or a mysterious "little black boy," he was an excellent musician who sang professionally early in his career and often accompanied singers in public and private. The musicians to whom he dictated his songs attested that he had a superb ear and could detect the slightest deviation from what he intended in a melody or piano accompaniment.

His first songs were written for a specific community, New York City's polyglot turn-of-the-century population of immigrants and first-generation Americans, and the style and content of these songs drew on the life and music of this community. But as his professional activity turned from the vaudeville stage to the more sophisticated revue and musical play, and then to the sound film and the Broadway musical, he found himself addressing national and international audiences. Accordingly, his later songs were written in a more generic style, tailored for listeners now defined not by region or ethnicity but by their common access to the mainstream mass media: the phonograph, network radio, sound film, and eventually television. Americans who through poverty and isolation (whether geographical or cultural) were without access to these channels of communication were not part of his audience.

Berlin had a penchant throughout his career for flavoring his songs with elements drawn from American vernacular dance music. Many writers of the 1910s hailed him as the king of ragtime, and journalists of the 1920s were under the impression that he wrote some of the best "jazz" songs of the era. These judgments are at odds with later scholarship and criticism, which argue that the popular music industry appropriated and diluted the African-American genres of ragtime, jazz, and blues. As Rudi Blesh put it in *Shining Trumpets: A History of Jazz* (1946, p. 11), "Commercialism [is] a cheapening and deteriorative force, a species of murder perpetuated on a wonderful music by whites and by those misguided negroes who, for one reason or another reason, choose to be accomplices to the deed."

To gain a better perspective on this issue, one must understand the Tin Pan Alley aesthetic. New songs were judged by audience acceptance or rejection, not by abstract analysis of their musical and lyrical components. As Wilder put it, for Berlin and his peers "a *good* song and a *hit* song [were] synonymous (p. 92)." To ensure that their songs would be immediately accessible to their audiences, composers drew on already familiar musical styles, including the most popular songs of the nineteenth and early twentieth centuries, widely disseminated pieces of the classical repertory, and social dances of the present and immediate past. Berlin himself wrote in the *Green Book Magazine* for April 1916, "There's no such thing as a new melody. Our work is to connect the old phrases in a new way, so that they will sound like a new tune."

Neither Berlin nor any other Tin Pan Alley songwriter pretended to write "authentic" pieces of ragtime, blues, or jazz; rather, they incorporated references to these and other styles and genres into a body of song that had its own style and its own cultural validity. Berlin's "Alexander's Ragtime Band" is not a ragtime composition but a song suggesting the idiom of ragtime, just as his "Opera Burlesque" is not an operatic composition but a song drawing on the materials and traditions of the operatic stage. As Isaac Goldberg put it in 1930 (pp. 320–21), American popular song is "a song of the city, synthetic in facture, as short-lived as a breath, yet not for these reasons any the less authentic."

Berlin's songs, like those of other songwriters of his generation, can be seen as homogenized products of the American melting pot, drawing on a wide range of musical styles to create a new genre with its own identity and authenticity. Woollcott (p. 215) quotes Jerome Kern on Berlin: "He honestly absorbs the vibrations emanating from the people, manners and life of his time, and in turn, gives these impressions back to the world—simplified—clarified—glorified."

• Berlin's papers, including business records of his publishing company and manuscript sketches and early versions of the lyrics and music of individual songs and complete shows, were deposited in the Library of Congress in 1992. Alexander Woollcott, *The Story of Irving Berlin* (1925), is a useful narrative of his childhood and early professional life by a close friend, and Mary Ellin Barrett, *Irving Berlin: A Daughter's Memoir* (1994), is the best account of the songwriter's middle and later life and career. Laurence Bergreen, *As Thousands Cheer: The Life of Irving Berlin* (1990), is a comprehensive biography, though flawed by a vituperative attitude toward its subject and a condescending view of popular music. Other biographies include Michael Freedland, *Irving Berlin* (1974) and *A Salute to Irving Berlin* (1986). Ian Whitcomb, *Irving Berlin and Ragtime America* (1988), is a lively and sometimes fanciful reconstruction of Berlin's early career and the environment in which he worked. Isaac Goldberg, *Tin Pan Alley: A Chronicle of the American Popular Music Racket* (1930), is a valuable contemporaneous view of the popular music industry. The best analysis and appreciation of Berlin's songs is in Alex Wilder, *American Popular Song: The Great Innovators, 1900–1950* (1972). Charles Hamm, *Irving Berlin: Early Songs, 1907–1914* (1994), is a complete critical edition of his first 200-odd songs, with an introductory essay discussing the social environment in which they were written. Vincent Motto, *The Irving Berlin Catalog* (1988; rev. ed., 1990) is an invaluable compendium of information about the songs and shows. Steven Suskin, *Berlin, Kern, Rodgers, Hart, and Hammerstein: A Complete Song Catalogue* (1990), contains the most complete and accurate listing of his songs, including many unpublished ones.

CHARLES HAMM

BERLINER, Emile (20 May 1851–3 Aug. 1929), inventor, was born Emil Berliner in the city of Hannover in the kingdom of Hannover (later a Prussian province), the son of Samuel Berliner, a merchant, and Sarah Fridman. His formal education ended in 1865 with four years at Samsonschule boarding school in Wolfenüttel, where he excelled in penmanship and drawing and evinced an early passion for classical music, a love that remained with him throughout his life. After graduation, his parents being hard pressed to provide for their large family, Berliner took employment in a print shop and then as clerk in a dry goods store. There, watching the handling of bolts of colored fabric, he took an interest in the weaving process and designed a weaving machine—the earliest evidence of his genius for invention.

An old family friend who had migrated to the United States and established a dry goods store in Washington, D.C., returned to Hannover for a visit and fascinated Berliner with his tales of America. In 1870 Berliner emigrated and settled in Washington, where he took a clerking job in his friend's establishment, learned English, and took lessons on piano and violin. The next six years were divided among Washington, D.C., New York City, and Milwaukee, Wisconsin, in various mercantile positions. Meanwhile, his interest in science grew, and in his spare time he taught himself the principles of acoustics and electricity.

During the winter of 1876–1877 he began tinkering with the telephone, Alexander Graham Bell's new invention, which was receiving a great deal of public attention. Bell's original device was electromagnetic in nature, with the electric current itself indirectly produced by the acoustic vibrations. As a result, the speaker had to shout at great volume in order to produce enough electric current to transmit speech useful distances. Berliner, convinced that the preferable means of transmitting speech was by a battery-produced current, worked at developing a means of superimposing acoustic vibrations on that electric current. The result of his experiments was the carbon transmitter (i.e., microphone), and it became the means of producing speech that could be carried over many miles, thus making long distance telephony a practical reality. Berliner filed patent applications on both the (telephone) transmitter and a continuous-current transformer, to increase the power of the microphone, in 1877, and the patent on the latter was granted the following year. Immediately he wrote the Telephone Company of New York (a subsidiary of the Bell Company), offering to sell his transmitter invention for $12,000, but the offer was rejected. Meanwhile, four other patent applications (two of the applicants were Bell and Thomas A. Edison) had been filed on the telephone transmitter, and not until 1897—after a lengthy lawsuit in which Berliner was accused of colluding with the patent office to delay issue of the patent in order to extend its useful life—was the patent issued to Berliner. During that period, Western Union decided to enter the telephone field itself with a battery transmitter designed by Edison. Bell Telephone, realizing the potential value of Berliner's inventions—especially in the face of Western Union's competitive threat—bought Berliner's patents and offered him a monthly retainer, and he remained associated with Bell for several years.

In 1877, while Berliner was still embroiled in the telephone controversy, Thomas Edison and Charles Cros of Paris independently publicized their ideas for the reproduction of speech from a recording made on a moving surface. Edison's invention, the "phonograph," modified and improved by Chichester A. Bell (Alexander Bell's cousin) and Charles Sumner Tainter working in Bell's laboratories, led to the "graphophone," the first practical sound-recording device, which engraved a groove of varying depth (i.e., vertical-cut grooves) in a rotating wax cylinder. Berliner set to work immediately to improve the process for what he described as "etching the human voice." Recognizing that distortion in the recording resulted from the nonlinear relation between cutting pressure and depth of groove, Berliner developed the lateral-cut method, in which vibrations are recorded as side-to-side motions. In order to facilitate the duplication process wherein many recordings could be manufactured from a single source recording (a task that posed formidable difficulties with cylinder recordings), Berliner replaced the cylinder with a flat disc. Because he used a hard material rather than the soft wax of Edison's cylinders, the tracking needle was self-propelled along the grooves; in the soft-wax cylinder a fine screw mechanism was required to propel the needle. These innovations constituted Berliner's "gramophone" machine, which he patented in 1887. Within four years he had perfected the technique for making matrices that could be used for the quantity production of commercial records. The Berliner Gramophone Company was established in Philadelphia to manufacture small hand-driven machines. Berliner's recording enterprise was later merged with machinist Eldridge R. Johnson's gramophone manufacturing business, to become, in 1901, the Victor Talking Machine Company.

Berliner's subsequent inventions included pioneering work in helicopter flight: in 1908 he designed the first lightweight radial aircraft engine and between 1919 and 1926, with his son, Henry, built and tested three experimental helicopters. In 1915, still concerned with the production and dissemination of sound and music, he studied the problem of acoustics in music halls and in 1925 invented the first acoustic tiles and acoustic cement cells to reduce undesirable reverberations.

In 1881 Berliner married Cora Adler of Washington, who subsequently bore him three sons and three daughters. The serious illness of his young daughter, Alice, in 1900, prompted Berliner to turn his attention to problems of public hygiene, and in 1890 he founded the Society for the Prevention of Sickness. In 1907 he organized the first milk conference in Washington and undertook an extensive effort to introduce pasteurization of raw milk as a health measure. He took out advertisements in Washington newspapers stressing the importance of scalding children's milk. In 1911 he founded the Sarah Berliner fellowship for scientific research by women. In 1919 he wrote *Rules of Health* as a collection of nursery rhymes to teach young children the importance of hygiene, and in 1921 he issued *The Bottle-Fed Baby* to inform young mothers of the value of bottle feeding. In 1902, under the pseudonym of Jerome du Barry, he published his ideas on love, philosophy, religion, immortality, prayer, monogamy, and other topics in *Conclusions*, early issued privately in 1899 under his own name. In 1919 he wrote "A Study towards the Solution of Industrial Problems in the New Zionist Commonwealth." Some of his talks on infant health and nutrition were published in pamphlet form in the early 1900s. He served as president of the District of Columbia Tuberculosis Association from 1915 to 1922. He died in Washington, D.C.

• The principal source of biographical information is Frederick W. Wile, *Emile Berliner, Maker of the Microphone* (1926). This highly adulatory account manages to bypass much of the incredibly complicated corporate and legal history of the early phonograph device and its protagonists that embroiled Berliner deeply; such details can be found in Roland Gelatt, *The Fabulous Phonograph: 1877–1977* (1955, 1977) and Oliver Read and Walter L. Welch, *From Tin Foil to Stereo: Evolution of the Phonograph* (1959, 1976). Welch being a longtime associate of the Edison enterprise, the latter study offers a counterbalance to Wile's pro-Berliner narrative. Some additional biographical material can be found in C. J. Hylander, *American Inventors* (1934). Information on Berliner's Jewish and Zionist activities is in *Encyclopedia Judaica* (1982). An obituary is in the *New York Times*, 4 Aug. 1929.

NORM COHEN

BERNARD, Francis (July 1712–16 June 1779), colonial governor, was born in Brightwell Parish, Berkshire, England, the son of Francis Bernard, an Anglican minister, and Margery Winlowe. When Bernard was three his father died. His mother married another Anglican minister, the Reverend Anthony Alsop. Alsop, a poet, died during Bernard's childhood, but the stepson later edited the definitive edition of Alsop's work. Bernard's mother died when he was six, and he was raised by an uncle, who was also a minister, and an aunt.

In 1725 Bernard entered St. Peter's College, Westminster, where he received a classical education. In 1729 he matriculated at Christ Church, Oxford, earning an M.A. degree in 1736. He became a member of the Middle Temple in 1733 and was admitted to the bar there in 1737. Following his entry into the legal profession, Bernard became a provincial counsel in Lincoln, where he maintained a successful practice until 1758. Bernard was appointed a public notary in 1738, and in 1740 he was appointed commissioner of bails for an area including Lincoln, York, and Nottingham. Also while in Lincoln, Bernard was elected steward of the city of Lincoln and recorder for the city of Boston in England.

In 1741 Bernard married Amelia Offley, with whom he had eight children. Bernard's wife provided him with excellent political connections; she was the niece of Colonel Samuel Shute, a former royal governor of Massachusetts, and a cousin of Viscount Barrington, with whom Bernard became good friends. Barrington's influence led to the appointment of Bernard in 1758 as the royal governor of New Jersey.

As governor of New Jersey, Bernard proved to be an energetic and capable leader. He ably reconciled opposing factions in East and West Jersey and successfully negotiated a treaty with the Delaware Indians. He convinced the colonial legislature to provide troops for the Canadian campaign during the French and Indian War and to give Quakers appropriate representation on the council. He also worked to convince British authorities to modify official policy prohibiting paper money in order to ease New Jersey's economic troubles. During Bernard's short tenure as governor, he managed to resolve most of New Jersey's major problems and to settle many of the controversies that divided the colony. His success produced a promotion. In 1760 Bernard was appointed royal governor of Massachusetts, a more prestigious post for the up-and-coming royal appointee. However, Bernard's experience in Massachusetts proved to be very different from his brief stint in New Jersey.

Bernard arrived in Massachusetts on 2 August 1760, and for several years he successfully governed that colony. He almost ruined his chances at success in the beginning of his tenure as governor by appointing Lieutenant Governor Thomas Hutchinson, a nonlawyer, as chief justice. The position had been promised to Colonel James Otis, long a practicing lawyer in Massachusetts, by Bernard's two predecessors, but he chose to ignore those promises. Bernard managed to overcome the political repercussions of this mistake and soon won popularity among many of the citizens of Massachusetts. Bernard wisely chose not to take sides in the Writs of Assistance Case in 1761, and he supported the passage of a paper money bill over the objection of Lieutenant Governor Hutchinson. In 1762 the General Court thanked him for his actions by voting him a salary of £1,300 and granting him the island of Mount Desert off the coast of Maine. Bernard also received accolades for his support of Harvard College. Following a fire that destroyed its library in 1764, he worked diligently to raise funds for its replacement and gave the college his private library. Bernard, an amateur architect, designed the new Harvard Hall to replace the destroyed building.

Bernard won some initial political approval for his criticism of British policy, particularly related to taxes in the colonies. He urged reduction or abolition of the duties in the Sugar Act of 1764 and proposed that the colonies be allowed to establish their own imperial taxes based on quotas set by Parliament. He also condemned the Stamp Act as misguided, but he refused to approve organized official resistance to imperial legislation. In the wake of the passage of the Stamp Act, Boston mobs destroyed several homes and forced the stamp commissioners to resign. Still Bernard insisted that British law must be obeyed. His insistence on enforcing unpopular laws and commands led to his loss of almost all support in Massachusetts.

Having failed in 1765 to enforce the Stamp Act, Bernard hoped to be more successful when Parliament passed the Townshend Acts in 1767. However, he failed to perceive accurately the determination of many in Massachusetts not to succumb to what they believed were unlawful acts of the British Parliament. On 11 February 1768, following the passage of the new taxes, the Massachusetts General Court invited other colonial legislatures to join in protesting the new duties and in developing a method for circumventing them. This invitation, the Massachusetts Circular Letter, marked the beginning of the end of Bernard's career as governor of Massachusetts. Bernard perceived the letter as an unlawful challenge to the authority of the royal government and forwarded it to Lord Hillsborough, the secretary of state for the colonies. Hillsborough told Bernard to order the general assembly to revoke the letter. The legislature refused, and Bernard was forced to dissolve the assembly in July 1768. Believing that further trouble was coming, Bernard hinted in correspondence to his superiors that British troops might be needed in Boston to aid in the enforcement of imperial legislation. Several public intimidations of the customs commissioners by mobs produced the order for troops to be sent to Boston. Their arrival on 1 October 1768 led to a rise in the intensity of the arguments between the colonials and government authorities, an intensity that would eventually result in the Boston Massacre of March 1770. Luckily for Bernard, he was no longer in Massachusetts by 1770.

In April 1769 the editors of the *Boston Gazette*, Benjamin Edes and John Gill, acquired six of Bernard's letters to Lord Hillsborough and published them in a pamphlet. In the letters, dated from 1 November to 5 December 1768, Bernard castigated the town of Boston and the General Court for refusing to obey a British law (the Quartering Act, 1766) to provide quarters for the troops that had recently arrived in Boston. Bernard wrote that the elected council, the upper house of the General Court, could no longer be depended on to support the Crown, and he urged the government to change the Massachusetts charter so that the council could be appointed directly by the king. Publication of these letters completely destroyed what remaining confidence the people had in Bernard. In their response, which also appeared in the pamphlet, the council stated that Governor Bernard had overstepped the powers of his office and officially requested that he be removed. The royal government apparently believed that Bernard's usefulness in Massachusetts was at an end, for they recalled him to London. Bernard left Boston on 1 August 1769, amid much rejoicing by the citizens of Boston.

Bernard continued as nominal governor of Massachusetts until 1770, but he never returned to the colony. The charges brought against him by the General Court were investigated by the Privy Council but found to be "groundless, vexatious and scandalous." As a reward for his "firmness and administrative ability," Bernard had been awarded a baronetcy in 1769, with the designation of "Francis Bernard of Nettleham in the County of Lincoln." He also was awarded an honorary doctorate from Oxford University in 1772. Bernard sought another royal appointment but did not receive a colonial post. For several years he served as a customs commissioner for Ireland, sending a substitute to do the work. In 1774 Bernard was placed on the pension list and retired from public service.

Bernard's major problem during his service in Massachusetts proved to be his inability to fully understand the colonial perspective. On one occasion he suggested that colonial representatives be admitted to Parliament in order to avoid a permanent rupture. However, in carrying out this change, he intended to restructure the colonies into several larger entities. The new setup would include a district comprising Massachusetts, New Hampshire, Rhode Island, and half of Connecticut, a plan that would clearly anger the colonists. Bernard also suggested the creation of a colonial nobility through royal appointment of life peers. He first made these proposals in 1764, but they received little attention before their publication in 1774 as *Select Letters on the Trade and Government of America, and the Principles of Law and Polity Applied to the American Colonies*. Bernard's actions helped exacerbate the growing conflict between Britain and the colonies, but he did not cause the disagreements, as stated by many contemporaries and historians, who claimed he was conspiring against colonial liberties. Bernard's inability to handle problems in Massachusetts led to his recall, but his successor, Thomas Hutchinson, proved no more successful.

Sir Francis Bernard's final years were spent as a semi-invalid. He began to experience seizures in 1771, and one of these finally proved fatal. He died at his home in Aylesbury.

• Bernard's correspondence as governor of Massachusetts is in the library of Harvard University. Bernard's other publications include *Letters to the Ministry* (1769) and *Letters to the Earl of Hillsborough* (1769). The first two volumes of T. E. Higgins, *The Bernards of Abington and Nether Winchendon* (1903), concentrate on Bernard's life and career. See also Francis G. Walett, "Governor Bernard's Undoing: An Earlier Hutchinson Letters Affair," *New England Quarterly* 38 (June 1965): 217–26; Jordan D. Fiore, "Sir Francis Bernard, Colonial Governor," *New England Social Studies Bulletin* 12 (1954): 13–18; and Ruth Owen Jones, "Governor Francis Bernard and his Land Acquisitions," *Historical Journal of Massachusetts* 16 (Summer 1988): 121–39. Standard histories of revolutionary Massachusetts, such as Bernard Bailyn, *The Ordeal of Thomas Hutchinson* (1974), and John J. Waters, Jr., *The Otis Family in Provincial and Revolutionary Massachusetts* (1968), have much information on Bernard. There is also an essential chapter on Bernard's ideas of colonial reform in Edmund S. Morgan and Helen M. Morgan, *Prologue to Revolution: Sources and Documents on the Stamp Act Crisis, 1764–1767* (1959).

CAROL SUE HUMPHREY

BERNARD, John (1756–29 Nov. 1828), actor and playwright, was born in Portsmouth, England, the son of John Bernard, a naval lieutenant, and Ann (maiden name unknown). From childhood, Bernard was fascinated with the stage. After seeing a play in London when he was seventeen, he ran away from home to join what he calls in his autobiography "a band of dramatic desperadoes." By the time he was in his mid-twenties, he had worked his way through the theatrical ranks in touring and small resident companies to become a popular low-comedy actor in London's Covent Garden Theater company. His repertoire, much of which would stand him in good stead for the rest of his life, included parts in *The Merry Wives of Windsor*, *The Comedy of Errors*, *The Merchant of Venice*, *She Stoops to Conquer*, and *The Rivals*. In 1786 Covent Garden produced two plays written by Bernard: *The Whimsical Ladies* and *The British Sailor*.

In 1774 Bernard married in Norwich an actress whose name was recorded only as Mrs. Cooper. They formed an acting team until her death in 1792. He married twice more, both actresses known only by their surnames: Mrs. Fisher in 1796 and, after her death in 1806, Miss Wright.

Invited to the United States by Thomas Wignell in 1797 to appear in his Chestnut Street Theater in Philadelphia, Bernard played a role in the development of the new country's burgeoning theater. He remained with the company as a leading comic actor until 1803, when he became manager of the Federal Street Theater in Boston. In 1811 Bernard began a theatrical tour of major U.S. cities, returning in 1816 to continue his acting career in Boston for three years before going back to England. With a large young family to support, Bernard soon fell on hard times in London, where he remained for the rest of his life, physically ill and utterly destitute. He died in London.

Bernard's chief contribution to American theater was in writing two memoirs published after his death, the first edited by his son, Bayle Bernard, a playwright and drama critic of some note, and the second by his son's wife. His first book, the two-volume *Retrospections of the Stage* (1830), recounts the everyday life of a touring theatrical company in England, including descriptions of lodgings, meals, landladies, provincial audiences, and what he calls the science of the stage. The account of London describes the famous social clubs beloved of the city's theater people. An officer in the famous Beefsteak Club, Bernard serves as a guide to other well-known clubs that welcomed actors in the eighteenth century.

Bernard's second book, *Retrospections of America* (1887), is one of the most extensive records of American theater in the Federal period. He describes the operation of theaters, theater buildings, the primary touring circuits at the time, and the economic circumstances and social standing of actors and managers. Although he testifies to the social ostracism frequently imposed on actors by certain circles, he also reveals the involvement of many theatrical folk in the full range of social activities. As a result, the book is much more than a theatrical memoir; it is a window on the broad political and cultural scene. Of particular interest are Bernard's descriptions of American cities, his characterization of American women and regional types, and his accounts of yellow fever epidemics. He also discusses U.S. involvement in the slave trade, the plight of black Americans, slave owners, and the institution of slavery, which he utterly deplored.

Bernard's involvement with the theater as well as his travels and interest in politics led to his friendship with George Washington and Thomas Jefferson, recounted in the memoir. He met Washington at the scene of a carriage accident, where he was impressed with Washington's physical power and his willingness to assist the accident victims personally rather than summoning his servants to help, as most other gentlemen would have done. Washington, an ardent theatergoer, welcomed Bernard's companionship and introduced him to Jefferson, with whom Bernard conversed about mutual interests such as the French Revolution, the United States' future as a democracy, and notables like Benjamin Rush, Mirabeau, and Joseph Priestley.

Through these two posthumously published works, John Bernard is remembered as a gifted observer and recorder of eighteenth- and nineteenth-century life in both England and the United States. Both works have been valuable sources for social historians for over a hundred years. Bernard is also known as a practicing theater man. Generally, he was more highly praised by American than English critics and was probably more popular with audiences than respected as an actor by his fellows. His vocations as actor, playwright, and manager have been recorded in the standard firsthand accounts of early American theater written by William Dunlap and William B. Wood. Dunlap not only praised him for his wide appeal but called him the finest comedian in the United States.

• British sources on Bernard include James Winston, *Theatric Tourist* (1805), and John Williams, *The Children of Thespis* (1786–1788). The primary nineteenth-century and early twentieth-century American sources of information about Bernard are T. Allston Brown, *A History of the New York Stage*, vol. 1 (1903); William Dunlap, *A History of the American Theatre* (1832); Laurence Hutton, *Curiosities of the American Stage* (1891); Noah Ludlow, *Dramatic Life As I Found It* (1880); George O. Seilhamer, *History of the American Theatre Before the Revolution* (1888); and William Wood, *Personal Recollections of the Stage* (1855). Also of interest are Thomas Clark Pollock, *The Philadelphia Theatre in the Eighteenth Century* (1933), and Francis Hodge, *Yankee Theatre* (1964).
CLAUDIA DURST JOHNSON

BERNARD, Luther Lee (29 Oct. 1881–23 Jan. 1951), sociologist, was born in Russell County, Kentucky, the son of Hiram H. Bernard and Julia Wilson, farmers. Although the senior Bernard showed courage fighting on the Union side in a border state, his petty tyranny contributed to the hardship and emotional turmoil of Luther's youth, which was spent mostly in West Texas and southwestern Missouri. A single bright spot was provided by two charismatic young teachers who introduced him to Charles Darwin and modern science at the ungraded high school he attended in Gordon, Texas. Otherwise, as his younger sister later commented, his attitude toward his family was "bitter" and "antagonistic."

Bernard earned a B.S. in 1900 at Pierce Baptist College in Missouri, where he taught science from 1901 to 1903. After two years as instructor of languages at Lamar (Mo.) College, he entered the University of Missouri, where he obtained a B.A. in 1907. There he studied with Charles A. Ellwood, a Chicago graduate already known for his theory that society possessed a "psychic" rather than a "real" unity, a psychological sociology influenced by Charles H. Cooley and John Dewey. Bernard's later attack on this view fueled a conflicted relationship with his mentor throughout his career, as Ellwood became an outspoken critic of what he termed sociological "objectivism."

At the University of Chicago, Bernard received the Ph.D. in 1910 for his thesis "An Objective Standard of Social Control," which was published in the *American Journal of Sociology* in 1911. In this work he drew upon the work of Emile Durkheim among others to attack the tradition of psychological sociology from Lester Ward through Albion Small, now Bernard's major professor. A scientific "social control," he argued, required that sociology focus on the group rather than the individual, and on concrete realities rather than abstractions such as "instincts" and "social processes." Although Small once ranked him with George Vincent and W. I. Thomas as the best of his students, Bernard in parting displayed his lifelong maverick tendencies in a blistering six-page letter criticizing the Chicago sociology department for being aloof toward students, top-heavy in theory, and inept in finding jobs for its graduates. This was the first of many such confrontations during his career.

After being exiled, as he saw it, to a position at the University of Florida for three years, Bernard eventually taught at more than half a dozen institutions, including the Universities of Minnesota (1918–1925) and North Carolina (1928–1929), Washington University in St. Louis (1929–1946), and Pennsylvania State (1947–1950). Although his onetime colleague Howard Odum dubbed him "America's favorite peripatetic professor of sociology," these frequent moves reflected a hypersensitive, often prickly personality, coupled with a penchant for womanizing that began soon after his first marriage in 1911, to Francis Fenton, a fellow graduate student at Chicago with whom he had one child. They were divorced in 1922. At Minnesota, Bernard finally resigned under pressure from administrators concerning charges of a common-law marriage, then illegal in the state. In September 1925, shortly before going to Cornell for a year, he married Jessie Ravitch, a brilliant undergraduate more than twenty years his junior, who later became a sociologist whose reputation as Jessie Bernard eclipsed his own. Although their marriage lasted until Bernard's death and produced three children, his continued philandering plagued their stormy union, while rumors of the events at Minnesota, combined with his combative personality, clouded his reputation for several years.

Despite difficulties securing a first-rate position, Bernard became a leading proponent of a radical variant of "objectivist" sociology. For William F. Ogburn, whom he regarded as his chief rival in the field, and F. Stuart Chapin, his chairman at Minnesota, "objectivity" demanded not only that sociologists confine their attention to the externals of human behavior and quantify wherever possible but also avoid value judgments. Bernard, in contrast, insisted that a positivistic sociology requires a "projective logic," akin to C. Wright Mills's later call for a "sociological imagination," whereby sociologists posit an ideal state as the goal of their analysis. For Bernard, this ideal was the perfect adjustment of individuals to their environment. In *Instinct* (1924), the work for which he was best known, he argued that since most so-called instincts are ossified customs and traditions, social progress is possible through manipulation of the environment.

During the 1930s Bernard turned his attention to the history of sociology, collecting "life histories" of his contemporaries and, with Jessie Bernard, researching the history of positivism presented in *Origins of American Sociology* (1943). He also played an active role in professional politics, mailing potential allies multiple carbons of letters on a variety of subjects—"L. L. B.'s onionskins," as they became

known. In 1930–1931 he mobilized a group of "rebels" to oppose the policies of the American Sociological Society, particularly the increasing emphasis on narrowly quantitative research. Elected president in 1932, he shaped the annual program to include papers on contemporary social issues and attempted with limited success to increase the number of women on the program. In his presidential address he attacked the research establishment and their increasing control of funds through educational foundations. In 1936 Bernard found himself excluded from a newly formed "Sociological Research Association," which he viewed as an elitist plot.

At war with the American Sociological Association and its leaders through the remainder of his career, Bernard resigned from the society in 1938, carrying on the battle in the pages of the *American Sociologist*, the journal he edited from 1938 to 1947. Although his call for an "objective standard" appeared at times to undercut his populist defense of the "little man," he opposed what he viewed as a business-dominated New Deal, once characterizing Franklin Roosevelt as "ninety percent Eleanor and ten percent mush." He later spoke against the rise of fascism at a time when many American sociologists remained silent. Perhaps the best-known North American sociologist in Latin America, he held a research grant in Argentina in 1926–1927 and helped disseminate the work of South American sociologists as a frequent reviewer for *Social Forces*. In *War and Its Causes* (1944; repr. 1972), a work that later attracted attention during the Vietnam era, he denounced the barbarity of war throughout history. Bernard died in State College, Pennsylvania.

Although Bernard trained relatively few graduate students, he counted among his disciples the sociologist George Lundberg, whose "operationalism" carried the tradition of sociological objectivism into the post–World War II decades. *Origins of American Sociology* remains a major study of the Comtean tradition in the United States, and the private and public papers Bernard carefully preserved constitute a major resource for histories of the discipline. As with many academic gadflies, his activities won him more critics than friends. To undergraduate students from Minnesota to Penn State, however, Bernard was an exciting, dedicated teacher. To his allies in the profession, as to his later defenders, "L. L. B." was an important if increasingly isolated voice for a more democratic, socially committed sociology in the interwar years.

• Bernard's papers are at the Pennsylvania State University. The manuscript divisions of the University of Chicago also holds many of the autobiographies Bernard collected for his unfinished history of contemporary American sociology. Other books by Bernard include *An Introduction to Social Psychology* (1926), *The Fields and Methods of Sociology* (1934), *Sociology and the Study of International Relations* (1934), and *Social Control in Its Sociological Aspects* (1939). Bernard's life and career are detailed in Robert C. Bannister, *Sociology and Scientism: The American Quest for Objectivity, 1880–1940* (1987), and *Jessie Bernard: The Making of a Feminist* (1991). For sympathetic assessments of Bernard's role as academic "radical," see Arthur J. Vidich and Stanford M. Lyman, *American Sociology: Worldly Rejections of Religion and their Directions* (1985), and John F. Galliher and Robert A. Hagan, "L. L. Bernard and the Original American Sociologist," *American Sociologist* 20 (1989): 134–43. Obituaries appear in the *American Sociological Review* 16 (1951): 262–63, 285–97, *Social Forces* 29 (1951): 480–81; *Sociology and Social Research* 36 (1952): 215–19; and the *New York Times*, 25 Jan. 1951.

ROBERT C. BANNISTER

BERNARD, Simon (26 Apr. 1779–5 Sept. 1839), military engineer, was born in Dôle, in the Franche-Comté region of eastern France, the son of an artisan. His parents' names are unknown. Although extremely poor, Bernard managed with the aid of a local priest to enter the École Central des Travaux Publics (soon renamed the École Polytechnique) in Paris, the basic school to train candidates for the technical branches of the French army. Graduating second in his class in 1797, he joined the Army of the Rhine, and for the next seventeen years he performed ably as an officer of engineers. He earned the notice of Emperor Napoleon I for a reconnaissance before the battle of Austerlitz in 1805, engaged in road building and counter-guerrilla operations in Dalmatia, and supervised the fortification of Antwerp. In 1809 he married Maria Anna von Lerchenfeld, with whom he had an unknown number of children. In 1813 Bernard was appointed an aide-de-camp to the emperor, and the following year he rose to *maréchal de camp*. A baron at the time of the empire's fall, Bernard received the rank of brigadier general in the Restoration army of Louis XVIII. During the Hundred Days, however, he rallied again to Napoleon and took part in the battle of Waterloo. Thus he was denied appointment in the army of the Second Restoration.

While an officer, Bernard had made the acquaintance of prominent Americans, notably William H. Crawford, minister to France in 1813–1815, and Crawford's successor, Albert Gallatin. In the aftermath of the War of 1812, the U.S. government launched an ambitious effort to reform the army and enhance national security, drawing on European models and expertise. A central feature of this program was the construction of permanent fortifications to defend the coastline from seaborne attacks. Through the influence of Crawford, who had become secretary of war, Congress passed a resolution in April 1816 that authorized the employment of a "skillful assistant" to be attached to the army Corps of Engineers, presumably to advise the government on fortification. Despite the opposition of high-ranking army engineers, who saw the employment of a foreign engineer as an adverse reflection on their corps and the U.S. Military Academy, the administration appointed Bernard to this position, granting him the rank and compensation of a brigadier general but no powers of command.

On his arrival in the United States, Bernard was assigned to the Board of Engineers for Fortification, a panel of engineering officers established by the War Department to designate sites and draft plans for new fortifications and to make recommendations on the design of existing works and those under construction. During the succeeding years the board conducted an extensive examination of the coastline and the Canadian border and submitted preliminary reports on its work. Bernard's appointment continued to rankle the Corps of Engineers, however, especially when John C. Calhoun, secretary of war in the James Monroe administration, favored the Frenchman's fortification plans over those of American engineers. In 1818 Chief Engineer Joseph G. Swift resigned from the army in protest, and Lieutenant Colonel William McRee, Bernard's senior colleague on the fortification board, soon did likewise.

Despite the controversy, the board continued its surveys, and in February 1821 it submitted a systematic plan of defense for the United States. Assuming Great Britain to be the most likely adversary, the board mentioned the importance of the navy, regular army, militia, and internal communication. It especially stressed the vital role of permanent seacoast fortifications, designed to secure bases and "rendezvous" for the American fleet, protect the vulnerable port cities, and prevent an enemy from gaining a foothold for an invasion. Once safe behind its permanent defenses, the nation could concentrate on expanding the navy, as its future wars would be fought entirely on the oceans. The report specified fifty sites to be fortified, dividing them into three classes according to their relative significance and urging that work on the first class begin immediately. In 1826 the fortification board compiled an updated and more comprehensive version of its defense plan, this time pointing to the danger to U.S. security posed by the implacable hostility of European despotism toward America's free institutions. Despite some skepticism in Congress about the expense and utility of large fortifications, the government adopted and gradually implemented the board's program. Occasionally revised and expanded, it remained a centerpiece of American defense policy into the post–Civil War era.

During the early 1820s the government increasingly assigned Bernard and his fellow engineers to transportation projects as well as to fortification work. Congress confirmed this trend with the General Survey Act of 1824, which authorized government surveys for roads and canals deemed of national importance. To implement this act, the War Department formed a second engineering board, entitled the Board of Engineers for Internal Improvement, and Bernard became its senior member. The new board's first assignment was to survey a route for the proposed Chesapeake and Ohio Canal, extending from Georgetown, District of Columbia, to Pittsburgh. The board's report enthusiastically endorsed the project, but its estimate of the cost, over $22 million, spurred controversy. Although launched at a lower funding level in 1828, the Chesapeake and Ohio Canal was soon superseded by less expensive railroads, and only the eastern section (to Cumberland, Md.) was completed. Among the other projects undertaken by Bernard as a member of the internal improvement board were surveys for the Delaware Breakwater to improve Philadelphia's harbor, a canal around Muscle Shoals on the Tennessee River, a waterway across northern Florida, and a second national road proposed to run from Buffalo, New York, to New Orleans.

In the aftermath of the July Revolution of 1830, Bernard visited France on leave and was encouraged by the prospect of employment in King Louis-Philippe's government. He resigned from the U.S. Army in July 1831 and returned permanently to his native land, where he soon acquired high honors, including aide-de-camp to the king, lieutenant general, grand officer of the Legion of Honor, and peer of France. Bernard also served as minister of war on two occasions, for three days in 1834 during the brief duc de Bassano ministry and from 1836 to 1839 under Count Louis-Mathieu Molé. He died in Paris while holding the office of governor of the royal palace.

Bernard was the most prominent of several Napoleonic veterans who contributed to the reform of the American military establishment after the War of 1812. His principal role in the United States was as chief architect of the system of seacoast fortifications that long remained a central component of U.S. defense policy.

• No collection of Bernard's personal papers is known to exist. The most reliable discussion of his American career is Joseph H. Harrison, Jr., "Simon Bernard, the American System, and the Ghost of the French Alliance," in *America, the Middle Period: Essays in Honor of Bernard Mayo*, ed. John B. Boles (1973). This work also includes citations of French sources on Bernard's life. For Bernard's role in planning the fortification system, see Jamie W. Moore, *The Fortifications Board 1816–1828 and the Definition of National Security* (1980); Robert S. Browning III, *Two If by Sea: The Development of American Coastal Defense Policy* (1983); and David A. Clary, *Fortress America: The Corps of Engineers, Hampton Roads, and United States Coastal Defense* (1990). The fortification board's reports of 1821 and 1826 are published in U.S. Congress, *American State Papers: Military Affairs*, vols. 2–3 (1832–1861). For Bernard's role in internal improvements, see Forest G. Hill, *Roads, Rails & Waterways: The Army Engineers and Early Transportation* (1957).

WILLIAM B. SKELTON

BERNARDI, Herschel (30 Oct. 1923–9 May 1986), actor, was born in New York City, the son of Bernard Bernardi and Helen (maiden name unknown), Yiddish actors. His parents came to New York in the early 1900s in the wake of the great Jewish migration from Eastern Europe and developed a modest professional career playing the Yiddish theater circuit.

Herschel was three months old when he made his theatrical debut at the McKinley Square Theatre in the Bronx as "a crying baby." At the age of three he won an amateur contest singing "Sonny Boy" at a Chinese restaurant in Philadelphia. He became an integral part of his working theatrical family and toured with them between the ages of three and thirteen. Later in life he reminisced that he had attended twenty-eight different primary and secondary schools in and around New York. One of his most famous roles as a child actor was in a Yiddish version of *The Champ* titled *Two Hearts*. In the production, presented at the National Theatre on Second Avenue in New York, the nine-year-old Herschel was advertised as the "Jewish Jackie Cooper." At the age of fourteen Herschel participated in *Green Fields* (1937), a Yiddish film based on Peretz Hirschbein's well-known play, which is considered one of the best Yiddish movies filmed in the United States. The film was directed by Edgar Ulmer who also directed Bernardi in his second Yiddish film, *The Singing Blacksmith* (1938), a musical drama written by prominent Yiddish dramatists Osip Dimow and David Pinski. Although Bernardi made his career as an adult actor in the English-language entertainment industry, he remained committed to his Yiddish theater legacy. In 1983 he paid tribute to it when he narrated *Almonds and Raisins*, a nostalgic documentary on the history of the Yiddish stage that was originally made for British television and shown often on Public Broadcasting Service TV stations in the United States.

Bernardi's English-language career developed slowly. Unable to get work in New York, he moved to Los Angeles in 1944. His first movie job was in a circus movie. Although he managed to appear in three movies, he failed to get any significant parts and returned to New York. During his stay in Hollywood Bernardi joined the Actors' Lab, a gathering place for Hollywood radicals in the 1940s. He paid for this association a decade later, during the McCarthy era, when he was blacklisted for two years by CBS television.

Back in New York, Bernardi began doing comedy monologues in Catskill hotels, playing summer stock, and performing at community centers and organizational functions. Much of his material was included in his 1960 album *Chocolate Covered Matzohs*, which traces the acculturation of the immigrant Jew in the United States through songs and anecdotes.

Bernardi's first big break came in 1954 when he was cast in the off-Broadway production of *The World of Sholom Aleichem*. The production was directed by Howard Da Silva, whom Bernardi had helped in 1944 with a recording of Sholom Aleichem stories. Written by Arnold Perl, the production featured some of the best-known actors of the New York stage, notably Will Lee, Jack Gilford, Morris Carnovsky, and Ruby Dee. Bernardi toured the country with the play and in 1955 returned to California. This time he was more successful and gained inroads into the new medium of television. He appeared on the early Matinee Theater, doing five live dramas a week from Hollywood's NBC studios, and made guest appearances on various television series. His parts were usually those of "ethnic" tough guys, perhaps, as Bernardi speculated, because he had a "great un-American face." His facility with languages allowed him to specialize in "playing dialects" such as French, German, Italian, Hungarian, and Russian. Bernardi first gained national recognition when he was engaged by Blake Edwards to play in the TV series "Peter Gunn" (1958–1961). In it he portrayed the dour-faced, sarcastic Lieutenant Jacoby, a part that earned him an Emmy nomination. He also starred in his own 1970–1971 TV series, "Arnie," in which he played a truck driver turned executive. On television Bernardi also appeared in "A Hatful of Rain," "But I Don't Want to Get Married," "No Place to Run," "Sandcastles," "The Miracle of Hannukah," "The Million Dollar Face," and "Hail to the Chief."

Bernardi's TV success paved the road for solid character roles in big-budget Hollywood movies. Most notably, he was featured as the sullen Inspector LeFevre in *Irma La Douce* (1963) and costarred with Natalie Wood and Steve McQueen in *Love with the Proper Stranger* (1964).

Bernardi made his debut on the Broadway stage on 23 November 1964 in *Bajour*, a musical comedy in which he originated the role of Johnny Dembo, the gypsy king. Bernardi's greatest success came a year later when he assumed the principal role of Tevye the Dairyman in the enormously successful musical *Fiddler on the Roof*, which had opened a year earlier. Although he was the third Tevye—the part had been originated by Zero Mostel, who was succeeded for a short while by Luther Adler—some critics claimed that Bernardi was the best Tevye. In creating the role the actor relied heavily on his family background and his experiences in the Yiddish theater. His finely detailed performance was a richly worked tapestry of gesture and sound that evoked the tragic and the comic elements that are at the heart of Tevye's appeal. Bernardi played the part on Broadway a record 702 times. He later participated in numerous revivals and regional productions of *Fiddler*. All told, he played the part more than 2,000 times. Following his great success, he was offered the leading role in the Broadway musical *Zorba the Greek*, a part he originated and played 600 times and for which he received a Tony nomination in 1968. Despite a partial disability in his left leg Bernardi performed the athletic Greek dances and leaps with zest. Bernardi's success was cut short when a serious throat ailment forced him to quit *Zorba* and into a long convalescence.

Bernardi continued to be one of the busiest and most versatile performers in the United States, slipping easily from musical comedy to drama, from radio to television to commercials. In 1976 he starred in *The Front*, with Woody Allen and Zero Mostel. The film, directed by Martin Ritt, dealt with the traumatic effect that blacklisting had on members of the entertainment world in the 1950s. He also scored a success in 1979 in Herb Gardner's *The Goodbye People*, playing Max, an angry Coney Island hot dog stand owner. For years Bernardi also played the "freeway circuit" in southern California, at college campuses and at community theaters.

Bernardi was active in TV commercials and specialized in voice overs. His voice was familiar to millions as the Jolly Green Giant and Charlie the Tuna. In a 1986 interview he stated that he had done 497 different commercials and counted 500 spots a year for more than 100 products.

Bernardi died in Los Angeles, California. He had been married three times and had three children with his second wife, Cynthia Griffith. At the time of his death he was married to Terry (maiden name unknown), the mother of his then fifteen-month-old baby.

• For background on Bernardi's family and his early life see Jack Bernardi, *My Father, the Actor* (1971), written by Bernardi's brother. The two best works on the Yiddish theater are Nahma Sandrow, *Vagabond Stars: A World History of Yiddish Theater* (1977), and David S. Lifson, *The Yiddish Theatre in America* (1963). An obituary is in the *New York Times*, 10 May 1986.

EDNA NAHSHON

BERNAYS, Doris Elsa Fleischman (18 July 1892–10 July 1980), pioneer public relations counsel and early feminist, was born in New York City, the daughter of Samuel E. Fleischman, an attorney, and Harriet Rosenthal. Doris studied music and planned to become an opera singer when she completed her bachelor's degree at Barnard College in 1913. Instead, that same year she joined the *New York Tribune*. Except for brief fundraising and freelance assignments in 1916, Doris was a reporter and assistant women's page and Sunday editor at the *Tribune* until 1919, when she left newspaper work and joined her future husband, Edward L. Bernays, in his new public relations firm. Edward married Doris in 1922. They had two daughters.

The couple joined the newly formed Lucy Stone League in 1921. The league sought to protect and ensure a married woman's right to use her own birth name on all occasions. The organization, dormant during World War II, was revived in 1950 with a broader mission of preserving and extending the civil and social rights of women. Doris Bernays served as vice president of the league until 1952. She was also president of the Woman Pays Club and active in Women in Communication. She participated in the first Women's Peace Parade in New York in 1917.

Edward Bernays generally considered the use of separate identities more critical than Doris. On their honeymoon, however, she attracted much publicity by registering at the Waldorf-Astoria hotel under her maiden name, Doris E. Fleischman. In 1923 the U.S. State Department granted her the first passport issued to a married woman under her maiden name. A great brouhaha erupted after their successful efforts in 1929 to get New York's health department to concede that a woman who keeps her maiden name after marriage may be registered by that name as the mother on a child's birth certificate.

In assessing the struggle to establish and maintain her separate identity, Bernays wrote in the *American Mercury* (1949), "Occasionally, use of my own name has given me a sense of separate individuality. . . . By and large, using my own name has been like swimming upstream through molasses. . . . A Lucy Stoner is mistaken in thinking that keeping her father's name is more significant than taking her husband's name. . . . We thought a name itself had power to confer a separate identity. It is the actions of women and the attitudes of men towards them that determine a woman's status." After 1955 she began using the name Mrs. Edward L. Bernays regularly.

After her marriage, Doris was considered an equal business partner. Edward, however, dominated their personal and professional lives. With her concurrence, Edward handled all client contacts and then consulted with Doris in private about strategies to pursue or avoid. Both have written that they respected each other, worked well together, and handled projects they probably could not have completed individually. Both agreed that theirs was a logical and practical arrangement.

Working as partners until Doris's death in Cambridge, Massachusetts, the Bernayses helped establish the principles, practices, and ethics of the new public relations profession. They advised many important men, women, governments, industries, corporations, and trade organizations. Clients included Dwight Eisenhower, Sigmund Freud (Edward Bernays's uncle), Thomas A. Edison, and Henry Ford.

In the early 1920s Doris Bernays developed *Contact*, a four-page house organ sent to 15,000 media people and community leaders. For a decade the quarterly publication helped attract new clients to the Bernayses' firm and improved the visibility of the new field of public relations.

Doris Bernays's major written work is her semiautobiographical book on women's roles, *A Wife Is Many Women* (1955). She effusively recommended that wives work alongside their husbands. She noted that "double partnership has made it possible for me to do the jobs that I am expected to do as a woman without conflicting with [Edward's] idea of my professional duties. . . . It seems to me that double partnership doubles everything, especially the pleasanter aspects—respect, loyalty, admiration, affection."

Edward Bernays valued Doris's advice. He described his wife as unassuming, caring little about public recognition, and usually seeking visibility only when he pressured her to do so. In *Biography of an Idea* (1965), he wrote that "over the years [Doris] has been my most valuable asset. She has contributed heavily to the policy and strategy we have advised our clients to carry out. Her balanced judgment carries overriding weight with me. And she has unique compassion and understanding."

In 1946 the Edward L. Bernays Foundation was established to further human relations, and Doris Bernays served as a vice president. In 1972 she received the National Headliner Award, the highest honor from Theta Sigma Phi, the national sorority of women in journalism and communications. She also received a leadership award in 1976 from the Chicago chapter of the Public Relations Society of America.

Through the 1970s she and her husband continued their public relations consulting. They also advocated causes such as pay for housewives and accelerated advancement for women working in the media.

Doris Bernays published several long articles in magazines such as *McCall's*, *American Mercury*, and *Ladies' Home Journal*. She contributed to several books and, in 1928, compiled and edited a book, *An Outline of Careers for Women: A Practical Guide to Achievement*, in which she assessed public relations as "an enthralling occupation for the woman who has constructive ideas and the desire and force to make them result in concrete activities, facts, laws, or products. She may have the satisfaction of working well and, if she desires, of receiving recognition. She may be a power for good. Her goal is of her own choosing."

In a 1930 *Ladies' Home Journal* article Bernays blamed women's lack of ambition, planning, and understanding of the working world for the fact that most women were poorly paid and held jobs with little authority. In an article for *Independent Woman* (Nov. 1941) she advised prospective public relations women that they should persuade men prejudiced against women of women's worth by "intelligent handling of problems, and not by slaying the dragon of antifeminism."

• Doris Fleischman Bernays's papers are held in her own name at the Arthur and Elizabeth Schlesinger Library on the History of Women in America at Radcliffe College. There are a few papers that relate directly to Bernays in her husband's papers in the Manuscript Division at the Library of Congress. Keith A. Larson, *Public Relations, the Edward L. Bernayses and the American Scene: A Bibliography* (1978), is an excellent source that lists books, articles, published talks, and mentions in books and periodicals for both Edward and Doris Bernays. An obituary is in the *New York Times*, 12 July 1980.

PETER E. MAYEUX

BERNAYS, Edward (22 Nov. 1891–9 Mar. 1995), public relations counsel, was born in Vienna, Austria, the son of Eli Bernays, a merchant and grain exporter, and Anna Freud, sister of Sigmund Freud. When he was one year old, his family immigrated to the United States, and he enjoyed a comfortable upbringing in New York City. At his father's request he attended Cornell University's school of agriculture and received a B.S. in 1912, but he soon abandoned agriculture, first for editing and then to work as a Broadway press-agent. His initial success came in promoting *Damaged Goods* (1913), a "social issues" play about the dangers of venereal disease. By 1917 he had built a successful business handling publicity for such acts as Enrico Caruso and Serge Diaghilev's Ballets Russes.

In 1918 he carried his skills to a new field when he joined George Creel's Committee on War Information (CWI), the U.S. government-sponsored propaganda organization. While there he directed Latin American News, utilizing American corporations' overseas offices to promote the Allied cause. In 1919 he was part of the CWI mission to the Paris Peace Conference though a growing backlash to Creel's work prevented it from handling American publicity there.

His work on the Creel Committee convinced Bernays that untapped opportunities existed in the management of public opinion. He soon established himself in a new field as a "counsel for public relations." He was careful to distinguish his work from that of the pressagent who, he claimed, merely sought publicity for his client. In contrast, the counsel for public relations would mediate between the client and the public, "interpret[ing] the client to the public . . . [and] the public to the client." Bernays's practice quickly prospered; during the 1920s many corporations were looking for better ways both to influence burgeoning consumer markets and to burnish their public image. Over the next few years Bernays built a client list that included the companies of General Motors, Liggett & Myers, Philco, Procter & Gamble, and the United Fruit Company. He did much of this in partnership with Doris E. Fleischman, whom he married in 1922; they had two daughters.

Bernays distinguished himself from competitors by claiming that public relations was an "applied social science" and that the public relations counsel should draw on the tools of social science, especially psychology. His own credentials in this field were seemingly guaranteed by his relationship to Freud—few interviewers missed the family tie, and many implied that the connection gave Bernays special insight into the public mind. Bernays helped establish respect for the emerging field of public relations by teaching the first college course in the field at New York University in 1923. He also wrote widely on the subject, most notably in his books *Crystallizing Public Opinion* (1923), *Propaganda* (1928), and his essay "The Engineering of Consent" (1947). These writings drew on the theories of Freud, Walter Lippmann, and French psychologist Gustave Le Bon and argued that mass publics were inherently irrational and relied on misleading stereotypes to guide their actions. In such circumstances, Bernays argued, the public relations counsel could not merely convey information to the public but had to engage in the "engineering of consent" to produce desired outcomes. In doing so, Bernays abandoned the approach to public relations of his predecessor Ivy L. Lee, who trusted the public sufficiently to argue that full disclosure was always the best policy.

Thus, Bernays's campaigns were often conducted behind the scenes, with his real aims and clients hidden behind a public-spirited goal. His 1930s campaigns for Dixie Cups, for instance, were designed not to promote Dixie Cups per se, but to convince consumers that only disposable cups were truly sanitary. Nowhere was his approach better demonstrated than in his involvement with "Light's Golden Jubilee," a 1929 commemoration apparently sponsored by Henry Ford to celebrate the fiftieth anniversary of Thomas Edison's invention of the light bulb. The Jubilee was, in fact, partially funded by several electric power companies, and Bernays used the hoopla surrounding it to impress upon Americans the benefits not only of Edison's invention, but of privately owned utilities.

Bernays's work attracted critics as well as clients. Journalists disputed his claim that a public relations counsel could "create news." *The Nation's* review of *Crystallizing Public Opinion* was titled "The Higher Hokum," and in his book *The American Language* (1919, rev. 1921, 1923, 1936), H. L. Mencken attacked the term "public relations" as a euphemism for press agentry. In the late 1930s the rise of totalitarian governments led some to compare Bernays's work to that of Nazi propagandist Joseph Goebbels. Despite such criticism, Bernays maintained a high public profile; Herbert Hoover named him to his Depression-fighting Emergency Committee for Employment in 1930. Bernays was also a longtime supporter of many liberal causes and occasionally handled publicity for the NAACP in the 1920s.

In 1946 Bernays began to cut back on his practice and started to devote half his time to non-profit organizations. He still served several clients, however, including the United Fruit Company. In the early 1950s he organized a public relations campaign for the firm designed to convince Americans that the Guatemalan government of Jacobo Arbenez, which was at that time involved in a bitter dispute with United Fruit, was riddled with Communism. The campaign helped generate support for the CIA-backed overthrow of Arbenez in 1954.

In 1962 Bernays closed his office and moved from New York City to Cambridge, Massachusetts. He continued working, however, and was still consulting for firms at age 100. He died in Cambridge, Massachusetts.

Observers described Bernays as a small, dapper man with a professorial air. He had a significant impact on both American business and culture. He was not, as some claimed, the "father of public relations," but he did help secure the field its place in American business and taught many corporations how to manage their public image. In the process, he developed a distinctively American variant of Freud's ideas and encouraged the belief that corporations could shape American public opinion.

• Bernays's papers are held at the Library of Congress. His autobiography, *Biography of an Idea: Memoirs of Public Relations Counsel Edward L. Bernays* (1968), provides a detailed account of his life, but it should be read with caution; he could exaggerate the events of his life and almost always placed himself in the most favorable light. Good accounts of his work can be found in histories of public relations by Alan R. Raucher, *Public Relations and Business, 1900–1929* (1968), Richard S. Tedlow, *Keeping the Corporate Image: Public Relations and Business, 1900–1950* (1979), and Stuart Ewen, *PR! A Social History of Spin* (1996). A useful guide to writings by and about Bernays is Keith A. Larson, *Public Relations, the Edward L. Bernayses, and the American Scene: A Bibliography* (1978). An obituary is in the *New York Times*, 10 Mar. 1995.
HARWELL WELLS

BERNBACH, William (13 Aug. 1911–2 Oct. 1982), advertising executive, was born in the Bronx, New York City, the son of Jacob Bernbach, a designer of women's clothes, and Rebecca Reiter. When he graduated from college (New York University, 1932), with a major in English, Bernbach faced the harsh facts of the depression. Jobs, especially in advertising, were few; the best he could do was take a position as an office boy with Schenley Distillers. Nevertheless, he mustered the enterprise to draft a promotional piece for Schenley's American cream whiskey and submitted it for consideration. Although the advertising department did in fact use the ad, no mention was made of Bernbach's having created it. But, his initiative having taken him this far, Bernbach went directly to the firm's president, Lewis Rosenthiel, to tell him that he had authored the ad. The effort paid off: Bernbach was taken on by the advertising department.

When Grover Whalen, the chairman of Schenley's board, became president of the 1938 New York World's Fair, he hired Bernbach to be a researcher and speech writer. That same year, Bernbach married Evelyn Carbone; they had two sons. From working for Whalen Bernbach went on, in 1941, to be a writer for the William H. Weintraub advertising agency. Thanks to the tutelage he received from the agency's art director, Paul Rand, he became much more attuned to questions of graphic design, and along with Rand he would play a major role in stimulating what Bernbach was to call "a new look in advertising."

In 1943 Bernbach had a short stint in the U.S. Army, but he was not in good enough physical condition to handle the rigors of service during World War II. After briefly working at Coty, Inc., he became a copywriter at Grey Advertising, the name of which suggested its somewhat lackluster performance in the business. Bernbach, who had persuaded the head of the agency to make him vice president for copy, proved able to win the kind of large accounts that would make for success in a highly competitive arena. An experienced account executive at Grey, Ned Doyle, shared with Bernbach the aspiration of establishing an ad agency that would be much more dynamic. The chance to do so arose when Ohrbach's, the New York chain of budget-priced women's fashion stores, let Bernbach know that they would forsake Grey if he and Doyle set up a new firm.

A third partner, an administrator and accountant named Maxwell Dane, added his stake to help form the Doyle Dane Bernbach agency in 1949. Right from the start, Ohrbach's was their high-profile account, with Bernbach showing the imagination and flair that would make his name in the advertising world. Other department stores in the New York area, such as Macy's and Gimbel's, had a far stronger presence in the market because they spent much more on ads and successfully promoted themselves as reliable outlets of quality goods. Bernbach, however, decided to capitalize on the idea of Ohrbach's as the store where the shopper would save money and still be able to dress fashionably. To do this as economically as possible, he emphasized advertising images that would grab attention. In the best known of the Ohrbach's ads he portrayed a cat with a large hat and long cigarette holder, affecting a la-di-da air as she comments on how a friend of hers, Joan, gets good clothes on the cheap at Ohrbach's. The store's name recognition soared. The

same technique of creating a strikingly memorable image or punchline was applied to the Henry S. Levy Bakery of Brooklyn, which, like Ohrbach's, could not afford an expensive ad campaign. The solution devised by Bernbach and his partners was to play with the idea of Levy's Jewish rye having universal appeal. Someone who was clearly not Jewish—perhaps an African American, an American Indian, or an Asian—would be pictured on a poster enjoying a sandwich made of rye, and the message would be spelled out in a caption no one would forget: "You don't have to be Jewish to love Levy's." Soon, Levy's outsold all other brands in the city. Now Doyle Dane Bernbach was positioned to acquire a major national account.

For Polaroid, the manufacturer of the first so-called instant camera, Bernbach once again set about creating a distinctive "hook" that would sell the product in the simplest, most economical terms possible. With the phrase "people take pictures of people they love" as the motto of the magazine ad campaign, which began in 1954, Bernbach used glossy images of friends and family gathered together where they would naturally feel comfortable and happy, where someone was ready to capture the moment on film, and where all would soon share in the pleasure of the photograph that would magically develop by itself. Once the ads became established, the scenes were so characteristic in style and tone that no explanatory text was needed.

In 1959 Doyle Dane Bernbach developed for the German automobile manufacturer Volkswagen one of the most celebrated product promotions of the era. The snub, little Volkswagen (literally, "people's car"), which came to be known colloquially as the beetle, seemed an unlikely challenger to the standard American sedan—the big, solid Chevrolets or Fords that dominated the highways. Again, Bernbach did not shy away from highlighting what others might have thought were a product's obvious liabilities. In a country where bigness seemed inherent to the national ethos, he dared to play up the diminutiveness of the Volkswagen. To emphasize the antithesis of bigness, the photo accompanying the text of the ad typically presented the car in a very large space, and the headline, set in modest type (though, again, with enough surrounding space to draw the eye to it), encapsulated the message in two economical words: "Think small." The virtues of the Volkswagen were, as Bernbach plainly expressed, rooted in its economical nature: a low-maintenance vehicle that far surpassed the average American car in gas mileage.

The Volkswagen ads had the same memorable directness that had stamped Bernbach's previous work, but now the spare, clean "look" that he had pioneered became recognized as a significant innovation in the general aesthetics of American advertising. That distinctiveness and creativity paid off handsomely for Doyle Dane Bernbach. From 1954, when the Polaroid campaign was kicked off, into the early 1960s, the firm's billings increased fivefold to about $40 million.

When the automobile rental company Avis went to Doyle Dane Bernbach, it was at perhaps an even greater disadvantage than Ohrbach's or Volkswagen. At the time, the largest company in the car rental business, Hertz, was barely challenged by the competition that Avis offered; Hertz's market share meant that Avis was a sliver on the pie chart. Once again, Bernbach's technique was not to deflect attention from what was patently the case. "Avis is only No. 2 in rent-a-cars," the ad began, but then added, "So why go with us? We try harder." The punchline was soon to be a ubiquitous phrase, and it was reproduced on immediately recognizable buttons in dozens of languages. In a red-colored, spare serif typeface on a white background, the words "We try harder" (followed by a decisive period) could be immediately understood whether they had been translated into French or Japanese. By the mid-1960s, Avis was enjoying an increase in revenues of nearly 30 percent.

In the same period of time, Doyle Dane Bernbach's annual billings jumped even more dramatically; at mid-decade, they amounted to $130 million. The firm was among the ten most successful in the advertising industry, and no one doubted that Bernbach was its guiding genius. Part of what set him apart was his keen sense of the purposes that advertising should serve. A basic tenet of his was that honesty sells. "Don't be slick," he advised. "Tell the truth." A corollary was his conviction that "nothing makes a bad product fail faster than a great advertising campaign." Another of his beliefs was that imagination and wit are of far greater value than market research. But he advocated a team-approach to creativity. A writer and an art director together were much more likely to develop a visually and verbally striking ad than they would be in isolation from each other. Synergy was the key to finding the right image to make an ad stand out.

Bernbach lived by his convictions outside the advertising business as well. Fervent in his desire for world peace, he developed for the Committee for a Sane Nuclear Policy (SANE) a print ad that he himself felt was a particularly good piece of work. To make his point, he used a simple photograph featuring Dr. Benjamin Spock, the world-famous pediatrician and author of books on the care and nurturing of babies. Shown with a child on his knee, he implicitly conveys what the caption says: "Dr. Spock is worried."

Ironically, when Bernbach decided to retire from his position as chief executive officer of Doyle Dane Bernbach in 1976, the firm was already drifting away from his tenets. Complacent in its attitude, it was losing major accounts, the first being Alka Seltzer early in the decade and then other prominent clients, such as Lever Brothers, Whirlpool, Sara Lee, Quaker Oats, and Cracker Jack. The ad agency that Doyle, Dane, and Bernbach founded as the contrary to the stodginess of a company like Grey Advertising was turning into a lackluster operation itself. Bernbach died in New York City.

• Useful additional material on Bernbach and his agency can be found in *Printers Ink*, 31 July 1959; "Meet Doyle Dane's Bernbach," *Newsweek*, 8 June 1964; *Advertising Age*, 8 Nov. 1976, 11 Oct. 1982, 8 Nov. 1982, 25 Apr. 1983, and 10 Dec. 1984; *Harper's*, Jan. 1983; and "Trying to Pull Doyle Dane Out of the Doldrums," *Business Week*, 5 Nov. 1984. Martin Mayer, *Madison Avenue, U.S.A.* (1958), calls Bernbach "the unquestioned hero of business today," while Stephen Fox, *The Mirror Makers* (1984), places Bernbach in historical perspective. An obituary is in the *New York Times*, 3 Oct. 1982.

JOHN N. INGHAM

BERNHARDT, Clyde Edric Barron (11 July 1905–20 May 1986), jazz trombonist and singer, was born Clyde Edric Barnhardt in Gold Hill, North Carolina, the son of Washington Michael Barnhardt, a miner, and Elizabeth Mauney. When Bernhardt was a child, he added the name Barron because his grandmother in slavery had been lent to a family named Barron who treated her kindly. He changed the spelling of his surname in 1930 on the advice of a psychic. In 1912, after his father suffered a heart attack and left mining, Bernhardt helped to peddle goods from a wagon. The family moved to New Hope (later absorbed into Badin), North Carolina, and in 1915 his father died. Bernhardt attended school for three months each year while holding various jobs, including work at Alcoa Aluminum in 1918.

The following year his mother took the family to Harrisburg, Pennsylvania, and then to Steeltown, Pennylvania. Bernhardt returned to Badin in November 1919 with the intent of resuming work at Alcoa, but instead he secured a better job, becoming a messenger boy for Western Union. After rejoining his mother and siblings in Steeltown in April 1921, he quit school, having reached eighth grade. He held various jobs over the next several years.

Although Bernhardt had been attracted to music in his preschool years, only in 1922 did he purchase a trombone and begin serious studies with teachers in Pennsylvania and Ohio, as his mother relocated the family and he moved out on his own. By 1925 he was working professionally, and in 1928, after affiliations with several little-known bandleaders, he joined the Whitman Sisters' show in Harlem and toured with them to June 1929. In March 1931 he joined cornetist King Oliver's band, touring for eight months, and with Oliver's encouragement he began doubling as a blues singer. He thought that he had married Barbara ("Bobby"; maiden name unknown) in 1931, only to discover a few months later that she was already married. He never attempted marriage again.

Bernhardt joined Marion Hardy's Alabamians in New York City in November 1931. He worked with Billy Fowler's band from September 1932 to April 1933, a gig that included jobs accompanying pianist and singer Fats Waller. He was a member of Vernon Andrade's dance orchestra from 1934 to 1937, and in September 1934 he made his first recordings, "Ain't It Nice?" and "Functionizin'," with Alex Hill's band. As a member of pianist Edgar Hayes's big band from February 1937, he performed in Europe in 1938 and made annual tours accompanying dancer Bill Robinson; he also worked with pianist Horace Henderson's big band in 1941.

After leaving Hayes, Bernhardt toured briefly with Waller's big band, but he was bored by the lack of challenging parts or solos. In September 1942 he joined pianist Jay McShann's big band, touring until July 1943. He played in tenor saxophonist Cecil Scott's band at the Ubangi Club in New York City for five months. In 1944 he joined the orchestra of pianist Luis Russell, who featured Bernhardt as a singer, most notably in well-received performances at the Apollo Theater in Harlem. Bernhardt suffered from bronchitis and was obliged to quit Russell's band in October. For the remainder of 1944 he worked in pianist Claude Hopkins's band at the Club Zanzibar in New York. He joined the Bascomb Brothers' orchestra in 1945, and he spent the first four months of 1946 with Scott again.

From 1946 to 1948 Bernhardt for the first time led his own group, the Blue Blazers. He rejoined Russell from 1948 to 1951 while also working with other bands. In 1952 he began recording under the pseudonym Ed Barron, and he had a hit rhythm-and-blues song with his own "Cracklin' Bread," but he was cheated out of royalties by the record company. From 1952 to 1970 he played in Joe Garland's dance orchestra. In the course of this lengthy affiliation he resumed day work and general studies. He passed the high school equivalency examination in 1963 and then took a job as a custodian in Newark, New Jersey.

Interest in Bernhardt's musical activities was rekindled by a series of articles published by Derrick Stewart-Baxter in 1967 and 1968 and by a recording that Stewart-Baxter produced in the latter year and issued in 1971. Bernhardt retired as a custodian in February 1972 and vacationed for a few weeks in England, where he was treated as a musical celebrity. He worked with bassist Hayes Alvis's band later that year, shortly before Alvis died. He recorded his own albums *Blues and Jazz from Harlem* (1972) and *More Blues and Jazz from Harlem* (1973), the latter with the Harlem Blues and Jazz Band, of which he eventually became the sole leader. A heart attack interrupted his new career in 1974, but he recovered and resumed playing and singing, touring Europe annually from 1976 to 1979 with his band. He spent his final years, from 1979 onward, as a member of drummer Barry Martyn's Legends of Jazz. He died in Newark.

While Bernhardt was not an important jazz or rhythm-and-blues performer, he is important for his detailed, level-headed reminiscences of dozens of African-American entertainers, including valuable essays on less well-known performers such as the Whitman Sisters, Hardy and his Alabamians, Andrade, Scott, and the Bascomb Brothers, among others, as well as important jazz musicians such as McShann and Russell. His several published recollections of a forceful, responsible, talented, shrewd King Oliver in late career provide an especially welcome antidote to the romantic but pathetic portrait of Oliver popularized in the famous early jazz book *Jazzmen* (1939).

• The definitive source, including discography and bibliography, is Clyde E. B. Bernhardt, as told to Sheldon Harris, *I Remember: Eighty Years of Black Entertainment, Big Bands, and the Blues* (1986). Stewart-Baxter's interviews appeared as "The Clyde Bernhardt Story," *Jazz Journal* 20 (Sept. 1967): 15, 40; (Oct. 1967): 11–12, 40; 21 (Jan. 1968): 31; and (Feb. 1968): 11. A further detailed interview is Gilbert Gaster, "Clyde Bernhardt," *Storyville*, no. 44 (1 Dec. 1972): 54–56, 58–70. See also Bernhardt, "Talking about King Oliver: An Oral History Excerpt," *Annual Review of Jazz Studies* 1 (1982): 32–38. An obituary is in the *New York Times*, 31 May 1986.

BARRY KERNFELD

BERNSTEIN, Aline Frankau (22 Dec. 1880–7 Sept. 1955), set and costume designer and author, was born in New York City, the daughter of Joseph Frankau, an actor, and Rebecca Goldsmith. Joseph Frankau, who was of German-Jewish ancestry, first named his daughter Hazel, but her mother changed it to Aline. Educated in the New York public schools and raised in the theater, as a child Aline wanted to be an actress, but her father encouraged her talent for drawing instead. After the early deaths of her parents (both had died by 1897), Aline became the ward of her aunt, Rachel, a drug addict. She attended Hunter College as a student of fine art. Tom Watson, a family friend and a member of the board of directors of the New York School of Applied Design, arranged for her to study drawing on scholarship at the school. She later studied portrait painting with Robert Henri, dedicating herself to this art form until she began to work in the theater.

In 1902 Aline married Theodore Bernstein, a successful Wall Street broker, with whom she had two children. She began volunteer work backstage at the Henry Street Settlement, where her friends Alice and Irene Lewisohn mounted pageants and plays. Eventually the Lewisohn sisters created the Neighborhood Playhouse (1915–1927) to bring the European "art theater" to America following the examples of designers Robert Edmond Jones, Lee Simonson, and Mordecai Gorelik. Steeped in "New Stagecraft" principles, Bernstein learned to interpret visually both script and character, to subordinate design to the values of the script, and to seek simplicity in the work. Critics frequently called her work unobtrusively "right" for the play.

Between 1915 and 1924 Bernstein served an apprenticeship at the Neighborhood Playhouse, first executing others' designs, then designing and executing her own costumes for at least fifteen plays. Her first design was for *The Queen's Enemies* in 1916. By 1924 she was also working part time for the Theatre Guild. But it was the 1924 production of *The Little Clay Cart* at the Neighborhood Playhouse that brought Bernstein to wider public attention. Her designs for *The Little Clay Cart*, an ancient Indian classic, captured with beauty and simplicity the essence of the Rajput style of miniature painting. For the American premiere of the classic Jewish folktale *The Dybbuk*, Bernstein's expressionistic designs grew progressively more distorted as the story action became increasingly mystical and supernatural. Also in 1924 Bernstein won acclaim with her stunning costume designs for Max Reinhardt's renowned production of *The Miracle*. From this time on Bernstein was considered one of the most influential of American set and costume designers.

In 1928 Bernstein began a four-year association with Eva Le Gallienne's Civic Repertory Theatre, for which her most innovative contribution was the creation of a unit set. Designed to suit the economic needs of a theater trying to stay alive as a repertory company during the depression, Bernstein's set was a neutral base that could change mood, tone, and style completely with the addition and subtraction of any number of possible insets, doors, windows, or flying scenery.

In 1925 Bernstein met Thomas Wolfe, a writer twenty years her junior, with whom she fell in love. The two carried on a stormy affair for more than five years, during which time Bernstein offered Wolfe social, artistic, and financial support. She urged him to write novels rather than plays, a decision that resulted in his autobiographical novels *Look Homeward Angel* (1929), *The Web and the Rock* (1939), and *You Can't Go Home Again* (1940). In the latter two works, Bernstein can be found in the character Esther Jack. Acting as Wolfe's agent, Bernstein found a publisher for his books. She in turn wrote novels—*Miss Condon* (1947), a bestseller, and *The Journey Down* (1938), as well as *Three Blue Suits* (1933), a collection of short stories. When her relationship with Wolfe ended, Bernstein attempted suicide. She recovered and continued to be surrounded by her family and a husband who remained loyal despite her affair.

In the thirties Bernstein continued to work with the Neighborhood Playhouse and the Civic Repertory Theatre (both of which closed by 1934) and the Theatre Guild. She also worked independently with Elmer Rice on *We the People* (1933) and designed Lillian Hellman's *The Children's Hour* (1934), *Days to Come* (1936), and *The Little Foxes* (1939) for director Herman Shumlin. She collaborated with Irene Lewisohn to establish the Museum of Costume Art, later absorbed by the Metropolitan Museum of Art as the Costume Institute. In 1944 she became president of the institute and remained in that office until her death.

During the forties Bernstein taught design at Vassar College, where she was also a consultant for the Experimental Theatre, and at both Yale University and Harvard College. At the age of seventy Bernstein collaborated with Robert Lewis on *Regina*, an operatic version of *The Little Foxes*, for which she won a Tony award. Her final project for the stage was costume design and execution for the off-Broadway production of *The World of Sholom Aleichem* in 1953. She died in New York City.

Bernstein was the first influential female set and costume designer in the United States. She was the first female designer to be invited to join the union, a triumph that took her two years to achieve; in 1926 she was sworn in as "Brother Bernstein," the first woman member of the United Scenic Artists Union of the American Federation of Labor. Bernstein's passion for design "burning in her breast" revealed itself in detailed artistry. The actress Helen Hayes once described a costume designed by Bernstein that she wore for a production of Shaw's *Caesar and Cleopatra* in 1925 as "hand-dyed blue taffeta appliques on cloth of gold in the form of little feathers like the wings of ibis. It was a work of art." Bernstein designed more than 100 plays in forty-one years. She was an artist, craftswoman, writer, historian, mentor, wife, and mother, a quintessential woman of the theater whose example still inspires.

• A collection of Bernstein's unpublished notebooks, drawings, photographs, and primary source clippings are in the Billy Rose Theatre Collection at the New York Public Library for the Performing Arts, Lincoln Center. Correspondence between Bernstein, Wolfe, and others is in the William B. Wisdom Collection housed in Harvard University's Houghton Library. Bernstein's other publications include her autobiography, *An Actor's Daughter* (1941), *Masterpieces of Woman's Costume of the Eighteenth and Nineteenth Centuries* (published posthumously in 1959), and *The Martha Washington Dollbook* (1945). Selected articles written by her include "Scissors and Sense," *Theatre Arts Monthly*, Aug. 1925, pp. 515–22; "The Costume Museum," *Theatre Arts Monthly*, Oct. 1937, pp. 812–17; "Women in Production," *Atlantic Monthly*, Sept. 1940, pp. 323–32; "The Theatre Takes Stock," *Atlantic Monthly*, May 1940, pp. 327–64; and "The Craftsmen," *Atlantic Monthly*, Apr. 1945, pp. 208–14.

Publications about Bernstein include Carole Klein, *Aline*, (1979); Norris Houghton, "Designer Sets the Stage: Jo Mielziner and Aline Bernstein," *Theatre Arts Monthly*, Feb. 1937, pp. 113–25; Florence Von Wien, "Women Who Are Stage Designers," *Independent Woman*, May 1946, pp. 134–36; Eva Le Gallienne, *At 33* (1934); Alice Lewisohn Crowley, *The Neighborhood Playhouse* (1959); and "Designer and Director," *Theatre Arts Monthly*, Feb. 1951, pp. 24–25. Works that discuss the Bernstein-Wolfe relationship include Elizabeth Nowell, *Thomas Wolfe: A Biography* (1960) and *The Letters of Thomas Wolfe* (1956); Richard S. Kennedy, *The Window of Memory: The Literary Career of Thomas Wolfe* (1962); Andrew Turnbull, *Thomas Wolfe* (1967); *The Notebooks of Thomas Wolfe*, ed. Richard S. Kennedy and Paschal Reeves (2 vols., 1970); and David Herbert Donald, *Look Homeward: A Life of Thomas Wolfe* (1987). An obituary is in the *New York Times*, 8 Sept. 1955.

KATHLEEN M. ROBBINS

BERNSTEIN, Herman (21 Sept. 1876–31 Aug. 1935), writer, was born in Neustadt-Scherwindt (Vladislavov), Lithuania, the son of David Bernstein, a merchant, and Maria Elsohn. When he was five, Bernstein's family moved to Mogilov, Belorussia, where he received a traditional Jewish education as well as a thorough grounding in secular subjects. The family emigrated to New York in 1893, where Bernstein rapidly mastered English well enough to create poems in the language, published in 1899 as *The Flight of Time*. He also contributed short stories to *Ainslee's Magazine*, the *New York Evening Post*, and the *Independent*. Over the years, he published translations of works by

Andreyev, Chekhov, Gorky, and Tolstoy, as well as adaptations of several Russian, Swedish, Austrian, and German plays.

In 1902 Bernstein married Sophie Friedman, with whom he was to have four children. The same year saw the publication of his collection of short stories, *In the Gates of Israel*, which has as its theme the inability of a diaspora Israel to maintain protective "gates" against a threatening New World. One such story, "The Disarmed Reformer," centers around a practical joke played aboard an immigrant ship on an Orthodox Jew, who is persuaded to have his earlocks, an essential element of his religious identity, removed as a condition for entry into the United States. While the man's aim in coming to America is to try to convert his Reform-Jewish son back to traditional Judaism, he fails to see that he is being tricked out of his Orthodoxy and loses his sense of moral authority with regard to his son. While one modern critic has dismissed Bernstein's short stories as literary pathos (Dittmar, p. 61), another has noted how refreshing it is to come across American-Jewish immigrant writing in which "familiar ghetto stereotypes like the cruel German-Jewish sweater, the consumptive sewing-machine operator, and the fiery young radical are absent" (Fine, p. 177). A moralistic novel, *Contrite Hearts*, showing how Orthodoxy leads to a fulfillment denied those who are governed by mere passion, was published in 1905.

Bernstein's career as a journalist took off in 1905 with the publication in the *New York Herald* of an account of the revolt aboard the armored cruiser *Potemkin*, sent to him by the sister of a high-ranking Russian diplomat, himself in New York at the time of publication. From 1908 Bernstein's reporting of foreign affairs as special correspondent of the *New York Herald*, *New York Sun*, *New York Times*, and William Randolph Hearst's papers took him all over Europe and allowed him to interview several cultural and political notables, such as Bergson, Einstein, Kropotkin, Nordau, Rathenau, Rodin, Shaw, Tolstoy, Trotsky, and Weizmann (partly collected in *With Master Minds* [1912], more fully in *Celebrities of Our Time* [1924]).

Bernstein's special strength, however, was a form of investigative international journalism that was motivated by a powerful desire to lay bare the operations of Russian totalitarianism, whether Czarist or Bolshevist, especially in so far as it affected the fate of Russian Jews. He managed to expose the involvement of the Russian secret police in the case of Mendel Beilis, the Jew wrongfully accused of the ritual murder of a gentile boy (1911–1913), a case fictionalized in Bernard Malamud's *The Fixer* (1966). In 1917 Bernstein had another scoop in the *New York Herald* when he brought to light the content of telegrams exchanged between Kaiser Wilhelm II and Czar Nicholas II from 1904 to 1907, revealing previously unknown intrigues against Britain (published as *The Willy–Nicky Correspondence* in 1918). Bernstein's personal achievement in securing this material may have been minor, given the fact that it was made available to him by Russian historians after the outbreak of the anticzarist revolu-

tion. Yet, over the ensuing months Bernstein managed to probe deep both into the exact course of events in Russia that preceded World War I and into conditions in the emergent Soviet Union. Interviews with both czarist and Communist leaders served as the basis for Bernstein's sharply critical pamphlet, *The Bolsheviki: The World Dynamiters* (1919), for the National Security League's Patriotism through Education series.

Bernstein's foreign affairs reporting did not prevent him from pursuing other interests simultaneously, prominent among which was his founding, in 1914, of the Yiddish daily, *Der Tog* (The Day), which he edited for two years. Bernstein left to become editor in chief (until Jan. 1919) of the Jewish-Orthodox weekly *American Hebrew*, while from 1925 to 1929 he was editor of the *Jewish Tribune*. His concern over the plight of Jews was made manifest on numerous occasions. Most conspicuously, Bernstein was one of the first to expose as a forgery *The Protocols of the Elders of Zion*, an influential anti-Semitic document circulating worldwide. His initial volume on the matter, *The History of a Lie* (1921), was followed by a more elaborate study, *The Truth About "The Protocols of Zion"* (1935). A lawsuit against Henry Ford, who had supported the distribution of the *Protocols* and published articles derived from them in his weekly *Dearborn Independent*, was settled out of court to Bernstein's advantage (1926–1928).

In 1928 Bernstein contributed to Herbert Hoover's election campaign by the publication in book form of his 1925 *McClure's* profile of the politician. He was rewarded with an appointment as minister to Albania (1930–1933), which enabled him to pursue his interest in European politics—he sent the State Department regular reports on the Balkan region—from a new vantage point. After his return to the United States, he published his final book, *Can We Abolish War?* (1935), a symposium that tended to answer the question less than optimistically. Bernstein died of a heart attack at Sheffield, Massachusetts.

At the time of publication, Bernstein's investigative foreign reporting had considerable impact. The British newspaper publisher Lord Northcliffe labeled his revelation of the imperial telegrams "one of the greatest journalistic coups of our time," and his success in suing Ford was generally regarded as a significant victory over anti-Semitism.

• On Bernstein's fiction, see Kurt Dittmar, *Assimilation und Dissimilation* (1976), and David M. Fine, "Immigrant Ghetto Fiction, 1885–1918: An Annotated Bibliography," *American Literary Realism* 6 (1973): 169–95. An obituary is in the *New York Times*, 1 Sept. 1935.

GERT BUELENS

BERNSTEIN, Leonard (25 Aug. 1918–14 Oct. 1990), conductor and composer, was born in Lawrence, Massachusetts, the son of Samuel Bernstein, a supplier of barber and beauty products, and Jenny Resnick. He began to pursue musical activities with abandon at about the age of ten and as a teen performed in classical and popular venues, including staged operettas with friends, as a jazz pianist at parties, as piano soloist with the Boston Public School Orchestra, and by playing light classics on the radio for thirteen weeks in 1934. Bernstein's consuming interest in music was not encouraged by his father, but he never seriously considered another career. In 1939 he received a B.A. cum laude in music from Harvard University, where his teachers included Heinrich Gebhard, Walter Piston, A. Tillman Merritt, and Edward Burlingame Hill. In 1951 Bernstein married Felicia Montealegre Cohn, a Chilean actress, with whom he had three children.

Bernstein's conducting career was launched under the tutelage and influence of three world-class conductors. He met Dimitri Mitropoulos while a student at Harvard and was impressed with Mitropoulos's demonstrative conducting and his performance of piano concertos while conducting from the keyboard. From 1939 to 1941 Bernstein studied conducting with Fritz Reiner at the Curtis Institute of Music in Philadelphia. During the summers of 1940 and 1941 he was a student of Serge Koussevitzky at the new Berkshire Music Center in Tanglewood, Massachusetts. A close friendship formed between the two men. Bernstein returned to Tanglewood as Koussevitzky's assistant in 1942, and in 1948 he joined the faculty, succeeding Koussevitzky as head of the conducting department in 1951. Bernstein returned to Tanglewood many times during his life, conducting his last concert there in 1990.

In 1943 Bernstein was named assistant conductor of the New York Philharmonic, making his debut on 14 November when he substituted for an ill Bruno Walter in a nationally broadcast concert. After another substitute appearance Bernstein was in demand, and his tenure as assistant at the Philharmonic lasted only one year. By the end of 1944 he had conducted orchestras in Pittsburgh, Boston, Montreal, Chicago, Cincinnati, Los Angeles, and Detroit.

From 1945 to 1948 Bernstein was music director of the New York City Symphony. In this position he showed his affinity for twentieth-century music and his flair for daring programming. But Bernstein's most important association was with the New York Philharmonic, which he frequently guest-conducted from 1944 to 1957. During the 1957–1958 season he was co-conductor with Mitropoulos and in 1958 was named music director, the youngest conductor ever to hold that position. He remained music director until 1969, when he became laureate conductor. With the addition of new concert series, the orchestra's audience tripled under Bernstein between the 1955–1956 season and the late 1960s. The Philharmonic became a regular feature on network television and recorded extensively for CBS Masterworks. Bernstein led it on many tours, including trips to South America in 1958 and to Europe, the Near East, and the Soviet Union in 1959. Bernstein frequently programmed music by American composers, and on a memorable tour of the United States and Europe in 1976 the orchestra performed exclusively American works.

Bernstein's international career began in the late 1940s. His long affiliation with the Israel Philharmonic Orchestra started in 1947; he served as its musical adviser in 1948–1949 and in 1988, after many collaborations, was named laureate conductor. In the late 1940s and early 1950s he conducted orchestras in Prague, London, Vienna, Paris, and other European cities. In 1953 he became the first American conductor to lead a performance at Milan's La Scala—a memorable version of Cherubini's *Medea* with Maria Callas in the title role. Bernstein's prominent international profile included frequent work as a guest conductor. A particularly fruitful relationship with the Vienna Philharmonic led to numerous recordings, among them a critically acclaimed set of Beethoven's nine symphonies and filmed performances of Mahler's nine completed symphonies.

The perception of Bernstein's conducting varied widely during his career. His early conducting was criticized as choreographic and vulgar, especially in regard to music from the nineteenth century. Although *New York Times* writer Harold Schonberg was a persistent critic of Bernstein's work, he recognized the conductor's growth. When Bernstein left the orchestra in 1969, Schonberg wrote in the *Times* (19 May) that he had begun "to conduct the big works of the repertory in a way that had shape as well as color, structural integrity as well as freedom within the phrase." Schonberg also described the conductor's wide range, from Mozart to moderns like Sergei Prokofiev, Igor Stravinsky, and Aaron Copland. Bernstein has been especially identified with the works of American composers from the midcentury and with the symphonies of Mahler, which he helped to popularize in the 1960s. He was also a fine pianist who often conducted piano concertos from the keyboard. In his later years, Bernstein was recognized as a master conductor and teacher, as popular in Europe as he was in the United States. His long association with Deutsche Grammophon began with a recording of the 1972 Metropolitan Opera production of *Carmen*, and he continued to record with the German company until his death.

Bernstein maintained an active profile as a composer throughout his life. His output cannot be called large, but he was one of the few composers to make significant contributions to both popular theater and classical music. His Jewish heritage exerts a strong influence on many compositions. The most important stylistic element in his music, however, is a wide-ranging eclecticism that allowed Bernstein to seek the best in all types of music. Despite his flexibility of expression, Bernstein forged a personal style recognizable to musicians and nonmusicians alike. In his finest works he fused jazz, popular music, and classical ideals in a way that captures the American consciousness. A prime example of this combination is the musical *West Side Story* (1957). When he chose his influences less carefully, the result was an uncomfortable mixture of styles, as may be heard in sections of *Mass* (1971). Another pervasive element in Bernstein's music is its theatricality, obvious in the staged vocal works but also present in the juxtaposition of disparate elements and vivid emotional contrasts in his symphonic music. Among Bernstein's influences one must name Aaron Copland, whom he met in 1937. Bernstein insisted that his work with Copland did not constitute formal study, but he showed Copland his music between 1937 and 1943, receiving comments and criticisms from the older master. Many of the decisive stylistic elements in Copland's music are also found in Bernstein's compositions. Bernstein once noted that, considering the variety of influences in his music, "you could . . . funnel all that through Aaron." Other important features of Bernstein's music are his lyrical melodies and extensive use of complex and spirited rhythms.

Bernstein composed in many genres, but his most lasting contributions were made in musical theater and symphonic works. His first significant work for the theater was the ballet *Fancy Free* (1944), commissioned by Ballet Theatre and choreographed by Jerome Robbins. Bernstein and Robbins then joined lyricists Betty Comden and Adolph Green in adapting the story from *Fancy Free* into the musical *On the Town*, a hit of the 1944–1945 New York season. In 1951 Bernstein composed the one-act opera *Trouble in Tahiti*, premiered at a festival at Brandeis University. Bernstein also wrote the libretto, and later composed as a sequel the full-length opera *A Quiet Place* (1983), commissioned by the Houston Grand Opera, Milan's La Scala, and Washington's Kennedy Center. Bernstein's work on Broadway continued in 1953 with *Wonderful Town*, another high-spirited collaboration with Comden and Green. Bernstein demonstrated his ease with various musical styles and the conventions of operetta in *Candide*, a collaboration with Lillian Hellman and others. Although the work was a box office failure when it premiered in 1956, it has enjoyed several revivals and contains some of Bernstein's best music.

Bernstein's best-known work is the musical play *West Side Story*, written in collaboration with director/choreographer Jerome Robbins, lyricist Stephen Sondheim, and the writer Arthur Laurents. Familiar as both a stage play and film, *West Side Story* demonstrated the possibilities of the unification of music with a story's dramatic structure. Bernstein brought the play's youthful sensibility to life through the use of jazz idioms and Latin rhythms, combining them with the dramatic use of themes and musical characterization that one usually associates with opera. His music, combined with the power and energy of Robbins's choreography, produced one of the monuments of the Broadway stage. In later years Bernstein did not repeat the success of *West Side Story*. A notable failure was *1600 Pennsylvania Avenue* (1976), written with lyricist Alan Jay Lerner. *Mass* (1971), a theatrical interpretation of the Roman Catholic ritual composed for the opening of the Kennedy Center in Washington, D.C., was Bernstein's most controversial work; it contains simultaneously some of his finest and most derivative music. Bernstein's theatrical output also includes the score to the film *On the Waterfront* (1954) and the ballet *Dybbuk* (1974).

Bernstein's concert works include three symphonies, a concerto for violin entitled *Serenade (after Plato's Symposium)* (1954), *Songfest* (1977), Divertimento for Orchestra (1980), and *Jubilee Games* (1986, later called Concerto for Orchestra), among other works. Each of his symphonies is programmatic. The Symphony no. 1, *Jeremiah*, for Mezzo-soprano and Orchestra (1942), a notable youthful effort. His most effective piece is the Symphony no. 2, *Age of Anxiety*, for Piano and Orchestra (1949), which refers to the poem of the same name by W. H. Auden. This symphony demonstrates Bernstein's concern with the role of faith in the modern world, a key theme that appears in various guises in many of his works, most prominently in *Chichester Psalms* (1965) and *Mass*. Dedicated to John F. Kennedy, the Symphony no. 3, *Kaddish*, for Speaker, Soprano, Chorus, Boys' Choir, and Orchestra (1963), takes its program from a crisis of faith and reflects the impact of Judaism on the composer. *Songfest* is a song cycle of American poems scored for soloists and orchestra. Divertimento for Orchestra and *Jubilee Games* demonstrate Bernstein's continued fertility in the symphonic arena. His output also includes songs, chamber music, and piano works.

Bernstein's work as an author and educator had an enormous impact on general audiences, especially his television broadcasts. These included performances with unforgettable narration on "Omnibus," "Leonard Bernstein and the New York Philharmonic," and "Young People's Concerts." His first three books—*The Joy of Music* (1959), *Leonard Bernstein's Young People's Concerts for Reading and Listening* (1962), and *The Infinite Variety of Music* (1966)—were largely based on scripts from his television shows. In academia, Bernstein was on the music faculty of Brandeis University from 1951 to 1954 and held the Charles Eliot Norton chair in poetry at Harvard University in 1973. These six Norton lectures were published in *The Unanswered Question* (1976). In the lectures, Bernstein applied the theories of linguist Noam Chomsky to a wide array of music, in the process asserting his own belief in the importance of tonality. Many essays and poems were included in his final book, *Findings* (1982). Bernstein was also important as a conducting pedagogue, teaching for many years at Tanglewood, in the 1980s at the Los Angeles Philharmonic Institute, and in other venues. He died in New York City.

With his supreme self-confidence and early success, Bernstein made his share of enemies in the musical and theatrical worlds, but he also had many friends and supporters who spoke of his importance as an educator and promoter of young talent. His almost manic nervous energy and intensity lasted throughout his life, leading him into a wide variety of projects and making him part of the social scene wherever he was. The public Bernstein combined these attributes with a notable interest in people and causes, producing a charisma matched by few others in his field. Among his voracious appetites were cigarettes, bourbon, and bisexual attractions, the latter becoming public knowledge in the 1980s.

Bernstein's role as the first American-born conductor with a significant international career looms large, as does his repertoire of recordings, many of which still receive critical acclaim. His music, superbly conceived for his time, includes genuine masterworks. Most memorable are his profound melodic gift seen in evocative tunes like "Maria," his profound expressions of faith like *Kaddish*, and his remarkable rhythmic invention. Without question, he was one of the most phenomenally talented American musicians of the twentieth century.

• A number of Leonard Bernstein's manuscript scores are held in the Music Division of the Library of Congress; in November 1993 the Bernstein estate also placed the bulk of his papers in a special Library of Congress repository. The majority of his compositions are available on recordings, many with the composer as conductor. Many of Bernstein's hundreds of recordings are commercially available; in the 1990s Sony Classical released a large number of his CBS Masterworks recordings from the 1950s to 1970s. His later recordings for Deutsche Grammophon will also remain an important legacy. The most complete listing of Bernstein's compositions and other works may be found in Jack Gottlieb, *Leonard Bernstein: A Complete Catalogue of His Works* (1978); an update of this work is in *Sennets & Tuckets: A Bernstein Celebration*, ed. Steven Ledbetter (1988), a collection of essays on the man and his work.

The most balanced biography is Michael Freedland, *Leonard Bernstein* (1987). Peter Gradenwitz, a lifelong friend, wrote the informative *Leonard Bernstein: The Infinite Variety of a Musician* (1987). Joan Peyser, *Bernstein: A Biography* (1987), is a poorly organized, mean-spirited examination of Bernstein's life. John Gruen, *The Private World of Leonard Bernstein* (1968), gives a personal account of Bernstein's work during his tenure with the New York Philharmonic and includes many photographs. A useful photographic tribute is *Bernstein Remembered*, ed. Jane Fluegel (1991). A delightful personal memory by Schuyler Chapin, a business associate of the composer and conductor, is *Leonard Bernstein: Notes from a Friend* (1992). An obituary by critic Donal Henahan is in the *New York Times*, 15 Oct. 1990.

PAUL R. LAIRD

BERNSTEIN, Philip Sidney (29 June 1901–3 Dec. 1985), Reform rabbi and Jewish leader, was born in Rochester, New York, the son of Abraham M. Bernstein, a wholesaler, and Sarah Steinberg. As a youth he was an enthusiastic member of Young Judea, a Zionist organization. In 1914 the national Zionist convention met in Rochester; there Bernstein met the leaders of American Zionism, among them his lifelong friend and mentor, Stephen S. Wise.

Bernstein graduated from Syracuse University in 1921 and was accepted by Harvard Law School in the same year; however, his father's illness kept him from enrolling. During the year that Bernstein ran his father's wholesale business and retail pants store, he became deeply involved in the activities of the Jewish community of Rochester. He decided to forego law

school and become a rabbi. Although raised in an Orthodox home, albeit a liberal one, his contact with the Temple Society of Concord in Syracuse while at the university drew him to the Reform movement. In 1926, as a member of the first graduating class, Bernstein was ordained by the Jewish Institute of Religion, New York. Postgraduate work followed at Columbia University, Cambridge University (England), and the Hebrew University (Jerusalem).

Beginning in 1927 Bernstein was the senior rabbi of Temple B'rith Kodesh in Rochester. A tireless worker for social improvement, he encouraged social reformers such as birth control advocate, Margaret Sanger and shared his pulpit with activist politicians, among them socialist Norman Thomas. A pacifist until the German invasion of Poland, Bernstein was the chairman of the Committee for International Peace of the Central Conference of American Rabbis. A committed Zionist, he served on the national executive board of the Zionist Organization of America and the American Jewish Congress, of which he was also the vice president.

During World War II, Bernstein served as the executive director of the committee on army and navy religious activities of the Jewish Welfare Board (Dec. 1942–Feb. 1946). In this capacity he traveled widely, visiting the 311 Jewish chaplains of the U.S. armed forces in Europe, Asia, and the Pacific who were under his supervision. Following the liberation of the concentration camps, President Harry Truman appointed Bernstein as the Jewish adviser to the U.S. Army military commanders in Europe, succeeding Simon H. Rifkind, the first to hold the office established by General Dwight D. Eisenhower. In this position (May 1946–Aug. 1947), Bernstein directly or indirectly advised the generals of the American Zone of Occupation (Lucius Clay, Mark Clark, Geoffrey S. Keyes, and Joseph T. McNarney) on Jewish affairs, including the care of the Jewish survivors in the custody of the U.S. Army. Bernstein visited the camps and talked to countless homeless, stateless, and politically disenfranchised Jewish persons, hearing their complaints and responding to their needs. He secured official recognition for the Central Committee of Liberated Jews, thereby enabling the establishment of the program for the restitution of Jewish property.

Bernstein's role as an advocate for the camp survivors brought him into personal contact with Pope Pius XII and the prime ministers of the United Kingdom, France, Italy, Czechoslovakia, and Poland. During this time Bernstein also testified before the U.S. Congress on behalf of the Stratton Bill and before the United Nations Special Commission on Palestine (1946–1947). He also interpreted the needs of the Jewish survivors to American Jews; for instance, he persuaded the army to print an edition of the Talmud for use in the refugee camps. The printing and distribution costs for this special edition were paid for with funds raised by the American Jewish community.

After the 1946 pogrom in Kielce, Poland, Bernstein was instrumental in persuading U.S. military commanders to countermand a previous order and to continue to keep open the borders of the American Zone of Occupation in Germany and Austria to Polish and other East European Jews fleeing mounting anti-Semitic violence and seeking emigration to Palestine. Unofficially, Bernstein used his office to aid *Bericha* (literally, "flight"), the underground Hagana organization created to move Jews from Eastern Europe to the western coastal ports for illegal transport (until May 1948) and entry into the Mandate. Bernstein's influence is credited with securing the rescue and protective care of over 110,000 European Jewish survivors.

After the war Bernstein returned to his pulpit at B'rith Kodesh. He married Sophie Rubin in 1952; they had three children. From 1954 to 1968, he was an honorary chairman of the America-Israel Public Affairs Committee (AIPAC). He was a close friend and adviser of Israeli leaders, among them David Ben-Gurion, Golda Meir, and Abba Eban. He was the recipient of the Solomon Bublick Award (Hebrew University). Bernstein's admirers established a chair in Jewish studies at the University of Rochester in his honor. He retired in 1973 and was a rabbi emeritus until his death in Rochester.

• Bernstein's papers are at the American Jewish Archives in Cincinnati, Ohio. He was the author of *What Jews Believe* (1951), a summary of the basic tenets of Judaism, and *Rabbis at War* (1971), his account of the Jewish chaplaincy in World War II; he also contributed numerous journal and magazine articles, including "The Fate of the German Jews," *Nation* 145 (1937): 423–25; "Pogroms or Partition," *Nation* 145 (1937): 607–9; "The Jews of Europe," *Nation* 156 (1943): 8–11, 48–51, 158–61, 196–200; and "Jewish Chaplains in World War II," *American Jewish Year Book* 47 (1945): 173–200. Other sources include Yehuda Bauer, *Flight and Rescue: Brichah* (1970); Thomas P. Liebschutz, "Rabbi Philip S. Bernstein and the Jewish Displaced Persons" (M.A. thesis, Hebrew Union College–Jewish Institute of Religion, Cincinnati, Ohio 1965); and Haim Genizi, "Philip S. Bernstein: Adviser on Jewish Affairs, May 1946–August 1947," *Simon Wiesenthal Center Annual* 3 (1986): 139–76. An obituary is Benjamin Friedman, "Philip S. Bernstein," *Central Conference of American Rabbis Yearbook* 96 (1986): 262–63.

ANN MANN MILLIN

BERNSTEIN, Theodore Menline (17 Nov. 1904–27 June 1979), newspaper editor, was born in New York City, the son of Saul Bernstein, a lawyer, and Sarah Menline, a high school teacher until her marriage. The family was well off, and as a child Bernstein was accustomed to seeing noted members of the professional community in his home. He went to Columbia College, where he was managing editor of the campus paper. He received an A.B. in 1924 and, despite his parents' wishes, continued on to the Columbia School of Journalism, earning a B.Litt. in 1925. He later told his niece that when anti-Semitism kept him from receiving one of the three prestigious Pulitzer Traveling Fellowships, a sympathetic faculty member gave him a compelling recommendation to the *New York Times*, and Bernstein went to work there as a copyeditor.

By 1930, the year he married Beatrice Alexander, he had become suburban editor, and two years later he shifted to the foreign copy desk; in 1939 he became foreign news editor, a post he held through World War II. He liked maps as a way of clarifying war developments, and he supervised their production; he also wrote the major war headlines and nightly instructions to correspondents.

With his promotion to news editor in 1951, and to first-ranked assistant managing editor in 1952, Bernstein won the authority to undertake the major achievement of his career, modernizing the writing, editing, and appearance of the paper. He led this effort for the next two decades, bringing what Turner Catledge, then managing editor, termed "a new element of daring to editing the paper." "He extended the use of maps and diagrams," Catledge said. "He even innovated in typography, against what had been unbreakable bounds of tradition."

When the *Times* was still in an eight-column format, Bernstein kept testing headline faces to replace the stodgy Latin Extra-Condensed heads, a time-honored hallmark of the *Times*, but he never found anything that combined a relatively generous word count with legibility. In the Bernstein period, the *Times* added a daily profile on a man or woman "in the News" and a quotation of the day. Analysis articles and other variations on straight newswriting also flourished. The news index underwent frequent change. When a satellite was put into orbit, Bernstein, who rejoiced in gimmicks, ordered maps of the globe to be printed back to back so that readers could hold the sheet to the light and see the satellite's path over both hemispheres.

Bernstein was precise but not prissy. He worked in a business shirt, sleeves carefully folded to the same level on his upper arms, and a four-in-hand necktie. He donned his jacket only to leave the building. His legible cursive writing was recognized by every printer, and his authority was so absolute that many associates believed that printers sawed the metal headline type to squeeze in tight counts rather than tell Bernstein his head would not fit. He smoked cigarettes and favored gin martinis without ice, habits that several heart attacks barely moderated. When he left work about 10 P.M., after the first edition was in hand, he took a dummy sketch of page one with him so that he could suggest changes if developing or breaking news required it. As one of the few things he did outside his regular job, he taught copyediting at Columbia, from 1925 to 1950. He took virtually no vacation, and when he did, it was always to the same places, frequently Longboat Key in Florida.

Bernstein's influence eventually widened beyond the *Times* to publications ranging from the *New Yorker* to the Abigail Van Buren column "Dear Abby." In 1951 he began issuing his admonitory in-house publication "Winners & Sinners," a single sheet that went every two weeks to the staff and eventually to a large free circulation of outside editors and journalism teachers. The authors of errors cited in W&S were permitted anonymity; writers of bright headlines, leads, captions, and passages were cited by name. No money, but considerable prestige, attached to being a "winner." The sheet was widely emulated, but imitators and successors learned that Bernstein set a standard so exhausting that it could not be matched by any editor with a personal life.

A Bernstein guideline was "don't tell me, show me." This item appeared in "Winners & Sinners" for 4 March 1960: "Natural infirmities often present a problem for the writer, the solution of which involves that elusive quality called taste. Here is a passage from a story about a reunion of the City College class of 1900: 'Some had canes. Some shook. Others could not hear perfectly.' (Jan. 31) To many readers that 'some shook' would be so jarringly harsh as to seem unfeeling. In contrast, notice how this passage delicately tells you that Fritz Kreisler's vision is failing: 'Mr. Kreisler brought his wrist close to his eyes and looked at his watch. "It is now 11:34," he said. "These reading glasses are very good."'"

The majority of Bernstein's seven books derived directly from Winners & Sinners, particularly the bulletin's discussions of the craft of editing, which he called "Helpful Hints for Hatchetmen." He sometimes reviewed books on usage for the *Times* and for trade publications; "Better Be a Mother Fudger" on obscenity in newspapers, for example, appeared in the newsletter of the American Society of Newspaper Editors for July 1969.

In 1960 Bernstein was sent to Paris as founding editor of the *Times*'s international edition. His account of the experience typically bore a title, "Bonjour, TTS," that was a pun on the title of the bestselling novel *Bonjour, Tristesse* and the Teletypesetting process used for the paper.

He returned to his job in New York the next year, staying in it until he was sixty-five, after which he spent two years as editorial head of the *Times* book division. After management declared him retired from his then-duties as a consultant in 1972, he kept an office in the building and wrote a column on language that was distributed by the *Times*'s special features service. He continued to write Winners & Sinners until the end of 1977.

The Bernsteins had one son, Eric. Bernstein's wife died in 1971, after which Bernstein lived with a longtime friend, Ethel C. Spiegel, in Greenwich Village, where he died.

• Bernstein's office files from 1952 until he retired in 1972, including confidential memorandums, have been archived by the *Times*'s history project. His first book, *Headlines and Deadlines*, a manual for copyeditors written with Robert E. Garst, was published in 1933 and stayed in print through many editions. It grew out of their experience teaching and is widely used as a textbook. Bernstein wrote the sections on headlines, including a short thesaurus, and Garst the sections on editing copy. Bernstein's later books were *Watch Your Language* (1958); *More Language That Needs Watching* (1962); his major work, *The Careful Writer* (1965); *Miss Thistlebottom's Hobgoblins* (1971); *Bernstein's Reverse Dictionary* (1975); and *Dos, Don'ts and Maybes of English Usage* (1977).

A vocal opponent of Webster's Third International, he was a consultant on the American Heritage and Random House dictionaries. *Miss Thistlebottom's Hobgoblins* was reissued in 1991 with a biographical introduction. Mrs. Bernstein's niece, Prof. Marylea Meyersohn, is an invaluable resource for personal and family data. The *Times* printed a major obituary, 28 June 1979.

BETSY WADE

BERRIEN, John Macpherson (23 Aug. 1781–1 Jan. 1856), politician and lawyer, was born in Rocky Hill, New Jersey, the son of John Berrien, a soldier, politician, and planter, and Margaret Macpherson. In 1783 the family moved to eastern Georgia, where Berrien's father started a plantation and pursued political office. He sent his five-year-old son to New York and later to New Jersey for his education, which culminated in graduation from Princeton in 1796 with a bachelor's degree.

Returning to Georgia, Berrien studied law under Joseph Clay, Jr., and was admitted to the bar in 1799. His distinguished and profitable law career began in Louisville, then the state capital of Georgia, but in 1802 Berrien moved to Savannah. Within seven years he was co-partner of the largest law practice in the city. He represented a diverse clientele but specialized in admiralty law. In 1803 he married Eliza Anciaux. They had nine children before her death in 1828.

Berrien's Federalist leanings and his coordination of the Federalist presidential campaigns in Georgia in 1800 and 1808 were political liabilities in a state heavily sympathetic to Thomas Jefferson and the Republicans. He was trounced in elections for state legislator and city alderman, but his proven legal talents led to his appointment as solicitor general of the Eastern District of Georgia in 1809. A year later the state legislature elected him judge of the Superior Court of the Eastern District of Georgia, a position he filled with distinction until his resignation in 1821. Berrien's nationalist and economic conservative decisions reflected his Federalist background, as did his advocacy of judicial review for Georgia legislation. During the War of 1812, however, Berrien abandoned the Federalist opposition and served as colonel of the First Georgia Cavalry. He saw no action.

Berrien's distinguished judicial career eased his move into politics. His vigorous support for the popular election of governor overcame lingering concerns about his reputation for aloofness and his Federalist past. Thus he was twice elected to the Georgia Senate from Chatham County, in 1822 and 1823, became allied with the Troup-Crawford faction, and secured election to the U.S. Senate, taking office in March 1825.

As did most Georgians, Berrien supported William Crawford for president in 1824 and then moved into the ranks of the Jacksonians. As senator he opposed John Quincy Adams's internal improvement and tariff measures. He fought for a national bankruptcy law and the abolition of imprisonment for debt. His fervent support for Georgia's removal of the Creek Indians received favorable notice from future secretary of war John Eaton and Andrew Jackson. Contrary to an oft-repeated myth that Berrien was a favorite of Vice President John C. Calhoun, Berrien conducted a rather independent political course. Even though Martin Van Buren was wary of Berrien, on the recommendations of Eaton and Richard Mentor Johnson, President-elect Jackson nominated Berrien for attorney general. Berrien's acceptance was a product of his ambition and his expectation of later securing a seat on the U.S. Supreme Court.

Berrien's service as attorney general was able and energetic but politically undistinguished. He diligently supported Jackson's American Indian policies, and his opinion on the legal status of Indian tribes was the basis of *Cherokee Nation v. Georgia* (1830). Never a close adviser of Jackson or Van Buren, Berrien remained independent. He tacitly supported the Bank of the United States and avoided the controversial Peggy Eaton. Berrien was consequently an easy victim of the "Eaton malaria," which produced a complete reorganization of the cabinet. On Jackson's request, Berrien graciously resigned in June 1831, but political enemies produced a complete falling out with Jackson soon thereafter.

Without a political party or popular support, Berrien reluctantly returned to his lucrative law practice. In the nullification crisis he tortuously and unsuccessfully attempted to rally Georgia against protective tariffs, President Jackson, and nullification. Although nominated for U.S. senator in 1833 and 1837, he was easily defeated by the Jacksonians both times. In 1833 he married Eliza Cecil Hunter. They had six children before her death in 1852.

In the presidential contest of 1840 Berrien early championed the candidacy of William Henry Harrison. The Whig success in Georgia propelled Berrien's return to the U.S. Senate, where he chaired the Judiciary Committee. As a close ally of Henry Clay, Berrien was an influential contributor to the national bank, bankruptcy, distribution, and tariff bills. His nationalism was fully evident in the Senate and on the stump for Clay in 1844. Bitterly disappointed in James K. Polk's election, Berrien joined the Whig resistance to the acquisition of Oregon and Texas and to the Mexican War. In part he feared expansion would fuel a destructive sectionalism. Soon after his reelection in 1847 Berrien encountered political opposition in Georgia from younger and more sectional Whigs, like Alexander Stephens, and in Washington, D.C., from President Zachary Taylor, who resented Berrien's support for Clay. Eventually Berrien's nationalism was tempered by the protection of slavery and Georgia's state rights. He unenthusiastically voted for an Oregon Territory without slavery but advocated slaveholders' rights throughout the Mexican Cession. Thus he came to reject Clay's Compromise of 1850. Instead he proposed the "Berrien platform," which repudiated secession but advocated southern economic resistance to the North. He found no support for his proposal from northern Whigs or from Georgians. Reluctantly Berrien backed the "Georgia Platform," which accepted the Compromise of 1850 but pledged firm resistance to any additional northern aggression. Not surprisingly, Berrien was not reelected to the Senate, and he resigned in May 1852. His last foray into politics was as president of the state convention of the American party in December 1855. Neither nativism nor anti-Catholicism motivated Berrien. He sought the chance to reunify the moderate elements of the Whig party in the North and South to stem the growing tide of sectionalism. He died in Savannah before he could shape the movement.

Political allies and foes often described Berrien as impeccably mannered and reserved, but friends knew him as a devoted family man. Berrien's greatest talents were legal. He augmented the prestige of Georgia's bench and bar. Opponents in Georgia and on the Supreme Court feared and respected him. As judge, senator, and attorney general, he was honest, energetic, and diligent. As a politician his greatest accomplishment was to lead anti-Jacksonian Georgians away from the despair of nullification into the national Whig party in the late 1830s and 1840s. Ultimately, Berrien demonstrated little skill at political machinations and lacked a devoted popular following in Georgia. Too often he sought compromise only on his own terms, but while they were intelligently and carefully constructed, they tended to be too cautious and legalistic. This was evident in his stands on the tariff and nullification crises, the annexation of Texas, the Compromise of 1850, and the growing sectionalism in the mid-1850s. His biographer astutely concludes, "Berrien's refusal to accept such a solution [secession and civil war] constituted his greatness; his failure to devise an alternative defined his inadequacy" (McCrary, "John Macpherson Berrien of Georgia," p. 415).

• Berrien's papers are scattered, with large deposits at the University of North Carolina, Chapel Hill, and the Georgia Historical Society, Savannah. The best biography is Royce Coggins McCrary, Jr., "John Macpherson Berrien of Georgia: A Political Biography" (Ph.D. diss., Univ. of Georgia, 1971). Other briefer but useful overviews include Stephen F. Miller, "John Macpherson Berrien, LL.D.," in *Bench and Bar of Georgia* (1858); Alexander R. MacDonell, "John Macpherson Berrien," *Georgia Historical Quarterly* 17 (1933): 1–12; and C. Jay Smith, Jr., "John McPherson [*sic*] Berrien," in *Georgians in Profile: Historical Essays in Honor of Ellis Merton Coulter*, ed. Horace Montgomery (1958). Studies that focus on important periods of Berrien's career include Thomas P. Govan, "John M. Berrien and the Administration of Andrew Jackson," *Journal of Southern History* 5 (1939): 447–67, which evaluates Berrien as attorney general. McCrary, "John Macpherson Berrien and the Know-Nothing Movement in Georgia," *Georgia Historical Quarterly* 61 (1977): 35–42, is a fair assessment of Berrien's association with the nativists. Richard Harrison Shryock, *Georgia and the Union in 1850* (1926), is dated but provides a broader perspective for Berrien's activities during that crisis.

M. PHILIP LUCAS

BERRY, Chu (13 Sept. 1908–30 Oct. 1941), tenor saxophonist, was born Leon Brown Berry in Wheeling, West Virginia; his parents's names and occupations are unknown. He played alto saxophone in high school and at West Virginia State College, which he attended for three years.

In 1929 Sammy Stewart hired Berry to play tenor in his Chicago band. In 1930 he moved to New York City and worked in several groups, including bands led by Benny Carter, Charlie Johnson, Spike Hughes, and Teddy Hill. An early highlight was a May 1933 recording for Hughes that included Coleman Hawkins, with the two tenor giants striving to surpass each other on tunes like "Fanfare." Berry recorded with a variety of groups during the second half of the 1930s, including those led by Gene Krupa, Benny Goodman, Henry Allen, Hot Lips Page, and Wingy Manone. His superb work with various Teddy Wilson groups is typified by his beautiful solo on Billie Holiday's 1935 recording of "Twenty-Four Hours a Day," with Wilson's orchestra. He also played and recorded with the Count Basie orchestra for a short while, soloing to particularly good effect on the 1939 Basie classic, "Lady Be Good."

Berry recorded much of his most important work with the Fletcher Henderson Orchestra in 1935 and 1936 and with Cab Calloway from 1937–1941. He established his reputation with Henderson; he wrote "Christopher Columbus," one of the band's biggest hits, and played propulsive solos on pieces like "Sing, Sing, Sing." With Calloway he soloed on practically every recorded performance by the band and was featured more often than any other player; he swapped arrangements with other groups, such as the Chick Webb band, and was personally responsible for keeping the group steeped in good music. Examples of his stellar work can be found on tunes like "Ghost of a Chance," "Lonesome Nights," and "Bye Bye Blues," and especially in his near-perfect solo on the 1939 recording of "Pluckin' the Bass."

While starring with the Calloway band, Berry also performed and recorded widely with his own groups. He recorded several sessions with his close friend Roy Eldridge. Among the best of these sides are four outstanding tunes the two musicians waxed for Commodore Records in 1938 (under the name Chu Berry and His Little Jazz Ensemble), in which they proved perfect foils for each other, particularly at the fast tempos at which both excelled. The Berry version of "Body and Soul" recorded at this time remains one of the few to rival the classic Coleman Hawkins rendition.

Berry's short life and compressed recording career provide a particularly accessible portrait of his playing style. From the beginning Hawkins loomed as his major influence—hardly an unusual situation, since he did so for nearly every other tenor player until Lester Young appeared. But Berry was more successful in carving out a clear stylistic niche for himself than any of the others. He had a less rounded, less "voluptuous" sound than Hawkins (though it was still full compared

to Young's) and was not as melodically imaginative as the older master, but he also had "a more emotive vibrato and a strange crying sound in his frequently-used upper register" (Carr, p. 40). He possessed a propulsive sense of swing and excelled at fast tempos that showed "an unerring sense of time" and a sophisticated "melodic-harmonic conception." On ballads he often played in double tempo with a wide, fast vibrato to compensate for his less warm tone. Towards the end of his life he grew less bombastic and more reflective in his ballad playing. Ballad recordings such as "A Ghost of a Chance" and "Lonesome Nights," both recorded with the Calloway band in 1940, and "On the Sunny Side of the Street," from his own 1941 session with Chu Berry and His Jazz Ensemble, illustrate this more subtle, sophisticated approach to balladry.

When Berry died in a car accident in Conneaut, Ohio, Calloway said it was "like losing a brother, someone I had joked with and hollered at. There was a quiet around the band for weeks and we left his chair empty" (Carr, p. 40). He had what some described as a "tubby and chuckling" personality. His friendship with Eldridge is legendary. The two often played together at after-hours jam sessions, taking on all comers and cutting them mercilessly. Musically, he just seemed to be coming into his own. A few months before his death, Hawkins ranked him among his favorite tenor players, second only to Ben Webster. Though long all but forgotten, Berry's music made something of a comeback in the 1970s and 1980s, influencing younger players like Frank Lowe.

• There are several excellent assessments of Berry's career and playing. Begin with Gunther Schuller, *The Swing Era: The Development of Jazz, 1930–1945* (1989). For Berry's association with Hawkins, see John Chilton, *The Song of the Hawk* (1990). For extensive discussions of his recordings, see Tom Piazza, *The Guide to Classic Recorded Jazz* (1995), and Dan Morgenstern, "The Complete Commodore Jazz Recordings," Vol. 1, in the booklet accompanying the 1988 reissues by Mosaic Records. The best short assessment is in Ian Carr et al., eds., *Jazz: The Essential Companion* (1987). Also see A. J. Bishop, "Chu Berry: An Appreciation," *Jazz Journal International* 29, no. 8 (1976): 18 and particularly the moving personal remembrances in Milt Hinton and David G. Berger, *Bass Line: The Stories and Photographs of Milt Hinton* (1988). An obituary is in the *New York Times*, 31 Oct. 1941.
RONALD P. DUFOUR

BERRY, Edward Wilber (10 Feb. 1875–20 Sept. 1945), paleobotanist, teacher, and university administrator, was born in Newark, New Jersey, the son of Abijah Conger Berry and Anna Wilber. Berry is a classic example of the self-trained scientist. He received elementary courses in biology and botany in high school that roused his interest in nature. Berry completed the three-year course in two years and finished his formal education at thirteen. From 1890 to 1897 he worked for a cotton goods company, rising from stock boy to traveling salesman. Berry then entered the newspaper world as business manager for the *Passaic (N.J.) Daily*

News. He advanced to managing editor, president, and treasurer. He absorbed the newspaper style of rapid composition with a minimum of rewrite, and this style remained with him throughout his life. In 1898 Berry married Mary Willard; both of their two sons became paleontologists.

While Berry was still in high school he began his career in geology, studying the cliffs around Raritan Bay and particularly collecting fossils from clays of Cretaceous age (about 65–135 million years old); his first short publication was in 1896, followed by three more in 1897 and a steady flow from 1900 through 1945. In all Berry has about 500 titles to his credit, totaling almost 8,000 printed pages. Although most of his works are short, significant longer works were published by the Maryland Geological Survey and the U.S. Geological Survey.

Some of his earliest papers were on living plants, but by the early 1900s he had become an authority on the plant fossils of New Jersey. During a field trip to Raritan Bay he so impressed W. B. Clark, a professor at the Johns Hopkins University, that in 1905 Clark offered him the opportunity to leave the newspaper business and pursue an academic career; by 1906 Berry was made an assistant in Hopkins's Department of Geology with the task of curating the fossil collections. Once in the university system, Berry flourished and advanced steadily, in part because of his increasing scientific productivity and partly because of his teaching ability and administrative skills. Within the Department of Geology he was an instructor in paleontology (1908–1910), associate in paleobotany (1910–1913), associate professor of paleobotany (1913–1917), professor (1917–1943), and finally professor emeritus from 1943 until his death.

From 1929 until 1942 Berry was dean of arts and sciences in addition to his association with the department. In 1930 he received his only advanced degree, an honorary doctorate from Lehigh University; he delighted in being known nationally as the "degreeless dean." Appointed to the deanship at the time Joseph S. Ames became university president, Berry also served informally as provost, and in 1935 when Isaiah Bowman succeeded to the presidency, Berry was formally appointed to that post. He continued as both dean and provost through 1942, and despite the administrative load he still taught part time.

In addition to his affiliation with the university, Berry was employed part time as a geologist with the U.S. Geological Survey in 1910 and retained this connection until 1942. In 1917 he was also appointed assistant state geologist of the Maryland Geological Survey and remained part of that organization also until 1942, contributing manuscripts and editing many of the publications.

During his lifetime Berry was the acknowledged expert on Cretaceous and the younger Cenozoic floras of eastern North America. He worked on all groups of fossil plants and all subdivisions of Cretaceous and Tertiary rocks exposed on the eastern and southern coastal plain of the United States. His works were mainly descriptive but were important for dating of the strata and critical to this advancing field. As his knowledge increased, Berry envisioned the plant fossils in terms of their life habitat, not as isolated specimens. He wrote on former climates, and his publications have provided the basic information for more detailed floristic investigations into paleoclimatology. Berry also wrote for newspapers and helped popularize geology and paleontology.

In addition to his investigations in the United States, Berry also described fossil plants of the Panama Canal Zone and other countries of Central America and throughout the Caribbean islands. He made three trips to South America, touring the Andean region in 1919, Ecuador and northern Peru in 1927, and Venezuela in 1933. His South American collections extended the geographic scope of his publications on extinct floras. Perhaps his single most important contribution to the study of evolution was the collection and description of Early Cretaceous angiosperms (flowering plants); these remain the oldest authentic flowering plants.

Berry's paleobotanic efforts were judged noteworthy by his professional colleagues. Among other organizations, he was a member of the American Philosophical Society, the National Research Council, and the National Academy of Sciences. In 1901, while still working for the *Passaic Daily News,* he received the Walker Prize from the Boston Society of Natural History. Venezuela awarded him a Medal Houra in 1933, and in 1944 he was given the Mary Clark Thompson Medal of the National Academy of Sciences. Berry was president of the Paleontological Society in 1924, and at the time of his death in Stonington, Connecticut, he had been elected president of the Geological Society of America.

• Berry's official papers are in the Milton Eisenhower Library, the Johns Hopkins University. His career and scientific achievements are mentioned in Henry N. Andrews, *The Fossil Hunters: In Search of Ancient Plants* (1980). For obituaries and memorials, see National Academy of Sciences, *Biographical Memoirs* 45 (1974): 57–95; *Science,* n.s. 102 (1945): 498–99; and *Proceedings of Geological Society of America, Annual Report for 1945* (1946): 193–214.

ELLIS L. YOCHELSON

BERRY, George Leonard (12 Sept. 1882–4 Dec. 1948), labor leader, was born in Lee Valley, Tennessee, the son of Thomas Jefferson Berry and Cornelia Trent. Berry claimed that his father was a judge and legislator, but this is not confirmed by state records. His father died when Berry was very young (some accounts indicate 1884, some 1888). Unable to support the family, his mother placed the boy in an orphan asylum; he was later moved to a foster home in Mississippi. Berry said that when he was only nine years old he ran away and began working as a newsboy for the Jackson, Mississippi, *Evening News.* He fought as a private in the Spanish-American War, then worked as a printer, first in St. Louis and next in San Francisco. He did some exhibition boxing on the side, and in 1903–1904 had a run of good luck prospecting for gold in Nevada. By 1907 he was back in San Francisco, running a substantial printing plant. That year he married Marie Margaret Gehres; the couple had no children.

Berry had joined the new International Printing Pressmen and Assistants' Union of North America (IPPAUNA) in 1899, and when he moved to San Francisco, he was chosen secretary and business agent of the IPPAUNA local there; he also became president of the city's Central Labor Council. In 1907 he represented San Francisco at the annual IPPAUNA convention in New York. When two stronger candidates deadlocked, Berry was elevated to the union presidency. During the next several years he moved the organization headquarters from Cincinnati, Ohio, to Rogersville, Tennessee, and launched a number of new services, including a union retirement home, a tuberculosis sanitarium, better death benefits, a pension system, more structured apprenticeships, and an office to advise union locals on collective bargaining. Berry also cooperated with other printing trade unions to found the International Allied Printing Trades Association, an organization that reinforced its position with a union label. In addition, he worked to keep the union abreast of changing technology, bringing lithographic offset printers into the union before they had established a strong foothold in the field and establishing a technical school to train members in new printing methods.

Berry participated in a number of international labor meetings during the years before World War I, and he published *Labor Conditions Abroad* in 1912. During World War I he served in France with the U.S. Army Corps of Engineers. He used his military title of major for the rest of his life, and in later years he helped found the American Legion. After serving as a labor adviser on the American Commission to the Paris Peace Conference in 1919, he returned to the union.

Berry's personal style was abrupt, but as a labor leader he followed Samuel Gompers's policy of "business unionism," much preferring conciliation to strikes and confrontation. Having won nationwide arbitration agreements with major employers, he was quite prepared to break strikes launched by his own locals in defiance of these contracts. Berry's policies evoked little criticism from his members, in part because of the union's prosperity. IPPAUNA expanded steadily, even during the 1920s when many unions lost ground; by 1929 its membership had passed 40,000.

Berry's members also supported his somewhat unorthodox blend of union business and private enterprise. During World War I he took $165,000 from the union pension fund to build a private power plant; he defied a 1921 federal court order to return the funds, and the charges were later dismissed. The membership backed him in this matter, as they did in 1927, when they agreed to loan Berry nearly $900,000 in union funds to launch the International Playing Card and Label Company on the understanding that the union would inherit Berry's share of the company when he

died. The company flourished and provided jobs for several hundred workers. Berry's other business ventures included banking, cattle raising, and producing cigarette wrappers; at one time he also owned several newspapers.

Berry was active in Tennessee's Democratic politics, unsuccessfully seeking his party's nomination for governor in 1914 and for U.S. senator in 1916. He came within three votes of winning the Democratic vice-presidential nomination in 1924, and in 1928 he worked for Al Smith's presidential campaign. Yet like many American Federation of Labor (AFL) leaders, he remained committed to the philosophy that government should stay out of labor affairs, leaving workers and management free to negotiate according to the "American way."

Only as the Great Depression took hold did Berry's position begin to change. In 1931 he observed, "Our capitalistic system requires a radical reorganization to meet the changing situation of the day." A few months later he came out in favor of unemployment insurance, a program that he and most of the AFL leadership had long opposed. Berry was one of the handful of national labor leaders who actively campaigned for Franklin D. Roosevelt in 1932. He was deeply disappointed when he was passed over for secretary of labor, but he did serve on two boards of the National Recovery Administration.

When a group of AFL unions seceded in 1935 to form the Congress of Industrial Organizations (CIO) Berry remained loyal to the AFL, but he maintained good relations with the insurgents, and in 1936 he worked with CIO leaders John L. Lewis and Sidney Hillman to found labor's Non-Partisan League (NPL) in support of Roosevelt. He served as the NPL president until 1937, when he was appointed to finish out the term of the recently deceased U.S. senator from Tennessee; he was defeated for renomination and left office in January 1939. Cooling toward the New Deal, which he now viewed as "state socialism," he supported Wendell Willkie for president in 1940.

Shortly before Berry died at the Pressmen's Home in Rogersville, Tennessee, he was convicted of income tax evasion. Berry's will left the union a half-interest in the local newspaper and extensive real estate (though not his share of the playing-card company). But once his legal fines were paid, hardly anything was left for his beneficiaries. Two years later a congressional investigation concluded that he had misused union funds.

George Berry built a strong union over the course of his life, although his commitment to labor seems always to have left considerable room for pursuing his own self-interest. He was generally classed with the more conservative labor leaders of his day, yet he developed many innovative services within his union, and he was among the first of the AFL leaders to recognize the need for a new relationship with government during the depression.

• Berry does not appear to have left any papers, but the *Rogersville (Tenn.) Review*, which he owned, contains considerable information about his career during the years 1932–1948. See also Elizabeth F. Baker, *Printers and Technology: A History of the International Printing Pressmen and Assistants' Union* (1957); Irving Bernstein, *The Lean Years* (1960) and *The Turbulent Years* (1970); Philip Taft, *The A.F.L. from the Death of Gompers to the Merger* (1959); Steven Fraser, *Labor Will Rule: Sidney Hillman and the Rise of American Labor* (1991); *Collier's*, 28 Aug. 1937; and *Newsweek*, 6 June 1949. An account of the congressional investigation appears in U.S. House of Representatives, 81st Cong., 1st sess. and 2d sess., *Hearings on Union Democracy before a Special Subcommittee of the Committee on Education and Labor* (1950).

SANDRA OPDYCKE

BERRY, George Packer (29 Dec. 1898–5 Oct. 1986), immunologist and medical educator, was born in Troy, New York, the son of the Reverend George Titus Berry and Carrie Electa Packer. Following preparatory education at the Hill School in Pottstown, Pennsylvania, he attended Princeton University, from which he received an A.B. with the highest honors in biology in 1921. After obtaining his M.D. from the Johns Hopkins Medical School in 1925, Berry trained as a house officer at the Johns Hopkins Hospital (1925–1927) and was afterwards assistant resident physician (1927–1928) and instructor in medicine at the Johns Hopkins Medical School (1928–1929). He joined the Rockefeller Institute for Medical Research in 1929, where he was assistant and later associate; he also served as assistant resident physician at the hospital of the Rockefeller Institute. At Rockefeller he worked with such well-known investigators as Richard E. Shope, Thomas M. Rivers, Cornelius P. Rhoads, and Jerome T. Syverton. In 1924 Berry had married Elizabeth L'Estrange Duncan of New Zealand, who died two years later; they had one daughter.

In 1932 Berry left Rockefeller to become professor of bacteriology and head of the Department of Bacteriology at the University of Rochester School of Medicine and Dentistry, serving also as associate professor of medicine (1932–1949), assistant dean (1941–1947), and associate dean (1947–1949). During World War II he was a member of the U.S. Naval Reserve, working on the medical aspects of the atomic bomb and, during 1946, in Operation Crossroads at Bikini.

In 1949 Berry was selected to be dean of the Faculty of Medicine of Harvard University. In his sixteen-year tenure, Berry strengthened the faculty, added at least twenty-six named chairs, more than doubled the school's endowment, embraced and increased scientific research, brought Harvard-affiliated hospitals closer together, and built the Francis A. Countway Library of Medicine, combining the Harvard Medical Library with the Boston Medical Library to form the largest academic medical library in the world. As president of the Association of American Medical Colleges (1951–1952) and as dean at Harvard (1949–1965), he was instrumental in shaping the quality of American medical education. His major report, "Medical Education in Transition," was a definitive evaluation of modern American medicine. He also coauthored a report for the Department of Health, Education and Welfare that set the stage for expansion of the National Institutes of Health.

During his years at Rockefeller, Berry became recognized nationally for his achievements in the field of animal virology and immunology. Between 1930 and 1949 he was a vigorous laboratory scientist. The range of his research interests encompassed bacteriophages, X-ray inactivation of viruses, and several bacterial diseases, such as Weil's disease and gonorrhea, caused by the gonococcus. He accomplished a series of studies on the virus of yellow fever, western equine encephalomyelitis virus, the virus of myxomatosis, the rabbit fibroma virus (also known as the Shope papilloma virus), and the psittacosis agent. During his extensive studies on psittacosis, he contracted the disease and suffered chronic sequelae. Berry wrote approximately 100 papers dealing with scientific problems and medical education.

Throughout his career Berry carried on a wide scope of professional activities in medical, educational, governmental, and military organizations, as well as in private foundations. From 1952 until his death he was a trustee of the American University of Beirut; he served as a director of the National Health Council and the National Society for Medical Research and served as a consultant on medical research and education to the Department of Health, Education and Welfare. He was also a director of the Josiah Macy, Jr. Foundation, the Louis T. Wright Memorial Fund, and the Commonwealth Fund and served on the Medical School Grants Committee of the Ford Foundation. Following his retirement from Harvard in 1965, Berry moved to Princeton, where he served as special consultant on the life sciences and as a charter trustee of the university. In 1969 he married Mariana Richardson Wilkinson. He died in Princeton, New Jersey.

Berry was a man of wide education and experience, with a deep interest in the history and culture of medicine. The descendant of several Princeton-trained ministers, he possessed pulpit eloquence as well as great intelligence and a commanding aspect, making many who knew him assert that he had been born to be a dean. A highly effective fundraiser, he is generally acknowledged to stand, along with David Linn Edsall, as Harvard's greatest and most effective medical dean.

• Press releases, newspaper and magazine interviews, obituaries, and other materials are contained in biographical files in the Harvard Medical Archives in the Francis A. Countway Library of Medicine, which also preserved Berry's Dean's Files and a large part of his personal papers. The most extensive biographical record of Berry was published in the spring 1987 issue of the *Harvard Medical Alumni Bulletin*, a special issue devoted to him. An earlier treatment is Greer Williams, "How Doctors Are Made," *Saturday Evening Post*, 25 Jan. 1958.

RICHARD J. WOLFE

BERRY, Martha McChesney (7 Oct. 1866–27 Feb. 1942), founder of Berry College, was born in Oak Hill, near Rome, Georgia, the daughter of Thomas Berry, a merchant, and Frances Rhea. Born in the post–Civil War South, Berry and her family lived in affluence compared with the mountain people of Floyd County. As a young girl, she often accompanied her father on excursions to the mountains, where she observed him encouraging the mountain people to help themselves. She received her formal education from a governess employed in the family. From this teacher she learned a love for nature and inspiration from heroic stories. Typical of southern young women of her class and race, Berry was sent to Madam Le Febvre's Edgeworth School in Baltimore to complete her studies at the age of sixteen. Unhappy far from the freedom of her country life in Georgia, she returned home after one year and remained in Rome for a lifetime.

Berry's future as an educator arose unexpectedly in the 1890s. She was a young woman, reared for a life of society and marriage, but with a vague goal to accomplish something more meaningful. One day, while reading in a small log cabin built by her father, she noticed several poorly clad children outside her window. She invited the mountain children in and read them stories from the Bible. The children returned with their families to hear her stories, play the melodeon, and sing. The deficient education of the children and their parents inspired Berry with a sense of mission. Against the wishes of her family and friends, she created a larger meetinghouse and school at the nearby settlement of Possum Trot. With the help of her sister, Frances, Berry organized Sunday schools, sewing classes, and day classes for children. She soon became dissatisfied with her day schools. The same conditions that inhibited attendance at the county public schools affected her classes. Poor roads, long distances between home and school, and, in her opinion, poor hygiene and habits convinced Berry that only in a boarding school could she make a difference in her students' lives.

In 1902 Berry used an inheritance of land and money from her father to open the Boys' Industrial School, renamed the Mount Berry School for Boys. To secure her first six pupils, she had to convince proud mountain parents that their sons needed a practical and academic education. In 1906 she was invited to speak at the Ninth Conference for Education in the South about her growing "industrial school for poor country boys." In 1909 she added a department for girls. Both the boys and girls wore uniforms and combined high school–level vocational and academic studies. Students were required to work a prescribed number of hours per week to help pay their tuition (most could not pay the entire fee), room, and board. The school was nondenominational but emphasized Christian values. In 1926 a junior college division was added, and in 1930 it could confer baccalaureate degrees.

Because of the social and economic distance between her own upbringing and the pupils who attended her school (she often traveled deep into the mountains looking for worthy pupils), Berry's writings and statements reflect a sense of noblesse oblige typical of her social class. For example, in one of her many appeals for equipment and money to aid the school, she described her students in a letter in 1938 as originating "from lonely, unpainted little mountain cabins . . . they come here to Berry—begging for a chance to work their way through school." Berry's hard work and vision for the schools created a deep sense of loyalty among many despite her tendency to view students as beneficiaries of charity. Students entered the Berry schools through a large archway inscribed with the words "Gate of Opportunity."

Berry's role shifted from teacher to director and fundraiser after the first decade of the school. At times exhausted and discouraged, particularly during the Great Depression of the 1930s, she nonetheless displayed a shrewd ability in her travels to the northern states each year to raise funds. Her efforts resembled that of other southern educators who tapped northern philanthropy during the first half of the twentieth century. She corresponded and visited with contemporary Booker T. Washington, whose Tuskegee Institute for African-American youth in Alabama shared her philosophy of practical training of the mind, heart, and hand. Berry also capitalized on the class and racial dynamics of the period to raise money. For example, in one of her many pamphlets circulated to potential donors, she appealed, "Can we perform a more patriotic service than to educate these boys and girls of the mountains in whose veins flow the best and purest Anglo-Saxon blood?" (*What the Berry Schools Are Doing for America*, 1917).

The public attention given to the Berry schools through national journals and newspapers, in addition to Berry's personal charm and skills in securing philanthropy, enabled her to expand the acreage and enrollment of the school. In 1910 she persuaded President Theodore Roosevelt to spend half a day touring the campus. She also successfully convinced automobile magnate Henry Ford of the school's usefulness; Ford donated almost $4 million for buildings and equipment to the school. Most benefactors, like Ford, praised the practical, rural nature of Berry—its dairy, its brickmaking equipment, and its fields for farming.

Berry received significant recognition for her work during a period when few women held positions of leadership. The Georgia legislature named her Distinguished Citizen of Georgia in 1924. The readers of *Good Housekeeping* voted her one of the nation's "Twelve Greatest Women" in 1931. She was the first woman in Georgia appointed a member of the board of regents of the state's university system (1932) and state planning board (1937). Berry, who remained single, died at St. Joseph's Hospital in Atlanta and is buried on the Berry College campus.

An educator in the milieu of the Progressive Era, Berry devoted her life to better educational and economic opportunities for the poor and illiterate white children of the mountains of Georgia. She developed the Berry schools during a period in southern educational history when philanthropic organizations stepped in to fill needs that the state neglected. At that time public schools in rural Georgia ranked among the lowest in the nation, and few public high schools existed outside of the cities.

Although critics emphasize Berry's authoritarian style and her sensitivity to criticism, few can dispute that she took action to correct injustice in her region of Georgia. In the 1990s Berry College encompassed almost thirty thousand acres of land, having begun with less than one hundred acres. It annually enrolled approximately fifteen hundred students working toward their bachelor's or master's degrees.

• Berry's correspondence and materials relating to the Berry schools are preserved at the Berry College Archives in Rome, Ga. Additional materials are maintained at the Martha Berry Museum near the college campus. Her correspondence reveals little about her personal thoughts and feelings. Laudatory accounts include Tracy Byers, *Martha Berry, the Sunday Lady of Possum Trot* (1932); Thomas Harnett Kane, *Miracle in the Mountains* (1956); and Evelyn Hoge Pendley, *A Lady I Loved* (1966). Articles about Berry and her schools during the first half of the century are Alice Booth, "Martha Berry (America's Twelve Greatest Women)," *Good Housekeeping*, Aug. 1931, pp. 50–51, 159–61; and Mary Watts Stanton, "What One Georgia Woman Is Doing for Poor Children," *Leslie's Weekly*, 27 Oct. 1910. A series of articles in the *New Republic* (1933–1934) raised questions about the amount of work and discipline required of Berry students. While director of the school, Berry published a promotional magazine, the *Southern Highlander*, which reveals her tactics for eliciting interest in the school from potential donors. An obituary is in the *New York Times*, 27 Feb. 1942.

VICTORIA-MARÍA MACDONALD

BERRYMAN, John (25 Oct. 1914–7 Jan. 1972), poet, was born John Allyn Smith, Jr., in McAlester, Oklahoma, the son of John Allyn Smith, a banker, and Martha Little, formerly a schoolteacher. The family moved frequently, finally settling in Tampa, Florida, where his father speculated in land, failed, and in 1926 committed suicide. Three months later his mother married John McAlpin Berryman, whose name was given to the son.

The new family moved to New York City, but hard times followed the 1929 stock market crash; young John attempted suicide in 1931. The next year he enrolled at Columbia College (later Columbia University), where he flourished under mentor Mark Van Doren, published poems in *Columbia Review* and *The Nation* (1935), and graduated Phi Beta Kappa in English. He studied two years at Cambridge University in England, meeting W. B. Yeats, T. S. Eliot, W. H. Auden, and Dylan Thomas. He tried playwriting, won the Oldham Shakespeare prize, and published poems in *Southern Review* (1937).

In 1939 Berryman taught at Wayne University (later Wayne State University) in Detroit and served as poetry editor of *The Nation*. By December he was hospitalized for epilepsy, although he was actually suffering from nervous exhaustion, a condition that would recur in future years, exacerbated by alcoholism. His first collected poems appeared in *Five Young American Poets* (1940), while Berryman taught at Harvard. Classified 4-F for the wartime draft, Berryman married Eileen Mulligan in 1942. The next year he published *Poems*. Unemployed and desperate enough to briefly teach English and Latin at a prep school, Berryman landed an instructorship at Princeton, having been invited by poet R. P. Blackmur; this became home for a decade.

For the next twenty years Berryman established his academic credentials, beginning with reviews of W. W. Greg's *The Editorial Problem in Shakespeare*, a critical edition of *King Lear* (never published), and articles on Henry James, F. Scott Fitzgerald, and Robert Lowell. He was promoted to associate in creative writing (1946) and resident fellow (1948) at Princeton, and his work *The Dispossessed* (1948) won the Poetry Society of America's Shelley Memorial award. He associated professionally and socially with Lowell, Saul Bellow, and others. He was also meeting women, and in 1946 he began his lifelong series of infidelities, recorded in *Sonnets to Chris* (written 1947, published 1967; also titled *Berryman's Sonnets*). His intense diary entries provide insight into his mania for sexual attention and adulation.

Berryman's poetic and academic lives continued apace. He published "The Poetry of Ezra Pound," defended Pound's Bollingen Prize in a letter (signed by seventy-three writers) to *The Nation* (1949), and published his psychological biography, *Stephen Crane* (1950), which reveals Berryman as well as Crane himself (see John Clendenning in *Recovering Berryman*, ed. Richard Kelley [1993]). He also wrote on Marlowe, Shakespeare, Monk Lewis, Walt Whitman, Theodore Dreiser, and Bellow. In 1950 he won the American Academy award for poetry.

In 1953 Berryman published *Homage to Mistress Bradstreet* in the *Partisan Review* (it appeared in book form in 1956). This difficult poem, a tribute to the Puritan poet of colonial America, took Berryman five years to complete and demanded much from the reader when it first appeared with no notes. The *Times Literary Supplement* hailed it as a path-breaking masterpiece; poet Robert Fitzgerald called it "the poem of his generation." In fifty-seven stanzas of eight rhymed lines each, the five sections of *Homage* were positioned symmetrically: Berryman's invocation of the dead poet, a Bradstreet monologue, a seductive dialogue between the two poets, a second Bradstreet monologue, and finally Berryman's peroration. Berryman addressed Bradstreet as both lover and listener, extending himself through her tribulations as an exile in the Rhode Island colony. He included personal tragedies such as her heart problems ("wandering pacemaker"), as well as identified with her situation, where he awaits "in a redskin calm." Their tension is evidenced even in the pauses:

You must not love me, but   I do not bid you cease.

With this work, Berryman emerged as a major literary figure.

During these years, when he won the National Institute of Arts and Letters Award (1950), the Levinson Prize (1950), and a Guggenheim Fellowship (1952), Berryman lectured at the Universities of Washington and Cincinnati and at the Writer's Workshop at Iowa, his teaching described by poet Philip Levine as "brilliant, intense, articulate" (*The Bread of Time* [1994]). Berryman's astounding memory allowed him to quote poetry at great length, and his short story, "Wash Far Away" (not published until 1975, *American Review*), showed how seriously he considered teaching. His private life, however, was crumbling on account of his alcoholism. He separated from Eileen in 1953 and was dismissed from Iowa after his arrest for public intoxication and disturbing the peace. His treatment by dream analysis he considered publishable. By 1955, assisted by poet Allen Tate, Berryman moved to Minneapolis and was appointed lecturer in humanities (separate from the English department) at the University of Minnesota, which became his home for life. The cycle was nearly complete, as he now lived thirty miles from his suicidal father's birthplace. At this time he began *The Dream Songs*, his most significant work.

Divorced in 1956, Berryman married 24-year-old Ann Levine a week later; the couple had a son. *Homage to Mistress Bradstreet* was nominated for a Pulitzer Prize in 1956; the next year Berryman was promoted to associate professor, and the State Department sponsored him on a lecture tour of India.

In 1958 Berryman was hospitalized for exhaustion; he also legally separated from Ann. In 1959 they divorced, and Berryman was again in the hospital for alcoholism and nerves; for the rest of his life he was hospitalized at least once a year. Over the next three years, Berryman taught at the University of California at Berkeley, at Bread Loaf in Vermont, and at Brown University, and he won awards, published a scholarly edition of Thomas Nashe's *The Unfortunate Traveller*, and married Kate Donahue, age twenty-two, in 1961. They had two daughters.

77 Dream Songs (1964) won the Pulitzer Prize. In all, *The Dream Songs*, published under that title in 1969, stretched to 385 songs and resembled a sonnet sequence, with each song composed in a three-stanza format, eighteen lines with rhyme. Their protagonist, Henry, is a white middle-aged American who talks about himself in first, second, and third voices and listens to his unnamed Friend, a white American in blackface speaking Negro dialect. Henry is greedy, lusty, petulant; he is essentially Freud's Id. His Friend is conscience, and their dialogue works itself out, as Helen Vendler argues in *The Given and the Made* (1995), as analysis in the therapist's office, each song approximating a session on the couch. Henry, speaking with all of Berryman's baggage—paternal suicide, shameless libido, drunkenness—is allowed to aggress and regress, throwing his anger, fears, and

blasphemy up against Friend, a blank wall of therapeutic response. Their comic poise is omnipresent, for example, when Friend condemns Henry for springing on another man's wife: "There ought to be a law against Henry" (Dream Song 4). At times, Henry's self-destruction is governed only by personified Ruin staring at him (Dream Song 45), and Henry remains "weeping, sleepless" (Dream Song 29).

To Henry, like Lord Byron's impetuous Don Juan, life is boring (Dream Song 14); however, Berryman's twentieth-century man resists rather than indulges. Unlike his Romantic predecessor, Berryman was disgusted with his isomorphic identification with the persona's desperate uncertainties, and in his volume of Kierkegaard, he underscored the passage: "This form of despair . . . lowest of all, in despair at willing to be another than himself."

Berryman was awarded a Guggenheim Fellowship in 1967 to complete *The Dream Songs*. He lived for a time in Ireland and continued to drink heavily, eventually checking into a Minneapolis hospital for alcohol treatment. Meanwhile, he won the Academy of American Poets and National Endowment for the Arts awards (1967). *His Toy, His Dream, His Rest* (1968) completed *The Dream Songs* and won the National Book Award (1969) and the Bollingen Prize. These awards celebrated his distinctive poetic voice, which the *New York Times* later described as "jaunty, jazzy, colloquial . . . full of awkward turns and bent syntax" (8 Jan. 1972). In his acceptance speech, Berryman explained his iconoclastic style: "I set up *The Dream Songs* as hostile to every visible tendency in both American and English poetry."

After checking into alcohol rehabilitation once in 1969 and three times in 1970, Berryman experienced "a sort of religious conversion" in 1970. He considered Judaism, professed Catholicism, and wrote *Recovery* (1971), a vague autobiography about alcoholic rehabilitation. His research on Shakespeare continued, but the fatal cycle refused to be broken: haunted by his father's suicide and with his youngest daughter just six months old, Berryman jumped to his death off the Washington Avenue Bridge in Minneapolis.

In a bathetic line, Berryman wrote, "For I am the penal colony's prime scribe" (Sonnet 73). Berryman's reputation varied over his lifetime, from rising star, to a poet of unrealized promise who was largely excluded from anthologies, and finally in the last eight years of his life to the first rank of American poets, whose *Dream Songs* became a rare book-club poetry selection. The poet's acute insecurities and neuroses manifested themselves in his public persona as a braggart, a womanizer, a drunk, and an intellectual. But he unleashed the range of colloquial American language in his verse with a lyrical intensity that Lowell called "more tearful and funny than we can easily bear."

• John Berryman's papers are found at the University of Minnesota, cataloged in Richard Kelly, *John Berryman: A Checklist* (1972). Berryman's letters to his mother are published in *We Dream of Honour* (1988). His essays and short stories are collected in *The Freedom of the Poet* (1976). An authorized biography is John Haffenden, *The Life of John Berryman* (1982). First wife Eileen Simpson's roman à clef, *The Maze* (1975), gives an insider's view of a manic poet; her *Poets in Their Youth* (1982) provides biographical detail. William Heyen, "John Berryman: A Memoir and an Interview," *Ohio Review* (Winter 1974): 46–65, presents a vivid picture of the vulnerable and frenzied poet. "Whiskey and Ink, Whiskey and Ink," *Life*, 21 July 1967, popularized Berryman in the Dylan Thomas image. Peter Stitt, "The Art of Poetry," *Paris Review* 53 (Winter 1972): 177–207, provides a famous interview Berryman gave shortly before his death. Joel Conarroe's *John Berryman* (1977) is an excellent overview. An obituary is in the *New York Times*, 8 Jan. 1972.

JOEL ATHEY

BERSON, Solomon Aaron (22 Apr. 1918–11 Apr. 1972), physician and medical scientist, was born in New York City, the son of Jacob Berson, the owner of a fur-dyeing company, and Cecilia Lieberman. Starting in high school and throughout his life, Berson was an avid violinist, mathematician, and chess player. He earned a B.S. from the City College of New York in 1938, reading widely in history and art during his undergraduate years. Following graduation Berson applied to twenty-one medical schools, only to be rejected by all. Forced to postpone his medical career, he entered a master of science program at New York University in the fall of 1938. While in this program Berson served as an assistant in anatomy at the NYU College of Dentistry. He received the M.Sc. in 1941 and was admitted to the NYU medical school the same year as a Blumenthal Fellow in Anatomy. While in medical school he lectured in physiology at Hunter College in New York City. In 1942 he married Miriam Gittleson; they had two children.

Berson received his M.D. in 1945 and began a year's internship at Boston City Hospital. In 1946 he joined the Army Medical Corps, rising from first lieutenant to captain in only two years. He returned to New York as a resident in internal medicine at the Bronx Veterans Administration Hospital in 1948. Following his residency Berson was hired as a medical researcher by Rosalyn Yalow, assistant chief of the hospital's radioisotope service. He also maintained a private practice in internal medicine for nearly a year before devoting himself full time to the rewarding and productive partnership with Yalow. They established a thyroid clinic at the radioisotope service in 1950 and began to conduct clinical research there in 1952.

One of the first research efforts Yalow and Berson undertook together was to examine the fundamental properties of human insulin circulation. By studying the mechanism of thyroid function and the response of the thyroid to the administration of insulin, Berson and Yalow determined that humans develop insulin antibodies upon treatment with the hormone. They then designed a radioimmunoassay technique to measure serum hormone levels. This technique, described in "Insulin-I 131 Metabolism in Human Subjects: Demonstration of Insulin Binding Globulin in the Circulation of Insulin-Treated Subjects" (*Journal of Clinical Investigation* 35 [1956]: 170–90), aided Berson and Yalow in further research on the mechanism of adult diabetes. In 1959 they demonstrated that adult diabetes is caused by the overly-rapid degradation of insulin rather than by flaws in the production or metabolism of the hormone. They published their results in several studies, the most important of which was "Assay of Plasma Insulin in Human Subjects by Immunological Methods" (*Nature* 184 [1959]: 1648–49). The radioimmunoassay developed by Berson and Yalow was utilized by countless other research groups for the analysis of previously unmeasurable chemical and peptide hormones, including parathyroid hormone, growth hormone, ACTH, and gastrin, in fields as diverse as endocrinology, clinical pharmacology, oncology, virology, and hematology.

In 1954 Berson was named chief of the radioisotope service of the Bronx Veterans Administration Hospital; he held that position for fourteen years. Berson and Yalow continued their work on radioisotopes as means of clinical investigation and published more than 200 papers in scientific and medical journals during their long and prosperous partnership. In addition, Berson served on the editorial boards of *Diabetes* (1965–1967), *Journal of Clinical Investigation* (1958–1968), *Diabetes Literature Index* (1966–1972), *Hormone and Metabolic Research* (1968–1972), and the *Mount Sinai Journal of Medicine* (1968–1972). In 1968 he was named professor and chairman of the Department of Medicine at Mount Sinai School of Medicine of the City University of New York; he was consistently commended as a gifted lecturer and dedicated member of the faculty. He served on the National Advisory Council, the Board of Scientific Counselors, and the National Institutes of Health and was a member of numerous medical and scientific societies. In 1966 he was the U.S. State Department American Specialist Grant Lecturer in South America, for which he was honored by several international and national bodies. In 1970 he traveled to Bombay, India, as World Health Organization consultant at the Radiation Medical Center. He amassed numerous other awards and invited lectureships during his career, including the Eli Lilly Award of the American Diabetes Association (1957), the William S. Middleton Medical Research Award (1960), the Banting Memorial Lecture and the Banting Medal of the American Diabetes Association (1965), and, in 1971, awards from the New York Academy of Medicine, the Gairdner Foundation, the University of Chicago, and the American College of Physicians. Berson died at a scientific meeting in Atlantic City, New Jersey. After his death Yalow won the 1973 Nobel Prize for developing the radioimmunoassay of peptide hormones. The products of their partnership revolutionized the conception of radioisotopes as resources for medical research, and the enthusiasm and dedication brought to medical science by Berson had a profound impact on his colleagues, students, and successors.

• Several articles in the *Mount Sinai Journal of Medicine* 40 (May–June 1973) are dedicated to Berson's memory. Other informative articles include J. E. Rall, "Solomon A. Berson," National Academy of Sciences, *Biographical Memoirs* 59 (1991): 55–70; E. Samols, "Solomon A. Berson: A Brief Biography," *Seminars in Nuclear Medicine* 9 (1979): 173–77; W. H. Daughaday, "Solomon A. Berson, 1918–1972," *Transactions of the Association of American Physicians* 85 (1972): 9–10; J. Roth, "Solomon A. Berson," *Diabetes* 22 (1973): 66–68; P. J. Randle, "Dr. Solomon A. Berson," *Diabetologia* 9 (1972): 311–12; and R. A. Arky and F. J. Ingelfinger, "Solomon A. Berson," *New England Journal of Medicine* 77 (1972): 477.

KRISTIN M. BUNIN

BERTHOLF, Guiliam (1656–1726?), Dutch Reformed minister, was born in Sluis, in the Dutch province of Zeeland, the son of Crijn Bertholf and Sara Guiliamse van Coperen. Bertholf was reared in the heartland of Dutch Pietism at a time when this movement was seriously roiling the Reformed Dutch Church. (Contrary to church traditionalists, Pietists favored an experiential approach to religion, emphasizing the necessity for personal conversion; stressed a literal reading of the Bible and the priesthood of all believers; and believed that spontaneous prayer and extemporaneous preaching were indications of the presence of the Holy Spirit.)

Bertholf's educational background has not been documented, but ordination in his day required facility in Latin, sufficient Greek and Hebrew for exegesis, and training in Reformed theology, doctrine, church history and polity, homiletics, and oratory. These foundations he probably obtained through self-study and private tutoring.

In Sluis, Bertholf was comfortably situated as the owner of a bakery, but at age twenty-eight he emigrated to America. Some have suggested that he was the object of harassment by Dutch ecclesiastical authorities as was his mentor, the Pietist preacher Jacobus Koelman. Bertholf sold his house in Sluis in September 1684 and set sail with his wife, Martina (also Martyntje) Hendrickse Vermeulen, whom he had married in 1676, and their three children. He joined the Reformed Dutch Church at Bergen (now Jersey City) the following month. He settled at first in nearby Acquackanonk (now Passaic), where he farmed and took up the trade of cooper and where his spiritual gifts and his talent for leadership soon became well known. In 1690 Bertholf was appointed clerk and "voorleser" (an order of lay readers and comforters of the sick) at Harlem Village on Manhattan Island, a position he held for a year before being invited in 1691 to become voorleser, clerk, and schoolmaster at Hackensack, New Jersey.

Bertholf resettled his growing family in Hackensack—he fathered at least eight children—and for the next two years he performed the duties of voorleser not only in this community but also in Bergen, Acquackanonk, Harlem Village, and Staten Island. These congregations had such a thirst for Bertholf's reverent and stirring preaching style and his spiritual guidance that he was persuaded by his listeners to return to the Netherlands to seek ordination. On 2 September 1693

Bertholf applied in person for ordination to the Classis of Walcheren in Middelburg, Province of Zeeland, and was subsequently examined, ordained, and invested with the pastoral care of the churches of Hackensack and Acquackanonk. Upon his return, Bertholf became the first ordained Dutch Reformed minister in America of Pietist background and was also the first resident ordained minister of any denomination to serve in colonial New Jersey (1694–1724).

Bertholf's ordination was greeted with uneasiness by his non-Pietist ministerial colleagues in the Reformed Dutch Church of New York, who viewed the rising tide of potentially separatist Pietism and Bertholf's following in the countryside as a threat both to their own authority and to the authority of the increasingly beleaguered church. Also, the non-Pietist clergy was well aware that the royal government had previously had reason to fear Bertholf's popularity and influence, for during the turbulent period of Leisler's Rebellion (1689–1691), he had taken a stand with the pro-Leislerian forces. In time, however, he came to be accepted by the New York clergy, both for his indefatigable evangelistic work in the countryside and for his attempts to moderate an ecclesiastical conflict that developed around the Pietist minister Theodorus Jacobus Frelinghuysen in the Raritan valley of New Jersey in the 1720s.

During his vigorous thirty-year pastorate, Bertholf was responsible for organizing congregations and establishing churches in communities in what are now Somerset, Hudson, Bergen, and Passaic counties in New Jersey, and Rockland and Westchester counties in New York. For his extensive travels, Bertholf was called the "itinerating apostle" of New Jersey. At the end of his career, he may have been influential in bringing to America the Pietist preacher Frelinghuysen, often described as a forerunner of the first Great Awakening in New Jersey.

Bertholf's spiritual and intellectual roots in Zeeland have been traced directly to the two pastors he had known in the Sluis pulpit, Pietists Jodocus van Lodenstein and Jacobus Koelman, and indirectly to the works of Pietist theologians Willem Teellinck and Gysbertus Voetius, Huguenot Jean Taffin, and English Puritans William Perkins and William Ames. The important Mennonite presence in Zeeland is also thought to have been a factor in Bertholf's development, as was the influence of the Huguenot community there. (The Huguenot congregation in New Milford, N.J., joined Bertholf's Hackensack church in 1694.) Koelman, a translator of English and Scottish Puritan writings into Dutch, and a prolific author on his own, exercised the single most significant influence on the theological thinking and style of the young Bertholf.

Though as a Pietist, Bertholf, like Koelman, advocated Bible study in homes, the practice of family devotions, and "conventicles" (private gatherings of born-again Christians for the purpose of witnessing and testifying to the glory of God), his Pietism remained within the church's confessional bounds, unlike that of either Koelman or, later, Frelinghuysen. None of Bertholf's sermons have surfaced to date, but in an introduction to a collection of Frelinghuysen's sermons Bertholf made a point of endorsing the "orthodox" doctrines, liturgy, and forms of the Dutch Reformed Church—which Frelinghuysen had been accused of violating—and in another context he urged moderation on the overly zealous Frelinghuysen.

In the religious history of New York and New Jersey, Bertholf is an obscure but pivotal figure who imparted the Pietist outlook and Spirit-filled theology to eager congregations in the Hudson, Hackensack, and Raritan valleys. As a link between Reformation Europe and Awakening America, he caught the winds of change in the old world and stirred the winds of change in the new. Bertholf probably died in Hackensack, where he is thought to be buried.

• Contemporary references to Bertholf can be found in E. T. Corwin, ed., *Ecclesiastical Records of the State of New York* (7 vols., 1901–1916), and in Joseph A. Loux, *Boel's "Complaint" against Frelinghuysen* (1979). Important articles are Howard G. Hageman, "William Bertholf: Pioneer Domine of New Jersey," *Reformed Review* 29 (1976), and Hageman, "Colonial New Jersey's First Domine," *de Halve Maen* 54, no. 3 (1969): 9–10, 14; and 55, no. 1 (1970): 17–18. Adrian C. Leiby devotes a chapter to Bertholf in *The United Churches of Hackensack and Schraalenburgh, New Jersey, 1686–1822* (1976). David Cole, *History of the Reformed Church of Tappan, N.Y.* (1894), pp. 8–20, and Firth Haring Fabend, *A Dutch Family in the Middle Colonies, 1660–1800* (1991), chap. 7, explore his pastorate in the church he organized in 1694 and served on a supply basis for three decades. Finally, James Tanis identifies the sources of Bertholf's Pietism in two works: *Dutch Calvinistic Pietism in the Middle Colonies: A Study of the Life and Theology of Theodorus J. Frelinghuysen* (1967), and "Reformed Pietism in Colonial America," in *Continental Pietism and Early American Christianity*, ed. F. Ernest Stoeffler (1976).

FIRTH HARING FABEND

BERTOCCI, Peter Anthony (1910–13 Oct. 1989), philosopher, was born in Gaeta, Italy, the son of Gaetano Bertocci and Annunziata Guglietta. His father had earlier settled in an immigrant quarter of Somerville, Massachusetts, and Peter was brought to Massachusetts by his mother when he was a few months old. The Bertocci family had its share of both tragedy and hard work. Of their thirteen children, only six survived childbirth. Both parents were relentless workers, rigorously frugal, and willing to undergo any sacrifice to make America the land of promise for their children. Peter himself was employed from the age of seven. He sold newspapers at the meat-packing plant where his father worked; tended a shoe-maker's shop; collected and repaired storage barrels; cleaned a neighbor's barn; and procured kindling, cooking wood, and coal.

With help from the Boston Rotary Club, earnings from summer jobs, and what he had managed to save, Bertocci enrolled at Boston University. The viewpoints of the professors there provided a sharp contrast to the fundamentalist approach to the Bible and

Christianity taught at the mission school in Somerville he had attended. He graduated in 1931, earning a B.A. in philosophy and a Phi Beta Kappa key.

Next he enrolled at Harvard University, where he earned a master's degree in psychology under Gordon W. Allport (1932). Then he returned to Boston University to work for a Ph.D. in philosophy. With guidance from a professor of his, Edgar Brightman, he spent a year of study (1934–1935) at Cambridge University under Frederick Robert Tennant, a theologian who sought to reconcile science with religion. He received his Ph.D. from Boston University in 1935. That same year he married Lucy Soldani; they were to have three sons.

In 1935 Bertocci took his first job teaching psychology at Bates College. While he was there, his dissertation written under Tennant was published as *The Empirical Argument for God in Late British Thought* (1938). It was the first of his fifteen books. In 1944 he rejoined Brightman as a faculty member at Boston University. In 1953 he was appointed to the Borden Parker Bowne Chair of Philosophy at the university, which he retained until his retirement in 1975. Thereafter, he continued a full schedule of research and lectures, writing two books—*The Goodness of God* (1981) and *The Person and Primary Emotions* (1988)—a dozen articles for philosophical journals, two essays for other books, and numerous reviews. Weakened by Parkinson's disease and other undiagnosed maladies, he died at home in Arlington, Massachusetts.

Bertocci was elected president of both the American Theological Society and the Metaphysical Society in the same year (1963–1964) and served as secretary-treasurer of the Personalistic Discussion Group for his entire career (1938–1975). In 1950–1951 he was a Fulbright scholar in Italy and in 1960–1961 a Fulbright research scholar in India. The scope of his work is indicated by his having published articles in psychology, education, ethics, religion, and philosophy.

Bertocci's major accomplishments include these aspects of his thought: his explanation and defense of the wider teleological argument for the existence of a personal God; his development of the finite/temporal concept of this personal God; the closely related account such a concept provides for excess natural and moral evil; his concept of "religion as creative insecurity" (to which he devoted a book by that name); and his discussion of virtue-ethics and its application to sex, love, and marriage.

It is important to note how Bertocci modifies and refines the teleological argument for God's existence. As Bertocci formulates this argument, it has five distinctive characteristics it did not have in its earlier classical forms as presented by the eighteenth-century English theologians Joseph Butler and William Paley. First, Bertocci's argument focuses on general or inclusive interrelationships rather than specific adaptations of, say, animals to their environment. It appeals to the general interconnectedness of physical nature to life and to human experience. The reciprocity, harmony, and interconnectedness of physical nature, life, and human experience requires, according to Bertocci, a purposive being or person for its explanation. Second, the argument appeals to empirical or factual evidence as indirect support for its primary hypothesis. The force or cogency of the argument arises from these inductive considerations rather than from any deductive steps or demonstrative proof. The indirect support, unlike any deductive inference, can only rely on its reasonableness as an interpretation of the facts. Third, the argument therefore offers its conclusion in terms of probability and reasonableness rather than certainty and necessity. It provides only a reasonable warrant for belief in a personal God. Fourth, the argument is cumulative in its cogency. Each of the links in the argument lends its persuasiveness to the whole line of reasoning. In its entirety the argument is persuasive even though individual links may not be completely convincing. Fifth, the argument relies on empirical coherence as an index of truth. Coherence requires that one be consistent, systematic, inclusive, analytic, and synoptic. It means being open to alternatives, active in one's search for truth, willing to test hypotheses, and willing to commit oneself to the best available hypothesis. The facts of an argument must fit together in accord with these standards.

Bertocci's most original contribution and insights are perhaps best captured in his *Religion As Creative Insecurity* (1958). For Bertocci, God's loving is an indication of God's commitment to the continual growth of human persons in community. This commitment involves suffering unto forgiveness, and forgiveness makes it possible for persons to attain self-fulfillment. By uniting people through mutual concern, forgiveness fosters improvement and growth. Knowledge acquired through forgiving love enables individuals to actualize their own potentiality and attain self-fulfillment through caring for others. Yet the goodness or love of God has a tragic dimension. God's moral perfection is a process that includes his "anguish" over his limited power to control his own nonrational aspects. In working against this obstacle in his own nature God expresses his commitment to creating the best compossible conditions for his human co-creators. God's creative insecurity is not free from frustration and disappointment, but neither of these factors totally prevents God's improving any situation. The goodness of God involves a suffering with and a suffering for that is integral to his nature. Part of the "tragic" aspect of God's goodness is the self-imposed requirement that God works for the good at the level of the specific choices made by free human agents. Because of his delegation of genuine freedom to human agents, God must work through the consequences of their use and abuse of each other and of natural resources. It is this "insecure" situation through which God realizes himself. God learns and is enriched through the experiences of human co-creators.

Bertocci's contributions to the philosophy of religion are of enduring significance. His revision of the traditional teleological argument for God's existence makes religious belief intellectually plausible, and his characterization of religion as creative insecurity has appeal to the modern world.

• Biographical material and correspondence related to Bertocci are in the archives of the Boston University Library. A brief essay by Bertocci, "Autobiographical Reflections," ed. John Howie, appears in the memorial issue of the *Personalist Forum* 7, 1 (Spring 1991): 5–36. A complete bibliography prepared by Howie with the assistance of Peter John Bertocci appears in the same memorial issue of the *Personalist Forum*, pp. 91–113. Among Bertocci's most important published writings, besides those mentioned above, are *Introduction to the Philosophy of Religion* (1951), *Free Will, Responsibility and Grace: Psychological and Ethical Perspectives* (1963, with Richard M. Millard), and *The Person God Is* (1970). Obituaries appear in the *Boston Globe*, 11 Nov. 1989; *American Philosophical Association Proceedings* 63, 5: 52–53; and *American Psychologist* 46 (Apr. 1991): 437.

JOHN HOWIE

BERTOIA, Harry (10 Mar. 1915–6 Nov. 1978), sculptor and designer, was born in San Lorenzo, near Udine, in northeastern Italy, the son of Giuseppe Bertoia, a miner and laborer. His mother's name is unknown. He was given his English name by his father, who had previously lived in Canada. As a teenager Bertoia emigrated with his father to Canada and then to Detroit, where his brother had earlier settled. Bertoia enrolled in Cleveland Junior High School in Detroit. Because of his talent in drawing he was allowed to enroll in a special class for artistically gifted students at Cass Technical High School, also in Detroit, where he received his first formal training in art, including metalsmithing. In 1936 he attended the School of the Detroit Society of Arts and Crafts on scholarship to study painting and drawing. In 1937 Bertoia received another scholarship based on his metalwork to attend the Cranbrook Academy of Art in Bloomfield Hills, Michigan.

Cranbrook had an enormous effect on Bertoia, especially through his contact with architects Charles Eames and Eero Saarinen, as well as the resident sculptor Carl Milles and the ceramist Maija Grotell. All were faculty members at Cranbrook and proponents of modernist Scandinavian design. Bertoia was appointed metal craftsman, a full-time teaching position, only one year after arriving at Cranbrook. With no rigid curriculum, the Cranbrook philosophy was characterized by an unstructured approach to materials and technique, as well as the rejection of the separation between fine and applied arts. Bertoia's metalwork at Cranbrook included highly polished, geometric holloware coffee/tea sets in the Scandinavian style, as well as jewelry characterized by the repetition of geometric and organic forms. Bertoia also became interested in printmaking at Cranbrook, and exhibitions of his monoprints and jewelry in New York in 1943 and 1945 were critically acclaimed.

In 1943 Bertoia married Brigetta Valentiner, the daughter of the renowned art historian Wilhelm Valentiner; they had three children. The same year the couple moved to southern California, where Bertoia collaborated with Charles Eames on the manufacture of Eames's famous plywood chair. Bertoia also worked for the defense industry, designing airplane parts for Evans Product Company.

Hans and Florence Knoll asked Bertoia to join Knoll Associates in 1950 because of his involvement with the Eames chair. (Other architects and designers at Knoll included Eero Saarinen, Mies van der Rohe, and Isamu Noguchi.) Bertoia and his family moved to Barto, a town in eastern Pennsylvania near a Knoll factory. His major design for Knoll was the "Bertoia chair," which came on the market in 1952. The chair was internationally popular, and it is still being sold by Knoll International. It consists of a web of chrome-plated or vinyl-coated wires welded in diamond shapes to form a graceful and functional cradle-like chair, which can be either completely upholstered or merely padded on the seat.

By 1953 Bertoia's involvement with furniture design was finished, even though he remained a consultant at Knoll. Instead, he turned full-time to sculpture. This was a natural progression, as his furniture designs were directly linked to contemporary sculpture. Bertoia's early works were tall, delicate wires topped with geometric forms. In the early 1950s he exhibited screenlike welded sculptures of repetitive geometric forms in the Knoll Showrooms in New York.

Bertoia's sculpture can be divided into four general categories: screens, bundles of wire strands, vaguely organic shapes with stems, and sound sculptures. He explored these categories both in large-scale architectural commissions and in smaller-scale works for collectors and museums. His smaller sculptures were often shown at the Staempfli Gallery in New York and the Mackler Gallery in Philadelphia during the 1960s.

Bertoia's first major sculpture commission was for the lobby of Eero Saarinen's GM Technical Center in Warren, Michigan. Completed in 1953, the sculpture is a rectangular screen consisting of gold-colored, textured rectangles in three planes with some open spaces. The sculpture's surface is enriched further by its own shadows. Bertoia created a larger variation of this screenlike sculpture in 1954 for the Manufacturers Hanover Trust Building in New York designed by Skidmore, Owings, and Merrill. The sculpture was acclaimed by the New York critics, and numerous major commissions followed.

The reredos (screen) for the altar of Eero Saarinen's interfaith chapel at the Massachusetts Institute of Technology (1954) was another acclaimed commission for Bertoia. Metal cords suspended from a dramatic skylight extend to the altar platform. On each cord are small, textured, flat rectangular brass plates, open rectangles, and triangles at different angles that change dramatically according to the weather.

For Minoru Yamasaki's National Life Insurance Building in Minneapolis, Bertoia produced his largest "bundle" sculpture in 1964. *Sunlit Straw*, which measures fourteen by forty-six by four feet, consists of thousands of steel rods coated with brass alloy and ar-ranged in bundles. Hung high above the lobby, the sculpture appears to float in space.

Bertoia's sculpture was often incorporated into fountains, as in his well-known large fountain for the Philadelphia Civic Center, completed in 1967. For it, he bronze-welded miles of copper tubing together to make an undulating floral form with a large stem. A total of eighty-six jets spray water into the sculpture from varying heights.

Another fountain he created for the 1966 River Oaks Shopping Center in Calumet City, Illinois, was his first to incorporate sound. It consists of welded bronze rods in different lengths placed side by side on a metal base. Free to move in the wind, the rods sound like bells when they strike each other. One of the most effective of Bertoia's sound sculptures, *Offering to the Wind* (1975), is located in a reflecting pool at the Amoco Building Plaza (formerly the Standard Oil Company Plaza) in Chicago in close proximity to the blustery shore of Lake Michigan.

Bertoia is remembered as a hard-working and quiet artist who was not afraid to cross the boundaries separating fine and applied arts, owing in large part to his Cranbrook education, as well as to his wide-ranging personal interests. Overall, his art is characterized by precise craftsmanship, and it ranges from the geometric to the painterly, usually incorporating color and light. According to Susan Montgomery, "Harry Bertoia was not simply a metalsmith or a furniture designer, sculptor or printmaker, artist or craftsman. He was all of these" (Montgomery, p. 23).

Bertoia's furniture design epitomizes postwar prosperity and a growing middle-class interest in quality design, and it was influenced by the availability of new affordable materials such as Fiberglas, plastic, and plywood. He was one of many postwar American sculptors who worked exclusively in abstraction, and his sculptures contributed to a new corporate and civic aesthetic that defined the interior and exterior spaces of many major American buildings built in the 1950s, 1960s, and early 1970s.

• The principal monograph on Bertoia is June Kompass Nelson, *Harry Bertoia, Sculptor* (1970). A 1972 interview conducted by Paul Cummings is available through the Archives of American Art, Smithsonian Institution. The archives also hold an illustrated booklet made by Bertoia when he was a teenager in Detroit. Background on Bertoia's education at Cranbrook is in Robert Judson Clark et al., *Design in America: The Cranbrook Vision, 1925–1950* (1983). A recent examination of Bertoia's smaller-scale work is Susan J. Montgomery, "The Sound and the Surface: The Metalwork and Jewelry of Harry Bertoia," *Metalsmith* (Summer 1987). A listing of the location of ninety-seven Bertoia sculptures is available through the Inventory of American Painting and Sculpture at the National Museum of American Art, Smithsonian Institution. An obituary is in the *New York Times*, 8 Nov. 1978.

KAY KOENINGER

BESSEY, Charles Edwin (21 May 1845–25 Feb. 1915), botanist, was born on a farm in Wayne County, Ohio, the son of Adnah Bessey, a schoolteacher and farmer, and Margaret Ellenberger. The boy attended country schools and an academy in Seville, Ohio. With the intention of studying civil engineering, Bessey entered Michigan Agricultural College (later Michigan State College) in East Lansing in 1866. Professor Albert Nelson Prentiss noted his enthusiasm for plants, however, and advised Bessey to study botany, a subject in which he received a B.S. in 1869. In February 1870 he became the first instructor of botany and horticulture at Iowa State College of Agriculture in Ames, which had been founded eighteen months earlier as the state's land-grant college. He advanced to professor in 1872.

Bessey corresponded with Asa Gray at Harvard, the foremost general botanist of that time, and met him at the 1872 meeting of the American Association for the Advancement of Science. At Gray's invitation, he spent three months in 1872 and 1873 at Harvard College Botanical Garden, where he learned plant morphology and the basics of systematic botany, the science on which the classification of plants is based. He married Lucy Athearn in December 1873; they had three sons.

In 1873 Bessey declined to include horticulture and pomology in his professorship of botany and zoology at Iowa State, because he did not favor applied courses. He believed that students of agriculture should be given courses in the natural and physical sciences, not in farming techniques. However, from 1871, at the urging of college president Adonijah Strong Welch, he participated in meetings between faculty members and farmers that came to be called Farmers' Institutes. In his classes, Bessey offered laboratory instruction with compound microscopes, the first or second teaching program to do so in undergraduate botany. He established a herbarium of plants collected in the state. He obtained varieties of potatoes and grasses from botanists elsewhere in the United States to try in Iowa, and he published on plant diseases, fungi injurious to agricultural crops, and insects that affected crops.

In 1875 Bessey gave a series of lectures on botany at the University of California at Berkeley. In 1875 he was one of the founders and first president of the Iowa Academy of Sciences. The next year, he studied plant physiology again at Harvard with Gray, whose *Manual of the Botany of the Northern United States* was the primary botany text of the day. At the request of a publisher, and at the urging of Harvard botanists George L. Goodale and Gray, Bessey wrote the textbook *Botany for High Schools and Colleges* (1880, revised three times to 1885). It was praised by the botanist John M. Coulter as "a new departure in American botanical text books" (*Botanical Gazette* 5 [1880]: 96). Bessey's second textbook, intended for a shorter and less technical course, was *The Essentials of Botany* (1884), which became the most widely used botany text in the United States, passing through seven editions to 1896. These were the first botany texts to include physiological plant anatomy and considerable information on the lower groups of plants. While writing them, Bessey

also became familiar with British and European botanical literature.

The regents of the University of Nebraska in Lincoln elected Bessey professor of botany in June 1884. After visiting the campus and finding that it had no program in botany, he declined, but two months later he accepted an expanded offer (promising increased facilities) there as professor of botany and dean of the industrial college, which included the school of agriculture. At the land grant college, he again introduced laboratory courses with microscopes and field trips in botany, and he started a herbarium and a botanical library. A new building in 1888 provided needed space. At the University of Nebraska Bessey was dean of the industrial college from 1884 to 1888 and from 1895 to 1909. He refused to be its chancellor but served as acting chancellor from 1888 to 1891 and simultaneously was dean of the college of literature, science, and the arts. He was acting chancellor again in 1899 and 1907.

Bessey's courses were very popular because of his own keen enthusiasm. Members of an informal club of his graduate students collected plants throughout Nebraska and in neighboring areas for a checklist. Bessey classified the native grasses and forage plants and determined the earlier distribution of trees. Always interested in the more primitive plants, he published on wheat rust, corn smut, and similar organisms. He gave many public lectures on the state's agricultural products, and he participated in groups like the Farmers' Institutes. From 1882, Bessey urged the establishment of state agricultural experiment stations supported by the federal government. This came to fruition as the Hatch Act of 1887, which included Bessey's definition of the duties of the stations and provided fifteen thousand dollars to each state. When the Nebraska Agricultural Experiment Station was established in 1888, Bessey served as its director for two years.

An advocate of Darwin's theory of evolution, about 1890 Bessey began analyzing the evolution of major plant groups. As other botanists of that time were doing, he tried to establish a natural system of plant classification, which he presented in "Evolution and Classification" (*Proceedings of the American Association for the Advancement of Science* 42 [1894]: 237–51); "Phylogenetic Taxonomy of Flowering Plants" (*Annals of the Missouri Botanical Garden* 2 [1915]: 109–64); and the last edition of *Essentials of College Botany* (1914, written with his son Ernst).

Bessey was a charter member of the Botanical Society of America, serving as its president in 1895. He was a founder of the Nebraska Academy of Sciences and its president (1892–1895 and 1914–1915). He was president of the American Association for the Advancement of Science in 1911. As botanical editor of *American Naturalist* (1880–1897) and of *Science* (1897–1915), he presented summaries of botanical studies, including European ones.

From the 1880s Bessey was a leader in a movement dubbed "the new botany" by Coulter, editor of the *Botanical Gazette*, that was a shift from an exclusive focus on taxonomy to physiological and environmental studies of plants. With others, he pushed for a more significant role for botany in the American Association for the Advancement of Science, which led to its establishment as a unit separate from biology in 1891. Bessey died in Lincoln, Nebraska.

• Many of Bessey's papers are at the University of Nebraska Archives and at the Nebraska Historical Society Archives; these include biographical material. In addition to the textbooks cited, Bessey wrote a laboratory manual for botany teachers, *Elementary Botanical Exercise* (1892, 1894), and about 150 scientific papers. Raymond J. Pool, "A Brief Sketch of the Life and Work of Charles Edwin Bessey," *American Journal of Botany* 2 (1915): 505–18, has a selected bibliography. A longer account is Richard A. Overfield, *Science with Practice: Charles E. Bessey and the Maturing of American Botany* (1993), with bibliography.

ELIZABETH NOBLE SHOR

BESSIE, Alvah (4 June 1904–21 July 1985), author and screenwriter, was born in New York City, the son of Daniel Bessie, a successful inventor and businessman, and Adeline Schlesinger. Bessie's rebelliousness was first expressed by his rejection of his father's values, which placed material achievement above human relationships. In 1924 Bessie was graduated from Columbia College, where he had begun writing poetry. He worked briefly as an actor with the Provincetown Players and as a journalist for the English-language *Paris-Times* before returning to New York in 1929.

In 1931 Bessie and his first wife, Mary Burnett, whom he had married a year earlier, were unable to find jobs in New York, so they went to Vermont for the summer to work as houseman and maid at a rich family's country house. They remained in Vermont for several years, with Bessie writing reviews and short stories and supplementing his income by digging potatoes for neighboring farmers. During this period he began his study of Marxist thought as a way of seeking to understand his own and society's condition.

Bessie published his first novel, *Dwell in the Wilderness*, in 1935, after completing it with the support of a Guggenheim Fellowship. Settled in New York again, he was an editor for the *Brooklyn Daily Eagle* from 1935 to 1937. He then devoted his energies to what he and other leftists perceived as the struggle against fascism in Spain. After a stint with the Spanish Information Bureau in New York, he left in 1938 to serve as a volunteer sergeant-adjutant in the Abraham Lincoln Battalion of the Fifteenth International Brigade in support of the Spanish Republic. His Spanish Civil War experiences are described in his nonfiction book *Men in Battle* (1939), which Al Richmond, writing in the *Nation* nearly forty years later, characterized as "the best descriptive narration of the Spanish Civil War to be written by a combatant, or by anyone else, for that matter."

In early 1943 Bessie was hired as a screenwriter by Warner Bros., known at the time for its socially progressive movies. Three of the four films he worked on while under contract—*Northern Pursuit* (1943), *Hotel Berlin* (1945), and *Objective, Burma!* (1945), for which

he was nominated for an Academy Award for original story—were war-related, delivering a pro-Allied, antifascist message. He was fired by Warner Bros. in 1945, reportedly for his pro-union activities in a bitter strike against the major studios. Bessie received co-writing credit on one other screenplay three years later, Allied Artists' *Smart Woman* (1948), before being blacklisted after his refusal to cooperate with the House Un-American Activities Committee (HUAC) in its 1947 investigation of Communist infiltration of the motion picture industry.

The Hollywood Ten—Bessie and nine other screenwriters, directors, and producers—were sentenced to six-month and one-year terms of imprisonment for "contempt" after pleading the First Amendment in their refusal to answer the investigating committee's questions about their Communist party membership. Bessie subsequently called his prison term and his service in the Spanish Civil War "the two activities in a lifetime of which I am particularly proud." He received a one-year sentence on 23 June 1950, of which he served ten months. While in federal prison in Texarkana, Texas, Bessie, under the pseudonym Nedrick Young, sold his original story "Cross of Gold" to Hollywood; it was made into the 1951 film *Passage West*. His only other Hollywood contribution was some uncredited rewrite work for *Executive Action* (1973), a film alleging the military-industrial complex's conspiracy to assassinate President John F. Kennedy.

Still blacklisted after his release from prison in 1951, Bessie worked as an editor of a labor newspaper, the International Longshoremen's and Warehousemen's Union's *Dispatcher*, and also as stage manager for the hungry i nightclub in San Francisco's North Beach. He resigned his membership in the Communist party in 1954 but continued to support left-wing causes for the rest of his life. He wrote two books drawn from his experiences under the blacklist, *The un-Americans* (1957), a novel, and *Inquisition in Eden* (1965), a memoir about the HUAC investigation. His work at the hungry i provided the background for his last novel, *One for My Baby* (1980).

Hollywood is the setting for Bessie's 1967 novel, *The Symbol*, about an exploited and lonely sex symbol strongly resembling Marilyn Monroe. He also wrote the teleplay for a TV movie (1974) that was based on his novel, but his script was heavily edited for fear of libel action. In 1968 he participated in the Spanish film *España otra vez*, collaborating on the screenplay and appearing on-screen; his book *Spain Again* (1975) includes part of the script and records his feelings about returning to Spain in the twilight of that country's fascist regime.

Bessie's marriage to Mary Burnett had ended in divorce in 1938; the dates of his second marriage, to Helen Clare Nelson, cannot be ascertained. He was married a third time, in 1963, to Sylviane Muller, a multilingual secretary. He had three children by these unions. From his prison release in 1951 until his death more than thirty years later, he lived in the San Francisco Bay area. A collection of short stories and a novella, *The Serpent Was More Subtil*, appeared in 1982. Bessie continued to write and, at the time of his death in Terra Linda, California, was working on an autobiography and a screen adaptation of one of his early novels.

• Alvah Bessie's papers are collected in Madison at the State Historical Society of Wisconsin. In addition to the films already mentioned, he received co-writing screen credit for *The Very Thought of You* (1944). His books not already mentioned are the novel *Bread and a Stone* (1941) and an edited volume, *The Heart of Spain* (1952). As indicated, *Inquisition in Eden* (1965) and *Spain Again* (1975) are memoirs of portions of his life, but a book-length autobiography was never published. The best biographical article is Gabriel Miller's introduction to *Alvah Bessie's Short Fiction* (1982), summarized by Miller in his article on Bessie in the *Dictionary of Literary Biography*, vol. 26 (1984).

LILLIAN S. ROBINSON

BEST, Charles Herbert (27 Feb. 1899–31 Mar. 1978), physiologist, was born in West Pembroke, Maine, the son of Herbert Huestis Best, a doctor, and Luella May Fisher. Best's parents were Canadian-born, and Best later spent his adult life in Canada. He graduated from the University of Toronto with a bachelor's degree in physiology and biochemistry in 1921 and worked for professor of physiology J. J. R. Macleod as a summer research assistant in preparation for enrolling in a master's program. Macleod asked Best and another student, E. C. Noble, to spend part of their time assisting physician Frederick Grant Banting, a recent alumnus who wanted to test an idea he had for isolating an antidiabetic substance thought to be secreted by the pancreas. Best won a coin toss with Noble to see who would help Banting first; Noble later found it convenient to let Best stay to do his share of the work.

For thirty years medical researchers had known that the pancreas played a crucial role in metabolism. Depancreatized animals could not properly metabolize their food, especially carbohydrates. These animals developed severe diabetes and soon died. In humans, the onset of diabetes before old age was almost invariably fatal too. Its course could only be retarded by rigid dieting, which in the young amounted to self-starvation. A diagnosis of diabetes in a child or young adult, like that of AIDS in a later generation, amounted to a sentence of certain and painful death. Hundreds of research attempts to isolate some kind of antidiabetic ingredient secreted by the pancreas had failed or proven inconclusive. But other internal secretions, including thyroxin and adrenalin, had been discovered, and the idea that the body contains an endocrine system, producing "hormones," made the hypothesis of a pancreatic secretion still seem attractive.

Banting, whose specialized training was in surgery, was restless in a faltering practice and enthusiastic about trying out research ideas. He knew little about diabetes but from reading journal articles thought it might be possible to isolate the supposed secretion by tying the pancreatic ducts in a living animal and waiting for the pancreas to atrophy. He persuaded Macleod, an international expert in carbohydrate metabolism, to give him lab space, a few dogs, and some student help for a few weeks.

Best did the chemical tests, measuring the sugar in the blood and urine of the dogs on which Banting did duct-ligations and pancreatectomies. The early results seemed exciting; the scientists were able to produce extracts of pancreas that appeared to reduce the blood sugar of diabetic dogs, suggesting that the metabolic function was being restored.

Banting and Best were inexperienced, enthusiastic researchers who tended to read all their results positively. Their notebooks and published papers show clearly that their extracts were no more advanced or effective than those of several other investigators, including Americans E. L. Scott and Israel Kleiner and Romanian N. C. Paulesco. The Toronto work was flawed by factual errors and misinterpretations, including a failure to realize that Banting's original hypothesis of some kind of antagonism between the external and internal secretions in the living animal was, in fact, unsound. His idea's main effect, and that of their summer's research, was to start the ball rolling.

In the autumn and winter of 1921–1922 Macleod, previously Banting's nominal supervisor, assumed active direction of the research. J. B. Collip, a trained biochemist with experience in tissue extraction, was added to the group—against the wishes of Best, now a master's student, who felt he was becoming marginalized. Banting also felt excluded and pressed hard to preserve a key role. Macleod allowed him and Best to make the first extract to be tested on a human diabetic, Leonard Thompson, in Toronto General Hospital, on 11 January 1922. The extract was not effective. On 23 January, however, Thompson was given extract purified by a process developed by Collip, and it eliminated the symptoms of his diabetes.

With that test the Toronto group knew they had made a very big discovery. They quickly expanded their clinical trials and by May 1922 were able to announce, triumphantly and credibly, their discovery of insulin and its impressive benefits for people with diabetes. (The name derives from the Latin root for the "islet" cells in the pancreas where insulin is made. Macleod suggested it; later the group found that previous researchers had given the hypothetical secretion that name, making insulin a substance named before it was discovered.)

The discovery team was riven with personality clashes and professional rivalries. Banting and Best were convinced that they had discovered insulin on their own in the summer of 1921 and that Macleod and Collip had only helped somewhat in its development. With much more justification, Macleod and Collip believed that their contributions were essential in allowing the group to go beyond the findings of others. Banting's penchant for verbally and sometimes physically attacking his associates, especially Collip, compounded the animosities. Collip's sudden failure to be able to make effective extract in the spring of 1922 caused a major crisis and further personal complications.

Best, who had been doing physiological studies of some of insulin's effects, appears to have been the first in the group to rediscover the ability to make crude insulin. When Collip left Toronto to return to the University of Alberta, Best was appointed director of insulin production at the university's small Connaught Laboratories. By this time, however, the Toronto group had decided to collaborate with Eli Lilly and Company of Indianapolis. Lilly researchers were largely responsible for the development of commercialized production of what became one of the era's most spectacular and important "wonder" therapies.

By the summer of 1922 insulin injections were reviving starved, dying children in scenes awed observers described as "miracles" and "resurrections." The most prominent early patient was Elizabeth Hughes, daughter of Charles Evans Hughes, then U.S. secretary of state. Regular insulin injections enabled her and millions of other diabetics around the world to aspire to a nearly normal life as opposed to certain early death. Because of the long-term complications of diabetes, even when controlled by insulin, and because insulin therapy is not a cure, the disease remains a major cause of suffering and death globally.

The 1923 Nobel Prize in physiology or medicine was awarded to Banting and Macleod for the discovery of insulin. Banting immediately announced that he was sharing his half of the prize money with Best. Macleod shared his money with Collip. Banting's generosity towards Best was sparked largely by the moral support Best had given him during bouts of insecurity and drinking Banting had suffered during the work. He did not credit Best with important scientific contributions and was often content to be honored as the single discoverer of insulin. Best quickly became unhappy at being so little recognized. In 1924 he married Margaret Mahon; they had two children.

Best completed a medical degree at Toronto, took a D.Sc. in England under H. H. Dale, and in 1929 succeeded Macleod (who returned to his native Scotland) as professor of physiology at Toronto. There he had a long and distinguished career, notable for his work on the role of choline in fat metabolism, his coordination in the 1930s of the development of the anticoagulant heparin, his wartime development of Canadian blood transfusion services, and later studies of insulin-related problems. With Norman B. Taylor, he coauthored a popular textbook, *The Physiological Basis of Medical Practice* (1937). He and Banting, who had become Canada's first professor of medical research, did no further work together and by the end of the 1930s were heading toward bitter professional and personal rivalry. Following Banting's accidental death in 1941, Best took over his department. He spent the rest of his life in Toronto.

Never a humble man, Best readily accepted laurels from diabetes organizations, universities, and other groups as a codiscoverer of insulin. He assiduously cultivated the idea that it had all been the work of Banting and Best, and tried systematically to blacken the reputations of Macleod and Collip, and that of the 1923 Nobel Prize Committee. His highly selective accounts of the insulin research were self-promotional to an ofttimes transparent degree. His wife, who hero-worshiped him, encouraged him in his overdramatization of his contribution to great events.

"In insulin there is glory enough for all," a speaker at University of Toronto's dinner for the Nobel laureates had said many years earlier. Best, who had provided useful support when the team reached for and grasped the golden ring of insulin in his youth, was never satisfied with the considerable glory he did get. Although he sometimes complained that his American birth hindered him in the political scramble for credit in Canada, there is no evidence to support that view.

• The Thomas Fisher Rare Books Library at the University of Toronto holds an incomplete collection of Best's papers. Also at the Fisher are the Banting papers, a much more important source for the insulin research, and small collections of Macleod and Collip papers. Toronto's University Archives has an extensive collection of the records of the university's Insulin Committee. The Fisher Library also holds the papers of W. R. Feasby, Best's designated biographer, and they are very revealing. So is the Best-Dale correspondence in the H. H. Dale Papers at the Royal Society of London. Most of Best's important publications were collected in *Selected Papers of Charles H. Best* (1963). The standard account of the discovery of insulin is Michael Bliss, *The Discovery of Insulin* (1982), supplemented by Bliss, *Banting: A Biography* (1984). For Best's later attempts to add to his glory, see Bliss, "Rewriting Medical History: Charles Best and the Banting and Best Myth," *Journal of the History of Medicine and Allied Sciences* 48 (1993): 253–74. An obituary is in the *New York Times*, 1 Apr. 1978.

MICHAEL BLISS

BEST, Denzil (27 Apr. 1917–25 May 1965), jazz drummer and composer, was born Denzil de Costa Best in New York City, the son of immigrant parents from Barbados; his mother was Josephine Best (his father's name is unknown). Best married Arline Riley (date unknown), with whom he had two daughters. Best began studying piano when he was six years old but later learned trumpet, which he played professionally in the mid-1930s with drummer Chris Columbus (Joe Morris). By the end of the decade he became associated with several seminal bop musicians playing at Minton's nightclub in New York, including Thelonious Monk, Kenny Clarke, and house bandleader Joe Guy. Because of a lung disorder Best stopped playing trumpet in 1941, returned to the piano, and later played string bass and drums.

After having worked as a drummer with locally led New York City bands (Saxie Payne, Eddie Williams, Leon Gross), Best made several recordings with saxophonist Ben Webster in September 1943. The next year he played drums on several recordings made by a number of well-known jazz musicians, including Coleman Hawkins (replacing Jimmy Crawford), Illinois Jacquet, Charlie Shavers, Clyde Hart, and Mary Lou Williams.

In 1947 Best was co-leader on several quartet recordings with Webster before joining bassist Chubby Jackson (with Conte Candoli, Frank Socolow, Terry Gibbs, and Lou Levy) on a Scandinavian tour. Throughout the late 1940s and into the 1950s Best played and recorded with Swing-era musicians such as Buck Clayton, Teddy Wilson, Shavers, Jimmy Jones, Stuff Smith, and Jack Teagarden. From 1949 to 1952 he played with the George Shearing quintet and helped originate the unique mellow sound that identified this group.

In an automobile accident in 1952 Best fractured his legs and was in temporary retirement until October of the next year, when he joined Artie Shaw's last Gramercy Five band, recording with the group in February and March 1954. Best then played with Erroll Garner in 1955–1956, recording on the pianist's milestone album *Concert by the Sea* (1955, Columbia CL883). During the late 1950s Best suffered from calcium deposits in his wrists, and although he continued to perform (with Lee Evans, Cecil Young, Nina Simone, Tyree Glenn, and Stuff Smith) his affliction seriously curtailed his professional career, and he worked sparingly during the 1960s. He died in New York City from head injuries he received in a fall down a flight of subway stairs.

Best was one of several bop-era drummers who personified the subtle, understated style of accompaniment drumming first demonstrated by Jo Jones and Dave Tough and later by Connie Kay and Chuck Flores. His playing, characterized by his facile brushwork on the recordings he made with Shearing and Garner, was in sharp contrast to the forceful style of most bop drummers of this period.

Although well known as a drummer, Best will most likely be remembered for his several compositions that have become bop standards. These include "Allen's Alley" ("Wee"), recorded first by Coleman Hawkins; "Dee Dee's Dance," recorded by Clyde Hart and Chubby Jackson; "Move," recorded by Miles Davis and later Fats Navarro; "Nothing but D Best," recorded by Shearing; and "Bemsha Swing," written with and recorded by Monk in 1952.

• Several articles have been written featuring Best, notably Pat Harris, "None Better Than Best with a Brush," *Down Beat* 18, no. 8 (Apr. 1951): 18, and Doug Stewart, "The Forgotten Ones: Denzil Best," *Jazz Journal International* 39, no. 11 (1986): 18. Best is also mentioned briefly in Ira Gilter, *Jazz Masters of the Forties* (1966). Other representative recordings include those Best made with Shearing, *I Hear Music* (1951, MGM 30624), and Phineas Newborn, *Fabulous Phineas* (1958, RCA LPM1873).

T. DENNIS BROWN

BESTOR, Arthur Eugene (19 May 1879–3 Feb. 1944), president of the Chautauqua Institution, was born in Dixon, Illinois, the son of Orson P. Bestor, a Baptist minister, and Laura Ellen Moore. Arthur Bestor attended Wayland Academy in Beaver Dam, Wisconsin, before moving to the University of Chicago, from which he received a bachelor's degree in 1901. From 1903 to 1905 Bestor pursued doctoral studies at the University of Chicago in history and political science but did not complete the degree. In 1905 he married Jeanette Louise Lemon; they had four children.

Bestor began his association with Chautauqua, an adult education center located at Chautauqua, New York, in 1905 as assistant director. He became director in 1907 and president of the institution in 1915. Under Bestor, Chautauqua underwent a series of changes, expansions, and crises. Because of continuing competition with other summer school programs and the growth of university extension, Bestor sought to establish preeminence for the Chautauqua Institution in a limited number of areas. He expanded the music and arts programs, increased the recreational activities available, and built up the summer lecture program. During his tenure, Chautauqua entered into an agreement with New York University to offer college credit for summer courses taken at the school.

The Great Depression had serious consequences for Chautauqua, which were exacerbated by the frenetic pace of Bestor's expansion program during the 1920s. The decline of income precipitated a crisis, and in 1933 Chautauqua went into receivership. Nevertheless, the board of trustees maintained its confidence in Bestor and he remained in the presidency; the debt was retired in 1936. Bestor devoted a large amount of his energies to fundraising activities.

In addition to his work with Chautauqua, Bestor was affiliated with a number of other adult education efforts. During World War I, he was appointed director of the Speakers' Division of the Committee on Public Information (1917–1918). Under his direction, the division became a giant lecture bureau, sending out speakers, coordinating with other offices, and setting up state organizations. In the 1930s Bestor was a member of the Advisory Committee on Emergency Education to the U.S. Commissioner of Education. In this capacity, he traveled around the country reporting on the condition of emergency education programs in individual states.

In addition to this government service, Bestor was active in a number of adult education agencies. Principal among these was the Town Hall, of which he was chairman of the board of trustees from 1935 to 1943. Town Hall, founded in 1894 to help educate independent voters, offered a series of lectures, forums, and discussion groups, and in 1935 began using radio as well. Bestor was particularly interested in Town Hall's educational work on international affairs and often acted as a moderator for its radio program, "America's Town Meeting of the Air." In 1926 Bestor participated in the founding of the American Association for Adult Education and served on its executive board continuously from 1926 until 1943.

Through the agencies he worked with and the lectures he gave throughout the United States, Bestor was committed to the use of education to bring about world peace and international understanding. Convinced that reason and national dialogue were possible, all of Bestor's work revolved around the development of education as the tool for bringing about enlightened public opinion. He was convinced that educators needed to use new technologies, particularly radio, because they contained the possibility for true national discussion.

Bestor died in New York City; he was still lecturing and seeking support for his vision of Chautauqua.

• Arthur Bestor's personal papers are in the library at the University of Illinois at Urbana-Champaign; his papers relating to the presidency of Chautauqua are at the Chautauqua Institution. There is no full-fledged biography of Bestor, but see the memoir by his daughter, Mary Frances Bestor Cram, *Chautauqua Salute* (1990), as well as the briefer account by his son, Arthur E. Bestor, Jr., "Arthur Eugene Bestor, 1879–1844. Biographical Sketch," *Chautauquan Daily Supplement* 4 Aug. 1944, p. 1. Marlene Wentworth, "From Chautauqua to Wastelands: The Bestors and American Education 1905–1955" (Ph.D. diss., Univ. of Illinois, 1992) focuses mostly on Arthur Bestor, Jr., but does discuss the work of Arthur Bestor, Sr., in some detail. His work at Chautauqua is discussed in Theodore Morrison, *Chautauqua: A Center for Education, Religion, and the Arts in America* (1974). In addition, Bestor's part in the Committee on Public Information is covered in Stephen Vaughn, *Holding Fast the Inner Lines: Democracy, Nationalism and the Committee on Public Information* (1980). An obituary is in the *New York Times*, 5 Feb. 1944.

AMY D. ROSE

BETHUNE, Joanna Graham (1 Feb. 1770–28 July 1860), founder of charitable societies, was born at Fort Niagara, Canada, the daughter of Isabella Marshall, a teacher and charitable worker, and John Graham, a surgeon for the British army. After John Graham's death in 1773, the family returned to Isabella Graham's native Scotland, where she supported herself and her four children by establishing schools in Paisley and in Edinburgh. Joanna attended both schools, completing her education at a French school in Rotterdam (1784–1786) under the patronage of her mother's friend, Lady Glenorchy. In 1789 the family immigrated to New York City, where Joanna and her sister Isabella taught in their mother's well-regarded school for young women.

The move to New York and her attraction to the social whirl precipitated in Joanna a religious crisis that she finally resolved in 1794, three years after joining the Cedar Street Scotch Presbyterian Church, spiritual home to her mother and her sister Isabella. In 1795 she cemented her commitment to evangelicalism by marrying Divie Bethune, a Scottish-born merchant whose friendship had sustained her during the religious crisis. In their 29-year marriage, during which Bethune bore six children, the couple enjoyed a close spiritual partnership that enabled them to use their comfortable economic position and growing social prestige in the service of evangelical and charitable causes, including foreign missions, tract distribution, Sunday schools, and public welfare. Along with Joanna's mother Isabella Graham, Joanna and Divie Bethune recruited members from New York City's mercantile and professional families—especially women—into religious and charitable enterprises and turned such activities

into acceptable, indeed admired, outlets for women's talents and ambitions.

Bethune's early ventures into charitable work were made in association with her mother. In 1797 the two women founded the Society for the Relief of Poor Widows with Small Children, which became active in helping the survivors of New York's 1798 yellow fever epidemic. In 1803, when Bethune returned from a visit to Scotland, they began a Sunday school, hiring teachers for the reading and writing classes but providing religious instruction themselves as volunteers. After 1806, Bethune increasingly devoted herself to the Orphan Asylum Society, an organization she founded for the children of Poor Widows' Society clients and which she served in various capacities until her retirement in 1858. Shortly before her mother's death in 1814, Bethune enlisted her aid to promote a House of Industry, which provided work as an alternative to charity for poor women. Funded in part by City Council donations, the House of Industry lasted until 1820. In this, as in other endeavors, Bethune relied on the assistance, financial contributions, and political connections of a group of friends and associates, including Susan Murray Ogden and Ogden's sister Hannah Murray, daughters of a wealthy merchant and former pupils of Isabella Graham. She was also assisted by Elizabeth Schuyler Hamilton, the widow of Alexander Hamilton.

After her mother's death, and especially after her husband's death ten years later, Bethune's concerns focused increasingly on children. In January 1816 she led the formation of the Female Union Society for the Promotion of Sabbath Schools (one month later Divie Bethune helped found a male counterpart), serving as its First Directress (president) until the society dissolved in 1828. Ever interested in educational trends, she sponsored the New York Infant School Society in 1827, acted as its head, and wrote several books for use in the schools. During the 1830s, she supported the American Colonization Society's efforts to relocate free blacks to Liberia, and became vice president of a women's group raising money for Liberian schools. The last twenty years of her life were devoted to the Orphan Asylum Society and Sunday school teaching. She died in New York City.

Bethune's full-time, if unpaid, career in benevolence enabled her to have a defining influence on the religious, educational, and charitable institutions she helped found and run. Convinced by personal experience that evangelical institutions could be powerful sources of meaning and of social discipline, she labored to bring their spiritual and secular influence to bear on poor children and women. The institutions with which she was involved combined meliorist approaches to social problems with faith in the transformative power of evangelical religion. Familial, religious, educational, and economic connections to New York City's growing commercial middle classes facilitated her work by providing her with female co-workers and with access to powerful and influential men in the city's political, business, and professional life. Using that access, she helped direct the energies of middle-class white women into religious and benevolent endeavors and shape the development of nineteenth-century charitable voluntarism.

• Bethune's spiritual diaries (1824–1853) and an autobiographical account of her religious conversion are at the Clements Library, University of Michigan. Her published works include a biography of her mother, compiled with Divie Bethune, *The Power of Faith: Exemplified in the Life and Writings of the Late Mrs. Isabella Graham, of New-York* (1816); the *Memoir of Miss Anna Goodale (1777–1811) with Familiar Letters* (1834); and texts designed for infant schools. The only complete biography is George Washington Bethune, *Memoirs of Mrs. Joanna Bethune* (1863), which contains lengthy excerpts from her spiritual writings. For a longer and more detailed biographical sketch, see the entry by Mary Sumner Benson in *Notable American Women*, vol. 1, pp. 138–40.

ANNE M. BOYLAN

BETHUNE, Louise Blanchard (21 July 1856–18 Dec. 1913), architect, was born in Waterloo, New York, the daughter of Dalson Wallace Blanchard, a schoolteacher and principal, and Emma Melona Williams, also a schoolteacher. Called Jennie by family and friends, Louise Blanchard was educated at home and then attended Buffalo High School, where she showed "great aptitude in planning houses and various other structures." After graduating in 1874, she spent two years in preparation for entering the newly established architecture program at Cornell University but eventually decided instead to become a draftsman for Buffalo architect Richard A. Waite. During her apprenticeship, she learned technical drawing and architectural design, visited construction sites, and studied a wide range of works in the office library. Eventually she became Waite's assistant. In 1881, recognizing Buffalo's prosperity and the need for practicing architects, Louise Blanchard decided to open her own office, an event that was announced at the Ninth Congress of the Association for the Advancement of Women and that made her the "first professional woman architect" in the United States. In December 1881 she married and formed a professional partnership with Robert Armour Bethune, a Canadian-born draftsman who had worked in Waite's office. The firm became Bethune, Bethune & Fuchs in 1883, the year she gave birth to her only child.

Louise Bethune's technical and aesthetic contributions to the architecture of the Buffalo area included industrial, commercial, and educational buildings, notably the Hotel Lafayette, the Offerman Baseball Stadium, a Buffalo Weaving Company factory, and the Denton & Cottier Music Store, which was constructed with a steel frame and poured concrete slabs. Between 1881 and 1904, the firm designed eighteen school buildings in Buffalo, including Lockport Union High School (1890), for which Louise Bethune is given sole design credit. Active in professional groups, Bethune joined the Western Association of Architects in 1885 and helped found the Buffalo Society of Architects. In 1888 she was the first woman elected to the American

Institute of Architects and became a Fellow one year later.

Unlike many of her contemporaries, Bethune disdained house commissions, calling domestic design "the most pottering and worst-paid work an architect ever does." Also, speaking in 1891 to the Women's Educational and Industrial Union, she emphasized that "dwelling house architecture, as a special branch for women, should be . . . out of the question." In general, Louise Bethune had strong feelings about women and architecture; she believed that "the future of woman in the architectural profession is what she herself sees fit to make it." However, she warned the few women then entering the field not to "shirk the brick-and-mortar-rubber-boot-and-ladder-climbing period of investigative education." She was adamant about equitable pay for women architects, and in protest against the unfair treatment of women architects she refused to submit a design for the Woman's Building at the 1893 World's Columbian Exposition, a competition won by Sophia G. Hayden, who had trained at the Massachusetts Institute of Technology.

Louise Bethune's professional activity was minimal after the mid-1890s, but she did not officially retire until 1908. During her final years, she lived with her son and pursued her interest in genealogy. She died in Buffalo.

• No drawings or papers from the career of Louise Blanchard Bethune are known to have been preserved. Bethune's 1891 speech was originally published as "Women in Architecture" in *Inland Architect and News Record* 17 (Mar. 1891): 20–21 and reprinted in *Inland Architect* 27 (July–Aug. 1983): 46–47. Biographical information is in Frances E. Willard and Mary A. Livermore, eds., *A Woman of the Century* (1893). The most complete recent sources are Adriana Barbasch, "Louise Blanchard Bethune: The AIA Accepts Its First Woman Member," in *Architecture: A Place for Women*, ed. Ellen Perry Berkeley and Mathilda McQuaid (1989), and Madeleine B. Stern, *We the Women: Career Firsts of Nineteenth-Century America* (1963). Bethune's relationship with the AIA is described in George Pettingill, "How the AIA Acquired Its First Woman Member," *AIA Journal* 63 (Mar. 1975): 35. For references to Bethune's buildings, see Francis R. Kowski et al., *Buffalo Architecture: A Guide* (1981), and Henry-Russell Hitchcock, "Buffalo Architecture in Review," *Art News* 38 (Jan. 1940): 8. Additional bibliographic sources on Bethune are noted in Lamia Doumato, *Architecture and Women* (1988).

LISA B. REITZES

BETHUNE, Mary Jane McLeod (10 July 1875–18 May 1955), organizer of black women and advocate for social justice, was born in Mayesville, South Carolina, the child of former slaves Samuel McLeod and Patsy McIntosh, farmers. After attending a school operated by the Presbyterian Board of Missions for Freedmen, she entered Scotia Seminary (now Barber-Scotia College) in Concord, North Carolina, in 1888 and graduated in May 1894. She spent the next year at Dwight Moody's evangelical Institute for Home and Foreign Missions in Chicago, Illinois. In 1898 she married Albertus Bethune. They both taught, briefly, at the Kindell Institute in Sumter, South Carolina. The marriage was not happy. They had one child and separated late in 1907. After teaching in a number of schools, Bethune founded the Daytona Normal and Industrial Institute for Training Negro Girls in Daytona, Florida, in 1904. Twenty years later the school merged with a boys' school, the Cookman Institute, and was renamed Bethune-Cookman College in 1929. Explaining why she founded the training school, Bethune remarked, "Many homeless girls have been sheltered there and trained physically, mentally and spiritually. They have been helped and sent out to serve, to pass their blessings on to other needy children."

In addition to her career as educator, Bethune helped found some of the most significant organizations in black America. In 1920 Bethune became vice president of the National Urban League and helped to create the women's section of its Commission on Interracial Cooperation. From 1924 to 1928 she also served as the president of the National Association of Colored Women. In 1935, as founder and president of the National Council of Negro Women, Bethune forged a coalition of hundreds of black women's organizations across the country. Bethune served from 1936 to 1950 as president of the Association for the Study of Negro Life and History, later known as the Association for the Study of Afro-American Life and History. In 1935 the National Association for the Advancement of Colored People awarded Bethune its highest honor, the Spingarn Medal. She received honorary degrees from ten universities, the Medal of Honor and Merit from Haiti (1949), and the Star of Africa Award from Liberia (1952). In 1938 she participated along with liberal white southerners in the annual meetings of the Southern Conference for Human Welfare.

Bethune's involvement in national government began in the 1920s during the Calvin Coolidge and Herbert Hoover presidential administrations when she participated in child welfare conferences. In June 1936 Bethune became administrative assistant and, in January 1939, director in charge of Negro Affairs in the New Deal National Youth Administration (NYA). This made her the first black woman in U.S. history to occupy such a high-level federal position. Bethune was responsible for helping vast numbers of unemployed 16- to 24-year-old black youths find jobs in private industry and in vocational training projects. The agency created work relief programs that opened opportunities for thousands of black youths, which enabled countless black communities to survive the depression. She served in this office until the NYA was closed in 1944.

During her service in the Franklin D. Roosevelt administration, Bethune organized a small but influential group of black officials who became known as the "Black Cabinet." Prominent among them were William Hastie of the Department of the Interior and the War Department and Robert Weaver, who served in Interior and several manpower agencies. The Black Cabinet did more than advise the president; they articulated a black agenda for social change, beginning with demands for greater benefit from New Deal programs and equal employment opportunities.

In 1937 in Washington, D.C., Bethune orchestrated the National Conference on the Problems of the Negro and Negro Youth, which focused on concerns ranging from better housing and health care for African Americans to equal protection of the laws. As an outspoken advocate for black civil rights, she fought for federal anti–poll tax and antilynching legislation. Bethune's influence during the New Deal was further strengthened by her friendship with first lady Eleanor Roosevelt.

During World War II Bethune was special assistant to the secretary of war and assistant director of the Women's Army Corps. In this post she set up the first officer candidate schools for the corps. Throughout the war she pressed President Roosevelt and other governmental and military officials to make use of the many black women eager to serve in the national defense program; she also lobbied for increased appointments of black women to federal bureaus. After the war she continued to lecture and to write newspaper and magazine columns and articles until her death in Daytona Beach, Florida.

Urged by the National Council of Negro Women, the federal government dedicated the Mary McLeod Bethune Memorial Statue at Lincoln Park in southeastern Washington, D.C., on 10 July 1974. Bethune's life and work provide one of the major links between the social reform efforts of post-Reconstruction black women and the political protest activities of the generation emerging after World War II. The many strands of black women's struggle for education, political rights, racial pride, sexual autonomy, and liberation are united in the writings, speeches, and organization work of Bethune.

• Essays written by Bethune include two pieces on the importance of Negro history: "Clarifying Our Vision with the Facts," *Journal of Negro History* 23 (Jan. 1938): 10–15, and "The Negro in Retrospect and Prospect," *Journal of Negro History* 35 (Jan. 1950): 9–19. The most insightful treatment of Bethune's multifaceted involvement in the New Deal remains B. Joyce Ross, "Mary McLeod Bethune and the National Youth Administration: A Case Study of Power Relationships in the Black Cabinet of Franklin D. Roosevelt," *Journal of Negro History* 60 (Jan. 1975): 1–28. More general information is available in Rackman Holt, *Mary McLeod Bethune: A Biography* (1964). Elaine M. Smith, "Mary McLeod Bethune and the National Youth Administration," in *Clio Was a Woman: Studies in the History of American Women*, ed. Mabel E. Deutrich and Virginia C. Purdy (1980), provides a lively and more detailed account of Bethune's political career. An obituary is in the *New York Times*, 19 May 1955.

DARLENE CLARK HINE

BETHUNE, Thomas Green. *See* Blind Tom.

BETTELHEIM, Bruno (28 Aug. 1903–13 Mar. 1990), therapist, educator, and author, was born in Vienna, Austria, the son of Anton Bettelheim, a lumber merchant, and Pauline Seidler. Following his father's death in 1926, he dropped out of the university to take over the family firm. Although successful in business, he re-enrolled ten years later to become, in February 1938, one of the last Jews to obtain a Ph.D. from Vienna University before World War II. While he was a philosophy student, aesthetics was his main subject, but he also studied psychology under Karl Bühler, director of the Psychology Institute and a pioneer in language theory (*Sprachtheorie*). Bettelheim's dissertation was "The Problem of the Beautiful in Nature and Modern Aesthetics."

In 1930 Bettelheim married Regina Altstadt, a nursery-school teacher interested in psychoanalysis. Bettelheim himself was in analysis with Richard Sterba, then secretary of the Vienna Psychoanalytic Society, when the Nazis invaded Austria in March 1938. In May he was arrested and sent to Dachau and later to Buchenwald concentration camp. He was released in April 1939 through the efforts of his family and of an American friend whose mentally-disturbed child had stayed at the Bettelheim home in Regina's care. Bettelheim immigrated to the United States two weeks later. (Regina Bettelheim had left Vienna before he was arrested.) He had lost his company and all his belongings.

Bettelheim's first jobs in the United States included the designing of a visual-arts test for the Eight Year Study of the Progressive Education Association and occasional tuition in the art department of the University of Chicago and work for its board of examiners. From 1941 to 1944 he also taught courses at Rockford College, Illinois, first in art history, and then, as the war called away more and more of his American colleagues, in philosophy, psychology, and German.

October 1943 saw the publication of Bettelheim's first major article, "Individual and Mass Behavior in Extreme Situations," a psychological study of concentration-camp inmates in which he notably used Anna Freud's concept of "identification with the aggressor." After being turned down by several publications for being too anti-German, his article was finally published in the *Journal of Abnormal and Social Psychology* (38 [1943]: 417–52); it would later serve as the basis for two of his books, *The Informed Heart* (1960) and *Surviving and Other Essays* (1979). In June 1945 Gordon Allport, editor of the *Journal*, informed Bettelheim that General Dwight D. Eisenhower had asked for permission to distribute the article to the Allied occupation forces in central Europe.

In 1944 Bettelheim was appointed director of the Orthogenic School of the University of Chicago, a decrepit institution for emotionally-disturbed children under the purview of the dean of education. Within a few years he turned it into a pioneering experiment in Freudian "milieu therapy." The school was organized as a family home, where erratic behavior was no longer viewed as a disturbance to be corrected, but as an expression of suffering—as signs to be read in order to understand what could help the troubled child. He reported on this experience in *Love Is Not Enough* (1950)

and *Truants from Life: The Rehabilitation of Emotionally Disturbed Children* (1955).

His early successes encouraged Bettelheim to try to treat what was then beginning to be identified as infantile autism. In "Childhood Schizophrenia as a Reaction to Extreme Situations" (*American Journal of Orthopsychiatry* 26 [July 1956]: 507–18), he drew a parallel that was to remain his hallmark: having witnessed sane men being driven mad by the conditions in the Nazi camps, he believed that a benevolent environment could bring profoundly disturbed children back to the world. This provided the basis for his approach to autism. His success rate was not as high as he reported in *The Empty Fortress: Infantile Autism and the Birth of the Self* (1967), especially when weighed against today's much stricter definition of autism; however, the book had a determining influence on the way psychotic children were viewed in psychiatric institutions worldwide. In a drastic departure from conventional thinking, Bettelheim portrayed even the most disturbed children as full-fledged individuals, stressing the meaningfulness of their actions rather than their deficiencies. He was totally opposed to the use of straitjackets or drugs.

After retiring in 1973, Bettelheim moved to California, where he held a few seminars, notably at Stanford, and gave many lectures but mostly wrote. *A Home for the Heart* (1974) summed up his work at the Orthogenic School. *The Uses of Enchantment* (1976), a study of the meaning of fairy tales for growing children, earned him the National Book Award for Contemporary Thought and immediately became a classic. In *Surviving*, Bettelheim brought together his main essays on Nazism, racism, and totalitarianism, subjects that remained alive for him throughout his life. For many years he had been the only thinker to tackle the psychological impact of the camp experience; however, his authority on the subject was being challenged, and it had taken him a long time to come to terms with the realization that what he had learned in Buchenwald had little relevance for those interned in Auschwitz, a camp where surviving was not an option. That controversy hurt him deeply.

Bettelheim had been divorced by his first wife in the United States. He soon married Gertrude Weinfeld, another refugee from Nazi Austria, in 1941. She was a Montessori teacher and a social worker; they had three children together.

Bettelheim never recovered from his wife's death in 1984. Although he kept lecturing and writing and was showered with honors, his health was failing and a deep depression gradually set in. On the fifty-second anniversary of Hitler's annexation of Austria, and shortly after Bettelheim published his last and most personal collection, *Freud's Vienna and Other Essays* (1990), he took his own life in the Maryland retirement home to which he had just moved. His suicide was soon followed by accusations in the press from half a dozen former patients who claimed he had mistreated them. Still under the shock of his suicide, the countless former students and associates who wanted to defend him were slow to react and later found the media uninterested in their stories.

Like the controversy sparked by his views on Nazism, however, this posthumous scandal goes to the heart of Bettelheim's most valuable contribution: his work on the inner violence of those in his care. His camp experience had made him realize the damage such archaic drives can do when circumstances force the subject to turn them against himself or herself. Thereafter, as a therapist as well as a teacher, his main aim had always been to bring that violence to the surface in order to show children and students its limits and to help them put it to life-oriented rather than destructive use.

This determination to deal with the "bad instincts" that are part of every human soul, coupled with a freedom of mind that led Bettelheim to pick and choose the concepts he needed from the various schools of Freudian psychology with little regard for their dogmatic differences (not to mention his difficult temper and his Socratic method of teaching), help to explain Bettelheim's outsider status with both the academic and psychoanalytic establishments. A good illustration of this can be found in *Freud and Man's Soul* (1982), a long essay in which Bettelheim demonstrated how the English translations of Freud's works betray him by giving them a scientific and therefore less human tone than was intended by the founder of psychoanalysis.

• Many of Bettelheim's papers, including some personal correspondence, are held in the Special Collections of the Regenstein Library at the University of Chicago. Other books by Bettelheim include *Symbolic Wounds: Puberty Rites and the Envious Male* (1954), a psychocultural study of circumcision; *Dialogues with Mothers* (1962); *The Children of the Dream* (1969), a study of kibbutz education; and *A Good Enough Parent* (1987). He also coauthored *Dynamics of Prejudice: A Psychological and Sociological Study of Veterans* (with Morris Janowitz, 1950), *On Learning to Read: The Child's Fascination with Meaning* (with Karen Zelan, 1981), and *The Art of the Obvious* (with Alvin A. Rosenfeld, 1993), a series of lessons in psychotherapy based on the Stanford seminars. The most complete assessment of his life and work is Nina Sutton, *Bettelheim: A Life and a Legacy* (1996). An illustration of the hatred he could stir up about himself can be found in the totally negative view of Richard Pollack, *The Creation of Dr. B* (1997). For an equally negative assessment of his work on concentration camps, see Terence Des Pres, *The Survivor* (1976), and for a more balanced assessment, *Psychoanalytic Review*'s special issue on Bettelheim, vol. 81 (Fall 1994). Students and co-workers who have written about Bettelheim's teaching and their working experience with him include Jerome M. Goldsmith and Jacquelyn S. Sanders, eds., *Milieu Therapy: Significant Issues and Innovative Applications* (1993); and Nathan M. Szajnberg, ed., *Educating the Emotions: Bruno Bettelheim and Psychoanalytic Development* (1992). For a fictional account of life at the Orthogenic School by a former resident, see Tom Lyons, *The Pelican and After* (1983).

NINA SUTTON

BETTENDORF, William Peter (1 July 1857–3 June 1910), inventor and manufacturer, was born in Mendota, Illinois, the elder of two sons of Michael Bettendorf, a schoolteacher and later a store clerk and then a federal government clerk, and Catherine Reck. Moving with his parents and three younger siblings to Sedalia, Missouri, and Fort Leavenworth, Kansas, he had only the most rudimentary schooling. While living at Fort Leavenworth, he attended St. Mary's Mission School, an institution established to educate Native Americans. For a time, his father also tutored him at home. About 1872 the family returned to Peru, Illinois. But Bettendorf's formal—and informal—education at the hands of others ended when at the age of fifteen he became totally self-supporting. Bettendorf had already been a messenger boy in Humboldt, Kansas, and a hardware store clerk in Peru. Next, in 1872 or 1873 he obtained a position as an apprentice machinist for a plow-manufacturing company in Peru. Leaving that town for a period of several years, he worked as a machinist for another plow company in Moline, Illinois, and then for a company in Canton, Ohio, that made a variety of agricultural implements. He married Mary Wortman in Peru in 1879. The couple had two children, both of whom died early. While in Canton, Bettendorf began an avid study of theoretical and practical aspects of mechanical engineering.

As a result, a dramatic change occurred in Bettendorf's life in 1878. He invented and patented a power lift for a sulky plow, that is, a plow with wheels and a seat for the driver. From 1882 to 1886 he was employed again by the plow company in Peru, as its shop superintendent. His next invention, the "Bettendorf metal wheel" for use in wagons and other farm vehicles, had a malleable iron hub with steel spokes secured in the hub by being "upset," that is, provided with a hammered head, inside the hub. This invention revolutionized wheels for farm machinery. Bettendorf also devised the necessary machinery to manufacture these new wheels. The plant in Peru was expanded to accommodate increased demand. In 1886 he and his brother Joseph William Bettendorf, with the assistance of E. P. Lynch, president of the Eagle Manufacturing Company in Davenport, Iowa, organized their own wheel-making company in that city. Soon incorporated as the Bettendorf Metal Wheel Company, it expanded, opened a branch in Springfield, Ohio, and eventually became the largest such manufacturing company in the United States, possibly in the world. In 1891 Bettendorf invented a self-oiling, hollow steel axle, bolster, and stakes for farm wagons, and designed and constructed the machinery necessary to produce such gear. In 1892 he resigned as vice president of the company and sold his interests to his associates, to devote more time to his inventions. He incorporated the Bettendorf Axle Company in 1895, with himself as president and his brother as secretary. Within a short while he was manufacturing not merely the gears but whole vehicles using them.

Next, the ingenious Bettendorf came to the conclusion that railway cars could easily be made stronger by the use of steel instead of wood in various parts. The devices he introduced to do so both lowered costs in the construction of rolling stock and made it more durable. His plant began to manufacture such parts. He planned the modification and shaping of steel I beams, joined them together with small ancillary parts sturdily bolted, and thus created a bolster useful in distributing and supporting the weight of railway cars and the weight of freight they transported. The Bettendorf bolster is still in use. He also invented a side frame for cars constructed of a single piece of cast steel. To go with all of these improvements, he modified the standard journal box, inventing in its place a metal box integral with the rigid side frame, to house and support car axles rotating on bearings. The unit was called the "Bettendorf frame." Finally, he began manufacturing entire railway cars. His unvarying intention was to combine fewer parts with greater strength, partly by means of less weight used more efficiently.

After two disastrous fires in 1902, Bettendorf built a new and larger manufacturing plant at Gilbert, Iowa, on farm land he persuaded the townspeople to purchase for this purpose. Gilbert was then a small agricultural marketing community, four miles northeast of Davenport and on the western bank of the Mississippi River. In 1903 the town was renamed and incorporated as Bettendorf, Iowa. In 1905 Bettendorf sold his wagon-building machinery to the International Harvester Company but continued to manufacture gears under contract with the larger company as long as he lived. In some twenty years Bettendorf was granted twenty-five patents. During the last few years of his life, he concentrated on the manufacture of better and better railroad cars. At the same time, he took ever-increasing delight in participating in the development and general welfare of the little city bearing his name, most notably by generously providing the means for schools and churches to be built. In 1908, seven years after the death of his first wife, he married Elizabeth H. Staby. The couple planned and began construction of a lavish, twenty-room mansion, which Bettendorf did not live to see in finished form. With twenty-five more patents pending in his name, he died in the town named after him.

• The Bettendorf Museum, in Bettendorf, Iowa, is the repository for Bettendorf's family and corporate papers. *Iowa: A Guide to the Hawkeye State* (1938), and Arthur J. Voelliger, *Bettendorf History* (1973), briefly describe Gilbert, Iowa, before and after it was renamed Bettendorf. Much Bettendorf family data is available in Hawthorne Daniel, "Bettendorf," *Railroad Workers Journal* (July/Aug. 1943): 6–9, 36, and in Darlene Paxton and L. T. Sloane, eds., *The Ancestors and Descendants of the Bettendorf-Kohrs and Related Families* (1984). Memorial essays on Bettendorf are in *Farm Machinery*, 7 June 1910, and *Farm Implement News*, 9 June 1910. An obituary is in the *Davenport Democrat and Leader*, 5 June 1910.

ROBERT L. GALE

BETTENHAUSEN, Tony (12 Sept. 1926–12 May 1961), auto racing driver, was born Melvin Eugene Bettenhausen in Tinley Park, Illinois, the son of Christian H. Bettenhausen, a soybean farmer. His mother's name is not known. Because he often defended himself against neighborhood bullies during his preteen years, the stubborn youngster was given the nickname "Tunney" after Gene Tunney, then world heavyweight boxing champion. Tunney soon evolved into Tony, the name by which he would be known for the rest of his life. In 1937 he married Valerie Rice; they had four children.

Bettenhausen's entry into motor racing came when he purchased a midget racing car from a friend in 1938. This form of racing, utilizing scaled-down cars on oval tracks usually a quarter of a mile or less in circumference, had begun in California in 1933 and had spread quickly to other regions of the country. Bettenhausen became one of the sport's most proficient performers, racing midget cars with success for the rest of his career.

In 1941 Bettenhausen moved up to an extremely dangerous form of racing, competing with "sprint" cars. At the time they were simply known as "big" cars, being very powerful, single-seated, open-wheel, front-engined machines, raced mostly on half-mile oval tracks in a series of short heats, capped by a "feature" of perhaps thirty laps in duration. He won three races and came in second or third several times to place second in the 1941 American Automobile Association–sanctioned Midwest "big" car championship. He also competed in two AAA national championship events, drawing plenty of attention by finishing second to the famed Rex Mays in a 100-mile event at Syracuse, New York.

U.S. involvement in World War II caused the temporary cessation of racing, and Bettenhausen spent the war years working at a Buick plant in Maywood, Illinois, assembling aircraft engines. His participation in the Indianapolis 500 was thus delayed until 1946. Although he eventually finished second there in 1955 and fourth in both 1958 and 1959, his real forte remained 100-mile races held on one-mile dirt tracks. Twenty of his twenty-one national championship victories between 1946 and 1959 (a postwar record until 1964) were on dirt tracks. His most successful year came in 1951, when he captured the season's title by winning eight out of fourteen races, all of his triumphs occurring on dirt tracks. Not confining himself to this series, he placed second in the AAA's stock car championship the same year.

In June 1952 Bettenhausen announced that he would compete only in the Indianapolis 500 plus selected midget and stock car events because he intended to devote more time to his farm and his recently acquired Chrysler car dealership. To the surprise of none of his friends, this semiretirement lasted for just over a year. In August 1953 he suddenly returned to national championship racing and began winning again almost immediately.

In June 1957 Bettenhausen joined a team of Indianapolis drivers who traveled to Monza, Italy, for a 500-mile race held on a steeply-banked 2.64-mile concrete oval. He drove a V-8 supercharged Novi racing car, qualifying with a then extraordinary speed of 176.818 miles per hour.

The veteran driver finally led the Indianapolis 500 for the first time in 1958, after having climbed as high as second place at one point during 500s of 1953, 1955, and 1956. He ended up fourth in the 1958 race and won his second national championship, achieving it with four second-place finishes and no victories. In 1959, however, he returned to his winning ways, registering his twentieth and twenty-first victories.

In May 1961 it appeared that Bettenhausen might finally achieve his two most cherished goals. He hoped to win both the coveted 500 "pole" position (for being the fastest qualifier on the first day of time trials) and the race itself. Poised as potentially the first driver ever to lap the 2½-mile Indianapolis Motor Speedway at an average speed in excess of 150 miles per hour, he recorded an unofficial 149.8 mph the day before the first day of qualifications. He then agreed to try out another car for a fellow driver, who was experiencing difficulty in achieving acceptable speed. A bolt dropped out of the steering arm while Bettenhausen was at top speed on the mainstraight. His car veered to the right, then climbed the outer retaining wall. The car barrel-rolled on top of it, fatally injuring Bettenhausen.

Despite this tragedy, all three Bettenhausen sons later became professional racing drivers; Gary and Tony competed in the Indianapolis 500 repeatedly. The senior Bettenhausen, who had driven in fourteen 500s, was inducted posthumously into the Indianapolis Motor Speedway–based Auto Racing Hall of Fame in 1974.

• Bettenhausen's overall career has been covered extensively in *Speed Age*, May 1947–Dec. 1953 and June 1954–Apr. 1959, and in Floyd Clymer's Indianapolis 500 yearbooks, 1946–1961. A feature devoted to Bettenhausen is "Mr. B Is Back," *Speed Age*, Mar. 1959. See also Robert Cutter and Bob Fendell, *Encyclopedia of Auto Racing Greats* (1973). An obituary is in the *New York Times*, 13 May 1961, along with other coverage of his accident.

DONALD DAVIDSON

BETTMAN, Alfred (26 Aug. 1873–21 Jan. 1945), lawyer, was born in Cincinnati, Ohio, the son of Louis Bettman, a clothing manufacturer, and Rebecca Bloom. After receiving his undergraduate degree from Harvard in 1894 and his law degree, also from Harvard, in 1898, Bettman returned to Cincinnati, where he embarked on the practice of law. In 1904 he married Lillian Wyler, forming a lifelong but childless union. At first, Bettman was drawn to criminal prosecution, serving as assistant prosecuting attorney for Hamilton County, Ohio (1909–1911), and as Cincinnati city solicitor (1912–1913). During World War I, he was appointed special assistant to the United States attorney general in charge of the division of prosecution in Cleveland, a post in which he was responsible for the prosecution of many aliens for alleged radicalism and communist agitation, although after the war he denounced the excesses of A. Mitchell Palmer's "Red Scare." Convinced that "in the field of criminal justice and crime reduction, accurate thinking is impossible without statistics," Bettman prepared several pioneering studies of Ohio law enforcement. In 1930

he served as an adviser to the prestigious National Commission on Law Observance and Enforcement chaired by George W. Wickersham.

Even as Bettman's reputation in the administration of criminal justice grew, he began to develop a new expertise in city and regional planning that was to bring him still greater prominence. First drawn to the area while serving as city solicitor, Bettman drafted a statute in 1917 that enabled Ohio cities to create planning boards. Although a Democrat, he was named to the national Advisory Committee on City Planning and Zoning by Herbert Hoover, then secretary of commerce, and took a leading role in drafting the Standard State Zoning Enabling Act of 1924 and the Standard City Planning Enabling Act of 1927. Legislation would be of no avail, however, if it were declared unconstitutional by the courts. Zoning necessarily limited the use to which land could be put, and judges in the 1920s were particularly zealous in the protection of the rights of property. Bettman's greatest contribution to the cause of planning was in devising legal arguments in defense of zoning. In 1926 in the landmark case *Village of Euclid v. Ambler Realty Company*, a closely divided Supreme Court upheld an Ohio zoning ordinance. Bettman, then counsel for the National Conference on City Planning, contributed an influential brief as *amicus curiae* that deflected the focus of argument away from the question of the taking of property rights, for which compensation would be required, to the question of public power to make regulations in the interest of health and safety.

Bettman went on to serve on many boards and commissions, always advocating the importance of regional rather than merely local planning. In 1933 President Franklin D. Roosevelt named him legal adviser to the commission that developed the Tennessee Valley Authority. At the time of his death he was returning to Cincinnati from Washington where he had appeared before a Senate subcommittee on behalf of the American Institute of Planners.

• A selection of Bettman's writings, including his brief in the *Euclid* case, is available in *City and Regional Planning Papers*, ed. Arthur C. Comey (1946). The volume also includes a brief biographical sketch and a comprehensive bibliography. The article on Bettman in the *Dictionary of American Biography*, suppl. 3, includes information supplied by his sister-in-law, Mrs. Gilbert Bettman (Iphigene Molony). An obituary is in the *New York Times*, 23 Jan. 1945.

JOHN V. ORTH

BEVAN, Arthur Dean (9 Aug. 1861–10 June 1943), surgeon and reformer of medical education, was born in Chicago, Illinois, the son of Thomas Bevan, a physician, and Sarah Elizabeth Ramsey. After attending high school in Chicago, Bevan earned his Ph.B. at Yale's Sheffield Scientific School in 1881. He then entered Rush Medical College in Chicago and obtained his M.D. in 1883. He finished first in the competitive examination for the U.S. Marine Hospital Service.

Assigned to Portland, Oregon, Bevan did not limit himself to the Marine Hospital during his five years there. He served as chief surgeon for the Oregon Railroad and Navigation Company and for the western region of the Union Pacific Railroad. He served in the Oregon National Guard as surgeon and major. In 1886–1887 he taught at the University of Oregon Medical School in Portland as professor of anatomy.

In 1888 Bevan resigned from his Oregon positions to accept an invitation from Rush to become professor of anatomy. The following year he was also appointed associate professor of surgery. He went to Europe in 1892–1893 for postgraduate education in Leipzig, Vienna, and Berlin. He held the positions in anatomy and surgery at Rush until 1902, when he became professor of surgery, the title he held until his retirement in 1934. In 1908 Bevan became head of the department of surgery. Upon retirement he was named the first Nicholas Senn Professor of Surgery.

In 1892 Bevan had also joined the surgical staff at Chicago's Presbyterian Hospital. In 1894 he became head of Presbyterian Hospital's surgical staff and remained so until 1934. Bevan married Anna Laura Barber of Akron, Ohio, in 1896. They had no children.

Bevan's major contribution was his work for the reformation of medical education. Poorly-prepared doctors were providing low quality, sometimes dangerous, medical care and were also cutting into the income of better-trained physicians. Bevan became the moving spirit behind the American Medical Association's (AMA) efforts to improve medical education.

In 1902 John A. Wyeth, president of the AMA, appointed a committee of three, with Bevan as chairman, to survey medical education in the United States and to make recommendations for the role of the AMA. At the 1903 annual meeting Bevan recommended the appointment of a permanent committee on education, with a salaried assistant secretary and an office at the AMA's headquarters. This report resulted in the formation in 1904 of the Council on Medical Education, of which Bevan was chairman from its beginning to 1928, except for his years (1918–1919) as president-elect and president of the AMA. The council collected pertinent statistics and slowly began to raise standards. Bevan's efforts eventually led to Abraham Flexner's survey, supported by the Carnegie Foundation, which resulted in an important 1910 report on medical education.

The council and the Flexner Report helped to raise admission requirements, eliminate many substandard schools, affiliate most good medical schools with universities, and improve related hospital facilities and internship programs. In 1920 the council began setting up committees to determine what preparation was needed for each specialty. This work eventually grew into the American Boards for the various specialties.

Bevan also served the AMA as a member of the House of Delegates (1902–1903); chairman, section on surgery and anatomy (1906–1907); and president (1918–1919). He was elected to the association's top post primarily in recognition of his work on the Council on Medical Education. At the 1917 annual meeting Bevan was named chairman of a committee to look into the best methods for using the records and activities of the AMA to support the war effort.

As an officer and representative of the AMA, Bevan spoke out on behalf of its role as the chief medical organization in the country. This led to his opposing the formation of a medical advisory committee (since this would lessen the AMA's power as the national spokesman for medicine) as part of the war effort in 1917–1918, and to several disagreements with the American College of Surgeons, even though Bevan had been a founder of the College and a member of its first board of governors. Bevan was also elected president of the Chicago Medical Society (1898), the Chicago Surgical Society (1908), the Inter-State Postgraduate Medical Association (1931), and the American Surgical Association (1932).

As a surgeon, Bevan built up a large practice and consultation. He specialized in the stomach and tumors of the breast. He was well known for the so-called hockey-stick incision, designed to avoid injuring major nerves in gallbladder operations. Bevan's name became attached to his operation for hydrocele of the testis. He also performed the first operation in which ethylene oxygen was used as the anesthetic.

As an author, Bevan edited Dean Lewis's translation of Erich Lexer's *General Surgery* in 1908. He wrote about 250 medical and surgical articles.

In 1929 Bevan and his wife donated $1 million to Presbyterian Hospital's expansion program. In addition, Bevan bequeathed more than $900,000 to the hospital. He died at his summer home in Lake Forest.

A colleague stated that Bevan "radiated strength and affluence and the joy of living." Although sometimes described as pompous, Bevan admitted mistakes in diagnosis and operative procedures. He was forthright in his opinions and fearless in personal or written debate. Although he was a competent surgeon, Bevan's outstanding contribution was widely recognized to be his efforts for the reformation of medical education.

• The Rush Medical Center Archives has a collection of Bevan's drafts of articles, speeches, and lectures, as well as reports of clinics. There is no collection of personal papers. Obituaries appeared in the *Journal of the American Medical Association* 122 (19 June 1943): 557, and the *Proceedings of the Institute of Medicine of Chicago* 14 (15 Nov. 1943): 499–501.

WILLIAM K. BEATTY

BEVERIDGE, Albert Jeremiah (6 Oct. 1862–27 Apr. 1927), U.S. senator and historian, was born in Highland County, Ohio, the son of Thomas Beveridge and Frances Parkinson, farmers. The family moved to Illinois when Beveridge was a child. Because of his father's financial difficulties, Beveridge worked as a plowboy, railroad section hand, logger, and teamster. He attended Asbury College (now DePauw University), graduating in 1885. He made his mark there in oratory, and he had a reputation throughout his life as a spellbinding public speaker. He was admitted to the bar in 1887. He married Katherine Langsdale that same year; she died in 1900. He married Catherine Eddy in 1907; they had two children.

Beveridge practiced law in Indianapolis, Indiana, until 1899, when his skillful lobbying of Republican state legislators won him election to the U.S. Senate. One of the youngest members ever of that body, he made no secret of his presidential ambitions. His quest for the limelight irritated many, in and out of the Senate. He would be involved in a continuing battle for control of the Indiana GOP with the faction headed by his senior colleague, Senator Charles W. Fairbanks.

Beveridge had first attracted public attention as an advocate of American imperialism at the time of the Spanish-American War. The depression of the 1890s had convinced him that continued prosperity required U.S. access to new markets and investment opportunities abroad. Along with championing the acquisition of the Philippines, he called for retaining Cuba despite the Teller Amendment of 1898, which prohibited its annexation. His major interest during the first term was the governance of the new American empire. He took a paternalistic approach, supporting generous treatment for Cuban and Puerto Rican exports in the U.S. market. Racist suspicions about the capacity of the native peoples for self-government led him to favor keeping political authority firmly in the hands of American officials. He had exaggerated hopes about the potential of the China market. He visited the Far East in 1901, decided that Japan would become the major rival to the United States in the region, and therefore took a pro-Russian line in his book *The Russian Advance* (1903).

Beveridge's major committee assignment was chair of the Senate Committee on Territories starting in December 1901. He was responsible for the 1906 legislation joining the Indian Territory with Oklahoma Territory to form one state. He opposed statehood for New Mexico and Arizona and blocked congressional approval until 1910. His public rationale was their sparse populations, but his opposition was at least partly motivated by his unhappiness over New Mexico's large Spanish-speaking population and Arizona's Democratic leanings.

Factional rivalries within the Hoosier State's GOP as much as personal and ideological affinities led Beveridge to align himself with Theodore Roosevelt (1858–1919) after Roosevelt became president in 1901. This alliance smoothed the path for Beveridge's reelection after the Republicans won the state in the 1904 elections.

In 1906 Beveridge became identified with the emerging progressive wing of the Republican party. He sponsored the Meat Inspection Act of 1906, designed to remedy the sanitary problems exposed by Upton Sinclair's *The Jungle* (1906). He championed a national child labor law banning shipment in interstate commerce of goods made with child labor, and he went on to call for tariff revision and the establishment of a tariff commission to separate tariff making from politics. He was alarmed by rising popular discontent with big business, and, at the same time, his passionate nationalism attracted him to German-style administrative reform and welfare measures promoting efficiency and social cohesion.

The turning point in Beveridge's political career came in 1909, when he joined the insurgent Republican revolt against the Payne-Aldrich tariff bill as a sellout to special interests. His vote against the tariff act not only alienated the GOP Old Guard but also the new president, William Howard Taft. This split was widened by his taking the insurgent side in the controversy between Gifford Pinchot and Secretary of the Interior Richard A. Ballinger over conservation, the struggle over new railroad regulation in the Mann-Elkins Act of 1910, and the fight over postal savings bank legislation.

Beveridge lost his seat in the Senate when the nationwide tide turned against the GOP in 1910, and the Democrats won control of the state legislature. At the lame duck session of the Senate, Beveridge led the unsuccessful fight to unseat Illinois Republican boss William Lorimer because his election had been tainted by bribery. Beveridge's loss of the federal patronage after his defeat cost him control of the Indiana Republican party. He not only supported Roosevelt for the Republican presidential nomination in 1912 but also followed him into the new Progressive party. He was the temporary chairman and keynote speaker at the Progressive party's national convention and its unsuccessful candidate for Indiana governor. In 1914 he was the Progressive party nominee for the U.S. Senate, but he ran third. In 1916, he returned to the Republican party.

During those years, Beveridge began moving politically to the right. He condemned passage of the Adamson Act of 1916, establishing the eight-hour day on interstate railroads, as a surrender to organized labor. Foreign policy issues most alienated him from President Woodrow Wilson. Beveridge attacked Wilson for failing to take a sufficiently hard line against Mexico. As was apparent from his 1915 book *What Is Back of the War*, he was pro-German in his sympathies in World War I and so was aggrieved at what he saw as Wilson's pro-Allied bias. He fulminated against U.S. membership in the League of Nations as meaning the loss of national independence.

After the 1912 campaign, Beveridge turned to a project he had been thinking about for some years—writing a life of Chief Justice John Marshall. At first, he appears to have had in mind no more than a popularization, but the project took on larger proportions as he proceeded. Houghton Mifflin published in 1916 the first two volumes of *The Life of John Marshall*, carrying Marshall up to his appointment as chief justice. The final two volumes appeared in 1919. Much of the praise that greeted the work was deserved. The writing was vivid and vibrant. Because of Beveridge's prodigious research, the volumes have remained the standard biography, but there were shortcomings. One was Beveridge's partisanship in contrasting Marshall's wisdom and foresight with Thomas Jefferson's villainies. A second was that Beveridge's emphasis on Marshall's nationalism as the primary, if not exclusive, determinant of his jurisprudence resulted in superficial treatment of his major decisions.

As his next historical project, Beveridge turned to a biography of another longtime hero, Abraham Lincoln. In 1922, however, he made a last bid to return to the political arena. He ran successfully in the Indiana Republican primary for the U.S. Senate nomination against the incumbent Harry S. New. His general election campaign featured denunciations of labor union power, attacks on high personal and corporate income taxes, and warnings against U.S. involvement with the League of Nations. Continuing Republican factionalism, coupled with the reaction against the GOP because of the 1921–1922 recession, led to Beveridge's defeat by Democratic nominee Samuel M. Ralston.

Throwing himself into work on the Lincoln biography, Beveridge built upon the experience he had acquired from working on the Marshall biography. As he had done with Marshall, he placed Lincoln within the context of the history of the period. Much of the material for Lincoln's life—like that for Marshall's—was scattered and often still in private hands. Beveridge spent time and money freely and exploited his contacts to consult all available primary sources. His biggest disappointment was the refusal by Robert Todd Lincoln to allow access to his cache of his father's papers. Working chapter by chapter, Beveridge rewrote and revised until he was satisfied with the result. As a final check, he sent drafts of the chapters to leading historians for their comments.

Because of his indefatigable efforts to strip away the myths and legends that had accumulated around Lincoln, the work is regarded as the first Lincoln biography to meet modern scholarly standards. In the process, however, Beveridge became increasingly disillusioned with what he thought was Lincoln's shiftiness and opportunism. The surprising new hero who came almost to overshadow Lincoln was Stephen A. Douglas.

Although envisaging another four-volume work, Beveridge was only partway through the chapter on the debates between Lincoln and Douglas during their 1858 senatorial contest when he died in Indianapolis. The historian Worthington S. Ford undertook the responsibility for seeing the manuscript through publication, and the resulting two-volume *Abraham Lincoln, 1809–1858* was issued by Houghton Mifflin in 1928. After his death, Beveridge's friends and admirers raised an endowment fund for the American Historical Association named in his honor.

• Beveridge's papers, a massive collection filling more than 300 boxes, are in the Library of Congress. John Braeman, *Albert J. Beveridge: American Nationalist* (1971), is a full-scale, critical biography. Claude G. Bowers's quasi-authorized biography, *Beveridge and the Progressive Era* (1932), remains worth reading. Beveridge's role in the insurgent Republican revolt is treated in Kenneth W. Hechler, *Insurgency: Personalities and Politics of the Taft Era* (1940), and James Holt, *Congressional Insurgents and the Party System, 1909–1916* (1967). Tracey E. Strevey, "Albert J. Beveridge," in *The Marcus W. Jernegan Essays in American Historiography*, ed. William T. Hutchinson (1937), is an admiring examination of Beveridge as a historian-biographer. More critical appraisals of the Marshall work are Landon C. Bell, "John Marshall: Albert J. Beveridge as a Biographer," *Virginia Law Register*, n.s. 12 (Mar. 1927): 641–55, and Max Lerner, "John Marshall and the Campaign of History," *Columbia Law Review* 39 (Mar. 1939): 396–431. Paul M. Angle, *A Shelf of Lincoln Books: A Critical, Selective Bibliography of Lincolniana* (1946), and Benjamin P. Thomas, *Portrait for Posterity: Lincoln and His Biographers* (1947), assess Beveridge's contributions to and place in Lincoln scholarship.

JOHN BRAEMAN

BEYER, Clara Mortenson (13 Apr. 1892–25 Sept. 1990), reformer and labor law administrator, was born in Middletown, California, the daughter of Danish immigrants Morten Mortenson, a carpenter and unsuccessful chicken farmer, and Mary Frederickson. Her father died in a trolley accident when she was fifteen. As the eldest of four children remaining at home, Beyer delayed further schooling until her mother sold the farm. She then worked her way through high school and the University of California, Berkeley, gaining firsthand understanding of labor conditions and unskilled workers' lives. At Berkeley she absorbed the institutional approach to labor economics, which emphasized the law and social institutions rather than market forces; she received a B.S. in 1915 and an M.S. in economics in 1916 with a thesis called "Organized Labor in San Francisco, from 1892–1902."

In 1916 Beyer went to teach at Bryn Mawr, where she had students join picket lines and investigate Philadelphia's tenement sweatshops. She became active in the National Consumers' League and found a mentor in its secretary, Florence Kelley. In 1917 she relinquished a fellowship at Columbia University and a job at Barnard College and chose instead to investigate wages, hours, and working conditions for Felix Frankfurter's War Labor Policies Board in Washington, D.C. She later commented that she found government work "much more exciting" than teaching.

Through Frankfurter, Beyer came under the wing of Supreme Court Justice Louis D. Brandeis and made friends with his daughter, Elizabeth, who became her assistant at the District of Columbia Minimum Wage Board. As secretary of the board, established in 1918 to set women's and children's wages in industries where existing rates were "inadequate to supply the cost of living," Beyer established procedures, set minimums, and enforced the law on a shoestring appropriation of $5,000. With a police badge under her lapel for protection against hostile employers, Beyer would go to the various mercantile houses and "stand on boxes at quitting time" to inform clerks about the District's minimum wage, the nation's highest at $16.50 a week. Employers challenged the law, however, applying freedom of contract doctrines to newly enfranchised women, and the Supreme Court declared the law unconstitutional in *Adkins v. Children's Hospital* (1923). This decision forced reformers to seek a fair wage rather than a living wage and to ground labor standards in the commerce clause of the Constitution. The Fair Labor Standards Act of 1938, which Beyer would help develop, reflected this change.

Beyer left the D.C. board and moved to New York in 1921, a year after her marriage to economist Otto Beyer, a pioneer in industrial conciliation. She had three sons in the early 1920s but continued her reform activities in part-time jobs with the Women's Joint Committee for the Minimum Wage and Hour Legislation, the American Federation of Labor, and the New York Consumers' League. In New York she developed lifelong friendships with Frances Perkins and Molly Dewson, future director of the Women's Division of the Democratic party. These labor-oriented reformers would become central members of a New Deal network that connected women in reform organizations with those in state and federal bureaus of labor and, through Eleanor Roosevelt, with the White House itself. Dewson and Beyer engineered the appointment of Perkins as secretary of labor in 1933. Beyer considered herself "a conniver," laboring behind the scenes for principles rather than seeking personal recognition.

In 1928 the Beyers returned to Washington, where Clara worked as an economist for the Children's Bureau. She became director of the bureau's industrial division in 1931 and worked there until 1934 when she was appointed associate director of the Department of Labor's new Division (later Bureau) of Labor Standards. Perkins had put a man in charge, to counter political concerns over too many women directors. Although Beyer essentially ran the agency, she served as acting director only in 1957, the year before her retirement. For the next sixteen years she advised the International Cooperation Administration and the Agency for International Development in labor law administration. She also reported on the condition of women throughout the world.

"Proud to be a bureaucrat," Beyer facilitated the passage and administration of labor standards legislation covering wages, hours, occupational health and safety, child labor, apprenticeship, vocational education, and elderly and migrant labor. She felt about industrial homework (piecework done at home) "like a preacher . . . towards sin" and spearheaded attempts to prohibit this practice because it undermined the enforcement of wage and hour laws. From the mid-1930s, Beyer offered technical counsel, model bills, moral support, and political advice while coordinating federal-state and interstate cooperation. During the early 1940s she initiated shop stewards' guides and other handbooks of federal and state legislation to streamline collective bargaining. She organized the Department of Labor for Puerto Rico and in later years aided other countries to develop and enforce labor laws. A lifelong Democrat, she remained active in the National Democratic party's women's club into her nineties.

Described in 1951 as "not one of those flag-waving-woman's right-crusaders," Clara Beyer combined paid labor and motherhood at a time when many of her companions in reform did not. She believed "this question of home-and-career is all an individual problem." In the early 1920s she defended sex-specific protective labor legislation and attacked the Equal Rights Amendment, arguing that women's social and biological differences necessitated state enforcement of special protections to gain "industrial equality with men." In the changed economic and political circumstances of the depression, she promoted the inclusion of men in minimum wage and other labor standards but retreated out of deference to the dominant opinion within the reform network that the courts first had to sustain the minimum wage for women. After *West Coast Hotel Co. v. Parrish* (1937), which upheld Washington State's minimum wage law, she renewed her efforts to pass and then enforce gender-neutral standards. She also supported extending labor protections to minority workers and in the 1960s organized the McLean, Virginia, community, where she had moved in 1931, for black civil rights and interracial cooperation. During her last years Beyer fought against the Reaganite dismantling of those New Deal labor regulations that were her legacy. She died in Washington, D.C.

• The major source for Beyer's life is the Clara Mortenson Beyer Collection at the Arthur and Elizabeth Schlesinger Library on the History of Women in America, Radcliffe College. Letters from Beyer appear in a number of other collections at Radcliffe, including those of Elizabeth Brandeis, Mary (Molly) Dewson, and the Consumers' League of Massachusetts. Her activities can be traced in agency papers at the National Archives, particularly the Children's Bureau (RG102); the Department of Labor, Frances Perkins Papers, especially materials relating to the Division of Labor Standards (RG174); and the Homework Committee of the National Recovery Administration (RG9). Beyer correspondence is also found in the Papers of the National Consumers' League, Library of Congress.

Her major studies were "History of Labor Legislation for Women in Three States," *Bulletin of the Women's Bureau*, no. 66 (1929), and "Children of Working Mothers in Philadelphia," *Bulletin of the Children's Bureau*, no. 204 (1931). Other published writing includes "What is Equality?" *Nation*, 31 Jan. 1921.

There is no book-length study of Beyer, but she is discussed in Susan Ware, *Beyond Suffrage: Women in the New Deal* (1981), and in Vivien Hart, "Feminism and Bureaucracy: The Minimum Wage Experiment in the District of Columbia," *Journal of American Studies* 26 (Apr. 1992): 1–22, which provides the best portrait of Beyer in action. She is also the subject of two oral interviews: Meg McGavran Murray, "The Work Got Done: An Interview with Clara Mortenson Beyer," in *Face to Face: Fathers, Mothers, Masters, Monsters—Essays for a Nonsexist Future*, ed. Meg McGavran Murray (1983), and "Conversation between Clara Mortenson Beyer and Vivien Hart, Washington, D.C., November 14, 1983, on Minimum Wage Legislation and Other Labor Laws," transcript available at the Schlesinger Library. Her fight against industrial homework is found in Eileen Boris, *Home to Work: Motherhood and the Politics of Industrial Homework in the United States* (1994). An obituary is in the *Washington Post*, 27 Sept. 1990.

EILEEN BORIS

BHAKTIVEDANTA, A. C. (1 Sept. 1896–14 Nov. 1977), founder of the International Society for Krishna Consciousness, was born Abhay Charan De in Calcutta, India, the son of Gour Mohan De, a cloth merchant, and Rajani (maiden name unknown). Abhay was brought up in a strict Bengali Vaishnava family, devoted to the worship of the god Krishna. His father had decided from the beginning not to send his son to England to be educated, lest his piety and moral purity be compromised. Instead Abhay entered the Scottish Churches College in Calcutta in 1916. During his schooling, a marriage was arranged for him with an eleven-year-old girl named Radharani Datta, with whom he would not live for several years. They later had three children.

While at college, Abhay was attracted by the Indian national independence movement and particularly inspired by the writings and exemplary life of Mohandas Gandhi. Despite having passed his college exams, Abhay refused to accept his degree, as a form of protest against British occupation. His father subsequently arranged employment for him as a department manager in a pharmaceutical laboratory.

In 1922 Abhay met the man who was to become his spiritual master, Bhaktisiddhanta Sarasvati Thakura, a leader of the Gaudiya Math Vaishnava movement, which derived its teachings from the sixteenth-century Hindu saint Caitanya. The Krishna devotionalism of the Caitanya sect had fallen into some obscurity until it was revived in the nineteenth century by Bhaktivinoda Thakura and his son, Bhaktisiddhanta Sarasvati. These teachers had hopes of spreading the ecstatic Caitanya message throughout the world, by means of the propagation of the *mahāmantra* or Hare Krishna chant. In 1932, after moving his work to Allahabad, Abhay received spiritual initiation and became a formal disciple of Bhaktisiddhanta Sarasvati. Before the latter's death in 1936 he had charged Abhay with the task of preaching Krishna devotion to English-speaking audiences. Abhay launched his efforts to fulfill this charge when he began to write and publish in India the magazine *Back to Godhead*.

In great financial difficulty, Abhay moved his wife and children back to Calcutta while he continued to live and work in Allahabad. Never satisfied with the life of the householder and spurred by the loss of his assets in a robbery, he finally abandoned both his business and his family in order to devote himself to his spiritual vocation.

In the 1950s, alone and impoverished, Abhay struggled to continue the publication of *Back to Godhead* and to translate the *Śrīmad-Bhāgavatam*, a Vaishnava text from the tenth century. Moving between New Delhi and Vrndāvana, the city most sacred to Krishna worshippers, Abhay took *sannyāsa*, the state of spiritual renunciation of the world, and was given the name Abhay Caranaravinda Bhaktivedanta Swami.

In 1965, with the sponsorship of a wealthy businessman, Bhaktivedanta, now nearly seventy years old, booked passage on a cargo ship to the United States. After a turbulent voyage in which he suffered two heart attacks, Bhaktivedanta Swami docked in New York on 19 September. Possessing only a two-month visa and $50 in cash, and wearing a cotton dhoti and rubber slippers, he took up residence on New York's Lower East Side. In spite of numerous setbacks, he slowly began to attract a group of young followers. With their help, he rented a storefront dwelling on Second Avenue where he began to lecture on the *Bhagavad Gītā* and conduct *kīrtana* (musical chanting) sessions. That spring, with a handful of followers, Bhaktivedanta (or Śrīla Prabhupāda as he was affectionately known) formed the International Society for Krishna Consciousness (ISKCON).

The numbers of Bhaktivedanta's followers began to increase dramatically when he and his disciples took to chanting, dancing, and serving vegetarian feasts in the local park. Among the youthful drug experimenters of the Lower East Side, the ecstasy produced by chanting rivaled the artificial high of psychedelics. In January 1967 Bhaktivedanta went to San Francisco to propagate his teachings in the fertile soil of the hippie-dominated Haight-Ashbury section, where another storefront temple had been acquired.

This was just the beginning of the rapid expansion of ISKCON. Between the time of his arrival in New York and 1975 Bhaktivedanta would travel around the world eight times to visit the ever-proliferating temples. Land was acquired for temples in India, as well as a 135-acre farm in Wheeling, West Virginia, headed by his closest disciple, Kīrtanānanda (Keith Ham). In 1970 Bhaktivedanta established a governing board of twelve disciples to manage the growing international concerns of ISKCON. Hundreds of thousands of dollars had been generated by the street distribution of Bhaktivedanta Book Trust publications. Stricken with ill health in May 1977, Bhaktivedanta returned to Vrndāvana with his disciples, who tended him until his death.

• Bhaktivedanta Swami's many translations of and commentaries on texts sacred to Vaishnava theology include *The Bhagavad Gītā as It Is* (1968), *Śrī Caitanya-caritāmrta* (17 vols., 1968), *KRSNA, The Supreme Personality of Godhead* (1970), *The Nectar of Devotion* (1970), *Śrīmad-Bhāgavatam* (30 vols., 1972–), *The Science of Self Realization* (1977), and *The Path of Perfection* (1979). His biography, by Satsvarūpa dāsa Gosvami, is *Śrīla Prabhupāda-līlāmrta* (3 vols., 1980–1983), or, in its condensed version, *Prabhupāda* (1983). A number of critical books about the Hare Krishna movement have been written, among them J. Stillson Judah, *Hare Krishna and the Counterculture* (1974), Faye Levine, *The Strange World of the Hare Krishnas* (1974), E. Burke Rochford, *Hare Krishna in America* (1985), and Larry D. Shinn, *The Dark Lord: Cult Images and the Hare Krishnas in America* (1987). Obituaries are in the *New York Times*, 16 Nov. 1977, and the *Los Angeles Times*, 15 Nov. 1977.

GAIL HINICH SUTHERLAND

BIANCO, Margery Winifred Williams (22 Jul. 1881–4 Sept. 1944), fiction writer and translator, was born in London, England, the daughter of Robert Williams, a barrister and classical scholar at Oxford, and Florence Harper. She spent her early childhood in London, where she enjoyed walks along the Thames and through Chelsea's Pensioners' Garden. In an autobiographical note, she recalled the old men, the flowers, and the natural scents of the latter place. Her enduring interest in animals, small pets, and stuffed toys began in these years. The youngest child in her family by six years, she felt much like an only child and developed self-reliance and creativity. She especially enjoyed John G. Wood's *Illustrated Natural History,* a three-volume work from her father's library, which offered models for a paper zoo she once constructed. Her independence came in part from her father's belief that children should be taught to read early but not to be formally taught until the age of ten. She did not attend school in England.

When Margery was seven, her father died. Two years later, in 1890, her mother moved the family to the United States. Her mouse Brownie accompanied her. The first summer, Bianco lived in New York City and enjoyed the foliage and animals of Central Park, which then still had some elements of wilderness. She would bring home grubs and caterpillars in cardboard boxes, creatures that mysteriously disappeared shortly after their arrival.

Bianco and her family moved to a farm in Pennsylvania, where she was able to continue her interest in animal and plant life. The farm country provided the rural delights like berry picking that were part of the dream life of an English child born in a city. Her only formal schooling occurred intermittently in these years; the longest and most pleasant stay was at the Convent of the Holy Child School in Sharon Hill, Pennsylvania, from 1896 to 1898. In the ensuing years, Bianco traveled frequently to England, with one stay lasting nearly a year.

In 1898 her literary career began with the writing and publishing of short stories. She remembers that she liked thinking and planning stories but that she did not like "sitting down and writing them out." Her audience, as she saw it then, would be adult readers. Writing under the name Margery Williams through 1925, she turned to the novel, her first, *The Late Returning,* being published in 1902. A second, *Spendthrift Summer,* followed in 1903; *The Price of Youth* in 1904; then, after her marriage, *The Bar* (1906) and *The Thing in the Woods* (1913). The long fiction explores the nature of loyalty and conflicts in human nature. About it is a sense of mystery, especially the mystery of Nature.

Bianco's children and the events of World War I altered the direction of her literary career. Her marriage to Francesco Bianco in 1904 brought her to London. Her son, Cecco Marco, was born on 15 August 1905; her daughter, Pamela, on 31 December 1906. The next year the family moved to Paris, where Francesco, a graduate of the University of Turin, managed the Rare Books Department of Brentano's. In 1910 she published *Peeps at Great Cities,* a year after which the family returned to London. Then war came. From 1914 to 1918 she and her family lived in Turin, Italy,

while her husband served as a captain in the Italian army.

After the war Bianco observed that she wanted to write something different. The summer of 1919 in San Remo, Italy, revived her energy and insight. She read English books for the first time in five years, especially the poetry collections of Walter de la Mare, whom she met. She felt the effect of his visual imagery and colors and delighted in the presence of the unexpected elements in the verse. That summer in Italy also revealed the power of her own daughter's artistic talent, her sketches inspiring de la Mare's *Flora.* In the fall the family traveled to London for an exhibition of Pamela's drawings. Two years later they journeyed to New York for another exhibition, and, a few months later, Cecco Marco enrolled at school in Maryland as preparation for entering Columbia.

If 1922 was an extraordinary year for the modernist movement—James Joyce's *Ulysses* and T. S. Eliot's *The Waste Land* were published—it was also Bianco's signal year of optimism in the face of widespread doubt following World War I. She wrote and published her first book for children, *The Velveteen Rabbit,* inspired by her childhood rabbit Fluffy. The transformation of a toy into a real being became a trademark of many of her later stories. An admirer of the stories of Hans Christian Andersen, Bianco regarded this book as "the beginning of all the stories written since."

The Little Wooden Doll, in which a discarded doll in an attic becomes a princess doll, and *Poor Cecco,* in which a wooden doll with her son's name explores the world, were published in 1925. Although *Poor Cecco* is considered by some to be more critically proficient, especially in its dialogue, than *The Velveteen Rabbit,* that first book with its message about the power of love still seems preferred by its intended readers. *The Apple Tree* (1926) echoes Bianco's interest in change somewhat differently as it emphasizes spring and renewal. Two subsequent children's books, *The Adventures of Andy* (1927) and *The Skin Horse* (1927; sequel to *The Velveteen Rabbit*), reflect on loss. In the former an owner leaves a doll after marriage, and the latter was inspired by Dobbin, the toy horse Bianco's brother left behind when the family moved to the United States.

In the next decade Bianco continued with the toy motif in several of her writings, but she also expanded her vision to include an exploration of the social community with *A Street of Little Shops* (1932) and *The Hurdy-Gurdy Man* (1933). Bianco's vision showed less optimism and a greater realism in *Winterbound* (1936; Newbery honor in 1937), in which the Ellis children brave a winter by themselves in a lonely farmhouse. Much darker is *Other People's Houses* (1939) as Dale, a working-class girl, attempts to earn a living in the city. Bianco wrote criticism for *Horn Book* magazine and translated works such as *Tales from a Finnish Tupa* (1936).

As Bianco experienced the Second World War, her writing exhibited even more the stress of the times in

Forward, Commandos! (1944). She died in New York City.

The author of *The Velveteen Rabbit* had a keen sense of the magic that comes from reading and a deep faith in the clear vision of youth. Although her novels for adults have some merit, her achievement lies in the books she wrote for children.

• The chief source of information about Bianco and her writings is Anne C. Moore and Bertha Miller *Writing and Criticism: A Book for Margery Bianco* (1951). The autobiographical sketch in Stanley Kunitz and Howard Haycroft *The Junior Book of Authors* (1940) is the basis of much information in the standard reference works. Kathryn Crabbe's essay in *American Women Writers* (1979) offers a balance of biographical and critical commentary. Marcus Crouch's essay in Tracy Chevalier's *Twentieth Century Children's Writers* (1989) has one of the stronger critical assessments of *Poor Cecco* and *The Velveteen Rabbit*. Also helpful are Martha E. Ward and Dorothy A. Marquardt *Authors of Books for Young People* (1971) and Constantine Georgiou *Children and Their Literature* (1969).

THOMAS BONNER, JR.

BIARD, Pierre (1567–17 Nov. 1622), Jesuit missionary to Canada, was born in Grenoble, France. His parents' names are unknown. He entered the Society of Jesus in 1583, studied philosophy at Tournon (1591–1592) and theology at Avignon (1596–1600), and was ordained to the priesthood in 1599 or 1600. He taught theology at Tournon from 1600 to 1604 and at Lyon from 1604 to 1607. In 1608 Henri IV summoned him, along with fellow Jesuit Ennemond Massé, to serve as missionary to the natives on the French colony of Acadia (now Nova Scotia).

The colonists of New France were motivated by commercial and patriotic interests. As a Jesuit, Biard was suspect to them on both accounts, and relations between Biard and the other colonists were unfriendly from the start. The owners of the colony's charter and Huguenot ship captains delayed his passage nearly three years, and his short stay on the island was marked by tension with the other French colonists. Jean de Biencourt, called Poutrincourt, who had been granted the Port Royal settlement, had bowed to pressure from persons close to King Henri IV to evangelize the natives and installed a secular priest, Jessé Fléché, to earn converts and thereby keep out the Jesuits. But Fléché performed mass baptisms of Indians, providing them with little instruction in the Christian faith. Biard's trip was finally made possible when the wealthy Marquise de Guercheville purchased a share in the trading expedition from the financially strapped Poutrincourt and gave her profits over to the Jesuit mission. Biard arrived on 22 May 1611.

On his arrival, Biard set about immediately learning Micmac, the local language, and scouting the island to find native populations and record their manners and customs. Continuing tension with the French traders forced the Marquise de Guercheville to move the Jesuits in 1613 to Pentagoët on the coast of present-day Maine, where they began to set up an entirely separate colony from which they could work without interference. Within weeks, however, an English fleet commanded by Samuel Argall arrived claiming British sovereignty over the area. After a brief battle that killed one of the Jesuits, Gilbert du Thet, he seized the Frenchmen and their ship. He offered passage to France for those who would work their trades in Virginia for a year, but on their arrival there Governor Thomas Dale revoked his offer and treated the captured French like pirates. He sent Argall back to Port Royal with his French prisoners who then watched the English plunder their settlement and burn it to the ground. Biard's own account of the affair insists that he successfully begged for the lives of his countrymen, but others accused him of guiding Argall to Port Royal and encouraging its destruction. He narrowly escaped danger again when a group of Frenchmen signed an affidavit falsely alleging that he was a Spanish Jesuit, and thus an enemy of England. Argall vowed to return the priest to Virginia for execution, but a storm separated the ships carrying the two men. Biard finally arrived in England in February 1614 and in April was given passage back to Calais. Some reports place him in Lyon in the following years, but it is certain that he served as superior to the mission at Paray-le-Monial from 1621 to 1622. He died at the Jesuit novitiate in Avignon after serving briefly as chaplain to army troops battling Huguenots on the German border.

Although he made no real converts among the Indians, Biard's account of his experience, *Relation de la Nouvelle France* (1616), was successful in several respects. He helped to raise interest in the New World, popularize the cause of missions, shape French impressions of American Indians, and influence the direction of missionary tactics. He also argued for the resumption of a missionary presence in the French New World. Moreover, his account of native culture was thorough. He praised the natives' honest and generous character and mourned with pity rather than indignation their somewhat debased moral condition. Although he warned that except for those few tribes friendly to the French, the Indians were fierce and warlike, he found "the nature of our Savages is in itself generous and not malicious" (Thwaites, vol. 3, p. 73). Biard was also instrumental in instituting what would become standard missionary practices in the next two centuries. He believed that learning native languages and studying their customs would facilitate a mutual understanding that would lead to a more lasting and genuine conversion. Despising the sort of nominal conversions wrought by Fléché, he insisted on full catechization of adult native converts prior to baptism so that they both possessed a complete knowledge of their new faith and were apprised of the moral demands that it made on them. His concerns were above all pastoral: it would be cruel to admit those to the church through baptism who would not have the sources available to nurture their new faith. In order to achieve a real Christianization of the Indians, he urged that the church "catechize, instruct, educate, and train the Savages properly and with long patience, and not expect that in one year, or in two, we can make Christians of people who have not felt the need of either a Priest or a Bishop" (Thwaites, vol. 3, p. 141).

• Biard's papers are in the Jesuit archives at the Curia for the Society of Jesus in Rome. In addition to his missionary pieces, he wrote *Librum pro Auctoritate Pontificis* (1619) in answer to an attack on the papacy. Much of his important correspondence and primary works are included in both their original languages and in English translation in *Jesuit Relations and Allied Documents: Travels and Explorations of the Jesuit Mission in New France, 1610–1791*, ed. Reuben Gold Thwaites (73 vols., 1959). Biard's contemporary and companion of Poutrincourt, Marc Lescarbot, chronicled the French experience in the New World, and in a late edition of his *Histoire de la Nouvelle France* (1618) he gives versions of events that often conflict with Biard's. Camille de Rochemonteix, *Les Jésuites et La Nouvelle-France au XVIIe Siècle* (1895–1896), and Pierre Francis Xavier de Charlevoix, *Historie et Description Générale de la Nouvelle-France* (1744), are the standard histories of early French Canada. Joseph de Jouvency, *Historia Societatis Jesu* (1710), gives some biographical information, and Auguste Carayon, ed., *Première Mission des Jesuites au Canada* (1864), contains some correspondence of both Massé and Biard. Although he often evinces a strong bias against the Jesuits, Francis Parkman provides a comprehensive and readable narrative of the French experience in *France and England in North America* (1865). J. H. Kennedy, *Jesuit and Savage in New France* (1950; repr. 1971), provides a good overview of Jesuit impressions and descriptions of Native Americans, for which Biard is a major source. Sean Patrick O'Neal's "Conversion on the Frontier: Attitudes of Jesuit Missionaries and American Indians toward Baptism in Seventeenth-Century New France" (Ph.D. diss., Univ. of California, Santa Barbara, 1991), contains discussion of Biard's experience, strategy, and impression of the Indians.

BRIAN K. PENNINGTON

BIBB, George Mortimer (30 Oct. 1776–14 Apr. 1859), jurist and politician, was born in Prince Edward County, Virginia, the son of Richard Bibb, a clergyman, and Lucy Booker. George attended Hampden-Sydney College in 1790–1791 and graduated in 1792 from the College of New Jersey (now Princeton University). He later attended the College of William and Mary, probably to study law, and apparently he also read law with Richard Venable and practiced briefly in Williamsburg. He moved to Lexington, Kentucky, in 1798, and in 1799 he married Martha Tabb, the daughter of Charles Scott, later governor of Kentucky.

Bibb was quickly successful as an attorney, and the young John J. Crittenden, who would become a U.S. senator from Kentucky, moved to Lexington to study under him. In 1806 Bibb was elected to the state legislature, but he soon resigned the position. In 1808 he was appointed a judge of the appeals court, and the following year his father-in-law made him chief justice. Bibb documented the activity of his bench in what became four published volumes of court reports.

Bibb resigned his judgeship in 1810 but was soon elected to the state legislature and then to the U.S. Senate, where he served from March 1811 to August 1814. In Washington, he was a solid supporter of war against Great Britain. In 1814, with that conflict underway, he resigned and returned to private life in Kentucky. He moved from Lexington to Frankfort in 1816, and the next year he served a term in the Kentucky legislature, vigorously supporting the unsuccessful effort to oust Gabriel Slaughter, a lieutenant governor who assumed the governorship at the death of his predecessor. In 1822 Bibb and Henry Clay acted as commissioners representing Kentucky in a land dispute with Virginia. Kentucky had passed laws to protect its claimants, but the Supreme Court found the measures unconstitutional. The Court reheard the matter, but despite the legal ability of the Kentucky team, the ruling reaffirmed the original position. Bibb supported the legislature against state courts in the struggle over debtor relief that dominated Kentucky politics from 1822 to 1826. The failure of the relief cause with which he was associated did not hurt his popularity, and he opposed the old appeals court, which had issued antirelief opinions. When the new, prorelief court was overturned, Governor Joseph Desha made Bibb chief justice of the old court, and the senate confirmed his appointment.

In 1828 Bibb was elected again to the U.S. Senate. Despite his friendship with Clay and Crittenden, he went to Washington as a supporter of the new president, Andrew Jackson. He voted against the Maysville Road Bill (May 1830) and supported Jackson's veto of the bank bill (July 1832). Gradually, however, Bibb turned against Jackson. He tried to give all newspapers the mailing privileges that the administration gave to pro-Jackson papers, and he supported an attack on the Jacksonian use of patronage. Most important, however, Bibb disagreed with the president over nullification. He felt that South Carolina had acted rashly in nullifying a federal law in November 1832, but he opposed protective tariffs and accepted the concept of states' rights under which South Carolina had acted. He felt that the Force Bill (Mar. 1833) was unconstitutional.

After serving a full six-year term, Bibb returned to Kentucky and worked to improve his personal finances. He took a position on the Louisville Chancery Court. In 1844 President John Tyler appointed Bibb secretary of the treasury, a position he held until Tyler left office in 1845. After that, "Chancellor Bibb," as he was known, stayed in Washington and practiced law there. He served as an assistant to Attorney General Crittenden in 1850 and later assisted John C. Frémont in his pursuit of land grants from the United States.

Bibb had ten children with his first wife and four or five with a second spouse, a Mrs. Dyer, whom he married in 1832. Family responsibilities may have accounted for the financial problems that plagued him, and in turn those concerns may explain why he so often resigned public positions to return to private life. In his later years he was known as a gentlemen who still wore the knee breeches of an earlier age and as an amiable man who talked fondly about the pleasure of fishing from the bank of a river. Bibb was a skilled jurist and politician who earned the respect of his well-known Kentucky colleagues. At his death in Georgetown, District of Columbia, the *Louisville Daily Courier* (19 Apr. 1859) called him "the last survivor of the old school of Kentucky statesmen."

• John S. Goff, "The Last Leaf: George Mortimer Bibb," *Register of the Kentucky Society* 59 (1961): 331–42, is a good biographical study. A number of other studies make references to Bibb, among them Albert D. Kirwan, *John J. Crittenden: The Struggle for the Union* (1962; repr. 1974), and Robert V. Remini, *Henry Clay: Statesman for the Union* (1991). An obituary is in *Harper's Weekly*, 30 Apr. 1859, pp. 273–74.

S. CHARLES BOLTON

BIBB, Henry Walton (10 May 1815–1854), author, editor, and antislavery lecturer, was born into slavery on the plantation of David White of Shelby County, Kentucky, the son of James Bibb, a slaveholding planter and state senator, and Mildred Jackson. White began hiring Bibb out as a laborer on several neighboring plantations before the age of ten. The constant change in living situations throughout his childhood, combined with the inhumane treatment he often received at the hands of strangers, set a pattern for life that he would later refer to in his autobiography as "my manner of living on the road." Bibb was sold more than six times between 1832 and 1840 and was forced to relocate to at least seven states throughout the South; later, as a free man, his campaign for abolition took him throughout eastern Canada and the northern United States. But such early instability also made the young Bibb both self-sufficient and resourceful, two characteristics that were useful against the day-to-day assault of slavery: "The only weapon of self defense that I could use successfully," he wrote, "was that of deception."

In 1833 Bibb met and married Malinda, a slave on William Gatewood's plantation in nearby Oldham County, Kentucky, and the following year she gave birth to Mary Frances, their only child to survive infancy. About this time Gatewood purchased Bibb from the Whites in the vain hope that uniting the young family would pacify their desire for freedom. Living less than ten miles from the Ohio River, Bibb made his first escape from slavery by crossing the river into Madison, Indiana, in the winter of 1837. He boarded a steamboat bound for Cincinnati, escaping the notice of authorities because he was "so near the color of a slaveholder," a trait deemed undesirable by prospective slave buyers, and for which he endured prolonged incarcerations at various slave markets. Bibb situated this first escape historically as "the commencement of what was called the underground railroad to Canada." Less than a year after achieving freedom, Bibb returned to Kentucky for his wife and daughter. He was captured and taken to the Louisville slave market, where he again escaped, returning to Perrysburg, Ohio.

In July 1839 Bibb once more undertook to free his wife and child. Betrayed by another slave, Bibb was again taken to Louisville for sale; this time his wife and child accompanied him on the auction block. While awaiting sale, Bibb received the rudiments of an education from white felons in the prison where he was forced to work at hard labor for a summer. Finally a speculator purchased the Bibbs for resale at the lucrative markets of New Orleans. After being bought by Deacon Francis Whitfield of Claiborn Parish, Louisiana, Bibb and his family suffered unimaginable cruelty. They were physically beaten and literally overworked to the point of death, and they nearly perished for lack of food and adequate shelter. Bibb attempted two escapes from Whitfield, preferring that his family risk the perils of the surrounding Red River swamps than endure eighteen-hour days in the cotton fields. The final escape attempt resulted in Bibb's permanent separation from his family in December 1840. First staked down and beaten nearly to death after his capture, Bibb was then sold to two professional gamblers who took him through Texas and Arkansas and finally into "Indian Territory," where they sold him to a Cherokee slave owner on the frontier of white settlement in what is probably present-day Oklahoma or southeastern Kansas. There Bibb received what he considered his only humane treatment in slavery. Because he was allotted a modicum of independence and respect, and because he was reluctant to desert his master, who was then terminally ill, Bibb delayed his final escape from slavery by a year, departing the night of his master's death. He traveled through wilderness, occasionally stumbling onto Indian encampments, before crossing into Missouri, where his route took him east along the Osage River into Jefferson City. From there he traveled by steamboat through St. Louis to Cincinnati, and on to freedom in 1841.

In Detroit in the winter of 1842, Bibb briefly attended the school of Rev. William C. Monroe, receiving his only formal education. Bibb's work as what he called an "advocate of liberty" began in earnest soon after his final escape from slavery; for the next decade he epitomized the black abolitionist, making his voice heard through lectures, a slave narrative, and the independent press. Like his contemporaries Frederick Douglass, William Wells Brown, and William Craft and Ellen Craft, Bibb was among a first generation of African-American fugitives from the South who used their firsthand experience in slavery as a compelling testimony against the atrocities of the southern institution. Although his highly regarded *Narrative of the Life and Adventures of Henry Bibb, An American Slave* was not published until the spring of 1849, Bibb began telling the story of his life before antislavery crowds in Adrian, Michigan, in May 1844. His story proved so poignant in its depiction of human suffering and endurance, so heroic in its accounts of ingenious escapes, and so romantic in its adventures in the territories of the West that the Detroit Liberty Association undertook a full-scale investigation to allay public incredulity, an unprecedented response to a nineteenth-century slave narrative. Through correspondence with Bibb's former associates, "slave owners, slave dealers, fugitives from slavery, political friends and political foes," the committee found the facts of Bibb's account "corroborated beyond all question."

Lecturing for the Michigan Liberty party, Bibb was sent to Ohio to lecture along the north side of the Mason-Dixon line, a region notorious for its proslavery sympathies. Bibb returned to the South one final time in the winter of 1845 in search of his wife and daughter. While visiting his mother in Kentucky, Bibb learned that his wife and daughter's escape from certain death on Whitfield's plantation came at the expense of their marriage; Malinda had been forced to become the mistress of a white southerner. In 1848, on a sabbatical from lecturing, Bibb met and married Mary E. Miles, an African-American abolitionist from Boston. It is not known whether they had children. With the passage of the 1850 Fugitive Slave Law, the Bibbs fled to Sandwich, West Canada, where in January 1851 Henry and Mary established the *Voice of the Fugitive*, a biweekly antislavery journal that reported on the condition of fugitives and advocated the abolition of slavery, black colonization to Canada, temperance, black education, and the development of black commercial enterprises.

With the aid of black abolitionists James Theodore Holly and J. T. Fisher, Bibb organized the North American League, an organization evolving out of the North American Convention of Colored People held in Toronto, and over which Bibb presided in September 1851. The league was meant to promote colonization to Canada and to serve as the central authority for blacks in the Americas. Although the league survived but a few short months, Bibb continued to work toward colonization, encouraging Michigan philanthropists a year later to help form the Refugee Home Society—a joint-stock company for the purpose of acquiring and selling Canadian farmland to black emigrants—to which Bibb attached his journal as its official organ. Tension among prominent black Canadians, however, brought about the society's demise. Bibb died in Windsor, Ontario, Canada, without realizing his vision for an African-American colony.

• For a collection of miscellaneous primary documents, see C. Peter Ripley, ed., *The Black Abolitionist Papers*, vols. 3–4 (1985, 1991). The most complete assessment of the slave narrative tradition and Bibb's role in it is William L. Andrews, *To Tell a Free Story: The First Century of Afro-American Autobiography, 1760–1865* (1988). Interpretations of and facts about his life can be found in David M. Katzman, *Before the Ghetto: Black Detroit in the Nineteenth Century* (1973); Floyd J. Miller, *The Search for Black Nationality: Black Colonization and Emigration, 1787–1863* (1975); Benjamin Quarles, *Black Abolitionists* (1969); Jason H. Silverman, *Unwelcome Guests: Canada West's Response to American Fugitive Slaves, 1800–1865* (1985); and Roger W. Hite, "Voice of a Fugitive: Henry Bibb and Ante-bellum Black Separatism," *Journal of Black Studies* 4 (Mar. 1974): 269–84.

GREGORY S. JACKSON

BIBB, William Wyatt (2 Oct. 1781–10 July 1820), U.S. senator and first governor of Alabama, was born in Amelia County, Virginia, the son of William Bibb, a planter and active revolutionary, and Sally Wyatt. William Bibb had served as a captain in the Continental army. In 1789 he moved his family, including young William Wyatt, to Elbert County, Georgia, to take up one of the land grants offered by Georgia to revolutionary veterans.

William Wyatt Bibb attended the College of William and Mary for two years and then transferred to the University of Pennsylvania, from which he received a medical degree in 1801. He returned to Petersburg, Georgia, and commenced practice as a physician. In 1803 he began as well to operate a tobacco plantation near Petersburg. In 1803 he married Mary Ann "Polly" Freeman. They would have two children.

Later in 1803 Bibb was elected to the lower house of the Georgia General Assembly and there sponsored an act to begin printing the state's legislative journals. He also took a leading part in establishing a school for the Petersburg area. In 1805 he was elected to the state senate as a Democratic Republican. The next year he was chosen in a special election to fill an unexpired term in the U.S. House of Representatives and took his seat on 26 January 1807.

In Congress, Bibb was an active member and was closely allied with his fellow Petersburg resident William H. Crawford. He denounced efforts to compensate the claimants under the Yazoo Fraud. In this affair, a New England company had bribed the Georgia legislature into granting it large sections of the future states of Alabama and Mississippi, and the U.S. Supreme Court had later held the grant binding, despite the corruption by which it had been obtained. Bibb fought the extension of Eli Whitney's patent on the cotton gin as an effort to impose a monopoly on the lower South. He opposed the embargo—a proposal of the Jefferson administration to forbid all trade with the warring nations of Europe until they would agree to cease interfering with neutral American shipping—on the ground that it was premature, but once it had been enacted, he opposed its repeal without a resort to arms. He supported Nathaniel Macon's nonintercourse proposals of 1811 and then joined the "War Hawks" in seeking the declaration of the War of 1812. As a member of the Ways and Means Committee, he played a significant role in placing the nation's finances on a wartime footing. When Crawford resigned his Senate seat to become minister to France, the Georgia legislature elected Bibb to the remainder of Crawford's term.

Bibb took the oath as senator on 6 December 1813. He vigorously supported the recharter of the Bank of the United States, though he reluctantly voted to sustain James Madison's veto of the initial recharter bill in 1815. He argued that without a central bank, America's currency would be regulated "by petty corporations and swindling individuals." He opposed the direct election of the president and vice president by the voters, because it would deprive the South of the influence it had in the electoral college by virtue of the three-fifths clause, which stated that three-fifths of the slave population, as well as the free, was counted in apportioning representation. He voted for the act of 1816 that converted the pay of congressmen from a per diem basis to an annual salary and was caught up in the whirlwind of national opposition to the measure. By condemning Bibb for his support of it, George M. Troup was able to defeat him for election to a full Senate term. Bibb at once resigned.

On the recommendation of Crawford and of Bibb's Senate colleague Charles Tait, President James Monroe appointed Bibb governor of the newly created Alabama Territory on 25 September 1817. Bibb purchased a plantation on the Alabama River in Autauga County and moved there at the end of the year. The territory had attracted a large number of wealthy immigrants from the Petersburg area, and they became the foundation of the Crawfordite political faction that quickly came together under the leadership of Bibb and John W. Walker of Huntsville. Bibb vetoed a bill sponsored by Walker that would have given the Huntsville Bank, headed by Walker's father-in-law, authority to create branches throughout Alabama and would have written into the bank's charter a pledge that Alabama would always receive the bank's notes for taxes. Bibb foresaw that the identification of his party with the particular financial interests of Huntsville capitalists could prove disastrous for its political fortunes. Nevertheless, the Bibb-Walker faction became increasingly associated with the bank in the public mind. That fact, together with the territorial assembly's repeal of the law against usury, would shape the course of Alabama's politics following the panic of 1819. In the years after Bibb's death, a political alliance headed by Israel Pickens and William Kelly succeeded in mobilizing the electorate's hostility to banks and creditors and in portraying the Crawfordites as wealthy enemies of democracy. The crusade against the Huntsville Bank became the foundation for Jacksonianism in the state.

In the meantime, unrest among the Creek Indians in the spring and summer of 1818 led Bibb to issue instructions to Andrew Jackson that were in part responsible for Jackson's controversial invasion of Florida, undertaken to eliminate the assistance that the Indians were receiving there. Settlers commanded by Samuel Dale crushed the final Creek resistance in September.

Almost from the creation of the territory, Bibb had been working through Charles Tait to have it admitted to statehood. An act of 2 March 1819, sponsored by Tait, authorized Alabama to write a state constitution and offered generous land grants, including a section, to be selected by Bibb, to serve as the state capital. Bibb's choice of Cahaba angered many residents of northern Alabama.

As a result, Tuscaloosa attorney Marmaduke Williams entered the new state's first gubernatorial election against Bibb. But Bibb was victorious, receiving 54 percent of the vote, and was inaugurated on 9 November 1819. In his message to the first legislature, he urged liberal support for public schools, to create an electorate able to distinguish demagogues from statesmen; adequate salaries for officials, to open office to the poor; and a survey of the state's rivers, to determine how to improve their navigation.

In February 1820 Bibb was thrown from a horse and suffered internal injuries. He lingered for five months, in great agony. During this period his duties as governor were largely performed by his brother Thomas, the president of the state senate, who succeeded him on his death. Bibb died on his Autauga County plantation.

• A small body of Bibb's personal papers from the period of his residence in Alabama is held by the Alabama Department of Archives and History, Montgomery; his papers from his Georgia years have been lost. For Bibb's term as territorial governor, see Clarence E. Carter, ed., *The Territorial Papers of the United States*, vol. 18, *The Territory of Alabama, 1817–1819* (1952). On Bibb's background, see E. Merton Coulter, *Old Petersburg and the Broad River Valley of Georgia: Their Rise and Decline* (1965). On the early history of Alabama, see Thomas Perkins Abernethy, *The Formative Period in Alabama, 1815–1828* (1922; repr. 1965). Bibb himself, however, has attracted little scholarly attention.

J. MILLS THORNTON III

BIBLE, Alan Harvey (20 Nov. 1909–12 Sept. 1988), U.S. senator, was born in Lovelock, Nevada, the son of Jacob Harvey Bible, a grocery clerk, and Isabel Welch, a schoolteacher. Bible graduated from the University of Nevada in 1930 with a B.A. in business. From 1931 to 1934 he attended Georgetown Law School and worked part-time for the U.S. Senate. After graduating in 1934, he returned to Nevada to practice law and to enter politics.

Bible began his political career as a member of the "McCarran machine" and remained a dedicated follower of Democratic senator Patrick McCarran until the "boss's" death in 1954. Bible was introduced to politics through a part-time job that Senator McCarran secured for him in 1933. Upon returning to Nevada, Bible went to work in McCarran's law firm in Reno until more attractive political opportunities presented themselves. He did not have to wait long. He was appointed district attorney of Storey County in 1935, elected to a full term in 1936, and resigned in 1938 to become Nevada's deputy attorney general. In 1939, he married Loucile Shields, and they raised four children. In 1942 he was elected Nevada's attorney general and was unopposed for reelection in 1946. During his second term, Bible was elected president of the National Association of Attorneys General.

In 1950 Bible declined to run for a third term and instead opened a law practice in Reno. In 1952 he was defeated in the Democratic primary for U.S. senator. Two years later he was chosen by the state Democratic party to succeed McCarran, who had died two months before the general election. Bible was elected in 1954 to fill McCarran's unexpired term and was elected to his first full term in 1956. He won reelection in 1962 and again in 1968. In 1974 Bible retired because of ill health.

Bible came to the Senate when Lyndon Johnson was taking control as majority leader. Thereafter, following the pattern of his earlier career as a "McCarran boy," Bible became a dedicated "Johnson man" and remained one until Johnson retired from the presidency in 1969. Johnson dominated Bible's early Senate career by arranging important committee assignments and helping to pass legislation vital to Nevada's economic future. It was Johnson who appointed Bible to the important Senate Appropriations Committee in 1959, assuring Bible's membership in the "Inner Club" of the Senate (the informal power structure then dominated by conservative southern committee chairmen).

Bible was an ideal senator for the 1950s. He was moderate on public policy issues, friendly, courteous, understanding of the constituent demands of his colleagues, and always willing to help solve the political problems of fellow senators. He accepted the customs and traditions of the Senate and never hesitated to engage in "pork barrel" politics. From Bible's perspective that was the essence of politics—avoid creating enemies and gain as much for Nevada as possible.

Bible's ability to acquire federal dollars for important state projects stimulated economic expansion in Nevada for twenty years. The key was water reclamation programs. In the 1950s he authored legislation for the Washoe Project in northern Nevada, providing for agricultural, municipal, industrial, and recreational use of dams and storage facilities. In the 1960s he was the prime mover in creating the Southern Nevada Water Project that brought water from Lake Mead to the Las Vegas valley. This prompted the phenomenal growth of Las Vegas, both in tourism and gaming, which soon made Las Vegas the center of Nevada's political and economic life.

While Bible played an important role in his own state's expanding economy, his most impressive work was at the national level, where he fostered the creation and preservation of national parks, monuments, and historic sites. In 1955 he asked to be assigned to the Senate Interior and Insular Affairs Committee, a position he held for twenty years. In 1964 he became chairman of the Parks and Recreation Subcommittee, which created forty-seven new national parks and an equal number of recreation sites and national monuments over the next decade. He helped establish the Cape Cod National Seashores Recreation Area, Indiana Dunes National Park, and the Redwoods National Park, just to name a few.

During the 1960s Bible was the most influential senator in the United States in the creation of recreational facilities because he held positions of power on both the Interior and Appropriations Subcommittees. George Hartzog, Jr., former director of the National Park Service, said, "Bible, more than any other in Congress, held the keys to life and death for the national park system." Henry "Scoop" Jackson, chairman of the full Senate Interior and Insular Affairs Committee, confirmed how effectively Bible used this power: "A listing of legislation Senator Bible has pilot-ed into enactment by Congress in the 1960s and 1970s reads like a roll call of the nation's national parks." Thus, Bible played an instrumental role in the establishment of a major component of Johnson's "Great Society"—national parks.

Bible's most enduring contribution came in 1971 when the Senate debated the Alaska Native Claims Settlement Act. After touring Alaska, he wrote Section 17(d) (2), which set aside eighty million acres for possible inclusion in four national interest categories: national parks, fish and wildlife preserves, forest service, and wild and scenic rivers. Congress was given until December 1978 to make the designations permanent. After much debate and White House pressure, Congress finally acted, and President Jimmy Carter signed the Alaska National Interest Land Conservation Act on 2 December 1980. As a result, 43.6 million acres were designated for national parks, 53.8 for fish and wildlife, 3.4 for national forests, and 56.4 for wilderness. Much of what was preserved in Alaska was due to Bible's foresight in 1971.

For two decades Bible stood at the center of the public debate over land-use policy. He continually emphasized the need for a balance between growth and development and preservation. He believed in multiple use of the public lands but stressed that not every acre should be open to exploitation. Some areas were suitable for public recreation, while others should be preserved in their pristine state. It was Bible's legislative leadership in the conservation decade of the 1960s that paved the way for the most dramatic expansion in the history of the National Park System. During this period Bible also contributed to the national welfare with his authorship of Section 17(d)(2), which gave preservationists the needed legislative authority to pursue their goal of protecting much of America's last frontier. He died in Auburn, California.

• Bible's Senate papers are located in the Special Collections Department, University of Nevada, Reno, Library. His oral history, "Recollections of a Nevada Native Son: The Law, Politics, the Nevada Attorney General's Office, and the United States Senate" (University of Nevada Oral History Project, 1981), is of limited value. For a detailed analysis of Bible's political career see Gary E. Elliott, "Land, Water, and Power: The Politics of Nevada Senator Alan Bible, 1934–1974" (Ph.D. diss., Northern Arizona Univ. 1990). On specific issues and aspects of Bible's career, the following articles by Elliott should be consulted: "A Work Horse, Not a Show Horse: Alan Bible and the Path to Power in the United States Senate, 1954 to 1974," *Halcyon*, 1993, pp. 149–60; "Nevada's Environmental Statesman: Alan Bible and the National Park System, 1954–1974," *Nevada Historical Society Quarterly* 34 (Winter 1991): 488–502; "Whose Land Is It: The Battle for the Great Basin National Park, 1956–1966," *Nevada Historical Society Quarterly* 34 (Spring 1991): 241–56; "Senator Alan Bible and the Southern Nevada Water Project, 1954–1971," *Nevada Historical Society Quarterly* 32 (Fall 1989): 181–97; and "A Legacy of Support: Senator Alan Bible and the Nevada Mining Industry," *Nevada Historical Society Quarterly* 31 (Fall 1988): 183–97.

GARY E. ELLIOTT

BIBRING, Grete Lehner (11 Jan. 1899–10 Aug. 1977), psychoanalyst, was born in Vienna, Austria, the daughter of Moritz Lehner, a businessman, and Victoria Stengel. She attended the Humanistic Gymnasium for Girls, where she became fluent in Greek and Latin. She first learned of the work of Sigmund Freud at age sixteen in a psychology class at the Gymnasium. On the way home from school that day she purchased two of his books.

Bibring received her baccalaureate in 1918 and then entered the University of Vienna to study medicine. At that time, medicine was a somewhat unusual career choice for a woman, and Bibring was one of only five women in her class. An avid student, she recalled her anatomy course as a "deeply esthetic experience in which everything hidden was made clear" (Gifford, 1976, p. 26). Sometime between 1918 and 1922 Bibring and three of her medical classmates started an informal group to study psychoanalysis. The group visited Freud to ask him to explain some of his concepts, and Freud invited them to attend the weekly meetings of the Vienna Psychoanalytic Society. Soon Bibring began her own psychoanalysis. In 1922 she married a fellow member of the study group, Edward Bibring; they had two children. Marrying while still in medical school was not customary. As Bibring recalled, she married at that time to relieve her mother's anxieties about "the free hours between classes." Her husband became a prominent psychoanalytic theoretician, and the couple formed a close professional collaboration.

Bibring received her M.D. in 1924. Her final anatomy examination went on for an entire day. Finally her professor, whose hostility to female medical students was well known, announced that he was "reluctantly obliged to give her the highest mark" (Gifford, 1976, p. 26). Her final exam in medicine, for which she also received highest honors, lasted only five minutes: as the patient was wheeled in, Bibring diagnosed an aortic aneurysm, a rare heart condition. Bibring's affinity for the science and practice of medicine foretold her interest in applying psychoanalytic understanding to medical practice.

Upon graduating from medical school, Bibring started a three-year residency in psychiatry and neurology at the Allgemeine Krankenhause under Wagner von Jauregg. At the same time she became formally associated with the Vienna Psychoanalytic Society and as part of her psychoanalytic training started to carry out analyses of low-fee patients. Bibring helped establish the world-renowned Vienna Psychoanalytic Institute and in 1933 became a training analyst and instructor there.

In 1938, after the Anschluss, Bibring and her family left for England, traveling with Freud, his family, and other members of the institute. Bibring was fluent in English and quickly became involved in the London psychoanalytic community. She was a consultant to a counseling service organized by the Society of Friends as well as a member and training analyst of the British Psychoanalytic Society and Institute.

In 1941 Bibring and her family emigrated to Boston, Massachusetts. She and her husband were among the wave of émigré psychoanalysts who established psychoanalysis in the United States and integrated it into both medicine and psychiatry. Bibring joined the Boston Psychoanalytic Institute as a training analyst and remained active in local and international psychoanalytic activities. She was the president of the Boston Psychoanalytic Society and Institute (1955–1958), the vice president of the International Psychoanalytic Association (1959–1963), and the president of the American Psychoanalytic Association (1962). Until shortly before she died she maintained a busy psychoanalytic practice.

In 1946 Herrman Blumgart, the chief of medicine at Beth Israel Hospital, asked Bibring to establish a department of psychiatry at the hospital. It was in her capacity as a clinician and teacher at Beth Israel Hospital that Bibring made the contributions for which she is best known. She brought a psychological perspective to the practice of medicine, emphasizing that successful medical care requires a physician to understand a patient's personality and psychological needs. She identified several patient personality types (for example, the "overconcerned, worrying" patient, and the "self-willed, independent" patient), described patients' underlying needs and conflicts, and made practical suggestions to doctors about how to best provide medical care to such patients ("Psychiatry and Medical Practice in a General Hospital," *New England Journal of Medicine* 254 [1956]: 366–72). In her teaching and writing, Bibring also stressed the importance of physician self-awareness, showing how a doctor's personality and attitudes influence his or her approach to patients.

In 1955 Bibring was named the psychiatrist in Chief and the director of psychiatric research at Beth Israel Hospital. Her psychiatry service became known for its practical helpfulness to both patients and physicians. A gifted teacher, she had a knack for clarifying complex psychoanalytic concepts and expressing them in ordinary, understandable terms.

In 1961 Bibring was appointed a clinical professor of psychiatry at the Harvard Medical School. She was the first woman to achieve a full professorship at Harvard Medical School and the first to serve as the head of a clinical department. In 1965 she retired from Beth Israel Hospital and Harvard. She continued to treat patients, taught a seminar for Radcliffe students on the professional development of women, and in her retirement published ten papers. Bibring died in Cambridge. Despite years of debilitating bone and heart disease, she treated patients until a few weeks before her death.

Bibring was prominent among the "second generation" students of Freud, who established the fundamental role of psychoanalytic concepts in the theory and practice of psychiatry. But Bibring also carried psychoanalytic understanding beyond psychoanalytic and psychiatric circles. In a singularly useful and lasting way, she brought a psychoanalytic perspective to the everyday practice of medicine.

• Bibring's papers are in the Francis A. Countway Library of Medicine at the Harvard Medical School. For further information, see the biographical sketches by her colleague Sanford Gifford, "Grete Bibring, a Professor in Retirement," *Harvard Medical Alumni Bulletin*, Spring 1976, pp. 23–28, and "Grete Bibring, 1899–1977," *Harvard Medical Alumni Bulletin*, Nov./Dec. 1977, pp. 18–22. An obituary is in the *New York Times*, 11 Aug. 1977.

WALTER A. BROWN

BICKEL, Alexander Mordecai (17 Dec. 1924–7 Nov. 1974), legal scholar, was born in Bucharest, Rumania, the son of Shlomo Bickel, a Rumanian lawyer who later became an essayist and literary critic principally for the Yiddish-language press in the United States, and Yetta Schaefer. He arrived in the United States with his family when he was fourteen years old and became a naturalized citizen five years later. Educated in the public schools of New York City, Bickel graduated at the top of his class both from the City College of New York in 1947 (interrupting his attendance to serve in the U.S. Army during World War II) and in 1949 from Harvard Law School, where he served as an editor of the *Harvard Law Review*.

After his law school graduation, Bickel served as law clerk to Chief Judge Calvert Magruder of the U.S. Court of Appeals for the First Circuit in Boston from 1949 to 1950. From 1950 to 1952 he worked for the State Department in the Office of the U.S. High Commissioner in Germany and as a U.S. observer to the European Defense Community Conference in Paris. He clerked for Justice Felix Frankfurter during the 1952–1953 Supreme Court term. While clerking for Frankfurter, Bickel helped draft questions for reargument in the pending school desegregation cases and prepared an extended memorandum concluding that the drafters of the Fourteenth Amendment did not determine for future generations the constitutionality of public school segregation. This conclusion helped persuade several members of the Supreme Court to strike down de jure public school segregation in *Brown v. Board of Education* (1954) and related cases. At the conclusion of his clerkship, Bickel returned briefly to the State Department in 1953 to join the Policy Planning staff but left a year later to become a research associate at the Harvard Law School.

Bickel's principal intellectual focus was on the use of institutional technique in shaping the role of the Supreme Court in a democratic society. His first book, *The Unpublished Opinions of Justice Brandeis* (1957), used the private working papers of Justice Louis D. Brandeis to explore the influence of internal memoranda on the Supreme Court. Bickel left Harvard in 1956 to join the faculty of the Yale Law School, where he became a full professor in 1960. In 1959 he married Josephine Ann "Joanne" Napolino; they had two daughters. In 1961 his article "The Passive Virtues" was published in the *Harvard Law Review* arguing that the Court's prudent use of various techniques to

avoid and delay reaching difficult and divisive legal questions was essential to developing a consensus for the ultimate resolution of the underlying issues, preferably by other institutions. The avoidance techniques Bickel endorsed were attacked by other scholars as unprincipled mechanisms to abrogate the responsibility of the courts to resolve important, even if unsettling, social and political problems. Bickel further developed his theme in his second book, *The Least Dangerous Branch: The Supreme Court at the Bar of Politics* (1963). At the core of Bickel's concern about the role of the Supreme Court was what he termed "the counter-majoritarian difficulty" presented by judicial review. In *The Least Dangerous Branch* he observed, "When the Supreme Court declares unconstitutional a legislative act or the action of an elected executive, it thwarts the will of representatives of the actual people of the here and now; it exercises control, not in behalf of the prevailing majority, but against it" (pp. 16–17).

Bickel was highly critical of the result-oriented jurisprudence of the Supreme Court under Chief Justice Earl Warren. Although in large measure he supported the results the Warren Court sought to achieve, he was wary about what he viewed as its neglect of institutional constraints and careful craftsmanship. He questioned whether such neglect would over the long run undermine the Court's authority. His sharp criticism of the judicial activism of the Supreme Court was published in *Politics and the Warren Court* (1965) and *The Supreme Court and the Idea of Progress* (1970), two collections of essays and lectures. His scholarly writings along with his regular contributions to popular journals of opinion, especially the *New Republic*, established him as among the most subtle and sophisticated proponents of judicial restraint.

Bickel's prominence as a scholar occasionally drew him into litigation as a consultant on important constitutional cases, most dramatically as counsel to the *New York Times* in the *Pentagon Papers Case* (1971). Characteristically avoiding an absolutist view of the fundamental legal issues, Bickel argued successfully against the injunction sought by the administration of Richard M. Nixon to block publication of its secret history of the Vietnam conflict by contending that the asserted threat to national security presented was too remote to justify a prior restraint and that the executive's position was violative of principles of separation of powers.

Throughout his career, Bickel, whose personal politics could generally be described as those of a liberal Democrat, demonstrated a willingness to rethink earlier views and a rigorously principled approach to partisan political issues. After attacking President John F. Kennedy's appointment of his brother Robert F. Kennedy as attorney general of the United States, Bickel later recanted that criticism in light of Robert F. Kennedy's record in the Justice Department and came to support his 1968 presidential campaign. Although Bickel successfully opposed the Nixon administration in the *Pentagon Papers Case*, he later defended President Nixon's constitutional authority to dismiss or limit the special prosecutor who was investigating him in connection with the Watergate scandal. Bickel steadfastly declined to compromise his principles to serve a partisan interest. "I would lose my way intellectually if I started thinking about the political impact of my position," he once told a Yale colleague.

Bickel died in New Haven, Connecticut, of cancer before publication of his two last books. *The Judiciary and Responsible Government 1910–1921* (1984), published ten years after Bickel's death, was coauthored with Benno Schmidt and deals with the history of the Supreme Court during part of the tenure of Justice Brandeis. *The Morality of Consent* (1975) is an outline of Bickel's approach to broader issues of political philosophy, in which he argued that the nation's institutions should "fix our eye on that middle distance where values are provisionally held, are tested, and evolve within the legal order derived from the morality of process, which is the morality of consent" (p. 142). Bickel's nuanced and thoughtful analyses of the institutional techniques a nonelected judiciary should deploy in a democratic society fully frame the issues presented by constitutional law and judicial power in American political philosophy.

• Bickel's papers are in the Yale University Library. A complete listing of books, articles, and book reviews that he had published at the time of his death is in "Writings of Alexander M. Bickel," *Yale Law Journal* 84 (1974): 201–4. A comprehensive article by Edward Purcell, "Alexander M. Bickel and the Post-Realist Constitution," *Harvard Civil Rights–Civil Liberties Law Review* 11 (1976): 521–64, provides a sympathetic yet skeptical discussion of Bickel's writings. Anthony M. Kronman, "Alexander M. Bickel's 'Philosophy of Prudence,'" *Yale Law Journal* (1985): 1567–1616, presents a full and supportive account of Bickel's political philosophy. Robert A. Burt, "Alex Bickel's Law School and Ours," *Yale Law Journal* 104 (1995): 1853–73, examines the continuities and discontinuities among generations of legal scholars as exemplified by the treatment of Bickel's work over time. Bickel's death generated a number of essays, including those by Anthony Lewis, *New York Times*, 18 Nov. 1974; Professor Charles L. Black, Jr., "Alexander Mordecai Bickel," *Yale Law Journal* 84 (1974): 199–200, and Albert M. Sachs, "A Tribute to Alexander M. Bickel," *Harvard Law Review* 88 (1975): 689–90. The Yale Law School Library has published a pamphlet, *Alexander Mordecai Bickel, 1924–1974* (1974), which includes eulogies delivered at Bickel's memorial service. A comprehensive obituary is in the *New York Times*, 8 Nov. 1974.

DOUGLAS P. WOODLOCK

BICKERDYKE, Mary Ann Ball (19 July 1817–8 Nov. 1901), Civil War nurse, was born in Knox County, Ohio, the daughter of Hiram Ball and Anne Rodgers, farmers. When her mother died in December 1818, Mary Ann, her sister, and her mother's two children from a previous marriage were sent to the farm of their Rodgers grandparents in Mansfield, Richland County, Ohio, about thirty miles north of Mount Vernon. Her father remarried in 1821 and subsequently moved to Belleville, about ten miles from Mansfield. Little is known of Mary Ann Ball's early life or education. She and her sister may have rejoined their father for a time, but after the death of their grandparents they also lived with their Ohioan uncle Henry Rodgers. Some accounts have her attending Oberlin College in 1833, studying in Cincinnati, caring for victims of a cholera epidemic in 1837, and participating in the Underground Railroad to Ohio. Recent research has found no evidence to corroborate these stories but rather suggests that she traveled with an aunt, evangelist Lydia Brown, and lived for a time in Cleveland working as a domestic servant. She may have also provided nursing assistance in the Cincinnati cholera epidemic in 1849.

The story picks up again with certainty in April 1847, when Mary Ann married an English widower, Robert Bickerdyke, a mechanic and sign painter, who played the bass viol with considerable skill. They lived in Cincinnati and had two children. In the 1850s the family moved to Keokuk, Iowa, and then to Galesburg, Illinois, in hopes of improving Robert's failing health. In 1859 Robert Bickerdyke died, and Mary Ann began working as a laundress, housekeeper, and nurse to support her children.

As a Congregationalist in Galesburg, Bickerdyke attended the church of Edward Beecher, brother of Catharine Beecher and Harriet Beecher Stowe. Shortly after the outbreak of the Civil War in 1861, the minister received a letter from Dr. Benjamin Woodward regarding the degraded state of soldiers' accommodations in Cairo, Illinois. The plea for medical help prompted Bickerdyke to leave her sons in the care of another family and travel to Cairo, bringing with her $100 worth of donated medical supplies and food. There she found soldiers ill from squalid living conditions, bereft of sanitation or a balanced diet. She proceeded to have them stripped and bathed, saw to the washing of clothes and bedding, and cooked meals, all in defiance of army regulations excluding women from its encampments without permission.

While army officials battled her presence with rules and regulations, Bickerdyke began a quiet medical revolution. The army medical department, preoccupied with pain control and amputations to forestall infection, did not consider cleanliness, fresh air, and diet as significant factors in the treatment of illness. Bickerdyke, though, persevered by sheer energy and force of character to treat the soldiers, and she was soon assisted by Cairo resident Mary Safford. Their success was such that when an army hospital building was finally designated in Cairo, Bickerdyke became its matron. There she dealt with the realities of an army staff that stole food and clothes and men who drank on the job.

Bickerdyke followed the army from one battle to another, improvising field hospitals wherever needed. In February 1862, again without official sanction, she and Mary Safford boarded the Sanitary Commission Hospital steamboat *City of Memphis*, which steamed up the Ohio and into the Cumberland River to provide hospital care for the wounded at the battle of Fort Donelson in Kentucky. From there she followed Ulysses S. Grant's army south, to the battle of Shiloh, where she again nursed the soldiers without any official standing. At that time Eliza Porter of the Sanitary Commission persuaded Bickerdyke to accept $50 monthly as a "Sanitary field agent," a position that allowed her legally to draw on Sanitary Commission stores. Grant also trusted her and provided her with a pass that enabled her to move within the ranks of his army. When Grant moved his army to Corinth, Bickerdyke opened a hospital there in the building of a female academy. The army moved to Memphis, where she rejoined it at the request of General Grant, and then on to Vicksburg, which fell on 4 July 1863. In Vicksburg she joined William Tecumseh Sherman's army for his planned march to Chattanooga. Sherman, a fellow Ohioan, also trusted Bickerdyke despite her irregular relationship to the army; he and Grant were both credited with the comment that "she ranks with me."

At Chattanooga, Bickerdyke argued with Sherman as to whether any civilians would accompany him on his march to Atlanta, Georgia, and she prevailed. She, Eliza Porter, and their requested sanitary supplies were allowed the use of the railroad between Chattanooga and Atlanta. Bickerdyke tended the wounded at the major battles of that march, which reached Atlanta on 2 September 1864. Sherman prevailed in a second confrontation with Bickerdyke, and she had to go north rather than accompany the army to Savannah.

When Sherman started marching north from Savannah, he wired Bickerdyke, then in New York, that he would again need her, and he provided a steamer for her and for needed supplies. She headed south immediately but stopped at Wilmington, North Carolina, where recently released prisoners from Andersonville had congregated. She stayed to help feed and clothe them and then rejoined Sherman as he came from Beaufort, North Carolina. After the war, Bickerdyke continued to serve the army as a nurse until all soldiers had been mustered out. She submitted her resignation as a sanitary agent on 21 March 1866.

Bickerdyke subsequently went to Chicago, where she worked a year in a home for the friendless. She then sought the aid of friends who had contact with the officers of the Chicago, Burlington and Quincy Railroad. She arranged for a number of veterans and their families to travel free from Illinois to Kansas, where they claimed land under the Homestead Act. Bickerdyke accompanied them to Kansas, where she ran a railroad hotel for a short time with her two sons. The hotel failed, however, and she fell ill, so her sons sent her to San Francisco for her health. There she received a patronage job in the San Francisco Mint and traveled the country helping soldiers obtain their pensions. She also served as a legal pension attorney. Bickerdyke remained a great heroine of the Grand Army of the Republic and often attended their frequent reunions. She died in Bunker Hill, Kansas. A memorial statue of her was erected in Galesburg, Illinois, in 1906.

• The Bickerdyke papers, which include extensive correspondence and miscellaneous biographical materials, are at the Library of Congress. Smaller holdings of books and articles may be found at the Galesburg Public Library and the Chicago Historical Society. A biography of Bickerdyke is Martin Litvin, *The Young Mary, 1817–1861: Early Years of Mother Bickerdyke, America's Florence Nightingale, and Patron Saint of Kansas* (1977). The standard published source is Nina Brown Baker, *Cyclone in Calico: The Story of Mary Ann Bickerdyke* (1952). Anecdotes may be culled from L. P. Brockett and Mary C. Vaughn, *Woman's Work in the Civil War: A Record of Patriotism, Heroism, and Patience* (1867); Sarah E. Henshaw, *Our Branch and Its Tributaries: Being a Story of the Work of the Northwestern Sanitary Commission and Its Auxiliaries, During the War of the Rebellion* (1868); Florence S. Kellogg, *Mother Bickerdyke as I Knew Her* (1907); Mary Livermore, *My Story of the War* (1887); and Agnes Brooks Young, *The Women and the Crisis: Women of the North in the Civil War* (1959).

SARAH H. GORDON

BICKERMAN, Elias Joseph (1 July 1897–31 Aug. 1981), ancient historian, was born in Kishinev, Ukraine, the son of Joseph Bikerman, a teacher, and Sarah Margulies. At the time of Bickerman's (to use the American spelling) birth, his father was beginning a rise that took him and his family first to Odessa and in 1905 to St. Petersburg, where the elder Bikerman became a celebrated journalist and political pamphleteer—one of the relatively few Jews active among the "Liberals." Elias Bickerman entered the University of St. Petersburg in 1915; there he studied with the great ancient historian Mikhail Ivanovich Rostovtzev, later his friend and protector. In 1917 Bickerman was wounded on the Persian frontier and upon recovery was at once drafted into the Red army; having obtained an administrative posting in St. Petersburg, he was able simultaneously to resume his studies, which he completed in 1921. He then moved with his family to Berlin, where he began graduate studies in 1922. In 1926 he received his Ph.D. for a thesis, written under the direction of the Greek papyrologist Ulrich Wilcken, on the so-called *Constitutio Antoniniana*, the empirewide grant of Roman citizenship made by the emperor Caracalla in A.D. 212 (published as *Das Edikt des Kaisers Caracalla in P. Giss. 40*). He completed his *Habilitation* (a thesis written after the Ph.D. that qualified its author for a professorial position in the German university system) the following year with a study of Greco-Egyptian diplomatics published in *Archiv für Papyrusforschung* (vols. 8 and 9, 1927–1930) and in 1929 was appointed to a teaching position at the University of Berlin.

In his Berlin period, which ended with the rise of the Nazis in 1933, Bickerman's interests already bifurcated in a way that would characterize the rest of his career. He began to publish extensively not only on questions of "general" (i.e., Greco-Roman) ancient history—especially diplomatics, chronology, and law, as well as a classic article on the postmortem deification of Roman emperors—but also on ancient Judaism and Christianity. This latter interest culminated in a major study of the Books of Maccabees, published in the *Pauly-Wissowa Realenzyklopädie der Classischen Altertumswissenschaft* (1930).

In 1933 Bickerman moved to Paris, where he was appointed *chargé de cours* at the École des Hautes Études, and was in 1937 made *chargé des recherches* at the Centre Nationale de la Recherche Scientifique. The seven years that Bickerman spent in Paris were in some respects the most fertile of his career. Many of the articles he published in this period, in both general and Jewish history, remained classics more than half a century. Of his books, *Institutions des Seleucides* (1938) is a still unsurpassed study of the institutional and administrative history of the Seleucid Empire, which ruled the Near East, except Egypt, from 312 to 63 B.C. *Der Gott der Makkabäer* (1937), Bickerman's most revolutionary, controversial, and influential work, argues that the Maccabean revolt (167–152 B.C.), traditionally represented as a successful Jewish national reaction to Seleucid persecution, was more likely to have been a civil war provoked by religious reforms instituted at the behest of a group of Hellenizing Jews. That Bickerman should have published such a book in 1937, in German (albeit with Schocken Verlag, a Jewish publishing house), testifies, among other things, to the rigor with which he adhered to the ideology of scholarly objectivity. It was, incidentally, the last thing Bickerman ever published in German.

Around 1941 Bickerman fled to the United States. In 1946 he was named research fellow at the Jewish Theological Seminary, in New York City, a position he held, with some interruptions, until 1952, when he was appointed professor of ancient history at Columbia University. Upon his retirement in 1967, he returned to the Jewish Theological Seminary as a research fellow and occasionally taught there. He held this position until his death, at Bat Yam, a suburb of Tel Aviv, Israel.

After a break in the 1940s, Bickerman resumed his intensive production of articles, now on the entire range of ancient history. These later books were either collections of articles, like *Four Strange Books of the Bible* (1967)—studies of Jonah, Daniel, Ecclesiastes, and Esther that were characterized by a profound sensitivity to the literary, intellectual, and social environments of these biblical books—or revisions of older works, like *Chronology of the Ancient World* (1968)—the standard discussion of and handbook on the topic. However, his final, posthumous, publication, *The Jews in the Greek Age* (1988), was a large-scale synthetic work, containing much new and entirely novel material—a conspicuous monument to Bickerman's rare ability to integrate legal, administrative, intellectual, and social history. Indeed, such integration—the insistence on considering the ancient Mediterranean world and Near East as a whole, in all its aspects—is the mark of Bickerman's entire *oeuvre*. His main influence has been felt in three fields. His minute studies of ancient documents, those preserved both on papyrus and stone, and in the literary tradition, have continued as standards, as has his discussion of personal status in Ptolemaic and Roman Egypt, which has broad legal and cultural implications.

The second area in which Bickerman's work has had enduring importance is the history of the Hellenistic kingdoms. Bickerman, while acknowledging the kingdoms' debt to Macedonian practice, also emphasized their continuity with their Near Eastern predecessors. He also always took for granted the social and especially cultural dynamism of the kingdoms and saw the boundary between conqueror and conquered as shifting, permeable, and obscure. In these respects he diverged sharply from most earlier scholarship, in which the conquered were invisible, and from much later, especially Marxist, scholarship, which saw the social, cultural, and political gulf between conqueror and conquered in the Hellenistic Near East as practically unbridged. Once again, the best work of the 1980s and 1990s on Hellenistic history has tended to reaffirm Bickerman's position. (Unlike many of his followers, Bickerman was not a cultural relativist: he assumed the superiority of Greek civilization.)

The central insights of Bickerman's work on the Hellenistic kingdoms informed in a crucially important way his work in the field in which he was perhaps most influential, ancient Judaism. To some extent, the iconoclasm of his work on ancient Judaism—a field always dominated by biblical scholars, most of them committed Christians, and Talmudists, most of them committed Jews—was simply the result of the fact that Bickerman was a historian trained in the classics, so the questions that concerned him differed from the norm. Nor was his work perfect: in the final analysis, Bickerman's ancient Jews are excessively pacific and scholastic; though his most celebrated book was about extremism and revolt, he displayed in his work little empathy with extremists and zealots, and certainly contributed little to the study of the apocalypses, magical books, and sectarian writings they produced. He was far more at home with the belletristic, the historiographical, and the legal, all of which he explicated brilliantly. His main contribution, though, was his insistence that the history and literary artifacts of the Jews be viewed as aspects of, and among the most important evidence for, the common culture of the Achaemenid, Hellenistic, and Roman Mediterranean and Near East.

It took some time for Bickerman's significance to be appreciated: he had few students and never established a "school." But revival of interest in the 1980s and 1990s in the Achaemenid and Hellenistic Near East, mainly in France and the Netherlands, and fueled by the massive syntheses produced by the Soviet scholar Mukhammad Dandamaev, himself patronized by Bickerman, surely owed something to, and helped to perpetuate, Bickerman's influence. His influence on Judaic scholarship with respect to method, as opposed to specific opinions, is most visible in the work of scholars associated with Columbia University; otherwise, it remains difficult to assess. The institutional base of Jewish studies in seminaries and special departments cannot be said to have favored general adoption of Bickerman's methods.

• Bickerman's papers are in the library of the Jewish Theological Seminary in New York City. A great deal of information about his early life is found in Joseph Bikerman and Jacob Bikerman, *Two Bikermans* (1975)—brief autobiographies by Elias's father and brother. This book, together with many years of personal acquaintance, served as the basis of the most accurate and complete biographical sketch of Bickerman, published by Morton Smith in *American Academy for Jewish Research Proceedings* 50 (1983): xv–xviii, reprinted in E. Bickerman, *Religions and Politics in the Hellenistic and Roman Periods*, ed. M. Smith and E. Gabba (1985), pp. ix–xii. Little is known about Bickerman's personal life after the 1920s: he was notoriously discrete and furthermore ordered his personal papers to be destroyed after his death. His main books have all been mentioned in the text. Also worth noting are the collections of his most important articles, *Studies in Jewish and Christian History* (3 vols., 1976–1985), and the aforementioned collection of papers on Hellenistic and Roman history. The latter contains a complete bibliography of Bickerman's work, excluding only the posthumous *Jews in the Greek Age*.

SETH SCHWARTZ

BICKMORE, Albert Smith (1 Mar. 1839–12 Aug. 1914), educator and museum director, was born in Tenant's Harbor, St. George, Maine, the son of John Bickmore, a sea captain and shipbuilder, and Jane Seavey. Bickmore's passion for natural history began during childhood, when he was an avid collector of shells, birds, and insects, and his enthusiasm for travel was ignited by a sailing trip with his father to Bordeaux. Following preparatory education at New London Academy in New Hampshire, Bickmore graduated from Dartmouth in 1860 with an A.B. He then enrolled in the Lawrence Scientific School at Harvard to study under the renowned zoologist Louis Agassiz. While at Harvard Bickmore was appointed as Agassiz's assistant at the Museum of Comparative Zoology (MCZ) in 1860. In 1862 he accompanied the showman P. T. Barnum on an expedition to Bermuda, where a large collection of marine specimens was obtained for the MCZ. Bickmore's education was interrupted by his military assignment with the Forty-fourth Massachusetts Volunteers in 1862–1863, although he used the tour of duty to procure an extensive collection of zoological material from the North Carolina coast. Unfortunately, Bickmore became frustrated with Agassiz's autocratic methods, and the relationship between the two grew increasingly strained. When Bickmore began raising his own funds for a collecting and research trip in 1863, Agassiz decided not to reappoint Bickmore as his assistant. Nevertheless, Bickmore received his A.M. in 1863 and his B.S. in 1864, both from Harvard.

With financial support from patrons in Boston and Cambridge, Bickmore departed in January 1865 for a lengthy trip through the Dutch East Indies, the Malay Archipelago, Java, Japan, China, and portions of Siberia. During his travels Bickmore discovered the Ainos of Yezo, a previously unknown culture that he identified as the remnant aboriginal peoples of Japan. Returning to Boston in 1867, Bickmore summarized the results of his expedition in a series of publications in the *Journal of the Royal Geographic Society* (1868), the

American Journal of Science (1868), and the *Proceedings of the Royal Geographical Society* (1867–1868). In addition to these technical papers, Bickmore published a book-length account of this sojourn, *Travels in the East Indian Archipelago* (1868), after which he was elected a life fellow of the Royal Geographical Society of London.

Although Bickmore served as professor of natural history at Madison University in 1868 and 1869, he concentrated his energy during these years primarily on establishing a natural history museum in New York City. He had begun developing these plans during his years with Agassiz at Harvard, where in 1863 Bickmore had received enthusiastic support for the concept from Sir Henry Wentworth Acland, founder of the Oxford Museum in England. Following his conversation with Acland, Bickmore "determined that I would work for nothing else by day and dream of nothing else by night" (Preston, p. 78). He discussed his ideas with botanist Asa Gray at Harvard, with William Earl Dodge in New York, and with Sir Richard Owen, the director of the Natural History Museum in London; but Bickmore began intense efforts on the project only after his return from abroad in 1867.

As a first step, Bickmore contacted a group of people who had attempted unsuccessfully in 1865 to raise money to build a museum for the scientific specimens of the Lyceum of Natural History of New York. In 1866 the Lyceum's collections were entirely destroyed by fire, but W. A. Haynes, D. Jackson Steward, and Robert L. Stuart continued their interest in establishing a science museum in New York City. In addition to their support, Bickmore received assistance from William E. Dodge, Jr., who introduced him to Theodore Roosevelt, father of the future president. Through Roosevelt's influence, informal conferences were held in the fall of 1868, and by December of that year Bickmore and his patrons drafted a letter to the commissioners of Central Park proposing the establishment of the museum. Under Bickmore's novel plan, the city would provide for the physical plant and its maintenance, while the collections would be acquired largely by private funding and donations. Joseph Choate drafted a charter, and at a meeting held in the home of Benjamin H. Field on 19 January 1869 a board of trustees was selected for the nascent museum. Bickmore received a Ph.D. from Hamilton College that same year.

Bickmore realized that the plans for the museum would almost certainly fail without the backing of Senator William M. "Boss" Tweed. After carefully obtaining letters of support from prominent men, including Samuel J. Tilden, Bickmore met with Tweed to urge his assistance with passage of the necessary legislation. Impressed with Bickmore's enthusiasm, Tweed reportedly said, "All right my young friend, I will see your bill safely through," and the bill passed without amendment on 9 April 1869 (Preston, p. 79). Bickmore quickly sought additional funding from wealthy patrons, and he persuaded the commissioners of Central Park to allocate space in the Arsenal Building near the south end of the park as the museum's initial facility. Subsequently, Bickmore was able to acquire the parcel of land known as Manhattan Square, which became the site of the American Museum of Natural History. Bickmore married Charlotte A. Bruce in New York in 1873; they had one son.

Following the establishment of the museum Bickmore was appointed superintendent in 1869, and he continued in the position until 1884, when he became director of the museum's department of public instruction. This department had been created in 1880 at Bickmore's recommendation in order to promote use of the museum's educational resources by public schools. Under Bickmore's leadership, the participation of city and state schools grew to the point that by 1884 New York state began to provide direct aid to the museum's programs. A very popular feature of Bickmore's lectures at the museum was his extensive collection of stereoptical slides, many obtained at his own expense during trips to Europe. In 1904 Bickmore was made curator emeritus because he was incapacitated by arthritis, although he continued as a trustee of the museum, a post he had held since 1885.

Known as the "father" of the American Museum of Natural History, Bickmore was described by his colleagues as "frank, fearless, generous, kind, energetic" (Kunz, p. 20) and "extremely optimistic, talkative, and articulate" (Preston, p. 76). He served as a trustee of Colgate University and of Vassar College, and he was elected a fellow of numerous scientific organizations, including the Geological Society of America, the American Geographical Society, the American Association for the Advancement of Science, and the New York Academy of Science. Bickmore died at his summer home in Nonquitt, Massachusetts.

• Many of Bickmore's papers are at the American Museum of Natural History in New York City. Major sources on Bickmore include L. P. Gratacap, "Memories of Professor Bickmore," *American Museum Journal* 15 (1915): 79–82; Edmund Otis Hovey, "Professor Albert S. Bickmore: Educator," *American Museum Journal* 11 (1911): 229–33; Douglas J. Preston, "The Museum and Professor Bickmore," *Natural History* 93 (Aug. 1984): 76–79, which features portraits of Bickmore; George Frederick Kunz, "Memoir of Albert Smith Bickmore," *Bulletin of the Geological Society of America* 26 (1915): 18–21; John Michael Kennedy, "Philanthropy and Science in New York City: The American Museum of Natural History, 1868–1968" (Ph.D. diss., Yale Univ., 1970); Geoffrey Hellman, *Bankers, Bones & Beetles* (1968); and Joseph H. Choate, "Reminiscences of a Founder of the American Museum," *American Museum Journal* 17 (1917): 285–87.

MARCUS B. SIMPSON, JR.

BIDDLE, Anthony Joseph Drexel, Jr. (17 Dec. 1896–13 Nov. 1961), diplomat, was born in Philadelphia, Pennsylvania, the son of Anthony Joseph Drexel Biddle, a wealthy publisher, lecturer, and evangelist, and founder of an international network of Bible schools, and Cornelia Rundell Bradley. The junior Biddle spent his childhood in Philadelphia, then attended St. Paul's School in Concord, New Hampshire, from which he graduated in 1915. Shortly after graduation

he married Mary Duke, the daughter of tobacco industrialist Benjamin Newton Duke; they had two children.

Following several brief jobs as a clerk in the shipping industry, Biddle enlisted in the U.S. Army and served in Europe during World War I, rising in rank from private to captain. During the 1920s, he held a number of positions in private business, including port superintendent (1920); member of a board of motion picture producers and distributors (1921); director of a real estate company and manager of the St. Regis Hotel in New York City (1922–1930); director of a Venezuelan oil company (1925–1926); and electrical research worker (1927–1930). In 1931 the Federal Bureau of Investigation commissioned him to conduct a survey of police systems in several European countries, a project that took four years to complete. In the same year he divorced his wife and married Margaret Thompson Schulze; they had no children.

Large financial contributions to the Pennsylvania Democratic party earned Biddle a number of diplomatic appointments during the administration of President Franklin D. Roosevelt. Biddle began his career as a diplomat in 1935, when Roosevelt appointed him U.S. ambassador to Norway. In 1937 he was given the same post in Poland. Two years later, when Germany invaded Poland, Biddle fled to Bucharest, Romania, and then resumed his duties as ambassador to the exiled Polish government in France. While in France, he also served as deputy ambassador to the French government, which at the time had moved from Paris to Tours, and subsequently to Bordeaux, following the German invasion of France in May 1940. This mission was terminated when the French government capitulated to Germany and moved to Vichy. Biddle maintained his position as ambassador to the Polish government in exile, which by this time had moved to England with the German invasion of France.

In late 1940 Biddle left France for Spain, where he directed relief efforts for American refugees. From there he was recalled to the United States for consultations with the State Department. During his brief stay, he gave a series of public lectures on the importance of military preparedness. In March 1941 he was sent to London, where he was American ambassador to the exiled governments of Belgium, the Netherlands, Norway, Yugoslavia, Czechoslovakia, Greece, and Luxembourg, as well as Poland.

In 1944 Biddle retired from diplomatic service and rejoined the army at the rank of lieutenant colonel. After a few months he was promoted to brigadier general and was named deputy chief of the European Allied Contact Section of the Supreme Headquarters of the Allied Expeditionary Force. The various contacts that he had developed as a diplomat in Europe proved valuable to the Allied war effort following the Normandy invasion in June 1944. In 1945 he was made chief of the European Allied Contact Section. That same year he and his second wife were divorced. In 1946 he married Margaret Loughborough, with whom he had two children.

Biddle continued to serve in the army following the end of World War II, maintaining the rank of brigadier general. From 1953 to 1955 he served as special assistant to Matthew B. Ridgway, chief of staff of the Department of the Army. In 1955 Biddle retired from military service and spent the next six years as adjutant general of the Pennsylvania National Guard, holding the rank of major general in the U.S. Army Reserve. In 1961 he resumed his diplomatic career when President John F. Kennedy appointed him U.S. ambassador to Spain. A few months later, Biddle died of a heart attack while undergoing treatment for lung cancer in Washington, D.C.

The variety and importance of the missions he served, especially during World War II, made Biddle one of the most distinguished and effective American diplomats of his generation.

• Duke University holds some papers, correspondence, and other Biddle materials. A collection of Biddle's papers was published as *Poland and the Coming of the Great War: The Diplomatic Papers of A. J. Drexel Biddle, U.S. Ambassador to Poland*, ed. Philip V. Cannistraro et al. (1976). Biddle's sister, Cordelia Drexel Biddle, wrote a biography of their father, *My Philadelphia Father* (1955), which contains information on the junior Biddle. An obituary is in the *New York Times*, 14 Nov. 1961.

THADDEUS RUSSELL

BIDDLE, Clement (10 May 1740–14 July 1814), merchant and army officer, was born in Philadelphia, Pennsylvania, the son of John Biddle, a shipping merchant, and Sarah Owen. Biddle's great-grandfather, who came to America in 1681, was one of the proprietors of West New Jersey. Biddle's father moved from Mount Hope, New Jersey, to Philadelphia in 1730. Except for some interruption from his army service, Clement Biddle was a lifelong merchant whose family eventually achieved great prominence in Philadelphia. He formed a partnership early in life with his father called John & Clement Biddle. On 6 June 1764 Biddle married Mary Richardson, daughter of Francis Richardson of Chester, Pennsylvania. They had one child, Frances, who died in infancy; Biddle became a widower in 1773. On 18 August 1774 he took as his second wife Rebekah Cornell, daughter of Gideon Cornell, who at the time of his death in 1765 was lieutenant governor and chief justice of Rhode Island. Rebekah lived until 18 November 1831, having borne thirteen children, two of whom died in infancy. Nine children married into prominent families, as did their successors, and this Biddle branch became one of Philadelphia's most powerful and wealthy families. Clement Biddle's sister, Ann, married General James Wilkinson. Clement Biddle was a liberal Quaker.

During the 1760s and 1770s, Biddle was active in Pennsylvania politics. In 1764 he organized a militia company to protect the Conestoga Indians who had fled to Philadelphia after the Lancaster massacre, seeking refuge from the "Paxton Boys." During the Stamp Act crisis, Biddle was among the principal merchants who signed the Non-Importation Act of 25 Oc-

tober 1765. Thereafter, he became a leader in the patriot cause. Biddle supported the democratic constitution of Pennsylvania in 1776 and after the war was known for his republican principles, even declining membership in the Society of the Cincinnati, the hereditary society of veteran revolutionary war officers.

When the Revolution began, Biddle helped to form the "Quaker Blues," two volunteer companies of light infantry. On 8 July 1776 he entered the Continental army service when Congress appointed him lieutenant colonel and deputy quartermaster general of the "Flying Camp," a volunteer militia for the protection of Pennsylvania, Maryland, New Jersey, and Delaware. In November 1776 General Nathanael Greene appointed Biddle a volunteer aide-de-camp, thus beginning a long friendship between the two men. He was involved in the military actions from Trenton to Monmouth. After the Trenton victory, Biddle was chosen by George Washington to receive the swords of the Hessian officer-prisoners. From July 1777 to June 1780, Biddle was commissary general of forage, working closely with General Greene, who during most of the period was quartermaster general.

During the war Biddle joined Greene in mercantile enterprises and land ownership, acquiring property near Catskill, New York. Greene's wife, Catherine, stayed with the Biddles during her frequent visits to her husband in Philadelphia. The Biddles became well known for their dinner parties, which Washington and his officers occasionally attended. One observer wrote that she was "pestered to death with ceremony and civility" during the Biddle social gatherings.

Biddle left the Continental army sometime between 15 September and 6 October 1780. On 10 November 1780 the Pennsylvania Executive Council appointed him marshal of the court of admiralty, a lucrative position. Biddle had charge of selling captured enemy vessels and their cargo. Upon Greene's recommendation, he was named quartermaster general and colonel of the Pennsylvania militia on 11 September 1781 and served in that position until the end of the war. Thereafter Biddle gave full time to his business as an importer of dry goods and served also as a merchant factor; during the 1780s and 1790s he handled produce from George Washington and also shipped various articles to him such as seed, clothes, books, and household goods.

He continued his public service after the Revolution. On 23 September 1788 he was appointed justice of the court of common pleas for the county of Philadelphia and served as U.S. marshal for Pennsylvania from 1789 to 1793. Among his duties as a notary public was adjustment claims for maritime losses. Biddle died in Philadelphia.

• Papers, mostly of a military nature, are found among collections of many libraries, including the papers of the Continental Congress at the National Archives and the George Washington Papers at the Library of Congress. Biddle was a frequent correspondent with Nathanael Greene; thus particularly useful are the numerous letters in Richard K. Showman, ed., *The Papers of Nathanael Greene* (6 vols., 1976–). Published letters may also be found in "Selections from the Correspondence of Colonel Clement Biddle," *Pennsylvania Magazine of History and Biography* 42 (1918): 310–42; and ibid., 43 (1919): 53–76, 143–62, and 193–207. There is no biography. There are, however, useful biographical notes. See, for example, Henry D. Biddle, "Owen Biddle," *Pennsylvania Magazine of History and Biography* 16 (1892): 299–329; Craig Biddle, *Autobiography of Charles Biddle* (1883), pp. 373–74, 376, and 421–23; and William F. Boogher, "Colonel Clement Biddle," in *Miscellaneous Americana: A Collection of History, Biography, and Genealogy* (1889), pp. 101–16.

HARRY M. WARD

BIDDLE, Francis Beverley (9 May 1886–4 Oct. 1968), lawyer, judge, and U.S. attorney general, was born in Paris, France, the son of Algernon Sydney Biddle, a law professor at the University of Pennsylvania, and Frances Robinson. Biddle attended Haverford Academy (1895–1899); Groton Academy (1899–1905), where he excelled at boxing and gymnastics; and Harvard University, from which he graduated with a B.A. cum laude in 1909 and an LL.B. in 1911. His first job upon graduating was as personal secretary to Associate Justice Oliver Wendell Holmes for the 1911–1912 Supreme Court term. Holmes influenced Biddle's political thought profoundly, imbuing him with a sense of noblesse oblige and a lifelong liberalism.

In 1912 Biddle moved to Philadelphia, was admitted to the Pennsylvania bar, and joined the family law firm of Biddle, Paul and Jayne. He became interested in politics for a short time and was a delegate to the 1916 Progressive party convention. He grew disenchanted when the party leadership voted to dissolve and endorsed the Republican presidential ticket. In 1917 Biddle moved to the law firm of Barnes, Biddle and Myers. The next year he married Katherine Garrison Chapin, a poet; they had two children.

In the summer of 1918 Biddle joined the army and began training to become an artillery officer, but World War I ended before he could go on active duty. After his discharge, Biddle returned to practicing law, becoming a partner at Barnes, Biddle and Myers in 1922. His caseload included such diverse clients as the Pennsylvania Railroad and the Dionne quintuplets. Later in 1922 he embarked on a four-year term as special assistant to the U.S. attorney for the Eastern District of Pennsylvania. In 1927 he published *Llanfear Pattern*, a novel critical of Philadelphia high society.

Although Biddle was officially a Republican, he grew increasingly disillusioned with the party's politics, especially its lack of concern for labor issues. He later wrote, "I saw the dark and dismal conditions under which the [Pennsylvania] miners lived, and the brutality that was dealt them if they tried to improve things" (*New York Times*, 5 Oct. 1968). Angry at President Herbert Hoover's neglect of labor issues during his first term, Biddle campaigned against his reelection in 1932. Biddle's efforts on behalf of the Pennsylvania coal miners, his concern for workers' rights, and his overall political support motivated the successful Democratic presidential candidate Franklin D. Roose-

velt to appoint him in 1934 chairman of the National Labor Relations Board. He served on that board until 1935. Following a brief return to his Philadelphia law practice, Biddle reentered politics in 1938, when he agreed to assist, as chief counsel, a congressional investigation into allegations of corruption and unfair competition at the Tennessee Valley Authority (TVA). The investigative group he headed clearly disproved these charges and restored the TVA's reputation, and Biddle later characterized his recovery of the TVA's name as his greatest contribution to the New Deal. In 1938–1939 he also served as a class c director and deputy chairman of the Federal Reserve Bank.

In 1939 Biddle was appointed to a judgeship on the Third Circuit of the U.S. Court of Appeals in Philadelphia. Soon bored with this job, he gave up his life tenure as judge after only one year and moved to Washington, D.C., to accept appointment as U.S. solicitor general. As the Roosevelt administration's legal advocate, Biddle vigorously defended New Deal legislation before the Supreme Court. He won all fifteen of the New Deal cases he argued, including *United States v. Darby* (1941), a suit concerning the Wage and Hour Act. In 1940 Biddle was placed in charge of the Immigration and Naturalization Service.

In September 1941 Biddle succeeded Robert Jackson as U.S. attorney general. Despite his liberal views and staunch belief in civil liberties, Biddle reluctantly implemented many wartime directives that seemed to threaten individual liberties, including the internment of Japanese Americans living on the West Coast in 1942 and the enforcement of the Alien Registration Act, later used during the Cold War to persecute Communists and other radicals. Reflecting on this legacy in his memoirs, he expressed regret for both actions. Biddle's single most memorable act as attorney general, however, was the physical removal of Sewell Avery from the chairmanship of Montgomery Ward in April 1944 while enforcing a decree from the War Labor Board. Avery had refused to recognize the "maintenance of membership" clause in wartime labor contracts, a government-supported compromise between closed and open shops. Because the goods produced at Montgomery Ward were considered useful to the war effort, the War Labor Board felt obliged to take strong steps to avoid labor conflicts. When implementing the board's decree, Biddle supervised as Avery was physically carried, still clinging to his office chair, from the company headquarters. In response to his forced removal, Avery cried, "You New Dealer!" To Avery, this was the supreme insult; to Biddle it was a great compliment. Roosevelt died in April 1945, elevating Harry Truman to the presidency. At Truman's request, Biddle resigned as attorney general in June 1945. In his memoirs, Truman claimed that Biddle's departure was voluntary, but Biddle remembered leaving under pressure.

Biddle was appointed to sit on the international tribunal at Nuremberg that, in the aftermath of World War II, tried Nazi leaders for "crimes against humanity." At the conclusion of these trials, he recommended to Truman that in the future the provocation of aggressive wars should be declared a crime under international law. Truman subsequently nominated Biddle as the American representative to the United Nations Educational, Scientific, and Cultural Organization (UNESCO). In 1947, when the Republican-controlled U.S. Senate hesitated to approve the nomination because Biddle was considered overly liberal, the nominee removed his name from consideration.

Although Biddle remained active in politics, he did not hold appointed office again, except for chairing a committee to plan Franklin D. Roosevelt's memorial (1955). Reflecting his liberal outlook, he chaired the Americans for Democratic Action (1950–1953). He had a noteworthy impact on national politics as an author, especially with *The Fear of Freedom* (1951), which attacked McCarthyism and denounced the House Committee on Un-American Activities, its assumptions of guilt by association, the censorship of school textbooks, and the excessive scrutiny of teachers suspected of Communist sympathies. His other works include the biographical *Justice Holmes, Natural Law, and the Supreme Court* (1961), an addition to his earlier biography, *Mr. Justice Holmes* (1942); and a two-volume autobiography, *A Casual Past* (1961) and *In Brief Authority* (1962). Biddle died on Cape Cod in Massachusetts. He is best remembered for his vigorous and unwavering support of Roosevelt's New Deal and for his staunch defense of labor interests and civil liberties.

• Biddle's correspondence is in the Franklin D. Roosevelt Library and the Harvard Law School Library. The best sources for information on Biddle are his two autobiographies. His other books include *Democratic Thinking and the War* (1944) and *World's Best Hope* (1949). Paul K. Conkin, *The New Deal* (1967), and Cabell B. H. Phillips, *The Truman Presidency: The History of a Triumphant Succession* (1966), briefly survey his attorney generalship. An obituary is in the *New York Times*, 5 Oct. 1968.

ELIZABETH ZOE VICARY

BIDDLE, George (24 Jan. 1885–6 Nov. 1973), artist, was born in Philadelphia, Pennsylvania, the son of Algernon Sydney Biddle, a lawyer, and Frances Robinson. Though the Biddles were a leading family of Pennsylvania, George's own immediate family, though quite comfortable, was never wealthy. Biddle attended Groton School in Massachusetts and Harvard College. After graduation in 1908, he spent a year in Texas and Mexico working on a cattle ranch to build up his fragile health. Returning to Harvard, he received a law degree in 1911, but, although he was admitted to the Pennsylvania bar, he never practiced.

Biddle spent the next five years shuttling between Europe and Philadelphia. In Paris, he attended the Académie Julian (1911–1912). During the academic years of 1912–1914, he studied at the Pennsylvania Academy of the Fine Arts. While studying printmaking (a medium in which he was to do some of his best work) in Munich in 1914–1915, he summered in Giverny, France, where he became acquainted with the

French art community. While in Paris, he studied with the much older impressionist painter Mary Cassatt, a fellow Philadelphian and family acquaintance who had done a posthumous portrait of Biddle's father.

Biddle's artistic development was interrupted by World War I. He enlisted in the U.S. Army and was commissioned a first lieutenant. Before shipping out to Europe, Biddle married Anne "Nancy" Coleman in 1917. Biddle fought in many battles, including that of the Marne, and was mustered out with the rank of captain in 1919. After returning to Philadelphia, he and Coleman separated, divorcing in 1922. They had no children.

In 1920 Biddle traveled to Tahiti, where he lived for much of the next two years. After returning to New York in 1922, Biddle again went to Paris. From 1923 to 1926 he mingled with members of the art world's avant-garde and attended Gertrude Stein's famed salons. His close contact with French modernism and such movements as cubism, dada, and surrealism reinforced his inherent "Americanism" and his belief in the primacy of realism in art. In his autobiography, Biddle wrote that "the average human being gets the maximum esthetic pleasure from representative art."

Biddle regularly exhibited at a number of galleries in New York and received polite and sympathetic reviews. Critics felt his work lacked a certain strength of design and was merely "decorative," lacking in the portrayal of deep emotions or great themes.

While in Paris in 1925, Biddle married Jane Belo. After traveling throughout the Caribbean, the couple returned to the United States and settled in Croton-on-Hudson, New York. In 1928 Biddle traveled with Mexican artist Diego Rivera on a sketching tour of Mexico. After his Mexican trip, Biddle's work began to reflect a deeper interest in the social and political aspects of American life. The *New York Times*, reviewing an exhibition of work from his Mexican sojourn, noted that Biddle was "no longer limited to the business of making amusing decorations" (3 Nov. 1929). In 1930 Biddle and Belo were divorced. They had no children. After the divorce, Biddle constructed a house and studio in Croton-on-Hudson, where, when he was not traveling, he lived for the rest of his life.

Biddle and the Belgian-born sculptress Hélène Sardeau were married in 1931. A son was born in 1934. Biddle and his wife traveled through Italy for much of 1931–1932. The trip resulted in his "Italian Series" of prints. Depicting the Italian countryside, these masterful lithographs reveal Biddle's facility in this medium.

The worsening economic climate of the depression and its effect on artists led Biddle to contact his former Groton schoolmate, President Franklin D. Roosevelt, with a proposal that the U.S. government create a program of federal aid to artists. (Biddle was inspired by a similar program begun in the 1920s by the Mexican government.) With the support of both Franklin and Eleanor Roosevelt, Biddle helped to organize the Public Works of Art Project (PWAP, 1933–1934). The

PWAP led to the Federal Art Project (1935–1943), a program of the Works Progress Administration and the Department of the Treasury's nonrelief fine art programs. Biddle was an active participant in the first American Artists Congress (1936), which fought for continuing and expanded support for the arts.

In 1936 Biddle joined his younger brother Francis, a member of the Roosevelt administration, in Washington. George came to Washington to work on a series of murals, which he designed around the theme of "society freed through justice," for the Department of Justice as part of the Department of the Treasury's mural program. Biddle's "radical" leanings, expressed in his penchant for portraying the working class in his art as well as his support for various social programs, caused him to be labeled, as he recounted in his autobiography, "a traitor to my class."

In 1940 Biddle and his wife undertook the decoration of the Mexican Supreme Court building in Mexico City with frescoes and sculptures. He also created murals for the Biblioteca Nacional in Rio de Janeiro in 1942.

Recalled to military service in 1943, Biddle served as chairman of the U.S. War Artists Committee. He traveled to North Africa and later published an account of his service in *Artist at War* (1944). In 1950 he was appointed by President Harry S. Truman to the influential Fine Arts Commission, where he was an advocate for representational art. In 1957 he published a collection of art criticism, *The Yes and No of Contemporary Art*, in which he argued that subject matter took precedence over technical innovation and the blind alleys of relentless self-examination.

An around-the-world trip in 1959 included a lengthy stop in India, where Biddle painted a portrait of the Indian prime minister, Jawaharlal Nehru. He also completed a series of lithographs that depicted both the crushing poverty of that nation as well as its capacity for spirituality. *Indian Impressions* (1960) describes his stay in India.

Biddle was the subject of a major retrospective at the Cober Gallery in New York in 1961. Summing up his approach to art on the occasion of this exhibit, Biddle told the *New Yorker* (13 Jan. 1962), "I'm not an abstract artist, as you know, and many critics regard my output as old-fashioned. I do think my idiom has remained the same, but I like to feel that in it I've expressed, as much as any other artist, the various phases our civilization has gone through."

Though semiretired, Biddle had further exhibitions throughout the 1960s. He died at his home at Croton-on-Hudson.

• Lithographs and paintings are in the collections of the Library of Congress, Washington, D.C.; the Philadelphia Museum of Art; the New York Public Library; and the Corcoran Gallery of Art, Washington, D.C. Major murals are in the Department of Justice, Washington, D.C.; the Biblioteca Nacional, Rio de Janeiro; and the Mexican Supreme Court Building, Mexico City. Biddle's extensive papers are held by the Library of Congress Manuscript Division; additional papers and those of his third wife, Hélène Sardeau, are available at the Archives of American Art, Smithsonian Institution. Biddle wrote an autobiography, *An American Artist's Story* (1939), which unfortunately covers only the earlier part of his life. Additional, though sketchy, biographical material may be gleaned from Biddle's *Tahitian Journal* (1968). Martha Pennigar, *The Graphic Work of George Biddle, with Catalogue Raisonné* (1979), contains biographical information as well as a complete catalog of Biddle's graphic work. Frank C. Waldrop, "The Biddle Boys in Washington," *New York Times-Herald*, 14 Mar. 1943, is an interesting source for Biddle's Washington career as well as a brief account of the Biddle antecedents. Obituaries are in the *Washington Post* and the *New York Times*, both 8 Nov. 1973.

MARTIN R. KALFATOVIC

BIDDLE, James (18 Feb. 1783–1 Oct. 1848), naval officer, was born north of Philadelphia, Pennsylvania, the son of Charles Biddle, an affluent mercantile entrepreneur and politician, and Hannah Shepard. Biddle attended the University of Pennsylvania, where he developed a lifelong love of literature. He and his younger brother, Edward, received their midshipmen's warrants on 14 February 1800 and joined the frigate *President* in September. They saw no action during the Quasi-War, and Edward died of a fever later that year. James was one of the 150 midshipmen who survived the naval reductions of 1801.

During the war with Tripoli, the Navy Department assigned Biddle to *Constellation*. After an uneventful eleven-month cruise, Biddle returned to Chesapeake Bay on 15 March 1803, but he left again in July for the Mediterranean in the frigate *Philadelphia*, under Captain William Bainbridge. In October 1803 *Philadelphia* grounded on uncharted shoals in Tripoli's harbor, and the Barbary pirates captured it and imprisoned the crew for nineteen months. Biddle returned to Philadelphia in late September 1805 after a treaty ended hostilities. Bainbridge spoke highly of Biddle in his evaluation for the Navy Department, writing, "James Biddle from his high sense of honor and talents must one day be conspicuous in the service of his Country" (*Naval Documents Related to the United States Wars with the Barbary Powers: Naval Operations*, 6 [1944]: 286).

For Biddle, a peacetime navy meant fewer opportunities for positions in large vessels. Consequently, the department assigned him in October 1805 to a gunboat flotilla off South Carolina and Georgia. Biddle commanded a gunboat, conducting a study of the suitability of Beaufort, South Carolina, as a naval base. He was on leave in Philadelphia from July 1806 to January 1807 and was promoted to lieutenant effective on 11 February 1807. He then took an extended furlough until March 1808, joining the crew of a China-bound merchant ship. On his return to America he was relegated to the command of Gunboat #120 in Chesapeake Bay.

The humiliation of the *Chesapeake–Leopard* affair of June 1807 and the increased demands placed on the navy by the Embargo and Non-Intercourse acts caused the Jefferson and Madison administrations to rethink their small-navy policy and take some of the larger vessels out of ordinary. This created more opportunities for officers like Biddle, who in early 1809 joined *President*, recently refitted by Captain Bainbridge, for several months of coastal cruising. Biddle spent the two years before the War of 1812 in uneventful posts—command of the sloop of war *Siren* and brief cruises on *Constitution* and *President*. He succumbed again to the lucrative lure of merchant service in spring 1811, receiving a furlough for a voyage to Portugal. After he returned to the United States in the fall of 1811, the State Department entrusted him with diplomatic dispatches for Britain and France. When Congress declared war on 18 June 1812, Biddle was not assigned to a ship, and it was not until October that he set sail in Master Commandant Jacob Jones's sloop of war *Wasp*. This vessel captured the British sloop *Frolic*, and Jones praised Lieutenant Biddle for his "intrepidity" in boarding the enemy vessel and hauling down her colors. The victory was short-lived, however; the British ship of the line *Poictiers* captured the two disabled warships just hours after their engagement. Biddle and his *Wasp* shipmates were prisoners for two weeks in Bermuda before being exchanged and returned to the United States.

Biddle spent the winter of 1812–1813 in Philadelphia, grudgingly accepting the command of the Delaware gunboat flotilla in early April until a more prestigious post, commanding the sloop of war *Hornet*, was offered to him later that month. Unfortunately, Master Commandant Biddle (his commission dated from 5 Mar. 1813) and the *Hornet* were blockaded in New London, Connecticut, in June 1813 along with Stephen Decatur's *United States* and Jacob Jones's *Macedonian*. *Hornet* escaped alone on 18 November 1814, but only to New York, where in January 1815 a squadron led by Decatur and including *Hornet* attempted to elude the British blockaders again. The British captured *President*, while the rest of the squadron rendezvoused at Tristan da Cunha in March 1815, just after *Hornet* captured the brig-sloop *Penguin*. *Peacock* and *Hornet* continued on their planned cruise to the Indian Ocean until the British ship of the line *Cornwallis* encountered them on 27 April and chose to pursue the slower vessel, *Hornet*. Biddle's excellent seamanship and his crew's efforts in lightening the sloop succeeded in evading *Cornwallis* after a grueling two-day chase. *Hornet*'s commerce-raiding days were over because she had jettisoned most of her provisions and gear and all but one gun. The ship headed for the neutral port of San Salvador, Brazil, where Biddle was informed on 9 June that the war was over. *Hornet* returned to New York on 29 July, and Biddle learned that during his last wartime cruise, the navy had promoted him to captain (28 Feb. 1815).

The postwar naval reduction left Biddle unemployed for almost two years until the Navy Department offered him the command of the sloop *Ontario* in May 1817. Biddle's cruise began in December 1817, with orders to deliver several American commissioners to their Latin American posts, to protect American shipping interests off Valparaiso and Lima, and to stake claim to the Oregon Territory. Biddle performed his diplomatic mission to the satisfaction of most, especially the mercantile community, and his planting the American flag on the southern bank of the Columbia River in August 1818 established the U.S. claim there for adjudication in the 1840s. After a cruise of 589 days, Biddle returned to Philadelphia for another period of forced unemployment.

In March 1822, with the frigate *Macedonian* as his flagship, Biddle assumed command of the West India Squadron, with orders to capture the pirates who were decimating American commerce in the Caribbean. As commander of a squadron, Biddle rated the courtesy title of commodore. The squadron seized thirty pirate vessels and established a convoy to Florida for American merchantmen, but it failed to stop the illegal traffic because it lacked authority to pursue the pirates onto Cuban territory. An outbreak of yellow fever among *Macedonian*'s crew forced Biddle to interrupt his West Indian tour during the summer of 1822 and return to the United States. He resumed command of the West India Squadron in the fall of 1822 in the frigate *Congress*, but he failed to curtail the piratical attacks and almost lost his flagship to a hurricane.

Biddle's most distasteful cruise, from June to December 1823, was transporting a diplomatic entourage of fourteen people; their furniture and luggage turned *Congress* into a junk-laden vessel. He then spent 1824 serving as a defense witness at a court-martial and taking a leave of absence to accompany an ailing cousin to Europe. He was commandant of the Philadelphia Navy Yard from May 1825 to April 1826.

Biddle's diplomatic skills shone as head of the newly established Brazil Squadron during his tenure from May 1826 to late summer 1828. He succeeded in protecting American commerce in the region in the midst of the war between Argentina and Brazil.

While he was in command of the Mediterranean Squadron from October 1829 to August 1832, Biddle and two other commissioners successfully negotiated America's first treaty with Turkey, which protected American commerce. The physical and mental strains of his Mediterranean command damaged his health severely. During the mid-1830s Biddle was on inactive status because of illness or because his seniority enabled him to reject assignments that did not offer either a sea command or shore duty in Philadelphia. In 1838 he accepted the governorship of the Naval Asylum at Philadelphia and within a year had added a school for midshipmen to his responsibilities. After leaving the asylum in 1842, he again took an extended leave to attend to his ailing brother Nicholas.

Never one to reject a sea command, the 62-year-old Biddle accepted "with pleasure" the command of the ship of the line *Columbus* and the sloop *Vincennes*, with orders to exchange ratifications of the Treaty of Wanghia, America's first diplomatic agreement with China. The vessels left New York in June 1845; after exchanging the ratified treaty on 31 December, Biddle spent the next six months establishing better trade relations with the Chinese. He left China in July 1846 to try to open Japanese ports to U.S. commerce, but the Japanese rejected his overtures.

Columbus left Japan on 29 July, and on reaching Honolulu on 9 September Biddle learned that the department had ordered him to command American naval forces in California. His administrative skills shone there: he sorted out a complicated command structure, replaced a paper blockade with a limited one, and established a moderate civil government. Biddle and his flagship *Columbus* left California on 25 July 1847 and entered Chesapeake Bay on 3 March 1848, ending a 33-month cruise around the world. He looked forward to retirement, but he died in Philadelphia within six months.

Biddle never married, but when not at sea he devoted his time to his large family in Philadelphia. He enjoyed his periods of leave between appointments, staying with his family at "Andalusia," the home of his brother Nicholas. He was paternalistic and a mild disciplinarian toward his crew, and he championed education for midshipmen. He excelled in gunnery and seamanship during his encounters with *Penguin* and *Cornwallis*. If Biddle received his hero status from the American people for his actions during the War of 1812, his peacetime service of twenty-three years was studded with many successes and only a few failures. He was independently wealthy and did not need his navy pay to subsist on, except during a short period of financial reverses in the early 1840s. Year after year his country called on him to undertake delicate diplomatic missions because it could rely on his discreet but forceful stance. He served in the navy until he was sixty-five, accepting a final, arduous mission to China because he loved the diplomatic challenge and sea command.

• Official naval correspondence between Biddle and the secretary of the navy is in the National Archives, Record Group 45, Naval Records Collection of the Office of Naval Records and Library, 1775–1910, M148 and M125; Letters to Biddle from the secretary are in M149. Also useful for the cruise of the *Ontario* is "Report of Capt. James Biddle, Commanding the U.S.S. *Ontario*, 1817–1819" in M902. Biddle's service record is in Record Group 24, Records of the Bureau of Naval Personnel, M330. Other Biddle correspondence is at Andalusia, the Biddle family estate near Philadelphia, with smaller collections at the Historical Society of Pennsylvania, the Historical Society of Delaware, the University of Michigan, the Library of Congress, and Yale University. A full-scale study of Biddle is David F. Long, *Sailor-Diplomat: A Biography of Commodore James Biddle, 1783–1848* (1983), a historical sketch of Biddle and the pre–Civil War navy. Theodore Roosevelt, *The Naval War of 1812* (1882; repr. 1987), and William S. Dudley et al., eds., *The Naval War of 1812: A Documentary History*, vols. 1 and 2 (1985, 1992), cover the operational themes of that war.

CHRISTINE F. HUGHES

BIDDLE, Nicholas (10 Sept. 1750–7 Mar. 1778), naval officer, was born in Philadelphia, Pennsylvania, the son of William Biddle, a merchant, and Mary Scull, a map purveyor. With only a basic academy education, he entered the merchant service at the age of thirteen on the *Ann and Almack*. His service on this British trader proved Biddle to be a courageous and determined seaman. During a voyage to the Caribbean the ship was lost at sea, and Biddle, along with other crew members, survived for two months on a desert island before being rescued by a Spanish sloop. Upon returning to Philadelphia, Biddle enlisted in the British Royal Navy in 1770 with the rank of midshipman. He later applied for service on a 1773 expedition to the Arctic Circle led by Captain Phipps, Lord Musgrave, but was turned down because of his youth. Determined to join the expedition, Biddle resigned from the navy and joined the cruise as an ordinary seaman. His messmate during this voyage was midshipman Horatio Nelson.

Biddle left the Royal Navy shortly after the Boston Tea Party as relations between Great Britain and her American colonies deteriorated. In 1775 he enlisted in the Continental navy and, due to his experience, received the rank of captain. The government of Pennsylvania assigned him to command the galley *Franklin* with orders to defend the Delaware coastline, but he soon tired of the post's inactivity and requested a transfer. To his delight, the navy assigned him command of the *Andrea Doria* under the direction of the united colonies' naval commander-in-chief, Esek Hopkins. In the spring of 1776 Hopkins's fleet set out to raid British shipping along the Virginia coast. The fleet instead used the opportunity to capture Forts Montague and Nassau in the Bahamas, despite the fact that the operation was, at best, a misinterpretation of orders. Hopkins then led the fleet to Rhode Island, where his poor leadership resulted in serious damage to the flotilla. This cruise led to Hopkins's eventual court-martial and censure, but it also led to recognition of Biddle as a superior naval officer. He continued to raid British shipping in the North Atlantic, and during an engagement off the coast of Newfoundland he captured two armed transports with a complement of over 400 Highlanders en route to Boston.

By April 1776 the Marine Committee of the Continental Congress had commissioned thirteen frigates, but only ten had been launched. Biddle received command of the first of these warships, the 32-gun *Randolph*, in October. The career of the *Randolph* began inauspiciously when, shortly after leaving port in February 1777, the main mast sheared away during a violent storm. Biddle's own inspection of the mast proved that it was rotten, having been warehoused for eighteen years. Repairs were made in Charleston, after which Biddle set sail for targets of opportunity in the West Indies. Only two weeks out, Biddle captured the twenty-gun *True Briton*, along with three accompanying merchantmen. The British navy enclosed the *Randolph* in Charleston from December 1777 through January 1778, but Biddle used the delay to secure funds and vessels from South Carolina for a new expedition. He also met and became engaged to Elizabeth Elliott Baker, the daughter of a local landholder.

Biddle's final cruise began in February 1778, when the *Randolph* and four smaller warships left Charleston outfitted with volunteers from the First South Carolina Continental Infantry. Upon discovering that the British blockade ships had withdrawn, Biddle swung his contingent toward the West Indies. On 7 March, sixty leagues east of Barbados, the *Randolph* met the 64-gun British ship of the line *Yarmouth*, commanded by Captain Nicholas Vincent. Biddle refused to show his ship's colors until the British frigate drew within hailing distance and demanded identification. Biddle responded, "This is the Continental frigate *Randolph!*" Instantly, the American ensign was raised in conjunction with a volley from the *Randolph*'s six- and twelve-pound guns. The *Yarmouth*, taken by surprise, was slow to respond. Biddle's tightly organized and well-trained crews fired three times faster than their opponent. The firepower of the *Yarmouth* proved to be superior, however, when, after a twenty-minute engagement, the *Randolph* disintegrated in a tremendous explosion resulting from a shot that landed in her forward magazine. Records indicate Biddle's powder may have been unusually volatile because it had been exposed to moisture while the ship was careened to scrape her bow in Charleston. Biddle died at his post, still issuing orders from a chair, as the ship's surgeon examined the wounds he had received from heavy enemy fire.

With Biddle's death the Continental navy lost one of its most experienced and courageous ship commanders. His career, though short, provided the young American navy with crucial tactical as well as morale-building victories. The manner of his death gave rise to one of the first legends of American naval tradition.

• Biddle's correspondence is located in various collections, the most useful of which is William B. Clark and William James Morgan, eds., *Naval Documents of the American Revolution* (1964). His personal papers are held by the estate of Edward Biddle in Philadelphia. Biddle's own surviving memoirs were published as "Biographical Memoirs of the Late Captain Nicholas Biddle," *Port Folio* 2 (Oct. 1809): 285–93. The Biddle family has also published several biographies, including James S. Biddle, ed., *Autobiography of Charles Biddle* (1883), which contains accounts of Nicholas's early life, and Edward Biddle, "Captain Nicholas Biddle," *United States Naval Institute Proceedings* 43 (Sept. 1917): 1993–2003. The most complete biography available is William Bell Clark, *Captain Dauntless: The Story of Nicholas Biddle of the Continental Navy* (1949). Biddle's service record in the Continental navy can be found in numerous sources, some of which are Gardner W. Allen, *A Naval History of the American Revolution* (1917; repr., 1962); John Van Duyn Southworth, *The Age of Sails: the Story of Naval Warfare under Sail, 1213 A.D.–1853 A.D.* (1968); Nathan Miller, *Sea of Glory: The Continental Navy Fights for Independence, 1775–1783* (1974); William M. Fowler, Jr., *Rebels Under Sail: The American Navy during the Revolution* (1976); and Edward L. Beach, *The United States Navy: 200 Years* (1986).

JAMES W. STENNETT

BIDDLE, Nicholas (8 Jan. 1786–27 Feb. 1844), banker, was born in Philadelphia, Pennsylvania, the son of Charles Biddle, a successful merchant and the vice president of the Supreme Executive Council of Pennsylvania, and Hannah Shepard. A precocious young man, serious beyond his years, Biddle hardly had a boyhood at all, entering the University of Pennsylvania at ten. Although he was ready to graduate at thirteen, his family sent him for further study to the College of New Jersey at Princeton, from which he graduated in 1801, the valedictorian of his class. He returned to Philadelphia to study law with his elder brother William Biddle and the well-known jurist William Lewis.

In 1804 Biddle accepted the invitation of John Armstrong, the newly appointed minister to France, to accompany him to Paris as his secretary. Biddle remained in Europe until 1807, traveling extensively, first through northern and eastern France and Switzerland and then across Italy, Sicily, Malta, and Greece, which aroused his enthusiasm for that country's language, history, and architecture. He returned to Paris in 1806 and resigned his position, intending to travel in Belgium, Germany, and Holland, but quickly tired of these areas. In London he accepted the offer of American ambassador James Monroe to act as his temporary secretary.

On his return to Philadelphia, Biddle rejoined the Tuesday Club, a literary society, regularly contributed to the *Port Folio*, and enjoyed the life of a man of letters. He also resumed his legal studies and was admitted to the Pennsylvania bar in December 1809. The following year he was elected to the lower house of the Pennsylvania legislature as an American Republican. In 1811 he married Jane Craig; they had five children. Upon Joseph Dennie's death in 1812, Biddle briefly became editor of the *Port Folio* and began work on the narrative *History of the Expedition of Captains Lewis and Clark* (1814). Biddle preferred writing to politics and refused to run for reelection so that he could finish this project, but he had made a name for himself in his brief career in the legislature as an advocate of public education and a learned defender of the Bank of the United States.

During the War of 1812 Biddle assisted his father, the chairman of the Philadelphia Committee of Defense, and was elected in 1814 to a four-year term in the state senate. In that body he prepared Pennsylvania's response to the antiwar and states' rights–oriented resolutions of the Hartford Convention, reflecting his strong nationalist views and ending his association with the Federalists. In part at the urging of his wife, Biddle attempted to obtain a foreign appointment from his friend President Monroe and twice ran unsuccessfully for Congress as a Republican. Eventually Monroe found him the federal job suited to his talents. In fact the president gave him two jobs in quick succession. One was to compile a volume on "the laws and regulations of foreign countries relative to commerce, moneys, weights and measures," which appeared as *The Commercial Digest* (1819). More importantly, Monroe nominated Biddle to serve as a government director of the Second Bank of the United States in an attempt to reform the institution that was plagued in its early years by political influence, mismanagement, and corruption.

Biddle cooperated with the new president of the bank, Langdon Cheves, but believed that the South Carolinian's severely deflationary measures, which turned public opinion in the South and the West against the bank, should have been tempered by greater use of bills of exchange purchased by the interior branches and drawn on the banks in the commercial centers. Increasingly Cheves's conservative policy alienated Biddle, who argued fruitlessly for a more flexible approach. Although he voted for Cheves's reelection in 1821, he strongly disapproved of his decision to placate the stockholders by the resumption of dividends, which seemed to reward those speculating in the bank's stock. In December 1821 Biddle retired from the board. That year he had been nominated as a candidate for the U.S. Senate, but the legislature failed to agree on anyone to fill the vacancy.

Out of government momentarily, Biddle became a gentleman farmer, developing the commercial potential of his wife's family estate, "Andalusia," on the Delaware River in Bucks County, Pennsylvania. He returned to the intellectual life of Philadelphia through active participation in the Wistar Association, the American Philosophical Society, and the Philadelphia Academy of Fine Arts. Biddle addressed the Philadelphia Society for Promoting Agriculture, helped organize the Historical Society of Pennsylvania, and served as a trustee of the University of Pennsylvania. On the death of Thomas Jefferson, he was chosen by the American Philosophical Society to deliver the eulogy.

When Cheves decided to resign as president of the bank in 1822, a faction among the stockholders approached Biddle, and both President Monroe and Secretary of the Treasury William Crawford urged him to take the position. After further maneuvering, he was elected by the stockholders' representatives as president of the Second Bank of the United States on 25 November 1822. At the time Biddle was thirty-six years old, and he served in the position for the next fourteen years. The first decade of his presidency of the bank was immensely successful, reviving the popularity of the bank and building his personal reputation as the nation's leading financier. Brilliantly managing the bank, he helped steer the American economy through one of its most spectacular periods of growth and development. Biddle set out to implement the changes in policy he had advocated while a member of the board. First, he carefully constructed the bank's board, influencing the choice of eight new private directors, while Monroe appointed Biddle and four others as the public directors. The most important addition was Thomas Cadwalader, Biddle's close friend and confidant, who served throughout as Biddle's "second in command," handling delicate financial and political negotiations and acting as a cautious and conservative counterweight to the impetuous and daring young president.

Biddle's initial actions were designed to spur the economy by increasing the business loans of the bank dramatically. But he intended generally to act countercyclically, tightening and easing credit to dampen the effects of outside forces. In 1825 and again in 1829 Biddle was able to relieve the constriction of credit by the Bank of England and cushion the American economy against the behavior of British capitalists. He was also concerned about the state of the national currency, made up in part of the notes of the bank and those of the state chartered banks. Because the bank was the largest and the only national institution with branches in practically every state and commercial center, Biddle controlled the uniform value of the notes of the bank and also forced the state banks to maintain their paper money at face value, thus guaranteeing a sound currency. By 1830 the Second Bank of the United States was more popular than at any other time during its existence.

Nevertheless, the bank continued to have enemies who believed that its existence violated the Constitution and that corporations were inherently monopolies at war with economic individualism and personal liberty. Unfortunately for Biddle, one such opponent of the bank was President Andrew Jackson. The bank had not been an issue in Jackson's election in 1828, and Biddle himself voted for him. Not until the new president's first annual message introduced a note of displeasure with the bank did Biddle become alarmed. Politicians in New Hampshire and Kentucky, attempting to influence branches of the bank for their own ends, brought charges of anti-Jackson activity against the bank and Biddle. He attempted to protect the bank from the politicians by providing as much information to the president as possible, investigating the various charges of partisan behavior and reporting his findings either through Jackson's intimate friend William Lewis or personally. Ironically, in one such meeting the president praised the bank and its management for helping to pay off the national debt but repeated his belief that the bank was unconstitutional. Jackson assured Biddle, "I do not dislike your bank any more than all banks."

Consequently, Biddle had to find ways to counter the president's prejudices if the bank were to be rechartered, which he believed crucial to the nation's economic well being. He conducted a campaign to inform the public by encouraging economically sophisticated men, like Jefferson's secretary of the treasury Albert Gallatin, to write articles defending the bank. James Madison wrote a public letter defending the bank, and Biddle penned an anonymous reply to the bank's critics. In Washington, Biddle's efforts to influence the situation involved lobbying by Cadwalader among Jacksonian congressmen and cabinet members, most of whom favored recharter. When informants in New York and Washington indicated that the time might be propitious, Biddle moved to obtain a new charter in early January 1832. Sure that Jackson would be reelected, he hoped to remove the question of recharter "from all party character" by concentrating on the probank Jacksonians, who were urging the president to either reverse his stand against recharter or leave the matter to Congress. Henry Clay, however, had advised Biddle to seek a new charter and made Jackson's veto an issue in the 1832 election.

The hard money forces initiated an investigation of the bank, hoping to turn up evidence to justify rejecting the bill to recharter. This was clearly a political exercise that altered few votes in Congress and only confirmed Jackson in his course. The majority of both houses of Congress passed the recharter bill, and Jackson responded with a veto on 10 July 1832. Biddle had expected that but was surprised by the tone of the president's message, which he thought had "all the fury of a chained panther biting the bars of his cage."

Unable to override the veto, Biddle operated the bank through 1833 in a manner he described as "inoffensive usefulness," but Jackson's decision to withdraw the government deposits from the bank to forestall any attempts to revive recharter initiated a new phase in his "war" against the bank. Biddle continued to hope that the deposits might be restored and that the bank would be rechartered. He made it clear to Jackson's friends and advisers that he and the directors were ready to compromise on changes in the charter but that he had to run the affairs of the bank with an eye to the behavior of the administration and Congress, whose economic policies and legislation were divided and contradictory. By 1834 Biddle was forced to wind up the bank's business, and the result was a contraction of credit. He tried to act in the interest of the economy as a whole, but at times in the process alienated not only the antibank element among the Jacksonians but also some of the richest and most powerful New York City financiers and leading members of the Whig coalition, who accused Biddle of trying to provoke a financial crisis.

In 1836 "Biddle's Bank," as Jackson called it, became the Bank of the United States of Pennsylvania under a new charter issued by that state's legislature. But no state bank had the impact on the economy of the national bank. Biddle's wings were clipped, and he has been criticized for his seeming refusal to understand this. He was forced also to function in a less favorable atmosphere than at any other time while he served as the president of the bank. At first Biddle succeeded in leading the response of American banks to the panic of 1837, which had been triggered by the Bank of England's sharp increase of interest rates. When he attempted a second time to play the role of a quasi-central banker in the crisis of 1839, managing a diminished institution in the midst of an economic crisis over which he had no control, his luck ran out. He could not stabilize the cotton market and weakened his institution at a time when every bit of its resources needed to be focused upon its own survival.

Biddle resigned in March 1839, and two years later, in the depths of the depression, "Biddle's Bank" closed its doors. Out of office he had continued to play a role in the bank's activities, but he was often overruled by other elements among the stockholders. When the bank failed, his enemies blamed Biddle, and they also circulated rumors that he had lent a large sum to a friend's wife with whom he was having an affair. His longtime personal friend, Democrat Charles J. Ingersoll, noted that the "dogs" that once "licked his hands and fawned on his footsteps" were now tearing him apart.

During his retirement, Andalusia, which Biddle had redesigned along Greek lines like the buildings of the Bank of the United States and Girard College, became something of a salon visited by both European exiles and notable Americans. Biddle had been quite ill for some time, and he showed the signs of clinical depression when he died at Andalusia of bronchitis accompanied by dropsy.

• Substantial collections of Biddle papers are at the Library of Congress, Princeton University, and the Historical Society of Pennsylvania. *The Correspondence of Nicholas Biddle Dealing with National Affairs, 1807–1844*, ed. Reginald C. McGrane (1919), remains useful. *Autobiography of Charles Biddle, Vicepresident of the Supreme Executive Council of Pennsylvania, 1745–1821* (1883) provides useful material on the Biddle family and Nicholas's youth and includes a brief sketch of his life. Thomas P. Govan, *Nicholas Biddle: Nationalist and Public Banker, 1786–1844* (1959), is a superb biography that serves as a brief in the subject's defense. Arthur M. Schlesinger, Jr., *The Age of Jackson* (1945), and Robert V. Remini, *Andrew Jackson and the Bank War: A Study in the Growth of Presidential Power* (1967), present the president's point of view. Jean A. Wilburn, *Biddle's Bank: The Crucial Years* (1967), details the popularity of the bank and the political problems faced by Biddle. Ralph C. H. Catterall, *The Second Bank of the United States* (1903); Fritz Redlich, *The Molding of American Banking: Men and Ideas* (2 vols., 1951); and Walter B. Smith, *Economic Aspects of the Second Bank of the United States* (1953), are excellent economic studies that favorably view Biddle's presidency. Bray Hammond, *Banks and Politics in America from the Revolution to the Civil War* (1957), is a classic economic and political history by a former director of the Federal Reserve. Hammond's claim that Biddle acted like a central banker is disputed by economist Peter Temin, *The Jacksonian Economy* (1969).

WILLIAM G. SHADE

BIDERMANN, Jacques Antoine (1790–8 June 1865), businessman, was born in Paris, France, the son of Jacques Bidermann, a wealthy financier, and Gabrielle Aimée Odier. So that he might escape the tumult of the French Revolution, the younger Bidermann—who went by the name Antoine—was raised at his family's home in Winterthur, Switzerland, and there trained for business. Back in Paris by 1804, he went to work for his father, who had invested in Eleuthère Irénée du Pont's gunpowder concern in Delaware.

In 1814, after Pierre Bauduy, a partner in the Delaware operation, had begun to suggest that du Pont was misusing investors' money, Bidermann's father sent Bidermann to the United States to review the situation. Examining the account books and finding them satisfactory, Bidermann sided with du Pont and eased the investors' qualms. He subsequently helped maneuver Bauduy out of the firm by purchasing part of his interest in it. Bidermann thereupon took Bauduy's place not only as du Pont's partner but also as his sales manager. This affiliation with du Pont became more than a matter of business in 1816, when Bidermann married his partner's daughter, Evelina Gabrielle du Pont. The couple had one son.

Through the next two decades Bidermann, headquartered at the du Pont works on Brandywine Creek, played a central role in the financial and commercial operations of a firm that had already become the largest gunpowder manufacturer in the Americas. Although not greatly involved in the actual making of the powder, Bidermann—who upon his father's death in 1817 had acquired an even larger share in the company—kept track of daily accounts, corresponded with established customers and tried to win new ones, angled for American and foreign government contracts, purchased supplies, supervised the firm's sales agents, and traveled on the company's behalf. By the early 1830s E. I. du Pont de Nemours & Co. was producing nearly one million pounds of gunpowder annually.

Bidermann had become such an important part of the business that when E. I. du Pont died in 1834, his heirs decided that control of the firm would first pass to Bidermann rather than to du Pont's sons, none of whom was yet prepared to take the helm. Bidermann presided as chief executive of E. I. du Pont de Nemours & Co. for three years, as one of his brothers-in-law, Alfred du Pont, involved himself in the manufacturing operations and another, Henry du Pont, learned to tend to the finances. The company thrived such that Bidermann was able to travel to France, settle up with the du Pont family's creditors, and buy out the du Pont Company's French shareholders. This allowed for the reorganization of the company into an entirely American firm whose ownership was vested exclusively with the du Pont family. Bidermann spurned a directorship, having determined to retire upon the considerable income his own and his wife's shares in the company generated. The presidency was at that point assumed by Alfred du Pont, to whom Bidermann loaned $56,000 to keep things running smoothly.

In 1837, the year of his retirement, Bidermann began construction of an estate on a 450-acre plot he had purchased not far from the du Pont site in Delaware. Named "Winterthur" after his family's Swiss home, it eventually encompassed a three-story Greek revival house, extensive gardens and orchards, and a model farm and dairy. Every bit the scientific farmer, Bidermann looked after the planting and livestock breeding until late in the 1850s, when ill health compelled him to rent out the fields.

After Evelina's death in 1863, Antoine Bidermann left Delaware to live with his son in Paris, where he died. He had played a crucial part in sustaining one of America's most prominent industrial concerns through its early decades. The year after Bidermann's death, Winterthur was purchased by Henry du Pont. Passed down through the family, the house was remodeled and much enlarged, and the estate was opened to the public as the Winterthur Museum in 1951. It houses one of the nation's outstanding collections of furniture and the decorative arts.

• Bidermann's papers are at the Eleutherian Mills Historical Library in Greenville, Del. Considerable information on Bidermann is in E. McClung Fleming, "History of the Winterthur Estate," *Winterthur Portfolio* 1 (1964): 9–51. See also Bessie du Pont, *E. I. du Pont de Nemours & Co., a History, 1802–1902* (1920); Leonard Mosely, *Blood Relations: The Rise and Fall of the du Ponts of Delaware* (1980); and Marc Duke, *The du Ponts: Portrait of a Dynasty* (1976). An obituary is in the *Delaware State Journal and Statesman*, 11 July 1865.

PATRICK G. WILLIAMS

BIDWELL, John (5 Aug. 1819–4 Apr. 1900), California pioneer, agriculturalist, and politician, was born on a farm in Chautauqua County, New York, the son of Abram Bidwell and Clarissa Griggs, farmers. The family moved to Pennsylvania and then Ohio. John was bookish, although he had only three winter months of schooling each year, at best. But he walked 300 miles to attend Kingsville Academy in 1836 and, after a year, was elected its principal. He returned home to teach, then went to Missouri to farm. There, a western trader told him of fertile California, a land of perpetual spring. So he helped organize a western emigration society.

At the jumping-off point of Independence, Missouri, Bidwell found that most of the 500 men who had signed up to emigrate had developed cold feet. Only a dozen or so wagons composed the first overland train to California. Later it came to be called the Bidwell-Bartleson Party because of the former's prominence. It was led by a mediocre captain, John Bartleson. The conscientious young Bidwell, named the party's secretary, showed natural leadership on the plains and demonstrated the qualities that would distinguish him all his life. He was not just active and courageous (without being reckless), but stable, self-disciplined, prudent, modest, quiet, and reticent and almost excessively honest.

The so-called Pilgrims of the Pacific had to leave their wagons in the desert east of the Sierra Nevada and reached California almost starving. Captain John Sutter not only took Bidwell in, he made him his trusted majordomo. Bidwell's first major job was to transfer property from Fort Ross, just bought by Sutter from the Russians, to New Helvetia, or Sutter's Fort, on the American River near its junction with the Sacramento River. In 1844 Bidwell imitated Sutter in becoming a Mexican citizen and a (very nominal) Catholic in order to secure a land grant, Ulpinos. But it and a later rancho, "Colusa," were low and marshy, full of mosquitoes. Bidwell did not develop either grant, but waited until he could buy a beautiful site (already granted to someone else) in the upper Sacramento Valley. In 1845 Bidwell was captured with Sutter in the latter's disastrous campaign on behalf of Governor Manuel Micheltorena. He was pardoned and, along with Sutter, allowed to return to pick up the pieces at New Helvetia. Bidwell only reluctantly participated in the Bear Flag Revolt of 1846, but he served as an officer in John C. Frémont's California Battalion during the Mexican War. He was alcalde, or magistrate, at

San Luís Rey mission, where he demonstrated his sympathy toward Indians.

After the war Bidwell left Sutter's employ amicably. He prospected for gold in 1848 and founded Bidwell's Bar on the Feather River. But his first love was agriculture, particularly horticulture. In 1849 he was able to buy 22,000 acres of flower-brightened grassland under great valley oaks near sycamore-shaded *Arroyo Chico* (Little Creek). He first imitated his mentor by herding cattle and sowing wheat. But he was much more of an experimental farmer than Sutter, and so he also planted oats, barley, corn, and grapevines. He dug irrigation ditches and brought in peach, pear, apple, and cherry trees. He secured better breeds of dairy cows and raised sheep, hogs, chickens, even honeybees, besides the usual cattle and horses. He experimented with figs, olives, quinces, English walnuts, sugarcane, and sorghum. He was one of the first to produce olive oil in California and a very early grower of both almonds and raisins, and he introduced casaba melons and "gyp" (Egyptian) corn to the state. He planted ornamental shrubs and trees, such as magnolias, started a nursery and cannery, and imported modern farm machinery, including threshing machines and fruit dryers. His Chico Ranch was the most successful in all California, and he was elected president of the State Agricultural Society.

Bidwell's prowess in agricultural activities led to his other, less successful, career in politics. He was always public-spirited and civic-minded, and he was chosen as a delegate to the 1849 constitutional convention and elected to the first state senate in 1850. A Stephen Douglas Democrat, he was a delegate to state conventions in 1854 and 1860 and to the national convention in the latter year. He suffered a setback in his failure to win reelection to the state senate, but he was chosen to chair San Francisco's railroad convention in 1859, and he founded the town of Chico in 1860. He was California's most resolute and outspoken Unionist among Democrats and opposed the Copperhead (prosecessionist) sentiment that was strong in the Sacramento Valley during the Civil War. Governor Leland Stanford rewarded his efforts with an appointment as brigadier general of militia. A delegate to the Union party convention, Bidwell was elected to the House of Representatives in 1864. He could do little as a junior congressman, but he fought to save the Department of Agriculture from budget trimmers and against taxation of California wine grape growers, although he had become a teetotaler himself. He declined being renominated for Congress in order to run for governor in 1867 as a Republican, but he was defeated.

Seemingly a confirmed bachelor, Bidwell married when he was forty-eight years old and his bride twenty-nine. She was Anne Kennedy, a strong-minded woman and even more straitlaced than her no-nonsense husband. She was a great influence on him. At her urging, he became a pious Presbyterian, gave up tobacco, and moved from temperance to hard-core Prohibition. He had already given up wine making

and then pulled up the vines and replanted with table and raisin grapevines.

So rigidly moral—incorruptible, and even suspicious of compromise in his devotion to lofty ideals—was Bidwell that he could never become successful in politics. One newspaperman wrote that he was too good a man to be governor. When he ran for governor again in 1875, it was on the ticket of the antimonopoly Peoples Independent party. He lost but ran again in 1890 and was again defeated. In 1892 he was the Prohibition party's presidential candidate. His hopeless race was a gesture of dissent. He identified not only with the party's antialcohol position but also with its other planks. He was in favor of an income tax, woman suffrage, labor arbitration, and government regulation of public utilities. He favored strong "regulation" of immigration, particularly of Chinese. Bidwell received 264,133 votes, the most ever cast for a Prohibition candidate.

The patriarch of Chico gave up politics in his seventies and redevoted himself to agriculture and horticulture. He was active in the fields and orchards to the very end, dying "in harness" as he cut cottonwood logs with a crosscut saw. His widow gave part of the ranch and their 25-room mansion to the people as Bidwell Park.

• Collections of Bidwell papers are at the California State Library and the Bancroft Library, UC-Berkeley. His own reminiscences have often been reprinted as *Echoes of the Past* (1962) and under other titles. The chapter on Bidwell in George R. Stewart's *Good Lives* (1967) is interesting but brief. A substantial study of his life is Rockwell D. Hunt, *John Bidwell: Prince of California Pioneers* (1942). The best account of his overland expedition is Doyce B. Nunis, *The Bidwell-Bartleson Party* (1991). Chad Hoopes, *What Makes a Man* (1973), is based on letters between Bidwell and his wife.

RICHARD H. DILLON

BIEBER, Margarete (31 July 1879–25 Feb. 1978), archaeologist and art historian, was born in Schoenau, Kreis Schwetz, West Prussia (now Przechowo, Kreis Swiece, Poland), the daughter of Jacob Heinrich Bieber, an industrialist, and Valli Bukofzer. In 1899 she went to Berlin, prepared privately and passed her *Abiturium* and *Maturitätsprüfung* (high school diplomas), and registered in classics at the University of Berlin, where she studied with the distinguished scholars Hermann Diels, Ulrich von Wilamowitz-Moellendorff, and Reinhard Kekulé von Stradonitz. In 1904 she transferred to the University of Bonn to become a student of Georg Loeschke; her other teachers there included Paul Clemen and Franz Buecheler. She received her doctorate in 1907, with a dissertation on a Dresden relief representing an actor.

From 1907 to 1914 she traveled in classical lands and lived in Rome, where she became friends with German scholars later noted for their work on ancient monuments, such as Walther Amelung and Gerhart Rodenwaldt, and where she met many international scholars, artists, and musicians, such as Ottorino Respighi. In 1909, as the first woman to receive the prestigious German Archaeological Institute's travel fellowship, she was introduced to the famous classical sites and their excavators, including Wilhelm Dörpfeld, who excavated Olympia, and Sir Arthur Evans, who discovered the Minoan civilization on Crete. Back in Rome, in 1912 and 1913, as a fellow of the German Archaeological Institute, she lived in the Institute building on the Capitoline Hill. Commissioned to write the catalogue of the important collection of ancient sculptures for the Kassel Museum, she pioneered in bringing ancient statues, such as the Kassel Apollo, back to their original state, removing nineteenth-century "restorations."

World War I brought her back to Germany and gave her the opportunity to teach Loeschke's courses at the University of Berlin. There her students included the art historian Erwin Panofsky and his wife, Dora, who, like Bieber, later emigrated to the United States. She became a member of the faculty at the University of Giessen and in 1932 was named full professor. She had just adopted a daughter, Inge, in 1933, when she was dismissed because she was Jewish and left Germany.

After an unhappy year in Oxford she was invited to come to New York (1934) to teach at Barnard College and Columbia University. Gisela Richter, of the Metropolitan Museum of Art, Mary Swindler, author of *Ancient Painting* (1929), and archaeologist Hetty Goldman recommended and helped her. Her colleagues included the foremost scholar on Greek architecture, William Dinsmoor, fellow refugee and art historian Meyer Schapiro, and medievalist Marion Lawrence. Bieber's *The History of the Greek and Roman Theater* (1939) and *Laocoon, the Influence of the Group since Its Rediscovery* (1942) remain basic texts. She reluctantly retired from Columbia in 1948 but continued to teach in its general studies division, at Barnard, the New School for Social Research, and Princeton. She continued to publish important surveys of ancient art, such as *Alexander the Great in Greek and Roman Art* (1964), *The Sculpture of the Hellenistic Age* (1955), and *Ancient Copies* (1977). In the latter work she dealt with Roman copies of Greek statues as Roman art rather than as reflections of Greek art. In numerous articles and reviews, including the series "Excavations in American Museums," she led the movement to place museum objects into a historical and archaeological context. Although fellow archaeologists sometimes criticized her works, many found them fruitful in their own research.

In 1974 Bieber was awarded the Archaeological Institute of America's gold medal for archaeological achievement. A special research grant from the National Endowment for the Humanities in 1976 received considerable attention in the press, but she never completed the projected work on Greek, Etruscan, and Roman dress. In 1976 she retired to her daughter's house in Connecticut, where she died.

In a predominantly male and highly specialized field, Bieber opened the way for women and for interdisciplinary study. While maintaining high standards of scholarship in her pioneering work on the restoration of ancient statues, in her teaching, and in her publications, she was also able throughout her long professional career to communicate archaeological findings to a broader audience.

• Correspondence from Bieber's former students, friends, and colleagues, as well as her personal library, are in the Tulane University Library. Larissa Bonfante-Warren and Rolf Winkes, eds., *Bibliography of the Works of Margarete Bieber: For Her 90th Birthday* (1969), contains 327 items. See also "Addenda, 1969–1974," *American Journal of Archaeology* 79 (1975): 147–48, and "Miscellaneous Additions," in *Women as Interpreters of the Visual Arts, 1820–1979*, ed. Claire Richter Sherman (1981), pp. 273–74. *Women as Interpreters*, pp. 238–74, includes an account of Bieber's life by Larissa Bonfante, based in part on Bieber's unpublished "Autobiography of a Female Scholar" (1959–1960). The necrology by Evelyn Harrison, *American Journal of Archaeology* 82 (1978): 573–75, has quotations from a published account of Bieber's German career to 1933.

LARISSA BONFANTE

BIEDERWOLF, William Edward (29 Sept. 1867–3 Sept. 1939), Presbyterian evangelist, was born in Monticello, Indiana, the son of German immigrants Michael Biederwolf and Abolona Schnetzer. At the age of eighteen, while teaching at a public school located near Monticello, he made a public profession of faith in Jesus Christ and joined the Presbyterian church at Monticello. His conversion was strongly influenced by his experience in Sunday school and also by his sister Kate, whose death of tuberculosis at the age of twenty thwarted her own plans to become a missionary.

After attending Wabash College in Crawfordsville, Indiana, Biederwolf went to Princeton College in 1890, receiving his B.A. in 1892, his M.A. in 1894, and his B.D. from Princeton Theological Seminary in 1895. During summer vacations he worked at rescue missions in the Bowery and Scranton, Pennsylvania. Following his graduation from the seminary, Biederwolf worked with evangelist B. Fay Mills for one year. After marrying his childhood classmate Ida Casad in 1896, Biederwolf spent eighteen months studying at the Universities of Berlin and Erlangen in Germany and at the Sorbonne in Paris. While at the University of Berlin he frequently preached at the city's American Church.

Biederwolf returned to the United States in 1897, was ordained as a Presbyterian minister, and became the pastor of the Broadway Presbyterian Church in Logansport, Indiana. Commissioned as a chaplain with the 161st Indiana Volunteers during the Spanish-American War in 1898, Biederwolf served six months with his regiment in the South and six months in Cuba, ministering to the sick and injured, holding daily chapel services, and working for conversions. He recorded the experiences of these Indiana soldiers in *History of the One Hundred and Sixty-first Regiment, Indiana Volunteer Infantry* (1899). After this military service, he pastored his congregation in Logansport for another two years, but, inspired by his success as an army chaplain, he decided in 1900 to become a professional evangelist.

For the next thirty years Biederwolf crisscrossed the United States, holding hundreds of revival meetings in cities and small towns and becoming one of the country's best-known and most respected evangelists. Like Billy Sunday, the most famous evangelist of the early twentieth century, Biederwolf stressed patriotism and prohibition and argued that American progress depended upon acceptance of revivalistic Christianity. He promoted civic reform much more than Sunday did, however, perhaps because of his experience with urban rescue missions. In 1911 and 1912 Biederwolf helped lead the Men and Religion Forward movement, which attempted to convert sinners, to inspire more men to participate in church life, and to motivate Christians to improve social conditions by holding eight-day crusades in seventy-six major North American cities and more than 1,000 towns.

After working as an assistant to another evangelist, J. Wilbur Chapman, for five years, Biederwolf began his own evangelistic ministry in 1906. For the next three decades he proclaimed the gospel throughout the country, concentrating on medium-sized cities in the American heartland. While Biederwolf used magical illusions and athletic feats (he had played four years of varsity football at Princeton) to attract and entertain listeners, it was primarily his powerful preaching and administrative skill that drew thousands each night to his services. In his sermons, Biederwolf combined the moving stories of the nineteenth-century evangelist Dwight Moody with the fiery oratory of Billy Sunday. He excelled at painting word pictures and at adapting his messages to different groups of listeners. Local committees were established in every city to prepare for and promote his crusades, extensive advertising was employed, and parades featuring a wide cross section of the community were often arranged to arouse interest. Always eager to improve evangelists' methods and to safeguard their reputations, Biederwolf served as the president of the Interdenominational Association of Evangelists, created in 1904 to unify and standardize the profession. Also, from 1914 to 1917 he served as executive director of the Federal Council of Churches' commission on evangelism. In 1923–1924 Biederwolf conducted well-attended crusades in Australia and many Asian countries. While visiting Korea, he saw firsthand the suffering of lepers and soon established a leper colony in that country and also became the director of the American Mission to Lepers.

In addition to his work as an evangelist, Biederwolf was involved in a number of other endeavors. In 1909 he established the Family Altar League to promote family devotions; for many years he served as its president. For seventeen years he also served as the director of the Winona Lake Bible Conference; its summer meetings featured many outstanding Bible teachers and preachers, including William Jennings Bryan. From 1923 until 1933 he was the director of the Winona Lake School of Theology, and in 1933 he became its

president. During the last ten years of his life he pastored the Royal Poinciana Chapel in Palm Beach, Florida, a nondenominational congregation of 1,500 members, many of whom were very wealthy.

Always interested in books, Biederwolf organized and owned the Winona Publishing Company, located in Chicago, which published religious literature and song books. He wrote more than thirty books himself on a variety of topics, many of which were collections of his sermons, illustrations for sermons, defenses of premillennialism, treatises on evangelism, discussions of practical theology, and critiques of cults. Most notable are *The Evangelistic Situation* (1920), *Evangelism* (1921), *Evangelistic Sermons* (1922), *The Millennium Bible* (1924), *Illustrations from Mythology* (1927), *Illustrations from Art* (1927), *Whipping-Post Theology* (1934), and *Frozen Assets* (1939).

An excellent administrator, an inspiring preacher, a popular author, and a highly successful evangelist, Biederwolf did much to help shape the methods and message of revivalism during the first thirty years of the twentieth century. Along with evangelists Reuben Torrey, J. Wilbur Chapman, and Billy Sunday, Biederwolf was a key link between the crusades of Dwight Moody in the late nineteenth century and the modern revivalism of Billy Graham in the years after 1950. He died at home in Monticello.

• Especially important for understanding Biederwolf's defense of revivalism and his attempt to reform the profession are his *The Evangelistic Situation* (1920) and his *Evangelism, Its Justification, Its Operation and Its Value* (1921). Ray E. Garrett, *William Edward Biederwolf: A Biography* (1948), is sketchy and laudatory, but it does contain excerpts from Biederwolf's sermons and books. William McLoughlin, *Modern Revivalism: Charles Grandison Finney to Billy Graham* (1959), provides more critical analysis of and context for Biederwolf's work. For Biederwolf's work with the Winona Lake Bible Conference, see Vincent H. Gaddis, *The Story of Winona Lake* (1949). An obituary is in the *New York Times*, 3 Sept. 1939.

GARY SCOTT SMITH

BIEMILLER, Andrew John (23 July 1906–3 Apr. 1982), labor lobbyist, was born in Sandusky, Ohio, the son of Andrew Frederick Biemiller, a traveling salesman who sold dry goods to small general stores, and Pearl Weber. Andrew Frederick was also chairman of the Republican Committee in Sandusky and a member of the Knights Templar. After her husband's death in the great flu epidemic in 1918, Pearl Biemiller ran a boardinghouse.

With the financial help of his grandmother, Anna Johanna Biemiller, Andrew attended Cornell University, receiving his B.A. in 1926. From 1926 to 1928 he was an instructor in history at Syracuse University. Then he pursued graduate studies (1928–1931) and taught (1929–1931) at the University of Pennsylvania, specializing in the British trade union movement. He was an Episcopalean in his early life, but he became a Quaker in 1929 as a result of the influence of his young radical Quaker friends in Philadelphia. He married Hannah Perot Morris in 1929. They had two children.

In 1932 the Biemillers moved to Milwaukee, Wisconsin, where Biemiller became a reporter on the *Milwaukee Leader*, a Socialist newspaper. From 1932 to 1942, in addition to serving on the executive board, he was labor counselor and general organizer for the Milwaukee Federation of Trade Councils and the Wisconsin State Federation of Labor. He was also a member of the Newspaper Guild and the American Federation of Teachers.

Biemiller resigned from the Socialist party in 1936 after being at odds with members who promoted isolationism. Nevertheless, that year he was elected as a Socialist-Progressive to the Wisconsin State Assembly, where he served as floor leader from 1939 to 1941. He was then appointed assistant to Joseph D. Keenan, vice chairman of the War Production Board (WPB) in Washington, D.C., and was responsible for labor production.

In 1944 Biemiller left the WPB to become a representative in the Seventy-ninth Congress. He lost his reelection bid in 1946, but two years later he again won a seat as a Socialist-Progressive in the Eighty-first Congress. At the 1948 Democratic National Convention, he was a member of the resolutions committee along with Hubert H. Humphrey of Minnesota, who was then running for his first term as U.S. senator. Biemiller drafted the party's revolutionary civil rights platform that Humphrey pushed to adoption. In response Strom Thurmond, then governor of South Carolina, led the Dixiecrats in walking out. After losing another reelection bid for Congress in 1950, and again in 1952, Biemiller abandoned participatory politics.

From 1951 to 1952 Biemiller served as a special assistant to the U.S. secretary of the interior and afterward became a public relations counselor in Washington, D.C. At the same time, he was appointed a legislative lobbyist for the American Federation of Labor, and in 1956 he became director of the newly merged American Federation of Labor–Congress of Industrial Organization's legislative department. Biemiller recalled that, upon appointing him the organization's lobbyist, AFL-CIO president George Meany admonished him, "Don't beg, don't threaten, and don't ever assume you are 100 percent right."

As a lobbyist Biemiller won widespread respect for his resourcefulness and effectiveness. Acknowledging the wisdom of the advice, he noted that "a lobbyist who misleads a member of Congress is through. Because they really do rely on us for information. In fact, make sure that the person you're talking to knows both sides of the argument. You can't ask someone to go out on the floor of the House or Senate with material you've given him unless he also knows the arguments he's going to run into." As chairman, Biemiller was brusque, stern, and effective, claiming "I know people who think the way to lobby is to call a congressman's office and ask some staff person how the congressman is going to vote on a particular bill. But that's not lobbying."

He was a diligent student of House Speaker Sam Rayburn in learning the parliamentary skills that made him an indispensable champion of labor's cause in Congress. In addition to actively pushing for a broad range of social legislation, including the minimum wage, comprehensive health insurance, and federal aid to education, he was an important force in getting the AFL-CIO to support the struggle for passage of civil rights legislation. Biemiller believed that union members were "American citizens as well as members of trade unions" and that labor must be "the people's lobby." For him, all labor issues—including health issues, occupational safety issues, trade issues, and congressional issues—were interelated. Biemiller argued, "And even on bills that don't directly involve your interests, you've got to be on the lookout for amendments that affect the group you're representing." For him, the basic force for progressive change, especially economic change, was "a strong labor movement and effective collective bargaining."

Another of Biemiller's accomplishments was leading organized labor's fight in blocking President Richard Nixon's appointments of Clement F. Haynsworth and G. Harrold Carswell to the Supreme Court. Not characteristically humble, Biemiller said of himself, "Meany used to tell me that if he picked a child to train as a lobbyist, and brought him all the way through, he couldn't have found anyone with a background better than I had."

Biemiller retired from the AFL-CIO in 1978 and lived quietly in Bethesda, Maryland, where he died.

• Biemiller's papers are in the AFL-CIO records at the George Meany Memorial Archives, Silver Spring, Md.; and at the Congressional Research Study Center, University of Oklahoma. Biemiller argues against the question "Should the American People Reject the Welfare State" in *Congressional Digest*, Aug.–Sept. 1950, and argues in favor of the topic "Viewpoint on Federal Aid to Education" in *Congressional Digest*, Nov. 1954. For information concerning Biemiller's life and career, see Gary Fink, ed., *Biographical Dictionary of American Labor* (1974; rev. ed., 1984); Joseph C. Goulden, *Meany: The Unchallenged Strong Man of American Labor* (1972); and "Andrew Biemiller: Labor's Man on the Hill," *Fortune*, Feb. 1959, p. 196. An extensive obituary is in the *AFL-CIO News Service*, 12 Apr. 1982. See also obituaries in the *New York Times* and the *Washington Post*, both 4 Apr. 1982.

DENTON L. WATSON

BIENVILLE, Sieur de. *See* Le Moyne, Jean-Baptiste.

BIERCE, Ambrose Gwinnett (24 June 1842–1914?), author and journalist, was born in the Horse Cave settlement in Meigs County, Ohio, the son of Marcus Aurelius Bierce and Laura Sherwood, farmers. The family was poor and moved several times, eventually settling in Elkhart, Indiana. His parents were strongly evangelical Protestant, but Bierce early resented his religious indoctrination and moved toward agnosticism. He briefly attended the Kentucky Military Institute in 1859. He enlisted at once in the Union army when the Civil War began in 1861 and was soon appointed a sergeant. He was later commissioned a second lieutenant and had risen to first lieutenant when invalided out of the army because of wounds in January 1865. He was brevetted major by President Andrew Johnson in August 1865.

Bierce had more firsthand war experience than any other important nineteenth-century writer. His first battle was at Philippi, and he subsequently fought at Laurel Hill, Carrick's Ford, Greenbrier, Buffalo Hill, Camp Allegheny, Shiloh, Corinth, Perrysville, Murfreesboro, Stone River, Chickamauga, Chattanooga, Lookout Mountain, Missionary Ridge, Rocky Face Ridge, Resaca, Dalton, New Hope Church, Pickett's Mill, Kenesaw Mountain, Coosa River, and Franklin. The Civil War, and the battle of Shiloh in particular, had a seminal influence on Bierce's philosophy and literature, ultimately convincing him that life itself, and not only military operations, was a condition of war.

Bierce worked with the Treasury Department in Alabama until he resigned in 1866, when he was invited by General W. B. Hazen, his former commanding officer, to join a four-man mapping expedition through Indian country in what is now the Dakotas, Montana, Utah, and Nevada. Failing to receive a captaincy in the regular army, Bierce quit when the expedition reached San Francisco and took a job with the U.S. Mint. Within the next year or two, he began to submit fiction and journalistic commentary to San Francisco periodicals, and thus launched his writing career.

Bierce married Mary E. "Mollie" Day on 25 December 1871. They had three children. After a separation beginning around 1888, they were divorced in 1905.

From approximately 1867 until 1900, Bierce lived and worked mostly in the San Francisco area. Several important exceptions were the years 1872 to 1875, when Bierce and his wife lived in London, where he wrote prolifically for a variety of English periodicals, and several months in 1880, when he served as an agent of a Black Hills gold-mining firm. In 1899, Bierce moved permanently to Washington, D.C., where he continued as a journalist until 1909. From 1909 to 1912, he edited the twelve-volume set of his collected works. He then put his affairs in order and in 1913 made a last sentimental visit to some Civil War battlegrounds, traveled to El Paso, and crossed the border into Mexico in late November or early December, ostensibly to observe Pancho Villa's revolution. A last letter from him dated 26 December 1913 was sent from Chihuahua. He then mysteriously disappeared.

Several generations of critics have fruitlessly speculated on Bierce's disappearance or repeated legends of his audacious personality but have largely ignored his outstanding literary achievements. For close to forty years, Bierce was one of the leading journalists of the nation. He wrote for or worked on a variety of periodicals: the *San Francisco News-Letter and California Advertiser, Alta California, Overland Monthly, Argonaut, Wasp,* San Francisco *Examiner, Wave,* and *Cosmopolitan.* Of these, the *Examiner* was the most important: it

became the leading newspaper of the West and the foundation on which William Randolph Hearst built his newspaper empire. Bierce's famous weekly column, "Prattle," became nationally syndicated. It usually consisted of controversial comments on personalities and events in the news, but it also frequently expressed his philosophical positions. In that column Bierce wrote a history of his own times. Though he was often at odds with the views of the majority, most of what were majority views are now dated, whereas Bierce's arguments have often endured as valid positions.

Bierce was a master of irony and invective, and his journalism sparkles with caustic wit. He was far more than a bitter or cantankerous gadfly, however. Bierce's writings were not only entertaining, they were also usually logical, consistent, and based on researched information. A moralist and social critic, he fearlessly attacked rascality, folly, and cruelty in high places but also characterized the public as ignorant, biased, and willful. In 1896, several years before the muckrakers began their investigative journalism, Bierce, supported by Hearst, led the campaign that caused the defeat of Collis P. Huntington's railroad Funding Bill by exposing the lies, bribes, and graft that attended it. In 1898, when the nation eagerly sought war with Spain, Bierce was one of a very few public figures courageous enough to warn against war. In so doing, Bierce contradicted the editorial policy of Hearst, who was instrumental in stirring up war fever. Once the war began, Bierce criticized its execution and turned out to be one of the country's best war correspondents. Although he wrote from San Francisco, he knew more about war than most of the correspondents on the scene, so he was able to sift the truth from the propagandistic battlefront communiques.

Bierce's fame, however, rests on his literary achievements rather than his journalism. A small group of short stories set in the Civil War—chiefly "An Occurrence at Owl Creek Bridge," "A Horseman in the Sky," and "Chickamauga"—have become classics both in America and abroad. Many of his other stories deal perceptively with death and terror. These stories have been widely misinterpreted as being technically brilliant but facetiously grisly, heartless, and pointless; some critics have attempted to link these stories to the cynical definitions of Bierce's popular *Devil's Dictionary.* The definitions are wickedly witty and delightfully quotable but represent too narrow a spectrum of his thought to reflect his philosophy accurately.

Although Bierce began writing short stories in 1871 and continued until 1908, most were written between 1887 and 1893 and were published in the *Examiner* in place of his regular columns. The best were collected in his most important book, *Tales of Soldiers and Civilians* (1891), and were republished and augmented in the collections *In the Midst of Life* (1892) and *Can Such Things Be?* (1893). His stories of war, terror, and death therefore had a gestation period of approximately twenty-five years. During all that time, Bierce was never free from the vivid and unhealed memories of the horrors and carnage he had witnessed in the Civil War. His stories represent his reflections on his experiences and are attempts to work out his philosophy.

Unable to believe in God, Bierce came close to being a Stoic and took seriously the Stoic adage *vivere est militare*, "to live is to be a soldier." As he saw it, although death comes to all, it comes soonest to those who underestimate the perils of life. Even stoicism failed him, however, for he realized that nothing could make humans invulnerable to pain, suffering, and death or always protect them from self-deception. An underlying compassion for humanity links his stories as tragic depictions of inevitable human failure before the indifference and deadliness of existence. Bierce wrote for careful and reflective readers. Beneath dazzling and ironic surfaces, both his fiction and nonfiction are based on well-thought-out positions and seek to challenge his readers with a serious and deeply moral view of life.

• The major collections of Bierce manuscripts, letters, and papers are at the Bancroft Library of the University of California at Berkeley and the Barrett Collection of the Alderman Library of the University of Virginia, Charlottesville. Important holdings of letters are at Stanford University, the Berg Collection of the New York Public Library, and the Library of Congress. Smaller collections of letters are found scattered around the country in such places as the University of Pennsylvania and the University of Cincinnati. The standard edition of Bierce is the twelve-volume *Collected Works* (1909–1912), but while it contains most of his fiction, verse, and satiric definitions in their best textual version, it is incomplete, fundamentally misrepresents his nonfiction, and has unreliable dates. The best biography is Carey McWilliams, *Ambrose Bierce: A Biography* (1929); the best general overview is M. E. Grenander, *Ambrose Bierce* (1971). Two useful unpublished Ph.D. dissertations are Lawrence I. Berkove, "Ambrose Bierce's Concern with Mind and Man" (Univ. of Pa., 1962), and Janet M. Francendese, "Ambrose Bierce as Journalist" (N.Y. Univ., 1977). A substantial sampling of Bierce's best journalism can be found in Lawrence Berkove, *Skepticism and Dissent: Selected Journalism, 1898–1901* (1980). Useful specialized works are Paul Fatout, *Ambrose Bierce and the Black Hills* (1956) and Cathy N. Davidson, ed., *Critical Essays on Ambrose Bierce* (1982). Important articles are Napier Wilt, "Ambrose Bierce and the Civil War," *American Literature* 1 (1929): 260–85; Edmund Wilson's chapter on Bierce in *Patriotic Gore* (1962); Jay Martin, "Ambrose Bierce," in *The Comic Imagination in American Literature*, (1973); F. J. Logan, "The Wry Seriousness of 'Owl Creek Bridge,'" *American Literary Realism* 10 (1977): 101–13; and Lawrence Berkove, "'Hades in Trouble': A Rediscovered Story by Ambrose Bierce," *American Literary Realism* 25, no. 2 (1993): 67–84.

LAWRENCE I. BERKOVE

BIERMAN, Bernard William (11 Mar. 1894–8 Mar. 1977), college athlete and football coach, was born in Springfield, Minnesota, the son of William August Bierman and Lydia Ruessler. His father worked at odd jobs, causing the family to live in three Minnesota towns, along with two years in Oklahoma, by the time Bierman graduated from high school. A bone infection in his leg prevented him from undertaking high school sports until his sophomore year. He then participated in football, basketball, and track.

At the University of Minnesota, Bierman won three letters in football, three in track, and one in basketball. In his senior year, 1915, he captained the football team, which won the Western (later Big Ten) Conference championship. To climax an undefeated season, he scored two touchdowns and made four interceptions in defeating Wisconsin. He won the Western Conference medal for athletic and scholarship proficiency, graduating with a bachelor's degree in education.

Bierman began his coaching career at Billings, Montana, high school in 1916. He left that position the following year to enlist in the U.S. Marine Corps as a private. After finishing basic training at Quantico, Virginia, he was commissioned a second lieutenant on 1 July 1917 and promoted to captain the next day. The rapid promotion was due to the need for special assignments, and the Marines felt these positions should be filled by college-educated officers.

Following his discharge from the service in 1919, Bierman became head football coach at the University of Montana. In 1922 he temporarily retired from coaching to enter the bond business in Minneapolis, Minnesota, but he returned to coaching in 1923 by becoming an assistant coach at Tulane University in Louisiana, serving under an old Minnesota teammate, Clark Shaughnessy. In 1925 Bierman moved to Mississippi Agricultural and Mechanical College (later Mississippi State University) as head coach, and in his first season his team defeated Tulane. When Shaughnessy moved to Loyola in 1927, Bierman became head coach at Tulane. His first two seasons there were lackluster, but from 1929 to 1931 his teams lost only two games, one to Southern California in the 1931 Rose Bowl game and the other to Northwestern. Bierman and Shaughnessy were both disciples of Dr. Henry Williams's system of football. When Shaughnessy advanced to a more important coaching job, he usually recommended Bierman as his successor. As they taught the same systems of offense and defense, the players did not have to learn entirely new systems.

Returning to the University of Minnesota as head coach in 1932, Bierman persuaded many players who had left the state to return home to play. His first Golden Gophers team won five games and lost three. From the close of the 1932 season until the game against Northwestern in 1936, his teams went undefeated with twenty-eight victories and four ties.

In 1934 Minnesota won the Big Ten championship and was proclaimed the national champion; that football team has been rated as one of the best teams of all time. The following season the Gophers tied Ohio State for the conference title and were again declared national champions. Despite a loss to Northwestern in 1936, Minnesota won its third consecutive national title. Bierman had two more national championship teams, in 1940 and 1941, for a record of five national titles in an eight-year span.

From 1942 to 1945, during World War II, Bierman served as a colonel in the U.S. Marine Corps. He coached the Iowa Sea Hawks during part of his Marine duty; the Marine football program was an integral part of the Marine program, and coaching teams was an important and legitimate duty assignment. (Many top coaches in the country had such assignments in the services.) Returning to Minnesota in 1945, Bierman coached for five years, retiring after the 1950 season. He had another great team in 1949, but it lost to Purdue and Michigan in successive weeks to spoil a bid for another national title.

Bierman employed a single-wing back formation with variations, often featuring an unbalanced line. His teams were always well conditioned and disciplined in the football basics. His teams were taught hard hitting, intelligent football, with no extra emotionalism, and they made few mistakes. During the season his teams did very little scrimmaging; practice sessions stressed execution of set plays, precision, crisp blocking, hard tackling and excellence in fundamentals.

Bierman's overall record included 162 victories, 57 losses, and 11 ties; his record for 16 seasons at Minnesota was 93 wins, 35 losses, and six ties as well as six Big Ten titles. He served as co-coach of the East team several times in the Shrine All-Star games, and twice he coached the College All-Stars in an annual exhibition game against the National Football League champions. He developed four All-America players at Tulane and fifteen at Minnesota, and his players at Minnesota included Bruce Smith, the 1941 Heisman Trophy winner.

Bierman was college coach of the year in 1936 and served as president of the American Football Coaches Association in 1935. He was enshrined in the National Football Foundation's College Football Hall of Fame in 1950. Called the "Silver Fox" or "Grey Eagle" for his prematurely grey hair, Bierman was a Blue Lodge Mason and active in many civic activities. He became a charter member of the State of Minnesota Sports Hall of Fame in 1957 and also a charter selection of the University of Minnesota Athletic Hall of Fame in 1991. The University of Minnesota named an athletic facility in his honor.

In 1921 Bierman married Clara McKenzie, a Minnesota graduate who lived in Havre, Montana. They had two sons, the older of whom later played for his father on Minnesota football teams. After retiring, Bierman retained an office on the campus for several years and served as a color commentator on radio broadcasts of games. He and his wife moved to California in 1949 and settled in the retirement community of Laguna Hills, California, in 1969, living there until his death.

• Bierman wrote a popular text on football with Frank Mayer, *Winning Football* (1937). See also George Barton, *My Lifetime in Sports* (1957); Stan W. Carlson, *Dr. Henry L. Williams, A Football Biography* (1938); *Minnesota Huddle Annual* (1936–1938); Richard Fisher, *Who's Who in Minnesota Athletics* (1941); James P. Quirk, *Minnesota Football; The Golden Years* (1984); University of Minnesota, *Gopher Gazette* (1976); and *One Hundred Years of Minnesota Football* (1981).

STAN W. CARLSON

BIERSTADT, Albert (7 Jan. 1830–18 Feb. 1902), artist, was born in Solingen, Germany, the son of Henry Bierstadt, a cooper, and Christina M. Tillmans. In 1832 his family emigrated to New Bedford, Massachusetts, where his father made barrels for the whaling trade. Showing no particular aptitude for art in his early years, Albert received a traditional New England education in the local grammar schools. His formal education did not extend beyond this level. By 1853 he was determined to become an artist and sailed that year for Düsseldorf, Germany, to study art. His limited means prevented him from formally enrolling in the academy at Düsseldorf, one of the most important centers for artistic study in the German states. Through friendships with Emanuel Leutze, Worthington Whittridge, Sanford S. Gifford, and Andreas Achenbach, who were formally studying at the Düsseldorf academy, Bierstadt gained knowledge of many of those color and compositional techniques that he would later use effectively in his large landscapes of the American West. Working diligently, Bierstadt began to master the portrayal of clouds, sunlight, shadows, and evening and morning skies. Returning to New Bedford in 1857, Bierstadt met with some success in selling his paintings, which were becoming increasingly large in size and frequently featured European themes.

Seeking both new subjects that might be portrayed and paintings that would be popular with an American audience, Bierstadt traveled west with the Lander's South Pass Wagon Road Expedition in 1859 as it sought a new route to California. In the Wind River country of the Rocky Mountains, Bierstadt found scenes that challenged his artistic imagination and furnished him with subjects for the balance of his life. In a letter to *The Crayon* (Sept. 1859) he reflected on his experiences in this region: "when we look up and measure the mighty perpendicular cliffs that rise hundreds of feet aloft, all capped with snow, we then realize that we are among a different class of mountains; and especially when we see the antelope stop to look at us, and still more the Indian, his pursuer, who often stands dismayed to see a white man sketching alone in the midst of his hunting grounds." Bierstadt established his reputation as a painter of this "different class of mountains" and gave the nation its initial vision of the majestic western landscape that awaited settlement. More than twenty-eight paintings resulted from this trip, including *The Rocky Mountains*; *The Rocky Mountains, Lander's Peak*; *Wasatch Mountains*; and *Wasatch Mountains, Wind River Country*. Bierstadt worked not only from field sketches but also from stereoscopic views that he made with early cameras; throughout his life he demonstrated a sustained interest in the development and use of photography by artists.

In 1860 Bierstadt established himself in New York, where he shared a studio with Leutze, Whittredge, William Stanley Haseltine, and Frederic E. Church. Paintings from his western trip began to be displayed at a number of eastern exhibitions. When his *Base of the Rocky Mountains, Laramie's Peak* was exhibited at the National Academy of Design's Annual Exhibition in 1860, it received significant praise in eastern newspapers, being described variously as "the *piece de resistance* of the landscape department" (*New York Tribune*, 12 Apr. 1860), "the largest and most elaborate painting in the exhibition" (*New York Herald*, 24 Apr. 1860), "the work of a powerful hand" (*The Crayon*, May 1860), and a painting "strongly, intelligently, faithfully done" (*Home Journal*, 5 May 1860). His reputation as a landscape artist was growing, and his work was beginning to be compared favorably with that of Church. That year Bierstadt was elected a full academician of the National Academy of Design. With the outbreak of the Civil War, Bierstadt made a brief sketching tour among the Union forces along the Potomac; nevertheless, his primary artistic interests lay in those lands beyond the Mississippi River.

Accompanied by Fitz Hugh Ludlow, Bierstadt traveled west once more in the late spring of 1863. The main incidents of this journey were published in Ludlow's articles, which appeared initially in the *Atlantic Monthly* and later in expanded form in *The Heart of the Continent* (1870). After passing through Kansas and Nebraska, the two men made their way to Denver, Colorado. While in Colorado Bierstadt made his studies for his famous *Storm in the Rocky Mountains, Mt. Rosalie*. After meeting Brigham Young in Salt Lake City, Ludlow and Bierstadt arrived in California. For six weeks Bierstadt sketched in Yosemite, producing ultimately from this experience the *Domes of Yosemite, In the Yosemite Valley*, and *Merced River*.

The decade from 1863 to 1873 was a period of great success for Bierstadt. He became more proficient in his compositions, accomplished in his use of color, and adept in his technical execution. His paintings commanded some of the most substantial prices paid for paintings in nineteenth-century America. *The Rocky Mountains, Lander's Peak* sold for $25,000, while *Storm in the Rocky Mountains, Mt. Rosalie* was purchased for $35,000. Bierstadt was becoming, with Church, one of the masters of the large "great picture." Bierstadt's paintings dwarfed in size many of the paintings of his contemporaries. Some of his landscape paintings reached more than nine feet in height and fifteen feet in length. In 1866 Bierstadt married Rosalie Osborne, Fitz Hugh Ludlow's former wife, and began plans for their great estate, "Malkasten," on the Hudson River. From 1867 to 1869 Bierstadt traveled in Europe. In 1872 and 1873 he worked once more in Yosemite and the Sierra Nevada. In the late 1870s Bierstadt's popularity began to wane, and it became more difficult for him to sell his paintings. His romantic and sublime interpretation of the American West was no longer acceptable to critics or desired by his former patrons. To maintain himself, he sought to sell not only his paintings but also photographic supplies, inventions, and guns. In 1889 his *Last of the Buffalo* was rejected by the American selection committee for the Paris Exposition. His wife died in 1893, and in 1894 he married a widow, Mrs. David Stewart. Bierstadt, who had no children, died in New York City.

The West that Bierstadt had loved to paint was experiencing rapid transformation. Industrialization and urbanization were altering the sublime natural world that he had so enthusiastically portrayed on his canvases. Bierstadt's landscapes complemented the rhetoric of the American frontier and imparted an imagined reality of the West that extended beyond the mere representation of the topography of those lands and responded to the nation's desire for visual images of the land of the buffalo, the world of the Indian, and the haunt of the mountain man. His smaller paintings are often more sensitive and less melodramatic than his large, heroic landscapes, but he was the first great landscape painter of the American West and the first to exploit the artistic potential of the majestic mountains of that region.

• Many of Bierstadt's personal papers, photographs, sketchbooks, and western artifacts were destroyed when Malkasten burned in 1882. Nancy K. Anderson and Linda S. Ferber's *Albert Bierstadt: Art & Enterprise* (1990) not only provides a solid introduction to his career and paintings but also is important for its extensive bibliography and for indicating the various archival locations for Bierstadt's extant manuscript materials. For a detailed assessment of his life and œuvre and good examples of his paintings, see Gordon Hendricks, *Albert Bierstadt: Painter of the American West* (1973). For a more succinct appraisal of Bierstadt, consult Matthew Baigell, *Albert Bierstadt* (1981). An examination of his relationship with Ludlow may be found in Ralph A. Britisch, *Bierstadt and Ludlow: Painter and Writer in the West* (1980). Bierstadt's experiences on his second western trip may be found in Fitz Hugh Ludlow, *The Heart of the Continent: A Record of Travel across the Plains and in Oregon with an Examination of the Mormon Principle* (1870). His paintings may be found in many American museums; significant collections are held by the Amon Carter Museum of Western Art, Fort Worth, Tex.; the Brooklyn Museum; the Buffalo Bill Historical Center, Cody, Wyo.; the Corcoran Gallery of Art, Washington, D.C.; the Metropolitan Museum of Art, New York City; the Museum of Fine Arts, Boston; and the Thomas Gilcrease Institute of American History and Art, Tulsa, Okla.

PHILLIP DRENNON THOMAS

BIFFLE, Leslie L. (9 Oct. 1889–6 Apr. 1966), Senate Democratic secretary to the majority and secretary of the Senate, was born in Boydsville, Arkansas, the son of Billie B. Biffle, a storekeeper, sheriff, and county clerk, and Ella Turner. Graduating from Piggott High School in 1908, Biffle enrolled at the Keys Business Institute in Little Rock before going to Washington, D.C., as secretary to Democratic representative Bruce Macon.

Following Macon's loss in 1912, Biffle became secretary to Arkansas senator James P. Clarke, president pro tempore of the Senate. When Clarke died in 1916, Arkansas senator Joseph T. Robinson secured for Biffle the superintendency of the Senate folding room, which prepared documents for mailing. During World War I, from 1917 to 1919, Biffle went to France as a War Department auditor. He married Mary Glade Strickling in 1921; they had no children.

Biffle's star rose with that of his patron, Robinson, who was elected Democratic minority leader in 1923. Robinson appointed Biffle assistant to Democratic secretary Edwin Halsey. After Democrats returned to the majority in 1933, Halsey became secretary of the Senate, while Biffle was promoted to secretary to the majority. Throughout the New Deal, Biffle worked the floor of the Senate as a "head counter," apprising majority leaders Robinson and Alben Barkley about how senators were likely to vote. Biffle discretely stopped senators as they entered and left the chamber to determine their leanings. He might take fifteen to twenty informal polls to identify the wavering senators and persuade them to side with Franklin D. Roosevelt's administration. In 1937, when Senate Democrats acrimoniously split over Roosevelt's proposal to "pack" the Supreme Court (to increase the Court's membership from nine to fifteen), Biffle as majority secretary managed to retain the confidence of both factions, sitting in meetings of those supporting and opposing the president's plan without divulging the other side's strategies.

As majority secretary, Biffle also served as secretary treasurer of the Senate Democratic Senatorial Campaign Committee, raising and distributing funds for Democratic candidates. In 1945, following the death of the incumbent Colonel Halsey, Biffle was elected secretary of the Senate. In an unprecedented gesture, the Republican minority made his election unanimous. When a controversy over the seating of Mississippi senator Theodore Bilbo prevented the Republicans from organizing the Senate at the beginning of the Eightieth Congress in 1947 and with the office of vice president vacant, Secretary of the Senate Biffle presided over Senate sessions for two days.

Known for his expressionless face and emotionless voice, Biffle had a habit of speaking with his left hand cupped over his mouth to keep his conversations confidential. Slightly built, dapper, and genial, he made himself a walking encyclopedia of Senate traditions, practices, and vote tallies. Biffle greeted new senators and ushered them through the rules and customs of the institution, urging them to listen, learn, and keep quiet for a while. "Easy, easy, Senator," he advised. "If there's anything you don't understand, come to me. I'm here to help you, and I'm glad to. Don't rush!"

In 1935 Biffle particularly befriended the new Missouri senator Harry Truman. Close in age and regional background, they thought similarly on most issues. In 1941 Biffle helped Truman become chairman of the Special Committee to Investigate the National Defense Program—better known as the Truman Committee—which propelled Truman into the national spotlight. In 1944, as sergeant at arms at the Democratic National Convention, Biffle boosted Truman for vice president; Truman won the nomination. When Franklin Roosevelt died in 1945, Truman placed his first telephone call from the White House to Biffle. The following day Biffle arranged a luncheon for the new president and senators in the secretary of the Senate's private dining room, a congenial meeting place where senators regularly gathered to relax over drinks. Throughout Truman's administration, Biffle arranged luncheons for cabinet officers, ambassadors, and other dignitaries to meet and lobby key senators.

"They don't make them any better than Les Biffle," Truman noted at his first press conference. Such praise and the direct line to the White House on his desk made Biffle a well-sought man in Washington. His office attracted crowds of favor-seekers, who left with nothing more than a handshake and an explanation that his influence had been greatly exaggerated. "My friendships in Washington are not for sale," Biffle said. "I'd rather go back to Arkansas and scratch gravel with the chickens."

In 1948, as sergeant at arms of the Democratic convention, Biffle promoted Barkley for vice president, buttonholing delegates and orchestrating a demonstration after Barkley delivered his keynote address. A suspicious Truman suspected Biffle of running Barkley for president instead but nevertheless endorsed him for the second place on the ticket. Biffle returned to Truman's good graces by predicting that Truman would score an upset victory in November. Dressed uncharacteristically in overalls and a straw hat, Biffle drove a truck through West Virginia, Ohio, Indiana, and Illinois, buying eggs and chickens and talking politics. The results of his widely publicized "Biffle poll" indicated that Truman had a fighting chance for reelection. Newsmen composed a parody for Truman: "People love me this I know, / For Les Biffle tells me so."

In 1952 Biffle retired from the Senate. In truth there was no place for him, since the new Democratic minority leader Lyndon Johnson wanted his own staff. Biffle's successor, Johnson protégé Bobby Baker, inherited both the post as secretary and Biffle's reputation as a legislative head counter. Biffle thereafter served as a business consultant but rarely did any congressional lobbying.

After his death in Washington, D.C., Biffle was eulogized by senators on both sides of the aisle, who remembered how he had welcomed and helped them fit into full-fledged membership in the Senate. Former Florida senator Claude Pepper hailed him as "the personification of the dedicated, unassuming, ever-diligent and faithful public servant," while the *Washington Post* commemorated Biffle as "the sort of indefatigable, tireless, self-effacing detail man that every official searches for and that few find."

• Although rumored to have kept a diary, Biffle left no papers. Useful articles are Lewis Wood, "Sage of Capitol Hill," *New York Times Magazine*, 26 Aug. 1945, p. 18; Ernest Barcella, "They Call Him Mr. Baffle," *Collier's*, 29 Jan. 1949, pp. 27, 61–62; and Jack Bell, "When Biffle's Phone Rings He

Knows Who It Is," *Washington Star*, 4 Mar. 1951. His "head counting" is discussed in Joseph Alsop and Robert Kintner, "Sly and Able: The Real Leader of the Senate, Jimmy Byrnes," *Saturday Evening Post*, 20 July 1940, pp. 18–19, 38–45; and in the Joseph Alsop Papers, Library of Congress. Obituaries are in the *New York Times* and the *Washington Post*, both 7 Apr. 1966.

DONALD A. RITCHIE

BIGARD, Barney (3 Mar. 1906–27 June 1980), jazz musician, was born Albany Leon Bigard in New Orleans, Louisiana, the son of Alexander Louis Bigard and Emanuella Marquez. Little is known of his family except that it produced musicians: his older brother Alex was a drummer, his uncle Emile was a violinist who played with musicians like King Oliver and Kid Ory, and his cousin Anatie ("Natty") Dominique was a trumpet player and band leader. Bigard studied clarinet under Lorenzo Tio, Jr., whose students included Johnny Dodds, Albert Nicholas, Omer Simeon, and Jimmie Noone.

Raised mostly by his grandparents, Bigard worked in his uncle Ulysses's cigar factory as a boy and also as a photoengraver, and he played music mostly with parade bands. At the age of sixteen, however, he joined Albert Nicholas's band as a tenor saxophonist. He continued playing the tenor with other New Orleans bands, including Luis Russell's. In 1924, on the recommendations of Russell and Nicholas, King Oliver asked Bigard to join his band in Chicago, and so, like many other young New Orleans musicians of the day, he left town and headed north. Bigard's first wife, Arthemise or Artemise (maiden name unknown), whom he married in about 1924, accompanied him to Chicago. They had four children, but the couple drifted apart, and the marriage ended some years later.

Bigard joined King Oliver's Dixie Syncopators as a tenor saxophonist, later switching to clarinet. While in Chicago, he recorded with Oliver, Louis Armstrong, Jelly Roll Morton, and Johnny Dodds. A young Doc Cheatham, at the time a budding saxophonist before he took up the trumpet, heard Bigard play in Chicago, and said years later, "I thought he was the greatest tenor player I ever heard in my life!" (*The World of Swing*, p. 307). It was with the clarinet, however, that Bigard's talent was fully realized. His sound is usually described as warm, clear, liquid, or woody and his style as fluid or articulate. His playing employed the full range of the instrument but with a particular resonance in the lower register, which some critics have ascribed to the fact that unlike most clarinetists he used the older Albert fingering system instead of the newer Boehm system. Haywood Henry, as a young sax and clarinet player, first heard Bigard playing with Duke Ellington in 1930 and remembered that "Barney Bigard was my model from the first. I loved his sound and the way he flowed on the clarinet. What he played always made a lot of sense, and he always told a story" (*The World of Swing*, p. 207).

Bigard played with the Oliver band, both in Chicago at the Plantation Cafe and on tour, until the summer of 1927, when, after a brief stint with Charlie Elgar's Creole Orchestra in Milwaukee, he went on to New York City, to join a group led by Luis Russell. He was spotted by Wellman Braud, the bassist for the Duke Ellington Orchestra, which was playing in Harlem at the Cotton Club. In January 1928 Ellington asked Bigard to join his band as the replacement for Rudy Jackson. Bigard remained with Ellington for fifteen years as a featured player on clarinet, working with such outstanding jazz musicians as Cootie Williams, Johnny Hodges, Sonny Greer, Harry Carney, and Sam Nanton. He contributed his distinctive New Orleans voice to the Ellington sound, and in return Ellington, as he did with other key musicians, wrote Bigard's voice into many of his classic arrangements, like "C-Jam Blues," "Azure," "Caravan," "Harlem Air Shaft," and "Clarinet Lament." Bigard claimed to have written one of the band's signature pieces, "Mood Indigo," based partly on a melody borrowed from Lorenzo Tio, Jr., although the published score bears Ellington's name and seems to give him credit for its composition.

In a highly segregated era, Ellington's band was an all-black group playing for all-white audiences. Bigard's obituary in the *New York Times* (28 June 1980) noted that "because he was fair-skinned, Mr. Bigard often purchased food for members of the Ellington band when the musicians toured in the Deep South during the years of the Jim Crow racial practices." Also, when the Ellington orchestra played on screen in a 1930 Amos 'n' Andy film titled *Check and Double Check*, Bigard and the band's valve trombonist, Juan Tizol, both being very light-skinned, were required to appear in blackface (Hasse, p. 129).

From 1931 on Ellington and his group were on the road much of the time. Finally, tired of the constant touring, which he found grueling, especially after 1941 when the war disrupted transportation schedules, Bigard left the Ellington orchestra in 1942 and headed to the West Coast, where he played with local groups, briefly formed a small band (with Kid Ory on trombone and Charlie Mingus on bass), and did studio work. Also in 1942 he married Dorothy Edgecombe; they did not have children. He returned to New York in 1944 and for a few months led his own group at the Onyx Club on Fifty-second Street. Then, in 1944 or 1945, it was back to California, where he played with Kid Ory. In 1947 he appeared in the film *New Orleans* with Armstrong. After the filming, Armstrong asked him to join Jack Teagarden, Cozy Cole, and Velma Middleton in a small Dixieland group to be called Louis Armstrong's All Stars. Bigard stayed with the All Stars for five years, making many tours and records, and later rejoined the group twice for shorter stints. By 1962 he had retired from full-time playing but continued to appear for brief engagements, concerts, and festivals, leading his own bands or playing with groups headed by Cozy Cole, Ben Pollack, Johnny St. Cyr, Muggsy Spanier, Rex Stewart, Earl Hines, Art Hodes, Eddie Condon, and Wild Bill Davison.

Bigard died in Culver City, California. Over a period of sixty years, he had been a quintessential sideman, playing in big bands and small, Dixieland and swing, associated with many of the great jazz figures of the first half of the twentieth century. He was in that group of fine young New Orleans clarinetists—among them Albert Nicholas, Buster Bailey, Omer Simeon, Edmond Hall, Sidney Bechet, and George Lewis—who brought their style of music north after the First World War and helped spread the gospel of jazz. A French critic, Jacques Morgantini, assessed Bigard's accomplishments this way: "Apart from those multiple qualities as an instrumentalist, improviser, and swingman . . . Barney Bigard possessed the remarkable talent of being able to adapt the typically New Orleans clarinet style to the big band context" (album notes, *Barney Bigard Story*, Jazz Archives, No. 12).

• The only extended account of Bigard's life is his tape-recorded reminiscences *With Louis and the Duke*, ed. Barry Martyn (1985). References in the form of anecdotes and appraisals can be found in Stanley Dance, *The World of Duke Ellington* (1970); Dance, *The World of Swing* (1974); Rex Stewart, *Jazz Masters of the Thirties* (1972); Charles Kinger, "The Tios of New Orleans and Their Influence on the Early Jazz Clarinet Style," *Black Music Research Journal* (Fall 1996); Duke Ellington, *Music Is My Mistress* (1973); and John Edward Hasse, *Beyond Category: The Life and Genius of Duke Ellington* (1993). The most complete bibliography of articles and interviews about Bigard is in *The New Grove Dictionary of Jazz*, ed. Barry Kernfeld (1988). An obituary is in the *New York Times*, 28 June 1980.

BRUCE R. CARRICK

BIGART, Homer (25 Oct. 1907–16 Apr. 1991), newspaper reporter, was born Homer William Bigart in Hawley, Pennsylvania, the son of Homer S. Bigart, a sweater manufacturer, and Anna Schardt. Bigart attended public schools and then went to Pittsburgh to study architecture at the Carnegie Institute of Technology. Carnegie quickly dropped him, and in 1927 Bigart went to New York to study journalism at New York University, holding a job as a part-time copy boy at the *New York Herald Tribune*.

With the stock market crash of 1929, Bigart became a full-time copy boy, which enabled him to send money home. In 1932, after advancing to head copy boy, he was promoted to reporter. He was improbable material, since he stammered in moments of tension and was a slow writer, a drawback on a daily paper. Moreover, as he later told Richard Kluger in interviews for *The Paper: The Life and Death of the New York Herald Tribune* (1986), his stories were labored. Eventually, though, he was given better assignments, and his work developed a flair; by developing a precise, rich vocabulary and occasionally displaying a mock-serious style, he was able to make something fresh out of such New York classics as the St. Patrick's Day Parade.

After the United States entered World War II, the *New York Herald Tribune* sent Bigart to cover the air war in Europe. In 1943 he was among the few reporters ever to fly on a daytime bombing raid over Germa-

ny; 25 percent of the aircraft in such raids were being lost. Then Bigart moved to the grueling ground war in Sicily, where he rode on muleback with the troops. He moved on to mainland Italy, where his work emerged as the benchmark for war correspondents, as has been noted by *Newsweek* correspondent Zeke Cook (*New York Herald Tribune*, 4 Oct. 1944). In 1944 he submitted reports for two months from the perilous Allied beachhead at Anzio, Italy, where he evoked the wrath of the Allied commander by reporting blunders as well as achievements. Although this was the first of many such clashes with the military brass, Bigart was allowed to enter Rome with the Allied troops on 4 June 1944.

After reporting on the campaign in southern France, Bigart was sent to the Pacific, where he covered the fighting for Leyte, Corregidor, and Luzon in the Philippines and for the Japanese strongholds of Iwo Jima and Okinawa. He flew with the Americans on their last air raid on Japan and covered the Japanese surrender on 2 September 1945. The next day, he was one of the first correspondents to view on the ground the destruction wrought by the atom bomb in Hiroshima. In 1946 Bigart won the first of his two Pulitzer Prizes, this one for foreign correspondence in the Pacific.

After World War II Bigart covered the Cold War in Europe and the Jewish struggle against British rule in Palestine before the establishment of Israel. Bigart, born a Presbyterian, was a favorite of the embattled Jews; he was taken secretly to see an induction of recruits by the Haganah, the Zionist underground.

In 1948, after the CBS correspondent George Polk was murdered trying to find the Greek insurgent known as General Markos, Bigart took up the chase and eventually interviewed Markos in the Grammos mountains. The first Polk Award, named for the lost correspondent, was given to Bigart for this feat.

Bigart's next major war was in Korea in 1950. The *Herald Tribune* sent two correspondents to Korea, Bigart and Marguerite Higgins. Their rivalry was legendary; and Bigart later said in an oral history interview for the *New York Times* (11 Aug. 1987) that he was afraid that Higgins's competitiveness was going to get both of them killed. In 1951 Bigart was awarded a second Pulitzer Prize, this one acknowledging his work in Korea; however, he had to share it with Higgins and four others. After his return from Korea in 1951, he married a fellow *Tribune* employee, Alice Kirkwood Veit. They were later divorced, and she died in 1959. In 1963 he married Alice Weel of CBS, who died in 1969. Bigart had no children in either marriage.

In October 1955, as the *Herald Tribune*'s future looked dim, Bigart shifted to the prosperous *New York Times*. He undertook major national stories there, including civil rights, native American rights, poverty in Appalachia, and strip-mining in Kentucky. Despite his age, Bigart continued to be a top choice for combat assignments. His most notable story overseas was the trial of the Nazi leader Adolf Eichmann in Israel in 1961.

Assigned to the Vietnam War for six months in 1962, Bigart gave counsel to younger correspondents that was described as invaluable by Neil Sheehan, then a competing reporter for United Press International; Sheehan, too, later moved to the *Times*. Bigart's last major Vietnam-related story was the longest military trial on record, the 1971 trial of First Lieutenant William L. Calley on charges growing out of the Mylai massacre.

Bigart's independence was frequently unwelcome in the countries he covered. He was ordered out of Hungary, Egypt, Syria, Lebanon, Jordan, Saudi Arabia, Oman, and Vietnam, although Saigon rescinded this order at the last minute, with the government saying the problem was a translation error.

In 1970 Bigart was married for a third time, to Else Holmelund Minarik, an author of children's books. Two years later he retired, and they settled on a farm in New Hampshire. They had no children together, but Bigart gained an adult stepchild in this marriage. Bigart died in Portsmouth, New Hampshire.

In 1973 an insurgent reporters' organization gave Bigart its award for "four decades of single-minded attention to his craft, persistent skepticism toward all forms of power and tenacious pursuit of social injustice long before such reporting became fashionable."

Although most newspaper accounts of World War II have lost their immediacy, according to Malcolm W. Browne, a former correspondent, Bigart's work "rings with genuine drama shorn of facile cliches, propaganda and self-congratulation" (*New York Times Book Review*, 11 Apr. 1993). In disputes over Pentagon restrictions on military coverage, the importance to the public of Bigart's untrammeled work was often cited. Harrison E. Salisbury wrote,

When the Vietnam war was lost, it did not surprise Bigart that the generals blamed the media, print and electronic, for their failure nor that the public took up the same cry. He had long since learned that if the reporter gets nothing but bouquets he must be missing part of the story—the important part. (*Forward Positions*, 1992)

• Bigart's few personal papers and overseas letters to his family are held by the State Historical Society of Wisconsin in Madison. This archive also includes a nearly complete file of Bigart byline clippings from the *New York Herald Tribune* (1934–1955), only available as part of a *Herald Tribune* microfilm file. Betsy Wade, ed., *Forward Positions: The War Correspondence of Homer Bigart* (1992), contains fifty war dispatches, a foreword by Harrison E. Salisbury, a biography by Wade, and the text of the *New York Times* obituary by Richard Severo, originally published 17 Apr. 1991. Wade owns letters from Bigart in Vietnam and his byline file from the *New York Times*. Richard Kluger, *The Paper: The Life and Death of the New York Herald Tribune* (1986), contains interviews with Bigart and details on the Bigart-Higgins clash. William Prochnau, *Once Upon a Distant War: Young War Correspondents and the Early Vietnam Battles* (1995), gives details on the impact of Bigart on the cadre of reporters who followed him to Saigon.

BETSY WADE

BIGELOW, Harry Augustus (22 Sept. 1874–8 Jan. 1950), attorney, law professor, and author, was born in Norwood, Massachusetts, the son of Erwin Bigelow, a merchant, and Amie Leighton Fischer. Bigelow attended high school in Norwood and then Harvard College (A.B., 1896) and Harvard Law School (LL.B., 1899), where he was an editor on the *Law Review*. For a year after his graduation, he taught criminal law at Harvard. He then worked for a brief period as a law clerk in a conveyancing office in Boston before moving to Honolulu, where he established a legal practice and spent three years as a junior member of the bar of the Hawaiian Islands. In 1902 he married Mary Parker; they had no children, and she died in 1920.

In January 1904 Bigelow joined the faculty of the University of Chicago and worked with Joseph H. Beale, a professor on leave from Harvard, and president of the college William Rainey Harper in organizing a law school there. Four years later he was admitted to the Illinois bar and the following year was made professor of law.

With his acute analytical mind, Bigelow earned the reputation of being a brilliant teacher. It was written of him after his death that "to sit in his classes was an experience highly prized by his students who developed a deep affection for him" (*Proceedings*, pp. 164–65). Though he was well liked, he was known for rendering stern reprimands to students whose work was "confused or slip-shod" (*Proceedings*, p. 165).

Although his clear, lively presentation of class material garnered him campus renown, Bigelow's legal influence spread beyond the University of Chicago with the publication of his casebooks, *The Law of Personal Property* (1917) and *The Law of Rights in Land*, published two years later. These books each went through three print editions and became standard classroom materials; Bigelow became known as an authority on the law of real and personal property. In addition to these books, he published *Introduction to the Law of Real Property* (1919), which provided a historical survey of the law of property and supplemented conventional references. Though a skilled instructor in case method, Bigelow believed that this approach was often cumbersome and time-consuming. Investigations of legal questions limited to the materials in law reports, he opined, often did little to enhance the students' perception of the issues. His book was not intended to replace standard textbooks but to supplement them. It became an essential reference source for the student of modern land law.

In addition to writing his own books, Bigelow assisted in the preparation of the American Law Institute's *Restatement of the Conflict of Laws* (1934) and *Restatement of the Law of Property* (1936). He became less involved with this project in 1929, when he was named dean of the University of Chicago Law School. Believing that a true understanding of the law required study in different areas, he reformed the school's curriculum to include subjects such as accounting, economics, and psychology. He also encouraged his faculty to begin a tutorial program aimed at enriching the law school experience for students.

Though he remained devoted to the school, Bigelow assumed new responsibilities in 1933 when he accepted an appointment as trustee in bankruptcy of Insull Utility Investments, Inc. Through the lengthy liquidation process, he demonstrated a sound knowledge of complex business concerns, earning the respect of those in the industry. In 1939 Bigelow, then having reached the university's retirement age, relinquished his position as dean but continued to teach conflict of laws and property classes. In 1947 President Harry S. Truman appointed him a member of the National Loyalty Review Board, an agency that passed on the loyalty of government employees. Bigelow served in this capacity for three years until his death in Chicago following a lengthy illness.

Throughout his life Bigelow was a big-game hunter and explorer. On expeditions in Africa in 1924 and 1925, along with Herbert E. Bradley and Mary Hastings Bradley, he was one of the first to cross the unexplored Belgian Congo west of Lake Edward. Bigelow was also a collector of fine art, and his collection of Japanese prints was excellent.

Bigelow devoted forty-six years of his life to the University of Chicago Law School and the legal profession at large. He was a member of many legal societies, including the American, Illinois, and Chicago bar associations, Phi Beta Kappa, Order of the Coif, and the Academy of Arts and Sciences. After his death, the University of Chicago established the Harry A. Bigelow Professorship and the Bigelow Tutorial Fellowship in his memory.

• Most of Bigelow's writings are preserved in his textbooks. Personal and professional information is available in the archives of the University of Chicago, the *Class Reports* of the Harvard College Class of 1896, obituaries published in *Proceedings* of the Association of American Law Schools (1950), the *Chicago Tribune* (9 Jan. 1950), and the death record of the Illinois Department of Health.

BETHANY K. DUMAS

BIGELOW, Henry Bryant (3 Oct. 1879–11 Dec. 1967), zoologist and oceanographer, was born in Boston, Massachusetts, the son of Joseph Smith Bigelow, a banker, and Mary Cleveland Bryant. Bigelow graduated from the Milton Academy at age sixteen. A year later he enrolled in Harvard College, from which he graduated cum laude with an A.B. in 1901, going on to earn an A.M. (1904) and a Ph.D. (1906). In 1906 he also married Elizabeth Perkins Shattuck; they had four children.

Bigelow had an early interest in birds and published his first papers, while still in school, on the American eider and the birds of Labrador. He had the opportunity to work with the noted naturalist Alexander Agassiz from 1901 until Agassiz's death in 1910. Their studies of marine life took them to the Indian Ocean, the eastern Pacific, and the West Indies. During their first venture, to the Maldive Islands, Bigelow was responsible for caring for the jellyfish and other medu-

soid animals that were collected. This led to his long-standing interest in siphonophores, which are marine invertebrates that live in colonies and are in the same class as jellyfish. Bigelow's dissertation, on the hydrozoan *Gonionemus vertens* reflected his particular interest in marine invertebrates.

Throughout his life Bigelow was an avid sportsman. After completing work on the trip to the Maldives, he stayed behind to hunt game in Ceylon. In his *Memories of a Long and Active Life* (1964) he recalled, "During the ten days or so that we were in 'game' country, my bag was two wild water buffaloes, a sambhar stag, two axis deer, one wild boar, an eight-foot crocodile, and a large python" (p. 11).

Bigelow was appointed in 1906 to the position of assistant at Harvard's Museum of Comparative Zoology. Over his career there he was promoted to curator of coelenterates (1913), research curator (1925), and eventually curator of oceanography (1927–1962). In 1921 he was appointed lecturer in zoology at Harvard, rising to associate professor in 1927 and full professor in 1931. He retired as professor emeritus in 1950.

Bigelow began one of his seminal works in 1912, conducting a series of studies on the Gulf of Maine and continuing through 1928. Little was known about the Gulf before these studies. His methods were groundbreaking because he covered the entire body of water and made a nearly comprehensive study of its fishes, plankton, and physical oceanography.

These investigations displayed Bigelow's recognition of the value of synthesizing the disciplines that comprise the marine sciences. In "A Developing View-point in Oceanography" (*Science* 71 [24 Jan. 1930]: 84–89), Bigelow remarked, "In the further development of sea science the keynote must be physical, chemical and biological unity, not diversity, for everything that takes place in the sea within the realm of any one of these artificially divorced sciences impinges on all the rest of them" (p. 86).

As secretary of the Committee on Oceanography of the National Academy of Sciences, Bigelow wrote the report that led to the founding of Woods Hole Oceanographic Institution. The report, titled "On the Scope, Problems and Economic Importance of Oceanography, on the Present Situation in America, and on the Handicaps to Development, with Suggested Remedies," was published in 1929. The NAS committee and the marine facility were both brain children of Frank Rattray Lillie, who was long affiliated with the Marine Biological Laboratory, also in Woods Hole.

Woods Hole Oceanographic Institution was established the following year, and Bigelow was its first director, serving from 1930 to 1939. The institution was equipped from the start with a research vessel, the *Atlantis*. For the first few years, Bigelow required all staff members to take at least one short cruise each year on the *Atlantis*, believing that fieldwork was paramount to oceanographic studies.

After leaving Woods Hole Bigelow was editor-in-chief of *Fishes of the Western North Atlantic*, to which he also contributed. The first part of the treatise was published nine years later, in 1948; subsequent volumes appeared in 1953, 1963, and 1964. Bigelow continued to contribute to this series until his death. At the request of the U. S. Navy, Bigelow and W. T. Edmondson wrote *Wind Waves at Sea, Breakers, and Surf* (1947), an introductory text on waves and their effect on seagoing vessels.

Bigelow was honored with appointments to several academic societies and committees. His students and colleagues prepared a festschrift for him in 1955, *Papers in Marine Biology and Oceanography*, which appeared as a supplement to volume 3 of *Deep-Sea Research*. He continued to work at the Museum of Comparative Zoology until his death, even though he had officially retired from it in 1962. He died in Concord, Massachusetts, his home for sixty years.

Over his long career Bigelow contributed substantially to the knowledge of Atlantic marine life, including such divergent forms as plankton, jellyfish, and sharks; completed a comprehensive oceanographic survey of the Gulf of Maine; and helped to establish Woods Hole Oceanographic Institution. In "The Oceanographic and How It Grew" (in *Oceanography: The Past: The Proceedings of the Third International Congress on the History of Oceanography* [1980]), Roger Revelle wrote, "Bigelow was certainly one of the fathers of oceanography in the United States in general and of the Woods Hole Oceanographic Institution in particular through his pioneering Gulf of Maine studies, his broadly-based, persuasive report to the Academy, and his work as the first Director of the Institution" (p. 12).

• A collection of Bigelow's correspondence is at the Harvard Museum of Comparative Zoology. The Woods Hole Oceanographic Institution maintains his director's files, and the Marine Biological Laboratory holds Bigelow's reprints. For an overview of Bigelow's career, including a detailed chronology, see Alfred C. Redfield's essay in National Academy of Sciences, *Biographical Memoirs* 48 (1976): 50–80. Michael Graham gives a rather personal account in an obituary, *Deep-Sea Research* 15 (1968): 126–32, which includes a bibliography. For Bigelow's recollections of the events leading to the founding of Woods Hole, see his "Dr. Lillie and the Founding of the Woods Hole Oceanographic Institution," *Biological Bulletin* 95 (1948): 157–58. An obituary is in the *New York Times*, 12 Dec. 1967.

SUE ANN LEWANDOWSKI

BIGELOW, Henry Jacob (11 Mar. 1818–30 Oct. 1890), surgeon and medical educator, was born in Boston, Massachusetts, the son of Jacob Bigelow, a physician, and Mary Scollay. After graduation from Harvard College in 1837, Bigelow studied medicine with his father, supplementing his preceptorship with attendance at medical lectures at Harvard and Dartmouth medical schools. Although Dr. James Jackson labeled Bigelow's decision to become a surgeon an immense mistake, Bigelow persisted in his choice and in 1838 was named house-surgeon at the Massachusetts General Hospital in Boston. He interrupted his surgical training in 1840 when he developed symptoms of pulmonary disease. He then traveled to Havana, Cuba, and spent the next four years in Europe, attending medical and surgical clinics in Paris and London. He returned to Harvard to receive his medical degree in 1841.

Upon his return to Boston in 1844, Bigelow incurred the disapproval of his professional colleagues by opening, with Dr. Henry Bryant, a small dispensary and advertising the availability of free medical advice and surgical services to the poor. Despite the inauspicious beginning, he earned a reputation as a skilled surgeon and impressive teacher. An essay on methods of orthopedic surgery earned him in 1844 the prestigious Boylston Prize from the Massachusetts Medical Society. In January 1846 he was named, at age twenty-seven, visiting surgeon at the Massachusetts General Hospital and in the same year embarked on a lifelong advocacy of ether anesthesia.

On 16 October 1846 Bigelow witnessed the administration of ether to a patient of Dr. John Collins Warren, surgeon at the Massachusetts General Hospital. The successful demonstration that inhaling ether could produce insensibility to pain during surgery would revolutionize medical practice. Quick to recognize the importance of this innovation, Bigelow took active steps to ensure its adoption by physicians. He published the first paper describing "Insensibility during Surgical Operations, Produced by Inhalation," in *Boston Medical and Surgical Journal* (35 [1846]: 309–17), and communicated news of the discovery to European physicians. After the introduction of chloroform as an anesthetic agent in 1848, Bigelow actively lobbied the medical community in support of ether as a less dangerous anesthetic agent. Although appreciative of the great benefit of ether anesthesia in surgery, Bigelow expressed concern that the availability of such anesthetic agents might prove an irresistible temptation for unscrupulous surgeons to attempt unnecessary operations. He continued to champion a conservative approach in surgery.

A surgical innovator, Bigelow performed the first known American excision of the hip joint in 1852 and explained the pathology and treatment of hip dislocations and fractures. He made numerous modifications of surgical instruments and developed an improved instrument (lithotrite) for the crushing of bladder stones, together with a new procedure he called litholapaxy, in which crushed fragments of the bladder stones were washed out through a catheter. His method for the rapid evacuation of the debris earned him in 1882 the Argenteuil Prize from the French Academy of Medicine. In 1850 Bigelow published a notable paper describing his studies of the injuries sustained in the "American crow-bar case," subsequently known as Bigelow's case, in which railroad foreman Phineas Gage survived the passage of an iron bar through the left side of his head. Although he was an early devotee of the microscope, Bigelow remained skeptical throughout his career about Glasgow surgeon Joseph Lister's introduction of antiseptic methods in the 1860s and 1870s.

A professor of surgery at Harvard Medical School from 1849 until his retirement in 1882, Bigelow was a staunch advocate of conservative medical education. In 1870–1871 he joined his powerful colleague Oliver Wendell Holmes, Sr., in opposing the educational reforms proposed by the newly installed Harvard president, Charles W. Eliot, including the admission of women to the medical school and the introduction of laboratory training into medical education. Although Holmes eventually reversed his stance, Bigelow remained hostile to laboratory instruction, which he believed distracted students from the acquisition of clinical knowledge. Requiring medical students to witness or inflict pain in animals, Bigelow warned, was not only therapeutically useless but morally corrupting. "If hospital service makes young students less tender of suffering," he observed in his 1871 address to the Massachusetts Medical Society, "[then] vivisection deadens their humanity and begets indifference to it." Despite the successful introduction of animal experimentation into the medical curriculum, he continued to reject the therapeutic optimism of American physiologists, believing that medical advances would result from observations at the patient's bedside rather than the laboratory. Bigelow's views on vivisection were frequently cited in literature circulated by American opponents of animal experimentation.

Bigelow had married Susan Sturgis, the daughter of Boston jurist William Sturgis, in 1847; the couple had one son. Bigelow did not remarry after his wife's death in 1853. He died at his country home in Newton, Massachusetts.

• The Countway Library of Medicine, Harvard Medical Library, has one box of Bigelow's papers, which includes correspondence concerning his surgical instrument collection and appointments at Massachusetts General Hospital. Bigelow's publications include "A History of the Discovery of Modern Anaesthesia," in *A Century of American Medicine, 1776–1876* (1876), pp. 75–112; *Medical Education in America* (1871); and *Surgical Anesthesia: Addresses and Other Papers* (1894). For biographical information, see, by his son, William Sturgis Bigelow, *A Memoir of Henry Jacob Bigelow* (1900), which includes a listing of Bigelow's publications; Oliver Wendell Holmes, "Memoir of Henry Jacob Bigelow," *Proceedings of the American Academy of Arts and Sciences* 26 (1890–1891): 339–50; William J. Mayo, "In the Time of Henry Jacob Bigelow," *Journal of the American Medical Association* 77 (1921): 597–603; George H. Jackson, "Henry Jacob Bigelow: Orthopedic Surgeon," *Archives of Surgery* 46 (1943): 666–72; M. J. V. Smith, "Henry Jacob Bigelow (1818–1890)," *Urology* 14 (1979): 317–22; and Stefan C. Schatski, "Dr. Henry Jacob Bigelow," *American Journal of Roentgenology* 163 (1994): 574. For Bigelow's opposition to experimental physiology, see John Harley Warner, *The Therapeutic Perspective: Medical Practice, Knowledge, and Identity in America, 1820–1885* (1986), and Thomas S. Huddle, "Looking Backward: The 1871 Reforms at Harvard Medical School Reconsidered," *Bulletin of the History of Medicine* 65 (1991): 340–65. The best treatment of anesthesia during Bigelow's lifetime is Martin S. Pernick, *A Calculus of Suffering: Pain, Professionalism, and Anesthesia in Nineteenth-Century America* (1985).

SUSAN E. LEDERER

BIGELOW, Jacob (27 Feb. 1787–10 Jan. 1879), physician and botanist, was born in Sudbury, Massachusetts, the son of Jacob Bigelow, a Congregationalist minister, and Elizabeth Wells. He grew up on the family farm, which provided the Bigelows with their primary means of support. During his early years, his father emphasized pragmatic concerns, disapproving of his attempts to learn Latin. He was an observer of nature and enjoyed tinkering on the farm, inventing miniature saw mills and better rat traps. In 1802, at age sixteen, he entered Harvard. After obtaining his bachelor's degree in 1806, he attended the medical lectures of John Gorham at Harvard. In 1809 he went to Philadelphia to study medicine and was influenced by Benjamin Smith Barton, a professor of botany at the University of Pennsylvania.

In 1811 Bigelow returned to Boston intent on establishing a medical practice in a large urban setting. He became associated in professional practice with James Jackson, whom he eventually succeeded as the president of the Massachusetts Medical Society and the president of the American Academy of Arts and Sciences. In 1812 Bigelow began teaching at Harvard. That same year, partially through his initiative, the university began offering lectures in botany. During his first year there, he colectured with the distinguished William D. Peck. The following year, he taught the class on his own. He was the first native-born botanist to collect and describe the flora of New England thoroughly. In 1814 he published *Florula Bostoniensis*, the first edition of which dealt only with the flora within a ten-mile radius of Boston. Later editions expanded the geographical area covered. *Florula Bostoniensis* remained the standard manual of New England botany until Asa Gray's manual was published in 1848. In describing the flora of his native land, Bigelow was the first to give generic names to plants, simplifying the system of nomenclature.

In 1815 Bigelow was appointed lecturer in materia medica and botany at Harvard, and two years later his title changed to professor. In 1817 he began to publish the three-volume *American Medical Botany*, for which he prepared the artwork. (Because hand-colored plates proved impracticable, he invented a method of doing color printing with a single, engraved plate.) That year he married Mary Scollay; they had five children, one of whom, Henry Jacob, became a prominent surgeon. He published *Pharmacopeia of the United States* (1820) along with three other botanists. Once again, Bigelow attempted to simplify the description of plants by giving a single name to a species whenever possible. His system for describing the materia medica was adopted nationally. After the publication of *Florula Bostoniensis*, he began exchanging correspondence and specimens with European naturalists, and Gray reported that thirty-six species of plants eventually bore his name.

Bigelow was also an energetic supporter of the reform of medical treatment. He published *Discourse on Self-Limited Diseases* (1835). In it he argued against heroic medical measures, then in vogue, which included aggressive treatment with drugs and bloodletting. He argued instead that many diseases, if left alone, would end naturally and that aggressive medical intervention often only prolonged the course of disease. Even in *American Medical Botany*, he asserted that his goal was to diminish, rather than enlarge, the plants used for medicinal purposes. Physician and author Oliver Wendell Holmes claimed that *Self-Limited Diseases* had a greater effect on medical practice than any short work published before it. During his career, Bigelow engaged in several projects relating to public health. He advocated the creation of a suburban cemetery because he believed that the burying of bodies within the city of Boston was a source of disease. The establishment of the Mt. Auburn cemetery typified Bigelow's endeavors to promote public health.

In spite of his continued passion for the classics, Bigelow was a staunch advocate of practical education, a position that was quite controversial. In 1816 he became Rumford Professor of Application of Science to the Useful Arts at Harvard. The purpose of the lectures was to teach utilitarian science and mathematics for the extension of industry and the well-being of society. He constructed many of the apparatuses that he used to illustrate his lectures, including architectural models, various windmills and steam engines, and three full-size working models of parts of the Waltham cotton factory. His *Elements of Technology* (1829) was taken from his lectures as Rumford Professor. He expanded this work and published *The Useful Arts* in 1840. Bigelow put his utilitarianism to use in supporting the newly created Massachusetts Institute of Technology in 1861. Only four years after its incorporation, he delivered a lecture there titled *The Limits of Education*, in which he launched his most vigorous attack on the hegemony of the classics in education. He claimed that the limits of classical education stymied progress, efficiency, virtue, and the general welfare of all people. While he revered the classics, he did not believe that they could be profitably put to use by the vast majority of people living in an expanding democracy. His valuation of utility even extended to his opinion of his friends. In his memorial of Jackson, his longtime confidante and mentor, he wrote that Jackson displayed "ready adaptation of knowledge to use." His utilitarian views met with great opposition, and one critic referred to them as "the glorification of the gospel of machinery." Bigelow died in Boston.

• Bigelow also published the following major works: *Nature in Disease* (1854); *Eolopoesis, American Rejected Addresses* (1855); *Brief Expositions of Rational Medicine* (1858); and *Modern Inquiries* (1867). The best biographical information is G. E. Ellis, *Memoir of Jacob Bigelow* (1880); Richard J. Wolfe, *Jacob Bigelow's American Medical Botany, 1817–1821* (1979); H. A. Kelly, *Some American Medical Botanists* (1914); J. G. Mumford, "Jacob Bigelow: A Sketch," *Johns Hopkins Hospital Bulletin* (1902); Mumford, *Surgical Memoirs* (1908); G. B. Howe, *Genealogy of the Bigelow Family of America* (1890); and Clark A. Elliott and Margaret W. Rossiter, eds., *Science at Harvard University: Historical Perspectives* (1992). Information regarding Bigelow's botany can be found in Asa

Gray, "Dr. Jacob Bigelow," *American Journal of Science* 17, no. 100 (Apr. 1879): 263–66, and L. H. Bailey's memorial in the *Boston Gazette*, May 1883. For a sample of Bigelow's tireless advocacy of the causes he held dear, see Walter J. Friedlander, "The Bigelow-Simpson Controversy: Still Another Early Argument over the Discovery of Anesthesia," *Bulletin of the History of Medicine* 66 (1992): 613–25. Holmes's obituary of Bigelow is in *Proceedings of the American Academy of Arts and Sciences* (1879).

OLIVIA WALLING

BIGELOW, John (25 Nov. 1817–19 Dec. 1911), writer, and diplomat, was born in Bristol (now Malden-on-Hudson), New York, the son of Asa Bigelow and Lucy Isham, successful farmers and merchants. At thirteen he entered Washington (later Trinity) College in Hartford, Connecticut, but transferred to Union College in Schenectady, New York, from which he was graduated in 1835. In New York City Bigelow studied law and was admitted to the bar in 1838.

Lacking the contacts for a profitable law practice and seeking friendship and intellectual stimulation, Bigelow began writing for literary magazines on the side, including the *Democratic Review*. Through this journal he met influential Democrats, including his lifelong friend Samuel J. Tilden. When a Democratic governor was elected in New York in 1844, Bigelow received an appointment as an inspector of Sing Sing Prison (1845–1848). Drawing upon current ideas of democratic and humane penal reform, he and his fellow inspectors instituted many changes (merit hiring, documentation of prisoners' punishments, elimination of graft in work programs), which they hoped would reform rather than merely punish inmates.

In politics Bigelow favored free trade and a money system based on coin rather than paper banknotes and opposed territorial expansion if it extended slavery. In 1848 he broke with the Democratic party when it refused to endorse a prohibition of slavery in the territory of the Mexican cession and became an organizer and campaigner for the new Free-Soil party. Following the election he accepted William Cullen Bryant's invitation to become a full-time partner in the antislavery and free trade *New York Evening Post*, leaving the practice of law for good. Although small and struggling, the paper was influential because of its elite readership. Bigelow helped put it on a sound financial footing and freed Bryant from his onerous editorial duties. In 1849 Bigelow participated in the negotiations that reunited many of the Free-Soilers with the Democratic party. The following year he married Jane Poultney; they had eight children.

Bigelow's strong antislavery beliefs convinced him to travel to Jamaica in 1850 to document the success of former slaves as free men. His letters to the *Evening Post* later appeared as *Jamaica in 1850* (1851). He made a similar visit to Haiti in 1853, which formed the basis for his *The Wit and Wisdom of the Haitians* (1877). Later, in 1854, Bigelow became a convert to the religious mysticism of Emanuel Swedenborg, whose teachings influenced several of his later writings; in 1888 he even published a book about the religious leader, *Emanuel Swedenborg Servus Domini*.

The renewal of the slavery issue in the mid-1850s led Bigelow, Bryant, and the *Evening Post* to cast their lot with the new Republican party. In 1856 Bigelow wrote a campaign biography for John C. Frémont, the party's first presidential nominee. As a reward for his constant labors for the *Post*, Bigelow began an eighteen-month European vacation in 1858 that provided him with contacts among liberal intellectuals and politicians who proved valuable to his later diplomatic career.

A friend of Secretary of State William H. Seward, Bigelow obtained an appointment as consul-general to Paris during the Civil War. Since the American minister, William L. Dayton, knew no French, Bigelow played an unusually large role for a consul. He excelled in propagandizing the Union cause in pamphlets and liberal newspapers throughout Europe but unwisely pleaded with Seward to lift the immensely unpopular Union blockade of Confederate ports. Bigelow's most notable success lay in cooperating with his diplomatic counterparts in Great Britain to stymie Confederate shipbuilding efforts, in particular the powerful Laird rams built to break the Union's blockade. Using documents he had purchased in France and others from the Richmond archives, Bigelow related the Confederate side of this story later in *France and the Confederate Navy, 1862–1868* (1888), an important study. Amid praise for his assiduous efforts on behalf of his country, Bigelow was named minister to France in April 1865. He warned Napoleon III against military intervention in Mexico but resigned in 1866 before this episode was resolved.

Before he left Europe Bigelow located and purchased the original manuscript of the autobiography of Benjamin Franklin (1706–1790). This enabled him to publish in 1868 the first accurate edition of this important work. Continuing his interest in Franklin, he also published a *Life of Benjamin Franklin* (1874; 2d ed., revised and corrected, 1879) and an important ten-volume edition of *The Complete Works of Benjamin Franklin* (1887–1888).

As a sign of his increased public stature, Bigelow was chosen a member of the exclusive Century Club made up of New York City's 100 most important public men in 1868. The following year he became managing editor of the *New York Times* upon the death of its founder, Henry J. Raymond, but had to resign almost immediately after an article secretly planted by Jay Gould helped to cause an abortive raid on the gold market (Black Friday). Intending to devote the rest of his life to writing, Bigelow lived in Germany from 1870 to 1873, publishing *Beaumarchais the Merchant* (1870) and *France and Hereditary Monarchy* (1871). Never an admirer of President Ulysses S. Grant, he nonetheless continued to find merit in Republican policies after the war, even when many of his friends joined the Liberal Republican revolt in 1872. New revelations of scandals in the Grant administration, coupled with rumors of a third term for Grant, though, increased Bigelow's disillusionment.

In 1875 Samuel Tilden, then governor of New York and soon the Democratic nominee for the upcoming presidential campaign, appointed Bigelow chair of a bipartisan commission to investigate frauds in the management of the Erie Canal. Unfortunately, the commission's report promoted Tilden's political career more than it brought justice to the perpetrators of the wrongdoing it documented. While the report was still in preparation, Bigelow changed his party allegiance once again and was elected New York's secretary of state as a Democrat. His breach with the Republicans was permanent and deeply resented by his former allies.

There seems little doubt that Bigelow never was able to maintain a sense of objectivity on Tilden. During the 1876 presidential campaign he defended Tilden's war record in a pamphlet he wrote—Tilden had been a noncombatant and administration critic. Later he explained away Tilden's inactivity during the negotiations that had cost him the presidency; the Democratic nominee, one vote short of an electoral college majority, allowed an electoral commission with a Republican majority to award twenty disputed votes, and the election, to Rutherford B. Hayes. When Tilden died in 1886, Bigelow was named executor of the estate and was charged with using the large fortune to found a public library in New York City. When Tilden's relatives successfully contested the will, Bigelow and the other library trustees combined the money that remained with other resources from the Lenox and Astor foundations to create what is now the New York Public Library. Bigelow also organized Tilden's papers, publishing his *Writings and Speeches* (1885) and *Letters and Literary Memorials* (1908). Despite suspicions that he had removed unflattering materials, these volumes are more valuable than his overly sympathetic and sometimes inaccurate *The Life of Samuel J. Tilden* (1895).

In his old age Bigelow traveled frequently to Europe, serving in 1888 as commissioner to the international exposition at Brussels. He continued writing on topics ranging from the Panama Canal to sewage in the Hudson River. In 1890 he published a biography of another old friend, William Cullen Bryant, for the American Men of Letters series. In 1909 he published three volumes of his discursive autobiography, *Retrospections of an Active Life*; his son completed the remaining two volumes (1913). Intellectual yet pragmatic, strong-minded and opinionated to the end, he died in New York City.

• Bigelow's lengthy personal journals and correspondence are located in the New York Public Library. Margaret Clapp, *Forgotten First Citizen: John Bigelow* (1947), is the only available biography; it contains a complete list of his publications. An obituary is in the *New York Times*, 20 Dec. 1911.

PHYLLIS F. FIELD

BIGELOW, Melvin Madison (2 Aug. 1846–4 May 1921), law professor and author, was born near Eaton Rapids, Michigan, the son of William Enos Bigelow, a Methodist clergyman, and Daphne Florence Madison or Mattison, as it was sometimes spelled. The family was descended from John Bigelow, who came from England and settled at Watertown, Massachusetts, before 1642. Bigelow attended public schools wherever his father was stationed in the territory of the Detroit Conference, most of which was sparsely populated frontier country. He went on to the University of Michigan in Ann Arbor, earning an A.B. in 1866, an LL.B. in 1868, and an A.M. in 1871. In 1879 he received additional degrees, an A.M. and a Ph.D., from Harvard University. He studied law in Pontiac, Michigan, for a short time, then joined an uncle, Joseph Enos Bigelow, who practiced law in Memphis, Tennessee. He was admitted to the Tennessee bar in 1868. A boyhood friend, Marshall Davis Ewell, later a well-known law teacher and writer himself, followed him to Memphis, and the two helped prepare the manuscript of H. Clay King's *Tennessee Digest*. It was when he traveled to Boston to read the proof of this manuscript that Bigelow met Elizabeth Chamberlain, whom he married in 1869. They had three children, two girls who died in early childhood and one son who died in his third year at Harvard Law School. Elizabeth died in 1881. In May 1883 Bigelow married Cornelia Frothington Read; she died in 1892. He then married Alice Bradford Woodward in November 1898; she survived him.

Interested in studying the deeper principles of the law, Bigelow decided to become a legal researcher rather than a practicing attorney. He moved to Boston in 1870 and was admitted to the Boston bar. He soon met a group of men, including Edmund H. Bennett, Justice Dwight Foster, Charles Theodore Russell, and others, who, like himself, were dissatisfied with the current method of teaching law. With these men, Bigelow helped establish the Boston University Law School, which opened in September 1872. It was the first law school to adopt a graded three-year course requiring regular attendance and the passing of systematic examinations as a prerequisite for a degree. Bigelow became a professor of law with the school and in 1902 was made dean. He resigned as dean in 1911 but remained on the faculty teaching postgraduate courses until his death. During his tenure at Boston University, he occasionally delivered special courses at the law schools of the University of Michigan and Northwestern University.

In addition to his skills in the classroom, Bigelow was also an accomplished writer. By the time he was twenty-six years old, he had published *The Law of Estoppel and Its Application in Practice* (1872). This was followed in 1875 with *Leading Cases on the Law of Torts*. Both of these books went through many editions and became conventional references. His *Elements of the Law of Torts* (1878) became a standard textbook in all American law schools for many years. A special edition of this book was published in 1889 by Cambridge University Press, the first American law textbook to be accorded such an honor. According to an American colleague, "The fact that [Bigelow] could make the same textbook, with slight changes, serve for both England and this country, shows how clear was his grasp of the fundamental principles of the law" (Harriman, p. 161). In addition, Bigelow was one of the few American contributors to Lord Acton's *Cambridge Modern History* (vol. 7), writing the articles on the Declaration of Independence and the Constitution of the United States. His ideas to the nature of law were English. When he visited that country, as he did on many occasions, he was honored by its foremost lawyers, judges, and legal scholars.

Bigelow wrote four additional textbooks, many of which were used throughout North America, England, China, Japan, India, and South America. Following his death, Dean Homer Albers of Boston University School of Law said of his writing, "He displayed such a capacity to think and analyze and concisely express himself that his works are generally recognized as the best expositions of the subjects which he treated" (Albers, p. 155). He further distinguished himself as a legal writer and historian when he published *Placita Anglo-Normannica* (1879) and *History of Procedure in England from the Norman Conquest* (1880). The first of these works, his doctoral thesis at Harvard, contains law cases from William I to Richard I and was said to give him his widest distinction as a scholar in Europe as well as in America. It is debatable whether Bigelow was better known in England than his own country, but it has been written that these works, along with others on English legal history, were better appreciated in that country. Nonetheless, Bigelow was "intensely American" and "never for a moment dreamed it possible that the United States should consent to sacrifice its sovereignty, its independence, and its own ideals in order to become part of . . . the League of Nations" (Harriman, p. 164).

Bigelow had a delicate humor, a philosophic understanding, and a poetic imagination. Often the press carried pieces of poetry bearing his initials, and a volume of original verse, *Rhymes of a Barrister*, was published in 1902. Brooks Adams, a colleague, said of Bigelow, "I have known few men of more charming manner, more agreeable disposition, more unselfishness, and more charity than [Melville Bigelow]. To know him is to love him" (Harriman, p. 167). Bigelow was a member of various societies, including the American Academy of Arts and Sciences, the Massachusetts Historical Society, and the Baronial Order of Runnymeade. He was also an honorary member of the Harvard chapter of Phi Beta Kappa. He died in Boston.

Bigelow made major contributions to legal scholarship; in particular, he produced at least two books, *Placita Anglo-Normannica* and *History of Procedure in England*, that are acknowledged as works of great permanent value. He helped to establish legal history as a field of study in its own right, defined the parameters of tort law in America and England, and addressed issues of procedure in an elegant and useful manner. Serving on the faculty of Boston University of nearly fifty years, Bigelow impressed his students with his knowledge and authority. Charles Jenney, a former student and later jurist of the Massachusetts Supreme Court, said, "He was modest and did not relish applause; but he loved his students and his affection was returned by them in abundant measure" (Jenney, p. 172).

• Principal published works by Bigelow not mentioned in the text include *Overruled Cases by Courts of America, England and Ireland* (1873), *Law of Fraud* (2 vols., 1878, 1890), *Elements of the Law of Equity* (1879), *Law of Bills, Notes and Cheques* (1880), *Mistakes of Law* (1885), *Law of Wills* (1898), *Law of Fraudulent Conveyances* (1911), *A False Equation: The Problem of the Great Trust* (1911), *Papers on the Legal History of Government* (1920), and *Centralization and the Law* (1906), with Brooks Adams, Edward Avery Harriman, and H. S. Haines. Information about Bigelow's ancestry may be found in Gilman Bigelow Hower, *Genealogy of the Bigelow Family of America* (1890), and Conrad Reno, *Memoirs of the Judiciary and Bar of New England*, vol. 2 (1901), p. 635. The best accounts of his life are in the *Boston Law Review* 1, no. 3 (June 1921), contributors as follows: Lemuel H. Murlin, Homer Albers, Harriman, Adams, and Charles M. Jenney.

BETHANY K. DUMAS
LISABETH G. SVENDSGAARD

BIGGERS, Earl Derr (26 Aug. 1884–5 Apr. 1933), novelist, short-story writer, and playwright, was born in Warren, Ohio, the son of Robert J. Biggers and Emma E. Derr, occupations unknown. He was a colorful student at Harvard, where he loudly voiced his preference for Franklin P. Adams, Richard Harding Davis, and Rudyard Kipling, among other writers, over faculty-endorsed Henry Fielding, Oliver Goldsmith, Horace, John Keats, Samuel Richardson, and Tobias Smollett. In 1908, a year after he had earned his B.A., Biggers began writing humor columns for the *Boston Traveler* and later wrote drama reviews for it, but in 1911 he lost his job for what was called "roasting bad plays." In 1912 he married Eleanor Ladd and moved with her to New York City. They had one child.

Biggers's first comedy, *If You're Only Human* (1912), was a flop. His first novel, published a year later, was *Seven Keys to Baldpate*, which combined farce, melodrama, mystery, and romance. George M. Cohan, the popular man of the theater, bought the dramatic rights to it and made a financially successful adaptation. Biggers published two more novels, *Love Insurance* (1914) and *The Agony Column* (1916).

Biggers gradually evolved into a writer of popular humor, magazine articles, short stories, and plays. His *Inside the Lines* ran 500 nights in London in 1915–1916. *A Cure for Curables*, which he coauthored with Lawrence Whitman, enjoyed a two-year run in New York, beginning in 1918. In 1919 his short story "See-Saw" was remade into a musical comedy, and he and Christopher Morley wrote a farce titled *Three's a Crowd*. From the early 1920s Biggers and his family made California their home. Although his stated reason was to improve his health and that of his bank account, in truth he disliked what rewrite men were doing to his plays. Once in Hollywood, he generated mystery, romance, comic relief, and suspenseful plotting for the Fox Corporation, Radio Pictures, and Warner Brothers.

Then pop-art fame came to Biggers by way of his famous fictional character Charlie Chan, a Chinese-born detective working in Honolulu. Biggers had vacationed in Hawaii in 1919, where stories of Chang Apana, a Chinese detective in Honolulu, triggered his imagination. Making his first appearance six years later, Chan grew in significance over the next eight years. Beginning with the 24 September 1925 issue, Biggers serialized "The House Without a Key" in the *Saturday Evening Post*; Charlie Chan was introduced in the second installment. *The House Without a Key* was published in book form in 1925. In the second Chan novel, *The Chinese Parrot*, which was serialized in the *Post* and published in book form in 1926, Chan emerges—thanks to *Post* illustrator W. H. D. Koerner—as young, clean-shaven, and slender despite being described in the first book as being fat. Biggers published two more non–Charlie Chan novels—*The Ruling Passion* (1924) and *Fifty Candles* (1926)—but put all of his creative energy for the remainder of his short life into four more novels that featured the detective. All first serialized in the *Post*, they are *Behind That Curtain* (1928), *The Black Camel* (1929), *Charlie Chan Carries On* (1930), and *Keeper of the Keys* (1932). *Behind That Curtain* is the first to include Charlie Chan's celebrated aphorisms, and *The Black Camel* is the first to include the gathering of suspects in a climactic scene. *Post* illustrations by Henry Raleigh for *Charlie Chan Carries On* first present the detective as fat, with sloping eyebrows, and sporting a moustache. By series end, Chan, an inspector since his *Black Camel* work, has become consummately observant, patient, and analytical.

Fully as popular as Biggers was the talented actor Warner Oland, made up to resemble the Raleigh illustrations, who starred in sixteen Charlie Chan movies, beginning with *Charlie Chan Carries On* and *The Black Camel* (both 1931), including *Charlie Chan's Greatest Case* (1933, based on *The House Without a Key*) and *Charlie Chan's Courage* (1934, based on *The Chinese Parrot*), and continuing through 1937, with other writers after Biggers's death of a sudden heart attack in Pasadena. So popular was the captivating detective that when Oland died in 1938, Sidney Toler starred in twenty-two more Charlie Chan movies, to 1947, after which Roland Winters played the leading role in six more movies, to 1949. A 1981 Charlie Chan movie starred Peter Ustinov. Charlie Chan was also featured in radio dramas and comic strips. Charlie Chan novels have been translated into at least ten foreign languages. John P. Marquand's Mr. Moto novels, beginning in 1935 and featuring a Japanese detective, owe more than a little to Biggers. (The bombing of Pearl Harbor in 1941 effectively ended Mr. Moto's career.) *Earl Derr Biggers Tells Ten Stories* is a posthumous collection of non–Charlie Chan pieces (1933).

Hollywood's Charlie Chan is only a fat shadow of Biggers's suave creation. On the screen, Chan is smug, ethnically stereotypical, and mainly memorable for his often silly pseudo-Chinese maxims and linguistic clichés. Biggers created his profoundly complex and engaging hero in large part to correct the old Fu Manchu image of the crafty, malevolent Chinese first popularized in 1913 by Sax Rohmer. Biggers's Charlie Chan is of abiding international significance for dramatizing East versus West: Eastern selfless contentment, a serene acceptance of enigmatic life, and a love of nature, on the one hand; Western ambition, curiosity, materialism and gadgetry, sick rush, and discontent, on the other. At the same time, Biggers presents emerging Western traits in his Asian sleuth. He is pleased with his growing command of the English language and grimaces at his Americanized sons' use of slang and his daughters' love of Hollywood values. Even as Chan criticizes the faltering English of his Chinese servant, he applauds the solid fellow's retention of Chinese ways.

To modern readers, Biggers's Charlie Chan novels are redolent of both nostalgia and ethnic stereotypes. Exotic and vivid old Honolulu and San Francisco locales of the 1920s come alive again. His rather routine plots feature animosities, shakedowns, revenge, knife and gunshot wounds, weak alibis, and disappearing items (including corpses). Romantic subplots often feature tired young male urbanites rejuvenated by contact not only with nature but also with ambivalent, liberated young females. Betraying Biggers's background as a playwright, his novels may now seem a bit too loaded with dialogue; but his central creation, the crosscultural Charlie Chan, grows more relevant as American culture becomes more global.

• Most of the very few letters by Biggers in repositories available to the public are in the Historical Society of Pennsylvania and the Humanities Research Center at the University of Texas. Walter Albert, *Detective and Mystery Fiction: An International Bibliography of Secondary Sources* (1985), pp. 322–23, covers Biggers. Howard Haycraft, *Murder for Pleasure: The Life and Times of the Detective Story* (1941; repr. 1984), offers early praise of Biggers. Chris Steinbrunner and Otto Penzler, eds., *Encyclopedia of Mystery and Detection* (1976), detail movies made from Biggers's non–Charlie Chan novels. Penzler, *The Private Lives of Private Eyes, Spies, Crime Fighters and Other Good Guys* (1977), presents a biography and personality profile of Biggers and a "biography" of Charlie Chan. Neil Ellman, "Charlie Chan Carries On," *Armchair Detective* 10 (1977): 183–84, shows how Biggers made Chan the first "domestic" detective in fiction. Jon L. Breen, "Murder Number One: Earl Derr Biggers," *New Republic*, 30 July 1977, pp. 38–39, traces the evolution of Charlie Chan in fiction and film. The best commentary on Biggers the writer is Henry Kratz, "Earl Derr Biggers," in *Critical Survey of Mystery and Detective Fiction*, ed. Frank N. Magill (1988), pp. 130–35. Ken Hanke, *Charlie Chan at the Movies: History, Filmography, and Criticism* (1989), provides data on forty-four Charlie Chan movies—both those deriving from Biggers's novels and those entirely by others. Francis Lacassin, "Charlie Chan ou le sage aux sept fleurs," in his *Mythologie du roman policier*, vol. 1 (1978), pp. 289–317, discusses ethnic and professional aspects of the characterization of Chan. Alfred Andriola,

Charlie Chan: 1938–1939 (1980), reprints Andriola's 1938–1939 McNaught Syndicate Charlie Chan comic strips. An obituary, with portrait, is in the *New York Times*, 6 Apr. 1933.

ROBERT L. GALE

BIGGS, E. Power (29 Mar. 1906–10 Mar. 1977), concert organist, was born Edward George Power Biggs in Westcliff-on-Sea, England, the son of Clarence Biggs, an auctioneer, and Alice Maud Tredgett. He was an only child and his father died three years after his birth. He grew up in Ventnor, on the Isle of Wight, where his mother ran a boardinghouse; at the age of seven he entered Hurstpierpoint College, a boarding school, where he took his first piano lessons. Upon graduation in 1922 he entered into an apprenticeship with an electrical engineering firm in London. At the age of eighteen he began taking organ lessons from J. Stuart Archer, a noted recitalist who was organist of a large Christian Science church. Archer encouraged his pupil to apply for a scholarship at the Royal Academy of Music, which Biggs did, winning the scholarship in 1926.

At the academy Biggs was again fortunate in his teacher. George D. Cunningham, municipal organist at Birmingham City Hall, was an outstanding recitalist and a gifted teacher who quickly became a role model for young Biggs. Late in his life, Biggs recalled that Cunningham "was not only a great player, he was also a great teacher." Upon Biggs's graduation in 1929 he signed on as organist and accompanist with a small concert company about to embark on a tour of the United States. The tour itself was rather disastrous, but Biggs saw a great deal of America and its varied organs, and in New York City at the end of the tour he played a recital at the Wanamaker store auditorium and made several important contacts. Although he returned to England, he was soon back in America, and in October 1930 he was hired as organist and choirmaster by Emmanuel Church in Newport, Rhode Island.

Biggs had made up his mind to become a recitalist very early on, and he was soon securing recital engagements and negotiating with a concert manager. In 1932 he moved to Cambridge, Massachusetts, where he would spend the rest of his life, and took the position of organist and choirmaster at Christ Church. He was also the organ teacher at the Longy School. Biggs was now under the management of Bernard Laberge and giving recitals on the national concert circuit. He was also developing an interest in contemporary music, particularly that of Leo Sowerby, whose difficult Symphony in G became one of his concert pieces, which he later recorded. In 1933 Biggs married Colette Lionne, a French pianist with whom he had collaborated on several organ-and-piano concerts, and in 1935 he became organist and choirmaster at the Harvard Congregational Church in Brookline, a position he held until 1960. In the choir of this church he was to meet his second wife, Margaret (Peggy) Allen, whom he married in 1945 after his divorce from Colette the previous year.

In 1937, the year Biggs became an American citizen, the Aeolian-Skinner Company placed an "experimental" organ in the gallery of the Germanic Museum on the Harvard University campus. Biggs liked its clean classic sound and proceeded to schedule recitals of early music on it. In 1939 he was engaged as a recording artist by Victor Red Seal and immediately began recording on the museum organ. In 1942 he went a step further, performing his popular Sunday morning radio broadcasts on the same instrument. Over the years, until the program was canceled in 1958, Biggs introduced his radio audience to a wealth of fine classical music, from Renaissance to contemporary, many of the pieces in the latter category having been requested or commissioned by him.

Around 1940 Biggs, a strong advocate for the secular role of the organ, became the official organist of the Boston Symphony Orchestra, and his influence was felt in two important areas. One was in programming: Biggs constantly lobbied for the inclusion of more organ-and-orchestra works, including new compositions. He was also very knowledgeable about organ design, and his expertise was almost immediately called upon when a new organ was built in 1940 for the Music Shed at Tanglewood, the orchestra's summer home. In 1947 he became involved in the design of a new organ for Boston's Symphony Hall. Shortly after its inauguration in 1949 Biggs instituted an annual series of organ recitals featuring well-known performers.

During the postwar years and into the 1960s, Biggs kept up a frenetic recital schedule, playing hundreds of recitals a year. He also stepped up his recording activity, having moved from Victor to Columbia in 1948, just as LP records were being developed. In 1954 he planned his first European concert tour, which, thanks to a suggestion from the Columbia management, also became a recording tour. As he later recalled in a taped interview, "playing the great historic organs of Europe had, for me, the impact of a revelation." Titled *The Art of the Organ*, the recording was the first to be made by an American on historic European organs, and it proved a revelation to listeners as well. It was followed by many more recordings, made in various countries and featuring works of Mozart, Bach, and French, Italian, and Spanish composers. One other tangible result of Biggs's exposure to European instruments was the replacement of the original organ in the Germanic Museum with a new instrument of classical design and mechanical action by the Dutch builder Flentrop. Although the radio broadcasts ended shortly after it was installed in 1958, it continued to be used by Biggs for recitals and recordings, including a projected (but never completed) series of the organ works of Bach.

Biggs enjoyed occasionally poking into the byways of music and instruments, with often interesting results. In 1960 he was one of the first to record some of the early American keyboard music and the first, in 1958–1959, to make recordings of the Handel organ concertos with a historic organ built in Handel's lifetime and a Handelian chamber orchestra. A similar recording of Haydn organ concertos was issued in 1964. The coincidence of anniversaries of the births of Mozart and Benjamin Franklin in 1956 led him to the glass armonica, an instrument of musical glasses invented by Franklin and written for by Mozart. With some foundation funding, Biggs sought to have made a modern replica of the instrument on which to record Mozart's music. The result was not entirely successful, however, and while the instrument was heard in only one concert, Biggs did record Mozart's "glass music" on the organ. Of greater importance was his discovery of the pedal harpsichord. In 1964 he commissioned a two manual and pedal instrument from John Challis, ostensibly for practice purposes. Before long, however, he had made several precedent-setting recordings on it, ranging from Bach trio sonatas to Scott Joplin rags.

One instrument that did not interest him was the electronic imitation of a pipe organ. To avoid having to play one with an orchestra in a venue where a pipe organ was not available, Biggs in 1954 commissioned a small movable organ with a detached console from the Schlicker Organ Company. It could be packed up and towed in a car trailer, and for several years Biggs used it for concerts and at least one television appearance before retiring it to his living room as a practice instrument. For Biggs the proper use of electronic technology was in the recording and faithful reproduction of authentic organ sound. He keenly followed every new development in this area, from LP discs to quadraphonic reproduction. When the latter development became reality in the early 1970s, Biggs was ready with plans for recording at the Cathedral of Freiburg-am-Breisgau in Germany, which had four organs controlled from a single console.

Although rheumatoid arthritis was beginning to affect Biggs's health in the 1960s, his recital and recording schedule barely slowed down. His series of recordings of historic organs continued, as did his Bach series, and in 1968 his recording of Gabrieli's music for organ, brass, and strings, made at St. Mark's in Venice, won him the coveted Grammy award. Shortly afterward he completed a long-planned project for an educational recording with a lavish liner booklet titled *The Organ in Sight and Sound*, issued in 1969.

By the 1970s Biggs had come to be regarded as the "elder statesman" of the American organ world, but he refused to rest on his laurels. Although he had by this time cut back significantly on recitals, he took part in 1975 in the dedication of the new organ in Alice Tully Hall in New York City and was at work on two very different recordings. One, a recording of lighthearted American music, was issued in 1976, the bicentennial year; the other, his last, was a lyrical performance of Bach's sinfonias, recorded in Bach's own church with members of the Leipzig Gewandhaus Orchestra. Biggs's last public performance, as soloist with the Boston "Pops" Orchestra, occurred in June 1976 as part of a national convention of the American Guild of

Organists. Biggs had been a lifelong supporter of this organization: he was active in the local chapter and had performed at countless other guild functions. In the last months of his life he wrote several somewhat autobiographical articles for various publications, and he was still planning new recording projects until a week before his death in Boston.

Biggs may without contradiction be called the most influential American organist of the middle decades of the twentieth century. He was a sincere believer in the power of the media and worked to advance the cause of the organ and its music through recordings, radio, and television. His standards were high and uncompromising, both in his choice of music and of organs; rather than lowering himself to the perceived standards of his public, he raised his audiences to his own standards simply by playing good music on good organs. His respect for the organs and music of the past was balanced by his active encouragement of young composers and players and by his advocacy of the best organ builders. As a performer, his legacy endures in his recordings, which continue to be issued as CDs.

• Biggs's correspondence and other material relating to him are in the Organ Library of the Boston Chapter, American Guild of Organists, Boston University School of Theology. Biggs was himself a prolific writer, and many of his articles appeared in *Music, Musical America, The Diapason, The Tracker, Organ Institute Quarterly, A.G.O. Quarterly,* and *Records and Recording.* Two of the most complete studies of Biggs's life and work are Barbara Owen, *E. Power Biggs, Concert Organist* (1987), and Eileen Hunt, *E. Power Biggs: Legacy of a Performing Artist* (D.M.A. diss., Boston Univ., 1986), which deals with his championing of new music. A detailed discography compiled by Andrew Kazdin appeared in *Music, The AGO-RCCO Magazine,* Mar. 1978, pp. 30–31, 42, and is reprinted as an appendix to Owen's book.

BARBARA OWEN

BIGGS, Hermann Michael (29 Sep. 1859–28 June 1923), pathologist, bacteriologist, physician, and public health official, was born in Trumansburg, New York, the son of Joseph Hunt Biggs and Melissa Pratt. Dr. Biggs married Frances M. Richardson, of Hornellsville, New York, in 1898; they had two children. Biggs received his primary education in Ithaca, New York, and matriculated into Cornell University, where he received the bachelor of arts degree in 1882. From Cornell Biggs went on to medical school at the Bellevue Hospital Medical College, where he received his M.D. the following year. He spent the next eighteen months (1882–1883) in the postgraduate course at Bellevue, where he served as a rotating intern and resident physician. Upon completion of this course, Biggs traveled to Europe and spent the next two years (1883–1885) studying bacteriology in Berlin and Griefswald. When he returned to New York City in 1886, Biggs was made director of the newly opened Carnegie Bacteriology Laboratory of the Bellevue Hospital. His rise in academic rank was meteoric; appointed a lecturer in pathology in 1886, Biggs was made a full professor of

pathology in 1889, professor of materia medica (pharmacology) in 1892, professor of therapeutics in 1898, and professor of medicine in 1912.

Biggs's professional career coincided with the bacteriological revolution of medicine; at this time the germ theory of disease began to be elaborated and the etiologic or causative agent of many infectious diseases, such as tuberculosis, cholera, whooping cough, and diphtheria, began to be identified. As a bacteriologist and physician, Biggs quickly appreciated the impact that these scientific findings would have on public health and preventive medicine. For example, during the late 1880s Biggs consulted with the New York Quarantine Station on the application of cholera culture methods to incoming immigrants. He continued to act as a consultant to the quarantine station and the New York City Department of Health throughout his career. In September 1892, when there was a fear of another cholera epidemic reaching American shores, Biggs was asked to organize and direct the Department of Pathology and Bacteriology of the New York City Health Department. Although medical historians frequently argue over which American city was the first to develop a bacteriological laboratory (Lawrence, Mass., Ann Arbor, Mich., and Providence, R.I., all had such laboratories established in the late 1880s), New York City's bacteriology laboratory was the first of its kind to not only test the purity of food and water but also to apply bacteriological methods to the diagnosis of disease.

Although Biggs maintained his academic appointment at the Bellevue Medical College throughout his career, it was his work with the New York City Health Department for which he is best known. In 1894, for example, with the assistance of William H. Park, Biggs introduced the use of diphtheria antitoxin to the United States. Diphtheria was a highly feared infectious disease of childhood; the bacteria in question attacks the child's throat, causing an intense inflammation and "pseudo-membrane" that can obstruct the child's breathing. If the child with diphtheria were fortunate enough to survive this phase of the illness, he had to be watched closely for the secondary effect of diphtheria, which was the secretion of a toxin that could cause the heart to stop beating. Diphtheria antitoxin, which was produced by injecting diphtheria organisms into a horse and subsequently purifying the horse serum into an antitoxin product, often prevented the cardiac complications of the disease. Under Biggs, the Health Department Bacteriology Laboratory was also quite entrepreneurial in that it licensed and sold its antitoxin product, as well as other biological products, to many other departments of health, physicians, and hospitals in the United States.

Biggs was also active in the prevention and amelioration of tuberculosis. During the early part of the twentieth century, tuberculosis was among the major killers of Americans between the ages of twenty and forty years. Biggs and his associates at the health department worked arduously to set up prevention programs based on analysis of the suspected patient's sputum, notification processes, and care facilities for those stricken with tuberculosis, including home nursing care. They also worked for the passage of public health laws that called for the isolation of "recalcitrant" tuberculosis patients. What appears especially amazing was that throughout Biggs's 22-year service with the New York City Health Department he was able to steer so many public health reforms within a milieu of political infighting and differing views of how to handle the ill, especially when those people happened to be among the urban poor or immigrant classes.

Biggs was appointed commissioner of the New York State Department of Health in 1914, which had been newly recreated by the New York state legislature to have much broader powers of public health reform and control than its predecessor. He remained at this post for nine years and developed some of the most novel and effective programs in epidemic disease control and maternal and infant health. Biggs also published widely on issues of public health and bacteriology. He died in New York City.

• Two of Hermann Biggs's more noteworthy publications are "The Diagnostic Value of the Cholera Spirillum, as Illustrated by the Investigation of a Case at the New York Quarantine Station," *New York Medical Journal* 46 (1887): 548–49, and "History of the Recent Outbreak of Epidemic Cholera in New York," *American Journal of Medical Science*, n.s., 105 (1893): 63–72. A biography of Biggs is Charles-Edward A. Winslow, *The Life of Hermann M. Biggs* (1929). Daniel M. Fox, "Social Policy and City Politics: Tuberculosis Reporting in New York City, 1889–1900," *Bulletin of the History of Medicine* 49 (1975): 169–95, and Howard Markel, *Quarantine: East European Jewish Immigrants and the New York City Epidemics of 1892* (1997), both discuss Biggs's contributions to public health. Biggs is mentioned in Wade Oliver, *The Man Who Lived for Tomorrow: A Biography of William Hallock Park* (1941). An obituary is in the *New York Times*, 29 June 1923.

HOWARD MARKEL

BIGLER, John (8 Jan. 1805–29 Nov. 1871), governor of California, was born near Carlisle, Pennsylvania, the son of Jacob Bigler and Susan Dock, farmers. He briefly attended Dickinson College until his family moved to Mercer County, where he was apprenticed to a printer. From 1827 to 1832 he edited the *Centre County Democrat* in Bellefonte, Pennsylvania. In addition, he read law, was admitted to the bar in 1840, and practiced law in Pennsylvania and Mount Sterling, Illinois. In mid-1849 he migrated with his wife and daughter to Sacramento, California (the name of his wife, the date of their marriage, and the total number of their children are unknown).

In Sacramento, at first a lack of opportunity forced Bigler to engage in manual labor and odd jobs while organizing the state Democratic party. In November 1849 he won a seat in the first California Assembly, to which he was reelected in 1850. His close, disputed elections led to charges of fraud, but he was always cleared by investigations. In each of his two assembly sessions, his colleagues voted him Speaker pro tem.

In May 1851 Bigler was nominated for governor at the Democratic party's first state convention. His victory in 1851 and reelection in 1853 made him the only California governor in the nineteenth century to win two terms of office. Simultaneously, his brother William Bigler was governor of Pennsylvania.

As governor Bigler upheld the Jefferson-Jackson tradition of states' rights and strict construction. He fought against imaginary banking monopolies, paper money, high taxes, and public debt. He was horrified that the state had raised revenue by issuing bonds that paid 3 percent interest, and he cut taxes to 30 cents per $100 of property. To reduce state spending, he recommended that the state legislature meet only every other year, abolish the state census, lower spending on hospitals, and trim the number of state officials.

Bigler spent much of his governorship fighting against the federal government. In his 1856 annual message, he blamed the state's empty treasury on California's never having enjoyed the "fostering care" of territorial status; its only federal ties had been supposedly oppressive customs collectors.

Most of these federal-state disputes centered on land. Since the birth of the republic, western lands were considered the public domain, the joint possession of the nation's citizens, of which farm lands could be purchased but mineral rights only leased, the proceeds going into the federal treasury. On the eve of the gold rush, President James K. Polk had scrapped this leasing system on the grounds that it cost more to maintain than it brought in. As a result, the gold discovered in California was ripe for plucking. An estimated $500,000 worth of gold from public land passed into private hands without its owners' paying a penny of tax or rent. Bigler applauded this transfer of wealth. His 1852 inaugural address urged that "the mines should be left as free as the air we breathe." Likewise, he championed squatters on agricultural lands, demanding not only preemption rights but a donation act, whereby Congress would allocate free 160-acre plots to settlers. All this was justified with Jeffersonian rhetoric "When by luxury and dissipation virtue and honesty take their flight from our cities," he declaimed in his first inaugural, "they will find a cherished home at the hearth of the generous farmer."

However, there were other claimants to the lands. The Treaty of Guadalupe Hidalgo, ending the Mexican War, had promised to honor Spanish and Mexican land claims. Bigler complained that the federal government's delays in adjudicating these claims were retarding the settlement of the state. As for the American Indians native to the area, in Bigler's eyes they had no rights. Although in 1851 federal agents had negotiated treaties with the tribes, by which one-seventh of the state would be Indian reservations, Bigler successfully fought against ratification of the treaties and demanded instead the removal of the natives.

As race relations deteriorated and violence escalated, Bigler excoriated the federal government for failing to protect the settlers. Rather than rely on federal troops, he sought to muster "volunteers," assuming that their expenses would be reimbursed by Congress. Indeed, he billed Congress for nearly $1 million for the state's prior Indian war debt, which he boasted would reduce the state debt by nearly half.

Though already governing a multiracial people, Bigler hoped to restrict future immigration to European whites. He particularly opposed Chinese immigration. In a special message of April 1852, he warned that the state was being flooded by a "tidal wave of Asiatic immigration." Pointing out that since 1790 naturalization had been restricted to white immigrants, he said in his 1856 annual message that Asians must "ever remain as the African a distinct and separate race, with marked peculiarities and characteristics, differing essentially from our own people, without the possibility of amalgamating or uniting with us in future." During his administration, a tax on foreign miners was enacted—and disproportionately enforced against the Chinese—and a tax on immigrants ineligible for citizenship was instituted as well. Rather than make allowances for the Hispanic population, Bigler opposed translating the legislative journal into Spanish.

Bigler did, however, sympathize with poor white settlers. He created state immigrant aid stations to assist the victims of the overland trail. California's public school system began while he was governor.

In other matters, he lobbied for a transcontinental railroad and signed the law making Sacramento the state capital. He had no qualms about slavery. In his first inaugural, he attacked abolitionists as "fanatical propagandists of mere moral tenets."

Defeated in his run for a third term, Bigler in 1856 visited the East Coast, where he campaigned for presidential candidate James Buchanan. After the election, Buchanan named him foreign minister to Chile, where he settled several longstanding maritime disputes. He held the post from 1857 to 1861.

Following his return to California, Bigler practiced law and reentered politics. Because California had shifted to the Republicans, he failed in a bid for a congressional seat in 1863 but was a delegate to Democratic national conventions. President Andrew Johnson appointed him to two minor public offices, though the Republican Senate rejected one of his appointments. In 1868 he founded the Democratic *State Capital Reporter*, a newspaper he edited until his death in Sacramento.

Bigler was a staunch party man in an age of bitter partisanship. While he was governor, the Democratic party and the nation split over sectionalism and slavery, issues for which he had little sensitivity. Though his political opponents repeatedly accused him of fraud and corruption, no evidence of malfeasance in office has been uncovered. The worst that can be said of him is that he was too blinded by a dying ideology to envision a special multi-ethnic future for the state.

• Scattered Bigler papers are at the California State Library, the California State Archives, and the Bancroft Library, University of California at Berkeley. Most of his speeches were published, occasionally with supplementary correspondence, copies of which may be found in the libraries cited above and in the Huntington Library, San Marino, Calif. Minor references to Bigler are published in the *California Historical Society Quarterly* and the *Southern California Quarterly*. A contemporary sketch is in Oscar T. Shuck, *Representative and Leading Men of the Pacific* (1870). A section on Bigler with a bibliography is in H. Brett Melendy and Benjamin F. Gilbert, *The Governors of California: Peter H. Burnett to Edmund G. Brown* (1965). The best account is Lionel Edward Freedman, "The Bigler Regime" (M.A. thesis, Stanford Univ., 1959). An obituary is in the *Sacramento Daily Union*, 30 Nov. 1871.

STEVEN J. NOVAK

BIGLER, William (1 Jan. 1814–9 Aug. 1880), governor and senator, was born at Shermansburg, Cumberland County, Pennsylvania, the son of Jacob Bigler and Susan Dock, farmers. Jacob Bigler died while William was a young boy, leaving the family in dire poverty. As a result, Bigler's education was cut short, and he was forced to seek employment at the age of fourteen. He left to work for his brother John Bigler, who became governor of California, in a printing office in Bellefonte, Centre County, where they published the *Centre Democrat*. At nineteen William decided to go into business for himself, and with the loan of a few hundred dollars and a secondhand printing press, he established the *Clearfield Democrat* as a pro-Jackson sheet in Clearfield, Pennsylvania.

In 1836 Bigler married Maria J. Reed, with whom he had five children. This prudent marriage permitted him to sell his paper and enter into a partnership with his wife's father. Bigler became one of the largest lumber merchants along the Susquehanna, and over the next few years he amassed a sizable fortune. In 1841 he entered politics and won election to the state senate, where he served until 1847, twice as Speaker (1843 and 1844).

During his tenure in the state legislature, Bigler distinguished himself by careful attention to repairing the state finances. The failure of the Bank of Pennsylvania in the late 1830s had caused severe financial hardship in the state. Therefore, he was primarily interested in rebuilding the state's solvency and in establishing railroad service westward to Pittsburgh.

In 1851 the Democratic party nominated Bigler for governor. His victory, which occurred shortly after the Christiana riots in Pennsylvania, was seen as a rebuke against abolitionists who defied the Fugitive Slave Law of 1850. During his tenure as governor, he created the office of county superintendent of schools and established a school for feeble-minded children and a "House of Refuge" for juvenile offenders. In his speech at the dedication of this reform school, he lauded the modern compassionate methods, combining gentleness with discipline and relying on environmental rather than on genetic explanations for delinquency. He also encouraged the institution to hire women as teachers. During his time in office, he saw the western Pennsylvania railroad completed and the North Branch Canal constructed. One of his most important contributions as governor was the consolidation of the city and county of Philadelphia. The numerous municipalities within the county's boundaries were brought together, which eliminated duplicate offices and simplified city management.

True to his Jacksonian roots, Bigler opposed the wholesale chartering of banks and imitated Andrew Jackson by becoming famous for vetoing bank charters. In one veto message he struck down eleven charters. Firmly convinced that each bill should only deal with one subject, he also vigorously opposed omnibus or logrolling bills. In 1854 Bigler was nominated for a second term but was defeated by the new Know Nothing party and by the growing Temperance movement in the state.

In 1855 Bigler became president of the Philadelphia & Erie Railroad Company. The following year he was elected to the U.S. Senate. As senator, he supported the Democratic nomination of James Buchanan for the presidency. Because of his close friendship with President Buchanan, Bigler exerted considerable influence on presidential appointments.

More active in committees than on the Senate floor, Bigler made few speeches. In the summer of 1857 he traveled to Kansas and, as a result of this trip, became more favorable in his stance toward the proslavery element in the territory. A supporter of states' rights, he endorsed the proslavery Kansas Lecompton constitution the following year. He called for the construction of an isthmus canal and for extending the railroad to the Pacific Coast. In his speeches on the latter subject, he always claimed to be less concerned with the precise location of the railroad, "a few degrees north or south," than with "protecting the rights of citizens on the Pacific side."

Bigler denied the southern states' right to secede, but he earnestly supported the Crittenden compromise, serving as a member of the Committee of Thirteen in the Senate. His moderate views led to his defeat for reelection and such harsh criticism that he retired in 1861 from national politics. One of his last speeches in the Senate pleaded for conciliatory measures. During the Civil War he remained outspoken against corruption and dishonesty in government and opposed the abolition of slavery.

In 1872 a statewide call arose for the reform of the Pennsylvania state constitution. The Pennsylvania legislature was notorious for corruption, bribery, rigged contracts, and legislators and, reputedly, senatorial offices for sale to the highest bidder. Both parties hoped to dismantle or at least manage the powerful machine of Simon Cameron. Ultimately, Bigler's influence failed to produce more than moderate changes, but he was considered, as a former governor and railroad promoter, one of the more prestigious members of the committee.

Bigler was also prominent in the Pennsylvania centennial celebrations for 1876 and was active on the committee's board of finance for the exposition. In 1876 he backed Samuel J. Tilden's bid for the presidency and traveled to Louisiana to defend the Democratic party against the Republican accusation of electoral fraud.

Bigler supported the Democratic party and attended most of the party's national conventions throughout the rest of his life. He remained an ardent railroad promoter and a successful capitalist in his hometown of Clearfield, where he died. Although one of his biographers has assessed his career as "wise rather than brilliant," during his tenure as governor Bigler was highly respected for his integrity and his scrupulously honest attention to state finances.

• Bigler's papers are in the collections of the Philadelphia Historical Society. Biographical information on Bigler is in William C. Armor, *Lives of the Governors of Pennsylvania, 1609–1872* (1872), and L. C. Aldrich, *History of Clearfield County, Pennsylvania* (1887). A brief summation and assessment of Bigler's career as governor is in Philip S. Klein and Ari Hoogenboom, *A History of Pennsylvania*, 2d ed. (1980). See also John F. Coleman, *The Disruption of the Pennsylvania Democracy, 1848–1860* (1975). Obituaries are in the *Philadelphia Press and Record* and the *New York Times*, both 10 Aug. 1880.

SILVANA SIDDALI

BIG WARRIOR (?–8 Mar. 1825), leader of the Upper Creeks whose Indian name has been rendered Tastanagi Tako or Tustunnugee Thlucco, was born probably at Tuckabatchee, an Indian town on the Tallapoosa River, in what is now Alabama. Nothing is known about the parentage or early career of Big Warrior. The Tuckabatchee Indians were one of several non-Muscogee–speaking groups incorporated in the Muscogee-dominated Creek confederacy that occupied much of present-day Alabama, Georgia, and Florida at the end of the eighteenth century.

Among the Creeks, *tastanagi tako* (big warrior) was a rank accorded the leading war chief in a town, but a contemporary report by Joseph V. Bevan explicitly stated that in this case Big Warrior was "the proper, and not the official name of the Indian." It appears that at his peak Big Warrior was the town civil chief, or *mico*, of Tuckabatchee rather than the head warrior, and it is possible that his name was related to his personal appearance: he was, recalled Thomas Woodward, a huge man, "almost as spotted as a leopard." Big Warrior probably inherited his office of *mico* through the female line, as was commonly the case among the Creeks.

Big Warrior was present at the treaty of Coleraine, on the St. Mary's River, in 1796, when the United States secured the right to establish trading and military posts in the Creek country. The treaty inaugurated a new period of Creek-American relations. Supervised by the Indian agent Benjamin Hawkins, the Creeks were encouraged by the United States to abandon hunting and the warrior society in favor of an improved agricultural economy. Although not entirely devoid of altruism, the "civilization" policy was intended to unlock Creek lands for white settlement by turning the Indians into independent farmers willing to sell surplus hunting ranges to buy equipment and supplies for their agriculture and manufacturing.

At the beginning of the nineteenth century Big Warrior was the "speaker" (spokesman) for the Upper Creeks of the Alabama, Coosa, and Tallapoosa rivers, and the most influential leader on the Creek National Council, which helped regulate affairs among both the Upper and the Lower Creeks, the latter principally settled on the Flint and Chattahoochee. Although Hawkins tried to strengthen the council and to use it to promote U.S. Indian policy, Big Warrior was never entirely amenable to the agent's influence, and the relationship between them was uneasy. Hawkins described Big Warrior as an ambitious and discontented man, and suspected his motives.

One reason for Big Warrior's resistance to Hawkins was his awareness of the growing threat to Creek land from both state and federal authorities. In 1805, by a treaty signed in Washington, D.C., by, among others, Big Warrior's eldest son, Tuskenau, the Creeks yielded some of their eastern territory to Georgia and permitted the United States to blaze a post road from Georgia to Mobile. Fears that border disputes between the Creeks and their Indian neighbors would be exploited by the Americans in order to secure more land encouraged Big Warrior to use Tuckabatchee as an intertribal forum where the Creeks, Cherokees, Chickasaws, and Choctaws could concert policy. It was hoped that there would be agreement that land sales would not be valid unless authorized by all the southern tribes. This strategy was referred to as early as 1798, was revived in 1803 and 1810, and contributed to the difficulties between Big Warrior and agent Hawkins. It may also have aroused Big Warrior's interest in the northern pan-Indian movement led by Tecumseh and Tenskwatawa (the Prophet), which also opposed land cessions. In 1810 a group of Creeks who visited Prophet's Town on the Wabash may have included Tuskenau.

When the Creek National Council met in September 1811, it was attended not only by Hawkins, imposing on the Creeks another road, from Tennessee to Mobile, but also representatives of the other southern tribes and a delegation of northern Indians under Tecumseh. Tecumseh's message was far more radical than Big Warrior had anticipated. He wanted the tribes to unite against American land hunger and to resist undue white influences, which the Prophet taught were displeasing to the Supreme Spirit. It was clear that Tecumseh's confederacy was ready to fight, and the divine authority he claimed for his mission seemed to be confirmed by the appearance of the comet of that fall and the first of the New Madrid earthquakes in December 1811. Soon an extreme anti-American nativist cult was developing among the Upper Creeks, especially on the Alabama. It demanded a purging of contaminating white influences, including the "civilization" program of Hawkins, and a resistance to further territorial encroachments. Such a policy, it was believed, would restore the Creeks to the favor of the Creator, the Maker of Breath.

According to a Lower Creek, William McIntosh, Big Warrior was "inimical in heart to the United States, but joined the friendly party through fear." His actions in the crucial years of 1812 and 1813 support this interpretation. Although he probably initially encouraged Tecumseh, Big Warrior quickly retreated as the forces he had unleashed grew more belligerent. The Creek leader was apparently taken by surprise by the sudden growth of religious fanaticism on the Alabama, but he was pushed further toward the United States when his political enemies, the Tallassees, made common cause with the militants. About 1807 Peter McQueen and Hopoithle Mico, the headmen at Tallassee, succeeded in ousting Big Warrior from the National Council. Assisted by Little Prince, Big Warrior had regained his position three years later and thrown the Tallassees out, but bitterness remained. When Big Warrior began dabbling in pan-Indianism, Hopoithle Mico had declared that he, and not the Tuckabatchee leader, was the head speaker for the four southern Indian nations. The growing alliance between the Tallassees and the Alabama nativists (McQueen led expeditions to Pensacola to secure arms and ammunition in May and July 1813) was a direct and formidable threat to Big Warrior's leadership.

Relations between the disaffected Creeks and the United States deteriorated, and Big Warrior tried to mediate. In 1812 he visited the governor of Georgia, assuring him of Creek friendship. In August his emissaries went into East Florida to dissuade the Seminoles and fugitive blacks from attacking Americans, and in October and November he brokered a conference at Tuckabatchee between the trading company of John Forbes of Pensacola and the Indians over the contentious issue of Creek debts. Much more significantly, and disastrously, Big Warrior followed Hawkins's advice and in 1812 and 1813 sent posses after Creeks who had committed occasional murders of white settlers and travelers. Hawkins, aware of expansionists in Tennessee and Georgia who awaited any pretext for invading Creek territory and seizing Indian lands, explained that Big Warrior must put the friendship of his nation for the United States beyond question and punish malefactors. Unfortunately, by executing fellow Creeks, the council incited their relatives to demand the lives of Big Warrior and his supporters in satisfaction and aroused the fury of the anti-American party. Some of the Creek murderers had been Tallassees, reputedly kin of McQueen. One, pursued by Big Warrior's police in 1812, claimed sanctuary in the house of Hopoithle Mico. Notwithstanding, he was shot dead in an act the Tallassees regarded as a gross insult to their band.

Big Warrior's culpability in the outbreak of the Creek War of 1813 prompted various assessments. Hawkins complained that Big Warrior acted complacently and should have preempted serious hostilities by attacking the Alabama prophets and crushing their movement in embryo, as Hawkins urged. On the other hand the chief's position was one of extreme difficulty. His execution of some seventeen Indians implicated in attacks on Americans was already raising a storm against him. In June 1813 Big Warrior tried to stay that rebellion by inviting the prophets to demonstrate their powers and by declaring the executions at an end. It was too late. The hostile Upper Creeks, increasingly known as Red Sticks, began killing pro-American chiefs and threatened the destruction of Big Warrior and his associates. "If I have done [w]rong in the course I have adopted," Big Warrior admitted, "I am sorry for it. I meant well."

The Creek war began as a civil war, with hundreds of Red Sticks besieging Big Warrior in Tuckabatchee in July 1813, determined to wipe out pro-American chiefs before turning on the United States. Reinforced by the party of Captain Isaacs, with his powder and lead, Big Warrior mustered 600 men in defense of his town. He appealed to the Lower Creeks for help and withstood attempts to storm and siege Tuckabatchee for almost a week. "Before we lose the Big Warrior we will all die for him," insisted one Lower Creek headman, and a relief force of 230 men eventually fought its way into the stricken town. They escorted Big Warrior's community to Coweta, a Lower Creek village, leaving the Red Sticks to burn Tuckabatchee and seize control of the upper part of the nation.

Expecting an attack on the Lower Creeks, Big Warrior solicited aid from Hawkins, Georgia, and the Cherokees. He also helped organize sorties against the hostiles, in October leading an attack on some Uchees on their way to join the Red Sticks, and the next month withstanding an attack on Coweta. After the rebel Creeks destroyed Fort Mims near Mobile in August, the United States entered the conflict, and Big Warrior offered his white allies lands on the Alabama as a reward for their help. He assisted the invading American armies. Under Mad Dog's Son his warriors accompanied the Georgian expedition against Auttose, and in 1814 they fought at the battles of Calebee Creek and Horseshoe Bend. The Red Sticks were crushed, and Big Warrior's rivals were eliminated. Hopoithle Mico was surrendered to the Americans in 1814, and McQueen and the leading prophet, Josiah Francis, fled with other hostile refugees to Florida.

Despite the defeat of the Red Sticks, the war was a disaster for pro- and anti-American Creeks alike. In August 1814 Andrew Jackson imposed on them the punitive treaty of Fort Jackson, seizing more than half of the nation's land for the United States. Big Warrior proved himself a capable orator during the proceedings. He protested the injustice of the treaty, which, he pointed out, contravened assurances already made by U.S. peace commissioner Thomas Pinckney, but was compelled to capitulate and signed as the speaker of the Upper Creeks. The treaty embittered Big Warrior, however. He loosed an Indian expedition against the fugitive Red Sticks in Florida in September 1814 but was simultaneously communicating with the British who had landed at Apalachicola Bay. The British were trying to recruit Indians in aid of their armed invasion of the South during the closing stages of the War of 1812. Had Britain gained the upper hand in the

conflict, it is likely that Big Warrior would have forsaken the United States. As it was, he could only brood and in November 1815 attempt to obstruct the survey of the Fort Jackson cession.

Big Warrior resumed his position as speaker for the Upper Creeks. He signed a treaty in January 1818 at the Creek agency defining the boundaries of the nation, continued his attempts to place Tuckabatchee at the center of intertribal affairs in the South, and sent delegations to Washington seeking, among other objectives, indemnification for the losses the friendly Creeks had suffered during the war. But he emerged most clearly again in 1824 when commissioners were appointed by the United States to seek the purchase of Creek lands within the limits of Georgia, which Big Warrior opposed. Encouraged, it was believed, by the Cherokee leader John Ross, he summoned the Upper Creeks to a meeting at his town in May, as a result of which threats were made against the lives of any who would sign a land cession.

Initial attempts to secure land from the Creeks failed, but in February 1825 William McIntosh and other Lower Creeks ceded most of the nation's lands in the East to the United States at the treaty of Indian Springs, Georgia. Through the influence of Big Warrior and his chiefs the Upper Creeks boycotted the treaty, although their attendance was not deemed necessary by the commissioners. McIntosh was assassinated by Upper Creeks in the recriminations that followed, but Big Warrior did not live to see the outcome. He led a delegation to Washington to get the treaty rescinded, and he died there of natural causes. Posterity has not been charitable. That he was self-seeking and ambitious is undeniable, but during the period of the Creek war he tried, if unsuccessfully, to steer the nation between two undesirable courses: military opposition to the Americans and uncritical compliance with the policies of the United States. He retained the confidence of many Creeks until his death and stood against the disposal of Indian land and their removal across the Mississippi. He was, in truth, a rather pathetic figure, broken by exceptionally difficult circumstances that would have defeated a far abler leader.

• Useful sources can be found in Letters Received by the Secretary of War, Registered and Unregistered Series (microfilms 221 and 222), RG 107, National Archives; *American State Papers, Class II, Indian Affairs* (2 vols., 1832–1834); *Letters, Journals and Writings of Benjamin Hawkins*, ed. C. L. Grant (2 vols., 1980); *Correspondence of Andrew Jackson*, ed. John S. Bassett, vols. 1–2 (1926–1935); Theron A. Nunez, ed., "Creek Nativism and the Creek War of 1813–14," *Ethnohistory* 5 (1958): 1–47, 131–75, 292–301; and Thomas S. Woodward, *Reminiscences of the Creek or Muscogee Indians* (1859; repr. 1939). Some notes, with late traditions of Big Warrior, are preserved in the Draper manuscripts, State Historical Society of Wisconsin, Madison, vol. 10U. Frank L. Owsley, *Struggle for the Gulf Borderlands* (1981), surveys the conflict but is thin on the Indians and contains surprising errors. Joel Martin, *Sacred Revolt* (1991), explores the religious dimensions of the war but gives little attention to underlying political tensions within the nation and has nothing to say about Big Warrior. Douglas Barber, "Council Government and the Genesis of the Creek War," *Alabama Review* 38 (1985): 163–74, contributes to a needed corrective. Although modest, Benjamin W. Griffith, *McIntosh and Weatherford, Creek Indian Leaders* (1988), makes a creditable reconstruction of many episodes. Some valuable insights may be gained from Merritt B. Pound, *Benjamin Hawkins: Indian Agent* (1951); Robert S. Cotterill, *The Southern Indians* (1954); Michael D. Green, *The Politics of Indian Removal* (1982); J. Leitch Wright, *Creeks and Seminoles* (1986); and Florette Henri, *The Southern Indians and Benjamin Hawkins, 1796–1816* (1986).

JOHN SUGDEN

BILBO, Theodore Gilmore (13 Oct. 1877–21 Aug. 1947), Mississippi governor and U.S. senator, was born in Juniper Grove, Mississippi, the son of James Oliver Bilbo, and Beedy (or Biddy) Wallace, farmers. Bilbo attended Peabody College in Nashville from 1897 to 1899 but left without receiving a degree. In 1898 he married Lillian S. Herrington; she died in 1900, leaving an infant daughter. Bilbo's second marriage, to Linda Gaddy Bedgood in 1903, produced one son. The marriage was troubled for many years and ended in divorce in 1938. After attending Peabody, Bilbo taught in Mississippi schools. His teaching career ended in 1905 following gossip about indiscretions with a female student. He then attended Vanderbilt Law School; though he again left without receiving a degree, he was admitted to the state bar in 1907.

That same year Bilbo was elected to the state senate from the Pearl River District in southern Mississippi. In the legislature he attacked railroads and supported prohibition. His rise to statewide power did not truly begin until 1910, when the legislature selected a replacement for deceased U.S. Senator Anselm McLaurin. The leading candidate was popular former governor James K. Vardaman. The legislature, meeting as a Democratic party caucus, selected the new senator in secret balloting. In an atmosphere of intrigue, voting continued for more than six weeks, until finally Vardaman was defeated by conservative LeRoy Percy, a wealthy planter and corporation lawyer. Shortly after the election, Bilbo announced that he had trapped Percy's manager, L. S. Dulaney, into offering Bilbo a bribe in return for a vote for Percy. Many observers thought the charge plausible, but the evidence was confused; following an investigation the senate voted 28 to 15, one short of the required two-thirds majority to expel Bilbo. The senators then voted 25 to 1 in favor of a resolution declaring Bilbo "unfit to sit with honest, upright men."

Bilbo responded by running for lieutenant governor in 1911. His principal campaign issue was the decision of the legislature to select a new senator in secret, rather than open, balloting. In his primary campaign the public discovered Bilbo's gifts for rhetorical display, which were extravagant even by Mississippi's standards. His speaking style owed much to his Baptist heritage and was perhaps compensation for his diminutive size. Crowds reveled in his vituperative denunci-

ations of the "secret caucus." Apparently in the mistaken belief that one J. J. Henry had authored an anti-Bilbo pamphlet, Bilbo in one speech denounced Henry as "a cross between a mongrel and a cur, conceived in a nigger graveyard at midnight, suckled by a sow, and educated by a fool." Shortly afterward the enraged Henry severely pistol-whipped Bilbo. A two-week stay in a hospital only increased the popularity of the now-martyred Bilbo, and he swept to victory.

Bilbo's term as lieutenant governor saw a replay of the bribe story. At the instigation of Governor Earl Brewer, Bilbo and Senator G. A. Hobbs were indicted in December 1913 for allegedly accepting a bribe from one Steve Castleman in return for a vote in favor of creating a new county. Hobbs replied that he had been trying to set a trap for Castleman, and Bilbo charged that Brewer's motives were purely political. In separate trials, both Hobbs and Bilbo were acquitted. Bilbo again rode controversy to higher office. In 1915 he ran for governor, again focusing his appeal on his core constituency, the small white farmers in southern and northeastern Mississippi. These voters, attracted by Bilbo's claim to represent their interests as against those of the rich Delta planters, sent him into office with an absolute majority of votes against four primary opponents. While in office (1916–1920), Bilbo presided over the enactment of a comprehensive progressive program highlighted by the creation of a new state tax commission, equalization of tax assessments throughout the state, and higher appropriations for education and state charitable institutions.

Unable to succeed himself, Bilbo ran for Congress in 1918 but was defeated. He failed in a second try for the governorship in 1923 but won election to that office once again in 1927. His second term as governor was not a success. Conflicts with the legislature blocked Bilbo's plans to establish a state-owned printing plant for textbooks, revamp highway funding, and move the state university from Oxford to Jackson. The frustrated governor forced out many administrators and faculty at the university as well as several state colleges, which then lost accreditation.

Despite the failures of his second term, Bilbo managed to win election as U.S. senator in 1934. In the Senate Bilbo compiled a strongly liberal voting record. His down-the-line support for President Franklin D. Roosevelt continued even in Roosevelt's second term, when many southern Democrats deserted the president. Bilbo's own legislative efforts focused on areas of special interest to his constituents, such as flood control and agriculture. He claimed to be proudest of sponsoring legislation to establish regional research centers to find new uses for agricultural products. He continued to intervene in Mississippi's factional politics, alternately supporting and opposing virtually every other major politician in the state in their races for governor or senator. Running as a strong supporter of Roosevelt, Bilbo easily won reelection in 1940.

Bilbo was a committed white supremacist, but unlike politicians such as Vardaman, he had always centered his appeal on economic rather than racial grounds. Only in the 1940s, in response to the increasing importance of civil rights in the agenda of the national Democratic party, did Bilbo make racism central to his message. He fought antilynching laws and tried to obstruct action by the Fair Employment Practices Commission, and he pushed a fantastic plan to establish a "Greater Liberia" as a "home" to which African Americans would voluntarily remove themselves. Following a crudely racist campaign for reelection in 1946, Bilbo rolled to his greatest victory, for the first time carrying even the conservative white votes of the Mississippi-Yazoo Delta. The next year he published *Take Your Choice: Separation or Mongrelization.* Following his reelection, several senators objected to his taking his seat, raising questions about Bilbo's relationships with defense contractors and his alleged threats to black voters in Mississippi. Before an investigation could be completed, however, Bilbo died in New Orleans. His final years as a defender of white supremacy, together with his incendiary political style, largely overshadowed the progressive and economically liberal nature of much of his public life.

• The only substantial collection of Bilbo papers is in the McCain Library at the University of Southern Mississippi, Hattiesburg. Two book-length treatments are Adwin Wigfall Green, *The Man Bilbo* (1963), a short biography, and Chester M. Morgan, *Redneck Liberal: Theodore G. Bilbo and the New Deal* (1985), which focuses on Bilbo's career in the U.S. Senate. See also Larry T. Balsamo, "Theodore G. Bilbo and Mississippi Politics, 1877–1932" (Ph.D. diss., Univ. of Missouri, 1967). An obituary is in the *New York Times,* 22 Aug. 1947.

J. WILLIAM HARRIS

BILLIKOPF, Jacob (1 June 1883–31 Dec. 1950), social worker and philanthropist, was born in Vilna, Russia (Vilnius, Lithuania), the son of Louis Billikopf and Glika Katzenelenbogen. Billikopf immigrated to the United States in 1897 and briefly attended Richmond College. With the support of a fellowship from the National Council of Jewish Women, he studied philanthropy at the University of Chicago, from which he received a Ph.B. in 1903. He also studied at the School of Philanthropy in New York in 1905. He married Ruth Marshall, the daughter of Louis Marshall, in 1920; they had a son and a daughter. His first wife died in 1936, and he married Esther Freeman in 1942.

Billikopf's first forays into the profession of social welfare occurred in New York's United Hebrew Charities, the Industrial Removal Office, and the Jewish settlement house in Cincinnati, where he was superintendent in 1904–1905. In 1907, after two years as head of the organized philanthropies in Milwaukee, he went to Kansas City, Missouri, where, during the next ten years, he honed his skills in social welfare. As head of the United Jewish Charities there, he worked in support of municipal baths, public night schools, a free legal bureau, remedial loans, public recreational facilities, and improved conditions for prisoners. Of particular importance was his work on behalf of dependent children: he was a leading spirit in calling for widows' pensions, which were formalized by the Mis-

souri legislature for Kansas City in 1911. He also taught sociology and economics at the University of Missouri, served as vice president of the Kansas City Board of Pardons and Paroles, and was a member of the Kansas City Board of Public Welfare. In 1911 he spent a year as president of the Missouri State Conference of Charities.

In 1918 Billikopf moved to New York City, where he became involved in efforts to raise money for European relief. For two years he served as executive director of the Joint Distribution Committee for the Relief of Jewish War Sufferers (JDC), directing the campaign to raise $25 million. In 1917, as a direct result of Billikopf's work, a new standard of giving was set with a gift of $1 million by Julius Rosenwald, on the condition that an additional $9 million be raised during that year. Indeed, Billikopf has been called "the brain behind the Joint Distribution Committee's fund-raising" (Marcus, p. 628). He showed such ingenuity in raising money, masterminding several of the JDC's multimillion-dollar campaigns in the 1920s and 1930s, that he was offered a job in the banking industry; he turned it down.

In 1919 Billikopf became executive director of the Federation of Jewish Charities in Philadelphia. He continued to work on behalf of relief efforts abroad, investigating conditions in Russia and Eastern Europe in the 1920s for the United Jewish Campaign. He became involved in labor issues, serving as chairman of the National Labor Board for the Philadelphia region in the 1930s, chairman of the Ladies Garment Industry of Philadelphia, vice president of the American Association for Old Age Security, and chairman of the Philadelphia Committee of One Hundred on Unemployment Relief in 1930–1931. He was a chairman of the Men's Clothing Industry in New York City in the 1920s and codirector of the Labor Standards Association from 1938 until his death.

During the 1930s and 1940s, Billikopf participated in efforts to help Jewish refugees from Nazi-occupied Europe; he was executive director of the National Coordinating Committee for Aid to Refugees and Emigrants from Germany and encouraged the formation of the University in Exile of the New School for Social Research, whose efforts helped to bring a large number of European scholars to the United States during the Nazi period. He had been a board member of the New School during its founding years in the 1920s.

Billikopf was a trustee of the *Nation* and the *Survey* and chairman of the Executive Committee of Howard University. He served as president of both the National Conference of Jewish Social Workers and its successor organization, the National Conference of Jewish Social Service. In 1938 he received an LL.D. from the University of Richmond, where he had established the Jacob Billikopf Foundation. In 1942 the alumni association of the University of Chicago cited him for his "service to community, nation and the world" (*New York Times,* 1 Jan. 1951). He died in Philadelphia.

• Billikopf's papers are in the American Jewish Archives in Cincinnati, Ohio. They include his voluminous correspondence, a veritable mine of information for those interested in American Jewish history. Further information on Billikopf is in Jacob Rader Marcus, *United States Jewry, 1776–1985* (1989). An obituary is in the *New York Times*, 1 Jan. 1951.

LAURA SMITH PORTER

BILLINGS, Charles Howland Hammatt (15 June 1818–14 Nov. 1874), artist and architect, was born in Milton, Massachusetts, the son of Ebenezer Billings, Jr., a tavern keeper and clerk, and Mary Demale Janes. Billings attended Boston's English High School in the early 1830s but did not graduate. He had begun instruction in drawing at the age of ten with an itinerant German master, Franz (or Francis) Graeter, and in the 1830s he apprenticed himself to Abel Bowen, a wood engraver, and to the architect Asher Benjamin, thus laying the groundwork for the two main occupations of his multifaceted career. In 1837–1838 Billings joined the architect Ammi B. Young in preparing the drawings for the Greco-Roman Boston Custom House; an engraved view of the building dated 1840 is Billings's earliest published work. By 1843 "Hammatt Billings," as he styled himself from then on, was established as an architect and designer in the first of a string of offices in downtown Boston. His one recorded trip abroad was to London in the summer of 1865.

Billings was married twice, in 1841 to Sarah Mason, who apparently died about 1859, and in about 1860 to Phoebe Warren. He had no children.

For three decades Billings worked as a jack-of-all-designs: as an architect, portrait painter, watercolorist, illustrator, graphic artist, and designer of sculpture, furniture, funereal and other monuments, gardens, pyrotechnical displays, and public spectacles. For versatility in the practice of *disegno* (design), he earned in his own day comparison to Michelangelo. As a designer, Billings gave visible form to the personal, civil, patriotic, and other public sentiments pervasive at the time in Boston and beyond. It was, however, as an architect and book illustrator, and to a lesser extent as a designer of monuments, that Billings chiefly made his mark.

Billings often worked with his brother Joseph E. Billings, an engineer. Their first major commission, the Boston Museum, was an extraordinary achievement. The museum, a combined exhibition hall and theater, was erected in 1846–1847 on Tremont Street and is one of the first examples of the Renaissance revival in the United States. The interior must have been one of the most impressive in Boston at the time, with its granite palazzo facade masking a stair hall lined with galleries that were supported by rows of colossal Corinthian columns. The museum was demolished in 1901. Working alone, with his brother, or as a "ghost" designer for other architects, Billings went on to design houses, churches, clubhouses, commercial blocks, and libraries from Maine to Connecticut in popular styles, from the classical to the picturesque.

Billings's crowning achievement, his designs for Wellesley College, was finished after his death. Between 1869 and 1875 he and his brother Joseph designed the grounds and the original buildings of the college. Abandoning the classicism of his teachers and his earlier work, he created a picturesque setting, through which a road snaked from quaint gatehouses to College Hall. College Hall, set high above Lake Waban, was an eclectic amalgamation of English- and French-inspired details, derived in part from James Renwick's recent building at Vassar College. For Henry Fowle Durant and his wife, Pauline, the founders of Wellesley, Billings created a building that efficiently centralized all the activities of the school and served as a major monument of picturesque eclecticism. The building burned in 1914.

Much of Billings's work as an illustrator of magazines, almanacs, advertisements, diplomas, certificates, and above all books remains extant, and it is probably the most important aspect of his career. In 1847 Henry Wadsworth Longfellow called Billings "the best illustrator of books we have yet had in this country." Longfellow's claim may be somewhat exaggerated, since the country's illustrators then included such fine artists as F. O. C. Darley, but Billings did in fact provide memorable illustrations for a number of important mid-nineteenth-century English and American writers. He created the original likenesses of Tom, Little Eva, Topsy, Legree, and other characters in Harriet Beecher Stowe's *Uncle Tom's Cabin*. The first edition (1852) contains seven wood engravings after Billings's drawings. The illustrated edition of the next year is filled with his vignettes; they are subtle but effective reinforcements of Stowe's impassioned attack on slavery, and they acted as guides for more famous artists who later illustrated *Uncle Tom's Cabin*, from George Cruikshank to Miguel Covarrubias. Billings went on to illustrate more than 225 titles, among them the writings of Nathaniel Hawthorne, John G. Whittier, Sir Walter Scott, Oliver Goldsmith, Charles Dickens, Louisa May Alcott, and Alfred, Lord Tennyson. One of Billings's earliest illustrated works was an edition of Mother Goose rhymes, and he is now chiefly remembered as an illustrator of children's literature. His output as an illustrator, however, like his career as a whole, was breathtakingly varied. During the 1850s he was a major contributor to the Boston illustrated newspaper *Gleason's* (later *Ballou's*) *Pictorial Drawing-Room Companion*. In this publication and in books, including William Barnes's *Rural Poems* (1869), Billings shared the pages with Winslow Homer.

As a designer of monuments, Billings provided cemetery art for private individuals, Civil War memorials for small towns like Concord, Massachusetts, and the now largely neglected National Monument to the Forefathers in Plymouth, Massachusetts. In 1855 Billings contracted to erect, from his designs, a baroque canopy over Plymouth Rock (now replaced by the pavilion erected in the 1920s) and a colossal figure of Faith. Billings designed a 70-foot-high granite figure on an 83-foot-high granite base, adorned with secondary figures and sculpted scenes, a worthy successor to the great colossi of the past. Although it was begun in 1859, the monument was not finished until 1889, long after Billings's death, and it was reduced in height and otherwise altered by other artists, including the sculptor William Rimmer, with whom Billings had studied. *Faith*, who holds a book against her left side and with her right arm points heavenward, seems a ponderous memorial now, but it stands in design, if not in meaning or technical achievement, as a forerunner of Frédéric Bartholdi's Statue of Liberty.

Billings's other tasks included designs for a Moorish arch that crossed Tremont Street, built to celebrate the arrival of the public water supply in 1848, a funereal float to adorn the procession mourning the death of President Zachary Taylor in 1850, and an arrangement of draped bunting on the State House in honor of the visit of the Prince of Wales in 1860. Billings was one of Boston's foremost mid-nineteenth-century designers, and his work could be seen virtually anywhere that the arts of design served private or public celebration. As an architect, he expressed rather than led his generation; as an illustrator, however, he contributed much to the literary luster of mid-nineteenth-century Boston. Billings died in New York City.

• There are four major repositories of Billings documents: architectural drawings are housed at the Stowe-Day Foundation in Hartford, Conn.; drawings for funereal and other monuments are located in the print room of the Boston Public Library; notes Billings took from lectures by William Rimmer are held in the Boston Medical Library of the Francis A. Countway Medical Library; and drawings for illustrations are contained in the Hammatt Billings Collection, Clapp Library, Wellesley College. The last also houses research notes and a collection of books illustrated by Billings. An inventory of his illustrations is in James F. O'Gorman, *A Billings Bookshelf: An Annotated Bibliography of Works Illustrated by Hammatt Billings (1818–1874)*, rev. ed. (1986). Billings's varied output has been discussed in scattered articles, beginning with Richard Stoddard, "Hammatt Billings, Artist and Architect," *Old-Time New England* 62 (Jan.–Mar. 1972): 57–65, 76–79. O'Gorman's articles include "H. and J. E. Billings of Boston: From Classicism to the Picturesque," *Journal of the Society of Architectural Historians* 42 (Mar. 1983): 54–73; "War, Slavery, and Intemperance in the Book Illustrations of Hammatt Billings," *Imprint* 10 (Spring 1985): 2–10; "Billings, Cruikshank, and *Uncle Tom's Cabin*," *Imprint* 13 (Spring 1988): 13–21; and "Hammatt Billings: Prolific, Protean, Important . . . and Forgotten," *Nineteenth Century* 10 (1991): 3–7. The most reliable obituary is in *Old and New* 2 (Mar. 1875): 355–57.

JAMES F. O'GORMAN

BILLINGS, Frederick (27 Sept. 1823–30 Sept. 1890), lawyer and railroad president, was born in Royalton, Vermont, the son of Oel Billings, a farmer and later register of probate, and Sophia Wetherbee. In 1835 Billings's father, a debtor, was instructed by the court to move to Woodstock, Vermont, as the law required that he live within a mile of a jail. Frederick Billings found schooling in Woodstock inadequate and persuaded his parents to send him to Kimball Union Academy. In 1840 he entered the University of Vermont, graduating in 1844. He studied law as an apprentice to Oliver Phelps Chandler in Woodstock and in 1846 became secretary of civil and military affairs to Horace Eaton, the Whig governor of the state. Eaton and Billings pressed in particular for school reform.

Restless and ambitious, Billings accompanied his sister Laura, to whom he was especially close, and her husband Bezer Simmons, who owned property in California, to the West Coast early in 1849. After a difficult journey via the Isthmus of Panama, the party reached San Francisco on 3 April. Laura had contracted fever aboard the *Oregon* and died three weeks after their arrival. In California, Billings made his first fortune. On his first day ashore he bought an old canal boat and sold its timbers at a profit; with this money he purchased real estate, especially "water lots." He was the first lawyer in California to hang out his shingle, and John Augustus Sutter, on whose estate the first gold strike had been made in 1848, was one of his earliest clients. Through a friend that Billings made aboard ship on the journey from the East, he met the military governor of California, Brigadier General Bennet Riley, who appointed him commissioner of deeds for San Francisco, chairman of the Board of Inspectors and Judges, and territorial legal adviser and attorney general, or procurador fiscal. As attorney general, Billings provided highly effective advice on how to maintain the public lands against squatters.

Though the junior partner, Billings was the driving force behind the law firm of Halleck, Peachy, and Billings, which opened its offices on 1 January 1850. The senior partner, Henry Wager Halleck, was intimately acquainted with Spanish land records and had written the leading treatise on Spanish and Mexican land law in California. The second partner, Archibald Cary Peachy, had been appointed professor of moral philosophy at the College of William and Mary; as a southerner, a Democrat, and an Episcopalian, he brought balance to the firm. Billings was a Yankee, a Whig, and a Presbyterian (the last only in California). (There was for a time a fourth partner, Trenor Park, a fellow Vermonter.) HPB, as the firm was known, specialized in litigating land claims at a time when this was the most complex and important legal endeavor in California, especially after the U.S. government established, early in 1852, a land commission to investigate and rule on conflicting claims.

HPB was centrally involved in two of California's most important land cases. The most complicated involved the world's second richest quicksilver mine, at New Almaden, which proved to be the single most valuable mine in California, producing more than $70 million in quicksilver. Seeking records and witnesses, Billings undertook a dangerous journey to Mexico City in 1859 at a time when that capital came under siege by the forces of Benito Juárez. HPB lost the case, despite Billings having completed what was regarded as possibly the most extensive research into a single land case anywhere in the nation up to that time. The second major controversy was over John C. Frémont's

Mariposa grant east of San Francisco. Here, too, HPB lost in the end, but the case (1857–1863) drew Billings into investment in mining and into a close working relationship with Frémont that extended through the Civil War. It was while at Bear Valley, Frémont's Mariposa seat, that Billings became an early advocate of the protection of the nearby Yosemite Valley for the use of future generations.

By the time he was thirty Billings was a millionaire from substantial legal fees; profits from land holdings in San Francisco, Sacramento, and elsewhere in California; and joint ownership of the Montgomery Block, the largest office property west of St. Louis when it opened in 1853. He was also developing a reputation for philanthropy to church, school, public park, and university. It was he who suggested the name of Berkeley for the seat of the new university of California; Billings helped clear the way for it legally and served as the first president of its board of trustees. He also spoke tirelessly against California separatism in the months prior to the outbreak of the Civil War. He might have remained in California had he not embarked on a series of European journeys to sell shares in the Mariposa mines and to purchase arms for Frémont's command. On his return from a European trip in 1861 Billings met Julia Parmly, daughter of Eleazar Parmly, a distinguished society dentist in New York City. They were married less than a month later, after which Billings returned to California just long enough to close down the law firm and to sell some of his properties before taking up residence in New York with his bride. The couple had seven children.

Billings made his second, and greater, fortune in railroads, in particular the Northern Pacific (NP), in which he purchased his first share in 1869. Ten years later he was president of the company and served it extraordinarily well. His first and most abiding contribution was as chairman of the land committee, on which he, with others, worked out plans for bringing settlers onto the land in Minnesota and the Dakota Territory. When Jay Cooke & Company, which was responsible for the sale of NP stocks, went under in the panic of 1873, it was Billings more than anyone else who fought off foreclosure, worked out a complex plan for reorganization, and began construction of the stalled rail line once again.

Elected president of the Northern Pacific in May 1879, Billings pressed ahead with construction. Under his leadership the NP became the largest single corporate enterprise in American history to that time. So intent was he on arranging for refinancing of the line, he did not see until too late the danger posed by Henry Villard, owner of the Oregon Railway & Navigation Company and proponent of a different route to the Pacific. In perhaps the first hostile takeover in corporate history, Villard acquired a controlling interest in the NP through the creation of a blind pool, and Billings resigned as president in June 1881. He remained on the board, however, and was present at the driving of the "last spike" in September 1883.

Despite his contributions to California, where he was seriously considered for a variety of high offices and pressed upon President Abraham Lincoln by the California delegation to be given a cabinet post, Billings is best remembered in Montana and Vermont. He was the largest individual landholder in the town that took his name, Billings, Montana; he played a significant role in promoting the concept of Yellowstone National Park, which was to be approached by the Northern Pacific; and he controlled banks, mines, ranches, and other railroads in the territory.

By 1869, however, his attention had turned back to Woodstock, Vermont, where he worked to put into effect the principles of George Perkins Marsh, author of *Man and Nature*, the "bible" of modern ecology first published in 1864. Billings purchased Marsh's home in Woodstock, into which he moved his family. He developed an extensive scientific farm on the estate, purchased Marsh's library for his alma mater, and became the driving force behind the state's first commission of reforestation. In 1872 Billings ran for governor, missing election by five votes. His contributions to conservation, while inchoate, were substantial for the time, as were his many benefactions in Woodstock, in particular to the Congregational church. He died in Woodstock.

Frederick Billings was a successful and honest businessman, lawyer, and entrepreneur at a time when many did not value the proprieties he held dear. Guided, perhaps even driven, by a sense of duty, by great pride in Vermont, and by his determination to see the Northern Pacific to completion, he strove to lead a life that was, as his friend Alfred Barstow remarked, "clean and entirely free from scandal." In the Gilded Age he demonstrated the possibility of being both financially successful and an honest man.

• Billings's papers are in the archives of the Billings mansion in Woodstock. The records of Halleck, Peachy, and Billings are divided among the Bancroft Library at the University of California, Berkeley; the library of the University of California, Los Angeles; and the Huntington Library, San Marino, Calif. Many fugitive items are to be found in numerous other collections set out in Robin W. Winks, *Frederick Billings: A Life* (1991). The records of the Northern Pacific Railroad are at the Minnesota Historical Society in St. Paul. In addition, see Jane Curtis et al., *Frederick Billings: Vermonter, Pioneer Lawyer, Business Man, Conservationist* (1986), and Eugene V. Smalley, *History of the Northern Pacific Railroad* (1883). An obituary is in the *New York Times*, 1 Oct. 1890.

ROBIN W. WINKS

BILLINGS, John Shaw (12 Apr. 1838–11 Mar. 1913), army medical officer, library organizer, and public health activist, was born near Allensville, Indiana, the son of James Billings, a farmer and storekeeper, and Abby Shaw. Despite spotty secondary schooling, he ultimately went to Miami College (Ohio), where he earned his B.A. in 1857. He was awarded the M.D. by the Medical College of Ohio in 1860. Billings remained with the latter institution for a year as an anatomical demonstrator, but after the outbreak of the

Civil War he joined the U.S. Army as a contract surgeon. In 1862 he was commissioned first lieutenant and assistant surgeon and went on to make army service his career. Also in 1862 he married Katharine Mary Stevens; they had five children.

During the war, Billings compiled a superior record as a field surgeon and hospital administrator and later as a troubleshooter and medical statistician. After the war he was retained for duty in Washington, D.C., on the staff of Joseph K. Barnes, the army surgeon general, where his colleagues included such prominent medical figures as Joseph J. Woodward and George Otis. Billings was initially responsible for settling the accounts of the excess contract surgeons, phasing out the large general hospitals, and otherwise helping dismantle the huge Civil War medical operation. Later, he organized two special hygienic surveys of the army's field posts, publishing the findings in 1870 and 1875.

After the Civil War, Billings steadily broadened his knowledge of military hospitals to become one of America's leading experts on hospital design and organization. As one result, between 1869 and 1870 he conducted a survey for the Treasury Department of the nation's far-flung network of marine hospitals. His recommendations for upgrading those institutions and creating a central supervisory agency to administer them were accepted. The agency that resulted, the Marine Hospital Service, subsequently evolved into today's U.S. Public Health Service.

By far the most lasting of Billings's military medical contributions was his work as officer-in-charge of the library of the surgeon general's office. Beginning in the mid-1860s he built up an institution that by 1895 held some 124,000 volumes and 210,000 pamphlets, the largest medical library in the Americas if not in the world. He early opened the library to all health professionals and in the late 1870s initiated two pioneering finding guides to the collection, the *Index Catalogue* and the *Index Medicus*. The latter remained through the twentieth century the principal finding guide to all elements of the world's medical literature.

In 1872 Billings joined the newly founded American Public Health Association and at the end of that decade served as its president. One of his initiatives in this body was a plan for a systematic sanitary survey of the United States. This plan was adopted in 1875, but it foundered when local funds proved difficult to raise.

In 1875 Billings was one of five experts invited to propose plans for the Johns Hopkins Hospital in Baltimore. The hospital trustees ultimately appointed Billings as their medical adviser to help work up and implement a final plan; he remained in this capacity throughout the construction period and until the hospital was opened in 1889. Billings's design incorporated the best of recent European and American hospital experience together with the results of his own innovative ideas, especially in ventilation and heating. During this time his numerous reports to the trustees dealt not only with the details of hospital design but with hospital organization, staffing, and other matters.

When completed, the Johns Hopkins Hospital became a model for other new large hospitals in the United States, while Billings's ideas rapidly passed into common currency among hospital organizers and planners.

In 1883 Billings was put in charge of the army's Medical Museum as well as the surgeon general's library. One of his museum contributions was to build up an outstanding collection of microscopes. However, of much greater importance for both the museum and the library were his efforts to obtain a new building to replace their badly outgrown facilities. Billings designed the structure and persuaded the American medical community to lobby Congress for the necessary funds. The building opened on the Mall in Washington in 1887, and he remained in charge of the two institutions until his retirement from the army in 1895. He also served for two years as professor of hygiene in the Army Medical School, on its establishment by Surgeon General George Sternberg in 1893. He served as consultant for the building of several hospitals, including the Memphis City Hospital in 1897 and Boston's Peter Bent Brigham Hospital between 1905 and 1908.

Billings was an effective spokesman for the idea of the modern university that was held by the early leadership of the Johns Hopkins University—an idea that helped revolutionize the shape and future of American higher education. While differing with President Daniel Gilman on some matters, he strongly endorsed the plan to develop the university's hospital in close relationship with its medical school. He lectured extensively on admission standards, curriculum, and course content for the school. He argued successfully for a central place for science in both institutions. And he helped select some of the key faculty, notably William H. Welch and William Osler. He taught the university's first courses in the history of medicine.

Billings's Civil War experiences also convinced him of the importance of sanitation and preventive medicine. Through his innovations in ventilation at army posts and at the Johns Hopkins Hospital, he became known as an expert in this aspect of sanitation. He also wrote extensively in plumbing and sanitary engineering journals, articles that he collected in his 1884 volume, *Principles of Ventilation and Heating*, enlarged in 1893. Meanwhile, his designs of hospitals, libraries, laboratories, and other large urban buildings brought him international recognition for their demonstrations of utilitarian principles, styles, and features in architecture. They also led to his service, from the 1870s, with an expert commission on the ventilation of the U.S. Capitol building.

Billings played a central role in the discussions and lobbying that led up to America's first federal public health body, the National Board of Health, created in 1879. As its vice president, he exerted a dominant influence during the first three years of the board's brief existence. While the board, under law, was chiefly obligated to build up and administer a national quarantine system, Billings pressed to broaden that mission.

He conducted for the board a comprehensive sanitary survey of Memphis, Tennessee, and subsequently helped initiate modest programs in communicable disease control, vital statistics improvement, hygiene, and health-related research. However, he was constantly frustrated by the failure of Congress to provide adequate funds for such programs as well as by the board's deplorable lack of statutory authority. His 1882 resignation from the board was also influenced by the vituperative opposition of states' rights interests and by the political maneuvering of the head of the Marine Hospital Service, Surgeon General John Hamilton.

Billings nevertheless remained active in public health. His later involvement in the field included organizational and scientific work between 1893 and 1903 for the Committee of Fifty on the Liquor Problem and, after 1906, as adviser to the Committee of One Hundred on National Health.

Many of Billings's contemporaries were struck by his propensity for quantifying medical facts and events and by his command of simple statistical methods. He applied this knowledge to the improvement of American local and state vital statistics and in the movement to obtain greater federal involvement in that field, particularly through the federal census. In the 1870 census Billings and his army colleague J. J. Woodward were assigned to analyze the imperfect mortality returns that were obtained. On the strength of that work, he was chosen to direct the entire work of planning, processing, interpreting, and publishing the vital statistics of the 1880 and 1890 censuses. While both censuses were criticized for the continuing inadequacy of their vital data, Billings's introduction of certified mortality data obtained from a few "registration area" states and cities was a major improvement. Of still more immediate value was his encouragement of Herman Hollerith's research on tabulation machines and his role in introducing Hollerith's machines into the 1890 census operation, as well as into the statistical work of local health departments.

Billings wrote extensively on mortality trends and other census findings for general and medical periodicals. He was deeply involved in international statistical organizations, and he lectured widely on the medical uses of statistics. The fullest statement of his ideas on the latter subject appeared in his Cartwright Lectures, "On Vital and Medical Statistics" (Medical Record, p. 36).

Billings was deeply persuaded of the basic importance of science as a key to the elevation of American medicine. He carried out modest microscopic researches for a time, though other duties soon took him permanently away from laboratory investigation. However, he became highly knowledgeable about the age's far-reaching developments in sanitary technologies, bacteriological research and discoveries, and changing concepts of the etiology of the infectious diseases. In his lectures and articles he passed on such information to members of the American medical and public health communities. In the process he spearheaded efforts (generally unheeded) among physicians and scientists to reconcile the older values and approaches of environmental sanitary science with the newer findings and methods of bacteriology.

Billings's most important contribution to science was as an administrator. In the National Board of Health, he organized modest but significant scientific activities, and as director of the Army Medical Museum, he supervised and built up the institution's research and teaching facilities in pathology, anthropology, microscopy, and sanitation. During the early 1890s he organized the University of Pennsylvania's Laboratory of Hygiene and, after retiring from the army in 1895, he joined the faculty as director of the laboratory for a year. He also directed Penn's University Hospital and planned its Pepper Laboratory of Clinical Medicine.

As personal adviser to Andrew Carnegie around the turn of the twentieth century, Billings played a central role in planning the Carnegie Institution of Washington and launching it as one of America's premier research support bodies. He served the new institution as executive committee member and vice president for the rest of his life and as chairman of the board of trustees for most of that time. He likewise participated in the scientific activities of such bodies as the Smithsonian Institution and the Philosophical Society of Washington and was a founder-member of the Cosmos Club, the social meeting place of Washington scientists. Elected to the National Academy of Sciences in 1883, he served that institution as treasurer between 1887 and 1898 and as council member from 1896 to 1907.

Billings made his final career move in 1896, when he became the first director of the New York Public Library. In that position he directed the effective merger of the former Astor, Lenox, and Tilden libraries. He drafted plans for the great central building to accommodate the consolidated collection, carried out the assimilation of some forty smaller free libraries into the system, and personally persuaded Andrew Carnegie to contribute funds sufficient for constructing buildings for them. The new central building was opened in 1911. Billings died in New York City two years later.

Widely honored both at home and abroad as an institution builder, Billings characterized the entire generation of doers who transformed post–Civil War America. As a library and science administrator, he helped define new parameters in the nation's intellectual life. As a physician, he was a transitional figure who presided over the transformation of the simple medicine of an earlier day into a specialized pursuit based increasingly in the hospital and in science. As the energizer of a cluster of national health agencies as well as contributor to the modern census, Billings was an insistent voice prodding America to turn from its long-held states' rights attitudes to a more appropriate federalism. As a professional man, he stood out as a role model for the swarms of other experts who came on the scene to shape American public and private life by the turn of the century.

Courtly, often humorous, and affectionate to his closest friends and family, Billings was generally perceived as strong-willed, self-assured, and sometimes abrupt in his professional relations. He became involved in a number of struggles for turf, as in the case of the National Board of Health, but if not invariably the victor, he emerged from them uncorrupted and mostly unscathed. He moved easily in the circles of power, in overlapping elites of the medical, governmental, scientific, academic, and professional leaders of his day, and gained his support and influence from them. And in the long run his impressive military bearing and ready exercise of authority proved to have been positive factors in pushing his generation to meet the taxing medical and sanitary challenges of the period.

• Extensive collections of Billings's papers are in the New York Public Library and the National Library of Medicine. Major works by Billings other than statistical reports, but not including items referred to in the text, include "*Bibliography of Cholera*," in House Doc. 95, *The Cholera Epidemic of 1873 in the United States* (1875), pp. 707–1025; *Physiological Aspects of the Liquor Problem* (2 vols., 1903); *The National Medical Dictionary* (2 vols., 1890); and "The History and Literature of Surgery," in *System of Surgery*, vol. 1, ed. Frederic Shepard Dennis (1895).

The long-standard biographical treatment is Fielding H. Garrison, *John Shaw Billings: A Memoir* (1915); but an important modern study is by Carleton B. Chapman, *Order Out of Chaos: John Shaw Billings and America's Coming of Age* (1994). A list of shorter works about Billings by title as well as an extensive but partial list of his writings is given in *Selected Papers of John Shaw Billings*, comp. Frank Bradway Rogers (1965). Important extended treatments of Billings, his circles, and his contributions to libraries and library science may be found in Wyndham B. Miles, *A History of the National Library of Medicine* (1981), pp. 25–183; and Phyllis A. Dain, *The New York Public Library: A History of Its Founding and Early Years* (1972).

JAMES H. CASSEDY

BILLINGS, Josh (21 Apr. 1818–14 Oct. 1885), humorist and author, was born Henry Wheeler Shaw in Lanesboro, Massachusetts, the son of Henry Shaw, a state and national legislator, and Laura Wheeler. Billings grew up in the Berkshire Hills in a prosperous, active family that enjoyed state and national political connections. Indeed, both his paternal grandfather, Dr. Samuel Shaw, and his father served in the U.S. Congress, and his father was a Massachusetts legislator for twenty-five years. Billings attended Hamilton College in Clinton, New York, during 1833–1834, but he was expelled during his sophomore year for climbing the lightning rod on the chapel and removing the bell clapper.

Billings's constant wanderlust led him into the Middle West for ten years, from 1835 to 1845, during which time he attempted a wide variety of endeavors, including an abortive exploration in the far West, working in a Norwalk, Ohio, law office, and delivering his first comic lecture, in Napoleon, Indiana, under the pseudonym Mordecai David. Back in Lanesboro in 1845, he married his childhood sweetheart, Zilpha Bradford, a descendant of William Bradford, the colonial governor of Plymouth Colony. For some nine years after their marriage, the couple moved about in the East and Midwest, Billings working at various jobs. The couple had two children. In 1854 they settled in Poughkeepsie, New York, where Billings worked as an auctioneer and realtor. He left Poughkeepsie for six months to operate an Ohio River steamboat from Pittsburgh, Pennsylvania. He sold the boat in July 1855 and returned to his business in Poughkeepsie. Elected alderman in 1858, Billings also began that year to submit humorous epigrams and articles to the *New Ashford Eagle* under the pen name Efrem Billings, a practice that continued into 1859 when Poughkeepsian newspapers started running his entries first under Si Sledlength and then Josh Billings.

By the middle 1860s Billings's popularity as a humorist was taking hold, mainly generated by early successes on the lecture platform and the publication of his first book, *Josh Billings, Hiz Sayings* (1865), a volume of witty aphorisms. Now moving to New York City, Billings established himself with publisher G. W. Carleton and the *New York Weekly*, for which he wrote a column that first appeared on 30 May 1867 and continued every Sunday for the rest of his life. These columns, under such headings as "The Josh Billings Papers," "Josh Billings' Spice Box," and "Josh Billings' Philosophy," consisted of aphorisms, essays, sketches, narratives, and travel accounts. These columns provided most of the material for his books. His writing was known for its comic phonetic misspellings and ungrammatical constructions, humorous techniques shared by many literary comedians of the day. The humor is also characterized by puns, understatement, hyperbole, and anticlimax. These techniques can preclude a modern appreciation of his wit, but it is important to see beyond the eccentric style of a Billings piece, for, as critic Joseph Jones wrote, the misspellings and distorted grammar are "not essential to the final effect" (p. 159). For his other New York column, titled "Uncle Esek's Wisdom," which ran in *Century Illustrated Monthly Magazine* from 1884 until 1888, Billings avoided the bizarre stylistics and wrote in standard English.

With his reputation established, book publications came quickly and friendships with noted writers and other personalities bloomed. Mark Twain, Charles Farrar Browne (a.k.a. Artemus Ward), the illustrator Thomas Nast, and poet William Cullen Bryant were a few of his most renowned friends. His second book of witty aphorisms and sketches, *Josh Billings on Ice, and Other Things*, was published in 1868, and the next year was to see the first installment of *Josh Billings' Farmer's Allminax*, a burlesque of the popular *Old Farmer's Almanac* that was to run through 1880. In its first four years, more than 100,000 copies of the *Allminax* were sold; in its remaining six years, more than 50,000 each year. Billings continued to lecture widely and successfully, and other publications followed suit, such as *Everybody's Friend; or, Josh Billings' Encyclopedia and Proverbial Philosophy of Wit and Humor* (a compendium of his writings to date, 1874), *The Complete Comical Writings of Josh Billings* (1876), *Josh Billings' Trump Kards* (a jest book, 1877), *Josh Billings' Cook Book and Picktorial Proverbs* (1880), and *Josh Billings Struggling with Things* (aphorisms, 1881).

Successful as a lecturer, journalist, and writer of almanacs, books of essays, and aphorisms, Billings became one of the most popular figures of his day. In his later years he remained highly active, writing and traveling, but his health began to decline in the summer of 1884. Taking the advice of physicians, Billings and his wife went to the Pacific coast in late summer 1885, settling in Monterey, California, where Billings died. He was buried in his hometown of Lanesboro, Massachusetts.

Billings's humor, replete with fresh, original wit and insights, places him squarely in the "crackerbarrel philosopher" strain of American humor practiced by Benjamin Franklin, Will Rogers, Garrison Keillor, and occasionally Mark Twain. His humorous aphorisms were often grounded in the classics: Shakespeare, Bryant, Goldsmith, Bunyan, Homer, Ovid, and Boccaccio, among others. Critic Max Eastman said that Billings's picturesque lines reflect the beginning of the imagist movement in letters, and Jennette Tandy believed that Billings's prose style may have influenced the type of modern prose written by Gertrude Stein. Certainly, Billings—along with the other literary comedians—played a role in the advancement of literary realism during the last half of the nineteenth century. Underneath his sometimes disarmingly comic lines are penetrating insights as poignant as the realistic observations of Mark Twain, H. L. Mencken, and Sinclair Lewis.

• The two most significant repositories of Billings's published writings are the *New York Weekly* (30 May 1867–27 Oct. 1888) and the *Century Magazine* (Mar. 1884–Aug. 1888). The standard biography of Billings is Cyril Clemens, *Josh Billings, Yankee Humorist* (1932). The standard critical study is David B. Kesterson, *Josh Billings* (1973). Also see Jennette Tandy, "The Funny Men: Artemus Ward and Josh Billings," in her *Crackerbox Philosophers in American Humor and Satire* (1925). An important article on Billings by Joseph Jones is "Josh Billings: Some Yankee Notions on Humor," *Studies in English* (1943): 148–61.

DAVID B. KESTERSON

BILLINGS, William (7 Oct. 1746–26 Sept. 1800), composer, singing teacher, and poet was born in Boston, Massachusetts, the son of William Billings, a shopkeeper, and Elizabeth Clark. Little is known of his early life and education, but he is thought to have attended common school and gained his musical education through attendance at singing schools (class lessons in choral singing). After the death of his father in 1760, Billings was apprenticed to a tanner, a trade he apparently followed off and on. Music, however, was his love and psalm-singing his passion. He began holding singing schools as early as 1769 and earned a high reputation throughout eastern New England as a teacher of choral singing. Billings was much in demand as a vocal teacher, particularly in the 1770s and 1780s, and he continued to teach as occasion permitted until his death.

Billings published his first collection of pieces, *The New-England Psalm-Singer*, in 1770. The tunebook, containing 126 works, all by Billings, was the first work to be devoted entirely to American compositions and to the music of a single American composer. Although musically and graphically flawed, the tunebook was a great success with the public. Billings used it as his singing-school textbook for about eight years. During this time he taught singing schools both around Boston and as far south as Providence, Rhode Island. In 1774 he held a singing school in Stoughton, Massachusetts, from which descended the Old Stoughton Musical Society. In 1774 Billings married Lucy Swan, a member of the Stoughton singing school; they had nine children. (This was Billings's only marriage, contrary to some earlier claims.)

In spite of the disruptions caused by the revolutionary war, in which he was an ardent patriot, the late 1770s and early 1780s were a time of considerable musical and financial success for Billings. He issued three collections of his music between 1778 and 1781, directed at three different clientele. *The Singing Master's Assistant* (1778), popularly known as "Billings's Best," was designed as his singing-school book, a revision of his earlier tunebook with many newly published pieces. It went through four editions to 1789. In 1779 Billings published *Music in Miniature*, a small collection of tunes for use in public worship. In his *The Psalm-Singer's Amusement* (1781), a collection of anthems, fuging-tunes, and set-pieces, he meant to challenge the musical abilities of the accomplished singers of his day. A musical tour de force, the collection has been called Billings's "most flamboyant performance" (McKay and Crawford, p. 114). By 1780 he was affluent enough to purchase a house at 89 Newberry Street in the commercial district of Boston.

During the mid- to late 1780s, Billings's fortunes appear to have declined. His editing of the first issue of the *Boston Magazine* in October 1783, with its colloquial language and off-beat humor, led to such a negative reaction from Boston's gentlemen that the publisher, John Norman, replaced Billings immediately. Nevertheless, Billings contributed some pieces to Norman's tunebook, *The Massachusetts Harmony* (1784), although they were not attributed to him. Billings's fifth tunebook, *The Suffolk Harmony* (1786), with more melodic, homophonic music, seemed to herald a stylistic change, but it drew little enthusiasm from the public. Billings again contributed new pieces to Norman's *The Federal Harmony* (1788) and to Isaiah Thomas's *The Worcester Collection* (2d ed., 1788). During these years he also issued several anthems and tunes as small pamphlets of eight or sixteen pages, including *An Anthem for Easter* (1787), his most enduringly popular piece.

By 1790 Billings's financial situation was desperate, probably due to the combined effects of his growing family, increased competition in the singing-school business, and possible illness. Although he held some minor municipal appointments—Sealer of Leather, scavenger, hogreeve—these apparently did not suffice to meet Billings's needs. A public concert was held for his benefit in December 1790, the notices assuring the public that his "distress is real." Shortly thereafter Billings mortgaged his house and offered to sell the rights to all his music to the publishing firm of Thomas and Andrews. When Isaiah Thomas, the senior partner, declined the offer, Billings's supporters among Boston's choristers devised the idea of publishing a collection of Billings's music and giving him the profits from its sale. Several years of negotiations between a committee representing the choristers and the firm of Thomas and Andrews followed before the publication of Billings's final tunebook, *The Continental Harmony* (1794). Billings himself seems to have played no direct role in the arrangements with the publishers and probably got little financial benefit from the publication. Nonetheless, *The Continental Harmony* offers an impressive compendium of Billings's musical accomplishments along with an amusing and enlightening prefatory essay discussing the technique and aesthetics of psalmody as Billings practiced it.

Following the publication of *The Continental Harmony*, Billings issued only one other work, a revised version of his *An Anthem for Easter*, that appeared in 1795. During the final five years of his life he published no more music, although he likely continued to compose. "A Piece on the Death of Washington, 1799" was noted among his compositions in a listing prepared by an acquaintance following Billings's death. Billings died in Boston, where he had lived his entire life. His estate was valued at slightly more than $800, approximately the value of his house. He was buried in an unmarked grave, probably in the Boston Common.

No portraits or pictorial images of Billings are known to exist (although the vignette of a singing master on the title page of *The Psalm-Singer's Amusement* may be an attempt to represent him). However, several contemporaries left verbal portraits of him. Shortly after his death, the Salem, Massachusetts, diarist Reverend William Bentley described him as "a singular man, of moderate size, short of one leg, with one eye, without any address, and with an uncommon negligence of person. Still he spake and sung and thought as a man above the common abilities" (Bentley, vol. 2, pp. 350–51). Nathaniel D. Gould, who began a career as a singing master shortly before Billings died, added that Billings had a stentorian voice, one arm somewhat withered, and took enormous quantities of snuff (Gould, p. 46).

Billings was acknowledged in his day as the premier American composer of sacred music. His pieces were frequently reprinted in contemporary American collections of psalmody and sung in singing schools, churches, and at public celebrations. His six published tunebooks, spanning the years 1770 to 1794, established him as the most gifted, imaginative, and innovative composer of psalmody in eighteenth-century America. He mastered a musical style, related more to Renaissance polyphony than to Classical Era art music, that allowed him to compose expressive melodies supported by deftly crafted contrapuntal voices. His psalm-tunes, fuging-tunes, and anthems take their substance from expressive settings of their texts, which are almost exclusively sacred and include the psalms and hymns of Isaac Watts, the psalms of Nahum Tate and Nicholas Brady, the hymns of James and John Relly, biblical passages from the Old and New Testaments, as well as a number of verses that Billings wrote himself. His own poetry, generally in the style of Watts, shows him to have been an imaginative if undistinguished versifier, fascinated with both the sound and the rhythm of words.

Following his death, the use of Billings's music declined in New England as tastes in sacred music changed. By 1820 few of his pieces were in use in fashionable churches, although many of them continued to be sung in the rural churches of the South and frontier West. During much of the nineteenth century Billings was denigrated by better-trained church musicians as a crude contrapuntist and musical bungler. During the mid-twentieth century Billings was rediscovered, as a musical pioneer forging a crude but independent path through a musical wilderness by the force of his own vision. More recently he has come to be viewed as a talented and imaginative master of a musical style only marginally related to the art and dance music of his day, in which he composed music of beauty, excitement, and significance. Billings was the first American composer to have a critically edited edition of his complete works published.

• Early notices of William Billings are found in "An Account of Two Americans of Extraordinary Genius in Poetry and Music," *Columbian Magazine, or Monthly Miscellany* (Philadelphia) 2 (Apr. 1788): 211–13; William Bentley, *The Diary of William Bentley, D.D., Pastor of East Church, Salem, Massachusetts* (4 vols., 1905–1914), vol. 2 (1905): 246, 350–51, 371, 378; and Nathaniel D. Gould, *Church Music in America* (1853, repr. 1972), pp. 42–51. A scholarly biography of Billings is David P. McKay and Richard Crawford, *William Billings of Boston: Eighteenth-Century Composer* (1975). Documents related to Billings's life and work are reproduced with a biographical commentary in Hans Nathan, *William Billings: Data and Documents* (1976). Information about Billings's style and musical milieu, as well as performance practices pertaining to his music, can be gained from the editors' prefaces to each of the four volumes of *The Complete Works of William Billings* (1977–1990). Important articles on Billings and his music include Richard Crawford and David McKay, "Music in Manuscript: A Massachusetts Tunebook of 1782," *Proceedings of the American Antiquarian Society* 84 (1974): 43; Gillian Anderson, "Eighteenth-Century Evaluations of William Billings: A Reappraisal," *Quarterly Journal of the Library of Congress* 35 (1978): 48; and Karl Kroeger, "William Billings's Music in Manuscript Copy and Some Notes on Variant Versions of His Pieces," *Notes* 39 (1982–1983): 316; "Word Painting in the Music of William Billings," *American Music* 6 (1988): 41; "William Tans'ur's Influence on William Billings," *Inter-American Music Review* 11 (1991): 12; and "William Billings and the Puritan Musical Ideal," *Studies in Puritan American Spirituality* 2 (1992): 31. See also *The New Grove Dictionary of American Music* (1986), which includes a complete works list.

KARL KROEGER

BILLINGSLEY, Sherman (10 Mar. 1900–4 Oct. 1966), nightclub owner and real estate developer, was born John Sherman Billingsley in Enid, Oklahoma Territory, the son of Robert Billingsley and Emily Collingsworth. Sherman Billingsley's parents were so poverty stricken that the youngster was forced to quit school after he finished the fourth grade. His first job was collecting discarded whiskey bottles for resale to bootleggers in the new "dry" state of Oklahoma. In 1912 the youth moved to Anadarko, Oklahoma, to join his two older brothers who had developed a chain of cigar shops and drugstores, establishments that also illegally sold whiskey. Later going into business for himself, he owned and managed a confectionery in Houston, Texas, before moving to Charleston, West Virginia, to take over a cigar store. After going into the drug business, he owned drugstores in Seattle and Omaha, successively. While still just a teenager, he moved to Detroit and opened a grocery store; soon, he had three. In 1923, after saving about $5,000 in capital, he moved to the Bronx, New York City, where he opened a drugstore.

Just as his brothers had done in Oklahoma, Billingsley began illegally selling whiskey to his steady customers. For some patrons he apparently wrote prescriptions for the alcohol; for others he just sold the liquor "under the counter." The successful Billingsley rapidly built or acquired a chain of twenty drugstores located in the Bronx or in adjacent Westchester County. As profits mounted, he went into the real estate business and soon built or acquired several apartment complexes and a number of rental houses. He also built several huge parking garages. Continuing to "ride" his success, in 1929 he (with partners) opened a ritzy speakeasy, the Stork Club, in midtown Manhattan. He soon bought out his partners, but events took a downturn when Prohibition agents closed the place. However, Billingsley had no intention of obeying the law. He soon reopened his club, but it reappeared at a different New York address. After the repeal of Prohibition in 1933, Billingsley moved the club to 3 East Fifty-third Street, where it would remain until its final closing in October 1965.

Billingsley's purpose in opening the new club was to present a rather exclusive restaurant-bar where celebrities such as Broadway entertainers, public figures, and professionals could mix and mingle with their own kind. Middle- and upper-class folk who wanted to see celebrities—or perhaps join their ranks—were also attracted to the club as were the ever-present tourists. Soon Billingsley and his club evolved into a status symbol; his was the "chic" place to be. Where else could one see H. L. Mencken, Eugene O'Neill, Ernest Hemingway, "Joltin'" Joe DiMaggio, Lana Turner, Ginger Rogers, and, at a later time, Grace Kelly and many other stars? Perhaps the best testimony about the elite club came from Paramount Pictures when it offered its posh 1945 movie, *The Stork Club*; Paramount paid Billingsley $100,000 for just the use of the name.

The original club, before its expansion, seated 374 people at one time. However, since the establishment never closed, observers estimated that about 2,000 people a day spent time at Billingsley's Stork Club. The L-shaped main dining room had a fifteen-by-twenty-foot dance floor. Playing in rotation, two bands gave the patrons uninterrupted music. The Cub Room was most exclusive. Only the most famous folk and the most important and beautiful of the clientele, who had Billingsley's personal invitation, could enter it. In the late 1940s and again in the early 1950s, the Oklahoman bought properties adjacent to his club, which was remodeled to take in the extra space.

While Billingsley was developing his "in" club that would eventually gross more than $3 million per year, he also acquired a family. After divorcing his first wife, Ina Dee, in 1924, he married Hazel Donnelly in August of that same year. Donnelly had once been a chorus girl at the Ziegfeld *Follies*. The couple had three children.

Concurrently, the Stork Club became an even greater success and seemed to have an ever-expanding clientele that included luminaries from Broadway and Hollywood. Grace Kelly and Prince Rainier announced their engagement at the club. The duke and duchess of Windsor visited the club. Billingsley feted General Douglas MacArthur on his return from the Pacific theater in World War II. Lana Turner and Artie Shaw announced their divorce from the Stork Club. J. Edgar Hoover and Ethel Merman were frequent visitors.

Although the club remained popular for many years, a noticeable decline occurred in the 1950s. First, a scandal developed that involved the black entertainer Josephine Baker. In 1951 she alleged discrimination when club waiters appeared to be slow in serving her. Subsequently Billingsley's place became the scene of protests by civil rights activists. Although New York City officials investigated the incident and "cleared" Billingsley and his establishment, damage was still done to the public image of the Stork Club. Six years later more negative press came when many of his employees joined a restaurant workers' union. Billingsley bitterly detested unions and made no secret of it; he fought unionization. The labor controversy dragged on from 1957 to 1962.

Between 1962 and 1965 the Stork Club lost piece after piece of its business. New trends in music and dance had led to the rise of the discotheque culture in Manhattan, a development that had swept the entire nation by the 1970s. Younger celebrities deserted first, with others following later. And when the "stars" left, so, too, did their followers. The Stork Club permanently closed on 5 October 1965.

After closing his once chic place, Billingsley concentrated more on Cigogne, Inc., a perfume company that he had earlier developed in partnership with entertainers Morton Downey and Arthur Godfrey. He wrote articles on nightclubs and restaurants for *Encyclopedia Britannica* and contributed articles to various magazines. Billingsley began writing his autobiography while continuing to work on plans to open a new club. But on the night of 4 October 1966, he awoke, complained of a headache, took some aspirin, and went back to sleep. He never woke up, his physician later reporting that he died of a massive heart attack in his New York City home.

• For more on Billingsley's career, see two early articles in *American Magazine*, June 1941, pp. 44–45, and Russell Whelan, "Inside the Stork Club," *American Mercury*, Sept. 1944 pp. 357–65; also see the *New York Journal-American*, 4 Sept. 1962; the *National Review*, 18 Oct. 1966; "Cafe Society," *Newsweek*, 18 Oct. 1965, pp. 42–47, and "Transition," *Newsweek*, 17 Oct. 1966, p. 73. Billingsley and his Stork Club are also covered in Miroslav Sasek, *This Is New York* (1960). An obituary is in the *New York Times*, 5 Oct. 1966.

JAMES M. SMALLWOOD

BILLINGTON, Ray Allen (28 Sept. 1903–7 Mar. 1981), historian, was born in Bay City, Michigan, the son of Cecil Billington, a private secretary, and Nina Allen. He attended the University of Michigan, planned to become a journalist, but transferred to the University of Wisconsin, where he became interested in history. After graduation in 1926 (Phi Beta Kappa), Billington returned to Michigan, where he earned an M.A. in 1927, and then moved to Harvard University for his doctorate. He married Mabel R. Crotty in 1928; the couple had two children.

At Harvard, Billington participated in the western history seminar of Frederick Merk, the foremost disciple of Frederick Jackson Turner, the founder of the Frontier School of American History. He wrote his dissertation—a study of nativism—with Arthur M. Schlesinger, a leading cultural and intellectual historian. He began teaching at Clark University in 1931 and received his Ph.D. in 1933.

In 1937 Billington joined the faculty of Smith College, and in 1938 he published his first book, *The Protestant Crusade, 1800–1860: A Study of the Origins of American Nativism*. Soon after, he published two textbooks. The first was *The United States: American Democracy in World Perspective*, which he coauthored with Samuel H. Brockunier and Bert J. Loewenberg. The second, which changed his career, came about when James B. Hedges of Brown University asked him to coauthor a text based on Turner's frontier course outline. Although initially skeptical of Turner's ideas, Billington accepted and in mastering the sources became a dedicated Turnerian. Hedges's interest waned, and Billington wrote 90 percent of the book. *Westward Expansion: A History of the American Frontier* (1949) also contained a superb annotated bibliography. The work went through five revisions (the last was published posthumously in 1982), and each reflected not only newer scholarship but also changing interpretations. It established Billington as a leading figure in the profession. He was Harmsworth Professor at Oxford University in 1953, and in 1956 he published *The Far Western Frontier*, a volume in the New American Nation series that covered the years 1830–1860. It was a fast-paced narrative based on wide reading, but it was little concerned with analysis.

In 1944 Billington moved to Northwestern University. His scholarship earned him the presidencies of the American Studies Association in 1959, the Organization of American Historians in 1962, and the Western History Association in 1962 (he was a cofounder and first president). He was also the plenary speaker, representing the United States, at the International Congress of Historical Sciences in 1975.

Billington left Northwestern in 1963 to become a senior research associate at the Henry E. Huntington Library in San Marino, California, a position once held by Turner, and he entered into the most productive period in his career. Although he often gave lectures (more than one hundred between 1963 and 1980), Billington devoted his thought and energy to explicating and elaborating Turner's contributions to American scholarship and to the meaning of the westering experience of the American people. After the publication of *Westward Expansion* Billington was also seen as Turner's leading advocate. Although he accepted Turner's general premise that the westward movement had a profound impact on national development and character, Billington gladly modified Turner's observations, such as the "safety valve" theory, when facts disproved them.

In 1966 Billington published *America's Frontier Heritage*, the first volume in the Histories of the American Frontier, a series that he established. Different from his other work, it was an analytical history in which he tested Turner's ideas about frontier traits and their persistence on the basis of extensive reading in sociology, psychology, anthropology, economics, and mobility theory. The book, intended to validate and update Turner's ideas about American exceptionalism, proved far more original. Critics pointed out that Billington paid scant attention to gender and environment.

At the Huntington, Billington gained access to the previously closed Turner papers. He abandoned western narrative history and began an unhurried intellectual quest for the sources of Turner's ideas and an explanation of his career. In 1970 he published *"Dear Lady": The Letters of Frederick Jackson Turner and Alice Forbes Perkins Hooper, 1910–1932* in which Turner not only shared his successes and failures at Harvard with a wealthy patron but also disclosed his political and historical views. This was followed in 1971 by *The Genesis of the Frontier Thesis: A Study in Historical Creativity*, which traced the evolution of Turner's thought and suggested that Turner's insight derived from his familiarity with the social thought of American intellectuals. In 1973 he published *Frederick Jackson Turner: Historian Scholar Teacher*, the first full-length biography of Turner. It demonstrated Turner's profound influence on American scholarship and academic life. The book won the coveted Bancroft Prize. Because Billington was captivated with the frontier thesis, he ignored Turner's ideas about sectionalism. These ideas, although far fetched, marked the origins of regional thinking. Billington's last book, *Land of Savagery / Land of Promise: The European Image of the American Frontier in the Nineteenth Century* (1981), juxtaposed the romantic image of the West depicted by foreign authors with the brutal narrative of violence and conquest. This book cast the frontier experience in a far darker hue than had Billington's earlier work and reflected a growing pessimism about the nation's future.

Billington's personality contributed in part to his professional success. His home was a mecca for foreign visitors and scholars. He tolerated people of widely different political and social views, but he was a social democrat throughout his life. He worked to end racial and religious discrimination, and he frequently lent his prestige to controversial causes and used his influence to effect change in the historical profession. Billington died in San Marino, California.

• Billington provided autobiographical material in many essays among the best of which is "The Frontier and I," *Western Historical Quarterly* 1 (Jan. 1970): 5–20. Of the essays critical of Billington's defense of the frontier thesis, the most vehement are in Richard Etulain, ed., *Writing Western History* (1991). Billington's role in western history is included in a scholarly work by Gerald D. Nash, *Creating the West: Historical Interpretations, 1890–1990* (1991). For a hostile account of Billington's career, see Wilbur Jacobs, *On Turner's Trail* (1994). Overall assessments are in Martin Ridge, "Ray Allen Billington," *Western Historical Quarterly* 12 (July 1981): 245–50; Ridge, "Ray Allen Billington, Western History, and American Exceptionalism," *Pacific Historical Review* 56 (Nov. 1987): 495–511; and Ridge, "Frederick Jackson Turner, Ray Allen Billington, and American Frontier History," *Western Historical Quarterly* 19 (Jan. 1988): 5–20. An obituary is in the *New York Times*, 8 Mar. 1981.

MARTIN RIDGE

BILLY (fl. 1781), a mulatto slave, also known as Will or William, was the subject of an alleged treason case during the American Revolution. The case is more significant for what it says about the ambivalence toward slavery of Thomas Jefferson and other Virginians than for the light it sheds on the life of Billy, or Will. Ironically, in 1710, another slave named Will had a brief flirtation with history. This earlier Will was freed for "his fidelity . . . in discovering a conspiracy of diverse negros . . . for levying war" in Virginia.

The Will, or Billy, of the treason case was the slave of Colonel John Tayloe, a resident of Richmond County, Virginia. Billy and others were arrested and convicted of seizing an armed vessel on 2 April 1781 in order to wage war against Virginia. He was condemned to death by the court of Oyer and Terminer in Prince William County on 8 May. Henry Lee and William Carr, dissenting justices, noted that he was not a citizen and owed no allegiance to Virginia. Furthermore, Billy argued that others had forced him onto the vessel, and there was no evidence that he had gone aboard voluntarily.

Only Governor Thomas Jefferson could grant Billy a reprieve. Jefferson was profoundly ambivalent about the institution of slavery; his actions and writings reveal his often contradictory impulses. Like many planters, Jefferson had a financial interest in perpetuating slavery and believed in the innate inferiority of Africans. He owned many slaves and offered a reward for the return of his escaped slave Sandy in 1769. Yet as a member of Virginia's House of Burgesses Jefferson also sought, albeit unsuccessfully, to permit slaveholders to free their slaves without approval of the legislature. When granting his own slaves freedom, he exiled them to the wilderness, providing them with the wherewithal for survival. In his draft of the Declaration of Independence Jefferson condemned the king of England for his involvement in the African slave trade.

When deciding whether to grant Billy a reprieve, Jefferson had to consider his own ambivalence toward slavery as well as Lord Dunmore's 1775 proclamation urging slaves and indentured servants to escape behind British lines to freedom. Even though he considered Dunmore's proclamation an attempt by the king to incite racial massacres, Jefferson did not let his fears of a slave uprising or the loss to the British of thirty of his own slaves deter him from seeking justice for Billy. In May 1781, after accepting the opinion of Mann Page, one of Tayloe's executors, Jefferson signed a temporary reprieve for Billy. After a joint resolution of the Virginia house and senate on 14 June 1781, Billy was granted a permanent reprieve. He was free to return to the anonymity he had known before his brief encounter with American justice.

• See Julian Boyd et al., eds., *The Papers of Thomas Jefferson*, vol. 5 (1952); Helen T. Catterall, ed., *Judicial Cases concerning American Slavery and Negro Slavery*, vol. 1 (1926); A. Leon Higginbotham, Jr., *In the Matter of Color: Race and the American Legal Process* (1977); and Matthew T. Mellon, *Early American Views on Negro Slavery* (1969).

WILLIAM SERAILE

BILLY BOWLEGS (1812?–1864?), Seminole chief who led the third and final Seminole war against the whites of Florida, also known as the Billy Bowlegs war of 1855–1858, was born on the Alachua savannah in Florida. He was a direct descendant of Secoffee, originally a Creek chief who migrated to Florida from the Creek homelands in Alabama and Georgia and later founded the Seminole nation. The names of Billy Bowlegs's father, mother, and other family members are unknown.

A striking feature of Bowlegs was his unusual style of dress. The Seminoles, admirers of distinctive costumes, were quite taken with the Scottish Highlanders who entered Florida in 1736. Both the Highlanders and the Indians shared common customs and attitudes. For instance, both were tribal and organized into clans, both preferred skirtlike clothing and refused to wear trousers, and both wore a similar style of garb in the form of breechcloths. In an 1852 daguerreotype portrait and an 1852 magazine portrait, Bowlegs, with a dash of Highland flair, is shown wearing three large silver gorgets (a distinctive emblem of authority), an embroidered bead bandolier, leggings with a wide strap and garters fingerwoven in diamond patterns, a calico frock, a short cloak, and a patterned paisley scarf attached to a scalloped turban with a profusion of protruding black ostrich feathers.

Bowlegs received his name not because of the curvature of his legs but from a family appellation, possibly from the corruption of the word "bolek" or "bowleck." Bowlegs spoke fluent English and Spanish and could sign his name. In fact his leadership name, "Halpatter-Micco [Micco meaning leader], appears for the first time in history" (Gifford, p. 26) when in an attempt to end hostilities before the second Seminole war, his signature appeared on the Treaty of Payne's Landing, 9 May 1832, in which he and fourteen other Seminoles agreed to cede their Florida lands and remove themselves to Indian Territory west of the Mississippi River. Later Bowlegs and the others denied this act. Bowlegs also was a Seminole representative in parleys to end hostilities during the final stages of the second Seminole war in 1842.

On 10 May 1842 President John Tyler ended any military action against the Seminoles, thereby concluding the second Seminole war. The Armed Occupation Act of 4 August 1842, however, became the beginning of the end for the Seminoles, as 200,000 acres of their homeland were taken by settlers coming into middle Florida. Even though on 14 August 1842 the Seminoles, in Military Order 28, were given 2.5 million acres for a "temporary" hunting and planting reserve and were protected with a corridor of land surrounding this reserve by President James Polk on 19 May 1845, the pioneer settlers kept infringing on the Seminoles' territory, often claiming some of this land as their own. Obviously the relations between the settlers and the Seminoles became strained, and the settlers would not be happy until all the Seminoles were forced out of Florida, even though the Seminoles, and not the whites, went to great lengths to respect the terms of the 1842 agreement.

As tensions kept rising, especially with the proposal for an early removal of the Seminoles, the Seminoles in 1848 started to acquire rifle powder and lead through trading, in order to prepare themselves for what they felt would become inevitable: war. Attacks and raiding occurred randomly from July 1849 to May 1850. Some attacks were done by outlaw Seminoles who were eventually turned over to the militia by Seminole chiefs such as Bowlegs and Sam Jones in order to keep the peace. However, both the settlers and the militia were tired of the ongoing attacks and raiding, so that it became more and more desirous for the Seminoles to be removed from Florida. In February 1851 Luther Blake, hired as a special agent to rid Florida of the Seminoles, enticed Bowlegs to go to Washington,

D.C., to meet President Millard Fillmore in the fall of 1852, in an endeavor to persuade Bowlegs to leave Florida. For a second time, on 20 September 1852, Bowlegs signed an agreement promising to move to Indian Territory, although he was still not ready to leave Florida. In January 1853 the Florida legislature signed a law making Seminole residence in Florida illegal and forbid trading with the Indians. By June 1854 the Indians were feeling the effects of the trade embargo and were running out of supplies.

As the settlers kept infringing on the Seminoles' territory, the Seminoles were forced to move deeper and deeper into the Florida everglades. In the fall of 1855 the Seminoles gathered to plan their warfare tactics against the white settlers. On 17 December 1855 First Lieutenant George L. Hartsuff took a reconnaissance into the Big Cypress Swamp, where Bowlegs's village was located. During their patrol they cut down and carried away bunches of bananas belonging to Bowlegs (there is some debate whether this was done maliciously or not). In anger Bowlegs led a war party of thirty Seminoles and attacked Hartsuff on 20 December 1855, thus igniting the last Seminole war in Florida. By 1 March 1856, in preparation for war, "Federal troops in south Florida numbered eight hundred men; state troops in federal service, two hundred and sixty men; state troops in state service, four hundred men; making a grand total of one thousand, four hundred and sixty men. Opposed to this force were about one hundred Seminole warriors; thus making a battlefield odds of one Indian to fourteen opponents" (Covington, *Bowlegs War*, p. 38). On 14 and 16 June 1856 two important Indian leaders were killed, ending the Seminoles' power in offensive strikes. On 19 November 1857 Bowlegs's village was discovered, and his food, animals, and crops were either taken or destroyed. As other villages were discovered, their food supplies were also demolished. A cessation of activity resulted, and white truce flags were soon displayed by the militia. On 15 March 1858 Bowlegs held council with the militia for the first round of negotiations, and on 27 March 1858 he accepted the terms of the proposal and began moving from the swamps. On 4 May 1858 Bowlegs and his followers met at Fort Myers and boarded the *Grey Cloud* and left Florida. They had a stopover in New Orleans, where Bowlegs was described "as possessing two wives, one son, five daughters, fifty slaves and one hundred thousand dollars in hard cash" (Covington, *Bowlegs War*, p. 79). The names of his two wives, one son, and four of his daughters are unknown. The only name mentioned is one daughter from his first wife, known as Lady Elizabeth Bowlegs. On 8 May 1858 Colonel Gustavus Loomis declared the third Seminole war officially ended.

Billy Bowlegs was known as an active, intelligent, and brave leader of the Seminoles and exercised great skill and good judgment during his war efforts. He wanted to remain in his homeland, saying that he was a little unhappy to leave, "for his navel cord had been cut in Florida, his blood spilled here and the peninsula was like a part of his body" (Covington, *Bowlegs War*,

p. 14). As a Seminole leader he was able to keep his band from being removed from Florida for approximately twenty-six years. Always a warrior, even in Indian Territory, he eventually played a prominent role in the Civil War, where he was appointed captain of an Indian regiment with the Union forces. Billy Bowlegs, king of the everglades and chief of the Seminoles, "died during the fall or winter of 1863–1864 from smallpox" (Covington, *Bowlegs War*, p. 82).

• Important sources on Billy Bowlegs and the Billy Bowlegs war are James W. Covington, *The Billy Bowlegs War, 1855–1858: The Final Stand of the Seminoles against the Whites* (1982) and *The Seminoles of Florida* (1993). Also see John C. Gifford, *Billy Bowlegs and the Seminole War* (1925), and Lieut.-Col. Hazelton (1865), "The Seminole Chief, or the Captives of the Kissimmee," in *The Garland Library of Narratives of North American Indian Captivities*, ed. Wilcomb E. Washburn, vol. 80 (1979). For a discussion of the term "Seminole" as derived from the Creek language, see William C. Sturtevant, "Creek into Seminole," in *North American Indians in Historical Perspective*, ed. Eleanor B. Leacock and Nancy O. Lurie (1971). A good account describing the attire of Billy Bowlegs and his band is in Dorothy Downs, *Art of the Florida Seminole and Miccosukee Indians* (1995). For details of Billy Bowlegs's life in Indian Territory, see Kenneth W. Porter, "Billy Bowlegs (Holata Micco) in the Civil War," pt. 2, *Florida Historical Quarterly* 45, no. 4 (1967): 391–401. Other articles include Kenneth Porter, "Billy Bowlegs (Holata Micco) in the Seminole Wars," *Florida Historical Quarterly* 45, no. 3 (1967): 219–42, and Carolyn T. Foreman, "Billy Bowlegs," *Chronicles of Oklahoma* 33 (1965): 512–22, as well as an account that started the Billy Bowlegs war, Ray B. Seley, Jr., "Lieutenant Hartsuff and the Banana Plants," *Tequesta* 22 (1962): 3–14.

DARLENE MARY SUAREZ

BILLY THE KID (15 Sept. 1859–14 July 1881), western outlaw and legendary figure in international folklore, was born Henry McCarty, probably in Brooklyn, New York, probably on the date given, and probably of Irish immigrants; all aspects of his origins, however, remain controversial. In 1873 his mother, Catherine, was remarried, to William Henry Antrim, whereupon the boy took his stepfather's name and became Henry Antrim. Later, for reasons that are obscure, he adopted the sobriquet William H. Bonney. In adolescence he was called simply Kid, but not until the final few months of his life was he known as Billy the Kid.

The Kid grew up in the mining camp of Silver City, New Mexico, where he was a good student and caused no more trouble than the average male adolescent. After his mother's death in 1874 he had a trivial run-in with the law, which landed him in jail. He escaped and took refuge in Arizona, where he became a petty horsethief. There in 1877, at the age of seventeen, he killed a bully who had been tormenting him and fled back to New Mexico to embark on the life of an outlaw.

The Kid gained experience and notoriety as a gunman in New Mexico's Lincoln County War of 1878. This was a conflict between rival mercantile firms seeking to dominate the county's economy, including federal contracts to supply the military post of Fort Stanton and the Apache Indian agency. The Tunstall-McSween faction sought to displace the entrenched monopoly of the Murphy-Dolan faction. As one of the Regulators, the fighting arm of the Tunstall-McSween faction, the Kid fought in all the skirmishes and battles of the war. With five others, he shared in the ambush slaying of Sheriff William Brady on Lincoln's main street. He also participated prominently in the archetypal western shootout with Buckshot Roberts at Blazer's Mill. The violent climax of the war took place in the town of Lincoln on 15–19 July 1878, when a sheriff's posse attempted to rout the Regulators. The final day featured a siege of the McSween house, in which the Kid and his cohorts were barricaded. The appearance of a military force from Fort Stanton, although it supposedly remained neutral, threw the advantage to the possemen. In a hail of gunfire, the Kid and three others escaped from the burning McSween house, leaving four of their comrades to be struck down and killed.

After the war the Kid pursued an ambivalent life of petty crime while also trying to free himself of legal entanglements in order to go straight. Based in the village of Fort Sumner, on the Pecos River, he and a handful of friends rustled Texas cattle from the nearby Staked Plains. A bargain with New Mexico governor Lew Wallace to turn state's evidence against other murderers collapsed when the Kid continued to rustle cows and Wallace failed to gain amnesty for him. Captured by a posse under Sheriff Pat Garrett after a gun battle at Stinking Springs in December 1880, the Kid was tried in Mesilla for the murder of Sheriff Brady during the Lincoln County War. He was found guilty and sent back to Lincoln to be hanged. Instead, in April 1881, he broke free from confinement, killing two guards as he went.

Billy the Kid remained free for three months, harbored by Hispanic sheepmen in the Fort Sumner area. On 14 July 1881, however, Sheriff Garrett confronted him in a darkened bedroom at Fort Sumner. Garrett fired first, and Billy died instantly, struck in the heart.

Billy the Kid did not marry. However, he was extremely popular with young women, especially the Hispanics who idolized him because he spoke their language and did not patronize them. Almost certainly he left an unrecorded progeny. His brother survived him by nearly fifty years and died a Denver derelict.

Even before his death, Billy the Kid had attained legendary stature. Legend credits him with killing twenty-one men, one for each of his twenty-one years. Actually, the number was four for certain plus six encounters in which he participated and may or may not have fired the fatal round. Nor was he the premier outlaw captain the press pictured. He and a few others rustled cows, but there was no organized gang under his leadership.

In history Billy the Kid rates hardly a footnote. In folklore he is a towering figure throughout the world. In the public imagination, two Kids have vied with each other since 1881. The first is the merciless outlaw killer; the other is the young Robin Hood whose guns blazed for the poor and downtrodden against the entrenched interests. The latter image, created by Walter Noble Burns's *Saga of Billy the Kid* (1926), was the model for subsequent books, articles, movies, and even an orchestral suite and ballet. For millions, Billy still rides as the ultimate symbol of the violence of the Old West.

• A vast body of literature focuses on Billy the Kid, but most of it is more legend than history. The standard biography is Robert M. Utley, *Billy the Kid: A Short and Violent Life* (1989). The legend is expertly treated in Stephen Tatum, *Inventing Billy the Kid: Visions of the Outlaw in America, 1881–1981* (1982). For the Lincoln County War, see Frederick Nolan, *The Lincoln County War: A Documentary History* (1992), and Robert M. Utley, *High Noon in Lincoln: Violence on the Western Frontier* (1987). Important as both history and legend is Pat Garrett's own version, ghostwritten by a creative journalist named Marshal A. Upson, *The Authentic Life of Billy the Kid*; first published in 1882, it has reappeared in many editions.

ROBERT M. UTLEY

BIMELER, Joseph Michael (c. 1778–27 Aug. 1853), Separatist and communitarian leader, was probably born in Württemberg, Germany, where he worked as a weaver. Little is known about his parents or his early years. He was self-educated and taught in Munich among a group of Pietist dissenters called Separatists. As the name suggests, these devout Protestants called for withdrawal from the official, state-supported Lutheran churches. A group of radical Pietists, including Bimeler, congregated in Württemberg between 1803 and 1805 under the mystical leadership of Barbara Grübermann. Their refusal to permit their children to be baptized, attend clergy-controlled schools, or serve in the military led to severe civil as well as ecclesiastical penalties, which forced them frequently to relocate.

In 1815 the Grübermann Separatists were allowed to live in peace in an isolated area near the southern boundary of Württemberg, but they were ordered to abandon this settlement in less than a year. By early 1817 preparations were complete for some 300 Separatists from Württemberg, Bavaria, and Baden, to seek their future in the United States. Grübermann died, however, before these plans were complete and Bimeler emerged as the group's spiritual leader.

After an arduous voyage the Separatists arrived in Philadelphia in mid-August 1817. Through the generosity of members of the Society of Friends (Quakers), they were housed and fed, and work was secured for those who were able. Also with the financial backing of Quakers, Bimeler purchased 5,600 acres of excellent timbered land on the east side of the Tuscarawas River in northeast Ohio. This tract (titled in Bimeler's name) was purchased for $16,500, with terms extended for fifteen years. Bimeler soon led a small company to the Tuscarawas Valley, cleared several acres for crops, laid out a village, and built a few log cabins. This village was called Zoar, named after the biblical place of refuge for Lot after fleeing the destruction of Sodom and Gomorrah. Those who had wintered in Philadelphia began to arrive in small groups the following spring.

Two harsh winters and the need to pay creditors, however, threatened the survival of the infant community. To ensure a livelihood for its members, a complete community of goods was introduced in 1819. Bimeler originally opposed this arrangement but their desperate financial situation forced him to reconsider. Articles for the "Society of Separatists of Zoar" were drawn up and signed by both male and female members. These were revised in 1824, and again in 1833 when a constitution was adopted. Bimeler was elected cashier and general agent with authority to administer all business transactions, positions which he held until his death.

Financial circumstances also led to the temporary abandonment of marriage. No new marriages were allowed and husbands and wives lived separately so that women could equally participate in work. The economic threat to Zoar eased in 1827, however, when the Ohio Canal was built through their property. The society contracted to build a portion of the canal, which netted them more than $21,000. By 1830 the debt for the land was settled and marriage was again permitted. Bimeler himself married twice. His first wife, whom he married in 1802, was Barbara Danzer; they had two children before her death in 1804. His second wife, whom he married in 1830, was Dorothea Huber.

Bimeler resided in the large and pretentious "Number One House," built in 1835 of brick, which stood in marked contrast with the modest Zoar homes. The most serious threat to his benevolent rule came in 1845. Two members were expelled for mismanagement and took him to court. Other unsatisfied members joined the two in an effort to break up the Society and distribute the assets. The case eventually reached the U.S. Supreme Court, which ruled in favor of Bimeler and found him to be a man of great business skill and above reproach. At the time of his death, Zoar was worth an estimated one million dollars, with herds, orchards, an iron works, several types of mills (wool, flour, and lumber), various shop industries including a pottery, brewery, and a hotel, general store, and jail that catered to visitors.

Bimeler, who also acted as Zoar's physician, guided the religious life of the community as well. Like the Quakers, the community frowned upon ritual. There was no baptism or confirmation, and marriage was not observed as a religious rite. Bimeler's discourses, later published and read at Sunday services, urged his flock to purge their souls of sinful thoughts and practice a pure Christianity. He died in Zoar.

• Bimeler's sermons are collected in three volumes: *Die Wahre Separation, oder die Wiedergeburt, Dargestellt in Geistreichen und Erbaulichen Versammlungs-Reden und Betrachtungen* (2 vols., 1856–1860); and *Etwas fürs Herz! oder Geistliche Brosamen von des Herrn Tisch Gefallen* (1860–1861). The best study of Zoar is Emilius O. Randall, *History of the Zoar Socie-*

ty 3d. ed. (1904), but see also Edgar B. Nixon, "The Society of Separatist of Zoar" (Ph.D. diss., Ohio State Univ., 1933); Catherine R. Dobbs, *Freedom's Will: The Society of the Separatists of Zoar—An Historical Adventure of Religious Communism in Early Ohio* (1947); and *Zoar: A Study in Ohio Communalism* (1953), a sixty-page pamphlet published by the Ohio Historical Society. Interpretative essays include George B. Landis, "The Separatists of Zoar," in American Historical Association, *Annual Report* (1898), pp. 165–220. See also, Charles Nordhoff, *The Communistic Societies of the United States* (1875), and William A. Hinds, *American Communities* (1878).

DAVID B. ELLER

BING, R. H. (20 Oct. 1914–28 Apr. 1986), mathematician, was born in Oakwood, Texas, the son of Rupert Henry Bing, a school district superintendent, and Lula May Thompson, a schoolteacher. Bing—who had no given names, only the initials R. H.—studied mathematics at Southwest Texas State Teachers College (now Southwest Texas State University) in San Marcos; his interest in the subject arose from his mother's influence. There he obtained the degrees of B.Ed. and B.S. in 1935. In order to receive an M.Ed., Bing took summer courses at the University of Texas in nearby Austin, where he came under the influence of the mathematician R. L. Moore. He received his education degree at Texas in 1938 and in the same year married fellow student Mary Blanche Hobbs; they had four children. Bing then taught mathematics and coached football and track at high schools for four years. He continued to take summer courses at Texas until Moore obtained an instructorship for him in the university's mathematics department in 1942. This position enabled Bing to concentrate on graduate work, and he obtained a Ph.D. in mathematics in 1945 with a dissertation in point-set topology on the topic of planar webs.

Bing quickly gained national recognition by solving a longstanding problem, not directly connected with his dissertation subject, known as the Kline sphere characterization problem. This was a problem, posed by J. R. Kline, which asked whether a surface can be determined to be a sphere from certain properties of curves and points on it. He published his solution along with ten other papers between 1945 and 1947, while he was an assistant professor at Texas. Solomon Lefschetz at Princeton University invited him to join the Princeton faculty but only on condition, as Bing recounted in an unpublished 1975 interview, that Bing abandon topology, a dying subject in Lefschetz's opinion. Instead, in 1947 Bing became an assistant professor at the University of Wisconsin at Madison, where he remained, except for visiting positions elsewhere, until returning to Texas as professor of mathematics in 1973. At Wisconsin Bing established, in effect, his own center for the study of point-set topology, published a further eighty-seven papers, and supervised thirty-three doctoral students. He was elected president of the Mathematical Association of America for 1963–1964. In 1970 he gave the American Mathematical Society Colloquium Lectures, later published as *The Geometric Topology of 3-Manifolds* (1983; repr. 1990).

Bing's election to the National Academy of Sciences in 1965 marked the beginning of a period of his extensive national and international service both within the mathematics profession and on behalf of it. His positions included chair in 1966–1967 of the Conference Board of Mathematical Sciences, an umbrella group sponsored by a number of mathematics-related organizations; U.S. delegate to the International Mathematical Union in 1966 and 1978; two-term member of the President's Committee on the National Medal of Science in 1966–1967 and from 1974 to 1976; and member of the National Science Board from 1968 to 1975. In the National Academy of Sciences he was chair of the Mathematics Section (1970–1973) and member of the council (1977–1980). In the National Research Council he served as chair of the Division of Mathematics (1967–1969) and on its governing board (1977–1980).

Returning to the University of Texas at Austin in 1973, Bing helped to build up the department's research status by recruiting new members. Over the next thirteen years, he published fifteen papers, oversaw two doctoral dissertations, and was elected president of the American Mathematical Society for 1977–1978. He died in Austin.

Friends have remarked on Bing's unfailing sense of humor, his loyalty, and a Texas accent that seemed to be more pronounced the farther from Texas he was. Always striving to make mathematics understandable and meaningful to others, he once complimented a speaker at a national AMS meeting by saying that where he came from "we appreciate a man who pitches the fodder where the calves can reach it." His teaching method was similar to that of his teacher Moore in that students were expected to prove theorems and, at the graduate level, develop their own thesis topics. Unlike Moore, whose classroom topics were restricted to those of interest to Moore, Bing chose topics that were more likely to be of general mathematical interest. However abstract Bing's mathematics was, he regarded its ultimate objective to be a better understanding of the space of physical intuition. The inspiration, and sometimes even key mathematical notions of much of his work, came from intuitions and methods in the physical world, such as the way the grid pattern on graph paper is used to make scaled drawings.

• The main collection of Bing's personal papers, which date primarily from the years 1973 to 1986, are in the Archives of American Mathematics at the University of Texas at Austin. Bing was instrumental in creating this national repository for historical materials on mathematics, the first of its kind in the United States. Another portion of his papers is in the Archives of Southwest Texas State University in San Marcos. His published papers are reprinted in *Collected Papers of R. H. Bing*, ed. S. Singh et al. (1988), which also includes a biographical sketch by Singh based on taped reminiscences by Bing, as well as photographs, a chronology of his life, and a bibliography. A memorial resolution committee at the University of Texas at Austin, chaired by Michael Starbird, prepared a biography that includes anecdotes giving insights into Bing's personality and working methods, a bibliography, and a listing of his doctoral students in *Documents and Minutes of the General Faculty* (1993), pp. 19185–202a. His many connections with the American Mathematical Society as well as his portrait are in Everett Pitcher, *A History of the Second Fifty Years, American Mathematical Society 1939–1988* (1988).

ALBERT C. LEWIS

BINGA, Jesse (10 Apr. 1865–13 June 1950), Chicago businessman, banker, and real estate investor, was born in Detroit, Michigan, the son of Robert Binga, Jr., a barber, and Adelphia Powers, a builder and real estate owner. (Nearly all sources cite William W. Binga as Jesse Binga's father, but all are based on a Dec. 1927 article by Inez V. Cantley in *Crisis*, which may not be reliable. A family member, Anthony J. Binga, Sr., after conducting research in the census records from the Courts of Records of the Dominion of Canada, claimed that Jesse Binga's father was Robert Binga, Jr. *Who's Who in Colored America* [1928–1929] also names Robert Binga as Jesse Binga's father.) The Binga family owned and managed real estate properties, and, according to a number of sources, it was Adelphia Binga who possessed most of the family's business acumen. As a youngster Binga helped his mother collect rents on the family's tenement properties along what was called "Binga Row." Tenants were mostly black migrants on their way to and from Canada.

Binga dropped out of high school after only two years to learn the barbering trade from his father. During this period he also worked for a young black attorney. In 1885 Binga left Detroit and set out on his own, working his way across the Northwest with the goal of becoming an entrepreneur. After working as a barber in Kansas City, Missouri; St. Paul, Minnesota; and Missoula, Montana; in Tacoma and Seattle, Washington, he opened his own barber shop. Each venture, however, was short-lived. In Oakland, California, he worked first as a barber and then as a porter for the Southern Pacific Railroad. Later, while in Ogden, Utah, he invested in a land deal on a former Indian reservation. The venture was profitable enough that, by the time he arrived in Chicago in 1893, Binga had enough capital to begin building his own empire.

He opened his first real estate office on State Street in 1898 and continued to prosper for the next three decades by acquiring rental properties throughout Chicago's South Side, regardless of racial restrictions. Binga would purchase the homes of more affluent whites who were fleeing the encroaching black population and then subdivide them into smaller units, which he would rent to single black men and families. In 1905 he leased a seven-story building on State Street and opened it to black tenants. Despite hostile reactions to his practice of "block busting" to bring black tenants into formerly white areas, Binga and others like him met housing needs that were not otherwise being addressed. Chicago's African-American population, which had grown rapidly since 1900, could no

longer be contained within the traditional black ghetto. Thus Binga's business activities served a crucial social need while at the same time turning a nice profit. By 1907 he was one of the most prosperous African-American real estate agents in the city. A year later he opened the Binga Bank in a newly constructed office building on State Street. It was the first private bank in the North to be owned, managed, directed, or controlled by blacks.

In 1912 Binga married Eudora Johnson, sister of John "Mushmouth" Johnson, the gambling kingpin of the South Side. Apparently Eudora Johnson was neither young nor attractive, and many Chicagoans were convinced that the handsome Binga married her for her money. Whatever the truth of that accusation, at the time of their marriage she had inherited from her father, after his death in 1906, an estate worth $200,000, which greatly enhanced Binga's economic prospects. According to Anthony J. Binga, Sr., the couple had two children. Anthony Binga has also claimed to have found a record of a second marriage in the U.S. Census records, but details are unknown.

Binga's bank and his personal fortune grew impressively in the wake of the massive black migration to northern cities in the years surrounding World War I, but white resentment in Chicago grew apace. His properties were vandalized on several occasions, and during the so-called "Red Summer" of 1919 both his real estate office and his home were bombed. Nonetheless, at one point in the mid-1920s Binga owned 1,200 leaseholds on flats and residences, and by 1926 the Chicago *Broad Ax* was reporting that he owned more frontage on State Street south of Twelfth Street than anyone else.

All of this made possible the opening of Binga State Bank in January 1921. The bank's board of directors was composed of the leading African-American businessmen in the community, and the *Broad Ax* viewed the bank's opening as a "history-making event among colored people residing in Chicago." By 1924 Binga had increased the capital and surplus of Binga State Bank to $235,000. He also opened the Binga Safe Deposit Company and organized a black insurance firm. However, although he had acquired a state charter for the bank, Binga continued to be its largest shareholder and ran the bank as if it were a private, solely owned corporation—practices for which he would later be severely criticized.

The pinnacle of Binga's success came in 1929 when he constructed the Binga Arcade, a five-story building and ballroom at the corner of Thirty-fifth and State streets. Once the center of black business in Chicago, the area had badly deteriorated. Binga hoped that his development would help to revitalize the area, but instead his empire soon began to unravel. When the Binga State Bank failed in 1930, Binga lost his personal fortune of $400,000 as well as the savings of thousands of black Chicagoans. Although the Great Depression was partly to blame for the failure, the state banking examiner concluded that Binga had managed the financial institution in an illegal and unwise manner.

Convicted of embezzlement in 1933, Binga was sentenced to ten years in prison; appeals delayed the start of his sentence until 1935.

Despite his mixed reputation in the community and the fact that many had lost their life savings when the bank failed, leading African Americans organized a petition drive to secure Binga's freedom. The effort was successful, and he was released from prison in 1938. Stripped of his former prominence, Binga spent the remainder of his life working as a custodian at St. Anselm's Catholic Church (having earlier converted to the faith). He died in Chicago after a fall at his nephew's home.

Binga's efforts to develop Chicago's black community brought him both praise and censure from the city's black and white communities. On the one hand, he was lauded for his business acumen and for his philanthropy, but he was also criticized for rent-gouging and for having a hard-driving personality. Many years after his death, the eminent African-American leader Earl Dickerson remembered Binga as "a mean son-of-a-bitch." In many ways Binga's career reflected the complex web of hope and despair that characterized the city's black business community during the early decades of the twentieth century.

• For information on Binga's parentage and marriages, see Anthony J. Binga, Sr., "Jesse Binga: Founder and President, Binga State Bank, Chicago, Illinois," *Journal of the Afro-American History and Genealogy Society* 2, no. 4 (1981): 146–52. For additional biographical information see the sketch by John N. Ingham in the *Biographical Dictionary of American Business Leaders*, vol. 1 (1983). Also see Carl Osthaus, "The Rise and Fall of Jesse Binga, Black Banker," *Journal of Negro History* 58 (Jan. 1973): 39–60; Abram L. Harris, *The Negro as Capitalist* (1936), pp. 153–64; and Gerri Major, *Black Society* (1976), pp. 304–6. Many articles on Binga appeared in the Chicago *Defender* and the *Broad Ax* during the period of his influence. See especially the *Defender*, 24 Feb. 1912, 16 Dec. 1916, 11 Oct. 1930, 24 Feb. 1931, 7 Mar. 1931, and 5 Mar. 1938; and the *Broad Ax*, 21 Sept. 1907 and 23 Oct. 1926. See also the *Freeman* (Indianapolis), 17 Apr. 1909. The social context for Binga's career is provided by St. Clair Drake and Horace R. Cayton, *Black Metropolis: A Study of Negro Life in a Northern City* (1945), and Allan H. Spear, *Black Chicago: The Making of a Negro Ghetto, 1890–1920* (1967). The effect of the great migration on Chicago is well treated in James R. Grossman, *Land of Hope: Chicago, Black Southerners, and the Great Migration* (1989). White hostility toward Binga and the civil unrest of 1919 are covered in William M. Tuttle, Jr., *Race Riot: Chicago in the Red Summer of 1919* (1970), and Chicago Commission on Race Relations, *The Negro in Chicago: A Study of Race Relations and a Race Riot* (1922). Two important editorials on the closing of Binga's bank are in *Opportunity*, Sept. 1930, p. 264, and (by W. E. B. Du Bois) in *Crisis*, Dec. 1930, pp. 425–26. A distressingly short obituary is in the Chicago *Herald American*, 14 June 1950; a longer one is in the *Defender*, 24 June 1950.

JOHN N. INGHAM

BINGHAM, Amelia (20 Mar. 1869–1 Sept. 1927), actress and theatrical manager, was born in Hicksville, Ohio, the daughter of John B. Smiley and Marie Schwille, owners of the town's only boardinghouse, which was frequented by touring theatrical companies. In the summer of 1887, at home from studies at Ohio Wesleyan College, Amelia acted in an amateur theatrical production, which was observed by Lloyd Bingham, the manager of a theatrical company. He persuaded her not only to join his company but to marry him that fall. She began to learn the ropes by taking small parts in his company, but her first real experience came in the early 1890s, when she joined the McKee Rankin Company and toured the Pacific Coast, accompanied by her husband, who was now serving as her personal manager. Here she gained confidence as an actress, playing successively larger and more important roles. She matured into an imposing, self-assured actress, popular with audiences, and appeared to be on her way to stardom.

On 18 December 1893 Amelia Bingham reached New York City, making her debut at Peoples Theatre on the Bowery in *The Struggle for Life*. For several years thereafter she acted leading roles in the popular melodramas of the day, notably in Dion Boucicault's *The Shaughraun* and *Colleen Bawn*, as well as in *The Village Postmaster*, *The Mummy*, *Captain Impudence*, and *Nature*. Her place on the New York stage became assured when she appeared in *The White Heather* in 1897 under the management of Charles Frohman, the leading theatrical producer of the time. Remaining with him for five years, she took roles in *The Pink Domino*, *On and Off*, *The Proper Caper*, *The Cuckoo*, *At the White Horse Tavern*, *His Excellency the Governor*, and *Hearts Are Trump*. She toured the country, returning often with her husband to her hometown in Ohio.

In 1900, finding herself financially successful but without an assignment, she organized the Amelia Bingham Company, leased the Bijou Theatre in New York, and took on the role of actress-manager in the manner of English and American actresses of a previous era. Her intelligence and executive skills made the company one of the foremost stock companies in New York for a few seasons at a time when they were in decline throughout the country. On 21 January 1901 she introduced both the new company and Clyde Fitch's play *The Climbers* to an enthusiastic Broadway audience. It ran for 163 performances, and she later revived it in 1904 and 1914. As Mrs. Sterling, the play's most sympathetic character, she probably played her greatest role. Fitch's play satirized the machinations of New York's parvenu society to achieve power and rank. During the next few seasons she produced and appeared in *Lady Margaret*, *A Modern Magdalen*, and *The Frisky Mrs. Johnson* (also by Fitch) at the Bijou and other theaters.

From 1904 to 1911 Bingham performed in New York, on the road, and with a stock company in St. Louis. In 1907 she put together a vaudeville sketch, "Big Moments from Great Plays," in which she toured both at home and in Britain, performing in the principal vaudeville houses and music halls for five years. In 1915 her husband joined Henry Ford's Peace Ship and died in Christiana, Norway, a few days after its arrival in Europe. Following his death, and while still a formidable figure on the stage, Bingham retired for a few seasons, but she returned in *The New Henrietta* in 1917, in *The Man Who Stayed at Home* in 1918, and with an all-star cast in *Out There* to benefit the Red Cross in the war effort of 1918. During World War I she became chair of the volunteers for the Stage Women's War Relief and entertained soldiers with her vaudeville sketch. She was a member of the Twelfth Night Club, the Professional Women's League of New York, and the Ohio Clubwomen of New York.

Throughout her long career on the stage, Bingham and her husband engaged in running battles with theater critics over her melodramatic style of acting, which they considered no longer suitable for the time. It culminated at one point in a fistfight at the Hoffman House between *New York Sun* critic Acton Davies and Lloyd Bingham, but a truce was later called during the final active years of Amelia Bingham's career. Although not a great actress, she was magnetic in melodrama, and audiences loved her. Schooled in the bravura acting styles of the nineteenth-century stock company, she tried to adapt to the new plays and the advances in stagecraft, particularly in scenery and lighting. Her acting became more subtle as she adjusted her technique to the increasingly realistic plays of the postwar stage and the smaller, intimate playhouses that were then being built. Her last roles were in *Mamma's Affair* (1920), *Ostriches* (1925), the revival of *Trelawney of the "Wells"* (1925), and *The Pearl of Great Price* (1926). She spent the last years of her life in New York City. Her house at 103 Riverside Drive, once owned by the famed actor Joseph Jefferson, was filled with theatrical curios and mementos of her career. She died there of complications from heart disease combined with pneumonia.

• For additional information on Bingham see the obituary and clipping file in the New York Public Library for the Performing Arts, Lincoln Center. For a list of her roles, see *Who Was Who in the Theatre*, vol. 1 (1978), and Lewis C. Strang, *Famous Actresses of the Day* (1902).

MARY C. HENDERSON

BINGHAM, Anne Willing (1 Aug. 1764–11 May 1801), leader of Philadelphia society during the Federalist period, was born in Philadelphia, Pennsylvania, the daughter of Thomas Willing, a wealthy importer and partner of Robert Morris (1734–1806), and Anne McCall, who oversaw Anne's education. Anne studied literature, writing, French, music, drawing, and embroidery. Her childhood and youth were filled with social engagements shared with children of elite families, including her relatives the Byrds and the Shippens. Though her father refused to sign the Declaration of Independence and her family remained in occupied Philadelphia during the Revolution, they remained socially aloof from General William Howe and other British officers. Her father's financial aid to America during the revolutionary period helped maintain the Willings's political and social position in Philadelphia. At the age of sixteen Anne glittered atop

Philadelphia society. She had many suitors, among them William Bingham (1752–1804), one of the richest men in America. She married him on 26 October 1780 in Christ Church, Philadelphia. They had three children, all of whom settled in England. Even after her marriage, Anne was chosen to dance with the comte de Dumas because she was one of the most beautiful women of Philadelphia.

In 1783 the Binghams went to Europe for three years, where they established friendships with French and English nobility, especially Lord Lansdowne, as well as with visiting Americans such as Thomas Jefferson. Anne quickly adopted French manners and fashions and dazzled the French and English courts. She became a public figure in England and an engraving of her was sold in London shops. Abigail Adams arranged that Anne be presented at court and recorded that Anne was very much admired. Gilbert Stuart began a painting of the family but it was never completed; the portrait of Anne, capturing her delicate beauty, has survived. The Binghams returned to Philadelphia in March 1786.

Upon their return, the Binghams completed building their large and elegant home, "Mansion House," which was modeled after the London townhouse of the duke of Manchester. It became the most admired house in Philadelphia, though some criticized it as ostentatious. Mansion House became a center for Philadelphia society, and Anne entertained impressively in the European fashion. The Binghams had two other homes, "Lansdowne" on the Schuylkill River and "Bellevue" on the Atlantic coast of New Jersey, where they entertained lavishly but in a more informal way.

Anne's wealth and European experience helped her achieve her goal of leadership of Philadelphia society. She used her status to solidify her own popularity and to position her daughters for successful marriages. Often her social activities reinforced her husband's successful business enterprises and sometimes they were connected to his political ambitions. For example, she entertained business leaders such as Thomas Twining and Alexander Baring and political dignitaries such as Jefferson and Talleyrand. George Washington was a frequent visitor to her home and she convinced him to have his portrait painted by Gilbert Stuart.

Anne was interested in politics, and her correspondence with Jefferson suggests that she hoped to become a political hostess like those she had met at the salons in Paris. She believed that French women had achieved a political influence that should be copied in the United States. Though her political opinions impressed John Quincy Adams and the Reverend William Coffin, her actual political influence was limited to her activities as a hostess. Indeed, her home became an important meeting place for Federalists, especially the followers of Alexander Hamilton (1755–1804). Though she also invited prominent Republican politicians to her balls and dinners, Anne Bingham, as the acknowledged leader of Federalist society and the wife of a Federalist senator, was often the focus of anti-aristocratic and anti-Federalist feeling. Her pretentious attempts to bring European formality to Philadelphia were a prime target for Republican critics.

Anne's social position was enhanced when her sixteen-year-old daughter married Alexander Baring in 1798. Anne achieved a social triumph with this alliance to one of England's wealthiest mercantile families. Her younger daughter Maria, however, plunged the Binghams into scandal when she eloped with the comte de Tilly, a notorious rake. Eventually Maria's marriage was annulled, but the incident put stress on Anne's delicate physical condition. She was further weakened by the birth of a son in 1800, and by March 1801 was seriously ill with tuberculosis. Her husband hoped she would regain her health in a warmer climate, so they set sail for the Caribbean, but Anne died in Bermuda.

Anne Willing Bingham never succeeded in establishing a political salon in the new republic, but she achieved her goal of dominating Philadelphia society. She remained a legend in Philadelphia throughout the nineteenth century, remembered by some for her charm and beauty and by others for her social ambition and aristocratic pretension.

• Few of Anne Bingham's letters survive, though there are references to her among her husband's and father's papers located at the Pennsylvania Historical Society. She is also mentioned in the collections of many prominent Americans of the Federalist era such as Thomas Jefferson, Abigail Adams, and John Jay. Anne's letter to Jefferson concerning the political influence of women is reprinted in Julian P. Boyd, ed., *The Papers of Thomas Jefferson*, vol. 11 (1955), pp. 392–94. Margaret L. Brown wrote a number of articles concerning Anne's life and influence, including "Mr. and Mrs. William Bingham of Philadelphia: Rulers of the Republican Court," *Pennsylvania Magazine of History and Biography* (July 1937): 286–324, and "Anne Willing Bingham," *Bermuda Historical Quarterly* 6 (1949): 123–34. Robert C. Alberts, *The Golden Voyage: The Life and Times of William Bingham 1752–1804* (1969), includes information about Anne Bingham.

ALLIDA SHUMAN MCKINLEY

BINGHAM, Barry (10 Feb. 1906–15 Aug. 1988), newspaper owner and editor, was born George Barry Bingham in Louisville, Kentucky, the son of Robert Worth Bingham, the mayor of Louisville, a newspaper owner, and the ambassador to Britain under Franklin D. Roosevelt, and Eleanor Miller. Bingham's mother died in a car-train accident in 1913; his father then married Mary Lily Kenan Flagler, the widow of Henry Morrison Flagler, a cofounder of Standard Oil and a Florida real estate tycoon. The marriage lasted just eight months, but Mary signed a codicil to her will, leaving $5 million to George Bingham even though he had waived all rights to any inheritance. Her death so closely followed the signing of the codicil that suspicions were aroused of possible foul play. Bingham's father used a portion of his inheritance to purchase two Louisville newspapers, *The Courier-Journal* and the *Louisville Times*, in 1918 from the Haldeman family.

Bingham attended private schools in Louisville and Concord, Massachusetts, going on to Harvard, from which he graduated with a degree in English in 1928.

During his college years he met Mary Clifford Caperton, whom he married in 1931; they had five children. After an unsuccessful attempt at novel writing financed by his father, Bingham began work at his father's newspapers as a police reporter. At the age of twenty-seven he was thrust to the top of his father's companies by the latter's appointment as ambassador to Great Britain. His father's death in 1937 left him owner of the family's companies, which by this time included a Louisville radio station purchased in 1922.

The year before his father's death Bingham had hired Mark Ethridge, a respected liberal southern publisher, to oversee the news operations of the papers, and Bingham took care of editorials. While Ethridge recruited more top talent to the newspapers, Bingham demonstrated an editorial courage that persisted throughout his years as owner. One of the locally unpopular causes Bingham embraced was his advocacy of the United States' entrance into World War II. In response to critics, Bingham decided to demonstrate the strength of his pro-war convictions by enlisting in the U.S. Navy in May of 1941—months before Pearl Harbor. Bingham left his papers under the control of his wife and Ethridge, and he served both in Europe and the Pacific, earning two bronze stars as director of navy information services. He was the head of the contingent of correspondents on the USS *Missouri* in Tokyo Bay in attendance at the Japanese surrender. In 1949 he served a year as chief of the Marshall Plan in France, and for his work the French government awarded him the rank of commander in the Legion of Honor.

In 1950 Bingham acquired a local television station, and his papers continued to gain recognition. Some of the innovations at Bingham's newspapers were influential in the industry; for instance, in 1967 his papers became the first to create the position of news ombudsman to handle readers' questions and complaints. In 1969 his newspapers were the first to correct errors in a conspicuous place on a regular basis. Other improvements included the use of a new and more readable typeface and publication of a Sunday newspaper magazine supplement printed in color. Under Bingham the amount of international coverage was unique for newspapers in a city the size of Louisville. The Bingham papers became famous for maintaining high ethical and reporting standards and for the promotion of local cultural activities and of humanitarian and reform causes such as civil rights, care of the mentally ill, improved public education, and protection of the environment.

The papers developed a reputation for supporting liberal causes in spite of a conservative readership. Bingham's papers took courageous editorial stands against corruption in local government, racial injustice, and the strip mining industry in Kentucky. In 1950 the *Reporter* commended Bingham's papers for helping to make Louisville free of graft and for editorial encouragement of improvements in local elementary and secondary education. Bingham also used his papers to promote the local arts, helping to create an environment in which a first-class symphony orchestra and a nationally admired regional theater were able to develop and thrive in Louisville. The city's Actors Theater was so successful that plays later awarded Pulitzer Prizes were first performed there.

Bingham was always politically active, supporting Franklin Roosevelt before and during World War II and later supporting Adlai Stevenson and other national, state, and local candidates, usually those of the Democratic party. John F. Kennedy and Jimmy Carter both offered Bingham diplomatic posts, but he felt he had a duty to stick with his papers.

Bingham was also a philanthropist; his companies donated 5 percent of pretax income to Louisville area charities. In 1954 Bingham used his television station to begin an annual tradition of charity telethons known as WHAS TV's Crusade for Children, which raises money for handicapped children. By 1986, when Bingham sold all of his companies, funds collected by the telethon totaled nearly $29 million. By 1993 this tradition was still thriving, raising more than $3 million annually. His generosity continued even after the sale of his papers, as he made commitments to donate more than $31 million to charity within two years of the sale.

In spite of great successes in his career, Bingham felt his family was star-crossed. In addition to the untimely deaths of his mother and two of his sons and the widely publicized suspicions connected to the acquisition of the newspapers by Bingham's father in 1918, there was another great controversy related to Bingham's decision to sell off all of his companies in an attempt to end bickering among his heirs. His son Barry, Jr., who had served as president of the newspapers since 1971, had become involved in a family dispute after asking all of the female members of the family to resign from the board of directors in 1984. His sister Sallie responded with charges of sexism and in 1989 published a memoir critical of her family. Even before this, the family tensions had mounted to such an extent that Bingham, over his son's strong objections, announced the sale of his family's businesses. Bingham's father's original investment of $1 million had grown by 1986 to a combined value of $435 million for all the businesses, including the two newspapers, a radio station, a television station, and a printing company. The two papers alone sold for $300 million to the Gannet Company in 1986. The large amount of money involved in the sales helped attract national attention to the family's problems, but Bingham himself managed at times to distance himself from these difficulties, saying of them, "Oh, what a soap opera!" Bingham died at his home in Louisville.

Under Barry Bingham the *Courier-Journal* was at times described as one of the top newspapers in the nation. John Gunther ranked it as one of the best in his book *Inside U.S.A.* (1946), and *Time* rated the paper one of the four best in the country in 1952 and one of the ten best in two subsequent rankings. A 1983 survey of editors, publishers, and journalism professors conducted by the Media Research Institute included the *Courier-Journal* among the best fifteen newspapers in the United States. The paper has won nine Pulitzer Prizes overall, most of them (seven) while owned by the Bingham family. Barry Bingham was primarily responsible for the sustained high regard for his papers, becoming well respected himself for what the *New York Times* called his "long-standing policy of sacrificing profit for editorial excellence."

After his death in 1988, a close adviser, corporate attorney Gordon Davidson, was one of many who expressed admiration for Bingham, saying, "Here was a fellow born to wealth and power, who, instead of sitting on his money, accepted the challenge of it, and lived to the highest code of ethics and morality." Katherine Graham, chairperson of the *Washington Post* Co., said of Bingham that he "ran a paper that was a model for the industry," and National Broadcasting Company (NBC) television's John Chancellor called Bingham "one of the class acts of American Journalism who cared deeply about responsibility to readers" and praised him for demonstrating that a newspaper need not be in the largest of cities to be good.

• Bingham's papers are at Schlesinger Library, Radcliffe University, and at Houghton Library, Harvard University. Three book-length works about Bingham and his family are David Leon Chandler, *The Binghams of Louisville: The Dark History behind One of America's Great Fortunes* (1987), Susan E. Tifft and Alex S. Jones, *The Patriarch: The Rise and Fall of the Bingham Dynasty* (1991); and the highly regarded Marie Brenner, *House of Dreams: The Bingham Family of Louisville* (1988). Bingham strongly challenged the possibility that his father was guilty of any misconduct in connection with the death of his second wife, theories about which are especially important ingredients in Chandler's book. Another book that presents Bingham's daughter's perspective on the family crisis that led to the sale of the communications empire is Sallie Bingham, *Passion and Prejudice: A Family Memoir* (1989). The *Courier-Journal Magazine*, 20 Apr. 1986, devotes twenty-three pages to a discussion of the history of Bingham and his family. The *Courier-Journal* also published a 64-page history of the paper in four sections to celebrate its 125th anniversary (19 Sept. 1993), which contains biographical material on Bingham as well as details about the accomplishments of his papers under his stewardship. The *Courier-Journal* printed two articles immediately after Bingham's death that include biographical information, 16 and 18 Aug. 1988. Additional obituaries are in the *New York Times* and the *Los Angeles Times*, both 16 Aug. 1988.

ALAN KELLY

BINGHAM, Caleb (15 Apr. 1757–6 Apr. 1817), textbook author and educator, was born in Salisbury, Connecticut, the son of Daniel Bingham and Hannah Conant, farmers. Though he was raised on the family farm, it is thought that Caleb was a rather frail youth who devoted most of his time to his studies. Caleb attended Dartmouth College, delivering the valedictory address in Latin in 1782. He served as the master of Moor's Indian Charity School at Dartmouth from 1782 to 1784. In 1784 he left New Hampshire, eventually settling in Boston, where he opened a school for girls on State Street. A pioneer in female education, Bingham taught the privileged girls who attended his school reading, writing, spelling, English grammar, and arithmetic, a much broader curriculum than had been offered previously to girls. He married Hannah Kemble in 1786; they had two daughters. Toward the end of 1789 he closed his school to become master of a Boston public reading school.

Bingham is best known as the author of numerous grammar and spelling textbooks. As a teacher he no doubt faced a dearth of suitable schoolbooks for his students (in the late eighteenth century the most commonly used texts were the Bible and psalter for reading and the *New England Primer*). Bingham thus dedicated himself to filling this void. *The Young Lady's Accidence; or, A Short and Easy Introduction to English Grammar, Designed Principally for the Use of Young Learners More Especially Those of the Fair Sex, Though Proper for Either* (1785) was only the second widely used grammar text in the United States (the first being Noah Webster's *Grammatical Institute of the English Language* [1784]). Bingham's 1794 *American Preceptor: Being a New Selection of Lessons for Reading and Speaking*, which emphasized the development of moral virtues as well as literary skills, was by far his most popular book, selling well over 600,000 copies. Other works include *The Child's Companion* (1792), a speller that passed through more than ten editions, and *The Columbian Orator* (1797), a combined reader and oratory text. Bingham's *Astronomical and Geographical Catechism* (1803) was one of the earliest texts to introduce the study of geography into public schools, and his *Juvenile Letters* (1803) was a collection of epistles between children designed to demonstrate various forms of letter writing and composition. Bingham was fond of the art of penmanship, and in 1796 he published what was probably the first set of copy slips, worksheets used for developing writing skills, in America. Bingham tried to make all his textbooks lively and entertaining for children, which he felt would facilitate their learning.

Bingham retired from the Boston school system in 1796 and went into business as a bookseller and printer in the city. He continued his strong commitment to free public education, allowing his small shop to serve as a meeting place for schoolteachers. He was also active in the formation of local libraries. Bingham helped organize in 1793 the Boston Society Library, where he volunteered his services as librarian for two years, and he established the first municipally funded library in the United States in his native Salisbury. In later years he was appointed by Governor Elbridge Gerry to be the director of the Massachusetts State Prison, where he took particular interest in the reform and education of young convicts.

In appearance and manners, Bingham was the quintessential (albeit somewhat antiquated) gentleman. He regularly wore his hair powdered and braided, in the style of George Washington, a cocked hat, black silk hose, and shoes with silver buckles. In religious matters, Bingham resisted the surging tide of Unitarianism and remained an orthodox Congregationalist his whole life. In political affairs, however, Bingham was

a liberal Jeffersonian and several times an unsuccessful candidate for the state senate. Scholarship was Bingham's hobby as well as his profession, and as an avid scholar of French Bingham translated François-Auguste-René de Chateaubriand's *Atala* (1802) into English. In his final years Bingham suffered greatly from an illness characterized as "dropsy of the brain." He died in Boston. His books continued to instruct and entertain schoolchildren well into the nineteenth century.

• Biographical sources on Bingham's life are few. See the memoir written by his former apprentice, William B. Fowle, "Memoir of Caleb Bingham," *American Journal of Education* 5 (1858): 325–49, for the most detailed account of Bingham's life and a good introduction to the state of elementary education in late eighteenth-century Boston. For discussions of Bingham's textbooks and his advocacy of public education and free libraries, see Charles Carpenter, *History of American Schoolbooks* (1963); George Littlefield, *Early Schools and School-Books of New England* (1904); John A. Nietz, *Old Textbooks* (1961); and Justin Winsor, *Memorial History of Boston* (1880).

KATHERINE M. GRANT

BINGHAM, George Caleb (20 Mar. 1811–7 July 1879), artist and politician, was born on a plantation near South River, in Augusta County, Virginia, the son of Henry Vest Bingham and Mary Amend, farmers. In 1819 the family moved to Franklin, Missouri, where Bingham's father opened a tavern and bought a farm near Arrow Rock, Missouri. In 1821 he became a county judge but died in 1823. A year later Bingham's mother established a girls' school in Franklin and two years after that moved with the family to a farm in Arrow Rock. In 1827 Bingham was apprenticed to a carpenter and Methodist minister in Boonville, Missouri, but when he saw a portrait painter at work, he decided to become one himself. He also studied religion, preached, and read law until 1830, after which he became an itinerant portrait painter. In Columbia, Missouri, he painted his four earliest surviving portraits (1834), including one of James Sidney Rollins (now in a private collection). He eventually painted at least five more portraits of Rollins, who became his patron and closest friend. In 1836 Bingham married Sarah Elizabeth Hutchison; they had four children.

In 1837 Bingham visited Philadelphia, Pennsylvania, and in 1838 New York City, where he exhibited his early genre painting *Western Boatmen Ashore* (location unknown) at the Apollo Gallery. In 1840 he began a four-year residence in Washington, D.C., and also submitted six paintings to the National Academy of Design in New York. After studying at the Pennsylvania Academy of the Fine Arts in Philadelphia (1843) and painting his grim *John Quincy Adams* (1844, private collection) in Washington, Bingham returned to Boonville, painted huge banners for the Whig convention there, and soon became so popular that he worked in two studios, one in Jefferson City, Missouri, the other in St. Louis, Missouri. In 1845 he registered with the American Art-Union in St. Louis, to which he sold four paintings, including *Fur Traders Descending the Missouri* (1845, Metropolitan Museum of Art), a luminous, mystical, haunting work, and *The Concealed Enemy* (1845, Stark Museum of Art, Orange, Tex.), depicting an armed Indian peering from behind rocks. He sold *The Jolly Flatboatmen* (1846, Pell Family Trust painting on loan to the National Gallery of Art), one of his most famous works, in St. Louis in 1846. In it a long-limbed central figure dances on the curved deck roof to the accompaniment of a drummer and a fiddler, with five well-posed idlers looking on. He later painted two more groups of such boatmen.

Bingham was elected as a pro-expansion Whig to the state legislature in 1846, but his victory was overturned in court. Two years later he won a seat without legal challenge. In 1849 he prepared a legislative report issued by the Committee on Federal Relations; it was in essence antislavery and antisecession while taking cognizance of the legitimate rights of states. In 1847 Bingham exhibited several new paintings in St. Louis and registered in the American Art-Union as a member artist residing in Arrow Rock. By this time his works were being praised in New York circles. Later that year his wife died of complications in childbirth, and the infant survived for only a month.

From 1849 until 1856 Bingham continued to combine painting, politics, and travel. In 1849 he completed *Country Politician* (Fine Art Museums of San Francisco), the portrayal of a fat, balding canvasser. The arrangement closely resembles that of William Sidney Mount's *The Tough Story—Scene in a Country Tavern* (1837, Corcoran Gallery of Art), which Bingham may have examined in New York. The two works achieve unity by an identical pyramidal form. Bingham later defined himself as Mount's Western equivalent because of his extensive genre work. In 1849 he married Eliza K. Thomas; they had one son.

After more genre efforts, he painted *The Emigration of Daniel Boone* (1851, Washington University, St. Louis), one of his most famous historical works. In it Boone is depicted as a latter-day Moses confidently walking at the head of a band of pioneers, some armed and afoot, others on horseback, one with a dog, and all advancing to the West—the land of great promise. Ever more popular and financially successful, Bingham opened a Columbia studio while continuing portrait work in St. Louis. In 1852 he was a delegate to the Whig convention in Baltimore, Maryland, completed *The County Election* (St. Louis Art Museum), and went to Philadelphia to arrange for it and his *Raftsmen Playing Cards* (1847, St. Louis Art Museum) to be engraved by the distinguished London-born artist John Sartain for sale by subscription. In 1844 he finished *Stump Speaking* (Boatmen's National Bank of St. Louis), in which a candidate blandishes a mostly attentive group while his portly rival awaits his turn under a tree.

Between forays to pursue political and commercial duties, for which he is largely forgotten, Bingham completed *The Verdict of the People* (Boatmen's National Bank of St. Louis) in 1855. The third in a trilogy including *Stump Speaking* and *The County Election*, this brilliant study in light and shadow portrays a dozen rural types animated or at rest, gesturing demonstratively or keeping their counsel. These three "Election Paintings," as they are frequently called, present altogether at least 150 human figures from crisp foreground to obscure distance, many deriving from Bingham's earlier painstaking sketches. In 1856 he began work on *Washington Crossing the Delaware* and copied for later use Gilbert Stuart's portraits of George Washington and Thomas Jefferson in Boston, Massachusetts.

In the fall of 1856 Bingham set sail for Europe with his wife and his daughter. After residing two months or so in Paris late in 1856 and examining masterpieces in the Louvre, Bingham proceeded in November to Düsseldorf to study and paint. He returned alone to Missouri in January 1859 with his portraits of Washington and Jefferson, which he had done for the Missouri legislature. He collected commissions for portraits of Andrew Jackson, Henry Clay, and the German scientist Alexander von Humboldt, and returned to Düsseldorf in May but the family returned home in September because of the death of his wife's father. In 1860 Bingham copied the painter Thomas Sully's head of Jackson in Washington and delivered his *Humboldt* to the St. Louis Mercantile Library Association. (This sensitive portrait was later damaged by fire and trimmed until only the face, neckpiece, and upper coat remain.) In 1861 Bingham's angular *Andrew Jackson* and *Henry Clay* were placed in the Hall of Representatives in Missouri's capitol building. (They were both destroyed by fire in 1911, as were several other paintings by Bingham displayed there.)

When the Civil War began, the orders for portraits came to a halt and in June 1861 Bingham became a captain in the U.S. Volunteer Reserve Corps. But he immediately felt unsuited for military service and tried unavailingly for a consulship. When he was appointed Missouri's state treasurer in January 1862, he gladly resigned his captaincy. He toiled at this post in Jefferson City until war's end. He did, however, receive a commission in 1862 to portray General Nathaniel Lyon, a Missouri hero killed in action the year before. Not completed until 1867, the flat, cartoonlike equestrian picture was to be another of the paintings lost in the 1911 fire.

Pro-Union though he was, Bingham was outraged by Union Brigadier General Thomas Ewing's infamous Order No. 11, dated 25 August 1863, evicting Missourians living just beyond the protection of Union military posts near the Kansas border. The Federals' scorched-earth operation left the Confederate raiders nothing of value. The confusion, uprooting, pillage, and bloodshed resulting from this harrowing exodus inspired Bingham to create his most dramatic work, *Order No. 11* (1865–1868, Cincinnati Art Museum). It shows, amid much else, a Union officer holding an irate crowd at bay after his brutal colleague has just shot a disobedient citizen, whose wife mourns hysterically while another woman collapses into the arms of a faithful black servant.

Bingham remained busy, though often troubled and less effective as an artist, during his final decade. In 1869 he was elected a school director in Independence, Missouri. That same year the surviving son from his first marriage died. A year later he moved to Kansas City, Missouri. In 1871 he visited Philadelphia to supervise the engraving of *Order No. 11*. In 1872 he and his wife vacationed for reasons of health in Colorado; this resulted in his mellow *View of Pike's Peak* (1872, Amon Carter Museum of Western Art, Fort Worth, Tex.). In 1873, though ill, he completed a big portrait of Rollins and traveled to Texas on family business and also to Louisville, Kentucky, to exhibit *Order No. 11* and his finally finished, lumpish, and congested *Washington Crossing the Delaware* (1856–1871, Chrysler Museum, Norfolk, Va.). In 1874 he was appointed president of the Kansas City Board of Police Commissioners for a brief term, agreed to run as a Democrat for Congress, but then changed his mind. In 1875 he was named adjutant general of Missouri, a position that sent him for a month the following year to Washington. While there, he met and painted two portraits of the sculptor Vinnie Ream. In October 1876 he requested indefinite leave as adjutant general because of poor health and to care for his deranged wife, who died a month later in a mental institution.

In 1877 Bingham was appointed the first professor of art at the University of Missouri, in Columbia, partly through the influence of his friend Rollins, who as a state legislator had helped found the university. In 1878 Bingham married Martha A. Livingston Lykins, the widow of a prominent Kansas City physician; they had no children. He journeyed to Richmond as a member of the board of commissioners to choose a design for a monument planned by the state of Virginia to honor Robert E. Lee. In February 1879 Bingham contracted pneumonia. he prepared an address on the ideals and utility of art, which Rollins read to the university faculty in March because of Bingham's worsening health. He visited Rollins again in May. Bingham died in Kansas City.

Bingham thought that art should imitate nature, express beauty and vigorous action, and especially record historical events and portray national leaders, so as to ensure what he called a "national immortality." He produced at least 494 paintings and 126 drawings. Long neglected by art historians as merely regional, Bingham is now seen as one of America's finest painters, at his robust best when preserving for posterity, in hearty strokes of old-fashioned realism, scenes of river commerce and rural election procedures—all this before the advent of railroad transportation, big-city politics, and more modern painterly techniques.

• Bingham's numerous letters to Rollins are at the State Historical Society, Columbia, Mo. Fern Helen Rusk, *George Caleb Bingham, the Missouri Artist* (1917), is commendable as a pioneering monograph but has been superseded by more thorough scholarship. The following detail Bingham's life and evaluate his best work: John Francis McDermott, *George Caleb Bingham: River Portraitist* (1959); E. Maurice Bloch, *George Caleb Bingham: The Evolution of an Artist* and *A Catalogue Raisonné* (2 vols., 1967). See also *The Paintings of George Caleb Bingham* (1986), Bloch's one-volume revision and expansion of his 1967 books. Two other worthwhile studies are Albert Christ-Janer, *George Caleb Bingham: Frontier Painter of Missouri* (1975), and Michael Edward Shapiro, *George Caleb Bingham* (1993). John Demos, "George Caleb Bingham: The Artist as Social Historian," *American Quarterly* 17 (Summer 1965): 218–28, discusses the sociology of Bingham's West. Nancy Rash, *The Paintings and Politics of George Caleb Bingham* (1991), relates Bingham's paintings and his Whig politics. James Thomas Flexner, *That Wilder Image: The Painting of America's Native School from Thomas Cole to Winslow Homer* (1962), pp. 142–55, is factually inaccurate but keenly analytical. Edward Lucie-Smith, *American Realism* (1994), places Bingham in the tradition of stylistically classical, emotionally sentimental pre–Civil War realists. Robert Hughes, *American Visions: The Epic History of Art in America* (1997), places Bingham briefly in the sweeping context of American painting and other art forms. Obituaries are in the *St. Louis Globe-Democrat*, 8 July 1879, and the *Jefferson City Weekly Democrat-Tribune*, 9 July 1879.

ROBERT L. GALE

BINGHAM, Hiram (30 Oct. 1789–11 Nov. 1869), Protestant missionary, was born in Bennington, Vermont, the son of Calvin Bingham and Lydia Denton, farmers. His family wanted him to take over the family farm, but instead he studied for the ministry, viewing it as a means to independence. He graduated from Middlebury College in 1816 and Andover Theological Seminary in 1819. That same spring he was accepted as a missionary with the American Board of Commissioners for Foreign Missions (ABCFM) on the condition that he be married. Bingham met his bride-to-be, Sybil Moseley, on 29 September 1819, the day he was ordained at Goshen, Connecticut. Moseley had been teaching in New York but was eager to join her husband as a missionary, and the couple were married on 11 October 1819. Twelve days later they set sail from Boston for Hawaii on the brig *Thaddeus*; arriving in Kailua-Kona on 4 April 1820, they were welcomed by Kamehameha II (Liholiho). The first company of missionaries to the islands was composed of two ordained ministers (Hiram Bingham and Asa Thurston) and twelve lay specialists with medical, farming, printing, and teaching abilities. The direction from the ABCFM to the missionaries was: "You are to aim at nothing short of covering those islands with fruitful fields and pleasant dwellings, and schools and churches; of raising up the whole people to an elevated state of Christian civilization; of bringing them to the mansions of eternal blessedness" (Feher, p. 172).

It was decided that the Binghams would go on to Honolulu on Oahu and that Asa Thurston would stay behind in Kailua-Kona to establish a mission. In Honolulu, the missionaries settled into temporary shelters, three thatched houses offered by some traders; the Binghams, who were to have seven children, occupied one house, its single room doubling as a schoolhouse. Led by Bingham, the missionaries worked together and shared common stores, receiving supplies from the ABCFM and living according to the common stock system. Later they moved into a frame house brought from New England and reconstructed in 1821. Kawaiahao Church, which came to be known as the Westminster Abbey of Hawaii, was built by native Hawaiians with money from the king and the chiefs on land given by the king to the Congregational mission.

Fighting for the "public good," Bingham introduced moral reforms, including a temperance in alcohol and tobacco campaign and programs encouraging chastity, single marriages, and an end to gambling. He translated portions of the Bible into Hawaiian, composed Hawaiian hymns, and led the congregation in singing. He also became a trusted adviser to the Hawaiian monarchy. After December 1821, when Kaahumanu, *kuhina-nui* (co-ruler), became a Christian, he developed a close friendship with the Binghams, giving them lands at Punahou for a cool retreat; this land was later used to create the Punahou School for the missionaries' children. The missionaries learned to speak Hawaiian and by committee designed a twelve-letter alphabet comprising the five vowels and seven consonants: *h, k, l, m, n, p,* and *w*. The first English-Hawaiian speller was printed at the Mission Frame House on 7 January 1822. Educational materials in Hawaiian now became available, and a second print shop was established in 1834 at Lahainaluna, a mission training school, on Maui.

The chiefs (*alii*) were first attracted to the new learning and were the first to be taught to read and write by Bingham's force. Then, at a special meeting held in Honolulu in April 1824, the chiefs, at the direction of Kaahumanu, decided that education would be offered to the commoners as well. Kaahumanu, Queen Mother Keopuolani, and Chiefess Kapiolani all supported the missionaries by donating land and by assisting in the establishment of schools and district churches. Bingham's education classes became so popular that "traders complained that they could get no one to cut sandalwood, or to raise the vegetables needed to supply ships" (Curtis, p. 76), especially right after a new book had come out. Bingham conducted a quarterly examination of his students, which was eagerly attended. "Some came from a long distance and lived in temporary shelters. A conch-shell trumpet sounded its clear call, and people crowded to the examination place. . . . Mr. Bingham announced a sentence to be written. A crier repeated this for all to hear. . . . Perhaps four hundred slate pencils (sea urchin spines) scratched together as the sentence was written (on bits of slate)" (Curtis, p. 77). Education was praised by the islanders and viewed by Bingham as the means for them to remain independent and defend themselves from foreign encroachment as well as read the Bible.

His wife's declining health due to tuberculosis forced Bingham to return to New England, and he was released from missionary service of the ABCFM in 1846. Sybil Bingham died in 1848; in 1852 he married Naomi Emma Morse. Bingham continued to preach in New England, but his son Hiram Bingham II contin-

ued on as a missionary in the Pacific, focusing on the Gilbert Islands in Micronesia. Before his death in New Haven, Hiram Bingham, Sr., published *A Residence of Twenty-one Years in the Sandwich Islands* (1847), a well-written analysis of his missionary life in Hawaii. In this work, he stated, "I have aimed to introduce to my readers the Hawaiian people and their country, with its mountain, valley, and volcanic scenery; their rulers, teachers, friends, and opposers; their habitations, schools, churches, revivals, etc., as they appeared to myself, and to show the footprints of the nation's progress in their uphill efforts to rise amid conflicting influences" (p. vi). In addition to the experiences of the missionaries themselves, Bingham vividly recounts pivotal events that had major historical consequences for the islands, for example, battles among the chiefs. His narratives lend fascinating details of early Hawaiian history.

Hiram Bingham proved to be an outstanding early Christian educator in Hawaii supported by native Hawaiian royalty, who offered him lands and friendship in return for his endeavors to promote education and Christianity, both of which they believed were valuable.

• The papers of Hiram Bingham are in the archives of the American Board of Commissioners for Foreign Missions (ABCFM) in Boston. Char Miller, *Fathers and Sons: The Bingham Family and the American Mission* (1982), is the definitive secondary source on the Bingham family. Caroline Curtis, *Builders of Hawaii* (1966), is another valuable secondary source. *The Missionary Album: Sesquicentennial Edition 1820–1970*, comp. Bernice Judd, contains a brief Bingham portrait. Barbara Bennett Peterson, ed., *Notable Women of Hawaii* (1984), contains biographical information on both Hiram and Sybil Bingham. Gavan Daws, *Shoal of Time: A History of the Hawaiian Islands* (1968), offers an excellent overview of the entire missionary period. Joseph Feher, *Hawaii: A Pictorial History* (1969), offers a brief discussion of the missionaries' development of the Hawaiian alphabet.

BARBARA BENNETT PETERSON

BINGHAM, Hiram (19 Nov. 1875–6 June 1956), explorer, was born Hiram Bingham III in Honolulu, Hawaii, the son of Hiram Bingham (1831–1908) and Clarissa Minerva Brewster, missionaries. Bingham's family assumed he would constitute the third generation of missionary service to the natives of the south Pacific and constantly pressured him to live the godly life. His few efforts as a missionary literally made him sick, and he seems to have had little interest in the salvation of the natives. Bingham (he appears to have dropped the III about the time his father died) instead sublimated the family's missionary zeal into a broad variety of interests.

In 1892 he was enrolled in Phillips Academy, Andover, Massachusetts. Once a stronghold of Congregationalism, Phillips had recently separated itself from its theological school and in many other ways was secularizing the curriculum as well as the student body. Hiram now dared to take such bold steps as to manage the football team, study Latin on Sunday, and participate in the burgeoning Student Volunteer Movement, an evangelical organization made up largely of eastern college boys who worked among the urban poor; it was much liberal-minded for his family.

Bingham moved even farther from the missionary field when, in the fall of 1894, he enrolled at Yale University. There Hiram experimented with many new interests, none to his parents' liking. He joined a fraternity and a debating society; he enjoyed sports. He wrote home criticizing the visiting evangelical preachers and lauding the exhilarating ideas of his teachers. He determined to become a college professor.

He also fell in love with Alfreda Mitchell, daughter of Alfred and Annie Mitchell, whom he had met in both Connecticut and Hawaii. The Mitchells, heirs to the Tiffany fortune, felt that a potential missionary might prove unable to support their daughter and withheld their approval of a marriage until Hiram had acquired an advanced college degree.

In 1899 Bingham commenced graduate work in history at the University of California at Berkeley. In 1900 he began his Ph.D. program in Latin American history at Harvard. That same fall he and Alfreda were married at the Mitchell estate in New London. He acquired his doctorate in 1905, occasionally teaching at Harvard and Princeton while completing his studies. In 1909 he received an appointment to Yale as assistant professor, rising through the usual ranks until 1922 when he entered politics.

The Tiffany wealth allowed him to acquire firsthand knowledge of his teaching subject matter. In 1906 he traveled to Venezuela and Colombia, attempting to retrace the routes of Simón Bolívar's military campaigns.

For the next few years exploring dominated his life far more than teaching. In 1908 and 1909 he traced old Spanish trade routes throughout southern South America, pausing long enough to serve as U.S. delegate to the first Pan American Scientific Congress at Santiago, Chile. In 1911 he made a major discovery high in the Peruvian Andes, the mysterious fortress, temple, and residence of ancient Incas—Machu Picchu. Unknown to all but a few Indians for hundreds of years, Machu Picchu made Bingham famous, and in spite of many other achievements, he continued to think of himself as an explorer for the rest of his life. He made many more trips to South America, finding new trails, climbing unknown mountains, and directing Yale's frequent Peruvian expeditions.

Prior to America's entrance into World War I, Bingham privately obtained his pilot's license and in 1917 obtained a commission in what was then called the U.S. Army Air Service. He organized schools of military aeronautics for the United States, then went to France as chief of air personnel, later commanding the Allies' largest flying school.

In 1922 he was easily elected lieutenant governor of Connecticut. After one term he won the gubernatorial campaign but served only two days; an incumbent U.S. senator committed suicide, forcing a special election that Bingham won. He was reelected in 1926 for a

full term but lost in 1932. In the Senate he specialized in measures concerning the Caribbean, the Pacific Islands, and air power. His behavior was often unusual. He once arrived at a press conference in a blimp and left another in an autogiro. In 1929 he became one of the few senators ever censured by the Senate, bringing to that body "dishonor and disrepute" for permitting a manufacturer's lobbyist to sit in on price-setting legislation. After the Democratic landslide of 1932 Bingham spent much of his remaining life pursuing business interests, including publishing.

In 1951 he was called from retirement by President Harry S. Truman to chair the new Loyalty Review Board, the final appeal of civil service loyalty cases. In the early years of the domestic Communist scare Bingham received much criticism from liberal circles for his decisions making it easier for the government to dismiss employees, among whom were several famous "old China Hands," accused of losing China to the Communists.

Bingham's role in his several careers was usually marked by controversy, often bitter. Even his explorations, which he considered his chief contribution, invoked complaints from Latin American nations; the government of Peru once accused him of smuggling Incan artifacts out of the country. In the Senate, where he considered himself an authority on the Far East, he opposed the independence of the Philippines on grounds of political immaturity, and he frequently upbraided other senators for their ignorance of Latin America. He favored sending the marines to Nicaragua, again because of what he viewed as the natives' backwardness. In his book *The Monroe Doctrine: An Absolute Shibboleth* (1913) Bingham called the Monroe Doctrine obsolete, provoking a national discussion among scholars and politicians. He later changed his mind, saying that the doctrine must still be applied to the small Caribbean states but not to the large nations of the southern cone of South America, which he thought had matured beyond the need for U.S. intervention.

Bingham was the author of a dozen or more books and many articles, mostly on his Latin American explorations, and he received many medals and honors from several Latin American governments. He frequently represented the United States in international congresses, especially those of a scientific nature.

His prolonged absences from home provoked serious family problems. He told Alfreda that their married life was better because of his absences and that he hoped she understood his need for other female companionship; he boldly acquired a mistress. In 1937 Alfreda divorced him, their seven children generally supporting their mother in the hearings. He died in Washington, D.C.

Bingham is highly praised in academic circles as a pioneer in Latin American history and geography. His major reputation lies in the exceptional and often solitary geographical discoveries he reported in *Across South America* (1911), *The Discovery of Machu Picchu* (1913), and *Inca Land* (1922). He had many "firsts," but in particular he should be recognized as the person who first popularized Latin America for the North American public.

• Archival material is in the Bingham family papers, the Mitchell-Tiffany papers, and the Yale Peruvian Expedition papers located at the Yale University Library. There is no biography of Hiram Bingham III, but a fine treatment of him and several generations of his family is in Char Miller, *Fathers and Sons: The Bingham Family and the American Mission* (1982). For a brief biographical sketch, see Jerry E. Patterson, "Hiram Bingham, 1875–1956." *Hispanic American Historical Review* 37 (1957): 131–37. Specific aspects of his career are delineated in Thomas L. Karnes, "Hiram Bingham and His Obsolete Shibboleth," *Diplomatic History* 3, no. 1 (1979): 39–57; Victor Von Hagen, "Hiram Bingham and His Lost Cities," *Archaeology* 2, no. 1 (1949): 42–46; and Carmelo Astilla, "The Latin American Career of Hiram Bingham" (M.A. thesis, Louisiana State Univ., 1967).

THOMAS L. KARNES

BINGHAM, John Armor (21 Jan. 1815–15 Mar. 1900), lawyer and politician, was born in Mercer, Pennsylvania, the son of Hugh Bingham, a carpenter, and Ester Bailey. His father was active in local politics, holding several offices including clerk of courts. After his mother's death in 1827, John went to Cadiz, Ohio, to live with his uncle Thomas Bingham. He returned to Mercer in 1831 and served two years as an apprentice to an anti-Masonic newspaper. He was a full-time student at Mercer Academy from 1834 to 1835 and enrolled in the antislavery Franklin College in New Athens, Ohio, in 1835. Though some sources suggest that an unspecified illness prevented Bingham from completing his course of study, he appears to have only missed the graduation ceremony. He moved back to Mercer in 1837 and studied law under two prominent local attorneys, John J. Pearson and William Stewart. Bingham was admitted to the practice of law in Pennsylvania and Ohio in 1840. He returned to Cadiz that same year campaigning on behalf of William Henry Harrison. During the campaign Bingham debated Edwin M. Stanton, who supported Martin Van Buren.

In 1843 Bingham moved to New Philadelphia, Ohio. He married his cousin, Amanda Bingham, in 1844. They had eight children. In 1846 he was elected prosecutor of Tuscarawas County and was a delegate to the Whig National Convention, where he unsuccessfully attempted to obtain the adoption of an antislavery resolution: "No more slave states; no more slave territories—the maintenance of freedom where freedom is and the protection of American industry." Although Bingham's role in the presentation of this resolution has been questioned, contemporary newspapers verify that he did present the resolution.

He campaigned for Zachary Taylor in 1848 and was himself narrowly reelected county prosecutor on the Whig ticket. In 1850 he moved to Cincinnati and entered into the practice of law with former Whig gubernatorial candidate William Johnston. In 1851 he moved back to Cadiz and ran unsuccessfully as a Whig candidate for judge of the Court of Common Pleas of Harrison County.

In 1854 he was active in the organization of the "Anti-Nebraska" movement and was its successful candidate to Congress. Serving as a Republican from 1854 to 1862, he opposed the admission of Oregon as a "free" state because of its discrimination against free African Americans and opposed the admission of Kansas as a slave state. He supported Salmon Chase for the Republican presidential nomination in 1860 and campaigned for Abraham Lincoln in the general election. At the time of secession Bingham opposed all compromise with the seceding states and reintroduced the Force Bill of 1832 that President Andrew Jackson had threatened to use against South Carolina during the nullification crisis.

During the Civil War Bingham was a strong supporter of President Lincoln's but urged the abolition of slavery before Lincoln was ready to embrace that action. In June 1862 he was the chairman of the managers for the House of Representatives in the Senate's trial of Tennessee's federal district judge West Humphreys, who had become a Confederate judge without resigning his U.S. commission.

Bingham was narrowly defeated for Congress in the election of 1862; he did not return to Congress until 1865. During that period he served as solicitor in the U.S. Court of Claims and then as a major in the Judge Advocate General's Office. In the latter capacity he successfully prosecuted the court-martial of the surgeon general of the United States, William A. Hammond, for corruption in office. When President Lincoln was assassinated, Secretary of War Edwin Stanton called Bingham to Washington to assist in the investigation and prosecution of those accused of conspiring to commit the assassination. He gave the closing argument for the prosecution. Though Bingham argued strenuously for conviction and argued that Jefferson Davis was ultimately responsible for the crime, he closed his argument by asking the court "out of tender regard and jealous care for the rights of the accused, to see that no error of mine, if any there be, shall work them harm."

Bingham again served in Congress from 1865 to 1872 and supported most of the postwar Reconstruction legislation including the Freedmen's Bureau, the Fourteenth and Fifteenth amendments, and the various enforcement acts. Though Bingham opposed the Civil Rights Act of 1866, he did so on the grounds that the act was beyond the constitutional power of Congress. He proposed to provide many of the same protections sought in the act by amending the Constitution.

Bingham was the author of section one of the Fourteenth Amendment protecting the privileges and immunities of citizens and guaranteeing due process of law and equal protection. Bingham's speeches make it clear that he thought the "chief" privileges and immunities of national citizens were those identified by the first eight amendments to the Constitution. That view has never been adopted by a majority of the Supreme Court, and scholars disagree whether his view was shared by other members of Congress, though most of the provisions of the Bill of Rights have been applied to the states through Bingham's due process clause. The due process clause and the equal protection clause are the foundations of much modern constitutional litigation and considered by many to be more important than any other provision of the Constitution.

In spite of his solid record in opposition to slavery and in support of civil rights, Bingham was not considered a Radical Republican. He thought ratification of the Fourteenth Amendment was the proper basis for readmitting the state representatives to Congress and led the fight against those radicals who wanted additional requirements. He opposed the impeachment of Andrew Johnson until Johnson violated the Tenure of Office Act. Bingham then joined the forces seeking impeachment. He became the chairman of the managers of the House of Representatives prosecuting the case in the Senate and gave the closing argument to the Senate. Though his argument spanned three days, he focused almost exclusively on Johnson's alleged violation of the statute and the issue of "whether the President is above the laws and can dispense with their execution with impunity in the exercises of what is adroitly called his judicial power of interpretation."

Bingham was involved, but cleared of any wrongdoing, in the Crédit Mobilier scandal of 1872, which had been prompted by revelations that congressmen held stock in a federally subsidized railroad company. He also voted for the "salary grab" of 1873 that increased many government salaries retroactively, including those of congressmen. He failed to win the Republican nomination to Congress in 1872 because of constituents' belief that the seat should be rotated among people from other counties in his district. In 1873 President Ulysses S. Grant nominated him to become U.S. minister to Japan. Bingham served in that capacity until 1885 when recalled by President Grover Cleveland. During that time he was a strong advocate of the rights of the Japanese to self-determination. Although this brought him in frequent conflict with the British and other Europeans, it won him the friendship of the Japanese.

After he returned to the United States, Bingham continued to be active in politics, attending Republican conventions and campaigning for Presidents Benjamin Harrison and William McKinley. He was not, however, a candidate for office. His wife died in 1891. In his last years he was in ill health and was unable to provide for himself financially. Congress passed a private bill in 1898 granting Bingham a pension of $25 per month. He died in Cadiz.

• The largest collection of Bingham papers is held privately in Cadiz, Ohio, but a microfilm copy is at the Ohio Historical Society, Columbus, Ohio. Another significant collection of his papers is in the Pierpont Morgan Library, New York City. A biography is Erving Beauregard, *Bingham of the Hills* (1989). Biographical articles include Walter Shotwell, "Bingham," *Driftwood: Being Papers on Old-Time American Towns and Some Old People* (1927), pp. 175–233; Donald Swift, "John Bingham and Reconstruction: The Dilemma of a Moderate," *Ohio History* 77 (1968): 76–94; and Richard Aynes, "The Antislavery and Abolitionist Background of John A. Bingham," *Catholic University Law Review* 37 (1988): 881–933. An analysis of Bingham's intent in drafting the Fourteenth Amendment is in Aynes, "On Misreading John Bingham and the Fourteenth Amendment," *Yale Law Journal* 103 (1993): 57–104. Obituaries are in the *Washington Evening Star*, 19 Mar. 1900; *Cleveland Leader*, 20 Mar. 1900; *Harrison News*, 21 Mar. 1900; and *Cadiz Sentinel* and *Cadiz Republican*, 22 Mar. 1900.

RICHARD L. AYNES

BINGHAM, Robert Worth (8 Nov. 1871–18 Dec. 1937), lawyer, newspaper publisher, and diplomat, was born in Mebane, North Carolina, the son of Robert Bingham, an educator, and Delphine Louise Worth. Bingham graduated from the Bingham School, a private school run by his father, and from 1888 to 1890 attended the University of North Carolina (no degree). He married Eleanor Everhart Miller in 1896; they had three children. He received a law degree from the University of Louisville a year later and, settling in Louisville, went into law practice with fellow North Carolinian W. W. Davies.

Bingham soon became part of the growing "good government" movement in the "River City." After the Kentucky Court of Appeals overturned the 1905 Louisville election results based on the fraudulent activities of the local Democratic party machine, Governor J. C. W. Beckham appointed Bingham interim mayor in late June 1907. Although he served only three months, Bingham removed the police and fire departments from city politics and ended other patronage abuses. A Democrat, he could not win the nomination of his party for the next mayoral race nor bring about long-lasting reform in such a short time.

Bingham's first wife died in an automobile accident in April 1913. In 1916 he married Mary Lily Kenan Flagler, the widow of multimillionaire Henry Flagler. They had no children, and less than a year later she died from heart problems. First rumors and then politically motivated public charges implicated Bingham in her death. The results of an autopsy ordered by her family were never made public, leading to the conclusion that she probably died as a result of acute alcoholism and not the action or inaction of her husband.

In 1918 Bingham purchased the *Courier-Journal* and the *Louisville Times* with money from the $5 million bequest from his second wife's estate. After sparring with Henry Watterson, the venerable editor of the *Courier-Journal*, for a few months, Bingham took over complete control of the papers. Over the next two decades he molded the papers into voices for liberalism in the upper South while modernizing the printing and distribution operations. By the late 1930s the circulation of each paper exceeded 200,000. In the early twenties the Bingham enterprises added WHAS radio to its holdings. In 1924 Bingham married Aleen Muldoon Hilliard; they had no children.

Bingham's wealth and media holdings catapulted him into state leadership. He allied himself with other progressive forces in the Kentucky Democratic party, particularly former governor Beckham and General

Percy Haly, a Louisville party figure. In the 1920s Bingham supported candidates who opposed the "bipartisan combine," a group determined to defeat any office seeker who supported legislation restricting racetrack gambling or a tax on coal production.

Bingham took an interest in the plight of tobacco farmers. When tobacco prices dropped after World War I, the future of farmers in Kentucky, North Carolina, Virginia, and surrounding states looked bleak. With the help of Aaron Sapiro, Bingham organized marketing cooperatives for the burley, dark-fired, and flue-cured varieties. He put up his own money as security for developing storage facilities, paid the salaries of tobacco cooperative employees, and aided in development of cooperative organizations for other commodities, ranging from wheat to potatoes. Like most such ventures, the tobacco cooperatives began to unravel in the mid-twenties.

When the Great Depression struck in its full fury, Bingham became one of the first prominent Democrats to support Franklin D. Roosevelt for president. Making substantial financial and editorial contributions to the 1932 campaign, Bingham was guaranteed an important appointment in the new administration. Roosevelt named him ambassador to the Court of St. James's in London in early 1933 but not before ugly rumors of the Louisvillian's complicity in Mary Lily Bingham's death surfaced again. Bingham could not immediately take up his post because of illness, but after his arrival in London, he devoted much time and energy to his diplomatic role while at the same time keeping firm control of his media holdings. In the mid-thirties his youngest son, Barry Bingham, Sr., began to assume more leadership over the newspapers. The addition of the experienced newspaperman Mark Ethridge as general manager added immeasurably to the success of "the Bingham newspapers" in coming years.

Often criticized as an Anglophile, Bingham blended an overall respect for things English with a healthy skepticism about British domestic and foreign policies in the thirties. He explained the United States, defending the New Deal to the English people and the British government. More important, he communicated to the State Department and Roosevelt significant attitude changes in Britain. Throughout his time in Britain he argued for closer Anglo-American relations but not if it meant a loss of independence for U.S. foreign policy. Bingham worked to reconcile Anglo-American differences over currency and trade issues. Before he died the British government had moved toward reconciliation. He developed a keen dislike for the totalitarian regimes in Berlin, Rome, and Tokyo and warned that their insatiable aggressiveness could be successfully opposed only by the concerted efforts of the United States, Great Britain, and other democracies. By 1937 he clashed with State Department officials by voicing strong opposition to Adolf Hitler in speeches in England while calling for stronger ties with that country. Apparently Roosevelt approved of Bingham's pronouncements and never considered asking

for his resignation. In late 1937, his health worsening, Bingham returned to the United States and died in Baltimore.

Throughout his life Bingham never overcame his devotion to southern tradition. He praised Margaret Mitchell's *Gone with the Wind* (1936) as the finest explication of the South of his father's generation. Yet, while retaining his prejudices, he opposed the Ku Klux Klan in the twenties and urged greater educational opportunities for African Americans. He used his fortune to support causes ranging from the League of Nations to the New Deal. His enlightened leadership laid the foundation for greater changes that would come with his son's generation.

• Bingham's papers are at the Library of Congress and the Filson Club in Louisville. Extensive files are also available in the Department of State collections at the National Archives and the Roosevelt Library at Hyde Park. Bingham did not publish widely, but his thoughts are carried in numerous unsigned *Courier* editorials and in farm cooperative pamphlets and journals. Published studies of Bingham and his children include David Leon Chandler and Mary Voelz Chandler, *The Binghams of Louisville: The Dark Story behind One of America's Great Fortunes* (1987); Marie Brenner, *House of Dreams: The Bingham Family of Louisville* (1988); Sallie Bingham, *Passion and Prejudice: A Family Memoir* (1989); Susan E. Tifft and Alex S. Jones, *The Patriarch: The Rise and Fall of the Bingham Dynasty* (1991); William E. Ellis, "Robert Worth Bingham and Louisville Progressivism, 1905–1910," *Filson Club History Quarterly* 54 (Apr. 1980): 169–95; Ellis, "Robert Worth Bingham and the Crisis of Cooperative Marketing in the Twenties," *Agricultural History* 56 (Jan. 1982): 99–116; and Ellis, "The Bingham Family: From the Old South to the New South and Beyond," *Filson Club History Quarterly* 61 (Jan. 1987): 5–33. Obituaries are in the *New York Times* and the London *Times*, both 19 Dec. 1937.

WILLIAM E. ELLIS

BINGHAM, Sybil Moseley (14 Sept. 1792–27 Feb. 1848), missionary and teacher, was born in Westfield, Massachusetts, the eldest child of Pliny Moseley and Sophia Pomeroy. Both parents had died by the time Sybil was nineteen, and she supported her three younger sisters by accepting teaching positions in Hartford, Connecticut; Canandaigua, New York; and Ontario Female Seminary. Invited by friends, she attended the ordination ceremony of Hiram Bingham (1789–1869) and Asa Thurston as missionaries, at Goshen, Connecticut, in 1819. A month later she married Hiram Bingham and joined the first company of Congregationalist missionaries that left in October 1819 for the Sandwich Islands (Hawaii).

The missionaries, under Hiram Bingham's direction, arrived in Hawaii in April 1820. They were greatly encouraged to learn that the ancient kapu (taboo) system and the native religion of Hawaii had just been abolished in 1819 and that the traditional pagan images and heiaus (places of worship) had been destroyed. Soon after the death of Kamehameha the Great in 1819, Kaahumanu, the kuhina-nui (coruler), and Keopuolani, Kamehameha's highest-ranking widow, had persuaded the new young king, Kamehameha II, known as Liholiho, to eat publicly with the women, thereby breaking one of the most stringent of the ancient taboos. This act had been followed by open revolt against the former religion, resulting in its destruction. The missionaries regarded these events as a miracle and centered their activities in Honolulu, on the island of Oahu. Kaahumanu and King Kamehameha II gave the missionaries permission to stay for one year and eventually allowed them permanent residence. Five families, including the Binghams, were given temporary shelter by traders and were moved into three thatched houses. The Bingham home was the center of activity, doubling as a meeting house and first schoolhouse. The missionaries lived on the common stock system, sharing possessions and the supplies sent to them by the American Board of Commissioners for Foreign Missions (ABCFM) located in Boston.

In her thatched home, and the frame house that replaced it after 1821, Bingham gave birth to seven children and established the first school for native Hawaiian chiefs and members of the alii (the chiefly class), who were mostly adults. Bingham's diary and letters of Bingham reflect the joy she felt in teaching as well as her fluency in the Hawaiian language. She worked with the other missionaries to develop a Hawaiian alphabet so that the Hawaiians might learn in their own language as well as in English. The missionaries prepared an eight-page English-Hawaiian speller for use in Bingham's school. After the book and the missionary teaching activities were praised by the alii and Kaahumanu at a public meeting in 1824, native Hawaiians flocked to the school and church in search of the palapala (reading and writing) and the pule (religious instruction). Two thousand pupils were enrolled under Bingham's direction in 1824 on Oahu, and fifty-two thousand throughout the islands by 1831.

Bingham's responsibilities, in addition to teaching school, included visiting mission women located on the outer islands to assist in childbirth and to aid generally those in need of medical attention. One of her outstanding contributions was the founding of the Poalima, or weekly prayer meeting, for adult Hawaiian women who were members of Kawaiahao Church, the first Christian church on the islands established by the Binghams and located adjacent to the mission house. More than fifteen hundred Hawaiian women attended these weekly sessions. Kaahumanu and Sybil Bingham became fast friends, as evidenced by Kaahumanu's gift of the 224-acre Punahou tract in 1829 as a cool retreat in Manoa valley. Here Bingham built another more secluded home and laid out a twenty-acre sugarcane and banana plantation for support of the mission. She surrounded this acreage with a stone wall and planted night-blooming cereus for adornment. The Punahou grant was later deeded to the mission board by the Binghams, and in 1841 Punahou School was established there to educate the children of the missionaries.

The Binghams returned to New England in 1840, because of Sybil's failing health, and settled in East-hampton, Massachusetts. Six years later, the Binghams were released from missionary service. Sybil Bingham died of tuberculosis and was initially buried in Easthampton. She was later placed beside her husband and his second wife in the New Haven city cemetery.

In sending the missionaries forth, the ABCFM gave them this charge: "You are to aim at nothing short of covering these islands with fruitful fields and pleasant dwellings, and schools and churches; of raising up the whole people to an elevated state of Christian civilization; of bringing them to the mansions of eternal blessedness." The American missionaries brought Christianity and Western education to the Sandwich Islands, and their successes and their progeny steered the future course of Hawaii toward eventual unification with the United States.

• The diaries and journals of Sybil Bingham are located in the Hawaiian Mission Children's Society Library and the Hawaiian Historical Society in Honolulu and offer the best insight into her life and times. The archives and records of the American Board of Commissioners for Foreign Missions may be found in the Houghton Library at Harvard University; the Bingham family papers are at the Yale University Sterling Memorial Library. Hiram Bingham, *A Residence of Twenty-One Years in the Sandwich Islands* (1847), is a record of the family's stay in Hawaii and considered an authoritative history; Lydia Bingham Coan, *A Brief Sketch of the Missionary Life of Mrs. Sybil Moseley Bingham* (1895), is an accurate and personal account by the Bingham's daughter. Char Miller, *Fathers and Sons: The Bingham Family and the American Mission* (1982), is a recent authoritative account. See also Henry Bond Restarick, *Sybil Bingham as a Youthful Bride* (1931), and Alfred M. Bingham, "Sybil's Bones, a Chronicle of the Three Hiram Binghams," *Hawaiian Journal of History* 9 (1975): 3–36. "Sybil Moseley Bingham," in Barbara Bennett Peterson, ed., *Notable Women of Hawaii* (1984), offers a more lengthy biography.

BARBARA BENNETT PETERSON

BINGHAM, Walter Van Dyke (20 Oct. 1880–7 July 1952), psychologist, was born in Swan Lake City, Iowa, the son of Lemuel Rothwell Bingham, a merchant and mining investor, and Martha Evarts Tracy. Bingham entered college at the University of Kansas at sixteen but transferred after a year to Beloit College, where he discovered the new experimental psychology. Bingham learned how to test sensory and motor abilities under Guy Allen Tawney, a student of Wilhelm Wundt, founder of the psychological research laboratory. After graduating in 1901, Bingham taught high school math and physics before enrolling in the University of Chicago's psychology program.

James R. Angell, leader of the Chicago school, led Bingham to consider the biological and social functions of mind, some of which help persons adapt to different environments. Bingham's 1908 dissertation utilized tests of finger tapping and breathing responses to describe melody as an interaction of biology and society: pitch sensation was innate, while melody perception depended on acculturation. It concluded that mind and body jointly anticipate the "feeling of completeness" that melodious pitch sequences offer.

Sharing the view that mental ability derives from both nature and nurture was Bingham's last mentor, E. L. Thorndike, leader of American educational psychology and Teachers College, Columbia University. As Thorndike adapted psychology to the needs of school administrators and teachers amid the rapid expansion of American public schools, Bingham helped him develop methods of classroom assessment. But the same year that he became an instructor at Teachers College (1908) he also joined "the Experimentalists," an exclusive professional fraternity whose leader, E. B. Titchener, denounced "applied psychology." Bingham soon began his attempt to reconcile the diverse purposes of scientific research and social utility; in 1910 he promoted the inclusion of laboratory methods in high school curricula.

Bingham further adapted experimental means to educational ends at Dartmouth, as an assistant professor in psychology and pedagogy from 1910 to 1915. Bingham's development of mental tests to assist admissions and advisement led the Carnegie Institute of Technology to hire him to organize the first American department of applied psychology in 1915. Bingham believed that psychological research could help unify the school's administrative, pedagogical, and socioeconomic functions. His plan to integrate Carnegie Tech's admissions, guidance, and placement activities paralleled the vertical integration of industrial functions (extraction, processing, and distribution of raw materials) that the school's namesake had achieved at Carnegie Steel.

Pittsburgh's corporate leaders recognized the usefulness of Bingham's plan and sponsored the Bureau of Salesmanship Research in 1916. Bingham hired Walter Dill Scott as director and offered Scott a distinction he eschewed for himself, first professor of applied psychology. Avoiding it helped him defend practical research before "colleagues of purity" at the American Psychology Association (APA) in 1916. Bingham claimed—a bit disingenuously—that "the college administrator's demands for student testing" had "forced upon us . . . problems of mental analysis, measurement, diagnosis and prognostication."

Experience with business clients prepared the faculty at Carnegie Tech to lead psychological service to the military during World War I. Bingham's diverse background helped him manage the relationship between psychology's two wartime organizations, which divided over so-called "pure" and "applied" psychology. Originally Bingham supported Scott's utilitarian proposal, which extended his salesmanship research and organized the commonsense personnel ratings of military leaders, but after APA president Robert M. Yerkes attempted to scuttle the project in favor of his own "pure scientific" system of individualized "general intelligence" tests, Bingham followed Yerkes and became secretary of his Committee on Psychological Examining.

Bingham was responsible for ensuring the participation of Lewis Terman, a professional rival of Yerkes and developer of the IQ test. Bingham agreed with Terman that a mass test of "general intelligence" might demonstrate the mental potential of "upper zone" recruits to succeed in various specialized positions of leadership and skill. After they persuaded Yerkes to allow the development of mass (and less scientific) intelligence testing, they collaborated in writing the first nationally standardized, multiple-choice group intelligence test, known later as Army Alpha. At Thorndike's direction, Bingham collected data from Scott's officer-rating scale to corroborate the new test's worth for the army in July 1917. This established the precedent for the modern psychological canon of test validation: testing tests against external criteria.

In August 1917, when the War Department established Scott's program instead of Yerkes's, Bingham became executive secretary of the Committee on the Classification of Personnel in the Army, which Scott and Thorndike directed. When the army chose to sponsor data collection on recruit skills per se, and not to support intelligence testing, Bingham reverted from Terman's belief in IQ to Thorndike's pluralist view and became the director of Trade (achievement) Testing. Measuring inherited general intelligence—at least for the normal majority—proved to be unworkable amid industrial specialization, and general intelligence theory did not prove to be functional. Ability to learn could no longer be considered merely as an inherited entity but as a general ability to learn a special, socially defined skill, which is the modern definition of "aptitude." The army commissioned Bingham as a lieutenant colonel just before the armistice.

Publicity of psychology's usefulness in both personnel selection and IQ tests brought renown to Bingham and produced a boom in psychological consulting. Colleagues elected Bingham first chairperson of the National Research Council Division on Anthropology and Psychology in 1919. Pittsburgh department stores developed the Research Bureau of Retail Training at Carnegie Tech; life insurance companies created their own salesmanship school; and bureaus in other practical fields soon emerged. After the boom ended with the depression of 1921–1922 and a liberal arts–oriented administration at Carnegie Tech terminated the Division of Applied Psychology in 1924, Bingham left academia to become a consultant to business and government. He moved to New York City with his wife, the former Millicent Todd, a geographer when they married in 1920. The couple had no children.

Although Bingham's original purpose—to manage students—nearly became lost in the shuffle of business consortia, Bingham did not lose his interest in linking education with business after he left higher education. His later publications addressed the concerns of both personnel managers (*Procedures in Employment Psychology* [1926], with Max Freyd, and *How to Interview* [1931], with Bruce V. Moore) and guidance counselors (*Aptitudes and Aptitude Testing* [1937]). Bingham was editor in chief of the *Journal of Personnel Research*

(1923–1935) as well as an editor of the *Journal of Applied Psychology* and the *Journal of Consulting Psychology*.

Bingham devoted much of his later career to administrative duties. He served as a director of the Psychological Corporation (1920–1952; president, 1926–1928) and of the Personnel Research Federation (1924–1934), and as president of the American Association of Applied Psychology (1941). He was chairperson of the Committee on Causes of Accidents for the National Conference on Street and Highway Safety (1925–1926) and of the Committee on the Driver for the National Safety Council between 1928 and 1933. As the U.S. Army prepared for another global war, the Adjutant General's Office named Bingham to chair the Committee on Classification of Military Personnel, which developed the main mental examination of World War II, the General Classification Test, in 1940. Bingham served as the army's chief psychologist until 1946, receiving the secretary of war's Emblem for Exceptional Civilian Service in 1944.

Bingham helped redefine the profession of psychology by demonstrating that the field could advance as a science when psychologists experimented in—and adapted their science of adaptationism to—socially useful contexts. The tension between purism and utilitarianism in Bingham's early career allowed him to become a conciliatory leader in psychology's departure from the ivory tower. His assertion that lay "demands" for psychology would provide "a powerful impetus to pure science, an augmented motive toward painstaking research, a stimulus and not a menace" became a truism well before he died (Bingham [1917]: 39–40). Furthermore, his successful failure at Carnegie Tech presaged a professional identity problem psychology has yet to solve: the attempt of modern applied psychologists to establish schools independently of academic psychology. Ultimately, underlying all of Bingham's contributions was his belief that the art and science of industrial psychology could compensate the modern world for the loss of small-town familiarity. Bingham died in Washington, D.C.

• Bingham's papers are in two collections at Hunt Library, Carnegie-Mellon University, Pittsburgh. In addition to the Walter Van Dyke Bingham Collection, several boxes of Bingham-related materials are in the collection of Leonard Ferguson, who wrote a thorough biographical chapter on Bingham in *The Heritage of Industrial Psychology* (1963). Autobiographical works include "Psychology Applied," *Scientific Monthly* 16 (1923): 141–59, and Bingham's contribution to Edwin G. Boring et al., eds., *A History of Psychology in Autobiography*, vol. 4 (1952); see also his "Mentality Testing of College Students," *Journal of Applied Psychology* 1 (1917): 38–45. For Bingham's military service, see Richard T. von Mayrhauser, "The Triumph of Utility: The Forgotten Clash of American Psychologies in World War I" (Ph.D. diss., Univ. of Chicago, 1986), and James Herbert Capshew, "Psychology on the March: American Psychologists and World War II" (Ph.D. diss., Univ. of Pennsylvania, 1986). An obituary is in the *New York Times*, 9 July 1952.

RICHARD T. VON MAYRHAUSER

BINGHAM, William (8 Apr. 1752–7 Feb. 1804), businessman and public official, was born in Philadelphia, Pennsylvania, the son of William Bingham, a saddler and merchant, and Mary "Molly" Stamper. Bingham graduated cum laude from the College of Philadelphia in 1768. Sometime after the death of his father in 1769, he served an apprenticeship with Philadelphia merchant Thomas Wharton. He toured Europe in 1773. By 1775 he owned several trading vessels. Although Bingham was apparently not active in the growing resistance to Great Britain, the Continental Congress's Committee on Secret Correspondence appointed him as its secretary in late 1775.

This committee sent Bingham to French Martinique as its agent in 1776, beginning his involvement in public affairs and helping him to obtain his large personal fortune. While in the West Indies, Bingham gathered political and military intelligence. He also secured munitions and produce, encouraged trade between the West Indies and the United States, authorized privateers, performed consular duties, and tried to persuade the French to support the Revolution. As expected by the Congressional Committee on Foreign Affairs, which oversaw him beginning in 1777, Bingham intermixed these public activities with his private business, financing one with the other. His business partner was Robert Morris, a member of the Committee on Foreign Affairs. Until late 1777 their partner was Thomas Willing, another prominent Philadelphia merchant. Although Bingham's business ventures in the West Indies were highly successful, they were to involve him in litigation for most of his life. These ventures also provoked suspicion and jealousy from some Americans. Anna Rawle, a Philadelphia Quaker, wrote that "the greatest part of his wealth [was] acquired by the sale of some guinea negroes, in the west indies," and that he lacked what she felt should be "disagreable [*sic*] sensations in using riches gained in that manner" (Letter to Mrs. Samuel Shoemaker, 4 Nov. 1870, Shoemaker Papers, vol. 1).

Bingham intermeshed business and public affairs with his private life. In 1780 he returned to Philadelphia and married Anne Willing, a daughter of his business partner. The couple had three children, including two daughters who would later marry sons of Sir Francis Baring, head of the British House of Baring, which invested in Bingham's Maine real estate. In Philadelphia Bingham broadened his business interests. When Morris, who had become Superintendent of Public Finance, organized the Bank of North America in 1781, Bingham became a major stock subscriber and was elected a director of the bank. (Willing was elected president.) Between 1792 and 1796 Bingham oversaw the construction and operation of a major commercial artery as president and manager of the Philadelphia and Lancaster Turnpike. The turnpike was modern in its engineering and crushed-stone surface and proved highly profitable as a business. In addition to these innovations, Bingham followed the traditional practice of wealthy American merchants with capital to invest: land speculation. He owned and attempted to develop large tracts in New York State and Maine. By reputation the wealthiest man in the United States, Bingham received the largest tax assessment in Philadelphia in 1800.

Bingham also continued to be active in public affairs. He participated in many local organizations, including the Abolition Society, the Pennsylvania Hospital, the Dancing Assembly, and the vestry of Christ Church and St. Peter's. A Republican in state politics in the 1780s, he supported the new state constitution of 1790 and won election to the state house of representatives, where he served as Speaker. On the national level, Bingham was a delegate to the Congress of the Confederation from 1786 to 1788. In October 1789 U.S. Treasury Secretary Alexander Hamilton solicited his advice, which anticipated in broad outline Hamilton's financial program of the following year. From 1795 to 1801 Bingham served as a U.S. senator. A moderate Federalist, he opposed war with France in 1798, and in 1801 he encouraged Federalist support for Thomas Jefferson rather than Aaron Burr when the House of Representatives chose the president.

The Binghams had toured Europe between 1784 and 1786 and returned to Philadelphia with many of the furnishings for the "mansion" they proceeded to build. An English traveler found it "a magnificent house and gardens in the best English style, with elegant and even superb furniture" and a dining room "papered in the French taste" (Alberts, p. 163). But Quaker Ann Warder dismissed it as "ungenteel." Bingham's mansion was the regular location of the Federalist senatorial caucus in the 1790s and the site of lavish entertainment.

During the 1790s Bingham's home was at the center of the Republican Court, a social network of wealthy and politically prominent Philadelphians and government officials. Bingham "affects to entertain in a style beyond everything in this place, or perhaps in America," admitted William Maclay, a political opponent. "[T]here is a propriety, a neatness, a cleanliness that adds to the splendor of his costly furniture and elegant apartments" (Maclay, p. 355). But a French traveler found only "a pomp which ought for ever to have been a stranger to Philadelphia" (Brissot de Warville, p. 318). Among the Court's detractors were national officials and Philadelphians who found that, in its imperfect and incongruous imitation of the aristocratic rituals of the English and neoclassical furnishings of the French, the Court seemed irrelevant to republican America. Philadelphia Federalist Samuel Breck admitted that, "There is too much sobriety in our American common sense to tolerate such pageantry" (Breck, p. 203).

The moment of the Republican Court was brief. The national capital moved to Washington in 1800, Bingham's term as senator ended in March 1801, and his wife died in May 1801. Distraught, Bingham moved with his daughter and his son-in-law Alexander Baring to England in August of that year. He later died at Bath, possibly following a stroke.

"He was pleasant in his manners, amiable in his temper" and "acquired his immense estate by his own ingenuity," reported Benjamin Rush (Rush, p. 269). But Abigail Adams stated this view: "Money, Money is his sole object." He has direct descendants in the Ashburton peerage and Baring baronetcy in Great Britain, but not in the United States. Bingham left only a small legacy as an author—two promotional pamphlets on business subjects. Binghamton, New York, is named for him.

Bingham was a traditional figure in some respects but modern in others. Although he married for business advantage, he showed strong affection for his wife, anticipating the manner of the nineteenth century. He was a multifaceted merchant of the eighteenth century, but his support for banking and internal improvements provided a foundation for nineteenth-century practices.

• There is no single large collection of Bingham papers. Some of his correspondence is found in the printed editions of the papers of prominent individuals in the revolutionary and early national periods, including Benjamin Franklin, Alexander Hamilton, and Robert Morris. The most significant Bingham manuscript is the "William Bingham Letter Book, 1791–1793," at the Historical Society of Pennsylvania (HSP), which contains copies of business correspondence. Also at the HSP, important manuscripts by or about Bingham are in the Tench Coxe, Shoemaker, Willing, and other papers and in the Society Miscellaneous and other collections. Robert C. Alberts, *The Golden Voyage: The Life and Times of William Bingham, 1752–1804* (1969), is comprehensive and reliable. Also useful is a series of three articles by Margaret L. Brown in the *Pennsylvania Magazine of History and Biography* (1937). On the Maine lands, see Frederick S. Allis, Jr., *William Bingham's Maine Lands, 1790–1820* (1954). Thomas Doerflinger, *A Vigorous Spirit of Enterprise: Merchants and Economic Development in Revolutionary Philadelphia* (1986), places Bingham in an entrepreneurial world of Philadelphia merchants who were creating preindustrial economic development. Assessments of Bingham are in *The Journal of William Maclay: United States Senator from Pennsylvania, 1789–1791* (1927), J. P. Brissot de Warville, *New Travels in the United States of America* (1792), Samuel Breck, *Recollections* (1877), and Benjamin Rush, *Autobiography* (1948).

ROBERT J. GOUGH

BINNEY, Amos (18 Oct. 1803–18 Feb. 1847), biologist and businessman, was born in Boston, Massachusetts, the son of Amos Binney, a businessman, and Hannah Dolliver. Interested early in natural history, Binney accumulated rocks, shells, and birds' eggs. He attended an academy at Hingham, Massachusetts, and at the age of fourteen entered Brown University, where he was especially interested in the natural sciences and expanded his collection of shells. After graduating in 1821, he studied medicine with a physician in Boston, then attended medical lectures at Dartmouth College.

There Binney became ill with pulmonary problems and was advised by doctors to take a long journey on horseback. In 1823 he rode from New Hampshire to Cincinnati, Ohio, where, in spite of persisting illness, he collected marine fossils from sedimentary rocks of the Silurian age before returning home. The next year he traveled to England and parts of Europe. There he observed exhibits of science and art, visited hospitals, obtained minerals, and collected seashells from the shores of the Mediterranean. In improved health, he entered Harvard University for medical studies and received the M.D. in 1826. He married Mary Ann Binney, a cousin, in 1827; they had five children.

Binney's primary interest in medicine was as a means of obtaining scientific knowledge to apply to natural history, so instead of practicing, he joined his father's businesses in real estate and mining. He thus amassed a considerable fortune. He devoted his leisure time to the sciences and was also interested in the arts.

In 1830 Binney and others, including physician Augustus Addison Gould, formed the Boston Society of Natural History. Binney prepared a draft of its constitution, was elected an honorary curator at the first meeting, and served as treasurer (1832–1834), corresponding secretary (1834–1837), vice president (1837–1843), and president (1843–1847). In 1831 he donated to the society 200 mineral specimens, 200 fossil specimens from Ohio, and 100 fossil specimens from foreign countries. His collection of approximately 1,500 species of mollusk shells was said by Gould (1851) to be "at that time by far the most complete collection in this country." Binney placed it in the society's collections in 1831 and donated it outright in 1840, along with 100 mounted specimens of American birds. He raised funds for a building for the society and donated generously to it.

From about 1835, Binney's primary scientific interest was terrestrial snails. Concentrating on those found in the United States, he obtained shells and living specimens of a great many species through the years, in part by hiring collectors in Florida, Texas, and the Southwest. He held living specimens in captivity for months in order to observe their habits and any changes brought about by age and diet. He arranged to have many specimens dissected by such experts in anatomy as Joseph Leidy of the University of Pennsylvania and Jeffries Wyman of Harvard. He also hired artists to illustrate the shells and animals for publication, often demanding changes before he was satisfied; the resulting illustrations are both scientifically accurate and artistic. The result of Binney's years of work was an almost-complete manuscript that defined many species, provided geographical ranges, and discussed the habits of this group of animals. He published a few papers on mollusks in the *Journal of the Boston Natural History Society*. Long in uncertain health, Binney provided in his will that his executors "employ some competent person or persons to prepare the same for the press, and shall publish the same at the expense of my estate" (1851, p. B). The work was completed by Gould after Binney's death and published in two volumes in 1851 as *The Terrestrial Air-Breathing Mollusks of the United States, and the Adjacent Territories of North America*.

Binney was elected to the legislative body of Massachusetts in 1836 for two years; in that position he gained state support for surveys of the state's geology, zoology, and botany. When biological specimens were sent from the U.S. Exploring Expedition of 1838–1842, he saw some of them in Washington, D.C., and advised that descriptions of new species should first be published in journals of scientific societies, rather than waiting for the final reports; this was done by several of the scientists involved. He was an active member of the American Association of Geologists and Naturalists from 1842 until his death, serving as chairman of its publishing committee from 1844 and contributing to its publishing costs. That organization expanded into the American Association for the Advancement of Science in 1848.

About 1842 Binney decided that his business affairs were in satisfactory condition and moved to the country outside Boston to restore his deteriorating health. Although still ailing, in 1846 he visited Europe to meet scientists and obtain scientific literature. His condition worsened, and he died in Rome.

Binney accumulated a library of zoology containing many hundred volumes. He also collected paintings, engravings, sculptures, and fine art books. Late in life, he commissioned four painters and two sculptors to create works related to American history, and several were completed before his death. He did outstanding work on land mollusks, and his philanthropic contributions were significant.

• Biographies of Binney include a sketch by Augustus A. Gould in Binney's *The Terrestrial Air-Breathing Mollusks of the United States, and the Adjacent Territories of North America* (1851), pp. xi–xxix; and William Healey Dall, "Some American Conchologists," *Proceedings of Biological Society of Washington* 4 (1888): 122–23.

ELIZABETH NOBLE SHOR

BINNEY, Horace (4 Jan. 1780–12 Aug. 1875), lawyer, was born in Philadelphia, Pennsylvania, the son of Barnabas Binney, a surgeon, and Mary Woodrow. Brought up in an elite neighborhood frequented by George Washington (1732–1799) and Alexander Hamilton (1755–1804), Binney attended Harvard College from 1793 to 1797 and graduated at the top of his class. In November 1797 he began to study law in the office of Jared Ingersoll (1749–1822), a prominent Philadelphia attorney, and in March 1800 he was admitted to the Philadelphia bar. While he was still struggling to establish a successful practice, he married Elizabeth Cox, daughter of a revolutionary army officer, in 1804. They had seven children.

Binney's first important case—*Gibson v. Philadelphia Insurance Company* (1808)—involved marine insurance law, a field that developed dramatically as a result of the Napoleonic wars. At a time when the Pennsylvania courts had to decide whether English precedents remained authoritative in a republican society, Binney's systematic research and lucid courtroom arguments enabled him to contribute significantly to the growth of a national jurisprudence, especially in matters of real property and commercial practice. By 1815 he had become an acknowledged leader of the Philadelphia bar, which was reputed to be the most distinguished in the nation.

Through his work as an early court reporter, Binney further confirmed his leadership status. In 1809 he published the first volume of his *Reports of Cases Adjudged in the Supreme Court of Pennsylvania*. Five other volumes followed, covering all major decisions handed down from 1799 to 1814. An invaluable research tool for practitioners, Binney's *Reports* provided Pennsylvania lawyers with an authoritative guide to the state's rapidly changing jurisprudence. With characteristic thoroughness Binney included the arguments of counsel as well as the opinions of the court. Critics praised his reports for their accuracy, and later reporters used them as models for their own publications.

Although Binney retired from courtroom practice in 1837, he continued to serve as legal consultant to banks and other corporations—an advisory role that would become increasingly common among elite lawyers after the Civil War. He also agreed, at the urging of the city councils, to argue one more case before the United States Supreme Court in 1844. *Vidal v. Philadelphia*, the Girard Will case, pitted Binney against Daniel Webster and proved to be the most celebrated case of his long career. Stephen Girard, a wealthy philanthropist, had bequeathed valuable property in trust to the city of Philadelphia for the establishment and maintenance of a school for poor white male orphans. Girard's heirs sought to have his will overturned, arguing that the trust provisions were too vague and against public policy, since they did not identify any specific orphans and, further, prohibited all clergymen from ever setting foot inside the school. In a learned and powerful argument for the Philadelphia trustees, Binney demonstrated that equity courts had historically exercised broad discretion in determining the beneficiaries of charitable trusts and that the students in Girard's school would learn religious values through required courses in ethics. The Supreme Court unanimously endorsed Binney's position and upheld Girard's will. As a result, equity courts in the United States—which handled cases for which the common law did not provide an adequate remedy—gained greater power over the administration of charitable trusts.

Unlike many other nineteenth-century lawyers, Binney had little interest in politics. Although he served one term in the state legislature (1806–1807) and another in the national House of Representatives (1833–1835), he deplored political partisanship and preferred instead to sit on the boards of municipal charities and cultural institutions. Originally a Federalist, he remained independent of party ties after the Federalists collapsed in the 1820s. During the Civil War his strong national sympathies led him to publish three influential pamphlets defending President Abraham Lincoln's power to suspend the writ of habeas corpus. In these publications Binney argued that the suspension issue was a matter of politics as much as law. Although the Constitution clearly authorized the suspension of habeas corpus "when in cases of rebel-

lion or invasion the public safety shall require it" (Art. I, sect. 9), no language indicated which branch of the government—legislative or executive—should exercise this power. Because the president is commander in chief of the armed forces and therefore responsible for suppressing a rebellion, Binney reasoned, the president might properly suspend the writ and order the arrest and detention of suspected disloyalists by military authorities. He died in Philadelphia.

• Letters from Binney are in the Horace Binney Papers, the John Sergeant Papers, and the James Gibson Papers at the Historical Society of Pennsylvania. Charles Chauncey Binney, *The Life of Horace Binney* (1903), is the standard biography. See also Hampton L. Carson, *A Sketch of Horace Binney* (1907). On the importance of Binney's Civil War pamphlets, see Phillip S. Paludan, *A Covenant with Death* (1975).

MAXWELL BLOOMFIELD

BINNS, Archie (30 July 1899–28 June 1971), novelist and historian, was born Archie Fred Binns in Port Ludlow, Washington, the son of Frank Binns, one of the early pioneers of western Washington, and Atlanta Sarah McQuah. Growing up in the Puget Sound area of northern Washington, Binns was nourished by both the soil and the sea. He spent his childhood working on the farm his father had cleared near Shelton and attending the district school he had established. Although Binns's upbringing was distinctly rural, the Puget Sound region—which he would later describe as the "Sea in the Forest"—helped to sustain his interest in seafaring. Family tradition may have also fueled his sea-interests; his mother had been born aboard the SS *Atlantic*, commanded by her father, a cotton-blockade runner during the Civil War who died at sea when he was just thirty-one. Shortly after graduating from Shelton High School, Binns joined the Umatilla Reef Lightship stationed off Cape Flattery near the treacherous waters of Washington's most northern coastal inlet. He spent nine months as a fireman on the steam-powered lightship, purportedly serving one stretch of 160 days without going ashore.

In 1918 Binns enlisted in the army and was commissioned a second lieutenant in the Field Artillery Reserve in 1923. Over the next several years he studied at college and spent time at sea. He received a B.A. in philosophy from Stanford University in 1922. Various accounts suggest that Binns sailed throughout the Atlantic, Pacific, and Indian Oceans as well as the Arabian Sea and on rivers within India during this period. In 1923 he boarded the SS *Ecuador* on the West Coast and sailed through the Panama Canal to New York City, where he quit the ship and embarked on a writing career. That September Binns married Mollie Windish. They had two children before her death in 1954.

Binns began working as a newspaper reporter, landing a job as Washington, D.C., correspondent for the Scripps-Howard newspapers in 1923. Eventually he returned to New York as an editor for the Leonard Scott Publication Company. His first book-length publication was *The Maiden Voyage* (1931), a collaborative effort with Felix Riesenberg, then a very popular writer of sea fiction. In September 1934 *Esquire* featured a short story written by Binns and offered a glowing review of his soon to be released *Lightship*. Based partly on experiences aboard the Umatilla Lightship, Binns's first novel won high critical praise. He constructed the novel around a set of nine characters—sailors of varying saltiness and experience—who reveal the stories of their lives to each other in the course of their monotonous duty on the Lightship, a vessel that never travels and is seldom relieved. In this limited setting, Binns weaves stories of sea and land, city and frontier, involving issues of philosophy, religion, evolution, lost innocence, love, and even such concerns as the plight of the American Indian. All of the sailors' experiences eventually intersect in a struggle to save the ship, broken from its moorings and adrift in a deadly storm.

Readers responded to *Lightship* so enthusiastically that the opening two chapters, forming a distinct episode in the novel, were separated for publication in 1936 as *Backwater Voyage*, an illustrated novella. Lincoln Colcord, another prominent writer of sea fiction at that time, wrote in his introduction to the reissue: "*Lightship* is the soundest and most vivid piece of nautical fiction produced by my generation in America. It is a great sea book because it is a great book about life, which makes it a great land book as well."

The early success of *Lightship* fostered a prolific period in Binns's career; he wrote five novels over the next eleven years. His second novel, *The Laurels Are Cut Down* (1937), received critical praise and was eventually awarded the Prix Femina Américain. Reprinted in 1967 as a selection of the Literary Guild of America, the story chronicles the journey of two brothers from their idyllic childhood home in northwestern Washington to war-torn Germany, Russian Siberia and, for the one who survives, back home. Binns's third novel, *The Land Is Bright* (1939), follows a more historic path, charting the hardships and triumphs of a family migrating west along the Oregon Trail in the early 1850s. His next three novels were all set in the Pacific Northwest: *Mighty Mountain* (1940) tells the story of a New Englander who abandons his dream to sail the world after visiting relatives in the Puget Sound area and decides to join them in settling the land; *The Timber Beast* (1944), a selection of the Book League, focuses on one family's struggle to survive in the competitive world of the modern lumber industry; *You Rolling River* (1947) weaves the stories of several characters and their experiences in a small port town near the mouth of the Columbia River.

While Binns was publishing successful novels during this period, he also managed to complete several historical and scholarly studies of subjects that interested him, mostly about Washington state history. *Northwest Gateway* (1941), *The Roaring Land* (1942), *Sea in the Forest* (1953), and a lengthy chapter in *Pacific Coast Ranges* (ed. Roderick Peattie, 1946) chronicle various aspects of the Pacific Northwest, especially the settling and development of Seattle and the Puget Sound wilderness. Binns also wrote (with Olive Kooken) *Mrs. Fiske and the American Theater* (1955), a biography of a popular turn-of-the-century stage actress. His last novel, *The Headwaters*, was published in 1957. During the 1950s he wrote several successful juvenile works, including *The Radio Imp* (1950), *Secret of the Sleeping River* (1952), *Sea Pup* (1954), and *The Enchanted Islands* (1956). In his final years, Binns wrote one more historical study, *Peter Skene Ogden, Fur Trader* (1967), and revisited one of his successful juvenile stories with *Sea Pup Again* (1965).

In addition to his prolific career as a writer, Binns also taught creative writing at the University of Washington from 1950 to 1956 and became an associate professor of creative writing at Western Washington College of Education, Bellingham, in 1957. In 1954 his wife died, and the next year he married Ellen Losey Goins. They had four children. Binns died in Sequim, Washington, near the Puget Sound wilderness where he was born and which he chronicled throughout his life.

• Biographical information regarding Archie Binns can be found in the *Wilson Bulletin for Librarians* 6 (Feb. 1935); Stanley J. Kunitz, ed., *20th Century Authors* (1942) and its first supplement (1955); and Harry R. Warfel, *American Novelists of Today* (1951; repr. 1972). The September 1934 issue of *Esquire* includes a photograph and short biography of Binns, his short story "What Do They Want?" and a review of *Lightship*. For an extensive treatment of Binns and his contribution to the tradition of American sea fiction—and a close reading of *Lightship*—see Bert Bender, *Sea-Brothers: The Tradition of American Sea Fiction from Moby Dick to the Present* (1988).

MATTHEW EVERTSON

BINNS, John (22 Dec. 1772–16 June 1860), newspaper editor, was born in Dublin, Ireland, the son of John Binns, a prosperous ironmonger, and Mary Pemberton. His childhood was shaped by tensions stemming from family differences, his father's relatives being Moravians and Irish patriots, his mother's Episcopalians and Loyalists. In 1774 his father drowned. On his mother's remarriage, the family moved to Drogheda, where the stepfather's maltreatment of Binns and his elder brother Benjamin led them in 1782 to run away to their father's family.

Binns's education was irregular and unfinished, but his inquisitiveness led him to read widely. He was exposed to the advanced ideas of the Irish patriots and Volunteers, making him a republican. Between 1792 and 1794 he played a small role in the Dublin Society of United Irishmen, which was seeking parliamentary reform and Catholic emancipation. In 1794 he moved to London, where he worked first in the plumbing trade, then lived off the fees from hiring out debating rooms that he rented in the Strand. He joined the radical London Corresponding Society and was soon prominent on its executive committee. In 1796 Binns traveled the provinces as an LCS delegate hoping to revive the movement for political reform. In Birmingham he was arrested for uttering seditious words in a public house. After long delays he was acquitted in 1797, probably because a sympathetic court official rigged the jury. Soon thereafter, Binns left the LCS, but almost certainly joined the underground revolutionary United Irishmen in London (his comments on this part of his life in his autobiography are disingenuous). He was arrested twice more, the most important occasion, in February 1798, leading to a charge of high treason. Again he was acquitted, although one of his associates, the Catholic priest James O'Coigley, was hanged. In March 1799 he was jailed under the Suspension of Habeas Corpus Act and released after nearly two years.

Binns emigrated to the United States in September 1801 and immediately traveled to Northumberland, Pennsylvania, settling close to Dr. Joseph Priestley and other English Unitarian refugees. In March 1802 he married Mary Ann Bagster, an Englishwoman. They had ten children. Binns's career in America revolved around Republican politics and his editorship of two long-running newspapers. He also established a printing shop and bookstore. His writings in the Northumberland *Republican Argus* (Dec. 1802–Dec. 1805) and the Philadelphia *Democratic Press* (Mar. 1807–Nov. 1829) reflect his slowly changing political views, from a championing of Thomas Jefferson's presidency by promoting a conventional "Jacobin" program, which emphasized democratic class harmony, popular sovereignty, law reform, and domestic manufacturing, through a reluctant support for James Madison (1751–1836), to a puzzled Whiggery and a principled anti-Jacksonianism in the 1820s (Binns seemed unable to explain his political declension even in the 1850s).

The explanation lies in the serpentine nature of Pennsylvania Republican politics, which began to fragment as early as 1803. A committed democrat, Binns placed his trust in the Country party led by Simon Snyder, who was governor for nine years from 1808. During these years Binns was an *éminence grise* on whom Snyder relied for political advice. Much of the state patronage flowed Binns's way, or was influenced by him. Inevitably he came into conflict not only with the moderate Republicans (Constitutional Republicans or "Quids," who evolved into the Family party, so-called for their leaders' close family connections), but also with his natural allies in Philadelphia, the Michael Leib–William Duane (1760–1835) radicals. The long-running feud between Duane and Binns—friends since 1795—fought out in the *Aurora* and the *Press,* was disastrous for them both, as it divided the Democrats in Philadelphia and thus reduced both men's political influence.

Binns's political career foundered when he was outmaneuvered by the Family party and lost his influence and his patronage with Snyder's successor, William Findlay. Never a good businessman, Binns slipped into debt. His political exclusion was completed by his refusal to support Andrew Jackson's presidential ambitions in 1823. He was convinced that Jackson was morally bankrupt and a murderer (Binns distributed thousands of prints of six coffins inscribed with the names of militiamen whom he believed Jackson had killed during the War of 1812). When his preferred candidate for president, William H. Crawford, died, he lent his support to John Quincy Adams (1767–1848). Thereafter Binns kept company with Whigs and Federalists, and his influence disappeared. Although the Democratic party made offers to him in 1828, on principle he could never endorse Jackson's candidature.

Elected an alderman in Philadelphia in 1822, Binns assiduously carried out his duties for twenty years, rekindling on the bench his friendship with Duane. He died in Philadelphia, having outlived most of his political opponents and his reputation for apostasy.

• The main source for Binns's life is his autobiography, *Recollections of the Life of John Binns* (1854), which includes only a cursory discussion of his political career in the United States. Additional information on his childhood can be found in letters written by his brother Benjamin in the Madden papers, Trinity College, Dublin. He is mentioned in various documents in the Home Office Papers and in the Treasury Solicitor's Papers, Public Record Office, London, and in the Place papers, British Library, London. For his time in the U.S., there are only a small number of letters in the Jones and Clarke Papers, Historical Society of Pennsylvania, Philadelphia. There is no full-length biography of Binns, but see Clive Emsley's essay, strong on Binns's radical career before 1801, in Joseph O. Baylen and Norbert J. Gossman, eds., *Biographical Dictionary of Modern British Radicals*, vol. 1 (1979), pp. 44–48. Binns's political life in the United States can best be studied in Sanford W. Higginbotham, *The Keystone of the Democratic Arch: Pennsylvania Politics, 1800–1816* (1952); Philip S. Klein, "John Binns and the Impeachment of Governor William Findlay," *Proceedings of the Northumberland County Historical Society* 11 (1939): 51–66; and—from an unsympathetic position—Kim Tousley Phillips, "William Duane, Revolutionary Editor" (Ph.D. diss., Univ. of California, Berkeley, 1968).

MICHAEL DUREY

BIRCH, Thomas (26 July 1779–13 Jan. 1851), landscape and marine painter, was born in Warwickshire, England, the son of William Russell Birch, an enamel painter and printmaker. The Birch family immigrated to the United States aboard *William Penn*, arriving in Philadelphia in September 1793. After first living in the city, the family later settled at Springland, near Neshaminy, Pennsylvania, in 1797.

Birch's father taught him to draw at an early age. "Master Birch" showed four views of London and an undisclosed number of local subjects at the first and only Columbianum Exhibition, a show organized by America's earliest art society in Philadelphia in May 1795. As a young man, Birch attended a classical academy in Burlington, New Jersey. He also sketched along the banks of the Schuylkill River in the company of artists John Lewis Krimmel, John Wesley Jarvis, David Edwin, and Thomas Sully.

Birch married Ann Goodwin in June 1802. Three years later he moved back to Philadelphia, where he lived for the rest of his life. He wed Sarah King in

March 1806; it is unclear if his first wife died or if the couple divorced. This second marriage produced two children: a daughter born in 1808, and Thomas, Jr., born in 1812, who was the founder of a major Philadelphia auction house that bore his name.

Birch initially prospered, supporting his family by painting watercolor portraits on bristol board. He also assisted his father and engraver Samuel Seymour in preparing the topographical portfolio *The City of Philadelphia* (1799–1800). In this project it seems likely that Birch played a major, although unacknowledged, role. Many prints in his father's *The Country Seats of the United States of North America with Some Scenes Connected with Them* (1808) also appear to have been based on paintings by Birch as well. William Dunlap dates Birch's first oil paintings to 1806. After a trip to the Delaware Capes the following year, Birch supposedly painted his first seascape. By 1813 Birch was no longer described as a "miniature painter" in the city directory but as "landscape and marine painter" or simply as "artist."

In 1810 Birch was made a fellow in the Society of Artists, a professional organization loosely associated with the Pennsylvania Academy of the Fine Arts. He sent several paintings to the academy's first annual exhibition the following year. Over the next twenty-three years Birch showed a total of ninety-three canvases at the academy, including landscapes, seascapes, ship portraits, topographical views, and scenes of shipwrecks.

By all accounts, the high point of Birch's career came during the War of 1812. Encouraged by the demand for representations of U.S. naval victories, he began painting battle scenes. He received a few commissions from key participants, such as James Biddle, a lieutenant aboard the USS *Wasp*. However, most of his battle scenes were painted on speculation or for exhibition. Engravers Cornelius Tiebout, Alexander Lawson, Francis Kearny, and Samuel Seymour all issued prints based on Birch's designs. Among his most popular subjects were *Constitution* versus *Guerrière* and *United States* versus *Macedonian*. Birch also contracted with publisher Joseph Delaplaine in April 1813 to produce a series of naval prints but apparently only one engraving resulted. Benjamin West, on seeing Tiebout's 1814 engraving of Oliver Hazard Perry's victory on Lake Erie, purportedly pronounced it "the best composition of a picture to have come from America" (Jackson, p. 293).

Following the war, as patriotic enthusiasm cooled and the economy weakened, the demand for paintings and prints waned. Birch began to supplement his income by decorating mirrors, restoring paintings, and trading prints. From July 1812 until February 1816 he was keeper of the academy, having succeeded engraver John Vallance. It is unclear why Birch was dismissed, but a committee including sculptor William Rush recommended closing the Pennsylvania Academy rather than letting Birch continue.

Birch's activities are obscure during the years 1816 to 1835. His early success was apparently fleeting.

Relatively few pictures sold from the Pennsylvania Academy's annual exhibitions during the late 1820s. Abel C. Thomas, a Unitarian minister and friend of Birch, wrote that many "took advantage of [Birch's] meager circumstances to obtain his pictures at a disheartening discount" (Thomas, p. 22). Like many other landscapists of his generation, Birch was apparently embittered by the lack of patronage and withdrew from all Philadelphia society except the company of other artists.

Frustrated by what they perceived to be the mismanagement of the Pennsylvania Academy, Philadelphia artists formed the Artists' Fund Society in 1835. Birch served as the first vice president and was a regular exhibitor at the society's annual exhibitions. He also exhibited with greater frequency during the late 1830s at the National Academy of Design in New York and at the Boston Athenaeum. Art unions, which gained popularity in the early 1840s, purchased dozens of Birch's compositions for distribution by lot. The American Art-Union in New York was the most active such institution, but Birch sold paintings to art unions as far away as Cincinnati. Birch died at his home in Philadelphia.

Birch introduced a tonal, Anglo-Dutch style of marine painting to North American audiences. His example profoundly affected later nineteenth-century marine artists. Although he seems to have had only one obscure pupil, Lemuel G. White, other landscape and marine painters such as George Robert Bonfield and James Hamilton emulated Birch's style. Noted landscape painter Thomas Cole later told Dunlap that his "heart sank as he felt his deficiencies in art" upon seeing Birch's work at the Pennsylvania Academy in 1824. Birch is considered to be the first professional marine artist to work in the United States.

• Birch left no papers of importance. Useful assessments of his life are found in William Dunlap, *History of the Rise and Progress of the Arts of Design in the United States*, vol. 2 (1834), pp. 259–60; J. Thomas Scharf and Thompson Westcott, *History of Philadelphia*, vol. 1 (1884), pp. 1266–67; and Joseph Jackson, *Encyclopedia of Philadelphia*, vol. 1 (1931), p. 293. William Gerdts's *Thomas Birch*, the catalog to the Philadelphia Maritime Museum's 1966 Birch exhibition, provides a good overview. Gerdt's catalog is largely based on Doris Jean Creer, "Thomas Birch: A Case Study of the Condition of Painting and the Artist's Position in Federal America" (M.A. thesis, Univ. of Delaware, 1958). The most recent discussion of Birch is Tony Lewis, "Interesting Particulars and Melancholy Occurrences: Thomas Birch's Representations of the Shipping Trade, 1799–1850" (Ph.D. diss., Northwestern Univ., 1994). Perhaps the best accounts of his life come from obituaries, most notably Abel C. Thomas, "Sketch of Thomas Birch," *Philadelphia Art Union Reporter* (Jan. 1851): 22.

TONY LEWIS

BIRCH, William Russell (9 Apr. 1755–7 Aug. 1834), enamelist, engraver, and painter, was born in Warwickshire, England, the son of Thomas Birch, a successful surgeon, and Mary Russell. Because Birch was unsuccessful at Latin school, his wealthy and paternalistic cousin, William Russell of Birmingham, took him into his care and eventually apprenticed him to his friend, the London jeweler and goldsmith Thomas Jeffreys. After six years, Birch left to study enamel painting with Henry Spicer. In 1775 he exhibited two enamel miniatures at the Society of Artists.

Enamel painting involves a painstaking technique in which vitreous glazes are fused to a metallic surface under extreme heat. Although the process and the final object are delicate, the medium is permanent. In his autobiography, written during his later years, Birch described the process as the unique art of "heightening and preserving the beauty of tints to futurity, as given in the works of the most celebrated Masters of Painting, without a possibility of their changing." His copies of works by his friend and mentor, Sir Joshua Reynolds, are of special interest because they preserve Reynolds's colors, which have proved fugitive. Birch's enamels are notable for their brilliant surfaces and the clarity and beauty of their colors. In 1784 and 1785 he received awards from the Society of Artists for technical improvements in enameling and excellence in his work. Among his technical improvements were a method of obtaining a warm white by underlaying the final coat of white with a thin coat of yellow and the discovery of a red-brown enamel. Between 1781 and 1794, Birch exhibited forty-one enamels at the Royal Academy. During his career, his miniature subjects encompassed both copies and original compositions, portraiture and still-life, and landscape and history painting. Often they were incorporated into enamel boxes or jeweled settings.

Birch moved easily among the educated and influential, enjoying considerable aristocratic patronage. Developing his skills as an engraver, he further utilized his gifts for translating large works to a smaller scale and in 1791 published a collection of thirty-six stipple engravings of landscapes "from the best masters of this country." It also included a few original scenes by Birch. His love of the landscape had been nurtured by jaunts with patrons through the English countryside in search of picturesque views, and he noted in the text that "A journey becomes a study to admirers of the landscape." He recalled that he titled the work *Délices de la Grande Bretagne* because it was considered "a compliment in England to France to adopt a french title to works of Art and elegance." His subscription list reveals that the duc d'Orleans was among his subscribers.

Birch had been successful in England, but uneasiness over the French Revolution, as well as the deaths of important friends and patrons, including Reynolds, left him bored and uncertain. Judge Samuel Chase of Maryland, whose stepmother was Birch's sister, encouraged him to relocate to America. When Birch moved to Philadelphia in 1794, he was thirty-nine and accompanied by his wife and four children. His fourteen-year-old son, Thomas Birch, would become a well-known American landscape and marine painter. A letter from Benjamin West to the influential William Bingham served as an introduction into an affluent and sophisticated segment of Philadelphia society, where he soon found patrons. Painting many notable social and political figures, he produced more than sixty enamel miniatures of Washington after Gilbert Stuart, most of which were based on that artist's Athenaeum head. Occasionally his likenesses were accompanied by decorative elements, such as his *Thomas Jefferson*, which was based on Stuart's profile portrait but accented by symbols of liberty and justice.

Birch's distinguished collection of European prints and paintings enriched Philadelphia's artistic resources, and he became a founder of the Columbianum, America's first organization to attempt to educate and provide exhibition opportunities for artists. In 1795 he displayed enamels, drawings, and prints in its only exhibition. Between 1811 and 1830, he periodically exhibited at the Pennsylvania Academy of the Fine Arts. He also exhibited in New York and Baltimore.

Birch is best known for his unique early record of an American city, *The City of Philadelphia in the State of Pennsylvania as It Appeared in 1800*. The series manifests both a high degree of technical skill and a number of original and dynamic compositions. Intended to be colored by hand, the publication was prepared between 1797 and 1798 with some assistance from Birch's son, Thomas, and his student, Samuel Seymour. Philadelphia was then America's largest city and its artistic, political, and cultural center. The views provided in *The City of Philadelphia* handsomely transcribed its impressive architecture while documenting a variety of occupations, industries, and amusements and providing a glimpse of the social differences between artisans, laborers, and the elite. Birch's nationalistic aim, according to his autobiography, was to "show early improvements of the country and convey [them] to Europe, to promote and encourage settlers to the establishment of trade and commerce." Among the many influential subscribers to the first edition was Thomas Jefferson, whose copy remained prominently displayed in his office throughout his presidency.

Birch's other collection of views, and the project closest to his heart, was *The Country Seats of the United States of North America*, which was first issued to subscribers in four parts but was reissued as one volume in 1809. Smaller in scale, but artistically distinguished and rarer because of the narrower subscriber interest of its subject matter, it included an introduction and twenty plates. As the first of many color-plate books on American scenery, its images of a calm, civilized rural landscape form an invaluable record of eighteenth- and early nineteenth-century estates, mostly in Pennsylvania, Maryland, and Delaware. Also assisted by his son on this project, Birch's purpose was "propagating Taste" in "rural retirement" (Snyder [1957]: 239). He felt that the "comforts and advantages of a Country Residence, after domestic accommodations are consulted, consist more in the beauty of the situation, than the massy magnitude of the residence" (Snyder [1957]: 249). Birch, himself, had moved from the city to the countryside in 1797. Over the years, he invested considerable time and money in attempting to emulate a genteel lifestyle and produce a model of landscape design at his beautifully situated property, "Springland," on the Neshaminy Creek near Bristol.

William Birch was also a professional practitioner of landscape design and small architectural projects. One patron, Baron Stier, in a letter to his daughter, described Birch as "an architect who is at the same time an artist." Birch returned to Philadelphia in 1828, where he remained until his death in 1834. Adaptable and multifaceted, Birch's technical expertise, design skills, and creativity greatly enriched his adopted country.

• The most important primary source on Birch is his autobiography, "The Life of William Russell Birch Enamel Painter. Written by Himself " (2 vols., Birch papers, Historical Society of Pennsylvania [HSP]). It includes annotations and a partial list of Birch's American enamel paintings. Also at HSP in the Society Collection is Birch's "List of Subscribers, Philadelphia Dissected," which records information on the various editions and subscribers to his *The City of Philadelphia*, a slightly different transcription of the autobiography without annotations, a partial list of Birch's art collection, and more information on Springland. The Library Company of Philadelphia owns a duplicate of the autobiography, copies of Birch's *Délices*, *The City of Philadelphia*, and *The Country Seats*, and related drawings. For works exhibited in England, see Algernon Graves, *A Dictionary of Artists Who Have Exhibited Works in the Principal London Exhibitions, 1760–1893*, 3d ed. (1901; repr. 1969), p. 26. For enamels, see Marvin C. Ross, "William Birch, Enamel Miniaturist," *American Collector* 9 (July 1940): 5, 20, and Jean Lambert Brockway, "William Birch: His American Enamel Portraits," *Antiques* 24 (Sept. 1933): 94–96. For prints, see Martin P. Snyder, "William Birch: His Philadelphia Views," *Pennsylvania Magazine of History and Biography* 73 (July 1949): 271–315, and Snyder, "Birch's Philadelphia Views: New Discoveries," *Pennsylvania Magazine of History and Biography* 88 (Apr. 1964): 164–73. These provide information on the various editions and restrikes of *The City of Philadelphia*. Snyder, "William Birch: His Country Seats of the United States," *Pennsylvania Magazine of History and Biography* 81 (July 1957): 225–54, gives an in-depth account of this series, its editions, and related works. It also discusses Springland and Birch's landscape design. For the latter, see "The Calvert-Stier Correspondence," ed. Wm. D. Hoyt, Jr., *Maryland Magazine* 45 (1950): 281–82, and *Mistress of Riverdale: The Plantation Letters of Rosalie Stier Calvert, 1795–1821*, ed. Margaret Law Callcott (1991), pp. 53–54, 134–35, 142, 148, 180. For Birch in the context of American landscape views, see Edward J. Nygren with Bruce Robertson, *Views and Visions, American Landscape before 1830* (1986). For an assessment of Birch's work, see Thomas P. Bruhn, *The American Print: Originality and Experimentation, 1790–1890* (1993), and Emily Cooperman, "'The Habit of Rural Retirement,' American Identity and William Birch's *Country Seats*" (Ph.D. diss., Univ. of Pennsylvania, 1997).

CAROL EATON SOLTIS

BIRD, Francis William (22 Oct. 1809–23 May 1894), radical reformer and antislavery politician, was born in Dedham, Massachusetts, the son of George Bird, a paper mill superintendent, and Martha C. Newell. Bird graduated from Brown College in 1831. He took an active interest in the welfare of his hometown of East Walpole, Massachusetts, where he continued the family paper manufacturing business. Bird lost his first wife and infant daughter to illness after one year of marriage. He married Abby Frances Newell in 1843; they had at least two children.

Bird's sincere, though at times idiosyncratic, enthusiasm in the cause of a wide range of reforms guided him through a remarkable career in Massachusetts and national politics. After converting to Sylvester Graham's regimen of healthful eating and then teaching in a mission school in an impoverished area of Boston, Bird embarked in 1847 on a political career as an antislavery or "Conscience" Whig. He joined the Free Soil party at its inception the following year. About this time he began inviting prominent political, intellectual, and business leaders to dine with him regularly on Saturday afternoons at a Boston hotel. This informal group, dubbed by outsiders as the "Bird Club," became in the 1850s the operative center of political antislavery radicalism in Massachusetts, if not in New England.

As a leader of the Massachusetts Free Soilers, Bird justified his party's anti-Whig coalition with the Democrats by accepting "sunday reforms in state policy" in exchange for electing his close friend and Bird Club member Charles Sumner to the U.S. Senate. After the political upheaval triggered by passage of the Kansas-Nebraska Act, Bird waged war with the suddenly popular anti-Catholic and anti-immigrant American or "Know Nothing" party. He never overcame his distrust of former associates, including Bird Club member Henry Wilson (1812–1875), who temporarily joined the Know Nothings. On election day in 1856 Bird fielded an "Honest Man's" Republican ticket in symbolic protest of his party's deal with the Know Nothings that gave Republican votes to the American gubernatorial candidate in exchange for Know Nothing support of John C. Frémont. (Bird's ticket polled about 4 percent of the ballots cast for governor.) Within Republican ranks the "pure" antislavery faction led by Bird repeatedly contended with the "time serving" nativist wing led by Nathaniel P. Banks, who won the governorship for the Republicans in 1857, 1858, and 1859. During these years the reaction of Bay Staters to national events, including President James Buchanan's acceptance of the Lecompton constitution for Kansas and endorsement of the Dred Scott decision, accelerated the popularity of the Bird Club radicals. In 1857 Bird, along with other Bird Club members, organized Sumner's near-unanimous return to the U.S. Senate by the state legislature.

According to contemporaries of the Civil War era, Bird exercised during the 1860s an "immense, informal influence" unmatched by any Republican who did not hold high public office. When Bird Club member John A. Andrew received the Republican nomination for governor in 1860, Bird and his followers celebrated their "complete and glorious victory over Banks, and the Know-Nothings, old Boston conservatism, and everything bad" (Robinson, p. 92). After Andrew's election in 1860, the Bird Club's political power was enhanced by the popularity of Governor Andrew. Through its control of the Republican State Committee and the highest state offices, the club was virtually able to dictate throughout the subsequent decade the strategy of the Massachusetts Republican party, with Bird as a primary power broker. He skillfully protected Senator Sumner's political interests at home, leaving Sumner free in the nation's capital to be the embodiment of uncompromising moral principles. While Bird's success hinged on the strong popular support that Sumner commanded, Bird, to a greater extent than Sumner, was responsible for holding together radical sentiment and leading it to victory by helping Sumner and injuring his opponents. In this endeavor Bird organized movements such as the Emancipation League, published radical viewpoints in sympathetic newspapers, and lobbied the influential. When the most revolutionary policy, including the use of black troops by the Union army, was discussed in detail in Washington, the Bird Club radicals had "already robbed it of its terror by making it familiar" (G. W. Curtis, *A Memorial of Charles Sumner* [1894], p. 158). Other concerns of Bird's included the abolition of slavery in the District of Columbia, equal pay for black soldiers, and repeal of all Massachusetts laws that discriminated against individuals on the basis of race, nationality, or religious affiliation.

During the war Bird grew exasperated with President Abraham Lincoln's slowness to implement Sumner's proposals. Anxious to pressure Lincoln to withdraw from the 1864 presidential race, Bird formed a movement for Salmon P. Chase in the Boston Customhouse, where many were loyal to the Treasury secretary. Bird rallied to Lincoln only after the fall of Atlanta. At the end of the war his early confidence in Andrew Johnson's administration quickly disappeared when it became clear that the new president desired a restoration and not a reconstruction of the white South. By the end of 1865 Johnson and the Bird Club radicals were engaged in a bitter debate that would dominate politics for the next three years. Bird welcomed the aid of former Democrat and Bird Club member Benjamin F. Butler (1818–1893) in the conflict with Johnson, but he became estranged from his longtime friend former governor Andrew, who, frustrated by Sumner's greater stature in the Republican party, supported Johnson's undemanding policies toward former Confederates.

At the height of his influence, Bird championed a host of causes other than civic and political equality for blacks. He advocated abolition of the franking privilege, endorsed woman suffrage, favored granting citizenship and naturalization rights to American Indians and Chinese immigrants, and opposed state support of private corporations—a position that led him to write vitriolic pamphlets against the Hoosac Mountain tunnel project. In the battle over prohibition of alcoholic beverages, he favored persuasion over compulsion. His fear of granting particular legal privileges to any

class of individuals rendered him lukewarm to the labor reform movement.

Although Bird successfully engineered in 1868 the nomination and election of Bird Club member William Claflin to the governorship, his last major triumph was denying the colorful and controversial Butler, who left the Bird Club in 1870, the Republican gubernatorial nomination in 1871. After the rift between Sumner and President Ulysses S. Grant over Santo Domingo annexation, the bulk of the Bird Club members joined the Liberal Republican movement. In 1872 Bird pressured Sumner to pronounce against Grant's reelection, destroyed the movement to nominate Sumner adversary Charles Francis Adams (1807–1886) for the presidency on a Liberal Republican ticket, and ran unsuccessfully as the "Liberal Republican and Democratic" candidate for the Massachusetts governorship. That same year Bird left the Republican party and for the remainder of his life acted with the Democratic party, having discovered that he had always been, in his words, "a Democrat of the Old School." With the death of Sumner in 1874, the political importance of the Bird Club ended, although its members continued to meet into the 1880s. Bird died at his home in East Walpole.

• Bird's papers, including his pamphlets and broadsides, are in the Houghton Library at Harvard University. His autobiographical essay detailing his personal crisis as a young man is found in the *Graham Journal of Health and Longevity* 1 (4 Apr. 1837): 2, and (17 Oct. 1837): 222–24. The account of his life written by his son, Charles Sumner Bird, *Francis William Bird: A Biographical Sketch* (privately printed, 1897), is less useful than the insights provided by his contemporaries contained in Mrs. William S. Robinson, ed., *"Warrington" Pen-Portraits: A Collection of Personal and Political Reminiscences from 1848 to 1876, from the Writings of William S. Robinson* (1877); Frank Preston Stearns, *Cambridge Sketches* (1905); and Henry Greenleaf Pearson, *The Life of John A. Andrew, Governor of Massachusetts, 1861–1865* (2 vols., 1904). The single best scholarly assessment is Donald B. Marti, "Francis William Bird: A Radical's Progress through the Republican Party," *Historical Journal of Massachusetts* 11 (1983): 82–93. See also James M. McPherson, *The Struggle for Equality: Abolitionists and the Negro in the Civil War and Reconstruction* (1964); David Montgomery, *Beyond Equality: Labor and the Radical Republicans, 1862–1872* (1981); and Dale Baum, *The Civil War Party System: The Case of Massachusetts, 1848–1876* (1984).

DALE BAUM

BIRD, Robert Montgomery (5 Feb. 1806–23 Jan. 1854), writer, was born in New Castle, Delaware, the son of John Bird, a merchant, and Elizabeth Van Leuvenigh, whose ancestors were among the early settlers of Delaware. Following the death of his father in 1810, Bird lived first with an uncle in New Castle and later with his mother in Philadelphia. In 1823 he entered the Germantown Academy to study for entrance to the University of Pennsylvania. After completing his work at this preparatory school, his developing interest in science led him to study for a summer in the office of a Philadelphia physician. In the fall of 1824 he entered the Medical School and College of Pharmacy at the University of Pennsylvania. He received his M.D. degree in 1827 and began his medical practice in Philadelphia.

As his papers and manuscript fragments attest, Bird had had ambitions to be a writer even before he received his medical degree. His evolving interest in poetry and (particularly) drama soon took priority: after one year, he gave up the practice of medicine and embarked on a literary career of astonishing activity. In addition to occasional verse and fiction, he wrote four extravagant tragedies between 1830 and 1833: *Pelopidas; or, The Fall of the Polemarchs* (set in ancient Thebes), *The Gladiator* (dramatizing the revolt of Roman slaves under Spartacus), *Oralloossa, Son of the Incas* (focusing on the Spanish conquest of Native Americans in Peru), and *The Broker of Bogota* (tracing the fate of a family in New Granada). Although the noted actor Edwin Forrest personally awarded *Pelopidas* a $1,000 prize as a notable American play, it was never produced, possibly because it had no appropriate role for Forrest. But Forrest starred in the other tragedies and helped to make *The Gladiator*—first performed in September 1831—one of the most popular American plays of the nineteenth century. Well aware that he had fashioned a role to feature Forrest's histrionic talents, Bird said that *The Gladiator* was "full of blood and thunder." In her later account of Bird's life and career, his wife praised the play's "quiet merits" as well as what she devotedly called its "glaring virtues."

Although he continued to publish poetry, short fiction, and essays, Bird turned primarily to the writing of novels in the middle and late 1830s. Both *Calavar; or, The Knight of the Conquest; A Romance of Mexico* (1834) and *The Infidel; or, The Fall of Mexico* (1835)—"exotic" romances, as Bird's biographer Curtis Dahl called them—evince his interest in the early history of Spanish America. Refashioned from an earlier and aborted narrative, *The Hawks of Hawk Hollow*, published in 1835, takes place in one of Bird's favorite settings, the Delaware Water Gap region he had visited the previous year. Perhaps for this reason, his wife later suggested, he preferred it to his other novels. The following year saw the publication of *Sheppard Lee*, a hallucinatory set of adventures involving the disembodied spirit of a young man who enters, consecutively, the bodies of six men who have recently died. And in what was an eventful year, 1837, Bird published *Nick of the Woods; or, The Jibbenainosay*, his most popular and interesting novel, broke with Forrest after repeated difficulties about royalties from his plays, and married Mary Mayer of Philadelphia (whose father was a trustee of the University of Pennsylvania). They had one child. The final two years of the decade saw the publication of a collection of sketches, *Peter Pilgrim*, and Bird's final novel, *The Adventures of Robin Day*.

In the 1830s Bird thus became a man of letters, recognizable if not prominent. As such he met the artist Washington Allston and the sculptor Hiram Powers, became acquainted with fellow writers Richard Henry Dana, Sr., and William Gilmore Simms, and came to the attention of Edgar Allan Poe, who asked him (in 1836) to write an article for the *Southern Literary Messenger*. Together with Edwin Forrest, he traveled extensively throughout the South in 1833, noting in his diary the geographical, economic, and social features of the region, marveling particularly at the wonders of Mammoth Cave in Kentucky. The following year he went to England in an unavailing effort to have *Calavar* published in that country—with the copyright protection that would come with such publication. In 1837 he became Philadelphia editor of the *American Monthly Magazine*, and he published two articles about Mammoth Cave during his tenure at the magazine. After six months, however, he was forced to resign because of ill health. With very little money after years of intense literary activity, he made a futile attempt at farming and then returned to his native New Castle in 1839.

When the Pennsylvania Medical College opened in Philadelphia in 1839, Bird accepted a faculty position out of need rather than commitment. Judging from the reports of his students, he was a successful teacher. But the college closed in 1843, and Bird was again in search of a livelihood. With the support of John M. Clayton, a Whig senator from Delaware, he tried to enter or at least be a part of political life during the final decade of his life. Testifying to his interest in national issues are his perceptive article on the newly established Smithsonian Institution in the *North American Review* (1846) and his campaign biography of Zachary Taylor (1848). Despite recurrent illness, Bird bought an interest in the Philadelphia *North American and United States Gazette* in 1847 (borrowing $30,000 from Senator Clayton to do so) and was an effective and perspicacious editor during the final years of his life. He died in Philadelphia of a brain tumor and was buried in Laurel Hill Cemetery.

Of the many works that came from Bird's pen, *Nick of the Woods* remains the most fascinating. Along with a set of stock characters and the comic bravado of Roaring Ralph Stackpole, this frontier novel features Nathan Slaughter, peaceful Quaker and man of violence, who is driven to avenge the death of his family at the hands of marauding Indians. Bird used his knowledge of medicine in the creation of Nathan Slaughter, who survived a scalping at the time of the massacre and in the course of the narrative undergoes seizures, literally foaming at the mouth, when he is transformed (always in private) from man of peace to vengeful killer, a mysterious figure whom the Indians regard as the Jibbenainosay or the devil, Nick of the woods. Almost fifty years before Robert Louis Stevenson fashioned the story of Dr. Jekyll and Mr. Hyde, Bird had explored the capacity of the civilized man to erupt into savagery. At the conclusion of *Nick of the Woods*, Nathan simply disappears. But his troubling legacy remains to haunt later generations of readers.

• A number of institutions contain documents relating to Bird's work, among them the Charles Patterson Van Pelt Library at the University of Pennsylvania, the Pennsylvania Historical Society in Philadelphia, and the Eleutherian Hills Historical Library in Greenville, Del. Mary Mayer Bird, *Life of Robert Montgomery Bird* (repr. 1945), is a basic source of information. Clement E. Foust, *The Life and Dramatic Works of Robert Montgomery Bird* (1919), not only presents a biographical account of the writer but reprints four of his plays. Curtis Dahl, *Robert Montgomery Bird* (1963), is a solid critical study, complete with an excellent annotated bibliography. For a contrast between James Fenimore Cooper's figure of Leatherstocking and Nathan Slaughter in Bird's *Nick of the Woods*, see Terence Martin, "Surviving on the Frontier: The Doubled Consciousness of Natty Bumppo," *South Atlantic Quarterly* 75 (1976): 447–59. Bird's obituary appears in the Philadelphia *North American and United States Gazette*, 24 Jan. 1854.

TERENCE MARTIN

BIRDSEYE, Clarence (9 Dec. 1886–7 Oct. 1956), inventor and entrepreneur, was born in Brooklyn, New York, the son of Clarence Frank Birdseye, an attorney and legal scholar, and Ada Underwood. When Birdseye was in his teens, his family moved to Montclair, New Jersey, where he completed his high school education. Interested in both food and natural history from an early age, he signed up for a cooking course in high school and trained himself to be a more than competent taxidermist, attempting for a time to earn some income by training others in that skill. Birdseye attended Amherst College on a sporadic basis between 1908 and 1910, but he left before graduating because of financial problems. In an attempt to pay his college bills, he had collected frogs to sell to the Bronx Zoo for feeding their snake population and caught rats in a butcher shop for a Columbia University faculty member who was conducting breeding experiments. Following his departure from Amherst in 1910, he worked as an office boy for an insurance agency in New York, and then briefly as a snow checker for the city's street cleaning department.

During summer vacations in college and on a full-time basis between 1910 and 1912, Birdseye was employed by the U.S. Biological Survey in the Department of Agriculture. Working as a field naturalist, he trapped wolves in Michigan and was involved in various projects in the western states, one of which led to the publication of *Some Common Mammals of Western Montana in Relation to Agriculture and Spotted Fever* (1912).

During his short tenure with the Biological Survey, Birdseye learned something of the fur trade and became involved for a time in the successful marketing of pelts. This led to a 1912 trip to Labrador, where he spent much of the next five years trading in furs and, for a brief period, helped to nurse ailing fishermen on Sir Wilfred Grenfell's hospital ship. During a trip home, he married Eleanor Gannett in August 1915, and she returned to Labrador with him and their five-week-old son a year later. The Birdseyes ultimately had two sons and two daughters.

While in Labrador, Birdseye made a discovery that would lead to his later great success in business. Observing natives fishing in temperatures of fifty degrees below zero, Birdseye noted that the fish froze solid as they left the water and reached the air. When thawed out some months later, Birdseye subsequently observed, certain of the fish showed signs of life. This observation and the need to feed fresh food to his infant child led him to make some preliminary experiments with cabbage, rabbits, ducks, and caribou meat. The results demonstrated that various kinds of meat, if frozen very rapidly and maintained at low temperatures, retained their fresh quality.

When Birdseye returned to the United States with his family in 1917, the American entry into World War I and other employment delayed further experimentation with food freezing for nearly six years. He was briefly a purchasing assistant for the Washington, D.C., offices of Stone and Webster, and then served as a purchasing agent for the U.S. Housing Corporation from 1917 to 1919. For the next three years he was assistant to the president of the U.S. Fisheries Association. Not until 1923 did Birdseye feel able to focus his attention on the experiments that would ultimately lead to a marketable product. His initial investment entailed seven dollars, which he spent on some ice, salt, and an electric fan. Some months later, he transferred his work to a space in a New Jersey icehouse made available to him by a friend. His objective was to avoid freezing foods too slowly, which destroyed their tastefulness and nutritional value.

Birdseye was not the first to come up with the concept of quick-freezing, nor was his company the first in the frozen food business. European companies had been marketing frozen whole fish before World War I. Birdseye's principal innovation was to develop a method of quick-freezing foods at less than fifty degrees below zero after they had been placed in small packages by pressing them rapidly between canvas belts that had been made extremely cold and later, after further experimentation, between metal plates that had been refrigerated. He achieved his first commercial success when he took frozen haddock, placed it in square blocks, and marketed it wrapped in cardboard containers.

With three partners, Birdseye organized the General Seafoods Company in Gloucester, Massachusetts, in 1924. There he continued his research while, beginning in 1925, he sold quick-frozen fish fillets and later expanded to include various meat products. Birdseye also developed a new and smaller freezer, which could more readily be taken to the source of the food he was packaging. In need of refinancing, however, Birdseye in 1929 sold 51 percent of his fresh-frozen process to the Postum Company for $10.75 million, while the Goldman Sachs Trading Corporation paid $12.75 million for the remaining 49 percent. The name Postum was changed to General Foods Corporation, to which Goldman Sachs later sold its interests. Birdseye continued as consultant to the new corporation.

From 1929, Birdseye was associated with Charles F. Seabrook in experimenting with the quick-freezing of vegetables at the latter's commercial farm and packing facilities near Bridgeton, New Jersey. In the challenge to make their products more saleable to the general public, Birdseye and his competitors had adopted more appealing packaging and improved marketing techniques by the early 1930s. In 1930 Birdseye formed Birds Eye Frosted Foods, of which he was president until 1934. His standards were high, and the first products to appear under the Birdseye brand were not made commercially available until 1932. Until 1935 all frozen fruits and vegetables marketed by the Birdseye firm were produced at the Bridgeton plant.

Despite the wealth his frozen food process had brought him, Birdseye continued inventing. Between 1935 and 1938 he was president of the Birdseye Electric Company, where his inventions included a reflector and infrared heat lamps, of which extensive use has been made in the food industry. Later, he also devised a recoilless harpoon for use in whaling and, in 1949, a dehydrated food process, which he termed the "anhydrous method." This latter procedure extracted water from food in a period of an hour and a half in contrast to the eighteen hours required by other methods then in use. The dried food could be packaged in containers the size of cigarette packs. While Birdseye did not pursue the commercial possibilities for this invention, other food-processing firms subsequently did so in the United States and abroad.

From 1953 to 1955 Birdseye worked under contract for a firm in Peru, where he perfected a continuous flow process that successfully translated sugar cane stalks (known as bagasse), straw, and other residual farm products into a paper pulp. This material was later used locally in the manufacture of a variety of paper products. In 1955–1956 he was president of the Process Evaluation and Development Corporation, which was designed to facilitate research and development in the several areas of food preservation in which Birdseye had pioneered.

Birdseye was the author of a number of papers on food preservation and made a number of presentations on the subject. He was active in a variety of technical and other organizations, including the American Chemical Society, the American Society of Refrigerating Engineers, the Institute of Food Technologists (he chaired the northeast section in 1945–1946), the International Association of Milk Sanitarians, and the Boston Horticultural Club.

Although he lacked formal technical training, Birdseye was a keen observer, a highly gifted experimenter, and an able entrepreneur. In 1941 he received an honorary master's degree from Amherst College.

In 1951 Birdseye, who never lost his fascination for nature and who devoted much of his spare time to a longtime interest in horticulture, collaborated with his wife on a small commercial publication, *Growing Woodland Plants*, which imparted some of the lessons he had learned concerning this subject.

While in Peru in the 1950s, Birdseye attributed a heart attack he had suffered there to the high altitudes at which he had been working. He died in New York City of a heart ailment.

• An interview with Clarence Birdseye is in the Food Processing Industry Collection, New York State Oral History Interviews, at the Cornell University Department of Manuscripts and Archives. Also at Cornell are the Harden Franklin Taylor Papers, which contain materials on Birdseye's career. Appreciations of Birdseye and his work include sketches in *Pathfinder*, 24 Oct. 1945; the *New York Post Magazine*, 20 Dec. 1945; H. Campbell, "The Father of Frozen Food," *Country Living*, May 1989; Leicester H. Sherrill, "Quick Freezing of Filleted Fish," *Food Industries* (Oct. 1928); "Quick Frozen Foods," *Fortune*, June 1939; Wambly Bald, "Lion Tidbit to Frozen Food Genius," *Quick Frozen Foods*, Sept. 1954, Mar. 1960, and Feb. 1977; William H. Clark and J. H. S. Moynahan, *Famous Leaders of Industry* (1955); and *Amherst College Biographical Record* (1973). Birdseye's insistence on high standards is mentioned in John L. Hess and Karen Hess, *The Taste of America* (1977). See also "December Almanac," *Life*, Dec. 1993. For a discussion of the takeover of Birdseye's initial enterprise by the Postum Company, see "The Reminiscences of Edwin T. Gibson," Columbia University Oral History Collections (1956). Obituaries are in the *New York Times* and *New York Herald Tribune*, 9 Oct. 1956.

KEIR B. STERLING

BIRGE, Edward Asahel (7 Sept. 1851–9 June 1950), limnologist and president of the University of Wisconsin, was born in Troy, New York, the son of Edward White Birge, a carpenter, farmer, and bookkeeper, and Ann Stevens. The family was Presbyterian and deeply religious. After completing high school, Birge was sent to Williams College from 1869 to 1873, with the expectation that he might become a physician. There he excelled in natural history (earning a B.A. in 1873 and an M.A. in 1876), and one of his professors advised him to study under Louis Agassiz at Harvard's Museum of Comparative Zoology, which he did until Agassiz died in December 1873. Birge then transferred to the Harvard Graduate School, where he remained until December 1875. In January he became an instructor of natural history and curator of the cabinet of the University of Wisconsin. He was hired by the university's president, John Bascom, who had taught English to him at Williams. In 1878 Birge returned to Harvard to receive his doctorate. He was promoted the following year to professor of biology. In 1880 he married a childhood friend, Anna Grant; they had two children. The couple honeymooned in Leipzig, where Birge spent a postdoctoral year studying under the physiologist Carl Ludwig.

Now a well-trained professor, Birge returned to Madison to offer courses in elementary zoology, botany, bacteriology, vertebrate anatomy, physiology, histology, and embryology. Although he had not become a physician himself, these courses were taken by many students who would become physicians. Training such students was not, however, his main interest. He had already developed an interest in invertebrate plankton while at Williams, and because the Madison campus adjoins a good-sized lake, Mendota, he continued to pursue research on plankton and other lake studies as a professor.

Equally interested in administration, he served as chairman of the zoology department from 1879 to 1906, dean of the College of Letters and Science from 1891 to 1918, acting president from 1900 to 1903, president from 1918 to 1925, and was president emeritus from 1925 to 1950. In addition, he served the state of Wisconsin as commissioner of fisheries from 1895 to 1915, director of the Geological and Natural History Survey from 1879 to 1919, and was a member of the Conservation Commission from 1908 to 1915. He was an efficient, hard-working administrator who maintained a formal style that was rather lacking in warmth. His enduring reputation is in limnology.

Although he published scientific papers on the plankton of Lake Mendota in the 1890s, Birge soon became interested in the physical factors—temperature, currents, transparency—and chemical factors—oxygen content, pH, dissolved substances—that influenced the distribution of species within lakes. He was the first American scientist to make extensive studies on the physics and chemistry of lakes, and he was probably more widely known for those investigations than for plankton studies. He took advantage of his administrative positions to advance this work. In 1900 he hired Chancey Juday as biologist with the Wisconsin Geological and Natural History Survey, and they collaborated on research until 1941—long after Birge had retired from the university. Many of their numerous scientific writings appeared either in the *Bulletin* of the Wisconsin Geological and Natural History Survey or in the *Transactions* of the Wisconsin Academy of Sciences, Arts and Letters, over which organization Birge also exerted much influence. Because of his prestige as both a leading scientist and a prominent administrator, he attracted other university scientists and graduate students as collaborators in his joint researches with Juday.

In 1925, after retiring, Birge established a university limnological research station in northern Wisconsin at Trout Lake, where he and Juday conducted much of their research with their collaborators. Its main attraction was its location in the midst of a great variety of pollution-free lakes. Birge hoped that if they conducted extensive surveys on those lakes they would find general principles that would apply to all lakes. Even though he found a few such general principles, Birge became prominent as America's first great limnologist. In 1950 the International Association of Limnology awarded him and Juday its Einar Naumann Medal for outstanding contributions to limnology. Birge died in Madison, Wisconsin. With the assistance of numerous collaborators, especially Juday, Birge not only investigated numerous aspects of the ecology of lakes, he established limnology as a significant field of study in the United States.

• Birge's papers are in the University of Wisconsin Archives. His bibliography is included in the works cited below by Sellery and by Frey. Three of his important studies (two coauthored by Juday) were reprinted in a 1977 volume under the title *Limnology in Wisconsin*. G. C. Sellery, *E. A. Birge: A Memoir* (1956), includes an appraisal of Birge, the limnologist, by C. H. Mortimer. A student of Juday has more broadly surveyed "Wisconsin: The Birge-Juday Era," in *Limnology in North America*, ed. David G. Frey (1963), pp. 3–54. Annamarie L. Beckel and Frank N. Egerton have drawn upon a wider historical background in *Breaking New Waters: A Century of Limnology at the University of Wisconsin* (1987). The most important obituary is John L. Brooks et al., "Edward Asahel Birge (1851–1950)," *Archiv für Hydrobiologie* 45 (1951): 235–43.

FRANK N. EGERTON

BIRGE, Edward Bailey (12 June 1868–16 July 1952), musician and educator, was born in Northampton, Massachusetts, the son of Edward Birge, an amateur musician, and Mary Thompson. Birge began teaching music in the Rhode Island public schools while he was still a student at Brown University. After completing his B.A. in 1891, he was appointed to music teaching positions in Easthampton and West Springfield, Massachusetts. In 1896 he became supervisor of music in the New Haven and New Britain normal schools. Birge's positions in these two Connecticut institutions of higher learning were the first in a series of appointments that progressively widened his sphere of influence as a teacher of teachers. In 1904 Birge received a bachelor of music degree from Yale University, where he had studied with composer and educator Horatio Parker. About this time, Birge began his long association with the Silver Burdett Company as an editor of children's song series.

As director of music in Indianapolis from 1901 to 1921, Birge was theoretically responsible for the musical education of every child in the city's public schools. For two decades he worked diligently to develop a music program that incorporated, and often anticipated, the most desirable aspects of public school music. At a time before specialized music teachers were commonly employed, Birge organized and directed teachers' choruses in an effort to arouse musical interest and to raise the general cultural level of the school system. In 1905 he organized the People's Concert Association, which presented outstanding musical programs and subsequently became one of the most vital forces in the musical life of the city. The People's Chorus was another organization that Birge established to extend the educational process into the community and thus provide a continuous musical program from the first grade through adulthood. Officials in Indiana and Indianapolis acknowledged his leadership by appointing him music chairman of the state and city centennial celebrations.

Through his participation in community affairs, Birge generated strong civic support for his programs in public school music. He developed the elementary program from weekly singing lessons into a coordinated course, in which every child was given daily instruction in music under the supervision of trained specialists. Other outstanding features of his program included ability grouping, special orchestral concerts for children, music testing programs for counseling purposes, music memory contests, an emphasis on appreciation and listening activities, and instrumental classes and orchestras.

Birge was a charter member of the Music Educators National Conference, founded in 1907. For more than forty years, he participated in MENC activities and served in all of its major positions. In 1965 the historian of the conference summarized Birge's devotion and service to the organization as "truly phenomenal."

Birge had already established a complete music curriculum in the Indianapolis secondary schools by the time MENC began exploring possibilities for high school music programs in the second decade of the twentieth century. Birge organized orchestras and bands and introduced courses in music theory, appreciation, and history. His program of awarding school credit for private music lessons received national recognition and acclaim. Birge's successor in the Indianapolis schools, Ernest G. Hesser, noted the high quality of the orchestras, the comprehensive courses in music theory, and the unusually large number of students participating in the music program.

In 1921 Birge was appointed to the faculty of Indiana University as head of the public school music department and director of the university chorus. For the next eighteen years, he trained students to become teachers and administrators and introduced them to major choral masterworks. After his retirement in 1938, Birge remained active in community music, edited and compiled music for children, and maintained a strong interest in public school music trends and developments. He also served as an adviser to MENC, and acted as chairman and, later, chairman emeritus of the editorial board of the *Music Educators Journal*.

Birge's contributions to the professional literature and materials in the field of music education span more than fifty years and include observations and information on practically every aspect of public school music. His writings appeared regularly in publications concerned with school music and music education in general. His *History of Public School Music in the United States* (1928; rev. ed., 1937) provided the first comprehensive account of the music education movement in the United States. Birge brought to every endeavor a consummate artistic taste combined with the highest ideals of character. He considered music a social heritage, an everyday occurrence that enriched the lives of children and adults. Birge's life was appropriately eulogized by his friend Guido Stempel, who referred to him as "music's humanist" (*Bloomington Star-Courier*, 25 July 1952).

• Birge's papers, including manuscripts, programs, and news clippings, are in the Music Education Historical Research Center, University of Maryland, College Park. Other publications by Birge include Birge et al., *A Book of Choruses for High School and Choral Societies* (1923), Will Earhart and Birge, eds., *The Master-Musician Series* (6 vols., 1909–1912), Earhart and Birge, eds., *Songs of Stephen Foster* (1947), Birge et al., eds., *The Music Hour Series* (14 vols., 1929–1938), Birge et al., eds., *New Music Horizons* (9 vols., 1944–1953), and Birge et al., *The Progressive Music Series* (13 vols., 1949–1925). See also Charles Frederick Schwartz, Jr., "Edward Bailey Birge, His Life and Contributions to Music Education" (Ph.D. diss., Indiana Univ., 1966). Obituaries are in the *Music Educators Journal* 39 (Sept. 1952), and the *Bloomington Star-Courier*, 25 July 1952.

CHARLES F. SCHWARTZ, JR.

BIRGE, Raymond Thayer (13 Mar. 1887–22 Mar. 1980), physicist, was born in Brooklyn, New York, the son of John Thaddeus Birge, a river transportation worker, and Caroline S. Raymond. In 1898 he moved with his family to Troy, New York, where his father took a management position with a washing machine manufacturer. After graduating from high school, he studied and taught bookkeeping at the local business college for a year before matriculating at the University of Wisconsin in 1906. Shortly thereafter he developed an interest in physics and received his A.B. in that discipline in 1909. He remained at Wisconsin to continue his studies in spectroscopy, the visual analysis of the spectra of electromagnetic radiation emitted by energized atoms, and received his M.A. and Ph.D. in physics in 1910 and 1914, respectively.

In 1913 Birge married Irene Adelaide Walsh, with whom he had two children. In that same year he became an instructor of physics at Syracuse University and was promoted to assistant professor two years later. He continued his work with spectroscopy by concentrating on the mathematical structure of band series, groups of spectral lines spaced so closely to one another that they appear to be wide bands. This avenue of investigation led him to calculate the precise value of the Rydberg constant, a number developed in 1890 by the Swedish physicist J. R. Rydberg to determine the wavelength and electromagnetic frequency of a given spectral line.

In 1918 Birge accepted a position at the University of California at Berkeley as an instructor of physics, and for the next fifteen years he devoted his research primarily to studying phenomena related to band series. He became interested in the spectral analysis of diatomic molecules, and in 1926, the same year he was promoted to full professor, he and the visiting German physicist Hertha Sponer devised a method to determine the amount of heat generated when these molecules dissociate into their constituent atoms. By 1929 he had derived from his observations of band series a complete set of molecular constants for diatomic molecules. This work led him to join the search for isotopes, forms of a chemical element with virtually identical physical properties but slightly different atomic masses. That same year he and the American physicist A. S. King used band series analysis to discover carbon-13, an isotope that possesses more mass than the typical carbon atom. In 1931 he and D. H. Menzel attempted to explain variations in the spectral line for hydrogen by postulating the existence of hydrogen-2, an isotope with more mass than the typical hydrogen atom and one that they estimated could be found approximately once among every 6,000 hydrogen atoms. Their postulation was verified later that same year by the American chemist Harold C. Urey, who discovered hydrogen-2, known today as deuterium.

As his work with spectral analysis continued to yield important results, Birge became increasingly aware that many of the day's accepted physical formulae resulted in theoretically expected values that differed significantly from laboratory observations. He attacked this problem on two fronts. Between 1924 and 1947 he published several papers on the value of least squares approximation, a tool of numerical analysis that is particularly useful for arriving at the linear function that describes experimental data most accurately. He also undertook a numerical analysis of the fundamental physical constants, such as the speed of light, the mechanical equivalent of heat, the charge of the electron, Avogadro's number, and Planck's constant, in an effort to arrive at the most precise values possible. In 1929 he published the results of this analysis in "Probable Values of the General Physical Constants" (*Reviews of Modern Physics* 1: 1–73). His values for these and other constants were so accurate that they went unchallenged until the late 1940s, when computers were employed to arrive at even more precise values.

Birge played a major role in the development of Berkeley's Department of Physics into one of the most important centers for physical experimentation in the country. In 1926 he and Leonard Loeb, a fellow Berkeley physicist, assumed the responsibility of recruiting new faculty members. In short order they succeeded in bringing to Berkeley a number of top-quality researchers, such as Ernest O. Lawrence, inventor of the cyclotron and winner of the 1939 Nobel Prize for Physics; and J. Robert Oppenheimer, director of the Manhattan Project, which resulted in the development of the first atomic bomb. In 1933 Birge became department chairman, a position he held until his retirement in 1955. During his tenure the number of faculty members and graduate students in the department quadrupled. His biggest challenge, which he met successfully, came during World War II when the department became involved in the Manhattan Project and enrolled large numbers of military personnel in war-related undergraduate physics courses in addition to its normal complement of students, without an increase in either faculty or facilities.

Birge was elected to the National Academy of Sciences in 1932. He played an active role in the American Physical Society and served as secretary of its Pacific Coast Division from 1942 to 1947, vice president in 1954, and president in 1955. In 1964 Berkeley's newly constructed physics building was named in his honor. He died in Berkeley.

Birge contributed to the advance of American physics in several ways. His pioneering studies in spectroscopy led to the discovery of two important isotopes as well as a better understanding of certain molecular behaviors. His interest in mathematics contributed to a more precise calculation of a number of important physical constants. His work as an administrator contributed significantly to the reputation of Berkeley's

physics department as one of the most important in the United States.

• Birge's papers are located in Berkeley's Bancroft Library. A biography, including a selected bibliography, is A. Carl Helmholz, "Raymond Thayer Birge," National Academy of Sciences, *Biographical Memoirs* 59 (1984): 73–84. An obituary is in *Physics Today*, Aug. 1980, pp. 68–70.

CHARLES W. CAREY, JR.

BIRKBECK, Morris (23 Jan. 1764–4 June 1825), pioneer and author, was born in Settle, Yorkshire, the son of Morris Birkbeck, apparently a businessman, and Hannah Bradford, both of whom were Quakers. In 1774 the Birkbecks moved to the hamlet of Wanborough, Surrey, where a community of Friends had been established and where Young Birkbeck was raised. He became a farmer, and by 1794 he was operating a 1,500-acre estate, which he leased. A slim, muscular, bald-headed man, Birkbeck was energetic, reflective, idealistic, and even-tempered. Frequently innovative, he was the first breeder of merino sheep in England. In 1794 he married Prudence Bush, also a Quaker, of nearby Wandsworth. She died in 1804, leaving him with seven children.

Ten years later Birkbeck traveled through France with his friend George Flower. His journal of that excursion became his first book, *Notes on a Journey through France* (1814). It reveals a fair-minded observer with broad interests, approving the social changes fostered by the French Revolution.

Returning to England, Birkbeck found himself unhappy in a country that denied him a vote, forced him to support an established church, and restricted his opportunities. So, in 1817 he emigrated to America, where he joined George Flower, his partner in a frontier settlement plan, and traveled to Illinois. Birkbeck bought 1,440 acres located forty-five miles north of Shawneetown; Flower bought a similar adjoining parcel, and in 1818 they laid out the village of Wanborough. The partners soon quarreled, however, and Flower established a separate community, Albion, a few miles away.

Together, the two communities were known as the English Settlement. Although neither hamlet prospered in the long run, the venture attracted considerable attention, chiefly because of Birkbeck's promotional efforts. He was an early advocate of farming the prairie, recommended scientific tilling of the soil, and promoted cattle raising. In the early 1820s he was president of the state's first agricultural society.

Birkbeck's two most important books record his immigrant experience. His journal of the trip from Virginia to southeastern Illinois, *Notes on a Journey in America* (1817), is a vivid chronicle of Birkbeck and Flower's search for a suitable place to establish their community, their version of the good society, devoted to freedom and prosperity. Birkbeck closes this book with a statement of their plans for the "colony" and invites interested readers to join them. His next book, *Letters from Illinois* (1818), describes the cultural condition of the frontier and reveals his reasons for emigrating. Taken together, the two books depict a man in the process of relocating himself in "a new country" (i.e., an undeveloped state) and redefining himself, psychologically, as an American. As he says in Letter XVI, "Liberty is no subject of dispute or speculation among us Back-woods men: it is the very atmosphere we breathe. I now find myself the fellow-citizen of about nine millions of persons, who are affording a sober and practical confutation of those base men, who . . . have dared to call this unalienable birthright of every human being a visionary scheme."

Both books were published in England and America, and they quickly went through several editions. Birkbeck produced two other slim volumes, *Extracts from a Supplementary Letter from the Illinois* (1819) and *An Address to the Farmers of Great Britain* (1822), and they also made emigration seem attractive to his former countrymen. Some of Birkbeck's contemporaries—notably journalist William Cobbett—criticized him for being too positive about his experience as a settler, but his enthusiastic depiction of a new beginning on the American frontier impressed thousands of readers and planted the American dream firmly on Illinois soil.

Birkbeck also struggled to maintain freedom in Illinois. During the early 1820s he vigorously opposed the drive for a constitutional convention that would have allowed slavery in Illinois, instead supporting the leadership of his friend Governor Edward Coles. Birkbeck's antislavery essays, published in 1823 under the pseudonym "Jonathan Freeman," appeared as letters to the editor in the *Illinois Gazette*.

Although Governor Coles appointed Birkbeck secretary of state late in 1824, he served only a few months. A proslavery majority in the state senate refused to confirm the appointment. On his return from a visit to social theorist Robert Owen at Harmony, Indiana, Birkbeck was drowned while crossing the Fox River.

Among students of Illinois history, Birkbeck remains well known as an early colonizer and antislavery advocate. *Notes on a Journey in America* and *Letters from Illinois* have been praised for depicting Birkbeck's quest to establish a community where the ideals of liberty and equality could be realized and for portraying his transformation into an American. He is regarded as the earliest significant Illinois author.

• *Notes on a Journey in America* was reprinted in 1966, and *Letters from Illinois* was reprinted in 1970, with an introduction by Robert M. Sutton. Charles Boewe prints selections from Birkbeck, Flower, and other residents of and visitors to the English Settlement in *Prairie Albion: An English Settlement in Pioneer Illinois* (1962). Studies that discuss Birkbeck include two volumes in the *Centennial History of Illinois*—Solon J. Buck, *Illinois in 1818* (1917), and Theodore Calvin Pease, *The Frontier State, 1818–1848* (1919)—as well as Jane Rodman, "The English Settlement in Southern Illinois, 1815–1825," *Indiana Magazine of History* 43 (1947): 329–62, and Gladys Scott Thomson, *A Pioneer Family: The Birkbecks in Illinois 1818–1827* (1953). The writings of Birkbeck and Flower are discussed by James Hurt in "Reality and the Picture of Imagination: The Literature of the English Prairie," *Great Lakes Review* 7 (1981): 1–24.

JOHN E. HALLWAS

BIRKHOFF, George David (21 Mar. 1884–12 Nov. 1944), mathematician, was born in Overisel, Michigan, the son of David Birkhoff, a physician, and Jane Gertrude Droppers. During much of his youth, George lived with his family in Chicago, where he studied at the Lewis Institute from 1896 to 1902 and attended the University of Chicago for one year. He then went to Harvard University, where he received a bachelor's degree in mathematics in 1905 and a master's degree in 1906. Birkhoff's mathematical interest and skill were revealed at a young age when in 1901 he began a correspondence with mathematician Harry S. Vandiver on a problem in number theory that resulted in the publication in 1904 of a joint paper in the *Annals of Mathematics*. He also presented results in analysis to the American Mathematical Society in 1904, prior to his return to the University of Chicago in the fall of 1905 in pursuit of a Ph.D. in mathematics. Birkhoff graduated in 1907 with a dissertation on asymptotic problems of ordinary differential equations.

After receiving his doctorate, Birkhoff spent two years in Madison as an instructor in mathematics at the University of Wisconsin. While there he met and married Margaret Elizabeth Grafius in 1908, with whom he had three children. In 1909 Birkhoff went to Princeton University as a preceptor in mathematics. He was promoted to a professorship there in 1911 but accepted a call to Harvard as an assistant professor in 1912. Harvard remained Birkhoff's academic home for the rest of his life. He was promoted to professor in 1919 and was named Perkins Professor in 1932. Birkhoff also served the university as dean of the Faculty of Arts and Sciences from 1935 to 1939.

Birkhoff's contemporaries held his work in the highest esteem; one prominent colleague memorialized him as "the leading American mathematician of his day." Birkhoff's research ranged over several important mathematical fields; he published nearly 200 papers and several monographs during the forty years of his career. His doctoral work on asymptotic problems of ordinary linear differential equations marks the beginning of one of three principal fields of Birkhoff's mathematical activity. Subsequently he extended that work to the study of a range of related areas, including expansion and boundary value problems, Sturm-Liouville theorems, difference equations, and a fundamental subject in the study of linear differential equations known as the generalized Riemann problem. The latter work was especially characterized by Birkhoff's skillful combined use of formal algebraic methods and numerical analysis.

The second major subject of Birkhoff's research, dynamics, includes perhaps his most significant contributions to mathematics. He began his work in this area in 1912 by extending the results of Poincaré on the "three-body problem." This work on a classic problem in celestial mechanics sought to show a connection between geometric conditions and the solutions of problems of motion. Among many important papers Birkhoff published in this area, "The Restricted Problem of Three Bodies" (1915) won the Querini-Stampalia Prize of the Royal Venice Institute of Science, and his "Dynamical Systems with Two Degrees of Freedom" (1917) received the first Bôcher Prize of the American Mathematical Society in 1923. His work on dynamics went far beyond the resolution of Poincaré's geometric problem to a generalized qualitative dynamical theory. For this work he was also awarded the annual prize of the American Association for the Advancement of Science in 1926, and his paper, "Nouvelles Récherches sur les Systèmes Dynamiques" received the biennial prize from the Pontifical Academy of Sciences in Rome in 1935. Birkhoff's discovery of what has come to be known as his "ergodic theorem" in 1931–1932 is his most well-known contribution of dynamics. This theory, which resolved in principle one of the fundamental problems arising in the theory of gases and statistical mechanics, has been influential not only in dynamics itself but also in probability theory, group theory, and functional analysis.

Much of Birkhoff's other work can be grouped in a third category, the applications of mathematics. Birkhoff pursued a somewhat idiosyncratic ideal of applying mathematical methods to fields including physics, aesthetics, and ethics. His work in mathematical physics included a serious interest in relativity theory, which resulted in the publication of a monograph (with R. E. Langer), *Relativity and Modern Physics*, in 1923 and later in some speculative research on a gravitational theory of his own. He was equally serious in his interest in applying mathematics outside the sciences. In 1933 he published a book documenting his ideas about the role of mathematics in art and music, *Aesthetic Measure*; in 1942 he published an article on the application of mathematics to ethics.

Birkhoff was not only a premier mathematical researcher. He also became a leader of the American mathematical community and displayed "a sort of religious devotion" to advancing mathematics in America (Veblen, p. 284). In addition, he maintained strong contacts within the international mathematical community, as was evidenced by his reports to the International Education Board and the Rockefeller Foundation in 1925 on the state of mathematics in Europe and opportunities for investment in mathematical research. He was also a member of the National Research Fellowship Board from 1925 to 1937, a position that gave him great influence on the development of younger scholars. Birkhoff was editor of the *Annals of Mathematics* from 1911 to 1913, and of the *Transactions of the American Mathematical Society* from 1920 to 1925. He received numerous honors, including membership in the National Academy of Sciences (1918), the American Philosophical Society, and the American Academy of Arts and Sciences, as well as thirteen honorary degrees. He was made an officer of the French Foreign Legion of Honor in 1936. He served

as president of the American Mathematical Society in 1925 and the American Association for the Advancement of Science in 1937. He was a foreign member of the Académie des Sciences de Paris, Accademia dei Lincei, Pontifical Academy, Circolo Matematico di Palermo, Royal Danish Academy of Sciences and Letters, Göttingen Academy of Sciences, Royal Institute of Bologna, Edinburgh Mathematical Society (honorary), London Mathematical Society (honorary), and the National Academy of Sciences of Lima, Peru. Birkhoff was selected to head the International Mathematical Congress in 1940, but it was cancelled due to war. He also worked to help establish the important American mathematical abstracting journal, *Mathematical Reviews*.

Birkhoff died at his home in Cambridge, Massachusetts. Recognized as "first among equals" (Stone, p. 71) in his generation of mathematical leaders in America, he left important legacies in both mathematical research and in the development of the mathematical community in America.

• A large collection of Birkhoff's papers, correspondence, bibliographies, and other materials is housed at Harvard University. His collected works were published as *Collected Mathematical Works of George David Birkhoff* (3 vols., 1950). Valuable sources on Birkhoff's life and work, all written by colleagues or students, include Marston Morse, "George David Birkhoff and his Mathematical Work," *Bulletin of the American Mathematical Society* 52 (1946); and Oswald Veblen, "George David Birkhoff (1884–1944)," *Yearbook of the American Philosophical Society* (1946). An account of Birkhoff's career to 1938, including a full bibliography of his works to that date, appears in Raymond Archibald, *Semicentennial History of the American Mathematical Society, 1888–1938* (1938). A personal assessment of Birkhoff's work and that of his contemporaries can be found in George David Birkhoff, "Fifty Years of American Mathematics," in *Semicentennial Addresses of the American Mathematical Society*, ed. Raymond Archibald (1938). An obituary is in the *New York Times*, 13 Nov. 1944.

LOREN J. BUTLER

BIRNEY, Alice Josephine McLellan (19 Oct. 1858–20 Dec. 1907), reformer, was born in Marietta, Georgia, the daughter of Leander C. McLellan, a small-scale cotton planter, and Harriet Tatem. The family soon moved to nearby Atlanta, where she enrolled in private school. She attended high school in Marietta and then, after teaching school for a short time in Atlanta, spent a year (1875–1876) at Mount Holyoke Seminary in Massachusetts. In 1879 she married Alonzo J. White, Jr., a lawyer then serving as city sheriff in his native Charleston, South Carolina. Alice dreamed of becoming a doctor, but in November 1880 her husband died of pleuropneumonia. A few months later Alice gave birth to their daughter, Alonsita, and returned to Atlanta to live with her family.

During the late 1880s Alice White tried to establish herself in New York City by selling advertising; failing, she returned to Atlanta. There she met Theodore Weld Birney, a lawyer and the grandson of the famed abolitionist James G. Birney. After marrying in 1892, the couple made their home in suburban Chevy Chase, Maryland. During the next three years they had two daughters.

As the wife of a prosperous and well-connected lawyer, Birney enjoyed all the advantages of a society matron, but her concern for her duties as a mother opened wider horizons in her life. Seeking advice on child-rearing, she learned that there was little authoritative information available for the general reader. She began to read widely on the subject, studying with particular care the works of psychologist G. Stanley Hall, philosopher Herbert Spencer, and the pioneer of the kindergarten idea, Friedrich Froebel. Mothers needed to be educated, she felt, but beyond that, the whole nation had to be awakened to "the supreme importance of the child." How to dramatize these ideas? Birney decided that there should be a national organization of mothers, starting with a convention in Washington. In 1895 she presented her proposal to a group of women at a summer session in Chautauqua, New York. When they responded with enthusiasm, she began to promote the idea among educational and civic leaders.

Early in her campaign, Birney had the good fortune to win the support of the wealthy Phoebe Apperson Hearst, who was then living in Washington. Hearst, who was already active in the kindergarten movement, set only one condition on her participation: men must be allowed to join, too. When Birney agreed, Hearst assumed most of the financial responsibility for launching the new organization. She also generated support among her friends, persuading Frances Cleveland, the wife of President Grover Cleveland, to hold a reception at the White House for those who attended the initial meeting, which was to be held on 17 February 1897. On the appointed day Birney and Hearst expected an attendance of about fifty. Instead, the convention attracted more than 2,000, including at least a few men. The unexpected turnout forced a frenzy of last-minute arrangements; the meetings were hastily moved to larger halls, while many overflow guests were accommodated in private homes. The event drew wide press coverage and culminated in the creation of the organization Birney had envisioned, the National Congress of Mothers, with Birney herself as president.

Various approaches were discussed at the founding meeting; some participants seemed to have an unclear view of the direction that the new organization should take. But Birney guided the congress firmly along the lines she believed most important. These were laid out in April 1897 in the congress's "Declaration of Principles." Groups of mothers would be organized in communities all across America to study child development, support local child welfare programs, and encourage improvement in their children's schools. "It is proposed to have the Congress consider subjects bearing upon the better and broader moral and physical, as well as mental training of the young," wrote Birney. "Of special importance will be the subject of the means of developing in children characteristics which will elevate and ennoble them." The mothers'

clubs were to be open to all, regardless of race, religion, or social status. Child-care arrangements would make it easier for poor women to attend; at the same time, upper-class participants would find their lives enriched. They hoped that, in time, the mothers' congress idea might spread to other countries and help foster world peace.

Within months of her organization's triumphant first meeting, Birney faced tragedy in her own life. Her husband fell gravely ill and died in July 1897. A widow once again, Birney threw herself into her work, traveling tirelessly to promote the creation of local mothers' clubs, as well as state-level affiliates. In the fall of 1897 Birney attended the organizing meeting of the first state group, the New York Assembly of Mothers. Over the next three years seven more states followed suit. By 1899 the National Congress of Mothers had 50,000 members. Birney placed particular emphasis on the need to build bridges between parents and teachers. Mothers' clubs, she said, should address "the physical and mental evils resulting from some of the present methods of our schools and the advantages to follow from a closer relation between the influence of the home and that of institutions of learning" (quoted in Robinson, p. 314). Birney's focus on children's schooling laid the groundwork for her organization's later evolution, first into the National Congress of Mothers and Parent-Teacher Associations (1908), and ultimately into the National Parent-Teacher Association (PTA).

At the conclusion of her five-year term as president in 1902, Birney resigned her office because of poor health. But she remained deeply interested in parenting and wrote a number of articles on the subject for *Delineator* magazine; these were later collected in her book *Childhood* (1905), for which G. Stanley Hall wrote the introduction. Birney died of cancer at her home in Chevy Chase.

Birney suffered repeated reversals in her life: she was forced to give up her dream of becoming a doctor, she failed to establish a foothold in New York, she lost one husband and then another after only a few years of marriage, and finally she contracted terminal cancer before she was fifty. Yet working within the accepted framework of her day, which placed its strongest emphasis on the maternal role of the woman, Birney built a national organization that addressed an issue she saw as central to the well-being of society. Her organization survives, though in altered form, nearly a century after her death.

• Birney left no personal papers, but clippings about her career are to be found in the Atlanta Public Library and in the papers of Myrta Lockett Avary, Atlanta Historical Society. For accounts of her life, see National Congress of Parents and Teachers, *Golden Jubilee History, 1897–1947* (1947); Helen C. Bennett and Alice D. Miller, "Making the Most of Motherhood," *Good Housekeeping*, Nov. 1913; Hannah K. Schoff, "Memories of Mrs. Theodore W. Birney," *Child Welfare*, Feb. 1930; Alonsita Walker, "My Mother," *National Parent-Teacher*, Feb. 1943; "The Work of the Mothers' Congress and Clubs," *Coming Age*, Sept. 1899, pp. 247–53; and Judith

Robinson, *The Hearsts: An American Dynasty* (1991). Obituaries are in the *New York Times* and the *Washington Post*, both 21 Dec. 1907, and in the *Atlanta Constitution* and *Atlanta Journal*, 22 Dec. 1907.

SANDRA OPDYCKE

BIRNEY, David Bell (29 May 1825–18 Oct. 1864), Union major general, was born in Huntsville, Alabama, the son of James Gillespie Birney, a lawyer. His mother's name is unknown. Birney's father, although a slaveholder, became an internationally known abolitionist and moved his family north when Birney was thirteen, eventually settling in Cincinnati. Birney received his education at Andover, Massachusetts, then returned to Cincinnati, where he entered business. When his company failed, Birney accepted a position as an agent for P. Choteau & Company in Upper Saginaw, Michigan, where he also studied law. Finding the Michigan climate too harsh, in 1848 Birney removed to Philadelphia, where in eight years he rose from clerk to chief manager and director of a mercantile agency. In 1856 he joined the Philadelphia bar and developed a successful law practice.

Birney's military experience prior to the Civil War was limited to service in two amateurish and ceremonial Philadelphia militia units. Abraham Lincoln's November 1860 election, however, motivated Birney to study military science in preparation for the war that he felt was likely.

Birney's militia outfit formed the nucleus for the Twenty-third Regiment of Pennsylvania Volunteers, a three-month regiment formed in April 1861. Birney served as its lieutenant colonel and saw action on 2 July 1861 at Falling Waters, Virginia. Upon the regiment's expiration in July, Birney returned to Philadelphia and recruited the new Twenty-third Pennsylvania Infantry, largely at his own expense. He led the regiment back to Virginia as its colonel.

Birney's promotion to brigadier general on 17 February 1862 originated primarily from his strong Republican political connections and the beliefs inherited from his father. His brigade of Maine and New York troops served in Brigadier General Philip Kearney's division of the Third Corps. Birney led his brigade during the Peninsula campaign, the Seven Days' battles, and the Second Manassas campaign. His corps commander, Major General Samuel P. Heintzelman, placed Birney under arrest following the battle of Fair Oaks for "halting his command a mile from the enemy." A court-martial exonerated Birney of this unfounded charge.

Following Kearny's death at the battle of Chantilly on 1 September 1862, Birney assumed command of the division. The Third Corps did not see action at Antietam, but Birney's division played a controversial role at the battle of Fredericksburg on 13 December 1862. Assigned to support an attack by Major General George G. Meade on the south end of the field, Birney's troops did not arrive in time to exploit the only Union success at that otherwise disastrous engagement. Meade complained bitterly of Birney's refusal to move forward (he was waiting for orders from his superiors), but other Union commanders did not endorse Meade's harsh judgment.

Birney performed well at the battle of Chancellorsville, cementing a close relationship with his immediate superior, Major General Daniel E. Sickles. The War Department rewarded Birney for his Chancellorsville generalship with promotion to major general to date from 20 May 1863. When Sickles fell seriously wounded on 2 July 1863 at the battle of Gettysburg, Birney temporarily assumed command of the Third Corps, despite suffering two slight wounds himself.

When the Army of the Potomac was consolidated in the spring of 1864, the Third Corps dissolved, and Birney's division transferred to the Second Corps. Birney led his men during the bloody Overland campaign of May and June 1864, particularly distinguishing himself during the famous fighting at the Spotsylvania "Mule Shoe" on 12 May. He led the Second Corps between 18 and 27 June at Petersburg, while the permanent corps commander, Major General Winfield S. Hancock, recuperated from wounds.

On 23 July 1864 Lieutenant General Ulysses S. Grant named Birney commander of the Tenth Corps in the Army of the James, then maneuvering against Richmond from the south and east. Birney led the corps during the operations at Deep Bottom in August and against Fort Harrison in September.

General Birney fell ill with malaria in the autumn and returned to Philadelphia on 11 October. He died in his home a week later. He had married Marie Antoinette Jennison; they had six children.

Birney's substantial political influence, cold, covert personality, and occasionally controversial relationship with fellow officers rendered him less than universally popular. He sided with his friend Sickles in the latter's bitter denunciation of Meade after Gettysburg, a stance that may have cost him command of the Third Corps. His ambition for advancement sometimes appalled his troops, who saw themselves disproportionately volunteered for dangerous missions. On balance, Birney proved to be a competent, brave, and energetic military leader, one of a minority of high-level Union officers whose prime motivation for fighting was emancipation of the slaves.

• A number of Birney's papers are in the James G. Birney Manuscripts at the University of Michigan Library. For information on Birney's Civil War career, including his military correspondence and battle reports, consult the index to *The War of the Rebellion: A Compilation of the Official Records of the Union and Confederate Armies* (128 vols., 1880–1901). The only biography is by Birney's law partner and close friend, Oliver Wilson Davis, *Life of David Bell Birney, Major-General United States Volunteers* (1867; repr. 1987). Obituaries are in the *Philadelphia Evening Telegraph*, 19 Oct. 1864, and the *New York Herald*, 20 Oct. 1864.

A. WILSON GREENE

BIRNEY, James Gillespie (4 Feb. 1792–18 Nov. 1857), lawyer and reformer, was born near Danville, Kentucky, the son of James Birney and Martha Reed (both of Irish extraction), owners of a prosperous plantation worked by slave labor. When James was three, his mother died, leaving him and an infant sister to be raised by a widowed aunt who came from Ireland. His aunt's opposition to slavery was one of the early influences on James's thinking, although he became a slave master himself at age six when he was given a slave his own age, Michael, as a birthday present. Michael remained with him until Birney's mid-life conversion to the abolitionist cause; he was then freed, given back wages for his years of service, and set up in a livery stable business. When James was seven his father and grandfather Reed both backed an unsuccessful attempt to write an emancipation clause into the state constitution.

While a student at Transylvania College in Lexington (1803–1805), one of Birney's teachers, Robert Hamilton Bishop, was one of the state's earliest outspoken opponents of slavery. At the College of New Jersey (later Princeton), from which he was graduated in 1810, its president, Samuel Stanhope Smith, preached the unity of the races, and Professor John MacLean spoke vigorously against enslaving fellow human beings. Birney himself participated in student debates on the subject. While in Philadelphia reading law (1810–1814) in the office of Alexander J. Dallas (later secretary of the U.S. Treasury under President James Madison), he heard the Quaker debates over slavery while enjoying friendship with a white antislavery Quaker, Abraham L. Pennock, and a prominent black businessman, James Forten, who employed both black and white workers and used his fortune to finance the antislavery cause.

Birney returned to Kentucky, where in 1816 he married Agatha McDowell; they had eleven children, five of whom died in infancy or early childhood. Birney was elected to the state legislature, served as one of the original trustees of Centre College, and took an active role in civic affairs. In 1818 he acquired land for a cotton plantation near Huntsville, Alabama, and increased the number of his slaves to forty-three. He believed as did his father and so many other planters that unless slavery was legally outlawed, one had to make the best of the "peculiar institution."

Although not a member of the Alabama Constitutional Convention, Birney was a leader in advocating that the new document should include a clause empowering the state legislature to prevent the commercial slave trade and also to provide for emancipation if the owners consented or were compensated. Treatment of slaves was to be regulated, and they were to be given some rights, such as trial by jury for certain crimes.

Birney, who was elected to the first state legislature in 1819, played a pivotal role in formulating procedures for the state's judicial system. Unfortunately, his unpopular support for his old family friend Henry Clay against Andrew Jackson, led to his defeat in the next election. Financial problems after the panic of 1819, compounded by an extravagant lifestyle, forced Birney to sell his plantation. His slaves, except for Mi-

chael and his family, were sold to a friend, and Birney returned to the practice of law.

Birney's lifelong concern about education continued in Alabama, where he became a trustee of Greene Academy in Huntsville. As mayor of the city, a post to which he was elected in 1829, Birney appointed a commission to establish a primary school for indigent children to be operated on the then-popular Lancastrian system. As a trustee of the University of Alabama he drew up the plan adopted in 1830 to admit as many students as possible free of charge, with allocation of funds on a county basis, a plan copied from Thomas Jefferson's for Virginia in which merit was to be determined by examination. His concern for the underprivileged was further expressed in service as counsel for the Cherokee Indians. His conversion to the Presbyterian church greatly influenced Birney's participation in reform causes. He became active in the Bible Society, the Tract Society, the Sunday school movement and, as mayor, used his political leadership to promote regulation of the sale of intoxicating beverages in Huntsville.

In 1832 Birney became an agent for the American Colonization Society, whose main goal was to arrange and finance the emigration of freed slaves to the new colony of Liberia in West Africa. In the spring of 1833 he supervised the departure of the *Ajax* from New Orleans, bound for Liberia with 150 settlers. He wrote essays, published in the Huntsville newspapers, aimed at winning further public support; instead they stirred up a vigorous local debate over the whole question of slaveholding.

Emancipation began to supersede colonization in Birney's thinking but, moderate that he was, he believed it would have to be a gradual process. He was realistic enough to see little chance of convincing many of his fellow slaveholders in the deep South. Prospects would be more favorable in the border states, he reasoned, and by the autumn of 1833 he returned to Kentucky, where his name ensured him a larger following. His plantation slaves had been sold before Birney's conversion; those who remained, including Michael's family of five and a small girl Birney had rescued from a cruel owner, were taken back to Kentucky and freed.

Shortly after his arrival in Kentucky, Birney joined with like-minded friends to form the Kentucky Society for the Gradual Relief of the State of Slavery, but by then he was considering the merits of "immediatism" as proclaimed by the American Anti-Slavery Society and especially in the debates at Lane Seminary in Cincinnati led by Theodore Dwight Weld in the spring of 1834. The result was that he resigned from the Kentucky gradualist society as well as the American Colonization Society. Two steps publicized his new position: the emancipation of his own slaves and the publication of his *Letter on Colonization, Addressed to the Rev. Thornton J. Mills, Corresponding Secretary of the Kentucky Colonization Society*, in which he argued that colonization was based more on the prejudices and self-interest of whites than on benevolent feelings toward blacks.

The attempt to find recruits for abolition proved disappointing. The churches could not be relied on to back it, Clay refused support, no emancipation bill succeeded in the legislature, and public agitation in the form of protest meetings and threats of violence (including death threats) thwarted Birney's efforts to publish an antislavery newspaper. He decided to move to Ohio, where despite death threats, he began publishing the *Philanthropist*. In the summer of 1836 a mob destroyed his press and extended its fury by ransacking the black residential section of Cincinnati. Although publication was resumed, Birney continued to feel the effects of public disfavor, reinforced when he was arrested and fined in 1837 for harboring a fugitive slave as a household servant. The verdict was eventually overturned. Meanwhile Birney and Salmon P. Chase used the opportunity to collaborate in laying the legal foundation for a subsequent decision on the unconstitutionality of the fugitive slave laws as they operated in Ohio.

Birney's criticism of the colonization society had attracted national attention; his standing up to the Cincinnati mobs further enhanced his reputation. He had become a champion of freedom of the press, and he was investigating the constitutionality of the state's fugitive slave laws. The American Anti-Slavery Society was eager to enlist Birney as one of its officers, and he moved his family to New York in 1837. Birney's tenure as corresponding secretary of the society was marked by growing disagreements between the New York and the Boston (Garrisonian) factions, which led to their formal separation in 1840. He opposed granting women equal rights to vote and hold office in antislavery organizations.

In 1840 Birney was nominated as the candidate of the Liberty party for the presidency of the United States, with Thomas Earle, a Philadelphia Quaker, as his running mate. He made no attempt to conduct the usual type of campaign; he was, in fact, in London as a delegate to the World Anti-Slavery Convention from May until after the November election. He polled only 7,059 votes.

At the London convention Birney, the highest-ranking American delegate, was named a vice president. As a former slaveholder he was an object of special interest. After the convention he, fellow delegate Henry B. Stanton, and British abolitionist John Scoble made lecture tours throughout the north of England, Scotland, and Ireland. Birney's important pamphlet, first published in England in 1840, *The American Churches: The Bulwarks of American Slavery*, was distributed to leading British churchmen.

Birney's wife had died in 1838, and in 1840 he married Elizabeth Fitzhugh of Geneseo, New York, a niece of well-known abolitionist Gerrit Smith. They had one child, a son. But personal financial problems as well as difficulty in raising money for the newly organized American and Foreign Anti-Slavery Society made it imperative that the Birneys leave New York. By November 1841 the Birney family was settling in Lower Saginaw (now Bay City), Michigan, where along with resuming his law practice, Birney worked as a land agent.

Although northern Michigan in the 1840s was not an ideal location for the Liberty party's nominee for the 1844 presidential election, Birney continued to speak and write. During this period his major contribution was his legal opinion on the *Creole* case, in which Birney argued that once a ship carrying slaves left the coastal waters of a state, it was under the exclusive jurisdiction of the federal government. Therefore, he argued, claiming those slaves as property under Virginia law was invalid. Congressman Joshua Giddings of Ohio presented Birney's arguments in a set of resolutions that were hotly debated in the House, with the result that Giddings was censured and resigned. But he was rewarded with reelection by his antislavery district.

In 1842 Birney ran on an antislavery ticket for the governorship of Michigan. Just prior to the 1844 presidential election, in which he was again the Liberty party candidate, he was on a speaking tour in the East when a letter purporting to be written by him was published, which "proved" him to be a secret Democrat. This "Garland Forgery," named for Jerome B. Garland of Michigan, the purported author of the letter, was later attributed to the Whigs, and may or may not have cost him votes. His vote total, though considerably higher than in 1840, was still only 2 percent of the national popular vote. His political career was ended and his antislavery activities were severely curtailed the following year when a horse-riding accident left him partially paralyzed. Nevertheless, he continued writing on political and constitutional issues regarding slavery.

Birney had been eager and optimistic in each move he made in life, then disappointed, sometimes bitterly. Only the final transplantation gave him peace: He died in a communal settlement in Eagleswood, New Jersey, where he had lived out his days in friendship with old antislavery colleagues.

As a former slaveholder Birney spoke with the voice of authority on race and slavery; as a lawyer he spoke as a moderate on constitutional issues. For him politics was a means to an end, never an end in itself. He died realizing that moderation on the race issue would not prevail but that civil war would tear the nation apart before emancipation could be proclaimed.

• Birney's papers are in the Manuscript Division, Library of Congress; the Boston Public Library; and the William L. Clements Library, University of Michigan, where his major pamphlets are also located. For his correspondence, see Dwight Lowell Dumond, ed., *The Letters of James Gillespie Birney, 1831–1857* (2 vols., 1938). The standard biography is Betty Fladeland, *James Gillespie Birney: Slaveholder to Abolitionist* (1955). Other biographical information can be found in Beriah Green, *Sketches of the Life and Writings of James Gillespie Birney* (1844), a campaign document, and William Birney, *James G. Birney and His Times: The Genesis of the Republican Party with Some Account of Abolition in the South before 1828* (1890).

BETTY FLADELAND

BIRNEY, William (28 May 1819–14 Aug. 1907), soldier, journalist, and lawyer, was born in Madison County, Alabama, the son of James Gillespie Birney, a lawyer, state legislator, and abolitionist leader, and Agatha McDowell. In 1818 his family had moved to Huntsville, Alabama, and in late 1835 they relocated to New Richmond, Ohio. Birney was educated at four colleges, including Yale University, and graduated from Cincinnati Law School in 1841. He began practicing law in that city and in 1845 married Catherine Hoffman. They would have nine children. For five years thereafter he resided on the Continent and in England. He contributed essays on the arts to English and American newspapers, and he upheld the activist reputation of his family by opposing French troops as a member of a Republican student battalion in Paris. In 1848 he accepted an appointment as professor of English literature at the lycée in Bourges.

Returning to the United States in 1852, Birney settled in Philadelphia, where in 1853 he founded and edited a daily newspaper. Upon the outbreak of the Civil War, he moved to New Jersey, raised a company of volunteers, and on 22 May 1861 entered Federal service as a captain of the First New Jersey Infantry. In September 1861 Birney became major of the Fourth New Jersey and on 13 January 1863, its colonel. He took part in the battles of First and Second Bull Run (Manassas) as well as the early battles of Major General George B. McClellan's Peninsula campaign. At Gaines' Mill, 27 June 1862, Birney and 436 other members of the Fourth New Jersey were captured when McClellan detached the regiment from its brigade and placed it in a precarious position. Released from a prison camp in early August, Birney returned to his decimated regiment, but at Second Bull Run (Manassas) he led the Fifty-seventh Pennsylvania Infantry and at Fredericksburg the Thirty-eighth New York. Both regiments were attached to a division commanded by his younger brother, Brigadier General David Bell Birney.

Long in favor of enlisting African Americans, Birney supervised the recruiting of the U.S. Colored Troops (USCTs) early in 1863. With characteristic energy, he personally raised seven regiments composed of black residents of Maryland, including the inmates of slave prisons he liberated. On 22 May Birney was appointed a brigadier general of volunteers. In this capacity he was able to fulfill an oft-stated desire "to give the colored troops a fair chance of distinction in the field." He was assigned a brigade of USCTs in the Department of the South, which he commanded at Beaufort, South Carolina, and later at Jacksonville, Florida. In both locales he protected government property and Unionist citizens while conducting limited offensives with white soldiers as well as Colored Troops. His preference for the latter, however, was never in doubt; on at least one occasion he offered to trade white units for an equal numbered of USCTs.

From April through July 1864 Birney was especially active in raiding outposts, guerrilla camps, railroads, mills, foundries, and other targets of opportunity. His expeditions cost the enemy millions of dollars in matériel, but the heavy hand he laid on his domain may have embarrassed his superiors. In August Birney was relieved of command of the District of Florida and sent to southeastern Virginia to join the X Corps in Major General Benjamin F. Butler's Army of the James. In this theater he again served under his brother, who commanded the corps from July until his death from disease in October.

Birney's record in the Army of the James was decidedly uneven. He performed well on the brigade level but only when closely supervised by his brother or other superiors. Given a larger command and granted wider latitude, he displayed a lack of tactical skill. Another of Birney's liabilities was a contentious disposition, which embroiled him in quarrels with numerous superiors and subordinates. At war's end, when commanding a division in the all-black XXV Army Corps, he shed rearguard duties to lead his troops in a furious pursuit of Robert E. Lee's Army of Northern Virginia, then in retreat from Petersburg to Appomattox Court House. On 8 April 1865, one day before his command overtook its enemy, Birney had a run-in with Butler's successor, Major General Edward O. C. Ord, whom Birney apparently accused of trying to deny his black troops a role in Lee's defeat. A resentful Ord summarily relieved his critic and sent him back to Petersburg in disgrace.

Despite this unseemly confrontation, Birney was brevetted major general of volunteers during the omnibus promotions that accompanied the war's close. Mustered out of the service in August 1865, he took up residence in Florida. In 1869 he moved to Washington, where he practiced law, contributed a column to the *New York Examiner*, and served briefly as U.S. attorney for the District of Columbia. He published numerous works, including religious tracts, volumes of church history, and a biography of his father. The general spent the last several years of his life in Forest Glen, Maryland, with his second wife, Mattie Ashby, whom he wed in 1891. They had no children. Birney died in Washington.

Birney was fluent in thirteen languages, but despite his impressive erudition and the variety of his pursuits and accomplishments, he is primarily remembered for his checkered military career. A zealous libertarian, he went to great lengths to combat what he termed "the preconceived idea on the part of many that a Negro has no rights" in or outside the army. But while he showcased the military abilities of African Americans, he failed to provide them with consistently capable leadership.

Birney rendered good service in expeditionary operations and, when closely supervised by his superiors, in battle. His shortcomings in semi-independent command were glaringly revealed during the Army of the James's September 1864 offensive north of the James River. On the 29th of that month, when attacking Forts Gregg and Gilmer, key points on the intermediate defense line of Richmond, Birney committed his command in piecemeal fashion. He ordered three regiments to advance beyond supporting distance of each other, each in a single line barely four companies strong. Predictably, the outfits were reduced to bloody fragments well short of their objective. Recriminations from the disaster soured Birney's relations with his colleagues and helped spawn a general perception that he was incompetent. Doubtless that perception played a role in his relief on the brink of final victory.

• A body of Birney's correspondence is among the James Gillespie Birney Papers at the University of Michigan's William L. Clements Library. Smaller groupings of his letters repose in the Elizur Wright Papers in the Library of Congress, Washington, D.C.; and the Simon Gratz, Ferdinand Dreer, and Salmon P. Chase papers at the Historical Society of Pennsylvania, Philadelphia. Reports of battles and expeditions in which Birney participated are in *The War of the Rebellion: A Compilation of the Official Records of the Union and Confederate Armies* (128 vols., 1880–1901). For an informative autobiographical sketch and an unobjective account of one of his many wartime quarrels, see *General William Birney's Answer to Libels Clandestinely Circulated by James Shaw, Jr.* (1878). Accounts by observers critical of Birney's generalship include Joseph M. Califf, *Record of the Services of the Seventh Regiment, U.S. Colored Troops* (1878); Joseph T. Wilson, *The Black Phalanx: A History of the Negro Soldiers of the United States* (1890); and O. W. Norton, *Army Letters, 1861–1865* (1903). An obituary is in the *Washington Post*, 15 Aug. 1907.

EDWARD G. LONGACRE

BISHOP, Abraham (5 Feb. 1763–28 Apr. 1844), politician and writer, was born in New Haven, Connecticut, the son of Samuel Bishop, a political notable of New Haven, and Mehetabel Bassett. Bishop graduated from Yale College in 1778, when he was fifteen, and was admitted to the bar on 6 April 1785. He did not practice law but followed eventually in the political footsteps of his father, who was a long-term officeholder, having served as town clerk, mayor, deputy in the state assembly, and judge of the county and probate courts. The younger Bishop visited Europe in 1787 and 1788, spending a lengthy period in France, an experience that one commentator suggested led to "the unsettlement of his religious views and the development of his passion for democracy" (Dexter, p. 17).

Back in the United States, Bishop attempted to reform the schools of New Haven by introducing a system of grades rather than having all students in one class. He was appointed director of public schools and of the private Hopkins Grammar School, but his project came to nought, and he lost the position. In 1791 he moved to Boston, Massachusetts, and for the next few years he taught school in various places in New England and spoke and wrote on political issues. In March 1792 he married Nancy Dexter of Newburyport, Massachusetts. She bore him a daughter, but the relationship was an unhappy one that soon ended in divorce. In 1795 he was back in New Haven, serving as clerk of the county court and the following year as clerk of the probate court. Bishop became an ardent supporter of Thomas Jefferson, however, and that al-

legiance cost him his local political office in Federalist New Haven.

Republicanism paid off for the Bishops, father and son. In 1801 President Jefferson replaced the Federalist collector of the port of New Haven and gave the position to the aging Samuel Bishop, with a tacit understanding that the work would be done by Abraham. At his father's death in 1803, Bishop received the appointment for himself and kept it until 1829, when Andrew Jackson replaced him. Bishop, a strong supporter of the tariff who had opposed Jackson's election in 1828, eventually became a Whig.

Bishop was an articulate and controversial political speaker and writer whose work was widely known in Connecticut and New England generally, in part because he attacked the entrenched structure of religious and political authority that dominated those societies. One of his early publications was a series of three short articles that appeared in the Boston *Argus* in 1791, in which Bishop praised the slave uprising in Haiti, comparing it to the American Revolution and arguing that from God's perspective the Rights of Man belonged to all races: "Whether white or black blood is spilt, is equal in the eye of that Being, who will never decide by their colour, the fate of the creatures, whom he has made" (Matthewson, p. 152).

Bishop's pamphlets were often Democratic-Republican tracts designed to weaken Federalist control of New England. *Connecticut Republicanism—An Oration on the Extent and Power of Political Delusion* was first delivered as an address to the Phi Beta Society at Yale at commencement in 1800. An important theme for him was the denial of religious freedom that resulted from the union of church and state in Connecticut. Beyond that the tone of the piece was partisan in the extreme. He warns the Federalists, those "*self-stiled* [sic] friends of order and good government" that they should "prepare their necks for the yoke" if Jefferson is elected and prepare to give up "funding system, federal city, foreign intercourse, army, navy." The tract may have helped Bishop's father win his post as collector. It was bitter enough to draw two published replies, one of them by Noah Webster, titled *A Rod for the Fool's Back*. In *Proofs of a Conspiracy, Against Christianity, and the Government of the United States* (1802), Bishop argued that the Federalists of New England were not really Protestants, having supported the Catholic church when it came under attack during the French Revolution.

Georgia Speculation Unveiled (1797), was a lengthy account of the Yazoo land frauds, which originated when the legislature of Georgia sold large amounts of land at bargain prices to land companies in which the lawmakers were heavily involved. After a public outcry, a new legislature rescinded the sales, but the original purchasers appealed to the courts. Bishop railed against the Georgia speculators, apparently motivated by the fact that many northerners had lost money. He warned his readers that the act repealing the fraudulent sales would stand, but the Supreme Court later ruled in *Fletcher v. Peck* (1810) that the contract clause of the Constitution protected the original grants.

Bishop's career as a political writer began to wane with his appointment as collector. He may also have mellowed as a result of marrying Betsy Law in 1802, with whom he had four daughters. She died in September 1817, and he took a third wife, Elizabeth Lynde, in January 1819. Bishop died one of the richest men in New Haven, but, other than the lucrative office of collector of the port of New Haven, exactly how he acquired his money is not clear. He gave books and fine furniture to the Yale library.

Bishop was a political writer of some influence in New England in the years before and after 1800, who exemplifies the influence of the Enlightenment in the United States and also the radicalism that was part of Jeffersonian Republicanism.

• There are no extant Bishop manuscripts. The best account of Bishop's life is in F. B. Dexter, *Biographical Sketches of the Graduates of Yale College*, vol. 4 (1907), which also lists all of his published pamphlets. The same author provides a fuller account of Bishop's publications in "Abraham Bishop of Connecticut and his Writing," *Proceedings of the Massachusetts Historical Society* (1905). See also Tim Matthewson, "Abraham Bishop, 'The Rights of Black Men,' and the American Reaction to the Haitian Revolution," *Journal of Negro History* 67 (1982): 148–54; and David Brion Davis, *The Problem of Slavery in the Age of Revolution, 1770–1828* (1966).
S. CHARLES BOLTON

BISHOP, Anna Rivière (9 Jan. 1810–18 Mar. 1884), soprano, was born in London, England, the daughter of Daniel Valentine Rivière and Henrietta Thunder. Her father, who had emigrated from France to England, was a drawing master and an amateur flutist. Bishop's musical talents were evident at an early age, and she studied with her mother before being selected as a foundation student at the Royal Academy of Music in early 1824. There she studied piano with Ignaz Moscheles. In the mid-1820s she abandoned study of the piano in favor of voice, which she studied under Henry Rowley Bishop, then one of the most popular English composers. Anna sang at a students' concert at St. James's Palace in 1828, in the presence of the king. Her public debut, with the Concerts of Antient Music, was at the New Rooms, Hanover Square, on 20 April 1831. She left the Royal Academy the same year, apparently without receiving a degree. In July 1831 she married Bishop, barely a month after the death of his first wife. The couple had three children.

During the early 1830s Anna Bishop sang at numerous music festivals in Gloucester, York, Hereford, and Worcester, usually under the direction of her husband. She also sang with the Concerts of Antient Music, the Philharmonic Concerts, and in the chorus at the coronation of Queen Victoria in 1838. During this period her repertory included primarily works by Haydn, Mozart, and Beethoven; she also sang compositions by Handel, no doubt prompted by the predominance of his works in the repertory of the Concerts of Antient Music. In the mid-1830s Bishop became acquainted with Robert Nicholas Charles Bochsa, an esteemed French harpist who had served as professor of harp and general secretary for the Royal Academy of Music from 1822 through 1826. Bochsa, who was also a composer, had been suspended by the academy following the discovery of his conviction in 1817 (in France) for forgery. Bishop was greatly influenced by Bochsa and consequently turned her attention to works in the Italian style. In 1839 she and Bochsa embarked on a provincial tour, performing "dramatic concerts" (operatic selections sung in character and in costume with instrumental interludes for harp) at the Queen's Theatre in Dublin, the Adelphi Theatre in Edinburgh, and Her Majesty's Theatre in London.

In August 1839 Bishop ran away with Bochsa; they never married and had no children. Henceforth, and for the rest of her life, "Madame Bishop," as she was known, traveled and performed almost incessantly. She and Bochsa first embarked on a lengthy European concert tour that lasted until 1846, during which time they performed in Denmark, Sweden, Russia, Moldavia, Austria, Italy, Hungary, and Bavaria. They did not, however, perform in France, where there was a standing warrant for Bochsa's arrest for forgery. In 1843 Bishop was engaged as *prima donna assoluta* at the San Carlo Opera House in Naples, where she gave 327 operatic performances over the course of the next twenty-seven months, performing in at least twenty different operas. Bishop briefly returned to England in 1846, and there she appeared in Michael Balfe's *The Maid of Artois*. In mid-1847, after having spent six months in Dublin, she sailed for the United States.

Although Bishop's concert tours of the United States were quite successful, she seems to have preferred to perform in opera. Over the course of her American career she performed as a visiting star with prominent East Coast theaters. Bishop was the featured artist around whom a resident opera company was assembled in 1854 at the Metropolitan Theatre in San Francisco, and she starred in her own itinerant opera troupes. Her American operatic debut was in Donizetti's *Linda di Chamounix* (in English) at the Park Theatre in New York on 4 August 1847. She later took part in the American premieres of *The Maid of Artois* (Park Theatre, 5 Nov. 1847) and Friedrich Flotow's *Martha* (Niblo's Garden, N.Y., 1 Nov. 1852).

Bishop and Bochsa traveled around and performed in the United States, Canada, and Mexico until 1855, appearing in concerts and opera productions wherever they could attract an audience. On 30 November 1855 they left San Francisco for Australia, where Bochsa died of dropsy on 6 January 1856. Bishop continued the tour, performing in Chile, Argentina, and Brazil before returning in 1858 to New York, where she married a diamond merchant named Martin Schultz (Henry Bishop had died of cancer in 1855); the couple had no children. She returned to England briefly in 1858–1859 and then embarked on another successful tour of North America in August 1859. In 1866 Bishop left California with her husband for the Sandwich Islands; en route from there to Hong Kong they were shipwrecked on a coral reef near Wake Island. The survivors of the shipwreck fashioned an open boat and made their way across 1,400 miles of ocean to the Ladrone Islands, where Bishop and Schultz resumed their tour. They traveled to Guam, Manila, Hong Kong, Singapore, and made an extended tour of India. In 1869 they returned to New York, via Australia and England. Bishop's final world tour—which included Australia, China, and South Africa—was made between 1874 and 1876. She retired to New York, where she made her last public appearance on 20 April 1883 at a Patrick Sarsfield Gilmore band concert—the final performance in a career that had spanned almost a half-century. Bishop died at her home in New York.

Bishop's soprano voice was sweet and pure and was characterized by great range, agility, and reliable intonation. Praised as brilliant, exquisite, and virtuosic, it was often compared to a bird or a flute. Although not powerful (some described it as thin), in all other ways her voice conformed to the mid-nineteenth-century ideal of soprano vocal beauty: light, supple, and perfectly suited to the seemingly effortless execution of the ornate *fiorature* (vocal embellishments) required of bel canto opera. A critic writing in the London *Morning Post* (9 Oct. 1846) declared that Bishop had a "soprano voice of excellent quality, unerring intonation, facile execution, [and] artistic feeling"; he also described her eyes as "large, lustrous, and full of fire" and her actions as "free, graceful, and dramatic."

Bishop's concert repertory—both in Europe and in the United States—consisted of arias and scenes from contemporary operas (*Tancredi, La Gazza Ladra, Romeo e Giulietta, Anna Bolena, La Sonnambula, Lucia di Lammermoor, L'Ambassadrice, Il Barbiere di Siviglia*) sung in both Italian and English and often performed in costume; occasional ballads ("The Last Rose of Summer," "John Anderson, My Jo," "On the Banks of the Guadalquivir," "Auld Robin Gray"); and works for harp, usually Bochsa's own virtuosic fantasias. Her reception by concert audiences all over the world was wildly enthusiastic; she was acclaimed for her beauty and exquisite costumes as well as for her vocal ability. Bishop was one of the most popular and best-known English singers of her generation and did much to further the increasing popularity of Italian operatic music in the United States. She was undoubtedly the most widely traveled vocalist of her time—and perhaps of the entire nineteenth century.

• Primary source materials about Bishop are readily available. Extensive scrapbooks containing information about her European and American travels are in the music department of the Boston Public Library; similar materials are in the archives of the New York Metropolitan Opera. Shortly before Bishop's death George Seilhamer interviewed her and published the results in *An Interviewer's Album*, no. 14 (1881). Several biographical studies of Bishop were written during her life, including C. G. Foster, *Biography of Anna Bishop* (1853), and the anonymous *Travels with Anna Bishop in Mexico, 1849* (1852). A useful and unexpected source of information is Frank Walker, *The Man Verdi* (1962); see also Richard Northcott, *The Life of Sir Henry R. Bishop* (1920). Informa-

tion about her activities in California can be found in Lawrence Estavan, ed., *San Francisco Theatre Research. History of Opera in San Francisco*, vol. 7 of the History of Music in San Francisco Series (1939); Katherine Preston also discusses Bishop's American activities prior to the Civil War in *Opera on the Road: Traveling Opera Troupes in the United States, 1825–1860* (1993). Obituaries are in the *New York Times*, 20 Mar. 1884, the *Musical Times*, Apr. 1884, and the *American Art Journal*, 1884.

KATHERINE K. PRESTON

BISHOP, Bernice Pauahi (19 Dec. 1831–16 Oct. 1884), native Hawaiian high chiefess and philanthropist, was born Pauahi in Honolulu, the daughter of Abner Paki and Konia (maiden name unknown), both of chiefly rank. She was the great-granddaughter of King Kamehameha I, who united the islands under his rule in 1810. Her father was an adviser to Kamehameha III and holder of numerous high offices in the kingdom. Pauahi's birth was celebrated in the traditional native Hawaiian way, with the composition and performance of chants to celebrate her sacred lineage. It was the final time that a descendant of Kamehameha I would be so honored, since she was the last of this royal line. Her native Hawaiian name, Pauahi, translates as "the fire is out." It was chosen to honor her maternal aunt, who had been badly burned in a gunpowder explosion when she was a child.

Pauahi spent her early childhood (1832–1839) as the adopted daughter of Kinau, kuhina-nui (coruler) of Hawaii and mother of Kamehameha IV and Kamehameha V. Pauahi returned to the home of her parents briefly in 1839. In 1840 she became one of the first students to live with Amos and Julia Cooke, an American missionary couple, at the Chief's Children's School. There she remained for ten years and received her missionary name, Bernice. A contemporary observer said of her during this time that she "had always been more under foreign influence than most of the pupils of her age [and was] the best educated of all the Hawaiian girls."

A prolific and highly skilled writer, Pauahi kept a journal of her years with the Cookes. In it she expressed her devotion to Julia Cooke as the model of Victorian womanhood she strove to emulate and evidenced what would become a lifelong concern for the moral and intellectual life of her people. She also wrote with respect and fondness of her native Hawaiian relatives and expressed her awareness of racism by recording an incident in which a native Hawaiian emissary was not allowed to eat with his Caucasian assistant during a diplomatic mission to the mainland United States. She did not include her reaction to this information, which she heard during a conversation at the Cooke home, but it may very well have contributed to her strong support for Hawaiian sovereignty, a position shared by her future husband and her royal cousins, Kamehameha IV and Kamehameha V.

On 4 June 1850 Pauahi married Charles Reed Bishop, a New York–born businessman to whom she had been introduced by the Cookes. At the time of their marriage he was collector of customs for the port of

Honolulu. This union was opposed by her parents, who wanted her to marry either Prince Alexander Liholiho (Kamehameha IV) or Prince Lot (Kamehameha V). A painful period of estrangement followed, but the marriage was such an obviously happy one, and Bishop himself so exemplary a skilled diplomat and businessman, that by the time her father died in 1855, they had reconciled their differences.

Abner Paki left Pauahi his entire estate, including "Hale'akala" (House of the Sun), a mansion located in what is now the center of Honolulu. There she cared for her mother during the last two years of Konia's life. Konia also left her estate, about 10,000 acres of land, to Pauahi. Thus by the age of twenty-six Pauahi possessed a considerable fortune and the responsibility for tenants and family retainers that her lands and her royal status entailed.

Hale'akala became a center of community life for both Caucasian and native Hawaiian residents of the islands and visiting dignitaries. In addition to her informal activities as a hostess and adviser, Pauahi was a lifetime member of Kawaihao (Congregational) Church, where she taught Sunday school. She also served as a vice president of one of the most important charitable organizations of the period, the Stranger's Friend Society.

In 1872 Pauahi refused King Kamehameha V's deathbed request that she succeed him as ruler of Hawaii. Her experience in the household of Kinau had shown her that ruling a nation in transition was filled with conflict, tension, and frustration. Through her training by the missionaries in the duties of a Victorian woman and wife, and through her own success at serving her people in other ways, she had already gained the love and admiration of both the native Hawaiian and Caucasian communities. Thus, although she left no written record, it is fair to speculate that she made her choice with minimal difficulty. As with other aspects of her life, it was a successful compromise between ancient Hawaiian and contemporary Christian values. By refusing to rule her people she continued to serve them—arguably better than if she had become queen—in a manner acceptable both to herself and to the increasingly westernized nation that was her home.

Having refused the crown without losing the devotion of her Hawaiian subjects, Pauahi was presented ten years later with a much more concrete responsibility to them that she could not avoid. Her cousin Princess Ruth, the richest woman in the kingdom, died on 24 May 1853 and designated Pauahi sole heir to an estate that included about 353,000 acres of land, several large homes, and other assets. Like Ruth, Pauahi was childless, so the disposition of the estate was a matter of primary importance. In making her decision to found an institution named after her royal lineage, she was guided both by traditional Hawaiian emphasis on the sacredness of the educational process and her concern for the fast-diminishing indigenous population. The majority of native Hawaiians were Protestants, so religion was not an issue. The damage that Western

diseases had caused since the time of Captain James Cook could not be reversed. Pauahi concluded that only by learning to cope with rapidly changing social and economic conditions—as she had done at the Chief's Children's School—could the remaining native Hawaiians survive and prosper. She therefore made provisions in her will for the establishment of the Kamehameha Schools, supported by a perpetual charitable trust and giving preferential enrollment to students of native ancestry.

Pauahi died of cancer and was buried in the Royal Mausoleum in Nuuanu Valley on the island of Oahu. A prophetic eulogy in the *Pacific Commercial Advertiser* stated that "her intense interest in, and strong influence over, the youth of her race has been most notable, and the future only can divulge the extent of her usefulness in this regard." The trustees of the estate, still known in the mid-1990s as the Bishop Estate and still one of Hawaii's largest landholders, opened a boys' school in 1887 and a girls' school in 1894. More than a century later the Kamehameha Schools remained as a testament to Pauahi, the last Kamehameha.

Additional institutions dedicated to Pauahi include the Bernice Pauahi Bishop Museum, established by her husband in 1889. In 1991 this internationally renowned, multipurpose museum devoted to the study and preservation of Hawaiian and Polynesian cultures and to all natural science disciplines that pertain to the Pacific basin was designated the State Museum of Natural and Cultural History. The Bishop Memorial Chapel at Kawaihao Church and the Pauahi Wing at Queen's Hospital in Honolulu also honor her memory.

• Pauahi's letters were destroyed in a hotel fire in San Francisco in 1906. "The Diary of Bernice Pauahi Bishop," written while she was at the Chief's Children's School and covering the years 1843–1846 (ms. and typescript), and a diary of her trip to Europe in 1875–1876 (ms. and handwritten transcription) are in the Bishop Museum Archives, along with miscellaneous papers and ephemera. *A Report of Voyages and Travels on Hawaii, Maui, and Molokai by the Students of the Chief's Children's School*, based on her diaries, was published by Bishop Museum Press in 1981. Pauahi's will, codicils, and probate records are available on microfilm at the Hawaii State Archives. Major biographies include Mary Hannah Krout, *The Memoirs of Hon. Bernice Pauahi Bishop* (1908), and Cobey Black and Kathleen D. Mellen, *Princess Pauahi and Her Legacy* (1965). Most recently, George Hu'eu Sanford Kanahele, *Pauahi: The Kamehameha Legacy* (1986), emphasized Pauahi's role as a link between the old (pre-contact) and new, Western-influenced Hawaii; it is the most complete biography to date. Biographical sketches may be found in Maxine Mrantz, *Women of Old Hawaii* (1975); Alfons L. Korn, *The Victorian Visitors* (1958); and Barbara Peterson, ed., *Notable Women of Hawaii* (1984). Mary A. Richard, *The Hawaiian Chief's Children's School* (1970), gives a firsthand account of Pauahi's years there and includes a biographical sketch. An extensive obituary is in the *Pacific Commercial Advertiser*, 21 Oct. 1884; it is valuable primarily for its expression of the esteem with which Pauahi was viewed by her contemporaries in the Caucasian community of Honolulu.

LINDA A. PETERSON

BISHOP, Charles Reed (25 Jan. 1822–7 June 1915), banker, cabinet minister, and philanthropist, was born near Glens Falls, New York, the son of Samuel Bishop, a toll collector on the Hudson River, and Maria Reed. Charles's mother died when he was two years old, and his father remarried. He was cared for first by an aunt and then by his paternal grandfather on whose farm he received an education in hard work and practical business. His only formal education was at Glens Falls Academy, which he attended in the seventh and eighth grades. Around 1838, after leaving school, he became a clerk in a mercantile house in Warrensburgh, New York, where he learned the intricacies of bookkeeping, inventory, and other business skills. In 1842 he moved to Sandy Hill, New York, to take a job as a bookkeeper and head clerk.

Bishop apparently yearned for far horizons, for in February 1846 he boarded the *Henry* in Newburyport, Massachusetts, bound for Oregon. It was a long and rough voyage around South America, and when the *Henry* put in at Honolulu on 12 October, he was delighted to accept a job in the Department of the Interior of the Kingdom of Hawaii and to settle down in the islands. Subsequently Bishop was hired as a clerk in the U.S. Consulate in Honolulu. In 1849, after becoming a naturalized citizen of the kingdom, he was appointed collector of customs and later, in 1853, commissioner of customs. During these years he began to acquire land and to invest in sugar and other business ventures.

In 1850 Bishop married Bernice Pauahi, a Hawaiian princess. They lived together happily until her death in 1884. Though childless, they were both concerned about the health and education of the young people of Hawaii. With Bishop's encouragement and assistance Princess Bernice set aside in her will her large inheritance of royal lands to form the Bishop Estate dedicated to the support of the Kamehameha Schools for Boys and Girls of Hawaiian ancestry.

While still serving the kingdom as commissioner of customs, Bishop developed an interest in a general store in Honolulu and made a number of other investments. What was to become the most important move of his business career came in August 1858, when he and a partner opened Bishop & Co., the first bank in Hawaii. An immediate success, Bishop & Co. furnished funds to the government and to private enterprise. It became the foundation of Bishop's personal fortune (which was enlarged by associated business interests in California) and a mainstay of the economy of the islands. After the Reciprocity Treaty between Hawaii and the United States went into effect in 1876, Bishop & Co. extended long-term loans that enabled the businessmen and planters of Hawaii to take full advantage of the economic possibilities offered by the treaty. Over the years Bishop had various partners, but he remained the primary banking officer and guiding genius of Bishop & Co. until he severed his main financial interests in Hawaii in June 1895.

While heavily engaged in the banking business, Bishop also held public office. In 1859, after resigning as commissioner of customs, he was appointed to the Privy Council, where he served until 1892 under five successive rulers. He was elected to the House of Representatives in 1853 and was appointed to the House of Nobles in 1859, holding a seat there until 1886. He was a member of the bureau of immigration, responsible for importing the labor vital to growing sugar in the islands, from 1869 to 1874; a member of the board of education from 1869 to 1891, serving part of the time as its president; minister of foreign affairs in 1873–1874; commissioner of Crown lands in 1873; and on the Commission to Increase the Original Hawaiian Race in 1876.

The Hawaiian sovereigns were grateful for Bishop's long and faithful labors on behalf of the kingdom and honored him with the Royal Order of Kamehameha I, Knight Commander, in 1869; the Knight Grand Cross in 1874; and the Royal Order of Kalakaua I, Knight Grand Cross, in 1875. He received numerous honors from Japan, Austria, Mexico, Bavaria, Baden, and Württemburg as well.

In addition to his business interests and his services to the Hawaiian Kingdom, Bishop undertook a number of civic responsibilities. He was president of the Chamber of Commerce (1883–1891), fostered the Pacific Cable (1890 on) and the introduction of telephones and electricity into the islands (1879 on), and beginning in 1876, supported the expansion of the Oahu Railway and Land Company, which eased transportation on Oahu and other islands.

Bishop also was active in local charities. In addition to his work in 1886–1887 in setting up Kamehameha schools under his wife's will, he was a trustee of Oahu College (now Punahou School) from 1867 to 1894, and he contributed generously to a number of major buildings on both school campuses. He also founded the Princess Bernice Pauahi Bishop Museum in Honolulu, which opened in 1890–1891. Originally envisioned as a memorial to his wife, to be filled with Hawaiian artifacts and personal memorabilia, it was gradually expanded to become the premier natural science museum in the Pacific.

In March 1894 Bishop left Honolulu for the last time. His ties to Hawaii had dwindled since his wife's death ten years earlier. His bank in Honolulu was in good hands, while his business interests in California were expanding and needed his personal attention. After the overthrow of the Hawaiian monarchy in 1893, he was no longer able to influence political events in the kingdom he had served for so long. With his finances in the islands in order he felt impelled to move to California. He lived in San Francisco until the earthquake of 1906, when he moved to Berkeley. He remained active in business and in civic affairs until his death in Berkeley. His ashes were returned to Hawaii, where they were buried, with those of his wife, in the Royal Mausoleum in Honolulu.

Harold W. Kent, his biographer, wrote that "Bishop combined judgment and restraint with a rare sense of propriety in business relations and an uncanny ability to visualize new business. . . . He also had a practical appreciation of the potential constructive effects of communications and transportation, which was manifested in his constant enterprise and interest in the ocean cable, good shipping lines, telephone service, and a sound currency and banking system" (p. 55).

• Many of Bishop's private papers were lost in the San Francisco fire of 1906. Many of his public papers are in the Archives of Hawaii; some private papers are in the Bishop Museum Archives. For additional information consult his biography, Harold W. Kent, *Charles Reed Bishop, Man of Hawaii* (1965), which also includes detailed accounts of the Kamehameha Schools for Boys and Girls and the Bernice Pauahi Bishop Museum. William T. Brigham, director of the museum, writing with personal knowledge of the museum's founder, contributed "Charles Reed Bishop, 1822–1915" to *The Hawaiian Annual for 1916* (1915), pp. 63–71. An obituary is in *The Friend* (Honolulu), July 1915.

RHODA E. A. HACKLER

BISHOP, Elizabeth (8 Feb. 1911–6 Oct. 1979), poet, was born in Worcester, Massachusetts, the daughter of Gertrude Bulmer and William Thomas Bishop, owners of the J. W. Bishop contracting firm. Bishop's childhood was filled with a sense of loss that pervades her poetry. Her father died from Bright's disease when she was eight months old. Her mother, psychologically distraught, spent the next five years in and out of psychiatric hospitals. With William's death, Gertrude lost her U.S. citizenship and, when she experienced the decisive breakdown in her family home in Nova Scotia, was hospitalized in a public sanatorium in Dartmouth, Nova Scotia. Elizabeth Bishop was five when this breakdown occurred; she later recounted it in her prose masterpiece "In the Village." Her mother, diagnosed as permanently insane, never saw Elizabeth again.

After her mother's hospitalization, Bishop lived in Great Village, Nova Scotia, with her mother's family, in a loving, comforting atmosphere. However, the equilibrium that she had gained was upset by her paternal grandparents' decision to raise the child with them in Worcester. In her prose memoir "The Country Mouse," Bishop writes, "I had been brought back unconsulted and against my wishes to the house my father had been born in, to be saved from a life of poverty and provincialism." There, in isolated wealth, Bishop keenly felt her lack of relations. She wrote, "I felt myself aging, even dying. I was bored and lonely with Grandma, my silent grandpa, the dinners alone. . . . At night I lay blinking my flashlight off and on, and crying."

When her mother's sister, Maud Bulmer Shepherdson, rescued Bishop in May 1918, even her paternal grandparents saw that their "experiment" had failed. Never a strong child, Bishop now suffered from eczema, asthma, St. Vitus's dance, and nervous ailments that made her nearly too weak to walk. Maud Shepherdson lived in an apartment in a South Boston tenement. An unpublished manuscript, "Mrs. Sullivan Downstairs," recounts Bishop's love for this neighbor-

hood. There, Bishop later recalled, she began to write poetry, influenced by Aunt Maud's love of literature.

As she grew stronger, Bishop spent her summers in Nova Scotia and attended Camp Chequesset on Cape Cod. Her unusual circumstances and poor health limited her formal schooling before age fourteen. However, she was an excellent student, and following her time at the Walnut Hill School for Girls, Bishop entered the Vassar College class of 1934.

At Vassar, Bishop, with novelist Mary McCarthy and others, began an underground literary magazine, *Con Spirito*, publishing a more socially conscious and avant-garde selection than the legitimate *Vassar Review*. In the spring of 1934, the year her mother died and the year of her graduation, Bishop met and became friends with poet Marianne Moore. Through Moore's influence, Bishop came to see poetry as an available, viable vocation for a woman. Moore recommended Bishop for the Houghton Mifflin Prize, and Bishop's manuscript *North and South* was chosen for publication in August 1946 from over 800 entries.

North and South introduces the themes central to Bishop's poetry: geography and landscape, human connection with the natural world, questions of knowledge and perception, and the ability or inability of form to control chaos. Before Robert Lowell reviewed *North and South*, he met Bishop at a dinner party, a meeting that marked the beginning of a crucial, if complicated, friendship. Lowell, like Moore, showed Bishop possibilities—practically, in the form of grants, fellowships, and awards, and artistically. In 1950 Lowell helped Bishop secure the post of poetry consultant for the Library of Congress while she worked on her second book.

Bishop won the Lucy Martin Donnelly Fellowship from Bryn Mawr College in 1950 and an award from the American Academy of Arts and Letters. In 1951 she traveled to South America to see the Amazon. However, before she could leave for the dreamed-of voyage, Bishop ate a cashew fruit to which she had a violent allergic reaction that kept her bedridden. As Bishop recovered her health, she fell in love, both with Lota de Macedo Soares, her friend and nurse, and with the landscape and culture of Brazil. For fifteen years Bishop lived with Soares, in the mountain town of Petropolis and in Rio de Janeiro. This new love and home offered Bishop happiness she had known only briefly in Great Village. She wrote to Lowell that she was "extremely happy for the first time in my life" (28 July 1953).

In April 1954 Bishop made an agreement with Houghton Mifflin to publish her second book, *A Cold Spring*, in a volume that included the poems from her first book, under the title *Poems: North and South—A Cold Spring*. This book won the 1956 Pulitzer Prize. When the book appeared in August 1955, the reviews were laudatory: Donald Hall called Bishop "one of the best poets alive."

After publishing *A Cold Spring*, Bishop spent the next three years translating a popular Brazilian work, the diary of "Helena Morely" (Dona Alice Brant) called *Minha Vida de Menina*. The story of Helena's life in the small town of Diamantina in 1893 reminded Bishop of her 1916 Great Village, and translating this work while reflecting on and writing about her own childhood helped Bishop explore her past as artistic material. The translation was published under the title *The Diary of Helena Morely* by Farrar, Straus, and Cudahy in 1957.

Bishop's third book, *Questions of Travel* (1965), includes both reflections on her childhood experiences and poems about her new home in Brazil. The book is divided into two sections, Brazil and Elsewhere, with the prose piece "In the Village" placed between the divisions. Bishop returns to themes of geography, form, and landscape, but here she allows more intimacy, both between viewer and landscape and between reader and poet. *Questions of Travel* garnered positive reviews. Robert Mazzocco in the *New York Review of Books* (Oct. 1967) called Bishop "one of the shining, central talents of our day." The book is filled with the description for which Bishop received so much praise, but it is also filled with an unmistakable sense of what Wyatt Prunty calls "the askew," moments in which the senses fail to report reality, slide off into the mysterious, terrifying, or ecstatic.

Throughout the mid-1960s, life in Brazil grew difficult for Bishop. Lota de Macedo Soares, involved in the politics of Rio, had taken charge of a public parks project that absorbed her time and attention. As the political situation worsened, Bishop felt more uncomfortable in her Brazilian home. In 1966 Bishop spent two semesters as poet in residence at the University of Washington but returned to Rio in the hope of reestablishing her life there. Both Bishop and Soares suffered physical and psychological distress and were hospitalized in Brazil. When Bishop grew stronger, she left for New York with the expectation that Soares, as soon as she was well enough, would join her. Soares arrived in New York on the afternoon of 19 September 1967 and later that evening took an overdose of tranquilizers and died at age fifty-seven.

This loss proved terribly difficult for Bishop personally, although she continued to write and publish. In 1969 Bishop published *Complete Poems*, a volume that included all of her previously published poems and several new pieces. This book won the National Book Award for 1970. When the ceremony took place, Bishop was once again trying to reestablish a Brazilian life. However, the politics, along with Bishop's inability to negotiate the culture without Soares's help, finally convinced her that a Brazilian life was impossible. In the fall of 1970 she returned to the United States to teach at Harvard. There Bishop met the woman who became a source of strength and love for the rest of her life, Alice Methfessel.

Bishop eventually signed a four-year contract with Harvard. Although she never felt completely comfortable as a teacher, her students report learning much from her precision, from the quiet conversation that constituted her class. In 1976 Bishop became the first American and the first woman to be awarded the

Books Abroad/Neustadt International Prize for Literature. In that year she also published her last collection of poetry, *Geography III*, which won the Book Critics' Circle Award for 1977. This volume of nine beautifully crafted poems returns to themes of *North and South* but with greater intimacy and immediacy. Alfred Corn, writing in the 1977 *Georgia Review*, gives a clear and insightful reading of *Geography III* that could apply to all Bishop's work. He praises

a perfected transparence of expression, warmth of tone, and a singular blend of sadness and good humor, of pain and acceptance—a radiant patience few people ever achieve and few writers ever successfully render. The poems are works of philosophic beauty and calm, illuminated by that "laughter in the soul" that belongs to the best part of the comic genius.

When Bishop submitted her application for a Guggenheim Fellowship on 1 October 1977, she indicated that she would work on a new volume, tentatively titled "Grandmother's Glass Eye," and a book-length poem, *Elegy*. Four poems of the new volume, "Santarem," "North Haven," "Pink Dog," and "Sonnet," were complete when Bishop died in Boston, Massachusetts. Bishop's poems have been collected in *The Complete Poems, 1927–1979*, published by Farrar, Straus and Giroux (1983).

• Elizabeth Bishop's papers are in both the Houghton Library, Harvard University, and Vassar College Library special collections. Brett C. Millier's biography *Elizabeth Bishop: Life and the Memory of It* (1993) is a valuable resource, as is Candace W. MacMahon's bibliography *Elizabeth Bishop: A Bibliography, 1927–1979* (1980). Other important critical assessments of Bishop's work include Bonnie Costello, *Elizabeth Bishop: Questions of Mastery* (1991); David Kalstone, *Becoming a Poet* (1989); Jeredith Merrin, *An Enabling Humility: Marianne Moore, Elizabeth Bishop, and the Uses of Tradition* (1990); Robert Dale Parker, *The Unbeliever: The Poetry of Elizabeth Bishop* (1988); and Thomas Travisano, *Elizabeth Bishop: Her Artistic Development* (1988). Her prose is in *The Collected Prose* (1984), with a helpful introduction by Robert Giroux. Giroux also edited and published Bishop's letters, masterpieces in themselves, in *One Art: Letters* (1994). An obituary is in the *New York Times*, 8 Oct. 1979.

ANNE AGNES COLWELL

BISHOP, George Holman (27 June 1889–12 Oct 1973), neurophysiologist, was born in Durand, Wisconsin, the son of George Stephen Bishop, who worked in lumber and farming, and Harriet Amanda Holman. The Bishop family lived in Wisconsin until 1905, when they moved to Ann Arbor, Michigan, for their children's schooling. Bishop displayed precocious abilities as a young child growing up on the family's farm outside of Ann Arbor. He was adept at creating solutions to any problem encountered, including a machine for faster preparation of beehives and the wiring of the farm house for electricity. His ability to visualize and create exacting measurements aided him during a stint at a saw mill run by his father in Louisiana, where at the age of fifteen Bishop took over the position of foreman and quickly accomplished the production of perfectly fitted tongue and groove boards.

Despite missing almost all of the seventh and eighth grades while in Louisiana, Bishop placed into the ninth grade upon returning to Michigan and completed the requirements for his high school diploma in just three years. Bishop read the works of John Milton and similar authors for pleasure, comprehended advanced Latin works with little or no difficulty, and demonstrated remarkable dexterity and innovation. Bishop enrolled at the University of Michigan in 1908, at first studying engineering. The relative mental boredom he felt caused him to transfer into the liberal arts school in 1910. Although none of his engineering credits transferred with him, Bishop received his B.A. two years later, graduating in 1912. Anxious to physically create once again, Bishop became a manual training teacher in a vocational school in Brookings, South Dakota, followed by a year in Milwaukee, Wisconsin, and two in Seattle, Washington.

During a visit to Ann Arbor in 1914, Bishop met A. S. Pearse, a neighbor of his parents and a professor at Michigan, who interested him in biology. Back in Seattle, Bishop took courses at the University of Washington in preparation for graduate school. With the aid of a laboratory assistantship in biology, he returned to the Midwest to study zoology at the University of Wisconsin where Pearse and another acquaintance, physiologist Percy Dawson, were now working. After two years of graduate study, Bishop enlisted in the Army during the latter part of World War I, for reasons that continued to escape him. From 1917 to 1918 he served in a medical unit stationed near Washington, D.C., attaining the rank of corporal and making the acquaintance of comparative neurologist C. J. Herrick. He gladly returned to graduate school, and in 1919 he completed his doctorate and married fellow student Ethel Ronzoni.

Bishop's first academic position was as an instructor in the zoology department of Northwestern University, leaving the following year for an assistant professorship of histology at the University of Tennessee Medical School. In 1921 he was invited to Washington University School of Medicine in St. Louis, Missouri, at the rank of associate professor in physiology. Stemming from his work with his father's beehives as a young boy, Bishop first studied the physiology of bees, a choice that baffled him in later years. Shortly after arriving in St. Louis, however, he was invited to join the ranks of Joseph Erlanger and Herbert S. Gasser, an offer that he promptly accepted. Erlanger and Gasser were intensely interested in electrophysiological recordings of the nerves, utilizing recently developed electroencephalography (EEG) methods to take measurements, introducing Bishop to his life's calling.

After his career with Erlanger and Gasser ended in the late 1920s, Bishop began his own investigations into the relationship between axon size, neuron function, and conduction rate in the peripheral nervous system. He eventually moved into the study of the central nervous system; this stemmed from an interest in the optic nerve and correlated with his appointment as a professor in applied physiology in ophthalmology from 1930 to 1932, after which he became a professor in biophysics in the laboratory of neurophysiology. In 1932 Bishop published his first studies with Howard Bartley concerning evoked potentials in the rabbit brain. Also during this time, James Lee O'Leary joined Bishop in his research concerning correlation of axon to function. Bishop voiced the opinion to longtime friend C. J. Herrick that there were possibly two separate components of the spinothalamic tract due to evolution, an idea resulting from a graduate student's discovery of nonmyelinated axons in advanced species.

During the 1920s and 1930s Bishop taught a number of courses, first for undergraduates and then primarily for graduate students and fellows. In 1947 he attained the position of professor of neurophysiology in the Department of Neuropsychiatry. He was elected to associate membership in the American Neurological Association in 1948 and was granted honorary status in 1964. Bishop was honored by Washington University with a doctor of science degree in 1959, and he was elected to the National Academy of Sciences in 1967. James Lee O'Leary noted that "several of [Bishop's] studies rate among the classics of electrophysiology" (O'Leary, *Transactions*). Bishop authored or coauthored over 200 works and penned at least twelve review articles prior to his death in St. Louis.

One of Bishop's most remarkable characteristics was his unlimited sense of humor. Quite apparent from an early age, his personal writings consist of numerous poems covering topics from the rainy weather of Seattle versus the clear weather in Wisconsin to a sarcastic commentary on the nature of World War I and who should be involved in it. This humorous side stretched into his work as well; he once conveyed critical opinions by recording them on a roll of toilet paper, stating that no other forum was suitable for his thoughts concerning the expressed idea. This humor undoubtedly made an impact on his students as well.

Bishop's work with Erlanger and Gasser in the early 1920s caused him to reflect later on the limits of research. He remarked in "My Life Among the Axons," "Why does it take so long to see what eventually appears inevitable?" (p. 1). He noted that Erlanger and Gasser were forced to overcome significant obstacles in the way of available electronics and technology in order to make the discoveries for which they won their Nobel Prize. Their work using the cathode-ray tube led to equipment that permitted faster developments by generations to come. Bishop's own major work, accomplished during the 1930s, 1940s, and 1950s, occurred during an era of substantial improvements in electrical engineering and in the machinery available for studying the brain and nervous system, allowing for more rapid discoveries. During the 1960s the flurry of activity in the arena in which Bishop and his contemporaries had once dominated, which was carried out by the next generation of physicians and scientists, did not distress him. Instead, he commented that "his generation is now privileged to watch the show from the sidelines, till death and transfiguration realize the prospect of working on angels instead of cats" (Bishop, p. 18). Bishop's abilities in a wide variety of arenas facilitated his excellence in the laboratory and his humanity outside of it.

• The most revealing of Bishop's works are poems that he wrote during his youth and career, and the reflections of his brother Frederick bring life to his childhood and depth to his personality. These works and others from his collection are held in the Bishop Papers in the Archives of the Becker Medical Library at Washington University School of Medicine. Providing insight into his personality as well as his work, Bishop's own account of his collaboration with Erlanger and Gasser, among others, is contained in "My Life Among the Axons," which appears as the prefatory chapter in the *Annual Review of Physiology* 27 (1965): 1–18. A useful reference that places Bishop in the history of neurology and neurophysiology is James Lee O'Leary and Sidney Goldring, *Science and Epilepsy: Neuroscience Gains in Epilepsy Research* (1976). Obituaries include two written by James Lee O'Leary, in the *Transactions of the American Neurological Association* 99 (1974): 278–79 and the *Journal of Neurophysiology* 37 (1974): 382–83, and one in the *New York Times*, 14 Oct 1973.

JOANNA B. DOWNER

BISHOP, Isabel (3 Mar. 1902–19 Feb. 1988), artist, was born in Cincinnati, Ohio, the daughter of John Remsen Bishop, a schoolmaster, and Anna Newbold Bartram. Younger by thirteen years than her siblings, in a family that included two sets of twins, Bishop's sense of isolation throughout her childhood was expressed in two of her own recollections: "My mother really wanted to be a scholar and writer rather than a homemaker and mother. She taught herself Italian in order to translate Dante's *Inferno*, a task which absorbed her attention entirely." Later, when the family moved to Detroit and lived, for financial reasons, in a working-class district, Bishop was forbidden to play with the neighborhood children. "I watched them from my window and thought that they had such a warmer life than I did; they all knew each other and saw each other every day. I think my being drawn to the Fourteenth Street people and my sympathetic fascination with them came partly from my isolation as a child." For over fifty years, Bishop continued to be a "watcher" from her studio window, as she sketched and painted the shoppers, shopgirls, and other transient inhabitants of Union Square in New York City.

After high school Bishop moved to New York and enrolled in the New York School of Applied Design for Women in order to study commercial art. A life drawing class there and exposure to the new atmosphere of excitement, controversy, and modernism in art inspired by the Armory Show of 1913 caused Bishop to leave commercial art studies and enroll, in 1920, at the Art Students League. Unhappy with Max Weber's class, she began working with Kenneth Hayes Miller—"My God, he has a mind, and I'm home!" she recalled later. Miller taught a Renaissance representational technique of suggesting a three-dimensional object in two-dimensional space, which he adapted to contemporary subject matter. He influenced not only Bishop's art but her conception that the pursuit of art was an absolute and meaningful commitment for the artist.

Bishop's friendship with artists Guy Pène Du Bois and Reginald Marsh, her dissatisfaction with the dark-toned, static, and repetitive quality of her earlier work (much of which she destroyed), and her first trip to Europe and study of works by Rembrandt and Rubens caused her to make a deliberate break from Miller's influence. Sketching figures in Union Square that she observed from her first studio at 9 West Fourteenth Street and beginning to etch as well as draw and paint, she developed a unique style designed to convey a sense of potential mobility—an innate ability to move rather than remain as static lines and shapes on a flat surface. Bishop's goal of infusing life into her work by suggesting the potential for movement and shifting change, rather than a frozen movement in time, was a dominant theme throughout her life. She accomplished this quality in her graphic works by the exquisite refinement and remarkable variety of her lines, ranging from vigorous and deliberate to a degree of delicacy suggestive of a fleeting spontaneous gesture. In her paintings, she sought to achieve the kinesthetic potential of figures by building up rich and semitransparent surface layers of glazes and colors to achieve an overall tonal balance across the canvas. In her later paintings of the 1960s and 1970s, the richness and luminosity of her surface glazes along with her loose brushwork and broken contours allow her figures to be perceived as moving within their own atmosphere, bathed in the warmth of shifting light. Her goal was to capture the movement, the flux and flow of life itself, as emblematic of the human condition. Her subjects were transient figures—the shopgirls on their lunch breaks, the unemployed men on park benches, the shoppers with their parcels, all indigenous to Union Square.

In 1932 Bishop had her first one-woman show at Midtown Galleries. This association with the dealer Alan D. Gruskin was to become a happy and productive relationship throughout her career. In 1934 she married a prominent neurosurgeon, Harold George Wolff, and in the same year she moved her studio to 857 Broadway (Union Square). Supportive of her goals as an artist, Wolff insisted on her returning to her daily routine shortly after the birth, in 1940, of their son and only child, Remsen, who became a professional photographer. Wolff died in 1962 of a cerebral hemorrhage. Bishop spoke of the marriage as a happy one, marked by mutual admiration and respect.

By 1940 Bishop had received wide acclaim for her work. Besides her shows at Midtown Galleries, she was represented in group exhibitions at the Art Students League, the Whitney Museum of American Art, the Virginia Museum of Fine Arts, and the Golden Gate International Exposition. She was appointed an instructor at the Art Students League. Her 1935 *Two Girls* was purchased by the Metropolitan Museum of

Art and first brought her to national public attention. She did a mural for a post office in New Lexington, Ohio, as part of the New Deal program for public art in America. In 1936 the art critic Emily Genauer in the *New York World Telegram* proclaimed, "Isabel Bishop, we say with vehemence and conviction, is one of the most important women painters in America today."

Many honors followed: Bishop was elected an academician of the National Academy of Design (1941), and she was elected a member of the National Institute of Arts and Letters (1944) and the vice president (first woman officer) of this organization in 1946. She received the gold medal of the National Arts Club and the Outstanding Achievement in the Arts Award (presented by President Jimmy Carter) in 1979.

The Whitney Museum held a retrospective of Bishop's work in 1974. Bishop served in 1959 and again in 1963 as an instructor at the Skowhegan School of Painting and Sculpture.

Until her final debilitating illness Bishop continued, through her graphic works and paintings, what she referred to as her "endless search" for complex imagery of the human figure in transition. Along with her contemporaries—Reginald Marsh, Miller, Raphael Soyer, and other artists of the so-called Fourteenth Street School—Bishop's primary reference was the colorful diversity of contemporary urban life in New York City. She is unique, however, in the vitality and empathetic qualities that infuse her portrayals of the human figure in her drawings, etchings, and paintings. Her sensitive rendition of humanity and her recognition of innate human decency without regard to economic or social status or stereotypical physical beauty have caused her to be compared with Rembrandt. Her earlier works represented people, and women especially, who had the potential to move both physically and in society. A second emphasis was on mobility through appearances—putting on or taking off a coat, for example, changes the viewer's perception as well as the self-image of a particular model. In her late works Bishop shows the figure in transformation between physical environments—the street, the subway—and their interrelationships in space. Working with live models in her studio, she created a "seamless web," as she called it, a hazy skein of tonality and texture of painted surface. Her expressive drawings and etchings also capture an elusive movement—the restless flow of human action and interaction—that defines her work as uniquely representative of urban life. Throughout the tumultuous period in America when abstract expressionism overshadowed the New York art world, Bishop remained true to her personal vision as a realist within a distinctly American tradition, which included Robert Henri, Everett Shinn, George Luks, John Sloan, Miller, Du Bois, and Marsh, of contemporary metropolitan life. Bishop died at her home in Riverdale, New York.

• Quotations in the above text are taken from personal interviews with Bishop conducted by Mary Sweeney Ellett on 2 Feb. 1985 and 24 Jan. 1986. The most comprehensive assessment of Bishop's achievements, one which includes a representative selection of reproductions, many in color and divided into categories by subject matter, is Helen Yglesias, *Isabel Bishop* (1989). Karl Lunde, *Isabel Bishop* (1975), also offers a good overall survey of her drawings, etchings, and paintings. Good color images, as well as illustrations of her graphic works, along with minimal descriptive text are in the catalog by Bruce St. John for the exhibition. *Isabel Bishop: The Affectionate Eye* (1985), at Laband Art Gallery, Loyola Marymount University, Los Angeles, Calif. See also Cindy Nemser, "Conversations with Isabel Bishop," *Feminist Art Journal* 5 (Spring 1976): 14–20. John Russell, "A Novelist's Eye in Isabel Bishop's Art," *New York Times*, 12 Apr. 1975, and Ernest Harmes, "Light Is the Beginning—The Art of Isabel Bishop," *American Artist* 25 (Feb. 1961): 28–33, 60–62. An obituary is in the *New York Times*, 22 Feb. 1988.

MARY SWEENEY ELLETT

BISHOP, James Alonzo (21 Nov. 1907–26 July 1987), journalist and author, was born in Jersey City, New Jersey, the son of John Michael Bishop, a police lieutenant, and Jenny Josephine Tier. The son of devout Catholics, Bishop attended St. Patrick's parochial school in Jersey City, graduating in June 1922. Except for a few courses in typing and shorthand at Drake Secretarial College in Jersey City, this ended Bishop's formal education. According to his 1981 autobiography, *A Bishop's Confession*, Bishop was a rebellious teen who fought with his parents and had difficulty holding a job, but he soon became fascinated with "facts," which "became the springboards from which my brain jumped." He read widely in psychology, history, biography, and the sciences and admired his father as he "watched him pirouette the black fountain pen in fine Spencerian letters, his head cocked to the right as he wrote police reports."

In 1929 Bishop's father helped him get a job as a copyboy with the *New York Daily News*, and a year later he was hired by the *Daily Mirror* as a reporter. Feature writer Mark Hellinger took Bishop on as an assistant from 1932 to 1934 and taught him rewriting and feature writing skills; in 1934 Bishop was promoted to the rewrite desk and became a feature writer. Hellinger trained Bishop to think and write his best "in the tick of a clock" because "additional thought might induce wordy, specious copy." In 1943 Bishop's first major news article, a story on Madame Chiang Kai-Shek, "ran with color" and brought the young reporter to the attention of his superiors.

Bishop left the *Mirror* in 1943 and during the next ten years held various editorial positions. From 1943 to 1946 he was associate editor and then war editor for *Collier's*; from 1946 to 1948, executive editor for *Liberty*; from 1948 to 1951, literary editor for the Music Corporation of America; in 1951, founding editor of Gold Medal Books, the juvenile division of Fawcett Books; and in 1953, executive editor of *Catholic Digest* and founder of the Catholic Digest Book Club.

During these years Bishop wrote the first five of the twenty-one books he would publish during his lifetime. The first, *The Glass Crutch: The Biographical Novel of William Wynne Wister* (1945), a fictionalized biography of an alcoholic, received some favorable review. The other four—*The Mark Hellinger Story* (1952), *Parish Priest* (1953), *The Girl in the Poison Cottage* (1953), and *The Making of a Priest* (1954)—received little notice, and by 1954 Bishop was deeply in debt. In addition his 1930 marriage to Elinor Dunning was increasingly troubled by personal difficulties and his wife's deteriorating physical and mental health.

At this time Bishop turned to a "crutch." He had been collecting notes on Abraham Lincoln's assassination for twenty-three years and used these to write an hour-by-hour account of Lincoln's last day. *The Day Lincoln Was Shot* (1955) was an immediate bestseller and was chosen by the Book-of-the-Month Club. The Lincoln book launched Bishop on his true career: writing a series of "day" books notable for the wealth of "you are there" detail and a terse, reportorial style. During his newspaper days Bishop had kept a copy of Ernest Hemingway's *The Sun Also Rises* in his desk drawer, and before writing Bishop would always read a few pages of it "hoping that some of the Hemingway magic would rub off on me."

The popularity of *The Day Lincoln Was Shot* prompted comedian Jackie Gleason to insist that Bishop write his biography, but *The Golden Ham: A Candid Biography of Jackie Gleason* (1956) created a rift between the two friends. More "day" books reflecting Bishop's concerns with American history and his Roman Catholic faith followed. *The Day Christ Died* (1957) was a Literary Guild selection that became a made-for-television movie in 1980, though Bishop was so unhappy with the film he insisted that his name be removed from the credits. Next came *The Day Christ Was Born: A Reverential Reconstruction* (1960). Bishop finished writing *A Day in the Life of President Kennedy* (1964) ten days before Kennedy was assassinated; he later produced *A Day in the Life of President Johnson* (1967). *The Day Kennedy Was Shot* (1968) is based primarily on the report of the Warren Commission and an interview with President Lyndon Johnson because the Kennedy family had asked other witnesses to cooperate exclusively with William Manchester, who was writing *Death of a President*. *The Days of Martin Luther King, Jr.* (1971) is a biography of the civil rights leader, a story, Bishop writes in the preface, that is "emotional, rather than intellectual or logical." In the book Bishop discusses the "elements which surrounded [King's] life work" and includes both "those who helped him [and] those who hurt him." Throughout his career Bishop continued to claim that he was neither historian, politician, nor theologian and refused to respond to critics who charged him with melodrama and superficiality. His aim was to make history vivid and graphic for the average reader, and his books successfully achieved this.

In 1957 Bishop signed a contract with King Features Syndicate for three columns per week. The column—predominantly human interest stories—ran for twenty-six years and was carried in 200 newspapers. Drawing on his experience at the rewrite desk, Bishop boasted that the average time spent writing each column was thirty-five minutes. A selection of these columns, whose topics include race relations, presidents, newspapers, family, and religion, are collected in *Jim Bishop, Reporter* (1966).

Bishop's wife Elinor died in 1957; the couple had two daughters. In 1961 he married a divorcée, Elizabeth Jame Kelly Stone, who became his assistant; he subsequently adopted her two daughters.

During the 1960s Bishop appeared on television in New York City as a commentator on "Byline—Jim Bishop," a weekly program on WABC-TV from 1961 to 1962, and as a moderator on "A Re-Examination of the Warren Commission Findings: A Minority Report," on WNEW-TV in 1966. He was given numerous awards and honors, including the Catholic Institute of the Press Award (1956), the Banshees Silver Lady Award (1956), the Northwestern University Award for the best writing of the year (1956), and the National Association of Independent Schools Award (1956). Although he rarely attended mass, Bishop described himself as a "deeply committed" Catholic, although his nightly prayers always included a petition that God forgive him for being a hypocrite. Bishop died in his Delray Beach, Florida, home.

• Bishop's papers and manuscripts of his books, columns, and magazine articles are in the Friedsham Memorial Library at St. Bonaventure University. Bishop published articles and excerpts of books in national magazines such as *Cosmopolitan*, *McCall's*, and *Good Housekeeping*. His other book-length works include *Fighting Father Duffy* (1956), a children's book; *Go with God* (1958) and *Some of My Very Best* (1960), both devotional works; *The Murder Trial of Judge Peel* (1962), an account of a 1950s Florida murder trial; *Honeymoon Diary* (1963), a novel; and *FDR's Last Year* (1974). The best source for biographical information is James Barron's 28 July 1987 *New York Times* obituary, in addition to Bishop's 1981 autobiography.

JUDITH E. FUNSTON

BISHOP, Joel Prentiss (10 Mar. 1814–4 Nov. 1901), legal treatise writer, was born in Volney, New York, the son of Amos Bishop and Fanny Prentiss, farmers. Joel Bishop was born in a remote farming community. His family was poor, and his mother died when he was an infant. Bishop worked on the farm while attending the local district school. At age sixteen he began teaching in lower schools while continuing his studies in various seminaries in Oneida County, New York. When he was twenty-one, Bishop joined the growing abolition movement and over the next seven years worked as an officer of the New York Anti-Slavery Society and as the assistant editor of the *Friend of Man*, an abolitionist newspaper. In 1842 Bishop moved to Boston, supporting himself by editing the *Social Monitor and Orphan's Advocate* and clerking in a law office. Two years later he was admitted to the Massachusetts bar.

In 1852 Bishop published *Commentaries on the Law of Marriage and Divorce*. Written to establish his reputation as a knowledgeable practitioner, it attracted such favorable attention that Bishop decided to abandon legal practice and devote himself to legal scholarship. Although practice offered large monetary rewards, he felt that through scholarship he could "make an impress for good on the law, and leave the world a gainer by my having lived in it" (*New Criminal Procedure* [1895], p. vi). As a result, Bishop composed one book on jurisprudence and legal study and a succession of treatises on family law, criminal law and procedure, statutory interpretation, contract, and tort law, many of which he shepherded through multiple thoroughly revised editions.

Treatise writing was the focus of Bishop's latter life. He lived nearly as a recluse, researching and writing on the law, and generally declining to address other issues of public concern. The only exceptions were pamphlets and speeches urging the constitutional propriety of enfranchising and arming southern slaves during the Civil War, the economic impropriety of strikes during the labor unrest of the 1880s, and the advantages of maintaining the common law system against efforts to supplant it with laws entirely premised upon legislative codes. Bishop died in Cambridge, Massachusetts.

Bishop's commentaries on marriage and divorce, on the rapidly shifting law of married women's property, and on criminal law and procedure were thorough and innovative works that significantly influenced their fields. In family law, for example, he helped establish the view that marriage was a status into which the parties contractually entered but over which they had little contractual power. In criminal law, he developed the notion that criminal law involved a network of consistent principles rather than a patchwork of disparate prohibitions. His treatise on statutory interpretation, *Commentaries on the Written Laws and Their Interpretation* (1882), was the first American treatment of the subject. His books on contracts and torts were less exhaustive works, more derivative of other scholars' presentations. Yet all of Bishop's writings were well received by his contemporaries. More than one legal periodical regarded him as "the foremost law writer of the age" (*Central Law Journal* 21 [1885]: 81), a writer whose "researches have been so original and exhaustive that his literary life affords a pattern to those who aspire to be called learned men" (*American Law Review* 18 [1884]: 854). In 1884, when the University of Berne in Switzerland celebrated its fiftieth anniversary by awarding honorary degrees to an international array of scholars, Bishop was the only American honoree.

Bishop's commentaries popularized the "formal" style of legal analysis then coming into vogue in England and America. He was among the first scholars to depict Anglo-American law as an ordered system in which the law's innumerable rules were the logical elaboration of a few initial principles, principles that jurists discovered through empirical study of decided cases. In Bishop's view, most legal disputes had "right" answers dictated by a small number of abstract principles. He envisioned law as a science that discovered preexisting, nondiscretionary solutions to social controversy. It was a comforting message to a nation beginning to view itself as divided into diverse, fractious religious, ethnic, and economic groups with fundamental disagreements over the direction of public policy.

In addition, Bishop's works presented American law as standing on a foundation of moral principle. Bishop said his scholarly task was to describe American law, believing that "he who undertakes to teach a system, must teach what he finds, and not, in its stead, another system which he may abstractly prefer" (*First Book of the Law* [1868], p. 108). Yet Bishop also was an evangelical Protestant who believed that God's "annunciations are through his works" (*Non-Contract Law* [1889], p. 33) and that Anglo-American law was one of those works. Bishop's view of American law was that "beneath, above, and around the rules of mere human invention, . . . woven into their very texture also, are the broad doctrines which an abstract science could draw from nature herself" (*Criminal Law*, 2d ed. [1858], p. 2).

Bishop also believed that humanity possessed a divinely implanted "moral sense" distinguishing right from wrong. The silently felt promptings of the moral sense indicated to morally upright judges the proper disposition of cases as surely as if "Almighty God appear[ed] in the midst of the tribunal . . . and reveal[ed] the right way to the understandings of the judges" (*First Book of the Law*, p. 129). Due to the judiciary's intuitive ability to decide cases properly, Bishop thought the pattern of case outcomes reflected underlying moral principles much as the pattern of physical events evidenced physical laws.

Blending the religious and the secular informed all of Bishop's lifework. He conceived legal scholarship as his "calling"; his vocation was to preserve, perfect, and defend America's legal heritage so that the nation might perform its divine mission in this world. Bishop was an empirical scholar who studied the pattern of American judicial activity and a theologically informed jurist who depicted law as the perfectible expression of the static precepts of divine governance.

• Bishop's major treatises are *Commentaries on the Law of Marriage and Divorce* (1852), *Commentaries on the Criminal Law* (1856–1858), *Commentaries on the Law of Criminal Procedure* (1866), *Commentaries on the Law of Married Women* (1871–1875), *Commentaries on the Written Laws and Their Interpretation* (1882), *Commentaries on the Law of Contracts* (1887), and *Commentaries on the Non-Contract Law* (1889). Although *The First Book of the Law* (1868) is the only volume specifically devoted to legal philosophy, Bishop frequently prefaced his treatises with lengthy jurisprudential discussions that he substantially revised from edition to edition. The prefaces to the last editions of the treatises on marriage and divorce, criminal law, and criminal procedure, published in the 1890s, are particularly revealing. See also his speech "The Common Law as a System of Reasoning," *American Law Review* 22 (1888): 1–29, republished as Joel Bishop, *The Common Law and Codification* (1888). Bishop's autobiographical sketch in *Central Law Journal* 20 (1885): 321–22 and the extended obituary notice in *American Law Review* 36 (1902): 1–9 are important sources. Michael Grossberg, *Governing the*

Hearth: Law and the Family in Nineteenth-Century America (1985), contains a thoughtful treatment of Bishop's work in family law.

STEPHEN A. SIEGEL

BISHOP, John Peale (21 May 1891–4 Apr. 1944), writer, was born in Charles Town, West Virginia, the son of Jonathan Peale Bishop, a physician and druggist, and Margaret Miller Cochran. His grandfather, a Yale graduate, had moved south from New York after the Civil War. Bishop considered himself a southerner, but he nevertheless maintained a high regard for his northern roots. When Bishop was ten his father died, and his mother remarried in 1906. His mother and stepfather moved to Hagerstown, Maryland, and Bishop entered Washington County High School. His health had not been robust during childhood, and in his senior year he had trouble with his eyesight; he was not able to attend school from 1910 to 1913. During these years his mother and sister read aloud to him, and he developed a fondness for poetry. Bishop published a poem, "To a Woodland Pool," in *Harper's Weekly* in 1912. When Bishop entered Princeton University in 1913, his vision finally improved, he was considerably older and more sophisticated than most of his classmates. While at Princeton he met two men who became lifelong friends of his, writers Edmund Wilson and F. Scott Fitzgerald (who modeled Tom D'Invilliers in *This Side of Paradise* on Bishop). Bishop published frequently in Princeton's *Nassau Literary Magazine*, and by the time he graduated in 1917 he had written enough poems to issue a privately published book, *Green Fruit*. That same year he accepted a commission in the U.S. Army. He did not experience combat, but he served in France until 1919. France always remained for him a land of cultural values, in which both contemporaneity and tradition were prized and in which, as he wrote in a 1941 essay, "the present was continuously enriched by the past" (Wilson, p. 174).

When he returned to civilian life Bishop was drawn to New York City. He became a junior editor, and eventually managing editor, of *Vanity Fair*. In 1922, the year he and Wilson published a joint collection of verse and prose titled *The Undertaker's Garden*, Bishop married Margaret Grosvenor Hutchins, a young woman from a wealthy New York family. Soon after their wedding the couple left for a sojourn in Europe. They returned to New York in 1924, and Bishop renewed his association with *Vanity Fair* and also worked as a caption writer for silent films in the New York office of Paramount Pictures. He grew increasingly unhappy with modern capitalism and industrialism and with the frenzy of jazz-age New York, and consequently Bishop and his wife returned to France in 1926. Taking advantage of Margaret's inheritance, they purchased and settled into a château in Orgeval, near Paris, devoting much of their time to the renovation and maintenance of their property and to the raising of their three children. During these expatriate years Bishop became well acquainted with writers such as Ezra Pound, Ernest Hemingway, E. E. Cummings, and Archibald MacLeish, and frequent correspondence nourished his friendship with American poet and critic Allen Tate. In the 1920s Bishop published only sporadically. Scribner's encouraged, but eventually did not publish, a disjointed romance of his titled *The Huntsmen Are Up in America*. In 1931, however, the publishing house issued a collection of stories, *Many Thousands Gone* (the title story won the 1930 *Scribner's Magazine* prize), and two years later it published a volume of Bishop's poetry, *Now with His Love*.

In 1933 the Bishops returned permanently to the United States, settling eventually on Cape Cod, where in 1937 they oversaw the building of a house in South Chatham. Bishop had begun to publish significantly, both poetry and criticism, in the last years of his stay in France, but the return to the United States seems to have further liberated his creative energies. The year 1935 saw the publication of a second book of poetry, *Minute Particulars*, as well as *Act of Darkness*, a novel about the dark undercurrents of life in a southern town just before World War I. Bishop was never a popular writer (the publication of *Act of Darkness* was overshadowed by the appearance three days later of Thomas Wolfe's *Of Time and the River*, also published, with much fanfare, by Scribner's), but his critical reputation was good during the final years of his life. He took part in several writers' conferences, published important essays in periodicals such as the *Virginia Quarterly Review* and the *Sewanee Review*, and he was a regular contributor to the *New Republic* and eventually the chief poetry reviewer for the *Nation*. Bishop was even invited to appear on the CBS radio program "Invitation to Learning." In 1941 his *Selected Poems* was published, and he began work as publications director in the New York office of the Council of National Defense, for which he oversaw the publication of an anthology of Latin American poetry and an anthology of American writing.

In 1943 Bishop was appointed a resident fellow at the Library of Congress. His health was poor, however, and a combination of high blood pressure and emphysema forced him to return to Cape Cod in November. He died in Hyannis, Massachusetts. *The Collected Poems of John Peale Bishop*, edited by Tate, and *The Collected Essays of John Peale Bishop*, edited by Wilson, were both published in 1948. In the introduction to the former, Bishop's longtime friend Tate remarked that his northern and southern heritage had helped to shape Bishop's outlook on life. Tate writes that this "split in loyalty" was "the condition of his special sensibility, liberating his powers of observation" (Tate, p. xii).

The opening lines of Bishop's 1925 poem "Speaking of Poetry," "The ceremony must be found / That will wed Desdemona to the huge Moor," suggest the thematic emphasis of Bishop's mature work, concerned with ambiguities, polarities, opposed tensions, and conflicting loyalties. Bishop once aphoristically described the poet, generically, as "the product of a border country, of the mixed race and the misalliance" (Wilson, p. 375). He did not, however, think that such tensions could, or should, be ultimately resolved. In a letter to Tate he wrote, "In a healthy society there are various tensions opposed. There is a continual effort necessary to maintain equilibrium which must be (this the Americans will not admit) an unstable equilibrium" (Young and Hindle, p. 47). Bishop's willingness to remain unsettled perhaps explains in part why his criticism is never programmatic, never harnessed to any particular body of critical theory. As Wilson writes in his introduction to the collected essays, Bishop's works are "not a series of literary critiques . . . but a set of discourses on various aspects of contemporary civilization" (Wilson, p. vii). In the essay "The Discipline of Poetry" Bishop argues that it is the goal of all the arts "to present the conflict of man with time. . . . And the famous release which the arts afford is essentially a release from time" (Wilson, p. 104). Bishop knew that humanity could not control time, but he felt that the artist could control "the consciousness of it," and that for the poet "the means . . . to that end is verse."

Early in his career Bishop was sometimes reproached for being too much influenced by other poets. By the mid-1930s, however, he had arrived at an individual poetic voice fully capable of treating man's relation to time, a subject masterfully dealt with in such late poems as "A Subject of Sea Change" and "The Hours," a moving elegy for Fitzgerald. The historical dimensions of time are also central to Bishop's fiction, particularly in *Many Thousands Gone* and *Act of Darkness*, which are both set in the fictional upper Shenandoah Valley town of Mordington and which epitomize Bishop's distinctive, if not major, accomplishments.

• Bishop's papers are in the Princeton University Library. His correspondence with Tate is in Thomas Daniel Young and John J. Hindle, *The Republic of Letters in America* (1981). A bibliography of works published in Bishop's lifetime is J. Max Patrick and Robert W. Stallman, "John Peale Bishop: A Checklist," *Princeton University Library Chronicle* 7 (1946): 62–79. A detailed but uncritical biography is Elizabeth Carroll Spindler, *John Peale Bishop* (1980). Also helpful are Jesse Bier, "A Critical Biography of John Peale Bishop" (Ph.D. diss., Princeton Univ., 1956), and Stephen C. Moore, "Variations on a Theme: The Poetry and Criticism of John Peale Bishop" (Ph.D. diss., Univ. of Michigan, 1963). Robert L. White, *John Peale Bishop* (1966), is a critical study. Joseph Frank published two excellent articles on Bishop: "Force and Form: A Study of John Peale Bishop," *Sewanee Review* 55 (1947): 71–107, and "The Achievement of John Peale Bishop," *Minnesota Review* 2 (1962): 325–44. An obituary is in the *New York Times*, 6 Apr. 1944.

ROBERT L. WHITE

BISHOP, Morris Gilbert (15 Apr. 1893–20 Nov. 1973), university professor and writer, was born in the Main Building of the Willard, New York, State Hospital for the Insane, the son of Edwin Rubergall Bishop, a Canadian physician, and Bessie E. Gilbert, a daughter of the institution's steward. His mother died when Bishop was a year old, and he and his brother were raised by his paternal grandparents in Brantford, Ontario, until they were reunited with their father and his new wife in Geneva, New York. After the death of their father and stepmother of tuberculosis when Morris was eight years old, the boys lived with their mother's family in Yonkers, where Bishop completed high school.

Admitted to Cornell University in 1910, Bishop won the Morrison Poetry Prize and admission to Phi Beta Kappa while graduating in three years. He earned an M.A. in romance languages from Cornell in 1914 and went to work as a salesman in Boston and San Francisco for Ginn and Company, textbook publishers. After cavalry service on the Mexican border in 1916 (which left him with a lifelong loathing for horses), World War I service as an army lieutenant, and a postarmistice stint in Finland as a member of the American Relief Administration mission, he worked for a year in a New York advertising agency before returning to Cornell in 1921 to teach French and Spanish. On earning his Ph.D. from Cornell in 1926, he was appointed assistant professor. He married Alison Mason Kingsbury in 1927. They had one daughter, Alison Bishop Jolly, who became an expert on lemurs. Promoted to full professor in 1936, Bishop was named Kappa Alpha Professor of Romance Literature two years later.

Early in life Bishop tried his hand at lyric poetry but found he preferred light verse, especially the limerick. He contributed frequently to *Life*, the *Saturday Evening Post*, and the *New Yorker*, and these pieces were collected in *Paramount Poems* (1929), *A Bowl of Bishop* (1954), and *The Best of Bishop: Light Verse from the "New Yorker" and Elsewhere* (1980). He also wrote a mystery novel, *The Widening Stain* (1942), under the pseudonym W. Bolingbroke Johnson. His scholarly forte was biography, and by the time of World War II he had published lives of an explorer, Núñez Cabeza de Vaca, a philosopher, Blaise Pascal, and a poet, Pierre de Ronsard.

From 1942 until 1944 Bishop served in New York and London with the Office of War Information, then, during 1944 and 1945, with the U.S. Army's Psychological Warfare Division. Returning to Cornell, he continued his scholarly output with biographies of another explorer, Samuel de Champlain, and a writer, François de la Rochefoucauld; a college textbook of French literature; and a translation of eight of Jean-Baptiste Molière's plays. In 1948 he was instrumental in finding Vladimir Nabokov a teaching position at Cornell and remained for the rest of his life a close friend, correspondent, and literary adviser of that writer. Bishop frequently bested Nabokov in jousting with limericks and quips. A good example of the latter is his query, "Vladimir, at your age are you not ashamed to live off a girl like Lolita?" During the 1951–1952 academic year, Bishop was visiting professor of American civilization at the University of Athens. From 1957 until his retirement from his chair in 1960, he served Cornell as a faculty trustee.

Bishop's career accelerated in the final dozen years of his life. He continued to serve until 1964 in the senate of Phi Beta Kappa, a term that had begun in 1958. In 1964 he was elected president of the Modern Language Association of America. After 1970 he was curator of the Cornell University Dante and Petrarch Collection. More biographies appeared, including another volume on Pascal; a life of the poet Francesco Petrarch, whose love poems Bishop had translated in 1932; a life of St. Francis of Assisi; and a book of vignettes of twenty-one extraordinary persons. He also published a history of the exploration of the St. Lawrence River, a history of Cornell University, a selection of Petrarch's letters, and a history of the Middle Ages. In addition he edited a series of classical, medieval, Renaissance, and romantic storybooks illustrated by his wife, and he produced numerous magazine articles on an astonishing range of topics. He died in Ithaca, New York.

Bishop's more than 400 publications are noteworthy not only by reason of their volume and their varied subject matter but also because of their charming style and formidable erudition. Bishop was fluent in German, French, Spanish, Swedish, modern Greek, and Latin; his command of the entire breadth of literature in the romance languages was exceptional. His scrupulous accuracy and keen insight gave substance not only to his core studies, those dealing with French language and civilization, but also to those in areas with which he was less familiar. Known as an urbane and witty teacher who brought a good deal of oratorical panache to his class lectures, Bishop acquired a somewhat different type of campus renown at the 1970 graduation exercises, when he stopped a student from disrupting the ceremony by thumping him soundly in the ribs with a fourteen-pound ceremonial mace.

• Bishop's papers, including classroom lecture notes, research notes, manuscripts, and correspondence, are in the Rare and Manuscript Collection of the Carl A. Kroch Library of Cornell University. Biographical information with comments from Bishop is in B. Asterlund, "Morris Bishop," *Wilson Library Bulletin*, Mar. 1943, p. 596; and Stanley J. Kunitz, *Twentieth Century Authors, Second Supplement* (1955). Appreciations of Bishop are Charlotte Putnam Reppert, "The Way He Said It," *Cornell Alumni News*, Nov. 1980; and David McCord, "The Arch Bishop," *Cornell Alumni News*, Nov. 1980, both reprinted from *The Best of Bishop: Light Verse from the "New Yorker" and Elsewhere*, ed. Reppert (1980). A photo is in Brian Boyd, *Vladimir Nabokov: The American Years* (1991). The most complete and useful obituary is in the *New York Times*, 22 Nov. 1973.

JOSEPH M. MCCARTHY

BISHOP, Robert Hamilton (26 July 1777–29 Apr. 1855), Presbyterian minister and educator, was born at Cult, Linlithgowshire, near Edinburgh, Scotland, the son of William Bishop and Margaret Hamilton, tenant farmers. His parents were devout Presbyterians, and his father was an elder in the Associate Reformed church. He entered Edinburgh University in 1793 and completed his A.B. in 1798 with some financial assistance from his professors. He studied under James Finlayson and Dugald Stewart and imbibed their liberal outlook. Afterward he completed studies at the Associate church's seminary at Selkirk. He was licensed by the presbytery of Perth in response to a call for ministers from the Associate Reformed church in the United States in 1802. Shortly before leaving for America that same year, he married Ann Ireland; they had eight children.

The synod of the Associate Reformed church assigned Bishop to Kentucky, where he engaged in an itinerant preaching for eighteen months before settling in Lexington. In 1804 he accepted a pastoral call from churches at Ebenezer and New Providence as well as a post in logic and moral philosophy at Transylvania University. The presbytery of Kentucky objected to his accepting the teaching position, and Bishop had to appeal to the synod before the presbytery would ordain him in 1808.

While Bishop's reputation as an educator grew, his ecclesiastical difficulties increased. His presbytery suspended him from the ministry for libel in 1815 as a result of an article in the *Evangelical Record and Western Review*, a monthly that he and other reform-minded Associate Reformed clergy published from 1811 to 1813. Appeals dragged out until 1818 when he was exonerated by the synod. Between 1815 and 1820 Bishop preached almost every Sunday to African Americans. While he was suspended, he had organized the first Sunday School for African Americans in Lexington, saying later that this was one of his most enjoyable ministries. Following years of contentious relationships with his presbytery, Bishop resigned and served as stated supply for the McChord Presbyterian Church in Lexington from 1820 to 1823.

Bishop served as acting president at Transylvania for two years (1816–1818), but his relations there grew strained after the arrival of a Unitarian president in 1818. In 1824 he became the first president of Miami University in Oxford, Ohio. The following year he was awarded the doctor of divinity by the College of New Jersey (now Princeton University) and reorganized a defunct Presbyterian congregation at Oxford, to which he preached regularly in the college chapel until it became large enough to secure a regular pastor in 1831. As president of Miami, Bishop was professor first of logic and moral philosophy, then of history and philosophy of social relations. His *Elements of the Science of Government* (1840) stressed religious and civil liberties rather than duties and obligations to government. He encouraged students to explore ideas even when their conclusions did not correspond with his and encouraged self-government in the student body, remarkable for his time. During his tenure as president, Miami became one of the leading universities in the old Northwest.

Bishop supported the formation of colonization (1827) and antislavery societies (1834) at Miami. He was active in both movements, throwing his support with evangelical abolitionists as the breach between the two positions widened. He was a friend and supporter of Lyman Beecher. His political outlook in his later years can be seen in his rejection of the Birney antislavery candidacy of 1840 on the grounds that it would reduce the force of the moral argument against slavery. In the presidential election of that year he supported the William Henry Harrison candidacy mainly as a means of opposition to Martin Van Buren.

The 1837 split of the Presbyterian church into Old and New School branches strained Bishop's relations with the Miami trustees, the majority of whom were Old School clergy. Bishop's sympathies were with the New School, but he deplored the division and worked for reunion of the two branches. His "A Plea for United Action" (1833) was an effort to head off the schism; and in the *Western Peacemaker and Monthly Religious Journal* (1839–1840) he carried on his efforts at reconciliation.

Charges of a lack of discipline among students, support of the antislavery cause, and attempts to reconcile the two branches of the Presbyterian church resulted in Bishop's dismissal from Miami in 1844. Although he remained as professor of history and political science, he and other New School sympathizers were finally ousted in 1844.

Bishop then moved to Pleasant Hill, Ohio, near Cincinnati and helped a former student, Freeman G. Cary, establish Farmer's College, which later became the Ohio Military Institute. At Miami, Bishop had unsuccessfully attempted a similar college, intended to enable those outside the professions to attain literary and scientific knowledge. Cary and Bishop brought the idea to reality at Pleasant Hill, where Bishop continued to teach and preach until his death in Coffe Hill, Ohio.

Contemporaries described Bishop as quick of temper, but just as quick to regret intemperate outbursts and seek reconciliation. While his reputation was primarily as an educator, he was always active in the life of the church, preaching regularly when he did not have a pastoral charge. His pastoral concerns carried over into his life as an educator and can be seen in the mutual affection that existed between him and his students. His financial assistance enabled many of them to have the opportunity for higher education. He exemplified a position that was at once theologically conservative and socially progressive, an outlook that was to divide into warring camps in the twentieth century.

• Correspondence, diaries (1805–1839), notes, accounts (1805–1823), and a memorandum book (1803–1852) are in the Bishop family papers, Miami University Library, Oxford, Ohio. His books also include *An Outline of the History of the Church in the State of Kentucky* (1824) and *Elements of Logic*, 2d ed. (1833). "Addresses to the Graduates of Miami University" (1840) and "Addresses Delivered at the Laying of the Corner-stone of the Farmer's College" (1846) present an assessment of his presidency of Miami and a statement of his educational philosophies. "An Outline of the Bible Argument against Slavery" in Thomas E. Thomas, *A Review of the Rev. Dr. Junkin's Synodical Speech in Defense of American Slavery* (1844), presents both Bishop's theological reasoning on the slavery issue and a polemic against Junkin. James H. Rode-

baugh, *Robert Hamilton Bishop* (1935), includes an extensive bibliography. Thorton A. Mills, *The Life and Services of Rev. R. H. Bishop, D.D.* (1889), includes an "Autobiographical Sketch" by Bishop.

BOYD T. REESE, JR.

BISHOP, Rufus (18 July 1774–2 Aug. 1852), Shaker leader, was born in Montague, Massachusetts, the son of Peter Bishop and Abigail (maiden name unknown). Bishop became a Shaker in childhood, joining with his parents and all but two of his siblings in 1780. On 9 March 1789 he became a fully covenanted member of the New Lebanon, New York, Shaker community. As a Shaker, Bishop committed himself to celibacy, pacifism, common ownership of property, and a physically active brand of Christian worship. Significantly, as a teenager Bishop was said to possess the humility and devotion that was sought in an elder of the group.

Beginning in 1812 Bishop composed *Testimonies of the Life . . . of Mother Ann Lee*, which was published in 1816. This compilation presented Ann Lee as a prophet who was divinely commissioned to found the United Society of Believers in Christ's Second Appearing, the group's formal name. Indeed, Bishop wrote, Lee *constituted* this second appearing, as she was "the First Spiritual Mother in Christ and the Second Heir of the covenant of life in the New Creation." *Testimonies* was a cornerstone for the development of later Shaker theology, as it embodied memories of the first generation of Shakers who had witnessed Lee's work and teaching. It remains the most important work about early Shakerism.

From 1808 to 1821 Bishop was second elder at the Church Family (an autonomous subunit at the center of the commune) of the New Lebanon community. After another Shaker's vision in 1821 in which his succession was prophesied, Bishop was promoted to the Central Ministry, the committee that led the entire Society. A remarkable period of twenty-seven years of joint leadership by four elders—Bishop and his brother Ebenezer and eldresses Mary Landon and Asanath Clark—followed. In the previous half-century the Society had been led by a series of charismatic figures, whose claims to authority were based on "gifts" received from God. The Central Ministry of Rufus Bishop, a generation removed from the Society's founders, sought authority through a well-defined organizational structure. Bishop's diaries record a steady routine of meetings and discussions with Shaker leaders, writers, and ordinary believers, all to create consensus on the issues of the day, such as fines imposed on the Shakers for nonobservance of militia duty, proposals to publish religious writings, and changes in Church Family leadership.

Bishop proved to be skilled at his management duties, compensating for his lack of charismatic gifts with a straightforward sensitivity. He maintained communication between the Central Ministry and distant communities from Maine to Kentucky by writing scores of letters each year and traveling many hundreds of miles to visit other Shaker communities. He reformed confession of sins to elders, an important part of Shaker practice, by introducing flexible times for members to confess in place of the previously required monthly confession. As Shaker leaders were required to do, he continued to practice his trade of tailoring.

Within the Society, leading by consensus was occasionally misconstrued as indecisiveness. In the early 1830s Bishop's tolerance of those who followed the vegetarian diet advocated by reformer Sylvester Graham was criticized by another elder as a concession to "ambitious fanatics." It was Bishop, however, who went west in 1834 to evaluate leaders at two troubled communities in Ohio and Kentucky. He determined in his four-month visit that the elders in question were unable to maintain discipline and order, and so after further consultations in New Lebanon, the Central Ministry recalled and replaced both of them. The episode reflects Bishop's willingness to confront disorder and to act to curb it, thus allowing the Shakers to maintain a virtually national network of communities.

Bishop's greatest challenge as elder may have been balancing the outburst of spiritualism between 1837 and 1844 with the order that the Society needed to continue. His detailed writings make clear that spiritual manifestations, a distinctive Shaker practice that dated from early in the group's history, occurred throughout the early nineteenth century. Spiritual phenomena became particularly intense in the late 1830s, especially among Shaker girls. Bishop and other leaders, while wanting to remain true to the earliest traditions of Shaker spiritualism, nonetheless feared ceding initiative to the ecstasies of the visionists. Bishop himself experienced a vision in 1839 in which an early Shaker elder, James Whittaker, gave him a gold box filled with "gifts." Seeking a middle ground between gift and order, Bishop endorsed some visions as "some of the sublimest sentences that ever entered my ears" but "urge[d] the necessity of keeping every order & counsel which had been given for our protection and increase" (quoted in Stein, 1992, pp. 186, 196). The effect was to direct the revivalist energies, as much as possible, toward reform and discipline in the Society as a whole.

Bishop remained an elder to the end of his life. In the summer of 1852 he again traveled west. When he arrived on 31 July at the small Shaker community of Whitewater, Ohio, near Cincinnati, he became ill with dysentery. He grew steadily weaker and died quietly there three days later.

The critical role of Rufus Bishop in Shaker history can be characterized by the notion of routinization of charisma. The translation of a new religious movement's initial burst of inspiration into organizational forms that will survive through time is an absolute necessity for a movement to continue. Bishop led the Shakers through a period of mild population growth in the East and the addition of three new communities in the West. His written contributions to Shaker institutional memory and his willingness to discipline western elders whom he saw as wayward suggest that he

emphasized the importance of order. His participation in the era of manifestations and his recognition that it could be directed toward the welfare of the Society shows that he also recognized the necessity of spiritual gifts for a charismatic religion such as the Shakers. Bishop's work to maintain the delicate balance between gift and order in Shaker organization was vital to the persistence of the Society.

• The best collection of Rufus Bishop's writings is in the Shaker Manuscript Collection, New York Public Library (his *Daily Journal of Passing Events* constitutes items 1–3). Other Bishop journals are in the Shaker Collection, Western Reserve Historical Society (see especially manuscript items V: B–85, a day book of the ministry kept from 1815 to 1829, and VI: A–6, testimonies on "Miraculous Gifts of Healing"). His *Testimonies of the Life, Character, Revelations and Doctrines of Our Ever Blessed Mother Ann Lee* (1816) was reprinted in 1888. On his birth and entrance into the Society with his family, see Anna White and Leila S. Taylor, *Shakerism: Its Meaning and Message* (1904). For more information on his death, see Western Reserve Historical Society manuscript V: B–153, "Daily Journal Kept by Daniel Boler," entries of 30 July–2 Aug. 1852. Close analysis of *Testimonies* appears in Susan M. Setta, "The Appropriation of Biblical Hermeneutics to Biographical Criticism: An Application to the Life of the Shaker Founder, Ann Lee," *Historical Methods* 16 (1983): 89–100. On Bishop's actions in the West, see Stephen J. Stein, "Community, Commitment, and Practice: Union and Order at Pleasant Hill in 1834," *Journal of the Early Republic* 8 (1988): 45–68. For other details, see Stein, *The Shaker Experience in America: A History of the United Society of Believers* (1992), and Priscilla J. Brewer, *Shaker Communities, Shaker Lives* (1986).

JOHN E. MURRAY

BISHOP, W. Howard (19 Dec. 1885–11 June 1953), Catholic priest and founder of the Glenmary Home Missioners, was born William Howard Bishop in Washington, D.C., the son of Francis Besant Bishop, a doctor, and Eleanor Theresa Knowles, both born and raised in North Carolina. Bishop was educated in public schools but in keeping with his family's social standing he attended Harvard College between 1906 and 1908. Originally motivated to pursue a career as a journalist, he took a year off from school to work and sort out his life. Ultimately, he enrolled at St. Mary's Seminary in Baltimore, Maryland. With six years of Latin, four years of Greek, and a familiarity with French, German, advanced mathematics, history, and literature, he was well-prepared academically to enter the six-year seminary education, which included two years of college and four years of theology.

Bishop's public school background, his Anglo-American heritage, and his Harvard experience set him apart from the typical seminarian of the period who had a parochial education, an immigrant background, and an immersion in the devotional Catholicism of a separatist subculture. With tendencies toward shyness and a slight limp because one leg was shorter than the other, Bishop excelled in writing and eventually became a good preacher. He was ordained in the spring of 1915 and spent two difficult years as an assistant pastor in a suburban Baltimore parish. In 1917 he convinced Cardinal James Gibbons, archbishop of Baltimore, to assign him to a rural parish. From 1917 to 1937 he was pastor of St. Louis Parish, Clarksville, Maryland, an assignment that included ministry at St. Mary's Chapel at Doughoregan Manor, the ancestral home of Charles Carroll, the Catholic signer of the Declaration of Independence.

With the help of the Catholic Daughters of the Americas, one of the women's counterparts to the Knights of Columbus, Bishop founded and headed the League of St. Louis (1922) to support a parochial school. It later became the League of the Little Flower (1924), an archdiocesan organization that supervised funding of catechetical programs and parochial education in rural parishes. He was also founder and editor of its quarterly publication, the *Little Flower* (1927–1937).

In accord with his pastoral activism, Bishop was engaged in several rural movements. He was a founding member of the National Catholic Rural Life Conference (NCRLC) in 1923 and served as its president (1928–1934). He founded and edited the NCRLC journal, *Landward* (1930), a quarterly dedicated to a back-to-the-land movement. He responded to the anti-Catholic prejudice vented in the 1928 defeat of Al Smith, the Democratic party candidate for president, by urging enlightened interfaith cooperation. In response to the Great Depression, Bishop lashed out at the capitalist free-market exploitation of the land. Indeed, he advocated federal legislation to promote the widest possible distribution of productive property. Bishop's policy to resolve urban unemployment entailed the establishment of rural colonies that would include cooperative ownership and management of small factories and a domestic system of craft enterprises.

Bishop unsuccessfully attempted to found in Clarksville a colony of the unemployed from Baltimore. Since he viewed his parish as encompassing non-Catholics as well as Catholics, his colony would have been open to people of all or no religious traditions. Hence, as a rural pastor he departed from the prevailing parish model that fostered Catholic separatism.

In 1935 he designed a plan for a religious community of Catholic rural missionaries. Influenced by the rural mission experiences of the Reverend Thomas F. Price in North Carolina, by the missionary bands of diocesan priests promoted by the Paulists, and by the foreign mission thrusts of the Maryknoll Missioners, Bishop's plan was based on direct-action evangelization. He aimed to convert the unchurched in the rural areas through "camp meetings" that would be led by a team of missioners who would represent Catholicity and establish mission parishes in some of the hundreds of counties in rural America. His famous mission map, titled "No Priest Land," featured more than 600 counties where there was no resident Catholic priest.

With the support of the founder-superior of Maryknoll, James A. Walsh, and Archbishop John T.

McNicholas of Cincinnati, Ohio, the Society of Home Missioners of America was founded in Cincinnati in 1939. Later called the Glenmary Home Missioners, the society was composed of priests, brothers, and sisters, who later formed a separate community. In 1938 Bishop founded the *Challenge*, the society's publication, which featured articles on the need for social and religious outreach to the rural poor. Approved by the Archdiocese of Cincinnati in 1939, the men missioners later received Vatican approval in 1947.

Even before the sister missioners were recognized as a viable community Bishop assigned three women aspirants to teach in vacation schools in the summer of 1944. In accord with their blend of education and social work these women made plans to establish a secondhand store and a clinic in a black neighborhood in Virginia. Eventually Dominican sisters served as novice directors, and the Glenmary Sisters received Vatican approval in 1952.

In the early 1950s Bishop was working on a paraliturgical service for what he referred to as the "faraways," families who have no Sunday Mass in their area. He was concerned that if the spiritual needs of faraways were not met, they might lose their faith. The core of the service was a simple English translation of the Mass; a lay leader would read aloud, and the community would respond as in the contemporary vernacular liturgy. Howard's service may be considered as a precursor to contemporary Catholic services for priestless parish communities and illustrates his prescience.

Bishop never lived to see his service in action. When he died in Norton, Virginia, the Glenmary Society included seven rural missions, twenty-one priests, eleven brothers, and twenty-nine sisters.

• An extensive collection of Bishop papers is at the Glenmary Archives in Cincinnati, Ohio. Useful sources on Bishop are Christopher J. Kauffman, *Mission to Rural America: The Story of W. Howard Bishop, Founder of Glenmary* (1991), and Herman W. Stauten, *Howard Bishop, Founder of the Glenmary Home Missions* (1961).

CHRISTOPHER J. KAUFFMAN

BISPHAM, David Scull (5 Jan. 1857–2 Oct. 1921), opera singer and recitalist, was the son of William D. Bispham and Jane Lippincott Scull, of Philadelphia. His father was a prosperous wool merchant who strayed from Quaker observance to such a point that his mother was disowned by her pious family for marrying "out of meeting." Still, the Bisphams considered themselves Quakers, and like many nineteenth-century Quakers, the family held the arts to be a laudable component of life, but not a centerpiece. They certainly did not see music as a suitable profession for a son. Bispham had only rudimentary exposure to music and appeared headed for a career in the family's wool business when he enrolled at Haverford College. At Haverford, however, he immersed himself in student theater and music, and his resonant voice and thespian talents flourished. He married Catherine Stricker Russell in 1885; they had three children. Later, in 1908, they separated.

In 1886 he ventured to Europe, studying voice for three years in Florence and Milan. In 1890 he settled in London, studying acting as well as singing in amateur performances. On 24 June 1892 his "big break" came when he successfully auditioned for the role of Kurwenal in Wagner's *Tristan und Isolde* at London's new Theatre Royal, Drury Lane; the conductor was composer Gustav Mahler. Bispham's success under Mahler's baton won him the notice of critics and other conductors and managers in London.

In 1896 Bispham became a lead baritone at Covent Garden in London and at the Metropolitan Opera in New York, and soon established himself as one of the leading baritones of the operatic world. He was celebrated particularly for his Wagnerian roles. A certain nasal character in Bispham's voice enhanced the effectiveness of some of his Wagnerian portrayals, particularly those of Kurwenal in *Tristan* and, even more, of Beckmesser in *Die Meistersinger von Nürnberg*, where the comic features of the role could thus be subtly underscored. Bispham himself boasted that his Beckmesser and Kurwenal were the greatest of their day.

Bispham was the first American-born opera singer to attain world stature. Critics in America and Europe commented upon both the rich resonances in the lower registers of Bispham's voice and the sophisticated level of acting he brought to the operatic stage—a dimension often missing among singers. Indeed, toward the end of his life, his voice having lost much of its strength, Bispham could still fill concert halls doing dramatic readings. Bispham once performed at the White House, and President Theodore Roosevelt (1858–1919) exclaimed to him: "By jove, Mr. Bispham, that was bully! With such a song as that you could lead a nation into battle."

In 1903 Bispham retired from regular operatic performing and turned to song recitals. He was equally successful here with both audiences and critics. His entry into this musical genre coincided with the birth of the recording industry, and Bispham was among the first to record many of the famous German *lieder*. His recording of Schubert's *Erl König*, set to Goethe's text, with its dramatic interplay of four characters, remains gripping despite the hissing and tinniness typical of early recordings. Bispham was the first major singer to perform the famous vocal literature of Beethoven, Schubert, Schumann and others in English. He also took part in English-language stagings of Mozart operas. With Bispham performing, critics could not summarily dismiss such presentations.

Bispham was critical of arts benefactors, such as Andrew Carnegie and J. P. Morgan (1837–1913), "who now direct the dramatic destinies of America [and fund] the masterpieces of other countries." Advocating a loosening of this tradition in order to promote national traditions, Bispham rejected the idea that the English language could not support serious art. "There is nothing bad in English," he declared, "as a medium for opera and song, except bad English." While nationalistic, Bispham remained openly elitist regarding the availability of musical training. Address-

ing a group of music teachers, he asserted that "no one should retain pupils who are not good enough at least to become fairly good amateurs." "How are we then to earn a living?" asked one. Bispham snorted: "Do something else."

Bispham's enthusiasm for English-language productions prompted the formation of the Society of American Singers, which continued the campaign for such work in art song and opera. The Opera Society of America, a Chicago-based organization, also promoted English productions. The Society regularly gives an award for excellence in American music making, an award fittingly named the David Bispham Medal. Bispham died in New York City.

• David Bispham's autobiography is *A Quaker Singer's Recollections* (1920). An informative entry on his career appears in *The New Grove Dictionary of Music and Musicians* (1980).

ALAN H. LEVY

BISSELL, Daniel (15 Aug. 1769–14 Dec. 1833), army officer, was born in Windsor, Connecticut, the son of Ozias Bissell and Mable Roberts. His father served in the American Revolution, and in 1781 Bissell, aged twelve years, joined the Connecticut militia as a drummer boy. Military life appealed to the young man, and on 19 May 1788 he enlisted as a private in the First Infantry. Bissell served throughout the western frontier and distinguished himself during several harrowing assignments as messenger. In 1791 he became sergeant, was present at General Arthur St. Clair's defeat by Indian forces on 4 November, and won a battlefield commission to ensign. Three years later Bissell commanded an artillery detachment during the Whiskey Rebellion and received personal commendation from General George Washington. In 1793 he married Deborah Seba; they had five children. Thereafter Bissell continually served on the frontier, rising to captain in 1799 and lieutenant colonel in 1808. By this time he had befriended the notorious General James Wilkinson and testified on his behalf at the Aaron Burr trial. Other accomplishments included command of Fort Massac, Illinois Territory, equipping the army's first company of horse artillery, and supervising construction of Fort Belle Fontaine near St. Louis. Bissell's peacetime career climaxed in 1809 when President Thomas Jefferson appointed him commander of the Eighth Military District. This vast wilderness region encompassed most of the Louisiana-Missouri territories, and he oversaw the victualing, training, and paying of scattered garrisons with efficiency.

The renewal of hostilities with Great Britain in 1812 provided Bissell with additional opportunities for advancement. He became colonel of the Fifth Infantry on 15 August 1812 and was appointed to defend the thinly guarded Missouri frontier. In June 1813 Bissell was succeeded by Governor Benjamin Howard and ordered to join his regiment at Fort George, Upper Canada. There he spent several weeks drilling his men in preparation for General Wilkinson's St. Lawrence expedition. Bissell served in the advance guard, acquitted himself well, and on 9 March 1814 received promotion to brigadier general. Shortly after he fought at La Colle Mill, Lower Canada, and subsequently accompanied General George Izard's Right Division on its controversial march from Plattsburgh, New York, to the Niagara frontier. There, on 19 October 1814, Bissell's brigade met and, after a stiff fight, defeated a British force at Cook's Mills on Lyon's Creek. This encounter is significant in being the last pitched battle between regular forces in Canada, and Izard commended Bissell in his official report.

Following the war, Bissell was retained in the peacetime establishment as colonel of the First Infantry with brevet rank of brigadier general. He took post with General Andrew Jackson's Division of the South until friction with other officers culminated in his court-martial in 1816. Bissell was charged with absenteeism and unofficerlike conduct, but he was cleared of all charges and returned to duty. He continued commanding a succession of important posts between St. Louis and New Orleans until 1821, when congressional reduction of the army resulted in an unexpected discharge. Angered by such treatment, Bissell sought reinstatement through the office of Missouri's influential senator, Thomas Hart Benton. Benton argued Bissell's case before Congress for twelve years but could not overcome the machinations of General Winfield Scott, who was believed to have engineered the discharge. Despite lengthy appeals to Presidents John Quincy Adams and Andrew Jackson, Bissell could not resecure his commission, and the dismissal became formal. It was a humiliating end to a 34-year military career spanning five administrations and every rank from private to general. Bissell soon after retired to his farm near St. Louis and emerged as a respected business and community leader. In April 1825 he chaired a committee supervising the arrival of General Lafayette to St. Louis and personally welcomed that esteemed visitor. Bissell continued his successful business and farming ventures until dying on his farm.

Bissell was neither a particularly dashing nor brilliant soldier and remains relatively obscure. His significance, however, lays less with battlefield activities than in the tenure and quality of his military administration. Throughout a period marked by incompetence, Bissell served diligently and effectively, without overt political favor. His lifelong devotion to the western frontier facilitated its settlement, particularly in Missouri, and establishes him as a major contributor to that process. Bissell's untimely and possibly illegal discharge is indicative of Congress's callous attitude toward military veterans, longevity notwithstanding, and was the only blot on an otherwise meritorious record.

• A large cache of Bissell manuscripts is in the St. Louis Mercantile Library Association. Other military records are in Record Group 94, Records of the Adjutant General, and Record Group 153, Records of the Judge Advocate General, National Archives. For correspondence highlighting his frontier administration consult Clarence E. Carter, ed., *Territorial Papers of the United States*, vol. 4 (1949), and W. Edwin Hemphill, ed., *The Papers of John C. Calhoun*, vols. 4 and 5 (1969). The most detailed biography remains Carl J. Zell, "General Daniel Bissell" (Ph.D. diss., St. Louis Univ., 1971). A more antiquarian treatment is Edith N. Jesop, *General Daniel Bissell* (1927). Additional details on his life and discharge are in two articles by Harold W. Ryan, "Daniel Bissell: His Story," Missouri Historical Society *Bulletin* 12 (Oct. 1955): 32–44, and "Daniel Bissell: Late General," Missouri Historical Society *Bulletin* 15 (Oct. 1958): 20–28; and in John Bakeless, "Spies in the Revolution," *American History Illustrated* 6 (Mar. 1971): 36–45.

JOHN C. FREDRIKSEN

BISSELL, Emily Perkins (31 May 1861–8 Mar. 1948), volunteer social worker and author, was born in Wilmington, Delaware, the daughter of Champion Aristarcus Bissell, a lawyer and banker, and Josephine Wales. Her forebears settled in Connecticut where her father, a Yale graduate, was reared. Her maternal grandfather, John Wales, served as a U.S. senator from Delaware from 1849 to 1851. Bissell was educated in Wilmington and at Miss Charlier's School in New York City.

Bissell's commitment to social work was sparked by a Sunday school trip to see urban poverty firsthand when she was fifteen years old. In 1883 she raised funds for a Presbyterian mission to serve immigrant mill workers on the outskirts of Wilmington. Responding to the problems posed by idle youth in the neighborhood, she created a youth club, incorporated in 1889 as the West End Reading Room. As the club's permanent secretary-treasurer, Bissell was responsible for developing the modest reading room into a full-scale settlement that became the West End Neighborhood House. In 1909 the settlement opened Delaware's first free kindergarten. It also provided a playground, a free milk station, classes for adults and children, a boys' brigade, and, in association with the State Board of Health, a well-baby clinic. In 1913 the West End Neighborhood House moved to larger quarters in a predominantly Italian section of the city. When funds ran short "Miss Bissell . . . would go sit in some businessman's office until he gave her the money" (Hulse, p. 19).

Bissell's national reputation rests primarily on her work as a crusader against tuberculosis. At the beginning of the twentieth century, scientists and physicians had determined the cause of this widespread disease, and the x-ray, developed in 1895, gave a reliable method of diagnosis. Prevention and early diagnosis depended on broad education of the public, and the only successful cure required lengthy rest and healthy diet in an atmosphere of clear air. Because few urban homes could supply these conditions, the rural sanatorium emerged as the most effective environment for isolation and recovery. In 1904 the newly founded Delaware Anti-Tuberculosis Society established a small sanatorium in a shack near Wilmington. When funds to maintain the facility were exhausted, Bissell recalled an article that she had read in the magazine *Outlook* in which Jacob Riis described how in Denmark Christmas stamps were sold to raise money to fight the disease.

Bissell secured permission from the American Red Cross, of which she was an active member, to use its name and, with a small sum of borrowed money, she sketched a design and had Christmas stamps printed locally, which volunteers sold in the vestibule of the Wilmington post office in 1907. When initial sales lagged, she convinced Leigh Mitchell Hodges, a crusading columnist for the *Philadelphia North American*, to write a newspaper article about the sale on the theme "stamp out tuberculosis." Held to raise at least $300 to keep the tuberculosis shack in operation, the stamps sale brought in $3,000, enough to purchase land that Bissell named "Hope Farm," where a larger, better-equipped facility was constructed. Bissell wrote magazine and newspaper articles to spread the word of Delaware's success throughout the United States. In 1908 the sale of the stamps, renamed Christmas seals, was extended nationally, and by 1916 the national sale raised over $1 million. These funds proved crucial to the Anti-Tuberculosis Society's efforts to build broad public support for its preventive, diagnostic, and curative programs. Because of her efforts, Bissell came to be called "the lady of the Christmas seal."

As permanent president of the Delaware Anti-Tuberculosis Society from 1908 until her death, Bissell successfully campaigned for state support of sanatoria for Delaware's black and white tuberculosis patients and oversaw the erection of a series of modern sanatorium buildings at Hope Farm, now collectively called the Emily P. Bissell Hospital. Her contribution to the fight against tuberculosis earned her the Trudeau Medal of the National Tuberculosis Association in 1942. She was the first person outside the medical profession to receive this honor.

Bissell's other interests included literature, child labor, and anti-suffrage. She was both a poet and the author of numerous magazine stories and essays that she began publishing in 1894 and that appeared principally in *Outlook* and *Harper's Bazaar* under the pen name "Priscilla Leonard." Her lifelong interest in philanthropy was inspired by religious faith, which she expressed poetically: "Teach me, through this world's strifery / to hold the heavenly harmony, / to soothe some sorrow, right some wrong, / transmute some discord into song."

Bissell lobbied the Delaware State General Assembly to enact protection for child laborers and later accepted an appointment to the State Child Labor Commission and the Children's Bureau. In 1906 she became the first president of the Consumers' League in Delaware and argued for the state's first law regulating employment for women. Although she was a forceful advocate for social reforms among Delaware's politicians, she did not support the ballot for women. As a leader of the National Association Opposed to Woman Suffrage, she gave speeches in several states, wrote articles, and testified before U.S. Senate committees in 1900, 1913, and 1916. In her view, the majority of American women did not want or need suffrage because they could influence public affairs through moral suasion.

Bissell lived in Wilmington where she collected antique china, furniture, and clocks. She summered in Paris Hill, Maine. She exemplified the volunteerism that sparked social reform movements in America in the early twentieth century. Her special talents were in fundraising and administering fledgling charitable organizations during the period before the professionalization of these responsibilities. Her fundraising on behalf of tuberculosis victims was instrumental in saving thousands of lives. She was honored by a U.S. stamp issued on the anniversary of her birthday, 31 May 1980. She died in Wilmington, Delaware.

• Bissell's papers can be found in several collections of the Historical Society of Delaware, Wilmington, including folders marked Emily P. Bissell, Red Cross, the Delaware Anti-Tuberculosis Society, and a file within the William P. Frank Papers. The major collection of the Delaware Anti-Tuberculosis Society Papers is at the Delaware State Archives, Dover, and includes correspondence from Bissell. Some of her poetry appeared in *Happiness and Other Verses* (1928). She wrote a brief account entitled "The Story of the Christmas Seal" for the fortieth-anniversary banquet of the Delaware Anti-Tuberculosis Society in 1947. For her role in tuberculosis work see also Richard H. Shryock, *National Tuberculosis Association 1904–1954* (1957), and Peter Welsh, "Delaware and the White Plague: Public Health Efforts against Tuberculosis to 1925," a seminar paper written in 1984 at the University of Delaware. On her work at the West End Neighborhood House see Lamont J. Hulse, *West End Neighborhood House, 100 Years of Service* (1983). Obituaries appear in the *Wilmington (Del.) Morning News*, 8 Mar. 1948, the *New York Times*, 9 Mar. 1948, and as "In Memoriam" in the minutes of the Delaware Anti-Tuberculosis Society, 20 Mar. 1948.

CAROL HOFFECKER

BISSELL, George Edwin (16 Feb. 1839–30 Aug. 1920), sculptor, was born in New Preston, Connecticut, the son of Hiram Bissell, a quarryman and marble worker, and Isabella Jones. In 1853 his father moved the family to Waterbury, where young George became a clerk in a general store. He was educated at the Northville Academy and at Dr. Gunn's Gunnery Academy in Washington, Connecticut. During the Civil War he served in the Twenty-third Regiment of Connecticut Volunteers and then in the U.S. Navy as paymaster. In 1865 he married Mary E. Welton of Waterbury. The number of their children, if any, is unknown.

Bissell then joined his father and brother in the marble business in Poughkeepsie, where he began to create elaborate designs for architectural decorations and gravestones. His first sculptural commission came in 1871 when he was asked to make a life-size marble figure of a fireman that was placed outside a fire station in Poughkeepsie. His latent talent thus awakened, he departed for Europe in 1875 to study art. In Paris he attended the Académie Julian and the Académie Colorossi, where his principal instructor was Aimé Millet. At the École des Beaux-Arts he took anatomy classes with Paul Dubois. In Rome, Bissell studied briefly at the English Academy and returned to America in 1876 ready to begin his career.

Bissell's first major commission was for the Soldiers' Monument for Waterbury, and to execute the figures for it he returned to Paris in 1883; until 1896 he spent almost as much time in the French capital as he did in the United States. But the figures for the Soldiers' Monument and the bronze image of Colonel John L. Chatfield (1887), also for Waterbury, reveal that Bissell did not adopt the lively, richly modeled style that then prevailed in the Parisian studios; rather, a carefully worked naturalism dominated his manner—the antithesis of the impassioned, impressionistic art of his French contemporary, Auguste Rodin. Naturalism had been established as the appropriate style for American sculpture by an earlier generation of sculptors, and although Bissell's work occasionally betrays the influence of the French Beaux-Arts style, in general he subscribed to the naturalistic tradition.

Bissell's bronze image of John Watts, congressman and judge, later erected in Trinity Churchyard in New York, was exhibited to general acclaim at the World's Columbian Exposition in Chicago in 1893; sculptor and historian Lorado Taft admired the figure's "air of great dignity and composure." That same year Bissell became a charter member of the National Sculpture Society, and his bronze statue of Abraham Lincoln was unveiled in Edinburgh, Scotland. One of his best-known works, a bronze statue of Abraham de Peyster in seventeenth-century attire, was set up in New York in 1896 to commemorate one of the city's early leaders. The de Peyster statue bears an obvious similarity to Michelangelo's *Moses*, which the American undoubtedly studied when he was in Rome. In that year the sculptor established his home and studio in Mount Vernon, New York.

Bissell's rather dry, naturalistic style is seen in his statue of President Chester Alan Arthur, which was dedicated in New York's Madison Square on 13 June 1899. The statue suited the taste of the times, for it was described as "impressive" and "noble," having captured, according to a review in the *New York Times* the following day, "the attitude so familiar to all who saw [President Arthur] in public and private life." The year 1899 also saw the completion of one of Bissell's finest works, the bronze statue of Chancellor James Kent, which was set up in the rotunda of the new Library of Congress in Washington. In style, the Kent piece has as much of the lively surface and rich modeling of the French school as Bissell ever achieved in his work. That same year he created the Army and Navy group for the great triumphal arch erected in New York to celebrate the return of Admiral George Dewey after his victory at Manila Bay; but the arch and its decorations were wrought of staff material (plaster and straw) and deteriorated under exposure to the weather. Bissell's *Lycurgus* (1900), for the Appellate Court Building in New York City, recalls an ancient Roman philosopher–type statue and also the work of the great Renaissance Florentine sculptors Ghiberti and Donatello.

Bissell was a part of the large corps of sculptors who worked at the great expositions of the turn of the century. For the Pan-American Exposition in Buffalo in 1901 he made the statue of Hospitality, while his *Science and Music*, also made of staff, adorned the 1904 Louisiana Purchase Exposition in St. Louis, where his work was awarded a silver medal. Bissell maintained one of the busiest sculpture studios in America during this period, and from 1903 to 1905 and 1907 to 1909 he had a studio in Florence, Italy. His works had a reserved dignity at the core of their design, and the artist's selective realism appealed to his patrons' equation of art and nature.

A quiet, good-natured, and kindly man, he was affectionately known as "Père Bissell" by sculptors of a younger generation. He lived to see the arrival of the modern movement in America, manifested through events such as the famous Armory show of 1913; but by then he was seventy-four years old and such work as he executed thereafter showed no recognition of the revolution that had occurred in art. He died at his home in Mount Vernon, New York.

• There is no known repository of Bissell papers. Brief accounts of his life and career are given in Lorado Taft, *History of American Sculpture* (1924), pp. 245–47, and Wayne Craven, *Sculpture in America* (1984), pp. 243–45. His obituary is in the *New York Times* and the *Hartford Times*, both 31 Aug. 1920.

WAYNE CRAVEN

BISSELL, Richard Mervin, Jr. (18 Sept. 1909–7 Feb. 1994), economics professor and government administrator, was born in Hartford, Connecticut, the son of Richard Bissell, a wealthy insurance executive, and Marie Truesdel. As a young man, Bissell studied at elite educational institutions, including Groton School; Yale University, where he received a B.A. in 1932; and the London School of Economics, where he began his postgraduate work. In 1933 he returned to Yale as an instructor and was promoted to assistant professor before earning his Ph.D. in economics in 1939. In 1940 he married Ann Cornelia Bushnell; they had five children. Described by one friend as "desperately shy," Bissell seemed destined in 1941 to remain a university educator and scholar. However, the outbreak of World War II dramatically changed his life, as he left Yale to become a member of Franklin D. Roosevelt's expanding wartime administration.

Bissell entered government service in 1941 as the chief economics analyst for the Department of Commerce and also as an executive in the War Shipping Administration, where he coordinated the acquisition and overseas distribution of supplies for American and Allied troops. As a result, he served as an early pioneer of policies and operations aimed at securing U.S. military strength through global economic intelligence gathering and strategic planning.

At the end of the war, Bissell resumed his academic career at the Massachusetts Institute of Technology (MIT). He returned to Washington, D.C., in 1948 along with hundreds of other scholars, business executives, and government bureaucrats who had been recruited to administer the largest foreign economic assistance program of their day, the European Recovery Plan. Hired as a midlevel executive, Bissell quickly distinguished himself amidst a tumultuous mix of free traders, global planners, and national security advocates working in the Economic Cooperation Administration (ECA). As an accomplished economic analyst, logistician, and government planner, he possessed the critical skills and prior experience necessary to administer programs for the ECA. By the end of 1949 Bissell assumed charge of one of the ECA's most sensitive operations—directing the compilation of classified reports on European economic and political conditions for White House and congressional review.

Bissell's government career took another decisive turn in the summer of 1950, as the ECA struggled to gear up North Atlantic Treaty Organization (NATO) military production for the Korean War and still maintain its original mission of European economic recovery and business reform. A longtime advocate of European remilitarization through Marshall Plan aid, he recommended that many of the ECA's programs be deflected away from European domestic recovery toward anti-Soviet defense. As a result of his Cold Warrior stance, Bissell was selected by the Harry Truman administration to serve as the chief assistant to business executive William C. Foster, who replaced automobile magnate Paul G. Hoffman as head of the ECA in August 1950. After Foster's departure to the Pentagon in 1951, Bissell was elevated to the position of acting administrator, and he continued to bring ECA economic aid programs in line with the Cold War military objectives of the Truman White House and NATO. He helped finalize the redirection of U.S. aid priorities toward Cold War defense by presiding over the subsumption of the ECA into the Mutual Security Administration in late 1952.

By the end of the ECA, Bissell had built a distinguished reputation as an able craftsman and bureaucrat of the U.S. modern security state. He had demonstrated over the course of his ten years in government service the valued ability to make decisions in an emotionally detached manner. One of a new breed of internal government experts, he used intelligence data, not political influence, to justify his decision making. His image as a brilliant, apolitical administrator was further enhanced by his success in carrying over U.S. aid policies and operations from Truman into the Dwight D. Eisenhower administration. As a trusted translator of inside knowledge and information, he helped establish a virtually seamless system of federal policy making and administration at the middle level following the end of World War II. In doing so, Bissell also created a bureaucratic power base that allowed him and other national security advocates to withstand presidential changeovers during the Cold War era.

However, the culmination of his career as a Cold War bureaucrat came in 1954, when, after serving briefly as an administrator at MIT and the Ford Foundation, Bissell reentered government service as the special assistant to Allen W. Dulles, director of the Central Intelligence Agency (CIA). While he had very little experience in covert intelligence work, Bissell quickly proved to be well suited to the clandestine nature of CIA administration and operations. Avidly loyal yet dispassionate and analytical in manner, Bissell was a typical member of the CIA's emerging culture of "agency men." His Ivy League educational and social background allowed him to rise rapidly within the elite cult of the CIA. However, he also possessed many special abilities—intellectual brilliance, high technical expertise, and an able managerial style—that enabled him to carve out a unique career in the CIA over the next six years.

Bissell first made his mark by guiding and shaping the entrance of technology into the surveillance and reconnaissance operations of the CIA. Appointed by Dulles to carry out new air defense initiatives set by the Intelligence Advisory Board in 1954, Bissell went on to organize the CIA's first aerospace project in foreign surveillance, the U-2 flights program. As project director, he excelled in building a diverse yet tightly knit team of military officers, civilian technicians, and business contractors while maintaining the utmost security for the U-2 project at its testing and construction facility, known as the "Skunk Works," in Burbank, California. By 1956 the Skunk Works team, under Bissell's leadership, had produced a breakthrough prototype aircraft, equipped with high-definition cameras, capable of flying over 3,000 miles at a world record altitude of 70,000 feet. While tainted by political controversy and public exposure after the Soviet downing and capture of American airman Gary Francis Powers in May 1960, the U-2 program was, nevertheless, an important first success for the CIA in the area of technical intelligence. Since 1956 the United States had gained invaluable military information, as twenty-two U-2 planes conducted frequent missions over the Soviet Union, the Middle East, Asia, and Western Europe. As a result, the CIA expanded its technical research beyond long-range flight to include computer science, electronics, and missile and aerospace engineering.

The U-2 project also acted as a watershed event in Bissell's career at the CIA. Along with controlling the technical side of the project, he had masterminded many of its covert operations, including the planning of surveillance flights and the secret delivery of U-2's to Great Britain and West Germany. Though he continued to manage technical projects, such as the development of the SR-71 aircraft and Corona spy satellite, Bissell increasingly became involved in the various political espionage activities of the CIA, particularly after his appointment as deputy director of plans (DDP) in 1958. While the extent of Bissell's complicity in CIA assassination plots prior to his promotion remains shrouded, he certainly continued plans previously devised by his predecessor Frank Wisner and Dulles. More importantly, Bissell assumed a leading role in planning the disastrous Bay of Pigs invasion launched in April 1961.

In December 1959, acting on a directive from Dulles that called for "the elimination of Fidel Castro," Bissell first devised an assassination scheme involving agency operatives and the Mafia. By the fall of 1960 the operation had expanded dramatically into a full-scale military invasion aimed at the overthrow and takeover of the Castro government. Employing World War II–styled tactics, Bissell arranged for the training of exiled Cuban rebels at a CIA camp in Guatemala. Supplied with U.S. B-26's, ships, and weapons, the guerrillas were to act, upon their invasion into Cuba, as an "underground" force, disabling communication and defense sites and sparking widespread popular rebellion and military confusion. Once underway, the invasion would then be supported by two U.S. air strikes, a naval blockade, and the landing of marine troops on the Cuban beach area known as the Bay of Pigs.

Bissell's plan was drawn up under the last days of the Eisenhower administration, but he gained approval from newly elected president John F. Kennedy to proceed with the Cuban invasion. Eager to make his mark as a Cold Warrior president, Kennedy agreed to the covert operation but refused, on the advice of his Pentagon advisers, to deploy U.S. armed forces in support of the initial invasion. Despite the lack of critical military support, Bissell enthusiastically launched the Bay of Pigs operation on 15 April 1961. Undersupplied and undermanned, the CIA-trained rebels were quickly overtaken, however, by Castro's military forces. The invasion was further disabled by Kennedy's decision to cancel a second wave of U.S.-assisted bombing attacks set for 17 April. For the next two days Bissell and CIA deputy director Charles P. Cabell argued unsuccessfully before Kennedy and his cabinet officials to lend further American military support for CIA rebel forces left fighting on the beaches at the Bay of Pigs. On 19 April, amidst mounting diplomatic pressure from the Soviet Union and media scrutiny, an embarrassed President Kennedy publicly conceded that the Cuban invasion had been a total failure but underplayed the role of his administration in its initiation.

The Bay of Pigs fiasco also proved disastrous for Bissell's government career. Once slated to succeed Dulles as head of the CIA, he offered his resignation to President Kennedy, who accepted it in February 1962. In March 1962 Bissell returned to civilian life after receiving from Kennedy the National Security Medal to mark his twenty-year career in U.S. government service. While he never returned to teaching, Bissell did spend the remaining thirty-two years of his life working as an analyst and management consultant for several Cold War defense-related companies, including the Washington-based Institute for Defense Analyses and United Aircraft Corporation of Connecticut. Despite his exit from the center of Washington policy making, he occasionally reemerged from his home in Farmington, Connecticut, to discuss his role in controversial CIA activities carried out in the late 1950s and 1960s. In the manner of a dedicated govern-

ment bureaucrat, Bissell never apologized for the CIA's conception of the Bay of Pigs crisis but did concede in a press interview in the *Washington Evening Star* in 1965 that frequent and "progressive moderation" in the plan should have led him and others in the Kennedy administration to cancel the invasion before its start. While his role in the Bay of Pigs remains the most notorious activity of Bissell's career in the CIA, a report by the Senate Select Committee on Intelligence Activities revealed in 1975 that he had also been involved in several plots to assassinate other world Communist figures, including Congolese leader Patrice Lumumba and Castro's brother Raul Castro.

When examined as a whole, Bissell's career as a government administrator helps shed light on the bureaucratic evolution of the U.S. national security state from its early roots in World War II through its buildup during the Cold War era. Also, Bissell can be credited with leading the CIA beyond its older tactics of political espionage into a new era of technical intelligence. He died at his home in Farmington, Connecticut.

• Bissell's papers are at Yale University. His memoirs were published as *Reflections of a Cold Warrior: From Yalta to the Bay of Pigs* (1996). He also wrote several articles relating to economic theory, U.S. foreign aid, Cold War policy, and the Bay of Pigs affair in *American Economic Review* 27, no. 1 (Mar. 1938); *American Economic Review* 42, no. 2 (May 1952); *Diplomatic History* 8, no. 4 (Fall 1984); *Foreign Affairs*, Apr. 1951; *Foreign Affairs*, Oct. 1952; *Fortune*, May 1952; and *Fortune*, June 1952. For further information on Bissell's career in the CIA, see Evan Thomas, *The Very Best Men* (1995); John Ranelagh, *The Agency* (1986); Thomas Powers, *The Man Who Kept the Secrets: Richard Helms and the CIA* (1979); Arthur Schlesinger, Jr., *A Thousand Days* (1965); and David Wise and Thomas B. Ross, *The Invisible Government* (1964). Additional information is in U.S. Senate, Select Committee to Study Intelligence Activities, *Alleged Assassination Plots Involving Foreign Leaders*, 1975. An obituary is in the *New York Times*, 8 Feb. 1994.

JACQUELINE McGLADE

BISSELL, William Henry (25 Apr. 1811–18 Mar. 1860), U.S. congressman and governor of Illinois, was born near Hartwick, Otsego County, New York, the son of Luther Bissell and Hannah Sheperd, farmers. He received an M.D. from Jefferson Medical College of Philadelphia in 1834 and practiced medicine in Painted Post, New York. In about 1837 he moved to Monroe County, Illinois, where he first taught school and then practiced medicine. In 1840 he married Emily Susan James, who bore two daughters before her death in 1844. In 1851 he married Elisabeth Kintzing Kane.

Bissell was elected as a Democrat to the lower house of the Illinois legislature in 1840. He was admitted to the Illinois bar in 1841 and practiced law in Belleville. He received an LL.B. from Transylvania University in 1844 and became highly successful as prosecuting attorney for the second Illinois judicial district. Volunteering for service in the Mexican War, he was elected colonel of the Second Illinois Regiment. At the battle of Buena Vista his troops engaged in heavy action and experienced many casualties. Returning to Belleville, he was elected in 1848 to the U.S. House of Representatives and served three continuous terms. While in Congress he also worked in Illinois as a lawyer and lobbyist for the Illinois Central Railroad. Bissell won national fame as a result of a powerful speech in the House on 21 February 1850 in which he dismissed southern charges of northern aggression, denounced secessionist threats, and declared that Illinois would raise regiments to preserve the Union. He also derided southern boasts of superior military prowess. Replying to a claim by Congressman James A. Seddon of Virginia that a Mississippi regiment under the command of Jefferson Davis had saved the day at Buena Vista, Bissell contended that his own and other northern units had repulsed the Mexicans while the Mississippi regiment had not been "within a mile and a half" of the engagement. Although Bissell acknowledged the "gallant conduct" of the Mississippians elsewhere on the field, his remarks nevertheless so angered Davis that he challenged Bissell to a duel, but third parties negotiated a settlement under which Bissell merely reiterated what he had said about the valor of Davis's regiment.

Throughout his six years in Congress, Bissell championed liberal land policies such as homesteads, bounties to veterans, and grants to railroads. On several occasions he introduced a bill embodying Dorothea Dix's plan for a federal allotment of ten million acres to the states to support institutions for the insane; the bill finally passed in 1854 but was vetoed by President Franklin Pierce. As chairman of the House Committee on Military Affairs, Bissell sought increased military pay and pensions and advocated defense of settlers in New Mexico. Although in 1850 he favored the Fugitive Slave Act and other compromise measures, in 1854 he broke with his party's leadership and refused to support the Kansas-Nebraska Bill because it repealed the Missouri Compromise. In May 1854 he was incapacitated by an illness of some years' standing, probably secondary syphilis affecting the sacrum. While acutely ill, he converted secretly to his wife's Roman Catholic faith. Unable to attend the final vote on the Kansas-Nebraska Bill on 22 May (although he declared his willingness to be carried into the House on a stretcher were his presence crucial to the outcome), or to participate at all in the second session of the Thirty-third Congress, he did not seek reelection in 1854. Thereafter his condition improved somewhat, but he never regained the ability to walk without crutches.

Because Abraham Lincoln and other founders of the Republican party of Illinois believed that only an antislavery Democrat had a prayer of leading their ticket to victory in the state elections of 1856, the party convention that met at Bloomington on 29 May unanimously nominated Bissell for governor. Despite his failed health, Bissell had declared himself available because, he said, "Slavery demands more room—more *scope and verge*. Shall she have it? . . . I say a thousand times, No!" Although unable to do much campaign-

ing, he won the November election by a plurality of nearly 5,000 votes, drawing support from Democrats, Whigs, abolitionists, and (his Catholicism not being known) nativists. At the inauguration on 12 January 1857, he was required by the state constitution to swear that he had never accepted a challenge to a duel. Democrats accused him of perjury, but he replied that it had never been legally established that he had accepted a challenge to a duel, and that in any case the oath could not encompass incidents that had occurred outside Illinois.

During Bissell's administration the government of Illinois was virtually paralyzed by partisan battles over organization of the legislature and apportionment of voting districts. Bissell was a conscientious governor but made two blunders. In 1857 he mistakenly signed an apportionment bill that he had meant to veto; Abraham Lincoln then won a ruling from the state supreme court upholding the right of the governor to withdraw his signature. In 1859 Bissell approved illegally the refunding of certain state securities (the Macallister-Stebbins bonds) then reversed his action; Lincoln and other Republican leaders complained that the bondholders had "besieged the Governor" and "dogged him in his afflicted condition." An ailing remnant of the brave soldier, talented orator, and ascendant politician he once had been, Bissell died in Springfield of pneumonia almost ten months before the end of his term.

• Valuable biographical material on Bissell gathered by John Francis Snyder is in the Snyder papers at the Illinois State Historical Library, Springfield; the library also has a few dozen important Bissell letters, most of them in the Joseph Gillespie Papers, as well as a series of letters (1851–1855) to Mrs. Bissell from her sister in Belleville. The William Henry Bissell Papers at the Missouri Historical Society, St. Louis, consist of approximately 220 items—almost entirely incoming letters, half of them responses to Bissell's 1850 speech. Bissell's gubernatorial papers, mostly incoming, are at the Illinois State Archives, Springfield. A few Bissell letters are in the Illinois Central Archives at the Newberry Library, Chicago. Scholarship on Bissell includes Robert P. Howard, *Mostly Good and Competent Men: Illinois Governors, 1818–1988* (1988); Robert P. Howard, "Abraham Lincoln, Governor William H. Bissell and Perjury: The Illinois Campaign of 1856," *Lincoln Herald* 87 (1985): 39–48; Donald Fred Tingley, "The Jefferson Davis-William H. Bissell Duel," *Mid-America* 38 (1956): 146–55; William U. Halbert, "William Henry Bissell, Eleventh Governor of Illinois," *Journal of the Illinois State Historical Society* 36 (1943): 41–49; Paul Wallace Gates, *The Illinois Central Railroad and Its Colonization Work* (1934). Obituaries are in the Springfield *Illinois State Journal*, 19 Mar. 1860; the Chicago *Press and Tribune*, 20 Mar. 1860; and the *Chicago Weekly Democrat*, 24 Mar. 1860.

DAVID L. LIGHTNER

BITTENBENDER, Ada Matilda Cole (3 Aug. 1848–15 Dec. 1925), lawyer and suffragist, was born in Bradford County, Pennsylvania, the daughter of Daniel Cole, an inventor and Civil War veteran, and Emily A. Madison. After some local schooling, she attended Lowell's Commercial College in Binghamton, New

York, graduating in 1869. She then attended the Pennsylvania State Normal School at Bloomsburg from 1874 to 1875, teaching there for one year after her graduation. From 1876 to 1877 she attended the Froebel Normal Institute in Washington, D.C. After graduating, she returned to Bloomsburg and served as principal of the Pennsylvania State Normal School, but she resigned after one year for reasons of health.

Ada Cole married Henry Clay Bittenbender, a Princeton graduate and lawyer, in August 1878 in Rome, Pennsylvania; in November 1878 the couple moved to Osceola, Nebraska. She taught school in Osceola for one year and then became editor of the *Osceola Record*, a newspaper owned and published by her husband and his partners. As the first woman delegate to the Nebraska State Board of Agriculture in 1881, she was asked to begin a farmers' paper. She saw this as a political opportunity, as a letter to Erasmus Correll (12 Mar. 1882) suggests: "The alliances of this Co. 14 in number, unanimously chose me to start their farmer's paper, which I will do. In this way I can dispose of our idle outfit and have an organ for woman suffrage established in the Co. Both of present papers are opposed. Will dispose of paper to first good woman suffragist who wants to buy. If you know of such who is also an Alliance man, send him this way."

Ada Bittenbender was a founding member of the Nebraska Woman Suffrage Association and became its first recording secretary in 1881. In 1882 she was elected president and also served as chairman of the State Woman Suffrage Campaign Committee. Stumping for woman's rights, she traveled extensively throughout the state. She attended local suffrage meetings and was reported to be "a fine speaker [who] presents the subject in such a manner as all are able to understand it" (*Western Woman's Journal*, Dec. 1881). She worked in booths at county fairs, encouraging women to join the organization, soliciting votes and signatures for a petition to encourage the legislature to adopt a constitutional amendment, and selling subscriptions to *Western Woman's Journal*, a newspaper devoted to the suffrage movement.

Bittenbender began reading law under the supervision of her husband in the early 1880s. She was admitted to practice in Nebraska District Court in 1882 after passing the bar examination in open court. The examination was to have been heard by six examiners, but the judge was so impressed with her skills that he waived the final three examiners. In December 1882 she and her husband moved to Lincoln, Nebraska, and began practicing law as Bittenbender and Bittenbender. She was admitted to practice before the Nebraska Supreme Court on 17 August 1883. On the motion of Senator Henry W. Blair of New Hampshire, she became the third woman admitted to practice before the U.S. Supreme Court on 15 October 1888. She was also a member of the Equity Club, a correspondence society for women lawyers.

A member of the Nebraska Women's Christian Temperance Union (WCTU), Bittenbender served as its superintendent of legislation and petitions from 1883 to 1889. She drafted bills, organized petition campaigns, and lobbied for compulsory temperance instruction in schools and a ban on the sale of tobacco to children. She also worked for the establishment of an institution for delinquent females and a bill granting women joint and equal legal guardianship of their children. In 1887 she was elected superintendent of legislation and petitions for the national WCTU, and in 1888 she was engaged as its attorney. In the latter capacity she spent most of her time in Washington, D.C., representing the organization in its attempt to secure temperance legislation and arguing before congressional committees in support of prohibition. She authored *The National Prohibitory Amendment Guide* (1889), a manual for activists. In 1890 she returned to Nebraska and private practice.

Both the Bittenbenders were active in local politics as members of the Nebraska Prohibition party. In 1887 Ada Bittenbender ran for a judgeship in the second judicial district; she received 1,109 votes, finishing fifth in a field of five. Undaunted by defeat, four years later she accepted the party's nomination to run for a vacancy on the Nebraska Supreme Court. Although she lost again, she receive nearly 5 percent of the vote.

In her later years Bittenbender retired from the practice of law and devoted her time to the study of philosophy and writing, long her avocation. In addition to her work on the *Osceola Record* and the Farmers' Alliance paper, she arranged the *Woman Suffrage Campaign Song Book* (1882), contributed similar essays titled "Woman and Law" to *Woman's Work in America* (1891) and *The National Exposition Souvenir: What America Owes to Women* (1893); and authored a work of allegorical fiction, *Tedos and Tisod: A Temperance Story* (1911). She had no children. She died in Lincoln, Nebraska.

• The Nebraska State Historical Society in Lincoln has documents related to Bittenbender, including microfilm copies of newspapers, the *Western Woman's Journal*, the *Osceola Record*, the *Daily Nebraska State Journal*, the *Lincoln State Journal*, and the *Lincoln Star*. The same archive holds the Erasmus W. Correll papers, with letters from Bittenbender, and a file on the Nebraska Woman's Christian Temperance Union. Information about her judicial candidacies is in *Abstract of Votes Cast, 1882–1970*. The most complete biographical sketches are in Edward T. James et al., eds., *Notable American Women 1607–1950: A Biographical Dictionary* (1971), pp. 153–54; Frances E. Willard and Mary A. Livermore, eds., *A Woman of the Century* (1893; repr. 1967), pp. 87–88; and Virginia G. Drachman, *Women Lawyers and the Origins of Professional Identity in America: The Letters of the Equity Club, 1887 to 1890* (1993), pp. 211–13. Drachman mentions Bittenbender frequently. Obituaries are in the *Lincoln Star*, 15 Dec. 1925, and the *Lincoln State Journal*, 18 Dec. 1925.

SANDRA B. PLACZEK

BITTER, Karl Theodore Francis (6 Dec. 1867–9 Apr. 1915), architectural sculptor, was born in Vienna, Austria, the son of Karl Johann Bitter, owner of a small household chemicals business, and Henriette Reitter. He attended the Volkschule in the suburb of Rudolfsheim and entered its Gymnasium at age nine. From 1881 to 1884 he attended the School of Applied Arts attached to the Austrian Museum of Art and Industry in Vienna, concentrating on ornamental drawing and modeling. In the spring of 1885 Bitter was enrolled in the Imperial Academy of Fine Arts where he attended primarily sculpture classes until the spring of 1888. His mentor, Edmund Heller, was a member of the liberal faction of the faculty which favored a naturalistic baroque style over the conservative tradition of neo-classicism inherited from Antonio Canova and Bertel Thorvaldsen.

During these years Bitter actively participated in the ornamentation of the grandiose public buildings inside the Ringstrasse of Vienna commissioned by the emperor, Franz-Josef. In the studio of Duell and Friedl, for example, he helped execute the sculpture on the Burgtheater and the large Horsebreaker groups in the court stables. By the time he was drafted into the army in 1887 he had essentially completed an apprenticeship in the techniques and style of sculpture that he employed throughout most of his career.

Having forfeited his student classification by leaving the Gymnasium without graduating, he was faced with three years of military service instead of one. Upon completing his first year of duty he deserted and fled to Berlin with the intention of emigrating to the United States. He arrived in New York City in November 1889 and almost immediately began to turn out a vast variety of decorative, figural sculpture for the highly successful Beaux-Arts architect Richard Morris Hunt and his student George B. Post. Mansions on Fifth Avenue and in Newport, Rhode Island, designed for the Astors and the Vanderbilts, among others, came complete with festive relief friezes and allegorical or mythological figures first modeled in clay then cast or carved by the young Viennese immigrant and his assistants. This productivity culminated in the sculpture for Hunt's last major residential commission, "Biltmore," a Beaux-Arts creation inspired by a French Renaissance chateau, southwest of Asheville, North Carolina, designed for George Washington Vanderbilt. In keeping with the estate's 125,000-acre landscape designed by Frederick Law Olmsted (1822–1903), Bitter's most pictorial marble frieze, *Return from the Chase*, spans the triple fireplace in the largest room of the house, the Banquet Hall. For the balustrade of an organ gallery at the opposite end of the hall he created a forty-foot-long, high-relief sculpture in oak with a cast of sixty figures performing Wagner's *Tannhäuser*. The rest of his Biltmore sculpture comprises individual figures: a bronze Goose Boy fountain for the Palm Court; over-life-size limestone statues of Saint Louis and Joan of Arc for the exterior of the grand spiral staircase; and paired wood figures of Hestia and Demeter to flank the chimneypiece in the library, along with Venus and Vulcan andirons for its hearth.

Eventually opened to tourists, Biltmore and its sculptures characterize Bitter's increased efforts to reach a wide audience through architectural collabora-tions. His first such effort was his enormous plaster allegorical groups for Hunt's domed administration building at Chicago's World's Columbian Exposition in 1893. Thereafter he continued to produce works in various materials for churches, office buildings, court houses, banks, museum buildings, two more world's fairs, and a state capitol building.

Until the last few years of his career, Bitter's work remained essentially baroque in style. Six painterly biblical reliefs framed by full standing saints and reclining allegorical figures enliven his 1894 bronze gates for Trinity Church across Broadway from Wall Street. An open-armed Christ flanked by six kneeling angels welcomes worshippers from a Gothic tympanum. The twelve niches that make up the base barely contain the restless apostles. Bitter's lively high-relief panels celebrated rail travel on Frank Furness's major addition to Philadelphia's Broad Street Station (1892–1895). A large plaster procession entitled *Progress of Transportation* that graced its waiting room is preserved in the Thirtieth Street Station built in 1933. In 1896 Bitter's three large atlantes in limestone knelt above the main entrance of what was then New York's tallest skyscraper, the St. Paul Building by George B. Post. This heavily burdened trio peering down on lower Broadway was followed in 1899 by a marble "Peace" group crowning the New York Apellate Court Building overlooking Madison Square, a naval artillery group for the temporary Admiral Dewey triumphal arch, and limestone figures representing the Arts on the Fifth Avenue façade of the Metropolitan Museum.

In 1896 Bitter built a new studio adjoining his protomodern concrete house perched on the Weehawken, New Jersey, bluffs above the Hudson, opposite mid-Manhattan. From it emerged portrait monuments of four historical heroes, four university presidents, and one businessman mingled with four plaintive family memorial figures, along with a huge Standard-Bearer on a rearing horse duplicated atop four towering pylons marking the Triumphal Causeway into the Pan-American Exposition in Buffalo (1901). In 1901 Bitter married Marie A. Schevill of Cincinnati; they had three children. The St. Louis World's Fair of 1904 featured his elongated, animated version of the Statue of Liberty rising as another "Peace" out of a Manifest Destiny globe supported by an enormous Doric-like column. The base of this classical support was decorated with various allegorical figures and an anecdotal relief, *The Signing of the Louisiana Purchase Treaty*. Examples of his historical portraits include the well-over-life-size, seated bronze figures of Thomas Jefferson and Alexander Hamilton (1755–1804) flanking the steps to the main entrance of the Cuyahoga County Courthouse in Cleveland, Ohio (1909–1911). A second interpretation of Jefferson in marble sits on a pedestal in the Jefferson Memorial at the Missouri Historical Society in Forest Park, St. Louis (1912–1913). More approachable are bronze wall-reliefs of James Angell and Henry Tappan, past presidents of the University of Michigan. These works are installed in campus buildings named for the two men.

During the last ten years of his career Bitter's most monumental architectural sculpture changed from academic baroque to neo-Greek archaic to Viennese Secessionist modernist. The first phase resulted from recent archaeological discoveries in early ancient Greek sculpture, the second from the contemporary revolt against his academy, both of which he could finally experience first hand in 1909 after receiving an amnesty for his desertion from the Austrian army. His archaism started in 1906 in the granite sculpture for the pediment of the Cleveland Trust bank building. It continued in two pediments and four free-standing allegorical groups in the same material for the new Wisconsin State Capitol designed by George B. Post and in the grey granite allegorical reliefs with which he decorated the exedra of his bronze Carl Schurz monument (1913) on Morningside Drive, New York City. His Secessionist figural style appeared in 1908 with three pairs of allegorical relief figures above the ground floor of a Beaux-Arts façade on the First National Bank in Cleveland. Inspired by the Viennese sculptor Franz Metzner, Bitter's modernist style ended prematurely with two recessed, yet open-spaced granite figures of Planting and Harvesting for the Thomas Lowry portrait monument in Minneapolis (1911–1915). His final work, the bronze "Abundance" figure (1915) on top of the Pulitzer fountain in front of the Plaza Hotel in New York punctuates the south end of the double square that he himself had conceived and planned in 1899.

In his 1916 commemorative sketch, Alexander Stirling Calder emphasized the "fluency" in Karl Bitter's art. "His work," wrote Calder of his friend, "covers a wide range in treatment, the earlier periods characterized by qualities more descriptive and pictorial; the later work by larger sculptural unity. Bitter viewed his art and considered all art from a social-political basis. . . . that the progressive democracy of a people must be expressed in its art." Bitter died from injuries he received in an automobile accident in New York City.

• Bitter's papers, including correspondence, a scrapbook-diary, travel journals, photographs of his work, and a few sketches are in the Archives of American Art, Smithsonian Institution, Washington, D.C. His brother-in-law, the historian Ferdinand Schevill, wrote a brief, commemorative biography published by the University of Chicago Press in 1917. See also the extensive art historical monograph by James M. Dennis, *Karl Bitter, Architectural Sculptor, 1867–1915* (1967). The most recent treatment of Bitter's stylistic development appears in Susan Rather, "Toward a New Language of Form: Karl Bitter and the Beginnings of Archaism in American Sculpture," *Winterthur Portfolio* 25 (Spring 1990): 1–19.

JAMES M. DENNIS

BITZER, Billy (21 Apr. 1872–29 Apr. 1944), motion picture cameraman, was born in the Roxbury section of Boston, Massachusetts, the son of Johann Martin Bitzer, a blacksmith and harness maker, and Anne Marie Schmidt. His brother John C. Bitzer became a well-known photographer. Baptized as Johann Gottlieb Wilhelm (recorded on his birth record as John William), Bitzer formally changed his name to George William but was known professionally as "G. W." or "Billy." Almost nothing is known of his early life or education. While in his early twenties Bitzer moved to New York and apparently attended night classes at Cooper Union, where he studied electrical engineering. He then worked as an electrician.

In 1896 Bitzer joined a maker of novelty movie shorts, the Magic Introduction Company, which changed its name to American Mutoscope and Biograph Company when it adopted William K. L. Dickson's Mutoscope movie camera and projection system. The company produced films and manufactured cameras, projecting equipment, and flip-card viewing machines. Working as a cameraman, Bitzer filmed presidential candidate William McKinley at his home in Canton, Ohio. On 12 October 1896 Bitzer ran the projector at the first showing of a Biograph motion picture in New York City.

During the early days of the motion picture the public's interest resided primarily in the novelty of the pictures actually "moving," while the subject matter remained secondary. Bitzer spent the next several years shooting news items and street scenes with such titles as *U.S.S. Maine*, *Havana Harbor*, *Children Feeding Ducklings*, and *Galveston Hurricane Shots*. But from the start Bitzer recognized that the possibilities of the new medium could be extended by experimenting with innovative lighting techniques and modifying the existing cameras. One of his earliest achievements was the shooting of the first artificially lighted indoor film, a recording of the boxing match between Tom Sharkey and Jim Jeffries in the fall of 1899. By 1900 Bitzer had become Biograph's chief cameraman, and in 1908 he was teamed up with a newly hired director, D. W. Griffith; this began a sixteen-year association that became one of the most remarkable in the history of the motion picture.

Within the next four years, with both Bitzer and Arthur Marvin as cameramen, Griffith directed or supervised the making of more than 300 one- and two-reel films. In many of these early shorts Bitzer extended his experiments with innovative lighting and camera techniques. For *A Drunkard's Reformation* (1909) he created a firelight effect using artificial light, a technique he repeated a few weeks later for *The Cricket on the Hearth*. For *Pippa Passes* (1909) Bitzer filmed the narrative's progress from dawn to dusk using indoor lighting exclusively. Bitzer shot *Politician's Love Story* (1909) directly into the sun and produced the halo effect of back lighting for the first time.

In addition to these innovations in lighting, Bitzer also made radical changes in the camera while working on these early Griffith films. He discovered the dramatic potential of the iris effect, which allowed him to mask out portions of the rectangular frame, focus attention, and produce fade-in and fade-out effects. He also fitted in front of the lens a matte box, which he subsequently used to matte out portions of the frame using a variety of filters. Whether or not Bitzer was actually the first to discover these innovations is uncertain, but he did use them in Griffith's films with great effect, establishing much of the aesthetic technique associated with early, silent film.

In January 1910 Griffith took the Biograph Company to California in order to continue shooting outside during an especially harsh eastern winter. He constructed in Los Angeles a modest studio, which was quickly expanded when he began to regularly alternate seasons between New York and California. Bitzer continued his experiments during these sojourns in California, where, for example, he made the first extreme long shot in *Ramona* (1910) and fast-moving traveling shots for *The Girl and Her Trust* (1912). Griffith left Biograph in 1913 after a disagreement over the cost of the production of the biblical epic *Judith of Bethulia*, and he signed a contract with the Mutual Film Corporation, taking Bitzer, as well as many of Biograph's stock players, including Lillian Gish and Dorothy Gish, with him to the new company.

Bitzer began work on Griffith's most famous film, *The Birth of a Nation* (1915), on 4 July 1914 at the Universal Ranch, which later became Universal City Studios, in California. Bitzer's camera work on the film is legendary. He devised the first "wide-screen" ratio, by masking the top and bottom of the frame, to emphasize the dramatic action of charging horsemen; he used a 100-foot tower to capture panoramic shots of the battlefield scenes; he mounted a camera on a racing car so that he could shoot close-ups of galloping horses and their riders; he devised a mobile camera that could move in front of charging soldiers and dart in and out of the hand-to-hand combat. His cinematography created a realistic documentary style that the critics compared to the work of Civil War photographer Matthew Brady. All of these effects were created with a single Pathe Studio Model camera. Because Griffith was so financially extended, Bitzer offered his services as a cameraman and even invested his life savings of $7,000 for a share of the film's profits. Eventually he received more than $240,000 from the film, making it probably the largest sum ever earned by a camera operator for shooting a single film.

Griffith began his next epic, *Intolerance* (1916), almost immediately after he completed shooting *The Birth of a Nation*. For the first time Bitzer had an official assistant, Karl Brown, to help him; in later years, Bitzer was most generous in praising Brown's contributions to the film. For the Babylon sequence in *Intolerance* Griffith erected the largest set ever built in Hollywood, and Bitzer and Brown invented ways to maximize the use of the enormous set, including the construction of a tower 140-feet-high, mounted on railroad car wheels, for the spectacular tracking shot that opens the feast of Belshazzar. Bitzer also used his matte technique to great effect to create the city of Babylon and later to shoot the miniatures when the city burned. Bitzer even went up in a hot air balloon in order to capture an aerial shot of the huge set. Al-

though he used as many as four different cameras for the crowd scenes, Bitzer still shot most of the film with a single camera. In spite of the film's eventual success, *Intolerance* proved to be the last epic film that Griffith made and that Bitzer photographed.

Some exterior filming of battle scenes for the World War I film *Hearts of the World* (1917–1918) was reported to have been done under fire on the western front, and *Way Down East* (1920) contains scenes shot outside during a severe New England winter; however, the best of Bitzer's later innovative work was done on studio sets. *Broken Blossoms* (1919), the last great work on which Bitzer and Griffith collaborated, displays marvelous interior lighting, all of which was created artificially. The film was released with both color tinting and toning, which gave it a subtle, nuanced effect. Perhaps no other silent film used this early color technique so effectively. Reviews from New York papers praised the film's tinting and Bitzer's camera work. However, the cooperative relationship between Griffith and Bitzer was strained during the 1920s when the director increasingly brought in younger cameramen to work alongside Bitzer. In the 1929 filming of *Lady of the Pavements* Bitzer worked for the last time with Griffith.

In 1926 Bitzer helped to organize the International Photographers of the Motion Picture Industry, a union of film technicians, and when a local was established in Hollywood in 1929 Bitzer was blacklisted by the industry. Not much is known about Bitzer's personal life, but he did have a common-law marriage with Elinore Farrell for some twenty years; when it failed, he married Ethel Boddy in 1923; the couple had one son. During the depression Bitzer worked for the Works Progress Administration preparing film strips and recording lectures. By 1939 he was restoring old prints and cameras for the Museum of Modern Art. After suffering a series of heart attacks he returned to California, where he lived at the Motion Picture Country Home in Los Angeles until his death there.

Billy Bitzer is the most famous cameraman of the motion picture's silent era and arguably one of the greatest of all time. He is credited with the perfection of many of the major cinematic techniques characteristic of silent movies. His best work has always been associated with D. W. Griffith, and in many ways the two men invented the grammar of the cinema and were largely responsible for creating the classic Hollywood film, which in its various forms dominates world cinema to this day.

• Bitzer's papers are housed in the D. W. Griffith Archives, Museum of Modern Art, New York City. In spite of Bitzer's importance to the development of the motion picture, little of a substantial nature has been written about him. His autobiography, *Billy Bitzer: His Story*, was published in 1973. Of the several general appreciations of his work, George J. Mitchell's two-part essay, "Billy Bitzer: Pioneer and Innovator," which appeared in the *American Cinematographer* (45, no. 12 [Dec. 1964]: 690–92, 708, 710–12; and 46, no. 1 [Jan. 1965]: 34, 36, 54–58), is probably the best. Several studies of

D. W. Griffith contain substantial mention of Bitzer and his work. Karl Brown, *Adventures with D. W. Griffith* (1973), and Robert M. Henderson, *D. W. Griffith: His Life and Work* (1972), are among the most comprehensive. "The Film Artistry of D. W. Griffith and Billy Bitzer," *American Cinematographer* 50, no. 1 (Jan. 1969): 86–91, 148–53, 172–73, also provides an appreciative analysis of the working relationship between these two pioneers of the motion picture.

CHARLES L. P. SILET

BIXBY, Horace Ezra (8 May 1826–1 Aug. 1912), steamboat pilot, was born in Geneseo, New York, the son of Sylvanus Bixby and Hannah Barnes, farmers. After running away from home when he was thirteen, Bixby made his way to Cincinnati, Ohio, where he first worked in a tailor shop. Like many river-town youths, he was attracted to steamboating, which was rapidly expanding in the 1840s. He started as a second, or mud, clerk on the *Olivia* and at age twenty became a pilot.

Bixby was regularly employed by various Mississippi and Ohio river lines during the 1850s, usually considered to have been the "Golden Age of Steamboating." In 1857, while navigating the *Paul Jones* from Cincinnati to New Orleans, he agreed to teach piloting to Samuel Langhorne Clemens, who later gained fame as Mark Twain. Their seventeen-month association earned Clemens a license as a Mississippi River pilot.

After the Civil War disrupted St. Louis–New Orleans commerce, Bixby piloted the Union gunboat *Benton* during the unsuccessful 1862 river campaign against Vicksburg, Mississippi. At the war's end Bixby, like many other St. Louisans, entered the Missouri River trade, which the Montana gold rush had made lucrative. With his talent for memorizing river-channel details, Bixby obtained a Missouri River piloting license and worked for the Montana and Idaho Transportation Company, the major St. Louis–Fort Benton, Montana, line. During his Missouri River career, Bixby had the misfortune of snagging and sinking the *Bertrand*, which he was piloting. After the short-lived Montana gold rush boom, Bixby returned to the Lower Mississippi River trade, which was seriously challenged by railroads. In 1860 Bixby married Susan Weibling of New Orleans. Their one child died while still very young. After his wife's death, Bixby married Mary Sheble of St. Louis on 2 January 1868; they had three children.

During the 1870s and 1880s, in partnership with his father-in-law and brother-in-law, Bixby owned and captained Anchor Line boats in the St. Louis–New Orleans business. In 1883 Mark Twain's *Life on the Mississippi* was published, and Bixby became a celebrity. This autobiographical work, in which Twain portrayed Bixby as a stern, precise, and profane master of the river, proved to be a mixed blessing for the veteran pilot. He received numerous letters from Twain fans, but he believed that even without Twain he had earned a place in riverboat history. Bixby also took pride in abstaining from vulgar language and objected to Twain's characterization of him as profane. Despite Bixby's feelings, it was Twain who made him famous as the quintessential pilot. Twain recalled that after observing Bixby complete a hazardous maneuver an awe-stricken fellow pilot exclaimed, "By the Shadow of Death, but he's a lightning pilot!" When commercial steamboating declined sharply, the small but able-bodied Bixby worked as a snagboat pilot in the federal government's river improvement service. He retired only two days before his death at his home in Maplewood, a suburb of St. Louis.

• Details of some of the steamboats piloted or commanded by Bixby, as well as biographical information on him, are in Frederick Way, Jr., comp., *Way's Packet Directory 1848–1983* (1983). For the Bixby-Twain association, see John Lauber, *The Making of Mark Twain: A Biography* (1985), and T. H. Watkins, *Mark Twain's Mississippi* (1974). The log abstract of the *U.S.S. Benton* for 11 Apr.–31 Dec. 1862 was published in *Official Records of the Union and Confederate Navies in the War of the Rebellion*, ser. 1, vol. 23 (1910). The story of the ill-fated *Bertrand* is thoroughly covered by Jerome E. Petsche in *The Steamboat Bertrand: History, Excavation, and Architecture* (1974). For coverage of the appeal of the Upper Missouri business to Mississippi River steamboatmen in the post–Civil War years, see William E. Lass, *A History of Steamboating on the Upper Missouri River* (1962). An obituary is in the *St. Louis Globe-Democrat*, 2 Aug. 1912.

WILLIAM E. LASS

BIXLER, Julius Seelye (4 Apr. 1894–28 Mar. 1985), educator, was born in New London, Connecticut, the son of James Wilson Bixler, a Congregational minister, and Elizabeth James. He studied at Amherst College, where his mother's father, for whom he was named, had been president. He graduated Phi Beta Kappa with an A.B. in 1916 and then went to Madura, India, to teach Latin and English for a year in its American college. He returned in 1917 to study for the ministry at Union Theological Seminary in New York City. However, he decided against becoming a minister because he preferred to study "all theologies rather than to bind himself to one creed." When the United States entered World War I, he left the seminary and joined the army but was not sent overseas.

With the defeat of Germany in 1918, he returned to do graduate work at Amherst and to be its director of religious activities. The same year he married Mary Harrison Thayer; they had four daughters. In 1920 he received his A.M. at Amherst and spent the next two years lecturing on philosophy at the American University in Beirut, Syria. He returned to the United States to continue his graduate studies in philosophy at Yale, where he received his Ph.D. in 1924. His thesis on William James was published in revised form in 1926 as *Religion in the Philosophy of William James*, and for the rest of his life he continued studying and writing on the philosopher.

Bixler commenced a long and distinguished teaching career at several leading American institutions of higher learning. From 1924 to 1933 he taught religion and biblical literature at Smith College, and from 1933 to 1942 he taught theology at Harvard Divinity

School, where he eventually was the Bussey Professor of Theology.

Bixler became president of Colby College in Maine soon after America entered World War II. He oversaw Colby's move from its downtown campus to its new quarters two miles away on Mayflower Hill. He accepted this challenge with relish as he was to do throughout his eighteen years at Colby. Bixler was responsible for the tripling of the college's endowment and physical plant, doubling the salaries of its teachers, doubling the student body, quintupling its operating budget, and starting its first departments of art and music, whose building was named for him. His enthusiasm for "the spirit that has always characterized the liberal arts college in the detachment of its search for truth" attracted energetic and creative people to the campus and eventually made the small college one of the more significant American liberal arts institutions.

Upon retiring in 1960 he continued to lecture at various colleges, including Thammasart University in Bangkok, the Universities of Canterbury and Aukland in New Zealand, the University of Hawaii, Wesleyan University's Center for Advanced Studies, Carleton and Bowdoin Colleges, and the University of Maine at Orono. He died in Weston, Massachusetts.

Throughout his life Bixler did research. While he worked on his thesis in 1924, he studied at Harvard; in 1928–1929 he was in Germany at the University of Freiburg; in 1938 he studied at the University of Zurich; and for four summers he was a lecturer at the Salzburg Seminar on American Studies in Austria. His research and reflection resulted in more than 100 articles, more than a half dozen books and countless book reviews. Several of Bixler's more important books were the result of invitations to give lectures: *Immortality and the Present Mood* (Ingersoll Lecture, 1931), *Religion for Free Minds* (Lowell Lectures, 1939), *Resources of Religion and Aims of Higher Education* (Hazen Lectures, 1942), *Conversations with an Unrepentant Liberal* (Terry Lectures, 1946), *A Faith that Fulfills* (Ayer Lectures, 1951), and *Education for Adversity* (Inglis Lecture, 1952). Even in his final illness Bixler was working on a book about the German philosophers whom he had known in the 1920s, including Ernst Cassirer, Rudolph Otto, Albert Schweitzer, Martin Heidegger, and Karl Jaspers.

Bixler was a trustee for Colby (1960–1985), Amherst (1952–1969), Radcliffe (1949–1961), and Smith (1962–1970) Colleges, a cofounder and first president of the Albert Schweitzer Fellowship (1940–1942), as well as president of the American Theological Society (1935–1936) and the National Council on Religion in Higher Education (1934–1939). In all his activity he was noted for his humor and humility.

In its 12 March 1941 issue the *Harvard Crimson* attacked the philosophy department but declared that Bixler was "a splendid teacher and wonderful with his students." Bixler believed that philosophy is a synthesis of the basic data of perception revealed by science and the various religious values that human experience has validated. As a teacher and college president he emphasized the impartial search for truth and knowledge, and as a philosopher he taught the values of toleration, understanding, and the need for wisdom in public and private living.

• Bixler's presidential papers and a videocassette interview are at Colby; additional small but helpful collections are at Amherst and Smith Colleges. For biographical details, see "Julius Seelye Bixler 1894–1985," *The Colby Alumnus* 74 (1985): 12–15; Virginia Corwin Brautigam, "Julius Seelye Bixler," *Smith Alumnae Quarterly* 76 (1985): 67–68; "Meet the Next President," *The Colby Alumnus* 30 (1941): 47. For his years at Colby, see Ernest Cummings Marriner, *The History of Colby College* (1963): 401–29. See also the *Colby Library Quarterly* (Sept. 1961) for a discussion of his philosophy, teaching, and presidency and for a bibliography of his publications. There is a brief account of his Harvard period in George Huntston Williams, ed., *The Harvard Divinity School* (1954). An obituary is in the *New York Times*, 2 Apr. 1985.

ALAN SEABURG

BJERKNES, Jacob Aall Bonnevie (2 Nov. 1897–7 July 1975), meteorologist, was born in Stockholm, Sweden, the son of Vilhelm Friman Koren Bjerknes, a physics professor at the University of Stockholm, and Honoria Sophia Bonnevie. Vilhelm, who studied hydrodynamics and meteorology, would eventually mathematically model the large-scale thermodynamics of the atmosphere and oceans alongside his son. Jacob was raised in Sweden, but moved to Norway when his father received a professorship of physics at the University of Christiana (Oslo) in 1905. Vilhelm was then appointed head of the new Geophysical Institute at the University of Leipzig in 1913; Jacob initially stayed in Norway to attend school but three years later joined his father in Germany as one of his research assistants. The following year the two moved again, this time to the newly founded Geophysical Institute of the Bergen Museum, where Vilhelm took up a professorship, and Jacob became a meteorologist in 1918 and chief forecaster in 1920.

During World War I, when weather forecasting information from Britain and Iceland was cut off, the father-and-son team organized a wide-ranging network of Norwegian weather stations linked by telephone and wireless telegraph. Based on data collected from these stations, and the work of meteorologists like Tor Bergeron, Bjerknes and his father together demonstrated the existence of adversarial long-term cold polar air masses and warm tropical air masses, separated by "fronts," named by analogy with the battle lines they had seen during the war. This theory readily explained the puzzling phenomena of cyclones, low pressure centers that came from atmospheric fronts between warm and cold air wedges. Jacob summarized their "Bergen theory" or "frontal theory" in a pioneering, eight-page paper, "On the Structure of Moving Cyclones," in *Geofysiske Publikasjoner* (1, no. 2 [1919]: 1–8).

During the 1920s Bjerknes worked out the consequences of the frontal theory and helped develop what came to be known as the "Bergen School" of meteorology. It included Bjerknes, his father, Bergeron, and Ernst Calwagen, along with Halvor Skappel Solberg (the coauthor of Jacob's influential 1923 paper, "Life Cycle of Cyclones and the Polar Front Theory of Atmospheric Circulation"), and others.

One of the puzzles of the Bergen theory was the nature of the upper portions of the fronts. Between 1922 and 1923 Bjerknes went to Zurich, both to promote the Bergen School among Swiss meteorologists, and to examine weather data from Alpine observatories to try to resolve the problem. The confirmation of the sloping nature of frontal surfaces led to Bjerknes's 1924 doctorate at the University of Christiania. His years in Switzerland also gave him opportunities to develop his lifelong hobbies, skiing and mountaineering.

After a brief stint as consultant to the Meteorological Office in London, England, in 1925–1926, Bjerknes returned to Bergen. In July 1928 he married Hedvig Borthen; the couple had two children. In 1931 he became professor of meteorology at the Geophysical Institute, where he continued his Bergen School research on upper-air currents, cyclones and anticyclones, air flows along frontal surfaces, and other atmospheric motions. In 1933 Bjerknes, his father, Bergeron, and Solberg collaborated in the writing of the popular 800-page treatise *Physikalische Hydrodynamik mit Awendung auf die Dynamische Meteorologie*, translated into French as *Hydrodynamique Physique* (3 vols., 1934); Bjerknes also collaborated with Finnish meteorologist Erik Palmén on a series of papers about the structure of cyclones.

During the 1930s Bjerknes also became a visiting lecturer and invited consultant at several institutions. He taught at the Massachusetts Institute of Technology in 1933–1934, returned to the London Meteorological Office in 1935–1936, and was a consultant to the Canadian weather office in Toronto, Ontario, in 1933 and 1939. While he was on a lecture trip in 1939 to the United States, World War II broke out in Europe; and when the Nazis occupied Norway, he was unable to return to Bergen.

Instead, Bjerknes decided to stay in the United States. He settled in Santa Monica, California, becoming a professor of meteorology at the University of California at Los Angeles (UCLA), a post he held until his 1965 retirement. During the war, Bjerknes helped to train more than a thousand U.S. Army and Navy weather officials. In 1940 he founded UCLA's faculty of meteorology, serving as its chair from 1945 to 1952; and under his leadership, the department became one of the world's leading centers for meteorological research.

In the 1940s Bjerknes continued his work on cyclone development, suggesting (with Jørgen Holmboe) that cyclones originated from changes of pressure and vorticity in air currents ("On the Theory of Cyclones," *Journal of Meteorology* 1, no. 1 [1944]: 1–22). This work was extended by Jul G. Charney, who earned UCLA's first doctorate in meteorology under Bjerknes in 1946.

Bjerknes became a U.S. citizen in 1946. He was elected to the National Academy of Sciences in 1947 and served as president of the International Union of Geodesy and Geophysics, Meteorological Association, from 1948 to 1951. He was awarded the Symons Medal of the Royal Meteorological Society of London in 1940 and the American Geophysical Union Bowie Medal in 1945. The 1950s brought him more honors, including the Swedish Society of Anthropology and Geography's Vega Medal in 1958, and the (World) International Meteorological Organization's Prize of 1959. During this decade, Bjerknes carefully examined upper-level air currents, especially the jet stream, a high-altitude stream of air flowing rapidly west to east, discovered by American bombers during World War II. He also pioneered in the use of space research in meteorology, by using cloud photographs taken from research rockets for weather prediction.

Bjerknes next studied the "El Niño" effect (a seasonal warming of the Pacific off the coast of Peru, named "the child" because of its arrival around Christmas). He also examined heat exchange between the atmosphere and the oceans. This research culminated in *Dynamic Meteorology and Weather Forecasting* (1957), coauthored with Bergeron, C. L. Godske, and R. C. Bundgaard.

Just before his retirement, Bjerknes joined the National Academy of Sciences' exchange program with the Soviet Academy of Sciences. In 1963 and 1965 he went to Leningrad (St. Petersburg) and Moscow as a guest lecturer; he also served as a Rand Corporation consultant for several years. He was awarded the Rossby Medal of the American Meteorological Society in 1960 and the National Medal of Science in 1966.

Bjerknes spent the final years of his life in Santa Monica. In 1975 he was asked to prepare a sampling of his most significant papers for his seventy-eighth birthday; one week before the *Selected Papers* went to press, however, he died in Los Angeles.

Bjerknes was one of the founders of the modern science of meteorology. Charney wrote that "his discovery of the front, the frontal wave and the upper wave each in its turn lay the groundwork for a major step forward in classifying and understanding the atmosphere" (*Selected Papers* [1975], p. 11); and historian of science Robert Marc Friedman pointed out that Bjerknes's work provided an important stimulus to the increasingly significant study of atmosphere and ocean as a united system. The joint theories of Bjerknes and his father, Vilhelm, have led directly to modern theories and techniques of weather prediction.

• Unpublished papers and correspondence of Bjerknes are in the Bergen District State Archive (Statsarchiv) and the University of Oslo Library. The most important source is *Selected Papers of Jacob Aall Bonnevie Bjerknes*, ed. M. G. Wurtele (1975), which contains Bjerknes's curriculum vitae, a 58-entry bibliography of his papers, of which twenty-six are reprinted in the volume, and several brief assessments of his career. This work includes "Life Cycle of Cyclones and the Polar Front Theory of Atmospheric Circulation," *Geofysiske Publikasjoner* 3, no. 1 (1923): 3–18, and his 1961 "El Niño" paper (*Inter-American Tropical Tuna Commission Bulletin 5*, no. 3: 219–73), among others. Bjerknes's early years at Bergen are well documented in Robert Marc Friedman, *Appropriating the Weather: Vilhelm Bjerknes and the Construction of a Modern Meteorology* (1989), esp. pp. 122–37.

JULIAN A. SMITH

BJERREGAARD, Carl Henrik Andreas (24 May 1845–28 Jan. 1922), librarian and philosopher, was born in Fredericia, Denmark, the son of Janus Bagge Friis, an educator, and Louise Nielsen. Bjerregaard attended the local Latin school, Fredericia College, in which his father was principal, but he did not graduate. He went on to study at, and apparently graduated from, the University of Copenhagen in 1863. After leaving Copenhagen, he volunteered as a Danish spy in the Danish–Schleswig-Holstein war. From 1865 to 1866 he went to St. Petersburg and other parts of Europe as a teacher in the household of a Danish minister to Russia. In 1866 he entered the Danish military as a candidate for reserve service and completed training at the Military Academy of Denmark. He served in the reserve army for seven years, achieving the rank of second lieutenant. In 1868 he married Mathilde Georgina Thomsen. They had seven children. From 1869 to 1870 he was professor of botany and curator of the natural history museum at Fredericia College. In the summer of 1873 Bjerregaard left the military and Denmark without permission. His hasty departure occurred the night before a police investigation into an allegation that he had violated the criminal code. Bjerregaard later offered two distinct defenses of his unauthorized exit. First, he claimed that he feared an unwanted military appointment to garrison duty in the Danish West Indies. Second, he proposed that his criminal offense consisted of having been witnessed with socialists while in uniform.

In August 1873 Bjerregaard arrived in New York. He first found a low-wage job at a linoleum factory in Salem, New Jersey. This job lasted only one month because of the economic panic of September 1873, which closed the factory. Bjerregaard persevered and found other temporary jobs. In the summer of 1874 his wife and two children were able to come to New York from Denmark.

Bjerregaard received a more lucrative and stabler position in 1879 when he was appointed to the staff of the Astor Library, which later became the New York Public Library, where he remained until his death. He was appointed librarian in 1881. Initially, he oversaw the reclassification of books at the library. In 1889 he became chief of the reading room, the largest section of the library that was open to the public. In this post he became familiar to thousands of readers.

Bjerregaard's position at the New York Public Library gave him the time and resources to devote to his own scholarly interests in philosophy. He became locally well known as a lecturer and author on mysticism and Eastern philosophy. He had six published works: *Lectures on Mysticism and Talks on Kindred Subjects* (1896); *Lectures on Mysticism and Nature Worship, Second Series* (1897); *Being and the Philosophical History of the Subject* (1899); *Sufi Interpretations of the Quatrains of Omar Khayyam and Fitzgerald* (1902); *The Inner Life and the Tao-Teh-King* (1912); *The Great Mother: A Gospel of the Eternally Feminine* (1913).

Bjerregaard was part of the theosophical movement that flourished in New York in the late nineteenth century. Theosophy is a form of monism in which all reality is a mode of some transcendent, fundamental source of being. Bjerregaard writes, "Unless we come to the perfect realization, that life is one, one glorious whole, and not split up into various antagonistic elements, we shall never come to sound and rational philosophies or religions" (*The Inner Life and the Tao-Teh-King*, p. 3). Bjerregaard sought to integrate Western and Eastern thought into one higher, overarching truth. This universal truth can be reached through mystical understanding and experience. Bjerregaard writes, "By Mysticism I understand a life directed towards the transcendental; a life not only free from illusions, but a life which has made its devotees living channels of themselves and filled them with the Universal" (*American-Scandinavian Review*, 9, no. 6 [1921]: 381).

Bjerregaard's most definitive historical influence was as a philosopher. While the theosophy that he espoused did not gain wide acceptance, it was an example of and an influence on reccurring syncretistic movements in American thought in which contradictory views of ultimate reality are subsumed beneath a more amorphous form. Bjerregaard's variety of syncretism claimed that no one way of looking at reality and truth was comprehensive or adequate. Instead, truth could be discovered only on an esoteric plane above the particular views of any religion or philosophy.

At the age of seventy-one Bjerregaard took up oil painting, feeling that he would use more of his inner power if he changed from the pen to the brush as a means of expression. On 11 September 1920 he was decorated a Knight of Dannebrog by King Christian of Denmark in recognition of his educational work among the Danes of New York. He died at his residence in New York.

• Other published works by Bjerregaard include *History and Doctrine of Mysticism* and *Jesus: A Poet, a Prophet, a Mystic, and a Man of Freedom* (1912). For evaluative comments on his publications, see the *Book Review Digest* 9 (Dec. 1913): 57, and the *New York Evening Post*, 11 Apr. 1914. Information on his duties at the library can be located in Harry Miller Lydenberg, *History of the New York Public Library* (1923). Further biographical items and an obituary are in the *Bulletin of the New York Public Library* 26, no. 2 (Jan.–Dec. 1922). Biographical information and pictures of his paintings can be found in the *American-Scandinavian Review* 9, no. 6 (June 1921). An obituary is in the *New York Times*, 29 Jan. 1922.

STEVEN L. PORTER

BLACK, Eugene Robert (1 May 1898–20 Feb. 1992), banking executive, was born in Atlanta, Georgia, the son of Eugene Robert Black, a lawyer and banker, and

Gussie King Grady. Black was the scion of a family that was both wealthy and well connected; his father served as president of the Atlanta Trust Company before becoming a governor of the Federal Reserve Board, and his mother was the daughter of Henry Woodfin Grady, the founder of the Atlanta *Herald*. Black attended the University of Georgia, and after graduating with a B.A. cum laude in 1918 served briefly in the U.S. Navy as an ensign during World War I. He married Dolly Blalock in 1918; they had one son before her death in 1928.

Following his discharge from the navy at the war's conclusion, Black returned to Atlanta. There he joined the local office of Harris, Forbes and Company, a New York investment firm, and quickly demonstrated his sales ability. When the firm was reorganized in the following year as Chase-Harris-Forbes Corporation, Black became the district manager for Atlanta. He managed branch offices in New Orleans, Houston, and Dallas, and he rose to assistant vice president before the firm fell victim to the depression in 1933. He remarried in 1930 to Susette Heath, with whom he had two children.

After weighing an offer to join former co-workers in the new firm of Starkweather and Company, Black decided instead to affiliate with Chase National Bank of New York. He joined Chase in June 1933 as second vice president, with responsibilities centered in eight southern states. Initially headquartered in Atlanta, he relocated to New York City in the following year and quickly became known as an expert on the bond market. He was successful enough to attract an offer to become under secretary of the U.S. Treasury in February 1936, which he initially accepted before rethinking his decision in light of the financial sacrifices he would be called to make. He became a senior vice president of Chase National Bank in 1937.

With the entry of the United States into World War II in 1941, Black took on additional responsibilities. He provided executive leadership on the New York Victory Bond Committee during its War Loan Drive of April 1943 and became director of the Banking and Investment Division of New York State's War Finance Committee two months later. During the latter part of the war Black became increasingly involved in the international dealings of Chase National Bank, and he made several trips to Europe between 1945 and 1947 to bolster Chase's activities in the area.

Black's increasingly visible activities in the world of international finance brought him to the attention of officials at the International Bank for Reconstruction and Development (more popularly known as the World Bank). Founded by a multinational group of delegates to a Bretton Woods, New Hampshire, conference in July 1944, the World Bank represented the hopes of many nations regarding postwar reconstruction and economic development. However, it had suffered growing pains during its first years of operation. Its first president, Eugene Meyer, resigned after fewer than six months on the job because of conflicts with the bank's executive directors (who represented the

nations with the greatest investment in the bank and who controlled much of the bank's day-to-day operations). His successor, John McCloy, felt that it was imperative that the next executive director from the United States command respect in the New York financial markets. Eugene Black fit the bill perfectly, and President Harry S. Truman appointed Black to the post in February 1947.

Truman's choice proved fortuitous. Initial plans to finance postwar worldwide reconstruction and development by guaranteeing repayment of loan funds from outside the organization soon proved unworkable, and Black proved to be just the man to reassure Wall Street investors, who feared not only the potential of default by overseas governments (the World Bank's primary customers) but the perception that the bank was overly liberal in its lending policies. The bank's initial attempt to raise capital through the bond markets in July 1947 was a smashing success; $250 million in bonds were soon oversubscribed. Having come on board in time to help approve the bank's first loan ($250 million to Crédit National of France in May 1947), Black also assisted in placing the bank's first loan to a developing country (Chile) in March of the following year.

Bank president McCloy resigned his post in May 1949 to become the U.S. high commissioner in Germany, and Black was the logical man to replace him. Taking office on 1 July of that year, Black held the presidency for more than thirteen years. During his tenure, the World Bank's membership (constituent nations) nearly doubled, and its lending portfolio increased fivefold. Staffing at the bank underwent similar growth, and as a result Black presided over the bank's internal reorganization. The newly restructured bank consisted of three area departments (Asia and Middle East; Europe, Africa, and Australia; and the Western Hemisphere) and a department of technical operations. The increasingly complex and diverse operations of the bank necessitated the development of additional operations as the years passed, and Black presided over the introduction of the Economic Development Institute in 1955 (which provided educational training to potential borrowers), the International Finance Corporation in 1956 (which expanded the bank's lending to the private sector of developing countries), and the International Development Association in 1960 (which expanded lending in poorer countries by offering loans on longer and more generous terms).

The advent of the Marshall Plan in the late 1940s removed the reconstruction of western Europe from the World Bank's list of priorities, and Black, who was appointed to a second five-year term as president in 1953, led the organization into an increasingly greater role in Third World economic development. A skilled negotiator, Black was often called in to mediate international disputes that threatened areas in which the bank was active. He sought to obtain joint financing for the Aswan High Dam in Egypt (1955–1956) between the United States, England, and the World Bank, only to see the proposed financing collapse in the face of American wariness over Egyptian president Gamal Nasser's close relationship with the Soviet Union. Black was more successful in negotiating a settlement to claims resulting from the Suez Canal crisis of 1956; his efforts resulted in a February 1959 agreement between Egypt and England that compensated the latter country for losses suffered during Nasser's nationalization of the waterway.

In his last years as World Bank president, Black served on a committee of American businessmen that reviewed Kennedy administration foreign aid policies. A long-time opponent of bilateral assistance, Black disappointed the administration by recommending that the total amount of assistance be reduced. He also attempted to mediate the 1962 dispute between India and Pakistan over Kashmir, but Indian rejection of his assistance ended the effort.

Suffering from declining health, Black left the World Bank at the end of 1962. He remained active, however, serving as the president of the Brookings Institution (a think tank) and as a trustee of Johns Hopkins University (1960–1970), the Institute for International Education, and the Ford Foundation. He also became a consultant for the United Nations, where he assisted in bond marketing and debt collection. Black also renewed his ties with Chase (which had become Chase Manhattan), serving as both consultant and director (1963–1970).

Black's most notable service after his tenure at the World Bank, however, occurred in Southeast Asia. Seeking to bolster support for his policies in the area, President Lyndon Johnson placed him in charge of the administration's economic program in the area in April 1965. Although his efforts resulted in the December 1965 creation of the multinational Asian Development Bank, other projects in the region (such as the Mekong River Redevelopment Commission) foundered with the continued escalation of American military involvement. Black received the Medal of Freedom in January 1969 from President Johnson for his efforts in the area.

Aside from serving as a consultant to American Express Corporation from 1970 to 1978, Black largely retired from active business affairs after 1970. He died in his sleep in Southampton, Long Island, New York. Although Black served in a variety of business-related capacities, his long presidency at a critical point in the World Bank's development was his greatest contribution to history. The continued development and growth of the World Bank is due in large part to the firm foundation that his leadership provided.

• Black's papers are held by the University of Georgia, Athens. Secondary literature on the World Bank abounds; among the best studies that discuss Black and his role are Edward S. Mason and Robert E. Asher, *The World Bank since Bretton Woods* (1973), and Catherine Gwin, *U.S. Relations with the World Bank, 1945–92* (1994). A succinct overview of the World Bank, its history, and its personnel is also available in Anne C. M. Salda, *Historical Dictionary of the World Bank* (1997). An obituary is in the *New York Times*, 21 Feb. 1992.
EDWARD L. LACH, JR.

BLACK, Frank Swett (8 Mar. 1853–22 Mar. 1913), lawyer and politician, was born in Limington, York County, Maine, the son of Jacob Black and Charlotte Swett, farmers. When Black was eleven years old, his family moved to Alfred, Maine, where he attended what later became the Limerick Academy. While still a youth he taught school to earn enough money to pursue his education at the Lebanon Academy in preparation for study at Dartmouth College. In 1875 he graduated from Dartmouth with honors and in his senior year married Lois B. Hamlin; they had one child.

Black's work as a schoolteacher, which he continued as a college student, gained him enough experience to be offered, at the time of his graduation, principalships in New Hampshire, Maine, and Iowa. He declined all of them and accepted the position of editor of the *Johnstown Journal* in Johnstown, Fulton County, New York. Always interested in the law, he began part-time legal studies. Within one year Black was forced to resign his editorship of the *Journal* over a political dispute with the owner and removed his family to Troy, New York, where he worked for a short time as a newspaperman and a law clerk. He completed his legal studies and in 1879 was admitted to the New York bar. He was associated for one year with the firm of Smith, Wellington, and Black and then opened his own practice. Black specialized in torts, contracts, and business law. He handled several highly publicized cases in Rensselaer County, including in 1893 an arrangement for receiverships of the Troy Steel and Iron Company and the Gilbert Car Company.

Black's contacts in the professional and business community of Troy gradually moved him into Republican politics. He served as a stump speaker for the Rensselaer County Republican Committee in the presidential campaigns of 1888 and 1892. In 1893 he became chairman of the committee, in which capacity he succeeded in unifying and solidifying the local organization. He also played a leading role in exposing election frauds involving the Democratic opposition in the county and helped steer to passage in the state legislature measures that were designed to prevent such misdeeds in the future. Black's activities earned him in 1894 the Republican nomination for Congress in a district that encompassed the counties of Rensselaer and Columbia, and he was easily elected over Democrat Charles D. Haines.

In Congress Black showed an interest in railroads and public land claims, and he was a member of committees that dealt with these subjects. In the meantime, Black developed a close relationship in New York with Republican leader Louis Payn of Columbia County, a confidant of state GOP boss Thomas C. Platt. Likewise he ingratiated himself with the party rank and file by regularly attending state nominating conventions and by working actively for William McKinley's presidential nomination at the 1896 Republican National Convention. He was temporary chairman of the Republican State Convention at Saratoga Springs in the summer of 1896, and there his political friend Payn persuaded the leaders, including Boss

Platt, to pass over Benjamin B. Odell, Jr., and nominate Black for governor. Black waged a strong campaign and defeated Democrat Wilbur F. Porter by a margin of almost 213,000 votes, the largest plurality in a New York gubernatorial election up to that time.

Black conducted his two-year term as governor in a highly partisan manner. Despite the clamor of independents and even some moderate Republicans, he insisted on the appointment of Payn, a corporate lobbyist, as superintendent of insurance. He devoted a substantial portion of his first message to the legislature to an attack on the civil service system. "Civil service will work better with less starch," he declared, and he sponsored a bill, which the legislature enacted, that gave appointing officers in state government greater leeway in determining the fitness of applicants for listed positions. Also in 1897 he approved the charter legislation that established the new borough-system government for greater New York, one of whose purposes was to secure Republican control of the consolidated city.

The rise of political independence in urban centers across the state together with a host of Democratic victories in the 1897 elections forced Black to relent somewhat his fiercely partisan approach to governing. In 1898 he urged the legislature to pass a measure that would reform the state's primary election law. "We want a fair, liberal, honest primary law, one against which no complaint can be made by a Mugwump or anybody else," he stated to a political ally. When the bill was subsequently enacted, it provided for the strict regulation of primary-election procedures and permitted party members to join nonpartisan organizations, like the recently created Citizens' Union in New York City. However, Black's lingering reputation as a partisan, his several disagreements with Boss Platt over patronage and certain legislative matters, including Black's opposition to an insurance bill that he believed would harm policyholders and his rejection of amendments to the state's railroad election laws, and his failure to prevent his subordinates' misuse of $9 million in canal-improvement monies rendered him vulnerable in 1898 for renomination as governor. Platt and his lieutenants turned to Theodore Roosevelt because they concluded that Roosevelt could better appeal to independent voters in the state. Black and his friends were criticized for their failure to work for Roosevelt's gubernatorial election, and the Black-Roosevelt relationship remained strained for many years.

After 1898 Black eased his way out of public life. He gave up his chairmanship of the Rensselaer County Republican Committee. In 1904 his name was mentioned as a possible successor to Platt as a U.S. senator, but he declined to be considered for the position. He ran a lucrative law practice in New York City until his retirement on his sixtieth birthday, at which time he returned to his home in Troy, where he died. In the legal profession Black enjoyed a reputation for superb preparation, mastery of detail, and clarity of argu-

ment. As a politician he was known for his personal integrity, fearlessness, and finely honed oratorial skill.

• A collection of Black papers is in the New York State Library in Albany. His gubernatorial messages are available in Charles Z. Lincoln, *State of New York, Messages from the Governors*, vol. 9 (1909). Biographical sketches appear in Edgar L. Murlin, *New York Red Book* (1899), and DeAlva Stanwood Alexander, *Four Famous New Yorkers* (1923). His political career is highlighted in Harold F. Gosnell, *Boss Platt and His New York Machine* (1924), and Richard L. McCormick, *From Realignment to Reform: Political Change in New York State, 1893–1910* (1981). An obituary is in the *New York Times*, 22 Mar. 1913.

ROBERT F. WESSER

BLACK, Hugo Lafayette (27 Feb. 1886–25 Sept. 1971), associate justice of the U.S. Supreme Court and senator from Alabama, was born in Harlan, near Ashland, Clay County, Alabama, the son of William Lafayette Black, a storekeeper, and Martha Ardella Toland. Although not raised in poverty, Black was a child of relatively humble antecedents. Through the depressions of the mid-1870s and 1890s, his father gradually acquired title to the property of debtors and left his children a sizable estate. Hugo used his inheritance to finance his education, attending medical school in Birmingham before switching to the law. He graduated from the University of Alabama Law School at Tuscaloosa in 1906. He then opened a law office in Clay County, but business was moribund, and in 1907 he moved to Birmingham. Black's first big case was the suit of a black convict who had been held in the convict lease program of a steel company for twenty-two days after his release date. Black won damages for his client and an enhanced reputation as well as his fee. Soon he became one of Birmingham's most successful plaintiffs' lawyers, a master of the jury trial, with an income of approximately $47,000, which was generated by hundreds of contingent-fee cases. He also earned the respect, even the friendship, of those in a position to judge his performance. Indeed, throughout his life, Black was renowned for his charm, his ability to withstand criticism with equanimity, and his generosity to opponents. He was polite, collegial, forgiving—and unswerving.

When Judge A. O. Lane, who had presided over the convict-lease case, was appointed city police commissioner in 1911, he chose Black as his police court judge. As a part-time judge, Black heard petty criminal cases, mostly involving black defendants, who were victimized by the city's corrupt fee system, which provided income for county officials who prosecuted impoverished residents for minor infractions. He was praised by local progressives for limiting fines and reducing fees that were generated by court appearances. Capitalizing on his reputation and campaigning hard, Black was elected Jefferson County prosecutor in 1914 on a platform that stressed "helpless people confronting the power of the big absentee corporations that dominated their lives." His record as a prosecutor was mixed, at least in part because his opponent in the election was appointed a criminal court judge, in whose court the newly elected prosecutor was given a chilly reception. He resigned to join the army in 1917 and attained the rank of captain before receiving an honorable discharge and returning to Birmingham in 1919.

Black's legal practice soon flourished once again, and he cemented his connections to the Birmingham elite by marrying the socially prominent Josephine Foster in 1921; they had three children. He conducted the successful prosecution of a ring of bootleggers and defended a Protestant minister who had been charged with murdering a Catholic priest. Both trials fit in well with the antiliquor and anti-Catholic politics of the Ku Klux Klan, which had achieved increasing importance throughout the South in the World War I era. Black, whose political ambitions were growing as fast as his legal practice, joined the Invisible Empire in 1923, even while condemning Klan violence. He resigned from the Klan two years later but was still supported by Klan leadership, which was widely viewed as a prerequisite to political success in Alabama in the 1920s.

As a candidate for the Senate in 1926, Black was an underdog, but his tireless campaigning ensured that voters knew his name. When he narrowly achieved victory in a three-way race in the Democratic primary, his election was assured. In the Senate, Black proved his party loyalty and backed the Democrat Al Smith (Alfred E. Smith) in the 1928 presidential election in spite of Smith's Catholicism. He also began an ambitious reading program, which included the works of Thucydides, Plutarch, Adam Smith, and John Locke, books that deeply influenced his thinking about the Constitution and human nature. With the onset of the Great Depression, Black's longstanding mistrust of big business was heightened. He attacked the Hoover administration's attempts to promote economic recovery through corporate consolidation as a sell-out to giant corporations without interest in the welfare of their employees or in democracy.

After defeating a challenge from a former Alabama governor in the Democratic primary for reelection in 1932, Black campaigned across the country for Franklin Delano Roosevelt. Following Roosevelt's election, Black was among the most loyal supporters of the New Deal in the Senate and even backed the so-called "Court-packing plan," which was designed to undermine the power of conservative justices to declare New Deal legislation unconstitutional. As a senator, he also made powerful enemies when, as chairman of an investigating subcommittee, his techniques included rousting witnesses out of bed at night and even jailing uncooperative witnesses. Finally, Black was a vehement opponent of the Wagner-Costigan antilynching bill, which he argued would replicate the mistakes of Reconstruction by angering white southerners. Although firmly committed to federal economic authority, he opposed interference with local "habits and customs."

When Roosevelt chose Black as his first Supreme Court appointment in August 1937, the nomination was therefore controversial. The confirmation vote was delayed as the Senate conducted a rare investigation of one of its own members. Even after the committee voted to confirm the nomination, debate in the Senate was heated, especially when the NAACP urged that Black be questioned about rumored membership in the Ku Klux Klan. Although Black did not deny Klan membership outright, Imperial Wizard Hiram Evans, a childhood friend of Black's and a fellow klansman in Birmingham, claimed that Black was neither a member nor a supporter. The controversy continued after his confirmation, and Black took the unusual step of taking the oath of office in August, before the traditional date on which new justices are sworn in. He then left on a trip to Europe. While he was gone, journalists uncovered solid evidence of his earlier Klan affiliation. The outcry that followed was loud and long. Even Roosevelt hinted that some explanation was in order. On his return, Black made an extraordinary radio address in which he admitted joining the Klan but said that he had never participated in Klan activities and promised that he would be a vigorous defender of the rights of all Americans. Response to the speech was mixed; one newspaper editorial called Black "a humbug and a coward," and another called him "a living symbol that here the cause of liberalism was unwittingly betrayed." Black nevertheless took his seat on the Court in October 1937. From then on, despite a lingering interest in politics, including a flirtation in the 1940s with a possible run for the presidency, Black devoted himself unstintingly to his judicial role.

Justice Black served for thirty-four years, during which time he articulated and defended a full-fledged philosophy of the Supreme Court's role in interpreting constitutional provisions. His vision was among the most influential, if hotly debated, constitutional theories in the nation's history. Not unexpectedly, he upheld the power of government to regulate economic affairs. His antitrust opinions, for example, construe the reach of federal legislation broadly. Less predictably, Black championed political and civil rights. From a senator who countenanced the flagrant violation of civil rights because of local "habits and customs," he grew into a passionate defender of the rights of minorities and political dissidents.

The evolution of Black's constitutional vision has confounded students of the Court. Some see his stance as a Supreme Court justice as fundamentally inconsistent with his life as a politician and his senatorial career as inconsistent with his life as a plaintiffs' lawyer. In this view, Black made several radical shifts, based primarily on the demands—or opportunities—presented by his various professional incarnations. Others argue that Black remained true to a central theme of the constancy of human nature throughout his long life and that the tension between community values (or government action) and individual rights was less of his making than a product of the tensions in American life in the twentieth century in general, and New Deal liberalism in particular. A third view reconciles apparent inconsistencies in Black's career as the expression of his "southern-ness"—a distrust of centralized power that recalled the populism of his roots, and a reverence for literalism that reflected his evangelical upbringing. Whatever the true explanation (and all three may have some validity), Black's mind—and his political instincts—were among the sharpest in the Supreme Court's history.

Black's most enduring contribution was in the field of constitutional adjudication, especially the law of the First Amendment. He believed profoundly in the efficacy of checks and balances of American government. Based in part on his reading of classical texts, he distrusted all abuses of power, including the potential for tyranny of the majority in a democracy. The Constitution, he believed, was the perfect solution to the problem of imbalances of power, and the Supreme Court was charged by the Constitution with correcting imbalances. He was famous for what he called his "constitutional faith" and always carried a copy of his text as a preacher would his Bible. Under the Constitution, Black maintained, the Court had great power, but the Constitution also guarded against an excess of power in the judiciary. Judges were responsible for carrying out the commands of the Constitution—nothing more, and nothing less. The Court was circumscribed by the text itself. This literal reading did not mean, however, that the Constitution should be interpreted narrowly to answer only those questions that had arisen in the late eighteenth century. The language of the document, although "literally" applied, according to Black, should be construed as "liberally" as possible. Thus, for example, freedom of speech included protection of forms of speech, such as radio broadcasts, that could not have been anticipated by the framers. A liberal reading of the Constitution, however, did not authorize judges to "gloss" constitutional language. Black categorically opposed the creation of rights that were not rooted in the Constitution and equally opposed protection of activities that were not clearly within the ambit of constitutional language.

Black's jurisprudence was heavily informed by his vast reading of Greek and Roman classics and of modern history and biography. He often referred to the writings of Aristotle and the life of Thomas Jefferson, and he was also devoted to Michel de Montaigne's essays, Charles Beard's story of the foundings of the United States, the longshoreman-philosopher Eric Hoffer, Will Durant, and Carl Sandburg. Black's other lifetime passion was tennis, which he found to be a tonic from day-to-day cares. He played well into his seventies with his sons, law clerks, and friends, sometimes seven sets at a clip.

When Black was appointed in 1937, his commitment to the literal words of the Constitution was a handy means of undercutting the "substantive due process" theory that had been a primary doctrinal tool of the Supreme Court's conservative majority when it invalidated social and economic legislation. This literalist approach also created difficulties for Black because the words of some of the Bill of Rights seemed to preclude application of the first nine amendments to the Constitution against state governments. For example, the First Amendment is addressed only to Congress. Black solved this dilemma by arguing that the Fourteenth Amendment's due process clause "incorporated" the Bill of Rights into protections against state as well as federal government. In effect, Black substituted one form of infusing the due process clause with meaning (the "substantive due process" model) for another—the "incorporation" model, which would tolerate significant economic regulation, but only if individual rights were not sacrificed to governmental efficiency or planning.

The difference, according to Black, was that his model was historically justified. The Reconstruction Congress that drafted the Fourteenth Amendment intended to apply the Bill of Rights against the states, Black maintained, so that his interpretation of the due process clause was faithful to Congress's intention. Thus Black entered the so-called "incorporation controversy," a heated debate over whether, and to what extent, the Bill of Rights applies to the states through the Fourteenth Amendment. Black's position was at once activist, since it would drastically increase the power of the Supreme Court to review state actions, and restrictive, because of its reliance on literal meaning. Historians and legal scholars continue to debate the validity of Black's research as well as the merits of his underlying philosophy. Labeled "simplistic" by some jurisprudents, Black's absolutism gave him the courage to take many unpopular, even extreme, positions: he was, for example, a consistent defender of the rights of pornographers, however abhorrent he found their product. This distinctive and, to some, idiosyncratic philosophy profoundly influenced the course of constitutional jurisprudence, but it was never accepted by a majority of the Court. It is fitting that his views were first announced in protest in *Adamson v. California* (1947), with Black dissenting, and he continued to leave his mark as much through dissents as through majority opinions.

For much of his tenure, Black's most potent intellectual and doctrinal opponent was Felix Frankfurter. Both justices were Roosevelt appointments, and both were adamant supporters of the New Deal. But Frankfurter's response to the problem presented by the "nine old men" was to develop a theory of judicial restraint in the interests of preserving and promoting majority rule. Legislation, in Frankfurter's view, was entitled to a strong presumption of validity, while in Black's perspective every piece of legislation that seemed to touch on specific constitutional limitations should be reviewed searchingly. The battles between two such titans are the stuff of Supreme Court legend. Although less cantankerous than his colleague, Black was no less relentless in fighting for his constitutional vision. Sublimely secure in the rightness of his own views, and possessing a steel will, Black loved a good scrap and was ever generous to his foes, Frankfurter among them. As the journalist and student of the First Amendment Anthony Lewis put it, "[Black] loved battling Felix Frankfurter. He also loved Felix Frank-furter."

Especially in cases involving freedom of speech, Black and Frankfurter were often at odds. In the Mc-Carthy era, Black was vigorous in defense of Communists, the Cold War notwithstanding. In three important dissents he argued that free association and free political debate should not be sacrificed to fear. The First Amendment, he wrote, was based on the conviction that the nation could survive without penalizing political belief and expression, "a far bolder philosophy than despotic rulers can afford" (*American Communications Association v. Douds*, 1950). See also *Dennis v. United States* (1951) and *Barenblatt v. United States* (1959).

Yet Black's record on political rights in general, and on speech in particular, is not uniformly supportive of individual liberty. He distinguished speech, which he argued was absolutely protected, from conduct, which he considered outside the ambit of the speech clause. Late in his career, for example, Black was horrified by the mass marches, sit-ins, and protests of the civil rights and anti-Vietnam War movements. As one scholar who watched television coverage of a protest rally with the aging Black in 1964 put it, Black distrusted the authoritarian and antidemocratic element of the protests. It is perhaps not surprising, then, that Black dissented in *Tinker v. Des Moines Independent Community School District* (1969), a case involving students who wore black armbands to school to protest the Vietnam War. Black's dissent argued that the armbands were a bar to the objective discussion of ideas; they were a form of conduct that was calculated to provoke an emotional response and likely to undermine school discipline. Even though the content of speech was "absolutely" protected, Black explained, speakers could validly be regulated through time, place, and manner restrictions. Allowing students to run amok, "conducting break-ins, sit-ins, lie-ins, and smash-ins," he wrote, undercut rather than undergirded respect for the training necessary to mold good citizens.

Black also was solicitous about questions of order and security in wartime, even in a case where the Bill of Rights would otherwise have dictated that the government had violated important constitutional rights. In *Korematsu v. United States* (1944), Black's opinion for the majority sustained the arrest of a Japanese American for violating an "exclusion" order, an order which, if obeyed, would have resulted in enforced confinement in a remote detention center without conviction, or even charge, of any crime. The hardships suffered by Korematsu, Black said, were "part of war, and war is an aggregation of hardships." In light of evidence that has since been released that the government knowingly concealed its awareness that all but a small number of Japanese Americans were loyal to the United States, the exclusion system in general, if not Black's opinion, was racist, and Congress formally apologized for it in 1988.

But despite *Korematsu*, his short-lived membership in the Ku Klux Klan, and his passionate opposition to the antilynching bill in the Senate, Black voted consistently in the majority for the desegregation of schools and the protection of African-American voting rights. He was a key advocate on the Court in overruling the notorious "separate but equal" doctrine that was first announced in *Plessy v. Ferguson* (1896) and enthusiastically joined the unanimous opinion of the Court in *Brown v. Board of Education* (1954), the landmark case that overturned the official racial segregation of public schools. As a southerner, Black understood that the court-ordered dismantling of America's version of apartheid would provoke resistance. He predicted that the *Brown* decision would revive the Klan and be the "end of political liberalism in the South." Despite this insight, he argued unsuccessfully within the Court for swifter implementation of desegregation than the "all deliberate speed" standard that was adopted in *Brown v. Board of Education II* (1955).

Black also understood that he and his family would pay a personal price for his decision. As the *Brown* case was under consideration, he wrote to his son Hugo Black, Jr., then a lawyer and aspiring congressional candidate in Birmingham: "This is your chance, son, but I've got to tell you something. . . . We've got some cases . . . challenging segregation. . . . I don't believe segregation is constitutional." Hugo Black, Jr., did indeed pay a price for his father's judicial conscience; not only was his candidacy immediately aborted, but he and his family were so harassed because of his father's "treason to the South" that he eventually left Alabama. Black himself was made aware that visits to the South, even to his hometown, were unwelcome, and he was not invited to his fiftieth law school reunion. Black never wavered and was author of the order that mandated the admission of James Meredith to "Ole Miss" in 1962. He also joined the Court's unprecedented action in *Cooper v. Aaron* (1958), which held the conduct of Governor Orval Faubus and the state of Arkansas unconstitutional after Faubus ordered the National Guard to prevent black students from attending Little Rock's Central High School. Years later, near the end of Black's service on the Court, he was honored at a large, emotional dinner that was attended by the community's political and business leaders.

In the 1960s, Black was placed in a quandary that was as vexing to him as was the Court's refusal to "incorporate" the Bill of Rights in earlier days. Deeply disturbed by civil disobedience, even in the name of social justice, he rejected the extension of First Amendment protection to a library "stand-in" that protested a segregated bookmobile system, complaining bitterly that nobody should have a "license to invade the tranquility and beauty of our libraries whenever they have a quarrel with some state policy that may or may not exist" (*Brown v. Louisiana* [1966]). He also protested the creation of a right of marital sexual privacy, saying that, although "I like my privacy as well as the next man, . . . [u]nlike my brethren, I am simply unable to find a constitutional right to it" (*Griswold v. Connecticut* [1965]). He also dissented in cases that invalidated poll taxes and sustained the provision in the Voting Rights Act of 1965 that required southern states to get the approval of the attorney general before establishing voter-qualification rules.

Some commentators speculate that Black in old age abandoned New Deal principles for a more conservative inclination to protect property rights and a disinclination to look behind outwardly neutral statutes that had racially discriminatory effects, such as the poll tax. The more widely accepted view is that the Court had simply moved beyond its most senior justice; the New Deal warrior's constitutional vision had been outlived. Black himself, as lectures he gave at New York University Law School and Columbia Law School illustrate, had not altered his constitutional philosophy. He believed until he died that judges should "support the Constitution as written, not as revised by the Supreme Court from time to time" (*A Constitutional Faith*, p. 22).

Black died at Bethesda Naval Hospital, only days after he resigned from the Court. He was survived by his second wife, Elizabeth Seay DeMeritte, whom he married in 1957 after the death of his first wife in 1951.

• Black's papers are in the Twentieth Century Collection of the Manuscripts Division of the Library of Congress. Hugo L. Black, *A Constitutional Faith* (1968), is a convenient summary of the justice's constitutional philosophy. Correspondence with Hugo Black, Jr., is published in *Mr. Justice and Mrs. Black: The Memoirs of Hugo L. Black and Elizabeth Black* (1986). Hugo L. Black, Jr., *My Father: A Remembrance* (1975), is a valuable source of insight and anecdotes. Tony Freyer, *Hugo L. Black and the Dilemma of American Liberalism* (1990); Gerald T. Dunne, *Hugo Black and the Judicial Revolution* (1977); and Roger K. Newman, *Hugo Black* (1994), are full-scale biographies. Among the most useful studies of Black's jurisprudence are Charles Reich, "Mr. Justice Black and The Living Constitution," *Harvard Law Review* 76 (1963): 673; Howard Ball and Phillip J. Cooper, *Of Power and Right: Hugo Black, William O. Douglas and America's Constitutional Revolution* (1992); Tony Freyer, ed., *Justice Hugo Black and Modern America* (1990); Wallace Mendelson, *Justices Black and Frankfurter: Conflict in the Court* (1961; 2d ed., 1966); G. Edward White, *The American Judicial Tradition: Profiles of Leading American Judges* (1976); and Daniel J. Meador, *Mr. Justice Black and His Books* (1974). A bibliography of works by and about Black is Cherry Lynn Thomas and Jean McCulley Holcumb, "Hugo Lafayette Black: A Bibliography of the Court Years, 1937–1971," *Alabama Law Review* 38 (1987): 381–499. Front-page obituaries are in the *Washington Post* and the *New York Times*, 25 Sept. 1971.

NORMAN DORSEN
SARAH BARRINGER GORDON

BLACK, Jeremiah Sullivan (10 Jan. 1810–19 Aug. 1883), U.S. attorney general, U.S. secretary of state, and attorney, was born near Stony Creek, Pennsylvania, the son of Henry Black, a judge and legislator, and Mary Sullivan. Black read law under Chauncey Forward in Somerset, Pennsylvania, passing his bar examination at age twenty. When Forward was elected to Congress in 1830, he left Black in charge of his office, and the young attorney assumed responsibilities

far beyond his experience. Black's practice in Forward's office became more secure when in 1836 he married Forward's daughter Mary Forward. They had five children. In 1843 Black was baptized into his father-in-law's faith, the Disciples of Christ church, and developed a close personal friendship with its founder Alexander Campbell.

Black also adopted the politics of his mentor and became during the 1830s an ardent Jacksonian Democrat, a commitment he retained permanently. A rising law career led to his appointment in 1842 as judge of the Court of Common Pleas for the Sixteenth District, a three-county area. In 1851 he was elected a judge of the Pennsylvania Supreme Court and was reelected three years later. During these years he earned a reputation as an outspoken yet fair jurist. Stories of his absentmindedness also grew. For example, before he departed on a judicial trip his wife admonished him to change shirts daily. On his return she asked for the dirty shirts, only to find her husband wearing all five at once, having carefully put on a clean one each day.

In 1857 Black attained national prominence when James Buchanan, a longtime associate of Black's in Pennsylvania Democratic politics, appointed him attorney general, a last-minute compromise choice among warring Pennsylvania Democratic factions. While not regarded as prosouthern, Black, like Buchanan, opposed any kind of radicalism, which for both included the Republican position of congressional containment of slavery. Much of Black's initial attention went to complex California land title cases stemming from Spanish and Mexican grants. He investigated thoroughly and convinced the Supreme Court to reverse several lower court decisions and restore to the public domain millions of acres fraudulently claimed by adventurers. On the more controversial sectional issues, Black tried to compel acceptance of his tightly argued legal views rather than the emotional political arguments of partisans in both the North and the South. Slavery, he believed, was a matter of law, and in the case of *Ableman v. Booth* (1859) he convinced the Court that a state (Wis.) could not defy the central government by declaring the Fugitive Slave Act of 1850 unconstitutional. He defended the proslavery Lecompton constitution for Kansas Territory, even though it had been rejected by the voters there. He led the administration's attack on Senator Stephen A. Douglas over the latter's opposition to Lecompton by arguing that, constitutionally, Congress had full authority over the territories. In an equally forceful argument, he defended constitutional law sanctioning slavery against the "higher law" arguments of Senator William H. Seward of New York.

The issue that above all others put Black in the center of sectional controversy was the Buchanan administration's response to South Carolina's secession in December 1860. The question split the cabinet into northern and southern factions. Although Black initially believed in the right of a state to secede, he backed away from urging endorsement of that position in response to the president's request for a legal opinion on secession. The attorney general responded that the federal government had a duty and right to collect duties and to defend public property and execute the laws. Yet this right could only be enforced peacefully, and if force were necessary, only Congress could legislate such procedures. Black asserted that Congress could not "arm one part of the people against another for any purpose beyond that of merely protecting the General Government in the exercise of its proper constitutional functions" (quoted in *Works of James Buchanan*, vol. 11). Black thus took an essentially conservative approach, which became the position of the administration, a stance that cynics argued was tantamount to saying, "You cannot do it, but we cannot stop you if you do." In essence, Black argued that secession was unconstitutional but that the federal government had no power to coerce a seceded state back into the Union.

Nevertheless, Black and Secretary of State Lewis Cass urged Buchanan to dispatch reinforcements to Major Robert Anderson, then in command of Fort Moultrie in Charleston Harbor. When southerners in the cabinet successfully prevented Buchanan from taking such action, Cass resigned in disgust, a move that was followed on 20 December by South Carolina's decision to secede. Further cabinet shuffling followed, and Buchanan appointed Black to fill the vacancy in the State Department and Edwin M. Stanton to become attorney general. The arrival in Washington of South Carolina commissioners determined on negotiations with the administration created a new cabinet crisis. In Black's eyes, Buchanan's response was not a firm enough rejection of negotiations, and Black threatened to resign. As a result, the president's resolve stiffened, and he rejected the commissioners' overtures. With Black writing the instructions to Major Anderson, the unarmed *Star of the West* sailed for Charleston on 5 January 1861 with relief supplies.

In the final confusing months of the Buchanan administration, Black's duties concentrated on preventing foreign recognition of the Confederacy. As a reward for Black's faithful service, Buchanan, in his last month in office, nominated him for the Supreme Court position vacated months earlier by the death of Peter V. Daniel. Senate confirmation was withheld, however, as southern states seceded, Douglas Democrats remained unenthusiastic, and Republicans showed open hostility. On 21 February 1861 the Senate voted 26 to 25 not to consider the nomination, and Black returned to private life upon Abraham Lincoln's inauguration.

During the early months of the Civil War, Black found himself in dire financial straits, having lost much of his money in a disastrous investment with his brother-in-law. Returning to Pennsylvania, he settled in York but spent part of his time in Washington in the humble position of reporter to the U.S. Supreme Court. Resuming his own law practice, he again took up the cause of clients who had become victims of fraudulent California land claims. Black was successful in most of these cases and in the process received

substantial fees. In the Quicksilver Mine case his fee was $180,000, said to be the largest ever paid to an attorney up to that time. By 1864 he could resign his reporter position and buy lands in his home state.

In the immediate postwar years Black combined Democratic politics with devotion to his constitutional principles, and through his involvement in a number of significant cases, he regained the prominence he had held as attorney general. Best known was his role in *Ex Parte Milligan* (1866), in which he argued for his client Lambdin P. Milligan, who had been convicted by a military court in Indiana for allegedly treasonous activities during the Civil War. Black's successful defense centered on the illegality of military law applying where civil courts functioned. He was prepared to offer similar arguments in relation to military rule in the South during Reconstruction in *Ex Parte McCardle* (1869) when Congress acted to deny court jurisdiction.

An opponent of Radical Reconstruction, Black supported Andrew Johnson's resistance to military government in the former Confederacy. He and Attorney General Henry Stanbery wrote the veto message for the First Reconstruction Act of February 1867, claiming it interfered with civil government and set up a military dictatorship. The federal government could not insist on black suffrage, since the franchise was a power belonging exclusively to the states. When Congress moved toward Johnson's impeachment, Black was initially included on the president's defense team. He later withdrew when Johnson sided with Secretary of State Seward in a dispute between the two that was unrelated to impeachment.

During Ulysses S. Grant's administration, Black remained active in both national and state issues. In the *Slaughterhouse Cases* (1873) he successfully defended Louisiana against enforcement of the Fourteenth Amendment. Pennsylvania Democrats pushed his name for presidential nominations in 1868 and 1872, but the eccentric, outspoken Black garnered little support outside of his home state. Actually, Black showed little interest in his own candidacy. In 1868 he campaigned enthusiastically for Horatio Seymour and in 1872 reluctantly campaigned for his old nemesis Horace Greeley. In May 1869 Black's right arm was crushed in a railroad accident, but he quickly learned to write with his left hand. In 1872–1873 he labored diligently for eleven months in Pennyslvania's constitutional convention, contributing significantly to the state's new constitution. His main efforts at the convention were directed against corporation lobbyists whom he regarded as comprising a corrupt ring and in effect a third house of the legislature that muzzled the governor and dictated legislation through bribery. He succeeded in persuading the delegates to endorse his "iron-clad oath," which required legislators to swear that they had not been a party to bribery. The convention, however, rejected his definition of bribery, and in general his unwillingness to compromise with the delegates left him frustrated.

A controversial writer, in 1870 Black attacked Henry Wilson over the latter's hostile account of the Buchanan administration and in 1881 defended Christianity against the attacks of the humanist and skeptic Robert G. Ingersoll. Effectively conbining invective with personal attack, Black remained constantly in the headlines through his writings and courtroom speeches. In 1877 he attacked the Republican majority on the commission that placed Rutherford B. Hayes in the presidency over Democrat Samuel J. Tilden, describing the result as "the Great Fraud."

Even in his declining years Black continued his outspoken defense of the Democratic party and his conservative interpretation of the Constitution. Despite his partisan views, he was an able and objective jurist, as witnessed by his appointment in 1874 to the commission to settle the longstanding boundary dispute between Virginia and Maryland. His constitutional views as attorney general and as a litigator of pivotal cases in public policy emphasized the limited nature of the federal government and the need to protect both individuals and states against the central government becoming too intrusive. His death in York ended a long and colorful career that rarely left Black in the background.

• Black's papers are in the Library of Congress, and a number of his important letters are included in *The Works of James Buchanan*, ed. John Bassett Moore (12 vols., 1908). His reminiscences were published in the *Philadelphia Press*, 7, 14, and 21 Aug. 1881. His son Chauncey F. Black edited *Essays and Speeches of Jeremiah S. Black* (1885). Biographies, all of which are appreciative in approach, are Mary Black Clayton, *Reminiscences of Jeremiah Sullivan Black* (1887), written by his daughter; Margaret C. Klingelsmith, "Jeremiah Sullivan Black, 1810–1883," in *Great American Lawyers*, vol. 6, ed. William D. Lewis (1909); and Francis N. Thorpe, "Jeremiah S. Black," *Pennsylvania Magazine of History and Biography* 50 (1926): 117–33, 273–86. William N. Brigance, *Jeremiah Sullivan Black: A Defender of the Constitution and the Ten Commandments* (1934), is well researched but lacks objectivity. More balanced views of Black's role as attorney general and secretary of state are in Elbert B. Smith, *The Presidency of James Buchanan* (1975); Philip S. Klein, *President James Buchanan, A Biography* (1962); Roy F. Nichols, *The Disruption of American Democracy* (1948); Harold M. Hyman and William M. Wiecek, *Equal Justice under Law: Constitutional Development, 1835–1875* (1982); and Nichols, "Jeremiah Sullivan Black," in *The American Secretaries of State and Their Diplomacy*, vol. 6, ed. Samuel F. Bemis (1928). Black's role in the Johnson impeachment is defended by Brigance in "Jeremiah Black and Andrew Johnson," *Mississippi Valley Historical Review* 19 (1932): 205–18. See also *Debates of the Convention to Amend the Constitution of Pennsylvania* (2 vols., 1873). An obituary is in the *New York Times*, 20 Aug. 1883.

FREDERICK J. BLUE

BLACK, John Donald (6 June 1883–12 Apr. 1960), agricultural economist, was born in Cambridge, Wisconsin, the son of Robert Black, a homestead farmer, and Margaret Scott, a schoolteacher. The family was of recent Scottish extraction. The fourth of ten children, Black grew up in a home where education was valued. Three of his siblings became teachers, one became a chemist, and one became a life insurance executive. Black graduated from the normal school at Oshkosh,

Wisconsin, in 1905 and taught high school in Rice Lake, Wisconsin, from 1905 to 1907. As a high school teacher he handled diverse subjects such as geography and algebra while also coaching the athletic teams.

In 1909 Black earned a B.A. in English (and membership in Phi Beta Kappa) from the University of Wisconsin; he followed that in 1910 with an M.A. from the same institution. He then embarked on a career of teaching rhetoric at the college level, first at Western Reserve University (1910–1911) and then at the Michigan College of Mines (1911–1915). It was at the latter school, which was located in a depressed mining district in the midst of labor unrest, that Black began to turn his attention to the economic questions that were more urgent to his students than English rhetoric. This would prove to be the turning point in Black's career. Returning to the University of Wisconsin to take summer courses in labor economics, Black was impressed by the work of economist Henry C. Taylor, the leading proponent of the new discipline of agricultural economics and a student of Richard T. Ely. Giving up English, Black went to study under Taylor and received a Ph.D. in agricultural economics in 1918. His dissertation on land tenure in Wisconsin was one of a number of University of Wisconsin studies at that time in the field of land economics. In 1917 he married Nina Van Steenberg; they had three children.

Black rose quickly to become a leader in agricultural economics. Between 1918 and 1927 he taught agricultural economics at the University of Minnesota, serving as chief of his division beginning in 1921. He attracted a number of scholars and students to Minnesota to study agricultural problems, which had become severe following a sharp price decline in 1920. Black's first book, *Introduction to Production Economics* (1926), was important in the development of the theory of the competitive firm. Meanwhile, in 1922 he had begun consulting with the U.S. Department of Agriculture's Bureau of Agricultural Economics in Washington, D.C., which was headed by Taylor. This led Black to further government work, including an assignment as chief economist for the Federal Farm Board in 1931–1932.

Black made contributions to a wide range of economic fields during this period, including input-output analysis, farm management, and the economics of agricultural cooperatives. Perhaps his most important public work, however, was his collaboration with economists W. J. Spillman and M. L. Wilson on the development of the domestic allotment plan for raising farm prices and controlling production. This plan became the basis of the price support and adjustment programs of the Agricultural Adjustment Act of 1933 and subsequent New Deal farm programs. Black's second book, *Agricultural Reform in the United States* (1929), was a catalyst in this debate. Black demurred, however, at the New Deal's granary plan for large-scale storage of surplus food and compulsory production controls.

In 1927 Black left Minnesota to join the faculty of Harvard University. He soon built a distinguished agricultural economics program there, which was unusual for a university that was not in the land-grant system. To attract students from farm backgrounds who might not otherwise have been able to afford Harvard, he sought research funds and other sources of money that could be used for student aid. In 1932 he was elected president of the American Farm Economics Association. From 1930 to 1933 he chaired the Social Science Research Council's advisory committee on agriculture. During World War II he consulted with the War Food Administration and served on the food and nutrition board of the National Research Council from 1941 to 1954.

In the postwar years Black published the notable studies *Farm Management* (coauthored with Marion Clawson, Charles R. Sayre, and Walter W. Wilcox, 1947) and *The Rural Economy of New England* (1951), as well as several other books. The American Economic Association elected him president in 1955 and chose him as one of its first fellows in 1957. He retired from Harvard in 1956, but he remained active as a visiting professor and as a consultant to the U.S. Forest Service and several foreign countries. In 1959 many of his shorter writings—often his most significant work— were collected in *Economics for Agriculture: Selected Writings of John D. Black*. Black died in Boston.

Black had a seminal influence on the development of agricultural economics. He was less concerned with refining economic theory or writing polished treatises than with staking out new territory. As two of his colleagues put it, Black was a pioneer with "a sense of timing that enabled him to 'open up' a field just when it needed to be opened up" (Cavin and Mighell, p. 223). Not a noted lecturer, Black's strength as a teacher came from the generous amount of time he spent with his advanced students. By energetically promoting the careers of his former students, he managed to spread his influence to nearly every academic department of agricultural economics in the country.

• Black's papers are at the Historical Society of Wisconsin in Madison. Additional letters from Black are in the Henry C. Taylor Papers there. Other significant books written or coauthored by Black include *The Dairy Industry and the AAA* (1935), *Future Food and Agriculture Policy* (1948), *Introduction to Economics for Agriculture* (1953), and *Biological Conservation with Particular Emphasis on Wildlife* (1954). Appreciations of Black's life include James P. Cavin and Ronald L. Mighell, "John Donald Black, 1883–1960," *Journal of Farm Economics* 42 (1960): 223–24, and John Kenneth Galbraith, "John D. Black: A Portrait," in *Economics for Agriculture: Selected Writings of John D. Black*, ed. James P. Cavin (1959). Black's early career is covered in Henry C. Taylor and Anne Dewees Taylor, *The Story of Agricultural Economics in the United States, 1840–1932* (1952). For his influence on the New Deal see Theodore Saloutos, *The American Farmer and the New Deal* (1982), and Richard S. Kirkendall, *Social Scientists and Farm Politics in the Age of Roosevelt* (1966). An obituary is in the *New York Times*, 13 Apr. 1960.

DOUGLAS E. BOWERS

BLACK, Max (24 Feb. 1909–27 Aug. 1988), philosopher, was born in Baku, Russia, the son of Lionel Black, a small trader and businessman, and Sophia Davinska. Because of the climate of anti-Semitism, Black's family left Russia when he was a young child, living a short while in Paris and finally settling in London in 1912. At an early age Black displayed a talent for mathematics, chess, and the violin and, at one time, contemplated a career as a pianist. It was his interest in mathematics, however, that led him to earn his B.A. in the subject at Queens College, Cambridge. While there, he became attracted to the analytic school of philosophy and, in particular, to the thought of Ludwig Wittgenstein, Bertrand Russell, G. E. Moore and F. P. Ramsey, all of whom were teaching at Cambridge while he was a student there and who were to have an influence on many of his subsequent ideas.

After completing his B.A. in 1930, Black received a one-year fellowship at Göttingen University, during which time he completed work on his first book, *The Nature of Mathematics*, which was published in 1933. That same year he married Michal Landsberg, with whom he had two children. He returned to London where, while working on his doctoral dissertation, "Theories of Logical Positivism," at the University of London, he lectured and tutored at the Institute of Education. Black soon grew tired of teaching mathematics and in 1940 accepted a position in the philosophy department at the University of Illinois at Urbana. He became coeditor of the *Journal of Symbolic Logic* in 1945 and of the *Philosophical Review* in 1946. Also in 1946 he became a professor of philosophy at Cornell University in Ithaca, New York. Two years later he became a U.S. citizen. A self-described "autodidact by necessity and a rover by inclination," Black found that his appointment at Cornell enabled him finally to pursue the varied interests that would make him a well-known figure in the social sciences, linguistics, literary criticism, and philosophy.

Black's interest in analytic philosophy can be traced back to the time he was introduced to the subject at Cambridge. Generally speaking, analytic philosophy examines the contexts in which logic, language, and reality are interrelated while shunning metaphysical speculations on the nature of existence. Black believed that the meaning of linguistic utterances could be revealed through logic and analysis. A more profitable philosophical inquiry, however, was one that investigated the rules that governed linguistic use. Black's commonsense approach to the rule-governing use of language led him to argue that in many cases the rules of discourse could not be rigidly followed. Thus, in his earliest philosophical work, *Language and Philosophy* (1949), he examined the indeterminacy or "vagueness" of certain rules, arguing that, while in logic and mathematics precision was essential, in many of the social sciences such exactness was only counterproductive. In later writings, he referred to this vagueness of concepts as the necessary "looseness" by which we think from rules without necessarily following what the rules dictate in every circumstance.

In addition to his emphasis on common sense and his use of everyday examples to illustrate his ideas, another defining feature of Black's written work was in its broad scope of subjects. In 1952 he published a translation of the philosophical papers of Göttlob Frege, one of the pioneers of analytical thought whose work on sense and reference Black had greatly admired. Shortly thereafter, in his *Problems of Analysis* (1954), Black tackled, among other perennial philosophical questions, the problem of induction, that is, the difficulty of making generalizations and future predictions based upon a series of known cases. Black did not attempt to overcome the problem that induction presents. He contended that there may be pragmatic reasons for accepting inductive reasoning but that these, too, would be difficult to defend when faced with the arguments of a skeptic. The most that can be claimed, according to Black, is that the rules of induction can generally be trusted to work if they meet the criterion of "self-supporting inferences." Otherwise, one must try to rely upon common sense.

In 1954 Black became the Susan Linn Sage Professor of Philosophy and Humane Letters at Cornell, a position he held until his retirement. In 1958 he was elected president of the Eastern Division of the American Philosophical Association.

As an analytic theorist, Black continually explored what language revealed about our thinking about the world. In 1962 he published *Models and Metaphors* wherein he characteristically argued that "the conception of language as a mirror of reality is radically mistaken" and that our linguistic utterances should strive to "conform to the discovered regularities of experience." By way of explication, he submitted that metaphorical language was more than an Aristotelian transitive or poetic figure of speech. Black argued that metaphors were examples of "conceptual archetypes" by which we learn to think and reason. In his "interactive" theory of metaphor, an analysis of the metaphor "man is a wolf" revealed that the word "man"—which Black called the "tenor"—interacted with the word "wolf"—the "vehicle." Thus, the reader is led not only to contemplate how men act like wolves, but how wolves can sometimes act like men. Moreover, Black argued that when conceived of in this fashion, the tenor and vehicle prompted a cognitive insight that could not be possible with any literal set of expressions. Although influential with some literary theorists, Black's cognitive theory of metaphor provoked some controversy in analytic circles, particularly when he and the American philosopher, Donald Davidson, debated Black's thesis in a series of journal articles and books, including Andrew Ortony, ed., *Metaphor and Thought* (1979), and Sheldon Sacks, ed., *On Metaphor* (1978).

In 1964 Black published his most important work, *A Companion to Wittgenstein's Tractatus*. Besides giving a useful annotation of Wittgenstein's work, he included explications of obscure and difficult passages, cross-referenced citations from relevant quotations from within and outside the *Tractatus*, and added critical commentaries on Wittgenstein's philosophy. In the chapter "Is the 'Tractatus' Self-Defeating?" Black suggested that Wittgenstein's thought resulted in "a negative metaphysics," for what it revealed was that metaphysical thought was impossible. To his critics, Wittgenstein's philosophy therefore rested on a contradiction, but not so for Black. He argued that even when philosophical examinations fail, they may still usefully illuminate the boundaries of thinking. In what can be taken for his own philosophical strategy, Black maintained that the philosopher must proceed by analogy and metaphor to "enlarge and extend the given concepts of science and ordinary life in a way that will allow him to arrive at a more extensive, more penetrating, and in some way more fundamental, view of the universe." In a similar vein to his earlier pronouncement that cognitive metaphors demonstrated how conceptual insights occur, he insisted that the value of Wittgenstein's work was in its showing the limits of our conceptual thinking.

Black devoted much of his later works to exploring, refining, and occasionally defending many of the ideas he sketched out earlier. Whether the subject was rational choice theory, justification theory, induction, metaphor, or the language theories of Noam Chomsky, John Dewey, or J. L. Austin, the distinctive quality that marks Black's later writings was an aspiration "not to prove anything, but to promote understanding and to provoke argument" (*Prevalence of Humbug* [1983]). After his retirement from Cornell in 1978, he continued to lecture at universities in the United States and abroad. From 1981 to 1984, he served as president of the International Institute of Philosophy, the second American ever to do so.

Black died in Ithaca. In his last book, published posthumously in 1990, he wrote that if he had to be classified he "would settle for logician, detached empiricist . . . and active skeptic." This is perhaps too clinical. A slightly more satisfying self-portrait is of a man who was a "lapsed mathematician, addicted reasoner, and devotee of metaphor and chess." Not only was Black a lifelong musician, but he was also a gifted chess player who, even in his late sixties, would play demonstration matches with as many as twenty opponents simultaneously. He was also fluent in six languages. So proficient in languages was he that, while lecturing in India in 1962, he was able to pick up the local dialect in only a month's time.

Black, who had no formal training in the subject, became chiefly known for his philosophical work. Although he was of Russian-Jewish extraction and acquired what might be called English cultural sensibilities, Black was thoroughly American in his thinking. As a philosopher, he was known for offering a commonsense, pragmatic approach to those theoretical issues that he knew required clarity. Highly skeptical of those who offered facile classifications, Black sought to confirm what can be known about the world and yet was ever mindful of the tentative nature that characterized most philosophical investigations.

• Black's papers are at Cornell University. His personal reflections on his life and work are in his introduction to *Perplexities* (1990). His *Critical Thinking* (1946) is a useful introductory textbook to logic. His philosophical ideas are compiled in several collections of essays, including *The Labyrinth of Language* (1968), *Margins of Precision* (1970), and *Caveats and Critiques* (1975). He also edited a number of philosophical texts, including *Philosophical Analysis* (1950), *Philosophy in America* (1965), *The Morality of Scholarship* (1967), and *Problems of Choice and Decisions* (1975). A partial treatment of his early childhood and family background is in Avril Blake, *Misha Black* (1984), a biography of Black's brother. The intellectual circles in which Black traveled while living in England are described in John Paul Russo, *I. A. Richards: His Life and Work* (1989), a biography of Black's mentor. An obituary is in the *New York Times*, 30 Aug. 1988.

JAMES WILSON-QUAYLE

BLACK, Winifred Sweet (14 Oct. 1863–25 May 1936), journalist known also as Annie Laurie and Winifred Bonfils, was born in Chilton, Wisconsin, the daughter of Benjamin Jeffrey Sweet, an attorney and Union army officer in the Civil War, and Lovisa Loveland Denslow. The fourth of five children, she was christened Martha Winifred. In 1869 the family moved to Illinois when her father was appointed U.S. pension agent for Chicago. Benjamin Sweet died in 1874 while serving in the Ulysses S. Grant administration in Washington, D.C. The death of Lovisa Sweet four years later left the orphaned Winifred to be raised by her elder sister. She received her education at the Sacred Heart Convent in Chicago, the Lake Forest Seminary, and Miss Burnham's Preparatory School at Northampton, Massachusetts.

Black first tried a career as an actress, joining the Black Crook touring company. Although her stage career was unsuccessful, she achieved her first success as a journalist when the *Chicago Tribune* published letters that she had written to her sister describing her adventures on tour. An 1890 trip to San Francisco to track down her runaway brother led to her decision to remain in California and pursue a career in journalism. She was hired by the *San Francisco Examiner*, whose managing editor, Sam Chamberlain, offered her instruction on how to write for a popular audience, telling her to imagine a cable car gripman reading his morning paper and ending with the advice, "Don't write a single word he can't understand and wouldn't read." Since it was customary for woman reporters at the time to write under a pseudonym, she chose the name "Annie Laurie," after a song her mother had sung. Her first major story in 1890, in which she exposed the rough treatment given to vagrants at San Francisco Receiving Hospital by pretending to be a patient, established her reputation. Her article also led to reforms that included the initiation of the city's first ambulance service.

Annie Laurie became known for her investigative journalism, including stories on the leper colony at Molokai, Hawaii; polygamy among the Mormons in Utah; and the juvenile court system in Chicago, but she was also given political and crime assignments. In 1892 she secured an exclusive interview with President Benjamin Harrison by reportedly sneaking aboard his private train and hiding under a table to surprise him.

Although she had married Orlow Black, a fellow *Examiner* reporter, in 1892 and had a small child, Winifred Black went to New York in 1895 to work with *Examiner* publisher William Randolph Hearst on his newly acquired *New York Journal*. New York was not to her liking, however, and she returned to California, where she was divorced from her husband in 1897. The same year, now writing as Winifred Black, she moved to Colorado to take a position with the *Denver Post*.

A second marriage in 1901 to Charles Alden Bonfils, brother of the copublisher of the *Denver Post*, gave Black two more children but did not interrupt her career. She continued to travel extensively, writing for both the *Denver Post* and the *New York Journal*. Bonfils, whose name Black rarely used, became managing editor of the *Kansas City Post* and then lived in New York City as a freelance writer; husband and wife rarely lived together after 1909.

Although she maintained her position at the *Denver Post*, Black continued to write feature stories for the *San Francisco Examiner*. It was for the *Examiner* that she wrote what has been called her greatest story: an eyewitness account of the Galveston flood of 1900. She wrote that she "begged, cajoled and cried" her way through lines of armed soldiers guarding the wharf at Texas City to board a boat for Galveston. She stayed on in the devastated city to help distribute the relief funds collected by the Hearst papers. Six years later she covered another disaster, the San Francisco earthquake. Reportedly, she rushed to San Francisco in response to a one-word telegram from Hearst: "Go!" In 1907 she went to New York to cover the sensational trial of playboy Harry K. Thaw for the murder of architect Stanford White. Black and three other women reporters sat together in the courtroom and wrote on the human interest side of the trial, leading a cynical colleague to label them "sob sisters." Black hated the nickname, but it followed her all of her life.

Black traveled to England to cover the suffragists and to Europe in 1918 to write on the aftermath of the First World War. She covered the Versailles peace conference in 1921 and the International Narcotics Convention in Geneva in 1931. During this period she continued to write her Annie Laurie column for the *San Francisco Examiner*.

Black's book in support of stronger drug control, *Dope: The Story of the Living Dead*, was published in 1928. In the same year she published a limited edition biography of Hearst's mother, *The Life and Personality of Phoebe Apperson Hearst*. A third book, *The Little Boy Who Lived on the Hill*, told the story of her invalid son. She continued to work as a journalist, although she suffered from diabetes and failing eyesight. When she died in San Francisco, her body lay in state in the city hall rotunda.

Black's career featured almost every kind of journalism and spanned more than thirty years. Her style could be crisp and direct or sentimental. She has been called the most versatile woman journalist of her time, writing with equal ease of disasters, murder, and everyday life in the city. She interviewed subjects as diverse as presidents and prostitutes, always emphasizing their humanity. "A woman has a distinct advantage over a man in reporting," she wrote, "if she has sense enough to balance her qualities."

• Much of what is known of the early life of Black is taken from a multipart autobiographical article, "Rambling through My Memories," *Good Housekeeping*, Jan.–May 1936. Barbara Belford, *Brilliant Bylines: A Biographical Anthology of Notable Newspaperwomen in America* (1986), contains a long biographical chapter on Black and reprints her 1900 article on the Galveston flood. The flood story, along with a short summary of Black's career, is also found in *Star Reporters and 34 of Their Stories*, ed. Ward Greene (1948). There are chapters on Black in Ishbel Ross, *Ladies of the Press* (1936); Madelon Schlipp and Sharon Murphy, *Great Women of the Press* (1983); and Marion Marzolf, *Up from the Footnote* (1977), although the last is quite brief. Black is briefly mentioned as "editorial page competition" for journalist Nellie Bly at the *New York Journal* in Brooke Kroeger's biography *Nellie Bly: Daredevil, Reporter, Feminist* (1994) and is also compared to Bly in Kay Mills, *A Place in the News: From the Women's Pages to the Front Pages* (1988). Obituaries are in the *Denver Post, San Francisco Chronicle*, and *San Francisco Examiner*, all 26 May 1936.

VIRGINIA ELWOOD-AKERS

BLACK BART (fl. 1875–1888), stagecoach robber, was born Charles E. Boles, probably in 1832 in either Norfolk, England, or upstate New York. His parents' names are unknown. He had a wife, Mary, and probably three children. He abandoned them all after the Civil War, in which he was wounded while serving as a first sergeant in the 116th Illinois Volunteer Infantry. He probably never saw any of his family again.

Between 1875 and 1883 Boles carried out twenty-nine holdups of stagecoaches, all in northern California. He came to epitomize the highwayman and popularized a new synonym for the latter, "road agent," a term remarked on by Robert Louis Stevenson in his *Silverado Squatters*. Boles took the name "Black Bart" from a character in a story that he had read. He fixed the nickname by deliberately leaving clues behind after two holdups. These were snippets of "poetry"—actually waggish doggerel—signed "Black Bart, P08."

Bart was the perfect bandit. He always worked alone, wearing a flour sack with eyeholes over his head and a duster over his clothing to hide his identity. He said nothing but "Throw down the [express] box!" so there was no accent or speech pattern to betray him. His victims only knew that his voice was deep and resonant. Bart never traveled on horseback but always afoot, with speed, stamina, and skill. Only once was a mounted sheriff's posse able to track him in the thick chaparral (brush) into which he had disappeared, and the deputies lost the trail in just six miles. James B. Hume, chief of detectives for Wells, Fargo, said Bart was "a person of great endurance, a thorough mountaineer, a remarkable walker; and [he] claims that he cannot be excelled in making quick transits over mountains and grades."

Bart's modus operandi never varied. He would "case" a stage from a temporary sleeping camp, to establish its schedule and memorize the terrain. His camps were never too close to a holdup site, he never built a fire at night, and he never slept over after a robbery. He rambled all over, from Redwood Coast to Sierra Nevada, and only once struck the same place twice. He always stopped a stage as it was forced to slow down on an upgrade, often at a curve that hid him from view until the last moment.

Bart was unique among badmen. He was something of a gentleman bandit and had a sense of humor. He did not smoke, drink, use drugs, or even curse drivers and guards to intimidate them. He does not even seem to have loaded the double-barreled shotgun that he used in robberies. He left the money and jewelry of travelers alone and was gallant toward female passengers. He stole only from Wells, Fargo & Co. and the U.S. Post Office, figuring that both could afford it.

Hume's study of the doggerel rhymes Bart left revealed only that he wrote each line in a different hand. The detective noted that Bart always opened "treasure" boxes with an old ax and slit mail pouches with a distinctive T-shaped cut near the bag's lock. Eventually Hume was able to put together a composite description of a suspect by interviewing people about strangers seen near the sites of stage robberies. The picture of Black Bart that he pieced together proved remarkably accurate but did him no good. The bandit struck, again and again, with impunity. Only once did a guard manage to get off a couple of shots at him.

Fate intervened when Bart, for the first time, made a holdup at the same site as an earlier robbery. In fact, it was the location of his very first robbery eight years earlier. It was on Funk Hill near Copperopolis in the mother lode. The driver, Reason McConnell, had no guard or passengers, so he gave a young deer hunter a lift. Jimmy Rolleri jumped off the stage to look for bucks before rejoining McConnell beyond the hill. Hume had bolted strongboxes inside the coaches, so Bart was still attacking the box with an ax when McConnell returned with Rolleri and the latter's Henry rifle. They took turns firing, and one of Rolleri's bullets nicked Bart in one knuckle. He dropped a bundle as he fled with his loot.

The local sheriff and Hume's assistant found a handkerchief among Bart's abandoned belongings. It bore the laundry mark F. X. O. 7. Hume sent a special investigator, Harry Morse, to check all of San Francisco's ninety-one laundries if he had to do so. Morse soon matched the mark with a middle-aged self-stated mining man who called himself Charles E. Bolton. Hume grilled him for hours and finally elicited a confession to (only) the last robbery.

William Randolph Hearst's *Examiner* protested about a "deal," and it is true that Black Bart received a mitigated sentence promised him by Hume for his cooperation. He drew only seven years in San Quentin and, a model prisoner, actually served only 4½ years, thanks to his good conduct. Still in good spirits while in his cell, he wrote McConnell and Rolleri, praising the former for his driving but adding, "I only regret that I am unable to compliment you on your marksmanship."

A legendary Black Bart grew up in newspapers and dime novels. His exploits and his loot were greatly exaggerated. The real Black Bart probably made far less than the $18,400 in "withdrawals" from Wells, Fargo that some writers estimated.

After his release from prison in 1888, Bart disappeared from public view, but there were stories that he had returned to crime, as new stage robberies were blamed on him. Another rumor had Wells, Fargo putting him on its payroll to *not* rob its express boxes. Bart was reportedly seen in various places, but Hume only stated that he had left California. Hume's assistant, Jonathan Thacker, in 1897 reported that Bart had sailed from Vancouver, British Columbia, on the *Empress of China*, bound for Japan. In any case, he utterly vanished.

• The best books on Black Bart are Richard H. Dillon, *Wells, Fargo Detective* (1969; repr. 1986), and William Collins and Bruce Levine, *Black Bart* (1993). Still useful are chapters in Joseph Henry Jackson, *Tintypes in Gold* (1939) and *Bad Company* (1949).

RICHARD H. DILLON

BLACKBEARD. *See* Teach, Edward.

BLACKBURN, Gideon (27 Aug. 1772–23 Aug. 1838), Presbyterian minister and missionary to Indians, was born in Augusta County, Virginia, the son of Robert Blackburn, a farmer. (His mother's name is not known.) Raised by his grandfather and then his uncle, Blackburn was fifteen years old when he became a Presbyterian, joining the church so dear to many of his Scotch-Irish predecessors. After rudimentary schooling, he migrated to eastern Tennessee and studied theology at the home of Robert Henderson. In 1792 the Abingdon Presbytery granted him a license to preach. His first pastorate centered on Fort Craig, later named Maryville, where Blackburn often accompanied soldiers in their efforts to forestall marauding Indians. He was not content to work in only one place, and so he ranged the countryside within a fifty-mile radius to organize new churches and preaching stations among the settlers. Blackburn was noted for carrying a loaded rifle along with his Bible as he sought to extend what he considered the blessings of civilization and religion in frontier regions. In 1793 he married Grizzel Blackburn, a second or third cousin, and they produced eleven children.

With a justified reputation as an Indian fighter, Blackburn experienced a change of heart and grew compassionate regarding Native Americans. He did not entertain much hope for Creek Indians, but he thought the Cherokees were willing to learn and seemed capable of progressive change. While still ministering to white congregations around Maryville, he began devoting a portion of his time to evangelical work among nearby Cherokee bands. Local presbyteries showed little enthusiasm for such efforts, but Blackburn persisted. In 1803 he appealed to the Tennessee General Assembly for support, and the following year he used its meager funding to begin a school on the Hiwassee River for native youths. The Christian gospel and white cultural standards were complementary features in his missionary enterprise. For seven years Blackburn affected the lives of some 300 pupils, teaching them the basics of arithmetic and English grammar, cleanliness, and the Shorter Catechism. By 1810, however, such activities had drained his health and personal finances to the point of collapse. Though reluctant to do so, he relinquished the school and churches in search of better conditions farther west.

Education and evangelism were twin occupations wherever Blackburn went, and in 1811 he began serving as first headmaster of Harpeth Academy in Franklin, Tennessee. He soon organized a Presbyterian church there and continued to preach in the surrounding area as well. These opportunities afforded better conditions for his growing family. Some Presbyterians opposed the revivals that began to occur in the early decades of the nineteenth century, but Blackburn favored such conversions among frontiersmen. His vivid oratory appealed to the imagination and conscience of his listeners, fitting the mold of preaching that emphasized human participation in the drama of salvation. In this way he contributed substantially to the Second Great Awakening in the trans-Allegheny West.

His reputation as an energetic preacher led to an invitation in 1823 to become minister of the First Presbyterian Church in Louisville, Kentucky. As before, he traveled around the area and organized several other churches and schools. Four years later he became president of Danville College, now known as Centre College. Blackburn encountered criticism there because he lacked an earned academic degree. More significantly, he had become an outspoken opponent of slavery and a champion of New School Presbyterianism, both minority views in his synod. Resigning in 1830, he served as pastor of a church in Versailles, Kentucky. Increasingly concerned about social reform, he also ranged the state speaking on behalf of the Kentucky Temperance Society. Over the years he had owned seven or eight slaves, but as his antislavery convictions grew, he emancipated them one by one and sent them to Liberia. In two cases, however, he considered the slaves too vicious and unfit for freedom and sold them into further servitude without regret.

Still, these views made the free soil of Illinois more appealing to Blackburn, and he moved there in 1833. He held no stated charge thereafter, but he remained vigorous in itinerant evangelical labors. He wanted to establish a theological school and devised a plan to raise funds through land speculation. He bought land for eastern investors and, with their approval, used a small portion of their payments to purchase land for the proposed school. The plan was not overly successful, but more than 16,000 acres became a legacy for the fledgling academy. It was not until 1857 that a school, later a college, bearing Blackburn's name actually opened in Carlinville, Illinois, the town where he died.

• No adequate biography of Blackburn exists. A sketch appears in William B. Sprague, *Annals of the American Pulpit (1857–1869)*, vol. 4 (1858). A somewhat larger study can be found in Earle W. Crawford, *An Endless Line of Splendor: Profiles of Six Pioneer Presbyterian Preacher-Educators* (1983).

HENRY WARNER BOWDEN

BLACKBURN, Joseph (fl. 1752–1778), portrait painter, was born probably in Great Britain. His parentage and details of his early life are unknown. The earliest record of Blackburn as a painter is his arrival in Bermuda in 1752. During his two-year stay there he painted at least twenty-five portraits for the Pigott, Jones, Harvey, Tucker, Gilbert, and Butterfield families. A number of these pictures remain on the island in the hands of descendants. In the best of these, such as *Mrs. Thomas Jones*, Blackburn exhibited a considerable skill at painting lace and ribbon and other details of dress. This ability has led some scholars to speculate that he was first trained as a drapery painter in a larger English studio.

Blackburn's whereabouts after leaving Bermuda for the American colonies on the mainland are well documented, as he signed and dated over half of the more than one hundred portraits by him that survive. He apparently arrived in Newport, Rhode Island, in 1754, then continued northward to Boston, where he spent the next few years. He brought with him to Boston at least one letter, which introduced "the bearor Mr. Blackburne to your favor & friendship, he is late from the Island of Bermuda a Limner by profession & is allow'd to excell in that science, has now spent some months in this place, & behav'd in all respects as becomes a Gentleman, being possess'd with the agreeable qualities of great modesty, good sence & genteel behaviour" (Stevens, p. 101).

Blackburn found little competition upon his arrival in Boston. John Smibert had died in 1751, Robert Feke had ceased painting there by 1752, and John Greenwood had gone to Surinam. Only three artists remained: Joseph Badger, an artist of only marginal skills, and two beginners, Nathaniel Smibert and John Singleton Copley. Blackburn quickly capitalized on this artistic vacuum and over the next five years painted several dozen portraits for many leading Boston families, such as the Olivers, Bowdoins, Pittses, and Winslows.

Blackburn's most ambitious painting, *Isaac Winslow and His Family* (1755), set a new standard for stylish group portraiture in colonial Boston. His style relied on the same light, pastel colors favored by Feke, but his poses are more fanciful and his modeling skills more adept. Bostonians embraced him enthusiastically, and around 1757 one patron wrote: "Tell Mr. Blackburn that Miss Lucy is in love with his pictures, wonders what business he has to make such extreme fine lace and satin, besides taking so exact a likeness" (Park, p. 273).

Although Blackburn produced a number of successful Boston portraits during the 1750s, among them *Andrew Oliver Jr.* (1755), *Susan Apthorp* (1757), and *Lieutenant General Jeffrey Amherst* (1758), Copley quickly assimilated the qualities of his more experienced competitor. By 1758 Copley had achieved technical parity with Blackburn. He also had begun to surpass Blackburn in his versatility, particularly his ability to capture a vigorous ruggedness, which Copley's increasingly numerous sitters welcomed. This probably contributed to Blackburn's decision to relocate to Portsmouth, New Hampshire, that year. There he had the opportunity to paint two formal and highly traditional full-length portraits of Governor Benning Wentworth and Lieutenant Governor John Wentworth (both 1760) to hang as a pair in the principal room of the Wentworth house. After five years in Portsmouth, during which time he made occasional trips to Exeter, New Hampshire, and Newburyport, Massachusetts, Blackburn went to England, perhaps because he was unable to sustain himself on the level of patronage he found in and around Portsmouth.

With his departure for England, Blackburn became an even more elusive artist, and knowledge of his career is limited to the handful of portraits from these last years (1763–1778). In 1767 he is known to have been in Dublin, where he signed and dated a *Portrait of a Young Girl Holding a Dublin Lottery Ticket*. He may be the same Mr. Blackburn who exhibited three history pictures at the Free Society of Artists (London) in 1769. His career continued at least until 1778, when documented examples of his work cease. Blackburn is among a handful of painters who achieved success in the American colonies before John Singleton Copley.

• The first important assessment of Blackburn is Lawrence Park, "Joseph Blackburn—Portrait Painter," *Proceedings of the American Antiquarian Society*, n.s., 32 (Oct. 1922): 270–329, which includes a checklist of his known work. This checklist was expanded and refined in John Hill Morgan and Henry Wilder Foote, "An Extension of Lawrence Park's Descriptive List of the Works of Joseph Blackburn," *Proceedings of the American Antiquarian Society*, n.s., 46 (Apr. 1936): 15–81. More recent articles focusing on his regional accomplishments in Newport, Portsmouth, and Boston are William B. Stevens, Jr., "Joseph Blackburn and His Newport Sitters, 1754–1756," *Newport History* 40 (Summer 1967): 95–107; Elizabeth Ackroyd, "Joseph Blackburn, Limner in Portsmouth," *Historical New Hampshire* 30 (Winter 1975): 231–43; and Andrew Oliver, "The Elusive Mr. Blackburn,"

Colonial Society of Massachusetts 59 (1982): 379–92. See also Richard H. Saunders and Ellen G. Miles, *American Colonial Portraits, 1700–1776* (1987).

RICHARD SAUNDERS

BLACKBURN, Joseph Clay Stiles (1 Oct. 1838–12 Sept. 1918), political leader, was born near Spring Station in Woodford County, Kentucky, the son of Edward Mitchell Blackburn, a farmer and thoroughbred breeder, and Lavina St. Clair Bell. Blackburn's brother Luke Blackburn would serve as governor of Kentucky from 1879 to 1883.

Blackburn graduated from Centre College in Danville in 1857. After studying privately, he was admitted to the bar in 1858. He then moved to Chicago, where he practiced law until 1860. Returning to Woodford County, Kentucky, he became active in politics as a speaker for John C. Breckinridge in the 1860 presidential campaign. After the Civil War began the next year, he joined the Confederate army and served as an officer in various capacities, including time as General William Preston's assistant adjutant general. He held an independent command in Mississippi from 1864 to the war's end. Following a three-year residence in Arkansas, where he practiced law and farmed, Blackburn returned to his native area in 1868. From that base, he started his long political career.

Blackburn served in the Kentucky House of Representatives as a Democrat from 1871 to 1875 then won election to Congress, where he represented the Central Bluegrass region in the U.S. House from 1875 to 1885. In 1884, in a hard-fought election for U.S. senator, Blackburn defeated his Democratic party rival John Stuart Williams, 73 to 67, on a joint legislative ballot. Reelection came easily in 1890.

In a decade in the U.S. House and a total of eighteen years in the U.S. Senate, Blackburn remained a devoted Democrat who forcefully supported the positions of his party and conservative white southerners. He spoke out and filibustered against the election commission's 1877 decision in the Hayes-Tilden election, (at one time crying out, "He who dallies is a dastard and he who doubts is damned") and traveled widely across the nation over the years as a sought-after party orator. A man who could be charming and witty, Blackburn also used his strong speaking skills and uncompromising words to attack Republicans without pause. He once quieted a loud, mostly Democratic crowd that was shouting down the opposition with these words: "My friends, listen to what he has to say, for God knows he has a hard enough task to try and defend the Republican Party, for the angels in Heaven weep and the devils in hell rejoice whenever a Republican gets up to speak."

Seeking reelection to the Senate in 1896, Blackburn could not unite his party behind his candidacy, partly because of his free silver views and support for William Jennings Bryan. Finally, after several months and 112 legislative ballots to break a deadlock, he lost in 1897 to William J. Deboe, who became the first Republican senator from Kentucky. Blackburn rebuilt his political base through an alliance with gubernatorial candidate William Goebel. He ran for the Senate in 1900 and won, 75–54, defeating former Republican governor William O. Bradley. The victor served as chairman of the Democratic caucus in the U.S. Senate from 1906 to 1907. Goebel's death and the factional opposition of his successor, John Crepps Wickliffe Beckham, doomed Blackburn's bid for reelection. In a three-way race for the Democratic caucus vote, "Old Jo" finished second to Thomas H. Paynter, the choice of the Beckham–Percy Haly faction, ending Blackburn's elective political career.

President Theodore Roosevelt (1858–1919) appointed Blackburn governor of the Panama Canal Zone, where he served from 1907 until December 1909. On his return to the United States, Blackburn was a member of the Lincoln Memorial Commission from 1914 until his death in Washington, D.C.

Blackburn married Therese Graham in 1858; they had four children. His first wife died in 1899, and he wed Mary E. Blackburn in 1901.

• Few printed sources exist on Blackburn, and manuscript materials are scarce. Standard national reference works and the following state sources provide the chief outline of his career: *Biographical Encyclopaedia of Kentucky* (1878); *Biographical Cyclopedia of the Commonwealth of Kentucky* (1896; repr. 1980); H. Levin, ed., *Lawyers and Lawmakers of Kentucky* (1897); E. Polk Johnson, *A History of Kentucky and Kentuckians*, vol. 2 (3 vols., 1912); and Hambleton Tapp and James C. Klotter, *Kentucky: Decades of Discord, 1865–1900* (1977). On his years in Congress, see the *Congressional Record*. A good newspaper summation of his life is the obituary in the Louisville *Courier-Journal*, 13 Sept. 1918.

JAMES C. KLOTTER

BLACKBURN, Luke Pryor (16 June 1816–14 Sept. 1887), physician and governor of Kentucky, was born in Woodford County, Kentucky, the son of Edward Blackburn and Lavina Bell, farmers. He graduated from Transylvania University's medical department in 1835, married Ella Gist Boswell of Lexington a few months later, and practiced medicine in Woodford and adjoining counties.

In 1846 Blackburn and his wife and son moved to Natchez, Mississippi. During the yellow fever epidemics of 1848 and 1854 Blackburn served as the city's health officer and established quarantines to prevent infected goods and passengers from entering the town. Believing his efforts were responsible for Natchez's relative freedom from the disease (the cause was unknown until 1900), he urged that similar measures be taken below New Orleans to prevent the malady's nearly annual introduction from the tropics. Unfortunately, quarantines hampered commerce, business interests controlled both states' legislatures, and Blackburn's advice was ignored.

Following his wife's death in 1856, Blackburn visited Europe to study hospital procedures and in Paris met Julia Churchill of Louisville. On their return to the United States in the fall of 1857 they married, resided briefly in Natchez, and then moved to New Orleans. Their only child died in infancy.

In the early months of the Civil War Blackburn served as a civilian agent for the Confederates, collecting arms and setting up hospitals. Shortly after the governor of Mississippi sent him to Canada in 1863 to collect supplies for blockade runners, Blackburn concocted a diabolical plan to create havoc in Union population centers by introducing yellow fever. Visiting Bermuda during the epidemic of 1864, he aided local physicians nursing the ill, and he gathered trunks full of bedding on which fever victims had died and sent them to metropolitan areas in the United States via Halifax. (Since the disease was mosquito-borne, no illnesses resulted, however.) The plot was revealed in April 1865 and the Bureau of Military Justice charged the doctor with conspiracy to commit murder and ordered his arrest. Living in Canada and beyond American jurisdiction, Blackburn was nevertheless detained by Montreal authorities and was tried but acquitted by a Toronto court for violating Canadian neutrality. The murder charge was neither dropped nor pursued.

Blackburn remained in Canada until 1867, operated a family farm near Helena, Arkansas, for five years, and in 1872 opened a medical practice in Louisville, Kentucky. During the 1873 yellow fever epidemic in Memphis and the 1877 outbreak in Florida, Blackburn earned accolades for aiding yellow fever victims. In March 1878 the doctor announced his candidacy for governor of Kentucky. Although his family was politically prominent, local politicians scoffed at his ambition. However, when he dropped his campaign in early September to help fever victims in the small Mississippi River town of Hickman, Kentucky, his philanthropic effort commanded the attention of the state's newspapers. Blackburn became the "Hero of Hickman," and many Kentuckians apparently believed that the executive office was a suitable reward. In the spring of 1879 he received the Democratic nomination. Throughout the summer campaign northern newspapers raised the issue of Blackburn's germ warfare activities, but the state's press chose to ignore the accusations. Blackburn easily won the general election over his Republican rival, Walter Evans of Hopkinsville, 125,790 to 81,882.

In his messages to the general assembly, Governor Blackburn urged the legislature to institute fiscal, judicial, and educational reforms. Acting on his suggestions, the legislators increased property taxes, revamped the district court system, established a superior court to relieve the overcrowded docket of the court of appeals by hearing cases involving less than $3,000, set salaries for judges and prosecuting attorneys whose remuneration previously had depended on the number of cases they tried and won, and created the University of Kentucky from the reorganized Agricultural and Mechanical College. At Blackburn's insistence the lawmakers also strengthened the state's newly formed Board of Health. Blackburn's appointee to that board, Joseph McCormack of Bowling Green, would serve for nearly forty years as its dynamic executive officer, drafting and enforcing legislation that advanced the course of public health.

Blackburn's major contribution resulted from his crusade to improve conditions at the overcrowded, unhealthy, and poorly administered eighty-year-old Kentucky Penitentiary. Using his executive pardoning power, Blackburn focused attention on the abominable prison by releasing the very young, the aged, the infirm, and those he believed were victims of injustice. Some Kentuckians speculated that "lenient Luke" might free everyone from "Kentucky's Black Hole of Calcutta." To prevent that, a few days before it adjourned the 1880 general assembly submitted to the governor two bills that incorporated most of his recommendations. One replaced the lessee (who leased the facility from the state and worked the inmates for profit) with a salaried administrator (warden) and called for a full-time physician, a part-time chaplain, and other employees paid by the state, and for the creation of a commission of prison directors to oversee the facility's administration. The other law established a committee to study the nation's prison system and make suggestions for a second (branch) penitentiary in Kentucky. The general assembly recommended that until the new facility was opened several hundred prisoners be leased to contractors to labor on public works. Because of the potential for abuse, Blackburn opposed this use of convicts, but he signed the bill to gain the other reforms. Consequently, he and other prison directors kept a close watch on the labor camps and reported substandard conditions under which the state's charges lived and worked. When the lawmakers refused to right these wrongs, Blackburn continued the liberal use of his pardoning power. Nevertheless, the legislature neither rescinded the law nor appropriated money for the Branch Penitentiary at Eddyville until the year after Blackburn left office.

Blackburn entered the executive office on a wave of gratitude, and as governor he achieved the first major reforms in more than twenty years. But he left the position in 1883 embittered by the derision heaped on him. Newspapers accused him of numerous irregularities, including selling pardons; politicos feared the expenditure of tax dollars on criminals harmed their careers; and taxpayers resented the threat created by pardoned convicts returning to their communities.

In the autumn of 1883 Blackburn resumed his medical practice until poor health curtailed his activities. He died in Frankfort. In 1971 the commonwealth named its newest minimum security facility for Blackburn, Kentucky's "father" of prison reforms.

• Blackburn's private papers apparently have not survived, but his governor's papers are housed in the Kentucky Department of Library and Archives (Frankfort). Era newspapers, the *Journals* of the Kentucky house and senate, and biennial reports of state officials and institutions, including Reports of the Prison Trustees, reveal much about Blackburn and his administration. For published biographical materials on Blackburn, see Nancy Disher Baird, *Luke Pryor Blackburn: Physician, Governor, Reformer* (1979); Baird, "Luke Pryor Blackburn's Campaign for Governor," *Register of the*

Kentucky Historical Society 74 (Oct. 1976): 300–313; and Baird, "The Yellow Fever Plot," *Civil War Times, Illustrated* 13 (Nov. 1974): 16–23.

NANCY DISHER BAIRD

BLACKBURN, Paul (24 Nov. 1926–13 Sept. 1971), poet and translator, was born in Saint Albans, Vermont, the son of William Blackburn and Frances Frost, a poet and novelist. Blackburn's parents separated in 1930. His father left for California; his mother pursued a literary career, eventually settling in New York City's Greenwich Village. Blackburn was left in the care of his strict maternal grandparents. His grandmother required little pretext for whipping him regularly, and his grandfather, who worked for the railroad, was away from home for long stretches at a time. In late poems such as "My Sainted," he reveals his bitterness about his early childhood.

However, Blackburn is primarily a poet of New York City life, and his contact with the New York literary scene came early. At age fourteen he joined his mother in Greenwich Village, where she lived with her lover, Paul's "Aunt" Carr. The bohemian environment was much more conducive to his creativity than life with his grandparents had been. His mother encouraged his interest in poetry, and Blackburn later acknowledged that her gift of W. H. Auden's *Collected Poems* was particularly helpful in giving him "a formal sense of musical structure." Blackburn entered New York University in 1945, but he left to join the army the following year.

In 1947 Blackburn reentered NYU, where he studied poetry under M. L. Rosenthal, who later became one of his most enthusiastic admirers. He served briefly as the editor of the *Apprentice*, the school literary magazine. It was here that Blackburn began reading Ezra Pound, who proved to be an enormous influence on him. In 1949 he transferred to the University of Wisconsin, where he graduated with a B.A. in 1950.

While studying at Wisconsin, Blackburn occasionally hitchhiked to Washington, D.C., to see Pound at St. Elizabeths Hospital. Pound helped Blackburn secure his first major publication, "The Innocents Who Fall Like Apples," in James Laughlin's *New Directions Annual* (1951). On Pound's advice Blackburn began corresponding with Robert Creeley, which developed into an important friendship. Blackburn's first book of translations, *Proensa* (1953), and his first book of original poems, *The Dissolving Fabric* (1955), were published by Creeley's Divers Press.

In his preface to Blackburn's *Against the Silences* (1980), Creeley acknowledges that Blackburn was "a far more accomplished craftsman." Of their first meeting Creeley writes, "I remember him showing me his edition of Yeats's *Collected Poems* with his extraordinary marginal notes, tracking rhythms, patterns of sounds, in short the whole tonal construct of the writing." Throughout his career other poets praised Blackburn highly for his understanding of the craft. In *Big Table* (Spring 1960), Paul Carroll wrote, "I don't suppose any poet our age handles a single line, a stanza, a whole poem with his skill and grace."

Friendship with Creeley led to contact with poets Charles Olson, Jonathan Williams, and Denise Levertov. Blackburn shared with them the ideas about poetry most notably articulated by Olson in his 1950 essay "Projective Verse." Their goal was a new musicality for modern poetry, which they believed suffered from the ascendancy of the metrical foot over the syllable and the breath. They felt a poet could correct this unhealthy emphasis by using the standardized spacing of the typewriter. A poem could be scored like a piece of music to preserve the poet's unique breath. Blackburn was adept at this technique, adjusting line breaks, margins, and spacing to reflect his desired reading pace and breathing patterns. Olson's gathering of Creeley, Williams, and others at Black Mountain College in North Carolina resulted in this approach becoming known as Black Mountain poetry. Blackburn, who remained in New York, always resisted the label "Black Mountain poet." He did, however, work briefly in the early 1950s as the New York distributor of Creeley's magazine *Black Mountain Review*. To support himself during the 1950s and 1960s he also worked a variety of jobs, including editing encyclopedias and writing book reviews.

Despite his inclusion in Donald Allen's influential anthology *The New American Poetry* (1960), for years Blackburn remained a little-known figure who continued to publish through small presses. His second book of original poetry, *Brooklyn-Manhattan Transit* (1960), contains some of his most memorable poems, including "Clickety-Clack" and "The Once-Over." Here, as in many of his poems, Blackburn plays the semidetached observer: "Clickety-Clack," for example, wryly describes an outrageous pass he makes at a woman on the subway. *The Nets* (1961) and two limited-edition books followed. Not until *The Cities* (1967), his first book issued by a major publisher, did Blackburn gain widespread attention. The only other full-length book of his poems to appear during his lifetime was *In, on, or about the Premises* (1968).

Chief among Blackburn's longer works are *The Selection of Heaven* (1980) and *The Journals* (1975). *The Selection of Heaven*, a mysterious poem commemorating both the death of his paternal grandparents and the breakup of his second marriage, was completed by 1967. *The Journals*, a record of the last four years of his life, including his stoic response to the cancer diagnosed in late 1970, has been faulted for its documentary quality. However, in a review for *Parnassus* (Spring–Summer 1976), poet Gilbert Sorrentino argues that *The Journals* represents a pinnacle, not a relaxation, of Blackburn's art: "That the poems seem, often, the thought of a moment, a brilliant or witty or dark response to still-smoking news, is the result of his carefully invented and released voice, a voice that we hear singing, virtuoso."

Blackburn published poems in little magazines constantly throughout his career. A prolific poet, at his death Blackburn had published or arranged for the publication of the 523 poems found in his *Collected Poems*, and he had written approximately 600 more. Of his eighteen books of original poetry, five were published posthumously.

In addition to writing poetry, Blackburn spent considerable time translating. Frustrated by his inability to read Provençal passages in Pound's epic poem the *Cantos*, Blackburn began to study that language. This led to his translations of the troubadours, collected in *Proensa* (1953; expanded ed. 1978). In 1954 his study of Provençal resulted in a Fulbright fellowship to the University of Toulouse, a city he satirizes in his poem "Sirventes." In 1956 Blackburn moved to Spain, where he bought a copy of poet Federico García Lorca's *Obras Completas*. His translations from it were collected posthumously as *Lorca/Blackburn* (1979). His translations also include *Poem of the Cid* (1966), Julio Cortázar's *Blow-Up and Other Stories* (1968), Cortázar's *Cronopios and Famas* (1969), and Pablo Picasso's *Hunk of Skin* (1968).

Blackburn's translations of the troubadours are provocative and have elicited both high praise and sharp criticism. Much of the debate has centered around their vernacular, occasionally vulgar, language. In an interview with the *New York Quarterly* (repr. in *The Journals*), Blackburn said that a translator must "be willing (& able) to let another man's life enter his own deeply enough to become some permanent part of his original author." Blackburn believed that the translator should strive for clarity above all else and should not fret over his inability to render into English the ambiguities present in the original text: "Let him approach polysemia crosseyed, coin in hand." Blackburn advised the translator to avoid the stiffness and artificiality that often accompany strict translation: "Occasionally, an adaptation will translate the spirit of the original to better use than any other method . . . Much depends upon the translator (also upon the reader)."

Blackburn was enormously generous to others and did much to create a mutually supportive community of poets in New York City. Newcomers found him ready to help them publish, give readings, find jobs, and locate places to stay. He moved the readings at Le Metro Café to St. Mark's Church-in-the-Bowery, where in 1966 he helped establish the Poetry Project (which in 1991 celebrated its twenty-fifth anniversary with the publication of the anthology *Out of this World*). From 1964 to 1965 Blackburn ran a radio show dedicated to poetry. His interest in the individual poet's unique breath led Blackburn to tape the many readings he attended and to popularize poetry recordings. In 1967 he won a Guggenheim fellowship, and he taught at the State University of New York at Cortland from the fall of 1970 until his death.

Despite the increasing readership Blackburn enjoyed at the end of his life, as well as the steady flow of posthumous publications, his poetry has yet to receive the attention his advocates believe it deserves. Aspects of his work that may contribute to this inattention include his frequent obscenity and his treatment of women, which to the feminist reader may seem un-pleasant or even cruel. Renewed interest in formalist poetry after his death was probably also detrimental. Perhaps Blackburn's most significant legacy is his sizable contribution to the popularization of poets and of the art of poetry.

Paul Blackburn was married three times: to Winifred Grey from 1954 to 1963 (they had been separated since 1958); to Sara Golden from 1963 to 1967; and to Joan Miller, with whom he had his only child, from 1968 until his death. He died of cancer of the esophagus in Cortland, New York.

• Blackburn's papers and recordings are in the Paul Blackburn Archive of the Archive for New Poetry at the University of California, San Diego. Kathleen Woodward, *Paul Blackburn: A Checklist* (1980), is the best single bibliography of Blackburn's writings. *The Collected Poems of Paul Blackburn*, ed. Edith Jarolim (1985), is the definitive collection of Blackburn's poetry. Selected volumes include *The Selected Poems of Paul Blackburn*, ed. Jarolim (1989), and Clayton Eshleman, *The Parallel Voyages* (1987), which offers forty-eight previously unpublished poems that span Blackburn's career. Jarolim's introduction to the *Collected Poems* and her entry on Blackburn in the *Dictionary of Literary Biography* together provide a reasonably detailed biographical treatment. Notable assessments of Blackburn's career include M. L. Rosenthal, "Paul Blackburn, Poet," *New York Times Book Review*, 11 Aug. 1974, and Marjorie Perloff's review of *Collected Poems*, repr. in her book *Poetic License* (1990). An obituary is in the *New York Times*, 15 Sept. 1971.

ROBERT M. WEST

BLACK ELK (Dec. 1863–19 Aug. 1950), Lakota holy man, was born on the Little Powder River (probably within the present-day borders of Wyoming), the son of Black Elk, a Lakota medicine man, and Mary Leggins Down (also called White Cow Sees). Black Elk, an Oglala Lakota, was raised in Big Road's Band, which lived and hunted in the territory west of the Black Hills through which white settlers blazed the Bozeman Trail in 1864. When he was only nine, Black Elk experienced a vision that would eventually give him distinction among his people: he was visited by Thunder-beings, which embodied the powers of the West and heralded his gift to cure and help his people in war. In 1877, after losing the cultural clash west of the Black Hills, the Oglala bands relocated to the Great Sioux Reservation in present-day South Dakota, and Black Elk's people fled to Canada after Crazy Horse was killed at Fort Robinson. Not until he was seventeen did Black Elk share his vision with an old and experienced medicine man, Black Road, and found the help he needed to cope with his great vision. The village medicine men were all astonished by the greatness of Black Elk's vision and advised him to sponsor a horse dance in which he could demonstrate the first part of his vision to his people. In the spring of 1881 Black Elk performed the horse dance at Fort Keogh, Montana, and thus began his life as a medicine man. In 1882 he and his family settled with the Oglalas at the Pine Ridge Agency. Here in South Dakota, Black Elk began the fasting and purification that preceded his cry for a vision. After asking for understanding to control his vision's power and thus help his people, Black Elk became a respected medicine man.

Reservation life rapidly changed traditional cultural patterns among the Lakota, and Black Elk chose to adapt and help his people do the same by learning about Euro-American ways. In 1886 he joined Buffalo Bill's Wild West Show to earn money and familiarize himself with the dominant American culture. Between 1886 and 1889 Black Elk traveled to New York, England, Germany, France, and Italy. Upon his return to South Dakota, Black Elk prepared to settle down, taking a job as a store clerk. The Ghost Dance, however, swept through his world and renewed his commitment to the great vision and the revitalization of his people. This hopeful religious movement ended tragically in the massacre at Wounded Knee in 1890, leaving Black Elk scarred but not broken. After the massacre, he settled in the Wounded Knee district of the Pine Ridge Reservation and married Katie War Bonnet in 1892. Black Elk remained a traditional healer but also showed an interest in the Roman Catholicism and the reservation mission established by the Jesuits during his trip to Europe. Black Elk and Katie, who died in 1903, had three children, and the last, Benjamin, survived and remained close to his father to his final days. Black Elk gave up his resistance to the Catholic church in 1904. While the holy man was treating a dying boy, Father Joseph Lindebner arrived to administer last rites. He threw Black Elk and his healing instruments out of the tent, commanding Satan to leave. A dejected Black Elk returned to the mission with Lindebner to begin two weeks of instruction before his baptism on 6 December 1904, when he became Nicholas Black Elk.

Nicholas Black Elk was a sincere and committed member of the Catholic church at Pine Ridge. He joined the St. Joseph Society in Manderson and helped the priests whenever he could. For his hard work and enthusiasm, the Jesuits appointed him a catechist and hoped he would help them speed conversions among his people. As a catechist, Black Elk substituted for unavailable priests, holding Sunday services, leading prayers and hymns, reading from the Scripture, and instructing his people—all in Lakota. In 1906 Black Elk married his second wife, Anna Brings White (also known as Brings White Horses). Although both had children from previous marriages, the couple had a daughter and two sons. In 1908 the Jesuits sent Black Elk and Joseph Redwillow on their first missionary trip to the Arapaho Wind River Reservation in Wyoming. They also made their way on a similar mission among the Nebraska Winnebago. In 1926, as a reward for their hard work and devotion, the Jesuits built a catechists' house near the church.

In 1930 John G. Neihardt, the poet laureate of Nebraska, appeared at Black Elk's home in Manderson and changed forever Black Elk's place in history. Neihardt began a friendship with Black Elk that eventually revealed the complexity of the latter's religious beliefs. Neihardt was visiting the Sioux in order to write the final volume of his epic poem *A Cycle of the West.*

He hoped the Sioux would share their story of the Ghost Dance and Wounded Knee. Black Elk responded to Neihardt with deep emotion, sensing a kindred spirit, and so agreed to teach the poet what he could. In May 1931 Neihardt returned with his daughters and began the slow process of interviewing, interpreting, note taking, and writing. During this month Black Elk, as the sixth grandfather (the spiritual representative of the earth and mankind), named Neihardt Flaming Rainbow and charged him with the responsibility of carrying his vision and Lakota culture to a larger audience. The details of the vision itself were recounted for the first time since Black Elk had shared it with the medicine men of his youth. Finally, when they finished, Black Elk with his son and interpreter, Ben, joined the Neihardts on a journey to Harney Peak in the Black Hills, where the old holy man prayed to the six grandfathers that the tree of his vision would finally bloom, that his people would flourish again. On 30 May the group climbed the peak, and Black Elk told his son if he had any of his old power, they would soon have thunder and rain. On that bright and clear day, clouds and rain did come during the old man's prayer. Neihardt's publication of *Black Elk Speaks* in 1932 represented the literary culmination of this extraordinary spiritual kinship between Black Elk and John G. Neihardt. Neihardt offered his readers a chance to understand the spiritual decline of the Lakota through the eyes of their holy man Black Elk. Because Neihardt's work ended with the Wounded Knee massacre in 1890, Black Elk's conversion to Catholicism and his remarkable adaptation to reservation life were noticeably absent. Despite an angry response to the book from the Jesuits, Black Elk continued to mesh his traditional Lakota culture with his Catholic faith, and he remained dedicated to teaching. He participated in Alex Duhamel's Sioux Indian Pageant every summer from 1935 until his death. As the pageant's main attraction, Black Elk demonstrated the role of the medicine man in traditional Lakota rituals. In 1941 Black Elk was hospitalized for nagging tuberculosis, but in 1944 he met again with Neihardt. This time the poet hoped to learn more about the general history of the Lakota people, interviewing Black Elk along with others. This material, *When the Tree Flowered*, was published in 1951. Black Elk died at Manderson, South Dakota, before he could see this second book.

Black Elk's place in history is complicated because so much of his biography is derived from John Neihardt's self-defined interpretive account of the holy man's life. Through Neihardt, Black Elk has come to represent for many "the vanishing American" and "the noble savage." Black Elk, however, was more complex, adapting to change and integrating old and new cultural forms to create a vibrant, living whole. The Lakota holy man remains a testament both to what America lost at Wounded Knee in 1890 and to the strength and flexibility of native cultures.

• While few papers written by Black Elk exist, some may be found in the collections of the Records of the Bureau of Catholic Indian Missions, Holy Rosary Mission Records at Marquette University in Milwaukee, and in the Western History Manuscripts Collections, John G. Neihardt Collection at the University of Missouri, Columbia. Black Elk's letters home from Europe were published in the Sioux language in the Santee, Nebr., monthly newspaper *Iapi Oaye* (the Word Carrier). The most straightforward sketch of Black Elk appears in Raymond J. DeMallie's edited collection of the notes taken during the interviews between Black Elk and John G. Neihardt, *The Sixth Grandfather: Black Elk's Teachings Given to John G. Neihardt* (1984). John G. Neihardt shaped these interviews into two books, *Black Elk Speaks: Being the Life Story of a Holy Man of the Oglala Sioux* (1932) and *When the Tree Flowered: An Authentic Tale of the Old Sioux World* (1951). Both books have fostered a significant debate about the relationship between the holy man and his interviewer and about methods for cross-cultural understanding. Joseph Eppes Brown, ed. and recorder, *The Sacred Pipe: Black Elk's Account of the Seven Rites of the Oglala Sioux* (1953), is also a significant rendering of Lakota teachings. More recently, Michael F. Steltenkamp published his interviews with Black Elk's daughter, Lucy, in *Black Elk: Holy Man of the Oglala* (1993), and Hilda Neihardt published her recollections of Black Elk and her father in *Black Elk and Flaming Rainbow* (1995).

A. KRISTEN FOSTER

BLACKFISH (1729?–1779), Shawnee war chief of the Chillicothe division, had the tribal name of Cot-ta-wa-ma-go or Mkah-day-way-may-qua. Because of his connections with Daniel Boone and Simon Kenton, Blackfish became one of the most legendary figures in the early history of Kentucky, but very little is known about him, and he appears in documents for only the last three years of his life. Blackfish appears in several stories and has been confused with later Shawnees of the same name.

During the Revolution most of the Shawnees decided to ally themselves with the British and to try to dislodge the infant American settlements in Kentucky. Despite the treaty of Fort Stanwix (1768), by which the Iroquois illegitimately ceded Indian claims to land south of the Ohio River, and the defeat of the Shawnees in Dunmore's war of 1774, Blackfish's people refused to acknowledge the loss of Kentucky, which they used for hunting. In 1777 a renewal of hostilities with the Americans seemed imminent, and most of the Shawnees abandoned their villages on the Scioto River (Ohio) and moved westward, settling on the Little and the Great Miami. The Chillicothe established a town on the Little Miami near present-day Xenia, Ohio. Blackfish was the leading war chief of the band. Then about fifty years of age, he was rated as a good orator as well as a successful warrior.

Encouraged by British officials in Detroit, Blackfish soon launched attacks across the Ohio, attempting to drive the Americans from their forts, Harrodsburg, Boonesborough, and St. Asaph's. Between March and September 1777 Blackfish's warriors harassed all three settlements, trying to lure the Kentuckians from behind their stockades, falling upon any they found outside, burning outbuildings, and killing livestock. Without artillery and sufficient manpower, Blackfish made little impression upon the settlements, and his prospects diminished with the arrival of reinforcements that gave the Kentuckians some 300 men. The Indians were able to create hardship, however, by disrupting the economic life of the colonists.

Blackfish surprised the Kentuckians in 1778 by leading a large war party against Boonesborough as early as February. Accompanied by two French Canadians, Charles Beaubien and Louis Lorimier, the Indians captured Daniel Boone and twenty-seven men who had been collecting salt on the Licking River. Foolishly the Indians then abandoned their attack upon the weakened Boonesborough and returned to the Shawnee towns. Blackfish was so pleased with his principal prisoner, Boone, that he took him to the British at Detroit in March but refused to allow them to ransom him. The story that Blackfish adopted Boone was spread by Boone's son, Nathan, and others but may be incorrect. Boone himself recalled that he "was adopted, according to their custom, into a family where I became a son, and had a great share in the affection of my new parents, brothers, sisters and friends." He also remarked that "the Shawanese King [presumably meaning Blackfish] took great notice of me and treated me with profound respect and entire friendship, often entrusting me to hunt at my liberty." This would suggest that Blackfish, in accordance with the best Shawnee custom, assigned Boone to a family who needed a son to provide for them but that he did not adopt the pioneer himself. In Shawnee society, chiefs often disposed the profits of hunting and war, including prisoners, to extend their influence or to express their responsibility for the community. If that is so, Nathan Boone's assumption that his father's young Indian "sisters" (Pom-me-pe-sy and Pim-me-pe-sy) were Blackfish's daughters may also be erroneous. The statement attributed to Benjamin Kelly, one of those captured with Boone, that Blackfish's adopted children included the famous Tecumseh and Tenskwatawa cannot be substantiated.

Boone's escape in June 1778, with his information about Shawnee preparations for another attack upon Boonesborough, postponed Blackfish's next campaign, but on 7 September he appeared before the fort with about 350 Indians and a handful of whites, including Fontenay DeQuindre, who had brought ammunition from the British. For two days Blackfish engaged Boone and others in negotiations outside the fort, hoping to persuade them to surrender, but after an unsuccessful attempt to seize the American negotiators the Indians attacked Boonesborough for nine days. The Indians tried to burn the settlement and even to tunnel into it but eventually withdrew, having achieved little. Shortly afterward Shawnees captured the noted pioneer Simon Kenton, who was attempting to take Indian horses north of the Ohio, and he was interrogated by Blackfish.

In 1779 the Kentuckians counterattacked. About 300 men under Colonel John Bowman attacked Blackfish's town, Chillicothe, in the night of 29–30 May. Many of the Shawnees were absent at a Mingo town, and others disgracefully fled, but while the women and children secured themselves in the village council-house, Blackfish led a party of warriors against the attackers. In a brief exchange of fire the chief was severely wounded, the ball entering his right knee and cutting upward into his thigh. Blackfish and his men fell back and forted up in the Indian cabins, the chief occupying one with three or four others. Throughout the night Bowman's men burned and looted but were unable to drive out the Shawnee. The next day they retreated with losses of ten killed. Blackfish had them shadowed to the Ohio and restored his town, the cornfields of which, although burned, had time to sprout anew and provide a harvest. The Indians admitted a loss of seven men killed or fatally wounded during the defense. One of them was Blackfish himself. It was reported that the chief planned to release and pay a prisoner, Chaplin, to bring medicine from the white settlements. According to one account he died after six weeks; by another account, he survived until the ensuing autumn.

Blackfish represented the more militant faction of the Shawnee, embittered by the white settlement of Kentucky and determined to use British aid to clear it. With the exception of his capture of Boone's party at the salt licks, he had little success, but he was respected by his enemies. He kept his promise to Boone that none of the prisoners taken on that occasion would be killed, and he made a gallant defense of Chillicothe. Blackfish's raids illustrated the difficulties Indians experienced in attacking fortified positions.

• Reminiscences relevant to Blackfish include the account of Daniel Boone in Willard Rouse Jillson, ed., *Filson's Kentucke* (1929), and three accounts in the Draper Manuscripts, State Historical Society of Wisconsin, Madison: Simon Kenton interviewed by John H. James (1832), series BB, vol. 5, pp. 106–25; the narrative of Joseph Jackson (1844), ser. C, vol. 11, p. 62 following; and Nathan Boone's interview (1851), ser. S, vol. 6, pp. 18–294. The fullest secondary account is John Bakeless, *Daniel Boone: Master of the Wilderness* (1939), although the details are sometimes unreliable. See also George W. Ranck, *Boonesborough* (1901), and John Mack Faragher, *Daniel Boone: The Life and Legend of an American Pioneer* (1992).

JOHN SUGDEN

BLACKFORD, Charles Minor (17 Oct. 1833–10 Mar. 1903), lawyer and author, was born in Fredericksburg, Virginia, the son of William Matthews Blackford, an editor, and Mary Berkeley Minor. He shaped his life by both emulating and rejecting his parents' lives and wishes. Although trained in law, Blackford's father pursued a career in politics and in 1846 moved the family to Lynchburg to take a job as a newspaper editor. Thus his father subjected the family to a precarious living based on party patronage but encouraged his five sons' interest in political and literary lives. His mother held strong antislavery beliefs and pressured her sons to seek their fortunes away from the taint of

the South. Charles was educated at home and at boarding schools; he completed his education at the University of Virginia, earning an L.L.B. in 1855.

In that year Blackford returned to Lynchburg, began the practice of law, and in 1856 married Susan Leigh Colston. They had two children. By this time, Blackford had lost much of his antislavery zeal, and during the crises of the 1850s—though never a fire-eater—he became militantly Virginian. He boasted of being proud that he had never gone above the Mason-Dixon line. After the raid at Harpers Ferry led by John Brown (1800–1859), he joined a volunteer company, which after the firing on Fort Sumter became incorporated into the Army of Virginia as the Second Virginia Cavalry. He rose to the rank of captain, serving mostly in the cavalry. In 1863 he was made judge advocate on General James Longstreet's staff.

At the conclusion of the war Blackford returned to Lynchburg where he resumed his legal practice. He also became a banker, eventually serving as president of the People's National Bank in Lynchburg. Blackford's postwar legal practice—first in partnership with Thomas J. Kirkpatrick and then as senior partner of Blackford, Horsely & Blackford—was dominated by corporate law. He became counsel to the three railroads that ran through Lynchburg and served as director of Old Virginia Midland Railway Company. As railroad counsel he often appeared in court defending railways against tort claims. His actions as a lawyer helped to establish the broad contours of negligence law in Virginia. Given his skills, the nature of his practice, and his second profession, Blackford was financially secure after the war.

In the last decade of Blackford's life, his affluence and his refusal to enter statewide politics (though he served as city councilman, member of the school board, and city solicitor in Lynchburg) gave him leisure time. Much of that time was consumed by his efforts to form and run the Virginia State Bar Association, of which he was president in 1894–1895. Blackford used the bar association as the means to pursue literary interests. His presidential address to the meeting in 1895 urged lawyers to escape the confines of their profession by reading more literature, cultivating their poetic impulses, and writing for posterity. Blackford also urged his colleagues to preserve, through literary efforts, the heroic history of Virginia, especially the incidents of the war.

In addition to preaching his doctrine of preserving history, Blackford practiced it through speeches and writings. His article, "The Trials and Trial of Jefferson Davis," originally delivered as a paper to the bar association in 1900 and then printed as a pamphlet, embodied the character of his writings. It showed his forensic skills in piecing together a tale from diverse sources and revealed his passion for the Lost Cause. The epitome of his literary effort was his *Memoirs of Life In and Out of the Army in Virginia* (1894–1896). This collection of family correspondence, diaries, and notes was compiled and edited by his wife Susan. That he urged her to undertake the task and aided her in preparing the work reveals their closeness, as nothing was more important to Blackford than preserving the heroic past. The thirty-five copies, privately printed, circulated among friends and family. Its heroic themes, high literary style, and idealization of Virginia are balanced by the mundane daily record of the war years. It is Blackford's chief contribution to American history.

• The Blackford family papers, including letters to and from Charles Minor, are collected in Alderman Library, University of Virginia, and in the Southern Historical Collection, University of North Carolina at Chapel Hill. The original two-volume compilation by Charles Minor Blackford and Susan Leigh Blackford, *Memoirs of Life In and Out of the Army in Virginia during the War between the States* (1894–1896), was reprinted on microcard in 1968. Selections from this work are in *Letters from Lee's Army*, ed. Charles Minor Blackford III (1947). Blackford's family is treated in L. Minor Blackford, *Mine Eyes Have Seen the Glory* (1954). John H. Lewis's "Memorial" in *Report of the Fifteenth Annual Meeting of the Virginia State Bar Association* (1903) summarizes Blackford's legal career.

RICHARD F. HAMM

BLACK HAWK (1767–3 Oct. 1838), Sauk war leader, was born at the village of Saukenuk, the present site of Rock Island, Illinois. He grew up hating the American invaders of his homeland, and during the War of 1812 he fought among Tecumseh's warriors on the British side. However, Black Hawk's fame rests primarily on the war bearing his name that was carried out during the spring and summer of 1832 in northwestern Illinois and southwestern Wisconsin. It ended in a bloody encounter near the confluence of the Bad Axe and Mississippi rivers north of Prairie du Chien, Wisconsin. The war had its genesis in a treaty signed by a delegation of Sauk and Fox Indians in 1804 at St. Louis. The signers thought the treaty was to establish peace after some settlers had been killed, but it really called for the tribes to cede a vast tract extending from southern Wisconsin through western Illinois and a strip along the Mississippi River in Missouri. The treaty allowed the Indians to occupy the land until it was opened for sale to whites, so the Indians did not realize they had signed away territory until settlers began buying up the land in the 1820s.

The allied Sauk and Fox had long supported the British, but after the War of 1812 they pledged their allegiance to the United States, which recognized Keokuk, a Sauk, as their primary chief. Keokuk did not think the tribes could prevail against the power of the United States and agreed that his people should remain west of the Mississippi in what is now Iowa.

Black Hawk refused to recognize the legality of the land cession, particularly in regard to the Saukenuk area. He continued to return there from Iowa with his band after the spring hunts, although settlers began moving in by 1829 and destroyed Indian gardens and homes. In 1831 Black Hawk agreed to remain in Iowa on the government's promise of corn to see his band through the winter. When supplies did not arrive, he considered the agreement invalid.

Although Black Hawk was not a hereditary chief, he enjoyed respect as a war leader. He was supported in his attachment to Saukenuk by Neapope, who was a recognized chief but, being younger than Black Hawk, deferred to Black Hawk's leadership. Another ally was White Cloud, known as the "Winnebago Prophet," whose village was upstream on the Rock River at present-day Prophetstown, Illinois. White Cloud assured Black Hawk that the Winnebago and Potawatomi would support him. White Cloud's prophesies and Neapope's wishful thinking convinced Black Hawk that the British would again fight the Americans and help him regain his homeland.

In early April 1832 Black Hawk led a band estimated at well over 1,000 people (including some dissident Fox and Kickapoo) across the Mississippi toward Saukenuk. Although there were 400 to 500 armed warriors in the group, the presence of many women and children signaled the peaceful intent to restore their dwellings and plant gardens. Learning that U.S. troops were ready to oppose him, Black Hawk bypassed Saukenuk and moved upstream along the Rock. He soon realized that he had been misled about expecting help from the British or even from the Potawatomi and Winnebago. Individuals in both tribes sided with Black Hawk, but the majority saw their best interests served by neutrality or alliance with the Americans.

Learning of an encampment of soldiers nearby as he moved beyond the Prophet's village, Black Hawk sent a delegation of three men under a white flag on 14 May to negotiate the safe return of his people to Iowa. Bellicose volunteers under Major Isaiah Stillman fired on the delegation, killing one man, and set off in pursuit of the Sauk. Black Hawk quickly set up an ambush and routed the whites. This unexpected victory for the greatly outnumbered Sauk warriors inspired independent attacks by parties of Winnebago and Potawatomi on isolated settlers, resulting in a massing of regular army and militia units. Black Hawk was now committed to a war he could neither avoid nor win. He led his people on a retreat up the Rock River and doubled back toward the northwest in Wisconsin to reach the Mississippi.

He again tried to surrender at Wisconsin Heights on the Wisconsin River near present-day Sauk City, but the American soldiers could not understand the terms shouted to them and opened fire. Holding the whites at bay, the Sauk escaped across the river when night fell. Part of the band tried to reach the Mississippi, going downstream on the Wisconsin River, but they were intercepted and most were killed.

Meanwhile, Black Hawk led the rest of the band over the extremely rugged terrain of southwestern Wisconsin, leaving a trail of abandoned belongings and exhausted dead. On 1 August they reached the Mississippi, where the steamboat *Warrior* was moving downstream. Black Hawk raised a white flag and by nightfall counseled a retreat north to find safety among the Chippewa, but only twenty to thirty people joined him. As the rest attempted to swim the Mississippi early on 2 August, troops under General Henry Atkinson caught up to them and began firing at them in the water. The *Warrior* also returned and added its firepower to the carnage. Those who managed the crossing were killed or captured within a week by some Sioux, traditional enemies of the Sauk.

Meanwhile, Black Hawk and his followers reached a small lake near the present city of Tomah, Wisconsin. They were spotted by a party of Winnebago hunters who returned to their village near La Crosse, Wisconsin, and reported their discovery to their chief, who coincidentally was also called Black Hawk. (Because of an interpreter's error, it was long believed that the Winnebago found Black Hawk at the dells of the Wisconsin River.) The Sauk accepted his offer of safe conduct to Prairie du Chien, where Black Hawk surrendered to the Indian agent, Joseph M. Street, on 27 August. Black Hawk, the Prophet, and his remaining warriors were imprisoned at Jefferson Barracks (St. Louis) until April 1833, when they were sent to Washington, D.C. They met President Andrew Jackson and were taken on a tour of eastern cities, where they attracted huge and generally sympathetic crowds. When Black Hawk returned to Iowa he asked the government interpreter, Antoine Le Claire, to write his story as he told it to present his side of the provocations and misunderstanding that had caused the hostilities of the previous summer. Black Hawk remained on the reservation until his death, always bitter toward Keokuk.

• Antoine Le Claire turned for help on the translation of Black Hawk's autobiography to John B. Patterson, a young newspaperman, who added literary flourishes typical of the period and published the account in 1833. Its authenticity was a matter of debate until the 1955 publication of *Black Hawk*, edited by Donald Jackson. Jackson published the complete 1833 text accompanied by meticulous research to establish that, despite problems inherent in any translation and Patterson's journalistic tinkering, the basic account had to have come from Black Hawk. Ellen M. Whitney, ed., *The Black Hawk War, 1831–32* (1970–1978), presents a compilation of all original and primary documents relating to the war, including testimony of Indian and non-Indian participants. A recently discovered manuscript written about 1920 by John Blackhawk, a great-grandson of the Winnebago chief named Black Hawk, proved that the Winnebago found the Sauk Black Hawk's camp near Tomah, not the Wisconsin dells. The manuscript and verifying research were published by Nancy Oestreich Lurie, "In Search of Chaetar: New Findings on Black Hawk's Surrender," *Wisconsin Magazine of History* 71, no. 3 (1988): 163–83.

NANCY OESTREICH LURIE

BLACK HOOF (fl. 1795–1831), head civil chief of the Ohio Shawnees and member of the Mekoche division of that tribe, had the Indian name Catecahassa or Cutthewekasaw. He died at an advanced age—estimates range up to an improbable 115 years—and references to his origins are contradictory. Indian agent John Johnston, who knew him well, said the chief remembered bathing in the sea off Florida as a boy, but he is represented to have told another acquaintance that he was born on the Monongahela River. Black Hoof told more than one person that he was present at Braddock's defeat in 1755, although no Shawnees are known to have participated in that action. He was probably at the battle of Point Pleasant (1774), as he said, and one witness recalled that Black Hoof helped Blackfish repulse John Bowman's attack on Chillicothe in Ohio in 1779. A reference to "Wapecashe—the White Hoof" by George Morgan in 1776 may be the first document to mention him. However, he does not figure clearly in records until 1795, when he complained to the British about the chiefly pretensions of a rival, Blue Jacket, and he signed the treaty of Greenville on 3 August 1795, agreeing to the cession of most of Ohio to the United States. In 1796 most of the Ohio Shawnees settled at Wapakoneta on the Auglaize River, Ohio, on the Indian side of the boundary, and there Black Hoof spent the rest of his life as their principal chief.

A small man, intelligent and compassionate, Black Hoof enjoyed the reputation of having been a brave warrior, but it was as a civil leader that he earned the respect of Indians and whites alike. He was an eloquent and entertaining speaker and could be devastatingly effective. Indian agent Johnston, recalling his rebuttal of an accusation at Lower Sandusky in 1804 that he had been forward in ceding land to the Americans, said Black Hoof "cut down his adversaries with wit and sarcasm; I never heard anything from the mouth of an Indian so cutting and severe" (Draper manuscripts, p. 22). By his later years he had a command of English. He had only one wife, but several children, one of whom married the Shawnee chief Shemenetoo (Big Snake). Black Hoof, Jr., born in 1795, migrated to Kansas in 1832.

In the first years of the nineteenth century the Shawnees were becoming increasingly impoverished. The hunting declined, treaty annuities were arbitrarily reduced on account of alleged horse thefts by the Indians, and the prices commanded by peltries fell. The tribe also feared that the United States would try to dispossess them of their remaining land. Encouraged by Quaker missionaries and U.S. officials, Black Hoof sought the answer in a selective use of the "civilization" plan favored by President Thomas Jefferson's administration. By improving the efficiency of Shawnee agriculture—for example, by fencing land and putting it beneath the plow—and by extending stock-raising and learning to spin and weave, the Shawnees could increase their prosperity and, in Black Hoof's thinking, reduce the incentive for the United States to take their land. As the warrior society declined and peaceful relations with white settlers were maintained, the Shawnees would become acceptable to their dominant American neighbors. In 1802, 1807, and 1808 the chief was in Washington, D.C., seeking recognition of Shawnee, as opposed to general Indian, limits and asking for instructors, tools, and livestock for his program.

The Quaker William Kirk worked at Wapakoneta in 1807 and 1808, but progress then lapsed until after the War of 1812. By 1832, however, the Shawnees had many frame houses, mills, a schoolhouse, fenced fields, and some 1,700 cattle and hogs. The basic pattern of Indian life, including the winter hunts, continued, but many men were taking a more active role in agriculture, formerly the task of the women. Instinctively conservative, this was probably as far as Black Hoof wanted to go. In preserving white-Indian relations, however, Black Hoof not only arbitrated occasional disputes but was led into cessions of land, albeit of areas marginal to the Shawnees: the treaties of Fort Wayne (7 June 1803), "Fort Industry" (4 July 1805), and Brownstown (25 Nov. 1808).

In addition, Black Hoof confronted three main tests of his policy: the return of the Shawnee Prophet (Tenskwatawa) and Tecumseh to Ohio in 1805, the War of 1812, and the U.S. postwar removal policy. By 1807 the Shawnee brothers Tecumseh and Tenskwatawa had established a rival community at Greenville, Ohio, espousing a religiously charged doctrine of social reform. It detracted from Black Hoof's personal influence but, in its espousal of more traditional Indian practices, directly challenged Wapakoneta's development plan. Worse, by alarming local settlers, it fractured the trust Black Hoof had been nurturing among his neighbors. Relations between the two factions were poor, with the Prophet declaring Black Hoof a witch to incite his assassination, and the Wapakoneta chiefs seeking the Prophet's removal from Greenville through the American Indian agent at Fort Wayne (Ind.). Although both parties achieved some reconciliation at Springfield, Ohio, on 24–25 June 1807, the problem eased only after Tecumseh and his brother moved to the Wabash in 1808.

During the War of 1812 the United States, after initially advocating neutrality on the part of the Indians, increasingly pressed those who had resisted joining the British to serve American forces as proof of their goodwill. Black Hoof had withdrawn his people from the war zone by moving them closer to Piqua (Miami County, Ohio) in 1813 but did not escape personal abuse. On 25 January 1813, while visiting U.S. general Edward Tupper at Camp McArthur on the Scioto, he was severely wounded in the face by a bullet fired through the chinking of a house. In July he was threatened with incarceration at Fort Amanda on the Auglaize until a Shawnee suspected of murder was surrendered. Despite this Black Hoof supported the Americans in numerous councils, and some of his warriors served in U.S. forces as scouts and skirmishers. He was a signatory to the treaties of Greenville (22 July 1814) and Spring Wells (8 Sept. 1814), guaranteeing Indian rights and privileges as they had existed before the war.

Afterward, pressure on Indian land increased. Black Hoof reluctantly signed the treaties of the Maumee Rapids (29 Sept. 1817) and the St. Mary's (17 Sept. 1818), leaving the Shawnees with only three small reservations in Ohio, at Wapakoneta, Hog Creek, and Lewistown. Long before the Indian Removal Act of 1830 some Shawnees, encouraged by officials such as Governor Lewis Cass of Michigan Territory, were abandoning Ohio for lands west of the Mississippi. Black Hoof believed that the supreme deity (to the Shawnees, Waashaa Monetoo) would not favor the tribe if they allowed themselves to be removed, and he strongly opposed the idea in a council of 23 May 1825. In 1831 the question arose again, when American commissioner James B. Gardner notified the Shawnees that he was coming to Wapakoneta with fresh proposals. Advised by the Quakers, Black Hoof and other chiefs determined to resist, but the old chief died before the matter was resolved. As he probably suspected, the proceedings led to a treaty being concluded on 8 August 1831 in which the Shawnees of Wapakoneta agreed to emigrate to Kansas. In the next two years all three bands quit Ohio, marking the ultimate failure of Black Hoof's strategies.

In some respects his career was more tragic than that of the militant Tecumseh, who had gone down fighting, and illustrated the futility of the Indian position in the early nineteenth century. Black Hoof had eschewed the overtures of the Prophet, Tecumseh, and the British; he had repeatedly shown friendship to the United States, and he had made sacrifices to follow the paths Americans advised. But he lost his land anyway and died a disillusioned man, believing that the whites had ruined his people.

• Thomas L. McKenney and James Hall, *The Indian Tribes of North America*, vol. 1 (repr. 1933), pp. 234–47, contains a portrait of Black Hoof with a sketch mainly derived from the information of John Johnston. Further comments by Johnston may be found in the Draper manuscripts, State Historical Society of Wisconsin, Madison, series YY, vol. 11. The Letters Received by the Secretary of War, Record Group 107, National Archives, contain several reports relating to Black Hoof's community at Wapakoneta for the years following 1800. Henry Harvey, *History of the Shawnee Indians* (1855), includes personal reminiscences of the chief, while Black Hoof's own account of Shawnee culture is printed in W. Vernon Kinietz and Erminie Wheeler Voegelin, eds., *Shawnese Traditions* (1939). The treaties signed by Black Hoof are given by Charles J. Kappler, ed., *Indian Affairs, Laws and Treaties* (4 vols., 1904–1929). For useful additional comment, see Carl G. Klopfenstein, "The Removal of the Indians from Ohio, 1820–1843" (Ph.D. diss., Western Reserve Univ., 1955); Leonard U. Hill, *John Johnston and the Indians of the Three Miamies* (1957); and R. David Edmunds, *The Shawnee Prophet* (1983).

JOHN SUGDEN

BLACK KETTLE (?–c. 1698), Onondaga chief, was originally from the Bay of Quinté (Ontario) region. Little is known about him before the 1680s. He was also called Dewadarondore and Chaudière Noire.

The peace signed between the French and the five Iroquois nations of present-day New York State and the Province of Ontario in 1665 began to break down by 1682. Black Kettle was among the influential leaders of the anti-French faction in Onondaga by this time. As a war chief, he headed a party that brought four Ottawa prisoners to François-Marie Perrot, local governor at Montreal, but he did not receive either the welcome or the presents he had expected. It is probable that, unlike the Ottawa traders, he was unwilling to comply with Perrot's control of bartering activities in Montreal in his own and Governor Buade de Frontenac's interests. To avenge himself of his poor reception, Black Kettle pillaged Fort Frontenac (present-day Kingston). In 1687 Governor Brisay de Denonville led an expedition into Seneca country that put a temporary stop to Iroquois raids on New France.

The following year Black Kettle was among the Iroquois delegates from three of the five Iroquois nations that met with the governor-general of New France, Brisay de Denonville, to negotiate peace terms. Peace terms had not been ratified when war broke out between England and France. In August 1691 Black Kettle and some six hundred Iroquois warriors, who were now allies of the British, terrorized some of the isolated villages near Montreal. Louis-Hector de Callière, governor of Montreal, organized a joint force of French regulars, Canadian militiamen, and Indian allies, which overtook the Iroquois war party a short day's march beyond Fort Frontenac and defeated them soundly. But the frontier raiding continued.

In the spring of 1692 Black Kettle's Onondagas were joined by some Senecas who planned to spend the summer hunting near the Chaudière rapids (Ottawa). They also intended to pillage French supply and fur brigades traveling the northern canoe route between Montreal and Michilimackinac. Black Kettle's combined force of about 140 warriors attacked a French party near the Long Sault on the lower Ottawa River. They captured three Indian boys and fourteen *habitant* farmers, who were drying hay at La Chesnaye, and carried them off to their deaths, enslavement, or adoption. The local governor, Callière, hurriedly organized a rescue party that included more than a score of "domiciled natives," mostly Iroquois from the *reductions* at La Montagne and Sault Saint-Louis. They overtook Black Kettle's party a couple of leagues above Long Sault, killed a number of them, freed nine colonists and the three Indian boys, and captured Black Kettle's wife but not Black Kettle.

In late 1697 the Treaty of Ryswick ended the war between England and France, but Callière maintained that the Iroquois must make separate treaties with the French and with their Ottawa and Huron allies. The new governor-general, Buade de Frontenac, who was returning for a second mandate, reopened peace overtures. Black Kettle sent a message to the commandant at Fort Frontenac, Dufrost de La Gemerais, saying the chiefs of his nation were ready to go to Quebec to finalize peace terms but they intended to continue their war against the Ottawa, New France's principal upper country allies. Black Kettle led a party of thirty or forty warriors intent on attacking parties of allied nations they might encounter. Along the Bay of Quinté beyond Fort Frontenac they came upon a band of thirty-four Algonkians, whom they immediately attacked. The latter responded with equal ferocity. The Algonkians killed Black Kettle, his new wife, and a number of his warriors and took eight prisoners to Montreal.

The loss of a renowned warrior chief did much to discourage the Iroquois. Already in July 1689 they had complained to the Earl of Bellemont, governor of New York, that since England and France had signed the peace treaty the Five Nations had suffered ninety-four casualties. The Covenant Chain between the British and the Iroquois needed renewing, as did trade conditions in the face of attractive conditions offered by the French. Neither this appeal nor Black Kettle's attempt to disrupt French activities in the upper country in order to win a more favorable position for the Five Nations succeeded. The Onondagas, Senecas, Cayugas, and Oneidas sent envoys to Montreal in 1700 to begin arrangements for a general peace with the French and their western allied nations. In 1701 the French succeeded in obtaining such a comprehensive pact of peace and friendship, and the Five Nations Iroquois adopted a policy of neutrality in the event of Anglo-French hostilities. Henceforth, the Anglo-American colonies would be subject to raids from their northern neighbors.

Although he was an enterprising war chief, Black Kettle is remembered more for the fear he inspired in the hearts of French colonists than for any significant advancement of Iroquois interests. He was so feared in New France that public prayers, reminiscent of western European medieval intercessions to be delivered from the scourge of the Norsemen, were recited in the colony for divine protection.

• The standard sources are E. B. O'Callaghan, ed., *Documents Relative to the Colonial History of the State of New-York; Procured in Holland, England and France, by John Romeyn Brodhead, Esq.*, vol. 9 (1855), pp. 678–81, 708–10; Cadwallader Colden, *The History of the Five Indian Nations of Canada* (1904), pp. 191–231; and Peter Wraxall, *An Abridgment of the Indian Affairs Contained in Four Folio Volumes . . .* (1968), p. 29. Readers should use O'Callaghan's laudable work with caution, as it contains translations of many incomplete documents for which he provides no context. For the published French documents of the events during Frontenac's second administration, a more reliable source is *Rapport de l'Archiviste de la Province de Québec, 1928–29* (1929), pp. 247–384. The best documentary sources in North America for the period of French colonization are the National Archives of Canada and the National Library in Ottawa, the Archives Nationales in Quebec, the Archives Acadiennes at the University of Moncton, and the archives of the Fortress of Louisbourg in Cape Breton. Robert Chevalier de Beauchêne, once a prisoner of Black Kettle, has some interesting things to say in *Histoire générale des Grands Aventuriers de la Mer*, vol. 7 (1968).

CORNELIUS J. JAENEN

BLACK KETTLE (1807?–Nov. 1868), Cheyenne chief, was a member of the Sutaio division of the Cheyenne until his marriage to Medicine Woman Later made him part of the Wotapio; Black Kettle's first wife was captured in a battle with the Utes in 1848. Little is known about his early years. Conflicting reports name his father as either Swift Hawk Lying Down or High-Backed Wolf. He had three sons and one daughter, according to George Bent, the mixed-blood husband of Black Kettle's niece, who lived with the Cheyenne for many years. Before whites began to spill into the American West, Black Kettle, spelled Me-tu-ra-to or Moka-ta-va-tah in the Cheyenne language, served as scout and warrior in combat against neighboring tribes. He began leading expeditions in the 1840s and rose to prominence among the Southern Cheyenne in the early 1850s. He emerged as a "principal chief" during the 1861 treaty negotiations at Fort Wise, Colorado. Black Kettle accepted an American flag offered by Commissioner of Indian Affairs A. H. Greenwood during the negotiations, symbolically accepting the notion of peace with white America. Despite several incidents of unprovoked violence against his people by federal troops and state militia, Black Kettle remained committed to peace until his death.

The first major incident was the murder of Chief Lean Bear, Black Kettle's longtime friend, who was shot in May 1864 by troops who had been ordered by Colonel John M. Chivington, a Methodist preacher, to "kill all Indians [they] came across." After Cheyenne warriors returned fire, Black Kettle rode among his people calling for an end to the fighting, thus averting a potential slaughter of the white soldiers. As violence between Indians and whites increased in the Colorado Territory and elsewhere on the central plains that summer, Black Kettle tried to secure peace with the aggressive territorial government, led by Colonel John Evans and Chivington, the territory's military commander. With George Bent's help, Black Kettle and other Cheyenne chiefs wrote to Major Edward W. Wynkoop, the commander of Fort Lyon (formerly Fort Wise), declaring their desire for peace. Black Kettle subsequently gave Wynkoop a peace offering: four white hostages procured at his expense. At a peace conference arranged by Wynkoop, held in Denver on 28 September 1864, Black Kettle told Evans, "All we ask is that we may have peace with the whites. . . . I want you to give all the chiefs of the soldiers here to understand that we are for peace, and that we have made peace, that we may not be mistaken by them for enemies" (Hoig, *Peace Chiefs*, p. 110). Evans in turn was belligerent, blaming the violence on Indians and telling Black Kettle that the Cheyenne must submit to the military authority at Fort Lyon. Black Kettle agreed to Evans's request, encamping near the fort at Sand Creek.

Evans and Chivington answered Black Kettle's call for peace with the Sand Creek massacre, one of the most ignominious incidents in the history of Indian-white relations. Major Scott J. Anthony, who suddenly replaced Wynkoop in early November, had promised Black Kettle that his people would be safe at their Sand Creek encampment, but Chivington, with Anthony's support, led his troops and Colorado volunteers in a brutal attack on the village on 29 November 1864. As the attack began, Black Kettle waved the American flag given him by Commissioner Greenwood, along with a white flag tied to a lodge pole, drawing hundreds of terrified Cheyennes to his tipi and soon hundreds of bullets from the charging mili-

tia. As Black Kettle and his wife fled the village, a bullet knocked her to the ground. Black Kettle, believing her dead, escaped; despite being shot eight more times, Medicine Woman Later survived. Chivington's order that no prisoners were to be taken resulted in the murder and mutilation of more than 100 Cheyennes, including several prominent chiefs; Arapahoe chief Left Hand and forty-six of his people also died in the attack.

The massacre at Sand Creek drove a wedge between Black Kettle and the Dog Soldiers, a Cheyenne warrior society distrustful of whites. As Cheyenne and Arapahoe warriors retaliated against whites in the north, Black Kettle and roughly 400 Cheyennes turned south. This tribal division ultimately prevented Black Kettle from achieving his objectives. Though distrustful of whites after Sand Creek, and no longer trusted by some within his tribe, Black Kettle tried to maintain peace and protect his people from other attacks by returning white hostages and negotiating with treaty councils. Black Kettle told the Little Arkansas treaty council in October 1865 that as a result of the Sand Creek massacre, "My shame is as big as the earth." It was difficult to "believe white men anymore," he said, but he felt he had no choice if he was to protect the Cheyenne from "young soldiers" who did not listen to their white chiefs. "Although wrongs have been done me I live in hopes," he told them (*Report of the Commissioner of Indian Affairs* [1865], pp. 704–5). Black Kettle signed the Treaty of the Little Arkansas, ceding the Cheyenne's remaining land in Colorado and their hunting grounds in western Kansas; but he warned the treaty commissioners that he could speak only for his followers, not for the Dog Soldiers. His participation in the Medicine Lodge treaty council aggravated the split with the Dog Soldiers, who responded to Black Kettle's peace offering by threatening to kill his horses if he did not participate in the sacred ceremony of the Medicine Arrows, which Black Kettle himself had carried into battle in 1853. Black Kettle persevered by seeking the full agreement of his tribe, knowing that no peace would last without the participation of the Dog Soldiers; after several days of negotiation with Black Kettle, they agreed to join the council after finishing their ceremony. The treaty, signed 21 October 1867, restricted Cheyenne settlement to a reservation in newly created Indian Territory. The Cheyenne were given the verbal promise that they could continue to hunt in their old territory, a false promise that ultimately led to renewed violence.

Black Kettle persisted in his efforts to protect his people from the U.S. Army the following year. Though Cheyenne raiding parties continued to operate near his village, Black Kettle made it clear to General William B. Hazen on 20 November 1868 that he wanted peace, offering to settle near Fort Cobb as a sign of goodwill; Hazen refused to offer the Cheyennes refuge. On 27 November, almost four years to the day of the Sand Creek massacre, Black Kettle and his wife were killed during the battle of the Washita, shot in the back trying to flee General George Custer's dawn attack. After reading newspaper accounts of the battle, Evan Connell wrote that it "sounds as though Black Kettle's village lay in the path of Genghis Khan" (*Son of the Morning Star* [1984], p. 187). The day after the battle, survivors hid Black Kettle's body from Custer's soldiers on a sandy knoll. In 1934 Works Progress Administration workers trying to stabilize a bridge over the Washita River uncovered a skeleton wearing Black Kettle's jewelry.

Though most historians do not call the Washita battle a massacre, it is difficult to view Custer's attack on Black Kettle and his wife and the killing of at least two dozen women and children as defensible. If Black Kettle had one weakness, it was an inability to control an aggressive tribal faction, but this shortcoming was mitigated by cultural and circumstantial factors that militated against such success. The U.S. Army and territorial militias, which lacked discipline, did not need a pretext to attack Indians during the 1860s. General Philip Sheridan ordered the attack on Black Kettle's village after deciding against negotiating the release of white hostages, negotiations sought by Black Kettle. There were alternatives to the killing of women and children and "the great peacemaker," as historian Stan Hoig called Black Kettle, who had strived for over eight years to fashion a lasting peace between his people and those whose actions at Sand Creek had given him every reason to lose faith in their words.

• Federal documents pertaining to Black Kettle include U.S. Congress, House of Representatives, "Massacre of Cheyenne Indians," in *Report on the Conduct of the War* (1865); and U.S. Congress, Senate, "The Chivington Massacre," in *The Reports of the Committees . . .* (1867), and "Report of the Secretary of War . . ." (1867), a report on the Sand Creek massacre. Also see U.S. Congress, Senate, "Letter of the Secretary of the Interior, Communicating . . . Information in Relation to the Late Battle of the Washita River" (1869). For treaty information, see Charles J. Kappler, ed., *Indian Affairs: Laws and Treaties* (1927). The best firsthand account of life with Black Kettle and the Cheyennes is George E. Hyde, *Life of George Bent: Written from His Letters* (1983); see also John Stands In Timber and Margot Liberty, *Cheyenne Memories* (1967). Stan Hoig provides the most complete history of Black Kettle in *The Peace Chiefs of the Cheyennes* (1980), chap. 8. For short biographical sketches, see Jason Gallman's entry in *Notable Native Americans* (1995), and John O'Leary, "Black Kettle: A Brief Profile," *American Indian Crafts and Culture* 7 (1973) 8–11. Vol. 1 of Peter J. Powell, *People of the Sacred Mountain: A History of the Northern Cheyenne Chiefs and Warrior Societies, 1830–1879* (1981), ends with an account of Black Kettle's death. For a bibliographical essay and reference work, see Powell, *The Cheyennes, Maheoo's People: A Critical Bibliography* (1980), which is part of the Newberry Library's bibliographical series.

The Sand Creek Massacre is covered in Hoig, *The Sand Creek Massacre* (1961); Duane Schultz, *Month of the Freezing Moon: The Sand Creek Massacre November 1864* (1990); and David P. Svaldi, *Sand Creek and the Rhetoric of Extermination* (1989). The battle of the Washita is covered in Jess C. Epple, *Custer's Battle of the Washita and a History of the Plains Indian Tribes* (1970); Charles J. Brill, *Conquest of the Southern Plains: An Uncensored Narrative of the Battle of the Washita*

and Custer's Southern Campaign (1975); and Hoig, *The Battle of the Washita: The Sheridan-Custer Indian Campaign of 1867–1869* (1976).

PAUL ROSIER

BLACKMER, Sidney (13 July 1895–5 Oct. 1973), actor, director, and producer, was born Sidney Alderman Blackmer in Salisbury, North Carolina, the son of Walter Steele Blackmer, a businessman, and Clara De Roulhac Alderman. He graduated from high school in 1908 and for the next three years studied liberal arts at academies in Warrentown, North Carolina, and Mercersburg, Pennsylvania. In 1913 he enrolled at the University of North Carolina to study law, made the varsity football team, and became a star fullback. By summer his priorities changed, and he left for a sabbatical in Europe.

On his return in 1914, Blackmer tried in vain to join the army. He drifted into community theater and that year made his stage debut playing an Indian in a Charlotte production of *The Trail of the Lonesome Pine*. He graduated in 1915 with a B.A. and LL.B. from North Carolina, but he never took the bar exam. He then worked briefly in the Southern Bell Telephone legal department in Atlanta. He relocated to New York City to pursue an acting career and took voice instruction to rid himself of his accent "so that I can pass for a New Yorker." Blackmer's first show business break was as an Indian and a cowboy in an episode of the Pearl White silent movie serial, *The Perils of Pauline* (filmed in Ithaca, N.Y., and Fort Lee, N.J.).

Blackmer made his New York stage debut at age twenty-two in a featured role in *The Morris Dance* (1917). That season he toured with the Ben Greet Players, doing "alfresco" performances of medieval and Shakespearean repertory, then joined the Broadway production of *The Thirteenth Chair*. At the outset of World War I, he enlisted in the U.S. Army Field Artillery Corps, in which he achieved the rank of lieutenant and served until 1919.

On returning to New York, Blackmer played his first lead when he took over the part of Napoleon Gibbs in the romantic comedy *39 East*. In 1920's *Trimmed in Scarlet*, even a temperature of 104 degrees could not stop him from taking the stage on opening night. "It was an important step in my early career," he reflected in an interview. The same year, opposite the legendary Eva Le Gallienne in *Not So Long Ago*, he received excellent notices. Directors recognized his talent and ease on stage and cast him in a variety of parts. Some seasons he did as many as three plays. He became known as an actor who approached his roles with seriousness. For 1921's *The Mountain Man*, Blackmer researched his character by living for several weeks in an isolated area of northern Georgia.

With his athletic build and a height just short of six feet, Blackmer became the Broadway matinee idol of the Roaring Twenties flapper era. He worked onstage in major New York productions for the next eight years. His versatility onstage gave him entrée to motion pictures. For the next decade he alternated between appearing on the stage with such luminaries as Helen Hayes and Tallulah Bankhead and in films. After two silent features (1928 and 1929), Blackmer made his "talkie" debut in *A Most Immoral Lady* (1929).

In 1928 Blackmer secretly wed actress Lenore Ulrich; they had no children. Their divorce in 1939 became a well-publicized affair when Ulrich declared his "constant traveling created a telegraph marriage." In 1942 Blackmer married stage actress Suzanne Kaaren; they had two sons.

Under contract to Warner Bros., MGM, and then as a freelance actor, Blackmer worked constantly. In 1937 and 1941 he had eleven films in release—double his usual output. On screen, often as a savvy politician, the "other man," or a suave criminal, Blackmer established himself as one of the most noted and popular character actors (there was only an occasional lead) from the 1930s to the 1960s. He costarred with the greats of Hollywood's "Golden Age." Blackmer said he grabbed the chance to play the villain, explaining that "the bad guy's character was always more colorful and interesting."

Blackmer's film highlights include *Kismet* (1930), *Little Caesar* (1930), *The Count of Monte Cristo* (1934), *The Little Colonel* (1935), *Heidi* (1937), *In Old Chicago* (1938), *Suez* (1938), *It's a Wonderful World* (1939), *Love Crazy* (1941), *Duel in the Sun* (1946), *The High and the Mighty* (1954), *The View from Pompey's Head* (1955), *High Society* (1956), and *Tammy and the Bachelor* (1957). From 1952 to 1960 he also appeared in and directed numerous stock productions. On Broadway, as the alcoholic husband in William Inge's *Come Back, Little Sheba* (1950), he won, among other honors, a Tony Award for best actor. He also won acclaim as Boss Finley in Tennessee Williams's *Sweet Bird of Youth* (1959). He expressed regret at losing both roles in the film adaptations. He succeeded Walter Pidgeon and costarred with Jackie Gleason in the Joseph Stein, Robert Russell, and Bob Merrill musical *Take Me Along* (1959).

Blackmer had another unique claim to fame: with wire-frame glasses and the proper makeup, he bore a resemblance to Theodore Roosevelt and played him in ten plays and films, including *The President Vanishes* (1934), *This Is My Affair* (1938), *The President's Mystery* (1936), and the short *Teddy, The Rough Rider* (n.d.). "It *was* my father!," exclaimed Alice Roosevelt Longworth, Roosevelt's daughter, after seeing one of Blackmer's performances. To avoid typecasting, he briefly left Hollywood in the late 1930s.

Blackmer was a founder of Actor's Equity, playing a major role in the hard fought battle over commissions and representation between actors and managers in 1919. He was a member of the national executive board of the American Federation of Television and Radio Artists (AFTRA). Blackmer was also a chairman of the board of the North Carolina School of the Arts (Winston-Salem) and on the board of the National Muscular Dystrophy Association, a charity he actively raised funds for from 1957 until his death. He received countless honors from politicians in North Carolina, where he was briefly the president of copper and gold manufacturing companies.

Blackmer's last film was *Rosemary's Baby* (1968); for his work in it he received outstanding reviews and was named as best supporting actor by the All-American Press Association. As the satanic warlock, Blackmer felt he gave his finest film performance, but he told the *New York Daily News* that "missing out [on being nominated for an Academy Award] isn't going to induce me to quit show business. The thought of dropping everything never enters my mind. I'm too damn old to retire. I'd just disintegrate if I did. I'm going to keep plugging until the last curtain falls" (Mar. 1969). Four years later, after a second bout with cancer, he died at New York City's Sloan-Kettering Institute for Cancer Research.

• Research material and Blackmer's personal papers are at the University of North Carolina at Chapel Hill and the North Carolina School of the Arts. An interview made after the 1968 Academy Awards nominations, at which Blackmer had been overlooked, is Bob Lardine, "The Elusive Prize," *New York Daily News Sunday Magazine*, 30 Mar. 1968. An obituary is in the *New York Times*, 6 Oct. 1973.

ELLIS NASSOUR

BLACKMUR, R. P. (21 Jan. 1904–2 Feb. 1965), literary critic, was born Richard Palmer Blackmur in Springfield, Massachusetts, the son of George Edward Blackmur, who failed at a variety of jobs, and Helen Palmer. His parents' marriage was unhappy; the family depended on his mother's earnings from the Cambridge, Massachusetts, boardinghouse in which they lived. Blackmur's formal education ended after about two years at the Cambridge High and Latin School. An omnivorous autodidact, he discovered while still a boy some of his lifelong masters, among them Henry James, Ezra Pound, and T. S. Eliot. From age fourteen to twenty-four he clerked in bookstores and Harvard University's Widener Library and became a partner in a Cambridge bookstore that failed after a year. Through friendship with Lincoln Kirstein and others, he became associated with *Hound & Horn*, one of the most important little magazines of the period. He was its editing manager from 1928 to 1930 and remained a contributor until it ended in 1934.

In 1930 Blackmur married the painter Helen Dickson. The childless marriage was difficult and ended in divorce in 1951. Until 1940, when he received a one-year appointment as assistant in the Creative Arts Program at Princeton University, Blackmur lived as a freelance poet and critic, for much of that time in extreme poverty. He published his first book of criticism, *The Double Agent*, in 1935, a collection of a dozen essays on such writers as Pound, Marianne Moore, E. E. Cummings, D. H. Lawrence, and Hart Crane. The dominant concern of these essays is how the artist can order "the chaos of private experience" in a form "external to the consciousness that entertained it in flux" by finding a language that is both traditional and conventional (Fraser, pp. 91–93). He published his first book of poetry, *From Jordan's Delight*, in 1937. From 1937 to 1939 he had Guggenheim fellowships to work on a biography of Henry Adams, a lifelong obsession that remained unfinished at his death, finally appearing in an edited version in 1980.

With his move to Princeton, Blackmur began a 25-year association with the university, though his position was not secure for some years. After two years as an assistant in Creative Arts, he was a Hodder fellow, for two years a fellow at the Institute for Advanced Study, then resident fellow in creative writing. Even after he was made associate professor of English in 1948, he was not fully accepted by some department colleagues who could not value his unorthodox education. Princeton raised Blackmur from extreme to genteel poverty, and he taught summers at the Cummington School in Massachusetts (1941, 1942), the University of Vermont's School of Modern Critical Studies (1951, 1952), and Indiana University's School of Letters (1952, 1954, 1958, 1959).

In 1940 he published another collection of criticism, *The Expense of Greatness*, and contracted to write a critical study of Henry James, a work he never completed. He published his second book of poetry, *The Second World*, in 1942 and his third and last book of poetry, *The Good European*, in 1947. In 1952 his best, most influential work of criticism, *Language as Gesture*, appeared. His biographer reported that this book sold only forty-eight copies in the United States in 1958 and was remaindered the next year. An abbreviated version, *Form and Value in Modern Poetry*, probably his best-known work, appeared in paperback in 1957.

In 1949 Blackmur created the Princeton Seminars in Literary Criticism, later renamed for Christian Gauss, which brought outstanding literary critics and scholars to the campus. Through these seminars he exercised his widest influence on the university community. In leading them, "he evoked an atmosphere of shared enquiry into which all members of the gathering felt drawn" (quoted in Cone et al., eds., p. 153). After World War II, he traveled extensively in Europe and the Middle and Far East under the auspices of the Rockefeller Foundation. What he learned led him to reconsider the work of the universities, and especially of the humanities, to overcome "the new illiteracy" of mass culture. *The Lion and the Honeycomb: Essays in Solicitude and Critique* (1955) and *A Primer of Ignorance*, posthumously published in 1967, contain what Edward W. Said has called "frankly speculative and theoretically administrative essays" that anticipated much of the development of cultural criticism and the study of literature later in the century. Blackmur's postwar criticism, Said argued, is "directly tied to a sense of American responsibility for the world after the dismantling of the old imperial systems" (Cone et al., eds., p. 113). In 1956 Blackmur lectured at the Library of Congress, publishing the lectures as *Anni Mirabiles, 1921–1925*. In 1959 he published *New Criticism in the United States*, based on lectures he gave in Japan, and in 1964 *Eleven Essays in the European Novel*.

Blackmur must be evaluated primarily in his two roles as critic and teacher. At its best, his criticism managed to be at once magisterial and provisional. Scrupulously detailed, it remained always, in his phrase from his 1935 article "A Critic's Job of Work," "the formal discourse of an amateur." His favorite form was the essay and frequently his essays were titled "notes." His writing was often difficult to follow, sometimes from the complexity of his ideas but often because of the autodidact's tendency to overelaborate. He loved to use strange words in strange settings: "surds," "aseity," "cumulus." He often quoted lines of poetry as a touchstone, then used them as a refrain several times in the essay.

Accounts of Blackmur as a teacher stressed many of the same qualities. E. D. H. Johnson described Blackmur's approach in seminars as "unfailingly oblique, tentative, exploratory, anything but dogmatic" (Cone et al., eds., p. 154). Working directly from a text and his notes in the margins, occasionally referring to a notebook, he would offer an exposition "in a consecutive and seemingly impromptu manner," which stimulated lively general discussion for the rest of the evening.

Though identified as a New Critic (popularly understood as one concerned with close exegetical reading of individual texts as opposed to placing texts in historical or biographical contexts), as early as "A Critic's Job of Work," Blackmur was concerned about the limitations of New Critical approaches. He always sought to anchor what he wrote about literature, poetry especially, in the details of the text. He also liked to deal with works and writers comparatively, showing how one's practice could throw light on the other's; for instance, he related Stevens to Pound or Eliot, Henry James to Proust. Only rarely would he make such comparisons in order to denigrate one of the paired writers. He was invariably interested in what a work could tell us of the writer's sensibility, which he defined in "In the Hope of Straightening Things Out" as "what you draw on to make fresh responses. Live language and particularly live poetry make the great objective reservoir of sensibility: the traditional and impersonal source of what power you have over your own sensibility" (*The Lion and the Honeycomb*, p. 173).

The work of the poet, he argued, was to get life, energy, and what he called "behavior" *into* the poem by the intensity and compression of language ("Unappeasable and Peregrine: Behavior and the 'Four Quartets,'" *Language as Gesture*, pp. 192–93). The poet must use "language as gesture"—the words must sound like music, make visual images, seem solid like sculpture and spacious like architecture, and have qualities of dance and acting. Yet, he claimed, "it is the fury in the words which we understand, and not the words themselves" ("Language as Gesture," in *Language as Gesture*, p. 12). Gesture in language was all the connotative power that words created under the pressures and tensions of association, the shaping forces of rhyme, meter, pattern, imagery, repetition, reduction, and condensation. The poet created or asserted value through form; we as readers or critics understood that human or moral value as the structures of the poem made them accessible to us. Such commitments on Blackmur's part explain not only the provisional qualities of his essays but also why he turned to wider considerations of modernism, the role of the humanities, and the social and political responsibilities of the United States in the postwar period. The psychological complexity, allusiveness, and intellectual demands of High Modernist writing required critics who read widely, deeply, and with subtlety. In R. P. Blackmur such literature found one of its earliest and most perceptive interpreters.

Blackmur died in Princeton, New Jersey.

• The most important collection of Blackmur material is in the Firestone and Mudd Libraries at Princeton University. See also Princeton's Scribner collection and the papers of Allen Tate, which contain further material on Blackmur. Scattered materials are also in the Beinecke Library at Yale University, in the *Hound & Horn* archive, the *Southern Review* papers, and the papers of Delmore Schwartz; the Regenstein Library at the University of Chicago, in the *Poetry Magazine* archive; and the Houghton Library at Harvard University. A selection of his poetry was published posthumously as *Poems of R. P. Blackmur* (1977). A comprehensive list of Blackmur manuscript collections appears in the full-length biography by Russell Fraser, *A Mingled Yarn: The Life of R. P. Blackmur* (1981). For critical analysis of his work and reflections on his professional career, see Edward T. Cone et al., eds., *The Legacy of R. P. Blackmur: Essays, Memoirs, Texts* (1986). Blackmur's contribution to the Gauss Seminars is detailed in Robert Fitzgerald, *Enlarging the Change: The Princeton Seminars in Literary Criticism, 1949–1951* (1985). Blackmur is also mentioned in Irving Howe, *A Margin of Hope* (1982), and Eileen Simpson, *Poets in Their Youth* (1982). An obituary is in the *New York Times*, 3 Feb. 1965.

PAUL A. LACEY

BLACKSTONE, Harry (27 Sept. 1885–16 Nov. 1965), magician, was born Harry Boughton in Chicago, Illinois, the son of Alfred Boughton, a florist and baker, and Barbara Degan. He began his career as a cabinetmaker, a skill applied later to the making of magic apparatus. Blackstone decided to become a magician when, at the age of 13, he was held spellbound by a performance by Harry Kellar at the McVicker's Theatre in Chicago. During the early 1900s Blackstone performed in vaudeville as an acrobat and later, with his brother Pete Boughton, as "Harry Bouton & Co., Straight and Crooked Magic," a name forecasting his theatrical style as "Blackstone the Great." Originally he had performed solo under the stage name of "Bouton." Briefly, he performed as "Fredrik the Great" when he was able to purchase a large number of playbills for Fredrik, another Midwestern magician. He adopted several more names until he finally chose "Blackstone." Depending on which story one chooses to believe, he adopted the name Blackstone from the Blackstone Hotel in Chicago, after Blackstone cigars, or from his grandmother's father.

Blackstone was first married to Inez Nourse, in Ingallston, Michigan, in 1919; they had no children. She had served as his show's music director and was later billed as "The Little Banjo Fiend." They were divorced in 1929. His second wife, Billie Matthews (Mildred Phinney), was also a member of the company, and they were married in 1933. She was the mother of Harry Blackstone, Jr., who achieved fame as a magician in his own right. They also were divorced after a short marriage. Blackstone met his third wife, Elizabeth Ross, while at a sanitarium, where he was recovering from asthma in 1950.

During the summers of the 1920s the troupe was headquartered in Colon, Michigan, a small town in Southwest Michigan, where the members built equipment, raised the many animals used in their show, and planned their new illusions. He was briefly in business with Percy Abbott, who founded Abbott's Magic Company, which still manufactures magic equipment and hosts a magic "get-together" in Colon each August.

Blackstone's two major competitor's were Howard Thurston and Harry Houdini. During the 1920s Blackstone, who was also an outstanding escape artist, often competed directly with Houdini for publicity and bookings. With Houdini's death in 1926 and Thurston's death in 1936, Blackstone remained the foremost American magician during the Great Depression. Blackstone's style was unique. He presented himself as a playful magician with a sense of humor that the audience loved. He might wear a white cowboy hat with formal tails as he swept a buzzsaw through a lady. Often, when performing the Disappearing Horse, one of his signature illusions, he would be left standing with a saddle between his legs, a surprised expression on his face. Other effects for which Blackstone was famous were a birdcage that vanished from his hands while it was being touched by spectators; an impish handkerchief that danced in his hands and on the stage, to the apparent consternation of Blackstone; and a lighted bulb that floated about the stage and over the audience and then vanished. He was known for giving away a magically produced rabbit to some lucky child at each show.

While performing at the Lincoln Theater in Decatur, Illinois, in 1942, Blackstone was informed that a neighboring building was on fire. Taking control of the situation with the calm of a master, Blackstone announced to the 3,200 fans that they were in for a special surprise and asked them to assemble at the front of the theater. Systematically he emptied each row of the audience while promising a special event outside. One overweight lady was stuck in her seat and so her chair was unbolted and she was carried out in it. While Blackstone watched the fire his devoted crew moved all of his invaluable props to the alley behind the theater, a fact that he did not learn until later.

During World War II Blackstone toured 165 U.S. military posts. He became the star of several comic book series written by his friend Walter Gibson (creator of "The Shadow" under the pseudonym Maxwell

Grant): *Super Magician Comics, Super Magician, Master Magician Comics*, and *Blackstone, the Magician Detective.* The last series became a radio show in 1944. Adapting well to television, in the 1950s he appeared on television specials, the "Tonight Show," the "Jackie Gleason Show," and Edward R. Murrow's "Person to Person."

In 1960 Blackstone retired and moved to Los Angeles, California. Shortly after his arrival the Magic Castle, an internationally known restaurant featuring magic theater, was opened and one of the rooms was named after him. He was elected to the Society of American Magicians' Hall of Fame. He died in Los Angeles.

• Blackstone's papers are at the American Museum of Magic in Marshall, Mich. Blackstone published two books (ghostwritten by Walter B. Gibson), *Blackstone's Secrets of Magic* (1929), and *Blackstone's Modern Card Tricks* (1929). More detailed information on Blackstone's life can be found in Harry Blackstone, Jr., *The Blackstone Book of Magic & Illusion* (1985). Additional material is also contained in Milbourne Christopher, *The Illustrated History of Magic* (1973). Obituaries are in the *New York Times* and the *Herald Tribune*, both 18 Nov. 1965.

R. DOUGLAS WHITMAN

BLACKSTONE, William (5? Mar. 1595–26 May 1675), Anglican clergyman, horticulturist, and first European settler in what is now Rhode Island, was born in Whickham, Durham, England, the son of John Blackstone, a wealthy landowner and poultryman, and Agnes Hawley. At Emmanuel College, Cambridge, Blackstone (sometimes Blackston or Blaxton) took his B.A. in 1617 and his M.A. in 1621. He at once took orders in the Church of England.

In 1623 Blackstone, tired of living under the constraints of the English bishops, joined the Robert Gorges expedition, whose members hoped to build a settlement at the current site of Boston. Within a year all but two of his fellow pioneers had given up and returned to England, but Blackstone decided to stay because he liked the solitude and had missionary hopes. He inherited some of the supplies the others left behind, including some cattle. Blackstone built a cottage on what is now Beacon Hill on the Shawmut peninsula and moved in with his 180-odd books. His cows pastured in the 46-acre clearing that later became Boston Common, where he cultivated the first apple orchard in Massachusetts. Blackstone befriended the local Native Americans and visited the two other Englishmen, who had settled in widely separated locales.

Blackstone lived the life of a scholarly missionary until 1630, when twelve ships appeared in Boston Harbor and disgorged nearly 1,000 Puritans from England. Philosophically and theologically at odds, Blackstone and the Puritans detested each other. Brandishing the charter of the Massachusetts Bay Colony, Puritan authorities confiscated all but fifty acres of Blackstone's land and imposed their religious views on him. The scholarly divine reportedly said, "I left England to get from under the power of the lord bish-

ops, but in America I am fallen under the power of the lord brethren."

In 1634 Blackstone sold all but six of his fifty acres to the Puritans. Packing apple tree shoots, his library, and other belongings, he headed southwest along the Native-American trail that someday would evolve into U.S. Route 1. With him were his cattle and a servant named Abbott. At the very edge of Rehoboth in the Plymouth Colony (present-day Cumberland, R.I.), Blackstone found a homesite at a bend in the river that was to bear his name. Dubbing the spot "Study Hill," Blackstone built a cabin and established a routine of gardening, apple cultivation, reading, walking, and preaching to the natives. At his new home Blackstone bred the first new strain of apples in North America, yellow sweetings.

In 1636 Roger Williams and a band of religious dissidents arrived at the head of Narragansett Bay, about six miles to the south, and established Providence. Blackstone and Williams, a crusader for religious tolerance, struck up a friendship, and the latter reportedly had him preach in Providence and at a trading post down the bay near modern Wickford. If this is true, it is a tribute to Williams's liberality, as the gulf between his and Blackstone's theologies was vast.

To Providence residents Blackstone became a familiar sight, walking (while still young) or riding his saddle-trained bull (as an older man) along the trails west of Narragansett Bay to preach, conduct monthly Anglican services, or to trade his apples for needed goods. Blackstone sometimes visited Boston, and it was there that in 1659, at the age of sixty-four, he married the widow Sarah Stevenson and fathered a son. Sarah died at Study Hill in 1673. Blackstone also died there.

Shortly after Blackstone's death, marauding natives engaged in King Philip's War burned the house at Study Hill and with it all of Blackstone's books and any writings he may have left. Blackstone's memory is preserved in the name of the river and valley between Providence and Worcester, Massachusetts, nearby Blackstone, Massachusetts, and many local streets and commercial firms.

Blackstone was more than a lovable recluse who simply wanted to read books and grow apples; few sought a life of bookish bliss by leaving the comforts of England for the terrors of the American wilderness. Blackstone's missionary zeal was almost certainly his motive and must have been far greater than most sources indicate. Certainly Blackstone's extensive travel, friendships, and missionary work hardly qualify him as a recluse. He used his apples to befriend the natives and settlers to whom he preached. A contemporary account repeated in most sources reports that Blackstone, before preaching in Providence, attracted an audience by distributing apples, a rare commodity at the time.

A monument in Cumberland, Rhode Island, believed to be at or near Blackstone's grave, bills him as "Founder of Boston." Blackstone, however, did not lead the Gorges expedition but stayed when it left and departed soon after the first permanent white settlers arrived. Blackstone simply was the first European to live on the site of Boston for any length. If Blackstone deserves a niche in American history, it is because at a time when conformity and tyranny were the rule, he was practical, resourceful, individualistic, and broad-minded.

• No writings by Blackstone are known to have survived, and secondary sources are few. Relatively complete accounts appear in sources available at the athenaeums and historical society libraries in Boston and Providence. One is in Leonard Bliss, *History of Rehoboth* (1836). Other sources include Richard M. Bayles, ed., *History of Providence County, Rhode Island* (2 vols., 1891); L. H. Tilton, *History of Rehoboth* (1918); and Charles Francis Adams, *Three Episodes in Massachusetts History* (1892). Genealogical sources are J. W. Blackstone, *Lineage and History of William Blackstone* (1907), and L. M. Sargent, *The Blackstone Family* (1857). More recent sources include a pamphlet by Louise Lind on Blackstone prepared for the Blackstone Valley Tourism Council (1989) and a monograph by Paul F. Eno in the Library of the Rhode Island Historical Society (1985).

PAUL F. ENO

BLACKSTONE, William E. (6 Oct. 1841–1935), Christian Zionist and author, was born in Adams, New York, the son of Andrew Blackstone, a tinsmith, and Sally (maiden name unknown). Born into a devout Methodist family, he had an evangelical conversion experience at the age of ten while attending a local Methodist revival meeting. He remained a Methodist for the rest of his life, although he criticized the denomination for the liberal or "modernist" direction it had taken by the turn of the twentieth century. Though he became a leading spokesperson for American fundamentalism and Zionism, Blackstone received no formal education or training. Rejected by the Union army on account of frailness, Blackstone spent the Civil War working for the Christian Commission, a missionary agency designed to provide spiritual counsel and medical aid to northern soldiers. He married Sarah Louis Smith in 1866; they had three children.

After settling in Rockford, Illinois, where he sold agriculture insurance, Blackstone moved to Oak Park, a suburb of Chicago, in 1870. While working as a businessman in Chicago, he became acquainted with a circle of fellow Christian businessmen who were active in promoting evangelical concerns. One of his acquaintances was Chicago-based revivalist Dwight L. Moody, who spurred Blackstone's thinking about biblical prophecy, especially the significance of prophecies about Israel.

Blackstone adopted a form of evangelical theology known as dispensationalism, which espoused a literal interpretation of the prophetic portions of the Bible and depicted human history in seven divinely ordained periods, or "dispensations." Adherents to this system affirmed that the future return of the Jews to Israel would serve as a harbinger for the second coming of Jesus Christ to inaugurate a millennial kingdom

of righteousness (the seventh dispensation) before the last judgment and the end of the world. Blackstone's relative success in business allowed him to finance the dissemination of dispensational theology. He lectured on dispensationalism at churches, Young Men's Christian Associations, and other religious forums throughout the country. In 1878 he began to devote himself to evangelism full time, although he maintained his business interests for the purpose of financially supporting his ministry.

In the same year, Blackstone published his most famous dispensationalist tract, *Jesus Is Coming*. The original 96-page pamphlet taught that Jewish people everywhere were the objects of biblical prophecy. The Jews had rejected Jesus as Messiah during his first earthly manifestation, but they now had the opportunity to place their faith in his imminent return to earth and the establishment of a millennial kingdom. The second coming of Christ, according to Blackstone's interpretation of biblical prophecies, would be preceded by a massive return of Jews to Israel, their rightful homeland. *Jesus Is Coming* was foremost an evangelistic tract, designed to prepare both Jews and non-Jews for the second coming of Jesus. Yet it could also be considered "Christian Zionist" literature, owing to its focus on the importance of a Jewish homeland. In 1908, for its third printing, *Jesus Is Coming* was expanded to 256 pages. The work was translated into forty-two languages and became one of the most popular dispensationalist tracts in the world.

As a logical outgrowth of his dispensationalism, Blackstone became a vigorous promoter of Zionism. His aggressive, evangelistic Christianity made Zionists in America somewhat skeptical of his views (especially his insistence that Jews convert to fundamentalist Christianity), but the movement nonetheless embraced him. In 1887 he helped found the Chicago Hebrew Mission and used the mission's magazine, *Jewish Era*, as a mouthpiece for his teachings on Zionism and the interpretation of biblical prophecy related to Israel. The following year Blackstone visited Palestine to encourage activism for a Jewish homeland, and in 1890 he organized the Conference on Christians and Jews to provide an interfaith discussion on the future of the Jewish nation.

Blackstone's most significant contribution to Zionism was his 1891 petition to President Benjamin Harrison advocating both a Jewish homeland and the relocation of persecuted Russian Jews to Palestine. Known as the "Blackstone Memorial," it was one of the first major articulations of Zionist thinking and appeared six years before Theodore Herzl, the acknowledged "father" of political Zionism, called his first Zionist Congress. The memorial was signed by 413 prominent Americans, including William McKinley, J. Pierpont Morgan, and John D. Rockefeller. The majority of the American Jewish community rejected Blackstone's petition, but it was supported by American Zionists. While the document was certainly "Zionist" in the sense that it championed the formation of a Jewish homeland in Palestine, its ultimate intellectual underpinnings lay within Blackstone's Christian dispensationalism.

In 1916 Blackstone drafted a similar "memorial" to President Woodrow Wilson urging him to support the Balfour Declaration, a recent proposal for a Jewish national homeland in Palestine. Although the 1916 memorial did not receive the same popular attention as the 1891 version, it drew support from the American Zionist community, including Louis Brandeis. It is unclear whether Blackstone's memorial had any effect on Wilson's eventual decision to support the Balfour proposal.

Blackstone spent most of his career and ministry speaking, writing, and organizing conferences to promote a Jewish homeland in Palestine. He remained active in both the Zionist and Protestant fundamentalist communities. He was one of the rare fundamentalists to promote Zionism actively and one of the few open supporters of Zionism to champion evangelical Christian doctrinal beliefs. His career reveals an unexplored link between Protestant evangelicalism and Zionist Judaism in late-ninteenth, early twentieth-century America. Blackstone died in Los Angeles.

• Collections of Blackstone's papers are at the Moody Bible Institute and the American Messianic Fellowship, both in Chicago. A biographical account of Blackstone's career is Beth M. Lindberg, *A God Filled Life: The Story of William E. Blackstone* (1985). The two best scholarly works on Zionism's relationship with fundamentalism are Yaakov Ariel, *On Behalf of Israel: American Fundamentalist Attitudes toward Jews, Judaism, and Zionism, 1865–1945* (1991), and David Rausch, *Zionism within Early American Fundamentalism, 1878–1918: A Convergence of Two Traditions* (1979). Works that address Blackstone briefly, but place his career and ideas in a broader historical context, include Paul Boyer, *When Time Shall Be No More: Prophecy Belief in Modern American Culture* (1992), George Marsden, *Fundamentalism and American Culture: The Shaping of Twentieth Century Evangelicalism* (1980), and Timothy P. Weber, *Living in the Shadow of the Second Coming: American Premillennialism, 1875–1925* (1979).

JOHN FEA

BLACKTON, James Stuart (5 Jan. 1875–13 Aug. 1941), motion picture pioneer, was born in Sheffield, England, the son of Henry Blackton, a carriage maker, and Jessie Stuart. After the family moved to the United States in 1886, Blackton worked several years as a carpenter while taking night classes at City College of New York. He then became an illustrator and reporter for the *New York World*. Sent to interview Thomas Alva Edison, Blackton so impressed the "Wizard of Menlo Park" with his drawing skills that the famed inventor asked him to do his "lightning sketches" for Edison's then new Kinetograph camera. An early motion picture, *Blackton, the Evening World Cartoonist* (1896), resulted. Blackton was fascinated by the experience. Almost immediately he purchased a Kinetograph camera from the Edison Company and went into partnership exhibiting films with Alfred E. Smith. In 1897 a third partner, William T. Rock, was added, and their Vitagraph Company began not only to exhibit, but to produce short motion pictures.

Before their involvement with the movies, Blackton and Smith had performed ventriloquism, magic, and magic lantern presentations on the Lyceum circuit. Blackton painted the slides and provided the monologue for the magic lantern show. But with the advent of their new film company, by 1897 Blackton and Smith had added motion pictures to their act. They met with success during the wave of interest in the Spanish-American War with such efforts as *Tearing Down the Spanish Flag* (1898). At first they tried to compile available war movie footage, but, with material hard to obtain, they filmed *The Battle of Manila Bay* on a table and in a homemade water tank in New York City, carefully manipulating photographs, models, gunpowder, and fireworks. They also recorded the New York Naval Parade in August 1898.

Soon, however, Vitagraph got into trouble duplicating Edison films, and rather than fight it became an Edison Company licensee. As the licensor, Edison now charged Vitagraph for making films and demanded that any exhibitor who booked them had to pay Edison an additional charge. For a time this symbiotic relationship thrived so that, by May 1899, Vitagraph was able to properly declare itself one of the largest movie-making concerns in the United States. Success came from films of boxing matches and public celebrations. For example, Vitagraph cameramen recorded Admiral George Dewey's successful return from the Philippines. Such films could be rushed to a theater and fully exploited before the competition could match them. Vitagraph also found success in imitating pioneer French filmmaker Georges Melies's "trick films" and in presenting distinctive comedies, in particular a series of "Happy Hooligan" adventures that starred Blackton.

But Edison wanted a monopoly and tried to shut Vitagraph down, suing for patent violations. As Vitagraph battled Edison in the courts through the first six years of the twentieth century, the Vitagraph company survived by importing films from abroad, especially from France. In the end Edison failed, and in 1906 Vitagraph built a Brooklyn studio and began to expand, free of expensive lawyers' fees. By 1910 Vitagraph was releasing some three reels per week, and establishing itself as a major film producer in the early motion picture business.

But the coming of Hollywood in the 1910s passed Blackton by. He survived the legal assault, but not a revolution in business practice. Despite some success with *The Battle Cry of Peace* (1915) and the filming of stage plays, he ended his movie-making career by trying to succeed as a line producer for pioneering Hollywood giant Famous Players-Lasky. Even with an early color film, *The Glorious Adventure* (1922), the Hollywood system he had helped inspire proved too difficult for him to enter in the early 1920s. Blackton returned to his native England in 1920 and made several films there. Before he turned fifty, however, his career effectively was over.

Blackton married four times: in the early 1890s, Isabelle Mabel MacArthur (two children); in 1908, actress Paula Dean (two children); in 1931, Helen Stahle; and, in 1936, Evangeline Russell, another actress.

When Warner Bros. purchased Vitagraph in 1925, Blackton, then retired, became a rich man, but only temporarily. He lost his entire fortune in the stock market crash of 1929 and finished his life as a minor craftsworker in the industry he had helped create. He died in Los Angeles.

• There are no Blackton papers. Blackton's own writings include "Awake America!," *Theatre*, Sept. 1915, and "The Movies Are Growing Up," *Motion Picture Magazine*, Feb. 1925. A biography by his daughter, Marian Blackton Trimble, *J. Stuart Blackton* (1985), is enlightening. The story of Vitagraph was told by his partner in Alfred E. Smith, with Phil A. Koury, *Two Reels and a Crank* (1952). The history of the Vitagraph Company can be found in *The Big V* by Anthony Slide (1987). The best history of the movies of this period is Charles Musser, *The Emergence of Cinema* (1990).

DOUGLAS GOMERY

BLACKWELDER, Eliot (4 June 1880–14 Jan. 1969), geologist, was born in Chicago, Illinois, the son of Isaac Simeon Blackwelder, a business executive, and Alice Gertrude Boughton, a prominent Chicago clubwoman. Even as a boy, Eliot displayed the inquisitive and orderly mind and the intense love of the natural world that are so evident in his later scientific work. A childhood interest in entomology led to a collection of more than 6,000 specimens of beetles and butterflies. By the age of fifteen his achievements in ornithology earned him membership in the American Ornithological Union, and this early interest in birds and insects continued throughout his life.

At the University of Chicago (1897–1901), a fascination with history inherited from his family plus enjoyable courses in Latin and Greek prompted a first choice of the classics as a probable major. This enthusiasm for classical antiquity remained with Blackwelder in later life, giving him a reputation as an amateur classicist and providing him with fitting quotations from the ancient authors. But in his senior year the brilliant teaching of geologist R. D. Salisbury led him back to his earlier interest in science. After graduation, two summers spent with Salisbury in the Rocky Mountains confirmed his commitment to the profession of geology. Much of his future work was conducted in the mountains and deserts of the American West, first introduced to him during these expeditions with Salisbury.

After graduating, Blackwelder taught geology at the University of Chicago for two years. In 1903 the noted geologist Bailey Willis invited Blackwelder to accompany him on a long trip to China. Together with topographer Harvey Sargent, Blackwelder and Willis took a roundabout path to the Orient by way of Europe and Russia. At numerous stops in Europe Blackwelder made personal contact with many noted geologists, contacts that were to form into the large network of acquaintance with fellow scientists that he maintained around the world. The visit in Europe was followed by an unforgettable voyage eastward on the newly completed trans-Siberian railroad. In China the travelers covered approximately 3,000 miles by foot, pony, boat, and train. The expedition made a profound impression on the young man's mind, giving him a valuable framework of personal and professional experience. Not only the geology but also the lives and social institutions of the people sparked his interest, an interest that remained strong through the later years of political unrest in China.

On returning to America Blackwelder in 1904 married a childhood acquaintance, Jean Bowersock, daughter of a well-known family from Kansas. The couple had seven children. From 1905 to 1916 he was on the faculty of the University of Wisconsin, where he became a full professor at the age of thirty, before earning his doctorate from Chicago in 1914. In 1916 he moved to the University of Illinois as head of its geology department. He was a visiting professor at Stanford University in 1919 but left in the same year for a job with the Argus Oil Company. He returned to an academic post at Harvard after working for two years as a petroleum geologist. In 1922 Blackwelder was invited by Stanford to succeed Bailey Willis as chairman of its geology department. He held this position for twenty-three years, until his retirement in 1945.

Before relocating to Stanford, Blackwelder had spent most summers doing fieldwork with the U.S. Geological Survey in the western states and in Alaska, work that led to the publication of many papers describing the geology of mountains in Wyoming and the glacial geology of the Alaskan coast. This extensive field experience also gave him the necessary background for more general papers on the geologic history of the continent and for some noteworthy shorter articles on a variety of subjects: the geologic behavior of phosphorus, the interpretation of unconformities (breaks in a sequence of sedimentary rocks indicating times when erosion was active), the origin of dolomitic limestone, and the effect of climate on continental sediments. These papers are notable for their clear language, their careful analysis of subjects that at the time were highly controversial, and their consistent marshaling of evidence from field observations to support or discredit theoretical ideas. The papers, although not profound, introduced much elucidation of basic geologic concepts at a time when such elucidation was badly needed.

The wide range of Blackwelder's interest, as shown by the subjects of these early papers, seems remarkable in view of the specialization to which geology, like other sciences, has become subject in more recent years. Geomorphology, the study of landscape forms, then as later, was his major concern; but he wrote lucidly about fossils, climate, structural geology, phosphate deposits, and ancient rocks of the Precambrian era. From his brief experience as a petroleum geologist came perceptive papers on the origin of oil domes and the movement of oil underground. At the early age of thirty-one he coauthored an elementary textbook, *Elements of Geology* (1911), with Harlan H. Brown. The text was unusual in that it tried to encompass the whole field of geology, both its physical and historical aspects.

The new base at Stanford after 1922 gave him an opportunity for research in two directions, which over the years became major emphases of his scientific work: the history of glaciation in the Sierra Nevada and the development of desert landscapes. In the Sierra Nevada, especially on its semiarid and unforested eastern slope, evidence for the advance and retreat of glaciers in the steep valleys during the Ice Age is particularly clear. From study of the debris and erosional forms left by the ice, Blackwelder could distinguish three major times of glacial advance and, less clearly, an earlier fourth stage recorded only by scant debris left on ridge crests. A similar periodic waxing and waning of glacial activity had long been recognized for the ice cap that once covered the north central part of the continent, and Blackwelder faced the problem of developing criteria for timing ice movements that would be applicable in the very different environment of mountain glaciers. The criteria he worked out and tested in the Sierra Nevada he then found useful in deciphering the glacial record in other ranges of the Great Basin and in the Rocky Mountains. Thus he could correlate glacial events over much of the West and more tentatively could suggest relations of these events with the better known chronology of ice movement in the midcontinent. The glacial history of the Sierra Nevada and other western ranges has been greatly refined since Blackwelder's work, but the major sequences of events that he established remain the framework for more recent research.

The peculiarities of erosional and depositional processes in deserts have long fascinated geologists, and Blackwelder's special gifts of keen observation and critical analysis proved well suited to their study. Few aspects of desert topography escaped his attention, but for four contributions he is particularly remembered: demonstrating the fallacy of the then-popular idea that much desert weathering results from day-to-night temperature changes, clarifying the part that wind plays in shaping desert landscape features, emphasizing the number and importance of mudflow deposits in desert sediments, and noting the distinction between broad erosional surfaces (pediments) and depositional surfaces (bajadas) as features of desert plains.

While Blackwelder's emphasis was on mountain glaciation and desert processes, his wide-ranging interests touched many other subjects during the years at Stanford. He marshaled evidence for an impact origin of Meteor Crater in Arizona, worked out details of the history of the great canyon carved by the Colorado River, pointed out the abundant but obscure evidence for the former presence of lakes in many now-dry valleys of the western states, and showed that certain peculiar sedimentary rocks exposed in some western mountains can best be explained as debris left by moving ice in another age of glaciation far back in geologic time. There were papers on earthquakes, landslides, finds of vertebrate fossils, exfoliation of rocks due to

weathering, and the small cliffs produced by movement of bedrock along faults. Some of these have become classics in geologic literature, not because of great originality or depth but more for their clear illumination of subjects that had been previously obscured by controversy.

Besides his involvement in scientific work, Blackwelder had interest in and deep concern for the social and political problems of his time. The great depression that dragged through the 1930s and the ominous events that were then occurring in Europe preyed increasingly on his mind. When in 1940 he needed a subject for his presidential address to the Geological Society of America, he abandoned geology for a topic that permitted him to express some of his social convictions and worries, "Science and Human Prospects." One theme of this address is a forceful expression of the old idea that education is the best cure for the troubles of democracy. This is coupled with worry about the meager training in science received by teachers in schools of education. In Blackwelder's view, a widespread knowledge of science is important because science will increasingly be called on to help solve social and political problems. Without an understanding of science, humanity faces a difficult and uncertain future. Blackwelder was so disturbed by the outbreak of war and the uncertainties of the postwar world that after retirement in 1945 he devoted most of his attention to possible ways of ensuring a durable peace, particularly a proposed political union of the principal democracies. Geologic activity was limited to occasional attendance at meetings, publication of a few abstracts based on earlier work, and preparation of articles for guidebooks and symposium volumes.

Blackwelder was active in many scientific organizations and served as an officer in three: president (1921) of the Geology and Geography Section of the American Association for the Advancement of Science; vice president (1934 and 1939) and president (1940) of the Geological Society of America; and vice president (1945–1946) and president (1947–1949) of the Seismological Society. He was honored by membership in the National Academy of Sciences (elected 1936), the American Philosophical Society, the Geological Society of London, the Geological Society of Belgium, the German Geological Association, and the Geological Society of China.

The last years of his life were troubled with Parkinson's disease, a debilitating illness that slowly undermined his physical strength but left his mind alert and active. To the end he retained an interest in national and international politics, in affairs of the university, in geologic organizations, and in the birds that came to the feeder outside his bedroom window. He died at the Stanford University hospital in Palo Alto.

Blackwelder considered himself primarily a field geologist, and it is certainly by long and careful observation in the field that he made his major contributions to science. His special talents were those of a disciplined observer—the ability to see at once the geologic essentials of a situation, to distinguish the important from the unimportant, and to sense what additional information should be sought in the field or in the laboratory. Added to this was a capacity for clear, direct thinking and for expressing complex ideas in simple language. His genius was not to generate spectacular or revolutionary concepts but patiently, unobtrusively, always with an eye for his own inadequacies, to bring order and good sense into disputed areas of science.

• Blackwelder's papers are preserved in the archives of the Hoover Institution at Stanford University. Scientific results of the expedition to China are described in a three-volume report, *Research in China*, Publication No. 54 of the Carnegie Institution of Washington (1907). His overall description of American geology appears in *Regional Geology of the United States of North America*, published as vol. 8, pt. 2, of the *Handbuch der regionalen Geologie* (1912). A sampling of important papers would include "Exfoliation as a Phase of Rock Weathering," *Journal of Geology* 33 (1925): 793–806; "Precambrian Geology of the Medicine Bow Mountains," *Geological Society of America Bulletin* 37 (1926): 615–58; "Desert Plains," *Journal of Geology* 39 (1931): 133–40; "Pleistocene Glaciation in the Sierra Nevada and Basin Ranges," *Geological Society of America Bulletin* 42 (1931): 865–922; "An Ancient Glacial Formation in Utah," *Journal of Geology* 40 (1932): 289–304; "The Insolation Hypothesis of Rock Weathering," *American Journal of Science* 26 (1933): 97–113; and "The Origin of the Colorado River," *Geological Society of America Bulletin* 45 (1934): 551–66. The sketch of Blackwelder in National Academy of Sciences, *Biographical Memoirs* 48 (1976), contains a complete bibliography.

KONRAD B. KRAUSKOPF

BLACKWELL, Alice Stone (14 Sept. 1857–15 Mar. 1950), women's rights advocate and humanitarian reformer, was born in Orange, New Jersey, the daughter of Henry Browne Blackwell, a hardware merchant, and Lucy Stone, a suffrage leader. Blackwell was surrounded by reform activity from her early childhood on. Both of her parents were prominent suffrage workers and founders of the American Woman Suffrage Association (AWSA). Elizabeth Blackwell, the first American woman to receive a medical degree, and Antoinette Brown Blackwell, the first female ordained minister in the United States, were her aunts, while figures like abolitionist leader and publisher William Lloyd Garrison and women's rights and peace advocate, reformer, lecturer, and writer Julia Ward Howe frequently visited her childhood home.

In 1869 Blackwell's family moved to Dorchester, Massachusetts, a Boston suburb. After completing her education at Boston's Chauncy Hall School, Blackwell enrolled in Boston University, graduating Phi Beta Kappa in 1881. She found immediate employment with the *Woman's Journal*, a women's rights periodical edited and published by her parents. By 1884 her name joined Henry Blackwell's and Lucy Stone's on the paper's masthead, and by the time of her mother's death in 1893, she had assumed almost sole editing responsibility. Blackwell's association with the *Woman's Journal* continued until its 1917 merger with two other papers. From 1887 to 1905 she also served as editor of the *Woman's Column*, a weekly suffrage-oriented broadside that was circulated free to newspapers with the hope that its articles would receive wider circulation. In both publications Blackwell's columns were noted by allies and opponents for their boldness, eloquence, and clarity.

Blackwell also assisted in the reunification of the suffrage movement in the 1880s. First factionalized in 1869 by disputes over the degree to which woman suffrage should remain tied to African-American male suffrage, the movement remained divided into the AWSA, which had retained its social conservatism and abolitionist ties, and Elizabeth Cady Stanton and Susan B. Anthony's more radical National Woman Suffrage Association (NWSA). As a prime negotiator in meetings with Anthony and other NWSA leaders, Blackwell played a considerable role in the 1890 formation of the National American Woman Suffrage Association (NAWSA). She served as the organization's recording secretary for almost twenty years after its founding.

Beginning in the 1890s and continuing throughout the rest of her life, Blackwell devoted herself to a multitude of social and humanitarian causes. She became an active member of organizations ranging from the Women's Trade Union League and the Women's Christian Temperance Union to the Anti-Vivisection League and the National Association for the Advancement of Colored People. She continued to work for women's rights. Believing that women brought a unique moral perspective to politics, Blackwell urged them to retain an independent voice once the franchise was achieved. A founding member of the Massachusetts League of Women Voters, she remained doggedly outside party politics. In 1935 she defended the right of Boston's married women to hold city jobs, denouncing as "a step in the direction of fascism" attempts to reserve the jobs for male candidates (*Boston Traveler*, 6 May 1935).

Blackwell's reform interests also began to take on an international character in the 1890s. After a short romance with an Armenian student, she became passionately involved with the Armenian refugee community. In addition to selling some of her possessions to feed Armenian children and providing job hunting assistance to adults, she discovered the country's literature, producing a collection of translated works, *Armenian Poems* (1896). Over the next forty years her interest in the literature of oppressed populations grew, and she produced pioneering translations of Hungarian, Russian, Yiddish, and Mexican poetry. Russian revolutionaries also attracted Blackwell's support. In 1904 she helped to found the Friends of Russian Freedom. After more than a decade of correspondence with revolutionary Catherine Breshkovsky, Blackwell edited *The Little Grandmother of the Russian Revolution: Reminiscences and Letters of Catherine Breshkovsky* (1914).

Blackwell was disheartened by what she viewed as political oppression in the United States in the wake of World War I. She lectured and wrote frequent letters to the editors of Boston papers on issues including racial discrimination, suppression of civil liberties, and the expulsion of radicals. In politics, Blackwell called herself "a socialist in opinion, but not a party member" (*Boston Post*, 13 May 1935) and threw her support to the Midwestern Non-Partisan League and to Robert La Follette's 1924 presidential campaign. Her support of controversially convicted anarchists Nicola Sacco and Bartolomeo Vanzetti extended to an active correspondence with Vanzetti until his 1927 execution. Throughout these years of activism, Blackwell also dedicated herself to writing a biography of her mother. *Lucy Stone* (1930) was the culmination of nearly four decades of research into the life and work of the woman who had sparked her first reform impulses.

Blackwell never married. After loaning her family home to a series of charities, she lived in a small Dorchester residence until retiring to Cambridge in 1936. In 1935 most of her savings were lost to an unscrupulous business agent. The contributions of thousands of supporters, including Eleanor Roosevelt and Carrie Chapman Catt, sustained her until her death in Cambridge.

• The Library of Congress holds Blackwell's papers and the papers of the NAWSA. Blackwell family papers are also in the Schlesinger Library, Radcliffe College. *Growing up in Boston's Gilded Age: The Journal of Alice Stone Blackwell, 1872–1874*, ed. Marlene Deahl Merrill (1990), reprints a portion of Blackwell's journal from her teenage years and includes a biographical introduction and afterword. Elinor Rice Hays, *Morning Star: A Biography of Lucy Stone* (1961), and Hays, *Those Extraordinary Blackwells* (1967), also provide biographical information. Shannon Smith, "From Relief to Revolution: American Women and the Russian-American Relationship," *Diplomatic History* 19 (Fall 1995): 601–17, explores Blackwell's support of Russian revolutionaries. Obituaries are in the *New York Times*, 16 May 1950, and the *Boston Globe*, 17 May 1950.

KATHLEEN FEENEY

BLACKWELL, Antoinette Louisa Brown (20 May 1825–5 Nov. 1921), minister, reformer, and author, was born in Henrietta, New York, the daughter of Joseph Brown, a farmer and justice of the peace, and Abigail Morse. Antoinette proved a precocious child, following her older siblings to school at the age of three. The preaching of evangelist Charles Grandison Finney in nearby Rochester during the Second Great Awakening deeply affected the family, and before she reached her ninth birthday, Antoinette Brown joined the Congregational church. The associated reform movements of the era—antislavery, temperance, and moral reform—also drew support from the Browns, who upheld the educational aspirations of both their sons and daughters. Antoinette attended local schools and the Monroe Academy before becoming a teacher in 1841.

In 1846 the family acceded to Antoinette's persistent desire to attend Oberlin College, known for its evangelical theology and its principled commitment to the equal education of women and African Americans.

There Brown began a lifelong friendship with Lucy Stone, who encouraged Brown's interest in woman's rights, but, as a radical abolitionist, did not approve of her commitments to orthodox religion and political abolition of slavery.

After receiving her literary degree in 1847, Brown remained at Oberlin for three more years, classified as a "resident graduate" because the faculty refused to allow her regular enrollment in the theology department while she trained for the ministry. Despite widespread opposition to public speaking by women, Brown accepted invitations in Ohio and New York to lecture against slavery and on woman's rights. To answer opponents who wished to exclude women from the pulpit, she completed an exegesis of 1 Corinthians 14:34–35 and 2 Timothy 11–12, published in the *Oberlin Quarterly Review* in July 1849. At commencement in 1850, the faculty refused to recognize Brown's studies and withheld the degree in theology; fearing further controversy, she chose not to seek ordination at that time, determining instead to wait to be ordained in a church for which she held pastoral responsibility.

Brown left Ohio for New York City, where she had been invited to undertake charitable work in the slums and to lecture to raise funds for this cause. But first she traveled to Worcester, Massachusetts, to attend the first National Woman's Rights Convention. Alarmed that their efforts might become associated with Brown's work for the equality of women, the New York supervisors cooled to the proposed arrangement, and Brown decided instead to take up a career as an independent lecturer. She spoke in Pennsylvania, Ohio, and New England on woman's rights, antislavery, and temperance, preaching church sermons on Sundays when invited.

In the fall of 1852 Brown received an invitation from the Congregational church in rural South Butler, New York, to take up its ministry. She accepted this call, turning down an offer from Horace Greeley and Charles H. Dana to support her preaching in New York City. Brown was ordained as minister of the Congregational Church of South Butler on 15 September 1853; on this ceremony rested her claim to be the first woman ordained in a regular Protestant denomination in the United States.

While attending to her pastorate, Brown continued her reform activities, becoming the center of a controversy at the 1853 World's Temperance Convention, where fellow delegates received her credentials but shouted her off the platform, refusing to permit a woman to speak. Growing religious doubts about the basis for her orthodox faith increasingly troubled her, and she resigned her pastorate in July 1854. After some months of rest she returned to New York City, working with Abby Hopper Gibbons for women criminals and prisoners and writing for Horace Greeley's *New York Tribune*. During this time she was courted by fellow reformer Samuel Charles Blackwell. Brown and Blackwell married in 1856.

The year of her marriage, Antoinette Brown Blackwell moved with the extended Blackwell family—many of whom were active in reform movements—from Cincinnati to New York and northern New Jersey. Between 1856 and 1869 she bore seven children; five daughters survived to adulthood. Except for brief periods of lecturing and travel and an interlude in New York City between 1896 and 1901, she resided in various communities in northern New Jersey for the rest of her life.

In 1860 Blackwell became embroiled in the controversy about divorce that engulfed the last national woman's rights convention held before the Civil War. Unlike her colleagues Susan B. Anthony and Elizabeth Cady Stanton, who agitated for easing the grounds on which women might seek divorce, Blackwell argued "that the married partner can not annul his obligations towards the other, while both live. . . . All divorce is naturally and morally impossible, even though we should succeed in annulling all legalities" (Stanton et al., vol. 1, p. 723). She reunited with Anthony and Stanton during the Civil War to found the Women's National Loyal League in support of African-American emancipation and enfranchisement. They argued again, however, in 1869 on the question of support for passage of the Fourteenth Amendment to the Constitution, which granted suffrage to all men irrespective of color but lacked similar guarantees for women. Blackwell joined Lucy Stone to found the American Woman Suffrage Association, which supported the amendment, while Stanton and Anthony's National Woman Suffrage Association opposed its ratification. Despite these political differences, Blackwell generally succeeded in maintaining cordial relationships with Stanton and Anthony for the rest of their lives.

In 1869 Blackwell published her first book, *Studies in General Science*. In it she set forth the outlines of the philosophical projects she pursued in her subsequent work: the reconciliation of natural and revealed religion, the relationship of mind and matter, and the unity of the physical and mental universe joined in an inexorable movement toward harmony. Much influenced by the evolutionary theories of Charles Darwin and Herbert Spencer, she drew on explorations in science to argue for the continued growth of "a perfected system of coöperations in which all sentient and unsentient forces mutually co-work in securing the highest ultimate good . . . by which successive generations . . . of being are mutually aiding each other into higher stages of existence" (p. 252). *The Sexes throughout Nature* (1875) proposed that equality of the sexes was an evolutionary necessity. In *The Physical Basis of Immortality* (1876) she further elaborated on what she viewed as scientific evidence of the "indivisible 'mind-body'" (p. 17), claiming on this basis the unalterable and timeless existence of souls. Her final works, *The Philosophy of Individuality* (1893), *The Making of the Universe* (1914), and *The Social Side of Mind and Action* (1915), further developed these themes, underscoring

the unity of nature accomplished through individual "correlated" actions. She also published a novel, *The Island Neighbors* (1871), and a book of poems, *Sea Drift* (1902).

Blackwell presented her philosophy regularly to a variety of organizations in which she was active. She helped found the Association for the Advancement of Women in 1873 to promote the general betterment of women, and she participated in meetings of the American Association for the Advancement of Science. She spoke regularly at suffrage meetings at the state and national levels and was elected president of the New Jersey Woman Suffrage Association in 1891. She was also active in the founding of the American Purity Association, which supported efforts to prevent state regulation of prostitution and to reform the social relations of the sexes.

In 1878 Blackwell requested and received recognition from the American Unitarian Association as a minister, and for a short time she actively sought a pulpit. The same year Oberlin belatedly recognized her theological studies by granting her an honorary A.M.; in 1908 it presented her with an honorary D.D. After she resettled in New Jersey, she worked with Unitarians in Elizabeth, New Jersey, and made a grant of land for a house of worship. In 1908 the Elizabeth Society recognized her as minister emeritus of All Souls Church.

Blackwell outlived her fellow suffrage pioneers; of all who attended the 1850 Woman's Rights Convention in Worcester, she alone survived to become enfranchised with the passage of the Nineteenth Amendment. She cast her vote in 1920 for Republican presidential candidate Warren G. Harding. She died in Elizabeth, New Jersey.

Blackwell was in the vanguard of antebellum reform, braving opposition to her ministerial career and her antislavery principles and persisting to build on the successes of her causes in the late nineteenth and early twentieth centuries. Synthesizing the evangelical orthodoxies of her childhood, the transcendental and romantic concern for nature, and the evolutionary science popularized by Darwin and Spencer, she built philosophical foundations on which she argued for the equality of the sexes.

• Antoinette Brown Blackwell's life is documented in the Blackwell Family Papers at the Library of Congress, as well as in two collections of Blackwell Family Papers at the Schlesinger Library, Radcliffe College. The Schlesinger collections include a partial typescript of Blackwell's memoirs, assembled and edited by Sarah Gilson. Elizabeth Cazden, *Antoinette Brown Blackwell: A Biography* (1983), is a more complete biography than two popular accounts, Laura Kerr, *Lady in the Pulpit* (1951), which concentrates on her early years, and Elinor Rice Hays, *Those Extraordinary Blackwells* (1967), which places her in the context of her family. Carol Lasser and Marlene Deahl Merrill, eds., *Friends and Sisters: Letters between Lucy Stone and Antoinette Brown Blackwell, 1846–93* (1987), includes the lifetime correspondence of the two reformers. Also useful are accounts in Elizabeth Cady

Stanton et al., *History of Woman Suffrage* (6 vols., 1881–1922). Additional, if unreliable, accounts underscoring the significance of Blackwell to her contemporaries appear in James Parton et al., *Eminent Women of the Age* (1868), and Frances Willard and Mary Livermore, *American Women* (1897).

CAROL LASSER

BLACKWELL, Betsy Talbot (1905?–4 Feb. 1985), fashion editor, was born in New York City, the daughter of Hayden Talbot, a playwright, and Benedict Bristow. After the Talbots were divorced in about 1913, Mrs. Talbot had to find a way to support herself, and her daughter later remembered: "When my mother divorced my father she wasn't trained for anything . . . had never worked . . . didn't have any experience, but what she did have was a flair for fashion. . . . Mother knew fashion and she was fortunate enough to be at the right place at the right time." Benedict Talbot went to work as a fashion stylist for Lord & Taylor department store, setting her daughter an example as a working woman as well as a fashion expert.

Betsy Talbot graduated from the Academy of St. Elizabeth in Convent Station, New Jersey, in 1923 and studied briefly at the College of St. Elizabeth on a part-time basis. During summer vacations she worked at a department store, and upon graduation from high school she obtained a job as a fashion reporter for a New York fashion publication titled the *Breath of the Avenue*. From there she went to *Charm* magazine, moving from assistant to the fashion editor to beauty editor to fashion editor between 1923 and 1931. In her tenure there, she later recalled, she "did everything but set type, and was even sent to Paris for the openings." In 1925 she married Bowden Washington, a radio engineer, whom she later divorced because he disapproved of a working wife, marrying (James) Madison Blackwell III, a Wall Street attorney, in 1930.

After working as advertising manager of Sisholz Brothers department stores in 1931, Blackwell had a baby and worked part time for the Tobe Fashion Service until 1935. In 1933 she volunteered her time for the Woman's Organization for National Prohibition Repeal.

In 1935 she went back to work full time as fashion editor of a new magazine, *Mademoiselle*. (She also served as beauty editor under the name Elizabeth Rich.) Intended as "a sort of junior Vogue," the magazine foundered for its first couple of years under editor Desmond Hall. In 1937 Blackwell stepped in as editor in chief and became, in the words of a *New York Times* profile from 1940, "the editor who raised *Mademoiselle* up from an awkward miss in pigtails." She remained with the magazine until her retirement in 1971, shaping *Mademoiselle* into a widely circulated American publication.

Blackwell pushed fashion to the fore of *Mademoiselle*'s editorial policy, breaking new ground by bringing a Boston nurse in for a glamorous makeover. She courted the college market by instituting an annual college issue written and edited by female college students—Sylvia Plath and Betsy Johnson becoming the most famous—during their summer vacations. She built issues around specific themes, a new strategy for a fashion magazine. The February 1954 issue, for example, dealt only with Welsh poet Dylan Thomas's radio play *Under Milk Wood*.

Blackwell did not consider herself a feminist and laughingly enjoined one reporter, "Please don't call me a career woman." Nevertheless, the magazine—and its editor—always supported working women. She dressed elegantly and was viewed as a mother figure by her staff as the years went by. In the mid-1950s *Mademoiselle* held a workshop about women's "Jobs and Futures" in conjunction with seven women's colleges, publishing the results.

Blackwell's editorial policy encompassed more than fashion and jobs, however. B. T. B., as she was called, threw humor into the *Mademoiselle* pot, publishing cartoons and humorous essays from the start of her editorship. In July 1961 she turned an issue over to the staff of the *Harvard Lampoon*. She also promoted serious writing and writers. Despite its light, youthful image, *Mademoiselle* published William Faulkner, Joyce Carol Oates, Truman Capote, Katherine Anne Porter, Robert Penn Warren, W. H. Auden, Colette, Gore Vidal, and Isaac Bashevis Singer under Blackwell's editorship.

When Blackwell retired in 1971, her colleagues paid tribute to her in a *New York Times* article. Although they dubbed her a "benevolent despot" and generally argued with her politically (the Republican editor was generally far to the right of her staff), her co-workers praised her strength, humor, and willingness to take chances. Betsy Talbot Blackwell died near her home in Connecticut.

• A number of articles focused on Blackwell and her relationship with *Mademoiselle*. *Time* ran "Success in Fashions" on 15 Apr. 1940. *Current Biography* profiled her in 1954. When Blackwell retired, Angela Taylor wrote "At Mademoiselle, Changing of the Guard" for the *New York Times* on 4 Apr. 1971. William P. Rayner, *Wise Women* (1983), devotes a chapter to the editor. Obituaries are in *Newsweek*, 18 Feb. 1985, and in the *New York Times*, 5 Feb. 1985.

TINKY "DAKOTA" WEISBLAT

BLACKWELL, Elizabeth (3 Feb. 1821–31 May 1910), physician, reformer, and medical educator, was born in Bristol, England, daughter of Samuel Blackwell, a prosperous sugar refiner, and Hannah Lane. Her father's interest in abolitionism and in "perfectionist reform," the belief that through education and spiritual regeneration human beings could achieve a just society on earth, coupled with a series of financial reversals, prompted a move to the United States in 1832 when Elizabeth was eleven.

In America the family struggled economically. Elizabeth's beloved father died in 1838 but not without leaving an activist legacy to his children: Elizabeth's brothers supported antislavery and women's rights. Henry married the feminist Lucy Stone, and Samuel wed Antoinette Brown, the first formally ordained woman minister in the United States. A poet and translator, sister Anna also dabbled in spiritualism. No doubt the family's move, shortly before her father's death, to Cinncinati, Ohio, a hotbed of revivalist congregationalism and avid abolitionism, further stimulated Elizabeth's liberal thinking. She formed friendships with a circle of New England Transcendentalists who had settled in the city, remembering most fondly the Reverend W. H. Channing, nephew of the minister Ellery Channing (1780–1842) of Boston and the group's spiritual and moral center.

As a young woman Blackwell struggled to cope with feelings that she viewed as contradictory—a powerful sexual attraction to men and the passionate desire to give purpose and direction to her life. For several years she taught school but had difficulty viewing teaching as her life's work. This period of uncertainty was resolved when a close friend, dying of cancer, urged on her the study of medicine, insisting that the ministrations of a woman physician during this trying time would have provided greater comfort and relief. An epiphany of sorts, this experience changed Blackwell's direction. After a year of reading medicine privately with physician friends in Charleston and Philadelphia, she finally found a school willing to accept her as a student. In 1847 Geneva Medical College in upstate New York admitted Blackwell after a reluctant faculty submitted the decision to a vote of the student body, which answered in the affirmative partially as a practical joke. When she received her medical degree in 1849, Blackwell was the first woman in the United States or Europe in the modern period to do so. Subsequently she attended clinics in London and Paris, studying midwifery at La Maternité for some months until she lost the sight in one eye when she contracted purulent ophthalmia while treating an infant suffering from the disease. Reluctantly giving up her original goal of becoming a surgeon, she returned to New York City in 1851 to hang out her shingle.

The next several years brought initial discouragement and ultimate success. In 1856 Blackwell was joined by her sister, Emily, fresh from studying surgery with James Y. Simpson in Edinburgh, and the talented Marie Zakrzewska, a German immigrant with extensive midwifery training in Berlin who had recently graduated from Western Reserve Medical School. A year later the three founded the New York Infimary for Women and Children, one of several female-run urban institutions being established by freshly minted women physicians. A fine medical school was added to the hospital complex a decade later, one that trained hundreds of women doctors before it merged with Cornell University Medical School in 1899.

Less interested in administration than in the larger implications of the women's medical movement, Blackwell left the management of the school to her sister while she herself emerged as the leading spokesperson for women physicians in the United States and in England, where she settled permanently in 1869. There she involved herself with the British cause,

serving on the executive council and as lecturer in midwifery at the new London School of Medicine for Women in 1875 and 1876.

When her health began to fail in the early 1870s, Blackwell gave up the active practice of medicine and devoted herself full time to reform. Her notion of medical reform was always broadly conceived, and she involved herself in Christian Socialism and Theosophy (intellectual movements emphasizing social justice and mystical-religious insight), the antivivisection movement, and moral and sexual purity. Her speeches and essays on these subjects, as well as on the topic of laboratory medicine, were eventually collected in a two-volume work titled *Essays in Medical Sociology* (1902; repr. 1972).

On the eve of the bacteriological revolution in the 1880s, Blackwell brooded long and hard about the dangers of "medical materialism," a term she used to accuse laboratory physicians of likening the body to a machine and turning real patients into objects. At the core of the new medicine was the "birth of the clinic"—the gathering together of vast patient populations into a hospital system that provided clinicians and students free access to sick bodies for physical examination, observation, the gathering of statistics, and autopsy. Laboratory medicine grew out of such changes and produced a new ideology of science consisting of an acceptance of the germ theory, the identification of specific disease, increasing specialization within medical practice, and a growing willingness to resort to evidence produced in a test tube. Blackwell, on the other hand, had been trained at an earlier time when sickness was viewed not as the specific affliction of a particular part of the body but as a condition affecting the entire organism. Therapy was consequently designed to treat the whole patient, and professional identity itself was embedded in ritualized interactions between doctors and patients during which intuitive and subjective factors were crucial in the diagnosis and treatment of disease. In addition, Blackwell believed there was a social, political, and moral component to illness. Prevention was even more important than cure, and insuring health meant comfortable housing, healthy food, and moral education for all. Indeed, she saw the practice of medicine as an opportunity to bring about fundamental social change.

Blackwell's thinking about medicine was deeply influenced by her conceptions of gender. She framed a discourse about the good practitioner that utilized the nineteenth-century ideology of domesticity, depicting the female qualities of nurturing, empathy, and moral superiority as naturally flowing from the experience of maternity. Motherhood, she claimed, much like the practice of medicine itself, was a "remarkable specialty" because of the spiritual principles that underlay the ordinary tasks most mothers performed daily. These principles she labeled collectively "the spiritual power of maternity," and they informed not only her notions of moral responsibility but her formulations of what constituted good science. Maternity as a force had much in common with the twentieth-century psychologist Erik Erikson's idea of generativity, which he defined as a concern for insuring the healthy moral and physical growth of future generations. Not only physicians but all mankind, Blackwell argued, must learn to harness it.

Blackwell modeled the doctor-patient relationship on the interactions between mother and child, and in doing so she gendered such behavior, though she was careful to assert that it was behavior that men could learn. She went even further in her construction of notions of gender in science by arguing that the new experimental science was too masculine in style, mode of thought, and orientation. She opposed the increased use of gynecological surgery to cure ailments of the female reproductive system, complaining that irresponsible male physicians were rendering women sterile unnecessarily. She blamed bacteriology on the "male intellect" and warned her students against the tyranny of male authority in medicine. Like many of her male colleagues, she was reluctant to deemphasize the importance of physician-patient interaction at the bedside. But although she was not alone in rejecting the new medical materialism or the increasingly reductionist approaches to patient care, she was innovative in using the language of gender to drive home her point. To later generations of women physicians, Blackwell's moralism appeared anachronistic, but we must concede her extraordinary prescience regarding the ambiguous legacy of the new science for the physician-patient relationship.

Blackwell never married, but in October 1854 she adopted a seven-year-old orphan, Katharine Barry, who played the various roles of daughter, companion, housekeeper, and amanuensis, as needed, for the rest of Blackwell's life. Barry often wrote letters for her to Elizabeth's extensive family, to which both remained quite close. Blackwell died in Argyllshire in the Highlands of Scotland.

• Elizabeth Blackwell's papers are in the Library of Congress and the Schlesinger Library, Radcliffe College. Columbia University holds a set of her letters written to the English reformer Barbara Leigh Smith Bodichon. Her autobiography, *Pioneer Work in Opening the Medical Profession to Women* (1895), reprinted in 1914, with a bibliography of her writings and an additional chapter by Robert Cochrane, and again in 1977, without the additions, is a helpful, if biased, source. The best biography of Blackwell remains Nancy Sahli, "Elizabeth Blackwell, M.D. (1821–1910): A Biography" (Ph.D. diss., Univ. of Pennsylvania, 1974). Also available are three popular works: Elinor Rice Hays, *Those Extraordinary Blackwells* (1967), Ishbel Ross, *Child of Destiny* (1944), and Mary St. J. Fancourt, *They Dared to Be Doctors: Elizabeth Blackwell, Elizabeth Garrett Anderson* (1965). See also Annie Sturgis Daniel, "'A Cautious Experiment': The History of the New York Infirmary for Women and Children and the Women's Medical College of the New York Infirmary," *Medical Woman's Journal* 46–48 (May 1939–Dec. 1942). For a list of the numerous short biographical sketches of Blackwell, see Sandra Chaff et al., *Women in Medicine: A Bibliography* (1977). Specific references to Blackwell are also in Regina Morantz, "Feminism, Professionalism and Germs: The Thought of Mary Putnam Jacobi and Elizabeth Blackwell,"

American Quarterly 34 (Winter 1982): 461–78, and Regina Morantz-Sanchez, "Feminist Theory and Historical Practice: Rereading Elizabeth Blackwell," *History and Theory* 31 (Dec. 1992): 50–69.

REGINA MORANTZ-SANCHEZ

BLACKWELL, Emily (8 Oct. 1826–7 Sept. 1910), physician and medical educator, was born in Bristol, England, the daughter of Samuel Blackwell, a prosperous sugar refiner, and Hannah Lane. Her father moved his family to the United States when Emily was five, primarily because of his interest in abolitionism, perfectionism, and reform. Although Samuel died in 1838, his children inherited his activist legacy: Elizabeth Blackwell, Emily's older sister, was the first woman to receive a medical degree (1849) in the United States or Europe; her brothers, Henry Blackwell and Samuel Blackwell, supported antislavery and women's rights. The former married the feminist Lucy Stone, and the latter wed Antoinette Brown, the first formally ordained woman minister in the United States. Sister Anna became a poet and translator who dabbled in spiritualism. Perhaps the family's move in 1844 to Cincinnati, Ohio, where they lived on the grounds of Lane Theological Seminary and developed friendships with radical evangelicals like Henry Ward Beecher and Harriet Beecher Stowe, further stimulated the children's liberal thinking.

Much like her sister, Emily cast about for work that would give purpose and direction to her life. In 1851 she wrote in her diary that she had "reached the age for action, for great deeds." Despite painful doubts, she followed her sister into medicine and, like Elizabeth, paid for her education through teaching. She first read medicine in 1848 with Dr. John Davis, demonstrator in anatomy at the Medical College of Cincinnati, and, after being rejected from eleven medical schools, including Geneva Medical College, the institution that had conferred a degree on Elizabeth in 1849, she finally won acceptance to Rush Medical College in Chicago in 1852. But when the state medical association censured the school's trustees for admitting a woman, Rush refused to allow Emily to return to complete her second term. Instead, she received her M.D., graduating with honors in 1854, from Western Reserve Medical School, which had recently opened its doors to women.

Blackwell spent her next two years in postgraduate education in Europe, where she studied surgery with Sir James Y. Simpson, already renowned for his use of chloroform in childbirth. Impressed with her surgical skill, he helped her win entry into clinics in Paris, London, Berlin, and Dresden, where she spent another year gaining valuable medical experience. In 1856 she returned to New York to join Elizabeth and Dr. Marie Zakrzewska, another graduate of Western Reserve, in expanding the little dispensary Elizabeth had established into a full-fledged hospital—the still extant New York Infirmary for Women and Children. A decade later came the hospital's medical school for women (1868), an institutional showcase that trained hundreds of female physicians before it merged with Cornell University Medical College in 1899. For thirty years Blackwell served as the school's dean and professor of obstetrics and diseases of women. She oversaw many of the school's curricular innovations—a required three-year graded course; a board of examiners consisting of some of the most distinguished male physicians in the city; the first course in hygiene (preventive medicine) offered anywhere in the country; and obligatory hospital residence or medical work, under the supervision of various clinics, for all candidates for graduation. Only a handful of medical schools could boast of such high standards in the 1870s. Because Blackwell was also respected for her surgical skill, the supporters of women physicians were disappointed in 1863 when J. Marion Sims passed over her and appointed a man to the position of assistant surgeon at the new Woman's Hospital of New York.

One of the leading female medical educators in the nineteenth century, Emily Blackwell's achievements have too often been overshadowed by those of her more outspoken sister. Modest and shy, but a woman of extraordinary dignity, she ran the hospital and medical school with intelligence and skill, especially after Elizabeth settled permanently in England in 1869. In addition, she proved an outstanding role model for a number of her students, who spoke of her with appreciation and respect. Recalled Dr. Sara Josephine Baker, one of her more famous protégés, "She inspired us all with the vital feeling that we were still on trial and that, for women who meant to be physicians, no educational standards could be too high."

Emily Blackwell never married, but she lived for over eighteen years in a "Boston marriage" with Dr. Elizabeth Cushier, a graduate of the New York Infirmary and a skilled gynecological surgeon. Blackwell adopted a daughter, who remained close to her mother throughout adulthood and whose own four children cherished and were cherished by their grandmother. Emily Blackwell died in the summer home that she shared with Cushier in York Cliffs, Maine, only three months after the death of her sister Elizabeth.

• The Blackwell family papers can be found in the Library of Congress, Columbia University, and the Radcliffe Women's Archives. Emily Blackwell's diary and letters to Barbara Bodichon are at Columbia. See also Elizabeth and Emily Blackwell, *Medicine as a Profession for Women* (1860), and Emily Blackwell, "Women in the Regular Medical Profession," *Report of the Association for the Advancement of the Medical Education of Women* (1878). There are a number of personal reminiscences of Emily Blackwell, many to be found in the New York Academy of Medicine, *In Memory of Dr. Elizabeth Blackwell and Dr. Emily Blackwell* (1911); see also three articles by Alice Stone Blackwell in the *Woman's Journal*, 6 Oct. 1906, and 10 and 17 Sept. 1910; several pieces in the *Woman's Medical Journal*, Apr. 1911; Annie Sturges Daniel, "'A Cautious Experiment,' The History of the New York Infirmary for Women and Children and the Woman's Medical College of the New York Infirmary," *Medical Woman's Journal*, May 1939–Dec. 1942; and Elise S. L'Esperance, "Influence of the New York Infirmary on Women in Medicine," *Journal of the American Medical Women's Association*, June 1949. Helpful as well are Frances E. Willard and Mary A. Livermore, eds., *American Women* (1897); Howard A. Kelly, *A Cyclopaedia of American Medical Biography* (1912); and Elizabeth H. Thomson's thorough entry in *Notable American Women* (1971). Obituaries can be found in the *New York Times*, 9 Sept. 1910, and *Lancet*, 24 Sept. 1910. In addition, Elizabeth B. Thelberg, ed., "Autobiography of Dr. Elizabeth Cushier," *Medical Review of Reviews*, Mar. 1933; Ishbel Ross, *Child of Destiny* (1919); and Elinor Rice Hays, *Those Extraordinary Blackwells* (1967), all have information on Emily Blackwell. For historical context, consult Elizabeth Blackwell, *Pioneer Work in Opening the Medical Profession to Women* (1895), and Regina Markell Morantz-Sanchez, *Sympathy and Science: Women Physicians in American Medicine* (1985).

REGINA MORANTZ-SANCHEZ

BLACKWELL, Henry Browne (4 May 1825–7 Sept. 1909), social reformer, editor, and entrepreneur, was born in Bristol, England, the son of Samuel Blackwell, a sugar refiner and antislavery reformer, and Hannah Lane. After business reversals the family moved in 1832 to New York, where their household became a haven for abolitionists, women's rights advocates, and self-emancipated slaves. In 1838 the debt-ridden Blackwells moved to Cincinnati, Ohio. When his father died a few months later, thirteen-year-old Henry went to work to support the family, initially as a clerk in a flour mill. In 1845 he joined the two illiterate millers as a partner, and two years later his brother made him a partner in a hardware firm. Within a few years the enterprising Henry ("Harry" to his friends) had his finger in many economic pies—among them an agricultural publishing firm, land speculation, and sugar beet production (perhaps after his father, who had sought an alternative to slave-based sugar cane). At the same time Harry moved to the forefront of women's rights agitation and abolitionism.

During this period Blackwell's quirks and character flaws emerged—among them his rashness, poor judgment, short attention span, and loathing of detail. In the land speculation enterprises, his inept bookkeeping and surveying resulted in lawsuits, while the hardware company steadily lost money. Around 1853 Blackwell decided to move east in a futile attempt to persuade a publisher to print his poetry; he also sought a "lady with a purpose, a character and a fortune." During this whirlwind wife-hunt several women rejected him. Blackwell's sister Elizabeth later compared him to a "comet that has not found its centre and goes wandering wildly through space."

But ultimately Blackwell did find a suitable woman. In 1853 he was elected secretary of the Fourth National Women's Rights Convention in Massachusetts. There he heard one of reformer Lucy Stone's brilliant speeches, from which she earned a handsome income, and he resolved to marry her. Within an hour of their first private meeting he proposed, but she refused. For months after, they exchanged long, searching letters. Stone feared marriage and distrusted Harry's principles, yet she had fallen in love. She began to loan him large sums of money and engaged him to manage her assets. On 1 May 1855, despite family members' misgivings, the pair were married at the Stone family home in Massachusetts.

At the ceremony the couple read their now-famous Wedding Protest (later printed in newspapers) in which Blackwell agreed to "*renounce* all the privileges which the law confers on me, which are not strictly *mutual*," to grant Stone full control over her own body, and to allow her to live wherever she wished. Against law, Stone retained her birthname, and the couple jointly condemned the husband's "custody of the wife's person," his "exclusive control and guardianship of their children," a man's "absolute right to the product of her industry" and a woman's property, and "the whole system" by which woman's identity vanished at marriage.

Thereafter, Blackwell came to be known mainly for his advocacy of women's rights, though his financial mismanagement continued to overshadow his activism. In April 1857, partly to protect their future children against poverty, Stone bought a cottage in Orange, New Jersey. Meanwhile, they traversed the country, both separately and together, to secure black freedom and votes for women. During this time, Blackwell moved restlessly between Chicago and New England. He took work with an agricultural book publishing company only to become dissatisfied; he then returned to a bookkeeping position in New York that held his attention only briefly. In September 1857 Stone and Blackwell celebrated the birth of their only child, Sarah (later called Alice), in New York. Soon after, Blackwell left for Chicago to resume work with the publishing company, leaving his wife with the newborn child.

Gradually the marriage foundered. Blackwell's speculations depleted family resources, and he began to yearn for a traditional home, admonishing Stone to live with him, mend his stockings, and accept primary responsibility for parenting. He also objected when she re-entered the lecture circuit. In early 1859, after months of temporary lodging and illness, Stone learned that she was again pregnant; the couple returned to New Jersey, where the child died. By 1860 Blackwell had opened real estate offices in both Orange and New York City. Financial exigency temporarily eased in 1862 when he accepted a clerkship in Ludlow Patton's brokerage firm. He moved into a New York City boarding house; Stone joined him. But because Blackwell still craved wealth and status, he often continued to speculate in lunatic schemes. Privately, Stone decried his "imperfect character, his imprudence," and his "restless unsatisfied aspirations."

While the couple periodically lived apart, their deep affection for each other and mutual commitment to social reform endured. During the Civil War they championed black suffrage and unionism. In 1869 after Blackwell's public infatuation with a mysterious "Mrs. P," Stone returned to public lecturing and procured separate lodgings in Boston. Blackwell may well have chafed under his wife's superior oratorical and breadwinning skills; whatever their differences, during these years Elizabeth Blackwell, along with many others, could say "nothing good about Harry."

Only in 1870 did Blackwell begin to right himself. Not only had Stone delivered an ultimatum, but they had also decided to establish a woman suffrage paper, the *Woman's Journal*. Blackwell divided his time between reform activities and doomed speculations; in one year alone he lost more than $20,000. But he assumed full responsibility for the *Journal* when Stone's work required long absences. The couple devoted much energy and money to aiding the badly divided woman suffrage movement in its state-by-state campaigns. They persisted even when their home (called "Pope's Hill") burned to the ground in 1871.

By 1871–1872 Stone had become the main editor of the *Journal* because Blackwell's businesses often took him to remote locations for long periods. During late Reconstruction both contributed mightily to the cause of woman suffrage. Ever the "loving warriors," they attended suffrage convocations to rouse audiences and raise money. In 1872 and each year thereafter, Blackwell labored to persuade Republican convention delegates to include a woman suffrage plank in party platforms, and during the depression of 1873 Blackwell and Stone published and mailed thousands of suffrage pamphlets. Meanwhile, at a rebuilt Pope's Hill the pair seemed to have settled into a comfortable domesticity, punctuated by travel.

By 1876–1877, however, Blackwell opened another sugar beet operation in Santo Domingo (which collapsed in 1878) and became infatuated with Colorado, while Stone decided to stay at Pope's Hill. In 1878–1879 he persuaded friends to sink over $100,000 in yet another ill-starred sugar venture, and by 1880 he had moved to Maine in a desperate effort to save the firm. He urgently suggested that Stone convert more property to his use, but she demurred, and he fell into one of his frequent depressions.

On the reform circuit Blackwell and other progressives sometimes resorted to expedient, racist arguments for woman suffrage. In 1867, for instance, he addressed a conciliatory essay to southern legislators, proposing in "What the South Can Do . . ." that southerners maintain white supremacy by enfranchising kindred women—that is, by "utilizing the intelligence and patriotism" of white southern "wives and daughters" to counteract black male ballots. At the same time he substantially advanced liberal causes. In 1869 he and Stone helped create the American Woman Suffrage Association—a group that agreed (in contrast to the National Woman Suffrage Association, which demanded black *and female* equality) to set "the woman question" aside long enough to secure black male freedom. Through the vehicle of the *Journal* they fanned the flames of reform into the twentieth century. They also organized grassroots campaigns for woman suffrage in Wisconsin, Nebraska, Kansas, Colorado, and other emerging states.

In 1889–1890, with Stone in ill health, Blackwell worked alone in North and South Dakota, Montana, and Washington; as conventions met to draft state constitutions, he lobbied for woman suffrage articles, and, failing that, for revised election laws. As of 1889 he was the only easterner working steadily in the West for women's rights. Still later he protested political atrocities, such as the Armenian massacre of 1895 and Russian pogroms, and championed political refugees. In his final years he developed an interest in economic relations with Canada, exemplified by *Reciprocity, a Republican Issue* (1904).

The high-minded, profligate Blackwell embodied both the glories and shortcomings of the early republic. Andrea Moore Kerr rightly concludes that, while he exhibited "a boundless idealism, a commitment to reform," and a "passion for politics," he also evinced an obsessive "desire for wealth, a preoccupation with . . . social superiority," recurring "moral myopia," and a "tendency to play fast and loose with the truth." He was a "would-be robber baron with a passion for the downtrodden," a "Don Quixote in pursuit of the City of Gold," and coarchitect of a tempestuous marriage notable, then as now, for its radical insistence upon gender equality. Perhaps ironically, when he died at Dorchester, Massachusetts, a decade before federalization of woman suffrage, Blackwell was serving without pay as editor of the *Woman's Journal*.

• The Library of Congress, Manuscripts Division, houses the Blackwell Family Papers; additional material can be found at the Arthur and Elizabeth Schlesinger Library, History of Women in America. Published primary sources include Leslie Wheeler, ed., *Loving Warriors: Selected Letters of Lucy Stone and Henry B. Blackwell, 1853–1893* (1981), and Carol Lasser and Marlene Deahl Merrill, eds., *Friends and Sisters: Letters between Lucy Stone and Antoinette Brown Blackwell, 1846–1893* (1987). Blackwell's writings in the *Woman's Journal*, from 1870 until his death, are also instructive. For scattered information, see Elinor Rice Hays, *Those Extraordinary Blackwells: The Story of a Journey to a Better World* (1967); Ellen DuBois, *Feminism and Suffrage: The Emergence of an Independent Women's Movement in America, 1848–1869* (1978); documents reprinted in Aileen S. Kraditor, ed., *Up from the Pedestal* (1968); and especially Andrea Moore Kerr, *Lucy Stone: Speaking Out for Equality* (1992), which provides detail about Harry Blackwell and the marriage. Obituaries are in the *Woman's Journal*, 11 Sept. 1909, and the *Boston Transcript*, the *Boston Post*, and the *Boston Daily Globe*, all 8 Sept. 1909.

DEBRA VILES
SANDRA F. VANBURKLEO

BLACKWELL, Randolph Talmadge (10 Mar. 1927–21 May 1981), attorney, educator, and civil rights activist, was born in Greensboro, North Carolina, the son of Joe Blackwell and Blanche Mary Donnell. He attended the city's public schools for African-American youth and earned a B.S. in sociology from North Carolina Agricultural and Technical University in Greensboro in 1949. Four years later Blackwell earned a J.D. degree from Howard University in Washington, D.C. In December 1954 he married Elizabeth Knox. The couple had one child. After teaching economics for a year at Alabama Agricultural and Mechanical College in Normal, Alabama, near Hunts-

ville, Blackwell became an associate professor of social sciences at Winston-Salem State Teachers College in North Carolina.

Because of his legal background, Wiley Branton, the director of the Voter Education Project (VEP), hired Blackwell as its field director in 1962. Secretly encouraged by the Kennedy administration, VEP was launched in April 1962 with funding from private foundations. Sheltered under the tax-exempt status of the Southern Regional Council, its purpose was to encourage voter registration among African Americans throughout the South by regranting funds to civil rights organizations to underwrite their voter registration efforts. In Mississippi, where only five percent of eligible black adults were registered, the prospect of funding from VEP encouraged the civil rights organizations to establish the Council of Federated Organizations (COFO) in order to coordinate voter registration efforts among African Americans. Faced with threats, the possibility of being jailed, beatings, bombings, or even death at the hands of determined white opposition, voter registration workers produced only 3,228 newly registered black voters in 1962, despite $50,000 worth of funding from VEP.

On 28 February 1963, eight days after an arsonist torched four black businesses in order to destroy COFO's voter registration office in Greenwood, Mississippi, Blackwell met with COFO organizers there. Jimmy Travis, a COFO worker, reported that three white men in a Buick with no license plates had staked out the COFO office. He then drove Blackwell and civil rights activist Robert Moses out of Greenwood toward Greenville. The Buick followed them. Seven miles out of Greenwood, white night riders pulled up beside them and fired on their car. Hit in both the shoulder and the back of his neck, Travis slumped into Moses's lap as he pulled the car to a halt. Two days later doctors at a Jackson hospital removed a bullet from his spine. Branton quickly wired Attorney General Robert Kennedy with a demand for "immediate action by the federal government" in Greenwood. An appeal to Martin Luther King Jr.'s Southern Christian Leadership Conference (SCLC) brought trained voter education workers to Greenwood for citizenship education classes. Blackwell revisited Greenwood in March 1963 and found twenty to thirty people working in the COFO office, helping with canvassing and voter registration, organizing clothing and food distribution, coordinating youth work, arranging both mass meetings and Sunday speaking engagements, and establishing citizenship schools.

When Wyatt Tee Walker left the staff of the SCLC in July 1964, Andrew Young became his successor, and Blackwell succeeded Young as program director. One of the few laymen to serve on SCLC's executive staff, Blackwell attempted to restructure the organization by employing various administrative techniques in order to establish clear lines of authority, thus avoiding the confusion and antagonism that previously permeated SCLC. Blackwell suggested separating the organization into specific departments with designated department heads who reported to Blackwell, who in turn answered to Young. The proposal had little effect, as charismatic preachers on the executive staff vied for control of the field staff and resented having to answer to anyone but King.

Blackwell was SCLC's program director during the Alabama voting rights campaign that led to the Selma to Montgomery march. After marchers were attacked at Selma's Edmund Pettus Bridge on "Bloody Sunday," 7 March 1965, Blackwell sent out two hundred telegrams in King's name inviting religious leaders from across the nation to join him for the march from Selma. By 9 March 450 white clergymen had gathered in Selma for the march to Montgomery. However, after the march Blackwell found little enthusiasm in black Selma for SCLC's continued presence there because of its staff's poor relationships with local community leaders.

In addition to fighting such external battles as the one in Selma, Blackwell was also plagued by internal battles within SCLC. Blackwell doubted the capacity of SCLC executive staff member Hosea Williams to manage its VEP-funded Southern Community Organization and Political Education (SCOPE) project in the summer of 1965. Later, his worst fears were confirmed by SCOPE's incompetence, by Williams's misconduct and mismanagement, and by the incredible waste of the organization as a whole. Blackwell accused Williams of "empire building" and begged King to end the program immediately. "It has cost freedom contributors ten times what it should have," Blackwell wrote. "The operation has raised suspicion of financial dishonesty." Later, Blackwell told King that "the conflict between myself and Mr. Williams . . . goes to the bottom of the philosophy of the organization. It raises in a very serious way the question of whether we can at this point develop the structural discipline needed" (Fairclough, p. 269). Although Blackwell agreed with Williams that SCLC should maintain its focus on the South rather than open a campaign in a major northern city like Chicago, by October he was talking about leaving SCLC. In February 1966 the conflict with Williams was so intense that he appealed to King for the resolution of a whole series of issues within the organization, and by August of that year, Blackwell had taken a leave of absence. As SCLC staff turmoil worsened after Blackwell's departure, King regretted not having dealt with his complaints, fearing that he would not return to the SCLC staff. As late as June 1967, SCLC's Septima Clark urged King to bring Blackwell back to the organization to ease his personal burdens and to bring more discipline to the staff.

When Blackwell left SCLC in 1966, he founded Southern Rural Action, Incorporated, an organization based in Atlanta that sought to develop black businesses and economic cooperatives. He was the director of this organization until 1977, when he became the director of the Department of Commerce's Office of Minority Business Enterprise in Washington, D.C. In 1979 Blackwell returned to Atlanta as director of the Office of Minority Enterprise Program and Develop-

ment. He remained in that position until his death from cancer in Atlanta. A recipient of the Martin Luther King, Jr., Peace Prize in 1976, Blackwell was also a member of the board of directors of the Martin Luther King, Jr., Center for Nonviolent Social Change and Southern Rural Action.

• The Randolph Blackwell Papers are at the Martin Luther King, Jr., Center for Nonviolent Social Change, Inc., Atlanta, Ga. Useful secondary sources on Blackwell's career in the civil rights movement are Steven F. Lawson, *Black Ballots: Voting Rights in the South, 1944–1969* (1976); David J. Garrow, *Bearing the Cross: Martin Luther King, Jr., and the Southern Christian Leadership Conference* (1986); Adam Fairclough, *To Redeem the Soul of America: The Southern Christian Leadership Conference and Martin Luther King, Jr.* (1987); and Thomas R. Peake, *Keeping the Dream Alive: A History of the Southern Christian Leadership Conference from King to the Nineteen-Eighties* (1987). See also Taylor Branch, *Parting the Waters: America in the King Years, 1954–1963* (1988); John Dittmer, *Local People: The Struggle for Civil Rights in Mississippi* (1994); and Charles M. Payne, *I've Got the Light of Freedom: The Organizing Tradition and the Mississippi Freedom Struggle* (1995). Obituaries are in the *Atlanta Constitution*, 22 May 1981, and the *New York Times*, 23 May 1981.

RALPH E. LUKER

BLAIK, Red (15 Feb. 1897–6 May 1989), college football coach, was born Earl Henry Blaik in Detroit, Michigan, the son of William Douglas Blaik, a real estate agent and housebuilder, and Margaret Jane Purcell. The family moved to Dayton, Ohio, in 1901, where at Steele High School Blaik lettered in football, basketball, and baseball. From 1914 to 1917 Blaik attended Miami University of Ohio, where he was a pre-law student and played four years of varsity football, starting at right end on teams that were undefeated in their 1916 and 1917 Ohio Conference championship seasons. In his senior year Blaik gained his first coaching experience under head coach George L. Rider, who had Blaik supervise the ends and tackles. Blaik also played basketball, and he won three letters as an outfielder on the baseball team, which he captained in 1917. He received an A.B. degree from Miami in 1918.

Blaik received an appointment to the U.S. Military Academy in 1918. At West Point he played end in football, left field in baseball, and center-forward in basketball. In 1919 he was named a third-team end on Walter Camp's All-America team, and he received West Point's Athletic Saber Award for the outstanding athlete in his class, in which he ranked 108th out of 271 graduating seniors.

At Fort Bliss, pursuing an army career, Blaik coached the post football team and played quarterback. He found promotion in the peacetime army too slow, however, and resigned his commission in March 1922. He returned to Dayton, where a year later he joined his father in the contracting business. In October 1923 he married Merle McDowell. They had two sons, the youngest of whom, Robert, played for Blaik at West Point and later became a college football assistant coach.

In 1926 Blaik served as an assistant coach at the University of Wisconsin under George Little, his coach at Miami. In 1927 Blaik returned to West Point as a part-time assistant in charge of the passing game and scouting. When the head coach at West Point resigned in 1932, Blaik was the logical choice for the job, but he was rejected because, by tradition, only a graduate who was an officer on regular duty could hold the position. He served one more season as an assistant coach.

At age thirty-seven, in 1934, Blaik took over a losing program at Dartmouth College and led the team to a 6–3 record that autumn. In the fourth game of the 1936 season Dartmouth began a 22-game unbeaten streak (with two ties) that lasted until the eighth game of 1938 with a 14–7 loss to Cornell. In seven seasons at Dartmouth, Blaik coached teams that compiled a 45–15–4 record and won unofficial Ivy League championships in 1936 and 1937. He and his assistants emphasized physical and mental toughness, pride in excellence, and the creation of spirited rivalries. He devised a "contain" defense at Dartmouth in which defenders did not charge the line of scrimmage but detected a play's direction and moved toward the ball carrier, thus holding the offense to short gains.

In 1941, Blaik returned to West Point to rebuild a declining program. He brought his Dartmouth assistants with him, and they instituted a demanding system of playbook study, practices, film study of games, and analysis and application of scouting reports. The players responded with a 5–3–1 record in 1941, including a 0–0 tie against highly ranked Notre Dame. After a 6–3 season in 1942, Blaik switched from the single wing to a T-formation offense to take advantage of the halfback speed and elusive running of Glenn Davis and other backs. The team compiled a 7–2–1 record in 1943, but Blaik suffered his third consecutive loss to the U.S. Naval Academy, Army's chief rival.

By 1944, however, Blaik's team had learned the T-formation system, and he had the experienced manpower to use different offensive and defensive units. The 1944 Army team went undefeated in nine games, with Army beating Navy 23–7 to decide the national championship. The 1944 team claimed the Eastern Champion Lambert Memorial Trophy, had six All-America selections, and featured the nation's collegiate scoring leader with halfback Davis, who tallied 120 points. The team totaled 504 points and gave up only 35, with no opponent scoring more than one touchdown.

In 1945, Army repeated as national champions with another 9–0–0 record and eight All-America selections, including the tandem of Davis and fullback Felix "Doc" Blanchard, popularly known as "Mr. Outside" and "Mr. Inside," respectively. Blanchard was awarded the Heisman Trophy, Maxwell Cup, Walter Camp Trophy, and Sullivan Award. The 1944 national championship began for Blaik's Army teams a remarkable seven years, in which they posted a 57–3–4 record and had undefeated strings of 32 and 28 games.

After consecutive national championships, the 1946 Army team finished 8–0–1, ranked second nationally behind Notre Dame, a team they tied 0–0. Blaik was named Coach of the Year for 1946 by the American Football Coaches Association, and he became director of athletics at West Point that year and chairman of the athletic board in 1949. Between 1944 and 1950, Blaik's Army teams had five undefeated seasons and claimed five Lambert trophies as Eastern champions. His approach was based on conditioning for speed and quickness, constant drilling and study for precision execution, effective use of players within the two-platoon system, and innovative variations of the T-formation offense.

During the 1951 season West Point was hit by a cheating scandal in which the tradition of the strict honor system was violated. Ninety cadets were expelled, including sixty varsity athletes, thirty-seven of whom were football players. Blaik's son, who played quarterback for the 1950 team, was one of those expelled. Blaik offered to resign, but he was persuaded to stay on. In his autobiography, *You Have to Pay the Price* (1960), he stated his belief that the ninety cadets expelled were "scapegoats" who took the blame for a mismanaged and overly demanding honor system.

Blaik's undermanned teams went 2–7 in 1951 and 4–4–1 in 1952 but came back with a 7–1–1 record in 1953 and were Eastern champions. In each of his last six seasons his teams had winning records. In 1958 Army was 8–0–1 and third-ranked nationally. On 13 January 1959 he resigned after eighteen years, with an overall coaching record of 166–48–14. He joined the Avco Corporation as a vice president and management board member and wrote weekly football articles for the Associated Press. In 1960 he became chairman of the executive committee and director of Avco.

In 1959, Blaik was elected to the College Football Hall of Fame, and in 1966 he received the National Football Foundation's Gold Medal Award. In 1974 he published a second autobiography, *The Red Blaik Story*, and after his retirement in the early 1980s he moved to Colorado Springs, Colorado. In May 1986 President Ronald Reagan presented him with the Presidential Medal of Freedom. Throughout his career Blaik was an effective proponent and defender of big-time collegiate football. He emphasized football's "showcase value" and its positive effect on undergraduate morale, its revenue-producing support of other intercollegiate sports, and its character-building value to participants. He died in Colorado Springs.

• Blaik's personal papers and military service records are located at the U.S. Military Academy, Alumni Records, Association of Graduates, West Point, N.Y. His coaching career is covered in Tim Cohane, *Great College Football Coaches of the Twenties and Thirties* (1973); Allison Danzig, *The History of American Football: Its Great Teams, Players, and Coaches* (1956); the chapters on Doc Blanchard, Glenn Davis, and Pete Dawkins in Dave Newhouse, *Heismen: After the Glory* (1985); Tom Perrin, *Football: A College History* (1987); and Edwin Pope, *Football's Greatest Coaches* (1956). Of the many periodical articles on Blaik, the best include Dave Camerer,

"The Toughest Coaching Job: Red Blaik Tackles the Army," *Saturday Evening Post*, 11 Oct. 1941; Marshall Smith, "Blaik and Son," *Look*, Oct. 1950; David B. Tinnin, "Head Master of Football Retires," *Sports Illustrated*, 26 Jan. 1959; and Stanley Woodward, "The Man behind the Army Team," *Sport*, Nov. 1950. Henry E. Maddox's *Army Football in 1945: Anatomy of a Championship Season* (1990) is a detailed study of what Maddox contends was the best college football team of all time.

DOUGLAS A. NOVERR

BLAIKIE, William (24 May 1843–6 Dec. 1904), physical fitness advocate, was born in York (Livingston County), New York, the son of Alexander Blaikie, a minister, and Nancy King. At an early age Blaikie moved to Boston with his family. He attended public schools there, graduating in 1862 from the Boston Latin School, where he captained the football team. He completed his formal education at Harvard University, earning a B.A. in 1866 and an LL.B. with honors in 1868.

A well-rounded athlete, Blaikie overcame tuberculosis in 1860 through vigorous outdoor exercises. His passion for physical activity led to his successful athletic career at Harvard, primarily in rowing. He was part of the first sophomore crew that captured first place at the Harvard Regatta, and in his senior year he captained the crew to victory over archrival Yale. But his contribution to rowing came more as a coach than as an oarsman. He traveled to England to study British rowing techniques and training regimens, which at that time were superior to American methods. On returning, he taught the British system to the Harvard crew. His approach to the sport enabled Harvard to dominate American rowing during the late 1860s and early 1870s.

In 1869 Blaikie accompanied the Harvard crew to London for a highly publicized challenge race against Oxford, which had the world's finest rowers. In addition to coaching the Harvard oarsmen, he was the correspondent to the *New York Herald* and starter of the race. Oxford easily won this first international intercollegiate race, which, to Englishmen and Americans alike, had become a symbol of cultural nationalism. The results, immediately transmitted via the newly laid transatlantic cable, dampened American pride.

Blaikie practiced law with private firms in Boston and New York City. He left Boston for Washington, D.C., in 1869 to serve as chief of the pardon bureau in the office of the U.S. attorney general. He then served as assistant U.S. attorney for the southern district of New York from 1870 until 1872. Thereafter, he returned to private practice in New York City. In 1872 he married Isabella Stuart Briggs of Harrisburg, Pennsylvania, with whom he had six children before her death in 1887. His second marriage, to Rebecca Wynne Scott of Elk Horn, Kentucky, took place in 1891.

An avid physical fitness advocate, Blaikie promoted exercise and physical education through his actions and writings. As a seventeen-year-old weighing 133 pounds, he had astonished the fitness world by lifting 1,019 pounds. He also held the long distance walking record for ten years when he covered 225 miles from Boston to New York in four and one-half days. He wrote numerous articles on exercise and athletic topics for newspapers and magazines along with two books, *How to Get Strong and How to Stay So* (1879) and *Sound Bodies for Our Boys and Girls* (1883). *How to Get Strong* underwent many printings, the last in 1902. Largely a treatise on Blaikie's concept that a strong body was the key to success for everyone, it was popular in both the United States and Europe. Physical fitness, the book contended, was the foundation on which a keen intellect and scrupulous morals could be built. Although the book is biased toward the benefits produced by crew and rowing exercises, Blaikie promotes a variety of physical activities to strengthen the body. He then analyzes the physiques of ninety-three of the Western world's great men, from Moses to Henry Ward Beecher, and he discusses how their strong bodies contributed to their greatness. Blaikie's writings, particularly *How to Get Strong*, influenced Luther Halsey Gulick, who became a prominent leader in physical education. Blaikie also helped Dudley A. Sargent, also a leader in physical education, become director of the Harvard University gymnasium. He was a popular speaker and frequently lectured on physical conditioning, morality, and temperance.

Blaikie's concern for strength and physical education brought him recognition from the newly organized American Association for the Advancement of Physical Education (later the American Alliance for Health, Physical Education, Recreation and Dance), which elected him as its second president in 1887. He served in that post until 1890. From 1873 until 1898 he resided in Englewood, New Jersey, and then in New York City, where he died.

A lawyer by profession, Blaikie was better known for his involvement in athletics, his lectures and writings on strength and exercise, and his promotion of physical education. His advocacy of exercise and physical activity for youth contributed to the emergence of physical education as a profession in the 1880s.

• The Harvard University Archives has a clipping file containing Blaikie's obituaries. Mabel Lee, *A History of Physical Education and Sports in the U.S.A.* (1983), briefly describes Blaikie's contributions to exercise and physical education, and Ronald A. Smith, *Sports and Freedom: The Rise of Big-Time College Athletics* (1988), discusses his influence on collegiate rowing. Obituaries are in the *New York Times*, 7 Dec. 1904, and the *Harvard Graduates Magazine* 13, no. 51 (Mar. 1905): 498–99.

J. THOMAS JABLE

BLAINE, Anita McCormick (4 July 1866–12 Feb. 1954), philanthropist, was born Anita Eugenie McCormick in Manchester, Vermont, the daughter of Cyrus Hall McCormick, an industrialist, and Nancy "Nettie" Fowler, a philanthropist. Cyrus McCormick had earlier invented the reaper and founded the Chicago-based McCormick Harvesting Machine, later International

Harvester Company. Anita spent her early years in New York City and Chicago isolated from most children except for her four siblings and her cousins. She was educated by governesses until age twelve, after which she attended female seminaries, graduating from the Kirkland Academy in Chicago in 1884. Typical for her social class at that time, Anita did not go to college. Whereas her three brothers were sent to Princeton and groomed to take over the family business, she was prepared for the social duties of wife, mother, and hostess. Although she was always independent-minded, Anita never rebelled against social convention. She had the traditional "coming out" event in 1887 and later that year embarked on a Grand Tour of Europe.

The robust Presbyterian faith of Anita's parents left an indelible imprint on her, though as an adult she became strongly nonsectarian. Thus her attitude toward the fortune she inherited after her father's death in 1884 was that of Christian stewardship—she was to use the money to do good for others. The management of her wealth, mostly shares in the family company, was left to others.

Cyrus McCormick had been a close associate of James G. Blaine, a presidential nominee and later secretary of state. Through that relationship, Anita met Blaine's son Emmons, a lawyer and railroad administrator eleven years her senior, and they were married in 1889. They initially lived in Baltimore until Emmons switched employers and joined the Chicago office of the Baltimore and Ohio railroad in 1891. The marriage was happy but brief; Emmons died unexpectedly in 1892 at the age of thirty-seven. Their son, Emmons, Jr., was born in 1890. Anita Blaine never remarried, but not for a lack of suitors. Widowhood propelled her into assuming a greater role in managing her affairs and raising her son. Returning to Chicago in 1893 after an extended stay in the East, she soon became deeply involved in the city's progressive reform activities and associated with such local and national leaders as social worker Jane Addams, educational reformers Francis W. Parker and John Dewey, and philanthropist Louise deKoven Bowen.

Common educational practices at the time emphasized routinized, rote learning. Blaine had disliked that teaching method when she was in school and was not going to allow her son to endure the same experience. When he was three she established a kindergarten in her home for him and other children. A few years later, while investigating elementary schools, she met Francis W. Parker, principal of the Cook County Normal School, an innovator famed for his child-centered approach to education. She enrolled her son in Parker's school in early 1896. Because it was several miles away from Chicago's North Side, Blaine soon asked Parker, and he consented, to establish a branch school in her neighborhood.

After oversight of Parker's normal school was transferred to the Chicago Board of Education, Parker began to chafe under the board's authority. Blaine offered to fund a new private school for teacher training

under his leadership. Parker accepted her offer and resigned from the school in 1899. The Chicago Institute, located in temporary quarters on the North Side of Chicago, began offering teachers' training classes in the summer of 1900 and elementary grade classes that fall. Of the five institute trustees Blaine was the dominant force; the others were trusted counselors selected by her. She was also the institute's major patron but was unwilling to be its sole benefactor. Severe cost overruns in the planned construction of a permanent building and school's operating expenses, coupled with Blaine's desire to economize, led the trustees of the institute to accept the offer of University of Chicago president William Rainey Harper to merge the Chicago Institute with the university's Department of Education.

The merger took place in 1901 after an endowment of $750,000 was raised by the university to match Blaine's contribution. Parker was to remain director of the Chicago Institute and to become head of the soon-to-be-established School of Education. Philosopher and educator John Dewey, who had been a friend of Blaine's for several years and was on friendly terms with Parker, was to run the proposed secondary school of the institute in addition to his innovative Laboratory School founded in 1896. This division of labor and authority was agreeable to all parties. However, after Parker died in 1902 and Dewey became director, problems arose between the two factions over the operation of the institute elementary school and the Laboratory School, which were combined in 1903. Blaine, still a trustee of the institute as well as a patron of the university, was appealed to by both sides. Through her influence an administrative arrangement was worked out that remained in effect until 1904, when Dewey left Chicago for Columbia University.

The merger and requisite move of the Chicago Institute to the South Side of Chicago had left affluent parents on the North Side without easy access to the school. Thus in 1901 Blaine became a prime mover in establishing the Francis W. Parker School on the original North Side site. Blaine persuaded the university, which owned the property, to relinquish it and again became deeply involved in funding the school. This time, however, she also played an active role in the educational program by substitute teaching and, for two years, serving as assistant principal. Blaine's patronage of the school continued for several decades during which she underwrote deficits and funded pensions for the teachers.

In 1905 Blaine and Jane Addams, founder of Hull House, were appointed to the Chicago Board of Education by the reform-minded mayor. The board became a battleground between the reformers and their enemies, however, and by 1908 most of the reformers had been replaced. Having fulfilled her duties in a nonconfrontational and less partisan manner, Blaine was asked to serve a second term, but she found the constant political infighting distasteful and declined. In 1900, concurrent with these events, Addams and Blaine established the City Homes Association, and in

1901 Blaine was named its president. The original purpose of the association was to document and publicize the crowded and unsanitary conditions of families in tenement housing. The association successfully agitated for changes in city housing ordinances but was less effective in securing their enforcement. During this same decade Blaine frequently worked with Louise deKoven Bowen at the city's Bureau of Charities, which assisted the needy and indigent, and at the Juvenile Protective Association, of which Bowen was president and which sought to protect youth from the harshness and hazards of urban life.

In 1912 Blaine was an unsuccessful candidate on the Republican ticket for trustee of the University of Illinois. About this time she withdrew from social welfare activism, believing that many of the goals of the progressive movement had been accomplished. The death of Emmons, Jr., however, during the influenza epidemic in 1918 rejuvenated her activist impulses. Because he had died while engaged in war work, she viewed his death as a war casualty and so began to direct her philanthropic efforts toward internationalist causes.

After the Republicans in Congress voted against U.S. membership in the League of Nations, Blaine joined nonisolationist Republicans in supporting the Democratic presidential ticket in 1920. Two years later she helped to organize the Chicago chapter of the League of Nations Non-Partisan Association and remained a patron of both the local and national organizations throughout the 1920s and 1930s. As the international crisis deepened in the 1930s she established a local discussion group, the World Citizen's Association, which included as members legal scholar Quincy Wright and author and foundation executive Edwin Embree, with the occasional participation of future governor Adlai Stevenson II. She served the association as vice president and coauthored its book *The World at the Crossroads* (1946). Before and during the war she served on the executive committee of the International Rescue Committee, aiding refugees fleeing from Europe. In 1945, when the League of Nations Association became the American Association for the United Nations, Blaine was named a director of the organization and later became its vice president.

Through her ardent support of President Franklin D. Roosevelt, Blaine came to know Vice President Henry Wallace, with whom she began a correspondence in 1941. Inspired by his ideas and earnestness, she helped establish the Progressive party and distributed more than $750,000 for his 1948 presidential campaign as the party's candidate. Most of the money went to state campaigns, literature, and radio advertising. Of a common mind, they believed that "democracy should be Christianity in action." That same year she also gave $1 million to set up the Foundation for World Government, whose organizers tried unsuccessfully to distance the new organization from Wallace and the Progressive party. In 1948 and 1949 Blaine provided initial crucial support for two newspapers that promoted Progressive party ideas, the *National Guardian* and *Daily Compass*. The former newspaper survives as *The Guardian*; the latter, a financial failure, folded in 1952.

Blaine's energies and activism were interrupted by ill health and old age in 1949. She died in Chicago. During her long life she had contributed to educational reform, international peace, and progressive politics both through activism and philanthropy. She was a woman of conscience, integrity, and determination that in combination with the McCormick name, money, and influence made her a considerable social force. Her educational involvements were to leave the most long-lasting mark—the Parker School and the university School of Education still survive—but her internationalist efforts endure as well. Of her $41 million estate $20 million was used to establish the New World Foundation to promote international peace and understanding. The foundation continues to operate from its New York City location.

• Blaine's voluminous papers are in the McCormick Collection, State Historical Society of Wisconsin in Madison. A useful resource is Margaret R. Hafstad, ed., *Guide to the McCormick Collection of the State Historical Society of Wisconsin* (1973). The Chicago Historical Society and the Newberry Library in Chicago have speeches and unpublished articles about Blaine. Details of the Chicago Institute merger with the University of Chicago can be found in Robert L. McCaul, "Dewey and the University of Chicago," *School and Society* 89 (1961): 152–57, 179–83, 202–6. Marie Stone Kirchner, ed., *Between Home and Community: Chronicle of the Francis W. Parker School, 1901–1976* (1976), complements McCaul and provides much information about Blaine and the Francis W. Parker School. The only book-length biography was written by Gilbert A. Harrison, the man who married Blaine's granddaughter, *A Timeless Affair: The Life of Anita McCormick Blaine* (1979). Among the most substantial of the numerous obituaries are ones in the *New York Times* and *Chicago Daily News*, 13 Feb. 1954.

MARK R. JORGENSEN

BLAINE, James Gillespie (31 Jan. 1830–27 Jan. 1893), Speaker of the House of Representatives and secretary of state, was born in West Brownsville, Pennsylvania, the son of Ephraim Blaine, a prosperous investor in land and trading goods, and Maria Gillespie. Blaine graduated from Washington and Jefferson College in 1847. While only seventeen years old, he began teaching at the Western Military Institute in Georgetown, Kentucky. Blaine married Harriet Stanwood in June 1850. They had six children. The following year he joined the faculty at the Pennsylvania Institute for the Education of the Blind in Philadelphia. In 1854 Blaine moved to Maine, where he became a newspaper editor and, in the political turmoil of the 1850s, served as one of the "founding fathers" of the new Republican party.

More than any other political figure of his time, Blaine seemed to symbolize the success—and occasional failure—of the Republican party in the Gilded Age of the late nineteenth century. He launched his political career in 1858, winning a seat in the state legislature, and became chair of the Republican State Committee in 1859. He chose, as many others did, to hire a substitute when drafted for the Civil War. Instead, Blaine was elected to the House of Representatives in 1862, beginning what has been described as a "long, colorful, and controversial national record" (Marcus, p. 7). After three terms in Congress, at the age of thirty-nine, he became Speaker of the House in 1869. Blaine served in that capacity until 1875, when the Republicans lost control of the House. This six-year term in a powerful and rewarding position represents the least controversial phase of his career on the national scene in what has been called "probably . . . the happiest period of Blaine's life" (Muzzey, p. 63).

Over and over again, contemporaries spoke of Blaine's "magnetism," the nineteenth-century equivalent of charisma. Many of the most sophisticated Republicans of the time indeed were drawn to him and devoted much of their political lives to a continuing crusade to put Blaine in the White House. With a "Blaine Legion" of devoted followers in place and Whitelaw Reid's powerful New York *Tribune* at his beck and call, Blaine emerged as "easily the GOP's most commanding public figure" by the late 1870s (Morgan, p. 22).

Blaine was the leading candidate for the presidential nomination when the Republicans gathered in Cincinnati in 1876. At the same time, allegations of financial misconduct damaged his chances of winning the nomination. He had been accused of using worthless bonds of the Little Rock & Fort Smith Railroad to secure a $64,000 loan. Blaine certainly maintained an upper-class life style, but he may have done so with income produced by returns from investments and from speculation in the stock market. As the leading figure in the Republican party over two decades, however, he made many enemies, and they never passed up an opportunity to bring charges against him.

This time, James Mulligan of Boston, who had been bookkeeper for Warren Fisher, Jr., builder of the Little Rock & Fort Smith, revealed that he had in his possession a collection of letters from Blaine to Fisher. Blaine's enemies assumed that the "Mulligan Letters" contained damaging information. Blaine then confronted Mulligan and demanded that he turn over what was private correspondence. Mulligan did so, but Blaine's actions seemed to confirm the charges. With the Republican National Convention only a week away, Blaine resorted to a dramatic gesture to attempt to clear himself, reading selected excerpts from the letters on the floor of the House of Representatives, but questions about his character remained a constant in the presidential politics of the late nineteenth century.

Blaine was presented to the Republican delegates in 1876 as the "Plumed Knight" who had defeated his enemies in battle, and he led all candidates for the nomination on the first ballot. On the seventh ballot, he came close to the prize with 351 votes, but those determined to stop Blaine rallied behind Rutherford B. Hayes, a former Civil War general who had served three terms as governor of Ohio. Hayes won the nomination with 384 votes on the same ballot.

Blaine would receive significant support for the presidential nomination at every subsequent Republican National Convention between 1880 and 1892, though he did not campaign for any nomination after 1876, one indication that he never recovered from that first defeat. At the time, Blaine went on with his life. He was given a vote of confidence by the governor of Maine, who chose him to fill out an unexpired term in the Senate. Shortly thereafter, the legislature elected him to a full term in the Senate. Blaine's service in the Senate, however, represents the least colorful phase of his career in Washington. He was distracted, watching in disbelief as the Republican party split into two informal wings, the "Stalwarts" and the "Half Breeds," by the end of the 1870s, after President Hayes had made it clear that he would not seek a second term.

The Stalwarts hoped to return Ulysses S. Grant to the White House for an unprecedented third term. Even in Blaine did not seek the presidential nomination at the Republican National Convention of 1880 in Chicago, he emerged as the acknowledged leader of the Half Breed opposition to another nomination for Grant and the only candidate who could stop Grant. On the first ballot for the presidential nomination, Grant received 304 votes to 284 votes for Blaine. The two leading candidates remained in much the same position through thirty-five ballots. Blaine then threw his support to James A. Garfield of Ohio, another former Civil War general who had served nine terms in the House of Representatives, providing most of the 399 votes that gave Garfield the nomination on the thirty-sixth ballot.

President-elect Garfield appointed Blaine secretary of state. Blaine, with Garfield's consent, would function as the "premier" of the president's short-lived administration. Though secretary of state for only nine and a half months, Blaine established an enduring reputation as "Jingo Jim," one of the architects of a new, more assertive foreign policy for the United States. He seemed to be attempting to implement his vision of an "American system," revolving around control of a Central American canal and aimed at expanding American influence and trade throughout the hemisphere.

In a three-week burst of activity, Blaine first informed the British government on 19 November that the United States hoped to terminate the Clayton-Bulwer Treaty of 1850, which provided for joint construction of any Central American canal. Blaine then extended invitations on 29 November for what would have been the first Pan-American conference. The invitations subsequently were withdrawn, but Blaine did preside over the first Pan-American Conference before the end of the decade. Finally, on 10 December, Blaine declared that Hawaii was "essentially a part of the American system." His resignation followed on 19 December.

Blaine seemed to retire in 1881, giving up his remaining political position when he resigned as chair of the Republican State Committee in Maine. Only fifty-one years old but suffering from gout, to many observers Blaine seemed "too apprehensive of the state of his health" (Muzzey, p. 184). Yet he remained the most popular Republican in the country in the early 1880s. While he concentrated on writing his memoirs, *Twenty Years of Congress: From Lincoln to Garfield*, published in two volumes of some 1,275 pages in 1884 and 1886, the Republican party seemed to be losing its edge. The Democrats captured control of the House of Representatives in 1882, and in New York a Democrat, Grover Cleveland, was elected governor. It quickly became apparent that Cleveland had a good chance of leading the Democrats back to the White House in 1884. An increasing number of Republicans became convinced that President Chester A. Arthur was not the best choice to withstand the Democratic challenge in 1884 and that only Blaine could lead the Republicans to victory.

On the first ballot for the presidential nomination at the Republican National Convention of 1884 in Chicago, Blaine received 334 votes to 278 votes for President Arthur. Blaine won the nomination easily on the fourth ballot. For two reasons the delegates then selected the controversial Senator John A. Logan of Illinois, a former Civil War general, as Blaine's running mate. Logan's presence on the ticket compensated for the fact that Blaine was the first Republican presidential candidate since the Civil War who had not served in the conflict. Furthermore, Logan, who had been a candidate for the presidential nomination as the "favorite son" from Illinois, yielded most of his votes to Blaine on the decisive fourth ballot. Unfortunately, Logan had damaged his reputation among Half Breed Republicans by playing a major role in the Stalwart effort to nominate Grant for president in 1880.

A small but very influential group of reform-minded Republicans refused to accept Blaine as the party's nominee. They felt no better about Logan, because many of these "Mugwumps" were the same upper-class intellectuals from the Northeast who had participated in the Liberal Republican movement against Grant in the presidential election of 1872. The Mugwumps were led by Carl Schurz, one of the most respected Republicans in the nation who had served as secretary of the interior in the Hayes administration. Schurz argued that Blaine lacked the moral character that should be expected from a president of the United States.

The Mugwump opposition to Blaine organized in Boston and received support from the *New York Times* and other newspapers in Boston, New York, and Philadelphia. In April a vicious editorial cartoon in *Puck* captioned "Tattooed Man" portrayed Blaine as a man with a checkered past. "Mulligan Letters" was among the phrases "tattooed" on Blaine. Then the Mugwumps produced new "Mulligan Letters," which appeared in the Boston *Journal* in mid-September. Under attack, Blaine decided to campaign for the nation's highest office, not standard practice in the late nineteenth century. For seven weeks before the election, he undertook a grueling travel schedule, covering the Northeast and the Midwest.

In two appearances in New York City on 29 October, with the election less than a week away, Blaine may have "self-destructed." Blaine first met with several hundred Protestant clergymen at the Fifth Avenue Hotel. When the Reverend Samuel D. Burchard described the Democrats as the party of "rum, Romanism and rebellion," the usually alert Blaine did not react. Perhaps he was weary after six weeks of travel, or perhaps something had temporarily distracted him. The Democrats moved quickly to inform New York's Irish Catholic community. Many among the normally Democratic Irish had been supporting Blaine because of the belief that as president he would "twist the lion's tail" by standing up to Great Britain in world affairs. After Burchard's denunciation of the Democratic party, many Irish voters decided to vote instead for Cleveland.

That evening Blaine joined some 200 of the wealthiest men in the nation for a lavish dinner at Delmonico's restaurant. The next day an editorial cartoon in the New York *World* depicted "Belshazzar Blaine and the Money Kings" dining on the finest food and wine while a poor family begged for scraps from the table. The *World*'s readers in that era surely could appreciate the significance of the biblical inscription in the background, "the handwriting on the wall." Blaine's attendance at the dinner may have solidified the opposition among the Mugwumps and their supporters, costing him still more votes in New York. As it turned out, Blaine lost New York by only 1,149 votes. New York's 36 electoral votes proved decisive, giving Cleveland the victory by a count of 219 to 182.

Though recognized as the leader of the Republican opposition to President Cleveland, Blaine seemed to retire once again to continue to work on his memoirs. He appeared to turn his back on the political scene when he sailed to Europe in June 1887 for what would be a fourteen-month stay. President Cleveland devoted his entire Annual Message in December to a call for lower tariff rates. In what may have been his "finest hour," Blaine opened the presidential campaign of 1888 when he provided an immediate Republican reply from Paris. Blaine insisted, as he had all along, that existing tariff rates provided benefits for business, labor, and farmers alike. More than any other Republican of his time, Blaine understood the protective tariff as a "safe" issue. In contrast, when Republicans became involved in more controversial social issues, for instance, the call for a prohibition on the Sunday sale of alcoholic beverages, they alienated various ethnic and religious groups among the voters.

Blaine insisted that he would not be a candidate for the presidential nomination. It is possible that he hoped the delegates to the Republican National Convention of 1888 would "draft" him. He did not act that way, however. Instead, he made it clear that he favored the nomination of former Civil War general Benjamin Harrison (1833–1901) of Indiana, who won the nomination on the eighth ballot. Harrison's debt to Blaine increased when Blaine returned to the United States in August to campaign for him. Harrison more or less had to ask Blaine to become secretary of state once again, but he did not want a "premier" for his administration. He did not consult Blaine about filling other positions in the cabinet. When Harrison also declined to allow Blaine's son, Walker Blaine, to serve as first assistant secretary of state, it was clear that Blaine's influence and power would be limited.

Nevertheless, both Blaine and Harrison have been credited with contributing the "strategic formulation" of the "new empire" that the United States created by the end of the nineteenth century. Indeed, they agreed on the objectives of American foreign policy: control of a Central American canal and establishment of a presence in both the Caribbean and the Pacific. In vain, the administration encouraged construction of a canal across Nicaragua, tried to obtain the first American naval base in the Caribbean in Haiti, and attempted the annexation of Hawaii. Blaine did preside over the first Pan-American Conference, which took place in Washington between October 1889 and April 1890.

As both agricultural and industrial production steadily increased in the late nineteenth century, many Americans became convinced that the nation needed an outlet for the surplus involved. Those who argued that downward revision of tariff rates would make the United States more competitive in world markets faced powerful opposition from the Republicans, who, in the period 1865–1890, controlled the White House for all but four years and the Senate for all but two years. The election of 1888 gave the party a majority in the House of Representatives as well, providing what was perceived to be an opportunity to carry out a Republican version of tariff "reform."

The Republican Congress passed the McKinley Tariff of 1890, raising rates to a record high level. Blaine, who in the early 1880s had talked in vague terms about a "Zollverein" or customs union as the basis for a free-trade policy among the nations of the hemisphere, had come to believe that bilateral treaties to establish commercial reciprocity with selected nations in the hemisphere represented a middle-ground position between a high tariff policy and free trade. This compromise might satisfy the demands for tariff reform. With support from Harrison, Blaine waged what has been called "the last great political effort of his career" (LaFeber, p. 115) to include a commercial reciprocity amendment in the McKinley Tariff, convinced that such a policy would open markets in the hemisphere.

The Harrison administration offered a unique brand of reciprocity to the nations of Latin America, removing the tariff from five of their major exports—animal hides, coffee, molasses, sugar, and tea—and expecting similar treatment for exports from the United States. Of all the nations in South America, only Brazil, which exported more than 300 million pounds of coffee to the United States in 1890, agreed to a reciprocity treaty. Nevertheless, Blaine accomplished his real goal, strengthening economic ties with the nations of Central America and the islands of the Caribbean. The United States concluded reciprocity treaties with El Salvador, Guatemala, Honduras, and Nicaragua in Central America and with the Dominican Republic, Great Britain for its West Indian colonies and British Guiana, and Spain for Cuba and Puerto Rico in the Caribbean. It is not possible, however, to determine whether reciprocity helped to increase exports. When the Democrats captured the White House and both houses of Congress in 1892, they abandoned reciprocity in the Wilson-Gorman Tariff of 1894.

Blaine's deteriorating health limited his ability to function as secretary of state on a day-to-day basis. As early as April-May 1889, while the United States participated in the Berlin Conference with Germany and Great Britain and established a three-power protectorate over Samoa, Blaine was confined to his bed with lumbago. After the tragic deaths from pneumonia of his son Walker in mid-January 1890 and his daughter Alice less than three weeks later, Blaine was never the same. He became ill in March 1891 and collapsed in April. Blaine did not return to the State Department until October. In the interval, he exhibited all the symptoms of a nervous breakdown.

Despite his continuing ill health, a group of powerful Republicans hoped to use Blaine at the Republican National Convention of 1892 to prevent the nomination of President Harrison for a second term. Harrison's independence had alienated several of the most important state "bosses," including Thomas C. Platt of New York, Senator Matthew Quay of Pennsylvania, and James S. Clarkson of Iowa. In the aftermath of a disastrous defeat in the congressional elections of 1890, when the Democrats won an overwhelming majority of the seats in the House of Representatives, the bosses insisted that Harrison could not win in 1892 and pressured Blaine to become a candidate for the presidential nomination.

Blaine suddenly resigned as secretary of state on 4 June, just a few days before the opening of the Republican National Convention in Minneapolis. He never explained why he resigned, but contemporaries described him as feeble, overwhelmed by the constant badgering of those involved in the scheme, and seemingly unable to resist being drawn into the machinations of the bosses. In any case, Harrison easily won the nomination. Blaine, the fading star of the party, and Governor William McKinley of Ohio, a rising star, each received 182 votes. Just a few days after the convention, another of Blaine's sons, Emmons, died from appendicitis. That may have been the final blow for Blaine. He made one brief speech during the campaign, in New York in October, and early in January became ill for the last time. He died in Washington.

Few men have so dominated the politics of an era as did Blaine. As Jingo Jim, the Plumed Knight, or the "Magnetic Man," he brought excitement to the political arena in the late nineteenth century. While it is difficult to distinguish among those who made it to the White House in the Gilded Age, Blaine, who did not, had the potential to bring the presidency into the modern era. He had the most important quality the others lacked, a charismatic personality, which could have allowed him to provide vigorous presidential leadership. In any case, Blaine contributed more than any other political figure of his time to the power and prestige of the Republican party in the post–Civil War era.

• The family papers of James G. Blaine, including some 7,000 items, are in the Manuscript Division of the Library of Congress. The two most important sources are dated. David S. Muzzey, *James G. Blaine: A Political Idol of Other Days* (1934), is the only scholarly biography. Alice Felt Tyler, *The Foreign Policy of James G. Blaine* (1927), is the only book-length treatment of his foreign policy. See also Justus D. Doenecke, *The Presidencies of James A. Garfield and Chester A. Arthur* (1981), and Allan Peskin, *Garfield* (1978), on his role in the Garfield administration; Walter LaFeber, *The New Empire: An Interpretation of American Expansion, 1860–1898* (1963), and David M. Pletcher, *The Awkward Years: American Foreign Relations under Garfield and Arthur* (1962), on his foreign policy; George H. Mayer, *The Republican Party, 1854–1964* (1964), Robert D. Marcus, *Grand Old Party: Political Structure in the Gilded Age, 1880–1896* (1971), and H. Wayne Morgan, *From Hayes to McKinley: National Party Politics, 1877–1896* (1969), on his role as a leading political figure in the late nineteenth century; and Homer Socolofsky and Allan Spetter, *The Presidency of Benjamin Harrison* (1987), on his role in the Harrison administration. A lengthy obituary is in the *New York Times*, 28 Jan. 1893.

ALLAN BURTON SPETTER

BLAINE, John James (4 May 1875–16 Apr. 1934), governor of Wisconsin and U.S. senator, was born near Castle Rock, in Grant County, Wisconsin, the son of James Ferguson Blaine and Elizabeth Johnson-Brunstad, farmers. Blaine attended Valparaiso University, from which he received a law degree in 1896. He began a law practice in Boscobel, Wisconsin, immediately after graduation. He married Anna C. McSpaden in 1904; they had one daughter.

In 1901 Blaine began his political career, which included three terms as mayor of Boscobel (1901–1904, 1906–1907) and four terms on the Grant County Board of Supervisors (1901–1904). In 1902 he entered state politics, winning election as a Robert La Follette (1855–1925) delegate to the Republican State Convention. For the rest of his life, he was both a follower and a leader in the Progressive wing of Republican politics in Wisconsin. In 1908 he won election to the Wisconsin state senate, where he initiated and led an investigation into corruption surrounding the reelection of Senator Isaac Stephenson. The investigation led to the passage of a drastic political corrupt practices act. Reelected to the state senate in 1910, he took a leading role in enacting a state life insurance fund, unemployment insurance, and the first state income tax. He served as a delegate to the national Republican conventions of 1912, 1916, 1920, 1924, and 1928.

In 1914 Blaine ran unsuccessfully as an independent candidate for governor, but in 1918 he was elected attorney general of the state on the Republican ticket. Subsequently he won three consecutive two-year terms as Republican governor of Wisconsin (1921–1927). His career as governor was highlighted by passage of laws granting equal rights to women, reduction of state expenditures, publication of income tax returns of political officials, and expansion of the number of state parks. He was also an outspoken critic of the Ku Klux Klan.

In 1926 Blaine was elected U.S. senator. In the United States Senate, he was a leading spokesman against Prohibition and introduced the resolution repealing Prohibition which led to the Twenty-first Amendment. He was a harsh critic of both the domestic and foreign policies of the Calvin Coolidge and Herbert Hoover administrations. Blaine cast the lone dissenting vote against the ratification of the Kellogg-Briand Pact, and he strongly opposed the use of injunctions against labor unions. Despite his nominal Republican affiliation, he supported Democratic presidential candidates in 1928 and 1932. Perhaps for this reason, he was defeated for reelection in the Republican primary of 1932. President Franklin D. Roosevelt appointed him a commissioner of the Reconstruction Finance Corporation in 1933. He died in Boscobel, Wisconsin, while holding that position.

Blaine was one of the key figures in the La Follette wing of the Republican party throughout his political career, and after the death of the elder Robert La Follette, he became one of its most important leaders. He was a natural politician who made friends easily and campaigned tirelessly. He was sharp in sensing changing public attitudes and adapted easily to new issues.

• The John Blaine Papers are at the State Historical Society of Wisconsin. There is no published biography of Blaine. There is material about his political career in Robert Nesbit, *Wisconsin: A History* (1973); *The Wisconsin Blue Book, 1927* (1927); Patrick G. O'Brien, "Senator John J. Blaine: An Independent Progressive during 'Normalcy,'" *Wisconsin Magazine of History* 60, no. 1 (1976): 25–41; and James H. Duffer, "Progressive Profile: John J. Blaine from 1873 to 1918" (Master's thesis, Univ. of Wisconsin, 1951). Extensive obituaries are in the *Milwaukee Sentinel*, 17 and 20 Apr. 1934; the Madison, Wis. *Capital Times*, 17 Apr. 1934; and the *New York Times*, 17 Apr. 1934.

ALBERT ERLEBACHER

BLAIR, Austin (8 Feb. 1818–6 Aug. 1894), governor of Michigan and congressman, was born in Caroline, New York, the son of George Blair and Rhoda Blackman Mann, farmers. Prior to graduating from Union College in 1839, he worked as a teacher in Speedsville, New York. He then studied law as a clerk with the firm of Sweet and Davis in Owego, New York. In 1841 he married Persis Lyman, a former student, and was admitted to the Tioga County bar. Unlikely to prosper in such a competitive legal environment and unable to support his bride as a law clerk, Blair decided his practice and family would both be better off in less crowded confines. Consequently, he followed his uncle to Jackson, Michigan, where he established a firm with Reule C. Baker in 1842.

Blair's partnership proved inauspicious, so his family migrated to neighboring Eaton Rapids, which was even less developed than Jackson. Although Blair found his services in greater demand there, his fortunes did not improve at a corresponding rate. Thus his subsequent entrance into politics was motivated as much by need as by principle. Failing to become a member of the Michigan House of Representatives in 1843 as a Whig, Blair bounced back to become clerk of Eaton County in 1844. However, he resigned from that office after the deaths of his wife and infant daughter and returned to Jackson, where he formed a partnership with Henry Frink in 1845.

Blair also reentered politics in 1845 when he was elected to Michigan's lower house. During his term, he played a pivotal role in abolishing the death penalty, although his efforts to amend the state constitution to extend the franchise to blacks were thwarted. His concern for civil rights was not dampened by this reversal, nor was his interest in justice limited to black suffrage. Disenchanted with the course of national politics, he abandoned the Whig party in favor of the Free Soil party in 1848, serving as a delegate to the party's national convention in Buffalo that same year. But just as Blair's political career began to flourish, he lost his second family. He had married Elizabeth Pratt in 1846; two years later his wife and infant son fell victim to another outbreak of the fever that claimed his first family. Bereft, Blair turned down the Free Soil party's nomination for lieutenant governor, returned to his law practice, and married Sarah Louise Ford in 1849. The couple had five children, four of whom reached adulthood.

In 1854, at the close of his first two-year term as prosecuting attorney of Jackson County, Blair rejoined the vanguard of third-party politics when he helped form the Republican party. He was a key participant in the party's organizational meetings in Jackson, Kalamazoo, and Detroit, and he helped draft the party's first platform. Fittingly, he was elected to the state senate later that year. As a member of the legislature's newly elected Republican majority, he worked on a litany of reform issues, including a temperance measure, a bill to establish an endowment for a women's college, and an act to establish property rights for married women. He also cowrote Michigan's personal liberty law, which obstructed federal enforcement of the Fugitive Slave Act of 1850.

William K. Gibson replaced Frink as Blair's partner in 1857. With a stable family life, a healthy practice, an accomplished record in public life, and a reputation as a skilled orator, Blair began to plan for a seat in the U.S. Senate. But intense party rivalries over the next fifteen years prevented him from being considered for one of Michigan's seats, so he had to be satisfied with lesser nominations. After declining the Republican gubernatorial nomination in 1858, he ran as the party's nominee in 1860. He went on to defeat Democrat John Barry by 20,727 votes out of 154,833 cast.

Upon assuming office, Blair faced a bankrupt state government and a Federal call for troops. After discovering that the previous state treasurer had fled with state funds, Blair immediately raised over $100,000 to equip and train Michigan's first units. A week later Michigan's first regiment was mustered into Federal service ahead of schedule. All told, the governor organized twenty-eight infantry regiments, fourteen artillery batteries, and eleven cavalry regiments, totaling some 83,347 men. He discerned that victory would be costly in other ways as well, so he took steps to husband Michigan's resources. Although he supplied the Federal government with 6,000 more men than President Abraham Lincoln requested in the war's first year, his recruits filled depleted regiments before new ones were formed. His economic policies put the state on a sound footing, and his arguments for emancipation—months before Lincoln signed the Emancipation Proclamation—helped convince the North that to protect the rebel's property was to "help him butcher our people" (quoted in Lanman, p. 155). At the close of his second term in 1865, Michigan's legislators passed a resolution commending his efforts unanimously.

Blair was elected to Congress in 1866. Over the next six years he dutifully supported Republican measures, but unfulfilled ambitions, declining popularity, and disgust with corruption in Washington led him to break with the party in 1872. That year he chaired an investigation of the Navy Department, supported Horace Greeley for President, and ran unsuccessfully for governor of Michigan as a Liberal Republican. He left Congress in 1873. Blair eventually returned to the Republican party in 1880. In 1885, during his second term as prosecuting attorney of Jackson County, he failed to gain a seat on Michigan's Supreme Court. He concluded public life as a two-term regent of the University of Michigan, serving from 1882 to 1890. His practice declining, he died virtually penniless in Jackson, Michigan.

Blair brought determination and skill to his careers in education, law, and politics. Ever the idealist, he struggled against personal hardship and for liberal reform throughout his public life, though he always will be best known for his pragmatic administration of Michigan during the Civil War.

• Blair's correspondence and papers are part of the Burton Historical Collection at the Detroit Public Library. His speeches are in George N. Fuller, ed., *Messages of the Governors of Michigan* (1925). Full-length studies include Earl O. Smith, "The Public Life of Austin Blair, War Governor of Michigan, 1845–1863" (M.A. thesis, Wayne State Univ., 1934); Vivian T. Messner, "The Public Life of Austin Blair, War Governor of Michigan, 1863–1894" (M.A. thesis, Wayne State Univ., 1937); Jean Joy L. Fennimore, "Austin Blair: Pioneer Lawyer, 1818–1844," *Michigan History* 48 (Mar. 1964): 1–17, "Austin Blair: Political Idealist, 1845–1860," *Michigan History* 48 (June 1964): 130–66, "Austin Blair: Civil War Governor, 1861–1862," Michigan History 49 (Sept. 1965): 193–227, and "Austin Blair: Civil War Governor, 1863–1864," *Michigan History* 49 (Dec. 1965): 344–69, and Robert Charles Harris, "Austin Blair of Michigan: A Political Biography" (Ph.D. diss., Michigan State Univ., 1969). Contemporaneous accounts include Charles Lanman, *The Red Book of Michigan: A Civil, Military, and Biographical History* (1871); and John Robertson, *Michigan in the War* (1882). An obituary is in the *Detroit Evening News*, 7 Aug. 1894.

ROBERT W. BURG

BLAIR, Eliza Violet Gist (1794–5 July 1877), newspaperwoman and political hostess, was born in either Virginia or in Bourbon County, Kentucky, the daughter of Nathaniel Gist, an Indian agent and planter, and Judith Cary Bell. Eliza's father died in 1797, and a decade later her mother married Charles Scott, who became the governor of Kentucky in 1808. Eliza's wedding to journalist Francis Preston Blair, the clerk of the state circuit court, on 21 July 1812 took place in the governor's mansion in Frankfort. Because Preston Blair, as he was called, was tubercular, neither Eliza's mother nor Scott approved the match. Headstrong and confident, Eliza declared that she would rather be Preston Blair's widow than any other man's wife. Aided by her lung remedy—special herbs in a honey and whiskey base—Preston Blair lived a long, productive life. The couple had six children, two of whom died in early childhood.

In November 1830 the Blairs, accompanied by their twelve-year-old daughter Lizzie, left Kentucky for the nation's capital. As a result of his newspaper articles that backed Andrew Jackson, Preston Blair had been asked to launch and edit a newspaper that would be the organ of President Jackson. The Washington *Globe* began production in 1830 and flourished. Preston Blair remained its editor until 1845. During these fifteen years, Eliza Blair was responsible for the newspaper's foreign news, human-interest items, and special features, which included short stories, poetry, book reviews, letters from diplomats and foreign travelers, and brief anecdotes. Openly acknowledging his wife's help, Preston Blair ignored the slurs of his political enemies, who claimed that Eliza Blair, who favored more rights and better wages for women, "was the head of the family in every sense and wrote" his editorials (*Evening Star*, 14 Sept. 1906). In truth, she wielded scissors more often than a pen, clipping interesting and pertinent materials from important periodicals for use in the *Globe*. Unlike her husband, who "had to be pursued in the garden & every where for his editorials," Blair "always had her work over before his ten o'clock breakfast" (June 1892, Breckinridge Long Papers).

Quite poor and living in rooming houses during their earliest Washington years, Blair and her family soon became intimates of President Jackson. On cold winter nights, he often insisted that young Lizzie, who like her father was tubercular, stay in the warm White House; during at least two summers the Blair family vacationed with Jackson at the "Rip Raps" near Fortress Monroe, Virginia; and during July 1834 they lived in the White House while he was in Tennessee. When he retired, Jackson thanked Blair for the comfortable stockings she had knitted for him and mentioned that his little granddaughter Rachel, who was accustomed to being cared for by Blair when ill during those White House years, had called out for her during a recent sickness.

Blair became known for her healing skills, which Lizzie Blair called her "*Simples* and kindness." She even administered her remedies to Henry Clay, her guardian and lawyer in Kentucky, whose hand she had earlier publicly refused to take. Not only had he denounced Jackson for dangerous, lawless, and unconstitutional behavior, he had urged fellow senators, for "the purity of the national character," to take the lucrative printing of the *Congressional Globe* (the publication of the daily proceedings of Congress) away from her husband and his partner (E. B. Smith, p. 145). The tubercular son and namesake of President Martin Van Buren remarked on the sweetness of Blair's liquid magnesia while taking the cure at "Silver Spring," the Blairs' country seat in Maryland. "In fact all her medicines have a most insinuating manner about them," he insisted, "& grow amazingly to ones liking" (2 May 1841, Blair Family Papers).

Wholeheartedly committed to the "noble political principles" of her husband and sons, Blair served willingly as their hostess. But she did not always see eye to eye with them. Despite her husband's enthusiasm for Van Buren, she, like his opponents, thought of him as the "Red Fox." Aware of Blair's "power . . . of persuasion . . . over her husband," Van Buren schemed with associates to keep her "from pulling Mr. Blair over" (W. E. Smith, vol. 1, p. 183). Before he left Washington, Van Buren presented her with his portrait and said, "Madam you will like it because it has rather a foxy look" (*Evening Star*, 14 Sept. 1906).

Although Preston Blair opposed the annexation of Texas, he supported James K. Polk when he won the Democratic nomination in 1844 on an expansionist platform. Despite Preston Blair's willingness to serve the victorious Polk as he had Jackson and Van Buren, Polk forced him to sell the *Globe*. Even without their newspaper, the Blairs remained influential. They considered themselves the keepers of the true Jacksonian democracy, and numerous politicians trekked out to Silver Spring to seek their advice and backing. Bitterly disillusioned with the 1854 Kansas-Nebraska Act—which opened those territories to slavery—Preston Blair became one of the chief organizers of the Republican party and succeeded in getting John C. Frémont nominated. Refusing to be infatuated with Frémont as was the rest of her family, Eliza Blair saw his foibles from the start and pointedly asked her husband in 1856 why he had "picked up that Turkey Gobbler for a candidate" (W. E. Smith, vol. 1, p. 367). Preston Blair advised Abraham Lincoln throughout his presidency, and Mary Lincoln felt especially comfortable visiting the Blairs, to whom she was slightly related and who, like she, were from Kentucky. Ever gracious, the Blairs were "run down with company" and entertained as often as six nights a week (1861, Blair Family Papers).

Continuing her acts of mercy, Blair cared for Senator Charles Sumner immediately after he was assaulted by Representative Preston Brooks and for Vice President Andrew Johnson, who had become intoxicated at President Lincoln's second inauguration, after dosing a mild illness with alcohol. Besides bringing medicines, flowers, fruit, vegetables, and dairy products to hospitalized soldiers during the Civil War, Blair opened her home to individual wounded servicemen. Working to ease the suffering on both sides, she asked President Johnson to let Varina Davis visit her husband, Confederate president Jefferson Davis, in prison.

Busy editing, nursing the sick, and managing a large household, Blair seldom wrote letters, even to her family, and pressed her daughter, house guests, and even invalids under her care to pen her notes. In one of these, she insisted that "none of my sons shall bully me" (E. B. Smith, pp. 183–84). Called "the Lioness" by her children, she was as proud of them as they were of her. She died at Silver Spring, surrounded by her children and grandchildren. Able and self-confident, Blair shaped and maintained seven sections of a major newspaper for a decade and a half, succored many of the nation's leaders in their time of need for more than four decades, and nurtured one of the nation's most influential political families for a lifetime.

• The principal collections of Blair's letters and papers are in the Blair Family Papers, Library of Congress, and the Blair-Lee Papers, Princeton University. References to her are also in the Levi Woodbury Papers and the Breckinridge Long Papers, Library of Congress. Biographical material is in Elbert B. Smith, *Francis Preston Blair* (1980); William E. Smith, *The Francis Preston Blair Family in Politics* (2 vols., 1933); Virginia Jeans Laas, ed., *Wartime Washington: The Civil War Letters of Elizabeth Blair Lee* (1991); and Elizabeth Blair Lee's obituary in the *Evening Star* (Washington, D.C.), 14 Sept. 1906. Blair's obituary is in the *New York Times*, 6 July 1877.

OLIVE HOOGENBOOM

BLAIR, Emily Newell (9 Jan. 1877–3 Aug. 1951), feminist, politician, and writer, was born in Joplin, Missouri, the daughter of Anna Cynthia Gray and James Patton Newell, a mortgage broker. She enrolled in the Woman's College of Baltimore (now Goucher College) in 1894, but her father's death cut short her education after just one year. Returning home, she helped raise her younger siblings, taught school, and attended classes at the University of Missouri without completing a degree. In 1900 she married Harry Wallace Blair, a former classmate at Carthage High School.

The Blairs settled in Carthage, Missouri, where her husband developed a successful law practice, and Blair bore a daughter and a son, managed the household, and participated in women's clubs and civic activities. The sale of her first story to *Woman's Home Companion* in 1909 marked the beginning of a writing career: over the years, her articles and short stories appeared in a host of periodicals, including *Cosmopolitan*, *Harper's*, *Century Magazine*, and *Woman Citizen*. She was associate editor of *Good Housekeeping* from 1925 to 1933 and published a book on home decorating, *The Creation of a Home*, in 1930, and a feminist novel, *A Woman of Courage*, in 1931. Obviously drawn from some of Blair's experiences, the novel recounts a woman's struggles in marriage, suffrage, politics, and business.

Blair's political activism began in 1914 with an appeal to an all-male civic club to support a county poor-house. At the same time, she joined the Missouri Equal Suffrage Association and managed press relations and publicity during the 1914 campaign for a state suffrage amendment. From 1914 to 1916 she served as founding editor of a monthly, the *Missouri Woman*, which had broad circulation after Blair persuaded the state Federation of Women's Clubs and the Parent-Teachers Association to endorse it as their official publication.

When the Democratic party held its 1916 national convention in St. Louis, Blair organized a suffrage demonstration, massing thousands of women for ten blocks along the street leading to the convention site. Dressed in white with yellow sashes and carrying yellow parasols, the silent women formed a "golden lane," a "walkless, talkless parade," through which delegates had to walk on the opening day of the convention.

During World War I Blair worked for the Council of National Defense, an agency designed to coordinate Red Cross work, bond sales, food conservation, and other home-front mobilization activities. She served first as district vice chair of the Missouri Woman's Committee and then moved to the executive office of the national Woman's Committee, working with other prominent suffragists in Washington, D.C., while her husband served with the YMCA in France. Blair was responsible for news and publicity, and she wrote the official history of the Woman's Committee of the Council of National Defense, published by the government in 1920.

After the war and the family's return to Joplin, Blair helped organize the League of Women Voters and instituted classes to introduce women to government and political activities. Her primary interest, however, was not in the nonpartisan approach of the league, but in party politics, in her view the most direct means to political power for women. In 1921 Blair was elected Democratic committeewoman from Missouri and soon thereafter became the highest-ranking woman in the party when she was elevated to vice chair of the Democratic National Committee, a post she held until 1928.

An energetic and creative organizer, Blair initiated a number of activities designed to bring women into party politics and to train them in speaking and other campaign activities. Beginning in 1922 she led a nationwide effort to establish more than 2,000 Democratic women's clubs. She organized "Schools of Democracy" around the country as well as a correspondence course to instruct women on party issues and principles. Blair also wrote a history of the party and produced campaign and organizing booklets and flyers. In 1924 she helped found the Women's National Democratic Club, a social and political gathering place for women in the nation's capital.

Blair combined a soft manner with shrewdness and strong determination. One male politician likened her to Southern Comfort, a liquor that "goes down easy, but packs a wallop." She pushed the Democratic National Committee to increase the number of female delegates to national conventions and made sure that her own position remained one elected by all the committeemen and -women. Her identification with social reform and women's rights placed her among a group of prominent women denounced by the right-wing Woman Patriots for being part of a feminist-Communist conspiracy.

Blair campaigned for Franklin D. Roosevelt in 1932, and when the Democrats captured the White House she became a member of the New Deal women's network. With common experiences in suffrage, social reform, and war work, these women cooperated in the 1930s to influence their party and government on patronage and policy issues. As a reward for the Blairs' contributions to the party, Roosevelt gave Blair's husband the post of assistant attorney general and appointed her to the Consumers' Advisory Board to the National Recovery Administration (NRA) in 1933. She chaired the board from February 1935 until the NRA was declared unconstitutional in May of that year. In 1942 Blair returned to public office, heading the women's interests section in the War Department's bureau of public relations. She remained there until 1944, when she was incapacitated by a stroke. She died in Alexandria, Virginia.

Along with other women who occupied a middle tier of leadership in the suffrage movement, Blair helped to gain full citizenship for women. She believed that women would achieve power by working within male institutions as citizens, not as women, insisting that "women's interests in politics are not essentially different from men's." As the most powerful woman in the Democratic party during the 1920s, she encouraged the politicization of women and pressured men to take them seriously. Disillusioned by the reluctance of men to share power, she turned from an emphasis on women's identity with men and toward alternative strategies for women to gain equality. In the economic realm, Blair suggested, women should give up their unsuccessful efforts to compete with men, develop their own enterprises, and "take over some part of the world's business as their own." In the political realm, she urged development of gender-conscious feminist blocs through which women would support one another until they achieved real power.

• Blair's papers, which include drafts of an autobiography, are housed in the Western Reserve Historical Society. Blair's most important reassessments of feminist strategy appear in "Wanted: A New Feminism," *Independent Woman*, Dec. 1930, pp. 498–99, 544; "Discouraged Feminists," *Outlook*, 8 July 1931, pp. 302–3, 318; "Putting Women into Politics," *Woman's Journal*, Mar. 1931, pp. 14–15, 29; and "Why I Am Discouraged about Women in Politics," *Woman's Journal*, Jan. 1931, pp. 20–22. For Blair's suffrage work, see Mary Semple Scott, "The Missouri Woman," *Missouri Historical Review* 14 (Apr.–July 1920): 281–384. Blair's political strategies are discussed in Estelle Freedman, "Separatism as Strategy," *Feminist Studies* 5 (Fall 1979): 522–24. For her place in the New Deal women's network, see Susan Ware, *Beyond Suffrage: Women in the New Deal* (1981). Obituaries are in the *New York Times* and the *Washington Post*, 4 Aug. 1951.

SUSAN M. HARTMANN

BLAIR, Francis Preston (12 Apr. 1791–18 Oct. 1876), newspaper editor and presidential adviser, was born in Abingdon, Virginia, the son of James Blair, a lawyer and, later, attorney general of Kentucky, and Elizabeth Smith; he was usually called Preston. Reared in Frankfort, Kentucky, Blair graduated with honors from Transylvania University in 1811. In 1812 he married Eliza Violet Gist, and for sixty-four years she was Blair's equal partner in every endeavor. They had four children who reached adulthood.

From 1813 to 1830 Blair, who studied law, was circuit court clerk of Franklin County, was deeply involved in state politics, and coedited *The Argus*, a local paper. To help debtors after the depression of 1819, the Kentucky legislature passed laws and created a bank, which the state supreme court declared unconstitutional. The legislature then created a new supreme court, and a bitter struggle ensued. Blair served as clerk of the new court and president of the new bank. Ultimately, the old court won. In 1824 Blair supported Henry Clay for president, but in 1828 he helped Andrew Jackson carry Kentucky. In 1830 Jackson called him to Washington to edit a new, pro-administration paper.

Blair's paper, *The Globe*, was a highly readable journal that idealized democracy and made Jackson its symbol. Democratic newspapers everywhere reprinted Blair's editorials, which helped spread the concept of America as a beacon of freedom for the world. Blair attacked the U.S. Bank as a threat to democracy because of its uncontrolled power over the national economy and its financial ties to various members of Congress and the Whig party, and he glorified Jackson's defense of the Union against South Carolina's effort to nullify the tariff laws. He was an adviser in Jackson's Kitchen Cabinet, helped organize the Democratic party into a national institution, and wielded great power in the dispensation of government jobs.

In 1840, when Martin Van Buren was defeated by Whig William Henry Harrison for the presidency, the *Globe* opposed Whig efforts to re-create the U.S. Bank and raise tariffs. Harrison soon died, however, and his successor, John Tyler, vetoed the policies of the party that had elected him. Blair supported Tyler's vetoes and hoped for the reelection of Van Buren in 1844.

In 1844 the major issue was the annexation of Texas, which had separated from Mexico eight years before. Many northerners feared the addition of a vast new slave area, and Texas was claiming a huge section of Mexico that had never been part of Texas. Although Blair and Van Buren feared that a premature annexation would bring war with Mexico and eventually provoke an American civil war, the *Globe*'s editor supported his party's candidate, James K. Polk, who advocated immediate annexation. Blair even won a $22,000 bet on Polk's election. Polk, however, forced Blair to sell the *Globe* to a more acceptable party editor.

Retiring to his Silver Spring, Maryland, country estate, Blair remained highly influential through his reputation and friendships. In 1848, although he owned a few slaves, he strongly supported Van Buren's Free Soil presidential candidacy. Blair was certain that slavery could not spread to the territories taken from Mexico and believed that southern radicals were misrepresenting the issue to promote disunion. In 1852 he wrote pamphlets supporting the Democratic candidacy of Franklin Pierce but was bitterly disappointed in him when Pierce promoted the Kansas-Nebraska Act, which repealed the Missouri Compromise and opened the western territories legally to slavery. Blair helped organize the new Republican party against slavery in Kansas, and when abolitionist senator Charles Sumner was caned by a congressman from South Carolina, Blair brought him to Silver Spring for recuperation. In 1856 Blair chaired the first Republican National Convention and later was instrumental in securing the nomination of John C. Frémont for president. In a widely distributed pamphlet published in April of that year, *A Voice from the Grave of Jackson*, Blair worked to convert northwestern Democrats by arguing that Jackson, if alive, would be a Republican.

In *Dred Scott v. Sandford* (1857), Blair's son Montgomery argued for the plaintiff's freedom, and another son, Frank (Francis Preston Blair, Jr.), a congressman from Missouri, made eloquent speeches advocating abolition and deportation of the freed slaves to Latin America. Blair and his sons were influential delegates at the 1860 Republican convention and were rewarded when Abraham Lincoln appointed Montgomery Blair postmaster general. Throughout Lincoln's presidency, Preston Blair and his son Frank were close friends and confidantes. Preston Blair argued passionately with Lincoln for reinforcing Fort Sumter, and Montgomery Blair was at first the only cabinet member opposed to its surrender. When the Civil War began, the Blairs persuaded Lincoln to make Frémont the western commander and helped get Frémont relieved from that command when he proved incompetent and rebellious. Frank Blair performed heroically as a general under William T. Sherman but returned to Congress briefly in 1864 to make speeches that destroyed Treasury Secretary Salmon P. Chase's effort to supplant Lincoln as the 1864 candidate. The Emancipation Proclamation did not apply to Maryland, but Preston Blair immediately freed his slaves and supported the emancipation movement in Maryland.

By supporting Lincoln's cautious approach to abolition and Reconstruction, the Blairs by 1864 had acquired numerous enemies. In September Montgomery Blair resigned from Lincoln's cabinet as part of the price for Frémont's withdrawal as a radical presidential candidate, but the Blairs and the Lincolns remained close. In December 1864, with Lincoln's approval, Preston Blair went to Richmond twice to implore Jefferson Davis to accept abolition and make peace. He brought back valuable information, and his efforts led to a subsequent conference between Lincoln and Confederate vice president Alexander H. Stephens at Hampton Roads, Virginia. Blair's daughter, Elizabeth Lee, was a trusted friend of Mary Lincoln

and was often with her during the difficult month after her husband's assassination.

After the Civil War, the Blairs, who favored an easy Reconstruction process that would not threaten states' rights or white supremacy, became influential confidants of President Andrew Johnson and broke with the Republican party. At this time their high hopes for political power rested primarily on Frank, who in 1868 was the Democratic vice presidential candidate and in 1871 was elected to the Senate. In 1875, however, Frank died, and his broken-hearted father followed a year later at Silver Spring.

As a partisan editor, Blair exaggerated the egalitarianism of the Democrats, but by glorifying democracy as the national ideal and by identifying the immensely popular Jackson with a coherent democratic philosophy, he contributed to the national spirit that saved the Union in 1861. On the Texas issue he sacrificed personal advantage for principle, and he worked tirelessly and effectively to prevent slavery's expansion and to preserve the American Union. The Pennsylvania Avenue home that he purchased in 1836 and gave to his son Montgomery fifteen years later still serves as a guesthouse for visiting foreign dignitaries.

• The Library of Congress has a large collection of Blair papers, but the vast Blair-Lee collection at Princeton University is much more extensive. Copies of Blair's various published pamphlets are in the Library of Congress. Blair is prominent in Virginia J. Laas, ed., *Wartime Washington: The Civil War Letters of Elizabeth Blair Lee* (1991). William E. Smith, *The Francis Preston Blair Family in Politics* (2 vols., 1933), is valuable, but the author did not see the Blair-Lee papers later given to Princeton and did little, if any, research in Kentucky. Elbert B. Smith, *Francis Preston Blair* (1980), is more accurate and complete.

ELBERT B. SMITH

BLAIR, Francis Preston, Jr. (19 Feb. 1821–9 July 1875), statesman and Union army officer, was born in Lexington, Kentucky, the son of Francis Preston Blair, the influential editor of the *Congressional Globe*, and Eliza Violet Gist. He was a brother of Montgomery Blair, a prominent lawyer, mayor of St. Louis, and cabinet member under Abraham Lincoln. As a private school student in Washington, D.C., Blair proved a gifted though undisciplined scholar, exhibiting both impetuosity and intensity—personality traits that would later define him as an adult. He was expelled from several academies and ultimately from both Yale and the University of North Carolina. While yet a struggling student, Blair contributed editorials to the *Globe*, which his father published willingly as a vital investment in his favorite son's political education and career. Blair eventually finished at Princeton University in 1841, but the faculty refused to allow him to graduate as a result of rash behavior. At the intercession of a ranking professor, he was granted his degree the following year.

After attending law school in 1842 at Transylvania University (his father's alma mater), Blair was admitted to the bar in Lexington and moved to St. Louis to share a practice with his brother Montgomery. For the next three years, Blair worked in the law office of Thomas Hart Benton while becoming active in local Democratic politics. In 1845, suffering from ill health and boredom, Blair traveled west to the Rocky Mountains. When the Mexican War broke out, he signed up with an American military unit. General Stephen Kearny, who captured what became New Mexico, chose Blair to be attorney general for the territory.

His health restored, Blair returned to the East in 1847, immediately marrying Appoline Alexander. They would have eight children. He then moved back to St. Louis to pursue his legal career. While a weak financial manager and a lifelong spendthrift, Blair showed himself a capable lawyer and aggressive politician who spoke his mind freely and quickly gained a solid local reputation. Though himself a slaveowner, Blair was avowedly opposed to opening up the western territories to slavery. His short-lived newspaper, the *Barnburner*, advocated free soil policies, and he established the Free Soil party in Missouri during the presidential election of 1848, supporting family friend Martin Van Buren. So vigorous were Blair's denunciations of slavery and supporters of its extension that in 1849 he was shot at by a would-be assassin in St. Louis. Nevertheless, Blair broke with his mentor, Benton, and endorsed the Compromise of 1850 in an effort to gain California, where his brother James Blair owned a shipping business.

In 1852 Blair gained election to the Missouri legislature, where for two terms he proved a stentorian champion of free soil politics. On one occasion he only narrowly avoided a duel as a result of his public tongue-lashing of a Benton detractor. In 1856 Blair was elected to the U.S. House as the only Free Soiler from a slave state. Though a Democrat, Blair supported John C. Frémont of the newly formed Republican party for the presidency. Only a month after taking his seat in the House, he gave his first speech to Congress. Authored in part by his father, Blair's speech portrayed the institution of slavery as a national problem rather than a sectional responsibility borne solely by the southern states. Forecasting the inevitable end to slavery, he promoted a policy of gradual emancipation. He also recommended that Congress support colonization of free blacks and those "who may hereafter become free."

In 1859, continuing his public opposition to slavery, particularly its extension into the territories, Blair once again collaborated with his father on an address presented in Boston supporting free labor and colonization, which was widely praised and published as *The Destiny of the Races on This Continent*. His national reputation thus gained, complemented by his strong oratorical skills and ability to speak extemporaneously, he won reelection in 1860 to Congress from St. Louis, though the election was so close that Congress itself was forced to vote to reseat Blair.

As national events hastened toward sectional division, Blair's Democratic affiliation gave way to political transience. He proved unyielding only in his support of the Constitution and of the Union. After losing his congressional bid as a Democrat in 1858, he had quickly affiliated with the Republican party to win his seat in 1860. Though initially a backer of presidential candidate Edward Bates, a Missouri Whig, Blair turned to the Republican, Lincoln, at the party's 1860 Chicago convention and campaigned tirelessly for the Illinoisan through the remainder of the campaign. Blair organized the Unconditional Unionist party in St. Louis and largely transformed it into the state's Republican party. As the specter of civil war hung over the nation, Blair organized the radical Unionist elements in St. Louis in preparation for the defense of the city. Blair formed paramilitary "Home Guard" units, made up of former Republican "Wide Awake" and German turnverein club members. He organized their training, supplied them with weapons, and drew on his family's important political connections in Washington in support of the Union cause.

Though Missouri voted to remain neutral (despite the efforts of its secessionist governor), Blair feared the anti-Union sentiment in St. Louis. After meeting Captain Nathaniel Lyon, a firebrand radical Unionist who commanded the garrison of the city's Federal arsenal, Blair used influence to remove the commanders of both the arsenal and the Western Department and in both cases succeeded in having Lyon appointed as replacement. Once that was done, Blair assisted Lyon in enlisting the city's Home Guard into Federal service and then marshaled their forces to capture a state militia encampment sympathetic with the Confederacy located outside the city. Rioting in St. Louis followed, and large numbers of hitherto neutral Missourians went over to the Confederate cause. Even so, the capture of the encampment ensured that St. Louis would remain in Union hands. In June, after his meeting with the state's secessionist leaders had resulted in the impetuous Lyon declaring war on the state, Blair led a brigade of troops under Lyon to Jefferson City, clearing militia from the center of the state and the secessionist government from its capital. While Lyon continued his campaign southward, Blair left Missouri and took his seat in Congress, chairing the House Committee on Military Defense.

Blair convinced Lincoln to appoint Frémont as commander of the Western Department, but, on returning to St. Louis and witnessing the new commander's conduct, he quickly criticized Frémont of incompetence. He was to become deeply embroiled in the controversy that led to Frémont's ouster. Blair then left Congress in 1862 and was appointed brigadier general in the Federal army. He managed to raise seven Missouri infantry regiments and led a brigade in battle at Vicksburg under William T. Sherman before being promoted to major general. As commander of an infantry corps through the remainder of the war, Blair on one occasion left the front to participate in a stormy session of Congress. He was the only nonregular army commander in attendance at the surrender of Confederate army commander Joseph E. Johnston.

Back in politics to offset his lost personal finances, Blair soon opposed the Radical Republican plan of Reconstruction. A supporter of Andrew Johnson and his lenient policies, Blair had no sympathy for test oaths, registry laws, disfranchisement of southern whites, and the provision of the vote to former slaves. His public stances drew the enmity of the Radicals, and Congress twice refused to confirm Blair's nomination by Johnson for government appointments. In 1868, after having reorganized the Democratic party in Missouri, Blair was chosen to be the running mate of presidential candidate Horatio Seymour, who lost to the Republican Ulysses Grant. Because of his cooperation with liberal Republicans, Blair was elected that same year to serve in the Missouri legislature; his fellow legislators eventually selected him to be a U.S. senator. Blair worked assiduously on behalf of Horace Greeley's nomination for president in 1872 and then helped to break Radical Republican power in his home state. He was defeated for reelection to the Senate in 1873 and served nominally as Missouri's state superintendent of insurance until his death. He died in St. Louis of head injuries incurred during a fall.

• The largest collection of letters to and from Blair is located in the Blair papers at the Library of Congress. Another large source of family papers is the Blair-Lee Collection at the Princeton University Library. Other important sources are at the Missouri Historical Society, the State Historical Society of Missouri, and in the Blair-Rives Collection at the Library of Congress. The most authoritative accounts of his life are in Elbert B. Smith, *Francis Preston Blair* (1980); and William E. Smith, *The Francis Preston Blair Family in Politics* (2 vols., 1933; repr. 1969). For Blair's services in Mo. during the early part of the Civil War, see also Christopher Phillips, *Damned Yankee: The Life of General Nathaniel Lyon* (1990); and James Peckham, *General Nathaniel Lyon and Missouri in 1861* (1866). Obituaries are in the *St. Louis Globe-Democrat* and the *St. Louis Dispatch*, both 10 July 1875.

CHRISTOPHER PHILLIPS

BLAIR, Henry William (6 Dec. 1834–14 Mar. 1920), U.S. representative and senator, was born in Campton, New Hampshire, the son of William Henry Blair and Lois Baker, schoolteachers. When Henry was two years old his father died, and his mother's straitened circumstances forced her to send him and several siblings to live with neighboring farmers. Engaged in farm work as a youth, he intermittently attended Plymouth Academy and New Hampshire Conference Seminary. He read law with William Leverett of Plymouth, New Hampshire, from 1856 to 1859 and was admitted to the bar in 1859. That same year he married Eliza Ann Nelson; they had at least one child. In 1860 he was appointed Grafton County solicitor. During the Civil War Blair rose to become lieutenant colonel of the Fifteenth New Hampshire Volunteers before severe wounding in the field in 1863 forced him to resign his commission.

Blair resumed the practice of law at Plymouth and entered active politics as a Republican. In 1866 he won election to the New Hampshire Assembly; the follow-

ing year voters chose him for a two-year term in the state senate. Blair's career in national politics began in 1874 with his election to the House of Representatives, where he served until 1879 when he moved over to the Senate. After two terms he was defeated for renomination to the Senate in 1891, but two years later he returned to the House for a single term in the Fifty-third Congress.

In Congress Blair faithfully advocated the central elements of the Republican party's program: a protective tariff, a stable currency based on coin, and generous pensions for Union veterans. But in both the House and the Senate he soon stood out as an example of that rarity in late nineteenth-century American politics, a passionate reformer who also managed to win and hold important public office. In 1876, during his first term in the House, he introduced a constitutional amendment to bar the manufacture, importation, and sale of liquor after 1900. During his tenure in Congress he repeatedly reintroduced this measure, and in 1888 he published a massive prohibitionist tome, *The Temperance Movement; or, The Conflict between Man and Alcohol*. In Congress he was equally persevering in pressing for a constitutional amendment for woman suffrage. In the mid-1880s, as chair of the Senate's Committee on Education and Labor, he headed an investigation into the relationship between capital and labor and held balanced hearings that offered a forum not only to business leaders but also to working people. In the aftermath of the committee's work, Blair sponsored legislation to create a bureau of labor statistics and a bill to bar the importation of contract labor.

Blair's most famous legislative initiative—the Blair bill—called for federal financial support for local common schools. Although he did not originate the idea of such federal aid, in the 1880s he became its most fervent advocate. The movement grew out of a deepening concern for the condition of the freedmen in the post–Civil War South. To Blair and others, blacks' high rates of illiteracy left them ill equipped to exercise their new responsibilities as citizens. Because the nation as a whole had freed the slaves and by the Fifteenth Amendment had enfranchised them, Blair argued that the national government should contribute to their education. He first introduced his federal aid bill in 1882. In a modified form it passed the Senate in 1884, 1886, and 1888.

The aid bill called for the national government to distribute $77 million to the states over eight years. The proportion of the funds assigned to each state would be determined by the degree of illiteracy among the state's people older than ten, thereby ensuring that the bulk of the funds would go to the South. To counter the argument that the proposal would encourage local and state authorities to shirk their responsibility to support education, the bill incorporated the matching principle, stipulating that in a given year no state could receive in federal funds a sum greater than it spent itself. Democratic opponents, including many from the South, argued against the bill as unconstitutional, extravagant, a threat to state and local control of education, and a drain on federal funds that would require maintaining high tariff rates. The bill never passed the House, and it failed in the Senate in 1890, largely because its opponents convinced enough members that southern states had made sufficient strides in supporting schools.

After Blair lost renomination to the Senate in 1891 to a Republican rival, he declined an appointment as federal district judge for New Hampshire. President Benjamin Harrison then appointed him minister to China. He accepted the post, but before he could take up his duties, the Chinese government rejected him as persona non grata because of his earlier support for legislation prohibiting Chinese immigration. After his last term in the House came to a close in 1895, he stayed on in Washington, practicing law until his death in that city.

Many of Blair's contemporaries dismissed him as a political gadfly. Noting his propensity for windy discourse on the House or Senate floor, the *New York Times* once stigmatized him as "a nuisance that calls for abatement" (21 Feb. 1890). Undeterred by such criticism, Blair cheerfully continued to back reforms. In doing so he offered an alternative voice in the generally conservative mainstream party politics of his times.

• The New Hampshire Historical Society holds a small collection of Blair's papers. In addition to his book on the temperance movement, Blair also published *National Aid in the Establishment and Temporary Support of Common Schools: The Education Bill* (1887), a collection of his speeches and other documents on the subject. The most important primary source for his public career is the *Congressional Record*. Secondary works have focused on his efforts in behalf of federal aid to education, including Gordon Canfield Lee, *The Struggle for Federal Aid: First Phase: A History of the Attempts to Obtain Federal Aid for the Common Schools, 1870–1890* (1949), and Daniel Wallace Crofts, "The Blair Bill and the Elections Bill: The Congressional Aftermath to Reconstruction" (Ph.D. diss., Yale Univ., 1968). For Blair's labor and capital hearings, see John A. Garraty, ed., *Labor and Capital in the Gilded Age* (1968), a compilation of selections from the testimony with a useful introduction. A brief biographical sketch of Blair is in Ezra S. Stearns, *History of Plymouth, New Hampshire* (1906).

CHARLES W. CALHOUN

BLAIR, James (May 1656?–18 Apr. 1743), founder and first president of the College of William and Mary, was born in Banffshire, Scotland, the son of Robert Blair, a Church of Scotland cleric. He was educated at Marischal College (now the University of Aberdeen) and in 1669 entered the University of Edinburgh, where he received an M.A. in 1673. Ordained in 1679 by a bishop of the Church of Scotland, Blair ministered to Cranston Parish until 1682, when he was displaced for refusing the Test Oath required of Scottish clergy under Catholic James II. He then went to London and served three years as clerk to the Master of the Rolls

before accepting appointment by Henry Compton, bishop of London, as missionary to Henrico Parish, Virginia.

Two years after his arrival in Virginia in 1685, Blair married seventeen-year-old Sarah Harrison, daughter of Benjamin Harrison II, a councilor and powerful planter. Marriage hastened his political rise. Appointed by Bishop Compton in 1689 as his commissary (deputy) in Virginia, Blair supervised the Anglican clergy sent to Virginia. His appointment as a councilor in 1694 further improved his status.

But Blair's chief achievement was the founding of the College of William and Mary, Virginia's first college (second in the colonies only to Harvard), chartered in 1693. Its liberal arts were designed to lead Virginians into theological studies and holy orders. Beginning his efforts in 1691, Blair spent two years in England, aided by Compton and other prelates, lobbying King William III and Queen Mary II to authorize and endow the college, which opened circa 1695.

Appointed college president for life, Blair moved in 1695 from Jamestown to Middle Plantation, which he and Lieutenant Governor Francis Nicholson in 1699 persuaded the General Assembly to rename Williamsburg and to designate it as Virginia's capital, succeeding Jamestown. In 1710 he also became rector of Bruton Parish in Williamsburg. Thereafter he was second in influence in Virginia only to the royal governor.

A red-faced, handsome, and combative churchman, Blair forced the recall to England of Francis Nicholson, Sir Edmund Andros, and Alexander Spotswood, governors whose autocracy angered him. Though sometimes vitriolic, he was admired for resisting tyranny. Reared with Scottish distaste for English imperialism, he voiced a whiggish concern for colonists' rights that anticipated the revolutionary spirit of Virginia.

A latitudinarian, Blair helped implant the low church Protestantism of Virginia's established church. He welcomed Wesleyan reformer George Whitefield to preach from Bruton's pulpit in 1739. As a doctrinarian, he was known chiefly for his five volumes of sermons, *Our Saviour's Divine Sermon on the Mount* (1722), republished in 1740 and translated into Danish in 1761. He was coauthor in 1697 of the highly critical *The Present State of Virginia, and the College*, published in 1727.

Childless, Blair died in Williamsburg and left his estate to the college and to his nephew, John Blair (1687–1771), who followed him as a councilor and as acting governor. James Blair's grandnephew, also named John Blair (1732–1800), was appointed by President George Washington in 1789 as associate justice of the United States Supreme Court.

• Few of Blair's personal letters survive, but letters and reports are in the Fulham Palace Papers, and other correspondence is in the Society for the Propagation of the Gospel Papers; both collections are at Rhodes House, Oxford. The Society for Promoting Christian Knowledge archives in London also contain Blair material. See also Parke Rouse, Jr., *James Blair of Virginia* (1971), and J. E. Morpurgo, *Their Majesties' Royall Colledge of William and Mary in the Seventeenth and Eighteenth Centuries* (1976).

PARKE ROUSE, JR.

BLAIR, John, Jr. (1732–31 Aug. 1800), associate justice of the Supreme Court of the United States, was born in Williamsburg, Virginia, the son of John Blair, a prominent colonial Virginia statesman, and Mary Monro. Educated at the College of William and Mary, from which he graduated with honors in 1754, Blair pursued the study of law at the Middle Temple in London (1755–1756), where in 1757 he was called to the bar. While in England, he married Jean Blair (no relation) on 26 December 1756.

Returning to Williamsburg, Blair took up the practice of law in the colony's General Court and became an active participant in Virginia's political affairs. Although as a representative of the College of William and Mary in the House of Burgesses he had opposed Patrick Henry's Stamp Act resolutions in 1765, four years later he assisted in drafting Virginia's nonimportation agreement. Thenceforth, Blair was a committed revolutionary even though he served as clerk to the royal governor's council in the early 1770s. In June 1776, after Virginia adopted a new constitution for the independent commonwealth, he became a member of the governor's council.

Blair's judicial career began in 1778 when he became one of five judges of the General Court, a post to which the state legislature had elected him. By 1779 he had become chief justice of the General Court, and by November of the next year he was chancellor of the three-member High Court of Chancery. Because he served on these two courts, he also sat on the Virginia Court of Appeals. As a member of that court, Blair, in the case of *Commonwealth v. Posey* (1787), joined the majority in a decision that supported the principle that long-settled English statutory constructions remained relevant to the interpretation of Virginia law. When Virginia reorganized its judicial system, the legislature appointed Blair in 1788 to the new supreme court of appeals.

Blair's judicial career advanced into a new arena after the adoption of the federal Constitution. In September 1789 George Washington nominated him to fill one of the six seats on the newly created Supreme Court of the United States. The Senate confirmed Blair two days later. As a delegate to both the constitutional convention in Philadelphia and the Virginia state ratifying convention, Blair had proven himself to be a staunch federalist and had apparently satisfied Washington's "solicitude for drawing the first characters of the Union in to the Judiciary." Blair felt some initial hesitation and wrote to Washington, "When I considered the great importance, as well as the arduous nature of the duties, I could not but entertain some fears, that I might find them well adapted neither to my domestic habits, my bodily constitution, nor my

mental capacity." He decided, however, to take the position on a trial basis: "I have determined to make an experiment, whether I may be able to perform the requisite services, with some degree of satisfaction, in respect both to the Public and my self."

Illness compelled Blair to resign from the Court in October 1795. He spent the years until his death at his home in Williamsburg. During his six years on the federal bench, Blair participated in several decisions, either as a justice of the Supreme Court or on a federal circuit court (a duty required of Supreme Court justices under the Judiciary Act of 1789), that established the national government as supreme in its sphere. In *Glass v. the Sloop Betsey* (1794) and *Penhallow v. Doane's Administrators* (1795), the Court affirmed the admiralty jurisdiction of federal district courts; in *Chisholm v. Georgia* (1793), as a member of the majority, Blair, in his opinion given seriatim, declared that states could be sued in the Supreme Court by citizens of other states, which, he argued, the language of Article III of the Constitution made clear. And, in *Georgia v. Brailsford* (1792; 1793; 1794), Blair was part of a unanimous Court that indicated, in jury instructions delivered by Chief Justice John Jay (1745–1829), that the Court believed that state confiscation and sequestration laws passed during the Revolution could not bar the recovery of debts by British subjects as specified in the 1783 Treaty of Peace.

More important, Blair contributed to the development of the idea that judicial review was a power that the Constitution intended federal judges to exercise, thereby advancing the establishment of the federal judiciary as a co-equal branch of the national government. As a U.S. Circuit Judge sitting in Pennsylvania, Blair, along with Justice James Wilson and Judge Richard Peters, refused to hear the petition of William Hayburn, who claimed that he was eligible for a federal pension under a 1792 statute. This action clearly indicated the circuit court's belief that the 1792 act was unconstitutional, although no official opinion to that effect was issued.

As an observer in a courtroom in which Justice Blair presided noted: "I think the President has been very fortunate in the appointment of Judges. We are much pleased with Judge Blair. His candor ease politeness and learning are acknowledged and I am no less pleased with his independence" (James Sullivan to William Bingham, 20 Oct. 1793). As a steadfast patriot in the American Revolution and an intelligent, erudite, and independent judge in the initial years of the nation's life, John Blair served his country well.

• No collection of Blair papers exists. A small number of letters can be found in the papers of other prominent founding generation figures, such as George Washington, John Jay, and James Wilson. A selection of Blair letters that pertain to the business of the Supreme Court and the federal circuit courts and two grand jury charges are published in Maeva Marcus, ed., *The Documentary History of the Supreme Court of the United States, 1789–1800* (1985–). No book-length biography of Blair has been written. Although marred by some inaccuracies, the best essay about Blair remains J. Elliott Drinard, "John Blair, Jr.," *Proceedings of the Thirty-Eighth Annual Meeting of the Virginia State Bar Association* (1927), pp. 436–49.

MAEVA MARCUS

BLAIR, Montgomery (10 May 1813–27 July 1883), postmaster general and lawyer, was born in Franklin County, Kentucky, the son of Francis Preston Blair and Eliza Violet Gist. His father, who served in the War of 1812 and was an assistant newspaper editor at the time of Montgomery's birth, later became the founder and editor of Andrew Jackson's official newspaper, the *Washington Globe*. His mother was the daughter of Nathaniel Gist, a revolutionary war hero, and Montgomery grew up in an influential family intensely concerned with public issues.

Educated in Kentucky schools and at Lexington's famous Transylvania College, Blair followed his father's wishes that he enter the U.S. Military Academy, graduating in 1836. Appointed a first lieutenant, he served a few months in the Seminole War in Florida, but he soon resigned his commission and studied instead for the more peaceful profession of the law. Admitted to the bar in 1839, he moved to St. Louis, where he became the protégé of Missouri's Democratic senator, Thomas Hart Benton.

Married in 1836 to Caroline Buckner, Blair had three children with his first wife, who died in childbirth in 1844. Three years later he married Mary Elizabeth Woodbury, who was the daughter of Levi Woodbury, a Democratic senator from New Hampshire and a member of Jackson's and Martin Van Buren's cabinets. They had five children. The lean, six-foot-tall Blair stood out among his contemporaries for the military posture he never lost and for the thin, reedy voice that sometimes detracted from the presentation of his powerful legal arguments, delivered, occasionally, to the U.S. Supreme Court.

In 1840 Blair was appointed the U.S. district attorney for Missouri, and though removed by the Whig John Tyler, he soon returned to public life as the mayor of St. Louis (1842–1843), followed by a four-year tenure as judge of the court of common pleas. He also developed a lucrative legal practice. By the time he moved in 1853 to Washington, D.C., where he and his wife resided in Blair House across from the White House before moving to Silver Spring, Maryland, he had prospered from the railroad cases he argued. In 1855 he was appointed U.S. solicitor for the U.S. Court of Claims, but he was removed from office by James Buchanan after he left the Democratic party over the issue of the repeal of the Missouri Compromise.

In 1856 Blair became the counsel for the plaintiff Dred Scott, and though he lost this case before the proslavery Roger B. Taney Supreme Court, Blair argued the important principle that the slave Scott was entitled to his freedom by virtue of his residence in free territory. Blair also held that the Missouri Compromise prohibited slavery in the territories and that

Congress had the authority to prohibit slavery there, a position that put him at odds with southern Democrats and that had been undermined in the 1854 Kansas-Nebraska Act.

Blair, along with his influential brother Francis Blair and his father, had come to oppose slavery and to support the return of freed blacks to Africa, the latter a policy that he believed would encourage southerners to free their slaves. Blair's views on slavery were representative of a body of border-state opinion, which opposed abolitionism and black equality as too extreme but which argued for a containment of slavery and its gradual end. In 1848 he was associated with the Free Soil party, attracted to that new organization during a period of party realignment by friends in New York. By 1852 he had returned to the Democratic party and was a delegate to its national convention. By 1860 he supported the Republican party and worked hard, though largely unsuccessfully, to organize this new political organization in Maryland.

Like his father and his brother, Blair favored Missourian Edward Bates for the Republican nomination in 1860. After Abraham Lincoln was elected, Blair's border-state residence and his pronounced Unionism led Lincoln to appoint him postmaster general in 1861. He served until the fall of 1864.

Methodical and hardworking, Blair made several contributions to the efficiency of his department, introducing the concept of prepaid letters, ending the postal service's deficit, fixing salaries for post office managers, and establishing free delivery in cities. Among his contributions to the war effort was the rapid creation of an effective military postal system.

As a cabinet officer Blair also became famous for his articulation of Unionist principles. "It is not right to suffer this noble fabric of freedom to be overthrown by demagoguery. . . . I am for the Union, now and forever, and against all its enemies, whether fire-eaters or abolitionists," he said shortly before taking office. Remembering his hero, the nationalist Jackson, Blair stood alone in counseling Lincoln that any abandonment of Fort Sumter would confirm the views of the South that the North would not fight, and he threatened to resign if the fort were not reinforced.

Caught amid the growing factionalism of the Republican party, Blair attacked what he called "the ambitions of the ultra-abolitionists" and their plans for the "amalgamation [of the races], equality and fraternity." On this basis he was especially critical of Lincoln's secretary of the Treasury, Salmon P. Chase. Blair denied that southern states had committed state suicide and should therefore be under federal control after the war had ended. As a result of his positions, more radical Republicans accused him of disloyalty, and Blair was the target of a resolution calling for a reorganization of the cabinet, which was approved by the Union National Convention that renominated Lincoln in 1864. After the president accepted his resignation and his home in Silver Spring was burned by Confederate marauders from Jubal Early's army, Blair returned to his law practice in Washington.

After the war Blair remained active in Maryland politics, returning to the Democratic party. In 1874 he was defeated for that party's nomination for Congress in the Sixth District because of his wartime associations with the Republicans. In 1882 he received the nomination but was defeated in the general election. Throughout the postwar period, along with his father and brother, he sought a realignment of parties so that middle-of-the-road Democrats and Republicans could undertake a more moderate policy toward the defeated South based on opposition to black voting and the repeal of laws that disenfranchised former Confederates. To this end he supported Andrew Johnson's efforts to form a Union party and in 1876 founded the *Washington Union*. That same year, during the controversy following the Hayes-Tilden election, Blair argued that the Democrat Samuel J. Tilden had been legally elected before the Electoral Commission, which eventually ruled for the Republican Rutherford B. Hayes. Blair died at his rebuilt estate near Silver Spring.

• The bulk of the Blair papers relating to Montgomery Blair are in the Library of Congress. Other manuscript materials are in the Lincoln papers (Robert Todd Lincoln Collection), the Levi Woodbury Papers, and the Blair Family Papers in Princeton University. The records of the post office are in the National Archives, and several of Blair's speeches and pamphlets are available in the Library of Congress. Given his prominence and long public life, useful materials appear in the *Diary of Gideon Welles* (3 vols., 1911) and David Donald, ed., *Inside Lincoln's Cabinet: The Civil War Diaries of Salmon P. Chase* (1954). William Ernest Smith's two-volume biography, *The Francis Preston Blair Family in Politics* (1933), is still invaluable.

JEAN H. BAKER

BLAKE, Eli Whitney (27 Jan. 1795–18 Aug. 1886), inventor and manufacturer, was born in Westboro, Massachusetts, the son of Elihu Blake, a farmer, and Elizabeth Whitney, sister of the cotton-gin inventor Eli Whitney. With the financing of his famous uncle, Blake graduated from Yale College in 1816. He then entered law school at Litchfield, Connecticut, but left when Whitney asked him to help run his arms factory near New Haven in the Whitneyville section of Hamden, Connecticut. As Whitney's right-hand man, Blake gained much practical experience in civil and mechanical engineering. In 1822 he married Eliza Maria O'Brien of New Haven; they had twelve children and sent five of their six sons through Yale.

After Whitney died in 1825, Blake and his brother Philos ran the Whitney Armory for ten years, modernizing its equipment to include what is now the oldest surviving milling machine. In 1835 they left the armory and joined another brother, John, in starting a hardware factory in nearby Westville. Blake Brothers made a variety of domestic hardware; the brothers invented and patented door locks (1833 and 1836), latches (1840), fasteners (1843), bedstead casters (1838), and corkscrews (1860). The firm closed about 1880, after the deaths of Philos and John. Eli had meanwhile turned to development of the Blake rock crusher,

which was granted a U.S. patent (# 20,542) in 1858, and formed the Blake Crusher Company to produce the machines.

While serving on a New Haven town committee that had been appointed in 1851 to build two miles of macadam road to Westville, Blake found that a hand hammer was the only means available to break stone for roads. For seven years he worked out every detail on paper before constructing a perfectly functioning machine to crush stones of varied sizes and shapes and release the desired-size fragments rapidly and automatically. The steam-powered machine had vertical jaws, one of which moved toward the other with sufficient pressure (27,000 pounds per square inch) to crush trap rock (dolerite). It found widespread use in crushing metal ores as well as stones used in road beds, railroad ballast, and concrete. In 1872, Blake estimated, his 509 machines had already saved their users over $55 million. Blake crushers are still used today. But after numerous lawsuits in the 1860s and 1870s, Blake, like his uncle, reaped little reward from his infringed-upon patent, which was reissued in 1866 and extended by seven years in 1872.

Blake's interests ran to science as well as technology. He was an early member, and president from 1850 to 1852, of the Connecticut Academy of Arts and Sciences and a fellow of the American Association for the Advancement of Science from 1874 to 1886. While still manufacturing muskets, he contributed articles on mechanics and fluid dynamics to Benjamin Silliman's *American Journal of Science and Arts*. Beginning in 1824 with an exhaustive treatise on cog wheel teeth, his topics included "The Crank Problem . . . " (1827) and "the Resistance of Fluids . . . " (1835). His 1848 article on " . . . the Flow of Elastic Fluids through Orifices" stemmed from disappointment in the power of a new steam engine at the Blake hardware factory. He concluded theoretically, and later experimentally, that the openings for the flow of steam from the cylinder should be twice as large as the rule then prescribed. In Britain Robert D. Napier and William J. M. Rankine later independently confirmed Blake's new rule. Blake propounded new views on the propagation of sound waves through the atmosphere in the *American Journal of Science and Arts* in 1848 and 1850. In 1882 he collected all his journal articles on the laws and properties of elastic fluids, together with a recently rejected paper on "sonorous waves," and printed them privately as *Original Solutions of Several Problems in Aero-dynamics*.

Blake died in New Haven. Since his time, the Blake stone crusher has not only paved the way to our modern highway system; its potential in skyscraper construction has become a concrete reality.

• Blake family papers are housed in the Yale University Archives. Annual *Patent Office Reports*, and a *Subject Matter Index of Patents for Inventions* (1874), list nineteenth-century patents. Blake's patent suits are indexed in the serial *Shepard's United States Patents and Trademarks Citations*. Models of the Blake stone crusher are in the collections of the Smithsonian Institution and the New Haven Colony Historical Society, which also houses the Whitneyville milling machine.

Blake's articles, letters, and notes in *American Journal of Science and Arts* appear from 1824 to 1860. Biographical sketches were written by Henry T. Blake, "Eli Whitney Blake, Scientist and Inventor," in *Papers of the New Haven Colony Historical Society* 7 (1914): 37–55; by Alida Blake Hazard, *The Blakes of Elm Street* (1925); and by Ralph Henry Gabriel in Richard S. Kirby, ed., *Inventors and Engineers of Old New Haven* (1939): 34–35. Robert Napier's acknowledgement of Blake's work on steam flow is in the *Engineer* 38 (1874): 478.

CAROLYN C. COOPER

BLAKE, Eubie (7 Feb. 1883–12 Feb. 1983), composer and pianist, was born James Hubert Blake in Baltimore, Maryland, the son of John Sumner Blake, a stevedore, and Emily Johnston, a launderer. His father was a Civil War veteran, and both parents were former slaves. While the young Blake was a mediocre student during several years of public schooling, he showed early signs of musical interest and talent, picking out tunes on an organ in a department store at about age six. As a result, his parents rented an organ for twenty-five cents a week, and he soon began basic keyboard lessons with Margaret Marshall, a neighbor and church organist. At about age twelve he learned cornet and buck dancing and was earning pocket change singing with friends on the street. When he was thirteen he received encouragement from ragtime pianist Jesse Pickett, whom he had watched through the window of a bawdy house in order to learn his fingering. By 1898 he had steady work as a piano player in Aggie Shelton's sporting house, a job that necessitated the lad's sneaking out of his home after his parents went to bed. The objections of his deeply religious mother when she learned of his new career were only overcome by the pragmatism of his sporadically employed father, once he discovered how much his son was making in tips.

In 1899 (the year Scott Joplin's famous *Maple Leaf Rag* appeared) Blake wrote his first rag, *Charleston Rag* (although he would not be able to notate it until some years later). In 1902 he performed as a buck dancer in the traveling minstrel show *In Old Kentucky*, playing briefly in New York City. In 1907, after playing in several clubs in Baltimore, he became a pianist at the Goldfield Hotel, built by his friend and the new world lightweight boxing champion Joe Gans. The elegant Goldfield was one of the first establishments in Baltimore where blacks and whites mixed, and there Blake acquired a personal grace and polish that would impress admirers for the rest of his life. Already an excellent player, he learned from watching the conservatory-trained "One-Leg Willie" Joseph, whom he often cited as the best piano player he ever heard. While at the Goldfield, Blake studied composition with Baltimore musician Llewellyn Wilson, and about the same time he began playing summers in Atlantic City, where he met such keyboard luminaries as Willie "The Lion" Smith, Luckey Roberts, and James P. Johnson. In July 1910 he married Avis Lee, the daughter of a black society family in Baltimore and a classically trained pianist.

In 1915 Blake met singer and lyricist Noble Sissle, and they quickly began a songwriting collaboration that would last for decades. One of their songs of that year, "It's All Your Fault," achieved success when it was introduced by Sophie Tucker. Sissle and Blake performed in New York with James Reese Europe's Society Orchestra. While Sissle and Europe were in the service during World War I, Blake performed in vaudeville with Henry "Broadway" Jones. After the war Sissle and Blake formed a vaudeville act called the Dixie Duo, which became quite successful. In an era when blacks were expected to shuffle and speak in dialect, they dressed elegantly in tuxedos, and they were one of the first black acts to perform before white audiences without burnt cork. By 1917 Blake had also begun recording on both discs and piano rolls.

In 1920 Sissle and Blake met the successful comedy and dance team of Flournoy Miller and Aubrey Lyles, who suggested combining forces to produce a show. The result was the all-black *Shuffle Along*, which opened on Broadway in 1921 and for which Blake was composer and conductor. The score included what would become one of his best-known songs, "I'm Just Wild about Harry." Mounted on a shoestring budget, the musical met with critical acclaim and popular success, running for 504 performances in New York followed by an extensive three-company tour of the United States. The show had a tremendous effect on musical theater, stirring interest in jazz dance, fostering faster paced shows with more syncopated rhythms, and paving the way in general for more black musicals and black performers. *Shuffle Along* was a springboard for the careers of several of its cast members, including Josephine Baker, Adelaide Hall, Florence Mills, and Paul Robeson.

Sissle and Blake worked for ten years as songwriters for the prestigious Witmark publishing firm. In 1922, through Julius Witmark, they were able to join ASCAP (American Society of Composers, Authors, and Publishers), which did not at that time include many blacks. They also appeared in an early sound film in 1923, *Sissle and Blake's Snappy Songs*, by electronics pioneer Lee De Forest. In 1924 they created an ambitious new show, *The Chocolate Dandies*. Unable to match the success of *Shuffle Along*, the lavish production lost money, but Blake was proud of its score and considered it his best.

The team returned to vaudeville, culminating in a successful eight-month tour of Great Britain in 1925–1926. The collaborators broke up when Sissle, attracted by opportunities in Europe, returned to work there, while Blake, delighted to be back home in New York, refused to accompany him. Over the next few years Blake collaborated with Harry Creamer to produce a few songs and shows, reunited with Broadway Jones to perform the shortened "tab show" *Shuffle Along Jr.* in vaudeville (1928–1929), and teamed with lyricist Andy Razaf to write songs for *Lew Leslie's Blackbirds of 1930*, including "Memories of You," later to be popularized by Benny Goodman. After Lyles's death in 1932, Sissle and Blake reunited with

Miller to create *Shuffle Along of 1933*, but the show failed, in part because of the depression. The remainder of the decade saw Blake collaborating with lyricist Milton Reddie on a series of shows, including the Works Progress Administration–produced *Swing It* in 1937, and with Razaf on several floor shows and "industrials" (promotional shows). Blake's wife died of tuberculosis in 1939, but despite his grief he managed to complete with Razaf the show *Tan Manhattan*.

During World War II Blake toured with USO (United Service Organizations) shows and worked with other collaborators. In 1945 he married Marion Gant Tyler, a business executive and former showgirl in several black musicals. She took over management of his financial affairs and saw to the raising of his AS-CAP rating to an appropriate level, enhancing their financial security considerably.

After the war, at the age of sixty-three, Blake took the opportunity to attend New York University, where he studied the Schillinger system of composition. He graduated with a degree in music in 1950. Meanwhile the presidential race of 1948 stirred renewed interest in "I'm Just Wild about Harry" when Truman adopted it as a campaign song. This resulted in a reuniting of Sissle and Blake and in a revival in 1952 of *Shuffle Along*. Unfortunately the producers' attempts to completely rewrite the show had the effect of eviscerating it, and the restaging closed after only four performances.

Following a few years of relative retirement, during which he wrote out some of his earlier pieces, a resurgence of popular interest in ragtime in the 1950s and again in the 1970s thrust Blake back into the spotlight for the last decades of his life. Several commemorative recordings appeared, most notably *The Eighty-six Years of Eubie Blake*, a two-record retrospective with Noble Sissle for Columbia in 1969. In 1972 he started Eubie Blake Music, a record company featuring his own music. He was much in demand as a speaker and performer, impressing audiences with his still considerable pianistic technique, as well as his energy, audience rapport, and his charm as a raconteur. Appearances included the St. Louis Ragfest, the Newport Jazz Festival, the "Tonight Show," a solo concert at Town Hall, and a concert in his honor by Arthur Fiedler and the Boston Pops in 1973, with Blake as soloist. In 1974 Jean-Cristophe Averty produced a four-hour documentary film on his life and music for French television. The musical revue *Eubie!*, featuring twenty-three of his numbers, opened on Broadway in 1978 and ran for a year. Blake was awarded the Medal of Freedom at the White House in 1981.

His wife Marion died in June 1982; Blake left no children by either of his marriages. A few months later his one-hundredth birthday was feted with performances of his music, but he was ill with pneumonia and unable to attend. He died five days later in New York City.

Over a long career as pianist, composer, and conductor, Blake left a legacy of more than 2,000 compositions in various styles. His earliest pieces were piano rags, often of such extreme difficulty that they were simplified for publication. As a ragtime composer and player he was, along with such figures as Luckey Roberts and James P. Johnson, a key influence on the Harlem stride-piano school of the 1930s. In the field of show music, Blake moved beyond the confines of ragtime, producing songs that combined rhythmic energy with an appealing lyricism. Particularly notable was his involvement with the successful *Shuffle Along*, which put blacks back on the Broadway stage after an absence of over ten years. Over his lifetime he displayed a marked openness to musical growth, learning from "all music, particularly the music of Mozart, Chopin, Tchaikovsky, Victor Herbert, Gershwin, Debussy, and Strauss," and indeed some of his less well-known pieces show these influences. Finally, his role in later years as an energetic "elder statesman of ragtime" provided a historical link to a time long gone, as well as inspiration to many younger fans.

• Blake's papers (ninety-four boxes of correspondence, photographs, and performance and legal records) are at the Maryland Historical Society in Baltimore. The best general biography of Blake, written by a longtime close friend, is Al Rose, *Eubie Blake* (1979). Robert Kimball and William Bolcom, *Reminiscing with Sissle and Blake* (1973), is lavishly illustrated with photographs and includes considerable background on both individuals while focusing on their collaborative efforts. Lawrence T. Carter, *Eubie Blake: Keys of Memory* (1979), contains many anecdotes, not all involving Blake; its value is diminished by a good many factual errors. Other valuable treatments are in Rudi Blesh and Harriet Janis, *They All Played Ragtime* (1950; 4th ed., 1971); David A. Jasen and Trebor Jay Tichenor, *Rags and Ragtime: A Musical History* (1978); and Eileen Southern, *The Music of Black Americans: A History* (1971; 2d ed., 1983).

WILLIAM G. ELLIOTT

BLAKE, Eugene Carson (7 Nov. 1906–31 July 1985), Presbyterian pastor, was born in St. Louis, Missouri, the son of Orville Prescott Blake, a steel company sales executive, and Lulu Carson. Because Blake's parents were active Presbyterians with fundamentalist leanings, their children attended weekly Bible study and fundamentalist summer conferences. In 1924 Blake went to Princeton University where he participated in the Philadelphian Society, a part of the Student Christian Movement. The society was then under the influence of Frank Buchman's First Century Christian Fellowship, which sought to deepen the spiritual experience of prominent young adults. While serving as the society's president, Blake broke with Buchman because Buchman's personal guidance was commonly identified with that of the Holy Spirit. Shortly thereafter, at a Christian conference in Northfield, Minnesota, Blake had a conversion experience that led him to enter the ministry.

After graduation from Princeton in 1928, Blake was uncertain what form his ministry would take. He first took a missionary position in Lahore, India (now Pakistan), where he taught English, philosophy, and Bible at the Forman Christian Church. The following year he married Valina Gillespie and began theological studies at the New College in Edinburgh. The couple had no children. In his academic work Blake expressed serious doubts about the Westminster Confession's adequacy as a statement of contemporary Presbyterian belief; he believed that the church must reinterpret its beliefs periodically. Many years later, as the stated clerk or executive officer of the United Presbyterian Church in the United States of America (UPCUSA), he acted on this early conviction by promoting the development of a new "Confession of 1967" and the substitution of a *Book of Confessions* for a single confession as the church's statement of belief.

In 1930 Blake attended Princeton Theological Seminary where he found his professors unwilling to recast Christian truth in new philosophical forms. He graduated from Princeton in 1932 and that year was ordained to the special ministry of "evangelist" by the Presbyterian Church in the United States of America (PCUSA). He served the next three years as assistant minister at the Collegiate Church of St. Nicholas in New York City. In 1935 Blake left to become senior pastor at the First Presbyterian Church in Albany, New York. While teaching Christian ethics part time at Williams College, he was deeply influenced by Reinhold Niebuhr's neo-orthodox theology. Despite his evangelical background and leanings, Blake rejected biblical fundamentalism, as did Niebuhr. He also appreciated neo-orthodoxy's focus on the need to reshape theology in contemporary thought forms, Niebuhr's interest in applying Christianity realistically to political and social affairs, and the neo-orthodox stress on the authority of Scripture without assuming biblical inerrancy or surrendering the Bible's truth claims.

Blake came to national prominence in 1940 when he was called to one of the largest Presbyterian congregations in the country, the Pasadena Presbyterian Church in California. Active with youth and a radio ministry, Blake became the chairman of the board of trustees for the Protestant Radio and Television Commission and was appointed to the Board of Christian Education for the PCUSA in 1939. As chair of a subcommittee on Educational Policies and Programs, he helped plan and promote the PCUSA's innovative Faith and Life Curriculum, which attempted to introduce contemporary biblical criticism and theology into adult lay education.

In 1951 Blake was elected stated clerk of the PCUSA. During his controversial tenure Blake transformed his office into a major executive position, which he used to oppose McCartheyism as well as state and federal aid to parochial schools. He also aggressively supported desegregation and assisted in the establishment of a Commission on Religion and Race in the UPCUSA in 1963. In two much-publicized events that same year, Blake was arrested while trying to integrate the Baltimore, Maryland, Gwynn Oak Amusement Park, and he spoke from the Capitol steps alongside Martin Luther King, Jr., during the March on Washington for Jobs and Freedom.

A vigorous proponent of ecumenism, Blake was instrumental in the union of the PCUSA with the United Presbyterian Church of North America that formed the UPCUSA in 1958. He also was elected president of the National Council of Churches, serving from 1954 to 1957, and general secretary of the World Council of Churches (WCC), serving from 1966 to 1972. His ecumenical involvement led him to adopt what he called an "ecumenical consensus theology." He suggested four primary convictions as the grounding for such a theology: that there is a transcendent God who is revealed in Jesus; that knowledge of God is found in reading Scripture and understanding its historical context; that the Christian faith is the same now as always, namely, God the creator is redeemer through Jesus and is working his purpose out; and that the Church must radically revise its understanding of God's expectations as time passes.

Blake's most famous contribution to ecumenism came in December 1960. From the pulpit of the Grace Episcopal Church in San Francisco Blake called for the merger of four mainline U.S. Protestant denominations. This proposal resulted in the creation of a Consultation on Church Union (COCU). Blake chaired the commission, which six years later proposed a plan of union, but the merger never materialized.

In 1961 Blake chaired the WCC's Division of Inter-Church Aid, Refugee and World Service when it took the unusual step of providing assistance to the Mississippi Delta Ministry. Later, as general secretary of the WCC, Blake reorganized WCC central structures into three program units; presided over the Fourth WCC Assembly in Uppsala, Sweden, in 1968; brought fifty new member churches into the WCC; challenged U.S. involvement in Vietnam; and led efforts to address the problems of racism and of economic inequities worldwide. One such effort involved controversial grants in 1970 to politically banned liberation movements in Africa that advocated the overthrow of white minority governments.

After leaving the WCC in 1972, Blake served on a COCU commission to develop a theological base for church union and as president of Bread for the World. Blake's wife died in 1973, and the following year he married Jean Ware Hoyt. In 1978 he chaired the UPCUSA Church and Society Task Force on peacemaking and American foreign policy. Blake died in Stamford, Connecticut.

By his own admission an "organization man," Blake was skilled at using established ecclesiastical channels to promote religious and social change. His critical eye for the moral oversight of the organizations he led, plus his professional credo that "ministers must risk being wrong rather than to be silent and safe," motivated his promotion of controversial civil rights advocacy and ecumenical union among Christians in the United States and abroad.

• Blake's papers are located at two repositories, the Archives of the Department of History for the Presbyterian Church (USA) in Philadelphia and the WCC Archives in Geneva, Switzerland. Blake published numerous addresses and essays but only five books. They are: *Christian Faith: Bulwark of Freedom* (1956), *The Church in the Next Decade* (1966), *He Is Lord of All* (1958), *Presbyterian Law for the Local Church* (1953), and *Presbyterian Law for the Presbytery* (rev. annually 1958–1962, 1964–1966).

The best biography of Blake's life, which includes both a primary and secondary bibliography, is R. Douglas Brackenridge, *Eugene Carson Blake: Prophet with Portfolio* (1978). See also Janet Harbison Penfield, "Ecumenist of Our Time: Eugene Carson Blake, a Whole Man for the Whole World," *Mid-Stream: An Ecumenical Journal* 18 (July 1979): 311–24, and Paul A. Crow, Jr., "Eugene Carson Blake: Apostle of Christian Unity," *Ecumenical Review* 38 (Apr. 1986): 228–36. An obituary is in the *New York Times*, 1 Aug. 1985.

MILTON J COALTER, JR.

BLAKE, Francis (25 Dec. 1850–19 Jan. 1913), scientist, inventor, and astronomer, was born in Needham, Massachusetts, the son of Francis Blake, a businessman and U.S. appraiser of Boston, and Caroline (maiden name unknown). Blake attended Brookline High School but left at age sixteen to take up a position as a draftsman in the U.S. Coast and Geodetic Survey. Blake remained with the survey team for thirteen years. The Coast Survey at that time hired young people out of high school or college in order to nurture the character values of morality, discipline, and loyalty in their employees. On-the-job training by knowledgeable instructors provided young men such as Blake with the skills to conduct research projects using the latest modern scientific techniques.

Blake engaged in survey work on the Susquehanna River in Maryland, on Florida's west coast, and in Cuba. His fieldwork focused on helping to determine the various points of longitude and latitude between the observatories at Greenwich, Paris, Cambridge, and Washington. For example, in 1869 Blake moved to Brest, France, in order to calculate the astronomical difference of longitude between Brest and the Cambridge University observatory. He did this by measuring the difference between local time at the two sites, using French telegraphic cables to communicate time signals. In 1870–1871 he served as astronomer on the Darien expedition, which studied the possibility of constructing a ship canal across the Panamanian isthmus. Blake was assigned the task of determining the astronomical latitudes and longitudes of points on the Atlantic and Pacific coasts, as well as in the interior between Colon and Panama. A study of the results of his transatlantic longitude work was published in Coast Survey reports (1872–1874). In 1875 Blake took part in a conference to determine the boundary between New York and Pennsylvania. He married Elizabeth Hubbard in 1873; they had two children.

In 1875 Blake resigned from the U.S. Coast and Geodetic Survey and moved back to Boston, where he soon became interested in the new field of commercial telephony. In the 1870s Alexander Graham Bell and Thomas Edison vied for dominance in establishing rival telephone businesses. Edison's company, American Speaking Telephone Company, was the first to patent a transmitter in 1878, but the National Bell Telephone Company management decided to go to court for patent infringement in 1878. Although they settled out of court, the rivalry continued.

Blake worked to perfect a voice transmitting device. He submitted the transmitter to the Bell Company in October 1878. Blake's telephone transmitter, in its simplest form, consisted of a battery (power supply), an electromechanical diaphragm, and an induction coil (amplifier). The electromechanical diaphragm resonated in response to the spoken voice (sound waves) and transmitted it electrically through a silver hair spring. A crude metal knob could be turned by the user to strengthen or lessen the pressure of the hair spring against the diaphragm, thus adjusting the transmitter's sensitivity. The use of platinum and carbon electrodes improved the volume of tone. Blake's device "increased the range and clarity of telephone transmission" (Wasserman, p. 56). The transmitter's output was estimated to be nearly twenty decibels higher than the previous electromagnetic model.

This "Blake transmitter" was an improvement over the designs of Edison and Emile Berliner, for it reduced the effects of mechanical vibration, helped to improve the strength of the signal, and reduced sound distortion. After 1878 the Blake transmitter became the Bell Company standard. The Blake transmitter represented "the peak development of single-contact transmitters." It was eventually superseded by the Henry Hunnings multiple-contact transmitter in the 1890s.

Blake continued to work for the Bell Company, where over the next nine years he patented more than eighteen devices, each improving or modifying telephone technology and electrical communication. These patents included numerous improvements in speaking telephones, the creation of an electric switchboard, and the creation of switchboards for telephone exchange.

Blake worked as a director with the American Bell Telephone Company and the American Telephone and Telegraph Company until he retired. During his retirement Blake pursued his interests in the fine arts, folklore, and forestry. He was a fellow of the American Association for the Advancement of Science and the American Academy of Arts and Sciences. He was also an honorary member of the Telephone Pioneers of America and a member of the American Institute of Electrical Engineers, the corporation of the Massachusetts Institute of Technology, the American Folk-Lore Society, the American Forestry Association, and the National Geographic Society. He died at his country home, "Keewaydin," in Weston, Massachusetts.

• The Francis Blake Papers, consisting of forty-seven diaries, are located at the Massachusetts Historical Society Library, Boston. References to Blake's life and work as an astronomer can be found in the coast survey manuals of the U.S. Coast and Geodetic Survey. Information on Blake's work as an inventor can be found in the *Biographical Index to American Science: The Seventeenth Century to 1920*, *American Men of Science*, and the *Twentieth Century Biographical Dictionary of Notable Americans*. A discussion of the Blake transmitter is found in Edward Byrn, *The Progress of Invention in the Nineteenth Century* (1900), and M. D. Fagen, ed., *A History of Engineering and Science in the Bell System: The Early Years, 1875–1925*, vol. 1 (1975). Neil Wasserman's *From Invention to Innovation: Long Distance Telephone Transmission at the Turn of the Century* (1985) gives information on the history of commercial telephony. Frederic William Wile's biography *Emile Berliner: Maker of the Microphone* (1974) claims that Blake suffered a nervous breakdown after his initial work on the transmitter and had to retire to his home for rest; therefore the "perfecting" of the Blake transmitter fell to Berliner. Obituaries are in the *New York Times*, the *Boston Transcript*, and the *Boston Daily Globe*, all 20 Jan. 1913.

VERONICA JUNE BRUCE

BLAKE, Harrison Gray Otis (10 Apr. 1º15–18 Apr. 1898), teacher and editor, was born in Worcester, Massachusetts, the son of Francis Blake, a successful lawyer, and Elizabeth Augusta Chandler. His father's death before Blake's first birthday sharply reduced the family's living standard. Blake graduated from Harvard College in 1835, ranking fourth and giving the Latin Salutatory Oration. Three years' study in Harvard's Divinity School ensued, during which he encountered the religious and ethical philosophy of the Transcendentalists. In 1838 a committee of Blake and two senior theology classmates invited Ralph Waldo Emerson to deliver the "customary discourse" ushering the graduates into ministerial careers. The oration would be Emerson's revolutionary Divinity School Address.

Blake's enthusiasm for the "Newness" and its principal apostle augured ill for his vocation as a Unitarian clergyman. For a year he "preached in various pulpits" and in July 1839 shared with Emerson his hesitations about the ministry. His views had been affected by Emerson and Thomas Carlyle, and, like other Transcendentalists trained for the clergy at Harvard, Blake determined to pursue self-development outside the church. He began a private school in Charlestown, the first of several Massachusetts schools with which Blake was associated as either master or paid assistant. He also tutored. His pupils, usually girls, received from him training in Latin, modern languages, and English. In 1840 he married a cousin, Sarah Chandler Ward. They had two children, one of whom died in infancy, before her death in 1846. He remarried in 1852—to Nancy Pope Conant of a wealthy Sterling, Massachusetts, family. A former student of Blake's, she brought him property and independence from teaching for his livelihood, though he continued to offer instruction for several years. She died childless in 1872.

Blake took two voyages to Europe: with his wife in 1869–1871 and again in 1882. Modest, gentle, and precise, he possessed such rectitude of word and deed that anecdotes circulated among his townsfolk and associates. Reportedly, after an absence "Harry" Blake greeted an acquaintance on the street, then rushed back and pointedly corrected his initial "I am very glad to meet you again" to "I am only glad to meet you."

Blake served his mentor Emerson by arranging lecture visits to Worcester. An industrial center with vigorous cultural institutions, Worcester rapidly became a center of religious and political dissent. Minister and writer Thomas Wentworth Higginson began the Free Church in 1852 and presided over a "Disunion Convention" in 1857 aiming to separate free states from the South. Edward Everett Hale headed another congregation of advanced social and religious beliefs. The exclusion of slavery from western territories (notably Kansas) and speedy abolition were shared commitments of the liberal community, whose leaders also included David Atwood Wasson, John Weiss, the Free Soil party activists Henry Harmon Chamberlin and Eli Thayer, and the antislavery-crusading Stephen S. Foster and Abigail Kelley Foster. Associated with this circle were Blake, the physician Seth Rogers, and Blake's intimate Theophilus Brown, a brilliant conversationalist. Visiting reformers orated in homes or in such auditoriums as Washburn Hall or Brinley's.

In March 1848, when Emerson was lecturing overseas, Blake had a philosophical conversation with Henry David Thoreau, to whom Emerson had introduced him, perhaps as early as 1838. Henceforward Blake's most intense intellectual relationship was with Thoreau. The tone of discipleship is set in the first known letter of their correspondence: Thoreau's spoken remarks had indicated to Blake "a depth of resources, a completeness of renunciation, a poise and repose in the universe, . . . to which I look up with veneration. . . . I would be roused by [your] words to a truer and purer life. . . . You would sunder yourself from society, from the spell of institutions, customs, conventionalities, that you may lead a fresh, simple life with God." Blake cherished Thoreau's letters to him, of which fifty-one survive: they comprise Thoreau's largest single correspondence, and they are typically long, idealistic, and aphoristic. When one of these missives arrived, Blake would assemble the faithful in his parlor or in Brown's tailor shop for recitation and discussion. Anticipating remarriage, Blake asked Amos Bronson Alcott, the Transcendental philosopher-educator, for guidance on the spiritual dimension of wedded union. Probably responding to a similar request, Thoreau presented Blake with "Love" and "Chastity & Sensuality," essays treating the relationship between sexuality and higher consciousness.

Among Thoreau's nine Worcester lectures (1849–1859) were "White Beans and Walden Pond," "Autumnal Tints," and "The Character of Captain John Brown." Blake made the arrangements, issued announcements, and often provided home accommodations. On their reciprocal visits they hiked and boated near Worcester and Concord. They made excursions to New Hampshire in 1858, to Mount Monadnock and to the White Mountains, where with Brown and Thoreau's friend Edward Sherman Hoar they camped in Tuckerman's Ravine, Mount Washington. When Thoreau developed active consumption, Blake had to decline his invitation (3 May 1861) to join him on a curative journey to Minnesota, but after Thoreau took to his deathbed Blake came skating with Brown to visit; they also attended the funeral. In old age Blake characterized his connection with Thoreau as "perhaps the highest privilege of my life."

Four of Thoreau's books were edited posthumously, 1863–1866, by his sister Sophia, while his *Letters to Various Persons* (1865) was edited by Emerson, who had nominated Blake for the job. Blake had declined, feeling himself inadequate to the task. Having shielded Thoreau's enormous manuscript journal from the publishing designs of several aspirants, Sophia at her death in 1876 bequeathed those notebooks and extensive additional papers to Blake, whom she regarded as the most loyal and sympathetic of Thoreau's friends. Quickly Blake decided how to present portions of the journal to readers, selecting passages from the same day of different years for a composite calendar of Thoreau's natural history observations. The first seasonal volume of selections was *Early Spring in Massachusetts* (1881); there followed *Summer* (1884), *Winter* (1888), and *Autumn* (1892), as well as *Thoreau's Thoughts* (1890), topically organized extracts from earlier books. At Alcott's Concord School of Philosophy, Blake sometimes gave inspirational readings from Thoreau. Blake died in Worcester, having willed the Thoreau manuscripts to his friend Elias Harlow Russell, principal of the State Normal School. After contracting for publication of the journal in extenso, Russell sold his bequest.

Blake's permanent importance is bound to the life and writings of Thoreau, of whom he was a devoted follower and a patient editor. While he lacked professional experience in textual scholarship and often misread Thoreau's difficult handwriting, Blake succeeded in issuing a substantial amount of Thoreau's heretofore unpublished journal. Thereby he helped advance Thoreau's reputation in the late nineteenth century and enabled consideration of Thoreau as naturalist.

• Letters by and to Blake may be found in *The Letters of Ralph Waldo Emerson*, ed. R. L. Rusk and E. M. Tilton (1939, 1990–1994); *The Correspondence of Henry David Thoreau*, ed. W. Harding and C. Bode (1958); Henry S. Salt, *Life of Henry David Thoreau* (1896); *Letters of Theo. Brown*, ed. S. T. Brown (1898); *The Letters of A. Bronson Alcott*, ed. R. L. Herrnstadt (1969); and Fritz Oehlschlaeger and George Hendrick, *Toward the Making of Thoreau's Modern Reputation* (1979). These sources are refined in Kenneth W. Cameron, "The H. G. O. Blake Correspondence—An Annotated Checklist," *American Renaissance Literary Report* 5 (1991): 150–71, and "Supplementing the Maimed Correspondence of . . . Theo Brown," *American Renaissance Literary Report* 6 (1992): 148–83. For references to Blake see, too, *The Journals and Miscellaneous Notebooks of Ralph Waldo Emerson*, ed. W. Gilman et al. (1960–1982); *The Writings of Henry David Thoreau: Journal*, ed. B. Torrey and F. H. Allen (1906); *The Writings of Henry D. Thoreau: Journal*, ed. J. C. Broderick et al. (1981–); *The Journals of Bronson Alcott*, ed. O. Shepard (1938); and *Daniel Ricketson and His Friends*, ed. A. and W. Ricketson (1902).

Blake wrote a brief autobiography in his college "Class Book" (1835) and another for *Memorials of the Class of 1835, Harvard University* (1886). Ruth H. Frost's study of Tho-

reau's Worcester friends appears in *American Renaissance Literary Report* 6 (1992): 130–47. The city's social and political life in the 1850s is detailed by Edmund A. Schofield in *Concord Saunterer* 17, no. 2 (1984): 14–48. For legal documents pertaining to Thoreau's manuscripts, see "The Will of H. G. O. Blake," *Thoreau Society Bulletin* 68 (1959): 2–3, and Cameron, "The Thoreau Family in Probate Records," *Emerson Society Quarterly* 11 (1958): 22. Obituaries of Blake in the *Worcester Daily Spy* and *Evening Gazette*, both 19 Apr. 1898, are unreliable; Daniel Gregory Mason memorialized him in "Harrison G. O. Blake, '35, and Thoreau," *Harvard Monthly* 26 (1898): 87–95.

JOSEPH J. MOLDENHAUER

BLAKE, James Vila (21 Jan. 1842–27 Apr. 1925), clergyman and author, was born in Brooklyn, New York, the son of Hamlin Blake, a successful merchant, and Elizabeth Dexter. After his graduation from Harvard University in 1862, Blake became secretary to Massachusetts governor John Andrew. Returning to Harvard, he graduated from the divinity school in 1866. At the time of his ordination, in January 1867, he was serving the Unitarian church at Haverhill, Massachusetts.

In 1869 Blake married Abbie Francis Hovey, with whom he had five children. That same year he was called to the Twenty-eighth Congregational Society in Boston, the former pulpit of Theodore Parker. His ministry there and elsewhere was firmly in the tradition of Parker's radicalism; in the spirit of the Transcendentalists, he built religious certainty on intuition rather than on biblical authority. In 1872 he left the ministry in order to pursue a career in business. This career change apparently took him to Illinois and perhaps to the job of superintendent of the Morgan and Wright rubber and tire factory in Chicago, although the chronology is unclear. In 1878 he returned to the Unitarian ministry with a pastorate in Quincy, Illinois, which he held for five years. He was settled at Third Unitarian Church in Chicago in 1883.

Blake quickly became a part of the "Unity men," a group of six ministers who were the leaders of the Western Unitarian Conference from 1878 until 1894. They were so called because, under the editorship of Jenkin Lloyd Jones, they made up the editorial board of *Unity*, the Western Conference's semi-official organ. The Unity men represented the most liberal wing of the Unitarians; transcending the Christian roots of the Unitarian church, they viewed religion as based in the acceptance of the broadest possible diversity and as amenable to the most up-to-date scientific conceptions. Blake and most of the others were also members of the Free Religious Association, an organization founded in 1867 by those Unitarians who felt excluded by what they viewed as the conservatism of the National Unitarian Conference.

Between 1878 and 1888, the most exciting years of the Unity men's activity, the Western Conference produced its own Sunday School materials to teach the religious conceptions it stood for. Blake wrote the lesson material on Asian religions, emphasizing that of China. His most substantial contribution to the conference came in the production of a conference hymnal, *Unity Hymns and Chorals*, with Frederick Hosmer and William C. Gannett, the three of them creating what they thought of as a "modern" Unitarian hymnody for the West. The hymns they collected blended scientific "modern" religion with a devotional and reverent spirit. The hymnal stayed in print and in use well into the 1920s. Blake's poetic productions are still occasionally found in contemporary hymnals. His particular genius was for the designing of worship. The orders of service in *Unity Festivals* and in the denomination's Sunday school publications were predominantly his.

During "The Issue in the West," the schism that troubled the Western Unitarian Conference from 1886 to 1892, Blake, determined to maintain the openness of the conference, unlimited by doctrinal definitions, stood firmly with the "ethical basis" position. He did not, however, follow Jenkin Lloyd Jones out of the conference when the position of the Unity men was defeated. Like that of the others, his participation in the conference almost ended with the loss of their influence after 1892.

During his pastorate at Third Unitarian Church in Chicago, Blake began the All Souls Unitarian Church in Evanston, Illinois, in 1892. He served both churches as pastor until 1897, when he relinquished his ministry in Chicago. From then until his retirement in 1916, he was minister only in Evanston.

The Unity men had regarded Blake as the scholarly and literary member of their number, and after the defeat of the "ethical basis" position in 1892, he seems to have turned to literature as his new form of expression. Blake published poetry, essays, Latin translations, sermons, and dramas. At his death in Chicago, he was engaged in a comprehensive study of English poetics. His output was large but did not cause much stir. The dramas were apparently not performed, and his poetry had a lukewarm reception.

• Some of Blake's letters can be found in the Jenkin Lloyd Jones collections at the Meadville-Lombard Theological School Library and at Joseph Regenstein Library, both in Chicago. His library was given to Meadville-Lombard. Blake's writings include *Manual Training in Education* (1886), *St. Solifer with Other Worthies and Unworthies* (1893), *Sonnets* (1902), *The Months* (1907), *Discoveries* (1904), *So Like Her Father* (1909), *Lady Bertha's Honeybroth* (1911), and *Sonnets from Marcus Aurelius* (1920). No biographical studies of him have been published to date, not even in the summary sketches of Unitarian ministers. The most complete obituary is in the *Christian Register*, 28 May 1925; a death notice is in the *Chicago Daily Journal*, 29 Apr. 1925.

THOMAS E. GRAHAM

BLAKE, John Lauris (21 Dec. 1788–6 Jul. 1857), clergyman and author, was born in Northwood, New Hampshire, the son of Jonathan Blake and Mary Dow, substantial farmers. An eager student, he attended Phillips Exeter Academy and graduated from Brown University in 1812. The following year he was licensed as a Congregational minister, but shortly thereafter he transferred to the Episcopal church. In 1814 Blake

married Louisa Gray Richmond. He fathered one child, but his wife died a year and a half later. In December 1916 he married Mary Howe, by whom he had three children. Ordained as a deacon in 1815, Blake established St. Paul's parish in Pawtucket, Rhode Island, serving as rector for five years. He later acted as rector in Hopkinton and Concord, New Hampshire. At Concord, Blake founded the Young Ladies' School, which he moved to Boston in 1822 when he became rector of St. Matthew's Church. In addition to his position as principal of the school, which he held until 1830, Blake served as editor of the *Gospel Advocate*, which was merged with the *Episcopal Watchman* in January 1827.

The author of numerous theological addresses, orations, and Christian "evidences," Blake resigned from the clergy in 1830 because of ill health. He moved to New York, devoting himself to writing and editing more general literature. Blake's past scholarly and clerical activities furnished him with a diversified stock of information, which he presented in nearly fifty books. Most of these works consisted of illustrated textbooks for use in his classes and small books for children. Some sense of his diligence and variety may be gained from a partial list of his works. Among his many titles are the following: *The Historical Reader* (1823), *A Geography for Children* (1830), *Conversations on Chemistry* (1831), *First Book in Astronomy* (1842), *Conversations in Natural Philosophy* (1843), *Adventures among the Indians* (1843), *A History of the American Revolution* (1844), and *Wonders of Art* (1845). Some of the texts carry the note, "Especially designed to prevent dullness and monotony in the reading and declamation of schools." Blake's books proved popular, running through several editions. Allibone's *Critical Dictionary* of 1858 observes, "Some of these works have been in use more than forty years, and to them we are indebted for a new feature in School-Book Literature; namely, an analysis of the text in printed Questions at the bottom of each page, which plan has since been frequently adopted."

Blake's literary reputation did not rest solely on his readers and children's library books. He was best known for his two useful reference works, *The General Biographical Dictionary* (1835), over 1,000 pages long, which was the basis of *Appleton's Cyclopaedia of American Biography*; and his equally lengthy *Family Encyclopedia of Useful Knowledge* (1834). Their popularity was amply attested to by their numerous successive editions: in twenty years, Blake's *Family Encyclopedia* went through ten editions, while his *Biographical Dictionary* had thirteen.

Most interesting, however, are Blake's forays into the science of agriculture. Having grown up on a farm, Blake was particularly interested in agricultural progress and rural instruction. His *Farmer's Every-Day Book* (1850), including "twelve hundred laconics and apothegms relating to ethics, religion, and general literature," moved a reviewer in the *New England Farmer* to declare, "It should hold a prominent place in the library of every family in the country." In 1853

Blake published *A Family Text-Book for the Country; or, The Farmer at Home, Being a Cyclopaedia of the More Important Topics in Modern Agriculture*, an alphabetical compilation of information, containing definitions, anecdotes, and facts and fancies from around the world. Since he termed agriculture "the basis of society, [that] constitutes the grand distinction between savage and civilized life," it is understandable that Blake allocated twice as much space to that entry as to practically any other.

Blake's entries are frequently interesting, and many are accompanied by illustrations, but occasionally one wonders about the need for, or the appropriateness of, the information. For example, he glosses the butterfly: "An insect well known, and much admired for its beauty; it is bred from the caterpillar. The wings of the butterfly are four in number, and though two of them be cut off, the animal can fly with the two others remaining." Also of note is Blake's *The Farm and the Fireside; or, The Romance of Agriculture* (1852). Concerned about the farmers' conception that their occupation requires "no more thought than that of the ox who is to toil in company with them," Blake endeavored to place agriculture on as thoroughly scientific a basis as possible. By providing his readers with a wealth of information about livestock, soils, tools, and crops, Blake attempted to invest the rural occupation with dignity and to demonstrate that successful farming required both knowledge and aptitude. Despite a tedious beginning, the work of this genial man is frequently entertaining, as for instance, in his "Anecdotes of the Goose."

Though the individual today would regard Blake's agricultural books only as curious relics of a bygone era, in the author's time they were widely valued. Considering that Blake also wrote or edited several ecclesiological works, numerous textbooks, and extensive reference books, he proved to be an important literary figure of the nineteenth century. His was a lifetime of service in many respects. All of his works focused on education, from birth (*Two Discourses on Christian Baptism* [1816]), through childhood and adolescence (*The Young Orator* [1833] and *Letters to an Only Daughter, on Confirmation* [1839]), to adulthood (*The Family Encyclopedia* [1834] and *Farmer's Every-Day Book* [1850]). A glance at these titles reveals how much Blake concentrated his attention on the needs of the whole person: mental, physical, social, and spiritual.

In the mid-1840s Blake moved to Orange, New Jersey. He served in the New Jersey legislature for the term 1857–1858 and received honorary A.M. degrees, one from Brown University and one from Burlington College. After a varied life "spent in self-sacrificing labors for the good of others," as his obituary declares, John Lauris Blake died in Orange.

• Among Blake's religious writings are his annotated *Every Day Scripture Readings* (1853); his Sunday-school book, *Evidences of Christianity* (1832); and his sermon, *The Gospel Minister's Farewell* (1820), occasioned by his departure from St. Paul's Church of North Providence, R.I., on 6 Aug. 1820. Blake's academic textbooks include a series of drills, such as *Questions Adapted to Aikin's Geography. By the author of Questions adapted to Murray's Grammar and Blair's Rhetoric* (1819). Blake also adapted and "improved" others' texts for school use, such as *Hutton's Book of Nature Laid Open* (1831) and Jane Haldimand Marcet's *Conversations on Natural Philosophy* (1831).

For academic information about Blake, consult the *Historical Catalogue of Brown University, 1764–1904* (1905); for general background, see E. C. Cogswell, *History of Nottingham, Deerfield, and Northwood, N. H.* (1878), pp. 645–47. An obituary is in the *Church Review and Ecclesiastical Register*, October 1857.

KAREN N. SCHRAMM

BLAKE, Lillie Devereux (12 Aug. 1835–30 Dec. 1913), author and feminist, was born in Raleigh, North Carolina, the daughter of George Pollok Devereux, a planter, and Sarah Elizabeth Johnson. Though she was christened Elizabeth Johnson, her father called her "Lilly," and she adopted that name with altered spelling. The Devereux were prominent slaveholders, and Lillie spent her early years on her father's cotton plantation. After George Devereux's death in 1837, she moved with her mother and sister to Connecticut, joining her mother's family there. She was raised in New Haven in an atmosphere of Episcopalian respectability and Whiggish political convictions. Her education at a girls' school was supplemented by private tutoring based on courses in the Yale curriculum.

Her family's active social life equipped Lillie Devereux with connections and social graces that she drew on throughout her career. As a young woman she was something of a belle, frankly recognizing that role as one of the few avenues toward exercising power as a female. "I live to redress the wrongs of my sex," she wrote at age sixteen, adding that to do so, "men's hearts must be attached and then trifled with." Later she wrote that her natural ambition in these years had been misdirected by the convention that, for women, "there was no arena but the drawing-room" (Blake and Wallace, p. 24). She married Frank Umsted, a Philadelphia lawyer, in 1855. The couple had two daughters and eventually settled in New York City. There Lillie began producing short stories for popular serials. Her successful first novel, *Southwold* (1859), denounced coquetry, linking it to male selfishness and domestic failure.

Soon after the novel's publication, Frank Umsted's apparent suicide shattered this comfortable life. Determined to support herself and her daughters, Lillie wrote at a desperate pace under multiple pseudonyms for newspapers and magazines. The coming of the Civil War expanded her opportunities. An ardent Unionist despite her southern ties, she moved to Washington, D.C., where she reported on wartime scenes for several eastern newspapers. She returned to the East in 1862. In 1866 she married Grinfill Blake, who worked for a manufacturing firm in New York. The couple had no children.

In 1869 Lillie Blake visited the recently established Woman's Bureau in New York. Long interested in women's issues but put off by popular stereotypes of suffragists, she found the stylish comportment of the bureau's leaders, Elizabeth Phelps and Elizabeth Cady Stanton, reassuring. She soon joined in the local activities of the National Woman Suffrage Association, developing a reputation as a dynamic speaker and organizer. In the early 1870s, concerned for the suffrage movement's respectability, she fought against the influence of the sexual radicals Victoria Woodhull and Tennessee Claflin. Her long career of legislative engagement began in 1873, when she testified on behalf of woman suffrage before the New York Constitutional Commission. A novel published the following year, *Fettered for Life; Or, Lord and Master*, emphasized women's unequal treatment in marriage and in the workplace.

Blake became the preeminent suffrage leader in late nineteenth-century New York, serving as president of both the New York State Woman Suffrage Association (1879–1890) and the New York City Woman Suffrage League (1886–1900). From these positions she kept constant watch on the legislature and in 1880 helped win the first step toward female suffrage in the state, a law permitting women to vote for school trustees. She undertook national duties as well, including lobbying at the major party conventions in 1880, speaking tours of other states, and frequent appearances at national suffrage meetings.

Blake strongly believed, however, that suffrage should be only one phase of a broader movement for women's rights. She took a keen interest in labor matters, speaking in support of striking workers and pressing for reforms such as better working conditions for female store clerks and improved status for police matrons. A talented controversialist, she attracted international attention for her response in 1883 to the antifeminist lectures of a conservative clergyman, Morgan Dix. In lectures published as *Woman's Place To-Day*, she denied that the Bible supported the subordination of women to men and argued that good "national housekeeping" demanded women's participation in public affairs.

Paralleling such actions, Blake also strove to heighten feminism's social status. She initiated a series of Pilgrim Mothers' Dinners, held annually in New York beginning in 1892, which promoted the feminist cause in high social circles, and she worked with the rising women's club movement to coordinate its suffrage work. In 1886 she founded her "kindergarten for suffrage," the Society for Political Study, which encouraged women to study politics and law from a feminist standpoint.

Blake's broad interest in legislation and women's rights brought her into conflict with suffrage leader Susan B. Anthony, who advocated focused concentration on obtaining the vote. An open break came in 1899, after Anthony dissolved the National American Woman Suffrage Association's Committee on Legislative Advice, which Blake chaired. Backed by Eliza-beth Cady Stanton, Blake challenged Anthony's chosen successor, Carrie Chapman Catt, for election to the presidency of NAWSA in 1900. Unfavorable rules forced Blake to drop the initiative. She then broke with NAWSA and established the National Legislative League, where she worked for causes such as equal treatment of women under inheritance and immigration laws. The NLL, however, failed to attract a large following. Blake continued her legislative activism until her health failed in 1906. She died in Englewood, New Jersey.

Lacking the background in antebellum moral reform that influenced many of her contemporaries, Blake brought a postwar concern for economic issues and political process to the women's movement. At the same time, though pressing far beyond its limits, she retained her mastery of the drawing-room. Her rare combination of talents strengthened the connections between the female reform tradition and the political system and broadened the appeal of feminism across class barriers both high and low. Her work presaged much of Progressive reform and helped sustain the suffrage cause through some of its most difficult years.

• Blake's papers, including her lifelong diaries and uncompleted autobiography, are at the Missouri Historical Society in St. Louis. Another small set of materials, dealing mainly with Blake's suffrage activities, resides in the Sophia Smith Collection, Smith College Library. Among Blake's voluminous journalistic writings, perhaps the most interesting is her column in the *Woman's Journal*, which appeared regularly between 1884 and 1904. For an informative memoir based on manuscript sources and her daughter's personal recollections, see Katherine Devereux Blake and Margaret Louise Wallace, *Champion of Women: The Life of Lillie Devereux Blake* (1943). Blake's activities are documented in Elizabeth Cady Stanton et al., *History of Woman Suffrage*, vols. 3 and 4 (1887–1902), though she felt, with some justification, that these volumes understated her role in the movement.

RONALD YANOSKY

BLAKE, Lyman Reed (24 Aug. 1835–5 Oct. 1883), inventor, was born in South Abington, Massachusetts, the son of Samuel Blake and Susannah Bates. In 1851, having completed his formal education at age sixteen, he went to work for his older brother Samuel, a "shoe boss." After the employees in his brother's shop cut out from leather the various pieces that comprise a shoe, the younger Blake put out these pieces to self-employed shoebinders—who hand-stitched together the uppers and then pegged or nailed the uppers to a sole—and collected the finished pairs, which his brother then sold.

In 1852 the I. M. Singer Company of Boston acquired the patent rights to a sewing machine that could stitch together leather uppers. Almost immediately, shoe bosses began buying upper-stitching machines and employing female operators in-house, although they still sent the finished uppers to outworkers to be attached by hand to soles. Within a year or two of this development, Blake became affiliated with Edmund Shaw, a salesman for Singer; after Shaw made a sale to a shoe boss, Blake installed the machines and taught the operators how to use them. In 1855 he married Susie V. Hollis, with whom he had no children.

In 1856 Blake became a partner in Gurney and Mears, a shoemaking concern, whereupon the firm became known as Gurney, Mears, and Blake. He expanded the company's operations by installing stitching machines and employing operators on a piecework basis. Despite his partners' initial skepticism, in 1857 he designed a shoe that could be stitched together by machine in its entirety. In 1858, having developed what was in effect the modern shoe, he invented and patented a machine capable of piercing the different thicknesses of shoe leather and securely fastening them together. In essence, this invention was a sewing machine with a curved needle that was mounted above a horn. After being molded to the desired shape, the upper, inner sole, and outer sole were positioned around the horn and then stitched together in one operation.

Poor health induced Blake to sell his patent in 1859 to Gordon McKay and move to Staunton, Virginia, where Blake opened a retail shoe store. Two years later, having regained his health (and no doubt uncomfortable over the prospects of being a Yankee in the South after the outbreak of the Civil War), he returned to Massachusetts and entered into a partnership with McKay. The two men tested and perfected Blake's invention, mostly by making the horn movable, while using it to manufacture shoes for the Massachusetts Light Artillery Battery and two regiments of Massachusetts volunteers. The following year the two men began selling Blake's invention, which became known in the United States as the McKay stitching machine, and modified it so that it could be powered by steam. They also developed a workable system for establishing and operating a factory centered around the use of their machine and then sold both machine and system to shoe manufacturers throughout New England. The entire concept was eagerly accepted; Blake later estimated that, between 1861 and 1876, more than 177 million pairs of shoes were made in the United States on "his" machine.

Between 1858 and 1872 Blake also received or shared in the receipt of fifteen additional patents for shoe-making machines and processes, including machines for waxing thread and channeling soles before stitching and devices for stitching uppers together with lasting, a closely woven fabric. In 1874 Blake renewed his patent on the McKay stitching machine, which he immediately reassigned for a sizable sum to the McKay Association, a group of New England shoe manufacturers. Blake then retired from the shoemaking industry and spent his remaining years traveling. He died in Abington.

Blake's invention of the shoe-stitching machine was an important stage in the transition from making shoes via a preindustrial system that employed home-based male hand-stitchers to manufacturing shoes via a factory system that employed centrally located female machine operators.

• Blake's contributions to the shoe industry are discussed in Mary H. Blewett, *Men, Women, and Work: Class, Gender, and Protest in the New England Shoe Industry, 1780–1910* (1988); William H. Mulligan, Jr., "The Family and Technological Change: The Shoemakers of Lynn, Massachusetts, during the Transition from Hand to Machine Production, 1850–1880" (Ph.D. diss., Clark Univ., 1982); Blanche Evans Hazard, *Organization of the Boot and Shoe Industry in Massachusetts before 1875* (1921); and F. A. Gannon, *Short History of American Shoemaking* (1912). Obituaries are in the *Boston Evening Transcript*, 6 Oct. 1883, and *Shoe and Leather Reporter*, 13 Mar. 1884.

CHARLES W. CAREY, JR.

BLAKE, Mary Elizabeth (1 Sept. 1840–26 Feb. 1907), author, was born Mary Elizabeth McGrath in Dungarven, Ireland, the daughter of Patrick McGrath, an artisan in marble, and Mary Murphy. Mary's family immigrated to Quincy, Massachusetts, when she was ten. Her father's trade prospered, enabling him to provide his children with good educations. Mary attended Quincy High School from 1855 to 1859, Emerson's Private School in Boston from 1859 to 1861, and the Academy of the Sacred Heart in Manhattanville from 1861 to 1863. Her major interests in school were music and modern languages. Upon graduating, Mary began teaching and writing poems, which were published in local newspapers. In 1865 she married John G. Blake, a prominent Boston physician; they had eleven children.

During the next several years, Blake devoted most of her energy to rearing her children. Despite her dedication to her family, however, she was aware of the importance of creative outlets for herself. She continued to write poems, some of which reflected her deep feelings over the deaths of five of her children. A devout Catholic, Blake included in even her most poignant poems lyrical and uplifting elements.

She did not dwell on poems of grief, however. Blake's poetry ran the gamut from keen observations of nature to fond remembrances of Ireland, overtures for religious festival days, translations of French and Mexican poems, romantic sonnets, celebrations of family life, and memorials to famous men and women, and stirring historical ballads. Blake's undying faith in God, her appreciation of the beauty of the world around her, her striving for a world of peace, and her recognition of a woman's role in both the private and public spheres were apparent in her verses. Reviewers applied adjectives such as "heartening," "cheerful," "entertaining," "inspirational," "stirring," and "thoughtful" to her poetry. Oliver Wendell Holmes (1809–1894) once said about Blake, "You are one of the birds that must sing."

Sometimes signed merely "M. E. B.," Blake's poetry was published in a variety of journals and newspapers, including the *Boston Gazette*, the *Boston Transcript*, the *Independent*, *Atlantic Monthly*, *Lippincott's Magazine*, *North American Review*, *Ave Maria*, *Peace Journal*, *Catholic World*, *Scribner's*, and the *Congregationalist*. Her books of poetry often were collections of poems that had been published previously in periodicals. Her first collection, *Poems*, was published in 1882. In 1885 and 1886 Blake wrote two books of poems for children, *The Merry Months All* and *Youth in Twelve Centuries*, respectively. Two collections of poetry for adults followed: *Verses along the Way* (1890) and *In the Harbour of Hope* (1907).

Although Blake's fame derived chiefly from her poetry, she also wrote a considerable amount of prose. Some essays were published in various periodicals, and her "Rambling Talks" appeared every two weeks in the *Boston Journal*, beginning in 1877. As the title suggests, the essays in this column covered a variety of general topics, such as biographical sketches, travel suggestions, views on public education, literary criticism, stances on moral and religious issues, historical discussions, and prescriptions for a simple life. Her pamphlet "The Coming Reform: A Woman's Word" (1887) was more specific in its purpose and reflected Blake's activism in the American Peace Society. It denounced "the absurdities of old fashioned militarism at home and abroad" and appealed to many readers during the Spanish-American War.

Blake's extensive excursions to the American West, to Mexico, and to Europe culminated in three books on travel: *On the Wing: Rambling Notes of a Trip to the Pacific* (serialized in the *Boston Journal* in 1882 and published in book form in 1883); *Mexico: Picturesque, Political, Progressive* (written with Margaret F. Sullivan and published in 1888), and *A Summer Holiday in Europe* (the result of five trips to Europe and published in 1890). Blake's travel writing was graceful, descriptive, and respectful of the terrain, the people, and the cultures she encountered. Comparisons with other locales sometimes found Boston wanting. Blake's travel books also included discussions of the literature of the various countries, for which her background in writing and modern languages provided a measure of expertise.

Despite the wide dissemination of her writings, Blake captivated the hearts of Bostonians most of all. There the city fathers asked her to write memorials for such celebrities as Wendell Phillips, Admiral David Dixon Porter, and the Reverend John J. Williams, archbishop of Boston. And there her home became the gathering place for Boston's eminent writers, artists, physicians, musicians, and intellectuals. Boston was also where Blake's full and meaningful life came to an end.

• Katherine E. Conway wrote a brief biography of Blake in her introduction to Blake's *In the Harbour of Hope* (1907). References to Blake are also included in J. B. Cullen, *The Story of the Irish in Boston*, rev. ed. (1893); Frances E. Willard and Mary A. Livermore, eds., *American Women* (1897; repr. 1973); and Lina Mainiero, ed., *American Women Writers* (1979). Obituaries are in the *Boston Globe*, 27 Feb. 1907, and *Publishers Weekly*, 9 Mar. 1907.

DOROTHY MCLEOD MACINERNEY

BLAKE, William Rufus (1805–22 Apr. 1863), actor and theater manager, was born in Halifax, Nova Scotia, Canada. Little is known of his parents except that his father was a descendant of the Blakes of Galway, Ireland. His father died when he was young; his mother apparently saw to his education, intending that he would either enter the mercantile trade or, as one obituary suggests, become a doctor or surgeon. When Blake was seventeen he attended a performance given by a strolling theater company visiting Halifax, and he decided to pursue a career in the theater. His first stage role was as the prince of Wales in *Richard III* for this unknown company. Blake traveled to Kingston, Jamaica, with the troupe; there he served his apprenticeship playing leading Shakespearean roles such as Iago, Othello, and Richard III—the results of the deaths of more established actors due to yellow fever. Theater historian Errol Hill has identified a notice of a Mr. Blake giving a recitation of "Lecture on Heads" in Kingston in March 1823. Sometime after this date Blake returned to North America.

The earliest stage appearance by Blake in the United States for which there is a record was in Albany, New York, on 29 December 1823 at the New Constitution Theatre (formerly the Thespian Hotel) in *The Stranger*. His New York City debut followed on 12 July 1824 as Frederick Bramble in *The Poor Gentleman* at the Chatham Garden Theatre. While acting in the company there he met Caroline Placide Waring (widow of actor Leigh Waring, who had died in 1817), whom he married in 1826. During this early phase of his acting career Blake, a handsome young man, excelled in such light comedic parts as Harry Dornton in *The Road to Ruin* and Captain Absolute in *The Rivals*.

For the next decade Blake acted throughout the Northeast and managed several theaters, beginning with Boston's new Tremont Theatre in 1827 (where he also appeared in its first production, *Wives as They Were*). According to theater lore, Blake was the first actor in the United States to be called before the curtain by the audience. Blake also managed Philadelphia's Walnut Street Theatre, beginning in 1829. With H. E. Willard he comanaged the Olympic Theatre in New York City, which they opened in 1837 but lost in 1839 because of an overly competitive entertainment market. In 1839, during a pleasure trip to Europe, Blake acted in *Three and Deuce* at London's Haymarket Theatre and considered management at Drury Lane. An unsatisfactory engagement and high renovation costs for the latter theater discouraged his efforts, and Blake returned to the United States. Later that same year he served as stage manager at the Walnut Street Theatre, and he assumed a similar position in 1848 at New York's Broadway Theatre.

For the remainder of his career Blake performed in the greatest companies of the day at Burton's, Laura Keene's, and Wallack's theaters as principal comedian. He is rumored to have received the highest salary of any actor in these stock companies. Blake, who had grown corpulent by the 1840s, wisely turned from the romantic leads of his youth to old comic uncles and fathers as well as to sentimental character roles.

Blake's last New York appearance, as Geoffrey Dale in *The Last Man*, was at Keene's theater on 16 April

1863, after which he left for a Boston engagement. After performing Sir Peter Teazle in *The School for Scandal* at the Boston Theatre on 21 April, Blake collapsed on the stage from an attack of "bilious cholic" and died suddenly the next day in Boston.

Blake was considered the finest performer of old-man parts on the American stage in the 1840s and 1850s. His interpretation of Lord Duberly in *The Heir at Law* was considered by one contemporary critic as a glorious performance. This writer noted that "one charm of his acting consists in bringing all the vulgarity of the 'old chandler' out in broad relief, and yet preserving his representation from being coarse—a great stroke of art." Critic William Winter described Blake as "noble in his dignity, so firm and fine and easy in his method, so copious in his natural humour," and historian-critic Joseph Ireland believed that no other contemporary could equal Blake's best roles (including Hardcastle, Old Dornton, Sir Peter Teazle, Sir Anthony Absolute), terming them "examples of perfection." One of Blake's fellow actors, Joseph Jefferson III, provides in his 1890 autobiography a vivid description of Blake and his art:

He was a superior actor, with the disadvantage of small eyes, a fat, inexpressive face, and a heavy and unwieldy figure. There must be something in the spirit of an actor that is extremely powerful to delight an audience when he is hampered like this. Without seeming to change his face or alter the stolid look from his eyes, Mr. Blake conveyed his meaning with the most perfect effect. He was delicate and minute in his manner, which contrasted oddly with his ponderous form. (1964 ed., p. 152)

Contemporary commentators writing at his death were unanimous in their estimation of Blake's unique position on the American stage, focusing in particular on the naturalness and spontaneity of his performances in a wide range of characters. Later historians have noted that many of Blake's roles, especially those from older comedies, died with him.

• Few sources deal specifically with Blake. His career can be pieced together from standard histories of the American stage, including W. Davenport Adams, *A Dictionary of the Drama* (1904); T. Allston Brown, *A History of the New York Stage* (1903); Laurence Hutton, *Plays and Players of This Century* (1875); Joseph N. Ireland, *Records of the New York Stage* (1866); George C. D. Odell, *Annals of the New York Stage* (1927–1949); Joseph Whitton, *Wags of the Stage* (1902); and William Winter, *Shadows of the Stage* (1892). Blake's early career is discussed in Henry P. Phelps, *Players of a Century* (1890), and in William Keese, *A Group of Comedians* (1901). A biographical sketch is in *Wilkes's Spirit of the Times*, 5 Apr. 1862. Useful obituaries are in the *New York Times*, 24 Apr. 1863, the *New York Clipper*, 2 May 1863, and the *Boston Evening Transcript*, 23 Apr. 1863.

DON B. WILMETH

BLAKELEY, Johnston (Oct. 1781–Oct. 1814), naval officer, was born near the village of Seaford, County Down, Ireland, the son of John Blakeley, a merchant. (His mother's name is unknown.) In 1783 the Blakeley family emigrated to the United States, settling in Wilmington, North Carolina. Johnston's mother and his only sibling, a brother, died after their arrival in Wilmington. In 1797 he enrolled at the University of North Carolina at Chapel Hill to study law. The death of his father in October 1797 and the destruction by fire in 1798 of the properties his father had bequeathed him prompted Blakeley to leave school and seek a career in the U.S. Navy.

Blakeley was appointed a midshipman on 5 February 1800. He first served in *President* during the Quasi-War with France. He next served in the Mediterranean Squadron in the war against Tripoli. He departed on the first of three cruises in that theater on 2 June 1801 in *President*; he later served in *John Adams*, *Congress*, and *Constitution*. After returning to the United States in September 1805, Blakeley was ordered to *Hornet*. In that vessel, and later in *Argus* and *John Adams*, he patrolled American waters enforcing the nation's trade laws. He was promoted to lieutenant on 10 February 1807 and on 4 March 1811 was given his first independent command, the schooner (later brig) *Enterprise*.

After the U.S. declaration of war against Great Britain in June 1812, Blakeley served briefly at New Orleans before being ordered to Portsmouth, New Hampshire. On 24 July 1813 he was promoted to master commandant, and on 6 August he was ordered to superintend the construction of the sloop of war *Wasp* at Newburyport, Massachusetts. Before resigning command of *Enterprise*, Blakeley made his first capture of the war, the British privateer schooner *Fly*. In December 1813 he married Jane Anne Hoope, in Boston's Trinity Episcopal Church. The couple's only child, Udney Maria, was born the following fall.

On 1 May 1814 Blakeley set sail from Portsmouth with orders to attack enemy shipping in the western approaches of the English Channel. Between 2 June and 6 July *Wasp* took eight prizes. The most notable capture occurred on 28 June when *Wasp* engaged HM brig-sloop *Reindeer* in ship-to-ship combat. Superior gunfire and a hard fought boarding action secured victory for the Americans. *Reindeer* was set afire the following day. After repairing and refitting his vessel at L'Orient, France, Blakeley set sail again on 27 August. Over the next five days *Wasp* captured three more ships. On the night of 1 September it engaged a second British warship, HM brig-sloop *Avon*. Although *Avon* struck its colors, Blakeley was forced to abandon his prize upon the appearance of additional enemy sail. The severely damaged *Avon* sank shortly afterward. During the next two weeks Blakeley's vessel took three more prizes. These were the North Carolinian's final captures, for sometime after 9 October, the last time *Wasp* was sighted, Blakeley and his command were lost at sea.

On 3 November 1814 Congress voted Blakeley a gold medal in recognition of his victory over *Reindeer*. He was promoted to captain three weeks later, before *Wasp*'s loss at sea became known. Blakeley was one of a number of outstanding ship commanders in the U.S.

Navy during the War of 1812. Only one other officer, William H. Allen, enjoyed greater success cruising in British home waters. And only one other captain, Charles Stewart, could claim two ship-to-ship victories over the enemy during the war.

• Papers relating to Blakeley are in the National Archives, including his correspondence with the Navy Department, in RG 45, and the logbooks and muster and pay rolls of the vessels he served in, in RG 24. An important document on *Wasp*'s 1814 cruise is the journal of David Geisinger in the Manuscript Division, Library of Congress.

Among the most reliable articles are the unattributed "Biographical Sketch of the Late Captain Johnston Blakeley," *Analectic Magazine* 9 (1817): 208–13, and William Johnson, "Biographical Sketch of Capt. Johnston Blakely, Late of the U.S. Sloop of War, *Wasp*," *North-Carolina University Magazine* 3 (1854): 1–16. Both include correspondence not found elsewhere. For information on Blakeley's only child, consult A. R. Newsome, "Udney Maria Blakeley," *North Carolina Historical Review* 4 (1927): 158–71. Works that provide insight into the naval context include Theodore Roosevelt, *The Naval War of 1812* (1882), and the multivolume collection by William S. Dudley, ed., *The Naval War of 1812: A Documentary History* (1985–).

CHARLES E. BRODINE, JR.

BLAKELOCK, Ralph Albert (15 Oct. 1847–9 Aug. 1919), landscape painter, was born in New York City, the son of Ralph Blakelock, a homeopathic physician, and Caroline Carey. Blakelock entered the Free Academy of the City of New York (later City College) in 1864, following his family's expectation that he would enter the practice of medicine. His personal interest lay in art and music, however, and Blakelock left the academy in 1866 without graduating. His only education in art consisted of the encouragement of James A. Johnston, a neighbor and friend of the family who was himself an amateur painter. Essentially, Blakelock can be regarded as self-taught. His work was accepted for exhibition by the National Academy of Design as early as 1867. In 1869 he began a trip to the western United States that took him through Kansas to Colorado, the Dakotas, Wyoming, Utah, and California. He returned in 1871 by way of Mexico and Panama with a stopover in Jamaica. During this trip his work was confined to landscape drawings, with very few references to the Native American tribes he is known to have visited and that figure prominently in later paintings.

In 1875 Blakelock married Cora Rebecca Bailey; they had eight children. The need to support his large family and his indifference to the marketplace frequently reduced Blakelock to hawking his work for any price that was offered. For a period of four years Blakelock was allowed to work in the studio of Harry W. Watrous, who was also his best customer.

The impact of the western frontier on Native American life is the single most important theme in Blakelock's painting. Interestingly, Blakelock, among all the painters of the American West, was the least concerned with documenting the varieties of aboriginal culture. There is no factual basis for his portrayals of

costume or ritual or the techniques of hunting and warfare. The Indian who appears in his paintings is a nomadic hunter, depicted almost exclusively in the domestic setting of his encampment. Blakelock's view of the frontier and its inhabitants is an entirely subjective record of his own romantic idealism.

Blakelock's best-known works are his many moonlight landscapes and Indian encampments, which epitomized the public's sentimental notion of the West. The landscapes are fantasy images, frequently reduced to the lace-like patterns of foliage against a lighted sky. The encampments present the Indians in a quiescent mood among their tepees, horses, and canoes, immersed in the atmosphere of twilight. In these paintings Blakelock achieved some of the definitive works of his career, as well as all too many mechanical repetitions, but it should be recognized that his range was not limited to these themes. There are numerous landscapes with no trace of Indians in them as well as some marine paintings that are quite unlike any other painting of the time. Works in the latter group suggest an increase in painterly concerns, such as the textural effects of nondescriptive brushwork, that are more characteristic of late twentieth-century painting.

Blakelock was, along with his contemporaries Albert Pinkham Ryder, William Morris Hunt, Homer Dodge Martin, George Fuller, Robert Loftin Newman, and John La Farge, part of a generation of artists who were devoted to the search for an alternative to the dramatic literalism of the Hudson River style, which had dominated the first half of the century. The artists were dedicated to a purely personal expression of their experience and to a greater freedom from the academy.

Although Blakelock's work is frequently compared with that of Ryder, there is no evidence of actual contact between the two men. Any stylistic influences that can be adduced are far more likely to be found among the painters of the French Barbizon school, who were enjoying considerable popularity among American collectors. The Barbizon school was a reaction against the academic classical landscape painting of Poussin and Claude Lorrain, emphasizing instead a realistic conception of nature, its topography and climate, and the ordinary details of rural life. Some of Blakelock's works contain traits of color and handling as well as an intimate response to nature that are very like those elements found in the works of Barbizon painters Theodore Rousseau, Virgile Diaz, and Adolphe Monticelli.

Blakelock's devotion to his own personal view of experience produced a style that was considerably ahead of contemporary taste and for which there was little or no market. Eventually the strain of his existence brought about a breakdown and commitment to a Long Island hospital in 1891 and again in 1899; finally, in 1901, he was admitted to the state hospital in Middletown, New York. A public campaign in 1916 to return Blakelock to normal activity and to provide support for his family was not successful. He continued to work sporadically in extremely limited circumstances but with no public success. He died in an Adirondack camp near Elizabethtown, New York.

The tragic irony of Blakelock's career took its final shape in 1916, with the Toledo Museum's purchase at auction of his *Brook by Moonlight* for the sum of $20,000, at that time the largest sum ever paid for the work of a living American artist. Recognition of Blakelock at the Universal Exhibition in Paris in 1900 and at the Pan-Pacific Exhibition in San Francisco in 1915, along with his election to the National Academy of Design in 1918 and multiple purchases of his works by wealthy collectors of the day, all came too late to revive his career and his physical and mental state.

Of his early work, *Sunrise* (1868; North Carolina Museum of Art, Raleigh) is probably the best. Of his works that directly reflect his travels on the western frontier, the most impressive is *Indian Encampment Along the Snake River* (1871; Phillips University, Enid, Okla.). *The Boulder and the Flume* (Metropolitan Museum of Art) represents Blakelock's closest adherence to the Hudson River style. The best known of his many Indian encampments is that in the Hearn Collection (also at the Metropolitan). The most famous of his moonlight landscapes is *The Brook by Moonlight* (Toledo Museum of Art). Also excellent is *Moonlit Lake* (Corcoran Gallery of Art). Blakelock's most extraordinary work is perhaps *The Sun Serene Sinks in the Slumbrous Sea* (Springfield [Mass.] Museum of Art).

• The Nebraska Blakelock Inventory in the Library of the University of Nebraska, Lincoln, is the most comprehensive collection of data pertaining to the artist's work. The archives of the Vose Galleries of Boston, the Babcock Galleries of New York, and the Macbeth Gallery archive in the Archives of American Art at the Smithsonian also are important sources of information. The earliest serious consideration of Blakelock's art is Frederick W. Morton, "Work of Ralph A. Blakelock," *Brush and Pencil*, Feb. 1902, pp. 257–69. Other contemporary writings are Elliott Daingerfield, *Ralph Albert Blakelock* (1914), and Frederick Fairchild Sherman, *Landscape and Figure Painters of America* (1917). Lloyd Goodrich's catalog text for the Blakelock Centenary exhibition at the Whitney Museum of American Art in 1947 remains the best biographical account. The research material compiled by Goodrich in preparation for the Whitney exhibition is in the custody of the Frick Art Reference Library in New York. Subsequent exhibition catalogs of importance are David Gebhard and Phyllis Stuurman, *The Enigma of Ralph Albert Blakelock* (Art Galleries of the University of California at Santa Barbara, 1969), and Norman A. Geske, *Ralph Albert Blakelock* (Sheldon Memorial Art Gallery, University of Nebraska, Lincoln, 1975). More recent considerations include Geske, "Ralph Albert Blakelock in the West," *American Art Review*, Jan.–Feb. 1976, pp. 123–35; Abraham Davidson, "The Wretched Life and Death of an American Van Gogh," *Smithsonian*, Dec. 1987, pp. 80–91; Dorinda Evans, "Art and Deception: Ralph Blakelock and His Guardian," *American Art Journal* 19, no. 1 (1987): 39–50; and Davidson, "Art and Insanity, One Case/Blakelock at Middletown," *Smithsonian Studies in American Art*, Summer 1989, pp. 55–71.

NORMAN A. GESKE

BLAKER, Eliza Ann Cooper (5 Mar. 1854–4 Dec. 1926), kindergarten and teacher educator, was born in Philadelphia, Pennsylvania, the daughter of Jacob Cooper and Mary Jane Gore, shopkeepers. Her Pennsylvania German mother largely carried the burden of supporting the family, which included Eliza and two younger children. Her Quaker father was not a financial success and suffered from ill health after he was wounded during the Civil War. Soon after his death, Eliza enrolled in the Girls Normal School of Philadelphia. Graduating as valedictorian in 1874, she served as a primary and grammar school teacher in the Philadelphia schools. For a short period, she supplemented this work with teaching in an artisans' night school.

A turning point in Eliza Cooper's life came in 1876 when she encountered the demonstration kindergarten run by Ruth Burritt at the Philadelphia Centennial Exposition. Through this exhibit, Cooper came into contact with the ideas of the German educator Friedrich Froebel, the originator of the kindergarten. Froebel's Romantic theories emphasized the innate goodness of the child and the unity of all things. Froebelian kindergartens also stressed the maternal role of the teacher and the need for play in aiding the child's development. When the Centennial Exposition ended, a group from the Religious Society of Friends (Quakers) persuaded Burritt to open a kindergarten and teacher-training school in Philadelphia. Eager to participate, Cooper enrolled in Burritt's Centennial Kindergarten Training School, graduating with honors in 1880. In that same year she married Louis J. Blaker, a friend since her childhood. She then taught briefly in Philadelphia's Vine Street Kindergarten.

In 1882, after receiving an invitation to establish a kindergarten in Indianapolis for the Hadley Roberts Academy, Blaker and her husband moved to Indiana. She soon left the academy, however, to work with the Indianapolis Free Kindergarten Society. At this time, urban reformers across the country were promoting free kindergartens in response to the suffering caused by the economic depression of the 1870s. Still felt in Indianapolis in the early 1880s, the effects of this depression spurred the free kindergarten movement there as well. Under Blaker, free kindergarten teachers emphasized habits of cleanliness and industry and used games, songs, and other activities in the classroom. Among one of the first free kindergartens that Blaker established was a school for African-American children. By 1900 there were twenty-three free kindergartens in Indianapolis, and by 1914 forty-seven were in operation. In the early years, Blaker and her associates worked constantly to acquire private funding for the free kindergartens. In 1901, however, after persuasive lobbying by Blaker and others, the state legislature allowed local taxation to fund the kindergartens.

Blaker's influence extended beyond Indianapolis, in particular because of the teacher-training school that she established. This normal school and its graduates helped to implement kindergarten programs in fourteen other cities by 1900. Blaker first opened the Kindergarten Normal Training School in 1882 as a one-year program to train teachers for the newly instituted kindergarten. Within a few years primary courses were added, and the school was renamed the Indiana Kindergarten and Primary Normal Training School. Still later known as the Teachers College of Indianapolis, it remained under the board of the Free Kindergarten Society until 1913. The normal school also offered classes in playground work, domestic skills, and the education of the blind and trained nursery governesses and Sunday school teachers. Under straitened circumstances after Blaker's death, Teachers College eventually became part of Butler University.

Blaker participated in the International Kindergarten Union, the National Education Association, the Indiana State Teachers Association, and numerous civic organizations in Indianapolis. She also chaired a committee to aid the victims of the terrible flood of 1913. She and her husband, a successful businessman, had no children, although they did take a number of young people under their care. While still president of Teachers College at the age of seventy-two, Eliza Blaker took ill suddenly and died in Indianapolis.

The kindergarten movement of the late nineteenth century had a major impact on American society. Over three million American children had received kindergarten schooling by 1907. Blaker was a key player in this significant social development in an important midwestern city. She was not a radical reformer, basing her activism instead on solid Presbyterian Christianity and the conservative image of the teacher as mother figure. Accordingly, she was not active in the woman suffrage movement. Through her increasing involvement in the work of teacher training, however, she exemplified the early stages of professionalization in education and the process by which the moral crusaders of the 1870s and 1880s became the professional educators of the early twentieth century.

• Although Blaker's personal papers no longer exist, notes to a number of her lectures and addresses as well as biographical sketches are in the Eliza A. Blaker Memorial Room, Butler University Library, Indianapolis. The Indiana Historical Society, Indianapolis, holds board minutes, salary ledgers, histories, and other materials related to the Indianapolis Free Kindergarten Society. For a biography of Blaker, see Emma Lou Thornbrough, *Eliza A. Blaker: Her Life and Work* (1956). See also Virginia Negley Hollingsworth, "History of the Teachers College of Indianapolis" (M.A. thesis, Butler Univ., 1946). On the history of the kindergarten movement, see Michael Steven Shapiro, *Child's Garden: The Kindergarten Movement from Froebel to Dewey* (1983), and Caroline Winterer, "Avoiding a 'Hothouse System of Education': Nineteenth-Century Early Childhood Education from the Infant Schools to the Kindergartens," *History of Education Quarterly* 32 (Fall 1992): 289–314. An obituary is in the *Indianapolis News*, 6 Dec. 1926.

AMY C. SCHUTT

BLAKESLEE, Albert Francis (9 Nov. 1874–16 Nov. 1954), botanist and geneticist, was born in Geneseo, New York, the son of Francis Durbin Blakeslee, a Methodist minister and school principal, and Augusta Miranda Hubbard, a teacher. He attended East Greenwich (R.I.) Academy, where his father was principal and his mother preceptress, and then Wesleyan University, Middletown, Connecticut, in the classical course; his freshman year was devoted solely to Greek, Latin, and mathematics, and his upperclass courses were mostly science. He won the Rice Prize in mathematics, played varsity football, was college tennis champion, and was elected to Phi Beta Kappa. He received the B.A. in 1896. Blakeslee's career was greatly influenced by his mentor, Wesleyan chemist Wilbur Olin Atwater, who (with physicist Edward Rosa and machinist Olin S. Blakeslee) was building an internationally publicized live-in respiration calorimeter to investigate human metabolism.

Blakeslee taught science and mathematics for two years at Montpelier Seminary, the Methodist institution that later became Vermont College, and at East Greenwich Academy. Enrolling at Harvard, he received the M.S. in biology in 1900. There he tackled several research projects of botanists Roland Thaxter and William G. Farlow, with little success. Then, while culturing bread molds, he made the startling observation that reproduction in several species of these fungi required sexual fusion. His thesis, "Sexual Reproduction in the *Mucorineae*," earned him a Ph.D. in 1904, Harvard's Bowdoin Medal in 1905, and a reputation as an original investigator. He received a postdoctoral grant from the Carnegie Institution to work for two years on molds with Georg Albrecht Klebs at Halle. He then taught botany for a year at Radcliffe.

In 1907 Blakeslee joined the experiment station and Connecticut Agricultural College at Storrs as the only Ph.D. on the faculty. During eight years there he was active in developing a farm school into a college, which twenty-four years later became the University of Connecticut. He established a botanic garden that he called a "field museum of agriculture"; his research turned toward flowering plants, with investigations of the genetics of the black-eyed Susan, *Rudbeckia hirta*, and the jimson weed, *Datura stramonium*. In 1914–1915 he was named professor of botany and genetics and taught what was probably the first undergraduate course in genetics in the country.

During his graduate studies, Blakeslee had been a teaching assistant (1901, 1902) in the summer botany course at the Biological Laboratory of the Brooklyn Institute of Arts and Sciences at Cold Spring Harbor, Long Island. In 1904 the Carnegie Institution opened its Station for Experimental Evolution adjacent to the Biological Laboratory. Blakeslee spent a year (1912–1913) at the station and joined the staff in 1915. He became assistant director in 1923 and was director from 1934 until his retirement in 1941. He was also for many years Cold Spring Harbor's school board chairman. As president of the Board of Trustees of *Biological Abstracts* from 1943 to 1946, he was credited with averting a financial catastrophe involving that journal.

At Cold Spring Harbor Blakeslee expanded his *Datura* research, demonstrating chemical mutagenesis caused by the alkaloid colchicine. He raised more than 70,000 *Datura* plants each summer in an exhaustive investigation of this genus. He also studied the genetics of human taste and smell, giving popular lectures on the inheritance of the ability to taste phenylthiocarbamide (PTC). He was also a consultant to the Beechnut Chewing Gum Company.

Blakeslee married Margaret Dickson Bridges, a nurse, on 26 June 1919. They had no children.

In 1942 Blakeslee was appointed William Allan Neilson Research Professor at Smith College in Northampton, Massachusetts. There he founded the Smith College Genetics Experiment Station, with initial funding from the Carnegie Institution. He brought with him Sophie Satina as assistant director and Amos G. Avery as associate geneticist. Satina had been his research associate since 1922. Amos Avery had taken the place of his brother, a Blakeslee student at Storrs and research assistant at Cold Spring Harbor who was killed in World War I.

For twelve years at Smith, Blakeslee expanded his *Datura* research to include investigations of the embryology and physiology of the plant. He also worked with *Rudbeckia* and developed its cultivated strain, Gloriosa daisy, for Burpee Seed Company during this period. He taught a course in genetics at Harvard in 1948 and 1949.

Personally, Blakeslee greatly influenced life on the Smith campus. He was elected president of the faculty club and found funds to expand its facilities. He was president of a town-and-gown club, invigorating cooperation between the campus and civic leaders. He founded and endowed the Out But Not Down Club to bring together retired members of the campus community. He endowed a hospitality fund for undergraduate Sigma Xi initiates, and his will provided a substantial endowment for genetics research at Smith.

Blakeslee was elected to the National Academy of Sciences, the American Philosophical Society, and the American Academy of Arts and Sciences. He served as president of the American Society of Naturalists (1930), the Torrey Botanical Club (1933), the American Association for the Advancement of Science (1940), the Society for the Study of Development and Growth (1946), and the Botanical Society of America (1950). He was elected to many foreign scholarly societies. He received the Morrison Prize of the New York Academy of Sciences twice (1926, 1936), the de Jouvenal Prize of the Palais de la Découverte (1938), and the gold medal of the Massachusetts Horticultural Society (1947). He died in Northampton.

• A large collection of Blakeslee's papers is at the American Philosophical Society, Philadelphia. The Cold Spring Harbor Laboratory Archives contain general correspondence files; the Smith College Archives contain information about the Smith College Genetics Research Station and Blakeslee's years at Smith, as well as reprints of most of his more than 300 publications. A biography with a list of his publications is Edmund Ware Sinnott, National Academy of Sciences, *Biographical Memoirs* 33 (1959): 1–38. An earlier biography is Burton E. Livingston in *Scientific Monthly* 50 (1940): 182–85. One of the most popular bulletins of the Storrs Agricultural Experiment Station was *New England Trees in Winter* by Blakeslee and Chester Deacon Jarvis (1911), republished as *Trees in Winter: Their Study and Identification* (1931). His lifetime research on the jimson weed was summarized in Amos Avery et al., *Blakeslee: The Genus Datura* (1959). An obituary is in the *New York Times*, 17 Nov. 1954.

GEORGE FLECK

BLAKEY, Art (11 Oct. 1919–16 Oct. 1990), jazz drummer and bandleader, was born Art William Blakey in Pittsburgh, Pennsylvania, the son of Burtrum Blakey, a barber, and Marie Roddericker. His father left home shortly after Blakey was born, and his mother died the next year. Consequently, he was raised by a cousin, Sarah Oliver Parran, who worked at the Jones and Laughlin Steel Mill in Pittsburgh. He moved out of the home at age thirteen to work in the steel mills and in 1938 married Clarice Stuart (four years his junior) the first of three wives. Other wives included Diana Bates and Ann Arnold. Blakey had at least ten children (the exact number is unknown), the last of whom was born in 1986.

As a teenager Blakey taught himself to play the piano and performed in local dance bands, but later switched to drums. Like many of his contemporaries, Blakey initially adapted the stylistic drumming techniques of well-known Swing Era drummers, including Chick Webb, Sid Catlett, and Ray Bauduc to whom he frequently paid tribute. As a result, his earliest playing experiences away from Pittsburgh centered around ensembles fronted by well-known big-band leaders.

Although some sources indicate Blakey first worked with the Fletcher Henderson Orchestra in 1939, it seems unlikely. Drummer Pete Suggs joined the Henderson band in June 1937 and remained with him until the group disbanded two years later, when Henderson became an arranger and pianist for the Benny Goodman band. However, Blakey did join a newly formed Henderson band in the spring of 1943 after playing with Mary Lou Williams's twelve-piece band and briefly leading his own group at a small Boston nightclub in 1942.

During the early 1940s Blakey was assimilating the innovative bop drumming styles of Kenny Clarke and Max Roach as evidenced by his selection as drummer for the Billy Eckstine big band organized in 1944. This group (with trumpeter Dizzy Gillespie as musical director) started at the Club Plantation in St. Louis and was among the first big bands to play bebop-influenced arrangements. Although somewhat unsuccessful as a commercial venture, the band rehearsed and recorded from 1944 to 1947. Blakey's playing with this ensemble indicates that regardless of the bebop bent of the repertoire, he played mainly late swing-style drums. But it was during his tenure with Eckstine that Blakey came in contact with several major bop luminaries, including Gillespie, Charlie Parker, Miles Davis, Dexter Gordon, and Kenny Dorham. His association with these musicians placed him firmly in the bop camp, where he remained throughout his career.

After the dissolution of Eckstine's band, Blakey joined Thelonious Monk for the pianist's first Blue

Note recordings in 1947; theirs was a complementary collaboration that continued off and on for the next decade. That same year Blakey organized a rehearsal band, the Seventeen Messengers, and in December made several recordings for Blue Note with his octet, Art Blakey's Jazz Messengers, which included Dorham on trumpet. This group was the first to bear the name through which Blakey would later become famous.

In 1948 Blakey made a brief, nonmusical trip to Africa at which time he accepted the Islamic religion, changing his name to Abdullah Ibn Buhaina. By mid-1948 he had returned to the United States, recording once again with Monk that July and with saxophonist James Moody in October. The next year he joined Lucky Millinder's rhythm-and-blues–based band and recorded with him in February. Although Blakey never recorded under his Muslim name, several of his children share this name with him, and later he was known to his musical friends as "Bu."

During the early 1950s Blakey solidified his bop drumming style by playing with well-known bop musicians such as Parker, Davis, Buddy DeFranco, Clifford Brown, Percy Heath, and Horace Silver. In the mid-1950s Blakey and Silver formed the first of the acclaimed Jazz Messengers ensembles that initially included Dorham, Hank Mobley, and Doug Watkins. When Silver left in 1956, Blakey retained leadership of the group that with constantly changing personnel became an important conduit through which many young, talented jazz musicians would pass. For the next twenty-odd years the Jazz Messengers' alumni would comprise a virtual list of who's who in modern jazz, including Donald Byrd, Bill Hardman, Jackie McLean, Junior Mance, Lee Morgan, Benny Golson, Bobby Timmons, Mobley, Wayne Shorter, Curtis Fuller, Freddie Hubbard, Cedar Walton, Reggie Workman, Keith Jarrett, Chuck Mangione, McCoy Tyner, Freddie Hubbard, Woody Shaw, Joanne Brackeen, Steve Turré, and Wynton and Branford Marsalis.

Despite impaired hearing, which ultimately left him deaf, Blakey continued to perform with the Jazz Messengers until shortly before his death in New York City. Throughout his dynamic and influential career he worked with nearly every major bop figure of the last half of the twentieth century and his Jazz Messengers ensembles provided a training ground for dozens more. He was inducted into the *Down Beat* Jazz Hall of Fame in 1981, and the Jazz Messengers received a Grammy award for best jazz instrumental group performance in 1984. The group recorded several film soundtracks (mainly overseas) from 1959 to 1972, and a documentary film, *Art Blakey: The Jazz Messenger* (Rhapsody Films), containing interviews with Blakey and other musicians as well as performances by the Jazz Messengers was released in 1988. Blakey also appears in *Art Blakey and the Jazz Messengers: Jazz at the Smithsonian* (1982) one video in a series produced by Sony.

Blakey's recorded legacy spans forty years and documents his prodigious and prolific career as drummer and leader. His earliest big-band recordings with Eckstine (De Luxe 2001, 1944) demonstrate an advanced swing style comparable to the best of the late Swing Era drummers. Although his early Monk recordings (*The Complete Blue Note Recordings of Thelonious Monk*, Mosaic, MR4-101) are clearly bop-oriented, he retains some of his earlier swing characteristics. By the beginning of the 1950s however, several of Blakey's well-defined playing characteristics emerge, including his heavy and constant high-hat rhythm and effective use of both bass drum and high-hat as additional independent rhythmic resources, which identify him as a progressive and influential bop drummer.

The Jazz Messengers' recordings are numerous and contain performances of varying degrees of success; however, Blakey's playing remains somewhat consistent, regardless of whom he is accompanying. The most impressive of the Messengers' playing is in a collection of recordings the group made in 1960 (*The Complete Blue Note Recordings of the 1960 Jazz Messengers*, Mosaic, MD6-141). Here, the group, consisting of Lee Morgan, Wayne Shorter, Bobby Timmons, Jymie Merritt, and Blakey, demonstrates exceptional talent and produces some of the Messengers' most memorable numbers, including Blakey's signature tune, "Night in Tunisia," composed by Gillespie. Later Messenger recordings with such notables as Jarrett and Mangione (*The Best of Art Blakey*, EmArcy 848245-2 CD, 1979) and the Marsalis brothers (*Keystone 3*, Concord CJ 196/CCD 4196, 1980) provide excellent examples of the continued influence Blakey's leadership had on the growth of jazz in the last quarter of the twentieth century.

Blakey's harshest criticism resulted from his loud, often overpowering drumming style, which developed in the 1950s and may have contributed to his early hearing loss. Nevertheless, he could also be a sensitive and unobtrusive drummer, as many of his ballad accompaniments demonstrate. Furthermore, his frequently recorded, unaccompanied improvised drum solo pieces provide numerous examples of his imaginative and flashy, but somewhat musically misdirected, solo ability.

• Lengthy interviews with Blakey appear in Wayne Enstice and Paul Rubin, *Jazz Spoken Here: Conversations with 22 Musicians* (1992); Chip Stern, "Art Blakey," *Modern Drummer* 8 (Sept. 1984): 8–13 ff.; and David H. Rosenthal, "Conversations with Art Blakey: The Big Beat," *Black Perspective in Music* 14 (1986): 267–89. A selected discography (to 1976) appears as a sidebar to John B. Litweiler, "Art Blakey: Bu's Delights and Laments," *Down Beat* 43 (June 1976): 15–17. See also Bob Blumenthal, "The Complete Blue Note Recordings of Art Blakey's 1960 Jazz Messengers," liner notes, Mosaic MD6-141. For discussions of Blakey, see Joe Goldberg, *Jazz Masters of the Fifties* (1965); Raymond Harricks et al., *These Jazzmen of Our Times* (1959); Herb Noland, "New Message from Art Blakey," *Down Beat* 46 (Nov. 1979): 19–22; Zan Stewart, "Art Blakey in His Prime," *Down Beat* 52 (July 1985): 20–22; John Tynan, "The Jazz Message,"

Down Beat 24 (Oct. 1957): 15; and Arthur Taylor, *Notes and Tones: Musician to Musician Interviews* (1977). Obituaries are in *Jazz Journal* 43, no. 12 (Nov. 1990): 2, and the *New York Times*, 17 Oct. 1990.

T. DENNIS BROWN

BLALOCK, Alfred (5 Apr. 1899–15 Sept. 1964), thoracic surgeon, was born in Culloden, Georgia, the son of George Z. Blalock, a merchant, and Martha Davis. Blalock's early years were spent in Culloden, but when he was eleven the family moved to Jonesboro, Georgia. By age fourteen Blalock had completed the ninth grade. He continued his education at the Georgia Military Academy; in 1915 he enrolled at the University of Georgia, receiving his A.B. in 1918. Blalock then decided to study medicine, and, despite his undistinguished grades, he was accepted by the Johns Hopkins Medical School in 1918. To defray the cost of his medical education he ran the school's medical bookstore.

After graduation Blalock was unable to obtain an internship on the general surgical service, so he accepted a position on Hugh Young's urology service. In spite of suffering partial paralysis of a facial nerve and an infection that led to the removal of a kidney, he earned a position on the general surgical service. Apparently, however, his performance as an assistant resident did not measure up to the standards of the service, and he was not reappointed to the surgical house staff (an occurrence over which he remained bitter). He worked during 1924 on the otology service of Samuel J. Crowe.

Tinsley Harrison, a medical resident, interested Blalock in medical research, and he began work on the lymphatic system in the early 1920s in the Hunterian Laboratory. In 1925 Blalock left Johns Hopkins and went to work as a resident on Barney Brook's surgical service at the Vanderbilt School of Medicine. He obtained this position through Harrison, who had moved to Vanderbilt to finish his training in internal medicine. He and Blalock began using the new VanSlyke method for measuring blood oxygen content to assess cardiac output. Although the two continued to help each other, Harrison drifted to studying cardiac output, while Blalock became interested in surgical shock. While at Vanderbilt, Blalock contracted tuberculosis; he spent 1927 at the Trudeau Sanatorium in Saranac Lake, New York.

To prevent the loss of Blalock's work, Harrison collected his data, organized it, and got it published. Upon his release from the sanatorium, Blalock spent a few months in England at Cambridge University, working in physiology with G. J. Anrep and Sir Joseph Barcroft. Upon his return to Vanderbilt he resumed his research on shock. In 1930 Vivien Thomas, a young black man, came to work in the surgical research laboratory at Vanderbilt. Within a short time he had mastered the experimental procedures as well as running the laboratory. This became an ideal arrangement, for Thomas allowed Blalock to carry on an active surgical practice as well as an innovative experimental program.

Blalock's experiments, begun in 1928 with Herbert Bradburn, established that the fundamental basis of traumatic shock was hypervolemia resulting from accumulation of fluid and blood at the site of injury; this disproved the accepted theory of Walter Cannon and William M. Bayliss that this type of shock was produced by a toxin.

At about the same time, Blalock accomplished the first successful transplantation of an adrenal gland. The importance of this experiment was that it showed that blood vessels could be cut and then sewn together, and remain open with survival of the organ they supplied. This result led Blalock to investigate whether pulmonary hypertension resulted after he anastomosed (surgically joined) the central end of the divided subclavian artery to the pulmonary artery. This experiment proved to be of great importance later.

In 1930 Blalock married Mary Chambers O'Bryan of Nashville, Tennessee. They had three children.

In 1938 DeWitt Lewis resigned as chairman of the Department of Surgery at the Johns Hopkins Hospital. The position was refused by several prominent surgeons, including Evarts A. Graham, who recommended Blalock. Blalock accepted the position in 1941 and brought George Duncan from Vanderbilt to continue his work on shock. Blalock's first research at Johns Hopkins was the removal of the thymus gland to treat myasthenia gravis, which he did in collaboration with A. McGehee Harvey and J. L. Lilenthal, Jr. With the encouragement of Edward A. Park, a professor of pediatrics, Blalock devised the first operative approach for the surgical management of coarctation of the aorta (a constriction of the aorta that blocks blood flow to the lower body) by anastomosing the subclavian to the aorta below the constriction. Blalock delayed using this operation in humans because he had observed that clamping the aorta while making the anastomosis produced a stroke in some of his experimental dogs. Because of this delay, the first coarctation operation is credited to Clarence Crafoord of Sweden and Robert Gross of Boston, who excised the aortic constriction and anastomosed the cut ends of the aorta.

Helen Brook Taussig, a professor of pediatric cardiology at Hopkins, had become a world authority on the diagnosis and treatment of congenital heart diseases. A particular interest of hers was the diagnosis and treatment of patients with the tetralogy of Fallot, a congenital condition characterized by pulmonary stenosis, intraventricular septal defect, an aorta that overrides the ventricular septum, and right ventricular hypertrophy. In this congenital anomaly oxygenation of the venous blood returning to the heart is shunted away from the lung by the constriction of the pulmonary artery and the intraventricular septal defect. Because of the distorted anatomy, dark blood with a low oxygen content flows into the left ventricle and is then pumped into the arterial circulation, producing cyanosis—hence the name of this condition, "blue baby syndrome." At a conference where Blalock presented his work on coarctation of the aorta, he mentioned earlier experiments in which he had sewn the subclavian artery into the pulmonary artery and found it did not produce pulmonary hypertension. This statement led Taussig to point out that the subclavian pulmonary artery anastomosis would be equivalent to a patent ductus (a blood vessel in the fetus through which blood bypasses the lungs; it closes at birth). Now the question was whether Taussig's suggestion to anastomose the subclavian vein to the pulmonary artery would relieve the cyanosis of "blue babies." Blalock and Vivien Thomas soon demonstrated that experimental cyanosis was relieved by subclavian pulmonary artery anastomosis. On 28 November 1944 Blalock undertook the first "blue baby" operation. The success of this operation brought patients and visiting physicians from all over the world to Johns Hopkins.

Blalock had a stimulating effect on the Johns Hopkins Medical School; he was demanding of his associates but supportive and quick to recognize and praise their accomplishments. These characteristics resulted in his training thirty-eight residents who held important academic positions and ten who became chairmen of departments of surgery in distinguished American medical schools. Blalock was always thoughtful, remarkably free of arrogance, courteous, and delightful company, so he was an effective leader at Hopkins as well as in the many organizations he served. In his last years he spent much time organizing the Children's Medical and Surgical Center in Baltimore, which was dedicated the year he retired. Blalock died in Baltimore in the Johns Hopkins Hospital three months after his retirement.

• Blalock's personal papers are in the Alan M. Chesney Archives of the Johns Hopkins Medical Institutions. A biographical sketch is A. McGehee Harvey, "Alfred Blalock, April 5, 1899–September 15, 1964," National Academy of Sciences, *Biographical Memoirs* 53 (1982). See also *The Papers of Alfred Blalock*, ed. Mark M. Ravitch (1966). Descriptions of Blalock's surgical contributions presented at the American Surgical Association are summarized in Mark M. Ravitch, *A Century of Surgery 1880–1980* (1981), pp. 890–92.

DAVID Y. COOPER

BLANC, Mel (30 May 1908–10 July 1989), radio, television, and film actor who specialized in voices for animated cartoons, was born Melvin Jerome Blanc in San Francisco, California, the son of Frederick Blanc and Eva Katz, sellers of women's apparel. He grew up in Portland, Oregon, and graduated from high school there in 1927. From an early age he exhibited a remarkable talent for vocal impersonation and for generating novel comic sounds. He entered show business in 1928, however, as a musician, playing both string and brass instruments for the NBC Radio Symphony Orchestra of San Francisco. Less than two years later he returned to Portland to become house conductor at the Orpheum Theater, which offered mixed vaudeville and film programs.

In 1933 Blanc married Estelle Rosenbaum, an actress, with whom he had one son. The couple produced and performed a daily variety hour, "Cobwebs and Nuts," broadcast live on a Portland radio station. Lacking money to hire other performers, each played multiple roles, creating a repertoire of voices. Blanc specialized in mimicking and exaggerating distinctive vocal features, especially ethnic and regional accents. The program's success inspired him to seek a career in Hollywood.

Blanc was hired in 1935 by Leon Schlesinger Productions, the Los Angeles animation studio where Looney Tunes and Merrie Melodies cartoons were produced for Warner Bros. He soon scored a major hit as the voice of Porky Pig in *Porky the Rain Maker* (1936). Porky became a star performer, appearing in more than thirty six-minute cartoons in the next three years. His stuttering closing line ("A-thee, a-thee, a-thee, a-that's all folks!") became a Warner Bros. trademark. "It's like a pig actually would talk," he told a reporter.

In *Porky's Hare Hunt* (1938) Blanc introduced his most famous character, Bugs Bunny, with a voice that he described as originating in the tough-guy Brooklyn accents of gangster movies. Bugs's famous greeting, "Eh, what's up, Doc?" became a household phrase. Blanc went on to create hundreds of voices for Warners. Some were caricatured accents, such as Foghorn Leghorn, a boisterous southern rooster; Speedy Gonzalez, a frenetic Mexican mouse; and Pepé le Pew, a romantic French skunk. Others exploited speech impediments, especially lisping. These included Daffy Duck and Sylvester the Cat ("Thuferring thuckatash!"). Blanc's voices could also be absurd linguistic concoctions, as was the case with Tweety-Pie ("I tawt I taw a puddy tat") and Road Runner ("Beep, beep"). A screen credit, "Voice Characterization by Mel Blanc," was conceded to the actor in 1937. It was the first such credit ever given in Hollywood cartoons.

Over a forty-year period Blanc created and performed the majority of voices in all Warner Bros. cartoons. Before signing an exclusive contract with Warners in 1950, he was also the voice of Woody Woodpecker for the Walter Lantz company. Blanc occasionally took supporting comic roles in non-animated features, including *Neptune's Daughter* (1949) and *Kiss Me, Stupid* (1964), but never appeared in a hit.

Blanc was a natural in radio, of course. During the late 1930s and 1940s he was best known in this regard as a regular on Jack Benny's popular comedy series, where he played several of Benny's recurring foils, including Professor Blanc, the violin teacher. Any Benny sketch set at a railway station included another Blanc trademark, the announcement of a train departing for "A-na-heim, A-zu-za and KOO-KA-MON-GA." Other top-rated radio series that made use of his talents were "Blondie" and "Abbott and Costello." "The Mel Blanc Show," in which he starred as a handyman, debuted on CBS Radio in 1946 but lasted only briefly. His association with Jack Benny continued when the star moved the series to television in the 1950s. Blanc also played a comically depressed postman on "The George Burns and Gracie Allen Show."

Blanc made scores of recordings during the 1940s and 1950s, doing comic voices for Spike Jones's novelty records and various types of comedy and children's albums. He recorded several songs in the voices of his characters, including "The Woody Woodpecker Song" and "I Tawt I Taw a Puddie Tat"; each sold over more than 2 million copies.

The production of animated series for television increased dramatically in the 1960s, and this proved to be a boon for the acknowledged master of the cartoon voice. "The Bugs Bunny Show," a half-hour of cartoons featuring many of Blanc's Warner Bros. creations, premiered on ABC in 1960. That same year the Hanna-Barbera studio produced the first animated prime-time situation comedy series, "The Flintstones." Blanc supplied the voices of Barney Rubble and Dino the Dinosaur. He also played Mr. Spacely in "The Jetsons."

One of the busiest performers in show business, Blanc also supplied voices to hundreds of TV and radio commercials over the years. In 1966 he formed Blanc Communications Corporation, which produced ads for major brands and services such as Chrysler, Kool-Aid, and Delta Airlines. The company also supplied sound effects and short comedy spots to radio stations.

Blanc resided for most of his life in Pacific Palisades, California, where he was a Shriner and a 32d-degree Mason. He trained his son, Noel, to take over many of his cartoon voices. In 1988 an autobiography, *That's Not All Folks!* written with Philip Basle, was published. Blanc died in Los Angeles.

• In addition to his autobiography, information on Blanc can be found in Leslie Halliwell, *The Filmgoer's Companion* (1989). An interview by Tom Shales is in the *Washington Post*, 3 Mar. 1975. An obituary is in *Variety*, 12 July 1989.

DAVID MARC

BLANCHARD, Jonathan (19 Jan. 1811–14 May 1892), educator and social reformer, was born in the township of Rockingham, Vermont, the son of Jonathan Blanchard, Sr., a farmer, and Polly Lovell. The relatively comfortable circumstances of Jonathan's upbringing on what he remembered as his father's "large stock farm" left him with an enduring affinity for rural life, though his ambitions for public life drew him away from farming. He taught district school to finance his education at an academy near his home and enrolled in 1828 at Middlebury College, Vermont, where he received a B.A. in 1832.

Blanchard graduated from college intending to prepare for the ministry. Having professed a "hope in Christ" at age sixteen, he joined the Congregationalist church during his college years and became a lifelong advocate of revivalism, influenced in part by famed evangelist Charles G. Finney's spectacular successes in the nearby "burned-over district" of New York. Also at Middlebury, Blanchard began his career as a reformer by lecturing on temperance and as a writer by publishing his poems and essays in the local press

and in *The Undergraduate*, a student newspaper that he helped to establish. He spent two years following graduation as the preceptor of an academy at Plattsburgh, New York, where he actively promoted common-school reform and temperance.

Entering Andover Theological Seminary in Massachusetts in 1834, Blanchard chafed at what he saw as the school's stultifyingly intellectualized Calvinist piety. He left Andover in the fall of 1836 to serve a year in southern Pennsylvania as an agent of the American Anti-Slavery Society. He remembered being "stoned" nearly every time he "crossed the street." This dramatic experience marked him forever as a radical reformer, both in his own mind and in the minds of others.

After his agent's commission expired, Blanchard enrolled in the fall of 1837 at Lane Theological Seminary in Cincinnati, Ohio, but never graduated. On 17 September 1838 he married Mary Avery Bent, a Middlebury, Vermont, native whom he had gotten to know during his year in Pennsylvania, where she was teaching school. Their marriage produced twelve children, two of whom died in infancy. On 31 October 1838 Cincinnati's Sixth Presbyterian Church (New School) installed Blanchard as its pastor, a post that he held until leaving the city in 1845. The congregation harbored abolitionist sympathies and endorsed Blanchard's outspoken advocacy of sabbatarianism and temperance as well.

A tireless publicist, Blanchard worked in 1840 to help establish a western Presbyterian newspaper, the *Cincinnati Observer*, which became the *Watchman of the Valley* in 1841. He contributed articles and occasionally served as editor, zealously promoting the paper in conjunction with revivalism and social reform on numerous tours through southern Ohio.

Wary of political abolitionism and repudiating the antislavery movement's "Christless" Garrisonian wing, Blanchard took it as his particular mission to establish the church's public witness against specific sins—intemperance, slavery, and sabbath-breaking—by "disfellowshipping" sinners and their apologists from Christian communion. His reputation among western abolitionists grew, and in 1843 the Ohio State Anti-Slavery Society sent him to the World's Anti-Slavery Convention in London, where he was one of the convention's American vice presidents.

Still drawn westward and believing that his "talents and turn of mind" qualified him as an educator, Blanchard was inaugurated president of Knox College at Galesburg, Illinois, in 1846. The financially troubled school was known for its abolitionism, having been founded by other reform-minded evangelicals from New England. An effective fundraiser, he restored Knox to fiscal stability and then used his position to crusade nationally for the exclusion of slaveholders and their apologists from the church and affiliated missionary organizations. Frustrated by what he called Presbyterianism's "four-story" church government, he turned Congregationalist soon after moving to Illinois. This action contributed to a bitter feud with Knox's founder, George Washington Gale, whose

Presbyterian supporters feared a Congregationalist takeover of the college. Blanchard's dictatorial personal style and propensity for invective helped fuel the controversy, which ended in his leaving Knox's presidency in 1858.

In 1860 Blanchard became the first president of Wheaton College at Wheaton, Illinois. The school had been established as Illinois Institute by Wesleyan Methodists but was foundering financially when Blanchard arrived to rename it and install a Congregationalist majority on the board of trustees. Once again, he proved to be an effective institution builder, passing Wheaton's presidency along to his son Charles when he retired in 1882.

Blanchard spent his final decades crusading against "secret societies," voluntary associations with covert rituals and oaths, particularly the Masonic Lodge. In 1868 he had been instrumental in launching the National Christian Association and its newspaper, the *Christian Cynosure*, which he edited until his death. Blanchard wrote prolifically in the *Cynosure*, using it to promote a sweeping program of Christian social reform that ranged from guaranteeing freed slaves their civil rights and international arbitration for peace to legal prohibition, Bible study in the public schools, and abolishing the electoral college. In addition to the *Cynosure*, Blanchard promoted his program by organizing the American party, a tiny third party that nominated presidential candidates in the elections of 1872, 1876, 1880, and 1884.

Jonathan Blanchard belonged to a generation of evangelical social reformers and educators who came of age amidst the religious revivals of the 1830s. More decided in his opinions and personally intense than most, Blanchard was described by an enemy as "a man to be watched by the safer part of the community," and he has been characterized retrospectively as a "violent" and bigoted moralist. Sympathizers, however, have remembered him for his courage, adherence to principle, and Christian concern for the poor and disenfranchised. When he died at his home in Wheaton, a friend likened him to the "ancient prophets of God."

• Blanchard's papers, including his journals and extensive family correspondence, are in the Wheaton College Archives, Wheaton, Ill. His most important published works include *A Debate on Slavery* (1846), *Secret Societies* (1850), *Memoir of Rev. Levi Spencer* (1856), *Sermons and Addresses* (1892), his voluminous writings in the *Christian Cynosure* (1868–1892), and numerous exposés of secret societies such as *Freemasonry Illustrated* (1879). Clyde S. Kilby's sympathetic *Minority of One: The Biography of Jonathan Blanchard* (1959) was written without access to most of Blanchard's personal papers, the story of which is told by Blanchard's grandson, Raymond P. Fischer, in *Four Hazardous Journeys of the Reverend Jonathan Blanchard, Founder of Wheaton College* (1987); Richard S. Taylor, "Seeking the Kingdom: A Study in the Career of Jonathan Blanchard, 1811–1892" (Ph.D. diss., Northern Illinois Univ., 1977), focuses on Blanchard's public life; Taylor, "Beyond Immediate Emancipation: Jonathan Blanchard, Abolitionism, and the Emergence of American Fundamentalism," *Civil War History* 25, no. 3 (Sept. 1981), on his social theology; and Taylor, "Religion and Higher Education in Gilded Age America: The Case of Wheaton College," *American Studies* 22, no. 1 (Spring 1981), on his shaping of Wheaton College's identity.

RICHARD S. TAYLOR

BLANCHARD, Theresa Weld (24 Aug. 1893–12 Mar. 1978), figure skater, was born in Brookline, Massachusetts, the daughter of Alfred Windsor Weld, a stockbroker, and Theresa Davis. Theresa Weld attended private schools and enjoyed the privileges of membership in the Country Club of Brookline, where she learned horsemanship, tennis, and figure skating. She won her first meet in a skating event intended for males only. While awaiting the scores, she overheard one judge remark, "Give it to the pretty girl."

Wishing to pursue figure skating year-round, several enthusiastic skaters, including Weld, her father, and her partner Nathaniel Niles, organized the Skating Club of Boston in 1911. It was Weld's home club throughout her competitive career. With the additional training provided by the club, she and Niles soon became America's premier skaters. She won the first U.S. women's title in 1914 and, following a World War I hiatus, won five consecutive singles titles beginning in 1920. She and Niles also began their eight-year reign as pairs champions in 1920 and captured the North American pairs title in 1925. They also took seven national dance championships including waltz in 1914, 1918, 1920, and 1921, fourstep in 1921 and 1922, and original dance in 1931. Although devastated by Niles's sudden death in 1932, Theresa Weld Blanchard continued to participate and won her last title as part of the national champion Boston Four in 1934.

In February 1920 she learned that figure skating would be included at the upcoming summer Olympic Games in Antwerp, Belgium. She convinced the United States Olympic Committee (USOC) to submit entries for herself and Niles in singles and pairs. The USOC, however, provided little additional support for the duo, who made up the entire U.S. skating team. They learned the compulsory figures only days before their departure and had to find their own practice rinks as they traveled to New York and then abroad. Wearing a daring new skirt that fell only six inches below her knees, Weld was the only woman in the games to perform jumps and salchows in her skating routine. Unfortunately several judges deemed those moves unsuitable for ladies and reduced her score accordingly. Although she got two first-place votes, Weld settled for the bronze medal while Magda Julen of Sweden won the gold medal despite receiving no first-place votes. The judging incensed Weld, who later remarked, "The girl who won didn't get any firsts at all! You can imagine this caused talk all over the world" (Blanchard, p. 9). She and Niles finished fourth in pairs, and the two gave a series of exhibitions abroad after the games. In October 1920 she married publisher Charles Blanchard, who supported her continued participation in the sport she loved. They had no children.

Although they competed in two more Olympics, Blanchard and Niles never repeated their 1920 success. Blanchard finished fourth in singles at the 1924 Olympics in Chamonix, France, while then-unknown Sonja Henie finished eighth. Blanchard fell to tenth place at the 1928 Olympics in St. Moritz, Switzerland, as Henie won the first of her three Olympic titles. Blanchard retired from international competition following those games but traveled in some official capacity with every U.S. Olympic figure skating team through the 1950s. She thereby befriended many individuals who would make up the elite of international skating for decades to come.

Soon after the 1923 founding of the United States Figure Skating Association (USFSA), Blanchard and Niles suggested that the organization needed an official publication. Charged with implementing the idea, they produced the first issue of *Skating* magazine in December 1923. They coedited the periodical until Niles's death, whereupon Blanchard assumed editorship. She often worked nine hours a day in the unpaid position she held through 1963. In this regard she was typical of wealthy women who devoted their time and energy to nonprofit, voluntary organizations. Blanchard, however, was different in that her cause was sport, and the organization she served was overwhelmingly dominated by men rather than women. To improve women's role in skating governance, in 1927 she helped found the Women's Committee of the USFSA. She also served as figure skating editor of the pioneering magazine *Sportswoman* through the 1930s.

By the time she retired from competition in 1935, Blanchard had become an international authority on the sport. She quickly moved from competitor to judge despite prejudice against women in that position. She helped train American judges while she herself attained the rank of world judge. Blanchard also became the first female member of the USFSA and served thirteen years on the executive committee. Still, she never achieved the honor she most deserved and by which she could have had her greatest impact: president of the USFSA. The gender barrier refused to yield, and the USFSA did not elect a woman president until 1992.

Blanchard remains one of the greatest champions in the history of American figure skating. Known as "Tee," she never turned professional, devoting her life to amateur skating until her death in Brookline. She captured twenty-five U.S. and North American figure skating championships in singles, pairs, and dancing, and she was the first U.S. Olympic figure skating medalist. Her versatility and longevity as an active competitor are unequaled, and she probably had more influence on American skating than anyone except perhaps Henie. Moreover, Blanchard, not Henie, pioneered shorter skirts and higher jumps in women's competition. Her other honors included being editor emeritus of *Skating* magazine and a lifetime member of the USFSA Executive Committee. She was also one of the first members elected to the Figure Skating Hall of Fame when it opened in 1976. Beloved by the skat-

ing fraternity as "Mrs. Figure Skating U.S.A." and "The Grand Dame of American Skating," Blanchard was truly America's first queen of the ice.

• Photos, records, and memorabilia of Blanchard's career are housed at the National Figure Skating Association Hall of Fame at Colorado Springs, Colo. Her most notable article is Theresa Blanchard, "The Olympics: 1920, 1924, and 1928," *Skating*, Dec. 1947, pp. 9, 10, 40, 41. Other sources include Frederick Goodridge, "The Figure Skating Championships of North America," *Sportswoman*, May 1929, pp. 20–21; Edith E. Ray, "A Tribute to Tee Blanchard," *Skating*, June 1953, pp. 23–24; and "The Women's Committee of the U.S.F.S.A.," *Sportswoman*, Nov. 1928, p. 20.

MARY LOU LeCOMPTE

BLANCHARD, Thomas (24 June 1788–16 Apr. 1864), inventor, was born in Sutton Township, Massachusetts, the son of Samuel Blanchard and Susanna Tenney, farmers. As a child he stammered, rarely attended school, avoided farm chores, and showed mechanical aptitude, making an apple-paring machine at the age of thirteen. Set to work in his older brother's tack-making shop in nearby Millbury, he invented a tack-counting device and then, after several years, during which he invented and patented a machine for shearing woolen cloth, he invented a machine that cut and headed 500 tacks per minute. He sold his tack-making patent rights for $5,000 and set up his own water-powered shop in West Millbury.

Among the diverse metal- and woodworking industries then at Millbury was the Waters gun manufactory, which made U.S. military muskets on contract. In early 1818 the proprietor, Asa Waters, Jr., called on Blanchard for help with a gun-barrel lathe Waters had invented. It eliminated the need for grinding the barrel cylindrical, but hand filing was still needed to shape the "ovals and flats" at the barrel's breech end. Blanchard solved the problem by adding a simple but wholly original cam motion to the lathe. This feat impressed not only Waters, but also Roswell Lee, the superintendent of the U.S. Armory in Springfield, Massachusetts. After Blanchard installed his improved barrel lathe at the U.S. armories at Springfield and at Harpers Ferry, Virginia, he went on to devise a machine to make gunstocks, which were much more irregular in shape than gun barrels. He obtained a patent for it in 1819 and had the patent revised and reissued on 20 January 1820. It also mechanized production of other irregular wooden shapes, such as shoe lasts, wheel spokes, and ax handles. The Blanchard irregular turning "lathe" coordinated the motions of a tracer pressing against a revolving model with those of a cutting wheel acting on a revolving workpiece, so that the machine cut a three-dimensional copy of the model.

In mid-1823 Blanchard began work as an inside contractor at the Springfield Armory, manufacturing gunstocks using armory facilities and materials but hiring his own helpers. In a few years he had devised a sequence of thirteen additional special-purpose machines for use with the irregular turning lathe in preparing the wooden stock for assembly with the musket's metal parts. This early production line, adopted also at Harpers Ferry Armory, was much admired as a model for modern factory methods. After Blanchard's "inside" contract ended at the close of 1827, he collected royalties on muskets produced at the two national armories during the fourteen-year term of his patent.

Also in the 1820s Blanchard set up water-powered machines for pulley-block manufacture near Hudson, New York, and built a steam carriage, which presumably incorporated his patent of 28 December 1825 for a "Traction Wheel for Regulating the Speed of Carriages." He also built and operated shallow-draft steamboats to navigate the rapids of the Connecticut River between Hartford and Springfield. In 1831 he obtained a patent for his stern-paddler "steamboat for the passage of rapids" and launched the 96 foot-long *Massachusetts*, thought to be the boat that Charles Dickens later took from Springfield to Hartford and scoffingly called "a warm sandwich about three feet thick." Blanchard pioneered by steamboat up the Allegheny from Pittsburgh and up the Kennebec to Waterville, Maine, before he moved to New York City in the early 1830s. There he resumed his interest in woodworking for nautical purposes and obtained patents in August 1836. The Winooski Patent Block Manufacturing Company put these machines into operation in an industrial-scale block mill near Burlington, Vermont.

On 30 June 1834 Congress passed an act granting Blanchard a fourteen-year extension of his irregular turning lathe patent. Thereafter he had to defend his patent in court against frequent infringers, especially makers of shoe lasts, who used the Blanchard lathe without paying royalties.

Blanchard lived in or near New York City and Newark, New Jersey, through the 1830s; around 1840 he moved to Boston, where he invented an improvement of his lathe, patented in 1843, for turning long items like ax handles and wheel spokes as well as gunstocks. His wood-bending machine, patented in 1849, found widespread use by makers of plow handles, carriage wheels, chair parts, and other bentwood objects, including even heavy ships' timbers. Blanchard resided in Boston for the rest of his life but traveled to New York, Newark, and Washington, D.C., to manage his patents. He lobbied Congress successfully in 1847 for yet another extension of his irregular turning lathe patent: he made marble busts of influential congressmen in a sculpture-copying machine that he misleadingly claimed was his old patented machine, in need of patent extension for this new use. Senator Rufus Choate of Massachusetts quipped that he had "turned the heads of Congress" to obtain the extension! By skillful patent management Blanchard not only achieved an unprecedented and unrepeated 42-year patent period for his lathe, he also acquired sufficient wealth by 1855 to move his family into a fashionable Charles Bulfinch–designed house overlooking the Boston Commons and to afford such luxuries as a trip to the Paris Exposition that summer, where he won medals for his wood-bending machine and his sculpture-copying machine. To attain this degree of affluence, however, he had to engage in protracted and expensive litigation on many occasions to claim recognition and royalties as patentee of the irregular turning lathe. A beneficial side effect of this activity was that he overcame his stutter.

Blanchard continued inventing through his sixties and into his seventies. His lifetime total of patents was more than the two dozen for which he is usually given credit. In 1862 he was depicted, along with Samuel Morse, Charles Goodyear, Elias Howe, and other famous inventors and scientists, in Christian Schussele's well-known collective portrait *Men of Progress* (National Portrait Gallery). His estate was valued at nearly $100,000 when he died.

Blanchard's family life was less successful than his inventive career. He married Sarah Segress in 1815; they had five children, all of whom died young. In 1834 his first wife died, and in about 1840 he married Marcia Pierce, with whom he had one child before her death. In 1863 Blanchard married his third wife, Laura A. Shaw. He died in Boston ten months later.

• Blanchard's patents are in Record Group 241, National Archives, Washington, D.C. Several incomplete biographical sketches were published in the nineteenth and early twentieth centuries, deriving almost wholly from Henry Howe, *Memoirs of the Most Eminent American Mechanics* (1840), pp. 197–210; Asa Holman Waters, *Biographical Sketch of Thomas Blanchard and His Inventions* (1878); Waters, "Thomas Blanchard," in *History of the Town of Sutton, Massachusetts, from 1704 to 1876*, ed. Rev. William A. Benedict and Rev. Hiram A. Tracy (1878), pp. 758–69, which differs from Waters's *Biographical Sketch* by the addition of six paragraphs; and [Waters], "Thomas Blanchard, the Inventor," *Harper's New Monthly Magazine*, July 1881, pp. 254–60. A more recent extended biographical sketch that draws on Waters is C. Meade Patterson, "Gunstocking Genius," *Gun Report* 6 (Sept. 1960): 6–10, 21–24; and 6 (Oct. 1960): 15–19, 24–30. See Carolyn C. Cooper, *Shaping Invention: Thomas Blanchard's Machinery and Patent Management in Nineteenth-Century America* (1991), for Blanchard's career in the context of the patent system and for further bibliographic information. For discussion of Blanchard's gunstocking production line at the U.S. armories, see Merritt Roe Smith, *Harpers Ferry Armory and the New Technology* (1977); David A. Hounshell, *From the American System to Mass Production* (1984); and Cooper, "'A Whole Battalion of Stockers': Thomas Blanchard's Production Line and Hand Labor at Springfield Armory," *IA, the Journal of the Society for Industrial Archeology* 14 (1988): 37–57. An obituary is in the *New York Times*, 24 Apr. 1864.

CAROLYN C. COOPER

BLANCHET, Francis Norbert (3 Sept. 1795–18 June 1883), Roman Catholic missionary and archbishop, was born in Saint-Pierre-Rivere-du-Sud, Quebec, the son of Pierre Blanchet and Rosalie (maiden name unknown), landowners whose ancestors were distinguished leaders in church and state in Canada. He received his initial education in Saint-Pierre and in 1810 entered, along with his younger brother Augustine, the minor seminary in Quebec.

Blanchet was ordained to the priesthood in July 1819 and assigned to serve in the cathedral parish in Quebec City. One year later he was assigned to the parish of Saint-Antoine in Richbouctou, New Brunswick, to minister to Micmac Indians and Irish immigrants. During his seven-year mission, Blanchet developed and successfully utilized an evangelization technique known as the "Catholic ladder" that presented Biblical teachings, Church history, and Christian doctrine in a pictorial compendium that could be memorized by illiterate converts.

In 1827 Blanchet returned to the province of Quebec as the pastor of Saint-Joseph-de-Soulanger parish near Montreal. There he served the main congregation and several outlying mission churches. He became widely known for his zeal, especially during the period between 1832 and 1834, when he ministered without regard to creed or race in combating an epidemic of Asiatic cholera.

The Hudson's Bay Company sent petitions to Joseph Provencher, the bishop of Juliopolis on the Red River in Manitoba, requesting that a priest be sent to the region of the Columbia River in the Oregon territory. In October 1836 Archbishop Joseph Signay of Quebec selected Blanchet to go to Oregon. In May 1838 he and another priest, Modeste Demers, set out for Oregon, arriving at Fort Vancouver on 24 November.

In January 1839 Blanchet blessed St. Paul's Chapel in the Willamette Valley, which became the headquarters for his mission. It soon became clear to Blanchet that more missionaries were needed to minister to the Indians and French Canadians of the region. Through the assistance of Pierre De Smet, a Jesuit missionary from St. Louis who visited Oregon in 1842, Jesuits and Sisters of Notre-Dame-de-Namur from Europe arrived in 1844 to teach.

Blanchet and De Smet discussed the mission's future and the difficulties experienced in its administration. Slow and unreliable communication between Oregon and Quebec, the ecclesiastical seat in the region, undermined the mission. Thus at De Smet's suggestion, Blanchet petitioned Signay that Oregon become an autonomous diocese. Jurisdictional changes required that the request be relayed to Archbishop John Rosati in St. Louis, who took the matter to the 1842 Baltimore Provincial Council. On 1 December 1843 the Holy See erected the vicariate of Oregon with Blanchet selected as vicar apostolic.

In July 1845 Blanchet was consecrated the bishop of Drusa and vicar apostolic in a ceremony in Montreal. Before returning to Oregon he toured Europe for one year in an effort to gain economic support and promote interest in his vicariate. While in Paris in July 1846, Blanchet learned that the ecclesiastical province had been divided into three sees at Oregon City, Walla Walla, and Vancouver Island. He was selected as the archbishop in the metropolitan see of Oregon City with Demers as the bishop in Vancouver and Blanchet's brother Augustine the bishop of Walla Walla.

When Blanchet arrived in Oregon in August 1847 he faced several problems. Persistent opposition from Methodist missionaries initially impeded the church's growth. Blanchet was able, however, to gain acceptance and successfully convert attitudes as noted by the historian Hubert Howe Bancroft: "The immediate effect of the arrival of Blanchet and Demers was to unite the French settlers in a community by themselves and weaken the power of the Methodist mission as a political body" (*History of Oregon*, vol. 1 [1886], p. 321). The massacre of Methodist minister Marcus Whitman, his wife, and twelve followers in late November 1847 by local Indians, falsely attributed to Catholic influence, raised the specter of anti-Catholicism in the region. The discovery of gold in California in 1848 prompted an exodus that reduced the already small Catholic population. Blanchet countered these setbacks and rallied the beleaguered Catholic population by calling the first Provincial Council of Oregon in February 1848. The council's three sessions enacted disciplinary regulations and recommended that the episcopal see of Walla Walla be transferred to Nesqually, the former site having been shut down in the wake of the Whitman massacre.

As archbishop, Blanchet developed the local church while also participating on national and international levels. He attended the 1852 and 1866 Plenary Councils of Baltimore. Between the fall of 1855 and December 1857 he traveled to South America and successfully raised sufficient funds to erase an archdiocesan debt and finance several projects. A recruiting trip to Canada in 1859 secured additional priests and sisters for service in the archdiocese. In 1862 he moved his see city to Portland and constructed a cathedral church. He supported the declaration of papal infallibility at the First Vatican Council (1869–1870). Returning to Oregon, Blanchet was responsible in February 1870 for the publication of the archdiocesan newspaper, the *Catholic Sentinel*, the foundation of St. Michael's College for boys in 1871, and the construction of St. Vincent's Hospital in 1875. Blanchet protested to Secretary of the Interior Columbus Delano that the "peace policy" of President Ulysses S. Grant, which associated religious denominations with various tribes and reservations, was unfair to Catholics, whom Blanchet felt were underrepresented in the pairings. Blanchet's protest resulted in the formation in 1874 of a permanent Catholic Indian Commission in Washington, D.C., with Charles Ewing as the first commissioner.

In 1879 Blanchet received an assistant, Charles John Seghers, who became coadjutor and succeeded to the archepiscopal office when Blanchet retired in 1881. Known as the "apostle of Oregon," Blanchet was a pioneer in establishing Catholicism in the West. His untiring labors and ability to direct diverse people toward a common goal in the face of opposition was a credit to the Catholic church and the nation. He died in Portland, Oregon.

• Blanchet's papers are in the archives of the Roman Catholic archdiocese of Portland, Oregon. His writings include *Fifti-*

eth Jubilee Sermon (1869), *Historical Sketches of the Catholic Church in Oregon* (1878), and *Historical Notes and Reminiscences* (1883). Sister Letitia Mary Lyons, *Francis Norbert Blanchet and the Founding of the Oregon Missions* (1838–1848) (1940), outlines Blanchet's early life in Canada, his travel to Oregon, and events until the formation of the archdiocese. Clarence B. Bagley, *Early Catholic Missions in Old Oregon* (2 vols., 1932), covers the same mission foundation years in greater depth. Harriet D. Munnick, *Priest's Progress: The Journey of Francis Norbert Blanchet from the Atlantic Ocean to the Pacific in Three Parishes* (1989), describes Blanchet's early years and ministry in Oregon before the formation of the archdiocese. M. Leona Nichols, *The Mantle of Elias: The Story of Fathers Blanchet and Demers in Early Oregon* (1941), provides details of the Oregon mission to the Indians and French-Canadian citizens. The work of Blanchet as archbishop is described in John R. Laidlaw, *The Catholic Church in Oregon and the Work of Its Archbishops* (1980), and Edwin V. O'Hara, *Pioneer Catholic History of Oregon* (1939).

RICHARD GRIBBLE

BLANCHFIELD, Florence Aby (1 Apr. 1884–12 May 1971), nurse and army officer, was born in Shepherdstown, West Virginia, the daughter of Joseph Plunkett Blanchfield, a stonemason and cutter, and Mary Louvenia Anderson, a nurse. In 1903 Blanchfield entered South Side Hospital Training School for Nurses in Pittsburgh, graduating in 1906. During postgraduate work at Johns Hopkins Hospital and Dr. Howard Kelly's Sanatorium in Baltimore in 1907, while working as a private-duty nurse, she studied surgical techniques and operating room supervision. In 1908 she served as surgical supervisor in the operating rooms of South Side and Montefiore hospitals in Pittsburgh. She became a nurse superintendent at Suburban General Hospital in Bellevue, Pennsylvania, in 1909.

In 1913 Blanchfield volunteered for the Panama Canal Zone as a civil service appointee, serving at Ancon Hospital as a staff nurse and nurse-anesthetist. Returning to the United States, she worked as an emergency surgical nurse for United States Steel in Bessemer, Pennsylvania, in 1915. She returned to her superintendent position at Suburban General, but after World War I broke out she joined the Army Nurse Corps (ANC). Assigned to the University of Pittsburgh's Base Hospital No. 27, Blanchfield sailed to France on 27 September 1917 as part of the American Expeditionary Forces. She served at Angers until November 1917; at Camp Coetquidan, an artillery training camp, as acting chief nurse until January 1919; and again at Angers until March 1919. When the war was over, Blanchfield returned to her superintendent position at Suburban Hospital, but she accepted reappointment in the ANC on 17 January 1920. From 1920 to 1935, Blanchfield's assignments were in Michigan, Indiana, California, the Philippines, Washington, D.C., Georgia, Missouri, and China.

On 1 July 1935 Blanchfield was assigned to the office of the chief nurse in the Office of the Surgeon General in Washington, D.C., where she remained for twelve years. She was promoted to captain on 1 February 1939, a rank that only five nurses could hold at one time. She became first assistant to the ANC superintendent, Major Julia Flikke, on 13 March 1942. On the next day Blanchfield was appointed to the relative rank of lieutenant colonel in the Army of the United States (AUS) and Flikke to colonel. Relative rank did not entitle nurses to full pay and privileges, although they received the courtesies due officers of that rank. Blanchfield and Flikke received pay at the lower ranks of major and lieutenant colonel, respectively. When Flikke left her position in January 1943, Blanchfield became acting superintendent. That June she became the seventh superintendent of the ANC and was promoted to the relative rank of colonel. The only other female colonel at that time was Oveta Culp Hobby, director of the Women's Army Corps.

During World War II, Blanchfield was superintendent of an ANC that numbered 57,000 nurses; she had been instrumental in raising their numbers from a peacetime level of 700. Her reputation as an effective administrator, human dynamo, and warm-hearted person gained her the affectionate title of the "Little Colonel"—she stood only five feet tall—from thousands of her charges. Blanchfield instituted a policy under which nurses were assigned to hospitals close to the front lines so that soldiers could be treated more quickly. She developed training schools at major commands for newly assigned nurses to learn how to perform their roles as officers. Blanchfield also initiated special courses for nurses-anesthetists, psychiatric nurses, and flight nurses. In the ANC headquarters office, she created a position for a public relations officer who kept Americans informed about nurses' roles in the military, which aided in recruiting. She obtained permission for nurses to wear battle fatigues in war zones. On 17 August 1945 Blanchfield received the Distinguished Service Medal for her work during World War II; she was the second woman to receive it in that war.

One of Blanchfield's primary goals was to eliminate the system of relative rank to which nurses had been tied since the beginning of the ANC. With help from Congresswoman Frances Payne Bolton, Blanchfield reached part of her goal in 1944 when temporary full military rank was given to women for the duration of the war plus six months. For women who had made careers out of the military, this was not enough. In 1947 Blanchfield was instrumental in the passing of the Army-Navy Nurse Act, which gave nurses permanent rank and commissions, with all rights and privileges that men had enjoyed, and incorporated the ANC into the regular army. Blanchfield was the first woman to receive a regular army commission, appointed to lieutenant colonel in the regular U.S. Army on 19 June 1947. In a Pentagon ceremony, General Dwight D. Eisenhower presented her with her commission and the serial number N-1. On 30 September 1947 she retired from the Army.

During her retirement, Blanchfield worked on a history of the ANC with Mary W. Standlee and wrote several articles on nursing. She remained concerned about the quality of nursing care and nurses' education and retained membership in a number of nursing organizations. She loved driving her car and traveled widely. She spent winters in Florida, making Inverness her home base, and summers in Goffstown, New Hampshire. During the rest of the year, she lived with a sister, Ruth M. Orndorff, and brother-in-law, Ford E. Orndorff, in Arlington, Virginia.

Recognition of Blanchfield's accomplishments did not end with her military retirement. The International Red Cross awarded her the Florence Nightingale Medal, the highest Red Cross award for nursing, in 1951. The army named an annual women's tennis trophy after Blanchfield, an avid sports fan, in 1956. Her home state of West Virginia awarded her its Distinguished Service Medal in 1963. She was buried in Arlington National Cemetery with full military honors following her death in Washington, D.C. As a final tribute, in 1982 the army dedicated The Colonel Florence A. Blanchfield Army Community Hospital at Fort Campbell, Kentucky, in honor of a woman considered one of the greatest humanitarians in the field of nursing.

• Blanchfield's papers are at Mugar Memorial Library, Department of Special Collections, Nursing Archives, Boston University. Her major writings are "The Needs of the Army Nurse Corps," *American Journal of Nursing* (Nov. 1943): 991–92, and "New Status in Military Nursing," *American Journal of Nursing* (Sept. 1947): 603–5. "R.N.: A Salute for Colonel Blanchfield," appeared in *Registered Nurse*, 10 Sept. 1947, pp. 31, 86. Edith A. Aynes, an assistant of Blanchfield, wrote "Colonel Florence A. Blanchfield," *Nursing Outlook* 7, no. 2 (Jan. 1959): 78–81. An interview by Evelyn Dent is in the *Washington Star*, 23 Feb. 1964. Doris W. Egge, "A Concise Biography of Colonel Florence Aby Blanchfield, ANC" (1974), is at the U.S. Army Center of Military History (CMH), Office of the Army Nurse Corps Historian, Nursing Archives. A transcript of interviews Blanchfield gave in 1964 to Major Katherine Jump, ANC, and Major Constance Ferebee, ANC, is also at CMH. Of numerous nursing histories, Edith A. Aynes, *From Nightingale to Eagle: An Army Nurse's History* (1973), gives Blanchfield the most attention. Mary M. Roberts, *The Army Nurse Corps Yesterday and Today* (1957), is also useful. "The History of the Army Nurse Corps," an unpublished CMH manuscript of eleven volumes, contains numerous references to Blanchfield's official actions and is located in the CMH Library. Blanchfield is included in Brooke Bailey, *The Remarkable Lives of 100 Women Healers and Scientists* (1994). Obituaries are in the *Washington Post*, 14 May 1971, and the *New York Times*, 13 May 1971.

CONNIE L. REEVES

BLAND, James Allen (22 Oct. 1854–5 May 1911), African-American minstrel performer and composer, was born in Flushing, Long Island, New York, the son of Allen M. Bland, an incipient lawyer, and Lidia Ann Cromwell of Brandywine, Delaware, of an emancipated family. Bland's father, whose family had been free for several generations, attended law school at Howard University in Washington, D.C., and in 1867 became the first black to be appointed an examiner in the U.S. Patent Office.

James Bland entered Howard University as a prelaw student in 1870 at the urging of his father, but the subject and the life associated with it did not appeal to him. He was attracted instead to the minstrel show that was approaching its peak during the 1870s. He played the guitar, danced the steps, sang the minstrel songs, and, most importantly, composed songs for the shows.

A free black man who attended college for two years, Bland did not have the speech or mannerisms of plantation blacks, but he learned from the workers at Howard University, mostly ex-slaves, something of the actions and the speech of plantation blacks. He was a good actor and a sweet singer and projected himself successfully into the minstrel milieu. In 1875 he left home to tour as a professional minstrel with the Black Diamond troupe of Boston; later he joined the Bohee Brothers, Sprague's Georgia Minstrels, and Haverly's Genuine Colored Minstrels.

It was with Haverly's group that Bland traveled in 1881 to London, where they played with great success at Her Majesty's Theatre. After a highly profitable year the Haverly troupe returned to the United States, but Bland and several others remained and enjoyed great success as music hall performers in England and Scotland. It was said that the prince of Wales showed special favor to Bland and once presented the actor with a gold-headed ebony cane. With these successes the performer-composer was able to indulge in lavish living (which sadly did not provide for his comforts in later life). Bland's career continued flourishing throughout the 1880s and part of the 1890s.

By 1901, however, Bland was back in the United States. He toured with W. S. Cleveland's Colossal Colored Carnival Minstrels, where he was billed as "the eccentric original James Bland." He and Tom McIntosh were called "the two greatest comedians of their race." In 1898 he appeared briefly with Black Patti's Troubadours. The minstrel show days were over, however, replaced in the public's affection by the musical comedy.

Bland made one try at writing a musical show, *The Sporting Girl*, but it was not a success. He had referred to himself as "the best Ethiopian song writer in the world," but that knack did not carry over into the new musical comedy. Many had called him "the Negro Stephen Foster," but in the early 1900s even Foster himself was not a great success. By 1911 Bland was in Philadelphia—out of fame, out of work, and out of money. He died there of pneumonia and was buried in an unmarked grave in the Merion Negro graveyard. Only in 1939 did James Francis Cooke, editor of the magazine *Etude*, find his grave (with the help of a long-memoried sister) and arrange for a proper gravestone, which was erected in 1946. Bland never married, so far as is known.

Bland's name has been kept alive by his music. The number of his compositions—minstrel songs, a few marching songs, a campaign song or two ("The Missouri Hound Dog")—has been estimated at 700, but this seems a considerable overestimate. The number of Bland's copyright deposits in the Library of Congress has been counted at only thirty-eight. (No doubt, of course, many songs and pieces were tossed off for particular occasions and did not always get published or even copyrighted.)

In 1875 Bland had written his best-known song, "Carry Me Back to Old Virginny," which as "Carry Me Back to Old Virginia" became the official state song of Virginia in 1940. Among his other best-known songs are "In the Evening by the Moonlight" (followed, of course, by "In the Morning by the Bright Light"), "Oh, Dem Golden Slippers" (which he sang with an especial dance routine), "Dancing on de Kitchen Floor," "The Colored Hop," and "Dandy Black Brigade." Many of Bland's songs were sung not only by him and other members of his troupe but also by members of other troupes. His songs have a combination of sentiment and lyric appeal that exemplified the spirit of the black minstrel show, which ironically was forwarded primarily by white performers in blackface makeup.

Bland is a prime example of the artist who happens to strike a subject at exactly the right time and succeeds without a long period of study and apprenticeship. His personality, musicianship, and acting ability—even acrobatic ability—gave him easy access to the top of his profession. When that profession dwindled in the eyes of the public, he lost his hold on success and had nothing with which to replace it. Perhaps because of faulty publishing habits he lost income from his compositions that would have helped him maintain some economic stability. "Easy come, easy go" was the long, sad story of Bland's life.

• Materials relating to Bland are in the Jesse E. Moorland Collection at Howard University. Black artists and blackface minstrelsy were seldom written about in the first half of the twentieth century. It was not until the July 1939 issue of *Etude* that editor James Francis Cooke published Kelly Miller's "The Negro 'Stephen Foster': The First Published Biography of James A. Bland," pp. 431–433, 472, accompanied by a photograph of Cooke standing by Bland's unmarked grave site in Philadelphia's Merion cemetery. A more substantial article by Charles Haywood, "James A. Bland, Prince of the Colored Songwriters," was published by the Flushing Historical Society as "A Discourse Delivered before the Flushing Historical Society," 25 Oct. 1944, and includes an account of Bland's career as a performer with minstrel troupes in the United States and Great Britain. "James Allen Bland, Negro Composer: A Study of His Life," (master's thesis, Howard Univ., 1968) by Lewis Horace Bland, a grandnephew, is available in the Founders' Library at Howard University, Washington, D.C. It contains much information gathered from the family. Other sources include John J. Daly, *A Song in His Heart* (1951); Langston Hughes, "James A. Bland: Minstrel Composer, 1854–1911," in *Famous Negro Music Makers* (1955); and Eileen Southern, *The Music of Black Americans: A History* (1971; rev. ed., 1983). Haywood's article on Bland in *The New Grove Dictionary of American Music*, vol. 1 (1986), pp. 231–32, lists about sixty of Bland's compositions and includes a bibliography of secondary sources.

WILLIAM LICHTENWANGER

BLAND, Richard (6 May 1710–26 Oct. 1776), colonial and revolutionary statesman, was born in Williamsburg, Virginia, the son of Richard Bland, a successful planter and local political leader, and Elizabeth Randolph. An exemplar of colonial Virginia's planter elite, he inherited a large James River estate and counted the Randolphs, Lees, Beverleys, and other first families among his relatives. At the College of William and Mary he received the best that Virginia could offer in the way of formal education. He qualified for the bar in 1746 and was recognized as an authority on constitutional law and Virginia's connections with the mother country. Thomas Jefferson, long after the Revolution, remembered him as "the most learned and logical man of those who took prominent lead in public affairs."

Bland's first wife and the mother of all of his twelve children was Anne Poythress, the daughter of one of Prince George County's leading planters, Peter Poythress. His first wife died in 1758, and Bland married Martha Macon, who also died a few years later. His third wife, Elizabeth Blair, the daughter of the president of the colonial council, John Blair, left him a widower in 1775. His marriages, first to respectable members of the local gentry and later to one of the prominent Blairs, helped to ensure his status.

As the first citizen of his county and one of the leading citizens of the province, Bland served as a vestryman of his local Anglican parish, as a justice of the peace for Prince George County, and as a colonel in the local militia. From 1742 until the Revolution he served as a member of the House of Burgesses, distinguishing himself as one of the two or three most important members of the colonial assembly.

Bland and his assembly colleagues accepted the habit of provincial self-rule. For over thirty years he was an exceptionally active burgess, playing a key role in virtually all of Virginia's internal affairs. He took the lead in opposition to the royal governor's 1753 plan to tax land patents, arguing that the "pistole fee" was an illegal tax because it did not have the consent of the elected representatives of the people of Virginia. In 1755 he took the lead again when the British Crown disallowed a law passed by the Virginia assembly that permitted colonists, during a tobacco crop failure, to pay their tobacco debts in paper money. In a satirical piece, "The Colonel Dismounted" (1764), he argued that only the representatives of Virginia could make laws for the internal affairs of the colony and that good laws made in the colony were beyond even the king's interference.

Bland was determined to defend a sphere of internal government reserved exclusively to the Virginia assembly, rationalizing in theory what he and his colleagues had long practiced: colonial self-rule. When Parliament began to threaten traditional legislative independence, Bland struck back with his effective pen. The 1765 Stamp Act was an especially perilous threat, which prompted his most important tract—and one of the important pamphlets of the American revolutionary era—*An Inquiry into the Rights of the British Colonies*, printed in 1766. This bold defense of colonial home rule advanced a theory of divided sovereignty within the British Empire, identifying the colonial assemblies as the supreme legislative bodies of the various colonies just as Parliament was the supreme legislature of Great Britain.

Bland based his theory on natural rights, including the right to resist if parliamentary power were used arbitrarily. He maintained that the colonists were the equals of the British; they had freedom to legislate their own affairs, and if the British government pushed too far they had the right to rebel. He advanced further into new ideological ground than any writer before him, presenting a theory of the British Empire that assured that Americans were masters in their own house. Thomas Jefferson admired Bland's closely argued tract, and his own *Summary View of the Rights America* was modeled closely on Bland's work.

Inherent in Bland's commonwealth theory of the empire was justification for revolution, but his preference was to see colonial self-government restored without breaking away from the British Crown. He opposed Patrick Henry's fiery resolves against the Stamp Act and his later call for immediately arming Virginia. Never a zealous revolutionary, Bland was a cautious elder statesman whose goal was to sustain the political and social way of life he had long known as a member of Virginia's elite. He opposed rebellion until it was clear that he had no other choice. He served as a delegate to the first two Continental Congresses, and in May 1776 the reluctant rebel voted both for Virginia's independence and the resolution that directed the Virginia delegation to the Continental Congress to declare for American independence. Just before his death he served on the committee that drew up the government of the independent state of Virginia.

Bland did as much as any leader of his generation to preserve self-government for Virginia and to articulate the colonists' discontent with British political interference. Although he died in Williamsburg in 1776, he had established a rationale for the American Revolution; his pamphlets were the initial papers of the rebellion. He distinguished himself in the struggle to preserve liberty in Virginia just as assuredly as more famous leaders—Thomas Jefferson, Patrick Henry, and George Mason—only he engaged in the struggle much earlier and gave them a philosophical base on which to build.

• The *Journals of the House of Burgesses* (13 vols., 1905–1915) provide the best primary source on Bland's political leadership over a period of thirty years. His political philosophy is laid out clearly in his tracts, particularly *An Inquiry into the Rights of the British Colonies* (1766), which established his important views on the rights of Americans within the British Empire. This tract is reprinted in William J. Van Schreeven and Robert L. Scribner, eds., *Revolutionary Virginia: The Road to Independence*, vol. 1 (1973). Regarding the records of the early Bland family see John Jester and Annie L. Hiden, *Adventurers of Purse and Person, Virginia 1607–1625* (1956; repr. 1964). Despite his contribution to the American Revolution, relatively little has been written about Bland. The most complete biography, placing him in the context of eighteenth-century Virginia political life, is Robert Detweiler, *Richard Bland and the Origins of the Revolution in Virginia* (1978). Clinton Rossiter, *Seedtime of the Republic* (1953), pp. 247–80, offers an interpretive characterization and summary of his contribution to revolutionary philosophy. Other secondary works on early American political thought offer brief discussion of Bland's writings; in particular, see Max Savelle, *Seeds of Liberty: The Genesis of the American Mind* (1948), and Bernard Bailyn, *The Ideological Origins of the American Revolution* (1967).

ROBERT DETWEILER

BLAND, Richard Parks (19 Aug. 1835–15 June 1899), congressman, was born near Hartford, Ohio County, Kentucky, the son of Stoughten Edward Parks Bland and Margaret Parks Nall, farmers. Orphaned in boyhood, Bland worked during the summer months to attend Ohio County schools. At eighteen he entered Griffin Academy in Hartford to complete a teacher's course. He then taught school before relocating to Missouri in the spring of 1855. For a year he taught in Wayne County, before removing to California, where he developed an interest in mining. For ten years, Bland lived in California, Colorado, and Nevada, teaching, prospecting, and studying law. He passed the bar in 1859. A Virginia City lawyer for a time, Bland served as treasurer of Carson County, Utah Territory, from 1860 until 1864. In 1865 Bland returned to Missouri, where he practiced law with his brother at Rolla. In 1869 he settled permanently in Lebanon, Missouri.

Bland had learned much about silver both as a metal and as a standard of value. He also sympathized with the frustrations of farmers during the postwar depression. In 1872, the year of President Ulysses S. Grant's reelection, Bland, a Democrat, won election to the U.S. House of Representatives with some Liberal Republican support. This heralded the beginning of a long career in the House, where he served continuously except for one term until his death. In 1873 he married Virginia Elizabeth Mitchell; they had nine children.

After the Democrats gained control of the House in 1875, Bland became chairman of the Committee on Mines and Mining, a position that enabled him to denounce the Coinage Act of 1873, which demonetized silver. With new discoveries in the West, silver production increased in the 1870s. Bland supported the expansion of silver production and advocated free and unlimited coinage of silver in relation to gold, but he stopped short of demanding a rigid ratio of coinage between the two metals. He sponsored a bill in 1876 that provided for free silver coinage, and the House, dominated by inflationist members, passed the measure that year and again in 1877. The Senate weakened the bill, but the Bland-Allison Act of 1878, passed over President Rutherford B. Hayes's veto, required the secretary of the treasury to make monthly purchases of between $2 and $4 million in silver and mint it into standard dollars. A compromise, the bill failed to attain the unlimited silver coinage that Bland had sought.

Over the next two decades, Bland led the struggle in the House for the restoration of bimetalism. A nationally known figure, he attended monetary conferences and wrote articles about the silver issue. Using his status as chairman of the Committee on Coinage, Weights, and Measures whenever the Democrats controlled the House, he continued to be a forceful spokesman for free silver coinage. In 1890 he opposed the Sherman Silver Purchase Act as a ridiculous representation of bimetalism, yet he vigorously fought against its repeal in 1893, and he did not substitute a free coinage act in its place. He warned President Grover Cleveland, a sound money Democrat, that free coinage Democrats would place the principle of silver coinage above party loyalty.

During the second Cleveland administration, economic depression enveloped the nation and lowered the living standards of virtually all farmers, laborers, and the middle class, whose debts skyrocketed. President Cleveland, whose political philosophy dictated a conservative response to the country's problems rather than social or economic experimentation, lost the support of many Democrats. Cleveland sympathized with the unemployed, but he entertained no notion of expanding the government's role to include providing jobs. Bland, who contended that all wealth came primarily from the soil, surfaced as an outspoken critic of Cleveland's fiscal policies. The struggle between rising industry and declining agriculture caused further party splits, and Bland fell victim to the times in 1894, when he lost his seat by seventy votes to Joel D. Hubbard, Republican clerk of Morgan County.

After his defeat, Bland concentrated on the upcoming 1896 presidential election. His fervent stand on silver made him a leading candidate among soft money Democrats and silver Republicans. Illinois governor John P. Altgeld, one of Bland's major supporters, wished to remove the vestiges of Clevelandism from the party. Bland, who wanted to reorganize the party on the principles of Thomas Jefferson and Andrew Jackson, saw the presidency as a place of trust and moral leadership, where he could execute policies that represented the will of the people. Declaring that laws should be made for "the protection of the weak," Bland considered his candidacy a matter of duty.

Several obstacles stood in Bland's way to the White House. He was sixty-one at the time and lacked the essential magnetism and the energy needed to mastermind a vigorous political crusade. Moreover, prominent Populists refused to support his presidential ambitions; Mrs. Bland was Catholic, and anti-Catholicism was extensive. At the Chicago convention, after momentum grew for the nomination of William Jennings Bryan, Bland, who had led on the first three ballots, withdrew his name from consideration. He refused the vice presidential position and when Arthur Sewall (1835–1900) received that nomination, Bland quickly announced his support of the party ticket. In an article in the *North American Review*, Bland asserted that Bryan's electoral triumph would mean "a complete, radical, and absolute change in the policies of administration" and that, under a bimetallic currency system, "there would be a revival of business throughout the land." The presidential victory of William McKinley, a sound money Republican, disheartened Bland.

Elected in 1896 to his former House seat, Bland focused his attention on McKinley's domestic and foreign policies and vigorously opposed high tariffs and monopolies. On 13 June 1898 Bland announced his opposition to the annexation of Hawaii to the United States in an address employing a wide array of constitutional and practical objections. Stating that Hawaiians could not comprehend the American political system, Bland recommended self-government for the islands. "We can do no more," he said, "than to turn over whatever territory comes under our jurisdiction [from the Spanish-American War] to their people. . . . And if . . . they are capable of self-government, they will succeed. Above all, our consciences will be free and our liberties not endangered."

Bland was sincere in his anti-imperialist position and bitterly opposed territorial expansion. Yet he declined to run for the Senate or for governor of Missouri, preferring to work in the House if he could not attain the nation's highest office.

Throughout his career, Bland lived modestly and always demonstrated real concern for the common people. He never wavered in his lifetime loyalty to free silver coinage. Nicknamed "Silver Dick" by friends and opponents, Bland, the dean of silver advocates in the House, was a prominent Gilded Age leader on the national scene. He died in Lebanon one year before Bryan's second presidential campaign.

• Bland left no personal papers. His letters are scattered in the manuscript collections of contemporaries, including the Grover Cleveland Papers and the William Jennings Bryan Papers, both at the Library of Congress. The speech on Hawaii is in the *Congressional Record*, 18 June 1898, pp. 6840–42. His articles in various periodicals provide a record of his ideas and positions on the issues of the day, especially free silver. See, for example, R. P. Bland, "The Duty of the Hour," *North American Review* 163 (1896): 368–76. The two major studies of Bland are William Vincent Byars, ed., *"An American Commoner": The Life and Times of Richard Parks Bland* (1900), and Harold Alanson Haswell, Jr., "The Public Life of Congressman Richard Parks Bland" (Ph.D. diss., Univ. of Missouri at Columbia, 1951). Obituaries are in the *New York Times* and the *St. Louis Globe-Democrat*, both 16 June 1899.

LEONARD SCHLUP

BLAND, Theodorick (21 Mar. 1742–1 June 1790), revolutionary soldier and politician, was born in Prince George County, Virginia, the son of Theodorick Bland, a planter, and Frances Bolling. In 1753 he was sent to Wakefield in Yorkshire, England, for schooling, remaining there until taking up medical studies in Liverpool in 1759. Two years later he transferred to the University of Edinburgh and received an M.D. degree in 1763. In Edinburgh and later in London Bland cut a fashionable figure, chivied by friends for his "monstrous large Whig." He was also known as "something of a politician," and it was with reluctance that he heeded his father's call to return to Virginia in 1764. There he began his medical practice with all its attendant "distresses, cares and anxieties," the "immense fatigue" of which caused him to retire from the profession in 1771. Wishing for a "calm, quiet, and philosophical life, in a rural situation," Bland became a planter in Prince George County.

In a distinctly unquiet way, however, Bland took an active part in the growing controversy with Great Britain. In 1774 he sold his tobacco in Great Britain to pay his debts but refused to purchase British items because the mother country "threatens us with a deprivation of our liberties." On 24 June 1775 he and twenty-four others, among them a future U.S. president (James Monroe) and a future governor of Virginia (Benjamin Harrison), looted the governor's mansion of weapons, after which Bland distributed the pistols, muskets, and swords to Whig partisans. In December 1775 he wrote two polemics published in the *Virginia Gazette* under the name "Cassius" attacking the governor, Lord Dunmore, for among other things, freeing slaves who ran away from their masters.

In June 1776 Bland responded to a call by the state of Virginia for volunteers to form a regiment of light dragoons. He was commissioned captain of the first troop and major commandant of the regiment. In January 1777 Bland's Horse was integrated into the Continental army as the First Regiment of Continental Light Dragoons, and Bland himself accepted a colonel's commission on 31 March 1777. He served with George Washington's army that year and fought in the battle of Brandywine on 11 September. Bland bears partial responsibility for the lack of reconnaissance that caused the American defeat there, and in the judgment of Henry Lee, one of his subordinates who later became a brilliant cavalry officer, the colonel, though "noble, sensible, honorable, and amiable," was "never intended for the department of military intelligence." Perhaps Bland felt this lack, for he tried to resign his commission in November 1777. His resignation was refused by Washington, who sent him to Virginia to acquire horses and recruit men for the regiment. In August 1778 he was recalled to headquarters at White Plains, and on 5 November he was ordered to conduct the Convention Army, British prisoners of war who had surrendered at Saratoga, from Boston to Charlottesville, Virginia. He was appointed commander of the barracks there in April 1779 and served until his resignation was accepted in November of that year.

In August 1780 Bland took his seat in the Continental Congress as a delegate from Virginia, a position he held, with some interruptions, for three years. He was a diligent legislator and a congenial companion whose letters are sprinkled with classical allusions and partisan zeal. He did not always see eye to eye with his Virginia colleague James Madison and toward the end of his term demonstrated an acute bias against France, allying himself with Arthur Lee, an old schoolmate from Edinburgh days, against Robert Morris and the more nationalist members of Congress. One colleague,

Thomas Rodney of Delaware, described him in his diary as "a Man of Moderate Talents, of Firmness & Candor and Much Attached To the Constitution of the States—Tho not very Systematical nor always of the best Judgment" and "rather rustic in debate" (Smith, vol. 17, p. 38). When his congressional term ended in 1783, Bland returned to his plantation, "Farmingdale," in Prince George County, which had suffered greatly during the British invasion of Virginia in 1781, and began to repair his fortune. By 1787, however, Bland ranked among the one hundred wealthiest Virginians.

Bland served in the House of Delegates in 1786, 1787, and 1788 and was considered for governor in 1786. In the 1788 Virginia ratifying convention Bland voted against the adoption of the U.S. Constitution. He stood for election to the U.S. House of Representatives in District Nine as an Antifederalist and as a strong advocate of amending the Constitution and won an overwhelming victory. In the House he was initially the only Virginia congressman to support Alexander Hamilton's plan for the assumption of state debts, but he did so, claimed William Maclay, to demonstrate "to the World. that our present Constitu[ti]on aimed directly at consolidation. and the sooner every body knew it the better." He died in New York City, however, before he could cast his vote for the measure. His marriage to Martha Daingerfield, who survived him, was childless.

• Bland's papers are found in a number of archives, most important of which are the Bland Family Papers in the Virginia Historical Society and the Tucker-Coleman papers at the College of William and Mary. A large part of the former collection is published in Charles Campbell, ed., *The Bland Papers* (2 vols. in one; 1840). Other letters can be found in the multivolume collection edited by Paul H. Smith, *Letters of Delegates to Congress, 1774–1789* (1976–); William T. Hutchinson et al., eds., *The Papers of James Madison* (1st ser., vols. 1–17, 1962–1991); and "Selections from the Campbell Papers," *Virginia Magazine of History and Biography* 9 (1901–1902): 59–77, 162–70, 298–306. Bland's Edinburgh thesis was published as *De Concoctione Alimentorum in Ventriculo* (1763). His social and financial standing is assessed in Jackson T. Main, "The One Hundred," *William and Mary Quarterly*, 3d ser., 11 (1954): 354–84. His will is printed in the *Virginia Magazine of History and Biography* 3 (1895–1896): 315.

DAVID B. MATTERN

BLANDING, Sarah Gibson (27 Nov. 1898–3 Mar. 1985), college administrator, was born on a farm near Lexington, Kentucky, the daughter of William de Saussure Blanding, a lawyer and storekeeper-gauger (internal revenue officer), and Sarah Gibson Anderson. When she was twelve, her father died in an accident, and because the family had little money, she abandoned plans to become a physician. She subsequently borrowed sufficient funds to pay the tuition for a two-year course in physical education at the New Haven, Connecticut, Normal School of Gymnastics (1917–1919).

Blanding was hired as a physical education instructor at the University of Kentucky in 1919, at the same time enrolling as an undergraduate in the A.B. program. When she graduated in 1923, she was appointed the university's acting dean of women, at age twenty-four the youngest university dean in the country. She subsequently undertook graduate studies, obtaining a master's degree in political science from Columbia University in 1926 and continuing her studies under Harold Laski at the London School of Economics in 1928–1929.

In 1929 Blanding returned to the University of Kentucky where she served as dean of women and professor of political science until 1941. During this time, she lived on a farm where she profitably raised tobacco, harvesting her own crop and taking it to market. She also founded and directed a girls' camp called Trail's End and was chair (1933–1935) of the university division of the National Association of Deans of Women.

Blanding was chosen in 1941 as the first dean of the Cornell University School of Home Economics, where she became known as an apt and aggressive administrator. She resigned from that position in 1946 to succeed Henry Noble MacCracken as Vassar College's first woman president. At the time of her inauguration, she was cited for her exceptional service as a consultant to the U.S. Secretary of War from March 1943 to June 1946, heading a program for women in the armed services, a position to which she was appointed, becoming the only woman member of the Joint Army and Navy Committee on Welfare and Recreation.

During Blanding's eighteen years as head of Vassar College, she made several significant institutional changes, including the advancement of faculty members on the basis of merit instead of time served. In 1949 she presided over the establishment of the Mary Conover Mellon Foundation for the Advancement of Education, created to encourage conditions in college life that would promote good mental and emotional health on campus. A new system of housefellows was established in Vassar dormitories under which faculty members and their families lived in the dormitories to activate the intellectual and cultural life of the students.

Blanding conducted a far-reaching development program at Vassar without professional assistance, tripling the college's investment portfolio by raising $25 million in nine years, overseeing construction of three new buildings, and achieving three major reconstructions of older buildings between 1955 and 1964. In 1957 she introduced a novel two-year study of every aspect of Vassar College, including its educational objectives and conditions of residential life. This was the first time that the college had subjected itself to such an extensive self-critical review, resulting in a new curriculum fostering increased independent work on the part of the students. During a period of political unrest and threats to academic freedom in the 1950s, she fearlessly defended several of her faculty members from attacks by political critics such as Senator Joseph R. McCarthy and Congressman B. Carroll Reece of Tennessee.

Speaking at a luncheon in New York City in 1961, Blanding predicted the demise of women's colleges, declaring that as a genre, they were on their way to extinction and that there would be no more than 200 of them left by the year 2000. In 1962, equally forthright but less tempered, she gave an impromptu and unguarded speech in a Vassar undergraduate assembly, decrying excessive use of alcohol, premarital sex, and vulgar conduct on the part of Vassar students. Although the speech represented her own moral values, it seemed to the students out-of-date and out-of-touch with the changing times; they resented what they considered a misrepresentation of their search for a new morality. The repercussions of the speech haunted the last years of Blanding's presidency.

Stemming from her early career as a tobacco farmer, Blanding often referred to herself as a "horse-trader." Her conduct showed independence of mind and a willingness to subject herself to the same critical evaluation to which her subordinates were held. She functioned effectively in the larger circles of higher education beyond Cornell and Vassar, and on both government and corporate business boards, where she was often the only woman. Indeed, she frequently told stories about how she got ahead in a man's world through cunning and aggressive action. Students often remarked about her salty language, which she explained was the result of her southern upbringing and youthful independence in running her tobacco farm, bidding her price up at sales, and having to fend for herself. She had an ear for the vernacular, including swear words, and peppered her language with what she heard.

Blanding was a member of the President's Commission on Higher Education under Harry Truman and the Public Advisory Board of the Economic Cooperation Administration. She also served on the board of directors of the Ford Foundation's Fund for Adult Education. After retirement from the Vassar presidency in 1964, Blanding traveled around the world to visit Vassar alumnae, then moved to Lakeville, Connecticut, with her sister Ellen Blanding, who had been her official hostess at Vassar. She died in Newtown Square, Pennsylvania, having spent her last years in a Quaker retirement center.

Blanding was a vigorous exponent of women. "I have no patience with women who are always talking about 'a man's world,' because they are the ones who make it so," she said early in her presidency. She encouraged college women to pursue professions, enter politics, develop independence of thought and action, and fight for an equal footing with men. She herself served as a formidable example of what it took to make the grade.

• There are two primary sources of information about Blanding. Her scanty personal papers are in the Schlesinger Library at Harvard University and include her manuscript about her family history as well as selected speeches, legal matters, and correspondence pertaining to her Vassar tenure. Other papers relating to Blanding's life and times are in the

Vassar College Library, along with the text of an oral history interview conducted at Vassar by Delores Greenberg on 11 June 1962. William Cooper, Jr., published "An Interview with Sarah Blanding" in *Kentucky Review* 1, no. 2 (Winter 1979–1980): 24–38. An obituary is in the *New York Times*, 4 Mar. 1985.

ELIZABETH ADAMS DANIELS

BLANKENBURG, Lucretia Longshore (8 May 1845–29 Mar. 1937), suffragist and reformer, was born near New Lisbon, Ohio, the daughter of Thomas Ellwood Longshore, a Quaker schoolteacher, and Hannah E. Myers, who also was from a Quaker family and who became the first woman doctor in Philadelphia. She was named for Lucretia Mott, an early advocate for women's rights. During her early years she lived near Attleboro, Pennsylvania, and in Philadelphia, where her mother completed her medical studies. When police had to prevent male medical students from breaking up her mother's graduation ceremony, Lucretia, an impressionable six-year-old, "resolved" to work "to free women from social and legal injustice" (Blankenburg, p. 156). She experienced "some persecution" as a child, with her teacher telling other children not to play with her because her mother, who had lectured to women on physiology and hygiene, "was an improper person" (Blankenburg, p. 104). Her childhood home, housing her mother's large medical practice and that of her mother's younger sister, Jane V. Myers (they were derisively called "she doctors"), was an exciting place. "Advanced thinkers and reformers" dropped in, a runaway slave once hid there for several days en route to freedom in Canada, and the abolitionist and reformer Sojourner Truth was a house guest (Blankenburg, p. 107).

After graduating from Bryant and Stratton Commercial College in Philadelphia, Lucretia attended her mother's alma mater for one semester but decided against studying medicine. In 1867 she married Rudolph Blankenburg, a German immigrant, who was a very successful textile salesman. They had three children, but none of them reached adulthood. In 1871 Blankenburg accompanied her husband to Europe to visit his family on the first of her eight trips there. When her husband started a dry goods store the next year, she worked with him, as she did in the textile firm he founded in 1875.

The 1876 Centennial Exhibition, held in Philadelphia, left new ideas in its wake, and Lucretia and Rudolph Blankenburg were among those determined to build upon the civic pride it quickened. To educate the householders living in her own district, Lucretia Blankenburg wrote a series of little primers with titles like "Do You Know the Tenth Ward?" "City Housekeeping," and "City Fathers." With her husband she joined a group organizing various Philadelphia charities, and she joined the New Century Club, which was founded by those involved in the Woman's Centennial Committee. This club became a "great factor in training" Blankenburg—who was too inhibited to read the first paper she prepared—"for a more ample life and

for a deeper interest in public affairs" (Blankenburg, p. 114). Long a member of the local suffrage association, she became more involved after Susan B. Anthony, who was writing a history of the woman's rights movement in the United States, asked her in 1884 to collect material for it in Philadelphia.

Through the New Century Club's Committee on Educational Affairs, which she chaired, Blankenburg helped Anna Hallowell introduce kindergartens to Philadelphia public schools in 1883. Blankenburg also arranged Hallowell's appointment as the first woman member of the Philadelphia Board of Education. When in 1884 the New Century Club started a New Century Guild for working-class women, Blankenburg became an active worker, director, and trustee. During two winters she taught evening bookkeeping classes to members of this association, which claimed to be the first in the United States to couple evening class instruction with the advantages of a social club.

Working through the New Century Club, Blankenburg and her associates successfully installed the first police matron in Philadelphia in 1886. As chair of the Smoke Nuisance Committee, Blankenburg managed to obtain the cooperation of some factory owners, and through the short-lived Woman's Health Protective Association she improved Philadelphia's drinking water with filtration and secured fenders on street cars and "vestibule protection from storm and cold for the street-car drivers" (Blankenburg, p. 119). In 1891 she launched a successful drive, backed by the New Century Club and suffrage and labor organizations, to get women appointed as factory inspectors.

When Blankenburg was elected president of the Pennsylvania Woman Suffrage Association in 1892, an office she held for sixteen years, Susan B. Anthony taught her how to project her voice so she could be heard in large auditoriums. An apt pupil, Blankenburg often pushed legislation for women in the halls of the state legislature and at hearings in the U.S. Congress. During her presidency, the state Woman Suffrage Association sponsored two bills in the Pennsylvania legislature. One, giving mothers equal guardianship with fathers over minor children, passed after being amended. The other, giving widows the same share of intestate estates as widowers, failed to pass, although a later bill improved a widow's lot by giving her $5,000 from her husband's estate before collateral heirs were considered. As chair of the Committee on Legislation and Civil Rights of the National Association, Blankenburg yearly reported on the changes in laws affecting women and children in the twenty-three states with suffrage associations.

After the death from diphtheria of their third daughter in 1892, Lucretia and Rudolph Blankenburg pledged themselves to do even more "to help others and if possible improve public affairs" (Blankenburg, p. 127). They were comforted in this third bereavement by Louise Adolphson, an art student, who began living with them that year and remained with them. Since they had earlier brought over a niece from Germany to be a companion to their daughter, their home was not childless, and a nephew later joined them.

On her seventh visit to Europe, Blankenburg was a delegate to the 1904 International Congress of Women in Berlin and the International Council of Women, which preceded it. During the congress, she gave a twenty-minute report on changes in U.S. laws increasing the rights of women.

In the 1890s Blankenburg began a campaign to enlist women's clubs in the cause of woman suffrage. First she gained the admittance of suffrage associations in the State Federation of Pennsylvania Women and then worked to secure the state and national federations' support for women's right to vote. In 1908 she became the auditor of the General Federation of Women's Clubs and arranged for the presentation of a suffrage resolution at its biennials in 1910, 1912, and 1914; it passed in 1914 over the protests of a bitter minority. After serving six years as auditor, Blankenburg became the federation's second and then its first vice president. She continued as an officer of the general federation for six years, following her auditorship with the second vice presidency and serving as first vice president from 1912 to 1914. Upon her retirement, she remained an honorary vice president for the rest of her life.

Blankenburg was also active in the peace and Prohibition movements and helped direct a coeducational school for industrial arts in Philadelphia. In addition, she always supported and cooperated with her husband. When Rudolph Blankenburg ran for mayor of Philadelphia in 1911, his wife's associates worked untiringly in the campaign. "It was the women and children of this city who elected me," he gratefully acknowledged (Bennett, p. 224). The Blankenburgs' "comradeship" in business, charity, and reform lasted fifty-one years until Rudolph Blankenburg's death in 1918.

Blankenburg in 1920 took an 11,000-mile auto trip to California and back, attending the biennial convention of the General Federation of Women's Clubs in Des Moines, Iowa, en route. A few years later 1,400 people shared her "two-story" eightieth birthday cake, decked with the goddess of liberty and eighty red candles. Attesting that "great changes" had taken place during her lifetime, Blankenburg rejoiced that women had become "athletic and alert" and that it was no longer "ladylike to be delicate, and to faint frequently" (Blankenburg, pp. 156–57). Three thousand women attended her ninetieth birthday dinner at her city's Convention Hall. She was "Philadelphia's grand old lady," who had kept her faith in America's youth, whom she insisted would "turn out all right" (Wainwright, p. 224). She was also America's oldest active clubwoman, who gave a speech at a testimonial luncheon a week before she died in Philadelphia.

• For Blankenburg's life story, see her autobiography, which she coupled with a biography of her husband, *The Blankenburgs of Philadelphia* (1928), and her twenty-four scrapbooks at the Historical Society of Pennsylvania. For short summaries of her life, see Nicholas B. Wainwright, "Lucretia Longshore Blankenburg, 1845–1937," *Notable Women of Pennsylvania* (1942), and Helen Christine Bennett, *American Women in Civic Work* (1915). Information on her work for woman suffrage can also be found in Ida Husted Harper, ed., *History of Woman Suffrage* (6 vols., 1900–1920). An obituary is in the *New York Times*, 29 Mar. 1937.

OLIVE HOOGENBOOM

BLANSHARD, Brand (27 Aug. 1892–19 Nov. 1987), rationalist philosopher and educator, was born Percy Brand Blanshard with a fraternal twin, Paul, in Fredericksburg, Ohio, the son of Francis George Blanshard, a Congregationalist minister, and Emily Coulter. In a tragic accident Emily Blanshard was burned to death when the twins were infants. Brand's father served for a few years as a minister of a Congregationalist church. Suffering from consumption, the young minister, on advice from his physician, went to live in a dry western state. Unfortunately, the move was to no avail and he died a short time later.

The Blanshard twins were raised by their grandmother, Orminda Blanshard, in northern Ohio and, later, for better schooling, in Michigan. She was head of the household for the next dozen years and managed to care for the boys on a very slim income. Her only source of income was a superannuation fund earned by her husband, Shem, because of his service as a minister to the Methodist church in Canada. Paul and Brand took their schooling in Edinburgh, Ohio, and Grand Rapids, Michigan. With their grandmother, they moved to Detroit, where the boys were enrolled at Central High School, and later to Ann Arbor, where they attended the University of Michigan. The brothers parted ways for several years when Brand, having received a Rhodes scholarship in 1913, set out for Merton College, Oxford University. Oxford created a lasting impression and had a profound influence on his philosophy. While there he was influenced by Harold H. Joachim, T. S. Eliot, F. H. Bradley, Hastings Rashdall, and other scholars. Blanshard stayed at Oxford until 1915 and then returned to New York, finishing an M.A. at Columbia University in 1918. His advanced academic work was interrupted in 1918–1919 while he served in the U.S. Army in France. The year 1919–1920 was again spent at Oxford, from which he received a B.Sc. in 1920. He received the Ph.D. from Harvard in 1921. Blanshard married Frances Margaret Bradshaw in 1918; they had no children. After her death in 1966, he married Roberta Yerkes in 1969.

Blanshard served as assistant professor and associate professor at the University of Michigan (1921–1928) and as professor of philosophy at Swarthmore College (1928–1945). During this period he published his two-volume work, *The Nature of Thought* (1939, 1940), together with important papers on education and ethics. A member of the Yale faculty from 1945 until his retirement in 1961, he was its philosophy chairman from 1945 to 1950, and 1959 to 1961.

Blanshard received numerous academic awards and honors. In the field of philosophy he was in constant demand as a speaker and lecturer. At Harvard he served as Dudleian Lecturer (1945), Noble Lecturer (1948), and Whitehead Lecturer (1961). He was one of two American philosophers (John Dewey was the other) to give both the famous Gifford Lectures (St. Andrews, Scotland, 1952–1953), and the Carus Lectures (1959), an honor conferred by members of the American Philosophical Association on only its most respected scholars. With these two high honors as bookends, he gave the Hertz Lecture to the British Academy (1952), the Adamson Lecture at Manchester University (1953), the Howison Lecture at the University of California, Berkeley (1954), and the Matchette Lecture at Wesleyan University (1957). Even fifteen years before his death, he had already lectured at 144 colleges or universities in the United States and abroad.

Blanshard served as president of the prestigious eastern division of the American Philosophical Association (1942–1944) and president of the American Theological Society (1955–1956). In addition he was a Rhodes Scholar (1913–1915, 1919–1920), Guggenheim Fellow (1929–1930), and recipient of a senior award from the American Council of Learned Societies (1958) as well as the medal of honor from Rice University (1962). He received honorary doctorate degrees from thirteen colleges and universities.

His writings and scholarship have been praised as both "lucid" and "elegant," terms rarely used to refer to philosophical essays. Blanshard is one of the small company of outstanding philosophers (including Dewey, Alfred North Whitehead, Gabriel-Honoré Marcel, and Albert Einstein) to have a volume in the Library of Living Philosophers devoted to his thought (*The Philosophy of Brand Blanshard*, ed. Paul Arthur Schilpp [1980]).

In much of his writing Blanshard is concerned to show the importance of reason as a guide and test for truth. In his earliest scholarly work, *The Nature of Thought*, Blanshard shows the rational movement of thought toward an end of its own and the correlative rationality or intelligibility of the world as a whole. He insists that in human experience there are some necessary connections and that it is a primary task of reason as coherence to discover and offer an account of these important connections. In his view, reason could not rest until it achieved an understanding that required seeing these matters clearly both in relation to each other and to the whole of which they were integral parts.

In a trilogy of volumes, *Reason and Goodness* (1961), *Reason and Analysis* (1962), and *Reason and Belief* (1974), Blanshard unfolds what he considers the basic task of philosophy. How is reason understood as coherence related to goodness? How is reason related to philosophical analysis? How is reason related to belief, especially religious belief? These questions provide focus for Blanshard's efforts and inquiry. But the pulsing heart in all of it is rationalism or the "reasonable temper."

For Blanshard rationalism characterizes a way of life that he admires. This rationalism is not confined to exercises in logic or mathematics, for it provides the foundation for choices among values and, in the final analysis, is the guide for practical living. And it is to rationalism that one turns for solutions to problems of race, gender, crime, the environment, and overpopulation.

In his final book, published when he was ninety-two years old, *Four Reasonable Men: Marcus Aurelius, John Stuart Mill, Ernest Renan, and Henry Sidgwick* (1984), Blanshard presents to his readers exemplars of reasonableness. Through this biographical study he insists that the crucial need of humankind is "the great grey virtue" or "a quiet habitual reasonableness." This alone will give integrity to divided selves, correct slipshod observation, rectify perversions of logic, assess egoistic quirks, correct family biases, depict religious dogmas in their proper hue, show rampant patriotism for the narrow-minded and myopic view it is, and function as a corrective for human prejudices based on race and gender. Blanshard died in New Haven, Connecticut.

• No collections of Blanshard's letters have been published in book form, although individual letters have appeared in the *New York Times* and elsewhere. Correspondence, interviews, and other Blanshard materials can be found in the Brand Blanshard Papers, Manuscript Group #1488, Sterling Library, Yale University. The most complete bibliography of Blanshard's writings (up to 1980, and with the cooperation and assistance of Brand and Roberta Blanshard) is found in *The Philosophy of Brand Blanshard*, pp. 1101–27. A list of Blanshard's writings for 1980 through 1987 appears in a special memorial issue of *Idealistic Studies* 20 (May 1990): 169–70. The compiler of both bibliographies is John Howie. Brand Blanshard gives an autobiographical account of his early life and development as a philosopher in *The Philosophy of Brand Blanshard*, pp. 1–185. Also useful is Israel Shenker, "At 80, Blanshard Twins Still Back the Unpopular," *New York Times*, 28 Aug. 1972, or the later interview with Seth Lerner in *Advocate* (Oct. 1984), housed with the Manuscript Group #1488.

JOHN HOWIE

BLANTON, Jimmy (18 Nov. 1918–30 July 1942), bass player, was born James Blanton in Chattanooga, Tennessee. Blanton is widely regarded as the most outstanding bass player of the late 1930s and early 1940s, almost single-handedly revolutionizing jazz bass playing both technically and conceptually. As a child, Blanton studied violin, making his first public appearance at age eight. Showing exceptional talent and a serious interest in music, he learned music theory from an uncle and later switched to string bass while studying at Tennessee State College (1934–1937). Precociously gifted on this instrument, Blanton was soon playing with local bands, including his mother's (a pianist and bandleader). In 1937 he moved to St. Louis to play with the Jeter-Pillars Orchestra and Fate Marable's Mississippi riverboat bands.

In late 1939 Blanton was heard by Duke Ellington, who immediately asked him to join the famous Ellington orchestra. Along with tenor saxophonist Ben Webster, Blanton contributed significantly to a revitalization of the Ellington orchestra, particularly in regard to its deep, rich sound and its strong sense of swing. Blanton recorded prolifically during his relatively brief tenure with the band, including a remarkable series of six bass and piano duets with Ellington, a format unprecedented and unheard of in the early 1940s and hardly ever assayed again since then. Within a short time, Blanton came to be regarded as the leading bass player in jazz. His influence is to a large extent attributable to the happy circumstance that his playing was superbly recorded as a result of new microphone and recording techniques, giving the bass a distinctive prominence on recordings. During his years with Ellington, Blanton also frequently played at Minton's Playhouse (Harlem) in informal jam sessions that were crucial in the development of the bop style.

In late 1941 signs of the illness (later diagnosed as tuberculosis) that was to cause Blanton's death began to show, forcing him to leave the Ellington orchestra and retire to a sanatorium in Los Angeles, California, where he died within a few months. He was never married.

Blanton's contribution to the development of jazz, particularly in regard to the full emancipation of the rhythm section, is immeasurable. He expanded jazz bass techniques by considerably extending the upper range of the bass; by developing greater agility in his solos and "walking" bass lines, both in his right-hand pizzicato dexterity and his left-hand nimbleness; by approaching improvisation more as a "horn" (brass or saxophone) player would; and by creating more harmonically explorative and wide-ranging (not just scalar) bass lines. In these ways Blanton contributed significantly to the greater musical independence of the rhythm section, thereby freed to make substantial contributions melodically, harmonically, contrapuntally, and texturally.

As the first major soloist on the bass, he elevated that instrument to a new and higher status. His strong, well-focused sound and his highly original walking bass lines, often exploring the uppermost range of the instrument, profoundly influenced all subsequent important jazz bass players long after his death (especially Ray Brown, George Duvivier, Oscar Pettiford, Milt Hinton, Eddie Safranski, Chubby Jackson, and Charles Mingus, among others).

• Of Blanton's many recordings with Ellington—many, considering the brevity of his career—especially notable are "Jack the Bear," "Concerto for Cootie," "Sepia Panorama," "In a Mellotone," "Cotton Tail," and the six duets with Ellington ("Plucked Again," "Blues," "Pitter Panther Patter," "Sophisticated Lady," "Body and Soul," and "Mr. J. B. Blues"). A discography of Blanton's recordings by I. Kanth was published in Stockholm, Sweden, in 1970. Blanton is also frequently and lovingly mentioned in Ellington's autobiography, *Music Is My Mistress* (1973). His work is also discussed in C. Carrère, *Pitter Panther Patter: les bassistes de Duke Ellington* (1975), and in Gunther Schuller, *Swing Era* (1989).

GUNTHER SCHULLER

BLASHFIELD, Edwin Howland (15 Dec. 1848–12 Oct. 1936), artist, writer, and lecturer, was born in Brooklyn, New York, the son of William Henry Blashfield, who was in the wholesale dry goods business, and Eliza Dodd, an amateur watercolorist. After some schooling in Hartford, Connecticut, he attended the Boston Latin School, and in 1863 he went to Hanover, Germany, where he intended to study engineering. However, three months later he was forced to return to the United States, where he enrolled in the Boston Institute of Technology (later Massachusetts Institute of Technology).

Although Blashfield's mother had always supported his artistic interests, his father was not persuaded to let him embark on a career as an artist until he heard that some of his drawings had been praised by the noted French artist Jean-Léon Gérôme. The leading art teacher in Boston at that time was William Morris Hunt, who urged Blashfield to study with one of his pupils, Thomas Johnson. Blashfield took Hunt's advice, and by April 1866 Hunt, who had been one of the first Americans to receive artistic training at the École des Beaux-Arts in Paris, felt that Blashfield was ready to follow in his footsteps. As Blashfield later recalled, Hunt told him to "go straight to Paris. All you learn here you'll have to unlearn" (Cortissoz, pages unnumbered). Hunt also allowed Blashfield to study with him for two months before leaving for Paris on 5 May 1867.

Blashfield had intended to study with Gérôme, but when he arrived at the artist's studio Gérôme told him that he needed further study before enrolling in the École and advised him to study in the atelier of Léon Bonnat. Blashfield remained with Bonnat until 1870, when the outbreak of the Franco-Prussian War forced him to leave Paris. After traveling in Belgium, Germany, and Italy, spending eight months in Florence, Blashfield returned to the United States in 1871 and opened up a studio in New York.

He returned to France in 1874 to continue his study with Bonnat and remained there until 1880. His work had some critical success; he began to exhibit at the Paris Salon of 1876 and also exhibited at the Royal Academy in London. Not many of his early works have come to light, but one painting of this period, *The Emperor Commodus Leaving the Arena at the Head of the Gladiators*, which was exhibited at the Salon of 1878, is now in the Hermitage Foundation Museum in Norfolk, Virginia.

In 1881 Blashfield married Evangeline Wilbour, a writer. Although they settled in New York, the couple made frequent visits to Italy, Greece, and Egypt. They had one child, who died in infancy. Blashfield continued to exhibit allegorical and religious paintings in the Paris salons, but he also did some illustrations for books and for *St. Nicholas Magazine*. In 1886 he was commissioned to paint a mural for the New York residence of H. McKown Twombly, a friend from his Boston Latin School days and later president of the New York Central Railroad. This was Blashfield's first mural, and it marked the beginning of what was to become his major field of activity.

In 1892 Blashfield and a number of other artists were asked to paint murals in the Manufactures and Liberal Arts Building of Chicago's World's Columbian Exposition of 1893. The work had to be done in six weeks, and although Blashfield had little experience in this type of work his dome murals illustrating the *Art of Metal Working* were awarded a bronze medal. At that time there were few murals in American public buildings, but the popularity of Blashfield's work and that of the other artists who worked at the 1893 exhibition marked the beginning of an enthusiasm for mural painting that continued unabated until the 1930s. State capitols, courthouses, libraries, and private homes were decorated with classicizing allegories and recreations of historic events that were enormously popular and considered by contemporary critics to be the most significant products of American artistic genius.

Blashfield was at the center of this "American Mural Renaissance." In 1895–1896 he carried out the murals illustrating the *Evolution of Civilization*, a band of twelve figures symbolizing the arts and sciences that surround the dome in the main reading room of the Library of Congress. This is his most important extant work and brought him great critical acclaim. In rapid succession followed his murals *The Power of the Law* (1899) in the Appellate Division Courthouse in New York City; *Washington Laying Down His Command at the Feet of Columbia* (1902) and *The Edict of Toleration of Lord Baltimore* (1904) in the courthouse in Baltimore, Maryland; and *Minnesota, Granary of the World* (1904), *Discoverers and Civilizers of the Mississippi* (1904), and *The Battle of Corinth, Mississippi* (1912) in the Minnesota State Capitol in St. Paul, to mention only a few of his major extant commissions. By the turn of the century Blashfield was acknowledged as one of the leading painters in the United States. In 1909 an exhibition of photographs of his work went on tour throughout the country, and his pendentive mural *The Law* (1910) in the Mahoning County Courthouse, Youngstown, Ohio, won him the New York Architectural League's gold medal of honor. He also designed some mosaics: *St. Matthew and the Angels of the Passion* in the sanctuary of the Church of St. Matthew the Apostle in Washington, D.C., was executed in 1914, but the pendentive decorations *The Four Evangelists* were not completed until 1926.

Blashfield was active as a writer and co-wrote, with his wife, and illustrated articles in *Scribner's Magazine* and *Century Magazine* from 1887 to 1896. In 1896, with Albert A. Hopkins, the Blashfields published a four-volume edited selection of seventy of sixteenth-century Italian artist Giorgio Vasari's biographies of Renaissance artists, a book that is still useful to scholars of Italian art. They also collaborated on *Italian Cities* (1902), and in 1913 Edwin Blashfield published *Mural Painting in America*, a work of considerable importance in the history of the American mural movement.

Blashfield promoted the development of the visual arts in the United States and was admired and respected by his fellow artists. He was elected a full member of the National Academy of Design in 1888 and served as its president from 1920 until 1926. In 1895–1896 he was the president of the Society of American Artists. In 1912 President William Howard Taft appointed him a member of the National Commission of Fine Arts, and he was president of the national Institute of Arts and Letters from 1914 until 1916. During World War I he was an associate chair of the Division of Pictorial Publicity, an organization of artists who volunteered their services to the government to create visual publicity to support the war effort. His allegorical painting *Carry On* was the first painting dealing with war themes that the Metropolitan Museum of Art purchased, and it was considered by some critics as the finest American painting of the war.

Blashfield's wife died in 1918, and in 1928 he married again. He and his second wife, Grace Hall, lived at 50 Central Park West in New York. Throughout the 1920s Blashfield continued to be honored for his work and his service to the profession; in 1926 he was awarded a doctorate in fine arts from New York University, and that same year the American Academy of Arts and Letters honored him with a major retrospective exhibition. He was also at various times vice president of the American Federation of Arts, a member of the Federation of Fine Arts of New York, and an honorary member of the American Institute of Architects. Blashfield lectured on art at Harvard, Yale, Columbia, and other universities, and in 1934 he received the gold medal from the National Academy of Design for "distinguished services to the fine arts," an honor that had previously been given only to Elihu Root and Samuel F. B. Morse.

But by then Blashfield's reputation was beginning to fade, and critics were already proclaiming that his work was hopelessly old-fashioned and out-of-date. He died at his summer home at South Dennis, Massachusetts, on Cape Cod. After his death his reputation continued to decline, and by the 1950s his work was considered by many to epitomize the art style that the progressive American artists of the early twentieth century had overthrown. In the late twentieth century, though, as art historians and critics began to reappraise the academic art of the late nineteenth century in Europe and the United States, there was a notable revival of interest in his work, particularly his murals. His role as a major spokesman for the American mural movement is now widely recognized, as is his importance in the formation of American artistic ideals during the Age of Elegance.

• Blashfield's correspondence, diaries, letters, notes on art, and miscellaneous papers are in the New-York Historical Society. Among the Lockman papers in the New-York Historical Society there is the text of a Blashfield interview with De-Witt McClellan Lockman in July 1927 (Archives of American Art microfilm). H. Barbara Weinberg, *The American Pupils of Jean-Léon Gérôme* (1984), has some information about Blashfield's student days in Paris. For Blashfield's mural paintings, see Frank J. Mather, *Edwin Blashfield and Mural Painting in America* (1913), and most important, Leonard N. Amico, *The Mural Decorations of Edwin Howland Blashfield (1848–1936)*, an exhibition catalog for the Sterling and Francine Clark Art Institute, Williamstown, Mass. (1978), which includes an extensive bibliography and a chronological list of the artist's known murals, extant and destroyed. Royal Cortissoz, *The Works of Edwin Howland Blashfield* (1937), is useful primarily for the illustrations. For the murals in the Library of Congress, see Sarah J. Moore, "In Search of an American Iconography: Critical Reaction to the Murals at the Library of Congress," *Winterthur Portfolio* 25 (Winter 1990): 231–39. Blashfield's obituary is in the *New York Times*, 13 Oct. 1936, and it remains the only attempt to compile a complete list of his works.

ERIC VAN SCHAACK

BLATCH, Harriot Stanton (20 Jan. 1856–20 Nov. 1940), woman suffrage leader, was born Harriot Eaton Stanton in Seneca Falls, New York, the daughter of Henry Brewster Stanton, a lawyer, state senator, and abolitionist, and Elizabeth Cady, a leader in the women's rights movement. Inspiration germinated within the Stanton household. Elizabeth Cady Stanton had been one of the initiators in writing the Declaration of Sentiments that was presented at the historic first convention for women's rights held in Seneca Falls in 1848. Harriot, the sixth of seven siblings, idolized her mother, a woman with a great imagination and a good amount of common sense who passed her fervor for the cause of woman suffrage on to her younger daughter.

Educated at private schools, Harriot Stanton attended Vassar College and graduated with honors in 1878. After a year at the Boston School of Oratory, she spent most of 1880–1881 in Germany, living with several young girls as their tutor and companion. She then returned to the United States to participate in compiling the *History of Woman Suffrage* with her mother and Susan B. Anthony. One of the actions for which she is best remembered was making sure that the history of the American Woman Suffrage Association (AWSA), the rival association to Stanton and Anthony's National Woman Suffrage Association (NWSA), was included in the account. Taking on the task herself, she amassed a chapter totaling nearly one hundred pages when it was printed in the second volume in 1881. Its inclusion did much to reconcile the two opposing factions in later years.

In 1881, on her return voyage to the United States, Stanton had met William Henry Blatch, an English businessman, later head of the May Brewing Company. The two were married in November 1882 and for the following two decades resided outside of London, where they had two daughters, one of whom died in childhood. While in England Harriot Blatch conducted a statistical study on the condition of working women in English villages through which she fulfilled requirements for an M.A. degree, awarded by Vassar in 1894. She also became affiliated with women's and social reform groups, serving on the executive committees of both the Women's Local Government Society and the socialist Fabian Society established in 1883. Through the Women's Franchise League, a group founded in 1889, Blatch developed techniques for suffrage organizing that would serve her well after she and her family returned to the United States in 1902.

Compared with the activity she had been a part of in Britain, the spark had gone out of the American woman suffrage movement; it had become stagnant, devoid of political awareness or activity. Blatch sought to change all that. Briefly a member on the executive board of the Women's Trade Union League (WTUL), Blatch knew that women workers would need to be recruited if the drive for suffrage was to be successful. Toward that end, in 1907 she founded the Equality League of Self-Supporting Women, which in 1910 was renamed the Women's Political Union. Although the league had elite members, its core consisted of 20,000 women factory, laundry, and garment workers from New York's Lower East Side. The group's forum was presented out-of-doors, and beginning in 1910 they marched in the first suffrage parades ever. League women also testified at legislative hearings, lobbied for their cause during electoral campaigns, and oversaw polling activity. With Blatch at the helm, the activist organization grew in strength and influence, and its drive for a state constitutional amendment for woman suffrage spurred women into action. Blatch used her influence to encourage legislative candidates to pledge their support, and after the 1913 election, most of the newly elected state legislators voted to submit a suffrage amendment to the electorate in 1915. In 1917, the year that New York women won the vote, she helped to unite the Women's Political Union and the Congressional Union, a national organization focused on passage of a federal suffrage amendment, which she had joined in 1913, the year it was founded by militant suffragists Alice Paul and Lucy Burns.

After her husband was accidentally electrocuted in 1915, Blatch regained her U.S. Citizenship, then returned briefly to England to settle his affairs. Blatch curtailed her fight for suffrage during the war years, devoting herself instead to the war effort as head of the Food Administration's Speakers' Bureau and as a director of the Woman's Land Army, organized to provide needed additional farm labor. In her book *Mobilizing Woman-Power*, published early in 1918, Blatch stated that war had given women the opportunity to go into "every line of service," and she urged women to "go to work." In her second book, *A Woman's Point of View*, published in 1920, a chastened Blatch wrote about the destruction of war, which she had witnessed firsthand, and the need for women to work to avoid further conflicts.

Blatch's dedication to women's causes continued after American women won the vote in 1920. Although a supporter of working women, she withdrew from the National WTUL and the National Consumers' League because she did not support their fight for protective legislation for women. Instead she joined the National Woman's Party in its bid for passage of the Equal Rights Amendment. She also joined the Socialist party. In the 1920s she made unsuccessful bids for controller of the city of New York on the Socialist party ticket and ran for New York Assembly for the Socialist and Farm Labor party. She later withdrew from the party, however, because it too supported protective legislation for women workers and because it failed to involve its women members in meaningful ways. She did continue to work on behalf of the League of Nations and world peace—creating a plan of improvements for the amendments to the League Covenant—until she fractured a hip and retired to a nursing home in Greenwich, Connecticut, in 1939. She died there the following year.

A powerful speaker, Harriot Blatch carried the spirit of her mother forward into the twentieth century. Militant in her course of action, Blatch infused new life into the cause of suffrage and thereby helped to bring about the passage of the Nineteenth Amendment.

• The Library of Congress has twelve volumes of Blatch's papers for the period 1903–1912. The best source for details on her life is her autobiography, written with Alma Lutz, *Challenging Years* (1940). For information on the various suffrage organizations see Rose Young, "The Women Who 'Get Together,'" *Good Housekeeping*, Dec. 1913; *Outlook*, 28 Dec. 1912, pp. 931–34; Charles A. Beard, "The Woman's Party," *New Republic*, 29 July 1916; and Eleanor Flexner, *Century of Struggle* (1959). The British suffrage movement that so influenced Blatch is detailed in Dame Christabel Pankhurst, *Unshackled: The Story of How We Won the Vote* (1959). An obituary is in the *New York Times*, 21 Nov. 1940.

MARILYN ELIZABETH PERRY